BRADFORD'S
CROSSWORD
COMPENDIUM

Collins

BRADFORD'S CROSSWORD COMPENDIUM

HarperCollins Publishers
Westerhill Road
Bishopbriggs
Glasgow
G64 2QT
Great Britain

first edition 2005

**Bradford's Crossword Solver's
Dictionary**
© Anne R. Bradford 1986, 1993, 1997,
2000, 2003, 2005

Bradford's Crossword Lists
© HarperCollins Publishers 2004

ISBN 0-00-721492-8

www.collins.co.uk

A catalogue record for this book is
available from the British Library

Computing support and typesetting
by Thomas Callan

Printed and bound in Germany by
Bercker

Preface

Since the *Bradford's Crossword Solver's Dictionary* was first published in 1986, it has proved an invaluable aid for countless cruciverbalists. Compiled as a daily task since 1957 by Anne R. Bradford, a true crossword lover and an active member of the Crossword Club who still solves around 20 crosswords a week, the book has gone from strength to strength over a number of editions, offering the user over 200,000 crossword solutions as well as advice on solving cryptic clues. The latest edition has proved to be the most successful and popular yet.

In 2004, *Bradford's Crossword Lists* provided the essential companion to *Bradford's Crossword Solver's Dictionary*. This title was compiled from the Collins thesaurus database with additional material and advice from Anne Bradford, giving useful word lists on hundreds of subjects, from **Artists, Birds,** and **Collectors** to **Winds, Shades of yellow,** and **Signs of the Zodiac**. The book provided vocabulary lists and encyclopaedic information – both of which are invaluable for crossword solving.

A key feature common to both books is the cross-reference. Where appropriate, these are included within entries, so that you can see at once that there are related entries elsewhere, which may provide further useful information to help you find your solution.

This *Collins Bradford's Crossword Compendium* brings together, in one single volume, the 6th edition of *Bradford's Crossword Solver's Dictionary* and *Bradford's Crossword Lists*, to provide an indispensable and comprehensive aid to those who tackle crosswords at any level.

Solving Crossword Clues

Crossword puzzles tend to be basically 'quick' or 'cryptic'. A 'quick' crossword usually relies on a one- or two-word clue which is a simple definition of the answer required. As has been stated, many words have different meanings, so that the clue 'ball' could equally well lead to the answer 'sphere', 'orb', or 'dance'. The way to solve 'quick' crosswords is to press on until probable answers begin to interlink, which is a good sign that you are on the right track.

'Cryptic' crosswords are another matter. Here the clue usually consists of a basic definition, given at either the beginning or end of the clue, together with one or more definitions of parts of the answer. Here are some examples taken from all-time favourites recorded over the years:

1. '*Tradesman who bursts into tears*' (**Stationer**)

Tradesman is a definition of stationer. *Bursts* is cleverly used as an indication of an anagram, which *into tears* is of stationer.

2. '*Sunday school tune*' (**Strain**)

Here *Sunday* is used to define its abbreviation S, *school* is a synonym for train, and put together they give strain, which is a synonym of *tune*.

3. '*Result for everyone when head gets at bottom*' (**Ache**)
(used as a 'down' clue)

This is what is known as an '& lit' clue, meaning that the setter has hit on a happy composition which could literally be true. *Everyone* here is a synonym for each, move the *head* (first letter) of the word to the *bottom*, and the answer is revealed, the whole clue being the definition of the answer in this case.

4. '*Tin out East*' (**Sen**)

In this example, *tin*, implying 'money', requires its chemical symbol Sn to go *out*(side) *East*, or its abbreviation, E, the whole clue being a definition of a currency (sen) used in the East.

5. '*Information given to communist in return for sex*' (**Gender**)

Information can be defined as gen; *communist* is almost always red, *in return* indicates 'reversed', leading to gen-der, a synonym for *sex*.

     6. '*Row about no enclosure of this with sardines*' (**Tin-opener**)

Row is a synonym for tier, *about* indicates 'surrounding', *no enclosure* can be no pen, leading to ti-no pen-er, and another '& lit' clue.

     7. '*Cake-sandwiches-meat, at Uncle Sam's party*' (**Clambake**)

Meat here is lamb, *sandwiches* is used as a verb, so we have C-lamb-ake, which is a kind of party in America. Uncle Sam or US is often used to indicate America.

     8. '*Initially passionate meeting of boy and girl could result in it*' (**Pregnancy**)

Initially is usually a sign of a first letter, in this case 'p' for *passionate* + Reg (a boy) and Nancy (a girl), and another clever '& lit'.

With 'cryptic' clues the solver needs to try to analyse the parts to see what he or she is looking for – which word or words can be the straight definition, and which refer to the parts or hint at anagrams or other subterfuges. Whilst it would be unrealistic to claim total infallibility, practice has shown that in most crosswords some 90% of the answers are to be found in this work.

Anne R Bradford

How to use the Dictionary

This dictionary is the result of over 45 years' analysis of some 300,000 crossword clues, ranging from plain 'quick' crosswords requiring only synonyms to the different level of cryptic puzzles. Therefore the words listed at each entry may be connected to the keyword in various ways, such as:

- a straightforward synonym
- a commonly-associated adjective
- an associated or proper noun
- a pun or other devious play on words

Keywords are listed alphabetically; in cases where the heading consists of more than one word, the first of these words is taken to be the keyword, and in cases where the end of a word is bracketed, the material up to the opening bracket is taken to be the keyword. Keywords marked with the symbol ▶ refer the user to other entries where additional information may be found. Keywords marked with the symbol ▷ give leads to anagrams and other ploys used by crossword setters. If the keywords found in the clue do not lead directly to the required answer, the solver should look under words given as cross-references to other entries. These are indicated by the symbol >, with the cross-referenced word shown in capitals.

As a completely innovative feature for this new edition, some entries have been divided into two parts – a general entry similar to the standard entries which appear elsewhere, and a panel entry which contains a list of more specific or encyclopedic material. So, for example, the entry 'Artist(ic)' includes not only a list of general words connected with 'Artist' or 'Artistic' in some way, such as 'Bohemian', 'Cubist', 'Fine' and 'Virtuoso', but also a panel with the heading 'Artists' containing a list of the names of specific artists, such as 'Bellini', 'Constable', and 'Rembrandt'. For added help, the words in these panels are arranged by length, with all three-letter words grouped together in alphabetical order, then all four-letter words, then all five-letter words, and so on.

How to use the Lists

This book gives useful vocabulary lists and information on hundreds of subjects which are likely to come up as part of crossword clues. The lists are arranged alphabetically by subject, so finding the one you want is as quick and easy as looking up a dictionary. A full table of the lists and the pages on which they appear is also given at the start of the Lists section of the book.

Where the entry consists of a straightforward list of words relevant to a given subject, such as **Shades of blue, Types of pasta,** or **Birds,** the words are arranged by length, with all three-letter words grouped together in alphabetical order, then all four-letter words, then all five-letter words, and so on.

Where an entry includes additional useful information – for example at **US States,** where not only the name of each state is shown, but also its **abbreviation, zip code, nickname,** and **capital** – the list is arranged in columns to allow you to find the relevant information you need to solve your clue. The book thus provides both vocabulary and encyclopaedic information, set out in whichever way will be most helpful to the user.

Lists such as **Artists** and **Composers,** which consist of people's names, are arranged by length of surname, or whichever part of the name the person is best known by, and then alphabetically within each length group. First names and other more 'optional' elements, such as nicknames and initials, are shown after the main part of the name, in italics. You can therefore find the person you are looking for straight away, and then choose the part of their name which is relevant to your crossword solution.

Cross-references are also included wherever appropriate at the ends of entries, so that if you happen to be looking up, for example, the entry for **Animals,** you can see straight away that there are also lists at **Amphibians, Birds, Insects,** and so on, which may provide further useful information to help you solve your clue. The cross-references are introduced by the line 'See also:' and each is preceded by the symbol ➤ with the cross-referenced list's title shown in bold type.

About the Author

Anne Bradford's love of words began to make itself evident even in her schooldays, when, as head girl of her school, she instituted a novel punishment – instead of making rulebreakers write lines, she had them write out pages from a dictionary, on the grounds that this was a more useful exercise. Little did she know this was soon to be her own daily routine!

In time, crosswords became a magnificent obsession for Anne. All lovers of crosswords can understand the irresistible lure of solving them, but Anne's interest went much deeper than most people's, and when she stopped work in 1957 to have her first child, she found herself starting to note down answers to particularly tricky clues as an aid to memory, in case she should come across them again in another puzzle. It was from this simple beginning that this crossword dictionary evolved.

Over the space of 25 years, Anne continued to build on her collection of solutions, analysing every crossword clue as she solved it and adding it to her steadily growing bank of entries. This unique body of material eventually reached such proportions that she had the idea of offering it to her fellow crossword-solvers as a reference book, and since then, the book has gone from strength to strength, providing valuable help to countless cruciverbalists over a number of editions.

Anne Bradford continues to devote time each day to solving crosswords, averaging some 20 a week – both quick and cryptic – and still avidly collects new solutions for her *Crossword Solver's Dictionary* at a rate of around 150 a week, compiling each solution by hand (without the use of a computer!). This latest edition therefore includes much new material, gleaned by a true crossword lover who not only solves crosswords but, as an active member of the Crossword Club, can offer the user an insight into the mind of a cunning crossword compiler.

The Crossword Club

If you are interested in crosswords, you might like to consider joining the Crossword Club. Membership is open to all who enjoy tackling challenging crosswords and who appreciate the finer points of clue-writing and grid-construction. The Club's magazine, Crossword, contains two prize puzzles each month. A sample issue and full details are available on request.

The Crossword Club
Coombe Farm
Awbridge
Romsey, Hants.
SO51 0HN
UK

email: bh@thecrosswordclub.co.uk
website address: www.thecrosswordclub.co.uk

BRADFORD'S CROSSWORD SOLVER'S DICTIONARY

Aa

A, An Ack, Adult, Ae, Alpha, Angstrom, Are, Argon, D, Ein, Her, If, L, One, Per, They

A1 Tiptop

AA Milne

Aardvark Ant-bear, Ant-eater, Earth-hog, Ground-hog

Aaron's Rod Hagtaper

Aba, Abba Patriarch

Abacus Counter, Soroban

Abaft Astern, Sternson

Abalone Ormer, Paua, Perlemoen

Abandon(ed), Abandonment Abdicate, Abnegate, Abort, Adrift, Amoral, Apostasy, Back down, Cade, Cancel, Castaway, Corrupt, Decommission, Defect, Derelict, > **DESERT**, Desuetude, Discard, Disown, Dissolute, Ditch, Drop, Dump, Elan, Evacuate, Expose, Flagrant, Forhoo(ie), Forhow, Forlend, Forsake, Gomorra, Immoral, Jack(-in), Jettison, Jilt, Leave, Loose, Louche, Maroon, Old, Orgiastic, Profligate, Quit, Rat, Relinquish, Renounce, Reprobate, Scrap, Shed, Sink, Strand, Vacate, Waive, Wanton, Yield

Abase Degrade, Demean, Disgrace, Grovel, > **HUMBLE**, Kowtow, Lessen

Abash Daunt, Discountenance, Mortify

Abate(ment) Allay, Appal, Decrescent, Defervescence, Diminish, Let up, Lyse, Lysis, Moderate, Reduce, Remit, > **SUBSIDE**

▷ **Abate** *may indicate* a contention

Abattoir Knackery, Slaughterhouse

Abbey Abbacy, Bath, Buckfast, Cloister, Downside, Fonthill, Fountains, Glastonbury, Je(r)vaulx, Medmenham, Melrose, Minster, Nightmare, Northanger, Priory, Rievaulx, Tintern, Westminster, Whitby, Woburn

Abbot Aelfric, Archimandrite, Brother, Friar

Abbreviate, Abbreviation Abridge, Ampersand, Compendium, Condense, Curtail, > **SHORTEN**, Sigla

ABC Absey

Abdicate, Abdication Cede, Demission, Disclaim, Disown, Resign

Abdomen Belly, C(o)eliac, Epigastrium, Gaster, Hypochondrium, Paunch, Pleon, > **STOMACH**, Tummy, Venter

Abduct(ed), Abduction Enlèvement, Kidnap, Rapt, Ravish, Shanghai, Steal

Aberdeen Granite City

Aberrant, Aberration Abnormal, Aye-aye, Deviant, Idolon, Perverse

Abet(tor) Aid, Back, Candle-holder, Second

Abeyance, Abeyant Dormant, Shelved, Sleeping, Store

Abhor(rent) > **DETEST**, Execrable, > **HATE**, Loathe, Odious, Shun

Abide Dwell, Inhere, > **LAST**, Lie, Live, Observe, Remain, Stand, Tarry

Abigail Maid, Masham

Ability Aptitude, Calibre, Capacity, Cocum, > **COMPETENCE**, Efficacy, ESP, Facility, Faculty, Ingine, Instinct, Lights, Potential, Prowess, Savey,

Savoir-faire, Savv(e)y, Skill, Talent

Abject Base, Craven, Grovel, Humble, Servile, Slave

Abjure Eschew, Forswear, Recant, Renege, Reny

Ablaze Afire, Ardent

Able Ablins, Accomplished, > **ADEPT**, Aiblins, Apt, Capable, > **COMPETENT**, Fere, Proficient, Seaman, Yibbles

Abnormal(ity) Anomalous, Atypical, > **DEVIANT**, Dysfunction, Ectopic, Erratic, Etypical, Freakish, Odd, Preternatural, > **QUEER**, Sport, Unnatural, Varus

Aboard On

Abode Domicile, Dwelling, Habitat, > **HOME**, Lain, Libken, Midgard, Remain

Abolish, **Abolition(ist)** Annihilate, Annul, Axe, > **BAN**, D, Delete, Destroy, Eradicate, Erase, Extirpate, John Brown, Nullify, Repeal, Rescind

Abomasum Read

Abominable, **Abominate**, **Abomination** Bane, Cursed, > **HATE**, Nefandous, Nefast, Revolting, Snowman, Vile, Yeti

Aboriginal, **Aborigine** Adivasi, Ainu, Aranda, Autochthon, Binghi, Boong, Buck, Bushmen, Carib, Evolué, Fringe-dweller, Gin, Gurindji, Indigenous, Jacky(-Jacky), Kamilaroi, Koori, Lubra, Maori, Mary, Motu, Myall, Piljantjatjara, Pintubi, Pre-Dravidian, Sakai, San, Sican, Siwash, Truganini, Vedda(h)

Abort(ion), **Abortive** Apiol, Cancel, Ecbolic, Miscarry, Moon-calf, Slip, Sooterkin, Teras, Termination

Abound(ing) Bristle, Copious, Enorm, Rife, Teem

About A, Almost, Anent, Around, C, Ca, Circa, Circiter, Concerning, Encompass, Environs, Going, Near, Of, On, Over, Re, Regarding, Soon at

▷ **About** *may indicate* one word around another

Above Abune, Aforementioned, Aloft, Over, Overhead, Overtop, Owre, Sopra, Superior, Supra-, Suspicion, Upon

Abracadabra Cantrip, Heypass

Abrade, **Abrasive** Carbanado, Carborundum®, Chafe, Emery, Erode, File, Garnet paper, > **GRATE**, Rub, Sand, Scrape, Scrat, Scuff

Abraham Lincoln, Patriarch, Urite

Abreast Alongside, Au courant, Au fait, Beside, Level, Up

Abridge(ment) Audley, Compress, Condense, Cut, Digest, Dock, Epitome, Pot, Shorten, Trim

Abroad Afield, Away, Distant, Forth, Offshore, Out, Overseas

▷ **Abroad** *may indicate* an anagram

Abrogate Abolish, Repeal, Replace

▷ **Abrupt** *may indicate* a shortened word

Abrupt(ly) Bold, Brusque, Curt, Gruff, Offhand, Premorse, Prerupt, Short, Staccato, Terse

Abscess Gumboil, Impost(h)ume, Ulcer, Warble

Abscond Absquatulate, Decamp, Desert, Elope, Flee, Leg-bail, Levant, Welch

Abseil(ing) Dulfer, Rappel

Absence, **Absent(ee)**, **Absent-minded(ness)** Abs, Abstracted, Away, Distant, Distracted, Distrait, Exile, Hookey, Mitch, Scatty, Skip, Truant, Vacuity, Void, Wanting, Wool-gathering

Absinthe Wormwood

Absolute(ly) Bang, Complete, Dead, Deep-dyed, Downright, Fairly, Implicit, Ipso facto, Just, Mere, Mondo, Nominative, Plenary, Plumb, Quite, Real, Sheer, Total, Truly, Unmitigated, Unqualified, Utter, Veritable, Very

Absolve, **Absolution** Acquit, Assoilzie, Clear, Exculpate, Excuse, Pardon, Shrive

Absorb(ed), Absorbent, Absorbing, Absorption Assimilate, Autism, Blot, Consume, Desiccant, Devour, Digest, Dope, Drink, > ENGROSS, Imbibe, Ingest, Intent, Merge(r), Occlude, Occupy, Osmosis, Porous, Preoccupation, Rapt, Sorbefacient, Spongy, Unputdownable

Absquatulate Skedaddle

Abstain(er), Abstemious, Abstinence, Abstinent Band of Hope, Celibacy, Chastity, Continent, Desist, Eschew, Forbear, Forgo, Maigre, Nazarite, Nephalism, Pioneer, Rechab(ite), Refrain, Resist, Sober, Temperate, TT

Abstract(ed), Abstraction Abrege, Abridge, Academic, Appropriate, Brief, Deduct, Digest, Discrete, Distrait, Epitome, Essence, Metaphysical, Musing, Notional, Précis, Prepossessed, Prescind, Remove, Resumé, Reverie, Stable, Steal, Summary, Syllabus, Tachism

Abstruse Deep, Esoteric, Obscure, Recondite

Absurd(ity) Alician, Apagoge, Fantastic, Farcical, Folly, Inept, Irrational, Laputan, Ludicrous, Madness, Nonsense, Paradox, Preposterous, Ridiculous, Silly, Solecism, Stupid, Toshy, Whim-wham

Abundance, Abundant A-gogo, Ample, Bounty, Copious, Excess, Flood, Flush, Fouth, Fowth, Fruitful, Galore, Lashings, Mickle, Mine, Mint, Oodles, Opulent, Over, Plenitude, Plenteous, > PLENTIFUL, Plenty, Pleroma, Plethora, Plurisie, Prolific, Relative, Replete, Rich, Rife, Routh, Rowth, Sonce, Sonse, Store, Tallents, Teeming, Tons, Uberous

Abuse, Abusive Assail, Billingsgate, Blackguard, Flak, Fustilarian, Fustil(l)irian, Hail, Insult, Invective, Limehouse, Maltreat, Miscall, > MISTREAT, Misuse, Obloquy, Opprobrium, Philippic, Rail, Rampallian, Rate, Rayle, Revile, Ritual, Satanic, Satire, Scarab(ee), Scurrilous, Serve, Sexual, Slang, Slate, Sledging, Snash, Solvent, Substance, Thersitical, Tirade, Vilify, Violate, Vituperation

Abut Adjoin, Border, Touch

Abysm(al), Abyss Avernus, Barathrum, Barranca, Chasm, Deep, Gulf, Swallet, Tartarean, Tartarus

AC Current, Erk

Acacia Bablah, Boree, Brigalow, Eumong, Eumung, Gidgee, Gidjee, Koa, Mimosa, Mulga, Myall, Sallee, Shittim, Wattle

Academic(ian) A, Acca, Acker, Della-Cruscan, Don, Erudite, Fellow, Hypothetic(al), Immortals, Literati, Master, Pedantic, PRA, Prof(essor), RA, Reader, Rector

Academy Athenaeum, Dollar, French, Loretto, Lyceum, Military, Naval, Royal, St Cyr, Sandhurst, School, Seminary, West Point

Acanthus Blankursine, Ruellia

Accelerate, Acceleration, Accelerator Antedate, Betatron, Bevatron, Collider, Cosmotron, Cyclotron, Festinate, G, Gal, Gun, Hasten, Increase, Linac, Linear, Rev, Signatron, Speed, Stringendo, Synchrotron

Accent(ed), Accentuate Acute, Beat, Breve, Brogue, Bur(r), Circumflex, Cut-glass, Doric, Drawl, Enclitic, Enhance, Grave, Hacek, Intonation, Kelvinside, Long, Macron, Martelé, Morningside, Mummerset, Nasal, Orthotone, Oxford, Oxytone, Paroxytone, Perispomenon, Pitch, Primary, Proparoxytone, Rhythm, Secondary, Stress, Tittle, Tone, Tonic, Twang

Accentor Dunnock

Accept(able), Acceptance, Accepted A, Accede, Admit, Adopt, Agree, Allow, Approbate, Bar, Believe, Buy, Can-do, Common, Consent, Cool, Cosher, Decent, Done, Grant, Kosher, Meet, Obey, On, Pocket, Putative, Settle, Stand, Swallow, Take, Tolerate, U, Wear, Widespread

Access(ible) Avenue, Card, Come-at-able, Credit, Direct, Door, Entrée, > ENTRY, Fit, Hack, Ingo, Key, Log in, Log on, Passe-partout, Password, Phreaking, Random, Recourse, Remote, Sequential, Spasm, Wayleave

Accessory, Accessories Abettor, Addition, Aide, Ally, Ancillary, Appendage, Appurtenance, Attribute, Bandanna, Bells and whistles, Cribellum, Findings, Fitment, Staffage, Trappings, Trimming

Accident(al) Adventitious, Bechance, Blowdown, Blunder, Calamity, > CHANCE, Circumstance, Contingency, Contretemps, Crash, Dent, Disaster, Fall, Fluke, Fortuitous, Hap, Hit and run, Mischance, Mishap, Promiscuous, Rear-ender, Shunt, Smash, Smash-up, Spill, Stramash, Wreck

Accidie Acedia, Sloth, Torpor

Acclaim Accolade, Applaud, Brava, Bravo, Cheer, Eclat, Fame, Fanfare, Hail, Kudos, Ovation, Praise, Salute

Accolade Award, Honour, Palm, Token, Tribute

Accommodate, Accommodation Adapt, B and B, Bedsit, Berth, Billet, Board, Botel, Bunkhouse, Camp, Chalet, Compromise, Crashpad, Digs, Flotel, Gaff, Gite, Grace and favour, Homestay, Hostel, Hotel, House, Lend, Loan, Lodge, Lodgement, Motel, > OBLIGE, Parador, Pension, Quarters, Rapprochement, Recurve, Room, Sheltered, Sorehon, Stabling, Stateroom, Steerage, Storage, Wharepuni, Xenodochium

▷ **Accommodating** *may indicate* one word inside another

Accompany(ing), Accompanied (by), Accompaniment, Accompanist Accessory, Alberti, And, Attend, Backing, Chaperone, Chum, Concomitant, Consort, Continuo, Descant, > ESCORT, Harmonise, Herewith, Obbligato, Obligate, Obligato, Repetiteur, Soundtrack, Trimmings, Vamp

Accomplice Abettor, Aide, > ALLY, Collaborator, Confederate, Federarie, Partner, Shill, Stale

Accomplish(ed), Accomplishment Able, > ACHIEVE, Arch, Attain, Clever, Complete, Consummate, Done, Effect, Master, Over, Perform, Polished, Realise, Ripe, Savant, Success, Tour de force

Accord(ingly), According to After, Agree, Ala, Allow, As per, Attune, Chime, Consensus, Give, Grant, Harmony, Jibe, Meech Lake, Meet, Sort, Thus

According to nature SN

Accordion Button, Concertina, Flutina, Piano, Squeeze-box

Accost Abord, Approach, Greet, Hail, Importune, Molest, Solicit, Tackle

Account(s) AC, Anecdote, Audit, Battels, Behalf, Bill, Cause, Charge, Checking, Chronicle, Current, Deposit, Discretionary, Drawing, Enarration, Expense, Explain, Exposition, Joint, Lawin, Ledger, Long, Memoir, Narration, Nostro, Numbered, Procès-verbal, Real, Reason, Recital, Regest, Register, > REPORT, Repute, Resumé, Sake, Short, Suspense, Swindlesheet, Tab, Tale, Thesis, Trust, Version, Vostro

Accountant Auditor, CA, Cost, Forensic, Hyde, Liquidator, Reckoner, Vestry-clerk

Accredit Attribute

Accumulate, Accumulation Accrue, Adsorb, Aggregate, > AMASS, Augment, Backlog, Build, Collect, Gather, Hoard, Lodg(e)ment, Pile, Rack up, Stockpile, Uplay

Accuracy, Accurate(ly) Bang-on, Cocker, > CORRECT, Dead-on, Fair, Fidelity, Minute, Precise, Right, Spot-on, True, Word-perfect

Accursed Argued, Blest, Blist, Sacred

Accusation, Accuse(d) Allege, Arraign, Attaint, Bill, Blame, Censure, Challenge, Charge, Criminate, Denounce, Dite, Gravamen, Impeach,

Incriminate, Panel, Suspect, Tax, Threap, Threep, Traduce, Wight, Wite, Wyte

Accustom(ed) Acquaint, Attune, Enure, General, Habituate, Inure, Teach, Wont, Woon

Ace(s) Basto, Crabs, Dinger, > EXPERT, Jot, Master, Mournival, One, Quatorze, Spadille, Spadill(i)o, Spot, Tib, Virtuoso, Wonderful

Acerbate Intensify

Ache, **Aching** Aitch, Die, Long, Mulligrubs, Nag, Otalgia, Pain, Stitch, Yearn, Yen

Achieve(ment) Accomplish, Acquisition, Attain, Come, Compass, > EFFECT, Exploit, Feat, Fulfil, Gain, Hatchment, Realise, Satisfice, Satisfy, Stroke, Succeed, Triumph, Trock, Troke, Truck

Acid(ity) Acrimony, Corrosive, Drop, EPA, Etchant, Hydroxy, Reaction, Ribosomal, Ribozyme, Solvent, Sour, Tart, Trans-fatty, Vinegar, Vitriol

ACIDS

2 letters:
PH

3 letters:
DNA
HCL
LSD
Oxo
RNA

4 letters:
Acyl
Dopa
Pyro
Uric
Wood

5 letters:
Amide
Amino
Auric
Boric
Caro's
Fatty
Folic
Iodic
L-dopa
Lewis
Malic
Mucic
Oleic
Orcin
Osmic
Trona

6 letters:
Adipic
Bromic
Capric
Cholic
Citric
Cyanic
Erucic
Formic
Gallic
Lactic
Lauric
Leucin
Lipoic
Lysine
Maleic
Marine
Niacin
Nitric
Oxalic
Oxygen
Pectic
Phenol
Picric
Quinic
Serine
Sialic
Sorbic
Tannic
Tiglic
Toluic
Valine

7 letters:
Abietic
Acrylic
Alanine
Alginic
Benzoic
Butyric
Caproic
Cerotic
Chloric
Chromic
Creatin
Cystine
Ellagic
Eugenic
Ferulic
Folacin
Fumaric
Fusidic
Glycine
Guanine
Leucine
Malonic
Meconic
Melanic
Muramic
Nitrous
Nucleic
Orcinol
Peracid
Proline
Prussic
Pteroic
Pyruvic
Racemic
Sebacic
Selenic
Silicic
Stannic

Stearic
Suberic
Terebic
Titanic
Valeric
Vanadic
Xanthic
Xylonic

8 letters:
Abscisic
Adenylic
Arginine
Ascorbic
Aspartic
Butanoic
Caprylic
Carbamic
Carbolic
Carbonic
Chlorous
Cinnamic
Creatine
Cresylic
Crotonic
Cyclamic
Cysteine
Decanoic
Ethanoic
Fulminic
Glutamic
Glyceric
Glycolic
Guanylic
Hippuric
Iopanoic

- Itaconic
- Linoleic
- Lysergic
- Manganic
- Margaric
- Muriatic
- Myristic
- Nonanoic
- Palmitic
- Periodic
- Phthalic
- Rhodanic
- Succinic
- Sulfonic
- Tantalic
- Tartaric
- Telluric
- Tungstic
- Tyrosine
- Uridylic
- Valproic

9 letters:
- Aqua-regia
- Citydylic
- Dichromic
- Histidine
- Hydrazoic
- Hydriodic
- Isocyanic
- Linolenic
- Methanoic
- Nalidixic

Nicotinic
Ornithine
Panthenic
Pentanoic
Polybasic
Propanoic
Propenoic
Saccharic
Salicylic
Sassolite
Selenious
Sulphonic
Sulphuric
Tellurous
Threonine

10 letters:
Aquafortis
Asparagine
Barbituric
Carboxylic
Citrulline
Dithionous
Dodecanoic
Glucoronic
Glutamatic
Glutaminic
Hyaluronic
Isoleucine
Margaritic
Methionine
Orthoboric
Pelargonic

Perchloric
Phosphoric
Proprionic
Pyrogallic
Ricinoleic
Thiocyanic
Thymidylic
Tryptophan

11 letters:
Arachidonic
Decanedioic
Ethanedioic
Ferricyanic
Ferrocyanic
Gibberellic
Hydnocarpic
Hydrobromic
Hydrocyanic
Hyponitrous
Methacrylic
Octanedioic
Pantothenic
Permanganic
Phosphorous
Ribonucleic
Sarcolactic
Taurocholic

12 letters:
Dicraboxylic
Hydrochloric
Hydrofluoric

Hypochlorous
Indoleacetic
Orthosilicic
Persulphuric
Phenylalanin
Polyadenalic
Propanedioic
Prostacyclin
Pyroligneous
Terephthalic

13 letters:
Galactosamine
Heptadecanoic
Indolebutyric
Phenylalanine
Prostaglandin
Pyrosulphuric
Thiosulphuric

14 letters:
Metaphosphoric
Pyrophosphoric

15 letters:
Orthophosphoric

16 letters:
Deoxyribonucleic

Acknowledge(ment) Accept, Admit, Allow, Answer, Avow, Confess, Credit, Grant, Mea culpa, Nod, Own, Receipt, Recognise, Resipiscence, Respect, Righto, Roger, Salute, Ta, Touché, Wilco, Yo
Acme Apex, Apogee, Climax, Comble, Crest, Peak, Summit, Top, Zenith
Acolyte Nethinim, Novice, Server, Thurifer
Acorn(s), Acorn-shell Balanus, Glans, Mast, Rac(c)ahout, Valonia
Acoustic(s) Harmonics, Phonics, Sonics
Acquaint(ance), Acquainted Advise, Cognisant, Enlighten, Familiar, > INFORM, Knowledge, Nodding, Notify, Tell, Versed
Acquiesce(nce), Acquiescent Accept, Bow, Conform, Resigned, Righto, Roger, Wilco, Yield
Acquire, Acquisition Acquest, Earn, Ern, Gain, > GET, Land, Obtain, Procure, Purchase, Steal, Take-over, Usucap(t)ion
Acquit(tal) Assoil, Cleanse, Clear, Exonerate, Free, Loose, Loste, Pardon
Acre(s) A, Area, Bigha, Hide, Rival, Rood
Acrid, Acrimony Bitter(ness), Empyreuma, Pungent, Rough, Sour, Surly
Acrobat(s), Acrobatics Equilibrist, Gymnast, Jerry-come-tumble, Ropedancer, Speeler, Splits, Trampoline, Tumbler, Wing-walker

Acropolis Citadel, Parthenon

Across A, Ac, Athwart, Opposite, Over, Through

Act(ing), **Action**, **Acts** A, Affirmative, Antic, Assist, Assumpsit, Auto, Barnstorm, Behave, Bit, Business, Camp, Campaign, Case, Cause, Charade, Come, Conduct, Coup, Daff, Deal, > DEED, Delaying, Deputise, Detinue, Direct, Do, DORA, Double, Enabling, Enclosure, Epistasis, Excitement, Exert, Exploit, Factory, Feat, Feign, Forth-putting, Function, Furthcoming, Habeas corpus, Histrionic, Homestead, Identic, Impersonate, Improbation, Incident, Industrial, Juristic, Lance-jack, Litigate, Locutionary, Measure, Method, Movement, Mum, Mutiny, Navigation, Partypiece, Pas, Perform(ance), Personate, Play, Positive, Pp, Practice, Pretence, Private, Procedure, Process, Qua, Qui tam, Reflex, Replevin, Represent, Riot, Rising, Routine, Sasine, Scenery, Secondary, Serve, Showdown, Shtick, Simulate, Stamp, Stanislavski, Statute, Steps, Suit, Synergy, Terminer, Test, Theatricise, Thellusson, Thing, Transitory, Treat, Trover, Truck, Turn, Twig, Uniformity, Union, Vicegerent, War, Windlass

Actinium Ac

Actinon An

Activate Arm, Engage, Goad, Spark, Spur, Stur, Styre, Trigger

Active, **Activist**, **Activity** A, Agile, Alert, At, Athletic, Brisk, Busy, Cadre, Deedy, DIY, Do(ing), Dynamited, Dynamo, Ecowarrior, Effectual, Energetic, Energic, Exercise, Extra-curricular, Floruit, Fluster, Game, Go-go, Goings-on, Hum, Hyper, Leish, Licht, Live, Mobile, Motile, Nimble, Ongo, On the go, Op, Operant, Play, Rambunctious, Residual, Sprightly, Springe, Spry, Sthenic, Surge, Third house, Vacuum, Voice, Wick, Wimble

Actor(s), **Actor-like** Agent, Alleyn, Artist, Ashe, Barnstormer, Benson, Betterton, Burbage, Cast, Character, Company, Diseur, Donat, Equity, Gable, Garrick, Gielgud, Guiser, Ham, Hamfatter, Heavy, Histrio(n), Jay, Juve(nile), Kean, Luvvie, MacReady, Mime, Mummer, Olivier, Performer, Player, Playfair, Roscian, Roscius, Savoyard, Sim, Stager, Strolling, Super, Thespian, Tragedian, Tree, Tritagonist, Trouper, Understudy, Wolfit

Actress Bankhead, Duse, Ingenue, Pierrette, Siddons, Soubrette, Terry, West

Actual(ity), **Actually** De facto, Entelechy, Literal, Live, Material, Real, Real-life, Tangible, True, Very

Acumen Insight

Acupressure Jin shin do, Shiatsu

Acupuncture Stylostixis

Acute Astute, Dire, Fitché, > INTENSE, Keen, Quick-witted, Sharp

Adage Aphorism, Gnome, Maxim, Motto, Paroemia, Proverb, Saw, Saying, Truism

Adam Bede, Delved

Adamant Inexorable, Insistent, Obdurate, Rigid, Unbending

Adapt(er), **Adaptable**, **Adaptor** Bushing, Ecad, Flexible, Pliant, Reorient, Resilient, Tailor, Timeserver, Transform, Versatile

Add(ed), **Addendum**, **Adder** Accrue, Adscititious, > APPENDIX, Attach, Cast, Coopt, Dub, Ech(e), Eik, Eke, Elaborate, Embroider, Enhance, Fortify, Insert, Lace, Puff, Reckon, Score, Spike, Sum, Summate, Tack on, Tot(e), Total, Viper

Addict(ion), **Addicted** Abuser, Acidhead, Base head, Buff, Couch potato, Dependency, Devotee, Dope-fiend, Etheromaniac, Fan, Fiend, Freak, Hophead, Hype, Jones, Joypopper, Junkie, Lover, Mainliner, Mania, Need, Pillhead, Pillpopper, Pothead, Shithead, Slave, Space-cadet, Speedfreak, User, Vinolent, Wino

Addison Spectator

Addition(al) Accession, Addend, Additive, Adscititious, Adulterant, Also, And, Annexure, (As an) in, Bolt-on, Braata, Codicil, Corollary, Eik, Eke, Encore, Epithesis, Etc, Extender, > **EXTRA**, Extramural, > **IN ADDITION**, Increment, Makeweight, Monkey, New, Odd, On, On top, Other, Padding, Paragog(u)e, Parergon, Plus, PS, Rider, Ripieno, Spare, Suffect, Suffix, Supplementary, Surcharge, Thereto, Top-up, Verandah

Address, Address system Accommodation, Accost, Adroit, Allocution, Apostrophe, Apostrophise, Appellation, Art, > **ATLAS**, Ave, Bub, Buster, Call, Compellation, Dedication, Delivery, Den, Diatribe, Direction, Discourse, Election, Epilogue, Epirrhema, Esquire, Gettysburg, Gospodin, Hail, Home, Homily, Lecture, Mester, Mister, Mush, Mynheer, Nkosi, Ode, Orate, Parabasis, Poste-restante, Prelection, Rig, Salute, Sermon, Sir(ree), Speech, Stance, Tact, Tannoy®, > **TITLE**, Towkay, Tuan, Valedictory, Wambenger, Wus, Y'all

Adduce Cite

Adelphic Adam

Adept Able, Adroit, Dab, Deacon, Don, > **EXPERT**, Fit, Handy, Mahatma

Adequate Condign, Does, Due, Egal, Equal, Ere-now, Passable, Proper, > **SUFFICIENT**, Tolerable, Valid

Adhere(nt), Adherence, Adhesive Allegiance, Ally, Araldite®, Bond, Burr, Child, Cling, Conform, Cow Gum®, Dextrin, Disciple, Epoxy, Fidelity, Follower, Glue, Goldsize, Guebre, Gum, Hot-melt, Impact, Jain(a), Mucilage, Partisan, Resin, Sectator, Servitor, Sticker, Supporter, Synechia, Waterglass

Adjacent, Adjoining Bordering, Conterminous, Contiguous, Handy, Nigh

Adjective Adnoun, Epithet, Gerundive

Adjourn(ment) Abeyance, Defer, Delay, > **POSTPONE**, Prorogate, Recess, Rise, Suspend

Adjudicate, Adjudicator Judge, Jury, Referee, Try, Umpire

Adjunct Addition, Aid, Ancillary, Rider

Adjust(able), Adjustment, Adjuster Accommodate, Adapt, Attune, Coapt, Dress, Ease, Fine-tune, Fit, Focus, Gang, Gauge, Gerrymander, J'adoube, Modify, Modulate, Orientate, Prepare, Reduce, Regulate, Reorientate, Reset, Scantle, Sliding, Suit, Tamper, Tram, Trim, True, Tune, Tweak, Vernier

▷ **Adjust** *may indicate* an anagram

Adjutant Aide, Argala, Officer, Stork

Adler Irene

Administer, Administration, Administrator Adhibit, Anele, Apply, Arrondissement, Bairiki, Bureaucrat, Control, Corridors of power, > **DIRECT**, Dispence, Dispense, Executive, Intendant, Intinction, > **MANAGE**, Raj, Regime, Registrar, Run, Secretariat, Soke, Steward

Admirable, Admiration, Admire(d), Admirer Clinker, Clipper, Conquest, Crichton, Esteem, Estimable, > **EXCELLENT**, Flame, Fureur, Ho, Iconise, Idolater, Laudable, Partisan, Regard, Ripping, Splendid, Toast, Tribute, Venerate, Wonder, Wow

Admiral Adm, Anson, Beatty, Beaufort, Benbow, Blake, Bligh, Boscawen, Butterfly, Byng, Byrd, Drake, Effingham, Fisher, Hood, Hornblower, Howard, Jellicoe, Keyes, Marrowfat, Navarch, Nelson, Raeder, Red, Rodney, Spee, Sturdee, Togo, Vanessa, Van Nieman, Van Tromp, White

Admission, Admit(ting), Admittance Accept, Access, Agree, Allow, Avow, Concede, > **CONFESS**, Enter, Entrée, Entry, Estoppel, Grant, Induct, Ingress, Initiate, Intromit, Ordain, Owe, Own, Recognise, Tho(ugh), ¥ield

Admonish, Admonition Chide, Lecture, Moralise, Pi-jaw, Rebuke, Reprimand,

> **SCOLD**, Tip, Warn

Ado Bother, Bustle, Fuss

Adolescent Developer, Grower, Halflin, Juvenile, Neanic, Teenager, Veal, Youth

Adonais Keats

Adonis Pheasant's Eye

Adopt(ed) Accept, Affect, Affiliate, Assume, Dalt, Embrace, Espouse, Father, Foster, Mother

Adoration, Adore Homage, Idolise, Latria, Love, Pooja(h), Puja, Revere, Venerate, Worship

Adorn(ed), Adornment Attrap, Banderol, Bedeck, Bedight, Bejewel, Caparison, Clinquant, Deck, Dight, Drape, Embellish, Emblaze, Emblazon, Embroider, Enchase, Equip, Festoon, Flourish, Furnish, Garnish, Grace, Graste, Ornament, Riband, Tattoo, Tatu, Tinsel, Trappings

Adrenaline Epinephrin(e)

Adroit Adept, Clever, Dextrous, Expert, Skilful

Adulate, Adulation Flatter(y), Praise, > **WORSHIP**

Adullam Cave

Adult Amadoda, Consenting, Grown-up, Man, Mature, Upgrown, X

Adulterant, Adulterate Cut, Debase, Impurify, Lime, Mix, Multum, > **POLLUTE**, Sophisticate, Weaken

Adulterer, Adultery Avoutery, Cuckold, Fornication, Francesca, Lenocinium

Advance(d) A, Abord, Accelerate, Anabasis, Ante, Approach, Assert, Charge, Develop, Extreme, Fore, Forge, Forward, Gain, Get on, Grubstake, Haut(e), Impress, Imprest, Incede, Late, Lend, > **LOAN**, March, Mortgage, On(ward), Overture, Pass, Piaffe, Posit, Postulate, Precocious, Prefer, Prest, Process, Progress, > **PROMOTE**, Propose, Propound, Ripe, Rise, Scoop, Sub, Submit, Tiptoe, Voorskot

Advantage(ous) Accrual, Aid, > **ASSET**, Avail, Batten, Benefit, Bisque, Boot, Edge, Emolument, Expedient, Exploit, Favour, Fruit, Gain, Grouter, Handicap, Handle, Head-start, Help, Interess, Interest, Lever(age), Odds, One-up, Pecuniary, Percentage, Plus, Privilege, Prize, Pro, Purchase, Salutary, Strength, Toe-hold, Upper-hand, Upside, Use, Van, Whiphand, Whipsaw

Advent(ist) Coming, Shaker

Adventure(r), Adventuress Argonaut, Assay, Aunter, Buccaneer, Casanova, Conquistador, Emprise, Enterprise, Escapade, > **EXPLOIT**, Filibuster, Gest, Lark, Mata Hari, Mercenary, Merchant, Picaresque, Picaro, Picaroon, Risk, Routier, Rutter, Swashbuckler, Vamp, Voyage

Adversary Antagonist, Cope(s)mate, Enemy, Foe

Adverse, Adversity Calamity, Cross, Down, Harrow, Misery, Reversal, Setback, Untoward, Woe

Advert(ise), Advertisement, Advertising Ad, Air, Allude, Bark, Bill, Blipvert, Circular, Classified, Coign(e), Coin, Commercial, Copy, Display, Dodger, Flier, Flyer, Flyposting, Flysheet, Hype, Infomercial, Jingle, Madison Avenue, Mailshot, Niche, Noise, > **NOTICE**, Packshot, Parade, Placard, Plug, > **POSTER**, Promo, Promote, Promulgate, Prospectus, Puff, Quoin, Refer, Semisolus, Sky-write, Splash, Spot, Stunt, Subliminal, Teaser, Tele-, Throwaway, Tout, Trailer, Trawl, Want(s) (ad)

Advice Conseil, Counsel, > **GUIDANCE**, Guideline, Information, Invoice, Opinion, Read, Recommendation, Re(e)de

Advise(d), Adviser, Advisable Acquaint, CAB, Cabal, Camarilla, Counsel, Egeria, Enlighten, Expedient, Genro, Induna, Inform, Instruct, Mentor, Oracle, Peritus, Politic, Prudent, > **RECOMMEND**, Tutor, Urge, Wise

Advocate(d) Agent, Argue, Attorney, Back, Counsel, Devil's, Exponent, Gospel, Lawyer, Move, Paraclete, Peat, Peddle, Pleader, Pragmatist, Preach, Proponent, Syndic, Urge

Aerial Aeolian, Aery, Antenna, Beam, Clover, Dipole, Dish, Ethereal, Ferriterod, Folded dipole, Frame, Ground plane, Long-wire, Loop, Parabolic, Rhombic, Satellite dish, Slot, Yagi

Aerobatics Stunt

Aerobics Pilates

▶ **Aeroplane** *see* AIRCRAFT

Aerosol Atomiser, Mace®

Aesir Loki

Aesthetic Arty, Tasteful

Affable Amiable, Avuncular, Benign, Suave, Urbane

Affair(s) Amour, Business, Concern, Current, Effeir, Effere, Event, External, Fight, Foreign, Go, Indaba, Internal, Intrigue, Matter, Pash, Pi(d)geon, Pidgin, Ploy, Relationship, Res, Romance, Shebang, Subject, Thing

Affect(ed), Affectation, Affection(ate) Air, Airtsy-mairtsy, Alter, Breast, Camp, Chi-chi, Concern, Crazy, Endearment, Euphuism, Foppery, Hit, Impress, Ladida, Lovey-dovey, Mimmick, Minauderie, Mincing, Minnick, Minnock, Mouth-made, Phoney, > POSE, Poseur, Precieuse, Preciosity, Pretence, Prick-me-dainty, Smitten, Spoilt, Stag(e)y, Storge, Susceptible, Sway, Sympathetic, Tender, Twee, Unction, Unnatural, Upend

Affiliate, Affiliation Adopt, Associate, Merge, Unite

Affinity Bro, Kin(ship), Penchant, Rapport, Tie

Affirm(ative), Affirmation Assert, Attest, Maintain, Predicate, Protestation, Uh-huh, > VERIFY, Yebo

Affix(ed) Append, Ascribe, > ATTACH, Connect, Fasten, On

Afflict(ed), Affliction Ail, Asthma, Cross, Cup, Curse, Disease, Furnace, Harass, Hurt, Lumbago, Molest, Nosology, Palsy, Persecute, Pester, Plague, Scourge, Smit, Sore, > SORROW, Stricken, Teen, Tene, Tic, Tribulation, > TROUBLE, Unweal, Visitation, Woe

Affluence, Affluent Abundance, Dinky, Fortune, Opulence, Wealth

Afford Allow, Bear, Give, Manage, Offer, Provide, Spare, Yield

Affray Brawl, Fight, Mêlée, Scuffle, Skirmish

Affront Assault, Defy, Facer, > INSULT, > OFFEND, Outrage, Scandal, Slight, Slur

Afghan(istan) Bactria, Dard, Hound, Kaf(f)ir, Pakhto, Pakhtu, Pashto, Pashtu, Pathan, Pushto(o), Pushtu

Afloat Aboard, Abroach, Adrift, Natant

Afoot Astir, Up

Aforesaid Above, Same

Afraid Adrad, Alarmed, Chicken, Fearful, Funk, Rad, Regretful, Scared, Timorous, Windy, Yellow

Africa(n) Abyssinian, Akan, Angolan, Ashanti, Baganda, Bambara, Bantu, Barbary, Barotse, Basotho, Basuto, Beento, Bemba, Beninese, Berber, Biafran, Bintu, Black, Boer, Botswana, Cairene, Carthaginian, Chewa, Chichewa, Congo(l)ese, Cushitic, Damara, Dinka, Duala, Dyula, Efik, Eritrean, Ethiopian, Eve, Fang, Fanti, Fingo, Flytaal, Fula(h), Gabonese, Galla, Gambian, Ganda, Gazankulu, Grikwa, Griqua, Gullah, Hamite, Hausa, Herero, Hottentot, Hutu, Ibibi, Ibo, Igbo, Impi, Kabyle, Kaffer, Kaf(f)ir, Kenyan, Khoikhoi, Kikuyu, Kongo, Lango, Lesotho, Liberian, Libyan, Lowveld, Lozi, Luba, Luo, Maghreb, Maghrib, Malawi, Malian, Malinke, Mande, Mandingo, Masai, Mashona, Matabele, Mende, Moor, Moroccan, Mossi, Mozambican, Mswahili,

Munt(u), Mzee, Nama, Nama(qua), Namibian, Negrillo, > **NEGRO**, Nguni, Nilot(e), Nubian, Nuer, Nyanja, Oromo, Ovambo, Pedi, Pied noir, Pondo, Rastafarian, Rhodesian, San, Shilluk, Shluh, Shona, Shono, Somali, Songhai, Sotho, Soweto, Sudanese, Susu, Swahili, Swazi, Temne, Tiv, Tonga, Transkei, Transvaal, Tshi, Tsonga, Tswana, Tuareg, Tutsi, Twi, Ugandan, Venda, Voltaic, Waswahili, Wolof, X(h)osa , Yoruban, Zairean, Zulu

Afrikaan(s), **Afrikaner** Crunchie, Hairyback, Mynheer, Taal, Volk, Voortrekker

After(wards) About, A la, At, Behind, Beyond, Eft, Epi-, > **LATER**, On, Once, Past, Rear, Since, Sine, Subsequent

Afterbirth Secundines, Sooterkin

▷ **After injury** *may indicate* an anagram

Aftermath Consequence, Fall out, Legacy, Mow(ing), Rawing, Rawn, Rowan, Rowen, Rowing, Sequel(a)

Afternoon A, Arvo, PM, Postmeridian, Undern

Afterpiece, **Afterthought** Addendum, Codicil, Epimetheus, Exode, Footnote, Note, PS, Supplement

Again Afresh, Agen, Anew, Back, Bis, De novo, Ditto, Do, Eft, Eftsoons, Encore, Iterum, More, Moreover, O(v)er, Re-, Recurrence, Reprise, Than, Then

Against A, Anti, Beside, Con, Counter, Gainsayer, Into, Nigh, On, Opposing, To, V, Versus

Agape Feast, Hiant, Ringent, Yawning

Agate Chalcedonyx, Moss, Murr(h)a, Onyx, Ruin

Agave Henequen, Lily, Maenad, Maguey

Age(d), **Ages**, **Aging** Achievement, Ae, Aeon, Aet, Alcheringa, Anno domini, Antique, Archaise, Atomic, Augustan, Azilian, Calpa, Century, Chellean, Coon's, Copper, Cycle, Dark, Day, Doddery, Eld, Elizabethan, Eon, Epact, Epoch(a), Era, Eternity, Generation, Gerontic, Golden, Grey, Heroic, Hoar, Hore, Ice, Information, Iron, Jazz, Jurassic, Kaliyuga, Kalpa, La Tene, Lias, Magdalenian, Maglemosian, Mature, Mental, Middle, Millennium, Neolithic, New, New Stone, Of, Old, Oligocene, Paleolithic, Passé, Periclean, Period, Phanerozoic, Progeria, Reindeer, S(a)eculum, Saros, Senescence, Silver, Solera, Space, Stone, Third, Villanovan, Yellow, Yonks, Yug(a)

Agency, **Agent** Agitator, Ambassador, Art, Bailiff, Barm, Bond, Broker, BSI, Bureau, Catalyst, Cat's paw, Cause, Commis, Complexone, Comprador(e), Consul, Countryside, Crown, Customs, Dating, Delcredere, Developing, Disclosing, Distributor, Doer, Double, Emissary, Environment, Envoy, Enzyme, Escort, Estate, Exciseman, Executor, Factor, Fed, Finger, Flack, Forwarding, Free, G-man, Go-between, Hand, Hirudin, House, Implement, Indian, Influence, Institorial, Instrument, Intermediary, Kinase, Law, Legate, Literary, Magic bullet, Man, Means, Medium, Mercantile, Mole, Mutagen, Narc, Narco, Nerve, Ninja, OO, -or, Order paper, Oxidizing, Parliamentaire, Parliamentary, Patent, Penetration, Pinkerton, Press, Procurator, Proxy, Realtor, Reducing, Rep(resentative), Resident, Reuters, Riot, Road, Runner, Salesman, Secret (service), Setter, Shipping, Sleeper, Solvent, Spy, Syndic, Tass, Teratogen, Third party, Ticket, Training, Travel, UNESCO, Vakeel, Vakil, Virino, Voice, Wetting, Wire service

Agenda Business, Hidden, Programme, Remit, Schedule

Aggie Agnes, Ines, Nessa, Nesta

Aggravate Annoy, Inflame, Irk, Needle, Nettle, Provoke, Try, Vex

Aggregate, **Aggregation** Ballast, Congeries, Detritus, Etaerio, Granulite, Gravel, Omnium, Ore, Sum, Total

Aggression, **Aggressive**, **Aggressor** Arsey, Attack, Belligerent, Bullish, Butch,

Defiant, Enemy, Feisty, Foe, Gungho, Hawk, Invader, In-your-face, Militant, On-setter, Pushing, Rambo, Rampant, Road rage, Shirty, Truculent, Wild

Agile Acrobatic, Deft, Lissom(e), Nifty, Nimble, Quick, Spry, Supple, Swank

Agitate(d), Agitation, Agitator Activist, Ado, Agitprop, Betoss, Boil, Bolshie, Bother, Chartist, Churn, Commotion, Commove, Convulse, Demagogue, Discompose, Distraught, > DISTURB, Doodah, Ebullient, Emotion, Excite, Extremist, Fan, Fantad, Fanteeg, Fantigue, Fantod, Ferment, Firebrand, Flurry, Fluster, Flutter, Fraught, Frenzy, Fuss, Goad, Heat, Hectic, Jabble, Lather, Militant, Panicky, Pedetic, Perturb, Poss, Pother, Rattle, Restless, Rouse, Ruffle, Seethed, Sod, Stir(-up), Swivet, Tailspin, Taking, Tew, Thermal, Tizzy, Toss, Tremor, Trepidation, Trouble, Turmoil, Tweak, Twitchy, Upset, Welter, Whisk, Wrought up, Ytost

▷ **Agitate** *may indicate* an anagram

Agley Awry, Unevenly

Aglow Alight, Tipsy

▶ **Agnes** *see* AGGIE

Agnostic Laodicean

Ago Lang syne

Agog Astir, Athirst, Eager, Keen, Pop-eyed

Agonise, Agony Ache, Anguish, Brood, Dread, Ecstasy, Heartache, > PAIN, Throe(s), Torment, Torture

Agree(ing), Agreed, Agreement Accede, Accept, Accord, Acquiescence, Allow, Amen, Analog(ue), Analogy, Apply, As one, Assent, Assort, Atone, Ausgleich, Aye, Bilateral, Bipartite, Bond, Cartel, Champerty, Chime, Closing, Coincide, Collective, Comart, Community, Compact, Comply, Comport, Concert, Concord(at), Concur, Conform, Congree, Congruent, Consension, Consensus, > CONSENT, Consonant, Contract, Contrahent, Convection, Correspond, Cotton, Covenant, Cushty, Dayton Accords, Deal, Deffo, Deign, Done, Entente, Equate, Escrow, Fadge, Gatt, Gentleman's, Handfast, Harmony, Homologous, Indenture, Jibe, Knock-for-knock, League, Like-minded, Mercosur, National, Net Book, Nod, Nudum pactum, Okay, Pact, Pair, Placet, Plant, Prenuptial, Procedural, Productivity, Rabat(te), Repurchase, Right(o), Right on, Roger, Sanction, Schengen, Service, Side, Sort(ance), Specialty, Sponsion, Square, Standstill, Substantive, Suit, Sweetheart, Sympathy, Synchronise, Synesis, Syntony, Tally, Technology, Threshold, Trade, Treaty, Uh-huh, Union, Unison, Unspoken, Wilco, Yea, Yes

Agreeable Amene, Harmonious, Pleasant, Sapid, Sweet, Well-disposed, Willing, Winsome

Agriculture, Agricultural(ist) Arval, Geoponic, Georgic, Inari, Permaculture, Smallholding, Tull

Aground Ashore, Beached, Sew, Stranded

Ague Dumb

▷ **Ague(ish)** *may indicate* an anagram

Ah Ach, Ay

Ahead Anterior, Before, Foreship, Forward, Frontwards, In store, Onward, Up

Aiblins Perhap, Perhaps, Yibbles

Aid(s), Aide Accessory, Adjutant, Assist, Decca, > DEPUTY, First, Foreign, Galloper, Grant, Hearing, Help, Key, Legal, Lend-lease, Monitor, Optophone, Orthosis, PA, Realia, Relief, Serve, Slim, Subsidy, Subvention, Succour, Support, Teaching, Visual, Yeoman('s) service

Ail(ment) Affect, Afflict(ion), Complaint, Croup, Disease, Malady, Narks, Pink-eye, Pip, Sickness

Aim Approach, Aspire, Bead, Bend, End, Ettle, Eye, Goal, Hub, Intent, Level, Mark, Mission, Object, Plan, Plank, Point, Purpose, Reason, Sake, Seek, Sight(s), Target, Tee, Telos, Train, View, Visie, Vizy, Vizzie, Zero-in

Aimless Adrift, Drifting, Erratic, Haphazard, Random, Unmotivated

Air(s), **Airer**, **Airy** Aerate, Aerial, Aero, Allure, Ambiance, Ambience, Aquarius, Arietta, Atmosphere, Attitude, Aura, Bearing, Calypso, Canzona, Canzone, Cavatina, Compressed, Dead, Demaine, Descant, Ditty, Draught, Dry, Emphysema, Ether(eal), Expose, Fan, Filmy, Front, Gemini, Heaven, Horse, Inflate, Libra, Lift, Light, Liquid, Look, Lullaby, Madrigal, Manner, Melody, Mien, Nitre, Oat, Open, Ozone, Parade, Periptery, Pneumatic, Radio, Screen, Scuba, Serenade, Serenata, Serene, Shanty, Side, Sky, Slipstream, Solo, Song, Strain, Swank, Thin, Trigon, > TUNE, Vent, Ventilate, Vital, Wake, Wind

Airborne Ab

Air-conditioning Plenum system

Aircraft, **Airship** Aerodyne, Aerostat, Angels, AST, Auster, Autoflare, Autogiro, Autogyro, Aviette, Avion, Biplane, Blimp, Brabazon, Bronco, Camel, Canard, Canberra, Chaser, Chopper, Coleopter, Comet, Concorde, Convertiplane, Corsair, Crate, Cropduster, Cyclogiro, Delta-wing, Dirigible, Doodlebug, Drone, Eagle, F, Ferret, Fixed-wing, Flying wing, Fokker, Freedom-fighter, Freighter, Galaxy, Glider, Gotha, Gyrodyne, Gyroplane, Hang-glider, Harrier, Hawkeeze, Heinkel, Helicopter, Hercules, Hunter, Hurricane, Interceptor, Intruder, Jet star, Jumbo, Jump-jet, Kite, Lancaster, Liberator, Lifting-body, Messerschmitt, Microlight, Microlite, MIG, Mirage, Monoplane, Mosquito, Moth, Multiplane, Nightfighter, Nightfinder, Oerlikon, Orion, Ornithopter, Orthopter, Parasol, Penguin, Phantom, > PLANE, Provider, Prowler, Ramjet, Rigid, Rotaplane, Runabout, Scramjet, Semi-rigid, Skyhawk, Sopwith, Sopwith Camel, Spitfire, SST, Starfighter, Starlifter, Stealth bomber, STOL, Stratocruiser, Stratotanker, Stuka, Super Sabre, Sweptwing, Swing-wing, Tankbuster, Taube, Taxiplane, Thunderbolt, Thunderchief, Tomcat, Tornado, Tracker, Trident, Tri-jet, Triplane, Tube, Turbo-jet, Turbo-prop, Turboramjet, Vigilante, Viking, Viscount, Voodoo, VTOL, Wild weasel, Zeppelin

Aircraftsman, **Airman** AC, Aeronaut, Erk, Fokker, Kiwi, LAC, RAF

Aircraftswoman Penguin, Pinguin

▶ **Airfield** *see* AIRPORT

Air force Luftwaffe

Airlift Thermal

Airline, **Airway** Aeroflot, Anthem, BAC, BEA, Duct, Larynx, Lot, Lyric, Qantas, SAS, S(ch)norkel, TWA, Weasand(-pipe), Windpipe

▶ **Airman** *see* AIRCRAFTSMAN, FLIER

Airport Drome, Entebbe, Faro, Gander, Gatwick, Heliport, Idlewild, Kennedy, Landing strip, Lod, Luton, Lydda, Lympne, Orly, Prestwick, Runway, Shannon, Stansted, Stolport, Vertiport, Wick

Air-raid Blitz, Mission

Air-tight Hermetic, Indisputable, Sealed

Aisle Gangway

Aitch Ache, Aspirate, H

Ajax Loo

Aka Alias

Akin Alike, Cognate, Congener, Kindred

Alarm Alert, Arouse, Bell, Bleep, Caution, Concern, Dismay, Eek, False, Fire, Fricht, Fright, Ghast, Larum, Panic, Perturb, Rock, Rouse, Siren, Smoke, Startle, Tirrit, Tocsin, Warn, Yike(s)

Alas Ah, Alack, Ay, Eheu, Ha, Haro, Harrow, Io, Lackadaisy, Lackaday, O, Oh, Ohone, O me, Ou, Sadly, Waesucks, Waly, Well-a-day, Wellanear, Wel(l)away, Woe

Alaskan AK, Sourdough

Alban Berg

Albanian Arna(o)ut

Albatross Alcatras, Golf, Gooney(-bird), Omen, Onus, Wandering

Albeit Tho(ugh)

Albert Chain, Chevalier, Consort, Hall, Herring, Slang

Album Autograph, Looseleaf, Photo, Record, Stamp

Albumen, Albumin Chalaza, Glair, Leucosin, Mucin, Myogen, Protein, Ricin, Serum, White

Alchemic, Alchemist, Alchemy Adept, Brimstone, Faust(us), Hermetic(s), Multiplier, Orpiment, Paracelsus, Quicksilver, Sal ammoniac, Sorcery, Spagyric, Spagyrist, Witchcraft

Alcides Hercules

Alcohol(ic) Absolute, Acrolein, Aldehyde, Amyl, Bibulous, Booze, Borneol, Catechol, Cetyl, Chaptalise, Cholesterol, Choline, Citronellol, Cresol, Denatured, Diol, Dipsomaniac, Drinker, Ethal, Ethanol, Ethyl, Farnesol, Feni, Fenny, Firewater, Fusel-oil, Geraniol, Glycerin(e), Grain, Hard, Hard stuff, Inebriate, Inositol, Isopropyl, Jungle juice, Lauryl, Linalool, Lush, Mahua, Mahwa, Mannite, Mannitol, Mercaptan, Mescal, Methanol, Meths, Methyl, Mow(r)a, Nerol, Phytol, Plonko, Propyl, Rotgut, Rubbing, Rubby, Secondary, Snake juice, Sorbitol, Sphingosine, Spirits, Spirits of wine, Spirituous, Sterol, Terpineol, Tincture, Tocapherol, Triol, Wino, Wood, Xylitol

Alcove Apse, Bay, Bole, Carrel(l), Dinette, Inglenook, Lunette, Niche, Recess, Tokonoma

Alcyonarian Sea-feather

Aldehyde Acrolein, Aldol

Alder Fothergilla

Alderman Bail(l)ie, CA

Alderney CI, Cow

Ale, Alehouse Audit, Barleybree, Barley wine, Beer, Church, Four, Heather, Humpty-dumpty, Lamb's wool, Light, Morocco, Nappy, Nog, Nogg, October, Pale, Plain, Purl, Real, Small, Stout, Swats, Tiddleywink, Tipper, White, Whitsun, Wort, Yard, Yill, Yorkshire stingo

Alert Arrect, Astir, Attentive, Aware, Gleg, Gogo, Intelligent, Open-eyed, Qui vive, Red, Scramble, Sharp, Sprack, Sprag, Stand-to, Vigilant, Volable, Wary, Watchful, Wide-awake

Alewife Barkeeper, Gaspereau

Alexander, Alexandrine Alex, Arius, Macedonian, Pope, Sandy, Sasha, Sawn(e)y, Selkirk, Senarius

Alfalfa Lucern(e), Luzern

Alfred Dreyfus, Garnet, Jingle

Alfresco Barbecue, Plein-air

Alga(e) Anabaena, Blanketweed, Chlorella, Conferva, Desmid, Diatom, Dulse, Heterocontae, Isokont, Jelly, Nostoc, Periphyton, Phycology, Pleuston, Pond scum, Prokaryon, Protococcus, Red, Seaweed, Spirogyra, Star-jelly, Stonewort, Ulothrix, Ulotrichales, Valonia, Volvox, Witches' butter, Zooxanthella

Algebra Boolean, Linear, Quadratics

Algerian Kabyle, Nimidian

Algonquin Innu

Alias Aka, Epithet, Moni(c)ker, Pen-name, Pseudonym

Alibi Excuse, Watertight

Alien(ate), **Alienation** A-effect, Amortise, Disaffect, Ecstasy, Estrange, ET, Exotic, External, Foreign, Forinsecal, Fremd, Hostile, Martian, Metic, Outlandish, Outsider, Philistine, Repugnant, Strange(r)

Alight Alowe, Availe, Detrain, Disembark, Dismount, In, Lambent, Land, Lit, Perch, Pitch, Rest, Settle

Align Arrange, Associate, Collimate, Dress, Juxtapose, Marshal, Orient, Straighten

▸ **Alike** *see* LIKE

Aliquot Submultiple

Alive Alert, Animated, Breathing, Extant, Quick

Alkali(ne), **Alkaloid** Antacid, Apomorphine, Atropine, Base, Bebeerine, Berberine, Betaine, Borax, Brucine, Capsaicin, Choline, Cinchon(id)ine, Codeine, Colchicine, Corydaline, Emetin(e), Ephedrine, Gelsemin(in)e, Guanidine, Harmaline, Harmin(e), Hyoscine, Lixivium, Lobeline, Lye, Mescalin, Narceen, Narceine, Nicotine, Papaverine, Pilocarpin, Piperine, Potash, Potass, Quinine, Reserpine, Rhoeadine, Scopolamine, Soda, Solanine, Sparteine, Thebaine, Theobromine, Theophylline, Tropine, Veratridine, Veratrin(e), Vinblastine, Vinca, Vincristine, Volatile, Yohimbine

Alkane Hexane

All A, > ENTIRE, Entity, Finis, Omni, Pan, Quite, Sum, > TOTAL, Toto, Tutti, Whole

Allah Bismillah, God

Allay Alleviate, Calm, Disarm, Lessen, Quieten, Soothe

Allegation, **Allege** Accuse, Assert, Aver, Claim, Obtend, Plead, Purport, Represent, Smear

Allegiance Faith, Foy, Loyalty

Allegory, **Allegorical** Apologue, Fable, Mystic, Myth, Parable

Allergy Atopy, Aversion, Bagassosis, Hay fever, Hives

Alleviate Allay, Allege, Calm, Mitigate, Mollify, Palliate, > RELIEVE, Temper

Alley Aisle, Blind, Bonce, Bowling, Corridor, Ennog, Ginnel, Lane, Laura, Marble, Passage, Silicon, Tin Pan, Twitten, Vennel, Walk, Wynd

Alliance Agnation, Axis, Bloc, Cartel, Coalition, Combine, Compact, Confederation, Dreibund, Dual, Federacy, > LEAGUE, Marriage, NATO, Quadruple, Syndicate, Triple, Union

Alligator Al(l)igarta, Avocado, Cayman

Alliteration Head-rhyme

Allocate, **Allocation** Allot, Apportion(ment), Assign, Designate, Earmark, Placement, Priorate, Ration, Share, Zone

Allot(ment), **Allow(ance)**, **Allowed**, **Allowing** Admit, Affect, Alimony, Allocation, Although, Aret(t), Assign, Award, Batta, Beteem(e), Budget, Charter, Cloff, Confess, Cor(r)ody, Diet, Discount, Dole, Enable, Entitle, Excuse, Expenses, Feod, Give, Grant, House-bote, Husbandage, Indulge, Jobseekers', Latitude, Legit(imate), Let, Licit, Luit(en), Machining, Mag, Mobility, Okay, Palimony, Parcel, Pension, Percentage, > PERMIT, Personal, Pittance, Plot, Portion, Quarterage, Quota, Ratio, Ration, Rebate, Rood, Salt-money, Sanction, Separation, Sequel, Share(-out), Shrinkage, Sizings, Stint, Stipend, Subsistence, Suffer, Tare, Tax, Teene, Though, Tolerance, Tolerate, Tret, Weighting, Yield

Allotment-holder Cleruch

▸ **Allow** *see* ALLOT

Alloy Albata, Alnico®, Amalgam, Babbit, Bell-metal, Billon, Brass, Britannia

metal, Bronze, Cermet, Chrome(l), Compound, Constantan, Cupronickel, Duralumin®, Electron, Electrum, Eutectoid, Ferrochrome, Gunmetal, Invar®, Iridosmine, Kamacite, Latten, Magnalium, Magnox, Manganin®, Marmem, Mischmetal, Mix, Monel®, Nichrome®, Nickel-silver, Nicrosilal, Nimonic, Nitinol, Occamy, Oreide, Orichalc, Ormolu, Oroide, Osmiridium, Paktong, Pewter, Pinchbeck, Platinoid, Porous, Potin, Pot metal, Prince's metal, Shakudo, Shibuichi, Similor, Solder, Spelter, Steel, Stellite®, Tambac, Terne, Tombac, Tombak, Tutenag, Zircal(l)oy, Zircoloy
▷ **Alloy** *may indicate* an anagram
Allright A1, Assuredly, Fit, Hale, Hunky(-dory), Jake, OK, Safe, Tickety-boo, Well
All-round Overhead, Versatile
All-seeing Panoptic
Allspice Jamaica pepper, Pimiento
Allude, **Allusion** Hint, Imply, Innuendo, Mention, Refer, Reference, Suggest
Allure, **Alluring** Agaçant(e), Charm, Circe, Decoy, Entice, Femme fatale, Glam, Glamour, Inviting, Magnet(ic), SA, Seduce, Seductive, Tempt, Trap, Trepan, Vamp
Ally, **Allied** Accomplice, Agnate, Aide, Alley, Alliance, Backer, Belamy, Cognate, Colleague, Dual, German(e), Holy, Marble, Marmoreal, Partner, Plonker, Related, Taw, Unholy
Almanac Calendar, Clog, Ephemeris, Nautical, Nostradamus, Whitaker's, Wisden, Zadkiel
Almighty Creator, Dollar, God, Jehovah, Omnipotent
Almond Amygdal, Emulsion, Jordan, Marchpane, Marzipan, Orgeat, Praline, Ratafia, Sugared, Valencia
Almost Anear, Anigh, Most, Near, Nigh(ly), Practically, Ripe, Une(a)th, Virtually, Well-nigh, Welly
Alms Awmous, Charity, Dole, Handout, Zakat
Aloe Agave, Pita
Alone Hat, Jack, Lee-lane, Onely, Pat, Secco, Separate, Single, Singly, Sola, Solo, Solus, Tod, Unaccompanied, Unaided, Unattended, Unholpen
Along, **Alongside** Abeam, Aboard, Abreast, Apposed, Beside, By, Parallel
Aloof Abeigh, Apart, Asocial, Cool, Detached, Distant, Hou inch, Indrawn, Mugwump, Offish, Remote, Reserved, Reticent, Skeigh, Snooty, Stand-offish, Toffee-nosed, Unapproachable
Alpaca Paco
Alphabet ABC, Black-out, Brahmi, Braille, Cyrillic, Deaf, Devanagari, Estrang(h)elo, Futhark, Futhorc, Futhork, Glagol, Glagolitic, Glossic, Grantha, Hangul, Horn-book, International, ITA, Kana, Kanji, Katakana, Kufic, Latin, Manual, Nagari, Og(h)am, Pangram, Phonetic, Pinyin, Romaji, Roman, Runic, Signary, Syllabary
Alpine, **Alps** Australian, Bernese, Cottian, Dinaric, Gentian, Graian, Julian, Laburnum, Lepontine, Maritime, Matterhorn, Pennine, Rhaetian, Savoy, Southern, Transylvanian, Tyrol
Also Add, And, Eke, Item, Likewise, Moreover, Too, Und
Altar, **Altar-cloth**, **Altarpiece** Butsudan, Dossal, Dossel, High, Polyptych, Retable, Shrine, Tabula
Alter Adapt, Adjust, Bushel, Change, Cook, Correct, Customise, Distort, Evolve, Falsify, Lib, Modify, Modulate, Mutate, Recast, Revise, Transpose, Up-end,
> VARY
Altercation Barney, Brawl, Fracas, Row, Words, Wrangle
Alternate, **Alternating**, **Alternation**, **Alternative** Boustrophedon, Bypass,

Exchange, Instead, Metagenesis, > OPTION, Ossia, Other, Rotate, Second string, Solidus, Staggered, Systaltic, Tertian, Variant

▷ **Alter(native)** *may indicate* an anagram

▷ **Alternately** *may indicate* every other letter

Althaea Mallow, Malva

Although Admitting, Albe(e), All-be, But, Even, Howsoever, Howsomever, Whereas, While

Altitude Elevation, Height

Alto Countertenor

Altogether Algate(s), All-to-one, Completely, Entirely, Holus-bolus, Idea, In all, Nude, Nudity, Purely, Slick, Tout, Uncut, Wholly

▷ **Altogether** *may indicate* words to be joined

Altruistic Heroic, Humane, Philanthropic, Selfless, Unselfish

Alum Potash

Aluminium, **Alumino-silicate** Al, Bauxite, Sillimanite, Stilbite

Alumnus Graduate, OB

Always Algate(s), Ay(e), Constant, E'er, Eternal, Ever(more), Forever, I, Immer, Semper, Sempre, Still

Amalgamate Coalesce, Consolidate, Fuse, Merge, Unite

Amalthea Cornucopia

Amarylli(d)s Leocojum, Lily, Polianthes

Amass Accumulate, Assemble, Collect, Heap, Hoard, Pile, Upheap

Amateur(s) A, AA, Armchair, Beginner, Corinthian, Dilettante, Diy, Enthusiast, Ham, Inexpert, L, Laic, Lay, Neophyte, Novice, Sunday painter, Tiro, Tyro

Amatory Eros, Erotic, Fervent

Amaze(d), **Amazement**, **Amazing** Astonish, Astound, Awe, Awhape, Cor, Criv(v)ens, Dumbfound, Far out, Flabbergast, Gee-whiz, Gobsmack, Goodnow, Grace, Incredible, Jesus wept, Magical, Monumental, O, Open-eyed, Open-mouthed, Perplex, Poleaxe, Pop-eyed, Stagger, Stupefaction, Stupendous, Thunderstruck

Amazon Ant, ATS, Brimstone, Britannia, Dragon, Hippolyta, Orellana, Penthesilea, Thalestris, Tupi, Virago

Ambassador Diplomat, Elchee, Elchi, Eltchi, Envoy, HE, Internuncio, Leaguer, Ledger, Legate, Leiger, Minister, Nuncio, Plenipo, Plenipotentiary

Amber Colophony, Lammer, Ligure, Resin, Retinite, Succinum

Ambience Aura, Milieu, Setting

Ambiguous, **Ambiguity** Amphibology, Cryptic, Delphic, Double, Double entendre, Enigmatic, Epicene, Equivocal, Loophole, Weasel words

Ambition, **Ambitious** Aim, Arrivisme, Aspiring, Careerism, Drive, Emulate, Goal, Go-getter, High-flier, Keen, Office-hunter, Purpose, Pushy, Rome-runner

Amble Meander, Mosey, Pace, Poddle, Saunter, Stroll

Ambrose Emrys

Ambrosia(l) Beebread, Fragrant, Odorant, Ragweed, Savoury

Ambulance, **Ambulanceman** Blood-wagon, Field, Pannier, Paramedic, Van, Yellow-flag, Zambu(c)k

Ambulatory Stoa

Ambush(ed) Ambuscade, Bushwhack, Embusque, Latitant, Lurch, Perdu(e), Trap, Waylay

Amelia Bloomer

Ameliorate Amend, Ease, Improve, Remedy

Amen Ammon, Approval, Inshallah, Verify

Amenable Putty

Amend(ment) Alter, Change, Expiate, Expurgate, Fifth, Redress, Reform, Repair, Restore, > REVISE, Satisfy

▷ **Amend** *may indicate* an anagram

Ament Catkin, Idiot

America(n) Algonki(a)n, Algonqu(i)an, Am, Caddo, Cajun, Carib, Chicano, Chickasaw, Copperskin, Digger, Doughface, Down-easter, Federalist, Flathead, Fox, Gringo, Interior, Joe, Jonathan, Latino, Mistec, Mixtec, Native, Norteno, Olmec, Paisano, Salish, Stateside, Statesman, Statist, Tar-heel, Tico, Tupi, Uncle Sam, US(A), WASP, Yankee, Yanqui

Americium Am

Amiable Friendly, Genial, Gentle, Inquiline, Sweet, Warm

Amid(st) Among, Atween, Between, Inter, Twixt

Amide Asparagine

Amino-acid Dopa, Tyrosine, Valine

Amiss Awry, Ill, Up, Wrong

Ammonia(c) Amide, Amine, Choline, Ethylamine, Hartshorn, Oshac

Ammonite Serpent-stone

Ammunition Ammo, Bandoleer, Bandolier, Buckshot, Bullets, Chain-shot, Dum-dum, Grape(shot), Grenade, Round, Shot, Slug, Tracer

Amnesia Fugal, Fugue, Lethe, Retrograde

Amnesty Oblivion

Amoeba Melboean

Amok Rampaging

Among Amid(st), In, Within

Amorous(ly) Casanova, Erotic, Fervent, Lustful, Smickly, Spoony, Warm

Amorphous Formless, Shapeless, Vague

Amount Come, Dose, Element, Figure, Lashings, Levy, Lot, Number, Ocean, Pot(s), Premium, Price, Quantity, Quantum, Span, Stint, Throughput, Volume, Whale, Wheel

Amour Affair(e), Intrigue, Love

Ampersand Tironian sign

Amphetamine Benny, Benzedrine, Speed

Amphibian, Amphibious Amb(l)ystoma, Amtrack, Anura, Axolotl, Batrachian, Caecilia, Caecilian, Desman, Eft, Frog, Guana, Hassar, Labyrinthodont, Mermaid, Mudpuppy, Newt, Olm, Proteus, Rana, Salamander, Salientia, Seal, Tadpole, Toad, Urodela(n), Urodele, Weasel

Amphipod Sand-screw, Shrimp

Amphitheatre Bowl, Circus Maximus, Coliseum, Colosseum, Ring, Stage

Ample Bellyful, Copious, Enough, Generous, Good, Large, Opulent, Profuse, Rich, Roomy, Round, Uberous, Voluminous

Amplifier, Amplify Booster, Double, Eke, Enlarge, Hailer, Laser, Loud hailer, Maser, Megaphone, Push-pull, Solion, Tannoy®, Transistor, Treble

Amulet Abraxas, Charm, Churinga, Fetish, Greegree, Grigri, Grisgris, Haemon, Pentacle, Periapt, Phylactery, Sea-bean, Talisman, Tiki, Toadstone, Token

Amuse(ment), Amusing(ly) Caution, Cottabus, Disport, Diversion, Divert, Divertimento, Divertissement, Drole, Droll, Game, Gas, Giocoso, Glee, Hoot, Killing, Levity, Light, Occupy, Pleasure, Popjoy, Priceless, Regale, Rich, Scream, Slay, Solace, > SPORT, Tickle, Titillate, Wacky

Amy Johnson, Robsart

▶ **An** *see* A

Ana(s) Story, Teal

Anabaptist Abecedarian, Dipper, Dopper, Hutterite, Knipperdolling

Anableps Four-eyes
Anachronism Archaism, Solecism
Anaconda Water boa
Anacreon Te(i)an
Anaemia Aplastic, Cooley's, Favism, Haemolytic, Megaloblastic, Pernicious, Sickle-cell, Thalassaemia
Anaesthetic, Anaesthetise, Anaesthetist Analgesic, Avertin®, Benzocaine, Bupivacaine, Caudal, Chloroform, Cocaine, Endotracheal, Epidural, Ether, Eucain(e), Freeze, Gas, General, Halothane, Infiltrate, Intravenous, Jabber, Ketamine, Lidocaine, Lignocaine, Local, Metopryl, Morphia, Novocaine, Number, Opium, Orthocaine, Pentothal, Procaine, Rhigolene, Special K, Spinal, Stovaine, Topical, Trike, Urethan(e)
Anagram Jumble
Anal Proctal, Tewel
Analgesic Aspirin, Bute, Codeine, Disprin, Ketamine, Menthol, Methadone, Morphia, Moxa, Painkiller, Pethidine, Phencyclidine, Quina, Salicin(e), Sedative
Analogous, Analogy Akin, Corresponding, Like, Parallel, Similar
Analyse(r), Analysis Alligate, Anagoge, Anatomy, Assess, Breakdown, Construe, Diagnosis, Emic, Eudiometer, Examine, Explication, Factor, Force-field, Fourier, Gravimetric, Harmonic, Input-output, Job, Kicksorter, Miscue, Parse, Pollen, Process, Psych out, Qualitative, Quantative, Quantitative, Risk, Rundown, Scan(sion), Semantics, Sift, Spectral, Spectroscopic, Spectrum, Systems, Test, Transactional, Volumetric
▷ **Analysis** *may indicate* an anagram
Analyst Alienist, Investment, Jung, Psychiatrist, Shrink, Trick cyclist
Anarchist, Anarchy Black Hand, Bolshevist, Chaos, Kropotkin, Nihilism, Provo, Rebel, Revolutionary, Trotskyite
Anathema Ban, Curse, Execration, Oath, Warling
Anatole, Anatolian France, Hittite
Anatomy, Anatomist Bones, Framework, Herophilus, Histology, Morbid, Worm
Ancestor, Ancestral, Ancestry Adam, Avital, Descent, Extraction, For(e)bear, Forefather, Gastraea, Humanoid, Lin(e)age, Parent, Predecessor, Proband, Profectitious, Progenitor, Propositus, Roots, Sire, Tipuna, Tree, Tupina
Anchor(age) Atrip, Bower, Cell, Deadman, Drag, Drift, Drogue, Eremite, Grapnel, Hawse, Hermit, Kedge, Kedger, Killick, Killock, Laura, Moor, Mud-hook, Mushroom, Nail, Ride, Roads(tead), Rode, Root, Scapa Flow, Sea, Sheet, Spithead, Stock, Stream, Toehold, Waist, Weather
Anchorite Recluse
Anchovy Fish, Pear
Ancient Antediluvian, Archaic, Auld-warld, Bygone, Early, Gonfanoner, Historic, Hoary, Iago, Immemorial, Lights, Neolithic, Ogygian, > OLD(ER), Old-world, Primeval, Primitive, Pristine, Ur, Veteran
Ancient city Carthage, Ur
Ancillary Adjunct, Secondary, Subservient
And Als(o), Ampassy, Ampersand, Amperzand, Ampussyand, Besides, Et, Furthermore, Item, 'n', Plus, Tironian sign, Und
Andalusite Macle
Andiron Chenet, Dog, Firedog
Andrew(es) Aguecheek, Lancelot, Merry
Androgynous Epicene

Android Automaton, Golem, Robot
Anecdote(s) Ana, Exemplum, Story, Tale, Yarn
Anemometer Wind-sleeve, Windsock
Anemone Actinia, Pasque-flower, Windflower
Angel(s) Abdiel, Adramelech, Apollyon, Archangel, Ariel, Arioch, Asmadai, Azrael, Backer, Banker, Beelzebub, Belial, Benefactor, Cake, Cherub, Clare, Destroying, Deva, Dominion, Dust, Eblis, Falls, Fuzzy-wuzzy, Gabriel, Guardian, Hierarchy, Host, Iblis, Investor, Israfel, Ithuriel, Lucifer, Michael, Power, Principality, Raphael, Recording, Rimmon, Seraph, Spirit, St, Throne, Uriel, Uzziel, Virtue, Watcher, Zadkiel, Zephiel
Angela Brazil
Angel's wings Begonia
Anger, Angry > ANNOY, Bile, Black, Bristle, Choler(ic), Conniption, Cross, Dander, Displeased, Dudgeon, Enrage, Exasperation, Face, Fury, Gram, Heat, Horn-mad, Incense, Inflame, Infuriate, Iracund, Irascible, Ire, Kippage, Livid, Mad, Monkey, Moody, Nettle, Pique, Provoke, Radge, Rage, Rampant, Ratty, Renfierst, Rile, Roil, Rouse, Sore, Spleen, Steam, Stroppy, Tamping, Tantrum, Tarnation, Teen(e), Temper, Tene, Tooshie, Vex, Vies, Waspish, Waxy, Wound up, Wrath, Wroth, Yond
Angina Sternalgia, Vincent's
Angle(d), Angular Acute, Altitude, Argument, Aspect, Axil, Azimuthal, Canthus, Cast, Catch, Chiliagon, Coign, Complementary, Conjugate, Contrapposto, Corner, Cos, Critical, Deidre, Diedral, Diedre, Dihedral, Elbow, Elevation, Ell, Fish, Fish-hook, Fork, Geometry, Gonion, Hade, Hip, In, L, Laggen, Laggin, Mitre, Oblique, Obtuse, Parallax, Pediculate, Perigon, Piend, Pitch, Plane, Quoin, Radian, Rake, Re-entrant, Reflex, Right, Sally, Sine, Sinical, Solid, Steeve, Steradian, Supplementary, Sweepback, Trotline, Vertical, Viewpoint, Washin, Weather
Angle(r) Attitude, Exterior, Facial, Hour, Hyzer, Interior, Mung, Negative, Peterman, Pitch-cone, Polyhedral, Position, Positive, Rodster, Round, Saltchucker, Spherical, Stalling, Straight, Visual, Walton, Wide-gab
Anglesey Mona
Anglican(s) CE-men, Conformist, Episcopal
Anglo-Catholic High-church
Anglo-Indian Qui-hi, Qui-hye, Topi-wallah
Angora Goat, Mohair, Rabbit
Angst Dread
Anguish(ed) Agony, Distress, Gip, Grief, Gyp, Hag-ridden, Heartache, Misery, > PAIN, Pang, Sorrow, Throes, > TORMENT, Torture, Woe
Angus Aberdeen
Animal(s) Acrita, Anoa, Armadillo, Atoc, Bag, Bandog, Barbastel, Beast, Bestial, Brute, Cariacou, Carnal, Chalicothere, Coati, Creature, Criollo, Critter, Ethology, Fauna, Felis, Gerbil, Herd, Ichneumon, Jacchus, Jerboa, Kinkajou, Klipdas, Mammal, Marmoset, Marmot, Menagerie, Moose, Noctule, Oribi, Pack, Parazoon, Pet, Protozoa, Pudu, Quagga, Rac(c)oon, Rhesus, Sensual, Sloth, Stud, Symphile, Tarsier, Teledu, Urson, Waler, Xenurus, Yapock, Zerda, Zoo
Animal-catcher Utricularia
Animate(d), Animation Activate, Actuate, Arouse, Biophor, Ensoul, Excite, Fire, Hortatory, Hot, Inspire, Live, Morph, Mosso, Pixil(l)ation, Rouse, Spritely, Suspended, Verve, Vivify
Animosity Enmity, Friction, Hostility, Ill-will, Malice, Pique, Rancour

Ankle Coot, Cuit, Cute, Hock, Hucklebone, Knee, Malleolus, Talus
Ankle(t), **Ankle covering** Cootikin, Cuitikin, Cutikin, Gaiter, Jess
Anna, **Anne**, **Annie** Boleyn, Hathaway, Laurie, Oakley, Page, Pavlova, Pice, Sewell, Sister
Annal(s) Acta, Archives, Chronicles, Register
Annatto Roucou
Annex(e) Acquire, Add, Affiliate, Attach, Codicil, Extension, Subjoin
Annihilate Destroy, Erase, Exterminate, Obliterate, Slay
Anniversary Birthday, Feast, Jubilee, Obit, Triennial, Wedding, Yahrzeit
Annotate, **Annotator** Comment, Interpret, Note, Postil, Scholiast
Announce(r), **Announcement** Banns, Bellman, Biil(ing), Blazon, Bulletin, Communiqué, Declare, Decree, Divulgate, Gazette, Herald, Hermes, Inform, Intimate, Meld, Newsflash, Noise, Post, Preconise, Proclaim, Promulgate, Pronunciamente, Publish, Release, > REPORT, Rescript, Speaker(ine), State, Toastmaster, Town crier, Trumpet
Annoy(ance), **Annoyed**, **Annoying** Aggravate, Aggrieve, Anger, Antagonise, Badger, Blight, Bother, Bug, Bugbear, Chagrin, Deuce(d), Disturb, Doggone, Doh, Drat, Fash, Fleabite, Frab, Fumed, Gall, Harass, Hatter, Hector, Hip, Huff, Hump, Humph, Incense, Irk, > IRRITATE, Mickey-taking, Miff, Mischief, Molest, Moryah, Nag, Nark, Nettle, Noisome, Peeve, Pesky, Pester, Pipsqueak, Pique, Rankle, Rats, Ratty, Resentful, Ride, Rile, Roil, Rub, Shirty, Tiresome, Tracasserie, Try, Vex, Wazzock
Annual, **Annuity** Book, Etesian, > FLOWER, Half-hardy, Hardy, Life, Pension, Perpetuity, Rente, Tontine, Yearbook, Yearly
Annul(ment) Abolish, Abrogate, Cashier, Cassation, Dissolution, Irritate, Negate, Recision, Repeal, Rescind, Reversal, Revoke, Vacatur, > VOID
Annular Toric
Anodyne Balm, Narcotic, Paregoric, Sedative
Anoint(ing) Anele, Cerate, Chrism, Embrocate, Grease, Hallow, Nard, Smear
Anomaly Eccentric, Gravity, Magnetic, Mean, True
▷ **Anomaly** *may indicate* an anagram
Anon Again, Anew, Later, Soon
Anonymous Adespota, Anon, A.N.Other, Faceless, Grey, Impersonal, Somebody, Unnamed
Anorak Wonk
Another Extra
Answer(ing), **Answer(s)** Account, Acknowledge, Amoebaean, Ans, Antiphon, Because, Comeback, Crib (sheet), Defence, Echo, Key, Lemon, Light, No, Oracle, Rebuttal, Rebutter, Rein, Rejoin(der), Repartee, Reply, Rescript, Respond, Response, Responsum, Retort, Return, Riposte, Serve, Sol, Solution, Solve, Verdict, Yes
Ant(s), **Anthill** Amazon, Army, Bull(dog), Carpenter, Colony, Driver, Dulosis, Emmet, Ergataner, Ergates, Ergatomorph, Fire, Formic, Formicary, Leafcutter, Legionary, Myrmecoid, Myrmidon, Nasute, Neuter, Pharaoh, Pismire, Sauba, Slave, Soldier, Termite, Thief, Umbrella, Velvet, White, Wood
Antacid Magnesia, Peptic
Antagonist(ic), **Antagonise** Estrange, Oppugnant, Peare, Peer
Antarctica Amelie Land, Graham land, Wilkes Land
Ant-bear Tamanoir
Ante Bet, Punt, Stake
Ant-eater Aardvark, Echidna, Edental, Manis, Numbat, Pangolin, S(e)ladang, Spiny, Tamandu, Tamandua, Tapir

Antelope Addax, Antilope, Blackbuck, Blaubok, Blesbok, Bloubok, Bluebuck, Bongo, Bontebok, Bubal(is), Bushbuck, Cabric, Chamois, Chikara, Chiru, Dikdik, Duiker, Duyker, Dzeren, Eland, Elk, Gazelle, Gemsbok, Gerenuk, Gnu, Goral, Grysbok, Harnessed, Hartbees, Hartebeest, Impala, Inyala, Kaama, Kid, Klipspringer, Kob, Kongoni, Koodoo, Kudu, Lechwe, Madoqua, Marshbuck, Mhorr, Mohr, Nagor, Nilgai, Nilgau, Nyala, Nylghau, Oribi, Oryx, Ourebi, Ox, Pale-buck, Pallah, Prongbuck, Pronghorn, Pronk, Puku, Pygarg, Reebok, Reedbuck, Rhebok, Sable, Saiga, Sasin, Sassaby, Serow, Sitatunga, Situtunga, Springbok, Steenbok, Steinbock, Stemback, Stembok, Suni, Takin, Thar, Topi, Tragelaph, Tsessebe, Waterbuck, Wildebeest

Antenna Aerial, Dipole, Dish, Horn, Sensillum, TVRO

Anterior Anticous, Earlier, Front, Prior

Anthelmintic Worm

Anthem Chant, Hymn, Introit, Isodica, Marseillaise, Motet(t), National, Psalm, Responsory, Song, Star Spangled Banner, Stem, Theme, Tract, Troparion

Anthology Album, Ana, Chrestomathy, Digest, Divan, Florilegium, Garland, Pick, Spicilege

Anthony Absolute, Adverse, Trollope

Anthracite Blind-coal

Anthrax Sang

Anthropo(i)d Peripatus, Sivapithecus

Anthropologist Mead

Anti Against, Agin, Con, Hostile

Anti-aircraft AA

Anti-bacterial, Antibiotic Actinomycin, Amoxicillin, Ampicillin, Aureomycin®, Bacitracin, Bacteriostat, Cephalosporin, Ciprofloxacin, Cloxacillin, Colistin, Cortisone, Co-trimoxazole, Doxorubicin, Doxycycline, Drug, Erythromycin, Gentamicin, Gramicidin, Griseofulvin, Interferon, Interleukin, Kanamycin, Lincomycin, Lineomycin, Methicillin, Mitomycin, Neomycin, Nystatin, Opsonin, Oxacillin, Oxytetracycline, Penicillin, Polymixin, Quinolone, Rifampicin, Rifamycin, Spectinomycin, Streptomycin, Streptothricin, Terramycin®, Tetracycline, Tyrocidine, Tyrothricin, Vancomycin, Wide-spectrum

Antibody Agglutinin, Amboceptor, Antitoxin, Blocker, Hybroid, Isoagglutinin, Lysin, Monoclonal, Opsonin, Precipitin, Reagin

Antic(s) Caper, Dido, Frolic, Gambado, Hay, Prank, Shenanigan, Stunt

Anti-carlist Queenite

Anticipate, Anticipation Antedate, Augur, Await, Drool, > **EXPECT**, Forecast, Foresee, Foresight, Forestall, Foretaste, Hope, Intuition, Prevenancy, Prolepsis, Prospect, Second-guess, Type

Anticlimax Bathos, Damp squib, Deflation, Letdown

Anticline Upwrap

Anticlockwise Dextrorse, Laevorotatory, Widdershins, Withershins

Anticoagulant C(o)umarin, Heparin, Hirudin, Prostacyclin, Warfarin

Anti-Communist McCarthyism

Anticyclone High

Antidote Adder's wort, Alexipharmic, Angelica, Antivenin, Arrowroot, Bezoar, Contrayerva, Cure, Dimercaprol, Emetic, Guaco, Interleukin, Mithridate, Nostrum, Orvietan, Remedy, Ribavirin, Senega, Theriac(a), (Venice)-Treacle

Anti-freeze Glycerol, Lagging

Antigen Hapten(e)

Antihistamine Dimenhydrinate

Anti-imperialist Guelf, Guelph
Antimacassar Tidy
Antimony Kohl, Sb, Stibium
Antioxidant Lycopene
Anti-parliamentarian Poujadist
Antipathy Allergy, Aversion, Detest, > DISLIKE, Enmity, Repugnance
Anti-perfectionist Cobden
Antiphon The Reproaches
Antipodean Abo, Antarctic, Antichthon, Enzed, Underworld
Antipope Novatian(us)
Anti-protectionist Cobden
Antiquated, Antique, Antiquarian Ancient, Archaic, A(u)stringer, Bibelot, Curio, Dryasdust, FAS, Fog(e)y, Fogram(ite), Fossil, Old-fangled, Ostreger, Relic
Anti-reformer Obscurant
Anti-revolutionary White
Anti-Roman Ghibel(l)ine
Anti-royalist Whig
Anti-semitic Pamyat
Antiseptic Acriflavine, Carbolic, Cassareep, Creosote, Disinfectant, Eupad, Eusol, Formaldehyde, Guaiacol, Iodine, Lysol®, Phenol, Sterile, Tar, Thymol, Tutty
Anti-slavery Free-soil, Wilberforce
Anti-smoker ASH, Misocapnic
Antisocial Hostile, Ishmaelitish, Misanthropic
Antithesis Contrary, Converse, Opposite
Anti-three Noetian
Antitoxin Antibody, Antivenin, Guaco, Serum, Vaccine
Anti-union Secesher
Antler(s) Bosset, Crown, Horn, Palm, Rights, Staghorn, Surroyal, Tine
Ant-proof Bilian
▶ **Anus** see ANAL
Anvil Bick-iron, Block, Incus, Stiddie, Stithy
Anxiety, Anxious Angst, Brood, Care(ful), Cark, Concern, Disquiet, Dysthymia, Fanteeg, Fantigue, Fantod, Fraught, Grave, Heebie-jeebies, Hypochondria, Inquietude, Jimjams, Jumpy, Reck, Restless, Scruple, Solicitous, Stress, Suspense, Sweat, Tension, Trepidation, Twitchy, Unease, Unquiet, Upset, Uptight, White-knuckle, Worriment
Any Arrow, Ary, Some
Anybody, Anyone Everyman, One, Whoso, You
Anyhow Anyway, Leastways
Anything Aught, Diddly-squat, Oucht, Owt, Whatnot
▷ **Anyway** may indicate an anagram
Apache Arizona, AZ
Apart Aloof, Aside, Asunder, Atwain, Beside, Separate
Apartheid Racism, Verkrampte
Apartment Ben, Condominium, Digs, Duplex, Efficiency, Flat, Insula, Mansion, Pad, Paradise, Penthouse, Pied-a-terre, Quarters, Room, Simplex, Solitude, Suite, Tenement, Unit, Walk-up
Apathetic, Apathy Accidie, Acedia, Incurious, Languid, Lethargic, Listless, Lobotomized, Pococurante, Torpid
Ape(-like), Apeman Anthropoid, Barbary, Big-foot, Bonobo, Catarrhine, Copy, Dryopithecine, Gelada, Gibbon, Gorilla, > IMITATE, Magot, Mimic, Orang,

Paranthropus, Pithecoid, Pongo, Proconsul, Sacred, Simian, Simulate, Yowie

Aperient Cascara, Laxative, Senna

Aperitif > DRINK, Pernod®

Aperture Balistraria, Chink, Fenestella, Hole, Keyhole, Osculum, Relative, Spiracle, Window

Apex Acme, Culmen, Keystone, Knoll, Knowe, Solar, Summit, Vortex

Aphid Ant-cow, Phylloxera

Aphorism Adage, Epigram, Gnome, Proverb, Sutra

Aphrodisiac, **Aphrodite** Cytherean, Erotic, Idalian, Paphian, Philter, Philtre, Spanish fly, Urania, Yohimbine

Aplomb Assurance, Cool, Equanimity, Poise, Sangfroid, Serenity

Apocryphal Spurious, Tobit

Apograph Roneo®

Apollo Belvedere, Pythian, Sun

Apology Excuse, Justifier, Mockery, Oops, Pardon, Scuse

Apostate Citer, > HERETIC, Pervert, Rat, Recreant, Renegade, Runagate, Turncoat

Apostle, **Apostolic** Cuthbert, > DISCIPLE, Evangelist, Johannine, Jude, Matthew, Pauline, Spoon, Twelve

Apostrophe, **Apostrophise** Elision, O(h), Soliloquy, Tuism

Apothegm Dictum, Maxim, Motto

Appal(ling) Abysmal, Affear(e), Dire, Dismay, Egregious, Frighten, Horrify, Piacular, Shock, Tragic

▷ **Appallingly** *may indicate* an anagram

Apparatus Alembic, Appliance, Autoclave, Caisson, Chemostat, Clinostat, Coherer, Colorimeter, Condenser, Cosmotron, Cryostat, Davis, Defibrillator, Device, Digester, Ebullioscope, Effusiometer, Electrograph, Electrophorus, Electroscope, Eprouvette, Equipment, Eudiometer, Exciter, Fixings, Gadget, Golgi, Graith, Helioscope, Hemocytometer, Hodoscope, Holophote, Hydrophone, Incubator, Injector, Instrument, Jacquard, Kipps, Kymograph, Lease-rod, Masora(h), Microreader, Mimeograph, Multi-gym, Oscillograph, Oxygenator, Pasteuriser, Percolator, Phonometer, Phytotron, Potometer, Proto®, Pulmotor®, Radiosonde, Replenisher, Respirator, Respirometer, Resuscitator, Retort, Rounce, Scintiscanner, Scuba, Set, Snorkel, Sphygmograph, Spirophore, Stellarotor, Steriliser, Still, Switchgear, Tackle, Tackling, Talk-you-down, Teleprinter, Thermopile, Tokamak, Transformer, Transmitter, Tromp(e), Ventouse, Wheatstone's bridge, Whip-and-derry

Apparel Attire, Besee, > COSTUME, Garb, Raiment, Wardrobe, Wardrop

Apparent(ly) Ap, Clear, Detectable, Manifest, Ostensible, Outward, Overt, Plain, Prima facie, Semblance, Visible

▷ **Apparent** *may indicate* a hidden word

Apparition Dream, Eidolon, Fetch, Ghost, > ILLUSION, Phantom, Shade, Spectre, Visitant, Wraith

Appeal(ing) Ad, Beg, Cachet, Catchpenny, Charisma, Charm, Cri de coeur, Cry, Entreat, Entreaty, Epirrhema, Fetching, Invocation, It, O, Oomph, Plead, SA, Screeve, Solicit, SOS, Suit

Appear(ance) Advent, Air, Apport, Arrival, Aspect, Broo, Brow, Burst, Cast, Compear, Debut, Emerge, Enter, Exterior, Eye, Facade, Facies, Far(r)and, Farrant, Fa(s)cia, Feature, Format, Garb, Guise, Habitus, Hue, Image, Kithe, Kythe, Loom, > MANNER, Mien, Occur, Ostensibly, Outward, Person, Phase, Phenomenon, Physiognomy, Presence, Prosopon, Represent, Rig, Rise, Seem, Semblance, Show, Spring, Superficies, Theophany, View, Visitation, Wraith

Appease(ment) Allay, Alleviate, Calm, Danegeld, Mitigate, > MOLLIFY, Munichism, Pacify, Placate, Propitiate, Satisfy, Soothe, Sop

Append(age) Adjunct, Affix, Aglet, Allantois, Aril, Arista, Cercus, Chelicera, Codpiece, Ctene, Fang, Flagellum, Hanger-on, Lobe, Lug, Palp(us), Paraglossa, Parapodium, Pedipalp, Stipel, Suffix, Swimmeret, Tail, Tailpiece, Tentacle, Ugly, Uropod, Uvula

Appendix Addendum, Apocrypha, Codicil, Grumbling, Label, Pendant, Pendent, Rider, Schedule, Vermiform

Appetite, Appetitive, Appetise(r) Antepast, Antipasto, Aperitif, Appestat, Bhagee, Bhajee, Bulimia, Bulimy, Canapé, Concupiscence, Concupy, Crudités, Desire, Dim-sum, Entremes(se), Entremets, Flesh, Hunger, Limosis, Malacia, Meze, Mezze, Nacho, Orectic, Orexis, Passion, Pica, Polyphagia, Relish, Tapa(s), Titillate, Twist, Yerd-hunger, Yird-hunger

Applaud, Applause Acclaim, Bravo, > CHEER, Clap, Claque, Eclat, Encore, Extol, Hum, Kentish fire, Olé, Ovation, Praise, Root, Ruff, Tribute

Apple Adam's, Alligator, Baldwin, Balsam, Biffin, Blenheim orange, Braeburn, Bramley, Charlotte, Codlin(g), Cooker, Costard, Crab, Custard, Dead Sea, Discord, Eater, Granny Smith, Greening, Jenneting, John, Jonathan, Leather-coat, Love, Mammee, May, McIntosh (red), Medlar, Nonpareil, Oak, Pacific Rose, Pearmain, Pippin, Pomace, Pome(roy), Pom(e)water, Pomroy, Potato, Punic, Pyrus, Quarantine, Quarenden, Quar(r)ender, Quarrington, Quodlin, Redstreak, Reinette, Rennet, Ribston(e), Ruddock, Russet, Seek-no-further, Snow, Sops-in-wine, Sorb, Sturmer, Sugar, Sweeting, Thorn, Toffee, Windfall, Winesap

Apple juice Malic

Apple-picker Atalanta

Applicant Ordinand, Postulant

Application, Apply, Appliance(s) Address, Adhibit, Appeal, Appose, Assiduity, Barrage, Blender, Devote, Diligence, Dressing, Exercise, Foment, Give, Implement, Inlay, Lay, Lotion, Mixer, Ointment, Opodeldoc, Petition, Plaster, Poultice, Put, Request, Resort, Respirator, Rub, Sinapism, Stupe, Truss, > USE, Vice, White goods

Appliqué Hawaiian

Appoint(ee), Appointment Advowson, Assign, Berth, Date, Delegate, Depute, Designate, Dew, Due, Executor, Induction, Installation, Make, Name, > NOMINATE, Nominee, Office, Ordain, Position, Post, Posting, Rendezvous, Room, Set, Tryst

▷ **Appointed** *may indicate* an anagram

Apportion(ment) Allocate, Allot, Mete, Parcel, Ration, Share, Weigh

Apposite Apt, Cogent, Germane, Pat, Pertinent, Relevant, Suitable

Appraise, Appraisal Analyse, > EVALUATE, Gauge, Guesstimate, Judge, Tape, > VALUE, Vet

Appreciate, Appreciation Acknowledgement, Cherish, Clap, Dig, Endear, Esteem, Gratefulness, Increase, Prize, Realise, Regard, Relish, Rise, Sense, Stock, Taste, Thank you, Treasure, > VALUE

Apprehend, Apprehension Afears, Alarm, Arrest, > CATCH, Collar, Fear, Grasp, Insight, Intuit, Perceive, Quailing, See, Take, Toey, Trepidation, Uh-oh, Unease, Uptake

Apprehensive Jumpy, Nervous, Uneasy

Apprentice(ship) Article, Commis, Cub, Devil, Garzone, Improver, Indent(ure), Jockey, L, Learner, Lehrjahre, Novice, Noviciate, Novitiate, Printer's devil, Pupillage, Snob, Tiro, Trainee, Turnover, Tyro(ne)

Approach(ing), Approachable Abord, Access, Accost, Advance, Affable, Anear, Appropinquate, Appulse, Avenue, Close, Come, Converge, Cost(e), Drive, Driveway, Fairway, Feeler, Gate, Imminent, Line, Near, Nie, Overture, Pitch, Procedure, Road, Run-up, Towards, Verge

Appropriate Abduct, Abstract, Annex, Apposite, Apt, Asport, Assign, Bag, Borrow, Collar, Commandeer, Commensurate, Confiscate, Convenient, Due, Embezzle, Expedient, Fit, Germane, Good, Happy, Hijack, Hog, Jump, Just, Meet, Nick, Pilfer, Plagiarise, Pocket, Pre-empt, Proper, Purloin, Right, Seize, Sequester, Sink, Snaffle, Steal, Suit, Swipe, Take, Timely, Trouser, Usurp

Approval, Approve(d) Adopt, Allow, Amen, Applaud, Attaboy, Aye, Blessing, Bravo, > COUNTENANCE, Credit, Dig, Endorse, Favour, Hear hear, Homologate, Hubba-hubba, Imprimatur, Initial, Kitemark, Laud, Nod, Okay, Olé, Orthodox, Plaudit, Rah, Ratify, Rubber-stamp, Sanction, Stotter, Thumbs-up, Tick, Tribute, Yay, Yes, Zindabad

Approximate(ly), Approximation Almost, Circa, Close, Coarse, Estimate, Guess, Imprecise, Near, Roughly

Apricot Mebos

April, April fool Apr, Hunt-the-gowk

Apron Barm-cloth, Bib, Blacktop, Brat, Bunt, Canvas, Dick(e)y, Ephod, Fig-leaf, Gremial, Ice, Pinafore, Pinner, Pinny, Placket, Stage, Tablier, Tier, Waist

Apse Concha, Exedra, Niche, Recess, Tribune

Apt(ly) Apposite, Appropriate, Apropos, Ben trovato, Capable, Evincive, Fit, Gleg, Happy, Liable, Pat, Prone, Suitable, Tends

Aptitude Ability, Bent, Faculty, Flair, Gift, Skill, Talent, Tendency

Aqua(tic) Euglena, Flustra, Lentic, Lotic, Regia, Zizania

Aqualung Scuba

Aqueduct Canal, Channel, Conduit, Hadrome, Xylem

Arab(ian), Arabia, Arabic Abdul, Adeni, Algorism, Ali, Baathist, Bahraini, Bahrein, Bedouin, Druse, Druz(e), Effendi, Fedayee(n), Gamin, Geber, Hashemite, Himyarite, Horse, Iraqi, Jawi, Lawrence, Mudlark, Nabat(a)ean, Nes(h)ki, Omani, PLO, Qatari, Rag(head), Saba, Sab(a)ean, Saracen, Saudi, Semitic, Sheikh, Street, UAR, Urchin, Yemen

Arabis Cress

Arachnid Podogona, Ricinulei, > SPIDER

Arbiter, Arbitrator ACAS, Censor, Daysman, Judge, Ombudsman, Ref(eree), Umpire

Arbitrary Despotic, Haphazard, Random, Wanton

Arboreal, Arbour Bower, Dendroid, Pergola, Trellis

Arc Azimuth, Bow, Carbon, > CURVE, Flashover, Fogbow, Halo, Island, Mercury, Octant, Quadrant, Rainbow, Reflex, Seadog, Trajectory, White rainbow

Arcade Amusement, Burlington, Cloister, Gallery, Loggia, Mall, Penny, Triforium

Arcadia(n) Idyllic, Nemoral, Sylvan

Arcane Esoteric, Obscure, Occult, Orphism, Recherché, Rune, Secret

Arch(ed) Acute, Admiralty, Arblaster, Arcade, Archivolt, Arcuate, Camber, Chief, Coom, Counterfort, Crafty, Cross-rib, Crown-green, Ctesiphon, > CUNNING, Curve, Elfin, Embow, Espiegle, Fallen, Flying buttress, Fog-bow, Fornicate, Fornix, Gill, Gothic, Hance, Haunch, Hog, Horseshoe, Instep, Intrados, Keel, Keystone, Lancet, Leery, Lierne, Limb-girdle, Marble, Norman, Ogee, Ogive, Order, Parthian, Pectoral, Pelvic, Portal, Proscenium, Relieving, Roach, Roguish, Roman, Safety, Saucy, Segmental, Shouldered, Skew, Soffit, Span, Squinch, Stilted, Trajan, Triumphal, Vault, Zygoma

Archaeological, **Archaeologist** Carter, Dater, Dig, Evans, Layard, Leakey, Mycenae, Petrie, Pothunter, Wheeler, Woolley ◆

Archangel Azrael, Gabriel, Israfeel, Israfel, Israfil, Jerahmeel, Michael, Raguel, Raphael, Sariel, Satan, Uriel

Arch-binder Voussoir

Archbishop Anselm, Augustine, Cosmo, Cranmer, Davidson, Dunstan, Ebor, Elector, Hatto, Lanfranc, Lang, Langton, Laud, Metropolitan, Primate, Temple, Trench, Tutu, Whitgift

Archdeacon Ven

Archduke Trio

Archer Acestes, Bow-boy, > BOWMAN, Cupid, Eros, Hood, Philoctetes, Sagittary, Tell, Toxophilite

Archetype Avatar, Form, Model, Pattern

Archibald, **Archie**, **Archy** Ack-ack, Cockroach, Oerlikon, Rice, Roach

Archilochian Epode

Archipelago Alexander, Antarctic, Azores, Bismarck, Camaguey, Fiji, Franz Josef Land, Gulag, Japan, Kerguelen, Malay, Marquesas, Mergui, Novaya Zemlya, Palmer, Paumotu, St Pierre and Miquelon, Severmaya Zemlya, Spitsbergen, Sulu, Svalbard, Tierra del Fuego, Tonga, Tuamoto, West Indies

Architect(ure), **Architectural** Arcology, Baroque, Bauhaus, Bricolage, Brutalism, Byzantine, Churrigueresque, Composite, Corinthian, Creator, Data-flow, Decorated, Designer, Domestic, Doric, Early English, Entablature, Federation, Flamboyant, Georgian, Gothic, Ionic, Jacobean, Landscape, Lombard, Mission, Moderne, Moorish, Moresque, Mudejar, Naval, Neoclassical, Neo-gothic, Norman, Palladian, Perpendicular, Planner, Plateresque, Prostyle, Romanesque, Saxon, Spandrel, Spandril, Tectonic, Tudor, Tuscan

ARCHITECTS

4 letters:	Soane	Columbo	Vitruvius
Adam	Utzon	Gropius	
Kent	Wyatt	Lutyens	10 letters:
Loos		Venturi	Inigo Jones
Nash	6 letters:	Vignola	Mackintosh
Shaw	Casson		Trophonius
Webb	Foster	8 letters:	Van der Rohe
Wood	Nissen	Bramante	
Wren	Repton	Palladio	11 letters:
	Spence	Piranesi	Abercrombie
5 letters:	Street	Saarinen	Butterfield
Gaudi	Wright	Vanbrugh	Le Corbusier
Inigo			
Nervi	7 letters:	9 letters:	12 letters:
Pugin	Behrens	Hawksmoor	Brunelleschi
Scott	Bernini	Macquarie	

Architrave Epistyle, Platband

Archive(s) Backfile, Muniment, PRO, Records, Register

Archon Draco

Arch-villain Ringleader

Arctic Estotiland, Frigid, Hyperborean, In(n)uit, Inupiat, Polar, Tundra

Ardent, Ardour Aflame, Aglow, Boil, Broiling, Burning, Fervent, Fervid, Fiery, Fire, Flagrant, Heat, Het, > **HOT**, Hot-brained, In, Mettled, Mettlesome, Passion(ate), Perfervid, Rage, Spiritous, Vehement, Warm-blooded, Zealous, Zeloso

Arduous Laborious, Uphill

Are A, 're

Area Acre, Aleolar, Apron, Are, Bailiwick, Belt, Bovate, Broca's, Carucate, Catchment, Centare, Centiare, Centre, Curtilage, Dec(i)are, Dedans, Development, Disaster, District, Domain, Endemic, Eruv, Extent, Farthingland, Gau, Goal, Grey, Growth, Heartland, Hectare, Henge, Hide, Husbandland, Imperium, Input, Karst, Landmass, Lathe, Latitude, Lek, Locality, Manor, Metroplex, Milieu, Morgen, Mush, No-go, Orb, Oxgang, Oxgate, Oxland, Parish, Patch, Penalty, Place, Pleasance, Plot, Precinct, Province, Purlieu, Quad, Quadrat, Quarter, Range, Redevelopment, Refugium, > **REGION**, Rest, Retrochoir, Rood, Sector, Service, Shire, Sterling, Subtopia, Support, Target, Technical, Terrain, Territory, Theatre, Tie, Tract, Tundra, Tye, Urban, White, Yard, Zone

Arena Circus, Cockpit, Dohyo, Field, Lists, Maidan, Olympia, > **RING**, Rink, Stadium, Tiltyard, Velodrome, Venue

Argal Ergo

Argent Ag, Silver

Argentina RA

Argon Ar

Argonaut Acastus, Jason, Lynceus, Meleager, Nautilus

Argot Flash, Idiom, Jargon, Lingo, Shelta

Argue, Argument Altercation, Antistrophon, Argie-bargie, Argle-bargle, Argy-bargy, Bandy, Beef, Blue, Brush, Case, Casuism, Choplogic, Conflict, Contend, Contest, Cosmological, Debate, Deprecate, Diallage, Difference, Dilemma, Dispute, Dissent, Elenchus, Elenctic, Enthymeme, Eristic, Exchange, Expostulate, Forensic, Free-for-all, Generalisation, Logic, Logomachy, Moot, Ob and soller, Ontological, Paralogism, Patter, Pettifog, Plead, Polemic, Polylemma, Premiss, Propound, Quarrel, Quibble, Quodlibet, Rammy, Ratiocinate, > **REASON**, Remonstrate, Row, Run-in, Sophism, Sorites, Spar, Stickle, Straw man, Summation, Syllogism, Teleological, Theme, Thetic, Tiff, Transcendental, Trilemma, Wrangle, Yike

Argyle Argathelian

Aria Ballad, Cabaletta, Melody, Song

Arid Dry, Parched

Ariel Pen

Arise Appear, Be, Develop, Emanate, Emerge, Upgo, Wax

Aristocracy, Aristocrat(ic) Blood, Boyar, Buckeen, Classy, Debrett, Duc, Elite, Eupatrid, Gentry, Grandee, High-hat, Junker, Nob, Noble, Optimate, Patrician, Thane, Tony, U-men, Upper-crust, Well-born

Aristotle Peripatetic, Stagirite, Stagyrite

Arithmetic(ian) Algorism, Algorith, Arsmetrick, Cocker, Euclid, Logistic, Modular, Sums

Ark(wright) Chest, Noah

Arly Thicket

Arm(ed), Arms Akimbo, Arsenal, Bearing, Brachial, Branch, Bundooks, Canting, Cove, Crest, Embattle, Equip, Escutcheon, Fin, Firth, Frith, Gnomon, Halbert, Hatchment, Heel, Heraldic, Inlet, Jib, Krupp, Limb, Loch, Long, Member, Olecranon, Pick-up, Quillon, Radius, Ramous, Rocker, Rotor, SAA,

Secular, Side, Small, Spiral, Tappet, Tentacle, Timer, Tone, Transept, Tremolo, Ulnar, > **WEAPON**, Whip

▷ **Arm** *may indicate* an army regiment, etc.

Armada Spanish

Armadillo Dasypod, Dasypus, Pangolin, Peba, Pichiciago, Tatou(ay), Xenurus

Armature Shuttle

Armenian Haikh

Armistice Truce

Armour(ed) Ailette, Armature, Armet, Barbette, Beaver, Besagew, Bevor, Brasset, Breastplate, Brigandine, Buckler, Byrnie, Camail, Cannon, Casspir, Cataphract, Chaffron, Chain, Chamfrain, Chamfron, Character, Chausses, Corium, Cors(e)let, Couter, Cuirass, Cuish, Cuisse, Culet, Curat, Curiet, Cush, Defence, Fauld, Garniture, Gear, Genouillère, Gere, Gorget, Greave, Habergeon, Hauberk, Hoplology, Jack, Jambeau, Jazerant, Jesserant, Lamboys, Loricate, Mail, Male, Mentonnière, Nasal, Nosepiece, Panoply, Panzer, Pauldron, Petta, Placcat, Placket, Plastron, Plate, Poitrel, Poleyn, Pouldron, Sabaton, Scale, Secret, > **SHIELD**, Solleret, Spaudler, Tace, Tank, Taslet, Tasse(t), Thorax, Tonlet, Tuille, Vambrace, Vantbrass, Ventail, Visor, Voider, Weed

Armpit Axilla, Oxter

Armstrong Satchmo

Army Arrière-ban, BEF, Church, Colours, Confederate, Crowd, Federal, Field, Fyrd, Golden (Horde), Horde, Host, IRA, Land, Landwehr, Lashkar, Legion, Line, Military, Militia, Multitude, New Model, Para-military, Red, SA, Sabaoth, Salvation, Sena, Service, Soldiers, Standing, Swarm, TA, Territorial, Volunteer, War, Wehrmacht

▷ **Army** *may indicate* having arms

Aroma(tic) Allspice, Aniseed, Aryl, Balmy, Coriander, Fenugreek, Fragrant, Odorous, Pomander, Spicy, Stilbene, Vanillin, Wintergreen

Around About, Ambient, Circa, Near, Peri-, Skirt, Tour

▷ **Around** *may indicate* one word around another

Arouse, Arousal Alarm, > **EXCITE**, Fan, Fire, Incite, Inflame, Must(h), Needle, Provoke, Stole, Touch up, Urolagnia, Waken

Arrange(r), Arrangement Adjust, Array, Attune, Bandobast, Bundobust, Concert, Concinnity, Configuration, Design, Display, Dispose, Do, Edit, Engineer, Fix, Foreordain, Formation, Grade, Ikebana, Layout, Marshal, Modus vivendi, Orchestrate, Orchestration, Ordain, > **ORDER**, Ordnance, Organise, Pack, Pattern, Perm, Permutation, Plan, Position, Prepare, Prepense, Quincunx, Redactor, Regulate, Run, Schedule, Schema, Scheme, Set, Settle, Sort, Spacing, Stereoisomerism, Stow, Straighten, Style, System, Tactic, Taxis, Transcribe

▷ **Arrange** *may indicate* an anagram

Arras Tapestry

Array(ed) Attire, Bedight, Deck, Herse, Marshal, Muster, Panoply, Phased, Seismic

Arrear(s) Aft, Ahint, Backlog, Behind, Debt, Owing

Arrest(ed), Arresting Abort, Alguacil, Alguazil, Ament, Apprehend, Attach, Attract, Blin, Book, Bust, Caption, Capture, Cardiac, Catch, Check, Citizen's, Collar, Detain, False, Furthcoming, Hold, House, Knock, Lift, Nab, Nail, Nick, Nip, Nobble, Pinch, Pull, Restrain, Retard, Riveting, Round-up, Run-in, Salient, Sease, Seize, Stasis, Stop, Sus(s)

Arris Groin

Arrival, Arrive, Arriving Accede, Advent, Attain, Come, Get, Happen, Hit,

Inbound, Influx, Johnny-come-lately, Land, Latecomer, Natal, Nativity, Reach, Show, Strike

Arrogance, **Arrogant** Assumption, Bold, Bravado, Cavalier, Cocksure, Disdain, Dogmatic, Effrontery, Haughty, Haut(eur), High, Hogen-mogen, Hoity-toity, Hubris, Imperious, Morgue, Overweening, Presumption, Proud, Side, Stuck-up, Surquedry, Toploftical, Turkeycock, Uppish, Uppity, Upstart

Arrogate Appropriate, Assume, Claim, Impute, Usurp

Arrow, **Arrow-head** Acestes, Any, Ary, Blunt, Bolt, Broad(head), Dart, Dogbolt, Filter, Flechette, Flight, Missile, Pheon, Pointer, Quarrel, Reed, Sagittate, Shaft, Sheaf

Arrowroot Kuzu, Maranta, Pia

Arsenal Ammo, Armo(u)ry, Depot, Magazine, Side

Arsenate, **Arsenic(al)**, **Arsenide** As, Erythrite, Realgar, Resalgar, Rosaker, Salvarsan, Scorodite, Skutterudite, Smaltite, Speiss, Zarnich

Arson(ist) Firebug, Pyromania

Art(s), **Arty**, **Art school**, **Art style** Abstract, Applied, Ars, Arte Povera, Bauhaus, Bloomsbury, Bonsai, Bricart, Brut, Chiaroscuro, Clair-obscure, Clare-obscure, Clip, Cobra, Commercial, Conceptual, Constructivism, Contrapposto, Craft, Cubism, Cunning, Dada, Daedal(e), Deco, Decorative, Dedal, De Stijl, Die Brucke, Diptych, Divisionism, Earth, Ekphrasis, Environmental, Es, Expressionism, Fauvism, Feat, Fine, Finesse, Flemish, Folk, Fugue, Futurism, Genre, Graphic, Guile, Impressionist, Jugendstil, Kakemono, Kano, Ka pai, Kinetic, Kirigami, Kitsch, Knack, Liberal, Mandorla, Mannerism, Martial, Minimal, Montage, Motivated, Music, Mystery, Nabis, Nazarene, Neoclassical, Neo-impressionism, New Wave, Norwich, Nouveau, Optical, Origami, Orphic cubism, Orphism, Outsider, Performance, Performing, Perigordian, Plastic, Pointillism, Pop, Postimpressionism, Postmodern, Practical, Pre-Raphaelite, Primitive, Psychedelic, Public, Quadratura, Quadrivium, Relievo, Sienese, > SKILL, Still-life, Supremation, Surrealism, Synchronism, Tachism(e), Tatum, Tenebrism, Toreutics, Trecento, Trivium, Trompe l'oeil, Trouvé, Tsutsumu, Useful, Verism, Virtu, Visual, Vorticism

▷ **Art** *may indicate* an -est ending

Artefact(s) Neolith, Tartanalia, Tartanry, Xoanon

▷ **Artefact** *may indicate* an anagram

Artemis Selene

Artemus Ward

Artery Aorta, Carotid, Coronary, Duct, Femoral, Frontal, Iliac, Innominate, M1, Maxillary, Phrenic, Pulmonary, Radial, Route, Spermatic, Temporal

Artful Cute, Dodger, Foxy, Ingenious, Quirky, Sly, Subtle, Tactician

Arthropod Limulus, Tardigrade, Water-bear

Artichoke Cardoon, Jerusalem

Article(s) A, An, Apprentice, Column, Commodity, Definite, Feature, Five, Indefinite, Indenture, Item, Leader, Paper, Piece, Pot-boiler, Sidebar, Specify, The, Thing, Thinkpiece, Thirty-nine, Treatise, Ware

Articulation, **Articulate(d)** Clear, Coherent, Coudé, Diarthrosis, Distinct, Eloquent, Enounce, Express, Fluent, Fortis, Gimmal, Gomphosis, Hinged, Jointed, Jymold, Lenis, Limbed, Lisp, Pretty-spoken, Pronounce, Schindylesis, Trapezial, Utter, Vertebrae, Voice

Artifice(r), **Artificial** Bogus, Chouse, Dodge, Ersatz, Factitious, Finesse, Guile, Hoax, In vitro, Logodaedaly, Man-made, Mannered, Opificer, Pretence, Prosthetic, Pseudo, Reach, Ruse, Sell, Sham, Spurious, Stratagem, > STRATEGY, Synthetic, Theatric, > TRICK, Unnatural, Wile, Wright

Artificial respiration Kiss of life, Schafer's method
Artillery Battery, Cannon, Field, Fougade, Fougasse, Guns, Mortar, Ordnance, Pyroballogy, RA, Rafale, Ramose, Ramus, Train
Artiodactyl Camel, Chevrotain, Deerlet
Artisan Craftsman, Joiner, Journeyman, Mechanic, Peon, Pioner, Pyoner, Shipwright, Workman
Artist(ic) Barbizon, Bohemian, Cartoonist, Colourist, Cubist, Dadaist, Daedal(e), Deccie, Decorator, Die Brucke, Etcher, Fauve, Fine, Gentle, Gilder, ICA, Impressionist, Left Bank, Limner, Linear, Maestro, Master, Miniaturist, > **MUSICIAN**, Nazarene, Oeuvre, Orphism, > **PAINTER**, Pavement, Paysagist, Piss, Plein-airist, Primitive, RA, Romantic, Screever, > **SCULPTOR**, Sien(n)ese, Tachisme, Trapeze, Trecentist, Virtuose, Virtuoso

ARTISTS

3 letters:
Arp
Cox
Rap

4 letters:
Cuyp
Dadd
Dali
Doré
Etty
Goya
Hals
John
Klee
Lely
Miró
Opie
Phiz

5 letters:
Aiken
Appel
Bacon
Bakst
Bosch
Corot
Crome
Degas
Dulac
Dürer
Ensor
Ernst
Hoare
Hooch
Klimt
Leech

Léger
Lippi
Lotto
Lowry
Manet
Monet
Munch
Nabis
Orpen
Redon
Riley
Rodin
Seago
Steen
Steer
Tatum
Watts

6 letters:
Boudin
Braque
Brucke
Calder
Callot
Derain
D'Orsay
Escher
Fuseli
Giotto
Greuze
Guardi
Haydon
Ingres
Knight
Le Nain
Millet
Renoir

Ribera
Rivera
Romney
Rothko
Rubens
Seurat
Signac
Sisley
Stubbs
Tissot
Titian
Turner
Warhol

7 letters:
Apelles
Audubon
Bellini
Bernini
Bonnard
Cézanne
Chagall
Chardin
Cimabue
Collier
Courbet
Cranach
Da Vinci
El Greco
Epstein
Gauguin
Hobbema
Hockney
Hogarth
Hokusai
Holbein
Hoppner

Kneller
Matisse
Millais
Morisot
Morland
Murillo
Nattier
Picasso
Pissaro
Poussin
Prudhon
Raeburn
Raphael
Rouault
Sargent
Sickert
Spencer
Tiepolo
Uccello
Utamaro
Utrillo
Van Dyke
Van Eyck
Van Gogh
Vermeer
Watteau
Zeuxian
Zoffany

8 letters:
Daubigny
Eastlake
Kirchner
Landseer
Leonardo
Magritte
Mantegna

Masaccio
Mondrian
Nevinson
Perugino
Piranesi
Reynolds
Rousseau
Topolski
Veronese
Whistler

9 letters:
Beardsley
Bonington

Canaletto
Carpaccio
Constable
Correggio
Delacroix
Donatello
Fragonard
Gericault
Giorgione
Grunewald
Hiroshige
Kandinsky
Rembrandt
Velasquez

10 letters:
Alma-Tadema
Botticelli
Burne-Jones
Guillaumin
Madox Brown
Modigliani
Rowlandson
Signorelli
Sutherland
Tintoretto
Van der Goes

12 letters:
Gainsborough
Lichtenstein
Michelangelo
Winterhalter

14 letters:
Jackson Pollock

15 letters:
Hieronymus
   Bosch
Toulouse-Lautrec

Artless Candid, Ingenuous, Innocent, Naive, Open, Seely, Simple
Arturo Toscanini
Arum Acorus, Green-dragon, Lily, Taro
As Aesir, Als, Arsenic, Coin, Eg, Forasmuch, Kame, Qua, Ridge, 's, Since, So, Thus, Ut, While
As above US
Asafoetida Hing
As before Anew, Ditto, Do, Stet
Asbestos Amiant(h)us, Amosite, Chrysolite, Crocidolite, Earthflax, Fireproof, Rockwood
Ascend(ant), Ascent Anabasis, Climb, Dominant, Escalate, Gradient, Lift, Pull, Ramp, Rise, Sclim, Sklim, Slope, Up, Upgang, Uphill, Uprise, Zoom
Ascertain Determine, Discover, > **ESTABLISH**, Prove
Ascetic Agapetae, Anchor(et), Anchorite, Ancress, Ashramite, Austere, Dervish, Diogenes, Encratite, Eremital, Essene, Fakir, Faquir, Gymnosophist, Hermit, Jain(ite), Monk, Nazarite, Nazirite, Nun's flesh, Sad(d)hu, Simeon Stylites, Stylite, Sufic, Therapeutae, Yogi(n)
Ascidian Chordate, Urochordate
Asclepiad Stapelia
Ascribe Assign, > **ATTRIBUTE**, Blame, Imply, Impute
Asdic Sonar
As far as Quoad
As good as Equal, Tantamount
Ash(es), Ashy Aesc, Aizle, Cinders, Cinereal, Clinker(s), Easle, Embers, Fly, Kali, Lahar, Pallor, Pearl, Pozz(u)olana, Prickly, Rowan, Ruins, Soda, Sorb, Spodo-, Tephra, Urn, Varec, Wednesday, Weeping, Witchen, Yg(g)drasil(l)
Ashamed Abashed, Embarrassed, Hangdog, Mortified, Repentant, Shent
Ashore Aland, Beached, Grounded, Stranded
Ash-pan Backet
Asia(n), Asiatic Altaic, Azari, Balinese, Bangladeshi, Bengali, Cantonese, E, Evenki, Ewenki, Gook, Hun, Hyksos, Indian, Kashmir, Korean, Kurd, Lao, Malay, Mongol, Naga, Negrito, Nepalese, Phrygian, Pushtu, Samo(y)ed, Shan, Siamese, Sogdian, Tamil, Tartar, Tibetan, Tocharian, Tokharian, Turanian, Turk(o)man
Asia Minor Anatolia, Ionic
Aside Apart, By, Despite, Private, Separate, Shelved, Sotto voce
Asinine Crass, Dull, Idiotic, Puerile, Stupid

Ask Beg, Beseech, Cadge, Demand, Desire, Enquire, Entreat, Evet, Implore, Intreat, Invite, Newt, Petition, Prithee, Pump, Quiz, Request, Rogation, Seek, Solicit, Speer, Speir, Touch

Askance Asconce, Askew, Oblique, Sideways

Askew Agee, Aglee, Agley, Ajee, Aslant, Awry, Crooked, Skivie

Asleep Dormant, Inactive, Napping

Asparagus Asperge, Sparrow-grass, Spear, Sprew, Sprue

Aspect Angle, Bearing, Brow, Face, Facet, Facies, Feature, Look, Mien, Nature, Outlook, Perfective, Perspective, Side, > VIEW, Visage, Vista

Aspersion Calumny, Innuendo, Libel, Slander, Slur, Smear

Asphalt Bitumen, Blacktop, Gilsonite®, Pitch, Pitch Lake, Uinta(h)ite

Aspirant, **Aspirate**, **Aspiration**, **Aspire** Ambition, Breath, Buckeen, Challenger, Desire, Dream, Endeavour, Ettle, Goal, H, Hope(ful), Pretend, Pursue, Rough, Spiritus, Wannabe(e), Yearn

Ass Buridan's, Burnell, Burro, Cardophagus, Chigetai, Clot, Couscous, Cuddie, Dick(e)y, Donkey, Dziggetai, Funnel, Golden, Hemione, Hemionus, Hinny, Jack, Jenny, Jerusalem pony, Kiang, K(o)ulan, Kourbash, Kourmiss, Kouskous, Kumiss, Kurbash, Kyang, Liripipe, Liripoop, Moke, Neddy, Nitwit, Onager, Quagga, Sesterce, Simp, > STUPID PERSON

Assail(ant) Assault, Attack, Batter, Bego, Belabour, Bepelt, Beset, Bombard, Impugn, Onsetter, Oppugn, Pillory, Ply, Revile

Assassin(ate), **Assassination** Booth, Brave, Bravo, Brutus, Casca, Character, Frag, Gunman, Highbinder, Hitman, Killer, Ninja, Sword, Thuggee, Tyrannicide

Assault Assail, Assay, Attack, Battery, Bombard, Hamesucken, Indecent, Invasion, Mug, > RAID, Scalade, Stoor, Storm, Stour, Stowre

Assay Cupel, Examine, Proof, Test, Wet

Assemble, **Assembly** Agora, Audience, Ball, Bundestag, Chapter, Chatuaqua, Cho(u)ltry, Co, Collation, > COLLECTION, Comitia, Company, Conclave, Concourse, Congeries, Congress, Consistory, Constituent, Convene, Conventicle, Convention, Convocation, Convoke, Cortes, Council, Court, Curia, Dail Eireann, Dewain, Diet, Divan, Donnybrook, Ecclesia, Eisteddfod, Erect, Feis(anna), Folkmoot, Folkmote, Force, Forgather, Gather(ing), Gemot(e), General, Gorsedd, Group, Headstock, Hoi polloi, Kgotla, Knesset, Landtag, Legislative, Levee, Loya jirga, Majlis, Make, Mass, > MEETING, Mejlis, Moot, Muster, National, Panegyry, Panoply, Parishad, Parliament, Patron, Pattern, Plenum, Pnyx, Powwow, Presence, Primary, Quorum, Rally, Rechate, Recheate, Reichstag, Repair, Resort, Sanghat, Sanhedrin, Sanhedron, Sejm, Senate, Skupshtina, Sobranje, Soc, Society, Stort(h)ing, Synagogue, Synedrion, Synod, T(h)ing, Tribunal, Troop, Unlawful, Vidhan Sabha, Volksraad, Wapens(c)haw, Wapins(c)haw, Wappens(c)haw, Wardmote, Weapon-s(c)haw, Witan, Witenagemot, Zemstvo

Assent Accede, Acquiesce, Agree, Amen, Aye, Comply, Concur, Nod, Placet, Royal, Sanction, Yea, Yield

Assert(ing), **Assertion** Affirm, Allege, Constate, Contend, > DECLARE, Ipse-dixit, > MAINTAIN, Pose, Predicate, Proclaim, Pronounce, Protest, Rumour, Thetical

Assess(ment) Affeer, Appraise, Audition, Cense, Estimate, Evaluate, Gauge, Guesstimate, > JUDGE, Levy, Means test, Measure, Perspective, Rating, Referee, Scot and lot, Special, Stent, Tax, Value, Weigh

Asset(s) Advantage, Capital, Chattel, Fixed, Floating, Goodwill, Intangible, Liquid, Net, Plant, Property, Resource, Talent, Virtue, Wasting

Assiduous Attentive, Busy, Constant, Diligent, Studious, Thorough

Assign(ation), Assignment Allocate, > ALLOT, Apply, Appoint, Aret, Ascribe, Attribute, Award, Date, Dedicate, Duty, Errand, Fix, Grant, Impute, Point, Quota, Refer, Transfer, Tryst

Assimilate(d) Absorb, Blend, Digest, Esculent, Fuse, Imbibe, Incorporate, Merge

Assist(ance), Assistant Acolyte, Adjunct, Aid(e), Aide-de-camp, Ally, Alms, Attaché, Best boy, Busboy, Cad, Chainman, Collaborate, Counterhand, Counter-jumper, Dresser, Ex parte, Facilitate, Factotum, Famulus, Feldschar, Felds(c)her, Gofer, > HAND, Headlanger, Help, Henchman, Legal aid, Mentor, National, Offsider, Omnibus, Public, Reinforce, Relief, Second, Server, Servitor, Shill, Sidesman, Smallboy, Social, Stead, Subsidiary, Subsidy, Suffragan, Supernumerary, > SUPPORT, Usher

Assize Botley, Circuit, Court, Maiden, Oyer

Associate, Association Accomplice, Affiliate, Alliance, Amphictyony, Ass, Attach, Bedfellow, Brotherhood, Cartel, Chapel, Chum, Clang, Club, Cohort, Combine, Comecon, Compeer, Complice, Comrade, Concomitant, Confrère, > CONNECT, Consort(ium), Co-partner, Correlate, Crony, Enclisis, Fellow, Fraternise, Free, Gesellschaft, Guild, Hobnob, Housing, Intime, Join, Kabele, Kebele, League, Liaison, Lloyds, Mell, Member, Mess, Mix, Moshav, Oddfellows, Pal, Parent teacher, Partner, Phoresy, Press, Professional, Relate, Residents', Ring, Round Table, Samit(h)i, Sangh(at), Sidekick, Sodality, Stablemate, Symbiosis, Syndicate, Toc H, Toenadering, Trade, Union, Verein, Whiteboy, Word, Yoke-mate

Assort(ed), Assortment Paraphernalia, Pick-'n'-mix, Various

▷ **Assorted** *may indicate* an anagram

Assuage Allay, Appease, Beet, Calm, Ease, Mease, Mitigate, Mollify, Slake, Soften

As such Qua

Assume, Assuming, Assumption Adopt, Affect, Arrogate, Attire, Axiom, Believe, Don, Donné(e), Feign, Hypothesis, Lemma, Occam's Razor, Posit, Postulate, Preconception, Premise, Premiss, Presuppose, Pretentious, Principle, Putative, Saltus, Suppose, Surmise, Take

▷ **Assumption** *may mean* attire

Assure(d), Assurance Aplomb, Aver, Belief, Calm, > CERTAIN, Confidence, Confirm, Earnest, Gall, Guarantee, Pledge, Poise, Warranty

Assuredly Indeed, Perdie, Verily, Yea

Astatine At

Astern Abaft, Apoop, Rear

Asteroid Ceres, Eros, Eros 433, Hermes, Hygiea, Juno, Pallas, Phaethon, Pholus, Star, Starfish, Trojan, Vesta

Astir Afoot, Agate, Agog

Astonish(ed), Astonishing, Astonishment, Astound Abash, Admiraunce, Amaze, Banjax, Bewilder, Confound, Corker, Crikey, Daze, Donnert, Dum(b)found, Dumbstruck, Eye-popping, Flabbergast, Gobsmack, Heavens, Mind-boggling, Open-eyed, Open-mouthed, Phew, Pop-eyed, Prodigious, Rouse, Singular, Stagger, Startle, Stun, Stupefaction, Stupefy, Stupendous, Surprise, Thunderstruck, Wow

Astray Abord, Amiss, Errant, Lost, Will, Wull

Astride Athwart, Spanning, Straddle-back

Astringent Acerbic, Alum, Catechu, Dhak, Gambi(e)r, Harsh, Kino, Krameria, Rhatany, Sept-foil, Severe, Sour, Styptic, Tormentil, Witch-hazel

Astrologer, Astrology Archgenethliac, Chaldean, Culpeper, Faust, Figure-caster, Genethliac, Judicial, Lilly, Moore, Nostradamus, Soothsayer,

Starmonger, Zadkiel

Astronaut Cosmonaut, Gagarin, Glenn, Lunarnaut, Spaceman, Spacer, Taikonaut

Astronomer, Astronomy, Astronomical Almagest, Aristarchus, Bessel, Bradley, Brahe, Callipic, Cassini, Celsius, Copernicus, Eddington, Encke, Eratosthenes, Eudoxus, Flamsteed, Galileo, Hale, Halley, Herschel, Hewish, Hipparchus, Hoyle, Hubble, Huggins, Infra red, Jeans, Kepler, Laplace, Leverrier, Lockyer, Lovell, Meton, Neutrino, Omar Khayyam, Oort, Physical, Planetology, Ptolemy, Radar, Radio, Reber, Roche, Schwarzschild, Selenography, Selenology, Sosigenes, Stargazer, Star read, Telescopy, Tycho Brahe, Ultraviolet, Urania, Uranic, X-ray, Zwicky

Astrophel Penthia

Astrophysicist Seifert

Astute Acute, Canny, Crafty, Cunning, Downy, Perspicacious, Shrewd, Subtle, Wide, Wily

As usual Solito

As well Additionally, Also, Both, Even, Forby, Too

Asylum Bedlam, Bin, Bughouse, Frithsoken, Funny-farm, Girth, Grith, Haven, Institution, Lunatic, Madhouse, Magdalene, Nuthouse, Political, Rathouse, Refuge, Retreat, Sanctuary, Shelter, Snake-pit

Asymmetric(al) Lopsided, Skew

At Astatine, In, To, Up-bye

Atahualpa Inca

At all Ava, Ever, Oughtlings

At all events Algate

Atavistic Reversion, Throw-back

Atheist Doubter, Godless, Infidel, Sceptic

Athenian, Athene Attic, Cleruch, Pallas, Pericles, Solon, Timon

Athlete, Athletic(s) Agile, Agonist, Blue, Coe, Discobolus, Field, Gymnast, Jock, Leish, Miler, Milo, Nurmi, Olympian, Pacemaker, Quarter-miler, Runner, Sportsman, Sprinter, Track

Athodyd Ram-jet

Athwart Across, Awry, Oblique, Traverse

Atlantic Pond

Atlas Dialect, Linguistic, Maps, Range, Silk

▷ **At last** *may indicate* a cobbler

Atmosphere Aeropause, Air, Ambience, Aura, Chemosphere, Elements, Epedaphic, Ether, F-layer, Geocorona, Ionosphere, Lid, Magnetosphere, Mesosphere, Meteorology, Miasma, Ozone, Standard, Thermosphere, Tropopause, Troposphere, Upper, Vibe(s)

At most Al piu

Atoll Bikini, Eniwetok, Kwajalein, Male, Motu, Tarawa

Atom(ic), Atoms Boson, Electron, Excimer, Free, Gram, Ion, Iota, Isobare, Isotone, Isotope, Labelled, Ligand, Molecule, Monad, Monovalent, Muonic, Nuclide, Odoriphore, Particle, Pile, Primeval, Radionuclide, Recoil, Sellafield, Side-chain, Steric, Stripped, Substituent, Tagged, Windscale, Xylyl

At once Ek dum, Holus-bolus, Immediate, Instanter, Presto, Statim, Straight away, Swith, Tight, Tit(e), Titely, Tyte

Atone(ment) Aby(e), Acceptilation, Appease, Expiate, Penance, Redeem, Redemption, Yom Kippur

Atop Upon

▷ **At random** *may indicate* an anagram

Atrocious, Atrocity Abominable, Brutal, Diabolical, Flagitious, Heinous, Horrible, Monstrous, Outrage, Vile

Atrophy Degeneration, Marasmus, Sudeck's, Sweeny, Wasting

▷ **At sea** *may indicate* an anagram

Attach(ed), Attachment Accessory, Accrete, Adhesion, Adhibition, Adnate, Adnation, Adscript, Affix, Allonge, Annexe, Bolt, Bro, Byssus, Cleat, Covermount, Devotement, Devotion, Distrain, Garnish, Glom, Glue, > JOIN, Netsuke, Obconic, Pin, Snell, Stick, Tie, Weld

Attack(ing), Attacker Access, Affect, Airstrike, Alert, Anti, Apoplexy, Asperse, Assail, Assault, At, Batten, Bego, Belabour, Beset, Bestorm, Blitz(krieg), Bodrag(ing), Bombard, Bordraging, Bout, Broadside, Bushwhack, Camisade, Camisado, Campaign, Cannonade, Charge, Clobber, Club, Counteroffensive, Coup de main, Denounce, Descent, Diatribe, Feint, Fit, Flèche, Foray, Get, Handbag, Iconoclast, Ictus, Impugn, Incursion, Inroad, Invade, Inveigh, Lampoon, Lese-majesty, Let fly, Maraud, Molest, Mug, Offensive, Onding, Onfall, Onrush, Onset, Onslaught, Oppugn, Panic, Pillage, Polemic, Predacious, Pre-emptive, Push, Quart(e), Raid, Rough, Sandbag, Savage, Seizure, Sic(k), Siege, Skitch, Snipe, Sortie, Storm, Strafe, Strike, Swoop, Thrust, Tilt, Vilify, Vituperate, Wage, Warison, Wolf-pack, Zap

Attain(ment) Accomplish, Arrive, Earn, Fruition, Get, Land, Reach

Attempt Bash, Bid, Burl, Crack, Debut, Effort, Endeavour, Essay, Go, Mint, Nisus, Seek, Shot, Show, Shy, Stab, Strive, > TRY, Venture, Whack, Whirl

Attend(ance), Attendant Accompany, Apple-squire, Await, Batman, Bearer, Be at, Behold, Bulldog, Caddy, Cavass, Chaperone, Chasseur, Checker, Corybant, Courtier, Cuadrilla, Cupbearer, Custrel, Entourage, Equerry, Escort, Esquire, Famulus, Footman, Gillie, Hand-maiden, Harken, Hear, > HEED, Hello, Holla, Iras, Kavass, Led captain, > LISTEN, Maenad, Marshal, Mute, Note, Outrider, Outrunner, Page, Panisc, Panisk, Paranymph, People, Presence, Pursuivant, Respect, Roll-up, Satellite, Second, Server, Sowar, Steward, Trainbearer, Turn-out, Valet, Varlet, Visit, Wait, Watch, Whiffler, Zambuck

Attention, Attentive Achtung, Assiduity, Court, Coverage, Dutiful, Ear, Gallant, Gaum, Gorm, Heed, Interest, Mind, Notice, Present, Psst, Punctilio, Qui vive, > REGARD, Selective, Solicitous, Spellbound, Tenty, Thought

Attenuate, Attenuation Lessen, Neper, Rarefy, Thin, Weaken

Attest Affirm, Certify, Depose, Guarantee, Notarise, Swear, > WITNESS

Attic Bee-bird, Cockloft, Garret, Greek, Koine, Loft, Mansard, Muse, Salt, Solar, Soler, Sollar, Soller, Tallat, Tallet, Tallot

Attila Etzel, Hun

Attire Accoutre, Adorn, Apparel, Clobber, > DRESS, Garb, Habit

Attitude Air, Aspect, Behaviour, Demeanour, Light, > MANNER, Mindset, Nimby, Outlook, Pose, Posture, Propositional, Sense, Song, Stance, Tone, Viewpoint

Attorney Advocate, Counsellor, DA, District, Lawyer, Proctor, Prosecutor

Attract(ion), Attractive Attrahent, Bait, Barrie, Becoming, Bewitch, Bonny, Bootylicious, Catchy, Charisma, > CHARM, Cheesecake, Clou, Crowd puller, Cute, Cynosure, Dipolar, Dish(y), Draught, > DRAW, Dreamboat, Duende, Engaging, Entice, Epigamic, Eye candy, Eye-catching, Eyeful, Fanciable, Fascinate, Feature, Fetching, Fox(y), Gravity, Groovy, Heartthrob, Himbo, Hunky, Inducement, Inviting, It, Loadstone, Lodestone, Looker, Lovable, Lovely, Lure, Luscious, Magnes, Magnet(ism), Mecca, Mediagenic, Meretricious, Nubile, Photogenic, Picturesque, Pull, Sematic, Sexpot, Shagtastic, Sideshow, Sightly, Slick, Soote, Speciosity, Spunk, Stotter, Striking,

Studmuffin, Taking, Taky, Tasteful, Theme-park, Weber, Winning, Winsome, Zaftig, Zoftig

Attribute Accredit, Allot, Ap(p)anage, Ascribe, Asset, Credit, Gift, Impute, Lay, Metonym, Owe, Quality, Refer, Shtick

Attune Accord, Adapt, Temper

Atypical Aberrant

Aubergine Brinjal, Brown Jolly, Egg-plant, Mad-apple

Aubrey Beardsley

Auburn Abram, Chestnut, Copper, Titian, Vill(age)

Auction(eer) Barter, Bridge, Cant, Dutch, Hammer, Knock out, Outcry, Outro(o)per, Roup, Sale, Subhastation, Tattersall, Vendue

Audacious, **Audacity** Bald-headed, Bold, Brash, Cheek, Chutspah, Der-doing, Devil-may-care, Effrontery, Face, Hardihood, Indiscreet, Insolence, Intrepid, Neck, Nerve, Rash, Sauce

Audience, **Auditorium** Assembly, Court, Durbar, Gate, Hearing, House, Interview, Pit, Sphendone, Tribunal

Audiovisual AV

Audit(or) Accountant, Check, Ear, Environmental, Examine, Green, Inspect, Listener, Position

Audition Cattle-call, Screen-test

Auditory Acoustic, Oral

Audrey Hoyden

Augment(ed) Boost, Eche, Eke, Ich, Increase, Supplement, Swell, Tritone

August Awe-inspiring, Grand, Imperial, Imposing, Lammas, Majestic, Noble, Solemn, Stately, Stern

Augustine, **Augustus** Austin, Hippo, John

Auk Guillemot, Ice-bird, Roch, Rotch(e)

Aunt(ie) Agony, Augusta, Beeb, Giddy, Maiden, Naunt, Sainted, Tia

Aura Aroma, Emanation, Mystique, Nimbus, Odour, Vibrations

Aureole Coronary, Halo, Nimbus

Auricle Ear, Otic

Aurora Eos, Leigh, Matutinal, Merry dancers, Northern lights

Auspice(s) Aegis, Patronage

Auster S-wind

Austere, **Austerity** Ascetic, Astringent, Bleak, Dantean, Hard, > HARSH, Moral, Plain, Rigour, Severe, Spartan, Stern, Stoic, Stoor, Strict, Vaudois, Waldensian

Austin Friar

Australia(n) Alf, Antipodean, Aussie, Balt, Banana-bender, Bananalander, Billjim, Canecutter, Cobber, Currency, Current, Darwinian, Digger, Gin, Godzone, Gumsucker, Gurindji, Jackie, Jacky, Koori, Larrikin, Lucky Country, Murree, Murri, Myall, Norm, Ocker, Oz, Pintupi, Roy, Sandgroper, Strine, Wallaby, Yarra-yabbies

Austrian Cisleithan, Tyrolean

Authentic(ate) Certify, Echt, Genuine, Honest, Notarise, Official, Real, Sign, Test, True, Validate

Author(ess) Anarch, Auctorial, Inventor, Me, Parent, Volumist, Wordsmith, > WRITER

▷ **Author** *may refer to* author of puzzle

Authorise(d), **Authorisation** Accredit, Clearance, Countersign, Delegate, Empower, Enable, Exequatur, Imprimatur, Legal, Legit, > LICENCE, Official, OK, Passport, > PERMIT, Plenipotentiary, Retainer, Sanction, Sign, Stamp, Warrant

Authority, Authoritarian, Authoritative Canon, Charter, Circar, Cocker, Commission, Commune, Crisp, Definitive, Domineering, Dominion, Establishment, Ex cathedra, Expert, Fascist, Free hand, Gravitas, Hegemony, Inquirendo, Jackboot, Licence, Magisterial, Mandate, Mantle, Mastery, Name, Oracle, Permit, > POWER, Prefect, Prestige, Pundit, Remit, Right, Rod, Say-so, Sceptre, Sircar, Sirkar, Source, Supremacy, Unitary, Warrant

Autobiography Memoir

Autocrat(ic) Absolute, Caesar, Cham, Despot, Khan, Neronian, Tsar, Tyrant

Autograph Signature

Autolycus Scrapman

Automatic, Automaton Android, Aut, Browning, Deskill, Instinctive, Machine, Mechanical, Pistol, Quarter-boy, Quarter-jack, Reflex, Robot, RUR, Zombi

Auto-pilot George

Autopsy Necropsy

Auto-suggestion Coueism

Autumn(al) Fall, Filemot, Leaf-fall, Libra, Philamot

Auxiliary Adjunct, Adjuvant, Adminicle, Aide, Be, Feldsher, Have, Helper, Ido, Subsidiary

Avail(able) Benefit, Dow, Eligible, Going, Handy, Off-the-shelf, On call, Open, Pickings, > READY, Serve, Use, Utilise

Avalanche Bergfall, Deluge, Landfall, Landslide, Landslip, Lauwine, Slide, Slip, Snowdrop

Avant-garde Modernistic, Spearhead

Avarice, Avaricious Cupidity, Golddigger, Greed, Money-grubbing, Pleonexia, Sordid

Avatar Epiphany, Incarnation, Rama

Avaunt Away, Go

Avenge(r) Eriny(e)s, Eumenides, Goel, Kurdaitcha, Nightrider, Punish, Redress, Requite, > REVENGE, Steed, Wreak

Avenue Alley, Arcade, Boulevard, Channel, Corso, Cradle-walk, Hall, Madison, Mall, Midway, Passage, Vista, Way, Xyst(us)

Aver Affirm, Asseverate, Depose, Swear, Vouch

Average Adjustment, Av, Batting, Dow Jones, Mean, Mediocre, Middle-brow, Middling, Moderate, Moving, Norm, Par, Particular, Run, Run-of-the-mill, Soso, Standard, Weighted

Averse, Aversion, Avert Against, Antipathy, Apositia, Disgust, Dislike, Distaste, Hatred, Horror, Opposed, Phobic, Scunner, Stave off

Avert Avoid, > DEFLECT, Forfend, Parry, Ward

Aviary Volary

Aviator Airman, Alcock, Bleriot, Brown, Byrd, Earhart, Flier, Hinkler, Icarus, Johnson, Lindbergh, Pilot, Red Baron, Richthofen

Avid Agog, > EAGER, Greedy, Keen

Avifauna Ornis

Avignon Pont

Avocado Aguacate, Guac(h)amole, Pear

Avocet Scooper

Avoid(er), Avoidance Abstain, Ba(u)lk, Boycott, Bypass, Cop-out, Cut, Dodge, Duck, Elude, Escape, Eschew, Evade, Evitate, Evite, Fly, Forbear, Gallio, Hedge, Miss, Obviate, Parry, Prevaricate, Scutage, Secede, Shelve, Shun, Sidestep, Skirt, Spare, Spurn, Waive

Avoirdupois Size, Weight

Avow(ed) Acknowledged, Affirm, Declare, Own, Swear

Await Abide, Bide, Expect, Tarry

Awake(ning) Aware, Conscious, Conversion, Fly, Rouse, Vigilant

Award Academy, Accolade, Addoom, Allot, Alpha, Aret(t), Bafta, Bestow, Bursary, Cap, Clasp, Clio, Crown, Emmy, Exhibition, Golden Raspberry, Golden Starfish, Grammy, Grant, Honours, Logie, Medal, Meed, Mete, Oscar, Padma Shri, Palme d'or, Premium, Present(ation), Prix Goncourt, > PRIZE, Queen's, Razzie, Scholarship, Tony, Trophy, Vir Chakra, Yuko

Aware(ness) Alert, C(o)enesthesis, Cognisant, Conscious, Conversant, ESP, Est, Hep, Hip, Informed, Liminal, Onto, Panaesthesia, Prajna, Presentiment, Samadhi, Scienter, Sensible, Sensile, Sensitive, Sentience, Streetwise, Switched on, Vigilant, Wot

Away Absent, Afield, Apage, Avaunt, By, For-, Fro(m), Go, Hence, Off, Out, Past

▷ **Away** *may indicate* a word to be omitted

Awe(d) D(o)ulia, Dread, Fear, Intimidate, Loch, Overcome, Popeyed, Regard, Respect, Reverent, Scare, Solemn

Awe-inspiring Numinous

Awful(ly) Alas, Deare, Dere, Dire, Fearful, Horrendous, O so, Piacular, Terrible

▷ **Awfully** *may indicate* an anagram

Awkward Angular, Bolshy, Bumpkin, Clumsy, Complicated, Corner, Crabby, Cubbish, Cumbersome, Cussed, Embarrassing, Farouche, Fiddly, Fix, Gangly, Gauche, Gawky, Handless, Howdy-do, Inconvenient, Inept, Kittle-cattle, Lanky, Loutish, Lurdan(e), Lurden, Maladdress, Mauther, Mawr, Naff, Nasty, Ornery, Perverse, Refractory, Slummock, Spot, Sticky, Stiff, Stroppy, Stumblebum, Swainish, Uneasy, Ungainly, Unwieldy, Wry

Awl(-shaped) Brog, Els(h)in, Nail, Stob, Subulate

Awn(ing) Barb, Beard, Canopy, Ear, Shade, Velarium

Awry Agley, Askew, Cam, Kam(me), Wonky

Axe Abolish, Adz(e), Bardiche, Bill, Celt, Chop(per), Cleaver, Curtal, Eatche, Gisarme, Gurlet, Halberd, Halbert, Hatchet, Ice, Jeddart staff, Jethart-staff, Labrys, Lochaber, Mattock, Palstaff, Palstave, Partisan, Piolet, Retrench, Sax, Slate, Sparth(e), Sperthe, Spontoon, Stone, Thunderbolt, Tomahawk, Twibill

Axiom Adage, Motto, Peano's, Proverb, Saw, Saying

Axis Alliance, Anorthic, Anticous, Axle, Caulome, Chital, Cob, Columella, Epaxial, Henge, Hinge, Major, Minor, Modiolus, Myelon, Neutral, Optic, Pivot, Polar, Principal, Rachis, Radical, Spindle, Sympodium, Visual, X, Y, Z

Axle, Axle-shoulder Arbor, Axis, Fulcrum, Hurter, Journal, Live, Mandrel, Mandril, Pivot, Stub

Ay I

Aye Always, Eer, Ever, Yea, Yes

Ayesha She

Azo-dye Para-red

Aztec Nahuatl

B Bachelor, Black, Book, Born, Boron, Bowled, Bravo

Babble(r) Blather, Brook, Chatter, Gibber, Haver, Lallation, Lurry, Prate, Prattle, Runnel, Tonguester, Twattle, Waffle

Babel Charivari, Confusion, Din, Dovercourt, Medley

Baboon Ape, Bobbejaan, Chacma, Dog-ape, Drill, Gelada, Hamadryas, Mandrill, Sphinx

Baby Bairn, Blue, Bub, Bunting, Changeling, Designer, Duck, Grand, Infant, Jelly, Neonate, Nursling, Pamper, Papoose, Plunket, Preverbal, Rhesus, Sis, Small, Sook, Suckling, Tar, Test tube, Thalidomide, Tot, War, Wean

Babylonian Mandaean, Semiramis, Sumerian

Bacchanalian, Bacchus Ivied, Upsee, Ups(e)y

Bacchantes Maenads

Bachelor BA, Bach, Benedict, Budge, Celibate, En garçon, Pantagamy, Parti, Seal, Single, Stag

Bacillus Comma, Germ, Klebs-Loffler, Micrococcus, Virus

Back(ing), Backward Abet, Accompany, Addorse, Again, Ago, Anticlockwise, Antimacassar, Arear, Arrear, Arrière, Assist, Baccare, Backare, Bankroll, Buckram, Champion, Chorus, Consent, Defender, Dorsal, Dorse, Dorsum, Dos, Ebb, Empatron, Encourage, Endorse, Finance, Frae, Fro, Fund, Gaff, Help, Hind, Historic, La-la, Late, Notaeum, Notal, Notum, On, Patronise, Poop, Pronotum, Punt, Rear(most), Retral, Retro(grade), Retrogress, Retrorse, Return, Rev, Reverse, Ridge, Root, Shy, Spinal, Sponsor, Stern, > **SUPPORT**, Sweeper, Tail, Telson, Tergum, Third, Thrae, Tonneau, Ulu, Uphold, Verso, Vie, Vo, Wager, Watteau

▷ **Back(ing)** *may indicate* a word spelt backwards

Back and forth Boustrophedon

Backbiter, Backbiting Catty, Defame, Detract, Libel, Molar, Slander

Backbone Chine, Grit, Guts, Mettle

Backchat Lip, Mouth, Sass

Backer Angel, Benefactor, Patron, Punter, Seconder, Sponsor

Backfire Boomerang

Backgammon Acey-deucy, Lurch, Tick-tack, Trick-track, Tric-trac, Verquere

Background Antecedence, Field, Fond, History, Horizon, Microwave, Muzak, Setting, Ulterior

Backhander Bribe, Payola, Reverso, Sweetener

Backroom Boffin, Boy, Moor

Backslide(r), Backsliding Apostate, Lapse, Regress, Relapse, Revert

Backwash Rift

Backwater Bogan, Ebb, Logan, Retreat, Slough, Wake

Backwoods Boondocks, Boonies, Hinterland

Backyard Court, Patio

Bacon Bard, Canadian, Collar, Danish, Essayist, Flitch, Francis, Gammon, Lardo(o)n, Pancetta, Pig, Pork, Rasher, Roger, Spec(k), Streaky, Verulam

Bacteria, Bacterium Aerobe, Amphitrica, Bacilli, Bacteriological, Botulinum, > BUG, Campylobacter, Chlamydia, Clostridia, Cocci, Coliform, Culture, Detritivore, Diplococcus, Escherichia, > GERM, Gonococcus, Gram-negative, Gram-positive, Intestinal flora, Klebsiella, Listeria, Lysogen, Meningococcus, Microbe, Mother, MRSA, Mycoplasma, Nitrous, Packet, Pasteurella, Pathogen, Probiotic, Prokaryote, Proteus, Pseudomonas, Pus, Ray-fungus, Rhizobium, Rickettsia, Salmonella, Schizomycete, Septic, Serotype, Serum, Shigella, Spirilla, Spirochaete, Spore, Staph, Staphylococcus, Strep(tococcus), Streptobacillus, Streptomyces, Sulphur, Superbug, Thermophil(e), Treponemata, Vibrio, Vinegar-plant, Yersinia, Zoogloea

Bad, Badness Addled, Chronic, Crook, Defective, Diabolic, Dud, Duff, Egregious, Execrable, Faulty, God-awful, Heinous, Ill, Immoral, Inferior, Injurious, Lither, Mal, Naughty, Nefandrous, Nefarious, Nice, Off, Ominous, Oncus, Onkus, Piacular, Poor, Rancid, Rank, Ropy, Scampish, Scoundrel, Sinful, Spoiled, Turpitude, Useless, Wack, Wick, > WICKED

▷ **Bad(ly)** *may indicate* an anagram

Badge Brassard, Brooch, Button, Chevron, Cockade, Cockleshell, Cordon, Crest, Emblem, Ensign, Epaulet, Episemon, Fáinne, Film, Flash, Garter, Gorget, ID, Insignia, Kikumon, Mark, Mon, Rosette, Scallop, Shield, Shouldermark, > SIGN, Symbol, Tiger, Token, Vernicle, Vine-rod, Wings

Badger > ANNOY, Bait, Bedevil, Beset, Brock, Browbeat, Bug, Bullyrag, Cete, Dassi(e), Ferret, Gray, Grey, > HARASS, Hassle, Heckle, Hog, Honey, Hound, Nag, Pester, Plague, Provoke, Ratel, Ride, Roil, Sow, Stinking, Teledu, Wisconsin

Bad habit Cacoethes, Vice

Badinage Banter, Chaff, Raillery

Bad luck Ambs-ace, Ames-ace, Deuce-ace, Hard cheese, Hard lines, Hoodoo, Jinx, Jonah, Shame, Voodoo

Bad-tempered Carnaptious, Curmudgeon, Curnaptious, Curst, Grouchy, Grum(py), Irritable, Moody, Nowty, Patch, Splenetic, Stroppy

Bad woman Harridan, Loose, Mort

Baffle(d), Baffling Anan, Balk, Bemuse, Bewilder, Confound, Confuse, Elude, Evade, Floor, Flummox, Foil, Fox, Get, Hush-kit, Mate, Muse, Mystify, Nark, Nonplus, Pose, Puzzle, Stump, Throw, Thwart

Bag(gage), Bags Acquire, Alforja, Allantois, Amaut, Amowt, Ascus, Ballonet, Besom, Bladder, Blue, Body, Bulse, Buoyancy, Caba(s), Caecum, Callet, Capture, Carpet, Carrier, Carryall, Case, Cecum, Clutch, Cly, Cod, Cool, Corduroy, Crone, Crumenal, Cyst, Daypack, Dilli, Dilly, Dime, Diplomatic, Ditty, Doggy, Dorothy, Douche, Duffel, Dunnage, > EFFECTS, Excess, Flannels, Flotation, Follicle, Galligaskins, Game, > GEAR, Gladstone, Grab, Grip, Gripsack, Grow, Holdall, Ice, Impedimenta, Jelly, Jiffy®, Kill, Lavender, Lithocyst, Marsupium, Meal-poke, Minx, Mixed, Monkey, Musette, Muzzle, Mystery, Nap, Net, Nunny, Overnight, Oxford, Packsack, Pantaloons, Plastic, Plus fours, Pochette, Pock(et), Pocketbook, Pockmanky, Pockmantie, Poke, Politzer's, Poly(thene), Port(manteau), Portmantle, Portmantua, Post, Pot, Pouch, Pounce, Pudding, Punch, Purse, Rake, Red, Reticule, Ridicule, Rucksack, Sabretache, Sac(cule), Sachet, Sack, Saddle, Sag, Satchel, Scent, Scrip, Scrotum, Sea, Shopper, Sick, Slattern, Sleeping, Sponge, Sporran, Stacks, Strossers, Sugar, Survival, Tea, Tote, > TRAP, Trews, Trollop, Trouse(r), Tucker (box), Udder, Unmentionables, Utricle, Valise, Vanity, Viaticals, Waist, Wallet, Water, Weekend, Win, Woolpack, Work, Ziplock

Bagatelle Bauble, Fico, Trifle, Trinket

Bagpipe Biniou, Chorus, Cornemuse, Drone, Musette, Pibroch, Piffero, Skirl,

Sourdeline, Uillean, Zampogna

Bahamas BS

Bail(er), Bailment Bond, Ladle, Mainpernor, Mainprise, Mutuum, Scoop

Bailey Bridge, Castle wall, Ward

Bailiff Adam, Bandog, Beagle, Bum, Factor, Foud, Grieve, Huissier, Hundreder, Hundredor, Land-agent, Nuthook, Philistine, Reeve, Shoulder-clapper, Shoulder-knot, Steward, Tipstaff, Water

Bairn Baby, > CHILD, Infant, Wean

Bait Badger, Berley, Brandling, Burley, Capelin, Chum, Dap, Decoy, Entice, Gentle, Gudgeon, Harass, Hellgram(m)ite, Incentive, Lobworm, Lug(worm), Lure, Mawk, > RAG, Ragworm, Sledge, Teagle, Tease

Bake(r), Baked, Baking Alaska, Batch, Baxter, > COOK, Fire, Kiln-dry, Roast, Scorch, Shirr

Baker's daughter Own

Baker Street Irregular

Balance Account, Beam, Compensation, Counterpoise, Counterweight, Equate, Equilibrium, Equipoise, Equiponderate, Even, Funambulate, Gyroscope, Gyrostat, Invisible, Isostasy, Launce, Libra, Librate, Meet, Otolith, Peise, Perch, Peyse, Poise, > REMAINDER, Remnant, Residual, Rest, Running, Scale, Sea-legs, Spring, Stand, Steelyard, Symmetry, Torsion, > TOTAL, Trial, Trim, Tron(e), Visible

Balcony Circle, Gallery, Loggia, Mirador, Moucharaby, Porch, Quarter-gallery, Sundeck, Tarras, Terrace, Veranda(h)

Bald, Baldness Alopecia, Apterium, Awnless, Barren, Calvities, Coot, Crude, Egghead, Fox-evil, Glabrous, Hairless, Madarosis, Open, Peelgarlic, Pilgarlic(k), Pollard, Psilosis, Slaphead, Smoothpate, Stark, Tonsured

Balderdash Drivel, Flapdoodle, Nonsense, Rot

Baldmoney Emeu, Meu, Spignel

Bale Bl, Bundle, Evil, Lave, Pack, Sero(o)n, Truss

Baleful Evil, Malefic, Malignant

▶ **Balk** see BAULK

Balkan Albanian, Bulgarian, Macedon, Rumanian, Serb, Vlach

Ball(s) Aelopile, Aelopyle, Aeolipile, Aeolipyle, Agglomerate, Alley, Ally, Ammo, Aniseed, Apple, Beach, Bead, Beamer, Birthing, Bobble, Boll, Bolus, Bosey, Bouncer, Break, Buzzer, Caltrap, Caltrop, Camphor, Cap, Cherry, Chin, Chinaman, Chopper, Clew, Clue, Condyle, Cotill(i)on, Cramp, Creeper, Croquette, Crystal, Cue, Curve, Daisy-cutter, > DANCE, Delivery, Dodge, Dollydrop, Dot, Dribbler, Eight, Ensphere, Eolipile, Eolipyle, Eolopile, Eolopyle, Falafel, Felafel, Gazunder, > GLOBE, Glomerate, Googly, Gool(e)ys, Goolies, Grub, Gutta, Gutter, Hank, Hop, Hummer, Inswinger, Ivory, Jump, Knur(r), Leather, Leg-break, Lob, Long-hop, Marble, Masked, Masque(rade), Matzo, Medicine, Minié, Mirror, Moth, Nur(r), O, Object, Off-break, Off-cutter, Off-spin, Orb, Outswinger, Overarm, Pakora, Pea, Pellet, Pill, Poi, Pomander, Pompom, Prom, Puck, Punch, Quenelle, Rabbit, Rissole, Round, Rover, Rundle, Seamer, Shooter, Shot, Sliotar, Sneak, Sphere, Spinner, Stress, Swinger, Taw, Testes, Thenar, Three, Tice, Track(er), Witches, Wood, Yorker

Ballad Bab, Bothy, Broadside, Bush, Calypso, Carol, Folk-song, Lay, Lillibullero, Lilliburlero, > SONG, Torch-song

Ballast Kentledge, Makeweight, Stabiliser, Trim, Weight

Ball-boy Dry-bob

Ballerina Coryphee, Dancer, Pavlova, Prima

Ballet, Ballet movement, Ballet-system Bharat Natyam, Bolshoi, Checkmate,

Développé, Don Pasquale, Écarté, Firebird, Giselle, Kirov, Laban, Labanotation, Leg business, Plie, Pointer, Swan Lake

Ballet-interlude Divertimento

Balloon(ist) Aeronaut, Aerostat, Airship, Bag, Barrage, Billow, Blimp, Bloat, Dirigible, Dumont, Fumetto, Hot air, Lead, Montgolfier, Pilot, Rawinsonde, Sonde, Trial, Weather, Zeppelin

Ballot Butterfly, Election, > POLL, Referendum, Suffrage, Ticket, Vote

Ballot-box Urn

Ballpoint Bic®, Biro®

Balm(y) Anetic, Arnica, Balsam, Calamint, Fragrant, Garjan, Gilead, Gurjun, Lemon, Lenitive, Lotion, > MILD, Mirbane, Myrbane, Nard, Oil, Opobalsam, Ottar, Redolent, Remedy, Soothe, Spikenard, Tiger, Tolu, Unguent

Balmoral Bonnet

Baloney Bunk, Hooey

Balsam Canada, Copaiba, Copaiva, Friar's, Nard, Peruvian, Resin, Spikenard, Tamanu, Tolu(ic), Touch-me-not, Tous-les-mois, Turpentine

Balt Esth, Lett

Baltic Estonian

Bamboo Split cane, Tabasheer, Whangee

Bamboozle(d) Cheat, Dupe, Flummox, Hoodwink, Mystify, Nose-led, Perplex, Trick

Ban Abolish, Accurse, Anathema, Black(ing), Censor, Debar, D-notice, Embargo, Estop, Excommunicate, Forbid, For(e)say, For(e)speak, Gate, Green, Moratorium, No, Outlaw, Prohibit, Proscribe, Taboo, Tabu, Test, Veto

Banal Corny, Dreary, Flat, Hackneyed, Jejune, Mundane, Platitudinous, > TRITE, Trivial

Banana(s) Abaca, Hand, > MAD, Matoke, Musa, Plantain, Scitamineae, Split, Strelitzia

Band(s) Alice, Ambulacrum, Anadem, Armlet, Barrulet, Belt, Border, Braid, Brake, Brass, Brassard, Brassart, Caravan, CB, Channel, Chromosome, Cingulum, Circlet, Citizen's, Clarain, Cohort, Collar, Collet, Combo, Company, Conduction, Corslet, Coterie, Crew, Deely boppers, Elastic, Endorse, Energy, Enomoty, Facia, Falling, Fascia, Fasciole, Ferret, Ferrule, Fess, Filament, Fillet, Frequency, Frieze, Frog, Frontlet, Galloon, Gamelan, > GANG, Garage, Garland, Garter, Gasket, Gaskin, Geneva, Gird, Girth, Guard, > HOOP, Hope, Iron, Jazz, Jug, Kitchen, Label, Laticlave, Lytta, Maniple, Mariachi, Massed, Military, Mourning, Myrmidon, Noise, One-man, Orchestra, Orchestrina, Pack, Parral, Parrel, Parsal, Parsel, Pass, Patte, Pipe, Plinth, Property, Purfle, Puttee, Retinaculum, Rib, Ribbon, Rigwiddie, Rigwoodie, Rim, Ring, Robbers, Rubber, Rymme, Sash, Scarf, Screed, Scrunchie, Scrunchy, Sect, Shadow, Shallal, Shash, Sheet, Shoe, Snood, Steel, Strake, Strap, Stratum, String, Stripe, Swath(e), Tambu-bambu, Tape, Tendon, Throat-latch, Tie, Tippet, Torques, Tourniquet, Train, Troop, Troupe, Tumpline, Turm, Tyre, Unite, Valence, Vinculum, Virl, Vitrain, Vitta, Wanty, Wedding, Weeper, Welt, With(e), Wristlet, Zona, Zone

Bandage Bind, Blindfold, Capeline, Dressing, Fillet, Ligature, Lint, Pledget, Roller, Scapular, Sling, Spica, Suspensor, Swaddle, Swathe, T, Tape, Truss, Tubigrip®, Wadding

Bandicoot Pig-rat

Bandit Apache, Bravo, Brigand, Desperado, Fruit-machine, Gunslinger, Klepht, Moss-trooper, Outlaw, Pirate, Rapparee, > ROBBER, Squeegee, Turpin

Bandsman, Band-leader Alexander, Bugler, Conductor, Maestro, Miller, Wait

Bandy Vie
Bane Curse, Evil, Harm, Poison
Bang(er) Amorce, Big, Cap, Chipolata, Clap, Cracker, Crock, Explode, Flivver, Fringe, Haircut, Heap, Implode, Jalopy, Maroon, Rattletrap, Report, Sausage, Sizzler, Slam, Sonic, Thrill, Wurst
Bangle Anklet, Armlet, Bracelet, Kara
Banish(ment) Ban, Deport, Depose, Exile, Expatriate, Expel, Extradition, Forsay, Maroon, Ostracise, > OUTLAW, Relegate, Rusticate
Banjo Ukulele
Bank(ing) An(n)icut, Asar, Backs, Bar, Bay, Bk, Blood, Bluff, Bottle, Brae, Brim, Bund, Camber, Cay, Central, Chesil, Clearing, Cloud, Commercial, Cooperative, Data, Depend, Deposit, Dogger, Down, Dune, Dyke, Earthwork, Escarp, Fog, Gene, Giro, Glacis, Gradient, Gradin(e), Hele, Hill, Home, Incline, Jodrell, Land, Left, Lender, Levee, Link, Memory, Merchant, Mound, Nap, National, Nore, Overslaugh, Parapet, Penny, Piggy, Pot, Private, Rake, Ramp, Rampart, Reef, > RELY, Reserve, Rivage, Riverside, Rodham, Row, Sandbar, Savings, Shallow, Shelf, Side, Slope, Soil, Sperm, Staithe, State, Sunk, Telephone, Terrace, Terreplein, Tier, Vault, West, World
Banker Agent, Financial, Fugger, Gnome, Lombard, Medici, > RIVER, Rothschild, Shroff
▷ **Banker** *may indicate* a river
Banknote Flimsy, Greenback
Bankrupt(cy) Break, Broke, Bung, Bust, Cadaver, Carey Street, Crash, Debtor, Deplete, Duck, Dyvour, Fail, Fold, Insolvent, Lame duck, Notour, Receivership, Ruin, Rump, Scat, Sequestration, Skatt, Smash
▷ **Bankrupt** *may indicate* 'red' around another word
Bank System Giro
Bann(s) Out-ask
Banner Banderol(e), Bandrol, Bannerol, > FLAG, Gumphion, Labarum, Oriflamme, Sign, Streamer
Banquet Beanfeast, Dine, Feast, Junket, Spread
Banquette Firestep
Bant Diet, Reduce
Banter Badinage, Borak, Chaff, Dicacity, Dieter, Jest, > JOKE, Persiflage, Picong, Rag, > RAILLERY, Rally, Ribaldry, Roast, Tease
Bantu Bosotho, Gazankulu, Herero, Qwaqwa, Shangaan, Sotho, Transkei, Tutsi, X(h)osa
Bap Bread, Roll, Tommy
Baptise(d), Baptism, Baptist Affusion, Amrit, Christen, Dip, Dipper, Dopper, Dunker, Illuminati, Immersion, Sabbatarian, Sprinkle, Tinker
Bar(s) Angle-iron, Anti-roll, Astragal, Asymmetric, Axletree, Bail, Ban, Barrelhouse, Baulk, Beam, Bierkeller, Bilboes, Billet, Bistro, Blackball, Blacklist, Block(ade), Bloom, Bolt, Boom, Bottega, Brasserie, Buffet, Bull, Bumper, But, Buvette, Café(-chantant), Café-concert, > CAGE, Came, Cantina, Capo, Capstan, Cocktail, Coffee, Colour, Counter, Cramp(on), Crow, Crush, Currency, Dive, Double-tree, Draw, Drift, Dumbbell, Espresso, Estop(pel), Except, Exclude, Fen, Fid, Flinders, Forbid, Foreclose, Forestall, Fret, Gad, Gemel, Grate, Grid, Grog-shop, Hame, Handspike, Heck, > HINDRANCE, Horizontal, Hound, Impediment, Ingoes, Ingot, Ingowes, Inn, Inner, Judder, Juice, Karaoke, Kickstand, Knuckleduster, Latch, Let, Lever, Limbo, Line, Local, Lounge, Macron, Mandrel, Mandril, Measure, Menu, Milk, Mousing, Muesli, Mullion, Nail, Nanaimo, No-go, Norman, Obstacle, Onely, Orgue, Outer,

Overslaugh, Oxygen, Parallel, Perch, Pile, Pinch, Pole, Private, Prohibit, Pub, Public, Putlog, Rabble, Rack, Rail, Ramrod, Rance, Randle-balk, Randle-perch, Randle-tree, Reach, Restrict, Rib, Risp, Rod, Roll, Roo, Rung, Saddle, Salad, Saloon, Sans, Save, Saving, Scroll, Semantron, Shaft, Shanty, Shet, Shut, Singles, Skewer, Slice, Slot, Snack, Snug, Spacer, Spar, Speakeasy, Sperre, Spina, Spit, Splinter, Sprag, Stancher, Stanchion, Status, Stave, Sternson, Stick, Stirre, Stretcher, Stripe, Sway, Swee, T, Tael, Tap(-room), Tapas, Taphouse, Tavern(a), Temple, Toll, Tombolo, Tommy, Tool, Torsion, Tow, Trace, Trangle, Transom, Trapeze, Triblet, Trundle, Type, Vinculum, Wall, Ward, Wet, Whisker, Window, Wine, Wire, Wrecking, Z, Zed, Zygon

Barabbas Robber

Barb(ed) Bur(r), Fluke, Harl, Herl, > HOOK, Jag(g), Jibe, Pheon, Prickle, Ramus, Tang, Vexillum

Barbados, **Barbadian** Bajan, Bim(m)

Barbara Allen, Major

Barbarian, **Barbaric** Boor, Crude, Fifteen, Foreigner, Goth, Heathen, Hottentot, Hun, Inhuman, Lowbrow, Outlandish, Philistine, Rude, Savage, Tartar, Tatar(ic)

Barbary Ape, Roan

Barbecue Braai vleis, Cook-out, Flame-grill, Grill, Hangi, Hibachi, Roast, Spit

Barbel Beard

Barber Epilate, Figaro, Scrape(r), Shaver, Strap, Todd, Tonsor, Trimmer

Barbiturate Goofball

Bard Ariosto, Griot, Heine, Meat, Minstrel, Muse, Ossian, Scald, Scop, Skald, Taliesin

Bare, **Bare-headed** Adamic, Aphyllous, Bald, Barren, Blank, Bodkin, Cere, Décolleté, Denude, Hush, Lewd, Marginal, Moon, > NAKED, Open, Plain, Scant, Sear, Stark, Uncase, Uncover, Unveil

Barefoot Discalced, Unshod

Barely At a pinch, At a stretch, Hand-to-mouth, Hardly, Just, Merely, Scarcely, Scrimp

Bargain(ing) Barter, Braata, Chaffer, Champerty, > CHEAP, Collective, Contract, Coup, Deal, Dicker, Distributive, Effort, Find, Go, Haggle, Higgle, Horse-trade, Huckster, Integrative, Option, > PACT, Plea, Productivity, Scoop, Snip, Steal, Supersaver, Time, Trade, Trock, Troke, Truck, Wanworth, Wheeler-dealing

Barge Birlinn, Bucentaur, Budgero(w), Butty, Gabbard, Gabbart, Galley-foist, Hopper, Intrude, Jostle, Keel, Lighter, Nudge, Obtrude, Pra(a)m, Ram, Scow, > SHIP, Trow, Wherry

▷ **Barge** *may indicate* an anagram

Bargee, **Bargeman** Keeler, Keelman, Legger, Lighterman, Ram, Trow

Barium Ba, Witherite

Bark Angostura, Ayelp, Azedarach, Bass, Bast, Bay, Bowwow, Calisaya, Cambium, Canella, Caribbee, Cascara, Cascarilla, Cassia, China, Cinchona, Cinnamon, Cork, Cortex, Cusparia, Honduras, Jesuit's, Kina, Kinakina, Latration, Liber, Myrica, Peel, Pereira, Peruvian, Phloem, Quebracho, Quest, Quillai, Quina, Quinquina, Red, Rind, Sagrada, Salian, Sassafras, Scrape, Scurf, > SHIP, Skin, Slippery elm, Tan, Tap(p)a, Totaquine, Waff, Waugh, Woof, Wow, Yaff, > YAP, Yellow, Yelp, Yip

Bar-keeper, **Barmaid**, **Barman** Advocate, Ale-wife, Bencher, Hebe, Luckie, Lucky, Tapster, Underskinker

Barley (water) Awn, Bear, Bere, Bigg, Hordeum, Malt, Orgeat, Pearl, Pot, Truce, Tsamba

Barm(y) Yeast
Barmecide, Barmecidal Imaginary
Barn Bank, Byre, Cowshed, Dutch, Farm, Grange, Mow, Perchery, Skipper, Tithe
Barnaby Rudge
Barnacle Acorn, Cypris, Goose(neck), Limpet
Barometer Aneroid, Glass, Orometer, Statoscope, Sympiesometer, Torricellian tube, Weatherglass
Baron B, Corvo, Drug, Munchausen, Noble, Thyssen, Tycoon
Baronet Bart
Baronne Dudevant Sand
Baroque Fancy, Gothic, Ornate, Rococo
▷ **Baroque** *may indicate* an anagram
Barrack(s), Barracking Asteism, Boo, Cantonment, Casern(e), Cat-call, Garrison, Heckle, Irony, Quarters
Barrage Balloon, Fusillade, Heat, Salvo
Barred Banned, Edh, Trabeculated
Barrel Bl, Butt, Cade, Capstan, Cascabel, Cask, Clavie, Drum, Hogshead, Keg, Kibble, Morris-tube, Oildrum, Organ, Pièce, Pork, Run(d)let, Tan-vat, Thrall, Tierce, Tun, Vat, Water, Wood
Barrel-organ Apollonicum, Hurdy-gurdy, Street piano
Barren Addle, Arid, Badlands, Blind, Blunt, Clear, Dry, Eild, > EMPTY, Farrow, Hirstie, Jejune, Sterile, Unbearing, Waste, Wasteland, Wilderness, Yeld, Yell
Barrier Bail, Barrage, Bayle, Block, Breakwater, Cauld, Checkrail, Cheval de frise, Chicane, Cordon (sanitaire), Crash, Crush, > DAM, Defence, Drawgate, Dyke, Fence, Fraise, Gate, Heat, Hedge, Hurdle, Mach, Obstruct, Pain, Rail(-fence), Rampart, Restraint, Revetment, Roadblock, Screen, Skreen, Sonic, Sound, Spina, Stockade, Thermal, Tollgate, Trade, Transonic, Turnpike, Turnstile, > WALL
Barrister Advocate, Attorney, Counsel, Devil, Lawyer, Rumpole, Sergeant (at law), Serjeant(-at-law), Silk, Templar, Utter
Barrow Dolly, Handcart, Henge, How, Hurley, Kurgan, Molehill, Mound, Pushcart, Tram, Trolley, Truck, Tumulus
Barrow-boy Coster, Trader
Bar-tail Scamel, Staniel, Stannel
Barter Chaffer, Chop, Coup, Dicker, > EXCHANGE, Haggle, Hawk, Niffer, Sco(u)rse, Swap, > TRADE, Traffic, Truck
Basalt Diabase, Tachylite, Tephrite, Toadstone, Traprock, Wacke
Base Adenine, Alkali, Bed, Beggarly, Billon, Bottom, Caitiff, Camp, Codon, Cytosine, Degenerate, Degraded, Dog, Down, E, Erinite, > ESTABLISH, First, Floor, Foot, Foothold, Footstall, Found, Fundus, Guanine, Harlot, Histamine, Ignoble, Indamine, Infamous, Install, Lewis, > LOW, > MEAN, Nefarious, Nook, Parasaniline, Partite, Patten, Platform, Plinth, Podium, Premise, Ptomaine, Purin(e), Pyrimidine, Pyrrolidine, Radix, Rascally, Rests, Ribald, Root, Rosaniline, Schiff, Servile, Shameful, Shand, Sheeny, Socle, Soda, Spaceport, Staddle, > STAND, Station, Substrate, Ten, Thymine, Torus, Triacid, Turpitude, Unworthy, Uracil, Vile
Baseball Apple, Nine
Baseless Idle, Unfounded, Ungrounded
Base-line Datum
Basement Bargain
Bash Belt, Clout, Go, Hit, Rave, Shot, Slog, Strike, Swat, Swipe
Bashful Awed, Blate, Coy, Modest, Retiring, Shamefast, Sheep-faced, Sheepish,

> SHY

Basic, **Basis** ABC, Abcee, Alkaline, Aquamanale, Aquamanile, Crude,
 > ESSENTIAL, Fiducial, Fond, Fundamental, Ground(work), Gut, Integral,
 Intrinsic, Logic, Nitty-gritty, No-frills, No-nonsense, Pou sto, Primordial,
 Principle, Radical, Rudimentary, Spit-and-sawdust, Staple, Substance,
 Underlying, Uracil

Basilica St Peter's

Basilisk Cannon, Lizard

Basin Aquamanale, Aquamanile, Artesian, Benitier, Bidet, Bowl, Canning,
 Catch, Catchment, Cirque, Corrie, Cwm, Dish, Dock, Doline, Donets, Drainage,
 Foxe, Geosyncline, Great, Impluvium, Kuzbass, Kuznetsk, Lavabo, Laver,
 Minas, Monteith, Pan, Park, Piscina, Playa, Porringer, Reservoir, River, Scapa
 Flow, Slop, Stoop, Stoup, Sugar, Tank, Tarim, Tidal

Bask Apricate, Revel, Sun, Sunbathe, > WALLOW

Basket, **Basket-work** Baalam, Bass, Bassinet, Bread, Buck, Cabas, Calathus,
 Canephorus, Car, Cesta, Cob, Coop, Corbeil(le), Corbicula, Corf, Creel, Cresset,
 Dosser, Fan, Flasket, Flax kit, Frail, Gabian, Hamper, Hask, Junket, Kago,
 Kajawah, Kipe, Kit, Leap, Maund, Mocock, Mocuck, Moses, Murlain, Murlan,
 Murlin, Osiery, Pannier, Ped, Petara, Pitara(h), Pollen, Pottle, Punnet, Rip,
 Scull, Scuttle, Seed-lip, Skep, Skull, Trolley, Trug, Van, Wagger-pagger(-bagger),
 Waste(-paper), Wattlework, Whisket, Wicker(-work), Will(e), Wisket, Work

Basket-bearer Canephor(a), Canephore, Canephorus

Basket-maker Alfa, Cane, Halfa, Wicker

Basque Euskarian

Bass Alberti, Ale, Alfie, B, Continuo, Deep, El-a-mi, Figured, Fish, Largemouth,
 Low, Ostinato, Serran, Smallmouth, Thorough, Walking

Bast Liber

Bastard, **Bastard-wing** Alula, Base, By-blow, Filius nullius, Git, Illegitimate,
 Mamzer, Momzer, Mongrel, Sassaby, Side-slip, Slink, Spuriae, Spurious,
 Whoreson

▷ **Bastard** *may indicate* an anagram

Baste Enlard, Sew, Stitch, Tack

Bastion Citadel, Lunette, Moineau

Bat, **Batter**, **Batting**, **Batsman**, **Batty** Aliped, Ames, Assail, Barbastelle, Baton,
 Belfry, Blink, Chiroptera, Close, Cosh, Crackers, Dad, Die Fledermaus, Eyelid,
 False vampire, Flittermouse, Flying fox, Fruit, Grace, Hammerhead, Hatter,
 Haywire, Hit, Hobbs, Hook, Horseshoe, In, Ink mouse, Insectivorous, Kalong,
 Language, Leisler, Man, Mastiff, Maul, May, Mormops, Mouse-eared, Myopic,
 Nictate, Nictitate, Night, Nightwatchman, Noctilio, Nora, Nurdle, Opener,
 Pinch-hit, Pipistrel(le), Poke, Pummel, Racket, Racquet, Ram, Rearmouse,
 Reremice, Reremouse, Roussette, Ruin, Sauch, Saugh, Scotch hand, Serotine,
 Sledge, Stick, Stonewall, Straight, Striker, Swat, Trap-stick, Vampire,
 Vespertilionid, Viv, Whacky, Willow, Wood

Batch Bake, Bunch

Bath(room) Aerotone, Aeson's, Bagnio, Bain-marie, Bed, Blanket, Blood,
 Bubble, Caldarium, Cor, Dip, En suite, Epha, Foam, Hammam, Hip,
 Hummaum, Hummum, Jacuzzi®, Laver, Mik vah, Mud, Mustard, Piscina,
 Plunge, Salt, Sauna, Shower, Sitz, Slipper, Soak, Spa, Sponge, Steam, Stew,
 Stop, Tepidarium, Therm, Tub, Turkish, Tye, Vapour, Whirlpool, Wife

Bathe, **Bathing** Balneal, Balneation, Balneology, Bay(e), Beath, Bogey, Bogie,
 Dip, Dook, Douk, Embay, Foment, Immerse, Lave, Lip, Skinny-dip, Souse,
 Splash, Stupe, > SWIM, Tub, > WASH

Batman Valet
Baton Mace, Rod, Sceptre, Staff, Truncheon
Batrachian Frog, Toad
▷ **Bats**, **Batting** *may indicate* an anagram
Battalion Bn, Corps, Troop
Batten Fasten, Tie
Batter(ed) Bombard, Bruise, Buffet, Decrepit, Pound
Battery Accumulator, Artillery, Drycell, Field, Galvanic, Henhouse, Nicad, Penlight, Pra(a)m, Primary, Solar, Storage, Troop, Voltaic, Waffle, Water
Battle(s), **Battleground** Action, Affair, Ben, Clash, Cockpit, Combat, > **CONFLICT**, Encounter, Engagement, Field, > **FIGHT**, Fray, Front, Hosting, Joust, Pitched, Royal, Sarah, Sciamachy, Skiamachy, Spurs, Stoor, Stour, Stowre, Theatre, Wage, > **WAR**

● **BATTLES**

3 letters:
Kut
Ulm

4 letters:
Alma
Ivry
Jena
Laon
Loos
Mons
Nile
Zama

5 letters:
Accra
Alamo
Allia
Arcot
Arras
Boyne
Bulge
Crecy
Ipsus
Issus
Lewes
Marne
Parma
Sedan
Somme
Ypres

6 letters:
Actium
Argyle
Arnhem

Barnet
Camlan
Cannae
Cressy
Crimea
Maldon
Naseby
Sadowa
Senlac
Shiloh
Tobruk
Varese
Verdun
Vigrid
Wagram
Wipers

7 letters:
Aboukir
Alamein
Beaches
Britain
Bull Run
Cambrai
Colenso
Coronel
Corunna
Dunkirk
Flodden
Flowers
Glencoe
Jericho
Jutland
Lepanto
Magenta
Marengo

Nations
Picardy
Plassey
Salamis
Warburg

8 letters:
Antietam
Ardennes
Blenheim
Borodino
Bosworth
Clontarf
Culloden
Edgehill
Flanders
Fontenay
Hastings
Inkerman
Jemappes
Manassas
Marathon
Navarino
Omdurman
Philippi
Poitiers
Ragnarok
Saratoga
Talavera
Waterloo

9 letters:
Agincourt
Balaclava
Caporetto
El Alemein

Gallipoli
Ladysmith
Otterburn
Oudenarde
Pharsalia
Ramillies
Sedgemoor
Solferino
Theomachy
Trafalgar
Worcester

10 letters:
Armageddon
Austerlitz
Bunker Hill
Camperdown
Gettysburg
Lundy's Lane
Stalingrad
Steenkerke

11 letters:
Bannockburn
Hohenlinden
Marston Moor
Prestonpans
Thermopylae
Wounded Knee

12 letters:
Flodden Field
Roncesvalles

13 letters:
Bosworth Field

- Little Bighorn
- Passchendaele

14 letters:
Stamford Bridge

15 letters:
Missionary Ridge

Battle-axe Amazon, Bill, Gorgon, Halberd, Ogress, Sparth(e), Termagant, Termagent, Turmagant, Turmagent

Battlement Barmkin, Crenellate, Merlon, Rampart

Battle-order Phalanx

Battleship Carrier, Destroyer, Dreadnought, Gunboat, Man-o'-war, Pocket, Potemkin

Bauble Bagatelle, Gaud, Gewgaw, Trifle

Bauhaus Gropius

Baulk Demur, Gib, Hen, Impede, Jib, Reest, Reist, Shy, Thwart

Bavardage Fadaise

Bawdy Raunchy, Sculdudd(e)ry, Skulduddery

Bawl Bellow, Gollar, Howl, Weep

Bay Ab(o)ukir, Aere, Arm, Baffin, Bantry, Bark, Bell, Bengal, Bight, Biscay, Bonny, Botany, Broken, Byron, Cardigan, Chesapeake, Cienfuegos, Cleveland, Colwyn, Corpus Christi, Cove, Covelet, Creek, Daphne, Delagoa, Delaware, Discovery, Dublin, Dvina, False, Famagusta, Fleet, Frobisher, Fundy, Galway, Gdansk, Georgian, Glace, Golden, Great Australian Bight, Green, Guantanamo, Gulf, Hangzhou, Harbour, Hawke's, Herne, Horse, > **HOWL**, Hudson, Inlet, James, Jervis, Jiazhou, Kavalla, Kuskokwim, Laura, Laurel, Layby, Loading, Lobito, MA, Manila, Massachusetts, Montego, Morton, Narragansett, New York, Niche, Oleander, Omaha, Oriel, Passamaquoddy, Pegasus, Pigs, Plenty, Port Phillip, Poverty, Recess, Red, Roan, St Michel, San Francisco, Santiago, Setubal, Shark, Sick, Sligo, Suvla, Table, Tampa, Tasman, Thunder, Tor, Toyama, Tralee, Ungava, Vae, Vlore, Voe, Waff, Walfish, Walvis, Wash, Whitley, Yowl

Bayonet Jab, Skewer, Stab, Sword

Bazaar Alcaiceria, Emporium, Fair, Fete, Market, Pantechnicon, Sale, Sook, Souk

BBC Auntie

Be Exist, Live, Occur

Beach Bondi, Coast, Daytona, Ground, Hard, Lido, Littoral, Machair, Miami, Omaha, Palm, Plage, Raised, Sand, Seaside, Shingle, Shore, Storm, Strand, Waikiki

Beachcomber Arenaria

Beacon Belisha, Fanal, Landing, Lightship, Need-fire, Pharos, Racon, Radar, Radio, Robot, Signal

Bead(s), Beaded Aggri, Aggry, Baily's, Ballotini, Bauble, Blob, Bugle, Cabling, Chaplet, Crab-stones, Drop, Droplet, Gadroon, Gaud, Kubaloi, Mala, Moniliform, Ojime, Passament, Passement, Paternoster, Poppet, Poppit, Prayer, Rosary, Se(a)wan, Subha, Sweat, Tear, Wampum(peag), Worry

Beadle Apparitor, Bederal, Bedral, Bumble, Herald, Paritor, Verger

Beagle Spy

Beak AMA, Bailie, Bill, Cad, Cere, Coronoid, Egg-tooth, Gar, JP, Kip(p), Magistrate, Master, Metagnathous, Mittimus, Nasute, Neb, Nose, Pecker, Prow, Ram, Rostellum, Rostrum, Shovel

Beaker Cup, Goblet

Beakless Erostrate

Beak-shaped Coracoid

Beam(ing) Arbor, Balance, Bar, Ba(u)lk, Binder, Boom, Bowstring, Box,

Beamish Breastsummer, Bressummer, Broadcast, Bum(p)kin, Cantilever, Carline, Carling, Cathead, Collar, Crosshead, Crosspiece, Deck, Girder, Grin, Hammer, Hatch, Herisson, Holophote, I, Irradiate, Joist, Ke(e)lson, Landing, Laser, Lentel, Lintel, Manteltree, Molecular, Needle, Outrigger, Particle, Pencil, Principal, Purlin, Putlock, Putlog, Radio, > **RAFTER**, > **RAY**, Rayon, Refulgent, Rident, Ridgepole, Rood, Roof-tree, Sandwich, Scantling, Searchlight, Shaft, Shine, Shore, Sleeper, Smile, Solive, Stanchion, Stemson, Sternpost, Straining, Streamer, Stringer, Stringpiece, Summer, Support, Tailing, Tie, Timber, Trabeate, Trabecula, Transom, Trave, Trimmer, Truss, Universal, Viga, Walking, Weigh-bauk, Yard, Yardarm

Beamish Galumphing, Nephew

Bean Abrus, Adsuki, Arabica, Asparagus pea, Baked, Berry, Black, Black-eye, Borlotti, Broad, Bush, Butter, Cacao, Calabar, Castor, Cocoa, Coffee, Cow-pea, Dwarf, Fabaceous, Fava, Flageolet, French, Frijol(e), Garbanzo, Goa, Gram, Green, Haricot, Harmala, Head, Horse, Jack, Jumping, Kachang putch, Kidney, Lablab, Lentil, Lima, Locust, Molucca, Moong, Moth, Mung, Nelumbo, Nib, Noddle, Ordeal, Pichurim, Pinto, Runner, Scarlet runner, Shell, Snap, Soy(a), String, Sugar, Sword, Tonga, Tonka, Tonquin, Urd, Wax, Winged, Yard-long

Beanfeast > **PARTY**, Spree, Wayzgoose

Bear(er), **Bear lover** Abide, Abrooke, Andean, Arctic, Arctophile, Baloo, Balu, Beer, Bigg, Breed, Brook, Brown, Bruin, Brunt, > **CARRY**, Cave, Churl, Cinnamon, Coati-mondi, Coati-mundi, Cub, Demean, Dree, Ean, > **ENDURE**, Engender, Exert, Fur-seal, Gonfalonier, Great, Grizzly, Hack, Ham(m)al, Harbinger, Have, Hold, Honey, Humf, Hump(h), Jampani, Keb, Kinkajou, Koala, Kodiak, Koolah, Lioncel(le), Lionel, Lug, Mother, Nandi, Nanook, Owe, Paddington, Panda, Polar, Pooh, Rac(c)oon, Roller, Rupert, Russia, Sackerson, Seller, Shoulder, Sit, Sloth, Spectacled, Stand, Stay, Stomach, > **SUFFER**, Sunbear, Sustain, Targeteer, Teddy, Teem, Thole, Throw, Tolerate, Tote, Transport, Undergo, Upstay, Ursine, Water, Whelp, White, Wield, Woolly, Yield

Bearberry Manzanita, Uva-ursi

Beard(ed) Aaron, Alfalfa, Anchor, Arista, Assyrian, Aureole, Awn, Balaclava, Barb, Barbiche, Beaver, Belgrave, Cadiz, Cathedral, Charley, Charlie, Confront, Defy, Ducktail, Face, Five o'clock shadow, Forked, Fungus, Goatee, Hair(ie), Hairy, Hear(ie), Imperial, Jewish, Kesh, Lincolnesque, Mephistopheles, Old Dutch, Olympian, Outface, Peak, Pencil, Raleigh, Rivet, Roman T, Screw, Shenandoah, Spade, Stibble, Stiletto, Stubble, Swallowtail, Tile, Trojan, Tuft, Uncle Sam, Vandyke, Whiskerando, Whiskery, Ziff

Beardless Callow, Clean, Tahr, Tehr

▷ **Bearhug** *may indicate* Teddy or similar around a word

Bearing(s) Air, Allure, Amenaunce, Armorial, Aspect, Azimuth, Babbitt, Ball, Behaviour, Bush, Carriage, Deportment, Direction, E, Endurance, Gait, Hatchment, Haviour, Hugger-mugger, Lioncel(le), Lionel, Manner, Mascle, Middy, Mien, N, Needle, Nor, Pheon, Port, Presence, Reference, Relevant, Roller, S, Tenue, Thrust, W, Yielding

▷ **Bearing** *may indicate* compass points

Beast > **ANIMAL**, Arna, Behemoth, Brute, Caliban, Caribou, Chimera, > **CREATURE**, Dieb, Dragon, Dzeren, Gayal, Genet, Grampus, Hippogriff, Hodog, Hog, Hy(a)ena, Hydra, Jumart, Kinkajou, Lion, Mammoth, Marmot, Mastodon, Mhorr, Monoceros, Oliphant, Opinicus, Oryx, Panda, Potto, Quagga, Rac(c)oon, Rhytina, Rother, Rumptifusel, Sassaby, Steer, Sumpter, Tarand, Teg, Theroid, Triceratops, Triton, Wart-hog, Whangam, Yahoo, Yak, Yale, Zizel

Beat(ing), Beaten, Beater Anoint, Arsis, Athrob, Bandy, Bang, Baste, Bastinado, Batter, Battue, Belabour, Belt, Bepat, Best, Blatter, Bless, Bo Diddley, Bubble, Cadence, Cane, Cat, Chastise, Clobber, Club, Clump, Conquer, Cream, Cudgel, Cuff, Curry, Debel, > **DEFEAT**, Ding, Donder, Dress, Drub, Duff up, Excel, Fatigue, Faze, Feague, Feeze, Fibbed, Firk, Flagellate, Flail, Flam, Float, Flog, Floor, Flush, Fly, Fustigate, Hipster, Hollow, Horsewhip, Ictus, Inteneration, Knock, Knubble, Lace, Laidie, Laidy, Lambast(e), Larrup, Lash, Laveer, Lay, Lick, Lilt, Lounder, Mall, Malleate, Mersey, Nubble, Outclass, Outdo, Outflank, Outstrip, Paik, Palpitate, Pash, Paste, Pommel, Pound, Prat, Pug, Pulsate, Pulse, Pulsedge, Pummel, Pun, Quop, Raddle, Ram, Ratten, Resolve, Retreat, Rhythm, Ribroast, Round, Rowstow, Ruff(le), Scourge, Scutch, Slat, Smight, Smite, Soak, Sock, Strap, Strap-oil, Strike, Swinge, Systole, Taber, Tabor, Tabrere, Tachycardia, Tact, Tala, Tattoo, Thesis, Thrash, Thresh, Throb, Thud, Thump, Thwack, Tick, Tired, Top, Torture, Tricrotic, Trounce, Tuck, Tund, Verberate, Vibrate, Wallop, Wappend, Welt, Wham, Whip, Whisk, Whitewash, Wraught, Ybet, Yerk, Yirk
▷ **Beaten-up** *may indicate* an anagram
Beat it Skedaddle, Vamo(o)se
Beatitude Macarism
Beau Admirer, Blade, Brummel, Cat, Damoiseau, Dandy, Flame, Geste, Lair, Lover, Masher, Nash, Spark, Tibbs
Beaufort Scale, Windscale
Beaut(y) Advantage, Bathing, Belle, Bombshell, Camberwell, Charmer, Colleen, Comeliness, Corker, Dish, Doll, Glory, Houri, Hyperion, Lana, Monism, Picture, Pride, Pulchritude, Purler, Sheen, Smasher, Stunner
Beautiful, Beautify Bonny, Bright, Embellish, Enhance, Fair, Fine, Gorgeous, Ornament, Pink, Radiant, Smicker, Specious, To kalon
Beauty spot Patch, Tempe, Tika
Beaver Beard, Castor, Eager, Grind, Mountain, Oregon, Rodent, Sewellel
Because (of) As, Forasmuch, Forwhy, Hence, In, Inasmuch, Sens, Since
Beckon Gesture, Nod, Summons, Waft, Wave
Become, Becoming Apt, Besort, Decent, Decorous, Enter, Fall, Fit, Flatter, Get, Go, Grow, Happen, Occur, Seemly, Suit, Wax, Worth
Bed(ding), Bedstead Air, Allotment, Amenity, Apple-pie, Arroyo, Base, Bassinet, > **BEDCOVER**, Berth, Bottom, Box, Bundle, Bunk, Caliche, Camp, Carrycot, Channel, Charpoy, Cill, Cot(t), Couch(ette), Counterpane, Couvade, Coverlet, Cradle, Crib, Cross, Cul(t)ch, Day, Divan, Doona, Doss, Duvet, Erf, False, Feather, Filter, Fluidized, Flying, Four-poster, Futon, Gault, Greensand, Hammock, Inlay, Kago, Kang, Kip, Knot, Knot garden, Layer, Lazy, Lilo®, Litter, Marriage, Mat, Matrix, Mattress, Murphy, Nap, Nest, Nookie, Oyster, Pad, Paillasse, Pallet, Palliasse, Pan, Parterre, Patch, Pavement, Pay, Pig, Plank, Plant, Plot, Procrustean, Puff, Quilt, Retire, Rollaway, Roost, Rota, Sack, Scalp, Settle, Shakedown, Sill, Sitter, Sleep, Sofa, Standing, Stratum, Stretcher, Sun, Tanning, Test, Thill, Trough, Truckle, Trundle, Twin, Wadi, Wady, Ware, Water, Wealden, Wedding
Bedaub Cake, Deck, Smear
Bed-bug B, B flat, Chinch, Flea, Louse, Vermin
Bedchamber, Bedroom Boudoir, Chamber, Cubicle, Dorm(itory), Dormer, Dorter, Ruelle, Ward
Bedcover Palampore, Palempore
Bedeck Adonise, Adorn, Array, Festoon
▷ **Bedevilled** *may indicate* an anagram

Bedjacket Nightingale

Bedlam Chaos, Furore, Madness, Nuthouse, Tumult, Uproar

Bed-rest Dutch-wife

Bedwetting Enuresis

Bee Athenia, Bumble, Carpenter, Cuckoo, Deseret, Drone, Drumbledor, Dumbledore, Group, Hiver, Honey, Humble, Killer, King, Lapidary, Leaf-cutter, Mason, Mining, Nurse, Queen, Quilting, Raising, Solitary, Spell, Spell-down, Spelling, Swarm, Worker, Working

Beech Antarctic, Copper, Fagus, Hornbeam, Mast, Taw(h)ai, Tree

Bee-eater Merops, Rainbow-bird

Beef(y) Baron, Bleat, Brawny, Bresaola, Bull(y), Bullock, Carpaccio, Charqui, Chateaubriand, Chuck, Complain, Corned, Filet mignon, Groan, Grouse, Hough, Jerk, Kobe, Liebig, Mart, Mice, Mousepiece, Muscle, Neat, Ox, Pastrami, Peeve, Porterhouse, Rother, Salt-junk, Sauerbraten, Sey, Silverside, Sirloin, Stolid, Stroganoff, Tournedos, Tranche, Undercut, Vaccine, Wellington

Beefeater Billman, Exon, Gin, Oxpecker, Warder, Yeoman

Bee-glue Propolis

Beehive Alveary, Apiary, Ball, Gum, Skep

Beelzebub Devil

Beer Ale, Alegar, Amber fluid, Bantu, Bitter, Black, Bock, Chaser, Draught, Drink, Dry, Entire, Export, Gill, Ginger, Granny, Grog, Guest, Heavy, Herb, Home-brew, Kaffir, Keg, Kvass, Lager, Lambic, Lite, Lush, Malt, March, Middy, Mild, Mum, Near, Nog, October, Pils(e)ner, Pint, Pony, Porter, Real, Root, Saki, Scoobs, Sherbet, Skeechan, Small, Spruce, Stingo, Stout, Swanky, Swats, Swipes, Switchel, Table, Taplash, Tinnie, Tipper, Tshwala, Tube, Wallop, Wheat, Zythum

Beer garden Brasserie

Bee's nest Bink

Beet Blite, Chard, Fat-hen, Goosefoot, Mangel(wurzel), Spinach, Sugar

Beetle Ambrosia, Anobiid, Argos tortoise, Asiatic, Bacon, Bark, Batler, Bee, Blister, Bloody-nosed, Boll weevil, Bombardier, Bruchid, Bug, Bum-clock, Buprestidae, Buprestus, Burying, Bustle, Buzzard-clock, Cabinet, Cadelle, Cane, Cantharis, Carabid, Cardinal, Carpet, Carrion, Chafer, Christmas, Churchyard, Cicindela, Click, Clock, Cockchafer, Cockroach, Coleoptera, Colorado, Coprophagan, Curculio, Darkling, Deathwatch, Dermestid, Devil's coach-horse, Diving, Dor(r), Dor-fly, Dumbledore, Dung, Dyticus, Dytiscus, Elater, Elytron, Elytrum, Firefly, Flea, Furniture, Glow-worm, Gold(smith), Goliath, Gregor, Ground, Hammer, Hangover, Hercules, Hop-flea, Hornbug, Huhu, Humbuzz, Impend, Japanese, Jewel, June, Khapra, Ladybird, Ladybug, Lamellicorn, Larder, Leaf, Leather, Longhorn, Longicorn, Mall(et), Maul, May-bug, Meloid, Museum, Musk, Oakpruner, Oil, Overhang, Pill, Pinchbuck, Pine, Potato, Project, Protrude, Race(-bug), Rhinoceros, Rhynchophora, Roach, Rosechafer, Rove, Sacred, Scamper, Scarab(ee), Scavenger, Scolytus, Scurry, Sexton, Shard, Skelter, Sledge(-hammer), Snapping, Snout, Soldier, Spanish fly, Spider, Spring, Stag, Tenebrio, Tiger, Toktokkie, Tortoise, Tumble-bug, Tumble-dung, Turnip-flea, Typographer, Vedalia, VW, Water, Weevil, Whirligig, Wireworm, Woodborer, Wood-engraver

Beetle-crushers Cops

Befall Happen, Occur

Before(hand) A, Advance, Ante, Avant, By, Coram, Earlier, Early, Ere, Erst(while), > **FORMER**, Or, Pre, Previously, Prior, Pro, Sooner, Till, To, Until, Van, Zeroth

Before food Ac

Befriend Assist, Cotton, Fraternise, Support

Befuddle Bemuse, Inebriate, Stupefy

Beg(gar), Beggarly, Begging Abr(ah)am-man, Ask, Badgeman, Beseech, Besognio, Bey, Bezonian, Blighter, Blue-gown, Cadge, Calendar, Clapper-dudgeon, Crave, > ENTREAT, Exoration, Flagitate, Fleech, Gaberlunzie, Gangrel, Hallan-shaker, Implore, Impoverish, Irus, Jarkman, Lackall, Lazar(us), Lazzarone, Lumpenproletariat, Maund, Mendicant, Mump, Niggardly, Obtest, Palliard, Panhandle, Pauper, Penelophon, Penniless, > PLEAD, Pled, Pray, Prig, Prog, Ptochocracy, Rag, Randie, Randy, Ruffler, Ruin(ate), Sadhu, Schnorr(er), Screeve, Scrounge, Shool(e), Skelder, Skell, Solicit, Sue, Supplicate, Thig(ger), Toe-rag, Touch, Undo, Whipjack

Beget Gender

Beggar rule Ptochocracy

Begging bowl Clackdish, Clapdish

Begin(ner), Beginning Ab ovo, Alpha, Author, B, Babyhood, Black, Cause, Clapdash, Commence, Daw, Dawn, Deb, Debut, Embryo, Enter, Exordium, Fall-to, Fledgling, Genesis, Germ, Go, Greenhorn, Inaugural, Inception, Inchoate, Incipient, Incipit, Initial, Initiate, Intro, L, Lead, Learn, Learner, Logos, Nascent, Neophyte, > NOVICE, Oncome, Onset, Ope(n), Ord, > ORIGIN, Outbreak, Pose, Prelim(inary), Presidium, Primer, Rookie, Seed, Set, > START, Startup, Takeoff, Tenderfoot, Tiro, To-fall, Tyro, Tyro(ne), Yearn

Begone Aroint, Aroynt, Avaunt, Scram, Shoo, Vamo(o)se

Begonia Elephant's-ear(s)

Begorrah Bedad, Musha

Begrudge Envy, Resent

Beguile(r) Charm, Coax, Divert, Enchant, Ensnare, Flatter, Gull, Intrigue, Jack-a-lantern, Wile

Behalf Ex parte, For, Part, Sake

Behave, Behaviour, Behaving Acquired, Act, Conduct, Convenance, Decorum, Demean, Deportment, Do, Epimeletic, Etepimeletic, Ethics, Goings-on, Horme, > MANNER, Nature, Netiquette, Noblesse oblige, Obey, Praxeology, Quit, React, Response, Satisficing, Strong meat, Tribalism, Unreasonable

Behead Decapitate, Decollate, Guillotine

Behind(hand) Abaft, Aft(er), Ahind, Ahint, Apoop, Arear, Arere, Arrear, Arse, Astern, Beneath, Bottom, Bum, Buttocks, Croup, Derrière, Fud, Late, Overdue, Post, Prat, > REAR, Slow, Tushie

Behold(en) Affine, Ecce, Eye, Here's, Indebted, La, Lo, Look, Observe, See, View

Beige Greige, Tan

Being Cratur, Creature, Ens, Entia, Entity, Esse, Essence, Existence, Human, Man, Metaphysics, Mode, Nature, Omneity, Ontology, > PERSON, Saul, Soul, Subsistent, Substance, Supreme, Ubiety, Wight

Bejabers Arrah

Belch Boak, Boke, Brash, Burp, Emit, Eruct, Rift, Spew, Yex

Belcher Foulard, Handkerchief, Toby

Beldam(e) Crone, Hag, Harridan, Scold

Belfry Campanile, Tower

Belgian Flemish, Walloon

Belief, Believe, Believed, Believer, Believing Accredit, Anata, Ativism, Bigot, Buy, Christian, Conviction, Credence, Credit, Creed, Cult, Culture, Deem, Deist, Doctrine, Doxastic, Doxy, Dukkha, Faith, Formulism, Gnostic, Heterodoxy, Hold, Holist, Idea, Islam, Ism, Ludism, Manichaeism, Meme, Messianist,

Methink, Notion, > **OPINION**, Orthopraxy, Ovist, Pacifism, Pantheism, Persuasion, Physicism, Pluralism, Presumption, Religion, Reputed, Seeing, Shema, Solfidian, Superstition, Suspect, Tenet, Theist, Think, Threap, Threep, Transcendentalism, Trinitarian, Trow, Trust, Ubiquitarianism, Unitarian, Universalism, Wear, Wis(t)

Belittle Cheapen, Cry down, Decry, Depreciate, Derogate, Discredit, Disparage, Downgrade, Humble, Pooh-pooh, Slight

Bell(s) Angelus, Ben, Big Ben, Bob, Bow, Bronte, Cachecope, Canterbury, Carillon, Chime, Chinese pavilion, Crotal, Curfew, Daisy, Diving, Division, Gong, Grandsire, Jar, Low, Lutine, Minute, Mort, Pancake, Passing, Pavilion, Peal, Peter, Pinger, Pudding, Ring, Roar, Sacring, Sanctus, Shark, Sleigh, Tailor, Tantony, Tenor, Tent, Tintinnabulum, Tocsin, Toll, Tom, Triple, Tubular, Vair, Vaire, Verry

Bell-bird Arapunga, Campanero

Belle Beauty, Starr, Toast, Venus

Bell-founder Belleter

Bellicose, **Belligerent** Chippy, Combatant, Gung-ho, Hostile, Jingoist, Martial, Militant, Truculent, Warmonger

Bellow(s) Buller, Holla, Holler, Moo, Rant, Rave, Roar, Rout, Saul, Thunder, Troat, Tromp(e), Trumpet, Windbag

Bell-ringer, **Bell-ringing** Bob, Campanology, Changes, Clapper, Course, Grandsire, Handstroke, Hunting, Maximus, Quasimodo, Rope, Sally, Tocsin, Toller

Belly Abdomen, Alvine, Bag, Beer, Bunt, Calipee, Celiac, Coeliac, Kite, Kyte, Pod, > **STOMACH**, Swell, Tum(my), Venter, Wame, Weamb, Wem(b), Womb

Belong, **Belonging(s)** Apply, Appurtenant, Chattels, Effects, Incident, Inhere, Intrinsic, Paraphernalia, Pertain, > **PROPERTY**, Relate, Traps

Beloved Acushla, Alder-lief, Boyfriend, David, Dear, Doy, Esme, Inamorata, Joy, Lief, Pet, Popular, Precious

Below Beneath, Inf(erior), Infra, Nether, Sub, Under, Unneath

Belt(ed) Baldric(k), Band, Bandoleer, Bandolier, Baudric(k), Bible, Black, Cartridge, Chastity, Clitellum, Clobber, Commuter, Conveyor, Copper, Cotton, Crios, Demolition, Equator, Fan, Fold and thrust, Gird(le), Girt, Great, Green, Hip, Inertial, Judoka, Kuiper, Larrup, Life, Lonsdale, Mitre, Money, Muesli, Orion's, Orogenic, Polt, Pound, Radiation, Roller, Rust, Safety, Sam Browne, Sanitary, Sash, Seat, Speed, Stockbroker, Storm, Strap, Stratosphere, Sun, Surcingle, Suspender, Swipe, Sword, Taiga, Tear, Tore, Tract, Van Allen, Wanty, Webbing, Wing, Zodiac, Zone, Zoster

Belt up Sh

Belvedere Gazebo, Mirador

Bemoan > **LAMENT**, Mourn, Sigh, Wail

Bemuse Infatuate, Stonn(e), Stun, Stupefy, Throw

Ben Battle, Hur, Jonson, Mountain, Nevis, Spence

Bench Banc, Banker, Bink, Bleachers, Counter, Court, Cross, Exedra, Form, Front, King's, Knifeboard, Magistrates, Optical, Pew, Queen's, Rusbank, > **SEAT**, Settle, Siege, Stillage, Thoft, Thwart, Treasury, Trestle, Widow's

Benchmark Criteria, Yardstick

Bend(er), **Bending**, **Bends** Angle, Arc, Arch, Articular, Becket, Bight, Binge, Buck(le), Bust, Camber, Carrick, Chicane, Circumflect, Corner, Crank(le), Cringe, > **CROOK**, Curl, Curve, Diffraction, Dog-leg, Double up, Elbow, Engouled, Epinasty, Es(s), Expansion, Falcate, Fawn, Flex(ural), Flexion, Flexure, Fold, Geller, Geniculate, Genu, Genuflect, Grecian, Hairpin, Hinge,

Hook, Horseshoe, Hunch, Incline, Inflect, Kink, Knee(cap), Kneel, Knot, Kowtow, Meander, Mould, Nutant, Ox-bow, Plash, Plié, Ply, Recline, Reflex, Retorsion, Retortion, Retroflex, Riband, S, Scarp, Sheet, Souse, Spree, Spring, Stave, Stoop, Swan-neck, Twist, U, Ups(e)y, Uri, Wale, Warp, > **YIELD**, Z

▷ **Bendy** *may indicate* an anagram

Beneath Below, Sub, Under, Unworthy

Benedict(ine) Black Monk, Cluniac, Dom, Eggs, Maurist, Olivetan, OSB, Tironensian, Tyronensian

Benediction Blessing, God-speed

Benefactor Angel, Backer, Barmecide, Carnegie, Donor, Maecenas, > **PATRON**, Promoter

Beneficial, Beneficiary, Benefit, Benefice > **AID**, Alms, Avail, Behalf, Behoof, Behove, Bonus, Boon, Boot, Charity, Collature, Commendam, Commensal, Devisee, Disablement, Dole, Donee, Endorsee, Enure, FIS, Fringe, Housing, Incapacity, Incumbent, Inheritor, Injury, Inure, Invalidity, Living, Manna, Maternity, Ménage, Neckverse, Pay, Perk, Perquisite, Plus, Portioner, Postulate, Prebend, Profit, Sake, Salutary, Sanative, Sickness, Sinecure, Spin-off, Stipend, Supplementary, Symbiotic, Unemployment, Use, Usufruct

Benevolence, Benevolent Charitable, Clement, Humanitarian, Kind, Liberal, Pecksniffian, Philanthropy

Benighted Ignorant

Benign Affable, Altruistic, Gracious, Kindly, Trinal

Benin DY

Benito Duce, Mussolini

Benjamin Franklin

Bennett Alan, Phil

Bent Akimbo, Bowed, Brae, Coudé, Courb, Crooked, Curb, Determined, Dorsiflex, Falcate, Fiorin, Flair, Geniculate, Habit, Heath, Inclination, Ingenium, Intent, Leant, Peccant, Penchant, Ply, Reclinate, Redtop, Round-shouldered, Scoliotic, Talent, Taste

▷ **Bent** *may indicate* an anagram

Bent grass Fiorin, Redtop

Bentham Utilitarian

Benzine Kinone, Phene, Toluene, Toluol

Bequeath, Bequest Bestow, Chantr(e)y, Demise, Endow, Heirloom, > **LEAVE**, Legacy, Mortification, Pittance, Transmit, Will

Berate(d) Censure, Chide, Jaw, Reproach, Scold, Shent, Slate, Vilify

Berber Almoravide, Kabyle, Rif(i), Riff, Shluh, Tuareg

Bereave(d), Bereavement Deprive, Loss, Mourning, Orb, Sorrow, Strip, Widow

Beret Green

Berg Alban, Floe

Bermuda Shorts

Bernard Levin, Shaw

Bernini Baroque

Berry Allspice, Bacca, Cubeb, Fruit, Goosegog, Haw, Pepo, Peppercorn, Pigeon, Pimento, Pottage, Rhein, Rhine, Sal(l)al, Slae, Sloe, Sop, Tomatillo

Berserk Amok, Ape-shit, Baresark, Frenzy, Gungho, Rage

Berth Anchorage, Bunk, Cabin, Couchette, Dock, Moor, Seat, Space

Beryl Aquamarine, Emerald, Heliodor, Morganite, Silica

Beryllium Be

Beseech Beg, Crave, Entreat, Implore, Invoke, Obsecrate

Beset Amidst, Assail, Assiege, Badger, Bego, Environ, Harry, Perplex, Scabrid,

Siege

Beside(s) Adjacent, Alone, And, At, Au reste, Else, Forby(e), Further(more), Moreover, Next, On, Withal, Yet

Besiege(d) Beset, Best(ed), Blockade, Gherao, Girt, Invest, Obsess, Plague, Surround

▷ **Besiege** *may indicate* one word around another

Besmirch Smear, Soil, Sully

Besom Cow, Kow

Besot(ted) Dotard, Infatuate, Intoxicate, Lovesick, Stupefy

Bespangle Adorn, Gem

Bespeak, Bespoken Address, Bee, Beta, Engage, Hint

Best A1, Ace, Aristocrat, Beat, Choice, Cream, Creme, Damnedest, Deluxe, Elite, Eximious, Finest, Flagship, Flower, Foremost, Greatest, Ideal, Optima, Outdo, Outwit, Overcome, Peak, Peerless, Pick, Pièce de résistance, Pink, Plum, Purler, Quintessence, Ream, Super, The, The tops, Tiptop, Top, Topper, Transcend, Wale

Bestiality Zoophalia

Bestiary Physiologus

Best man Paranymph

Bestow Accord, Bequeath, Donate, > GIVE, Impart, Present

Bestride Cross

Bet(ting), Betting System A cheval, Ante, Back, Banco, Chance, Double, Each way, Flutter, Gaff, Gamble, Go, Hedge, Impone, Lay, Long shot, Martingale, Mise, Note, Pari-mutuel, Perfecta, Pip, Punt, Quadrella, Quinella, Ring, Risk, Roll up, Saver, Set, Spec, Sport, Spread, Stake, Superfecta, Tattersalls, Tatts, Totalisator, Totalise, Tote, Treble, Treble chance, Triella, Trifecta, > WAGER, Yankee

Betel Catechu, Pan, Pawn, Siri(h)

Betimes Anon, Early, Soon

Betise Solecism

Betray(al), Betrayer Abandon, Abuse, Belewe, Cornuto, Desert, Divulge, Dob, Double-cross, Gethsemane, Giveaway, Grass, Judas, Renegade, Renege, Rumble, Sell, Sellout, Shop, Sing, Sinon, Stab, Traditor, Traitor, Treachery, Treason, Turncoat

Betroth(ed), Betrothal Assure, Engage, Ensure, Espouse, Fiancé(e), Pledge, Subarr(h)ation

Better Abler, Amend, Apter, Bigger, Buck, Cap, Convalescent, Fairer, Finer, Gambler, Gamester, Imponent, Improve, Meliorate, Mend, Outdo, Outpoint, Outshine, Outsmart, Outstrip, Outwit, Preponderate, Punter, Race-goer, Reform, Superior, Surpass, Throw, Top, Turfite, Worst

Between Amid, Bet, Betwixt, Inter, Interjacent, Linking, Mesne, Twixt

Bevel Angle, Cant, Oblique, Slope, Splay

Beverage Ale, Cocoa, Coffee, Cordial, Cup, > DRINK, Hydromel, Nectar, Tea

Bevy Flock, Group, Herd, Host

Beware Cave, Fore, Heed, Mind, Mistrust, Pas op

Bewilder(ed), Bewilderment Amaze, At sea, Baffle, Buffalo, Confuse, Consternation, Daze, Flummox, Mate, Maze, Mystify, Perplex, Stun, Taivert, Will, Wull

Bewitch(ed), Bewitching Charm, Delight, Elf-shot, Enchant, Ensorcell, Glam(orous), Hex, Hoodoo, Jinx, Obeah, Obiah, Strike

Beyond Above, Ayont, Besides, Farther, Outwith, Over, Thule, Trans, Ulterior

Bias(ed) Angle, Aslant, Bent, Chauvinism, Discriminatory, Grid, Imbalance,

Loaded, One-sided, Partial, Parti pris, Partisan, Penchant, Predilection,
> **PREJUDICE**, Prepossess, Sexism, Skew, Slope, Tendency, Unjust, Warp

Bib, **Bibulous** Apron, Beery, Feeder, Pout, Tope, Tucker

Bibelot Objet d'art

Bible Adulterous, Alcoran, Alkoran, Antilegomena, Apocrypha, Authority, AV, Avesta, Bamberg, Book, Breeches, Bug, Coverdale, Cranmer, Cromwell, Douai, Douay, Family, Ferrara, Fool, Forgotten sins, Gemara, Geneva, Gideon, Good book, Goose, Gospel, Gutenberg, Hagiographa, Hexapla, Holy, Idle, Isagogic, Itala, Italic, King James (version), Leda, Matthew Parker, Mazarin(e), Midrash, Missal, Murderer, New English, NT, Omasum, Ostrog, OT, Pentateuch, Peshito, Peshitta, Peshitto, Polyglot, Psalter, Revised Version, RSV, RV, Scriptures, Septuagint, Stomach, Talmud, Tanach, Tantra, Targum, Taverner, Taverners, Thirty-six-line, Treacle, Tyndale, Unrighteous, Vinegar, Vulgate, Whig, Wicked, Wife-hater, Wyclif(fe), Zurich

Biblical scholar Rechabite, USPG, Wycliffe

Bibliophagist, **Bibliophile** Bookworm

Bicarb Saleratus

Bicker Argue, Bowl, Brawl, Coggie, Dispute, Tiff, Wrangle

Bicycle, **Bike(r)** Bambi, Bone-shaker, Coaster, Dandy-horse, Dirt, Draisene, Draisine, Exercise, Fixed-wheel, Hobby, Hobbyhorse, Mixte, Moped, Mount, Mountain, Multicycle, Ordinary, Pedal, Penny-farthing, Quad, Raleigh®, Recumbent, Roadster, Safety, Scooter, Spin, Tandem, Trail, Tree, Velocipede

Bid(der), **Bidding system** Acol, Apply, Call, Canape, Command, Contract, Declare, Double, Forcing, Gone, Hostile, Invite, Jump, Misère, Nod, NT, > **OFFER**, Order, Pass, Pre-empt, Proposal, Psychic, Puffer, Redouble, Shut-out, Summon, Take-over, Tell, Tender, Vied, White bonnet

Biddy Gammer

Biennial Trieteric

Bier Hearse, Litter

Big Beamy, Bulky, Bumper, Burly, Cob, Enormous, Fat, Ginormous, Gross, > **LARGE**, Loud, Mansize, Massive, Mighty, Obese, Skookum, Slockdoliger, Slockdologer, Soc(k)dologer, Sogdolager, Sogdoliger, Stonker, Thumping, Tidy, Vast, Whacker, Whopper

Bigamy, **Bigamist**, **Bigamous** Bluebeard, Diandrous

Bight Canterbury, Heligoland

Bigot(ed) Chauvinist, Dogmatist, Fanatic, Hide-bound, Intolerant, Narrow-minded, Racialist, Sexist, Wowser, Zealot

Bigshot, **Bigwig** Cheese, Law lord, Nib, Nob, Oner, Oneyer, Oneyre, Swell, > **VIP**

Bijou Doll-like

▶ **Bike** *see* **BICYCLE**

Bikini Atoll, Tanga

Bile, **Bilious(ness)** Cholaemia, Choler, Gall, Icteric, Melancholy, Scholaemia, Venom, Yellow

Bilge Leak, Pump, Rot, Waste

Bilingual Diglot

Bilk Default

Bill(y) Ac(c), Accommodation, Accompt, Account, Act, Ad, Addition, Barnacle, Beak, Becke, Budd, Buffalo, Can, Carte, Chit(ty), Cody, Coo, Coronoid, Demand, Dixy, Docket, Double, Due, Exactment, Fin, Finance, Foreign, Gates, Goat, Hybrid, Invoice, Kaiser, > **LAW**, Lawin(g), Legislation, Liam, Liar, List, Measure, Menu, Neb, Ness, Nib, > **NOTE**, Notice, Pork barrel, Portland, Poster, Private, Programme, Public, Reckoning, Reform, Remanet, Rhamphotheca, Rostral,

Rostrum, Score, Short, Shot, Show, Sickle, Silly, Sparth(e), Sperthe, Spoon, Sticker, Tab, Tomium, Trade, Treasury, True, Twin, Victualling, Willy

Billet Berth, Casern, Cess, Chit, Coupon, Note, Quarter

Billet doux Capon, Valentine

Billiards, **Billiards player**, **Billiards stroke** Bar, Cannon-game, Cueist, Jenny, Long jenny, Massé, Pocket, Pool, Potter, Pyramids, Snooker, Whitechapel

Billion Gillion, Milliard, Tera

Bill of sale Bs

Billow Roil, Roller, Rule, Surge, Swell, Wave

Bin Bing, Box, Container, Crib, Dump, Hell, Receptacle, Sin, Snake-pit, Stall, Wagger-pagger, Wheelie, Wheely

Binary ASCII, Semidetached

Bind(er), **Binding** Adherent, Adhesive, Akedah, Alligate, Apprentice, Astrict, Astringent, Bale, Bandage, Bandeau, Bandster, Bias, Bibliopegist, Brail, Burst, Calf, Chain, Cinch, Circuit, Clamp, Colligate, Complain, Cord, Cummerbund, Deligation, Drag, Edge, Embale, Enchain, Engage, > **FASTEN**, Fetter, Galloon, Gird, Girdle, Grolier, Hay-wire, Hold, Incumbent, Indenture, Iron, Keckle, Lash(er), Law-calf, Leash, Ligament, Ligature, Mail, Marl, Morocco, Muslin, Obi, Obligate, Oblige, Oop, Organdie, Oup, Parpen, Perfect, Pinion, Raffia, Restrict, Ring, > **ROPE**, Roxburghe, Sheaf, Spiral, Strap, Stringent, Stygian, Swathe, Syndesis, Tape, Tether, Thirl, Thong, Three-quarter, Tie, Tree-calf, Truss, Twine, Valid, Whip, Withe, Yapp, Yerk, Yoke

Bindweed Bearbine, Convolvulus, With(y)wind

Bing Crosby, Go, Heap

Binge Bat, Beano, Bend(er), Blind, Carouse, > **DRINK**, Drinking-bout, Party, Riot, Soak, Souse, Splore, Spree, Toot, Tout

Bingo Beano, Housey-housey, Keno, Lotto, Tombola

Binocular(s) Glasses, OO, Stereoscope

Biochemical, **Biochemist(ry)** Ames, DNA, Proteomics

Biographer, **Biography** Boswell, CV, Hagiography, History, Life, Memoir, Plutarch, Potted, Prosopography, Suetonius, Vita

Biology, **Biologist** Cladistics, Mendel, Phenetics, Photodynamics, Somatology, Teratology

Bioscope Kinema

Birch Birk, Cane, Cow, Flog, Hazel, Kow, Larch, Reis, Rice, Rod, Silver, Swish, Twig, Weeping, Whip, White, Withe

Bird(s) Al(l)erion, Aves, Avian, Bertram, Brood, Damsel, Doll, Early, Flier, Fowl, Gal, > **GIRL**, Grip, Hen, Jail, Left, Ornis, Pecker, Pen, Poultry, Quod, Raptor, Roaster, Sis, Skirt, Time

BIRDS

2 letters:	Jay	Ree	Cobb
Ka	Kae	Roc	Coly
	Kea	Ruc	Coot
3 letters:	Maw	Tit	Crax
Ani	Mew	Tui	Crow
Auk	Moa		Dodo
Boo	Nun	4 letters:	Dove
Cob	Owl	Barb	> DUCK
Emu	Pea	Chat	Emeu
Fum	Pie	Cirl	Erne

- Eyas
- Fung
- Gled
- Gnow
- Guan
- Guga
- Gull
- Hawk
- Hern
- Huia
- Huma
- Ibis
- Iynx
- Jynx
- Kagu
- Kaka
- Kite
- Kiwi
- Knot
- Kora
- Lark
- Loom
- Loon
- Lory
- Mina
- Monk
- Myna
- Nene
- Otis
- Pavo
- Pawn
- Pern
- Piet
- Pink
- Pown
- Pyot
- Rail
- Rhea
- Roch
- Rook
- Ruff
- Ruru
- Rype
- Shag
- Smee
- Sora
- Swan
- Taha
- Teal
- Tern
- Tick
- Tody

Tuli
Weka
Wren
Xema
Yale
Yite

5 letters:
Agami
Ardea
Ariel
Bennu
Booby
Bosun
Capon
Colin
Colly
Crake
Crane
Diver
Egret
Finch
Fleet
Galah
Glede
Goose
Goura
Grebe
Heron
Hobby
Homer
Isaac
Junco
Kight
Liver
Lowan
Macaw
Madge
Manch
Mavis
Merle
Mimus
Monal
Murre
Mynah
Nandu
Nelly
Noddy
Ousel
Ox-eye
Peggy
Pekan

Pewit
Picus
Pilot
Piper
Pipit
Pitta
Poaka
Poker
Potoo
Prion
Quail
Quest
Quist
Raven
Reeve
Rifle
Robin
Rotch
Ryper
Saker
Scape
Scart
Scaup
Scops
Scray
Scrub
Serin
Shama
Sitta
Skart
Snipe
Solan
Soree
Spink
Sprug
Squab
Stare
Stilt
Stint
Stork
Swift
Sylph
Terek
Tewit
Topaz
Twite
Umber
Umbre
Urubu
Veery
Vireo
Wader

Whaup
Widow
Wonga
Yaffa

6 letters:
Aquila
Avocet
Avoset
Bantam
Barbet
Bishop
Bittor
Bittur
Bonxie
Boubou
Brolga
Bulbul
Canary
Chough
Chukar
Condor
Corbie
Coucal
Cuckoo
Curlew
Cushat
Darter
Dikkop
Dipper
Drongo
Duiker
Dunlin
Duyker
Elanet
Evejar
Falcon
Fulmar
Gambet
Gander
Gannet
Garuda
Gentle
Gentoo
Go-away
Godwit
Gooney
Goslet
Grakle
Hagden
Hagdon
Haglet

Hermit	Quoist	Apteryx	Hagbolt
Hoopoe	Redcap	Babbler	Hagdown
Houdan	Reeler	Bécasse	Halcyon
Jabiru	Roller	Bee-kite	Harrier
Jacana	Scamel	Bittern	Hemipod
Jaegar	Scarth	Bittour	Hoatzin
Kakapo	Scaury	Bluecap	Humming
Kotuku	Scraye	Blue-eye	Ice-bird
Lanner	Sea-cob	Blue jay	Jacamar
Leipoa	Sea-mew	Bluetit	Kamichi
Linnet	Seapie	Boobook	Kestrel
Lintie	Shrike	Bullbat	Killdee
Loerie	Simara	Bunting	Kinglet
Loriot	Simorg	Buphaga	Lapwing
Lourie	Simurg	Bush-tit	Leghorn
Lungie	Siskin	Bustard	Limpkin
Magpie	Skarth	Buzzard	Manakin
Martin	Smeath	Cacique	Maribou
Menura	Soland	Cariama	Martlet
Merlin	Sorage	Cheeper	Mesites
Merops	Strich	Chewink	Minivet
Missel	Sultan	Coal-tit	Oilbird
Mistle	Sylvia	Cole-tit	Ortolan
Monaul	Tailor	Colibri	Oscires
Mopoke	Takahe	Corella	Ostrich
Mossie	Tarcel	Cotinga	Pandion
Motmot	Tassel	Courlan	Peacock
Musket	Tewhit	Courser	Pelican
Mutton	Thrush	Cow-bird	Penguin
Nandoo	Tom-tit	Creeper	Phoenix
Oriole	Toucan	Crombec	Pickmaw
Oscine	Towhee	Cropper	Piculet
Osprey	Trogon	Diamond	Pinnock
Oxbird	Turaco	Dinorus	Pintado
Parrot	Turbit	Dottrel	Pintail
Parson	Tyrant	Dovekie	Pochard
Pavone	Tystie	Dunnock	Pockard
Peahen	Verdin	Emu-wren	Poe-bird
Peewee	Walker	Fantail	Poy-bird
Peewit	Waxeye	Fern-owl	Quetzal
Pernis	Whidah	Figbird	Rainbow
Petrel	Whydah	Finfoot	Rasores
Phoebe	Willet	Flicker	Redpoll
Pigeon	Woosel	Frigate	Redwing
Plover	Yaffle	Gobbler	Regulus
Pouter	Ynambu	Goburra	Rooster
Progne	Yucker	Gorcrow	Rosella
Puffin	Zoozoo	Goshawk	Rotchie
Pukeko		Grackle	Ruddock
Pullet	**7 letters:**	Grallae	Sakeret
Queest	Anhinga	Hacklet	Sawbill
Quelea	Antbird	Hadedah	Scooper

Scourie
Sea-mell
Simurgh
Sirgang
Sitella
Skimmer
Skylark
Snow-cap
Spadger
Sparrow
Squacco
Staniel
Stinker
Sturnus
Sunbird
Swallow
Tanager
Tanagra
Tarrock
Tattler
Teacher
Teuchat
Tiercel
Tinamou
Titanis
Titlark
Titling
Tokahea
Totanus
Touraco
Tumbler
Tweeter
Vulture
Vulturn
Wagtail
Warbler
Waxbill
Waxwing
Whooper
Widgeon
Wimbrel
Witwall
Woosell
Wren-tit
Wrybill
Wryneck
Yang-win

8 letters:
Aasvogel
Accentor
Adjutant

Aigrette
Alcatras
Altrices
Amadavat
Aquiline
Arapunga
Avadavat
Barnacle
Bellbird
Blackcap
Bluebird
Blue-wing
Boatbill
Boattail
Bobolink
Bob-white
Buln-buln
Caracara
Cardinal
Cargoose
Cheewink
Chirn-owl
Cockatoo
Cockerel
Coquette
Curassow
Dabchick
Didapper
Dip-chick
Dobchick
Dotterel
Estridge
Fauvette
Fernbird
Fish-hawk
Flamingo
Gambetta
Gang-gang
Garefowl
Garganey
Greenlet
Grosbeak
Guacharo
Hackbolt
Hangbird
Hangnest
Hawfinch
Hazelhen
Hemipode
Hernshaw
Hoactzin
Hornbill

Killdeer
Kingbird
Kiskadee
Landrail
Lanneret
Laverock
Longspur
Lorikeet
Lyrebird
Magotpie
Megapode
Mire-drum
Morepork
Murrelet
Nightjar
Notornis
Nuthatch
Ovenbird
Oxpecker
Paradise
Parakeet
Peetweet
Percolin
Petchary
Pheasant
Philomel
Podargus
Poorwill
Prunella
Puffbird
Quarrian
Quarrion
Rainbird
Rallidae
Redshank
Redstart
Reedling
Reed-wren
Rice-bird
Rifleman
Ringtail
Riroriro
Sandpeep
Scolopar
Screamer
Shake-bag
Shoebill
Silktail
Skua-gull
Snowbird
Stanniel
Struthio

Surfbird
Swiftlet
Tantalus
Tapacolo
Tapaculo
Teru-tero
Thrasher
Thresher
Throstle
Ticklace
Titmouse
Tom-noddy
Toucanet
Tragopan
Trembler
Troopial
Troupial
Tubenose
Umbrella
Umbrette
Water-hen
Wheatear
Whimbrel
Whinchat
Whipbird
Whitecap
White-eye
Wildfowl
Wirebird
Woodchat
Woodcock
Woodlark
Woodwale
Yoldring

9 letters:
Accipiter
Aepyornis
Albatross
Aylesbury
Baldicoot
Baltimore
Beccaccia
Beccafico
Bergander
Blackbird
Blackhead
Blackpoll
Bower-bird
Brambling
Broadbill
Bullfinch

- Campanero
- Cassowary
- Chaffinch
- Chatterer
- Chickadee
- Coachwhip
- Cockatiel
- Cormorant
- Corncrake
- Cross-bill
- Currawong
- Dowitcher
- Estreldid
- Fieldfare
- Fig-pecker
- Fire-crest
- Fledgling
- Francolin
- Friarbird
- Frogmouth
- Gallinule
- Gerfalcon
- Gier-eagle
- Goldcrest
- Goldfinch
- Goosander
- Grassquit
- Grenadier
- Guillemot
- Happy Jack
- Helldiver
- Heronshaw
- Hornywink
- Icteridae
- Impundulu
- Jack-snipe
- Kittiwake
- Lintwhite
- Mallemuck
- Merganser
- Mistletoe
- Mollymawk
- Mousebird
- Night-hawk
- Nutjobber
- Olive-back
- Ossifraga
- Ossifrage
- Pardalote
- Peaseweep
- Peregrine
- Phalarope

Pictarnie
Porphyrio
Ptarmigan
Razorbill
Rosy-finch
Salangane
Sandpiper
Sapsucker
Satinbird
Scansores
Sea-turtle
Secretary
Seedeater
Sheldrake
Shoveller
Skunk-bird
Solitaire
Spoonbill
Standgale
Stonechat
Stormbird
Storm-cock
Sugarbird
Swart-back
Sword-bill
Talegalla
Thickhead
Thick-knee
Thornbill
Trochilus
Trumpeter
Turnstone
Volucrine
Water-rail
Wind-hover
Woodspite
Xanthoura

10 letters:
Aberdevine
Bearded tit
Bluebreast
Bluethroat
Brain-fever
Bubbly-jock
Budgerigar
Butter-bump
Chiff-chaff
Demoiselle
Dickcissel
Didunculus
Dive-dapper

Dollarbird
Ember-goose
Eyas-musket
Fallow-chat
Fly-catcher
Fringillid
Goatsucker
Gobemouche
Grassfinch
Greenfinch
Greenshank
Hen-harrier
Honey-eater
Honey guide
Kingfisher
Kookaburra
Locust-bird
Mallee fowl
Marsh-robin
Meadowlark
Night-churr
Noisy miner
Nutcracker
Peckerwood
Pettichaps
Pettychaps
Pratincole
Quaker-bird
Racket-tail
Rafter-bird
Regent-bird
Rhampastos
Rhinoceros
Roadrunner
Ruby-throat
Saddleback
Saddlebill
Sanderling
Sandgrouse
Shearwater
Sheathbill
Sicklebill
Silverbill
Spatchcock
Stone-snipe
Tanagridae
Tropicbird
Wattlebird
Weaver bird
Whisky-jack
Whisky-john
Wonga-wonga

Woodpecker
Woodpigeon
Yaffingale
Yellowbird
Yellowhead
Yellowlegs
Yellowyite

11 letters:
Apostlebird
Bokmakierie
Bristlebird
Butcherbird
Fallow-finch
Fringilline
Gnatcatcher
Grallatores
Happy-family
Honey-sucker
Humming-bird
Ichthyornis
Java sparrow
Leatherhead
Mockingbird
Moss-bluiter
Moss-cheeper
Nightingale
Pied wagtail
Plantcutter
Pyrrhuloxia
Reed-warbler
Scissortail
Snowbunting
Sparrow-hawk
Stilt-plover
Stone-curlew
Storm petrel
Stymphalian
Thunderbird
Tree-creeper
Wall creeper
Whitethroat
Woodcreeper
Woodswallow
Woodwarbler
Yellow-ammer

12 letters:
Bronze-pigeon
Drongo-cuckoo
Drongo-shrike
Flowerpecker

- Hedge-warbler
- Honey creeper
- Peppershrike
- Ring-dotterel
- Sage-thrasher
- Sedge-warbler
- Serpent-eater
- Standard-wing
- Stonechatter

Stormy petrel
Throstle-cock
Whippoorwill
Willy wagtail
Yellow-hammer
Yellow-yowley

13 letters:
Archaeopteryx

Cetti's warbler
Cock-of-the-rock
Oyster-catcher
Pipiwharauroa
Plantain-eater
Willow-wagtail
Willow warbler
Wilson's petrel

14 letters:
Manx shearwater
Tawny frogmouth

16 letters:
Tyrant flycatcher

17 letters:
Pectoral sandpiper

▷ **Bird** *may indicate* a prison sentence
Bird-catcher Avicularia, Fowler, Papageno
Bird-like Hirundine, Sturnine
Bird's nest(ing) Caliology, Monotropa, Soup
Bird-watcher Augur, Twitcher
Birkenhead F.E.Smith
Birmingham Brum(magem)
Birth Burden, Congenital, Delivery, Drop, Extraction, Genesis, Happy event, Jataka, Lineage, Nativity, Natural, Origin, Parage, Parity, Virgin
Birthday Anniversary, Genethliac
Birthmark Blemish, Mole, Mother-spot, Naevus, Stigmata, Strawberry
Birthright Heritage, Mess, Patrimony
Birthwort Aristolochia
Biscuit Abernethy, Bath-oliver, Bourbon, Brandysnap, Butterbake, Captain's, Charcoal, Cookie, Cracker, Cracknel, Crispbread, Dandyfunk, Digestive, Dog, Dunderfunk, Fairing, Flapjack, Florentine, Fortune cookies, Four-by-two, Garibaldi, Ginger nut, Gingersnap, Hardtack, Kiss, Langue de chat, Lebkuchen, Macaroon, Marie, Mattress, Matza(h), Matzo(h), Nut, Oatcake, Oliver, Osborne, Parkin, Perkin, Petit four, Petticoat tails, Pig's ear, Pilot, Poppadom, Poppadum, Pretzel, Ratafia, Rusk, Rye-roll, Shortbread, Soda, Sweetmeal, Tack, Tararua, Tea, Wafer, Water, Wine, Zwieback
Bisexual AC/DC, Freemartin, Switch-hitter
Bishop Aaronic, Abba, Aidan, Ambrose, Bench, Berkeley, Bp, Cambrensis, Cantuar, Chad, Coverdale, Diocesan, Dunelm, Ely, Eparch, Episcopate, Eusebian, Exon, Golias, Hatto, Henson, Latimer, Lord, Magpie, Metropolitan, Norvic, Odo, Ordainer, Patriarch, Peter, Piece, Polycarp, Pontiff, Prelate, Priest, Primate, Primus, Proudie, RR, Sleeve, Suffragan, Titular, Tulchan, Weaver, Weed
Bismarck Otto
Bismuth Bi
Bison Bonas(s)us, Buffalo, Ox, Wisent
Bit Baud, Cantle(t), Centre, Chad, Cheesecake, Chip, Crumb, Curb, Curn, Drib, Excerpt, Flibbert, Fraction, Gag, Haet, Hate, Ion, Jaw, Jot, Mite, Modicum, Morsel, Mote, Mu, Nit, Ort, Ounce, Pelham, Peni, Penny, > PIECE, Port, Rap, Rare, Ratherish, Scintilla, Scrap, Section, Shaving, Shiver, Shred, Smidgen, Snaffle, Snatch, Snippet, Some, Soupcon, Spale, Speck, Splinter, Spot, Spudding, Suspicion, Tad, Tait, Tate, Threepenny, Trace, Unce, Whit
Bite(r), **Biting**, **Bitten** Caustic, Chelicera, Chew, Eat, Engouled, Erose, Etch, Gnash, Gnat, Hickey, Hickie, Incisor, Knap, Masticate, Midge, Molar, Mordacious, Mordant, Morsel, Morsure, Nibble, Nip(py), Occlude, Peck, Pium, Rabid, Remorse, Sarcastic, Sharp, Shrewd, Snap, Sound, Spammie, Tart
Bitter(ness) Absinth, Acerb, Acid, Acrid, Acrimonious, Ale, Aloe, Angostura,

Bile, Cassareep, Caustic, Eager, Ers, Fell, Gall, Keen, Marah, Maror, Myrrh, Pique, Rancorous, Rankle, Resentful, Sarcastic, Sardonic, Snell, Sore, Spleen, Tart(aric), Venom, Verjuice, Virulent, Vitriolic, Wersh, Wormwood
Bittern Boomer, Bull-of the-bog, Butterbump, Heron, Sedge, Siege
Bittersweet Dulcamara
Bitumen Albertite, Asphalt, Blacktop, Elaterite, Gilsonite®, Maltha, Mineral tar, Pissasphalt, Pitch, Tar, Uintaite
Bivalve Clam, Cockle, Lamellibranch, Mollusc, Muscle, Mussel, Oyster, Pelecypod, Piddock, Razorshell, Scallop, Whelk
Bivouac Camp
Bizarre Antic, Curious, Eccentric, Exotic, Fantastic, Far-out, Freaky, Gonzo, Grotesque, Odd, Off-the-wall, Outlandish, Outré, Pythonesque, Queer, Strange, Surreal, Weird
▷ **Bizarre** *may indicate* an anagram
Blab Babble, Gossip, Prate, Squeal
Black(en), **Blackness**, **Black-out** Amadoda, Atramental, B, BB, Bess, Blae, Boong, Cape Coloured, Carbon, Char, Charcoal, Cilla, Coloured, Coon, Cypress, Darkie, Darky, Death, Denigrate, Dinge, Dwale, Ebon(y), Eclipse, Ethiop, Fuzzy-wuzzy, Geechee, Gladwellise, Graphite, Heben, Hole, Ink(y), Ivory, Japan, Jeat, Jet, Jim Crow, Kohl, Lepidomelane, Malign, Market, Melanic, Melano, Moke, Moor, Muntu, Myall, Negritude, Negro, Niello, Niger, Nigrescent, Nigritude, Obliterate, Obscure, Outage, Oxford, Piceous, Pitch, Platinum, Pongo, Prince, Pudding, Puke, Quashee, Quashie, Raven, Sable, Sambo, Scab, School, Sericon, Sheep, Slae, Sloe, Snowball, Sodium, Solvent, Sombre, Soot, Sooterkin, Spode, Spook, Stygian, Swart(y), Swarth(y), Tar, Uncle Tom, Weeds
Black art Necromancy, Nigromancy
Blackball Ban, Exclude, Pip, Reject
Blackberry Acini, Bramble, Mooch, Mouch
Blackbird Crow, Jackdaw, Ousel, Raven, Woosel
Blackcurrant Quinsy-berry
Black eye(d) Half-mourning, Mouse, Shiner, Susan
Blackguard Leg, Nithing, Raff, Revile, Rotter, Scoundrel, Sweep
Blackhead Comedo
Black hole Collapsar
Blackjack Billie, Billy, Cosh, Flag, Sphalerite, Tankard, Truncheon, Vingt(-et)-un
Blackleg Fink, Scab, Snob
Black-letter Gothic
Black magic Goety
Blackmail(er) Bleed, Chantage, Chout, Exact, Extort, Ransom, Shakedown, Strike, Vampire
Blackout ARP, Eclipse, Faint, Swoon
Black Sea Pontic
Black sheep Neer-do-well, Reprobate
Blacksmith Brontes, Burn-the-wind, Farrier, Forger, Harmonious, Shoer, Vulcan
Blackthorn Sloe
Bladder Air, Balloon, Blister, Cholecyst, Cyst, Gall, Hydatid, Isinglass, Sac, Sound, Swim, Urinary, Utricle, Varec(h), Vesica, Vesicle
Blade Acrospire, Bilbo, Brand, Brown Bill, Cleaver, Co(u)lter, Cutlass, Dandy, Espada, Faible, Foible, Forte, Gleave, Gouge, Guillotine, Hydrofoil, Knife, Lance, Leaf, Man, Mouldboard, Oar, Omoplate, Palmetto, Peel, Propellor,

Rachilla, Rapier, Razor, Rip, Rotor, Scimitar, Scull, Scythe, Skate, Spade-, Spatula, Spatule, Spear, Spoon, Stiletto, Stock, Strigil, > **SWORD**, Symitar, Toledo, Turbine, Vane, Vorpal, Web

Blair Eric, Tony

Blame(worthy) Accuse, Censure, Condemn, Confound, Decry, Dispraise, Fault, Guilt, Inculpate, Odium, Rap, Reprehensible, Reproach, Reprove, Stick, Thank, Twit, Wight, Wite, Wyte

Blameless Innocent, Irreproachable, Unimpeachable

Blanch Bleach, Etiolate, Scaud, Whiten

Blancmange Carrageen, Flummery, Mould, Shape, Timbale

Bland Anodyne, Glop, Mild, Pigling, Sleek, Smooth, Spammy, Suave, Tame, Unctuous

Blandish(ment) Agremens, Agrement, Cajole, > **COAX**, Flatter, Treacle, Wheedle

Blank Cartridge, Empty, Erase, Flan, Lacuna, Mistigris, Planchet, Shot, Space, Tabula rasa, > **VACANT**

Blanket Afghan, Bluey, Chilkat, Counterpane, Cover, Electric, Fire, General, Hudson's Bay, Kaross, Mackinaw, Manta, Obscure, Overall, Poncho, Quilt, Rug, Saddle, Sarape, Security, Serape, Shabrack, Smog, Space, Stroud, Wagga, Wet, Whittle

Blare Horn, Trumpet

Blarney Cajolery, Flattery, Nonsense, Sawder, Taffy

Blasé Worldly

Blaspheme, Blasphemous Abuse, > **CURSE**, Defame, Profanity, Revile

Blast(ed) Blight, Blore, Blow, Bombard, Dang, Darn, Dee, Drat, Dynamite, Explode, Fanfare, Flaming, Flurry, Fo(e)hn, Gale, Gust, Noser, Oath, Parp, Pryse, Rats, Scarth, Scath(e), Sere, Shot, Sideration, Skarth, Tantara, Toot, Tromp(e), Trump(et), Volley

Blatant Flagrant, Hard-core, Noticeable, Open, Strident, Vulgar

Blather Baloney, Gabble

Blaze(r) Beacon, Bonfire, Burn, Cannel, Conflagration, Firestorm, > **FLAME**, Flare, Glare, Jacket, Low(e), Lunt, Palatinate, Race, Ratch, Star, Sun, Tead(e)

Bleach Agene, Blanch, Chemic, Chloride, Decolorate, Etiolate, Janola®, Keir, Kier, Peroxide, Whiten, Whitster

Bleak Ablet, Bare, Blay, Bley, Cheerless, Dour, Dreary, Dreich, Raw, Wintry

Bleary Blurred, Smudged

Bleat Baa, Blat, Bluster, Maa

Bleed(er), Bleeding Cup, Ecchymosis, Epistaxis, Extravasate, Fleam, Haemorrhage, Leech, Menorrhagia, Menorrh(o)ea, Metrorrhagia, Milk, Purpura, Root-pressure

Bleep Earcon, Pager

Blefuscudian Big-endian, Little-endian

Blemish Birthmark, Blot, Blotch, Blur, Botch, Defect, Flaw, Mackle, Mark, Mote, Naevus, Scar, Smirch, Spot, Stain, Sully, Taint, Tash, Vice, Wart, Wen

Blench Flinch, Recoil, Wince

Blend(ing) Amalgam, Coalesce, Commix, Contemper, Contrapuntal, Counterpoint, Electrum, Fuse, Go, Harmonize, Hydrate, Interfuse, Interlace, Liquidise, Meld, Melt, > **MERGE**, Mingle, Mix, Osmose, Portmanteau, Scumble, Sfumato, Synalepha

▷ **Blend** *may indicate* an anagram

Blenny Eel-pout, Gunnel, Shanny

Bless(ing), Blessed(ness) Amen, Approval, Asset, Beatitude, Benedicite, Benediction, Benison, Benitier, Bensh, Bismillah, Boon, Brachah, Brocho,

Bless me Consecrate, Cup, Damosel, Darshan, Elysium, Ethereal, Felicity, Gesundheit, Godsend, Grace, Gwyneth, Holy (dam), Kiddush, Luck, Macarise, Mercy, Mixed, Sain, Saint, Sanctify, Sanctity, Sheva Brachoth, Sheva Brochos, Toronto, Urbi et orbi, Xenium

Bless me Lawk(s)

Blight Afflict, Ague, Bespot, Blast, Destroy, Eyesore, Fire, Planning, Potato, Rot, > RUIN, Rust, Shadow, Viticide, Wither

Blighter Cuss, Perisher, Varment, Varmint

Blimey Coo, Cor, Crimini, O'Riley, Strewth

Blimp Airship, Colonel

Blind(ness), **Blind spot** Amaurosis, Amblyopia, Artifice, Austrian, Beesome, Bisson, Blend, Blotto, Carousal, Cecity, Chi(c)k, Cog, Concealed, Dazzle, Eyeless, Feint, Festoon, Gravel, Hemeralopia, Hood, Jalousie, Legless, Meropia, Mole, Night, Nyctalopia, Onchocerciasis, Persian, Persiennes, Pew, Prestriction, Rash, Roller, Roman, Scotoma, Seel, Shade, Shutter, Snow, Stimie, Stimy, Stymie, Sun, Teichopsia, Typhlology, Venetian, Window, Word, Yblent

Blindfish Amblyopsis

Blindfold Bandage, Hoodwink, Muffle, Seal, Wimple

Blindworm Anguis

Blink(er), **Blinkered**, **Blinking** Bat, Blepharism, Bluff, Broken, Eye-flap, Flash, Haw, Idiot, Insular, Nictate, Owl-eyed, Owly, Twink, Wapper, Wink

Bliss(ful) Beatitude, Bouyan, Composer, Delight, > ECSTASY, Eden, Happy, Idyll, Ignorance, Married, Millenium, Nirvana, Paradise, Rapture, Sion, Tir-na-nog, Valhalla, Walhalla, Wedded

Blister(ed), **Blistering** Blab, Blain, Bleb, Bubble, Bullate, Cold sore, Epispastic, Herpes, Pemphigus, Phlyctena, Scorching, Tetter, Vesicant, Vesicle, Visicate, Water

Blitz Attack, Bombard, Onslaught, Raid

Blizzard Buran, Gale, Snowstorm, Whiteout

Bloat(er) Buckling, Puff, Strout, Swell, Tumefy

Blob Bead, Bioblast, Drop, Globule, O, Spot, Tear

Bloc Alliance, Cabal, Cartel, Party

Block(er), **Blockage**, **Blocked**, **Blocking** Altar, Anvil, Ashlar, Atresia, > BAR, Barricade, Barrier, Brake, Breeze, Brick, Briquette, Building, Bung, Bunt, Catasta, Cavity, Chinese, Choke, Chunk, Clint, Clog, Clot, Cloy, Compass, Congest, Constipated, Cut-off, Cyclopean, Cylinder, > DAM, Dead-eye, Debar, Dentel, Dentil, Die, Dit, Domino, Electrotint, Embolism, Emphractic, Encompass, Euphroe, Fipple, Hack-log, High-rise, Hunk, Ice, Ileus, Impasse, Impede, Impost, Ingot, Insula, Interclude, Interrupt, Investment, Jam, Line, Lingot, Lodgment, Log-jam, Lump, Mental, Ministroke, Mitre, Mutule, Nerve, Nifedipine, Nog, Notepad, Oasis®, Obstacle, > OBSTRUCT, Occlude, Office, Opossum, Oppilate, Pad, Page, Parry, Perched, Pile-cap, Pile-up, Pillow, Plinth, Plummer, Power, Pre-empt, Prevent, Process, Psychological, Quad, Ram, Saddle, Scotch, Sett, Siege, Snatch, Stalemate, Stap, Starting, Stenosis, Stimie, Stimy, Stone, Stonewall, Stop, Stumbling, Stymie, Swage, Tamp, Thwart, Tower, Tranche, Trig, Triglyph, Uphroe, Upping-stock, Wood(cut), Wrest, Writer's, Zinco, Zugzwang

Blockbuster Epic

Blockhead Jolterhead, Mome, Nitwit, Noodle, Pig sconce, Stupid

Bloke Beggar, Chap, Cove, Fellow, Gent, Man, Oik

Blond(e) Ash, Cendré, Fair, Flaxen, Goldilocks, Peroxide, Platinised, Platinum, Strawberry, Tallent, Tow-haired, Towhead

Blood(y) Ancestry, Bad, Bally, Blue, Blut, Claret, Clot, Cruor, Cup, Ecchymosis, Ensanguine, Epigons, Factor, First, Full, > GORE, Haemal, Haemorrhage, Ichor, Internecine, Introduce, Kin, Kinship, Knut, Menses, New, Nut, Opsonin, Parentage, Persue, Pigeon's, Plasma, Platelet, Plurry, Properdin, Pup, Race, Rare, Red, Rh negative, Rh positive, Ruby, Sang, Serum, Show, Stroma, Toff, Welter, Whole, Young

Blood disease, **Blood-poisoning** Hypinosis, Isch(a)emia, Leukemia, Lipaemia, Purpura, Pyaemia, Sapraemia, Septicemia, Spanaemia, Thalassemia, Thrombocytopenia, Toxaemia, Uraemia

Bloodhound Lime, Lyam, Sleuth, Spartan

Bloodless Anaemic, Isch(a)emic, Wan, White

Blood-letter Leech, Phlebotomist, Sangrado

▶ **Blood-poisoning** *see* BLOOD DISEASE

Blood-pressure Hypertension, Hypotension

Bloodshot Red-eyed

Blood-sport Hunting, Shooting, Venery

Blood-sucker Asp, Dracula, Flea, Gnat, Ked, Leech, Louse, Mosquito, Parasite, Reduviid, Sponger, Tick, Vampire(-bat)

Bloom(er), **Blooming** Anthesis, Bally, Blossom, Blow, Blush, Boner, Dew, Effloresce, Error, Film, Florescent, Flowery, Flush, Gaffe, Glaucous, Heyday, Knickers, Loaf, Miscalculation, Out, Pruina, Rationals, Reh, Remontant, Rosy, Underwear

▷ **Bloomer** *may indicate* a flower

Blossom Blow, Burgeon, Festoon, Flourish, Flower, May, Orange, Pip

Blot Atomy, Blob, Cartel, Delete, Disgrace, Dry, Eyesore, Obscure, Smear, Smudge, Southern, Splodge, Splotch

Blotch(y) Blemish, Giraffe, Monk, Mottle(d), Spot, Stain

Blotto Legless

Blouse Choli, Garibaldi, Gimp, Guimpe, Kerbaya, Middy, Pneumonia, Sailor, Shirtwaist, Smock, Tunic, Windjammer

Blow(er) Appel, Bang, Bash, Bat, Bellows, Biff, Billow, Blip, Bloom, Brag, Breeze, Buckhorse, Buffet, Burst, Calamity, Clap, Clat, Claut, Clip, Clout, Clump, Conk, Coup, Cuff, Dad, Daud, Dev(v)el, Dinnyhayser, Dint, Douse, Dowse, Estramacon, Etesian, Facer, Fan, Fillip, Gale, Grampus, Gust, Hammer, Haymaker, Hit, Hook, Ictus, Impact, Insufflate, Karate, Kibosh, Knuckle sandwich, KO, Lame, Lander, Lick, Lounder, Muff, Neck-herring, Northerly, Noser, Oner, One-two, Paddywhack, Paik, Pash, Phone, Piledriver, Plague, Plug, Plump(er), Polt, Pow, Puff, Punch, Purler, Rats, Rattler, Rib-roaster, Roundhouse, Sas(s)arara, Scat, Settler, Short, Sideswipe, Side-winder, Sis(s)erary, Skiff, Skite, Skyte, Slat, Slog, Slug, Snot, Sock, Sockdolager, Sockdologer, Southwester, Spanking, Spat, Spout, Squall, Squander, Stripe, Stroke, Strooke, Stunning, Sufflate, Supercharger, Swash, Swat, Swinger, Telephone, Thump, Thwack, Tingler, Tootle, Trump(et), Tuck, Undercut, Upper-cut, Waft, Wallop, Wap, Waste, Welt, Whammy, Whample, Whang, Whap, Wheeze, Wherret, Whiffle, Whirret, > WIND, Winder, Wipe, Wuther

Blown-up Elated, Enlarged, Exploded

Blow-out Binge, Bloat, Exhale, Feast, Feed, Flat, Lava, Nosh-up, Snuff, Spiracle, > SPREAD

Blowpipe Hod, Peashooter, Sarbacane, Sumpit(an)

Blub(ber) Cry, Fat, Snotter, Sob, Speck, > WEEP, Whimper

Bludge Sinecure

Bludgeon Bully, Club, Cosh, Cudgel, Sap

Blue(s) Abattu, Accablé, Adult, Anil, Aquamarine, Azure, Beard, Berlin, Bice, Bleuâtre, Blow, Bottle, Butterfly, C, Caesious, Cafard, Cambridge, Cantab, Celeste, Cerulean, Clair de lune, Cobalt, Coomassia, Copenhagen, Cornflower, Coventry, Cyan, Danish, Danube, Dejected, Dirty, Disconsolate, Doldrums, > **DOWN**, Duck-egg, Eatanswill, Eggshell, Electric, Facetiae, Firmament, Fritter, Gentian, Germander, Glaucous, Glum, Hauyne, Heliotrope, Hump, Indecent, Indigo, Indol(e), Iron, Isatin(e), Lapis lazuli, Lavender, Lewd, Lionel, Low, Mazarine, Methylene, Midnight, Monastral®, Mope, Morose, Murder, Nattier, Naughty, Navy, Nile, Ocean, Off-colour, Oxford, Peacock, Periwinkle, Perse, Petrol, Phycocyan, Porn, Powder, Prussian, Rabbi, Ribald, Riband, Right, Ripe, Robin's egg, Royal, Sad, Sapphire, Saxe, Saxon(y), Scurrilous, > **SEA**, Shocking, Sky, Slate, Smalt(o), Smutty, Sordid, Spirit, Splurge, Squander, Stafford, Steel, Stocking, Teal, Thenard's, Tony, Tory, Trist, True, Trypan, Turnbull's, Turquoise, Ultramarine, Unhappy, Urban, Verditer, Washing, Watchet, Wedgwood®, Welkin, Woad, Zaffer, Zaffre
▷ **Blue** *may indicate* an anagram
Bluebell Blawort, Blewart, Campanula, Harebell
Bluebottle Blawort, Blewart, Blowfly, Blowie, Brommer, Brummer, Cop, Cornflower, Fly, Policeman
▶ **Blue-legged** *see* **BLUESTOCKING**
Blueprint Cyanotype, Draft, Plan, Recipe
Bluestocking, **Blue-legged** Basbleu, Carter, Erudite, Femme savante, Hamburg(h), Mrs Montagu, Précieuse, Sheba
Bluff(ing) Blunt, Cle(e)ve, Cliff, Clift, Crag, Fake, Flannel, Frank, Hal, Headland, Height, Hoodwink, Kidology, Pose, Precipice, Steep, Trick
Blunder(er), **Blundering** Betise, Bévue, Bish, Bloomer, Blooper, Boob, Break, Bull, Bumble, Clanger, Clinker, Cock-up, Err, Faux pas, Floater, Flub, Fluff, Gaff(e), Goof, Howler, Inexactitude, Irish, Josser, Malapropism, > **MISTAKE**, Muddle, Mumpsimus, Slip, Solecism, Stumble, Trip
Blunt(ed), **Bluntly** Abrupt, Alleviate, Bate, Bayt, Brash, Brusque, Candid, Deaden, Disedge, Downright, Forthright, Frank, Hebetate, Mole, Morned, Obtund, Obtuse, Outspoken, Pointblank, Rebate, Retund, Retuse, Roundly, Snub, Straight-out, Stubby
Blur(ring) Cloud, Confuse, Fog, Fuzz, Halation, Mackle, Macule, Pixilation, > **SMUDGE**, Stump, Tortillon
Blurb Ad, Puff
Blush(ing) Colour, Cramoisy, Crimson, Erubescent, Erythema, Incarnadine, Mantle, > **REDDEN**, Rouge, Rubescent, Ruby, Rufescent, Rutilant
Bluster(ing), **Blusterer**, **Blustery** Arrogance, Bellow, Blore, Hector, Rage, Rant, Rodomontade, Roister, Sabre-rattler, Squash, Swagger, Vapour, Windbag, Wuthering
Boar Barrow, Calydonian, Erymanthian, Hog, Pentheus, Sanglier, Sounder, Tusker, Wild
Board(s), **Boarding** Abat-voix, Admiralty, Banker, Barge, Beaver, Billet, Bristol, Bulletin, Catchment, Centre, Cheese, Chevron, Circuit, Collegium, Committee, Contignation, Counter, Cribbage, Dagger, Dart, Daughter, Deal, Directors, Diving, Draft, Draining, Drawing, Embark, Embus, Emery, Enter, Entrain, Fare, Fascia, Featheredge, Fibro, Flannelgraph, Full, Gibraltar, Gutter, Hack, Half, Half-royal, Hawk, Hoarding, Idiot, Instrument, Ironing, Kip, Lag, Ledger, Lodge, Magnetic, Malibu, Masonite®, Match, Mill, Mortar, Moulding, Notice, Otter, Ouija, Palette, Pallet, Panel, Parochial, Particle, Patch, Pedal, Peg(board), Pension, Planch(ette), Plank, Ply(wood), Quango, Running,

Sandwich, Sarking, Scaleboard, School, Screed, Sheathing, Shelf, Shingle, Side-table, Sign, Skirting, Sleeve, Snow, Sounding, Splasher, Spring, Stage, Strickle, Stringboard, Supervisory, Surf, > TABLE, Telegraph, Thatch, Theatre, Trencher, Verge, Wainscot, Wobble

▷ **Board** *may refer to* chess or draughts

Boarder Interne, PG, Roomer

Boarding house Digs, Lodgings, Pension

Boast(er), Boasting Big-note, Blew, Blow, Blowhard, Bluster, Bobadil, Bounce, Brag, Braggadocio, Breeze, Crake, Crow, Fanfaronade, Gas, Gascon(nade), Glory, Hot air, Jactitation, Line, Ostent(atious), Prate, Rodomontade, Scaramouch, Skite, Swagger, Swank, Tall, Thrasonic, Vainglory, Vaunt, Yelp

Boat Ark, Barge, Bark, Canal, Cat, Coaster, Codder, Corvette, Cott, Cruiser, Curragh, Dragon, Eight, Flagship, Flatboat, Fly(ing), Fore-and-after, Four, Foyboat, Goldie, Gravy, Hooker, Isis, Jolly, Keel, Kit, Lapstrake, Launch, Long, Lymphad, Mackinaw, Monkey, Monohull, Mosquito, Motor, Narrow, Outrigger, Pair-oar, Pedalo, Pont, Privateer, PT, Pucan, Puffer, Sailer, Sauce, Sculler, Shallop, She, > SHIP, Skiff, Slogger, Smack, Swing, Tangle-netter, Tanker, Tender, Torpid, Trek-ox, Vaporetto, Vedette, > VESSEL, Wager, Weekender

Boater > HAT, Punter, Straw

Boatman Bargee, Charon, Cockswain, Coxswain, George, Gondolier, Harris, Hoveller, Phaon, Voyageur, Waterman, Wet-bob

Boat population Tank(i)a

Boat-shaped Carina, Scaphoid

Boatswain Bosun, Serang, Smee

Bob Acres, Beck, Curtsey, Deaner, Dip, Dock, Dop, Duck, Float, Hod, Hog, Jerk, Page-boy, Peal, Plumb, Plummet, Popple, Rob, S, Shingle, Sled(ge), Sleigh

Bobbin Reel, Shuttle, Spindle, Spool

Bobble Pompom

Bobby Bluebottle, Busy, Copper, Flatfoot, Patrolman, Peeler, Pig, > POLICEMAN

Bobby-dazzler Dinger, Stunner

Bock Stein

Bode Augur

Bodice Basque, Bolero, Bustier, Chemise, Chemisette, Choli, Corsage, Gilet, Halter, Jirkinet, Liberty, Plastron, Polonie, Polony, Spencer, Tucker, Watteau

Bodkin Eyeleteer, Needle, Poniard, Stilet(to)

Body, Bodies, Bodily Administration, Amount, Anatomic, Astral, Barr, Board, Bouk, Buik, Buke, Bulk, Cadaver, Cadre, Carcase, Carcass, Carnal, Caucas, Centrosome, Chapel, Chapter, Chassis, Chondriosome, Ciliary, Clay, Coachwork, Coccolite, Cohort, Column, Comet, Committee, Contingent, Cormus, Corpor(e)al, Corps, Corpse, Corpus, Corse, Cytode, Detail, Earth, Flesh, Food, Frame, Fuselage, Gazo(o)n, Golgi, Goner, Grey, > GROUP, Heavenly, Hull, Incarnate, Inclusion, Ketone, Lewy, Lich, Like, Lithites, Malpighian, > MASS, Militia, Moit, Mote, Mummy, Nacelle, Nucleole, Nucleolus, Pack, Personal, Phalanx, Pineal, Plant, Platelet, Platoon, Polar, Politic, Posse, Purview, Quango, Relic(t), Ruck, Senate, Solid, Soma, Soredium, Sound-box, Soyle, Spinar, Spore, Squadron, Square, Staff, Statoblast, Stiff, Syndicate, Tagma, Testis, Thallus, Torse, Torso, Trunk, Turm, Ulema, Vitreous, Wolffian, X

▷ **Body** *may indicate* an anagram

Body builder Steroid

Bodyguard Amulet, > ESCORT, Gentleman-at-arms, House-carl, Minder, Praetorian, Protector, Retinue, Schutzstaffel, > SHIELD, SS, Triggerman,

Varangian, Yeomen

Body segment Arthromere, Metamere

Boer Afrikaner, Kruger

Bog(gy) Allen, Blanket, Can, Carr, Clabber, Fen, Gents, Glaur, Hag, Lair, Latrine, Loo, Machair, Marsh, Merse, Mire, Morass, Moss(-flow), Mud, Muskeg, Peat, Petary, Quag, Raised, Serbonian, Slack, Slade, Slough, Spew, Spouty, Stodge, Sump, Vlei, Washroom, WC, Yarfa, Yarpha

Bog(e)y Boggart, Bug(aboo), Bugbear, Chimera, Eagle, Mumbo jumbo, Nis(se), Par, Poker, Rawhead, Scarer, Spectre, Troll

Boggle Astonish, Bungle, Demur, Hesitate, Perplex, Shy

Bog-trotter Tory

Bogus Assumed, Counterfeit, Fake, False, Histrionic, Phoney, > SHAM, Snide, Snobbish, Spoof, Spurious

Bohemian Arty, Beatnik, Gypsy, Hippy, Hussite, Mimi, Offbeat, Taborite, Trustafarian

Boil(er), Boiled, Boiling (point) Angry, Anthrax, Blain, Botch, Brew, Bubble, C, Carbuncle, Coction, Cook, Cree, Dartre, Decoct, Ebullient, Foam, Furuncle, Gathering, Hen, Herpes, Kettle, Leep, Ligroin, Pimple, Pinswell, Poach, Poule, Rage, Reflux, Samovar, Seethe, Simmer, Sod, Sore, Steam, Stew, Stye, Tea-kettle

Boisterous Gilp(e)y, Goustrous, Gusty, Hoo, Knockabout, Noisy, Rambunctious, Randy, Riotous, Rorty, Rough, Stormy, Strepitoso, Termagant, Turbulent, Wild

Bold(ly), Boldness Assumptive, Brash, Brass, Bravado, Bravery, Bravura, Brazen, Brussen, Caleb, Crust, Daredevil, Defiant, Derring-do, Diastaltic, Familiar, Free, Gallus, Hardihood, Heroics, High-spirited, Impudent, Intrepid, Malapert, Mature, Outspoken, Parrhesia, Pert, Plucky, Presumptive, Rash, Risoluto, Sassy, Temerity, Unshrinking

Bole Stem, Trunk

Bolivar Liberator

Bollard Cone, Kevel

Bolshevik Communist, Maximalist, Soviet

Bolster Cushion, Dutch wife, Pillow, > PROP

Bolt Arrow, Coach, Cuphead, Dash, Dead, Eat, Elope, Expansion, Explosive, Fish, Flee, Gobble, Gollop, Gorge, Gulp, Latch, Levant, Levin, Lightning, Lock, Machine, Missile, Panic, Pig, Pintle, Ragbolt, Rivet, Roll, Scoff, Slot, Snib, Sperre, Stud, Tap, Thunder, Toggle, U, Wing, Wolf

Bolus Ball

Bomb(er), Bombing Atom, Attack, B, Blitz, Blockbuster, Borer, Buzz, Candle, Carpet, Cluster, Cobalt, Daisycutter, Depth charge, Deterrent, Dirty, Doodlebug, Egg, Fission, Flop, Flying, Fragmentation, Fusion, Glide, Greek fire, Grenade, H, Harris, Hydrogen, Lancaster, Land-mine, Letter, Liberator, Loft, Logic, Megaton, Millennium, Mills, Minnie, Mint, Molotov cocktail, Mortar, Nail, Napalm, Neutron, Nuclear, Nuke, Parcel, Petar, Petard, Petrol, Pineapple, Pipe, Plaster, Plastic, Prang, Precision, Radium, Ransom, Robot, Shell, Skip, Smart, Smoke, Sneak-raid, Stealth, Stick, Stink, Stratofortress, Stuka, Tactical, Terrorist, Thermonuclear, Time, Torpedo, Turkey, V1, Volcanic, Walleye

Bombard(ment) Attack, Battery, Blitz, Cannonade, Drum-fire, Mortar, Pelt, Shell, Stone, Stonk, Strafe, Straff

Bombardon Tuba

Bombast(ic) Euphuism, Fustian, Grandiose, Hot air, Magniloquence, Orotund, Pomp, Rant, Timid, Tumid, Turgent

Bombay Nasik
Bombay duck Bum(m)alo
▶ **Bomber** *see* BOMB
Bonanza Luck, Windfall
Bonaparte Boney, > NAPOLEON, Plon-plon
Bond(age) Adhesive, Agent, Assignat, Bail, Cedula, Cement, Chain, Compact, Connect, Copula, Corporate, Duty, Escrow, Flemish, Gilt, Hyphen, Ionic, James, Knot, Liaise, Ligament, Link(age), Manacle, Mortar, Nexus, Noose, > PLEDGE, Rapport, Shackle, Starr, Thral(l)dom, > TIE, Valence, Vinculum, Yearling, Yoke
Bond(s), Bondsman Affinity, Baby, Bail, Bearer, Consols, Coordinate, Covalent, Covenant, Daimyo, Dative, Debenture, Deep-discount, Double, Electrovalent, English, Ernie, Esne, Fetter, Fleming, Flemish, Geasa, Grammy, Granny, Heart, Herringbone, Hydrogen, Income, Investment, Ionic, Junk, Long, Managed, Metallic, Municipal, Nexus, Pair, Peptide, Performance, Post-obit, Premium, Property, Recognisance, Relationship, Revenue, Running, Samurai, Security, Semipolar, Serf, Shogun, Single, Slave, Solder, Stacked, Superglue, Surety, Thete, Treasury, Triple, Vassal, Zebra
Bone(s), Bony Acromion, Anableps, Apatite, Astragalus, Atlas, Axis, Baculum, Calcaneus, Caluarium, Cannon, Capitate, Capitellum, Carina, Carpel, Carpus, Catacomb, Centrum, Chine, Clavicle, Cly, Coccyx, Coffin, Columella, Concha, Condyle, Coracoid, Coral, Costa, Coxa, Crane, Cranium, Cuboid, Cunciform, Dentary, Diaphysis, Dib, Dice, Diploe, Endosteal, Ethmoid, Femur, Fetter, Fibula, Fillet, Frontal, Funny, Ganoid, Gaunt, Haunch, Hause-bane, Horn, Humerus, Hyoid, Ilium, Incus, Innominate, Involucrum, Ischium, Ivory, Jugal, Kneecap, Knuckle, Lacrimal, Lamella, Luez, Luz, Malar, Malleolus, Malleus, Mandible, Manubrium, Marrow, Mastoid, Maxilla, Medulla, Membrane, Metacarpal, Metatarsal, Napier's, Nasal, Navicular, Occipital, Olecranon, Omoplate, Orthopaedics, Os, Ossicle, Palatine, Parasphenoid, Parietal, Patella, Pecten, Pectoral, Pedal, Pelvis, Pen, Percoid, Perone, Petrous, Phalanx, Pisiform, Premaxilla, Pubis, Pygostyle, Quadrate, Rachial, Rack, Radialia, Radius, Relic, Rib, Sacrum, Scaphoid, Scapula, Sclere, Sepium, Sequestrum, Sesamoid, Skeleton, Skull, Sphenoid, Splint, Splinter, Spur, Squamosal, Stapes, > STEAL, Sternebra, Sternum, Stifle, Stirrup, Suboperculum, T, Talus, Tarsus, Temporal, Tibia, Tibiotarsus, Tot, Trapezium, Triquetral, Trochanter, Trochlea, True-rib, Tympanic, Ulna, Vertebrae, Vomer, Whirl, Wish, Wormian, Zygomatic
Bone-head Capitellum, Capitulum
Bonehouse Ossuary
Boneshaker Dandy-horse, Draisene, Draisine
Bonfire Bale-fire, Beltane, Blaze, Chumping, Clavie, Feu de joie, Pyre
Boniface Inn-keeper, Landlord, Taverner
Bonne-bouche Cate
Bonnet Balmoral, Bongrace, Cap, Cornette, Cowl, Easter, Glengarry, Hood, Hummel, Hummle, Kiss-me, Mobcap, Mutch, Poke, Scotch, Sun, Toorie, War
Bonny Blithe, Gay, Merry, Sonsy, Weelfar'd
Bonsai Saikei
Bonus Bounty, Bye, Christmas box, Danger money, Dividend, Escalator, Extra, Hand-out, Lagniappe, No-claim, > PREMIUM, Reversionary, Reward, Scrip, Spin-off, Windfall
Boob Gaffe, Nork, Simpleton, Stumer
Booby Dunce, Hick, Patch, Patchcocke, Patchoke, > STUPID
Boojum Snark

Book(s), **Bookish**, **Bookwork** Academic, Acts, Album, Amos, Antilegomena, Antiphonary, Apocalypse, Apocrypha, Atlas, Audio, B, Backlist, Baruch, Bestiary, Bestseller, Bible, Black, Blotter, Blue, Bodice-ripper, Breviary, Caxton, Chrestomathy, Chron(icles), Chumash, Classic, Closed, Coffee-table, Commonplace, Compendium, Concordance, Cookery, Corinthians, Course, Cyclopedia, Dan(iel), Deuteronomy, Diary, Dictionary, Digest, Directory, Domesday, Doomsday, Eccles, Ecclesiastes, Edda, Ench(e)iridion, Encyclopedia, Engage, Enter, Eph, Ephesians, Erudite, Esdras, Esther, Exercise, Exeter, Exodus, Ezek(iel), Ezra, Facetiae, Folio, Gal, Galatians, Gazetteer, Genesis, Good, Gradual, Gradus, Grimoire, Grolier, Guide, Hag(gai), Haggadah, Haggadoh, Hagliographa, Hardback, Heptameron, Herbal, Hitopodesa, Hosea, Hymnal, I Ching, Imprint, Incunabula, Isaiah, Issue, Jashar, Jasher, Joel, John, Joshua, Jud(ges), Jude, Kama Sutra, Kells, Kings, Lam(entations), Lectionary, Ledger, Leviticus, Lib, Liber, Libretto, Literary, Log, Luke, Macc, Maccabees, Malachi, Manga, Manual, Mark, Martyrs, Matthew, Micah, Missal, Monograph, Mook, Nahum, Nomenclator, NT, Numbers, Octavo, Octodecimo, Omnibus, Open, Orarium, Order, Ordinal, Ordinary, OT, Page-turner, Paperback, Paralipomena, Pass, Passionary, Pedantic, Penny dreadful, Pharmacopoeia, Philemon, Philippians, Phrase, Pica, Plug, Polyglot, Pop-up, Porteous, Portesse, Potboiler, Prayer, Primer, Prompt, Prophet, Proverbs, Psalms, Psalter, Pseudepigraphia, Publication, Quair, Quarto, Quire, Rag, Ration, Reader, Red, Reference, Remainder, > **RESERVE**, Responsorial, Revelations, Road, Rom, Romans, Satyricon, Script, Scroll, Sext, Sextodecimo, Sibylline, Sir, Sixteenmo, Sketch, Snobs, Softback, Spelling, Statute, Studious, Study, Style, Sus, Susanna, Sutra, Table, Tablet, Talking, Telephone, Teratology, Text(ual), Thriller, Title, Titule, To-bit, Tome, Trade, Transfer, Triodion, Tripitaka, Twelvemo, Twelve Tables, Vade-mecum, Veda, Vercelli, Vesperal, Visiting, Visitor's, Vol(ume), Waste, White, Work, Year, Zephadiah

Bookbinder, **Bookbinding** Fanfare, Grolier, Mutton-thumper, Organdie

Book-case Credenza, Press, Satchel

Bookie(s), **Bookmaker** John, Layer, Librettist, Luke, Mark, Matthew, Printer, Ringman, To-bit

Booking Reservation

Bookkeeper, **Bookkeeping** Clerk, Double entry, Librarian, Posting, Recorder, Satchel, Single-entry

Booklet B, Brochure, Folder

Book-like Solander

Book-lover Incunabulist

Bookmark Tassel

Book-scorpion Chelifer

Bookseller Bibliopole, Colporteur, Conger, Sibyl, Stallman

Bookworm Sap, Scholar

Boom(ing) Baby, Beam, Boost, Bowsprit, Bump, Fishpole, Increase, Jib, Orotund, Prosper, Resound, Roar, Sonic, Spar, Supersonic, Swinging, Thrive, Torpedo, Wishbone

Boomer Bittern, Bull-of the-bog, Butter-bump, Kangaroo, Mire-drum

Boomerang Backfire, Kiley, Kyley, Kylie, Recoil, Ricochet, Throwstick, Woomera

Boon Bene, Benefit, Blessing, Bounty, Cumshaw, Gift, Godsend, Mills, Mitzvah, Prayer, Windfall

Boor(ish) Bosthoon, Chuffy, Churl, Clodhopper, Crass, Goth, Grobian, Hog, Ill-bred, Jack, Keelie, Kern(e), Kernish, Kill-courtesy, Lob, Lout, Lumpen, Ocker, Peasant, Philistine, Trog, Uncouth, Yahoo, Yob, Yokel

Boost(er) Afterburner, Bolster, Ego, Encourage, Fillip, Help, Hoist, Impetus, Increase, Injection, Lift, Promote, Raise, Rap, Reheat, Reinforce, Reinvigorate, Spike, Supercharge, Tonic, Wrap

Boot(s) Addition, Adelaide, Ankle-jack, Avail, Balmoral, Beetle-crushers, Benefit, Blucher, Bottine, Bovver, Brogan, Brogue, Buskin, Cerne, Chukka, Cockers, Cold, Combat, Concern, Cothurn(us), Cowboy, Cracowe, Crowboot, Denver, Derby, Desert, Dismiss, Field, Finn(e)sko, Finsko, Fire, Football, Galage, Galosh, Gambado, Go-go, Granny, Gum, Hessian, High shoe, Hip, Jack, Jemima, Jodhpur, Kamik, Kletterschuh, Lace-up, Larrigan, Last, Mitten, Moon, Muchie, Muc(k)luc(k), Mukluk, Pac, Para, Profit, Riding, Rock, Russian, Sabot, > SACK, Seven league, > SHOE, Surgical, Thigh, Toe, Tonneau, Tops, Trunk, Ugh, Vibram®, Vibs, Wader, Warm, Weller, Wellie, Wellington, Welly

Booth Assassin, Crame, Kiosk, Polling, Stall, Stand, Telephone, Voting

Bootlegger Cooper, Coper, Runner

Bootless Futile, Idle, Vain

Booty Creach, Creagh, Haul, Loot, Prey, Prize, Spoil(s), Spolia optima, Swag

Booze(r) > DRINK, Liquor, Pub, Spree, Tipple

Borage Bugloss, Comfrey, Gromwell, Myosote

Borax Tincal

Border(s), **Borderland**, **Borderline** Abut, Adjoin, Apron, Bed, Bind, Bound, Braid, Checkpoint, Coast, Cot(t)ise, Dado, Dentelle, > EDGE, Engrail, Fimbria, Frieze, Fringe, Frontier, Furbelow, Guilloche, Head-rig, Hedgerow, Hem, Herbaceous, Impale, Kerb, Lambrequin, Limb, Limbo, Limen, Limes, Limit, Limitrophe, Lip, List, March, Marchland, > MARGIN, Mat, Mattoid, Meith, Mete, Mount, Neighbour, Orle, Pand, Pelmet, Penumbra, Perimeter, Purfle, Purlieu, Rand, Rim, Roadside, Roon, Royne, Rubicon, Rund, Rymme, Scottish, Selvage, Selvedge, Side, Skirt, Skirting, Strand, Strip, Surround, Swage, The Marches, Trench, Tressure, Valance, Valence, > VERGE

▷ **Borders** *may indicate* first and last letters

Bore(d), **Boredom**, **Borer**, **Boring** Aiguille, Anobium, Anorak, Apathy, Aspergillum, Aspergillus, Aspersoir, Auger, Awl, Beetle, Bind, Bit, Broach, Brog, Bromide, Calibre, Chokebore, Deadly, Drag, > DRILL, Dry, Dusty, Dweeb, Eagre, Eat, Eger, Elshin, Elsin, Endured, Ennui, Ennuye, Foozle, Gim(b)let, Gouge, Gribble, Grind, Had, Heigh-ho, Ho-hum, Irk, Jumper, Listless, Longicorn, Longueur, Miser, Mole, Nerd, Noyance, Nudni(c)k, Nuisance, Nyaff, Oporose, Pain, Pall, Penetrate, Perforate, Pest, Pholas, Pierce, Pill, Probe, Prosaic, Prosy, Punch, Ream(ingbit), Rime, Sat, Schmoe, Scolytus, Screw, Severn, Shothole, Snooze, Snore, Sondage, Spleen, Sting, Stob, Stupid, Tediosity, Tedious, Tedisome, Tedium, Tedy, Terebra, Teredo, Termes, Termite, Thirl, Tire, Trepan, Trocar, Tunnel, > WEARY, Well, Wimble, Windbag, Wonk, Woodworm, Worldweary, Xylophoga, Yawn

Borgia Cesare, Lucretia

Boric Sassolin, Sassolite

Born B, Free, Great, Nascent, Nat(us), Né(e)

Boron B

Borough Borgo, Pocket, Port, Quarter, Rotten, Township, Wick

Borrow(ed), **Borrowing** Adopt, Appropriate, Cadge, Copy, Derivative, Eclectic, George, Hum, Leverage, Scunge, Straunge, > TAKE, Touch

Bosh Humbug, Nonsense, Rot

Bosom Abraham's, Breast, Close, Gremial, Inarm, Intimate, Poitrine

Boss(ed), **Bossy** Blooper, Burr, Cacique, Director, Dominate, Gadroon, Governor, Headman, Honcho, Hump, Inian, Inion, Jewel, Knob, Knop, Knot, Leader,

Maestro, > **MANAGER**, Massa, > **MISTAKE**, Mistress, Netsuke, Noop, Nose-led, Omphalos, Overlord, Overseer, Owner, Pannikin, Pellet, Protuberance, Ruler, Run, Sherang, Straw, Stud, Superintendent, Taskmaster, Umbo(nate)

Boston Hub

Bot Oestrus

Botanist, **Botany** Banks, Bryology, Candolle, Carpology, Cockayne, Dendrologist, Frees, Garden, Godet, Herbist, Linnaeus, Phytology, Tradescant, Weigel

Botch(ed) Bungle, Clamper, Cock-up, Flub, Fudge, Mismanage, Pig's ear, Spoil, Tink

Both Together, Two

Bother(some) Ado, Aggro, Care, Deave, Deeve, Disturb, Drat, Fash, Fluster, Fuss, Get, Hassle, Hector, Incommode, Irk, Irritate, Moither, Nuisance, Perturb, Pesky, Pest(er), Pickle, Reke, Todo, > **TROUBLE**

Bottle(s) Ampul(la), Bacbuc, Balthasar, Balthazar, Belshazzar, Borachio, Bundle, Carafe, Carboy, Cock, Cork, Costrel, Courage, Cruet, Cruse, Cucurbital, Cutter, Dead-men, Decanter, Demijohn, Fearlessness, Feeding, Fiasco, Flacket, Flacon, Flagon, Flask, Goatskin, Gourd, Guts, Half-jack, Hen, Imperial, Jeroboam, Klein, Lachrymal, Lagena, Magnetic, Magnum, Marie-Jeanne, Matrass, Medicine, Methuselah, Mettle, Mickey, Nansen, Nebuchadnezzar, > **NERVE**, Nursing, Phial, Pilgrim, Pitcher, Pooter, Pycnometer, Rehoboam, Resource, Retort, Salmanaser, Salmanazar, Screwtop, Siphon, Smelling, Split, Squeeze, Squeezy, Sucking, Tear, Tube, Twenty-sixer, Vial, Vinaigret(te), Wad, Water, Weighing, Winchester, Wine, Woulfe

▷ **Bottle(d)** *may indicate* an anagram or a hidden word

Bottom Anus, Aris, Arse, Ass, Base, Beauty, Bed, Benthos, Bilge, Breech, Bum, Butt, Buttocks, Croup(e), Croupon, Demersal, Derrière, Doup, End, Fanny, Floor, Foot, Foundation, Fud, Fundus, Haunches, Hunkers, Hurdies, Keel(son), Kick, Lumbar, Nadir, Nates, Podex, Posterior, Pottle-deep, Prat, Pyramus, Rear, Rock, Root, Rump, Seat, Ship, Sill, Sole, Staddle, Tail, Tush, Weaver

Bottom drawer Glory box

Bottomless Subjacent

Botulism Limberneck

Boudoir Bower, Room

Bouffant Pouf

Bough Branch, Limb

Bought Coft

Boulder Gibber, Niggerhead, Rock, > **STONE**

Boule Senate

Bounce(r), **Bouncing**, **Bouncy** Bang, Blague, Bound, Caper, Dap, Dead-cat, Doorman, Dop, Dud, Eject, Evict, Fib, Jounce, Keepy-uppy, Kite, Lie, Lilt, Resilient, Ricochet, Spiccato, Spring, Stot, Tale, Tamp, Verve, Vitality, Yorker, Yump

▷ **Bouncing** *may indicate* an anagram

Bound(er), **Boundary** Adipose, Apprenticed, Articled, Bad, Barrier, Beholden, Border, Bourn(e), Bubalis, Cad, Cavort, Certain, Circumference, Curvet, Decreed, Demarcation, Demarkation, Dool, Dule, Duty, End, Engirt, Entrechat, Erub, Eruv, Event horizon, Exciton, Fence, Four, Frape, Galumph, Gambado, Gambol, Girt, Harestane, Hedge, Heel, Held, Hoarstone, Hops, Hourstone, Ibex, Interface, Izard, Jump, Kangaroo, K/T, > **LEAP**, Limes, Limit, Linch, Lollop, Lope, March-stone, Meare, Meer, Meith, Mere, Merestone, Mete, Moho, Muscle, Obliged, Ourebi, Outward, Pale, Parameter, Perimeter, Periphery,

Plate, Prance, Precinct, Prometheus, Purlieu, Redound, Ring-fence, Roller, Roo, Roped, Rubicon, Scoup, Scowp, Serf, Side, Sideline, Six(er), Skelp, Skip, Spang, Spring, Sten(d), Stoit, Stylolite, Terminator, T(h)alweg, Tied, Touchline, Upstart, Vault, Verge, Wallaby

▷ **Bounds** *may indicate* outside letters

Bounty, **Bountiful** Aid, Bligh, Boon, Christian, Generosity, > **GIFT**, Goodness, Grant, Head money, Honorarium, Largess(e), Lavish, Queen Anne's

Bouquet Aroma, Attar, Aura, Compliment, Corsage, Fragrancy, Garni, Nose, Nosegay, Plaudit, Posy, Spiritual, Spray

Bourbon Alfonso

Bourgeois Biedermeier, Common, Pleb(ian), Pooter(ish)

Bout Bender, Bust, Contest, Dose, Go, Jag, Match, Spell, Spree, Turn, Venery, Venewe, Venue

Boutique Shop

Bovine Stolid

Bow(ing), **Bower**, **Bowman** Alcove, Arbour, Arc, Arch, > **ARCHER**, Arco, Arson, Bandy, Beck, Bend, Boudoir, Butterfly, Clara, Congé(e), Crescent, Crook, Cupid, > **CURVE**, Defer, Dicky, Drail, Droop, Duck, Echelles, Eros, Eugh, Eye, Fiddle(r), Fiddlestick, Foredeck, Halse, Hawse, Jook, Jouk, Kneel, Kotow, Laval(l)ière, Lean, Long, Lout, Lowt, Martellato, Moulinet, Namaste, Nameste, Nod, Nutate, Obeisance, Obtemper, Paganini, Pergola, Prore, Quarrel, Reverence, Salaam, Seamer, Shelter, Slope, Sound, Spiccato, Stick, > **SUBMIT**, Tie, Yew, Yield

Bowdler(ize) Edit(or), Water

Bowels Entrails, Guts, Innards, Viscera

▷ **Bower** *may indicate* using a bow

Bowl(ing), **Bowler**, **Bowl over**, **Bowls** B, Basin, Begging, Bicker, Bocce, Bocci(a), Boccie, Bodyline, Bool, Bosey, Bouncer, Cage-cup, Calabash, Candlepins, Cap, Carpet, Caup, Chalice, Cheese, Chinaman, Christie, Christy, Cog(g)ie, Coolamon, Crater, Cup, Deliver, Derby, > **DISH**, Dismiss, Dome, Drake, Dumbfound, Dust, Ecuelle, End, Finger, Fivepin, Goldfish, Googly, Grub, Hog, Hoop, Jack, Jeroboam, Jorum, Kegler, Krater, Lavabo, Laver, Leg-spin, Lightweight, Lob, Locke, Mazer, Monteith, Night, Offbreak, Old, Over-arm, Pace, Pan, Pétanque, Piggin, Porringer, Pot-hat, Pottinger, Punch, Raku, Rice, Rink, Roll, Roundarm, Seam(er), Skip, Skittle(s), Spare, Speed, Spinner, Spofforth, Stadium, Stagger, Stummel, Sucrier, Super, Ten-pin, Tom, Underarm, Underhand, Underwood, Voce, Wassail, Wood, York(er)

Box(ing) Baignoire, Ballot, Bandbox, Bareknuckle, Bento, Bijou, Bimble, Binnacle, Black, Blue, Bonk, Buist, Bunk, Bush, Caddy, Call, Camera, Canister, Case, Cash, Casket, Cassolette, Chest, Chinese, Christmas, Ciborium, Clog, Coach, Coffer, Coffin, Coffret, Coin, Confessional, Cool, Crate, Cuff, Deed, Dialog(ue), Dispatch, Ditty, Dog, Drawer, Encase, Enclose, > **FIGHT**, File, Fist, Fund, Fuse, Fuzz, Glory, Glove, Go-kart, Grass, Hat, Hay, Hedge, Honesty, Humidor, Hutch, Ice, Idiot, Inro, Jewel, Journal, Junction, Jury, Keister, Kick, Kiosk, Kite, Knevell, Ladle, Letter, Light, Live, Locker, Lodge, Loge, Match, Mill, Mitre, Mocock, Mocuck, Musical, Nest(ing), Omnibus, Orgone, Package, Paint, Pandora's, Papeterie, Patch, Peepshow, Peg, Penalty, Petara, Pew, Phylactery, Pill, Pillar, Pitara, Pix, Poor, Post, Pouncet, Powder, Press, Prompt, Protector, Puff, Pugilism, Pyxis, Register, Ring, Royal, Saggar(d), Sagger, Sand, Savate, Scrap, Seggar, Sentry, Set-top, Shadow, Shoe, Shooting, Signal, Skinner, Skip(pet), Slipcase, Smudge, Soap, Solander, Sound, > **SPAR**, Spice, Spring, Squeeze, Strong, Stuffing, Swell, Tabernacle, Tefillin, Telephone, Telly, Thai, Tin, Tinder, Tool, Touch, Trunk, Tube, Tuck, TV, Vanity, Vasculum, Vinaigrette,

Voice, Weather, Window, Wine, Witness, Yakhdan

Boxer Ali, Amycus, Babyweight, Bantamweight, Bruiser, Bruno, Canine, Carnera, Carpentier, Carthorse, Chinaman, Cooper, Crater, Cruiserweight, Dog, Eryx, Farr, Featherweight, Flyweight, Ham, Heavyweight, Lightweight, McCoy, Middleweight, Mosquito-weight, Pandora, Pollux, Pug, Pugil(ist), Rebellion, Rocky, Shadow, Southpaw, Strawweight, Welterweight, Wilde

Boxing-glove Hurlbat, Muffle, Whirlbat, Whorlbat

Boy(s) Amoretto, Apprentice, Ball, Bevin, Blue-eyed, Breeches, Bub(by), Cabin, Callant, Catamite, Champagne, Chiel(d), > CHILD, Chokra, Chummy, Cub, Cupid, Dandiprat, Errant, Galopin, Garçon, Gorsoon, Gossoon, Green Mountain, Groom, Ha, Hansel, Jack, Kid, Klonkie, Knave, Knave-bairn, Kwedien, Lackbeard, > LAD, Loblolly, Loon(ie), Minstrel, Nibs, Nipper, Office, Page, Pot, Prentice, Principal, Putto, Rent, Roaring, Shaver, Son, Spalpeen, Sprig, Stripling, Tad, Tar, Ted(dy), Tiger, Toy, Urchin, Whipping, Wide, > YOUTH

▷ **Boy** *may indicate* an abbreviated name

Boycott Avoid, Ban, Bat, Black, Blacklist, Exclude, Hartal, Isolate, Ostracise, Shun, Swadeshi

Boyfriend Beau, Date, Fella, Fellow, Steady

Boyle Juno

Bp Bishop, DD, RR

Brace(s), Bracing Accolade, Couple, Crosstree, Fortify, Gallace, Gallows, Gallus(es), Gird, Hound, Invigorate, Pair, Pr, Rear-arch, Rere-arch, Skeg, Spider, Splint, Steady, Stiffener, Strut, > SUPPORT, Suspenders, Tauten, Thorough, Tone, Tonic, Two

Bracelet Armil(la), Armlet, Bangle, Cuff, Darbies, Handcuff, Identity, Manacle, Manilla

Brachiopod Ecardines, Lamp-shell, Spirifer

Bracken Brake, Fern, Pteridium, Tara

Bracket Angle-iron, Bibb, Brace, Cantilever, Console, Corbel, Couple, Cripple, Lance rest, Misericord(e), Modillion, Mutule, Parenthesis, Potence, Pylon, Rigger, Sconce, Square, Straddle, Strata, > STRUT, Trivet, Truss

Bract Glume(lla), Involucel, Involucre, Leaf, Lemma, Palea, Palet, Phyllary, Spathe

Brad Nail, Pin, Rivet, Sprig

Brag(gart), Bragging Basilisco, Birkie, Bluster, Boast, Bobadil, Braggadocio, Bull, Cockalorum, Crow, Falstaff, Fanfaronade, Gab, Gascon, Hot-air, Loudmouth, Parolles, Puckfist, Puff, Rodomontader, Skite, Slam, Swagger, Thrason, Thrasonic, Tongue-doubtie, Tongue-doughty, Vainglorious, Vaunt

Brahma(n) Sannyasi(n)

Braid A(i)glet, Aiguillette, Fishbone, French, Frog, Galloon, Lacet, Plait, Plat, Rickrack, Rick-rack, Ricrac, Seaming-lace, Sennet, Sennit, Sinnet, Soutache, Tress, Trim, Twist, Weave

Braille (system) Moon

Brain(s), Brainy, Brain disease, Brain-power Amygdala, Appestat, Bean, Bright, Cerebellum, Cerebrum, Cortex, Diencephalon, Dura mater, Encephalon, Epencephalon, Fornix, Genius, Gyrus, Harn(s), Head, Hippocampus, Hydrocephalus, Hypothalamus, Insula, Intelligence, IQ, Kuru, Left, Limbic, Loaf, Lobe, Mastermind, Mater, Medulla, Medulla oblongata, Metencephalon, Mind, Noddle, Noesis, Nous, Peduncle, Pericranium, Pia mater, Pons, Pontile, Prosencephalon, Rhinencephalon, Rhombencephalon, Sconce, Sense, Sensorium, Striatum, Subcortex, Tapagnosia, Tectum, Telencephalon, Thalamencephalon, Thalamus, Upper stor(e)y, Vermis, Wetware

▷ **Brain(s)** *may indicate* an anagram

Brainless Anencephaly, Bimbo, Stupid, Thick

Brainwash(ing) Indoctrinate, Menticide, Propaganda

Brake ABS, Adiantum, Air, Antilock, Bracken, Curb, Disc, Dive, Drag, Drum, Fern, Foot, Grove, Hand, Hydraulic, Nemoral, Overrun, Ratchet, Rein, Shoe, Shooting, > SLOW, Spinney, Sprag, Tara, Thicket, Vacuum, Westinghouse

Bramble, Brambly Batology, Blackberry, Boysenberry, Brier, Cloudberry, Rubus, Thorn, Wait-a-bit, Youngberry

Bran Cereal, Chesil, Chisel, Oats, Pollard

Branch(ed), Branches, Branching, Branch Office Affiliate, Antler, Arm, BO, Bough, Cladode, Cow, Dendron, Dept, Diversify, Diverticulum, Divide, Filiate, Fork, Grain, Jump, Kow, Lateral, Leaf-trace, Limb, Lobe, Loop, Lye, Lylum, Offshoot, Olive, Patulous, Raguly, Ramate, Ramulus, Reis, Rice, Shroud, Special, Spray(ey), Sprig, Spur, Tributary, Turning, Turn-off, Twig, Wattle, Yard

Branch-rib Lierne

Brand Broadsword, Buist, Burn, Cauterise, Chop, Class, Denounce, Earmark, Ember, Excalibur, Falchion, Faulchin, Faulchion, Idiograph, Inust, Iron, Label, Line, > MARK, Marque, Own, Power, Sear, Sere, Stigma, Sweard, Sword, Torch, Wipe

Brandish Bless, Flaunt, Flourish, Waffle, Wampish, Wave

Brandy Aguardiente, Applejack, Apricot, Aqua vitae, Armagnac, Bingo, Calvados, Cape Smoke, Cold without, Dop, Eau de vie, Fine, Framboise, Grappa, Mampoer, Marc, Mobbie, Mobby, Nantes, Nantz, Napoleon, Palinka, Peach, Quetsch, Slivovic(a), Slivovitz, Smoke

Bras Arms

Brash Impudent, Jumped-up, Pushy, Rain, Rash

Brass(y), Brassware Benares, Brazen, Cheek, Club, Corinthian, Cornet, Dinanderie, Face, Front, Harsh, High, Horn, Horse, Latten, Lip, Loot, Lota(h), Loud, Matrix, > MONEY, Moola(h), Oof, Oricalche, Orichalc, Pyrites, Sass, Snash, Sopranino, Talus, Top, Trombone, Wood

Brassard Armlet

Brass hat Brig

Brassica Brussels (sprout), > CABBAGE, Colza, Turnip

Brat Bairn, Enfant terrible, Gait(t), Gamin, Geit, Git, Gyte, Imp, Lad, Terror, Urchin

Brave(ry) Amerind, Apache, Bold, Conan, Corragio, Courage, Creek, Dare, > DEFY, Doughty, Dress, Face, Fearless, Gallant, Game, Gamy, Gutsy, Hardy, Heroism, Indian, Injun, Intrepid, Lion, Manful, Manly, Nannup, Plucky, Prow(ess), Sannup, Skookum, Spunk, Stout, Uncas, Valiant, Valour, Wight

Bravo Acclaim, B, Bandit, Bully, Desperado, Euge, Murderer, Olé, Spadassin, Villain

Brawl(er) Affray, Bagarre, Bicker, Brabble, Donnybrook, Dust, Fight, Flite, Flyte, Fracas, Fratch, Fray, Melee, Prawl, Rammy, Roarer, Roughhouse, Row, Scuffle, Set-to, Shindig, Stoush, Tar, Wrangle

Brawn Beef, Burliness, Headcheese, He-man, Might, Muscle, Power, Rillettes, Sinew

Bray Cry, Heehaw, Stamp, Vicar, Whinny

Brazen Bold, Brassy, Flagrant, Impudent, Shameless, Unabashed

Brazier Brasero, Fire, Hibachi, Mangal, Scaldino

Brazil(ian) Caboclo, Carioca, Para

Breach Assault, Break, Chasm, Cleft, Gap(e), Infraction, Redan, Rupture, Saltus, Schism, Solution, Trespass, Violate

Bread, Bread crumbs Afrikomen, Azym(e), Bagel, Baguette, Bannock, Bap, Barmbrack, Batch, Baton, Brewis, Brioche, Brownie, Bun, Cash, Chal(l)ah, Chametz, Chapati, Cheat, Ciabatta, Cob, Coburg, Corn, Corsned, Croissant, Crostini, Croute, Crouton, Crumpet, Crust, Damper, Dibs, Dika, Doorstep, Elephant's-foot, Eulogia, Flatbread, Focaccia, French, Garlic, Gluten, Graham, Granary, Grissino, Guarana, Hallah, Hametz, Hometz, Horse, Host, Indian, Injera, Jannock, Johnny-cake, Kaffir, Laver, Leavened, Loaf, Long tin, Manchet, Maori, Milk-sop, > **MONEY**, Monkey, Na(a)n, Pain, Panada, Panary, Pane, Paneity, Paratha, Pikelet, Pit(t)a, Pone, Poppadom, Poultice, Pumpernickel, Puree, Puri, Raspings, Ravel, Roll, Rooty, Roti, Round, Rusk, Rye, Sally Lunn, Schnecken, Shive, Simnel, Sippet, Smor(re)brod, Soda, Soft-tommy, Sourdough, Staff of life, Standard, Stollen, Stottie, Sugar, Sweet, Tartine, Tea, Tommy, Tortoise-plant, Twist, Wastel, Zakuski, Zwieback

Breadfruit Ja(c)k

Breadwinner Earner, Pa

Break, Break-down, Break-in, Break-up, Broken Adjourn, Aposiopesis, Bait, Breach, Caesura, Caesure, Cantle, Cark, Cesure, Chinaman, Chip, Cleave, Coffee, Comb, Comma, Commercial, Comminute, Compost, Conk, Crack, Crock, Crumble, Deave, Debacle, Deeve, Demob, Destroy, Diffract, Disintegrate, Disperse, Disrupt, Erupt, Exeat, Fast, Fault, Four, > **FRACTURE**, Fragment, Fritter, Frush, Gaffe, Give, Greenstick, Half-term, Half-time, Hernia, Hiatus, Holiday, Infringe, Interim, Interlude, Intermission, Interrupt, > **INTERVAL**, Irrupt, Knap, Knickpoint, Lacuna, Lapse, Leave, Lysis, Moratorium, Nickpoint, Nooner, Outage, Part, Pause, Phreak, Playtime, Poach, Polarise, Price, Reave, Recess, Recrudescent, Relief, Rend, Resorption, Respite, Rest, Rift, Ruin, Rupture, Saltus, Schism(a), Secede, Shatter, Shiver, Smash, Smokeho, Smoko, Snap, Split, Stave, Stop, Stop-over, Stove, Sunder, Tame, Tea-ho, Tear, Time-out, Torn, Transgress, Truce, Vacation, Violate

Breakable Brittle, Delicate, Fissile, Frail, Friable

Breakdown Analyse, Autolysis, Cataclasm, Collapse, Conk, Glitch, Glycolosis, Histolysis, Hydrolysis, Lyse, Lysis, Nervous, Ruin

Breaker Billow, Comber, Ice, Roller, Smasher, Surf

Breakfast B, Brunch, Chota-hazri, Continental, Disjune, English, Kipper, Petit déjeuner, Power, Wedding

Breakneck Headlong

Breakwater Groyne, Jetty, Mole, Pier, Tetrapod

Bream Fish, Porgy, Sar(gus), Tai

Breast(s), Breastbone, Breastwork Bazuma, Blob, Bosom, Brave, Brisket, Bristols, Bust, Counter, Diddy, Duddy, Dug, Falsies, Garbonza, Gazunga, Heart-spoon, Jubbies, Jugs, Knockers, Norg, Nork, Pigeon, Rampart, Redan, Sangar, Stem, Sternum, Sungar, Supreme, Tit, Xiphisternum

Breastplate Armour, Byrnie, Curat, Curiet, Pectoral, Plastron, Rational, Rest, Shield, Thorax, Xiphiplastron

Breath(e), Breathing, Breather Aerobe, Aspirate, Branchia, Caesural, Cheyne-Stokes, Circular, Cypress-knee, Eupnoea, Exhalation, Expiration, Flatus, Gasp, Gill, H, Halitosis, Hauriant, Haurient, Hobday, Hypernoea, Hyperventilation, Hypopnoea, Inhale, Inspiration, Lung, Nares, Nostril, Orthopnoea, Oxygenator, Pant, Pneuma, Prana, Pulmo, Rale, Respire, Respite, Rest, Rhonchus, Rough, Scuba, Snore, Snorkel, Snortmast, Snuffle, Spiracle, Spirit, Spiritus, Stertor, Stridor, Vent, Wheeze, Whiff, Whift, Whisper, Whist, Wind, Windpipe

Breathless(ness) Anhelation, Apnoea, Asthma, Dyspnoea, Emphysema,

Orthopnoea, Puffed-out, Tachypnoea, Wheezing

Breathtaking Amazing, Asphyxia

Breech(es) Bible, Buckskin, Chaps, Flog, Galligaskins, Hose, Jodhpurs, Kneecords, Knickerbockers, Plushes, Riding, Smallclothes, Smalls, Trews, Trouse(rs), Trusses

Breed(er), Breeding(-place) Bear, Beget, Cleck, Endogamous, Engender, Engend(r)ure, Eugenics, Fast, Generation, Gentilesse, Gentrice, Hetero, Hotbed, In-and-in, Lineage, > MANNERS, Origin, Panmixia, Procreate, Propagate, Pullulate, Race, Raise, Rear, Seminary, Sire, Species, Stock, Strain, Stud, Telegony, Thremmatology, Tribe, Voltinism

Breeze, Breezy Air, Breath, Brisk, Catspaw, Chipper, Doctor, Fresh, Gentle, Gust, Light, Mackerel, Moderate, Sea, Slant, Sniffler, Tiff, Zephyr

Brethren Bohemian, Darbyite, Elder, Exclusive, Herrnhuter, Kin, Open, Plymouth, Trinity

Breton Armoric, Brezonek

Breve Minim, Note, O

Breviary Portesse, Portous

▶ **Brevity** *see* BRIEF

Brew(ery), Brewer, Brewing Ale, Billycan, Brose, Browst, Bummock, > CONCOCT, Contrive, Dictionary, Distillery, Ferment, Infusion, Liquor, Malt, Potion, Steep, Witches', Yeast, Yill, Zymurgy

Briar Bramble, Canker, Lawyer

Bribe(ry) Backhander, Bonus, Boodle, Bung, Carrot, Dash, Embracery, Get at, Graft, Grease, Hush-money, Insult, Kickback, Oil, Palm, Palm-grease, Palm-oil, Payola, Schmear, Slush, Soap, Sop, Square, Straightener, Suborn, Sweeten(er), Tamper, Tempt, Tenderloin, Vail, Vales

Bric-a-brac Bibelot, Curio, Rattle-trap, Smytrie, Tatt, Virtu

Brick(s), Brickwork Adobe, Air, Bat, Bath, Boob, Bullnose, Bur(r), Clanger, Clinker, Closer, Course, Dutch clinker, Fletton, Gaffe, Gault, Gold, Hard stocks, Header, Ingot, Klinker, Lateritious, Lego®, Malm, Nogging, Red, Soldier, Sport, Stalwart, Stretcher, Terra-cotta, Testaceous, Tile, Trojan, Trump

Brickbat Missile

Bricklayer Churchill

Bride(s) Bartered, Danaides, Ellen, Hen, Spouse, War, Wife, Ximena

Bridesmaid Paranymph

Bridge(head), Bridge player Acol, Al Sirat, Aqueduct, Auction, Bailey, Balance, Barre, Bascule, Bestride, Bifrost, Biritch, Bridle-chord, Brig, Brooklyn, Cantilever, Capo, Capodastro, Capotasto, Catwalk, Chevalet, Chicago, Chicane, Clapper, Clifton, Contract, Counterpoise, Cross, Cut-throat, Deck, Declarer, Drawbridge, Duplicate, Flying, Foot, Four-deal, Gangplank, Gangway, Gantry, Girder, Hog's back, Humber, Humpback, Humpbacked, Ice, Irish, Jigger, Land, Lattice, Leaf, Lifting, Ligger, Link, London, Menai, Nasion, Overpass, Pivot, Plafond, Ponceau, Ponticello, Pontifice, Pont Levis, Pontoon, Rainbow, Rialto, Rubber, Sighs, Sinvat, Skew, Snow, > SPAN, Spanner, Stamford, Straddle, Suspension, Swing, Tay, Temper, Tête-de-pont, Through, Transporter, Traversing, Trestle, Truss, Turn, Vertical lift, Viaduct, Vint, Waterloo, Weigh, Wheatstone, Wire

Bridge pair EW, NS, SN, WE

Bridge protector Ice-apron

Bridge system Acol

Bridle Bit, Branks, Bridoon, Bristle, Browband, Crownpiece, Curb, Hackamore, Halter, Headstall, Musrol, Noseband, Rein, Scold's

Bridle path Orbit, Track

Brief(s), **Briefing**, **Briefly**, **Brevity** Awhile, Barristerial, Bluette, Brachyology, Breviate, Cape, Compact, > **CONCISE**, Conspectus, Crisp, Curt, Dossier, Fill in, Fleeting, Instruct, Laconic, Nearly, Pants, Pennorth, Pithy, Prime, Scant, > **SHORT(EN)**, Short-term, Short-winded, Sitrep, Succinct, Summing, Tanga, Terse, Transient, Undies, Update, Watching

Brig Br, Hermaphrodite, Jail, Nancy Bell, > **SHIP**, Snow

Brigade Boys', Corps, Fire, Fur, Girls', Green-ink, International, Naval, Red, Troop

Brigand Bandit, Bandolero, Cateran, Haiduck, Heiduc, Heyduck, Klepht, Pillager, Pirate, > **ROBBER**, Rob Roy, Trailbaston

Bright, **Brightness** Afterglow, Alert, Ashine, Brainy, Breezy, Brilliant, Brisk, Cheery, Cla(i)re, Clear, Clever, Effulgent, Elaine, Facula, Fair, Floodlit, Florid, Garish, Gay, Glad, Glow, Helen, Hono(u)r, Light, Lit, Loud, Lucid, Luculent, Lustre, Net(t), Nit, Radiant, Rorie, Rosy, Scintillating, Sematic, Sharp, Sheeny, Sheer, Shere, Skyre, Smart, Spark(y), Stilb, Sunlit, Sunny, Vive, Vivid, White

Bright spot Facula

Brilliant, **Brilliance** Ace, Blaze, Brainy, Def, Effulgent, Flashy, Galaxy, Gay, Gemmy, Glossy, Inspired, Lambent, Lucent, Lustre, Mega-, Meteoric, Nitid, Pear, > **RADIANT**, Refulgent, Resplendent, Shiny, Spangle, Splendour, Star, Virtuoso, > **VIVID**, Water

Brim Edge, Lip, Rim, Ugly

Brimstone Hellfire, S, Sulphur

Brindisi Skolion, Toast

Brindled Piebald, Tabby, Tawny

Brine Muriatic, Ozone, Pickle, Saline, Salt

Bring Afferent, Bear, Carry, Cause, Conduct, Convey, Earn, Evoke, Fet, Fetch, Foist, Hatch, Induce, Land, Produce, Wreak

Bring up Breed, Educate, Exhume, Foster, Nurture, Raise, > **REAR**

Brink > **EDGE**, Lip, Rim, Shore, > **VERGE**

Brio Elan

Brisk(ness) Active, Alacrity, Alert, Allegro, Breezy, Busy, Chipper, Crank, Crisp, Crouse, Fresh, Gaillard, Galliard, Jaunty, Kedge, Kedgy, Kidge, Lively, Peart, Perk, Pert, Rattling, Roaring, Scherzo, Sharp, Smart, Snappy, Spanking, Spirited, Sprightly, Vivace, Yare, Zippy

Bristle, **Bristling**, **Bristly** Aciculum, Arista, Awn, Barb, Birse, Bridle, Campodeiform, Chaeta, Flurry, Fraught, Frenulum, Glochidium, Gooseflesh, Hackles, Hair, Hérissé, Hispid, Horrent, Horripilation, Nereid, Polychaete, Seta, Setose, Striga, Strigose, Stubble, Styloid, Vibraculum, Villus, Whisker

Bristle-tail Campodea

Brit Silt

Brit(ish), **Briton(s)**, **Briton** All-red, Anglo, Herring, Iceni, Insular, Isles, Kipper, Limey, Pict, Pom, Rooinek, Saxon, Silurian, UK

Britain Alban(y), Albion, GB

Britannia, **Britannia metal** Tutania

Brittany Armorica

Brittle Bruckle, Crackly, Crimp, Crisp, Delicate, > **FRAGILE**, Frush, Hot-short, Redsear, Red-share, Red-shire, Redshort, Shivery, Spall, Spalt

▷ **Brittle** *may indicate* an anagram

Broach Approach, Open, Raise, Spit, Suggest, Tap, Widen

Broad(ly) Crumpet, Dame, Doll, Doxy, Drab, General, Generic, Largo, Latitudinous, Loose, Outspoken, Ovate, Pro, Roomy, Spatulate, Thick, Tolerant,

Wide, Woman

Broad-beaked Latirostrate

Broadcast(ing), Broadcaster Ad(vertise), Air, Announce, Beam, Breaker, CB, Disperse, Disseminate, Downlink, Emission, Ham, IBA, Network, Newscast, OB, On, Outside, Pirate, Programme, Promulgate, Radiate, Radio, Relay, Satellite, > SCATTER, Scattershot, Screen(ed), SECAM, Seed, Simulcast, Sky, Sow, Sperse, Spread, Sprinkle, Transmission, Ventilate, Wavelength

Broad-nosed Platyrrhine

Broadside Barrage, Criticism, Salvo, Tire

Broadway Boulevard, Esplanade, Motorway

Brocade Arrasene, Baldachin, Baldaquin, Baudekin, Bawdkin, Kincob, Zari

Brochure Leaflet, Pamphlet, Programme, Tract

Brogue Accent, > SHOE

Broke(n) Bankrupt, Bust(ed), Duff, Evans, Fritz, Impoverished, Insolvent, Kaput, On the rocks, Puckeroo, Shattered, Skint, Stony, Stove, Strapped

▷ **Broken** *may indicate* an anagram

Broken off Prerupt

Broker Agent, Banian, Banyan, Go-between, Jobber, Mediator, > MERCHANT, Shadchan, Uncle

Bromide Halide, Haloid, Truism

Bromine Br

Bronchitis, Bronchitic Chesty, Husk

Bronte(s) Bell, Cyclops

Brontosaurus Apatosaurus

Bronze, Bronze age Bell, Bras(s), Brown, Eugubine, Gunmetal, Hallstatt(ian), Helladic, Kamakura, Manganese, Minoan, Mycenean, Ormolu, Phosphor, Schillerspar, Sextans, Talos, Tan, Third

Brooch Cameo, Clasp, Fibula, Luckenbooth, Ouch, Owche, Pin, Preen, Prop, Spang, Sunburst

Brood(y) Clock, Clucky, Clutch, Cogitate, Covey, Eye, Eyrie, Hatch, Hover, Incubate, Introspect, Kindle, Litter, Meditate, Mill, Mull, Nest, Nid, Perch, Pet, > PONDER, Repine, Roost, Sit, Sulk, Team

Brook Abide, Babbling, Becher's, Beck, Branch, Burn, Countenance, Creek, Endure, Ghyll, Gill, Kerith, Kill, Pirl, Purl, Rill(et), River, Rivulet, Runlet, Runnel, Stand, Stomach, Stream, Suffer, Tolerate

Broom Besom, Brush, Cow, Cytisus, Genista, Gorse, Greenweed, Knee-holly, Kow, New, Orobranche, Retama, Spart, Sweeper, Whisk

Broth Bouillon, Brew(is), Cullis, Dashi, Kail, Kale, Muslin-kale, Pot liquor, Pottage, Scotch, Skilly, > SOUP, Stock

Brothel Bagnio, Bordel(lo), Cathouse, Corinth, Crib, Den, Flash-house, Honkytonk, Hothouse, Kip, Knocking shop, Red-light, Seraglio, Stew, Vaulting-house

Brother(hood) Ally, Bhai, Billie, Billy, Blood, Boet, Brethren, Bro, Bud, Comrade, Fellow, Fra, Freemason, Lay, > MONK, Moose, Pre-Raphaelite, Sib(ling), Theatine, Trappist, Worker

Brow Crest, Forehead, Glabella, Ridge, Sinciput, Tump-line

Browbeat Badger, Bully, Butt, Hector, Nut

Brown(ed) Abram, Adust, Amber, Apricate, Auburn, Au gratin, Bay, Biscuit, Bisque, Bister, Bistre, Bole, Br, Braise, Brindle, Bronzed, Brunette, Burnet, Burnt umber, Capability, Caramel, Caromel, Chamois, Cinnamon, Cook, Coromandel, Dun, Fallow, Filemot, Fulvous, Fusc(ous), Grill, Hazel, Infuscate, Ivor, John, Khaki, Liver, March, Meadow, Mocha, Mousy, Ochre, Olive,

Oxblood, Philamot, Rufous, Rugbeian, Russet, Rust, Scorch, Seal, Sepia, Sienna, Soare, Sore, Sorrel, Tan, Tawny, Tenné, Testaceous, Toast, Tom, Umber, Vandyke, Wholemeal, Windsor

Browne Sam

Brownie Dobbie, Dobby, Dobie, Goblin, Hob, Kobold, Leprechaun, Nis(se), Rosebud, Sprite

Browse(r) Graze, Netscape®, Pasture, Read, Scan, Stall-read, Surf

Bruce Robert

Bruise Contund, Contuse, Crush, Damage, Ding, Ecchymosis, Frush, Golp(e), Hurt, Intuse, Livedo, Lividity, Mark, Mouse, Pound, Purpure, Rainbow, Shiner, Ston(n), Stun, Surbate

Brummagen Tatty

Brunette Dark, Latin

Brush (off), **Brushwood** Bavin, Bottle, Brake, Broom, Carbon, Chaparral, Clash, Dandy, Dismiss, Dust, Encounter, Fan, Filbert, Filecard, Firth, Fitch, Frith, Grainer, Hag, Hog, Kiss, Liner, Loofah, Mop, Paint, Pig, Pope's head, Putois, Rebuff, Rice, Rigger, Sable, Scrub, Scuff, Skim, Striper, Thicket, Touch, Whisk, Wire

Brusque Abrupt, Blunt, Curt, Downright, Pithy, Short

Brussels Carpet, Lace

Brutal, **Brute** Animal, Barbaric, Beast, Bête, Caesar, Caliban, Cruel, Hun, Iguanodon, Inhuman, Nazi, Nero, Ostrogoth, Pitiless, Quagga, Rambo, Roughshod, Ruffian, Thresher-whale, Yahoo

Brutus Wig

Bryophyte Moss, Tree-moss

Bubble(s), **Bubbly** Air-bell, Air-lock, Barmy, Bead(ed), Bell, Bleb, Blister, Boil, Buller, Cavitate, Champagne, Cissing, Ebullition, Effervesce, Embolus, Enthuse, Espumoso, Foam, > **FROTH**, Gassy, Globule, Gurgle, Head, Magnetic, Mantle, Mississippi, Popple, Rale, Reputation, Roundel, Rowndell, Seed, Seethe, Simmer, South Sea, Vesicle, Widow

Bubble and squeak Colcannon

Buccaneer Corsair, Dampier, Drake, Freebooter, Morgan, Picaroon, Pirate

Buck (up) Bongo, Brace, Cheer, Dandy, Deer, Dollar, Elate, Encheer, Hart, Jerk, Leash, Male, Ourebi, Pitch, Pricket, Ram, Rusa, Sore, Sorel(l), Sorrel, Spade, Spay(a)d, > **STAG**, Staggard, Stud, Water, Wheel

Buckaroo Cowboy, Cowpoke

Bucket(s) Bail, Bale, Clamshell, Ice, Jacob's ladder, Kibble, Noria, Pail, Piggin, Rust, Scuttle, Situla, Slop, Stoop(e), Stope, Stoup, Tub

Buckeye Ohio

Buckle Artois, Clasp, Contort, Crumple, Deform, Dent, Fasten, Warp

▷ **Buckle** *may indicate* an anagram

Buckle-beggar Patrico

Buckler Ancile, Rondache, > **SHIELD**, Targe

▷ **Bucks** *may indicate* an anagram

Buckshee Free

Buckthorn Cascara, Wahoo

Buckwheat Brank, Sarrasin, Sarrazin

Bucolic Aeglogue, Eglogue, Idyllic, Pastoral, Rural, Rustic

Bud(ding), **Buddy** Botoné, Bottony, Bulbil, Burgeon, Clove, Cobber, Deb, Eye, Gem(ma), Germinate, Holly, Knop, Knosp, Knot, Nascent, Pal, Scion, Serial, Shoot, Sprout, Taste, Turion

Buddha, **Buddhism**, **Buddhist** Abhidhamma, Ahimsa, Amitabha, Anata,

Anatta, Anicca, Arhat, Asoka, Bodhisattva, Dalai Lama, Dukkha, Esoteric, Foism, Gautama, Hinayana, Jain, Jataka, Jodo, Kagyu, Mahatma, Mahayana, Maya, Nichiren, Pali, Pitaka, Pure Land, Rinzai, Ryobu, Sakya-muni, Sangha, Shinto, Siddhartha Gautama, Sila, Soka Gakkai, Soto, Theravada, Tripitaka, Triratna, Vajrayana, Zen(o)

Budge Jee, Move, Stir, Submit

Budget Allocation, Estimate, Operating, Plan, Programme, Shoestring

Buff Beige, Birthday suit, Eatanswill, Fan, Fawn, Nankeen, Nude, Nut, Polish, > RUB, Streak

Buffalo African, Anoa, Arna, Asiatic, Bison, Bonasus, Bugle, Cap, Cape, Carabao, Ox, Perplex, Takin, Tamarao, Tamarau, Timarau, Water, Zamouse

Buffer Bootblack, Cofferdam, Cutwater, Fender, Sleek-stone

Buffet Bang, Blow, Box, Carvery, Counter, Cuff, Finger-food, Hit, Lam, Maltreat, Perpendicular, Shove, Sideboard, Smorgasborg, Strike, Strook(e)

Buffoon(ery) Antic, Clown, Droll, Goliard, Harlequin, Horseplay, Iniquity, Jester, Mime(r), Mome, Mummer, Nutter, Pantagruel, Pantaloon(ery), Pickle-herring, Pierrot, Punchinello, Scaramouch, Scogan, Scoggin, Scurrile, Slouch, Tomfool, Vice, Wag, Zany

Bug(s) Anoplura, Arthropod, Assassin, Bacteria, Bedevil, Beetle, Berry, Capsid, Chinch, Cimex, Coccidae, Cockchafer, Corixid, Croton, Damsel, Debris, Dictograph®, Eavesdrop, Germ, Ground, Harlequin, Hassle, Hemiptera, > INSECT, Jitter, June, Kissing, Lace, Lightning, Listeria, Maori, May, Mealy, Micrococcus, Mike, Milkweed, Millennium, Mite, Nettle, Pill, Reduviid, Rhododendron, Shield, Skeeter, Squash, Tap, Vex, Wheel, Wiretap

Bugbear Anathema, Bogey, Bogle, Bogy, Eten, Ettin, Poker, Rawhead

Buggy Beach, Car, Cart, Pushchair, Shay, Tipcart, Trap

Bughouse Fleapit, Loco

Bugle, Bugle call Chamade, Clarion, Cornet, Hallali, Last post, Ox, Reveille, Taps, > TRUMPET, Urus

Build(ing), Building site Accrue, Anabolism, Ar(a)eostyle, Assemble, Bhavan, Big, Bricks and mortar, Capitol, Chapterhouse, Colosseum, Commons, Corncrib, Cot, > CREATE, Cruck, Curia, Develop, Dipteros, Drystone, Duplex, Edifice, Edify, Erect, Fabric, High-rise, Hut, Infill, Insula, Kaaba, Ken, Linhay, Listed, Low-rise, Lyceum, Minaret, Monopteron, Mould, Observatory, Outhouse, Palazzo, Phalanstery, Phalanx, Pile, Portakabin®, Premises, Prytaneum, Quonset®, Raise, Ribbon, Rotunda, Skyscraper, Stance, Structure, Synthesis, System, Tectonic, Telecottage, Temple, Tenement, Tholos, Tower, Triplex®

Builder Brick, Constructor, Engineer, Mason, Millwright, Stonemason, Waller

▷ **Building** *may indicate* an anagram

Bulb Camas(h), Camass, Chive, Cive, Corm, Flash, Globe, Lamp, Light, Olfactory, Pearl, Rupert's drop, Scallion, Set, Shallot, Squill

Bulge, Bulging Astrut, Bag, Bias, Biconvex, Bug, Bulbous, Bunchy, Cockle, Entasis, Expand, Exsert, Inion, Protrude, Protuberant, Relievo, Rotund, Strout, Strut, > SWELL, Tumid

Bulk(y) Aggregate, Ample, Big, Body, Corpulent, Density, Extent, Gross, Hull, Massive, Preponderance, Roughage, Scalar, > SIZE, Stout, Vol(ume), Weight

Bull(s), Bullock, Bully Anoa, Apis, Bakha, Beef, Blarney, Bludgeon, Bluster, Bovine, Brag, Brave, Browbeat, Buchis, Bucko, Despot, Dragoon, Drawcansir, Encierro, Englishman, Eretrian, Fancyman, Farnese, Flashman, Flatter, Gold, Gosh, Hapi, Harass, Hawcubite, Haze(r), Hector, Hoodlum, Huff, Intimidate, Investor, Iricism, Irish(ism), John, Killcow, Lambast, Maltreat, Merwer,

Mick(e)(y), Mistake, Mithraism, Mohock, Nandi, Neat, Pamplona, Papal, Piker, Pistol, Placet, Poler, Rhodian, Roarer, Rot, Ruffian, Sitting, Souteneur, Stag, Stale, Strong-arm, Swash-buckler, Taurine, Taurus, Toitoi, Tommy-rot, Tosh, Trash, Twaddle, Tyran(ne), Tyrannise, Tyrant, Unigenitus, Winged, Zo(bo)

Bulldog Marshal, Tenacious

Bulldoze(r) Angledozer, Coerce, Earthmover, Leveller, Overturn

Bullet Ammo, Balata, Ball, Baton round, Biscayan, Dumdum, Fusillade, Magic, Minié, Minié ball, Missile, Pellet, Percussio, Plastic, Round, Rubber, Shot, Slug, Soft-nosed, Tracer

Bulletin Memo, Message, Newsletter, Report, Summary

Bull-fight(er) Banderillero, Banderillo, Corrida, Cuadrilla, Escamillo, Matador, Picador, Rejoneador, Tauromachy, Toreador, Torero

Bull-head Cottoid, Father-lasher, Pogge, Sea-poacher

Bull-rider Europa

Bull-roarer Rhombos, Tu(r)ndun

Bull's eye Carton, God, Humbug, Target

Bulrush Pandanaceous, Reed, Reed-mace, Tule

Bulwark Bastion, Defence, Rampart, Resistor

Bum Ass, Beg, Prat, Sponge, Thumb, Tramp, Vagabond

Bumble Beadle, Bedel(l)

▷ **Bumble** *may indicate* an anagram

Bumboat woman Buttercup

Bumf Spam

Bump(er), Bumps Big, Blow, Bradyseism, Bucket, Clour, Collide, Dunch, Encephalocele, Fender, Hillock, Immense, Inian, Inion, Joll, Jo(u)le, Jowl, Keltie, Kelty, Knar, Knock, Mamilla, Mogul, Organ, Overrider®, Phrenology, Reveille, Rouse, Speed, Thump

Bumpkin Bucolic, Bushwhacker, Clodhopper, Hawbuck, Hayseed, Hick, Jock, Lout, Oaf, Put(t), Rube, Rustic, Yokel, Zany

Bumptious Arrogant, Brash, Randie, Randy, Uppity

Bun Barmbrack, Bath, Black, Chelsea, Chignon, Chou, Currant, Devonshire split, Hot-cross, Huffkin, Mosbolletjie, Roll, Teacake, Toorie, Wad

Bunch Acinus, Anthology, Bob, Botryoid, Bouquet, Byndle, Cluster, Fascicle, Finial, Flock, > GROUP, Hand, Handful, Lot, Lump, Nosegay, Panicle, Raceme, Spray, Staphyline, Tassel, Tee, Truss, Tuft

Bundle Axoneme, Bale, Bavin, Bluey, Bottle, Byssus, Desmoid, Dorlach, Drum, Fag(g)ot, Fascicle, Fascine, Fibre, Fibrovascular, Kemple, Knitch, Lemniscus, Matilda, > PACK(AGE), Parcel, Sack, Sheaf, Shiralee, Shock, Shook, Stook, Swag, Tie, Top, Trousseau, Truss, Vascular, Wad, Wadge, Wap

Bung Cork, Dook, Obturate, Plug, Stopgap, Stopper

Bungalow Dak

Bungle(r) Blunder, Blunk, Bodge, Boob, Botch, Bumble, Bummle, Dub, Duff, Fluff, Foozle, Foul, Foul up, Goof, Mash, Mess, Mis(h)guggle, Muddle, Muff, Mull, Prat, Screw, Spoil

Bunk(er), Bunkum Abscond, Absquatulate, Balderdash, Baloney, Berth, Blah, Bolt, Casemate, Claptrap, Clio, Entrap, Guy, Hazard, History, Hokum, Humbug, Malarky, Nonsense, Rot, Sandtrap, Scuttle, Stokehold, Tosh, Trap, Tripe

Bunter Billy, Owl

Bunthorne Aesthete, Poet

Bunting Bird, Cirl, Flag, Fringilline, Ortolan, Snow, Streamer, Yellow-hammer, Yowley

Buoy Bell, Breeches, Can, Dan, Daymark, Dolphin, Float, Life, Marker, Nun,

Raft, Ring, Seamark, Sonar, Sonobuoy, Spar, Sustain, Wreck

Buoyant Afloat, Blithe, Floaty, Resilient

Burble Blat, Gibber

Burden Albatross, Beare, Bob, Cargo, Cark, Chant, Chorus, Cross, Cumber, Deadweight, Drone, Droore, Encumber, Encumbrance, Fa-la, Fardel, Folderol, Fraught, Freight, Gist, Handicap, Hum, Lade, > **LOAD**, Lumber, Millstone, Monkey, Oercome, Onus, Oppress, Put-upon, Refrain, Rumbelow, Saddle, Servitude, Shanty, Substance, Tax, Tenor, Torch, Trouble, Weight, Woe, Yoke

Burdensome Irksome, Onerous, Oppressive, Weighty

Burdock Clote(-bar), Clothur, Cockle-bar, Weed

Bureau Agency, Agitprop, Cominform, Davenport, Desk, Interpol, Kominform, Marriage, > **OFFICE**, Volunteer

Bureaucracy, **Bureaucrat(ic)** CS, Impersonal, Jack-in-office, Mandarin, Red tape, Tapist, Wallah

Burgeon(ing) Asprout, Blossom, Bud, Grow, Sprout

Burgess, **Burgher** Citizen, Freeman

Burglar, **Burgle** Area-sneak, Cat, Crack(sman), House-breaker, Intruder, Peterman, Picklock, Raffles, Robber, Screw, Thief, Yegg

Burgundy Macon, Vin

Burial(place) Catacomb, Charnel, Committal, Crypt, Cubiculum, Darga, Funeral, God's acre, Golgotha, Grave, Interment, Kurgan, Lair, Last rites, Sepulchre, Sepulture, Tomb, Tumulus, Vault, Zoothapsis

Burin Graver

Burlesque Caricatura, Caricature, Comedy, Farce, Heroicomical, Hudibrastic(s), Hurlo-thrumbo, Lampoon, Macaronic, Parody, Satire, Skimmington, Skit, Spoof, Travesty

Burlington RA

Burly Bluff, Stout, Strapping

Burmese Karen(ni), Naga, Shan

Burn(er), **Burning**, **Burnt** Adust, Afire, Alow(e), Ardent, Argand, Arson, Ash, Auto-da-fé, Bats-wing, Beck, Bishop, Blaze, Blister, Blowtorch, Brand, Bren(ne), Brent, Brook, Bunsen, Causalgia, Caustic, Cauterise, Char, Chark, Chinese, Cinder, Coal, Coke, Combust, Conflagration, Cremate, Crozzled, Crucial, Deflagrate, Destruct, Eilding, Ember, Emboil, Empyreuma, Fervid, Fircone, > **FIRE**, Fishtail, Flagrant, Flare, Flash, Fresh(et), Gleed, Gut, Holocaust, Ignite, In, Incendiary, Incense, Incinerate, Inure, Inust(ion), Kill, Live, Lunt, Offering, On, Oxidise, Oxyacetylene, Plo(a)t, Powder, Pyric, Pyromania, Rill, Sati, Scald, Scorch, Scouther, Scowder, Scowther, Sear, Sienna, Sike, Singe, Sizzle, Smart, Smoulder, Suttee, Swale, Third-degree, Thurible, Torch, Umber, Urent, Ustion, Ustulation, Weeke, Welsbach, Wick

Burp Belch

Burr(ing) Brei, Brey, Clote, Croup, Dialect, Knob, Rhotacism

Burrow(er), **Burrowing** Dig, Earth, Fossorial, Gopher, Groundhog, Hole, How, Howk, Mole, Nuzzle, Root, Sett, Tunnel, Viscacha, Warren, Wombat, Worm

Bursar(y) Camerlengo, Camerlingo, Coffers, Grant, Purser, Scholarship, Treasurer

Bursitis Beat

Burst(ing) Blowout, Brast, Break, Dehisce, Disrupt, Dissilient, Ebullient, Erumpent, Erupt, > **EXPLODE**, Flare-up, Fly, Implode, Pop, Sforzato, Shatter, Spasm, Spirt, Split, Sprint, Spurt, Stave, Tetterous

Bury Cover, Eard, Earth, Embowel, Engrave, Enhearse, Graff, Graft, Imbed, Inearth, Inhearse, Inhume, Inter, Inurn, Landfill, Repress, Sepulture, Sink,

Ye(a)rd, Yird

Bus Aero, Bandwagon, Car, Charabanc, Coach, Double-decker, Greyhound, Hondey, Hopper, ISA, Jitney, Mammy-wagon, Rattletrap, Single-decker, Tramcar, Trolley, Walking

Bus conductor Cad, Clippy

Bush(y) Bramble, Brier, Bullace, Busket, Calico, Clump, Cotton, Dumose, Firethorn, Hawthorn, Hibiscus, Kapok, Mallee, Matagouri, Mulberry, Outback, Poinsettia, Poly-poly, President, Sallee, Shepherd, Shrub, Sugar, Thicket, Tire, Tod(de)

Bush-baby Durukuli, Galago, Nagapie, Night-ape

Bushel Ardeb, Bu, Co(o)mb, Cor, Ephah, Fou, Homer, Peck, Weight, Wey

Business Affair, Agency, Biz, Bus, Cartel, Cerne, Co, Commerce, Company, Concern, Conglomerate, Craft, Duty, Enterprise, Ergon, Establishment, Exchange, Fasti, Firm, Funny, Game, Gear, Hong, Industry, Line, Métier, Monkey, Office, Palaver, Pi(d)geon, Pidgin, Practice, Professional, Racket, Shebang, Shop, Show, To-do, Trade, Traffic, Transaction, Tread, Turnover, Unincorporated, Vocation, Zaikai

Businessman Babbitt, Capitalist, City, Entrepreneur, Financier, Realtor, Taipan, Trader, Tycoon

Busk(er) Bodice, Corset, Entertainer, German-band

Buskin(s) Brod(e)kin, Cothurn(us), Shoe

Buss Kiss, Osculate, Smack

Bussu Troelie, Troely, Troolie

Bust Beano, Boob, Brast, Break, Chest, Falsies, Figurehead, Herm(a), Insolvent, Sculp, Shatter(ed), Spree, Statue, Term(inus), To-tear, To-torne, Ups(e)y

▷ **Bust** *may indicate* an anagram

Bustard Bird, Otis, Turkey

Buster Keaton

Bustle Ado, Beetle, Do, Dress-improver, Flap, Pad, Scurry, > STIR, Swarm, Tournure, Whew

Busy Active, At (it), Deedy, > DETECTIVE, Dick, Eident, Employ, Ergate, Eye, Goer, Hectic, Hive, Humming, Occupied, Ornate, Prodnose, Stir, Tec, Throng, Worksome

Busybody Bustler, Meddler, Noser, Pragmatic, Snooper, Trout, Yenta

But Aber, Bar, Except, However, Keg, Merely, Nay, Only, Save, Sed, Simply, Tun

Butch He-man, Macho

Butcher(y) Cumberland, Decko, Dekko, Flesher, Kill, Killcow, Look, Massacre, Ovicide, Sever, Shambles, Shochet, Shufti, Slaughter, Slay

Butler Bedivere, Bread-chipper, Jeeves, Khansama(h), Major-domo, RAB, Rhett, Samuel, Servant, Sewer, Sommelier, Steward

Butt (in) Aris, Barrel, Bumper, Bunt, Clara, Dimp, Dunch, Enter, Geck, Glasgow kiss, Goat, Header, Horn, Jesting-stock, Laughing-stock, Mark, Nut, Outspeckle, Pantaloon, Pipe, Push, Ram, Roach, Scapegoat, Snipe, Stompie, > STOOGE, Straight man, Stump, Target, Tun, Ups

Butter Adulation, Billy, Brandy, Butyric, Cocoa, Coconut, Drawn, Flatter, Galam, Garcinia, Ghee, Ghi, Goa, Goat, Illipi, Illupi, Kokum, Mahua, Mahwa, Maitre d'hotel, Mow(r)a, Nut, Nutter, Pat, Peanut, Print, Ram, Scrape, Shea, Spread, Vegetable

▷ **Butter** *may indicate* a goat or such

Buttercup Bumboat woman, Crow-foot, Crow-toe, Goldilocks, Ranunculus, Reate, Thalictrum

Butterfingers Muff

Butterfish Nine-eyes
Butterfly Apollo, Argus, Birdwing, Blue, Brimstone, Brown, Cabbage white, Camberwell beauty, Cardinal, Chequered skipper, Cleopatra, Clouded yellow, Comma, Common blue, Dilettante, Eclosion, Emperor, Fritillary, Gate-keeper, Grayling, Hair-streak, Heath, Hesperid, Imaginal, Kallima, Large copper, Large white, Leaf, Lycaena, Marbled-white, Meadow brown, Milk-weed, Monarch, Morpho, Mourning-cloak, Nerves, Nymphalid, Nymphean, Orange-tip, Owl, Painted lady, Papilionidae, Peacock, Pieris, Psyche, Purple emperor, Red admiral, Rhopalocera, Ringlet, Satyr(idae), Satyrinae, Silverspot, Skipper, Small white, Speckled wood, Stamper, Sulphur, Swallow-tail, Thecla, Thistle, Tiger swallowtail, Tortoiseshell, Two-tailed pasha, Vanessa, Wall brown, White admiral
Buttermilk Bland, Lassi
Butternut Souari
Butter-tree Mahua, Mahwa, Mow(r)a
Buttocks Arse, Ass, Bahookie, Booty, Bottom, Can, Coit, Derrière, Doup, Duff, Fanny, Fundament, Gluteus maximus, Hinder-end, Hinderlan(d)s, Hurdies, Jacksie, Jacksy, Keester, Keister, Mooning, Nache, Nates, Prat, Quoit, Seat, Tush
Button(s) Barrel, Bellboy, Fastener, Frog, Hot, Knob, Mute, Netsuke, Olivet, Page(boy), Panic, Pearl, Push, Snooze, Stud, Switch, Toggle
Buttonhole Accost, Boutonniere, Detain, Eye, Flower
Buttress Brace, Counterfort, Flying, Hanging, Pier, Prop, Stay, Support, Tambour
Buxom Bonnie, Busty, Plump, Sonsy
Buy(ing), Buyer Believe, Bribe, Coff, Corner, Customer, Emption, Engross, Impulse, Monopsonist, Oligopsony, Panic, Purchase, Regrate, Shop, Shout, Spend, Take, Trade, Vendee
▷ **Buyer** *may indicate* money
Buzz(er) Bee, Bombilate, Bombinate, Button, Fly, Hum, Rumour, Scram, Whirr, Whisper, Zed, Zing, Zoom
Buzzard Bee-kite, Bird, Buteo, Hawk, Pern, Puttock, Vulture
By Alongside, At, Gin, Gone, In, Near, Neighbouring, Nigh, Of, Past, Per, Through, With, X
Bye Extra
Bye-bye Adieu, Farewell, Tata
Bygone B.C., Dead, Departed, Past, Yore
By Jove Egad
Bypass Avoid, Circuit, Coronary, ▷ DETOUR, Evade, Ignore, Omit, Shunt, Skirt
By-product Epiphenomenon, Spin-off
Byre Cowshed, Manger, Stable, Trough
By so much The
By the way Apropos, Incidentally, Obiter
Byway Alley, Lane, Path
Byword Ayword, Phrase, Proverb, Slogan
Byzantine Catapan, Complicated, Exarch, Intricate, Intrince, Theme

Cc

C Around, Caught, Celsius, Cent, Centigrade, Charlie, Conservative, San

Cab Boneshaker, Crawler, Drosky, Fiacre, Four-wheeler, Growler, Gurney, Hackney, Hansom, Mini, Noddy, Taxi, Vettura

Cabal(ler) Arlington, Ashley, Buckingham, Clifford, Clique, Conspiracy, Coterie, Faction, Junto, Lauderdale, Party, Plot

Cab(b)alistic Abraxis, Mystic, Notarikon, Occult

Cabaret Burlesque, Floorshow

Cabbage(-head), Cabbage soup Book choy, Borecole, Brassica, Castock, Cauliflower, Cavalo nero, Chinese, Choucroute, Cole, Collard, Crout, Custock, Drumhead, Kerguelen, Kohlrabi, Kraut, Loaf, Loave, Pak-choi, Pamphrey, Pe-tsai, Sauerkraut, Savoy, Shchi, Shtchi, Skunk, Thieve, Turnip, Wild, Wort

Caber Fir, Janker, Log, Sting

Cabin Berth, Bibby, Bothy, Box, Cabana, Caboose, Camboose, Coach, Cottage, Crannog, Crib, Cuddy, Den, Gondola, Hovel, Hut, Izba, Lodge, Loghouse, Long-house, Pod, Pressure, Room, Roundhouse, Saloon, Shanty, Stateroom, Trunk

Cabin-boy Grummet

Cabinet Bahut, Cabale, Case, Closet, Commode, Console, Cupboard, Filing, Kitchen, Ministry, Secretaire, Shadow, Shrinal, Vitrine

Cabinet maker Chippendale, Ebeniste, Hepplewhite, Joiner, PM

Cable(way), Cable-car Chain, Coax(ial), Extension, Flex, Halser, Hawser, Jumper, Jump leads, Junk, Landline, Lead, Lead-in, Lifeline, Null-modern, Oil-filled, Outhaul, Rope, Slatch, Snake, Téléférique, > TELEGRAM, Telegraph, Telepherique, Telpher(age), Topping lift, Trunking, Wire, Yoke

Cache Deposit, Hidlin(g)s, > HOARD, Inter, Stash, Store, Treasure

Cachet Prestige

Cackle Cluck, Gaggle, Gas, Haw, Snicker, Titter

Cacography Scrawl

Cacophony Babel, Caterwaul, Charivari, Discord, Jangle

Cactus, Cactus-like Alhagi, Barel, Cereus, Cholla, Christmas, Dildo, Easter, Echino-, Hedgehog, Jojoba, Maguey, Mescal, Nopal, Ocotillo, Opuntia, Organ-pipe, Peyote, Prickly pear, Retama, Saguaro, Stapella, Star, Strawberry, Torch-thistle, Tuna, Xerophytic

Cad Base, Boor, Bounder, Churl, Cocoa, Heel, Oik, Rascal, Rotter, Skunk

Cadaver(ous) Body, Corpse, Deathly, Ghastly, Goner, Haggard, Stiff

Caddy Porter, Tea, Teapoy

Cadence Beat, Close, Euouae, Evovae, Fa-do, Flow, Lilt, Meter, Perfect, Plagal, Rhythm

Cadenza Fireworks

Cadet(s) Junior, OTC, Scion, Syen, Trainee, Younger

Cadge(r) Bludge, Bot, Bum, Impose, > SCROUNGE, Sponge

Cadmium Cd

Caesar Nero

Caesium Cs

Cafe(teria) Automat, Bistro, Brasserie, Buvette, Canteen, Commissary, Cybercafe, Diner, Dinette, Donko, Eatery, Estaminet, Filtré, Greasy spoon, Hashhouse, Internet, Juke joint, Pizzeria, Pull-in, Tearoom, Transport

Cage Bar, Battery, Box, Cavie, Confine, Coop, Corf, Dray, Drey, Enmew, Faraday, Fold, Frame, Grate, Hutch, Keavie, Mew, Pen, > PRISON, Safety, Squirrel, Trave

Cahoots Hugger-mugger

Cairn Barp, Dog, Horned, Man, Mound, Raise

Caisson Bends

Caitiff Meanie

Cajole(ry) Beflum, Beguile, Blandish, Blarney, Carn(e)y, > COAX, Cuittle, Humbug, Inveigle, Jolly, Persuade, Wheedle

Cake Agnus dei, Angel, Baba, Babka, Baklava, Banbury, Bannock, Bara brith, Barmbrack, Battenberg, Birthday, Brioche, Brownie, Buckwheat bun, Carcake, Cattle, Chapat(t)i, Chillada, Chupati, Chupattie, Chupatty, Clapbread, Clot, Coburg, Corn dodger, Cotton, Croquette, Cruller, Crumpet, Dainty, Devil's food, Drizzle, Dundee, Eccles, Eclair, Fancy, Farl(e), Filter, Fish, Flapjack, Frangipane, Frangipani, Fritter, Galette, Genoa, Gingerbread, Girdle, > HARDEN, Hockey, Hoe, Idli, Jannock, Jumbal, Jumbles, Koeksister, Kruller, Kuchen, Kueh, Lamington, Lardy, Latke, Layer, Linseed, Macaroon, Madeira, Madeleine, Maid of honour, Marble, Meringue, Millefeuille, Mud, Muffin, Napoleon, Nut, Oatmeal, Oil, Pan, Panettone, Paratha, Parkin, Parliament, Pat, Patty, Pavlova, Petit four, Pikelet, > PLASTER, Pomfret, Pone, Pontefract, Poori, Popover, Pound, Profiterole, Puff, Puftaloon(a), Puri, Queencake, Ratafia, Ready-mix, Religieuse, Rice, Rock, Rosti, Roti, Rout, Rum baba, Rusk, Sachertorte, Saffron, Sally Lunn, Salt, Sandwich, Savarin, Scone, Seed, Set, Simnel, Singing-hinny, Slab, Slapjack, Soul, Spawn, Spice, Sponge, Stollen, Stottie, Sushi, Swiss roll, Tablet, Tansy, Tea(bread), Tipsy, Torte, Tortilla, Twelfth, Upside down, Vetkoek, Wad, Wafer, Waffle, Wedding, Wonder, Yeast

▷ **Cake** *may indicate* an anagram

Cake-shaped Placentiform

Cakestand Curate

Cakewalk Doddle

Calaboose Jail, Loghouse

Calamitous, Calamity Blow, Catastrophe, Dire, > DISASTER, Distress, Fatal, Ill, Jane, Ruth, Storm, Tragic, Unlucky, Visitation, Woe

Calcareous Ganoin, Lithite

Calcium Ca, Colemanite, Dogger, Dripstone, Otolith, Quicklime, Scawtite, Whewellite

Calculate(d), Calculation, Calculator Abacus, Actuary, Compute(r), Cost, Design, Estimate, Extrapolate, Log, Napier's bones, Prorate, Quip(p)u, Rate, > RECKON, Slide-rule, Sofar, Soroban, Tactical, Tell

Calculus Cholelith, Differential, Functional, Infinitesimal, Integral, Lambda, Lith, Lithiasis, Predicate, Propositional, Science, Sentential, Sialolith, Stone, Tartar, Urolith

Caledonian Kanak

Calendar Advent, Agenda, Almanac, Chinese, Diary, Fasti, Gregorian, Hebrew, Intercalary, Jewish, Journal, Julian, Luach, Lunisolar, Menology, Newgate, New Style, Ordo, Perpetual, Revolutionary, Roman, Sothic

Calender(ing) Dervish, Mangle, Swissing

Calf Ass, Bobby, Box, Cf, Deacon, Dogie, Dogy, Freemartin, Golden, Leg, Maverick, Poddy, Sleeper, Stirk, Sural, Tollie, Tolly, Tree, Veal, Vitular

Caliban Moon-calf

Calibrate, **Calibre** Bore, Capacity, Graduate, Mark, > QUALITY, Text

Californium Cf

Caliph Abbasid(e), Vathek

Call(ed), **Calling**, **Call on**, **Call up** Adhan, Appeal, Arraign, Art, Awaken, Azan, Banco, Bawl, Beck, Behote, Bevy, Bid, Boots and saddles, Business, Buzz, Career, Chamade, Cite, Claim, Clang, Clarion, Cleep, Clepe, Close, Cold, Conference, Conscript, Convene, Convoke, Cooee, Cry, Curtain, Dial, Drift, Dub, Evoke, Gam, Go, Hail, Hallali, Haro, Heads, Heave-ho, Hech, Hete, Hey, Hight, Ho, Hot(e), Howzat, Huddup, Hurra(h), Job, Junk, Last (post), Line, Local, Métier, Misère, Mobilise, Mot, Name, Nap, Need, Nemn, Nempt, Nominate, Olé, Page, Phone, Photo, Post, Proo, Pruh, Pursuit, Rechate, Recheat, Retreat, Reveille, Ring, Roll, Rort, Rouse, Route, Sa-sa, Sennet, > SHOUT, Shut-out, Slam, Slander, Slogan, Soho, Sola, SOS, STD, Style, Subpoena, Summon(s), Tails, Tantivy, Taps, Telephone, Term, Toho, Toll, Trumpet, Trunk, Visit, Vocation, Waken, Wake-up, Whoa-ho-ho, Wo ha ho, Yell, Yo, Yodel, Yodle, Yo-ho(-ho), Yoicks, Yoo-hoo

Calla(s) Aroid, Lily, Maria

Caller Fresh, Guest, Herring, Inspector, Muezzin, Rep, Traveller, > VISITOR

Calligraphy Kakemono

Callipers Odd legs

Callosity, **Call(o)us** Bunion, Cold, Corn, Hard, Horny, Obtuse, Ringbone, Seg, Thylose, Tough, Tylosis, Unfeeling

Callow Crude, Green, Immature, Jejune

Calm Abate, Alegge, Aleye, Allay, Allege, Appease, Ataraxy, Composed, Cool, Doldrums, Easy, Easy-osy, Eevn, Equable, Equanimity, Even, Eye, Flat, Glassy, Halcyon, Loun(d), Lown(d), Lull, Mellow, Mild, Milden, Millpond, Nonchalant, Pacify, Peaceful, Philosophical, Phlegmatic, Placate, Placid, Quell, Quiet, Relax(ed), Repose, Seraphic, Serene, Settle, Simmer down, Sleek, > SOOTHE, Sopite, Still, Stilly, Subside, Tranquil(lise), Unturbid, Windless

Calorie Gram, Kilogram

Calumniate, **Calumny** Aspersion, Backbite, Defame, Libel, Malign, Slander, Slur

Calvary Golgotha

Calvin(ist) Accusative, Coolidge, Genevan, Hopkins, Huguenot, Infralapsarian, Predestination, Sublapsarian, Supralapsarian

Calydonian Boar

Calypso Ogygia, Siren, > SONG

Cam Cog, River, Snail, Tappet

Camaraderie Fellowship, Rapport, Team spirit

Camber Hog, Slope

Cambium Phellogen

Cambodian Khmer (Rouge)

Cambria(n) Menevian, Wales

Cambridge Cantab, Squat, Uni

Came Arrived

Camel, **Camel train** Aeroplane, Arabian, Artiodactyla, Bactrian, Caisson, Colt, Dromedary, Kafila, Llama, Oont, Sopwith, Tulu

Cameo Anaglyph, Camaieu, Carving

Camera, **Camera man** Box, Brownie®, Camcorder, Candid, Chambers, Cine, Compact, Digital, Disc, Electron, Flash, Gamma, Grip(s), Iconoscope, Kodak®, Miniature, Minicam, Movie, Obscura, Orthicon, Palmcorder, Panoramic,

Pantoscope, Pinhole, Polaroid®, Process, Programmed, Reflex, Retina, Schmidt, SLR, Somascope, Speed, Steadicam®, Stop-frame, Video, Vidicon, Viewfinder, Webcam

Camouflage Conceal, > DISGUISE, Mark, Maskirovka, War-dress

▷ **Camouflaged** *may indicate* an anagram

Camp(er) Affectation, Aldershot, Banal, Base, Belsen, Bivouac, Boma, Boot, Caerleon, Cantonment, Castral, Colditz, Concentration, David, Death, Depot, D(o)uar, Dumdum, Epicene, Faction, Fat, Flaunt, Gulag, Happy, Health, High, Holiday, L(a)ager, Labour, Lashkar, Leaguer, Low, Manyat(t)a, Oflag, Outlie, Peace, Prison, Side, Siwash, Stagey, Stalag, Stative, Swagman, Tent, Theatrical, Transit, Treblinka, Valley Forge, Work, Zare(e)ba, Zariba, Zereba, Zeriba

Campaign(er) Barnstorm, Battle, Blitz, Blitzkreig, Canvass, Crusade, Doorknock, Drive, Field, Jihad, Lobby, Mission, Promotion, Run, Satyagraha, Smear, Stint, Strategist, Tree-hugger, Venture, Veteran, War, Warray, Warrey, Whispering, Whistle-stop, Witchhunt

Campanula Rampion

Campeador Chief, Cid

Camp-follower Lascar, Leaguer-lady, Leaguer-lass, Sutler

Camphor Menthol

Campion Knap-bottle, Lychnis, Ragged robin, Silene

▷ **Camptown** *may indicate* de-

Can(s) Able, Billy, Bog, Capable, Churn, Cooler, Dow, Gaol, Garbage, Gents, Headphones, Is able, Jerry, Jug, Karsy, Loo, May, Nick, Pail, Pot, Preserve, > PRISON, Privy, Stir, Tank, Tin, Trash, Watering

Canada, Canadian Abenaki, Acadian, Canuck, Comox, Dene, Dogrib, Hare, Herring choker, Inuit, Johnny Canuck, Maliseet, Montagnais, Naskapi, Nuxalk, Péquiste, Quebeccer, Quebecker, Québecois, Salteaux, Slavey, Stoney, Tsimshian, Ungava, Yukon

Canal Alimentary, Ampul, Anal, Birth, Caledonian, Channel, Conduit, Corinth, Duct, Duodenum, Ea, Enteron, Erie, Foss(e), Gota, Grand (Trunk), Grande Terre, Grand Union, Groove, Gut, Haversian, Kiel, Klong, Labyrinth, Lode, Manchester Ship, Meatus, Midi, Mitelland, Navigation, New York State Barge, Oesophagus, Panama, Pharynx, Pipe, Pound, Resin, Ring, Root, Scala, Schlemm's, Semi-circular, Ship, Shipway, Spinal, Stone, Suez, Suo, Urethra, Waterway, Welland, Zanja

Canal-boat Barge, Fly-boat, Gondola, Vaporetto

Canapé Cate, Snack, Titbit

Canary Bird, Grass, Roller, Serin, Singer, Yellow

Cancel Abrogate, Adeem, Annul, Counteract, Countermand, Cross, Delete, Destroy, Erase, Kill, Negate, Nullify, Obliterate, Override, Remit, Repeal, Rescind, Retrait, Revoke, Scrub, Undo, Unmake, Void, Wipe, Write off

Cancer(ian) Moon Child

Cancer(ous) Big C, Carcinoma, Crab, Curse, Kaposi's Sarcoma, Leukaemia, Oat-cell, Tropic, Tumour, Wolf

Candela Cd

▸ **Candelabra** *see* CANDLE(STICK)

Candid, Candour Albedo, Blunt, Camera, Franchise, Frank, Honesty, Open, Outspoken, Plain(-spoken), Round, Upfront

Candida Fungus

Candidate(s) Agrege, Applicant, Aspirant, Contestant, Entrant, Field, Nominee, Ordinand, Postulant, Running mate, Stalking horse, Testee

Candied, Candy Angelica, Caramel, Cotton, Eryngo, Eye, Glace, Maple, Rock,

Snow, Succade, Sugar, > **SWEET**

Candle(stick), **Candelabra** Amandine, Bougie, C(i)erge, Dip, Fetch, Girandole, Hanukiah, International, Jesse, Lampadary, Light, Long-sixes, Menorah, Mould, Padella, Paschal, Pricket, Roman, Rushlight, Sconce, Serge, Shammash, Shammes, Slut, Sperm, Standard, Tace, Tallow, Tallow-dip, Taper, Torchère, Tricerion, Wax, Waxlight

Candlefish Eulachon, Oolakon, Oulachon, Oulakon, Ulic(h)an, Ulic(h)on, Ulikon

▶ **Candy** *see* **CANDIED**

Cane Arrow, Baculine, Bamboo, Baste, Beat, Birk, Crabstick, Dari, Dhurra, Doura, Dur(r)a, Ferula, Ferule, Goor, Gur, Jambee, Malacca, Narthex, Penang-lawyer, Pointer, Raspberry, Rat(t)an, Rod, Stick, Sugar, Swagger-stick, Swish, Switch, Swordstick, Tan, Tickler, Vare, Wand, Whangee, Wicker(-work)

Canine Biter, C, Dog, Eye-tooth

Canker Corrosion, Curse, Lesion, Ulcer

Cannabis Benj, Bhang, Bifter, Boneset, Durban poison, Ganja, Ganny, Grass, Hash, Hemp, Henry, Louie, Pot, Skunk, Zol

Cannibal Anthropophagus, Heathen, Long pig, Man-eater, Ogre, Thyestean, Wendigo

Cannon Amusette, Barrage, Basilisk, Bombard, Breechloader, Carom, Carronade, Chaser, Collide, Criterion, Culverin, Drake, Drop, Falcon, Gun, Howitzer, Kiss, Long-tom, Loose, Monkey, Mons Meg, Nursery, Saker, Stern-chaser, Water, Zamboorak, Zomboruk, Zumbooru(c)k

Cannot Canna, Cant, Downa(e), Downay

Canny Careful, Frugal, Prudent, Scot, Shrewd, Slee, Sly, Thrifty, Wice, Wily, Wise

Canoe(ist) Bidarka, Bidarkee, Canader, Dugout, Faltboat, Kayak, Log, Mokoru, Monoxylon, Montaria, Oomiack, Paddler, Peterborough, Piragua, Pirogue, Rob Roy, Surf, Waka, Woodskin

Canon(ise) Austin, Besaint, Brocard, Camera, Cancrizens, Chapter, Chasuble, Code, Crab, Infinite, Isidorian, > **LAW**, Line, Mathurin(e), Minor, Nocturn, Norbertine, Nursery, Pitaka, Polyphony, Prebendary, Precept, Premonstratensian, Retrograde, Rota, Round, Rule, Square, Squier, Squire, Standard, Tenet, Unity, White

Canopy Awning, Baldachin, Baldaquin, Chuppah, Ciborium, Clamshell, Dais, He(a)rse, Huppah, Majesty, Marquee, Marquise, Pavilion, Shamiana(h), State, Tabernacle, Tent, Tester

Cant Argot, Bevel, Heel, Incline, Jargon, Mummery, Patois, Patter, Rogue's Latin, Shelta, Slang, Slope, Snivel, Snuffle, Tip

Cantankerous Cussed, Fire-eater, Ornery, Querulous, Testy, Tetchy

Cantata Kinderspiel, Motet, Tobacco

Canteen Chuck-wagon, Mess, Munga, Naafi

Canter Amble, Hypocrite, Jog, Lope, Tit(t)up, Tripple

Canto Air, Fit(te), Fitt, Fytte, Melody, Verse

Canton Aargau, Appenzell, Basle, District, Eyalet, Fribourg, Glarus, Graubunden, Jura, Lucerne, Neuchatel, Quarter, St Gall, Schaffhausen, Schwyz, Solothurn, Thurgau, Ticino, Unterwalden, Uri, Valais, Vaud, Zug, Zurich

Cantred Commot(e)

Canvas Awning, Burlap, Dra(b)bler, Fly-sheet, Lug-sail, Mainsail, Marquee, Oil-cloth, Paint, Raven's-duck, Reef, > **SAIL**, Staysail, Stuns(ai)l, Tent, Trysail, Wigan

Canvass(er) Agent, Doorstep, Drum, Poll, Solicit

▷ **Canvasser** *may indicate* a painter or a camper
Canyon Box, Canada, Defile, Grand, Grand Coulee, Nal(l)a, Nallah, Submarine
Cap(ped) Abacot, Amorce, Balaclava, Balmoral, Barret, Baseball, Bathing, Bellhop, Bendigo, Ber(r)et, Biggin, Biretta, Blakey, Blue, Blue-bonnet, Bonnet-rouge, Bycoket, Call, Calotte, Calpac(k), Calyptrate, Capeline, Caul, Chaco, Chape, Chapeau, Chaperon, Chapka, Chechia, Cheese-cutter, Cloth, Cockernony, Coif, Cope, Cornet, Cowl, Cradle, > **CROWN**, Czapka, Davy Crockett, Deerstalker, Dunce's, Dutch, Fatigue, Ferrule, Filler, Flat, Fool's, Forage, Gandhi, Garrison, Gimme, Glengarry, Grannie, Granny, > **HAT**, Havelock, Hummel bonnet, Iceberg, International, Jockey, Juliet, Kalpak, Kepi, Kilmarnock, Kippa, Kippoth, Kipput, Kiss-me(-quick), Knee, Liberty, Lid, Mob, Monmouth, Monteer, Montero, Mor(r)ion, Mortar-board, Muffin, Mutch, Newsboy, Night, Outdo, Pagri, Patellar, Percussion, Perplex, Phrygian, Pile, Pileus, Pinner, Polar, Puggaree, Quoif, Root, Schapska, Shako, Skullcap, Square, Statute, Stocking, Summit, > **SURPASS**, Taj, Tam(-o'-shanter), Thimble, Thinking, Thrum, Toe, Toorie, Top, Toque, Toy, Trenchard, Trencher, Tuque, Turk's, Watch, Wishing, Yarmulka, Yarmulke, Zuchetto
Capable, **Capability** Able, Brown, Capacity, Competent, Deft, Effectual, Efficient, Firepower, Qualified, Skilled, Susceptible, Up to
Capacitance, **Capacity** Ability, Aptitude, C, Cab, Competence, Content, Cor, Cubic, Endowment, Function, Gift, Limit, Log, Power, Qua, Receipt, Scope, Size, Skinful, Tankage, Thermal, Tonnage, Valence, Vital, Volume
Caparison Robe, Trap(pings)
Cape Agulhas, Almuce, Bon, Burnouse, Byron, Calimere Point, Canaveral, Canso, Cloak, Cod, Comorin, Delgado, Dezhnev, Domino, Dungeness, East(ern), Fairweather, Faldetta, Fanion, Fanon, Farewell, Fear, Fichu, Finisterre, Flattery, Good Hope, Guardafui, Harp, Hatteras, Head(land), Helles, Hoe, Hogh, Hook of Holland, Horn, Inverness, Kennedy, Leeuwin, Lindesnes, Lizard, Manteel, Mant(e)let, Mantilla, Mantle, Matapan, May, Miseno, Mo(z)zetta, Muleta, Naze, Ness, Nordkyn, North, Northern, Ortegal, Palatine, Parry, Pelerine, Peninsula, Point, Poncho, Promontory, Race, Ras, Ray, Reinga, Roca, Ruana, Runaway, Sable, St Vincent, Sandy, Scaw, Skagen, Skaw, Sontag, Southwest, Talma, Tippet, Trafalgar, Ushant, Verde, Waterproof, Western, Wrath
Caper(ing) Antic, Bean, Boer, Capparis, Capriole, Cavort, Dance, Dido, Flisk, Frisk, Frolic, Gambado, Gambol, Harmala, Harmalin(e), Harmel, Harmin(e), Prance, Prank, Saltant, Scoup, Scowp, Skip, Tit(t)up
Capet Marie Antoinette
Cape Town SA
Capitalist Financier, Moneyer, Sloane
▷ **Capitalist** *may indicate* one living in a capital
Capitals A1, Assets, Block, Boodle, Bravo, Bully, Cap, Chapiter, Chaptrel, Doric, Equity, Euge, Excellent, Fixed, Flight, Float, Floating, Fonds, Great, Helix, Human, Initial, Ionic, Lethal, Lulu, Metropolis, Principal, Risk, Rustic, Seat, Seed, Social, Splendid, Sport, Stellar, Stock, Super, Topping, UC, Upper case, Venture, Working

CAPITALS

3 letters:	Ufa	4 letters:	Baku
Jos		Acra	Bari
Rio		Apia	Bern

Bida	Enugu	Bangui	Moroni
Bonn	Hanoi	Banjul	Moscow
Brno	Harar	Bastia	Munich
Caen	Jammu	Batumi	Muscat
Cali	Jinan	Beirut	Nagpur
Chur	Kabul	Berlin	Nassau
Cork	Kazan	Bhopal	Nevers
Dili	Konia	Bogota	Niamey
Doha	Konya	Bruges	Nouméa
Faro	Lagos	Brunei	Ottawa
Graz	Lassa	Colima	Oviedo
Homs	Lhasa	Cracow	Owerri
Hums	Lille	Darwin	Palmas
Ipoh	Lyons	Denver	Pamjin
Kiel	Macao	Dessau	Panaji
Kiev	Meroe	Dodoma	Peking
Kobe	Minsk	Dublin	Pierre
Laos	Monza	Geneva	Prague
Lima	Nancy	Giyani	Ranchi
Lomé	Nukus	Gondar	Regina
Male	Palma	Habana	Riyadh
Metz	Paris	Harare	Roseau
Nuuk	Patna	Havana	Ryazan
Oslo	Pella	Hobart	Sendai
Pegu	Perth	Hohhot	Skopje
Riga	Pinsk	Ibadan	Sokoto
Rome	Poona	Ilorin	St Paul
San'a	Praha	Imphal	Taipei
Sion	Praia	Jaipur	Tallin
Susa	Quito	Jalapa	Tehran
Suva	Rabat	Johore	Thebes
Xian	Salem	Kaduna	Thimbu
	Sanaa	Kigali	Tirana
5 letters:	Seoul	Kohima	Tobruk
Abiya	Simla	Lahore	Topeka
Abuja	Sofia	Lisbon	Umtata
Accra	Sucré	Loanda	Vienna
Agana	Tokyo	London	Warsaw
Amman	Tunis	Luanda	Xining
Berne	Turin	Lusaka	Yangon
Bisho	Vaduz	Macapá	Zagreb
Boise	Zomba	Maceió	
Cairo		Madrid	**7 letters:**
Cuzev	**6 letters:**	Maikop	Abidjan
Dacca	Abakan	Malabo	Ajaccio
Dakar	Albany	Manama	Algiers
Delhi	Ankara	Manila	Antioch
Dhaka	Asmara	Maputo	Atlanta
Dijon	Astana	Maseru	Baghdad
Dilli	Athens	Mekele	Bangkok
Dutse	Austin	Merano	Barnaul
Emisa	Bamako	Merida	Beijing

Belfast	Tel Aviv	Kirkwall	Nuku'alofa
Bikaner	Thimphu	Kishinev	Perigueux
Bishkek	Toronto	Lausanne	Perpignan
Caracas	Trieste	Lilongwe	Port Blair
Cardiff	Tripoli	Mandalay	Port Louis
Cayenne	Vilnius	Monrovia	Porto Novo
Colombo	Vilnyus	Monterey	Port Royal
Conakry	Xanthus	Narbonne	Putrajaya
Cordoba	Yaounde	Ndjamena	Pyongyang
Cuttack	Yerevan	Pamplona	Reykjavik
Douglas		Pergamum	Samarkand
Funchal	**8 letters:**	Port Said	St Georges
Gangtok	Abu Dhabi	Pretoria	Stockholm
Goiania	Adelaide	Saltillo	Stuttgart
Hanover	Agartala	Salzburg	Thorshavn
Honiara	Asuncion	Santiago	Trebizond
Huhenot	Belgrade	Sarajevo	Ulan Bator
Isfahan	Belmopan	Shanghai	Vientiane
Jackson	Beyrouth	Shenyang	
Jakarta	Boa Vista	St Helier	**10 letters:**
Kaesong	Brasilia	Tashkent	Addis Ababa
Kampala	Brisbane	Usumbura	Basse-terre
Karachi	Brussels	Valletta	Baton Rouge
Khartum	Budapest	Victoria	Bratislava
Konakri	Cagliari	Windhoek	Bridgetown
Lansing	Calcutta	Winnipeg	Charleston
Louvain	Canberra		Copenhagen
Lucknow	Cape Town	**9 letters:**	Eisenstadt
Madison	Castries	Amsterdam	Frauenfeld
Malacca	Columbia	Annapolis	Georgetown
Managua	Columbus	Ashkhabad	Kragujevac
Mathura	Culiacan	Bangalore	Libreville
Mbabane	Curitiba	Benin City	Little Rock
Memphis	Djibouti	Bucharest	Mexico City
Morelia	Edmonton	Bujumbura	Montevideo
Munster	Eraklion	Cartagena	Montgomery
Nairobi	Florence	Chihuahua	Montpelier
Nicosia	Freetown	Des Moines	Nouakchott
Nineveh	Gaborone	Edinburgh	Panama City
Palermo	Godthaab	Fongafale	Paramaribo
Papeete	Golconda	Heraklion	Persepolis
Pishpek	Hannover	Innsbruck	Porto Velho
Plovdiv	Hargeisa	Islamabad	Providence
Potsdam	Hartford	Jerusalem	Rawalpindi
Rangoon	Helsinki	Kathmandu	Trivandrum
San José	Honolulu	Leningrad	Valladolid
San Juan	Istanbul	Ljubljana	Washington
Stanley	Jayapura	Magdeburg	Wellington
Taiyuan	Katmandu	Maiduguri	Whitehorse
Tallinn	Khartoum	Melbourne	Willemstad
Tbilisi	Kingston	Mogadishu	Yashkar-Ola
Teheran	Kinshasa	Nashville	

- **11 letters:**
- Brazzaville
- Buenos Aires
- Campo Grande
- Charlestown
- Guadalajara
- Johore Bahru
- Kuala Lumpur
- Nakhichevan
- Ouagadougou
- Pandemonium
- Pondicherry

Port Moresby
Port of Spain
Saarbruchen
San Salvador
Tegucigalpa
Yellowknife

12 letters:
Antananaviro
Bloemfontein
Fort-de-France
Pandaemonium

Port-au-Prince
Port Harcourt
Salt Lake City
Santo Domingo
Tenochtitian
Williamsburg
Yamoussoukro

13 letters:
Hertogenbosch
Jefferson City

14 letters:
Constantinople

15 letters:
Charlotte Amalie

16 letters:
Pietermaritzburg

Capitulate Acquiesce, Comply, > SURRENDER
Capless Bare
▷ **Capless** *may indicate* first letter missing
Capone Al, Scarface
▷ **Capriccioso** *may indicate* an anagram
Caprice, **Capricious** Arbitrary, Boutade, Capernoitie, Conceit, Desultory, Erratic, Fancy, Fitful, Freak, Humoresk, Humoresque, Irony, Megrim, Mood, Perverse, Quirk, Vagary, Wayward, Whim(sy)
Capsize Crank, Overbalance, Purl, Tip, Turn turtle, Upset, Whemmle, Whomble
▷ **Capsized** *may indicate* a word upside down
Capstan Sprocket, Windlass
Capsule Amp(o)ule, Bowman's, Cachet, Habitat, Internal, Ootheca, Orbiter, Ovisac, Pill, Space, Spacecraft, Spansule, Spermatophore, Suppository, Time, Urn
Captain Ahab, Bligh, Bobadil, Bones, Brassbound, Capt, Channel, Chief, Cid, Commander, Condottiere, Cook, Copper, Cuttle, Flint, Group, Hornblower, Kettle, Kidd, Leader, Macheath, Master, Nemo, Old man, Owner, Patron, Patroon, Post, Privateer, Protospatharius, Skip(per), Standish, Subah(dar), Subedar, Swing, Trierarch
Caption Cutline, Heading, Headline, Inscription, Masthead, Roller, Sub-title, Title
Captious Critical, Peevish
Captivate(d), **Captivating** Beguile, Bewitch, Charm, Enamour, Enthrall, Epris(e), Take, Winsome
Captive, **Captivity** Bonds, Duress, POW, Prisoner, Slave
Capture Abduct, Annex, Bag, Catch, Collar, Cop, Electron, Enchain, Enthral(l), Grab, Land, Motion, Net, Prize, Rush, Seize, Snabble, Snaffle, Snare, > TAKE
Capuchin Cebus, Monkey, Sajou
Car Astra, Audi, Auto, Banger, Beetle, Berlin, Biza, BL, Bluebird, Bomb, Brake, Bubble, Buffet, Bugatti, Buick, Bumper, Bus, Cab(riolet), Cadillac, Catafalco, Catafalque, Chariot, Classic, Clunker, Coach, Company, Concept, Convertible, Cortina, Coupé, Courtesy, Crate, Daimler, Diner, Dodgem®, Drag(ster), Drophead, Dunger, Elf, Estate, E-type, Fastback, Fiat, Flivver, Ford, Formula, Freight, Ghost, Gondola, Griddle, GT, Hardtop, Hatchback, Heap, Hearse, Hillman, Hot-rod, Irish, Jalop(p)y, Jamjar, Jammy, Jaunting, Jim Crow, Kart, Kit, Knockabout, Lada, Lagonda, Lancia, Landaulet, Landrover, Lift-back, Limo, Limousine, Merc(edes), MG, Mini, Model T, Morris, Nacelle, Notchback, Observation, Opel, Panda, Parlour, Patrol, Popemobile, Prowl, Racer, Ragtop, Railroad, Rattletrap, Restaurant, Roadster, Roller, Rolls, RR,

Runabout, Rust bucket, Saloon, Scout, Sedan, Service, Shooting-brake, Skoda, Sleeper, Sleeping, Soft-top, Speedster, Sports, Squad, Station wagon, Steam, Stock, Stretch-limo, Subcompact, Sunbeam, Tank, Telepherique, Telpher, Three-wheeler, Tin Lizzie, Tonneau, Tourer, Tram, Trolley, Turbo, Two-seater, Vehicle, Veteran, Vintage, Voiture, VW, Wheeler, Wheels

Caramel Brûlé

Carat Point

Caravan Caf(f)ila, Convoy, Fleet, Kafila, Safari, Trailer

Caravanserai Choltry, Choutry, Inn, Khan

Caraway Aj(o)wan, Carvy, Seed

Car-back Boot, Dick(e)y, Tonneau

Carbamide Urea

Carbide Silicon

Carbine Gun, Musket

Carbohydrate Agarose, Carrageenan, Cellulose, Chitin, Dextran, Disaccharide, Glycogen, Heptose, Hexose, Inulin, Ketose, Laminarin, Mannan, Mucilage, Pectin, Pectose, Pentosan(e), Pentose, Saccharide, Sorbitol, Starch, Sucrose, Sugar

Carbolic Orcin

Carbon(ate) Activated, Ankerite, Austenite, Buckminsterfullerene, Buckyball, C, Charcoal, Coke, Dialogite, Diamond, Flame, Flimsy, Fullerene, Gas black, Graphite, Lampblack, Natron, Scawtite, Soot, Spode, Spodium, Urao, Witherite, Zaratite

Carbon deficiency Acapnia

Carboy Demijohn

Carbuncle Anthrax, Ruby

Carcase, Carcass Body, Cadaver, Carrion, Corpse, Cutter, Krang, Kreng, Morkin, Mor(t)ling

Card(s), Cardboard Ace, Affinity, Amex®, Baccarat, Basto, Bill, Birthday, Bower, Business, Calling, Canasta, Cartes, Cash, Caution, Charge, Cheque, Chicane, Cigarette, Club, Comb, Compass, Court(esy), Credit, Cue, Curse of Scotland, Dance, Debit, Deck, Deuce, Devil's (picture) books, Diamond, Donor, Drawing, Ecarté, Eccentric, Euchre, Expansion, Face, False, Flash, Flaught, Flush, > **GAME**, Gold, Green, Hand, Hard, Health, Heart, Hole, Honour, ID, Identification, Identity, Intelligent, Jack, Jambone, Jamboree, Joker, Kanban, Key, King, Laser, Leading, Letter, Loo, Loyalty, Magnetic, Manille, Master, Matador, Maximum, Meishi, Meld, Memory, Mise, Mistigris, Mogul, Mournival, Oddity, Ombre, Pack, Past, Pasteboard, Payment, PC, Picture, Placard, Place, Plastic, Playing, Proximity, Punch(ed), Quatorze, Quatre, Queen, Queer, Quiz, Race, Rail, Red, Rippler, Rove, Scraperboard, Scribble, Shade, Show, Sim, Singleton, Smart, Soda, Solo, Sound, Spade, Spadille, Squeezer, Stiffener, Store, Strawboard, Swab, Swipe, Swish, Switch, Swob, Swot, Talon, Tarok, Tarot, Tease(r), Tenace, Test, Thaumatrope, Ticket, Tiddy, Time, Tose, Toze, Trading, Trey, Trump, Union, Valentine, Visa, Visiting, Wag, Weirdie, Wild, Yellow, Zener

Cardigan Jacket, Wam(m)us, Wampus, Woolly

Cardinal Camerlingo, Chief, College, Eight, Eminence, Eminent, Grosbeak, Hat, HE, Hume, Legate, Manning, Mazarin, Newman, Number, Pivotal, Polar, Prelate, Radical, Red, Red-hat, Richelieu, Sacred college, Sin, Spellman, Virtue, Vital, Wolsey, Ximenes

Card-player Dealer, Pone

Care(r), Caring Attention, Burden, Cark, Caution, Cerne, Cherish, Community,

> **CONCERN**, Cosset, Grief, Heed, Intensive, Kaugh, Keep, Kiaugh, Maternal, Mind, Pains, Palliative, Parabolanus, Providence, Reck(e), Reke, Residential, Respite, Retch, Solicitude, > **TEND**, Tenty, Worry

Careen(ing) Parliament-heel

Career Course, Hurtle, Life, Line, Run, Rush, Speed, Start, Tear, Vocation

▷ **Career** *may indicate* an anagram

Carefree > **CARELESS**, Irresponsible, > **NEGLIGENT**, Oops, Perfunctory, Rollicking, Thoughtless

Careful(ly) Canny, Chary, Discreet, Gentle, Hooly, Meticulous, Mindful, Painstaking, Pernickety, Provident, Prudent, Scrimp, Studious, Tentie, Tenty, Thorough, Vigilant, Ware, Wary

Careless(ly) Casual, Cheery, Debonair, Easy, Free-minded, Gallio, Improvident, Imprudent, Inadvertent, Insouciance, Irresponsible, Lax, Lighthearted, Négligé, > **NEGLIGENT**, Nonchalant, Oops, Oversight, Perfunctory, Raffish, Rash, Remiss, Resigned, Riley, Rollicking, Slam-bang, Slapdash, Slaphappy, Slipshod, Sloven(ly), Slubber, Taupie, Tawpie, Thoughtless, Unguarded, Unmindful, Untenty, Unwary

▷ **Carelessly** *may indicate* an anagram

Caress Bill, Coy, Embrace, Fondle, Kiss, Lallygag, Lollygag, Noursle, Nursle, Pet, Touch

Caretaker Concierge, Curator, Custodian, Granthi, Guardian, Interim, Janitor, Nightwatchman, Sexton, Shammash, Shammes, Superintendent, Verger, Warden

Careworn Haggard, Lined, Tired, Weary

Cargo Bulk, Burden, Fraught, Freight, Lading, Last, > **LOAD**, Payload, Shipload, Shipment

Caribbean Belonger, Puerto Rican, Soca, Sokah, Taino, WI

Caribou Tuktoo, Tuktu

Caricature, **Caricaturist** Ape, Beerbohm, Burlesque, Caron d'Ache, Cartoon, Cruikshank, Doyle, Farce, Gillray, Rowlandson, Skit, Spy, Tenniel, Travesty

Carlin Pug

Carmelite Barefoot, White (Friar)

Carmen AA, BL, Chai, RAC

Carnage Butchery, Massacre, Slaughter

Carnal Bestial, Lewd, Sensual, Sexual, Worldly

Carnation Clove pink, Dianthus, Gillyflower, Malmaison, Picotee, Pink

Carnival Fair, Fasching, Festival, Fete, Mas, Moomba, Revelry

Carnivore Cacomistle, Cacomixl, Creodont, Fo(u)ssa, Genet, Glutton, Grison, Meerkat, Ratel, Suricate, Viverridae, Wolverine

Carob Algarroba, Locust, St John's bread

Carol Noel, Sing, Song, Wassail, Yodel

Carousal, **Carouse** Bend, Birl(e), Bouse, Bride-ale, Compotation, Drink, Mallemaroking, Mollie, Orge, Orgy, > **REVEL**, Roist, Screed, Spree, Upsee, Upsey, Upsy, Wassail

Carp(er) Beef, Censure, Complain, Crab, Critic, Crucian, Crusian, Gibel, Goldfish, Id(e), Koi, Kvetch, Mirror, Mome, Nag, Nibble, Nitpick, Roach, Roundfish, Scold, Twitch, Yerk, Yirk

Carpenter Cabinet-maker, Carfindo, Chips, Fitter, Joiner, Joseph, Menuisier, Quince, Tenoner, Woodworker, Wright

▷ **Carpenter** *may indicate* an anagram

Carpet Aubusson, Axminster, Beetle, Berate, Bessarabian, Broadloom, Brussels, Castigate, Chide, Dhurrie, Drugget, Durrie, Dutch, Kali, Kelim, Khilim,

Kidderminster, Kilim, Kirman, Lecture, Lino, Magic, Mat, Moquette, Persian, Rate, Red, Reprimand, Reproach, Rug, Runner, Shagpile, Shark, Shiraz, Stair, Turkey, Wall-to-wall, Wig, Wilton

Carrageen Sea-moss

Carriage Air, Bandy, Barouche, Bearing, Berlin(e), Bier, Brake, Brit(sch)ka, Britska, Britzka, Brougham, Buckboard, Buggy, Cab, Calash, Calèche, Car, Cariole, Caroche, Carriole, Carryall, Cartage, Chaise, Charet, Chariot, Chassis, Chay, Clarence, Coach, Coch, Composite, Conveyance, Coupé, Curricle, Demeanour, Dennet, Deportment, Désobligeante, Diner, Dormeuse, Dos-a-dos, Do-si-do, Drag, Dros(h)ky, Ekka, Equipage, Fiacre, Fly, Four-in-hand, Gait, Gig, Gladstone, Go-cart, Growler, Gun, Haulage, Herdic, Horseless, Hurly-hacket, Landau(let), Limber, Mien, Non-smoker, Norimon, Observation-car, Phaeton, Pick-a-back, Pochaise, Pochay, Poise, Port(age), Portance, Postchaise, Posture, Poyse, Pram, Pullman, Railcar, Railway, Random, Ratha, Remise, Rickshaw, Rockaway, Shay, Sled, Sleeper, Smoker, Sociable, Spider, Stanhope, Sulky, Surrey, Tarantas(s), Taxi, Tender, Tenue, Tilbury, Tim-whiskey, Tonga, Trail, Trap, Vetture, Victoria, Voiture, Wagonette, Waterage, Whirligig, Whisk(e)y

Carrier Airline, Arm, Baldric, Barkis, Barrow, Bomb-ketch, Caddy, Cadge, Camel, Coaster, Conveyor, Escort, Fomes, Fomites, Frog, Grid, Hamper, Haversack, Hod, Janker, Jill, Minority, Nosebag, Noyade, Obo, Packhorse, Pigeon, Porter, Rucksack, Satchel, Schistosoma, Semantide, Sling, Straddle, Stretcher, > **TRAY**, Vector

Carrion Cadaver, Carcase, Carcass, Flesh, Ket, Stapelia

Carrots Seseli, Titian

Carry(ing) Bear, Chair, Convey, Enlevé, Escort, Ferry, Frogmarch, Hawk, Hent, Hump, Kurvey, Land, Pack, Pickaback, Port, Stock, Sustain, Tide over, Tote, > **TRANSPORT**, Trant, Wage, With, Yank

Carry on Continue, Create, Wage

Carry out Execute, Pursue

Cart Bandy, Barrow, Bogey, Buck, Cape, Car(r)iole, Chapel, Democrat, Dog, Dolly, Dray, Furphy, Gambo, Gill, Golf, Governess, Gurney, Hackery, Jag, Jill, Lead, Mail, Pie, Rickshaw, Scotch, Shandry, T, Tax(ed), Telega, Trolley, Tumbrel, Tumbril, Village, Wag(g)on, Wain, Whitechapel

Cartel Duopoly, Ring, Syndicate

Carthaginian Punic

Carthorse Shire

Carthusian Bruno

Cartilage Antitragus, Arytenoid, Chondrin, Chondrus, Cricoid, Darwin's tubercle, Disc, Epiglottis, Gristle, Hyaline, Lytta, Meniscus, Semilunar, Tendron, Thyroid, Tragus, Worm, Xiphoid

Cartload Seam

Cartographer Cabot, Chartist, Mercator, OS, Speed

Carton Box, Case, Crate, Sydney, Tub

Cartoon(ist) Animated, Bairnsfather, Caricature, Comic, Disney, Drawn, Emmet, Fougasse, Fumetto, Garland, Goldberg, Leech, Low, Manga, Mel, Partridge, Popeye, Robinson, Short, Spy, Strip, Tenniel, Thurber, Tidy, Tintin, Trog

Cartridge Blank, Bullet, Cartouche, Cassette, Doppie, Magazine, QIC, Shell

Cart-track Rut

Cartwheel Handspring

Caruncle Aril, Carnosity

Carve(d), Carver, Carving Alcimedon, Armchair, Bas relief, Camaieu, Cameo, Chisel, Cilery, Crocket, Cut, Dismember, Doone, Enchase, Engrave, Entail, Entayle, Fiddlehead, Gibbons, Glyptic, Hew, Incise, Inscribe, Insculp, Intaglio, Knotwork, Netsuke, Nick, Petroglyph, Scrimshaw, Sculp(t), Slice, Tondo, Truncheon, Whittle

Caryatid Column, Telamon

Casanova Heartbreaker, Leman

Cascade Cataract, Fall, Lin(n), Stream, Waterfall

Cascara Buckthorn, Honduras bark, Rhamnus, Wahoo

Case(s), Casing Abessive, Ablative, Accusative, Action, Adessive, Allative, Altered, Appeal, Aril, Ascus, Assumpsit, Attaché, Basket, Beer, Bere, Bittacle, Blimp, Box, Brief, Bundwall, Burse, C, Ca, Cabinet, Calyx, Canister, Canterbury, Capsule, Cartouch(e), Cartridge, Cause celebre, Cellaret, Chase, Chitin, Chrysalis, Cocoon, Compact, Crate, Croustade, Crust, Dative, Declension, Detinue, Dispatch, Dossier, Dressing, Elative, Elytron, Enallage, Essive, Etui, Etwee, Example, Flan, Flapjack, Frame, Genitive, Grip, Hanaper, Hard, Hatbox, Hold-all, Housewife, Hull, Humidor, Husk, > IN CASE, Index, Indusium, Inessive, Instance, Keister, Locative, Locket, Lorica, Manche, Matter, Mezuzah, Nacelle, Nominative, Non-suit, Nutshell, Objective, Oblique, Ochrea, Ocrea, Papeterie, Patient, Pencil, Penner, Phylactery, Plight, Plummer-block, Pod, Port, Possessive, Prima facie, Quiver, Recce, Reconnoitre, Sabretache, Sad, Scabbard, Sheath(e), Shell, Situation, Six-pack, Sporran, Stead, Sted, Subjunctive, Suit, Tantalus, Tea-chest, Telium, Test, Theca, Tichborne, Trial, Trunk, Valise, Vasculum, Vocative, Volva, Walise, Walking, Wallet, Wardian, Wing, Writing

Case-harden Nitrode

Casein Curd

Casement Frame, Roger, Sash, Window

Cash Blunt, Bonus, Bounty, Change, Coin, Dosh, Dot, Float, Hard, Imprest, Lolly, > MONEY, Needful, Ochre, Oscar, Pence, Petty, Ready, Realise, Rhino, Spondulicks, Spot, Stumpy, Tender, Tin, Wampum, Wherewithal

Cashier Annul, Break, Depose, Disbar, Dismiss, Oust, Teller, Treasurer

Cashmere Circassienne

Cask(et) Armet, Barrel, Barrico, Bas(i)net, Box, Breaker, Butt, Cade, Casque, Cassette, Drum, Firkin, Galeate, Harness, Heaume, Hogshead, Keg, Leaguer, Octave, Pin, Pipe, Puncheon, Pyxis, Run(d)let, Salade, Sallet, Sarcophagus, Scuttlebutt, Shrine, Solera, Tierce, Tun, Wine

Cask-stand Stillion

Cassava Manioc, Tapioca, Yucca

Casserole Diable, Osso bucco, Pot, Salmi, Terrine, Tzimmes

Cassette Cartridge, Tape, Video

Cassia Cleanser, Senna

Cassio Lieutenant

Cassiterite Needle-tin, Tinstone

Cassock Gown, Soutane, Subucula

Cast (down, off, out), Casting Abattu, Actors, Add, Appearance, Bung, Die, Discard, Ecdysis, Ectype, Eject, Endocranial, Exorcise, Exuviae, Exuvial, Fling, Found, Fusil, Grape, Heave, Hob, Hue, Hurl, Impression, Ingo(w)es, Keb, Look, Lose, Mew, Molt, Moulage, Mould, Pick, Plaster(stone), Players, Put, Reject, Shed, Shoot, Sling, Slive, Slough, Spoil, Stookie, Tailstock, > THROW, Toss, Tot, Warp, Wax, Ytost

▷ **Cast** *may indicate* an anagram or a piece of a word missing

Castanet Crotal(um), Knackers
Castaway Adrift, Crusoe, Gunn, Left, Outcast, Selkirk, Stranded, Weft
▷ **Cast by** *may indicate* surrounded by
Caste Brahmin, Class, Dalit, Group, Harijan, Hova, Kshatriya, Rajpoot, Rajpout, Rank, Scheduled, Sect, Sudra, Vaisya, Varna
Caster Truckle
Castigate Berate, Chastise, Criticise, Denounce, Keelhaul, Lash, Punish
Cast-iron Spiegeleisen
Castle(d) Adamant, Arundel, Balmoral, Bamburgh, Bastille, Belvoir, Berkeley, Bouncy, Braemar, Broch, C, Calzean, Canossa, Carbonek, Carisbrooke, Casbah, Chateau, Chepstow, Chillon, Citadel, Colditz, Conwy, Corfe, Culzean, Dangerous, Despair, Doubting, Dunsinane, Edinburgh, Egremont, Eileen Donan, Elephant, Elsinore, Fastness, Fort, Fotheringhay, Glamis, Gormenghast, Harlech, Herstmonceux, Hever, Howard, Kasba(h), Kenilworth, Lancaster, Leeds, Lincoln, Ludlow, Maiden, Malperdy, Man, More, Mot(t)e, Motte and bailey, Otranto, Perilous, Rackrent, Raglan, Rook, Sand, Schloss, Sherborne, Sissinghurst, Spain, Stirling, Stokesay, Stormont, Stronghold, Tintagel, Trim, Urquhart, Villa, Wartburg, Warwick, Windsor
Castor-oil Ricinus
Castrate(d) Alter, Cut, Doctor, Emasculate, Eunuch, Evirate, Geld, Glib, Lib, Mutilate, Neuter, Spado, Spay, Swig
Castro Fidel
Casual Accidental, Adventitious, Airy, Blasé, Chance, Flippant, Grass, Haphazard, Idle, Incidental, Informal, Jaunty, Lackadaisical, Nochalant, Odd(ment), Offhand, Off-the-cuff, Orra, Passing, Promiscuous, Random, Scratch, Sporadic, Stray, Temp, Throwaway
Casualty Caduac, Chance-medley, > VICTIM
Casuist Jesuit
Cat Abyssinian, Alley, American curl, American wirehair, Angora, Asian shorthair, Asparagus, Australian mist, Balinese, Baudrons, Binturong, Birman, Bluepoint, Bobcat, Burmese, Cacomistle, Cacomixl, Caracal, Chantilly, Chartreux, Cheetah, Cheshire, Civet, Clowder, Colourpoint, Cop, Cornish Rex, Cougar, Dandy, Dasyure, Delundung, Devon Rex, Domestic, Egyptian Mau, Eyra, Fat, Felid, Feline, Felix, Flog, Foss(a), Foumart, Foussa, Genet(te), Gib, Gossip, Grimalkin, Gus, Havana Brown, Himalayan, Hipster, Hodge, Jaguar(ondi), Jaguarundi, Jazzer, Kilkenny, Kit, Korat, Lair, La Perm, Lash, Leopard, Linsang, Lion, Long-hair, Lynx, Maine coon, Malkin, Maltese, Manul, Manx, Margay, Marmalade, Mehitabel, Mewer, Mog, Mountain, Mouser, Munchkin, Musang, Musk, Nandine, Neuter, Nib, Norwegian Forest, Ocelot, Ocicat, Oriental, Ounce, Painter, Pallas's, Palm, Panther, Pard, Pardal, Persian, Pharaoh, Polecat, Practical, Puma, Puss, Quoll, Ragdoll, Rasse, Rex, Ringtail, Rumpy, Russian blue, Sacred, Scottish Fold, Scourge, Sealpoint, Selkirk Rex, Serval, Shorthair, Siamese, Siberian Forest, Sick, Singed, Snowshoe, Somali, Spew, Sphynx, Spue, Swinger, Tabby, Tibert, Tiffanie, Tiffany, Tiger, Tigon, Tigress, Tobermory, Tom, Top, Tortoise-shell, Turkish Angora, Turkish Van, Tybalt, Viverra, Weasel, Zibet(h)
Catacomb Cemetery, Crypt, Hypogeum, Vault
Catalepsy Catatony, Trance
Catalogue Cattle dog, Dewey, Dictionary, Index, Inventory, List, Litany, Magalog, Messier, Ragman, Ragment, Raisonné, Record, Register, Specialogue, Subject, Table, Tabulate, Union
Catalyst Accelerator, Agent, Influence, Unicase, Ziegler

Catamite Ingle

Catapult Ballista, Ging, Launch, Mangon(el), Perrier, Petrary, Propel, Scorpion, Shanghai, Sling, Slingshot, Stone-bow, Tormentum, Trebuchet, Wye, Y

Cataract Cascade, Film, Pearl, Pearl-eye, Torrent, Waterfall, Web and pin

Catarrh Coryza, Rheum

Catastrophe Apocalypse, Calamity, > DISASTER, Doom, Epitasis, Fiasco, Meltdown

Catatonia Stupor

Cat-call Boo, Mew, Miaow, Miaul, Razz, Wawl, Wrawl

Catch(y), Caught Air, Apprehend, Attract, Bag, Benet, Bone, C, Capture, Chape, Clasp, Cog, Collar, Contract, Cop, Corner, Cotton on, Ct, Deprehend, Detent, Dolly, Engage, Enmesh, Ensnare, Entoil, Entrap, Fang, Field, Fumble, Gaper, Get, Glee(some), Grasp, Had, Hank, Haud, Haul, Hear, Hitch, Hold, Hook, Inmesh, Keddah, Keight, Kep(pit), Kheda, Kill, Land, Lapse, Lasso, Latch, Lime, Lock, Morse, Nab, Nail, Net, Nick, Nim, Nobble, Noose, Overhear, Overhent, Overtake, Parti, Pawl, Rap, Release, Rope, Round, Rub, Safety, Sean, Sear, See(n), Seize, > SNAG, Snap, Snare, Snib, Snig, > SONG, Surprise, Swindle, Tack, Take, Tickle, Trammel, Trap, Trawl, Trick, Tripwire, Troll, Twig, Understand, Wrestle

Catchword Motto, Shibboleth, Slogan, Tag

Catechism Carritch, Test

Categorise, Category > CLASS, Etic, Genre, Genus, Label, Order, Pigeonhole, Range, Taxon

Cater(er) Acatour, Cellarer, Feed, Manciple, > PROVIDE, Purveyor, Serve, Steward, Supply, Victualler, Vivandière

Caterpillar Army worm, Aweto, Boll worm, Cotton-worm, Cutworm, Eruciform, Geometer, Gooseberry, Hop-dog, Hornworm, Inchworm, Larva, Looper, Osmeterium, Palmer, Tent, Webworm, Woolly-bear

Catfish Hassar, Woof

Cathartic Turbeth

Cathedral Basilica, Chartres, Chester, Cologne, Dome, Duomo, Ely, Guildford, Lateran, Lichfield, Lincoln, Minster, Notre Dame, Rheims, Ripon, St Paul's, Salisbury, Sens, Up(p)sala, Wells, Westminster, Winchester, Worcester, York

Catherine Braganza, Parr

Catherine-wheel Girandole

Cathode Electrode, Filament, Ray

Catholic Broad, Defenders, Doolan, Eclectic, Ecumenical, Fenian, General, Irvingism, Jebusite, Latin, Left-footer, Liberal, Marian, Opus Dei, Ostiary, Papalist, Papaprelatist, Papist, Passionist, Recusant, Redemptionist, Roman, Salesian, Spike, Taig, Te(a)gue, Teigue, Thomist, Tike, Tory, Tridentine, Tyke, Universal, Ursuline, Waldenses, Wide

Catkin Amentum, Chat, Lamb's tail, Pussy-willow, Salicaceous

Cat-lover Ailurophile

Catmint Nep, Nepeta

Cato Porcian, Uticensis

Cats-eye Chatoyant, Cymophane

Catsmeat Lights

Catspaw Pawn, Tool

Cat's tail Reed-mace, Typha

Cat's whiskers Vibrissa

Cattle(pen) Aberdeen Angus, Africander, Ankole, Aver, Ayrshire, Beefalo, Bestial, Brahman, British white, Buffalo, Carabao, Charbray, Charol(l)ais,

Chillingham, Dexter, Drove, Durham, Fee, Friesland, Galloway, Gaur, Gayal, Guernsey, Gyal, Heard, Herd, Hereford, Highland, Holstein (Friesian), Illawara, Jersey, Kerry, Kine, Kouprey, Kraal, Ky(e), Kyloe, Lairage, Limousin, Lincoln, Longhorn, Luing, Neat, Nout, Nowt, Owsen, Oxen, Piemontese, Rabble, Redpoll, Rother, Santa Gertrudis, Shorthorn, Simment(h)al, Soum, Sowm, Steer, Stock, Store, Stot, Sussex, Tamarao, Tamarau, Teeswater, Welsh black

Cattle disease Anthrax, Black water, Footrot, Hoove, Johne's, Listeriosis, Lumpy jaw, Mange, Mastitis, Milk lameness, Moorill, Quarter-ill, Red-water, Rinderpest, Scours, Scrapie, Texas fever, Wire-heel, Woody-tongue

Cattle food Fodder

Cattleman Cowboy, Herder, Maverick, Rancher, Ringer, Stock-rider

Catty Kin, Spiteful

Caucasian Aryan, Azabaijani, European, Melanochroi, Paleface, Semite, Shemite, White, Yezdi, Yezidee, Zezidee

Caucus Assembly, Cell, Gathering, Race

▶ **Caught** *see* CATCH

Caul Baby-hood, Kell, Membrane, Sillyhow

Cauldron Kettle, Pot

Cauliflower Curd, Ear, Floret

Caulk Fill, Pitch, Snooze

Causation, Cause(d), Causes Aetiology, Agent, Beget, Breed, Bring, Compel, Create, Crusade, Determinant, Due, Effect, Efficient, Encheason, Engender, Factor, Final, First, Flag-day, Formal, Gar(re), Generate, Ideal, Induce, Lead, Lost, Make, Material, Motive, Movement, > OCCASION, Parent, Probable, Provoke, Reason, Root, Sake, Source, Teleology, Topic, Ultimate, Wreak

Causeway Tombolo

Caustic Acid, Acrimonious, Alkaline, Burning, Erodent, Escharotic, Lime, Moxa, Pungent, Sarcastic, Scathing, Seare, Tart, Vitriol, Waspish, Withering

Cauterise Brand, Burn, Disinfect, Inustion, Sear

Caution, Cautious (person) Achitophel, Admonish, Ahithophel, Alert, Amber, Awarn, Beware, Cagey, Card, Care, Cave, Caveat, Chary, Circumspect, Credence, Cure, Defensive, Deliberate, Discretion, Fabian, Gingerly, Guard(ed), Heedful, Leery, Prudent, Rum, Scream, Skite, Tentative, Vigilant, Ware, > WARN, Wary, Yellow card

Cavalcade Pageant, Parade, Procession, Sowarree, Sowarry

Cavalier Brusque, Cicisbeo, Devil-may-care, Gallant, Lively, Malignant, Offhand, Peart, Rider, Royalist

Cavalry(man) Blues, Car(a)bineer, Car(a)binier, Cornet, Cossack, Dragoon, Equites, Heavies, Horse, Household, Hussar, Ironsides, Knights, Lancers, Light-horse, Plunger, Ressaldar, Risaldar, Rough-rider, Rutter, Sabres, Silladar, Spahi, Uhlan, Yeomanry

Cave(rn), Caves, Cave-dwelling Acherusia, Alert, Altamira, Antar, Antre, Beware, Cellar, Collapse, Corycian, Den, Domdaniel, Erebus, Fingal's, Fore, Grot(to), Hollow, Jenolan, Lascaux, Look-out, Lupercal, Mammoth, Nix, Pot-hole, Proteus, Sepulchre, Snow, Spel(a)ean, Speleology, Spelunker, Speos, Tassili, Vault, Waitomo, Ware, Weem

Cave-dweller Troglodyte

Caveman Adullam, Aladdin, Fingal, Neanderthal, Primitive, Troglodyte, Troll

Caviare Beluga, Roe, Sevruga, Sturgeon

Cavil Carp, Haggle, Quibble

Cavity Acetabulum, Amygdale, Amygdule, Androclinium, Atrial, Camera,

Cavort(ing) | 104

Camouflet, Celom, Chamber, Clinandrium, Coelenteron, Coelom(e), Concepticle, Concha, Countermark, Crater, Crypt, Dent, Domatium, Druse, Enteron, Follicle, Foss, Gap, Geode, Glenoid, Hold, Hole, Lacuna, Locule, Mediastinum, Orbita, Orifice, Pocket, Resonant, Segmentation, Sinus, Tear, Tympanum, Vacuole, Vein, Ventricle, Vesicle, Vitta, Vomica, Vug, Vugg, Vugh, Well

Cavort(ing) Jag

Cavy Agouti, Capybara, Hograt, Paca

Cease(fire) Abate, Blin, Cut, Desist, Die, Disappear, Halt, Intermit, Lin, Lose, Pass, Refrain, Remit, Sessa, > **STOP**, Truce

Ceaseless Eternal, Incessant

Cecil Rhodes

Cedar(wood) Arolla, Atlas, Deodar, Incense, Japanese, Toon

Cede Grant, Yield

Ceiling Absolute, Barrel, Coffered, Cove, Cupola, Dome, Glass, Lacunar, Laquearia, Limit, Plafond, Roof, Service, Soffit

Celebrate(d), **Celebration**, **Celebrity** Ale, Beanfeast, Besung, Bigwig, Binge, Carnival, Cel, Chant, Commemorate, Distinguished, Do, Emblazon, Encaenia, Epithalamion, Epithalamium, Fame, Feast, Fest, Festivity, Fete, Fiesta, Gala, Gaudeamus, Gaudy, Glorify, Grog-up, Harvest home, Hold, Holiday, Honour, Jamboree, Jollifications, Jollities, Jubilee, Keep, Laud, Legend, Lion, Loosing, Lowsening, Maffick, Mardi gras, Mass, Mawlid al-Nabi, Megastar, Monstre sacre, Name, Noted, Nuptials, Observe, Occasion, Orgy, Panathenaea, Praise, Randan, Rejoice, Renown, Repute, Revel, Roister, Saturnalia, Sing, Spree, Star, Storied, Sung, Superstar, Treat, Triumph, Wassail, Wet

Celerity Dispatch, Haste, Speed, Velocity

Celery Alexanders, Smallage, Stick

Celestial Chinese, Divine, Ethereal, Heavenly, Supernal, Uranic

Celibate, **Celibacy** Bachelor, Chaste, Paterin(e), Rappist, Rappite, Shakers, Single, Spinster

Cell(s), **Cellular** Battery, Bullpen, Cadre, Chamber, Chapel, Condemned, Crypt, Cubicle, Death, Dungeon, Group, Laura, Padded, Peter, > **PRISON**, Strip, Tank, Unit

CELLS

1 letter:
T

3 letters:
Dry
Pec
Sex
Wet

4 letters:
Axon
Comb
Cone
Cyte
Fuel
Germ

Hair
HeLa
Mast
Oxum
Soma
Stem
Zeta

5 letters:
Ascus
Basal
Canal
Clark
Flame
Giant
Gland

Guard
Linin
Lymph
Nerve
Nicad
Solar
Spore
Stone
Swarm
Water
X-body

6 letters:
Button
Censor
Collar

Cybrid
Cytoid
Diaxon
Gamete
Goblet
Killer
Morula
Neuron
Oocyte
Plasma
Sensor
Sickle
Somite
Target
Zygote

7 letters:
Cadmium
Cambium
Cathode
Daniell
Energid
Gemmule
Gravity
Helper T
Lithite
Myotome
Myotube
Neurite
Neurone
Neutron
Plastid
Primary
Schwann
Sertoli
Somatic
Spireme
Sporule
Storage
Tapetum
Vesicle
Voltaic

8 letters:
Akaryote
Auxocyte
Basidium
Basophil
Blasteme
Blastula
Congenic
Cytology
Daughter
Defensin
Ectomere
Endoderm
Endosarc
Epiblast
Eukaryon
Galvanic
Gonidium
Gonocyte
Hapteron
Hemocyte

Meiocyte
Meristem
Monocyte
Myoblast
Neoblast
Palisade
Parietal
Platelet
Purkinje
Receptor
Retinula
Schizont
Selenium
Seredium
Squamous
Standard
Sweatbox
Symplast
Synergid
Tracheid
Unipolar
Zoosperm
Zoospore

9 letters:
Adipocyte
Antipodal
Astrocyte
Athrocyte
Auxospore
Basophile
Coenocyte
Companion
Corpuscle
Desmosome
Ectoplasm
Embryo-sac
Fibrocyte
Haemocyte
Hybridoma
Idioblast
Internode
Iridocyte
Karyology
Laticifer
Leclanché
Leucocyte
Macromere

Merozoite
Microcyte
Myelocyte
Myofibril
Organelle
Periplasm
Periplast
Phagocyte
Phellogen
Proembryo
Secondary
Spermatid
Sporocyte
Suspensor
Syncytium
Synkaryon
Thymocyte
Trabecula
Tracheide

10 letters:
Ameloblast
Archespore
Blastoderm
Blastomere
Centrosome
Choanocyte
Chromaffin
Chromosome
Cnidoblast
Eosinophil
Epithelium
Fibroblast
Gametocyte
Histiocyte
Leucoblast
Leukoblast
Lymphocyte
Macrophage
Melanocyte
Mesenchyme
Myeloblast
Neuroblast
Neutrophil
Normoblast
Osteoblast
Osteoclast
Perikaryon

Phelloderm
Protoplast
Spermatium
Spherocyte
Totipotent

11 letters:
Aplanospore
Arthrospore
Endothelium
Erythrocyte
Granulocyte
Interneuron
Kinetoplast
Megaloblast
Melanoblast
Microgamete
Microvillus
Motor neuron
Odontoblast
Poikilocyte
Propoceptor
Schistocyte
Spheroplast

12 letters:
Aplanogamete
Chondroblast
Electrolytic
Haematoblast
Interstitial
Paraphysisis
Photovoltaic
Reticulocyte
Spermatocyte
Spermatozoid
Spermatozoon
Spongioblast

13 letters:
Chromatophore
Mitochondroin
Photoelectric
Photoreceptor

14 letters:
Spermatogonium
Weston standard

Cellar Basement, Bodega, Coalhole, Dunny, Hypogeum, Ratskeller, Storm, Vault, Vaut, Wine
Cell division Amitosis

Cellist, **Cello** Hermit, Prisoner, Tortelier
Celluloid, **Cellulose** Acetate, Cel, Viscose, Xylonite
Celt(ic) Belgic, Breton, Brython, Druid, Gadhel, Gael, Goidel, Helvetii, Kelt, Taffy, Welsh
Cement Araldite®, Compo, Concrete, Fix, Flaunch, Glue, Grout, High-alumina, Hydraulic, Lute, Maltha, Mastic, Mortar, Paste, Pointing, Porcelain, Portland, Putty, Rice-glue, Roman, Rubber, Slurry, > STICK, Trass, Water
Cemetery Aceldama, Arenarium, Arlington, Boneyard, Boot Hill, Campo santo, Catacomb, Churchyard, God's Acre, Golgotha, Graveyard, Musall, Necropolis, Père Lachaise, Potter's field, Saqqara, Urnfield
Censer Cassolette, Navicula, Thurible
Censor(ious), **Censure** Accuse, Admonition, Animadvert, Appeach, Ban, Banner, Berate, Blame, Blue-pencil, Bowdler, Braid, Cato, Comstockery, > CONDEMN, Critical, Criticise, Damn, Dang, Decry, Dispraise, Edit, Excommunicate, Excoriate, Expurgate, Gag, Obloquy, Opprobrium, Rap, Repress, Reprimand, Reproach, Reprobate, Reprove, Satirise, Scold, Scrub, Slam, Slate, Stricture, Suppress, Tax, Tirade, Traduce, Wig
Census Count, Poll
Cent Bean, Coin, Ct, Penny, Red
Centaur Ch(e)iron, Horseman, Nessus, Sagittary, Therianthropic
Centenary, **Centennial** Anniversary, Colorado
Centipede Chilopoda, Earwig, Polypod, Scolopendra, Scutiger
Central, **Centre** Active, Amid, Attendance, Axis, Broca's, Bunt, Call, Cardinal, Chakra, Civic, Community, Contact, Core, Cost, Day, Daycare, Dead, Detention, Detoxification, Deuteron, Deuton, Downtown, Drop-in, Epergne, Eye, Field, Focus, Frontal, Garden, Health, Heart, Hotbed, Hothouse, Hub, Incident, Inmost, Internal, Interpretive, Kernel, Kingpin, Law, Leisure, Lincoln, Live, Main, Mecca, Median, Medulla, Mid(st), Music, Nave, Nerve, Nucleus, Omphalus, Pompidou, Profit, Property, Reception, Rehabilitation, Remand, Shopping, Social Education, Storm, Teachers', Trauma, Visitor, Waist, Weather
Central heating Cen, CH
▷ **Centre** *may indicate* middle letters
Centrepiece Epergne
Century Age, C, Era, Magdeburg, Period, Ton
Cephalopod Ammonite, Calamary, Cuttle, Loligo, Nautilus, Octopus, Sepia, Squid
Ceramic(s) Agateware, Arcanist, China, Earthen, Ferrite, Porcelain, Pottery, Sialon, Tiles
Cereal Amelcorn, Barley, Blé, Bran, Buckwheat, Bulgar, Bulg(h)ur, Cassava, Corn, Cornflakes, Couscous, Emmer, Farina, Gnocchi, Grain, Granola, Groats, Hominy, Maize, Mandioc(a), Mandiocca, Mani(h)oc, Manihot, Mealie, Millet, Muesli, Oats, Paddy, Popcorn, Rye(corn), Sago, Samp, Sarassin, Seed, Semolina, Sorghum, Spelt, Tapioca, Tef(f), Triticale, Triticum, Wheat, Zea
Cerebrate, **Cerebration** Pore, Thought
Ceremonial, **Ceremony** Amrit, Barmitzvah, Chado, Chanoyu, Common Riding, Coronation, Doseh, Durbar, Encaenia, Enthronement, Etiquette, Eucharist, Flypast, Form(al), Gongyo, Habdalah, Havdalah, Havdoloh, Heraldry, Investiture, Matsuri, Maundy, Mummery, Observance, Occasion, Ordination, Pageantry, Parade, Pomp, Powwow, Protocol, Rite, Ritual, Sacrament, Sado, Seder, Service, State, Tea, Unveiling, Usage
Cerium Ce
Cert(ain), **Certainty** Absolute, Actual, Assured, Banker, Bound, Cast-iron,

Cinch, Cocksure, Confident, Convinced, Decided, Exact, Fact, Fate, Indubitable, Inevitable, Infallible, Keen, Monte, Moral, Nap, One, Positive, Poz, Precise, Shoo-in, Siccar, Sicker, Snip, Some, > SURE, Sure-fire, Truth, Yes

Certainly Agreed, Ay, Certes, Fegs, Forsooth, Indeed, Iwis, Jokol, OK, Oke, Pardi(e), Pardy, Perdie, Siccar, Sicker, > SURE, Truly, Verily, Yea, Yes, Yokul, Ywis

Certificate, **Certified**, **Certify** Affirm, Attest, Bene decessit, Bond, Chit, Cocket, Confirm, Credential, Death, Debenture, Depose, Diploma, Docket, Document, Enseal, Gold, Guarantee, Landscrip, Licence, Lines, Medical, MOT, Notarise, Paper, Patent, Proven, Savings, School, Scrip, Scripophily, Share, Stock, Sworn, Talon, Testamur, Testimonial, Treasury, U, Unruly, Voucher, Warrant

Cesspit Bog, Dungmere, Sinkhole, Slurry

Cetacean Dolphin, Porpoise, Whale

Ceylon(ese) Serendip, Vedda(h)

Chafe, **Chafing** Chunter, Fray, Fret, Harass, Intertrigo, Irritate, > RUB, Seethe, Worry

Chaff(y) Badinage, Banter, Bran, Chip, Dross, Hay, Husk, Rag, Raillery, Rally, Ramentum, Refuse, Roast, Rot, Tease, Twit

Chaffer(ing) Bandy, Bargain, Haggle, Higgle, Hucksterage, Traffic

Chaffinch Whitewing

Chagrin Envy, Mortify, Spite, Vexation

Chain(ed) Acre's-breadth, Albert, Anklet, Band, Bind, Bond, Bracelet, Branched, Bucket, Cable, Catena, Chatelaine, Choke, Cistron, Cordillera, Cyclic, Daisy, Decca, Dixie, Drive, Duplex, Dynasty, Engineer's, Esses, Fanfarona, Fetter, Fob, Food, Furlong, Gleipnir, Golden, Grand, Gunter's, Gyve, Heavy, Learner's, Markov, Mayor, Micella(r), Micelle, > MOUNTAIN, Noria, Open, Pennine, Pitch, Range, Rockies, Roller, Safety, Seal, > SERIES, Shackle, Side, Slang, Snigging, Sprocket, Straight, String, Strobila, Supply, Surveyor's, Suspensor, Team, Tug, Voluntary, Watch

Chain-gang Coffle

Chair Basket, Bath, Bench, Bentwood, Berbice, Bergère, Birthing, Bosun's, Butterfly, Camp, Cane, Captain's, Carver, Club, Curule, Deck, Dining, Director's, Easy, Electric, Emeritus, Estate, Fauteuil, Fiddle-back, Folding, Frithstool, Garden, Gestatorial, Guérite, High, Jampan, Jampanee, Jampani, Ladder-back, Lounger, Love-seat, Merlin, Morris, Musical, Personal, Pew, Preside, Recliner, Rocker, > SEAT, Sedan, Stool, Sugan, Swivel, Throne, Wainscot, Wheel, Windsor, Wing

Chair-back Ladder, Splat

Chairman Convener, Emeritus, Landammann, Mao, MC, Pr(a)eses, Prof, Prolocutor, Sheraton, Speaker

Chalaza Albumen, Treadle, Treddle

Chaldean Babylonian, Ur

Chalet Cabana, Cot, Skio

Chalice Poisoned

Chalk(y) Calcareous, Cauk, Cawk, Crayon, Credit, Cretaceous, French, Senonian, Soapstone, Spanish, Steatite, Tailor's, White(n), Whit(en)ing

Challenge(r), **Challenging** Acock, Assay, Call, Cartel, Champion, Confront, Contest, Dare, Defy, Gage, Gauntlet, Glove, Hazard, Hen(ner), Iconoclasm, Impugn, Oppugn, Provoke, Query, Question, Recuse, Sconce, Shuttle, Tackle, Taker, Tall order, Tank, Threat, Vie, Wero, Whynot

Chamber(s) Airlock, Atrium, Auricle, Bubble, Camarilla, Camera, Casemate, Cavern, Cavitation, Cavity, Cell(a), Chanty, Close-stool, Cloud, Cofferdam, Combustion, Cubicle, Decompression, Dene-hole, Dolmen, Echo, Float,

Fumatorium, Gas, Gazunder, Gilded, Hall, Horrors, Hypogea, Inspection, Ionization, Jerry, Jordan, Kiva, Lethal, Locule, Lok Sabha, Lower, Magma, Mattamore, Mesoscaphe, Plenum, Po(t), Presence, Privy, Reaction, Resonance-box, Roum, Second, Serdab, Silo, Spark, Star, Swell-box, Synod, Thalamus, Undercroft, Upper, Utricle, Vault, Ventricle, Wilson cloud, Zeta

Chamberlain Camerlengo, Camerlingo, Censor

Chameleon Ethiopian, Lizard, Tarand

Chamfer Bevel, Groove

Chamois Ibex, Izard, Shammy

Champ Bite, Chafe, Chew, Chomp, Eat, Gnash, Gnaw, Hero, Mash, Morsure, Munch

Champagne Boy, Bubbly, Charlie, Fizz, Gigglewater, Pop, Sillery, Simkin, Simpkin, Stillery, Troyes, Widow

Champion(s) Ace, Adopt, Ali, Apostle, Belt, Campeador, Cid, Cock, Crusader, Cupholder, Defend, Don Quixote, Doucepere, Douzeper, Dymoke, Enoch, Espouse, Gladiator, Harry, > HERO, Horse, Kemp, Kemper(yman), King, Knight, Maintain, Matchless, Messiah, Messias, Neil, Paladin, Palmerin, Peerless, Perseus, Promachos, Proponent, Protagonist, Roland, St Anthony, St David, St Denis, St George, St James, St Patrick, Spiffing, Spokesman, Star, Support, Tribune, Upholder, Victor, Wardog, > WINNER, Yokozuna

Championship Open, Seven, Super Bowl, Title

Chance (upon), Chancy Accident, Aleatory, Aunter, Bet, Break, Buckley's, Cast, Casual, Cavel, Coincidence, Contingent, Dice, Earthly, Even, Fat, > FATE, Fighting, First refusal, Fluke, Fortuitous, Fortuity, Fortune, > GAMBLE, Game, Hap, Happenstance, Hobnob, Iffy, Kevel, Light, Loaves and fishes, Look-in, Lot, > LOTTERY, Luck, Main, Meet, Mercy, Occur, Odds, Odds-on, Opening, Opportunity, Outside, Posse, Potluck, Probability, Prospect, Random, Rise, Risk, Run into, Russian roulette, Serendipity, Slant, Spec, Sporting, Stake, Stochastic, Sweep, Toss-up, Treble, Turn, Tychism, Ventre, Venture, Wager

Chancel Adytum, Bema, Nave

Chancellor Adolf, Bismarck, Dollfuss, Kohl, Logothete, Minister, More

Chancery Court, Hanaper

Chandelier Candlestick, Corona, Drop, Electrolier, Gasolier, Girandole, Lustre, Pendant

Chandler Acater, Raymond

Chaney Lon

Change(able), Changes, Changing Adapt, Adjust, Agio, > ALTER, Amendment, Attorn, Backtrack, Barter, Become, Bob-major, Capricious, Cash, Catalysis, Chameleon, Chop, Cline, Commute, Convert, Coppers, Denature, Departure, Dichrony, Edit, Enallage, Esterify, Eustatic, Evolve, Exchange, Fickle, Find, Flighty, Float, Fluctuate, Flux, Guard, Gybe, Inflect, Innovate, Kembla, Killcrop, Labile, Loose, Make-over, Menopause, Metabolic, Metabolise, Metamorphose, Metamorphosis, Mobile, Modify, Mutable, Mutalis mutandis, Mutanda, Mutation, Parallax, Peal, Peripet(e)ia, Permute, Port, Prophase, Protean, Quantum leap, Realise, Recant, Rectify, Reform, Refraction, Regime, Rejig, Resipiscence, Rest, Reverse, Revise, Revolutionise, Rework, Sandhi, Scourse, Sd, Sea, Seesaw, Sere, Sex, Shake-out, Shake-up, Shift, Silver, Small, Sublimation, Substitute, Swap, Swing, Switch, Tempolabile, Tolsel, Tolsey, Tolzey, Transfer, Transfiguration, Transform, Transition, Transmogrify, Transmute, Transpose, Transubstantial, Turn, Uncertain, Upheaval, U-turn, Vagary, Variant, Variation, Vary, Veer, Vicissitude, Volatile, Volte-face, Wankle, Washers, Waver, Wheel, Wow

▷ **Change(d)** *may indicate* an anagram

Changeling Auf, Killcrop, Oaf, Turncoat

Channel Access, Aflaj, Aqueduct, Artery, Beagle, Bed, Billabong, Bristol, Canal, Canaliculus, Chimb, Chime, Chine, Chute, Conduit, Culvert, Cut, Cutting, Distribution, Ditch, Drain, Duct, Dyke, Ea, English, Estuary, Euripus, Fairway, Falaj, Flume, Foss, Funnel, Furrow, Gat, Geo, Gio, Glyph, Grough, Gully, Gut, Gutter, Head-race, Ingate, Katabothron, Katavothron, Khor, Kill, Kos, Lane, Leat, Leet, Limber, Major, Meatus, Medium, Minch, Moat, Mozambique, Multiplex, Narrows, North, Penstock, Pentland Firth, Pescadores, Pipeline, Qanat, Race, Rebate, Rigol(l), Rivulet, St George's, Sea-gate, Seaway, Sewer, Shunt, Sinus, Sky, Sloot, Sluice, Sluit, Sny(e), Solent, Solway Firth, Sound, Sow, Spillway, Sprue, Strait, Suez, Sure, Swash, Tailrace, Tideway, Tracheole, Trough, Ureter, Vallecula, Watercourse, Wireway, Yucatan

Chant Anthem, Antiphon, Canticle, Cantillate, Cantus, Chaunt, Daimoku, Decantate, Euouae, Evovae, Gregorian, Haka, Harambee, Hymn, Intone, Introit, Motet, Pennillion-singing, Plainsong, Psalm, Sing, Slogan, Te deum, Yell

Chantilly Cream, Lace

Chaos, **Chaotic** Abyss, Anarchy, Confusion, Disorder, Fractal, Hun-tun, Jumble, Mess, Mixter-maxter, Muss, Shambles, Shambolic, Snafu, Tohu bohu

▷ **Chaotic** *may indicate* an anagram

Chap(s) Beezer, Bloke, Bo, Bod, Bor, Chafe, Cheek, Chilblain, Chop, Cleft, Cod, Codger, Cove, Crack, Customer, Dog, Fella, Fellow, Flews, Genal, Gent, Gink, Guy, Hack, Joll, Jowl, Kibe, Lad, > **MAN**, Mouth, Mum, Ocker, Rent, Rime, Spray, Spreathe, Spreaze, Spreethe, Spreeze, Wang

Chapel Bethel, Bethesda, Beulah, Cha(u)ntry, Ebenezer, Feretory, Galilee, Lady, Oratory, Parabema, Prothesis, Sacellum, Sistine

Chaperon(e) Beard, Cap, Duenna, Escort, Gooseberry, Griffin, Griffon, Gryphon, Muffin

Chaplain CF, Ordinary, Padre, Priest, Skypilot, Slope

Chaplet Anadem, Coronet, Fillet, Garland, Wreath

▷ **Chaps** *may indicate* an anagram

Chapter Accidents, C, Canon, Cap, Capitular, Ch, Chap, Cr, Division, Episode, Lodge, Phase, Section, Social, Sura(h), Verse

Char(woman) Adust, Burn, Cleaner, Coal, Daily, Duster, Mop(p), Mrs Mop(p), Scorch, Sear, Singe, Smoulder, Toast, Togue, Torgoch

Charabanc Bus, Chara, Coach

Character(s) Aesc, Alphabet, Ampersand, Ampussyand, Atmosphere, Aura, Backslash, Brand, Calibre, Case, Cipher, Clef, Cliff, Climate, Coloration, Complexion, Contour, Credit, Delimiter, Deuteragonist, Devanagari, Digamma, Digit, Dramatis personae, Eta, Ethos, > **FEATURE**, Fish, Fist, Form, Grain, Graphics, Grit, Hieroglyphic, Homophone, Ideogram, Ideograph, Italic, Kanji, Kern, Kind, La(m)bda, Letter, Logogram, Make-up, Mark, Mu, Nagari, > **NATURE**, Non-person, Nu, Ogam, Ogham, Pahlavi, Pantaloon, Part, Pehlevi, Person(a), Personage, > **PERSONALITY**, Phonogram, Physiognomy, Pi, Polyphone, Protagonist, Psi, Raisonneur, Reference, Repute, Rho, Role, Rune, Runic, Sampi, San, Self, Sirvente, Slash, Sonancy, Space, Sphenogram, Stamp, Subscript, Superscript(ion), Swung dash, Syllabary, Symbol, Testimonial, Ton(e), Trait, Uncial, Unit, Vav, Vee, Waw, Wen, Wild card, Wyn(n), Yogh, Zeta

Characterise(d), **Characterism**, **Characteristic(s)** Acquired, Attribute, Aura, Cast, Colour, Distinctive, Ethos, Facies, Feature, Hair, Hallmark, Has, Headmark, Idiomatic, Idiosyncrasy, Jizz, Lineament, Mien, Nature, Notate,

Peculiar, Persona, Phenotype, Point, Property, Quality, Signature, Stigma, Strangeness, Streak, Style, > TRAIT, Transfer, Typical, Vein

Characterless Anon, Inane, Wet

Charade Enigma, Pretence, Riddle

Charcoal Carbon, Coke, Fusain, Sugar

Charge(s), Charged, Charger Accusal, Accuse, Aerate, Agist, Allege, Annulet, Arraign, Ascribe, Assault, Baton, Bear, Behest, Blame, Brassage, Brush, Buckshot, Bum rap, Care, Cathexis, Commission, Community, Complaint, Congestion, Cost, Count, Cover, Criminate, Damage, Debit, Delate, Delf, Delph, Demurrage, Depth, Depute, Directive, Dittay, Dockage, Due, Duty, Electric, Electron, Entrust, Entry, Exit, Expense, Fare, Fee, Fill, Fixed, Fleur-de-lis, Floating, Flock, Freight, Fullage, Fuse, Fuze, Gazump, Gravamen, > HERALDIC, Hot, Hypothec, Impeach, Impute, Indict, Inescutcheon, Inform, Instinct, Ion, Isoelectric, Last, Lien, Lioncel(le), Lionel, Live, Load, Mandate, Mine, Mount, Objure, Obtest, Onrush, Onslaught, Onus, Ordinary, Orle, Overhead, Pervade, Pew-rent, Plaint, Positive, Premium, Prime, Prix fixe, Q, Rack-rent, Rap, Rate, Red-dog, Rent, Report, Reprise, Roundel, Run, > RUSH, Saddle, Service, Specific, Steed, Tariff, Tax, Tear, Terms, Tilt, > TRAY, Tressure, Trickle, Trust, Tutorage, Upfill, Vaire, Vairy, Verdoy, Vigorish, Ward, Warhead, Wharfage

Chariot(eer) Auriga, Automedon, Biga, Cart, Curricle, Hur, Phaethon, Quadriga, Vimana, Wagon, Wain

Charisma Oomph, Personality

Charitable, Charity Alms, Awmous, Benign, Caritas, Cause, Dole, Dorcas, Eleemosynary, Largesse, Leniency, Liberal, Lion, Love, Mercy, Oddfellow, Openhanded, Oxfam, Pelican, Zakat

Charivari Rough music, Uproar

Charlatan Cheat, Crocus, Empiric, Escroc, Faker, Imposter, Katerfelto, Mountebank, Poseur, Quack(salver), Saltimbanco

Charlemagne Carlovingian

Charles, Charley, Charlie Beard, Car, Champagne, Chan, Chaplin, Checkpoint, Elia, Lamb, (Old) Rowley, Pretender, Rug-gown, Sap, Tail-end, Watchman

Charles de Gaulle Airport

Charlotte Bronte, Russe, Yonge

Charm(er), Charming Abracadabra, Abrasax, Abraxas, Allure, Amulet, Appeal, Aroma, Attraction, Beguile, Bewitch, Captivate, Charisma, Circe, Comether, Cute, Cutie, Delectable, Emerods, Enamour, Enchant, Engaging, > ENTRANCE, Fascinate, Fay, Fetish, Grace, Greegree, Gri(s)gris, Hand of glory, Houri, Juju, Magnetic, Mascot, Mojo, Obeah, Obi(a), Periapt, Phylactery, Porte-bonheur, Pretty, Prince, Quaint, Quark, Ravish, Siren, Smoothie, Spellbind, Suave, Sweetness, Taking, Talisman, Tefillah, Telesm, Tephillah, Tiki, Trinket, Unction, Voodoo, Winning, Winsome

▷ **Charming** *may indicate* an anagram

Chart(ed), Charting Abac, Bar, Breakeven, Card, Control, Diagram, Eye, Flip, Flow, Gantt, Graph, Histogram, Hydrography, Isogram, Isopleth, List, Magna Carta, > MAP, Mappemond, Nomogram, Organisation, Pie, Plane, Plot, Portolano, Ringelmann, Social, Table, Timetable, Waggoner, Weather, Z

Charta, Charter Atlantic, Book, Citizen's, Covenant, Hire, Lease, Novodamus, Rent, Social (chapter), Tenants', Time, Voyage

Chary Cagey, Careful, Cautious, Frugal, Shy, Wary

Charybdis Maelstrom, Whirlpool

Chase(r), Chasing Cannock, Chace, Chevy, Chivy, Ciseleur, Ciselure, Course, Cranbome, Decorate, Drink, Game, Harass, Hound, > HUNT, Jumper, Oxo,

Pursuit, Race, Scorse, Sic(k), Steeple, Sue, Suit, Wild-goose

Chasm Abyss, Crevasse, Fissure, Gap, Gorge, Gulf, Schism, Yawn

Chaste, Chastity Agnes, Attic, Celibate, Classic, Clean, Florimell, Ines, Innocent, Modesty, Nessa, > PURE, Vestal, Virginal, Virtue

Chasten, Chastise(d), Chastisement Beat, Correct, Discipline, Disple, Lash, Rib-roast, Rollicking, Scold, Scourge, Shame-faced, Spank, Strap, Whip

Chat, Chatter(box) Babble, Bavardage, Blab(ber), Blether, Campanero, Causerie, Chelp, Chinwag, Clack, Clishmaclaver, Confab(ulate), Converse, Cosher, Coze, Crack, Dialogue, Froth, Gab(ble), Gas, Gossip, Gup, Hobnob, Jabber, Jargon, Jaw, Kilfud, Madge, Mag(pie), Natter, Patter, Pie, Pourparler, Prate, Prattle, Rabbit, Rabble, Rap, Rattle, Scuttlebutt, Shmoose, Talk, Talkee-talkee, Tattle, Tongue-work, Twattle, Waffle, Windbag, Witter, Wongi, Yacketyyak, Yak, Yap, Yarn, Yatter, Yoking

Chateau Castle, Cru, Malmaison, Schloss

Chateaubriand René

Chattel Asset, Chose, Deodand

Chaucer(ian) Dan, OE

Chauffeur Cabby, Coachy, Driver, Sice, Syce

Chauvinist Alf, Bigot, Jingo, MCP, Partisan, Patriot, Sexist

Cheap Bargain, Base, Catchpenny, Cheesy, Chintzy, Cut-price, Downmarket, Giveaway, Ignoble, Knockdown, Low, Off-peak, Poor, Sacrifice, Shoddy, Stingy, Tatty, Tawdry, Ticky-tacky, Tinhorn, Tinpot, Tinselly, Trivial, Tuppenny, Two-bit, Twopenny, Undear, Vile

▷ **Cheap** *may indicate* a d- or p- start to a word

Cheapside Bow

Cheat(ers), Cheating Bam, Bamboozle, Beguile, Bilk, Bite(r), Bob, Bonnet, Bucket, Bullock, Cardsharp(er), Charlatan, Chiaus, Chicane(ry), Chisel, Chouse, Clip, Cod, Cog(ger), Colt, Con, Cozen, Crib, Cross, Cross-bite(r), Cuckold, Cully, Defraud, Delude, Diddle, Dingo, Dish, Do, Doublecross, Duckshove, Dupe, Escroc, Faitor, Fiddle, Finagle, Flam, Fleece, Fob, Foister, Fox, Fraud, Gaff, Gip, Glasses, Gull-catcher, Gum, Gyp, Hoax, Hocus, Hoodwink, Hornswoggle, Horse, Intake, Jockey, Leg, Magsman, Mulct, Mump, Nick, Pasteboard, Picaro(on), Poop, Queer, Rib, Rig, Rogue, Rook, Rush, Scam, Screw, Shaft, Sharper, Short-change, Slur, Smouch, Snap, Stack, Stiff, Sting, Swindle, Thimble-rigging, Trepan, Trim, Two-time, Welsh, Wheedle

Check Arrest, Audit, Bauk, Ba(u)lk, Bill, Bridle, Collate, Compesce, Control, Count, Cramp, Cross-index, Curb, Dam, Damp, Detain, Detent, Discovered, Dogs-tooth, Examine, Foil, Frustrate, Halt, Hamper, Hobble, Houndstooth, Inhibit, Jerk, Jerque, Let, Limit, Mate, Monitor, Observe, Overhaul, Party, Perpetual, Prevent, Rain, Reality, Rebuff, Rebuke, Rein, Repress, Reprime, Repulse, Reread, > RESTRAIN, Revoke, Saccade, Screen, Service, Setback, Shepherd's, Shorten, Sit-upon, Sneap, Sneb, Snib, Snub, Sound, Spot, > STEM, Stop, Stunt, Tab, Tally, Tartan, Tattersall, Test, Thwart, Tick, Trash, Verify, Vet

Checkers Chinese, Piece

Check-out Till

Cheddar Cheese, Gorge

Cheek(y) Alforja, Audacity, Brass-neck, Buccal, Chap, Chollers, Chutzpah, Cool, Crust, Flippant, Fresh, Gum, Hard-faced, Hussy, Impertinent, Impudent, Joll, Jowl, Lip, Malapert, Malar, Masseter, Neck, Nerve, Noma, Pert, Presumption, Quean, Sass, Sauce, Sideburns, Wang, Yankie, Zygoma

Cheep Chirp, Chirrup, Peep

Cheer(s), Cheerful(ness), Cheering Acclaim, Agrin, Applaud, Banzai, Barrack,

Blithe, Bonnie, Bravo, Bright, Bronx, Bubbly, Buck, Buoy, Cadgy, Canty, Carefree, Cherry, Chin-chin, Chipper, Chirpy, > **COMFORT**, Crouse, Debonair, Drink, Ease, Elate, Elevate, Enliven, Exhilarate, Festive, Genial, Gladden, Happy-go-lucky, Hearten, Hilarity, Holiday, Hooch, Hoorah, Hurra(h), Huzzah, Insouciance, Jocund, Jovial, Kia-ora, Light-hearted, Lightsome, Lively, Meal, Ovate, Peart, Perky, Please, Praise, Prosit, Rah, Riant, Rivo, Root, Rumbustious, Shout, Sko(a)l, Slainte, Sonsie, Sunny, Ta, Tata, Thanks, Three, Tiger, Tiggerish, Toodle-oo, Warm, Winsome, Yell

Cheerless Dismal, Drab, Drear, Gloomy, Glum

Cheese, Cheesy American, Amsterdam, Appenzell, Asiago, Bel Paese, Blue, Boursin, Brie, Caboc, Caerphilly, Camembert, Cantal, Casein, Caseous, Cheddar, Cheshire, Chessel, Chèvre, Colby, Cottage, Coulommiers, Cream, Crowdie, Curd, Damson, Danish blue, Derby, Dolcelatte, Double Gloucester, Dunlop, Edam, Emmental(er), Emmenthal(er), Ermite, Esrom, Ewe, Fet(a), Fontina, Fromage frais, Fynbo, Gloucester, Goat, Gorgonzola, Gouda, Grand Panjandrum, Gruyère, Halloumi, Hard, Havarti, Huntsman, Ilchester, Islay, Jarlsberg®, Junket, Kebbock, Kebbuck, Kenno, Killarney, Lancashire, Leicester, Limburg(er), Lymeswold®, Macaroni, Mascarpone, Mousetrap, Mozzarella, Mu(e)nster, Mycella, Neufchatel, Oka, Orkney, Paneer, Parmesan, Pecorino, Pont l'Eveque, Port Salut, Pot, Provolone, Quark, Raclette, Rarebit, Reblochon, Rennet, Ricotta, Romano, Roquefort, Sage Derby, Samso, Sapsago, Skyr, Stilton®, Stone, Stracchino, Swiss, Tilsit, Tofu, Truckle, Vacherin, VIP, Wensleydale

Cheesecake Pin-up, Talmouse

Cheese-scoop Pale

Chef Commis, Escoffier

Chekhov Anton

Chemical Acanthin, Acid, Acrolein, Adrenalin®, Agent orange, Alar, Aldehyde, Alkali, Allomone, Alum, Amide, Anabolic, Barilla, Bradykinin, Bute, Carbide, Carnallite, Caseose, Catalyst, Cephalin, Cerebroside, Depside, Developer, Dopamine, Encephalin, Enkephalin(e), Enol, Fixer, Fluoride, Formyl, Freon, Fungicide, Gamone, Glutamine, Glycol, Halon, Harmin, Heavy, Hecogenin, Heptane, Hexylene, Hexylresorcinol, Histamine, Hypo, ICI, Imine, Imipramine, Indican, Interleukin, Larvicide, Morphactin, Natron, Nitre, Oestregen, Olefin, Olein, Oxide, Oxysalt, Pentane, Pentene, Pentyl, Peptide, Periclase, Phenol, Phenyl, Pheromone, Potash, Potassa, Psoralen, Ptomaine, Reagent, Resorcin, Resorcinol, Restrainer, Serotonin, Soman, Soup, Strontia, Sulphide, Thio-salt, Toner, Trimer, Weedicide, Weedkiller

Chemise Cymar, Sark, Serk, Shift, Shirt, Simar(re), Smock, Symar

Chemist(ry) Alchemy, Alchymy, Analyst, Apothecary, Bunsen, Butenandt, Cavendish, Cleve, Davy, Debye, Dewar, Dispenser, Druggist, Drugstore, FCS, Gahn, Hevesy, Inorganic, Lavoisier, Liebig, LSA, MPS, Nernst, Newlands, Nobel, Nuclear, Organic, Paracelsus, Pasteur, Pharmacist, Physical, Pothecary, Pottingar, Proust, Prout, Redwood, RIC, Sabatier, Sanger, Schiff, Spageric, Spagiric, Spagyric, Spicer, Stinks, Stoich(e)iometry, Technical, Urey, Zymurgy

Cheops Khufu

Cheque Blank, Giro, Gregory, Open, Rubber, Stumer, Tab, Traveller's

Chequer Dice

Cherish(ed) Dear, Dote, Enshrine, Entertain, Esteem, Foment, Foster, Harbour, Inshrine, Nestle, Nurse, Pamper, Pet, Precious, Treasure

Cheroot Cigar, Manil(l)a

Cherry (tree) Amarelle, Ball, Bigaroon, Bigarreau, Bird, Blackheart, Cerise,

Cornelian, Gean, Ground, Heart, Jerusalem, Kearton, Kermes, Kermesite, Malpighia, Marasca, Maraschino, May-duke, Maz(z)ard, Merry, Morel(lo), Red, Sweet, Whiteheart

Cherry-pie Heliotrope

Cherub Angel, Putto, Seraph

Chess (move), **Chess player**, **Chess term** Black, Blindfold, Endgame, Euwe, Fianchetto, FIDE, J'adoube, Karpov, Lightning, Miranda, Patzer, Plank, Shogi, Speed, White, Zugzwang, Zwischenzug

Chessman Bishop, Black, Castle, Horse, King, Knight, Pawn, Pin, Queen, Rook, White

Chest(y) Ark, Bahut, Bosom, Box, Breast, Buist, Bunker, Bureau, Bust, Caisson, Cap-case, Case, Cassone, Chapel, Chiffonier, Coffer, Coffin, Coffret, Commode, Community, Cub, Dresser, Hope, Inro, Kist, Larnax, Locker, Lowboy, Meal-ark, Medicine, Ottoman, Pectoral, Pereion, Pigeon, Pleural, Safe, Scrine, Scryne, Sea, Shrine, Slop, Steam, Sternum, Tallboy, Tea, Thorax, Toolbox, Trunk, Wangan, Wangun, Wanigan, War, Wind

Chester Deva

Chestnut Auburn, Badious, Ch, Chincapin, Chinese, Chinkapin, Chinquapin, Cliché, Conker, Dwarf, Favel(l), Hoary, Horse, Marron, Marron glacé, Moreton Bay, Russet, Saligot, Soare, Sorrel, Spanish, Sweet, Water

Chest protector > ARMOUR, Bib

Chevalier Bayard, Knight, Pretender

Chevron Dancette, Stripe

Chew(ing) Bite, Champ, Chaw, Cud, Eat, Fletcherism, Gnaw, Gum, Manducate, Masticate, Maul, Meditate, Moop, Mou(p), Munch, Ruminate, Siri(h), Spearmint

Chewink Ground-robin

Chiastolite Macle

Chic Dapper, Elegant, In, Kick, Modish, Posh, Radical, Smart, Soigné, Stylish, Swish, Tonish, Trim

Chicago Windy City

Chicane(ry) Artifice, Deception, Fraud, Wile

Chichester Yachtsman

Chichi Precious

Chick(en) Australorp, Battery, Biddy, Boiler, Broiler, Capon, Cheeper, Chittagong, Chuckie, Clutch, Cochin, Coronation, Coward, Cowherd, Eirack, Gutless, Hen, Howtowdie, Kiev, Layer, Marengo, Minorca, Mother Carey's, Niderling, Poltroon, Poot, Poult, Pout, Prairie, Precocial, Pullus, Quitter, Roaster, Spatchcock, Spring, Squab, Supreme, Timorous, Unheroic, Windy, Wyandotte, Yellow

Chickenfeed Maize

Chickenpox Varicella

Chickpea Garbanzo

Chickweed Snow-in-summer

Chicory Endive, Radiccio, Succory, Witloof

Chide Admonish, Berate, Objurgate, Rate, Rebuke, Reprove, Row, Scold, Tick off, Twit, Upbraid

Chief(tain) Arch, Ardrigh, Ariki, Boss, Caboceer, Cacique, Calif, Caliph, Capital, Capitan, Capitayn, Capo, Caradoc, Cazique, Ch, Chagan, Dat(t)o, Dominant, Emir, Finn (MacCool), First, Foremost, Geronimo, Grand, Haggis, > HEAD, Hereward, Jarl, Kaid, King, Leader, > MAIN, Mass, Mugwump, Nizam, Oba, Overlord, Paramount, Pendragon, Premier, Primal, Prime, Principal, Quanah,

Raja(h), Rajpramukh, Rangatira, Rangatiratanga, Ratoo, Ratu, Sachem, Sagamore, Sarpanch, Sudder, Supreme, Tanist, Tank, Top

Chiffonier Cabinet, Commode

Chilblain Kibe

Child(ish), **Childhood**, **Children** Aerie, Alannah, Ankle biter, Babe, Baby, Badger, Bairn, Bambino, Bantling, Boy, Brat, Brood, Butter-print, Ch, Changeling, Cherub, Chick, Chickabiddy, Chit, Collop, Cub, Dream, Elfin, Eyas, Foster, Foundling, Gait, Gangrel, Ge(i)t, Girl, Gyte, Heir, Hellion, Hurcheon, Imp, Infancy, Infant, Inner, Issue, It, Jailbait, Jejune, Juvenile, Kid(die), Kiddie(wink), Kiddy, Kinder, Lad, Latchkey, Limb, Litter, Littlie, Littling, Love, Mamzer, Mardy, Minion, Minor, Mite, Munchkin, Naive, Nipper, Nursling, Offspring, Papoose, Piccaninny, Pickin, Progeny, Puerile, Puss, Putto, Ragamuffin, Rip, Rug rat, Scion, Second, Small fry, Smout, Smowt, Sprog, Street arab, Subteen, Tacker, Ted, Teeny-bopper, Tike, Toddle(r), Tot(tie), Totty, Trot, Tweenager, Tyke, Urchin, Waif, Wean, Weanel, Weanling, Weeny-bopper, Whelp, Younker, Youth

Childbearing, **Childbirth** Couvade, Intrapartum, Lamaze, Parity, Puerperal, Tocology, Tokology

Child-killer Herod

Childless Atocous, Atokous, Barren, Nullipara, Sp

Chill(er), **Chilly** Bleak, Cauldrife, > **COLD**, Frappé, Freeze, Freon®, Frigid, Frosty, Gelid, Ice, Iciness, Mimi, Oorie, Ourie, Owrie, Parky, Raw, Refrigerate, Rigor, Scare

Chilli Bird's eye

Chime(s) Bell, Cymar, Jingle, Peal, Semantron, Tink, > **TOLL**, Wind

Chimera Graft

Chimney (pot), **Chimney corner** Can, Cow(l), Femerall, Flare stack, Flue, Funnel, Lamp, Lug, Lum, Smokestack, Stack, Stalk, Steeplejack, Tallboy, Tunnel

Chimp Ape, Jocko

Chin, **Chinwag** Chitchat, Double, Genial, Jaw, Jowl, Mentum

China(man), **Chinese** Ami, Amoy, Boxer, Cameoware, Cantonese, Cathay, Celestial, Ch, Chelsea, Chink(y), Chow, Coalport, Cochin, Cock, Communist, Confucius, Crackle, Crockery, Delft, Derby, Dresden, Eggshell, Etrurian, Flowery land, Friend, Fukien, Google, Googly, Goss, Hakka, Han, Hizen, Hmong, Imari, Kanji, Kaolin, Kuo-yu, Limoges, Manchu, Mandarin, Mangi, Maoist, Mate, Meissen, Min, Ming, Minton, National, Oppo, Pal, Pareoean, Pekingese, Pe-tsai, Pinyin, Porcelain, > **POTTERY**, Putonghua, Queensware, Red, Rockingham, Royal Worcester, Seric, Sèvres, Shanghai, Sinic, Spode®, Sun Yat-sen, Tai-ping, Taoist, Teng, Tocharian, Tungus, Uigur, Wal(l)y, Ware, Wedgwood®, Whiteware, Willowware, Worcester, Wu

Chine Chink, Chynd, Ridge

Chink Chinaman, Chop, Cleft, Clink, Cloff, Crack, Cranny, Crevice, Gap, Rent, Rift, Rima, Sinic, Window

Chintz Kalamkari

Chip(s) Blue, Bo(a)st, Carpenter, Counter, Cut, Deep-fried, EPROM, EROM, Fish, Flake, Fragment, Game, Hack, Knap, Log, Nacho(s), Neural, Nick, Pin, Potato, Shaving, Silicon, Spale, Spall, Span, Teraflop, Tortilla, Transputer

▷ **Chip** *may indicate* an anagram

Chipmunk Gopher, Hackee, Suslik, Zizel

Chipper Jaunty, Spry, Wedge

Chiron Centaur

Chiropody Podiatry
Chiropractic McTimoney
Chirp(y), **Chirrup** Cheep, Cherup, Chirm, Chirr, Cicada, Peep, Pip, Pipe, Pitter, Stridulate, Trill, Tweet, Twitter
Chisel(ler), **Chisel-like** Bam, Boaster, Bolster, Bur, Burin, Carve, Cheat, Clip, Drove, Firmer, Gad, > GOUGE, Half-round, Mason, Paring, Scalpriform, Scauper, Scorper, Sculpt, Socket, Sting
Chit Docket, Girl, Note, Voucher
Chivalry, **Chivalrous** Brave, Bushido, Courtly, Gallant, Quixotic
Chivvy Badger, Harass, Pursue
Chloride, **Chlorine** Calomel
Chlorophyll Leaf-green
Chock Trig
Chocolate Aero, Brown, Cacao, Carob, Cocoa, Dragee, Ganache, Milk, Neapolitan, Noisette, Pinole, Plain, Theobroma, Truffle, Vegelate
Choice, **Choose**, **Choosy**, **Chosen** Adopt, Anthology, Appoint, Aryan, Cherry-pick, Cull, Dainty, Decide, Druthers, Eclectic, Elect, Elite, Esnecy, Fine, Fork, Free will, Hobson's, Leet, Leve, Lief, List, Multiple, Opt, Option, Or, Ossian, Peach, Peculiar, > PICK, Picking, Plum(p), Precious, Predilect, Prefer, Proairesis, Rare, Recherché, > SELECT, Superb, Try(e), Via media, Volition, Wale
Choiceless Beggar
Choir, **Choral**, **Chorister**, **Chorus** Antiphony, Antistrophe, Anvil, Apse, Burden, Choragus, Choregus, Dawn, Decani, Faburden, Fauxbourdon, Group, Hallelujah, Harmony, Hymeneal, Motet, Ninth, Parabasis, Precentor, > REFRAIN, Ritual, Singing, Stop, Strophe, Treble, Triad, > UNISON
Choir-master Choragus, Choregus, Precentor
Choke(r) Block, Clog, Gag, Garotte, Glut, Silence, Smoor, Smore, Smother, Stap, Stifle, Stop, Strangle(hold), Strangulate, > THROTTLE
Choky Can, Prison
Cholera Hog
Cholesterol Squalene
Choliamb Scazon
▶ **Choose** *see* CHOICE
Chop(per), **Chops**, **Chopper(s)**, **Choppy** Adze, Ax(e), Celt, Charge, Cheek, Chump, Cleave, Côtelette, Cuff, Cutlet, Dice, Fell(er), Flew, Hack, Helicopter, Hew, Ivory, Karate, Lop, Mince, Mouth, Rotaplane, Rough, Suey, Teeth, To-rend, Wang
Chopin Pantoufle, Shoe
Chopstick(s) Waribishi
Chord(s) Arpeggio, Barré, Broken, Common, Diameter, Eleventh, Harmony, Intonator, Latus rectum, Neapolitan sixth, Nerve, Ninth, Picardy third, Riff, Seventh, Submediant, Thirteenth, Triad, Vocal
Chore Darg, Duty, Fag, Task
Choreographer Arranger, Ashton, Balanchine, Cecchetti, Cranko, Fokine, Laban, Massine
Chorus Antistrophe, Dawn, Ninth, Stop, Strophe
Chosen Korea
Chough Chewet
Chowder Bouillabaisse, Skink, Soup
Christ > CHRIST, Ecce homo, Messiah, Pantocrator, Prince of Peace, Saviour, The Good Shepherd, The Redeemer, X, Xt
Christen(ing) Baptise, Launch, Name-day

Christian(ity) Abcee, Abecedarian, Absey, Adventist, Albigenses, Anabaptist, Beghard, Believer, Cathar(ist), Charismatic, Coptic, Dior, Donatist, D(o)ukhobor, Ebionite, Galilean, Giaour, Gilbertine, Gnostic, Godsquad, Goy, Heteroousian, Holy roller, Homo(i)ousian, Hutterite, Jehovah's Witness, Lutheran, Marrano, Melchite, Melkite, Methodist, Moral, Mozarab, Muscular, Mutineer, Nazarene, Nestorian, Phalange, Pilgrim, Presbyterian, Protestant, Quaker, Quartodeciman, RC, Sabotier, Scientist, SCM, Shambe, Traditor, Uniat(e), Unitarian, Valdenses, Waldensian, Wesleyan, Xian, Zwinglian

Christian Scientist Eddy

Christmas(time) C(h)rimbo, Dec, Island, Nativity, Noel, Yuletide

Christopher Kit, Robin, Sly, Wren

Chromatin Karyotin

Chromium Cr

Chromosome Aneuploid, Autosome, Centromere, Cistron, Euchromatin, Genome, Haploid, Homologous, Id(ant), Karyotype, Lampbrush, Operon, Philadelphia, Ploid(y), Polytene, Prophage, Trisomy, X, Y

Chronicle(r) Anglo-Saxon, Annal, Brut, Calendar, Diary, Froissart, Hall, History, Holinshed, Logographer, Moblog, Paralipomena, Parian, Paris, > **RECORD**, Register, Stow

Chrysalis Nymph, Pupa

Chrysanthemum Corn-marigold, Feverfew

Chrysolite Olivine, Peridot

Chub Cheven, Chevin, Fish

Chubby Butterball, Plump

Chuck (out) Berry, Buzz, Chook(ie), Discard, Eject, Food, Grub, Pat, Pitch, Shy, Sling, Three-jaw, Toss, Turf

Chuckle Chortle, Giggle, Gurgle

Chukka Polo

Chum(my) Buddy, Cobber, Cock, Companion, Crony, Mate, Pal, Sociable, Sodality

Chump Mug(gins), Noddle, Sap, Stupid

Chunk(y) Boxy, Chubby, Gob, Piece, Slab, Squat, Wad

Church Abbey, Armenian, Autocephalous, Basilica, Bethel, Bethesda, Broad, Brood, Byzantine, CE, Ch, Chapel, Chevet, Clergy, Collegiate, Congregational, Coptic, Delubrum, Eastern, EC, Ecumenical, Episcopal, Episcopalian, Established, Faith, Fold, Free, Greek, High, House, Kirk, Lateran, Latin, Low, Lutheran, Maronite, Methodist, Minster, Moravian, Mormon, New, New Jerusalem, Orthodox, Pentecostal, Preaching-house, Prebendal, Presbyterian, RC, Reformed, Relief, Rome, Russian Orthodox, Shrine, Smyrna, Station, Stave, Steeple, Temple, Triumphant, Unification, Unitarian, United Reformed, Visible, Wee Free, Western, Wool

Churchgoer, **Churchman**, **Churchwarden** Antiburgher, Azymite, Baptist, Believer, Classis, Clay, Cleric, Clerk, Congregation, Deacon, Dom, Dopper, Elder, Evangelist, Hatto, Ignorantine, Incumbent, Invisible, Knox, Lector, Lutheran, Methodist, Militant, Moderator, Moonie, Mormon, MU, Newman, Oncer, Parson, PE, Pipe, Pontiff, Prebendary, Precentor, Predicant, Predikant, Prelate, Presbyterian, Priest, Protestant, Puritan, Rector, Ruridecanal, Sacristan, Sidesman, Sim, Simeonite, Subdeacon, Succentor, Swedenborgian, Tantivy, Triumphant, Ubiquitarian, Unitarian, Verger, Visible, Wesleyan, Worshipper, Wren

Church house Deanery, Manse, Parsonage, Presbytery, Rectory, Vicarage

Churchill Tank, Winston

Churchyard God's acre
Churl(ish) Attercop, Boor, Crabby, Curmudgeonly, Cynical, Ethercap, Ettercap, Gruff, Ill-natured, Nabal, Peasant, Rustic, Serf, Surly
Churn Bubble, Kirn, Seethe
Chute Flume, Runway
CIC Shogun, Sirdar
Cicada Greengrocer, Locust, Tettix
Cicatrix Scar
Cicely Myrrh, Sweet
Cicero Cic, Tully
Cid Campeador, Chief, Hero
Cider Drink, Perry, Scrumpy
Ci-devant Ex
Cigar(ette), Cigarette cards Beedi(e), Bumper, Burn, Cancer stick, Caporal, Cartophily, Cheroot, Cigarillo, Claro, Coffin nail, Conch, Concha, Corona, Dog-end, Doob, Durry, Fag, Filter-tip, Gasper, Giggle(-stick), Havana, Joint, Locofoco, Long-nine, Loosies, Maduro, Manilla, Panatella, Paper-cigar, Perfecto, Puritano, Reefer, Regalia, Roach, Roll-up, Smoke, Snout, Splif(f), Stog(e)y, Stogie, Stompie, Twist, Weed, Whiff, Zol
Cinch Belt, Certainty, Duck soup, Girth
Cinchona Kina, Quina
Cinder(s) Ash, Breeze, Clinker, Dander, Embers, Slag
Cinderella Drudge, Stepdaughter
Cinema(s) Art house, Big screen, Biograph, Bioscope, Circuit, Drive-in, Films, Fleapit, Flicks, Megaplex, Movies, Multiplex, Mutoscope, New Wave, Nickelodeon, Nouvelle Vague, Odeon, Plaza, Theatre, Tivoli
Cinnabar Vermilion
Cinnamon, Cinnamon stone Canella, Cassia(bark), Essonite, Hessonite, Spice
Cipher Chi-rho, Code, Cryptogram, Nihil, Nobody, > **NOTHING**, Number, O, Steganogram, Zero
Circle Almacantar, Almucantar, Annulet, Antarctic, Arctic, Circassian, Co, Colure, Company, Compass, Corn, Corolla, Coterie, Cromlech, Crop, Cycloid, Cyclolith, Dip, Disc, Druidical, Eccentric, Ecliptic, Embail, Enclose, Epicyclic, Equant, Equator, Equinoctial, Euler's, Family, Fraternity, Full, Galactic, Girdle, Gloriole, Great, Gyre, Halo, Hoop, Horizon, Hour, Hut, Inner, Inorb, Lap, Longitude, Loop, Magic, Malebolge, Mandala, Meridian, Mohr's, Nimbus, O, Orb, Orbit, Parhelic, Parquet, Parterre, Penannular, Peristalith, Pitch, Polar, Quality, Rigol, > **RING**, Rondure, Rotate, Roundlet, Sentencing, Set, Setting, Small, Sphere, Stemme, Stone, Striking, Surround, Tinchel, Traffic, Transit, Tropic, Turning, Umbel, Upper, Vertical, Vicious, Vienna, Virtuous, Volt, Wheel
Circuit(ous) Ambit, AND, Autodyne, Bypass, Closed, Comparator, Daughterboard, Diocese, Discriminator, Dolby®, Equivalent, Eyre, Gyrator, IC, Integrated, Interface, Lap, Limiter, Logic, Loop, Microprocessor, Motherboard, NAND, NOR, NOT, Open, OR, Perimeter, Phantom, Phase, Printed, Quadripole, Reactance, Ring, Round, Scaler, Series, Short, Smoothing, Three-phase, Tour, Windlass
Circuit-breaker Fuse
Circular Annular, Court, Folder, Leaflet, Mailshot, Orby, Round, Spiral, Unending, Wheely
Circulate, Circulation Astir, Bloodstream, Cyclosis, Disseminate, Flow, Gyre, Issue, Mingle, Mix, Orbit, Pass, Publish, Report, Revolve, Rotate, Scope, Spread,

Stir, Troll, Utter

▷ **Circulating** *may indicate* an anagram

Circumcise(r), **Circumcision** Bris, Brith, Brit milah, Infibulate, Milah, Mohel, Pharaonic

Circumference Boundary, Girth, Perimeter, Size

Circumlocution Periphrasis, Tautology

Circumnavigation Periplus

Circumscribe Define, Demarcate, Enclose, Restrain

Circumspect Chary, Guarded, Prudential, Wary

Circumstance(s), **Circumstantial** Case, Detail, Event, Fact, Formal, > **INCIDENT**, Mitigating, Precise, Shebang, Situation

Circumvent Bypass, Dish, Evade, Outflank, Outwit, Usurp

Circus, **Circus boy** Arena, Big top, Eros, Flea, Flying, Harrier, Hippodrome, Marquee, Maximus, Media, Monty Python, Ring, Sanger, Slang, Three-ring

Cistercian Trappist

Cistern Feed-head, Flush-box, Sump, Tank, Tub, Vat

Citadel Acropolis, Alhambra, Castle, Fort(ress), Keep, Kremlin

Citation, **Cite** Adduce, Allegation, Mention, Name, Quote, Recall, Reference, Repeat, Sist, Summon

Citizen(s), **Citizenship** Burgess, Burgher, Civism, Cleruch, Denizen, Dicast, Ephebe, Franchise, Freeman, Jus sanguinis, Jus soli, Kane, National, Oppidan, Patrial, People, Quirites, Resident, Roman, Second-class, Senior, Snob, Subject, Trainband, Trierarch, Venireman, Voter

Citroen DS

Citron, **Citrous** Bergamot

Citrus Acid, Calamondin, Cedrate, Lemon, Lime, Mandarin, Min(n)eola, Orange, Pomelo, Tangerine, Ugli

City Agra, Athens, Atlantis, Babylon, Burgh, Carthage, Cosmopolis, Ctesiphon, Dodge, EC, Empire, Eternal, Forbidden, Free, Garden, Gath, Hilversum, Holy, Imperial, Inner, LA, Leonine, Medina, Megalopolis, Metropolis, Micropolis, Mycenae, NY, Persepolis, Petra, Pompeii, Rhodes, Salem, Smoke, Sparta, Tech, Teheran, Town, Ur, Vatican, Weldstadt, Wen

Civet Binturong, Cat, Fo(u)ssa, Genet(te), Herpestes, Linsang, Musang, Nandine, Palm, Paradoxine, Paradoxure, Rasse, Suricate, Toddy-cat, Viverra, Zibet

Civil(ian), **Civilisation**, **Civilised**, **Civility** Amenity, Christian, Cit, Citizen, Civ(vy), Comity, Courtesy, Culture, Fertile crescent, Humane, Indus Valley, Kultur, Maya, Municipal, Nok, Non-combatant, Polite, Politesse, Secular, Temporal, Urbane

Civil Service CS

Clad(ding) Sarking, Weatherboard

Clag(gy) Stickjaw

Claim Appeal, Arrogate, Assert, Asseverate, Bag, Challenge, Charge, Darraign(e), Darrain(e), Darrayn, Demand, Deraign, Droit, Encumbrance, Haro, Harrow, Lien, List, Maintain, Nochel, Plea, Pose, Posit, Postulate, Pretence, Pretend, Profess, Pulture, Purport, Puture, Revendicate, Right, Set-off, Sue, Title

Claimant Irredentist, Petitioner, Pot-waller, Pretender, Prospector, Tichborne, Usurper

Clairvoyance, **Clairvoyancy** ESP, Fey, Insight, Lucidity, Psiphenomena, Taisch, Taish, Tel(a)esthesia, Telegnosis

Clam Bivalve, Cohog, Geoduck, Giant, Gweduc, Littleneck, Mollusc, Mya,

Quahang, Quahog, Soft-shell, Tridacna, Venus

Clamant Vociferous

Clamber Climb, Crawl, Scramble, Spra(i)ckle, Sprauchle

Clammy Algid, Damp, Dank, Moist, Sticky, Sweaty

Clamour(ing), Clamorous Blatant, Brouhaha, Din, Hubbub, Hue, Outcry, Racket, Raird, Reird, Rout, Shout, Strepitant, Uproar, Utis, Vociferate

Clamp Beartrap, Clinch, Coupler, Denver boot, Fasten, Grip, Holdfast, Jumar, Pinchcock, Potato-pit, Serrefine, Stirrup, Tread, Vice, Wheel

Clan(sman) Cameron, Clique, Gens, Gentile, Group, Horde, Kiltie, Kindred, Name, Phratry, Phyle, Sect, Sept, Society, Stewart, Stuart, Tribe

Clandestine Covert, Furtive, Secret, Underhand

Clang(er), Clanging, Clank Bell, Belleter, Boob, Boo-boo, Clash, Gong, Jangle, Plangent, Ring

Clap(per), Clapping Applaud, Blow, Castanet, Chop, Crotal, Dose, Jinglet, Peal, Thunder, Tonant

Claptrap Bilge, Blab, Bombast, Bunkum, Eyewash, Hokum, Rot, Tripe

Claque(ur) Fans, Hat, Laudator, Sycophant

Clara Bow, Butt

Claret Blood, Loll-shraub, Loll-shrob, Vin

Clarify, Clarifier Clear, Despumate, Dilucidate, Explain, Explicate, Finings, Purge, Refine, Render, Simplify

Clarinet Reed

Clarion Brassy, Clear, Trumpet

Clary Orval, Sage

Clash(ing) Bang, Clangour, Clank, Claver, Coincide, Collide, Conflict, Friction, Gossip, > IMPACT, Incident, Irreconcilable, Jar, Loud, Missuit, Shock, Showdown, Strike, Swash

Clasp(ing) Adpress, Agraffe, Amplexus, Barrette, Brooch, Button, Catch, Chape, Clip, Embrace, Fibula, Grasp, Hasp, Hesp, Hook, Hug, Inarm, Interdigitate, Link, Morse, Ochreate, Ouch, Tach(e), Tie, Unite

Class(ification), Classify, Classy Acorn, Arrange, Assort, Bourgeois(ie), Bracket, Brand, Breed, Business, Cabin, Canaille, Caste, > CATEGORY, Chattering, Cheder, Cl, Clan, Clerisy, Clinic, Club, Course, Criminal, Dewey, Digest, Division, Economy, Estate, Evening, Faction, First, Form, Genera, Gentry, Genus, > GRADE, Group, Harvard, Heder, Hubble, Ilk, Keep-fit, Kohanga Reo, League, Life, Linn(a)ean, List, Lower, Mammal, Master, Middle, Number, Order, Phonetics, Phylum, Pigeon-hole, Pleb(eian), Proper, Race, Range, Rank, Rate, Rating, Reception, Remove, Salariat, Second, Seminar, Shell, Siege, Social, Sort(ation), Spectral, Steerage, Stratum, Stream, Syntax, Taxonomy, Teach-in, Third, Tony, Tourist, Tribe, Tutorial, > TYPE, U, Universal, Upper, Varna, Water, Working, World, Year

Classic(al), Classics, Classicist Ageless, Ancient, Basic, Derby, Elzevir, Grecian, Greek, Humane, Leger, Literature, Pliny, Purist, Roman, Standard, Traditional, Vintage

Clatch Blunk, Smear, Spoil

Clatter Bicker, Charivari, Clack, Din, Noise, Rattle

Clause Apodosis, Article, Basket, Condition, Conscience, Coordinate, Dependent, Disability, Endorsement, Escalator, Escape, Exclusion, Exemption, Filioque, Four, Golden parachute, Grandfather, Independent, Main, Member, Omnibus, Option, Poison-pill, Principal, Protasis, Proviso, Reddendum, Reported, Reservation, Rider, Salvo, Saving, Sentence, Subordinate, Tenendum, Testatum, Testing, Warrandice

Claw Chela, Claut, Crab, Dewclaw, Edate, Falcula, Grapple, Griff(e), Hook, Nail, Nipper, Pounce, Scrab, Scramb, Sere, Talent, > **TALON**, Tear, Telson, Tokay, Unguis

Clay Allophane, Argil, Argillite, Barbotine, B(e)auxite, Bentonite, Blaes, Blaise, Blaize, Bole, Calm, Cam, Caum, Ceramic, Charoset(h), China, Cimolite, Cloam, Clunch, Cob, Cornish, Earth, Engobe, Fango, Figuline, Fire, Fuller's earth, Gault, Glei, Gley, Gumbotil, Hardpan, Haroset(h), Illite, Kaolin, Laterite, Lithomarge, Loam, Lute, Malm, Marl, Meerschaum, Mire, Mortal, Mud, Papa, Pipeclay, Pipestone, Pise, Plastic, Plastilina, Porcelain, Potter's, Pottery, Puddle, Pug, Saggar(d), Sagger, Scroddle(d), Seggar, Sepiolite, Slip, Slurry, Smectite, Thill, Till(ite), Tumphy, Varve, Warrant, Warren, Wax

Clean(er), **Cleaning** Absterge, Bathbrick, Besom, Bleach, Bream, Broom, Careen, Catharise, Catharsis, Chaste, Clear, Daily, Debride, Decontaminate, Dentifrice, Depurate, Deterge(nt), Dhobi, Dialysis, Dicht, Douche, Dust(er), Eluant, Emunge, Enema, Erase, Ethnic, Evacuant, Evacuate, Expurgate, Fay, Fettle, Fey, Floss, Flush, Full, Grave, Groom, Gut, Heels, Hoover®, Hygienic, Immaculate, Innocent, Launder, Lave, Lustrum, Lye, Mouthwash, Mrs Mop(p), Mundify, Net, Overhaul, Porge, Pull-through, Pumice, Pure, Purgative, Purge, Ramrod, Rebite, Rub, Rump, Sandblast, Scaffie, Scavenge, Scour, Scrub, Shampoo, Snow-white, Soap, Soogee, Soogie, Soojey, Sponge, Spotless, Squeaky, Squeegee, Sterile, Sujee, Swab, Sweep, Tidy, Toothpick, Ultrasonic, Vac(uum), Valet, > **WASH**, Whistle, Wipe

Clear(ance), **Clearly** Absolve, Acquit, Aloof, Apparent, Bell, Berth, Bold, Bore, Brighten, Bus, Categorical, Clarify, Crystal, Decode, Definite, Delouse, Diaphanous, Dispel, Distinct, Downright, Earn, Eidetic, Evacuate, Evident, Exculpate, Exonerate, Explicit, Fair, Five-by-five, Gain, Headroom, Hyaline, Intelligible, Iron, Laund, Leap, Legible, Limpid, Lucid, Luculent, Manifest, Mop, Neat, Negotiate, Net(t), > **NOT CLEAR**, Observable, Obvious, Ope(n), Overleap, Palpable, Pellucid, Perspicuous, Plain, Play, Pratique, Predy, Pure, Quit, Rack, Realise, Remble, Rid, Ripple, Serene, Sheer, Shere, Slum, Sweep, Thro(ugh), Thwaite, Transire, Translucent, Transparent, Unblock, Vault, Vivid, Well, Windage, Wipe

Clearing Assart, Glade, Opening, Shire, Slash

Cleat Bitt, Wedge

Cleave, **Cleavage**, **Cleft** Adhere, Bisulcate, Chimney, Chine, Cling, Cloff, Cohere, Cut, Divide, Division, Divorce(ment), Gap, Ghaut, Goose-grass, Grike, Gryke, Pharynx, Rift, Riva, Scissure, Severance, Slack, Space, Spathose, Split

Clef Treble

Clematis Montana, Old man's beard, Traveller's joy, Virgin's-bower

Clemenceau Tiger

Clemency, **Clement** Ahimsa, Grace, Lenience, Lenity, Mercy, Mildness, Quarter, Temperate

Cleopatra Needle

Clergy(man), **Cleric(al)** Abbé, Canon, Cantor, Cardinal, Chaplain, Cleric, Clerk, Cloth, Curate, Curé, Deacon, Dean, Ecclesiast(ic), Goliard, Incumbent, Josser, Levite, Ministerial, Ministry, Non-juror, Non-usager, Notarial, Paperwork, Parson, Pastor, Pontifex, Pontiff, Preacher, Prebendary, Precentor, Prelate, Presbyter, Presenter, Priest, Primate, Prior, Proctor, Rabbi, Rector, Red-hat, Reverend, Rome-runner, Scribal, Secretarial, Shaveling, Shepherd, Sky pilot, Slope, Spin-text, Spirituality, Squarson, Subdeacon, Theologian, Vartabed, Vicar

Clergy-hater Misoclere

Clerk(s) Actuary, Baboo, Babu, Basoche, Cleric, Cratchit, Cursitor, Filing, Heep, Lay, Limb, Notary, Parish, Pen-driver, Penman, Penpusher, Poster, Prot(h)onotary, Protocolist, Recorder, Salaryman, Scribe, Secretariat, Shipping, Tally, Vicar, Writer

Clever(ness) Able, Adroit, Astute, Brainy, Bright, Canny, Cool, Cute, Daedal(e), Deep-browed, Deft, Genius, Gleg, Ingenious, Intellectual, Jackeen, Know-all, Natty, Nimblewit, Sage(ness), Shrewd, Skilful, Smart(y), Smarty-pants, Souple, Subtle

Clevis Becket

Cliché Banality, Boilerplate, Commonplace, Corn, Platitude, Saying, Tag

Click(er), Clicking Castanet, Catch, Forge, Pawl, Rale, Ratch(et), Snick, Succeed, Tchick, Ticktack

Client Customer, Gonk, John, Patron, Trick

Cliff(s) Beachy Head, Bluff, Cleve, Corniche, Crag, Craig, Escarp, Palisade, Precipice, Sca(u)r

Cliffhanger Samphire, Serial, Thriller

Climate Atmosphere, Attitude, Continental, Mood, Sun, Temperament, Temperature, Weather

Climax Apex, Apogee, Catastasis, Come, Crescendo, Crest, Crisis, Edaphic, End, Head, Heyday, Orgasm, Top, Zenith

Climb(er) Alpinist, Aralia, Aristolochia, Ascend, Breast, Briony, Bryony, Clamber, Clematis, Clusia, Cowage, Cowhage, Cowitch, Crampon, Creeper, Cucumber, Dodder, Heart-pea, Hedera, Ivy, Kie-kie, Kudzu, Lawyer, Layback, Liana, Liane, > MOUNT, Munro-bagger, Pareira, Parvenu, Prusik, Rat(t)an, Rise, Root, Scale, Scan, Scandent, Scansores, Sclim, Scramble, Shin, Shinny, Sklim, Smilax, Social, Speel, Steeplejack, Sty(e), Swarm, Timbo, Tuft-hunter, Udo, Up(hill), Uprun, Vine, Wistaria, With(y)wind, Woodbine, Zoom

Clinch Attach, Carriwitchet, Ensure, Fix, Quibble, Rivet, Secure, Settle

Cling(er), Clinging Adhere, Bur(r), Cherish, Cleave, Embrace, Hold, Hug, Ring, Tendril

Clinic Dental, Dispensary, Hospital, Hospitium, Mayo, Well-woman

Clink Gingle, Jail, Jingle, Lock up, Prison, Stir, Ting, Tinkle

Clinker Ash, Slag

Clip(ped), Clipper, Clipping Banana, Barrette, Brash, Bulldog, Butterfly, Cartridge, Clasp, Crocodile, Crop-ear, Crutch, Curt, Curtail, Cut, Cutty Sark, Dag, Dock, Dod, Excerpt, Fleece, Jubilee, Jumar, Krab, Lop, Pace, Paper, Pare, Peg, Prerupt, Prune, Roach, Scissel, Secateur, Shear, Ship, Shore, Shorn, Snip, Spring, Staccato, Tie, Tie-tack, Tinsnips, Topiarist, Trim

Clippy Cad, Conductor

Clique Cabal, Clan, Club, Coterie, Faction, Gang, Junta, Ring, Set

Clive Arcot

Cloak(room), Cloaks Aba, Abaya, Abba, Abolla, Amice, Bathroom, Buffalo-robe, Burnous, Capa, Cape, Capote, Caracalla, Cardinal, Cassock, Chasuble, Chimer(e), Chlamydes, Chlamys, Chuddah, Chuddar, Conceal, Cope, Cover, Disguise, Dissemble, Djellaba(h), Domino, Gabardine, Gaberdine, Gal(l)abea(h), Gal(l)abi(y)a(h), Gal(l)abi(y)eh, Gentlemen, Gents, Grego, Hall-robe, Heal, Hele, Himation, Hood, Inverness, Jelab, Jellaba, Joseph, Kaross, Manta, Manteel, Mant(e)let, Mantle, > MASK, Mourning, Mousquetaire, Mozetta, Opera, Paenula, Paletot, Pallium, Paludamentum, Pelisse, Pilch, Poncho, Powder-room, Rail, Revestry, Rocklay, Rokelay, Roquelaure, Sagum, Sarafan, Scapular, > SCREEN, Shroud, Swathe, Talma, Toga, Vestiary, Vestry, Visite

Clobber Anoint, Dress, Garb, Habiliments, Lam, Tack

Clock Alarm, Ammonia, Analogue, Astronomical, Atomic, Beetle, Big Ben, Biological, Blowball, Body, Bracket, Bundy, Caesium, Carriage, Clepsydra, Cuckoo, Dandelion, Digital, Doomsday, Floral, Grandfather, Grandmother, Hit, Knock, Long case, Meter, Parliament, Quartz, Repeater, Sandglass, Solarium, Speaking, Speedo, Strike, Sundial, Tell-tale, Time(r), Turret, Wag at the wa', Water

Clockmaker Fromanteel, Graham, Harrison, Knibb, Mudge, Tompion

Clockwise Deasil, Deasiul, Deasoil, Deiseal, Deisheal

Clockwork Precision, Regular

Clod Clumsy, Divot, Glebe, Lump, Mool, Mould, Put(t), Scraw, Sod, Stupid, Turf

Clog Accloy, Ball, Block, Clam, Crowd, Dance, Fur, Galosh, Golosh, Hamper, Jam, Lump, Mire, Obstruct, Overshoe, Patten, Sabot

Cloisonné Shippo

Cloister Arcade, Confine, Cortile, Immure, Monastery, Mure, Refuge

Clone, **Cloning** Ramet, Reproduce, Therapeutic

Cloots Worricow

Close(d), **Closing**, **Closure** Airless, Alongside, Atresia, Block, Boon, By, Cadence, Clammy, Clap, Clench, Complete, Cone off, Court, Dear, Debar, Dense, > **END**, Epilogue, Ewest, Finale, Gare, Grapple, Handy, Hard, Hard by, Imminent, Inbye, Infibulate, Intent, Intimate, Lock, Lucken, Marginal, Mean, Miserly, Muggy, Mure, Narre, Narrow, Near, Nearhand, Neist, Nie, Niggardly, Nigh, Nip and tuck, Obturate, Occlude, Occlusion, Oppressive, Parochial, Precinct, Reserved, Reticent, Seal, Secret, Serre, Serried, Serry, Shet, Shut(ter), Shutdown, Silly, Slam, Snug, Stap, Sticky, Stuffy, Sultry, Tailgate, Temenos, Tight, Uproll, Warm, Yard

Close-cropped Crewcut, Not-pated

Close-fitting Skintight, Slinky, Tight

Closet Cabinet, Confine, Cubicle, Cupboard, Dooket, Earth, Locker, Safe, Wardrobe, WC, Zeta

Close-up Detail, Fill, Shut, Stop, Zoom

Closing-time Eleven, End

Clot(ting) Agglutinate, Ass, Clag, Clump, Coagulate, Congeal, Crassamentum, Cruor, Curdle, Dag, Embolism, Embolus, Gel, Globule, Gob, Gout, Grume, Incrassate, Incrust, Jell, Lapper, Lopper, > **LUMP**, Mass, Prothrombin, Splatch, Stupid, Thicken, Thrombosis, Thrombus

Cloth Antependium, Carmelite, Clergy, Cloot, Clout, Dishrag, Duster, > **FABRIC**, > **FELT**, Frocking, Frontal, Gremial, Loin, Lungi, > **MATERIAL**, Nap, Napery, Napje, Nappie, Needlework, Netting, Pall, Pane, Pilch, Priesthood, Print(er), Purificator, Puttee, Putty, Rag, Raiment, Roll, Sashing, Scarlet, Serviette, Sheet, Sheeting, Shoddy, Stripe, Stuff, Sudarium, Supper, Sweatband, T, Tapestry, Tea, > **TEXTILE**, Throw, Tissue, Vernicle, Veronica, Washrag, Whole

● **CLOTHS**
●
●

1 letter:	Web	Drab	Ikat
J®		Duck	Kelt
	4 letters:	Fent	Knit
3 letters:	Aida	Gair	Lamé
Abb	Baft	Haik	Lawn
Rep	Ciré	Harn	Leno
Say	Doek	Hyke	Line

Mull
Nude
Pina
Puke
Rund
Shag
Slop
Sulu
Wire
Wool

5 letters:
Atlas
Baize
Beige
Binca
Budge
Chino
Crash
Crepe
Denim
Dobby
Drill
Duroy
Fanon
Foulé
Frisé
Gauze
Gazar
Grass
Gunny
Haick
Honan
Jaspe
Kanga
Kente
Khadi
Khaki
Kikoi
Linen
Llama
Loden
Lurex®
Lycra®
Moiré
Mongo
Monks
Mummy
Mungo
Ninon
Orlon®
Panel

Panne
Perse
Pilot
Piqué
Plaid
Plush
Poult
Rayon
Scrim
Serge
Slops
Stupe
Surah
Surat
Surge
Tabby
Tamin
Tammy
Terry
Tibet
Toile
Towel
Tulle
Tweed
Tweel
Twill
Union
Voile
Wigan

6 letters:
Aertex®
Alpaca
Angora
Armure
Barège
Beaver
Bouclé
Broche
Burlap
Burnet
Burrel
Byssus
Caddis
Calico
Camlet
Camlot
Canvas
Chintz
Cilice
Cloqué
Coburg

Coutil
Covert
Crepon
Cubica
Cyprus
Damask
Devoré
Dialon®
Dimity
Domett
Dossal
Dossel
Dowlas
Duffel
Duffle
Dupion
Durrie
Etamin
Faille
Fannel
Frieze
Gloria
Greige
Gurrah
Haique
Harden
Herden
Hodden
Hoddin
Humhum
Hurden
Jersey
Kersey
Khanga
Kincob
Lampas
Madras
Medley
Melton
Merino
Mohair
Mongoe
Moreen
Muleta
Muslin
Mutton
Nankin
Oxford
Pongee
Rateen
Ratine
Runner

Russel
Samite
Satara
Sateen
Saxony
Sendal
Shalli
Sherpa
Sindon
Soneri
Stroud
Tamine
Tartan
Tencel®
Thibet
Tricot
Velour
Velure
Velvet
Vicuna
Wadmal
Wincey
Winsey

7 letters:
Abattre
Alamode
Alepine
Baracan
Batiste
Brocade
Cabbage
Cambric
Camelot
Challie
Challis
Cheviot
Chiffon
Crombie
Cypress
Delaine
Dhurrie
Doeskin
Dorneck
Dornick
Drabbet
Drapery
Droguet
Drugget
Duvetyn
Etamine
Faconné

- Fannell
- Fishnet
- Flannel
- Foulard
- Fustian
- Galatea
- Genappe
- Gingham
- Gore-tex®
- Grogram
- Hessian
- Holland
- Hopsack
- Jaconet
- Jamdani
- Khaddar
- Kitenge
- Lockram
- Mockado
- Nankeen
- Oilskin
- Organza
- Orleans
- Ottoman
- Paisley
- Percale
- Rabanna
- Raploch
- Raschel
- Ratteen
- Rattine
- Sacking
- Sagathy
- Schappe
- Silesia
- Sinamay
- Spandex®
- Stammel
- Tabaret
- Tabinet
- Taffeta
- Tiffany
- Tussore
- Viyella®
- Wadmaal
- Webbing
- Woolsey
- Worsted
- Zanella

8 letters:
- Aircraft

Algerine
American
Armozeen
Armozine
Arresine
Bagheera
Barathea
Barracan
Bayadere
Bobbinet
Brocatel
Cameline
Cashmere
Casimere
Celanese
Chambray
Chamelot
Chenille
Ciclaton
Corduroy
Corporal
Coteline
Coutille
Cretonne
Drabette
Duchesse
Dungaree
Duvetine
Duvetyne
Eolienne
Gambroon
Gossamer
Homespun
Jacquard
Jeanette
Lava-lava
Lustring
Mackinaw
Mantling
Marcella
Marocain
Mazarine
Moleskin
Moquette
Nainsook
Organdie
Osnaburg
Pashmina
Prunella
Rodevore
Sarcenet
Sarsenet

Shabrack
Shalloon
Shantung
Sicilian
Swanskin
Tabbinet
Tarlatan
Toilinet
Whipcord
Wild silk
Zibeline

9 letters:
Aeroplane
Balzarine
Bengaline
Bombasine
Calamanco
Cassimere
Cerecloth
Charmeuse®
Ciclatoun
Corporale
Cottonade
Crepoline
Crimplene®
Crinoline
Evenweave
Fabrikoid®
Farandine
Filoselle
Folk-weave
Gaberdine
Georgette
Grenadine
Grosgrain
Haircloth
Horsehair
Indiennes
Levantine
Longcloth
Mandilion
Mandylion
Marseille
Matelassé
Messaline
Open-weave
Overcheck
Paramatta
Penistone
Percaline
Persienne

Pinstripe
Polyester
Ravenduck
Sailcloth
Sharkskin
Silkaline
Stockinet
Swansdown
Tarpaulin
Tricotine
Velveteen
Wire gauze
Worcester
Zibelline

10 letters:
Balbriggan
Broadcloth
Brocatelle
Candlewick
Farrandine
Fearnought
Ferrandine
Florentine
Geotextile
Kerseymere
Lutestring
Mousseline
Needlecord
Parramatta
Polycotton
Ravensduck
Seersucker
Shabracque
Sicilienne
Tattersall
Toilinette
Tuftaffeta
Winceyette

11 letters:
Abercrombie
Cloth of gold
Dotted Swiss
Drap-de-berry
Dreadnought
Hammercloth
Interfacing
Kendal green
Marquisette
Nun's veiling
Sempiternum

- Stockinette
- Stretch knit
- Swiss muslin

12 letters:
Brilliantine
Crepe de chine

Leather-cloth

13 letters:
Linsey-woolsey

Cloth-designing Batik
Clothe(s), Clothing, Clothed Apparel, Array, Attire, Baggies, Besee, Bib and tucker, Cape, Casuals, Chasuble, Choli, Cits, Clad, Clericals, Clobber, Coat, Combinations, Coordinates, Costume, Cour, Cover, Croptop, Dicht, Dight, Don, Drag, > DRESS, Duds, Emboss, Endue, Finery, Frippery, Garb, Garments, Gear, Gere, Get-up, Glad rags, Grave, Habit, Haute couture, Innerwear, Judogi, Jumps, Kimono, Layette, Mocker, Outfit, Pannicle, Plain, Raggery, Rag trade, Raiment, Rami, Rigout, Robes, Samfoo, Samfu, Schmutter, Scungies, Shmatte, Shroud, Slops, Sunday best, Swaddling, Swathe, Swothling, Tackle, Togs, Tracksuit, Trappings, Trousseau, Tweeds, Two-piece, Vernicle, Vestiary, Vestiture, Vestment, Wardrobe, Watteau, Weeds, Widow's weeds, Workwear, Yclad, Ycled
Clothes horse Airer, Winterhedge
Cloud(ing), Clouded, Cloudiness, Cloudy Altocumulus, Altostratus, Banner, Benight, C, Cataract, Cirrocumulus, Cirrostratus, Cirrus, Coalsack, Coma, Contrail, Crab Nebula, Cumulonimbus, Cumulus, Dim, Dull, Emission nebula, Fog, Fractocumulus, Fractostratus, Funnel, Goat's hair, Haze, Horsehead Nebula, Infuscate, Magellanic, Mare's tail, Milky, Mist, Molecular, Mushroom, Nacreous, Nephele, Nephelometer, Nepho-, Nimbostratus, Nimbus, Nubecula, Nubilous, Nuée ardente, Obscure, Octa, Okta, Oort, Overcast, Pall, Pother, Rack, Stain, Storm, Stratocumulus, Stratus, Thunderhead, Turbid, Virga, War, Water-dog, Woolpack, Zero-zero
Cloudberry Mountain bramble
Cloudless Serene
Clough Dale, Gorge, Ravine
Clout Belt, Cloth, Hit, Influence, Lap(pie), Lapje, Pull, Raddle
Clove Chive, Eugenia, Rose-apple, Split
Clover Alfalfa, Alsike, Berseem, Calvary, Cinque, Cow-grass, Four-leaf, Hare's foot, Japan, Ladino, Lespedeza, Medic(k), Melilot, Owl's, Pin, Rabbit-foot, Red, Serradella, Serradilla, Shamrock, Souple, Sucklers, Sweet, Trefoil, Trilobe, White
Clown(ish) Antic, Antick, August(e), Boor, Bor(r)el, Buffoon, Carl, Chough, Chuff, Clout-shoe, Coco, > COMEDIAN, Comic, Costard, Daff, Feste, Froth, Girner, Gobbo, Goon, Gracioso, Grimaldi, Harlequin, Hob, Idiot, Jack-pudding, Jester, Joey, Joker, Joskin, Leno, Merry Andrew, Mountebank, Nedda, Nervo, Peasant, Pickle-herring, Pierrot, Put, Rustic, Slouch, Thalian, Touchstone, Trinculo, Wag, Zany
Cloy(ing) Choke, Clog, Glut, Pall, Satiate, Surfeit, Sweet
Club(s), Club-like Adelphi, Airn, Almack's, Alpeen, Apex, Army and Navy, Artel, Association, Athen(a)eum, Baffy, Band(y), Basto, Bat, Bath, Beefsteak, Blackjack, Blaster, Bludgeon, Boodles, Bourdon, Brassie, Brook's, Bulger, C, Card, Carlton, Caterpillar, Cavalry, Chigiriki, Clavate, Cleek, Clip-joint, Combine, Conservative, Constitutional, Cordeliers, Cosh, Cotton, Country, Crockford's, Cudgel, Devonshire, Disco(theque), Driver, Driving iron, Drones, Fan, Fascio, Feuillant, Fustigate, Garrick, Glee, Golf, Guards, Guild, Hampden, Hell-fire, Honky-tonk, Indian, Investment, Iron, Jacobin, Jigger, Jockey, Junior Carlton, Kennel, Kierie, Kiri, Kitcat, Kiwanis, Knobkerrie, Landsdowne, Lathi, League, Leander, Lions, Lofter, Luncheon, Mace, Mallet, Mashie, Maul, Mell,

Mere, Meri, Mess, Midiron, Monday, National Liberal, Niblick, Night(stick), Nightspot, Nitery, Nulla(-nulla), Oddfellows, Patu, Pitching wedge, Polt, Priest, Provident, Pudding, Putter, Quarterstaff, RAC, Reform, Ring, Rota, Rotarian, Rotary, Round Table, Sand wedge, Savage, Savile, Shillelagh, Slate, Society, Soroptimist, Sorosis, Spoon, Spot, Spurs, Strike, Strip, Thatched House, Tong, Travellers, Trefoil, Truncheon, Trunnion, Union, United Services, Variety, Waddy, Wedge, White's, Wood, Youth

Club-foot Kyllosis, Polt-foot, Talipes, Varus

Clubman Member

Club-rush Deer-hair, Scirpus, Sedge

Cluck Chirrup, Dent

Clue Across, Anagram, Ball, Charade, Clave, Dabs, Down, > HINT, Inkling, Key, Lead, Light, Rebus, Scent, Scooby(doo), Signpost, Thread, Tip

Clueless Ignorant

Clump Cluster, Finial, Knot, Mass, Mot(te), Patch, Plump, Tread, Tuft, Tump, Tussock

▷ **Clumsily** *may indicate* an anagram

Clumsy Artless, Awkward, Bauchle, Bungling, Butterfingers, Cack-handed, Calf, Chuckle, Clatch, Clodhopper, Cumbersome, Dub, Dutch, Galoot, Gauche, Gimp, Ham(-fisted), Heavy-handed, Horse-godmother, Inapt, Inelegant, Inept, Inexpert, Klutz, Lob, Loutish, Lubbard, Lubber, Lummox, Lumpish, Maladroit, Mauther, Mawr, Mawther, Messy, Mor, Nerd, Nurd, Off-ox, Palooka, Plonking, Rough, S(c)hlemiel, Schlemihl, Spastic, Spaz(zy), Squab, Stot, Swab, Swob, Taupie, Tawpie, Two-fisted, Ungain, Unskilful, Unwieldy

Cluster Assemble, Bunch, Clump, Collection, Constellate, Conurbation, Corymb, Cyme, Gather, Globular, Glomeration, Knot, Oakleaf, Packet, Plump, Raceme, Sheaf, Sorus, Strap, Thyrse, Truss, Tuffe, Tuft, Umbel, Verticillaster

Clutch Battery, Brood, Chickens, Clasp, Cling, Eggs, Friction, Glaum, Grab, > GRASP, Gripe, Nest, Seize, Sitting, Squeeze

Clutter Confusion, Litter, Mess, Rummage

Coach Battlebus, Berlin, Bogie, Bus, Car, Carriage, Chara, Clerestory, Crammer, Diligence, Dilly, Double-decker, Drag, Edifier, Fly, Four-in-hand, Gig, Hackney, Landau(let), Life, Microbus, Phaeton, Post chaise, Pullman, Railcar, Rattler, Repetiteur, Saloon, Shay, Sleeper, Slip, Sobriety, Stage, Surrey, Tally(-ho), Teach(er), Thoroughbrace, Train(er), Tutor, Voiture

Coach-horse Rove-beetle

Coachman Automedon, Bunene, Coachy, Dragsman, Jarvey, Jehu, John

Coagulant, **Coagulate**, **Coagulation** Cautery, Clot, Congeal, Curds, Jell, Rennet, Run, Runnet, Set, Solidify

Coal Anthracite, Bituminous, Black diamonds, Brown, Burgee, Cannel, Cherry, Clinker, Coom, Crow, Culm, Dice, Eldin, Ember, Fusain, Gas, Gathering, Hard, Jud, Knob, Lignite, Maceral, Mineral, Nut, Open-cast, Paper, Purse, Sapropelite, Score, Slack, Soft, Splint, Steam, Vitrain, Wallsend, White, Wood

Coalesce(nce) Amalgamate, Concrete, Fuse, Merge, Sintery, Synaloepha, Unite

Coalfish Saith

Coalition Alliance, Bloc, Janata, Merger, Rainbow, Tie

Coal-tar Cresol, Indene

Coal-tub Corf, Dan, Scuttle

Coarse(ness) Base, Blowzy, Bran, Broad, Common, Crude, Dowlas, Earthy, Fisherman, Foul, Grained, Grobian, Gross, Grossièreté, Haggery, Ham, Illbred, Indelicate, Low-bred, Plebeian, Rabelaisian, Rank, Rappee, Raunchy, Ribald, Rough, Rudas, Rude, Sackcloth, Semple, Slob, Sotadic, Unrefined, Vulgar

Coast(al) Barbary, Beach, Bight, Caird, Causeway, Coromandel, Costa, Drift, Freewheel, Glide, Gold, Hard, Ivory, Littoral, Longshore, Malabar, Maritime, Murman(sk), Orarian, Riviera, Seaboard, Seafront, Seaside, > **SHORE**, Slave, Sledge, Strand, Toboggan

Coaster Beermat, Drog(h)er, Mat, Roller, Ship

Coastguard CG, Gobby

Coastline Watermark

Coast-road Corniche

Coat(ing) Abaya, Ab(b)a, Achkan, Acton, Admiral, Anarak, Anodise, Anorak, Balmacaan, Barathea, Bathrobe, Belton, Benjamin, Blazer, Box, British warm, Buff, Buff-jerkin, Calcimine, Car, Chesterfield, Cladding, Claw-hammer, Clearcole, Cloak, Clutch, Cocoon, Coolie, Cover, Covert, Creosote, Crust(a), Cutaway, Doggett's, Dress, Duffel, Duster, Electroplate, Enamel, Encrust, Exine, Extine, Fearnought, Film, Fleece, Frock, Fur, Gabardine, Galvanise, Gambeson, Ganoin, Glaze, Grego, Ground, Ha(c)queton, Hair, Happi, Impasto, Integument, Inverness, Jack(et), Jemmy, Jerkin, Jodhpuri, Joseph, Jump, Jupon, Lacquer, Lammie, Lammy, Layer, Loden, Mac, Mackinaw, Matinee, Metallise, Morning, Newmarket, > **OVERCOAT**, Paint, Paletot, Palla, Parka, Parkee, Passivate, Patinate, Pebbledash, Pelage, Pelisse, Perfuse, Peridium, Petersham, Plate, Polo, Pos(h)teen, Primer, Primine, Prince Albert, Raglan, Redingote, Resin, Resist, Riding, Roquelaure, Sack, Saque, Sclera, Seal, Sheepskin, Shellac, Sherardise, Sherwani, Silver, Skinwork, Spencer, Sports, Stadium, Surtout, Swagger, Swallowtail(ed), Tabard, Taglioni, Tail, Tar, Teflon, Tent, Top, Trench, Truss, Trusty, Tunic, Tuxedo, Ulster(ette), Underseal, Veneer, Verdigris, Warm, Wash, Windjammer, Wool, Wrap-rascal, Zamarra, Zamarro, Zinc

Coat of arms Crest, Hatchment

Coat-tail Flap

Coax Blandish, Blarney, Cajole, Carn(e)y, Cuittle, Flatter, Lure, Persuade, Wheedle, Whilly(wha), Whillywhaw

Cob Hazel(nut), Horse

Cobalt Co, Zaffer, Zaffre

Cobble(s), Cobblers Claptrap, Cosier, Cozier, Mend, Patch, Rot, Snob, Soutar, Souter, Sowter, Stone, Sutor, Twaddle, Vamp

Cobra King

Cobweb(by) Arachnoid, Araneous, Gossamer, Snare, Trap

Cocaine Basuco, C, Charlie, Coke, Crystal, Freebase, Moonrock, Nose candy, Number, Ready-wash, Snow

Coccid Wax-insect

Cock(y) Alectryon, Ball, Capon, Chanticleer, Chaparral, Erect, Escape, Fighting, Flip, Fowl, France, Fugie, Half, Hay, Heath, Jack-the-lad, Jaunty, Midden, Penis, Roadrunner, Robin, Rooster, Shake-bag, Snook, Strut, Swaggering, Tilt, Turkey, Vain, Valve, Vane

Cock-a-hoop Crowing, Elated

Cockatoo Bird, Corella, Galah, Leadbeater's, Major Mitchell, Parrot

Cockboat Cog

Cockchafer Humbuzz, Maybug

Cocker Blenheim, Cuiter, Spaniel

Cockeyed Agee, Askew, Skewwhiff

Cockfight Main

Cockle Bulge, Crease, Wrinkle

▷ **Cockle(s)** *may indicate* an anagram

Cockney 'Arriet, 'Arry, Bow, Eastender, Londoner, Londonese
▷ **Cockney** *may indicate* a missing h
Cockpit Greenhouse, Well
Cockroach Archy, Beetle, Black beetle, Croton bug, German, Oriental, Orthoptera
▶ **Cockscomb** *see* COXCOMB
Cocktail Alexander, Aperitif, Atomic, Bellini, Bloody Mary, Buck's fizz, Bumbo, Cobbler, Cold duck, Crusta, Daiquiri, > DRINK, Egg-flip, Fruit, Fustian, Gibson, Gimlet, Harvey Wallbanger, Highball, > HORSE, Julep, Manhattan, Margarita, Martini®, Melange, Mix, Molotov, Old-fashioned, Piña colada, Pink lady, Prawn, Punch, Rickey, Rusty nail, Sangaree, Sangria, Sazerac®, Screwdriver, Sherry cobbler, Side-car, Snowball, Spritzer, Stengah, Stinger, Swizzle, Tom Collins, Twist, White-lady
Cocoa Criollo, Nib(s)
Coconut Coco-de-mer, Coir, Copra, Head, Madafu, Toddy-palm
Cocoon Dupion, Mother, Swathe, Trehala
Cod Bag, Cape, Coalfish, Fish, Gade, Gadus, Haberdine, Keeling, Kid, Lob, Man, Morrhua, Murray, Red, Saith, Saltfish, Stockfish, Torsk, Tusk, Whiting
Coda End(ing), Epilogue, Rondo, Tail
Coddle Cosset, Molly, Nancy, Pamper, Pet, Poach
Code, Coding Access, Alphanumeric, Amalfitan, Area, Bar, Binary, Bushido, Canon, Character, Cipher, City, Civil, Clarendon, Codex, Colour, Computing, Condition, Country, Cryptogram, Cryptograph, Dialling, Disciplinary, Dogma, Dress, DX, EBCDIC, Enigma, Error, Escape, Ethics, Fuero, Genetic, Gray, Green Cross, Hammurabic, Highway, Hollerith, Iddy-umpty, Justinian, MAC, Machine, Morse, Napoleon(ic), Object, Omerta, Opcode, Penal, PGP, Pindaric, Postal, Price, Rulebook, Scytale, Signal, Sort, Source, STD, Talmud, Time, Twelve Tables, Zip
Code-breaker Malpractitioner
Codger Buffer, Fellow
Codicil Addition, Label, PS
Codon Initiator
Coefficient Correlation, Diffusion, Partition, Pearson's correlation, Spearman's rank-order, Transmission, Young modulus
Coelacanth Latimeria
Coerce, Coercion Bully, Compel, Dragoon, Gherao, Pressure, Railroad, Restrain, Threaten
Coffee, Coffee beans, Coffee pot Arabica, Brazil, Cafetiere, Cappuccino, Decaff, Demi-tasse, Espresso, Expresso, Filter, Gaelic, Gloria, Granules, Instant, Irish, Java, Latte, Macchiato, Mocha, Peaberry, Robusta, Rye, Tan, Triage, Turkish
Coffee-house Lloyd's
Coffer Ark, Box, Casket, Cassone, Chest, Lacunar, Locker
Coffin Bier, Casket, Hearse, Kist, Larnax, Sarcophagus, Shell, Wooden kimono, Wooden overcoat
Cog(ged) Contrate, Mitre-wheel, Nog, Pinion, Tooth
Cogent Compelling, Forceful, Good, Sound, Telling
Cogitate Deliberate, Mull, Muse, Ponder
Cognate Paronym
Cohabit Bed, Indwell, Share
Co-heir Parcener
Cohere(nt) Agglutinate, Clear, Cleave, Cling, Logical, Stick
Cohort Colleague, Crony, Soldier

Coif Calotte, Cap, Hood
Coiffure Hairdo, Pompadour, Tête
Coil(s), **Coiled** Armature, Bight, Bought, Choke, Clew, Clue, Curl, Fake, Fank, Furl, Hank, Helix, Ignition, Induction, Loading, Mortal, Moving, Primary, Rouleau, Scorpioid, Solenoid, Spark, Spiral, Spiraster, Spire, Tesla, Tickler, Toroid, Twine, Twirl, > WIND, Wound, Wreath, Writhe, Yoke
Coin Base, Bean, Bit, Cash, Change, Coign(e), Copper, Create, Doctor, Double-header, Dump(s), Fiver, Han(d)sel, Imperial, Invent, Make, Mill, Mint, Mite, > MONEY, Neoterise, Numismatic, Nummary, Piece, Plate, Proof, Shiner, Slip, Smelt, Specie, Stamp, Sterling, Strike, Tenner, Thick'un, Thin'un, Touchpiece, Unite, Unity

COINS

1 letter:
D

2 letters:
As
DM
Kr
Rd
Xu

3 letters:
Ban
Bar
Bob
Cob
Dam
Ecu
Fen
Fil
Fin
Flu
Hao
Jun
Kip
Lat
Lei
Lek
Leu
Lev
Lew
Mil
Mna
Moy
Ore
Pul
Pya
Red
Sen
Sol
Som
Sou
Won
Yen
Zuz

4 letters:
Anna
Baht
Bani
Birr
Buck
Cedi
Cent
Chon
Dibs
Dime
Doit
Dong
Dram
Duro
Euro
Fiat
Fils
Inti
Jack
Jane
Jiao
Kina
Kobo
Kuna
Kyat
Lari
Lion
Lira
Loti
Maik
Mark
Merk
Mina
Obol
Para
Paul
Peag
Peni
Peso
Pice
Pula
Puli
Punt
Rand
Real
Reis
Rial
Riel
Rock
Ryal
Sene
Sent
Slog
Tael
Taka
Tala
Toea
Tray
Trey
Vatu
Yuan
Zack

5 letters:
Agora
Angel
Asper
Aurar
Baiza
Bekah
Belga
Bodle
Broad
Brown
Butat
Butut
Chiao
Colon
Conto
Crore
Crown
Daric
Dibbs
Dinar
Dobra
Ducat
Eagle
Eyrir
Franc
Fugio
Gazet
Gerah
Groat
Grosz
Haler
Krona
Krone
Kroon
Kurus
Laari
Laree
Leone
Liard
Litas
Livre
Louis

- Lyart
- Maile
- Manat
- Maneh
- Mohur
- Mongo
- Mopus
- Naira
- Nakfa
- Ngwee
- Noble
- Obang
- Oscar
- Paisa
- Paolo
- Pence
- Pengo
- Penie
- Penni
- Penny
- Plack
- Pound
- Razoo
- Rider
- Royal
- Ruble
- Rupee
- Sceat
- Scudo
- Scute
- Semis
- Sente
- Shand
- Soldo
- Souon
- Sucre
- Sycee
- Tenge
- Thebe
- Tical
- Ticky
- Tolar
- Toman
- Tyiyn
- Zaire
- Zimbi
- Zloty

6 letters:
- Aureus
- Balboa
- Bawbee

Bender
Bezant
Boddle
Byzant
Canary
Centas
Colone
Copeck
Couter
Dalasi
Danace
Deaner
Décime
Denier
Derham
Dirham
Dirhem
Dodkin
Dollar
Double
Drachm
Ekuele
Escudo
Filler
Florin
Forint
Gilder
Gourde
Guinea
Gulden
Halala
Heller
Hryvna
Jitney
Kobang
Koruna
Kroner
Kroona
Kruger
Kwacha
Kwanza
Lepton
Likuta
Loonie
Makuta
Mancus
Markka
Mawpus
Pa'anga
Pagoda
Pataca
Pennia

Peseta
Pesewa
Qintar
Rappen
Rouble
Rupiah
Santum
Satang
Sceatt
Seniti
Sequin
Shekel
Sickle
Siglos
Somoni
Stater
Stiver
Stotin
Talent
Tanner
Tester
Teston
Thaler
Tickey
Toonie
Tugrik
Turner
Vellon
Wakiki

7 letters:
Afghani
Austral
Bolivar
Cardecu
Carolus
Centavo
Chetrum
Cordoba
Crusado
Drachma
Ekpwele
Guarani
Guilder
Hryvnya
Jacobus
Joannes
Kopiyka
Kreuzer
Lemoira
Metical
Millime

Milreis
Moidore
Ostmark
Ouguiya
Patrick
Piastre
Piefort
Pistole
Pollard
Quarter
Quetzal
Ringgit
Ruddock
Rufiyaa
Sextans
Solidus
Spanker
Tambala
Testoon
Testril
Thrimsa
Thrymsa
Tughrik
Unicorn
Xerafin

8 letters:
Brockage
Cardecue
Cruzeiro
Denarius
Doubloon
Ducatoon
Emalengi
Farthing
Groschen
Johannes
Kreutzer
Llangeni
Louis d'or
Maravedi
Millieme
Napoleon
Ngultrum
Picayune
Pistolet
Planchet
Portague
Portigue
Quadrans
Rigmarie
Semuncia

Sesterce
Shilling
Skilling
Solidare
Spur-rial
Spur-ryal
Stotinka
Xeraphim
Zecchino

9 letters:
Boliviano
Britannia
Centesimo
Dandiprat

Dandyprat
Didrachma
Dupondius
Half-eagle
Luckpenny
Pistareen
Rennminbi
Rix-dollar
Rose noble
Schilling
Sou marque
Sovereign
Spur-royal
Yellowboy
Zwanziger

10 letters:
Broadpiece
Chervonets
Krugerrand
Portcullis
Reichsmark
Siege-piece

11 letters:
Bonnet-piece
Deutschmark
Double eagle
Sword-dollar
Tetradrachm

12 letters:
Antoninianus

13 letters:
Rennminbi yuan

14 letters:
Three-farthings

18 letters:
Maria Theresa
   dollar

Coinage Currency, Invention, Nonce-word
Coincide(nt), **Coincidence** Accident, Chance, Consilience, Fit, Fluke, Homotaxis, Overlap, Rabat(to), Simultaneous, Synastry, Synchronise, Tally
Coke Chark, Coal, Cocaine, Kola
Col Pass, Poort, Saddle
Cold(-blooded) Ague, Algid, Arctic, Austere, Biting, Bitter, Bleak, C, Catarrh, Cauld(rife), Charity, Chill(y), Colubrine, Common, Coryza, Ectotherm, Frem(d), Fremit, Frigid, Frost(y), Gelid, Glacial, Hiemal, Icy, Impersonal, Jeel, Nippy, Nirlit, Parky, Passionless, Perishing, Piercing, Poikilotherm(ic), Polar, Psychro-, Remote, Rheumy, Rigor, Rume, Snap, Snell, Sniffles, Sour, Standoffish, Streamer, Subzero, Taters, Weed, Wintry
Cold sore Herpes, Shiver
Coldstream Borderer, Guard
Cole Colza, King, Nat, Porter
Colic Batts, Bots, Botts, Gripe, Lead, Painter's, Upset, Zinc
Collaborate, **Collaborator**, **Collaboration** Assist, Combine, > COOPERATE, Quisling, Synergy, Vichy
Collapse Apoplexy, Buckle, Cave, Conk, Crash, Crumble, Crumple, Debacle, Downfall, Fail(ure), Fall, Fold, Founder, Give, Implode, Inburst, Landslide, Meltdown, Phut, Purler, Rack, Rot, Ruin, Scat(ter), Sink, Slump, Stroke, Subside, Sunstroke, Swoon, Telescope, Tumble, Wilt, Wrack, Zonk
> **Collapsing** *may indicate* an anagram
Collar(ed) Arrest, Astrakhan, Bermuda, Bertha, Berthe, Bib, Bishop, Blue, Brecham, Buster, Butterfly, Button-down, Buttonhole, Capture, Carcanet, Chevesaile, Choke(r), Clerical, Collet, Dog, Esses, Eton, Falling-band, Flea, Gorget, Grandad, Hame, Head(stall), Holderbat, Horse, Jabot, Jampot, Karenni, Mandarin, Moran, Mousquetaire, Nab, Nail, Neckband, Necklet, Ox-bow, Peter Pan, Piccadell, Piccadillo, Piccadilly, Pikadell, Pink, Polo, Puritan, Rabato, Rebater, Rebato, Revers, Rollneck, Roman, Ruff, Sailor, Seize, Shawl, Steel, Storm, Tackle, Tappet, Tie-neck, Torque, Turndown, Turtleneck, Vandyke, Whisk, White, Wing, Yoke
Collation Comparison, Meal, Repast
Colleague Ally, Associate, Bedfellow, Confrère, Mate, Oppo, Partner
Collect(ion), **Collective(ly)**, **Collector** Accrue, Agglomerate, Aggregate, Album, Alms, Amass, Amildar, Ana, Anthology, Arcana, Assemble, Aumil, Bank, Bow, Budget, Bunch, Bundle, Burrell, Caboodle, Calm, Cap, Cete, Clowder,

Compendium, Compile, Congeries, Conglomerate, Covey, Cull, Dossier, Dustman, Earn, Egger, Exaltation, Exordial, Fest, (Fest)schrift, Florilegium, Gaggle, Garner, Gather, Gilbert, Glean, Glossary, Grice, Heap, Herd, Hive, Idant, In all, Jingbang, Job lot, Kit, Kitty, Levy, Loan, Magpie, Meal, Meet, Mein(e)y, Meinie, Menagerie, Menyie, Miscellany, Mish-mash, Montem, Murmuration, Museum, Muster, Nide, Offertory, Omnibus, Omnium-gatherum, Paddling, Pile, Plate, Pod, Post, Prayer, Quest, Raft, Raise, Recheat, Sedge, Serene, Set, Shoe, Siege, Skein, Smytrie, Sord, Sottisier, Sounder, Spring, Stand, Tahsildar, Team, Troop, Unkindness, Watch, Whipround, Wisp

▷ **Collection** *may indicate* an anagram

Collection-box Brod, Ladle, Rammle

Collectorate Taluk

College(s) Academy, All Souls, Alma Mater, Ampleforth, Balliol, Brasenose, Business, C, Caius, Campus, CAT, Cheltenham, Clare, Classical, Coed, Commercial, Community, Corpus, Cow, Cranwell, Downing, Electoral, Emmanuel, Eton, Exeter, Foundation, Girton, Hall, Herald's, Jail, Junior, Keble, King's, Lancing, Linacre, Lincoln, LSE, Lycée, Lyceum, Madras(s)a(h), Madressah, Magdalen(e), Medrese, Medresseh, Merton, Newnham, Nuffield, Open, Oriel, Poly, Polytechnic, Pontifical, Protonotariat, Queen's, Ruskin, Sacred, St Johns, Saliens, Sandhurst, Selwyn, Seminary, Sixth-form, Somerville, Sorbonne, Staff, Tech(nical), Technikon, Tertiary, Theologate, Training, Trinity, Tug, UMIST, Up, Village, Wadham, Winchester, Yeshwa(h)

Collide, Collision Afoul, Barge, Bird-strike, Bump, Cannon, Carom(bole), Clash, Dash, Fender-bender, Foul, Head-on, Impact, Into, Kiss, Meet, Pile-up, Rencounter, Strike, Thwack

Collie Bearded, Border, Dog, Kelpie, Kelpy, Rough, Sheepdog

Collier Geordie, Hoastman, Miner, Necklace, Patience, Ship

Colloid Gel, Lyophil(e), Sol

Collude, Collusive Abet, Cahoots, Conspire, Deceive

Colon Aspinwall, Sigmoid, Spastic, Transverse

Colonel Blimp, Bogey, Chinstrap, Col, Everard, Goldstick, Newcome, Nissen, Pride

Colonial, Colonist Ant, Antenatal, Boer, Creole, Emigré, Oecist, Oikist, Overseas, Phoenician, Pioneer, Planter, Polyp(e), Settler, Sicel(iot), Sikel(ian), Sikeliot, Stuyvesant, Swarm, Territorial

Colonnade Eustyle, File, Gallery, Porch, Portico, Stoa

Colony Aden, Charter, Cleruchy, Crown, Dependency, Hive, Hongkong, Nudist, Penal, Presidio, Proprietary, Rookery, Settlement, Swarm, Termitarium, Warren, Zambia

Colophony Rosin

Colossal > ENORMOUS, Epochal, Gigantic, Huge, Vast

Colosseum Amphitheatre

Colour(ed), Colouring, Colours Achromatic, Alizarin(e), Anil, An(n)atta, An(n)atto, Anthocyan, Aquamarine, Arnotto, Auburn, Bay, Bedye, Bice, Bisque, Bister, Bistre, Blee, Blue, Blush, Buff, Burgundy, C, Camel, Cap, Cappagh-brown, Cardinal, Cerise, Chica, Chromatic, Chrome, Complementary, Complexion, Coral, Crayon, Criant, Cyan, Day-Glo®, Distort, Dye, Ecru, Eosin, False, Filemot, Film, Flag, Florid, Flying, French navy, Gamboge, Gouache, Gules, Haem, > HUE, Ink, Irised, Isabel, Jet, Kalamkari, Lake, Leer, Lemon, Lilac, Lime, Local, Lovat, Lutein, Magenta, Maroon, Mauve, Metif, Nankeen, Navy, Oatmeal, Ochre, Olive, Or, Orange, Orpiment, Palette, Pastel, Peach, Philamot, Philomot, Pied, Pigment, Pochoir, Polychrome,

Primary, Prism, Prismatic, Process, Puke, Queen's, Reddle, Regimental, Reseda, Rince, Riot, Roucou, Rouge, Ruddle, Sand, Secondary, Sematic, Sepia, Shade, Sienna, Solferino, Solid, Spectrum, Startle, Tartrazine, Taupe, Teal, Tenne, Tenny, Tertiary, Tie-dye, Tinc(ture), Tinge, Tint, Titian, Tone, Ultramarine, Umber, Umbrage, Uvea, Vert

Colour blindness Daltonism, Deuteranopia, Dichrom(at)ism, Monochromatic, Protanomaly, Protanopia, Protanopic, Tritanopia

▷ **Coloured** *may indicate* an anagram

Colourful Abloom, Brave, Flamboyant, Flowery, Iridescent, Kaleidoscope, Opalescent, Splashy, Vivid

Colourless Albino, Bleak, Drab, Dull, Hyalite, Pallid, Pallor, Wan, White

Colt Cade, Foal, Gun, Sta(i)g, Teenager, Two-year-old

Columbine Aquilegia

Column(s), **Column foot** Agony, Anta, Atlantes, Clustered, Commentary, Control, Corinthian, Correspondence, Cylinder, Decastyle, Diastyle, Doric, Editorial, Eustyle, Fifth, File, Geological, Gossip, Hypostyle, Impost, Lat, Lonelyhearts, Monolith, Nelson's, Newel, Obelisk, Pericycle, Peristyle, Persian, Personal, Pilaster, > PILLAR, Pilotis, Prostyle, Rouleau, Row, Short, Spina, Spinal, Spine, Stalactite, Stalagmite, Steering, Stylobate, Systyle, Tabulate, Telamone, Third, Tige, Tore, Torus, Trajan's, Vertebral

Columnist Advertiser, Caryatid, Newsman, Stylite, Telamon, Writer

Coma(tose) Apoplexy, Crown, Sedated, Sleep, Torpor, Trance

Comb(er), **Combed**, **Combing** Alveolate, Beehive, Breaker, Card, Copple, Crest, Curry, Dredge, Fine-tooth, Hackle, Heckle, Hot, Kaim, Kame, Kangha, Kemb, Noils, Pecten, Rake, Red(d), Ripple(r), Scribble, Search, Small tooth, Smooth, Tease(l), Toaze, Tooth, Tose, Toze, Trawl, Wave

Combat(ant), **Combative** Argument, > BATTLE, Competitor, Conflict, Contest, Dispute, Duel, > FIGHT, Gladiator, Joust, Jujitsu, Just, Karate, Kendo, List, Mêlée, Militant, Oppose, Paintball, Protagonist, Spear-running, Unarmed, War

Combination, **Combine(d)**, **Combining** Accrete, Alligate, Ally, Amalgam, Associate, Axis, Bloc, Cartel, Cleave, Clique, Coalesce, Coalition, Composite, Concoction, Conflated, Conglomerate, Consortium, Coordinate, Crasis, Fuse, Group, Harvester, Integration, Join, Junta, Kartell, League, Meld, Merge(r), Mingle, Mixture, Perm(utation), Piece, Pool, Quill, Ring, Solvate, Splice, Syncretize, Synthesis, Terrace, Trona, Unite, Valency, Wed, Zaibatsu

Comb-like Ctenoid, Pecten

Combustible, **Combustion** Ardent, Fiery, Inflammable, Phlogistic, Phlogiston, Spontaneous, Wildfire

▷ **Combustible** *may indicate* an anagram

Come, **Coming (back)**, **Coming out** Advent, Anear, Anon, Appear, Approach, Ar(r), Arise, Arrive, Attend, Debouch, Derive, Emerge, Future, Happen, Iceman, Issue, Millenarian, Orgasm, Parousia, Pass, Pop, Respond, Second, Via

Comeback Boomerang, Bounce, Echo, Homer, Quip, Rally, Rearise, Rebound, Recovery, Repartee, Reply, Retort, Retour, Return, Reversion, Riposte

Comedian Benny, Buffoon, Chaplin, > CLOWN, Comic, Durante, Emery, Goon, Groucho, Hope, Joker, Karno, Leno, Quipster, Robey, Scream, Screwball, Tate, Tati, Tummler, Wag, Wise, Yell

Comedo Blackhead

Comedown Avale, Bathetic, Bathos, Disappointment, Drop, Letdown, Shower

Comedy Black, Com, Drama, Errors, Farce, High, Humour, Keystone, Knockabout, Lazzo, Low, Millamant, Musical, Situation, Slapstick, Thalia,

Travesty

Comely Beseen, Bonny, Fair, Goodly, Graceful, Jolly, Likely, Pleasing, Pretty, Proper

Comestible(s) Cate, Eats, Fare

Comet Geminid, Halley's, Kohoutek, Meteor, Oort cloud, Reindeer, Shoemaker-Levy 9, Vomet, Xiphias

Come through Weather

Comfort(er), Comforting Amenity, Analeptic, Balm, Bildad, Calm, Cheer, Cherish, Clover, Cold, Consolation, Console, Creature, Crumb, Dummy, Ease, Eliphaz, Featherbed, Reassure, Relief, Relieve, Scarf, Solace, Soothe, Succour, Zophar

Comfortable, Comfy Armchair, Bein, Canny, Cose, Cosh, Cosy, Couthie, Couthy, Cushy, Easy, Gemutlich, Heeled, Homely, Mumsy, Plum, Plushy, Relaxed, Rug, Snug, There, Tosh, Trig, Warm, Well, Well-to-do

Comic(al) Beano, Buff, Buffo(on), Bumpkin, Buster, Chaplin, Clown, > COMEDIAN, Dandy, Droll, Eagle, Facetious, Fields, > FUNNY, Gagster, Hardy, Horror, Jester, Knock-about, Laurel, Leno, Mag, Manga, Quizzical, Rich, Robey, Strip, Tati, Trial, Zany

Comma Inverted

Command(eer), Commanding, Commandment(s) Behest, Bid, Categorical imperative, Charge, Coerce, Control, Decalogue, Direction, Dominate, Domineer, Easy, Edict, Fiat, Fighter, Firman, Haw, Hest, High, Imperious, Impress, Instruction, Jussive, Mandate, Maritime, Mastery, Mitzvah, Mobile, > ORDER, Precept, Press, Requisition, Rule, Seize, Ukase, Warn, Warrant, Will, Wish, Writ

Commander Admiral, Ag(h)a, Barleycorn, Bey, Bloke, Blucher, Boss, Brennus, Brig, Caliph, Centurion, Cid, Decurion, Emir, Emperor, Field cornet, Generalissimo, Hetman, Hipparch, Imperator, Killadar, Leader, Manager, Marshal, Master, Meer, Mir, Moore, Officer, Overlord, Pendragon, Raglan, Seraskier, Shogun, Sirdar, Taxiarch, Trierarch, Turcopolier, Vaivode, Voivode, Waivode, Warlord, Wing

Commando Chindit(s), Fedayee(n), Green Beret, Raider, Ranger, SAS

Commemorate, Commemoration Encaenia, Epitaph, Eulogy, Keep, Memorial, Monument, Plaque, Remember

Commence Begin, Initiate, Open, Start

Commend(ation) Belaud, Bestow, Encomium, Entrust, Laud, Panegyric, > PRAISE, Roose, Tribute

Commensal Epizoon, Messmate

Commensurate Adequate, Enough, Equivalent, Relevant

Comment(ary), Commentator Analyst, Animadvert, Annotate, Apercu, Comm, Coryphaeus, Critic, Critique, Descant, Discuss, Editorial, Essay, Explain, Exposition, Expound, Footnote, Gemara, Gloss(ographer), Glosser, Hakam, Kibitz, Margin, Midrashim, Note, Par, Platitude, Postil, Remark, Running, Scholiast, Zohar

Commerce, Commercial Ad, Barter, Cabotage, Jingle, Marketable, Mercantile, Mercenary, Merchant, Shoppy, Simony, Trade, Traffic

Commercial traveller Drummer, Rep

Commiserate, Commiseration Compassion, Pity, Sympathise

Commission(er), Commissioned Authorise, Brevet, Brokerage, Charge, Charity, Countryside, Delegation, Depute, ECE, Employ, Engage, Envoy, Errand, European, Factor, High, Husbandage, Job, Kickback, Law, Magistrate, Mandate, Office(r), Official, Ombudsman, Order, Percentage, Perpetration,

Place, Poundage, Price, Rake-off, Resident, Roskill, Roving, Royal, Task, Task force, Trust, Wreck

Commit(al), **Commitment** Consign, Contract, Decision, Dedication, Delegate, Devotion, Do, Engage, Entrust, Enure, Impeachment, Perpetrate, Pledge, Rubicon

Committee Board, Body, Commission, Council, Group, Joint, Junta, Politburo, Presidium, Propaganda, Review body, Samiti, School, Select, Standing, Steering, Syndicate, Table, Vigilance, Watch, Works

Commode, **Commodious** Ample, Closestool, Roomy, Spacious

Commodities, **Commodity** Article, Futures, Gapeseed, Item, Physicals, Soft, Staple, Ware

Common(ly), **Commoner**, **Commons** As per usual, Average, Cad, Conventional, Diet, Dirt, Doctor's, Ealing, Eatables, Enclosure, Epicene, Everyday, Familiar, Fare, Folk, General, Green, Greenham, House, Law, Lay, Low, Lower House, Mark, Mere, MP, Mutual, Naff, Non-U, Normal, People, Pleb, Prevalent, Prole, Public, Related, Rife, Roturier, Ryfe, Scran, Sense, Shared, Stray, Tie, Tiers d'état, Trite, Tritical, Tuft, Tye, Use, > USUAL, Vile, Vul(gar), Vulgo, Vulgus, Widespread, Wimbledon

Commonplace Banal, Copybook, Hackneyed, Homely, Humdrum, Idée reçue, Mot, Ordinary, Philistine, Plain, Platitude, Prosaic, Quotidian, Trite, Workaday

Commonsense Gumption, Nous, Smeddum, Wit

Commonwealth Puerto Rico

Commotion Bluster, Bustle, Carfuffle, Clangour, Clatter, Curfuffle, Dirdam, Dirdum, Do, Dust, Ferment, Flap, Flurry, Fraise, Fuss, Hell, Hoo-ha(h), Hurry, Pother, Racket, Romage, Rort, Ruckus, Ruction, Rumpus, Shemozzle, Shindig, Shindy, Shivaree, Steery, Stir, Storm, Stushie, Tirrivee, Tirrivie, To-do, Toss, Tumult, Turmoil, Upheaval, Uproar, Whirl, Wroth

Communal, **Commune** Agapemone, Collective, Com, Meditate, Mir, Paris, Phalanstery, Public, Talk, Township

Communicate, **Communication** Ampex, Announce, Baud, Boyau, Cable, Channelling, Conversation, Convey, Cybernetic, E-mail, Expansive, Impart, Infobahn, Inform, Intelpost, Intelsat, Internet, Message, Nonverbal, Note, Oracy, Prestel®, Proxemics, Reach, Road, Semiotics, Signal, Tannoy®, Telepathy, Telex, Telstar, Tieline, Transmit, Utraquist, Viewdata

Communion Creed, Fellowship, Host, Housel, Intinction, Lord's Supper, Species, Viaticum

Communiqué Announcement, Statement

Communism, **Communist** Apparat(chik), Aspheterism, Bolshevist, Com, Comecon, Cominform, Comintern, Commo, Comsomol, Deviationist, Essene, Fourier, Khmer Rouge, Komsomol, Leninite, Maoist, Nomenklatura, Perfectionist, Pinko, Politburo, Populist, Red, Revisionism, Soviet, Spartacist, Stalinism, Tanky, Titoist, Trot, Vietcong, Vietminh

Communities, **Community** Alterne, Ashram, Biome, Body, Brook Farm, Brotherhood, Clachan, Climax, Coenobitism, Coenobium, Colonia, Colony, Consocies, Ecosystem, EEC, Enclave, European, Frat(e)ry, Global, Kahal, Kibbutz, Mesarch, Neighbourhood, People, Phyle, Public, Pueblo, Seral, Sere, Shtetl, Sisterhood, Society, Street, Toon, Town, Tribe, Ujamaa, Village, Virtual, Volost, Zupa

Commute(r) Change, Convert, Reduce, Straphanger, Travel

Como Lake, Perry

Compact Agreement, Cement, Concise, Conglobe, Covenant, Covin, Coyne, Dense, Entente, Fast, Firm, Flapjack, Hard, Knit, League, Match, Neat, Pledge,

Powder, Solid, Terse, Tight, Treaty, Well-knit

Companion(able) Achates, Arm candy, Associate, Attender, Barnacle, Bedfellow, Bonhomie, Bud(dy), Butty, CH, China, Comate, Comrade, Consort, Contubernal, Crony, Cupman, Duenna, Ephesian, Escort, Felibre, > **FELLOW**, Fere, Handbook, Helpmate, Mate, Pal, Pard, Playmate, Sidekick, Skaines mate, Stable, Thane, Thegn, Trojan, Vade-mecum

Company, **Companies** Actors, Artel, Ass, Assembly, Band, Bank, Battalion, Bevy, > **BUSINESS**, Bv, Cahoot, Cartel, Cast, Cavalcade, Chartered, CIA, Circle, City, Close, Club, Co, Conger, Consort, Cordwainers, Core, Corporation, Corps, Coy, Crew, Crowd, Decury, Dotcom, East India, Enterprise, Entourage, Faction, Finance, Fire, > **FIRM**, Flock, Free, Gang, Garrison, Ging, Guild, Haberdashers, Heap, Holding, Hudson's Bay, ICI, Inc, Indie, In-house, Intercourse, Investment, Jingbang, Joint-stock, Limited, Listed, Livery, Management, Maniple, Muster, Order, Organisation, Parent, Plc, Private, Public, Quoted, Rep(ertory), Room, SA, Sedge, Set, Set out, Shell, Siege, Sort, SpA, Stock, Subsidiary, Syndicate, Table, Team, Thiasus, Touring, Troop, Troupe, Trust, Twa, Two(some), Visitor, White

Compare(d), **Comparison** Analogy, Balance, Beside, Bracket, Collate, Confront, Contrast, Correspond, Cp, Equate, Liken, Match, Odious, Parallel, Relation, Simile, Weigh

Compartment Ballonet, Bay, Booth, Box, Carriage, Casemate, Cell, Chamber, Cofferdam, Cubbyhole, Cubicle, Dog box, Locellate, Loculament, Loculus, Panel, Partition, Pigeonhole, Pocket, Pod, Room, Room(ette), Severy, Stall, Till, Watertight

Compass Ambit, Area, Beam, Binnacle, Bounds, Bow, Gamut, Goniometer, Gyro, Gyromagnetic, Gyroscope, Infold, Magnetic, Mariner's, Needle, Orbit, Pelorus, Perimeter, Prismatic, Radio, > **RANGE**, Reach, Rhumb, Room, Scale, Sweep, Tessitura, Width

Compassion(ate) Aroha, Bleed(ing), Clemency, Commiseration, Empathy, Humane, Mercy, Pity, Samaritan, Sympathy

Compatible Consistent, Fit, Harmonious

Compatriot National

Compel(led), **Compulsion**, **Compulsive**, **Compulsory** Addiction, Coact, Coerce, Command, Constrain, Dragoon, Duress, Enforce, Extort, Fain, > **FORCE**, Gar, Make, Mandatory, Oblige, Pathological, Steamroller, Strongarm, Tyrannise

Compendium Breviate

Compensate, **Compensation** Amend(s), Balance, Boot, Comp, Counterbalance, Counterpoise, Damages, Demurrage, Guerdon, Offset, Payment, Recoup, Redress, Reparation, Reprisal, Requital, Restitution, Restore, Retaliation, Salvage, Satisfaction, Solatium, Wergild, X-factor

Compère Emcee, Host, MC, Presenter

Compete Contend, Emulate, Enter, Match, Outvie, Play, Rival, Vie

Competence, **Competent** Ability, Able, Adequate, Can, Capacity, Dab, Efficient, Fit, Responsible, Sui juris, Worthy

Competition, **Competitive**, **Competitor** Agonist, Backmarker, Bee, Biathlon, Candidate, Comper, Contest, Cup, Drive, Entrant, Event, Field, Freestyle, Gymkhana, Head-to-head, Heptathlon, Imperfect, Judoka, Karateka, Knockout, Match, Match-play, Open, Opponent, Pairs, Panellist, Pentathlon, Perfect, Player, Pro-am, Puissance, Race, Rally, Regatta, Repechage, Rival(ise), Rodeo, Show-jumping, Super G, Tension, Test, Tiger, Tournament, Tourney, Trial, Triallist, Wap(p)enshaw

Compile(r), **Compilation** Anthology, Arrange, Collect, Edit, Prepare, Segue,

Zadkiel

Complacent Babbitt, Fatuous, Joco, Pleasant, Self-satisfied, Smug

Complain(t), **Complainer** Adenoids, Affection, Affliction, Alas, Alastrim, Alopecia, Anaemia, Angashore, Angina, Asthma, Barrack, Beef, Bellyache, Bitch, Bleat, BSE, Carp, Cavil, Charge, Chorea, Colic, Crab, Cramp, Criticise, Diatribe, Disorder, Dropsy, Epidemic, Ergot, Exanthema, Girn, Gout, Gravamen, Groan, Grouch, Grouse, Growl, Grudge, Grumble, Grutch, Harangue, Hives, Hone, Hypochondria, > **ILLNESS**, Jeremiad, Kvetch, Lupus, Malady, Mange, Mean(e), Mein, Mene, Moan, Morphew, Mumps, Murmur, Nag, Natter, Neuralgia, Ologoan, Pertussis, Plica, Poor-mouth, Protest, Pule, Pyelitis, Querimony, Rail, Remonstrate, Repine, Rickets, Sapego, Sciatica, Scold, Sigh, Silicosis, Squawk, Staggers, Thrush, Tic, Tinea, Upset, Wheenge, Whimper, Whine, Whinge, Yammer, Yawp

Complaisant Agreeable, Flexible, Suave, Supple

Complement Alexin, Amount, Balance, Finish, Gang, Lot, Reciprocate

Complete(ly), **Completion** Absolute, Accomplish, Achieve, All, Arrant, Attain, Clean, Congenital, Consummate, Crown, Do, End, Entire, Finalise, Finish, Follow through, Fruition, Fulfil, Full, Full-blown, Hollow, Incept, Integral, In toto, One, Ouroboros, Out, Out and out, Perfect, Plenary, Quite, Ready, Sew-up, Sheer, Spang, Sum, Teetotal, Thorough, Total, Unanimous, Uncut, Unequivocal, Unmitigated, Whole (hog)

Complex(ity) Abstruse, Arcane, Castration, Compound, Difficult, Electra, Golgi, Hard, Heath Robinson, Immune, Inferiority, Intricate, Intrince, Involute, Knot, Manifold, Mixed, Multinucleate, Nest, Network, Obsession, Oedipus, Paranoid, Persecution, Phaedra, Superiority, Syndrome, Web

Complexion Aspect, Blee, Hue, Leer, Temper, Tint, View

Compliance, **Compliant**, **Comply** Agree, Assent, Conform, Deference, Docile, Follow, Hand-in-glove, Obey, Observe, Obtemper, Sequacious, Surrender, Wilco, Yield

Complicate(d), **Complication** Bewilder, Complex, Deep, Elaborate, Embroil, Implex, Intricate, Involve, Inweave, Node, Nodus, Perplex, Ramification, Rigmarole, Sequela, Snarl, Tangle, Tirlie-wirlie

▷ **Complicated** *may indicate* an anagram

Compliment(s) Baisemain, Bouquet, Congratulate, Devoirs, Douceur, Encomium, Flatter, Flummery, Praise, Soap, Trade-last, Tribute

Component Coherer, Constituent, Contact, CRT, Element, Factor, Guidance, Impedor, Inductor, Ingredient, Longeron, > **PART**, Pre-amp, Subunit, Tensor

Compose(d), **Composure** Aplomb, Arrange, Calm, Choreograph, Consist, Cool, > **CREATE**, Equanimity, Even, Face, Improvise, Indite, Lull, Notate, Orchestrate, Placid, Poise, Produce, Reconcile, Sangfroid, Sedate, Serenity, Settle, Soothe, Tranquil, Unruffled, Write

Composer Contrapunt(al)ist, Hymnist, Inditer, Inventor, Maker, Melodist, Musician, > **POET**, Serialist, Six, Songwriter, Symphonist, Triadist, Tunesmith, Writer

COMPOSERS

3 letters:	Arne	Bull	Ives
Bax	Bach	Byrd	Kern
	Berg	Cage	Lalo
4 letters:	Blow	Dima	Monk
Adam	Brel	Graf	Nono

Orff
Peri
Raff
Wolf

5 letters:
Auber
Auric
Balfe
Berio
Bizet
Bliss
Bloch
Boito
Boyce
Brian
Bruch
Crumb
D'Indy
Dukas
Elgar
Fauré
Field
Finzi
Glass
Gluck
Grieg
Harty
Haydn
Henze
Holst
Ibert
Lasso
Lehar
Liszt
Loewe
Lully
Parry
Prout
Ravel
Reger
Rossi
Satie
Sousa
Suppe
Tosti
Verdi
Watts
Weber
Weill
Zappa

6 letters:
Alfven
Arnold
Azione
Barber
Bartók
Berlin
Boulez
Brahms
Bridge
Burney
Busoni
Chopin
Coates
Delius
Duparc
Dvorák
Flotow
Franck
German
Glière
Glinka
Gounod
Handel
Hummel
Joplin
Kodaly
Lassus
Ligeti
Mahler
Mingus
Morley
Mozart
Ogolon
Pierne
Rameau
Rubbra
Schutz
Tallis
Varese
Wagner
Walton
Webern

7 letters:
Albeniz
Alberti
Allegri
Bantock
Bellini
Berlioz
Berners

Borodin
Britten
Brubeck
Copland
Corelli
Debussy
De Falla
Delibes
Dohnany
Dowland
Gibbons
Ireland
Janácek
Lambert
Mancini
Martinu
Milhaud
Nielsen
Novello
Ormandy
Poulenc
Puccini
Purcell
Purnell
Quilter
Rodgers
Rodrigo
Romberg
Rossini
Roussel
Salieri
Smetana
Stainer
Strauss
Tartini
Tippett
Vivaldi
Warlock
Xenakis
Youmans

8 letters:
Alaleona
Albinoni
Boughton
Bruckner
Chabrier
Chausson
Couperin
Gershwin
Gesualdo
Glazunov

Grainger
Granados
Honegger
Kreutzer
Marcello
Mascagni
Massenet
Messager
Messiaen
Paganini
Respighi
Schubert
Schumann
Scriabin
Sessions
Sibelius
Sondheim
Sullivan
Taverner
Telemann

9 letters:
Bacharach
Balakirev
Beethoven
Bernstein
Boulanger
Broughton
Buxtehude
Chaminade
Cherubini
Donizetti
Dunstable
Hindemith
Meyerbeer
Offenbach
Pachelbel
Pergolesi
Prokofiev
Scarlatti
Schnittke
Zemlinsky

10 letters:
Birtwistle
Boccherini
Carmichael
Cole Porter
Monteverdi
Mussorgsky
Palestrina
Ponchielli

- Rawsthorne
- Saint-Saëns
- Schoenberg
- Stravinsky
- Villa-Lobos
- Williamson

11 letters:
- Charpentier

Frescobaldi
Humperdinck
Leoncavallo
Mendelssohn
Stockhausen
Tchaikovsky
Wolf Ferrari

12 letters:
Khachaturian
Rachmaninoff
Shostakovich

13 letters:
Havergal Brian
Maxwell Davies

14 letters:
Rimsky-Korsakov

15 letters:
Vaughan
  Williams

▷ **Composing** *may indicate* an anagram

Composite Aster, Costmary, Foalfoot, Gerbera, Groundsel, Hybrid, Integral, Motley, Opinicus, Rag(weed), Sphinx, Synthesized, Thistle

Composition, **Compositor** Albumblatt, Aleatory, Azione, Bagatelle, Beaumontage, Beaumontague, Canon, Capriccio, Caprice, Cob, Concerto, Creation, Dite, Essay, Etude, Exaration, Fantasia, Inditement, Ingredient, Line, Loam, Met, Montage, Morceau, Nonet(te), Opus, Oratorio, Part-writing, Pastiche, Piece, Pieta, Poem, Polyphony, Printer, Quartette, Raga, Rhapsody, Round, Ship, Sing, Smoot, Sonata, Sonatina, Structure, Suite, Symphony, Synthesis, Terracotta, Texture, Toccata, Treatise, Typesetter, Verismo, Voluntary, Work

Compost Dressing, Fertilizer, Humus, Vraic, Zoo doo

Compound, **Compound stop** Admixture, Amalgam, Bahuvrihi, Blend, > **CAMP**, Composite, Constitute, Coordination, Cpd, Cutting, Derivative, Ethiops, Mix, Mixture, Multiply, Racemate, Rooting, Type

COMPOUNDS

3 letters:
Azo

4 letters:
Alum
EDTA
Enol
Haem
Heme
TEPP
Urea

5 letters:
Allyl
Aloin
Amide
Amino
Azide
Azine
Azole
Diazo
Diene
Dimer
Diode

Erbia
Ester
Furan
Halon
Imide
Imine
Lipid
Nitro
Olein
Oxide
Oxime
Potin
Pyran
Salol
Sarin
Tabun
Thiol
Trona
Vinyl

6 letters:
Acetal
Alkane
Alkene

Ammine
Arsine
Baryta
Borane
Calque
Cetane
Chrome
Cresol
Epimer
Fluate
Glycol
Halide
Haloid
Hexene
Isatin
Isomer
Ketone
Kinone
Lithia
Niello
Octane
Phenol
Pinene
Potash

Purine
Pyrone
Retene
Silane
Speiss
Tannin
Tartar
Tetryl
Thymol
Triene
Trimer
Uranyl

7 letters:
Acetone
Acridin
Aglycon
Ammonia
Benzene
Betaine
Bromide
Caliche
Calomel
Camphor

- Carbide
- Chelate
- Choline
- Cinerin
- Creatin
- Cumarin
- Cyanide
- Diamine
- Diazine
- Diazole
- Dioxide
- Dvandva
- Epoxide
- Erinite
- Ethanol
- Eugenol
- Fenuron
- Ferrite
- Flavone
- Hormone
- Hydrate
- Hydride
- Indican
- Indoxyl
- Lactate
- Lactone
- Menthol
- Metamer
- Monomer
- Niobite
- Nitride
- Nitrite
- Oxazine
- Oxonian
- Pentane
- Peptone
- Polyene
- Polymer
- Protein
- Quassia
- Quinoid
- Quinone
- Realgar
- Skatole
- Steroid
- Sulfide
- Syncarp
- Taurine
- Terpene
- Toluene
- Tritide
- Uridine

Wolfram
Zymogen

8 letters:
Acridine
Aglycone
Aldehyde
Alizarin
Arginine
Astatide
Butyrate
Catenane
Chloride
Chromene
Coenzyme
Coumarin
Creatine
Cyanogen
Datolite
Dieldrin
Dopamine
Ethoxide
Farnesol
Fluoride
Furfuran
Glycogen
Hydroxyl
Indoform
Isologue
Ketoxime
Lecithin
Luteolin
Massicot
Melamine
Monoxide
Oligomer
Pentosan
Peroxide
Piperine
Ptomaine
Purpurin
Pyrazole
Rock-alum
Rotenone
Selenate
Silicide
Siloxane
Sodamide
Stilbene
Sulphide
Sulphone
Tautomer

Tetroxid
Thiazide
Thiazine
Thiazole
Thiophen
Thiotepa
Thiourea
Titanate
Tolidine
Triazine
Triazole
Trilling
Tyramine
Urethane
Xanthate
Xanthine
Zirconia

9 letters:
Aflatoxin
Alicyclic
Aliphatic
Anhydride
Biguanide
Carbazole
Carnitine
Celloidin
Cellulose
Cementite
Cetrimide
Chromogen
Copolymer
Cortisone
Deuteride
Dibromide
Dipeptide
Disulfram
Endorshin
Ferrocene
Flavanone
Fulleride
Glycoside
Greek fire
Guanosine
Haematein
Histamine
Hydrazide
Hydroxide
Imidazole
Impsonite
Ionophore
Menadione

Merbromin
Methoxide
Monoamine
Organotin
Pentoxide
Phenazine
Phenoxide
Pheromone
Phosphide
Piperonal
Polyamine
Porphyrin
Qinghaosu
Quercetus
Quinidine
Serotonin
Tetroxide
Veratrine

10 letters:
Amphoteric
Argyrodite
Cellosolve®
Cytochroma
Dichloride
Dimethoate
Disulphide
Enkephalin
Ethambutol
Isocyanate
Lumisterol
Mercaptide
Nitrazepam
Nucleoside
Phenocaine
Picrotoxin
Piperazine
Piperidine
Propionate
Putrescine
Pyrimidine
Tatpurusha
Thimerosal
Tocopherol

11 letters:
Acetanilide
Amphetamine
Coprosterol
Dimercaprol
Electrolyte
Fluorescein

Ghitathione
Hydrocarbon
Neostigmine
Sesquioxide
Sphingosine

12 letters:
Carbohydrate
Formaldehyde
Haematoxylin

Hydroquinone
Permanganate
Phenanthrine
Polyurethane
Thiosinamine
Triglyceride
Trimethadine

13 letters:
Catecholamine

Cycloheximide
Isoproterenol
Metronidazole
Nortriptyline
Phenothiazine
Trinucleotide

14 letters:
Cyanocobalamin
Oxyhaemoglobin

Phenolphthalin
Polycarboxylic
Polyunsaturate
Trohalomethane

17 letters:
Pentachloro-
phenol

▷ **Compound(ed)** *may indicate* an anagram
Comprehend, Comprehensive All-in, Catch-all, Catholic, Compass, Compendious, Contain, Exhaustive, Fathom, Follow, Full-scale, General, Global, Grasp, Include, Indepth, Ken, Large, Omnibus, Panoramic, Perceive, School, Sweeping, Thoroughgoing, > **UNDERSTAND**, Wide
Compress(ed), Compression, Compressor Astrict, Astringe, Bale, Coarctate, Contract, Pack, Solidify, Squeeze, Stupe, Thlipsis, Turbocharger
Comprise Contain, Embody, Embrace, Include
Compromise Avoision, Brule, Commit, Concession, Endanger, Give and take, Happy medium, Involve, Settlement, Time-server, Trade off
▶ **Compulsion** *see* COMPEL
Compunction Hesitation, Regret, Remorse, Scruple, Sorrow
Computation, Computer (language), Computer term, Computer user ActiveX, Ada, Algol, Algorism, Analog(ue), Anorak, Antialising, Apple, Arpa, ASCII, Authoring, Autosave, Basic, Bloatware, Boot, Bootstrap, Brain, Browser, Busbar, C, CADMAT, Calculate, Calculus, Cast(er), Checksum, Chiphead, Clickstream, Clipboard, COBOL, COL, CORAL, Counter, Crippleware, Cyber(netics), Cyberpunk, Cybersurfer, Desktop, Digerati, Digital, DRAM, Earcon, Earom, Eniac, EPROM, ERNIE, Estimate, Ethernet, E-wallet, Extranet, FAT, Figure, Fileserver, Firewall, Floptical, Fortran, Freenet, GIGO, Gopher, Groupware, Hacker, HAL, Hardware, High-end, Holmes, Hybrid, Hypermedia, ICL, IDE, Integrator, Interface, Internet, IT, JANET, Java®, Kludge, Laptop, Linker, Linux, LISP, Luser, Macro, Mail merge, Mainframe, MARC, Measure, Micro, MIDI, Modem, Morphing, Mouse potato, Nerd, Network, Neural, Notebook, Number-cruncher, Numlock, OCCAM, OCR, On-line, Otaku, Palmtop, PASCAL, Patch, PC, Peer-to-peer, Perl, Personal, Pixel, Platform, Processor, Program, PROM, Pushdown, RAM, README file, Read-out, Realtime, Reboot, Reckoner, RISC, ROM, Scratchpad, Server, Shareware, SNOBOL, Software, Spreadsheet, Sprite, Stand-alone, String, Subroutine, Superserver, TALISMAN, Tally, Tape streamer, TAURUS, Thick client, Thin client, Toggle, Tower, Track(er)ball, Turing machine, Unix, Vaccine, Voxel, WIMP, WORM, Wysiwyg
Comrade Achates, Ally, Buddy, Butty, China, Fellow, Friend, Kamerad, Mate, Oliver, Pal, Pard, Roland, Tovarich, Tovaris(c)h
Con(man) Against, Anti, Bunco, Diddle, Dupe, Fleece, Hornswoggle, Jacob, Lag, Learn, Peruse, Read, Scam, Scan, Steer, Sucker, Swindle, Tweedler
Concave Dished, Invexed
Conceal(ed), Concealment Blanket, Blind, Closet, Clothe, Cover, Curtain, Dissemble, Doggo, Drown, Feal, Heal, Heel, Hele, > **HIDE**, Latent, Misprision, Occult, Palm, Perdu(e), Recondite, Screen, Scriene, Secrete, Shroud, Sleeve, Smother, Snow job, Stash, Subreption, Ulterior, Wrap

Concede, **Concession** Acknowledge, Admit, Allow, Budge, Carta, Charter, Compromise, Confess, Favour, Forfeit, Franchise, Munich, Ou, Owe, Own, Privilege, Ship, Sop, Synchoresis

Conceit(ed) Bumptious, Caprice, Carriwitchet, Cat-witted, Concetto, Crank, Crotchet, Device, Dicty, Egomania, Fancy, Fastuous, Figjam, Flory, Fop, Fume, Hauteur, Idea, Mugwump, Notion, Podsnappery, Prig, Princock, Princox, Puppyism, Quiblin, Self-assumption, Side, Snotty, Stuck-up, Swellhead, Toffee-nose, Vain(glory), Wind

Conceive, **Conceivable** Beget, Create, Credible, Imagine, Possible, Surmise

Concentrate(d), **Concentration** Aim, Attend, Bunch, Cathexis, Centre, Collect, Condense, Dephlegmate, Distil, Elliptical, Essence, Extract, Focalise, Focus, Intense, Kurtosis, Listen, Major, Mantra, Mass, Molality, Molarity, Navel-gazing, Potted, Rivet, Samadhi, Titrate, Titre

Concept(ion) Brain, Hent, Ideal, Ideation, Image, Immaculate, Myth, Notion, Stereotype

Concern(ing) About, After, Ail, Altruism, Anent, As to, Bother, Business, Care, Cerne, Company, Disturb, Firm, Going, Heed, In re, Intéressé, Interest, Into, Lookout, > MATTER, Mell, Misease, Over, Part, Pidgin, Pigeon, Re, Reck, Regard, Reke, Respect, Retch, Solicitude, Touch, Trouble, Worry

▷ **Concerned** *may indicate* an anagram

Concert (place) Agreement, Benefit, Chamber, Charivari, Cooperation, Device, Dutch, Gig, Hootananny, Hootenanny, Hootnannie, Odeon, Odeum, Pop, Prom(enade), Recital, Singsong, Smoker, Symphony, Together, Unison, Unity, Wit

Concertina Bandoneon, Pleat, Squeezebox, Squiffer

Concerto Brandenburg, Emperor, Grosso

▶ **Concession** *see* CONCEDE

Conch Shell, Strombus

Conchie CO

Conciliate Allay, Calm, Disarm, Ease, Mollify, Placate, Reconcile

Concise Compact, Curt, Encapsulated, Laconic, Short, Succinct, Terse, Tight

Conclave Assembly, Caucus, Confab, Meeting

Conclude(d), **Conclusion**, **Conclusive** Achieve, A fortiori, Afterword, Amen, Binding, Cease, Clinch, Close, Complete, Dead, Decide, Deduce, > END, Envoi, Explicit, Finding, Fine, Finis, > FINISH, Foregone, Gather, Illation, Infer, Lastly, Limit, Omega, Peroration, Point, Postlude, Punchline, Reason, Resolve, Settle, Summary, Upshot, Uptie

Conclusive Cogent, Convincing, Estoppel, Final

Concoct(ion) Brew, Compound, Creation, Plan, Trump (up)

Concord Consonance, Harmony, Peace, Plane, Sympathy, Treaty, Unity

Concorde SST

Concourse Assembly, Confluence, Esplanade, Throng

Concrete, **Concretion** Actual, Aggregate, Beton, Bezoar, Cake, Calculus, Clot, Dogger, Gunite, Hard, Lean, Mass, Minkstone, No-fines, Pile-cap, Positive, Prestressed, Reify, Reinforced, Siporex, Solid, Tangible, Tremie

Concubine Apple-squire, Campaspe, Harem, Hetaria, Madam, Mistress, Odalisk

Concur Accord, Agree, Coincide, Comply, > CONSENT, Gree

Concurrent(ly) Meantime

Concuss(ion) Clash, Shock, Stun

Condemn(ation) Accuse, Blame, Blast, Cast, Censor, Censure, Convict, Damn, Decry, Denounce, Deprecate, Doom, Judge, Kest, Obelise, Proscribe, Revile,

Sentence, Theta, Upbraid

Condense(d), **Condenser** Abbe, Abbreviate, Abridge, Brief, Capacitator, Compress, Contract, Distil, Encapsulate, Epitomise, Jet, Liebig, Précis, Rectifier, Reduce, Shorten, Shrink, Summarise, Vernier, Vinifactor

Condescend Deign, Patronise, Stoop, Vouchsafe

Condiment Caraway, Cayenne, Chutney, Cum(m)in, Flavour, Horse radish, Kava, Relish, Sambal, Sambol, Sauce, Tracklement, Turmeric, Vinegar

Condition(al), **Conditioning** Circ(s), Congenital, Connote, Fettle, Going, Hammertoe, Hood, If, > **IN GOOD CONDITION**, Kelter, Kilter, Necessary, Nick, Order, Pass, Pavlovian, Plight, Pliskie, Ply, Point, Position, Predicament, Prepare, Prerequisite, Presupposition, Protasis, Proviso, Provisory, Repair, Reservation, Reserve, Rider, Ropes, Sine qua non, Sis, Standing, State, Sted, Stipulation, String, Sufficient, Term, Tid, Tox(a)emia, Trim, Trisomy, Unless

Condom Blob, Cap, Franger, French letter, Gumboot, Johnny, Letter, Prophylactic, Rubber, Safe, Scumbag, Sheath

Condone Absolve, Excuse, Forgive, Overlook

Conduct(or), **Conductress** Accompany, Anode, Arm, Arrester, Barbirolli, Bearing, Beecham, Behaviour, Bulow, Bus-bar, Cad, Chobdar, Clippie, Coil, Comport, Demean(our), Deportment, Direct, Disorderly, Drive, Editor, Electrode, Escort, Feedthrough, Fetch, Goings-on, Haitink, Hallé, Ignitron, Karajan, Kempe, Klemperer, Lark, Lead, Liber, Lightning, Maestro, Mho, Microchip, Nerve, N-type, Officiate, Outer, Parts, Photodiode, > **PILOT**, Previn, Probe, Prosecute, Protocol, Psychopomp, P-type, Rattle, Safe, Sargent, Scudaller, Scudler, Shunt, Skudler, Solicit, Solti, Tao, Thermistor, Toscanini, Transact, > **USHER**, Varactor, Varistor, Wave guide, Wire, Wood, Zener diode

▷ **Conducting** *may indicate* an '-ic' ending

Conduit Aqueduct, Canal, Carrier, Duct, Main, Penstock, Pipe, Tube, Utilidor

Cone(s), **Conical** Cappie, Circular, Female, Fir, Fusion, Moxa, Nose, Pastille, Peeoy, Pineal, Pingo, Pioy(e), Puy, Pyramid, Retinal, Seger, Spire, Storm, Strobilus, Taper, Tee, Traffic, Volcanic, Wind, Windsock

Coney Daman, Doe, Hyrax

Confection(er) Candy, Caramel, Chocolate, Concoction, Conserve, Countline, Ice, Kiss, Marzipan, Noisette, Nougat, Quiddery, Rock, Sweet, Sweetmeat, Tablet

Confederal, **Confederacy**, **Confederate**, **Confederation** Accessory, Alliance, Ally, Association, Body, Bund, Bunkosteerer, Cover, Illinois, League, Partner, Senegambia, Union

Confer(ence) Bestow, Bretton Woods, Cf, Collogue, Colloqium, Colloquy, Congress, Council, Diet, Do, Dub, Fest, Forum, Grant, Huddle, Hui, Imparlance, Imperial, Indaba, Intercommune, Lambeth, Meeting, Munich, Negotiate, News, Palaver, Parley, Pawaw, Pear, Potsdam, Pourparler, Powwow, Press, Pugwash, Quadrant, Seminar, Settle, Summit, Symposium, Synod, > **TALK**, Teach-in, Video, Vouchsafe, Yalta

Confess(ion), **Confessor** Acknowledge, Admit, Agnise, Avowal, Concede, Declare, Disclose, Edward, Own, Peccavi, Recant, Shrift, Shriver, Sing, Whittle

Confide(nce), **Confident(ial)**, **Confidant** Aplomb, Aside, Assertive, Assured, Bedpost, Belief, Bottle, Certitude, Cocksure, Cocky, Cred, Crouse, Entre nous, Entrust, Faith, Feisty, Gatepost, Hardy, Hope, Hush-hush, Intimate, Morale, Nerve, Pack, Private, Privy, Sanguine, Secret, Secure, Self-possessed, Sub rosa, Sure, Tell, Trust, Unbosom, Under the rose, Vaulting

Confine(d), **Confines**, **Confinement** Ambit, Bail, Bale, Cage, CB, Chain, Constrain, Cramp, Crib, Detain, Emmew, Encase, Enclose, Endemic, Enmew,

Ensheath, Gaol, Gate, House arrest, Immanacle, Immew, Immure, Impound, > **IMPRISON**, Incage, Incarcerate, Incommunicado, Inhoop, Intern, Local, Mail, March, Mew, Mure, Narrow, Pen, Pent, Pinion, Poky, Restrict, Rule 43, Rules, Section, Solitary, Tether, Thirl, Trammel

Confirm(ed), Confirmation Addict, Ascertain, Assure, Attest, Bear, Certify, Chrisom, Christen, Chronic, Clinch, Corroborate, Endorse, Homologate, Obsign, OK, Ratify, Sacrament, Sanction, Seal, Strengthen, Ten-four, Tie, Validate, Vouch

Confiscate, Confiscation Attainder, Deprive, Dispossess, Distrain, Escheat, Garnishee, Impound, Infangenethef, Raupatu, Seize, Sequestrate

Conflagration Blaze, Holocaust, Inferno, Wildfire

Conflict(ing) Agon, Armageddon, Battle, Camp, Clash, Close, Contend, Contravene, Controversy, Disharmony, Encounter, Feud, Fray, Inconsistent, Jar, Lists, Mêlée, Muss, Oppose, Rift, Scrape, Strife, > **STRUGGLE**, Tergiversate, War

Conform(ity) Accord, Adjust, Comply, Consistence, Correspond, Normalise, Obey, Observe, Propriety, Standardize, Stereotype(d), Suit, Trimmer, Yield

Confound(ed) Abash, Amaze, Astound, Awhape, Baffle, Bewilder, Blamed, Blasted, Blest, Blinking, Bumbaze, Contradict, Darn, Drat, Dumbfound, Elude, Floor, Jigger, Mate, Murrain, Nonplus, Perishing, Perplex, Rabbit, Spif(f)licate, Stump, Throw

▷ **Confound** *may indicate* an anagram

Confrère Ally

Confront(ation) Appose, Beard, Breast, Eyeball, Face, Loggerheads, Mau-mau, Meet, Nose, Oppose, Showdown, Tackle

Confuse(d), Confusedly, Confusion Addle, Anarchy, Astonishment, Babel, Baffle, Bazodee, Bedevil, Befog, Befuddle, Bemuse, Bewilder, Blur, Bobby-die, Burble, Bustle, Chaos, Cloud, Clutter, Complicate, Debacle, Didder, Discombobulate, Disconcert, Disorient, Distract, Dither, Dizzy, Dudder, Dust, Egarement, Embrangle, Embroglio, Embroil, Farrago, Flap, Flat spin, Flummox, Flurry, Fluster, Fog, Fox, Fuddle, Galley-west, Hash, Havoc, Hazy, Helter-skelter, Hubble-bubble, Huddle, Hugger-mugger, Hurly-burly, Hurry-scurry, Hurry-skurry, Imbrangle, Imbroglio, > **IN CONFUSION**, Indistinct, Litter, Lost, Lurry, Maelstrom, Maffled, Mayhem, Maze, Melange, Melee, Mess, Mingle, Mish-mash, Mixtie-maxtie, Mix-up, Mizzle, Mizzy maze, Moider, Moither, Moonstruck, Morass, > **MUDDLE**, Mudge, Muzzy, Overset, Pellmell, Perplex, Pi(e), Pose, Ravel, Razzle-dazzle, Razzmatazz, Rout, S(c)hemozzle, Scramble, Skimble-skamble, Snafu, Spin, Stump, Stupefy, Synchysis, Tangle, Throw, Tizzy, Topsy-turvy, Tzimmes, Welter, Whemmle, Whomble, Whummle, Woolly, Woozy

▷ **Confuse(d)** *may indicate* an anagram

Confute Confound, Contradict, Deny, Disprove, Infringe, Redargue, Refel

Congeal Coagulate, Freeze, Gel, Gunge, Set, Solidify

Congenial Agreeable, Amiable, Compatible, Connate, Couthie, Couthy, Happy, Kindred, Simpatico, Sympathique

Congenital Connate, Inborn, Innate, Inveterate

Congest(ed), Congestion Coryza, Cram, Crowd, Engorge, Impact, Jam, Logjam, Turgid

Conglomerate, Conglomeration Aggregate, Banket, Gather, Heap, Mass

Congo(u) Shaba, Tea

Congratulate, Congratulation Applaud, Felicitate, Laud, Mazeltov, Preen, Salute

Congregate, **Congregation(alist)** Assembly, Barnabite, Body, Brownist, Class, Community, Conclave, Ecclesia, Flock, Fold, Gathering, Host, Laity, Oratory, Propaganda, Synagogue

Congress(man) ANC, Assembly, Conclave, Continental, Council, Eisteddfod, Intercourse, Legislature, Pan-Africanist, Rally, Senator, Solon, Synod, Vienna

Conifer(ous) Araucaria, Cedar, Cypress, Cyrus, Evergreen, Larch, Picea, Pine, Spruce, Taiga, Taxus, Thuja, Yew

Conject(ure) Fancy, Goldbach's, Guess, Speculate, Surmise, Theory, View

Conjoin Alligate, Ally, Connect, Knit

Conjugate, **Conjugation** Couple, Hermitian, Join, Nuptial, Synopsis, Typto, Zygosis

Conjunction Alligation, Ampersand, And, Combination, Consort, Nor, Polysyndeton, Synod, Syzygy, Together, Union, Unless

Conjure, **Conjuror** Angekkok, Charm, Contrive, Heypass, Heypresto, Hocus-pocus, Illusionist, Imagine, Invoke, Mage, Magic, Palmer, Prestidigitator, Prestigiator, Thaumaturgus

Connect(ed), **Connection**, **Connector** About, Accolade, Adaptor, Affinity, Agnate, Anastomosis, And, Associate, Attach, Band, Bind, Bridge, Bridle, Cable, Clientele, Coherent, Colligate, Conjugate, Couple, Cross-link, Delta, Dovetail, Drawbar, Fishplate, Fistula, Hook-up, > IN CONNECTION WITH, Interlink, Interlock, Join, Jumper, Kinship, Liaison, Lifeline, Link, Marry, Merge, Mesh, Nexus, On, Online, Patch, Pons, Raphe, Rapport, Relate, Relative, Respect, Shuttle, Splice, S-R, Synapse, Syntenosis, Syssarcosis, Tendon, Through, Tie, Tie-in, Union, Y, Yoke, Zygon

Connecticut Ct

Connive, **Connivance** Abet, Cahoots, Collude, Condone, Conspire, Plot

Connoisseur Aesthete, Cognoscente, Epicure, Expert, Fancier, Gourmet, Judge, Maven, Mavin, Oenophil

Connotate, **Connotation** Imply, Infer, Intent, Meaning

Conquer(or), **Conquest** Beat, Conquistador, Crush, Debel, Genghis Khan, Hereward, > MASTER, Moor, Norman, Ostrogoth, Overcome, Overpower, Overrun, Pizarro, Subjugate, Tame, Tamerlane, Vanquish, Victor

Conquistador Cortes, Cortez

Conscience, **Conscientious** Casuistic, Duteous, Heart, Inwit, Morals, Painstaking, Pang, Remorse, Scruple(s), Sense, Superego, Syneidesis, Synteresis, Thorough, Twinge

Conscious(ness) Awake, Aware, Chit, Limen, Mindful, On to, Persona, Sensible, Sentient

Conscript(ion) Blood-tax, Choco, Commandeer, Draft(ee), Impress, Landsturm, Levy, Nasho, > RECRUIT, Register

Consecrate, **Consecration** Bless, Hallow, Noint, Oint, Sacring, Sanctify, Venerate

Consecutive Sequential, Successive

Consensus Agreement, Harmony, Unanimity

Consent Accord, Acquiesce, Affo(o)rd, Agree, Approbate, Comply, Concur, Grant, Informed, Permit, Ratify, Volens, Yes-but, Yield

Consequence, **Consequent(ial)** Aftermath, Consectaneous, Corollary, Effect, End, Importance, Issue, Karma, Knock-on, Logical, Moment, Outcome, Ramification, Repercussion, > RESULT, Sequel, Upshot

Conservative Blimpish, Blue, C, Cautious, Diehard, Disraeli, Fabian, Hard-hat, Hidebound, Hunker, Neanderthal, Old guard, Old-line, Preppy, Progressive, Rearguard, Redneck, Right(-wing), Safe, Square, Thrifty, Tory, True blue,

Unionist, Verkramp

Conservatory Hothouse, Orangery, Solarium

Conserve, Conservation(ist) Can, Comfiture, Husband(ry), Jam, Jelly, Maintain, Maintenance, Noah, NT, Protect, Save

Consider(able), Consideration Animadvert, Attention, Avizandum, By-end, Case, Cerebrate, Chew over, Cogitate, Contemplate, Count, Courtesy, Debate, Deem, Deliberate, Entertain, Envisage, Factor, Fair, Feel, Forethought, Heed, Importance, Inasmuch, Judge, Many, Meditate, Muse, Pay, Perpend, Poise, Ponder, Premeditate, Pretty, Rate, Reckon, Reflect, Regard, Respect, See, Several, Shortlist, Solicitous, Song, Speculate, Steem, Study, Substantial, Think, Tidy, Vast, View, Ween, Weigh

Consign(ment) Allot, Award, Batch, Bequeath, Delegate, Deliver, Drop shipment, Entrust, Lading, Ship, Transfer

Consist(ent), Consistency Agree, Coherent, Comprise, Enduring, Even, Liaison, Rely, Steady

Consolation, Console Ancon, Appease, Balm, Comfort, Relief, Solace, Sop

Consolidate Coalesce, Combine, Compact, Gel, Merge, Pun, Unify

Consommé Julienne, Soup

Consonant(s) Affricate, Agma, Agreeing, Cacuminal, Cerebral, Explosive, Fortis, Fricative, Harmonious, Implosive, Labial, Lateral, Lenis, Media, Mouillé, Plosive, Sonorant, Spirant, Surd, Tenuis, Velar

Consort Ally, Associate, Maik, Mate, Moop, Moup, Partner, Spouse

Consortium Coalition, Combine, Ring

Conspicuous Arresting, Blatant, Clear, Eminent, Glaring, Kenspeck(le), Landmark, Light, Manifest, Patent, Salient, Signal, Striking

Conspiracy, Conspirator, Conspire, Conspiring Cabal, Casca, Cassius, Catiline, Cato St, Champerty, Cinna, Collaborate, Colleague, Collogue, Collude, Complot, Connive, Covin, Covyne, Guy, Highbinder, In cahoots, Intrigue, Oates, Omerta, > **PLOT**, Ring, Scheme

Constable Beck, Catchpole, Cop, Dogberry, Dull, Elbow, Harman(-beck), Headborough, High, John, Officer, Painter, Petty, Pointsman, Posse, Special, Thirdborough, Tipstaff, Verges

Constancy, Constant Abiding, Boltzmann, C, Changeless, Chronic, Coefficient, Devotion, Dielectric, Diffusion, Dirac, Eccentricity, Eternal, Faith, Firm, Fundamental, G, Gas, Gravitational, H, Honesty, Hubble's, K, Lambert, Leal(ty), Logical, Loyal, Magnetic, Often, Parameter, > **PERPETUAL**, Planck's, Pole star, Resolute, Sad, Solar, Staunch, Steadfast, Steady, Time, True, Unfailing, Uniform, Usual

Constellation Andromeda, Antlia, Apus, Aquarius, Aquila, Ara, Argo, Aries, Auriga, Bootes, Caelum, Canis major, Canis minor, Carina, Cassiopeia, Centaurus, Cepheus, Cetus, Cham(a)eleon, Circinus, Columba, Coma Berenices, Coma Cluster, Corvus, Crater, Cygnus, Cynosure, Delphinus, Dolphin, Dorado, Draco, Equuleus, Eridanus, Fornax, Galaxy, Gemini, Gru(i)s, Hercules, Horologium, Hydra, Hydrus, Indus, Lacerta, Leo, Leo minor, Lepus, Libra, Lupus, Lynx, Lyra, Mensa, Monoceros, Musca, Norma, Octans, Ophiuchus, Orion, Pavo, Pegasus, Perseus, Phoenix, Pictor, Piscus Austrinus, > **PLANET**, Puppis, Pyxis, Reticulum, Sagitta, Sagittarius, Scorpius, Sculptor, Scutum, Serpens, Sextans, Southern Cross, Spica, > **STAR**, Telescopium, Triangulum (Australe), Tucana, Twins, Unicorn, Vela, Virgin, Virgo, Volans, Vulpecula, Wag(g)oner, Whale, Zodiacal

Consternation Alarm, Dismay, Doodah, Fear, Horror

Constipate(d), Constipation Astrict, Bind, Block, Costive, Stegnotic, Stenosis

Constituency, **Constituent** Borough, Component, Element, Immediate, Part, Principle, Seat, Voter

> **Constituents** *may indicate* an anagram

Constitute, **Constitution(al)** Appoint, Charter, Compose, Comprise, Congenital, Creature, Establishment, Form, Fuero, Health, Physique, Policy, Polity, Seat, State, Synthesis, Upmake, Walk

Constrain(ed), **Constraint** Bind, Bondage, Boundary, Coerce, Confine, Coop, Curb, Duress(e), Hard, Oblige, Pressure, Repress, Stenosis, Taboo, Trammel

Constrict(ed), **Constriction** Bottleneck, Choke, Coarctate, Contract, Cramp, Hour-glass, Impede, Limit, Phimosis, Squeeze, Stegnosis, Stenosis, Strangulate, Thlipsis, Tighten, Venturi

Construct(ion), **Constructor**, **Constructive** Build, Compile, Engineer, Erect, Fabricate, Facture, Fashion, Form, Frame, Idolum, Make, Manufacture, Seabee, Tectonic, Weave

Construe Deduce, Explain, Expound, Infer

Consul Ambassador, Attaché, Horse, Praetor

Consult(ant), **Consultation** Confer, Deliberate, Discuss, Emparl, Imparl, Joint, Peritus, See, Surgery, Vide

Consume(r), **Consumption**, **Consumptive** Bolt, Burn, Caterpillar®, Decay, Devour, Diner, Eat, Engross, Exhaust, Expend, Feed, Glutton, Hectic, Mainline, Scoff, Spend, Swallow, TB, Use, Waste, Wear

Consummate, **Consummation** Keystone, Seal

Contact Abut, Adpress, Contingence, Hook-up, Lens, Liaise, Liaison, Meet, Reach, Shoe, Taction, > TOUCH, Touchy-feely, Wiper

Contagious, **Contagion** Infection, Noxious, Poison, Taint, Variola, Viral

Contain(er) Amphora, Ampulla, Aquafer, Aquifer, Barrel, Bass, Bidon, Bin, Bottle, Box, Buddle, Cachepot, Can, Canakin, Canikin, Canister, Cannikin, Cantharus, Capsule, Carafe, Carboy, Carry, Carton, Case, Cask, Cassette, Chase, Chest, Churn, Coffer, Comprise, Coolamon, Crate, Crater, Crucible, Cup, Cupel, Decanter, Dracone, Dredger, Enclose, Encompass, Enseam, Esky®, Feretory, Flagon, Flask, Gourd, > HOLD, House, Igloo, Include, Incubator, Intray, Jar, Jeroboam, Jerrican, Jerrycan, Jug, Keg, Kirbeh, Leaguer, Lekythos, Monkey, Monstrance, Mould, Olpe, Pail, Pinata, Piscina, Pitcher, Pithos, Pod, Pottle, Reliquary, Repository, Restrain, Sac(k), Saggar, Scyphus, Shaker, Situla, Skin, Skip, Snaptin, Spittoon, Stamnos, Tank, Tantalus, Terrarium, Tinaja, Trough, Tub, Tun, Tupperware®, Urn, Vessel, Vinaigrette, Wineskin, Woolpack, Workbag

Contaminate(d) Adulterate, Corrupt, Defile, Denature, Flyblown, Impure, Infect, Pollute, Soil, Stain, Tarnish

Contemplate, **Contemplation** Consider, Ecce, Envisage, Hesychasm, Meditate, Muse, Ponder, Reflect, Retrospection, Rue, Samadhi, Spell, Study, Think, Watch

Contemporary AD, Coetaneous, Current, Equal, Fellow, Modern, Present, Verism

Contempt(ible), **Contemptuous** Abject, Ageism, Aha, Arsehole, Bah, BEF, Cheap, Contumely, Crud, Crumb, Cullion, Cynical, Derision, Despisal, Disparaging, Dog-bolt, Fig, Hangdog, Ignominious, Insect, Low, Mean, Measly, Misprision, Odious, Paltry, Phooey, Pish, Poxy, Pshaw, Ratfink, Rats, Razoo, Scabby, Scarab, Schlub, > SCORN, Scumbag, Sexism, Shabby, Shithead, Slimeball, Sneeze, Sniff, Snooty, Snot, Soldier, Sorry, Squirt, Squit, Supercilious, Toad, Toerag, Vilipend, Weed, Whipster, Wretched

Contend(er) Argue, Candidate, Claim, Clash, Compete, Cope, Debate, Dispute,

Fight, Grapple, Oppose, Stickle, > **STRIVE**, Struggle, Submit, > **VIE**, Wrestle

Content Apaid, Apay, Appay, Blissful, Happy, Inside, Please, Satisfy, Volume

▷ **Content** *may indicate* a hidden word

Contention, Contentious Argument, Bellicose, Cantankerous, Case, Combat, Competitive, Perverse, Polemical, Rivalry, Strife, Struggle, Sturt

Contest(ant) Agon, Battle, Beauty, Biathlon, Bout, Catchweight, Challenge, Championship, Combat, Competition, Concours, Darraign, Decathlon, Defend, Deraign, Dogfight, Duel(lo), Entrant, Eurovision, Event, Examinee, Free-for-all, Fronde, Handicap, Heptathlon, Kriegspiel, Lampadephoria, Match, Matchplay, Olympiad, Pancratium, Paralympics, Pentathlon, Pingle, Play-off, Prizer, Race, Rival, Roadeo, Rodeo, Set-to, Skirmish, Slam, Slugfest, Strife, Struggle, Tenson, Tetrathlon, Tournament, Triathlon, Vie, War, With

Context Opaque, Transparent

Continent(al) Abstinent, Asia, Atlantis, Austere, Chaste, Dark, Epeirogeny, Euro, European, Gallic, Gondwanaland, Laurasia, Lemuria, Mainland, Moderate, Pang(a)ea, Shelf, Teetotal, Temperate, Walloon

Contingency, Contingent Accident, Arm, Casual, Chance, Conditional, Dependent, Event, Fluke, Group, Prospect

Continual(ly), Continuous Adjoining, Away, Chronic, Connected, Eer, Endlong, Eternal, Ever, Frequent, Incessant, Non-stop, On(going)

Continue, Continuation, Continuing, Continuity Abye, Duration, Dure, During, Enduring, Enjamb(e)ment, Follow-on, Go on, Hold, Keep, Last, Link, Ongoing, Onward, Persevere, Persist, Proceed, Prolong, Remain, Resume, Sequence, Stand, Subsist, Survive, Sustain, Synaphe(i)a, Tenor

▷ **Continuously** *may indicate* previous words to be linked

Contort(ion) Deform, Gnarl, Jib, Twist, Warp, Wry

Contour Curve, Graph, Isallobar, Isobase, Isocheim, Isochime, Isogeothermal, Line, Profile, Silhouette, Streamline, Tournure

Contraband Hot, Illicit, Prohibited, Smuggled

Contraception, Contraceptive Cap, Coil, Condom, Diaphragm, Dutch cap, IU(C)D, Loop, Minipill, Oral, Pessary, Pill, Prophylactic, Rubber(s), Sheath, Vimule®

Contract(ion), Contractor Abbreviate, Abridge, Agreement, Appalto, Astringency, Bargain, Biceps, Bottomry, Braxton-Hicks, Bridge, Builder, Catch, Champerty, Charter, Clonus, Condense, Consensual, Constringe, Contrahent, Covenant, Cramp, Crasis, Curtail, Debt, Diastalsis, Dupuytren's, Dwindle, Engage, Entrepreneur, Escrow, Fitzgerald-Lorentz, Flex, Gainsay, Gooseflesh, Guarantee, Hand-promise, Hire, Incur, Indenture, Jerk, Ketubah, Knit, Lease, Levator, Lorentz-Fitzgerald, Make, Miosis, Myosis, Narrow, Obligee, Party, Peristalsis, Promise, Pucker, Purse, Restriction, Risus (sardonicus), Service, Shrink, Shrivel, Sign, Slam, Social, Spasm, Specialty, Steelbow, Stenosis, Stipulation, Supplier, Sweetheart, Syngraph, Systole, Tetanise, Tetanus, Tic, Tighten, Time bargain, Tonicity, Treaty, Triceps, Wrinkle, Yellow-dog, Z

Contradict(ion), Contradictory Ambivalent, Antilogy, Antinomy, Belie, Bull, Contrary, Counter, Dementi, Deny, Disaffirm, Disprove, Dissent, > **GAINSAY**, Negate, Oxymoron, Paradox, Sot, Stultify, Sublate, Threap, Threep, Traverse

Contrarily, Contrary Adverse, A rebours, Arsy-versy, But, Captious, Converse, Counter, Counterfleury, Crosscurrent, Cross-grained, Cross-purpose, Froward, Hostile, Inverse, Mary, Opposite, Ornery, Perverse, Rebuttal, Retrograde, Wayward, Withershins

Contrast Chiaroscuro, Clash, Colour, Compare, Differ, Foil, Relief

Contravene Infringe, Oppose, Thwart, Violate

Contribute, **Contribution** Abet, Add, Assist, Chip in, Conduce, Donate, Dub, Furnish, Go, Help, Input, Kick in, Mite, Offering, Share, Sub, Subscribe, Whack, Widow's mite

▷ **Contributing to** *may indicate* a hidden word

Contrite, **Contrition** Penance, Penitent, Remorse, Repentant, Rue, > SORRY

Contrivance, **Contrive** Art, Contraption, Deckle, Deus ex machina, Device, Dodge, Engine, Finesse, Gadget, Gin, Hokey, Invention, Page, Plot, Rest, Wangle

Contrive(r) Chicaner, Cook, Devise, Engineer, Frame, Hatch, Intrigue, Machinate, Manage, Manoeuvre, Plan, Procure, Scheme, Secure, Stage, Trump, Weave

Control(ler), **Controllable** Ada, Appestat, Big Brother, Birth, Boss, Bridle, Cabotage, Chair, Check, Christmas tree, Corner, Corset, Cybernetics, Descendeur, Dirigible, Dirigism(e), Dominate, Dominion, Dynamic, Etatiste, Fast-forward, Fet(ch), Finger, Flood, Fly-by-wire, Gain, Gar, Gerent, Govern, Ground, Gubernation, Harness, Have, Heck, Helm, Influence, Influx, Joystick, Knee-swell, Lead, Lever, > MANAGE, Martinet, Mastery, Moderate, Mouse, Nipple, Numerical, Operate, Override, Pilot, Placebo, Police, Population, Possess, Power, Preside, Price, Process, Puppeteer, Quality, Radio, Regulate, Regulo®, Rein, Remote, Rent, Repress, Restrain, Rheostat, Ride, Ripple, Rule, Run, School, Servo, Snail, Solion, Steady, Steer, Stop, Stranglehold, Stringent, Subdue, Subject, Subjugate, Supervise, Suzerain, Sway, Takeover, Thermostat, Throttle, Tiller, Tone, Valve, Weld, Wield, Zapper

Controversial, **Controversy** Argument, Contention, Debate, Dispute, Eristic(al), Furore, Hot potato, Polemic(al), Tendentious

Conundrum Acrostic, Egma, Enigma, Puzzle, Riddle, Teaser

Convalesce(nt), **Convalescence** Anastatic, Mend, Rally, Recover, Recuperate, Rest-cure

▶ **Convene** *see* CONVOKE

Convenience, **Convenient** Behoof, Commode, Eft, Expedient, Facility, Gain, Gents, > HANDY, Hend, Lav, Leisure, Near, Opportune, Pat, Privy, Public, Suitable, Toilet, Use, Well

Convent Cloister, Fratry, Friary, House, > MONASTERY, Motherhouse, Nunnery, Port-royal, Priory, Retreat

Convention(al) Academic, Accepted, Babbitt, Blackwood, Bourgeois, Caucus, Conclave, Conformity, > CUSTOMARY, Diet, Done, Formal, Geneva, Habitude, Iconic, Lingua franca, Meeting, Middlebrow, Middle-of-the-road, More, National, Nomic, Orthodox, Pompier, Proper, Schengen, Staid, Starchy, Stereotyped, Stock, Synod, Uptight, Usage, Warsaw

Converge Approach, Focus, Meet

Conversation(alist), **Converse**, **Conversant** Abreast, Antithesis, Board, Buck, Cackle, Causerie, Chat, Chitchat, Colloquy, Commune, Confab, Crosstalk, Deipnosophist, Dialogue, Discourse, Eutrapelia, Eutrapely, Hobnob, Interlocution, Jaw-jaw, Natter, Opposite, Palaver, Parley, Persiflage, Rap, Rhubarb, Shop, Socialise, > TALK, Transpose, Wongi, Word

Conversion, **Converter**, **Convert(ible)** Adapt, Alter, Assimilate, Azotobacter, Bessemer, Catalytic, Catechumen, Change, Commute, Cyanise, Diagenesis, Disciple, Encash, Etherify, Exchange, Expropriate, Fixation, Gummosis, Hodja, Kho(d)ja, L-D, Liquid, Marrano, Metanoia, Neophyte, Noviciate, Novitiate, Persuade, Prill, Proselyte, Put, Ragtop, Realise, Rebirth, Recycle, Revamp, Souper, Tablet, Taw, Torque, Transduce, Transform, Transmute, Try

▷ **Conversion**, **Converted** *may indicate* an anagram

Convex(ity) Arched, Bowed, Camber, Curved, Entasis, Extrados, Gibbous, Lenticle, Nowy

Convey(ance) Assign, BS, Carousel, Carriage, Carry, Charter, Coach, Conduct, Cycle, Deed, Eloi(g)n, Enfeoffment, Giggit, Grant, Guide, Lease, Litter, Lorry, Mailcar(t), Pneumatic, Re-lease, Sac and soc, Screw, Tip, Title deed, Tote, Tram, Transfer, Transit, Transmit, Transport, Vehicle

Convict(ion) Attaint, Belief, Bushranger, Certitude, Cockatoo, Cogence, Crawler, Credo, Creed, Criminal, Demon, Dogma, Faith, Felon, Forçat, Lag, Magwitch, Old chum, > **PERSUASION**, Plerophory, Ring, Trusty, Vehemence, Yardbird

Convince(d), **Convincing** Assure, Cogent, Doubtless, Luculent, Persuade, Satisfy, Sold, Sure

Convivial(ity) Boon, Bowl, Festive, Gay, Genial, Jovial, Social

Convoke Assemble, Call, Convene, Summon

Convolute(d), **Convolution** Coiled, Gyrus, Helical, Intricate, Spiral, Tortuous, Twisty, Whorl, Writhen

Convolvulus Bindweed, Dodder

Convoy Caravan, Column, Conduct, Escort, Pilot, Train, Wagon-train

Convulsion(s), **Convulsive** Agitate, Clonic, Commotion, Disturb, DT, Eclampsia, > **FIT**, Galvanic, Paroxysm, Spasm, Throe, Tic

Cook(s), **Cooker**, **Cooking** Aga®, Babbler, Bake, Balti, Beeton, Benghazi, Bhindi, Bouche, Braise, Broil, Cacciatore, Calabash, Captain, Charbroil, Chargrill, Chef, Coddle, Concoct, Cordon bleu, Cuisine, Deep-fry, Devil, Do, Doctor, Dumple, Edit, Escoffier, Fake, Falsify, Fiddle, Flambé, Forge, Fricassee, Fry, Fudge, Greasy, Grill, Haute cuisine, Haybox, Marinière, Meunière, Microwave, Nouvelle cuisine, Poach, Prepare, Pressure, Provencale, Ribroast, Rig, Ring, Roast, Roger, Sous-chef, Spit, Steam, Stew, Stir-fry, Tandoori, Tikka, Tire

▷ **Cook** *may indicate* an anagram

Cool(er), **Cooling**, **Coolness** Aloof, Aplomb, Calm, Can, Chill, Collected, Composed, Cryogen, Cryostat, Defervescence, Desert, Dispassionate, Distant, Esky®, Fan, Frappé, Fridge, Frigid, Frosty, Gaol, Goglet, Ice(box), Jail, Jug, Keel, La Nina, Phlegm, Prison, Quad, Quod, Reefer, Refresh, Regenerative, Reserved, Sangfroid, Serene, Skeigh, Stir, Temperate, Thou(sand), Trendy, Unruffled, Wint(e)ry

Coop Cage, Cavie, Confine, Gaol, Hutch, Mew, Pen, Rip

Cooper Gary, Henry, Tubman

Cooperate, **Cooperation**, **Cooperative** Collaborate, Combine, Conspire, Contribute, Coop, Give and take, Liaise, Play, Synergy, Teamwork, Together, Worker's

Coordinate(d), **Coordination** Abscissa, Abscisse, Agile, Arrange, Cartesian, Ensemble, Harmony, Nabla, Orchestrate, Ordonnance, Peer, Polar, Right ascension, Spherical, Synergy, Teamwork, X, Y, Z

Coot Stupid, Sultan

Cop(s) Bag, Bull, Catch, Dick, Keystone, Peeler, Peon, > **POLICEMAN**, Silent

Copal Dammar, Resin

Cope Chlamys, Deal, Face, Handle, Make do, > **MANAGE**, Mantle, Meet, Negotiate, Pallium, Poncho

Coping (stone) Balustrade, Capstone, Skew

Copious Abundant, Affluent, Ample, Fecund, Fluent, Fruitful, Fulsome, Plentiful, Profuse

Copper As, Atacamite, Blister, Bluebottle, Bobby, Bornite, Busy, Cash, Cent, Chessylite, > **COIN**, Cu, D, Dam, Double, Erinite, Flatfoot, Lawman, Lota(h),

Malachite, Mountain-blue, Ormolu, Peacock, Pence, Penny, Pfennig, Pie, Pig, Plack, Policeman, Red, Rosser, Rozzer, S, Sen(s), Slop, Special, Traybit, Venus, Verdet, Washer, Washtub, Wire bar

Copse Thicket

Copulate Intercourse, Line, Mate, Roger, Tup

Copy(ing), Copier, Copyist Aemule, Ape, Apograph, Autotype, Calk, Calque, Camera-ready, Carbon, Clerk, Clone, Counterpart, Crib, Cyclostyle, Diazo, Ditto, Download, Dyeline, Echo, Echopraxia, Ectype, Edition, Eidograph, Electro, Emulate, Engross, Estreat, Example, Facsimile, Fair, Fax, Flimsy, Forge, Hard, Hectograph, > IMITATE, Issue, Jellygraph, Knocking, Manifold, Manuscript, Match, Me-tooer, Milline, Mimeograph®, Mimic, Mirror, MS, Offprint, Parrot, Photostat®, Plagiarism, Polygraph, Read-out, Replica, Repro, Reproduce, Review, Roneo®, Scribe, Script, Scrivener, Sedulous, Show, Simulate, Spit, Stencil, Stuff, Telautograph®, Tenor, Tenure, Trace, Transcribe, Transume, Vidimus, Xerox®

Copyright C

Coquette Agacerie, Flirt, Rosina, Tease, Vamp

Cor Bath, Crumbs, Ephah, Homer

Coracle Currach, Curragh

Coral (reef) Alcyonaria, Aldabra, Atoll, Brain, Cup, Deadman's fingers, Gorgonia(n), Laccadives, Madrepore, Millepore, Pink, Precious, Red, Reef, Sea fan, Sea ginger, Sea-pen, Sea whip, Seed, Stony, Zoothome

Cord, Cord-like Aiguillette, Band, Bedford, Bind, Boondoggle, Cat-gut, Chenille, Communication, Creance, Drawstring, Flex, Fourragère, Funicle, Gasket, Heddle, Lace, Laniard, Lanyard, Ligature, Line, Moreen, Myelon, Net, Ocnus, Piping, Quipo, Quipu, Rep(s), Restiform, Rip, Rope, Sash, Sennit, Service, Shroudline, Spermatic, Spinal, > STRING, Tendon, Tie, Torsade, Twine, Umbilical, Vocal, Wick

Cordial Anise(ed), Anisette, Benedictine, Cassis, Drink, Gracious, Grenadine, Hearty, Hippocras, Kind, Neighbourly, Oporice, Orangeade, Persico(t), Pleasant, Ratafia, Rosa-solis, Roso(g)lio, Shrub, Tar-water, Warm

Cordon Picket, Ring, Sanitaire, Surround

Corduroy Rep(p)

Cordyline Ti-tree

Core Barysphere, Calandria, Campana, Centre, Chog, Essence, Filament, Hard, Heart, Hub, Kernel, Nife, Nitty-gritty, Plerome, Quintessence, Slug

Co-religionist Brother

Coriander Cilantro

Corinthian(s) Casuals, Caulis, Epistolaters

Cork(ed), Corker Balsa, Bouché, Bung, Float(er), Humdinger, Mountain, Oner, Phellem, Phellogen, Plug, Seal, Shive, Stopper, Suber(ate)

Corkscrew Bore, Opening, Spiral

Cormorant Duiker, Duyker, Scart(h), Skart(h)

Corn(y) Bajr(a), Banal, Blé, Cereal, Cob, Emmer, Epha, Flint, Gait, Graddan, Grain, Green, Grist, Guinea, Icker, Indian, Kaffir, Mabela, Maize, Mealie, Muid, Negro, Nubbin, Pickle, Pinole, Posho, Rabi, Rye, Seed, Shock, Stitch, Straw, Sugar, Sweet, Thrave, Trite, Zea

Corncrake Landrail

Cornel Dogberry, Tree

Corner Amen, Angle, Bend, Cantle, Canton, Cranny, Dangerous, Diêdre, Elbow, Entrap, Hole, Hospital, Lug, Monopoly, NE, Niche, Nook, NW, Penalty, Predicament, Quoin, SE, Short, Speakers', Spot, SW, Tack, Tight, Trap, Tree,

Vertex

Cornerstone Coi(g)n, Encoignure, Skew-corbel, Skew-put, Skew-table

Cornet Cone, Cornopean, Field, Horn

Cornice Surbase

Cornish(man) Cousin Jack

Cornstalks Strammel, Straw, Strummel, Stubble

Cornucopia Amalthea, Horn

Cornwall SW

Corollary Conclusion, Dogma, Porism, Rider, Theory, Truism

Corona Aureole, Cigar, Larmier, Nimbus, Wreath

Coroner Procurator fiscal

Corporal Bardolph, Bodily, Bombardier, Brig(adier), Lance-pesade, Lance-prisade, Lance-prisado, Lance-speisade, Naik, NCO, Nym, Pall, Physical, Trim

Corporation Belly, Body, Close, Commune, Company, Conglomerate, Guild, Kite, Kyte, Paunch, Public, Stomach, Swag-belly, Tum, Wame, Wem

Corps Body, C, Crew, Diplomatic, Peace, RAC, REME, Unit

Corpse Blob, Body, Cadaver, Carcass, Carrion, Goner, Like, Mort, Relic, Remains, Stiff, Zombi(e)

Corpulence, **Corpulent** Adipose, Fat, Gross, Obese, Stout, Tubby

Corpuscle Cell, Erythrocyte, Malpighian, Meissner's, Microcyte, Neutrophil, Pacinian, Phagocyte

Correct(ing), **Correctly**, **Correctness**, **Correction**, **Corrector** Accurate, Alexander, Align, Amend, Aright, Blue-pencil, Bodkin, Castigate, Chasten, Chastise, Check, Decorous, Diorthortic, Emend, Exact, Fair, Grammatical, Legit, Mend, Politically, Preterition, Probity, Proofread, Proper, Propriety, Punctilious, Punish, Purism, Rebuke, Rectify, Rectitude, Redress, Remedial, Reprove, Revise, Right(en), Scold, Spot-on, Sumpsimus, Trew, True, U

▷ **Corrected** *may indicate* an anagram

Correspond(ence), **Correspondent**, **Corresponding** Accord, Agree, Analogy, Assonance, Coincident, Communicate, Congruence, Counterpart, Equate, Equivalence, Eye-rhyme, Fit, Foreign, Hate mail, Homolog(ue), Identical, Match, On all fours, One to one, Par, Parallel, Relate, Snail mail, Symmetry, Tally, Veridical, War, Write

Corridor Air, Aisle, Berlin, Entry, Gallery, Lobby, Passage, Polish, Re-entry

Corroborate Confirm, Support, Verify

Corrode(d), **Corrosion**, **Corrosive** Acid, Brinelling, Burn, Canker, Decay, Eat, Erode, Etch, Fret, Gnaw, Hydrazine, Mordant, > **ROT**, Rubiginous, Rust, Waste

Corrugate Gimp

Corrupt(er), **Corrupting**, **Corruption** Abuse, Adulterate, Bastardise, Bent, Bobol, Bribable, Canker, Debase, Debauch, Debosh, Decadent, Defile, Degenerate, Depravity, Dissolute, Dry rot, Emancipate, Embrace(o)r, Embrasor, Empoison, Etch, Fester, Gangrene, Graft(er), Immoral, Impure, Inquinate, Jobbery, Leprosy, Malversation, Nefarious, Obelus, Payola, Perverse, Poison, Pollute, Power, Putrid, Ret(t), Rigged, Rot, Scrofulous, Seduce, Sepsis, Septic, Sleaze, Sodom, Sophisticate, Spoil, Suborn, Tammany, Twist, Venal, Vice, Vitiate

Corsage Buttonhole, Pompadour, Posy, Spray

Corsair Barbary, Picaroon, Pirate, Privateer, Robber, Rover

Corset, **Corslet** Belt, Bodice, Busk, Girdle, Lorica, Roll-on, Stays, Thorax, Waspie

Corsican Napoleon

Cortege Parade, Retinue, Train

Cortex Cerebral, Renal

Cortisone Hecogenin
Corundum Emery, Sapphire
Corvo Rolfe
Corybant Roisterer
Cosh Sap
Cosmetic Beautifier, Blusher, Bronzer, Eye-black, Eyeliner, Eye-shadow, Face-pack, Foundation, Fucus, Highlighter, Kohl, Liner, Lip gloss, Lip liner, Lipstick, Lotion, Maquillage, Mascara, Mousse, Mudpack, Paint, Pearl-powder, Powder, Reface, Rouge, Talcum, Toner
▶ **Cosmic** *see* COSMOS
Cosmonaut Gagarin, Spaceman, Tereshkova
Cosmopolitan International, Urban
Cosmos, Cosmic Globe, Heaven, Infinite, Nature, Universe, World
Cossack Ataman, Hetman, Mazeppa, Russian, Tartar, Zaporogian
Cosset Caress, Coddle, Fondle, Pamper
Cost(s), Costly Bomb, Carriage, Charge, Damage, Direct, Earth, Escuage, Estimate, Exes, > EXPENSE, Factor, Fixed, Hire, Indirect, Loss, Marginal, Opportunity, Outlay, Overhead, Precious, Price, Prime, Quotation, Rate, Sacrifice, Sumptuous, Toll, Unit, Upkeep, Usurious, Variable
Costa Rica(n) Tico
Costermonger Barrow-boy, Kerb-merchant, Pearly
Costume Apparel, Attire, Camagnole, Cossie, Dress, Ensemble, Get-up, Gi(e), Guise, Judogi, Livery, Maillot, Motley, Nebris, Polonaise, Rig, Surcoat, Tanga, Togs, Uniform, Wear
Cosy Cosh, Intime, Snug
Cot Moses basket
Coterie Cell, Cenacle, Circle, Clan, Clique, Club, Ring, Set, Society
Cottage(r) Bach, Bordar, Bothie, Bothy, Box, Bungalow, Cabin, Chalet, Cot, Crib, Dacha, Home-croft, Hut, Lodge, Mailer
Cotton Agree, AL, Alabama, Balbriggan, Batiste, Batting, Bengal, Calico, Candlewick, Ceiba, Chambray, Chino, Chintz, Collodion, Coutil(le), Cretonne, Denim, Dho(o)ti, Dimity, Ducks, Fustian, Galatea, Gossypine, Gossypium, Humhum, Ihram, Jaconet, Lavender, Lawn, Lea, Lille, Lint, Lisle, Manchester, Marcella, Muslin, Nainsook, Nankeen, Nankin, Osnaburg, Pongee, Sea-island, Seersucker, Silesia, Stranded, Surat, T-cloth, Thread, Twig, Upland
Cotton soil Regar, Regur
Cotyledon Seed-leaf
Couch Bed, Casting, Davenport, Daybed, > DIVAN, Express, Grass, Lurk, Palanquin, Palkee, Palki, Quick, Recamier, Sedan, Settee, Sofa, Studio, Triclinium, Winnipeg, Word
Coué Auto-suggestion
Cougar Cat, Painter
Cough(ing) Bark, Croup, Expectorate, Hack, Hawk, Hem, Hoast, Hooping, Kink, Pertussis, Phthisis, Rale, Tisick, Tussis, Ugh, Whooping
Could Couth
Council (meeting), Councillor, Counsel(lor) Achitophel, Admonish, Admonitor, Advice, Advocate, Ahithophel, Alfred, Amphictryon, Anziani, Aread, A(r)re(e)de, Assembly, Attorney, Aulic, Aunt, Ayuntamiento, Board, Body, Boule, Bundesrat, Burgess, Cabinet, Casemate, Committee, Consistory, Corporation, County, Cr, Decurion, Dergue, Devil, Dietine, Divan, Douma, Duma, Ecumenical, Egeria, European, Executive, Exhort, Great, Greenbag, Hebdomadal, Indaba, Induna, Industrial, Info, Islands, Jirga, Junta, Kabele,

Kebele, King's, Kite, Landst(h)ing, Lateran, Leader, Legislative, Loan, Majlis, Mentor, Nestor, Nicaean, Nicene, Panchayat, Paraclete, Parish, Powwow, Press, Privy, Provincial, Queen's, Rede, Regional, Reichsrat, Robber, Samaritan, Sanhedrim, Sanhedrin, Security, Senate, Shoora, Shura, Sobranje, Sobranye, Soviet, Syndicate, Synedrion, Synod, Thing, Town, Trades, Trent, Tridentine, Trullan, Vatican, Volost, Wages, Whitley, Witan, Witenagemot, Works, Zemstvo, Zila, Zillah

Count(ed), Counter, Counting Abacus, Add, Algoriam, Anti, Bar, Basie, Blood, Buck, Buffet, Calculate, Cavour, Census, Chip, Compute, Coost, Desk, Dracula, Dump, Earl, Enumerate, Fish, Geiger, Geiger-Muller, Graf(in), Grave, Itemise, Jet(t)on, Landgrave, Margrave, Marker, Matter, Merel(l), Meril, Milton Work, Nobleman, Number, Obviate, Olivia, Oppose, Palatine, Palsgrave, Paris, Pollen, Presume, Proportional, Rebut, **> RECKON**, Refute, Rejoinder, Rely, Retaliate, Retort, Rhinegrave, Scintillation, Score, Sperm, Squail, Statistician, Stop, Sum, Table, Tally, Tell, Tiddleywink, Ugolino, Weigh, Zeppelin

Countenance Approve, Brow, Endorse, Face, Favour, Mug, Sanction, Support, Visage

Counteract(ing) Ant-, Antidote, Cancel, Correct, Frustrate, Offset, Talion

Counterbalance Bascule, Offset, Undo, Weigh

Counter-charge Recrimination

Counterclockwise L(a)evorotatory

Counterfeit(er) Belie, Bogus, Boodle, Brum, Coiner, Duffer, Dummy, Fantasm, Flash, Forge, Imitant, Phantasm, Phoney, Pinchbeck, Postiche, Pseudo, Queer, Rap, Schlenter, Sham, Shan(d), Simulate, Slang, Slip, Smasher, Snide, Spurious, Stumer

Counterfoil Stub

Counterglow Gegenschein

Counter-irritant Seton

Countermand Abrogate, Annul, Cancel, Override, Rescind, Retract, Revoke

Counterpart Copy, Double, Obverse, Oppo, Parallel, Shadow, Similar, Spit(ting), Tally, Twin

Counterpoint Contrapuntal, Descant

Countersign Endorse, Password

Counterthrust Riposte

Counties, County Antrim, Armagh, Avon, Barset, Beds, Berkshire, Buteshire, Carlow, Cavan, Ceredigion, Champagne, Clare, Cleveland, Co, Comital, Cork, Cornwall, District, Donegal, Dorset, Down, Dublin, Durham, Dyfed, Fermanagh, Fife, Flint, Gwent, Gwynedd, Hampshire, Herefordshire, Herts, Hunts, Kent, Kerry, Kesteven, Kildare, Kilkenny, Kincardineshire, Kinrossshire, Kirkcudbrightshire, Lanarkshire, Laois, Leicestershire, Leitrim, Limerick, Lincolnshire, Loamshire, Londonderry, Longford, Louth, Mayo, Meath, Merionithshire, Merseyside, Metropolitan, Midlothian, Monaghan, Monmouthshire, Montgomeryshire, Moray, Nairnshire, Neath Port Talbot, NI, Norfolk, Northamptonshire, Northumberland, North Yorkshire, Notts, Offaly, Omagh, Oxfordshire, Palatine, Parish, Peeblesshire, Pembrokeshire, Perth(shire), Powys, Radnorshire, Renfrewshire, Roscommon, Ross, Ross and Cromarty, Rutland, Seat, Selkirkshire, Shire, Shropshire, Six, Som(erset), South Glamorgan, Staffordshire, Stirlingshire, Suffolk, Surrey, Sussex, Sutherland, Sy, The Mearns, Tipperary, Torfaen, Tyne and Wear, Tyrone, Vale of Glamorgan, Warwickshire, Waterford, West Glamorgan, West Lothian, Westmeath, West Midlands, Westmoreland, West Sussex, West Yorkshire, Wexford, Wicklow, Wigtownshire, Wilts, Worcs, Yorkshire

Countless Infinite, Innumerable, Myriad, Umpteen, Untold
Country(side), **Countrified** Annam, Bangladesh, Boondocks, Bucolic, Champaign, Clime, Colchis, Edom, Enchorial, Fatherland, Greenwood, High, Karoo, Karroo, > LAND, Lea, Lee, Low, Mongolia, Motherland, Nation, Parish, Paysage, People, Province, Realm, Region, Republic, Rural, Satellite, Scenery, Soil, State, Sultanate, Thrace, Tundra, Tweedy, Weald, Wold, Yemen
Country girl Amaryllis
Country house Hall, Manor, Quinta
Countryman Arcadian, Bacon, Boor, Culchie, Hick, Hillbilly, Hodge, National, Native, Peasant, Un, Yokel
Coup Blow, Deal, KO, Move, Putsch, Scoop, Stroke
Coupé Cabriolet, Landaulet
Couple(r), **Coupling** Ally, Band, Brace, Bracket, Connect, Direct, Duet, Duo, Dyad, Fishplate, Flange, Galvanic, Gemini, Geminy, Hitch, Item, > JOIN, Marrow, Marry, Mate, Meng(e), Ment, Ming, Octave, Pair, Pr, Relate, Shackle, Tie, Tirasse, Turnbuckle, Tway, Union, Universal, Voltaic, Wed, Yoke
Couple of ducks Spectacles
Couplet Distich, Heroic
Coupon(s) Ration, Ticket, Voucher
Courage(ous) Balls, Bottle, Bravado, Bravery, Bulldog, Cojones, Dutch, Fortitude, Gallantry, Game, Gimp, Grit, Gumption, Guts, Hardihood, Heart, Heroism, Lion-heart, Macho, Mettle, Moxie, Nerve, Pluck, Prowess, Rum, Spirit, Spunk, Stalwart, Steel, Valiant, Valour, Wight
Courgette Zucchini
Courier Estafette, Guide, Harbinger, Herald, > MESSENGER, Postillion, Postman
Course(s) Access, Afters, Aim, Aintree, Antipasto, Appetiser, Arroyo, Ascot, Assault, Atlantic, Barge, Bearing, Beat, Belt, Canal, Career, Chantilly, Chase, Circuit, Collision, Consommé, Correspondence, Crash, Current, Curriculum, Cursus, Daltonism, Dessert, Diadrom, Dish, Dromic, Entrée, Epsom, Fish, Food, Foundation, Going, Golf, Goodwood, Greats, Heat, Isodomon, Lane, Lap, Layer, Leat, Leet, Line, Lingfield, Links, Longchamp, Magnetic, Main, Meal, Meat, Mess, Newbury, Newmarket, Nine-hole, Nulla, > OF COURSE, Orbit, Period, Policy, PPE, Procedure, Process, Programme, Progress, Pursue, Quadrivium, Race, Raik, Refresher, Regimen, Rhumb, Ride, Ring, Rink, Road, Rota, Route, Routine, Run, Rut, Sandown, Sandwich, Semester, Seminar, Series, Sorbet, Soup, Stadium, Starter, Stearage, Steerage, Step(s), Stratum, Streak, Stretch, Stretching, String, Syllabus, Tack, Tanride, Tenor, Track, Trade, Trend, Troon, Vector, Via media, Water table, Way, Wearing, Wentworth
Court(ier) Address, Admiralty, Appellate, Arches, Areopagus, Atrium, Attention, Audience, Audiencia, Aula, Banc, Bar, Basecourt, Bench, Beth Din, Bishop's, Boondock, Camelot, Caravanserai, Cassation, Centre, Chancery, Chase, Clay, Consistory, County, Criminal, Crown, CS, Ct, Curia, Curia Regis, Curtilage, Cutcher(r)y, Date, Dedans, Dicastery, Diplock, District, Doctor's Commons, Domestic, Duchy, Durbar, Dusty Feet, En tout cas, Evora, Eyre, Federal, Fehm(gericht), Fehmgerichte, Forensic, Forest, Forum, Friars, Fronton, Galleria, Garth, Go steady, Grass, Guildenstern, Halimot(e), Hampton, Hard, High, Hof, Holy See, Hustings, Hypaethron, Inferior, Intermediate, Invite, Jack, Justice, Juvenile, Kachahri, Kacheri, Kangaroo, Keys, King, King's Bench, Kirk Session, Knave, Law, Leet, Lobby, Lyon, Magistrate's, Majlis, Marshalsea, Mash, Moot, Old Bailey, Open, Parvis, Patio, Peristyle, Petty Sessions, Philander, Piepowder, Police, Porte, Praetorium, Presbytery, Prize, Probate, Provincial, Provost, Quad, Quarter Sessions, Queen,

Queen's Bench, Retinue, Rosenkrantz, Royal, Sanhedrim, Sanhedrin, See, Service, Session, Sheriff, Shire-moot, Spoon, Stannary, Star Chamber, Sue, Superior, Supreme, Swanimote, Sweetheart, Thane, Thegn, Traffic, Trial, Tribunal, Vehm, Vehmgericht(e), Vestibulum, Walk out, Ward, Wench, Woo, World, Wow, Yard, Youth

Courteous, Courtesy Affable, Agrement, Bow, Chivalry, Civil, Comity, Devoir, Etiquette, Genteel, Gracious, Hend, Polite, Refined, Urbanity

Courtesan Aspasia, Bona-roba, Delilah, Demi-monde, Demi-rep, Geisha, Hetaera, Lais, Lampadion, Lorette, Madam, Phryne, Plover, Pornocracy, Prostitute, Stallion, Thais

Courtly Chivalrous, Cringing, Dignified, Flattering, Refined

Court-martial Drumhead

Courtyard Area, Cortile, Enceinte, Garth, Marae, Patio, Quad

Cousin(s) Bette, Cater, Country, Coz, Cross, German, Kin, Kissing, Robin, Skater

Couturier Dior, Dressmaker

Cove Abraham's, Arm, Bay, Bight, Buffer, Creek, Cure, Gink, Grot, Guy, Hithe, Hythe, Inlet, Lulworth, Nook

Covenant(er) Abrahamic, Alliance, Appurtenant, Bond, Contract, Hillmen, Pledge, Restrictive, Warranty, Whiggamore

Coventry Isolation

Cover(ed), Covering Adventitia, A l'abri, Amnion, Antependium, Antimacassar, Apron, Aril, Attire, Awning, Barb, Bard(s), Bark, Bedspread, Bestrew, Bind, Blanket, Bodice, Brood, Bubblewrap, Bury, Camouflage, Canopy, Cap, Caparison, Cape, Capsule, Casing, Casque, Catch-all, Caul, Ceil, Ciborium, Cladding, Clapboard, Cleithral, Clithral, Coat, Cocoon, Coleorhiza, Conceal, Cope, Copyright, Cosy, Counterpane, Cour, Covert, Cowl, Curtain, Deadlight, Deck, Deputise, Dividend, Dome, Drape(t), Dripstone, Duchesse, Dust-sheet, Duvet, Eiderdown, Encase, Endue, Enguard, Enlace, Enshroud, Envelop(e), Enwrap, Exoderm(is), Exoskeleton, Extra, Face, Falx, Fanfare, Felting, Fielder, Figleaf, Fingerstall, First-day, Flashing, Fother, Front, Gaiter, Gambado, Grolier, Ground, Hap, Harl, Hat, Hatch, Havelock, Heal, Heel, Hejab, Hele, Hell, Helmet, Hijab, Hood, Housing, Hubcap, Immerse, Incase, Indusium, Inmask, Insulate, Insurance, Insure, Jacket, Lag, Lay, Leap, Leep, Legging, Legwarmer, Lid, Liner, Loose, Manche, Mantle, Mask, Metal, Mount, Muffle, Mulch, Notum, Numnah, Obscure, OC, Occlude, On, Operculum, Orillion, Orlop, Overlay, Palampore, Palempore, Pall, Pand, Parcel, Pasties, Patch, Pebbledash, Pelmet, Periderm, Pillow sham, Plaster, Plate, Pleura, Point, Pseudonym, Pullover, Quilt, Radome, Regolith, Robe, Roof, Roughcast, Rug, Sally, Screen, Serviette, Setting, Sheath, Sheet, Shell, Shelter, Shield, Shrink-wrap, Shroud, Shuck, Skin, Smokescreen, Solleret, Span, Spat, Stand-by, Stifle, Swathe, Tampian, Tampion, Tapadera, Tapis, Tarpaulin, Teacosy, Tectorial, Tegmen, Tegument, Tent, Test(a), Tester, Thatch, Thimble, Thumbstall, Tick(ing), Tile, Tilt, Tonneau, Top, Trapper, Trench, Trip, Turtleback, Twill, Twilt, Umbrella, Upholster, Valance, Veil, Vele, Veneer, Ventail, Vesperal, Vest, Visor, Volva, Wainscot, Waterdeck, Whelm, Whitewash, Wrap, Wrapper, Yapp

Covert(ly) Clandestine, Copse, Privy, > **SECRET**, Shy, Sidelong, Sub rosa, Surreptitious, Tectrix, Ulterior

Covet(ed), Covetous Avaricious, Crave, Desiderata, Desire, Eager, Envy, Greedy, Hanker, Yearn

Cow Adaw, Alderney, Amate, Appal, Awe, Ayrshire, Bovine, Brahmin, Browbeat, Cash, Charolais, Colly, Crummy, Danton, Daunt, Dexter, Dsomo, Dun, Galloway, Gally, Goujal, Guernsey, Hawkey, Hawkie, Heifer, Hereford,

Intimidate, Jersey, Kouprey, Kyloe, Mart, Milch, Mog(gie), Moggy, Mooly, Muley, Mulley, Overawe, Redpoll, Red Sindhi, Rother(-beast), Sacred, Santa Gertrudis, Scare, Simmental, Springing, Stirk, Subact, Teeswater, Threaten, Unnerve, Vaccine, Zebu, Z(h)o

Coward(ly) Bessus, Cat, Chicken, Cocoa, Craven, Cuthbert, Dastard, Dingo, Dunghill, Fraidy-cat, Fugie, Funk, Gutless, Hen, Hilding, Jessie, Lily-livered, Meacock, Milk-livered, Niddering, Nidderling, Nidering, Niderling, Niding, Nithing, Noel, Panty-waist, Poltroon, Pusillanimous, Recreant, Scaramouch, Sganarelle, Slag, Sook, Squib, Viliaco, Viliago, Villagio, Villiago, Yellow, Yellow-belly

Cowboy, Cowgirl Broncobuster, Buckaroo, Cowpoke, Cowpuncher, Gaucho, Inexpert, Io, Jerrybuilder, Leger, Llanero, Puncher, Ranchero, Ritter, Roper, Vaquero, Waddie, Waddy, Wrangler

Cow-catcher Fender, Reata

Cower Croodle, Crouch, Fawn, Quail, Skulk, Wince

Cowl Bonnet, Capuchin, Granny, Hood, Kilmarnock

Cowpox Vaccinia

Cowshed, Cowstall Byre, Crib, Shippen, Shippon, Stable, Stall, Staw

Cowslip Culver-key, Pa(i)gle

Cox Steerer

Coxcomb Copple, Crest, Dandy, Dude, Fop, Jackanapes, Popinjay, Yellow-rattle

Coy Arch, Coquettish, Demure, Laithfu', Mim, Shamefast, > SHY, Skeigh, Skittish

Coyote SD

CPRS Think tank

Crab(by), Crablike Apple, Attercop, Blue swimmer, Calling, Cancer, Cancroid, Cantankerous, Capernoity, Cock, Coconut, Daddy, Decapoda, Diogenes, Ethercap, Ettercap, Fiddler, Ghost, Grouch, Hard-shell, Hermit, Horseman, Horseshoe, King, Land, Limulus, Mantis, Mitten, Mud, Nebula, Ochidore, Oyster, Pagurian, Partan, Pea, Perverse, Podite, Roast, Robber, Rock, Sand, Saucepan-fish, Scrawl, Sentinel, Sidle, Soft-shell, Soldier, Spectre, Spider, Velvet, Woolly-hand, Xiphosura, Zoea

▷ **Crab** *may indicate* an anagram

Crab-apple Scrog-bush, Scrog-buss

Crab-eater Urva

Crabs-eye Abrus

Crack(ed), Cracker(s), Cracking Ad-lib, Admirable, Bananas, Biscuit, Bonbon, Break, Cat, Catalytic, Chap, Chasm, Chat, Chink, Chip, Chop, Clap, Cleave, Cleft, Cloff, Confab, Cranny, Craquelure, Craqueture, Craze, Cream, Crepitate, Crevasse, Crevice, Crispbread, Dawn, Decode, Doom, Dunt, Elite, Expert, Fatiscent, Fent, Firework, First-rate, Fisgig, Fissure, Fizgig, Flaw, Flip-flop, Fracture, Go, Graham, Grike, Gryke, Gully, Hairline, Hit, Jibe, Joint, Knacker, Leak, Liar, Little-endian, Matzo, Moulin, Oner, Peterman, Pore, Praise, Prawn, Quarter, Quip, Rap, Report, Rhagades, Rictus, Rift, Rille, Rima, Rime, Rimous, Rive, Rock, Saltine, Sand, Seam, Shake, Snap, Soda, Solve, Split, Squib, Sulcus, Toe, Top, Try, Waterloo, Yegg

Crackerjack Ace, Nailer, Trump

Crackle, Crackling Craze, Crepitation, Crepitus, Crinkle, Decrepitate, Fizz, Glaze, Rale, Skin

Crackpot Nutter

Cracksman Burglar, Peterman, Raffles

Cradle Bassinet, Berceau, Cat's, Cot, Crib, Cunabula, Hammock, Knife, Nestle,

Newton's, Rocker

Craft(y) Arch, Art, Aviette, Barbola, Boat, Canal boat, Cautel, Cunning, Disingenuous, Finesse, Fly, Guile, Hydroplane, Ice-breaker, Insidious, Kontiki, Landing, Machiavellian, Mister, Mystery, Oomiack, Reynard, Saic, Shallop, Ship, Shuttle, > SKILL, Slee, Sleeveen, Slim, Slippy, Sly, Slyboots, State, Subdolous, Subtil(e), Subtle, Suttle, Triphibian, Umiak, Underhand, Versute, > VESSEL, Wile, Workmanship

▷ **Craft** *may indicate* an anagram

Craftsman AB, Artificer, Artisan, Artist, Chippy, Cutler, Ebonist, Fabergé, Finisher, Gondolier, Guild, Hand, Joiner, Journeyman, Mason, Mechanic, Morris, Opificer, Wainwright, Wright

Crag(gy) Eyrie, Height, Heuch, Heugh, Krantz, Noup, Rock

Cram(mer) Bag, Candle-waster, Cluster, Craig, Fill, Gag, Gavage, Neck, Pang, Prime, Rugged, Scar(p), Shoehorn, Spur, Stap, Stodge, Stow, Swat, Tuck

Cramp(ed) Agraffe, Charleyhorse, Confine, Constrict, Crick, Hamper, Hamstring, Incommodious, Myalgia, Pinch, Poky, Potbound, Restrict, Rigor, Squeeze, Stunt, Tetany, Writer's

Crane Brolga, Cherry picker, Davit, Deck, Demoiselle, Derrick, Dragline, Gantry, Gooseneck, Grabbing, Herd, Heron, Hooper, Ichabod, Jib, Jigger, Kenworthy, Luffing-jib, Rail, Sarus, Sedge, Shears, Sheer, Siege, Stork, Stretch, Tower, Tulip, Whooper, Whooping, Winch

Crane-fly Leatherjacket, Tipulidae

Crank(y) Eccentric, Grouch, Handle, Lever, Mot, Perverse, Whim, Wince, Winch, Wind

Crash Bingle, Collapse, Disk, Dush, Fail, Fall, Fragor, Intrude, Linen, Nosedive, Pile up, Prang, Rack, Ram, Rote, Shunt, Slam, Smash, Thunderclap, Topple

▷ **Crashes** *may indicate* an anagram

Crass Coarse, Crude, Rough, Rude

Crate Biplane, Box, Case, Ceroon, Crib, Hamper, Sero(o)n, Soapbox, Tube

Crater Alphonsus, Aristarchus, Aristotle, Askja, Autolycus, Bail(l)y, Blowhole, Caldera, Cavity, Cissing, Clavius, Copernicus, Fra Mauro, Grimaldo, Hipparchus, Hole, Hollow, Kepler, Kilauea, Maar, Meteor, Newton, Plato, Ptolemaeus, Pythagoras, Schickard, Sinus iridium, Theophilus, Tycho

Cravat Ascot, Neckatee, Neck-cloth, Oerlay, Overlay, Scarf, Soubise, Steenkirk, Tie

Crave, Craving Appetite, Aspire, Beg, Beseech, Covet, Desire, Entreat, Gasp, Greed, Hanker, Hunger, Itch, Libido, Long, Lust, Malacia, Methomania, Munchies, Opsomania, Orexis, Pica, Polyphagia, Sitomania, The munchies, Thirst, Yearn, Yen

Craven Abject, Coward, Dastard, Hen, Recreant

Crawl(er) All fours, Clamber, Creep, Cringe, Drag, Grovel, Lag, Lickspittle, Pub, Reptile, Scramble, Scrome, Skulk, Snail, Swim, Sycophant, Tantony, Trail, Trudgen, Yes-man

Crayfish Astacology, Gilgie, Jilgie, Yabbie, Yabby

Crayon Chalk, Colour, Conté®, Pastel, Pencil, Sauce

Craze(d), Crazy Absurd, Ape, Barmy, Bats, Batty, Berserk, Bonkers, Break, Cornflake, Crack(ers), Crackpot, Cult, Daffy, Dement, Derange, Dingbats, Dippy, Distraught, Doiled, Doilt, Doolally, Dottle, Dotty, Fad, Flake, Flaw, Folie, Frantic, Furious, Furore, Gaga, Geld, Gonzo, Gyte, Haywire, Headbanger, Insane, Loco, Loony, Lunatic, Madden, Maenad(ic), Mania, Manic, Mattoid, Melomania, Meshug(g)a, Nuts, Porangi, Potty, Psycho(path), Rage, Rave, Scatty, Screwball, Skivie, Slatey, Stunt, Unhinge, Wacko, Wacky, Wet,

W(h)acky, Whim, Wowf, Zany

▷ **Crazy** *may indicate* an anagram

Creak(y) Cry, Grate, Grind, Rheumatic, Scraich, Scraigh, Scroop, Seam, Squeak

Cream(y) Barrier, Bavarian, Best, Chantilly, Clotted, Cold, Cornish, Crème fraiche, Devonshire, Double, Elite, Foundation, Glacier, Ivory, Jollop, Lanolin, Liniment, Lotion, Mousse, Off-white, Ointment, Opal, Paragon, Pick, Ream, Rich, Salad, Salve, Sillabub, Single, Skim, Smitane, Sour, Sun(screen), Syllabub, Vanishing, Whipped, Whipping

Crease Crumple, > **FOLD**, Lirk, Pitch, Pleat, Popping, Return, Ridge, Ruck(le), Ruga, Rugose, Wrinkle

Create, **Creation**, **Creative** Arty, Build, Coin, Compose, Continuous, Devise, Dreamtime, Engender, Establish, Fabricate, Forgetive, Form, Found, Generate, Genesis, Godhead, Ideate, Imaginative, > **INVENT**, Oratorio, Originate, Produce, Shape, Universe

Creator Ahura Mazda, Author, Demiurge, God, Inventor, Maker, Ormazd, Ormuzd

Creature Animal, Ankole, Basilisk, Beast, Being, Chevrotain, Cratur, Critter, Crittur, Man, Nekton, Saprobe, Sasquatch, Sphinx, Whiskey, Wight

Credence, **Credential(s)** Certificate, Document, Papers, Qualifications, Shelf, Testimonial

Credibility Street

Credible, **Credit(s)**, **Creditor** Ascribe, Attribute, Belief, Billboard, Byline, Carbon, Crawl, Esteem, Extended, Family, Honour, HP, Kite, Kudos, LC, Lender, Mense, Post-war, Probable, Reliable, Renown, Revolving, Shylock, Social, Strap, Street, Tally, Tick, Title, Trust, Weight, Youth

Credulous Charlie, Gullible, Naive, Simple, Trusting

Creed Apostle's, Athanasian, Belief, Doctrine, Faith, Ism, Nicene, Ophism, Outworn, Sect, Tenet

Creek Bay, Breaches, Cooper, Cove, Crick, Dawson, Estuary, Fleet, Geo, Goe, Indian, Inlet, Kill, Pow, Slough, Vae, Voe, Wick

Creel Basket, Hask, Scull, Skull

Creep(er), **Creeping**, **Creeps** Ai, Ampelopsis, Arbutus, Aseismic, Boston ivy, Cleavers, Crawl, Grew, Grovel, Grue, Heebie-jeebies, Heeby-jeebies, Herpetic, Honey, Inch, Insect, Ivy, Mission, Nerd, Nuthatch, Pussyfoot, Repent, Reptant, Sarmentous, Sittine, Skulk, Slink, Snake, Sneak(sby), Sobole(s), Soil, Toad, Tropaeolum, Truckle, Vinca, Vine, Virginia, Wickthing, Willies

Creeping Jenny Moneywort

Cremate, **Cremation**, **Crematorium** Burn, Char, Cinerarium, Ghat, Ghaut, Incinerate, Pyre, Sati, Suttee, Ustrinium

Creole Gullah, Haitian, Kriol, Papiamento, Tok Pisin

Crepe Blini, Blintz(e), Canton, Pancake

Crescent Barchan(e), Bark(h)an, Fertile, Growing, Lune(tte), Lunulate, Lunule, Meniscus, Moon, Red, Sickle, Waxing

Cress Cardamine, Garden, Hoary, Isatis, Pepperwort, Wart, Water, Yellow

Crest(ed) Acme, Chine, Cimier, Cockscomb, Comb, Copple, Crista, Height, Kirimon, Knap, Mon, Peak, Pileate, Pinnacle, Plume, Ridge, Summit, Tappit, Tee, > **TOP**, Tufty

Cretaceous Chalky, Senonian

Cretan Candiot(e), Minoan, Teucer

Crevasse Bergschrund, Chasm, Gorge, Rimaye

Crew Boasted, Company, Core, Eight, Equipage, Four, Lot, Manners, Men, Oars, Prize, Sailors, Salts, Seamen, Team, Teme, Torpid

Crew-cut Not(t)

Crib Cheat, Cot, Cowhouse, Cratch, Filch, Horse, > KEY, Manger, Pony, Purloin, Putz, Shack, Stall, Steal, Trot

Crick Cramp, Kink, Spasm

Cricket(ers) Balm, Bat, Botham, Bowler, Bradman, CC, Cicada, Dry-bob, French, Grade, Grasshopper, Grig, Hopper, Jerusalem, Katydid, Keeper, Knott, Leg, Long-leg, Long-off, Long-on, Longstop, March, May, Mid-on, Mole, Muggleton, Nightwatchman, Opener, Packer, Point, Pyjama, Shield, Single-wicket, Slip, Stool, Stridulate, Tate, Test, Tettix, Tip and run, Vigoro, Warner, Windball, Windies, Wisden, XI(gent)

Crier Bellman, Herald, Muezzin, Niobe, Outrooper

Crime Attentat, Barratry, Caper, Chantage, Chaud-mellé, Computer, Corpus delicti, Ecocide, Fact, Felony, Fraud, Graft, Hate, Heist, Iniquity, Inside job, Malefaction, Mayhem, Misdeed, Misdemeanour, > OFFENCE, Organised, Ovicide, Peccadillo, Perjury, Pilferage, Ram raid, Rap, Rape, Rebellion, > SIN, Tort, Transgression, Treason, Victimless, War, Wrong

Crimea Balaclava

Criminal Bandit, Bent, Bushranger, Chummy, Con, Cosa Nostra, Counterfeiter, Crack-rope, > CROOK, Culpable, Culprit, Delinquent, Escroc, Felon, Flagitious, Forensic, Gangster, Heavy, Heinous, Highbinder, Hitman, Hood(lum), Jailbird, Ladrone, Lag, Larcener, Lifer, Looter, Lowlife, Maf(f)ia, Malefactor, Maleficent, Malfeasant, Mob(ster), Mobster, Ndrangheta, Nefarious, Nefast, Outlaw, Perp(etrator), Racketeer, Receiver, Recidivist, Reprehensible, Rustler, Sinner, Snakehead, Thug, Triad, Underworld, Villain, Wicked, Wire, Yakuza, Yardie, Yegg

▷ **Criminal** *may indicate* an anagram

Crimp Pleat

Crimson Carmine, Incarnadine, Modena, Red, Scarlet

Cringe, Cringing Cower, Creep, Crouch, Fawn, Grovel, Shrink, Sneaksby, Truckle

Crinkle, Crinkly Rugate, Rugose

Crinoline Farthingale, Hoop

Cripple(d) Damage, Debilitate, Disable, Game, Hamstring, Handicap, Injure, > LAME, Lameter, Lamiter, Maim, Paralyse, Polio, Scotch, Spoil

Crisis Acme, Crunch, Drama, Emergency, Exigency, Fastigium, Fit, Flap, Head, Identity, Make or break, Midlife, Panic, Pass, Quarterlife, Shake-out, Solution, Test

Crisp Brisk, Clear, Crimp, Crunchy, Fresh, Potato, Sharp, Short, Succinct, Terse

Crispin Sutor(ial)

Criss-cross Alternate, Fret, Interchange, Vein

Criteria, Criterion Benchmark, Gauge, Koch's postulates, Measure, Precedent, Proof, Rayleigh, Rule, Shibboleth, > STANDARD, Test, Touchstone

Critic(al), Criticise, Criticism Acute, Agate, Animadversion, Archer, Aristarch, Armchair, Arnold, Attack, Badmouth, Bagehot, Barrack, Bellettrist, Berate, Bird, Blame, Boileau, Boo, Captious, Carp, Castigate, Cavil, Censor(ious), > CENSURE, Climacteric, Clobber, Comment, Condemn, Connoisseur, Crab, Criticaster, > CRUCIAL, Crunch, Dangle, Decisive, Denigrate, Denounce, Deprecate, Desperate, Diatribe, Dutch uncle, Earful, Etain, Exacting, Excoriate, Fastidious, Fateful, Feuilleton, Flak, Flay, Fulminous, Gosse, Harrumph, Important, Impugn, Inge, Inveigh, Judge, Judgemental, Knife-edge, Knock(er), Lash, Leavis, Literary, Masora(h), Mas(s)orete, Mordacious, Nag, Nasute, Nibble, Nice, Niggle, Overseer, Pan, Pater, Puff, Pundit, Quibble, Rap, Rebuke, Reprehend, Review(er), Rip, Roast, Ruskin,

Scalp, Scarify, Scathe, Scorn, Second guess, Serious, Severe, Shaw, Sideswipe, Slag, Slam, Slashing, Slate, Sneer, Snipe, Stick, Stricture, Strop, Tense, Textual, Threap, Touch and go, Ultracrepidate, Urgent, Vet, Vitriol, Vituperation, Watershed, Zoilism

Croak Creak, Crow, Die, Grumble, Gutturalise

Croatian Cravates, Glagolitic, Serb

Crochet Lace, Weave

Crock Chorrie, Crate, Jar, Mug, Pig, Pitcher, Pot, Potshard, Potshare, Potsherd, Stean(e)

Crockery Ceramics, China, Dishes, Earthenware, Oddment, Sunbeam, Ware

▷ **Crocks** *may indicate* an anagram

Crocodile Cayman, File, Flat dog, Garial, Gavial, Gharial, Line, Mud gecko, Mugger, River-dragon, Saltwater, Sebek, Teleosaur(ian)

Crocus Autumn, Naked lady, Prairie, Saffron

Croesus Lydia

Cromwell Ironside, Lord Protector, Noll, Oliver, Protector, Richard, Roundhead

Crone(s) Beldam(e), Ewe, Graeae, Hag, Mawkin, Ribibe, Rudas, Sibyl, Sybil, Trot, Trout, > WITCH

Crony Anile, Chum, Intimate, Mate, Pal, Sidekick

Crook(ed) Adunc, Ajee, Aslant, Awry, Bad, Bend, Bow, Cam, Camsheugh, Camsho(ch), Criminal, Cromb, Crome, Crosier, Crummack, Crummock, Crump, Curve, Elbow, Fraud, Heister, Hook, Indirect, Kam(me), Kebbie, Lituus, Malpractitioner, Operator, Shyster, Sick, Skew(whiff), Slick(er), Squint, Staff, Swindler, Thraward, Thrawart, Thrawn, Twister, Wonky, Yeggman

▷ **Crooked** *may indicate* an anagram

Croon(er), Crooning Bing, Como, Lament, Lull, Monody, Murmur, Sing

Crop(s), Cropped Basset, Browse, Cash, Catch, Clip, Cover, Craw, Cut, Distress, Dock, Emblements, Energy, Epilate, Eton, Foison, Forage, Harvest, Hog, Ingluvies, Kharif, Milo, Not(t), Plant, Poll, Produce, Rabi, Riding, Rod, Root, Shingle, Silage, Stow, Subsistence, Succession, Top, Truncate, White

Cropper Downfall, Header, Purler

Croquet (term) Peel, Rover

Croquette Kromesky, Quenelle, Rissole

Cross(ing), Crossbred Angry, Ankh, Ansate, Archiepiscopal, Banbury, Basta(a)rd, Beefalo, Bois-brule, Boton(n)e, Burden, Calvary, Cantankerous, Canterbury, Capital, Cattalo, Celtic, Channel, Chi, Chiasm(a), Cleche, Clover-leaf, Compital, Constantine, Crosslet, Crotchety, Crucifix, Crux, Decussate, Demi-wolf, Dihybrid, Double, Dso(mo), Dzobo, Eleanor, Encolpion, Faun, Fiery, Fitché, Fleury, Foil, Footbridge, Ford, Frabbit, Fractious, Frampold, Franzy, Funnel, Fylfot, Geneva, George, Grade, Greek, Holy rood, Humette, Hybrid, Ill, Imp, Indignant, Interbreed, Intersect, Intervein, Iona, Iracund, Irate, Irked, Iron, Jerusalem, Jomo, Jumart, Kiss, Krest, Ladino, Latin, Level, Liger, Lorraine, Lurcher, Maltese, Mameluco, Market, Mermaid, Military, Mix, Moline, Mongrel, Mule, Narky, Nattery, Node, Norman, Northern, Nuisance, Obverse, Ordinary, Orthodox, Overpass, Overthwart, Papal, Patonce, Patriarchal, Pattée, Pectoral, Pedestrian, Pelican, Plumcot, Plus, Pommé, Potence, Potent, Preaching, Puffin, Quadrate, Ratty, Reciprocal, Red, Roman, Rood, Rose, Rouen, Rouge, Rubicon, Ruthwell, Sain, St Andrew's, St Anthony's, St George's, St Patrick's, St Peter's, Saltier, Saltire, Satyr, Shirty, Sign, Snappy, Southern, Strid, Svastika, Swastika, T, Tangelo, Tau, Tayberry, Ten, Testy, Thraw, Thwart, Tiglon, Tigon, Times, Transit, Transom, Transverse, Traverse, Tree, Urdé, Vexed, Vext, Victoria, > VOTE, Weeping, Whippet, Wry, X,

Yakow, Zambo, Zebra(ss), Zebrinny, Zebroid, Zebrula, Zebrule, Zedonk, Z(h)o, Zobu

▷ **Cross** *may indicate* an anagram

▸ **Cross-bar** *see* CROSSPIECE

Cross-bearer Crucifer

Cross-bill Metagnathous

Cross-bones Marrowbones

Cross-bow Arbalest, Bal(l)ista

Cross-country Langlauf, Overland

Cross-dressing Eonism

Cross-examine Grill, Interrogate, Question, Targe

Cross-eyed Skelly(-eyed), Squint

Crossfertilisation Allogamy, Heterosis, Hybrid vigour, Xenogamy

Cross-grained Ill-haired, Mashlam, Mashlim, Mas(h)lin, Mashlock, Mashlum, Stubborn

Crosspiece, **Cross-bar**, **Cross-timber** Bar, Cancelli, Footrail, Inter-tie, Lierne, Phillipsite, Putlock, Putlog, Quillon, Serif, Seriph, Stempel, Stemple, Stretcher, Stull, Swingle-tree, Toggle, Transom, Whiffle-tree, Whipple-tree, Yoke

Crossroads Carfax, Carfox, Carrefour, Compital, Soap

Crossword Cryptic, Grid, Puzzle, Quickie

Crotchet(y) Eccentric, Fad, Fancy, Grouch, Kink, Quarter-note, Toy

Crouch Bend, Cringe, Falcade, Fancy, Lordosis, Ruck, Set, Squat, Squinch

Croup Angina, Cough, Kink, Rump

Crow Boast, Brag, Carrion, Chewet, Chough, Corbie, Corvus, Crake, Currawong, Daw, Flute-bird, Gorcrow, Hooded, Hoodie, Huia, Jackdaw, Jim(my), Murder, Piping, Raven, Rook, Saddleback, Skite, Squawk, Swagger, Vaunt

Crowbar Gavelock, James, Jemmy, Lever

Crowd(ed) Abound, Army, Bike, Boodle, Bumper, Bunch, Byke, Caboodle, Clutter, Concourse, Congest(ed), Cram, Crush, Crwth, Dedans, Doughnut, Drove, Fill, Flock, Galere, Gate, Gathering, Herd, Horde, > HOST, Huddle, Hustle, Jam, Lot, Mein(e)y, Meinie, Menyie, Mob, Mong, Multitude, Ochlo-, Pack, Pang, Press, Rabble, Raft, Ram, Ratpack, Ring, Ruck, Scrooge, Scrouge, Scrowdge, Scrum, Serr(é), Shoal, Shove, Slew, Slue, Squeeze, Stuff, Swarm, Swell, Three, Throng, Trinity, Varletry

Crowfoot Gilcup, Reate

Crown Acme, Bays, Bull, Camp, Cantle, Cap, Capernoity, Cidaris, Civic, Coma, Corona, Cr, Diadem, Ecu, Engarland, Enthrone, Fillet, Garland, Gloria, Haku, Head, Headdress, Instal, Iron, Ivy, Krantz, Laurel, Monarch, Mural, Naval, Nole, Noll, Noul(e), Nowl, Olive, Optical, Ore, Ovation, Pate, Peak, Pschent, Sconce, Taj, Tiara, > TOP, Triple, Triumphal, Trophy, Vallary, Vertex

Crucial Acute, Critical, Essential, Key, Pivotal, Quintessential, Vital, Watershed

Crucible Cruset, Melting-pot, Vessel

Crucifix(ion), **Crucify** Calvary, Cross, Golgotha, Mortify, Rood, Torment, Torture

Crude(ness) Bald, Brash, Brute, Coarse, Earthy, Halfbaked, Immature, Incondite, Primitive, Raunch, Raw, Rough, Rough and ready, Rough-hewn, Rough-wrought, Tutty, Uncouth, Vulgar, Yahoo

Cruel(ty) Barbarous, Bloody, Brutal, Dastardly, De Sade, Draconian, Fell, Fiendish, Flinty, Hard, Heartless, Immane, Inhuman, Machiavellian, Mental, Neronic, Pitiless, Raw, Remorseless, Sadistic, Stern, Tormentor, Vicious

▷ **Cruel** *may indicate* an anagram

Cruet Ampulla, Condiments, Decanter

Cruise(r) Booze, Busk, Cabin, Nuke, Prowl, Rove, Sail, Ship, Tom, Travel, Trip,

Voyager

Crumb(le), **Crumbly**, **Crumbs** Coo, Decay, Disintegrate, Ee, Fragment, Friable, Law, Leavings, Moulder, Mull, Murl, Nesh, Nirl, Ort, Particle, Ped, Raspings, Rot, Rotter

Crumpet Dish, Girl, Muffin, Nooky, Pash, Pikelet

Crumple Collapse, Crunkle, Crush, Raffle, Scrunch, Wrinkle

Crunch(y) Chew, Craunch, Crisp, Gnash, Graunch, Grind, Munch, Occlude, Scranch

Crusade(r) Baldwin, Campaign, Cause, Pilgrim, Tancred, Templar

Crush(ed), **Crusher** Acis, Anaconda, Annihilate, Bow, Champ, Comminute, Conquer, Contuse, Cranch, Crunch, Defeat, Destroy, Graunch, Grind, Hug, Jam, Knapper, Levigate, Mangle, Mash, Mill, Molar, Mortify, Oppress, Overcome, Overwhelm, Pash, Policeman, Pound, Press, Pulp, Pulverise, Quash, Ruin, Schwarmerei, Scotch, Scrum, Scrumple, Smash, Squabash, Squash, Squeeze, Squelch, Squish, Stamp, Stave, Steam-roll, Stove, Suppress, Telescope, Trample, Tread

Crust(y) Argol, Beeswing, Cake, Coating, Coffin, Continental, Cover, Crabby, Craton, Fur, Gratin, Heel, Horst, Kissing, Kraton, Lithosphere, Oceanic, Osteocolla, Pie, Reh, Rind, Rine, Sal, Salband, Scab, Shell, Sial, Sima, Sinter, Sordes, Surly, Tartar, Teachie, Terrane, Tetchy, Upper, Wine-stone

Crustacea(n) Amphipod, Barnacle, Brachyuran, Branchiopoda, Camaron, Cirriped, Cirripede, Cirripid, Cladoceran, Copepod, Crab, Crayfish, Cumacean, Cyclops, Cyprid, Cypris, Decapod(a), Entomostraca, Euphausia, Fishlouse, Foot-jaw, Gribble, Isopod, Krill, Langoustine, Lobster, Macrura, Malacostracan, Marron, Nauplius, Ostracoda, Pagurian, Phyllopod, Prawn, Rhizocephalan, Sand-hopper, Scampi, Scampo, Schizopod, Sea slater, Shellfish, Shrimp, Slater, Squilla, Stomatopod, Woodlouse, Yabbie, Yabby

Crutch Morton's, Potant

Crux Essence, Nub

Cry(ing) Aha, Alalagmus, Alew, Banzai, Bark, Battle, Bawl, Bell, Blat, Bleat, Bleb, Blub(ber), Boo, Boohoo, Bray, Bump, Caramba, Caw, Cheer, Chevy, Chirm, Chivy, Clang, Crake, Croak, Crow, Dire, Euoi, Eureka, Evoe, Exclaim, Fall, Field-holler, Gardyloo, Gathering, Geronimo, Gowl, Greet, Halloo, Harambee, Haro, Harrow, Havoc, Heigh, Hemitrope, Herald, Hinny, Hoicks, Holler, Honk, Hoo, Hoop, Hosanna, Hout(s)-tout(s), Howl, Humph, Io, Kaw, Low, Mewl, Miaou, Miau(l), Miserere, Mourn, Night-shriek, O(c)hone, Oi, Olé, Ow, Pugh, Rallying, Rivo, Sab, Scape, Scream, Screech, Sell, Sese(y), Sessa, > **SHOUT**, Shriek, Slogan, Snivel, Snotter, Sob, Soho, Sola, Squall, Squawk, Street, Tally-ho, Tantivy, Umph, Vagitus, View-halloo, Vivat, Vociferate, Wail, War, Watchword, Waul, Wawl, Weep, Westward ho, Whee(ple), Whimper, Whine, Whinny, Whoa, Whoop, Winge, Wolf, Yammer, Yelp, Yicker, Yikker, Yip, Yippee, Yodel, Yo-heave-ho, Yo-ho-ho, Yoick, Yoop, Yowl

Crypt(ic) Catacomb, Cavern, Chamber, Crowde, Encoded, Favissa, Grotto, Hidden, Obscure, Occult, Secret, Sepulchre, Short, Steganographic, Tomb, Unclear, Undercroft, Vault

Cryptogam Acotyledon, Acrogen, Fern(-ally), Moss, Pteridophyte

Cryptographer Decoder, Ventris

Crystal(lise), **Crystal-gazer**, **Crystalline** Allotriomorphic, Axinite, Baccara(t), Beryl, Candy, Citrine, Clathrate, Clear, Copperas, Coumarin, Cumarin, Dendrite, Druse, Effloresce, Elaterin, Enantiomorph, Epitaxy, Erionite, Fuchsin(e), Geode, Glass, Hemihedron, Hemimorphic, Hemitrope, Ice-stone, Ideal, Imazadole, Jarosite, Lead, Liquid, Lithium, Love-arrow, Macle,

Macro-axis, Melamine, Mixed, Nicol, Orthogonal, Orthorhombic, Pellucid, Phenocryst, Piezo, Piezoelectric, Pinacoid, Pinakoid, Prism, Pseudomorph, Purin(e), Quartz, R(h)aphide, R(h)aphis, Rhinestone, Rock, Rotenone, Rubicelle, Scryer, Shoot, Skryer, Smectic, Snowflake, Sorbitol, Spar, Spicule, Table, Trichite, Trilling, Twin(ned), Watch-glass, Xanthene, Xenocryst

Cub Baby, Kit, Novice, Pup, Whelp, Wolf

Cube, **Cubic**, **Cubist** Bath, Braque, Cu, Die, Necker, Nosean, Quadrate, Rubik's®, Serac, Smalto, Snub, Solid, Stere, Stock, Tesseract

Cubicle Alcove, Booth, Carrel(l), Stall

Cuckold Actaeon, Cornute, Graft, Homer, Lenocinium, Vulcan's badge, Wittol

Cuckoo Ament, Ani, April fool, Bird, Brain-fever bird, Gouk, Gowk, Inquiline, Insane, Koel, > **MAD**, Mental, Piet-my-vrou, Stupid

▷ **Cuckoo** *may indicate* an anagram

Cuckoopint Arum

Cucumber Bitter-apple, Choko, Colocynth, Coloquintida, Dill, Elaterium, Gherkin, Pickle, Sea-slug, Squirting, Trepang, Wolly

Cuddle Canoodle, Caress, Clinch, Embrace, Fondle, Hug, Nooky, Smooch, Smuggle, Snuggle

Cudgel Alpeen, Ballow, Bludgeon, Brain, Club, Cosh, Drub, Fustigate, Plant, Rack, Shillelagh, Souple, Stick, Swipple, Tan, Towel, Truncheon

Cue Cannonade, Catchword, Feed, Feed-line, Half-butt, Hint, Mace, > **PROMPT**, Reminder, Rod, Sign, Signal, Wink

Cuff Box, Buffet, Clout, French, Iron, Muffettee, Strike, Swat

Cuirass Armour, Corselet, Lorica

Cuisine Bourgeoise, Cookery, Food, Lean, Menu, Minceur, Nouvelle

Cul-de-sac Blind, Dead-end, Impasse, Loke

Cull Gather, Pick, Select, Thin, Weed

Culminate, **Culmination** Apogean, Apogee, Climax, Conclusion, Crest, End, Head

Culpable Blameworthy, Guilty

Cult Aum Shinrikyo, Cabiri, Candombie, Cargo, Creed, Fertility, Macumba, Personality, Rastafarian, Sect, Shango, Shinto, Wicca, Worship

Cultivate(d), **Cultivation** Agronomy, Arty, Civilise, Dig, Dress, Ear, Ere, Farm, Genteel, Grow, Hoe, Hydroponics, Improve, Labour, Pursue, Raise, Refine, Sative, Sophisticated, Tame, Tasteful, Till, Tilth

Culture(d), **Cultural** Acheulean, Acheulian, Agar, Art(y), Aurignacian, Azilian, Bel esprit, Brahmin, Capsian, Civil(isation), Corporate, Ethnic, Experiment, Explant, Gel, Grecian, Hallstatt, Hip-hop, Humanism, Kultur(kreis), La Tène, Learning, Maglemosean, Maglemosian, Minoan, Mousterian, Organisational, Perigordian, Polish, Pure, Refinement, Solutrean, Sophisticated, Starter, Strepyan, Suspension, Tardenoisian, Tissue, Villanovan, Water

Cumbersome Clumsy, Heavy, Lumbering, > **UNWIELDY**

Cunctator Dilatory

Cuneiform Wedge(d)

Cunning Arch, Art, Artifice, Cautel, Craft(y), Deceit, Deep, Devious, Down, Finesse, Foxy, Insidious, Leery, Machiavellian, Quaint, Skill, Slee(kit), Sleight, Slim, Sly(boots), Smart, Sneaky, Subtle, Vulpine, Wile

Cup(s), **Cupped** Aecidium, America's, Beaker, Calcutta, Calix, Calyculus, Cantharus, Chalice, Claret, Cotyle, Cruse, Cupule, Cyathus, Cylix, Davis, Demitasse, Deoch-an-doruis, Deuch-an-doris, Dish, Doch-an-dorach, Dop, Egg, European, FA, Fairs, Final, Fingan, Finjan, Fruit, Gemma, Glenoid, Goblet, Grace, Grease, Hanap, Horn, Kylix, Loving, Melbourne, Merry, Monstrance,

Moustache, Mug, Noggin, Nut, Pannikin, Parting, Planchet, Plate, Poley, Posset, Pot, Procoelous, Quaff, Quaich, Quaigh, Rhyton, Rider, Ryder, Sangrado, Scyphus, Stem, Stirrup, Tantalus, Tass(ie), Tastevin, Tazza, Tea-dish, Tig, Tot, > **TROPHY**, Tyg, UEFA, Volva, Waterloo, World

Cup-bearer Ganymede, Hebe

Cupboard Almery, Almirah, A(u)mbry, Beauf(f)et, Cabinet, Chiffonier, Chiff(o)robe, Closet, Court, Credenza, Dresser, Fume, Livery, Locker, Meat-safe, Press, Walk-in

Cup-holder Hanaper, Hebe, Plinth, Saucer, Zarf, Zurf

Cupid Amoretto, Amorino, Archer, Blind, Cherub, Dan, Eros, Love, Putto

Cupola Belfry, Dome, Tholos

Cup-shaped Poculiform

Cur Dog, Messan, Mongrel, Mutt, Pi-dog, Scab, Scoundrel, Wretch, Yap

Curare, **Curari** Ourali, Poison, Wourali

Curassow Crax

Curate Minister, Nathaniel, Padré, Priest

Curb Bit, Brake, Bridle, Check, Clamp, Coaming, Dam, Edge, Puteal, Rein, Restrain, Rim, Snub, Well

Curd(s) Bean, Cheese, Junket, Lapper(ed)-milk, Lemon, Skyr, Tofu

Curdle Clot, Congeal, Earn, Erne, Lopper, Posset, Ren, Rennet, Run, Set, Sour, > **TURN**, Whig, Yearn

Cure(d), **Curative** Ameliorate, Amend, Antidote, Antirachitic, Bloater, Cold turkey, Dry-salt, Dun, Euphrasy, Ginseng, Heal, Hobday, Hydropathy, Jadeite, Jerk, Kipper, Laetrile, Medicinal, Nature, Nostrum, Panacea, Park-leaves, Prairie oyster, > **PRESERVE**, Reast, Recover, Recower, Reest, Remede, Remedy, Restore, Salt, Salve, Serum, Smoke, Smoke-dry, Tan, > **TREATMENT**, Tutsan, Water

▷ **Cure** *may indicate* an anagram

Curfew Gate, Prohibit, Proscribe

Curie Ci

Curio, **Curiosity**, **Curious** Agog, Bibelot, Freak, Inquisitive, Into, Meddlesome, Nos(e)y, Objet d'art, Objet de vertu, Odd, Peculiar, Prurience, Rarity, Rum, > **STRANGE**

▷ **Curious(ly)** *may indicate* an anagram

Curium Cm

Curl(s), **Curler**, **Curling**, **Curly** Bev, Bonspiel, Cirrus, Coil, Crimp, Crimple, Crinkle, Crisp, Crocket, Dildo, Earlock, Friz(z), Frizzle, Heart-breaker, Hog, Inwick, Kiss, Leaf, Loop, Love-lock, Outwick, Perm, Pin, Quiff, Repenter, Ringlet, Roll, Roulette, Scroll, Shaving, Spiral, Spit, Tong, Trunk, Twiddle, > **TWIST**, Ulotrichous, Wave, Wind

Curlew Bird, Whaup, Whimbrel

Curmudgeon Boor, Churl, Grouch, Route, Runt

Currant Berry, Flowering, Raisin, Rizard, Rizzar(t), Rizzer

Currency Cash, Circulation, > **COIN**, Coinage, Decimal, Euro, Finance, Fractional, Jiao, Kip, Koruna, Monetary, > **MONEY**, Prevalence, Reserve, Soft

▷ **Currency** *may indicate* a river

Current Abroad, AC, Actual, Alternating, Amp(ere), Amperage, California, Canary, Contemporaneous, Cromwell, DC, Direct, Draught, Drift, Dynamo, Ebbtide, Eddy, Electric, El Nino, Equatorial, Euripus, Existent, Flow, Foucault, Going, Gyre, Humboldt, Hummock, I, Immediate, Inst, Intermittent, Japan, Kuroshio, Labrador, Millrace, Modern, Newsy, North Atlantic, Now, Ongoing, Output, Peru, Present, Prevalent, Pulsating, Race, Rapid, Rife, Rip, Roost,

Running, Stream, Thames, Thermal, Thermionic, Tide, Tideway, Topical, Torrent, Turbidity, Underset, Undertow, Updraught

Curriculum Cursal, National, Programme

Curry Bhuna, Brush, Comb, Cuittle, Dhansak, Fawn, Groom, Ingratiate, Korma, Madras, Spice, Tan, Tandoori, Turmeric, Vindaloo

Curse Abuse, Anathema, Badmouth, Ban, Bane, Beshrew, > **BLASPHEME**, Blast, Chide, Dam(me), Damn, Dee, Drat, Ecod, Egad, Excommunicate, Execrate, Heck, Hex, Imprecate, Jinx, Malison, Maranatha, Mau(l)gré, Mockers, Moz(z), Mozzle, Nine (of diamonds), Oath, Paterson's, Pize, Plague, Rant, Rats, Scourge, 'Snails, Spell, Swear, Upbraid, Weary, Winze, Wo(e)

Cursive Estrang(h)elo, Run

Cursor Mouse, Turtle

Cursorily, Cursory Casual, Hasty, Lax, Obiter, Passing, Sketchy, Speedy, Superficial

Curt Abrupt, Blunt, Crusty, Laconic, Offhand, Short, Snappy

Curtail(ment) Apocope, Crop, Cut, Reduce, Shorten

Curtain(s), Curtain-rod Arras, Backdrop, Bamboo, Canopy, Caudle, Cloth, Cyclorama, Death, Demise, Drape, Drop, Dropcloth, Dropscene, Fatal, Hanging, Iron, Louvre, Net, Pall, Portière, Purdah, Safety, Scene, Screen, Scrim, Shower, Tab, Tormentor, Tringle, Upholstery, Vail, Valance, Veil, Vitrage, Window

Curtsey Bob, Bow, Dip, Dop

Curvature, Curve(d), Curvaceous, Curvy Adiabatic, Aduncate, Anticlastic, Apophyge, Arc, Arch, Archivolt, Axoid, Bend, Bight, Bow, Camber, Cardioid, Catacaustic, Catenary, Caustic, Characteristic, Cissoid, Conchoid, Contrapposto, Crescent, Cycloid, Diacaustic, Dogleg, Entasis, Epicycloid, Epinastic, Epitrochoid, Ess, Evolute, Exponental, Extrados, Felloe, Felly, Folium, French, Gaussian, Geodesic, Gooseneck, Growth, Hance, Helix, Hodograph, Hollow-back, Hook, Hyperbola, Hypocycloid, Inswing, Intrados, Isochor, J, Jordan, Kyphosis, Laffer, Learning, Lemniscate, Limacon, Liquidus, Lituus, Lordosis, Loxodrome, Normal, Nowy, Ogee, Parabola, Phillips, Pothook, Pott's disease, Pulvinate, Reclinate, Record, Rhumb, Roach, Rotundate, Scoliosis, Sheer, Sinuate, Sinusoid, Slice, Spiral, Spiric, Strophoid, Survival, Swayback, Synclastic, Tautochrone, Tie, Tractrix, Trajectory, Trochoid, Tumble-home, Twist, Undulose, U-turn, Volute, Witch (of Agnesi)

Cushion(s) Air, Allege, Bolster, Buffer, Frog, Ham, Hassock, Kneeler, > **PAD**, Pillow, Pin, Pouf(fe), Pulvillus, Scatter, Soften, Squab, Upholster, Whoopee

Cusp Horn, Spinode, Tine

Custard (apple) Creme caramel, Flam(m), Flan, Flaune, Flawn, Flummery, Pa(w)paw, Zabaglione

Custodian, Custody Care, Claviger, Guard, Hold, Janitor, Keeping, Sacrist, Steward, Trust, Ward

Custom(ised), Customs (officer), Customary Agriology, Coast-waiters, Consuetude, Conventional, Couvade, Dedicated, De règle, Dhamma, Dharma, Douane, Exciseman, Familiar, Fashion, Folklore, > **HABIT**, Land-waiter, Lore, Manner, Montem, Mores, Nomic, Octroi, Ordinary, Practice, Praxis, Relic, Rite, Routine, Rule, Sororate, Spanish, Sunna, Tax, Thew, Tidesman, Tide-waiter, Tikanga, Tradition, Unwritten, Usance, Used, Usual, Won, Wont, Woon, Zollverein

Customer Client, Cove, Patron, Prospect, Purchaser, Shillaber, Shopper, Smooth, Stiff, Trade, Trick, Ugly

Cut(ter), Cutting Abate, Abjoint, Abridge, Abscission, Abscond, Acute, Adeem,

Adze, Aftermath, Ali Baba, Amputate, Apocope, Axe, Bang, Bisect, Bit, Bite, Bowdlerise, Boycott, Brilliant, Broach, Caesarean, Caique, Canal, Cantle, Caper, Carver, Castrate, Caustic, Censor, Chap, Chisel, Chopper, Chynd, Circumscribe, Cleaver, Clinker-built, Clip, Colter, Commission, Concise, Coppice, Coulter, Coupé, Crew, Crop, Cruel, Culebra, Curtail, Deadhead, Decrease, Dedekind, Dicer, Die, Director's, Discide, Disengage, Dismember, Dissect, Division, Divorce, Dock, Dod, Edge, Edit, Emarginate, Embankment, Engraver, Entail, Entayle, Epistolary, Epitomise, Eschew, Estrepe, Excalibur, Excide, Excise, Exscind, Exsect, Exude, Fashion, Fell, Fillet, Flench, Flense, Flinch, Form, Froe, Frow, Gaillard, Garb, Gash, Go-down, Grater, Graven, Gride, Gryde, Hack, Handsaw, Hew(er), Ignore, Incision, Incisor, Indent, Intersect, Jigsaw, Joint, Junk, Kerf, Kern, Kirn, Lacerate, Lance, Leat, Lesion, Lin, Lop, Math, Medaillon, Microtome, Milling, Mohel, Mortice, Mortise, Mower, Nache, Nick, Not, Notch, Nott, Occlude, Omit, Open, Operate, Osteotome, Oxyacetylene, Padsaw, Pare, Pink, Plant, Pliers, Ploughshare, Pollard, Pone, Power, Precisive, Press, Proin, Quota, Race, Rake off, Rase, Razor, Reap, Rebate, Reduction, Re-enter, Resect, Retrench, Revenue, Ring, Ripsaw, Roach, Rose, Rout, Saddle, Sarcastic, Sarky, Saw(n), Scarf, Scathing, Scion, Scission, Scissor, Score, Sculpt, Scye, Scythe, Secant, Secateurs, Sect, Section, Sever, Sey, Share(out), Shaver, Shears, Shingle, Ship, Shorn, Short, Shred, Shun, Sickle, Sirloin, Skin, Skip, Slane, Slash, Slicer, Slip, Slit, Sloop, Sned, Snee, Snib, Snick, Snip, Snub, Spade, Speedy, Spin, Spud, Steak, Stencil, Stereotomy, Stir, Stramac, Stramazon, Strimmer®, Style, Surgeon, Swath(e), Tailor(ess), Tart, Tenderloin, Tenotomy, Tomial, Tomium, Tonsure, Tooth, Topside, Transect, Trash, Trench, Trenchant, Trepan, Trim, Truant, Truncate, Urchin, Whang, Whittle, Winey

▷ **Cut** *may indicate* an anagram
▷ **Cutback** *may indicate* a reversed word
Cute Ankle, Pert, Pretty, Taking
Cuticle Epidermis, Eponychium, Periplast, Pleuron, Skin
Cut in Interpose, Interrupt
Cutlass Machete, Sword
Cutlery Canteen, Flatware, Fork, Knife, Setting, Silver, Spoon, Tableware, Trifid
Cutlet Schnitzel
Cut off Elide, Enisle, Estrange, Inisle, Insulate, Intercept, > ISOLATE, Lop, Prune
Cut-throat Razor, Ruinous
Cuttlebone, Cuttlefish Octopus, Pen, Polyp(e)s, Polypus, Sea-sleeve, Sepia, Sepiost(aire), Sepium, Squid
CV Biodata
Cyanide Acrylonitrile, Nitrile, Prussiate
Cycad Coontie, Coonty
Cyclamen Sow-bread
Cycle, Cyclist Anicca, Arthurian, Bike, Biorhythm, Cal(l)ippic, Calvin, Carbon, Carnot, Cell, Circadian, Closed, Daisy, Diesel, Eon, Era, Fairy, Four-stroke, Freewheel, Frequency, Geological, Gigahertz, Heterogony, Hydrologic, Indiction, Ko, Krebs, Life, Light-year, Lunar, Metonic, Moped, Nitrogen, Oestrus, Orb, Otto, Pedal, Peloton, Period, Rankine, Repulp, Revolution, Ride, Roadster, Rock, Rota, Round, Samsara, Saros, Scorch, Series, Sheng, Solar, Song, Sonnet, Sothic, Spin, Sunspot, TCA, Trade, Trick, Trike, Turn, UCI, Urea, Water, Wheeler, Wheelman, Wu
Cyclone Cockeye(d) bob, Storm, Tornado, Typhoon, Willy-willy
Cyclops Arges, Arimasp(i), Brontes, Polyphemus, Steropes

Cylinder, Cylindrical Clave, Column, Drum, Master, Pipe, Pitch, Roll, Rotor, Slave, Spool, Steal, Stele, Terete, Torose, Treadmill, Tube

Cymbal(s) High-hat, Hi-hat, Zel

Cynic(al) Crab, Diogenes, Doubter, Hard-bitten, Hard-boiled, Menippus, Pessimist, Sardonic, Sceptic, Thersites, Timon

Cynosure Centre, Focus

Cynthia Artemis, Moon

Cypress Bald, Leyland(ii), Monterey, Retinospora, Swamp, Tree

Cypriot Enosis, Eoka

Cyst Atheroma, Bag, Blister, Chalazion, Dermoid, Hydatid, Impost(h)ume, Meibomian, Ranula, Sac, Sebaceous, Vesicle, Wen

Czechoslovakia CZ, Sudetenland

Dd

D Daughter, Delta, Died, Edh, Eth, Penny

Dab(s) Bit, Daub, Fish, Flounder, Pat, Print, Ringer, Smear, Spot, Stupe, Whorl

Dabble(r) Clatch, Dally, Dilettante, Plouter, Plowter, Potter, Smatter, Splash, Stipple, Trifle

Dachshund Teckel

Dactyl Anapaest

Dad(dy) Blow, Dev(v)el, Father, Generator, Hit, Male, Pa(pa), Pater, Polt, Pop, Slam, Sugar, Thump

Daddy-longlegs Crane-fly, Jennyspinner, Leather-jacket, Spinning-jenny, Tipula

Daffodil Asphodel, Jonquil, Lent-lily, Narcissus

Daft Absurd, Crazy, Potty, Ridiculous, Silly, Simple, Stupid

Dag Jag, Pierce, Pistol, Prick, Stab, Tag, Wool

Dagger(s) An(e)lace, Ataghan, Baselard, Bayonet, Bodkin, Crease, Creese, Da(h), Diesis, Dirk, Double, Dudgeon, Han(d)jar, Hanger, Jambiya(h), Katar, Khanjar, Kindjahl, Kirpan, Kreese, Kris, Lath, Misericord(e), Obelisk, Obelus, Poi(g)nado, Poniard, Pugio, Puncheon, Pusser's, Quillon, Rondel, Sgian-dubh, Skean, Skene(-occle), Spanish, Stiletto, Swordbreaker, W(h)inger, Whiniard, Whinyard, Yatag(h)an

Dahlia Cosmea

Daily Adays, Char, Circadian, Diurnal, Domestic, Guardian, Help, Journal, Mail, Mirror, Paper, Per diem, Quotidian, Rag, Regular, Scotsman, Sun, Tabloid

Dainty Cate(s), Cute, Delicacy, Elegant, Elfin, Entremesse, Entremets, Exquisite, Junket, Lickerish, Liquorish, Mignon(ne), > **MORSEL**, Neat, Nice, Particular, Petite, Pussy, Sunket, Twee

Dairy Creamery, Loan, Parlour

Dairymaid Dey, Patience

Dais Estate, Machan, Platform, Podium, Pulpit, Stage, Tribune

Daisy African, Barberton, Bell, Felicia, Gowan, Hen and chickens, Livingstone, Marguerite, Marigold, Michaelmas, Moon, Ox-eye, Shasta, Transvaal, Vegetable sheep

Dale(s) Dell, Dene, Dingle, Glen, Vale, Valley, Yorkshire

Dally Coquet(te), Dawdle, Finger, Flirt, Play, Spoon, Sport, Toy, Trifle, Wait

Dam An(n)icut, Arch, Aswan, Bar, Barrage, Barrier, Block, Boulder, Bund, Cabora Bassa, Cauld, Check, Gravity, Hoover, Kariba, Kielder, Ma, Mater, Obstacle, Obstruct, Pen, Stank, > **STEM**, Sudd, Turkey nest, Weir, Yangtze

Damage(d), Damages, Damaging Bane, Banjax, Bruise, Buckle, Charge, Chip, Collateral, Contuse, Cost, Cripple, Dent, Desecrate, Detriment, Devastate, Devastavit, Estrepe, Exemplary, Fault, Flea-bite, Foobar, Fubar, Fuck up, Harm, Havoc, Hit, Hole, Hurt, Impair, Injury, Insidious, Loss, Mar, Mayhem, Moth-eaten, Mutilate, Nobble, Prang, Price, Punitive, Ratten, Ravage, Retree, Sabotage, Scaith, Scath(e), Scotch, Scratch, Skaith, Smirch, Solatium, > **SPOIL**, Tangle, Toll, Value, Vandalise, Violate, Wear and tear, Wing, Wound, Wreak,

Wreck

▷ **Damage(d)** *may indicate* an anagram

Dambuster Ondatra

Dame Crone, Dowager, Edna, Gammer, Lady, Matron, Nature, Naunt, Partlet, Peacherino, Sis, Title(d), Trot, Woman

Damn(ation), Damned Accurst, Attack, Blame, Condemn, Curse, Cuss, Darn, Dee, Execrate, Faust, Hell, Hoot, Jigger, Malgre, Perdition, Predoom, Sink, Swear, Tarnal, Tarnation, Tinker's, Very

Damp(en), Damping Aslake, Black, Blight, Check, Clam(my), Dank, Dewy, Fousty, Fusty, Humid, Moist, Muggy, Raw, Rheumy, Rising, Roric, Soggy, Sordo, Sultry, Unaired, Viscous, > WET, White

Damper Barrier, Check, Dashpot, Killjoy, Mute

Damsel Girl, Lass, Maiden, Wench

Damson Plumdamas

Dan Box, Cupid, Leno, Olivetan, Scuttle, Tribe

Dance(r), Dancing Astaire, Baladin(e), Ballabile, Ballant, Ballerina, Ballroom, Bayadère, Bob, Body-popping, Caper, Chorus-girl, Contredanse, Corybant, Coryphee, Dervish, Diaghilev, Dinner, Dolin, Exotic, Figurant, Foot, Gandy, Gigolo, Hetaera, Hetaira, Hoofer, Kick-up, Knees-up, Leap, Maenad, Modern, Nautch-girl, Night, Nijinsky, Nureyev, Oberek, Old-time, Partner, Pavlova, Petipa, Pierette, Raver, Ring, St Vitus, Salome, Saltatorious, Skipper, Spring, Step, Strut, Table, Tea, Terpsichore, Tread, Trip(pant), Vogue(ing), Whirl

● **DANCES**
●
●
● **3 letters:**
● Bop
● Fan
● Gig
● Hay
● Hey
● Hop
● Ice
● Jig
● Lap
● Pas
● Poi
● Sun
● Tap
● Toe
● War
●
● **4 letters:**
● Alma
● Ball
● Barn
● Clog
● Dump
● Fado
● Folk
● Frug
● Giga

3 letters:	Go-go	**5 letters:**	Ragga
Bop	Haka	Bamba	Robot
Fan	Hora	Belly	Round
Gig	Hula	Bogle	Rumba
Hay	Jive	Brawl	Salsa
Hey	Jota	Carol	Samba
Hop	Juba	Ceroc®	Shake
Ice	Juke	Conga	Skank
Jig	Kolo	Disco	Snake
Lap	Line	Fling	Stomp
Pas	Lion	Furry	Sword
Poi	Loup	Galop	Tango
Sun	Nach	Ghost	Twist
Tap	Pogo	Gigue	Valse
Toe	Polo	Glide	Volta
War	Reel	Gopak	Waltz
	Rope	Horah	
4 letters:	Sand	Limbo	**6 letters:**
Alma	Shag	Loure	Almain
Ball	Slam	Mambo	Apache
Barn	Spin	Mooch	Ballet
Clog	Spot	Natch	Bolero
Dump	Stag	Paspy	Boogie
Fado	Taxi	Pavan	Boston
Folk	Wire	Paven	Branle
Frug		Pavin	Bubble
Giga		Polka	Canary

Can-can
Cha-cha
Fading
Floral
German
Hustle
Jump-up
Kathak
Lavolt
Maxixe
Minuet
Morris
Pavane
Redowa
Shimmy
Smooch
Square
Toy-toy
Trophe
Valeta
Veleta
Waggle

7 letters:
Bambuca
Beguine
Bourrée
Bransle
Brantle
Cantico
Capuera
Carioca
Coranto
Cossack
Country
Courant
Csardas
Farruca
Forlana
Foxtrot
Furlana
Gavotte
Halling
Hoe-down
Lambada
Lancers
Landler
Lavolta
Macabre
Mazurka
Measure
Moresco

Morisco
Morrice
Moshing
One-step
Pericon
Planxty
Polacca
Pyrrhic
Ridotto
Ringlet
Romaika
Roundel
Roundle
Routine
Sardana
Sashaya
Shuffle
Tanagra
Tordion
Toyi-toy
Toy-toyi
Trenise
Two-step
Ziganka

8 letters:
Alegrias
Bunnyhop
Bunnyhug
Cachucha
Cakewalk
Canticoy
Capoeira
Chaconne
Cotillon
Courante
Egg-dance
Excuse-me
Fandango
Flamenco
Flip-flop
Galliard
Habanera
Hay-de-guy
Haymaker
Headbang
Hey-de-guy
Heythrop
Hoolican
Hornpipe
Hula-hula
Irish jig

Joncanoe
Junkanoo
Kantikoy
Kazachok
Kazatzka
Lindy hop
Macarena
Marinera
Matachin
Medicine
Merengue
Murciana
Orchesis
Rigadoon
Robotics
Ronggeng
Saraband
Snowball
Soft-shoe
Taglioni
Toyi-toyi
Trucking

9 letters:
Allemande
Bergamask
Bergomask
Bossanova
Caballero
Cha-cha-cha
Chipaneca
Cotillion
Ecossaise
Eightsome
Farandole
Formation
Gallopade
Hoolachan
Jitterbug
Kathakali
Malaguena
Pas de deux
Paso doble
Passepied
Paul Jones
Polonaise
Poussette
Quadrille
Quickstep
Ring-shout
Roundelay
Siciliano

Sink-a-pace
Tambourin
Tripudium
Variation
Zapateado

10 letters:
Antimasque
Breakdance
Carmagnole
Charleston
Cinque-pace
Corroboree
Gay Gordon's
Hay-de-guise
Hay-de-guyes
Hey-de-guise
Hey-de-guyes
Hokey-cokey
Passamezzo
Petronella
Rug-cutting
Saltarello
Seguidilla
Sicilienne
Sinke-a-pace
Strathspey
Tarantella
Thé dansant
Tripudiate
Turkey trot
Tyrolienne
Walk-around

11 letters:
Antistrophe
Black bottom
Buck and wing
Comprimario
Cracovienne
Lambeth walk
Palais glide
Passacaglia
Pastourelle
Progressive
Schottische
Shimmy-shake
Varsovienne

12 letters:
Bharat Natyam
Labanotation

- Passemeasure
- Passy-measure
- Virginia reel

13 letters:
Highland fling

14 letters:
Divertissement
Jack-in-the-green

18 letters:
Sir Roger de
Coverley

Dance movement Arabesque, Balancé, Battement, Batterie, Brisé, Chassé, Dos-à-dos, Dosido, Entrechat, Fishtail, Fouetté, Glissade, Jeté, Lassu, Pantalon, Pas de basque, Pas de chat, Pas seul, Pigeonwing, Pirouette, Plié, Poule, Poussette, Routine, Sauté, Step

Dance tune Toy

▷ **Dancing** *may indicate* an anagram

Dancing party Ball, Ridotto

Dandelion Kok-saghyz, Piss-a-bed, Scorzonera, Taraxacum

Dander Anger, Gee, Passion, Saunter, Temper

Dandle Dance, Doodle, Fondle, Pet

Dandruff Furfur, Scurf

Dandy Adonis, Beau, Blood, Boulevardier, Buck(een), Cat, Coxcomb, Dapper, > DUDE, Exquisite, Fantastico, Fop, Gem, Jay, Jessamy, Johnny, Kiddy, Knut, Lair, Macaroni, Masher, Modist, Monarcho, Muscadin, Nash, Nut, Posh, Roy, Smart, Spark, Spiff, Swell, Ted, Toff, U, Yankee-doodle

Dandy-horse Draisene, Draisine

Dane(s) Clemence, Dansker, Ogier, Ostmen

Danger(ous) Apperil, Breakneck, Chancy, Crisis, Dic(e)y, Dire, Dodgy, Emprise, Fear, Hairy, Hazard, Hearie, High-risk, Hot, Insecure, Jeopardy, Lethal, Menace, Mine, Nettle, Nocuous, Objective, Parlous, Periculous, > PERIL, Pitfall, Precarious, Quicksand, Risk, Serious, Severe, Snag, Snare, Tight, Trap, Wonchancy

Dangle A(i)glet, Aiguillette, Critic, Flourish, Hang, Loll, Swing

Daniel Dan, Defoe, Deronda, Lion-tamer, Portia, Quilp

Dank Clammy, Damp, Humid, Moist, Wet, Wormy

Daphne Agalloch, Agila, Eaglewood, Lace-bark, Laura, Laurel, Mezereon

Dapper Dressy, Natty, Neat, Smart, Spiff, Spruce, Sprush, Spry, > TRIM

Darbies Cuffs, Irons, Snaps

Dare, **Dare-devil**, **Daring** Adventure, Bold, Brave, Challenge, Courage, Da(u)nton, Defy, Durst, Emprise, Face, Gallant, Gallus, Hardihood, Hazard, Hen, Intrepid, Moxie, Neck, Prowess, Racy, Stuntman, Taunt, Venture

Dark(en), **Darkie**, **Darkness** Aphelia, Aphotic, Apophis, Black, Blind, Cimmerian, Cloud, Depth, Dim, Dingy, Dirk(e), Dusky, Eclipse, Erebus, Evil, Gloom, Glum, Inumbrate, Mare, Maria, Melanous, Mulatto, Murk(y), Negro, Night, Obfuscate, Obscure, Ominous, Ousel, Ouzel, Pall, Phaeic, Pitch-black, Pit-mirk, Rooky, Sable, Sad, Secret, Shady, Shuttered, Sinister, Solein, Sombre, Sooty, Sphacelate, Stygian, Sullen, Swarthy, Tar, Tenebr(i)ous, Tenebrose, Unfair, Unlit, Wog, Woosel, Yellowboy, Yellowgirl

Darling Acushla, Alannah, Asthore, Beloved, Charlie, Cher, Chéri(e), Chick-a-biddy, Chick-a-diddle, Chuck-a-diddle, Dear, Dilling, Do(a)ting-piece, Duck(s), Favourite, Grace, Honey, Idol, Jarta, Jo(e), Lal, Love, Luv, Mavourneen, Mavournin, Minikin, Minion, Oarswoman, Own, Peat, Pet, Poppet, Precious, Sugar, Sweetheart, Yarta, Yarto

Darn Begorra, Blow, Doggone, Hang, Mend, Repair, Sew

Dart(er) Abaris, Arrow, Banderilla, Dace, Dash, Deadener, Dodge, Fleat, Fléchette, Flit, Harpoon, Javelin, Launch, Leap, Scoot, Skrim, Speck, Spiculum, Sprint, Strike, Thrust, Wheech

Dash(ing), **Dashed** Backhander, Bally, Blade, Blight, Blow, Buck, Charge,

Collide, Cut, Dad, Dah, Damn, Dapper, Dart(le), Daud, Debonair, Ding, Elan, En, Fa(s)cia, Flair, Fly, Go-ahead, Hang, Hurl, > **HURRY**, Hustle, Hyphen, Impetuous, Jabble, Jaw, Jigger, Lace, Line, Minus, Morse, Natty, Nip, Panache, Pebble, Rakish, Ramp, Rash, Rule, Run, Rush, Sally, Scamp(er), Scart, Scoot, Scrattle, Scurry, Scuttle, Shatter, Showy, Soupçon, Souse, Spang, Speed, Splash, Splatter, Sprint, Strack, Streak, Stroke, > **STYLE**, Swung, Throw, Touch, Viretot

Dashboard Fascia

Dashwood Hell-fire club

Dastard(ly) Base, Coward, Craven, Nid(d)erling, Poltroon

Data(base), **Datum** Archie, Cyberspace, Donne(e), Evidence, Facts, Fiche, File, Floating-point, Gen, HOLMES, Info, Input, Material, Matrix, News, Soft copy

Date(d), **Dates**, **Dating** AD, Age, AH, Almanac, Appointment, Blind, Boyfriend, Calendar, Carbon, Carbon-14, Computer, Court, Deadline, Engagement, Epoch, Equinox, Era, Escort, Exergue, Expiry, Fixture, Girlfriend, Ides, Julian, Meet, Outmoded, > **OUT OF DATE**, Passé, Past, Radioactive, Radio-carbon, Radiometric, Rubidium-strontium, See, System, > **TRYST**, Ult(imo), Value

Daub Begrime, Blob, Dab, Gaum, Mess, Moil, Noint, Plaister, Plaster, > **SMEAR**, Smudge, Splodge, Teer, Wattle

Daughter (in law) Child, D, Elect, Girl, Jephthah's, Niece, Offspring, Skevington's

Daunt Adaw, Amate, Awe, Deter, Dishearten, Intimidate, Overawe, Quail, Stun, Stupefy, Subdue

Dauphin Delphin

David Dai, Psalmist

Davit Crane, Derrick, Hoist

Davy Crockett, Jones

Daw Bird, Magpie, Margery

Dawdle(r) Dally, Draggle, Drawl, Idle, Lag(gard), > **LOITER**, Potter, Shirk, Slowcoach, Tarry, Troke, Truck

Dawn Aurora, Cockcrow, Daw, Daybreak, Daylight, Day-peep, Dayspring, Eoan, Eos, False, Light, Morrow, Occur, Prime, Roxane, Start, Sunrise, Ushas

Day(s) Account, Ahemeral, All Fools', All Hallows', All Saints', All Souls', Anniversary, Annunciation, Anzac, April Fool's, Armistice, Ascension, Australia, Bad hair, Baker, Banian, Bastille, Boxing, Calendar, Calends, Calpa, Canada, Civil, Columbus, Commonwealth, Contango, D, Daft, Date, Decoration, Degree, Distaff, Dog, Dominion, Duvet, Early, Ember, Empire, Epact, Fast, Fasti, Father's, Feast, Ferial, Field, Flag, Fri, Gang, Gaudy, Groundhog, Guy Fawkes', Halcyon, High, Hogmanay, Holy, Holy Innocents', Holy-rood, Hundred, Ides, Inauguration, Independence, Intercalary, Judgment, Judicial, Kalends, Kalpa, Labo(u)r, Lady, Laetare, Lammas, Law(ful), Lay, Leap, Mardi, May, Memorial, Michaelmas, Midsummer, Mon, Morrow, Mother's, Muck-up, Mufti, Mumping, Name, New year's, Nones, Nychthemeron, Oak-apple, Octave, Open, Orangeman, Pancake, Paper, Pay, Poppy, Pound, Present, Primrose, Pulvering, Quarter, Rag, Rainy, Red-letter, Remembrance, Rest, Robin, Rock, Rogation, Rood(-mas), Rosh Chodesh, Sabbath, Saint's, St Swithin's, St Valentine's, Salad, Sat, Settling, Shick-shack, Show, Sidereal, Snow, Solar, Solstice, Speech, Sports, Station, Sun, Supply, Tag, Term, Thanksgiving, Thurs, Ticket, Time, Transfer, Trial, Tues, Twelfth, Utas, Valentine's, Varnishing, VE, Veterans', Victoria, Visiting, VJ, Waitangi, Wed, Wedding, Working

Daybreak Cockcrow

Daydream(er) Brown study, Dwam, Fancy, Imagine, Muse, Reverie, Rêveur,

Walter Mitty

Daylight Artificial, Dawn, Space, Sun

Daze(d) Amaze, Bemuse, Confuse, Dwaal, Gally, Muddle, Muzzy, Punch drunk, Reeling, Spaced out, > STUN, Stupefy, Stupor, Trance

Dazzle(d), **Dazzling** Bewilder, Blend, Blind, Eclipse, Foudroyant, Glare, Meteoric, Outshine, Radiance, Resplendent, Splendour, Yblent

Deacon Cleric, Doctor, Minister

Deactivate Unarm

Dead(en) Abrupt, Accurate, Alamort, Asgard, Asleep, Blunt, Brown bread, Bung, Cert, Cold, Complete, D, Deceased, Defunct, Doggo, Expired, Extinct, Gone(r), Inert, Infarct, Late, Lifeless, Morkin, Muffle, Mute, Napoo, Niflheim, Numb, Obsolete, Obtund, Ringer, She'ol, Slain, Smother, Stillborn, True, Utter, Waned

Dead end, **Deadlock** Blind alley, Cut-off, Dilemma, Impasse, Logjam, Stalemate, Stoppage

Dead-leaf colour Filemot, Philamot, Philomot

Deadline Date, Epitaph, Limit

Deadlock Stand-off, Sticking-point

Deadly Baleful, Dull, Fell, Funest, Internecine, > LETHAL, Malign, Mortal, Mortific, Pestilent, Unerring, Venomous

Deadly Nightshade Belladonna, Dwale

Deadpan Expressionless

Dead reckoning Dr

Dead tree Rampick, Rampike

Deaf(en), **Deafness** Adder, Asonia, Deave, Deeve, Dunny, Heedless, Paracusis, Presbyc(o)usis, Surd(ity)

Deal(er), **Dealings**, **Deal with** Address, Agent, Agreement, Allot(ment), Arb, Arbitrageur, Bargain, Breadhead, Brinjarry, Broker, Business, Cambist, Chandler, Chapman, Commerce, Cope, Coup, Cover, Croupier, Dispense, Distributor, Do, Dole, Eggler, Exchange, Fripper, Goulash, Hand(le), Help, Inflict, Insider, Interbroker, Jiggery-pokery, Jobber, Lashing, Lay on, Lay out, Let, Manage, Mercer, Merchant, Mickle, Middleman, Monger, Mort, Negotiate, New, Operator, Package, Pine, Productivity, Pusher, Raft, Raw, Sale, Serve, Side, Sort, Spicer, Square, Stockist, Stockjobber, Takeover, Tape, Timber, Tout(er), > TRADE, Traffic, Transaction, Treat, Truck, Wheeler, Wholesaler, Wield, Woolstapler, Yardie

Dean Acheson, Arabin, Colet, Decani, Doyen, Forest, Head, Inge, Nellie, Provost, RD, Rural, Rusk, Slade, Spooner, Swift, Vale, Vicar-forane

Dear(er), **Dearest**, **Dear me** Ay, Bach, Beloved, Cara, Caro, Cher(e), Cherie, Chou, Chuckie, Darling, Duck(s), Expensive, High, Honey(bun), Lamb, Leve, Lief, Lieve, Loor, Love, Machree, Mouse, My, Pet, Pigsney, Pigsnie, Pigsny, Steep, Sweet, Sweetie, Toots(ie), Up

Dearth Famine, Lack, Paucity, Scantity, Scarcity, > SHORTAGE

Deaspiration Psilosis

Death(ly) Auto-da-fe, Bane, Bargaist, Barg(h)est, Biolysis, Black, Cataplexis, Charnel, Clinical, Cot, Curtains, Cypress, Demise, Departure, Dormition, End, Eschatology, Euthanasia, Exit, Extinction, Fatality, Funeral, Fusillation, Gangrene, Grim Reaper, Hallal, Heat, Infarction, Jordan, Karoshi, Lead colic, Lethee, Leveller, Living, Mors, Napoo, Necrosis, Nemesis, Night, Obit, Quietus, Reaper, Sati, Sergeant, SIDS, Small-back, Strae, Sudden, Suttee, Terminal, Thanatism, Thanatopsis, Thanatos

Death-flood Styx

Deathless(ness) Athanasy, Eternal, Eterne, Immortal, Struldberg, Timeless,

Undying

Debacle Cataclysm, Collapse, Disaster, Fiasco

Debar Deny, Exclude, Forbid, > PREVENT, Prohibit

Debase(d) Adulterate, Allay, Bemean, Cheapen, Corrupt, Demean, Depreciate, Dialectician, Dirty, Grotesque, Hedge, Lower, Pervert, Traduce, Vitiate

Debate Argue, Combat, Contention, Contest, Deliberate, Dialectic, Discept, Discuss(ion), > DISPUTE, Flyte, Forensics, Full-dress, Moot, Polemics, Powwow, Reason, Teach-in, Warsle, Wrangle, Wrestle

Debauch(ed), **Debauchee**, **Debauchery** Corrupt, Decadent, Defile, Degenerate, Dissipate, Dissolute, Heliogabalus, Libertine, Licence, Orgy, Profligate, Rake-hell, Riot, Roist, Royst, Seduce, Spree, Stuprate, Wet, Whore

Debenture Bond, Security

Debilitate(d), **Debility** Asthenia, Atonic, Cachexia, Feeble, Languid, Weak

Debit Charge, Debt, Direct

Debonair Cavalier, Gay, Gracious, Jaunty

Debris Bahada, Bajada, Detritus, Eluvium, Moraine, Moslings, Refuse, > RUBBLE, Ruins, Tephra, Waste

▷ **Debris** *may indicate* an anagram

Debt(or) Alsatia, Arrears, Arrestee, Dr, Due, Floating, Funded, Insolvent, IOU, Liability, Moratoria, National, Obligation, Poultice, Public, Queer Street, Score, Tie, Unfunded

Debt-collector Bailiff, Forfaiter, Remembrancer

Debut Launch, Opening, Outset, Presentation

Debutante Bud, Deb

Decade Rosary, Ten

Decadence, **Decadent** Babylonian, Decaying, Degeneration, Dissolute, Effete, Fin-de-siècle, Libertine

Decamp Abscond, Absquatulate, Bolt, Bunk, Depart, Flee, Guy, Levant, Mizzle, Slide, Slope, Vamoose

Decant Pour, Unload

Decapitate, **Decapitation** Aphesis, > BEHEAD, Guillotine

▷ **Decapitated** *may indicate* first letter removed

Decay(ed), **Decaying** Alpha, Appair, Beta, Biodegrade, Blet, Canker, Caries, Caseation, Consenescence, Crumble, Decadent, Declension, Decline, Decompose, Decrepit, Dieback, Disintegrate, Dissolution, Doat, Doddard, Doddered, Dote, Dricksie, Druxy, Dry rot, Fail, F(o)etid, Forfair, Gangrene, Heart-rot, Impair, Moulder, Pair(e), Perish, Plaque, Putrefy, Radioactive, Ret, Rot, Saprogenic, Sap-rot, Seedy, Sepsis, Spoil, Tabes, Wet-rot

Decease(d) Death, Decedent, Demise, Die, Stiff

Deceit(ful), **Deceive(r)** Abuse, Artifice, Bamboozle, Barrat, Befool, Bitten, Blind, Bluff, Braide, > CHEAT, Chicane, Chouse, Con, Cozen, Cuckold, Defraud, Delude, Diddle, Dike, Dissemble, Do brown, Double-cross, Double-tongued, Dupe, Duplicity, False(r), Fastie, Fast-talk, Fiddle, Flam, Fox, Fraud, Gag, Gerrymander, Gloze, Guile, Gull, Hoax, Hoodwink, Hornswoggle, Humbug, Hype, Illusion, Imposition, Inveigle, Invention, Jiggery-pokery, Kid, Malengine, Mata Hari, Mendacious, Mislead, Mislippen, Phenakism, Poop, Poupe, Pretence, Punic, Rig, Ruse, Sell, Sham, Sinon, Sleekit, Snow job, Spruce, Stratagem, Subreption, Swindle, Swizzle, Tregetour, Trick, Trump, Two-faced, Two-time, Wile

Decency, **Decent** Chaste, Decorum, Fitting, Healsome, Honest, Kind, Modest, Passable, Seemly, Sporting, Wholesome

Decentralise Disperse

Deception, **Deceptive** Artifice, Bluff, Catchpenny, Catchy, Cheat, Chicanery, Codology, > DECEIT, Disguise, Dupe, Duplicity, Eyewash, Fallacious, False, Flam, Fraud, Gag, Gammon, Guile, Have-on, Hocus-pocus, Hokey-pokey, Hum, Hunt-the-gowks, Hype, Ignes-fatui, Ignis-fatuus, Illusion, Insidious, Lie, Moodies, Runaround, Ruse, Sell, Sleight, Smoke and mirrors, Specious, Sting, The moodies, > TRICK, Trompe l'oeil, Two-timing, Underhand

Decide(r), **Decided** Addeem, Agree, Ballot, Barrage, Cast, Clinch, Conclude, > DECISION, Deem, Definite, Determine, Distinct, Engrenage, Firm, Fix, Jump-off, Mediate, Opt, Parti, Predestination, Pronounced, Rescript, > RESOLVE, Rule, Run-off, See, Settle, Sudden death, Tiebreaker, Try

Decimal Mantissa, Recurring, Repeating, Terminating

Decimate Destroy, Lessen, Weaken

Decipher(ing) Cryptanalysis, Decode, Decrypt, Descramble, Discover, Interpret

▷ **Decipher(ed)** *may indicate* an 'o' removed

Decision Arbitrium, Arrêt, Crossroads, Crunch, Decree, Engrenage, Fatwa, Fetwa, Firman, Judg(e)ment, Placit(um), Referendum, Resolution, Resolve, Responsa, Ruling, Sentence, Sudden death, Verdict

Decisive Climactic, Clincher, Critical, Crux, Definite, Final, Pivotal

Deck Adorn, Array, Attrap, Bejewel, Boat, Cards, Clad, Daiker, Daub, Decorate, Dizen, Embellish, Equip, Flight, Focsle, Forecastle, Garland, Hang, Helideck, Hurricane, Lower, Main, Monkey poop, Orlop, Ornament, Pack, Platform, Poop, Prim, Promenade, Quarter, Saloon, Spar, Sun, Tape, Upper, Void, Well

Declare, **Declaration**, **Declaim**, **Decree** Absolute, Affidavit, Affirm, Air, Allege, Announce, Annunciate, Assert, Asseverate, Aver, Avow, Balfour, Bann(s), Breda, Dictum, Diktat, Doom, Edict, Elocute, Enact, Fatwa(h), Fiat, Firman, Go, Grace, Harangue, Hatti-sherif, Independence, Indulgence, Insist, Interlocutory, Irade, Law, Mandate, Manifesto, Mecklenburg, Meld, Motu proprio, Mou(th), Nisi, Noncupate, Novel(la), Nullity, Nuncupate, Orate, Ordain, Order, Ordinance, Parlando, Pontificate, Predicate, Proclaim, Profess, Promulgate, Pronounce, Protest, Psephism, Publish, Rant, Recite, Rescript, Resolve, Rights, Rule, Ruling, SC, Sed, Senecan, Shahada, Signify, Speak, Spout, State, Statutory, Testify, Testimony, UDI, Ultimatum, Unilateral, Vie, Voice, Vouch, Word

▷ **Declaring** *may indicate* a word beginning 'Im'

Decline, **Declining** Age, Ail, Atrophy, Catabasis, Comedown, Decadent, Degeneration, Degringoler, Deny, Descend, Deteriorate, Devall, Die, Dip, Dissent, Downhill, Downtrend, Downturn, Droop, Dwindle, Ebb, Fade, Fall, Flag, Forbear, Paracme, Quail, Recede, Recession, Refuse, Retrogression, Rot, Rust, Sag, Senile, Set, Sink, Slide, Slump, Stoop, Wane, Welke, > WILT, Withdraw, Wither

Decoct(ion) Apozem, Cook, Devise, Ptisan, Tisane

Decode(d) En clair

Decolleté Low, Neckline

Decompose, **Decomposition** Biodegradable, Crumble, Decay, Disintegrate, Hydrolysis, Mor, Pyrolysis, Rot, Wither

Decompression Bends

Decor Background, Scenery

Decorate(d), **Decoration**, **Decorative** Adorn, Angelica, Aogai, Arpillera, Attrap, Award, Baroque, Beaux-arts, Biedermeier, Bordure, Braid, Brattishing, Braze, Brooch, Cartouche, Centrepiece, Chambranle, Champlevé, Chinoiserie, Christingle, Cinquefoil, Cloissoné, Cresting, Crocket, Cul-de-lampe, Dentelle, Diamante, Doodad, Dragée, Dragging, Emblazon, Emboss, Embrave, Engrail,

Enrich, Epergne, Etch, Fancy, Festoon, Filigree, Finial, Fleuret(te), Fleuron, Floriated, Flushwork, Fluting, Fourragère, Frieze, Frill, Frog, Furbish, Gammadion, Garniture, Gaud, Gild, Goffer, Gradino, Grecque key, Guilloche, Historiated, Ice, Illuminate, Impearl, Inlay, Intarsia, Intarsio, Interior, Knotwork, Linen-fold, Linen-scroll, Marquetry, MC, Medal(lion), Mola, Motif, Moulding, Oath, OBE, Order, > ORNAMENT, Ornate, Orphrey, Ovolo, Paint, Paper, Parament, Pâté-sur-pâté, Pinata, Pipe, Pokerwork, Pompom, Prettify, Prink, Purfle, Purple heart, Quilling, Rag-rolling, Rangoli, Repoussé, Rich, Rosemaling, Ruche, Scallop, Schwarzlot, Scrimshander, Scrimshaw, Serif, Set-off, Sgraffito, Skeuomorph, Soutache, Spangle, Staffage, Stomacher, Storiated, Strapwork, Studwork, Tailpiece, Tattoo, TD, Titivate, Tool, Topiary, Trim, Veneer, Wallpaper, Well-dressing

Decorous, **Decorum** Becoming, Demure, Etiquette, Fitness, Parliamentary, Prim, > PROPER, Propriety, Seemlihe(a)d, > SEEMLY, Staid

Decoy Allure, Bait, Bonnet, Button, Call-bird, Coach, Crimp, Entice, Lure, Piper, Roper, Ruse, Shill, Stale, Stalking-horse, Stool-pigeon, Tole, Toll, Trap, Trepan

Decrease Decrew, Diminish, Dwindle, Iron, Lessen, Press, Reduce, Rollback, Slim, Step-down, Subside, Wane, Wanze

Decree > DECLAIM, Saw

Decrepit Dilapidated, Doddery, Failing, Feeble, Frail, Moth-eaten, Time-worn, Tumbledown, Warby, Weak

Decry Condemn, Crab, Denounce, Derogate, Detract, Downgrade

Dedicate(d), **Dedication** Corban, Devote, Endoss, Hallow, Inscribe, Oblate, Pious, Sacred, Votive

Deduce, **Deduction**, **Deductive** A priori, Assume, Conclude, Consectary, Corollary, Derive, Discount, Dockage, Gather, Illation, Infer(ence), Obvert, Off-reckoning, Reason, Rebate, Recoup, Reprise, Stoppage, Surmise, Syllogism

Deed(s) Achievement, Act(ion), Atweel, Backbond, Charta, Charter, Derring-do, Disposition, Escrol(l), Escrow, Exploit, Fact(um), Feat, Indeed, Indenture, Manoeuvre, Mitzvah, Muniments, Premises, Specialty, Starr, > TITLE, Trust

Deem Consider, Opine, Ordain, Proclaim, Repute, Think

Deep(en), **Deeply** Abstruse, Bass(o), Brine, Briny, Enhance, Excavate, Grum, Gulf, Hadal, Intense, Low, Mindanao, Mysterious, > OCEAN, Profound, Re-enter, Rich, Sea, Sonorous, Throaty, Upsee, Ups(e)y

Deep-rooted Inveterate

Deer(-like) Axis, Bambi, Barasing(h)a, Barking, Blacktail, Brocket, Buck, Cariacou, Caribou, Carjacou, Cervine, Chevrotain, Chital, Doe, Elaphine, Elk, Fallow, Gazelle, Hart, Hog, Moose, Mouse, Mule, Muntjac, Muntjak, Musk, Père David's, Pricket, Pudu, Pygarg, Red, Rein, Roe, Rusa, Sambar, Sambur, Selenodont, Sika, Sorel(l), Spade, Spay(d), Spayad, Spitter, Spottie, Stag(gard), Tragule, Ungulate, Virginia, Wapiti, Water, White-tailed

Deer-hunter Tinchel

Deface Disfigure, Spoil

▷ **Defaced** *may indicate* first letter missing

Defame, **Defamatory**, **Defamation** Abase, Bad mouth, Blacken, Calumny, Cloud, Denigrate, Detract, Dishonour, Impugn, Libel, Malign, Mud, Mudslinging, Scurrilous, Slander, Smear, Stigmatise, Traduce, Vilify

Default(er) Absentee, Bilk, Dando, Delinquent, Flit, Levant, Neglect, Omission, Waddle, Welsh

Defeat(ed), **Defeatist** Beat, Best, Caning, Capot, Codille, Conquer, Counteract, Debel, Defeasance, Demolish, Discomfit, Dish, Ditch, Fatalist, Floor, Foil, Foyle, Hammer, Hiding, Kippered, Laipse, Lick, Loss, Lurch, Marmelize,

Master, Mate, Negative, Out, Outclass, Outdo, Outplay, Outvote, Outwit, > **OVERCOME**, Overpower, Overreach, Overthrow, Overwhelm, Pip, Reverse, Rout, Rubicon, Scupper, Set, Shellacking, Sisera, Squabash, Stump, Tank, Thrash, Thwart, Tonk, Trounce, Vanquish, War, Waterloo, Whap, Whip, Whitewash, Whop, Whup, Wipe-out, Worst

Defecate, **Defecation** Horse, Mute, Poop, Shit, Tenesmus

Defect(ion), **Defective**, **Defector** Abandon, Amateur, Apostasy, Bug, Coma, Crack, Faulty, Flaw, > **FORSAKE**, Frenkel, Halt, Hamartia, Kink, Manky, Mote, Natural, Paralexia, Point, Psellism, Rachischisis, Renegade, Renegate, Ridgel, Ridgil, Rig, Rogue, Runagate, Schottky, Shortcoming, Spina bifida, Terrace, Treason, Trick, Want, Weakness, Wreath

Defence, **Defend(er)**, **Defensible** Abat(t)is, Alibi, Antibody, Antidote, Antihistamine, Apologia, Back, Back four, Bailey, Barbican, Barmkin, Barricade, Bastion, Battery, Battlement, Berm, Bestride, Bridgehead, Bulwark, Calt(h)rop, Catenaccio, CD, Champion, Chapparal, Civil, Curtain, Demibastion, Ditch, Embrasure, Hedgehog, Herisson, Hold, J(i)u-jitsu, Justify, Kaim, Keeper, Laager, Laer, Last-ditch, Linebacker, Maintain, Martello Tower, MIDAS, Miniment, Moat, Muniment, Outwork, Palisade, Parapet, Perceptual, Propugnation, Rampart, Redan, Redoubt, Resist, Ringwall, > **SHELTER**, Shield, Stonewall, Support, Sweeper, Tenable, Tenail(le), Testudo, Tower, Trench, Trou-de-loup, Uphold, Vallation, Vallum, Vindicate, Wall, Warran(t), Zonal

Defenceless Helpless, Inerm, Naked, Sitting duck, Vulnerable

Defendant Accused, Apologist, Respondent, Richard Roe

Defer(ence), **Deferential** Bow, Complaisance, Delay, Dutiful, Homage, Morigerous, Obeisant, Pace, Polite, Postpone, Procrastinate, Protocol, Respect, Shelve, Submit, Suspend, Waive, Yield

Defiance, **Defiant**, **Defy** Acock, Bold, Brave, Contumacy, Dare, Daring, Disregard, Do or die, Outbrave, Outdare, Recusant, Resist, Stubborn, Titanism, Truculent, Unruly

Deficiency, **Deficient** Absence, Acapnia, Anaemia, Beriberi, Defect, Inadequate, Incomplete, Kwashiorkor, Lack, Osteomalacia, Scant, Scarcity, SCID, Shortage, Shortfall, Spanaemia, Want

▷ **Deficient** *may indicate* an anagram

Deficit Anaplerotic, Arrears, Defective, Ischemia, Loss, Poor, Shortfall

Defile(ment) Abuse, Array, Barranca, Barranco, Besmear, Col, Conspurcation, Desecrate, Dishonour, Donga, Enseam, > **FOUL**, Gate, Gorge, Gully, Inquinate, Inseem, Kloof, Moil, Pass, Pollute, Poort, Ravine, Ray, Roncesvalles, Smear, Spoil, > **SULLY**

Define(d), **Definition**, **Definitive** Decide, Demarcate, Determine, Diorism, Distinct, Explain, Fix, Limit, Parameter, Set, Tangible, Term

Definite(ly) Classic, Clear, Emphatic, Firm, Hard, Pos, Positive, Precise, Specific, Sure, Yes

Deflate Burst, Collapse, Flatten, Lower, Prick, Puncture

Deflect(or), **Deflection** Avert, Bend, Detour, Diverge, Divert, Glance, Otter, Paravane, Refract, Snick, Swerve, Throw, Trochotron, Veer, Windage

Deform(ed), **Deformity** Anamorphosis, Blemish, Crooked, Disfigure, Distort, Gammy, Hammer-toe, Harelip, Misborn, Mishapt, Mooncalf, Mutilate, Phocomelia, Phocomely, Polt-foot, Saddle-nose, Stenosed, Talipes, Valgus, Varus, Warp

▷ **Deformed** *may indicate* an anagram

Defraud Bilk, Cheat, Cozen, Gull, Gyp, Mulct, Shoulder, Sting, Swindle, Trick

Defray Bear, Cover, Meet

Defrost Thaw

Deft Adept, Agile, Dab, Dexterous, Elegant, Handy, Nimble

Defunct Deceased, Extinct, Obsolete

Defy *see* DEFIANCE

Degenerate, **Degeneration**, **Degenerative** Acorn-shell, Ascidian, Atrophy, Balanus, Base, Cirrhipedea, Cirrhipedia, Cirrhopod(a), Cirripedea, Cirripedia, Decadent, Deprave, Descend, Deteriorate, Eburnation, Fatty, Kaliyuga, Necrobiosis, Pejorate, Pervert, Rakehell, Relapse, Retrogress, Salp, Tunicate

Degrade, **Degradation** Abase, Cheapen, Culvertage, Debase, Demote, Depose, Diminish, Disennoble, Embase, Humble, Imbase, Lessen, Lower, > SHAME, Waterloo

Degree(s) Aegrotat, As, Azimuthal, BA, Baccalaureate, BCom, BD, B es S, C, Class, D, Desmond (Tutu), Doctoral, Douglas (Hurd), Engler, Extent, External, F, First, German, Gradation, Grade, Grece, Gree(s), Greece, Gre(e)se, Grice, Griece, Grize, > IN A HIGH DEGREE, K, Lambeth, Latitude, Letters, Level, Levitical, Licentiate, MA, Measure, Mediant, Nth, Nuance, Peg, PhD, Pin, Poll, Rate, Remove, Second, Stage, Status, Step, Third, Trevor (Nunn), Water

Dehiscence Suture

Dehydrate Exsiccate

Deification, **Deify** Apotheosis

Deign Condescend, Stoop

Deity Avatar, Demogorgon, Divine, Faun, > GOD, > GODDESS, Idolise, Immortalise, Numen, Pan, Satyr, Zombi(e)

Deject(ed), **Dejection** Abase, Abattu, Alamort, Amort, Blue, Chap-fallen, Crab, Crestfallen, Despondent, Dismay, Dispirited, Down, Downcast, Gloomy, Hangdog, Humble, Melancholy

Delay(ed) Ambage, Avizandum, Behindhand, Check, Cunctator, Defer, Demurrage, Detention, Fabian, Filibuster, For(e)slow, Forsloe, Frist, Hesitate, Hinder, Hitch, Hold up, Hysteresis, Impede, Laches, Lag, Late, Laten, Let, Linger, Loiter, Mora(torium), Obstruct, Procrastinate, Prolong, Prorogue, Remanet, Reprieve, Respite, Retard, Setback, Slippage, Sloth, Slow, > STALL, Stand-over, Stay, Stonewall, Temporise, Wait

Delectable Delicious, Luscious, Tasty

Delegate, **Delegation** Agent, Amphictyon, Apostolic, Appoint, Assign, Decentralise, Depute, Devolution, Mission, Nuncio, Offload, Representative, Secondary, Transfer, Vicarial, Walking

Delete Cancel, Cut, Erase, Excise, Expunge, Purge, Rase, Scratch, Scrub, Twink out

Deliberate(ly) Adagio, Consider, Debate, Intentional, Meditate, Moderate, Ponder, Prepensely, Studied, Voulu, Weigh, Witting

Delicacy, **Delicate** Airy-fairy, Beccafico, Blini, Canape, Cate, Caviare, Dainty, Difficult, Discreet, Ectomorph, Eggshell, Elfin, Ethereal, Fastidious, Fine, Finespun, Finesse, Flimsy, Fragile, > FRAIL, Friand, Gossamer, Guga, Hothouse, Inconie, Incony, Kickshaw, Kidglove, Ladylike, Light, Lobster, Morbidezza, Nesh, Nicety, Niminy-piminy, Ortolan, Oyster, Reedy, Roe, Sensitive, Soft, Subtle(ty), Sunket, Sweetmeat, Taste, Tender, Tenuous, Ticklish, Tidbit, Titbit, Truffle

Delicious Ambrosia, Delectable, Exquisite, Fragrant, Goloptious, Goluptious, Gorgeous, Lekker, Lip-smacking, Mor(e)ish, Mouthwatering, Scrummy, Scrumptious, Tasty, Toothsome, Yummo, Yummy, Yum-yum

> **Delight** *may indicate* 'darken'

Delight(ed), **Delightful** Bliss, Chuff, Delice, Dreamy, Elated, Elysian, Enamour,

Enjoyable, Enrapture, Exuberant, Felicity, Fetching, Frabjous, Gas, Glad, Glee, Gratify, Honey, Joy, Nice, Overjoy, Over the moon, Please, Pleasure, > **RAPTURE**, Regale, Scrummy, Super, Taking, Tickle, Turkish, Whacko, Whee, Whoopee, Wizard, Yippee, Yum-yum

Delineate Draft, Sketch, Trace

Delinquent Bodgie, Criminal, Halbstarker, Juvenile, Negligent, Offender, Ted

Delirious, Delirium Deranged, DT, Frenetic, Frenzy, Insanity, Mania, Phrenetic, Spazz, Wild

Deliver(ance), Deliverer, Delivery Accouchement, Ball, Birth, Bowl, Breech, Caesarean, Consign, Convey, Deal, Drop, Elocution, Escape, Express, Extradition, Give, Jail, Lead, Liberate, Lob, Orate, Over, Pronounce, Recorded, Redeem, Release, Relieve, Render, Rendition, > **RESCUE**, Rid, Round(sman), Salvation, Save, Say, Seamer, Sell, Shipment, Speak, Special, Tice, Transfer, Underarm, Underhand, Utter, Wide, Yorker

Dell Dale, Dargle, Dene, Dimble, Dingle, Dingl(e)y, Glen, Valley

Delphic Pythian

Delphinium Larkspur

Delta Camargue, D, Del, Flood-plain, Kronecker, Nabla, Nile, Oil Rivers, Triangle

Delude, Delusion Bilk, Cheat, Deceive, Fallacy, Fool, Hoax, > **MISLEAD**, Paranoia, Schizothymia, Trick

Deluge Avalanche, Flood, Ogygian, Saturate, Submerge, > **SWAMP**

De luxe Extra, Plush, Special

Delve Burrow, Dig, Excavate, Exhume, Explore, Probe, Search

Demagogue Agitator, Fanariot, Leader, Mobsman, Phanariot, Speaker, Tribune

Demand(ing) Appetite, Call, Claim, Cry, Dun, Exact, Excess, Exigent, Fastidious, Final, Hest, > **INSIST**, Mandate, Market, Need, Order, Postulate, Pressure, Request, Requisition, Rush, Sale, Stern, Stipulate, Stringent, Summon, Ultimatum, Want

Demean(ing) Belittle, Comport, Debase, Degrade, Humble, Infra dig, Lower, Maltreat

Demeanour Air, Bearing, Conduct, Expression, Front, Gravitas, Mien, Port

Dement(ed) Crazy, Hysterical, Insane, Mad, Wacko

Demi-god Aitu, Daemon, Garuda, Hero

Demi-mondaine Cocotte, > **LOOSE WOMAN**, Prostitute

Demise Death, Decease, Finish

Demo March, Parade, Protest, Rally, Sit-in

Democracy, Democrat D, Hunker, Industrial, Locofoco, Montagnard, Popular, Republic, Sansculotte, Social, Tammany

Demoiselle Crane, Damselfish

Demolish, Demolition Bulldoze, Devastate, Devour, Dismantle, Floor, KO, Level, Rack, > **RAZE**, Smash, Wreck

▶ **Demon** *see* DEVIL

Demoness Lilith

Demonstrate, Demonstration, Demonstrator Agitate, Barrack, Display, Endeictic, Evènement, Evince, Explain, Hunger march, Maffick, Manifest, March, Morcha, Ostensive, Portray, Protest, Prove, Provo, Send-off, > **SHOW**, Sit-in, Touchy-feely

Demoralize Bewilder, Corrupt, Destroy, Shatter, Unman, Weaken

Demote, Demotion Comedown, Degrade, Disbench, Disrate, Embace, Embase, Reduce, Relegate, Stellenbosch

Demur Hesitate, Jib, Object

Demure Coy, Mim, Modest, Prenzie, Primsie, Sedate, Shy

Den Dive, Domdaniel, Earth, Hell, Hide-away, Holt, Home, Lair, Lie, Opium, Room, Shebeen, Study, Sty, Wurley

Denial, **Deny**, **Denier** Abnegate, Antinomian, Aspheterism, Bar, Contradict, Démenti, Disavow, Disenfranchise, Disown, Forswear, > GAINSAY, Nay, Negate, Nick, Protest, Refuse, Refute, Renague, Renay, Reneg(e), Renegue, Reney, Renig, Renounce, Reny, Repudiate, Sublate, Traverse, Withhold

Denigrate Besmirch, Blacken, Defame, Tar

Denim Jeans

Denizen Diehard, Inhabitant, Resident

Denomination Category, Cult, Sect, Variety

Denote Import, Indicate, Mean, Signify

Denouement Anagnorisis, Climax, Coda, Exposure, Outcome, Showdown

Denounce, **Denunciation** Ban, Commination, Condemn, Criticise, Decry, Delate, Diatribe, Hatchet job, Hereticate, Proclaim, Proscribe, Shop, Stigmatise, Upbraid

Denry Card

Density Compact, Current, D, Double, Firm, Flux, Neutral, Opaque, Optical, Reflection, Relative, Solid, Spissitude, Tesla, Thick, Transmission, Vapour, Woofy

Dent(ed) Batter, Concave, Dancette, Depress, Dimple, Dinge, Dint, Nock, V

Dental, **Dentist(ry)** DDS, Entodontics, Extractor, Kindhart, LDS, Odontic, Periodontic, Toothy

Dentures Biteplate, Bridge, Bridgework, False teeth, Plate, Store teeth, Wallies

► **Deny** *see* DENIAL

Deodorant Anti-perspirant

Deoxidise Outgas, Reduce

Depart(ed), **Departing**, **Departure** Abscond, Absquatulate, Bunk, D, Dead, Decession, Defunct, Die, Digress, Divergence, Exit, Exodus, Flight, > GO, Leave, Lucky, Outbound, Rack off, Remue, Vade, Vamoose, Walkout

Department Achaea, Ain, Aisne, Allier, Alpes Maritimes, Angers, Arcadia, Ardeche, Ardennes, Argo, Argolis, Ariege, Arrondissement, Arta, Attica, Aube, Aude, Aveyron, Bas-Rhin, Belfort, Beziers, Bouches-du-Rhone, Branch, Bureau, Calvados, Cantal, Charente, Cher, Commissariat, Corrèze, Cote d'Or, Cotes d'Armor, Cotes du Nord, Creuse, DEFRA, Deme, Deux-Sevres, Division, Dordogne, Doubs, Drôme, El(e)ia, Essonne, Eure, Eure-et-Loir, Faculty, Finistere, Fire, FO, Gard, Gers, Gironde, Greencloth, Guadeloupe, Gulag, Hanaper, Haute-Garonne, Haute-Loire, Haute-Marne, Haute-Normandie, Hautes-Alpes, Hautes-Saône, Hautes-Savoie, Haute-Vienne, Haut-Rhin, Hauts-de-Seine, Herault, Home, Ille-et-Vilaine, Indre, Indre-et-Loire, Isere, Jura, Landes, Loire, Loir-et-Cher, Lot, Lot-et-Garonne, Lozere, Maine-et-Loire, Manche, Mayenne, Meurthe-et-Moselle, Meuse, Ministry, Morbihan, Moselle, Nièvre, Nome, Nomos, Nord, Office, Oise, Orne, Pas-de-Calais, Province, Puy de Dôme, Pyrénées(-Atlantique), Pyrénées-Orientales, Region, Rehabilitation, Rhône, Sanjak, Saône-et-Loire, Sarthe, Savoie, Secretariat(e), Section, Seine-et-Marne, Seine Maritime, Seine St Denis, Somme, Sphere, State, Tarn(-et-Garonne), Treasury, Tuscany, Val de Marne, Val d'Oise, Var, Vaucluse, Vendée, Vienne, Voiotia, War, Wardrobe, Yonne, Yvelines

Depend(ant), **Dependency**, **Dependent** Addicted, Child, Client, Colony, Conditional, Contingent, Count, Dangle, Fief, Habit, Hang, Hinge, Icicle, Lean, Minion, Pensioner, Relier, Rely, Retainer, Ross, Sponge, Subject, Trust, Turn on, Vassal

Dependable Reliable, Reliant, Secure, Sheet-anchor, Solid, Sound, Staunch, Sure, > **TRUSTWORTHY**

Depict Delineate, Display, Draw, Limn, Paint, Portray, Present, Represent

Depilate, Depilatory Grain, Rusma, Slate

Deplete Diminish, Drain, Exhaust, Reduce

Deplorable, Deplore Base, Bemoan, Chronic, Complain, Deprecate, Dolorous, Grieve, Lament, Mourn, Piteous, Regret, Rue

Deploy(ment) Extend, Herse, Unfold, Use

▷ **Deploy(ment)** *may indicate* an anagram

Depopulate Deracinate

Deport(ment) Address, Air, Banish, > **BEARING**, Carriage, Demeanour, Mien, Renvoi, Renvoy

Depose, Deposition Affirm, Banish, Dethrone, Displace, Dispossess, Overthrow, Pieta, Testify

Deposit Alluvial, Alluvium, Arcus, Argol, Atheroma, Bank, Bathybius, Bergmehl, Calc-sinter, Calc-tuff, Caliche, Cave-earth, Coral, Crag, Delta, Depone, Diluvium, Drift, Evaporite, Fan, File, Firn, Fur, Gyttja, Kieselguhr, Land, Lay, Lodge(ment), Loess, Löss, Measure, Moraine, Natron, Outwatch, Park, Pay dirt, Placer, Plank, Plaque, Precipitate, Put, Repose, Residuum, Saburra, Saprolite, > **SEDIMENT**, Silt, Sinter, Sludge, Stockwork, Stratum, Surety, Tartar, Terramara, Terramare, Till, Time, Tophus, Turbidite

Depot Barracoon, Base, Camp, Depository, Station, Terminus, Treasure-city, Warehouse

Deprav(ed), Depravity Bestial, Cachexia, Cachexy, > **CORRUPT**, Dissolute, Evil, Immoral, Low, Reprobate, Rotten, Sodom, Total, Turpitude, Ugly, Vice, Vicious, Vile

Deprecate Censure, Deplore, Expostulate, Reproach

Depreciate Abase, Belittle, Derogate, Detract, Discount

Depredate, Depredation Pillage, Plunder, Rob

Depress(ed), Depressing, Depression Accablé, Alamort, Alveolus, Amort, Astrobleme, Attrist, Black dog, Blight, Blues, Cafard, Caldron, Canada, Canyon, Chill, Col, Combe, Couch, Crab, Crush, Cyclone, Dampen, Deject, Dell, Dene, Dent, Despair, > **DIMPLE**, Dip, Dismal, Dispirit, Dolina, Doline, Doomy, Downlifting, Drear, Drere, Dumpish, Endogenous, Exanimate, Flatten, Fonticulus, Foss(ula), Fossa, Fovea, Frog, Geosyncline, Ghilgai, Gilgai, Gilgie, Glen, Gloom, Graben, Grinch, Ha-ha, Hammer, Hilar, Hilum, Hilus, Hollow, Howe, Hyp, Joes, Kettle, Kick(-up), Lacuna, Leaden, Low(ness), Low-spirited, Moping, Neck, Ocean basin, Pan, Pit, Polje, Postnatal, Prostrate, Qattara, Recession, Re-entrant, Sad, Saddle, Salt-cellar, Salt-pan, Scrobicule, Sink, Sinkhole, Sinus, Sitzmark, Slot, > **SLUMP**, Slumpflation, Soakaway, Spiritless, Stomodaeum, Sump, Swag, Swale, Swallowhole, Trench, Trough, Umbilication, Vale, Vallecula, Valley, Wallow, Weigh down, Wet blanket

Deprivation, Deprive(d) Bereft, Deny, Disenfranchise, Disfrock, Disseise, Disseize, Expropriate, Famine, Foreclose, Geld, Have-not, Hunger, Reduce, Remove, Rob, Withhold

Depth Draught, Draw, F, Fathom, Gravity, Intensity, Isobath, Pit, Profundity

Deputise, Deputy Act, Agent, Aide, Assistant, Commis(sary), Delegate, Legate, Lieutenant, Locum, Loot, Mate, Number two, Prior, Proxy, Represent, Secondary, Standby, Sub, Substitute, Succentor, Surrogate, Vicar, Vice, Viceregent, Vidame

Derange(d) Craze, Détraqué, Disturb, Insane, Manic, Troppo, Unhinge, Unsettle

Derby Demolition, Donkey, Eponym, Hat, Kentucky, Kiplingcotes, Race, Roller

Derek Bo

Derelict Abandoned, > DECREPIT, Deserted, Negligent, Outcast, Ramshackle

Deride, Derision, Derisive Contempt, Gup, Guy, Hoot, Jeer, Mock, Nominal, Raspberry, > RIDICULE, Sardonic, Scoff, Scorn, Snifty, Snort, Yah, Ya(h)boo

Derive, Derivation, Derivative Ancestry, Creosote, Deduce, Descend, Extract, Get, Kinone, Of, Offshoot, Origin, Pedigree, Secondary

Dermatitis *see* SKIN DISEASE

Derogate, Derogatory Belittle, Decry, Defamatory, Demeaning, Detract, Discredit, Pejorative, Personal, Slighting, Snide

Deronda Daniel

Derrick Crane, Davit, Hoist, Jib, Spar, Steeve

Dervish Calender, Doseh, Mawlawi, Mevlevi, Revolver, Santon, Whirling

Descant Comment, Discourse, Faburden, Melody, Song

Descartes René

Descend(ant), Descent Ancestry, Avail, Avale, Bathos, Blood, Chute, Cion, Decline, Degenerate, Derive, Dismount, Dive, Drop, Epigon, Extraction, Heir, Heraclid, > LINEAGE, Offspring, Pedigree, Prone, Rappel, Said, Say(y)id, Scarp, Scion, Seed, Shelve, Sien(t), Sink, Stock, Syen, Vest, Volplane

Describe, Description, Descriptive Blurb, Define, Delineate, Depict, Designate, Draw, Epithet, Exposition, Expound, Graphic, Job, Narrate, Outline, Paint, Portray, Rapportage, Recount, Relate, Report, Sea-letter, Sketch, Specification, Synopsis, Term, Trace

Describing *may indicate* 'around'

Descry Behold, Discern, Get, Notice, Perceive

Desecrate, Desecration Abuse, Defile, Dishallow, Profane, Sacrilege, Unhallow

Desecrated *may indicate* an anagram

Desert(er), Deserted, Desert(s) Abandon, Apostasy, Arabian, Arid, Ar Rimal, Arunta, Atacama, AWOL, Badland, Barren, Bledowska, Bug, Bunk, Colorado, Come-uppance, D, Dahna, Defect, Desolate, Dissident, Due, Empty, Eremic, Etosha Pan, Factious, Fail, Fezzan, Foresay, Forhoo, Forhow, Forlorn, Forsake, Forsay, Frondeur, Garagum, Gibson, Gila, Gobi, Great Basin, Great Indian, Great Sandy, Great Victoria, Heterodox, Indian, Jump ship, Kalahari, Kara Kum, Kavir, Kyzyl Kum, Libyan, Lurch, Meeds, Merit, Mohave, Mojave, Nafud, Namib, Negev, Nubian, Ogaden, Painted, Pategonian, Pindan, Rat, Refus(e)nik, Reg, > RENEGADE, Reward, Rub'al-Khali, Run, Runaway, Sahara, Sahel, Sands, Secede, Shamo, Simpson, Sinai, Sonoran, Sturt, Syrian, Tacna-Arica, Tergiversate, Thar, Turncoat, Ust(y)urt, Victoria, Void, Wadi, Waste, Western Sahara, Wilderness, Worthiness

Deserve(d) Condign, Earn, > MERIT, Well-earned, Worthy

Desiccate(d) Dry, Sere

Design(er) Adam, Aim, Architect, Ashley, Batik, Broider, Cardin, Cartoon, Castrametation, Chop, Cloisonné, Create, Cul de lampe, Damascene, Decal(comania), Decor, Depict, Devise, Dévoré, Dior, Draft, Embroidery, End, Engender, Engine(r), Engineer, Erté, Etch, Fashion, Feng-shui, Former, Hepplewhite, Hitech, Iconic, Impresa, Imprese, Industrial, Intend(ment), Intent(ion), Interior, Issigonis, Layout, Linocut, Logo, Marquetry, Mascle, Mean, Meander, Millefleurs, Modiste, Monogram, Morris, Mosaic, Motif, Pattern, > PLAN, Plot, Propose, Pyrography, Quant, Retro, Ruse, Schema, Scheme, Seal, Sheraton, Sketch, Specification, Stencil, Stubble, Stylist, Sunburst, Tatow, Tattoo, Tattow, Tatu, Think, Tooling, Trigram, Versace, Vignette, Watermark, Whittle

Designate Earmark, Note, Style, Title

Desirable, **Desire**, **Desirous** Ambition, Appetite, Aspire, Avid, Best, Cama, Conation, Concupiscence, Covet, Crave, Cupidity, Dreamboat, Earn, Eligible, Epithymetic, Fancy, Gasp, Hanker, Hope, Hots, Hunger, Itch, Kama(deva), Le(t)ch, Libido, List, Long, Luscious, Lust, Mania, Nymphomania, Orectic, Owlcar, Plum, Reck, Request, Residence, Salt, Streetcar, Thirst, Velleity, Vote, Wanderlust, Want, Whim, Will, Wish, Yearn, Yen

Desist Abandon, Cease, Curb, Pretermit, Quit, Stop

Desk Almemar, Ambo, Bureau, Carrel(l), Cash, Check-in, Cheveret, City, Copy, Davenport, Desse, Devonport, Enquiry, E(s)critoire, Faldstool, Lectern, Lettern, Litany, Pay, Pedestal, Prie-dieu, Pulpit, Reading, Roll-top, Scrutoire, Secretaire, Vargueno, Writing

Desman Pyrenean

Desolate, **Desolation** Bare, Barren, Desert, Devastate, Disconsolate, Forlorn, Gaunt, Godforsaken, Gousty, Moonscape, Waste, Woebegone

Despair, **Desperate**, **Desperation** Acharne, Anomy, De profundis, Despond, Dire, Dismay, Extreme, Frantic, Gagging, Giant, Gloom, Hairless, Headlong, Last-ditch, Last-gasp, Life and death, Reckless, Unhopeful, Urgent, Wanhope

▶ **Despatch** *see* DISPATCH

Desperado Bandit, Bravo, Ruffian, Terrorist

Despicable Abject, Base, Caitiff, Cheap, Churl, Contemptible, Heinous, Ignoble, Ignominious, Mean, Moer, Puke, Ratfink, Scumbag, Shabby, Toerag, Wretched

Despise Condemn, Contemn, Forhow, Hate, Ignore, Scorn, Spurn, Vilify, Vilipend

Despite For, Malgré, Notwithstanding, Pace, Though, Venom

Despoil Mar, Ravage, Vandalise

Despondent Dejected, Downcast, Forlorn, Gloomy, Sad

Despot(ism) Autarchy, Autocrat, Caesar, Darius, Dictator, Napoleon, Nero, Satrap, Stratocrat, Tsar, Tyrant, Tzar

Dessert Afters, Baked Alaska, Baklava, Bavarian Cream, Bavarois, Bombe, Charlotte, Charlotte russe, Cobbler, Compote, Coupe, Crème brulée, Crème caramel, Entremets, Flummery, Fool, Junket, Kissel, Knickerbocker glory, Kulfi, Marquise, Mousse, Mud pie, Nesselrode, Parfait, Pashka, Pavlova, Peach Melba, Pud(ding) Sawine, Sabayon, Semifreddo, Shoofly pie, Strudel, Sundae, Syllabub, Tiramisu, Tortoni, Trifle, Vacherin, Zabaglione

Destine(d), **Destination** Design, End, Fate, Foredoom, Goal, Home, Intend, Joss, Meant, Port, Purpose, Weird

Destiny Doom, > FATE, Karma, Kismet, Lot, Manifest, Moira, Yang, Yin

Destitute Bankrupt, Bare, Broke, Devoid, Dirt-poor, Helpless, Indigent, Needy, Poor, Sterile

Destroy(er) Annihilate, Antineutrino, Antineutron, Antiparticle, Apollyon, Atomise, Blight, D, Decimate, Deep-six, Deface, Delete, Demolish, Denature, Destruct, Dish, Dismember, Dissolve, Eat, Efface, End, Eradicate, Erase, Estrepe, Exterminate, Extirpate, Flivver, Fordo, Harry, Iconoclast, > KILL, Murder, Obliterate, Overkill, Perish, Predator, Ravage, Raze, Ruin, Saboteur, Scuttle, Slash, Smash, Spif(f)licate, Spoil, Sterilize, Stew-can, Stonker, Subvert, Trash, Undo, Uproot, Vandal, Vitiate, Whelm, Wreck, Zap

Destruction, **Destructive** Adverse, Autolysis, Bane, Can, Collapse, Deathblow, Deleterious, Devastation, Doom, Downfall, End, Götterdämmerung, Grave, Havoc, Holocaust, Insidious, Internecine, Kali, Lethal, Loss, Pernicious, Quelea, Rack, Ragnarok, Ravage, Sabotage, Speciocide, Stroy, Wrack

Desultory Aimless, Cursory, Fitful, Idle

Detach(ed), **Detachment** Abstract, Alienate, Aloof, Body, Calve, Clinical, Cut,

Detail, Discrete, Insular, Isle, Isolate, Loose, Outlying, Outpost, Patrol, Picket, Picquet, Separate, Sever, Staccato, Stoic, Unfasten, Unhinge

Detached work Ravelin

Detail(s), **Detailed** Annotate, Dock, Elaborate, Embroider, Expatiate, Explicit, Expound, Instance, > ITEM, Itemise, Minutiae, Nicety, Particular(ise), Pedantry, Point, Recite, Relate, Respect, Send, Spec, Special, Specification, Technicality

▷ **Detailed** *may indicate* last letter missing

Detain(ee), **Detention** Arrest, Buttonhole, Collar, Custody, Delay, Detinue, Gate, Glasshouse, Hinder, Intern, Keep, POW, Preventive, Retard, Stay, > WITHHOLD

Detect(or), **Detective** Agent, Arsène, Asdic, Bloodhound, Brown, Bucket, Busy, Catch, Chan, CID, Cuff, Dick, Discover, Divine, Doodlebug, Dupin, Espy, Eye, Fed, Find, Flambeau, Flic, Fortune, French, Geigercounter, Geophone, Gumshoe, Hanaud, Hercule, Holmes, Interpol, Investigator, Jack, Lecoq, Lupin, Maigret, Metal, Microwave, Mine, Minitrack®, Nose, Peeper, PI, Pinkerton, Plant, Poirot, Private eye, Prodnose, Radar, Reagent, Rumble, Scent, Scerne, Sense, Sensor, Shadow, Shamus, Sherlock, > SLEUTH, Sofar, Sonar, Sonobuoy, Spot, Tabaret, Take, Tec, Thorndyke, Toff, Trace, Trent, Vance, Wimsey, Yard

Detent Pawl, Trigger

Deter(rent) Block, Check, Daunt, Dehort, Delay, Dissuade, Prevent, Restrain, Turn-off

Detergent Cationic, Cleaner, Solvent, Surfactant, Syndet, Tepol, Whitener

Deteriorate, **Deterioration** Decadence, Degenerate, Derogate, Entropy, Pejoration, Rust, Worsen

▷ **Deterioration** *may indicate* an anagram

▷ **Determination** *may indicate* 'last letter'

Determine(d), **Determination** Arbitrament, Ardent, Ascertain, Assign, Assoil, Bent, Condition, Dead-set, > DECIDE, Define, Doctrinaire, Dogged, Dour, Drive, Earnest, Fix, Govern, Grit(ty), Headstrong, Hell-bent, Indomitable, Influence, Intent, Judgement, Law, Out, Point, Purpose, Quantify, > RESOLUTE, Resolve, Rigwiddie, Rigwoodie, Self-will, Set, Settle, Shape, Stalwart, Steely, Type, Weigh

Detest(able) Abhor, Despise, Execrable, Execrate, Hate, Loathsome, Pestful, Vile

Detonate, **Detonator** Blast, Explode, Fire, Fuse, Fuze, Ignite, Kindle, Plunger, Primer, Saucisse, Saucisson, Tetryl, Trip-wire

Detour Bypass, Deviate, Divert

Detract Belittle, Decry, Diminish, Discount, Disparage

Detriment(al) Adverse, Damage, Harm, Injury, Loss, Mischief

Deuce Dickens, Old Harry, Twoer

Deuteron Diplon

Devalue Debase, Reduce, Undermine

Devastate Demolish, Destroy, Lay waste, Overwhelm, Ravage, Ruin, Sack, Traumatise, Waste, Wreck

Develop(er), **Developed**, **Developing**, **Development** Advance, Amidol®, Aplasia, Breakthrough, Breed, Bud, Build, Burgeon, Catechol, Creep, Educe, Elaborate, Enlarge, Epigenetic, Escalate, Evolve, Expand, Expatriate, Foetus, Full-fledged, Fulminant, Genesis, Germinate, Gestate, Grow, Hatch, Hydroquinone, Hypo, Imago, Improve, Incipient, Incubate, Lamarckism, Larva, Mature, Metamorphose, Metol, Morphogenesis, Oidium, Ontogenesis, Pathogeny, Pullulate, Pupa, Pyro, Pyrogallol, Quinol, Ribbon, Ripe(n), Shape, Soup, Speciation, Sprawl, Teens, Tone, Unfold, Upgrow

▷ **Develop** *may indicate* an anagram

Deviant, **Deviate**, **Deviation** Aberrance, Abnormal, Anomaly, Average, Brisure, Deflect, Depart, Derogate, Digress, Diverge, Divert, Error, Kinky, Kurtosis, List, Mean, Pervert, Quartile, Sheer, Solecism, Sport, Standard, Stray, Swerve, Transvestite, > **TURN**, Valgus, Varus, Veer, Wander, Wend

Device Appliance, Artifice, Contraption, Contrivance, Deus ex machina, Dodge, Emblem, Expedient, Gadget, Gimmick, Gubbins, Instrument, Logo, Mnemonic, Pattern, Plan, > **STRATAGEM**, Subterfuge, Tactic, Tag, Trademark, Trick

DEVICES

3 letters:	Relay	Reverb	Lighter
Bug	Saser	Roller	Machine
FET	Scart	Router	Minicom
LED	Servo	Selsyn	Monitor
Mux	Shear	Sensor	Pelorus
Zip	Sonde	Switch	Pickoff
	Sprag	Swivel	Plunger
4 letters:	SQUID	Temple	Ratchet
Capo	Timer	Tipple	Rotator
Fret	Tromp	Tracer	Scanner
Fuse	Valve	Tremie	Shut-off
Gobo	V-clip	Triode	Shuttle
Orle	Waldo	Trompe	Sniffer
Plug		Turtle	Snorkel
Rest	**6 letters:**	Tympan	Snuffer
Tram	Atlatl	Viewer	Sounder
Trap	Biodot	Wafter	Spoiler
	Bungee	Widget	Stinger
5 letters:	Buzzer		Storage
Audio	Charge	**7 letters:**	Sundial
Balun	Cotter	Bearing	Swatter
Chaff	Cut-out	Bendlet	Synchro
Cleat	Dasher	Cleaver	Tokamak
Cramp	Deckle	Clicker	Tonepad
Diode	De-icer	Compass	Vernier
Frame	Detent	Counter	Vocoder
Gizmo	Dimmer	Coupler	
Gland	Dongle	Dashpot	**8 letters:**
Input	Elevon	Digibox®	Atomiser
Maser	Engine	Divider	Autodial
Meter	Etalon	Doubler	Barostat
Mixer	Filter	Fuzzbox	Betatron
Modem	Friend®	Genlock	Bootjack
Mouse	Kludge	Gimbals	Calutron
Optic®	Petard	Grapnel	Conveyor
Pager	Pick-up	Imprese	Demister
Petar	Pinger®	Inhaler	Detector
Prism	Possum	Isotron	Diestock
Probe	Quippu	Jetpack	Ecraseur
Quipu	Rabble	Krytron	Enlarger

Episcope
Episemon
Geophone
Ignitron
Monogram
Odograph
Paravane
Pulsator
Pyrostat
Resister
Shoehorn
Snow-eyes
Snowshoe
Solenoid
Spreader
Squeegee
Sweatbox
Swellbox
Terminal
Thin-film
Trembler
Varactor
Vibrator

9 letters:
Aspirator
Capacitor
Compasses
Converter
Delayline
Detonator
Dynamotor
Eccentric
Excelsior
Exerciser
Generator
Gyroscope
Hendiadys
Hodoscope
Hydrofoil
Hydrostat
Hygrostat
Konimeter
Kymograph
Megaphone

Mekometer
Metronome
Nebuliser
Octophone
Optophone
Overdrive
Pacemaker
Parachute
Periscope
Photocell
Pitchbend
Polygraph
Propeller
Rectifier
Regulator
Remontoir
Resonator
Responsor
Rheotrope
Rotachute
Rotameter
Satellite
Scrambler
Separator
Sequencer
Simulator
Smokejack
Sonograph
Sprinkler
Steadicam
Tabulator
Tasimeter
Telemeter
Thyristor
Tonometer
Trackball
Tremulant

10 letters:
Applicator
Autowinder
Centrifuge
Chronotron
Commutator
Comparator

Cyclometer
Derailleur
Descendeur
Groundprox
Humidistat
Hygroscope
Jawbreaker
Jaws of Life
Metrostyle
Microphone
Microscope
Peripheral
Phonoscope
Phonospore
Remontoire
Respirator
Siderostat
Snowplough
Spirograph
Stabiliser
Stimpmeter
Suppressor
Switchgear
Tachograph
Tachometer
Telewriter
Thermistor
Thermopile
Thermostat
Tourniquet
Transducer
Transistor
Turnbuckle
Ventilator
Vertoscope®
Videophone
Viewfinder
Viscometer

11 letters:
Afterburner
Autochanger
Baffle-plate
Carburettor
Epidiascope

Fluoroscope
Insufflator
Multiplexer
Smokerlyzer
Snickometer
Spectograph
Speedometer
Swingometer
Trackerball
Transceiver
Transformer
Transponder

12 letters:
Breathalyser
Concentrator
Intrauterine
Lithotripter
Oscillograph
Sensitometer
Snooperscope
Spectroscope
Supercharger
Teleprompter
Thermocouple
Turbidimeter
Viscosimeter

13 letters:
Baton-sinister
Phonendoscope
Rack and pinion

14 letters:
Anamorphoscope
Dead man's
    handle
Interferometer
Intervalometer
Plethysmograph
Scintillometer
Spinthariscope

Devil(ish), Demon Abaddon, Afree, Afrit, Ahriman, Amaimon, Apollyon,
Asmodeus, Atua, Auld Hornie, Azazel, Barbason, Beelzebub, Belial, Buckra,
Clootie, Cloots, Dasyure, Davy Jones, Deev, Deil, Demogorgon, Demon, Deuce,
Devling, Diable, Diabolic, Dickens, Div, Drudge, Dust, Eblis, Falin, Familiar,
Fend, Fiend, Fient, Ghoul, Goodman, Goodyear, Grill, Hangie, Hornie, Iblis,
Imp, Incubus, Infernal, Lamia, Legion, Lilith, Lord of the Flies, Lori, Lucifer,

Mahoun(d), Manta, Mara, Maxwell's, Mazikeen, Mephisto(pheles), Mischief, Nick, Old Bendy, Old Nick, Old One, Old Pandemonium, Old Poker, Old Roger, Old Split-foot, Old Toast, Printer's, Ragamuffin, Rahu, Ralph, Satan, Sathanas, Satyr, Scour, Scratch, Screwtape, Season, Setebos, Shaitan, Shedeem, Snow, Sorra, Succubine, Succubus, Tailard, Tasmanian, Tempter, Titivil, Tutivillus, Wendigo, Wicked, Wicked One, Wirricow, Worricow, Worrycow, Zernebock

Devious Braide, Cunning, Deep, Eel(y), Erroneous, Evasive, Implex, Indirect, Scheming, Shifty, Stealthy, Subtle, Tortuous, Tricky

Devise(d) Arrange, Contrive, Decoct, Hatch, Hit-on, Imagine, Invenit, Invent, Plot, Thermette

Devitrified Ambitty

Devoid Barren, Destitute, Empty, Vacant, Wanting

Devolve Occur, Result, Transmit

Devote(e), Devotion(al), Devoted Addiction, Aficionado, Angelus, Attached, Bhakti, Consecrate, Corban, Dedicate, Employ, Fan, Fervid, Fiend, Holy, Hound, Loyalty, Novena, Ophism, Passion, Pious, Puja, Religioso, Sea-green incorruptible, S(h)akta, Solemn, True, Zealous

Devour(ing) Consume, Eat, Engorge, Engulf, Manducate, Moth-eat, Scarf, Scoff, > SWALLOW, Vorant

▷ **Devour** *may indicate* one word inside another

Devout Holy, Pia, Pious, Reverent, Sant, Sincere

Dew(y) Bloom, Moist, Mountain, Rime, Roral, Roric, Rorid, Roscid, Serein, Serene, Tranter

Dexterity, Dexterous Adept, Adroit, Aptitude, Cleverness, Craft, Deft, Feat(e)ous, Featuous, > HANDY, Knack, Shrewd, Sleight, Slick

Diabolic Cruel, > DEVILISH, Infernal

Diacritic (mark) Acute, Angstrom, Cedilla, Circumflex, Diaresis, Eth, Grave, Háček, Thorn, Tilde, Umlaut

Diadem Coronet, Fillet, Garland, Tiara

Diagnose, Diagnosis Fetal, Findings, Identify, Scan, Scintigraphy

Diagonal(ly) Bend(wise), Bias, Cater(-corner), Catty-cornered, Counter, Oblique, Slant, Solidus, Twill

Diagram Argand, Block, Butterfly, Chart, Compass rose, Decision tree, Dendogram, Drawing, Fault-tree, Feynman, Figure, Flow, Graph, Graphics, Grid, Hertzsprung-Russell, Indicator, Logic, Map, Plan, Plat, Run-chart, Scatter, Schema, Stem-and-leaf, Stemma, Stereogram, Tephigram, Venn, Wind rose

Dial(ling) Card, Face, Mug, Phiz, Phone, Pulse, STD, Visage

Dialect Accent, Aeolic, Alemannic, Arcadic, Attic, Basuto, Burr, Doric, Eldin, Eolic, Erse, Eye, Franconian, Friulian, Gallo-Romance, Gascon, Geechee, Geordie, Greenlander, Hegelian, Idiom, Ionic, Isogloss, Jargon, Jockney, Joual, Khalka, Koine, Konkani, Ladin, Lallans, Landsmaal, Langobardic, Langue d'oc, Langue d'oil, Langue d'oui, Lingo, Low German, Mackem, Norman, Norn, Parsee, Patois, Prakrit, Riffian, Romansch, Scouse, Sesotho, Syriac, Taal, Talkee-talkee, Tongue, Tshi, Twi, Vernacular, Wu, Yealdon, Yenglish, Yinglish

Dialogue Colloquy, Conversation, Critias, Discussion, Exchange, Interlocution, Lazzo, Pastourelle, Speech, Stichomythia, Talk, Upspeak

Dialysis Kidney, Peritoneal

Diameter Breadth, Calibre, Gauge, Systyle, Tactical, Width

Diamond(s), Diamond-shaped Adamant, Black, Boart, Brilliant, Bristol, Carbonado, Cullinan, D, DE, Delaware, Eustace, Florentine, Hope, Ice, Industrial, Isomer, Jim, Koh-i-noor, Lasque, Lattice, Lozenge, Paragon, Pick,

Pitch, Pitt, Quarry, Rhinestone, Rhomb, Rock, Rose-cut, Rosser, Rough, Rustre, Sancy, Solitaire, Spark, Sparklers, Squarial, Suit

Diana Artemis, Di

Diapason Normal, Open, Ottava, Stopped

Diaphanous Clear, Sheer, Translucent

Diaphoretic Sweater

Diaphragm Cap, Iris, Mid-riff, Phrenic, Stop

Diaresis Trema

Diarist *see* DIARY

Diarrhoea Collywobbles, Gippy tummy, Lientery, Montezuma's revenge, Runs, Scours, Squitters, The shits, Trots, Verbal, Weaning-brash, Wood-evil

Diary, Diarist Chronicle, Dale, Day-book, Evelyn, Hickey, Journal, Kilvert, Log, Nobody, Pepys, Pooter, Record, Video

Diaspora Exodus, Galuth

Diatribe Harangue, Invective, Philippic, Tirade

Dice(r), Dicey Aleatory, Astragals, Bale, Bones, Chop, Craps, Cube, Doctor, Dodgy, Fulham, Fullams, Fullans, Gourd(s), Highman, Jeff, Mandoline, Poker, Shoot, Snake-eyes, Tallmen

Dichotomy Split

Dick(y), Dickey Clever, Deadeye, Front, Moby, OED, Policeman, Rumble, Shaky, Shirt, Spotted, Tec, Tonneau, Tucker, Tumbledown, Unstable, Wankle, Weak, Whittington

▸ **Dick** *may indicate* a dictionary

Dickens Boz, Deuce, Devil, Mephistopheles

Dicker Bargain, Barter, Haggle, Trade

▸ **Dicky** *may indicate* an anagram

Dictate, Dictator(ial) Amin, Authoritarian, Autocrat, Big Brother, Caesar, Castro, Cham, Command, Czar, Decree, Demagogue, Despot, Duce, Franco, Fu(e)hrer, Gauleiter, Hitler, Impose, Lenin, Ordain, Overbearing, Peremptory, Peron, Salazar, Shogun, Stalin, Tell, Tito, Totalitarian, Tsar, Tyrant, Tzar

Diction Language, Lexis, Speech, Style

Dictionary Alveary, Calepin, Chambers, Data, Etymologicon, Fowler, Gazetteer, Glossary, Gradus, Hobson-Jobson, Idioticon, Johnson's, Larousse, Lexicon, Lexis, OED, Onomasticon, Thesaurus, Vocabulary, Webster, Wordbook

Dictum Obiter

Did Began, Couth, Fec(it), Gan

Didactic Sermonical

Diddle Cheat, Con, Hoax

Dido Antic, Caper, Carthaginian, Elissa

Die(d), Dying Ache, Cark, Choke, Crater, Croak, Cube, D, Decadent, Desire, End, Evanish, Exit, Expire, Fade, Fail, Flatline, Forfair, Fulham, Fulhan, Fullam, Go, Go west, Highman, Hop, Kark, Long, Morendo, Moribund, Ob(iit), Orb, Pass, Peg out, Perdendosi, Perish, Peter, Snuff, Snuff it, Solidum, Sphacelation, Stamp, Sterve, Succumb, Suffer, Swage, Swelt, Tine, Wane

Diehard Blimp, Fanatic, Intransigent, Reactionary, Standpatter, Zealot

Diet(er) Assembly, Bant(ing), Cacatrophy, Council, Dail, Eat, Fare, Hay, Intake, Kashrut(h), Ketogenic, Landtag, Lent, Macrobiotic, Parliament, Pleading, Reduce, Regimen, Reichstag, Slim, Solid, Sprat, Staple, Strict, Tynwald, Vegan, Vegetarian, Weightwatcher, Worms

Dietetics Sit(i)ology

Differ(ence), Differing, Different(ly) Allo, Barney, Change, Cline, Contrast, Deviant, Diesis, Disagree, Discord, Discrepant, Disparate, Dispute,

Dissent, Dissimilitude, Distinct, Diverge, Diverse, Else, Elsewise, Nuance, Omnifarious, Other, Othergates, Otherguess, Otherness, Otherwise, Potential, Separate, Several, Symmetric, Tiff, Unlike, Variform, Various, Vary

Differential, **Differentiate** Calculus, Del, Distinguish, Nabla, Secern, Taxeme, Wage

Difficult(y) Abstruseness, Ado, Aporia, Arduous, Augean, Badass, Balky, Ballbuster, Bitter, Block, Bolshie, Bother, Catch, Choosy, Complication, Corner, Deep, Depth, Dysphagia, Extreme, Fiddly, Formidable, Gordian, > **HARD**, Hassle, Hazard, Hiccup, Hobble, Hole, Ill, Impasse, Indocile, Intractable, Jam, Kink, Knot, Lurch, Mulish, Net, Nodus, Obstacle, Parlous, Pig, Pitfall, Plight, Predicament, Quandary, Queer St, Recalcitrant, Rough, Rub, Scrape, Scrub, Setaceous, Shlep, Snag, Soup, Steep, Stick, Sticky, Stiff, Strait, Stubborn, Stymie, Ticklish, Tight spot, Trial, Tricky, Troublous, Une(a)th, Uphill, Via dolorosa

Diffident Bashful, Meek, Modest, Reserved, Shy

Diffuse, **Diffusion** Barophoresis, Disperse, Disseminate, Endosmosis, Exude, Osmosis, Pervade, Radiate, Spread, Thermal

Dig(s), **Digger**, **Digging**, **Dig up** Antipodean, Australian, Backhoe, Beadle, Bed(e)ral, Bedsit, Billet, Bot, Burrow, Costean, Delve, Enjoy, Excavate, Flea-bag, Fossorial, Gaulter, Gibe, Gird, Graip, Grub, Howk, Jab, Kip, Lair, Like, Lodgings, Mine, Navvy, Nervy, Nudge, Pad, Pioneer, Probe, Prod, Raddleman, Resurrect, Root, Ruddleman, Sap, See, Spade, Spit, Spud, Star-nose, Taunt, Tonnell, Trench, Tunnel, Undermine, Unearth

Digest(ible), **Digestion**, **Digestive** Abridgement, Absorb, Abstract, Aperçu, Archenteron, Assimilate, Codify, Concoct, Endue, Epitome, Eupepsia, Eupepsy, Gastric, Indew, Indue, Light, Pandect, Pem(m)ican, Pepsin(e), Peptic, Précis, Salt-cat, > **SUMMARY**

Digit(s) Binary, Bit, Byte, Dactyl, Finger, Hallux, Mantissa, Number, Pollex, Prehallux, Thumb, Toe

Dignified, **Dignify** August, Elevate, Exalt, Handsome, Honour, Lordly, Majestic, Manly, Proud, Solemn, Stately

Dignitary Bigwig, Dean, Name, Personage, Provost, > **VIP**

Dignity Aplomb, Bearing, Cathedra, Decorum, Face, Glory, Grandeur, Maestoso, Majesty, Nobility, Poise, Pontificate, Presence, Scarf, Tiara

Digraph Eng, Ng

Digress(ion) Apostrophe, Deviate, Diverge, Ecbole, Episode, Excurse, Excursus, Maunder, Veer, Wander

Dike Bank, Channel, Cludgie, Dam, Ditch, > **DYKE**, Embank(ment), Estacade, Lav(atory), Levee, Wall

Dilapidated, **Dilapidation** Decrepit, Desolate, Disrepair, Eroded, Ruined, Rust bucket, Tumbledown

Dilate, **Dilation**, **Dilatation** Amplify, Develop, Diastole, Ecstasis, Enlarge, Expand, Increase, Mydriasis, Sinus, Swell, Telangiectasia, Tent, Varix

Dilatory Protracting, Slow, Sluggish, Tardy

Dilemma Casuistry, Choice, Cleft, Dulcarnon, Fix, Horn, Predicament, Quandary, Why-not

Dilettante Aesthete, Amateur, Butterfly, Dabbler, Playboy

Diligence, **Diligent** Active, Application, Assiduous, Coach, Conscience, Eident, Industry, Intent, Painstaking, Sedulous, Studious

Dill Anise, Pickle

Dilute, **Dilution** Adulterate, Delay, Diluent, Lavage, Simpson, Thin, Water, Weaken

Dim(ness), Dimming, Dimwit Becloud, Blear, Blur, Brownout, Caligo, Clueless, Crepuscular, Dense, Dusk, Eclipse, Fade, Faint, Feint, Gormless, Ill-lit, Indistinct, Mist, Nebulous, Ninny, Obscure, Overcast, Owl, Pale, Shadow, Unsmart

Dimension Area, Breadth, Extent, Fourth, Height, Length, Measure, Size, Volume, Width

Diminish(ed), Diminuendo, Diminution, Diminutive Abatement, Assuage, Baby, Bate, Calando, Contract, Cot(t)ise, Deactivate, Decrease, Détente, Detract, Disparage, Dissipate, Dwarf, Dwindle, Erode, Fourth, Hypocorism(a), Lessen, Lilliputian, Minify, Minus, Mitigate, Petite, Pigmy, Scarp, Small, Stultify, Subside, Toy, Trangle, Wane, Whittle

Dimple(d) Dent, Depression, Hollow, Orange-peel

Din Babel, Charivary, Chirm, Commotion, Deen, Discord, Gunga, Hubbub, > NOISE, Rackct, Racket, Raird, Randan, Reel, Reird, Uproar, Utis

Dine(r), Dining Aristology, Eat, Feast, Refect, Sup, Trat(toria)

Dingbat Doodad

Dinghy Pram, Shallop, Ship, Skiff

Dingo Warrigal

Dingy Crummy, Dark, Dirty, Drear, Dun, Fusc(ous), Grimy, Isabel(la), Isabelline, Lurid, Oorie, Ourie, Owrie, Shabby, Smoky

Dining-room Cafeteria, Cenacle, Commons, Frater, Hall, Langar, Refectory, Restaurant, Triclinium

Dinner Banquet, Collation, Feast, Hall, Kail, Kale, Meal, Prandial, Progressive, Repast, Spread

Dinosaur Allosaurus, Ankylosaur, Apatosaurus, Brachiosaurus, Brontosaurus, Ceratopsian, Chalicothere, Coelurosaur, Cotylosaur, Cynodont, Dinothere, Diplodocus, Dolichosaurus, Duck-billed, Elasmosaur, Glyptodon, Hadrosaur, Ichthyosaur(us), Iguanodon, Megalosaur, Mosasaur, Omithosaur, Ornithischian, Ornithopod, Oviraptor, Pelycosaur, Placoderm, Plesiosaur, Prehistoric, Prosauropod, Pteranodon, Pterodactyl, Pterosaur, Saurischian, Sauropod, Smilodon, Stegadon(t), Stegosaur, Teleosaurus, Theropod, Titanosaurus, Titanothere, Triceratops, Tyrannosaurus, Uintothere, Velociraptor

Dint Brunt, Dent, Depression, Force, Means, Power

Diocese Bishopric, District, Eparchate, See

Diode Zener

Diogenes Cynic

Dioxide Cassiterite, Needle-tin

Dip(per) Bagna cauda, Baptise, Basin, Bathe, Bob, Brantub, Dabble, Dap, Dean, Dib, Diver, Dop, Double, Duck, Dunk, Foveola, Geosyncline, Guacomole, H(o)ummus, Houmous, Hum(m)us, Immerse, Intinction, Ladle, Lucky, Magnetic, Ouzel, Paddle, Rinse, Rollercoaster, Sag, Salute, Star, Submerge, Tapenade, Taramasalata, Tzatziki, Ursa

Diphthong Synaeresis, Synizesis

Diploma Charter, Parchment, Qualification, Scroll, Sheepskin

Diplomacy, Diplomat(ic) Altemat, Ambassador, Attaché, CD, Chargé d'affaires, Chateaubriand, Cheque-book, Consul, DA, Dean, Dollar, Doyen, El(t)chi, Envoy, Fanariot, Finesse, Gunboat, Legation, Lei(d)ger, Megaphone, Phanariot, Plenipotentiary, Shuttle, Suave, > TACT

▷ **Dippy** *may indicate* a bather

Dipsomania Oenomania

Dire Dreadful, Fatal, Fell, Hateful, Ominous, Urgent

Direct(or), Directly Administer, Advert, Aim, Airt, Auteur, Aventre, Board, Boss, Cann, Channel, Charge, Command, Compere, Con(n), Conduct, Control, Cox, Dead, Due, Eisenstein, Enjoin, Executive, Explicit, Fast-track, Fellini, First-hand, Forthright, Frontal, Guide, Helm, Hitchcock, Immediate, Impresario, Instruct, Intendant, Kappelmeister, Lead, Lean, Manager, Mastermind, Navigate, Nonexecutive, Outright, Pagnol, Pilot, Play, Point-blank, Ready, Refer, Régisseur, Rudder, Set, Signpost, Stear, > **STEER**, Straight, Teach, Tell, Truffaut, Unvarnished, Vector, Welles

Direction Aim, Airt, Arrow, Astern, Bearings, Course, Cross-reference, E, End-on, Guidance, Guide, Heading, Keblah, L, Line, N, Orders, Passim, R, Route, Rubric, S, Sanction, Send, Sense, Side, Slap, Tack, Tenor, Thataway, Tre corde, Trend, W, Way, Wedelns

Direction-finder Asdic, Compass, Decca, Quadrant, Radar, Sextant, Sonar

Directory Crockford, Debrett, Encyclop(a)edia, Kelly, List, Red book, Register, Yellow pages®

Dirge Ballant, Coronach, Dirige, Epicedium, Knell, Monody, Requiem, Song, Threnody

Dirigible Airship, Balloon, Blimp, Zeppelin

Dirk Anelace, Dagger, Skean, Whinger, Whiniard, Whinyard

Dirt(y) Begrime, Bemoil, Cacky, Chatty, Clag, Clarty, Colly, Contaminate, Coom, Crock, Crud, Draggle, Dung, Dust, Earth, Festy, Filth, Foul, Gore, Grime, Grufted, Grungy, Impure, Manky, Moit, Mote, Muck, Obscene, Ordure, Pay, Pollute, Ray, Sculdudd(e)ry, Scum, Scungy, Scuzzy, Skanky, Skulduddery, Smirch, Smut(ch), Soil, Sooty, Sordes, Sordor, Squalid, Stain, Trash, Unclean, Unsatisfactory, Warb, Yucky, Yukky

Dis Hades, Hell

Disability, Disable Cripple, Incapacitate, Lame, Maim, Paralyse, Scissor-leg, Scotch, Wreck

Disadvantage Detriment, Downside, Drawback, Handicap, Mischief, Out, Penalise, Penalty, Supercherie, Upstage, Wrongfoot, Zugswang

Disagree(ing), Disagreeable, Disagreement Argue, Argy-bargy, Bad, Clash, Conflict, Contest, Debate, Differ, Discrepant, Dispute, Dissent, Dissonant, Evil, Fiddlesticks, Friction, Heterodoxy, Pace, Plagu(e)y, Rift, Unpleasing

Disallow Forbid, Overrule

Disappear(ing) Cook, Dispel, Evanesce, Evanish, Evaporate, Fade, Kook, Latescent, Melt, Occult, Pass, Skedaddle, Slope, > **VANISH**

Disappoint(ment), Disappointed Anticlimax, Balk, Bombshell, Bummer, Chagrin, Comedown, Crestfallen, Delude, Disgruntle, Frustrate, Gutted, Heartsick, Lemon, Letdown, Regret, Sell, Shucks, Sick, Suck-in, Sucks, Swiz(zle), Thwart

Disapproval, Disapprove Ach, Animadvert, Boo, Catcall, Censure, Deplore, Deprecate, Discountenance, Expostulate, Frown, Harrumph, Hiss, Napoo, Object, Pejorative, Po-faced, Raspberry, Razz, Reject, Reproach, Reprobate, Squint, Tush, Tut, Tut-tut, Umph, Veto, Whiss

Disarm(ament), Disarming Bluff, Defuse, Demobilise, Nuclear, Winsome

Disarrange Disturb, Muddle, Ruffle, Tousle, Unsettle

Disarray Disorder, Mess, Rifle, Tash, Undress

Disaster, Disastrous Adversity, Apocalypse, Bale, Calamity, Cataclysm(ic), Catastrophe, Debacle, Dire, Doom, Evil, Fatal, Fiasco, Flop, Impostor, Meltdown, Mishap, Pitfall, Rout, Ruin, Screw-up, Seism, Shipwreck, Titanic, Tragedy, Wipeout

Disavow Abjure, Deny, Disclaim, Recant, Retract

Disbelief, Disbelieve(r) Acosmism, Anythingarian, Atheism, Gawp, Incredulity, Mistrust, Nothingarianism, Occamist, Phew, Phooey, Puh-lease, Puh-leeze, Question, Sceptic, Shoot, Voetsak

Disburse Distribute, Expend, Outlay, Spend

Disc, Disk Bursting, Button, CD, Cheese, Compact, Coulter, Counter, Diaphragm, Dogtag, EP, Epiphragm, Flexible, Floppy, Frisbee®, Gold, Gong, Hard, Harrow, Intervertebral, Laser, LP, Magnetic, Mono, O, Optical, Parking, Paten, Patin, Planchet, Plate, Platinum, Puck, RAM, Rayleigh, Record, Rosette, Roundel, Roundlet, Rowel, Sealed unit, Silver, Slipped, Slug, Stereo, Stylopodium, Swash plate, System, Tax, Token, Video, Wafer, Whorl, Winchester, Wink, WORM

Discard(ed) Abandon, Burn, Crib, Defy, Dele, Jettison, Kill, Leave, Obsolete, Off, Offload, Oust, > REJECT, Scrap, Shed, Shuck, Slough, Sluff, Supersede, Trash

Discern(ing), Discernment Acumen, Acute, Descry, Discrimination, Eagle-eyed, Flair, Insight, Perceive, Percipient, Perspicacity, Realise, Sapient, Scry, See, Skry, > TASTE, Tell, Wate

Discharge Absolve, Acquit, Arc, Assoil, Blennorrhoea, Brush, Cashier, Catamenia, Catarrh, Conditional, Corona, Dejecta, Deliver, Demob, Disembogue, Disgorge, Dismiss, Disruptive, Dump, Efflux, Effusion, Egest, Ejaculate, Eject, Embogue, Emission, Emit, Encopresis, Enfilade, Evacuate, Excrete, Execute, Exemption, Expulsion, Exude, Fire, Flashover, Flower, Flux, Frass, Free, Gleet, Glow, Lava, Lay off, Leak, Let off, Leucorrhoea, Lochia, Loose, Maturate, Menses, Mitimus, Mute, Offload, Otorrhoea, Oust, Ozaena, Pay, Perform, Period, Planuria, Purulence, Pus, Pyorrhoea, Quietus, Rheum, Rhinorrhoeal, Sack, Salvo, Sanies, Secretion, Show, Shrive, Snarler, Spark, Suppurate, Teem, Unload, Vent, Void, Water, Whites

Disciple(s) Adherent, Apostle, Baruch, Catechumen, Follower, John, Judas, Luke, Mark, Matthew, Peter, Simon, Son, Student, The Seventy, Thomist, Votary

Disciplinarian, Discipline Apollonian, Ascesis, Chasten, Chastise, Correct, Despot, Drill, Exercise, Feng Shui, Inure, Martinet, Mathesis, Punish, Regimentation, Regulate, Sadhana, School, Science, Spartan, Stickler, Subject, Taskmaster, Train, Tutor

Disc jockey *see* DJ

Disclaim(er) Deny, Disown, No(t)chel, Recant, Renounce, > REPUDIATE, Voetstoots

Disclose, Disclosure Apocalypse, Confess, Divulge, Expose, Impart, Leak, Manifest, Propale, > PUBLISH, Report, Reveal, Spill, Tell, Unheal, Unhele, Unrip, Unveil

Discoloration, Discolour(ed) Bruise, Cyanosis, Dyschroa, Ecchymosis, Livid, Livor, Stain, Streak, Tarnish, Tinge, Weather

Discomfit(ure) Abash, Confuse, Disconcert, Disturb, Frustrate, Lurch, Shend

Discomfort Ache, Angst, Dysphoria, Gyp, Heartburn, Pain, Unease

Disconcert(ing) Abash, Confuse, Disturb, Embarrass, Faze, Feeze, Flurry, Fluster, Nonplus, Off-putting, Phase, Pheese, Pheeze, Phese, > RATTLE, Shatter, Throw, Upset, Wrong-foot

Disconcert(ed) *may indicate* an anagram

Disconnect(ed) Asynartete, Detach, Disjointed, Off-line, Sever, Staccato, Uncouple, Undo, Unplug

Disconsolate Desolate, Doleful, Downcast, > GLOOMY

Discontent(ed) Disquiet, Dissatisfied, Humph, Repined, Sour, Umph

Discontinuance, Discontinue Abandon, Cease, Desist, Desuetude, Drop,

Prorogue, Stop, Terminate

Discord(ant) Absonant, Ajar, Conflict, Din, Dispute, Eris, Faction, Hoarse, Jangle, Jar, Raucous, Ruction, Strife

▷ **Discord(ant)** *may indicate* an anagram

Discount Agio, Cashback, Deduct, Disregard, Forfaiting, Invalidate, > REBATE, Trade

Discountenance Disfavour, Efface, Embarrass

Discourage(ment) Caution, Chill, Dampen, Dash, Daunt, Demoralise, Deter, Dishearten, Disincentive, Dismay, Dissuade, Enervate, Frustrate, Opposition, Stifle, Unman

Discourse Address, Argument, Conversation, Descant, Diatribe, Dissertate, Eulogy, Expound, Homily, Lecture, Lucubrate, Orate, Preach, Relate, Rigmarole, Sermon, Wash

Discourteous, **Discourtesy** Impolite, Insult, Rude, Slight, Uncivil, Unmannerly

Discover(y), **Discoverer** Amundsen, Anagnorisis, Ascertain, Betray, Breakthrough, Columbus, Cook, Descry, Detect, Discern, Discure, Eureka, > FIND, Heureka, Heuristic, Learn, Locate, Manifest, Moresby, Protege, Rumble, Serendip, Serendipity, Spy, Tasman, Trace, Treasure trove, Unearth, Unhale, Unmask, Unveil

▷ **Discovered in** *may indicate* an anagram or a hidden word

Discredit(able) Debunk, Decry, Disgrace, Explode, Infamy, Scandal, Smear, Unworthy

Discreet, **Discretion** Cautious, Circumspect, Freedom, Option, Polite, Politic, Prudence, Prudent, Trait, Wise

Discrepancy Difference, Gap, Lack, Shortfall, Variance

Discrete Distinct, Separate, Unrelated

Discriminate, **Discriminating**, **Discrimination** Ag(e)ism, Colour bar, Diacritic, Differentiate, Discern, Distinguish, Elitism, Invidious, Nasute, Racism, Secern, Segregate, Select, Sexism, Siz(e)ism, Speciesism, Subtle, Taste

Discursive Roving

Discuss(ed), **Discussion** Agitate, Air, Canvass, Commune, Conf(erence), Debate, Dialectic, Dialogue, Dicker, Disquisition, En l'air, Examine, Excursus, Expatiate, Handle, Hob and nob, Interlocution, Korero, Moot, Over, Palaver, Parley, Pourparler, Prolegomenon, Quodlibet, Rap, Re, Symposium, Talk, Tapis, Treatment, Ventilate, Vex

Disdain(ful) Belittle, Contempt, Coy, Deride, Despise, Geck, Poof, Pooh-pooh, Puh, Sassy, > SCORN, Scout, Sdei(g)n, Sniffy, Spurn, Supercilious, Ugh

Disease(d) Affection, Ailment, Epidemic, Fever, Functional, Industrial, Infection, Malady, Noso-, Nosocomial, Organic, Pest(ilence), Rot, Scourge, Sickness

● **DISEASES**
●
● **2 letters:**
● CD
● MS
● TB
● VD
●
● **3 letters:**
● BSE
● Flu

Haw
Pip
Pox
> STD
TSE
Wog

4 letters:
Aids

Boba
Bunt
Clap
Conk
Gout
Keel
Kuru
Loco
Lues

Lyme
Roup
Yaws

5 letters:
Bang's
Black
Borna
Brand

Dread
Dutch
Ebola
Edema
Ergot
Favus
Fifth
Gapes
Lupus
Lurgi
Lurgy
Mesel
Mumps
Ngana
Palsy
Pinta
Polio
Pott's
Rabid
Scall
Sprue
Surra
Tinea
Virus
Weil's
Worms

6 letters:
Anbury
Blight
Blotch
Border
Canker
Chagas'
Chorea
Cowpox
Crohn's
Cruels
Dartre
Dengue
Eczema
Farcin
Graves'
Income
Johne's
Mad cow
Marck's
Meazel
Mildew
Morbus
Mosaic
Nagana

Oedema
Paget's
Rabies
Sapego
Scurvy
Social
Still's
Thrush
Tunnel
Typhus
Ulitis
Urosis
Yuppie
Zoster

7 letters:
Ascites
Batten's
Bright's
British
Caisson
Cholera
Coeliac
Crewels
Dieback
Dourine
Endemic
English
Frounce
Hansen's
Hardpad
Hydatid
Icterus
Leprosy
Maidism
Malaria
Marburg
Moor-ill
Murrain
Mycosis
Myiasis
Pébrine
Podagra
Porrigo
Purples
Rickets
Rosette
Scabies
Sequela
Serpigo
Tetanus
Tetters

Typhoid
Variola
Wilson's
Zymosis

8 letters:
Addison's
Alastrim
Beri-beri
Bornholm
Clubroot
Cushing's
Cynanche
Diabetes
Dutch elm
Economo's
Fishskin
Gaucher's
Glanders
Glaucoma
Gummosis
Hodgkin's
Hookworm
Impetigo
Jaundice
Kala-azar
Leaf-roll
Loose-cut
Menières
Minamata
Myxedema
Nosology
Pandemic
Pathogen
Pellagra
Phthisis
Phytosis
Progeria
Pullorum
Rachitis
Raynaud's
Rose-rash
Scrofula
Shingles
Smallpox
Suppeago
Swayback
Swinepox
Syphilis
Tay-Sachs
The bends
Venereal

Vincent's
Zoonosis

9 letters:
Brown lung
Chancroid
Chlorosis
Christmas
Cirrhosis
Contagion
Diathesis
Distemper
Dysentery
Enteritis
Exanthema
Filanders
Gonorrhea
Ideopathy
Ixodiasis
Kawasaki's
Lathyrism
Leucaemia
Leukaemia
Loose smut
Myxoedema
Nephritis
Nephrosis
Newcastle
New Forest
Pellagrin
Pemphigus
Porphyria
Seborrhea
Siderosis
Silicosis
Toxicosis
Trichosis
Tularemia

10 letters:
Acromegaly
Alzheimer's
Amoebiasis
Asbestosis
Autoimmune
Babesiosis
Bagassosis
Bluetongue
Byssinosis
Chickenpox
Dandy-fever
Deficiency

- Diphtheria
- Erysipelas
- Filariasis
- Framboesia
- Gonorrhoea
- Heartwater
- Hemophilia
- Iatrogenic
- Ichthyosis
- Impaludism
- Leuchaemia
- Limber-neck
- Lou Gehrig's
- Louping ill
- Moniliasis
- Muscardine
- Nosography
- Ornithosis
- Parkinson's
- Scarlatina
- Seborrhoea
- Tularaemia

11 letters:
Anthracosis
Brittle-bone
Cardiopathy
Consumption
Green Monkey
Haemophilia
Hebephrenia
Huntington's
Kwashiorkor
Listeriosis
Myxomatosis
Parasitosis
Psittacosis
Rickettsial
Septicaemia
Thalassemia
Trichinosis
Yellow-fever

12 letters:
Enterobiasis
Fascioliasis
Finger and toe

Foot and mouth
Furunculosis
Legionnaires'
Molybdenosis
Motor neurone
Osteomalacia
Osteoporosis
Scheuermann's
Shaking palsy
Slapped cheek
Thalassaemia
Tuberculosis
Uncinariasis

13 letters:
Elephantiasis
Leichmaniasis
Leptospirosis
Osteomyelitis
Poliomyelitis
Sclerodermata
Syringomyelia
Toxoplasmosis
Tsutsugamushi

14 letters:
Cystic fibrosis
Histoplasmosis
Leucodystrophy
Onchocerciasis
Pneumoconiosis
Sporotrichosis
Trichomoniasis
Trichophytosis

15 letters:
Schistosomiasis
Trypanosomiasis

16 letters:
Pneumonoco-
niosis
Sleeping sickness
Sweating sickness

17 letters:
Multiple sclerosis

▷ **Diseased** *may indicate* an anagram
Disembark Alight, Detrain, Land
Disembarrass Extricate, Rid, Unthread
Disembowel Eviscerate, Exenterate, Gralloch, Gut
Disenchant Disabuse, Dismay, Embitter
Disencumber Free, Rid, Unburden
Disengage(d), **Disengagement** Clear, Divorce, Liberate, Loosen, Release, Untie
Disentangle Debarrass, Extricate, Red(d), Solve, Unravel, Unsnarl
Disestablishmentarian Cosmist
Disfavour Maugre
Disfigure(ment), **Disfigured** Agrise, Agryze, Camsho, Deface, Deform, Goitre,
    Mutilate, Scar, Spoil, Tash, Ugly
▷ **Disfigured** *may indicate* an anagram
Disgorge Discharge, Spew, Spill, Vent, Void
Disgrace Atimy, Attaint, Baffle, Blot, Contempt, Contumely, Degrade, Discredit,
    Dishonour, Dog-house, Ignominy, Indignity, Infamy, Obloquy, Opprobrium,
    Scandal, Shame, Shend, Slur, Soil, Stain, Stigma, Yshend
Disgraceful Diabolical, Fie, Ignoble, Ignominious, Indign, Infamous, Mean,
    Notorious, Shameful, Turpitude
Disgruntled Malcontent, Resentful, Sore
▷ **Disgruntled** *may indicate* an anagram
Disguise(d) Alias, Blessing, Camouflage, Cloak, Colour, Conceal, Cover, Covert,
    Dissemble, Hide, Hood, Incog(nito), Mantle, Mask, Masquerade, Obscure,
    Peruke, Pretence, Pseudonym, Ring, Shades, Travesty, Veil, Vele, Veneer,
    Visagiste, Visor, Vizard
▷ **Disguised** *may indicate* an anagram
Disgust(ing) Ach-ŷ-fi, Ad nauseam, Aversion, Aw, Bah, Cloy, Discomfort,

Execrable, Faugh, Fie, Foh, Fulsome, Grody, Irk, Loathsome, Manky, Mawkish, Minging, Nauseous, Noisome, Obscene, Odium, Oughly, Ouglie, Pah, Pho(h), Pish, Pshaw, Pugh, Repel, Repugnant, > **REVOLT**, Revulsion, Scomfish, Scumfish, Scunner, Scuzz, > **SICKEN**, Si(e)s, Squalid, Tush, Ugsome, Vile, Yech, Yu(c)k, Yucko, Yukky

Dish(y) Allot, Apollo, Ashet, Basin, Belle, Bowl, Chafing, Charger, Cocotte, Cook-up, Cutie, Dent, Dole, Dreamboat, Epergne, Flasket, Grail, Kitchen, Laggen, Laggin, Lanx, Luggie, Muffineer, Ovenware, Pan, Pannikin, Paten, Patera, Patin(e), Petri, Plate, Platter, Porringer, Ramekin, Ramequin, Receptacle, Sangraal, Sangrail, Sangreal, Satellite, Saucer, Scallop, Serve, Service, Side, Smasher, Special, Watchglass

DISHES

3 letters:
Poi

4 letters:
Fool
Mess
Olla
Puri
Sate
Soss
Taco
Toll

5 letters:
Adobo
Balti
Bhaji
Bitok
Brose
Champ
Curry
Dolma
Gomer
Kasha
Kibbe
Kofta
Korma
Laksa
Maror
Pilau
Pilow
Poori
Raita
Ramen
Salmi
Satay
Sushi
Tamal

Tikka

6 letters:
Bhagee
Bharta
Cou-cou
Cuscus
Diable
Entrée
Fondue
Haggis
Hotpot
Kimchi
Kishke
Mornay
Mousse
Muesli
Nachos
Paella
Pakora
Panada
Quiche
Ragout
Regale
Salmis
Sowans
Sowens
Subgum
Surimi
Tamale
Tsamba

7 letters:
Biriani
Bobotie
Burrito
Calzone
Cassava

Ceviche
Comport
Compote
Crowdie
Crubeen
Crumble
Custard
Cuvette
Dariole
Dhansak
Dopiaza
Egg roll
Fajitas
Fal-a-fel
Fel-a-fel
Foo Yung
Friture
Grav lax
Marengo
Mousaka
Padella
Poutine
Rarebit
Ravioli
Sashimi
Seviche
Soufflé
Stovies
Tempura
Terrine
Timbale
Tostada

8 letters:
Brandade
Caponata
Chop suey
Chow mein

Coolamon
Coq au vin
Coquille
Couscous
Crostini
Dog's-body
Entremes
Feijoada
Flummery
Frittata
Gado-gado
Halloumi
Kedgeree
Keftedes
Kickshaw
Kouskous
Kreplach
Mazarine
Meuniere
Moussaka
Pandowdy
Pastrami
Porridge
Pot-au-feu
Pot-roast
Raclette
Shashlik
Sillabub
Souvlaki
Squarial
Sukiyaki
Syllabub
Teriyaki
Tzatziki
White-pot
Yakimono
Yakitori

- **9 letters:**
- Carbonara
- Carpaccio
- Compotier
- Egg-fo-yang
- Enchilada
- Entremets
- Fricassee
- Galantine
- Gravad lax
- Guacamole
- Howtowdie
- Jambalaya
- Manicotti
- Pastitsio
- Pepper-pot
- Reistafel
- Rijstafel
- Shashlick

Souvlakia
Succotash

10 letters:
Blanquette
Cacciatore
Couscousou
Doner kebab
Egg-foo-yung
Jugged hare
Koulibiaca
Mousseline
Nasi goreng
Parmigiana
Plat du jour
Provencale
Quesadilla
Rijsttafel
Salmagundi

Sauerkraut
Shish kebab
Spitchcock
Spring roll
Stroganoff

11 letters:
Buck-rarebit
Fritto misto
Saltimbocca
Sauerbraten
Spanakopita
Surf and turf
Welsh rabbit

12 letters:
Eggs Benedict
Shepherd's pie
Steak tartare

Sweet and sour
Taramasalata
Welsh rarebit

13 letters:
Rumbledethump
Solomon Grundy
Toad-in-the-hole

14 letters:
Chilli con carne
Rumbledethumps
Scotch woodcock

15 letters:
Bubble and
   squeak

Dishabille Disarray, Négligé, Undress
Dishearten Appal, Core(r), Cow, Daunt, Depress, Discourage, Dispirit
Dishevel(led) Blowsy, Blowzy, Daggy, Mess, Rumpled, Touse, Tousle, Touzle, Tumble, Uncombed, Unkempt, Windswept
Dishonest(y) Bent, Crooked, Cross, Dodgy, False, Fraud, Graft, Hooky, Hot, Improbity, Jiggery-pokery, Knavery, Malpractice, Malversation, Shonky, Stink, Twister, Underhand, Venal
Dishonour Defile, Disgrace, Disparage, Ignominy, Seduce, > **SHAME**, Violate, Wrong
Disillusion Disenchant, Sour
Disincline(d), Disinclination Apathy, Loth, Off, Reluctant
Disinfect(ant) Acriflavin(e), Carbolic, Cineol(e), Cleanse, Eucalyptole, Formalin, Formol, Fuchsine, Fumigate, Lysol®, Phenol, Purify, Sheep-dip, TCP, Terebene
Disingenuous Insincere, Mask, Oblique, Two-faced
Disinherit Deprive, Dispossess
Disintegrate, Disintegration Break, Collapse, Crumble, Decay, Erode, Fragment, Lyse, Lysis, Osteoclasis, Rd, Rutherford
Disinter Exhume, Unearth
Disinterested Apathetic, Impartial, Incurious, Mugwump, Unbiased
Disjointed Bitty, Incoherent, Rambling, Scrappy
▶ **Disk** *see* **DISC**
Dislike Allergy, Animosity, Animus, Antipathy, Aversion, Derry, Disesteem, Displeasure, Distaste, Lump, Mind, Needle, Scunner, Warling
Dislocate, Dislocation Break, Diastasis, Displace, Fault, Luxate, Slip
Dislodge Budge, Displace, Expel, Luxate, Oust, Rear, Tuft, Unship, Uproot
Disloyal(ty) False, Treason, Unfaithful, Untrue
Dismal Black, Bleak, Cheerless, Dark, Dowie, Dowly, Drack, Dreary, Funereal, > **GLOOMY**, Grey, Long-faced, Morne, Obital, Sepulchral, Sombre, Sullen, Trist(e), Wae
Dismantle(d), Dismantling Decommission, Derig, Divest, Get-out, Sheer-hulk, Strike, Strip, Unrig

Dismast Unstep

Dismay Amate, Appal, Confound, Consternation, Coo, Daunt, Fie, Ha, Horrify, Lumme, Qualms

Dismiss(al) Annul, Ax, Boot, Bounce, Bowl(er), Bum's rush, Cancel, Cashier, Catch, Chuck, Congé, Constructive, Daff, Discard, Discharge, Expulsion, Fire, Heave-ho, Kiss-off, Lay off, Marching orders, Mitten, Och, Prorogue, Push, Recall, Reform, Remove, R.O., Road, Sack, Scout, Send, Shoo, Spit, Spurn, Stump, Via, Voetsak, Voetsek, Walking papers, York

Dismount Alight, Hecht

Disobedience, Disobedient, Disobey Contumacy, Defy, Flout, Insubordination, Rebel, Wayward

Disorder(ly), Disordered Ague, Ailment, Anarchy, Ariot, Asthma, Ataxia, Catatonia, Chaos, Chlorosis, Clutter, Confuse, Contracture, Defuse, Derange, Deray, Diabetes, Dishevel, Dissociative, Dysthymic, Dystrophy, Echolalia, Entropy, Epilepsy, Farrago, Grippe, Haemophilia, Hallucinosis, Huntingdon's chorea, Hypallage, Inordinate, Irregular, Mange, ME, Mental, Mess, Mistemper, > **MUDDLE**, Muss(y), Neurosis, Oncus, Onkus, Pandemonium, Panic, Para-, Pell-mell, Personality, Porphyria, Psychomatic, Psychosis, Ragmatical, Rile, Roughhouse, Rowdy, SAD, St Vitus' Dance, Schizophrenia, Seborrh(o)ea, Shell-shock, Slovenly, Sydenham's chorea, Tarantism, Thalass(a)emia, Tousle, Turbulence, Unhinge, Unruly, Upset, Virilism

▷ **Disorder(ed)** *may indicate* an anagram

Disorganised At sea, Deranged, Scatterbrain, Shambolic, Structureless

Disown Deny, Disclaim, Disinherit, Renounce, Repudiate, Unget

Disparage, Disparaging Abuse, Belittle, Decry, Defame, Denigrate, Depreciate, Detract, Discredit, Lessen, Pejorative, > **SLANDER**, Slur, Snide, Traduce, Vilify

Dispassionate Calm, Clinical, Composed, Cool, Impartial, Objective, Serene

Dispatch Bowl, Celerity, Consign, Destroy, Dismiss, Expede, Expedite, Express, Gazette, Kibosh, Kill, Missive, Post, Pronto, Remit, Report, > **SEND**, Ship, Slaughter, Slay

Dispel Disperse, Scatter

Dispensation, Dispense(r), Dispense with Absolve, Administer, Aerosol, Apothecary, Automat, Ax(e), Cashpoint, Chemist, Container, Distribute, Dose, Dropper, Exempt, Handout, Indult, Scrap, Visitation

Dispersable, Disperse, Dispersion Diaspora, Diffract, Diffuse, Disband, Dissolve, Lyophil(e), Scail, Scale, > **SCATTER**, Skail, Sow, Strew

Dispirit(ed) Dampen, Dash, Daunt, Discourage, Dishearten, Exorcism, Listless, Sackless

Displace(ment), Displaced Antevert, Blueshift, Depose, Disturb, Ectopia, Ectopy, Fault, Heterotopia, Lateroversion, Luxate, Move, Oust, Proptosis, Ptosis, Reffo, Shift, Stir, Subluxation, Unseat, Unsettle, Uproot, Valgus, Varus, Volumetric

Display, Display ground Air, Array, Blaze, Blazon, Brandish, Bravura, Depict, Eclat, Epideictic, Etalage, Evidence, Evince, Exhibition, Exposition, Express, Extend, Extravaganza, Exude, Fireworks, Flaunt, Float, Gondola, Hang, Head-down, Head-up, Heroics, LED, Lek, Liquid crystal, Manifest, Mount, Muster, Ostentation, Outlay, Overdress, Pageant, Parade, Paraf(f)le, Peepshow, Pixel, Pomp, Propale, Pyrotechnics, Rode, Rodeo, Roll-out, Scene, Shaw, > **SHOW**, Sight, Spectacle, Splash, Splurge, Sport, Spree, State, Stunt, Tableau, Tattoo, Tournament, Up, Vaunt, Wear

Displease(d), Displeasure Anger, Dischuffed, Humph, Irritate, Provoke, Umbrage

Disport Amuse, Divert, Play
Dispose(d), Disposal, Disposition Apt, Arrange, Bestow, Cast, Despatch, Dump, Eighty-six, Kibosh, Lay(-out), Ordonnance, Prone, Sale, Sell, Service, Settle, Stagger
▷ **Disposed, Disposition** *may indicate* an anagram
Disposition Affectation, Attitude, Bent, Bias, Humour, Inclination, Kidney, Lie, Nature, Penchant, Talent, Temper(ament), Trim
Dispossess(ed) Abate, Attaint, Bereft, Depose, Deprive, Evict, Oust
Disproportion(ate) Asymmetric, Extreme, Imbalance, Unequal
Disprove, Disproof Debunk, Discredit, Negate, Rebut, Rebuttal, Redargue, Refel, Refute
Dispute(d), Disputant Argue, Barney, Brangle, Cangle, Case, Chaffer, Challenge, Chorizont(ist), Contend, Contest, Contravene, Contretemps, Controversy, Debate, Deny, Differ, Discept, Discuss, Eristic, Fray, Haggle, Kilfud-yoking, Lock-out, Militate, Ob and soller, Odds, Oppugn, Plea, Polemic, Pro-and-con, > QUESTION, Quibble, Rag, Resist, Spar, Stickle, Threap(it), Threep(it), Tiff, Tissue, Variance, Wrangle
Disqualify Debar, Incapacitate, Recuse, Reject, Unfit
Disquiet(ed) Agitate, Concern, Discomboberate, Discombobulate, > DISTURB, Pain, Perturb(ation), Solicit, Turmoil, Uneasy, Unnerve, Vex
Disraeli Dizzy, Tancred
Disregard(ed) Anomie, Anomy, Contempt, Defy, Disfavour, Flout, Forget, Ignore, Oblivion, Omit, Overlook, Oversee, Pass, Pretermit, Slight, Spare, Violate, Waive
Disrepair Dilapidation, Ruin
Disreputable, Disrepute Base, Disgrace, Grubby, Louche, Low, Lowlife, Raffish, Ragamuffin, Reprobate, Rip, Scuzz(ball), Seamy, Shady, Shameful, Shy, Sleazy
Disrespect(ful) Contempt, Derogatory, Discourtesy, Flip(pant), Impiety, Impolite, Irreverent, Profane, Slight, Uncivil
Disrupt(ion) Breach, Cataclasm, Disorder, Distract, Hamper, Interrupt, Jetlag, Mayhem, Perturb, Quonk, Screw, Upheaval
▷ **Disruption** *may indicate* an anagram
Dissatisfaction Displeasure, Distaste, Humph, Umph
Dissect(ion) Analyse, Dismember, Examine, Necrotomy, Zootomy
Dissemble(r) Conceal, Feign, Fox, Hypocrite, Impostor
Dissension, Dissent(er), Dissenting Contend, Differ, Disagree, Discord, Dissident, Faction, Heretic, Jain, Lollard, Noes, Non-CE, Non-con(formist), Pantile, Protest, Raskolnik, Recusant, Separat(ion)ist, Splinter group, > STRIFE, Vary
Dissertation Essay, Excursus, Lecture, Thesis, Treatise
▶ **Dissident** *see* DESERTER
Dissimilar Different, Diverse, Heterogeneous, Unlike
Dissipate(d) Debauch, Diffuse, Disperse, Dissolute, Gay, Revel, Scatter, Shatter, Squander, Waste
▷ **Dissipated** *may indicate* an anagram
Dissociate Separate, Sever, Withdraw
Dissolute Degenerate, Demirep, Falstaffian, Hell, Lax, Libertine, Licentious, Loose, Rake-helly, Rakish, Rip, Roué, Wanton
▷ **Dissolute** *may indicate* an anagram
Dissolution Dismissal, Divorce, End, Repeal, Separation
Dissolve Deliquesce, Digest, Disband, Disunite, Liquesce, Melt, Repeal, Terminate, Thaw

Dissonance Wolf

Dissuade Dehort, Deter, Discourage

Distaff Clotho, Female, Lady, Rock, Stick

Distance Absciss(a), Afield, Apothem, Breadth, Coss, Declination, Eloi(g)n, Farness, Foot, Headreach, Height, Hyperfocal, Interval, Klick, Kos(s), Latitude, League, Length, Mean, Mean free path, Mileage, Northing, Outland, Parasang, Parsec, Range, Reserve, Rod, Span, Spitting, Stade, Striking, Way, Yojan, Zenith

Distant Aloof, Far, Frosty, Hyperfocal, Icy, Long, Northing, Offish, Outland, Polar, Remote, Tele-, Timbuctoo, Yonder

Distaste(ful) Gross-out, Repugnant, Ropy, Scunner, Unpalatable, Unpleasant, Unsavoury

Distemper Ailment, Colourwash, Hard-pad, Paint, Panleucopenia, Tempera

Distend(ed), **Distension** Bloat, Dilate, Ectasia, Emphysema, Expand, Hoove, Inflate, > **STRETCH**, Swell, Turgid, Tympanites, Varicocele, Varicose

Distil(late), **Distillation**, **Distiller**, **Distilling** Alcohol, Alembic, Anthracine, Azeotrope, Brew, Condense, Drip, Pelican, Pyrene, Pyroligneous, Rosin, Turps, Vapour

> **Distillation** *may indicate* an anagram

Distinct(ive) Apparent, Characteristic, Clear, Determinate, Different, Evident, Grand, Individual, Peculiar, Plain, Separate, Several, Signal, > **SPECIAL**, Stylistic, Vivid

Distinction Beaut(y), Blue, Cachet, Credit, Diacritic, Difference, Dignity, Diorism, Disparity, Division, Eclat, Eminence, Honour, Lustre, Mark, Mystique, Note, Nuance, OM, Prominence, Quiddity, Rank, Renown, Speciality, Style, Title

Distinguish(ed), **Distinguishing** Classify, Demarcate, Denote, Diacritic, Different(iate), Discern, Discriminate, Divide, Elevate, Mark, Notable, Perceive, Prestigious, Prominent, Signal, Stamp

Distort(ion), **Distorted** Anamorphosis, Bend, Colour, Contort, Deface, Deform, Dent, Fudge, Garble, Helium speech, Jaundiced, Mangle, Misshapen, Pervert, Rubato, Thraw, Travesty, Twist, > **WARP**, Wow, Wrest, Wring, Wry

> **Distort(ed)** *may indicate* an anagram

Distract(ed), **Distraction** Absent, Agitate, Amuse, Avocation, Bewilder, Divert, Embroil, Éperdu, Forhaile, Frenetic, Lost, Madden, Mental, Nepenthe, Perplex, Sidetrack, Sledge, Upstage

> **Distract(ed)** *may indicate* an anagram

Distrain(t) Na(a)m, Poind, Sequestrate, Stress

Distraught Deranged, Elfish, Elvan, Frantic, Mad, Troubled

Distress(ed), **Distressing** Afflict, Ail, Alack, Anger, Anguish, Antique, Distraint, Dolour, Exigence, Extremity, Grieve, Harass, Harrow, Heartbreak, Hurt, Ill, > **IN DISTRESS**, Irk, Misease, Misfortune, Need, Oppress, Pain, Poignant, Prey, Sad, Shorn, Sore, SOS, Straits, Traumatic, Tribulation, > **TROUBLE**, Une(a)th

Distribute(d), **Distribution** Allocate, Allot, Binomial, Busbar, Carve, Chi-square, Colportage, Deal, Deliver(y), Deploy, Dish, Dispense, Dispose, Exponential, F, Frequency, Gamma, Gaussian, Geometric, Issue, Lie, Lot, Mete, Normal, Out, Pattern, Poisson's, Prorate, Repartition, Serve, Share

> **Distributed** *may indicate* an anagram

District Alsatia, Amhara, Arcadia, Ards, Area, Arrondissement, Bail(l)iwick, Banat, Barrio, Belt, Canton, Cantred, Classis, Community, Diocese, End, Exurb, Federal, Gau, Ghetto, Hundred, Lathe, Liberty, Locality, Loin, Manor, Metropolitan, > **NEIGHBOURHOOD**, Oblast, Pachalic, Pale, Parish(en), Paroch,

Pashalik, Patch, Phocis, Province, Quarter, Quartier, Rape, > **REGION**, Ride, Riding, Ruhr, Rural, Sanjak, Section, Sheading, Sircar, Soc, Soke(n), Stannary, Suburb, Sucken, Talooka, Taluk, Tenderloin, Township, Venue, Vicinage, Walk, Wapentake, Way, Wealden, Zila, Zillah, Zone

Distrust Caution, Doubt, Suspect, Wariness

Disturb(ance), Disturbed Ado, Aerate, Affray, Agitate, Atmospherics, Autism, Betoss, Brabble, Brainstorm, Brash, Brawl, Broil, Carfuffle, Collieshangie, Concuss, Delirium, Dementia, Derange, Desecrate, Disquiet, Dust, Dysfunction, Feeze, Firestorm, Fracas, Fray, Fret, Harass, Hoopla, Incommode, Infest, Interrupt, Jee, Kerfuffle, Kick-up, Kurfuffle, Muss, Outbreak, Perturb(ation), Prabble, Rammy, Ramp, Ripple, Romage, Rook, Roughhouse, Rouse, Ruckus, Ruction, Ruffle, Rumpus, Shake, Shellshock, Shindy, Shook-up, Stashie, Static, Steer, Stir, Sturt, Tremor, Trouble, Turbulent, Unquiet, Unrest, Unsettle, Upheaval, Uproot, > **UPSET**, Vex

▷ **Disturb(ed)** *may indicate* an anagram

Disunite Alienate, Dissever, Divide, Divorce, Split

Disuse Abandon, Abeyance, Desuetude, Discard, Lapse

Ditch Barathron, Barathrum, Channel, Crash-land, Cunette, Delf, Delph, Dike, Discard, Donga, Drainage, Drop, Dyke, Euripus, Foss(e), Graft, Grip, Gully, Ha(w)-ha(w), Haw-haw, Jettison, Khor, Level, Lode, Moat, Na(l)la(h), Nulla(h), Rean, Reen, Rhine, Rid, Sea, Sheuch, Sheugh, Sike, Sloot, Sluit, Spruit, Stank, Syke, Trench

Dither(ing) Agitato, Bother, Faff, Hesitate, Indecisive, Pussyfoot, Twitter

Dittany Gas-plant

Ditty, Ditties Air, Arietta, Canzonet, Departmental, Jingle, Lay, Song

Diuretic Frusemide, Furosemide

Diva Callas, Patti, Singer

Divan Compilement, Congress, Couch, Council, Settee, Sofa

Dive(r), Diving Armstand, Backflip, Belly-flop, Crash, Dart, Den, Duck, Full-gainer, Half-gainer, Header, Honkytonk, Jackknife, Joint, Ken, Nitery, Nose, Pass, Plummet, Plunge, Plutocrat, Power, Saturation, Scoter, Skin, Sound, Stage, Stoop, Submerge, Swallow, Swan, Swoop, Tailspin, Urinant

Diver(s) Didapper, Duck, Embergoose, Flop, Frogman, Gainer, Grebe, Guillemot, Loom, Loon, Lungie, Many, Merganser, Pearl, Pike, Plong(e), Pochard, Poker, Puffin, Sawbill, Scuba, Snake-bird, Speakeasy, Sundry, Urinator, Various, Zoom

Diverge(nce) Branch, Deviate, Divaricate, Spread, Swerve, Variant, Veer

Divers Miscellaneous, Some

Diverse, Diversify Alter, Chequer, Dapple, Different, Eclectic, Interlard, Intersperse, Manifold, Motley, Multifarious, Separate, Variegate, Various, Vary

Diversion, Divert(ing) Amuse, Avocation, Beguile, Deflect, Detour, Disport, Dissuade, Distract, Entertain, Game, Hare, Hobby, Interlude, Pastime, Pleasure, Prolepsis, Ramp, Red-herring, Refract, Reroute, Ruse, Shunt, Sideshow, Sidetrack, Sport, Stalking-horse, Steer, Stratagem, Sway, Switch, Tickle, Upstage, Yaw

▷ **Diverting** *may indicate* an anagram

Divest Denude, Rid, Strip, Undeck, Undress

Divide(d) Apportion, Balk, Band, Bipartite, Bisect, Branch, Cantle, Cleft, Comminute, Commot(e), Continental, Counter-pale, Cut, Deal, Demerge, Digital, Dimidiate, Dissever, Estrange, Fork, Great, Indent, Parcel, Part, Partitive, Polarise, Rend, Rift, Separate, Sever, Share, > **SPLIT**, Sunder, Watershed, Zone

Dividend Bonus, Div, Interim, Into, Peace, Share

Divination, **Diviner** Augury, Auspices, Axinomancy, Belomancy, Bibliomancy, Botanomancy, Capnomancy, Cartomancy, Ceromancy, Chiromancy, Cleromancy, Coscinomancy, Crithomancy, Crystal-gazing, Crystallomancy, Doodlebug, Dowser, Empyromancy, Geomancy, Gyromancy, Hariolation, Haruspex, Hepatoscopy, Hieromancy, Hieroscopy, Hydromancy, I Ching, Intuition, Lampadomancy, Lithomancy, Magic, Mantic, Myomancy, Omphalomancy, Oneiromancy, Ornithomancy, Ornithoscopy, Palmistry, Pyromancy, Rhabdomancy, Scapulimancy, Sciomancy, Seer, Sibyl, Sortes, Sortilege, Spae(man), Spodomancy, Taghairm, Tais(c)h, Theomancy, Tripudiary, Vaticanator, Xylomancy

Divine, **Divine presence**, **Divinity** Acoemeti, Atman, Avatar, Beatific, Clergyman, Conjecture, Curate, DD, Deduce, Deity, Douse, Dowse, Ecclesiastic, Forecast, Foretell, Fuller, > **GOD**, > **GODDESS**, Godhead, Guess, Hariolate, Heavenly, Holy, Immortal, Inge, Isiac, Kami, Mantic, Numen, Numinous, Olympian, Pontiff, Predestinate, Predict, Presage, Priest, RE, Rector, RI, Rimmon, Scry, Sense, Seraphic, Shechinah, Shekinah, Spae, Superhuman, Supernal, Theanthropic, Theologise, Theology, Triune

Division, **Divisible** Amitosis, Angiosperm, Arcana, Arm, Arrondissement, Bajocian, Banat(e), Bannet, Bar, Bizone, Branch, Brome, Caesura, Canton, Cantred, Cantref, Cassini's, Caste, Category, Cell, Champart, Chapter, Classification, Cleft, Cloison, Clove, Comitatus, Commot(e), Commune, Compartment, Coralline Crag, Corps, County, Crevasse, Curia, Department, Dichotomy, Disagreement, Disunity, Duan, Eyalet, Family, Farren, Fissile, Fork, Grisons, Guberniya, Gulf, Gulph, Hedge, Hide, Hundred, Inning, Isogloss, Keuper, Kim(m)eridgian, Lathe, Leet, Legion, Lindsey, List, Lobe, Long, M(e)iosis, Mitosis, Mofussil, Nome, Pachytene, Pargana, Part, Partition, Passus, Pergunnah, Period, Phratry, Phyle, Phylum, Pipe, Pitaka, Platoon, Polarisation, Presidency, Queen's Bench, Quotition, Rape, Red Crag, Reduction, Region, Replum, Reservation, Riding, Sanjak, Schism, Section, Sector, Segment, Semeion, Sept(ate), Sever, Share, Sheading, Shed, Shire, Short, Stage, Subheading, Tahsil, Tanach, Taxis, Telophase, Tepal, Thanet, Trichotomy, Trio, Trivium, Troop, Tuath, Unit, Vilayet, Volost, Wapentake, Ward, Watershed

Divisor Aliquant, Aliquot

Divorce(d) Diffarreation, Disaffiliate, Dissolve, Disunion, Div, Estrange, Get(t), Part, Separate, Sequester, > **SUNDER**, Talak, Talaq

Divot Clod, Sod, Turf

Divulge Confess, Disclose, Expose, Publish, Reveal, Split, Tell, Unveil, Utter

DIY Flatpack

Dizziness, **Dizzy** Beaconsfield, Ben, Capricious, Dinic, Disraeli, Giddy, Giglot, Lightheaded, Mazey, Mirligoes, Swimming, Vertiginous, > **VERTIGO**, Woozy

DJ Deejay, Monkey-suit, Selecta, Shockjock, Tuxedo, Veejay

DNA Antisense, Centromere, Chromatin, Cistron, Codon, Complementary, Cytosine, Exon, Gene, Heteroduplex, Homopolymer, Intron, Junk, Microsatellite, Muton, Nucleosome, Plasmid, Procaryote, Profiling, Prokaryote, Purine, Recombinant, Replicon, RNA, Satellite, Selfish, Southern blot, Telomere, Thymidine, Transposon, Vector, Watson-Crick model

Do(es), **Doing** Accomplish, Achieve, Act, Anent, Banquet, Beano, Begin, Char, Cheat, Chisel, Cod, Con, Cozen, Deed, Dich, Dish, Div, Doth, Dupe, Effectuate, Enact, Execute, Function, Gull, Handiwork, Hoax, Mill, Perform, Same, Serve, Settle, Shindig, Spif(f)licate, Suffice, Thrash, Ut

▷ **Do** *may indicate an anagram*

Do away Abolish, Banish, Demolish, Kill

Docile Agreeable, Amenable, Biddable, Dutiful, Facile, Meek, Submissive, Tame, Tractable, Yielding

Dock(er), Docked, Docks Abridge, Barber, Basin, Bistort, Bob, Camber, Canaigre, Clip, Curta(i)l, Cut, Deduct, De-tail, Dry, Floating, Grapetree, Graving, Knotweed, Lop, Marina, Moor, Off-end, Pare, Patience, Pen, Pier, Quay, Rhubarb, Rumex, Rump, Scene, Seagull, Shorten, Snakeweed, Sorrel, Sourock, Stevedore, Tilbury, Watersider, Wet, Wharf, Wharfie, Yard

Docket Invoice, Label, Tag

Dockyard Arsenal, Rosyth

Doctor(s) Allopath, Alter, Arnold, Asclepiad, Barefoot, Barnardo, Bleeder, BMA, Bones, Breeze, Bright, Brighton, Brown, Caius, Castrate, Chapitalize, Clinician, Cook, Cup(per), Cure(r), Dale, Diagnose, Dr, Dryasdust, Erasmus, Extern(e), Fake, Falsify, Family, Faustus, Feldsher, Fell, Finlay, Flying, Foster, Fundholder, Galen, Geriatrician, Geropiga, GP, Hakeem, Hakim, Healer, Homeopath, Houseman, Hyde, Imhotep, Intern, Internist, Jekyll, Jenner, Johnson, Kildare, Lace, Leach, Leech, Linacre, Load, Locum, Luke, Manette, Massage, MB, MD, Medicate, Medico, Middleton, Mindererus, Minister, Misrepresent, MO, MOH, Molla(h), Moreau, Mulla(h), Neuter, No, Ollamh, Ollav, Paean, Panel, Pangloss, Paracelsus, Paramedic, Pedro, PhD, Physician, Pill(s), Practitioner, Quack, Quacksalver, Rabbi, RAMC, Registrar, Resident, Rig, Salk, Sangrado, Saw, Sawbones, School, Shaman, Slammer, Slop, Spin, Stum, Surgeon, Syn, Syntax, Thorne, Treat, Vaidya, Vet, Water, Watson, Who, Witch

▷ **Doctor(ed)** *may indicate* an anagram

Doctrine Adoptianism, Adoptionism, Antinomian, Apollinarian, Archology, Arianism, Averr(h)oism, Bonism, Brezhnev, Cab(b)ala, Calvanism, Chiliasm, Consubstantiation, Credo, Creed, Determinism, Ditheletism, Docetism, Dogma, Doxie, Doxy, Esotery, Federalism, Fideism, Finalism, Functionalism, Gnosticism, Gospel, Holism, Infralapsarianism, Islam, Ism, Jansenism, Krypsis, Laches, Lore, Malthusian, Manich(a)eism, Metempsychosis, Molinism, Monergism, Monism, Monroe, Nestorianism, Neutral monism, Nihilism, Pragmatism, Predestination, Pythagorean(ism), Reformism, Satyagrahi, Sharia, Sheria, Shibboleth, Strong meat, Subjectivism, Sublapsarianism, Subpanation, Substantialism, Swedenborgianism, Syndicalism, Synergism, System, Teleology, > **TENET**, Terminism, Theory, Theravada, Thomism, Transubstantiation, Tutiorism, Utilitarianism, Voluntarism, Wasm, Weismannism, Whiteboyism, Zoism, Zwinglian

Document(s), Documentary Bumf, Bumph, Carta, Certificate, Charter, Contract, Conveyance, Covenant, Daftar, Deed, Diploma, Docket, Doco, Dompass, Dossier, Fiat, Form, Grand Remonstrance, Holograph, Latitat, Logbook, Mandamus, Offer, Papers, Precept, Production, Public, Ragman, Ragment, Record, Resort, Roll, Roul(e), Screed, Source, Stamp note, Warrant, Waybill, Writ, Write up

Dod Pet, Poll

Dodder(y) Old, Shake, Stagger, Strangleweed, Totter, Tremble

Doddle Easy

Dodge, Dodgy Artful, Avoid, Bell-ringing, Column, Elude, Evade, Evasion, Iffy, Jink, Jook, Jouk, Racket, Ruse, Shirk, Sidestep, Skip, Slalom, Slinter, Tip, Trick, Twist, Urchin, Weave, Welsh, Wheeze, Wire, Wrinkle

Doe(s) Deer, Faun, Hind

Doff Avail(e), Avale, Remove, Rouse, Shed, Tip

Dog(s) Bowwow, Canes, Canidae, Canine, Feet, Fire, Fog, Heading, Hot, Hunter, Kennel, Leading, Nodding, Pursue, Sea, Search, Seeing-eye, Shadow, Sleeve, Spotted, Stalk, Sun, Tag, Tail, Top, Tracker, Trail, Wammul, Water, Yellow

DOGS

3 letters:
Cur
Eye
Gun
Pig
Pom
Pug
Rab
Yap

4 letters:
Barb
Bird
Brak
Bran
Bush
Cant
Chow
Dane
Fido
Heel
Iron
Kuri
Mutt
Oath
Peke
Puli
Rach
Sled
Stag
Tike
Toby
Tosa
Tray
Tyke
Wolf

5 letters:
Alans
Apsos
Argos
Boots
Boxer
Brach
Cairn
Coach

Dhole
Dingo
Guard
Guide
Haunt
Hound
Husky
Hyena
Kurre
Laika
Lorel
Luath
Moera
Pidog
Pluto
Pooch
Rache
Rover
Shock
Spitz
Spoor
Whelp
Zorro

6 letters:
Afghan
Bandog
Barbet
Barker
Basset
Beagle
Bitser
Blanch
Borzoi
Bounce
Bowler
Briard
Caesar
Canaan
Chenet
Cocker
Collie
Dangle
Eskimo
Gelert
Goorie

Heeler
Jackal
Katmir
Kelpie
Kennet
Ketmir
Kratim
Lassie
Mauthe
Messan
Moppet
Pariah
Piedog
Police
Poodle
Pye-dog
Ranger
Saluki
Setter
Shaggy
Shough
Sirius
Sothic
Talbot
Teckel
Touser
Towser
Vizsla
Westie
Yapper
Yorkie

7 letters:
Andiron
Basenji
Bobbery
Boerbul
Bouvier
Brachet
Bulldog
Courser
Griffon
Harrier
Hearing
Iceland
Lurcher

Maltese
Maremma
Mastiff
Mongrel
Orthrus
Pointer
Prairie
Raccoon
Reynard
Samoyed
Sapling
Sausage
Shar-Pei
Sheltie
Shih tzu
Showghe
Sniffer
Spaniel
Starter
>TERRIER
Volpino
Whiffet
Whippet
Yapster

8 letters:
Aardwolf
Aberdeen
Airedale
Alsatian
Blenheim
Bouvrier
Bratchet
Brittany
Carriage
Cerberus
Chow-chow
Doberman
Elkhound
Hovawart
Huntaway
Kangaroo
Keeshond
Komondor
Labrador
Landseer

- Malamute
- Malemute
- Papillon
- Pekinese
- Pembroke
- Pinscher
- Samoyede
- Sealyham
- Sheepdog
- Springer
- Turnspit
- Warragal
- Warrigal

9 letters:
- Buckhound
- Chihuahua
- Coonhound
- Dachshund
- Dalmatian
- Deerhound
- Dobermann
- Gazehound
- Great Dane
- Greyhound
- Harlequin
- Kerry blue
- Lhasa apso
- Molossian
- Pekingese

Retriever
Schnauzer
Staghound
Strong-eye
Wolfhound

10 letters:
Bedlington
Bloodhound
Blueheeler
Fox terrier
Otterhound
Pomeranian
Rottweiler
Schipperke
Shin-barker
Tripehound
Weimaraner

11 letters:
Bichon frise
Jack Russell
Montmorency
Skye terrier
Sleuthhound
Tibetan apso
Trendle-tail
Trindle-tail
Trundle-tail
Wishtonwish

12 letters:
Border collie
Gazelle hound
Japanese chin
Newfoundland
Saint Bernard
West Highland

13 letters:
Affenpinscher
Dandie Dinmont
Scotch terrier
Sussex spaniel

14 letters:
Italian spinone
Tibetan mastiff

15 letters:
Bernese Mountain
Estrela Mountain
Mexican hairless
Norwegian
 buhund
Portuguese water
Swedish vallhund

16 letters:
Doberman-
 pinscher

Pyrenean
 mountain
Russian
 wolfhound
Shetland
 sheepdog

17 letters:
Anatolian
 Shepherd
Dobermann-
 pinscher

18 letters:
Large
 Munsterlander
Old English
 sheepdog
Rhodesian
 ridgeback

20 letters:
Landseer
 Newfoundland

21 letters:
Polish Lowland
 sheepdog

Dog-bane Apocynum
Doge Dandolo
Dogfish Huss, Rigg
Dogged Determined, Die-hard, Dour, Indefatigable, Pertinacious, Stubborn, Sullen
Doggerel Crambo, Jingle, Laisse, Rat-rhyme
Dog Letter R
Dogma(tic) Assertive, Belief, Conviction, Creed, Doctrinal, Ideology, Ipse dixit, Opinionated, Pedagogic, Peremptory, Pontifical, Positive, > TENET
Do-gooder Piarist, Reformer, Salvationist, Samaritan, Scout
Dogsbody Bottle-washer, Gofer, Skivvy
Dog star Canicula, Lassie, Sirius, Sothic
Do it Dich
Dolce Stop, Sweet
Dole Alms, Batta, B(u)roo, Give, Grief, Maundy, Payment, Pittance, Pog(e)y, Ration, > SHARE, Tichborne, Vail, Vales
Doll(y) Barbie®, Bimbo, Common, Corn, Creeper, Crumpet, Dress, Dutch, Golliwog, Kachina, Kewpie®, Maiden, Marionette, Matryoshka, Maumet, Mommet, Mummet, Ookpik®, Ornament, Paris, Parton, Poppet, Puppet, Ragdoll, Russian, Sis(ter), Sitter, Tearsheet, Toy, Trolley, Varden, Washboard, Wax

Dollar(s) Balboa, Boliviano, Buck, Cob, Cob money, Euro, Fin, Greenback, Iron man, Peso, Petrol, Piastre, Pink, S, Sand, Sawbuck, Sawhorse, Scrip, Smacker, Spin, Sword, Top, Wheel

Dollop Glob, Helping, Share

▷ **Dolly** *may indicate* an anagram

Dolly-bird Dish

Dolour Grief, Pain, Sorrow

Dolphin Amazon, Arion, Beluga, Bottlenose, Cetacean, Coryphene, Delphinus, Grampus, Lampuka, Lampuki, Meer-swine, Porpess(e), Risso's, River, Sea-pig

Dolt Ass, Blockhead, Clodhopper, Noodle, Oaf, Owl, > STUPID

Domain Archaea, Bacteria, Bourn(e), Demain, Demesne, Eminent, Emirate, Empire, Estate, Eukarya, Manor, Predicant, Public, Rain, Realm, Region, Reign

Dome(-shaped) Al-Aqsa, Cap, Cupola, Cupula, Dagoba, Geodesic, Head, Imperial, Louvre, Millennium, Onion, Periclinal, Rotunda, Salt, Stupa, Tee, Tholos, Tholus, Tope, Vault, Xanadu

Domestic(ate) Char, Cleaner, Dom, Esne, Familiar, Home-keeping, Homely, House, Housetrain, Humanise, Interior, Internal, Intestine, Maid, Menial, > SERVANT, Tame, Woman

Domicile Abode, Dwelling, Hearth, Home, Ménage

Dominate, **Dominance**, **Dominant** Ascendancy, Baasskap, Ballbreaker, Bethrall, Clou, Coerce, Control, Hegemony, Henpeck, Maisterdome, Mesmerise, Monopolise, O(v)ergang, Override, Overshadow, Power, Preponderant, Preside, Rule, Soh, > SUBDUE, Subjugate, Tower

Domineer Boss, Henpeck, Lord, Ride, Swagger, Tyrannize

Dominica(n) Jacobite, Monk, OP, Preaching friar, Predicant, Savonarola, WD

Dominie Maister, Master, Pastor, Sampson, Schoolmaster

Dominion Dom, Empire, Khanate, NZ, Realm, Reame, Reign, > RULE, Supremacy, Sway, Territory

Domino(es) Card, Fats, Mask, Matador

Don Academic, Address, Assume, Caballero, Camorrist, Endue, Fellow, Garb, Giovanni, Indew, Juan, Lecturer, Mafia, Prof, Quixote, Reader, Senor, Spaniard, Tutor, Wear

Dona(h) Duckie, Love

Donate, **Donation** Aid, Bestow, Contribution, Gift, Give, Peter's pence, Present, Wakf, Waqf

Done Achieved, Complete, Crisp, Ended, Executed, Had, Over, Spitcher, Tired, Weary

Donjon Dungeon, Keep

Donkey Ass, Burro, Cardophagus, Cuddie, Cuddy, Dapple, Dick(e)y, Dunce, Eeyore, Fussock, Genet(te), Jennet, Jerusalem pony, Kulan, Modestine, Moke, Mule, Neddy, Nodding, Onager, Stupid, Years

Donor Benefactor, Bestower, Settlor, Universal

Doo Dove

Doodle(r) Scribble, Yankee

Doodlebug Antlion, Larva, V1

Doom(ed) Condemned, Damnation, Date, Destine, Destiny, > FATE, Fay, Fey, Fie, Goner, Ill-starred, Lot, Predestine, Preordain, Ragnarok, Ruined, Sentence, Spitcher, Star-crossed, Weird

Doone Carver, Lorna

Door(s), **Doorstep**, **Doorway** Aperture, Communicating, Damnation, Drecksill, Dutch, Elephant, Entry, Exit, Fire, Folding, Front, Haik, Hake, Hatch, Heck, Ingress, Jib, Lintel, Louver, Louvre, Muntin, Oak, Open, Overhead, Portal,

Postern, Revolving, Rory, Screen, Sliding, Stable, Stage, Storm, Street, Swing, Trap, Up and over, Vomitory, Wicket, Yett

Doorkeeper, Doorman Bouncer, Commissionaire, Guardian, Janitor, Ostiary, Porter, Tiler, Tyler, Usher

Doormat Subservient, Weakling

Doorpost Architrave, Dern, Durn, Jamb, Yate, Yett

Dope Acid, Amulet, Bang, Coke, Crack, > DRUG, Gen, Goose, Info, Lowdown, Narcotic, Nobble, Rutin, Sedate, Soup, > STUPID PERSON, Tea

Dorcas Gazelle, Needle, Shepherdess

Dorian, Doric Metope, Mutule

Doris Day, Lessing, Mollusc

Dormant Abed, Comatose, Hibernating, Inactive, Inert, Joist, Latent, Resting, > SLEEPING, Torpescent

Dormitory Barrack, Dorter, Dortour, Hall, Hostel, Quarters

Dormouse Loir

Dorothy Bag, Dot, Sayers

Dorsal Back, Neural, Notal

Dory Fish, John

Dosage, Dose Acute, Administer, Booster, Cascara, Cumulative, Drachm, Draught, Drench, Drug, Hit, Kilogray, > MEASURE, Physic, Posology, Potion, Powder, Rem, Threshold, Tolerance

Doss (house) Dharmsala, Dharmshala, Kip, Padding-ken, Spike

Dossier File, Record

Dot(s), Dotted, Dotty Absurd, Bind(h)i, Bullet, Centred, Criblé, Dit, Dower, Dowry, Ellipsis, Engrailed, Leader, Lentiginose, Limp, Micro, Morse, Occult, Or, Particle, Pixel, > POINT, Polka, Precise, Punctuate, Punctulate, Punctum, Schwa, Semé(e), Set, Speck, Spot, Sprinkle, Stigme, Stipple, Stud, Tap, Tittle, Trema, Umlaut

Dote, Dotage, Doting, Dotard Adore, Anile, Anility, Cocker, Dobbie, Idolise, Imbecile, Pet, Prize, Senile, Tendre, Twichild

Double(s) Amphibious, Ancipital, Bi-, Bifold, Binate, Clone, Counterpart, Crease, Dimeric, Doppel-ganger, Doppio, Dual, Duo, Duple(x), Duplicate, Equivocal, Fetch, Fold, Foursome, Geminate, Gimp, Image, Ingeminate, Ka, Look-alike, Loop, Martingale, Pair, Parlay, Polyseme, Reflex, Replica, Ringer, Run, Similitude, Spit, Trot, Turnback, Twae, > TWIN, Two(fold)

Double-barrelled Tautonym

Double-cross, Double dealing Ambidext(e)rous, Two-time

Double-entendre Polyseme, Polysemy

Doublet Peascod, Pourpoint, TT

Doubt(ful), Doubter Ambiguous, Aporia, Askance, But, Debatable, Distrust, Dubiety, Dubitate, Hesitate, Hum, Iffy, Incertitude, Misgiving, Mistrust, > NO DOUBT, Precarious, Qualm, Query, > QUESTION, Rack, Scepsis, Sceptic, Scruple, Shady, Shy, Sic, Skepsis, Sus, Suspect, Suspicious, Suss, Thomas, Thos, Umph, Uncertain, Unsure, Waver

Doubtless Probably, Sure, Truly

Douceur Bonus, Sop, Sweetener

Douche Bath, Gush, Rinse, Shower, Wash

Dough(y) Boodle, Cake, Calzone, Cash, Duff, Hush-puppy, Knish, Loot, Magma, Masa, Money, Paste, Pop(p)adum, Ready, Sad, Sour, Spondulicks, Strudel

Doughboy Dumpling, Soldier

Doughnut Beavertail®, Cruller, Knish, Koeksister, Olycook, Olykoek, Sinker, Torus

Doughty Brave, Intrepid, Resolute, Stalwart, Valiant

Dour Glum, Hard, Mirthless, Morose, Reest, Reist, Sinister, Sullen, Taciturn

Douse Dip, Drench, Extinguish, Snuff, Splash

Dove Collared, Columbine, Culver, Cushat, Diamond, Doo, Ice-bird, Mourning, Pacifist, > PIGEON, Queest, Quoist, Ring, Rock, Stock, Turtle

Dove-cot(e) Columbarium, Columbary, Louver, Louvre, Lover

Dovetail Fit, Lewis(son), Mortise, Tally, Tenon

Dowager Elder, Widow

Dowdy Frumpish, Mums(e)y, Shabby, Sloppy, Slovenly

Dowel Peg, Pin

Down(s)s, Down(beat), Downsize, Downward, Downy A bas, Abase, Abattu, Alow, Amort, Bank, Below, Berkshire, Blue, Cast, Catabasis, Chapfallen, Comous, Cottony, Crouch, Darling, Dejected, Dowl(e), Drink, Epsom, Feather, Fledge, Floccus, Flue, Fluff, Fly, Fuzz, Goonhilly, Ground, Hair, Hill, Humble, Humiliate, Jeff, Kennet, Lanugo, Losing, Low, Lower, Nap, Oose, Ooze, Owing, Pappus, Pennae, Pile, Plumage, Powder, Quash, Repress, Sebum, Slim, Thesis, Thistle, Tomentum, Unserviceable, Urinant, Vail, Wold, Wretched

Downcast Abject, Chapfallen, Despondent, Disconsolate, Dumpish, Hangdog, Hopeless, Melancholy, Woebegone

Downfall, Downpour Cataract, Collapse, Deluge, Fate, Flood, Hail, Onding, Overthrow, Rain, Ruin, Shower, Thunder-plump, Torrent, Undoing, Waterspout

Downgrade(d) Déclassé, Disrate

Downright Absolute, Arrant, Bluff, Candid, Clear, Complete, Flat, Plumb, Plump, Pure, Rank, Sheer, Stark, Utter

Downstairs Below

Dowry Dot, Dower, Lobola, Lobolo, Merchet, Portion, Settlement, Tocher

Dowse(r), Dowsing Divine, Enew, Fireman, Rhabdomancy, Water-witch

Doxology Gloria, Glory

Doxy Harlot, Loose woman, Wench

Doyen Dean, Senior

Doze Ca(u)lk, Dove(r), Nap, Nod, Semi-coma, Sleep, Slip, Slumber

Dozen(s) Baker's, Long, Round, Thr(e)ave, Twal, Twelve

Dr Debtor, Doctor, Dram

Drab Ash-grey, Cloth, Dell, Dingy, Dull, Dun, Isabel(line), Lifeless, Livor, Mumsy, Prosaic, Pussel, Quaker-colour, Rig, Road, Slattern, Sloven, Subfusc, Tart, Trull, Wanton, Whore

Drabble Bemoil, Draggle

Dracula Bat, Count, Vampire

Draft Cheque, Draw, Ebauche, Essay, Landsturm, Minute, MS, Outline, Plan, Press, Projet, Rough, Scheme, Scroll, Scrowle, > SKETCH

Drag Car, Drail, Dredge, Drogue, Elicit, Eonism, Epicene, Extort, Fiscal, Form, Hale, Harl, > HAUL, Induced, Keelhaul, La Rue, Lug, Parasite, Pressure, Profile, Puff, Pull, Rash, Sag, Schlep, Shoe, Skidpan, Sled, Snig, Sweep, Toke, Tote, Trail, Train, Travail, Travois, Trawl, Treck, Trek, Tump, Vortex

Draggle Drail, Lag, Straggle

Dragon Basilisk, Bel, Bellemère, Chaperon(e), Chindit, Draco, Drake, Fafnir, Fire-drake, Gargouille, Komodo, Kung-kung, Ladon, Lindworm, Opinicus, Peist, Puk, Python, Rouge, Safat, Shrew, Typhoeus, Wantley, Wivern, Worm, Wyvern

Dragonfly Aeschna, Demoiselle, Devil's darning needle, Nymph, Odonata

Dragon's teeth Cadmus, Spartae, Sparti

Dragoon Coerce, Force, Press, Trooper

Drain(ed), Drainage, Draining, Drainpipe Bleed, Brain, Buzz, Catchment, Catchwater, Channel, Cloaca, Cundy, Delf, Delph, Dewater, Ditch, Dry, Ea(u), > EMPTY, Emulge(nt), Exhaust, Field, Fleet, Grating, Grip, Gully, Gutter, Ketavothron, Kotabothron, Lade, Leach, Leech, Limber, Lose, Milk, Mole, Nala, Nulla(h), Penrose, Pump, Rack, Rone, Sap, Scupper, Seton, Sew(er), Sheuch, Sheugh, Silver, Sink, Siver, Sluice, Sluse, Soakaway, Sough, Spend, Stank, Storm, Sump, Sure, Syver, Tile, Trench, Trocar, Unwater, Ureter, U-trap, Weary, Well

Dram Drink, Drop, Nipperkin, Nobbler, Portion, Snifter, Tickler, Tiff, Tot, Wet

Drama(tic), Drama school Auto, Catastasis, Charade, Closet, Comedy, Drastic, ER, Farce, Heroic, Histrionic, Kabuki, Kathakali, Kitchen sink, Legit, Mask, Masque, Mime, Moralities, No, Nogaku, Noh, Piece, Play, RADA, Scenic, Sensational, Singspiel, Stagy, Striking, Tetralogy, Theatric, Thespian, Tragedy, Unities, Wagnerian, Wild

Dramatist Adamov, Aeschylus, Albee, Aristophanes, Beaumarchais, Beaumont, Brecht, Bridie, Calderon, Congreve, Corneille, Coward, Drinkwater, Eumenides, Euripides, Fletcher, Frisch, Fry, Gay, Genet, Goldoni, Havel, Ibsen, Ionesco, Jarry, Kyd, Lyly, Massinger, Menander, Middleton, Molière, Odets, O'Neill, Osborne, Otway, Pinero, Pirandello, Plautus, > PLAYWRIGHT, Racine, Rostand, Rowe, Rowley, Schiller, Seneca, Shadwell, Shaffer, Sherriff, Sophocles, Stoppard, Strindberg, Synge, Terence, Udall, Vanbrugh, Voltaire, Webster, Wedekind, Wesker, Wilde, Wilder, Will, > WRITER, Yeats

Dram-shop Bar, Boozingken, Bousingken

Drape(ry) Adorn, Coverlet, Coverlid, Curtain, Festoon, Fold, Hang, Mantling, Swathe, Valance, Veil, Vest

Draper Gilpin, Hosier, Mercer, Ruth, Scotch cuddy

Drastic Dire, Dramatic, Extreme, Harsh, Purge, Senna, > SEVERE, Violent

Drat Bother, Dang, Darn

Draught(s), Draughtsman Aloetic, Aver, Breeze, Dam, Design, Drench, Drink, Fish, Gulp, Gust, Haal, Hippocrene, King, Men, Nightcap, Outline, Plan, Potation, Potion, Pull, Quaff, Sketch, Sleeping, Slug, Swig, Tracer, Up-current, Veronal, Waucht, Waught, Williewaught

▷ **Draught** *may refer to* fishing

Draught-board Dam-board, Dambrod

Dravidian Tamil

Draw (off), Drawer(s), Drawing, Drawn Adduct, Allure, Attract, Bleed, Bottom, Cock, Crayon, Dead-heat, Delineate, Derivation, Describe, Dis(em)bowel, Doodle, Dr, Draft, Drag, Dress, Educe, Entice, Equalise, Evaginate, Extract, Fetch, Gather, Gaunt, Glorybox, Gut, Haggard, Hale, Halve, Haul, Induce, Indue, Inhale, Lengthen, Limn, Longbow, Lottery, Pantalet(te)s, Panty, Perpetual check, Petroglyph, Protract, Pull, Rack, Raffle, Remark, Scent, Score, Sesquipedalian, Shottle, Shuttle, Siphon, Sketch, Slub, Snig, Spin, Stalemate, Stumps, Sweepstake, Syphon, Tap, Taut, Technical, Tempt, Tenniel, Tie, Till, Toke, Tole, Tombola, Top, Tose, Tow(age), Toze, Trice, Troll, Tug, Unsheathe, Uplift

▷ **Draw** *may indicate* something to smoke

Drawback Catch, Downside, Ebb, Impediment, > OBSTACLE, Rebate, Retraction, Shrink, Snag

Drawbridge Bascule, Pontlevis

Drawing Cartoon, Charcoal, Crayon, Dentistry, Detail, Diagram, Elevation, Freehand, Fusain, Graphics, Indraft, Line, Mechanical, Monotint,

Orthograph, Pastel, Petroglyph, Profile, Seductive, Sepia, Silverpoint, Study, Technical, Traction, Wash, Working
Drawl Dra(u)nt, Haw, Slur, Twang
Drawn *may indicate* an anagram
Drawn up Atrip, Drafted
Dray Cart, Lorry, Wagon
Dread(ed) Angst, Anxiety, Awe, Fear, > HORROR, Rasta, Redoubt, Thing
Dreadful Awful, Chronic, Dearn, Dire, Formidable, Ghastly, Horrendous, Penny, Sorry, Terrible
Dream(er), **Dream home**, **Dream state**, **Dreamy** Alchera, Alcheringa, Aspire, Castle, Desire, Drowsy, Dwalm, Dwa(u)m, Fantast, Fantasy, Faraway, Gerontius, Idealise, Illusion, Imagine, Languor, Long, Mare, Mirth, Moon, Morpheus, Muse, Nightmare, On(e)iric, Pensive, Phantasmagoria, Pipe, > REVERIE, Rêveur, Romantic, Somniate, Spac(e)y, Stargazer, Surreal, Sweven, Trance, Trauma, Vague, Vision, Walter Mitty, Wet
Dreary Bleak, Desolate, Dismal, Doleful, Dreich, Dull, Gloom, Gray, Grey, Oorie, Ourie, Owrie, Sad
Dredger Caster
Dregs Bottom, Draff, Dunder, F(a)eces, Fecula, Gr(e)aves, Grounds, Lees, Legge, Mother, Mud, Riffraff, Scaff, Sediment, Settlings, Silt, Snuff, Ullage
Dreikanter Ventifact
Drench Dowse, Soak, Souse, Steep, Submerge
Dress(ing), **Dressed** Academic, Accoutre, Adorn, Aguise, Align, Ao dai, Array, Attire, Attrap, Bandage, Bandoline, Bedizen, Black-tie, Bloomer, Blouson, Boast, Bodice, Boun, Bowne, Brilliantine, Busk, Caftan, Cataplasm, Charpie, Cheongsam, Chimer, Cimar, Clad, > CLOTHING, Coat, Cocktail, Comb, Compost, Compress, Corsage, Corset, Costume, Court, Curry, Cymar, Dandify, Dashiki, Deck, Deshabille, Dight, Dirndl, Dizen, Doll, Dolly Varden, Dolman, Don, Drag, Dub, Dubbin, Elastoplast®, Empire, Endue, Enrobe, Evening, Fancy, Far(r)andine, Farthingale, Fatigues, Ferrandine, Fertiliser, Fig, Finery, Flamenco, French, Frock, Full, Gamgee tissue, Garb, Garnish, Gauze, Girt, Gown, Graith, Granny, Guise, Gymslip, > HABIT, Highland, Ihram, Italian, Jaconet, Kabuki, Ketchup, K(h)anga, Kimono, Kirtle, Kitenge, Line, Lint, Lounger, Maxi, Mayonnaise, Merveilleuse, Midi, Mineral, Mob, Morning, Mother Hubbard, Mufti, Mulch, Muu-muu, Oil, Ore, Patch, Peplos, Pinafore, Plaster, Pledget, Plumage, Polonaise, Pomade, Poultice, Power, Prank, Preen, Prepare, Princess (line), Rag, Raiment, Rainbow, Ranch, Ray, Rehearsal, Rémoulade, Rig, Robe, Russet, Russian, Rybat, Sack, Sacque, Salad, Samfoo, Samfu, Sari, Sarong, Sartorial, Sauce, Scutch, Seloso, Separates, Sheath, Shift, Shirt, Shirtwaister, Simar(re), Smock, Sterile, Stole, Stupe, Subfusc, Subfusk, Suit, Sundress, Symar, Tartan, Tasar, Taw, Tent, Tenue, Tew, Thousand Island, Tiff, Tire, Tog, Toga, Toilet, Tonic, Top, Treat, Trick, Trim, Trollopee, Tunic, Tusser, Tussore, Tuxedo, Uniform, Vest, Vinaigrette, Wear, Wedding, Well, White-tie, Wig, Yclad, Ycled
Dressage Demivolt(e), Manège, Passade, Passage, Pesade, Piaffe
> **Dressed up**, **Dressing** *may indicate* an anagram
Dresser Adze, Almery, Bureau, Chest, Couturier, Deuddarn, Dior, Lair, Lowboy, Sideboard, Transvestite, Tridarn, Welsh
Dressing-gown Bathrobe, Negligee, Peignoir
Dressing-room Apodyterium, Vestiary, Vestry
Dressmaker Costumier, Dorcas, Modiste, Seamstress, Tailor
Drew Steeld, Stelled

Dribble Drip, Drivel, Drop, Seep, Slaver, Slobber, Slop, Trickle

Dried Fish Bum(m)alo, Bummaloti, Haberdine, Speld(r)in(g), Stockfish

▶ **Dried Fruit** *see* DRY FRUIT

Drift(ing), Drifter Becalmed, Continental, Cruise, Current, Digress, Diluvium, Float, Genetic, Heap, Impulse, Longshore, Maunder, Natant, North Atlantic, Plankton, Purport, Rorke, Slide, Tendence, Tendency, > **TENOR**, Waft, Wander, Zooplankton

Drill(ing) Appraisal, Auger, Bore, Burr, Close order, Directional, Educate, Exercise, Fire, Form, Hammer, Jackhammer, Jerks, Kerb, Monkey, Pack, PE, Pierce, Pneumatic, Power, PT, Radial, Reamer, Ridge, Rimer, Seeder, Sow, Square-bashing, Teach, Train, Twill, Twist, Usage, Wildcat

Drink(er), Drunk(enness) AA, Absorb, Adrian Quist, Alkie, Alky, Babalas, Bacchian, Barfly, Bender, Beverage, Bev(v)y, Bezzle, Bib(ite), Binge, Birl(e), Bland, Blatted, Blind, Blitzed, Bloat, Blotto, Bombed, Boose, Booze, Bosky, Bottled, Bouse, Bowl, Bracer, Brandy, Bumper, Burst, Carafe, Carousal, Cat-lap, Chaser, Compotation, > **CORDIAL**, Corked, Crapulent, Crapulous, Cratur, Crocked, Cuppa, Cut, Demitasse, Digestif, Dipsomaniac, Double, Down, Drain, Draught, Drop, Ebriate, Ebriose, Elixir, Entire, Eye-opener, Finger, Fleein', Flying, Fou, Fuddle-cap, Fuddled, Full, Glug, Half-seas-over, Heart-starter, High, Hogshead, Honkers, Hophead, Imbibe, Indulge, Inhaust, Intemperate, Irrigate, Ivresse, Jag, Jar, Juice, Juicehead, Knock back, Lap, Legless, Lethean, Libation, Lit, Loaded, Lord, Lower, Lush(y), Maggoty, Maltworm, Maudlin, Merry, Methomania, Methysis, Mixer, Moony, Mortal, Mug, Nog(gin), Obfuscated, Oenomania, Oiled, One, Oppignorate, Overshot, Paid, Paint, Partake, Particular, Peg, Pickled, Pick-me-up, Pie-eyed, Pint(a), Piss-artist, Pissed, Pisshead, Pisspot, Pixil(l)ated, Plonk(o), Plottie, Potation, Poteen, Potion, Primed, Quaff, Rat-arsed, Ratted, Roaring, Rolling, Rotten, Round, Rouse, Rumfustian, Rummer, Screwed, Sea, Shebeen, Shicker, Shotover, Silenus, Sip(ple), Skinned, Slake, Slewed, Sloshed, Slued, Slug, Slurp, Smashed, Smoothie, Snort, Soak, Soused, Sozzled, Sponge, Spongy, Spunge, Squiffy, Steaming, Stewed, Stimulant, Stinko, Stocious, Stoned, Stonkered, Stotious, Stuporous, Sup, Swacked, Swallow, Swig, Swill, Tank, Temulence, Tiddl(e)y, Tiff, Tift, Tight, Tipper, Tipple, Tipsy, Tope, Toss, Tossicated, Tost, Two-pot screamer, Usual, Wash, Wat, Wauch, Waught, Well-oiled, Wet, Whiffled, Williewaught, Winebag, Wino, Wrecked, Zonked

● **DRINKS**

2 letters:			
It	Kir	Coke®	Sack
	L&P	Flip	Sake
	Mum	Grog	Saki
3 letters:	Pop	Homa	Soda
Ale	Rum	Kava	Soft
Ava	Rye	Kola	Soma
Bub	Tea	Malt	Sour
Cha	Tot	Mead	Sura
Cup	Vin	Neck	Tape
Dop		Nipa	Tass
Fap		Ouzo	Tent
Gin	**4 letters:**	Port	Yill
G&T	Asti	Purl	
Hom	Bock	Raki	
	Bull		

5 letters:

Assai
Bingo
Bombo
Bumbo
Cider
Cocoa
Copus
Crush
Doris
Float
Glogg
Haoma
Hogan
Hooch
Joram
Jorum
Julep
Kefir
Kelty
Kvass
Lassi
Mâcon
Malwa
Mauby
Meath
Medoc
Meths
Mobby
Morat
Mulse
Nappy
Negus
Pekoe
Pepsi®
Perry
Pimms
Polly
Pombe
Punch
Rakee
Rummy
Sarsa
Sarza
Shake
Short
Shrub
Skink
Sling
Smile
Stout
Toddy

Tonic
Totty
Vodka
Xeres

6 letters:

Amrita
Apozem
Arrack
Bishop
Burton
Busera
Cassis
Caudle
Cauker
Chasse
Coffee
Cognac
Cooler
Cooper
Doctor
Eggnog
Enzian
Gimlet
Grappa
Gutrot
Hobnob
Hootch
Kalied
Keltie
Kephir
Kirsch
Kumiss
Kümmel
Maotai
Meathe
Mescal
Mickey
Mobbie
Nectar
Obarni
Old Tom
Oolong
Orgeat
Oulong
Pastis
Pernod®
Plotty
Porter
Posset
Pulque
Rickey

Rotgut
Saloop
Samshu
Shandy
Sherry
Smiler
Squash
Stingo
Strega
Strunt
Taffia
Tisane
Waragi
Yaqona
Zythum

7 letters:

Absinth
Akvavit
Alcopop
Amoroso
Aquavit
Bacardi®
Bitters
Campari®
Caribou
Chablis
Chianti
Cobbler
Curaçao
Curaçoa
Daquiri
Eggflip
Fairish
Fustian
Guarana
Italian
Koumiss
Malmsey
Mineral
Nobbler
Oenomel
Oloroso
Persico
Philter
Philtre
Pilsner
Pink gin
Quickie
Ratafia
Reviver
Rosiner

Rosolio
Sangria
Sazerac
Screech
Scrumpy
Sherbet
Sherris
Sloe gin
Snifter
Stengah
Swizzle
Tequila
Tio Pepe®
Wassail

8 letters:

Absinthe
Aleberry
Ambrosia
Anisette
Aperitif
Armagnac
Borachio
Bordeaux
Brown cow
Burgundy
Calvados
Champers
Charneco
Ciderkin
Coca-cola®
Cold duck
Daiquiri
Dog's nose
Dubonnet®
Eau de vie
Geropiga
Ginsling
Gluhwein
Highball
Hollands
Homebrew
Hydromel
Lemonade
Mahogany
Nepenthe
Nightcap
Persicot
Pilsener
Ragmaker
Red biddy
Regmaker

Resinata
Resinate
Rice beer
Riesling
Rosoglio
Sangaree
Schnapps
Skokiaan
Snowball
Spritzer
Switchel
Tequilla
Tincture
Vermouth
Witblits

9 letters:
Applejack
Aqua-vitae
Ayahuasco
Badminton
Buck's fizz
Calabogus
Champagne
Chocolate

Claret cup
Cream soda
Cuba libre
Eccoccino
Febrifuge
Firewater
Gingerade
Grenadine
Hippocras
Lambswool
Manhattan
Metheglin
Milk punch
Milkshake
Mint julep
Moose milk
Nipperkin
Refresher
Sauternes
Slivovica
Slivovitz
Snakebite
Stiffener
Sundowner
The cratur

Whisky mac

10 letters:
Blackstone
Bloody Mary
Buttermilk
Chartreuse®
Lolly water
Maraschino
Mickey Finn
Piña colada
Pousse-café
Shandygaff
Tom Collins

11 letters:
Aguardiente
Amontillado
Benedictine
Black and tan
Black velvet
Boiler-maker
Doch-an-doris
Half-and-half
Niersteiner

Screwdriver
Soapolallie
Tom and Jerry
Whiskey sour

12 letters:
Deoch-an-doris
Doch-an-dorach
Doch-an-doruis
Humpty-dumpty
Jimmy Woodser
Marcobrunner
Old-fashioned
Sarsaparilla

13 letters:
Deoch-an-doruis
Mops and brooms
Prairie oyster

14 letters:
John Barleycorn

Drink store Cellar
Drip Bore, Dew-drop, Dribble, Drop, Gutter, IV, Leak, Post-nasal, Saline, Seep, Splatter, Stillicide, Trickle, Wimp
Dripstone Label, Larmier
Drive(r), Driving, Drive out AA, Acquired, Actuate, Amber gambler, Ambition, Backseat, Banish, Beetle, Bullocky, Ca', Cabby, Campaign, Carman, Chain, Charioteer, Chauffeur, Coachee, Coact, Crankshaft, Crew, Crowd, Designated, Disk, Dislodge, Dr, Drover, Drum, Economy, Eject, Emboss, Energy, Enew, Enforce, Engine, Expatriate, Faze, Feeze, Ferret, Fire, Firk, Flexible, Fluid, Force, Four-stroke, Four-wheel, Front-wheel, Fuel, Gadsman, Goad, Hack, Hammer, Haste, Heard, Helmsman, Herd, Hie, Hoon, Hoosh, Hot-rod, Hoy, Hunt, Hurl, Impact, Impel, Impetus, Impinge, Impulse, Jarvey, Jehu, Jockey, Juggernaut, Lash, Libido, Locoman, Lunge, Mahout, Make, Mall, Miz(z)en, Motor, Motorman, Offensive, Overland, Peg, Penetrate, Phase, Piston, Power, Powertrain, Propel, Puncher, Put, RAC, Rack, Ram, Rebut, Reinsman, Ride, Road, Roadhog, Run, Scorch, Screw, Scud, Shepherd, Shoo, Spank, Spin, Spur, Start, Stroke, Sumpter-horse, Sunday, Sweep, Tape, Task-master, Teamster, Tee, Test, Thrust, Toad, Tool, Torrential, Trot, Truckie, Tup, Two-stroke, Urge, Urgence, Vetturino, Wagoner, Whist, Wood, Wreak
Drivel Balderdash, Blether(skate), Drip, Drool, Humbug, Maunder, Nonsense, Pabulum, Pap, Rot, Salivate, Slaver
Driving club AA, Iron, RAC
Drizzle Drow, Haze, Mist, Mizzle, Roke, Scouther, Scowther, Serein, Skiffle, Smir(r), Smur, Spit
Droll Bizarre, Comic, Funny, Jocular, Queer, Waggish
Drone Bee, Buzz, Dog-bee, Doodle, Dor(r), Drant, Draunt, Drawl, Hanger-on,

Hum, Idler, Parasite, Tamboura, Thrum, Windbag

Drool Drivel, Gibber, Salivate, Slaver

Droop(y), **Drooping** Cernuous, Decline, Flaccid, Flag, Languish, Lill, Limp, Lob, Loll, Lop, Nutate, Oorie, Ourie, Owrie, Peak, Ptosis, > **SAG**, Slink, Slouch, Weeping, Welk(e), Wilt, Wither

Drop(s), **Dropping** Acid, Airlift, Apraxia, Bag, Bead, Beres, Blob, Cadence, Calve, Cascade, Cast, Chocolate, Cowpat, Dap, Delayed, Descent, Deselect, Dink, Dip, Downturn, Drappie, Drib(let), Ease, Ebb, Escarp(ment), Fall, Floor, Flop, Fruit, Fumet, Gallows, Globule, Gout(te), Guano, Gutta, Guttate, Instil, Knockout, Land, Minim, Modicum, Muff, Mute, Omit, Pilot, Plonk, Plummet, Plump, Plunge, Plunk, Precepit, Precipice, (Prince) Rupert's, Rain, Scat, Scrap, Shed, Sip, Skat, Spraint, Stilliform, Tass, Taste, Tear, Virga, Wrist

Drop-out Beatnik, Hippie, Hippy

Drop-shot Dink

Dropsy Anasarca, Ascites, Edema, Oedema

Dross Chaff, Dregs, Recrement, Scoria, Scorious, Scum, Sinter, Slack, Slag, Waste

Drought Dearth, Drouth, Lack, Thirst

Drove(r) Band, Crowd, Flock, Herd, Host, Masses, Overlander, Puncher

Drown(ed), **Drowning** Drench, Drent, Drook, Drouk, Engulf, Inundate, Noyade, Overcome, Sorrows, Submerge

Drowse, **Drowsiness**, **Drowsy** Blet, Comatose, Doze, Hypnagogic, Hypnopompic, Lethargic, Nap, Narcolepsy, Narcosis, Nod, Snooze

Drub Anoint, Thrash

Drudge(ry) Devil, Dogsbody, Donkey-work, Fag, Grind, Hack, Jackal, Johnson, Plod, Scrub, Slave(y), Snake, Sweat, Swink, Thraldom, Toil, Trauchle, Treadmill

Drug(ged) Acaricide, ACE inhibitor, Anti-depressant, AZT, Bag, Barbiturate, Base, Blow, Bolus, Bomber, Boo, Botanical, Cholagogue, Deck, Depressant, Designer, DET, Diuretic, Dope, Downer, E, Ecbolic, Ecphractic, Elixir, Emmenagogue, Errhine, Euphoriant, Fantasy, Fertility, Fig, Galenical, Gateway, Hallucinogen, Hard, High, Homeopathy, Immunosuppressant, Knockout drops, Largactic, Lifestyle, Line, Load, Mainline, Medicine, Miracle, Nervine, Nobble, OD, Opiate, Painkiller, Paregoric, Parenteral, Peace, Pharmaceutics, Pharmacopoeia, Poison, Popper, Prophylactic, Psychedelic, Psychoactive, Psychodelic, Recreational, Scag, Sedate, Sialogogue, Snort, Soft, Soporific, Sorbefacient, Speedball, Spermicide, Spike, Statin, Stimulant, Stone(d), Stupefacient, Stupefy, Substance, Synthetic, Tranquiliser, Truth, Upper, Vermicide, Weed, White stuff, Wonder, Wrap, Zeolitic

DRUGS

1 letter:	Tea	Soma	Grass
Q		Toot	Hocus
	4 letters:		Intal®
3 letters:	Acid	**5 letters:**	L-dopa
Eve	Adam	Aloes	Mummy
Hop	Bang	Benny	Opium
Ice	Bute	Bhang	Quina
INH	Dopa	Candy	Rutin
LSD	Hemp	Crank	Salep
PCP®	Junk	Dagga	Salop
Tab	Sida	Ganja	Senna

- Speed
- Sugar
- Sulfa
- Taxol
- Zyban

6 letters:
- Amulet
- Ativan®
- Charas
- Curare
- Dragée
- Heroin
- Inulin
- Joypop
- Mescla
- Mummia
- Nubain®
- Peyote
- Pituri
- Prozac®
- Saloop
- Sulpha
- Valium®
- Viagra®

7 letters:
- Atabrin
- Atebrin®
- Botanic
- Cascara
- Charlie
- Churrus
- Codeine
- Damiana
- Dapsone
- Ecstasy
- Eucaine
- Guarana
- Hashish
- Henbane
- Hypnone
- Insulin
- Jellies
- Librium®
- Metopon
- Miltown®
- Mogadon®
- Morphia
- Nebutal®
- Patulin
- Quinine

- Relenza®
- Ritalin®
- Seconal®
- Septrin®
- Seroxat®
- Steroid
- Suramin
- Trional
- Turpeth
- Veronal®
- Xenical®

8 letters:
- Adjuvant
- Ataraxic
- Banthine
- Curarine
- Diazepam
- Fentanyl
- Goofball
- Hyoscine
- Ketamine
- Laetrile
- Laudanum
- Mersalyl
- Mescalin
- Methadon
- Miticide
- Moonrock
- Morphine
- Naloxone
- Narcotic
- Nepenthe
- Nystatin
- Oxytocic
- Psilocin
- Retrovir®
- Rifampin
- Roborant
- Rohypnol®
- Scopolia
- Serevent®
- Snowball
- Tetronal
- Thiazide
- Varidase
- Veratrin
- Viricide
- Zerumbet

9 letters:
- Acyclovir

- Analeptic
- Angel-dust
- Anovulant
- Antrycide
- Augmentin
- Barbitone
- Biguanide
- Busulphan
- Captopril
- Carbachol
- Cisplatin
- Clozapine
- Compound Q
- Corticoid
- Cyclizine
- Digitalis
- Dramamine®
- Electuary
- Ephedrine
- Foscarnet
- Frusemide
- Ibuprofen
- Iprindole
- Isoniazid
- Jaborandi
- Lorazepam
- Mepacrine
- Methadone
- Mydriasis
- Novocaine
- Nux vomica
- Oxycontin®
- Paludrine®
- Pethidine
- Phenytoin
- Practolol
- Quinidine
- Quinquina
- Reserpine
- Sudorific
- Synergist
- Tamoxifen
- Temazepam
- Teniacide
- Totaquine
- Trinitrum
- Verapamil
- Veratrine
- Vermifuge
- Wobbly egg

10 letters:
- Amantadine
- Ampicillin
- Antagonist
- Anxiolytic
- Atracurium
- Belladonna
- Benzedrine
- Bufotenine
- Cimetidine
- Clofibrate
- Clomiphene
- Colestipol
- Disulfiram
- Ergotamine
- Ethambutol
- Fluoxetine
- Formestane
- Imipramine
- Indapamide
- Isoniazide
- Ivermectin
- Mefloquine
- Nalbuphine
- Nifedipine
- Nitrazepam
- Papaverine
- Paroxetine
- Penicillin
- Pentaquine
- Phenacetin
- Prednisone
- Primaquine
- Probenecid
- Propanolol
- Psilocybin
- Rifampicin
- Salbutamol
- Selegiline
- Stramonium
- Sucralfate
- Taeniacide
- Zidovudine

11 letters:
- Aminobutene
- Amphetamine
- Beta-blocker
- Carbimazole
- Chloroquine
- Ciclosporin
- Cinnarizine

Clenbuterol
Clindamycin
Cyclosporin
Deserpidine
Distalgesic
Fluconazole
Fluvoxamine
Galantamine
Gemfibrozil
Haloperidol
Ipratropium
Isoxsuprine
Magic bullet
Meprobamate
Nikethamide
Paracetamol
Pentamidine
Pentazocine
Pravastatin

Purple heart
Succedaneum
Thalidomide
Theobromine
Tolbutamide
Tous-les-mois
Tropomyosin
Vinblastine
Vincristine

12 letters:
Alpha-blocker
Anthelmintic
Antiperiodic
Arsphenamine
Azathioprine
Chlorambucil
Fluphenazine
Gonadotropin

Guanethidine
Indomethacin
Methaqualone
Methotrexate
Mifepristone
Perphenazine
Physotigmine
Promethazine
Salicylamide
Streptomycin
Trimethoprim

13 letters:
Amitriptyline
Anthelminthic
Antihistamine
Carbamazepine
Flunitrazepam
Materia medica

Nitroglycerin
Penicillamine
Phencyclidine
Pyrimethamine
Sulphadiazine
Thiabendazole
Triamcinolone

14 letters:
Bendrofluozide
Butyrhophenone
Flucloxacillin
Norethisterone
Pentobarbitone
Phenacyclidine
Phenobarbitone
Phenylbutazone
Sulphanilamide

Druid Gorsedd
Drum(mer), Drumming, Drumbeat Arête, Atabal, Barrel, Beatbox, Bodhran, Bongo, Brake, Carousel, Chamade, Conga, Dash-wheel, Devil's tattoo, Dhol, Djembe, Dr, Drub, Ear, Flam, Gran cassa, Kettle, Lambeg, Mridamgam, Mridang(a), Mridangam, Myringa, Naker, Ngoma, Oil, Pan, Paradiddle, Percussion, Rappel, Rataplan, Reel, Rep, Ridge, Rigger, Roll, Ruff, Ruffle, Salesman, Side, Skin, Snare, Steel, Tabla, Tabour, Tabret, Tambourine, Tam-tam, Tap, Tattoo, Thrum, Timbal, Timp(ano), Tom-tom, Touk, Traps, Traveller, Tuck, Tymbal, Tympanist, Tympano, Whim, Winding, Work
Drum-belly Hoven
Drumstick Attorney, Leg, Rute
Drunk(ard) see **DRINK**
Drunken may indicate an anagram
Drupe Tryma
Druse Crystal
Dry(ing), Drier Air, Anhydrous, Arefaction, Arefy, Arid, Blot, Bone, Brut, Corpse, Crine, Dehydrate, Desiccate, Detox, Drain, Dull, Ensear, Evaporate, Exsiccator, Firlot, Fork, Harmattan, Hasky, Hi(r)stie, Humidor, Hydrate, Jejune, Jerk, Khor, Kiln, Mummify, Oast, > **PARCH**, Prosaic, Reast, Reist, Rizzar, Rizzer, Rizzor, Sciroc, Scorch, Sear, Sec(co), Seco, Sere, Shrivel, Siccative, Siroc(co), Sober, Sponge, Steme, Stove, Ted, Thirsty, Thristy, Toasted, Torrefy, Torrid, Towel, Tribble, Trocken, TT, Unwatery, Watertight, Welt, Wilt, Win(n), Wipe, Wither, Wizened, Xeransis, Xerasia, Xero(sis), Xerostomia
Dryad Eurydice, Nymph
Dry fruit, Dried fruit Achene, Akene, Currant, Mebos, Prune, Raisin, Samara, Silicula, Siliqua, Silique, Sultana
Dry mouth Xerostoma
DT's Dingbats, Hallucinations, Zooscopic
Dual Double, Twin, Twofold
Dub Array, > **CALL**, Entitle, Hete, Knight, Name
Dubious Doubtful, Equivocal, Fishy, Fly-by-night, Hesitant, Iffy, Improbable, Questionable, Scepsis, Sceptical, Sesey, Sessa, > **SHADY**, Shonky, Suspect, Touch

and go, Unlikely

▷ **Dubious** *may indicate* an anagram

Dubliner Jackeen

Duce Leader, Musso(lini)

Duchess Anastasia, Malfi, Peeress, Titled

Duchy Brabant, Cornwall, Dukedom, Franconia, Grand, Limburg, Luxembourg, Nassu, Omnium, Realm, Swabia, Valois, Westphalian

Duck(ling), Ducked Amphibian, Avoid, Aylesbury, Bald-pate, Bargander, Bergander, Blob, Blue, Bluebill, Bob, Broadbill, Bufflehead, Bum(m)alo, Canard, Canvasback, > **COUPLE OF DUCKS**, Dead, Dearie, Decoy, Dip, Diving, Dodge, Dodo, Douse, Drook, Drouk, Dunk(er), Eider, Enew, Escape, Evade, Ferruginous, Flapper, Gadwall, Garganey, Garrot, Golden-eye, Goosander, Greenhead, Hareld, Harlequin, Heads, Herald, Immerse, Indian runner, Jook, Jouk, Lame, Long-tailed, Mallard, Mandarin, Muscovy, Musk, Nil, Nodding, Nun, O, Oldsquaw, Old Tom, Orpington, Paddling, Palmated, Paradise, Pekin(g), Pintail, Plunge, Pochard, Poker, Redhead, Ruddy, Runner, Rush, Scaup, Scoter, Sheld(d)uck, Shieldrake, Shovel(l)er, Shun, Sitting, Smeath, Smee(th), Smew, Sord, Spatula, Spirit, Sprigtail, Steamer, Surf(scoter), Teal, Team, Tufted, Tunker, Ugly, Velvet scoter, Whistling, Widgeon, Wigeon, Wood, Zero

Duckbill Ornithorhynchus, Platypus

Duckwalk Waddle

Duckweed Lemna

Ducky Sweet, Twee

Duct Bile, Canal(iculus), Channel, Conduit, Diffuser, Diffusor, Emunctory, Epididymus, Fistula, Gland, Lachrymal, Lacrimal, Laticifer, Lumen, Parotid, Pipe, Tear, Thoracic, Tube, Ureter, Vas deferens

Dud Bouncer, Failure, Flop, Shan(d), Stumer

Dude Cat, Coxcomb, Dandy, Fop, Lair, Macaroni, Popinjay, Roy

Dudgeon Anger, Hilt, Huff, Pique

Due(s) Adequate, Arrearage, Claim, Debt, Deserts, Forinsec, Geld, Heriot, Just, Lot, Mature, Owing, Reddendo, Rent, Right, > **SUITABLE**, Thereanent, Toll, Tribute, Worthy

Duel(list) Mensur, Monomachy, Principal, Tilt

Duenna Chaperone, Dragon

Duff Bungle, Dough, Nelly, NG, Plum, Pudding, Rustle

Duffer Bungler, Rabbit, Useless

Dug Ploughed, Teat, Titty, Udder

Dugong Halicore, Sea-cow, Sea-pig, Sirenian

Dug-out Abri, Canoe, Piragua, Pirogue, Shelter, Trench, Trough

Duke(dom) Alva, Clarence, D, Ellington, Fist, Iron, Milan, Orsino, Peer, Prospero, Rohan, Wellington

Dulcimer Cembalo, Citole, Cymbalo, Santir, Sant(o)ur

Dull(ard), Dullness Anorak, Bald, Banal, Barren, Besot, Bland, Blear, Blunt, Boeotian, Boring, Cloudy, Commonplace, Dead (and alive), Deadhead, Dense, Dim, Dinge, Dingy, Ditchwater, Doldrums, Dowf, Dowie, Drab, Drear, Dreich, Dry, Dunce, Faded, Flat, Fozy, Grey, Heavy, Hebetate, Ho-hum, Humdrum, Illustrious, Insipid, Jejune, Lacklustre, Lifeless, Log(y), Lowlight, Mat(t), Matte, Monotonous, Mopish, Mull, Obtund, Obtuse, Opacity, Opiate, Ordinary, Overcast, Owlish, Pall, Pedestrian, Perstringe, Podunk, Prosaic, Prose, Prosy, Rebate, Rust, Slow, Sopite, Staid, Stick, Stodger, Stodgy, Stolid, Stuffy, Stultify, > **STUPID**, Sunless, Tame, Tarnish, Tedious, Ticky-tacky,

Toneless, Torpor, Treadmill, Tubby, Vapid, Wonk, Wooden, Zoid

Dumb(ness) Alalia, Aphonic, Crambo, Hobbididance, Inarticulate, Mute, Silent, Stupid

Dumbfound(ed) Amaze, Astound, Flabbergast, Stun, Stupefy, Stupent

Dumb ox Aquinas

Dummy Comforter, Copy, Effigy, Fathead, Flathead, Mannequin, Mannikin, Mock-up, Model, Pacifier, Quintain, Soother, Table, Teat, Waxwork

Dump(ing), Dumps Abandon, Blue, Core, Dejection, Dispirited, Doldrums, Empty, Fly-tipping, Hole, Jettison, Junk, Mine, Scrap, Shoot, Store(house), Tip, Unlade, Unload

Dumpling Dim sum, Dough(boy), Gnocchi, Knaidel, Knaidloch, Kneidlach, Knish, Kreplach, Matzoball, Norfolk, Quenelle, Ribaude, Suet, Won ton

Dumpy Pudgy, Squat

Dun Annoy, Cow, Importune, Pester, > SUE, Tan

Duncan Isadora

Dunce Analphabet, Booby, Dolt, Donkey, Dullard, Fathead, Schmo, Schmuck, Schnook, Stupid

Dune Areg, Bar, Barchan(e), Bark(h)an, Erg, Sandbank, Seif, Star, Whaleback

Dung(hill) Argol, Buttons, Chip, Coprolite, Cowpat, Droppings, Fewmet, Fumet, Fumiculous, Guano, Hing, Manure, Midden, Mixen, Mute, Ordure, Puer, Pure, Scat, Scumber, Shard, Sharn, Siege, Skat, Skummer, Sombrerite, Sombrero, Spraint, Stercoraceous, Tath

Dungarees Overalls

Dung-eating Merdiverous

Dungeon Bastille, Cell, Confine, Donjon, Durance, Oubliette, Souterrain

Dunk Immerse, Sop, Steep

Dunnock Accentor

Duo Couple, Pair, Twosome

Dupe Catspaw, Chiaus, Chouse, Cony, Cully, Delude, Geck, Gull, Hoax, Hoodwink, Mug, Pawn, Pigeon, Plover, Sitter, Sucker, Swindle, > TRICK, Victim

Duplex Twofold

Duplicate, Duplicator Clone, Copy, Cyclostyle, Double, Facsimile, Match, Ozalid®, Replica, Reproduce, Roneo®, Spare

Durable Enduring, Eternal, Eterne, Hardy, Lasting, Permanent, Stout, Tough

Duralumin® Y-alloy

Duration Extent, Period, Span

Duress Coercion, Pressure, Restraint

Durham Palatine

During Amid, Dia-, For, In, Over, Throughout, While, Whilst

Dusk(y) Dark, Dewfall, Dun, Eve, Gloaming, Gloom, Owl-light, Phaeic, Twilight, Umbrose

Dust(y) Arid, Ash, Bo(a)rt, Calima, Clean, Coom, Cosmic, Culm, Derris, Devil, Duff, Earth, Fuss, Khaki, Lemel, Limail, Lo(e)ss, Miller, Nebula, Pellum, Pollen, Pother, Pouder, Poudre, Powder, Pozz(u)olana, Pudder, Rouge, Seed, Shaitan, Slack, Stour, Talc, Volcanic, Wipe

> **Dusted** *may indicate* an anagram

Duster Cloth, Feather, Red, Talcum, Torchon

Dustman Doolittle, Garbo(logist), Scaffie

Dust measure Konimeter, Koniscope

Dutch(man), Dutchwoman Batavian, Boor, Cape, Courage, D(u), Double, Elm, Erasmus, Flying, Frow, Kitchen, Knickerbocker, Middle, Mynheer, Parnell shout, Patron, Pennsylvania, Sooterkin, Taal, Wife

Dutiful, Duty Active, Ahimsa, Average, Blench, Bond, Charge, Corvee, Customs, Death, Debt, Deontology, Devoir, Docile, Drow, Due, Duplicand, End, Estate, Excise, Fatigue, Feu, Function, Heriot, Homage, Imposition, Impost, Incumbent, Lastage, Likin, Mission, Mistery, Mystery, Obedient, Obligation, Octroi, Office, Onus, Pia, Picket, Pious, Point, Prisage, Probate, Rota, Sentry-go, Shift, Stamp, Stillicide, Stint, Succession, Tariff, > **TASK**, Tax, Toll, Transit, Trow, Watch, Zabeta

Duvet Doona, Quilt

Dwarf(ism) Achondroplasia, Agate, Alberich, Andvari, Ateleiosis, Bashful, Belittle, Bes, Black, Bonsai, Brown, Doc, Dopey, Droich, Drow, Durgan, Elf, Gnome, Grumpy, Happy, Hobbit, Homuncle, Hop o' my thumb, Knurl, Laurin, Little man, Man(n)ikin, > **MIDGET**, Mime, Minikin, Minim, Nanism, Nectabanus, Ni(e)belung, Nurl, Overshadow, Pacolet, Pigmy, Pygmy, Red, Regin, Ront, Rumpelstiltskin, Runt, Skrimp, Sleepy, Sneezy, > **STUNT**, Tiddler, Titch, Tokoloshe, Tom Thumb, Toy, Troll, Trow, White

Dwell(er), Dwelling Abide, Be, Bungalow, Cabin, Cell, Cot(tage), Descant, Discourse, Domicile, Habitation, Harp, Heteroscian, Hogan, House, Hut, Laura, Lavra, Live, Lodge, Longhouse, Maison(n)ette, Mansion, Messuage, Palafitte, Pied-à-terre, Pueblo, Reside, Roof, Tenement, Tepee, Terramara, Tipi, Weem, Wigwam, Won(ing), Woon

Dwindle Decline, Diminish, Fade, Lessen, Peter, Shrink, Wane

Dye(ing), Dyestuff Acid, Alkanet, Amaranth, Anil, Anthracene, Anthraquinone, Archil, Azo(benzine), Azurine, Bat(t)ik, Brazil(e)in, Burnt umber, Camwood, Canthaxanthin, Carthamine, Catechin, Chay(a), Chica, Chicha, Chico, Choy, Cinnabar, Cobalt, Cochineal, Colour, Congo, Corkir, Crocein, Crotal, Crottle, Cudbear, Dinitrobenzene, Direct, Embrue, Engrain, Envermeil, Eosin, Flavin(e), Fluoxene, Fuchsin(e), Fustic, Fustoc, Gambi(e)r, Gentian violet, Grain, Haematoxylin, Henna, Hue, Ikat, Imbrue, Imbue, Incardine, Indamine, Indican, Indigo, Indigocarmine, Indirubin, Indoxyl, Indulin(e), Ingrain, Kalamkari, Kamala, Kermes, Kohl, Korkir, Madder, Magenta, Mauvein(e), Methyl violet, Murex, Myrobalan, Nigrosin(e), Orcein, Orchel(la), Orchil, Para-red, Phenolphthalein, Phthalein, > **PIGMENT**, Primuline, Puccoon, Purpurin, Pyronine, Quercitron, Quinoline, Raddle, Resorcinol, Rhodamine, Rosanilin(e), Safranin(e), Shaya, > **STAIN**, Stone-rag, Stone-raw, Sumac(h), Sunfast, Tannin, Tartrazine, Tie-dye, Tinct, Tint, Tropaeolin, Turnsole, Valonia, Vat, Wald, Weld, Woad, Woald, Wold, Xanthium, Xylidine

▶ **Dying** *see* DIE

Dyke Aboideau, Aboiteau, Bund, Devil's, > **DIKE**, Gall, Offa's

Dynamic Ballistics, Energetic, Forceful, Gogo, High-powered, Potent

Dynamite Blast, Explode, Gelignite, Giant-powder, TNT, Trotyl

Dynamo Alternator, Armature

Dynasty Angevin, Bourbon, Capetian, Carolingian, Chin(g), Ch'ing, Chou, Era, Gupta, Habsburg, Han, Hapsburg, Honan, House(hold), Hyksos, Khan, Manchu, Maurya, Merovingian, Ming, Pahlavi, Ptolemy, Qajar, Q'ing, Rameses, Romanov, Rule, Safavid, Saga, Sassanid, Seleucid, Seljuk, Shang, Song, Sui, Sung, Tai-ping, Tang, Tudor, Wei, Yi, Yuan, Zhou

Dysentery Bloody flux, Slugellosis

Dyslexia Strephosymbolia

Dyspeptic Cacogastric

Dysprosium Dy

Dystrophy Duchenne's, Muscular

Ee

E Boat, East, Echo, Energy, English, Spain

Each All, Apiece, Ea, > **EVERY**, Ilka, Per, Severally

Eager(ly) Agog, Antsy, Ardent, Avid, Beaver, Bore, Earnest, Enthusiastic, Fain, Fervent, Fervid, Frack, Gung-ho, Hot, Intent, > **KEEN**, Perfervid, Race, Raring, Rath(e), Ready, Roost, Sharp-set, Sore, Spoiling, Thirsty, Toey, Wishing, Yare

Eagle Al(l)erion, American, Aquila, Bald, Bateleur, Berghaan, Bird, Double, Erne, Ethon, Fish, Gier, Golden, Harpy, Hawk, Legal, Lettern, Nisus, Ossifrage, Sea, Spread, Tawny, Wedge-tailed

Ear(drum), Ear trouble Ant(i)helix, Attention, Audience, Auricle, Barotitis, Cauliflower, Cochlea, Concha, Conchitis, Deafness, Dionysius, Dolichotus, External, Glue, Hearing, Helix, Icker, Incus, Inner, Internal, Jenkins, Kieselguhr, Labyrinth, Labyrinthitis, Listen, Locusta, Lop, Lug, Malleus, Middle, Modiolus, Myringa, Myringitis, Nubbin, Otalgia, Otalgy, Otic, Paracusis, Paramastoid, Parotic, Pavilion, Periotic, Petrosal, Phonic, Pinna, Prootic, Spike, Thick, Tin, Tragus, Tympanitis, Utricle

Earl(dom) Belted, Mar, Peer, Sandwich

Earlier, Early Above, Ago, Ahead, Alsoon, AM, Antelucan, Auld, Betimes, Cockcrow, Daybreak, Ere-now, Ex, Germinal, Incipient, Or, Precocious, Precursor, Prehistoric, Premature, Prevernal, Previous, Primeval, Primordial, Prior, Rath(e), Rath(e)ripe, Rear, Rudimentary, Soon, Timely, Tim(e)ous

> **Early** *may indicate* belonging to an earl

Early man Eoanthropus, Flat-earther

> **Early stages of** *may indicate* first one or two letters of the word(s) following

Earmark Allocate, Bag, Book, Characteristic, > **RESERVE**, Tag, Target

Earn(er), Earnings Achieve, Addle, Breadwinner, Deserve, Digerati, Gain, Income, Invisible, Make, Merit, O.T.E., Win

Earnest Ardent, Arle(s)(-penny), Deposit, Fervent, Imprest, Intent, Promise, Serious, Token, Zealous

Earring Drop, Hoop, Keeper, Pendant, Sleeper, Snap, Stud

Earshot Hail, Hearing

Earth(y) Alkaline, Antichthon, Art, Asthenosphere, Brown, Capricorn, Clay, Cloam, Cologne, Craton, Diatomite, Dirt, Drey, Dust, E, Eard, Edaphic, Epigene, Foxhole, Friable, Fuller's, Gaea, Gaia, Gault, Ge, Globe, Ground, Horst, Infusiorial, Kadi, Lair, Leaf-mould, Lemnian, Lithosphere, Loam, Malm, Mankind, Mantle, Mools, Mould, Mouls, Papa, Pise, Planet, Rabelaisian, Racy, Rare, Red, Seat, Sett, Sod, > **SOIL**, Subsoil, Taurus, Telluric, Tellus, Terra, Terrain, Terramara, Terrene, Topsoil, Tripoli, Virgo, Wad, Ye(a)rd, Yellow, Yird

Earth-bound Chthonian

Earthenware Arretine, Biscuit, Ceramic, Creamware, Crock(ery), Delf(t), Della-robbia, Delph, Faience, Figuline, Maiolica, Majolica, Pig, Pot, Queen's ware, Raku, Samian, Terracotta

Earthquake Aftershock, Bradyseism, Foreshock, Mercalli, Richter, Seism, Shake, Shock, Temblor, Tremor

Earth's surface Sal, Sial
Earthwork Agger, Bank, Cursus, Gazon, Parados, Rampart, Remblai, Vallum
Earthworm Angledug, Angletwitch, Angleworm, Annelid, Bait, Night-crawler
Earwig Clipshear(s), Forkit-tail, Forky-tail
Ease, Easing, Easygoing Alleviate, Carefree, Clear, Clover, Comfort, Content, Defuse, Deregulate, Détente, Facility, Hands down, Informal, Lax, Mellow, Mid(dy), Mitigate, Palliate, Peace, Pococurante, Quiet, Relieve, Reposal, Repose, Soothe
East(erly), Eastward Anglia, Asia, Chevet, E, Eassel, Eassil, Eothen, Eurus, Levant, Middle, Near, Orient, Ost, Sunrise
Easter Festival, Island, Pace, Pasch, Pasque
Eastern(er), Eastern language Asian, Kolarian, Oriental, Virginian
East European Lettic, Slovene
Easy, Easily ABC, Breeze, Cakewalk, Carefree, Child's play, Cinch, Cushy, Dagage, Doddle, Eath(e), Ethe, Facile, Free, Gift, Glib, Hands down, Independent, Jammy, Lax, Light, Midshipman, Natural, Nimps, Oldster, Picnic, Pie, Pushover, Simple, Sitter, Snotty, Soft, Tolerant, User-friendly, Walk-over, Well, Yare
▷ **Easy** *may indicate* an anagram
Eat(able), Eater, Eating Bite, Bolt, Champ, Chop, Commensal, Consume, Corrode, Edible, Edite, Endew, Endue, Erode, Esculent, Etch, Fare, Feast, > **FEED**, Fret, Gastronome, Gnaw, Go, Gobble, Graze, Grub, Hog, Hyperphagia, Ingest, Manducate, Munch, Nosh, Nutritive, Omnivore, Partake, Phagophobia, Predate, Refect, Scoff, Stuff, Sup, Swallow, Syssitia, Take, Taste, Trencherman, Trophesy, Whale
Eavesdrop(per) Cowan, Earwig, Icicle, Listen, Overhear, Pry, Snoop, Stillicide, Tab-hag, Tap, Wiretap
Ebb(ing) Abate, Decline, Recede, Refluent, Sink, > **WANE**
Ebony Black, Cocus-wood, Coromandel, Hebenon, Jamaican
Ebullient Brash, Effervescent, Exuberant, Fervid
Eccentric Abnormal, Cam, Card, Character, Crank, Curious, Daffy, Dag, Deviant, Dingbat, Ditsy, Ditzy, E, Farouche, Fey, Fie, Freak, Fruitcake, Geek, Gonzo, Iffish, Irregular, Kinky, Kook(y), Mattoid, Nutcase, Nutter, Odd(ball), Offbeat, Off-centre, Off the wall, Original, Outré, > **PECULIAR**, Phantasime, Pixil(l)ated, Queer, Quirky, Quiz, Rake, Raky, Recondite, Rum, Scatty, Screwball, Screwy, Squirrelly, Wack(y), Way-out, Weird(o), W(h)acko
▷ **Eccentric** *may indicate* an anagram
Ecclesiastic Abbé, Clergyman, Clerical, Lector, Secular, Theologian
Echelon Formation
Echinoderm Asteroidea, Basket-star, Brittle-star, Comatulid, Crinoid, Heart-urchin, Sea-egg, Sea-lily, Sea-urchin, Starfish
Echo Angel, Answer, Ditto, E, Imitate, Iterate, Rebound, Repeat, Repercussion, Reply, Resonant, > **RESOUND**, Respeak, Reverb(erate), Revoice, Ring, Rote, Tape
Eclat Flourish, Glory, Prestige, Renown
Eclectic Babist, Broad, Complex, Liberal
Eclipse Annular, Block, Cloud, Deliquium, Hide, Lunar, Obscure, Occultation, Outmatch, Outweigh, Overshadow, Partial, Penumbra, Solar, Total, Transcend
Eclogue Bucolic, Idyll, Pastoral
Eco-community Seral
Economic(s), Economise Budget, Conserve, Dismal science, Eke, Entrench, Husband, Intrench, Pinch, Retrench, Scrimp, Skimp, Spare, Sparing, Stagflation, > **STINT**, Supply-side, Welfare

Economist Angell, Bentham, Chrematist, Cole, Friedman, Keynes, Malthus, Marginalist, Meade, Mill, Pareto, Physiocrat, Ricardo, Tinbergen, Toynbee, Veblen, Webb

Economy, Economic(al), Economics Agronomy, Black, Careful, Cliometrics, Command, Conversation, Frugal, Knowledge, Market, Mixed, Neat, New, Parsimony, Planned, Political, Retrenchment, Shoestring, Siege, Stakeholder, Thrift, Tiger, Token

Ecstasy, Ecstatic Bliss, Delight, Delirious, Dove, E, Exultant, Joy, Liquid, Lyrical, Nympholepsy, Rapture, Rhapsodic, Sent, Trance, Transport

Ecumenical Catholic, Lateran

Eczema Pompholyx

Eddy Backset, Curl, Gurge, Maelstrom, Nelson, Pirl, Purl, Rotor, Sousehole, Swelchie, Swirl, Vortex, Weel, Well, Whirlpool, Wiel

Eden Bliss, Fall, Heaven, Paradise, PM, Utopia

Edentate Ant-eater, Armadillo, Sloth, Tatou, Xenarthra

Edge, Edging, Edgy Advantage, Arris, Border, Bordure, Brim, Brink, Brittle, Brown, Burr, Chamfer, Chimb, Chime, Chine, Coaming, Costa, Cutting, Dag, Deckle, End, Flange, Flounce, Frill, Fringe, Frontier, Furbelow, Gunnel, Gunwale, Hem, Hone, Inch, Inside, Kerb, Knife, Leading, Leech, Limb(ate), Limbus, Limit, Lip, List, Lute, Marge(nt), Margin, Nosing, Orle, Outside, Parapet, Periphery, Picot, Pikadell, Piping, Rand, Rim, Rund, Rymme, Selvage, Selvedge, Sidle, Skirt, Strand, Trailing, Trim, Tyre, Verge, Wear

▸ **Edible** *see* EAT(ABLE)

Edict Ban, Bull, Decree, Decretal, Extravagantes, Fatwa, Firman, Interim, Irade, Nantes, Notice, Pragmatic, Proclamation, Pronunciamento, Rescript, Ukase

Edifice Booth, Building, Structure

Edify Instruct, Teach

Edinburgh Auld Reekie

Edit(or), Editorial Abridge, Article, City, Copy (read), Cut, Dele, Emend, Expurgate, Garble, Leader, Prepare, Recense, Redact, Revise, Seaman

> **Edited** *may indicate* an anagram

Edition Aldine, Bulldog, Bullpup, Ed, Extra, Ghost, Hexapla(r), Impression, Issue, Library, Limited, Number, Omnibus, Trade, Variorium, Version

Edmond, Edmund Burke, Gosse, Ironside(s), Rostand, Spenser

Educate(d) Baboo, Babu, Enlighten, Evolué, Informed, Instruct, Learned, Noursle, Nousell, Nousle, Nurture, Nuzzle, Polymath, Preppy, Scholarly, School, > TEACH, Train, Yuppie

Education(alist) Adult, B.Ed, Classical, Conductive, Didactics, Further, Heurism, Learning, Mainstream, Montessori, Paedotrophy, Pedagogue, Pestalozzi, Physical, Piarist, Primary, Schooling, Steiner, Teacher, Tertiary, Upbringing

Educe Elicit, Evoke, Extract, Infer

Edward Confessor, Ed, Elder, Lear, Martyr, Ned, Ted

Eel Conger, Congo, Electric, Elver, Glass, Grig, Gulper, Gunnel, Hagfish, Kingklip, Lamper, Lamprey, Lant, Launce, Leptocephalus, Moray, Murray, Murr(e)y, Olm, Paste, Sand(ling), Silver belly, Snig, Spitchcock, Tuna, Vinegar, Wheat, Wolf

Eerie Spooky, Uncanny, Unked, Weird

Efface Cancel, Delete, Dislimn, > ERASE, Expunge, Obliterate

Effect(s), Effective(ness), Effectual Able, Achieve, Acting, Auger, Babinski, Bags, Barkhausen, Belongings, Bit, Bohr, Border, Bricolage, Butterfly, Causal, C(h)erenkov, Chromakey, Coanda, Competent, Compton, Consequence,

Coriolis, Domino, Doppler, Dr(y)ice, Eclat, Efficacious, Enact, End, Estate, Experimenter, Foley, Fringe, Functional, Fungibles, Gear, Goods, Greenhouse, Ground, Gunn, Halo, Hawthorne, Home, Horns and halo, Impact, Implement(al), Impression, Introgenic, Josephson, Joule(-Thomson), Kerr, Keystone, Knock-on, Magnus, Meissner, Moire, Mossbauer, Neat, Nisi, Notch, Operant, Optical, Outcome, Ovshinsky, Oxygen, Parallax, Peltier, Perficient, Personal, Phi, Photoelectric, Photovoltaic, Piezoelectric, Piezomagnetic, Pinch, Placebo, Pogo, Position, Potent, Primary, Promulgate, Raman, Ratchet, Recency, Repercussion, > RESULT, Ripple, Schottky, Seebeck, Side, Skin, Sound, Sovereign, Special, Spectrum, Spin-off, Stark, Striking, Stroop, Submarine, Tableau, Teeth, Telling, Thermoelectric, Thomson's, Toxic, Tunnel, Tyndall, Upshot, Valid, Viable, Virtual, Win, Withdrawal, Work, Zeeman

Effeminate Camp, Carpet-knight, Carpet-monger, Cissy, Cookie-pusher, Dildo, Epicene, Female, Gussie, Jessie, Milksop, (Miss) Nancy, Molly(coddle), Panty-waist, Poovy, Prissy, Punce, Sissy, Swish, Tender, Tenderling, Tonk, Unman, Wuss(y)

Effervescence, **Effervescent** Bubbling, Ebullient, Fizz, Frizzante, Pétillant, Soda

▷ **Effervescent** *may indicate* an anagram

Effete Camp, Epigon(e)

Efficacious, **Efficacy** Effective, Operative, Potent, Sovereign, Value

Efficiency, **Efficient** Able, Capable, Competent, Current, Despatch, Electrode, Ergonomics, Luminous, Productivity, Quantum, Smart, Streamlined, Strong, Thermal, Volumetric

Effigy Figure, Guy, Idol, Image, Statua, Statue

Efflorescence Bloom, Blossom, Reh

Effluence, **Effluent**, **Effluvia** Air, Aura, Billabong, Discharge, Fume, Gas, Halitus, Miasma, Odour, Outflow, Outrush

Effort Achievement, Attempt, Best, Conatus, Drive, Essay, Exertion, Fit, Herculean, Labour, Molimen, Nisus, Pains, Rally, Spurt, Stab, Strain, Struggle, > TRY, Work, Yo

Effortless Lenis

Effrontery Audacity, Brass, Cheek, Face, Gall, Neck, Nerve, Temerity

Effulgent Bright, Radiant, Shining

Effuse, **Effusion**, **Effusive** Emanate, Exuberant, Exude, Gush, Lyric, Ode, Outburst, Prattle, Rhapsody, Sanies, Screed, Spill

Eft After

Eg As, Example

Egest Eliminate, Evacuate, Excrete, Void

Egg(s) Abet, Benedict, Berry, Bomb, Caviar(e), Chalaza, Cleidoic, Clutch, Cockney, Collop, Coral, Curate's, Darning, Easter, Edge, Fabergé, Fetus, Flyblow, Foetus, Free-range, Glair(e), Goad, Goog, Graine, Hoy, Incite, Instigate, Layings, Mine, Nest, Nidamentum, Nit, Oocyte, Oophoron, Ostrich, Ova, Ovum, Pace, Plover's, Prairie oyster, Press, Raun, Roe, Scotch, Scrambled, Seed, Spat, Spawn, Spur(ne), Tar(re), Thunder, Tooth, Tread(le), Urge, Whore's, Wind, Yelk, Yolk, Zygote

Egghead Don, Highbrow, Intellectual, Mensa, Pedant

Egg-plant Aubergine, Brinjal

Egg-producer Gametophyte, Hen, Ovipositor

Egg-shaped Obovate, Oval, Ovate

Egg-white Albumen, Glair

Ego(ism), **Egoist** Che, Conceit, I, Narcissism, Not-I, Pride, Self, Solipsism, Ubu,

Vanity

Egocentric Solipsistic

Egregious Eminent, Flagrant, Glaring, Shocking

Egypt(ian), Egyptologist Arab, Cairene, Carter, Cheops, Chephren, Copt(ic), ET, Gippo, Goshen, Gyppo, Imhotep, Nasser, Nefertiti, Nilote, Nitrian, Osiris, Ptolemy, Rameses, Syene, UAR, Wafd, Wog

Eiderdown Bedspread, Duvet, Quilt

Eight(h), Eighth day Acht, Byte, Crew, Cube, Middle, Nundine, Octa, Octad, Octal, Octastrophic, Octave, Octet, Ogdoad, Okta, Ottava, Ure

Eighteen Majority

Eighty R

Einsteinium Es

Either Also, Both, O(u)ther, Such

Ejaculate Blurt, Discharge, Emit, Exclaim

Eject Bounce, Disgorge, Dismiss, Emit, Erupt, Expel, Oust, Propel, Spew, Spit, Spue, Vent

Eke Augment, Eche, Enlarge, Husband, Supplement

Elaborate Detail, Develop, Dressy, Enlarge, Evolve, Florid, Imago, Improve, Intricate, Ornate, Rich, Stretch

Elan Dash, Drive, Esprit, > FLAIR, Gusto, Lotus, Panache, Spirit, Vigour

Elapse Glide, Intervene, Pass

Elastic(ity) Adaptable, Bungee, Buoyant, Dopplerite, Elater, Flexible, Give, Resilient, Rubber, Spandex®, Springy, Stretchy, Tone, Tonus

Elate(d), Elation Cheer, Euphoric, Exalt, Exhilarate, Gladden, Hault, Ruff(e), Uplift

Elbow, Elbow tip Akimbo, Ancon, Angle, Bender, Cubital, Hustle, Joint, Jostle, Justle, Kimbo, Noop, Nudge, Olecranon, Tennis

Elder(ly), Eldest Ancestor, Ancient, Bourtree, Chief, Classis, Eigne, Geriatric, Guru, Kaumatua, Kuia, OAP, Presbyter, > SENIOR, Sire, Susanna, Wallwort

Eldorado Ophir

Eleanor(a) Bron, Duse, Nora(h)

Elect(ed), Election(eer), Electoral Choice, Choose, Chosen, Eatanswill, Elite, General, Gerrymander, Hustings, In, Israelite, Khaki, Off-year, Opt, Pick, PR, Primary, Psephology, Rectorial, Return, Select, Stump

Electrical discharge Corposant, Ion, Zwitterion

Electrical instrument Battery, Charger, Galvaniser, Mains, Resistor, Rheostat, Shoe

Electrical unit Amp(ere), Coulomb, Farad, Kilowatt, Ohm, Volt, Watt

Electric eye Pec

Electrician Gaffer, Lineman, Ohm, Siemens, Sparks, Tesla

Electricity Galvanism, HT, Juice, Mains, Negative, Positive, Power, Static, Vitreous

Electrify Astonish, Galvanise, Startle, Stir, Thrill

Electrode Anode, Cathode, Dynode, Element, Photocathode

Electrolyte Ampholyte

Electromagnet(ic) Abampere, Armature, Oersted, Solenoid, Weber

Electron(ics), Electronic device Cooper pairs, Exciton, FET, Linac, Lone pair, Martenot, Polaron, Quantum, Thermionics, Valence, Valency

Elegance, Elegant Artistic, Bijou, Chic, Classy, Debonair, Fancy, Feat, Finesse, Gainly, Galant, Grace, Jimp, Luxurious, Polished, Recherche, Refined, Ritzy, > SMART, Soigné(e), Suave, Swish, Tall, Urbane

Elegy Dirge, Lament, Poem

Element(s), **Elementary** Abcee, Abecedarian, Absey, Barebones, > COMPONENT, Detail, > ESSENCE, Essential, Factor, Feature, Fuel, Heating, Ideal, Identity, Milieu, Pixel, Primary, Principle, Rare Earth, Simple, Trace, Transition, Weather

ELEMENTS

3 letters:
Air
Tin (Sn)

4 letters:
Atom
Fire
Gold (Au)
Iron (Fe)
Lead (Pb)
Neon (Ne)
Ylem
Zinc (Zn)

5 letters:
Alloy
Argon (Ar)
Boron (B)
Earth
Morph(eme)
Niton
Radon (Rn)
Terra
Water
Xenon (Xe)

6 letters:
Barium (Ba)
Carbon (C)
Cerium (Ce)
Cesium
Cobalt (Co)
Copper (Cu)
Curium (Cm)
Erbium (Er)
Helium (He)
Indium (In)
Iodine (I)
Nickel (Ni)
Osmium (Os)
Oxygen (O)
Radium (Ra)
Silver (Ag)
Sodium (Na)

7 letters:
Arsenic (As)
Bismuth (Bi)
Bromine (Br)
Cadmium (Cd)
Caesium (Cs)
Calcium (Ca)
Dubnium (Db)
Fermium (Fm)
Gallium (Ga)
Hafnium (Hf)
Hahnium (Hn)
Halogen
Hassium (Hs)
Holmium (Ho)
Iridium (Ir)
Isotope
Krypton (Kr)
Lithium (Li)
Mercury (Hg)
Niobium (Nb)
Peltier
Rhenium (Re)
Rhodium (Rh)
Silicon (Si)
Sulphur (S)
Terbium (Tb)
Thorium (Th)
Thulium (Tm)
Uranide
Uranium (U)
Wolfram
Yttrium (Y)

8 letters:
Actinide
Actinium (Ac)
Antimony (Sb)
Astatine (At)
Chlorine (Cl)
Chromium (Cr)
Didymium
Europium (Eu)
Fluorine (F)
Francium (Fr)

Hydrogen (H)
Illinium
Inchoate
Lutetium (Lu)
Masurium
Nebulium
Nitrogen (N)
Nobelium (No)
Platinum (Pt)
Polonium (Po)
Rubidium (Rb)
Samarium (Sm)
Scandium (Sc)
Selenium (Se)
Tantalum (Ta)
Thallium (Tl)
Titanium (Ti)
Tungsten (W)
Vanadium (V)

9 letters:
Alabamine
Aluminium (Al)
Americium (Am)
Berkelium (Bk)
Beryllium (Be)
Brimstone
Columbium
Germanium (Ge)
Joliotium
Lanthanum (La)
Magnesium (Mg)
Manganese (Mn)
Metalloid
Neodymium (Nd)
Neptunium (Np)
Palladium (Pd)
Plutonium (Pu)
Potassium (K)
Ruthenium (Ru)
Strontium (Sr)
Tellurium (Te)
Virginium
Ytterbium (Yb)
Zirconium (Zr)

10 letters:
Dysprosium (D)
Gadolinium (Gd)
Lanthanide
Lawrencium (Lr)
Meitnerium (Mt)
Molybdenum (Mo)
Phlogiston
Phosphorus (P)
Promethium (Pm)
Rudimental
Seaborgium (Sg)
Technetium (Tc)

11 letters:
Californium (Cf)
Einsteinium (Es)
Mendelevium
   (Md)
Transuranic
Unnilennium
   (Une)
Unnilhexium
   (Unh)
Unniloctium
   (Uno)
Ununquadium
   (Uuq)

12 letters:
Kurchatovium
Nielsbohrium
Praseodymium
   (Pr)
Protactinium (Pa)
Unnilpentium
   (Unp)
Unnilseptium
   (Uns)

13 letters:
Rutherfordium
Transactinide
Unniliquadium
   (Unq)

Elephant African, Babar, Hathi, Indian, Jumbo, Kheda, Mammoth, Mastodon, Oliphant, Pachyderm, Pad, Pink, Rogue, Subungulata, Trumpeter, Tusker, White

Elephant-headed Ganesa

Elephant's ears Begonia

Elevate(d), **Elevation**, **Elevator** Agger, Attitude, Cheer, Colliculus, El, Eminence, Ennoble, Foothill, Grain, Heighten, Hoist, Jack, Lift, Machan, Montic(u)le, Monticulus, Promote, > RAISE, Random, Relievo, Ridge, Rise, Steeve, Sublimate, Up(lift), Uplying, Upraise, Wallclimber

Eleven Elf, Hendeca-, Legs, Side, Tail-ender, Team, XI

Elf, **Elves** Alfar, Chiricaune, Fairy, Goblin, Imp, Kobold, Ouph, Pigwiggen, Pixie, Ribhus, Sprite

Elicit Evoke, Extract, Toase, Toaze, Tose, Toze

Eligible Available, Catch, Fit, Nubile, Parti, Qualified, Worthy

Eliminate, **Elimination** Cull, Delete, Discard, Exclude, Execute, Extirpate, Heat, Liquidate, Omit, Preclude, Purge, Red-line, Rid, Separate, Slay, Void, Zap

Elision Synal(o)epha, Syncope

Elite Best, Choice, Crack, > CREAM, Elect, Flower, Liberal, Meritocracy, Ton, U, Zaibatsu

Elixir Amrita, Arcanum, Bufo, Cordial, Daffy, Essence, Medicine, Panacea, Quintessence, Tinct

Elizabeth Bess(ie), Gloriana, Oriano

Elk Deer, Gang, Irish, Moose

Elkoshite Nahum

Ellipse, **Elliptic** Conic, Oblong, Oval

Elm Dutch, Slippery, Wahoo, Weeping, Wich, Winged, Wych

Elmer Gantry

Elongate Extend, Lengthen, Protract, Stretch

Elope Abscond, Decamp

Eloquence, **Eloquent** Articulate, Demosthenic, Facundity, Fluent, Honey-tongued, Oracy, Rhetoric, Vocal

Else(where) Absent, Alibi, Aliunde, Other

Elucidate Explain, Expose, Interpret

Elude, **Elusive** Avoid, Dodge, Escape, > EVADE, Evasive, Foil, Intangible, Jink, Slippy, Subt(i)le, Will o' the wisp

Elves see ELF

Elysium Tir-nan-Og

Em Mut(ton), Pica

Emaciated, **Emaciation** Atrophy, Erasmus, Gaunt, Haggard, Lean, Skinny, Sweeny, Tabid, Thin, Wanthriven, Wasted

Emanate, **Emanation** Arise, Aura, Discharge, Exude, Issue, Miasma, Radiate, Spring

Emancipate, **Emancipation** Deliver, Forisfamiliate, Free, > LIBERATE, Manumission, Uhuru

Emasculate Castrate, Debilitate, Evirate, Geld, Unsex

Embalm Anoint, Mummify, Preserve

Embankment Berm, Bund, Causeway, Dam, Dyke, Earthwork, Levee, Mattress, Mound, Rampart, Remblai, Sconce, Staith(e), Stopbank, Terreplein

Embargo > BAN, Blockade, Edict, Restraint

Embark Begin, Board, Enter, Inship, Launch, Sail

Embarrass(ed), **Embarrassing**, **Embarrassment** Abash, Ablush, Barro, Chagrin, Cheap, Disconcert, Gêne, Haw, Mess, Mortify, Pose, Predicament, Shame,

Sheepish, Squirming, Straitened, Toe-curling, Upset, Writhing

▷ **Embarrassed** *may indicate* an anagram

Embassy Consulate, Embassade, Legation, Mission

Embed(ded) Fix, Immerse, Inlaid, Set

Embellish(ed), Embellishment Adorn, Beautify, Bedeck, Deck, Decorate, Dress, Embroider, Enrich, Frill, Garnish, Garniture, Mordent, > ORNAMENT, Ornate, Rel(l)ish, Roulade, Turn

Ember(s) Ash, Cinder, Clinker, Gleed

Embezzle(ment) Defalcate, Malversation, Peculate, Purloin, > STEAL

Embitter(ed) Acerbate, Aggravate, Enfested, Rankle, Sour

Emblem(atic) Badge, Bear, Colophon, Daffodil, Device, Figure, Ichthys, Impresa, Insignia, Kikumon, Leek, Lis, Maple leaf, Oak, Rose, Roundel, Shamrock, Sign, Spear-thistle, > SYMBOL, Tau-cross, Thistle, Token, Totem(ic), Triskelion, Wheel

Embody, Embodied, Embodiment Epitome, Fuse, Incarnation, Incorporate, Personify, Quintessence

Embolism Clot, Infarct

Emboss(ed) Adorn, Chase, Cloqué, Engrave, Matelassé, Pounce, Raise, Repoussé, Toreutic

Embrace(d) Abrazo, Accolade, Arm, Canoodle, Clasp, Clinch, Clip, Coll, Complect, Comprise, Cuddle, Embosom, Encircle, Enclasp, Enclose, Enfold, Enlacement, Envelop, Espouse, Fold, Grab, Halse, Haulst, Hause, Hesp, Hug, Imbrast, Inarm, Inclasp, Inclip, Include, Kiss, Lasso, Neck, Press, Stemme, Twine, Welcome, Wrap

▷ **Embraces, Embracing** *may indicate* a hidden word

Embrocate, Embrocation Anoint, Arnica, Liniment

Embroider(y) Appliqué, Arrasene, Assisi, Battalia-pie, Braid, Brede, Couching, Crewel-work, Cross-stitch, Cutwork, Drawn threadwork, Embellish, Exaggerate, Eyelet, Fag(g)oting, Fancywork, Featherstitch, Filet, Framework, Gros point, Handiwork, Knotting, Lace(t), Mola, Needlepoint, Needlework, Open-work, Opus anglicanum, Orfray, Ornament, Orphrey, Orris, Petit point, Pinwork, Pulled threadwork, Purl, Sampler, Sew, Smocking, Stitch, Stumpwork, Tambour, Tent, Wrap

Embroideress Mimi

Embroil Confuse, Entangle, Involve, Trouble

Embryo(nic) Blastocyst, Blastula, Conceptus, Epicotyl, Fo(e)tus, Gastrula, Germ, Mesoblast, Morula, Nepionic, Neurula, Origin, Rudiment, Undeveloped

Emend Adjust, Alter, Edit, Reform

Emerald Beryl, Gem, Green, Oriental, Smaragd, Uralian

Emerge(ncy), Emerging Anadyomene, Arise, Craunch, Crise, Crisis, Crunch, Debouch, Eclose, Emanate, Enation, Erupt, Exigency, Issue, Lash-up, Last-ditch, Loom, Need, Outcrop, Pinch, Spring, Stand-by, Stand-in, Strait, Surface

▷ **Emerge from** *may indicate* an anagram or a hidden word

Emerson Waldo

Emetic Apomorphine, Cacoon, Epicac, Evacuant, Ipecacuanha, Puke, Sanguinaria, Stavesacre, Tartar, Vomitory

Emigrant, Emigration Chozrim, Colonist, Italiot, Jordim, Redemptioner, Settler, When-we, Yordim

Emile Zola

Emily Ellis

Eminence, Eminent Alp, Altitude, Cardinal, Distinguished, Eximious, Grand,

Height, Hill, Inselberg, Knoll, Light, Lion, Lofty, Luminary, Noble, > **NOTABLE**, Note, Palatine, Prominence, Renown, Repute, Stature, Tor, Trochanter, > **VIP**, Wallah

Emissary Agent, Envoy, Legate, Marco Polo

Emission, **Emit** Discharge, Emanate, Field, Give, Issue, Spallation, Thermionic, Utter

Emmer Amelcorn, Wheat

Emollient Paregoric

Emolument Income, Perk, Remuneration, Salary, Stipend, Tip, Wages

Emotion(al) Affection, Anger, Anoesis, Atmosphere, Breast, Chord, Ecstasy, Empathy, Excitable, Feeling, Freak-out, Gusty, Hysteria, Joy, Limbic, Passion, Reins, Roar, Sensibility, Sensitive, Sentiment, Spirit, Torrid, Transport, Weepy

Emotionless Deadpan, Glassy

Empathy Identifying, Rapport, Rapprochement, Sympathy

Emperor Agramant(e), Akbar, Akihito, Antoninus, Augustus, Babur, Barbarossa, Bonaparte, Caligula, Caracalla, Charlemagne, Claudius, Commodus, Concerto, Constantine, Diocletian, Domitian, Ferdinand, Gaius, Genghis Khan, Gratian, Hadrian, Heraclius, Hirohito, Imp, Imperator, Inca, Jimmu, Justinian, Kaiser, Keasar, Kesar, King, Maximilian, Menelik, Mikado, Ming, Mogul, Montezuma, Mpret, Napoleon, Negus, Nero, Nerva, Otho, Otto, Penguin, Peter the Great, Purple, Pu-yi, Rex, Rosco, Ruler, Severus, Shah Jahan, Shang, Sovereign, Sultan, Tenno, Theodore, Theodosius, Tiberius, Titus, Trajan, Tsar, Valens, Valentinian, Valerian, Vespasian, Vitellius, Wenceslaus

Emphasis, **Emphasize**, **Emphatic** Accent, Birr, Bold, Dramatise, Forcible, Foreground, Forzando, Hendiadys, Italic, Marcato, Positive, Sforzando, > **STRESS**, Underline, Underscore, Vehement

Empire Assyria, British, Byzantine, Celestial, Chain, Chinese, Domain, Empery, First, Georgia, Holy Roman, Indian, Kingdom, NY, Ottoman, Parthia, Persian, Principate, Realm, Reich, Roman, Russian, Second, Turkish, Western

Empiricism Positivism

Emplacement Battery, Platform

Employ(ment) Business, Calling, Designated, Engage, Exercitation, Hire, Occupy, Pay, Place, Portfolio, Practice, Pursuit, Service, Shiftwork, Trade, Use, Using, Utilise, Vocation

Employee(s) Factotum, Hand, Help, Hireling, Intrapreneur, Minion, Munchkin, Networker, Payroll, Pennyboy, Personnel, Rainmaker, Servant, Staff, Staffer, Valet, Walla(h), Worker

Employer Baas, Boss, Malik, Master, Melik, Padrone, User

▸ **Employs** *may indicate* an anagram

Emporium Bazaar, Shop, Store

Empower Authorise, Enable, Entitle, Permit

Empress Eugenie, Josephine, Messalina, Queen, Sultana, Tsarina

Empty Addle, Bare, Barren, Blank, Boss, Buzz, Claptrap, Clear, Deplete, Deserted, Devoid, Disembowel, Drain, Exhaust, Expel, Forsaken, Futile, Gousty, Gut, Hent, Hollow, Inane, Jejune, Lade, Lave, Null, Phrasy, Pump, Shallow, Teem, Toom, Tume, Unfurnished, Unoccupied, Unpeople, Vacant, Vacate, Vacuous, Vain, Viduous, > **VOID**

▸ **Empty** *may indicate* an 'o' in the word or an anagram

Emulate Ape, Copy, Envy, Equal, Imitate, Match

Emulsion Pseudosolution, Tempera

Enable Authorise, Empower, Potentiate, Qualify, Sanction

Enact Adopt, Effect, Ordain, Personate, Portray

Enamel(led), **Enamel work** Aumail, Champlevé, Cloisonné, Della-robbia, Dentine, Fabergé, Ganion, Lacquer, Polish, Porcelain, Schwarzlot, Shippo, Smalto, Stoved, Vitreous

Encampment Bivouac, Douar, Dowar, Duar, Laager, Laer, Settlement

Encase(d), **Encasement** Box, Crate, Emboîtement, Encapsulate, Enclose, Obtect

Enchant(ing), **Enchanted**, **Enchantment** Bewitch, Captivate, Charm, Delight, Gramary(e), Incantation, Magic, Necromancy, Orphean, Rapt, Sorcery, Spellbind, Thrill

Enchanter, **Enchantress** Archimage, Archimago, Armida, Circe, Comus, Fairy, Lorelei, Magician, Medea, Mermaid, Prospero, Reim-kennar, Sorcerer, Vivien, Witch

Encircle(d) Belt, Enclose, Encompass, Enlace, Entrold, Gird, Inorb, Introld, Orbit, Pale, Ring, > **SURROUND**, Wreathe

Enclave Cabinda, Ceuta, > **ENCLOSURE**, Melilla, Pocket, San Marino

Enclose(d), **Enclosing**, **Enclosure** Bawn, Beset, Boma, Box, Cage, Carol, Carrel, Case, Common, Compound, Corral, Court, Embale, Embowel, Embower, Enceinte, Encircle, Enclave, Enshrine, Fence, Fold, Forecourt, Garth, Haggard, Haw, Hem, Henge, Hope, Impound, In, Incapsulate, Infibulate, Insert, Interclude, Lairage, Pale, Peel, Pele, Pen(t), Petavius, Pightle, Pin, Pinfold, Pit, Playpen, Plenum, Rail, Rath, Recluse, Ree(d), Ring, Run, Saddling, Seal, Sekos, Sept, Seraglio, Serail, Several, Sin bin, Steeld, Stell, Stockade, Sty, > **SURROUND**, Tine, Unsaddling, Vibarium, Ward, Winner's, Wrap, Yard

Encode Cipher, Scramble

Encomium Eulogy, Praise, Sanction, Tribute

Encompass Bathe, Begird, Beset, Environ, Include, Surround

Encore Again, Agen, Ancora, Bis, Ditto, Do, Iterum, Leitmotiv, Recall, Repeat

Encounter Battle, Brush, Combat, Contend, Cope, Dogfight, Face, Hit, Incur, Intersect, Interview, > **MEET**, One-one, Rencontre, Ruffle, Skirmish, Tilt

Encourage(ment), **Encouraging** Abet, Acco(u)rage, Alley-oop, Animate, Attaboy, Bolster, Boost, Brighten, Buck, Cheer, Cohortative, Comfort, Commend, Dangle, Egg, Elate, Embolden, Empatron, Exhort, Fillip, Fire, Fortify, Foster, Fuel, Gee, Hearten, Heigh, Help, Hope, Hortatory, Incite, Inspirit, Nourish, Pat, Patronise, Proceleusmatic, Prod, Protreptic, Push, Reassure, Root, Support, Tally-ho, Train, Upcheer, Uplift, Urge, Wean, Yo

Encroach(ment) Impinge, Infringe, Inroad, Intrude, Invade, Overlap, Overstep, Poach, Purpresture, Trespass, Usurp

Encrypt(ion) CODING, Public key

Encumber, **Encumbrance** Burden, Charge, Clog, Deadwood, Dependent, > **HANDICAP**, Impede, Load, Obstruct, Saddle

Encyclopaedic Comprehensive, Diderot, Extensive, Universal, Vast

End(ing) Abolish, Abut, Aim, Ambition, Amen, Anus, Arse, Big, Bitter, Bourn(e), Butt, Cease, Climax, Close, Closure, Cloture, Coda, Conclude, Crust, Culminate, Curtain, Curtains, Cut off, Dead, Death, Decease, Denouement, Desinence, Desistance, Destroy, Determine, Dissolve, Domino, Effect, Envoi, Envoy, Epilogue, Exigent, Expire, Explicit, Extremity, Fatal, Fattrels, Feminine, Final(e), Fine, Finis, > **FINISH**, Finite, Gable, Grave, Heel, Ish, Izzard, Izzet, Kill, Kybosh, Last, Let up, Little, Loose, Masculine, Mill, Nirvana, No side, Ort, Outro, Period, Peter, Pine, Point, Purpose, Quench, Receiving, Remnant, Rescind, Result, Roach, Scotch, Scrag, Shank, Slaughter, Sopite, Split, Sticky, Stub, Supernaculum, Surcease, Swansong, Tag, Tail, Tailpiece, Telesis, Telic, Telos, Term, Terminal, Terminate, Terminus, Thrum, Tip, Toe, Top, Ultimate, Up, Upshot, West, Z

Endanger Hazard, Imperil, Periclitate, Risk

Endear(ing), Endearment Adorable, Affection, Asthore, Caress, Cariad, Ducky, Enamour, Hinny, Honey (-bunch), Honey-chile, Ingratiate, Jarta, Luv, Machree, Mavourneen, Peat, Pet

Endeavour Aim, Effort, Enterprise, Morse, Strive, Struggle, Try, Venture

Endemic Local, Prevalent

Endive Escarole

Endless Continuous, Ecaudate, Eternal, Eterne, Infinite, Interminable, Perpetual, Undated

▷ **Endlessly** *may indicate* a last letter missing

End of the world Ragnarok

Endorse(ment) Adopt, Affirm, Allonge, Approve, Assurance, Back, Confirmation, Initial, Okay, Oke, Ratify, Rubber stamp, Sanction, Second, Sign, Subscript, > **SUPPORT**, Underwrite, Visa

Endow(ment) Assign, Bequeath, Bestow, Bless, Cha(u)ntry, Dot, Dotation, Enrich, Foundation, Gift, Leave, Patrimony, State, Vest, Wakf, Waqf

Endurance, Endure(d), Enduring Abought, Aby(e), Bear, Bide, Brook, Dree, Face, Fortitude, Have, Hold, > **LAST**, Livelong, Lump, Patience, Perseverance, Pluck, Ride, Stamina, Stand, Stay, Stomach, Stout, Support, Sustain, Swallow, Tether, Thole, Timeless, Tolerance, Undergo, Wear

Endymion Bluebell

Enema Catharsis, Clyster, Purge

Enemy Adversary, Antagonist, Boer, Devil, Fifth column, Foe(n), Fone, Opponent, Public, Time

Energetic, Energise, Energy Active, Alternative, Amp, Animation, Arduous, Atomic, Cathexis, Chakra, Chi, Dash, Drive, Dynamic, Dynamo, E, Enthalpy, Entropy, EV, Fermi, Fireball, Firebrand, Firecracker, Force, Fossil, Free, Fructan, Geothermal, Gism, Go, Graviton, Hartree, H.D.R., Horme, Input, Instress, Internal, > **JET**, Jism, Jissom, Joie de vivre, Joule, Kinetic, Kundalini, Lattice, Libido, Lossy, Luminous, Magnon, Moxie, Nuclear, Orgone, Pep, Phonon, Potency, Potential, > **POWER**, Powerhouse, Prana, QI, Quantum, Rad, Radiant, Radiatory, Renewable, Roton, Rydberg, Sappy, Solar, Stamina, Steam, Sthenic, Stingo, Tidal, Trans-uranic, Vehement, Verve, Vibrational, Vigour, Vim, Vital, Wave, Wind (-farm), Zappy, Zing, Zip

Enfold Clasp, Embrace, Envelop, Stemme, Swathe, Wrap

Enforce(ment) Administer, Coerce, Control, Exact, Implement, Impose

Eng Agma

Engage(d), Engagement, Engaging Absorb, Accept, Appointment, At, Attach, Bespoken, Betrothal, Bind, Book, Busy, Contract, Date, Embark, Employ, Engross, Enlist, Enmesh, Enter, Fascinate, Gear, Gig, Hire, Hold, Interest, Interlock, Lock, Mesh, Met, Occupy, Pledge, Promise, Prosecute, Reserve, Residency, Skirmish, Sponsal, Sponsion, Spousal, Sprocket, Trip, Wage, Winsome

▷ **Engagement** *may indicate* a battle

Engender Beget, Breed, Cause, Occasion, Produce

Engine, Engine part Athodyd, Beam, Booster, Bricole, Bypass, Carburettor, Catapult, Compound, Diesel, Donkey, Dynamo, Fan-jet, Fire, Four, Gas, Gin, Heat, Ion, Jet, Lean-burn, Light, Locomotive, Machine, Mangonel, > **MOTOR**, Nacelle, Onager, Orbital, Outboard, Petard, Petrary, Petrol, Petter, Pilot, Plasma, Podded, Pony, Pug, Pulp, Pulsejet, Push-pull, Put-put, Radial, Ramjet, Reaction, Reciprocating, Retrorocket, Rocket, Rotary, Scorpion, Scramjet, Search, Side-valve, Stationary, Steam, Stirling, Tank, Terebra, Testudo,

Traction, Trompe, Turbine, Turbofan, Turbojet, Turbo-prop, Turboprop, Two-handed, Two-stroke, V, Vernier, Wankel, Warwolf, Water, Winch, Winding

Engineer(ing), Engineers AEU, Arrange, Barnes Wallis, BE, Brindley, Brinell, Brunel, CE, De Lessops, Genetic, Greaser, Ground, Heinkel, Junkers, Kennelly, Manoeuvre, Marconi, Marine, Mastermind, McAdam, Mechanical, Mechatronics, Military, Mime, Operator, Organise, Otto, Planner, Process, RE, Repairman, Rig, Sapper, Scheme, Siemens, Smeaton, Social, Stage, Stephenson, Strauss, Systems, Telford, Tesla, Traffic, Wangle, Wankel, Watt, Whittle, Whitworth

England Albany, Albion, Blighty, Demi-paradise, Eden, John Bull, Merrie, Merry, Middle, The Old Dart

English(man) Anglican, Anglice, Baboo, Babu, Basic, Brit, Bro talk, Choom, E, Eng, Estuary, Gringo, Hawaiian, Hong Kong, Indian, Irish, Jackeroo, John Bull, King's, Kipper, Limey, Middle, Mister, Modern, Newspeak, Norman, Officialese, Oxford, Philippine, Pidgin, Pom(my), Pommie, Pongo, Pork-pudding, Queen's, Qui-hi, Qui-hye, Rock, Rooinek, Sassenach, Saxon, Scotic, Shopkeeper, Side, Singapore, Singlish, South African, South Asian, Southron, Standard, Strine, Wardour Street, Woodbine, Yanqui, Yinglish

Engorge Devour, Glut, Swallow

Engraft Inset

Engrave(r), Engraving Aquatint, Blake, Carve, Cerography, Cerotype, Chalcography, Character, Chase, Cut, Die-sinker, Dry-point, Durer, Enchase, Eng, Etch, Glyptic, Glyptograph, Hogarth, Impress, Inciser, Inscribe, Insculp, Intagliate, Inter, Lapidary, Line, Mezzotint, Niello, Photoglyphic, Plate, Scalp, Scrimshander, Scrimshandy, Scrimshaw, Steel, Stillet, Stipple, Stylet, Stylography, Turn, Wood, Xylographer

Engross(ed) Absorb, Engage, Enwrap, Immerse, Monopolise, > OCCUPY, Preoccupy, Prepossess, Rapt, Sink, Writ large

Engulf Overwhelm, Swamp, Whelm

Enhance Add, Augment, Better, Elevate, Embellish, Exalt, Heighten, Intensify

Enigma(tic) Charade, Conundrum, Dilemma, Gioconda, Mystery, Oracle, Poser, Problem, > PUZZLE, Quandary, Question, Rebus, Riddle, Secret, Sphinxlike, Teaser

Enjoin Command, Direct, Impose, Prohibit, Require

Enjoy(able), Enjoyment Apolaustic, Appreciate, Ball, Brook, Delectation, Fruition, Glee, Groove, Gusto, Have, Lekker, Like, Own, Possess, Relish, Ripping, Savour, Taste, Wallow

Enlarge(ment), Enlarger Accrue, Acromegaly, Add, Aneurism, Aneurysm, Augment, Blow-up, Diagraph, Dilate, Exostosis, Expand, Expatiate, Explain, Increase, > MAGNIFY, Piece, Ream, Rebore, Sensationalize, Swell, Telescope, Tumefy, Upbuild, Varicosity

Enlighten(ed), Enlightenment Awareness, Bodhisattva, Dewali, Divali, Edify, Educate, Explain, Haskalah, Illumine, Instruct, Nirvana, Revelation, Satori, Verlig(te)

Enlist Attest, Conscript, Draft, Engage, Enrol, Induct, Join, Levy, Muster, Prest, Recruit, Roster, Volunteer

Enliven(ed) Animate, Arouse, Brighten, Cheer, Comfort, Exhilarate, Ginger, Invigorate, Merry, Pep, Refresh, Warm

Enmity Animosity, Aversion, Hatred, Malice, Nee(d)le, Rancour, Spite

Ennoble(ment) Dub, Elevate, Ermine, Exalt, Honour, Raise

Ennui Boredom, Tedium

Enormous Colossal, Exorbitant, Googol, Huge, Humongous, Humungous, >IMMENSE, Jumbo, Mammoth, Mega, Plonking, Vast

Enough Adequate, >AMPLE, Anow, Basta, Belay, Enow, Fill, Geyan, Nuff, Pax, Plenty, Qs, Sate, Satis, Suffice, Sufficient, Via, When

Enounce Affirm, Declare, State

Enquire, Enquiring, Enquiry Ask, Check, Curious, Eh, Examine, Inquest, Inquire, Organon, Request, Scan, See, Steward's, Trial

Enrage(d) Emboss, Enfelon, Imboss, >INCENSE, Inflame, Infuriate, Livid, Madden, Wild

Enrapture(d) Enchant, Ravish, Sent, Transport

Enrich Adorn, Endow, Enhance, Fortify, Fructify, Oxygenate

Enrol(ment) Attest, Empanel, Enlist, Enter, Incept, >JOIN, List, Matriculate, Muster, Register

Ensconce(d) Establish, Settle, Shelter, Snug

Ensemble Band, Octet(te), Orchestra, Outfit, Ripieno, Set, Tout, Whole

Enshrine Cherish, Sanctify

Ensign Ancient, Badge, Banner, Duster, >FLAG, Gonfalon, Officer, Pennon, Red, White

Enslave(ment) Addiction, Bondage, Captivate, Chain, Enthral, Thrall, Yoke

Ensue Follow, Result, Succeed, Supervene, Transpire

Entail Involve, Necessitate, Require

Entangle(ment) Ball, Cot, Elf, Embrangle, Embroil, Encumber, Ensnarl, Entrail, Fankle, Implicate, >KNOT, Mat, Ravel, Retiarius, Taigle, Trammel

Enter Admit, Board, Broach, Come, Enrol, Infiltrate, Ingo, Inscribe, Insert, Invade, Lodge, Log, Penetrate, Pierce, Record, Run, Submit, Table

Enterprise, Enterprising Adventure, Ambition, Aunter, Cash cow, Dash, Emprise, Free, Go ahead, Goey, Go-getter, Gumption, Industry, Minefield, Plan, Private, Public, Push, Spirit, Starship, Stunt, Up and coming, Venture

Entertain(er), Entertaining, Entertainment Accourt, Acrobat, Afterpiece, All-nighter, Amphitryon, Amuse, Balladeer, Ballet, Beguile, Burlesque, Busk, Cabaret, Carnival, Cater, Charade, Cheer, Chout, Circus, Comedian, Comic, Concert, Conjure, Consider, Cottabus, Crack, Craic, Cuddy, Diseur, Diseuse, Distract, Divert, Divertissement, ENSA, Extravaganza, Fete, Fleshpots, Floorshow, Foy, Fun, Gaff, Gala, Gas, Gaudy, Gig, Harbour, Harlequin, Have, Hospitality, Host(ess), Impressionist, Interest, Interlude, Intermezzo, Jester, Juggler, Karaoke, Kidult, Kursaal, Lauder, Levee, Light, Masque, Melodrama, Minstrel, Musical, Olio, Opera, Palladium, Panto, Pap, Party, Peepshow, Performer, Piece, Pierrot, Play, Raree-show, Reception, Regale, Review, Revue, Ridotto, Roadshow, Rodeo, Serenade, Showbiz, Sideshow, Singer, Snake-charmer, Soirée, Son et lumière, Striptease, Table, Tamasha, Tattoo, Treat, Variety, Vaudeville, Ventriloquist, Wattle

Enthral(l) Charm, Enchant, Enslave, Spellbind

Enthuse, Enthusiasm, Enthusiast(ic) Acclamatory, Amateur, Ardent, Ardour, Buff, Bug, Buzz, Cat, Cheerleader, Crazy, Crusader, Delirium, Demon, Devotee, Ebullience, Ecstatic, Estro, Fandom, Fiend, Fire, Flame, Freak, Furor(e), Get-up-and-go, Gung-ho, Gusto, Hacker, Hearty, Hype, Into, Keen, Lyrical, Mad, Mania, Muso, Nethead, Nympholept, Oomph, Outpour, Overboard, Passion, Perfervid, Preoccupation, Rah-rah, Raring, Rave, Rhapsodise, Schwärmerei, Sold, Spirit, Teeny-bopper, Verve, Warmth, Whole-hearted, Wonk, Zealot, Zest

Entice(ment), Enticing Allure, Angle, Cajole, Carrot, Decoy, Lure, Persuade, Seductive, >TEMPT, Tole, Toll

Entire(ly), **Entirety** Absolute, All, Bag and baggage, Clean, Complete, Full Monty, Inly, Intact, Integral, In toto, Livelong, Lot, Purely, Systemic, Thorough, Total, Tout, > WHOLE

Entitle(ment) Empower, Enable, Legitim, Name, Right

Entity Being, Body, Existence, Holon, Monad, Tao, Tensor, Thing, Virino

Entomologist Fabré

Entourage Cortège

Entrail(s) Bowels, Chawdron, Giblets, Gralloch, Guts, Ha(r)slet, Humbles, Lights, Numbles, Offal, Quarry, Tripe, Umbles, Viscera

Entrance(d), **Entrant**, **Entry** Access, Adit, Anteroom, Arch, Atrium, Attract, Avernus, Bewitch, Charm, Closehead, Contestant, Door, Doorstop, Double, Dromos, Eye, Fascinate, Foyer, Gate, Ghat, Hypnotise, In-door, Infare, Inflow, Ingress, Inlet, Introitus, Jawhole, Jaws, Jib-door, Mesmerise, Mouth, Narthex, Pend, Porch, Portal, Porte-cochère, Postern, Propylaeum, Propylon, Ravish, Reception, Record, Regest, Registration, Single, Spellbound, Starter, Stem, Stoa, Stoma, Stulm, Torii

Entreat(y) Appeal, Ask, Beg, Beseech, Flagitate, Impetrate, > IMPLORE, Orison, Petition, Plead, Pray, Precatory, Prevail, Prig, Rogation, Solicit, Sue, Supplicate

Entrée Access, Dish, Entry, Ingate

Entrench(ment) Coupure, Encroach, Fortify, Trespass

Entrepreneur Businessman, Executor, Impresario, Wheeler-dealer

Entrust Aret(t), Confide, Consign, Delegate, Give

▶ **Entry** *see* ENTRANCE

Entwine Complect, Impleach, Intervolve, Lace, Twist, Weave

Enumerate, **Enumeration** Catalogue, Count, Detail, Fansi, List, Tell

Enunciate, **Enunciation** Articulate, Declare, Deliver, Diction, Proclaim

Envelop(e) Arachnoid, Bangtail, Chorion, Corolla, Corona, Cover(ing), Cuma, Enclose, Entire, First day cover, Floral, Invest, Involucre, Jiffy(bag)®, Muffle, Mulready, Perianth, Sachet, Sae, Serosa, Smother, Surround, Swathe, Window

Envious, **Envy** Begrudge, Covet, Jaundiced, Jealousy, Penis

Environment(s), **Environmental(ist)** Ambience, Ecofreak, Econut, Eco-warrior, Element, Entourage, Ergonomics, Green, Greenpeace, Habitat, Milieu, Realo, Setting, Sphere, Surroundings, Umwelt, Vicinity

Envisage Contemplate, Imagine, Suppose

Envoi Farewell, RIP

Envoy Agent, Diplomat, Elchee, El(t)chi, Hermes, Legate, Plenipotentiary

Enzyme ACE, Aldolase, Allosteric, Amylase, Amylopsin, Apyrase, Arginase, Asparaginase, Autolysin, Bromel(a)in, Carbohydrase, Carboxylase, Casease, Catalase, Cathepsin, Cellulase, Chimotrypsin, Cholinesterase, Chymopapain, Coagulase, Collagenase, Constitutive, Cyclase, Cytase, Deaminase, Decarboxylase, Diastase, Dipeptidase, Elastase, Enolase, Enterokinase, Erepsin, Esterase, Fibrinolysin, Flavoprotein, Guanase, Histaminase, Hyaluronidase, Hydrase, Hydrolase, Inducible, Inulase, Invertase, Isomerase, Kallikrein, Kinase, Lactase, Lecithinase, Ligase, Lipase, Luciferase, Lyase, Lysin, Lysozyme, Maltase, Mutase, Neuraminidase, Nuclease, Oxdoreductase, Oxidase, Oxygenase, Papain, Pectase, Pectinesterase, Pepsin(e), Peptidase, Permease, Peroxidase, Phosphatase, Plasmin, Polymerase, Protease, Proteinase, PSA, Ptyalin, Reductase, Ren(n)in, Restriction, Ribonuclease, Saccharase, Steapsin, Streptodornase, Streptokinase, Subtilisin, Sulfatase, Sulphatase, Thrombin, Thrombokinase, Thromboplastin, Transaminase, Transcriptase, Transferase, Trehalase, Trypsin, Tyrosinase, Urease, Urokinase, Zymase

Eon Arch(a)ean
Epaminondas Theban
Ephemera(l) Brief, Day, Drake, Fungous, Mayfly, Momentary, Passing, Transient, Transitory, Trappings
Epic Aeneid, Ben Hur, Beowulf, Calliope, Colossal, Dunciad, Edda, Epopee, Epyllion, Gilgamesh, Heroic, Homeric, Iliad, Kalevala, Lusiad(s), Mahabharata, Nibelungenlied, Odyssey, Ramayana, Rhapsody, Saga
Epicene Hermaphrodite
Epicure(an) Apicius, Apolaustic, Connoisseur, Friand, Gastronome, Gastrosopher, Glutton, > GOURMAND, Gourmet, Hedonist, Sybarite
Epidemic Pandemic, Pestilence, Plague, Prevalent, Rampant, Rash
Epigram Adage, Apophthegm, Gnomic, Mot, Proverb
Epigraph Citation, Inscription, RIP
Epilepsy, **Epileptic** Clonic, Eclampsia, Falling evil, Falling sickness, Fit, Grand mal, Petit mal, Turn
Epilogue Appendix, Coda, Postscript
Epiphenomenon ESP
Epiphyte Air-plant
Episcopalian PE, Prelatic
Episode, **Episodic** Chapter, Incident, Page, Picaresque, Scene
Epistle(s) Lesson, Letter, Missive, Pastoral, Titus
Epitaph Ci-git, Hic jacet, Inscription, RIP
Epithet Adj(ective), Antonomasia, Apathaton, Byword, Curse, Expletive, Panomphaean, > TERM, Title
Epitome, **Epitomise** Abridge, Abstract, Digest, Image, Model, Summary, Typify
Epoch Age, Eocene, Era, Holocene, Magnetic, Miocene, Neogene, Oligocene, Palaeocene, Palaeolithic, Perigordian, Period, Pl(e)iocene, Pleistocene
Epsom salts Kieserite
Equable, **Equably** Calm, Just, Pari passu, Smooth, Tranquil
Equal(ly), **Equality**, **Equal quantities** Alike, A(n)a, As, Balanced, Commensurate, Compeer, Egal(ity), Emulate, Equinox, Equiparate, Equity, Even, Even-steven, Fifty-fifty, For, Identical, Identity, Is, Iso-, Isocracy, Isonomy, Level, Level-pegging, Maik, Make, Match, Mate, Owelty, Par, Pari passu, > PEER, Peregal, Pheer(e), Rise, Rival, > SO, Square, Upsides, Wyoming, Ylike
Equanimity Aplomb, Balance, Poise, Serenity
Equate, **Equation(s)** Balance, Cubic, Differential, Diophantine, Dirac, Exponential, Gas, Identity, Linear, Logistic, Maxwell, Parametric, Personal, Polar, Quadratic, Reduce, Relate, Rhizic, Schrödinger, Simultaneous, Van der Waals', Wave
Equator(ial) Celestial, Galactic, Line, Magnetic, Thermal, Tropical
Equerry Courtier, Officer, Page
Equilibrium Balance, Composure, Homeostasis, Isostasy, Poise, Punctuated, Stable, Stasis, Steady state, Tautomerism, Thermodynamic
Equinox Autumnal, Vernal
Equip(ment), **Equipage** Accoutrement, Adorn, Aguise, Aguize, Apparatus, Apparel, Appliance, Armament, Array, Attire, Carriage, Codec, Deadstock, Deck, Dight, Expertise, > FURNISH, Gear, Gere, Get-up, Graith, Habilitate, Kit, Material, Matériel, Mechanise, Muniments, Outfit, Paraphernalia, Retinue, Rig, Sonar, Spikes, Stock, Stuff, Tack(le), Tool, Trampet(te), Trampoline, Turn-out
Equity Actors, Equality, Justice, Law, Negative, Union
Equivalence, **Equivalent** Correspondent, Equal, Equipollent, Ewe, Formal,

In-kind, Same, Tantamount

Equivocal Ambiguous, Dubious, Evasive, Fishy, Oracular, Vague

Equivocate Flannel, Lie, Palter, Prevaricate, Quibble, Tergiversate, Waffle, Weasel

Er Um

Era Age, Archaean, C(a)enozoic, Christian, Common, Cretaceous, Cryptozoic, Decade, Dynasty, Eozoic, Epoch, Hadean, Hegira, Hej(i)ra, Hijra, Jurassic, Lias, Mesozoic, Palaeozoic, Period, Precambrian, Proterozoic, Republican, Vulgar

Eradicate, **Erase** Abolish, Delete, Demolish, Destroy, Efface, Expunge, Extirp, Obliterate, Purge, Root, Scrat, Scratch, Stamp-out, Strike off, Uproot, Uptear

Erasmus Humanist

Erbium Er

Erect(ion), **Erector** Attolent, Build, Construct(ion), Elevate, Hard-on, Henge, Horn, Perpendicular, Priapism, Prick, Rear, Rigger, Stiffy, Straight-pight, Tentigo, Upright, Vertical

Ergo Argal, Hence, Therefore

Erica Heather, Ling

Ermine Fur, Minever, Miniver, Stoat

Ernie Bondsman

Erode, **Erosion** Abrade, Corrasion, Denude, Destroy, Deteriorate, Etch, Fret, Planation, Spark, Wash, Wear, Yardang

Eros, **Erotic(a)** Amatory, Amorino, Amorous, Aphrodisiac, Carnal, Cupid, Curiosa, Lascivious, Philtre, Prurient, Salacious, Steamy

Err(or) Aliasing, Anachronism, Bish, Blip, Blooper, Blunder, Boner, Bug, Clanger, Comedy, Corrigendum, EE, Fault, Glaring, Heresy, Human, Jeofail, K'thibh, Lapse, Lapsus, Literal, Mackle, Mesprise, Mesprize, Misgo, Misprint, Misprise, Misprize, Misstep, > **MISTAKE**, Mumpsimus, Out, Probable, Rounding, Rove, Sampling, Semantic, Sin, Slip, Slip-up, Solecism, Standard, Stray, Trip, Truncation, Typo, Typographical, Wander

Errand Chore, Commission, Fool's, Message, Mission, Sleeveless, Task

Errand-boy Cad, Galopin, Page

Erratic Haywire, Temperamental, Unstable, Vagary, Vagrant, Wayward

Erroneous False, Inaccurate, Mistaken, Non-sequitur

Ersatz Artificial, Synthetic

Erudite, **Erudition** Academic, Didactic, Learned, Savant, Scholar, Well-read, Wisdom

Erupt(ion), **Erupture** Belch, Brash, Burst, Ecthyma, Eject, Emit, Emphlysis, Exanthem(a), Exanthemata, > **EXPLODE**, Fissure, Flare, Fumarole, Hives, Hornito, Lichen, Mal(l)ander, Mallender, Morphew, Outbreak, Outburst, Papilla, Paroxysm, Pompholyx, Pustule, Rash, Rose-drop, Scissure

Escalate, **Escalator** Accrescence, Expand, Granary, Grow, Lift, Travolator

Escape(e), **Escapade**, **Escapist** Abscond, Atride, Avoid, Bale out, Bolt, Bolthole, Breakout, Caper, Eject, Elope, Elude, Elusion, Esc, Evade, Exit, Fire, Flee, Flight, Frolic, Gaolbreak, Hole, Hoot, Houdini, Hout, Lam, Leakage, Leg-it, Let-off, Levant, Loop(-hole), Meuse, Mews, Muse, Narrow, Near thing, Outlet, Prank, Refuge, Rollick, Runaway, Sauve qui peut, Scapa, Scarper, Seep(age), Shave, Slip, Vent, Walter Mitty, Wilding, Wriggle

Escapement Anchor, Foliot, Recoil

Eschew Abandon, Avoid, For(e)go, Ignore, > **SHUN**

Escort Accompany, Attend, Bodyguard, Chaperone, Comitatus, Conduct, Convoy, Cortege, Corvette, Date, Destroyer, Entourage, Frigate, Gallant, Gigolo, Guide, Lead, Outrider, Protector, Retinue, See, Send, Set, Squire, Take, Tend,

Usher, Walker

Escutcheon Achievement, Crest, Shield

Esker OS

Eskimo Aleut, Caribou, Husky, In(n)uit, Inuk, Inukitut, Thule, Yupik

Esoteric Abstruse, Acroamatic, Arcane, Inner, Mystic, Occult, Orphic, Private, Rarefied, Recondite, Secret

ESP Psi

Especial(ly) Chiefly, Esp, Espec, Outstanding, Particular

Esperanto Ido, Zamenhof

Espionage Industrial, Spying, Surveillance

Esplanade Promenade, Walk

Esprit Insight, Spirit, Understanding, Wit

Esquire Armiger(o), Esq, Gent

Essay(s) Article, Attempt, Causerie, Critique, Dabble, Disquisition, Dissertation, Endeavour, Festschrift, Go, Paper, Prolusion, Stab, Theme, Thesis, Tractate, Treatise, Try

Essayist Addison, Bacon, Carlyle, Columnist, Elia, Ellis, Emerson, Hazlitt, Holmes, Hunt, Huxley, Lamb, Locke, Montaigne, Pater, Prolusion, Ruskin, Scribe, Steele, > WRITER

Essence Alma, Atman, Attar, Aura, Being, Core, Element, Entia, Esse, Extract, Fizzen, Flavouring, Foison, Gist, Heart, Hom(e)ousian, Inbeing, Inscape, Kernel, Marrow, Mirbane, Myrbane, Nub, Nutshell, Oil, Ottar, Otto, Perfume, Per-se, Pith, Quiddity, Ratafia, Soul, Ylang-ylang

Essential(ly) Basic, Central, Crucial, Entia, Formal, Fundamental, Imperative, In, Indispensable, Inherent, Integral, Intrinsic, Kernel, Key, Lifeblood, Linch-pin, Marrow, Material, Must, Necessary, Need, Nitty-gritty, Nuts and bolts, Part-parcel, Per-se, Prana, Prerequisite, Quintessence, Radical, Requisite, Sine qua non, Vital, Whatness

Establish(ed) Abide, Anchor, Ascertain, Base, Build, Create, Deploy, Embed, Enact, Endemic, Engrain, Ensconce, Entrench, Evince, Fix, > FOUND, Haft, Imbed, Ingrain, Instal(l), Instate, Instil, Institute, Inveterate, Ordain, Pitch, Pre-set, Prove, Raise, Root(ed), Set, Stable, Standing, Substantiate, Trad, Trite, Valorise, Verify

Establishment Building, Business, CE, Church, Co, Concern, Creation, Hacienda, Household, Institution, Lodge, Proving ground, Salon, School, Seat, System, Traditional

Estate Allod(ium), Alod, Assets, Commons, Demesne, Domain, Dominant, Dowry, Fazenda, Fee-simple, Fee-tail, Fen, First, Fourth, General, Hacienda, Hagh, Haugh, Having, Hay, Housing, Industrial, Land-living, Latifundium, Legitim, Life, Manor, Messuage, Odal, Personal(ity), Plantation, Press, > PROPERTY, Real, Runrig, Second, Situation, Spiritual, Standing, Talooka, Taluk(a), Temporal, Thanage, Third, Trading, Trust, Udal, Zamindari, Zemindari

Estate agent Realtor

Esteem(ed), Estimable Account, Admiration, Appreciation, Count, Have, Honour, Izzat, Los, Precious, Prestige, Price, Pride, Prize, Rate, > REGARD, Reputation, Respect, Store, Value, Venerate, Wonder, Worthy

Ester Depside, Glyceride, Olein, Palmitin, Phthalate, Psilocybin, Urethan(e)

▶ **Estimable** *see* ESTEEM

Estimate, Estimation Appraise, Assess, Calculate, Carat, Conceit, Cost, Esteem, Extrapolation, Forecast, Gauge, Guess, Guess(timate), Inexact, Interval, Opinion, Point, Projection, Quotation, Rate, Rating, Reckon, Regard, Sight,

Value, Weigh

Estrange Alienate, Disunite, Wean

Estuary Bay, Creek, Dee, Delta, Firth, Gironde, Humber, Inlet, La Plata, Mouth, Ostial, Para

Esurient Arid, Insatiable

Etc(etera) Et al(ia), So on

Etch(ing) Aquafortis, Aquatint(a), Bite, > **ENGRAVE**, Incise, Inscribe

Eternal, Eternity Aeonian, Ageless, Endless, Everlasting, Eviternal, Ewigkeit, Forever, Immortal, Infinity, Never-ending, Perdurable, Perpetual, Sempiternal, Tarnal, Timeless

Ether Atmosphere, Ch'i, Crown, Gas, Petroleum, Sky, Yang, Yin

Ethereal Airy, Delicate, Fragile, Heavenly, Nymph

Ethic(al), Ethics Deontics, Marcionite, Moral, Principles, Work

Ethiopia(n) African, Amharic, Asmara, Cushitic, Galla, Geez, Kabele, Kebele

Ethnic Racial, Roots

Ethyl ET

Etiquette Code, Conduct, Kawa, > **MANNERS**, Politesse, Propriety, Protocol, Ps and Qs, Punctilio

Etna Empedocles, Vessel, Volcano

Etonian Oppidan, Victim

Etruscan Tyrrhenian

Etymologist Hobson-jobson, Isodore

Eucalyptus Bloodwood, Coolabah, Gum-tree, Ironbark, Jarrah, Mallee, Marri, Morrell, Sallee, Stringybark, Sugar gum, Tewart, Tooart, Tuart, Wandoo, Yate

Eucharist Communion, Housel, Mass, Supper, Viaticum

Eugene Aram, Onegin

Eugenia Jambal, Jambolan(a), Jambu(l)

Eulogy Encomium, Panegyric, Praise, Tribute

Euphausia Krill, Shrimp

Euphemism Fib, Gosh, Gracious, Heck, Hypocorism

Euphoria, Euphoric Cock-a-hoop, Ecstasy, Elation, High, Jubilation, Mindfuck, Rapture, Rush

Euphrasia Eyebright

Eurasian Chee-chee, Chi-chi

Europe(an) Balt, Bohunk, Catalan, Community, Continent, Croat, E, Faringee, Faringhi, Feringhee, Fleming, Hungarian, Hunky, Japhetic, Lapp, Lithuanian, Palagi, Polack, Ruthene, Ruthenian, Serb, Slavonian, Slovene, Topi-Wallah, Transleithan, Tyrolean, Vlach, Yugoslav

Europium Eu

Eustace Diamonds

Euthanasia Exit

Evacuate, Evacuation Excrete, Expel, Getter, Planuria, Planury, Scramble, Stercorate, Stool, Vent, Void, Withdraw

Evade, Evasion, Evasive Ambages, Avoid, Cop-out, Coy, Dodge, Duck, Elude, Equivocate, Escape, Fence, Fudge, Hedge, Loophole, Mealymouthed, Parry, Prevaricate, Quibble, Quillet, Scrimshank, Shack, Shifty, Shirk, Shuffling, Sidestep, Skive, Skrimshank, Slippy, Stall, Subterfuge, Tergiversate, Waive, Weasel, Weasel out, Whiffler

Evaluate, Evaluation Appraise, Assess, Estimate, Gauge, Job, Rate, Review, Waid(e), Weigh

Evanescent Cursory, Fleeting, Fugacious

Evangelical, Evangelist(ical) Converter, Crusader, Fisher, Gospeller,

Happy-clappy, Jesus freak, John, Luke, Marist, Mark, Matthew, Moody, Morisonian, Peculiar, Preacher, Revivalist, Salvationist, Sankey, Sim(eonite), Stundist, Wild

Evaporate, **Evaporation** Condense, Dehydrate, Desorb, Dry, Exhale, Steam, Steme, Ullage, Vaporise

Evelyn Diarist, Hope

Eve(n), **Evening** Albe(e), Albeit, All, All Hallow's, Average, Balanced, Clean, Drawn, Dusk, Een, Ene, Equable, Equal, Erev, Fair, Flush, Forenight, Iron, J'ouvert, Level, Level-pegging, Meet, Nightfall, Pair, Par, Plain, Plane, Plateau, Quits, Rib, St Agnes's, Smooth, Soirée, Subfusc, Subfusk, Sunset, Tib(b)s, Toss-up, Twilight, Vesperal, Vespertinal, Vigil, Yester, Yet

Evening flight Ro(a)ding

Evensong Vespers

Event Case, Circumstance, Contingency, Discus, Encaenia, Episode, Fest, Field, Gymkhana, Happening, Happy, Heat, Incident, Iron man, Landmark, Leg, Media, Milestone, Occasion, Occurrence, Ongoing, Outcome, Pass, Regatta, Result, Stick-on, Three-day, Three-ring circus, Track, Triple

Even-toed Artiodactyl

Eventual(ity), **Eventually** Case, Contingent, Finally, Future, In time, Nd, Sooner or later

Ever Always, Ay(e), Constantly, Eternal, Eviternity

Everglade Vlei

Evergreen Abies, Ageless, Arbutus, Cembra, Cypress, Gaultheria, Ivy, Myrtle, Olearia, Periwinkle, Pinaster, Privet, Thuja, Thuya, Washington, Winterberry, Yacca

Everlasting Cat's ear, Changeless, Enduring, Eternal, Immortal, Immortelle, Perdurable, Recurrent, Tarnal

Every(one), **Everything** All, Complete, Each, Existence, Full Monty, Ilk(a), In toto, Monty, Sum, The works, To a man, Tout, Tout le monde, Universal, Varsal

Everyday Banal, Informal, Mundane, Natural, Ordinary, Plain

Everywhere Omnipresent, Passim, Rife, Throughout, Ubiquity

Evict Disnest, Eject, Expel, Oust

Evidence, **Evident** Adminicle, Apparent, Argument, Axiomatic, Circumstantial, Clear, Confessed, Credentials, Direct, Distinct, Document, Empirical, Exemplar, Flagrant, Hearsay, Indicate, Internal, King's, Manifest, Marked, Obvious, Overt, > **PATENT**, Plain, Premise, Prima facie, Probable, Proof, Queen's, Record, Sign, Smoking gun, State's, Surrebuttal, Testimony, Understandable

Evil Ahriman, Alastor, Amiss, Badmash, Bale, Beelzebub, Budmash, Corrupt, Depraved, Eale, Guilty, Harm, Heinous, Hydra, Ill, Immoral, Iniquity, King's, Malefic, Mare, Mischief, Necessary, Night, Perfidious, Rakshas(a), Shrewd, Sin, > **SINISTER**, Turpitude, Vice, Wicked

Evil eye Jettatura

Evince Disclose, Exhibit, Indicate, > **MANIFEST**, Show

Eviscerate(d) Debilitate, Disembowel, Drawn, Gralloch

Evoke Arouse, Awaken, Elicit, Move, Stir

Evolution(ary) Countermarch, Development, Emergent, Growth, Holism, Lamarck, Moner(on), Neo-Lamarckism, Orthogenesis, Phylogeny, Social, Spencerman, Stellar, Transformism, Turning

▷ **Evolution** *may indicate* an anagram

Ewe Crone, Gimmer, Keb, Sheep, Teg, Theave

Ewer Aquamanale, Aquamanile

Ex Former, Late, Quondam, Ten

Exacerbate Aggravate, Embitter, Exasperate, Irritate, Needle

Exact(ing), **Exactitude**, **Exactly** Accurate, Authentic, Careful, Dead, Definite, Due, Elicit, Estreat, Even, Exigent, Extort, Fine, Formal, It, Jump, Literal, Literatim, Mathematical, Meticulous, Nice(ty), Pat, Point-device, > **PRECISE**, Require, Slap-bang, Spang, Specific, Spot-on, Strict, Stringent, T, To a 't', Verbatim

Exaction Blackmail, Extortion, Impost, Montem, Sorelion, Tax

Exaggerate(d), **Exaggeration** Agonistic, Amplify, Ballyhoo, Boast, Brag, Camp, Colour, Distend, Dramatise, > **EMBROIDER**, Goliathise, Hoke, Hyperbole, Inflate, Lie, Line-shoot, Magnify, Munch(h)ausen, Mythomania, Overdo, Overdraw, Overpaint, Overplay, Overrate, Overstate, Over-the-top, Romance, Steep, Stretch, Tall, Theatrical

Exalt(ed), **Exaltation** Attitudes, Deify, Dignify, Elation, Enhance, Ennoble, Erect, Extol, Glorify, High, Jubilance, Larks, Lofty, Magnific, > **PRAISE**, Raise, Rapture, Ruff(e), Sama, Sublime, Supernal, Throne

Exam(ination), **Examine**, **Examinee**, **Examiner** Agrégé, A-level, Analyse, Analyst, Appose, Audit, Auscultation, Autopsy, Baccalauréat, Biopsy, Case, Check-out, Check-up, Cognosce, Collate, Comb, Common Entrance, Consideration, Cross-question, CSE, Deposal, Depose, Disquisition, Dissect, Docimasy, Endoscopy, Entrance, Expiscate, Explore, Eyeball, Finals, GCE, GCSE, Going-over, Grade(s), Great-go, Greats, Gulf, Haruspex, Hearing, Inspect, Inter, Interrogate, Interview, Introspection, Jerque, Jury, Little-go, Local, Mark, Matriculation, Medical, Mocks, Moderator, Mods, Mug, O-level, Once-over, Oral, Ordalian, Ordeal, Overhaul, Palp(ate), Paper, Peruse, Physical, Post-mortem, Prelim, Probe, Pry, Psychoanalyse, Pump, > **QUESTION**, Quiz, Ransack, Recce, Reconnaissance, Responsions, Review, Sayer, Scan, Schools, Scrutator, Scrutineer, Scrutinise, Search, Seek, Shroff, Sift, Sit, Smalls, Sus(s), Test, Trial, Tripos, Try, Unseen, Vet, Viva, Voir dire

Example Apotheosis, Assay-piece, Byword, Epitome, Foretaste, > **FOR EXAMPLE**, Illustration, Instance, Lead, Lesson, Model, Paradigm, Paragon, > **PATTERN**, Praxis, Precedent, Prototype, Role model, Say, Shining, Showpiece, Specimen, Standard, Stormer, Such as, Touchstone, Type, Typify

Exasperate, **Exasperating**, **Exasperation** Anger, Embitter, Galling, Irk, Irritate, Nettle, Provoke

Excavate, **Excavation**, **Excavator** Armadillo, Burrow, Catacomb, Crater, Cutting, Delf, Delph, > **DIG**, Dike, Disinter, Ditch, Dragline, Dredge, Drive, Earthwork, Gaulter, Hollow, JCB, Mine, Pichiciago, Pioneer, Pioner, Pyoner, Quarry, Shaft, Sink, Sondage, Steam-shovel, Stope, Well

Exceed, **Exceeding(ly)** Amain, Not half, Outdo, Overstep, Surpass, Transcend, Very

Excel(lence), **Excellency**, **Excellent** A1, Ace, Admirable, A-per-se, Assay-piece, Bangin(g), Beat, Beaut, Better, Bitchin, Blinder, Bodacious, Boffo, Bonzer, Booshit, Boss, Bottler, Bravo, Brill, Bully, Capital, Castor, Champion, Cheese, Choice, Class(y), Classical, Copacetic, Copesettic, Copybook, Corking, Crack, Crackerjack, Crucial, Daisy, Def, Dic(k)ty, Dilly, Dominate, Doozy, Elegant, Excelsior, Exemplary, Eximious, Exo, Extraordinaire, Fab, Fantastic, Five-star, Great, Grit, Grouse, HE, High, Humdinger, Hunky(-dory), Inimitable, Jake, Jammy, Jim-dandy, Knockout, Lalapalooza, Laudable, Lollapalooza, Lummy, Matchless, Mean, Mega-, Merit, Neat, Noble, Out and outer, Outbrag, Outdo, Outstanding, Outtop, Overdo, Overtop, Paragon, Peachy, Phat, Prime, Pure, Rad, Rare, Rattling, Ring, Rinsin', Ripping, Ripsnorter, Say-piece, > **SHINE**,

Shit-hot, Sick-dog, Sik, Spanking, Spiffing, Stellar, Stonking, Stupendous, Sublime, Superb, Super-duper, Superior, Supreme, Swell, Terrific, Tip-top, Top flight, Top-hole, Topnotch, Topping, Transcend, Transcendant, Triff, Virtue, Wal(l)y, War, Way-out, Wicked, Worth

Except(ion) Bar, But, Else, Exc, Nobbut, Omit, Save, Than, Then, Unless

Exceptional Abnormal, Anomaly, Cracker, Egregious, Especial, Extraordinary, Gas, Rare, Ripsnorter, Select, Singular, Special, Uncommon, Zinger

Excerpt(s) Digest, Extract, Passage, Scrap

Excess(ive), Excessively All-fired, Basinful, Exorbitant, Extortionate, Extravagant, Flood, Fulsome, Glut, Hard, Inordinate, > LAVISH, Mountain, Nimiety, OD, Old, OTT, Outrage, Over, Overage, Overblown, Overcome, Overdose, Overkill, Overmuch, Overspill, Over-the-top, Owercome, Plethora, Preponderance, Profuse, Salt, Satiety, Spate, Spilth, Steep, Superabundant, Superfluity, Surfeit, Surplus, Terrific, Troppo, Ultra, Undue, Unequal, Woundily

Exchange Baltic, Bandy, Barter, Bourse, Cambist, Catallactic, Change, Chop, Commute, Contango, Convert, Cope, Corn, Ding-dong, Employment, Enallage, Excambion, Foreign, Inosculate, Interplay, Ion, Labour, Logroll, > MARKET, Mart, Needle, Niffer, Paraphrase, PBX, Post, Rally, Rate, Recourse, Rialto, Royal, Scorse, Scourse, Stock, Swap, Switch, Swop, Telephone, Tolsel, Tolsey, Tolzey, > TRADE, Traffic, Transfusion, Trophallaxis, Truck

Exchequer Remembrancer

Excise(man), Excise district Ablate, Bobbitt, Crop, Expunge, Gauger, Resect, Ride, Tax

Excitable, Excite(d), Excitement, Exciting Ablaze, Aboil, Abuzz, Aerate, Agitate, Agog, Amove, Animate, Aphrodisiac, Arouse, Athrill, Atwitter, Awaken, Brouhaha, Buck-fever, Climatic, Combustible, Commotion, Delirium, Electrify, Emove, Enthuse, Erethism, Feisty, Fever, Fire, Flap, Flat spin, Frantic, Frenzy, Frisson, Furore, Fuss, Galvanise, Gas, Grip, Headiness, Heat, Hectic, Het, Hey-go-mad, Hilarity, Hobson-Jobson, Hoopla, Hothead, Hyped, Hyper, Hysterical, Impel, Incite, Inebriate, Inflame, Intoxicate, Jimjams, Kick, Kindle, Metastable, Must, Neurotic, Oestrus, Orgasm, Overheat, Overwrought, Panic, Passion, Pride, Prime, Provoke, Racy, Radge, Red-hot, Rile, Roil, > ROUSE, Rousement, Ruff(e), Rut, Send, Sexy, Spin, Spur, Startle, Stimulate, Stir(e), Suscitate, Temperamental, Tetany, Tew, Thrill, Titillate, Trickle, Turn-on, Twitter, Upraise, Va-va-voom, Waken, Whee, Whet, Whoopee, Yahoo, Yerk, Yippee, Yoicks

Excite(d) *may indicate* an anagram

Exclaim, Exclamation (mark) Ahem, Begorra, Blurt, Bo, Ceas(e), Crikey, Criv(v)ens, Dammit, Ecphonesis, Eina, Ejaculate, Epiphonema, Eureka, Expletive, Fen(s), Good-now, Hadaway, Haith, Halleluiah, Hallelujah, Heigh-ho, Hem, Hip, Hookey Walker, Hosanna, Inshallah, Interjection, Oops, Pling, Protest, Pshaw, Sasa, Screamer, Sese(y), Sessa, Vociferate, Walker, Whau, Whoops, Wow, Yippee, Zounds

Exclude, Excluding, Exclusion Ban, Bar, Block, Debar, Deforcement, Disbar, Drop, Eliminate, Ex, Except, Excommunicate, Freeze out, Omit, Ostracise, Outbar, Outwith, Pauli, Shut out, Social

Exclusive Cliquish, Closed-shop, Complete, Debarment, Elect, Monopoly, Particular, Pure, Rare, Scoop, Select, Single, Sole

Excommunicate Curse

Excoriate Flay, Slam

Excrement, Excretion Dirt, Doo-doo, Dung, Faeces, Frass, Jobbie, Keech,

Meconium, Oliguria, Ordure, Poo(p), Poo-poo, Puer, Pure, Refuse, Scatology, Shit(e), Sir-reverence, Stercoraceous, Strangury, Turd, Urea, Waste

Excrescence Aril, Carnosity, Caruncle, Enate, Gall, Growth, Knob, Knurl, Lump, Nurl, Pimple, Pin, Spavin(e), Strophiole, Talpa, Twitter(-bone), Wart

Excruciate, **Excruciating** Agonising, Rack, Torment, Torture

Exculpate Acquit, Clear, Forgive

Excursion Airing, Cruise, Dart, Digression, Jaunt, Junket, Outing, Road, Sally, Sashay, Sortie, Tour, Trip

Excusable, **Excuse** Absolve, Alibi, Amnesty, Bunbury, Condone, Essoin, Essoyne Evasion, Exempt, Exonerate, Faik, Forgive, Mitigate, Occasion, Off come, Out, Overlook, Palliate, > **PARDON**, Pretext, Release, Salvo, Venial, Viable, Whitewash

Execrate Abhor, Ban, Boo, Curse

Execute(d), **Executioner**, **Executive**, **Executor** Abhorson, Accomplish, Account, Administrate, Behead, Carnifex, Deathsman, Despatch, Discharge, Dispatch, Exor, Finish, Fry, Gan, Gar(r)otte, Gin, Guardian, Hang, Headsman, Implement, Ketch, Kill, Koko, Lynch, Management, Noyade, Official, Perform, Pierrepoint, Politburo, Scamp, Top, Trustee, Tyburn

Exemplar(y) Byword, Impeccable, Laudable, Model, Paragon, St, Warning

Exemplify Cite, Epitomise, Illustrate, Instantiate, Satisfy

Exempt(ion) Dispensation, Exclude, Exeem, Fainites, Fains, Free, Immune, Impunity, Indemnity, Overslaugh, Quarter, Spare, Vains

Exercise(s) Aerobics, Air, Antic, Apply, Callanetics®, Cal(l)isthenics, Chi kung, Cloze, Constitutional, Drill, Employ, Enure, Eurhythmics, Exert, Floor, Gradus, Inure, Isometrics, Kata, Kegel, Krav Maga, Lesson, Limber, Manual, Medau, Op, Operation, PE, Physical jerks, Pilates, Ply, Popmobility, Practice, Practise, Press-up, PT, Pump iron, Push-up, Qigong, Shintaido, Sit-up, Solfeggi(o), Step (aerobics), Stretch, Tai chi (ch'uan), Thema, Theme, Thesis, Train, Trampoline, Use, Vocalise, Warm-up, Wield, Work, Work-out, Xyst(us), Yomp

▷ **Exercise(d)** *may indicate* an anagram

Exert(ion) Conatus, > **EFFORT**, Exercise, Labour, Operate, Strain, Strive, Struggle, Trouble, Wield

Ex-European Japhetic

Exhalation, **Exhale** Breath, Fume, Miasma, Reek, Steam, Transpire, Vapour

Exhaust(ed), **Exhausting**, **Exhaustion**, **Exhaustive** All-in, Beaten, Beggar, Bugger(ed), Burn, Burn-out, Bushed, Clapped out, Consume, Deadbeat, Debility, Deplete, Detailed, Dissipate, Do, Done, Drain, Eduction, Effete, Emission, Empty, End, Enervate, Fatigue, Forfeuchen, Forfochen, Forfoughen, Forfoughten, Forjaskit, Forjeskit, Forspent, Forswink, Frazzle, Gruelling, Heat, Heatstroke, Inanition, Jet-lagged, Jet-stream, Jiggered, Knacker, Mate, Milk, Out, Outwear, Poop, Powfagged, Puckerood, Puggled, Rag, Ramfeezle, Rundown, Sap, Shatter, Shot, Shotten, Spend, Spent, Stonkered, Tailpipe, Tire, Trauchled, Use, Used up, Wabbit, Wappend, Warby, Washed-up, Wasted, Waygone, > **WEARY**, Wind, Worn, Zonked

Exhibit(ion), **Exhibitioner** Circus, Concours, Demo, Demonstrate, Demy, Diorama, Discover, Display, Evince, Expo, Expose, Fair, Hang, Indicate, > **MANIFEST**, Olympia, Pageant, Panopticon, Parade, Present, Retrospective, Salon, Scene, Set forth, Show(piece), Showcase, Viewing

Exhilarate(d) Bubble, Cheer, Elate, Enliven

Exhort(ation) Admonish, Allocution, Caution, Counsel, Incite, Lecture, Par(a)enesis, Persuade, Urge

Exhume Delve, Disinter, Resurrect, Unearth

Exigency, **Exigent** Emergency, Pressing, Taxing, Urgent, Vital

Exile Adam, Babylon, Banish, Deport, Emigré, Eve, Expatriate, Exul, Galut(h), Ostracise, Outlaw, Relegate, Tax, Wretch

Exist(ence), **Existing** Be(ing), Corporeity, Dwell, Enhypostasia, Entelechy, Esse, Extant, Identity, In esse, Life, Live, Ontology, Perseity, Solipsism, Substantial, Ubiety

Existentialist Camus, Sartre

Exit Débouché, Door, Egress, Gate, Leave, Log off, Log out, Outlet

Exodus Book, Departure, Flight, Hegira, Hejira

Ex-official Outler

Exogamous Outbred

Exonerate(d) Absolve, Acquit, Clear, Excuse, Exempt, Shriven

Exorbitant Excessive, Expensive, Steep, Tall, Undue

Exorcise, **Exorcist** Benet, Lay

Exordium Opening, Preface, Prelude

Exotic Alien, Ethnic, Fancy, Foreign, Free, Outlandish, Strange

Expand, **Expanse**, **Expansion** Amplify, Boom, Branch out, Develop, Diastole, Dilate, Distend, Ectasis, Elaborate, > **ENLARGE**, Escalate, Flesh out, Grow, Increase, Magnify, Ocean, Outspread, Snowball, Spread, Stretch, Swell, Wax, Wire-draw

Expatiate Amplify, Descant, Dwell, Enlarge, Perorate

Expatriate Banish, Colonial, Emigrate, Émigré, Exile, Outcast

Expect(ant), **Expectation**, **Expected**, **Expecting** Agog, Anticipate, Ask, Await, Due, Foresee, Gravid, Hope, Lippen, Look, Natural, Par, Pip, Pregnant, Presume, Prim, Prospect, Require, > **SUPPOSE**, Tendance, Think, Thought, Usual, Ween

Expectorant, **Expectorate** Expel, Guaiacol, Hawk, Spit

Expedient Advisable, Artifice, Contrivance, Fend, Make-do, Makeshift, Measure, Politic, Resort, Resource, Shift, Stopgap, Suitable, Wise

Expedite, **Expedition**, **Expeditious** Advance, Alacrity, Anabasis, Celerity, Crusade, Dispatch, Excursion, Fastness, Field trip, Hasten, Hurry, Kon-tiki, Pilgrimage, Post-haste, Quest, Safari, Short cut, Speed, Trek, Trip, Voyage

Expel Amove, Dispossess, Drum out, Egest, Evacuate, Evict, Exile, Exorcize, Hoof, Oust, Out(cast), Read out, Void

Expend(iture) Budget, Consume, Cost, Dues, Gavel, Goings-out, Mise, Occupy, Oncost, Outgo(ing), Outlay, Poll, Squander, Tithe, Toll, Use, Waste

Expendable Cannon-fodder

Expense(s) Charge, Cost, Current, Exes, Fee, Law, Oncost, Outgoing, Outlay, Overhead, Price, Sumptuary

Expensive Chargeful, Costly, Dear, Executive, High, Salt, Steep, Upmarket, Valuable

Experience(d) Accomplished, A posteriori, Assay, Blasé, Discovery, Empiric, Encounter, Expert, > **FEEL**, Felt, Find, Freak-out, Gust, Hands-on, Have, Incur, Know, Learn, Live, Mature, Meet, Mneme, Near-death, Old hand, Old-stager, Ordeal, Out-of-body, Pass, Plumb, Seasoned, See, Senior, Sense, Sensory, Stager, Stand, Street-smart, Streetwise, Taste, Transference, Trial, Trip, Trocinium, Try, Undergo, Versed, Work

Experiment(al) Attempt, Avant-garde, Control, Empirical, Essay, Peirastic, Pilot, Sample, Taste, Tentative, > **TRIAL**, Try, Venture, Vivisection

Expert(ise) Accomplished, Ace, Adept, Adroit, Arch, Authority, Boffin, Buff, Cambist, Cocker, Cognoscente, Connoisseur, Crack, Craft, Dab(ster), Dan, Deft, Don, Egghead, Finesse, Fundi, Gourmet, Gun, Hotshot, Karateka, Know-all, Know-how, Luminary, Maestro, Masterly, Maven, Mavin, Meister, Nark, Oner,

Oneyer, Oneyre, Peritus, Practised, Pro, Proficient, Pundit, Ringer, Savvy, Science, Shroff, Skill(y), Sly, Specialist, Technique, Technocrat, Troubleshooter, Ulema, Used, W(h)iz

Expiate, Expiation, Expiatory Amends, Atone, Penance, Piacular

Expire(d), Expiry Blow, Collapse, Croak, > DIE, End, Exhale, Invalid, Ish, Lapse, Neese, Pant, Sneeze, Terminate

Explain(able) Account, Annotate, Aread, Arede, Arreede, Clarify, Conster, Construe, Decline, Define, Describe, Elucidate, Explicate, Exponible, Expose, Expound, Extenuate, Gloss, Gloze, Justify, Parabolize, Salve, Solve, Upknit

Explanation, Explanatory Apology, Commentary, Exegesis, Exegetic, Exposition, Farse, Gloss, Gloze, Hypothesis, Key, Note, Preface, Reading, Rigmarole, Solution, Theory

Expletive Arrah, Darn, Exclamation, Oath, Ruddy, Sapperment

Explicit Clean-cut, Clear, Definite, Express, Frank, Full-on, Outspoken, > PRECISE, Specific

Explode, Explosion, Explosive Agene, Airburst, Amatol, Ammonal, ANFO, Antimatter, Aquafortis, Backfire, Bang, Bangalore torpedo, Big bang, Blast, Burst, Cap, Cheddite, Chug, Cordite, Cramp, Crump, Cyclonite, Debunk, Detonate, Dualin, Dunnite, Dust, Egg, Erupt, Euchloric, Euchlorine, Fireball, Firecracker, Firedamp, Firework, Fulminant, Fulminate, Gasohol, Gelatine, Gelignite, Grenade, Guncotton, Gunpaper, Gunpowder, HE, High, Iracund, Jelly, Landmine, Low, Lyddite, Megaton, Melinite, Mine, Nail-bomb, Napalm, Nitroglycerine, Outburst, Ozonide, Paravane, Payload, Petar(d), Petre, Phut, Plastic, Plastique, Pluff, Pop, Population, Pow, Priming, Propellant, Ptarmic, Pustular, Report, Roburite, SAM, Semtex®, Sheet, Shrapnel, Snake, Sneeze, Soup, Squib, Supernova, Tetryl, Thunderflash, Tinderbox, TNT, Tonite, Trinitrobenzene, Trotyl, Volatile, Volcanic, Warhead, Xyloidin(e)

Exploit(s), Exploiter, Exploitation Act, Adventure, Deed, Develop, Escapade, Feat, Gest, Harness, Ill-use, Impose, Kulak, Manoeuvre, Milk, Mission, Parlay, Rachmanism, Ramp, Res gestae, Stunt, Sweat, Tap, Use, Utilise

Explore(r), Exploration Amerigo, Amundsen, Baffin, Balboa, Bandeirante, Banks, Barents, Bering, Boone, Burton, Cabot, Cartier, Chart, Columbus, Cook, Cortes, Da Gama, Dampier, Darwin, De Soto, Dias, Diaz, Discover, Dredge, Eric, Eriksson, Examine, Feel, Field trip, Frobisher, Fuchs, Humboldt, Investigate, Livingstone, Magellan, Map, Marco Polo, Mungo Park, Nansen, Navigator, Pathfinder, Peary, Pioneer, Potholer, Probe, Przewalski, Rale(i)gh, Research, Rhodes, Ross, Scott, Scout, Search, Shackleton, Spaceship, Speke, Stanley, Sturt, Tasman, Vancouver, Vasco da Gama, Vespucci

▷ **Explosive** *may indicate* an anagram

Exponent Advocate, Example, Index, Interpreter, Logarithm

Export(s) Despatch, Invisible, Klondike, Klondyke, Ship, Visible

Expose(d), Exposure Air, Anagogic, Bare, Bleak, Blot, Blow, Burn, Debag, Debunk, Denude, Desert, Disclose, Double, Endanger, En prisé, Exhibit, Flashing, Glareal, Indecent, Insolate, Moon, Nude, Object, Open, Out, Over, Propale, Reveal, Showdown, Snapshot, Streak, Strip, Subject, Sun, Time, Uncover, Unmask, Windswept

Exposition Aperçu

Expostulate, Expostulation Argue, Arrah, Protest, Remonstrate

Expound(er) Discourse, Discuss, Exegete, Explain, Open, Prelict, Red, Scribe, Ulema

Express(ed), Expression, Expressive Air, APT, Aspect, Breathe, Cacophemism, Circumbendimus, Cliché, Colloquialism, Conceive, Concetto, Couch,

Countenance, Declare, Denote, Eloquent, Embodiment, Epithet, Explicit, Face, Fargo, Formulate, Good-luck, Gup, Hang-dog, Hell's bells, Idiom, Limited, Locution, Lyrical, Manifest, Metonym, Mien, Mot (juste), Neologism, Non-stop, Orient, Paraphrase, Phrase, Pleonasm, Pony, Precise, Pronto, Put, Quep, Register, Say(ne), Show, Soulful, > SPEAK, State, Strain, Succus, Term, Token, Tone, Topos, Utterance, Vent, > VOICE

Expressionless Aphasia, Blank, Boot-faced, Deadpan, Impassive, Inscrutable, Po(ker)-faced, Vacant, Wooden

Expressman Fargo

Expropriate Dispossess, Pirate, Seize

Expulsion Discharge, Eccrisis, Ejection, Eviction, Exile, Sacking, Synaeresis

Expunge Cancel, Delete, Erase, Obliterate

Expurgate Bowdlerize, Castrate, Censor, Purge

Exquisite Beautiful, Choice, Ethereal, Fine, Intense, Lair, Macaroni, Pink, Princox, Refined, Soigné(e), Too-too

Ex-serviceman Vet

Extemporise Ad lib, Improvise, Pong

Extend(ed), Extension Add, Aspread, Augment, Conservative, Cremaster, Draw, Eke, Elapse, Ell, Elongate, Enlarge, Escalate, Expand, Exsert, Fermata, Grow, Increase, Jumboise, Length, Long, Long-range, Long-stay, Long-term, Offer, Outgrowth, Overbite, Overlap, Porrect, Proffer, Prolong, Propagate, Protract, Reach, Retrochoir, Span, Spread, Steso, > STRETCH, Substantial, Widen

Extensive, Extent Ambit, Area, Capacious, Catch-all, Compass, Comprehensive, Distance, Duration, Large, Latitude, Length, Limit, > MAGNITUDE, Panoramic, Range, Reach, Scale, Size, Spacious, Span, Spread-eagle, Sweeping, Wide, Widespread

Extenuate Diminish, Lessen, Mitigate, Palliate

Exterior Aspect, Crust, Derm, Facade, Outer, > OUTSIDE, Shell, Surface, Veneer

Exterminate, Extermination Abolish, Annihilate, Destroy, Holocaust, Uproot

External Exoteric, Exterior, Extraneous, Foreign, Outer

Extinct(ion) Archaeopteryx, Bygone, Chalicothere, Creodont, Dead, Death, Defunct, D(e)inothere, Dodo, Obsolete, Quagga, Rasure, Saururae, Theodont

Extinguish Douse, Dout, Dowse, Dowt, Extirpate, Obscure, Quash, Quell, Quench, Slake, Smother, Snuff, Stamp out, Stifle, Suppress

Extirpate End, Erase, Excise, Obliterate, Root, Uproot

Extol Commend, Enhance, Eulogise, Exalt, Laud, Puff

Extort(ion), Extortioner Barathrum, Blackmail, Bleed, Bloodsucker, Chantage, Chout, Churn, Compel, Exact, Force, Gombeen, Montem, Rachman, Rack, Racketeer, Ransom, Screw, Shank, Squeeze, Sweat, Urge, Vampire, Wrest, Wring

Extra Accessory, Additament, Addition(al), Additive, Adjunct, And, Annexe, Attachment, Bisque, Bonus, By(e), Debauchery, Encore, Etcetera, Further, Gash, Lagniappe, Left-over, Leg bye, Make-weight, More, Nimiety, Odd, Optional, Out, Over, Overtime, Perk, Plus, Plusage, Reserve, Ripieno, > SPARE, Spilth, Staffage, Sundry, Super, Supernumerary, Supplementary, Suppletive, Surplus, Trop, Undue, Walking-gentleman, Walking-lady, Wide, Woundy

Extract(ion), Extractor Apozem, Bleed, Breeding, Catechu, Clip, Corkscrew, Decoction, Descent, Distil, Draw, Educe, Elicit, Emulsin, Enucleate, Essence, Estreat, Excerpt, Exodontics, Extort, Gist, Gobbet, Insulin, Kino, Liver, Milk, Mine, Oust, Parentage, Passage, Pericope, Pick, Piece, Pituitary, Pry, Pyrene, Pyrethrin, Quintessence, Retour, Smelt, Squeeze, Stope, Suck, Summary, Tap, Trie, Try, Vanilla, Ventouse, Winkle, Worm, Wring, Yohimbine

Extradition Renvoi

Extraneous Extrinsic, Foreign, Irrelevant, Outlying, Spurious

Extraordinary Amazing, By-ordinar, Case, Curious, Humdinger, Important, Phenomenal, Preternatural, Rare, Singular, Startling, Strange, Unusual

Extravagance, **Extravagant**, **Extravaganza** Bombastic, Excessive, Fancy, Feerie, Glitzy, Heroic, High-flown, Hyperbole, Lavish, Luxury, Outré, Prodigal, Profligate, Profuse, Rampant, Reckless, Riotise, Romantic, Splash, Splurge, Squander, Sumptuous, Superfluous, Waste

Extreme(ly), **Extremist** Acute, Almighty, Butt, Deep-dyed, Desperate, Die-hard, Drastic, Edge, Exceptional, Farthermost, Gross, In spades, > INTENSE, Jacobin, Mega-, Mondo, Nazi, Opposite, Parlous, Pretty, Radical, Root and branch, Steep, Thule, Too, Tremendous, Ultimate, Ultima thule, Ultra, Unco, Utmost, Utter, > VERY, Vitally, Wing

▷ **Extreme** *may indicate* a first or last letter

Extremity Bourn(e), Crisis, Digit, Ending, Finger(-tip), Limb, Limit, Outrance, Pole, Tip, Toe, Utterance

Extricate Liberate, Loose, Rescue, Untangle

Extrinsic Aliunde, External, Irrelevant, Outward

Extrovert Lad, Outgoing

Extrude Debar, Eject, Project

Exuberance, **Exuberant** Brio, Copious, Ebullient, Effusive, Gusto, Hearty, Lavish, Mad, Profuse, Rambunctious, Rumbustious, Skippy, Streamered

Exudation, **Exude** Bleed, Ectoplasm, Emit, Extravasate, Guttate, Ooze, Secrete, Still, Sweat, Swelter, Ulmin, Weep

Exult(ant) Crow, Elated, > GLOAT, Glorify, Jubilant, Paeonic, Rejoice, Triumphant, Whoop

Eye(ful), **Eye-ball**, **Eyes**, **Eyepiece** Beady, Canthus, Compound, Cringle, Eagle, Ee, Eine, Electric, Emmetropia, Evil, Glad, Glass, Glim, Glom, Goggles, Hurricane, Huygen's, Iris, Jack, Keek, Klieg, Lamp, Lazy, Lens, London, Magic, Mincepie, Mind's, Mongoloid, Naked, > OBSERVE, Ocellar, Ocular, Ogle, Ommateum, Ommatidium, Optic, Orb, Pedicel, Peeper, PI, Pigsn(e)y, Pigsnie, Pineal, Pupil, Regard, Retina, Rhabdom, Roving, Sclera, Screw, Shufti, Shufty, Sight, Spy, Storm-centre, Tec, Third, Uvea, Watch, Water-pump, Weather, Whally, Windows, Winker

Eyebright Euphrasy

Eyebrow Bree, Brent-hill, Glib, Penthouse, Superciliary

Eyeglass Loupe

Eyelash Cilium

Eyelet Cringle, Grommet, Hole

Eyelid Canthus, Ectropion, Haw, Palpebral

Eye-rod Rhabdom

Eye-shadow Kohl

Eyesore Blot, Disfigurement, Sty(e)

Eye-stalk Ommatophore, Stipes

Eye trouble Amblyopia, Ametropia, Aniseikonia, Anisomatropia, Aphakia, Asthenopia, Astigmatism, Cataract, Ceratitis, Coloboma, Cycloplegia, Diplopia, Entropion, Erythropsia, Exophthalmus, Glaucoma, Hemeralopia, Hemi(an)op(s)ia, Hypermetropia, Hyperopia, Iritis, Keratitis, Leucoma, Lippitude, Micropsia, Miosis, Monoblepsis, Muscae volitantes, Myosis, Nebula, Nyctalopia, Nystagmus, Ommateum, Palinop(s)ia, Photophobia, Photopsia, Pink-eye, Presbyopia, Private, Retinitis, Retinoblastoma, Scotoma(ta), Seeing, Shiner, Stigmatism, Strabismus, Strephosymbolia,

Strong, Stye, Synechia, Teichopsia, Thylose, Thylosis, Trachoma, Trichiasis, Tritanopia, Tylosis, Wall-eye, Xeroma, Xerophthalmia

Eye-wash Collyrium

Eyrie Nest

Ezra Pound

Ff

F Fahrenheit, Fellow, Feminine, Fluorine, Following, Force, Foxtrot

Fab Super

Fabian, Fabius Dilatory, Washington

Fable(s) Aesop, Allegory, Apologue, Exemplum, Fiction, Hitopadesa, La Fontaine, Legend, Marchen, Milesian, Myth, Panchatantra, Parable, Romance, Tale, Tarand

Fabric > CLOTH, Contexture, Framework

Fabricate, Fabrication Artefact, Concoct, Construct, Contrive, Cook, Fake, Fangle, Figment, Forge, > INVENT, Lie, Porky, Trump, Weave, Web

Fabulous (beast), Fabulous place Apocryphal, Apologue, Chichevache, Chimera, Cockatrice, Eldorado, Fictitious, Fung, Gear, Griffin, Hippogriff, Hippogryph, Huma, Incredible, Jabberwock(y), Kylin, Legendary, Magic, Manticora, Manticore, Merman, Monoceros, Mythical, Opinicus, Orc, Phoenix, Roc, Romantic, Simorg, Simurg(h), Snark, Sphinx, Tarand, Tragelaph, Unicorn, Unreal, Utopia, Wivern, Wyvern, Yale

Facade Front(age), Frontal, Mask, Pretence

Face, Facing Abide, Affront, Ashlar, Ashler, Aspect, Audacity, Brave, Brazen, Caboched, Caboshed, Cheek, Chiv(v)y, Coal, Countenance, Culet, Dalle, Dare, Dartle, Deadpan, Dial, Eek, Elevation, Encounter, Facade, Fat, Favour, Features, Fineer, Fortune, > FRONT, Gardant, Girn, Gonium, Grid, Groof, Groue, Grouf, Gurn, Hatchet, Head-on, Jib, Kisser, Light, Lining, Look, Lore, Mascaron, Meet, Metope, Moe, Mug, Mush, Obverse, Opposite, Outstare, Outward, Pan, Paper tiger, Phisnomy, Phiz(og), Physiognomy, Poker, Puss, Revet, Revetment, Roughcast, Rud, Rybat, Side, Snoot, Socle, Straight, Stucco, Type, Veneer, Vis(age), Visnomy, Withstand, Zocco(lo)

Face-ache Noli-me-tangere

Face-lift Rhytidectomy

Face-saving Redeeming, Salvo

Facet(ed) Angle, Aspect, Bezel, Culet, Face, Pavilion, Polyhedron

Facetious Frivolous, Jocular, Waggish, Witty

Facile Able, Adept, Complaisant, Ductile, Easy, Fluent, Glib

Facilitate, Facility Amenity, Assist, Benefit, Capability, > EASE, Expedite, Fluency, Gift, ISO, Knack, Skill

Facsimile Copy, Photostat®, Replica, Repro

Fact(s), Factual Actual, Case, Corpus delicti, Correct, Data, Datum, Detail, Griff, Info, Literal, Mainor, Nay, Really, Truism, Truth, Veridical, Yes

Faction Bloc, Cabal, Camp, Caucus, Clique, Contingent, Ghibelline, Guelph, Junto, Red Army, Schism, Sect, Tendency, Wing

Factor Agent, Aliquot, Broker, Cause, Chill, Clotting, Coagulation, Co-efficient, Common, > COMPONENT, Divisor, Edaphic, Element, F, Feel-good, Growth, House, Intrinsic, Load, Modulus, Power, Q, Quality, Representative, Rh, Rhesus, Risk, Safety, Steward, Wind chill, X

Factory Cannery, Gasworks, Glassworks, Hacienda, Maquiladora, Mill, Plant,

Refinery, Sawmill, Steelworks, Sweatshop, Tinworks, Works, Workshop

Factotum Circar, Handyman, Servant, Sircar, Sirkar

Faculty Aptitude, Arts, Capacity, Department, Ear, Ease, Indult, Knack, Power, School, Sense, Speech, > **TALENT**, Teachers, Wits

Fad(dish) Crank, Craze, Cult, Fashion, Foible, Ismy, Thing, Vogue, Whim

Fade(d), **Fading** Blanch, Die, Diminuendo, Dinge, Elapsion, Etiolate, Evanescent, Fall, Filemot, Lessen, Mancando, Pale, Passé, Perdendo(si), Peter, Smorzando, Smorzato, Stonewashed, Vade, Vanish, Wallow, Wilt, Wither

Faeces Dingleberry, Dung, Kak, Meconium, Motion, Mute, Scybalum, Skatole, Stercoraceous, Stools

Fag(ging) Chore, Cigarette, Drag, Drudge, Fatigue, Gasper, Homosexual, Menial, Pennalism, Quean, Reefer, Snout, Tire, Toil, Weary

Fag-end Ash, Butt, Dout, Lag, Snipe, Stub

Fag(g)ot(s) Bavin, Bundle, Fascine, Firewood, Homosexual, Kid, Knitch, Twigs

Fail(ing), **Failure** Ademption, Anile, Anuria, Blemish, Blow, Bomb, Bummer, Cark, > **COLLAPSE**, Conk, Crack up, Crash, Cropper, Debacle, Decline, Defalcation, Default, Defect, Demerit, Die, Dog, Dry, Dud, Fault, Feal, Fiasco, Fink out, Flame out, Flivver, Flop, Flow, Flunk, Fold, Founder, Frost, Glitch, Gutser, Infraction, Lapse, Lemon, Lose, Malfunction, Manqué, Mis-, Miscarry, Miss, Muff, Nerd, No-hoper, No-no, Omit, Outage, Oversight, Pip, Plough, Pluck, Pratfall, Reciprocity, Refer, Refusal, Respiratory, Shambles, Short(coming), Short circuit, Slippage, Smash, Spin, Stumer, Turkey, Vice, Wash-out, Weakness, White elephant, Wipeout

Fain Lief

Faineant Gallio

Faint(ness) Black-out, Conk, Darkle, Dim, Dizzy, Dwalm, Fade, Lassitude, Pale, Stanck, Swarf, Swarve, Swelt, Swerf, Swerve, Swoon, Swound, Syncope, Unclear, Wan, Whitish

Faint-heart Coward, Craven, Timid, Wet

Fair Adequate, A(e)fald, Aefauld, Aefwld, Barnet, Bartholomew, Bazaar, Beauteous, Beautiful, Belle, Blond, Bon(n)ie, Bonny, Brigg, Decent, Dishy, Donnybrook, Equal, Equitable, Evenhanded, Exhibition, Expo(sition), Feeing-market, > **FESTIVAL**, Fine, Funfair, Gaff, Gala, Gey, Goose, Gwyn, Hiring, Honest, Hopping, Isle, > **JUST**, Kermess, Kermis, Kirmess, Market, Mart, Mediocre, Mela, Mop, Nundinal, Objective, OK, Paddington, Passable, Play, Pro rata, Rosamond, Sabrina, Sporting, Square, Statute, Steeple, Straight, Tavistock, Tidy, Tolerable, Tow-headed, Trade, Tryst, Unbias(s)ed, Vanity, Wake, Widdicombe

Fair-buttocked Callipygean

Fairing Ornament, Spat

Fairly Clearly, Enough, Evenly, Midway, Moderately, Pari passu, Pretty, Properly, Quite, Ratherish

Fairway Dog-leg, Pretty

Fairy, **Fairies** Banshee, Befana, Cobweb, Dobbie, Dobby, Elf(in), Fay, Gloriana, Good people, Hob, Hop o' my thumb, Leprechaun, Lilian, Little people, Mab, Morgane(tta), Morgan le Fay, Moth, Nis, Peri, Pigwidgin, Pigwiggen, Pisky, Pixie, Pouf, Puck, Punce, Sandman, Seelie, Sidhe, Spirit, Sprite, Sugar-plum, Tink(erbell), Titania, Tooth, Unseelie, Urchin-shows

Faith(ful) Accurate, Achates, Belief, Constant, Creed, Devoted, Doctrine, Faix, Fay, Feal, Fegs, Fideism, Fiducial, Haith, Implicit, Islam, Lay, Loyal, Plerophory, Punic, Puritanism, Quaker, Religion, Shahada, Shema, Solifidian, Staunch, Strict, Troth, > **TRUE**, True-blue, Trust, Truth, Umma(h)

Faithless Atheist, Disloyal, False, Hollow, Nullifidian, Perfidious, Punic

Fake(r), Faking Bodgie, Bogus, Copy, Counterfeit, Duff(er), Ersatz, False, Fold, Fraud, Fudge, Imitation, Imposter, Impostor, Paste, Phoney, Postiche, Pretend, Sham, Spurious, Trucage, Truquage, Truqueur, Unreal

Falcon Gentle, Hawk, Hobby, Iceland, Kestrel, Lanner(et), Merlin, Nyas, Peregrine, Prairie, Saker, Sakeret, Spar-hawk, Sparrow-hawk, Stallion, Staniel, Stannel, Stanyel, Tassel-gentle, Tassell-gent, Tercel-gentle, Tercel-jerkin

Falklander Kelper

Fall(s), Fallen, Falling Abate, Accrue, Angel, Arches, Astart, Autumn, Boyoma, Cadence, Cascade, Cataract, Churchill, Chute, Collapse, Crash, Cropper, Cross press, Declension, Decrease, Degenerate, Descent, Dip, Domino effect, Douse, Downswing, Dowse, > **DROP**, Ebb, Firn, Flag, Flop, Flump, Folding press, Free, Grabble, Grand, Gutser, Gutzer, Horseshoe, Idaho, Iguaçu, Incidence, Kabalega, Kaieteur, Lag, Landslide, Lapse, Lin(n), Niagara, Oct(ober), Onding, Owen, Perish, Plonk, Plummet, Plump, Plunge, Prolapse, Purl(er), Rain, Reaction, Relapse, Ruin, Sheet, Sin, Sleet, Snow, Soss, Spill, Stanley, Sutherland, Tailor, Takakkau, Topple, Toss, Trip, Tugela, Tumble, Victoria, Voluntary, Wipeout, Yellowstone, Yosemite

Fallacious, Fallacy Elench(us), Error, Gamblers', Idolum, Ignoratio elenchi, Illogical, Illusion, Material, Naturalistic, Pathetic, Sophism, Specious, Unsound

Fallible Human, Imperfect

▷ **Falling** *may indicate* an anagram or a word backwards

Fallow Barren, Lea, Tan, Uncared, Uncultivated, Untilled

False, Falsify Adulterate, Bastard, Bodgie, Bogus, Braide, Canard, Cavil, Charlatan, Cook, Deceitful, Disloyal, Dissemble, Doctor, Fake, Feigned, Fiddle, Forge, Illusory, Knave, Lying, Meretricious, Mock, Perjury, Pinchbeck, Postiche, Pretence, Pseudo, Rap, Roorback, Sham, Specious, Spoof, Spurious, Treacherous, Two-faced, Untrue, Veneer

False notions Idola

Falter Hesitate, Limp, Stoiter, Totter, Waver

Fame, Famous Bruit, Celebrity, Distinguished, Eminent, Glitterati, Gloire, Glory, Greatness, History, Humour, Illustrious, Kudos, Legendary, Luminous, Name, Noted, Notorious, Prestige, Reclamé, Renown, Repute, Rumour, Splendent, Spur, Stardom, Word

Familiar(ise), Familiarity Accustom, Acquaint, Assuefaction, Au fait, Auld, Chummy, Comrade, Conversant, Crony, Dear, Demon, Easy, Free, Friend, Habitual, Homely, Homey, Incubus, Intimate, Known, Liberty, Maty, Old, Old-hat, Privy, Python, Used, Versed, Warhorse

Family Ancestry, Bairn-team, Blood, Breed, Brood, Clan, Class, Close-knit, Cognate, Consanguine, Descent, Dynasty, Extended, House(hold), Issue, Kin, Kind, Line, Mafia, Medici, Name, Nuclear, One-parent, Orange, People, Phratry, Progeny, Quiverful, Race, Sept, Sib(b), Sibship, Stem, Stirps, Strain, Taffy, Talbot, Tribe, Whanau

Family tree Pedigree, Stemma

Famine Dearth, Lack, Scarcity

Famish(ed) Esurient, Hungry, Ravenous, Starving

▷ **Famished** *may indicate* an 'o' in the middle of a word

Fan(s), Fan-like Admirer, Aficionado, Alligator, Alluvial, Arouse, Bajada, Blow, Cat, Clapper, Claque, Colmar, Cone, Cool, Cuscus, Devotee, Diadrom, Dryer, Enthusiast, Extractor, Fiend, Flabellum, Following, Groupie, Hepcat, Khuskhus, Nut, Outspread, Partisan, Punka(h), Rhipidate, Ringsider,

Sail, Spectator, Spread, Supporter, Tail, Tifosi, Ventilate, Votary, Voteen, Washingtonia, Wind machine, Wing, Winnow, Zealot, Zelant

▸ **Fan** *may indicate* an anagram

Fanatic(al) Bigot, Devotee, Energumen, Enthusiastic, Extremist, Fiend, Frenetic, Glutton, Mad, Maniac, Nut, Partisan, Phrenetic, Picard, Rabid, Santon, Ultra, Wowser, Zealot

Fancy, Fanciful Caprice, Chim(a)era, Conceit, Concetto, Crotchet, Daydream, Dream, Dudish, Elaborate, Fangle, Fantasy, Fit, Flam, Florid, Frothy, Guess, Hallo, Idea(te), Idolon, > IMAGINE, Inclination, Lacy, Liking, Maya, Mind, My, Nap, Notion, Ornamental, Ornate, Picture, Pipe dream, Predilection, Reverie, Rococo, Suppose, Thought, Urge, Vagary, Visionary, Ween, Whigmaleerie, Whigmaleery, Whim(sy), Woolgather

▸ **Fancy** *may indicate* an anagram

Fane Banner, Pronaos

Fanfare Flourish, Sennet, Show, Tantara, Trump, Tucket

Fang Tooth, Tusk

Fanny Adams, Bottom, Gas-lit, Price

Fantasist, Fantasy, Fantastic Absurd, Antic, Bizarre, Caprice, Chimera, Cockaigne, Cockayne, Escapism, Fab, Fanciful, Grotesque, Hallucination, Idol, Kickshaw(s), Lucio, Myth, Outré, Phantasmagoria, Queer, Romance, Unreal, Untrue, Walter Mitty, Wannabe(e), > WHIM, Whimsical, Wild

Far Apogean, Away, Distal, Distant, Extreme, Outlying, Remote, Thether, Thither

Farce(ur) Burletta, Charade, Comedy, Exode, Feydeau, Lazzo, Mime, Mockery, Pantomime, Rex, Sham

Fare Apex, Charge, Cheer, Commons, Do, Eat, Excess, Excursion, > FOOD, Go, Passage, Passenger, Rate, Table, Traveller

Farewell Adieu, Adios, Aloha, Apopemptic, Bye, Cheerio, Departure, Godspeed, > GOODBYE, Leave, Prosper, Sayonara, Send off, So long, Toodle-oo, Toodle-pip, Totsiens, Vale, Valediction

Far-fetched Fanciful, Improbable, Recherché

Farm(ing), Farmhouse Agronomy, Arable, Bocage, Bowery, City, Cold Comfort, Collective, Cooperative, Croft, Cultivate, Dairy, Deep-litter, Dry, Emmerdale, Estancia, Extensive, Factory, Fat, Fish(ery), Funny, Geoponical, Grange, Hacienda, Health, Home, Homestead, Husbandry, Intensive, Kibbutz, Kolkhoz, Land, Ley, Loaf, Location, Mailing, Mains, Mas, Mixed, No-tillage, Onstead, Orley, Pen, Plaas, Plough, Poultry, Ranch, Rent, Sewage, Shamba, Sheep station, Smallholding, Sovkhoz, Station, Stead(ing), Sted(d), Stedde, Steed, Stock, Store, Stump, Subsistence, Tank, Till, Toon, Toun, Town, Trash, Tree, Truck, Wick, Wind

Farmer Blockie, Boer, Campesino, Carl, Cockatoo, Cocklaird, Cocky, Collins Street, Colon, Cow cocky, Crofter, Estanciero, Gebur, Gentleman, George, Giles, Hick, Hobby, Macdonald, Metayer, Nester, NFU, Peasant, Pitt Street, Queer St, Ryot, Share-cropper, Smallholder, Sodbuster, Squatter, Stubble-jumper, Tenant, Tiller, Whiteboy, Yeoman, Zeminda(r)

Farmhand Cadet, Cottar, Cotter, Cottier, Ditcher, Hand, He(a)rdsman, Hind, Ploughman, Redneck, Rouseabout, Roustabout, Shearer

▸ **Farmhouse** *see* FARM

Farmyard Barton, Homestall, Villatic

Farouche Awkward, Shy, Sullen

Farrago Hotch-potch, Jumble, Medley, Mélange

Farrier Marshal, Smith

Farrow Litter, Mia, Sow

Far-sighted Presbyte

Fart Poep

Farthing Brass, F, Fadge, Har(r)ington, Mite, Q, Quadragesimal, Rag

Fascia Band, Fillet, Platband

Fascinate, **Fascinating** Allure, Attract, Bewitch, > CHARM, Dare, Enchant, Engross, Enthral(l), Fetching, Inthral, Intrigue, Kill, Mesmeric, Rivet, Siren, Witch

Fascist Blackshirt, Blue shirt, Brownshirt, Dictator, Falange, Falangist, Iron Guard, Lictor, Nazi, Neo-nazi, NF, Rexist, Sinarchist, Sinarquist

Fashion(able), **Fashioned** Aguise, A la (mode), Bristol, Build, Chic, Construct, Convention, Corinthian, Craze, Create, Cult, Custom, Cut, Dernier cri, Design, Directoire, Elegant, Entail, Fad, Feat, Feign, Forge, Form, Genteel, Go, Hew, High, Hip, Hot, In, Invent, Kitsch, Look, > MAKE, Man-about-town, Manière, Manners, Mode, Mondain(e), Mould, Newgate, Pink, Preppy, Rage, Rag trade, Rate, Roy, Sc, Shape, Smart, Smith, Snappy, Snazzy, Stile, Stylar, Style, Swish, Tailor, Ton, Ton(e)y, Tonish, > TREND(Y), Turn, Twig, Vogue, Way, Wear, With-it, Work, Wrought

Fast(ing), **Faster** Abstain, Apace, Ashura, Breakneck, Citigrade, Clem, Cracking, Daring, Dharna, Dhurna, Double-quick, Elaphine, Express, Fizzer, Fleet, Immobile, Lent, Lightning, Loyal, Maigre, Meteoric, Moharram, Muharram, Muharrem, Pac(e)y, Posthaste, Presto, Pronto, Quadragesimal, Quick, Raffish, Raking, Ramadan, Ramadhan, Rash, Relay, Siyam, Spanking, Speedy, Stretta, Stretto, Stuck, Supersonic, Swift, Tachyon, Thick, Tight, Tisha b'Av, TishaBov, Tishah-Baav, Tishah-b(e)Ab, Tishah-b(e)Av, Whistle-stop, Yarer, Yom Kippur

Fast and loose Fickle, Pick-the-garter, Strap-game

Fasten(er), **Fastening** Anchor, Attach, Bar, Belay, Bind, Bolt, Buckle, Button, Chain, Clamp, Clasp, Click, Clinch, Clip, Cramp, Cufflink, Dead-eye, Diamond-hitch, Dome, Espagnolette, Eye-bolt, Frog, Gammon, Hasp, Hesp, Hook, Lace, Latch, Lock, Moor, Morse, Nail, Netsuke, Nut, Padlock, Parral, Patent, Pectoral, Pin, Preen, Press stud, Reeve, Rivet, Rope, Rove, Seal, > SECURE, Sew up, Shut, Spar, Sprig, Staple, Stitch, Tach(e), Tag, Tape, Tassel, Tether, Tintack, Toggle, U-bolt, Velcro®, Wedge, Zip

Fastidious Chary, Critical, Dainty, Fussy, Neat, Nice, Particular, Precieuse, Precious, Squeamish

Fat(s), **Fatten**, **Fatty** Adipic, Adipocere, Adipose, Aldermanly, Aliphatic, Arcus, Atheroma, Bard, Batten, Battle, Blubber, Brown, Butter, Calipash, Calipee, Cellulite, Cholesterol, Chubbed, Chubby, Corpulent, Creesh, Degras, Dika-oil, Dosh, Dripping, Embonpoint, Enarm, Endomorph, Flab, Flesh, Flick, Fozy, Fubsy, Galam-butter, Grease, Gross, Keech, Kitchen-fee, Lanolin, Lard, Leaf, Lipaemia, Lipid, Lipoma, Love handles, Margarine, Marge, Marrow, Obese, Oil, OS, Palmitin, Pinguid, Plump, Poddy, Podgy, Polyunsaturated, Portly, Puppy, Pursy, Rich, Rolypoly, Rotund, Saddlebags, Saginate, Saim, Saturated, Schmal(t)z, Seam(e), Sebacic, Sebum, Shortening, Soil, Spare tyre, Spe(c)k, Squab, Stearic, Steatopygia, Steatorrhea, Suberin, Suet, Tallow, Tin, Tomalley, Triglyceride, Tub, Unsaturated, Vanaspati, Waller, Wool

Fatal(ism), **Fate(s)**, **Fated**, **Fateful** Apnoea, Atropos, Cavel, Chance, Clotho, Deadly, Death, Decuma, Destiny, Doom, End, Fay, Fell, Joss, Karma, Kismet, Lachesis, Lethal, Lot, Meant, Moira, Mortal, Mortiferous, Nemesis, Norn(a), Parca, Pernicious, Portion, Predestination, Skuld, Urd, Verdande, Waterloo, Weird, Weird sisters

Father(ly) Abba, Abbot, Abuna, Adopt, Apostolic, Bapu, Begetter, Breadwinner, Brown, City, Curé, Dad, Engender, Foster, Founding, Fr, Generator, Genitor, Getter, Gov, Governor, Guv, Male, Pa, Padre, Papa, Pappy, Parent, Pater(nal), Paterfamilias, Patriarch, Père, Pilgrim, Pop(pa), Popper, Priest, Rev, Sire, Stud, Thames, Tiber, William

Father-lasher Sea-scorpion

Fathom Delve, Depth, Dig, F, Plumb, Plummet, Understand

Fatigue Battle, Combat, Exhaust, Fag, Jade, Jet lag, ME, Metal, Neurosthenia, Overdo, Tire, Weariness, Weary

Fatuous Gaga, Idiotic, Silly, Stupid

Faucet Cock, Spigot, Tap

Fault(y) Arraign, Bad, Beam, Blame(worthy), Blunder, Bug, Cacology, Carp, Culpable, Defect, Demerit, Dip, Dip-slip, Drop-out, Duff, > **ERROR**, Failing, Flaw, Frailty, Gall, Glitch, Gravity, Henpeck, Hitch, Imperfect, Literal, Massif, > **MISTAKE**, Nag, Nibble, Niggle, Nit-pick, Oblique, Out, Outcrop, Overthrust, Para, Peccadillo, Rate, Reprehend, Rift, Rupes Recta, San Andreas, Sclaff, Set-off, Short, Slip, Step, Strike, Strike-slip, Technical, Thrust, Trap, Underthrust, Upbraid, Vice

Faultless Immaculate, Impeccable, Lily-white, Perfect

Fauna Mesobenthos, Wild life

Fauvist Matisse

Faux pas Blunder, Boner, Gaffe, Leglen-girth, Solecism

Favour(able), **Favoured**, **Favourite** Advance, Advantage(ous), Aggrace, Agraste, Alder-liefest, Approval, Back, Befriend, Behalf, Benign, Bless, Boon, Bribe, Cert, Chosen, Cockade, Curry, Darling, Ex gratia, Fancy, Favodian, Form horse, Good turn, Grace, Graste, Gratify, Gree, Hackle, Hot, In, Indulge, Kickback, Minion, Odour, Particular, Peat, Persona grata, Pet, Pettle, Popular, > **PREFER**, Promising, Propitious, Resemble, Rib(b)and, Roseate, Rose-knot, Rosette, Smile, Toast, Token, Win-win

Fawn(er), **Fawning** Adulate, Bambi, Beige, Blandish, Brown-nose, Crawl, Creep, Cringe, Deer, Ecru, Flatter, Fleech, Grovel, Ko(w)tow, Lickspittle, Obsequious, Servile, Smarm, Smoo(d)ge, Subservient, Sycophant, Tasar, Toady, Truckle, Tussah, Tusseh, Tusser, Tussore

Fay Fairy, Korrigan, Peri

FBI G-men

Fear Aichmophobia, Angst, Apprehension, Awe, Bête noire, Bugbear, Claustrophobia, Cold sweat, Crap, Creeps, Cyberphobia, Dismay, Doubt, Drad, Dread, Foreboding, > **FOR FEAR**, Fright, Funk, Hang-up, Horror, Kenophobia, Mysophobia, Nyctophobia, Ochlophobia, > **PHOBIA**, Photophobia, Redoubt, Revere, Taphephobia, Taphophobia, Terror, Thalassophobia, Trepidation, Willies

Fearful Afraid, Cowardly, Dire, Horrific, Nervous, Pavid, Rad, Redoubtable, Timorous, Tremulous, Windy

Fearless Bold, Brave, Courageous, Gallant, Impavid, Intrepid

Fearsome Dire, Formidable

Feasible Goer, Likely, On, Possible, Practical, Probable, Viable

Feast Adonia, Agape, Assumption, Banquet, Barmecide, Beano, Belshazzar's, Blow-out, Candlemas, Carousal, Celebration, Dine, Do, Double, Eat, Encaenia, Epiphany, Epulation, Festival, Fleshpots, Fool's, Gaudeamus, Gaudy, Halloween, Hallowmas, Hockey, Hogmanay, Holy Innocents, Id-al-Adha, Id-al-Fitr, Immaculate Conception, Isodia, Junket, Kai-kai, Lady Day, Lamb-ale, Lammas, Love, Luau, Lucullus, Martinmas, Michaelmas, Midnight, Movable,

Noel, Passover, Pentecost, Pig, Potlatch, Purim, Regale, Revel, Roodmas, Seder, Shindig, Spread, Succoth, Sukkot(h), Tabernacles, Tuck-in, Wake, Wayzgoose, Weeks, Yule, Zagmuk

Feast-day Mass

Feat Achievement, Deed, Effort, Exploit, Gambado, Handspring, Stunt, Trick

Feather(ed), **Feathers** Alula, Barbicel, Boa, Braccate, Cock, Contour, Covert, Crissum, Down, Duster, Filoplume, Flags, Fledged, Fletch, Flight, Gemmule, Hackle, Harl, Hatchel, Herl, Lei, Lure, Macaroni, Manual, Oar, Ostrich, Pen(na), Pin, Pinna, Pith, Plumage, Plume, Plumule, Pteryla, Ptilosis, > QUILL, Rectrix, Remex, Remiges, Rocket-tail, Saddle-hackle, Scapular, Scapus, Secondary, Semiplume, Shaft, Shag, Sickle, Standard, Stipa, Swansdown, Tectrix, Tertial, Vibrissa, White, Wing covert

Feather-worker Plumassier

Feature(s) Acoustic, Amenity, Appurtenance, Article, Aspect, Attribute, Brow, Character, Chin, Depict, Double, Eye, Eyebrow, Face, Figure, Hallmark, Highlight, Item, Jizz, Landmark, Lineament, Neotery, Nose, Nucleus, Overfold, Phiz(og), Physiognomy, Spandrel, Star, Temple, Trait, Underlip

Featureless Flat

Febrifuge Atabrin, Atebrin®, Mepacrine, Quina

February Fill-dyke

Fecund(ity) Fertile, Fruitful, Prolific, Uberty

Federal, **Federation** Alliance, Axis, Bund, Commonwealth, Interstate, League, Russian, Statal, Union

Fee Charge, Chummage, Commitment, Common, Contingency, Corkage, Drop-dead, Dues, Duty, Faldage, Fine, Groundage, Hire, Honorarium, Interchange, Mortuary, Mouter, Multure, Obvention, Pay, Premium, Refresher, Retainer, Sub, Subscription, Transfer, Tribute

Feeble Banal, Characterless, Daidling, Debile, Decrepit, Droob, Effete, Feckless, Fizzenless, Flaccid, Foisonless, Footling, Fragile, Fus(h)ionless, Geld, Ineffective, Infirm, Jessie, Namby-pamby, Pale, Puny, Sassy, Sickly, Slender, Slight, Tailor, Tame, Thin, Tootle, Wallydrag, Wallydraigle, Washy, Wastrel, Weak, Weak-kneed, Weak-minded, Weed, Weedy, Wersh, Wet, Wimpish, Worn

Feed(er), **Feeding** Battle, Bib, Break, Browse, Cake, Cater, Cibation, Clover, Cowfeteria, Cram, Cue, Demand, Dine, Dressing, Drip, > EAT, Fatten, Filter, Fire, Fishmeal, Flushing, Fodder, Food, Force, Gavage, Graze, Hay, Lunch, Meal, Nourish, Paid, Pecten, Provender, Refect, Repast, Sate, Soil, Stoke, Stooge, Stover, Sustain, Tire, Tractor, Wean, Wet nurse

Feedback Negative, Positive

Feel, **Feeling(s)** Aesthesia, Affetuoso, Artificial, Atmosphere, Ballottement, Compassion, Darshan, Déja vu, > EMOTION, Empathy, Empfindung, Euphoria, > EXPERIENCE, Fellow, Finger, Flaw, Frisk, Grope, Groundswell, Handle, Heart, Heartstrings, Hunch, Intuit, Knock, Know, Palp, Passible, Passion, Phatic, Pity, Premonition, Presentiment, Probe, Realise, Sensate, Sensation, > SENSE, Sensitive, Sentiment, Somesthesis, Spirit, Tactual, Touch, Turn, Undercurrent, Vehemence, Vibes, Vibrations, Zeal

Feeler Antenna, Barbel, Exploratory, Overture, Palp, Sensillum, Tentacle

▸ **Feet** *see* FOOT

Feign Act, Affect, Colour, Fake, Malinger, Mime, Mock, > PRETEND, Sham, Simulate

Feint Deke, Disguise, Dodge, Faint, Fake, Spoof, Trick

Fel(d)spar Adularia, Albite, Anorthite, Gneiss, Hyalophane, Moonstone, Orthoclase, Petuntse, Petuntze, Plagioclase, Sun-stone

Felicity Bliss, Happiness, Joy, Relevance
Feline *see* CAT
Fell Axe, Chop, Cruel, Deadly, Dire, Dread, Fierce, Heath, Hew, Hide, Hill, Inhuman, Knock-down, KO, Lit, Log, Malign, Moor, Pelt, Poleaxe, Ruthless, Sca, Shap, Skittle
Fellow(s), Fellowship Academic, Associate, Bawcock, Birkie, Bloke, Bo, Bro, Buffer, Carlot, Cat, Chal, Chap, Chi, China, Cock, Cod(ger), Collaborator, Co-mate, Communion, Companion, Comrade, Confrère, Cove, Cully, Cuss, Dandy, Dean, Dog, Don, Dude, Equal, F, Fogey, Fop, Gadgie, Gadje, Gaudgie, Gauje, Gink, Guy, Joe, Joker, Josser, Kerel, Lad, Like, M, Mall, Man, Mate, Member, Mister, Mun, Partner, Peer, Professor, Rival, Seniority, Sister, Sociate, Sodality, Swab, Twin, Waghalter, Wallah
Felon(y) Bandit, Convict, Crime, Gangster, Offence, Villain
Felt Bat(t), Drugget, Knew, Met, Numdah, Numnah, Pannose, Roofing, Sensed, Tactile, Underlay, Velour
Female (bodies), Feminine, Feminist Anima, Bint, Bit, Dame, Distaff, Doe, F, Filly, Girl, Harem, Hen, Her, Kermes, Lady, Libber, Maiden, Muliebriety, Pen, Petticoated, Riot girl, Sakti, Shakti, She, Sheila, Shidder, Soft, Spindle, Thelytoky, -trix, > WOMAN, Yin
Female, Feminine *may indicate* an -ess ending
Fen Bog, Carr, Ea, Jiao, Marsh, Morass
Fence(r), Fencing (position) Balestra, Bar, Barrier, Botte, Carte, Croisé, Cyclone®, Derobement, Dogleg, Enclose, Epee, Feint, Flanconade, Flèche, Foils, Fraise, Froissement, Haha, Hay, Hedge, Hot, Hurdle, Iaido, Imbrocate, Inquartata, Kendo, Link, Mensur, Molinello, Montant, Netting, Obstacle, Ox, Oxer, Pale, Paling, Palisade, Palisado, Parry, Passado, Pen, Picket, Post and rail, Quart(e), Quinte, Rabbit-fence, Raddle, Rail, Rasper, Receiver, Reset, Ring, Scrimure, Seconde, Sept(um), Septime, Singlestick, Sixte, Snow, Stacket, Stockade, Stramac, Stramazon, Sunk, Swordplay, Tac-au-tac, Tierce, Touché, Trellis, Virginia, Wattle, Wear, Weir, Weldmesh®, Wire, Worm
Fend(er) Buffer, Bumper, Cowcatcher, Curb, Mudguard, Parry, Provide, Resist, Skid, Ward, Wing
Fennel Finnochio, Finoc(c)hio, Herb, Love-in-a-mist, Narthex, Ragged lady
Fent Offcut, Remnant, Slit
Feral Brutal, Fierce, Savage, Wild
Ferdinand Archduke, Bull
Ferment(ation) Barm, Enzym(e), Leaven, Mowburn, Protease, Ptyalin, Seethe, Solera, Storm, Stum, Trypsin, Turn, Vinify, Working, Ye(a)st, Zyme, Zymo-, Zymology, Zymosis, Zymurgy
Fermium Fm
Fern Acrogenous, Adder's-tongue, Adiantum, Archegonial, Asparagus, Aspidium, Asplenium, Azolla, Barometz, Bird's nest, Bladder, Bracken, Brake, Bristle, Buckler, Bungwall, Ceterach, Cinnamon, Coral, Cryptogam, Cyathea, Cycad, Dicksonia, Door, Elkhorn, Fairy moss, Filicales, Filices, Filmy, Fishbone, Grape, Hard, Hart's-tongue, Ice, Isoetes, Lady, Maidenhair, Male, Marattia, Marsh, Marsilea, Marsilia, Meadow, Moonwort, Mosquito, Mulewort, Nardoo, Nephrolepis, Oak, Ophioglossum, Osmunda, Parsley, Pepperwort, Pig, Pillwort, Polypod, Polystichum, Ponga, Pteridology, Pteris, Punga, Rachilla, Rhizocarp, Rockbrake, Royal, Salvinia, Schizaea, Scolopendrium, Seed, Shield, Silver, Snowbrake, Spleenwort, Staghorn, Sword, Tara, Tree, Venus's hair, Walking, Wall rue, Water, Woodsia
Ferocious Brutal, Cruel, Fell, Predatory, Rambunctious

Ferret Albin, Black-footed, Business, Fesnyng, Gill, Hob, Jill, Nose, Polecat, Ribbon, Rootle, Snoop, Trace, Unearth

Ferry(man) Charon, Convey, Hovercraft, Passage, Plier, Pont, Roll-on, RORO, Sealink, Shuttle, Soyuz, Train, Traject, Tranect

Fertile, **Fertility (symbol)** Battle, Fat, Fecund, Fruitful, Linga, Priapus, Productive, Prolific, Rhiannon, Rich, Uberous

Fertilise(r), **Fertilisation** Ammonia, Auxin, Bee, Bone-ash, Bone-earth, Bone-meal, Caliche, Caprify, Compost, Cross, Fishmeal, Guano, Heterosis, Humogen, Humus, In-vitro, IVF, Kainite, Manure, Marl, Nitrate, Nitre, Nitro-chalk, Pearl-ash, Phosphate, Pollen, Pollinator, Potash, Potassa, Self, Sham, Stamen, Superphosphate, Top dressing

Fervent, **Fervid**, **Fervour** Ardent, Burning, Earnest, Heartfelt, Heat, Hwyl, Intense, Keen, Passionate, White-hot, Zeal, Zeloso

Fester Beal, Putrefy, Rankle, Rot, Suppurate

Festival, **Festive**, **Festivity** Adonia, Aldeburgh, Ale, Al Hijra(h), All Saints' Day, Ambarvalia, Anniversary, Anthesteria, Ashora, Bairam, Baisak(h)i, Bayreuth, Beano, Beltane, Biennale, Candlemas, Carnival, Celebration, Cerealia, Chanuk(k)ah, Childermas, Church-ale, Circumcision, Commemoration, Convivial, Corpus Christi, Corroboree, Crouchmas, Dassehra, Dewali, Dionysia, Divali, Diwali, Doseh, Druid, Easter, Eisteddfod, Encaenia, En fête, Epiphany, > FAIR, Feast, Feis, Fete, Fête-champêtre, Fete-Dieu, Fete-galante, Fiesta, Fringe, Gaff, > GALA, Gaudy, Gregory, Hallowmas, Hanukkah, Harvest, Harvest home, Hock-tide, Hogmanay, Holi, > HOLIDAY, Holy-ale, Hosay, Hosein, Id-al-fitr, Imbolc, Imbolg, Kermess, Kermiss, Kirmess, Kumbh Mela, Kwanzaa, Lady-day, Lailat-ul-Qadr, Lammas, Laylat-al-Miraj, Lemural, Lemuria, Lesser Bairam, Let-off, Lughnasadh, Lupercalia, Matsuri, Mayday, Mela, Merry-night, Michaelmas, Miraj, Mod, Moombah, Navaratra, Navaratri, Noel, Obon, Palilia, Panathenaean, Panegyry, Pardon, Pasch, Passover, Pentecost, Pesa(c)h, Play, Pongal, Pooja(h), Pop, Potlach, Puja, Purim, Quirinalia, Revel, Rosh Hashanah, Rush-bearing, Samhain, Saturnalia, Seder, Semi-double, Shabuath, Shavuath, Shemini Atseres, Shrove(tide), Simchas Torah, Simchat(h) Torah, Simchat Torah, Slugfest, Terminalia, Tet, Thargelia, Thesmophoria, Tide, Transfiguration, Up-Helly-Aa, Utas, Vesak, Vinalia, Visitation, Vulcanalia, Wake, Wesak, Yom Tob, Yomtov, Yuan Tan, Yule(tide)

Festoon Deck, Decorate, Encarpus, Garland, Swag, Wreathe

Fetch(ing) Arrive, Attract, Bring, Charming, Fet(t), Get, Gofer, Realise

Fete Bazaar, Champetre, Entertain, > FESTIVITY, Gala, Honour, Tattoo

Fetish(ist) Charm, Compulsion, Gimp, Idol, Ju-ju, Obeah, Obi(a), Talisman, Totem, Voodoo

Fetter Basil, Bilboes, Chain, Gyve, Hamshackle, Hopple, Iron, Leg-iron, Manacle, Shackle

Fettle Arrange, Condition, Frig, Potter, Repair

Feud Affray, Blood, Clash, Feoff, Fief, Quarrel, Strife, > VENDETTA

Feudal (service) Arriage, Auld-farrant, Forinsec, Old

Fever(ish) African coast, Ague, Beaver, Blackwater, Brain, Breakbone, Buck, Cabin, Calenture, Cat-scratch, Cerebrospinal, Childbed, Dengue, East coast, Enteric, Ferment, Fog, Frenetic, Gastric, Gate, Glandular, Haemorrhagic, Hay, Heatstroke, Hectic, Hyperpyretic, Insolation, Intense, Intermittent, Jail, Japanese river, Jungle, Kala-azar, Lassa, Malaria, Malta, Marsh, Mediterranean, Miliary, Milk, Mono, Mud, Paratyphoid, Parrot, Parturient, Passion, Puerperal, Putrid, Pyretic, Pyrexia, Pyrogenic, Q, Quartan, Quintan, Quotidian, Rabbit, Ratbite, Recurrent, Relapsing, Remittent, Rheumatic, Rift

Valley, Rock, Rocky mountain spotted, Roseola, Sandfly, Scarlatina, Scarlet, Sextan, Spotted, Spring, Sunstroke, Swamp, Swine, Tap, Temperature, Tertian, Texas, Tick, Trench, Typhoid, Typhus, Undulant, Verruga, Vomito, West Nile, Whot, Worm, Yellow(jack)

Few(er) Handful, Infrequent, > LESS, Limited, Scarce, Some, Wheen

Fey Clairvoyant, Eccentric, Elfin, Weird

Fez Tarboosh, Tarboush, Tarbush

Fiancé(e) Betrothed, Intended, Promised

Fiasco Bomb, Debacle, Disaster, Failure, Flask, Flop, Lash-up, Wash-out

Fiat Command, Decree, Edict, Order, Ukase

Fib Gag, > LIE, Prevaricate, Story, Taradiddle, Untruth

Fibre, Fibrous Abaca, Acrilan®, Acrylic, Aramid, Arghan, Backbone, Bass, Bast, Beta, Buaze, Bwazi, Cantala, Carbon, Coir, Constitution, Cotton, Courtelle®, Cuscus, Dietary, Dralon®, Elastane, Elastin, Filament, Filasse, Flax, Funicle, Gore-Tex®, Graded-index, Hair, Hemp, Henequen, Henequin, Herl, Hypha, Ispaghula, Istle, Ixtle, Jute, Kapok, Kenaf, Kevlar®, Kittul, Lemniscus, Manilla, Monkey-grass, Monofil, Monomode, Multimode, Mungo, Muscle, Myotube, Nap, Natural, Nerve, Noil(s), Nylon, Oakum, Olefin(e), Optic(al), Orlon®, Peduncle, Piassaba, Piassava, Pina, Pita, Polyarch, Pons, Pontine, Pulu, Raffia, Ramee, Rami, Rhea, Rock-cork, Roughage, Rove, Sida, Silk, Sisal, Slagwool, Sleave, Slub(b), Spandex, Splenium, Staple, Sterculia, Strand, Strick, Sunn-hemp, Tampico, Toquilla, Tow, Uralite, Viver, Vulcanized, Wallboard, Watap, Whisker, Wood pulp

Fibula Bone, Brooch, Perone

Fickle(ness) Capricious, Change, False, Inconstant, Light, Mutable, Protean, Shifty, Varying, Volage, Volatile

Fiction(al), Fictitious Bogus, Cyberpunk, Fable, Fabrication, Legal, Pap, Phoney, Picaresque, Romance, Science, Slash, Splatterpunk, > STORY

Fiddle(r), Fiddling Amati, Bow, Calling-crab, Cello, Cheat, Crab, Cremona, Croud, Crouth, Crowd, Crwth, Fidget, Fix, Gju, Ground, Gu(e), Jerrymander, Kit, Launder, Nero, Peculate, Petty, Potter, Racket, Rebec(k), Rig, Rote, Sarangi, Saw, Sawah, Scam, Scotch, Scrape, Scrapegut, Second, Spiel, Strad, Sultana, > TAMPER, Tinker, Toy, Trifle, Tweedle(-dee), Twiddle, Viola, > VIOLIN, Wangle

Fidelity Accuracy, Faith, Fealty, Loyalty, Troth

Fidget(y) Fantad, Fanteeg, Fantigue, Fantod, Fike, Fuss, Fyke, Hirsle, Hotch, Jimjams, Jittery, Niggle, Trifle, Twiddle, Twitch, Uneasy

Fiduciary Trustee

Fief Benefice, Fee

Field(er), Fielding, Fields(man) Aalu, Aaru, Abroad, Aceldama, Aerodrome, Area, Arena, Arish, Arpent, Arrish, Campestral, Campestrian, Catch, Champ(s), Close, Coulomb, Cover, Domain, Electric, Electromagnetic, Electrostatic, Elysian, Entry, Fid, Flodden, Flying, Forte, Fylde, Glebe, Gracie, Gravitational, Grid(iron), Gully, Hop-yard, Ice, Keep wicket, Killing, Land, Landing, Lare, Lay, Lea(-rig), Leg slip, Ley, Line, Long leg, Long-off, Long-on, Longstop, Lords, Magnetic, Mead(ow), Mid-off, Mid-on, Mid-wicket, Mine, Oil, Padang, Paddock, Paddy, Parrock, Pasture, Pitch, Playing, Point, Potter's, Province, Realm, Runners, Salting, Sawah, Scarecrow, Scope, Scout, Shamba, Short leg, Shortstop, Short stop, Silly, Slip, Sphere, Square leg, Stage, Stray, Stubble, Territory, Tract, Unified, Vector, Visual, W.C., World

> **Field** *may indicate* cricket

Field marshal Allenby, Bulow, French, Haig, Ironside, Kesselring, Kitchener, Montgomery, Roberts, Robertson, Rommel, Slim, Wavell

Fieldwork Lunette, Ravelin, Redan, Redoubt, Tenaillon

Fiend Barbason, Demon, > **DEVIL**, Enthusiast, Flibbertigibbet, Frateretto, Hellhound, Hobbididance, Mahn, Modo, Obidicut, Smulkin, Succubus

Fierce(ly) Billyo, Breem, Breme, Cruel, Draconic, Dragon, Grim, Hard-fought, Intense, Ogreish, Rampant, Renfierst, > **SAVAGE**, Severe, Tigerish, Tigrish, Violent, Wild, Wood, Wud

Fiery Ardent, Argand, Aries, Con fuoco, Dry, Fervent, Hot, Igneous, Leo, Mettlesome, Phlogiston, Sagittarius, Salamander, Zealous

Fiesta Festival, Fete, Gala, Holiday

Fife Piffero

Fifth Column, Diapente, Hemiol(i)a, Nones, Perfect, Quint, Sesquialtera, Sextans

Fifty Demi-c, Jubilee, L

Fig Bania, Benjamin-tree, Caprifig, Fico, Figo, Footra, Fouter, Foutra, Foutre, Hottentot, Indian, Moreton Bay, Mouldy, Sycamore, Sycomore, Syncomium, Trifle

Fight(er), Fighting Affray, Agonistics, Aikido, Alpino, Altercate, Bandy, Barney, > **BATTLE**, Bicker, Biffo, Blue, Bout, Box, Brave, Brawl, Bruiser, Bundeswehr, Bush-whack, Campaign, Chaud-mellé, Chindit, Combat, Conflict, Contest, Crusader, Cuirassier, Defender, Dog, Donnybrook, Duel, Encounter, Engagement, Extremes, Faction, Fecht, Fence, Fisticuffs, Flyting, Fray, Freedom, Free-for-all, Fund, Ghazi, Gladiator, Grap(p)le, Gunslinger, Gurkha, Hurricane, Kite, Kumite, Lapith, Marine, Med(d)le, Medley, Mêlée, Mercenary, MIG, Militate, Mill, Mujahed(d)in, Mujahidin, Naumachy, Night, Partisan, Pellmell, Pillow, PLO, Prawle, Press, Pugilist, Pugnacity, Punch up, Rammy, Repugn, Resist, Ring, Ruck, Ruction, Rumble, Savate, Sciamachy, Scold, Scrap, Scrimmage, Scuffle, Shadow, Shine, Skiamachy, Skirmish, Slam, Soldier, Spar, Spitfire, Squabble, Stoush, Straight, Strife, Struggle, Sumo, Swordsman, Tar, Tatar, Thersites, Toreador, Tuilyie, Tuilzie, Tussle, Umbrella, War(-dog), War-horse, War-man, Warrior, Wraxle, Wrestle, Yike, Zero

Figment Delusion, Fiction, Invention

Figure(s), Figurine Arabic, Aumail, Bas-relief, Body, Build, Caganer, Canephorus, Caryatid, Cast, Chladni, Cinque, Cipher, Cone, Cube, Cypher, Decahedron, Digit, Ecorché, Effigy, Eight, Ellipse, Enneagon, Enneahedron, Epanadiplosis, Escher, > **FORM**, Fusil, Girth, Gnomon, Graph, Heptagon, Hexagon, Hour-glass, Icon, Icosahedron, Idol, Ikon, Image, Impossible, Insect, Intaglio, Integer, Interference, Lay, Lissajous, Magot, Matchstick, Moai, Motif, Nonagon, Number, Numeral, Numeric, Octagon, Octahedron, Orant, Outline, Parallelogram, Pentacle, Pentalpha, Plane, Polygon, Poussette, Prism, Puppet, Pyramid, Reckon, Repetend, Repoussoir, Rhomboid, See, > **SHAPE**, Sheela-na-gig, Significant, Simplex, Solid, Sonorous, Statistics, Statue(tte), String, Tanagra, Telamon, Tetragon, Torus, Triangle, Trihedron, Triskele, Triskelion, Ushabti, Waxwork

Figure of speech Allegory, Alliteration, Analogy, Antimask, Antimasque, Antimetabole, Antithesis, Asyndeton, Catachresis, Chiasmus, Deixis, Diallage, Ellipsis, Euphemism, Hendiadys, Hypallage, Hyperbaton, Hyperbole, Hysteron proteron, Irony, Litotes, Meiosis, Metalepsis, Metaphor, Metonymy, Onomatopoeia, Oxymoron, Paral(e)ipsis, Prosopoea, Simile, Solecism, Syllepsis, Synecdoche, Taxeme, Tmesis, Trope, Tropology, Zeugma

Figure study Arithmetic, Mathematics, Numeration

Figure-weaver Draw-boy

Filament Barbule, Byssus, Cirrus, Fibre, Fimbria, Floss, Gossamer, Hair, Hypha,

Mycor(r)hiza, Myofibril, Paraphysis, Protonema, > **THREAD**, Whisker, Wreath

Filch Appropriate, Drib, Pilfer, Pinch, Prig, Purloin, Smouch, > **STEAL**

File, Filing(s) Abrade, Archive, Back up, Batch, Binary, Box, Burr, Clyfaker, Coffle, Croc(odile), Crosscut, Database, Data set, Disc, Disk, Dossier, Enter, Floatcut, Generation, Half-round, Index, Indian, Limation, Line, Lodge, Nail, Pigeon-hole, Pollute, Quannet, Rank, Rasp, Rat-tail, README, Riffler, Risp, Row, Scalprum, Scratch, Single, Single-cut, String, Swarf, Text, Tickler, TIF(F)

Filial generation F1

Filibuster Freebooter, Hinder, Obstruct, Run on, Stonewall

Filigree Delicate, Fretwork, Sheer

Filipino Igorot, Moro, > **PHILIPPINE(S)**

Fill(ing), Filler Anaplerosis, Balaam, Banoffee, Banoffi, Beaumontag(u)e, Beaumontique, Billow, Bishop, Bloat, Brick-nog, Brim, Bump, Centre, Charge, Cram, Fat-lute, Gather, Gorge, Heart, Imbue, Impregnate, Inlay, Instill, Jampack, Line, Mastic, Occupy, Pabulous, Packing, Permeate, Plug, Repletive, Salpicon, Sate, Satisfy, Shim, Stack, Stock, Stocking, Stopping, > **STUFF**, Tales, Tank-up, Teem, Top up, Ullage

Fillet(s) Anadem, Annulet, Band, Bandeau, Bandelet, Bone, Cloisonné, Flaunching, Fret, Goujons, Grenadine, Headband, Infula, Label, Lemniscus, List(el), Mitre, Moulding, Reglet, Regula, Ribbon, Rollmop, Slice, Snood, Sphendone, Stria, Striga, Taeniate, Tape, Teniate, Tilting, Tournedos, Vitta

Fillip Boost, Kick, Snap, Stimulus

Filly Colt, Foal, She

Film(s), Filmmaker, Filmy, Filming Acetate, Actioner, Amnion, Biopic, Blaxploitation, Blockbuster, Bollywood, Buddy, Carry On, Casablanca, Caul, Cel, Chick-flick, Chiller, Cine, Cinema vérité, Cinerama®, Circlorama®, Cliffhanger, Cling, Clip, Coat, Compilation, Creature feature, Deepie, Dew, Diorama, Docudrama, Documentary, Dogma, Dust, Epic, ET, Exposure, Feature, Fiche, Flick, Floaty, Footage, Gigi, Gossamer, Hammer, Haze, Hollywood, Horror, Horse opera, Infomercial, Kell, Kidult, Lacquer, Layer, Loid, Mask, Membrane, Microfiche, Mist, Molecular, Montage, Movie, Neo-noir, Newsreel, Noddy, Noir, Non-flam, Oater, Omnimax®, Outtake, Panchromatic, Patina, Pellicle, Photo, Pilot, Plaque, Prequel, Psycho, Quickie, Quota-quickie, Reel, Release, Reversal, Roll, Romcom, Rush, Safety, Scale, Scent-scale, Screen, Scum, Sheet, Shoot-'em-up, Short, Shot, Silent, Skin, Skin flick, Slasher-movie, Slick, Slo-mo, Snuff, Spaghetti western, Splatter, Studio, Talkie, Tear-jerker, Technicolor, Titanic, Trailer, Travelogue, Trippy, Two-shot, Ultrafiche, Varnish, Video, Video-nasty, Vitaphone®, Web, Weepie, Weepy, Weft, Western

Film star Extra, Vedette

Filter(ing) Band-pass, Clarify, Colour, Dialysis, Dichroic, Leach, Low-pass, Percolate, Perk, Seep, Sieve, > **SIFT**, Skylight, Strain

Filth(y) Addle, Augean, Bilge, Colluvies, Crock, Crud, Defile, Dirt, Dung, Feculent, Foul, Grime, Lucre, Mire, Muck, Obscene, Pythogenic, Refuse, Slime, Smut(ch), Soil, Squalor, Stercoral, Sullage, Yuck

Fin Adipose, Anal, Caudal, Ctene, Dollars, Dorsal, Fluke, Pectoral, Pelvic, Pinna, Pinnule, Rib, Skeg, Skegg, Stabiliser, Ventral

Final(e), Finalise Absolute, Closing, Coda, Conclusive, Cup, Decider, End, End-all, Eventual, Exam, Extreme, Grand, Last, Net(t), Peremptory, Sew up, Swansong, Terminal, Ultimate, Utter

Finance, Financial, Financier Ad crumenan, Angel, Back, Banian, Banker, Bankroll, Banyan, Bottomry, Cambism, Chrematistic, Equity, Exchequer,

Fiscal, Gnome, Grubstake, Mezzanine, Monetary, Revenue, Sponsor, Subsidise, Treasurer, Underwrite

Finch Bird, Brambling, Bunting, Canary, Charm, Chewink, Crossbill, Darwin's, Fringillid, Gouldian, Grosbeak, Linnet, Marsh-robin, Peter, Redpoll, Rosy, Serin, Siskin, Spink, Twite, Zebra

Find(er), Finding Ascertain, Come across, Detect, Direction, Discover(y), Get, Hit, Inquest, > **LOCATE**, Meet, Provide, Rumble, Trace, Track down, Trouvaille, Unearth, Verdict

Fine, Fine words Amende, Amerce, Amerciament, Arts, Assess, Beau(t), Bender, Blood-wit(e), Bonny, Boshta, Boshter, Boss, Brandy, Brave, Braw, Champion, Dainty, Dandy, Dick, End, Eriach, Eric(k), Estreat, F, Fair, Famous, Forfeit, Gate, Godly, Good(ly), Gossamer, Gradely, Graithly, Grand, Grassum, Hair, Hairline, Handsome, Heriot, Hunkydory, Immense, Impalpable, Inconie, Incony, Infangthief, Issue, Keen, Leirwite, Log, Maritage, Merchet, Mooi, Mulct, Nifty, Niminy-piminy, Noble, OK, Oke, Outfangthief, > **PENALTY**, Phat, Precise, Pure, Relief, Safe, Sconce, Sheer, Sicker, Slender, Spanking, Subtle, Summery, Super, Tax, Thin, Ticket(t)y-boo, Tiptop, Topping, Unlaw, Wally, Waly, Wer(e)gild

Fine-collector Cheater

Finery Braws, Fallal, Frills, Frippery, Gaudery, Ornament, Trinket, Wally, Warpaint

Finesse Artifice, Artistry, Delicacy, Skill, Strategy

Fine-weather All-hallond, All-hallow(e)n, All-hollown

Finger(s), Fingernail Dactyl, Digit, Fork, Green, Handle, Index, Lunula, Medius, Name, Nip, Piggy, Pinky, Pointer, Potato, Prepollex, Pusher, Ring(man), Shop, Sponge, Talaunt, Talon, Tot, Trigger, White

Finger-hole Lill, Ring

Fingerprint(ing) Dabs, Dactylogram, DNA, Genetic, Loop, Whorl

Fingerstall Hutkin

Finial Bunch, Knob, Ornament, Tee

Finical, Finicky Faddy, Fastidious, Fussy, Particular, Pernickety, Precise

Finis, Finish(ed), Finishing touch Arch, Blanket, Calendar, Close, Coating, Coda, Complete, > **CONCLUDE**, Crown, Die, Dish, Do, Dope, Dress, > **END**, Epilog(ue), Epiphenomena, Exact, Full, Grandstand, Kibosh, Lacquer, Log off, Matt, Mirror, Neat, Outgo, Outwork, Pebbledash, Peg out, Perfect, Photo, Refine, Ripe, Round, Satin, Settle, Shot, Spitcher, Surface, Terminate, Through, Top out, Up (tie), Veneer, Wau(l)k, Wind-up

Finite Bounded, Limited

Finn(ish) Esth, Huck(leberry), Karelian, Lapp, Mickey, Mordvin, Suomic, Udmurt, Votyak

Fiord Bay, Hardanger, Inlet, Oslo, Randers, Trondheim

Fir Abies, Balsam, Douglas, Larch, Oregon, Scotch, Silver, Spruce, Umbrella

Fire(side) Accend, Agni, Animate, Ardour, Arouse, Arson, Atar, Axe, Bake, Bale, Barbecue, Barrage, Beacon, Behram, Blaze, Boot, Brand, Brazier, Brush, Burn, Bush, Chassé, Conflagration, Corposant, Covering, Delope, Discharge, Dismiss, Elan, Electric, Element, Embolden, Ena, Energy, Enfilade, Enkindle, Enthuse, Flak, Flame, Friendly, Furnace, Greek, Gun, Hearth, Hob, Ignite, Inferno, Ingle, Inspire, Kentish, Kiln, Kindle, Launch, Let off, Light, Liquid, Lowe, Pop, Prime, Prometheus, Pull, Pyre, Quick, Rake, Rapid, Red, Red cock, Sack, St Anthony's, St Elmo's, Scorch, Shell, Shoot, Smudge, Spark, Spirit, Spunk, Stoke, Stove, Strafe, Tracer, Trial, Wake, Watch, Wisp, Zeal

▶ **Firearm** *see* **GUN**

Fireback Reredos

Fireball Bolide
Firebird Phoenix
Fire-break Epaulement, Greenstrip
Fire-dog Andiron
Fire engine Green Goddess
Fire-extinguisher Halon, Hell-bender, Salamander
Firefly Glow-worm, Lightning-bug, Luciferin, Pyrophorus
Fire-guard Fender
Fireman Abednego, Brigade, Deputy, Prometheus, Stoker, Visiting
Fire-opal Girasol
Fireplace Camboose, Chimney, Grate, Hearth, Hob, Ingle, Loop-hole, Range
Fireplug H, Hydrant
Fireproof Abednego, Asbestos, Incombustible, Inflammable, Meshach, Salamander, Shadrach, Uralite
Firewalker Salamander
Firewood Billet, Faggot, Knitch, Tinder
Firework(s) Banger, Bengal-light, Bunger, Cherry bomb, Cracker, Devil, Fisgig, Fizgig, Flip-flop, Fountain, Gerbe, Girandole, Iron sand, Jumping Jack, Maroon, Pastille, Peeoy, Petard, Pharaoh's serpent, Pinwheel, Pioy(e), Pyrotechnics, Realgar, Rocket, Roman candle, Serpent, Skyrocket, Sparkler, Squib, Tantrum, Throwdown, Tourbill(i)on, Volcano, Wheel, Whizzbang
Fire-worshipper Parsee
Firing Baking, Fusillade, Mitten, Salvo, Touchpaper
Firm Adamant, Agency, Binding, Business, Collected, Compact, Company, Concern, Concrete, Conglomerate, Constant, Crisp, Decided, Determined, Duro, Faithful, Fast, Fixed, Hard, Inc, Oaky, Obdurate, Obstinate, > RESOLUTE, Sclerotal, Secure, Set, Siccar, Sicker, > SOLID, Stable, Stalwart, Staunch, Ste(a)dfast, Steady, Steely, Steeve, Stern, Stieve, Stiff, Strict, Sturdy, Sure, Tight, Tough, Well-knit
Firmament Canopy, Empyrean, Heaven, Sky
First Ab initio, Alpha, Arch, Archetype, Best, Calends, Champion, Chief, Earliest, E(a)rst, Foremost, Former, Front, Head, I, Ideal, Imprimis, Initial, 1st, Kalends, Led, Maiden, No 1, One, Opener, Or, Original, Pioneer, Pole, Pole position, Premier, Prima, Primal, Prime, Primo, Principal, Prototype, Rudimentary, Senior, Starters, Top, Uppermost, Victor, Yama
First-aid(ers) Zambu(c)k
First born Ariki, Eigne, Eldest, Heir, Major, Senior
First class, **First rate** A1, Crack, Prime, Supreme, Tiptop, Top(notch)
First day Calends
First fruits Annat, Arles, Primitiae, Windfalls
First man Adam, Ask, Gayomart, Premier, President, Yama, Ymer, Ymir
First offender Eve, Probationer
▶ **First rate** *see* FIRST CLASS
First woman Embla, Eve, Pandora, Premier
Firth Estuary, Forth, Inlet, Moray, Pentland, Solway, Tay
Fish(ing) Angle, Bob, Bottom, Cast, Catch, Chowder, Coarse, Cran, Creel, Dredge, Dry, Dry-fly, Episcate, Fly, Flying, Frozen, Fry, Game, Gefilte, Goujons, Guddle, Halieutics, Haul, Inshore, Ledger, Mess, Net, Otterboard, Overnet, Piscine, Queer, Roe, Rough, Sashimi, Shoal, Snigger, Sniggle, Spin, Spot, Trawl, Troll, Tub, Walking, Wet, White
Fish-basket Creel, Hask, Kipe
Fish disease Argulus

FISH

2 letters:
Ai
Id

3 letters:
Ayu
Bar
Bib
But
Cat
Cod
Cow
Dab
Dib
Dog
Eel
Gar
Ged
Hag
Ide
Koi
Lax
Lob
Par
Pod
Ray
Rig
Sar
Tai
Top

4 letters:
Bass
Blay
Bley
Brit
Butt
Carp
Cero
Chad
Char
Chub
Chum
Coho
Cray
Cusk
Dace
Dare
Dart
Dory

Fugu
Gade
Goby
Gump
Hake
Harl
Hoki
Huso
Huss
Ikan
Jack
Kelt
Keta
Lant
Leaf
Ling
Luce
Lump
Maid
Maze
Moki
Mola
Mort
Opah
Orfe
Parr
Peal
Peel
Pike
Pope
Pout
Raun
Rawn
Rigg
Rudd
Ruff
Scad
Scar
Scat
Scup
Seer
Seir
Shad
Sild
Slip
Snig
Sole
Star
Tope
Trot

Tuna
Tusk
Woof

5 letters:
Ablet
Allis
Angel
Apode
Aspro-
Basse
Blain
Bleak
Bream
Brill
Bully
Capon
Charr
Cisco
Clown
Cobia
Cohoe
Coley
Cuddy
Danio
Dorad
Doras
Doree
Dorse
Elops
Elver
Fluke
Gadus
Gibel
Grunt
Jewie
Jurel
Laker
Lance
Loach
Lythe
Maise
Maize
Manta
Masus
Mease
Molly
Murre
Murry
Nerka

Padle
Perai
Perca
Perch
Pilot
Piper
Pirai
Platy
Pogge
Powan
Prawn
Roach
Roker
Royal
Ruffe
Saith
Sargo
Saury
Scrod
Sewen
Sewin
Shark
Sheat
Skate
Slope
Smelt
Snoek
Snook
Solen
Speck
Sprat
Sprod
Tench
Tetra
Togue
Torsk
Trout
Tunny
Umber
Wahoo
Whiff
Wirra
Witch
Yabby
Zebra

6 letters:
Alevin
Allice
Anabas

Angler
Archer
Ballan
Barbel
Belone
Beluga
Big-eye
Blenny
Bonito
Bounce
Bowfin
Braise
Braize
Bumalo
Burbot
Callop
Caplin
Caranx
Caribe
Cheven
Clupea
Cockle
Comber
Conger
Conner
Cottus
Cudden
Cuddie
Cuddin
Cunner
Cuttle
Darter
Dentex
Diodon
Dipnoi
Discus
Doctor
Dorado
Dun-cow
Espada
Finnac
Finnan
Fogash
Fumado
Gadoid
Garvie
Gilgie
Goboid
Goramy
Grilse
Groper
Gulper

Gunnel
Gurami
Gurnet
Haddie
Hapuka
Hassar
Inanga
Jerker
Jilgie
Kipper
Labrus
Lancet
Launce
Lizard
Louvar
Lunker
Mad Tom
Mahsir
Maigre
Marlin
Meagre
Medaka
Medusa
Megrim
Milter
Minnow
Morgay
Mudcat
Mullet
Murena
Nerite
Oyster
Paddle
Paidle
Pakoko
Parrot
Pholas
Piraya
Plaice
Podley
Pollan
Porgie
Puffer
Redfin
Remora
Robalo
Roughy
Saithe
Salmon
Samlet
Sander
Sardel

Sargus
Sauger
Saurel
Scampi
Sea-bat
Sea-owl
Seeder
Serran
Shanny
Sheath
Shiner
Skelly
Sparid
Splake
Sucker
Tailor
Tarpon
Tautog
Tinker
Toitoi
Tomcod
Trygon
Twaite
Ulicon
Ulikon
Vendis
Weever
Wirrah
Wrasse
Yabbie
Zander
Zingel

7 letters:
Ale-wife
Anchovy
Anemone
Asterid
Azurine
Batfish
Bellows
Bergylt
Bloater
Bluecap
Boxfish
Brassie
Buffalo
Bummalo
Cabezon
Capelin
Cavalla
Cavally

Ceviche
Cichlid
Codfish
Copepod
Cottoid
Crappie
Croaker
Crucian
Crusian
Cutlass
Dogfish
Eelfare
Eel-pout
Escolar
Findram
Finnack
Finnock
Flattie
Garfish
Garvock
Geelbek
Gemfish
Goldeye
Gourami
Grouper
Growler
Grunion
Gudgeon
Gurnard
Gwiniad
Gwyniad
Haddock
Hagdown
Hagfish
Halibut
Herling
Herring
Hirling
Hogfish
Homelyn
Houting
Ichthys
Inconnu
Jewfish
Kahawai
Keeling
Koi carp
Lampern
Lamprey
Lampuki
Lantern
Lingcod

- Lobster
- Lyomeri
- Mahseer
- Matelot
- Medacca
- Merling
- Mojarra
- Moon-eye
- Morwong
- Muraena
- Oarfish
- Old-wife
- Oolakan
- Opaleye
- Osseter
- Oulakan
- Oulicon
- Panchax
- Pandora
- Peacock
- Pegasus
- Pigfish
- Pinfish
- Piranha
- Pollack
- Pomfret
- Pompano
- Ragfish
- Rasbora
- Ratfish
- Rat-tail
- Redfish
- Rorqual
- Roughie
- Sand dab
- Sardine
- Scalare
- Scallop
- Sculpin
- Sea-bass
- Sea-cock
- Sea-dace
- Sea-moth
- Sea-pike
- Sea-star
- Sea-wife
- Sevruga
- Sillock
- Silurid
- Skegger
- Skitter
- Snapper

Sock-eye
Sparoid
Speldin
Sterlet
Sunfish
Sunstar
Surgeon
Teleost
Tiddler
Tilapia
Titling
Torgoch
Torpedo
Tubfish
Ulichon
Vendace
Wall-eye
Whipray
Whistle
Whiting
Wide-gab

8 letters:
Albacore
Anableps
Arapaima
Asteroid
Atherine
Billfish
Blennius
Bloodfin
Blowfish
Blueback
Bluefish
Bluegill
Brisling
Bullhead
Bullhorn
Cabezone
Cabrilla
Carangid
Cardinal
Cavefish
Characid
Characin
Chimaera
Coalfish
Corkwing
Cucumber
Cyprinid
Dealfish
Dragonet

Drumfish
Eagle-ray
Escallop
Eulachon
Fallfish
Fighting
Filefish
Flathead
Flounder
Four-eyes
Frogfish
Ganoidei
Gillaroo
Gilthead
Goatfish
Gobiidae
Graining
Grayling
Hackbolt
Hair-tail
Half-beak
Hard-head
Holostei
Hornbeak
Hornpout
Kabeljou
Killfish
Kingfish
Kingklip
Kukukuma
Lionfish
Luderick
Lumpfish
Lungfish
Mackerel
Mahi-mahi
Mata Hari
Menhaden
Milkfish
Monkfish
Moonfish
Mosquito
Mulloway
Nannygai
Nennigai
Nine-eyes
Oulachon
Paradise
Patutuki
Pickerel
Pilchard
Pipefish

Pirarucu
Redbelly
Rock-cook
Rockfish
Rockling
Roncador
Rosefish
Saibling
Sailfish
Saltfish
Sardelle
Scabbard
Sciaenid
Scorpion
Scuppaug
Sea-devil
Seahorse
Sea-lemon
Sea-raven
Sea-robin
Sergeant
Serranus
Skipjack
Smear-dab
Snake-eel
Sparling
Spelding
Speldrin
Stenlock
Sting-ray
Stonecat
Sturgeon
Tarakihi
Tarwhine
Teraglin
Terakihi
Tile-fish
Toadfish
Trevally
Tropical
Tubenose
Tullibee
Weakfish
Whitling
Wolffish

9 letters:
Amberjack
Anchoveta
Barracuda
Blackfish
Butterfly

Carangoid
Cascadura
Ceratodus
Chaetodon
Chavender
Clingfish
Clupeidae
Coregonus
Coryphene
Devilfish
Gaspereau
Glassfish
Globefish
Goldfinny
Goldsinny
Golomynka
Goosefish
Greenbone
Greenling
Grenadier
Haberdine
Hornyhead
Hottentot
Houndfish
Ichthyoid
Jacksmelt
Jewelfish
Kabeljouw
Killifish
Labyrinth
Latimeria
Matelotte
Menominee
Mudhopper
Neon tetra
Pikeperch
Porbeagle
Porcupine
Quillback
Roussette
Scaldfish
Scalefish
Schnapper

Scorpaena
Selachian
Shubunkin
Siluridae
Slickhead
Snailfish
Snakehead
Snipefish
Spadefish
Spearfish
Speldring
Stargazer
Steenbras
Stingaree
Stockfish
Stonefish
Surfperch
Surmullet
Swellfish
Swordfish
Sword-tail
Thornback
Threadfin
Tittlebat
Topminnow
Trachinus
Troutfish
Trunkfish
Whitebait
White-bass
Wreckfish

10 letters:
Barracoota
Barracouta
Barramunda
Bitterling
Bombay duck
Bottlehead
Butterfish
Candlefish
Cockabully
Cornetfish

Cyclostome
Damselfish
Demoiselle
Dollarfish
Etheostoma
Fingerling
Flutemouth
Groundling
Horned pout
Lumpsucker
Maskalonge
Maskanonge
Maskinonge
Midshipman
Mossbunker
Mudskipper
Needlefish
Nurse-hound
Rabbitfish
Red emperor
Red-snapper
Ribbonfish
Rudderfish
Scopelidae
Sea-poacher
Sea-surgeon
Serrasalmo
Sheepshead
Ship-holder
Shovelnose
Silverside
Springfish
Squeteague
Teleostome
Titarakura
Tripletail
Yellowtail

11 letters:
Chondrostei
Dolly Varden
Istiophorus
Lapidosteus

Lepidosiren
Lophobranch
Maskallonge
Moorish idol
Muskellunge
Ostracoderm
Oxyrhynchus
Plagiostome
Plectognath
Scolopendra
Seventy-four
Soldierfish
Stickleback
Stoneroller
Surgeonfish
Triggerfish
Trumpetfish
Water souchy
Yellowbelly

12 letters:
Ballan-wrasse
Elasmobranch
Father-lasher
Heterosomata
Histiophorus
Mangrove Jack
Miller's thumb
Mouthbreeder
Orange roughy
Plectognathi
Rainbow-trout
Squirrelfish

13 letters:
Leatherjacket
Musselcracker
Sailor's choice
Sergeant Baker

15 letters:
Crossopterygian

Fisher(man) Ahab, Andrew, Angler, Black cat, Caper, Codder, Dragman, High-liner, Liner, Pedro, Peter, Piscator, Rodster, Sharesman, Walton
Fisherwoman *see* FISHSELLER
Fish-hawk Osprey
Fishing-ground Haaf
Fishing-line G(u)imp, Gymp, Paternoster
Fishpond Ocean, Stew, Vivarium
Fishseller, Fisherwoman Fishwife, Molly Malone, Ripp(i)er, Shawley, Shawlie

Fishy Botargo, Suspicious, Vacant

Fission Multiple, Nuclear

Fissure Chasm, Cleft, Crack, Crevasse, Crevice, Gap, Grike, Gryke, Lode, Rent, Rolando, Sand-crack, Scam, Sylvian, Sylvius, Vallecula, Vein, Zygon

Fist Clench, Dukes, Hand, Iron, Join-hand, Mailed, Neaf(fe), Neif, Neive, Nief, Nieve, Pud, Punch, Thump

Fit(s), Fitful, Fitting(s), Fitness Able, Access, Adapt, Ague, Appointment, Appropriate, Apropos, Apt, Babbitt, Bout, Canto, Capable, Cataleptic, Cataplexy, Click, Concinnous, Condign, Congruous, Conniption, Convulsion, Culver-tail, Darwinian, Decent, Decorous, Desultory, Dod, Dove-tail, Due, Eclampsia, Egal, Eligible, Ensconce, Epilepsy, Equip, Exies, Expedient, Fairing, Fay, Fiddle, Furniment, Furnishing, Fytte, Gee, Germane, Habile, Hale, Hang, Health, Hinge, Huff, Hysterics, Ictus, Inclusive, In-form, Interference, Intermittent, In trim, Just, Kashrut(h), Lune, Marry, Mate, Meet, Mood, Nest, Paroxysm, Passus, Pertinent, Prepared, Press, > **PROPER**, Queme, Ready, Rig, Rind, Ripe, Rynd, Seemly, Seizure, Set, Shrink, Sit, Snotter, Sort, Sound, Spasm, Spell, Start, Suit(able), Syncope, Tantrum, Throe, To prepon, Turn, Up to, Well, Wobbler, Wobbly, Worthy, Wrath

▷ **Fit(ting)** *may indicate* a 't'

Fitment Adaptor, Unit

Fitzgerald Edward, Ella, Scott

Five(s) Cinque, Mashie, Pallone, Pedro, Pentad, Quinary, Quintet, Sextan, Towns, V

Five years Lustre, Lustrum

Fix(ed), Fixer, Fixative Affeer, Anchor, Appoint, Appraise, > **ARRANGE**, Assess, Assign, Attach, Bind, Brand, Cement, Clamp, Clew, Clue, Constant, Corking-pin, Cure, Decide, Destinate, Destine, Determine, Do, Embed, Empight, Encastré, Engrain, Establish, Fast, Firm, Fit, Freeze, Gammon, Hold, Hypo(sulphite), Immutable, Impaction, Imprint, Inculcate, Ingrain, Jag, Jam, Locate, Lodge, Nail, Name, Narcotic, Nobble, Orientate, Peg, Persistent, Pin, Point, Quantify, Repair, Resolute, Rig, Rigid, Rivet, Rove, Rut, Scrape, Screw, Seat, Seize, Set, Settle, Ship, Shoo, Skatole, Skewer, Splice, Stage, Staple, Static, Stell, Step, Stew, Stuck, Tie, Valorize, Weld

Fixture Attachment, Event, Match, Permanence, Rawlplug®, Unit

Fizz(ed), Fizzy Buck's, Effervesce, Gas, Hiss, Pop, Sherbet, Sod, Soda

Fizzle Failure, Flop, Hiss, Washout

▶ **Fjord** *see* **FIORD**

Flabbergast(ed) Amaze, Astound, Floor, Thunderstruck

Flabby Flaccid, Lank, Lax, Limp, Pendulous, Saggy

Flaccid Flabby, Lank, Limp, Soft

Flag(gy), Flags Acorus, Ancient, Ashlar, Banderol, Banner, Black, Blackjack, Blue (ensign), Blue Peter, Bunting, Burgee, Calamus, Chequered, Colour(s), Dan(n)ebrog, Decline, Droop, Duster, Ensign, Fail, Falter, Fane, Fanion, Field colours, Gladdon, Gonfalon, Green, Guidon, Hail, Hoist, Irideal, Iris, Jack, Jade, Jolly Roger, Kerbstone, Languish, Lis, Old Glory, Orris, Pave(ment), Pavilion, Pencel, Pennant, Pennon, Penoncel(le), Pensel, Pensil, Peter, Pilot, Pin, Prayer, Quarantine, Rag, Red, Red Duster, Red Ensign, Sag, Sedge, Semaphore, Sick, Sink, Slab(stone), Slack, Standard, Stars and bars, Stars and stripes, Streamer, Tire, Tricolour, Union (Jack), Vane, Vexillology, Waif, Whift, White (ensign), Wilt, Wither, Yellow (Jack)

Flagday Tagday

Flagellate Beat, Mastigophora, Scourge, Trypanosome, Whip

Flagon Bottle, Carafe, Jug, Stoop, Stoup, Vessel
Flagpole Pin, Staff
Flagrant Egregious, Glaring, Heinous, Patent, Wanton
Flagship Admiral, Victory
Flail Beat, Drub, Swingle, Swip(p)le, Threshel
Flair Art, Bent, Elan, Gift, Knack, Panache, Style, > TALENT
Flak AA, Attack, Criticism
Flake Chip, Flame, Flaught, Flaw, Floccule, Flocculus, Fragment, Peel, Scale, Smut, Snow
Flam Impose
Flamboyant Baroque, Brilliant, Florid, Garish, Grandiose, Ornate, Ostentatious, Paz(z)azz, Piz(z)azz, Swash-buckler
Flame, Flaming Ardent, Blaze, Fire, Flake, Flambé, Flammule, Glow, Kindle, Leman, Lover, Lowe, Musical, Olympic, Oxyacetylene, Sensitive, Sweetheart
Flan Pastry, Quiche, Tart
Flanders Mare, Moll
Flange Border, Collar, Collet, Lip, Rim
Flank(s) Accompany, Anta, Flange, Flitch, Ilia, Lisk, Loin, Side, Spur
Flannel Blather, Canton, Cloth, Cotton, Face, Outing, Soft-soap, Waffle, Zephyr
Flap(ped), Flapper, Flapping Agnail, Aileron, Alar, Alarm(ist), Aventail(e), Bate, Beat, Bird, Bobbysoxer, Bustle, Chit, Dither, Elevon, Epiglottis, Fipple, Flacker, Flaff, Flag, Flaught, Flutter, Fly, Fuss, Giglet, Giglot, Hover, > IN A FLAP, Labium, Labrum, Lapel, Loma, Louvre, Lug, Operculum, Panic, Spin, Spoiler, Tab, Tag, Tailboard, Tailgate, Tiswas, To-do, Tongue, TRAM, Volucrine, Wave, Whisk
Flare(d), Flare up Bell, Fishtail, Flame, Flanch, Flaunch, Godet, Magnesium, Scene, Signal, Solar, Spread, Spunk, Ver(e)y, Widen
Flash(y), Flasher Coruscate, Cursor, Electronic, Essex man, Fire-flag, Flare, Flaught, Fulgid, Fulgural, Garish, Gaudy, Glaik, Gleam, Glisten, Glitzy, Green, Green ray, Helium, Indicate, Instant, Jay, Lairy, Levin, Lightning, Loud, Magnesium, Meretricious, Mo, Ostentatious, Photopsy, Raffish, Ribbon, Ring, Roary, Scintillation, Second, Sequin, Showy, Sluice, Snazzy, Spark, Streak, Strobe, Swank(e)y, Tick, Tigrish, Trice, Twinkle, Vivid, Wire
► **Flashing** *may indicate* an anagram
Flask(-shaped) Ampulla, Aryballos, Bottle, Canteen, Carafe, Conceptacle, Costrel, Cucurbit, Dewar, Erlenmeyer, Fiasco, Flacket, Flacon, Florence, Goatskin, Hip, Lekythos, Matrass, Mick(e)(y), Pocket-pistol, Powder, Reform, Retort, Thermos®, Vacuum, Vial
Flat(s), Flatten(ed), Flattener Ancipital, Apartment, Bachelor, Bald, Banal, Beat, Bed-sit, Blow-out, Bulldoze, Callow, Complanate, Compress, Condominium, Corymb(ose), Cottage, Coulisse, Dead, Demolish, Dorsiventral, Double, Dress, Dull, Even, Feeble, Flew, Floor, Flue, Fool, Gaff, Garden, Granny, Guyot, Haugh, High-rise, Homaloid, Home-unit, Horizontal, Insipid, Ironed, Jacent, Key, KO, Law, Level, Lifeless, Llano, Marsh, Monotonous, Mud, Nitwit, Norfolk, Oblate, Pad, Pancake, Pedestrian, Peneplain, Peneplane, Penthouse, Pentice, Pied-à-terre, Plain, Planar, Plane, Planish, Plat, Plateau, Press, Prone, Prostrate, Recumbent, Rooms, Salt, Scenery, Service, Smooth, Splayfoot, Spread-edged, Squash, Studio, Tableland, Tabular, Tame, Tasteless, Tenement, True, Vapid, Walk-up
Flat-chested Cithara
Flat-faced Socle
Flat-foot(ed) Policeman, Splay
Flat-nosed Camus

Flatter(ing), Flatterer, Flattery Adulate, Becoming, Beslaver, Blandish, Blarney, Bootlick, Butter, Cajole, Candied, Carn(e)y, Claw(back), Complimentary, Comprabatio, Earwiggy, En beau, Eyewash, Fawn, Fillibrush, Flannel, Flannen, Fleech, Flummery, Fulsome, Gloze, Gnathonic(al), Honey, Imitation, Lip-salve, Moody, Palp, Phrase, Poodle-faker, Proneur, Puffery, Sawder, Smarm, Snow job, Soap, Soft soap, Soother, Souk, Spaniel, Stroke, Sugar, Sweet talk, Sycophant, Taffy, Toady, Treacle, Unction, Wheedle, Word

Flatulence Belch, Borborygmus, Burp, Carminative, Colic, Gas, Wind

Flaunt Brandish, Flourish, Gibe, Parade, Skyre, Strout, Strut, Wave

Flavour(ed), Flavouring Absinth(e), Alecost, Anethole, Angostura, Anise, Aniseed, Aroma, Benne, Bold, Borage, Bouquet garni, Clove, Coriander, Cumin, Dill, Essence, Fenugreek, Flor, Garlic, Garni, Gingili, Marinate, Mint, Orgeat, Piperonal, Quark, Race, Ratafia, Relish, Rocambole, Sair, Sassafras, Sesame, Tack, Tang, Tarragon, > **TASTE**, Til, Tincture, Twang, Vanilla

Flaw Blemish, Brack, Bug, Chip, Crack, Defect, Fallacy, > **FAULT**, Gall, Hamartia, Imperfection, Kink, Knothole, Lophole, Red-eye, Rima, Spot, Taint, Tear, Thief, Tragic, Windshake

Flawless Impeccable

Flax(en) Aleseed, Blonde, Codilla, Harden, Hards, Herden, Herl, Hurden, Line, Linseed, Lint, Lint-white, Linum, Mill-mountain, Poi, Tow

Flay Excoriate, Fleece, Flense, Scourge, Skin, Strip, Uncase, Whip

Flea Aphaniptera, Chigger, Chigoe, Chigre, Daphnid, Hopper, Itch-mite, Lop, Pulex, Sand, Turnip, Water

Flea-bane Erigeron

Fleabite Denier

Fleck Dash, Freak, Spot, Streak

Fledgling Aerie, Eyas, Sorage

Flee Abscond, Bolt, Decamp, Escape, Eschew, Fly, Lam, Loup, Run, Scapa, Scarper, Scram

Fleece, Fleecy Bleed, Coat, Despoil, Flocculent, Golden, Jib, Lambskin, Lanose, Pash(i)m, Pashmina, Plot, Pluck, Rifte, Ring, Rob, Rook, Shave, Shear, Sheepskin, Skin, > **SWINDLE**, Toison

Fleer Ogle

Fleet(ing) Armada, Brief, Camilla, Ephemeral, Evanescent, Fast, First, Flit, Flota, Flotilla, Fugacious, Fugitive, Hasty, Hollow, Lightfoot, Navy, Pacy, Passing, Prison, Spry, Street, Transient, Velocipede

Flesh(y) Beefy, Body, Carneous, Carrion, Corporeal, Corpulent, Creatic, Dead-meat, Digastric, Finish, Goose, Gum, Hypersarcoma, Joint, Longpig, Lush, Meat, Mons, Mummy, Muscle, Proud, Pulp, Sarcous, Spare tyre, Tissue

Flesh-eating Cannibalism, Carnassial, Creophagus, Omophagic

Fleshless Dry, Maigre, Pem(m)ican

Flex(ible), Flexibility Adaptable, Bend(y), Compliant, Double-jointed, Elastic, Genu, Limber, Lissom(e), Lithe, Pliant, > **RESILIENT**, Rubato, Rubbery, Squeezy, Supple, Tensile, Tonus, Wieldy, Willing, Wiry

▷ **Flexible, Flexuous** *may indicate* an anagram

Flick(er), Flicks Bioscope, Cinema, Fillip, Film, Flip, Flirt, Flutter, Glimmer, Gutter, Movie, Movy, Snap, Snow, Spang-cockle, Switch, Talkie, Twinkle, Waver

Flickertail ND

Flier Aerostat, Airman, Alcock, Amy, Aviator, Bleriot, Blimp, Brown, Crow, Daedalus, Erk, Fur, George, Gotha, Handout, Icarus, Leaflet, Lindbergh, Montgolfier, Pilot, RAF, Scotsman, Spec, Speedy

Flier *may indicate* a bird

Flight(y) Backfisch, Birdbrain, Bolt, Bubble-headed, Capricious, Charter, Contact, Dart, Departure, Escalier, Escape, Exaltation, Exodus, Fast, Fickle, Flaught, Flibbertigibbet, Flip, Flock, Flyby, Fly-past, Free, Fugue, Giddy, Grese, Gris(e), Guy, Hegira, Hejira, Hejra, Hellicat, Hijra, Lam, Mercy, Milk-run, Mission, Open-jaw, Pair, R(a)iser, Redeye, Ro(a)ding, Rode, Rout, Skein, Sortie, Stairs, > **STAMPEDE**, Stayre, Steps, Swarm, Test, Top, Tower, Trap, Vol(age), Volatile, Volley, Whisky-frisky, Wing

Flightless Kakapo, Ostrich, Rhea, Struthious

Flighty *may indicate* an anagram

Flimsy Finespun, Gimcrack, Gossamer, Jimcrack, Lacy, Sleazy, Sleezy, Tenuous, Thin, Weak, Wispy

Flinch Blench, Cringe, Funk, Quail, Recoil, Shrink, Shudder, Start, Wince

Fling Dance, Flounce, Highland, Hurl, Pitch, Shy, Slat, Slug, Slump, Spanghew, Spree, Throw, > **TOSS**

Flint Chert, Firestone, Granite, Hag-stone, Hornstone, Microlith, Mischmetal, Optical, Pirate, Rock, Silex, Silica, Stone, Touchstone

Flip(pant), **Flipping** Airy, Bally, Brash, Cocky, Flick, Frivolous, Impudent, Jerk, Nog, Pert, Purl, Sassy, Saucy, Toss, Turn

Flipper(s) Fin-toed

Flirt(ation), **Flirting**, **Flirtatious** Bill, Buaya, Carve, Chippy, Cockteaser, Come-hither, Come-on, Coquet(te), Dalliance, Demivierge, Footsie, Gallivant, Heart-breaker, Lumber, Mash, Minx, Neck, Philander(er), Prick-teaser, Rig, Toy, Trifle, Vamp, Wow

Flit Dart, Decamp, Flicker, Flutter, Moonlight, Scoot

Float(er), **Floating**, **Flotation** Balsa, Bob, Buoy, Caisson, Camel, Carley, Clanger, Drift, Fleet, Flotsam, Flutterboard, Froth, Fucus, Jetsam, Jetson, Levitate, Lifebuoy, Milk, Natant, Neuston, Oropesa, Outrigger, Planula, Pontoon, Pram, Quill, Raft, Ride, Sail, Skim, Sponson, Stick, Trimmer, Vacillate, Waft, Waggler, Waterwings

Floating garden Chinampa

Flock(s) Assemble, Bevy, Charm, Chirm, Company, Congregation, Drove, Flight, Fold, Forgather, Gaggle, Gather, Gregatim, Herd, Mob, Rally, Sedge, Sord, Spring, Trip, Troop, Tuft, Vulgar, Wing, Wisp, Wool

Flog(ger), **Flogging** Beat, Birch, Breech, Cane, Cat, Exert, Flay, Hawk, Hide, Knout, Lace, Lambast, Larrup, Lash, Lather, Lick, Orbilius, Rope's end, Scourge, Sell, Strap, Tat, > **THRASH**, Thwack, Tout, Vapulate, Welt, Whip

Flood(ed) Awash, Bore, Cataclysm, Deluge, Deucalion's, Diffuse, Diluvium, Drown, Dump, Eger, Flash, Freshet, Gush, Inundate, Irrigate, Noachic, Overflow, Overwhelm, Pour, Rage, Smurf, Spate, Speat, Swamp, Tide, > **TORRENT**, Undam

Floodgate St(a)unch

Floodlight Ashcan, Blond(e), One-key

Floor(ing) Area, Astound, Baffle, Barbecue, Beat, Benthos, Chess, Deck, Dev(v)el, Down, Entresol, Etage, Fell, Flags(tone), Flatten, Flight, Gravel, Ground, Kayo, KO, Mezzanine, Parquet, Pelvic, Piano nobile, Pit, Planch, Platform, Puncheon, Screed, Shop, Stage, Story, Stump, Terrazzo, Tessella, Tessera, Thill, Woodblock

Flop Belly-landing, Bomb, Collapse, Dud, Failure, Fizzer, Fosbury, Lollop, Mare's-nest, Misgo, Phut, Plump, Purler, Washout, Whap, Whitewash

Flora Benthos, Biota, Cybele, Flowers, Intestinal

Florence, **Florentine** Tuscan

Florid Coloratura, Cultism, Flamboyant, Fresh, Gongorism, High, Red, Rococo, Rubicund, Ruddy, Taffeta

Florida Fa

Floss(y) Dental, Flashy, Florence, Ornate, Silk

▸ **Flotation** *see* FLOAT

Flotilla Armada, Escadrille

Flotsam Detritus, Driftwood, Flotage, Waift, Waveson, Weft

Flounce Falbala, Frill, Furbelow, Huff, Prance, Ruffle, Sashay, Toss

Flounder Blunder, Fluke, Reel, Slosh, Struggle, Stumble, Tolter, Toss, Wallow

Flour Cassava, Couscous(ou), Cribble, Crible, Farina, Graham, Gram, Kouskous, Meal, Middlings, Pinole, Plain, Powder, Red-dog, Rock, Rye, Self-raising, Soy(a), Wheatmeal, White, Wholegrain, Wholemeal, Wholewheat, Wood

Flourish(ed), Flourishing Blague, Bless, Bloom, Blossom, Boast, Brandish, Bravura, Burgeon, Cadenza, Epiphonema, Fanfare, Fiorita, Fl, Flare, Floreat, Grow, Kicking, Lick, Melisma, Mort, Omar, Palmy, Paraph, Prosper, Rubric, Scroll, Swash, Tantara, Thrive, Tucket, Veronica, Vigorous, Wampish, Wave, Welfare

Flout Disdain, Disobey, Insult, Malign, Mock, Profane, Scorn, Scout

Flow(ing) Abound, Afflux, Cantabile, Cash, Current, Cursive, Cusec, Distil, Ebb, Emanate, Estrang(h)elo, Fleet, Fluent, Fluid, Flush, Flux, Freeform, Gene, Gush, Knickpoint, Laminar, Liquid, Loose-bodied, Nappe, Nickpoint, Obsequent, Onrush, Ooze, Popple, Pour, Purl, Rail(e), Rayle, Rill, Rin, Run, Scapa, Seamless, Setter, Slip, Slur, Spate, Spurt, Stream, Streamline, Teem, Tidal, Torrent, Trickle, Turbulent, Viscous

Flower (part), Flowering, Flowers, Flower bed Best, Bloom, Bloosme, Blossom, Cream, Develop, Efflorescence, Elite, Inflorescence, Parterre, Passion, Plant, Pre-vernal, Prime, Remontant, > RIVER, Spray, Square, Stalked, Stream, Trumpet, Vernal, Wreath

FLOWERS

4 letters:
Arum
Cyme
Disc
Flag
Gold
Gool
Gule
Irid
Iris
Knot
Lily
Pink
Rose

5 letters:
Agave
Aster
Brook
Bugle
Camas

Daisy
Enemy
Hosta
Padma
Phlox
Poppy
Spink
Tansy
Toran
Tulip
Umbel
Yulan

6 letters:
Adonis
Arabis
Camash
Camass
Corymb
Crants
Dahlia

Gollan
Henbit
Madder
Maguey
Nuphar
Onagra
Orchid
Paeony
Pompom
Pompon
Protea
Scilla
Sesame
Silene
Smilax
Spadix
Tassel
Torana

7 letters:
Aconite

Alyssum
Anemone
Astilbe
Bugloss
Campion
Cowslip
Freesia
Fumaria
Gentian
Gilt-cup
Glacier
Gladdon
Godetia
Golland
Gowland
Ipomoea
Kikumon
Melilot
Nosegay
Petunia
Picotee

Quamash
Rampion
Sulphur
Verbena

8 letters:
Abutilon
Amaranth
Argemone
Asphodel
Bindi-eye
Bluebell
Carolina
Clematis
Cyclamen
Daffodil
Floscule
Foxglove
Gardenia
Geranium
Gillyvor
Glory-pea

Hepatica
Hibiscus
Kok-sagyz
Larkspur
Leucojum
Magnolia
Marigold
Myosotis
Oleander
Primrose
Scabious
Stapelia
Trollius
Tuberose
Turnsole
Valerian

9 letters:
Bald-money
Belamoure
Buttercup
Columbine

Edelweiss
Eglantine
Galingale
Gessamine
Hellebore
Hydrangea
Jessamine
Melampode
Pimpernel
Rudbeckia
Santonica
Saxifrage
Speedwell
Strobilus

10 letters:
Bellamoure
Buttonhole
Coronation
Granadilla
Heliotrope
Immortelle

Nasturtium
Pentstemon
Poinsettia
Snapdragon
Stavesacre
Tibouchine
Touch-me-not

11 letters:
Boutonniere
Bur-marigold
Gillyflower
Loose-strife
Meadow-sweet

12 letters:
Hortus siccus
None-so-pretty
Tradescantia

Flower *may indicate* a river
Flower arrangement, Flower work Barbola, Ikebana, Lei
Flowery Anthemia, Damassin, Orchideous, > ORNATE, Pseudocarp, Verbose
Flu Asian, Gastric, Grippe, Lurgi, Yuppie
Fluctuate(r), Fluctuation Ambivalence, Balance, Seiche, Trimmer, Unsteady, Vacillate, Vary, Waver
Flue Chimney, Duct, Funnel, Pipe, Tewel, Uptake, Vent
Fluent(ly) Eloquent, Facile, Flowing, Glib, Liquid, Oracy, Verbose, Voluble
Fluff(y) Bungle, Dowl(e), Down, Dust, Feathery, Flocculent, Floss, Flue, Fug, Fuzz, Girl, Lint, Mess-up, Muff, Noil, Oose, Ooze, Thistledown
Fluid Amniotic, Anasarca, Ascites, Broo, Chyle, Cisterna, Colostrum, Condy's, Coolant, Edema, Enema, Fixative, Fl, Humour, Joint-oil, Juice, Latex, > LIQUID, Lymph, Movable, Mucus, Oedema, Perfect, Perilymph, Plasma, Sap, Seminal, Serous, Serum, Shifting, Spermatic, Spittle, Succus, Synovia, Vitreum, Vril, Water
Fluid *may indicate* an anagram
Fluke Accident, Anchor, Chance, Fan, Flounder, Ga(u)nch, Grapnel, Killock, Liver, Lobe, Redia, Schistosome, Scratch
Flummox Baffle, Bamboozle, Floor, Nonplus
Flunk Fail
Flunkey Chasseur, Clawback, Haiduck, Heyduck, Jeames, Lackey, Servant, Toady
Fluorescence, Fluorescent Bloom, Day-glo, Epipolism, Glow, Phosphorescence
Fluorine F
Flurry Bustle, Fluster, Haste, Hoo-ha, Shower
Flush(ed) Affluent, Beat, Busted, Even, Ferret, Florid, Flow, Gild, Hectic, Heyday, Hot, Level, Red, Rolling, Rose, Royal, Rud, Scour, Sluice, Spaniel, Start, Straight, Sypher, Thrill, Tierce, Vigour, Wash
Fluster Befuddle, Confuse, Disconcert, Faze, Flap, Pother, Rattle, Shake

Flute (player) Bellows-maker, Bohm, Channel, Claribel(la), Crimp, Fife, Fipple, Flageolet, German, Glass, Glyph, Groove, Marsyas, Nose, Ocarina, Piccolo, Pipe Poogye(e), Quena, Shakuhachi, Sulcus, Thisbe, Tibia, Toot, Transverse, Whistle

Flutter Bat, Bet, Fan, Fibrillate, Flacker, Flaffer, Flaught, Flichter, Flicker, Flitter, Fly, > **GAMBLE**, Hover, Palpitate, Play, Pulse, Sensation, Twitter, Waft, Winnow

Flux D, Electric, Flow, Fusion, Luminous, Magnetic, Maxwell, Melt, Neutron, Panta rhei, Radiant, Tesla, Weber

Fly(ing), Flies Abscond, Agaric, Airborne, Alder, Alert, Antlion, Assassin, Astute, Aviation, Awake, A-wing, Baker, Bedstead, Bee, Blister, Blowfly, Blue-arsed, Bluebottle, Bolt, Bot, Breese, Breeze, Brize, Brommer, Bulb, Bush, Cab, Caddis, Carriage, Carrot, Cecidomyia, Chalcid, Cheesehopper, Cheese skipper, Cleg, Cluster, Cock-a-bondy, Crane, Cuckoo, > **CUNNING**, Decamp, Deer, Diptera, Dobson, Doctor, Dolphin, Doodlebug, Dragon, Drake, Drone, Drosophila, Dry, Dung, Dutchman, Escape, Face, Fiacre, Flee, Flesh, Flit, Fox, Frit, Fruit, Glide, Glossina, Gnat, Grannom, Greenbottle, Greenhead, Hackle, Harvest, Hedge-hop, Hessian, Homoptera, Hop, Horn, Horse, Hover, Hurtle, Ichneumon, Instrument, Jenny-spinner, Jock Scott, Lace-wing, Lamp, Lantern, Laputan, March brown, Mosquito, Moth, Motuca, Murragh, Musca, Mutuca, Needle, New Forest, Nymph, Onion, Opening, Ox-warble, Palmer, Para, Pilot, Pium, Plecopteran, Pomace, Rapid, Robber, Saucer, Sciaridae, Scorpion, Scotsman, Screwworm, Scud, Sedge, Silverhorn, Simulium, Smart, Smother, Snake, Snipe, Soar, Spanish, Speed, Spinner, Stable, Stream, Syrphidae, Tabanid, Tachina, Tear, Thrips, Tipula, Trichopteran, Tsetse, Tube, Turkey brown, Vamoose, Vinegar, Volatic, Volitate, Warble, Watchet, Water, Welshman's button, Wet, Wheat, Wide-awake, Willow, Wily, Wing, Yellow sally, Yogic, Zebub, Zimb, Zipper

Fly-catcher Attercop, Cobweb, Darlingtonia, Dionaea, King-bird, Phoebe, Spider, Tanrec, Tyrant

Flying-fox Fruit-bat, Kalong

Flying saucer UFO

Fly-killer Chowri, Chowry, DDT, Swat

Foam(ing) Barm, Bubble, Froth, Lather, Mousse, Oasis®, Polystyrene, Ream, Scum, Seethe, Spindrift, Spooming, Spume, Sud(s), Surf, Wake, Wild water, Yeast, Yest

Fob Chain, Defer, Fub, Pocket, Slang

Focal, Focus Centre, Converge, Fix, Hinge, Hub, Narrow, Pinpoint, Point, Prime Principal, Spotlight, Train

Fodder Alfalfa, Browsing, Buckwheat, Cannon, Clover, Eatage, Emmer, Ensilage, Foon, Forage, Gama-grass, Grama, Guar, Hay, Lucerne, Oats, Oilcake, Pasture, Provender, Rye-grass, Sainfoin, Silage, Soilage, Stover

Foe Contender, > **ENEMY**, Opponent, Rival

Foetus Embryo

Fog Aerosol, Brume, Cloud, Damp, Fret, Haar, (London) Particular, Miasm(a), Mist, Murk, Obscure, Pea-soup(er), Roke, Sea-fret, Sea-haar, Smog, Smoke, Soup, Thick, Vapour, Yorkshire

Fogey Die-hard

Fogg Phileas, Solicitor

Foible Failing, Flaw, Idiosyncrasy, Quirk, Weakness

Foil(ed) Ba(u)lk, Chaff, Cross, Dupe, Epée, Fleurette, Frustrate, Gold, Lametta, Leaf, Offset, Paillon, Pip, Scotch, Scupper, Silver, Stooge, Stump, Tain, Thwart, Touché

Foist Fob, Insert, Suborn, Wish

Fold(er), **Folding**, **Folded**, **Folds** Anticline, Bend, Binder, Close, Collapse, Concertina, Convolution, Corrugate, Cote, Crash, Crease, Crimp, Crinkle, Crunkle, Diapir, Diptych, Dog-ear, Double, Duo-tang®, Epicanthus, Epiploon, Fake, Fan, File, Fr(a)enum, Frill, Furl, Gather, Groin, Gyrus, Jack-knife, Lap, Lapel, Lap(p)et, Lirk, Mesentery, Monocline, Nappe, Nympha, Obvolute, Octuple, Omentum, Origami, Pastigium, Pen, Pericline, Pintuck, Pleach, > PLEAT, Plica, Plunging, Ply, Pran(c)k, Prancke, Ptyxis, Recumbent, Ruck(le), Ruga, Sheep-pen, Syncline, Triptych, Tuck, Vocal, Wrap

Foliage Coma, Finial, Frond, Greenery, Leafage

Folio(s) Elephant, F(f), File, Percy

Folk(sy) Beaker, Homespun, Kin, People, Public

Follicle Graafian

Follow(er), **Following** Adhere, After, Agree, And, Anthony, Attend(ant), Believer, Clientele, Consequence, Copy, Dangle, Disciple, Dog, Echo, Ensew, Ensue, Entourage, Epigon(e), Equipage, F, Fan, Groupie, Heel(er), Henchman, Hereon, Hunt, Man, Merry men, Muggletonian, Myrmidon, Neist, Next, Obey, Pan, Post, Pursue, Rake, Road, Run, Satellite, School, Secundum, Seewing, Segue, Sequel, Seriation, Servitor, Shadow, Sheep, Sidekick, Stag, Stalk, Stear, Steer, Subsequent, Succeed, Sue, Suivez, Supervene, Tag, Tail, Tantony, Trace, Track, Trail, Train, Use, Vocation, Votary

Follower 'a follower' *may indicate* B

Folly Antic, Bêtise, Idiocy, Idiotcy, Imprudence, Lunacy, Mistake, Moria, Unwisdom, Vanity

Foment(ation) Arouse, Brew, Embrocation, Excite, Poultice, Stupe

Fond(ness) Amatory, Ardour, Dote, Keen, Loving, Partial, Penchant, Tender, Tendre

Fondant Ice, Sweet

Fondle Canoodle, Caress, Dandle, Grope, Hug, Nurse, Pet, Snuggle

Font Aspersorium, Bénitier, Delubrum, Ennage, Source

Food Aliment, Ambrosia, Bakemeat, Balti, Batten, Battill, Battle, Bellytimber, Board, Bolus, Bord, Broth, Browse, Bully, Burger, Cate, Chametz, Cheer, Cheese, Chop, Chow, Chuck, Chyme, Cocoyam, Collation, Comestible, Comfort, Commons, Convenience, Course, Curd, Deutoplasm, Dietetics, > DISH, Dodger, Dog's body, Dunderfunk, Eats, Esculents, Eutrophy, Falafel, Fare, Fast, Fast casual, Felafel, Fodder, Forage, Frankenstein, Freedom, Fuel, Functional, Grub, Hangi, Hometz, Incaparina, Ingesta, Jootha, Jorts, Junk, Kai, Keep, Langar, Leben, Lerp, Long-pig, Maigre, Manna, Mato(o)ke, Matzoon, Meal, Meat, Muckamuck, Nacho, Nardoo, Nosebag, Nosh, Nourishment, Nourriture, Oven-ready, Pabulum, Pannage, Pap, Parev(e), Parve, Pasta, Peck, Pemmican, Pizza, Prog, Provender, Provision, Ration(s), Rysttafel, Sambal, Sap, Sashimi, Scaff, Scoff, Sitology, Sizings, Skin, Slow, Snack, Soil, Soul, Staple, Stodge, Sushi, Table, Tack, Takeaway, Tamale, Taro, Tempura, Teriyake, Tofu, Trimmings, Trophallaxis, Tuck(er), Vegeburger, Veggie-burger, Viand, Victuals, Vivers, Waffle, Yantia, Yittles, Yog(h)urt

Food-plant Laser, Silphium

Foodstore Delicatessen, Grocery, Larder, Pantry, Silo

Fool(hardy), **Foolish(ness)** Air-head, Anserine, April, Assot, Berk, BF, Bob, Brainless, Brash, Buffoon, Cake, Capocchia, Chump, Clot, Clown, Cockeyed, Coxcomb, Cully, Daft, Dagonet, Daw, Delude, Dessert, Dummy, Dunce, Empty, Etourdi, Fatuous, Feste, Flannel(led), Folly, Fon, Fond, Fox, Gaby, Gaga, Galah, Git, Glaikit, Goat, Gobbo, Goon, Goose, Gooseberry, Groserts, Gubbins, Gull,

Gullible, Halfwit, Hanky-panky, Hare-brained, Highland, Huntiegowk, Hunt-the-gowk, Idiotic, Imbecile, Inane, Ineptitude, Injudicious, Jest, Joke, Kid, Kissel, Lark, Loon, Mamba, Mislead, Mome, Moron, Muggins, Niaiserie, Nignog, Ni(n)compoop, Ninny, Nong, Oanshagh, Omadhaun, Patch, Poop, Poupe, Punk, Rash, Sawney, Scogan, Scoggin, Senseless, Shallow, Snipe, Soft, Sot, Spoony, > **STUPID**, Sucker, Tom (noddy), Trifle, Unwitty, Vice, Wantwit, Yorick, Yoyo, Zany

Foolproof Fail-safe

Foot(ing), Footwork, Feet Amphibrach, Amphimace, Anap(a)est, Antibacchius, Antispast, Athlete's, Bacchius, Ball, Base, Choliamb, Choree, Choriamb, Club, Cold, Cretic, Dactyl, Dance, Dochmii, Dochmius, Epitrite, F, Hephthemimer, Hoof, Hoppus, Iamb(us), Immersion, Infantry, Ionic, Molossus, Ockodols, Pad, Paeon, Palama, Pastern, Paw, Pay, Pedate, Pedicure, Pes, Plates, Podium, Proceleusmatic, Pyrrhic, Roothold, Scazon, Semeia, Serif, Shanks's mare, Shanks's pony, Spade, Spondee, Standing, Syzygy, Tarsus, Terms, Tootsie, Tootsy, Tootsy-wootsy, Tread, Trench, Tribrach, Trilbies, Triseme, Trochee, Trotter, Tube, Verse, Wrong

Football(er) Aerial pingpong, Australian Rules, Back, Barbarian, Ba'spiel, Camp, Canadian, Centre, Fantasy, FIFA, Five-a-side, Flanker(back), Fly-half, Gaelic, Goalie, Gridder, Keeper, Kicker, League, Libero, Lineman, Lock, Midfield, Pack, Pele, Pigskin, RU, Rugby, Rugger, Rules, Safety, Seven-a-side, Sevens, Soccer(oos), Sport, Stand-off, Striker, Subbuteo®, Sweeper, Table, Tight-end, Togger, Total, Touch(back), Wallgame, Wing, Wingman

Footboard Stretcher

Foot-fault Bunion, Corn, Hammer-toe, Verruca

Foothold Lodgement, Purchase, Stirrup

Footlights Floats

Footloose Peripatetic

Footman Attendant, Flunkey, Lackey, Pedestrian, Pompey, Yellowplush

Footnote Addendum, PS

Footpad Land-rat, Mugger, Robber

Footpath, Footway Banquette, Catwalk, Clapper, Track

Footplate Horseshoe

Footprint Ecological, Ichnite, Ichnolite, Pad, Prick, Pug, Seal, Slot, Trace, Track, Tread, Vestige

Footrest, Footstool Coaster, Cricket, Hassock, Stirrup, Stool, Tramp

Footrot, Footsore Blister, Bunion, Corn, Halt, Surbate, Surbet, Weary, Wire-heel

Footslogger Infantryman

Footwashing Maundy, Nipter

Footwear Gumboot, > **SHOE**, Slipper, Sock, Spats, Stocking

Fop(pish) Apery, Barbermonger, Beau, Buck, Cat, Coxcomb, Dandy, Dude, Exquisite, Fallal, Fangled, Fantastico, Finical, La-di-da, Macaroni, Monarcho, Muscadin, Popinjay, Skipjack, Toff

For Ayes, Because, Concerning, Cos, Pro, Since, To

Forage Alfalfa, Fodder, Graze, Greenfeed, Ladino, Lucern(e), Pickeer, Prog, Raid, Rummage, Sainfoin, Search

Foray Attack, Creach, Creagh, Raid, Sortie, Spreagh

Forbear(ance), Forbearing Abstain, Clement, Endure, Indulgent, Lenience, Lineage, Longanimity, Mercy, Pardon, Parent, Patient, Quarter, > **REFRAIN**, Suffer, Tolerant, Withhold

Forbid(den), Forbidding Ban, Bar, City, Denied, Don't, Dour, Enjoin,

For(e)speak, Gaunt, Grim, Haram, Hostile, Loury, NL, Prohibit, Stern, Taboo, Tabu, Tapu, Tref(a), Verboten, Veto

Force(d), **Forceful**, **Forces**, **Forcible** Activist, Agency, Air-arm, Army, Back emf, Bathmism, Bind, Birr, Bludgeon, Body, Bounce, Brigade, Bring, Brunt, Bulldoze, Cadre, Capillary, Cascade, Centrifugal, Centripetal, Chi, Coerce, Cogency, Commando, Compel, Constrain, Coriolis, Cram, Delta, Detachment, Dint, Domineer, Downflow, Dragoon, Drive, Duress(e), Dynamic, Dyne, E, Edge, Electromotive, Emphatic, Energetic, Equilibrant, Erdgeist, Erg, Exchange, Expeditionary, Extort, Extrude, F, Farci, Fifth, Fire brigade, Frogmarch, G, Gar, Gendarmerie, Gilbert, Gism, Gouge, Gravitational, Hale, Host, Hurricane, Impetus, Impose, Impress, Inertial, Instress, Intense, Irgun, Irrupt, Jism, Juggernaut, Kinetic, Kundalini, Labour, Land, Lashkar, Legion, Life, Linn, Lorentz, Magnetomotive, Magnus, Make, Mana, Manpower, Market, Militia, Moment, Momentum, Muscle, Navy, Newton, Numen, Oblige, Od, Odyl(e), OGPU, Old Contemptibles, Orgone, Orotund, Personnel, Phrenism, Physical, Pigs, Pion, Pithy, Plastic, Police, Posse, Potent, Pound, Poundal, Prana, Press(gang), Pressure, Prise, Procrustean, Psyche, Pull, Put, Qi, Railroad, Rape, Ravish, Reave, Regular, Require, Restem, Route, Rush, SAS, Sforzando, Shear, Snorting, Spetsnaz, Squirt, Steam(roller), Stick, Stiction, Strained, > STRESS, Strong-arm, Subject, TA, Task, Telergy, Telling, Thrust, Torque, Tractive, Troops, Van der Waals', Vehement, Vigorous, Vim, Violence, Vires, Vis, Vis visa, Vital, Vively, Vociferous, Vril, Wrench, Wrest, Wring, Zap

Force(d) *may indicate* an anagram
Forced labour Begar
Force-feeding Gavage
Forceps Bulldog, Capsule, Crow(s)bill, Hemostatic, Mosquito, Obstetrical, Pedicellaria, Pincers, Rongeur, Tenaculum, Thumb, Vulsella
Ford Anglia, Car, Crossing, Drift, Escort, Sierra, Strid, Tin Lizzy, Wade
Forearm Cubital, Radius, Ulna
Forebear *see* FORBEAR
Foreboding Anxiety, Augury, Cloudage, Croak, Feeling, Freet, > OMEN, Ominous, Premonition, Presage, Presentiment, Sinister, Zoomantic
Forecast(er), **Forecasting** Augury, Auspice, Divine, Extrapolation, Horoscope, Metcast, Numerical, Perm, Portend, Precurse, Predict, Presage, Prescience, Prognosis, Prognosticate, Prophesy, Rainbird, Shipping, Soothsay, Spae, Tip, Weather
Foreclose Bar, Block, Obstruct, Preclude
Forefather(s) Ancestor, Elder, Forebear, Parent, Rude
Forefront Van
Forehead Brow, Front(let), Glabella(r), Sincipitum, Temple
Foreign(er) Alien, Amakwerekwere, Arab, Auslander, Barbarian, Easterling, Ecdemic, Eleanor, Ethnic, Exclave, Exotic, External, Extraneous, Extrinsic, Forane, Forinsecal, Forren, Fraim, Fremit, Gaijin, German, Gringo, Gweilo, Malihini, Metic, Moit, Mote, Outlander, Outside, Oversea, Peregrine, Remote, > STRANGE, Stranger, Taipan, Tramontane, Uitlander, Unfamiliar, Wog
Foreman Baas, Boss, Bosun, Chancellor, Gaffer, Ganger, Manager, Overseer, Steward, Superintendent, Topsman
Foremost First, Front, Leading, Primary, Prime, Supreme, Van
Foremost *may indicate* first letters of words following
Forenoon Undern
Forepart Cutwater, Front
Forerunner Augury, Harbinger, Herald, Messenger, Omen, Pioneer, Precursor,

Prequel, Trailer, Vaunt-courier

Foresee Anticipate, Divine, Preview, Prophesy, Scry

Foreshadow Adumbrate, Augur, Bode, Forebode, Hint, Portend, Prefigure, Presage, Type

Foreshow Betoken, Bode, Signify

Foresight Ganesa, Prescience, Prophecy, Prospect, Providence, Prudence, Taish, Vision

Foreskin Prepuce

Forest(ry) Arden, Ashdown, Black, Bracknell, Bush, Caatinga, Charnwood, Chase, Cloud, Dean, Epping, Fontainebleau, Gallery, Gapo, Glade, Greenwood, Igapo, Jungle, Managed, Monte, Nandi, Nemoral, New, Petrified, Rain, Savernake, Selva, Sherwood, Silviculture, Taiga, Thuringian, Urman, Virgin, Waltham, > **WOOD**, Woodcraft

Forestall Anticipate, Head-off, Obviate, Pip, Pre-empt, Prevent, Queer, Scoop

Forester Foster, Lumberjack, Verderer, Walker, Woodman, Woodward

Foretaste Antepast, Antipasto, Appetiser, Pregustation, Prelibation, Preview, Sample, Trailer

Foretell(ing), Forewarn Augur, Bode, Caution, Divine, Fatidic, Forecast, Portend, Predict, Premonish, Presage, Prognosticate, Prophecy, Soothsay, Spae

Forethought Anticipation, Caution, Prometheus, Provision, Prudence

Forever Always, Amber, Ay(e), Eternal, Evermore, Keeps

▶ **Forewarn** see **FORETELL**

Foreword Introduction, Preamble, Preface, Proem, Prologue

For example Eg, Say, Vg, ZB

For fear Lest

Forfeit Deodand, Fine, Forgo, > **PENALTY**, Relinquish, Rue-bargain, Sconce

Forge(d), Forger(y) Blacksmith, Copy, Counterfeit, Drop, Dud, Fabricate, Fashion, Foundry, Hammer, Heater, Horseshoe, Ireland, Lauder, Mint, Paper-hanger, Pigott, Progress, Rivet-hearth, Smith(y), Smithery, Spurious, Stiff, Stithy, Stumer, Tilt, Trucage, Truquage, Utter, Valley, Vermeer, Vulcan

Forget(ful), Forget-me-not Amnesia, Dry, Fluff, Lethe, Myosotis, Neglect, Oblivious, Omit, Overlook

Forgive(ness), Forgiving Absolution, Amnesty, Clement, Condone, Merciful, Overlook, Pardon, Placable, Remission, Remittal

Forgo(ne) Abstain, Expected, Refrain, Renounce, Waive

Forgotten Bygone, Missed, Sad

Forjeskit Overscutched

Fork(ed) Bifurcate, Biramous, Branch, Caudine, Cleft, Crotch, Crutch, Divaricate, Forficate, Fourchette, Grain, Graip, Morton's, Osmeterium, Prong, Replication, Runcible, Sucket, Tine, Toaster, Tormenter, Tormentor, Trident, Trifid, Tuner, Tuning, Y

Forlorn(ness) Abject, Aidless, Desolate, Destitute, Drearisome, Miserable, Nightingale, Sad, Woebegone

Form(s) Alumni, Bench, Bumf, Cast, Ceremonial, Class, Constitute, Coupon, Create, Document, Dress, Experience, Fashion, Feature, Fig, > **FIGURE**, Formula, Free, Game, Gestalt, Hare, Image, Keto, Lexicalise, Logical, Mode, Mood, Morph(ic), Morphology, Mould, Order, Originate, > **OUT OF FORM**, P45, Physique, Protocol, Questionnaire, Redia, Remove, Rite, Ritual, Schedule, Shape, Shell, Stage, Stamp, State, Stereotype, Structure, Style, Symmetry, Ternary, Version

Formal Ceremonious, Conventional, Dry, Exact, Fit, Literal, Methodic, Official, Pedantic, Precise, Prim, Routine, Set, Solemn, Starched, Stiff, Stodgy, Tails

Formality Ceremony, Ice, Pedantry, Protocol, Punctilio, Starch
Formation Battalion, Configuration, Diapyesis, Echelon, Eocene, Fours, Growth, Line, Manufacture, Origin, Pattern, Phalanx, Prophase, Reaction, Riss, Wedge
Former *may indicate* something that forms
Former(ly) Ance, Auld, Before, Ci-devant, Earlier, Ere-now, Erst(while), Ex, Late, Maker, Matrix, Old, Once, One-time, Past, Previous, Prior, Pristine, Quondam, Sometime, Then, Umquhile, Whilom
Formidable Alarming, Armipotent, Battleaxe, Fearful, Forbidding, Gorgon, Powerful, Shrewd, Stoor, Stour, Stowre, Sture, Tiger
Formless Amorphous, Invertebrate, Nebulous, Shapeless
Form of, **Forming** *may indicate* an anagram
Formosan Tai
Formula(te) Define, Devise, Doctrine, Empirical, Equation, Frame, Incantation, Invent, Kekule, Lurry, Molecular, Paternoster, Prescription, Protocol, > RECIPE, Reduction, Rite, Ritual, Stirling's, Structural
Forsake Abandon, Desert, Quit, Renounce
Forsooth Certes, Certy, Even, Marry, Quotha
Forswear Abandon, Abjure, Disavow, Renounce, Reny
Forsyte Fleur, Saga
Fort(ification), **Fortress** Acropolis, Alamo, Alhambra, Balclutha, Bastille, Bastion, Battlement, Bawn, Blockhouse, Bonnet, Breastwork, Bridgehead, Burg, Casbah, Castellated, Castellum, Castle, Citadel, Contravallation, Crémaillère, Demilune, Deva, Dun, Earthwork, Edinburgh, Enceinte, Epaule, Escarpment, Fastness, Fieldwork, Flanker, Flèche, Fortalice, Fortilage, Fortlet, Fraise, Ft, Gabion(ade), Garrison, Golconda, Haven, Hedgehog, Hornwork, Kaim, Kame, Kasba(h), Keep, Knox, La(a)ger, Lauderdale, Louisbourg, Maiden, Malakoff, Martello tower, Masada, Merlon, Mile-castle, Moineau, Motte and bailey, Orillion, Pa(h), Peel, Pele, Pentagon, Place, Rampart, Rath, Ravelin, Redoubt, Reduit, Ring, Salient, Sallyport, Sangar, Sconce, Stronghold, Sumter, Talus, Tenaille, Terreplein, Tete-du-pont, Tower, Trench, Vallation, Vitrified, William, Worth
Forte F, Metier, Specialty, Strength
Forth Away, From, Hence, Out
Forthright Candid, Direct, Frank, Prompt
Forthwith Anon, Directly, Eft(soons), Immediately
Fortify Arm, Augment, Brace, Casemate, Embattle, Lace, Munify, Steel, > STRENGTHEN
Fortitude Endurance, Grit, Mettle, Patience, Pluck, > STAMINA
Fortunate Auspicious, Blessed, Blest, Godsend, Happy, > LUCKY, Opportune, Providential, Well
Fortune (teller), **Fortune-telling** Auspicious, Bonanza, Bumby, Cartomancy, Chaldee, Cha(u)nce, Destiny, Dukkeripen, Fame, Fate, Felicity, Genethliac, Geomancy, Hap, Hydromancy, I Ching, Lot, Luck, Mint, Motser, Motza, Oracle, Packet, Palmist, Peripety, Pile, Prescience, Pyromancy, Sibyl, Soothsayer, Sortilege, Spaewife, Success, Taroc, Tarok, Tarot, Tyche, Wealth, Windfall
Forty, **Forties** Capot, F, Hungry, Kemple, Roaring
Forty-ninth Parallel
Forum Arena, Assembly, Debate, Platform, Tribunal
Forward(s) Accede, Advanced, Ahead, Along, Anterior, Arch, Assertive, Assuming, Bright, Early, Flanker, Forrad, Forrit, Forth, Fresh, Future, Hasten, Hooker, Immodest, Impudent, Insolent, Lock, Malapert, On(wards), Pack, Pert,

Petulant, Porrect, Precocious, > **PROGRESS**, Promote, Prop, Readdress, Redirect, Scrum, Send, Stem, To(ward), Van, Wing

Fossil(ised), Fossils Amber, Ammonite, Baculite, Belemnite, Blastoid(ea), Calamite, Ceratodus, Chondrite, Conodont, Corallian, Cordaites, Derived, Encrinite, Eohippus, Eozoon, Eurypterus, Exuviae, Fairy stone, Florula, Florule, Fogy, Goniatite, Graptolite, Hipparion, Ichnite, Ichnolite, Ichthyodurolite, Ichthyolite, Index, Jew's stone, Lepidostrobus, Lingulella, Living, Mosasauros, Nummulite, Odontolite, Olenus, Oligocene, Orthoceras, Osteolepis, Ostracoderm, Oxfordian, Pal(a)eo-, Pentacrinus, Petrifaction, Phytolite, Plesiosaur, Pliohippus, Pliosaur, Psilophyton, Pteridosperm, Pterodactyl(e), Pterygotus, Pythonomorph, Relics, Reliquiae, Remanié, Reworked, Sigillaria, Sinanthropus, Sivatherium, Snakestone, Stigmaria, Stromatolite, Taphonomy, Teleosaurus, Titanotherium, Trace, Trilobite, Uintatherium, Wood-opal, Zinganthropus, Zoolite

Foster (child, mother), Fostering Adopt, Cherish, Da(u)lt, Develop, Farm out, Feed, Fornent, Further, Harbour, Incubation, Metapelet, Metaplot, Nourish, Nourse(l), Noursle, Nousell, Nurse, Nurture, Nuzzle, > **REAR**

Foul, Foul-smelling Base, Beray, Besmirch, Besmutch, Bewray, Bungle, > **DEFILE**, Dreggy, Drevill, Enseam, Evil, Feculent, Funky, Gross, Hassle, Hing, Mephitic, Mud, Noisome, Olid, Osmeterium, Professional, Putid, Putrid, > **RANK**, Reekie, Rotten, Sewage, Soiled, Squalid, Stagnant, Stain, Stapelia, Technical, Unclean, Unfair, Vile, Violation, Virose

▷ **Foul** *may indicate* an anagram

Found (in) Among, Base, Bed, Bottom, Build, Cast, Caught, Emong, Endow, > **ESTABLISH**, Eureka, Institute, Introduce, Met, Occur, Plant, Recovered, Rest, Start, Table

Foundation(s) Base, Bedrock, Corset, Cribwork, Establishment, Footing, Girdle, Grillage, Ground, Groundwork, Hard-core, Hypostasis, Infrastructure, Institution, Matrix, Panty girdle, Pile, Roadbed, Rockefeller, Root, Scholarship, Stays, Stereobate, Substrata, Substructure, Trackbed, Underlie, Underlinen

▷ **Foundations** *may indicate* last letters

Founder Author, Collapse, Crumple, Fail, Inventor, Iron-master, Miscarry, Oecist, Oekist, Patriarch, Perish, Settle, Sink, Steelman, Stumble

Fount Aonian, Digital, Source, Springlet, Wrong

Fountain Acadine, Aganippe, Arethusa, Bubbler, Castalian, Cause, Conduit, Drinking, Fauwara, Forts, Gerbe, Head, Hippocrene, Jet, Pant, Pirene, Salmacis, Scuttlebutt, Soda, Spring, Trevi, Youth

Fountain basin Laver

Four(times), Foursome Cater, Georges, Horsemen, IV, Mess, Qid, Quartet, Quaternary, Quaternion, Reel, Tessara, Tessera, Tetrad, Tetralogy, Tiddy, Warp

Fourpence Groat

Fourteenth Bastille, Trecento, Valentine

Fourth Deltaic, Estate, Fardel, Firlot, Forpet, Forpit, July, Perfect, Quarter, Quartet, Quaternary, Quintan, Sesquitertia, Tritone

Fowl Barnyard, Biddy, Boiler, Brahma, Brissle-cock, Burrow-duck, Capon, Chicken, Chittagong, Cob, Cock, Coot, Domestic, Dorking, Duck, Ember, Gallinaceous, Gallinule, Game, Gleenie, Guinea, Hamburg(h), Heather-bleat(er), > **HEN**, Houdan, Jungle, Kora, Leghorn, Mallee, Moorhen, Orpington, Partridge, Pheasant, Pintado, Plymouth Rock, Poultry, Quail, Rooster, Rumkin, Rumpy, Solan, Spanish, Spatchcock, Spitchcock, Sultan, Sussex, Teal, Turkey, Wyandotte

Fox(y) Alopecoid, Arctic, Baffle, Blue, Charley, Charlie, Corsac, Cunning, Desert,

Fennec, Flying, Fool, Friend, Fur, Grey, Kit, Lowrie(-tod), Outwit, Pug, Puzzle, Quaker, Red, Reynard, Rommel, Russel, Silver, Skulk, > **SLY**, Swift, Tod, Uffa, Uneatable, Vixen, White, Zerda, Zoril(le), Zorro

Foxglove Cowflop, Deadmen's bells, Digitalis, Witches-thimble

Foxhole Earth

Foyer Hall, Lobby

Fracas Brawl, Dispute, Mêlée, Prawle, Riot, Rumpus, Scrum, Shindig, Uproar

Fraction Common, Complex, Compound, Continued, Improper, Ligroin, Mantissa, Packing, Part, Partial, Piece, Proper, Scrap, Simple, Some, Vulgar

Fracture Break, Colles, Comminuted, Complicated, Compound, Crack, Fatigue, Fault, Fissure, Greenstick, Hairline, Impacted, Pathological, Pott's, Rupture, Simple, Split, Stress

Fragile Brittle, Crisp, Delicate, Frail, Frangible, Nesh, Slender, Tender, Vulnerable, Weak

Fragment(s) Atom, Bit, Bla(u)d, Brash, Breccia, Brockram, Cantlet, Clastic, Crumb, End, Flinder, Fritter, Frust, Graile, Lapilli, Mammock, Mite, Morceau, Morsel, Ort, > **PARTICLE**, Piece, Potshard, Potsherd, Relic, Restriction, Rubble, Scrap, Segment, Shard, Shatter, Sheave, Shiver, Shrapnel, Shred, Skerrick, Sliver, Smithereens, Smithers, Snatch, Splinter

Fragment of *may indicate* a hidden word

Fragrance, Fragrant Aromatic, Attar, Bouquet, Conima, Nosy, Odour, Olent, > **PERFUME**, Pot-pourri, Redolent, > **SCENT**, Sent, Spicy, Suaveolent

Frail Brittle, Creaky, Delicate, Feeble, Flimsy, > **FRAGILE**, Puny, Slight, Slimsy, Weak

Framboesia Morula, Yaws

Frame(work) Adjust, Airer, Angle, Armature, Bail, Bayle, Body, Bow, Brickbat, Build, Cadge, Cadre, Cage, Case, Casement, Casing, Cent(e)ring, Centreing, Chase, Chassis, Clamper, Climbing, Cold, Compages, Companion, Cowcatcher, Cradle, Cratch, Cribwork, Deckel, Deckle, Draw, Entablature, Everest pack, Fabric, Fiddley, Flake, Form, Frisket, Gallows, Gambrel, Gantry, Garden, Gate, Gauntry, Grid-iron, Heck, Horse, Hull, Jungle gym, Lattice, Limit, Louvre, Mantel, Mixter, Mood, Mount, Mullion, Muntin(g), Newsreel, Ossature, Outrigger, Oxford, Pannier, Pantograph, Parameter, Partners, Passe-partout, Pergola, Physique, Pillory, Plant, Plot, Plummer-block, Poppet head, Portal, Puncheon, Rack, Rave, Redact, Retable, Rib(bing), Rim, Sampling, Sash, Scaffold, Scuncheon, Sect(ion), Set, Setting, Skeleton, Spring-box, Stanchion, Still(age), Stocking, Stocks, Straddle, Stretcher, Stretching, Stroma, > **STRUCTURE**, Studwork, Surround, Tabernacle, Taboret, Tambour, Tent(er), Tepee, Time, Trave, Trellis, Tress, Tressel, Trestle, Tribble, Trussing, Vacuum, Victimize, Walking, Wattle, Ways, Window, Yoke, Zarf, Zimmer®

Framley Parsonage

Franc Fr, Leu, Lev, Lew

France Anatole, Marianne, RF, Thibault

Franchise Charter, Contract, Liberty, Privilege, Right, Suffrage, Vote, Warrant

Franciscan Custos, Minorite, Observant, Salesian, Scotist, Tertiaries

Francium Fr

Franck Cesar

Frank(ish) Artless, Austrasia, Blunt, > **CANDID**, Direct, Easy, Free, Free-spoken, Honest, Ingenuous, Man-to-man, Merovingian, Natural, Open, Outspoken, Overt, Postage, Postmark, Ripuarian, Salian, Sincere, Stamp, Straight, Straightforward, Sty, Upfront

Frankincense Laser, Olibanum, Thus

Frans, Franz Hals, Lehar
Frantic Demoniac, Deranged, Distraught, Frenzied, Hectic, Mad, Overwrought Phrenetic, Rabid, Violent, Whirl(ing)
▷ **Frantic** *may indicate* an anagram
Frappé Iced
Fraternise, Fraternity Affiliate, Brotherhood, Burschenschaft, Consort, Elk, Fellowship, Lodge, Mingle, Moose, Order
Fratricide Cain
Fraud(ulent) Barratry, Bobol, Bubble, Charlatan, Cheat, Chisel, Collusion, Covin, Cronk, Deceit, Diddle, Do, Fineer, Gyp, Humbug, Hypocrite, > IMPOSTOR Imposture, Jiggery-pokery, Jobbery, Knavery, Liar, Peculator, Piltdown, Pious, Pseud(o), Put-up, Ringer, Rip-off, Roguery, Rort, Scam, South Sea Bubble, Stellionate, Supercherie, Swindle, Swiz(z), Swizzle, Tartuffe, Trick
Fraught Perilous
Fray(ed) Bagarre, Brawl, Contest, Feaze, Frazzle, Fret, Fridge, Ravel, Riot, Scrimmage
Freak Cantrip, Caprice, Chimera, Control, Deviant, Geek, Jesus, Mooncalf, Sport, Teras, Whim, Whimsy
Freckle Ephelis, Fern(i)tickle, Fern(i)ticle, Heatspot, Lentigines, Lentigo, Spot, Sunspot
Frederick Barbarossa, Carno, Great
Free(d), Freely Acquit, Assoil, Buckshee, Candid, Canny, Church, Clear, Complimentary, Cuffo, Dead-head, Deregulate, Devoid, Disburden, Disburthen, Disengage, Disentangle, Eleutherian, Emancipate, Enfranchise, Enlarge, Excuse, Exeem, Exeme, Exempt, Exonerate, Extricate, Familiar, Footloose, Frank, French, Gratis, House, Idle, Immune, Independent, Kick, Large, Lavish, Lax, Leisure, Let, Liberate, Loose, Manumit, Open, Parole, Pro bono, Quit(e), Range, Ransom, Redeem, > RELEASE, Relieve, Rescue, Reskew, Rick, Rid, Sciolto, Scot, Solute, Spare, Spring, Stald, Stall, Trade, Unlock, Unloosen, Unmew, Unmuzzle, Unshackle, Unsnarl, Untangle, Untie, Untwist, Vacant, Verse, Voluntary
▷ **Free** *may indicate* an anagram
Freebooter Cateran, Corsair, Franklin, Marauder, Moss-trooper, Pad, Pindaree, Pindari, Pirate, Rapparee, Snapha(u)nce, Snaphaunch, Thief, Viking
Freedom Abandon, Autonomy, Breadth, Carte blanche, Eleutherian, Exemption, Fear, Fling, Four, Immunity, Impunity, Laisser aller, Laisser faire, Laissez aller, Laissez faire, Latitude, Liberty, Licence, Moksha, Play, Range, Releasement, Speech, Uhuru, UNITA, Want, Worship
Free gift Bonus, Charism, Perk
Freehold(er) Enfeoff, Franklin, Frank tenement, Odal(l)er, Seisin, Udal(ler), Yeoman
Freelance Eclectic, Independent, Mercenary, Stringer
Freeloader Sponge
▷ **Freely** *may indicate* an anagram
Freeman Burgess, Ceorl, Churl, Franklin, Liveryman, Thegn, Thete, Villein
Freemason(ry), Freemason's son Craft, Lewis, Lodge, Moose, Templar
Free-range Eggs, Outler
Free State Orange
Freethinker Agnostic, Bradlaugh, Cynic, Libertine, Sceptic
Free-trade(r) Cobdenism, Wright
Free-wheel Coast
Freeze(s), Freezer, Freezing Alcarrazo, Benumb, Congeal, Cool, Cryogenic,

Cryonics, Eutectic, Freon®, Frost, Harden, Ice, Lyophilize, Moratoria, Nip, Numb, Paralyse, Regelate, Riss, Stiffen, Wage

Freight Cargo, Carriage, Fraught, Goods, Load

French(man), Frenchwoman Alsatian, Aristo, Basque, Breton, Cajun, Crapaud, Creole, Dawn, Dreyfus, Frog, Gallic(e), Gaston, Gaul, Gombo, Grisette, Gumbo, Huguenot, Joual, Jules, M, Mamselle, Marianne, Midi, Monsieur, Mounseer, Neo-Latin, Norman, Parleyvoo, Pierre, René, Rhemish, Savoyard

Frenetic Deranged, Frantic, Overwrought

Frenzied, Frenzy Amok, Berserk, Corybantic, Deliration, Delirium, Demoniac, Enrage, Enrapt, Euhoe, Euoi, Evoe, Feeding, Fit, Fury, Hectic, Hysteric, Lune, Maenad, Mania, Must, Nympholepsy, Oestrus, Phrenetic, Rage

Frequency, Frequent(er), Frequently Angular, Attend, Audio, Bandwidth, Channel, Common, Constant, Expected, Familiar, Forcing, Formant, FR, Fresnel, Gene, Habitué, Hang-out, Haunt, Hertz, High, Incidence, Intermediate, Medium, Megahertz, Natural, Often, Penetrance, Pulsatance, Radio, Recurrent, Regular, Relative, Resort, Spatial, Spectrum, Superhigh, Thick, Ultrahigh, Video

Fresco Intonaco, Sinopia, Tempera

Fresh(en), Freshness Airy, Aurorean, Brash, Caller, Chilly, Clean, Crisp, Dewy, Entire, Forward, Green, Hot, Insolent, Lively, Maiden, New, Novel, Quick, Rebite, Recent, Roral, Roric, Rorid, Smart, Span-new, Spick, Sweet, Tangy, Uncured, Verdure, Vernal, Virent

Freshman Bajan, Bejan(t), Fresher, Pennal, Recruit, Student

Fret(ful) Chafe, Filigree, Fray, Grate, Grecque, Haze, Impatient, Irritate, Ornament, Peevish, Repine, Rile, Ripple, Roil, Rub, Stop, Tetchy, Tracery, Whittle, Worry

Friable Crisp, Crumbling, Powdery

Friar(s) Augustinian, Austin, Bacon, Barefoot, Black, Brother, Bungay, Capuchin, Carmelite, Conventual, Cordelier, Crutched, Curtal, Dervish, Dominican, Fra(ter), Franciscan, Frate, Grey, Jacobin, Laurence, Limiter, Lymiter, Minim, Minor, Minorite, > **MONK**, Observant, Observantine, Predicant, Recollect, Recollet, Redemptionist, Rush, Tuck, White

Friction Attrition, Conflict, Dissent, Drag, Rift, Rub, Skin, Sliding, Stiction, Stridulation, Tribology, Tripsis, Wear, Xerotripsis

Friday Black, Girl, Golden, Good, Holy, Man, Savage

Fridge Esky®, Freezer, Icebox, Rub

Fried cake Croquette, Cruller

Friend(ly), Friends Achates, Affable, Ally, Alter ego, Ami(cable), Amigo, Approachable, Associate, Avuncular, Belamy, Benign, Boet(ie), Bosom, Bud(dy), Buster, Butty, Cackermander, Cater-cousin, China, Choma, Chum, Circle, Cobber, Cock, Cohort, Compadre, Companion, Companionable, Comrade, Confidant, Cordial, Couthie, Crony, Cully, Damon, Downhome, Edwin, En ami, Fairweather, False, Familiar, Feare, Feathered, Feer, Fere, Fiere, Gemütlich, Gossib, Gossip, Gregarious, Hail-fellow-well-met, Ingle, Intimate, Inward, Jong, Kith, Litigation, Marrow, Mate, Mentor, Mucker, Near, Outgoing, Paisano, Pal, Paranymph, Pen, Penn, Pheere, Privado, Prochain ami, Prochein ami, Pythias, Quaker, Sidekick, Sociable, Societal, Sport, Steady, Tillicum, Tonga, Tosh, Wack(er), Warm, Well-wisher, Wus(s)

Friendliness, Friendship Amity, Bonhomie, Camaraderie, Contesseration, Entente, Platonic, Sodality

Frieze Dado, Metope, Zoophorus

Fright(en), Frightened, Frightful Afear, Affear(e), Agrise, Agrize, Agryze,

Alarm, Aroint, Aroynt, Ashake, Chilling, Cow, Dare, Da(u)nt, Deter, Eek, Eerie, Faceache, Fear(some), Flay, Fleg, Fleme, Fley, Flush, Gallow, Gally, Ghast, Gliff, Glift, Grim, Grisly, Hairy, Horrid, Horrific, Intimidate, Ordeal, Panic, Scar, > **SCARE**, Scarre, Scaur, Schrecklich, Shocking, Sight, Skear, Skeer, Skrik, Spine-chilling, Spook, Stage, Startle, Terrible, Terrify, Terror, Tirrit, Unco, White-knuckle, Windy, Yitten

Frigid Bleak, Cold, Dry, Frory, Frosty, Ice, Indifferent, Serac, Stiff

Frill Armil, Armilla, Bavolet, Falbala, Furbelow, Jabot, Oriental, Ornament, Papillote, Ruche, Ruff(le), Tucker, Valance

▷ **Frilly** *may indicate* an anagram

Fringe(s), Fringed Bang, Border, Bullion, Ciliated, Ciliolate, Edge, Fall, Fimbria, Frisette, Interference, Laciniate, Loma, Lunatic, Macramé, Macrami, Pelmet, Peripheral, Robin, Ruff, Run, Thrum, Toupee, Toupit, Tsitsith, Tzitzith, Valance, Verge, Zizith

Frisian Holstein

Frisk(y) Caper, Cavort, Curvet, Fisk, Flimp, Frolic, Gambol, Search, Skip, Wanton

Fritillary Snake's-head

Fritter Batter, Beignet, Dribble, Dwindle, Fragment, Fribble, Pakora, Piddle, Potter, Puf(f)taloon, Squander, Waste

Frivolous Butterfly, Empty(-headed), Featherbrain, Flighty, Flippant, Frothy, Futile, Giddy, Idle, Inane, Light, Light-minded, Lightweight, Playboy, Skittish, Trifling, Trivial

Frizz(le), Frizzly Afro, Crape, Crimp, Crinkle, Curly, Fry, Fuzz, Hiss

Frock Dress, Gown, Ordain, Robe, Smock

Frog Anoura, Anura, Batrachia(n), Braid, Bullfrog, Crapaud, Depression, Flying, Fourchette, Frenchman, Frush, Goliath, Hairy, Hyla, Marsupial, Mounseer, Nic, Nototrema, Paddock, Paradoxical, Peeper, Pelobatid, Platanna, Puddock, Puttock, Rana, Ranidae, Tree, Wood, Xenopus

Frogman Diver

Frogmouth Mo(re)poke, Podargus

Frog spawn Redd, Tadpole

Frolic(some) Bender, Bust(er), Cabriole, Caper, Cavort, Curvet, Disport, Escapade, > **FRISK(Y)**, Fun, Galravage, Galravitch, Gambol, Gammock, Gil(l)ravage, Jink, Kittenish, Lark, Play, Pollick, Prank, Rag, Rand, Rig, Romp, Scamper, Skylark, Splore, Sport, Spree, Tittup, Wanton

From A, Against, Ex, For, Frae, Off, Thrae

Frond Fern, Leaf, Tendril

Front(al), Frontman Antependium, Anterior, Bow, Brass, Brow, Cold, Cover, Dead, Dickey, Dicky, Esplanade, Facade, Face, Fore(head), Forecourt, Foreground, Groof, Grouf, Head, Home, Metope, National, Newscaster, Occluded, Paravant, People's, Plastron, Polar, Popular, Pose, Preface, Pro, Prom, Prow, Sector, Sinciput, Stationary, Tabula, Temerity, Van, Vaward, Ventral, Warm, Western

Frontier(sman) Afghan, Barrier, Border, Boundary, Checkpoint, Limit, Limitrophe, List, March, North-west, Pathan, Wild West

Front page P1

Front-ranker Pawn

Frost(ing), Frosty Alcorza, Chill, Cranreuch, Cryo-, Freon®, Frigid, Frore(n), Frorne, Glacé, Ground, Hoar, Hore, Ice, Icing, Jack, Mat, Nip, Rime, White

Froth(y) Barm, Bubble, Cuckoospit, Cuckoospit(tle), Despumate, Foam, Frogspit, Gas, Head, Lather, Mantle, Off-scum, Ream, Saponin, Scum, Seethe, Shallow, Spoom, Spoon, Spume, Sud, Yeasty, Yest, Zephir

Frown Glower, Lour, Lower, Scowl

Frozen Froren, Gelid, Glacé, Graupel, Ice-bound, Static, Tundra

Fructification, **Fructify**, **Fructose** Aeci(di)um, Basidium, Fertilise, Flower, Fruit, Inulin

Frugal Meagre, Parsimonious, Provident, Prudent, Scant, Skimpy, Spare, Spartan, Thrifty

Fruit(ing), **Fruit tree**, **Fruity** Accessory, Achene, Acinus, Akene, Autocarp, Bacciform, Cedrate, Coccus, Compot(e), Confect, Conserve, Crop, Dessert, Drupe, Eater, Encarpus, Etaerio, First, Follicle, Forbidden, Fritter, Harvest, Issue, Orchard, Poof, Product(ion), Pseudocarp, Result, Return, Rich, Ripe, Schizocarp, Seed, Soft, Stoneless, Sweetie, Sweety, Syconium, Syncarp, Utricle, Valve, Wall, Xylocarp, Yield

FRUIT

3 letters:
Fig
Haw
Hep
Hip
Hop
Jak
Key
Nut

4 letters:
Akee
Bael
Bito
Date
Gage
Gean
Jack
Kaki
Lime
Pepo
Pome
Sloe
Sorb
Star
Tuna
Ugli

5 letters:
Ackee
Anana
Anona
Apple
Assai
Berry
Bread
Choko

Genip
Gourd
Guava
Jaffa
Lotus
Mango
Nancy
Naras
Nashi
Nelis
Olive
Papaw
Prune
Regma
Rowan
Whort

6 letters:
Almond
Ananas
Babaco
Banana
Banian
Banyan
Carica
Cherry
Chocho
Citron
Citrus
Comice
Durian
Durion
Emblic
Feijoa
Lichee
Litchi
Longan

Lychee
Mammee
Medlar
Narras
Nelies
Papaya
Pawpaw
Pepino
Pomace
Pomelo
Pruine
Quince
Raisin
Rennet
Replum
Russet
Samara
Sapota
Sharon
Squash
Tomato
Wampee

7 letters:
Apricot
Avocado
Bullace
Chayote
Crab-nut
Cypsela
Geebung
Genipap
Gherkin
Kumquat
Leechee
Litchee
Manjack

Morello
Passion
Pimento
Pinguin
Poperin
Pupunha
Regmata
Ruddock
Satsuma
Silicle
Siliqua
Silique
Sorosis
Soursop
Succade
Tangelo
Winesap

8 letters:
Abricock
Apricock
Bergamot
Bilberry
Blimbing
Calabash
Dewberry
Fraughan
Goosegog
Hagberry
Hastings
Hedgehog
Kalumpit
Minneola
Mulberry
Plantain
Prunello
Rambutan

- Rathripe
- Sebesten
- Shaddock
- Silicula
- Sunberry
- Tamarind
- Tayberry
- Waxberry

9 letters:
- Algarroba
- Allocarpy
- Apple-john
- Aubergine
- Bakeapple
- Blueberry
- Canteloup
- Carambola
- Caryopsis
- Cherimoya
- Cranberry
- Cremocarp

- Freestone
- Haanepoot
- Hackberry
- Mirabelle
- Myrobalan
- Naseberry
- Nectarine
- Neesberry
- Ortanique
- Persimmon
- Plumdamas
- Poppering
- Ratheripe
- Saskatoon
- Shadberry
- Sorb-apple
- Star-apple
- Tomatillo
- Victorine
- Whimberry
- Whinberry

10 letters:
- Apothecium
- Blackberry
- Canteloupe
- Cherimoyer
- Clementine
- Clingstone
- Elderberry
- Granadilla
- Grenadilla
- Jargonelle
- Mangosteen
- Pick-cheese
- Punicaceae
- Scaldberry
- Watermelon
- Youngberry

11 letters:
- Boysenberry
- Hesperidium
- Huckleberry

- Marionberry
- Pampelmoose
- Pampelmouse
- Pomegranate
- Pompelmoose
- Pompelmouse
- Salmonberry

12 letters:
- Blackcurrant
- Checkerberry
- Custard-apple
- Service-berry
- Whortleberry

13 letters:
- Bullock's heart

14 letters:
- Worcesterberry

Fruitful(ness) Calathus, Ephraim, Fat, Fecund, Feracious, Fertile, Productive, Prolific, Uberty, Worthwhile

Fruitless Bare, Futile, Sisyphean, Sterile, Useless, Vain

Frump(ish) Dowdy, Judy, Shabby, Unkempt

Frustrate Baffle, Ba(u)lk, Beat, Blight, Bugger, Check, Confound, Dash, Disappoint, Discomfit, Dish, Foil, Hogtie, Outwit, Scotch, Stymie, Tantalise, Thwart

Fry, **Fried** Blot, Brit, Christopher, Elizabeth, Fricassee, Fritter, Frizzle, Parr, Sauté, Sizzle, Small, Spawn, Whippersnapper, Whitebait

Fuddle(d) Drunk, Fluster, Fuzzle, Maudlin, Ta(i)vert, Tosticated, Woozy

▷ **Fuddle(d)** *may indicate* an anagram

Fudge Cook, Doctor, Dodge, Drivel, Evade, Fiddlesticks, Nonsense, Rot, Stop-press

Fuel Anthracite, Argol, Astatki, Atomic, Avgas, Biodiesel, Biogas, Briquet(te), Bunker, Butane, Candle-coal, Cannel, Carbonette, Charcoal, Coal, Coke, Derv, Diesel, Eilding, Eldin(g), Ethane, Faggot, Fire(wood), Fossil, Gasohol, Gasoline, Go-juice, Haxamine, Hydrazine, Hydyne, Kerosene, Kerosine, Kindling, Knitch, Lignite, Mox, Napalm, Naphtha, Nuclear, Orimulsion, Paraffin, Peat, Propane, Propellant, Smokeless, Solid, Stoke, Triptane, Unleaded, Yealdon

Fug Frowst

Fugitive Absconder, Ephemeral, Escapee, Fleeting, Hideaway, Lot, Outlaw, Refugee, Runaway, Runner, Transient

Fugue Ricercar(e), Ricercata

Fulcrum Key-pin, Pivot

Fulfil(ment) Accomplish, Complete, Fruition, Honour, Implementation, Meet, Pass, Realise, > SATISFY, Steed, Subrogation

Fulgent Bright, Shining

Full(ness), **Fully** Abrim, Ample, Arrant, Bouffant, Capacity, Chock-a-block, Chocker, Complete, Copious, Embonpoint, Engorged, Entire, Fat, Fed, Flush,

Fou, Frontal, German, High, Hoatching, Hotch, Mill, Plein, Plenary, Plenitude, Pleroma, Plethora, Replete, Rich, Sated, Satiated, Thorough, Toss, Turgid, Turgor, Ullage, Up, Wau(l)k, Wholly

Full-faced Caboched, Caboshed

Full-throated Goitred

Fulminate, **Fulmination** Detonate, Explode, Levin, Lightning, Rail, Renounce, Thunder

Fumarole Mofette

Fumble Blunder, Faff, Grope, Misfield, Muff

Fume(s) Bluster, Gas, Halitus, Nidor, Rage, Reech, Reek, Settle, Smoke, Stum, Vapours

Fumigate Disinfect, Smoke

Fun(ny), **Funny bone** Amusing, Antic, Boat, Buffo, Caper, Clownery, Comedy, Comic(al), Delight, Droll, Frolic, Gammock, Gig, Giocoso, Glaik, Guy, Hilarity, Humerus, Humorous, Hysterical, Ill, Jest, Jouisance, Jouysaunce, Killing, Kinky, Lark, Music, Play, Pleasure, Priceless, Rag, Rich, Rummy, Scream, Sidesplitting, Skylark, Sport, Uproarious, Weird(o), Yell

Funambulist Blondin, Equilibrist, Tight-rope

Function(al) Act, Algebraic, Antilog, Apparatchik, Arccos, Arcsine, Arctan, Bunfight, Ceremony, Characteristic, Cosec, Cosh, Cotangent, Coth, Density, Discriminant, Distribution, Dynamic, Exponential, Gamma, Gibbs, Hamilton(ian), Helmholtz, Hyperbolic, Integrand, Inverse, Jacobian, Job, Logarithm, Map(ping), > OPERATE, Periodic, Polymorphic, Probability, Propositional, Quadric, Quantical, Recursive, Role, Run, Secant, Sech, Sentential, Service, Sine, Sinh, State, Ste(a)d, Step, Surjection, Tan(h), Tick, Transcendental, Trigonometric, Use, Utensil, Utility, Versin, Vital, Wave, > WORK

Functionless Otiose

Fund(s), **Funding**, **Fundraising** Bank, Bankroll, Barrel, Capital, Chest, Consolidated, Emendals, Endow, Evergreen, Finance, Fisc, Fisk, Gild, Hedge, Imprest, Index, Jackpot, Kitty, Managed, Mutual, Nest-egg, Pension, Pool, Pork-barrel, Prebend, Private, Public, Purse, Revolving, Roll-up, Sinking, Slush, Social, Sou-sou, Stabilisation, Stock, Subsidise, Sustentation, Susu, Telethon, Treasury, Trust, Vulture, Wage(s), War chest, Wherewithal

Fundamental(ist) Basic(s), Bedrock, Cardinal, Essence, Grass-roots, Hamas, Missing, Nitty-gritty, Organic, Prime, Principle, Radical, Rudimentary, Taliba(a)n, Ultimate

Fund-holder Rentier

Funeral, **Funereal** Charnel, Cortege, Dismal, Exequy, Feral, Hearse, Obit, Obsequy, Sad-coloured, Solemn, Tangi

Fungicide Biphenyl, Bordeaux mixture, Burgundy mixture, Captan, Diphenyl, Ferbam, Menadione, PCP, Thiram, Zineb

Fungoid, **Fungus** Agaric, Amadou, Amanita, Ambrosia, Anthersmut, Anthracnose, Apothecium, Asci(us), Asomycete, Aspergillus, Barm, Basidium, Beefsteak, Black, Blackknot, Blewits, Blue-mould, Blue-rot, Boletus, Bootlace, Botrytis, Bracket, Bread-mould, Bunt, Candida, Ceps, Chantarelle, Chanterelle, Cladosporum, Clubroot, Conk, Coral spot, Corn smut, Craterellus, Cryptococcus, Cup, Death-cap, Death-cup, Dermatophytosis, Destroying angel, Discomycetes, Dutch elm, Earth-star, Elf-cup, Empusa, Endophyte, Ergot, Eumycetes, Favus, Funnel-cap, Fuss-ball, Fuzz-ball, Gall, Gibberella, Gill, Honey, Horsehair, Hypersarcoma, Hypha, Imperfect, Ink-cap, Ithyphallus, Jelly, Jew's ear, Liberty cap, Lichen, Magic mushroom, Merulius,

Mildew, Milk cap, Monilia, Morel, Mould, Mucor(ales), Mushroom, Mycelium, Mycetes, Mycology, Noble rot, Oak-leather, Oidium, Orange-peel, Penicillium, Pest, Peziza, Phallus, Phycomycete, Pileum, Plica, Polonica, Porcino, Pore, Prototroph, Puccinia, Puckfist, Puffball, Pythium, Rhizopus, Rhytisma, Russula, Rust, Saccharomyces, Saprolegnia, Saprophyte, Sariodes, Scab, Shaggy cap, Shaggy mane, Shoestring, Slime, Smut, Sooty mould, Spunk, Stinkhorn, Stipe, Stromata, Sulphur tuft, Tarspot, Thalline, Thallophyte, Toadstool, Torula, Tremella, Trichophyton, Truffle, Tuckahoe, Uredine, Ustilago, Velvetshank, Wax cap, Wheat rust, Witches' butter, Wood hedgehog, Yeast, Yellow brain, Yellow rust, Yellows, Zygomycete, Zygospore

Fungus-eater Mycophagist

Funicular Cable-car

Funk(y) Blue, Dodge, Dread, Fear, Scared, Stylish

Funnel Buchner, Chimney, Choana, Drogue, Flue, Hopper, Infundibulum, Separating, Smokestack, Stack, Stovepipe, Tun-dish, Wine

Fur Astrakhan, Astrex, Beaver(skin), Boa, Broadtail, Budge, Calabre, Caracul, Castor, Chinchilla, Coonskin, Crimmer, Ermelin, Ermine, Fitchew, Flix, Flue, Fun, Galyac, Galyak, Genet, Kolinsky, Krimmer, Lettice, Minever, Miniver, Mink, Mouton, Musquash, Ocelot, Otter, Pashm, Pean, Pekan, Rac(c)oon, Roskyn, Sable, Sealskin, Sea-otter, Stole, Tincture, Tippet, Vair(e), Victorine, Wolverine, Zibeline, Zorino

Furbish Polish, Renovate, Spruce, Vamp

Furl Fold, Roll, Stow, Wrap

Furlough Congé, Leave

Furnace Arc, Athanor, Blast, Bloomery, Bosh, Calcar, Cockle, Cremator, Cupola, Destructor, Devil, Electric, Finery, Firebox, Forge, Glory-hole, Kiln, Lear, Lehr, Lime-kiln, Oast, Oon, Open-hearth, Oven, Pot, Producer, Reverberatory, Scaldino, Solar, Tank, Wind

Furnish(ing) Appoint, Array, Deck, Decorate, Endow, Endue, Equip, Feed, Fledge, Gird, Lend, Produce, Provision, Soft, Stock, Supply, Tabaret, Upholster

Furniture Biedermeier, Chattels, Chippendale, Duncan Phyfe, Encoignure, Escritoire, Etagère, Flatpack, Hepplewhite, Insight, Lumber, Moveable, Queen Anne, Sheraton, Sideboard, Sticks, Stoutherie, Street, Tire, Unit, Washstand, Whatnot

Furore Brouhaha, Commotion, Outburst, Stink, Storm, Uproar

Furrier Trapper

Furrow(ed) Crease, Feer, Feerin(g), Furr, Groove, Gutter, Plough, Pucker, Rill(e), Rugose, Rut, Stria, Sulcus, Vallecula, Wrinkle

Fur-seal Seecatch(ie)

Further(more), Furthest Additional, Advance, Again, Aid, Also, Besides, Deeper, Else, Expedite, Extend, Extra, Extreme, Fresh, Infra, Longer, Mo(e), Mow, Other, Promote, Serve, Speed, Subserve, Then

Furtive(ly) Clandestine, Cunning, Hole and corner, Secret, Sly, Sneaky, Stealthy, Stowlins, Stownlins

Fury, Furies, Furious Acharné, Agitato, Alecto, > ANGER, Apoplexy, Atropos, Avenger, Eriny(e)s, Eumenides, Exasperation, Frantic, Frenzied, Furor, Hectic, Incensed, > IRE, Livid, Maenad, Megaera, Rabid, Rage, Savage, Seething, Tisiphone, Virago, Wood, Wrath, Yond

Furze Gorse, Whin

Fuse(d), Fusion Anchylosis, Ankylosis, Blend, Coalesce, Cohere, Colliquate, Conflate, Encaustic, Endosmosis, Flow, Flux, Match, Merge, Merit, Nuclear, Percussion, Portfire, Proximity, Rigelation, Run, Safety, Saucisson, Short,

5

287 | **Fuzz(y)**

Slow-match, Syncretism, Syngamy, Time, Tokamak, Unite

Fuselage Body, Monocoque, Structure

Fuss(y) Ado, Agitation, Anile, Ballyho, Bobsie-die, Bother, Br(o)uhaha, Bustle, Carfuffle, Chichi, Coil, Commotion, Complain, Cosset, Create, Cu(r)fuffle, Dust, Faff, Fantad, Fantod, Fiddle-faddle, Finical, Finikin, Hairsplitter, Hoohah, Hoopla, Mither, Niggle, Nit-pick, Old-womanish, Overexact, Overnice, Overwrought, Palaver, Particular, Perjink, Pernickety, Picky, Pother, Precise, Prejink, Primp, Prissy, Racket, Razzmatazz, Rout, Song, Song and dance, Spoffish, Spoffy, Spruce, Stashie, Stickler, Stink, > STIR, Stishie, Stooshie, Stushie, Tamasha, To-do, Tracasserie

Fustian Bombast, Gas, Pompous, Rant

Futile Empty, Feckless, Idle, Inept, No-go, Nugatory, Null, Otiose, Pointless, Sleeveless, Stultified, Trivial, Useless, > VAIN

Future(s), Futurist Again, Be-all, Coming, Demain, Financial, Hence, Horoscope, Index, Interest-rate, Later, Long-range, Offing, Ovist, Paragogic, Posterity, Prospect, To-be, Tomorrow

Fuzz(y) Blur, Crepe, Fluff, Foggy, Lint, Pig, Policeman

Gg

G George, Golf, Gravity

Gab(ble), **Gabbler** Chatter, Dovercourt, Jabber, Pie, Prattle, Talkative, Yabber

Gable Clark, Corbie, Jerkinhead, Pediment, Pine end

Gabriel Angel, Walter

Gad(about), **Gadzooks** Gallivant, Lud, Rover, Sbuddikins, Sdeath, Traipse, Trape(s), Viretot

Gadfly Breese, Breeze, Brize

Gadget Appliance, Artifice, Device, Dingbat, Dingus, Doodad, Doodah, Doofer, Doohickey, Gismo, Gizmo, Gubbins, Hickey, Jimjam, Notion, Possum, Tool, Utility, Waldo, Widget

Gadolinium Gd

Gadzooks Odsbobs

Gaekwar Baroda

Gael(ic) Celt, Erse, Goidel, Scottish, Teague

Gaff(e), **Gaffer** Bêtise, Blague, Bloomer, Error, Floater, Foreman, Gamble, Game, Solecism, Spar, Throat, Trysail, Yokel

Gag Brank, Choke, Estoppel, Joke, Pong, Prank, Retch, Silence(r), Smother, Wheeze

Gage Challenge, Pawn, Pledge, Plum

▸ **Gaiety** *see* GAY

Gain(s), **Gained** Acquire, Appreciate, Attain, Avail, Boodle, Boot, Bunce, Capital, Carry, Catch, Chevisance, Clean-up, Derive, Earn, Edge, Fruit, > GET, Good, Gravy, Land, Lucre, Obtain, Plus, Profit, Purchase, Rake-off, Reap, Thrift, Use, Velvet, Wan, Win, Windfall, Winnings

Gainsay Contradict, Deny

Gait Bearing, Canter, Pace, Piaffer, Rack, Trot

Gaiter(s) Cootikin, Cu(i)tikin, Gambado, Hogger, Legging(s), Puttee, Spat(s), Spattee, Spatterdash, Vamp

Gala Banquet, Festival

Galaxies, **Galaxy** Active, Andromeda, Great Attractor, Heaven, Magellanic cloud, Milky Way, Radio, Seyfert, Spiral, Stars

Galbanum Ferula

Gale(s) Backfielder, Equinoctial, Fresh, Moderate, Peal, Ripsnorter, Sea turn, Snorter, Squall, Storm, Tempest, Whole, Winder

Gall Aleppo, Bedeguar, Bitterness, Canker, Ellagic, Enrage, Fell, Irritate, Mad-apple, Maugre, Maulgre, Oak(nut), Saddle, Sage-apple, Sandiver, > SAUCE, Tacahout, Vine

Gallant(ry) Admirer, Amorist, Beau, Blade, Buck, Cavalier, Chevalier, Cicisbeo, Courtliness, Lover, Prow, Romeo, Sigisbeo, Spark, Valiance

Galleon Galloon, Ghostly, Ship

Gallery Accademia, Alure, Amphitheatre, Arcade, Assommoir, Belvedere, Brattice, Bretasche, Bretesse, Brettice, Brow, Catacomb, Celestials, Cupola, Dedans, Fly, Gods, Hayward, Hermitage, Jube, Ladies', Loft, Loggia, Louvre,

Machicolation, Mine, Minstrel, National, Organ, Pawn, Pinacotheca, Pinakothek, Pitti, Prado, Press, Public, Rogues', Serpentine, Shooting, Strangers', Tate, Terrace, Tribune, Triforium, Uffizi, Veranda(h), Whispering, Whitechapel, Winning

Galley Bireme, Bucentaur, Caboose, Drake, Galliot, Kitchen, Lymphad, Penteconter, Proof

Gallimaufry Macedoine, Mishmash, Stew

Gallium Ga

Gallon(s) Bushel, Cong(ius), Cran, Hin, Imperial, Tierce

Galloon Lace, Osiris

Gallop(er) Aide, Canter, Career, Lope, Trot, Wallop

Gallows Bough, Cheat, Drop, Dule-tree, Forks, Gibbet, Nub, Nubbing-cheat, Patibulary, Three-legged mare, Tree, Tyburn, Tyburn-tree, Widow, Woodie

Gallows-bird Crack-halter, Crack-hemp, Crack-rope

Gall-stone Cholelith

Galore Abundance, A gogo, Plenty, Whisky

Galosh Overshoe, Rubber

Galvanise Buck up, Ginger, Rouse, Zinc

Gam Pod

Gambit Manoeuvre, Ploy, Stratagem

Gamble(r), **Gambling (place)** Adventure, Ante, Back, Bet, Casino, Chance, Dice(-play), Flutter, Gaff, Hold, Jeff, Martingale, Mise, Pari-mutuel, Parlay, Partingale, Piker, Plunge, Policy, Punter, Raffle, Reno, Risk, Roulette, School, Spec, Speculate, Speculator, Sweep(stake), Throw(ster), Tinhorn, Tombola, Tontine, Treble chance, Two-up, > **WAGER**

Gambol Frisk, Frolic

Game(s) Away, Closed, Commonwealth, Computer, Decider, Electronic, Frame, Gallant, Gammy, Ground, Gutsy, High-jinks, Highland, Home, Intrepid, Isthmian, Jeu, > **LAME**, Match, Middle, Nemean, Numbers, Olympic, On, Open, Panel, Paralympic, Parlour, Perfect, Platform, Play, Plaything, Preference, Pythian, Raffle, Road, Round, Rubber, Saving, Secular, Spoof, Sport, Square, String, Table, Tie-break, Vie, Waiting, Willing

GAMES

2 letters:	Swy	I-spy	Solo
Eo	Tag	Keno	Taws
Go	Tig	Kino	Vint
PE	War	Laik	Wall
RU		Loto	Word
	4 letters:	Ludo	
3 letters:	Base	Main	**5 letters:**
Cat	Brag	Mora	Bingo
Hob	Bull	Palm	Bocce
Loo	Crap	Polo	Bowls
Maw	Dibs	Pool	Cards
Nap	Fa-fi	Putt	Catch
Nim	Fair	Ruff	Chess
Pam	Faro	Scat	Cinch
Pit	Goff	Skat	Craps
Put	Golf	Slam	Darts
Sim	Grab	Snap	Fives

Gleek
Goose
Halma
House
Jacks
Keeno
Lotto
Lurch
Merel
Meril
Monte
Morra
Noddy
Novum
Omber
Ombre
Poker
Quino
Roque
Rummy
Shogi
Tarok
Tarot
Trugo
Two-up
Video
Whisk
Whist

6 letters:
Basset
Beetle
Boston
Boules
Casino
Chemmy
Clumps
Crambo
Ecarté
Euchre
Fantan
Footer
Gammon
Gobang
Gomoku
Hockey
Hoopla
Hurley
Kitcat
Merell
Pelota
Piquet

Quinze
Quoits
Shinny
Shinty
Soccer
Socker
Squash
Tenpin
Tipcat
Uckers
Vigoro

7 letters:
Ba'spiel
Bezique
Braemar
Camogie
Canasta
Cassino
Charade
Chicken
Codille
Conkers
Coon-can
Croquet
Curling
Diabolo
Doubles
Hangman
Hurling
In-and-In
Jai Alai
Jukskei
Kabaddi
Lottery
Mahjong
Mancala
Marbles
Matador
Muggins
Murphy's
Netball
Old Maid
Pachisi
Pallone
Passage
Peekabo
Pharaoh
Pinball
Plafond
Pontoon
Primero

Push-pun
Pyramid
Rackets
Reversi
Ring-taw
Seven-up
Singles
Snooker
Squails
Tenpins
Vingt-un

8 letters:
All-fives
All-fours
Baccarat
Bumpball
Buzkashi
Canfield
Chouette
Conquian
Cottabus
Cribbage
Dominoes
Draughts
Fivepins
Football
Forfeits
Four-ball
Foursome
Gin rummy
Goalball
Handball
Handicap
Hardball
Kickball
Klondike
Klondyke
Korfball
Leapfrog
Mahjongg
Monopoly®
Napoleon
Ninepins
Nintendo®
Octopush
Pachinko
Pall-mall
Pastance
Patience
Peekaboo
Penneech

Penneeck
Penuchle
Petanque
Ping-pong
Pinochle
Pintable
Pope Joan
Push-ball
Reversis
Rolypoly
Roulette
Rounders
Scrabble®
Skittles
Slapjack
Softball
Sphairee
Subbuteo®
Teetotum
Trap-ball
Tray-trip
Tredille
Tric-trac
Verquere
Verquire

9 letters:
Acey-deucy
Badminton
Bagatelle
Billiards
Black-cock
Black-jack
Broomball
Cutthroat
Duplicate
Fillipeen
Hopscotch
Jingo-ring
Lanterloo
Level-coil
Matrimony
Mistigris
Mournival
Mumchance
Newmarket
Paintball
Parcheesi®
Pelmanism
Punchball
Quadrille
Quidditch®

Shoot'em-up
Solitaire
Spoilfive
Stoolball
Tip-and-run
Tredrille
Trick-trac
Tric-track
Twenty-one
Vingt-et-un
Water polo

10 letters:
Angel-beast
Basketball
Battledore
Bouillotte
Candlepins
Cat's cradle
Deck tennis
Dumb Crambo
Five-stones
Flapdragon
Handy-dandy
Horseshoes
Hot cockles
Jackstones
Jackstraws
Knurr-spell
Lansquenet

Paddleball
Phillipina
Phillipine
Philopoena
Punto-banco
Put and take
Snapdragon
Spillikins
Strip poker
Tablanette
Tchoukball
Thimblerig
Trick-track
Troll-madam
Trou-madame
Volley-ball

11 letters:
Barley-brake
Bumble-puppy
Catch-the-ten
Chemin de fer
Fox and geese
General post
Gerrymander
Mumbletypeg
Puncto-banco
Racquetball
Rouge et noir
Sancho-pedro

Shovelboard
Speculation
Tick-tack-toe
Tiddlywinks
Troll-my-dame

12 letters:
Consequences
Fast and loose
Hoodman-blind
Knucklebones
One-and-thirty
Pitch and putt
Pitch and toss
Shuffleboard
Span-farthing
Troll-my-dames

13 letters:
Blind Man's Buff
Chicken-hazard
Double or quits
French cricket
Musical chairs
Postman's knock
Prisoner's base
Space Invaders
Tenpin bowling
Tickly-benders

14 letters:
Crown and anchor
Ducks and drakes
Fives and threes
Follow-my-leader
Hunt-the-slipper
Pig-in-the-middle
Prick-the-garter
Shove-halfpenny
Snip-snap-
    snorum
Tenpins bowling
Three-card monte

15 letters:
Chinese Whispers

16 letters:
Piggy-in-the-
    middle
Snakes and
    ladders
Trente-et-
    quarante

20 letters:
Kiss-me-quick-in-
    the-ring

Game, Game birds Bag, Fowl, Grouse, Guan, Hare, Meat, Partridge, Pheasant, Prairie chicken, Ptarmigan, Quail, > QUARRY, Rype(r), Snipe, Spatchcock, Woodcock

Gamekeeper Mellors, Velveteen, Venerer, Warrener

Gaming place Bucket-shop, Casino, Saloon, Table

Gammerstang Taupie, Tawpie

Gammon Baloney, Bilge, Tosh

Gamut Compass, Range

Gander Airport, Look-see

Gandhi Mahatma

Gang Band(itti), Bing, Bunch, Canaille, Chain, Coffle, Core, Crew, Crue, Droog, Elk, Go, Horde, Mob, Mods, Nest, Outfit, Pack, Posse, Press, Push, Ratpack, Rockers, Triad, Tribulation, Troop, Yardie

Ganglia Basal

Gangrene Canker, Gas, Noma, Phaged(a)ena, Sphacelate, Thanatosis

Gangster Al, Bandit, Capone, Crook, Dacoit, Dakoit, Hatchet-man, Highbinder, Hood, Mafioso, Mobster, Ochlocrat, Scarface, Skollie, Skolly, Tsotsi, Yakuza, Yardie

Gangway Brow, Catwalk, Road

Gannet Booby, Guga, Solan(d)

Gantry Elmer

Ganymede Cupper

▸ **Gaol(er)** *see* JAIL(ER)

Gap Aperture, Belfort, Breach, Chasm, Chink, Credibility, Day, Deflationary, Diastema, Dollar, Embrasure, Energy, F-hole, Financing, Flaw, Fontanel(le), Gender, Generation, Gulf, Gulph, Hair-space, Hiatus, Hole, Inflationary, Interlude, Interstice, Kirkwood, Lacunae, Leaf, Lin(n), Loophole, M(e)use, Mews, Muset, Musit, Opening, Ostiole, Pass, Rest, Rima, Shard, Sherd, Skills, Slap, > SPACE, Spark, Street, Synapse, Trade, Truth-value, Water, Wind

Gape(r), **Gaping** Comber, Dehisce, Fatiscent, Gant, Ga(u)p, Gerne, Hiant, Mya, Outstare, Rictal, Rictus, Ringent, Rubberneck, Stare, Yawn, Yawp

Garage Carport, Chopshop, Hangar, Lock-up

Garb Apparel, Costume, Gear, Gere, Guise, Ihram, Invest, Leotard, Raiment, Toilet

Garbage Bunkum, Junk, Refuse, Rubbish, Trash

Garble Edit, Jumble, Muddle

▷ **Garble** *may indicate* an anagram

Garden(ing), **Gardens** Arbour, Area, Babylon(ian), Bagh, Bear, Beer, Botanic, Chinampa, Colegarth, Cottage, Covent, Cremorne, Dig, Eden, Erf, Floriculture, Garth, Gethsemane, Hanging, Hesperides, Hoe, Italian, Kailyard, Kew, Kitchen, Knot, Landscape, Lyceum, Market, Monastery, NJ, Olitory, Paradise, Parterre, Physic, Pleasance, Plot, Potager, Ranelagh, Rockery, Roji, Roof, Rosary, Rosery, Tea, Tilth, Topiary, Tuileries, Vauxhall, Welwyn, Window, Winter, Yard, Zoological

Gardener Adam, Capability Brown, Fuchs, Jekyll, Landscape, Mali, Mallee, Mary, Nurseryman, Topiarist, Tradescant, Trucker

Gargantuan Enormous, Huge, Pantagruel, Vast

Gargle Gargarism, Mouthwash

Gargoyle Waterspout

Garish Criant, Flashy, Gaudy, Glitzy, Jazzy, Painty, Roary, Rorie, Rory, Technicolour

Garland Anadem, Anthology, Chaplet, Coronal, Crants, Festoon, Lei, Stemma, Toran(a), Vallar(y), Wreath

Garlic Clove, Elephant, Hedge, Rams(on), Rocambole

Garment Aba(ya), Abba, Alb, Ao dai, Barrow, Blouse, Blouson, Bodice, Body warmer, Bolero, B(o)ub(o)u, B(o)urk(h)a, Breeks, Burnous, Burqa, Busuuti, Caftan, Catsuit, Cerements, Chador, Chasuble, Chimer, Cilice, Cimar, Clout, Cote-hardie, Cotta, Cover-slut, Dalmatic, Dashiki, Dirndl, Djibbah, Doublet, Dreadnought, Ephod, Exomion, Exomis, Fanon, Foundation, Gambeson, G-suit, Habiliment, Habit, Hand-me-down, Himation, Hug-me-tight, Ihram, Izar, Jeistiecor, Jibbah, Jubbah, Jumpsuit, Kaftan, Kanzu, Kaross, K(h)anga, Kittel, Levis, Lingerie, Mandilion, Mandylion, Mantle, Negligee, One-piece, Pallium, Pantihose, Pantyhose, Partlet, Pelerine, Pelisse, Penitential, Peplos, Pilch, Popover, Rail, Ramée, Rami(e), Reach-me-down, Rochet, Rompers, Ruana, Sackcloth, Salopettes, Sanbenito, Sari, Sarong, Scapular, Shroud, Singlet, Slop, Soutane, Step-in, Stola, Stole, Sulu, Surcoat, Surplice, Swimsuit, Tabard, Tank-top, Thong, Toga, Togs, Tunic(le), Unitard, Vestment, Vesture, Waistcoat, Weed, Woolly, Wrapper, Zephyr

Garnet Alabandine, Almandine, Andradite, Carbuncle, Demantoid, Essonite, Grossular(ite), Hessonite, Melanite, Pyrenite, Pyrope, Rhodolite, Spessartite, Topazolite, Uvarovite

Garnish Adorn, Attach, Crouton, Decorate, Gremolata, Lard, Parsley, Sippet, Staffage

Garret Attic, Loft, Sol(l)ar, Sol(l)er

Garrison Fort, Man, Presidial

Garrulity, **Garrulous** Babbling, Gas, Gushy, Windbag

Garter Bowyang, Crewel, Flash, G(r)amash, Gramosh, Nicky-tam

Gary Glitter, Player

Gas(sy) Acetylene, Afterdamp, Air, Ammonia, Argon, Argonon, Arsine, Azote, Blah(-blah), Blather, Blether, Bottle(d), Butadiene, Butane, Butene, BZ, Calor®, Carrier, Chat, Chlorine, Chokedamp, Chrom(at)osphere, CN, Coal(-oil), Crypton, CS, Cyanogen, Damp, Diphosgene, Dispersant, Electrolytic, Emanation, Ethane, Ethene, Ether(ion), Ethine, Ethylene, Firedamp, Fizz, Flatulence, Flatus, Flocculus, Flue, Fluorin(e), Formaldehyde, Fugacity, Gabnash, Greenhouse, H, Halitus, He, Helium, Hot-air, Hydrogen, Ideal, Inert, Jaw, Ketene, Kr(ypton), Laughing, Lewisite, Lurgi, Mace®, Marsh, Methane, Mofette, Mustard, Napalm, Natural, Ne, Neon, Nerve, Nitrogen, Noble, North Sea, Nox, O, Oil, Olefin(e), Orotund, Oxyacetylene, Oxygen, Perfect, Petrol, Phosgene, Phosphine, Plasma, Poison, Prate, Producer, Propane, Propellant, Propene, Propylene, Protostar, Radon, Rare, RN, Sarin, Sewage, Sewer, Silane, Solfatara, Soman, Sour, Stibine, Sulphur dioxide, Swamp, Synthesis, Tabun, > **TALK**, Taraniki wind, Tear, Tetrafluoroethene, Therm, Thoron, Town, V-agent, Vapour, Waffle, War, Water, Whitedamp, > **WIND**, Xenon, Yackety-yak

Gasbag Blimp, Envelope, Prattler

Gascon(ade) Boast, Braggart, Skite

Gash Incise, Rift, Score, Scotch, > **SLASH**

Gas-mask Inhaler

Gasp(ing) Anhelation, Apn(o)ea, Chink, Exhale, Kink, Oh, Pant, Puff, Singult, Sob

Gast(e)ropod Conch, Cowrie, Cowry, Dog-whelk, Dorididae, Euthyneura, Fusus, Glaucus, Haliotis, Harp-shell, Limpet, Mitre, Mollusc, Murex, Nerita, Nerite, Nudibranch, Opisthobranch, Ormer, Pelican's foot, Periwinkle, Pteropod, Purpura, Sea-ear, Sea-hare, Slug, Snail, Spindle-shell, Stromb, Top, Triton, Turbo, Turritello, Wentletrap, Whelk

Gate(s), **Gateway** Alley, Attendance, Brandenburg, Caisson, Cilician, Crowd, Decuman, Entry, Erpingham, Golden, Head, Ivory, Kissing, Lock, Lych, Mallee, Menin, Moravian, Nor, Pearly, Portal, Portcullis, Postern, Praetorian, Propylaeum, Propylon, Pylon, Starting, Tail, Taranaki, Toran(a), Torii, Traitor's, Turnout, Turnstile, Waste, Water, Wicket, Yate, Yet(t)

Gatecrash(er) Interloper, Intrude, Ligger, Sorn, Unasked

Gatepost Sconcheon, Scontion, Scuncheon

Gateshead *may indicate* 'g'

Gather(ed), **Gathering** Accrue, Amass, Assemble, Bee, Braemar, Cluster, Collate, > **COLLECT**, Colloquium, Concourse, Conglomerate, Congregate, Conventicle, Corral, Corroboree, Crop, Crowd, Cull, Derive, Eve, Fest, Function, Gabfest, Galaxy, Get together, Glean, Glomerate, Harvest, Hootenanny, Hotchpot, Hui, Husking, In, Infer, Jamboree, Kommers, Learn, Lek, Lirk, Love-in, Meinie, Menyie, Pleat, Plica, Plissé, Pucker, Purse, Raft, Rake, Rally, Reef, Reunion, Round-up, Rout, Ruche, Ruff(le), Salon, Shindig, Shir(r), Shoal, Shovel, Singsong, Social, Spree, Take, Tuck, Vindemiate, Vintage, Wappensc(h)aw

Gauche Awkward, Clumsy, Farouche, Graceless

Gaudy Criant, Fantoosh, Flash, Garish, Glitz(y), Meretricious, Tacky, Tinsel

Gauge Absolute, Alidad(e), Anemometer, > **ASSESS**, Bourdon, Broad, Calibre, Denier, Dial, Estimate, Etalon, Evaluate, Feeler, Judge, Lee, Limit, Loading, Manometer, Marigraph, Measure, Meter, Narrow, Ombrometer, Oncometer,

Perforation, Plug, Pressure, Rain, Rate, Ring, Scantle, Size, Slip, Standard, Strain, Tape, Template, Tonometer, Tram, Tread, Tyre, Udometer, Vacuum, Water, Weather, Wind, Wire

Gauguin Paul

Gaul Asterix, Cisalpine, Vercingetorix

Gaunt Haggard, Lancaster, Lean, Randletree, Ranneltree, Rannletree, Rantletree, Rawbone, > **THIN**, Wasted

Gauntlet C(a)estus, Gantlope

Gauss G

Gautama Buddha

Gauze, Gauzy Gas mantle, Gossamer, Muslin, Sheer, Tiffany, Wire

Gawky Clumsy, Cow, Gammerstang

Gawp Rubberneck

Gay, Gaiety Blithe, Bonny, Boon, Buxom, Camp, Canty, Daffing, Debonair, Festal, Frolic, Gallant, Gladsome, Glee, Gordon, Grisette, Inverted, Jolly, Lightsome, May, Merry, Nitid, Out, Rackety, Riant, Rorty, Tit(t)upy, Volatile

Gaze Moon, Pore, Regard, Stare

Gazelle Ariel, Gerenuk, Goa, Mhorr, Mohr, Tabitha, Thomson's

Gazette London, Paper

Gear(ing) Angel, Arrester, Attire, Bags, Bevel, Capital, Clobber, Dérailleur, Differential, Draw, Duds, Engrenage, Epicyclic, Fab, Finery, Granny, Harness, Helical, Herringbone, Hypoid, Involute, Kit, Landing, Lay-shaft, Mesh, Mess, Mitre, Neutral, Overdrive, Ratio, Reverse, Rig, Riot, Rudder, Spur, Steering, Sun and planet, Synchromesh, > **TACKLE**, Timing, Top, Trim, Tumbler, Valve, Worm(-wheel)

Gecko Tokay

Gee Horse, Hump, My, Reist, Sulk, Tout, Towt, Urge

Geiger-counter Scintillator

Geisha Maiko

Gel Hair, Pectin, Pectose, Silica

Gelatine, Gelatinous Calipash, Collagen, Glutinous, Isinglass, Size, Tunicin

Geld(ing) Castrate, Lib, Neuter, Spado

Gelignite Jelly

Geller Uri

Gem Abraxas, Agate, Alexandrite, Almandine, Amazonite, Andradite, Asteria, Baguette, Birthstone, Bloodstone, Boule, Brilliant, Briolette, Cabochon, Cachalong, Cairngorm, Carnelian, Cat's eye, Chrysolite, Chrysoprase, Cornelian, Cymophane, Demantoid, Diamante, Diamond, Dumortierite, Emerald, Girasol(e), Girosol, Grossular(ite), Hawk's eye, Heliodor, Heliotrope, Hessonite, Hiddenite, Hyacinth, ID, Idaho, Indicolite, Iolite, Jacinth, Jargo(o)n, Jasper, Jaspis, > **JEWEL**, Kunzite, Lapis lazuli, Ligure, Marquise, Melanite, Menilite, Moonstone, Morganite, Onyx, Pearl, Peridot(e), Plasma, Prase, Pyrope, Rhinestone, Rhodolite, Rose-cut, Rubellite, Ruby, Sapphire, Sard, Sardius, Sardonyx, Scarab, Scarabaeoid, Smaragd, Solitaire, Sparkler, Spessartite, Starstone, Stone, Tiger's eye, Tourmaline, Turquoise, Uvarovite, Verd antique, Zircon

Gemination, Gemini Diplogenesis, Twins

Gen Info

Gendarme Flic

Gender Form, Natural, Sex

Gene(tics) Allel(e), Allelomorph, Anticodon, Codon, Complementary, Creation, Designer, Disomic, Episome, Exon, Factor, Gay, Genome, Hereditary,

Heterogamy, Holandric, Hologynic, Intron, Jumping, Lysenkoism, Mendel, Michurinism, Molecular, Muton, Oncogene, Operon, Regulatory, Selfish, Structural, Telegony, Terminator, Transposon, Weismannism

Genealogist, **Genealogy** Armory, Family, Heraldry, Line, Pedigree, Seannachie, Seannachy, Sennachie, Whakapapa

General Agamemnon, Agricola, Agrippa, Alcibiades, Allenby, Antigonus, Antipater, Antony, Ataman, Banquo, Blucher, Booth, Boulanger, Broad, C in C, Clive, Common, Communal, Conde, Cornwallis, Crassus, Current, Custer, De Gaulle, De Wet, Diadochi, Eclectic, Ecumenical, Election, Fairfax, Franco, Gamelin, Gen, GOC, Gordon, Grant, Hadrian, Hannibal, Holofernes, Ike, Inspector, Joshua, Kitchener, Lafayette, Lee, Leslie, Macarthur, Main, Marshall, Massena, Montcalm, Napier, Napoleon, Omnify, Overall, Overhead, Patton, Pershing, Pompey, Prevailing, Raglan, Regulus, Rife, Rommel, Scipio, Sherman, Shrapnel, Smuts, Stilwell, Strategist, Structural, Sulla, Tom Thumb, Turenne, > **UNIVERSAL**, Vague, Wide, Wolfe

Generate, **Generation**, **Generator** Abiogenetic, Age, Beat, Beget, Boomerang, Breeder, Charger, Create, Dynamo, Electrostatic, Epigon, Father, Fuel-cell, House, Kipp, Lost, Magneto, Motor, Noise, Olds, Powerhouse, Signal, Sire, Spawn, Spontaneous, Stallion, Van de Graaff, Windmill, X, Yield

Generosity, **Generous** Bounty, Charitable, Free-handed, Free-hearted, Handsome, Kind, Largess(e), > **LAVISH**, Liberal, Magnanimous, Munificent, Noble(-minded), Open, Open-handed, Open-hearted, Philanthropic, Plump, Profuse, Selfless, Sporting, Unstinting

Genetic *see* GENE

Geneva(n) Calvinist, Gin, Hollands

Genial(ity) Affable, Amiable, Benign, Bluff, Bonhomie, Chin, Human, Kindly, Mellow

Genie Mazikeen, Shedeem

Genipap Lana

Genital(s) Ballocks, Bol(l)ix, Bollocks, Box, Crack, Crotch, Cunt, Fanny, Minge, Muff, Naff, Private parts, Privates, Pubes, Pudendum, Pussy, Quim, Secrets, Tackle, Tail, Twat, Vagina, Vulva, Yoni

Genius Agathodaimon, Brain, Daemon, Einstein, Engine, Flash, Inspiration, Ka, Michaelangelo, Numen, Prodigy

Genteel Conish, Polite, Proper, Refined

Gentian European, Felwort, Violet, Yellow

Gentile(s) Aryan, Ethnic, Goy, Nations, Shi(c)ksa

Gentle Amenable, Amenage, Bland, Clement, Delicate, Gradual, Grub, Light, Maggot, Mansuete, Mild, Tame, Tender

Gentleman(ly), **Gentlemen** Amateur, Baboo, Babu, Caballero, Cavalier, Duni(e)wassal, Dunniewassal, Esq(uire), Gemman, Gemmen, Ja(u)nty, Knight, Messrs, Milord, Mister, Mr, Nob, Proteus, Ritter, Runner, Rye, Sahib, Senor, Signor, Sir, Sirra(h), Smuggler, Squire, Sri, Stalko, Stir(rah), Swell, Tea, Toff, Tuan, Von, Yeoman

Gentry County, Landed, Quality, Squir(e)age

Gents Bog, John, Lav, Loo

Genuflexion Bend, Curts(e)y, Kowtow, Salaam

Genuine Authentic, Bona-fide, Dinkum, Dinky-di, Echt, Frank, Heartfelt, Honest, Intrinsic, Jannock, Jonnock, Kosher, Legit(imate), McCoy, Nain, Proper, Pucka, Pukka, Pure, Pusser, > **REAL**, Real McCoy, Right, Simon-Pure, Sincere, Square, Sterling, True, Veritable

Genus Class, Form, -ia, Mustela

Geode Druse

Geographer, **Geography** Chorography, Dialect, Economic, Hakluyt, Linguistic, Mercator, Pausanias, Physical, Political, Strabo

Geology Economic, Isotope, Seismology, Self-rock, Tectonics

Geometer, **Geometrician**, **Geometry** Analytical, Conics, Descriptive, Differential, Elliptic, Euclid(ean), Hyperbolic, Moth, Non-Euclidean, Plane, Porism, Projective, Riemannian, Solid, Spherics, Topologist

Geordie Guinea, Tynesider

George(s) Autopilot, Best, Borrow, Eliot, Farmer, Lloyd, Orwell, Pilot, Sand

Georgia(n) Ga, Hanover, Iberian

Geraint Knight

Geranium Dove's foot, Rose, Stork's bill, Yellow

Gerbil Jird

Germ(s) Bacteria, Bug, Culture, Klebsiella, Seed, Spirilla, Strep, Virus, Wheat, Zyme

German(y) Al(e)main(e), Alemannic, Angle, Anglo-Saxon, Bavarian, Berliner, Blood-brother, Boche, Cimbri, Composer, Cousin, Denglish, Franconian, Frank, Fritz, G, Goth, Habsburg, Hans, Hapsburg, Herr, Hessian, High, Hun, Jerry, Jute, Kaiser, Kraut, Landgrave, Low, Lusatian, Neanderthal, Ossi, Ostrogoth, Otto, Palsgrave, Plattdeutsch, Pruce, Prussian, Salic, Saxon, Squarehead, Tedesco, Teuton(ic), Vandal, Visigoth, Wessi, Wolfgang

Germane Apt, > **PERTINENT**, Relevant

Germanium Ge

Germ-free Aseptic

Germinate Grow, Pullulate, Sprout

Gesticulate, **Gesticulation**, **Gesture(s)** Ameslan, Beck(on), Ch(e)ironomy, Fico, Gest(e), Harvey Smith, Mime, Motion, Mudra, Salute, > **SIGN**, Signal, Snook, Token

Get, **Get by**, **Get On** Acquire, Advance, Aggravate, Annoy, Attain, Bag, Become, Brat, Bring, Capture, Cop, Cope, Derive, Fet(ch), Fette, Gain, Gee, Learn, Make, Manage, Milk, Net, Noy, > **OBTAIN**, Peeve, Procure, Progress, Reach, Realise, Rile, Roil, Secure, See, Sire, Twig, Understand, Win

Getaway Escape, Vamoose

▷ **Getting** *may indicate* an anagram

Getting better Convalescing, Improving, Lysis

Get-up Tog(s)

Geum Avens

Gewgaw Bagatelle, Bauble, Doit, Tat, Trifle

Geyser Soffioni, Therm

Ghanaian Ashanti, Fantee, Fanti, Tshi, Twi

Ghastly Gash, Grim, Hideous, Lurid, Macabre, Pallid, Ugsome, Welladay, White

Gherkin Cornichon

Ghetto Barrio, Slum

Ghost(ly) Acheri, Apparition, Apport, Caddy, Chthonic, Duende, Duppy, Eerie, Eery, Fantasm, Fetch, Gytrash, Haunt, Hint, Holy, Jumbie, Jumby, Larva(e), Lemur, Malmag, No'canny, Paraclete, Pepper's, Phantasm(agoria), Phantom, Revenant, Sampford, Shade, Shadow, Spectre, > **SPIRIT**, Spook, Trace, Truepenny, Umbra, Vision, Visitant, Waff, Wraith

Ghoul Fiend

GI Joe, Yankee

Giant(ess) Alcyoneus, Alifanfaron, Anak, Antaeus, Archiloro, Argus, Ascapart, Atlas, Balan, Balor, Bellerus, Blunderbore, Bran, Briareus, Brobdingnagian,

Cacus, Colbrand, Colbronde, Colossus, Coltys, Cormoran, Cottus, Cyclop(e)s, Despair, Enceladus, Ephialtes, Eten, Ettin, Ferragus, Gabbara, Galligantus, Gargantua, Géant, Gefion, Geirred, Gigantic, Gog, Goliath, Grim, Harapha, Hrungnir, Hymir, Idris, Irus, Jotun(n), Jumbo, Krasir, Lestrigon, Leviathan, Magog, Mammoth, Mimir, Monster, Oak, Og, Ogre, Otus, Pallas, Pantagruel, Patagonian, Polyphemus, Pope, Red, Rounceval, Skrymir, Slaygood, Talos, Talus, Thrym, Titan, Tityus, Tregeagle, Triton, Troll, Tryphoeus, Typhon, Urizen, Utgard, Ymir, Yowie

Gibberish Claptrap, Double Dutch, Greek, Jargon

Gibbet Gallows, Patibulary, Potence, Ravenstone, Tree

Gibbon(s) Hoolock, Hylobate, Orlando, Siamang, Stanley, Wou-wou, Wow-wow

Gibe Barb, Brocard, Chaff, Fleer, Glike, Jeer, Jibe, Shy, Slant, Wisecrack

Gibraltar Calpe

Giddy (girl), **Giddiness** Dizzy, Fisgig, Fishgig, Fizgig, Giglot, Glaikit, Glaky, Haverel, Hellicat, Hoity-toity, Jillet, Light, Light-headed, Skipping, Staggers, Sturdy, Turn, Vertigo, Volage(ous), Wheel, Woozy

Gift(s), **Gifted** Ability, Alms, Aptitude, Bef(f)ana, Bequest, Blessing, Blest, Bonbon, Bonsel(l)a, Boon, Bounty, Charism(a), Congiary, Corban, Covermount, Cumshaw, Dash, Deodate, > **DONATION**, Etrenne, Fairing, Flair, Foy, Freebie, Gab, Garnish, Godsend, Grant, Greek, Handout, Han(d)sel, Hogmanay, Indian, Knack, Koha, Kula, Lagniappe, Largesse, Legacy, Manna, Ne'erday, Nuzzer, Offering, Parting, Peace-offering, PET, Potlatch, > **PRESENT**, Presentation, Prezzie, Propine, Reward, Sop, Talent, Tongues, Treat, Wakf, Waqf, Windfall, Xenium

Gig Cart, Dennet, Moze, Whisk(e)y

Gigantic Atlantean, Briarean, Colossal, Goliath, > **HUGE**, Immense, Mammoth, Monster, Patagonian, Rounceval, Titan, Vast

Giggle Cackle, Ha, Keckle, Simper, Snicker, Snigger, Tehee, Titter

Gigolo Gallant, Ladykiller, Pimp

Gilbert Bab, Gb, White, WS

Gild(ed), **Gilding** Checklaton, Embellish, Enhance, Inaurate, Ormolu, S(c)hecklaton, Vermeil

Gill(s) Beard, Branchia, Cart, Ctenidium, Jill, Noggin, Spiracle

Gillman's Aqualung

Gilpin Draper, John, Renowned

Gilt Elt, Sow

Gimcrack Gewgaw, Tawdry, Trangam

Gimmick Doodad, Doodah, Hype, Ploy, Ruse, Stunt

Gin Bathtub, Geneva, Genever, Hollands, Juniper, Lubra, Max, Mother's ruin, Noose, Old Tom, Pink, Ruin, Schiedam, Schnapp(s), Sloe, Snare, Springe, Toil, Trap, Trepan, Twankay

Ginger Activist, Amomum, Asarum, Cassumunar, Costus, Curcuma, Galanga(l), Galengale, Galingale, Gar, Malaguetta, Nut, Pachak, Pep, Pop, Putchock, Putchuk, Race, Rase, Red(head), Root, Spice, Stem, Turmeric, Zedoary, Zingiber

Gingerbread D(o)um-palm, Lebkuchen, Parkin, Parliament(-cake), Pepper-cake

Gingivitis Ulitis

Gipsy *see* GYPSY

Giraffe Camelopard, Okapi

Gird Accinge, Belt, Equip, Gibe, Jibe, Quip

Girder Beam, Binder, H-beam, I-beam, Lattice, Loincloth, Spar

Girdle Baldric, Center, Cestus, Chastity, Cincture, Cingulum, Corset, Enzone, Hippolyte, Hoop, Mitre, Pectoral, Pelvic, Sash, Shoulder, Surcingle, Surround,

Zona, Zone, Zonulet

Girl(s) Backfisch, Ball, Bimbo, Bint, Bird, Bit, Bobby-dazzler, Bobby-soxer, Bohemian, Broad, Burd, Call, Charlie, Chit, Chorus, Coed, Colleen, Cover, Crumpet, Cummer, Cutey, Cutie, Cutty, Dam(o)sel, Deb, Dell, Demoiselle, Dish, Doll, Dollybird, Essex, Filly, Fisgig, Fizgig, Flapper, Fluff, Fraulein, Frippet, Gaiety, Gal, Gammerstang, Geisha, Gibson, Gill(et), Gilp(e)y, Gouge, Gretel, Grisette, Hen, Hoiden, Hoyden, Hussy, Italian, Judy, Kimmer, Kinchinmort, Land, Lass(ock), Lorette, Maid(en), Mauther, Mawr, Mawther, May, Miss(y), Moppet, Mor, Mot, Mousmé, Mousmee, Mystery, Nautch, Number, Nymph(et), Oanshagh, Peach, Petticoat, Piece, Pigeon, Popsy, Principal, Puss, Quean, Queyn, Quin(i)e, Randy, Senorita, Sheila, Shi(c)ksa, Sis(s), Smock, Sweater, Tabby, Taupie, Tawpie, Teddy, Tiller, Tit, Trull, Weeny-bopper, Wench, Widgie, Wimp

▷ **Girl** *may indicate* a female name

Girlfriend Baby, Chérie, Confidante, Date, Flame, Hinny, Leman, Moll, Peat

Girth Cinch, Compass, Exploitable, Size, Surcingle

Gist Essence, Kernel, > **NUB**, Pith, Substance

Give, **Give up**, **Giving** Abandon, Abstain, Accord, Administer, Afford, Award, Bend, Bestow, Buckle, Cede, Confiscate, Dative, Dispense, Dole, > **DONATE**, Duck, Elasticity, Enable, Enfeoff, Forswear, Gie, Grant, Impart, Jack, Largition, Render, Resign, Sacrifice, Sag, Spring, Stop, Tip, Vacate, Vouchsafe, Yeve

Give-away Freebie, Gift-horse

Given If

Give out Bestow, Dispense, Emit, Exude, Peter

Give over Cease, Lin

Glacial, **Glaciation** Gunz, Mindel, Riss, Wurm

Glacier Aletsch, Crevasse, Drumline, Fox, Franz-Josef, Hanging, Iceberg, Ice-cap, Icefall, Moraine, Muir, Rhône, Riss, Serac, Stadial, Tasman

Glad(ly), **Gladden** Cheer, Fain, > **HAPPY**, Lief, Willing

Glade La(u)nd

Gladiator Retiarius, Spartacus

Glamour(ise), **Glamorous** Charm, Glitter(ati), Glitz, Halo, It, Prestige, SA, Sexy, Spell

Glamour girl Cheesecake, Odalisk, Odalisque, Pin-up

Glance Allusion, Amoret, Argentite, Blink, Browse, Carom(bole), Coup d'oeil, Dekko, Draw, Eld, Eliad, Eye-beam, Galena, Glimpse, Illiad, Inwick, Lustre, Oeillade, Once-over, Peek, > **PEEP**, Ray, Redruthite, Ricochet, Scan, Sheep's eyes, Shufti, Shufty, Skellie, Skelly, Snick, Squint, Squiz, Twire, Vision

Gland Acinus, Adenoid, Adenoma, Adrenal, Apocrine, Bartholin's, Bulbourethral, Colleterial, Conarium, Cowper's, Crypt, Digestive, Ductless, Duodenal, Eccrine, Endocrine, Epiphysis, Exocrine, Goitre, Green, Helocrine, Hypophysis, Hypothalamus, Ink-sac, Lachrymal, Lacrimal, Liver, Lymph, Mammary, Meibomian, Musk-sac, Nectary, Oil, Osmeterium, Ovary, Pancreas, Paranephros, Parathyroid, Parotid, Parotis, Parotoid, Perineal, Pineal, Pituitary, Pope's eye, Preen, Prostate, Prothoracic, Salivary, Scent, Sebaceous, Shell, Silk, Sublingual, Submaxillary, Suprarenal, Sweat, Sweetbread, Tarsel, Tear, Testicle, Testis, Thymus, Thyroid, Tonsil, Uropygial, Vesicle, Zeiss

Glanders Farcy

Glandular (trouble) Adenitis

Glare, **Glaring** Astare, Blare, Dazzle, Flagrant, Garish, Gleam, Glower, Holophotal, Iceblink, Lour, Low(e), Naked, Shine, Vivid, Whally

Glass(es), **Glassware**, **Glassy** Amen, Ampul(la), Aneroid, Avanturine,

Aventurine, Baccara(t), Barometer, Bifocals, Bins, Bottle, Brimmer, Bumper, Burmese, Burning, Calcedonio, Case, Cheval, Cloche, Cocktail, Cooler, Copita, Cordial, Coupe, Cover, Crookes, Crown, Crystal, Cullet, Cupping, Cut, Dark, Delmonico, Diminishing, Eden, Euphon, Favrile, Fibre, Field, Flint, Float, Flute, Frigger, Frit, Fulgurite, Gauge, Glare, Goblet, Goggles, Granny, Green, Ground, Hand, Highball, Horn-rims, Humpen, Hyaline, Iceland agate, Jar, Jena, Jigger, Lace, Lalique, Laminated, Lanthanum, Latticinio, Lead, Lens, Liqueur, Liquid, Log, Lorgnette, Loupe, Lozen(ge), Lunette, Magma, Magnifying, Metal, Mica, Middy, Milk, Millefiori, Minimizing, Mirror, Moldavite, Monocle, Mousseline, Multiplying, Murr(h)ine, Musical, Object, Obsidian, One-way, Opal, Opal(ine), Opera, Optical, Pane, Parison, Paste, Pearlite, Pebble, Peeper, Pele, Pele's hair, Perlite, Perspective, Pier, Pince-nez, Pinhole, Pitchstone, Plate, Pon(e)y, Pressed, Prospective, Prunt, Psyche, Pyrex®, Quarrel-pane, Quarry, Quartz, Reducing, Roemer, Ruby, Rummer, Safety, Schmelz, Schooner, Seam, Seidel, Sheet, Silex, Silica, Sleever, Slide, Smalt(o), Snifter, Soluble, Specs, > SPECTACLES, Spun, Stained, Stein, Stemware, Stone, Storm, Strass, Sun, Supernaculum, Tachilite, Tachylite, Tachylyte, Tektite, Telescope, Tiffany, Tiring, Toilet, Trifocals, Triplex®, Tumbler, Uranium, Varifocals, Venetian, Venice, Vernal, Vita, Vitrail, Vitreous, Vitrescent, Vitro-di-trina, Volcanic, Watch, Water, Waterford, Weather, Window (pane), Wine, Wire

Glass-gall Sandiver

Glass-house Conservatory, Orangery

Glassite Sandemania

Glass-maker Annealer, Blower, Glazier, Lalique, Pontie, Pontil, Ponty, Puntee, Punty

Glaze(d), **Glazing** Aspic, Ciré, Coat, Double, Eggwash, Film, Flambé, Frit, Glost, Ice, Majolica, Peach-blow, Sancai, Slip, Tammy, Temmoku, Velatura

Gleam(ing) Blink, Flash, Glint, Glisten, Glitter, Gloss, Leme, Light, Ray, Relucent, Sheen, Shimmer, > SHINE

Glean(er) Gather, Harvest, Lease, Stibbler

Glee Exuberance, Joy, Mirth, Song

Glen Affric, Ghyll, Gill, Rushy, Silicon, Vale

Glib Flip, Slick, Smooth

Glide(away), **Glider**, **Gliding** Aquaplane, Coast, Elapse, Float, Illapse, Lapse, Luge, Microlight, Off, On, Portamento, Rogallo, Sail, Sailplane, Sashay, Scorrendo, Scrieve, Skate, Ski, Skim, Sleek, Slide, Slip, Slur, Swim, Volplane

Glimmer(ing) Gleam, Glent, Glint, Glow, Inkling, Light, Stime, Styme, Twinkle, Wink

Glimpse Aperçu, Flash, Glance, Glisk, Stime, Styme, Waff, Whiff

Glint Flash, Shimmer, > SPARKLE, Trace, Twinkle

Glisten(ing) Ganoid, Glint, Sheen, Shimmer, > SHINE, Sparkle

Glitter(ing) Clinquant, Garish, Gemmeous, Glee, Paillon, Sequin, Spang(le), Sparkle, Tinsel

Gloat(ing) Crow, Drool, Enjoy, Exult, Schadenfreude

Globe, **Globule** Artichoke, Ball, Bead, Celestial, Drop, Earth, Orb, Shot, Sphear, Sphere

Globulin Legumin, Protein

Gloom(y) Atrabilious, Benight, Blues, Cheerless, Cimmerian, Cloud, Crepuscular, Damp, Dark, > DESPAIR, Dingy, Disconsolate, Dismal, Dool(e), Downbeat, Drab, Drear, Drumly, Dump(s), Dyspeptic, Feral, Funereal, Glum, Grey, Louring, Mirk, Misery, Mopish, Morne, Morose, Mumps, Murk,

Obscurity, Overcast, Sable, Sad, Saturnine, Sepulchral, Solein, Solemn,
> **SOMBRE**, Stygian, Sullen, Tenebrous, Unlit

Glorification, **Glorify** Aggrandise, Apotheosis, Avatar, Bless, > **EXALT**, Extol, Halo
Laud, Lionise, Praise, Radiance, Splendour

Glorious, **Gloria**, **Glory** Chorale, Grand, Halo, Hosanna, Ichabod, Knickerbocker
Kudos, Lustre, Magnificent, Nimbus, Strut, Sublime, Twelfth

Glory-pea Kaka-beak, Kaka-bill, Kowhai

Gloss(y) Ciré, Enamel, Gild, Glacé, Japan, Lustre, Patina, > **POLISH**, Postillate,
Sheen, Sleek, Slick, Slide, Slur, Supercalendered, Veneer, Wetlook, Whitewash

Glossary Catalogue, Clavis, Index, K'thibh

Gloucester Cheese

Glove Boxing, Cestus, Dannock, Gage, Gauntlet, Kid, Mermaid's, Mitten,
Mousquetaire, Muffle, Oven, Velvet

Glow(er), **Glowing** Aflame, Ashine, Aura, Bloom, Burn, Calescence, Candent,
Candescence, Firefly, Flush, Foxfire, Gegenschein, Gleam, Halation, Iceblink,
Incandescence, Lambent, Leam, Leme, Luculent, Luminesce, Lustre, Perspire,
Phosphorescence, Radiant, Reflet, Rushlight, Shine, Snowblink, Translucent,
> **WARMTH**

Glucin(i)um Gl

Glucose, **Glucoside** Aesculin, Amygdalin, Dextrose, Digitalin, Indican,
Saponin, Solanine

Glue(y) Alkyd, Araldite®, Bee, Cement, Colloidal, Gelatin(e), Ichthyocolla,
Isinglass, Marine, Paste, Propolis, Size, Spetch

Glum Dour, Livery, Lugubrious, Moody, Morose, Ron, Sombre

Glut Choke, Gorge, Sate, Satiate, Saturate, Surfeit

Gluten, **Glutinous** Goo, Ropy, Seiten, Sticky, Tar, Viscid, Zymome

Glutton(ous), **Gluttony** Bellygod, Carcajou, Cormorant, Edacity, Gannet, Gorb,
Gourmand, Greedyguts, Gulosity, Gutser, Gutsy, Gutzer, Lurcher, Pig, Ratel,
Scoffer, Sin, Trencherman, Trimalchio, Wolverine

Glyceride, **Glycerine** Ester, Olein

Glycoside Hesperidin

Gnarl(ed) Knot, Knuckly, Knur, Nob

Gnash(ing) Bruxism, Champ, Grate

Gnat Culex, Culicidae, Midge, Mosquito

Gnaw(ing) Corrode, Erode, Fret, Lagomorph, Rodent

Gnome Adage, Bank-man, Chad, Cobalt, Financier, Kobold, Motto, Proverb, Saw
Sprite

Gnostic Archontic, Cainite, Mand(a)ean, Marcionism, Ophite, Sabian, Tsabian,
Zabian

Gnu Wildebeest

Go, **Going (after, for, off, on, up, etc)** Advance, Afoot, Anabasis, Animation,
Assail, Attempt, Bash, Betake, Bing, Brio, Choof, Clamber, Continuance,
Crack, Depart, Die, Do, Energy, Fare, Gae, Gang, Gee, Gonna, Green, Hamba,
Hark, Hence, Hie, Imshi, Imshy, Ish, > **LEAVE**, March, Match, Off, Path, Pep,
Perpetual, Ply, Quit, Raik, Repair, Resort, Resume, Run, Scat, Scram, Segue,
Shoo, Skedaddle, Snick-up, Sour, Spank, Stab, Success, Transitory, Trine, Try,
Turn, Vam(o)ose, Verve, Via, Viable, Wend, Work, Yead, Yede, Yeed, Zap, Zing,
Zip

Goad Ankus, Brod, Gad, Impel, Incite, > **NEEDLE**, Prod, Rowel, Spur, Stimulate,
Stimulus, Taunt

Goal(posts) Ambition, Basket, Bourn(e), Destination, Dool, Dream, Drop, Dule,
End, Ettle, Field, Golden, Grail, Hail, Home, Horme, Hunk, Limit, Mission,

Moksha, Own, Score, Target, Tip-in, Touch-in, Ultima Thule, Uprights

Goat(-like) Alpine, Amalthea, Angora, Antelope, Antilope, Billy, Bok, Buck, Caprine, Cashmere, Gait, Gate, Giddy, Goral, Hircine, Ibex, Izard, Kashmir, Kid, Libido, Markhor, Mountain, Nan(ny), Nubian, Rocky mountain, Saanen, Sassaby, Serow, Serpent-eater, Steenbok, Steinbock, Tahr, Takin, Tehr, Thar, Toggenburg

Goatsucker Fern-owl, Nightjar

Gob Clot, Mouth, Yap

Gobble Bolt, Devour, Gorge, Gulp, Slubber, Wolf

Gobelin Tapestry

Go-between Broker, Factor, Intermediate, Link, Mediate, Middleman, Pandarus, Pander, Shuttle

Goblet Chalice, Hanap

Goblin Bargaist, Barg(h)est, Bodach, Bogey, Bogle, Bogy, Brownie, Bucca, Croquemitaine, Empusa, Erl-king, Esprit follet, Genie, Gnome, Gremlin, Knocker, Kobold, Lutin, Nis(se), Phooka, Phynnodderree, Pooka, Pouke, Puca, Pug, Red-cap, Red-cowl, Shellycoat, > **SPRITE**, Troll, Trow

Goby Dragonet

God(s) All-seer, Divine, Gallery, Gracious, Holy One, Household, Immortals, Light, Maker, Od(d), Olympian, Prime Mover, Principle, Providence, Serpent, The Creator, Trinity, Truth, Unknown, War

GODS

1 letter:	Tyr	Mors	Khnum
D		Nebo	Liber
	4 letters:	Odin	Lludd
2 letters:	Abba	Ptah	Mimir
An	Agni	Rama	Momus
As	Aitu	Seth	Njord
Ra	Amun	Siva	Numen
Re	Apis	Soma	Orcus
	Ares	Thor	Orixa
3 letters:	Asur	Tyrr	Pales
Anu	Aten	Yama	Picus
Bel	Atum	Zeus	Pluto
Bes	Baal		Rudra
Dis	Brag	**5 letters:**	Satyr
Gad	Bran	Aesir	Sebek
Geb	Cama	Ammon	Shiva
Jah	Deva	Bragi	Sinis
Lar	Dieu	Comus	Surya
Lir	Eros	Cupid	Thoth
Lug	Faun	Dagan	Titan
Mot	Frey	Dagon	Vanir
Pan	Joss	Donar	Woden
Set	Kama	Freyr	Yahve
Sol	Kami	Haoma	Yahwe
Tin	Llyr	Horus	
Tiu	Loki	Hymen	**6 letters:**
Tiw	Lugh	Indra	Adonai
Tum	Mars	Janus	Aeolus

Amen-ra
Amon-ra
Anubis
Apollo
Ashtar
Asshur
Avatar
Balder
Boreas
Brahma
Cabiri
Chemos
Cronus
Delian
Elohim
Faunus
Ganesa
Garuda
HaShem
Helios
Hermes
Hughie
Hypnos
Kronos
Mammon
Marduk
Mexitl
Mextli
Mithra
Molech
Moloch
Nereus
Njorth
Oannes
Orisha
Ormazd
Ormuzd

Osiris
Panisc
Panisk
Plutus
Rimmon
Saturn
Somnus
Tammuz
Teraph
Teshup
Thamiz
Thunor
Triton
Uranus
Varuna
Vishnu
Vulcan
Yahweh
Zombie

7 letters:
Alastor
Alpheus
Angus Og
Anteros
Bacchus
Chemosh
Daikoku
Ganesha
Hanuman
Heimdal
Jehovah
Jupiter
Krishna
Kuan Yin
Kwan Yin
Mercury

Mithras
Neptune
Nisroch
Oceanus
Penates
Phoebus
Priapus
Proteus
Rameses
Sarapis
Sat guru
Serapis
Setebos
Shamash
Silenus
Thammuz
Zagreus

8 letters:
Achelous
Dionysus
Heimdall
Hyperion
Kamadeva
Mahadeva
Morpheus
Mulciber
Nataraja
Pantheon
Poseidon
Quirinus
Silvanus
Sylvanus
Terminus
Trimurti
Wahiguru
Zephyrus

9 letters:
All-father
Asclepius
Fabulinus
Heimdallr
Jagganath
Promachos
Tetragram
Thunderer
Vertumnus
Zernebock

10 letters:
Demogorgon
Elegabalus
Hephaistos
Juggernaut
Karttikaya
Mumbo-jumbo
Prometheus
Trophonius

11 letters:
Adrammelech
Aesculapius
Bodhisattva

12 letters:
Quetzalcoati
Supreme Being

14 letters:
Tetragrammaton

God-bearing Deiparous
Goddess(es) Divine, Green, Muse

GODDESSES

2 letters:
Ge

3 letters:
Ate
Eos
Hel
Mut
Nox

Nut
Nyx
Ops
Pax

4 letters:
Dian
Eris
Gaea

Gaia
Hera
Idun
Iris
Isis
Juno
Kali
Leda
Leto

Luna
Maat
Maut
Nike
Norn
Pele
Rhea
Sita
Thea

5 letters:
Aruru
Ceres
Diana
Dione
Durga
Erato
Flora
Freya
Grace
Horae
Houri
Hulda
Iduna
Irene
Kotys
Pales
Tanit
Terra
Tyche
Ushas
Venus
Vesta

6 letters:
Aglaia
Ashnan
Athene
Aurora
Bastet
Cybele
Cyrene
Eastre
Freyja
Frigga
Graeae
Graiae
Hathor
Hecate
Hertha
Hestia
Huldar
Hyaeia
Idalia
Ishtar
Ithunn
Lucina
Pallas
Parcae

Phoebe
Pomona
Satyra
Selene
Semele
Tellus
Tethys
Themis
Thetis

7 letters:
Artemis
Astarte
Astraea
Bellona
Cotytto
Cynthia
Demeter
Fortuna
Kotytto
Lakshmi
Megaera
Minerva
Nemesis
Nepthys

Parvati
Sabrina
Strenia
Victory

8 letters:
Cloacina
Libitina
Valkyrie
Victoria
Walkyrie

9 letters:
Aphrodite
Ashtaroth
Ashtoreth
Eumenides
Mnemosyne
Sarasvati

10 letters:
Amphitrite
Proserpina
Proserpine

Godfather, **Godmother** Capo, Cummer, Fairy, Gossip, Kimmer, Rama, Sponsor, Woden
Godless Agnostic, Atheistic, Atheous, Impious, Profane
Godly Deist, Devout, Holy, Pious
Godown Hong
God-willing Deo volente, DV, Mashallah
Go-getter Arriviste, Hustler
Goggle(s) Snow-eyes, Stare
Going wrong Aglee, Agley, Misfiring
> **Going wrong** *may indicate* an anagram
Goitre Derbyshire neck, Exophthalmic, Graves' disease, Struma
Gold(en) Age, Amber, Apple, Ass, Au, Aureate, Auriferous, Bendigo, Bough, Bull, Bullion, California, Doubloon, Dutch, Eagle, Electron, Electrum, Emerods, Filigree, Filled, Fleece, Fool's, Free, Fulminating, Gate, Gule, Handshake, Hind, Horde, Horn, Ingot, Leaf, Lingot, Moidore, Mosaic, Muck, Nugget, Oaker, Obang, Ochre, Ophir, Or, Oreide, Ormolu, Oroide, Pistole, Placer, Pyrites, Red, Reef, Rolled, Silence, Silver-gilt, Sol, Standard, Stream, Stubborn, Talmi, Tolosa, Treasury, Venice, Virgin, White, Witwatersrand, Yellow
Gold-digger Forty-niner, Prospector
Golden Fleece Phrixus
Goldfield Rand
Goldfinch Charm, Chirm, Redcap
Gold leaf Ormolu
Gold rush Kalgoorlie, Klondike
Goldsmith Cellini, Fabergé, Oliver
Golf (ball) Better-ball, Clock, Crazy, Foursome, Gutta, Matchplay, Medal play,

Repaint, Round, Stableford

Golfer Alliss, Braid, Cotton, Els, Faldo, Hogan, Pivoter, Rees, Roundsman, Seve, Snead, Teer, Trevino, Wolstenholme, Yipper

Golly Crumbs, Gosh

Gondolier Balloonist, Bargee

Gone Ago, Dead, Defunct, Napoo, Out, Past, Ygo(e), Yod

▷ **Gone off** *may indicate* an anagram

Gone west Had it

Gong Bell, DSO, Medal, Tam-tam, VC

Gonorrhoea Clap

Goo Gleet, Gunge, Poise, Ulmin

Goober Monkey nut

Good(ness), **Goody-goody** Agatha, Agathodaimon, Altruism, Angelic, Bad, Bein, Benefit, Blesses, Bon, Bonzer, Bosker, Bounty, Brod, Budgeree, Canny, Castor, Civil, Clinker, Common, Coo, Cool, Crack(ing), Credit, Dab, Dandy, Def, Dow, Enid, Estimable, Fantabulous, Finger lickin', First-class, G, Gear, Giffen, Gosh, Guid, Humdinger, Lois, Lor, Ma foi, Nobility, > NO GOOD, Pi, Plum, Proper, Purler, Rattling, Rectitude, Riddance, Right, Rum, Sake, Salutary, Samaritan, Sanctity, Slap-up, Smashing, Spiffing, St, Suitable, Super, Taut, Tollol, Topping, Valid, Virtue, Virtuous, Weal, Welfare, Whacko, Wholesome, Worthy

Goodbye Addio, Adieu, Adios, Aloha, Apopemptic, Arrivederci, Cheerio, Ciao, Congé, Farewell, Hooray, Hooroo, Sayonara, Tata, Toodle-oo, Toodle-pip, Vale

Good evening Den

Goodfellow Brick, Puck, Robin, Samaritan, Worthy

Good-for-nothing Bum, Donnat, Donnot, Dud, Idler, Layabout, Lorel, Lorrell, Losel, Napoo, Sca(l)lawag, Scallywag, Scant o'grace, Sculpin, Shot-clog, Useless, Vaurien, Waff, Waster, Wastrel

Good Friday Parasceve

Good-humour(ed), **Good-natured** Amiable, Bonhomie, Gruntled, Kind

Good-looking Bon(n)ie, Bonny, Bonwie, Comely, Fair, Handsome, Personable, Pretty, Wally

Good news Evangel

Good number Thr(e)ave

Good order Eutaxy, Shipshape

Goods Bona, Brown, Cargo, Consumer, Disposable, Durables, Fancy, Flotsam, Freight, Futures, Gear, Hardware, Insight, Ironware, Lagan, Lay-away, Line, Piece, Products, Property, Schlock, Soft, Sparterie, Truck, Wares, White

Goodwill Amity, Bonhom(m)ie, Favour, Gree

Goody Wrong'un

Goon Secombe, Sellers

Goose, Geese Anserine, Barnacle, Bernicle, Blue, Brent, Canada, Capr Barren, Colonial, Daftie, Ember, Gander, Gannet, Golden, Greylag, Grope, Harvest, Hawaiian, Idiot, Juggins, MacFarlane's, Magpie, Michaelmas, Mother, Nana, Nene, Pink-footed, Quink, Roger, Saddleback, Silly, Simpleton, Skein, Snow, Solan, Strasbourg, Stubble, > STUPID PERSON, Swan, Team, Wav(e)y, Wawa, Whitehead

Gooseberry Cape, Chaperon(e), Chinese, Detrop, Fool, Gog, Groser(t), Groset, Grossart, Grozer, Honey blob, Kiwi, Physalis, Tomato

Gooseflesh Horripilation

Goosefoot Allgood, Amarantaceae, Beet, Blite, Fat-hen, Mercury, Orache, Saltbush

Gooseherd Quill-driver

Gopher Camass-rat, Minnesota

Gordian Knot

Gordon Chinese, Flash, Rioter

Gore Blood, Cloy, Gair, Horn, Toss

Gorge(s) Abyss, Arroyo, Barranca, Barranco, Canyon, Chasm, Cheddar, Cleft, Couloir, Cram, Defile, Donga, Flume, Gap, Ghyll, Glut, Grand Canyon, Grand Coulee, Gulch, Iron Gate, Khor, Kloof, Lin(n), Nala, Nalla(h), Nulla(h), Olduvai, Overeat, Overfeed, Pass, Ravine, Snarf, Staw, > STUFF, Throat, Tire, Tums, Valley, Yosemite

Gorgeous Delectable, Grand, Splendid, Superb

Gorgon Euryale, Medusa, Ogress, Stheno

Gorilla *see* MONKEY

Gorse Broom, Furze, Gosse, Ulex, Whin

Gosh Begad, Begorra, Blimey, Coo, Cor, Gadzooks, Gee, Gum, Heavens, Lor, My, Och, Odsbobs, Odso

Gospel(s), **Gospeller** Apocryphal, Creed, Diatessaron, Evangel, Fact, John, Kerygma, Luke, Mark, Matthew, Nicodemus, Prosperity, Protevangelium, Synoptic, Truth, Waldensian

Gossamer(y) Araneous, Byssoid, Cobwebby, Gauzy

Gossip Ana(s), Aunt, Backbite, Blether, Cackle, Cat, Causerie, Chat, Chin, Chitchat, Clash, Claver, Cleck, Clish-clash, Clishmaclaver, Confab, Coze, Crack, Cummer, Dirt, Flibbertigibbet, Gab(nash), Gabfest, Gas, Goster, Gup, Hen, Jaw, Loose-tongued, Maundrel, Nashgab, Natter, Noise, On dit, Pal, Personalist, Prattle, Quidnunc, Reportage, Rumour, Scandal(monger), Schmooze, Scuttlebutt, Shmoose, Shmooze, Sweetie-wife, Tabby(cat), Talk(er), Tattle, Tibby, Tittle(-tattle), Twattle, Yatter, Yenta

Got Gat, Obtained

Goth(ic) Alaric, Moesia

Gothamite Abderian, New Yorker

Gouge Chisel, Groove, Scoop

Gourd Bottle, Calabash, Courgette, Dishcloth, Guiro, Hercules' club, Loofa, Melon, Monkeybread, Pumpkin, Squash, Zucchini

Gourmand, **Gourmet** Apicius, > EPICURE, Gastronome, Gastrosopher, Lickerish, Table, Trencherman, Ventripotent

Gout Chiragra, Hamarthritis, Podagra, Taste, Tophus

Govern(or), **Government** Adelantado, Administer, Ag(h)a, Agricola, Alderman, Amban, Amman, Amtman, ANC, Autarchy, Autocrat, Autonomy, Bahram, Ban, Beehive, Beg, Beglerbeg, Bencher, Bey, Bridler, Bureaucracy, Burgrave, Cabinet, Caretaker, Castellan, Catapan, Cham, Circar, Classics, Coalition, Command, Commonweal, Condiminium, Congress, Constable, Constitution, Consulate, Cybernetic, Darogha, Democracy, Dergue, Despotism, Dey, Diarchy, Dictatorship, Dinarchy, Directoire, Directory, Dominate, Downing St, Duarchy, Dulocracy, Duumvirate, Dyarchy, Dynast, Earl, Empery, Eparch, Ergatocracy, Escapement, Ethnarch, Exarch, Fascism, Federal, G, Gauleiter, Gerontocracy, Gov, Grieve, Gubernator, Hagiocracy, Hague, Hajjaz, Hakim, Haptarchy, Harmost, HE, Helm, Hexarchy, Hierocracy, Honcho, Hospodar, Imperialism, Ins, Inspector, Isocracy, Junta, Kaimakam, Kakistocracy, Kamalism, Kebele, Khalifate, Khan, Kremlin, Legate, Local, Majlis, Majorism, Monarchy, Monocracy, Mudir, Nabob, Naik, Nomarch, Nomocracy, Ochlocracy, Oireachtas, Oligarchy, Optic®, Pa, Pacha, Padishah, Pasha, Pater, Pentarch, Père, Petticoat, Physiocracy, Pilate, Placemen, Plutocracy, Podesta, Polity,

Polyarchy, Porte, Power, Priest-king, Proconsul, Propraetor, Proveditor, Provedor(e), Providor, Ptochocracy, Quadrumvirate, Quirinal, Raj, Realpolitik, Rection, Rector, Rectrix, Regency, Regié, Regime(n), Reign, Rein, Ride, > **RULE**, Satrap, Senate, Serkali, Shogun, Signoria, Sircar, Sirkar, Stad(t)holder, Stakhanovism, Statecraft, Steer, Stratocracy, Subadar, Sway, Technocracy, Tetrarchy, Thatcherism, Thearchy, Theonomy, Timocracy, Totalitarianism, Triumvirate, Tuchun, Tyranny, Vali, Viceregal, Viceroy, Vichy, Wali, Warden, Wealsman, Whitehall, White House, Witan

Governess Duenna, Eyre, Fraulein, Griffin, Mademoiselle, Prism, Vicereine

Government revenue Jaghir(e), Jagir

Gown Banian, Banyan, Dressing, Empire, Geneva, Green, Johnny, Kirtle, Manteau, Manto, Mantua, Morning, Mother Hubbard, Peignoir, Polonaise, Robe, Silk, Slammakin, Slammerkin, Slop, Stola, Stuff, Tea, Wrap(per)

Grab Annexe, Bag, Clutch, Cly, Collar, Glaum, Grapnel, Hold, Holt, Rap, Seise, Seize, > **SNATCH**, Steal, Swipe

Gracchi Jewels

Grace(s), Graceful Aglaia, Airy, Amnesty, Anna, Bad, Beauty, Become, Benediction, Bethankit, Blessing, Charis(ma), Charites, Charity, Darling, Dr, Elegance, Euphrosyne, Fluent, Gainly, Genteel, Genty, Godliness, Grazioso, Light, Mense, Mercy, Molinism, Mordent, Omnium, Ornament, Pralltriller, Sacrament, Saving, Streamlined, Style, Thalia, Thanks, WG, Willowy

Gracious Benign, By George, Charismatic, Generous, Good, Handsome, Hend, Merciful, Polite

Gradation Cline, Degree, Nuance, Stage

Grade, Gradient Alpha, Analyse, Angle, Assort, Beta, Class(ify), Dan, Degree, Delta, Echelon, Gamma, Geothermal, Gon, Gride, Hierarchy, Inclination, Kyu, Lapse, Measure, Order, Ordinary, Pressure, Rank, Score, Seed, Slope, Stage, Standard, Status, Temperature

Gradual Gentle, Grail, Imperceptible, Inchmeal, Piecemeal, Slow

Graduate, Graduation Alumnus, BA, Bachelor, Calibrate, Capping, Classman, Incept, Laureateship, Licentiate, LlB, MA, Master, Nuance, Optime, Ovate

Graffiti Bomb, Doodle, Tag, Tagger

Graft Anaplasty, Autoplasty, Boodle, Bribery, Bud, Bypass, Crown, Dub, Enarch, Enrace, Flap, Hard, Heteroplasty, Imp, Implant, Inarch, Inoculate, Payola, Pomato, Racket, Scion, Shoot, Skin, Slip, Transplant, Whip, Ympe

Grail Chalice, Cup, Sangraal, Sangrail, Sangreal

Grain(y) Bajra, Bajree, Bajri, Bear, Bere, Boll, Bran, Cereal, Corn, Couscous, Crop, Curn, Curn(e)y, Cuscus, Distiller's, D(o)urra, Extine, Frumentation, Gr, Graddan, Granule, Groats, Grumose, Intine, Kaoliang, Knaveship, Malt, Mashlam, Mashlin, Mashloch, Mashlum, Maslin, Mealie, Millet, Milo, Minim, Mongcorn, Oats, Panic(k), Pannick, Pickle, Pinole, Pollen, Polynology, Popcorn, Puckle, Quarter, Rabi, Raggee, Raggy, Ragi, Rhy, Rye, Sand, Scruple, Seed, Semsem, Sorghum, Thirlage, Tola, Touch, Wheat, Wholemeal

Gram Black, Chich, Chick-pea, Green, Teen, Tene, Urd

Grammar(ian), Grammatical Ablative absolute, Accidence, Amphibology, Anacoluthia, Anacoluthon, Anaphora, Anastrophe, Case, Cataphora, Categorical, Donat, Donet, Generative, Gr, Linguistics, Montague, Paradigm, Pivot, Primer, Priscianist, Scholiast, Stratificational, Syndetic, Syndeton, Synectics, Synesis, Syntax, Systemics, Tagmeme, Transformational, Trivium, Typto, Universal, Valency

Gramophone Record player, Victrolla®

Grampus Orc, Thresher-whale, Whale

Granary Barn, Girnel, Silo

Grand(eur), **Grandiose** Canyon, Epical, Flugel, G, Gorgeous, Guignol, High-faluting, Hotel, Imposing, La(h)-di-da(h), Long, Lordly, Magnificent, Majestic, Megalomania, Palatial, Piano(forte), Pompous, Regal, Splendid, Stately, Stoor, Stour, Stowre, Sture, Sublime, Swell, Tour

Grandchild Mokopuna, Niece, Oe, Oy(e)

Grandee Adelantado, Don, Magnifico

Grandfather Ancient, Avital, Clock, Goodsire, Gramps, Gudesire, Gutcher, Luckie-dad, Oldster, Old-timer, Oupa

Grandmother Babushka, Beldam, Gran(nie), Granny, Moses, Nan(a), Ouma

Grandparent(al) Aval, Avital

Grand Prix Race(-cup)

Grandsire Peal

Grange Moated

Granite Aberdeen, Chinastone, Graphic, Greisen, Luxul(l)ianite, Luxulyanite, NH, Pegmatite, Protogine

Grannie Forebear, Knot, Nan(a)

Grant(ed) Accord, Aid, Award, Bestow, Beteem(e), Bounty, Bursary, Carta, Cary, Charta, Charter, Concession, > **CONFER**, Cy, Datum, Endow, Exhibition, Feoff, Give, Land, Lend, Let, Munich, Obreption, Patent, President, Regium donum, Send, Sop, Subsidy, Subvention, Teene, Vouchsafe, Yeven, Yield

Granule, **Granulate(d)** Kern, Otolith, Pearl, Plastid, Pound, Prill

Grape(s) Aligoté, Botros, Botryoid, Cabernet, Cabernet Sauvignon, Catawba, Chardonnay, Chenin blanc, Concord, Delaware, Diamond, Fox, Gamay, Gewurztraminer, Grenache, Haanepoot, Hamburg(h), Hanepoot, Honeypot, Hyacinth, Lambrusco, Malmsey, Malvasia, Malvesie, Malvoisie, Merlot, Muscadel, Muscadine, Muscat(el), Noble rot, Oregon, Petite Syrah, Pinot, Pinot Blanc, Pinot Chardonnay, Ptisan, Racemose, Raisin, Rape, Riesling, Sauvignon, Scuppernong, Sémillon, Sercial, Shiraz, Sour, Staphyline, Steen, Sultana, Sweet-water, Sylvaner, Syrah, Tokay, Uva, Verdelho, Véronique, Vino, Wineberry, Zinfandel

Grapefruit Pampelmoose, Pomelo, Pompelmouse, Pompelo, Pumple-nose, Ugli

Grapeshot Mitraille

Grape-sugar Glucose

Grapevine Hearsay, Moccasin telegraph

Graph(ic) Bar, Chart, Contour, Diagram, Histogram, Learning curve, Nomograph, Ogive, Picturesque, Pie (chart), Profile, Sonogram, Table, Vivid

Graphite Kish, Plumbago

Grapple Clinch, Close, Hook, Lock, Struggle, Wrestle

Grasp(ing) Apprehend, Catch, Clat, Claut, Clinch, > **CLUTCH**, Compass, Comprehend, Fathom, Get, Grab, Grapple, Greedy, Grip(e), Hent, Hug, Prehend, Prehensile, Raptorial, Realise, Rumble, Sense, Snap, Snatch, Twig, Uptak(e)

Grass(land), **Grass roots**, **Grassy** Agrostology, Alang, Alfa(lfa), Arrow, Avena, Bahia, Bamboo, Bang, Barbed wire, Barley, Barnyard, Beard, Bennet, Bent, Bermuda, Bhang, Blade, Blady, Blue(-eyed), Bristle, Brome-grass, Bromus, Buffalo, Buffel, Bunch, Bush, Canary, Cane, Canna, Cannach, Carpet, Cat's tail, Chess, China, Citronella, Cleavers, Clivers, Clover, Cochlearia, Cocksfoot, Cockspur, Cogon, Cord, Cortaderia, Cotton, Couch, Cow, Crab, Culm, Cuscus, Cutty, Dactylis, Danthonia, Dari, Darnel, Deergrass, Dhur(r)a, Diss, Divot, Dogstail, Dog's tooth, Dogwheat, Doob, Doura, Dura, Durra, Eddish, Eel, Eelwrack, Elephant, Emmer, Esparto, Feather, Fescue, Finger, Fiorin, Flinders, Floating, Flote, Fog, Foggage, Foxtail, Gage, Gama-grass, Ganja, Glume,

Glumella, Goose, Grama, Green(sward), Hair, Halfa, Harestail, Hassock, Haulm, Hay, Haycock, Heath(er), Hemp, Herbage, High veld, Holy, > **INFORM**, Jawar(i), Job's tears, Johnson, Jowar(i), Kangaroo, Kans, Kentucky blue, Khuskhus, Kikuyu, Knoll, Knot, Lalang, Laund, Lawn, Lemon, Locusta, Lolium, Lop, Lucern(e), Lyme, Machair, Manna, Marram, Marrum, Mary Jane, Mat, Materass, Matweed, Mead, Meadow (-fescue), Melic, Melick, Millet, Milo, Miscanthus, Monkey, Moor, Nark, Nassella tussock, Nose, Oat, Orchard, Oryza, Painted, Palet, Pamir, Pampas, Panic, Paspalum, Pasturage, Peach, Pennisetum, Pepper, Persicaria, Phleum, Plume, Poa, Porcupine, Pot, Puszta, Quack, Quaking, Quick, Quitch, Ramee, Rami(e), Rat, Rat on, Redtop, Reed, Rescue, Rhodes, Rib, Ribbon, Rice, Rips, Roosa, Rough, Rumble(r), Rusa, Rye, Rye (-brome), Sacaton, Sago, Salt, Savanna(h), Saw, Scorpion, Scraw, Scurvy, Scutch, Sea-reed, Sedge, Seg, Sesame, Sheep's fescue, Shop, Sing, Sinsemilla, Sisal, Sneak(er), Snitch, Snout, Snow, Sorghum, Sour-gourd, Sourveld, Spanish, Spear, Spelt, Spike, Spinifex, Splay, Split, Squeal, Squirrel-tail, Squitch, Stag, Star(r), Stipa, Stool-pigeon, Storm, Sudan, Sugar, Sward, Swath(e), Sword, Tape, Tath, Tea, Tef(f), Tell, Teosinte, Timothy, Toad, Toetoe, Toitoi, Triticale, Triticum, Tuffet, Turf, Tussac, Tussock, Twitch, Veld(t), Vernal, Vetiver, Whangee, Wheat, Whitlow, Windlestraw, Wire, Witch, Wood melick, Worm, Yard, Yellow-eyed, Yorkshire fog, Zizania, Zostera, Zoysia

Grasshopper Cicada, Cricket, Grig, Katydid, Locust, Long-horned, Meadow, Tettix, Wart-biter, Weta

Grate(r), **Grating** Abrade, Burr, Cancelli, Chirk, Crepitus, > **FRET**, Graticule, Gravelly, Grid, Grill, Guichet, Guttural, Hack, Hearth, Heck, Hoarse, Ingle, Jar, Mort-safe, Portcullis, Rasp, Risp, Rub, Ruling, Scrannel, > **SCRAPE**, Scrat, Shred, Siver, Strident, Syver

Grateful Beholden, Cinders, Indebted, Obliged

Gratification, **Gratify(ing)** Aggrate, Indulge, Kick, Masochism, Oblige, Pleasure, Regale, Reward, Sadism

Gratitude God 'a mercy, Ta, Thanks

Gratuitous, **Gratuity** Baksheesh, Beer-money, Bonsella, Bonus, Bounty, Cumshaw, Free, Glove-money, Gratis, Tip

Grave(yard) Accent, Arlington, Bass, Bier, Burial, Charnel, Chase, Darga, Demure, Dust, God's acre, Heavy, Heinous, Important, Ingroove, Kistvaen, Kurgan, Long home, Mound, Passage, Pit, Sad, Saturnine, Serious, Sober, Sombre, Speos, Staid, Stern, Tomb, Watery

Grave-digger Bederal, Fossor, Sexton

Gravel(ly) Calculus, Channel, Chesil, Chisel, Eskar, Esker, Glareous, Grail(e), Grit, Hoggin(g), Murram, Nonplus, Pay, Pea, Pingo, Shingle

Gravity Barycentric, G, Geotaxis, Geotropism, Great Attraction, Magnitude, Mascon, Quantum, Specific, Weight, Zero

Gravy Baster, Browning, Coin, Jus, Sauce

Gravy-boat Argyle, Argyll

▶ **Gray** *see* GREY

Grayling Umber

Graze, **Grazing** Abrade, Agist, Bark, Brush, Crease, Crop, Feed, Herdwick, Leasow(e), Machair, Pascual, Pasture, Rake, Rangeland, Scrape, Scrawn, Shave, Shieling, Zero

Grease, **Greasy** Bribe, Creesh, Dope, Dubbing, Elaeolite, Elbow, Enseam, Glit, Lanolin, Lard, Lubricate, Seam(e), Shearer, Sheep-shearer, Smarm, Suint, Unctuous

Great(s), **Greater**, **Greatest** Ali, Astronomical, Bully, Colossus, Extreme,

Gargantuan, Gay, Gey, Gran(d), Grit, Gt, Guns, Helluva, Immortal, Important, Lion, Macro, Main, Major, Massive, Mega, Mickle, Mochell, Modern, Much, Muchel(l), Muckle, OS, Profound, Rousing, Stoor, Stour, Stupendous, Sture, Sublime, Super, Superb, Swingeing, Synergy, Tall, Titan(ic), Tremendous, Unco, Untold, Utmost, Vast, Voluminous, Zenith

Great deal Mort

Grebe Cargoose

Grecian Bend, Nose

Greed(y) Avarice, Avid, Bulimia, Bulimy, Cupidity, Edacious, Esurient, Gannet, Gare, Gulosity, Harpy, Killcrop, Lickerish, Mercenary, Piggery, Pleonexia, Rapacity, Selfish, Solan, Voracity, Wolfish

Greek(s) Achaean, Achaian, Achilles, Aeolic, Agamemnon, Ajax, Aonian, Arcadia, Archimedes, Argive, Aristides, Athenian, Attic, Cadmean, Cleruch, Corinthian, Cretan, Cumae, Cyzicus, Delphian, Demotic, Ding, Diomedes, Dorian, Doric, Eoka, Eolic, Epaminondas, Ephebe, Epirus, Euclid, Evzone, Fanariot, Gr, Helladic, Hellene, Hellenic, Homer, Hoplite, Ionian, Isocrates, Italiot(e), Javan, Katharevousa, Klepht, Koine, Laconian, Lapith, Leonidas, Linear B, Locrian, Lucian, Macedonia, Middle, Modern, Molossian, Momus, Nestor, Nike, Nostos, Orestes, Paestum, Patroclus, Pelasgic, Pelopid, Perseus, Phanariot, Pythagoras, Romaic, Samiot, Seminole, Spartacus, Spartan, Stagirite, Strabo, Sybarite, Tean, Teian, Theban, Thersites, Theseus, Thessal(on)ian, Thracian, Timon, Typto, Uniat, Xenophon, Zorba

Green(ery) Almond, Apple, Avocado, Baggy, Bice, Biliverdin, Bottle, Bowling, Caesious, Callow, Celadon, Cerulein, Chard, Chartreuse, Chlorophyll, Chrome, Citron, Cole, Collard, Common, Copper, Corbeau, Crown, Cyan, Dioptase, Eau de nil, Eco-, Ecofriendly, Emerald, Emerande, Envious, Erin, Fingers, Foliage, Forest, Fundie, Fundy, Gaudy, Glaucous, Go, Goddess, Grass, Gretna, Gull, Immature, Inexpert, Jade, Jungle, Kendal, Kensal, Khaki, Lawn, Leafage, Lime, Lincoln, Loden, Lovat, Mead, Monastral®, Moss, Moulding, Naive, New, Nile, Oasis, Olive, Paris, Pea, Peridot, Pistachio, Porraceous, Putting, Raw, Realo, Reseda, Rifle, Rink, Sage, Scheele's, Sea, Sludge, Smaragdine, Sward, Teal, Tender, Terre-vert, Turacoverdin, Tyro, Unfledged, Uninitiated, Unripe, Uranite, Verdant, Verd antique, Verdigris, Verdure, Vert, Virent, Virid, Vir(id)escent, Young

Greenheart Bebeeru

Greenhorn Baby, Dupe, Put(t), Rookie, Sucker

Greenhouse Conservatory, Orangery, Phytotron, Polytunnel

Greens Broccoli, Cabbage, Calabrese, Cash, Money, Sprout, Vegetable(s)

Greet(ing) Abrazo, Accost, All hail, Arvo, Banzai, Benedicite, Blubber, Chimo, Ciao, Hail, Hallo, Halse, Handclasp, Handshake, Haway, Heil, Heita, Hello, Herald, Hi, High-five, Hiya, Hongi, How, How d'ye do, Howsit, Jai Hind, Jambo, Kia ora, Kiss, Kissagram, Mihi, Namaskar, Namaste, Respects, Salaam, Salam Alaikum, Salute, Salve, Sd, Shalom, Shalom aleichem, Sorry, Strippagram, Strippergram, Tena Koe, Wave, > **WELCOME**, Wotcher, Yo

Gregarious Social

Gregorian Chant, NS, Plagal

Gremlin *see* **GOBLIN**

Grenade Bomb, Egg, Hand, Pineapple, Rifle, Stun

Greta Garbo

Grey(ing), Gray Age, Agnes, Argent, Ashen, Ashy, Battleship, Beige, Bloncket, Charcoal, Cinereous, Dapple, Dorian, Dove, Drab, Ecru, Feldgrau, Field, Glaucous, Gloomy, Gr, Gridelin, Griesie, Gries(l)y, Grise, Grisy, Grizzled,

Gunmetal, Gy, Hoary, Hodden, Hore, Inn, Iron, Leaden, Liard, Livid, Lucia, Lyart, Mouse-coloured, Neutral, Olive drab, Oyster, Pearl, Perse, Pewter, Poliosis, Putty, Sclate, Slaty, Steel, Taupe, Zane

Greyfriars Bunter, Magnet

Greyhound Crew, Italian, Longtail, Ocean, Persian, Saluki, Sapling, Whippet

Grey matter Cinerea

Grid(dle), Gridiron Bar, Barbecue, Brandreth, Cattle, Control, Dot matrix, Crate, Graticule, Grating, National, Network, Reseau, Reticle, Roo-bar, Screen, Starting, Suppressor, Tava(h), Tawa, Windscale

Gride Creak, Grate

Grief, Grievance, Grieve, Grievous Axe, Bemoan, Bitter, Complaint, Condole, Cry, Dear(e), Deere, Distress, Dole, Dolour, Gram(e), Gravamen, Heartbreak, Hone, Illy, Io, > **MISERY**, Monody, O(c)hone, Pain, Pathetic, Plaint, Rue, Score, Sore, Sorrow, Teen, Tene, Tragic, Wayment, Weeping, Woe, Wrong

Griffin Gripe, Grype, Novice, Pony

Grill(er), Grilling Braai, Brander, Broil, Carbonado, Crisp, Devil, Gridiron, Inquisition, Interrogate, Kebab, Mixed, Pump, Question, Rack, Radiator, Reja, Yakimona

Grim Dire, Dour, Gaunt, Glum, Gurly, Hard, Macabre, Stern

▷ **Grim** *may indicate* an anagram

Grimace Face, Girn, Moe, Mop, Moue, Mouth, Mow, Murgeon, Pout

Grime(s), Grimy Colly, Dirt, Peter, Rechie, Reechie, Reechy, Soil, Sweep

Grin Fleer, Girn, Risus, Simper, Smirk, Sneer

Grind(ing), Grinder Bray, Bruxism, Chew, Crunch, > **CRUSH**, Droil, Gnash, Grate, Graunch, Grit, Home, Kern, Kibble, Levigate, Mano, Metate, Mill, Mince, Molar, Muller, Pug, Pulverise, Slog, Stamp, Triturate

Grip(ping), Gripper Ascendeur, Bite, Chuck, Clam, Clamp, Clip, Clutch, Craple, Embrace, Enthral, Get, Grapple, > **GRASP**, Haft, Hair, Hairpin, Hand(fast), Handhold, Hend, Hold, Hug, Key, Kirby®, Lewis, Obsess, Pincer, Pinion, Pistol, Prehensile, Purchase, Raven, Rhine, Sally, Setscrew, Sipe, Strain, Streigne, Twist, Valise, Vice, Walise, Wrestle

Gripe(s) Colic, Complain, Ditch, Grasp, Griffin, Ileus, Pain, Tormina

Grisly Gory

Grist Burden

Gristle, Gristly Cartilage, Chondroid, Lytta

Grit(s), Gritty Blinding, Clench, Gnash, Granular, Grate, Guts, Hominy, Nerve, Pluck, Resolution, Sabulose, Sand, Shingle, Swarf, Valour, Yorkshire

Grizzle(d) Grey

Groan(er) Bewail, Bing, Moan

Grocer Grasshopper, Jorrocks, Pepperer, Symbol

Groggy Dazed, Shaky

Groin Gnarr, Inguinal, Lisk

Groom(ed) Brush, Coistrel, Coistril, Comb, Curry, Dress, Fettler, Kempt, Ostler, Palfrenier, Paranymph, Preen, Prink, S(a)ice, Smarten, Spouse, Strapper, Syce, Tiger, Tracer, Train, Wrangler

▷ **Groom** *may indicate* an anagram

Groove(d), Groovy Bezel, Canal, Cannelure, Chamfer, Channel, Chase, Clevis, Coulisse, Croze, Dièdre, Exarate, Fissure, Flute, Fuller, Furr, Furrow, Glyph, Gouge, Kerf, Key-seat, Keyway, Lead-in, Lead-out, Oche, Pod, Rabbet, Race(way), Raggle, Raphe, Rebate, Rif(f)le, Rigol(l), Rout, > **RUT**, Scrobe, Sipe, Slot, Sulcus, Throat, Track, Trough, Vallecula

Grope(r) Feel, Fumble, Grabble, Hapuka, Ripe, Scrabble

Gross All-up, Coarse, Complete, Crass, Dense, Earn, Earthy, Flagrant, Frankish, Fustilugs, Gr, Loathsome, Material, Obese, Outsize, Overweight, Pre-tax, Rank, Ribald, Rough, Stupid, Sum, Whole

Gross *may indicate* an anagram

Grotesque Antic, Bizarre, Fantastic, Fright, Gargoyle, Magot, Outlandish, Rabelaisian, Rococo, Teras

Grotto Cave, Lupercal

Ground(s) Abthane, Arena, Astroturf, Basis, Bottom, Breeding, Campus, Cause, Common, Criterion, Crushed, Deck, Dregs, Eard, Earth, Edgbaston, Epig(a)eal, Epig(a)ean, Epig(a)eous, Floor, Footing, Gathering, Grated, Grist, Grouts, High, Hunting, Lees, Leeway, Lek, Lords, Lot, Marl, Mealed, Middle, Occasion, Oval, Parade, Piste, Pitch, Plat, Pleasure, Plot, Policy, Proving, Quad, > REASON, Recreation, Réseau, Ring, Sediment, Slade, Soil, Solum, Sports, Stadium, Stamping, Terra, Terrain, Tom Tiddler's, Touch, Tract, Turf, Udal, Vantage, Venue, Waste(land), Yard, Yird

Ground *may indicate* an anagram

Groundbait Chum

Ground-crew Erk

Ground-rent Crevasse

Groundsheet Hutchie

Groundsman Greenkeeper

Group Abelian, Acyl, 'A'list, Band, Batch, Beatles, Bee, Bevy, Bloc(k), Blood, Bloomsbury, Body, Bracket, Bratpack, Bruges, Caboodle, Cadre, Camarilla, Camp, Cartel, Category, Caucus, Cave, Cell, Chain, Chordata, Circle, Clade, Class(is), Clique, Cluster, Cohort, Colony, Combo, Commune, Community, Concertina, Congregation, Consort(ium), Contact, Contingent, Control, Convoy, Coterie, Covey, Crew, Deme, Demi-monde, Denomination, Detail, Enclave, Encounter, Ensemble, Faction, Fascio, Focus, Fold, Fraternity, Front, Galère, Gang, Gemeinschaft, Gender, Genus, Gesellschaft, Ginger, Globe, Guild, Hapu, Heading, Hexad, Hirsel, House, Income, In-crowd, Ketone, Kit, Knot, League, Marathon, Marshal, Nexus, Order, Outfit, Oxford, Pack(et), Panel, Parti, Party, Passel, Peer, Phalange, Phratry, Phylum, Platoon, Pleiad, Pocket, Pod, Point, Pool, Pop, Pressure, Prosthetic, Push, Quincunx, Raceme, Racemose, Rap, Reading, Ring, Rush, School, Sector, Seminar, Series, Set, Several, Sex, Shower, Society, Sort, Sorus, Splinter, Strain, Stream, String, Study, Sub-general, Sub-order, Support, Syndicate, T, Tales, Taxon, Tetrad, Tithing, Trainband, T-Rex, Tribe, Tribune, Trilogy, Trio, TU, Umbrella, Unit, User, Vigilante, Workshop, Zaibatsu, Zupa

Grouse Black, Blackcock, Bleat, Blue, Caper(caillie), Capercailzie, Covey, Gorcock, Greyhen, Gripe, Growl, Grumble, Hazel-hen, Heath-cock, Heath-hen, Jeremiad, Moan, Moorcock, Moorfowl, Moor-pout, Muir-poot, Muir-pout, Mutter, Natter, Peeve, Pintail, Prairie-hen, Ptarmigan, Red, Resent, Ruffed, Rype(r), Sage, Sharp-tailed, Snarl, Spruce, Twelfth, Wheenge, W(h)inge, Willow

Grove Academy, Arboretum, Bosk, Bosquet, Copse, Glade, Hurst, Lyceum, Motte, Nemoral, Orchard, Orchat, Silva, Tope

Grovel Cheese, Crawl, Creep, Fawn, Ko(w)tow

Grow(ing), **Grow out**, **Growth** Accrete, Accrue, Acromegaly, Adenoma, Aggrandisement, Angioma, Apophysis, Arborescence, Auxesis, Bedeguar, Boom, Braird, Breer, Burgeon, Car(b)uncle, Cholelith, Chondroma, Compensatory, Condyloma, Crescendo, Crop, Culture, Cyst, Ectopia, Edema, Ellagic, Enate, Enchondroma, Enlarge, Epinasty, Epitaxy, Excrescence,

Grow(n) Exostosis, Expansion, Fibroid, Flor, Flourish, Flush, Gain, Gall, Germinate, Get
Goitre, Hepatocele, Hummie, Hyponasty, Increase, Keratosis, Knur(r), Lichen,
Lipoma, Mole, Mushroom, Myoma, Nur(r), Oedema, Oncology, Osselet,
Osteoma, Osteophyte, Polyp, Proleg, Proliferate, Rampant, Rank, Scirrhus,
Septal, Snowball, Spavin, > **SPROUT**, Stalagmite, Stipule, Sympodial, Tariff,
Thrive, Tylosis, Vegetable, Wart, Wax, Wox

▷ **Grow(n)** *may indicate* an anagram

Growl(ing) Fremescent, Gnar, Groin, Grr, Gurl, Roar(e), Roin, Royne, Snar(l)

Grown up Adult, Mature, Risen

Grub(by) Assart, Aweto, Bardy, Bookworm, Caddis, Caterpillar, Cheer, Chow,
Chrysalis, Dig, Eats, Fare, Fodder, > **FOOD**, Gentle, Groo-groo, Gru-gru, Larva,
Leatherjacket, Mawk, Mess, Nosh, Palmerworm, Peck, Pupa, Root(le), Rout,
Rowt, Sap, Slave, Stub, Tired, Wireworm, Witchetty, Wog, Worm

Grudge, Grudging Chip, Derry, Envy, Grutch, Resent, Score, Sparse, Spite, Spleen

Gruel Brochan, Bross, Loblolly, Skilligalee, Skilligolee, Skilly

Gruesome Ghastly, Grisly, Grooly, Horror, Livid, Macaberesque, Macabre,
> **MORBID**, Sick

Gruff Guttural, Hoarse, Surly

Grumble Beef, Bellyache, Bitch, Bleat, Chunter, Crab, Croak, Girn, Gripe,
Grizzle, Groin, Growl, Moan, Murmur, Mutter, Nark, Natter, Repine, Rumble,
Whinge, Yammer

Grump(y) Attercop, Bearish, Cross, Ettercap, Grouchy, Moody, Sore-headed,
Surly

Grunt Groin, Grumph, Humph, Oink, Pigfish, Spanish, Ugh, Wheugh

Guano Dung, Sombrerite

Guanoco Llama

Guarantee Accredit, Assure, Avouch, Certify, Ensure, Gage, Hallmark, Insure,
Mainprise, Money-back, Pignerate, Pignorate, > **PLEDGE**, Plight, Seal, Secure,
Sponsion, Surety, Underwrite, > **VOUCHSAFE**, Warn, Warrandice, Warrant(y)

Guard(ed), Guards Acolouthos, Advance, Apron, Beefeaters, Blues, Bostangi,
Bouncer, Bracer, Cabiri, Cage, Cag(e)y, Cerberus, Chaperon(e), Chary,
Cheesemongers, Cherry-pickers, Coast, Coldstream, Colour, Cordon, Crinoline,
Curator, Custodian, Custos, Diehards, Dragoons, Duenna, Equerry, Escort,
Eunuch, Excubant, Exon, Fence, Fender, Gaoler, Grenadiers, Greys, Hedge,
Home, Horse, INS, Jaga, Jailer, Keep, Lancers, Life, Lilywhites, Look out, Mask,
Mort-safe, National, Nightwatch(man), Nutcrackers, Out-rider, Out-sentry,
Pad, Palace, Patrol, Picket, Point, Praetorian, > **PROTECT**, Provost, Quillon, Rail,
Red, Ride, Screw, Secure, Security, Sentinel, Sentry, Shadow, Shield, Shopping,
Shotgun, SS, Strelitz, Streltzi, Swiss, Switzer, Tapadera, Tapadero, Tile, Toecap,
Tsuba, Turnkey, Vambrace, Vamplate, Varangian, Vigilante, Visor, Wage,
Wait(e), Ward, Wary, Watch (and ward), Watchdog, Watchman, Wear, Weir,
Wire, Yeoman

Guardian Altair, Argus, Curator, Custodian, Custos, Dragon, Gemini, Granthi,
Hafiz, Janus, Julius, Miminger, Templar, Trustee, Tutelar(y), Warder,
Watchdog, Xerxes

Gudgeon Fish, Pin, Trunnion

Guenon Grivet, Vervet

Gue(r)rilla Bushwhacker, Chetnik, Contra, ETA, Fedayee, Gook, Irregular,
Khmer Rouge, Komitaji, Maquis, Mujahadeen, Mujaheddin, Mujahed(d)in,
Mujahedeen, Mujahideen, Partisan, Red Brigade, Terrorist, Tupamaro, Urban,
Viet cong, Zapata

Guess Aim, Aread, Arede, Arreede, Conjecture, Divine, Estimate, Harp, Hazard,

Imagine, Infer, Level, Mor(r)a, Mull, Shot, Speculate, Suppose, Surmise, Theorise

Guessing game Handy-dandy, Mor(r)a, Quiz

Guest(s) Caller, Company, House-party, Inquiline, Parasite, Paying, PG, Symbion(t), Symphile, Synoecete, Umbra, Visitant, > **VISITOR**, Xenial

Guesthouse Minshuku, Xenodochium

Guff Bosh, Gas

Guianian S(a)ouari

Guidance, Guide, Guideline, Guiding Advice, Antibarbus, Auspice, Baedeker, Bradshaw, Cicerone, Clue, Concordance, Conduct, Counsel, Courier, Curb, Cursor, Director(y), Docent, Dragoman, Drive, > **ESCORT**, Field, Gillie, Graticule, Helm, Heuristic, Index, Inertial, Inspire, Itinerary, Jig, Key, Lad, Landmark, Lead, Lodestar, Map, Mark, Marriage, Mentor, Model, Navaid, Navigate, Nose, Pelorus, Pilot, Pointer, Postil(l)ion, Principle, Queen's, Range, Ranger, Reference, Rein, Relate, Rudder, Sabot, Shepherd, Sherpa, Shikaree, Shikari, Sight, Sign, Sixer, Stear, Steer, Stire, Template, Templet, Terrestrial, Tiller, Train, Travelogue, Tutelage, Vocational, Voyageur, Waymark, Weise, Weize, Wise

Guild Artel, Basoche, Company, Freemason, Gyeld, Hanse, Hoastman, League, Mistery, Mystery, Society, Tong, Union

Guile Art, Cunning, Deceit, Dole, Malengine

Guillotine Closure, Louisiette, Maiden, Marianne

Guilt(y) Angst, Blame, Cognovit, Flagitious, Mea culpa, Nocent, Peccavi, Remorse, Wicked

Guinea(s) Canary, Geordie, Gns, Job, Ls, Meg, Spade

Guinea-fowl Pintado

Guinea-pig Abyssinian, Agoute, Agouti, Cavie, Cavy, Paca

Guinea-worm Dracunculus

Guise Form, Manner, Shape

Guitar(ist) Acoustic, Axe(man), Bottleneck, Cithern, Cittern, Dobro®, Electric, Fender®, Gittarone, Gittern, Hawaiian, Humbucker, Lute, Lyre, Pedal steel, Plankspanker, Samisen, Sancho, Sanko, Shamisen, Sitar, Slide, Spanish, Steel, Uke, Ukulele

Gulf Aden, Aqaba, Bay, Bothnia, California, Cambay, Carpentaria, Chasm, Chihli, Corinth, Cutch, Darien, Dvina, Exmouth, Fonseca, Genoa, Gonaives, Hauraki, Honduras, Joseph Bonaparte, Kutch, Lepanto, Leyte, Lingayen, Lions, Mannar, Martaban, Maw, Mexico, Persian, Queen Maud, Saronic, Siam, Sidra, Spencer, Taganrog, Tongking, Tonkin, Trieste, Tunis, Van Diemen, Vorago

Gull(s) Black-backed, Bonxie, Cheat, Cob(b), Cod, Cony, Cozen, Dupe, Fool, Geck, Glaucous, Have, Hoodwink, Ivory, Kittiwake, Laridae, Larus, Maw, Mew, Mollyhawk, Pickmaw, Pigeon, Queer, Rook, Sabine's, Saddleback, Scaury, Scourie, Scowrie, Sea-cob, Sea-mew, Sell, Simp, Skua, Sucker, Swart-back, Tern, Tystie, Xema

Gullet Crop, Enterate, Maw, Oesophagus, Throat, Weasand-pipe

Gullible Green, Naive, Sucker

Gulliver Lemuel

Gully Couloir, Donga, Geo, Gio, Goe, Grough, Gulch, Pit, Rake, Ravine, Sloot, Sluit, Wadi

Gulp Bolt, Draught, Gollop, Quaff, Slug, Sob, > **SWALLOW**, Swig, Swipe, Wolf

Gum (tree) Acacia, Acajou, Acaroid, Agar, Algin, Angico, Arabic, Arabin, Arar, Arctic, Asafoetida, Bablah, Balata, Balm, Bandoline, Bdellium, Benjamin, Benzoin, Bloodwood, Blue, Boot, Bubble, Cerasin, Chicle, Chuddy, Chutty,

Coolabah, Courbaril, Cow®, Dextrin(e), Dragon's-blood, Ee-by, Eucalyptus, Euphorbium, Flooded, Frankincense, Galbanum, Gamboge, Ghost, Gingival, > **GLUE**, Goat's-thorn, Gosh, Grey, Guar, Ironbark, Karri, Kauri, La(b)danum, Lac, Lentisk, Mastic(h), Mucilage, Myrrh, Nicotine, Olibanum, Opopanax, Oshac, Red, Sagapenum, Sarcocolla, Scribbly, Size, Sleep, Snow, Spearmint, Spirit, Starch, Sterculia, Stringybark, Sugar, Sweet, Tacamahac, Tragacanth, Tupelo, Ulmin, Water, White, Xanthan

Gumbo Okra

Gumboil Parulis

Gumption Nous, Spirit

Gun(fire), Guns Amusette, Archibald, Archie, Arquebus, Automatic, Barker, Baton, Bazooka, Beanbag, Beretta, Big Bertha, Biscayan, Blunderbuss, Bofors, Bombard, Breech(-loader), Bren, Broadside, Brown Bess, Browning, Bulldog, Bullpup, Bundook, Burp, Caliver, Cannonade, Carbine, Carronade, Cement, Chokebore, Coehorn, Colt®, Dag, Derringer, Electron, Elephant, Escopette, Falcon(et), Field, Fieldpiece, Firearm, Fire lock, Flame, Flash, Flintlock, Four-pounder, Fowler, Fowlingpiece, Garand, Gat(ling), Gingal(l), Grease, HA, Hackbut, Half-cock, Harquebus, Heater, Hired, Howitzer, Jezail, Jingal, Kalashnikov, Lewis, Long Tom, Luger®, Machine, Magazine, Magnum, Maroon, Martini-Henry®, Matchlock, Mauser®, Maxim, Metal, Minnie, Minute, Mitrailleuse, Morris Meg, Mortar, Musket(oon), Muzzle-loader, Neutron, Noonday, Oerlikon, Ordnance, Over and under, Owen, Paderero, Paterero, Ped(e)rero, Pelican, Perrier, Petronel, Piece, Pistol(et), Pompom, Pump (action), Punt, Purdey®, Quaker, Radar, Ray, Repeater, Rev, Riot, Rod, Roscoe, Saker, Sarbacane, Self-cocker, Shooter, Sidearm, Siege, Smoothbore, Snapha(u)nce, Spear, Spray, Squirt, Staple, Starting, Sten, Sterculia, Sterling, Stern-cannon, Stern-chaser, Stun, Swivel, Taser®, Tea, Thirty eight, Thompson, Tier, Time, Tommy, Tool, Tupelo, Turret, Uzi, Walther, Wesson, Young, Zip

Gunge Gowl

Gunman Ace, Assassin, Bandit, Earp, Greaser, Pistoleer, Sniper, Starter

Gunner, Gunner's assistant Arquebusier, Arsenal, Artillerist, Cannoneer, Cannonier, Culverineer, Gr, Matross, RA

Gunpowder Charcoal, Pebble-powder, Saucisse, Saucisson

Gunwale Gunnel, Portland, Portlast, Portoise

Guppy Million

Gurgle Clunk, Glug, Gobble, Gollar, Goller, Guggle, Ruckle, Squelch

Gurnard Tubfish

Guru Lifestyle, Sadhu, Teacher

Gush(ing) Blether, Effusive, > **FLOOD**, Flow, Jet, Outpour, Rail, Raile, Regurgitate, Rhapsodize, Scaturient, Spirt, Spout, Spurt, Too-too

Gusset Godet, Gore, Insert, Inset, Mitre

Gust Blast, Blore, Flaught, Flaw, Flurry, Puff, Sar, Waff

Gusto Elan, Relish, Verve, Zest

Gut(s), Gutty Archenteron, Balls, Beer, Bowel(s), Chitterlings, Cloaca, Disembowel, Draw, Duodenum, Enteral, Enteron, Entrails, Gill, Ileum, Insides, Kyle, Mesenteron, Minikin, Omental, Omentum, Purtenance, Remake, Sack, Sand, Snell, Stamina, Staying-power, Strip, Thairm, Tripe, Ventriculus, Viscera

Gutta-percha Jelutong, Pontianac, Pontianak

Gutter(ing) Arris, Channel, Conduit, Coulisse, Cullis, Grip, Kennel, Rhone, Rigol(l), Roan, Rone, Sough, Spout, Strand, Sweal, Sweel

Guttersnipe Arab, Gamin, Thief
Guttural Faucal, Throaty
Guy Backstay, Bo, Burgess, Chaff, Clewline, Decamp, Deride, Effigy, Fall,
  Fawkes, Fellow, Gink, Josh, Mannering, Parody, Rib, Rope, Scarecrow, Stay,
  Tease, Vang, Wise
Guzzle(d) Gannet, Gorge, Go(u)rmandize, Overeat
Gwyn Nell
Gym(nasium), **Gymnast(ic)** Acrobat, Akhara, Arena, Contortionist, Dojo,
  Jungle, Lyceum, Palaestra, PE, PT, Rhythmic, Sokol, Tumbler, Turner
Gymnosophist Yogi
Gypsum Alabaster, Gesso, Plaster, Satin-stone, Selenite, Terra alba
Gypsy, **Gipsy** Bohemian, Cagot, Caird, Caqueux, Chai, Chal, Chi, Collibert,
  Egyptian, Esmeralda, Faw, Gipsen, Gitano, Hayraddin, Lavengro, Meg,
  Rom(any), Rye, Scholar, Tinker, Traveller, Tsigane, Vagabond, Vlach, Walach,
  Wanderer, Zigan, Zigeuner, Zincala, Zincalo, Zingaro
Gyrate Revolve, Rotate, > SPIN, Twirl

Hh

H Ache, Aitch, Aspirate, Height, Hospital, Hotel, Hydrant, Hydrogen

Haberdasher(y) Clothier, Ferret, Hosier, Notions

Habit(s), Habitual, Habituate, Habitué Accustom, Addiction, Apparel, Assuefaction, Assuetude, Bent, Cacoethes, Chronic, Clothes, Coat, Consuetude, Crystal, Custom, Diathesis, Dress, Ephod, Frequenter, Garb, Inure, Inveterate, Motley, Mufti, Nature, Outfit, Pathological, Practice, Raiment, Regular, Riding, Robe, Rochet, Routine, Scapular, Schema, Season, Set, Soutane, Suit, Surplice, Toge, Trait, Tway, Usual, Way, Won, Wont, Xerotes

Habitat Element, Environment, Haunt, Home, Locality, Station

Hacienda Ranch

Hack(er) Chip, Chop, Cough, Cut, Drudge, Garble, Gash, Ghost, Grub-street, Hag, Hash, Hedge-writer, Heel, Hew, Horse, Journo, Mangle, Mutilate, Nag, Notch, Pad, Paper-strainer, Penny-a-liner, Pot-boiler, Rosinante, Spurn, Steed, Tadpole, Taper, Tussis, Unseam, White hat

Hackle(s) Comb, Rough

Hackneyed Banal, Cab, Cliché, Corny, Percoct, Stale, Threadbare, Tired, Trite

Haddock Arbroath smokie, Findram, Finnan, Fish, Norway, Rizzered, Smoky, Speldin(g), Speldrin(g), Whitefish

Hades Dis, Hell, Orcus, Pit, Tartarus

Had (to) Moten, Must, Obliged, Threw

Haematite Oligist

Haemorrhoids Farmer Giles, Piles

Hafnium Hf

Hag(-like) Anile, Beldame, Besom, Carlin(e), Crone, Harpy, Harridan, Hell-cat, Hex, Nickneven, Occasion, Rudas, Runnion, Trot, Underwood, Witch

Haggard Drawn, > GAUNT, Pale, Rider

Haggis Kishke

Haggle Argue, Badger, > BARGAIN, Barter, Chaffer, Dicker, Horse-trade, Niffer, Palter, Prig

Ha-ha Dike, Sunk-fence

Hahnium Hn

Hail(er) Acclaim, Ahoy, Ave, Bull-horn, Cheer, Fusillade, Graupel, Greet, Hi, Ho, Megaphone, Salue, Salute, Shower, Signal, Skoal, Skol, Sola, Stentor, Storm, Trumpet, Whoa-ho-ho

Hair (cut), Hair problem/condition, Hair style, Hairlike, Hairy Afro, Ailes de pigeon, Ainu, Alopecia, Baldy, Bang, Barnet, Beard, Beehive, Bezoar, Bingle, Bob, Bouffant, Braid, Brede, Bristle, Brutus, Bumfluff, Bun, Bunches, Butch, Cadogan, Camel, Capillary, Catogan, Chignon, Cilia, Cleopatra, Coat, Cockernony, Coif, Coiffure, Comal, Comate, Comb-over, Cornrow, Corymbus, Cowlick, Crepe, Crew-cut, Crinal, Cronet, Crop, Cue, Curlicue, DA, Dangerous, Dreadlocks, Dubbing, Duck's arse, Ducktail, Earmuffs, Elf locks, En brosse, Esau, Feather, Feather-cut, Fetlock, Filament, Flat-top, Floccus, Forelock, French pleat, French roll, Frenulum, Fringe, Fur, Garconne, Glib(s),

Glochidium, Guard, Hackles, Heard, Heer(i)e, Hispid, Hog, Indumentum, Kemp, Kesh, Lanugo, Lash, List, Lock, Lovelock, Lowlights, Madarosis, Mane, Marcel, Mohican, Mop, Mullet, Muttonchops, Not(t), Number two, Pageboy, Pappus, Pashm, Pele(s), Pelt, Perm(anent), Pigtail, Pika, Pile, Pilus, Plait, Plica, Pompadour, Ponytail, Poodle cut, Porcupine, Pouf(fe), Pow, Psilosis, Puberulent, Pubescent, Pudding basin, Punk, Queue, Quiff, Radicle, Rat-tail, Red mullet, Rhizoid, Roach, Root, Scalp lock, Scopate, Scopula, Set, Shag, Shingle, Shock, Sideburns, Sidelock, Snell, Spikes, Stinging, Strammel, Strand, Strigose, Strummel, Switch, Sycosis, Tête, Thatch, Tomentose, Tonsure, Topknot, Tragus, Tress, Trichoid, Trichology, Trichome, Trim, Velutinous, Vibrissi, Villi, Villosity, Villus, Wedge, Widow's peak, Wig, Wisp, > **WOOL**, Xerasia

Hair-cream, **Hair-oil** Conditioner, Pomade

Hairdresser Barber, Coiffeur, Comb, Crimper, Friseur, Marcel, Salon, Stylist, Trichologist

Hairless Bald, Callow, Glabrate, Glabrescent, Glabrous, Irate

Hairnet Kell, Snood

Hairpiece Frisette, Merkin, Postiche, Strand, Toupee, > **WIG**

Hairpin Bodkin, Slide, U, U-turn

Hair-shirt Ab(b)a, Cilice

Haiti RH

Hal Prince

Halberd Spontoon

Halcyon Calm, Kingfisher, Mild

Hale(r) Drag, Healthy, Koruna, Robust, Well

Half, **Halved** Bifid, Demi, Dimidiate, Dirempt, Divide, Hemi, Moiety, Semi, Share, Split, Stand-off, Term

Half-a-dozen Six, VI

Half-asleep, **Half-conscious** Dove, Dozy

Half-baked Foolish, Mediocre, Samel, Slack-bake

Half-breed, **Half-caste** Bastard, Baster, Creole, Eurasian, Mameluco, Mestee, Mestiza, Mestizo, Metif, Métis(se), Mongrel, Mulatto, Mustee, Octaroon, Quadroon, Quarteroon, Quintero, Quintroon, Sambo, Yellow-boy, Yellow-girl, Zambo

Half-guinea Smelt

Half-hearted Reluctant, Tepid

Half-hour Bell

Half-pence, **Half-penny** Mag, Maik, Mail(e), Make, Obolus, Patrick, Portcullis, Posh, Rap, Wood's

Half-turn Caracol(e), Demivolt

Half-wit Changeling, Mome, Simpleton, > **STUPID**

Hall Anteroom, Apadana, Atrium, Auditorium, Aula, Basilica, Carnegie, Casino, Chamber, Citadel, City, Concourse, Corridor, Dance, Dojo, Domdaniel, Dome, Dotheboys, Ex(h)edra, Festival, Foyer, Gallen, Hardwick, Holkham, Kedleston, Liberty, Lobby, Locksley, Megaron, Mess, Moot, Music, Narthex, Newby, Odeon, Palais, Palais de danse, Passage, Prytaneum, Rathaus, Salle, Saloon, Stationer's, Tammany, Tara, Tolsel, Town, Valhalla, Vestibule, Walhall(a), Wildfell

Hallmark(ed) Brand, Contrôlé, Logo, Seal, Stamp

Hallo *see* **HELLO**

Hallow Revere, Worship

Hallucinate, **Hallucination**, **Hallucinogen** Autoscopy, DT's, Fantasy,

Formication, Freak, Freak out, Illusion, Image, Mirage, Photism, Psilocin, Psilocybin, Psychedelic, Trip

Halo Antheolion, Areola, Aura, Aureola, Corona, Galactic, Gloria, Gloriole, Mandorla, Nimbus, Rim, Vesica, Vesica piscis

Halogen Iodine

Halt(er) Abort, Arrest, Block, Brake, Bridle, Cavesson, Cease, Check, Full stop, Game, Hackamore, Heave-to, Hilch, Lame(d), Limp, Noose, Prorogue, Rope, Stall, Standstill, Staw, > **STOP**, Stopover, Toho, Tyburn-tippet, Whoa

Ham(s) Amateur, Barnstormer, Flitch, Gammon, Haunch, Hock, Hoke, Hough, Hunker, Jambon, Jay, Nates, Overact, Overplay, Parma, Prat, Prosciutto, Radio, Tiro, Westphalian, York

Hamfisted Maladroit, Unheppen

Hamite Berber, Nilot(e)

Hamlet Aldea, Auburn, Cigar, Clachan, Dane, Dorp, Hero, Kraal, Stead, Thorp(e), Vill(age), Wick

Hammer(ed), **Hammerhead** About-sledge, Ballpeen, Ballpein, Beetle, Bully, Bush, Celt, Claw, Drop, Excudit, Flatten, Fore, Fuller, Gavel, Hack, Incuse, Jack, Kevel, Knap, Knapping, Kusarigama, Lump, Madge, Mall(et), Malleate, Martel, Maul, Mjol(l)nir, Monkey, Nevel, Oliver, Pane, Pean, Peen, Pein, Pene, Percussion, Piledriver, Planish, Plessor, Plexor, Pneumatic, Rawhide, Repoussé, Rip, Sheep's-foot, Shingle, Sledge, Steam, Stone, Strike, Tack, Tenderizer, Tendon, Tilt, Trip, Umbre, Water, Wippen

▷ **Hammered** *may indicate* an anagram

Hammerthrower Thor

Hammock Cott

▷ **Hammy** *may indicate* an anagram

Hamper Basket, Cabin, Ceroon, Cramp, Cumber, Delay, Encumber, Entrammel, Hamstring, Handicap, Hobble, Hog-tie, Obstruct, Pad, Pannier, Ped, Pinch, Restrict, Rub, Sero(o)n, Shackle, Tangle, Trammel, Tuck

Hamster Cricetus, Idea

Hamstring Cramp, Hock, Hox, Lame, Popliteal, Thwart

Hand(s), **Hand over**, **Hand down**, **Hand-like**, **Handwriting** Assist(ance), Bananas, Bequeath, Cacography, Calligraphy, Charge, Chicane, Chirography, Clap(ping), Claque, Club, Clutch, Copperplate, Court, Crew, Cursive, Daddle, Danny, Dawk, Dead, Deal, Deck, Deliver, Devolve, Donny, Dukes, Dummy, Famble, Fin, Fist, Flipper, Flush, Free, Glad, Graphology, Help, Helping, Hond, Hour, Impart, Iron, Israel, Italian, Jambone, Jamboree, Jemmy, Kana, L, Lone, Man, Manual, Manus, Maulers, Medieval, Minute, Mitt(en), Nes(h)ki, Niggle, Operative, Orthography, Pad, Palm(atifid), Part, Pass, Paw, Podium, Post, Pud, R, Referral, Rein (arm), Round, Script, Second, Signature, Span, Spencerian, Stage, Station, Straight, Sweep, Text, Tiger, Upper, Whip, Widow, Worker, Yarborough

Handbag Caba(s), Grip, Indispensable, Pochette, Purse, Reticule, Valise

Handbook Baedeker, Companion, Enchiridion, Guide, Manual, Vade-mecum

Handcuff(s) Bracelet, Darbies, Golden, Irons, Manacle, Mittens, Nippers, Snaps, Wristlet

Handful Few, Gowpen, Grip, Problem, Pugil, Rip(p), V

Handicap Bisque, Burden, Cambridgeshire, Ebor, Encumber, Hamper, Impede, Impost, Lame, Liability, Lincolnshire, Mental, > **OBSTACLE**, Off, Physical, Restrict, Weigh(t), Welter-race

Handicraft Marquetry

Handkerchief, **Hanky** Bandan(n)a, Belcher, Billy, Buffon, Clout, Fogle, Foulard,

Kleenex®, Madam, Madras, Monteith, Mouchoir, Muckender, Napkin, Nose-rag, Orarium, Romal, Rumal, Sudary, Tissue, Wipe(r)

Handle(d) Ansate, Bail, Bale, Behave, Bitstock, Brake, Broomstick, Cope, Crank, Dead man's, Deal, Doorknob, Dudgeon, Ear, Feel, Finger, Forename, Gaum, Gorm, Grab, Grip, Haft, Helve, Hilt, Hold, Knob, Knub, Lug, > MANAGE, Manipulate, Manubrium, Maul, Moniker, Name, Nib, Palp, Paw, Pommel, Process, Rounce, Shaft, Snath, Snead, Sneath, Sned, Staff, Staghorn, Stale, Steal(e), Steel, Steil, Stele, Stilt, Stock, Tiller, Title, To-name, Touch, Transact, Treat, Use, Whipstock, Wield, Withe

Handmaid(en) Iras, Manicurist, Valkyrie

Hand-out Alms, Charity, Dole, Gift, Release, Sample

Handshake Golden

Hand-signal Beck(on), Point, Wave

Handsome Adonis, Apollo, Bonny, Brave, Comely, Dashing, Dishy, Featuous, Gracious, Liberal

Handspring, **Handstand** Cartwheel, Diamodov

Hand-warmer Muff, Pome

Hand-washer Pilate

Handwriting *see* HAND

Handy(man) Accessible, Close, Convenient, Deft, Dext(e)rous, Digit, Factotum, Jack(-of-all-trades), Near, Nigh, Palmate, Palmist, Ready, Skilful, Spartan, Useful

Hang, **Hanger**, **Hanging(s)** Append, Arras, Aweigh, Chick, Chik, Coat, Dangle, Darn, Depend, Dewitt, Dossal, Dossel, Dosser, Drape, Droop, Execute, Frontal, Gobelin, Hinge, Hoove, Hove(r), Kakemono, Kilt, Lime, Lobed, Loll, Lop, Lynch, Mooch, Noose, Nub, Pend(ant), Sag, Scenery, Scrag, Set, Sit, Sling, Suspend, Suspercollate, Swing, Tapestry, Tapet, Tapis, Toran(a)

Hanger-on Bur, Lackey, Leech, Limpet, Liripoop, Parasite, Satellite, Sycophant, Toady

Hangman, **Hangmen** Bull, Calcraft, Dennis, Derrick, Gregory, Ketch, Marwood, Nubbing-cove, Pierrepoint

Hangnail Agnail

Hangover Canopy, Cornice, Crapulence, Drape, DT's, Head, Hot coppers, Katzenjammer, Mistletoe, Remnant, Tester

Hank Bobbin, Coil, Fake, Skein

Hanker(ing) Desire, Envy, Hunger, Itch, Long, Yearn, Yen

Hannibal Punic

Hansard Minutes

Haphazard Casual, Chance, Helter-skelter, Higgledy-piggledy, Hit and miss, Hitty-missy, Promiscuous, > RANDOM, Rough and tumble, Slapdash, Willy-nilly

Happen(ing), **Happen to** Afoot, Be, Befall, Befortune, Betide, Come, Event(uate), Fall-out, Materialise, > OCCUR, Pan, Pass, Prove, Subvene, Thing, Tide, Transpire, Worth

Happiness, **Happy** Apposite, Ave, Beatific, Beatitude, Blessed, Bliss, Bluebird, Bonny, Carefree, Cheery, Chuffed, Cock-a-hoop, Dwarf, Ecstatic, Elated, Eud(a)emony, Exhilarated, Felicity, Felix, Fool's paradise, Fortunate, Glad(some), Gleeful, Golden, Goshen, Gruntled, Halcyon, Half-cut, Hedonism, Jovial, Joy, Larry, Light-hearted, Merry, Opportune, Radiant, Rapture, Sandboy, Seal, Seel, Sele, Serene, Sunny, Tipsy, Trigger, Warrior

Hara-kiri Eventration, Seppuku, Suicide

Harangue Declaim, Diatribe, Earwigging, Lecture, Oration, Perorate, Philippic,

Sermon, Speech, Spruik, Tirade

Harass(ed) Afflict, Annoy, Badger, Bait, Beleaguer, Bother, Chivvy, Distract, Dun, Gall, Grill, Grind, Grounden, Hassle, Haze, Heckle, Hector, Hound, Irritate, Needle, Persecute, Pester, Plague, Press, Thwart, Trash, Vex

Harbinger Herald, Omen, Precursor, Usher

Harbour(ed) Alee, Anchorage, Basin, Brest, Cherish, Dock, Entertain, Foster, Herd, Hide, Hythe, Lodge, Manukau, Marina, Mulberry, Pearl, PLA, Poole, Port, Quay, Reset, Scapa Flow, > **SHELTER**, Watemata, Wellington

Hard(en), Hardness Abstruse, Adamant(ine), Adularia, Augean, Bony, Brindell, Brinell, Brittle, Bronze, Cake, Calcify, Callous, Caramel, Cast-iron, Chitin, Concrete, Cornute, Crusty, Dentin(e), Difficult, Dour, Draconian, Ebonite, Endure, Enure, Firm, Flint(y), Geal, Granite, Gruelling, H, Hellish, Herculean, HH, Horny, Indurate, Inure, Iron(y), Jasper, Knotty, Liparite, Lithoid, Metallic, Metally, Moh, Moh's scale, Nails, Obdurate, Obdure, Osseous, Ossify, Permafrost, Permanent, Petrify, Picrite, Raw, Rugged, Ruthless, Schist, Scleral, Set, Severe, Solid, Sore, Steel(y), Steep, Stereo, Stern, Stoic, Stony, Teak, Temper, Tough, Wooden

Hardback Case-bound

Hard-core Riprap, Scalpins

Hard-headed Stegochepalian

Harding Warden

Hardliner Hawk

Hardly Borderline, Ill, Just, Scarcely, Uneath(es), Unnethes

Hard-pressed Strait, Taxed

Hardship Affliction, Grief, Mill, Mishap, Penance, Privation, Rigour, Trial, Trouble

Hardware Gear, Ironmongery

Hardy Brave, Dour, Durable, Manful, Oliver, Ollie, Rugged, Spartan, Sturdy, Thomas

Hare Arctic, Baud(rons), Bawd, Belgian, Doe, Dolicholis, Down, Electric, Husk, Jack-rabbit, Jugged, Lam, Leporine, Malkin, Mara, March, Mawkin, Mountain, Ochotona, Pika, Puss, Scut, Snowshoe, Spring, Wat

Hare-brained Giddy, Madcap, Scatty

Harem Gynaeceum, Gynoecium, Seraglio, Serai(l), Zenana

Hark(en) Ear, Hear, List(en)

Harlequin Chequered, Columbine, Pantaloon

Harlot Blue gown, Drab, Hussy, Loon, Loose, Paramour, Plover, Pusle, Pussel, Quail, Rahab, Scrubber, Slut, Strumpet, Whore

Harm(ed), Harmful Aggrieve, Bane, Blight, Deleterious, Detriment, Endamage, Evil, Hurt, Inimical, Injury, Insidious, Maleficent, Malignant, Maltreat, Mischief, Nocuous, Noxious, Pernicious, Sinister, Spoil, Wroken, Wrong

Harmless Benign, Canny, Drudge, Informidable, Innocent, Innocuous, Innoxious, Inoffensive

Harmonica Harp

Harmonious, Harmonise, Harmonist, Harmony Agree(ment), Alan, Assort, Atone, Attune, Balanced, Blend, Chord, Close, Concent, Concentus, Concert, Concinnity, Concord, Congruous, Consonant, Consort, Coordinate, Correspondence, Counterpoint, Descant, Diapason, Diatessaron, Doo-wop, Euphony, Eur(h)ythmy, Faburden, Feng-shui, Go, Jibe, Match, Melody, Mesh, Musical, Rappite, Solidarity, Symmetry, Sympathy, Symphonious, Sync, Thorough-bass, Tone, Tune, Unanimity, Unison, Unity

Harmotome Cross-stone

Harness(maker) Breeching, Bridle, Cinch, Equipage, Frenum, Gear, Girth, Hitch, Inspan, Lorimer, Loriner, Pad-tree, Partnership, Swingletree, Tack(le), Throat-stop, Trace, Whippletree, Yoke

Harp(sichord) Aeolian, Clairschach, Clarsach, Clavier, Drone, Dwell, Irish, Lyre, Nebel, Trigon, Virginal, Welsh, Wind, Zither

Harpagon L'avare, Miser

Harpoon(er) Bart, Fis(h)gig, Fizgig, Grain, Iron, Lily iron, Peg, Spear, Specktioneer, Toggler, Tow-iron, Trident

Harpy Aello, Celeno, Eagle, Ocypete

Harridan Hag, Harpy, Shrew, Xantippe, Zantippe, Zentippe

Harrier Hen, Montagu's

Harriet Hetty, Martineau

Harrow Alas, Appal, Brake, Disc, Frighten, Herse, Pitch-pole, Plough, Rake, Rend, Shock

Harry Aggravate, Badger, Bother, Champion, Chase, Chivvy, Coppernose, Dragoon, Flash, Fret, Hal, Harass, Hassle, Hector, Herry, Houdini, Hound, Lauder, Lime, Maraud, Molest, Nag, Pester, Plague, Rag, Reave, Reive, Rieve, Rile, Tate, Tchick, Torment

> **Harry** *may indicate* an anagram

Harsh(ness) Abrasive, Acerbic, Austere, Barbaric, Brassy, Cacophonous, Cruel, Desolate, Discordant, Draconian, Extreme, Glary, Grating, Gravelly, Grim, Gruff, Guttural, Hard, Inclement, Raucle, Raucous, Raw, Rigour, Rude, Scabrid, Screechy, > SEVERE, Sharp, Spartan, Stark, Stern, Stoor, Stour, Stowre, Strict, Strident, Unkind

Hart Deer, Spade, Spay, Spay(a)d, Venison

Harte Bret

Hartebeest Bubal, Kaama, Kongoni

Harum-scarum Bayard, Chaotic, Madcap, Rantipole

Harvest(er), Harvest home Combine, Crop, Cull, Fruit, > GATHER, Hairst, Hawkey, Hay(sel), Hockey, Horkey, In(ning), Ingather, Kirn, Lease, Nutting, Pick, Produce, Rabi, Random, Reap, Shock, Spatlese, Tattie-howking, Thresh, Vendage, Vendange

Has Habet, Hath, Owns, 's

Has-been Effete, Ex, Outmoded

Hash(ish) Bungle, Charas, Discuss, Garble, Garboil, Hachis, Lobscouse, Mince, Pi(e), Ragout

> **Hashed** *may indicate* an anagram

Hasn't Hant, Nas

Hassle Aggro, Bother

Hassock Kneeler, Pouf(fe), Stool, Tuffet

Haste(n), Hastening, Hastily, Hasty Cursory, Despatch, Expedite, Express, Festinately, Fly, Hare, Headlong, Hie, Hotfoot, > HURRY, Hurry-scurry, Impetuous, Precipitant, Race, Ramstam, Rash, Rush, Scuttle, Speed, Spur, Stringendo, Subitaneous, Sudden, Tear, Tilt, Urge

Hastings Banda, Bustles, Senlac, Warren

Hat Akuba, Ascot, Astrakhan, Balibuntal, Balmoral, Basher, Beanie, Beany, Bearskin, Beaver, Beret, Billycock, Biretta, Boater, Bollinger, Bonnet, Bowler, Boxer, Brass, Breton, Broad-brim, Busby, Cap, Capotain, Cartwheel, Castor, Chapeau, Cheese-cutter, Chimneypot, Christie, Christy, Claque, Cloche, Cocked, Cockle-hat, Coolie, Cossack, Cowboy, Crusher, Curch, Deerstalker, Derby, Dolly Varden, Dunstable, Envoy, Fedora, Fez, Flat-cap, Fore-and-after, Gaucho, Gibus, Gimme, Glengarry, Hard, Hattock, Headdress, Head-rig,

Hennin, Homburg, Kamelaukion, Kepi, Lamington, Leghorn, Lid, Lum, Matador, Mitre, Mob-cap, Mountie's, Mushroom, Nab, Opera, Pagri, Panama, Petasus, Picture, Pilion, Pill-box, Pilleus, Pilos, Pith, Planter's, Plateau, Plug, Poke(-bonnet), Pork-pie, Potae, Profile, Puggaree, Puritan, Ramil(l)ies, Red, Runcible, Safari, Sailor, Scarlet, Shako, Shovel, Silk, Skimmer, Skull-cap, Slouch, Snap-brim, Snood, Sola(-helmet), Solah, Sola-topi, Sombrero, Songkok, Souwester, Steeple-crown, Stetson®, Stovepipe, Straw, Sugarloaf, Sunbonnet, Sundown, Sunhat, Tam(o'shanter), Tarboosh, Tarb(o)ush, Tarpaulin, Ten-gallon, Terai, Thrummed, Tile, Tin, Tit(fer), Toorie, Top(per), Topee, Topi, Toque, Tricorn(e), Trilby, Turban, Tyrolean, Ugly, Wide-awake, Witch's

Hat-band Weeper

Hatch(ment), **Hatching** Achievement, Altricial, Booby, Breed, Brood, Cleck, Clutch, Companion, Concoct, Cover, Devise, Eclosion, Emerge, Escape, Incubate, Set, Trap-door

Hatchet(-shaped) Axe, Bill, Chopper, Cleaver, Dolabriform, Tomahawk

▷ **Hatching** *may indicate* an anagram

Hatchway (surround) Companionway, Fiddley, Guichet, Porthole, Scuttle, Service

Hate(ful), **Hatred** Abhor, Abominable, Abominate, Anims, Aversion, Bugbear, Detest, Enmity, Haterent, Loathe, Misogyny, Odium, Phobia, Racism, Resent, Spite, Ug(h), Vitriol

Hat-plant S(h)ola

Hatter Mad

Hatty Etta

Haughty Aloof, Aristocratic, Arrogant, Bashaw, Cavalier, Disdainful, Fastuous, High, Hogen-mogen, Hoity-toity, Hye, Imperious, Lofty, Orgillous, Orgulous, Paughty, > PROUD, Scornful, Sdeignful, Sniffy, Toplofty, Upstage

Haul(age), **Haulier** Bag, Bouse, Bowse, Brail, Carry, Cart, Catch, Drag, Heave, Hove, Kedge, Loot, Plunder, Pull, Rug, Sally, Scoop, Snig, TIR, Touse, Touze, Tow(se), Towze, Transporter, Trice, Winch, Yank

Haunch Hance, Hip, Huckle, Hunkers, Quarter

Haunt(s) Catchy, Den, Dive, Frequent, Ghost, Hang-out, Honky-tonk, Houf(f), Howf(f), Infest, Obsess, Purlieu, Resort, Spot, Spright

Hauteur Bashawism, Height, Morgue, Vanity

Have, **Having** Bear, Ha(e), Han, Hoax, Hold, Of, > OWN, Possess, Sell

Haven Asylum, Harbour, Hithe, Hythe, Oasis, Port, Refuge, Refugium, Retreat, Shelter, Tax

Haver(s) Blether, Clanjamfray, Dither, Gibber, Nigel

▸ **Haversack** *see* RUCKSACK

Havoc Desolation, Devastation, Hell, Ravage, Waste

▷ **Havoc** *may indicate* an anagram

Haw Hip, Sloe

Hawaiian Kanaka

Hawk(er), **Hawkish** Accipitrine, Auceps, Badger, Bastard, Buzzard, Cadger, Camelot, Caracara, Cast, Cheapjack, Cooper's, Cry, Duck, Eagle, Elanet, Eyas, Falcon, Fish, Gerfalcon, Goshawk, Haggard, Hardliner, Harrier, Harrumph, Hobby, Honey-buzzard, Keelie, Kestrel, Kite, Lammergeier, Lanner(et), Marsh, Merlin, Molla(h), Monger, Moolah, Mosquito, Mullah, Musket, Nyas, Osprey, Ossifrage, Passage, Pearlie, Pearly, Peddle, Pedlar, Peregrine, Pigeon, Ringtail, Sacre(t), Sell, Slab, Slanger, Soar(e), Sorage, Sore(-eagle), Sparrow, Spiv, Staniel, Sutler, Tallyman, Tarsal, Tarsel(l), Tassel, Tercel(et), Tiersel, Trant(er), Trucker,

Warlike
Hawkeye IA, Iowa
Hawk-keeper Austringer, Ostreger
Hawser Line, Rope
Hawthorn Albespine, Albespyne, May(flower), Quickset
Hay(cock), **Hey** Antic, Cock, Contra-dance, Fodder, Goaf, Hi, Kemple, Math, Mow, Pleach, Pook, Salt, Stack, Straw, Windrow
Hayfever Pollenosis
Haymaker Blow, Slog
Hayseed Chaw-bacon, Hodge, Joskin, Rustic
Hazard(ous) Breakneck, Bunker, Chance, Danger, Dare, Die, Dye, Game, Gremlin, Guess, Imperil, In-off, Jeopardy, Losing, Main, Moral, Nice, Occupational, Peril, Pitfall, Play, Pothole, Queasy, > RISK, Stake, Trap, Venture, Vigia, Wage, Winning
Haze, **Hazy** Blear, Cloud, Filmy, Fog, > MIST, Mock, Muzzy, Nebulous, Smaze, Smog, Tease
Haze *may indicate* an anagram
Hazel(wort) Amenta, Asarabacca, Catkin, Cob, Corylus, Filbert
HC Encomia, Encomium
He, **HE** A, Helium, Tag, Tig, > TNT, Tom
Head(s), **Heading**, **Headman**, **Head shaped**, **Heady** Aim, Apex, Ard-ri(gh), Beachy, Bean, Behead, Bill, Block, Bonce, Boss, Brain, Brainpan, Bregma, Brow, But(t), Caboceer, Cape, Capitani, Capitate, Capitulum, Capo, Captain, Caption, Caput, Caudillo, Cephalic, Chaton, Chief, Coarb, Coconut, Coma, Commander, Conk, Cop, Coppin, Costard, Cranium, Crest, Crisis, Crown, Crumpet, Cylinder, Director, Dome, Dummy, Each, Ear, Exarch, Figure, Flamborough, Foam, Foreland, Froth, General, Glomerate, Grand Mufti, Hegumen(os), Herm(a), Hoe, Hogh, Jowl, Karmapa, Knob, Knowledge-box, Lead(er), Lid, Lizard, Loaf, Loave, Loo, Lore, Malik, Manager, Mayor, Maz(z)ard, Melik, Mocuddum, Mogul, Mokaddam, Mr Big, Mull, Muqaddam, Nab, Nana, Napper, Nappy, Ness, Nob, Noddle, Noggin, Noll, Noup, Nowl, Nut, Obverse, Occiput, Onion, Panicle, Parietal, Pash, Pate, Pater(familias), Patriarch, Pick-up, Point, Poll, Pow, Prefect, President, Pressure, Principal, Promontory, Provost, Ras, Read-write, Ream, Rubric, Sarpanch, Scalp, Scaup, Scaw, Scholarch, Scolex, Sconce, Short, Sinciput, Skaw, Skull, Sound, Source, Spume, Squeers, Starosta, Superior, Taipan, Tanadar, Tete, Thanadar, Throne, Tight, Title, Toilet, Top, Topic, Tsantsa, Twopenny, Upperworks, Vaivode, Velocity, Voivode, Yorick, Zupan
Head *may indicate* the first letter of a word
Headache Cephalalgia, Encephalalgia, Hangover, Megrim, Migraine, Neuralgia, Red out, Scotodinia, Splitter
Headband Fillet, Garland, Infula, Sphendone
Headdress, **Head cover** Ampyx, Balaclava, Bandeau, Bas(i)net, Bonnet, Burnous(e), Busby, Calotte, Caul, Chaplet, Circlet, Comb, Cor(o)net, Cowl, Coxcomb, Crownet, Curch, Doek, Dopatta, Dupatta, Fascinator, Fontange, Fool's cap, Frontlet, Hat(tock), Helm(et), Juliet cap, Kaffiyeh, Kell, Kerchief, Kuffiyeh, Kufiah, Kufiya(h), Mantilla, Mitre, Mobcap, Modius, Mortarboard, Nubia, Periwig, Pill-box, Plug-hat, Porrenger, Porringer, Romal, Sakkos, Ship-tire, Silly-how, Skullcap, Sphendome, Stephane, Taj, Tarbush, Tiara, Tower, Tulban, Turban, War bonnet, Wig, Wimple
Header Bonder, Dive, Fall, Rowlock
Headhunter Naga

Headland Beachy Head, Bill, Cape, Cape Horn, Dungeness, Finisterre, Head-rig, Hoe, Hogh, Morro, Naze, Ness, Noup, Promontory, Ras, Ross, St Vincent, Scaw, Skaw

Headless Acephalous

Headlight Beam, Dip, Halo

Headline Banner, Caption, Drophead, Frown, Kicker, Ribbon, Scare-head, Screamer, Streamer, Title

Headlock Chancery

Headlong Breakneck, Pell-mell, Precipitate, Ramstam, Reckless, Steep, Sudden, Tantivy, Tearaway

▶ **Headman** *see* HEAD

Headmaster Principal, Squeers

Headphone(s) Cans, Earpiece, Walkman®

Headquarters Base, Command, Depot, Guildhall, Pentagon, SHAEF, SHAPE, Station

▷ **Heads** *may indicate* a lavatory

Headstrong Obstinate, Rash, Stubborn, Unruly, Wayward, Wilful

Head-to-tail Tête-bêche

Headway Advancement, Headroom, Progress

Head-word Lemma

Heal(ing) Aesculapian, Balsam, Chiropractic, Cicatrise, Cleanse, Cure, Esculapian, G(u)arish, Hele, Hippocratise, Intention, Knit, Mend, Mental, New Thought, Olosis, Osteopathy, Restore, Sain, Salve, Sanitary, Spiritual, Therapeutic, Vulnerary

Healer Asa, Doctor, Homeopath, Naturopath, Osteopath, Sangoma, Shaman, Time

Health(y) Bouncing, Bracing, Chin-chin, Doer, Fit, Flourishing, Gesundheit, Hail, Hale, Hartie-hale, Heart, Holism, Kia-ora, L'chaim, Lustique, Lusty, Medicaid, Medicare, Pink, Prosit, Robust, Rosy, Salubrious, Sane, Slainte, Sound, Toast, Tope, Valetudinarian, Vigour, Well, WHO, Wholesome

Heap(ed) Acervate, Agglomerate, Amass, Bing, Boneshaker, Bulk, Car, Clamp, Coacervate, Cock, Congeries, Cumulus, Drift, Hog, Jalopy, Lot, Pile, Raff, Raft, Rick(le), Ruck, Scrap, Slag, Stash, Tass, Toorie, Up-piled

Hear(ing) Acoustic, Attend, Audience, Audile, Avizandum, Captain's mast, Catch, Clairaudience, Dirdum, Ear, Harken, Learn, List(en), Oyer, Oyez, Panel, Paracusis, Try

▷ **Hear(say)** *may indicate* a word sounding like one given

Hearsay Account, Gossip, Report, Rumour, Surmise

Hearse Bier, Catafalco, Catafalque, Shillibeer

Heart(en), Heartily, Hearty, Heart-shaped AB, Agood, Auricle, Backslapping, Beater, Bleeding, Bluff, Bosom, Bradycardia, Cant, Cardiac, Centre, Cheer, Cockles, Columella, Cordate, Cordial, Core, Courage, Crossed, Daddock, Embolden, Essence, Gist, H, Hale, Herz, Inmost, Jarta, Kernel, Lepid, Lonely, Memoriter, Mesial, Mid(st), Middle, Nub, Nucleus, Obcordate, Purple, Robust, Root, Sacred, Sailor, Seafarer, Seaman, Sinoatrial, Staunch, Tachycardia, Tar, Ticker, Yarta, Yarto

Heart-break Crève-coeur, Grief, Sorrow

Heartburn Brash, Cardialgia, Pyrosis

Heartfelt Deep, Genuine, Real, Sincere

Hearth Cupel, Fireside, Home, Ingle, Killogie

Heartless Callous, Cored, Cruel, Three-suited

Heart's ease Pansy

Heart trouble Bradycardia, Fallot's tetralogy, Fibrillation, Murmur, Tachycardia

Heat(ed), **Heater**, **Heating** Anneal, Ardour, Arousal, Atomic, Barrage, Beath, Blood, Brazier, Calcine, Califont, Caloric, Calorifier, Central, Chafe, Convector, Dead, Decay, Dielectric, Dudgeon, Eccaleobion, Element, Eliminator, Endothermic, Enthalpy, Estrus, Etna, Excite, Exothermic, Fan, Ferment, Fever, Fire, Fluster, Fug, Furnace, Het, Hibachi, Hyperthermia, Hypocaust, Immersion, Incalescence, Induction, J, Kindle, Latent, Liquate, Lust, Moxibustion, Normalise, Oestrus, Panel, Prelim, Prickly, Q, Radiant, Radiator, Rankine, Recalescence, Red, Render, Repechage, Rut, Salt, Scald, Sinter, Sizzle, Solar, Space, Specific, Spice, Stew, Storage, Stove, Swelter, Teend, Temperature, Tind, Tine, Torrefy, Total, Tynd(e), Underfloor, Warming-pan, Warmth, White

Heath(land) Bearberry, Bent, Briar, Brier, Egdon, Epacrid, Erica, Geest, Lande, Manoao, Manzanita, Moor, Muir, Stead, Ted

Heathen(s) Ethnic, Gentile, Infidel, Litholatrous, Nations, Pagan, Pa(i)nim, Paynim, Philistine, Primitive, Profane, Proselyte of the gate

Heather Bell, Broom, Calluna, Epacrid, Erica, Ling, Rhodora, Sprig

Heating *may indicate* an anagram

Heave(d) Cast, Fling, Frost, Heeze, Hoist, Hump, Hurl, Popple, Retch, Shy, Sigh, Vomit

Heave *may indicate* 'discard'

Heaven(s), **Heavenly** Air, Aloft, Ama, Ambrosial, Asgard, Bliss, Celestial, Celia, Divine, Ecstasy, Elysian, Elysium, Empyrean, Ethereal, Fiddler's Green, Firmament, Hereafter, Himmel, Holy, Land o' the Leaf, Leal, Lift, Mackerel, Olympus, Paradise, Pole, Rapture, Seventh, Shangri-la, Sion, Sky, Supernal, Svarga, Swarga, Swerga, Tur-na-n'og, Uranian, Welkin, Zion

Heavy(weight), **Heavily**, **Heaviness** Ali, Clumpy, Dutch, Elephantine, Embonpoint, Endomorph, Grave, Hefty, Last, Leaden, Lumpish, Onerous, Osmium, Pesante, Ponderous, Sad, Scelerate, Stout, Top, Upsee, Ups(e)y, Weighty, Wicked

Hebe Barmaid

Hebrew Aramaic, Eli, Heb, Jesse, Karaism, Levi, Mishnayoth, Modern, Yid

Hebridean Harris

Heckle Badger, Gibe, Harass, Hatchel, Needle, Spruik

Hectic Ding-dong, Feverish, Frenetic

Hector Badger, Bluster, Browbeat, Bully, > **HARASS**, Nag

Hedge, **Hedging** Box, Bullfinch, Enclosure, Equivocate, Haw, Hay, Lay off, Meuse, Mews, Muse, Pleach, Privet, Quickset, Raddle, Sepiment, Shield, Stonewall, Texas, Thicket, Waffle

Hedgehog Gymnure, Hérisson, Tenrec, Tiggywinkle, Urchin

Hedge-parson Bucklebeggar, Patercove

Hedge-sparrow Accentor

Hedonist Cyreniac, Epicurean, Playboy, Sybarite

Heed(ed), **Heedful** Attend, Listen, > **MIND**, Notice, Observe, Rear, Reck, Regard(ant), Reke, Respect, Rought, Tent

Heedless Careless, Incautious, Rash, Scapegrace, Scatterbrain

Heel Achilles, Cad, Calcaneum, Cant, Careen, Cuban, Dogbolt, Foot, French, Kitten, List, Louse, Rogue, Seel, Spike, Stacked, Stiletto, Tilt, Wedge

Heel-tap Snuff

Hefty Brawny, Heavy, Solid, Weighty

Heifer Io, Quey, Stirk

Height(en), **Heights** Abraham, Altitude, Cairngorm, Ceiling, Dimension,

Elevation, Embroider, Eminence, Enhance, Golan, H, Hill, Hypsometry, Level, Might, Peak, Procerity, Spot, Stature, Stud, Sum, > **SUMMIT**, Tor, X

Heinous Abominable, Atrocious, Flagrant

Heir Alienee, Claimant, Coparcener, Dauphin, Devisee, Distributee, Eigne, H(a)eres, Institute, Intitule, Legatee, Parcener, Scion, Sprig, Tanist

Heirless Escheat, Intestate

Held Captive, Hostage, Sostenuto

▷ **Held by** *may indicate* a hidden word

Helen Elaine, Nell(y)

Helicopter, Heliport Airstop, Chopper, Egg-beater, Gunship, Hover, Iroquois, Medevac, Rotodyne, Sea Cobra, Sea King, Sea Knight, Sea Sprite, Sea Stallion, Sikorsky, Sky-hook, Whirlybird

Helios Hyperion

Heliotrope Cherry-pie

Helium He

Helix Alpha, Double

Hell(ish) Abaddon, Ades, Agony, Amenthes, Annw(yf)n, Avernus, Ayss, Below, Chthonic, Dis, Erebus, Furnace, Gehenna, Hades, Heck, Inferno, Jahannam, Lower regions, Malebolge, Naraka, Orcus, Pandemonium, Perditious, Pit, Ruin, Sheol, Stygian, Tartar(ean), Tartarus, Tophet, Torment

Hellbender Menopome, Mud-puppy

Hellebore Itchweed, Setterwort

Hellespont Dardanelles

Hello, Hallo, Hullo Aloha, Chin-chin, Ciao, Dumela, Golden, Hi, Ho(a), Howdy, Howzit, Yoo-hoo

Helm(sman) Cox, Pilot, Steer, Tiller, Timon(eer)

Helmet Armet, Balaclava, Basinet, Beaver, Burganet, Burgonet, Cask, Casque, Comb, Crash, Galea, Heaume, Knapscal, Knapscull, Knapskull, Montero, Mor(r)ion, Nasal, Pickelhaube, Pith, Plumed, Pot, Pressure, Salade, Sal(l)et, Shako, Skid-lid, Smoke, Topee, Topi

Helot Esne, Slave

Help(er), Helping, Helpful Abet, Accomplice, Adjuvant, Advantage, Aid(ance), Aidant, Aide, Alleviate, Ally, Asset, > **ASSIST**, Avail, Back, Beet-master, Beet-mister, Befriend, Benefit, Bestead, Boon, Brownie, Char(woman), Coadjutor, Complice, Conducive, Daily, Dollop, Dose, Forward, Further(some), Go, Hand, Henchman, Hint, Home, Instrumental, Leg-up, Life-saver, Maid, Mayday, Monitor, Obliging, Order, Patronage, Ration, Recourse, Relieve, Servant, Serve, Slice, SOS, Stead, Sted, Subserve, Subvention, Succour, Taste, Therapeutic, Use

Helpless(ness) Adynamia, Anomie, Feeble, Impotent, Paralytic, Useless

Helpmate Consort

Hem Border, Fringe, Hoop, List

He-man Adonis, Hunk, Jock, Macho

Hemisphere, Hemispherical Dominant, Magdeburg, Rose-cut, Western

Hemlock Conia, Cowbane, Insane root, Tsuga

Hemp Abaca, Bhang, Boneset, Bowstring, Carl(ot), Choke-weed, Codilla, Dagga, Fimble, Ganja, Hards, Henequen, Hiniquin, Indian, K(a)if, Kef, Love-drug, Manil(l)a, Moorva, Murva, Neckweed, Pita, Sida, Sunn, Tat, Tow

Hen Ancona, Andalusian, Australorp, Biddy, Buff Orpington, Chock, Cochin, Dorking, Eirack, Fowl, Grig, Houdan, Langshan, Layer, Leghorn, Maori, Marsh, Mud, Orpington, Partlet, Pertelote, Plymouth Rock, Poulard, Pullet, Ree(ve), Rhode Island Red, Sitter, Sultan, Tappit, Welsummer, Wyandotte

Hence Apage, Avaunt, Ergo, Go, Hinc, So, Therefore, Thus
Henchman Attendant, Follower, Myrmidon, Satellite
Hen-house Battery, Eggery
Henna Camphire
Hennery Run
Hen-pecked Spineless, Woman-tired
Henry Eighth, H, Hal, Hank, Hooray, Hy, James, Navigator, O
Hep Bacca, Berry, Hip
Hepatic Scale-moss
Hepatitis Favism, Jaundice
Herald(ic), Heraldry Abatement, Argent, Armory, Azure, Bagwyn, Bars,
  Baton sinister, Bend, Bendwise, Blazonry, Bloody Hand, Blue Mantle,
  Bordure, Caboched, Calygreyhound, Chevron, Chief, Cicerone, Cinquefoil,
  Clarenc(i)eux, Compone, Compony, Couchant, Coue, Counter-passant, Couped,
  Coward, Crest, Crier, Degraded, Difference, Displayed, Dormant, Endorse,
  Enfield, Erased, Fecial, Fess(e), Fetial, File, Flory, Forerunner, Gardant, Garter,
  Gironny, Golp(e), Gules, Gyronny, Hauriant, Hermes, Issuant, King-of-arms,
  Lionel, Lodged, Lyon, Manchet, Martlet, Messenger, Minocaine, Morne,
  Mullet, Naiant, Naissant, Nascent, Nombril, Norroy, Nowed, Nowy, Opinicus,
  Or, Ordinary, Pale, Pallet, Paly, Passant, Pile, Portcullis, Portend, Potant,
  Precursor, Proclaim, Purpure, Pursuivant, Quartering, Rampant, Red Hand,
  Regardant, Rouge Croix, Rouge Dragon, Roundel, Roundle, Sable, Salient,
  Scarp, Sea lion, Segreant, Sejant, Statant, Stentor, Subordinary, Trangle,
  Tressure, Trick, Trippant, Trundle, Umbrated, Urinant, Usher, Vaunt-courier,
  Verdoy, Vert, Vol(ant), Vorant, Wivern, Wyvern, Yale
Herb(s) Aconite, Ajowan, Allspice, Angelica, Anise, Aristolochia, Arugula,
  Avens, Basil, Bay, Bennet, Bergamot, Borage, Capers, Cardamom, Centaury,
  Chamomile, Chervil, C(h)ive, Cilanto, Comfrey, Coriander, Costmary,
  Cum(m)in, Dill, Dittany, Echinacea, Eruca, Exacum, Eyebright, Felicia, Fennel,
  Fenugreek, Ferula, Feverfew, Fireweed, Fitch, Fluellin, Forb, Garlic, Garnish,
  Gentian, Germander, Good-King-Henry, Gunnera, Haworthia, Hyssop, Inula,
  Kalanchoe, Knapweed, Lamb's ears, Laserpicium, Laserwort, Lewisia, Lovage,
  Madder, Madwort, Mandrake, Marjoram, Maror, Medic, Mint, Moly, Mustard,
  Oca, Oleraceous, Oregano, Origan(e), Origanum, Ornithogalum, Orval,
  Paprika, Parakeelya, Parakelia, Parsley, Paterson's curse, Pia, Pipsissewa,
  Plantain, Purpie, Purslane, Pussytoes, Rest-harrow, Rhizocarp, Rodgersia,
  Rosemary, Rue, Saffron, Sage, Salad, Saloop, Salsify, Savory, Senna, Sesame,
  Soapwort, Sorrel, Southernwood, Spearmint, Staragen, Sweet cicely, Tacca,
  Tansy, Tarragon, Thyme, Tormentil, Turmeric, Typha, Valerian, Vervain,
  Vetch, Weed, Willow, Wormwood, Wort, Yarrow, Yerba
Herbert Alan, AP(H), Lom, Spencer
Herbicide Agent Orange, Atrazine, Defoliant, Picloram
Herbivore Iguanodon, Sauropod
Hercules Alcides, Huge, Rustam, Rustem
Herd(er), Herdsman Band, Corral, Drive, Drover, Flock, Gang, Marshal, Mob,
  Pod, Raggle-taggle, Round-up, Shepherd, Tinchel, Vaquero
Here Adsum, Hi, Hic, Hither, Local, Now, Present
Hereditary, Heredity Ancestry, Blood, Breeding, Codon, Dynastic, Eugenics,
  Exon, Genetics, Id(ant), Idioplasm, Mendelism
Herein *may indicate* a hidden word
Here is laid HS
Heresiarch Nestor

Heresy, Heretic(al) Agnoitae, Albi, Albigensian, Apollinaris, Apostasy, Arian, Bab, Bogomil, Bugger, Cathar, Cerinthus, Docete, Donatist, Dulcinist, Eudoxian, Giaour, Heresearch, Heterodoxy, Lollard, Manichaean, Montanism, Nestorian, Nonconformist, Origen, Patarin(e), Pelagius, Phrygian, Racovian, Rebel, Unitarian, Zendik

Heritage Birthright, Due, Ottilie, Patrimony

Hermaphrodite Androgynous, Gynandromorph, Monochinous, Monoecious

Hermes (rod) Caduceus, Mercury

Hermetic Alchemist, Sealed

Hermit(age) Anchoret, Anchorite, Ascetic, Ashram(a), Augustinian, Austin, Cell, Cloister, Crab, Eremite, Grandmontine, Marabout, Monk, Museum, Nitrian, Peter, Recluse, Retreat, Robber-crab, Sannyasi, Soldier-crab, Solitary, Troglodyte

Hernia Bubonocele, Cystocoele, Diverticulum, Enterocele, Hiatus, Inguinal, Rupture

Hero(ic) Achilles, Agamemnon, Aitu, Ajax, Alcides, Amadis, Bader, Bellerophon, Beowulf, Brave, Bunyan, Champ(ion), Cid, Couplet, Crockett, Cuchulain, Cuchullain, Cyrano, Dambuster, Demigod, Drake, Epic, Eponym, Eric, Everyman, Faust, Fingal, Finn, Finn MacCool, Folk, Garibaldi, Glooscap, Gluscap, Gluskap, God, Goody, Great, Hector, Heracles, Hercules, Hiawatha, Howleglass, Hudibrastic, Icon, Ideal, Idol, Ivanhoe, Jason, Kaleva, Kami, Leonidas, Lion, Lochinvar, Lothair, Marmion, Meleager, Nestor, Noble, Oliver, Onegin, Orion, Owl(e)glass, Ow(l)spiegle, Paladin, Parsifal, Pericles, Perseus, Philoctetes, Priestess, Principal, Rambo, Raven, Resolute, Revere, Rinaldo, Roderego, Roderick, Roland, Rustem, Rustum, Saladin, Sheik, Siegfried, Sigurd, Superman, Tam o'Shanter, Tancred, Tarzan, Tell, Theseus, Tragic, Triptolemus, Tristan, Trist(r)am, Ulysses, Valiant, Vercingetorix, Virago, Volsung, White knight, Zorro

Herod Agrippa, Antipas

Heroin Dogfood, Doojie, Dynamite, Gumball, H, Harry, Henry, Horse, Jack, Junk Scag, Shit, Skag, Smack, Snow, Snowball, Speedball, Sugar

Heroine Andromeda, Ariadne, Candida, Darling, Hedda, Imogen, Isolde, Juliet, Leda, Leonora, Manon, Mimi, Nana, Norma, Pamela, Star, Tess, Una

Heron(s) Ardea, Bird, Bittern, Butter-bump, Egret, Green, Handsaw, Kotuko, Screamer, Sedge, Siege, Squacco

Herpes Cold sore, Dartre, Shingles, Shiver

Herring Bismarck, Bloater, Brisling, Brit, Buckling, Caller, Cisco, Clupea, Digby chick(en), Gaspereau, Kipper, Lake, Ma(a)tjes, Maise, Maize, Mattie, Maze, Mease, Menhaden, Norfolk capon, Ox eye, Rabbitfish, Red, Rollmop, Sea-stick Shotten, Sild, Silt, Sparling, Teleost, White

Herringbone Sloping

Hesitant, Hesitate, Hesitation Balance, Boggle, Cunctation, Delay, Demur, Dicker, Dither, Doubtful, Dubitate, Er, Falter, Halting, Haver, Haw, Irresolute, Mammer, > PAUSE, Qualm, Scruple, Shillyshally, Shrink, Stagger, Stammer, Swither, Tarrow, Teeter, Tentative, Um, Ur, Vacillate, Wait, Waver

Hesperus Vesper

Hessian Burlap, Hireling

Heterodoxy Heresy

Heterogeneous Diverse, Motley, Piebald

Heterosexual Straight

Hew Ax, Chop, Cut, Hack, Sever

Hex Bewitch, Jinx, Voodoo

Hexameter Dolichurus
Hey *see* HAY
Heyday Prime, Summer
Hi Cooee, Hello, Howdie
Hiatus Caesura, Entr'acte, Gap, Hernia, Interact, Interregnum, Interval, Lacuna, Lull
Hibernate, **Hibernating** Estivate, Hole up, Latitant, Sleep, Winter
Hibernian Irish
Hibiscus Okra, Roselle, Rozelle
Hiccup Glitch, Singultus, Snag, Spasm, Yex
Hick Jake, Oaf, Podunk, Rube, Yokel
Hickory Black, Jackson, Mockernut, Pecan, Scaly-bark, Shagbark
Hidden Buried, Cabalistic, Covert, De(a)rn, Doggo, Hooded, Latent, Obscure, Occult, Pentimento, Recondite, Screened, Secret, Shuttered, Sly, Ulterior, Unseen, Veiled, Wrapped
Hidden *may indicate* a concealed word
Hide, **Hiding (place)** Abscond, Befog, Bield(y), Box-calf, Burrow, Cache, Camouflage, Ceroon, Coat, > CONCEAL, Cootch, Cordwain, Couch, Cour, Crop, Curtain, Cwtch, Deerskin, Doggo, Earth, Eclipse, Encave, Ensconce, Enshroud, Envelop, Epidermis, Fell, Flaught, Flay, Gloss over, Harbour, Heal, Heel, Hele, Hell, Hole-up, Incave, Inter, Kip, Kipskin, Lair, Leather, Mai-mai, Mask, Mobble, Nebris, > OBSCURE, Parfleche, Pell, Pelt, Plank, Plant, Priest's hole, Robe, Saffian, Screen, Secrete, Shadow, Shellac(k), Shroud, Skin, Spetch, Stash, Strap-oil, Tappice, Thong, Thrashing, Trove, Veil, Wallop, Whang, Wrap
Hideous(ness) Deform(ed), Enormity, Gash, Grotesque, Horrible, Monstrous, Odious, Ugly, Ugsome
Hierarchic, **Hierarchy** Byzantine, Elite, Theocracy
Hieroglyph Cipher, Pictogram
Higgledy-piggledy Mixtie-maxtie
High(er), **Highly**, **Highness** Alt(a), Altesse, Altissimo, Apogee, Atop, Brent, Climax, Doped, Drugged, E-la, Elation, Elevated, Eminent, Exalted, Excelsior, Frequency, Gamy, Haut(e), Intoxicated, Lofty, Maggotty, Mind-blowing, Orthian, Prime, Rancid, Ripe, School, Senior, Sent, Shrill, So, Steep, Stenchy, Stoned, String-out, Strong, Superior, Swollen, Tall, Tension, Tipsy, Top-lofty, Topmost, Treble, Up(per), Very, Wired
High *may indicate* an anagram
High and mighty Haughty, Hogen-mogen
Highball Drink, Lob, Loft
Highbrow Brain, Egghead, Intelligentsia, Long-hair
High-class Best, Superior, U
High-crowned Copataine
Highest Best, Climax, Mostwhat, Ne plus ultra, Progressive, Supreme
Highest note E-la
High-flown Bombastic, Euphuism
Highland(er), **Highlands** Blue-bonnet, Blue-cap, Cameron, Cat(h)eran, Down, Duniwassal, Dun(n)iewassal, Gael, Karoo, Kiltie, Masai, Nainsel(l), Plaid(man), Redshank, Riff, Scot, Seaforth, Shire, Teuchter
Highlight Feature, Focus, Heighten, Stress
High-pitched *see* HIGH
High-spirited Extravert, Extrovert
High tension HT
Highway Alaska, Alcan, Autobahn, Autopista, Autostrada, Divided, Flyover,

Freeway, Interstate, Motorway, Overpass, Pass, Queen's, Road, Rode, Tarseal, Thoroughfare, Tightrope

Highwayman, **Highway robber(y)** Bandit, Bandolero, Duval, Footpad, Fraternity, Gilderoy, Jack Sheppard, Land-pirate, Land-rat, Latrocinium, MacHeath, Motorist, Rank-rider, Road-agent, Scamp, Skyjacker, Toby, Tobyman, Turpin, Twitcher, Wheel

Hijack(er) Abduct, Pirate

Hike(r) Backpack, Bushbash, Bushwalk, Raise, Rambler, Ramp, Rise, Traipse, Tramp, Trape(s), Upraise

Hilarious, **Hilarity** Hysterical, Jollity, Mirth, Riot

Hilary Term

Hill(ock), **Hills**, **Hillside** Arafar, Areopagus, Aventine, Barrow, Beacon, Ben, Bent, Berg, Beverly, Black, Bluff, Bombay, Brae, Breed's, Broken, Bunker, Butte, Caelian, Calvan, Capitol(ine), Cheviots, Chiltern, Chin, Cleve, Cone, Coteau, Crag-and-tail, Crest, Djebel, Drumlin, Dun(e), Dunsinane, Eminence, Esquiline, Fell, Flodden, Gebel, Golan Heights, Golgotha, Gradient, Grampians, Hammock, Height, Helvellyn, Highgate, Holt, Horst, How, Hummock, Incline, Inselberg, Janiculum, Jebel, Kip(p), Knap, Knoll, Knot, Kop(je), Koppie, Lammermuir, Lavender, Law, Loma, Low, Ludgate, Mamelon, Man, Matopo, Mendip, Merrick, Mesa, Monadnock, Monte Cassino, Monticule, Morro, Mound, Mount Lofty Ranges, Nab, Naga, Nanatak, Nilgiri(s), North Downs, Otway Ranges, Palatine, Pennines, Pike, Pingo, Pnyx, Quantocks, Quirinal, Rand, Range, Saddleback, Savoy, Scaur, Seven, Silbury, Sion, Stoss, Tara, Tel(l), Toft, Toot, Tump, Tweedsmuir, Valdai, Viminal, Wolds, Wrekin, Zion

Hillbilly Yap

Hill-dweller Ant

Hillman Areopagite, Nepalese

Hilltop Crest, Knoll, Nab

Hilt Basket, Coquille, Haft, Handle, Hasp, Shaft

Him(self) He, Ipse, Un

Himalaya(n) Nepali, Panda, Sherpa, Tibetan

Hind(most) Back, Deer, Lag, Rear

Hinder, **Hindrance** Back, Bar, Block, Check, Counteract, Cumber, Debar, > DELAY, Deter, Estop, Hamper, Harass, Holdback, Impeach, Impede, Obstacle, Overslaugh, Posterior, Pull-back, Rear, Rein, Remora, Rump, Shackle, Slow, Stop, Stunt, Taigle, Thwart, Trammel

Hindi, **Hindu(ism)** Arya Samaj, Babu, Bania(n), Banyan, Brahman, Brahmin, Dalit, Gentoo, Gurkha, Harijan, Jaina, Kshatriya, Maharishi, Nagari, Pundit, Rajpoot, Rajput, Rama, Sad(d)hu, Saiva, Sanatana Dharma, Sankhya, Shaiva, S(h)akta, Sheik(h), Shudra, Smriti, Sudra, Swami, Swinger, Trimurti, Untouchable, Urdu, Vaishnava, Vais(h)ya, Varna, Vedanta

Hindquarters Backside, Crupper, Haunches

Hinge(d) Butt, Cardinal, Cross-garnet, Drop-leaf, Garnet, Gemel, Gimmer, Ginglymus, Joint, Knee, Mount, Parliament, Pivot, Stamp, Strap

▷ **Hinge(s)** *may indicate* a word reversal

Hingeless Ecardinate

Hinny Ass, Donkey, Joe

Hint Allude, Clew, Clue, Cue, Element, Gleam, Hunch, Idea, Imply, Inkle, Inkling, Innuendo, Insinuate, Intimate, Key, Mint, Nuance, Office, Overtone, Pointer, Preview, Scintilla, Shadow, Soupçon, > SUGGEST, Tang, Tip, Touch, Trace, Trick, Wind, Wink, Wisp, Word, Wrinkle

Hint *may indicate* a first letter

Hip(pie), **Hippy**, **Hips** Cafard, Cheer, Coxa(l), Drop-out, Huck(le), Hucklebone, Hunkers, Informed, Ischium, Sciatic, Tonish

Hippopotamus Behemoth, River-horse, Sea-cow, Sea horse

Hire(d), **Hiring** Affreightment, Charter, Employ, Engage, Fee, Freightage, Job, Lease, Merc(enary), Never-never, Pensionary, Rent, Shape-up, Ticca, Wage

Hirsute Hairy, Pilose, Shaggy

His *may indicate* greetings

Hiss Boo, Fizzle, Goose, Hish, Sibilant, Siffle, Sizzle, Swish

Historian Acton, Adams, Antiquary, Archivist, Arrian, Asellio, Bede, Biographer, Bryant, Buckle, Camden, Carlyle, Centuriator, Chronicler, Etain, Froude, Gibbon, Gildas, Green, Griot, Herodotus, Knickerbocker, Livy, Macaulay, Oman, Paris, Pliny, Plutarch, Ponsonby, Renan, Roper, Sallust, Spengler, Starkey, Strachey, Suetonius, Tacitus, Taylor, Thiers, Thucydides, Toynbee, Trevelyan, Wells, Xenophon

History, **Historical** Account, Anamnesis, Ancient, Annal, Bunk, Case, Chronicle, Clio, Epoch(a), Ere-now, Ever, Heritage, Legend, Life, Living, Mesolithic, Modern, Natural, Ontogency, Oral, Past, Record, Renaissance

Histrionic Operatic, Theatrical

Hit Bang, Bash, Baste, Bat, Bean, Belt, Blip, Blockbuster, Bloop, Blow, Bludgeon, Boast, Bolo, Bonk, Bunt, Clobber, Clock, Clout, Club, Collide, Cuff, Dot, Flail, Flick, Flip, Foul, Fourpenny-one, Fungo, Get, Hay, Head-butt, Home(-thrust), Impact, Knock, Lam, Lob, Magpie, Mug, Pandy, Paste, Pepper, Pistol-whip, Polt, Prang, Punto dritto, Ram, Roundhouse, Sacrifice, Score, Sensation, Six, Skier, Sky, Slam, Slap, Slosh, Smash(eroo), Smit(e), Sock, Spank, Stoush, Straik, Stricken, Strike, Strook, Struck, > **SUCCESS**, Swat, Switch, Thwack, Tip, Tonk, Touché, Undercut, Venewe, Venue, Volley, Wallop, Wham, Wing, Ythundered, Zap, Zonk

Hitch(ed) Catch, Contretemps, Edge, Espouse, Hike, Hirsle, Hoi(c)k, Hotch, Jerk, Lorry-hop, Rub, Sheepshank, Sheet bend, Shrug, Snag, Technical, Thumb, Wed

Hitherto Before, Yet

Hittite Uriah

Hive(s) Nettlerash, Skep, Spread, Swarm, Wheal

Hoar(y) Ashen(-grey), Canescent, Froren, Frost, Gaudy-day, Grizzled, Rime

Hoard(ing) Accumulate, Amass, Bill, Billboard, Cache, Coffer, Eke, Heap, Hoord, Husband, Hutch, Mucker, Plant, Pose, Salt away, Save, Sciurine, Snudge, Squirrel, Stash, Stock, Store, Stow, Treasure

Hoarse(ness) Croupy, Frog, Grating, Gruff, Husky, Raucous, Roar(er), Roopit, Roopy, Throaty

Hoax April-fish, Bam, Canard, Cod, Do, Doff, Fub, Fun, Gag, Gammon, Gull, Hum, Huntie-gowk, Kid, Leg-pull, Piltdown, Put-on, Sell, Skit, Spoof, String, Stuff, Supercherie, > **TRICK**

Hobble, **Hobbling** Game, Hamshackle, Hilch, Hitch, Lame, Limp, Pastern, Picket, Spancel, Stagger, Tether

Hobby Avocation, Fad, Falcon, Interest, Pastance, > **PASTIME**, Predator, Pursuit, Recreation, Scrimshaw

Hobby-horse Dada, Obsession, Play-mare

Hobgoblin Bog(e)y, Puck

Hobnail Clinker, Tacket

Hobnob Chat, Mingle

Hobo Bum, > **TRAMP**, Vagrant

Hock Cambrel, Dip, Gambrel, Gambril, Gammon, Ham, Heel, Hough,

Hypothecate, Pawn, Pledge, Rhenish, Wine

Hockey Grass, Hurling, Pond, Shinny, Shinty

Hod Carrier, Tray

Hodge Peasant, Rustic, Yokel

Hoe Claut, Dutch, Grub, Jembe, Nab, Pecker, Prong, Rake, Scuffle, Thrust, Weed

Hog Babiroussa, Babirussa, Boar, Glutton, Guttle, Peccary, Pig, Porker, Road, Shoat, Shott, Whole

Hogmanay Ne'erday

Hog-rat Hutia

Hogshead Butt, Cask, Muid

Hogwash Bull, Nonsense, Swill, Twaddle

Hoi-polloi Prole(tariat), Rabble

Hoist Boom, Bouse, Crane, Davit, Derrick, Gin, Heft, Hills, Jack, Lewis, Lift, Raise, Shearlegs, Shears, Sheerlegs, Sheers, Sway, Teagle, Trice, Whip-and-derry, Wince, Winch, Windas, Windlass

Hold(er), **Holding**, **Hold back**, **up**, **etc** Absorb, Anchor, Backbreaker, Belay, Believe, Boston crab, Canister, Cease, Cement, Cinch, Clamp, Clasp, Cling, Clutch, Contain, Cotland, Delay, Detain, Display, Dog, Embrace, Engross, Er, Facebar, Fast, Fief, Fistful, Frog, Full nelson, Garter, > **GRASP**, Grip, Grovet, Half-nelson, Hammerlock, Handle, Haud, Have, Headlock, Heft, Heist, Hiccup, Hinder, Hitch, Ho(a), Hoy, Hug, Impedance, Impede, Impediment, Impound, Incumbent, Intern, Intray, Japanese stranglehold, Keep, Keepnet, Lease, Maintain, Manure, Nelson, Own, Port, Proffer, Rack, Reluct, Reserve, Rivet, Rob, Rundale, Runrig, Save, Scissors, Shelve, Shore, Sleeve, Sostenuto, Stand, Suplex, Suspend, Tenancy, Tenement, Tenure, Toehold, Toft, Tray, Tripod, Wristlock, Zarf, Zurf

Hole(s), **Holed**, **Holey** Agloo, Aglu, Albatross, Antrum, Aubrey, Beam, Birdie, Black, Cat, Cave, Cavity, Cenote, Coal, Coalsack, Crater, Cubby, Dell, Den, Dene, Dog-leg, Dolina, Doline, Dormie, Dormy, Dreamhole, Dry, Dugout, Eagle, Earth, Ethmoid, Eye(let), Faveolate, Finger, Foramen, Funk, Gap, Geat, Glory, Gnamma, Gutta, Hag(g), Hideout, Kettle, Knot, Lenticel, Lill, Limber, Loop, Loup, Lubber's, Lumina, Maar, Mortise, Moulin, Namma, Nineteenth, Oillet, > **OPENING**, Orifex, Orifice, Ozone, Perforate, Pierce, Pigeon, Pinprick, Pit, Pocket, Pore, Port, Pot, Potato, Priest's, Punctuate, Punctum, Puncture, Rowport, Sallyport, Scupper, Scuttle, Scye, Situation, Slot, Snag, Snow, Soakaway, Socket, Sound, Spandrel, Spider, Spiraculum, Starting, Stead, Stew, Stop, Stove, Swallow, Tear, Thirl, Touch, Trema, Vent, Ventage, Ventige, Voided, Vug, Watering, Well, White, Wookey

Holiday(s) Bank, Benjo, Break, Busman's, Childermas, Ferial, Festa, > **FESTIVAL**, Fete, Fiesta, Furlough, Gala, Half(term), High, Honeymoon, Lag b'Omer, Laik, Leasure, Leave, Legal, Leisure, Long, Minibreak, Off-day, Off-time, Outing, Packaged, Pink-eye, Play-day, Playtime, Public, Purim, Recess, Repose, Rest, Roman, Seaside, Shabuoth, Shavuot, Sojourn, Statutory, Stay, Sunday, Tax, Trip, > **VACATION**, Villegiatura, Wake(s), Whitsun

Holinshed Chronicler

Holland(s) Batavia, Genevese, Gin, Hogen-mogen, Netherlands, NL

Hollow Acetabulum, Alveary, Antar, Antre, Antrum, Armpit, Axilla, Blastula, Boss, Bowl, Cave(rn), Cavity, Chasm, Chott, Cirque, Cleché, Comb(e), Concave, Coomb, Corrie, Crater, Cup(mark), Cwm, Deaf, Dean, Dell, Delve, Den(e), Dent, Dimple, Dingle, Dip, Dish(ing), Dolina, Doline, Empty, Fossette, Frost, Gilgai, Glenoid, Gnamma-hole, Gowpen, Grot(to), Hole, How, Igloo, Incavo, Insincere, Keck(sy), Kex, Khud, Lip-deep, Mortise, Namma-hole, Niche, Omphaloid,

Orbita, Pan, Pit, Punt, Redd, Rout, Rut, Scoop, Shott, Sinus, Slade, Sleepy, Slot, Slough, Socket, Swire, Thank-you-ma'am, Trematic, Trough, Vlei, Vola, Wame, Wem

Holly Aquifoliaceae, Eryngo, Ilex, Mate, Yaupon
Hollyhock Althaea, Rose mallow
Hollywood Bowl, Tinseltown
Holm Isle
Holmes Sherlock, Wendell
Holmium Ho
Holocaust Churban, Shoah
Hologram, Holograph Laser, MS
Holothurian Trepang
Holster Sheath
Holy(man), Holiness Adytum, Alliance, Blessed, > DIVINE, Godly, Grail, Halidom, Helga, Hery, Khalif, Loch, Mountain, Orders, Pan(h)agia, Pious, Sacred, Sacrosanct, Sad(d)hu, Saintly, Sanctitude, Sannayasi(n), Santon, Sekos, Sepulchre, Shrine, Starets, Staretz, SV, Tirthankara, War
Holy Books, Holy writing Adigranth, Atharvaveda, Bible, Gemara, Granth, Hadith, Koran, Mishnah, NT, OT, Pia, Purana, Rigveda, Sama-Veda, > SCRIPTURE, Shaster, Shastra, Smriti, Sura(h), Tanach, Writ, Yajur-Veda
Holy building, Holy place Chapel, Church, Kaaba, Penetralia, Synagogue, Temenos, Temple
Holy Ghost Paraclete
Holy water Amrit
Homage Bow, Cense, Honour, Kneel, Manred, Obeisance, Tribute, Vail
Home Abode, Base, Blighty, Burrow, Cheshire, Chez, Clinic, Community, Domal, Domicile, Earth, Eventide, Family, Fireside, Gaff, Goal, Habitat, Harvest, Heame, Hearth, Heme, Hospice, House, In, Lair, Libken, Mental, Mobile, Montacute, Nest, Nursing, Pad, Plas Newydd, Remand, Res(idence), Rest, Starter, Stately, Villa
Homecoming Nostos
Home counties SE
Homeless Outler, Rootless, Skell
Homer(ic) Comatose, Cor, Epic(ist), Nod, Pigeon, Somnolent
Home-rule Parnellism, Swaraj
Homesick(ness) Heimweh, Mal du pays
Homespun Plain, Raploch, Russet, Simple
Homestead Ranch, Toft
Homework Prep, Preparation
Homicidal, Homicide Chance-medley, Justifiable, Killing, Manslaughter
Homily Lecture, Midrash, Pi, Postil, Prone, Sermon, Tract
Homing *may indicate* coming back
Hominid Oreopitheous
Homogeneous Indiscrete
Homosexual(ity) Auntie man, Bardash, Batty boy, Bender, Bent, Camp, Cat, Closet queen, Cocksucker, Cottaging, Dike, Dyke, Fag(got), Fairy, Fruit, Gay, Gaydar, Ginger, Homophile, Invert, Lesbian, Moffie, Muscle Mary, Ponce, Poof(tah), Poofter, Poove, Pouf(fe), Poufter, Puff, Quean, Queer, Quiff, Rough trade, Shirt-lifter, Swish(y), Tonk, Tribade, Uranism, Urning, Woofter
Hone Grind, > SHARPEN, Whet
Honest(y) Aboveboard, Afauld, Afawld, Candour, Clean, Fair dinkum, Genuine, Incorruptible, Injun, Jake, Legitimate, Lunaria, Lunary, Open-faced,

Penny, Probity, Rectitude, Reputable, Righteous, Round, Sincere, Square, Squareshooter, Straight, Straight-arrow, Trojan, > **TRUE**, Upfront, Upright, Upstanding

Honey Comb, Flattery, Hybla, Hymettus, Mel, Melliferous, Nectar, Oenomel, Oxymel, Palm, Peach, Popsy-wopsy, Sis, Sugar, Sweetheart, Sweetie, Wood

Honeycomb(ed) Cellular, Faveolate, Favose, Waxwork

Honey-eater Bear, Blue-eye

Honeypot Haanepoot

Honeysuckle Abelia, Anthemion, Caprifoil, Caprifole, Lonicera, Rewa rewa, Suckling, Woodbind, Woodbine

Honorary, Honour(able), Honours, Honorific Accolade, Ace, Adore, Birthday, Blue, CBE, Commemorate, Credit, Dan, Elate, Emeritus, Ennoble, > **ESTEEM**, Ethic, Face-card, Fame, Fete, Glory, Grace, Greats, Homage, Insignia, Invest, Izzat, King, Knave, Knight, Kudos, Laudation, Laurels, MBE, Mention, Military, OBE, Pundonor, Queen, Remember, Repute, Respect, Revere, Reward Ten, Tenace, Titular, Tripos, Venerate, Worship

Honourable companion CH

Honourless Yarborough

Hooch Moonshine

Hood(ed) Almuce, Amaut, Amice, Amowt, Apache, Balaclava, Bashlik, Biggin, Blindfold, Calash, Calèche, Calyptra, Capeline, Capuccio, Capuche, Chaperon(e), Coif, Cope, Cowl, Cucullate(d), Gangster, Jacobin, Kennel, Lens, Liripipe, Liripoop, Mantle, Mazarine, Pixie, Robin, Rowdy, Snood, Trot-cosey, Trot-cozy

Hoodlum Gangster, Roughneck, Thug

Hoodoo Mozz

Hoodwink(ed) Blear, Bluff, Cheat, > **DECEIVE**, Gull, Nose-led, Seel

Hoof(ed) Artiodactyla, Cloot, Coffin, Frog, Trotter, Ungula

Hoohah Humdudgeon

Hook(er), Hooked, Hooks Addict, Adunc, Aduncous, Barb(icel), Becket, Butcher's, Cant(dog), Catch, Chape, Claw, Cleek, Clip, Corvus, Crampon, Cromb, Crome, Crook, Crotchet, Cup, Drail, Fifi, Fish, Fluke, Fly, Gab, Gaff, Gig, Grapnel, Hamate, Hamose, Hamulus, Heel, Hitch, Inveigle, Kype, Meat, Pot, Prostitute, Pruning, Retinaculum, Sister, Snell, Sniggle, Swivel, Tala(u)nt, Tart, Tenaculum, Tenter, Tie, Trip, Uncus, Wanton, Welsh

Hookah Chillum, Hubble-bubble, Pipe

Hooligan Apache, Casual, Desperado, Droog, Hobbledehoy, Keelie, Larrikin, Lout, Ned, Rough(neck), Ruffian, Skollie, Skolly, Tearaway, Ted, Tough, Tsotsi, Yahoo, Yob(bo)

Hoop Bail, Band, Circle, Farthingale, Garth, Gird, Girr, Hula®, O, > **RING**, Tire, Trochus

Hooray Whoopee, Yippee

Hoot(er) Conk, Deride, Honk, Madge, Nose, Owl, Riot, Screech-owl, Siren, Ululate

Hoover Dam

Hop(per) An(o)ura, Ball, Bin, Cuscus, Dance, Flight, Jeté, Jump, Kangaroo, Leap, Lilt, Opium, Pogo, Saltate, Scotch, Skip, Spring, Tremié, Vine

Hope(ful) Anticipate, Aspirant, Contender, Daydream, Desire, Dream, Esperance, Evelyn, Expectancy, Forlorn, Gleam, Good, Pipe-dream, Promising, Roseate, Rosy, Sanguine, Trust, Valley, White, Wish

Hopeless(ness), Hopeless quest Abattu, Anomie, Anomy, Black, Buckley's chance, Despair, Despondent, Forlorn, Goner, Perdu, Pessimist

Hopscotch Peever
Horace Flaccus, Ode, Satirist
Horatio Nelson
Horatius Cocles
Horde Golden, Many, Mass, Swarm
Horizon Artificial, B, C, Celestial, Event, Gyro, Rational, Scope, Sea-line, Skyline
Horizontal Advection, Flat, Level, Prone, Supine
Hormone ACTH, Adrenalin®, Adrenaline, Aldosterone, Androgen,
   Androsterone, Angiotensin, Autacoid, Auxin, Biosynthesis, Bursicon,
   Calcitonin, Catecholamine, Corticoid, Corticosteroid, Cortisone, Cytokinin,
   Ecdysone, Endocrine, Erythropoietin, Estrogen, Florigen, Folliculin,
   Gastrin, Gibberellin, Glucagon, Gonadotrophic, Gonadotrop(h)in, Growth,
   Hydrocortisone, IAA, Inhibin, Insulin, Intermedin, Juvenile, Kinin,
   Lipotropin, Luteinizing, Melanotropine, Melatonin, Noradrenalin(e),
   Oestradiol, Oestriol, Oestrogen, Oestrone, Oxytocin, Parathyroid,
   Progesterone, Progestin, Progestogen, Prolactin, Prostaglandin, Relaxin,
   Secretagogue, Secretin, Secretion, Serotonin, Sex, Somatomedin,
   Somatostatin, Somatotrop(h)in, Steroid, Stilboestrol, Testosterone, Thymosin,
   Thyroid, Thyrotrop(h)in, Thyroxine, Triiodothyronine, TSH, Vasopressin
Horn(y) Advancer, Amalthea, Antenna(e), Antler, Baleen, Basset, Bez, Brass,
   Bugle, Cape, Ceratoid, Cor, Cornet, Cornett, Cornopean, Cornu(a), Cornucopia,
   Cromorna, Cromorne, Cusp, Dilemma, Exponential, Flugel-horn, French,
   Frog, Golden, Gore, Hooter, > **HORNBLOWER**, Hunting, Ivory, Keratin, Klaxon,
   Lur, Morsing, Mot, Oliphant, Periostracum, Plenty, Post, Powder, Pryse, Ram's,
   Scur, Shofar, Shophor, Spongin, Tenderling, Trey, Trez, Trumpet, Waldhorn
Hornblower Brain, Horatio, Peel, Triton, Trumpeter
Hornbook Battledoor, Battledore
Horned (sheep) Cabrié, Cabrit, Cornute, Hamate, Lunate, Mouflon, Muflon
Hornless Doddy, Humbel, Humlie, Hummel, Mooly, Mul(l)ey, Poley, Polled
Hornpipe Matelote
Horoscope Figure, Future, Prophecy, Star-map
Horrible, Horror Aw(e)some, Brat, Dire, Dread(ful), Execrable, Ghastly, Grisly,
   Gruesome, Hideous, Loathsome, Odious, Shock, Terror, Ugh, Vile
Horrid, Horrific, Horrify(ing) Dire, Dismay, Dreadful, Frightful, Ghastly, Gothic,
   Grim, Grisly, H, Loathy, Odious, Spiteful, Ugly
Hors d'oeuvres Antipasto, Canapé, Carpaccio, Ceviche, Hoummos, Houmus,
   Hummus, Mez(z)e, Pâté, Smorgasbord, Smor(re)brod, Smør(re)brød,
   Zak(o)uski
Horse Airer, Bidet, Bloodstock, Carriage, Cut, Cutting, Dark, Doer, Dray,
   Drier, Drug, Equine, H, > **HEROIN**, High, Hobby, Iron, Knight, Kt, Light,
   Malt, Outsider, Pack, Pantomime, Plug, Ride, Rocking, Sawbuck, Screen,
   Selling-plate, Sense, Stalking, Standard-bred, Stayer, Steeplechaser, Stock,
   Trestle, Vaulting, Willing, Wooden

HORSES

2 letters:	Cob	Rip	Barb
GG	Dun	Tit	Buck
	Gee		Cert
3 letters:	Nag	**4 letters:**	Colt
Ass	Pad	Arab	Crib
Bay	Pot	Aver	Dale

Fell
Foal
Hack
Jade
Mare
Pole
Pony
Post
Prad
Roan
Scag
Snow
Span
Stud
Taki
Trot
Yale
Yaud

5 letters:
Arion
Arkle
Bevis
Borer
Caple
Capul
Favel
Filly
Genet
Morel
Mount
Neddy
Pacer
Pinto
Poler
Punch
Rogue
Screw
Seian
Shire
Steed
Tacky
Takhi
Troop
Waler
Wheel
White

6 letters:
Ambler
Bayard
Bronco

Brumby
Calico
Canuck
Cayuse
Chaser
Cooser
Crollo
Curtal
Cusser
Dobbin
Entire
Exmoor
Favell
Ganger
Garran
Garron
Gennet
Hogget
Hunter
Jennet
Kanuck
Keffel
Lampos
Livery
Morgan
Mudder
Novice
Pad-nag
Plater
Pommel
Poster
Quagga
Randem
Remuda
Roarer
Rouncy
Runner
Sabino
Saddle
Shoo-in
Sorrel
String
Stumer
Summer
Tandem
Tarpan
Tracer
Trojan
Vanner

7 letters:
Bobtail

Breaker
Cavalry
Centaur
Charger
Clipper
Coacher
Courser
Cuisser
Dappled
Draught
Eclipse
Eventer
Gelding
Hackney
Hobbler
Liberty
Marengo
Marocco
Morocco
Mustang
Palfrey
Pegasus
Piebald
Quarter
Remount
Saddler
Sheltie
Spanker
Starter
Sumpter
Swallow
Swinger
Trigger
Trotter
Walking
Wheeler
Xanthos
Xanthus

8 letters:
Aquiline
Bangtail
Bathorse
Boerperd
Buckskin
Camargue
Chestnut
Clay-bank
Cocktail
Dartmoor
Destrier
Eohippus

Friesian
Galloway
Highland
Holstein
Hyperion
Kochlani
Lusitano
Palomino
Schimmel
Shetland
Skewbald
Sleipnir
Springer
Stallion
Stibbler
Warragal
Warragle
Warragul
Warrigal
Welsh cob
Whistler
Yarraman
Yearling

9 letters:
Appaloosa
Black Bess
Caballine
Clavileno
Coldblood
Connemara
Gringolet
Houyhnhnm
Icelandic
Incitatus
Knabstrup
Percheron
Rosinante
Rozinante
Warmblood

10 letters:
Andalusian
Bucephalus
Buckjumper
Buttermilk
Clydesdale
Copenhagen
Lipizzaner
Lippizaner
Pliohippus
Przewalski

Svadilfari Przewalskis Thoroughbred **16 letters:**
Tennessee
Walking

11 letters: **12 letters:** **13 letters:**
Daisy-cutter Hambletonian Perissodactyl
High-stepper Suffolk punch

Horseback Croup
Horse-box Stable, Stall
Horse-chestnut Aesculus, Conker
Horse collar Brecham, Hame
Horse complaint, **Horse disease**, **Horse trouble** Blind staggers, Bogspavin,
   Cracked heels, Curb, Dourine, Equinia, Eweneck, Farcy, Fives, Founder, Frush,
   Glanders, Gourdy, Head staggers, Heaves, Hippiatric, Knee spawn, Laminitis,
   Lampas, Lampers, Malander, Mallander, Mallender, Megrims, Miller's
   disease, Mooneye, Mud fever, N(a)gana, Poll-evil, Quitter, Quittor, Ringbone,
   Sallenders, Scratches, Seedy-toe, Spavie, Spavin, Strangles, Stringhalt,
   Summer sores, Surra, Sway-back, Sween(e)y, Thorough-pin, Thrush,
   Toe-crack, Vives, Windgall, Wind-sucking, Wire-heel, Yellows
Horse-dealer Buster, Coper
Horse-lover Philip
Horseman Ataman, Caballero, Cavalry, Centaur, Conquest, Cossack, Cowboy,
   Death, Dragman, Famine, Farrier, Hobbler, Hussar, Knight, Lancer, Nessus,
   Ostler, Parthian, Picador, Pricker, Quadrille, Revere, > RIDER, Slaughter, Spahi,
   Stradiot, Tracer
Horsemanship Manège
Horseplay Caper, Chukka, Knockabout, Polo, Rag, Rant, Romp
Horsepower Hp, Ps
Horseradish Ben, Moringa
Horseshoe(-shaped) Henge, Hippocrepian, King-crab, Lunette, Manilla,
   Oxbow, Plate
Horsetail Equisetum
Horse thief Blanco, Rustler
Horticultural, **Horticulture**, **Horticulturist** Grower, Pomology, RHS
Hose Chausses, Fishnet, Galligaskins, Gaskins, Lisle, Netherstock(ing), Nylons,
   Panty, Sock, Stockings, Tabi, Tights, Trunk, Tube
Hospitable, **Hospitality** Convivial, Entertainment, Euxine, Lucullan, Open
   house, Philoxenia, Social, Xenial
Hospital Ambulance, Asylum, Barts, Base, Bedlam, Clinic, Cottage, Day,
   ENT, Field, General, Guys, H, Home, Hospice, Imaret, Karitane, Lambarene,
   Lazaretto, Leprosarium, Leprosery, Lock, Loony bin, Lying-in, MASH, Mental,
   Nosocomial, Ozzie, Pest-house, Polyclinic, San, Scutari, Sick bay, Snake-pit,
   Special, Spital, Spittle, Teaching, Trust, UCH
Host(s), **Hostess** Amphitryon, Army, Barmecide, Chatelaine, Compere,
   Crowd, Definitive, Emcee, Entertainer, Eucharist, Heavenly, Hirsel, Hotelier,
   Innkeeper, Intermediate, Laban, Landlady, Landlord, Legend, Legion,
   Lion-hunter, Lot, Mass, Mavin, MC, Publican, Quickly, Sabaoth, Swarm,
   Taverner, Throng, Trimalchio
Hostage Gherao, Pawn, Pledge, POW
Hostel Asylum, Dharms(h)ala, Dorm, Entry, Halfway house, Inn, YHA, Youth
Hostile, **Hostility** Adverse, Aggressive, Alien, Animus, Bellicose, Bitter,
   Chilly, Currish, Diatribe, Feud, Hating, Icy, Ill, Ill-will, Inimical, Inveterate,
   Oppugnant, Unfriendly, Vitriolic, War

Hot (tempered) Ardent, Big, Blistering, Breem, Breme, Cajun, Calid, Candent, Dog days, Enthusiastic, Facula, Fervid, Feverish, Fiery, Fuggy, Gospeller, In, Incandescent, Irascible, Lewd, Live, Mafted, Mustard, Pepper, Piping, Potato, Randy, Red, Roaster, Scorcher, Sizzling, Spicy, Stewy, Stifling, Stolen, Sultry, Sweaty, Sweltering, Sweltry, Tabasco®, Thermidor, Torrid, Toustie, Tropical, Zealful

Hotchpotch Bricolage, Farrago, Mish-mash, Powsowdy, Welter

Hotel, **Hotelkeeper** Bo(a)tel, Fleabag, Flophouse, Gasthaus, Gasthof, H, Hilton, Host, Hydro, Inn, Motel, Parador, Patron(ne), Posada, Private, Ritz, Roadhouse, Savoy, Tavern, Temperance, Trust

Hothead(ed) Impetuous, Rash, Spitfire, Volcano

Hot-house Conservatory, Nursery, Orangery, Vinery

Hot plate Salamander

Hot rod Dragster

Hotspur Harry, Hothead, Rantipole

Hottentot Griqua, Khoikhoi, Strandloper

Hot water Soup, Therm

Hound(s) Afghan, Basset, Beagle, Bellman, Brach, Cad, Canine, Cry, > DOG, Entry, Gabriel's, Hamiltonstovare, Harass, Harrier, Hen-harrier, Ibizan, Javel, Kennet, Lyam, Lym(e), Mute, Otter, Pack, Pharaoh, Pursue, Rache, Ranter, Reporter, Saluki, Talbot, True, Tufter

Hound's bane Palay

Hour(s) Canonical, Complin(e), Elder's, Eleventh, Golden, H, Happy, Holy, Hr, Little, Lunch, None(s), Orthros, Peak, Prime, Rush, Sext, Sidereal, Small, Staggered, Terce, Tide, Time, Undern, Vespers, Visiting, Witching, Working, Zero

House(s), **Housing**, **Household(er)** Abode, Accepting, Admiralty, Althing, Astrology, Audience, Auditorium, B, Bach, Bastide, Beehive, Beth, Bhavan, Bhawan, Biggin, Bingo, Block, Boarding, Bondage, Bourbon, Broadcasting, Broiler, Brownstone, Bundestag, Burghley, Bush, Casa, Chalet, Chamber, Chapter, Charnel, Chateau, Chatsworth, Chattel, Chez, Clapboard, Clearing, Coffee, Commercial, Commons, Concern, Convent, Cote, Cottage (orne), Council, Counting, Country, Crankcase, Crib, Custom(s), Dacha, Dail, Demain, Demesne, Derry, Des res, Discount, Disorderly, Domal, Domicile, Donga, Door, Dower, Drostdy, Drum, Duplex, Dwelling, Dynasty, Edifice, Entertain, Establishment, Este, Familial, Fashion, Fibro(cement), Finance, Firm, Forcing, Frame, Fraternity, Free, Frontager, Full, Gaff, Gambling, Garage, Gite, Government, Habitat, Habitation, Hacienda, Halfway, Hanover, Harbour, Harewood, Hatfield, Heartbreak, Hearth, HK, Ho, Holyrood, Home, Homestead, Ice, Igloo, Inn, Insula, Isuing, Joss, Ken, Kenwood, Keys, Knebworth, Knesset, Lagthing, Lancaster, Leo, Lockwood home, Lodging, Longleat, Lords, Lot(t)o, Maison(ette), Malting, Manor, Manse, Mansion, Mas, Meeting, Meinie, Meiny, Ménage, Messuage, Mobility, Montagne, Nacelle, Odelst(h)ing, Open (-plan), Opera, Orange, Osborne, Pad, Parliament, Pent, Petworth, Picture, Pilot, Plantagenet, Pole, Pondokkie, Post, Prefab, Public, Quinta, Radome, Ranch, Ratepayer, Register, Residence, Rooming, Rough, Russborough, Safe, Sandringham, Satis, Scala, Schloss, Seanad (Eireann), Seat, Semi, Shanty, Sheltered, Show, Sign, Social, Software, Somerset, Sporting, Stable, Station, Steeple, Stewart, Storey, Stuart, Succession, Syon, Tavern, Tea, Terrace, Theatre, Third, Tied, Toft, Tombola, Tower, Town, Tract, Treasure, Tree, Trinity, Trust, Tudor, Upper, Usher, Vaulting, Vicarage, Villa, Wash, Watch, Weather, Weatherboard, Weigh, Wendy, Whare, Wheel, White,

Wilton, Windsor, Work, York, Zero, Zodiac
House-boat Wangun, Wan(i)gan
House-builder Jack
House-keeper Chatelaine, Matron, Publican
House-leek Sengreen
Housemaid's knee Bursa
Houseman Betty, Doctor, Intern, Peer
House-warming Infare
Housewife Etui, Needlecase
Housework Chore, Diy
Housing Case, Crankcase, Shabrack, Shelter, Slum, Tenement
Hova Malagash
Hove Plim, Swell
Hovel Cru(i)ve, Den, Pigsty, Shack, Shanty
Hover Hang, Levitate, Lurk, Poise
How Hill, Hollow
How'dyedo, **How d'ye do** Hallo, Pass, Salve
However As, But, Leastwise, Sed, Still, Though, Yet
Howitzer Gun
Howl(er) Banshee, Bawl, Bay, Bloop, Clanger, Hue, Mycetes, Squawk, Ululate, Wow, Yawl, Yowl
How much The
Hoy Bilander, Ship
HP Never-never
HQ Centre, Headquarters, SHAPE
Hub Boss, Centre, Focus, Hob, Nave, Pivot, Tee
Hubbub Charivari, Chirm, Coil, Din, Level-coil, Palaver, Racket, Row, Stir
Hubris Pride
Huckster Hawker, Kidd(i)er, Pedlar
Huddle Cringe, Gather, Hunch, Ruck, Shrink
Hudson River, Rock
Hue Colour, Dye, Outcry, Proscription, Steven, Tincture, Tinge, Utis
Huff Dudgeon, Hector, Pant, Pet, Pique, Snuff, Strunt, Umbrage, Vex
Hug Bear, Cuddle, > EMBRACE, Squeeze
Huge (number) Astronomical, Brobdingnag, Colossal, Enorm(ous), Gargantuan, Giant, > GIGANTIC, Gillion, Ginormous, Humongous, Humungous, Immane, Immense, Leviathan, Lulu, Mega-, Milliard, Monolithic, Monster, Octillion, Prodigious, Socking, Tall, Titanian, Tremendous, Vast, Whacking
Hugo Victor
Huguenot Camisard
Hulk Lout, Ruin, Shale, Shell, Ship
Hull Bottom, Framework, Husk, Inboard, Monocoque, Pod, Sheal, Sheel, Shell, Shiel, Shill, Shiplap
Hullabaloo Outcry, Razzamatazz, Raz(z)mataz(z)
Hullo *see* HELLO
Hum(ming) Bombilate, Bombinate, Bum, Chirm, Drone, Lilt, Moan, Murmur, Nos(e)y, Pong, Ponk, Rank, Reek, Sowf(f), Sowth, Stink, Stir, Whir(r), Zing
Human(e), **Humanist**, **Humanity** Anthropoid, Bang, Colet, Earthling, Erasmus, Incarnate, Kindness, Mandom, Merciful, Mortal, Philanthropic, Species, Sympathy, Ubuntu, Virtual, Wight
Humble Abase, Abash, Afflict, Baseborn, Chasten, Cow, Degrade, Demean,

Demiss(ly), Lower, Lowly, Mean, > **MEEK**, Modest, Morigerate, Obscure, Poor, Rude, Small, Truckle

Humbug Berley, Blague, Blarney, Buncombe, Bunk(um), Burley, Cant, Claptrap, Con, Delude, Flam, Flummery, Fraud, Fudge, Gaff, Gammon, Gas, Guff, Gum, Hoax, Hoodwink, Hookey-walker, Kibosh, Liar, Maw-worm, Nonsense, Shenanigan, Wind

Humdinger Lulu

Humdrum Banal, Bourgeois, Monotonous, Mundane, Ordinary, Prosaic, Tedious

Humid(ity) Clammy, Damp, Dank, Machie, Machy, Muggy, Saturation, Steam, Sticky, Sultry

Humiliate, Humiliation, Humility Abase, Abash, Baseness, Degrade, Disbench, Eating crow, Fast, Indignity, Mortify, Put-down, > **SHAME**, Skeleton, Take-down, Wither

Humming-bird Colibri, Hermit, Rainbow, Sabre-wing, Sapphire-wing, Sappho, Sylph, Thornbill, Topaz, Trochilus

Hummock Tump

Humorist Cartoonist, Comedian, Jester, Leacock, Lear, Punster, Twain, Wodehouse

Humour, Humorous Aqueous, Bile, Blood, Caprice, Cardinal, Chaff, Coax, Cocker, Coddle, Cosher, Cuiter, Cuittle, Daut, Dawt, Dry, Facetious, Fun, Gallows, Ichor, Indulge, Irony, Jocose, Jocular, Juice, Kidney, Levity, Light, > **MOOD**, Observe, One-liner, Pamper, Phlegm, Pun, Pythonesque, Ribaldry, Salt, Serum, Temper, Trim, Vein, Vitreum, Wetness, Whim, Wit

Humourless Dry, Po(-faced)

Hump(ed) Boy, Bulge, Dorts, Dowager's, Gibbose, Gibbous, Hog, Huff, Hummock, Hunch, Middelmannetje, Pip, Ramp, Road, Speed bump, Tussock

▶ **Humpback** *see* **HUNCHBACK**

Humphrey Bogart

Humus Compost, Leafmould, Moder, Mor, Mull

Hun Alaric, Atli, Attila, Fritz, German

Hunch, Hunchback Camel, Chum, Crookback, Gobbo, Intuition, Kyphosis, Premonition, Quasimodo, Roundback, Sense, Urchin

Hundred(s), Hundredth Burnham, C, Cantred, Cantref, Cent, Centesimal, Centum, Century, Chiltern, Commot, Days, Desborough, Great, Host, > **IN A HUNDRED**, Long, Northstead, Old, Shire, Stoke, Ton, Wapentake

Hundred and fifty CL, Y

Hundred and sixty T

Hundredweight Centner, Quintal

Hung Displayed, Executed, Framed, High

Hungarian, Hungary Bohunk, Cheremis(s), Csardas, Magyar, Nagy, Szekely, Tzigane, Ugric, Vogul

Hunger, Hungry Appestat, Appetite, Bulimia, Bulimy, Clem, > **CRAVE**, Desire, Edacity, Empty, Esurient, Famine, Famish, Fast, Hanker, Hunter, Pant, Peckish, Rapacious, Raven, Ravin, Sharp-set, Unfed, Yaup, Yearn

▷ **Hungry** *may indicate* an 'o' in another word

Hunk(s) Beefcake, Chunk, Dry-fist, Miser(ly), Slab

Hunt(er), Hunting, Huntress, Huntsman Actaeon, Alew, Archer, Artemis, Atalanta, Battue, Beagle, Bellman, Bounty, Calydon, Chace, Chase(r), Chasseur, Chevy, Cool, Coursing, Crockett, Cynegetic, Dog, Drag(net), Esau, Ferret, Fox, Free-shot, Gun, Halloo, Herne, Hound, Jager, Lamping, Leigh, Lurcher, Montero, National, Nimrod, Orion, Peel, Pig-sticking, Poot, Pout,

Predator, Pursue, Quest, Quorn, Rabbit, Rach(e), Rake, Ran, Rancel, Ranzel, Ride, Rummage, Run, Scavenge(r), Scorse, > **SEARCH**, Seek, Shikar(ee), Shikari, Skirter, Slipper, Stag, Stalk, Sticker, Still, Swiler, Terrier, Thimble, Tinchel, Tower, Trail, Trap, Treasure, Venatic, Venator, Venerer, Venery, > **WATCH**, Whip, Whipper-in, Witch, Wolfer, Woodman, Woodsman, Yager

Hunting-call Rechate, Recheat, Tally-ho, View-halloo

Hunting-ground Forestation, Walk

Hurdle(r) Barrier, Doll, Fence, Flake, Gate, Hemery, Raddle, Sticks, Wattle

Hurdy (gurdy) Barrel-organ, Hainch, Haunch, Vielle

Hurl(ing) Camogie, Cast, Dash, > **FLING**, Heave, Put(t), Throw, > **TOSS**

Hurly-burly Furore, Noise

Hurrah Cheers, Huzza, Io, Whee

Hurricane Baguio, Tornade, Tornado, Typhoon, > **WIND**

Hurry Belt, Bustle, Chivvy, Chop-chop, Dart, Dash, Drive, Festinate, Fisk, Frisk, Gad, Gallop, Giddap, Giddup, Giddy-up, Hadaway, Hare, Haste, Hie, Hightail, Induce, Mosey, Post-haste, Press, Push, Race, Railroad, > **RUSH**, Scamper, Scoot, Scramble, Scur(ry), Scutter, Scuttle, Skelter, Skurry, Spank, Speed, Streak, Tear

Hurt(ful) Abuse, Ache, Ake, Bruise, Cutting, Damage, De(a)re, Disservice, Harrow, Hit, > **INJURE**, Lesion, Maim, Nocent, Nocuous, Noxious, Noyous, Pain, Pang, Prick(le), Scaith, Wound, Wring

Hurtle Rush, Spin, Streak, Streek

Husband(ry), Husbands Add, Baron, Breadwinner, Consort, Darby, Ear, Eche, Economy, Eke, Ere, Farm, Gander-mooner, Georgic, Goodman, Groom, H, Hoddy-doddy, Hodmandod, Hubby, Ideal, Man, Manage, Mate, Partner, Polyandry, Retrench, Save, Scrape, Scrimp, Spouse, Squirrel, > **STORE**, Tillage

Hush(-hush) Bestill, Gag, Sh, Silent, Smug, St, Tace, Wheesh(t), Whisht

Husk(s), Husky Acerose, Bran, Draff, Eskimo, Hoarse, Hull, Malemute, Seed, Sheal, Shuck

Hussar Cherry-picker, Cherubim

Hussite Calixtin(e)

Hussy Besom, Hen, Loose, Minx, Vamp

Hustle(r) Frogmarch, Jostle, Pro, Push, Railroad, Shoulder, Shove, Skelp

Hut(s) Banda, Booth, Bothie, Bothy, Bustee, Cabin, Caboose, Chalet, Choltry, Gunyah, Hogan, Humpy, Igloo, Mia-mia, Nissen, Pondok(kie), Quonset®, Rancheria, Rancho, Rondavel, Shack, Shanty, Sheal(ing), Shebang, Shed, Shiel(ing), Skeo, Skio, Succah, Sukkah, Tilt, Tolsel, Tolsey, Tolzey, Tramping, Wan(n)igan, Whare, Wi(c)kiup, Wigwam, Wil(t)ja, Wurley, Wurlie

Hutch Buddle, Crate, Pen

Hyacinth Cape, Grape, Starch, Wild

Hybrid Bigener, Bois-brûlé, Catalo, Centaur, Chamois, Chichi, Chimera, Citrange, Cockatrice, Cross, Dso, Funnel, Geep, Graft, Hippogriff, Hircocervus, Interbred, Jersian, Jomo, Jumart, Lurcher, Mameluco, Mermaid, Merman, Metis, Mongrel, Mule, Mutation, Opinicus, Ortanique, Ox(s)lip, Percolin, Plumcot, Pomato, Ringed, Tangelo, Tiglon, Tigon, Topaz, Ugli, Zho(mo)

Hybrid *may indicate* an anagram

Hydra Polyp

Hydrant Fireplug, H

Hydrocarbon Acetylene, Aldrin, Alkane, Alkene, Alkyl, Alkyne, Amylene, Arene, Asphaltite, Benzene, Butadiene, Butane, Butene, Camphane, Camphene, Carotene, Cetane, Cubane, Cycloalkane, Cyclohexane, Cyclopropane, Cymogene, Decane, Diene, Dioxin, Diphenyl, Ethane, Gutta, Halon, Hatchettite, Hemiterpene, Heptane, Hexane, Hexene, Hexyl(ene), Indene,

Isobutane, Isoprene, Ligroin, Limonene, Mesitylene, Naphtha, Naphthalene, Nonane, Octane, Olefine, Paraffin, Pentane, Pentene, Pentylene, Phenanthrene, Phene, Picene, Polyene, Propane, Pyrene, Retene, Squalene, Stilbene, Styrene, Terpene, Toluene, Triptane, Wax, Xylene, Xylol

Hydrogen Deut(er)on, Diplon, Ethene, H, Muonium, Protium, Replaceable, Tritium

Hydrophobic Rabid

Hydroplane Skid

Hydroponic Soil

Hydrozoa(n) Campanularia, Millepore, Portuguese man-of-war, Siphonophore

Hyena Aard-wolf, Earthwolf, Laughing, Spotted, Strand-wolf, Tiger-wolf

Hygiene, Hygienic Aseptic, Oral, Sanitary, Sepsis, Sleep

Hymen Maidenhead

Hymn(s) Anthem, Benedictine, Bhajan, Canticle, Carol, Cathisma, Choral(e), Coronach, Dies Irae, Dithyramb, Doxology, Gloria, Hallel, Introit(us), Ithyphallic, Lay, Magnificat, Mantra, Marseillaise, Nunc dimittis, Ode, P(a)ean, Psalm, Recessional, Rigveda, Sanctus, Secular, Sequence, Stabat mater, Sticheron, Tantum ergo, Te deum, Trisagion, Troparion, Veda

Hymnographer, Hymnologist David, Faber, Heber, Moody, Neale, Parry, Sankey, Watts

Hyperbole, Hyperbolic Auxesis, Exaggeration, Sech

Hypercritical Captious

Hyperion Titan

Hypersensitive Allergic, Idiosyncratic

Hypha(e) Conidiophore, Stroma

Hyphen(ated) Dash, Parasyntheton, Soft

Hypnosis, Hypnotise, Hypnotic, Hypnotism, Hypnotist Braidism, Chloral, Codeine, Enthral, Entrance, Hypotonia, Magnetic, Meprobamate, Mesmerism, Svengali

Hypochondria(c) Hyp, Nosophobia, Phrenesiac, Valetudinarian

Hypocrisy, Hypocrite, Hypocritical Archimago, Bigot, Byends, Cant, Carper, Chadband, Deceit, Dissembler, Heep, Holy Willie, Humbug, Insincere, Janus-faced, Mucker, Nitouche, Pecksniff, Pharisaic, Pharisee, Prig, Sanctimony, Self-pious, Sepulchre, Tartuf(f)e, Two-faced, Whited sepulchre

Hypothesis, Hypothetical Biophor, Continuum, Gluon, Graviton, Nebular, Notional, Null, Plantesimal, Sapir-Whorf, Suppositious, Virtual, Working

Hyrax Cony, Daman, Dassie, Klipdas

Hysteria, Hysteric(al) Achiria, Astasia, Conniption, Delirium, Frenzy, Meemie, Mother

Ii

I A, Ch, Cham, Che, Dotted, Ego, Ich, Indeed, India, Iodine, Italy, J, Je, Me, Muggins, One, Self

Ian Scot

Ibex Izard

Ibis Hadedah, Sacred, Waldrapp

Ice(d), Ice-cream, Icing, Icy Alcorza, Anchor, Arctic, Ballicatter, Banana split, Berg, Black, Brash, Camphor, Cassata, Coconut, Cone, Cool, Cornet, Coupe, Cream, Crystal, Diamonds, Drift, Dry, Floe, Frappé, Frazil, Freeze, Frigid, Frore, Frosting, Frosty, Gelato, Gelid, Gems, Glacé, Glacial, Glacier, Glare, Glib, Granita, Graupel, Ground, Growler, Hailstone, Hok(e)y-pok(e)y, Hommock, Hummock, Knickerbocker glory, Kulfi, Lolly, Macallum, Marzipan, Neapolitan, Pack, Pancake, Pingo, Polar, Popsicle®, Rime, Rink, Royal, Sconce, Serac, Shelf, Sherbet, Slay, Slider, Slob, Sludge, Sorbet, Spumone, Spumoni, Stream, Sugar, Tickly-benders, Topping, Tortoni, Tutti-frutti, Verglas, Virga, Wafer, Water, Wintry

Ice-axe Piolet

Iceberg Calf, Floe, Growler

Ice-box Cooler, Freezer, Fridge, Frig, Yakhdan

Ice-cream *see* ICE

Iceland IS

Ice-skating Choctaw, Figure, Glide

Icicle Tangle

Icon Idol, Image, Madonna, Sprite

Icterus Jaundice

Id(e) Ego, Fish, Orfe

Idea(s) Archetype, Brainchild, Brainwave, Clou, Clue, Conceit, Concept, Fancy, Fixed, Germ, Hunch, Idée fixe, Idolum, Image, Inkling, Inspiration, Interpretation, Keynote, Light, > **NOTION**, Obsession, Plan, Plank, Rationale, Recept, Theory, Thought, Whimsy, Zeitgeist

Ideal(ise) A1, Abstract, Bee's knees, Cat's whiskers, Dream, Eden, Ego, Goal, Halo, Hero, Model, Monist, Nirvana, Notional, Paragon, Pattern, > **PERFECT**, Romantic, Siddhi, Sidha, Sublimate, Transcendental, Utopian, Vision

Idealism, Idealist(ic) Dreamer, More, Perfectionist, Quixotic, Romantic, Visionary

Identical Alike, Clone, Congruent, Equal, Menechmian, Same, Selfsame, Verbatim, Very

Identification, Identify Bertillonage, Codeword, Credentials, Designate, Diagnosis, Differentiate, Discern, Document, Dog-tag, Earmark, Empathy, Espy, Finger(print), ID, Label, Mark, Name-tape, Password, Pin, Pinpoint, Place, Recognise, Reg(g)o, Secern, Spot, Swan-hopping, Swan-upping, Verify

Identikit® E-fit

Identity Alias, Appearance, Corporate, Credentials, Equalness, Likeness, Numerical, Oneness, Qualitative, Seity, Self, Selfhood

Ideologue Hard-liner

Idiom Americanism, Argot, Britishism, Cant, Expression, Idioticon, Jargon, Language, Pahlavi, Parlance, Pehlevi, Syri(a)cism, Syrism

Idiosyncrasy Foible, Mannerism, Nature, Quirk, Way

Idiot(ic), Idiocy Congenital, Dingbat, Dolt, Eejit, Fool, Goose, Half-wit, Imbecile Inane, Maniac, Moron, Natural, Nerk, Nidget, Noncom, Oaf, Ouph(e), > **STUPID (PERSON)**, Tony, Twit, Zany

Idle(ness), Idler Bludger, Boondoggle, Bum, Bumble, Bummle, Cockaigne, Dally, Deadbeat, Diddle, Dilly-dally, Dole-bludger, Donnat, Donnot, Do-nothingism, Drone, Fainéant, Fallow, Farnarkel, Fester, Flaneur, Flim-flam, Footle, Frivolous, Groundless, Hawm, Inaction, Indolent, Inert, Lackadaisical, Laesie, Lallygag, Layabout, Laze, Lazy, Lead-swinger, Lie, Light, Limer, Loaf, Lollop, Lollygag, Lotophagus, Lounge, Lusk, Micawber, Mike, Mollusc, Mooch, Mouch, Otiose, Otium, Patagonian, Piddle, Ride, Scapegrace, Shiftless, Skive, Sloth, Sluggard, Spiv, Stalko, Stock-still, Stooge, Stroam, Tarry, Transcendental, Trock, Troke, Truant, Truck, Twiddle, Unbusy, Unoccupied, Vain, Vegetate, Veg out, Waste

Idol(ise) Adore, Adulate, Baal(im), Baphomet, Bel, Crush, Fetich(e), Fetish, God, Heartthrob, Hero, Icon, Image, Joss, Juggernaut, Lion, Mammet, Manito, Manitou, Matinee, Maumet, Mawmet, Molech, Moloch, Mommet, Moorish, Mumbo-jumbo, Stotter, Swami, Teraph(im), Termagant, Vision, Wood, Worship

Idyll(ic) Arcady, Eclogue, Pastoral, Peneian

Ie Sc

If, If it All-be, An('t), Condition, Gif, Gin, In case, Pot, Provided, Sobeit, Whether

Igloo Snowden

Ignis-fatuus Elf-fire, Fire-dragon, Fire-drake, Friar's lanthorn, Wildfire

Ignite, Ignition Coil, Electronic, Flare, Kindle, Lightning, Spark, Starter

Ignoble Base, Inferior, Mean, Vile

Ignominious, Ignominy Base, Dishonour, Fiasco, Infamous, Scandal, > **SHAME**

Ignorance, Ignorant Analphabet, Anan, Artless, Benighted, Blind, Clueless, Darkness, Green, Hick, Illiterate, Inerudite, Ingram, Ingrum, Inscient, Know-nothing, Lewd, Lumpen, Misken, Nescience, Night, Oblivious, Oik, Philistine, Purblind, Red-neck, Unaware, Uneducated, Unlettered, Unread, Unschooled, Untold, Unversed, Unwist

Ignore Ba(u)lk, Blink, Bypass, Connive, Cut, Discount, Disregard, Forget, Neglect, Omit, Overlook, Override, Overslaugh, Pass, Pass-up, Rump, Slight, Snub

Igor Prince

I Know Iwis, Ywis

Ill Adverse, All-overish, Bad, Bilious, Cronk, Crook, Evil, Inauspicious, Income, Off-colour, Poorly, Queer, Sea-sick, > **SICK**, Unweal, Unwell, Valetudinarian, Wog, Wrong

▷ **Ill** *may indicate* an anagram

Ill-balanced Lop-sided

Ill-bred Churlish, Plebeian, Uncouth, Unmannerly

▷ **Ill-composed** *may indicate* an anagram

Ill-defined Diagnosis, Hazy, Unclear, Vague

Ill-dressed Frumpish

Illegal, Illicit Adulterine, Black, Bootleg, Breach, Furtive, Ill-gotten, Malfeasance, Misbegotten, Pirated, Shonky, Unlawful

Illegitimate Bastard, By-blow, Come-o'-will, Fitz, Irregular, Love-child,

Lucky-piece, Mamzer, Misbegotten, Misborn, Misfortunate, Momzer, Natural, Scarp, Spurious, Unlineal

Ill-favoured Lean, Offensive, Thin, Ugly

Ill-feeling, Ill-humour Bad blood, Bile, Curt, Dudgeon, Glum, Hate, Miff, Peevish, Pique, Rheumatic

Illiberal Insular

Illicit *see* ILLEGAL

Illiterate Ignoramus, Unlettered, Unread

Ill-looking Peaky, Poorly

Ill-luck Ambs-ace, Ames-ace, Bad trot, Deuce-ace, Misfortune

Ill-mannered, Ill-natured Attercop, Bitchy, Crabby, Ethercap, Ettercap, Guttersnipe, Huffy, Stingy, Sullen, Ugly, Uncouth, Unkind

Illness Aids, Ailment, Attack, Autism, Brucellosis, Complaint, Croup, Death-bed, Diabetes, Disease, DS, Dwalm, Dwaum, Dyscrasia, Eclampsia, Grippe, Hangover, Hypochondria, Lockjaw, Malady, ME, Scarlatina, Sickness, Terminal, Toxaemia, Urosis, Weed, Weid, Wog

Ill-nourished Emaciated

Illogical Non-sequitur

Ill-smelling F(o)etid, High, Hing, Miasmic, Stinking

Ill-tempered *see* ILL-MANNERED

Ill-timed Inopportune, Unseasonable

Illuminate(d), Illumination Brighten, Clarify, Cul-de-lampe, Decorate, Enlighten, Floodlit, Lamplight, Langley, Light, Limn, Miniate, Nernst, Pixel, Radiate, Rushlight

Illusion, Illusory Air, Apparition, Barmecide, Deception, Deja vu, Fallacy, Fancy, Fantasy, Hallucination, Ignis-fatuus, Mare's-nest, Maya, Mirage, Muller-Lyer, Optical, Phantom, Phi-phenomenon, Specious, Trompe l'oeil, Unreality, Will o'the wisp

Illustrate(d), Illustration, Illustrator Case, Centrefold, Collotype, Demonstrate, Drawing, Eg, Elucidate, Epitomise, Exemplify, Explain, Figure, Frontispiece, Grangerize, Graphic, Half-tone, Illume, Illumin(at)e, Instance, Instantiate, Limner, Lithograph, Pictorial, Plate, Show, Sidelight, Spotlight, Tenniel, Vignette

Illustrious Bright, Celebrated, Famous, Legendary, Renowned

Ill-will Animosity, Enmity, Grudge, Hostility, Malice, Maltalent, Spite

I'm I'se

Image(s) Atman, Blip, Brand, Corporate, Discus, Effigy, Eidetic, Eidolon, Eikon, Eiluned, Emotion, Enantiomorph, Graphic, Graven, Hologram, Hypnagogic, Icon, Iconograph, Ident, Idol, Invultuation, Joss, Latent, Likeness, Matte, Mirror, Murti, Paranthelium, Pentimento, Phantasmagoria, Photogram, Photograph, Pic(ture), Pixel(l)ated, Pixil(l)ated, Poetic, Profile, Public, Recept, Representation, Scintigram, Search, Shadowgraph, Simulacrum, Spectrum, Spitting, Split, Stereotype, Symbol, Teraph(im), Tiki, Tomogram, Totem, Video, Virtual, Xoanon

Imaginary (land), Imagination, Imaginative, Imagine(d) Assume, Believe, Boojum, Cloud-cuckoo-land, Cockaigne, Cockayne, Conceive, Conjure, Cyborg, Dystopia, Envisage, Esemplasy, Faery, Faine, Fancy, Feign, Fictional, Fictitious, Fictor, Figment, Figure, Hallucinate, Hobbit, Ideate, Invent, Mind's eye, Oz, Picture, Poetical, Prefigure, Pretend, Recapture, Replicant, Scotch mist, Snark, Straw, > SUPPOSE, Surmise, Think, Vicarious, Visualise, Whangam

Imbecile Anile, Fool, Idiot, > STUPID

> **Imbecile** *may indicate* an anagram

Imbibe Absorb, Drink, Lap, Quaff, Suck, Swallow
Imbricate Overlie
Imbroglio Complication, Maze
Imbrue, Imbue Colour, Impregnate, Indoctrinate, Infuse, Inoculate, Permeate, Soak, Steep
Imitate, Imitation, Imitator Act, Ape, Copy(cat), Counterfeit, Dud, Echo, Echopraxia, Emulate, Epigon(e), Ersatz, Fake, False, Faux, Follow, Marinist, Me-too, Mime, Mimetic, Mimic(ry), Mockery, Monkey, Parody, Parrot, Paste, Pastiche, Pinchbeck, Potichomania, Rip-off, Sham, Simulate, Stumer, Take-off, Travesty
Immaculate Conception, Flawless, Lily-white, Perfect, Pristine, Spotless, Virgir
Immanentist Pantheist
Immaterial Insignificant, Spiritual, Trifling
Immature(ly), Immaturity Callow, Crude, Embryo, Ergate(s), Green, Inchoate, Larval, Neotenic, Non-age, Puberal, Puberulent, Pupa, Raw, Sophomoric, Tender, Unbaked, Unripe, Young
▷ **Immature** *may indicate* a word incompleted
Immediate(ly) Alsoon, At once, B(e)live, Direct, Eftsoons, Ekdum, First-time, Forthwith, Imminent, Incontinent, Instantaneous, Instanter, Near, > **NOW**, Outright, Present, Pronto, Right-off, Short-term, Slapbang, Spontaneous, Stat Straight, Straight off, Sudden, Then, Tout de suite
Immense Brobdingnag, Cosmic, Enormous, > **GIGANTIC**, Huge, Vast, Wide
Immerse Baptise, Demerge, Demerse, Drench, Embathe, Emplonge, Enew, Engage, Imbathe, Plunge, Soak, Steep
Immigrant, Immigration Aliya(h), Aussiedler, Carpet-bagger, Chalutz, Greener, Greenhorn, Halutz, Illegal, Incomer, Issei, Merino, Metic, Nisei, Olim, Outsider, Pilgrim, Pommy, Redemption(er), Reffo, Sanei, Sansei, Settler, Wetback, Whenwe
Imminent Approaching, Close, Immediate, Pending
Immobility, Immobilize Cataplexy, Catatonia, Hog-tie, Inertia, Pinion, Rigidity, Tether
Immoderate Excessive, Extreme, Inordinate, Intemperate, Lavish, Undue
Immodest Brash, Brazen, Forward, Indelicate, Unchaste
Immolation Sacrifice, Sati, Suttee
Immoral(ity) Corrupt, Dissolute, Evil, Lax, Libertine, Licentious, Loose, Nefarious, Peccable, Reprobate, Turpitude, Unsavoury, Wanton
Immortal(ity) Agelong, Amarant(h), Amarantin, Amritattva, Athanasy, Deathless, > **DIVINE**, Enoch, Eternal, Ever-living, Famous, Godlike, Memory, Sin, Struldbrug, Timeless, Undying
Immovable Fast, Firm, Obdurate, Rigid, Stable, Stubborn
Immune, Immunisation, Immunise(r), Immunity Acquired, Anamnestic, Anergy, Bar, Cree, Diplomatic, Free, Inoculate, Klendusic, Natural, Non-specific, Pasteurism, Pax, Premunition, Properdin, Serum, Vaccine
Immure Confine, Encloister, Imprison
Imp(ish) Devilet, Elf, Flibbertigibbet, Gamin(e), Hobgoblin, Limb, Lincoln, Litherly, Nickum, Nis(se), Puck, Ralph, Rascal, Sprite
Impact Bearing, Bump, Clash, Collision, Feeze, Impinge, Jar, Jolt, Pack, Percuss, Pow, Slam, Souse, Wham
Impair(ed), Impairment Cripple, Damage, Disease, Enfeeble, > **HARM**, Injure, Lame, Mar, Mental, Odd, Paralogia, Stale, Vitiate
Impala Pallah
Impale Elance, Ga(u)nch, Skewer, Spike, Transfix

Impart Bestow, Convey, Divulge, Impute, Infect, Shed, Tell

Impartial Candid, Detached, Equitable, Even-handed, Fair, Just, Neutral, Unbiased

Impassable, **Impasse** Deadlock, Dilemma, Invious, Jam, Snooker, Stalemate, Zugzwang

Impassioned Emotional, Fervid, Fiery, Heated, Zealous

Impassive Apathetic, Deadpan, Stoical, Stolid

Impatience, **Impatient** Chafing, Chut, Dysphoria, Fiddle-de-dee, Fiddlesticks, Fidgety, Fretful, Hasty, Irritable, Och, Peevish, Peremptory, Petulant, Pish, Till(e)y-vall(e)y, Tilly-fally, Tut

Impeach Accuse, Challenge, Charge, Indict

Impeccable Faultless, Novice

Impecunious Penniless, Poor, Short

Impedance, **Impede**, **Impediment** Burr, Clog, Dam, Diriment, Encumber, Halt, Hamstring, Handicap, > **HINDER**, Hog-tie, Let, Log, Obstacle, Obstruct, Reactance, Rub, Shackle, Snag, Stammer, Stymie, Tongue-tie, Trammel, Veto, Z

Impel(led) Actuate, Coerce, Drave, Drive, Drove, Goad, Inspire, > **URGE**

Impend(ing) Imminent, Looming, Toward

Impenetrable Adamantine, Air-tight, Dense, Hard, Impervious, Proof

Imperative Categorical, Dire, Jussive, Mood, Need-be, Pressing, Vital

Imperceptible Intangible, Invisible, Latent, Subtle

Imperfect(ion) Aplasia, Aplastic, Blotch, Defect, Deficient, Faculty, Feathering, Flawed, Half-pie, Kink, Kinkle, Lame, Poor, Rough, Second, Unideal

Imperial(ist), **Imperious** Beard, C(a)esarian, Commanding, Haughty, Majestic, Masterful, Mint, Peremptory, Regal, Rhodes, Royal, Tuft

Imperil Endanger, Risk

Imperishable Eternal, Immortal, Indestructible

Impermeable Airtight, Athermanous, Proof, Resistant

Impersonal Abstract, Cold, Detached, Inhuman

Impersonate, **Impersonation**, **Impersonator** Amphitryon, Ape, As, Double, Imitate, Impression, Mimic, Pose, Spoof

Impertinence, **Impertinent** Crust, Flip(pant), Fresh, Impudent, Irrelevant, Rude, Sass, Sauce

Imperturbable Cool, Placid, Stoic, Tranquil

Impervious(ness) Athermancy, Callous, Hardened, Obdurate, Proof, Tight

Impetigo Scrumpox

Impetuous, **Impetuosity** Birr, Brash, Bullheaded, Elan, > **HASTY**, Headstrong, Heady, Hothead, Impulsive, Rash, Tearaway, Vehement, Violent, Young Turk

Impetus Birr, Drift, Incentive, MacGuffin, Momentum, Propulsion, Slancio, Steam, Swing

Impious Blasphemous, Godless, Irreverent, Unholy

Implant(ation) AID, Embed, Engraft, Enroot, Graft, Inset, Instil, Nidation, Sow

Implausible Lame, Off-the-wall

Implement Agent, Celt, Cultivator, Disgorger, Eolith, Execute, Flail, Follow out, Fork, Fulfil, Hacksaw, Harrow, Hayfork, Muller, Pin, Pitchfork, Plectrum, Plough, Pusher, Rest, Ripple, Scarifier, Scythe, Seed drill, Shoehorn, Sickle, Spatula, Spayd®, Squeegee, Strickle, Tongs, > **TOOL**, Toothpick, Utensil

Implicate, **Implication** Accuse, Concern, Connotation, Embroil, Incriminate, Innuendo, > **INVOLVE**, Material, Overtone

Implore Beg, Beseech, Crave, > **ENTREAT**, Obsecrate, Petition, Plead, Pray

Imply, **Implied** Hint, Insinuate, Involve, Predicate, Signify, > **SUGGEST**, Tacit

Impolite Ill-bred, Rude, Uncivil

Import(s) Convey, Denote, Drift, Invisible, Mean, Parallel, Sense, Signify, Spell, Visible

Importance, Important (person) Big, Big cheese, Big wheel, Calibre, Cardinal, Central, Cheese, Cob, Coming, Considerable, Core, Cornerstone, Count, Critical, Crucial, Crux, Earth-shaking, Earth-shattering, Eminent, Epochal, Grave, Gravitas, Greatness, Heavy, High, High-muck-a-muck, Honcho, Hotshot, Huzoor, Key, Keystone, Macher, Magnitude, Main, Major, Material, Matters, Megastar, Mighty, Milestone, Moment(ous), Nabob, Nib, Note, Numero uno, Obbligato, Personage, Pivotal, Pot, Preponderate, Prime, Principal, Salient, Seminal, Serious, Significant, Something, Special, Stature, Status, Stress, Substantive, Tuft, Urgent, VIP, Weight, Weighty, Worth

Importune, Importunate Beg, Coax, Flagitate, Press(ing), Prig, Solicit, Urgent

Impose, Imposing, Imposition Allocate, Assess, August, Burden, Charge, Cheat, Diktat, Dread, Enforce, Enjoin, Epic, Fine, Flam, Foist, Fraud, Grand(iose), Hidage, Homeric, Hum, Impot, Inflict, Kid, Levy, Lumber, Majestic, Obtrude, Pensum, Pole, Scot, Sponge, Stately, Statuesque, Sublime, Whillywhaw

Impossible Hopeless, Incorrigible, Insoluble, Insurmountable, No-go, No-no, Unacceptable

Impost Excise, Levy, Tax, Toll

Imposter, Impostor Bunyip, Charlatan, Disaster, Faitor, Faitour, > FAKE, Fraud, Idol, Pretender, Sham, Triumph, Warbeck

Impotent Barren, Helpless, Spado, Sterile, Weak

Impound(er) Appropriate, Bond, Confiscate, Intern, Pen, Pinder, Poind

Impoverish(ed) Bankrupt, Bare, Beggar, Exhaust, Indigent, Straiten

Impractical Absurd, Academic, Chim(a)era, Idealist, Inoperable, Laputan, Not on, Other-worldly, Quixotic, Useless

Imprecation Oath, Pize

Imprecise Approximate, Inaccurate, Indeterminate, Loose, Nebulous, Rough, Sloppy, Vague

Impregnate Conceive, Enwomb, Imbue, Inseminate, Milt, Permeate, Resinate

Impresario Maestro, Manager, Producer, Showman

Impress(ive), Impression(able) Air, Astonish, Awe, Blur, Blurb, Bowl over, Brand, Cliché, Commanding, Conscript, Crimp, Deboss, Dent, Dramatic, Edition, Effect, Engram(ma), Engrave, Enstamp, Epic, Feel(ing), Fingerprint, Fossil, Frank, Gas, Grab, Grandiose, Heroic, Homeric, Idée, Impinge, Imprint, Incuse, Intaglio, Kick ass, Knock, Let, Niello, Noble, Note, Palimpsest, Plastic, Plate, Pliable, Powerful, Prent, Presence, Press(gang), Print, Proof, Recruit, Repute, Responsive, Ripsnorter, Rotund, Seal, Seize, Sense, Shanghai, Slay, Smite, Soft, Spectacular, Stamp, Stereotype, Strike, Susceptible, Sway, Tableau, Touch, Vibrant, Watermark, Weal, Weighty, Wow

Impressionist Cezanne, Liebermann, Lumin(ar)ist, Manet, Matisse, Monet, Morisot, Renoir

Imprint Edition, Engrave, Etch, Stamp

Imprison(ment) Cape, Committal, Confine, Constrain, Custody, Durance, False, Immure, Incarcerate, Intern, Jail, Penal servitude, Quad, Quod, Time

Improbable Buckley's chance, Buckley's hope, Dubious, Far-fetched, Unlikely

Impromptu Ad lib, Extempore, Improvised, Offhand, Spontaneous, Sudden, Unrehearsed

Improper, Impropriety Abnormal, Blue, Demirep, False, Illegitimate, Indecent, Indecorum, Outré, Prurient, Solecism, Undue, Unmeet, Unseemly, Untoward

▷ **Improperly** *may indicate* an anagram

Improve(ment), Improver, Improving Advance, Ameliorate, Beet, Benefit, Bete, Break, Buck, Cap, Chasten, Conditioner, Cultivate, Détente, Didactic, Ease, Edify, Edutainment, Embellish, Emend, Enhance, Enrich, Eugenic, Euthenics, File, Gentrify, Kaizen, Meliorate, Mend, Potentiate, Promote, Rally, Refine, Reform, Resipiscence, Retouch, Sarvodaya, Slim, Streamline, Surpass, Tart, Tatt, Titivate, Top, Touch-up, Turn round, Tweak, Uptrend, Upturn

Improvident Feckless

Improvise(d), Improvisation Adlib, Break, Devise, Drumhead, Extemporise, Invent, Knock-up, Lash-up, Noodle, Ride, Scratch, Sudden, Vamp, Wing

Imprudent Foolhardy, Foolish, Impetuous, Impolitic, Indiscreet, Injudicious, Rash, Reckless, Unwary, Unwise

Impudence, Impudent Audacious, Backchat, Bardy, Bold, Brash, Brassy, Brazen, Cheeky, Cool, Crust, Effrontery, Forward, Gall, Gallus, Impertinent, Insolent, Jackanapes, Lip, Malapert, Neck, > NERVE, Pert, Sass(y), Sauce, Saucebox, Saucy, Temerity, Whippersnapper, Yankie

Impugn Censure, Challenge, Defame, Impeach, Malign

Impulse, Impulsive Compelling, Conatus, Dictate, Drive, Efferent, Headlong, Horme, Ideopraxist, Impetus, Instigation, > INSTINCT, Libido, Madcap, Nerve, Nisus, Premature, Premotion, Send, Signal, Snap, Specific, Spontaneous, Tendency, Thrust, Tic, Urge, Whim

Impure, Impurity Adulterated, Donor, Faints, Feints, Indecent, Lees, Lewd, Regulus, Scum, Unclean

Imputation, Impute Ascribe, Attribute, Charge, Scandal, Slander, Slur

In A, Amid, Chic, Home, Hostel, I', Inn, Intil, Occupying, On, Pop(ular), Pub, Trendy, Within

Inability Anosmia, Aphagia, Aphasia, Apraxia

Inaccessible Abaton, Impervious, Remote, Unattainable

Inaccurate Distorted, Erroneous, Faulty, Imprecise, Inexact, Out, Rough, Slipshod, Unfaithful

Inactive, Inaction, Inactivity Acedia, Cabbage, Comatose, Dead, Dormant, Extinct, Fallow, Hibernate, Idle, Inert, Moratorium, Passive, Quiescent, Rusty, Sedentary, Sluggish, Torpid, Veg(etate)

In addition Eke, Else, Further, Moreover, Plus, To boot, Too

Inadequate Derisory, Feeble, Inapt, Inferior, Pathetic, Poor, Ropy, Scanty, Thin

Inadvertent(ly) Accidental, Careless, Chance, Unwitting

In a flap *may indicate* an anagram

In a high degree So

In a hundred Percent

Inane Empty, Fatuous, Foolish, Imbecile, Silly, Vacant

Inanimate Abiotic, Lifeless

Inappropriate Amiss, Infelicitous, Malapropos, Off-key, Unapt, Unbecoming, Undue, Unsuitable, Untoward

Inapt Maladroit, Unsuitable

Inarticulate(ness) Indistinct, Mumbling, Psellism

Inartistic Artless, Crude

Inattentive, Inattention Asleep, Deaf, Distrait, Dwaal, Dwa(l)m, Dwaum, Heedless, Loose, Slack, Unheeding, Unobservant

Inaudible Silent, Superhet

Inaugurate Han(d)sel, Initiate, Install, Introduce

Inauspicious Adverse, Ominous, Sinister

In a whirl *may indicate* an anagram

In a word *may indicate* two clue words linked to form one

Inborn, Inbred Homogamy, Inherent, Innate, Native, Selfed, Sib
Incalculable Endless, Unpredictable, Untold
Incandescent Alight, Bright, Brilliant, Excited
Incantation Charm, Magic, Mantra, Spell
Incapable Can't, Powerless, Unable, Useless
Incarnation Advent, Avatar, Embodiment, Fleshing, Krishna, Rama, Ramachandra
In case Lest, So
Incautious Foolhardy, Rash, Reckless, Unwary
Incendiary Arsonist, Combustible, Firebug, Fire-lighter, Fireship, Napalm
Incense(d), Incenser Anger, Aroma, Elemi, Enfelon, Enrage, Homage, Hot, > INFLAME, Joss-stick, Navicula, Onycha, Outrage, Pastil(le), Provoke, Thurible Thus, Vex, Wrathful
Incentive Carrot, Carrot and stick, Fillip, Impetus, Motive, Premium, Spur, Stakhanovism, Stimulus, Wage
Incessant Constant, Endless
Incest Backcross
Inch(es) Ait, Column, Edge, Isle, Mil, Sidle, Tenpenny, Uncial
Inchoate Formless, Immature, Incipient
Incident(al) Affair, Baur, Bawr, Carry-on, Chance, Circumstance, Episode, Event, Facultative, Handbags, Negligible, Occasion, Occurrent, Page, Scene, Throwaway
Incinerate, Incinerator Burn, Combust, Cremate, Destructor
Incipient Beginning, Germinal, Inchoate
Incise, Incision, Incisive(ness) Bite, Cut, Engrave, Incavo, Lobotomy, McBurney's, Mordant, Notch, Phlebotomy, Punchy, Scarf, Scribe, Slit, Surgical Tracheotomy, Trenchant
Incisor Foretooth
Incite(ment) Abet, Drive, Egg, Fillip, Hortative, Hoy, Impassion, Inflame, Instigate, Kindle, Motivate, Prod, Prompt, Provoke, Put, Rouse, Sa sa, Sedition, Set, Sic(k), Sool, > SPUR, Sting, Suborn, Suggest, Tar, Urge
Incline(d), Inclination Acclivity, Angle, Aslope, Atilt, Bank, Batter, Bent, Bias, Bow, Camber, Clinamen, Declivity, Dip, Disposed, Drift, Enclitic, Glacis, > GRADIENT, Grain, Hade, Heel, Hill, Kant, Kip, Lean, Liking, List, Maw, Minded, Nod, On, Partial, Peck, Penchant, Proclivity, Prone, Propensity, Rake, Ramp, Ready, Rollway, Set, Shelve, Slant, > SLOPE, Steep, Steeve, Stomach, Supine, Tend, Tilt, Tip, Trend, Upgrade, Velleity, Verge, Weathering, Will
Include(d) Add, Bracket, Compass, Comprise, Connotate, Contain, Cover, Embody, Embrace, Enclose, Involve, Subsume, Therein
Incognito Anonymous, Disguised, Faceless, Secret, Unnamed
Incoherent Confused, Disconnected, Disjointed, Gabbling, Inarticulate, Rambling, Spluttering
Incombustible Clinker
Income Annuity, Benefice, Disposable, Dividend, Earned, Entry, Fixed, Franked Livelihood, Living, Meal-ticket, Milch cow, Notional, OTE, Penny-rent, Prebend, Primitiae, Private, Proceeds, Rent, Rente, Rent-roll, Returns, Revenue, Salary, Stipend, Unearned, Unfranked, Wages
Incommunicado Isolated, Silent
Incomparable Supreme, Unequalled, Unmatched
Incompatible, Incompatibility Contradictory, Dyspathy, Incongruous, Inconsistent, Mismatched, Unsuited
Incompetent Bungler, Deadhead, Helpless, Ill, Inefficient, Inept, Palooka,

Unable, Unfit

Incomplete Broadbrush, Cagmag, Catalectic, Deficient, Inchoate, Lacking, Partial, Pendent, Rough, Unfinished

Incomprehensible Double Dutch, Hard, Unbelievable

Inconceivable Impossible, Incredible

In confusion *may indicate* an anagram

Incongruous, **Incongruity** Absurd, Discordant, Heterogenous, Irish, Ironic, Sharawadgi, Sharawaggi

In connection with Re

Inconsiderable Light, Slight

Inconsiderate High-handed, Hog, Petty, Presumptuous, Roughshod, Thoughtless, Unkind

Inconsistency, **Inconsistent** Alien, Anacoluthon, Anomaly, Contradictory, Discrepant, Oxymoronic, Paradoxical, Unequal, Unsteady, Variance

Inconsolable Heartbroken, Niobe

Inconspicuous Unobtrusive

Inconstant Chameleon, Desultory, Fickle, Light, Mutable, > VARIABLE

Inconvenience, **Inconvenient** Awkward, Bother, Discommode, Fleabite, Incommodious, > TROUBLE, Unseemly, Untoward

Incorporate(d), **Incorporation** Absorb, Embody, Inc, Integrate, Introgression, Join, Merge, Subsume

Incorporeal Aery, Airy, Spiritual

Incorrect Catachresis, False, Improper, Invalid, Naughty, Wrong

Incorrigible Hopeless, Obstinate

Incorruptible Copper-bottomed, Honest, Immortal, Pure, Robespierre, Sea-green

Increase, **Increasing** Accelerando, Accelerate, Accession, Accrue, Add, Additur, Aggrandise, Amplify, Amp up, Appreciate, Approve, Augment, Auxetic, Bolster, Bulge, Crank up, Crescendo, Crescent, Crescive, Deepen, Dilate, Double, Ech(e), Eech, Eik, Eke, Enhance, Enlarge, Escalate, > EXPAND, Explosion, Greaten, > GROW, Heighten, Ich, Increment, Interbreed, Jack, Jack up, Lift, Magnify, Mark up, Mount, Multiply, Plus, Proliferate, Propagate, Ramp up, Redshift, Reflation, Regrate, Rise, Snowball, Swell, Thrive, Up, Upswing, Wax

Incredible Amazing, Cockamamie, Extraordinary, Fantastic, Steep, Stey, Tall

Incredulity, **Incredulous** Distrust, Infidel, Suspicion, Thunderstruck, Unbelief

Increment Accrual, Augment, Growth, Increase

Incriminate Accuse, Implicate, Inculpate

Incubate, **Incubator** Brooder, Develop, Eccaleobion, Hatch

Incubus Demon, Load, Nightmare

Inculcate Implant, Infuse

Incumbent Lying, Obligatory, Occupier, Official

Incur Assume, Earn, Involve

Incursion Foray, Inroad, Invasion, Raid, Razzia

Indecent Bare, Blue, Fescennine, Free, Immodest, Immoral, Improper, Lewd, Obscene, Rabelaisian, Racy, Scurril(e), Sotadic, Spicy, Sultry, Unproper, Unseem(ly), X-rated

Indecision, **Indecisive** Demur, Dithery, Doubt, Hamlet, Havering, Hung jury, Inconclusive, Suspense, Swither, Weakkneed

Indeclinable Aptote

Indecorous Graceless, Immodest, Outré, Unbecoming

Indeed Atweel, Ay, Da, Een, Even, Faith, Haith, Insooth, Ja wohl, La, Marry, Quotha, Truly, Verily, Yah, Yea

Indefensible Implausible, Inexcusable, Vincible

Indefinite(ly) A, An, Any, Evermore, Hazy, Nth, Some, Undecided, Vague

Indelible Fast, Permanent

Indelicate Broad, Coarse, Improper, Vulgar, Warm

Indemnify, Indemnification, Indemnity Assythement, Compensation, Double, Insurance

Indent(ed), Indentation Apprentice, Contract, Crenellate, Dancetty, Dimple, Impress, Niche, Notch, Order, Philtrum, Subentire

Independence, Independent Autocephalous, Autogenous, Autonomy, Crossbencher, Detached, Extraneous, Free(dom), Free-lance, Free spirit, I, Liberty, Maverick, Mugwump, Perseity, Self-sufficient, Separate, Separatist, Sui juris, Swaraj, Udal, UDI, Uhuru

Indescribable Incredible, Ineffable

Indestructible Enduring, Impenetrable, Inextirpable

Indeterminate Borderline, Formless, Incalculable, Open-ended, Unknown

Index Alidad(e), Catalogue, Cephalic, Colour, Cranial, Dial, Dow Jones, Exponent, Facial, Finger, Fist, Fog, Footsie, Forefinger, Gazetteer, Glycaemic, Hang Seng, Kwic, Librorum Prohibitorum, Margin, Nasal, Nikkei, Opsonic, Power, Price, Refractive, > **REGISTER**, Rotary, Share, Table, Thumb, TPI, UV, Verborum

India(n) Adivisi, Asian, Ayah, Baboo, Babu, Bharat(i), Bihari, Canarese, Carib, Chin, Dard, Dravidian, File, Gond(wanaland), Gujarati, Harijan, Harsha, Hindu, Indic, Ink, Jain, Jat, Jemadar, Kafir, Kanarese, Kannada, Khalsa, Kisan, Kolarian, Kshatriyas, Lepcha, Ma(h)ratta, Maratha, Mazhbi, > **MEXICAN**, Mofussil, Mogul, Mulki, Munda, Munshi, Naga, Nagari, Nair, Nasik, Nation, Nayar, > **NORTH AMERICAN**, Nuri, Ocean, Oriya, Pali, Panjabi, Pargana, Parsee, Parsi, Peshwa, Plains, Prakrit, Punjabi, Punja(u)bee, Sanskrit, Sepoy, Shri, Sikh, Sind(h), > **SOUTH AMERICAN**, Sowar, Summer, Swadeshi, Tamil, Telegu, Vakeel, Vakil

Indiaman Clive

Indicate, Indication, Indicative, Indicator Adumbrate, Allude, Argue, Blinker, Cite, Clue, Cursor, > **DENOTE**, Design, Desine, Dial, Endeixis, Evidence, Evince, Fluorescein, Gesture, Gnomon, Litmus, Manifest, Mean, Mood, Nod, Notation, Performance, Pinpoint, Point, Portend, Proof, Ray, Register, Remarque, Representative, Reveal, Show, > **SIGN**, Signify, Specify, Symptom, Tip, Token, Trace, Trafficator, Trait, Winker

Indictment Accusation, Caption, Charge, Dittay, Reproach

Indifference, Indifferent Adiaphoron, Aloof, Apathetic, Apathy, Blasé, Blithe, Callous, Cavalier, Cold, Cool(th), Dead, Detached, Disdain, Easy-osy, Empty, Incurious, Insouciant, Jack easy, Mediocre, Neutral, Nonchalant, Perfunctory, Phlegm, Pococurante, Sangfroid, So-so, Stoical, Supercilious, Supine, Tepid, Unconcerned

Indigence, Indigent Need, Pauper, Penury, Poverty, Want

Indigenous Aboriginal, Endemic, Native

▷ **Indi-gent** *may indicate* Baboo or Babu

Indigestion Apepsia, Apepsy, Dyspepsia, Heartburn

Indignant, Indignation Anger, Annoyed, Incensed, Irate, Pique, Resentful, Wrathful

Indignity Affront, Outrage

Indigo Anil, Blue, Bunting, Carmine, Indole, Isatin(e)

Indirect Back-handed, By(e), Devious, Implicit, Mediate, Oblique, Remote, Roundabout, Sidelong, Zig-zag

Indiscreet, **Indiscretion** Blabbermouth, Folly, Gaffe, Imprudence, Indelicate, Injudicious, Loose cannon, Rash, Unguarded, Wild oats
Indiscriminate Haphazard, Random, Scattershot, Sweeping
Indispensable Basic, Essential, King-pin, Necessary, Sine qua non, Vital
Indispose(d), **Indisposition** Adverse, Disincline, Ill, Incapacitate, Sick, Unwell
Indisputable Evident
Indistinct Ambiguous, Bleary, Blur, Bumble, Bummle, Faint, Fuzzy, Hazy, Pale, S(c)hwa, Sfumato, > VAGUE
In distress *may indicate* an anagram
Indite Compose, Pen, Write
Indium In
Individual(ist), **Individuality** Being, Discrete, Exclusive, Free spirit, Gemma, Haecceity, Identity, Ka, Libertarian, Loner, Man, Man-jack, One-to-one, Own, Particular, Person, Poll, Respective, Separate, Single, Singular, Solo, Soul, Special, Unit, Zoon
Indoctrinate Brainwash, Discipline, Instruct
Indo-European Aryan, Jat(s)
Indolence, **Indolent** Bone idle, Fainéance, Inactive, Languid, Lazy, Otiose, Sloth, Sluggish, Supine
Indomitable Brave, Dauntless, Invincible
Indonesia(n) Batavian, Nesiot, RI
Indoor(s) Within
Indubitably Certainly, Certes, Manifestly, Surely
Induce(ment) Bribe, Carrot, Cause, Coax, Draw, Encourage, Get, Inveigle, Lead, Motivate, > PERSUADE, Prevail, Suasion, Suborn, Tempt
Induct(ion), **Inductance** Epagoge, Henry, Inaugurate, Initiate, Install, L, Logic, Prelude, Remanence
Indulge(nce), **Indulgent** Absolution, Binge, Coddle, Drink, Favour, Gratify, Humour, Law, Luxuriate, Oblige, Pamper, Pander, Pardon, Pet, Pettle, Please, > SATISFY, Splurge, Spoil, Spoonfeed, Surfeit, Tolerant, Venery, Voluptuous, Wallow
Industrial, **Industrious**, **Industry** Appliance, Application, Business, Busy, Cottage, Deedy, Diligence, Eident, Energetic, Labour, Ocnus, Operose, Ruhr, Service, Smokestack, Sunrise, Technical, Tourism, Zaibatsu
Inebriate *see* INTOXICATE
Inedible Inesculent, Noisome, Rotten
Ineffective, **Ineffectual** Clumsy, Deadhead, Drippy, Droob, Dud, Empty, Fainéant, Fruitless, Futile, Idle, Ill, Impotent, Mickey Mouse, Neutralised, Null, Powerless, Resty, Sterile, Toothless, > USELESS, Void, Weak, Wet
Inefficient Clumsy, Incompetent, Lame, Shiftless, Slack
Inelegant Awkward, Inconcinnity, Stiff, Turgid, Unneat
Ineligible Unqualified
Inept Absurd, Anorak, Cack-handed, Farouche, Nerd, Otaku, Sad sack, Schlimazel, Unskilled, Wet
Inequality Anomaly, Chebyshev's, Disparity, Injustice, Odds, Tchebyshev's
Inert(ia) Catatonia, Comatose, Dead, Dull, Excipient, Inactive, Leaden, Mollusc, Neon, Oblomovism, Potato, Sluggish, Stagnant, Stagnation, Thowless, Torpid
Inestimable Incalculable, Invaluable, Priceless
Inevitable, **Inevitably** Automatic, Certain, Fateful, Inexorable, Needs, Perforce, TINA, Unavoidable
Inexact(itude) Cretism, Incorrect, Terminological, Wrong
Inexorable Relentless

Inexpedient Impolitic, Imprudent, Unwise

Inexpensive Bargain, Cheap, Dirt-cheap, Economic

Inexperience(d), Inexpert Amateur, Callow, Colt, Crude, Fresh, > GREEN, Greenhorn, Ham, Ingénue, Jejune, Raw, Rookie, Rude, Tender, Unconversant, Unseasoned, Unseen, Unversed, Yardbird, Youthful

Inexplicable Magical, Mysterious, Paranormal, Unaccountable

Infallible Foolproof, Right, Sure-fire, Unerring

Infamous, Infamy Base, Ignominious, Notorious, Opprobrium, Shameful, Villainy

Infant Babe, Baby, Innocent, Lamb, Minor, Oral, Rug rat

Infantry(man) Buff, Foot, Grunt, Jaeger, Phalanx, Pultan, Pulto(o)n, Pultun, > SOLDIER, Tercio, Turco, Zouave

▷ **Infantry** *may refer to* babies

Infatuate(d), Infatuating, Infatuation Assot, Besot, Circean, Crush, Enamoured, Engou(e)ment, Entêté, Fanatic, Foolish, Lovesick, > OBSESSION, Rave, Turn

Infect(ed), Infecting, Infection, Infectious Angina, Anthrax, Candidiasis, Catching, Catchy, Cholera, Communicable, Contagious, Contaminate, Corrupt, Cowpox, Diseased, Fascioliasis, Fester, Focal, Fomes, Giardiasis, Gonorrhoea, Herpes, Leishmaniasis, Listeria, Lockjaw, NSU, Orf, Overrun, Poison, Polio(myelitis), > POLLUTE, Py(a)emia, Quittor, Ringworm, Roup, Salmonella, Sarcoid, Septic, Shingles, Smit(tle), Strongylosis, Taint, Tetanus, Thrush, Tinea, Toxocariasis, Trichuriasis, Typhoid, Typhus, Virion, Virulent, Whitlow, Wog, Yersiniosis, Zymosis

Infeftment Sasine, Seisin

Infer(ence), Inferred Conclude, Conjecture, Deduce, Divine, Educe, Extrapolate, Generalise, Guess, Illation, Imply, Judge, Obversion, Putative, Surmise, Syllogism

▷ **Infer** *may indicate* 'fer' around another word

Inferior Base, Bodgier, Cheap-jack, Cheesy, Coarse, Crummy, Degenerate, Dog, Ersatz, Gimcrack, Grody, Grub-street, Indifferent, Infra, Jerkwater, Less, Lo-fi, Lower, Low-grade, Minor, Naff, Nether, One-horse, Ornery, Paravail, Petty, Poor, Rop(e)y, Schlock, Second, Second-best, Shlock, Shoddy, Sprew, Sprue, Subjacent, Subordinate, Substandard, Surat, Tatty, Tinpot, Trashy, Under(man), Underneath, Understrapper, Untermensch, Waste, Worse

Infernal Demogorgon, Diabolic, Hellish, Phitonian, Tartarean, Unholy

Infertile Barren, Sterile

Infest(ed), Infestation Acariasis, Acrawl, Beset, Blight, Dog, Hoatching, Overrun, Pediculosis, Phthiriasis, > PLAGUE, Stylopised, Swarm, Torment, Trombiculiasis, Trombidiasis, Uncinariasis

Infidel Atheist, Caffre, Giaour, Heathen, Heretic, Kafir, Pagan, Paynim, Saracen

Infield Intown

Infiltrate Encroach, Enter, Instil, Intrude, Pervade

Infinite, Infinity Cosmic, Endless, Eternal, N

Infinitive Split

Infirm Decrepit, Doddery, Feeble, Lame, Shaky

▷ **Infirm** *may indicate* 'co' around another word

Infirmary Hospital, Sick bay

Inflame(d), Inflammable, Inflammation Acne, Adenitis, Afire, Ancome, Anger, Angina, Aortisis, Appendicitis, > AROUSE, Arteritis, Arthritis, Asbestosis, Balanitis, Blepharitis, Bloodshot, Bronchitis, Bronchopneumonia, Bubonic, Bunion, Bursitis, Carditis, Catarrh, Cellulitis, Cervicitis, Cheilitis,

Colitis, Colpitis, Conjunctivitis, Coryza, Croup, Cystisis, Dermatitis, Diverticulitis, Duodenitis, Ecthyma, Eczema, Enamoured, Encephalitis, Encephalomyelitis, Enchafe, Endocarditis, Endometrisis, Enfire, Enkindle, Enteritis, Enterocolitis, Erysipelas, Farmer's lung, Fasciitis, Felon, Fever, Fibrosis, Fibrositis, Fire, Folliculitis, Founder, Frostbite, Garget, Gastritis, Gastroenteritis, Gingivitis, Gleet, Glossitis, Golfer's elbow, Gout, Hepatitis A, Hepatitis B, Hyalitis, Ignatis, Ignite, Ileitis, Impassion, Incense, Infection, Intertrigo, Ire, Iritis, Keratitis, Labyrinthitis, Laminitis, Laryngitis, Lymphadenitis, Lymphangitis, Mastitis, Mastoiditis, Meningitis, Meningocephalitis, Metritis, Misenteritis, Mycetoma, Myelitis, Myocarditis, Myositis, Napalm, Naphtha, Nephritis, Neuritis, Noma, Onychia, Oophoritis, Ophthalmia, Orchitis, Osteitis, Osteoarthritis, Osteomyelitis, Osteoporosis, Otitis, Ovaritis, Panarthritis, Pancreatitis, Papillitis, Paronychia, Parotitis, Pericarditis, Perihepatitis, Perinephritis, Periodontisis, Peritonitis, Perityphlitis, Pharyngitis, Phlebitis, Phlegmasia, Phlegmon, Phlogistic, Phrenitis, Pinkeye, Pleurisy, Pneumonia, Pneumonitis, Polyneuritis, Proctitis, Prostatitis, Prurigo, Pyelitis, Pyelonephritis, Pyorrhoea, Quinsy, Rachitis, > RED, Retinitis, Rhinitis, Rosacea, Salpingitis, Sandy blight, Scleritis, Sclerotitis, Shin splints, Sinusitis, Splenitis, Spondylitis, Stimulate, Stomatitis, Strumitis, Sty(e), Sunburn, Swelling, Swimmer's itch, Sycosis, Synovitis, Tendinitis, Tennis elbow, Tenosynovitis, Thoroughpin, Thrombophilia, Thrombosis, Thrush, Thyroiditis, Tonsillitis, Touchwood, Tracheitis, Trichomoniasis, Tylosis, Tympanitis, Typhlitis, Ulitis, Urethritis, Utriculitis, Uveitis, Uvulitis, Vaginitis, Valvulitis, Vasculitis, Vincent's angina, Vulvitis, Whitlow, Windburn, Woody-tongue

Inflate(d), Inflation Aerate, Aggrandise, Bloat, Bombastic, Cost-push, Dilate, Distend, Distent, Exaggerate, Grade, Increase, Pneumatic, Pump, Remonetise, RPI, Spiral, Stagflation, Stagnation, Swell

Inflect(ion) Accidence, Conjugation

Inflexible, Inflexibility Adamant(ine), Byzantine, Doctrinaire, Hard-ass, Hard-liner, Iron, Obstinate, Ossified, Relentless, Resolute, Rigid, Rigour, Set, Stubborn, Unbending

Inflict(ion) Deal, Force, Give, Impose, Subject, Trouble, Visit, Wreak

Inflorescence Bostryx, Catkin, Ci(n)cinnus, Drepanium, Glomerule, Panicle, Pleiochasium, Polychasium, Raceme, Umbel, Verticillaster

Inflow Affluence, Influx

Influence(d), Influential Act, Affect, After, Backstairs, Charm, Clout, Credit, Determine, Drag, Earwig, Embracery, Eminence grise, Factor, Force, Get at, Govern, Hold, Hypnotise, Impact, Impress, Incubus, Inspire, Interfere, Lead, Leverage, Lobby, Macher, Mastery, Militate, Mogul, Octopus, Operation, Power, Pressure, Prestige, > PULL, Push, Reach, Rust, Say, Seminal, Significant, Star, Star-blasting, Stimulus, Suggest, Svengali, Sway, Swing, Telegony, Undue, Will, Work, Wull

Influenza Flu, Grippe, Wog

Inform(ation), Informed, Informer Acquaint, Advise, Agitprop, Apprise, Au fait, Aware, Beagle, Bit, Burst, Canary, Ceefax®, Clype, Contact, Cookie, Datum, Delate, Dob(ber), Dope, Education, Exposition, Facts, Fact sheet, Feedback, Fink, Fisgig, Fiz(z)gig, Gen, Genome, Grapevine, Grass, Griff, Gunsel, Hep, Input, Inside, Instruct, Izvesti(y)a, Light, Lowdown, Media, Moiser, Nark, Nepit, Nit, Nose, Notify, Occasion, Oracle®, Peach, Pem(m)ican, Pimp, Poop, Prestel®, Prime, Printout, Propaganda, Prospectus, Rat, Read-out, Revelation, Rheme, Rumble, Shelf, Shop, Sidelight, Sing, Sneak, Snitch, Squeak, Squeal,

Stag, Stoolie, Stool-pigeon, Supergrass, Sycophant, Teletext®, Tell, Tidings, Tip-off, Up, Videotext®, Viewdata®, Whistle(-blower), Wire

Informal Casual, Intimate, Irregular, Outgoing, Unofficial

Infra Under

Infra dig Ignominious

Infrequent Casual, Occasional, Rare, Scant, Seldom, Sparse

Infringe Contravene, Violate

Infuriate Anger, Bemad, Bepester, Enrage, Exasperate, Incense, Madden, Pester, Provoke

Infuse(r), Infusion Brew, Distill, Gallise, Instil, Mash, Saloop, Saturate, Steep, Tea, Tea-ball, Tea-egg, Tisane, Toddy, Uva-ursi

Ingenious, Ingenuity Adept, Adroit, Art, Artificial, Clever, Cunning, Cute, Inventive, Natty, Neat, Resourceful, Smart, Subtle, Wit

Ingenuous Artless, Candid, Green, Innocent, Naive, Open

Ingest Eat, Endue, Incept, Indue, Swallow

In good condition Fit, Shipshape, Taut, Trim

Ingot Bar, Billet, Bullion, Lingot, Sycee

Ingrain Fix, Impregnate, Train

Ingrate Thankless, Viper

Ingratiate, Ingratiating Butter, Court, Flatter, Greasy, Silken, Smarm(y)

Ingredient(s) Additive, Admixture, Basis, Content, Element, Factor, Formula, Makings, Staple

Ingrowing, Ingrowth Onychocryptosis, T(h)ylosis

Inhabit(ants) Affect, Children, Denizen, Dweller, Inholder, Inmate, Live, Native, Occupant, People, Resident

Inhale, Inhalation Aspirate, Breath(e), Draw, Gas, Inspire, Sniff, Snort, Snuff, Take

Inharmonious Out, Patchy

Inherent Characteristic, Essential, Immanent, Inbred, Innate, Native

Inherit(ance), Inherited, Inheritor Accede, Birthright, Borough-English, Congenital, Feoffee, Gene, Genom, Heirloom, Inborn, Legacy, Legitim, Meek, Mendelism, Particulate, Patrimony, Portion, Reversion, Succeed, Tichborne, Ultimogenitive

Inhibit(ing), Inhibition, Inhibitor Captopril, Chalone, Chalonic, Deter, Enalapril, Forbid, Hang-up, Protease, Restrain, Retard, Retroactive, Stunt, Suppress

Inhuman Barbarous, Brutal, Merciless

Inimical Adverse, Harmful, Hostile

Iniquity, Iniquitous Diabolical, Evil, Offence, Sin, Vice

Initial Acronym, First, Letter, Monogram, Paraph, Prelim(inary), Primary, Rubric

▷ **Initially** *may indicate* first letters

Initiate(d), Initiation, Initiative Baptism, Begin, Bejesuit, Blood, Bora, Bring, Ceremony, Debut, Demarche, Enter, Enterprise, Epopt, Esoteric, Gumption, Induct, Instigate, Instruct, > **LAUNCH**, Nous, Spark, > **START**

Inject(or), Injection Bang, Booster, Collagen, Enema, Epidural, Fuel, Hypo, Implant, Innerve, Inoculation, Instil, Introduce, Jab, Mainline, Pop, Reheat, Serum, Shoot, Skin-pop, Solid, Syringe, Transfuse, Venipuncture

Injunction Command, Embargo, Mandate, Mareva, Swear, Writ

Injure(d), Injury, Injurious, Injustice ABH, Abuse, Aggrieve, Bale, Bled, Bruise, Concuss, Contrecoup, Damage, De(a)re, Forslack, Frostbite, Gash, GBH, Harm, > **HURT**, Ill-turn, Impair, Iniquity, Lesion, Malign, Mar, Mayhem, Mistreat,

Mutilate, NAI, Nobble, Nocuous, Noxal, Nuisance, Oppression, Outrage, Packet, Paire, Prejudice, Rifle, RSI, Scaith, Scath(e), Scotch, Sore, Sprain, Teen(e), Tene, Tort, Trauma, Umbrage, Whiplash, Wound, Wrong

Injury *see* AFTER INJURY

Ink(y) Atramental, Black, Bray, China, Chinese, Cyan, Gall, Gold, Indian, Invisible, Magnetic, Marking, Printer's, Sepia, Stained, Sympathetic, Tusche

Inkling Clue, Glimpse, Hint, Idea

Inkpot Standish

Inlaid, Inlay(er) Boulle, Buhl, Damascene, Emblemata, Empaestic, Enamel, Enchase, Incrust, Intarsia, Intarsio, Koftgar(i), Marquetrie, Marquetry, Pietra-dura, Piqué, Set, Tarsia, Veneer

Inland Hinterland, Interior, Up

Inlet Arm, Bay, Bohai, Cove, Creek, Entry, Estuary, Fiord, Firth, Fjord, Fleet, Geo, Gio, Gusset, Infall, Ingate, McMurdo Sound, Moray Firth, Pamlico Sound, Pearl Harbor, Plymouth Sound, Pohai, Port Jackson, Solway Firth, Sullom Voe, Table Bay, Tor Bay, Wash, Zuyder Zee

Inlet *may indicate* 'let' around another word

Inmate Intern(e), Lodger, Patient, Prisoner, Resident

Inn(s), Innkeeper Albergo, Alehouse, Auberge, Barnard's, Boniface, Caravanserai, Chancery, Change-house, Coaching, Court, Gray's, Halfway-house, Host, Hostelry, Hotel, House, Imaret, In, Inner Temple, Jamaica, Khan, Ladin(ity), Law, Licensee, Lincoln's, Lodging, Luckie, Lucky, Middle Temple, Motel, Padrone, Parador, Patron, Porterhouse, Posada, Posthouse, Pothouse, Publican, Roadhouse, Ryokan, Serai, Tabard, Taphouse, Tavern(er), Victualler

Inn *may refer to* the law

Innards Entrails, Giblets, Gizzard, Guts, Harigals, Harslet, Haslet, Rein, Viscera

Innate Congenital, Essential, Inborn, Inbred, Inbuilt, Instinctive, Natural

Inner(most) Bencher, Esoteric, Internal, Intima, Intimate, Lining, Man, Medulla, Private, Woman

Innings Chance, Knock, Turn

Innkeeper *see* INN

Innocent Absolved, Angelic, Arcadian, Babe, Blameless, Canny, Chaste, Cherub, Childlike, Clean, Doddypoll, Dodipoll, Dove, Encyclical, Green, Idyllic, Ingenue, Lamb, Lily-white, Maiden, Naive, Opsimath, Pope, > PURE, Sackless, Seely, Simple, St, Unwitting, White

Innocuous Harmless, Innocent

Innovate, Innovative, Innovation, Innovator Alteration, Ground-breaking, Newell, Novelty, Pioneer

Inn-sign Bush

Innumerable Countless, Infinite, Myriad, N

Inoculate, Inoculation Engraft, Immunise, Jab, Protect, Vaccine, Variolate

Inoffensive Mild, Pleasant

Inoperative Futile, Nugatory, Silent, Void

Inopportune Inconvenient, Intempestive, Untimely

Inordinate Excessive, Irregular, Undue

Inordinately *may indicate* an anagram

In place of For, Qua, Vice, With

Input Direct, OCR

Inquest Debriefing, Hearing, Inquiry, Investigation

Inquire, Inquiring, Inquiry Ask, Demand, Investigation, Maieutic, Nose, Organon, Probe, Query, Question, See, Speer, Speir

Inquisition, Inquisitive, Iniquisitor Curious, Interrogation, Meddlesome, Nosy, Prying, Rubberneck, Snooper, Spanish, Stickybeak, Torquemada

▷ **In revolt, In revolution** *may indicate* an anagram

Inroad(s) Breach, Encroachment, Honeycomb, Invasion

Insane, Insanity Absurd, Batty, Crack-brained, Crazy, Deranged, Headcase, Hebephrenia, Loco, Lune, Mad, Manic, Mattoid, Nutso, Paranoia, Pellagra, Psycho, Schizo, Yarra

Insatiable Greedy, Ravenous, Voracious

Insatiate child Killcrop

Inscribe(d), Inscription Chisel, Chronogram, Colophon, Dedicate, Emblazon, Engrave, Enter, Epigraph, Epitaph, Exergue, Graffiti, Hic jacet, Hierograph, Lapidary, Legend, Lettering, Neum(e), Posy, Writ

Inscrutable Deadpan, Esoteric, Mysterious, Sphinx

Insect(s) Entomic, Nonentity, Non-person

INSECTS

3 letters:
Ant
Bee
Bot
Bug
Fly
Ked
Lac
Nit
Wax
Wog

4 letters:
Flea
Gnat
Grig
Lice
Mite
Moth
Pium
Pupa
Tick
Wasp
Weta
Zimb

5 letters:
Aphis
Borer
Brise
Cimex
Emmet
Gogga
Louse
Midge

Nymph
Ox-bot
Scale
Stick
Zebub

6 letters:
Acarid
Breese
Breeze
Capsid
Chigoe
Cicada
Cicala
Day-fly
Earwig
Elater
Gadfly
Hopper
Hornet
Instar
Locust
Maggot
Mantid
Mantis
Mayfly
Noctua
Psocid
Psylla
Punkie
Redbug
Sawfly
Scarab
Slater
Spider

Tettix
Thrips
Vespid
Walker
Weevil

7 letters:
Antlion
Bristle
Buzzard
Chalcid
Chigger
Cornfly
Cricket
Culicid
Cutworm
Daphnid
Ergates
Firefly
Gallfly
Girdler
Grayfly
Hexapod
Hive-bee
Humbuzz
Katydid
Ladybug
Odonata
Oestrus
Oniscus
Phasmid
Pill-bug
Pyralis
Sandfly
Spectre

Stylops
Termite

8 letters:
Alderfly
Bookworm
Circutio
Coccidae
Crane-fly
Dipteras
Firebrat
Gall-wasp
Glossina
Greenfly
Horntail
Horsefly
Itchmite
Lacewing
Ladybird
Lygus bug
Mealybug
Metabola
Milliped
Mosquito
Myriapod
Puss-moth
Reduviid
Ruby-tail
Scarabee
Silkworm
Snowflea
Stinkbug
Stonefly
Symphile
Waterbug

Whitefly
Wireworm
Woodworm

9 letters:
Ametabola
Booklouse
Caddis-fly
Centipede
Cochineal
Cockroach
Compodeid
Damselfly
Dobsonfly
Dor-beetle
Dragonfly
Ephemeron
Hemiptera
Homoptera
Leaf-miner
Mecoptera
Millepede
Millipede

Rearhorse
Robber-fly
Songololo
Synoekete
Tabanidae
Tiger-moth
Woodlouse
Xylophage

10 letters:
Apterygota
Bark mantis
Bluebottle
Casebearer
Chironomid
Cockchafer
Coleoptera
Collembola
Fan-cricket
Fen-cricket
Froghopper
Greendrake
Harvestman

Leaf-cutter
Leafhopper
Mallophaga
Orthoptera
Phylloxera
Plant-louse
Pond-skater
Psocoptera
Rhipiptera
Silverfish
Springtail
Thysanuran
Treehopper
Web spinner

11 letters:
Bristletail
Dermapteran
Grasshopper
Greenbottle
Hymenoptera
Mole-cricket
Neuropteran

Tiger-beetle
Trichoptera

12 letters:
Bishop's mitre
Creepy-crawly
Dictyopteran
Heteropteran
Rhipidoptera
San Jose scale
Strepsiptera
Thousand-legs
Thysanoptera
Water boatman

13 letters:
Daddy-long-legs
Jenny-longlegs
Leatherjacket
Praying mantis
Staphylinidae
Water scorpion

Insecticide Allethrin, Aphicide, Carbaryl, Chromene, DDT, Deet, Derris, Dieldrin, Endosulfan, Endrin, Flycatcher, Gammexane®, Ivermectin, Lindane®, Malathion®, Menazon, Methoxychlor, Miticide, Naphthalene, Parathion, Paris green, Pyrethrin, Pyrethrum, Rotenone, Spray, Timbo, Toxaphene, Zineb

Insectivore Agoura, Desman, Donaea, Drosera, Hedgehog, Jacamar, Nepenthaceae, Otter-shrew, Sarracenia, Tanrec, Tenrec(idae), Venus flytrap, Zalambdodont

Insecure Infirm, > LOOSE, Precarious, Shaky, Unsafe, Unstable, Unsteady, Vulnerable

Insensitive, **Insensitivity** Analgesia, Blunt, Callous, Dead, Log, Numb, Obtuse, Pachyderm, Stolid, Tactless, Thick-skinned

Inseparable Indiscrete, One, United

Insert(ed), **Insertion**, **Inset** Cue, Empiecement, Enchase, Enter, Entry, Foist, Fudge, Godet, Gore, Graft, Gusset, Immit, Imp, Implant, Inject, Inlay, Input, Intercalar, Interject, Interpolate, Interpose, Intersperse, Introduce, Intromit, Lexical, Mitre, Pin, Sandwich

Inside(r) Content, Core, Entrails, Gaol, Heart, Indoors, Interior, Internal, Interne, Inward, Inwith, Mole, Tum, > WITHIN

Insidious Artful, Crafty, Sly

Insight Acumen, Anagoge, Aperçu, Enlightenment, Hunch, Inkling, Intuition, > PERCEPTION, Tais(c)h

Insignia Armour, Arms, Badger, Charge, Chevron, Mark, Regalia, Ribbon, Roundel, Tab

Insignificant (person) Dandiprat, Fico, Fiddling, Flea-bite, Fractional, Gnat, Inconsiderable, Insect, Mickey Mouse, Minimus, Miniscule, Minnow, Nebbich, Nobody, Nominal, Nonentity, One-eyed, Petit, Petty, Pipsqueak, Quat, Scoot, Scout, Scrub, Shrimp, Slight, Small potatoes, Small-time,

Squirt, Squit, Tenuous, Trifling, Trivial, Two-bit, Unimportant, Venial, Warb, Whippersnapper

Insincere Affected, Artificial, Barmecide, Cant, Double, Double-faced, Empty, Factitious, Faithless, False, Glib, Greenwash, Hollow, Janus-faced, Lip service, Mealy-mouthed, Meretricious, Mouth-made, Pseudo, Shallow, Synthetic, Two-faced

Insinuate, Insinuating, Insinuation Allude, Hint, Imply, Innuendo, Intimate, Sleek, Sneck-draw

Insipid Banal, Blab, Bland, Drippy, Fade, Flat, Insulse, Jejune, Lash, Mawkish, Shilpit, Tame, Tasteless, Vapid, Weak, Wearish, Wersh

Insist(ent) Assert, Demand, Dogmatic, Exact, > STIPULATE, Stress, Swear, Threap, Threep, Urge

Insolence, Insolent Audacity, Bardy, Brassy, Cheek, Contumely, Effrontery, Gum, Hubris, Hybris, Impudence, Lip, Rude, Snash, Stroppy, Wanton

Insoluble Cerasin, Hard, Irresolvable, Mysterious

Insolvent Bankrupt, Broke, Destitute, Penniless

Insomnia Agrypnotic, Sleeplessness, Wakefulness, White night

Insouciant Carefree, Careless, Cavalier

Inspect(ion), Inspector Alnage(r), Auditor, Case, Comb, Conner, Darogha, Examine, Go-over, Government, Investigator, Jerque, Keeker, Lestrade, Look-see, Morse, Muster, Once-over, Peep, Perlustrate, Proveditor, Rag-fair, Recce, Review, Sanitary, Scrutinise, Spot check, Survey, Test, Vet, Vidimus, Visitation

Inspiration, Inspire(d), Inspiring Actuate, Aerate, Afflatus, Aganippe, Animate, Brainstorm, Brainwave, Breath(e), Castalian, Draw, Duende, Elate, Exalt, Fire, Flash, Hearten, Hunch, Idea, Illuminate, Impulse, Induce, Inflatus, Infuse, Kindle, Move, Muse, Pegasus, Prompt, Prophetic, Satori, Sniff(le), Stimulus, Taghairm, Theopnautic, Theopneust(y), Uplift, Vatic, Verbal

In spite of Augre

Instability Anomie, Anomy

Install(ation) Enchase, Enthrone, Inaugurate, Induction, Infrastructure, Insert, Invest, Put (in)

Instalment Episode, Fascicle, Fascicule, Heft, Insert, Livraison, Never-never, Part, Serial, Tranche

Instance, Instant As, Case, Chronon, Example, Flash, Jiffy, Moment, Present, Say, Shake, Spur, Tick, Trice, Twinkling, Urgent

Instead (of) Deputy, For, Lieu, Locum, Vice

Instigate Arouse, Foment, Impel, Incite, Prompt, Spur

Instil(l) Implant, Inculcate, Infuse, Teach, Transfuse

Instinct(ive) Automatic, Flair, Herd, Id, Impulse, Inbred, Innate, Intuition, Nature, Nose, Pleasure principle, Talent, Tendency, Visceral

Institute, Institution Academy, Activate, Asylum, Bank, Begin, Bring, Broadmoor, Charity, College, Erect, Found(ation), I, Inaugurate, Mechanical, MORI, Orphanage, Poorhouse, Protectory, Raise, Redbrick, Retraict, Retrait(e), Retreat, Royal, Smithsonian, Start, University, Women's, Workhouse

Instruct(ed), Instruction, Instructor ADI, Advice, Apprenticeship, Brief, CAI, Catechism, Clinic, Coach, Course, Didactic, Direct(ive), Document, Edify, Educate, Enjoin, Ground(ing), Inform, Lesson, Loop, Macro, Manual, Mystagogue, Mystagogus, Notify, Order, Percept, Prescription, Program, Recipe, Rubric, Script, Swami, > TEACH, Train, Tutelage, Tutorial, Up

Instrument(al) Ablative, Act, Agent, Dash(board), Helpful, Kit, Mean(s), Mechanical, > MUSICAL INSTRUMENT, Negotiable, > RESPONSIBLE, > TOOL,

Transit, Transposing, > UTENSIL

INSTRUMENTS

3 letters:
Fan
Gad

4 letters:
Celt
Clam
Dupe
Fork
Mike
Prog
Rasp
Rote
Tram

5 letters:
Brake
Curet
Fleam
Float
Gadge
Groma
Meter
Miser
Organ
Probe
Sonde
Wecht

6 letters:
Bougie
Broach
Etalon
Megger®
Opener
Pallet
Pestle
Scythe
Strobe
Trocar

7 letters:
Alidade
Cadrans
Caliper
Caltrop
Cautery
Curette

Diopter
Flesher
Forceps
Organic
Pelican
Plotter
Pointel
Probang
Scriber
Sextant
Spatula
Stapler
Strigil
Swazzle
Swingle
Swozzle
Syringe
Trammel

8 letters:
Barnacle
Burdizzo
Diagraph
Dividers
Ecraseur
Enlarger
Iriscope
Odometer
Ohmmeter
Otoscope
Oximeter
Quadrant
Scalprum
Scissors
Snuffler
Strickle
Trephine
Tweezers
Waywiser

9 letters:
Alphonsin
Arcograph
Astrolabe
Atmometer
Auxometer
Barometer
Baryscope

Bolometer
Coelostat
Crows-bill
Cryoscope
Cymograph
Depressor
Dermatome
Dip-circle
Dosemeter
Dosimeter
Dropsonde
Endoscope
Ergograph
Eriometer
Extractor
Fadometer
Fetoscope
Flowmeter
Fluxmeter
Haemostat
Heliostat
Hodometer
Hourglass
Konimeter
Lysimeter
Machmeter
Manometer
Marigraph
Megascope
Metronome
Microtome
Milometer
Nocturnal
Nut-wrench
Oedometer
Ondograph
Optometer
Optophone
Osmometer
Osteotome
Periscope
Polygraph
Potometer
Pyrometer
Raspatory
Retractor
Rheometer
Skiascope

Sonograph
Tasimeter
Telemeter
Telescope
Tellurian
Tellurion
Tenaculum
Tonometer
Toothpick
Tripmeter
Voltmeter
Wavemeter
Xylometer
Zymometer

10 letters:
Almacantar
Almucantar
Altazimuth
Anemometer
Ceilometer
Clinometer
Colposcope
Comparator
Cryophorus
Cystoscope
Drosometer
Fibrescope
Goniometer
Gonioscope
Gravimeter
Heliograph
Hydrometer
Hydroscope
Hygrometer
Hypsometer
Iconometer
Integrator
Micrograph
Micrometer
Microphone
Mileometer
Nephograph
Nephoscope
Nitrometer
Orthoscope
Oscillator
Osteoclast

Pantograph
Photometer
Piezometer
Pilliwinks
Planimeter
Protractor
Pulsimeter
Pulsometer
Pycnometer
Radiometer
Radiophone
Radioscope
Radiosonde
Siderostat
Spirograph
Spirometer
Tachigraph
Tachometer
Tensometer
Theodolite
Thermopile
Thorascope
Tribometer
Tromometer
Urinometer
Variometer

11 letters:
Auxanometer
Chronograph
Chronometer
Chronoscope
Coercimeter

Colonoscope
Dilatometer
Fluorometer
Fugitometer
Gastroscope
Gradiometer
Helicograph
Intoximeter
Jacob's staff
Laparoscope
Nephroscope
Opeidoscope
Pinnywinkle
Polarimeter
Polariscope
Proctoscope
Psychograph
Pyranometer
Pyrgeometer
Quantometer
Rangefinder
Rocketsonde
Screwdriver
Seismograph
Seismoscope
Solarimeter
Spherometer
Stactometer
Stadiometer
Stauroscope
Stereometer
Stereoscope
Stethoscope

Stroboscope
Synthesizer
Tacheometer
Tensiometer
Thermometer
Thermoscope
Urethoscope
Vectorscope
Voltammeter

12 letters:
Aethrioscope
Bronchoscope
Camera lucide
Cephalometer
Electrometer
Galactometer
Galvanometer
Galvanoscope
Harmonometer
Inclinometer
Keraunograph
Myringoscope
Nephelometer
Oscilloscope
Penetrometer
Pinniewinkle
Respirometer
Scarificator
Sensitometer
Snooperscope
Spectroscope
Sphygmograph

Synchroscope
Tellurometer
Turbidimeter
Zenith-sector

13 letters:
Phonendoscope
Pneumatograph
Pneumatometer
Potentiometer
Pyrheliometer
Reflectometer
Refractometer
Sigmoidoscope
Stalagmometer
Tachistoscope
Weatherometer

14 letters:
Diffractometer
Interferometer
Ophthalmoscope
Phosphoroscope
Synchronoscope

15 letters:
Phenakestoscope

16 letters:
Sphygmoma-
nometer

Insubordinate Contumacious, Faction, Mutinous, Rebel, Refractory

Insubstantial Airy, Brief, Flimsy, Frothy, Illusory, Jackstraw, Slight, Thin, Wispy, Ye(a)sty

Insufferable Egregious

Insufficient Exiguous, Inadequate, Poor, Scant, Shortfall

Insular Isolated, Moated, Narrow, Xenophobe

Insulate, **Insulation**, **Insulator** Biotite, Dielectric, Electret, Enwind, Grommet, Haybox, Inwind, Lagging, Mica, Non-conductor, Padding, Pugging, Sleeving, Tog

Insult(ing) Abuse, Affront, Aspersion, Barb, Charientism, Contumely, Cut, Dyslogistic, Embarrass, Facer, Fig, Injurious, Lese-majesty, Mud, Mud-pie, Offend, Opprobrious, Rip on, Skit, Slagging, Slight, Slur, Snub, Trauma, Uncomplimentary, Verbal, Yenta, Yente

Insurance, **Insure(r)** Abandonee, Cover, Fidelity, Fire, Guarantee, Hedge, Indemnity, Knock-for-knock, Life, Lloyds, Marine, Medicare, Mutual, National, Participating, Pluvius, Policy, Reversion, Security, Social, Term, Underwrite, Whole-life

Insurgent, **Insurrection** Cade, Jacquerie, Mutiny, Outbreak, Pandy, Rebel,

Revolt, Sedition, Whisky

Intact Complete, Entire, Inviolate, Unused, Whole

Intaglio Diaglyph

Intake Absorption, Entry, Fuel

Integer, Integral Component, Definite, Entire, Improper, Inbuilt, Indefinite, Needful, Number, Organic, Unitary

Integrate(d), Integration Amalgamate, Assimilate, Combine, Fuse, Harmonious, Holistic, Large-scale, Mainstream, Merge, Tightknit

Integrity Honesty, Principle, Probity, Rectitude, Strength, Uprightness, Whole

Integument Coat, Sheath, Skin, Velum

Intellect, Intellectual(s) Academic, Aptitude, Brain, Cerebral, Dianoetic, Egghead, Eggmass, Far-out, Genius, Highbrow, Intelligent, Intelligentsia, -ist, Learned, Literati, Luminary, Mastermind, Mental(ity), Mind, Noesis, Noetic, Noology, Nous, Profound, Reason, Titan

Intelligence, Intelligent Advice, Artificial, Boss, Brains, Bright, CIA, Discerning, Dope, Eggmass, Emotional, Esprit, G, Grey matter, GRU, Info, Ingenious, IQ, Knowledgeable, Machiavellian, Machine, MI, Mossad, Mother wit, News, Pate, Pointy-headed, Rational, Sconce, Sense, Sharp, Shrewd, Spetsnaz, Spetznaz, Tidings, Wit

Intelligible Exoteric

Intemperance Acrasia, Crapulent, Excess, Gluttony, Immoderation

Intend(ed), Intending Allot, Betrothed, Contemplate, Design, Destine, Ettle, Fiancé(e), Going, > MEAN, Meditate, Propose, Purpose

Intense, Intensify, Intensity Acute, Aggravate, Ardent, Depth, Earnest, Earthquale, Emotional, Enhance, Escalate, Estro, Excess, Extreme, Fervent, Keen, Luminous, Might, Profound, Radiant, Redouble, Sharpen, Vehement, Vivid

Intent, Intention(al) A dessein, Animus, Deliberate, Dole, Earnest, Hellbent, Manifesto, Mens rea, Mind, Paradoxical, Purpose, Rapt, Resolute, Set, Studious, Systematic, Thought, Tire, Witting, Yrapt

Inter Bury, Entomb

Interaction Chemistry, Enantiodromia, Solvation

Interbreed(ing) Miscegenation

Intercalation Embolism

Intercede, Intercession Mediate, Negotiate, Plead, Prayer

Intercept Absciss(a), Abscisse, Check, Hack, Meet

Interchange(d) Altercation, Alternate, Clover-leaf, Crossing, Equivalent, Mutual, Permute, Reciprocate, Substitute

Intercourse Ball, Bang, Bed, Boff, Bonk, Coition, Coitus, Commerce, Commixture, Congress, Consummation, Converse, Copulation, Cottaging, Cunnilingus, Deflowering, Enjoy, Fluff, Fornication, Gamahuche, Gamaruche, Greens, Hochmagandie, Hochmagandy, Jass, Jazz, Jiggy, Jump, Knee-trembler, Know(ledge), Laying, Leg-over, Lie with, Make, Marriage bed, Naughty, Necrophilia, Nookie, Nooky, Poontang, Pussy, Quickie, Ride, Rim, Roger, Root, Rumpy(-pumpy), Screw, Sexual, Shaft, Shag, Shtup, Sixty-nine, Sociality, Sodomy, Stuff, Swive, Tail, Tie, Trade, Trock, Troilism, Truck, Whoredom

Interdict Ban, Forbid, Prohibit, Taboo

Interest(ed), Interesting Amusive, APR, Attention, Behalf, Benefit, Clou, Compound, Concern, Contango, Coupon, Dividend, Ear-grabbing, Engage, Engross, Enthusiasm, Fad, Fee-simple, Fee-tail, Grab, Hot, Human, Import, Income, Insurable, Int(o), Intrigue, Landed, Life, Line, Negative, Part, Partisan, Percentage, Readable, Rente, Respect, Revenue, Scene, Share, Side, Sideline,

Simple, Spice, Stake, Topical, Usage, Usance, Usure, Usury, Vested, Vig(orish), Warm

Interfere(r), Interference Busybody, Clutter, Disrupt, Hamper, Hinder, Intrude, Mar, > **MEDDLE**, Molest, Officious, Pry, Radio, Shash, Static, Tamper, Teratogen

Interferometer Etalon

Intergrowth Perthite

Interim Break, Meantime, Meanwhile, Temporary

Interior Backblocks, Cyclorama, Domestic, Innards, Innate, Inner, Inside, Outback, Plain, Up-country, Vitals

Interject(ion) Ahem, Begorra(h), Gertcha, Haith, Hoo-oo, Interpolate, Lumme, Nation, Sese(y), Sessa, 'Sheart, 'Slid, Tarnation, Tush

Interlace Mingle, Pleach, Weave, Wreathe

Interlock Dovetail, Engage, Knit, Tangle

Interlocutor Elihu, MC, Questioner

Interloper Gate-crasher, Intruder, Trespasser

Interlude Antimask, Antimasque, Divertimento, Entr'acte, Interruption, Kyogen, Lunch-hour, Meantime, Pause, Verset

Intermediary, Intermediate Agent, Bardo, Comprador(e), Go-between, Instar, Mean, Medial, Mesne, Mezzanine, Middleman, Middle-of-the-road, Thirdsman

Interminable Endless, Infinite, Unending

Intermission Apyrexia, Break, Interval, Pause, Recess

Intermittent Broken, Fitful, Off-on, Periodic, Random, Spasmic, Spasmodic, Sporadic

Intern(e) Confine, Doctor, Impound, Restrict, Trainee

Internal Domestic, Inner, Internecine, Inward, Within

International Cap, Cosmopolitan, Lion, Test, UN, Universal

Internet Infobahn, URL, WWW

Interpolate(r), Interpolation Diaskeuast, Insert, Intercalate, Interrupt, Tmesis

Interpose Butt in, Horn in, Interject, Interlay, Interprone, Intervene, Spatchcock, Stickle

Interpret(er) Conster, Construe, Decipher, Decode, Dobhash, Dragoman, Exegete, Explain, Exponent, Expositor, Expound, Glossator, Hermeneutist, Hierophant, Jehovist, Latiner, Lingster, Linguistic, Linkster, Medium, Moonshee, Moonshi, Munshi, Oneirocritic, Origenist, Prophet, Read, Rede, Render, Represent, Spokesman, Textualist, > **TRANSLATE**, Truchman, Ulema

Interpretation Anagoge, Anagogy, Construction, Copenhagen, Eisegesis, Euhemerism, Exegesis, Exegete, Gematria, Gloss(ary), Gospel, Halacha(h), Halakah, Hermeneutics, Midrash, Portray, Reading, Rede, Rendition, Spin, Targum, Translation, Tropology

Interrogate, Interrogation Catechism, Debrief(ing), Enquire, Examine, Grill, Maieutic, Pump, > **QUESTION**, Quiz

Interrupt(ion), Interrupter Ahem, Aposcopesis, Blip, Break, Butt, Chequer, Chip in, Disturb, Entr'acte, Heckle, Hiatus, Intercept, Interfere, Interpellate, Interpolate, Interpose, Interregnum, Intrusion, Overtalk, Pause, Portage, Rheotome, Stop, Suspend, Time-out

Intersect(ion) Carfax, Carfox, Carrefour, Chiasm(a), Cross, Crunode, Cut, Decussate, Divide, Groin, Metacentre, Orthocentre, Trace

Intersperse Dot, Interpose, Scatter, Sprinkle

Interstice Areole, Interlude, Pore, Space

Intertwine Braid, Impleach, Knit, Lace, Plait, Splice, Twist, Writhe

Interval Between, Break, Breather, Class, Closed, Comma, Contour, Diapente,

Diastaltic, Diatesseron, Diesis, Distance, Ditone, Duodecimo, Entr'acte, Fifth, Gap, Half-time, Hiatus, Hourly, Interim, Interlude, Interregnum, Interspace, Interstice, Lunitidal, Meantime, Meantone, Meanwhile, Microtone, Ninth, Octave, Ottava, Perfect, Pycnon, Respite, Rest, Schisma, Semitone, Sixth, Space, Span, Spell, Tritone, Unison, Wait

Intervene, Intervention Agency, Arbitrate, Interfere, Interjacent, Interrupt, Mediate, Mesne, Theurgy, Up

Interview Audience, Audition, Beeper, Conference, Doorstep, Examine, Hearing, Oral, Press conference, See, Vox pop

Interweave, Interwoven, Interwove Entwine, Interlace, Monogram, Pirnit, Plait, Plash, Pleach, Raddle, Wreathed

Intestate Heirless, Unwilling

Intestinal, Intestine(s) Bowel, Chit(ter)lings, Derma, Duodenum, Enteric, Entrails, Guts, Harigals, Innards, Jejunum, Kishke, Large, Mesenteron, Omenta, Rectum, Small, Splanchnic, Thairm, Viscera

Intimacy, Intimate(ly) Achates, Boon, Bosom, Communion, Connote, Familiar, Friend, Heart-to-heart, Inmost, Innuendo, Intrigue, Nearness, Opine, Pack, Private, Signal, Special, Thick, Throng, Warm, Well

Intimation Clue, Hint, Implication, Inkling, Innuendo, Si quis

Intimidate, Intimidating Awe, Browbeat, Bulldoze, Bully, Cow, Daunt, Dragon, Hector, Niramiai, Psych, Threaten, Tyrannise, Unnerve

Into At, Intil, Within

Intolerable, Intolerant Allergic, Bigotry, Excessive, Illiberal, Impossible, Ombrophobe, Self-righteous

Intone, Intonation Cadence, Just, Twang

In touch Au fait

Intoxicant, Intoxicate(d), Intoxicating, Intoxication Alcoholic, Areca-nut, Benj, Bhang, Coca, Corn, Cup, Disguise, Fuddle, Ganja, Heady, > HIGH, Hocus, Hou high, Inebriate, Jag, Merry, Mescal, Peyote, Pixil(l)ated, Rumbullion, Slewed, Soma, Sozzle, Spirituous, Swacked, Temulent, Whiskeyfied, Whiskified, Zonked

Intractable Disobedient, Kittle, Mulish, Obdurate, Perverse, Surly, Unruly, Wilful

Intransigent Adamant, Inflexible, Rigid, Uncompromising

Intransitive Neuter, Objectless

Intrepid Aweless, Bold, Brave, Dauntless, Doughty, Firm, Gallant, > RESOLUTE, Valiant

Intricate Complex, Daedal(ian), Daedale, Dedal, Gordian, Intrince, Involute, Knotty, Pernickety, Sinuous, Tirlie-wirlie, Tricky, Vitruvian

Intrigue(r), Intriguing Affaire, Artifice, Brigue, Cabal, Camarilla, Cloak and dagger, Collogue, Conspiracy, Fascinate, Hotbed, Ignatian, Jesuit, Jobbery, Liaison, Machinate, Plot, Politic, Rat, > SCHEME, Strategy, Traffic, Trinketer

Intrinsic(ally) Basically, Genuine, Inherent, Innate, Inner, Per se

Intrinsically *may indicate* something within a word

Introduce(r), Introduction, Introductory Acquaint, Anacrusis, Curtain-raiser, Emcee, Enseam, Exordial, Foreword, Immit, Import, Induct, Initiate, Inject, Insert, Instil(l), Intercalate, Interpolate, Intrada, Introit, Isagogic, Lead-in, Opening, Phase in, Plant, Preamble, Preface, Preliminary, Prelude, Prelusory, Preparatory, Present, Presentment, Proem, Prolegomena, Prolegomenon, Prologue, Proponent, Referral, Standfirst, Start, Usher

Introduction *may indicate* a first letter

Intromission Vicious

Introspective Musing, Reflex, Ruminant

▷ **In trouble** *may indicate* an anagram

Introvert(ed) Cerebrotonic, Ingrow, In-toed, Reserved, Shy

Intrude(r), Intrusion, Intrusive Abate, Aggress, Annoy, Bother, Burglar, Disturb, > **ENCROACH**, Gatecrash, Hacker, Interloper, Invade, Meddle, Nosey, Porlocking, Presume, Raid, Sorn, Trespass

Intuition, Intuitive Belief, ESP, Hunch, Insight, Instinct, Inwit, Noumenon, Premonition, Presentiment, Seat-of-the-pants, Telepathy, Theosophy, Visceral

▷ **In two words** *may indicate* a word to be split

Inuit Eskimo, Yupik

Inundate, Inundation Flood, Overflow, Overwhelm, Submerge, Swamp

Inure Acclimatise, Accustom, Harden, Season, Steel

Invade(r), Invasion Angle, Attack, Attila, Dane, Descent, Encroach, Hacker, Hengist, Horsa, Hun, Infest, Inroad, Intruder, Irrupt, Jute, Lombard, Martian, Norman, Norsemen, Ostrogoth, Overlord, Overrun, Permeate, Raid, Trespass, Vandal, Visigoth

Invalid(ate), Invalidation Bad, Bogus, Bunbury, Cancel, Chronic, Clinic, Defunct, Diriment, Erroneous, Expired, False, Inauthentic, Inform, Inoperative, Irritate, Lapsed, Nugatory, Null, Nullify, Refute, Shut-in, Terminate, Valetudinarian, Vitiate, Void

Invaluable Essential, Excellent, Precious, Useful

Invariable, Invariably Always, Constant, Eternal, Habitual, Perpetual, Steady, Uniform

Invective Abuse, Billingsgate, Diatribe, Philippic, Reproach, Ribaldry, Tirade

Inveigh Declaim, Denounce, Protest, Rail

Invent(ion), Inventive Adroit, Babe, Baby, Brainchild, Chimera, Coin, Contrive, Cook up, > **CREATE**, Daedal, Design, Device, Excogitate, Fabricate, Fain, Fantasia, Feign, Figment, Imaginary, Improvise, Ingenuity, Mint, Originate, Patent, Pretence, Resourceful, Synectics, Whittle, Wit

Inventor Archimedes, Arkwright, Artificer, Author, Babbage, Baird, Bell, Biro, Boys, Bramah, Cartwright, Celsius, Coiner, Creator, Crompton, Daedalus, Edison, Engineer, Galileo, Geiger, Hansom, Jubal, Marconi, Maxim, Minié, Mint-master, Morse, Nernst, Newcomen, Nobel, Patentee, Savery, Siemens, Tesla, Torricelli, Tull, Watt, Wheatstone, Whitney

Inventory Account, Index, Itemise, List, Perpetual, Personality, Register, Steelbow, Stock

Inversion, Invert(ed) Anastrophe, Antimetabole, Antimetathesis, Capsize, Chiasmus, Entropion, Entropium, First, Homosexuality, Opposite, Overset, Resupinate, Reverse, Second, Tete-beche, Turn, Upset

Invertebrate Annelida, Anthozoan, Arrowworm, Arthropod, Brachiopod, Coelenterate, Cridarian, Crinoid, Ctenophore, Decapod, Echinoderm, Echinoid, Euripterid, Feather star, Gast(e)ropod, Globigerina, Hydrozoan, Mollusc, Onychophoran, Parazoan, Pauropod, Peritrich, Polyp, Poriferan, Protostome, Rotifer, Roundworm, Scyphozoan, Sea-cucumber, Sea-lily, Spineless, Starfish, Tardigrade, Trepang, Trochelminth, Unio, Water bear, Worm, Zoophyte

Invest(or), Investment Agamemnon, Ambient, Angel, Bate, Beleaguer, Besiege, Bet, Blockade, Blue-chip, Capitalist, Collins Street farmer, Contrarian, Dignify, Dub, Embark, Empanoply, Enclothe, Endow, Enrobe, Ethical, Financier, Flutter, Gilt, Girt, Holding, Infeft, Install, On, Pannicle, Panniculus, Parlay, Place, Portfolio, Put, Ring, Robe, Saver, Share, Siege, Sink, Spec, Speculation, Stag, Stake, Stock, Surround, Tessa, Trust, Trustee, Venture, Zaitech

Invest *may indicate* one word surrounding another

Investigate, **Investigator**, **Investigation** Canvass, Case, Chart, CID, Delve, Examine, Explore, Fed, Ferret, Fieldwork, Go into, Hunt, Inquest, Inquirendo, Inquiry, Inquisition, McCarthyism, Nose, Organon, Organum, Probe, Pry, Quester, Rapporteur, Research, Scan, Scout, Screen, Scrutinise, Search, Sleuth, Snoop, Study, Suss, Tec, Test, T-man, Track, Try, Zetetic

Investiture Award, Inauguration

Inveterate Chronic, Double-dyed, Dyed-in-the-wool, Engrained, Habitual, Hardened

Invidious Harmful, Hostile, Malign

Invigilator Proctor

Invigorate, **Invigorating**, **Invigoration** Analeptic, Brace, Brisk, Cheer, Elixir, Energise, Enliven, Fortify, Insinew, Pep, Refresh, Renew, Stimulate, Tonic, Vital

Invincible Almighty, Brave, Stalwart, Valiant

Inviolatable, **Inviolate**, **Inviolable** Intemerate, Sacred, Sacrosanct

Invisible Hidden, Imageless, Infra-red, Secret, Tusche, Unseen

Invite, **Invitation**, **Inviting** Ask, Attract, Bid, Call, Card, Overture, > **REQUEST**, Solicit, Stiffie, Summons, Tempt, Toothsome, Woo

Invocation, **Invoke** Appeal, Call, Conjure, Curse, Entreat, Epiclesis, Solicit

Invoice Account, Bill, Docket, Itemise, Manifest, Pro forma

Involuntary Automatic, Instinctive, Unwitting

Involve(d), **Involvement** Commitment, Complicate, Complicit, Concern, Embroil, Engage, Entail, Envelop, Imbroglio, Immerse, > **IMPLICATE**, Include, Intricate, Meet, Necessitate, Participate, Tangle

Involved *may indicate* an anagram

Inward(s) Afferent, Centripuntal, Homefelt, Introrse, Mental, Private, Varus, Within

Iodine I, Kelp, Thyroxin(e)

Ion Ammonium, Anion, Carbanion, Carborium, Hydroxyl, Isomer, Onium, Zwitterion

Ionian Iastic, Te(i)an

Iota Atom, Jot, Subscript, Whit

IOU Cedula, Market, PN, Shinplaster, Vowels

IOW Vectis

IRA Provisional, Provo

Iran(ian) Babist, Kurd, Mede, Osset, Parsee, Ta(d)jik, Tadzhik

Irascible Choleric, Crusty, Fiery, Peevish, Snappy, Tetchy, Toustie

Irate Angry, Cross, Infuriated, Wrathful

Ire Anger, Bait, Cholera, Fury, Rage, Wrath

Ireland Composer, Deirdre, Gaeltacht, Hibernia, Innisfail, Irena, IRL, Iverna

Iridescence, **Iridescent** Chatoyant, Flambé, Opaline, Reflet, Shimmering, Shot, Water-gall

Iridium Ir

Iris Areola, Eye, Flag, Fleur-de-lis, Gladdon, Ixia, Lily, Lis, Orris, Rainbow, Roast-beef plant, Sedge, Seg, Stinking, Sunbow

Irish(man) Bark, Bog-trotter, Boy, Celt(ic), Clan-na-gael, Defender, Dermot, Dubliner, Eamon(n), Eirann, Erse, Fenian, Gael, Gaeltacht, Goidel, Greek, Keltic, Kern(e), Mick(e)(y), Middle, Milesian, Mulligan, Ogamic, Orange(man), Ostmen, Paddy(-whack), Partholon, Pat(rick), Rapparee, Redshank, Reilly, Riley, Rory, Ryan, Sean, Shoneen, Teague, Temper, Ultonian, Whiteboy, Wildgeese

Irk(some) Annoy, Bother, Irritate, Needle, Tedious
Iron(s), **Ironwork(s)** Airn, Alpha, Angle, Beta, Carron, Cautery, Chains, Chalybeate, Chancellor, Channel, Climbing, Coquimbite, Corrugated, Cramp(on), Crampon, Crimp, Cross, Curling, Curtain, Delta, Derringer, Dogs, Eagle-stone, Fayalite, Fe, Ferredoxin, Ferrite, Fetter, Fiddley, Flip-dog, Galvanised, Gamma, Gem, Golfclub, Goose, Grappling, Grim, Grozing, > GUN, Gyve, Horse, Ingot, Italian, Kamacite, Laterite, Lily, Maiden, Malleable, Marcasite, Mars, Martensite, Mashie, Mashy, Meteoric, Pea, Pig, > PRESS, Pro-metal, Rabble, Rations, Rod, Sad, Shooting, Smoother, Soft, Soldering, Spiegeleisen, Steam, Stirrup, Stretching, Strong, Taconite, Taggers, Terne, Tin terne, Toggle, Tow, Wafer, Waffle, Wear, Wedge, White, Wrought
Iron age Latene, Villanovan
Ironic, **Irony** Antiphrasis, Asteism, Dramatic, Meiosis, Metal, Ridicule, Sarcasm, Satire, Socratic, Tongue-in-cheek, Tragic, Trope, Wry
Ironside Edmund
Ironwood Pyengadu
▶ **Ironwork(s)** *see* IRON
Irrational Absurd, Brute, Delirious, Foolish, Illogical, Number, Superstitious, Surd, Wild
Irreconcilable Poles apart
Irrefutable Evident, Positive, Undeniable
Irregular(ity) Abnormal, Alloiostrophus, Anomaly, Aperiodic, A salti, Asymmetric, Atypical, Bashi-bazouk, Blotchy, Crazy, Erratic, Evection, Fitful, Flawed, Formless, Free-form, Guerilla, Heteroclitic, Incondite, Inordinate, Kink, Occasional, Orthotone, Para-military, Partisan, Patchy, Rambling, Random, Scalene, Scrawl, Sebundy, Sharawadgi, Sharawaggi, Snatchy, Solecism, Sporadic, TA, Uneven, Unsteady, Unwonted, Variable, Wayward, Zigzag
▷ **Irregular** *may indicate* an anagram
Irrelevant Academic, Digression, Extraneous, Gratuitous, Immaterial, Inept, Non sequitur, Unrelated
Irreligious Heathen, Impious, Pagan, Profane
Irremedial Hopeless, Incurable, Laches
Irrepressible Resilient
Irreproachable Blameless, Spotless, Stainless
Irresistible Almighty, Endearing, Inevitable, Mesmeric, Overwhelming
Irresolute, **Irresolution** Aboulia, Doubtful, Hesitant, Timid, Unsure, Weak-willed
Irresponsible Capricious, Feckless, Flighty, Fly-by-night, Slap-happy, Strawen, Trigger-happy, Wanton, Wildcat
Irreverent Blasphemous, Disrespectful, Impious, Profane
Irrigate, **Irrigation** Canalise, Colonic, Douche, Enema, Flood, Get, Water
Irritable, **Irritability**, **Irritant**, **Irritate(d)**, **Irritation** Acerbate, Anger, Annoy, Bête noire, Blister, Bug, Chafe, Chauff, Chippy, Chocker, Crabby, Cross-grained, Crosspatch, Crotchety, Crusty, Dod, Dyspeptic, Eat, Edgy, Enchafe, Erethism, Ewk, Exasperate, Fantod, Feverish, Fiery, Fleabite, Frabbit, Fractious, Fraught, Fretful, Gall, Get, Goad, Grate, Gravel, Hasty, Heck, Intertrigo, Irk, Itch, Jangle, Livery, Mardy, Narky, Needle, Nettle, Niggly, Ornery, Peckish, Peevish, Peppery, Pesky, Pestilent(ial), Pet, Petulance, Pinprick, Pique, Prickly, Provoke, Rag'd, Ragde, Rankle, Rasp, Rattle, Ratty, Rile, Roil, Rub, Ruffle, Savin(e), Scratchy, Shirty, Snappy, Snit, Snitchy, Splenetic, Sting, Tease, Techy, Testy, Tetchy, Thorn, Tickle, Toey, Touchy, Uptight, > VEX, Waxy, Yuke

Irritated *may indicate* an anagram
Irving Actor, Berlin
Is Est, Ist
Isaiah Is
Isinglass Carlock, Fish-glue, Mica, Sturgeon
Islam(ic) Al Queda, Crescent, Druse, Druz(e), Hamas, Kurd(ish), Senus(si), Sheriat, Shia(h), Shiite, Sunni(te), Taleban, Taliban, Wah(h)abi
Island, Isle(t) Ait, Archipelago, Atoll, Cay, Char, Desert, Eyot, Floating, Holm, I, Inch, Is, Key, Lagoon, Mainland, Motu, Refuge, Traffic

ISLANDS

2 letters:
TT

3 letters:
Aru
Cos
Diu
Fyn
Hoy
Kos
Man
May
Rat
Rum
Sea
Yap

4 letters:
Amoy
Aran
Arru
Attu
Bali
Biak
Bute
Calf
Cebu
Coll
Cook
Cuba
Dogs
Eigg
Elba
Erin
Fair
Fiji
Guam
Heat
Herm
Holy

Hova
Idse
Iona
Java
Jolo
Jura
Keos
King
Line
Long
Mahe
Maui
Mazu
Mona
Muck
Mull
Niue
Oahu
Saba
Sark
Skye
Spud
Truk
Uist
Unst
Wake
Yell

5 letters:
Aland
Apple
Arran
Aruba
Banka
Banks
Barra
Batan
Belle
Bioko
Bohol

Bonin
Canna
Capri
Ceram
Cheju
Chios
Clare
Cocos
Coney
Coral
Corfu
Crete
Delos
Disko
Ellis
Faial
Farne
Faroe
Fayal
Funen
Haiti
Ibiza
Islay
Isola
Jerba
Kiska
Kuril
Lanai
Lewis
Leyte
Lundy
Luzon
Maewo
Malta
Matsu
Melos
Nauru
Naxos
Nevis
North

Oland
Ormuz
Palau
Panay
Paros
Pelew
Pemba
Pines
Qeshm
Qishm
Reil's
Rhode
Samar
Samoa
Samos
Saria
Seram
South
Spice
Sumba
Sunda
Thera
Thule
Timor
Tiree
Tonga
Upolu
Whale
White
Wight
Youth
Zante

6 letters:
Achill
Aegean
Aegina
Amager
Andros
Avalon

Azores	Majuro	Barbuda	Pacific
Baffin	Marajo	Basilan	Palawan
Banaba	Mercer	Battery	Phoenix
Bangka	Midway	Bedloe's	Rathlin
Barrow	Negros	Bermuda	Reunion
Bikini	Ogygia	Bonaire	Roanoke
Borneo	Paphos	Cartier	Rockall
Bounty	Patmos	Celebes	Salamis
Butung	Penang	Channel	San Juan
Caicos	Pharos	Chatham	Sheppey
Canvey	Philae	Cipango	Shikoku
Cayman	Phuket	Corsica	Society
Ceylon	Pladdy	Crannog	Socotra
Chiloe	Quemoy	Curacao	Sokotra
Cyprus	Ramsey	Cythera	Solomon
Devil's	Rhodes	Diomede	Stewart
Diomed	Rialto	Emerald	St Kilda
Djerba	Robben	Eriskay	St Kitts
Easter	Ryukyu	Falster	St Lucia
Eelpie	Safety	Frisian	Sumatra
Ellice	Saipan	Fur Seal	Sumbawa
Euboea	Savage	Gambier	Suqutra
Flores	Savaii	Gilbert	Surtsey
Fraser	Scilly	Gotland	Tenedos
Hainan	Sicily	Grenada	Tokelau
Harris	Skerry	Hawaiki	Tortola
Hawaii	Skyros	Iwa Jima	Tortuga
Hobart	Snares	Jamaica	Tutuila
Honshu	Soenda	Keeling	Visayan
Hormuz	Staffa	Laaland	Volcano
Imbros	Staten	Ladrone	Waihake
Indies	Tahiti	La Palma	Watling
Insula	Taiwan	Leeward	Western
Ionian	Thanet	Liberty	Wrangel
Ischia	Thasos	Lofoten	Zealand
Ithaca	Tobago	Lolland	Zetland
Jersey	Tresco	Madeira	
Kodiak	Tubuai	Majorca	**8 letters:**
Kurile	Tuvalu	Mariana	Alcatraz
Kvaloy	Unimak	Masbate	Alderney
Kyushu	Ushant	Mayotte	Aleutian
Labuan	Veneti	Mindoro	Anglesey
Laputa	Virgin	Minorca	Anguilla
Lemnos		Molokai	Antilles
Lesbos	**7 letters:**	Moreton	Atlantis
Leucas	Aeolian	Mykonos	Auckland
Leukas	Aldabra	Nicobar	Balearic
Levkas	Andaman	Norfolk	Barbados
Lipari	Antigua	Oceania	Bathurst
Lizard	Austral	Okinawa	Billiton
Lombok	Bahamas	Orcades	Blefuscu
Madura	Baranof	Orkneys	Bora-Bora

Bornholm
Canaries
Caroline
Catalina
Choiseul
Colonsay
Cyclades
Dominica
Falkland
Farquhar
Flinders
Foulness
Friendly
Gothland
Gottland
Guernsey
Hamilton
Hatteras
Hebrides
Hokkaido
Jan Mayen
Kangaroo
Kermadec
Kiribati
Ladrones
Lilliput
Lord Howe
Luggnagg
Mackinac
Maldives
Mallorca
Marianas
Marquesa
Marshall
Melville
Mindanao
Miquelon
Moluccas
Mustique
Northern
Pelagian
Pitcairn
Pleasant
Portland
Pribilof
Principe
Sakhalin
Sandwich
Sardinia
Schouten
Shetland
Somerset

South Sea
Sporades
Sri Lanka
St Helena
St Martin
St Thomas
Sulawesi
Svalband
Sverdrup
Tasmania
Tenerife
Terceira
Thousand
Thursday
Trinidad
Tsushima
Unalaska
Venetian
Victoria
Viti Levu
Windward
Zanzibar

9 letters:
Admiralty
Andreanof
Anticosti
Antipodes
Ascension
Barataria
Benbecula
Chichagof
Christmas
Elephanta
Ellesmere
Falklands
Fortunate
Galapagos
Governors
Greenland
Hainan Tao
Halmahera
Innisfree
Jamestown
Kerguelen
Lampedusa
Lanzarote
Macquarie
Manhattan
Margarita
Marquesas
Mascarene

Mauritius
Melanesia
Nantucket
New Guinea
Polynesia
Rangitoto
Rarotonga
Runnymede
Sao Miguel
Shetlands
Sjaelland
Stromboli
St Vincent
Teneriffe
Trobriand
Vancouver
Vanua Levu
Walcheren

10 letters:
Basse-Terre
Bermoothes
Campobello
Cape Barren
Cape Breton
Cephalonia
Corregidor
Dodecanese
Formentera
Grand Manan
Grand Terre
Grenadines
Heligoland
Hispaniola
Isle Royale
Kiritimati
Langerhans
Madagascar
Manitoulin
Marinduque
Martinique
Micronesia
Montsarrat
New Britain
New Georgia
New Ireland
Pescadores
Poor Knight
Puerto Rico
Saint Croix
Samothrace
Sandalwood

Seychelles
Three Kings
Vesteralen
West Indies
Whitsunday

11 letters:
Austronesia
Dry Tortugas
Glubdubdrib
Grand Bahama
Grand Canary
Guadalcanal
Lakshadweep
Lesser Sunda
Lindisfarne
Mount Desert
New Siberian
Pantelleria
Philippines
San Salvador
Southampton
Spitsbergen

12 letters:
Bougainville
Cassiterides
Glubbdubdrib
Greater Sundo
Marie Galante
New Caledonia
Newfoundland
Nusa Tenggara
Prince Edward
San Cristobal
Santa Barbara
Seringapatam
South Georgia
Torres Strait

13 letters:
Espiritu Santo
Forneaux Group
Fuerteventura
Juan Fernandez
New Providence
Prince of Wales
Santa Catalina

14 letters:
Amboina oceanic
D'Entrecasteaux

- Lesser Antilles
- Queen Charlotte
- Queen Elizabeth
- Tristan da Cunha
- Turks and Caicos

Vestmannaeyjar

15 letters:
Greater Antilles

Mont-Saint-
Michel
Wallis and Futuna

16 letters:
Heard and
McDonald

Islander Chian, Cretan, D(a)yak, Filipino, Kanaka, Kelper, Laputan, Madeiran, Maltese, Mauritian, Native, Nesiot, Newfie, Orcadian, Parian, Rhodian, Samiot, Sican, Singalese, Taiwanese

Isle of Wight Vectis

Isn't Aint, Nis, Nys

Isolate(d) Ancress, Apart, Backwater, Cleidoic, Cut off, Enclave, Enisle, Incommunicado, Inisle, In vacuo, Island, Lone, Maroon, Pocket, Quarantine, Sea-girt, Seclude, Secret, Segregate, Separate, Sequester, Solitary, Sporadic, Stray

Isomer Carvacrol, Geranial, Neral, Pinene, Theophylline

Isosceles Triangle

Isotope Actinon, Deuterium, Iodine-131, Muonium, Protium, Strontium-90, Thoron, Tritium

Israel(i) Beulah, IL, Meir, Sabra

Issue(s) Children, Come, Crux, Debouch, Denouement, Derive, Disclose, Dispense, Edition, Effluence, Egress, > **EMANATE**, Emerge, Emit, Escape, Exit, Exodus, Family, Feigned, Fiduciary, Flotation, Fungible, General, Governmen, Gush, Ish, Litter, Material, Number, Offspring, Outflow, Part, Proof, Publish, Result, Rights, Sally, Seed, Side, Son, Spawn, Special, Spring, Stream, Subject, Topic, Turn, Utter

Istanbul Byzantium, Constantinople

Isthmus Darien, Karelian, Kra, Neck, Panama, San Blas, Tehuantepec

It A, Chic, Hep, Id, Italian, Oomph, SA, 't, Vermouth

Italian, Italy Alpini, Ausonia, Bolognese, Calabrian, Chian, Dago, Ding, Este, Etnean, Etrurian, Etruscan, Eyeti(e), Eytie, Faliscan, Florentine, Genoese, Ghibelline, Guelf, Guelph, Hesperia, Irredentist, It, Latian, Latin, Lombard, Medici, Mezzogiorno, Moro, Oscan, Paduan, Patarin(e), Rocco, Roman, Sabine, Samnite, Sicel, Sienese, Signor(i), Sikel, Spag, Tuscan, Umbrian, Venetian, Vermouth, Volscian, Wop

Italic Swash

Itch(ing), Itchiness Acariasis, Annoy, Cacoethes, Dhobi, Euk, Ewk, Hanker, Joc, Miliaria, Photopsy, Prickle, Prurience, Prurigo, Pruritis, Psora, Scabies, Scrapi, Seven-year, Tickle, > **URGE**, Urtication, Yeuk, Youk, Yuck, Yuke

Item(ise) Also, Article, Bulletin, Detail, Entry, Flash, List, Number, Piece, Point, Spot, Too, Topic

Iterate Repeat

Itinerant, Itinerary Ambulant, Didakai, Didakei, Did(d)icoy, Gipsy, Gypsy, Hob, Journey, Log, Pedlar, Peripatetic, Pie-powder, Roadman, Roamer, Romany, Rootless, Route, Stroller, Traveller

Itself Per se

Ivan Russian, Terrible

Ivory (tower) Black, Bone, Dentine, Distant, Eburnean, Impractical, Incisor, Key, Solitude, Teeth, Tower, Tusk, Vegetable, Whale's bone

Ivy Ale-hoof, Angelica-tree, Aralia, Boston, Bush, Cat's-foot, Climber, Creeper, Evergreen, Gill, Grape, Ground, Hedera, Helix, Japanese, Panax, Poison, Shiel, Udo, Weeping

Jj

J Curve, Juliet, Pen

Jab(ber) Chatter, Foin, Gabble, Immunologist, Inject, Jaw, Jook, Nudge, One-two, Poke, Prattle, Prod, Proke, Punch, Puncture, Sook, Sputter, Stab, Stick, Venepuncture, Yak

Jack(s) AB, Apple, Artocarpus, Ass, Ball, Boot, Bower, Bowl(s), Boy, Card, Cheap, Coatcard, Crevalle, Deckhand, Dibs(tones), Five stones, Flag, Frost, Hoist, Honour, Hopper, Horner, Hydraulic, Idle, J, Jock, Ketch, Kitty, Knave, Knucklebones, London, Lumber, Mark, Matlow, Mistress, Nob, Noddy, Pilot, Point, Pot, Pur, Rabbit, Raise, Rating, Ripper, Robinson, Russell, Sailor, Salt, Screw, Shaun, Sprat, Spring-heeled, Springtail, Steeple, Sticker, Straw, Tar, Tee, Tradesman, Turnspit, Union, Uplift, Wood, Yellow

Jackal Anubis, Dieb, Hack, Stooge

Jackass Aliboron, Goburra, Kookaburra, Stupid

Jackdaw Bird, Chawk, Chough, Daw, Kae, Raven, Rheims, Thief

Jacket Acton, Afghanistan, Amauti(k), Anorak, Bainin, Baju, Bania(n), Banyan, Barbour®, Basque, Battle, Bawneen, Bed, Bellhop, Blazer, Blouson, Body-warmer, Bolero, Bomber, Brigandine, Bumfreezer, Bush, Cagoul(e), Camisole, Can, Caraco, Cardigan, Carmagnole, Casing, > **COAT**, Dinner, Dolman, Donkey, Drape, Dressing, Duffel coat, Duffle coat, Dust-cover, Dustwrapper, Fearnought, Flak, Fleece, Gambeson, Gendarme, Grego, Habergeon, Hacking, Ha(c)queton, Half-kirtle, Hug-me-tight, Jerkin, Jupon, Kagool, Kaross, Life, Life preserver, Lumber, Mackinaw, Mae West, Mandarin, Mandilion, Mao, Matinée, Mess, Monkey, Nehru, Newmarket, Norfolk, Parka, Pea, Petenlair, Pierrot, Pilot, Polka, Potato, Railly, Reefer, Safari, Sayon, Shearling, Shell, Shortgown, Simar(re), Sleeve, Slip-cover, Smoking, Spencer, Sports, Steam, Strait, Tabard, Tailcoat, Toreador, Tunic, Tux(edo), Tweed, Vareuse, Waistcoat, Wam(m)us, Wampus, Water, Windbreaker®, Windcheater, Windjammer, Wrapper, Zouave

Jackknife Dive, Fold, Jockteleg, Pike

Jackpot Cornucopia, Kitty, Pool

Jackson Stonewall

Jackstraw Spellican, Spil(l)ikin

Jacobite(s) Non-compounder, Non juror, Wild Geese

Jacquard Matelasse

Ja(c)ques Melancholy, Tati

Jade(d) Axe-stone, Bidet, Cloy, Crock, Disjaskit, Exhaust, Fatigue, Greenstone, Hack, Hag, Horse, Hussy, Limmer, Minx, Nag, Nephrite, Pounamu, Rip, Rosinante, Sate, Screw, Slut, Spleenstone, Stale, Tired, Trite, Weary, Yaud, Yu(-stone)

Jag(ged) Barbed, Cart, Drinking, Erose, Gimp, Injection, Laciniate, Ragde, Ragged, Serrate, Snag, Spree, Spur, Tooth

Jagger Mick, Pedlar

Jaguar American tiger, Car, Caracal, Cat, E-type, Ounce, Tiger

Jail(er) Adam, Alcaide, Alcatraz, Bedford, Bin, Bridewell, Can, Clink, Commit, Cooler, Gaol, Hoosegow, Imprison, Incarcerate, Jug, Keeper, Kitty, Lockup, Marshalsea, Newgate, Nick, Pen, Pokey, > **PRISON**, Screw, Shop, Slammer, Spandau, Strangeways, Tronk, Turnkey, Warder

Jailbird Con, Lag, Lifer, Trusty

Jain(ism) Mahavira

Jakarta Batavia

Jake Honest, Hunkydory, OK, Rube

Jalopy Banger, Boneshaker, Buggy, Car, Crate, Heap, Shandry(dan), Stock-car

Jam(my) Apple butter, Block, Choke, Clog, Confiture, Crush, Cushy, Dilemma, Gridlock, Hold-up, Jeelie, Jeely, Lock, Log, Plight, > **PREDICAMENT**, Preserve, Press, Quince, Seize, Snarl-up, Spot, Squeeze, Stall, Stick, Tailback, Tangle, Traffic, Vice, Vise, Wedge

Jamaica(n) Rasta(farian), Rastaman, Yardie

Jamb Doorpost, Durn, Sconcheon, Scontion, Scuncheon, Upright

James Agee, Bond, Bothwell, Henry, Jacobite, Jemmy, Jesse, Jim, Joyce, Screw, Seamus, Seumas, Sid, Watt

Jane Austen, Calamity, Eyre, Seymour, Shore, Sian

Jangle Clank, Clapperclaw, Clash, Rattle, Wrangle

Janitor Doorman, Porter, Servitor, Tiler

Jankers KP

Jansky Jy

Janus Two-faced

Japan(ese), Japanese drama Ainu, Burakumin, Daimio, Eta, Geisha, Genro, Gloss, Haiku, Heian, Hondo, Honshu, Issei, Kabuki, Kami, Kana, Kirimon, Lacquer, Mandarin, Meiji, Mikado, Mousmé, Mousmee, Nippon, Nisei, No(h), Resin, Sansei, Satsuma, Shinto, Shogun, Togo, Tycoon, Yamato

Jape Jeer, Joke, Prank, Trick

Jar(ring) Albarello, Amphora, Bell, Canopus, Churr, Clash, Crock, Cruet, Din, Dissonant, Distune, Dolium, Enrough, Gallipot, Grate, Greybeard, Gride, Grind, Gryde, Humidor, Hydria, > **JOLT**, Kalpis, Kang, Kilner®, Leyden, Mason, Off-key, Olla, Pint, Pithos, Pot(iche), Quarrel, Rasp, Shelta, Shock, Stamnos, Start, Stean, Steen, Stein, Tankard, Tinaja, Turn, Vessel, Water-monkey

Jargon Argot, Baragouin, Beach-la-mar, Buzzword, Cant, Chinook, Eurobabble, Eurospeak, Gobbledegook, Gobbledygook, Jive, Kennick, Legalese, Lingo, Lingoa geral, Lingua franca, Mumbo-jumbo, Newspeak, Officialese, Parlance, Patois, Patter, Patter-flash, Psychobabble, Shelta, Shoptalk, > **SLANG**, Technobabble, Technospeak, Vernacular

Jasmine Cape, Frangipani, Gelsemine, Gessamine, Jessamy, Madagascar, Olea

Jasper Basanite, Bloodstone, Egyptian, Porcelain

Jaundice(d) Cynical, Icterus, Prejudiced, Sallow, Yellow

Jaunt Journey, Outing, Sally, Stroll, Swan, Trip

Jaunty Airy, Akimbo, Chipper, Debonair, Perky, Rakish

▷ **Jaunty** *may indicate* an anagram

Java man Pithecanthropus

Javelin Dart, Gavelock, Harpoon, Jereed, Jerid, Pile, Pilum, Spear

Jaw(s), Jawbone Blab, Chaft, Chap, Chat, Chaw, Cheek, Chide, Chin, Entry, Glass, Gnathic, Gnathite, Gonion, Hypognathous, Jobe, Lantern, Lumpy, Mandible, Masseter, Maxilla, Mesial, Muzzle, Mylohyoid, Natter, Opisthognathous, Overshot, Phossy, Pi, Premaxillary, Prognathous, Ramus, Rubber, Shark, Stylet, Underhung, Undershot, Wapper-jaw, Ya(c)kety-Ya(c)k

Jay Bird, J, Sirgang, Whisky-jack, Whisky-john

Jazz(er), Jazzman Acid, Barber, Barrelhouse, Basie, Bebop, Blues, Boogie,
Boogie-woogie, Bop, Cat, Cool, Dixieland, Enliven, Gig, Gutbucket, Hardbop,
Hipster, Jive, Latin, Lick, Mainstream, Modern, New Orleans, Progressive,
Ragtime, Riff, Scat, Skiffle, Stomp, Swinger, Trad, Traditional, West Coast
Jealous(y) Envious, Green(-eyed), Green-eyed monster, Grudging, Zelotypia
Jean(s) Chinos, Denims, Levis®, Pants, Trousers, Wranglers®
Jeer(ing) Ballyrag, Barrack, Belittle, Birl, Boo, Burl, Digs, Fleer, Flout, Gird, Hoot,
Jape, Jibe, > MOCK, Rail, Razz, Ridicule, Scoff, Sling off, Sneer, Taunt, Twit, Yah
Jeeves Valet
Jehovah God, Lord, Yahve(h), Yahwe(h)
Jehovah's Witness Russellite
Jehu Charioteer, Driver
Jejune Arid, Barren, Dry, Insipid, Juvenile
Jelly Acaleph(a), Acalephe, Agar(-agar), Aspic, Brawn, Calf's foot, Chaudfroid,
Comb, Cow-heel, > EXPLOSIVE, Flummery, Gel, Isinglass, Jam, Kanten,
Macedoine, Medusa, Mineral, Mould, Napalm, Neat's foot, Petroleum,
Quiddany, Royal, Shape, Tunicin, Vaseline®, Vitreous humour
Jelly *may indicate* an anagram
Jellyfish Acaleph(a), Acalephe, Aurelia, Blubber, Box, Cnidaria, Discomedusae,
Discophora, Hydromedusa, Irukandji, Medusa, Mesogloea, Planoblast,
Portuguese man-of-war, Quarl, Scyphistoma, Scyphozoan, Sea-blubber,
Sea-nettle, Sea-wasp, Strobila
Jemmy Betty, Crowbar, Lever
Jenkins Ear, Roy, Up
Jenny Ass, Lind, Long, Mule, Short, Spinner, Spinning, Spinster, Wren
Jeopardise, Jeopardy Danger, Double, Expose, Hazard, Peril, Risk
Jerboa Desert rat
Jeremiad Lament, Tragedy, Woe
Jeremy Fisher, Jerry
Jerk(y), Jerkily, Jerking, Jerks Aerobics, A salti, Bob, Braid, Cant, Diddle,
Ebrillade, Flirt, Flounce, Gym(nastics), Hike, Hitch, Hoi(c)k, Jut, Kant, Knee,
PE, Peck, Physical, Saccade, Shove, Spasm, Start, Strobe, Surge, Sydenham's
chorea, Tic, Toss(en), Tweak, > TWITCH, Wrench, Yank
Jerkin Jacket, Tabard
Jerome Kern, Vulgate
Jerry, Jerry-built Boche, Flimsy, Fritz, Hun, Kraut, Mouse, Po(t)
Jersey(s) CI, Cow, Frock, Gansey, Guernsey, Kine, Lily, Maillot, Polo, Roll-neck,
Singlet, > SWEATER, Sweatshirt, Yellow, Zephyr
Jerusalem Ariel, Hierosolymitan, Sion, Zion
Jess(e) James, Strap
Jest(er), Jesting Badinage, Barm, Baur, Bawr, Bourd(er), Buffoon, Clown, Cod,
Comic, Droll, Goliard, Inficete, Jape, Jig, Joker, Josh, Merryman, Miller, Motley,
Patch, Quip, Raillery, Ribaldry, Rigoletto, Scogan, Scoggin, Sport, Toy, Trinculo,
Wag, Wit, Yorick
Jesuit Bollandist, Ignatius, Loyola, SJ
Jesus > CHRIST, Emmanuel, IHS, Immanuel, INRI, Isa, Jabers, Lord
Jet Airbus®, Aircraft, Beadblast, Black, Burner, Chirt, Douche, Fountain, Geat,
Harrier, Ink, Jumbo, Plane, Pump, Soffione, Spirt, Spout, Spray, Spurt, Squirt,
Stream, Turbine, Turbo, Vapour, Water
Jettison Discard, Dump, Flotsam, Jetsam, Lagan, Ligan
Jetty Groin, Mole, Pier, Wharf
Jew(ish), Jews Ashkenazi, Chas(s)id, Diaspora, Essene, Falasha, Grecian,

Greek, Has(s)id, Hebrew, Kahal, Karaite, Karta, Landsman, Levite, Lubavitch, Maccabee, Marrano, Misnaged, Mitnag(g)ed, Nazarite, Neturei, Peculiar people, Pharisee, Refusenik, Sabra, Sadducee, Semite, Sephardim, Sheeny, Shemite, Shtetl, Smouch, Smouse, Tobit, Wandering, Yid(dish), Zealot

Jewel(s), Jeweller(y) Agate, Almandine, Artwear, Beryl, Bijouterie, Brilliant, Chrysoprase, Cloisonné, Cornelian, Costume, Crown, Diamond, Earbob, Ear-drop, Emerald, Ewe-lamb, Fabergé, Fashion, Ferron(n)ière, Finery, Garnet > **GEM**, Girandole, Gracchi, Jade, Junk, Lherzolite, Marcasite, Navette, Olivine, Opal, Parure, Paste, Pavé, Pearl, Pendant, Peridot, Rivière, Rubin(e), Ruby, Sapphire, Sard, Scarab, Smaragd, Solitaire, Stone, Sunburst, Tom, Tomfoolery, Topaz, Torc, Treasure, Trinket

Jezebel Harlot, Loose, Whore

Jib Ba(u)lk, Boggle, Boom, > **DEMUR**, Face, Flying, Foresail, Genoa, Milk, Reest, Reist, Stay-sail, Storm

Jibe Bob, Correspond, Dig, Fling, > **JEER**, Mock, Quip, Sarcasm, Slant, Taunt

Jiffy Mo, Pronto, Twinkling

Jig(gle) Bob, Bounce, Dance, Fling, Frisk, Hornpipe, Jog, Juggle, Morris

Jigger(ed) Beat, Chigoe, Jolley, Ruin

Jill Ferret

Jilt Discard, Reject, Shed, Throw-over

Jim(my) Diamond, Dismal, Jas, Lucky, Pee, Piddle, Riddle

Jingle(r) Clerihew, Clink, Ditty, Doggerel, Rhyme, Tambourine, Tinkle

Jingo(ism) Odzooks, Patriot, War-rant

Jink Elude

Jinn(i) Afreet, Eblis, Genie, Marid, Spirit

Jinx Curse, Hex, Jonah, Kibosh, Moz(z), Spoil, Voodoo, Whammy

Jitter(s), Jittery Coggly, DT, Fidgets, Funk, Jumpy, Nervous, Willies

▷ **Jitter(s)** *may indicate* an anagram

Jo > **LOVER**, Sweetheart

Job(bing) Agiotage, Appointment, Berth, Career, Chore, Comforter, Crib, Darg, Errand, Gig, Hatchet, Homer, Inside, Metier, Nixer, Oratorio, Patient, Pensum Place(ment), Plum, Position, Post, Problem, Pursuit, Put-up, Sinecure, Snow, Spot, Steady, > **TASK**, Ticket, Trotter, Undertaking, Work

▷ **Job** *may indicate* the biblical character

Jock Deejay, DJ, Mac, Sawn(e)y, Scot

Jockey Carr, Cheat, Diddle, Disc, Jostle, Jump, Lester, Manoeuvre, Rider, Steve, Suicide, Swindle, Trick, Video, Winter

▷ **Jockey** *may indicate* an anagram

Jocose, Jocular, Jocund Cheerful, Debonair, Facete, Facetious, Jesting, Lepid, Scurril(e), Waggish

Joe(y), Joseph Addison, Dogsbody, GI, Kangaroo, Pal, Roo, Sloppy, Stalin, Surface, Trey

Jog(ger), Joggle, Jog-trot Arouse, Canter, Dog-trot, Dunch, Dunsh, Heich-how, Heigh-ho, Hod, Jiggle, Jolt, Jostle, Memo, Mosey, Nudge, Piaffe, Prompt, Ranke Remind, Run, Shake, Shog, Tickle, Trot, Whig

John(ny) Ajax, Augustus, Barleycorn, Bog, Bright, Brown, Bull, Bunyan, Cloaca Collins, Doree, Dory, Elton, Evan, Gaunt, Gents, Gilpin, Groats, Halifax, Ia(i)n, Ivan, Lackland, Latecomer, Lav, Little, Loo, Peel, Prester, Stage-door, Throne, Toot, Tout, WC

Johnson Cham, Doctor, Idler

Join(er), Joined, Joining Abut, Accede, Accompany, Add, Ally, And, Annex, Associate, Attach, Braze, Butt-end, Cement, Cleave, Combine, Conflate,

Conglutinate, Conjugate, Connect, Cope, > COUPLE, Dovetail, Engraft, Enlist, Enrol, Enter, Federate, Fuse, Glue, Graft, Hasp, Hitch, Hyphen, Include, Inosculate, Jugate, Knit, Link, Marry, Meet, Member, Menuisier, Merge, Mix, Mortar, Mortise, Oop, Oup, Overlaunch, Piece, Piecen, Rebate, Regelation, Rivet, Scarf, Seam, Se-tenant, Sew, Siamize, Snug, Solder, Splice, Spot-weld, Squirrel, Staple, Stylolite, Tenon, Unite, Wed, Weld, Yoke

Joint(ed) Ancon, Ankle, Arthrosis, Articular, Ball and socket, Bar, Baron, Butt, Cardan, Carpus, Chine, Clip, Co, Cogging, Colonial goose, Commissure, Conjunction, Cuit, Cup and ball, Cut, Dive, Dovetail, Drumstick, Elbow, Enarthrosis, Entrecôte, Expansion, Fish, Gambrel, Gimmal, Gimmer, Ginglymus, Hainch, Haunch, Heel, Hinge, Hip, Hough, Huck, Hunker, J, Joggle, Jolly, Junction, Knee, Knuckle, Lap(ped), Lith, Loin, Marijuana, Meat, Mitre, Mortise, Mouse (buttock), Mouse-piece, Mutton, Mutual, Phalange, Phalanx, Pin, Popliteal, Psoas, Rabbet, Rack, Raphe, Reducer, Reefer, Rhaphe, Ribroast, Roast, Saddle, Scarf, Schindylesis, Seam, Shoulder, Silverside, Sirloin, Splice, Spliff, Stifle, Straight, Strip, Symphysis, Syndesmosis, T, Tarsus, T-bone, Tenon, Together, Toggle, Tongue and groove, Topside, Trochanter, Undercut, Universal, Vertebra, Water, Weld, Wrist

Joist Accomplement, Bar, Beam, Dormant, Groundsill, H-beam, I-beam, Rib, Rolled-steel, Sleeper, Solive, String, Trimmer

Joke(r), **Joke-book** Banter, Bar, Booby-trap, Bourdon, Card, Chaff, Chestnut, > CLOWN, Cod, Comedian, Comic, Crack, Cut-up, Farceur, Farceuse, Fool, Fun, Funster, Gab, Gag, Glike, Guy, Have-on, Hazer, Hoax, Hum, Humorist, Jape, Jest, Jig, Lark, Legpull, Merry-andrew, Merryman, Mistigris, One, One-liner, Pleasantry, Practical, Prank(ster), Pun, Punchline, Pundigrion, Quip, Sally, Scherzo, Scogan, Scoggin, Sick, Skylark, Sottisier, Squib, Standing, Wag, Wheeze, Wild, Wisecrack, Wit

Jollity, **Jolly** 'Arryish, Bally, Convivial, Cordial, Do, Festive, Galoot, Gaucie, Gaucy, Gawcy, Gawsy, Gay, Hilarious, Jocose, Jovial, Marine, Mirth, Rag, RM, Roger, Sandboy, Tar, Very

Jolt Bump, Jar, Jig-a jig, Jostle, Jounce, Shake, Shog, Start

Jonah Hoodoo, Jinx, Moz(z)

Jones Davy, Emperor, Inigo

Jordan Pot, Urinal

Joris Horseman

Joseph *see* JOE

Josh Chaff, Kid, Rib, Tease

Josiah Stamp, Wedgewood

Joss Incense, Luck, Stick

Jostle Barge, Bump, Compete, Elbow, Hog-shouther, Hustle, Push, Shoulder, > SHOVE

Jot(ter), **Jotting(s)** Ace, Fig, Iota, Memo, Mite, Note, Pad, Stime, Styme, Tittle, Whit

Journal Daily, Daybook, Diary, Ephemeris, Gazette, Hansard, Lancet, Log, Noctuary, Organ, Paper, Periodical, Pictorial, Punch, Rag, Record, TES, TLS, Trade, Weblog

Journalism, **Journalist** Cheque-book, Columnist, Commentariat, Contributor, Diarist, Diurnalist, Ed, Fleet St, Freelance, (GA) Sala, Gonzo, Hack, Hackery, Hackette, Hatchetman, Inkslinger, Investigative, Keyhole, Lobby, Muckraker, Newshound, Northcliffe, NUJ, Pepys, Press(man), Reporter, Reviewer, Scribe, Sob sister, Stead, Stringer, Wireman, > WRITER, Yellow

Journey Circuit, Cruise, Errand, Expedition, Eyre, Foray, Grand Tour, Hadj, Hop,

Jaunce, Jaunse, Jaunt, Mush, Odyssey, Passage, Periegesis, Ply, Raik, Rake, Red-eye, Ride, Run, Sentimental, Tour, Travel, Trek, Viatical, Walkabout

Journeyman Artisan, Commuter, Craftsman, Sterne, Yeoman

Joust Giust, Tilt, Tournament, Tourney

Jove Egad, Gad, Igad, Jupiter, Thunderer

Jovial Bacchic, Festive, Genial, Jolly

Jowl Cheek, Chops, Jaw

Joy(ful), Joyous Bliss, Blithe, > DELIGHT, Dream, Ecstasy, Elation, Exulting, Fain, Felicity, Festal, Frabjous, Glad, Glee, Gloat, Hah, Hey, Jubilant, Nirvana, Rapture, Schadenfreude, Sele, Tra-la, Transport, Treat, Yippee

Joyce Haw Haw, Traitor

JP Beak, Quorum

Jubilant, Jubilation, Jubilee Celebration, Cock-a-hoop, Diamond, Ecstatic, Elated, Exultant, Holiday, Joy, Triumphant

Judaism Semitism

Judas Double-crosser, Iscariot, Traitor, Tree

Judder Put-put, Shake, Vibrate

Jude Obscure

Judge(ment), Judges Addoom, Adjudicator, Agonothetes, Alacus, Alcalde, Arbiter, Areopagite, Aret(t), Arrêt, Assess, Assize, Auto-da-fé, Avizandum, Banc, Brehon, Cadi, Calculate, Censure, Centumvirus, Circuit(eer), Common Serjeant, Comparative, Connoisseur, Consider, Coroner, Court, Critic(ise), Daniel, Daysman, Deborah, Decern(e), Decide, Decision, Decreet, Deem(ster), Dempster, Dicast, Differential, Dikast, Discern(ment), District, Ephor, Ermined, Estimate, Evaluate, Gauge, Gesse, Gideon, Good-sense, Guess, Hakeem, Hakim, Hearing, Hold, Honour, Inky-smudge, Interlocutor, J, Jeffreys, Jephthah, Justice, Justicier, Last, Lud, Lynch, Minos, Mufti, Non prosequitur, Nonsuit, Official Referee, Old Fury, Opine, Opinion, Ordinary, Outfangthief, Panel, Paris, Podesta, Providence, Puisne, Puny, Reckon(ing), Recorder, Ref(eree), Regard, Rhadamanthus, Ruler, Samson, Samuel, Sapience, Scan, See, Sentence, Sentiment, Shallow, Sheriff, Sober, Solomon, Sound, Suppose, Surrogate, Syndic, Tact, Think, Touch, Trior, Try, Umpire, Value, Verdict, Weigh up, Wig, Wik, Wisdom, Worship

Judicious Critical, Discreet, Politic, Rational, Sage, Sensible, Shrewd, Sound

Judo, Judo costume Dojo, Gi(e), Shiai

Jug(s) Amphora, Bellarmine, Bird, Blackjack, Bombard, Breasts, Can, Cooler, Cream(er), Crock, Enghalskrug, Ewer, Gaol, Gotch, Greybeard, Growler, John Roberts, Malling, Measuring, Olpe, Pitcher, Pound, Pourer, Pourie, > PRISON, Quad, Quod, Shop, Stir, Tits, Toby, Urceolus

Juggle(r) Conjuror, Cook, Escamotage, Fake

Juice, Juicy Bacca, Cassareep, Cassaripe, Cremor, Current, Fluid, Fruity, Gastric, Hypocist, Ichor, Jungle, La(b)danum, Laser, Latex, Lush, Moist, Must, Oil, Pancreatic, Perry, Rare, Sap, Soma, Spanish, Succ(o)us, Succulent, Tarantula, Thridace, Vril, Walnut, Zest

Juju Charm, Fetish

Jujube Lotus, Padma, Sweet

Jukebox Nickelodeon

Julian Apostate

July Dogdays

Jumble Chaos, Conglomeration, Farrago, Garble, Huddle, Jabble, Lumber, Mass, Medley, Mingle-mangle, Mish-mash, Mixter-maxter, Mixtie-maxtie, Mixture, Mix(t)y-max(t)y, Pastiche, Printer's pie, Raffle, Ragbag, Scramble, Shuffle,

Wuzzle

Jumbled *may indicate* an anagram

Jumbo Aircraft, Elephant, Jet, Large-scale, Mammoth, OS

Jump(er), Jumping, Jumpy Aran, Assemble, Axel, Bate, Batterie, Boomer, Bound, Bungee, Bungy, Caper, Capriole, Cicada, Cicata, Crew-neck, Cricket, Croupade, Daffy, Desultory, Entrechat, Euro, Eventer, Flea, Fosbury flop, Gansey, Gazump, Gelande (sprung), Guernsey, Halma, Helicopter, Hurdle, Impala, Itchy, Jersey, Joey, Kangaroo, Katydid, Knight, Lammie, Lammy, Leap(frog), Lep, Lope, Lutz, Nervous, Nervy, Ollie, Parachute, Pig, Pogo, Polo-neck, Pounce, Prance, Prank, Pronking, Puissance, Quantum, Quersprung, Rap, Salchow, Saltatory, Saltigrade, Saltus, Scissors, Scoup, Scowp, Skip, Skipjack, Skydiver, > **SPRING**, Start, Sweater, Toe (-loop), Trampoline, Triple, Turtle-neck, Vau(l)t, Water, Western roll

Jumping jack Pantine

Junction Abutment, Alloyed, Angle, Box, Bregma, Carfax, Close, Clover-leaf, Connection, Crewe, Crossroads, Diffused, Gap, Intersection, Joint, Josephson, Knitting, Meeting, P-n, Point, Raphe, Spaghetti, Suture, T, Tight, Union

Juneberry Saskatoon, Shadbush

Jungle Asphalt, Blackboard, Boondocks, Bush, Concrete, Forest, Shola, Tangle

Junior Cadet, Chota, Cion, Dogsbody, Fils, Minor, Name-son, Petty, Puisne, Scion, Sub(ordinate), Underling, Understrapper, Younger

Juniper Red-cedar, Savin(e)

Junk(shop) Bric-a-brac, Chuck in, Jettison, Litter, Lorcha, Lumber, Refuse, Ship, Tagareen, Tatt, Trash

Junk *may indicate* an anagram

Junker Prussian

Junket(ing) Beano, Creel, Custard, Feast, Picnic, Rennet, Spree

Junta Cabal, Council

Jupiter Jove, Newspaper

Jurassic Lias, Rhaetic

Jurisdiction Authority, Bailiwick, Domain, Province, Soke(n)

Juror(s), Jury Assize, Dicast, Grand, Hung, Inquest, Judges, Mickleton, Old Fury, Pais, Panel, Party, Petit, Petty, Sail, Special, Tales, Tribunal, Venire, Venireman, Venue

Just(ice) Alcalde, All, Aristides, Astraea, Balanced, Condign, Cupar, Deserved, Equal, Equity, E(v)en, Fair, Fair-minded, Forensic, Honest, Impartial, J, Jasper, Jeddart, Jethart, Jurat, Mere, Natural, Nemesis, Newly, Nice, Only, Palm-tree, Piso, Poetic, Provost, Puisne, Pure and simple, Recent, Restorative, Right(ful), Righteous, Rightness, Rough, Shallow, Silence, Simply, Sommer, Street, Themis, Tilt, Upright

Justifiable, Justification, Justify Apology, Autotelic, Avenge, Aver, Avowry, Clear, Darraign(e), Darrain(e), Darrayn, Defend, Deraign, Excusable, Explain, Grounds, Rationale, Vindicate, Warrant

Just so Exactly, Sic, Stories

Jut Beetle, Bulge, Overhang, Project, Protrude, Sail

Jute Burlap, Corchorus, Gunny, Hengist, Hessian, Horsa, Urena

Juvenile Childish, Teenage(r), Yonkers, Young, Younkers

Juxtaposition Parataxis

Kk

K Kelvin, Kilo, King, Kirkpatrick
K2 Dapsang, Godwin Austen
Kaffir Shares, Xosa
Kail, **Kale** Borecole, Cabbage, Cole, Curly-greens, Ninepins
Kaiser Doorn
Kaleidoscope Dappled, Motley, Myrioscope, Various
Kangaroo Bettong, Boomer, Boongary, Bounder, Brush, Cus-cus, Diprotodont, Euro, Forester, Joey, Macropodidae, Nototherium, Old man, Potoroo, Rat, Red, Steamer, Tree, Troop, Wallaby, Wallaroo
Kansas Sunflower
Kaolin Lithomarge
Karate Kung Fu, Wushu
Karma Destiny, Fate, Predestination
Kate Greenaway, Shrew
Kayak Bidarka
Kebab Cevapcici, Doner, Gyro, Satay, Sate, Shashli(c)k, Sosatie, Souvlakia
Keel Bilge, Bottom, Carina, Centreboard, Faint, False, Fin, List, Overturn, Skeg(g), Sliding
Keen(ness), **Keener** Acid, Acute, Agog, Argute, Aspiring, Astute, Athirst, Avid, Aygre, Bemoan, Bewail, Breem, Breme, Cheap, Coronach, Dash, Devotee, Dirge, Eager, Elegy, Enthusiastic, Fanatical, Fell, Greet, Grieve, Hone, Hot, Howl, Into, Lament, Mourn, Mustard, Mute, Narrow, Ochone, Ohone, Partial, Peachy, Perceant, Persant, Raring, Razor, Ready, Red-hot, Rhapsodic, Sharp, Shrewd, Shrill, Snell, Thirsting, Threnodic, Thrillant, Trenchant, Ululate, Wail, Whet, Zeal(ous)
Keep(er), **Keeping** Ames, Armature, Austringer, Castellan, Castle, Celebrate, Chatelain(e), Citadel, Conceal, Conserve, Curator, Custodian, Custody, Depositary, Depository, Detain, Donjon, Escot, Finder, Fort, Gaoler, Goalie, Guardian, Have, Hoard, > **HOLD**, Maintain, Nab, Net, Observe, Ostreger, Park, Pickle, Preserve, Retain, Safeguard, Stay, Stet, Stock, Store, Stow, Stumper, Support, Sustain, Tower, Warden, Withhold
Keep back Detain, Recoup, Reserve, Retard, Stave
Keepsake Memento, Souvenir, Token
Keep under Cow, Subdue, Submerge
Keg Barrel, Cask, Powder, Tub, Tun, Vat
Kelly('s) Eye, Gene, Ned
Kelvin Absolute, K
Ken Eyeshot, Know(ledge), Purview, Range
Kennel(s) Guard, Home, House, Shelter
Kent Lathe, SE, Superman
Kentuckian, **Kentucky** Chicken, Corn-cracker, Derby, KY
Kenya(n) Masai, Mau Mau
Kerala Nair, Nayar

Kerb Edge, Gutter, Roadside

Kerchief Babushka, Bandan(n)a, Headcloth, Romal, Scarf

Kernel Copra, Core, Corn, Grain, Nucleus, Pine, Praline, Prawlin

Kestrel Bird, Hawk, Keelie, Stallion, Staniel, Stannel, Stanyel, Windhover

Ket Carrion, Wool

Ketch Jack

Ketchup Relish, Sauce, Tomato

Kettle Boiler, Cauldron, Dixie, Dixy, Drum, Fanny, Pot, Tea, Turpin, War, Whistling

Key(s), Keyhole A, Ait, Allen, Alt, Ash, B, Basic, C, Cay, Central, Chip, Church, Cipher, Clavis, Clew, Clink, Clue, Control, Crib, D, Dichotomous, Digital, Dital, Dominant, E, Enter, Esc(ape), Essential, F, Flat, Florida, Fruit, Function, G, Greek, High, Holm, Hot, Ignition, Important, Inch, Index, INS, Instrumental, Islet, Ivory, Kaie, King-pin, Latch, Legend, Linchpin, Locker, Low, Main, Major, Master, Minor, Note, Nut, Octachord, Opener, Oustiti, Outsiders, Pass(word), Passe-partout, Piano, Pipe, Pivot, Pony, Prong, Reef, Return, Semibreve, Shift, Signature, Skeleton, Spanner, Spline, Stimulate, Supertonic, Tab, Table, Tipsy, Tonal, Turning, Vital, Watch, Water, Wedge, Woodruff, Yale®

Keyboard, Keypad Azerty, Console, Digitorium, DVORAK, Electronic, Manual, Martenot, Numeric, Piano, Pianola®, Qwerty, Spinet

Keyholder Occupant, Resident, Tenant, Warder

Key man Islander, Kingpin

Keynote Line, Mese, Theme, Tonic

Keystone Cops, Crux, PA, Pennsylvania, Quoin, Sagitta, Voussoir

Keyword Kwic, Sesame

Khan Aga, Chagan, Cham, Serai, Shere

Kick(ing) Back-heel, Bicycle, Boot, Buzz, Corner, Dribble, Drop, Fling, Flutter, Fly, Free, Frog, Garryowen, Goal, Grub, Hack, Hitch, Hoof, Lash, Nutmeg, Pause, Penalty, Pile, Punce, Punt, Recalcitrate, Recoil, Recoyle, Savate, Scissors, Sixpence, Speculator, Spot, Spur, Spurn, Squib, Stab, Tanner, Tap, Thrill, Toe, Up and under, Vigour, Volley, Wince, Yerk, Zip

Kid(s) Arab, Befool, Billy, Brood, Cheverel, Chevrette, Child, Chit, Cisco, Con, Delude, Goat, Hircosity, Hoax, Hocus, Hoodwink, Hum, Joke, Leather, Misguide, Nipper, Offspring, Outwit, Pretend, Rag, Rib, Spoof, Suede, Sundance, > **TEASE**, Tot, Trick, Whiz(z), Wiz

Kidnap Abduct, Hijack, Plagium, Shanghai, Snatch, Spirit, Steal

Kidney(-shaped) Character, Mettle, Nature, Reins, Renal, Reniform, Sort

Kill(ed), Killer, Killing Assassin, Attrit, Battue, Behead, Biocidal, Boojum, Butcher, Carnage, Carnifex, Category, Chance-medley, Choke, Comical, Croak, Crucify, Cull, Despatch, Destroy, Electrocute, Euthanasia, Execute, Exterminate, Extirpate, For(e)do, Frag, Garotte, Germicide, Gun, Handsel, Hatchet man, Hilarious, Homicide, Ice, Immolate, K, Knacker, Knock off, Liquidate, Lynch, Mactation, Matador(e), Mercy, Misadventure, Mortify, Murder, Napoo, Necklace, Ninja, NK, Off, Orc(a), Penalty, Pesticide, -phage, Pick off, Pip, Predator, Prolicide, Quell, Quietus, Regrate, Sacrifice, Serial, Settle, Shochet, Slaughter, Slay(er), Slew, Smite, Snuff, Spike, Stifle, Stonker, Strangle, Swat, Tailor, Thagi, Thug(gee), Top, Toreador, Total, Vaticide, Veto, Waste, Zap

Killjoy Crab, Puritan, Sourpuss, Spoilsport, Wowser

Kiln Oast, Oven

Kilometre Km, Verst

Kilt Drape, Filabeg, Fil(l)ibeg, Fustanella, Phil(l)abeg, Phil(l)ibeg, Plaid, Tartan

Kimono Yukata
Kin(sman) Ally, Family, Kith, Like, Nearest, Relation, Sib(b), Sybbe
Kind(ly) Akin, Amiable, Avuncular, Benefic, Benevolent, Benign, Boon, Breed, Brood, Brotherly, Category, Class, Clement, Considerate, Favourable, Gender, Generic, Generous, Genre, Gentle, Genus, Good, Humane, Ilk, Kidney, Kin, Lenient, Manner, Modal, Nature, Nice, Sisterly, > SORT, Species, Strain, Strene, Trine, Type, Understanding, Variety, Well-disposed, Ylke
Kindle, **Kindling** Accend, Fire, Ignite, Incense, Incite, Inflame, > LIGHT, Litter, Lunt, Stimulate, Teend, Tind, Tine, Touchwood, Tynd(e)
Kindness Aloha, Benevolence, Clemency, Favour, Humanity
Kindred Allied, Blood, Like, Related
King(s), **Kingly** Coatcard, Cobra, Elvis, English, ER, Evil, Highness, Kong, Majesty, Monarch, Pearly, Penguin, Potentate, R, Ransom, Reigner, Rex, Rial, Roi, Royalet, Ruler, Ryal, Seven, Shilling, Sovereign, Stork

KINGS

2 letters:	5 letters:	Amasis	7 letters:
GR	Apple	Arthur	Acestes
Og	Ard-ri	Atreus	Admetus
Re	Balak	Attila	Ard-righ
	Brute	Baliol	Athamas
3 letters:	Creon	Brutus	Baldwin
Asa	Cyrus	Canute	Balliol
Erl	David	Cheops	Beowulf
Ine	Edgar	Clovis	Busiris
Lir	Edwin	Darius	Butcher
Log	Etzel	Duncan	Caradoc
Lud	Gyges	Edmund	Cecrops
Zog	Herod	Egbert	Cepheus
	Hiram	Farouk	Croesus
4 letters:	Idris	Fergus	Danaiis
Agag	Ixion	Harold	Diomede
Agis	James	Hellen	Elidure
Ahab	Laius	Hyksos	Evander
Brut	Lludd	Josiah	Gunther
Ceyx	Louis	Lucomo	Kenneth
Cnut	Midas	Ludwig	Macbeth
Cole	Minos	Lycaon	Malcolm
Edwy	Mpret	Memnon	Oedipus
Fahd	Negus	Nestor	Peishwa
Inca	Ninus	Oberon	Pharaoh
Jehu	Penda	Ogyges	Porsena
Knut	Priam	Paphos	Ptolemy
Lear	Rufus	Peleus	Pyrrhus
Nudd	Uther	Peshwa	Rameses
Numa		Philip	Servius
Offa	6 letters:	Ramses	Sigmund
Olaf	Aegeus	Rhesus	Solomon
Otto	Alaric	Sailor	Stephen
Saul	Alfred	Xerxes	Tarquin
Shah	Alonso		Telamon

Umberto	Porsenna	Florestan	Erechtheus
	Rehoboam	Frederick	Ozymandias
8 letters:	Sarpedon	Gambrinus	Wenceslaus
Adrastus	Sisyphus	Gargantua	
Aegyptus	Tantalus	Gilgamesh	**11 letters:**
Alberich	Thutmose	Idomeneus	Charlemagne
Cambyses	Thyestes	Lionheart	Hardicanute
Cophetua	Tigranes	Nabonidus	Jehoshaphat
Diomedes	Zedekiah	Pygmalion	Melchizedek
Endymion		Ras Tafari	Sennacherib
Ethelred	**9 letters:**	Rodomonte	Tutenkhamen
Hezekiah	Agamemnon	Sigismund	
Jereboam	Ahasuerus	Tarquinus	**12 letters:**
Jonathan	Alexander	Tyndareus	Wayland Smith
Leonidas	Athelstan	Vortigern	
Menander	Bretwalda	Wenceslas	**14 letters:**
Menelaus	Brian Boru		Nebuchadnezzar
Milesian	Conchobar	**10 letters:**	Sweyn Forkbeard
Odysseus	Cunobelin	Belshazzar	Uther Pendragon
Peishwah	Cymbeline	Cadwaladar	
Pentheus	Ethelbert	Caractacus	

Kingdom, Kingship Animal, Aragon, Barataria, Bhutan, Bohemia, Brunel, Castile, Cilicia, Connacht, Connaught, Dalriada, Dominion, Edom, Elam, Fes, Fez, Fife, Granada, Heptarchy, Jordan, Leon, Lesotho, Lydia, Mercia, Meroe, Middle, Mineral, Moab, Morocco, Navarre, Nepal, Netherlands, Neustria, Noricum, Northumbria, Norway, Parthia, Plant, Pontic, Realm, Reame, Reign, Royalty, Ruritania, Saba, Samaria, Saudi Arabia, Sennar, Sheba, Spain, Sphere, Swaziland, Sweden, Thailand, Throne, Tonga, Two Sicilies, Vegetable, Wessex, World

Kingfisher Alcyone, Halcyon
Kingmaker Neville, Warwick
King-of-arms Clarenc(i)eux, Garter, Lyon, Norroy (and Ulster)
King's evil Crewels, Cruels, Scrofula
Kingsley Amis, Charles
King's son Dauphin, Delphin, P, Prince
Kink(y) Bent, Buckle, Crapy, Curl, Enmeshed, Flaw, Gasp, Knurl, Null, Nurl, Odd, Perm, Perverted, Quirk, Twist, Wavy
Kink(y) *may indicate* an anagram
Kinkajou Honey-bear, Potto
Kip(per) Cure, Dosser, Doze, Limey, Nap, > SLEEPER, Smoke
Kipling Beetle
Kirkpatrick K
Kismet Destiny, Fate, Karma, Predestination
Kiss(er), Kissing Buss, Butterfly, Caress, Contrecoup, Cross, Deep, French, Lip, Mouth, Neck, Osculate, Pax(-board), Pax-brede, Peck, Pet, Plonker, Pree, Salue, Salute, Smack(er), Smooch, Smouch, Snog, Spoon, Thimble, X, Yap
Kit Accoutrement, Christopher, Clobber, Clothes, Housewife, Layette, Marlowe, Mess, > OUTFIT, Rig, Set, Slops, Sportswear, Tackle, Uniform
Kitchen Caboose, Cookhouse, Cuisine, Galley, Scullery, Soup, Thieves
Kite Belly, Bird, Box, Chil, Crate, Dragon, Elanet, Forktail, Gled(e), Hawk, Milvus, Paunch, Puttock, Rokkaku

Kitten(ish) Cute, Kindle, Sexy
Kittiwake Bird, Gull, Hacklet, Haglet
Kitty Ante, Cat, Fisher, Float, Fund, Jackpot, Pool, Pot, Tronc
Kiwi Apteryx, Chinese gooseberry, NZ, Ratitae
Klu-Klux-Klan Nightrider
Knack Art, Flair, Forte, Gift, Hang, Instinct, > TALENT, Technique, Trick
Knacker Castanet, Exhaust
Knapsack Musette
Knapweed Matfelon
Knave(ry) Bezonian, Bower, Boy, Card, Coatcard, Coistril, Coystril, Custrel, Dog, Drôle, Fripon, Jack(-a-napes), Jock, Loon, Makar, Maker, Nob, Noddy, Pam, Pur, Rapscallion, > RASCAL, Recreant, Ropery, Scoundrel, Taroc, Tarot, Tom, Treachery, Varlet, Villain
Knead Conch, Malax(ate), Massage, Mould, Pug, Pummel, Work
Knee(s), Knee-cap, Knee-pan Genicular, Genu, Hock, Housemaid's, Lap, Marrowbones, Patella, Poleyn, Popliteal, Punch, Rotula, Whirl bone
Kneel(er) Defer, Genuflect, Hassock, Kowtow, Prie-dieu, Truckle
Knell Bell, Curfew, Dirge, Peal, Ring, Toll
Knicker(bocker), Knickers Bloomers, Culottes, Directoire, Irving, Panties, Plus-fours, Shorts, Trousers
Knick-knack Bagatelle, Bibelot, Bric-a-brac, Gewgaw, Pretty(-pretty), Quip, Smytrie, Toy, Trangam, Trifle, Victoriana
Knife Anelace, Barlow, Barong, Bistoury, Blade, Boline, Bolo, Bolster, Bowie, Carver, Carving, Case, Catling, Chakra, Clasp, Cleaver, Couteau, Cradle, Cuttle, Cutto(e), Da(h), Dagger, Fleam, Flick, Fruit, Gull(e)y, Hay, Hunting, Jockteleg, Kard, Keratome, Kukri, Lance(t), Machete, Matchet, Moon, Oyster, Palette, Pallet, Panga, Paper, Parang, Pen, Pigsticker, Pocket, Putty, Scalpel, Scalping, Sgian-dubh, Sheath, Shiv, Simi, Skean-dhu, Slash, Snee, Snickersnee, Spade, Stab, Stanley, Steak, Sticker, Switchblade, Table, Tranchet, Trench
Knight Accolon, Aguecheek, Alphagus, Amfortas, Artegal, Balan, Banneret, Bayard, Bedivere, Black, Bliant, Bors, Britomart, Caballero, Calidore, Cambel, Caradoc, Carpet, Cavalier, Chevalier, Companion, Crusader, Douceper, Douzeper, Dub, Equites, Errant, Galahad, Gallant, Gareth, Garter, Gawain, Geraint, Grey, Guyon, Hospitaller, Kay, KB, KBE, Kemper, KG, La(u)ncelot, Launfal, Lionel, Lochinvar, Lohengrin, Maecenas, Malta, Medjidie, Melius, Modred, Mordred, N, Noble, Orlando, Paladin, Palmerin, Parsifal, Perceforest, Perceval, Percival, Pharamond, Pinel, Precaptory, Preux chevalier, Ritter, Round Table, St Columba, Samurai, Sir, Tannhauser, Templar, Teutonic, Trencher, Tristan, Tristram, Valvassor, Vavasour, White
Knit(ting), Knitwear Aran, Contract, Crochet, Double, Entwine, Fair Isle, Hosiery, Interlock, K, Mesh, Porosis, Purl, Seam, Set, Stockinet, Weave, Wrinkl
Knob(by) Berry, Boll, Boss, Botoné, Bottony, Bouton, Bur(r), Cam, Caput, Cascabel, Croche, Gear, Handle, Hill, Inion, Knub, Knur(r), Node, Noop, Pellet, Pommel, Protuberance, Pulvinar, Push-button, Snib, Snub, Snuff, Stud, Torose, Tuber, Tuner
Knobless Enodal
Knock(er), Knock down, off, out Bang, Beaut, Biff, Blow, Bonk, Bump, Ca(a), Chap, Clash, Clour, Collide, Con, Criticise, Daud, Dawd, Degrade, Denigrate, Deride, Dev(v)el, Ding, Dinnyhauser, Etherise, Eyeful, Floor, Grace-stroke, > HIT, Innings, KO, Lowse, Lowsit, Mickey Finn, Opportunity, Pan, Pink, Quietus, Rap, Rat-tat, Six, Skittle, Spat, Steal, Stop, Strike, Stun(ner), Tap, Technical, Thump, Tonk, Wow

Knock-kneed Valgus

Knot(ted), **Knotty** Apollo, Baff, Bend, Blackwall hitch, Bow, Bowline, Bur(r), Burl, Carrick-bend, Cat's paw, Clinch, Clove hitch, Cluster, Crochet, Diamond hitch, Englishman's, Entangle, Figure of eight, Fisherman's (bend), Flat, French, Gnar, > GNARL, Gordian, Granny, Half-hitch, Harness hitch, Hawser-bend, Herculean, Hitch, Interlace, Knag, Knap, Knar, Knur(r), Loop, Love(r's), Macramé, Macrami, Magnus hitch, Marriage-favour, Matthew Walker, Mouse, Nirl, Node, Nowed, Nub, Nur(r), Overhand, Picot, Porter's, Problem, Prusik, Quipu, Reef, Rolling hitch, Rosette, Running, Seizing, Sheepshank, Sheetbend, Shoulder, Shroud, Sleave, Slip, Slub, Spurr(e)y, Square, Stevedore's, Surgeon's, Sword, Tangle, Tat, Thumb, Tie, Timberhitch, Torose, Truelove, Tubercle, Turk's head, Virgin, Wale, Wall, Weaver's (hitch), Windsor, Witch

Know(how), **Knowing(ly)**, **Knowledge(able)**, **Known** Acquaintance, Autodidactic, Aware, Carnal, Cognition, Common, Compleat, Comprehend, Cred, Epistemics, Erudite, Expertise, Famous, Fly, Gnosis, Gnostic, Have, Hep, Hip, Info, Information, Insight, Intentional, Intuition, Jnana, Ken, Kith, Kydst, Lare, Light, Lore, Mindful, Omniscience, On, On to, Pansophy, Paragnosis, Party, Polymath, Positivism, Privity, Recherché, > RECOGNISE, Sapient, Savvy, Science, Scienter, Scilicet, Sciolism, Shrewd, Smattering, Understand(ing), Up, Versed, Wat(e), Weet(e), Well-informed, Well-read, Wise, Wist, Wit, Wot

Know-all Arrogant, Besserwisser, Bumptious, Cognoscenti, Pansophist, Polymath, Poseur, Smart alec(k), Smart-arse, Smart-ass, Wiseacre

Knuckle (bone) Apply, Dolos, Fist, Joint, Ossein, Submit

Koko List

Kookaburra Laughing jackass, Settler's clock

Kop Spion

Koran Scripture, Sura(h)

Korea(n) Chosen, ROK

Kosher Approved, Genuine, Legitimate, Real

Kremlin Fortress

Kri Masora

Krypton Kr

Kudos Credit, Glory, Praise

Kurd Yezidi

Kyanite Disthene

Ll

L Latitude, League, Learner, Left, Length, Liberal, Lima, Litre, Long, Luxembourg, Pound

La Indeed, My

Label Badge, Band, Book-plate, Brand, Crowner, Designer, Docket, File, Identifier, Mark, Own, Seal, Sticker, Style, Tab, Tag, Tally, Ticket, Trace

Labiate Catmint, Hoarhound, Horehound

Laboratory Lab, Language, Skylab, Space-lab, Studio, Workshop

Labour(er), **Laboured**, **Laborious** Aesthetic, Arduous, Begar, Birth, Carl, Casual, Chirl, Chore, Coolie, Corvée, Cottager, Cottar, Culchie, Dataller, Day, Direct, Docker, Dwell, Forced, Gandy-dancer, Ganger, Gibeonite, Grecian, Grind, Hard, Hercules, Hodge, Hodman, Ida, Indirect, Job, Journeyman, Kanaka, Katorga, Leaden, Manpower, Militant tendency, Moil, Navvy, Okie, Operose, Opposition, Pain, Peon, Pioneer, Prole, Redneck, Roll, Rouseabout, Roustabout, Rouster, Sisyphean, Slave, Spalpeen, Statute, Stint, Strive, Sudra, Swagman, Sweated, Task, The grip, The lump, > **TOIL(S)**, Toss, Travail, Uphill, Vineyard, > **WORK(ER)**, Workmen, Yakka

Labrador Innu, Retriever, Tea

Labyrinth Daedalus, Maze, Mizmaze, Warren, Web

▷ **Labyrinthine** *may indicate* an anagram

Lac Lacquer, Lakh, Resin, Shellac, Tomans

Lace, **Lacy** Alençon, Babiche, Beat, Blonde, Bobbin, Bone, Bourdon, Brussels, Chantilly, Cluny, Colbertine, Dash, Dentelle, Duchesse, Filet, Galloon, Guipure, Honiton, Inweave, Irish, Jabot, Lash, Macramé, Malines, Mechlin, Mignonette, Mode, Net, Orris, Pearlin, Picot, Pillow, Point, Reseau, Reticella, Ricrac, Rosaline, Seaming, Shoestring, Shoe-tie, Spike, Stay, Tat(ting), Tawdry, Thrash, Thread, Torchon, Trim, Trol(le)y, Valenciennes, Venise, Weave, Welt, Window-bar

Lacerate(d) Ganch, Gash, Gaunch, Maul, Rent, Rip, Slash, Tear

Lachrymose Maudlin, Niobe, Tearful, Water-standing, > **WEEPY**

Lack(ing), **Lacks** Absence, Aplasia, Bereft, Dearth, Famine, Ha'n't, Insufficiency, Manqué, Minus, > **NEED**, Poverty, Privation, Remiss, Sans, Shortfall, Shy, Void, Want

Lackadaisical Languid, Listless, Torpid

Lackaday Haro

Lackey Boots, Flunkey, Moth, Page, Poodle, Satellite, Skip-kennel

Lacklustre Dull, Insipid, Matt

Lack of confidence Doubt, Scepsis

Laconic Blunt, Close-mouthed, Curt, Spartan, Succinct, Terse

Lacquer Coromandel, Enamel, Hair(spray), Japan, Shellac, > **VARNISH**

Lad Boy(o), Bucko, Callan(t), Chiel(d), Child, Geit, Gyte, Knight, Loonie, Master, Nipper, Shaver, Stableman, Stripling, Tad, Whipper-snapper

Ladder(y) Accommodation, Aerial, Bucket, Companion, Companionway, Etrier, Fish, Jack, Jacob's, Pompier, Potence, Rope, Run, Salmon, Scalado, Scalar,

Scaling, Sea, Squash, Stie, Sty, Trap, Turntable

Ladle Bail, Dipper, Punch, Scoop, Shank

Lady Baroness, Bevy, Bountiful, Burd, Dame, Dark, Dinner, Don(n)a, Duenna, Female, First, Frau, Frow, Gemma, Godiva, Hen, Khanum, Luck, Maam, Madam(e), Memsahib, Muck, Nicotine, Peeress, Senora, Shopping bag, Signora, Tea, White, Windermere

▸ **Lady** *may indicate* an '-ess' ending

Ladybird Cushcow, Hen, Vedalia

▸ **Ladybird** *may indicate* a female of a bird family

Ladykiller Bluebeard, Lothario, Masher, Wolf

Lady of the lake Vivian

Lady's Fingers Gumbo, Okra

Lady's maid Abigail

Lag(gard) Culture, Dawdle, Delay, Drag, Flag, Hysteresis, Inmate, Jailbird, Jet, Leng, > **LINGER**, Loiter, Prisoner, Retard, Slowcoach, Slowpoke, Time, Tortoise, Trail

Lager Pils(e)ner

Lagoon Barachois, Haff, Pontchartrain, Pool, Salina, Saline

Laic, Laid *see* **LAY**

Lair Couch, Den, Earth, Haunt, Hideaway, Kennel, Lodge, Warren

Lake(s) Alkali, Basin, Bayou, Carmine, Cirque, Cowal, Crater, Crimson, Cut off, Finger, L, Lacustrine, Lagoon, Lagune, > **LOCH**, Lochan, Lough, Madder, Mead, Mere, Nyanza, Ox-bow, Poets, Pool, Red, Reservoir, Salina, Salt, Shott, Soda, Tarn, Turlough, Vlei, Wine

LAKES

2 letters:
No

3 letters:
Ewe
Van

4 letters:
Amin
Bala
Biel
Bled
Chad
Como
Erie
Erne
Eyre
Kivu
Nyos
Pink
Tana
Thun

5 letters:
Atlin

Chott
Cowan
Frome
Garda
Gatun
Great
Huron
Ilmen
Leman
Leven
Lower
Malar
Morar
Mungo
Mweru
Myall
Nam Co
Neagh
Nyasa
Onega
Playa
Poopo
Pskov
Sevan
Tahoe

Taupo
Tsana
Urmia

6 letters:
Albert
Argyle
Averno
Baikal
Barlee
Bitter
Broads
Cayuga
Corrib
Edward
Geneva
Kariba
Kittle
Ladoga
Lugano
Malawi
Miveru
Mobutu
Nakura
Nam Tso

Nyassa
Oneida
Peipus
Poyang
Rudolf
Saimaa
Te Anau
Tekapo
Vanern
Zurich

7 letters:
Amadeus
Aral Sea
Avernus
Axolotl
Balaton
Bizerte
Iliamna
Katrine
Koko Nor
Lucerne
Manapua
Nipigon
Ontario

Rotonia
Sempach
Toronto
Torrens
Turkana
Vattern

8 letters:
Balkhash
Bodensee
Carnegie
Dongting
Gairdner
Grasmere
Kinneret
Maggiore
Manitoba
Masurian
Menindee
Michigan
Naumachy
Okanagan
Onondaga
Regillus

Reindeer
Superior
Tiberias
Titicaca
Tonle Sap
Tungting
Veronica
Victoria
Wakatipu
Wanawaka
Winnipeg

9 letters:
Athabasca
Bangweulu
Champlain
Constance
Ennerdale
Everglade
Genfersee
Great Bear
Great Salt
Innisfree
Killarney

Macquarie
Manapouri
Maracaibo
Naumachia
Nipissing
Serbonian
Thirlmere
Trasimene
Trasimono
Ullswater
Wairarapa
Wastwater
Winnebago
Ysselmeer

10 letters:
Buttermere
Clearwater
Great Slave
Hawes Water
Ijsselmeer
Miraflores
Mistassini
Okeechobee

Okefenokee
Saint Clair
Serpentine
Tanganyika
Windermere

11 letters:
Lesser Slave
Paralimnion
Stanley Pool

12 letters:
Derwentwater
Memphremagog
Waikaremoana
Winnipegosis

13 letters:
Coniston Water
Crummock Water

14 letters:
Disappointment
Ennerdale Water

Lake-dwelling Crannog
Lakeland Cumbria
Lam Flee, Scram
Lama Dalai, Karmapa, Panchen
Lamb(skin) Baa, Barometz, Budge, Bummer, Cade, Canterbury, Caracul, Cosset, Ean(ling), Elia, Fat, Grit, Innocent, Keb, Larry, Noisette, Paschal, Persian, Rack, Shearling, Target, Yean(ling)
Lambent Flickering, Glowing, Licking
Lambert Constant
Lame(ness) Accloy, Claude, Cripple, Crock, Game, Gammy, Gimp(y), Halt, Hamstring, Hirple, Hors de combat, Maim, Main, Spavined, Springhalt, Stringhalt, Weak
Lament(able), Lamentation, Lamenter Bemoan, Bewail, Beweep, Complain, Croon, Cry, Dirge, Dumka, Dump, Elegy, Funest, Jeremiad, Jeremiah, Keen, Meane, Mein, Mene, Moon, Mourn, Ochone, Paltry, Piteous, Plain, Repine, Sigh, Sorry, Threne, Threnody, Ululate, > WAIL, Welladay, Wel(l)away, Yammer
Lamia Deadnettle
Lamina(te) Film, Flake, Folium, Formica®, Lamella, Layer, Plate, Scale, Table
Lamp(s) Aldis, Anglepoise, Arc, Argand, Bowat, Bowet, Buat, Cru(i)sie, Cru(i)zie, Crusy, Davy, Eye, Eyne, Flame, Fluorescent, Fog, Geordie, Glow, Head, Hurricane, Incandescent, Induction, Kudlik, Lampion, Lantern, Lava, Lucigen, Mercury vapour, Miner's, Moderator, Neon, Nernst, Nightlight, Padella, Photoflood, Pilot, Platinum, Quartz, Reading, Riding, Safety, Sanctuary, Scamper, Searchlight, Signal, Sodium, Sodium-vapour, Spirit, Standard, Street, Stride, Stroboscope, Sun, Tail, Tantalum, Tiffany, Tilley, Torchier(e), Tungsten, Uplight(er), Veilleuse, Xenon
Lamplighter Leerie, Spill

Lampoon Caricature, Parody, Pasquil, Pasquin(ade), Satire, Skit, Squib

Lamprey Hag, Lampern, Sandpride

Lancaster Burt, Osbert

Lance Dart, Harpoon, Morne, Pesade, Pike, Prisade, Prisado, Rejôn, Spear, Speisade, Thermic, White arm

Lancelet Amphious

Lancer Bengal, Picador, Uhlan

Lancet Fleam

Land(s), Landed Acreage, Aina, Alight, Alluvion, Arpent, Bag, Beach, Bigha, Bovate, Byrd, Carse, Carucate, Cavel, Conacre, Corridor, Country, Croft, Crown, Demain, Demesne, Disbark, Disembark, Ditch, Doab, Dock, Earth, Edom, Enderby, Estate, Fallow, Farren, Farthingland, Fee, Feod, Feoff, Feud, Fief, Freeboard, Gair, Glebe, Gondwanaland, Gore, Graham, Ground, Hide, Holding, Holm, Holy, Horst, Ind, Innings, Isthmus, Kingdom, La-la, Laurasia, Lea, Leal, Ley, Light, Link, Machair, Maidan, Manor, Marginal, Marie Byrd, Mesnalty, Métairie, Moose pasture, Morgen, Mortmain, Nation, Never-never, Nod, No man's, Odal, Onshore, Oxgang, Oxgate, Pakahi, Palmer, Pangaea, Panhandle, Parcel, Pasture, Peneplain, Peneplane, Peninsula, Piste, Plot, Ploughgate, Point, Polder, Pr(a)edial, Promised, Property, Purlieu, Queen Maud, Real estate, Realm, Realty, Reservation, Roman candle, Rundale, Rupert's, Savanna(h), Set-aside, Settle, Spit, Swidden, Tack, Taluk, Terra(e), Terra-firma, Terrain, Territory, Thwaite, Tie, Tir na n'Og, Touchdown, Turbary, Tye, Udal, Unship, Ure, Van Diemen's, Veld(t), Victoria, Wainage, Waste, Whenua, Wilkes, Yird

Landfall *see* **LANDSLIDE**

Landing (craft, stair, system) Autoflare, Crash, Forced, Gallipoli, Gha(u)t, Half, Halfpace, Hard, Instrument, LEM, Module, Pancake, Pier, Quay, Soft, Solar, Splashdown, Three-point, Three-pricker, Touchdown, Undercarriage

Landlock Embay

Landlord, Land owner Absentee, Balt, Boniface, Bonnet laird, Copyholder, Eupatrid, Fiar, Franklin, Herself, Host, Innkeeper, Junker, Laird, Lessor, Letter, Licensee, Patron, Patroon, Proprietor, Publican, Rachman, Rentier, Squattocracy, Squire, Squirearchy, Squireen, Thane, Zamindar(i), Zemindar

Landmark Meith, Watershed

Landmass Laurasia

Land right Emphyteusis

Landscape Karst, Paysage, Picture, Saikei, Scene, Vista

Landslide, Landfall Avalanche, Earthfall, Eboulement, Lahar, Scree, Slip

Landsman Lubber

Land-tenure Frankalmoign, Raiyatwari, Ryotwari

Lane Boreen, Bus, Corridor, Crawler, Drangway, Drury, Express, Fast, Fetter, Gut, Inside, Loan, Lois, Loke, Memory, Mincing, Outside, Overtaking, Passage, Petticoat, Pudding, Ruelle, Sea-road, Slow, Twitten, Twitting, Vennel, Wynd

Langerhans Insulin, Islets

Language(s) Argot, Artificial, Assembly, Auxiliary, Basic, Body, Cant, Command, Dead, Dialect, Formal, Georgian, Hobson-Jobson, Humanities, Idioglossia, Idiolect, Idiom, Inclusive, Jargon, Langue, Ledden, Lingo, Lingua franca, Macaroni, Machine code, Mellowspeak, Mixed, Modern, Mother tongue, Native, Natural, Neo, Newspeak, Novelese, Object, Officialese, Page description, Parlance, Philology, Pidgin, Polysynthetic, Pragmatics, Private, Procedural, Programming, Prose, Query, Relay, Rhetoric, Sea-speak, Second, Sign, Sociolect, > **SPEECH**, Style, Symbolic, Synthetic, Target, Technobabble, Telegraphese, Tone, > **TONGUE**, Union, Vedic, Verbiage, Vernacular, Vocabulary,

LANGUAGES

3 letters:
Ada
Bat
Fur
Giz
Gur
Ibo
Ido
Kwa
Luo
Mon
Reo
Tai
Tiv
Twi

4 letters:
Ainu
Avar
Cham
Daru
Erse
Geez
Igbo
Inca
Komi
Krio
Lozi
Maya
Motu
Naga
Nuba
Nupe
Pali
Pedi
Pict
Shan
Taal
Thai
Tshi
Tupi
Urdu
Wawa
Xosa
Zulu
Zuni

5 letters:
Aleut
Aryan
Azeri
Balti
Bantu
Batak
Cajun
Carib
Chewa
Cobol
Dogon
Doric
Fanti
Farsi
Ganda
Gondi
Hausa
Hindi
Hokan
Indic
Joual
Kafri
Koine
Kriol
Kuo-yu
Ladin
Lamba
Lamut
Latin
Lubon
Lunda
Lyele
Malay
Maori
Mayan
Munda
Nguni
Norse
Oriya
Oscan
P-Celt
Sakai
Sango
Satem
Shona
Shono
Sioux

Sotho
Suomi
Swazi
Taino
Tajik
Tamil
Te reo
Tigre
Tonga
Turki
Ugric
Vogul
Welsh
Wolof
Xhosa
Yakut
Yuman
Yupik

6 letters:
Adyahe
Adygei
Adyghe
Altaic
Arabic
Aranda
Aymara
Basque
Basutu
Bokmal
Brahui
Breton
Celtic
Centum
Chadic
Coptic
Creole
Cymric
Dardic
Divehi
Eskimo
Evenki
Fantee
Fijian
Finnic
Fulani
Gaelic
Gagauz

German
Gullah
Hebrew
Herero
Italic
Ladino
Lahnda
Lakota
Lu wian
Lydian
Manchu
Micmac
Mishmi
Na-Dene
Nepali
Novial
Nubian
Ostyak
Pahari
Paiute
Pakhti
Papuan
Pashto
Pashtu
Pushto
Pushtu
Romany
Rwanda
Salish
Shelta
Sindhi
Siouan
Somali
Strine
Tanoan
Tartar
Telegu
Telugu
Tuareg
Tungus
Turkic
Udmurt
Ugrian
Uralic
Yoruba
Zyrian

7 letters:

Adamawa
Amerind
Amharic
Aramaic
Austric
Bengali
Bislama
Caddoan
Catalan
Chaldee
Chinook
Chuvash
Cushite
Dzongka
Flemish
Frisian
Gagauzi
Hamitic
Hin Motu
Hittite
Janlish
Japlish
Kannada
Khoisan
Kirundi
Kurdish
Kushite
Lallans
Laotian
Lingala
Luganda
Marathi
Miao-Yao
Mingrel
Nahuatl
Nilotic
Nyungar
Oceanic
Ossetic
Ottoman
Pahlavi
Pehlevi
Pictish
Prakrit
Punjabi
Pushtoo
Quechua
Romance
Romansh
Samnite
Samoyed

Semitic
Sesotho
Sinhala
Sinitic
Slovene
Sornian
Sudanic
Swahili
Swedish
Tagalog
Tahitan
Tibetan
Tlingit
Turkish
Turkmen
Umbrian
Uralian
Venetic
Volapuk
Voltaic
Walloon
Wendish
Yerkish
Yiddish

8 letters:

Akkadian
Albanian
Arawakan
Assamese
Bulgaric
Cherkess
Chibchan
Chichewa
Croatian
Cushitic
Dzongkha
Ethiopic
Etruscan
Faliscan
Fanagalo
Filipino
Frankish
Friesian
Gujarati
Gujerati
Gurkhali
Illyrian
Japhetic
Jugoslav
Kashmiri
Kingwana

Kolarian
Kwakiuti
Landsmal
Mandarin
Mongolic
Mon-Khmer
Nez Perce
Penutian
Pilipino
Polabian
Rhaetian
Romansch
Rumansch
Rumonsch
Sanscrit
Sanskrit
Scythian
Setswana
Shemitic
Slavonic
Sumerian
Tahitian
Teutonic
Thracian
Tigrinya
Tshiluba
Tungusic
Turanian
Turkoman
Ugaritic
Wakashan
Warlpiri
Yugoslav

9 letters:

Abkhazian
Algonkian
Algonquin
Anatolian
Brythonic
Cantonese
Chari-Nile
Diglossia
Dravidian
Esperanto
Esthonian
Euskarian
Franglais
Gujarathi
Gujerathi
Hottentot
Inuktitut

Iroquoian
Kamilaroi
Kiswahili
Landsmaal
Langue d'oc
Leizghian
Malayalam
Messapian
Muskogean
Nostratic
Onondagan
Provencal
Putonghua
Roumansch
Sabellian
Semi-Bantu
Sinhalese
Tocharian
Tokharian
Tokharish
Ukrainian
Winnebago

10 letters:

Algonquian
Athabascan
Azerbayani
Circassian
Diachronic
Eteocretan
Finno-Ugric
Gallo-Roman
Himyaritic
Hindustani
Langue d'oil
Malayalaam
Melanesian
Mingrelian
Muskhogean
Niger-Congo
Papiamento
Proto-Norse
Rajasthani
Serbo-croat
Singhalese
Synchronic
Ural-Altaic
Uto-Aztecan
Vietnamese

11 letters:

Dagestanian

- Interglossa
- Interlingua
- Kordofanian
- Langobardic
- Nilo-Saharan
- Osco-Umbrian
- Pama-Nyungan

Sino-Tibetan
Sranantongo
Tessaraglot
Tupi-Guarani

12 letters:
Billingsgate

Gallo-Romance
Idiom neutral
Indo-European
Platt-deutsch
Tibeto-Burman
Volga-Baltaic

13 letters:
Neo-Melanesian
Semito-Hamitic

14 letters:
Thraco-Phrygian

Languid, Languish Die, Divine, Droop, Feeble, Flagging, Listless, Lukewarm, Lydia, Melancholy, Quail, Torpid, Wilt

Languor Lassitude

Lanky Beanpole, Gangly, Gawky, Spindleshanks, Windlestraw

Lanolin Woolfat, Yolk

Lantern Aristotle's, Bowat, Bowet, Buat, Bull's eye, Chinese, Dark(e)y, Epidiascope, Episcope, Friar's, Glim, Japanese, Jaw, Lanthorn, Magic, Sconce, Stereopticon, Storm, Turnip

Lanthanum La

Laodicean Lukewarm

Lap Circuit, Gremial, Leg, Lick, Lip, Luxury, Override, Pace, Sypher

Lapdog Messan, Shough, Showghe

Lapel Revers

Laplander, Lapp Saam(e), Sabme, Sabmi, Sami

Lappet Infula

Lapse Backslide, Drop, Error, Expire, Fa', Fall, Nod, Sliding, Trip

Lapwing Teru-tero

Larceny Grand

Larch Hackmatack, Tamarack

Lard Enarm, Leaf, Saim, Seam(e)

Larder Buttery, Pantry, Spence, Springhouse

Large(ness), Largest Ample, Astronomical, Big, Boomer, Bulky, Buster, Colossus, Commodious, Decuman, Enormous, Epical, Extensive, Gargantuan > GIGANTIC, Ginormous, Great, Grit, Gross, Hefty, Helluva, Huge, Hulking, Humdinger, Humongous, Humungous, Kingsize, L, Lunker, Macrocephaly, Massive, Maximin, Maximum, Outsize, Plethora, Prodigious, Rounceval, Rouncival, Skookum, Slew, Slue, Sollicker, Spacious, Spanking, Stonker, Stout Swingeing, Tidy, Titanic, Vast, Voluminous, Whopping

Large number Centillion, Fermi, Giga, Gillion, Googol, Googolplex, Grillion, Infinitude, Jillion, Legion, Mille, Nation, Nonillion, Quadrillion, Quintillion, Raft, Regiment, Ruck, Scads, Sea, Septillion, Sextillion, Slather, Slew, Slue, Squillion, Toman, Trillion, Zillion

Largess Alms, Charity, Frumentation, Generosity

Lariat Lasso, Reata, Riata

Lark Adventure, Aunter, Caper, Dido, Dunstable, Exaltation, Fool, Giggle, Guy, Laverock, Magpie, Mud, Pipit, Prank

Larkspur Stavesacre

Larva Ammacoete, Aphid lion, Army-worm, Augerworm, Axolotl, Bagworm, Bloodworm, Bot(t), Budworm, Cabbage worm, Caddice, Caddis, Cankerworm, Caterpillar, Cercaria, Chigger, Chigoe, Coenurus, Doodlebug, Grub, Hellgram(m)ite, Hydatid, Indusium, Instar, Jigger, Jointworm, Leather-jacket Leptocephalus, Maggot, Mealworm, Measle, Miracidium, Muckworm, Naiad, Nauplius, Nigger, Nymph, Ox-bot, Planula, Pluteus, Porina, Redia, Screwworm, Shade, Silkworm, Strawworm, Tadpole, Trochophore,

Trochosphere, Veliger, Water penny, Wireworm, Witchetty, Witchetty grub, Woodworm, Zoea

Laryngitis Croup, Hives

Lascar Seacunny, Tindal

Lascivious(ness) Crude, Goaty, Horny, Lewd, Lubric, Paphian, Satyric, Sotadic, Tentigo, Wanton

Lash(ed), **Lashings** Cat, Cilium, Firk, Flagellum, Frap, Gammon, Knout, Mastigophora, Oodles, Oup, Quirt, Riem, Rope's end, Scourge, Secure, Sjambok, Stripe, Swinge, Tether, Thong, Trice, Whang, > WHIP

Lass(ie) Damsel, Maid, Quean, Queyn, Quin(i)e

Lassitude Accidie, Acedie, Languor, Lethargy

Lasso Lariat, Reata, Rope

Last(ing) Abide, Abye, Aftermost, > AT LAST, Boot-tree, Bottom, Chronic, Coda, Dernier, Dure, Endurance, Endure, Extend, Extreme, > FINAL, Hinder, Latest, Linger, Live, Long-life, Model, Nightcap, Outstay, Perdure, Permanent, Perpetuate, Persist, Spin, Stable, Stay, Supper, Survive, Swan-song, Thiller, Thule, Tree, Trump, Ult(imate), Ultimo, Utmost, Wear, Weight, Whipper-in, Yester, Z

Last drop Supernaculum

Last resort Pis aller

Last syllable Ultima

Last word(s) Amen, Envoi, Farewell, Ultimatum, Zythum

Latch Bar, Clicket, Clink, Espagnolette, Lock, Night, Sneck

Late(r), **Latest** After(wards), Afterthought, Behindhand, Chit-chat, Dead, Deid, Ex, Former, Gen, Infra, Lag, Lamented, New(s), Overdue, Overrunning, Past, Recent, Sine, Slow, State-of-the-art, Stop-press, Syne, Tardive, Tardy, Top shelf, Trendy, Umquhile

Late-learner Opsimath

Latent Concealed, Delitescent, Dormant, Maieutic, Potential

Lateral Askant, Edgeways, Sideways

Latex Antiar, Gutta-percha, Jelutong, Ule

Lath Lag, Splat

Lathe Capstan, Mandrel, Mandril, Turret

Lather Flap, Foam, Froth, Sapples, Suds, Tan

Latin(ist) Biblical, Criollo, Dago, Dog, Erasmus, Eyeti, Greaseball, High, Humanity, Italiot, L, Late, Law, Low, Medieval, Neapolitan, New, Pig, Romanic, Romish, Scattermouch, Silver, Spic, Vulgar, Wop

Latin-American Criollo, Tico

Latitude Breadth, Celestial, Ecliptic, Free hand, Horse, L, Leeway, Liberty, Licence, Meridian, Parallel, Play, Roaring forties, Scope, Tropic, Width

Latrine Ablutions, Bog, Cloaca, Furphy, Garderobe, Loo, Privy, Rear

Latter Last, Previous

Latter-day Recent, Saints, Young

Lattice Bravais, Clathrate, Espalier, Grille, Space, Treillage, Trellis

Lattice-leaf Ouvirandra

Latvian Lett

Laud(er) Commend, Eulogist, Extol, Harry, Praise

Lauderdale Caballer

Laugh(ing), **Laughable**, **Laughter** Belly, Cachinnate, Cackle, Chortle, Chuckle, Cod, Corpse, Democritus, Deride, Derision, Fit, Fou rire, Gelastic, Giggle, Goster, Guffaw, Ha, He-he, Ho-ho, Homeric, Hoot, Horse, Hout, Howl, Irrision, Last, Lauch, Leuch, Levity, Ludicrous, > MIRTH, Mock, Nicker, Peal, Present,

Riancy, Riant, Rich, Rident, Ridicule, Risus, Scream, Snigger, Snirt(le), Snort, Tehee, Titter, Yo(c)k
Laughing-stock Outspeckle, Sport
Launcelot Gobbo
Launch(ing), Launch pad Begin, Blast-off, Catapult, Chuck, Cosmodrome, ELV, Fire, Float, Hurl, Initiate, Lift-off, Moonshot, Motoscalp, Opening, Pioneer, Presentation, Release, Roll out, Shipway, Slipway, Start, Steam, Unstock, Upsend, VTO
Launder, Laundry Bagwash, Clean, Lav, Steamie, Tramp, Transfer, Wash, Washhouse, Whites
Laurel(s) Aucuba, Bay, Camphor, Cherry, Daphne, Japan, Kalmia, Kudos, Mountain, Pichurim, Rose (bay), Sassafras, Spicebush, Spotted, Spurge, Stan, Sweet-bay, True
Laurence Sterne
Lava Aa, Block, Bomb, Coulee, Cysticercus, Dacite, Flood basalt, Lahar, Lapilli, Magma, Nuée ardente, Pahoehoe, Palagonite, Pillow, Pitchstone, Plug, Pumice, Pyroclast, Scoria, Tephra, Toadstone
Lavatory Ajax, Bogger, Brasco, Can, Carsey, Carzey, Cludgie, Comfort station, Convenience, Cottage, Dike, Dunnakin, Dunny, Dyke, Earth closet, Elsan®, Facilities, Forica, Furphey, Gents, Heads, Jakes, Jane, John, Kars(e)y, Karzy, K(h)azi, Kleinhuisie, Kybo, Ladies, Lat(rine), Loo, Necessary, Netty, Office, Outhouse, Privy, Rear(s), Reredorter, Shithouse, Shouse, Siege, Smallest room, Throne, Thunderbox, Toot, Tout, Urinal, Washroom, WC
Lave Lip, Wash
Lavender Aspic, Spike
Lavengro Borrow
Laver Moabite, Nori, Ore-weed
Lavish Barmecidal, Copious, Excessive, Exuberant, Flush, Free, Fulsome, Generous, Liberal, Lucullan, Lush, Prodigal, Shower, Slap-up, Sumptuous, Wanton, Waste
Law(s) Abingdon, Act, Agrarian, Anti-trust, Ass, Association, Avogadro's, Babo's, Bar, Barratry, Bernoulli's, > **BILL**, Biogenetic, Bode's, Bonar, Boyle's, Bragg's, Brehon, Brewster's, Brocard, Buys Ballot's, Byelaw, Cain, Canon, Capitulary, Case, Chancery, Charles's, Civil, Code, Common, Constitution, Corn, Coulomb's, Criminal, Cupar, Curie's, Curie-Weiss, Cy pres, Dalton's, Dead-letter, Decree, Decretals, De Morgan's, Deodand, Dharma, Dictate, Digest, Din, Distributive, Dry, Edict, Einstein's, Enact, Excise, Forest, Fuero, Fundamental, Fuzz, Game, Gas, Gay-Lussac's, Gresham's, Grimm's, Grotian, Haeckel's, Halifax, Hardy-Weinberg, Henry's, Homestead, Hooke's, Hubble's, Hume's, International, Irade, Iure, Joule's, Jura, Jure, Jus, Kain, Kashrut(h), Kepler's, Kirchhoff's, Labour, Lay, Leibniz's, Lemon, Lenx's, Lien, Lor(d), Losh, Lydford, Lynch, Magdeburg, Mariotte's, Martial, May, Mendel's, Mercantile, Military, Mishna(h), Mishnic, Moral, Mosaic, Murphy's, Natural, Newton's, Noahide, Nomistic, Nomothetic, Ohm's, Oral, Ordinance, Pandect, Parity, Parkinson's, Pass, Penal, Periodic, Planck's, Plebiscite, Poor, Principle, Private, Public, Roman, Rubric, Rule, Salic, Salique, Scout, Sharia(h), Sheria(t), Shield, Shulchan Aruch, Snell's, Sod's, > **STATUTE**, Stefan's, Stokes, Sumptuary, Sunna, Sus(s), Sword, Table, Talmud, Tenet, Thorah, Thorndike's, Torah, Tort, Tradition, Ulema, Unwritten, Use, Verner's, Vigilante, Written
Lawless(ness) Anarchy, Anomie, Anomy, Antinomian, Piratical
Lawmaker, Lawman, Lawyer Alfaqui, Ambulance chaser, Attorney, AV, Barrack room, Barrister, Bencher, BL, Bluebottle, Bramble, Bush, Canon, Coke,

Counsel, DA, Defence, Doge, Draco, Earp, Enactor, Fiscal, Greenbag, Grotius, Hammurabi, Jurisconsult, Jurist, Legal eagle, Legist, Mooktar, Moses, MP, Mufti, Mukhtar, Nomothete, Notary, Penang, Pettifoggers, Philadelphia, Proctor, Procurator fiscal, Prosecutor, Rabbi, Shirra, Shyster, Silk, Solicitor, Spenlow, Stratopause, Talmudist, Templar, Thesmothete, Vakil, WS

Lawn Cloth, Grass, Green, Linen, Sward, Turf

Lawrence DH, Ross, Shaw, TE

Lawrencium Lr

Lawsuit Case, Cause, Plea, Trover

Lawyer(s), Lawman *see* **LAWMAKER**

Lax *may indicate* an anagram

Lax(ity) Freedom, Inexact, Laissez-aller, Latitude, Loose, Remiss, > **SLACK**, Wide, Wide-open

Laxative Aloin, Aperitive, Cascara, Cathartic, Eccoprotic, Elaterin, Elaterium, Glauber's salt, Gregory (powder), Loosener, Physic, Purgative, > **PURGE**, Saline, Senna-pod, Taraxacum

Lay(ing), Layman, Laic, Laid Air, Amateur, Aria, Ballad, Bed, Bet, Blow, Chant, Civil, Ditty, Drop, Earthly, Egg, Embed, Fit, Impose, Lied, Lodge, Man, Minstrel, Oat, Oblate, Ode, Ordinary, Outsider, Oviparous, Oviposit, Parabolanus, Secular, Set, Sirvente, > **SONG**, Sypher, Tertiary, Tribal, Wager, Warp

Layabout Loafer, Lotophagus

Lay-by Rest stop

Layer(s) Abscission, Ancona, Appleton, Battery, Boundary, Cake, Caliche, Cladding, Coating, Crust, D, Depletion, E, Ectoplasm, Ectosarc, Ekman, Epiblast, Epilimnion, Epitaxial, Epithelium, Erathem, Exine, Exocarp, Film, Flake, Friction, Ganoin, Germ, Gossan, Gozzan, Granum, Ground, Heaviside, > **HEN**, Herb, Kennelly(-Heaviside), Kerf, Lamella, Lamina, Lap, Leghorn, Lie, Malpighian, Media, Miocene, Ozone, Pan, Patina, Paviour, Photosphere, Ply, Retina, Scale, Sclerite, Screed, Skin, Sliver, Spathic, Stratify, Stratum, Substratum, Tabular, Tapetum, Tier, Tremie, Trophoblast, Trophoderm, Varve, Vein, Velamen, Veneer

Lay-off Dismiss, Hedge, Redundance

Lay-out Ante, Design, Fell, Format, Map, Mise, Pattern, Spend, Straucht, Straught, Streak, Streek, Stretch

Laze, Laziness, Lazy (person) Bed-presser, Bummer, Cabbage, Faineant, Hallian, Hallion, Hallyon, Indolent, Inert, Lackadaisical, Languid, Layabout, Lie-abed, Lig(ger), Lime, Lither, Loaf, Lotus-eater, Lusk, Mollusc, Ne'er-do-well, Oblomovism, Resty, Sloth, Slouch, Slug(-a-bed), Sluggard, Susan, Sweer, Sweir, Workshy

> **Lazily** *may indicate* an anagram

Lea Grass, Meadow

Leach(ing) Cheluviation, Lixivial, Ooze

Lead(er), Leading, Leadership Ag(h)a, Ahead, Akela, Anglesite, Article, Atabeg, Atabek, Ayatollah, Bab, Bellwether, Black, Bluey, Brand, Cable, Cade, Calif, Caliph, Came, Capitano, Capo, Captain, Castro, Caudillo, Causal, Centre, Ceruse, Cheer, Chieftain, Chiliarch, Chin, China white, Choragus, Choregus, CO, Codder, Condottiere, Conducive, Conduct, Coryphaeus, Coryphee, Demagogue, Dictator, Duce, Dux, Editorial, Escort, Ethnarch, Extension, Figurehead, Floor, Foreman, Foremost, Frontrunner, Fu(e)hrer, Fugleman, Gaffer, Garibaldi, Gerent, Go, Graphite, Guide(r), Halter, Hand, Headman, Headmost, Headnote, Hegemony, Heresiarch, Hero, Hetman, Honcho, Idi, Imam, Imaum, Jason, Jefe, Jump, Juve(nile), Kabir, Kame, King, Ksar, Leam,

Litharge, Livid, Loss, Lost, Lyam, Mahatma, Mahdi, Main, Market, Marshal, Massicot, Masticot, Mayor, Meer, Mehdi, Minium, Mir, Nanak, No 1, Nomarch Nose, Numero uno, Omrah, Open, Pacemaker, Pacesetter, Padishah, Pb, Pilot, Pioneer, Pit, Plumb(um), Plummet, PM, Precentor, Premier(e), President, Price Ratoo, Rebbe, Rebecca, Red, Role, Ruler, Sachem, Sagamore, Saturn, Saturn's tree, Scotlandite, Scout, Scuddaler, Scudler, Sharif, Sheik(h), Sixer, Skipper, Skudler, Soaker, Soul, Sounding, Spearhead, Staple, Star, Sultan, Supremo, Taoiseach, Tecumseh, Tetraethyl, Top banana, Trail(blazer), Tribune, Tsaddik, Tsaddiq, Tzaddik, Up, Usher, Vaivode, Van(guard), Vanadinite, Va(u)nt, Vaunt-courier, Voivode, Vozhd, Waivode, Warlord, White, Whitechapel, Wulfenite, Youth, Zaddik, Zia

▷ **Lead(s)**, **Leaders** *may indicate* first letters of words

Leaden Flat, Plumbeous, Saturnine

Lead-glance Galena

Leading to Pre

Leaf(y), **Leaves** Acanthus, Acrospire, Amphigastrium, Amplexicaul, Betel, Blade, Bract, Carpel, Cataphyll, Cladode, Coca, Consent, Corolla, Costate, Cotyledon, Dolma, Drop, Duff, Fig, Finial, Foil, Foliage, Foliar, Folio(se), Folium, Frond, Glume, Gold, Holiday, Induviae, Jugum, K(h)at, Maple, Megaphyll, Needle, Nervate, Out, P, Pad, Page, Pan, Phyllid, Phyllome, Qat, Repair, Riffle, Rosula, Scale, Sclerophyll, Secede, Sepal, Siri(h), Skip, Spathe, Sporophyll, Stipule, Tea, Title, TTL, Valve, Vert, Vine, Withdraw

Leafhopper Thrip

Leafless Ebracteate, Scape

Leaflet At(t)ap, Bill, Bracteole, Circular, Dodger, Fly-sheet, Foliolose, Handbill, Pinna, Pinnula, Prophyll, Stipel, > **TRACT**

League Achaean, Alliance, Arab, Band, Bund, Compact, Delian, Entente, Federation, Gueux, Guild, Hanse(atic), Holy, Ivy, Land, Major, Minor, Nations, Parasang, Primrose, Redheaded, Rugby, Super, Union, Ypres, Zollverein, Zupa

Leak(y) Bilge, Drip, Escape, Extravasate, Gizzen, Holed, Holey, Ooze, Pee, Porous, Seepage, Sype, Trickle, Wee, Weep, Wee-wee

Leak-proof Airtight

Leamington Spa

Lean(ing) Abut, Barren, Batter, Bend, Careen, Carneous, Carnose, Griskin, Heel, > **INCLINE**, Lie, Lig(ge), Minceur, Prop, Propend, Rake, Rely, Rest, Scraggy, Scrawny, Skinny, Spare, Stoop, Taste, Tend, Tilt, Tip, Walty

Leander Abydos

Lean-to Skillion

Leap(ing), **Leapt** Assemblé, Bound, Brise, Cabriole, Caper, Capriole, Cavort, Clear, Croupade, Curvet, Echappé, Entrechat, Falcade, Fishdive, Frisk, Galumph, Gambado, Gambol, Jeté, Jump, Loup, Luppen, Ollie, Over, Pigeon-wing, Pronk, Quantum, Sally, Salto, Somersa(u)lt, Somerset, > **SPRING**, Stag, Transilient, Vault, Volte

Leap year Bissextile, Penteteric

Lear Edward, King, Nonsense

Learn(ed), **Learner** Beginner, Blue, Bluestocking, Chela, Con, Discover, Distance, Doctor, Don, Erudite, Gather, Get, Glean, Hear, Instrumental, Kond, L, Lear(e), Leir, Lere, Literate, Literati, Literato, Lucubrate, Master, Memorise, Mirza, Mug up, > **NOVICE**, Pandit, Polymath, Programmed, Pundit, Pupil, Rookie, Savant, Scan, Scholar, Scient, See, Starter, Student, > **STUDY**, Tiro, Trainee, Tutee, Tyro, Wise

Learning Culture, Discipline, Discrimination, Erudition, Index, Insight, Latent

Lore, Machine, New, Open, Opsimathy, Rep, Wit

Lease(-holder) Charter, Farm, Feu, Gavel, Hire, Let, > RENT, Set(t), Tack, Tacksman

Leash Lead, Lune, Lyam, Lym(e), Slip, Three, Trash, Triplet

Least Minimum

Leather(y) Artificial, Bouilli, Bouilly, Box-calf, Buckskin, Buff, Cabretta, Calf, Capeskin, Chammy, Chamois, Checklaton, Cheverel, Chevrette, Cordovan, Cordwain, Corium, Cowhide, Crispin, Cuir(-bouilli), Deacon, Deerskin, Diphthera, Doeskin, Dogskin, Durant, Fair, Goatskin, Hide, Hog-skin, Horsehide, Japanned, Kid, Kip(-skin), Lamp, Levant, Marocain, Maroquin, Mocha, Morocco, Mountain, Nap(p)a, Neat, Nubuck®, Ooze, Oxhide, Paste-grain, Patent, Pigskin, Plate, Rand, Rawhide, Rexine®, Riem(pie), Roan, Rock, Rough-out, Russia, Saffian, Shagreen, Shammy, Sharkskin, Shecklaton, Sheepskin, Shoe, Skiver, Slinkskin, Spetch, Split, Spur, Stirrup, Strand, Strap, Suede, Tan, Taw, Thong, Upper, Wallop, Wash, Waxed, White, Whitleather, Yuft

Leatherneck Marine, RM

Leave(r), Leavings, Leave off Abandon, Abiturient, Abscond, Absit, Absquatulate, Acquittal, Adieu, Bequeath, Blessing, Bug, Compassionate, Congé, Congee, Decamp, Depart, Desert, Desist, Devisal, Devise, Ditch, Exeat, Exit, Exodus, Forego, Forgo, Forsake, French, Furlough, Garlandage, > GO, Inspan, Ish, Legate, Liberty, Licence, Maroon, Maternity, Mizzle, Omit, Orts, Pace, Park, Part, Paternity, > PERMISSION, Permit, > QUIT, Residue, Resign, Sabbatical, Scapa, Scat, Scram, Shore, Sick, Skedaddle, Skidoo®, Stick, Strand, Vacate, Vade, Vamo(o)se, Will, Withdraw

Leaven Barm, Ferment, Yeast

Lebanese, Lebanon Druse, RL

Lecher(ous), Lechery Gate, Goaty, Lascivious, Libertine, Lickerish, Lustful, Profligate, Rake, Roué, Salaciousness, Satirisk, Satyr, Silen, Whoremonger, Wolf

Lectern Ambo, Desk, Eagle, Oratory

Lecture(r), Lectures, Lecturing Address, Aristotelian, Chalktalk, Creed, Curtain, Dissert(ator), Don, Earful, Erasmus, Expound, Homily, Hulsean, Jaw, Jawbation, Jobe, L, Lector, Pi-jaw, Prelect, Privatdocent, Prone, Rate, Read(er), Rede, Reith, Scold, Sententious, > SERMON, Spout, Talk, Teacher, Teach-in, Wigging, Yaff

Ledge Altar, Berm, Channel, Fillet, Gradin(e), Linch, Misericord(e), Scarcement, Settle, > SHELF, Window (sill)

Ledger Book, Purchase, Register

Lee(s) Dregs, Dunder, Heeltaps, Sediment, Shelter, Ullage

Leech Bleeder, Gnathobdellida, Horse, Medicinal, Parasite, Rhynchobdellida

Leek Allium, Fouat, Fouet, Porraceous, Rocambole

Leer Eliad, Fleer, Oeillade, Ogle

Leeway Drift

Left(-handed), Left-hander, Left-winger Adrift, Balance, Bolshy, Corrie-fisted, Dolly-push, Gallock, Hie, High, Inherited, L, Laeotropic, Laevorotation, Larboard, Links, Lorn, Near, New, Other, Over, Pink, Port, Portsider, Quit, Rad, Red, Relic, Residuum, Resigned, Sinister, Soc(ialist), Southpaw, Thin, Titoism, Trot, Verso, Vo, Went, West, Wind, Yet

Left-over End, Lave, Oddment, Orra, Remanet, > REMNANT, Waste

Leg(s), Leggings, Leggy, Leg-wear Antigropelo(e)s, Bandy, Barley-sugar, Breeches, Cabriole, Cannon, Chaparajos, Chaparejos, Chaps, Crural, Crus, Dib,

Drumstick, Fine, Fly-sail, Gaiter, Galligaskins, Gam(b), Gamash, Gambado, Garter, Gaskin, Giambeux, Gigot, Gramash, Gramosh, Ham, Haunch, Hest, Hock, Jamb, Jambeau, Knock-knee(d), Limb, Long, Member, Myriapod, Oleo, On(side), Peg, Peraeopod, Periopod, Pestle, Pin, Podite, Proleg, Puttees, Pylon, Relay, Section, Shanks, Shanks's pony, Shaps, Shin, Short, Spats, Spatterdash, Spider, Spindleshanks, Square, Stage, Stump, Thigh, Tights

Legacy Bequest, Cumulative, Demonstrative, Dowry, Entail, General, Heirloom, Residuary, Specific, Substitutional

Legal(ism), **Legally**, **Legitimate** Bencher, Forensic, Halacha, Halaka(h), Halakha, Lawful, Licit, Nomism, Scienter, Statutory

Legal book Halacha, Halaka(h), Halakha, Talmud

Leg-armour, **Leg-covering** Cootikin, Cu(i)tikin, Gambado, Jamb(e), Pad

Legate, **Legator** Ambassador, Consul, Devisor, Emissary, Envoy, Nuncio

Legend Arthurian, Caption, Edda, Fable, Folklore, Motto, Myth, Saga, Story

▷ **Legend** *may indicate* leg-end, (e.g. foot, talus)

Leger Swindler

Leghorn Livorno

Legible Clear, Lucid, Plain

Legion(ary), **Legionnaire** Alauda, American, Army, British, Cohort, Countless, Deserter, Foreign, Geste, Honour, > **HOST**, Maniple, Many, Throng, Thundering Zillions

Legislate, **Legislator**, **Legislature** Assemblyman, Congress, Decemvir, Decree, MP, Nomothete, Oireachtas, > **PARLIAMENT**, Persian, Solon, Zemstvo

Legitimate Loyal

Legless Amelia, Blotto, Boozy, Caecilia, Psyche

Leg-pull Chaff, Joke, Rise, Rot

Legume, **Leguminous** Bean, Guar, Lentil, Pea, Pipi, Pod, Pulse

Leibniz Monadism

Leigh Amyas

Leisure(ly) Adagio, Ease, Lento, Liberty, Moderato, Otium, Respite, Rest, Vacation

Lemon Answer, Cedrate, Citron, Citrus, Smear-dab, Sole, Yellow

Lemur Angwantibo, Aye-aye, Babacoote, Bush-baby, Colugo, Galago, Half-ape, Indri(s), Loris, Macaco, Malmag, Mongoose, > **MONKEY**, Potto, Ringtail, Sifaka, Spectre, Tana, Tarsier

Lend Advance, Loan, Prest, Vaunce

Length(y), **Lengthen(ing)**, **Lengthwise** Archine, Arsheen, Arshin(e), Aune, Barleycorn, Braccio, Cable, Chain, Cubit, Distance, Eke, Ell, > **ELONGATE**, Endways, Epenthetic, Expand, Extensive, Focal, Foot, Furlong, Inch, Ley, Mile, Nail, Passus, Perch, Piece, Plethron, Pole, Prolate, Prolix, Prolong, Protract, Reach, Remen, Rod, Rope, Slow, Span, Stadium, Toise, Vara, Verbose, Yard

Lenient Clement, Exurable, Lax, Mild, Permissive, Soft, Tolerant

Lens Achromatic, Anamorphic, Anastigmat, Aplanatic, Apochromat(ic), Bifocal, Compound, Contact, Corneal, Crookes, Crown, Crystalline, Dielectric, Diopter, Dioptre, Diverging, Electron, Electrostatic, Eye, Eyeglass, Eye-piece, Facet, Fish-eye, Fresnel, Gravitational, Hard, Immersion, Lentil, Macro, Magnetic, Metallic, Mirror, Object-glass, Optic, Pantoscope, Phacoid, Piano-concave, Piano-convex, Soft, Soft-focus, Stanhope, Sunglass, Telephoto, Toric, Trifocal, Varifocal, Water, Wide-angle, Zoom

Lent Careme, Fast, Laetare, Out, Quadragesimal, Term

Lentil(s) D(h)al, Dholl, Ervalenta, Lens, Phacoid, Pulse, Revalenta

Leonora Overture

Leopard Clouded, Hunting, Leap, Libbard, Ounce, Panther, Pard, Snow, Spots

Leopold Bloom

Leotard Maillot

Leper, **Leprosy**, **Leprous** Gehazi, Lazar, Leontiasis, Lionism, Meazel, Mesel, Outcast, Pariah

Lepidopterist Aurelian, Moth-er, Pendleton, Treacler

Leprechaun Elf, Gremlin, Imp

Lepton Muon

Lesbian Bull dyke, Crunchie, Diesel, Dike, Dyke, Homophile, Lipstick, Sapphist, Tribade

Lesion Cut, Gash, Pannus, Scar, Serpiginous, Sore

Less(en), **Lesser**, **Lessening** Abate, Alaiment, Bate, Contract, Deaden, Decline, Deplete, Derogate, Dilute, > **DWINDLE**, Extenuate, Fewer, Junior, Littler, Minus, Reduce, Relax, Remission, Subordinate, Subsidiary, Under

Lesson Example, Lear(e), Lection, Leir, Lere, Life, Moral, Object, Parashah, Period, Sermon, Shiur, Tutorial

Let (go, off, out), **Letting** Allow, Cap, Charter, Conacre, Displode, Divulge, Enable, Entitle, Explode, Hire, Impediment, Indulge, Lease, Litten, Loot(en), Luit(en), Lutten, Net, Obstacle, Obstruct, > **PERMIT**, Rent, Reprieve, Sett, Tenancy, Unhand, Warrant

Let down Abseil, Betray, Lower, Sell, Vail

Let-down Non-event

Lethal Deadly, Fatal, Fell, Mortal

Lethargic, **Lethargy** Accidie, Apathy, Coma, Drowsy, Ennui, Hebetude, Inertia, Lassitude, Listless, Passive, Sleepy, Sluggish, Stupor, Supine, Torpid

Letter(s) Ache, Aerogam, Aesc, Airgraph, Aleph, Alif, Alpha, Ascender, A(y)in, Bayer, Begging, Beta, Beth, Block, Breve, Cadmean, Caph, Capital, Capon, Casket, Chain, Cheth, Chi, Circular, Col, Collins, Consonant, Covering, Cue, Cuneiform, Daled, Daleth, Dead, Dear John, Delta, Digamma, Digraph, Dominical, Edh, Ef(f), Emma, Encyclical, Ep(isemon), Epistle, Epsilon, Eta, Eth, Fan, Favour, Fraktur, French, Gamma, Gimel, Grapheme, He, Heth, Initial, Iota, Izzard, Jerusalem, Kaph, Kappa, Koppa, Kufic, Labda, Lambda, Lamed(h), Landlady, Landlord, Lessee, Lessor, Literal, Love, Mail, Mail-shot, Majuscule, Mem, Memo, Miniscule, Minuscule, Missive, Monogram, Mu, Night, Note, Notelet, Nu, Nun, Og(h)am, Omega, Omicron, Open, Pahlavi, Paston, Pastoral, Patent, Pe, Pehlevi, Phi, Pi, Plosive, Poison-pen, Polyphone, Postbag, Psi, Pythagorean, Qoph, Resh, Rho, Rom, Runestave, Sad(h)e, Samekh, Samian, Sampi, San, Scarlet, Screed, Screwtape, Script, See, Shin, Siglum, Sigma, Sign, Signal, Sin, Sort, Swash, Tau, Tav, Taw, Teth, Theta, Thorn, Toc, Tsade, Typo, Uncial, Upsilon, Vau, Vav, Versal, Vowel, Waw, Wen, Wyn, Wynn, Xi, Yod(h), Yogh, Ypsilon, Zayin, Zed, Zeta

Lettering Cufic, Kufic

Lettuce Butterhead, Cabbage, Chicon, Corn-salad, Cos, Frog's, Iceberg, Lactuca, Lamb's, Lollo rosso, Mizuna, Romaine, Salad, Thridace

Leucoma Albugo

Levant(ine) Coptic, Go, Israelite, Jew, Ottamite, Ottomite

Levee Bank, Dyke, Embankment, Party

Level(ler) A, Abney, Abreast, Aclinic, Ad eundum, Aim, Awash, Base, Break even, Bulldoze, Champaign, Countersink, Degree, Dumpy, Echelon, Energy, Equal, > **EVEN**, Extent, Flat, Flight, Flush, Fog, Grade, Logic, O, Occupational, Ordinary, Par, Plane, Plat(eau), Point, Price, Race, Rank, Rase, Raze, Reduced, Savanna, Sea, Spirit, Split, > **SQUARE**, Stratum, Street, Strew, Strickle,

Subsistence, Support, Surveyor's, Tier, Top, Trophic, True, Water, Y

Lever(age) Backfall, Bell-crank, Cock, Crampon, Crowbar, Dues, Gear, Handspike, Jemmy, Joystick, Key, Knee-stop, Landsturm, Pawl, Peav(e)y, Pedal Prise, Prize, Pry, Purchase, Stick, Sweep, Swipe, Tappet, Tiller, Treadle, Tremolo arm, Trigger, Tumbler, Typebar

Leviathan Whale

Levitate Float, Hover, Rise

Levity Flippancy, Glee, Humour, Jollity

Levy Capital, Estreat, Impose, Imposition, Leave, Militia, Octroi, Raise, Scutage Talliate, Tax, Tithe, Toll

Lewd(ness) Bawdy, Blue, Impure, Libidinous, Lubricity, Obscene, Priapism, Prurient, Silen(us), Unclean

Lewis Carroll, Tenon

Lexicographer, Lexicon Compiler, Craigie, Drudge, Etymologist, Florio, Fowler, Glossarist, Grove, Johnson(ian), Larousse, Liddell, Mental, Murray, OED, Thesaurus, Vocabulist, Webster, Words-man

Liability, Liable Anme, Apt, Current, Debt, Employer's, Incur, Limited, Open, Product, Prone, Subject, Susceptible

Liaison Affair, Amour, Contact, Link

Liana Guarana

Libel(lous) Defamatory, Malign, Slander, Smear, Sully, Vilify

Liberal(ity) Abundant, Adullamites, Ample, Besant, Bounteous, Bountiful, Breadth, Bright, Broad, Free(hander), Free-hearted, > **GENEROUS**, Giver, Grey, Grimond, Grit, Handsome, Indulgent, L, Largesse, Lavish, Octobrist, Open, > **PROFUSE**, Rad(ical), Samuelite, Simonite, Steel, Tolerant, Trivium, Unstinted, Verlig, Verligte, Whig

Liberate(d), Liberation, Liberator Bolivar, Deliver, Emancipate, Fatah, > **FREE**, Inkatha, Intolerant, Messiah, PLO, Release, Save, Sucre, Unfetter, UNITA, Women's

Liberian Kroo, Kru

Libertarian, Libertine Chartered, Corinthian, Debauchee, Laxist, Lecher, Lothario, Lovelace, Playboy, Rake, Rip, Roué, Wencher, Wolf

Liberty Bail, Civil, Discretion, Franchise, Freedom, Hall, Mill, Sauce

Library Bibliothecary, BL, Bodleian, Bookmobile, Circulating, Cottonian, Film, Gene, Harleian, Laurentian, Lending, Mazarin, Mobile, Morgue, PL, Public, Radcliffe, Reference, Subscription, Tauchnitz

Librettist Boito, Gilbert, Lyricist

▸ **Lice** *see* **LOUSE**

Licence, License Abandon, Allow, Authorisation, Carnet, Charter, Dispensation Driving, Enable, Exequatur, Fling, Franchise, Free(dom), Gale, Imprimatur, Indult, > **LATITUDE**, Let, Marriage, Occasional, Passport, > **PERMIT**, Poetic, Pratique, Provisional, Road-fund, Rope, Slang, Special, Table

Licentious Artistic, Corinthian, Debauchee, Hot, Immoral, Large, Lax, Liberal, Loose, Prurient, Ribald, Sensual, Wanton

Lichen Apothecia, Archil, Corkir, Crotal, Crottle, Cup, Epiphyte, Epiphytic, Graphis, Korkir, Lecanora, Litmus, Orchel, Orchil(la), Orcine, Orseille, Parella, Parelle, Roccella, Rock tripe, Sea-ivory, Stone-rag, Stone-raw, Tree-moss, Usnea, Wartwort

Lick(ing) Bat, Beat, Deer, Lambent, Lap, Leather, Salt, Slake, Speed, Tongue, Whip

▸ **Licorice** *see* **LIQUORICE**

Lid Cover, Hat, Kid, Maximum, Opercula, Screwtop, Twist-off

Liddell Alice

Lido Beach, Pool

Lie(s), **Liar**, **Lying** Abed, Accubation, Accumbent, Ananias, Bam, Bare-faced, Bask, Billy, Bounce(r), Braide, Cau(l)ker, Cellier, Clipe, Clype, Concoction, Contour, Couchant, Cracker, Cram(mer), Cretism, Cumbent, Deception, Decubitous, Decumbent, Direct, Doggo, Fable, False(r), Falsehood, Falsify, Falsity, Fib, Fiction, Figment, Flam, Gag, Gonk, Incumbent, Invention, Inveracity, Kip, Lair, Leasing, Lee(ar), Lig(ge), Lurk, Mythomania, Obreption, Oner, Perjury, Plumper, Porky, Porky (pie), Procumbent, Prone, Prostrate, Pseudologia, Recline, Recumbent, Repent, Repose, Reptant, Ride, Romance(r), Sham, Sleep, Strapper, Stretcher, Supine, Swinger, Tale, Tappice, Tar(r)adiddle, Thumper, Tissue, Try, Untruth, Whacker, Whid, White, Whopper, Yanker

Lied Art-song, Song

Lie-detector Polygraph

Lien Mortgage, Title

Lieu Locus, Place

Lieutenant Cassio, Flag, Loot, Lt, No 1, Sub(altern)

Life Age, Animation, Being, Bio, Biog(raphy), Brian, Brio, C'est la vie, Clerihew, CV, Esse, Existence, Good, Heart, High, Mean, Pep, Plasma, Private, Real, Shelf, Span, Spirit, Still, Subsistence, Time, True, Useful, Vita, Zoe

Life-blood Essence, Lethee

Lifeboat Ark

Life-cell Energid

Life-cycle Redia

Life-force Ch'i, Chi, Qi

Lifeguard Cheesemonger

Lifeless(ness) Abiosis, Algidity, Amort, Arid, Azoic, Barren, Catatonic, Cauldrife, > DEAD, Dull, Flat, Inanimate, Inert, Log, Mineral, Possum, Sterile, Stonen, Wooden

Lifelike Breathing, Speaking

Lifeline Umbilicus

Life-rent Usufruct

Life-saver Preserver, Raft

Lift(ed), **Lifter**, **Lifting** Arayse, Arsis, Attollent, Bone, Cable-car, Camel, Chair, Cly, Copy, Crane, Davit, Dead, Dumb waiter, Elate, Elevator, Enhance, Extol, Filch, Fillip, Fireman's, Heave, Heeze, Heezie, Heft, Heist, Hitch, Hoise, Hoist, Hove, Jack, Jigger, Kleptomania, Leaven, Lefte, Lever, Lewis, Nab, Nap, Paternoster, Pilfer, Press, Pulley, > RAISE, Ride, Scoop, Ski, Sky, Snatch, Stair, Steal, T-bar, Teagle, Theft, Thumb, Up, Winch, Windlass

Ligament Annular, Fr(a)enum, Paxwax, Spring, Suspensory, Tendon, Urachus

Ligation, **Ligature** Aesc, Bandage, Bind, Tubal

Light(en), **Lighting**, **Lighter**, **Lights** Aerate, Airy, Albedo, Ale, Alow, Alpenglow, Amber, Ancient, Ans(wer), Arc, Aurora, Batswing, Beacon, Beam, Bengal, Bezel, Bleach, Brake, Bude, Bulb, Candle, Cannel, Casement, Chiaroscuro, Cierge, Clue, Courtesy, Day, Dewali, Diffused, Direct, Diwali, Dream-hole, Drop, Drummond, Earth-shine, Eddystone, Electrolier, Ethereal, Fairy, Fall, Fan, Fantastic, Fastnet, Fetch-candle, Fidibus, Fill, Fire, First, Fixed, Flambeau, Flame, Flare, Flax(y), Flicker, Flippant, Flit(t), Floating, Flood, Fluorescent, Fog (lamp), Frothy, Fuffy, Gegenschein, Gleam, Glim(mer), Glow, Gossamer, Green, Guiding, Gurney, Haggis, Hazard, Head, House, Ignite, Illum(in)e, Incandescence, Indirect, Induction, Inner, Irradiate, Junior, Key, Kindle, Klieg, Lamp, Land, Lantern, Lanthorn, Laser, Leading, Leerie, Leggiero,

Levigate, Lime, Link, Loadstar, Lobuli, Lodestar, Lozen, Lucarne, Lucigen, Luminaire, Lumine, Luminescence, Luminous, Lustre, Lux, Mandorla, Match, Mercurial, Merry-dancers, Mithra(s), Moon, Naphtha, Navigate, Neon, Nit, Northern, Obstruction, Od(yl), Offal, Optics, Pale, Pane, Parhelion, Pavement, Phosphene, Phosphorescence, Phot, Photon, Pilot, Pipe, Polar, Portable, Producer-gas, Range, Rear, Red, Reflex, Relume, Rembrandt, Reversing, Riding, Rocket, Running, Rush, Satori, Scoop, Sea-dog, Search, Shy, Southern-vigil, Spill, Spot, Spry, Steaming, Strip, Strobe, Stroboscope, Subtle, Sun, Sunshine, Suttle, Svelte, Tail, Tally, Taper, Taps, Threshold, Tind, Tine, Torch, Torchère, Touchpaper, Traffic, Trivial, Ultraviolet, Unchaste, Unoppressive, UV, Ver(e)y, Vesica, Vesta, Vigil, Watch, Wax, White, Windock, Window, Winnock, Zodiacal

▷ **Light** *may indicate* an anagram

Lighter Barge, Birlinn, Casco, Gas-poker, Keel, Linstock, Lunt, Match, Pontoon, Pra(a)m, Spill, Taper

Lighthouse Beacon, Caisson, Eddystone, Fanal, Fastnet, Phare, Pharos, Sea-mark, Signal

Lightless Aphotic, Dark, Obscure, Unlit

Lightness Buoyancy, Galant, Levity, Pallor

Lightning Ball, Catequil, Chain, Dry, Eclair, Enfouldered, Fireball, Fire flag, Forked, Fulmination, Heat, Levin, Sheet, Thunderbolt, Wildfire, Zigzag

Lightship Nore

Lightweight Nobody, Oz, Trivial

Lignite Jet, Surtarbrand, Surturbrand

Like(ness), Liking As, Broo, Care, Corpse, Dig, Duplicate, Effigy, Eg, Egal, Enjoy, Equal, Fancy, Fellow, Lich, Palate, Parallel, Peas, Penchant, Please, Predilection, Semblant, Shine, Similar, Simile, Sort, Speaking, Taste, Tiki

Likely, Likelihood Apt, Fair, Maximum, Odds-on, Offchance, On, Plausible, Possible, Probable, Probit, Prone

Likewise Also, Do, Eke, Item, So, Too, Tu quoque

Lilac Laylock, Mauve, Pipe-tree, Syringa

Lilliputian Minute

Lilt Swing

Lily African, Agapanthus, Aloe, Amaryllis, Annunciation, Arum, Asphodel, Aspidistra, Belladonna, Blackberry, Calla, Camas(h), Camass, Canada, Candock, Chincherinchee, Colchicum, Colocasia, Convallaria, Corn, Crinum, Dale, Day, Easter, Elaine, Fawn, Fleur de lys, Fritillary, Galtonia, Guernsey, Haemanthus, Hemerocallis, Herb-paris, Jacob's, Jersey, Kniphofia, Laguna, Lent, Leopard, Lote, Lotos, Lotus, Madonna, Mariposa, Martagon, Meadow, Moorva, Mount Cook, Nelumbo, Nenuphar, Nerine, Nuphar, Orange, Padma, Phormium, Pig, Plantain, Pond, Quamash, Regal, Richardia, Sabadilla, Sansevieria, Sarsa, Scilla, Sego, Skunk cabbage, Smilax, Solomon's seal, Spider, Star of Bethlehem, Stone, Sword, Tiger, Trillium, Tritoma, Turk's cap, Vellozia, Victoria, Water, Yucca, Zephyr

Lily-maid Elaine

Lima Sugar bean

Limb Arm, Bough, Branch, Crural, Exapod, Flipper, Hindleg, Imp, Leg, Leg-end, Member, Phantom, Proleg, Pterygium, Ramus, Scion, Shin, Spald, Spall, Spaul(d), Wing

Limbless Amelia

Limbo Bardo, Isolation

Lime Bass(wood), Beton, Calc, Lind(en), Malm, Mortar, Slaked, Soda, Teil, Tilia,

Trap, Unslaked, Viscum, Whitewash

Limerick Doggerel, Twiner, Verse

Limestone Calp, Ca(u)m, Clint, Coquina, Coral Rag, Cornbrash, Cornstone, Forest Marble, Grike, Karst, Kentish rag, Kunkar, Kunkur, Muschelkalk, Oolite, Pisolite, Rottenstone, Scaglia, Travertin(e)

Limey Rooinek

Limit(ation), **Limited**, **Limiting** Ambit, Bind, Border, Borné, Bound, Bourn(e), Brink, Cap, Cash, Ceiling, Chandrasekhar, Circumscribe, Climax, Compass, Confine, Deadline, Define, Demark, Determine, Earshot, Eddington, Edge, End, Entail, Esoteric, > EXTENT, Extreme, Finite, Frontier, Gate, Goal, Gole, Impound, Induciae, Insular, Limes, Lynchet, March, Maximum, Meare, Mete, Minimum, Nth, Outedge, Pale, Parameter, Perimeter, Periphery, Predetermine, Qualify, Range, Rate-cap, Ration, Reservation, Restrict, Rim, Roche, Roof, Scant, Shoestring, Sky, Speed, Stint, String, Sumptuary, Tail(lie), Tailye, Tailzie, Term(inus), Tether, Three-mile, Threshold, Thule, Tie, Time, Tropic, Twelve-mile, Utmost, Utter, Verge

Limit *may indicate* 'surrounding'

Limner RA

Limousine Daimler, Rolls, Zil

Limp Claudication, Dot, Droopy, Flabby, Flaccid, Flimsy, Floppy, Hilch, Hirple, Hitch, Hobble, Hop, Lank, Lifeless, Spancel, Tangle

Limpet Keyhole, Patella, Slipper, Streptoneura

Limpid Clear, Lucid, Pure

Linch Terrace

Lincoln(shire) Abe, Poacher, Yellow-belly

Linden Baucis, Lime, Tilia

Line(d), **Lines**, **Lining** Abreast, Aclinic, Agate, Agonic, Allan, Anacreontic, > ANCESTRY, Anent, Angle, Apothem, Arew, Asclepiadean, Assembly, Asymptote, Axis, Babbitt, Bakerloo, Bar, Barcode, Battle, Baulk, Becket, Bikini, Bluebell, Bob, Bombast, Bottom, Boundary, BR, Brail, Branch, Bread, Bush, Canal, Carolingian, Carriage, Casing, Cell, Ceriph, Chord, Ciel, Club, Coach, Coffle, Colour, Column, Contour, Cord(on), Coseismal, Course, Crease, Credit, Crocodile, Crowsfoot, Curve, Cushion, Dancette, Date, Datum, Deadball, Delay, Descent, DEW, Diagonal, Diameter, Diffusion, Directrix, Distaff, Dotted, Doublure, Downhaul, Downrigger, Dress, Dynasty, Earing, E-la-mi, Encase, Equator, Equinoctial, Equinox, Faint, Fall(s), Fault, Feint, Fess(e), Fettle, File, Finishing, Firing, Firn, Flex, Flight, Frame, Fraunhofer, Front, Frontier, Frost, Furr(ow), Geodesic, Germ, Gimp, Giron, Goal, Graph, Grass, Green, Gridiron, Gymp, Gyron, Hachure, Halyard, Hard, Hatching, Hawser, Hemistich, Heptameter, Hexameter, Hexapody, High-watermark, Hindenburg, Hockey, Hogscore, Hot, House, Impot, Inbounds, Inbred, Incase, Interfluve, Intima, Isallobar, Isentrope, Isobar, Isobath, Isobront, Isocheim, Isochime, Isochron(e), Isoclude, Isocryme, Isogloss, Isogonal, Isogram, Isohel, Isohyet, Isolex, Isomagnetic, Isonome, Isopach(yte), Isophone, Isophote, Isopiestic, Isopleth, Isopyenal, Isotach, Isothere, Isotherm, Knittle, L, Land, Lane, Lansker, Lap, Lariat, Latitude, Lead, Leash, Le(d)ger, Ley, Lie, Ling, LMS, Load, Log, Longitude, Loxodrome, Lubber, Lye, Macron, Maginot, Main, Mainsheet, Mark, Marriage, Mason-Dixon, Median, Meridian, Mesal, Miurus, Monorail, Multiplet, Naman, Nazca, Nidation, Noose, Norsel, Northern, Number, Oche, Octastichon, Ode, Oder-Meisse, Og(h)am, Omentum, Onedin, Ordinate, Orphan, Painter, Parallel, Parameter, Parastichy, Party, Paternoster, Path, Penalty, Pencil, Phalanx, Picket, Pinstripe, Plimsoll, Plumb, Poetastery, Police,

Policy, Popping-crease, Poverty, Power, Product(ion), Profession, Punch, Pure, Queue, Race, Radial, Radius, Rail, Rank, Raster, Ratlin(e), Ratling, Rattlin, Ray, Red, Retinue, Rew, Rhumb, Ripcord, Rope, Route, Row, Rugose, Rugous, Rule, Ry, Sarking, Scazon, Score, Script, Secant, Seperatrix, Serif, Seriph, Service, Set, Siding, Siegfried, Sield, Sight, Silver, Slur, Snood, Snow, Soft, Solidus, Sounding, Spectral, Spring, Spunyarn, Squall, SR, Staff, Stance, Stanza, Starting, Static, Stave, Stean, Steen, Stein, Stem, Stich(os), Stock, Story, Strap, Streak, Striate, String, Stripe, Stuff, Subtense, Swifter, Symphysis, Syzygy, Tag, Tailback, Talweg, Tangent, Teagle, Tea lead, Terminator, Tetrameter, Thalweg, Thin blue, Thin red, Thread, Throwaway, Tidemark, Tie, Timber, Touch, Trade, Transmission, Transoceanic, Transversal, Tree, Trimeter, Tropic, Trot, Trunk, Tudor, Variety, Verse, Vinculum, Virgule, Wad, Wallace's, Washing, Water(shed), White, Widow, Wire, Wrinkle, Yellow, Zag, Zip, Zollner's

Lineage Ancestry, Descent, Extraction, Parage, Pedigree

Linen Amice, Amis, Barb, Bed, Byssus, Cambric, Crash, Damask, Dornick, Dowlas, Ecru, Flax Table, Harn, Huckaback, Inkle, Lawn, Lint, Lockram, Moygashel, Napery, Percale, Seersucker, Sendal, Silesia, Toile

Liner Artist, Bin-bag, Eye, Ocean greyhound, RMS, Ship, Sleeve, Steamer, Steen, Titanic

Linesman Parodist, > POET, Touch-judge

Linger(ing) Chronic, Dawdle, Dwell, Hang, Hove(r), Lag, > LOITER, Straggle, Tarry, Tie

Lingerie Bra, Drawers, Undies

Lingo Argot, Bat, Cant, Jargon, Speech

Linguist(ic), Linguistics Glottic, Historical, Philological, Phonemics, Polyglot, Semantics, Structural, Stylistics, Syntax, Tagmemics, Taxeme

Liniment Balm, Carron-oil, Embrocation, Ointment, Opodeldoc, Salve

Link(ing), Links Associate, Between, Bond, Bridge, Chain, Cleek, Colligate, Concatenation, Copula, Couple, Cross-reference, Desmid, Drag, Ess, Flambeau, Golf, Hookup, Hot, Hotline, Incatenation, Interface, Internet, Intertwine, Karabiner, Krab, Liaise, Machair, Missing, Nexus, Pons, Preposition, Relate, Tead(e), > TIE, Tie-in, Tie-line, Torch, Unite, Weakest, Yoke

Linkman Lamplighter, Mediator

Linnet Finch, Lintie, Lintwhite, Twite

Linoleum Waxcloth

Lint Charpie, Dossil

Lintel Summer, Transom

Lion(ess) Androcles, Aphid, Chindit, Elsa, Glitterati, Hero, Leo, Maned, Mountain, Nemean, Opinicus, Personage, Pride, Simba

Lionel Trilling

Lion-tamer Dan(iel)

Lip(py), Lips Beestung, Cheek, Fat, Fipple, Flews, Hare, Helmet, Jib, Labellum, Labiate, Labret, Labrum, Ligula, Muffle, > RIM, Rubies, Sass, Sauce, Slack-jaw, Submentum

Lipstick Chapstick

Liquefy Dissolve, Fuse, Melt

Liqueur, Liquor Abisante, Absinthe, Advokaat, Ale, Almondrado, Amaretto, Anise, Anisette, Apry, Benedictine, Bree, Brew, Broo, Broth, Calvados, Cassis, Cerise, Chartreuse, Chasse, Cherry marnier, Cher-suisse, Chicha, Choclair, Chococo, Cocoribe, Cointreau®, Creature, Crème, Crème de menthe, Curaçao, Drambuie®, Eau des creoles, Elixir, Enzian, Feni, Fenny, Fraises, Framboise, Fumet, Fustian, Galliano, Geropiga, Grand Marnier, Hogan, Hogan-mogen,

Hooch, John Barleycorn, Jungle juice, Kahlua, Kaoliang, Kir, Kirschwasser, Kirsh(wasser), Kummel, Lager, Lap, Malt, Maraschino, Mastic, Metheglin, Mickey Finn, Midori, Mirabelle, Mobbie, Mobby, Noyau, Oedema, Ooze, Ouzo, Parfait d'amour, Pasha, Pastis, Pernod, Persico, Pot, Potation, Pousse-café, Prunelle, Rakee, Raki, Ratafia, Roiano, Roncoco, Rose, Rotgut, Rum, Sabra, Sambuca, Samshoo, Schnapps, Sciarada, Shypoo, Skink, Stingo, Stock, Stout, Strega®, Strunt, Stuff, Supernaculum, Tape, Taplash, Tequila, Tia Maria, Tickle-brain, Tiff, Van der Hum, White lightning, Wine, Witblits, Wort

Liquid(ate), Liquidity, Liquids, Liquefaction Acetal, Amortise, Annihilate, Apprize, Azeotrope, Bittern, Bouillon, Bromine, Butanal, Butanol, Butyraldehide, Butyrin, Cacodyl, Cadaverine, Cash, Cash flow, Chloramine, Cinerin, Clyster, Court-bouillon, Creosol, Creosote, Decoction, Dispersant, Dope, Eluate, Erase, Ethanol, Ether, Eucalyptol, Eugenol, Flow, Fluid, Fural, Furfural, Furol, Halothene, Jaw, Kakodyl, Lewisite, Limonene, Linalool, Lye, Massacre, Mess, Minim, Mouillé, Picamar, Pipe, Potion, Protoplasm, Ptisan, Pyrrole, Pyrrolidine, Raffinate, Rhigolene, Safrole, Serum, Solution, Solvent, Syrup, Terebene, Thixotropy, Titer, Titre, Tuberculin, Tusche, Ullage, Verjuice, Whey, Wort

Liquorice Indian, Jequirity, Nail, Nail-rod, Pomfret, Pontefract-cake, Spanish juice, Sugarallie, Sugarally

Lis Iris, Lily

Lisa Mona

Lisp(er) Ephraimite, Sibilance

Lissom(e) Agile, Lithe, Nimble, Svelte

List *may indicate* 'listen'

List(s), Listing Active, Agenda, Antibarbarus, Appendix, Army, Atilt, Barocco, Barrace, Bead-roll, Bibliography, Canon, Cant, Catalog(ue), Categorise, Catelog, Cause, Check, Civil, Class, Compile, Credits, Danger, Debrett, Docket, Entry, Enumerate, Front, Glossary, Hark, Hearken, Heel, Hit, Hit-parade, Honours, Index, Indian, Interdiction, Inventory, Itemise, Lean, Leet, Line-up, Linked, Lloyds, Mailing, Manifest, Navy, Notitia, Official, Panel, Paradigm, Party, Prize, Register, Repertoire, Reserved, Roin, Roll, Roon, Roster, Rota, Rund, Schedule, Short, Sick, Slate, Slope, Strip, Syllabus (of Errors), Table, Tariff, Tick, Ticket, Tilt, Timetable, Tip, Transfer, Union, Waiting, Waybill, White, Wine, Wish

Listen(er) Attend, Auditor, Auscultate, Ear, Eavesdropper, Gobemouche, Hark, > **HEED**, Lithe, Lug, Monitor, Oyez, Sithee, Wire-tap, Yo-ho(-ho)

Listen to *may indicate* a word sounding like another

Listless(ness) Abulia, Accidie, Acedia, Apathetic, Atony, Dawney, Draggy, Inanition, Indolent, Lackadaisical, Languor, Mooning, Mope, Mopus, Sloth, Thowless, Torpor, Waff

Lit Alight, Landed

Lit *may indicate* an anagram

Litany Eirenicon

Literacy Emotional

Literal(ly), Literal sense Etymon, Misprint, Simply, Typo, Verbatim

Literary Academic, Bas bleu, Booksie, Erudite, Lettered

Literary girls Althea, Jenny, Maud, Pippa

Literature Belles lettres, Corpus, Fiction, Gongorism, Midrash, Page, Picaresque, Polite, Prose, Responsa, Splatterpunk, Wisdom

Lithe Flexible, Limber, Pliant, Souple, > **SUPPLE**, Svelte, Willowy

Lithium Li

Litigant Barrator, John-a-Nokes, John-a-Stiles, John Doe, Party, Richard Roe, Suer, Suitor

Litmus Indicator, Lacmus, Lichen

Litre L

Litter Bed, Brancard, Brood, Cacolet, Cubs, Debris, Doolie, Duff, Emu-bob, Farrow, Jampan, Kago, Kajawah, Kindle, Mahmal, Mor, Nest, Norimon, Palankeen, Palanquin, Palkee, Palki, Pup, > **REFUSE**, Scrap, Sedan, Stretcher, Sweepings, Team

Little Bagatelle, Billee, Brief, Chota, Curn, Dorrit, Drib, Drop, Fewtrils, Insect, Iota, John, Jot, Leet, Lilliputian, Limited, Lite, Lyte, Mini, Miniscule, Minnow, Minuscule, > **MINUTE**, Modicum, Morceau, Nell, Paltry, Paucity, Petite, Pink, Pitttance, Ronte, Runt, Scant, Scut, Shade, Shoestring, Shred, Shrimp, Slight, Sma', > **SMALL**, Smattering, Smidge(o)n, Smidgin, Some, Soupçon, Spot, Tad, Tich, Tine, Titch, Touch, Tyne, Vestige, Wee, Weedy, Whit, Women

Liturgical, Liturgy Doxology, Hallel, Rite, Versicle

Live(d), Livelihood, Living, Liveliness, Lively, Lives Active, Alert, Allegretto, Allegro, Am, Animated, Animation, Animato, AV, Awake, Be, Birkie, Bouncy, Breezy, Brio, Brisk, Cant(y), Capriccio(so), Cheery, Chipper, Chirpy, Cohabit, Con moto, Crouse, Durante vita, > **DWELL**, Ebullient, Entrain, Exist, Feisty, Frisky, Galliard, Gamy, Gay, Giocoso, Gracious, Grig, Hang-out, Hard, High jinks, Hijinks, Hot, Is, Jazz, Kedge, Lad, Lead, Mercurial, Merry, Outgo, Pacey, Peart, Pep, Piert, Quicksilver, Rackety, Racy, Reside, Rousing, Salt, Saut, Scherzo, Skittish, Spiritoso, Spirituel(le), Sprack, Spry, Spunky, Sustenance, Swinging, Vibrant, Vigoroso, Vital, Vitality, Vivace, Vive, Vivo, > **VOLATILE**, Vyvyan, Zappy, Zingy, Zippy, Zoe

▶ **Livelihood** *see* LIVE(D)

Liver(ish) Foie gras, Hepar, Hepatic(al), Porta, Puce, Resident, Tomalley

Liverpool, Liverpudlian Scouse

Liverwort Gemma-cup, Hepatica, Riccia

Livery(man) Ermine, Flunkeydom, Goldsmith, Skinner, Tiger, Uniform

Livid Blae, Bruised, Cross, > **FURIOUS**, Pale

Living Advowson, Benefice, Biont, Bread, Canonry, Crust, Glebe, Inquiline, Lodging, Quick, Resident, Simony, Subsistence, Symbiotic, Vicarage, Vital

Livingstone Doctor, Ken

Liza, Lizzie Bess, Betty, Flivver, Hexam, Tin

Lizard Abas, Agama, Amphisboena, Anguis, Anole, Basilisk, Bearded, Bearded-dragon, Blindworm, Blue-tongued, Brontosurus, Chameleon, Chuckwalla, Dinosaur, Draco, Eft, Evet, Fence, Flying, Frilled, Full-necked, Galliwasp, Gecko(ne), Gila, Gila monster, Glass snake, Goanna, Gotcha, Guana Hatteria, Hellbender, Horned, Iguana, Jew, Kabaragoya, Komodo (dragon), Lacerta, Legua(a)n, Lounge, Mastigure, Menopome, Moloch, Monitor, Mosasaur(us), Mountain devil, Newt, Perentie, Perenty, Reptile, Sand, Sauria, Scincoid, Seps, Skink, Slow-worm, Snake, Stellio(n), Sungazer, Tegu(exin), Thorny devil, Tokay, Tuatara, Tuatera, Varan, Wall, Whiptail, Worm, Worral, Worrel, Zandoli, Zonure

Llama Alpaca, Alpaco, Guanaco, Huanaco, Paco, Vicuna

Load(ed), Loader, Loading, Loads Accommodation, Affluent, Ballast, Base, Boot-strap, Burden, Cargo, Charge, Cobblers, Dead weight, Disc, Dope, Drunk, Dummy, Fardel, Fother, Freight, Front-end, Fulham, Full, Gestant, Heap, Input, Jag, Lade, Lard, Last, Live, Onus, Pack, Packet, Pay, Peak, Power, Prime, Rich, Seam, Shipment, Some, Span, Super, Surcharge, > **TIGHT**, Tod, Traction, Ultimate, Useful, Wealthy, Weight, Wharfinger, Wing

Loaf(er), Loaves Baguette, Batch, Baton, Bloomer, Bludge, Brick, Bum, Bu(r)ster, Cad, Cob, Coburg, Cottage, Danish, Farmhouse, French stick, Hawm, Hoe-cake, Idle, > LAZE, Long tin, Lusk, Manchet, Miche, Mouch, Pan, Pan(h)agia, Plain, Quartern, Roll, Roti, Shewbread, Showbread, Slosh, Split tin, Square tin, Sugar, Tin, Vantage, Vienna, Yob

Loam Clay, Loess, Loss, Malm

Loan(s) Advance, Balloon, Benevolence, Bottomry, Bridging, Debenture, Droplock, Imprest, Lane, Mutuum, Omnium, Out, Prest, Respondentia, Roll-over, Soft, Start-up, Sub, Time, War

Loathe, Loathing, Loathsome Abhor(rent), Abominate, Carrion, Detest, Hate, Nauseate, Scunner, Ug(h)

Lob Loft, Sky, Underarm

Lobby Demo, Division, Entry, Foyer, Gun, Hall, Press, Urge

Lobe(d) Anisocercal, Fluke, Frontal, Insula, Jugum, Lacinia, Lap, Occipital, Optic, Palmate, Parietal, Pinnule, Runcinate, Segment, Temporal, Uvula, Vermis

Lobster Cock, Crawfish, Crayfish, Crustacean, Decapoda, Langouste, Newburg, Norway, Pot, Rock, Scampo, Spiny, Thermidor, Tomalley

Local(ity) Area, Endemic, Home, Inn, Insider, Landlord, Native, Near, Nearby, Neighbourhood, Number, Parochial, Pub, Regional, Resident, Swadishi, Tavern, Topical, Vicinal

> **Local** *may indicate* a dialect word

Locale Scene, Site

Locate Connect, Find, Fix, Lay, Pinpoint, Plant, Site, Spot

Location Address, Milieu, Node, Place, Recess, Site, Situation, Sofar, Ubiety, Website, Zone

Loch, Lough Allen, Ashie, Awe, Derg, Earn, Eil, Erne, Etive, Fine, Gare, Garten, Holy, Hourn, Katrine, > LAKE, Larne, Leven, Linnhe, Lomond, Long, Moidart, Morar, More, Nakeel, Neagh, Ness, Rannoch, Ryan, Shiel, Strangford, Tay, Torridon

Lock(ing), Locker, Locks, Lock up Bar, Bolt, Canal, Central, Chubb®, Clinch, Combination, Cowlick, Curlicue, Davy Jones, Deadbolt, Detent, Drop, Fastener, Fermentation, Foretop, Gate, Haffet, Haffit, Handcuff, Hasp, Hold, Intern, Key, Latch, Lazaretto, Man, Mortise, Percussion, Prison, Quiff, Ragbolt, Ringlet, Sasse, Scalp, Scissors, > SECURE, Sluice, Snap, Spring, Stock, Strand, Tag, Talon, Time, Trap, Tress, Tuft, Vapour, Villus, Ward, Wheel, Wrestle, Yale®

Locket Lucy

Lockjaw Tetanus, Trismus

Locksmith Garret-master, Hairdresser

Locomotive Banker, Bogie, Bul(l)gine, Engine, Iron horse, Mobile, Rocket, Steam, Steamer, Train

Locum Deputy, Relief, Stopgap

Locus Centrode, Horopter, Lemniscate, Place, Spot

Locust, Locust tree Anime, Carob, Cicada, Hopper, Nymph, Robinia, Seventeen-year, Voetganger

Lode Comstock, Lodge, Mother, Reef, Vein

Lodestone Magnes, Magnet

Lodge(r) Billet, Board(er), Box, Cosher, Deposit, Dig, Doss, Entertain, Freemason, Grange, Guest, Harbour, Host, Inmate, Layer, Lie, Masonic, Nest, Orange, Parasite, PG, Quarter, Rancho, Room(er), Roomie, Stay, Storehouse, Stow, Sweat, Tenant, Tepee, Wigwam

Lodging(s) Abode, B and B, Chummage, Dharms(h)ala, Digs, Dosshouse, Ferm,

Grange, Grove, Hostel, Inquiline, Kip, Minshuku, Pad, Padding-ken, Pension, Pied-à-terre, Quarters, Resiant, Rooms, Singleen, YHA

Loft(iness), Lofty Aerial, Airy, Arrogant, Attic, Celsitude, Chip, Choir, Garret, Grand, Haymow, High, Jube, Lordly, Magniloquent, Noble, Olympian, Pulpitum, Rarefied, Rigging, Rood, Roost, Tallat, Tallet, Tallot

Log Billet, Black box, Cabin, Chip, Chock, Diarise, Diary, Hack, Ln, Mantissa, Nap(i)erian, Neper, Patent, > **RECORD**, Stock, Yule

Logarithm Common, Lod, Mantissa, Nap(i)erian, Natural

Logic(al) Alethic, Aristotelian, Chop, Dialectic(s), Distributed, Doxastic, Epistemics, Formal, Fuzzy, Heuristics, Iff, Mathematical, Modal, Organon, Philosophical, Premise, Pusser's, Ramism, Rational(e), Reason, Sequacious, Sorites, Symbolic, Tense, Trivium

Logo Colophon

Loin(s) Flank, Inguinal, Lungie, Lunyie, Reins

Loincloth Dhoti, Lungi, Pareu, Waist-cloth

Loiter(ing) Dally, Dare, Dawdle, Dilatory, Dilly-dally, Idle, Lag, Lallygag, Leng, Lime, > **LINGER**, Mooch, Mouch, Potter, Saunter, Scamp, Suss, Tarry

Lola Dolores

Loll Hawm, Lounge, Sprawl

Lollipop, Lolly Ice pole, Lulibub

Lolly Money, Sweetmeat

London(er) 'Arry, Big Smoke, Cockaigne, Co(c)kayne, Cockney, East-ender, Flat-cap, Jack, Roseland, Smoke, Town, Troynovant, Wen

London pride None-so-pretty

Lone(r), Lonely Remote, Rogue, Secluded, Sole, Solitary, Unked, Unket, Unkid

Long(er), Longing, Longs Ache, Aitch, Ake, Appetent, Aspire, Brame, Covet, Desire, Die, Earn, Erne, Far, Greed, Green, Grein, > **HANKER**, Huey, Hunger, Inveterate, Island, Itch, L, Lanky, Large, Lengthy, Longa, Lust, Macron, Miss, More, > **NO LONGER**, Nostalgia, Option, Pant, Parsec, > **PINE**, Prolix, Sesquipedalian, Side, Sigh, Tall, Thirst, Trews, Weary, Wish, Wist, Yearn, Yen

Long-eared Spicate

Longitude Celestial, Ecliptic, Meridian

Long-lashed Mastigophora(n)

Long live(d) Banzai, Macrobian, Viva, Zindabad

Longshoreman Hobbler, Hoveller, Wharfinger

Long-suffering Job, Patient, Stoical

Long-tailed Macrural

Long-winded Prolix, Verbose, Wordy

Loo Ajax, Bog, Can, Chapel, Dike, Game, Gents, Jakes, John, Privy, Toilet

Look(s), Look at Air, Aspect, Behold, Belgard, Bonne-mine, Busk, Butcher's, Butcher's hook, Clock, Close-up, Crane, Daggers, Decko, Deek, Dekko, Ecce, Ecco, Expression, Eye, Face, Facies, Gander, Gawp, Gaze, Geek, Glance, Glare, Gledge, Glimpse, Glom, Goggle, Good, Grin, Hallo, Hangdog, Hey, Iliad, Inspect, Keek, La, Leer, Lo, Mien, New, Ogle, Peek, Peep, Prospect, Ray, Recce, Refer, > **REGARD**, Scan, Scrutinise, Search, See, Seek, Shade, Sheep's eyes, Shufti, Shufty, Spy, Squint, Squiz, Survey, Toot, V, Vista, Wet

Look-out (man) Cockatoo, Crow's nest, Dixie, Huer, Mirador, Sangar, Sentinel, Sentry, Sungar, Toot(er), Watch, Watchtower

▷ **Look silly** *may indicate* an anagram

Loom Beamer, Dobby, Emerge, Impend, Jacquard, Lathe, Menace, Picker, Temple, Threaten, Tower

Loon Diver

Loop(ed), **Loophole**, **Loopy** Articulatory, Becket, Bight, Billabong, Bouclé, Carriage, Chink, Closed, Coil, Eyelet, Eyesplice, Fake, Frog, Frontlet, Grom(m)et, Ground, Grummet, Hank, Henle's, Hysteresis, Infinite, Kink, Knop, Lasket, Lippes, Lug, Noose, Oillet, Parral, Parrel, Pearl(-edge), Picot, Prusik, Purl, Scrunchie, Staple, Stirrup, Tab, Terry, Toe, Twist

Loos Anita

Loose(n), **Loose woman** Absolve, Abstrict, Afloat, Anonyma, Baggage, Bail, Besom, Bike, Chippie, Chippy, Cocotte, Cutty, Demi-mondaine, Demirep, Demivierge, Desultory, Dissolute, Dissolve, Doxy, Draggletail, Dratchell, Drazel, Emit, Flirt-gill, Floosie, Floozie, Floozy, Floppy, Franion, Free, Gangling, Gay, Hussy, Insecure, Jade, Jezebel, Lax, Light-heeled, Loast, Mob, Mort, Naughty pack, Pinnace, Profligate, Quail, Ramp, > RELAX, Sandy, Scrubber, Skanky-ho, Slag, Slapper, Streel, Tart, Tramp, Trull, Ungyve, Unhasp, Unhitch, Unknit, Unknot, Unlace, Unpin, Unreined, Unscrew, Unthread, Untie, Vague, Waistcoateer, Wappend, Whore

Loot Boodle, Booty, Cragh, Creach, Foray, Haul, Mainour, Peel, Pluck, > PLUNDER, Ransack, Rape, Reave, Rieve, Rob, Sack, Smug, Spoils, Spoliate, Swag, Treasure, Waif

Lop Behead, Clop, Curtail, Detruncate, Droop, Shroud, Sned, Trash

Lope Stride

Loquacious Chatty, Gabby, Garrulous, Rambling

Lord(s), **Lordship**, **Lordly** Adonai, Arrogant, Boss, Byron, Cyril, Dieu, Domineer, Dominical, Duc, Earl, Elgin, Gad, God, Haw-haw, Herr, Imperious, Jim, Justice, Kami, Kitchener, Landgrave, Law, Ld, Liege, Lonsdale, Losh, Lud, Mesne, Misrule, Mynheer, Naik, Oda Nobunaga, Omrah, Ordinary, Ormazd, Ormuzd, Peer, Sea, Seigneur, Seignior, Shaftesbury, Sire, Spiritual, Taverner, Temporal, Tuan, Ullin

Lords and ladies Wake-robin

Lore Cab(b)ala, Edda, Lair, Lare, Riem, Upanis(h)ad

Lorelei Siren

Lorgnette Starers

Lorna Doone

Lorry Artic(ulated), Camion, Crummy, Drag, Flatbed, Juggernaut, Low-loader, Rig, Tipper, Tonner, > TRUCK, Wagon

Lose(r) Also-ran, Decrease, Drop, Elude, Forfeit, Hesitater, Leese, Misère, Mislay, Misplace, Nowhere, Tank, Throw, Tine(r), Tyne, Underdog, Unsuccessful, Waste, Weeper

Loss, **Lost** Anosmia, Aphesis, Aphonia, Apocope, Apraxia, Astray, Attainder, Boohai, Chord, Cost, Dead, Decrease, Depreciation, Detriment, Disadvantage, Elision, Extinction, Foredamned, Forfeited, Forgotten, Forlorn, Gone, Lore, Lorn, Lurch, Missing, Omission, Outage, Pentimento, Perdition, Perdu, Perished, Preoccupied, Privation, Psilosis, Reliance, Tine, Tinsel, Tint, Toll, Traik, Tribes, Tyne(d), Ullage, Unredeemed, Wastage, Wasted, Will, Write-off, Wull

Loss of memory Amnesia, Black-out, Fugue, Infonesia, Paramnesia

▷ **Lost** *may indicate* an anagram or an obsolete word

Lot(s) Abundant, Amount, Aret(t), Badly, Batch, Boatload, Caboodle, Cavel, Chance, Deal, Dole, Doom, Drove, Due, > FATE, Fortune, Group, Hantle, Hap, Heaps, Horde, Host, Item, Job, Kevel, Kismet, Lashings, Legion, Luck, Manifold, Many, Mass, Moh, Moira, Mony, Mort, Myriad, Oceans, Omnibus, Oodles, Pack, Parcel, Parking, Plenitude, Plenty, Portion, Power, Purim, Raft, Rich, Scads, Set, Sight, Slather, Slew, Slue, Sortilege, Sortition, Stack, Sum, Tall order, The works, Tons, Vole, Wagonload, Weird

Loth Averse, Circumspect, Sweer(t), Sweir(t)

Lothario Lady-killer, Libertine, Poodle-faker, Rake, Womaniser

Lotion After-shave, Blackwash, Calamine, Collyrium, Cream, Eye-wash, Humectant, Setting, Suntan, Unguent, Wash, Yellow wash

Lottery, Lotto Art union, Ballot, Bingo, Cavel, Draw, Gamble, National, Pakapoo, Pools, Postcode, Punchboard, Raffle, Rollover, Scratchcard, Sweepstake, Tattersall's, Tombola

Lotus (eater), Lotus land Asana, Djerba, Lotophagus, Padmasana

Loud(ness), Loudly Bel, Big, Blaring, Booming, Brassy, Decibel, F, FF, Flashy, Forte, Fracas, Full-mouthed, Garish, Gaudy, Glaring, Hammerklavier, High, Lumpkin, Noisy, Orotund, Plangent, Raucous, Roarie, Siren, Sone, Stentor(ian), Strident, Tarty, Vocal, Vociferous, Vulgar

Loudspeaker Action, Boanerges, Bullhorn, Hailer, Megaphone, Stentor, Subwoofer, Tannoy®, Tweeter, Woofer

▸ **Lough** *see* LOCH

Louis Baker, Roi

Louisianian Cajun

Lounge(r) Cocktail, Da(c)ker, Daiker, Departure, Hawm, Idle, Laze, Lizard, Loll, Lollop, Parlour, Paul's man, Sitkamer, Slouch, Sun, Transit

Louse (up), Lousy, Lice Acrawl, Argulus, Bolix, Bollocks, Chat, Cootie, Crab, Crummy, Fish, Head, Isopod(a), Kutu, Nit, Oniscus, Pedicular, Phthiriasis, Plant, Psocoptera, Psylla, Slater, Snot, Sowbug, Sucking, Vermin, Whale

Lout Clod(hopper), Coof, Cuif, Hallian, Hallion, Hallyon, Hick, Hob, Hobbledehoy, Hooligan, Hoon, Jack, Jake, Keelie, Lager, Larrikin, Litter, Lob(lolly), Loord, Lubber, Lumpkin, Oaf, Oik, Rube, Swad, Tout, Tripper, Yahoo, Yob(bo)

Love(r) Abelard, Adore, Adulator, Affection, Agape, Amant, Amateur, Ami(e), Amoret, Amoroso, Amour, Antony, Ardour, Ariadne, Aroha, Aucassin, Beau, Bidie-in, Blob, Calf, Care, Casanova, Chamberer, Cicisbeo, Concubine, Coquet, Court, Courtly, Cupboard, Cupid, Dona(h), Dotard, Dote, Doxy, Duck(s), Ducky, Dulcinea, Eloise, Eloper, Emotion, Enamorado, Eros, Fan, Fancy man, Flame, Frauendienst, Free, Goose-egg, Greek, Idolise, Inamorata, Inamorato, Isolde, Jo, Kama, Lad, Leman, Like, Lochinvar, Loe, Loo, Lurve, Nihility, Nil, Nothing, Nought, O, Pairs, Paramour, Pash, Passion, Philander, -phile, Platonic, Protestant, Psychodelic, Puppy, Revere, Romance, Romeo, Sapphism, Spooner, Stale, Storge, Suitor, Swain, Thisbe, Touch, Toyboy, Troilus, True, Turtle(-dove), Valentine, Venus, Virtu, Worship, Zeal, Zero

Love-apple Tomato, Wolf's-peach

Love-bite Hickey

Love-child By-blow, Come-by-chance

Love-in-a-mist Nigella

Love letter Capon

Lovely Adorable, Belle, Dishy, Dreamy, Exquisite, Nasty

Love-making > INTERCOURSE, Kama Sutra, Sex, Snog

Love-sick Smit(ten), Strephon

Loving(ly) Amoroso, Amorous, Fond, Tender

Low(est), Low-cut, Lower(ing) Abase, Abate, Abysmal, Amort, Area, Avail(e), Avale, B, Basal, Base(-born), Bass(o), Beneath, Caddish, Cartoonist, Cheap, Church, Condescend, Contralto, Cow, Croon, Crude, Darken, Debase, Décolleté, Deepmost, Degrade, Demean, Demit, Demote, Depress, Devalue, Dim, Dip, Dispirited, Doldrums, Drawdown, Drop, Early, Embase, Flat, Foot, Frown,

Gazunder, Glare, Guernsey, Gurly, Hedge, Humble, Ignoble, Imbase, Inferior, Jersey, Laigh, Lallan, Law, Light, Lite, Mass, Mean, Menial, Moo, Mopus, Morose, Nadir, Net, Nether, Nett, Ostinato, Paravail, Plebeianise, Profound, Prole, Relegate, Ribald, Rock-bottom, Sad, Scoundrel, Scowl, Settle, Shabby, Short, Soft, Stoop, Subordinate, Sudra, Undermost, Unnoble, Vail, Vulgar, Weak, Wretched

Lowbrow Philistine

Lowdown Gen, Info

Lower *may refer to* cattle

Lowland(er) Carse, Gallovidian, Glen, Laigh, Lallans, Merse, Mudflat, Plain, Polder, Sassenach, Vlei

Low-lying Callow, Epigeous, Fens, Inferior, Sump

Low person Boor, Bunter, Cad, Caitiff, Cocktail, Demirep, Ratfink, Snot

Loyal(ty) Adherence, Allegiant, Brick, Dependable, Esprit de corps, Faithful, Fast, Fidelity, Gungho, Leal, Patriotic, Stalwart, Staunch, > TRUE, True blue, Trusty

Loyalist Hard core, Paisley, Patriot, Tory

Lozenge Cachou, Catechu, Fusil, Jujube, Mascle, Pastille, Pill, Rhomb, Rustre, Tablet, Troche

LSD Acid, Money

Lubber(ly), Lubbers Booby, Clod, Clumsy, Gawky, Hulk, Lob, Looby, Oaf, Slowback, Swab, Swads

Lubricant, Lubricate, Lubrication Carap-oil, Coolant, Derv, Fluid, Force-feed, Grease, Oil, Petrolatum, Sebum, Unguent, Vaseline®, Wool-oil

Luce Ged

Lucerne Alfalfa, Medick, Nonsuch

Lucia Mimi

Lucid Bright, Clear, Perspicuous, Sane

Lucifer Devil, Match, Proud

Luck(y) Amulet, Auspicious, Beginner's, Bonanza, Break, Caduac, Cess, Chance, Charmed, Chaunce, Daikoku, Dip, Fate, Fluke, > FORTUNE, Godsend, Hap, Heather, Hit, Jam(my), Joss, Lady, Lot, Mascot, Mozzle, Pot, Prosit, Providential, Pudding-bag, Purple patch, Seal, Seel, Sele, Serendipity, Sess, Sonsie, Sonsy, Star(s), Streak, Success, Talisman, Tinny, Tough, Turn-up, Windfall

Luckless Hapless, Wight

Lucre Money, Pelf, Tin

Lucy Locket

Lud Gad

Luddite Saboteur, Wrecker

Ludicrous Absurd, Bathetic, Bathos, Farcical, Inane, Irish, Jest, Laughable, Risible

Ludo Uckers

Luff Derrick

Lug Ear, Earflap, Sea-worm, Sowle, Tote, Tow

Luggage Bags, Carryon, Cases, Dunnage, Excess, Grip, Hand, Kit, Petara, Suiter, Traps, Trunk

Luggage-carrier Grid

Lugubrious Dismal, Drear

Luke-warm Laodicean, Lew, Tepid

Lull, Lullaby Berceuse, Calm, Cradlesong, Hushaby, Respite, Rock, Sitzkreig, Soothe, Sopite

Lulu Stunner

Lumber(ing) Clump, Galumph, Jumble, Pawn, Ponderous, Raffle, Saddle, Scamble, Timber

Lumberjack Bushwhacker, Feller, Logger

Luminance, **Luminous**, **Luminosity**, **Luminescence** Aglow, Arc, Foxfire, Glow, Ignis-fatuus, L, Light, Nit, Phosphorescent, Sea-dog, Wildfire, Will o' the wisp

Lumme Coo, Lor

Lump(y) Aggregate, Bubo, Bud, Bulge, Bur(r), Caruncle, Chuck, Chunk, Clat, Claut, Clod, Clot, Cob, Combine, Dallop, Da(u)d, Dollop, Enhydros, Epulis, Flocculate, Ganglion, Geode, Gnarl, Gob(bet), Goiter, Goitre, Grape, Hunch, Hunk, Inium, Knarl, Knob, Knub, Knur(r), Knurl, Lob, Lunch, Malleolus, Mass, Mote, Mott, Myxoma, Neuroma, Nibble, Nirl, Node, Nodule, Nodulus, Nub, Nubble, Nugget, Nur(r), Nurl, Osteophyte, Plook, Plouk, Quinsy, Raguly, Sarcoma, Scybalum, Sitfast, Slub, Strophiole, Tragus, Tuber(cle), Wart, Wodge

Lumpsucker Sea-owl

Lunacy, **Lunatic** Bedlam, Dementia, Demonomania, Folly, Insanity, Mad(ness), Psychosis

Lunar Evection, Mascon

▷ **Lunatic** *may indicate* an anagram

Lunch(time) Dejeune, Déjeuner, L, Nacket, Nocket, Nuncheon, Packed, Piece, Ploughman, Pm, Power, Tiff(in), Working

Lung(s) Bellows, Coalminer's, Farmer's, Green, Iron, Lights, Pulmo, Pulmonary, Soul

Lung disease Anthracosis, Byssinosis, Emphysema, Farmer's lung, Pneumoconiosis, Siderosis, Silicosis, Tuberculosis

Lunge Breenge, Breinge, Dive, Stab, Thrust, Venue

Lungfish Dipnoi(an)

Lupin Arsene

Lurch Reel, Stoit, Stumble, Swee

Lure Bait, Bribe, Carrot, Decoy, Devon minnow, Entice, Horn, Inveigle, Jig, Judas, Roper, Spinner, Spoonbait, Spoonhook, Stale, Temptation, Tice, Tole, Toll, Train, Trepan, Wormfly

Lurid Gruesome, Purple

Lurk(ing) Dare, Latitant, Skulk, Slink, Snoke, Snook, Snowk

Lusatia(n) Wend(ic), Wendish

Luscious Succulent

Lush Drunk, Fertile, Green, Juicy, Lydian, Sot, Tosspot, Verdant

Lust(ful), **Lusty** Cama, Concupiscence, Corflambo, Desire, Eros, Frack, Greed, Kama, Lech(ery), Lewd, Megalomania, Obidicut, Randy, Rank, Raunchy, Salacious, Venereous

Lustre, **Lustrous** Brilliance, Census, Galena, Gaum, Gilt, Gloss, Gorm, Inaurate, Lead-glance, Pentad, Reflet, Satiny, Schiller, > SHEEN, Water

Lute, **Lutist** Amphion, Chitarrone, Cither, Dichord, Orpharion, Pandora, Theorbo, Vielle

Lutetium Lu

Lutheran Adiaphorist, Calixtin(e), Pietist

Lux Lx

Luxemburg L

Luxuriant, **Luxuriate**, **Luxurious**, **Luxury (lover)** Bask, Clover, Cockaigne, Cockayne, Copious, Deluxe, Dolce vita, Extravagant, Fleshpots, Lavish, Lucullan, Lush, Mollitious, Ornate, Pie, Plush, Posh, Rank, > RICH, Ritzy, Sumptuous, Sybarite, Wallow

Lycanthropist Werewolf

Lydia Languish
Lye Buck
Lying *see* LIE
Lymph Chyle
Lymphoma Burkett's
Lynch(ing) Dewitt, Hang, Necktie party
Lynx Bobcat, Caracal, Rooikat
Lyre Cithern, Harp, Psaltery, Testudo
Lyric(al), **Lyricist**, **Lyrist** Cavalier, Dit(t), Epode, Gilbert, Melic, Ode, Orphean, Paean, Pean, Poem, Rhapsodic, Song

Mm

M Married, Member, Metre, Mike, Mile, Thousand
Mac Mino, Scot, Waterproof
Macabre Gothic, Grotesque, Sick
Macaroni Beau, Blood, Cat, Dandy, Elbow, Exquisite, Fop, Jack-a-dandy, Olio,
    Pasta, Petitmaitre
Macaroon Biscuit, Signal
Macaulay Layman
Mace Club, Nutmeg, Sceptre, Spice
Mace-bearer Beadle, Bedel, Poker
Macedonian Philip, Stagirite, Stagyrite
Machine(ry) Apparat(us), Appliance, Automaton, Bathing, Bulldozer, Calender,
    Centrifuge, Cycle, > DEVICE, Dialyser, Dredge(r), Drum, Engine, Enginery,
    Facsimile, Fax, Fruit, Gin, Hawk-eye®, Heck, Hopper, Hot-press, Instrument,
    Jawbreaker, Lathe, Life-support, Loom, Milling, Moulinet, Mule, Nintendo®,
    Party, Planer, Plant, Press, Processor, Propaganda, Pulsator, Robot, Rowing,
    Sewing, Slicer, Slot, Spinning jenny, Tape, Tedder, Throstle, Time, Transfer,
    Turbine, Turing, Twin tub, Typewriter, Vending, Virtual, War, Washing,
    Weighing, Wimshurst, Wind(mill), Wringer
Macho Jock
Mackerel Albacore, Brack, Dory, Fish, Horse, Pacific, Pimp, Scad, Scomber, Sky,
    Spanish, Spotted, Trevally
Mackintosh Burberry®, Mac, Mino, Oilskin, Slicker, Waterproof
Macropus Euro, Wallaroo
Mad(den), Madman, Madness Angry, Balmy, Bananas, Barking, Barmy,
    Bedlam, Besotted, Bonkers, Crackbrained, Crackpot, Crazy, Cuckoo, Cupcake,
    Daffy, Delirious, Dement, Distract, Dotty, Enrage, Fay, Fey, Folie, Folly,
    Frantic, Frenetic(al), Fruitcake, Furioso, Fury, Gelt, Gyte, Harpic, Hatter,
    Idiotic, Incense, Insane, Insanie, Insanity, Into, Irritate, Kook, Loco, Lunatic,
    Lycanthropy, Madbrained, Maenad, Mania, Mattoid, Mental, Meshug(g)a,
    Midsummer, Motorway, Mullah, Psycho, Rabid, Rasputin, Raving, Redwood,
    Redwud, Scatty, Screwy, Short-witted, Starkers, Tonto, Touched, Troppo,
    Unhinged, Wacko, Wood, Wowf, Wrath, Wud, Xenomania, Yond, Zany
▷ **Mad(den)** *may indicate* an anagram
Madagascan, Madagascar Aye-aye, Hova, Indri, Lemur, Malagasy, RM
Madam(e) Baggage, Lady, Proprietress
Madcap Impulsive, Tearaway
Madder Alizari, Chay(a), Gardenia, Genipap, Rose, Rubia, Shaya
Made (it) Built, Did, Fec(it), Ff, Gart, Invented
Madge Pie
▷ **Madly** *may indicate* an anagram
Madonna Lady, Lily, Mary, Pietà, Sistine, Virgin
Madrigal Ballet, Fala, Song
Maelstrom Voraginous, Vortex, Whirlpool

Maenad Devotee, Fan

Maestro Artist, Toscanini, Virtuoso

Mafia Camorra, Capo, Cosa nostra, Godfather, Mob, Ndrangheta, Omerta, The Mob

Mag Mail

Magazine Arsenal, Clip, Colliers, Contact, Cornhill, Cosmopolitan, Digizine, Economist, Field, Girlie, Glossy, Granta, Jazz mag, Lady, Lancet, Listener, Magnet, Organ, Periodical, Pictorial, Playboy, Pulp, Punch, She, Skin, Slick, Spectator, Store, Strand, Tatler, Time, Vogue, Warehouse, Weekly, Yoof

Magdalene St. Mary

Maggie Rita

Maggot Bot, Flyblow, Gentiles, Gentle, Grub, Larva, Mawk, Myiasis, Whim, Worm

Magi Balthazar, Gaspar, Melchior

Magic(al), Magician, Magic square Archimage, Art, Baetyl, Black, Black art, Charm, Circle, Conjury, Diablerie, Diablery, Enchanting, Faust, Faustus, Genie, Goetic, Goety, Gramary(e), Grimoire, Hermetic, Houdini, Illusionist, Incantation, Math, Medea, Merlin, Mojo, Moly, Morgan le Fay, Myal, Nasik, Natural, Necromancer, Obeah, Pawaw, Powwow, Prospero, Reim-kenner, Rhombus, Shamanism, Sorcery, Sortilege, Spell, Speller, Supernatural, Sympathetic, Talisman, Thaumaturgics, Theurgy, Voodoo, White, Wizard, Zendik

Magistracy, Magistrate Aedile, Amman, Amtman, Archon, Avoyer, Bailie, Bailiff, Bailli(e), Burgess, Burgomaster, Cadi, Censor, Consul, Corregidor, Demiurge, Doge(ate), Draco, Edile, Effendi, Ephor, Field cornet, Finer, Foud, Gonfalonier, JP, Judiciary, Jurat, Kotwal, Landamman(n), Landdrost, Lord Provost, Maire, Mayor, Mittimus, Novus homo, Podesta, Portreeve, Pr(a)efect, Pr(a)etor, Prior, Proconsul, Propraetor, Provost, Qadi, Quaestor, Recorder, Reeve, Shereef, Sherif, Stad(t)holder, Stipendiary, Syndic, Tribune, Worship

Magnanimity, Magnanimous Big, Charitable, > GENEROUS, Largeness, Lofty, Noble

Magnate Baron, Bigwig, Industrialist, Mogul, Onassis, Randlord, Tycoon, Vanderbilt, VIP

Magnesia, Magnesium Humite, Kainite, Mg, Periclase

Magnet(ic), Magnetism Animal, Artificial, Attraction, Bar, Charisma, Field, Gauss, Horseshoe, It, Loadstone, Lodestone, Maxwell, Od, Oersted, Permanent, Personal, Polar, Pole, Pole piece, Poloidal, Pull, Remanence, Retentivity, Solenoid, Terrella, Terrestrial, Tesla, Tole

Magnificence, Magnificent Gorgeous, Grandeur, Imperial, Laurentian, Lordly, Noble, Pride, Regal, Royal, Splendid, Splendo(u)r, State, Superb

Magnifier, Magnify(ing) Aggrandise, Augment, Binocle, > ENLARGE, Exaggerate, Increase, Loupe, Megaphone, Microscope, Teinoscope, Telescope

Magniloquent Bombastic, Orotund

Magnitude Absolute, Abundance, Extent, Muchness, Photoelectric, Scalar, Size, Visual

Magnolia An(n)ona, Beaver-tree, Champac, Champak, Mississippi, Sweet bay, Umbrella-tree, Yulan

Magpie Bell, Bird, Chatterer, Madge, Mag, Margaret, Outer, Pica, Piet, Pyat, Pyet, Pyot

Magus Artist

Magyar Hungarian, Szekel(y), Szekler, Ugrian, Ugric

Mahogany Acajou, Carapa, Cedrela, Philippine, Wood

Mahommedan Dervish, Shiah

Maid(en) Abigail, Aia, Amah, Biddy, Bonibell, Bonne, Bonnibell, Chamber, Chloe, Clothes-horse, Damosel, Dell, Dey, Femme de chambre, First, Girl, Guillotine, Ignis-fatuus, Imago, Inaugural, Io, Iras, Iron, Lorelei, M, Marian, May, Miss, Nymph, Opening, Over, Parlour, Pucelle, Rhine, Skivvy, Soubrette, Suivante, Thestylis, Tirewoman, Tweeny, Valkyrie, Virgin, Walkyrie, Wench, Wicket

Maidenhair Fern, Ginkgo

Mail Air, > ARMOUR, Byrnie, Cataphract, Chain, Da(w)k, Direct, E(lectronic), Express, Fan, Habergeon, Hate, Hauberk, Helm, Junk, Letter, Metered, Panoply, Pony express, Post, Ring, Send, Snail, Spam, Surface, Tuille(tte), Voice

Mailboat Packet

Maim Cripple, Impair, Lame, Main, Mayhem, Mutilate, Vuln

Main(s) Atlantic, Brine, Briny, > CENTRAL, Chief, Cockfight, Conduit, Essential, Foremost, Gas, Generally, Grid, Gross, Head, > KEY, Lead(ing), Major, Pacific, Palmary, Predominant, Prime, Principal, Ring, > SEA, Sheer, Spanish, Staple, Water

Mainland Continent, Pomona

Mainstay Backbone, Bastion, Pillar, Support

Maintain, Maintenance Alimony, Allege, Ap(p)anage, Argue, Assert, Aver, Avouch, Avoure, Avow, Claim, Contend, Continue, Defend, Escot, Insist, Keep (up), Preserve, Run, Sustain, Upbear, Uphold, Upkeep

Maize Corn, Hominy, Indian, Indian corn, Mealie, Popcorn, Samp, Silk, Stamp, Zea

Majestic, Majesty August, Britannic, Dignity, Eagle, Grandeur, Imperial, Maestoso, Olympian, Regal, SM, Sovereign, Stately, Sublime, Tuanku

Major (domo) Barbara, Drum, > IMPORTANT, Pipe, PM, Seneschal, Senior, Sergeant, Star, Trumpet, Wig

Majority Absolute, Age, Body, Eighteen, Landslide, Latchkey, Maturity, Moral, Most, Preponderance, Relative, Silent, Working

Make(r), Make do, Making Amass, Brand, Build, Clear, Coerce, Coin, Compel, Compulse, Concoct, Creant, Create, Devise, Earn, Execute, Fabricate, Factive, Fashion, Faute de mieux, Fet(t), Forge, Form, Gar(re), God, Halfpenny, Mail(e), Manage, Marque, Prepare, Production, Reach, Render, Shape, Sort, Temporise, Wright

▷ **Make** *may indicate* an anagram

Make believe Fantasy, Fictitious, Pretend, Pseudo

Make good Abet, Compensate, Remedy, Succeed, Ulling

Make hay Ted

Make off Bolt, Leg it, Mosey, Run, Scarper

Makeshift Bandaid, Crude, Cutcha, Expedient, Jury-rigged, Kacha, Kludge, Kutcha, Lash-up, Mackle, Pis-aller, Rude, Stopgap, Timenoguy

Make up Ad lib, Compose, Concealer, Constitution, Cosmetics, Fucus, Gaud, Gawd, Gene, Greasepaint, Identikit®, Kohl, Liner, Lipstick, Maquillage, Mascara, Metabolism, Paint, Pancake, Powder, Reconcile, Rouge, Slap, Tidivate, Titivate, Toiletry, Visagiste, War paint, White-face

Maladroit Awkward, Clumsy, Graceless, Inelegant, Unperfect

Malady Disease, Illness

Malagas(e)y Hova, RM

Malaise Affluenza

Malapropism Catachresis, Slipslop

Malaria Ague, Marsh-fever, Paludism, Tap, Vivax

Malawi Nyasa

Malay(an), Malaysian Austronesian, Datuk, D(a)yak, Jawi, Madurese, Moro, Sakai, Tokay, Tuan

Male Arrhenotoky, Buck, Bull, Butch, Dog, Ephebe, Ephebus, Gent, Hob, John Doe, Macho, Mansize, Masculine, Ram, Rogue, Spear(side), Stag, Stamened, Telamon, Tom

Malediction Curse, Cuss, Oath, Slander

Malefactor Criminal, Felon, Villain·

Malevolent, Malevolence Evil, Fell, Malign, Pernicious

Malformation Teratogenesis

Malfunction Glitch, Hiccup

Mali RMM

Malice, Malicious Bitchy, Catty, Cruel, Despiteous, Envy, Hatchet job, Malevolent, Malign, Narquois, Prepense, Schadenfreude, Serpent, Snide, Spite, Spleen, Venom, Virulent, Vitriol

Malign(ant), Malignity Asperse, Backbite, Baleful, Defame, Denigrate, Gall, Harm, Hate-rent, Hatred, Libel, Poor-mouth, Sinister, Slander, Spiteful, Swart(h)y, Toxin, Vicious, Vilify, Vilipend, Viperous, Virulent

Malinger(er) Dodge, Leadswinger, Scrimshank, Shirk, Skrimshank, Truant

Mall Parade

Mallard Duck, Sord

Malleable Clay, Ductile, Fictile, Pliable

➤ **Malleable** *may indicate* an anagram

Mallet Beetle, Club, Hammer, Mace, Maul, Serving, Stick

Mallow Abutilon, Dwarf, Musk, Sida, Urena

Malodorous Mephitic

Malpractice(s) Sculduggery, Skulduggery

Malt Brewer's grain, Diastase, Grains, Grist, Wort

Maltese (cross) Falcon, GC

Maltreat Abuse, Harm, Maul, Mishandle, Misuse

Mammal Animal, Armadillo, Artiodactyl, Binturong, Bobcat, Cacomistle, Cacomixle, Caracal, Cervid, Cetacean, Charronia, Chevrotain, Chiropteran, Ciscus, Colugo, Creodont, Dhole, Dinothere, Dolphin, Dugong, Eutheria, Fisher, Glires, Glutton, Grison, Guanaco, Hydrax, Hyrax, Indri, Jaguarondi, Jaguarundi, Kinkajou, Lagomorph, Leporid, Linsang, Loris, Lynx, Manatee, Margay, Marten, Meerkat, Mongoose, Monotreme, Musteline, Numbat, Olungo, Otter, Pachyderm, Pangolin, Peccary, Pekan, Perissodactyl, Pika, Pine marten, Pinniped, Platypus, Polecat, Porpoise, Primate, Pronghorn, Pudu, Raccoon, Rasse, Rhytina, Sable, Shrew, Sirenian, Skunk, Sloth, Solenodon, Springhaas, Taguan, Tahr, Takin, Tamandu(a), Tanrec, Tapir, Tayra, Teledu, Tenrec, Theria(n), Titanothere, Tylopod, Uintathere, Vicuna, Viverrid, Weasel, Whale, Wolverine, Zorilla

Mammon Money, Riches, Wealth

Mammoth Epic, Gigantic, Huge, Jumbo, Mastodon, Whopping, Woolly

Man(kind) Ask(r), Best, Betty, Bimana(l), Biped, Bloke, Bo, Boxgrove, Boy, Cad, Cairn, Calf, Castle, Cat, Chal, Chap, Checker, Chequer, Chiel, Cockey, Cod, Contact, Continuity, Crew, Cro-Magnon, Cuffin, Cully, Dog, Don, Draught, Dude, Emmanuel, Essex, Everyman, Family, Fancy, Fella, Feller, Fellow, Folsom, Friday, Front, G, Gayomart, Geezer, Gent, Grimaldi, Guy, He, Heidelberg, Himbo, Hombre, Hominid, Homme, Homo, Homo sapiens, Inner, IOM, Iron, Isle, Jack, Java, Joe (Bloggs), Joe Blow, Joe Sixpack, John(nie), John Doe, Josser, Limit, Lollipop, M, Male, Medicine, Microcosm, Mister,

Mon, Mondeo, Mr, Muffin, Mun, Neanderthal, Nutcracker, Oreopithecus, Organisation, Ou, Paleolithic, Party, Pawn, Peking, Person, Piece, Piltdown, Pin, Pithecanthropus, Property, Raff, Remittance, Renaissance, Resurrection, Rhodesian, Right-hand, Rook, Sandwich, Servant, Servitor, Ship, Sinanthropus, Sodor, Soldier, Solo, Spear, Staff, Stag, Straw, Third, Thursday, Trinil, Twelfth, Tyke, Type, Utility, Valet, Vir, White van, Wight

Man-about-town Boulevardier

Manacle Fetter, Handcuff, Iron, Shackle

Manage(r), Manageable, Management, Managing Adhocracy, Administer, Agent, Amildar, Attain, Aumil, Behave, Boss, Chief, Come by, Conduct, Contrive, Control, Cope, Darogha, Direct, Docile, Exec(utive), Fare, Fend, Find, Floor, Fund, Gerent, Get by, Govern, Grieve, Handle, Head bummer, Honcho, IC, Impresario, Intendant, Line, Logistical, MacReady, Maitre d('hotel), Manipulate, Manoeuvre, Middle, Nomenklatura, Organise, Proctor, Procurator, Regisseur, Rig, Roadie, > RUN, Scrape, Shift, Steward, Succeed, Suit, Superintend, Swing, Tawie, Top, Tractable, Transact, Treatment, Trustee, Wangle, Wield(y), Yare

Manatee Lamantum, Mermaid, Sea-ape

Manchu Fu

Mandarin Bureaucrat, Chinaman, Kuo-Yu, Nodding, Satsuma, Yamen

Mandate Authority, Decree, Fiat, Order

Mandrake Springwort

Mandrel Triblet

Mane(d), Manes Crest, Encolure, Jubate, Larva(e), Shades

Manege Horseplay, Train

Manganese Mn, Synadelphite, Wadd

Manger Cratch, Crib, Hack, Stall

Mangle Agrise, Butcher, Distort, Garble, Hack, Hackle, Haggle, Wring(er)

▷ **Mangle** *may indicate* an anagram

Mango Dika

Manhandle Frogmarch, Maul, Rough

Manhater Misanthrope

Manhattan Bowery

Mania Cacoethes, Craze, Frenzy, Passion, Rage

Manichaean Albi

Manifest(ation), Manifestly Attest, Avatar, Epiphany, Evident, Evince, Exhibit, Extravert, Extrovert, Feat, List, Marked, Mode, Notably, Obvious, Open, Show

Manifesto Plank, Platform, Policy, Pronunciamento

Manifold(ness) Many, Multeity, Multiple

Manila Abaca, Cheroot

Manioc Cassava

Maniple Fannel, Fanon

Manipulate, Manipulative, Manipulator, Manipulation Chiropractor, Cog, Control, Cook, Demagogic, Diddle, Fashion, Finagle, Gerrymander, Handle, Jerrymander, Juggle, Legerdemain, Logodaedalus, Masseuse, Osteopath, Play off, Ply, Rig, Tweeze, Use, Wangle, > WIELD

▷ **Manipulate** *may indicate* an anagram

Manna Alhagi, Food, Trehala, Turkish

Manner(ism), Mannerly, Manners Accent, A la, Appearance, Attitude, Bedside, Behaved, Behaviour, Bon ton, Breeding, Carriage, Conduct, Couth, Crew, Custom, Deportment, Ethos, Etiquette, Farand, Farrand, Farrant, Habit, How, Mien, Mister, Mode, Morality, Mores, Of, Ostent, Panache, Politesse,

Presentation, P's & Q's, Quirk, Rate, Sort, Style, Table, Thew(s), Thewe(s), Trick, Upsee, Upsey, Upsy, Urbanity, Way, Wise

Manoeuvre(s) Campaign, Castle, Christie, Christy, Engineer, Exercise, Faena, Fianchetto, Fork, Gambit, Half-board, Heimlich, Hot-dog, Jink(s), Jockey, Manipulate, Op(eration), Pendule, Pesade, Ploy, Renversement, Ruse, Skewer, Use, U-turn, Valsalva, Wear, Wheelie, Whipstall, Wile, Zigzag

Manoeuvre *may indicate* an anagram

Man-of-war Armada, Bluebottle, Destroyer, Ironclad, Portuguese

Manor (house) Area, Demain, Demesne, Estate, Hall, Kelmscott, Vill(a), Waddesdon

Mansion Casa, Knole, Luton Hoo, Mentmore, Penshurst Place, Queen's House, Seat, Stourhead, Stowe

Mantle Asthenosphere, Authority, Burnous(e), Capote, Caracalla, Chlamydate, Dolman, Elijah, Gas, Pall, Pallium, Paludament, Pelisse, Rochet, Sima, Toga, Tunic, Veil

Mantuan Maro, Virgil

Manual Blue collar, Bradshaw, Cambist, Console, Enchiridion, Great (organ), Guide, Hand, Handbook, How-to, Portolan(o), Positif, Sign

Manufacture, Manufacturing Fabricate, Industrial, Kanban, Make, Produce

Manure Compost, Dressing, Dung, Fertiliser, Green, Guano, Hen-pen, Lime, Muck, Sha(i)rn, Tath

Manuscript(s) Book of Kells, Codex, Codicology, Folio, Hand, Holograph, Longhand, Miniscule, MS, Opisthograph, Palimpsest, Papyrus, Parchment, Script, Scroll, Scrowl(e), Vellum

Manx(man) Cat, IOM, Kelly, Kelt

Manx *may indicate* a last letter missing

Many C, CD, Countless, D, Hantle, Herd, Horde, Host, L, Lot, M, Manifold, Mony, Multi(tude), Myriad, Scad, Sight, Stacks, Tons, Umpteen

Many *may indicate* the use of a Roman numeral letter

Maoist Naxatile, Red Guard

Maori (house) Hauhau, Hori, Mallowpuff, Moa hunter, Tangata whenua, Te reo, Wahine, Whare

Map(ping) Atlas, Card, Cartogram, Chart, Chorography, Chromosome, Cognitive, Contour, Digital, Face, Genetic, Inset, Key, Loxodromic, Mappemond, Mental, Mosaic, Moving, Mud, OS, Perceptual, Plan, Plot, Relief, Road, Sea-card, Sea-chart, Strip, Topography, Weather

Maple Acer, Flowering, Manitoba, Mazer, Norway, Plane, Silver, Sugar, Sycamore, Syrup

Map-maker Cartographer, OS, Speed

Maquis Queach, Underground

Mar Blight, Denature, Dere, Impair, Soil, Spoil, Taint

Marabout Sofi, Sufi

Marathon Comrades, Huge, London, Race, Two Oceans

Marauder Amalekite, Attacker, Bandit, Pillager, Pirate, Predator, Prowler

Marble(s), Marbling Aeginetan, Agate, All(e)y, Arch, Arundelian, Bonce, Bonduc, Bool, Boondoggle, Bowl, Carrara, Chequer, Cipollino, Commoney, Devil's, Dump, Elgin, Humite, Hymettus, Knicker, Languedoc, Lucullite, Marl, Marmarosis, Marmoreal, Marver, Mottle, Nero-antico, Nickar, Nicker, Onychite, Onyx, Paragon, Parian, Pavonazzo, Pentelic(an), Petworth, Phigalian, Plonker, Plunker, Purbeck, Rance, Ringer, Ring-taw, Ruin, Sanity, Scagliola, Spangcockle, Taw, Variegate, Xanthian

Marcel Proust

March(ing) Abut, Adjoin, Advance, Anabasis, Border(er), Borderland, Dead, Defile, Demo, Etape, File, Footslog, Forced, Freedom, Fringe, Galumph, Go, Goosestep, Hikoi, Hunger, Ides, Jarrow, Lide, Limes, Lockstep, Long, Meare, Music, > PARADE, Procession, Progress, Protest, Quick, Rogue's, Route, Slow time, Step, Strunt, Strut, Trio, Tromp, Wedding, Yomp

▷ **March** *may indicate* 'Little Women' character, Amy, Beth, Jo, Meg

Marco Il Milione, Polo

Mare Dam, Flanders, Horse, M, MacCurdle's, Shanks's, Spanish, Yaud

Margaret Anjou, Meg, Peg, Rita

Margarine Oleo

Marge, Margin(al) Annotate, Border, Brim, Brink, Curb, Edge, Fimbria, Hair's breadth, Kerb, Lean, Leeway, Limit, Lip, Littoral, Neck, Nose, Peristome, Profit, Rand, Repand, > RIM, Selvedge, Sideline, Tail, Term

Marginal note Apostil(le), K'ri

Margosa Melia, Nim

Maria(nne) France, Tia

Marie Dressler, Tempest

Marigold Calendula, Kingcup, Tagetes

Marijuana Alfalfa, Camberwell carrot, Dagga, Gage, Ganja, Grass, Greens, Gungeon, Ha-ha, Hay, Herb, Jive, Kaif, Kef, Kif, Leaf, Locoweed, Mary-Jane, Pot, Roach, Rope, Shit, Sinsemilla, Splay, Spliff, Tea, Toke, Weed

Marina Wharf

Marine (creature) Aquatic, Bootie, Bootneck, Cephalopod, Chaetognath, Cnidarian, Coelenterate, Comatulid, Ctenophora, Cunjevoi, Enteropneusta, Flustra, Foram(inifer), Galoot, Graptolite, Harumfrodite, Hemichorda, Holothurian, Horse, Hydrocoral, Hydroid, Hydromedusa, Jolly, Leatherneck, Lobster, Mercantile, Mere-swine, Mistress Roper, Oceanic, Physalia, Pollywag, Pollywog, Salpa, Sea-soldier, Seston, Thalassian, Ultra

Mariner AB, Ancient, MN, Noah, RM, Sailor, Salt, Seafarer, Spacecraft, Tar

Marionette(s) Fantoccini, Puppet

Marjoram Amaracus, Origan, Pot, Sweet, Wild, Winter-sweet

Mark(ing), Marked, Marks Accent, Antony, Apostrophe, Asterisk, Astrobleme, Badge, Banker, Bethumb, Birth, Blaze, Blot, Blotch, Brand, Bruise, Bull, Butt, Cachet, Caract, Caret, Caste, CE, Cedilla, Charter, Chequer, Cicatrix, Class, Clout, Colon, Comma, Coronis, Crease, Criss-cross-row, Dash, Denote, Dent, Diacritic, Diaeresis, Dieresis, Distinction, DM, Duckfoot quote, Ensign, Enstamp, Exclamation, Expression, Feer, Fleck, Glyph, Gospel, Grade, Guillemet, Hacek, Hair-line, Hash, Hatch, Heed, High water, Hyphen, Impress(ion), Indicium, Ink, Inscribe, Insignia, Interrogation, Keel, Kite, Kumkum, Lentigo, Line, Ling, Livedo, Logo, Lovebite, Low water, M, Macron, MB, Merk, Mottle, NB, Notal, Note, Notice, Obelisk, Observe, Oche, Paginate, Paraph, Period, Pilcrow, Pit, Plage, Pling, Point, Popinjay, Port wine, Post, Presa, Printer's, Proof, Punctuation, Question, Quotation, Record, Reference, Register, Regulo, Ripple, Roundel, Sanction, Scar, Score, Scratch, Section, See, Service, Shadow, Shilling, Sigil, Sign, Smit, Smut, Smutch, Speck, Splodge, Splotch, Stain, Stencil, Stigma(ta), Strawberry, Stress, Stretch, Sucker, Swan-upping, Symbol, Tag, Target, Tatow, Tattoo, Tee, Theta, Thread, Tick, Tika, Tikka, Tilak, Tilde, Tittle, Token, Touchmark, Trace, Track, Trout, Tug(h)ra, Twain, Umlaut, Ure, Victim, Wand, Warchalking, Watch, Weal, Wel

Marker Bollard, Buck, Cairn, Fanion, Flag, Ink, Inukshuk, Label, Scorer, Tie

Market(ing), Market day, Market place Agora, Alcaiceria, Baltic, Bazaar, Bear, Billingsgate, Black, Borgo, Bull, Buyer's, Capital, Captive, Cattle, Change,

Chowk, Common, Denet, Direct, Discount, Dragon, EC, Emerging, Emporium, Errand, Exchange, Fair, Feeing, Flea, Forum, Forward, Free, Grey, Growth, Internal, Kerb, Lloyds, Main, Mandi, Mart, Mercat, Money, Niche, Nundine, Open, Outlet, Piazza, Relationship, Sale, Sellers', Share, Shop, Single, Social, Sook, Souk, Spot, Stance, Staple, Stock, Stock Exchange, Tattersall's, Terminal, Test, Third, Tiger, Trade, Tron, Tryst, Vent, Viral, Wall Street

Marksman Sharpshooter, Shootist, Shot, Sniper, Tell

Marlborough Blenheim

Marlene Lilli

Marmalade Cat, Mammee-sapota, Preserve, Squish

Marmoset Jacchus, Mico, Midas, Monkey, Wistiti

Marmot Bobac, Bobak, Dassie, Groundhog, Hoary, Hyrax, Rodent, Whistler, Woodchuck

Maroon Brown, Castaway, Enisle, Firework, Inisle, Isolate, Strand

Marquee Pavilion, Tent, Top

Marquess, Marquis Granby, Lorne, Sade

Marquetry Boul(l)e, Buhl, Inlay

Marriage > ALLIANCE, Bed, Beenah, Bigamy, Bridal, Buckle-beggar, Civil, Coemption, Common law, Confarreation, Conjugal, Connubial, Coverture, Digamy, Endogamy, Espousal, Exogamy, Gandharva, Genial, Group, Hedge, Hetaerism, Hetairism, Hymen(eal), Jugal, Ketubah, Knot, Levirate, Match, Mating, Matrilocal, Matrimony, Mésalliance, Mixed, Monandry, Monogamy, Morganatic, Noose, Nuptial, Open, Pantagamy, Patrilocal, Punalua, Putative, Sacrament, Shidduch, Shotgun, Tie, Trial, > UNION, Wedding, Wedlock

Marriageable Marrow, Nubile, Parti

Marriage-broker Shadchan

Marrow Courgette, Friend, Gist, Medulla, Myeloid, Pith, Pumpkin, Squash, Vegetable

Marry, Married Ally, Amate, Buckle, Cleek(it), Confarreate, Couple, Coverture, Espouse, Feme covert, Forsooth, Goody, Hitch, Join, Knit, M, Mate, Matron, Memsahib, Pair, Pardie, Quotha, Splice, Tie, Troggs, Troth, Unite, W, Wed, Wive

Mars Areography, Ares, Red (planet)

Marsh(y) Bayou, Bog, Chott, Corcass, Emys, Everglades, Fen, Hackney, Maremma, Merse, Mire, Morass, Ngaio, Paludal, Plashy, Pontine, Pripet, Quagmire, Romney, Salina, Salt, Shott, Slade, Slough, Sog, Spew, Spue, Swale, Swamp, Taiga, Terai, Vlei, Wetlands

Marshal Arrange, Array, Commander, Earp, Foch, French, Hickok, MacMahon, Muster, Neil, Ney, Order, Pétain, Provost, Shepherd, Tedder, Usher, Yardman

Marshmallow Althaea, Mallowpuff

Marsupial Bandicoot, Bilby, Cuscus, Dasyure, Dibbler, Didelphia, Diprotodont, Dunnart, Honey mouse, Honey possum, Kangaroo, Koala, Macropod, Metatheria, Notoryctes, Nototherium, Numbat, Opossum, Pad(d)ymelon, Pademelon, Petaurist, Phalanger, Polyprodont, Possum, Potoroo, Pouched mouse, Pygmy glider, Quokka, Quoll, Roo, Tammar, Tasmanian devil, Theria, Thylacine, Tuan, Wallaby, Wambenger, Wombat, Yapo(c)k

Marten Fisher, Mustela, Pekan, Pine, Sable, Woodshock

Martha Vineyard

Martial (arts) Bellicose, Budo, Capoeira, Capuera, Chopsocky, Dojo, Iai-do, Judo, Ju-jitsu, Karate, Kick boxing, Kung Fu, Militant, Muay thai, Ninjutsu, Shintaido, Tae kwon do, T'ai chi (chuan), Warlike, Wushu

Martin Bird, Luther, Swallow

Martinet Captious, Ramrod, Stickler

Martini® Cocktail, Henry

Martyr(dom), Martyrs Alban, Alphege, Colosseum, Donatist, Justin, Latimer, Metric, MM, Passional, Persecute, Sebastian, Stephen, Suffer, Tolpuddle, Wishart

Marvel(lous) Bodacious, Bully, Epatant, Fab, Lulu, Magic, Marl, Miracle, Mirific, Phenomenon, Prodigious, Superb, Super-duper, Swell, Terrific, Wonder

Marx(ism), Marxist Aspheterism, Chico, Comintern, Commie, Groucho, Gummo, Harpo, Karl, Menshevik, Revisionism, Tanky, Tipamaro, Zeppo

Mary Bloody, Celeste, Madonna, Moll, Morison, Our Lady, Tum(my), Typhoid, Virgin

Marylebone Station

Marzipan Marchpane

Mascara Eye-black

Masculine, Masculinity He, He-man, Linga(m), M, Machismo, Macho, Male, Manly, Virile

Maser Laser

Mash(er) Beat, Beau, Beetle, Brew, Lady-killer, Pap, Pestle, Pound, Sour, Squash

Mask(ed) Bird cage, Camouflage, Cloak, Cokuloris, Death, Disguise, Dissemble, Domino, False face, Gas, Hide, Larvated, Life, Loo, Loup, Mascaron, Matte, Oxygen, Persona, Respirator, Screen, Semblance, Shadow, Stalking-horse, Stocking, Stop out, Template, Visor, Vizard

Mason(ry) Ashlar, Ashler, Brother, Builder, Cowan, Emplecton, Isodoma, Isodomon, Lodge, Moellon, Nogging, Opus, Perry, Random, Squinch, Stylobate

Masque(rade), Masquerader Comus, Domino, Guisard, Mum(m), Pose, Pretend

Mass(es) Aggregate, Agnus dei, Anniversary, Banket, Bezoar, Bike, Body, Bulk, Cake, Chaos, Clot, Congeries, Conglomeration, Consecration, Core, Crith, Critical, Crowd, Demos, Density, Flake, Flysch, Folk, Geepound, Gravitational, Great, Herd, High, Horde, Hulk, Inertial, Jud, Kermesse, Kermis, Kilo(gram), Kirmess, Low, Lump, M, Majority, Missa, Month's mind, Mop, Nest, Phalanx, Pile, Plumb, Pontifical, Populace, Proper, Raft, Requiem, Rest, Ruck, Salamon, Salmon, Scrum, Sea, Serac, Service, Shock, Sicilian, Size, Slub, Slug, Solar, Solemn, Solid, Stack, Stroma, Sursum corda, Te Igitur, Tektite, Trental, Vesper, Vigil, Volume, Wad, Weight, Welter

Massacre Amritsar, Blood-bath, Butcher, Carnage, Glencoe, Havock, Manchester, Peterloo, Pogrom, Purge, St Bartholomew's Day, Scullabogue, Scupper, September, Sicilian vespers, Slaughter, Slay, Wounded Knee

Massage, Masseur An mo, Chafer, Do-in, Effleurage, Hellerwork, > **KNEAD**, Malax, Palp, Petrissage, Physio, Rolf(ing), Rubber, Shampoo, Shiatsu, Stone, Stroke, Swedish, Tapotement, Thai, Tripsis, Tui na

Massive Big, Bull, Colossal, Gargantuan, Heavy, Herculean, Huge, Monumental, Strong, Titan

Mast(ed), Masthead Acorn, Banner, Captain's, Crosstree, Flag, Foretop, High top, Hounds, Jigger, Jury, M, Mizzen, Mooring, Pannage, Pole, Racahout, Royal, Ship-rigged, Spar, Top-gallant, Truck, Venetian

Master(ly) Artful, Baalebos, Baas, Beak, Beat, Boss, Buddha, Bwana, Careers, Checkmate, Conquer, Control, Dan, Dominate, Dominie, Employer, Enslave, Exarch, Expert, Gov, Grand, Harbour, Herr, Himself, International, Learn, Lord, MA, Maestro, Mas(s), Massa, Mes(s), Nkosi, Old, Ollamh, Ollav, Oner, Oppress, Original, Overcome, Overlord, Overpower, Overseer, Passed, Past, Pedant, Rabboni, Seigneur, Seignior, Signorino, Sir(e), Skipper, > **SUBDUE**, Subjugate,

Superate, Surmount, Swami, Tame, Task, Thakin, Towkay, Tuan, Usher, Vanquish, Virtuoso

Mastermind Brain, Conceive, Direct

Masterpiece Chef d'oeuvre, Creation

Master-stroke Coup, Triumph

Masturbate, Masturbation Abuse, Frig, Gratify, Jerk off, Jock, Onanism, Toss off, Wank, Whack off

Mat(ted), Matting Bast, Coaster, Doily, Dojo, Doyley, Felt, Inlace, Pad, Paunch, Place, Plat, Prayer, Rug, Table, Taggy, > TANGLE, Tat(ami), Tatty, Taut, Tawt, Tomentose, Welcome, Zarf

Matador Card, Espada, Ordonez, Theseus, Torero

Match(ed) Agree, Alliance, Amate, Balance, Besort, Bonspiel, Bout, Carousel, Compare, Congreve, Contest, Cope, Correlate, Correspond, Counterpane, Doubles, Emulate, Engagement, Equal(ise), Equate, Even, Exhibition, Fellow, Fit, Fixture, Four-ball, Friction, Friendly, Fusee, Fuzee, Game, Go, Greensome, International, Joust, Light, Locofoco, Love, Lucifer, Main, Marrow, Marry, Meet, Mouse, Needle, Pair(s), Paragon, Parti, Pit, Prizefight, Promethean, Reproduce, Return, Rival, Roland, Rubber, Safety, Shield, Singles, Slanging, Slow, Spunk, Striker, Suit, Sync, > TALLY, Team, Test, Tie, Twin, Union, Venue, Vesta, Vesuvian, Wedding

Matchbox label (collecting) Phillumeny

Match girl Bride

Match-holder Lin(t)stock

Matchless Non(e)such, Orinda

Matchmaker Blackfoot, Broker, Pairer, Promoter, Shadchan

Mate, Mating Achates, Adam, Amigo, Amplexus, Bedfellow, Bo, Breed, Buddy, Buffer, Butty, Check, Chess, China, Chum, Cobber, Cock, Comrade, Consort, Crony, Cully, Digger, Eve, Feare, Feer, Fellow, Fere, Fiere, First, Fool's, Husband, Ilex, Maik, Make, Marrow, Marry, Match, Mister, Nick, Oldster, Oppo, > PAIR, Pal, Panmixia, Panmixis, Paragon, Partner, Pheer(e), Pirrauru, Running, Scholar's, Second, Serve, Sex, Skaines, Smothered, Soul, > SPOUSE, Tea, Wack, Wacker, Wife, Wus(s)

Material Agalmatolite, Aggregate, Agitprop, Apt, Armure, Ballast, Blastema, Bole, Borsic, Byssus, Celluloid, Cellulose, Ceramic, Cermet, > CLOTH, Cob, Compo, Copy, Corfam®, Corporeal, Data, Documentation, Earthy, > FABRIC, Factual, Fallout, Fettling, Fibrefill, Fibreglass, Fines, Flong, Frit(t), Fuel, Gang(ue), Germane, Hylic, Illusion, Illuvium, Interfacing, Lambskin, Macintosh, Matter, Metal, Oilskin, Papier-maché, Pertinent, Physical, Pina-cloth, Plasterboard, Positive, Pug(ging), Raw, Relevant, Sackcloth, Sagathy, Skirting, Stuff, Substance, Swish, Tangible, Tape, Textile, Thingy, Towelling, Tusser, Wattle and daub

Materialise Appear, Apport, Click, Reify

Materialist(ic) Banausian, Hylist, Hyloist, Philistine, Somatist

Mathematician Apollonius, Archimedes, Archytas, Bernoulli, Bessel, Boole, Briggs, Cantor, Cocker, Descartes, Diophantus, Dunstable, Eratosthenes, Euclid, Euler, Fermat, Fibonacci, Fourier, Gauss, Godel, Goldbach, Gunter, Hawking, Laplace, Leibniz, Lie, Mercator, Napier, Newton, Optime, Pascal, Penrose, Playfair, Poisson, Ptolemy, Pythagoras, Pytheas, Riemann, Torricelli, Turing, Wrangler, Zeno

Mathematics, Mathematical, Maths Algebra, Applied, Arithmetic, Arsmetrick, Calculus, Geometry, Higher, Logarithms, Mechanics, New, Numbers, Porism, Pure, Topology, Trig, Trigonometry

Matilda Liar, Swag, Untruthful, Waltzing
Matinee Coat, Idol, Show
Mating Pangamy
Matins Nocturn
Matricide Orestes
Matrimony Bed, Conjugal, Marriage, Sacrament, Spousal, Wedlock
Matrix Active, Array, Boston, Hermitian, Jacobian, Mould, Orthogonal, Pattern
   Scattering, Square, Uterus
Matron Dame, Hausfrau, Lucretia, Nurse, Warden
Matt(e) Dense, Dingy, Dull
Matter Alluvium, Bioblast, Biogen, Body, Concern, Consequence,
   Dark, Degenerate, Empyema, Epithelium, Gear, Gluon, Go, Grey, Hyle,
   Impost(h)ume, Issue, Mass, Material, Molecule, Phlegm, Pith, Point, Positron,
   Protoplasm, Pulp, Pus, Quark, Reck, Reke, Scum, Shebang, Signify, Solid,
   Subject, > **SUBSTANCE**, Thing, Topic, Tousle, Touzle, White, Ylem
Matthew Arnold
Mattress Bed(ding), Biscuit, Dutch, Featherbed, Foam, Futon, Lilo®, Pallet,
   Palliasse, Spring, Tick
Mature, **Maturity** Adult, Age, Blossom, Bold, Concoct, Develop, Mellow,
   Metaplasis, Old, Puberty, Ripe(n), Rounded, Seasoned, Upgrow(n)
Maudlin Fuddled, Mawkish, Sentimental, Sloppy, Too-too
Maul Hammer, Manhandle, Paw, Rough
Maundy Money, Nipter, Thursday
Mauretanian, **Mauritania(n)** Moor, RIM
Mausoleum Helicarnassus, Mole, Sepulchre, Taj Mahal, Tomb
Mauve Lilac, Mallow, Perkin's
Maverick Misfit, Nonconformist, Rogue
Mavis Throstle
Maw Crop, Gorge, Gull(et), Oesophagus
Mawkish Sickly
Maxim Adage, Aphorism, Apo(ph)thegm, Axiom, Byword, Gnome, Gorki, Gun,
   Hiram, Moral, Motto, Proverb, Restaurateur, > **RULE**, Saw, Saying, Sentence,
   Sentiment, Watchword
Maximum All-out, Full, Highest, Most, Peak, Utmost
May Blossom, Can, Hawthorn, Merry, Might, Month, Mote, Quickthorn, Shall,
   Whitethorn
Maybe Happen, Mebbe, Peradventure, Percase, Perchance, Perhaps, Possibly
▷ **May become** *may indicate* an anagram
May day Beltane, SOS
Mayfair WI
Mayfly Ephemera, Ephemeroptera, Green-drake, Sedge
Mayhem Chaos, Crime, Damage, Havoc, Pandemonium
Mayonnaise Aioli, Rémoulade
Mayor Alcaide, Burgomaster, Casterbridge, Councilman, Porteeve, Provost,
   Whittington
Maze Labyrinth, Meander, Warren, Wilderness
MC Compere, Host, Ringmaster
MD Doctor, Healer
ME Yuppie flu
Me I, Mi
Mead(ow) Flood, Grass, Haugh, Hydromel, Inch, Lea(se), Ley, Meath(e),
   Metheglin, > **PASTURE**, Runnymede, Saeter, Salting, Water

Meadowsweet Dropwort

Meagre Bare, Exiguous, Measly, Paltry, Pittance, Scant, Scrannel, Scranny, Skimpy, Skinny, Spare, Sparse, Stingy, Thin

Meal(s) Banquet, Barbecue, Barium, Beanfeast, Blow-out, Board, Breakfast, Brunch, Buffet, Cassava, Cereal, Cholent, Chota-hazri, Collation, Corn, Cornflour, Cottoncake, Cottonseed, Cou-cou, Cribble, Dejeune(r), Deskfast, Dinner, Drammock, Ervalenta, Fare, Farina, Feast, Flour, Food, Grits, Grout, Hangi, High tea, Iftar, Indian, Lock, Lunch, Mandioc, Mandioc(c)a, Mani(h)oc, Matzo, Melder, Meltith, Mensal, Mess, Mush, No-cake, Nosh, Nuncheon, Obento, Ordinary, Picnic, Piece, Plate, Poi, Polenta, Porridge, Prandial, Prix fixe, Rac(c)ahout, Refection, Repast, Revalenta, Rijst(t)afel, Salep, Scambling, Scoff, Seder, Smorgasborg, Snack, Spread, Square, Supper, Table d'hote, Takeaway, Tea, Thali, Tiffin, Tightener, Twalhours, Undern

Meal-ticket LV

Mean(ing), Meant Aim, Arithmetic(al), Average, Base, Betoken, Bowsie, Caitiff, Connotation, Curmudgeon, Definition, Denotate, Denote, Design, Dirty, Drift, Essence, Ettle, Feck, Footy, Foul, Geometric(al), Gist, Golden, Hang, Harmonic, Humble, Hunks, Ignoble, Illiberal, Imply, Import, Inferior, Insect, Intend, Intermediate, Lexical, Low, Mang(e)y, Marrow, Medium, Mesquin, Method, Mid, Miserly, Narrow, Near, Norm, Nothing, One-horse, Ornery, Paltry, Par, Penny-pinching, Petty, Piker, Pinch-penny, Pith, Point, Purport, > **PURPOSE**, Quadratic, Ratfink, Revenue, Roinish, Roynish, Scall, Scrub, Scurvy, Semanteme, Semantic(s), Sememe, Sense, Shabby, Signify, Slight, Small, Sneaky, Snoep, Snot, Sordid, Sparing, Spell, Stingy, Stink(ard), Stinty, Substance, Symbol, Thin, Threepenny, Tightwad, Two-bit, Value, Whoreson

Meander Fret, Ring, Sinuate, Stray, Wander, Weave, Wind

Meaningless Ducdame, Empty, Hollow, Hot air, Insignificant, Nonny, Rumbelow

Means Agency, Dint, Income, Media, Method, Mode, Opulence, Organ, Private, Resources, Staple, Substance, Tactics, Visible, Ways, Wherewithal

Meantime, Meanwhile Among, Emong, Greenwich, Interim

Measles Morbilli, Roseola, Rose-rash, Rubella, Rubeola

Measure(d), Measuring, Measurement By(e)law, Calibre, Circular, Crackdown, > **DANCE**, Demarche, > **DIMENSION**, Distance, Dose, Dry, Gavotte, Gross, Imperial, Limit, Linear, Moratorium, Of, Offset, Precaution, Prophylactic, Quickstep, Ration, Share, > **SIZE**, Standard, Statute, Step, Strike, Struck, Survey, Token, Wine

MEASURES

2 letters:		4 letters:	
As	Erg	Acre	Foot
Em	Fat	Aune	Gage
En	Hin	Bath	Gill
Mu	Lay	Boll	Hide
	Lea	Bolt	Inch
	Ley	Comb	Koss
3 letters:	Log	Cord	Last
Are	Lug	Coss	Line
Bel	Mil	Cran	Link
Cab	Rod	Dram	Maze
Cor	Tot	Epha	Mete
Ell	Wey		Mile

Mole
Mott
Muid
Nail
Omer
Pace
Peck
Pint
Pole
Pood
Ream
Reau
Rood
Rope
Shot
Span
Tape
Thou
Unit
Vara
Volt
Warp
Yard

5 letters:
Anker
Ardeb
Barye
Bekah
Bigha
Caneh
Carat
Chain
Clove
Combe
Coomb
Crore
Cubit
Cumec
Cusec
Depth
Ephah
Fermi
Float
Gauge
Grain
Groma
Hanap
Homer
Joule
Kaneh
Lento

Liang
Ligne
Lippy
Loure
Mease
Meter
Metre
Optic®
Perch
Plumb
Quart
Romer
Ruler
Scale
Sound
Stade
Stere
Tesla
Therm
Toise
Verst
Wecht
Yojan

6 letters:
Albedo
Alnage
Arpent
Arshin
Barrel
Barren
Beegha
Bovate
Bushel
Chenix
Chopin
Cicero
Cubage
Denier
Double
Etalon
Fathom
Firkin
Firlot
Gallon
Height
Hemina
Jigger
Kelvin
Kilerg
League
Lippie

Liquid
Metage
Modius
Morgan
Noggin
Oxgang
Parsec
Pascal
Pottle
Radius
Runlet
Sazhen
Stadia
Tierce
Yojana

7 letters:
Aneroid
Arshine
Breadth
Burette
Caliper
Candela
Chalder
Choenix
Coulomb
Cyathus
Decibel
Drastic
Entropy
Furlong
Geodesy
Lambert
Leaguer
Pelorus
Quarter
Rundlet
Sleever
Spondee
Venturi
Virgate

8 letters:
Angstrom
Calliper
Carucate
Chaldron
Crannock
Desyatin
Diameter
Fistmele
Foot rule

Hogshead
Kilogray
Luxmeter
Mutchkin
Odometer
Oximeter
Parasang
Puncheon
Tape-line
Teraflop
Waywiser

9 letters:
Astrolabe
Bolometer
Cryometer
Decalitre
Decastere
Dosimeter
Ergometer
Eriometer
Kilometre
Lysimeter
Manometer
Mekometer
Nipperkin
Oenometer
Potometer
Steradian
Tappet-hen
Telemeter
Titration
Tonometer
Yardstick

10 letters:
Amphimacer
Anemometer
Barleycorn
Bathometer
Centimetre
Cyclometer
Densimeter
Dessiatine
Dessyatine
Drosometer
Eudiometer
Goniometer
Gravimeter
Humidistat
Hydrometer
Hygrometer

Lactometer
Micrometer
Millimetre
Opisometer
Photometer
Piezometer
Resistance
Touchstone
Tromometer

Winchester

11 letters:
Actinometer
Auxanometer
Colorimeter
Dioptometer
Dynamometer
Intoximeter

Jacob's staff
Stereometer
Venturi tube
Weighbridge

12 letters:
Cathetometer
Densitometer
Electrometer

Electronvolt
Extensimeter
Extensometer
Galactometer
Nephelometer
Tellurometer
Viscosimeter

Meat(s) Aitchbone, Bacon, Bard, Beef, Biltong, Brawn, Brisket, Brown, Burger, Cabob, Carbonado, Carrion, Charcuterie, Chop, Collop, Confit, Croquette, Cut, Devon, Easy, Edgebone, Entrecote, Escalope, Essence, Fanny Adams, Fleishig, Fleishik, Flesh, Flitch, Force, Galantine, Gigot, Gobbet, Gosht, Griskin, Ham, Haslet, Jerky, Joint, Junk, Kabab, Kabob, Kebab, Kebob, Lamb, Loin, Luncheon, Mart, Mince, Mutton, Noisette, Offal, Olive, Pastrami, Pem(m)ican, Piccata, Pith, Pork, Processed, Rack, Red, Rillettes, Roast, Saddle, Sasatie, Satay, Scaloppino, Schnitzel, Scran, Scrapple, Sey, Shashlik, Shishkebab, Side, Sirloin, Sosatie, Spam®, Spare rib, Spaul(d), Steak, Tenderloin, Tongue, Variety, Veal, Venison, Vifda, Virgate, Vivda, Weiner schnitzel, White, Wurst

Meatball(s) Cecils, Croquette, Faggot, Falafel, Felafel, Fricadel, Goujon, Knish, Kofta, Kromesky, Quenelle, Rissole

Meat extract Brawn, Gravy, Juice, Stock

Meatless Banian, Lent, Maigre, Vegetarian

Mecca Centre, Kaaba, Keblah, Kibla(h), Qibla

Mechanic(s) Apron-man, Artificer, Artisan, Banausic, Bottom, Engineer, Fitter, Fluid, Fundi, Grease monkey, Greaser, Hand, Journeyman, Kinematics, Kinetics, Newtonian, Operative, Quantum, Rock, Soil, Statics, Statistical, Technician, Wave

Mechanic(al) *may indicate* characters from 'A Midsummer Night's Dream'

Mechanical, Mechanism Action, Apparatus, Auto, Banausic, Defence, Derailleur, Escape, Escapement, Gimmal, Instrument, Machinery, Movement, Organical, Pulley, Pushback, Servo, Synchromesh, Trippet, Works

Medal(lion)(s) Award, Bar, Bronze, Congressional, Decoration, Dickin, DSM, GC, George, Gold, Gong, Gorget, Military, MM, Numismatic, Pan(h)agia, Purple Heart, Putty, Roundel, Silver, Tony, Touchpiece, VC, Vernicle

Meddle(r), Meddlesome Busybody, Dabble, Finger, Hen-hussy, > **INTERFERE**, Interloper, Marplot, Mell, Monkey, Officious, Potter, Pragmatic, Pry, Snooper, Spoilsport, Tamper, Tinker, Trifle

Media Mass, Mixed, New, PR

Mediate, Mediator ACAS, Arbitrate, Intercede, Interpose, Intervene, Liaison, Muti, Referee, Thirdsman, Trouble-shooter

Medical, Medicament, Medication, Medicine (chest) Allopathy, Alternative, Andrology, Anodyne, Antacid, Antibiotic, Antidote, Antisepsis, Antiseptic, Arnica, Asafetida, Ayurveda, Bi, Bismuth, Brunonian, Buchu, Bucku, Calumba, Carminative, Charm, Chiropody, Chlorodyne, Chrysarobin, Clinician, Complementary, Cordial, Corpsman, Cubeb, Curative, Defensive, Diapente, Diascordium, Diatessaron, Dose, Draught, Drops, > **DRUG**, Dutch drops, Electuary, Elixir, Emmenagogue, Empirics, Enema, Epulotic, Excipient, Expectorant, Fall-trank, Febrifuge, Feldsher, Folk, Forensic, Fringe, Galen, Galenism, Genitourinary, Gutta, Herb, Herbal, Hesperidin, Holistic,

Hom(o)eopathy, Horse-drench, Iatric(al), Imhotep, Industrial, Inhalant, Inro, Internal, Iodine, Ipecac(uanha), Iron, Ko cycle, Lariam®, Laxative, Leechcraft, Legal, Loblolly, Lotion, Magnesia, Menthol, Mishmi, Mixture, Moxar, Muti, Nephritic, Nervine, Nostrum, Nuclear, Nux vomica, Officinal, Oporice, Orthopoedics, Osteopath, Palliative, Panacea, Paregoric, Patent, Pathology, Pharmacy, Physic, Physical, Pill, Placebo, Polychrest, Posology, Potion, Poultice, Preparation, Preventive, Proctology, Psionic, Psychiatry, Quinacrine, Quinine, Quin(quin)a, Radiology, Relaxative, > **REMEDY**, Salve, Sanative, Sanguinaria, Senna, Serology, Simple, Space, Specific, Sports, Steel, Stomachic, Stramonium, Stupe, Suppository, Synergast, Syrup, Tabasheer, Tabashir, Tablet, Tar-water, Tetracycline, Therapeutics, TIM, Tisane, Tonic, Totaquine, Trade, Traditional Chinese, Traumatology, Treatment, Troche, Valerian, Veronal, Veterinary, Virology

Medicine man Koradji

Medick Snail

Medieval Archaic, Feudal, Gothic, Med, Old, Trecento

Mediocre Fair, Indifferent, Middling, Ordinary, Pap, Respectable, So-So, Undistinguished

Meditate, **Meditation**, **Meditator**, **Meditative** Brood, Chew, Cogitate, Gymnosophy, Hesychast, Muse, Mystic, Pensive, Ponder, Reflect, Reverie, Revery, Ruminate, Thanatopsis, Transcendental, Vipassana, Weigh, Yoga, Zazen

Mediterranean Levant, Midi

Medium Agency, Average, Channel, Clairvoyant, Contrast, Culture, Dispersive, Element, Ether, Even, Happy, Home, Intermediary, Interstellar, M, Magilp, Mean, Megilp, Midsize, Midway, Milieu, Oils, Organ, Ouija, Planchette, Press, Radio, Regular, Shaman, Spiritist, Spiritualist, Television, Telly, TV, Vehicle

Medley Charivari, Collection, Gallimaufry, Jumble, Macedoine, Melange, Mix, Pastiche, Patchwork, Pi(e), Pot-pourri, Quodlibet, Ragbag, Salad, Salmagundi, Series, Tat

▷ **Medley** *may indicate* an anagram

Medusa Planoblast

Meek Docile, Griselda, Humble, Milquetoast, Patient, Tame

Meerschaum Sepiolite

Meet(ing), **Meeting place** Abide, Abutment, AGM, Appointment, Apropos, Assemble, Assembly, Assignation, Audience, Baraza, Bosberaad, Camporee, Caucus, Chapterhouse, Chautauqua, Clash, Conclave, Concourse, Concur, Confluence, Confrontation, Congress, Connivance, Consistory, Consulta, Contact, Conterminous, Convene, Convent(icle), Convention, Converge, Conversazione, Convocation, Correspond, Cybercafé, Defray, Demo, EGM, Encounter, Ends, Experience, Face, Find, Fit, For(e)gather, Forum, Fulfil, Gemot, Giron, Gorsedd, Guild, Gyeld, Gymkhana, Gyron, Howf(f), Hunt, Hustings, Imbizo, Indaba, Infall, Interface, Interview, Join, Junction, Kgotla, Korero, Lekgotla, Liaise, Marae, Moot, Obviate, Occlusion, Occur, Oppose, Overflow, Pay, Plenary, Plenum, Pnyx, Pow-wow, Prayer, Prosper, Quadrivial, Quaker, Quorate, Quorum, Race, Races, Rally, Rencontre, Rencounter, Rendezvous, Reunion, Sabbat(h), Satisfy, Seance, See, Seminar, Session, Sit, Social, Sports, Suitable, Summit, Symposium, Synastry, Synaxis, Synod, Tackle, Talkfest, Town, Track, Tryst, Venue, Vestry, Wapinshaw, Wardmote, Wharepuni, Workshop

Megalith(ic) Sarsen, Skara Brae, Stonehenge

Megalomaniac Monarcho

Megaphone Bull-horn

Megapode Mound-bird, Talegalla

Meiosis Understatement

Melancholy, **Melancholic** Adust, Allicholy, Allycholly, Anatomy, Atrabilious, Cafard, Despond(ency), Dreary, Dump(s), Gloom, Heart-sore, Hipped, Hump, Hyp, Hypochondria, Jaques, Lienal, Pensieroso, Pensive, Saturnine, Sombre, Spleen, Splenetic, Triste, Tristesse, Weltschmerz

Melanesian Kanak

Mêlée Brawl, Commotion, Fracas, Rally, Salmagundi, Scrum

Melia Margosa, Neem, Nim

Mellifluent, **Mellifluous** Cantabile, Melodic

Mellow Fruity, Genial, Mature, Ripe, Smooth

Melodrama(tic) Bathos, Histrionic, Sensation, Transpontine

Melody, **Melodious** Air, Arioso, Cabaletta, Cantabile, Cantilena, Canto (fermo), Cantus, Conductus, Counterpoint, Descant, Dulcet, Euphonic, Fading, Musical, Orphean, Plainsong, Ranz-des-vaches, Refrain, Songful, Strain, Theme, Tunable, > **TUNE(S)**

Melon(like) Cantaloup(e), Cas(s)aba, Gourd, Honeydew, Mango, Musk, Nar(r)as, Ogen, Pepo, Persian, Rock, Spanspek, Winter

Melt(ed), **Melting** Ablate, Colliquate, > **DISSOLVE**, Eutectic, Eutexia, Flux, Found, Fuse, Fusil(e), Liquescent, Liquid, Run, Smectic, Syntexis, Thaw, Touch

Member Adherent, Arm, Branch, Bro(ther), Chin, Confrère, Cornice, Coulisse, Crossbeam, Crypto, Direction, Felibre, Fellow, Forearm, Forelimb, Founder, Gremial, Insider, Keel, Leg, Limb, Lintel, Longeron, M, MBE, Montant, MP, Organ, Part, Partisan, Private, Rood-beam, Soroptomist, Stile, Stringer, Strut, Syndic, Toe

Membrane, **Membranous** Amnion, Arachnoid, Axilemma, Caul, Cell, Chorioallantois, Chorion, Choroid (plexus), Chromoplast, Conjunctiva, Cornea, Cyst, Decidua, Dissepiment, Dura (mater), Endocardium, Endometrium, Endosteum, Ependyma, Exine, Extine, Film, Fr(a)enum, Frenulum, Haw, Hyaloid, Hymen, Indusium, Intima, Intine, Involucre, Mater, Mediastinum, Meninx, Mesentery, Mucosa, Mucous, Nictitating, Patagium, Pellicle, Pericardium, Pericarp, Perichondrium, Pericranium, Periost(eum), Periton(a)eum, Pia mater, Pleura, Putamen, Retina, Rim, Sarcolemma, Scarious, Schneiderian, Sclera, Serosa, Serous, Skin, Synovial, Tectorial, Tela, Third eyelid, Tissue, Tonoplast, Trophoblast, Tympan(ic), Vacuolar, Velamen, Velum, Vitelline, Web, Yolk-sac

Memento, **Memoir** Keepsake, Locket, Relic, Remembrancer, Souvenir, Token, Trophy

Memo(randum) Bordereau, Cahier, Chit, IOU, Jot, Jurat, Minute, Note, Notepad, > **REMINDER**

Memoirist Casanova

Memorable, **Memorise**, **Memory** Bubble, Cache, Catchy, Collective, Con, Core, Echoic, Engram(ma), Extended, Flash (bulb), Folk, Get, Historic, Iconic, Immortal, Immunological, Learn, Living, Long-term, Main, Memoriter, Mind, Mneme, Mnemonic, Mnemosyne, Non-volatile, Notable, Pelmanism, Photographic, RAM, Recall, Recovered, > **REMEMBER**, Retention, Retrospection, Ro(a)te, ROM, Samskara, Screen, Semantic, Short-term, Souvenir, Sovenance, Static, Virtual, Volatile, Word, Working

Memorial Cenotaph, Cromlech, Ebenezer, Gravestone, Hatchment, Headstone, Marker, Monument, Mount Rushmore, Obelisk, Plaque, Relic, Statue, Tomb, Trophy, War

▶ **Memory loss** *see* **LOSS OF MEMORY**

Men(folk) Amadoda, Chaps, Chess, Cuffins, Male, Mortals, OR, Race, Troops

Menace, Menacing Danger, Endanger, Foreboding, Minatory, Peril, Pest, Threat(en)

Menagerie Ark, Circus, Zoo

Mend Beet, Bete, Bushel, Cobble, Correct, Darn, Fix, Heal, Improved, Patch, Piece, Recover, Remedy, > **REPAIR**, Set, Sew, Solder, Trouble-shoot

Mendelevium Md

Mendicant Beggar, Fakir, Franciscan, Servite

Menial Bottlewasher, Drudge, Drug, Eta, Fag, Flunkey, Lowly, Scullion, Servile, Toady, Underling

Meninx (D)jerba

Menopause Andropause

Menstruation Menarche, Menses

Mental (condition), Mental disorder Alienism, Doolally, Eject, Hallucinosis, Insane, Noetic, Paranoia, Psychic

▷ **Mental** *may indicate* the chin

Mention(ed) Allusion, Bename, Benempt, Broach, Bynempt, Citation, Hint, Name, Notice, Quote, Refer, Speech, State, Suggest, Touch

Mentor Rebbe, Tutor

Menu Agenda, Card, Carte, Carte du jour, Cascading, Drop-down, Fare, List, Table d'hôte, Tariff

Mercantile Commercial, Trade

Mercator Cartographer

Mercenary Arnaout, Condottiere, Freelance, Greedy, Hack, Hessian, Hireling, Landsknecht, Legionnaire, Pindaree, Pindari, Rutter, Sordid, Spoilsman, Venal, Wildgeese

Merchandise Cargo, Goods, Line, Produce, Ware(s)

Merchant(man) Abudah, Antonio, Broker, Bun(n)ia, Burgher, Chandler, Chap, Crare, Crayer, Dealer, Factor, Flota, Hoastman, Importer, Jobber, Law, Magnate, Marcantant, Mercer, Monger, Négociant, Pedlar, Polo, Retailer, Shipper, Speed, Stapler, Sutler, Trader, Vintner, Wholesaler

Mercia Offa

Merciful, Mercy Amnesty, Charity, Clement, Compassionate, Corporal, Grace, Humane, Kind, Kyrie, Lenient, Lenity, Miserere, Misericord(e), Pacable, Pity, Quarter, Ruth, Sparing, Spiritual

Merciless Cruel, Hard, Hard-hearted, Inclement, Pitiless

Mercurial, Mercuric sulphide, Mercury Azoth, Cyllenius, Fulminating, Herald, Hermes, Hg, Horn, Hydrargyrum, Messenger, Quicksilver, Red-man, Spurge, Tiemannite, Volatile

Mere(ly) Allenarly, Bare, Common, Lake, Pond, Pool, Pure, Sheer, Tarn, Very

Merge(r), Merging Amalgamate, Blend, Coalesce, Conflate, Consolidate, Die, Elide, Fusion, Incorporate, Interflow, Liquesce, Meld, Melt, Mingle, Syncretism, Synergy, Unify, Unite

Meridian Magnetic, Noonday, Prime

Meringue Pavlova

Merit(ed) CL, Condign, Deserve, Due, Earn, Found, Rate, Virtue, Worth(iness)

Mermaid Dugong, Halicore, Merrow, Siren, Tavern, Undine

Merriment, Merry Andrew, Bonny, Boon, Cant, Cherry, Chirpy, Crank, Elated, Full, Gaudy, Gay, Gean, Gleesome, Greek, Jocose, Jocular, Jocund, Jolly, Joyous, L'allegro, Lively, Nitid, On, Page, Riant, Sportive, Sunny, Vogie, Waggery, Wassail

Merry Andrew Clown, Jack-pudding, Pickle-herring
Merry-go-round Carousel, Whirligig
Merry-making Cakes and ale, Carnival, Festivity, Gaiety, Gaud, Gawd, Revel
Merrythought Clavicle, Collarbone, Wishbone
Mesh Cancellate, Chain, Entangle, Net, Reseau
Mess(y) Balls-up, Bedraggled, Boss, Botch, Canteen, Caudle, Chaos, Clamper, Clutter, Cock-up, Failure, Farrago, Fiasco, Flub, Garboil, G(l)oop, Glop, Gory, Guddle, Gunge, Gunk, Gun-room, Hash, Horlicks, Hotch-potch, Hugger-mugger, Imbroglio, Lash-up, Louse, Mash, Meal, Mismanage, Mix, Mixter-maxter, Modge, Muck, Muff, Muss, Mux, Pi(e), Piss-up, Plight, Pollute, Pottage, Screw-up, Scungy, Shambles, Shambolic, Shemozzle, Sight, Slaister, Smudge, Snafu, Soss, Sty, Sully, Untidy, Wardroom, Whoopsie, Yuck(y)
Message(s) Aerogram, Bull, Bulletin, Cable, Contraplex, Dépêche, Despatch, Dispatch, Email, Errand, Error, Flame, Missive, News, Note, Pager, Posting, Postscript, Radiogram, Rumour, Signal, Slogan, SOS, Stripagram, Strippergram, Subtext, Telegram, Telephone, Telex, Text, Tidings, Wire, >WORD
Messenger Angel, Apostle, Azrael, Caddie, Caddy, Chaprassi, Chuprassy, Courier, Culver, Despatch-rider, Emissary, Envoy, Forerunner, Gaga, Gillie-wetfoot, Gillie Whitefoot, Hatta, Herald, Hermes, Internuncio, Iris, Ladas, Mercury, Nuncio, Page, Peon, Post, Pursuivant, Runner, Send, Shellycoat, Valkyrie
Messiah Christ, Emmanuel, Immanuel, Mahdi, Mashiach, Saviour, Son of man
Met Old Bill, Weather
Metabolism Basal
Metal(s), **Metallic**, **Metalware** Ag, Aglet, Aiglet, Aiguillette, Al, Aluminium, Antimony, Babbitt, Base, Bell, Billon, Brassy, Britannia, Cadmium, Chrome, Chromium, Cobalt, Copper, Death, Dutch, Dysprosium, Er(bium), Europium, Expanded, Filler, Foil, Fusible, Gallium, Germanium, Gib, Heavy, Hot, Ingot, Invar®, Iridium, Iron, Jangling, Leaf, Magnolia, Manganese, Mineral, Misch, Mitis, Monel(l), Muntz, Natrium, Nickel, Noble, Nonferrous, Ore, Osmium, Parent, Perfect, Planchet, Platinum, Precious, Prince's, Protore, Regulus, Rhenium, Road, Ruthenium, Samarium, Scrap, Sheet(-iron), Slug, Sm, Sn, Sodium, Speculum, Speiss, Sprue, Steel, Strontium, Taggers, Tantalum, Terbic, Terbium, Terne, Thallium, Thorium, Thrash, Tin, Tole, Tramp, Transition, Tutania, Tutenag, Type, White, Wolfram, Yellow, Zinc
Metal-worker Founder, Lorimer, Smith, Spurrier, Tubal Cain
Metamorphose Transmogrify
> **Metamorphosing** *may indicate* an anagram
Metamphetamine Ice
Metaphor Conceit, Figure, Image, Kenning, Malonym, Mixed, Symbol, Trope, Tropical
Metaphysics Ontology
Mete Inflict
Meteor(ic), **Meteorite** Achondrite, Aerolite, Aerosiderite, Bolide, Chondrite, Comet, Drake, Falling star, Fireball, Germinid, Leonid, Perseid, Quantrantid, Siderite, Siderolite, Star(dust), Stony, Tektite
Meter Alidad(e), Electric, Exposure, Gas, Light, Orifice, Parking, Postage, Postal, Torque, Torsion, Water, White
Methane Alkane
Methedrine Speed
Method(ology), **Methodical** Art, Billings, Buteyko, Direct, Feldenkrais,

Formula, Gram's, Historical, Hi-tec(h), Kenny, Line, Manner, Mode, Modus, Modus operandi, Monte Carlo, Montessori, Neat, Orderly, Ovulation, Painstaking, Ploy, Procedure, Process, Q, Rhythm, Schafer's, Scientific, Socratic, Stanislavski, > SYSTEM, Tactics, Technique, Way

Methodism, Methodist Huntingdonian, Jumper, Methody, Primitive, Ranter, Scientism, Southcottian, Swaddler, Wesley

Methuselah Bottle, Macrobiote

Meticulous Careful, > EXACT, Finicky, Minute, Precise, Punctilious, Quiddler, Scrupulous, Thorough

Metier Line, Trade, Vocation

Metre Alexandrine, Amphibrach, Amphimacer, Anapaest, Antispast, Arsis, Ballad, Cadence, Choliamb, Choree, Choriamb, Common, Dipody, Galliambic, Iambic, Long, M, Prosody, Rhythm, Sapphic, Scansion, Scazon, Service, Short, Spondee, Strophe, Tripody, Trochee

Metric (system) MKS

Metroland Subtopia

Metropolitan Eparch

Mettle Ardour, Bravery, Courage, Ginger, Guts, Pith, > PLUCK, Pride, Smeddum, Spirit, Spunk, Steel

Mew Caterwaul, Miaou, Miaow, Pen, Purr, Seagull, Waul, Wrawl

Mews Meuse, Muse(t), Musit, Stables

Mexican (Indian) Atlalt, Aztec, Carib, Chicano, Chichibec, Diaz, Greaser, Gringo, Hairless, Hispanic, Maya, Mixe-Zoque, Mixtec, Montezuma, Nahuatl, Nortéño, Olmec, Otomi, Pachuco, Spic, Spik, Taino, Toltec, Wetback, Zapotec, Zuni

Mezzanine Entresol

Mezzo-soprano Tessa

Mica Biotite, Daze, Fuchsite, Glimmer, Lepidolite, Lepidomelane, Muscovite, Paragonite, Phlogopite, Rubellan, Sericite, Talc, Verdite, Vermiculite

Micawber Wilkins

Mick(ey) Greek, Mouse

Micro Mu

Microbe, Microorganism Germ, Lactobacillus, Organism

Microphone Bug, Carbon, Crystal, Lavaliere, Lip, Mike, Radio, Ribbon, Throat

Microscope Compound, Confocal, Dissecting, Electron, Engyscope, Lens, Optical, Phase-contrast, Proton, Reflecting, SEM, Simple, Solar, TEM, Ultraviolet

Mid(st) Amongst, Mongst

Midas Goldinger, Tamarin

Midday Meridian, N, Noon, Noon-tide, Noon-time

Middle, Middling Active, Basion, Centre, Core, Crown, Enteron, Excluded, Eye, Girth, Heart, Loins, Median, Mediocre, Meridian, Meseraic, Mesial, Mesne, Meso, Midriff, Moderate, Noon, Passive, Turn, Twixt, Wa(i)st

Middle age Menopause

Middle-cambrian Menevian

Middle class Bourgeois, Hova

Middle Eastern Arab, Iraqi, Omani

Middleman Broker, Comprador(e), Diaphragm, Interlocutor, Intermediary, Jobber, Median, Navel, Regrater, Regrator

Middlesex Hermaphrodite

Midge Gall, Gnat

Midget Dwarf, Homunculus, Lilliputian, Pygmy, Shrimp

Midianite Prowler
Midlands Mercia
Midnight G, O am
Midnight *see* PAST MIDNIGHT
Midriff Phrenic, Skirt, Waist
Midshipman Brass-bounder, Easy, Middy, Oldster, Reefer, Snottie, Snotty
Midst *see* MID
Midwife Accoucheur, Doula, Gran(nie), Granny, Howdie, Howdy, Lucina, Mab, Obstetric
Mien Air, Bearing, Demean, Manner
Might(iness), Mighty Force, Main, Mote, Nibs, Potence, > POWER, Prowess, Puissant, Should, Strength
Mignon(ette) Dyer's rocket, Fillet, Reseda, Weld
Migraine Megrim, Scotodinia, Teichopsia
Migrant Externe, Gastarbeiter, Lemming, Traveller
Migrate, Migration, Migratory Colonise, Diapedesis, Diaspora, Drift, Eelfare, Exodus, Fleet, Great Trek, Run, Tre(c)k, Volkwanderung
Mikado Emperor, Kami
Mike Bug, Stentorphone
Milanese Patarine
Mild(ly) Balmy, Benign, Bland, Clement, Euphemism, Genial, Gentle, Lenient, Litotes, Mansuete, Meek, > MODERATE, Pacific, Patient, Sarcenet, Sars(e)net, Temperate
Mildew Downy, Foxing, Fungus, Mould, Oidium, Powdery, Vine
Mile(s) Admiralty, Coss, Coverdale, Food, Geographical, Knot, Kos, Li, Milliary, Nautical, Passenger, Roman, Royal, Sea, Soldier, Square, Standish, Statute, Swedish, Train
Milesian Teague
Milestone Milliary, MS
Milfoil Yarrow
Militant, Military Activist, Aggressive, Battailous, Black Panther, Commando, Hawkish, Hezbollah, Hizbollah, Hizbullah, Hostile, Ireton, Landwehr, Mameluke, Martial, Presidio, Provisional, Provo, Soldatesque, West Point
Militia Fyrd, Guard, Haganah, Minuteman, Reserve, Tanzim, Trainband, Yeomanry
Milk(er), Milky Acidophilus, Beestings, Bland, Bleed, Bonny-clabber, Bristol, Casein, Colostrum, Condensed, Creamer, Crud, Curd, Emulge, Evaporated, Exploit, Galactic, Glacier, Goat's, Jib, Kefir, Kephir, K(o)umiss, Lactation, Lacteal, Latex, Madzoon, Magnesia, Malted, Matzoon, Mess, Opaline, Pasteurised, Pinta, Posset, Raw, Sap, Semi-skimmed, Shedder, Skim(med), Soya, Squeeze, Strippings, Stroke, Suckle, UHT, Whig, Whole, Yaourt, Yogh(o)urt
Milking-machine, Milking parlour Loan, Tapper
Milking-pail Leglan, Leglen, Leglin
Milkless Agalactic, Dry, Eild
Milkmaid, Milkman Chalker, Dey, Emulge, Kefir, Kephir, Radha, Rounder, Roundsman, Skimmed
Milksop Coward, Meacock, Namby-pamby, Nance, Pance, Weakling
Milk-vetch Loco
Milkweed Asclepias
Milkwort Senega
Milky Way Via Lactea

Mill(ing), **Mills** Aswarm, Barker's, Boxing, Coffee, Economist, Gang, Gastric, Grind(er), Hayley, Kibble, Knurl, Mano, Melder, Molar, Nurl, Paper, Pepper, Post, Powder, Press, Pug, Quern, Reave, Rob, Rolling, Satanic, Scutcher, Smock, Stamp, Stamping, Strip, Sugar, Surge, Thou, Tide, Tower, Tuck, Water, Wool(len), Works

Miller Dusty, Glen, Grinder, Jester, Joe, Molendinar, Multurer

Millet Bajra, Bajree, Bajrii, Couscous, Dari, Dhurra, Doura, Dur(r)a, Grain, Miliary, Negro-corn, Pearl, Proso, Ragee, Raggee, Ragi, Whisk

Millionaire Astor, Carnegie, Rockefeller, Rothschild, Vanderbilt

Millions, **Millionth** Crore, Femto-, Milliard, Muckle, Pico-

Millipede Songololo

Millstone Ligger, Rind, Rynd

Mim Perjink

Mime, **Mimic(ry)** Ape, Batesian, Copycat, Farce, Imitate, Impersonate, Lipsync, Mina, Mullerian, Mummer, Parody, Sturnine

Mimosa Cacoon, Saman

Mince Cecils, Chop, Dice, Grate, Grind, Prance, Rice

Mind(er) Aide, Beware, Brain, Genius, Handler, > **HEED**, Herd, Id, Intellect, Noology, Noosphere, One-track, Phrenic, Psyche, Psychogenic, Resent, Sensorium, Tabula rasa, Tend, Thinker, Wit, Woundwort

Mine, **Mining** Acoustic, Antenna, Bomb, Bonanza, Bottom, Bouquet, Burrow, Camouflet, Chemical, Claymore, Colliery, Contact, Creeping, Dane-hole, Data, Dig(gings), Drifting, Egg, Eldorado, Excavate, Explosive, Floating, Flooder, Fougade, Fougasse, Gallery, Gob, Golconda, Gold, Gopher, Grass, Homing, Land, Limpet, Magnetic, Naked-light, Nostromo, Open-cast, Open-cut, Ophir, Pit, Placer, Pressure, Prospect, Rising, Sap, Set(t), Show, Sonic, Stannary, Stope, Strike, Strip, Undercut, Wheal, Win, Workings

Mine-deflector Otter, Paravane

Mine-owner Operator

Miner, **Mine-worker**, **Mine-working** Butty-gang, Collier, Continuous, Cutter, Digger, Forty-niner, Geordie, Leaf, Molly Maguire, NUM, Oncost(man), Pitman, Shot-firer, Stall, Tributer, UDM

Mineral Accessory, Essential, Index

MINERALS

3 letters:	Emery	Galena	Silica
YAG	Flint	Gangue	Sphene
	Fluor	Garnet	Spinel
4 letters:	Macle	Glance	Tincal
Gang	Mafic	Gypsum	Zircon
Mica	Nitre	Hauyne	
Sard	Prase	Illite	7 letters:
Spar	Topaz	Jargon	Alunite
Talc	Trona	Lithia	Anatase
Trap	Umber	Natron	Apatite
Urao		Nosean	Axinite
	6 letters:	Pinite	Azurite
5 letters:	Acmite	Pyrite	Barytes
Balas	Albite	Quartz	Biotite
Borax	Augite	Rutile	Bornite
Chert	Blende	Schorl	Brucite

Calcite
Calomel
Catseye
Cuprite
Cyanite
Diamond
Dysodil
Epidote
Euclase
Eucrite
Fahlore
Felspar
Gahnite
Göthite
Gummite
Hessite
Ice spar
Jadeite
Jargoon
Kainite
Kernite
Kyanite
Leucite
Mellite
Mullite
Nacrite
Olivine
Pennine
Peridot
Pyrites
Realgar
Rosaker
Sylvine
Sylvite
Thorite
Thulite
Tripoli
Turgite
Ulexite
Uralite
Uranite
Uranium
Zeolite
Zincite
Zoisite
Zorgite

8 letters:
Adularia
Allanite
Analcime
Analcite

Andesine
Ankerite
Antimony
Aphanite
Asbestos
Autunite
Blue john
Boehmite
Boracite
Braunite
Bronzite
Brookite
Calamine
Cerusite
Chlorite
Chromite
Cinnabar
Cleveite
Corundum
Crocoite
Cryolite
Datolite
Dendrite
Diallage
Diaspore
Disthene
Dolomite
Dysodile
Dysodyle
Epsomite
Erionite
Euxenite
Fayalite
Feldspar
Flinkite
Fluorite
Galinite
Gibbsite
Goethite
Gyrolite
Hematite
Idocrase
Ilmenite
Iodyrite
Jarosite
Lazulite
Lazurite
Lewisite
Limonite
Massicot
Meionite
Melilite

Mimetite
Monazite
Nephrite
Noselite
Orpiment
Petuntse
Picotite
Prehnite
Pyroxene
Resalgar
Rock-salt
Sanidine
Saponite
Siderite
Smectite
Sodalite
Stannite
Stibnite
Stilbite
Taconite
Tenorite
Titanite
Troilite
Xenotime
Zaratite

9 letters:
Alabaster
Allophane
Amazonite
Amphibole
Anglesite
Anhydrite
Anorthite
Aragonite
Argentite
Atacamite
Blackjack
Blacklead
Carnelian
Carnotite
Celestine
Celestite
Cerussite
Chabazite
Chalybite
Cheralite
Chondrule
Cobaltine
Cobaltite
Coccolite
Columbate

Columbite
Covellite
Cystolith
Dolomitic
Elaeolite
Endomorph
Enhydrite
Enstatite
Erythrite
Fibrolite®
Fluorspar
Gehlenite
Germanite
Geyserite
Gmelinite
Goslarite
Haematite
Harmotome
Hercynite
Hiddenite
Hornstone
Kaolinite
Kermesite
Kieserite
Magnetite
Malachite
Manganite
Marcasite
Margarite
Marialite
Microlite
Microlith
Millerite
Mispickel
Mizzonite
Moonstone
Muscovite
Natrolite
Nepheline
Nephelite
Niccolite
Nitratine
Olivenite
Ottrelite
Paramorph
Pargasite
Pectolite
Periclase
Pericline
Perimorph
Phenacite
Pleonaste

Polianite
Pollucite
Powellite
Proustite
Rhodonite
Rubellite
Scapolite
Scheelite
Scolecite
Spodumene
Sylvanite
Tantalite
Tremolite
Troostite
Tungstite
Uraninite
Uvarovite
Variscite
Vulpinite
Wavellite
Wernerite
Willemite
Witherite
Wulfenite
Zinkenite

10 letters:
Actinolite
Alabandine
Alabandite
Andalusite
Bastnasite
Calaverite
Carnallite
Chalcocite
Chessylite
Chrysolite

Colemanite
Cordierite
Crocoisite
Dyscrasite
Forsterite
Gadolinite
Garnierite
Glauconite
Halloysite
Heulandite
Honey-stone
Hornblende
Indicolite
Indigolite
Jamesonite
Laurdalite
Meerschaum
Microcline
Oligoclase
Orthoclase
Perovskite
Phosgenite
Polybasite
Polyhalite
Pyrolusite
Pyrrhotite
Redruthite
Riebeckite
Ripidolite
Samarskite
Sapphirine
Saussurite
Serpentine
Smaragdite
Sperrylite
Sphalerite
Staurolite

Tennantite
Thaumasite
Thenardite
Thorianite
Tiemannite
Torbernite
Tourmaline
Triphylite
Vanadinite
Wolframite

11 letters:
Alexandrite
Annabergite
Apophyllite
Baddeleyite
Bastnaesite
Cassiterite
Chiastolite
Chrysoberyl
Clinochlore
Crocidolite
Dendrachate
Franklinite
Greenockite
Hypersthene
Idiomorphic
Josephinite
Molybdenite
Pentlandite
Phosphorite
Piedmontite
Pitchblende
Plagioclase
Pseudomorph
Psilomelane
Pyrargyrite

Sillimanite
Smithsonite
Tetradymite
Vermiculite
Vesuvianite
Ythro-cerite

12 letters:
Adularescent
Arfvedsonite
Arsenopyrite
Babingtonite
Chalcanthite
Chalcopyrite
Cristobalite
Dumortierite
Feldspathoid
Fluorapatite
Hemimorphite
Pyromorphite
Pyrophyllite
Senarmontite
Skutterudite
Strontianite
Synadelphite
Tetrahedrite
Wollastonite

13 letters:
Cummingtonite
Rhodochrosite

15 letters:
Gooseberry-stone
Montmorillonite

Mineral water Apollinaris, Tonic
Minesweeper Oropesa, Unity
Mingle Blend, Circulate, Consort, Interfuse, Mell, > MIX, Participate, Socialise, Unite
Mini Cab, Car, Skirt, Teen(s)y
Miniature, Miniaturist Cosway, Microcosm, Midget, Model, Toy, Young
Minimise, Minimum (range) Bare, Downplay, Fewest, Least, Neap, Shoestring, Stime, Styme, Threshold, Undervalue
▷ **Minimum of** *may indicate* the first letter
Minion Flunkey, Lackey, Pet, Subordinate, Tool, Vassal
Minister Ambassador, Attend, Buckle-beggar, Cabinet, Chancellor, Chaplain, Cleric, Coarb, Commissar, Deacon, Dewan, Diplomat, Divine, D(i)wan, Dominee, Dominie, Envoy, First, Foreign, Holy Joe, Mas(s)john, Mes(s)john, Moderator, Nurse, Officiant, Padre, Parson, Pastor, Peshwa, Preacher,

Predikant, Presbyter, Prime, Rector, Secretary, Seraskier, > SERVE, Stickit, Subdeacon, Tend, Visier, Vizier, Wazir, Wizier

Ministry Defence, Department, Dept, DoE, MOD, MOT, Orders, Service

Mink Kolinsky, Mutation, Vison

Minnow Penk, Pink, Tiddler

Minoan Knossus

Minor(ity) Child, Comprimario, Ethnic, Faction, Few, Infant, Junior, Less, Minutia, Nonage, One-horse, Petty, Pupillage, Slight, Small-time, Trivial, Ward

Minotaur Bull-headed

Minstrel Allan-a-dale, Bard, Blondel, Bones, Busker, Cantabank, Christy, Cornerman, Gleeman, Hamfatter, Joculator, Jongleur, Minnesinger, Nigger, Pierrot, Scop, Singer, Taillefer

Mint Aim, Bugle-weed, Catnip, Coin, Ettle, Fortune, Herb, Horse, Humbug, Labiate, Monarda, Monetise, Nep, New, Penny-royal, Polo®, Poly, Royal, Selfheal, Stamp, Strike, Unused, Utter

Minute(s), Minutiae Acta, Alto, Degree, Detailed, Diatom, Entry, Infinitesimal, Little, Micron, Mo, Mu, Nano-, Pinpoint, Resume, Small, Teen(t)sy, Teeny, Tine, Tiny, Trivia, Tyne, Wee

Minx Hellion

Miracle, Miraculous Cana, Marvel, Merel(l), Meril, Morris, Mystery, Phenomenon, Supernatural, Thaumaturgic, Theurgy, Wirtschaftswunder, Wonder, Wonderwork

Mirage Fata morgana, Illusion, Loom, Northern lights

Mire Bog, Glaur, Lair(y), Latch, Lerna, Lerne, Loblolly, Marsh, Mud, Quag, Sludge, Soil

Mirky Dark, Dirk(e)

Mirror(ed) Alasnam, Busybody, Cambuscan, Catoptric, Cheval, Claude Lorraine glass, Coelostat, Conde, Dare, Enantiomorph, Glass, Image, Imitate, Lao, Magnetic, Merlin, One-way, Pierglass, Primary, Psyche, Rearview, > REFLECT, Reynard, Shisha, Siderostat, Sign, Specular, Speculum, Stone, Two-way, Vulcan, Wing

Mirror-image Perversion

Mirth(ful) Cheer, Dream, Festive, Hilarity, Joy, Laughter, Spleen

> **Misalliance** *may indicate* an anagram

Misanthrope Cynic, Timon

Misapplication Catachresis, Misuse

Misappropriate, Misappropriation Asport, Detinue, Purloin, Steal

Miscarry Abort, Backfire, Fail, Slink

Miscegenation Allocarpy

Miscellaneous, Miscellany Assortment, Chow, Collectanea, Diverse, Etceteras, Misc, Odds and ends, Odds and sods, Olio, Omnium-gatherum, Potpourri, Raft, Ragbag, Sundry, Varia, Variety, Various

Mischief(-maker), Mischievous Ate, Bale, Bane, Cantrip, Cloots, Devilment, Diablerie, Dido, Disservice, Gremlin, Harm, Hellery, Hellion, Hob, Imp, Injury, Jinks, Larrikin, Litherly, Malicho, Mallecho, Monkey-tricks, Nickum, Owl-spiegle, Pestilent, Pickle, Prank, Puckish, Rascal, Scally(wag), Scamp, Scapegrace, Shenanigans, Spriteful, Tricksy, Wag, Wicked, Widgie

Misconception Delusion, Idol(on), Idolum, Misunderstanding

Misconduct Impropriety, Malfeasance, Malversation

Miscreant Reprobate, Sinner

Misdeed Offence, Peccadillo, Trespass, Wrong

▷ **Misdelivered** *may indicate* an anagram

Misdemeanour Delict, Offence, Peccadillo, Tort, Wrongdoing

Miser(ly) Carl, Cheapskate, Cheese-parer, Close, Curmudgeon, Gare, Grasping, Harpagon, Hunks, Marner, Meanie, Mingy, Niggard, Nipcheese, Nipcurn, Nipfarthing, Pennyfather, Pinch-commons, Puckfist, Runt, Scrape-good, Scrape-penny, Screw, Scrimping, Scrooge, Skinflint, Snudge, Storer, Tightwad, Timon

Miserable, **Misery**, **Miserably** Abject, Angashore, Bale, Cat-lap, Crummy, Distress, Dole, Forlorn, Gloom, Grief, Hell, Joyless, Lousy, Perdition, Punk, Sad, Scungy, Sorry, Sourpuss, Tragic, Triste, > **UNHAPPY**, Woe(begone), Wretched

Misfire Dud

Misfit Drop-out, Geek, Loner, Maverick, Sad sack

Misfortune Accident, Affliction, Bale, Calamity, Curse, Disaster, Distress, Dole, Hex, Ill, Reverse, Rewth, Ruth, Wroath

Misgiving(s) Anxiety, Doubt, Dubiety, Qualms, Scruples

Misguide(d) Impolitic

▷ **Misguided** *may indicate* an anagram

Mishandle Abuse

Mishap Accident, Contretemps, Misaunter, Misfortune, Wroath

Mishit, **Misstroke** Crab, Draw, Edge, Fluff, Muff, Sclaff, Shank, Slice, Thin, Top

Misinterpret(ation) Mondegreen, Wrest

Mislay Leese, Lose

Mislead(ing) Blind, Bum steer, Cover-up, Deceive, Delude, Dupe, Equivocate, Fallacious, False, Gag, Red herring, Runaround, Smoke and mirrors

▷ **Misled** *may indicate* an anagram

Mismanage Blunder, Bungle, Muddle

Mismatch Kludge

Misplace(ment) Ectopia

Misplay Fluff, Whitechapel

Misprint Error, Literal, Slip, Typo

Mispronunciation Cacoepy, Lallation, Lambdacism

Misrepresent(ation) Abuse, Belie, Calumny, Caricature, Colour, Distort, Falsify, Garble, Lie, Slander, Subreption, Traduce

Miss(ing) Abord, Avoid, AWOL, Colleen, Desiderate, Dodge, Drib, Err(or), Fail, Forego, Gal, > **GIRL**, Kumari, Lack, Lass, Link, Lose, Mademoiselle, Maid, Maiden, Mile, Muff(et), Near, Neglect, Negligence, Omit, Otis, Overlook, Senorita, Shy, Skip, Spinster, Stoke, Unmeet, Wanting, Whiff

▷ **Miss** *may refer to* Missouri

Missal Breviary, Te igitur, Triodion

Misshapen Crooked, Deformed, Dysmelia, Gnarled

Missile Air-to-air, Ammo, Anti-ballistic, Arrow, Artillery, Atlas, Ball, Ballistic, Beam Rider, Blue streak, Bolas, Bolt, Bomb, Boomerang, Brickbat, Bullet, Condor, Cruise, Dart, Dingbat, Doodlebug, Dum-dum, Exocet®, Falcon, Fléchette, Genie, Grenade, Guided, HARM, Harpoon, Hawk, Hellfire, Hound Dog, ICBM, Interceptor, Jired, Kiley, Kyley, Kylie, Lance, Mace, MARV, Maverick, Minuteman, MIRV, Missive, Mx, Onion, Patriot, Pellet, Pershing, Phoenix, Polaris, Poseidon, Qual, Quarrel, Rocket, SAM, Scud, Sea Skimmer, Sergeant, Shell, Shillelagh, Shot, Shrike, Side-winder, Smart bomb, Snowball, Sparrow, Spartan, Spear, Sprint, SSM, Standard Arm, Standoff, Styx, Subroc, Surface to air, Surface to surface, Talos, Tartar, Terrier, Thor, Titan, Tomahawk, Torpedo, Tracer, Trident, UAM, Warhead

Mission(ary) Aidan, Alamo, Antioch, Apostle, Assignment, Augustine, Bethel,

Caravan, Charge, Delegation, Embassage, Embassy, Errand, Evangelist, Foreign, Iona, Legation, Livingstone, LMS, Message, NASA, Ninian, Op, Paul, Quest, Reclaimer, Redemptionist, Schweitzer, Task, Vocation, Xavier

Missis, Missus, Mrs Devi, Maam, Mrs, Wife

Missive Letter, Message, Note

Missouri Mo

Misstroke *see* MISHIT

Mist(y) Blur, Brume, Cloud, Dew, Drow, Dry-ice, Film, Fog, Haar, Haze, Hoar, Miasma, Moch, Nebular, Niflheim, Rack, Red, Roke, Scotch, Sea-fret, Sfumato, Smir(r), Smog, Smur, Vapour

Mistake(n) Barry (Crocker), Bish, Bloomer, Blooper, Blunder, Boner, Boob, Booboo, Boss, Botch, Clanger, Clinker, Confound, Deluded, Domino, Erratum, Error, Fault, Floater, Flub, Fluff, Gaffe, Goof, Howler, Identity, Incorrect, Lapse, Malapropism, Miss, Muff, Mutual, Nod, Off-beam, Oversight, Plonker, Pratfall, Screw-up, > SLIP, Slip-up, Solecism, Stumer, Trip, Typo

▸ **Mistake(n)** *may indicate* an anagram

Mister Babu, Effendi, Mr, Sahib, Senor, Shri, Sir, Sri

Mistletoe Album, Missel, Parasite, Viscum

Mistreat Abuse, Attrite, Manhandle, Violate

Mistress Amie, Aspasia, Canary-bird, Chatelaine, Concubine, Courtesan, Demimondaine, Devi, Doxy, Goodwife, Herself, Hussif, Inamorata, Instructress, Lady, Leman, Maintenon, Martha, Montespan, Mrs, Natural, Paramour, Stepney, Teacher, Wardrobe, Wife

Mistrust(ful) Askant, Doubt, Gaingiving, Suspect, Suspicion

Misunderstand(ing) Disagreement, Discord, Mistake

Misuse Abuse, Catachresis, Defalcate, Malappropriate, Malapropism, Maltreat, Perversion, Torment

Mite Acaridian, Acarus, Bit, Cheese, Child, Flour, Forage, Fowl, Gall, Harvest, Itch, Lepton, Little, (Red) spider, Rust, Sarcoptes, Speck, Sugar, Trombiculid, Tyroglyphid, Varroa, Widow's

Mitigate, Mitigating Abate, Allay, Allieve, Ameliorate, Assuage, Extenuating, Lenitive, Lessen, Mease, Palliate, Quell, Relief, Relieve

Mitosis Anaphase

Mitre Hat, Tiar(a)

Mitt(en), Mittens Fist, Glove, Hand, Paw, Pockies

Mix(ed), Mixer, Mixture, Mix-up Alloy, Amalgam, Associate, Assortment, Attemper, Balderdash, Bigener, Bland, Blend, Blunge, Bordeaux, Brew, Carburet, Card, Caudle, Chow, Cocktail, Co-meddle, Compo, Compound, Conglomerate, Consort, Cross, Cut, Disperse, Dolly, Drammock, Embroil, Emulsion, Entectic, Farrago, Fold-in, Freezing, Garble, Grill, Griqua, Heather, Hobnob, Hotchpotch, Hybrid, Imbroglio, Interlace, Intermingle, Isomorphous, Jumble, Lace, Lard, Lignin, Linctus, Load, Macedoine, Matissé, Meddle, Medley, Melange, Mell, Meng(e), Ment, Mess, Mestizo, Metis, Ming(le), Miscellaneous, Miscellany, Mishmash, Mong, Motley, Muddle, Muss(e), Neapolitan, Octaroon, Octoroon, Olio, Olla, Pi(e), Potin, Pousowdie, Powsowdy, Praiseach, Promiscuous, Raggle-taggle, Ragtag, Salad, Scramble, Spatula, Stew, Stir, Temper, Through-other, Trail, Vision, Yblent

▸ **Mixed** *may indicate* an anagram

Mizzle Decamp, Scapa, Scarper

Mnemonic Quipo, Quipu, Reminder

Moab(ite) Balak, Ruth, Wash-pot

Moan(ing) Beef, Bleat, Complain, Groan, Hone, Keen, > LAMENT, Meane,

Plangent, Sough, Wail, W(h)inge

Moat Dike, Ditch, Foss(e)

Mob(ster) Army, Assail, Canaille, Crew, Crowd, Doggery, Faex populi, Gaggle, Gang, Herd, Hoi-polloi, Hoodlum, Lynch, Ochlocrat, Press, Rabble, Raft, Ragtag, Ribble-rabble, Riff-raff, Rout, Scar-face

Mobile, Mobilise, Mobility Donna, Downward, Fluid, Horizontal, Movable, Plastic, Rally, Thin, Upward(ly), Vagile, Vertical

Mob-rule Ochlocracy

Mocassin Larrigan, Shoe, Snake

Mock(ery), Mocking Ape, Banter, Chaff, Chyack, Cod, Cynical, Deride, Derisory, Dor, Ersatz, False, Farce, Fleer, Flout, Gab, Geck, Gibe, Gird, Guy, Imitation, Irony, Irrisory, Jape, > **JEER**, Jibe, Lampoon, Laugh, Mimic, Narquois, Parody, Paste, Pillorise, Rail(lery), Rally, Ridicule, Sacrilege, Sardonic, Satirise, Scout, Sham, Simulate, Slag, Travesty, Wry

Mocking-bird Mimus, Sage-thrasher

Mode Aeolian, Convention, Dorian, Ecclesiastical, Fashion, Form, Formal, Greek, Gregorian, Iastic, Ionian, Locrian, Lydian, Major, Manner, Material, Medieval, Minor, Mixolydian, Phrygian, Plagal, Rate, Real-time, Sleep, Step, Style, Ton

Model(ler), Modelling Archetype, Bozzeto, Cast, Copy, Demonstration, Diorama, Doll, Dummy, Ecorché, Effigy, Epitome, Example, Exemplar, Fictor, Figure, Figurine, Icon, Ideal, Image, Instar, Jig, Last, Lay-figure, Layman, Madame Tussaud, Manakin, Manikin, Mannequin, Maquette, Mark, Mock-up > **MOULD**, Norm, Original, Orrery, Papier-mache, Parade, Paragon, Pattern, Phelloplastic, Pilot, Plasticine, Pose(r), Posture-maker, Prototype, Replica, Role, Scale, Sedulous, Sitter, Specimen, Standard, Superwaif, T, Template, Templet, Terrella, Toy, Trilby, Twiggy, Type, Typify, Waif, Waxwork, Working

▷ **Model(s)** *may indicate* an anagram

Modem Subset

Moderate(ly), Moderation Abate, Allay, Alleviate, Assuage, Average, Centre, Chasten, Continent, Diminish, Discretion, Ease, Gentle, Girondist, Ho, Lessen, Lukewarm, Measure, Mediocre, Medium, Menshevik, Mezzo, Middling, Mild, Mitigate, OK, Politique, Reason(able), Slake, So-so, Sumptuary, Temper(ate), Temperance, Tolerant, Tone, Via media, Wet

Modern(ise) AD, Aggiornamento, Contemporary, Fresh, Latter(-day), Neonomian, Neoterical, > **NEW**, Present-day, Progressive, Recent, Retrofit, Swinger, Update, Up-to-date

Modest(y) Aidos, Blaise, Chaste, Decent, Demure, Discreet, Humble, Ladylike, Maidenly, Mim, Mussorgsky, Propriety, Prudish, Pudency, Pure, Reserved, Shame, Shy, Unassuming, Unpretending, Unpretentious, Verecund

Modicum Dash

Modifiable, Modification, Modifier, Modify Adapt, Adverb, Alter, Backpedal, Change, Enhance, Extenuate, H, Leaven, Misplaced, Plastic, Qualify, Retrofit, Sandhi, Scumble, Soup, Streamline, Temper, Vary

Modulation, Module, Modulus Accent, Bulk, Cadence, Command, Frequency, Habitat, Inflexion, Lem, Lunar, Mitigate, Phase, Pulse, Service, Tune, Unit, Vary, Velocity, Young's

Mogul Bigwig, Magnate, Padishah, Plutocrat, Taipan, VIP

Mohair Moire

Mohammed, Mohammedan (era) Hadith, Hegira, Hejira, Hejra, Hijra, Islamite, Mahdi, Mahoun(d), Moslem, Muezzin, Mussulman, Prophet, Said, Shiite, Sunna(h)

Moist(en), Moisture Baste, Bedew, Damp, Dank, De(a)w, Humect, Latch, Love-in-a-mist, Madefy, Mesarch, Moil, Nigella, Oozy, Slake, Slocken, Sponge, Wet

Moither *may indicate* an anagram

Molar Grinder, Mill-tooth, Secodont, Tooth, Wang

Molasses Blackstrap, Sorghum, Treacle

Mole(hill) Breakwater, Fen-cricket, Golden, Hydatidiform, Jetty, Marsupial, Miner, Mo(u)diewart, Moudi(e)wart, Mouldiwarp, Naeve, Notoryctes, Orology, Pier, Sea-wall, Shrew, Sleeper, Spot, Spy, Star-nose(d), Talpa, Want(hill), Want knap, Warp

Molecular, Molecule Acceptor, Atom, Buckyball, Carbene, Cavitand, Chiral, Chromophore, Closed chain, Cobalamin, Codon, Coenzyme, Cofactor, Dimer, DNA, Electrogen, Enantiomorph, Footballene, Fullerene, Gram, Hapten, Iota, Isomer, Kinin, Ligand, Long-chain, Metabolite, Metameric, Monomer, Peptide, Polymer, Polysaccharide, Quark, Replicon, Ribozyme, Semantide, Stereoisomer, Trimer, Uridine, Vector

Molendinar Mill

Molest(er) Annoy, Bother, Harass, Nonce, Scour

Moll(y), Mollie Bloom, Bonnie, Carousal, Cutpurse, Flanders, Girl, Maguire, Malone, May, Sissy

Mollify Appease, Fob, Mease, Mitigate, Pacify, Relax, Soften, Temper

Mollusc(s) Ammonite, Amphineura, Arca, Argonaut, Ark-shell, Belemnite, Bivalve, Bulla, Capiz, Cephalopod, Chiton, Clam, Cockle, Conch, Cone-shell, Cowrie, Cowry, Cuttle(fish), Dentalium, Doris, Gaper, Gast(e)ropod, Goniatite, Heart-cockler, Heart-shell, Helix, Horse mussel, Lamellibranch, Limpet, Malacology, Marine boxer, Money cowry, Murex, Mussel, Mya, Nautilus, Neopilina, Octopod, Octopus, Olive, Opisthobranch, Oyster, Pandora, Paper nautilus, Paper-sailor, Pearly nautilus, Pecten, Pelican's-foot, Pholas, Piddock, Pinna, Polyp, Poulpe, Pteropod, Quahaug, Quahog, Razor-clam, Razor-fish, Razorshell, Saxicava, Scallop, Scaphopoda, Sea-hare, Sea-lemon, Sea-slug, Sepia, > SHELLFISH, Shipworm, Slug, Snail, Solen, Spat, Spirula, Spoot, Squid, Strombus, Tectibranch, Tellen, Tellin, Teredo, Toheroa, Top-shell, Triton, Trochophore, Trochus, Trough-shell, Turbo, Tusk-shell, Unio, Univalve, Veliger, Venus, Venus shell, Vitrina, Wentletrap, Whelk, Wing-shell, Winkle

Mollycoddle Indulge, Nanny, Pamper

Moloch Thorn-devil

Molten Dissolved, Fusil, Melted

Molybdenum Mo

Moment(s), Momentous Bending, Bit, Dipole, Electromagnetic, Flash, Hogging, Import, Instant, Jiffy, Magnetic, > MINUTE, Mo, Nonce, Psychological, Pun(c)to, Sands, Sec, Shake, Stound, Stownd, Tick, Time, Trice, Twinkling, Weighty, Wink

Momentum Impetus, L, Speed, Thrust

Mona(s) I, IOM

Monaco Grimaldi

Mona Lisa La Gioconda

Monarch(y) Autocrat, Butterfly, Constitutional, Crown, Emperor, HM, K, Karling, King, Limited, Merry, Potentate, Q, Queen, R, Raine, Reign, Ruler, Tsar

Monarchist Cavalier

Monastery Abbey, Abthane, Charterhouse, Chartreuse, Cloister, Community, Gompa, Hospice, Lamaserai, Lamasery, La Trappe, Laura, Priory, Vihara, Wat

Monastic Abthane, Celibate, Holy, Monkish, Oblate, Secluded

Monday Black, Collop, Handsel, J'ouvert, Meal, Oatmeal, Plough, Whit

Mondrian Piet

Monetary, Money Ackers, Akkas, Allowance, Annat, Ante, Appearance, Assignat, Banco, Batta, Blood, Blunt, Boodle, Bottle, Brass, Bread, Bread and honey, Broad, Cabbage, Capital, Cash, Caution, Change, Chink, Cob, > COIN, Collateral, Conscience, Crackle, Cranborne, Crinkly, Currency, Danger, Dib(s), Dingbat, Dosh, Dust, Earnest, Easy, Even, Fat, Fee, Fiat, Float, Folding, Fonds, Fund, Funny, Gate, Gelt, Gilt, Gold, Grant, Gravy, Greens, Hard, Head, Hello, Hoot, Hot, Housekeeping, Hush, Idle, Ingots, Investment, Kale, Key, L, Lolly, Loot, Lucre, M, Mammon, Maundy, Mazuma, Means, Mint, Monopoly, Moola(h), Narrow, Necessary, Needful, Nest-egg, Note, Numismatic, Nummary, Oaker, Ochre, Offertory, Oof, Option, Outlay, P, Packet, Paper, Passage, Payroll, Peanuts, Pecuniary, Pelf, Pin, Pine-tree, Pittance, Plastic, Plum, Pocket, Posh, Press, Prize, Proceeds, Profit, Protection, Purse, Push, Ready, Rebate, Resources, Revenue, Rhino, Rogue, Rowdy, Salt(s), Scratch, Scrip, Seed, Shin-plaster, Ship, Short, Siller, Silly, Silver, Slush, Smart, Soap, Soft, Spondulicks, Stake, Sterling, Stipend, Stuff, Subsistence, Sugar, Sum, Table, Takings, Tender, Tin, Toea, Token, Tranche, Treaty, Tribute, Turnover, Viaticum, Wad, Wealth, Wonga

Money-box Penny-pig, Piggy bank

Moneylender Gombeen, Shylock, Usurer

Moneymaking Earner, Profitable, Quaestuary

Mongol(ian) Bashkir, Buriat, Buryat, Calmuck, Chuvash, Evenski, Golden Horde, Kalmuck, Kara-Kalpak, Kazak(h), Khalkha, Kubla(i) Khan, Kyrgyz, Lapp, Lepcha, Manchoo, Manchu, Mishmi, Mogul, Samoyed, Shan, Sherpa, Tamerlane, Tatar, Tungus(ic), Uig(h)ur, Ural-altaic, Uzbak

Mongoose Ichneumon, Mangouste, Meerkat, Suricate, Urva

Mongrel Bitser, Cross(bred), > DOG, Goorie, Goory, Hybrid, Kuri, Lurcher, Mutt, Quadroon, Tyke, Underbred, Zo

Monitor Detect, Goanna, Iguana, Lizard, Observe, Offer, Ofgas, Ofgem, Oflot, Ofsted, Oftel, Ofwat, Prefect, Record, Screen, Track, Warship, Watchdog, Whole-body, Worral, Worrel

Monk(s) Abbey-lubber, Abbot, Acoemeti, Angelico, Archimandrite, Arhat, Asser, Augustinian, Austin, Basilian, Bede, Beghard, Benedictine, Bernardine Bethlehemite, Bhikhu, Black, Bonaventura, Bonze, Brother, Bruno, Caedmon, Caloyer, Carthusian, Celestine, Cellarist, Cenobite, Cistercian, Cluniac, Coenobite, Cowl, Culdee, Dan, Dervish, Dom, Dominican, Félibre, Feuillant, Fraticelli, Friar, General, Gyrovague, Hegumen, Hermit, Hesychast, Hildebrand, Ignorantine, Jacobin, Jacobite, Jerome, Lama, Maurist, Mechitharist, Mekhitarist, Mendel, Norbertine, Obedientiary, Oblate, Olivetan, Order, Pelagian, Prior, Rakehell, Rasputin, Recluse, Recollect, Religieux, Roshi, Salesian, Sangha, Savonarola, Simeon Stylites, Sub-prior, Talapoin, Theatine, Thelemite, Thelonius, Thomas à Kempis, Tironensian, Trappist, Votary

Monkey Anger, Ape, Aye-aye, Baboon, Bandar, Bobbejaan, Bonnet, Bushbaby, Capuchin, Catar(r)hine, Cebidae, Cebus, Chacma, Coaita, Colobus, Cynomolgus, Diana, Douc, Douroucouli, Drill, Durukuli, Entellus, Galago, Gelada, Gibbon, Gorilla, Grease, Green, Grison, Grivet, Guenon, Guereza, Hanuman, Hoolock, Howler, Hylobates, Indri, Jacchus, Jackey, Jocko, Kippage, Langur, Leaf, Lemur, Loris, Macaco, Macaque, Magot, Malmag, Mandrill, Mangabey, Marmoset, Meddle, Meerkat, Mico, Midas, Mona, Mycetes, Nala,

Nasalis, New World, Old World, Orang-utang, Ouakari, Ouistiti, Phalanger, Platyrrhine, Powder, Primate, Proboscis, Pug, Puzzle, Rage, Ram, Rhesus, Sago(u)in, Saguin, Sai(miri), Sajou, Saki, Sapajou, Satan, Semnopithecus, Siamang, Sifaka, Silen(us), Silverback, Simian, Simpai, Slender loris, Spider, Squirrel, Talapoin, Tamarin, Tamper, Tana, Tarsier, Tee-tee, Titi, Toque, Trip-hammer, Troop, Tup, Uakari, Vervet, Wanderoo, White-eyelid, Wistiti, Wou-wou, Wow-wow, Wrath, Zati

Monkey-nut Earth-pea
Monkey-puzzle Araucaria, Bunya-bunya
Monkshood Aconite
Monocle Eye-glass, Gig-lamp, Lorgnon, Quiz(zing-glass)
Monocot(yledon) Araceae, Endogen, Tradescantia
Monodon Narwhal
Monogram, **Monograph** Chi-rho, Cipher, Study, Treatise, Tug(h)ra
Monolith Ayers Rock, Cenotaph, Chambers Pillar, Uluru
Monologue Interior, Patter, Rap, Recitation, Soliloquy, Speech
Monopolise, **Monopoly** Appalto, Bloc, Bogart, Cartel, Corner, Engross, Octroi, Régie, Trust
Monotonous, **Monotony** Boring, Dull, > FLAT, Grey, Humdrum, Same(y), Sing-song, Tedious
Monsoon Hurricane, Typhoon, > WIND
Monsoon *may indicate* weekend (Mon soon)
Monster, **Monstrous** Alecto, Apollyon, Asmodeus, Bandersnatch, Behemoth, Bunyip, Caliban, Cerberus, Cete, Chichevache, Chim(a)era, Cockatrice, Colossal, Cyclops, Dabbat, Deform, Dinoceras, Dismayd, Div, Dragon, Echidna, Enormous, Erebus, Erinys, Erl-king, Eten, Ettin, Evil-one, Fiend, Fire-drake, Frankenstein, Freak, Geryon, Ghost, Giant, Gila, Golem, Gorgon, Green-eyed, Grendel, Harpy, Hippocampus, Hippogriff, Huge, Hydra, Jabberwock, Kraken, Lamia, Leviathan, Lilith, Lusus naturae, Mastodon, Medusa, Minotaur, Misbegotten, Moloch, Mylodont, Nessie, Nicker, Nightmare, Ogopogo, Ogre, Ogr(e)ish, Opinicus, Orc, Outrageous, Pongo, Sarsquatch, Satyral, Scylla, Serra, Shadow, Simorg, Simurg(h), Siren, Skull, Snark, Spectre, Sphinx, Spook, Stegodon, Stegosaur, Succubus, Taniwha, Teras, Teratoid, Triceratops, Troll, Typhoeus, Typhon, Unnatural, Vampire, Vast, Wasserman, Wendego, Wendigo, Wer(e)wolf, Wyvern, Xiphopagus, Yowie, Ziffius
Month(ly) Ab, Abib, Adar, Anomalistic, April, Asadha, Asvina, August, Bhadrapada, Brumaire, Bul, Calendar, Cheshvan, Chislev, December, Dhu-al-Hijjah, Dhu-al-Qadah, Diaconic, Elul, February, Floreal, Frimaire, Fructidor, Germinal, Hes(h)van, Iy(y)ar, January, July, Jumada, June, Jysaitha, Kartuka, Kisleu, Kislev, Lide, Lunar, Lunation, Magha, March, Margasirsa, May, Messidor, Mo, Moharram, Moon, Muharram, Muharrem, Nisan, Nivose, Nodical, November, October, Periodical, Phalguna, Pluviose, Prairial, Rabia, Rajab, Ramadan, Ramazon, Rhamadhan, Safar, Saphar, September, Sha(a)ban, Shawwal, S(h)ebat, Sidereal, Sivan, Solar, Stellar, Synodic, Tammuz, Tebeth, Thermidor, Tisri, Tropical, Vaisakha, Veadar, Vendemiaire, Ventose
Monument Ancient, Arch, Archive, Cenotaph, Charminar, Column, Cromlech, Dolmen, Henge, Megalith, Memorial, Menhir, Monolith, National, Pantheon, Pyramid, Sacellum, Stele(ne), Stone, Stonehenge, Stupa, Talayot, Tombstone, Trilith, Trilithon, Urn
Mood(y) Active, Anger, Atmosphere, Attitude, Capricious, Conjunctive, Dudgeon, Enallage, Fettle, Fit, Glum, Grammar, Humour, Hump, Imperative,

Indicative, Mercurial, Morale, Optative, Passive, Peat, Pet, Revivalist, Sankey, Spleen, Subjunctive, Temper, Tid, Tone, Tune, Vein, Vinegar, Whim

Moon(light), Moony Aah, Alignak, Aningan, Apogee, Artemis, Astarte, Blue, Callisto, Calypso, Cheese, Cynthia, Diana, Epact, Eye, Flit, Full, Gander, Ganymede, Gibbous, Glimmer, Grimaldi, Harvest, Hecate, Hunter's, Hyperion, Inconstant, Juliet, Leda, Lucina, Luna(r), Mani, Mascon, McFarlane's Buat, Midsummer, Mock, Month, Mope, New, Nimbus, Nocturne, Octant, Oliver, Paddy's lantern, Paraselene, Paschal, Pasiphaë, Phoebe, Plenilune, Proteus, Raker, Satellite, Selene, Set, Shepherd, Shot, Sickle, Sideline, Silvery, Sonata, Stargaze, Stone, Syzygy, Thebe, Thoth, Titan, Triton, Umbriel, Wander

Moonraker Astrogeologist, Gothamite

Moonshine(r) Hootch, Poteen, Rot, Shebeener

Moor(ing), Moorish Berth, Culloden, Dock, Fen, Heath, Iago, Ilkley, Makefast, Marston, Moresque, Moroccan, Mudéjar, Othello, Palustrine, Roadstead, Ryepeck, Saracen, Tether, > TIE, Wold

Mop(ping) Dwile, Flibbertigibbet, Girn, Glib, Shag, Squeegee, Squilgee, Swab, Swob, Thatch, > WIPE

Mope Boody, Brood, Peak, Sulk

Mor Humus

Moral(ity), Morals Apologue, Austere, Deontic, Ethic(al), Ethos, Everyman, Fable, High-minded, Integrity, Precept, Principled, Puritanic, Righteous, Sittlichkeit, Tag, Upright, Virtuous, Well-thewed

Morale Ego, Mood, Spirit, Zeal

Moralise, Moralising Preach, Sententious

Moralist Prig, Prude, Puritan, Whitecap

Morass Bog, Fen, Flow, Marsh, Moss, Quagmire, Slough

Morbid(ity) Anasarca, Ascites, Cachaemia, Dropsy, Ectopia, Ghoul(ish), Gruesome, Pathological, Plethora, Prurient, Religiose, Sick, Sombre

Mordant Biting, Caustic, Critic(al), Sarcastic, Tooth

Mordent Inverted, Pralltriller, Upper

More Added, Additional, Else, Extra, Increase, Less, Mae, Merrier, Mo(e), > NO MORE, Over, Piu, Plus, Stump, Utopia

Moreover Also, Besides, Eft, Either, Eke, Further, Too, Yet

Morgan Buccaneer, Pirate

Moribund Dying, Stagnant, Withered

Mormon Danite, Latter-day Saint, Salt Lake City, Utah, Young

Morning Ack-emma, Am, Antemeridian, Dawn, Daybreak, Early, Forenoon, Matin(al), Morrow, Sparrowfart

Morning-glory Bindweed, Ipomoea, Turbith, Turpeth

Morning-star Morgenstern, Phosphor(us), Threshel, Venus

Moroccan, Morocco Agadir, French, Leather, Levant, MA, Mo(o)r, Persian, Riff, Tangerine, Venus

Moron Fool, Idiot, Schmuck, > STUPID

Morose Acid, Boody, Churlish, Crabby, Cynical, Disgruntled, Gloomy, Glum, Grum, Moody, Sour-eyed, Sullen, Surly

Morph Phase

Morris Car, Dance, Fivepenny, Merel(l), Meril, Nine Men's, Ninepenny

Morrow Future

Morse Code, Endeavour, Iddy-umpty, Walrus

Morsel Bit, Bite, Bouche, Canape, Crumb, Dainty, Morceau, Ort, Scrap, Sippet, Sop, Tidbit, Titbit

Mortal(ity) Averr(h)oism, Being, Deathly, > FATAL, Grave, Human, Lethal, Yama

Mortar, **Mortar-board** Bowl, Cannon, Cement, Co(e)horn, Compo, Grout, Gunite, Hawk, Life, Metate, Mine-thrower, Minnie, Moaning (Minnie), Parget, Plaster, Pot gun, Screed, Square, Squid, Toc emma, Trench(er)

Mortgage(e) Balloon, Bond, Cedula, Chattel, Debt, Dip, Encumbrance, Endowment, First, Hypothecator, Loan, Pension, Pledge, Wadset(t)

Mortification, **Mortified**, **Mortify** Abash, Ashame, Chagrin, Crucify, Crush, Gangrene, Humble, Humiliate, Infarct, Necrose, Penance, Sick, Sphacelus, Wormwood

Mosaic Buhl, Cosmati, Inlay, Intarsia, Musive, Opus musivum, Pietra dura, Screen, Tarsia, Terrazzo, Tessella(te), Tessera, Tobacco, Venetian

Moscow Dynamo

Moses Grandma

Moslem *see* MUSLIM

Mosque Dome of the Rock, El Aqsa, Jami, Masjid, Medina

Mosquito Aedes, Anopheles, Culex, Culicine, Gnat, Parasite, Stegomyia

Moss(y) Acrogen, Agate, Bryology, Carrag(h)een, Ceylon, Club, Fog, Fontinalis, Hag(g), Hypnum, Iceland, Irish, Lecanoram, Lichen, Litmus, Liverwort, Long, Lycopod, Marsh, Musci, Muscoid, Parella, Peat, Polytrichum, Reindeer, Rose, Scale, Selaginella, Spanish, Sphagnum, Staghorn, Tree, Usnea, Wall, Wolf's claw

Most Largest, Major, Maxi(mum), Optimum

Mot Quip, Saying

Mote Atom, Particle, Speck

Moth(s) Abraxas, Antler, Arch, Arctiidae, Atlas, Bag, Bee, Bell, Bobowler, Bogong, Bombycid, Brown-tail, Buff-tip, Bugong, Burnet, Cabbage, Cactoblastus, Carpenter, Carpet, Cecropia, Cinnabar, Clearwing, Clifden nonpareil, Clothes, Codlin(g), Corn (-borer), Dagger, Dart-moth, Death's head, Diamondback, Drepanid, Drinker, Eggar, Egger, Emerald, Emperor, Ermine, Flour, Fox, Geometer, Geometrid, Ghost, Giant peacock, Gipsy, Goat, Goldtail, Gooseberry, Grass, Gypsy, Hawk, Herald, Honeycomb, Hook-tip, House, Hummingbird, Imago, Io, Kentish glory, Kitten, Lackey, Lappet, Large Emerald, Lasiocampidae, Leafroller, Leopard, Lepidoptera, Lichen, Lobster, Luna, Lymantriidae, Magpie, Meal, Mother of pearl, Mother Shipton, Muslin, Noctua, Noctuid, Notodonta, Nun, Oak-egger, Owl, Owlet, Peppered, Pine-beauty, Pine-carpet, Plane, Plume, Polyphemus, Privet hawk, Processionary, Prominent, Psyche, Pug-moth, Purple Emperor, Puss, Pyralidae, Red underwing, Sallow-kitten, Saturnia, Saturniid, Scavenger, Silkworm, Silver-Y, Sphingid, Sphinx, Swift, Tapestry, Thorn, Tiger, Tinea, Tineidae, Tortrix, Turnip, Tussock, Umber, Underwing, Unicorn, Vapourer, Veneer, Wainscot, Wave, Wax, Wheat, Winter, Woodborer, Yellow underwing, Y-moth, Zygaena

Mothball(s) Abeyance, Camphor, Naphtha, Preserver

Mother Bearer, Church, Cognate, Cosset, Courage, Dam(e), Dregs, Ean, Earth, Eve, Foster, Generatrix, Genetrix, Genitrix, Goose, Hubbard, Lees, Ma, Machree, Madre, Mam(a), Mamma, Mater, Maya, Minnie, Mom, Multipara, Mum, Native, Nature, Nourish, Nursing, Parity, Pourer, Primipara, Reverend, Shipton, Superior, Surrogate, Wit

Mother *may indicate* a lepidopterist (moth-er)

Motherless Adam, Orphan

Motif Anthemion, Design, Gist, Idée, Theme

Motion Contrary, Diurnal, Early day, Fast, Gesture, Harmonic, Impulse, Kepler, Kinematics, Kinetic, Link, Move, Oblique, Offer, Parallactic, Peculiar,

Perpetual, PL, Proper, Proposal, Rack and pinion, Rider, Similar, Slow, Spasm, Wave

Motionless Doggo, Frozen, Immobile, Quiescent, Stagnant, Stasis, Still, Stock-still

Motive, **Motivate**, **Motivation** Actuate, Cause, Ideal, Impel, Incentive, Intention, Mainspring, Mobile, Object, > PURPOSE, Spur, Ulterior

Motley Jaspé, Medley, Piebald, Pied

Motor(boat) Auto, Car, Dynamo, Electric, Engine, Hot rod, Inboard, Induction, Jato, Linear, Outboard, Scooter, Stator, Synchronous, Thruster, Turbine, Universal, Water

Motorcycle, **Motorcyclist** Bikie, Chookchaser, Farm-bike, Hell's Angel, Moped, Pipsqueak, Scooter, Scramble, Trail bike, Yamaha®

Motorist(s) AA, Driver, Petrolhead, RAC

Motorman Austin, Benz, Ford, Morris

Motor race Rally, Scramble, TT

Motorway Autobahn, Autopista, Autoput, Autoroute, Autostrada, Expressway, M(1), Throughway, Thruway

Mottle(d) Brindled, Chiné, Jaspé, Marbled, Marly, Mirly, Pinto, Poikilitic, Tabby

Motto Device, Epigraph, Gnome, Impresa, Imprese, Impress(e), Legend, Maxim, Mot, Poesy, Posy, Saw

Mou(e) Grimace, Mim

Mould(ed), **Mouldable**, **Moulding**, **Mouldy** Accolade, Architrave, Archivolt, Astragal, Baguette, Balection, Beading, Bend, Black, Blow, Blue, Bolection, Bread, Briquet(te), Cabling, Casement, Cast(ing), Cavetto, Chessel, Chill, Cornice, Coving, Cyma, Cymatium, Dariole, Die, Die-cast, Dogtooth, Doucine, Dripstone, Ductile, Echinus, Egg and dart, Emboss, Flong, > FORM, Foughty, Fousty, Fungose, Fungus, Fusarol(e), Fust, Gadroon, Godroon, Green, Hood-mould, Hore, Humus, Injection, Iron, Jelly, Leaf, Machine, Matrix, Mildew, Model, Mool, Moulage, Mucid, Mucor, Must, Myxomycete, Nebule, Noble rot, Ogee, Ovolo, Palmette, Papier-mâché, Phycomycete, Picture, Pig, Plasm(a), Plastic, Plat, Platband, Plate, Prototype, Prunt, Quarter-round, Reeding, Reglet, Rhizopus, Rot, Rust, Sandbox, Scotia, Shape, Slime, Smut, Soil, Soot(y), Storiated, Stringcourse, Stucco, Surbase, Tailor, Talon, Template, Templet, Timbale, Tondino, Torus, Trochilus, Vinew, Water table

Moult(ing) Cast, Metecdysis, Mew, Shed

Mound Agger, Bank, Barp, Barrow, Berm, Cone, Dike, Dun, Embankment, Heap Hog, Kurgan, Mogul, Molehill, Monticule, Mote, Motte, Orb, Pile, Pingo, Pome Rampart, Rampire, Remblai, Tel(l), Teocalli, Teopan, Tuffet, Tumulus, Tussock

Mound-bird Megapode

Mount(ed), **Mounting**, **Mountain (peak)**, **Mountains** > ALPINE, Aspiring, Back, Barp, Ben, Berg, Board, Breast, Butter, Chain, Charger, > CLIMB, Colt, Cordillera Cradle, Dew, Display, Djebel, Dolly, Escalade, Frame, Hinge, Horse, Inselberg, Jebel, Massif, Monture, Mt, Nunatak, Orography, Orology, Passe-partout, Pike, Pile, Pin, Pownie, Quad, Ride, Saddlehorse, Scalado, Scale, Set, Soar, Stage, Stanley, > STEED, Stie, Strideways, Tel, Tier, Tor, Turret, Upgo, Volcano

MOUNTAINS

2 letters:	3 letters:	Ore	Blue
K2	Apo		Bona
	Ida	4 letters:	Cook
	Kaf	Alai	Etna

Fuji
Harz
Hoss
Jaya
Jura
Meru
Nebo
Oeta
Ossa
Rigi
Ubac
Zeil

5 letters:
Abora
Adams
Aldan
Altai
Amara
Andes
Aneto
Athos
Atlas
Badon
Black
Blanc
Coast
Djaja
Eiger
Ellis
Ghats
Green
Guyot
Hekla
Horeb
Idris
Kamet
Kenya
Logan
Munro
Ozark
Rocky
Rydal
Sayan
Serra
Sinai
Siple
Smoky
Snowy
Table
Tabor
Tatra

Tyree
Tyrol
Uinta
Urals
Welsh
White

6 letters:
Ala Dag
Amhara
Anadyr
Arafat
Ararat
Averno
Balkan
Bogong
Carmel
Cho Oyu
Dragon
Egmont
Elbert
Elberz
Elbrus
Erebus
Gilead
Hermon
Hoggar
Hoosac
Katmai
Kazbek
Kunlun
Lhotse
Makalu
Mourne
Olives
Ortles
Pamirs
Pelion
Pindus
Pisgah
Pocono
Robson
Scopus
Sintra
Sorata
Steele
Tasman
Taunus
Taurus
Umbria
Vernon
Vosges

Zagros

7 letters:
Aetolia
Ala Dagh
Aorangi
Aragats
Arcadia
Bernina
Brocken
Buffalo
Calvary
Cariboo
Cascade
Chianti
Corbett
Dapsang
Everest
Helicon
Kennedy
Khingan
Kuenlun
Lebanon
Lucania
Manaslu
Markham
Nan Shan
Olympic
Olympus
Palomar
Perdido
Pilatus
Rainier
Rhodope
San Juan
Scafell
Selkirk
Skiddaw
Snowdon
Sperrin
Sudeten
Tibesti
Travers
Whitney
Wicklow

8 letters:
Ben Nevis
Cambrian
Carstenz
Catskill
Caucasus

Cevennes
Cumbrian
Demavend
Grampian
Hymettus
Illimani
Jungfrau
Kinabalu
King Peak
Leibnitz
McKinley
Mulhacen
Ngaliema
Pennines
Pyrenees
Rushmore
St Helen's
Taraniki
Tien Shan
Vesuvius
Victoria
Wrangell

9 letters:
Aconcagua
Allegheny
Annapurna
Apennines
Ben Lomond
Blue Ridge
Cairngorm
Catskills
Caucasian
Connemara
Demavrand
Dolomites
El Capitan
Grampians
Guadalupe
Helvellyn
Highlands
Himalayas
Hindu Kush
Jebel Musa
Karakoram
Lenin Peak
Longs Peak
Marmolada
Mont Blanc
Nanda Devi
Parnassus
Pikes Peak

Shivering
Sugarloaf
Tirich Mir
Tupungato
Vancouver
Venusberg
Voralberg
Weisshorn
Woodroffe
Yablonovy
Zugspitze

10 letters:
Arakan Yoma
Armageddon
Black Hills
Cantabrian
Carpathian
Delectable
Dhaulagiri
Equatorial
Erymanthus
Erzgebirge
Great Gable
Great Smoky
Harney Peak
Horselberg
Laurentian
Matterhorn
Monte Corno
Montserrat
Pentelikon
Puncak Jaya
Puy de Sancy
St Michael's

Tengri Khan
Teton Range
Waziristan
Wellington
Wetterhorn

11 letters:
Adirondacks
Alaska Range
Appalachian
Bartle Frere
Bimberi Peak
Brooks Range
Drakensberg
Fairweather
Gerlachovka
Kilimanjaro
Kirkpatrick
Kolyma Range
Nanga Parbat
Salmon River
Scafell Pike
Sierra Madre

12 letters:
Albert Edward
Cascade Range
Eastern Ghats
Godwin Austen
Gran Paradiso
Ingleborough
Kanchenjunga
Ruahine Range
Sierra Morena
Sierra Nevada

Slieve Donard
Tararua Range
Victoria Peak
Vindhya Range
Vinson Massif
Wasatch Range
Western Ghats

13 letters:
Carrantuohill
Croagh Patrick
Flinders Range
Grossglockner
Humphrey's Peak
Kangchenjunga
Massif Central
Petermann Peak
San Bernardino
Stanovoi Range
Tibesti Massif

14 letters:
Admiralty Range
Bohemian Forest
Carnarvon Range
Finsteraarhorn
Hamersley Range
Kaikoura Ranges
Kommunizma
 Peak
Liverpool Range
Musgrove Ranges
Ruwenzori Range
Stirling Ranges
Thadentsonyane

Wind River Range

15 letters:
New England
 Range
Teutoburger Wald

16 letters:
Emperor
 Seamounts
Macdonnell
 Ranges
Thabana-
 Ntlenyana

17 letters:
Continental
 Divide
Transylvanian
 Alps

18 letters:
Great Dividing
 Range

19 letters:
Macgillicuddy's
 Reeks

20 letters:
Salmon River
 Mountains

Mountain-building Orogenesis
Mountaineer(ing) Abseil, Alpinist, Arnaut, Climber, Hunt, Sherpa, Smythe,
 Upleader
Mountebank Antic(ke), Baladin(e), Charlatan, Jongleur, Quack, Saltimbanco
Mourn(er), Mournful, Mourning Adonia, Black, Dirge, Dole, Elegiac, Grieve,
 Grone, Half-mast, Hatchment, Jamie Duff, Keen, Lament, Niobe, Omer,
 Ovel, Plangent, Saulie, Shibah, Shivah, Shloshim, Sorrow, Tangi, Threnetic,
 Threnodial, Weeds, Weep, Willow
Mouse(like), Mousy Black eye, Deer, Dun(nart), Fat, Field, Flitter, Harvest,
 Honey, House, Icon, Jumping, Marsupial, Meadow, Muridae, Murine, Pocket,
 Pouched, Rodent, Shiner, Shrew, Vermin, Waltzer, White-footed
Mousse Styling
Moustache Boxcar, Burnside, Charley, Charlie, Chevron, Excrement, Fu
 Manchu, Handlebar, Hindenburg, Horseshoe, Kaiser, Mistletoe, Pencil,
 Pyramid, Regent, Roman T, Soupstrainer, Toothbrush, Walrus, Waxed, Wings,
 Zapata

Mouth(piece) Aboral, Bazoo, Bocca, Brag, Buccal, Cakehole, Chapper, Check, Crater, Debouchure, Delta, Embouchure, Estuary, Fipple, Gab, Gam, Geggie, Gills, Gob, Gum, Hard, Kisser, Labret, Lawyer, Lip, Manubrium, Maw, Neb, Orifex, Orifice, Os, Oscule, Ostium, Outfall, Outlet, Port, Potato trap, Rattle-trap, Speaker, Spokesman, Spout, Stoma, Swazzle, Swozzle, Teat, Trap, Trench, Uvula

Mouthful Bite, Gob, Morceau, Morsel, Sip, Sup, Taste

Mouthless Astomatous

Mouth-organ Harmonica, Harp, Palp, Sang

Move(d), **Mover**, **Movable**, **Moving** Act, Actuate, Affect, Andante, Astir, Budge, Carry, Catapult, Chattel, Coast, Counter-measure, Coup, Decant, Démarche, Displace, Disturb, Ease, Eddy, Edge, Evoke, False, Flit, Flounce, Fluctuate, Forge, Frogmarch, Gambit, Gee, Go, Gravitate, Haulier, Hustle, Inch, Instigate, Jee, Jink, Kedge, Kinetic, Knight's progress, Link, Mill, Mobile, Mosey, Motivate, Nip, Opening, Overcome, Pan, People, Poignant, Prime, Proceed, Progress, Prompt, Propel, Quicken, Qui(t)ch, Rearrange, Redeploy, Relocate, Remuage, Retrocede, Roll, Rouse, Roust, Sashay, Scoot, Scramble, Scroll, Scuttle, Sealed, Sell, Shift, Shog, Shoo, Shunt, Sidle, Skelp, Slide, Soulful, Spank, Steal, Steer, Step, Stir, Styre, Sway, Swish, Tack, Tactic, Taxi, Transfer, Translate, Translocate, Transplant, Transport, Travel, Troll, Trundle, Turn, Unstep, Up, Upsticks, Vacillate, Vagile, Veronica, Vire, Volt(e), Waft, Wag, Wapper, Whirry, Whish, Whisk, Whiz, Wuther, Yank, Zoom, Zwischenzug

Movement(s) Action, Advection, Aerotaxis, Al Fatah, Allegro, Allemande, Almain, Andantino, Antic, Azapo, Badinerie, Bandwagon, Brownian, Cadence, Capoeira, Cell, Charismatic, Chartism, Chemonasty, Constructivism, Course, Crusade, Dadaism, Diaspora, Diastole, Ecumenical, Enlightenment, Eoka, Eurhythmics, Expressionism, Faction, Feint, Fianchetto, Fris(ka), Gait, Gallicanism, Geneva, Gesture, Groundswell, Hip-hop, Honde, Imagism, Indraught, Inkatha, Intermezzo, Jhala, Jor, Kata, Keplarian, Kin(a)esthetic, Kinesis, Kinetic, Larghetto, Largo, Lassu, Ligne, Logistics, Manoeuvre, Mudra, Nastic, Naturalism, Naziism, New Wave, Nihilism, Official, Operation, Orchesis, Oxford, Pantalon, Parallax, Pase, Passade, Pedesis, Photokinesis, Photonasty, Piaffer, Pincer, Play, Populist, Poule, Poulette, Procession, Progress, Provisional, Punk, Puseyism, Reformation, REM, Renaissance, Resistance, Ribbonism, Risorgimento, Romantic, Rondo, Saccade, Scherzo, Seiche, Sinn Fein, Solifluction, Solifluxion, Spuddle, Stir(e), Sturm und Drang, Swadeshi, Swing, Symbolist, Tachism, Tamil Tigers, Tantrism, Taxis, Tectonic, Telekinesis, Tide, Tractarianism, Transhumance, Trend, Trenise, Ultramontanism, UNITA, Verismo, Veronica, Wheel, Women's, Zionism

Movie Bioscope, Buddy, Cine(ma), Disaster, Film, Flick, Nudie, Popcorn, Road, Slasher, Snuff, Splatter, Talkie

Mow(er), **Mowing** Aftermath, Cut, Grimace, Lattermath, Lawn, Math, Rawing, Rawn, Rowan, Rowen, Rowing, Scytheman, Shear, Sickle, Tass, Trim

MP Backbencher, Commoner, Gendarme, Member, Politico, Provost, Redcap, Retread, Snowdrop, Stannator, Statist, TD

Mr *see* MISTER

Mrs *see* MISSIS

Mrs Copperfield Agnes, Dora

Mrs Siddons Tragic muse

Much Abundant, Far, Glut, Great, Lots, Mickle, Scad, Sore, Viel

Mucilage Gum, > MUCUS, Putty, Resin

Muck (up), **Mucky** Bungle, Dirt, Dung, Island, Leep, Manure, Midden, Mire, Rot,

Sludge, Soil, Sordid, Spoil, Stercoral

Mucker Fall, Pal, Purler

Mucus Phlegm, Pituate, Pituita, Snivel, Snot, Sputum

Mud(dy) Adobe, Clabber, Clart, Clay, Cutcha, Dirt, Drilling, Dubs, Fango, Glaur, Glob, Gutter, Kacha, Lahar, Lairy, Limous, > **MIRE**, Moya, Ooze, Peloid, Pise, Riley, Roily, Salse, Slab, Slake, Sleech, Slime, Slob, Slough, Sludge, Slur(ry), Slush, Stulch, Tocky, Trouble, Turbid, Volcanic

Muddle Befog, Bemuse, Botch, Cock up, Confuse, Disorder, Embrangle, Fluster, Gump, Mash, Mêlée, Mess, Mix, Mull, Pickle, Puddle, Shemozzle, Snarl-up, Stupefy, Tangle

▷ **Muddled** *may indicate* an anagram

Mudfish Lepidosiren

Mudguard Splashboard, Wing

Mudlark Ragamuffin, Urchin

Muesli Granola

Muff Boob, Botch, Bungle, Drop, Snoskyn

Muffin Bun, Mule, Popover

Muffle(d), Muffler Damp, Envelop, Hollow, Mob(b)le, Mute, Scarf, Silencer, Sourdine, Stifle

Mug(ger), Muggy Assault, Attack, Bash, Beaker, Bock, Can, Club, Con, Croc(odile), Cup, Dial, Dupe, Enghalskrug, Face, Fool, Footpad, Gob, Humid, Idiot, Latron, Learn, Mou, Noggin, Pan, Pot, Puss, Rob, Roll, Sandbag, Sap, Sconce, Simpleton, Steamer, Stein, Sucker, Swot, Tankard, Tax, Thief, Thug(gee), Tinnie, Tinny, Toby, Trap, Ugly, Visage, Yap

Mulatto Griff(e)

Mulberry Artocarpus, Breadfruit, Cecropia, Contrayerva, Cow-tree, Jack, Morat, Morus, Murrey, Overlord, Sycamine

Mulch Compost

Mulct Fine

Mule Ass, Bab(o)uche, Barren, Donkey, Funnel, Hybrid, Mocassin, Moccasin, Moyl(e), Muffin, Muil, Pack, Rake, Shoe, Slipper, Spinning, Sumpter

Muleteer Arriero

Mull Brood, Chew, Kintyre, Ponder, Promontory, Study

Mullein Aaron's rod

Mullet Goatfish

Mullion Monial

Multi-coloured Scroddled

Multiform Allotropic, Diverse, Manifold

Multiple, Multiplication, Multiplied, Multiplier, Multiply Augment, Breed, Double, > **INCREASE**, Modulus, Populate, Product, Proliferate, Propagate, Scalar, Severalfold

Multi-purpose Polychrest

Multitude Army, Crowd, Hirsel, Horde, Host, Legion, Populace, Shoal, Sight, Throng, Zillion

Mum(my) Boutonné, Carton(n)age, Corpse, Egyptian, Embalm, Mamma, Mine Mute, Quiet, Sh, Silent, Tacit, Whisht, Wordless

Mumble Grumble, Moop, Moup, Mouth, Mump, Mushmouth, Mutter, Royne, Slur

Mumbo jumbo Hocus pocus, Mammet, Maumet, Mawmet, Mommet

Mummer Actor, Mime, Scuddaler, Scudler, Skudler

Mumps Parotitis

Munch Champ, Chew, Chomp, Scranch

Mundane Banal, Common, Earthly, Nondescript, Ordinary, Prosaic, Quotidian, Secular, Subcelestial, Trite, Workaday, Worldly
Municipal Civic
Munificent Bounteous, Generous, Liberal, Profuse
Munition(s) Arms, Artillery, Matériel, Ordnance
Munro Saki
Mural(s) Fresco, Graffiti
Murder(er), Murderess, Murderous Aram, Assassin, Blue, Bluebeard, Bravo, Burke, Butcher, Butler, Cain, Cathedral, Crackhalter, Crippen, Cutthroat, Do in, Eliminate, Filicide, First degree, Fratricide, Genocide, Hare, Hit, Hitman, Homicide, Internecine, Judicial, > KILL, Liquidate, Locusta, Made man, Massacre, Matricide, Modo, Parricide, Patricide, Petty treason, Poison, Red, Regicide, Ripper, Ritual, Ritz, Second degree, Sikes, Slaughter, Slay, Strangle(r), Take out, Thagi, Throttle, Thug(gee), Whodun(n)it
Murk(y) Black, Dirk(e), Gloom, Obscure, Rookish, Stygian
Murmur(ing) Brool, Bruit, Bur(r), Burble, Coo, Croodle, Croon, Grudge, Heart, Hum, > MUTTER, Purr, Repine, Rhubarb, Rumble, Rumour, Souffle, Sowf(f), Sowth, Sturnoid, Undertone, Whisper
Murphy Chat, Potato, Pratie, Spud, Tater
Muscle, Muscular Abductor, Abs, Accelerator, Accessorius, Adductor, Anconeus, Aryepiglottic, Arytaenoid, Athletic, Attollens, Beef(y), Beefcake, Biceps, Bowr, Brachialus, Brawn, Buccinator, Ciliary, Clout, Complexus, Corrugator, Creature, Cremaster, Deltoid, Depressor, Diaphragm, Digastric, Dilat(at)or, Duvaricator, Effector, Elevator, Erecter, Erector, Evertor, Extensor, Eye-string, Flexor, Force, Gastrocnemius, Gemellus, Glut(a)eus, Gluteus maximus, Gracilis, Hamstring, Hiacus, Iliacus, Intrinsic, Involuntary, Kreatine, Lat, Latissimus dorsi, Laxator, Levator, Lumbricalis, Masseter, Mesomorph, Might, Motor, Mouse, Myalgia, Mylohyoid, Nasalis, Oblique, Occlusor, Omohyoid, Orbicularis, Pathos, Pec(s), Pectoral, Perforans, Perforatus, Peroneus, Plantaris, Platysma, Popliteus, > POWER, Pronator, Protractor, Psoas, Pylorus, Quad(riceps), Quadratus, Rambo, Rectus, Retractor, Rhomboid, Risorius, Rotator, Sarcolemma, Sarcous, Sartorius, Scalene, Scalenus, Serratus, Sinew, Smooth, Soleus, Sphincter, Spinalis, Splenial, Sthenic, Striated, Striped, Supinator, Temporal, Tenaculum, Tendon, Tensor, Teres, Thenar, Thew, Tibialis, Tonus, Trapezius, Triceps, Vastus, Voluntary, Zygomatic
Muscovite Mica, Talc
Muse(s), Muse's home, Musing Aglaia, Aonia(n), Attic, Calliope, Clio, Cogitate, Consider, Erato, Euphrosyne, Euterpe, Helicon, Inspiration, IX, Melpomene, Mull, Nine, Nonet, Pensée, Pierides, Poly(hy)mnia, Ponder, > REFLECT, Ruminate, Study, Teian, Terpsichore, Thalia, Tragic, Urania, Wonder
Museum Alte-Pinakothek, Ashmolean, BM, British, Fitzwilliam, Gallery, Getty, Guggenheim, Heritage centre, Hermitage, Hunterian, Louvre, Metropolitan, Parnassus, Prado, Repository, Rijksmuseum, Science, Smithsonian, Tate, Uffizi, VA, V and A, Waxworks
Mush Cree, Goo, Mess, Porridge, Puree, Schmaltz, Slop
Mushroom Agaric, Blewits, Boletus, Burgeon, Button, Cep, Champignon, Chanterelle, Darning, Enoki, Expand, Fly agaric, > FUNGUS, Gyromitra, Horse, Hypha(l), Ink-cap, Liberty cap, Magic, Matsutake, Meadow, Morel, Oyster, Parasol, Penny-bun, Pixy-stool, Porcino, Russula, Sacred, St George's, Scotch bonnet, Shaggymane, Shiitake, Sickener, Spread, Start-up, Straw, Truffle, Upstart, Velvet shank, Waxcap
Music Absolute, Light, Medieval, Minstrelsy, > MUSICAL INSTRUMENTS, Phase,

Piece, Pop(ular), Post-rock, Score

MUSIC

3 letters:
Air
AOR
Art
Dub
Emo
Gat
Jor
Pop
Rag
Rai
Rap
Rug
Ska
Son

4 letters:
Alap
Duet
Folk
Funk
Go-go
Jazz
Loco
Meno
Note
Opus
Prom
Raga
Riff
Rock
Romo
Soca
Soul
Surf
Tala
Trad
Trio
Tune
Zouk

5 letters:
Alaap
Alapa
Bebop
Canon
Chant
Cliff

Cu-bop
Disco
Dream
Early
Fugue
Funky
House
Indie
Jhala
Kwela
Largo
March
Motet
Muzak®
Neume
Nonet
Outro
Piped
Ragga
Rondo
Roots
Rough
Salon
Salsa
Sheet
Sokah
Staff
Suite
Swing
Thema
Tonal
Truth
Vocal
World

6 letters:
Arioso
Bebung
Bouree
Decani
Doo-wop
Enigma
Equali
Facade
Fugato
Gagaku
Galant
Garage

Gospel
Gothic
Grunge
Hip-hop
Jungle
Khayal
Kwaito
Lydian
Mantra
Marabi
Mashup
Melody
Motown®
New Age
Pycnon
Ragini
Redowa
Reggae
Rhythm
Rootsy
Sextet
Sonata
Strain
Techno
Techno
Thrash
Trance
Verset
Zydeco

7 letters:
Allegro
Andante
Ars nova
Ballade
Baroque
Bhangra
Bluette
Bourree
Britpop
Cadenza
Calypso
Cantata
Ceilidh
Chamber
Chorale
Country
Dad rock

Euterpe
Fanfare
Gangsta
Hardbag
Introit
Klezmer
Landler
Marcato
Melisma
Messiah
Morceau
New Wave
Numbers
Organum
Orphean
Partita
Passion
Pecking
Pibroch
Prelude
Qawwali
Quartet
Quintet
Ragtime
Rastrum
Requiem
Reverse
Romanza
Rondeau
Rondino
Rosalia
Roulade
Sanctus
Scherzo
Setting
Skiffle
Soukous
Toccata
Trip hop
Ziganka

8 letters:
Acid rock
Aleatory
Berceuse
Chaconne
Cock rock
Concerto

Concrete
Coranach
Coronach
Entracte
Fantasia
Flamenco
Folk rock
Glam rock
Hard core
Hard rock
High life
In nomine
Janizary
Karnatak
Lollipop
Madrigal
Maggiore
Mariachi
Mbaqanga
Modality
Nocturne
Notation
Old skool
Oratorio
Parlando
Partitur
Pastiche
Postlude
Psalmody
Punk rock
Rhapsody
Ricercar
Saraband

Serenade
Serenata
Symphony
Synth-pop

9 letters:
Acid-house
Allemande
Antiphony
Arabesque
Bagatelle
Bluegrass
Breakbeat
Cantilena
Capriccio
Dixieland
Drum'n'bass
Fioritura
Grandioso
Hillbilly
Honky-tonk
Interlude
Obbligato
Partitura
Pastorale
Plainsong
Polyphony
Prick-song
Quodlibet
Ricercare
Rock'n'roll
Septimole
Spiritual

Swingbeat
Tambourin
Technopop
Toccatina
Voluntary
Warehouse

10 letters:
Albumblatt
Anacrustic
Chopsticks
Coloratura
Desert rock
Electronic
Gangsta rap
Gothic rock
Heavy metal
Hindustani
Humoresque
Incidental
Intermezzo
Jam session
Martellato
New Country
Percussion
Polyhymnia
Ritornello
Rockabilly
Rocksteady
Seguidilla
Toccatella
Twelve-tone
Urban blues

11 letters:
Motor rhythm
Passacaglia
Psychobilly
Raggamuffin
Renaissance
Sinfonietta
Solmisation
Stadium rock
Third stream
Thrash metal

12 letters:
Boogie-woogie
Concertstuck
Contrapuntal
Divertimento
Electroclash
Nunc Dimittis
Pralltriller

13 letters:
Detroit techno
Progressional

14 letters:
Rhythm and blues

15 letters:
Musique concrete
Progressive rock

Musical Arcadian, Azione, Brigadoon, Cats, Chess, Euphonic, Evergreen, Evita, Gigi, Grease, Hair, Harmonious, Kabuki, Kismet, Lyric, Mame, Melodic, Oliver, Opera, Operetta, Orphean, Revue, Showboat
Musical box Juke-box, Polyphon(e)
Musical chairs Level-coil

MUSICAL INSTRUMENTS

2 letters:
Ax
Gu

3 letters:
Axe
Gue
Kit
Oud
Saz

Uke
Zel

4 letters:
Buva
Chyn
Crwd
Drum
Fife
Gong

Harp
Horn
Kora
Koto
Lure
Lute
Lyre
Moog®
Oboe
Pipa

Rate
Reed
Rote
Sang
Tuba
Vina
Viol
Zeze

5 letters:
Aulos
Banjo
Cello
Clave
Cobza
Corno
Crowd
Crwth
Esraj
Flute
Gazog
Guiro
Gusla
Gusle
Gusli
Kazoo
Mbira
Naker
Nebel
Organ
Piano
Quena
Rebec
Regal
Sanko
Sansa
Sarod
Shalm
Shawm
Sitar
Stick
Tabla
Tabor
Tibia
Veena
Viola
Zanze
Zinke

6 letters:
Antara
Bisser
Bongos
Citole
Cornet
Cymbal
Euphon
Flugel
Guitar
Kanoon
Maraca
Poogye
Racket
Rebeck
Ribibe
Sancho
Santir
Santur
Shalme
Shofar
Sittar
Spinet
Syrinx
Tom-tom
Trigon
Vielle
Violin
Zither
Zufolo

7 letters:
Anklong
Bagpipe
Bandore
Bandura
Baryton
Bassoon
Bazooka
Celesta
Celeste
Cembalo
Chikara
Cithara
Cittern
Clarino
Clarion
Clavier
Console
Cornett
Dichord
Dulcian
Fagotto
Flutina
Gamelan
Gazogka
Gittern
Hautboy
Helicon
High-hat
Kalimba
Kantela
Kantele
Kithara
Klavier
Lyricon
Mandola
Marimba
Musette
Ocarina
Pandora
Pandore
Pandura
Pianola®
Piccolo
Poogyee
Posaune
Rackett
Sackbut
Sambuca
Samisen
Santour
Sarangi
Saxhorn
Saxtuba
Serpent
Tambour
Tambura
Theorbo
Timbrel
Timpano
Trumpet
Tympany
Ukelele
Vihuela
Violone
Zuffolo

8 letters:
Angklung
Archlute
Autoharp®
Barytone
Berimbau
Bouzouki
Calliope
Canorous
Carillon
Charango
Cimbalom
Clarinet
Clarsach
Clavecin
Cornetto
Cornpipe
Cromorna
Cromorne
Crumhorn
Dulcimer
Gemshorn
Guarneri
Guimbard
Handbell
Hautbois
Humstrum
Jew's harp
Key-bugle
Langspel
Lyra-viol
Mandolin
Manzello
Martenot
Melodeon
Melodica
Mirliton
Oliphant
Ottavino
Pan pipes
Phorminx
Polyphon
Psaltery
Recorder
Reco-reco
Slughorn
Spinette
Sticcado
Sticcato
Surbahar
Tamboura
Tamburin
Tenoroon
Theremin
Triangle
Trombone
Virginal
Vocalion
Zambomba
Zampogna

9 letters:
Accordion
Aerophone
Alpenhorn
Balalaika
Bandoneon
Bandurria
Banjulele
Bombardon

Chalumeau
Cornemuse
Decachord
Dulcitone®
Euphonium
Flageolet
Flexatone
Gittarone
Gutbucket
Harmonica
Harmonium
Idiophone
Kent-bugle
Krummhorn
Langspiel
Mandoline
Monochord
Mouth-harp
Nose flute
Orpharion
Pantaleon
Pastorale
Polyphone
Saxophone
Seraphine
Slughorne
Snare-drum

Sopranino
Stockhorn
Trompette
Vibraharp
Washboard
Xylophone
Xylorimba

10 letters:
Bullroarer
Chitarrone
Clavichord
Colascione
Concertina
Cor anglais
Didgeridoo
Flugelhorn
French horn
Gramophone
Hurdy-gurdy
Kettledrum
Lagerphone
Mellophone
Nun's fiddle
Ophicleide
Orpheoreon
Pentachord

Shakuhachi
Squeeze-box
Stylophone®
Symphonium
Tambourine
Thumb piano
Vibraphone
Wokka board

11 letters:
Chordophone
Clairschach
Contrabasso
Harmoniphon
Harpsichord
Heckelphone
Nickelodeon
Orchestrina
Orchestrion
Phonofiddle
Straduarius
Synthesizer
Trump-marine
Violincello
Wobble-board

12 letters:
Chapman stick
Chinese block
Clavicembalo
Glockenspiel
Harmoniphone
Metallophone
Penny-whistle
Sarrusophone
Stock and horn
Stradivarius
Tromba-marina
Tubular bells

13 letters:
Contrabassoon
Ondes Martenot
Panharmonicon
Physharmonica

14 letters:
Glass harmonica
Jingling Johnny
Ondes musicales
Piano accordion

Music-hall Alhambra, Disco, Empire, Odeon
Musician(s), **Musicologist** Accompanist, Arion, Arist, Beiderbecke, Brain, Chanter, Clapton, Combo, > **COMPOSER**, Conductor, Crowder, Duet, Ensemble, Executant, Flautist, Gate, Grove, Guido d'Arezzo, Guslar, Handel, Jazzer, Jazzman, Joplin, Mahler, Mariachi, Menuhin, Minstrel, Muso, Noisenik, Nonet, Octet, Orphean, Pianist, Quartet, Quintet, Rapper, Reed(s)man, Répétiteur, Rubinstein, Septet, Session, Sextet, Sideman, Spohr, String, Techno, Tortelier, Troubador, Trouvère, Violinist, Wait
Musk Civet, Mimulus, Must
Musket Brown Bess, Caliver, Carabine, Eyas, Flintlock, Fusil, Hawk, Jezail, Nyas, Queen's-arm, Weapon
Musketeer Aramis, Athos, D'Artagnan, Fusilier, Ja(e)gar, Porthos, Rifleman, Sam
Muslim (ritual), **Moslem** Alaouite, Alawite, Ali, Almohad(e), Balochi, Baluchi, Berber, Black, Caliph, Dato, Dervish, Druse, Fatimid, Ghazi, Hadji, Hafiz, Hajji, He'zbolah, Iranian, Islamic, Ismaili, Karmathian, Khotbah, Khotbeh, Khutbah, Mahometan, Mogul, Mohammedan, Moor, Morisco, Moro, Mufti, Mus(s)ulman, Mutazilite, Nawab, Panislam, Paynim, Pomak, Said, Saracen, Say(y)id, Senus(s)i, Shafiite, Shia(h), Shiite, Sofi, Sonnite, Sufi, Sulu, Sunna, Sunni(te), Tajik, Turk, Ummah, Wahabee, Wahabi(te), Wahhabi
Muslin Butter, Cloth, Coteline, Gurrah, Jamdani, Leno, Mousseline, Mull, Nainsook, Organdie, Tarlatan, Tiffany
Musquash Ondatra
Mussel(s) Bearded, Bivalve, Clabby-doo, Clam, Clappy-doo, Deerhorn, Moules

mariniéres, Mytilus, Niggerhead, Pearl, Swan, Unio, Zebra

Mussorgsky Modest

Must(y) Amok, Essential, Foughty, Froughy, Frowsty, Frowy, Funky, Fust, Man, Maun(na), Mote, Mould, Mucid, Mun, Need(s)-be, Shall, Should, Stum, Wine

▷ **Must** *may indicate* an anagram

Mustard Black, Charlock, Cress, English, Erysimum, French, Garlic, Nitrogen, Praiseach, Quinacrine, Runch, Sauce-alone, Senvy, Treacle, Wall, White, Wild

Mustard plaster Sinapism

Muster Array, Assemble, Bangtail, Call up, Mass, Raise, Rally, Really, Recruit, Round-up, Wappenshaw

Mutability Wheel

Mutate, **Mutant**, **Mutation** Auxotroph(ic), Change, Somatic, Sport, Suppressor, Terata, Transform

▷ **Mutation** *may indicate* an anagram

Mute(d) Deaden, Dumb, Harpo, Noiseless, Silent, Sordino, Sordo, Sourdine, Stifle

Mutilate(d), **Mutilation** Castrate, Concise, Deface, Dismember, Distort, Garble, Hamble, Injure, Maim, Mangle, Mayhem, Obtruncate, Riglin, Tear

▷ **Mutilate(d)** *may indicate* an anagram

Mutineer, **Mutiny** Bounty, Caine, Christian, Curragh, Indian, Insurrection, Meerut, Nore, Pandy, > REVOLT, Rising, Sepoy

Mutter(ing) Chunter, Fremescent, Grumble, Mumble, Mump, Murmur, Mussitate, Rhubarb, Roin, Royne, Rumble, Whittie-whattie, Witter

Mutton Colonial goose, Em, Ewes, Fanny Adams, Gigot, Macon, Saddle, Sheep, Theave, Traik

Mutual (aid) Common, Log-roll, Reciprocal, Symbiosis

Muzzle Decorticate, Gag, Jaw, Mouth, Restrain, Snout

My Coo, Gemini, Golly, Gosh, Ha, Lor, Lumme, Musha, Odso, Oh, Our, Tush

Mynah Stare, Starling

Mynheer Stadholder

Myopia, **Myopic** Hidebound, Mouse-sight, Narrow, Short-sighted, Thick-eyed

Myriad Host, Zillion

Myristic Nutmeg

Myrrh Stacte

Myrtle Callistemon, Crape, Crepe, Eucalyptus, Gale, Jambolana, Tasmanian, Tooart, Tuart

Mysterious, **Mystery** Abdabs, Abdals, Acroamatic, Arcane, Arcanum, Cabbala, Closed book, Craft, Creepy, Cryptic, Dark, Deep, Delphic, Eleusinian, Enigma, Esoteric, Grocer, G(u)ild, Incarnation, Inscrutable, Miracle, Mystagogue, Numinous, Occult, Original sin, Orphic, Penetralia, Riddle, > SECRET, Telestic, Trinity, UFO, Uncanny, Whodunit

▷ **Mysterious(ly)** *may indicate* an anagram

Mystic (word), **Mystical** Abraxas, Agnostic, Cab(e)iri, Epopt, Fakir, Familist, Hesychast, Mahatma, Occultist, Quietism, Rasputin, Secret, Seer, Sofi, Sufi, Swami, Tantrist, Theosophy, Transcendental, Zohar

Mystify Baffle, Bamboozle, Bewilder, Metagrabolise, Metagrobolise, Puzzle

Myth(ology), **Mythical (beast)** Allegory, Behemoth, Bunyip, Centaur, Cockatrice, Dragon, Euhemerism, Fable, Fantasy, Fictitious, Folklore, Garuda, Geryon, Griffin, Hippocampus, Impundulu, Kelpie, Kylin, Legend, Leviathin, Lore, Otnit, Pantheon, Pegasus, Phoenix, Sea horse, Selkie, Solar, Speewah, Sphinx, Sun, Thunderbird, Tokoloshe, Unicorn, Urban, Wivern, Wyvern, Yale, Yeti

Nn

N Name, Nitrogen, Noon, North, November
Nab Arrest, Capture, Collar, Grab, Seize
Nabob Deputy, Nawab, Wealthy
Nadir Bottom, Depths, Dregs, Minimum
Nag(ging) Badger, Bidet, Brimstone, Callet, Cap, Captious, Complain, Fret, Fuss, Harangue, Harp, Henpeck, Horse, Jade, Jaw, Keffel, Peck, Pester, Plague, Rosinante, Rouncy, > **SCOLD**, Tit, Xant(h)ippe, Yaff
Nail(ed) Brad, Brod, Catch, Clinker, Clout, Coffin, Fasten, Hob, Keratin, Onyx, Pin, Rivet, Screw, Secure, Shoe, Sisera, Sparable, Sparrow-bill, Spick, Spike, Sprig, Staple, Stub, Stud, Tack(et), Talon, Tenpenny, Tenterhook, Thumb, Tingle, Toe, Unguis, Wire
Naive(té) Artless, Green, Guileless, Gullible, Ingenuous, Innocence, Open, Pollyanna, Simpliste, Simplistic, Unsophisticated, Wide-eyed
Naked Adamical, Artless, Bare, Blunt, Buff, Clear, Cuerpo, Defenceless, Encuerpo, Exposed, Gymno-, Kaal gat, Nuddy, Nude, Querpo, Raw, Scud, Simple, Skyclad, Stark(ers), Uncovered
Namby-pamby Milksop, Nance, Sissy, Weak, Weakling, White-shoe
Name(d), Names Agnomen, Alias, Allonym, Anonym, Appellation, Appoint, Baptise, Behight, Byline, Call, Celeb(rity), Christen, Cite, Cleep, Clepe, Cognomen, Day, Designate, Dinges, Dingus, Dit, Domain, Dub, Epithet, Eponym, Exonym, Family, First, Generic, Given, Handle, Hete, Hight, Hypocorism, Identify, Identity, Label, Maiden, Marque, Masthead, Mention, Metronymic, Middle, Moni(c)ker, Mud, N, Nap, Nemn, Nom, Nomen(clature), Noun, Onomastics, Onymous, Patronymic, Pennant, Personage, Pet, Place, Proper, Proprietary, Pseudonym, Quote, Red(d), Repute, Scilicet, Sign, Signature, Sir, Specify, Stage, Street, Substantive, Tag, Teknonymy, Term, > **TITLE**, Titular, Titule, Toponymy, Trade, Trivial
Name-dropper Eponym
Nameless Anon, Unchrisom
Namely Ie, Scilicet, To-wit, Videlicet, Viz
Namesake Homonym
Name unknown Anon, A N Other, NU
Nancy Coddle, Effeminate, Milksop
Nanny Ayah, Foster, Goat, Nurse
Naos Cell(a)
Nap(py) Ale, Bonaparte, Diaper, Doze, Drowse, Fluff, Frieze(d), Fuzz, Happen, Hippin(g), Kip, Moze, Oose, Ooze, Oozy, Power, Put(t), Shag, Siesta, > **SLEEP**, Slumber, Snooze, Tease, Teasel, Teaze, Tipsy, Tuft
Nape Niddick, Noddle, Nucha, Scrag, Scruff, Scuff, Scuft
Napier Logarithm
Napkin Cloth, Diaper, Doily, Doyley, Linen, Muckender, Paper, Sanitary, Serviette, Table
Napless Threadbare

Napoleon Badinguet, Bonaparte, Boustrapa, Cognac, Coin, Consul, Corporal Violet, Corsican, December, Little Corporal, Nantz, Nap, Pig, Rantipole
Napper Bonce, Shearman
Narcissus Echo, Egocentric, Jonquil
Narcotic Ava, Benj, B(h)ang, Charas, Churrus, Coca, Codeine, Datura, Dope, > DRUG, Heroin, Hop, Kava, Laudanum, Mandrake, Marijuana, Meconium, Methadone, Morphia, Opiate, Pituri, Sedative, Tea, Trional
Nark Grass, Inform, Irritate, Nose, Pique, Roil, Squealer, Stag
Narrate, **Narration**, **Narrative**, **Narrator** Allegory, Anecdote, Cantata, Describe, Diegesis, Fable, History, Oblique, Periplus, Plot, Raconteur, Récit, Recite, Recount, Saga, Scheherazade, Splatterpunk, Story, Tell, Voice-over
Narrow(ing), **Narrow-minded** Alf, Bigoted, Borné, Constringe, Cramp, Ensiform, Grundy(ism), Hidebound, Illiberal, Insular, Kyle, Limited, Meagre, Nary, One-idead, Parochial, Phimosis, Pinch, Provincial, Prudish, Puritan, Scant, Sectarian, Shrink, Slender, Slit, Specialise, Squeak, Stenosed, Strait, Suburban, Verkramp, Waist
Narwhal Monodon
Nasal Adenoidal, Twang
Nash Beau
Nashville Bath
Nastiness, **Nasty** Disagreeable, Drevill, Filth, Fink, Ghastly, Lemon, Lo(a)th, Malign(ant), Noxious, Obscene, Odious, Offensive, Ribby, Sordid, Vile
Nat(haniel) Hawthorne, Winkle
Natal Inborn, Native, Patrial
Natant Afloat, Swimming
Nation(s), **National(ist)** Anthem, Baathist, Casement, Chetnik, Country, Cuban, Debt, Eta, Federal, Five, Folk, Grand, Indian, IRA, Israeli, Jingoist, Land, Mexican, Pamyat, Patriot, > PEOPLE, Plaid Cymr, Polonia, Race, Rainbow, Risorgimento, Scottish, Six, SNP, Subject, Swadeshi, United, Verkrampte, Vietminh, Wafd, Yemini, Young Ireland, Zionist
Native(s) Abo(rigin), Aborigine, African, Amerind, Annamese, Arab, Ascian, Australian, Autochthon, Aztec, Basuto, Belonging, Bengali, Boy, Bushman, Cairene, Carib, Carioca, Chaldean, Citizen, Colchester, Conch, Creole, Criollo, Domestic, Dyak, Edo, Enchorial, Eskimo, Fleming, Fuzzy-wuzzy, Genuine, Habitual, Home-bred, Inborn, Inca, Indigene, Indigenous, Inhabitant, Intuitive, John Chinaman, Kaffir, Libyan, Local, Malay, Maori, Micronesian, Moroccan, Norwegian, Oyster, Polack, Portuguese, Scythian, Son, Spaniard, Te(i)an, Thai, Tibetan, Uzbeg, Uzbek, Whitstable, Yugoslav
Nativity Birth, Jataka, Putz
Natron Urao
Natter Chat, Gossip, Jack, Prate
Natty Bumppo, Chic, Dapper, Leatherstocking, Smart, Spruce
Natural(ly), **Naturalised**, **Naturalism** Artless, Ass, Denizen, Easy, Genuine, Homely, Idiot, Illegitimate, Inborn, Inbred, Indigenous, Ingenerate, Inherent, Innate, Moron, Native, Nidget, Nitwit, Nude, Ordinary, Organic, Prat, Real, Simpleton, Simpliciter, Sincere, True, Undyed, Untaught, Verism
Naturalist Buffon, Darwin, Wallace, White
Nature Adam, Akin, Character, Disposition, Esse(nce), Ethos, Haecceity, Human, Inscape, Mould, Quiddity, Quintessence, Second, SN, Temperament
Naught Cypher, Failure, Nil, Nothing, Zero
Naughty Bad, Disobedient, Girly, Improper, Light, Marietta, Nonny, Rascal, Remiss, Spright, Sprite, Wayward

Nausea, **Nauseous** Disgust, Fulsome, Malaise, Queasy, Sickness, Squeamish, Wamble, Wambly

Nave Aisle, Apse, Centre, Hub, Nef

Navel Belly-button, Naff, Nave, Omphalos, Umbilicus

Navigate, **Navigator** Albuquerque, Bougainville, Cabot, Cartier, Columbus, Control, Da Gama, Dias, Direct, Franklin, Frobisher, Gilbert, Hartog, Haul, Henry, Hudson, Keel, Magellan, Navvy, Orienteer, Pilot, Sail, Star-read, > **STEER**, Tasman, Traverse, Vancouver, Vespucci

Navigation (aid, system) Asdic, Cabotage, Celestial, Decca, Dectra, Fido, Gee, Inland, Loran, Loxodromics, Navarho, Omnirange, Portolan(o), Portulan, Radar, Satnav, Shoran, Tacan, Teleran®, Vor

Navvy Workhorse

Navy, **Naval** AB, Armada, Blue, Fleet, French, Maritime, Merchant, N, Red, RN, Senior Service, Wren

Nawab Huzoor, Nabob, Viceroy

Nazi Brownshirt, Gauleiter, Hess, Hitler, Jackboot, SS, Stormtrooper, Wer(e)wolf

NB Niobium, Nota bene

NCO Bombardier, Corp(oral), Havildar, Noncom, Orderly, Sergeant, SM

Neanderthal Mousterian

Neap Low, Tide

Neapolitan Ice

Near(er), **Nearest**, **Nearby**, **Nearly**, **Nearness** About, Adjacent, All-but, Almost, Anigh, Approach, Approximate, Beside, By, Close, Cy pres, Degree, Even, Ewest, Feckly, Forby, Gain, Handy, Hither, Imminent, Inby(e), Mean, Miserly, Narre, Neist, Next, Nie, Niggardly, Nigh, Outby, Propinquity, Proximity, Short-range, Stingy, Thereabout(s), To, Upon, Warm, Well-nigh

Neat(ly) Bandbox, Cattle, Clean-cut, Clever, Dainty, Dapper, Deft, Dink(y), Doddy, Donsie, Elegant, Feat(e)ous, Featly, Featuous, Gayal, Genty, Gyal, Intact, Jemmy, Jimpy, Lower, Nett, Ninepence, Orderly, Ox(en), Preppy, Pretty, Rother, Shipshape, Short, Smug, Snod, Spruce, Straight, > **TIDY**, Trig, Trim, Unwatered

Neb Beak, Bill, Nose, Snout

Nebula, **Nebulous** Aeriform, Celestial, Cloudy, Gum, Hazy, Horsehead, Obscure, Planetary, Shadowy, Vague

Necessary, **Necessarily** Bog, Cash, De rigueur, > **ESSENTIAL**, Estovers, Important, Indispensable, Intrinsic, Money, Needful, Ought, Perforce, Prerequisite, Requisite, Vital, Wherewithal

Necessitate, **Necessity** Ananke, Compel, Constrain, Cost, Emergency, Entail, Exigent, Fate, Indigence, Logical, Mathematical, Must, Natural, Need, Need-be, Oblige, Perforce, Require, Requisite

Neck(ed) Bottle, Brass, Canoodle, Cervical, Cervix, Channel, Col, Crag, Craig, Crop, Cuff, Embrace, Ewe, Gall, Gorgerin, Halse, Hawse, Inarm, Inclip, Isthmus, Kiss, Mash, Nape, Pet, Polo, Rack, Rubber, Scoop, Scrag, Scruff, Smooch, Snog, Stiff, Strait, Surgical, Swan, Swire, Theorbo, Torticollis, Trachelate, Vee

Necking *may indicate* one word around another

Necklace Anodyne, Brisingamen, Chain, Choker, Collar, Corals, Lava(l)lière, Lunula, Mangalsutra, Negligee, Pearls, Rope, Sautoir, String, Torc, Torque

Neckline Boat, Collar, Cowl, Crew, Décolletage, Lanyard, Palter, Plunging, Sweetheart, Turtle, Vee

Neckwear Ascot, Barcelona, Boa, Bow, Collar, Cravat, Fur, Rail, Steenkirk, Stock, Tie

Necromancer Goetic, Magician, Ormandine, Osmand, Witch, Wizard

Necrosis Infarct, Sphacelus
Nectar Ambrosia, Amrita, Honey, Mead
Ned(dy) Donkey, Kelly, Ludd
Need(ed), Needy Beggarly, Call, Demand, Desiderata, Egence, Egency, Exigency, Gap, Gerundive, Impecunious, Indigent, > LACK, Mister, Pressing, PRN, Require, Strait, Strapped, Want
Needle(s) Acerose, Acicular, Aciform, Between, Bodkin, Cleopatra's, Darning, Dip, Dry-point, Electric, Goad, Gramophone, Hagedorn, Hype, Hypodermic, Ice, Icicle, Inoculate, Leucotome, Magnetic, Miff, Monolith, Neeld, Neele, Netting, Obelisk, Pine, Pinnacle, Pique, Pointer, Prick, R(h)aphis, Sew, Sharp, Spanish, Spicule, Spike, Spine, Stylus, Tattoo, Tease, Thorn, Wire
Needlewoman Cleopatra, Seamstress
Needlework Baste, Crewel, Drawn(-thread), Embroidery, Fag(g)oting, Fancy work, Mola, Patchwork, Petit point, Plainwork, Rivière, Sampler, Smocking, Spanish, Tapestry, Tattoo, Woolwork, Worsted-work
Ne'er-do-well Badmash, Budmash, Bum, Good-for-nothing, Scullion, Shiftless, Skellum, Wastrel
Negation, Negative Ambrotype, Anion, Apophatic, Cathode, Denial, Double, Enantiosis, False, Ne, No, Non, Nope, Nullify, Pejorative, Photograph, Refusal, Resinous, Unresponsive, Veto, Yin
Neglect(ed), Neglectful, Negligence, Negligent Careless, Casual, Cinderella, Contributory, Cuff, Default, Dereliction, Disregard, Disuse, Failure, Forget, Forlorn, Heedless, Inadvertence, Inattention, Incivism, Laches, Malpractice, Misprision, Omission, Oversight, Pass, Pass-up, > REMISS, Shirk, Slight, Slipshod, Undone, Waif, Wanton
▷ **Neglected** *may indicate* an anagram
Negligee Déshabillé, Manteau, Mob, Nightgown, Peignoir, Robe
Negligible Fig, Minimal
Negotiate, Negotiator Arbitrate, Arrange, Bargain, Clear, Confer, Deal, Diplomat, Haggle, Intermediary, Liaise, Manoeuvre, Mediator, Parley, Trade, Transact, Treat(y), Weather
Negro(id) > AFRICAN, Baganda, Bambara, Barotse, Bemba, Bergdama, Bini, Black, Buck, Chewa, Creole, Cuffee, Cuffy, Damara, Dinge, Duala, Dyula, Ebon(y), Edo, Efik, Ethiop, Ewe, Fang, Ga, Ganda, Gullah, Hausa, Hottentot, Hutu, Ibibio, Ibo, Igorot, Jim Crow, Kikuyu, Kongo, Luba, Luganda, Malinke, Maninke, Mestee, Moke, Moor, Mossi, Mustee, Ndebele, Nilote, Nupe, Nyanja, Nyoro, Ovambo, Pondo, Quashee, Quashie, Sambo, Snowball, Spade, Susu, Temne, Thick-lips, Tiv, Tonga, Tsonga, Tswana, Twi, Uncle Tom, Vanda, Watu(t)si, Wolof, Xhosa, Yoruba, Zambo, Zulu
Negus Emperor, Rumfruction, Selassie
Nehru Pandit
Neigh Bray, Hinny, Nicker, Whicker, Whinny
Neighbour(ly), Neighbouring, Neighbours Abut(ter), Adjoin, Alongside, Amicable, Bor, Border, But, Friendly, Joneses, Nearby, Next-door, Vicinal
Neighbourhood Area, Community, District, Environs, Locality, Precinct, Vicinage, Vicinity
Neither Nor
Nell(ie), Nelly Bly, Dean, Trent
Nelson Columnist, Eddy, Horatio
Nemesis Alastor, Avenger, Deserts, Downfall, Fate, Retribution, Revenge
Neodymium Nd
Neolithic Avebury, Halafian, Stonehenge

Neon Ne
Nepalese Gurkha
Neper N
Nephrite Yu
Nepotism Kin, Partisan, Patronage
Neptune God, Planet, Poseidon
Neptunium Np
Nerd Anorak, Otaku
Nereid Cymodoce, Nymph, Panope
Nerve(s), **Nervous(ness)**, **Nervure**, **Nerve centre**, **Nervy** Abdabs, Abducens, Accessory, Acoustic, Afferent, Aflutter, Afraid, Alveolar, Appestat, Auditory, Axon, Baroreceptor, Bottle, Bouton, Buccal, Chord, Chutzpah, Collywobbles, Column, Commissure, Cones, Courage, Cranial, Cyton, Depressor, Edgy, Effector, Efferent, Electrotonus, Epicritic, Excitor, Facial, Gall, Ganglion, Glossopharyngeal, Grit, Guts, Habdabs, Heart-string, High, Highly-strung, Hyp, Hypoglossal, Impudence, Jitters, Jittery, Median, Mid-rib, Motor, Myelon, Nappy, Neck, Nidus, Octulomotor, Olfactory, Optic, Pavid, Perikaryon, Proprioceptor, Rad, Radial, Receptor, Restiform, Restless, Sacral, Sangfroid, Sauce, Sciatic, Screaming abdabs, Screaming meemies, Sensory, Shaky, Shpilkes, Solar plexus, Splanchnic, Spunk, Squirrel(l)y, Steel, Strung-up, Synapse, Tense, Tizzy, Toey, Tongue-tied, Trembler, Tremulous, Trigeminal, Trochlear, Twitchy, Ulnar, Uptight, Vagus, Vapours, Vestibulocochlear, Wandering, Willies, Windy, Yips
Nervous disease, **Nervous disorder** Chorea, Epilepsy, Neuritis, Tetany
Nervously *may indicate* an anagram
Ness Cape, Headland, Ras
Nessus Centaur
Nest Aerie, Aery, Aiery, Ayrie, Bike, Bink, Brood, Byke, Cabinet, Cage, Caliology, Clutch, Dray, Drey, Eyrie, Eyry, Lodge, Love, Nid, Nide, Nidify, Nidus, Norwegian, Sett, Termitarium, Wurley
Nestle Burrow, Coorie, Cose, Courie, Cuddle, Nuzzle, Snug(gle)
Nestor Counsellor, Kea, Sage
Net(ting), **Nets**, **Network** Anastomosis, Bamboo, BR, Bunt, Butterfly, Cast, Casting, Catch, Caul, Clap, Clathrate, Clear, Cobweb, Crinoline, Crossover, Drift, Earn, Eel-set, Enmesh, Equaliser, Ethernet, Fetch, Filet, Final, Fish, Flew, Flue, Fyke, Gill, > **GRID**, Hammock, Heliscoop, Internet, Intranet, JANET, Kiddle, Lace, LAN, Land, Landing, Lattice, Leap, Line, Linin, Mains, Malines, Maze, > **MESH**, Mosquito, Neural, Neuropic, Old boys', PCN, Plexus, Portal system, Pound, Pout, Purse-seine, Quadripole, Reseau, Rete, Retiary, Reticle, Reticulate, Reticulum, Ring, Safety, Sagene, Screen, Sean, Seine, Set(t), Shark, Snood, Sweep-seine, System, Tangle, Tela, Telex, Toil, Torpedo, Trammel, Trap, Trawl, Tulle, Tunnel, Usenet, WAN, Web, Wide-area, Wire
Netball Let
Nether Below, Inferior, Infernal, Lower, Under
Nettle(rash) Anger, Annoy, Day, Dead, Hemp, Hives, Horse, Irritate, Labiate, Nark, Pellitory, Pique, Ramee, Rami, Ramie, Rile, Roman, Ruffle, Sting, Urtica(ceae), Urticaria
Neuralgia, **Neuritis** Migraine, Sciatica, Tic
Neurosis Compulsion, Obsessive-compulsive, Shellshock
Neuter Castrate, Gib, Impartial, Neutral, Sexless, Spay
Neutral(ise) Alkalify, Angel gear, Buffer zone, Counteract, Grey, Impartial, Inactive, Schwa, Sheva, Shiva, Unbiased

Neutron(s) Fast, Nucleon, Thermal, Virgin
Never(more) Nary, Nathemo(re), No more, Nowise, St Tibb's Eve
Never-ending Age-long
Nevertheless Algate, Anyhow, But, Even, However, Quand même, Still, Tout de même, Yet
▷ **New** *may indicate* an anagram
New(s), News agency Bulletin, Copy, Coranto, Dope, Euphobia, Evangel, Flash, Forest, Fresh, Fudge, Gen, Green, Griff, Info, Innovation, Intelligence, Item, Kerygma, Latest, Mint, Modern, N, Novel, Oil(s), Original, PA, Paragraph, Pastures, Pristine, Propaganda, Recent, Report, Reuter, Scoop, Span, Split, Star Tass, Tass, Teletext®, Tidings, Ultramodern, Unco, Usenet, Wire service, Word
New boy Gyte
Newcomer Dog, Freshman, Griffin, Immigrant, Jackaroo, Jackeroo, Jillaroo, Johnny-come-lately, Novice, Parvenu, Pilgrim, Settler, Tenderfoot, Upstart
Newfoundland Dog, Nana, Vinland
Newgate Calendar
Newly wed Benedick, Benedict, Bride, Groom, Honeymooner, Neogamist
Newman Cardinal, Noggs
New moon Rosh Chodesh
Newsman, News-reader Announcer, Editor, Journalist, Press, Reporter, Sub, Sysop
Newsmonger, News-vendor Butcher, Gossip, Quidnunc
Newspaper Blat(t), Broadsheet, Courier, Daily, Express, Fanzine, Feuilleton, Freesheet, Gazette, Guardian, Herald, Journal, Jupiter, Le Monde, Mercury, National, Organ, Patent inside, Patent outside, Post, Pravda, Press, Print, Rag, Red-top, Scandal sheet, Sheet, Spoiler, Squeak, Sun, Tabloid, Today
Newsreel Actualities
Newt(s) Ask(er), Eft, Evet, Swift, Triton, Urodela
Newton N
New world USA
New year Hogmanay, Neer-day, Rosh Hashana(h), Tet
New York(er) Big apple, Gotham, Knickerbocker
New Zealand(er) Aotearoa, Enzed, Jafa, Kiwi, Maori, Mooloo, Moriori, Pakeha, Pig Island, Shagroon, Zelanian
Next Adjacent, Adjoining, After, Alongside, Beside, Following, Immediate, Later, Nearest, Neist, Proximate, Proximo, Sine, Subsequent, Syne
Nib J, Pen, Point, Tip
Nibble Bite, Brouse, Browse, Byte, Crop, Eat, Gnaw, Knap(ple), Moop, Moup, Munch, Nag, Nepit, Nosh, Peck, Pick, Snack
Nice(ty) Accurate, Amene, Appealing, Cool, Dainty, Fastidious, Fine, Finical, Genteel, Lepid, Mooi, Ninepence, Pat, Pleasant, Precise, Quaint, Rare, Refined, Subtil(e), Subtle, Sweet, T
Niche Alcove, Almehrahb, Almery, Ambry, Apse, Aumbry, Awmrie, Awmry, Columbarium, Cranny, Exedra, Fenestella, Mihrab, Recess, Slot
Nicholas Santa
Nick(ed) Appropriate, Arrest, Bin, Blag, Can, Chip, Cly, Colin, Copshop, Cut, Denay, Dent, Deny, > DEVIL, Erose, Groove, Hoosegow, Kitty, Knock, Nab, Nap, Nim, Nock, Notch, Pinch, Pook, Pouk, Prison, Scratch, > STEAL, Steek, Swan-upping, Swipe, Thieve, Whip, Wirricow, Worricow, Worrycow
Nickel (silver) Coin, Garnierite, Jitney, Millerite, Ni, Packfong, Paktong, Zaratite
Nicker Bonduc, Neigh, Whinny
Nickname Alias, Byname, Byword, Cognomen, So(u)briquet, To-name

Nicotine Tobacco, Weed

Nifty Smart, Stylish

Nigeria(n) Biafran, Efik, Hausa, Ibibio, Ibo, Igbo, Nupe, WAN, Yoruba

Niggard(ly) Dry-fist, Illiberal, Mean, Miser, Near-(be)gaun, Nippy, Nirlit, Parsimonious, Pinchcommons, Pinchgut, Pinchpenny, Scrunt, Skinflint, Tightwad

Niggle Carp, Gripe, Nag, Trifle

Night(s), Nightfall Acronychal, Arabian, Darkmans, First, Gaudy, Guest, Guy Fawkes, Hen, Leila, Nacht, Nicka-nan, Nutcrack, Nyx, School, Stag, Twelfth, Twilight, Walpurgis, Watch, White

Night-blindness Day-sight, Nyctalopia

Night-cap Biggin, Cocoa, Kilmarnock cowl, Nip, Pirnie, Sundowner

Nightclub Clip joint, Dive, Honkytonk

Night-dew Serein, Serene

Nightdress Wylie-coat

Nightingale Bulbul, Florence, Jugger, Lind, Philomel, Scutari, Swedish, Watch

Nightjar Evejar, Fern-owl, Goatsucker, Poorwill, Potoo

Night-light Moonbeam

Nightmare, Nightmarish Cacod(a)emon, Ephialtes, Incubus, Kafkaesque, Oneirodynia, Phantasmagoria

Night-rider Revere

Nightshade Belladonna, Bittersweet, Black, Circaea, Deadly, Dwale, Enchanter's, Henbane, Morel, Solanum, Woody

Nightwatchman Charley, Charlie, Rug-gown

Nightwork Lucubrate

Nihilist Anarchist, Red, Sceptic

Nil Nothing, Nought, Zero

Nile Albert, Blue, Luvironza, Victoria, White

Nimble, Nimbly Active, > AGILE, Alert, Deft, Deliver, Fleet, Light, Light-footed, Lissom(e), Lithe, Quiver, Sciolto, Springe, Spry, Supple, Swack, Wan(d)le, Wannel, Wight, Ya(u)ld

Nimbus Aura, Aureole, Cloud, Gloriole, Halo

Nimrod Hunter

Nincompoop Ass, Imbecile, Ninny, Stupid

Nine, Ninth Choral, Ennead, Muses, Nonary, Nonet, Novenary, Pins, Sancho, Skittles, Tailors, Worthies

Nine hundred Sampi

Nine of Diamonds Curse of Scotland

Nineteen(th) Bar, Decennoval

Ninetieth, Ninety N, Nonagesimal

Ninevite Assyrian

Ninny (hammer) Fool, Goose, Idiot, Stupid, Tony

Ninon Nan

Niobium Nb

Nip(per) Bite, Check, Chela, Chill, Claw, Dram, Fang, Gook, Jap, Lad, Lop, Nep, Nirl, Peck, Pincers, Pinch, Pook, Pop, Scotch, Sneap, Susan, Taste, Tot, Tweak, Urchin, Vice, Vise

Nipa At(t)ap, Palm

Nipple Dug, Grease, Jogger's, Mastoid, Pap, Teat

Nis Brownie, Goblin, Kobold, Sprite

Nit Egg, Insect, Louse

Nitre Saltpetre

Nitric, Nitrogen Azote, Azotic, Gas, N, Quinoline

Nitroglycerine Glonoin

Nitwit Ass, Flat, Fool, Simpleton, > STUPID

No Aikona, Denial, Na(e), Nah, Negative, Nix, Nope, Nyet, O, Refusal

Noah Arkite, Beery, Utnapishtim

Nob(by) Grandee, Parage, Prince, Swell, Toff

Nobble Dope, Hilch, Injure, Interfere

▷ **Nobbled** *may indicate* an anagram

Nobelium No

Noble(man), Noblewoman, Nobility Adeline, Aristocrat, Atheling, Baron(et), Bart, Boyar, Brave, Bt, Burgrave, Childe, Count, County, Daimio, Dom, Don, Doucepere, Douzeper(s), Duc, Duke, Duniwassal, Earl, Empress, Eorl, Ethel, Eupatrid, Fine, Gent, Glorious, Graf, Grandee, Grandeur, Great, Heroic, Hidalgo, Highborn, Infant, Jarl, Junker, King, Landgrave, Lord, Magnate, Magnifico, Manly, Margrave, Marquis, Nair, Nayar, Palatine, Patrician, Peer, Rank, Seigneur, Seignior, Sheik(h), Stately, Sublime, Thane, Thegn, Titled, Toiseach, Toisech, Vavasour, Vicomte, Vidame, Viscount

Nobody Gnatling, Jack-straw, Nebbish, Nemo, None, Nonentity, Nyaff, Pooter, Quat, Schlepp, Scoot, Shlep

Nocturnal (creature) Bat, Galago, Moth, Night, Owl

Nod(ding) Agree, Assent, Beck(on), Bob, Browse, Catnap, Cernuous, Doze, Headbang, Mandarin, Nutant, Somnolent

Node, Nodular, Nodule Ascending, Boss, Descending, Enhydros, Geode, Knot, Lump, Lymph, Milium, Pea-iron, Ranvier, Root, Swelling, Thorn, Tubercle

No doubt Iwis, Ywis

Noel Christmas, Coward, Yule

Nog(gin) Ale, Cup, > DRINK, Peg

No good Dud, NG, Ropy

No-hoper Gone goose

Noise, Noisy Ambient, Babel, Bedlam, Big, Blare, Bleep, Blip, Bobbery, Boing, Boink, Bruit, Cangle, Charm, Chellup, Clamant, Clamour, Clangour, Clash, Clatter, Clitter, Clutter, Coil, Crackle, Creak, Deen, Din, Dirdum, Euphonia, Euphony, F, Flicker, Fuss, Hewgh, Hubbub, Hue, Hullabaloo, Hum, Hurly-burly, Knocking, Loud, Mush, Obstreperous, Ping, Pink, Plangent, Quonk, Racket, Report, Roar, Robustious, Rorie, Rort, Rory, Row(dow-dow), Rowdedow, Rowdy(dow)(dy), Rucous, Schottky, Scream, Screech, Shindig, Shindy, Shot, Shreek, Shreik, Shriech, Shriek, Solar, Sone, Sonorous, Sound, Strepent, Strepitation, Strepitoso, Stridor, Surface, Thermal, Thunder, Tinnitus, Top, Tumult, > UPROAR, VIP, Vociferous, White, Zoom

Noisome Fetid, Invidious, Noxious, Offensive, Rank

No longer Ex, Past

Nomad(ic) Amalekite, Ammonites, Bedawin, Bed(o)uin, Bedu, Berber, Chal, Edom(ite), Fula(h), Gypsy, Hottentot, Hun, Hunter-gatherer, Itinerant, Kurd, Kyrgyz, Rom, Rootless, Rover, Saracen, Sarmatian, Strayer, Tsigane, Tsigany, Tuareg, Turk(o)man, Unsettled, Vagabond, Vagrant, Zigan

Noman Ta(r)tar

Nome Province

Nominal Formal, Onomastic, Titular, Trifling

Nominate, Nomination Appoint, Baptism, Designate, Elect, Present, > PROPOSE, Slate, Specify, Term

Nomogram Abac

No more Gone, Napoo

Nomothete Enactor, Legislator
Non-attender Absentee, Recusant
Non-believer Atheist, Cynic, Infidel, Sceptic
Non-catalyst Zymogen
Nonchalance, **Nonchalant** Blasé, Casual, Cool, Debonair, Insouciant, Jaunty, Poco
Noncommittal Trimmer
Non-communist West
Non-conformist, **Non-conformity** Beatnik, Bohemian, Chapel, Deviant, Dissent(er), Dissident, Ebenezer, Heresiarch, Heretic, Maverick, Odd-ball, Outlaw, Pantile, Patarine, Rebel, Recusant, Renegade, Renegate, Sectarian, Wesleyan
Nondescript Dull, Grey, Insipid, Neutral, Nyaff
None Nada, Nary, Nil, Nought, Zero
Nonentity Cipher, Nebbich, Nebbish(er), Nebish, Nobody, Pipsqueak, Quat
Non-essential Adiaphoron, Extrinsic, Incidental
Nonesuch Model, Nonpareil, Paradigm, Paragon, Rarity
Nonetheless Mind you
▷ **Nonetheless** *may indicate* an 'o' to be omitted
Non-finite Verbid
Non-gypsy Gajo, Gorgio
Non-interference Laissez faire
Non-Jewish Goy, Shi(c)ksa, Shkitzim, Sho(y)getz
Non-juror Usager
Non-Maori Tangata tiriti, Tauiwi
Non-Muslim Raia, Rayah
No-nonsense Hardball
Nonpareil Nonesuch, Pearl, Peerless, Type, Unequal, Unique
Nonplus(sed) Baffle, Bewilder, Blank, Perplex, Stump
Non-professional Amateur, Laic
Non-radiative Auger
Non-resident Extern, Outlier
Non-runner Scratched, Solid
Nonsense Absurdity, Amphigon, Amphigory, Balderdash, Baloney, Bilge, Bizzo, Blague, Blah, Blarney, Blat(her), Blether, Bollocks, Boloney, Bora(c)k, Borax, Bosh, Bull, Bulldust, Bullshit, Bull's wool, Buncombe, Bunkum, Clamjamfr(a)y, Clamjamphrie, Claptrap, Cobblers, Cock, Cockamamie, Cod, Codswallop, Crap, Crapola, Drivel, Dust, Eyewash, Faddle, Falderal, Fandangle, Fiddlededee, Fiddle-faddle, Fiddlesticks, Flannel, Flapdoodle, Flim-flam, Folderol, Footling, Fudge, Gaff, Galimatias, Gammon, Get away, Gibberish, Guff, Gum, Hanky-panky, Haver, Hogwash, Hokum, Hooey, Horsefeathers, Humbug, Jabberwocky, Kibosh, Kidstakes, Malark(e)y, Moonshine, Mouthwash, My eye, Niaiserie, Phooey, Piffle, Pishogue, Pshaw, Pulp, Ratbaggery, Rats, Rhubarb, Rigmarole, Rot, Rubbish, Scat, Shenanigans, Shit(e), Squit, Stuff, Tom(foolery), Tommy-rot, Tosh, Trash, Tripe, Tush, Twaddle, Unreason, Waffle
Non-sequitur Anacoluthia, Irrelevant
Non-stick Tusche
Non-stop Through
Non-U Naff
Non-violence Ahimsa, Pacificism, Satyagraha
Non-white Coloured, Yolk

Noodle(s) Capellini, Crispy, Daw, Fool, Head, Laksa, Lokshen, Manicotti, Mee, Moony, Pasta, Sammy, Simpleton, Soba, Udon
Nook Alcove, Angle, Corner, Cranny, Niche, Recess, Rookery
Noon Am end, M, Midday, N, Narrowdale
No one Nemo, None
Noose Fank, Halter, Lanyard, Loop, Necktie, Rope, Rope's end, Snare, Twitch
▶ **Nor** *see* NOT
Nordic, Norse(man) Icelander, Norn, Scandinavian, Viking
▶ **Nordic** *see* NORWAY, NORWEGIAN
Norm Canon, Criterion, Rule, Standard
Normal Average, Conventional, Customary, Everyday, General, Natural, Norm, Ordinary, Orthodox, Par, Perpendicular, Regular, Standard, Unexceptional, Usu(al)
Normal eyes Emmetropia
Norman French, Rufus
▶ **Norse** *see* NORWAY, NORWEGIAN
North(ern), Northerner Arctic, Boreal, Cispontine, Copperhead, Doughface, Eskimo, Geographic, Hyperborean, Magnetic, N, Norland, Runic, Septentrion, True, Up
North American (Indian) Ab(e)naki, Algonki(a)n, Algonqui(a)n, Apache, Arapaho, Assiniboine, Basket Maker, Blackfoot, Brave, Caddoan, Cajun, Cayuga, Cherokee, Cheyenne, Chibcha, Chickasaw, Chinook, Chipewyan, Choctaw, Comanche, Copperskin, Creek, Crow, Delaware, Dene, Erie, Fox, Galibi, Geronimo, Haida, Hiawatha, Hopi, Huron, Injun, Iroquois, Kiowa Apache, Kootenai, Kootenay, Kutenai, Kwakiuti, Lakota, Mahican, Malecite, Mandan, Manhattan, Massachuset(ts), Melungeon, Menominee, Mescalero, Micmac, Mikasuki, Miniconjou, Minneconjou, Mission, Mogollon, Mohave, Mohawk, Mohegan, Mohican, Montagnais, Montagnard, Mound Builder, Mugwump, Muskogee, Narraganset, Natchez, Navaho, Nez Percé, Nootka, Northern P(a)iute, Oglala, Ojibwa(y), Okanagon, Okinagan, Omaha, Oneida, Onondaga, Osage, P(a)iute, Palouse, Papago, Papoose, Pawnee, Pequot, Pima, Plains, Pocahontas, Pomo, Ponca, Pontiac, Potawatom, Pueblo, Quapaw, Red(skin), Sachem, Sagamore, Sahaptan, Sahapti(a)n, Salish, Sannup, Sauk, Scalper, Seminole, Senecan, Serrano, Shawnee, Shoshone, Sioux, Sitting Bull, Siwash, Southern P(a)iute, Status, Suquamash, Susquehannock, Tahitan, Taino, Tarahumara, Teton, Tewa, Tiwa, Tlingit, Tribe, Tsimshian, Tuscarora, Ute, Wampanoag, Wichita, Winnebago, Wyandot(te), Yalkama, Yanqui, Yuman, Zuni
Northwestern Aeolis
Norway, Norwegian Bokmal, Fortinbras, Landsma(a)l, N, Nordic, Norweyan, Nynorsk, Rollo
Nose, Nosy A(d)jutage, Aquiline, Beak, Bergerac, Boko, Bouquet, Catarrhine, Conk, Cromwell, Curious, Desman, Droop, Fink, Flair, Gnomon, Grass, Grecian, Greek, Grog-blossom, Honker, Hooter, Index, Informer, Leptorrhine, Meddle, Muffle, Muzzle, Nark, Neb, Nozzle, Nuzzle, Parker, Platyrrhine, Proboscis, Prying, Pug, Rhinal, Roman, Schnozzle, Shove, Smelly, Sneb, Sniff, Snoot, Snout, Snub, Squeal, Stag, Stickybeak, Toffee
Noseband Barnacle, Cavesson, Musrol
Nose-bleed Epistaxis
Nosh Eat, Food, Nibble, Snack
Nostalgia Longing, Retrophilia, Yearning
Nostril(s) Blowhole, Cere, Choana, Nare

Nostrum Elixir, Medicine, Remede, Remedy

Not, Nor Dis-, Na(e), Ne, Neither, Never, No, Pas, Polled, Taint

Notable, Notability Conspicuous, Distinguished, Eminent, Especial, Landmark, Large, Lion, Memorable, Signal, Striking, Unco, VIP, Worthy

Not allowed NL

Not allowed *may indicate* a word to be omitted

Notary Escribano, Scrivener

Notation(al) Benesh, Cantillation, Descriptive, Entry, Hexadecimal, Memo, Octal, Polish, Positional, Romic, Staff, Tablature

Notch(ed) Crena(l), Crenel, Cut, Dent, Erode, Erose, Gain, Gap, Gimp, Indent, Jag, Kerf, Nick, Nock, Raffle, Score, Sinus, Snick, Tally, Vandyke

Not clear Blocked, NL, Obscure, Opaque, Pearl

Note(s), Notebook A, Acciaccatura, Accidental, Adversaria, Advice, Agogic, Apostil(le), Apparatus, Appoggiatura, Arpeggio, Auxiliary, B, Bill(et), Bradbury, Breve, C, Cedula, Chit(ty), Chord, Cob, Comment, Conceit, Continental, Cover, Credit, Crotchet, Currency, D, Debit, Delivery, Demand, Dig, Dominant, E, E-la, F, Fa(h), Fame, Fiver, Flat, Flim, G, Gamut, Gloss(ary), Gold, Grace, Greenback, Heed, Hemiole, Identic, Index rerum, IOU, Item(ise), Jot(tings), Jug(-jug), Key, Kudos, La, Large, Leading, Lichanos, Line, Log, Long, Longa, Marginalia, Masora(h), Me, Melisma, Melody, Memo(randum), Mese, Mi, Minim, Minute, > MONEY, Mordent, Nachschlag, Natural, NB, Nete, Neum(e), Oblong, Observe, Octave, Oncer, Ostmark, Outline, Parhypate, Passing, Post-it®, Pound, Promissory, Prompt, Prosiambanomenos, Protocol, PS, Quarter, Quaver, Rag-money, Re, Record, Remark, Renown, Request, Root, Scholion, Scholium, Semibreve, Semiquaver, Semitone, Sextolet, Sharp, Shinplaster, Shoulder, Si, Sick, Smacker, Sol, Stem, Strike, Subdominant, Submediant, Subtonic, Supertonic, Te, Ten(ner), Third, Tierce, Tonic, Treasury, Treble, Undecimole, Ut, Variorum, Verbal, Wad, Warison, Whole

Note-case Pochette, Purse, Wallet

Notes *may indicate* the use of letters A-G

Noteworthy Eminent, Extraordinary, Memorable, Particular, Signal, Special

Nothing, Nought Cipher, Devoid, Diddlysquat, Emptiness, FA, Gratis, Nada, Napoo, Naught, Nihil, Niks-nie, Nil, Nix(-nie), Noumenon, Nowt, Nuffin, Nullity, O, Rap, Rien, Sweet FA, Void, Zero, Zilch, Zip(po)

Notice(able) Ad(vertisement), Advice, Affiche, Apprise, Attention, Avis(o), Banns, Bill, Blurb, Caveat, Circular, Cognisance, Crit, D, Descry, Discern, Dismissal, Enforcement, Gaum, Get, Gorm, Handbill, > HEED, Intimation, Marked, Mensh, Mention, NB, No(t)chel, Obit, Observe, Oyez, Placard, Plaque, Playbill, Poster, Press, Proclamation, Prominent, > REMARK, Review, See, Short, Si quis, Spot, Spy, Sticker, Tent, Whip

Notify Acquaint, Advise, Apprise, Awarn, Inform, > TELL, Warn

Notion(al) Academic, Conceit, > CONCEPT, Crotchet, Fancy, Hunch, Idea, Idee, Idolum, Inkling, Opinion, Reverie, Vapour, Whim

Notoriety, Notorious Arrant, Byword, Crying, Egregious, Esclandre, Fame, Flagrant, Infamous, Infamy, Notour, Proverbial, Reclame, > RENOWN, Repute

No trump Laical, Lay, NT

Notwithstanding Although, Despite, Even, For, Howbeit, However, Nath(e)less, Natheless(e), Naythles, Nevertheless, Spite

Nougat Montelimar, Sundae

Nought *see* NOTHING

Noughts and crosses Tic(k)-tac(k)-to(e)

Noun Abstract, Agent, Aptote, Collective, Common, Count, Gerund, Mass, N,

Proper, Substantive, Tetraptote, Verbal

Nourish(ing), Nourishment Aliment, Battill, Cherish, Cultivate, Feed, Ingesta, Meat, Nurse, Nurture, Nutrient, Promote, Replenish, Sustenance, Trophic

Nous Intellect, Intelligence, Reason

Nova Scotia(n) Acadia, Blue-nose

Novel(ty) Aga-saga, Bildungsroman, Bonkbuster, Book, Campus, Change, Different, Dime, Dissimilar, Emma, Epistolary, Fad, Fiction, Fresh, Gimmick, Gothic, Graphic, Historical, Horror, Idiot, Innovation, Ivanhoe, Kenilworth, Kidnapped, Kim, Middlemarch, > NEW, Newfangled, Original, Outside, Page-turner, Pamela, Paperback, Pendennis, Penny dreadful, Persuasion, Picaresque, Pot-boiler, Primeur, Pulp, Rebecca, Roman-à-clef, Romance, Roman fleuve, Sex and shopping, Shilling-dreadful, Shilling-shocker, Ulysses Unusual, Whodun(n)it, Yellowback

▷ **Novel** *may indicate* an anagram

▶ **Novelist** *see* WRITER

Novice Acolyte, Apprentice, Beginner, Cadet, Chela, Colt, Cub, Greenhorn, Griffin, Jackaroo, Jillaroo, Johnny-raw, Kyu, L, Learner, Neophyte, Patzer, Postulant, Prentice, Rookie, Tenderfoot, Tyro(ne), Unweaned

Now(adays) AD, Alate, Anymore, Current, Here, Immediate, Instanter, Interim Nonce, Nunc, Present, Pro tem, This

Nowhere Limbo

Nowt Cattle, Cows, Ky(e), Neat, Nothing

Noxious Harmful, Offensive, Poisonous, Venomous

Nozzle A(d)jutage, Fishtail, Nose, Nose-piece, Rose, Spout, Stroup, Syringe, Tewel, Tuyere, Tweer, Twier, Twire, Twyer(e)

Nuance Gradation, Nicety, Overtone, Shade

Nub Crux, Gist, Knob, Lump, Point

Nubile Beddable, Marriageable, Parti

Nuclear, Nucl(e)ide, Nucleus Cadre, Calandria, Centre, Core, Crux, Daughter, Deuteron, Eukaryon, Euratom, Even-even, Even-odd, Heartlet, Hub, Isomer, Isotone, Karyon, Kernel, Linin, Mushroom, Nuke, Pith, Prokaryon, Synkaryon Triton

▷ **Nucleus** *may indicate* the heart of a word

Nude, Nudism, Nudist, Nudity Adamite, Altogether, Aphylly, Bare, Buff, Eve, Exposed, Full-frontal, Gymnosophy, > NAKED, Nuddy, Scud, Stark, Stripped, Undress

Nudge Dunch, Dunsh, Elbow, Jostle, Poke, Prod

Nudibranch Sea-slug

Nugget Chunk, Cob, Gold, Lump

Nuisance Bore, Bot, Bugbear, Chiz(z), Drag, Impediment, Inconvenience, Mischief, Pest, Plague, Public, Terror, Trial

Null(ification), Nullify Abate, Cancel, Counteract, Defeasance, Destroy, Diriment, Disarm, Invalid(ate), Negate, Neutralise, Recant, Terminate, Undo, Veto, Void

Numb(ness) Asleep, Blunt, Dead(en), Stun, Stupor, Torpefy, Torpescent, Torpid, Unfeeling

Number(s) Abscissa, Abundant, Accession, Air, Aleph-null, Aleph-zero, Algebraic, Algorithm, Aliquant, Aliquot, Amicable, Anaesthetic, Antilog, Apocalyptic, Apostrophus, Army, Atomic, Augend, Avogadro, Babylonian, Binary, Box, Brinell, Calculate, Cardinal, Cetane, Chromosome, Class, Cocaine Coefficient, Cofactor, Complex, Composite, Concrete, Constant, Coordination, Count, Cyclic, Decillion, Deficient, Deficit, Diapason, Digit, Drove, E, Edition,

Epidural, Ether, Eucaine, Ex-directory, F, Feck, Frost(bite), Froude, Gas, Gobar, Golden, Googol, Handful, Hantle, Hash(mark), Hemlock, Host, Imaginary, Include, Index, Infimum, Integer, Irrational, Isospin, Item, Lac, Lakh, Legion(s), Lepton, Livraison, Local, Mach, Magazine, Magic, Mass, Melodic, Milliard, Minuend, Minyan, Mixed, Mort, Muckle, Multiple, Multiplex, Multiplicity, Multitude, Myriadth, Nasik, Natural, Neutron, No(s), Nonillion, Nth, Nucleon, Num, Numerator, Numerical, Octane, Octillion, Opiate, Opium, Opposite, Opus, Ordinal, OT, Paginate, Par, Paucal, Peck, Perfect, Pile, PIN, Plural, Prime, Proton, Quantum, Quarternion, Quorum, Quotient, Radix, Raft, Random, Rational, Real, Reckon, Registration, Regulo®, Repunit, Reynolds, Sampi, Scads, Serial, Sight, Slew, Slue, Some, Square, Strangeness, Strength, Subtrahend, Summand, Surd, T, Tale, Telephone, Tell, Thr(e)ave, Totient, Totitive, Transcendental, Transfinite, Troop, Turn-out, Umpteen, Umpty, Urethane, Verse, Wave, Whole, Wrong, Zeroth
Number *may indicate* a drug
Numeral(s) Arabic, Chapter, Figure, Ghubar, Gobar, Integer, Number, Roman
Numerous(ness) Divers, Galore, Legion, Lots, Many, Multeity, Myriad
Numskull Blockhead, Booby, Dunce, Stupid
Nun Beguine, Bhikkhuni, Clare, Cluniac, Conceptionist, Dame, Minim, Minoress, Mother Superior, Pigeon, Poor Clare, Prioress, Religeuse, Sister, Top, Ursuline, Vestal, Vowess, Zelator, Zelatrice, Zelatrix
Nun *may indicate* a biblical character, father of Joshua
Nuptial (chamber) Bridal, Marital, Marriage, Thalamus
Nurse(ry) Aia, Alice, Amah, Ayah, Bonne, Caledonia, Care(r), Cavell, Charge, Cherish, Crèche, Day, Deborah, District, Dry, EN, Flo(rence), Foster, Gamp, Glumdalclitch, Harbour, Karitane, Mammy, Midwife, Minister, Mother, Mrs Gamp, Nan(n)a, Nanny, Night, Nightingale, Nourice, Nourish, Parabolanus, Phytotron, Playroom, Playschool, Plunket, Probationer, RN, Seminary, SEN, Sister, Staff, Suckle, Tend, VAD, Visiting, Wet
Nursery(man) Conservatory, Crèche, Garden, Hothouse, Rhyme, Seedsman, Slope
Nursing *may indicate* one word within another
Nurture Cultivate, Educate, Feed, Foster, Suckle, Tend
Nut(s), Nutcase, Nutshell, Nut tree, Nutty Acajou, Acorn, Almond, Amygdalus, Anacardium, Aphorism, Arachis, Areca, Arnut, Babassu, Barcelona, Barking, Barmy, Bats, Beech-mast, Bertholletia, Betel, Brazil, Briefly, Buffalo, Butterfly, Butternut, Cashew, Cob, Coffee, Cola, Coquilla, Coquina, Core, Cranium, Cuckoo, Dukka(h), En, Filberd, Filbert, Gelt, Gilbert, Gland, Glans, Goober, Gum, Hazel, Head, Hickory, Illipe, Ivory, Kernel, Kola, Lichee, Li(t)chi, Litchi, Loaf, Lug, Lunatic, Lychee, Macadamia, Macahuba, Macaw-palm, Macoya, Manic, Marking, Mast, Mockernut, Monkey, Noisette, Noodle, Nucule, Palmyra, Para, Pate, Pecan, Philippina, Philippine, Philopoena, Physic, Pili, Pine, Pistachio, Praline, Prawlin, Quandang, Quantong, Queensland, Rhus, Sapucaia, Sassafras, Shell, Skull, Slack, Sleeve, Stuffing, Supari, Thumb, Tiger, Walnut, Weirdo, Wing, Zany, Zealot
Nut *may indicate* Egyptian god, father of Osiris
Nutcase, Nutshell *see* NUT
Nutmeg Connecticut, CT, Mace, Myristica
Nutrient, Nutriment, Nutrition Eutrophy, Food, Ingesta, Protein, Sustenance, Trace element, Trophic
Nuts *may indicate* an anagram
Nuzzle Snoozle

Nyasaland Malawi

Nymph(et) Aegina, Aegle, Amalthea, Arethusa, Callisto, Calypso, Camenae, Carme, Clytie, Constant, Cymodoce, Daphne, Doris, Dryad, Echo, Egeria, Eurydice, Galatea, Hamadryad, Hesperides, Houri, Hyades, Ida, Insect, Larva, Liberty, Lolita, Maelid, Maia, Maiden, Mermaid, Naiad, Nereid, Oceanid, Oenone, Oread, Pupa, Rusalka, Sabrina, Scylla, Siren, Sylph, Syrinx, Tessa, Tethys, Thetis, Water, Wood

Oo

O Blob, Duck, Nought, Omega, Omicron, Oscar, Oxygen, Spangle, Tan, Zero

Oaf Auf, Changeling, Dolt, Fool, Ocker, Stupid, Twit

Oak(s) Bog, Bur, Cerris, Classic, Cork, Desert, Dumbarton, Durmast, Flittern, Fumed, Gabriel, Herne, Holly, Holm, Honour, Ilex, Jerusalem, Kermes, Live, Major, Parliament, Pedunculate, Philemon, Poison, Quercus, Red, Roble, Royal, Sessile, Silky, Swamp, Swilcar, > TREE, Turkey, Watch, White

Oakley Annie

Oar(s), Oarsmen Blade, Ctene, Eight, Leander, Organ, Paddle, Palm, Propel, Rower, Scull, Spoon, Stroke, Sweep

Oasis Buraimi, Haven, Hotan, Refuge, Spring, Tafilalet, Tafilelt

Oat(meal), Oats Ait, Athole brose, Avena, Brome-grass, Fodder, Grain, Grits, Groats, Gruel, Haver, Loblolly, Parritch, Pilcorn, Pipe, Porridge, Quaker®, Rolled, Wild

Oatcake Bannock, Clapbread, Farle, Flapjack, Jannock

Oath Affidavit, Begorrah, Curse, Dang, Demme, Doggone, Drat, Ecod, Egad, Expletive, God-so, Gospel, Halidom, Hippocratic, Igad, Imprecation, Jabers, Lumme, Lummy, Nouns, Oons, Promise, Sacrament, Sal(a)mon, Sapperment, Saucer, Sdeath, Sfoot, Sheart, 'slid, Strewth, Stygian, Swear, Tarnation, Tennis-court, Voir dire, Vow, Zbud, Zounds

Obdurate Adamant, Cruel, Hard, Intransigent, Stony, Stubborn, Tenacious

Obedient, Obedience, Obey Bent, Bridlewise, Canonical, Comply, Dutiful, Follow, Hear, Mindful, Obsequious, Observe, Obtemper, Passive, Perform, Pliant, Servant, Yielding

Obeisance > BOW, Salaam

Obelisk, Obelus Aguilla, Column, Dagger, Monument, Needle, Pillar

Oberon King, Merle

Obese, Obesity Bariatrics, Corpulent, Fat, Stout

Object(s), Objection(able), Objective(ness), Objector Ah, Aim, Ambition, Argue, Article, Bar, Beef, Case, Cavil, Challenge, Clinical, Complain(t), Conchy, Conscientious, Cow, Demur, Direct, End, Exception, Fuss, > GOAL, Her, Him, Impersonal, Improper, Indifferent, Indirect, Intensional, Intention, It, Item, Jib, Loathe, Mind, Moral, Niggle, Non-ego, Noumenon, Obnoxious, Offensive, Oppose, Outness, Plan, Plot, Point, Protest, Question, Quibble, Quiddity, Rebarbative, Recuse, Refuse, Resist, Retained, Sake, Scruple, Sex, Subject, Sublime, Target, Thing, Transitive, Tut, Ultimate, Unbiased, Virtu, Wart

Object *may indicate* a grammatical variant

Objectless Intransitive

Oblate, Oblation Gift, Monk, Offering, Sacrifice

Oblige, Obliging, Obligation, Obligatory Accommodate, Affable, Behold, Binding, Burden, Charge, Compel, Complaisant, Compliant, Contract, Corvée, Debt, De rigueur, Duty, Easy, Encumbent, Force, Giri, Gratify, Impel, Incumbent, IOU, Mandatory, Must, Necessitate, Obruk, Promise, Recognisance, Sonties, Synallagmatic, Tie, Wattle

Oblique(ly) Askance, Askew, Asklent, Asquint, Athwart, Awry, Cross, Diagonal, Indirect, Perverse, Plagio-, Separatrix, Sidelong, Skew, Slanting, Solidus, Squint, Virgule

▷ **Oblique** *may indicate* an anagram

Obliterate(d) Annul, Blot, Dele(te), Efface, Expunge, Exterminate, Rase, Rast, Raze, Wipe

Oblivion, **Oblivious** Forgetful, Lethe, Limbo, Nirvana, Obscurity

Oblong Rectangular

Obnoxious Foul, Horrid, Offensive, Pestilent, Repugnant, Septic, Sod

Obscene(ly), **Obscenity** Bawdy, Blue, Fescennine, Gross, Hard-core, Indecent, Lewd, Lubricious, Paw(paw), Porn(o), Salacious, Smut, Vulgar

Obscure, **Obscurity** Abstruse, Anheires, Becloud, Befog, Blend, Blot out, Cloud, Cobweb, Conceal, Cover, Cryptic, Darken, Deep, Dim, Disguise, Eclipse, Encrypt, Envelop, Esoteric, Filmy, Fog, Hermetic, Hide, Indistinct, Mantle, Mist, Murk, Nebular, Night, Nubecula, Obfuscate, Obnubilate, Opaque, Oracular, Overcloud, Overshade, Overshadow, Recherché, Recondite, Shadowy, Tenebrific, Twilit, Unclear, > **VAGUE**, Veil, Vele, Wrap

▷ **Obscure(d)** *may indicate* an anagram

Obsequious Bootlicker, Brown nose, Creeping Jesus, Fawn, Fulsome, Grovelling, Menial, Parasitic, Pig, Servile, Sleeveen, Slimy, Subservient, Suck-hole, Sycophantic, Tantony, Toady

Observance, **Observant**, **Observation** Adherence, Alert, Attention, Comment, Custom, Empirical, Espial, Eyeful, Holy, Honour, Lectisternium, Mass, > **NOTICE**, Obiter dicta, Percipient, Recce, Remark, Right, Rite, Ritual, Vising

Observatory Arecibo, Atalaya, Greenwich, Herstmonceux, Hurstmonceux, Jodrell Bank, Lookout, Mount Palomar, Tower

Observe(d), **Observer** Behold, Bystander, Celebrate, Commentator, Detect, Espy, Eye, Fly-on-the-wall, Heed, Keep, Mark, NB, Note, Notice, Obey, Onlooker, Optic, Regard(er), Remark, Rite, Scry, See, Sight, Spectator, Spial, Spot, Spy, Study, Take, Twig, View, Voyeur, Witness

Obsess(ed), **Obsession**, **Obsessive** Besot, Bug, Bugbear, Craze, Dominate, Fetish, Fixation, Hang-up, Haunt, Hobbyhorse, Hooked, Idée fixe, Infatuation, Mania, Monomania, Necrophilia, Neurotic, One-track, Preoccupy, Thing

Obsolete, **Obsolescence**, **Obsolescent** Abandoned, Antique, Archaic, Dated, Dead, Defunct, Disused, Extinct, Latescent, Obs, Outdated, Outworn, Passé, Planned

Obstacle Barrage, Barrier, Boyg, Cheval de frise, Chicane, Dam, Drag, Dragon's teeth, Drawback, Gate, Handicap, Hindrance, Hitch, Hurdle, Node, Oxer, Remora, Rock, Sandbank, Snag, Stimie, Stumbling-block, Stymie, Tank-trap

Obstetrics Gynaecology, Midwifery, Tocology, Tokology

Obstinacy, **Obstinate** Asinine, Buckie, Bullish, Contumacious, Cussed, Die-hard, Dour, Entêté, Froward, Headstrong, Inflexible, Intractable, Intransigent, Mule, Persistent, Perverse, Pervicacious, Pig-headed, Recalcitrant, Refractory, Restive, Rusty, Self-will, Stiff(-necked), Stubborn, Thraward, Thrawart, Wilful

Obstreperous Noisy, Truculent, Unruly

Obstruct(ion) Bar, Block, Bottleneck, Chicane, Clog, Crab, Cross, Cumber, Dam, Embolus, Fil(l)ibuster, Gridlock, Hamper, Hedge, Hinder, Hurdle, Ileus, Impede, Let, Obstacle, Occlude, Sab(otage), Snooker, Stall, Stap, Stonewall, Stop, Stymie, Sudd, Thwart, Trammel, Trump

Obtain Achieve, Acquire, Cop, Exist, Gain, Get, Land, Pan, Prevail, Procure, Realise, Secure, Succeed, Wangle, Win

Obtrude, Obtrusive Expel, Impose, Loud, Prominent, Push, Sorn, Thrust

Obtuse Blunt, Dense, Dull, Purblind, Stupid, Thick

Obverse Complement, Cross, Face, Front, Head

Obviate Forestall, Preclude, Prevent

Obvious Apparent, Axiom, Blatant, Brobdingnag, Clear, Distinct, Evident, Flagrant, Frank, Inescapable, Kenspeck(le), Manifest, Marked, Open(ness), Open and shut, Overt, Palpable, Patent, Pikestaff, Plain, Pronounced, Salient, Self-evident, Stark, Transparent, Truism, Visible

Occasion Call, Cause, Ceremony, Encheason, Event, Fete, Field day, Nonce, > OPPORTUNITY, Reason, Ride, Sometime, Tide, Time

Occasional(ly) Casual, Chance, Daimen, Intermittent, Irregular, Motive, Orra, Periodic, Sometimes, Sporadic, While

Occident(al) West, Western(er)

Occlude, Occlusion Absorb, Clog, Coronary, Embolism, Obstruct

Occult(ist) Angekkok, Arcane, Art, Esoteric, I-ching, Magic, Mysterious

Occupant, Occupation, Occupy(ing) Absorb, Activity, Avocation, Beset, Business, Busy, Denizen, Embusy, Employ, Engage, Engross, Fill, Hold, In, Incumbent, Indwell, Inhabitant, Inmate, Involve, Line, Metier, People, Profession, Pursuit, Reserved, Resident, Runrig, Sideline, Squat, Stay, Tenancy, Tenant, Tenure, Thrift, Trade, Upon, Use, Vocation, Walk of life

Occur(rence) Arise, Be, Betide, Betime, Case, Contingency, Crop up, Event, Fall, Happen, Incident, Instance, Outbreak, Outcrop, Pass, Phenomenon

Ocean(ic), Oceania Abundance, Abyssal, Antarctic, Arctic, Atlantic, Blue, Deep, German, Hadal, Herring-pond, Indian, Melanesia, Micronesia, Pacific, Panthalassa, Pelagic, Polynesia, Sea(way), Southern, Thalassic, Waves, Western

Och aye Troggs

Ochre Keel, Ruddle, Sienna

Octave Diapason, Diminished, Eight, Great, Ottava, Perfect, Small, Utas

Octopus Blue-ringed, Cephalopod, Cuero, Devilfish, Paper nautilus, Polyp, Poulp(e), Scuttle, Squid

Octoroon Mestee, Mestizo, Mustee

Od Energy, Force

Odd (person), Oddity Abnormal, Anomaly, Bizarre, Card, Cure, Curio, Droll, Eccentric, Eery, Erratic, Gink, Impair, Imparity, Jimjam, Offbeat, Original, Orra, Outré, Paradox, Parity, Peculiar, Queer, Quiz, Random, Rare, Remote, Rum, Screwball, Singular, > STRANGE, Unequal, Uneven, Unmatched, Unusual, Weird, Whims(e)y

Odd(s) *may indicate* an anagram or the odd letters in words

Odd job man Joey, Orraman, Rouster, Smoot, Thronner

Odds, Oddments Bits, Carpet, Chance, Gubbins, Handicap, Line, Long, Price, Short, SP, Tails, Variance

Ode Awdl, Dit, Epicede, Epicedium, Epinicion, Epinikion, Genethliacon, Horatian, Hymn, Lay, Lyric, Monody, Paeon, Pindaric, Poem, Sapphic, Song, Stasimon, Strophe, Threnody, Verse

Odin One-eyed, Woden

Odium, Odious Comparison, Disestimation, Disgrace, Foul, Hatred, Heinous, Invidious, Ponce, Repugnant, Stigma

Odorous, Odour Air, Bad, BO, Flavour, Funk, Good, Hum, Opopanax, Perfume, Quality, Redolence, Sanctity, Scent, Smell, Whiff

Odourless Silent

Odyssey Epic, Journey, Wandering

Oedipus Complex, Parricide

Oeillade Glance, Leer, Ogle, Wink

Oesophagus Crop

Oestrogen, Oestrus Frenzy, Heat, Mestranol, Must, Rut, Stilb(o)estrol

Of (me) About, Among, Aus, By, De, From, My, Re

▷ **Of** *may indicate* an anagram

Of course Certainly, Natch, Yes

Off Absent, Agee, Ajee, Away, Discount, Distance, Far, From, High, Inexact, Licence, Odd, Reasty, Reesty, Relache, Start

▷ **Off** *may indicate* an anagram

Offal Cagmag, Carrion, Chitterling, Entrails, Fry, Gralloch, Gurry, Haggis, Ha(r)slet, Heart, Innards, Kidney, Lamb's fry, Lights, Liver, Numbles, Sweetbread, Tripe, Variety meat

Off-beat Zoppo

Off-colour Pale, Seedy, Wan

▷ **Off-colour** *may indicate* an anagram

Offence Attack, Crime, Delict, Delinquency, Distaste, Fault, Huff, Hurt, Lapse, Miff, Misdemeanour, Misprision, Outrage, Peccadillo, Pip, Pique, Piracy, Regrate, Sedition, > SIN, Summary, Trespass, Umbrage, Violation

Offend(ed), Offender Affront, Anger, Annoy, Boobhead, Bridles, Culprit, Default, Disoblige, Displease, Distaste, Hip, Huff, Hurt, Hyp, Infringe, Inveigh Miffy, Miscreant, Nettle, Nonce, Nuisance, Peeve, Provoke, Sin(ner), Stray, Transgress, Twoccer, Violate, Wrongdoer

Offensive Affront, Aggressive, Alien, Attack, Bombardment, Campaign, Cruel, Embracery, Execrable, Eyesore, Foul, Hedgehog, Hedgepig, Indelicate, Miasmic, Nasty, Noisome, Obnoxious, Obscene, Peccant, Personal, Push, Putrid, Rank, Repugnant, > RUDE, Scandalous, Scurrilous, Sortie, Storm, Ugly, Unbecoming

Offer(ing) Alms, Altarage, Anaphora, Bargain, Bid, Bode, Bouchée, Cadeau, Corban, Deodate, Dolly, Epanophora, Extend, Ex voto, Gift, Godfather, Hold, Inferiae, Invitation, Oblation, Overture, Peddle, Plead, Potla(t)ch, Present, Propine, > PROPOSAL, Propose, Propound, Sacrifice, Shewbread, Shore, S(h)raddha, Special, Stamp, Stand, Submit, Tender, Utter, Volunteer, Votive, Wave, Xenium

Offhand Airy, Banana, Brusque, Casual, Cavalier, Curt, Extempore, Impromptu, Indifferent, Snappy

Office(s) Agency, Bedelship, Box, Branch, Broo, Bucket shop, Bureau, Buroo, Caliphate, Chair, Colonial, Complin(e), Consulate, Crown, Daftar, Dataria, Dead-letter, Deanery, Den, Divine, Employment, Evensong, Foreign, Function, Holy, Home, Job, Land, Last, Left luggage, Lieutenancy, Little, Mayoralty, Met(eorological), Ministry, Missa, Mistery, Mudiria, Mutessarifat, Mystery, Nocturn, Nones, Obit, Oval, Palatinate, Papacy, Patent, Personnel, Pipe, Place, Plum, Portfolio, Position, Post, Prelacy, Press, Prime, Printing, Provosty, Record, Regency, Register, Registry, Rite, See, Seraskierate, Shogunate, Sinecure, Situation, Stationery, Tariff, Tenebrae, Terce, Ticket, Tierce, Tol(l)booth, Tribunate, Vespers, War, Yamen

Officer(s) Acater, Adjutant, Admiral, Ag(h)a, Agistor, Aide, Apparitor, Bailiff, Beatty, Bimbashi, Black Rod, Blimp, Blue Rod, Bombardier, Bos(u)n, Brass-hat, Brigadier, Bumbailiff, Capt(ain), Catchpole, Catchpoll, Cater, Centurion, Chamberlain, Chancellor, CIGS, Colonel, Commander, Commissioner, Commodore, Compliance, Constable, Cop(per), Co-pilot, Cornet, Coroner, Counter-round, Cursitor, Darogha, Datary, Deacon, Decurion, Duty, Earl

Marshal, Ensign, Equerry, Exciseman, Executive, Exon, Field Marshal, Filacer, Filazer, First, Flag, Flying, Gallant, Gazetted, Gen(eral), GOC, Group, Gunner, Havildar, Hayward, Hetman, Ima(u)m, Incumbent, Infirmarian, Intendant, Jamadar, Janty, Jauntie, Jaunty, Jemadar, Jemidar, Jonty, Jurat, Justiciar, Lance-sergeant, Liaison, Lictor, Lord High Steward, Lt, Marshal, Mate, Moderator, NCO, Number one, Nursing, Official Solicitor, Orderly, Oxon, Petty, Pilot, Pipe major, PO, Posse, Prefect, Prison, Probation, Proctor, Provost, Provost-marshal, Purser, Pursuivant, Quartermaster, Relieving, Remembrancer, Returning, Rodent, Rupert, Samurai, Sbirro, Schout, Sea Lord, Second mate, Select-man, Serang, Sergeant-major, Sewer, Sexton, Sheriff, Silver-stick, Skipper, SL, SM, Speaker, Staff, Striper, Sub(altern), Suba(h)dar, Subchanter, Sublieutenant, Supercargo, Superintendent, Tahsildar, Tidewaiter, Tindal, Tipstaff, Treasurer, Tribune, Usher, Varlet, Waldgrave, Warden, Wardroom, Warrant, Watch, Yeoman

Official(s), **Officiate**, **Officious** Aga, Agent, Amban, Amtman, Atabeg, Atabek, Attaché, Authorised, Beadle, Bossy, Bureaucrat, Catchpole, Censor, Chamberlain, Chancellor, Chinovnik, Claviger, Commissar, Commissioner, Consul, Count, Dean, Diplomat, Dogberry, Ealdorman, Ephor, Equerry, Escheater, Eurocrat, Executive, Fonctionnaire, > **FORMAL**, Functionary, Gauleiter, Gymnasiarch, Hayward, Incumbent, Inspector, Intendant, Jack-in-office, Jobsworth, Keeper, Landdrost, Lictor, Linesman, Mandarin, Marplot, Marshal, Mayor, MC, Meddlesome, Mirza, Mueddin, Mukhtar, Nazir, Notary, Ombudsman, Omlah, Overbusy, Palatine, Paymaster, Pleaseman, Plenipotentiary, Polemarch, Pontificate, Poohbah, Postmaster, Pragmatic, Prefect, Proctor, Procurator, Prog, Proveditor, Reeve, Regisseur, Registrar, Remembrancer, Shammash, Shammes, Sherpa, Silentiary, Souldan, Staff, Steward, Suffete, Suit, Syndic, Timekeeper, Tipstaff, Tribune, Trier, Trior, Turncock, Valid, Valuer General, Veep, Verderer, Verger, Vizier, Walla(h), Whiffler, Whip, Woodward, Yamen, Yeoman

Offprint Separate

Off-putting Dehortative, Discouraging, Manana, Negative, Procrastination, Rebarbative, Repellent, Yips

Offset Balance, Cancel, Compensate, Counter(act), Counterbalance

Offshoot Bough, Branch, Limb, Lye, Member, Outgrowth, Plant, Scion, Sien, Swarm

Offspring Boy, Burd, Chick, Children, Daughter, Descendant, Family, Fry, Get, Girl, Heir, Procreation, Product, Progeny, Seed, Sient, Son, Spawn

Offstage Wings

Often Frequent, Habitual, Repeated

Often *may indicate* 'of ten'

Ogee Cyma, Moulding, Talon

Ogle Drake, Eliad, Eye, Glance, Leer, Oeillade, Wodewose

Ogre(ss) Baba yaga, Boyg, Brute, Eten, Etten, Fiend, Giant, Monster, Orc

Ohio Buckeye

Oil(y), **Oil producer** Aj(o)wan, Aleuritis, Anele, Anoint, Apiezon®, Argan, Attar, Balm, Balsam, Banana, Bath, Beech-mast, Ben, Benne, Benni, Bergamot, Bittern, Bone, BP, Bribe, Brilliantine, Butter, Cajeput, Cajuput, Camphire, Camphor, Camphorated, Canola, Carapa, Carron, Carvacrol, Castor, Chaulmoogra, Chaulmugra, Chinese wood, Chrism, Citronella grass, Clove, Coal, Coconut, Cod-liver, Cohune, Colza, Copra, Corn, Cotton-seed, Creasote, Creosote, Croton, Crude, Derv, Diesel, Dittany, Drying, Elaeis, El(a)eoptene, Essence, Essential, Ethereal, Eucalyptus, Eugenol, Evening primrose,

Extra virgin, Fatty, Fish, Fixed, Fuel, Fusel, Gas, Gingelli, Gingelly, Gingili, Golomynka, Good, Grapeseed, Grass, Groundnut, Guttiferae, Hazelnut, Heavy, Jojoba, Kerosene, Kerosine, Lamp, Lavender, Linalo(o)l, Linseed, Lipid, Long, Lubricant, Lumbang, Macassar, Magilp, Megilp, Menthol, Midnight, Mineral, Mirbane, Moringa, Multigrade, Musk, Mustard, Myrbane, Myrrhol, Naphtha, Neat's-foot, Neem, Neroli, Niger, Nim, Nimb, Nut, Oint, Oiticica, Oleo, Olive, Ottar, Otto, Palm, Paraffin, Parathion, Patchouli, Peanut, Pellitory, Petroleum, Picamar, Pomade, Poon, Poppy, Pristane, Pulza, Pyrrole, Ramtil, Rape, Rapeseed, Retinol, Ricinus, Rock, Rose, Rosin, Rusa, Safrole, Sandalwood, Sassafras, Savin(e), Sebum, Seed, Semsem, Sesame, Shale, Short, Sleek, Slick, Slum, Smalmy, Smarmy, Smeary, Snake, Spearmint, Sperm, Spike(nard), Spindle, Stand, Star-anise, Sunflower, Sweet, Tall(ow), Tolu, Train, Tung, Turpentine, Ulyie, Ulzie, Unction, Vanaspati, Vegetable, Verbena, Virgin, Vitriol, Volatile, Wallaba, Walnut, Whale, Wintergreen, Wood, Wool, Ylang-ylang, Yolk

Oilcake Poonac

Oilcan Pourie

Oilcloth American, Lino

Oilman Driller, Prospector, Rigger, Texan

Oil painting Master, Titian

Ointment Balm, Basilicon, Boracic, Boric, Cerate, Cream, Nard, Pomade, Pomatum, Salve, Spikenard, Theriac, Unguent, Vaseline®, Zinc

OK Agree(d), Approve, Authorise, Clearance, Copacetic, Copesettic, Go-head, Green light, Hunky-dory, Initial, Kosher, Right(o), Sanction, Sound, U, Vet

Okra Bhindi, Lady's fingers

Old(er), **Oldie** Ae(t), Aged, Aine(e), Ancient, Antique, Auld, Bean, Decrepit, Dutch, Fogram, Former, Gaffer, Geriatric, Glory, Golden, Gray, Grey, Hills, Hoary, Immemorial, Major, Methusaleh, Moore, Nestor, Nick, O, OAP, Obsolete, Off, Ogygian, One-time, Outworn, Palae-, Passé, Primeval, Ripe, Rugose, Sen(escent), Senile, Senior, Shot, Signeur, Stale, Trite, Venerable, Veteran, Victorian(a), Worn

Old boy, **Old girl** Alumnae, Alumnus, Fossil, OB

Old days Once, Past, Yore

Old English OE

Old-fashioned Aging, Ancient, Antediluvian, Antwackie, Arch(aic), Arriere, Bygone, Corn(y), Dated, Dowdy, Fuddy-duddy, Medieval, Museum piece, Neanderthal, No tech, Obsolete, Ogygian, Oldfangled, Outdated, Outmoded, Passé, Primeval, Quaint, Relic, Retro, Rinky-dink, Schmaltzy, Shot, Square, Square-toes, Steam, Stick-in-the-mud, Traditional, Uncool, Vieux jeu, Worm-eaten

Old hat Clichéd

Old maid Biddy, Spinster

Old man, **Old woman** Anile, Aunty, Bodach, Burd, Cailleach, Crow, Faggot, Fantad, Fantod, Fogey, Fogramite, Fogy, Fussy, Gammer, Geezer, Grandam, Grannam, Greybeard, Greyhen, Husband, Kangaroo, Luckie, Lucky, Methuselah, Mort, Mzee, OAP, Oom, Presbyte, Rudas, Trot, Trout, Wife, Wight, Woopie, Wrinkly

Old-timer Hourglass, Sundial, Veteran

Olid Fetid, Foul, High, Rancid, Rank

Olio Hash, Medley, Mess, Potpourri, Stew

Olive (grove), **Olivine** Calamata, Cerulein, Drupe, Dunite, Gethsemane, Kalamata, Olea(ster), Peridot, Queen

Oliver Bath, Cromwell, Goldsmith, Hardy, Noll, Protector, Twist

Olympian, Olympus Asgard, Athlete, Celestial, Elis, Pantheon, Quadrennium, Zeus

Omelette Crepe, Foo yong, Foo yung, Frittata, Fu yung, Pancake, Spanish, Tortilla

Omen Abodement, Absit, Augury, Auspice, Foreboding, Forewarning, Freet, Freit, Portent, Presage, Prodrome, Sign, Token, Warning

Omentum Caul, Epiploon

Ominous Alarming, Baleful, Bodeful, Dire, Dour, Forbidding, Grim, Inauspicious, Oracular, Sinister, Threatening

Omission, Omit Aph(a)eresis, Apocope, Apospory, Apostrophe, Asyndeton, Caret, Disregard, Drop, Elide, Elision, Ellipse, Ellipsis, Failure, Haplography, Haplology, Lipography, Loophole, Miss, Neglect, Nonfeasance, Oversight, Paral(e)ipomenon, Senza, Skip

Omnibus Anthology, Coach, Collection

Omniscient Encyclopedia

Omnivorous Pantophagous

On (it) Aboard, About, Agreed, An, An't, At, Atop, By, Game, In, Leg, O', Of, Oiled, Over, Pon, Re, Tipsy, Up(on)

On *may indicate* an anagram

On account of Over

On board *may indicate* chess, draughts, or 'SS' around another word

Once(r) Ance, > AT ONCE, Bradbury, Earst, Erst(while), Ever, Ex, Fore, Former, Jadis, Oner, Onst, Secular, Sole, Sometime, Whilom

One(self) A, Ace, Ae, Alike, An(e), Any, Body, Chosen, Eeny, Ego, Ein, Formula, Individual, Integer, Me, Monad, Per se, Single(ton), Singular, Solo, Tane, Un, Unit(y), Unitary, United, Us, Yin, You

One-act-er Playlet

One-eared Monaural

One-eyed Arimasp(ian), Cyclops

One-man band Moke

One o'clock 1 am, NNE

One-off Ad hoc

One-rayed Monact

Onerous Arduous, Exacting, Taxing, Tedious, Weighty

Onion(s) Bengi, Bonce, Bulb, Chibol, Chive, Cibol, Cive, Eschalot, Green, Head, Ingan, Jibbons, Leek, Lyonnaise, Moly, Pearl, Ramp, Ramson, Rocambole, Ropes, Scallion, Scilla, Shal(l)ot, Soubise, Spanish, Spring, Squill, Sybo(e), Sybow, Tree, Welsh

Onlooker Bystander, Kibitzer, Rubberneck, Spectator, Witness

Only Allenarly, Anerly, But, Except, Just, Meer, Merely, Nobbut, Seul, Singly, Sole

Onset Affret, Attack, Beginning, Charge, Dash, Ending, Rush, > START, Thrust

Onslaught Attack, Dead-set, Onset, Raid, Spreagh, Storm

On time Pat, Prompt, Punctual

Onus Burden, Charge, > DUTY, Responsibility

Onward Advance, Ahead, Away, Forth, Forward, Progress

Oodles Heaps, Lashings, Lots, Slather

Oolite Pisolite, Roestone

Oomph Energy, It, SA, Verve

Ooze Drip, Exhale, Exude, Gleet, Mud, Percolate, Pteropod(a), Seep, Sew, Sipe, Slime, Slob, Spew, Spue, Sweat, Sype, Transude

Opal(escent) Cymophanous, Fire, Gem, Girasol, Girosol, Hyalite, Hydrophane,

Liver, Menilite, Noble, Potch, Wood

Opaque, Opacity Dense, Dull, Intense, Leucoma, Obscure, Obtuse, Onycha, Roil, Thick

Open(er), Opening, Openness Adit, Ajar, Antithesis, Anus, Apert(ure), Apparent, Apse, Autopsy, Bald, Bare, Bat, Bay, Bole, Breach, Break, Broach, Buttonhole, Candid, Cardia, Cavity, Champaign, Chance, Chasm, Chink, Circumscissile, Clear, Crevasse, Dehisce, Deploy, Dispark, Door, Dup, Embrasure, Exordium, Expansive, Eyelet, Fair, Fenestra, Fissure, Fistula, Flue, Fontanel(le), Foramen, Frank, Free, Gambit, Gap, Gaping, Gat, Gate, Give, Glasnost, Glottis, Guichet, Gullwing, Hagioscope, Hatch, Hatchback, Hiatus, Hilus, > HOLE, Inaugural, Intake, Interstice, Intro, Key, Lacy, Lance, Lead, Loid, Loophole, Loose, Machicolation, Manhole, Meatus, Micropyle, Mofette, Moongate, Mouth, Oillet, Orifice, Oscule, Osculum, Ostiole, Ostium, Overture, Patent, Peephole, Pert, Pervious, Pick(lock), Placket, Plughole, Pore, Port(age), Porta, Porthole, Preliminary, Premiere, Prise, Pro-am, Public, Pylorus, Receptive, Rent, Riva, Room, Scuttle, Scye, Sesame, Sicilian, Sincere, Slit, Spare, Spirant, Squint, Start, Stenopaic, Stoma, Syrinx, Thereout, Touchhole, Trapdoor, Trema, Trou, Truthful, Unbar, Unbolt, Unbutton, Uncork, Undo, Unfurl, Unhasp, Unlatch, Unscrew, Unsubtle, Untie, Unzip, Vent, Vulnerable, Window

Open air Alfresco, Sub divo, Sub Jove

Opera Aida, Ariadne, Ballad, Bouffe, Buffo, Burletta, Carmen, Comic, Comique, Dramma giocoso, Electra, ENO, Ernani, Falstaff, Faust, Fedora, Fidelio, Glyndebourne, Grand, Hansel and Gretel, Horse, Idomineo, Iolanthe, Light, Lohengrin, Lulu, Macbeth, Met, Musical, Nabucco, Norma, Oater, Oberon, Onegin, Open Wingrave, Orfeo, Otello, Parsifal, Pastorale, Patience, Pinafore, Rienzi, Rigoletto, Ruddigore, Savoy, Scala, Seria, Singspiel, Soap, Space, Tell, The Met, Threepenny, Tosca, Turandot, Verismo, Werther, Work, Zarzuela

Opera-glasses Jumelle

Opera-lover Wagnerite

Opera-singer Baritone, Bass, Contralto, Diva, Savoyard, Soprano

Operate, Operation(s), Operative Act(ion), Activate, Actuate, Agent, Artisan, Attuition, Barbarossa, Caesarean, Campaign, Conduct, Couching, Current, Desert Storm, Detective, Exercise, Function, Game, Hobday, Holding, Keystroke, Liposuction, Logical, Manipulate, Mechanic, Mules, Overlord, Practice, Run, Sealion, Shirodkar's, Sortie, Strabotomy, Ure, Valid, Wertheim, Work

Operator Agent, Conductor, Dealer, Laplace, Manipulator, Nabla, Sparks, Surgeon

Opiate, Opium Dope, Drug, Hop, Laudanum, Meconin, Meconium, Narcotic, Religion, Soporific, Thebaine

Opinion, Opinionative Attitude, Belief, Bet, Consensus, Cri, Dictum, Dogma, Doxy, Entêté, Esteem, Feeling, Groundswell, Guess, Judgement, Mind, Parti pris, Private, Public, Pulse, Say, Second, Sense, Sentence, Sentiment, Tenet, Utterance, View, Viewpoint, Voice, Vox pop, Vox populi

Opossum Lie, Marmose, Phalanger, Tarsipes, Vulpine, Yapo(c)k

Oppidan Cit, Townsman, Urban

Opponent(s) Adversary, Antagonist, Anti, E-N, Enemy, E-S, Foe, Gainsayer, N-E, N-W, S-E, S-W, W-N, W-S

Opportune, Opportunist, Opportunity Appropriate, Apropos, Break, Carpetbagger, > CHANCE, Day, Equal, Facility, Favourable, Ganef, Ganev, Ganof, Godsend, Go-go, Golden, Gonif, Gonof, Heaven-sent, Occasion, Opening, Pat,

Photo, Room, Seal, Seel, Sele, Snatcher, Tide, Timely, Timous, Well-timed, Window

Oppose(d), Opposer, Opposing, Opposite, Opposition Against, Agin, Anti, Antipathy, Antipodes, Antiscian, Antithesis, Antithetic, Antonym, Argue, At, Au contraire, Averse, Battle, Black, Breast, Colluctation, Combat, Confront, Contradict, Contrary, Converse, Counter, Diametric, Dis(en)courage, Disfavour, Dissent, Distance, E contrario, Face, Foreanent, Fornen(s)t, Hinder, Hostile, Impugn, Inimical, Inverse, Militate, Mugwump, Noes, Object, Overthwart, Polar, Reaction, Reluct, Repugn, Resist, Retroact, Reverse, Rival, Shadow, Subtend, Syzygy, Teeth, Terr, Thereagainst, Thwart, Toto caelo, Traverse, V, Versus, Vis-a-vis, Withstand

Oppress(ion), Oppressive Airless, Bind, Burden, Close, Crush, Despotic, Incubus, Jackboot, Onerous, Overpower, Persecute, Ride, Stifling, Sultry, Tyrannise

Opprobrium Disgrace, Envy, Odium, Scandal

Oppugn Attack, Criticise

Opt, Option(al) Alternative, > CHOICE, Choose, Crown-jewel, Default, Elect, Facultative, Fine, Leipzig, Local, Menu, Pick, Plump, Select, Share, Soft, Trade(d), Traditional, Voluntary, Votive, Wale, Zero(-zero)

Optic(al), Optics Active, Adaptive, Electron, Fibre, Fire, Lens, Prism, Reticle, Visual

Optimism, Optimist(ic) Bull, Chiliast, Expectant, Feelgood, Hopeful, Morale, Pangloss, Pollyanna, Rosy, Sanguine, Upbeat, Utopiast, Yea-sayer

Opulent Abundant, Affluent, Moneyed, Rich, Wealthy

Opus Piece, Study, Work

Or Au, Either, Ere, Gold, Ossia, Otherwise, Sol

Oracle(s), Oracular Delphi, Dodonian, Mirror, Prophet, Pythian, Pythoness, Sage, Seer, Sibyl(line), Thummim, Urim, Vatic

Oral Acroamatic, Sonant, Spoken, Verbal, Viva, Viva voce, Vocal

Orange An(n)atta, Annatto, Arnotto, Aurora, Bergamot, Bigarade, Bilirubin, Bitter, Blood, Blossom, Calamondin, Chica, Claybank, Clockwork, Croceate, Flame, Flamingo, Fulvous, Jaffa, Kamala, Kamela, Kamila, Karaka, Kumquat, Mandarin, Mock, Naartje, Nacarat, Nartjie, Navel, Osage, Pig, Roucou, Ruta, Satsuma, Seville, Shaddock, Sour, Sweet, Tangerine, Tenné, Ugli, Ulsterman

Orang-utan Ape, Monkey, Satyr

Orate, Oration Address, Declaim, Eloge, Elogium, Elogy, Eulogy, Harangue, Panegyric, Philippics, Speech

Oratorio, Orator(y) Boanerges, Brompton, Brougham, Cantata, Cicero, Creation, Demosthenes, Diction, Elijah, Hwyl, Isocrates, Lectern, Morin, Nestor, Prevaricator, Proseucha, Proseuche, Rhetor, Samson, Spellbinder, Stump, Tub-thumper, Windbag, Yarra-banker

Orb Ball, Eyeball, Firmament, Globe, Mound, Pome, Sphere

Orbit Apse, Apsis, Circuit, Dump, Eccentric, Ellipse, Eye, Graveyard, Osculating, Parking, Path, Periastron, Perigee, Perihelion, Perilune, Periselenium, Polar, Revolution, Stationary, Synchronous

Orcadian Hoy

Orchard Arbour, Grove, Holt

Orchestra(te), Orchestration Chamber, Charanga, Concertgebouw, Concerto, ECO, Ensemble, Gamelan, Hallé, LPO, LSO, Palm-court, Pit, Ripieno, Score, SNO, String, Symphony

Orchid Adam and Eve, Adder's mouth, Arethusa, Bake-in-a-cradle, Bee, Bee-orchis, Bird's nest, Bog, Burnt-tip, Butterfly, Calanthe, Calypso, Cattleya,

Cooktown, Coralroot, Cymbidium, Cypripedium, Disa, Epidendrum, Fly, Fly orchis, Fragrant, Fringed orchis, Frog, Helleborine, Lady, Lady's slipper, Lady's tresses, Lizard, Man, Marsh, Military, Moccasin-flower, Monkey, Musk, Naked lady, Odontoglossum, Oncidium, Pogonia, Purple-fringed, Puttyroot, Pyramidal, Rattlesnake plantain, Salep, Scented, Slipper, Snakemouth, Soldier, Spider, Spotted, Swamp pink, Twayblade, Vanda, Vanilla

Ord Beginning, Point

Ordain Arrange, Command, Decree, Destine, Enact, Induct, Japan, Priest

Ordeal Corsned, Disaster, Preeve, Test, > **TRIAL**, Via Dolorosa

Order(ed), Orderly, Orders Acoemeti, Adjust, Affiliation, Alphabetical, Anton Piller, Apollonian, Apple-pie, Arrange, Array, Attendant, Attention, Attic, Avast, Bade, Banker's, Bankruptcy, Bath, Batman, Battalia, Bed, Behest, Benedictine, Bespoke, Bid, Book, Call, Camaldolite, Canon, Category, Caveat, CB, Chaprassi, Charter, Cheque, Chit, Chuprassy, Class, Coherent, Command(ment), Committal, Compensation, Composite, Corinthian, Cosmos, Court, Decorum, Decree, Demand, Dictate, Diktat, Direct(ion), Directive, Dispone, Distringas, Dominican, Doric, DSO, Edict, Embargo, Enclosed, Enjoin, En règle, Establishment, Eutaxy, Eviction, Exclusion, Feldsher, Fiat, Firing, Firman, Form(ation), Franciscan, Fraternity, Freemason, Garnishee, Garter, Gilbertine, Ginkgo, Grade, Habeas corpus, Heast(e), Hecht, Hest, Holy, Indent, Injunction, Interdict, Ionic, Irade, Khalsa, Kilter, Kosmos, Language, Lexical, Loose, Mail, Mandamus, Mandate, Marching, Market, Marshal, Masonic, Medjidie, Merit, Methodical, Minor, Mittimus, Monastic, Monitor, Natural, Neatness, Nunnery, OBE, Oddfellows, Official, OM, Open, Orange, Ord, Ordain, Organic, Pecking, Possession, Postal, Precedence, Precept, Premonstrant, Prescribe, Preservation, Provisional, Pyragyrite, Rank, Receiving, Reception, Règle, Regular, Religious, Restraining, Return, Right, Rule, Ruly, Sailing, Sealed, Search, Series, Settle, Shipshape, Short, Side, Standing, State, Statutory, Stop(-loss), Straight, Subpoena, Summons, Supersedere, Supervision, System, Tabulate, Tall, Taxis, Tell, Templar, Third, Thistle, Tidy, Trim, Tuscan, Ukase, Uniformity, Warison, Warrant, Word, Writ

▷ **Ordering** *may indicate* an anagram

Ordinal Book, Number, Second, Sequence

Ordinance Byelaw, Decree, Edict, Law, Prescript, Rescript, Rite, Statute

Ordinary Average, Banal, Bog standard, Canton, Chevron, Comely, Common (or garden), Commonplace, Cot(t)ise, Everyday, Fess(e), Flanch, Flange, Folksy, Grassroots, Hackneyed, Mediocre, Middling, Mundane, > **NORMAL**, O, OR, Plain, Prosy, Pub, Rank and file, Run-of-the-mill, Saltier, Saltire, Simple, Tressure, Trivial, Unexceptional, Uninspired, Usual, Workaday, Your

Ordnance Artillery, Cannon, Guns, Supply

Ordure Cess, Dung, Fertiliser, Manure

Ore Alga, Babingtonite, Bauxite, Bornite, Breunnerite, Calamine, Calaverite, Cerusite, Chalcocite, Chalcopyrite, Coffinite, Coin, Coltan, Copper, Crocoite, Element, Galenite, Glance, Haematite, Hedyphane, Horseflesh, Ilmenite, Iridosmine, Ironstone, Kidney, Limonite, Mat, Melaconite, Middlings, Millhead, Milling grade, Mineral, Minestone, Niobite, Oligist, Peacock, Phacolite, Pipe, Pitchblende, Proustite, Psilomelane, Pyrargyrite, Pyromorphite, Realgar, Red-lead, Schlich, Seaweed, Siderite, Sinoptite, Slime, Slug, Smaltite, Speiss, Sphalerite, Stephanite, Stilpnosiderite, Stream-tin, Tenorite, Tetrahedrite, Tin, Wad(d), White-lead, Yellow cake

Organ(s), Organic Adnexa, Anlage, Apollonicon, Appendix, Archegonium, Barrel, Biogenic, Calliope, Carpel, Chair, Chamber, Chemoreceptor, Chord,

Claspers, Clave, Conch(a), Console, Corti's, Cribellum, Ctene, Ear, Echo, Electric, Electronic, Electroreceptor, End, Essential, Exteroceptor, Feeler, Fin, Flabellum, Fundus, Gametangium, Gill, Glairin, Gonad, Hammond®, Hand, Hapteron, Harmonica, Harmonium, House, Hydraulos, Imine, Isomere, Kerogen, Kidney, Lien, Light, Liver, Lung-book, Means, Mechanoreceptor, Media, Medulla, Melodion, Ministry, Nasal, Natural, Nectary, Nephridium, Newspaper, Oogonia, Ovipositor, Palp, Pancreas, Parapodium, Part, Pedal, Photophore, Photoreceptor, Physharmonics, Pipe, Pipeless, Placenta, Plastid, Portative, Positive, Prothallus, Pulmones, Purtenance, Pyrophone, Radula, Receptor, Recit, Reed, Regal, Relict, Sang, Saprobe, Scent, Sense, Sensillum, Serra, Siphon, Spinneret, Spleen, Sporangium, Sporophore, Stamen, Steam, Stratocyst, Swell, Syrinx, Tentacle, Textual, Theatre, Theca, Thymus, Tongue, Tonsil, Tool, Tympanum, Uterus, Vegetative, Velum, Viscera, Viscus, Vitals, Voice, Voluntary, Womb, Wurlitzer®

Organise(d), **Organisation**, **Organiser** Activate, Anatomy, > ARRANGE, Association, Brigade, Caucus, Collect, Comecon, Company, Constitution, Coordinate, Design, Embody, Entrepreneur, Fascio, Firm, Impresario, Infrastructure, Jaycee, Ku Klux Klan, Logistics, Machine, Mafia, Marshal, Mobilise, Octopus, Orchestrate, Outfit, Personal, Quango, Rally, Regiment, Resistance, Rosicrucian, Run, Setup, Social, Soroptimist, Sort, Stage, Steward, System, Tidy, Together, UN

Organise(d) *may indicate* an anagram

Organism Aerobe, Agamic, Being, Biont, Biotic, Cell, Chimeric, Chlamydia, Ciliate, Clade, Coral, Diplont, Ecad, Endogenous, Entity, Epizoite, Epizoon, Eucaryote, Euglena, Eukaryote, Germ, Halobiont, Halophile, Haplont, Holophyte, Holoplankton, Homeotherm, Incross, Infauna, Infusoria(n), Lichen, Macrobiote, Medusa, Meroplankton, Microbe, Moneron, Morphology, Nekton, Neuston, Paramecium, Pathogen, Phenetics, Plankter, Plankton, Protist, Protozoan, Radiolarian, Saprobe, Streptococcus, Symbion(t), Torula, Virino, Volvox

Organ-part, **Organ-stop** Bourdon, Clarabella, Diapason, Gamba, Montre, Nasard, Principal, Pyramidon, Quint, Salicet

Organ-tuner Reed-knife

Orgy Bacchanalia(n), Binge, Blinder, Bust, Carousal, Dionysian, Feast, Revel, Saturnalia, Spree, Wassail

Orient(al) Adjust, Annamite, Chinoiserie, Dawn, Dayak, E, East(ern), Fu Manchu, Hindu, Levant, Leyton, Malay, Mongolian, Pareoean, Shan, Sunrise, Tatar, Thai, Tibetan, Turk(o)man

Orifice Aperture, Blastosphere, Gap, Hole, Micropyle, Nare, Opening, Pore, Spiracle, Trema, Vent

Origen's work Tetrapla

Origin(al), **Originate**, **Originating** Abo, Adam, Arise, Beginning, Birth, Come, Cradle, Creation, Derive, Editio princeps, Elemental, Emanate, Epicentre, Etymon, Extraction, First, Firsthand, Focus, Found, Generic, Genesis, Genetical, Germ, Grow, Hatch, Incunabula, Initial, Innovate, Invent, Master, Mother, Nascence, Natality, New, Novel, Ord, Primal, Primary, Primigenial, Primordial, Pristine, Prototype, Provenance, Rise, Root, Seminal, Source, Spring, Start, Ur, Ylem, Zoism

Oriole Firebird, Hangbird

Orison Blessing, Prayer

Ormer Abalone, Haliotis

Ornament(al), **Ornamentation** Acroter(ia), Adorn, Anaglyph, Antefix,

Anthemion, Aplustre, Arabesque, Bahuti, Ball-flower, Barbola, Baroque, Barrette, Bead, Bedeck, Bez(z)ant, Billet, Blister, Boss, Bracelet, Breloque, Broider, Bugle, Bulla, Cartouche, Chase, Clock, Cockade, Corbeil(le), Cornice, Crocket, Cross-quarters, Curin, Curlicue, Decorate, Decoration, Diamanté, Die-work, Diglyph, Dog's-tooth, Doodad, Embellish, Emblem(a), Enrich, Epaulet(te), Epergne, Fallal, Fandangle, Fiddlehead, Figuration, Figurine, Filagree, Filigrain, Filigree, Fleuret, Fleurette, Fleuron, Florid, Fret, Fretwork, Frill, Frounce, Furbelow, Furnish, Gadroon, Gaud, Gingerbread, Gorget, Griff(e), Guilloche, Gutta, Headwork, Heitiki, Helix, Illustrate, Inlay, Knotwork, Labret, Lambrequin, Leglet, Macrome, Mantling, Mense, Millefleurs, Mordent, Moresque, Motif, Nail-head, Netsuke, Nicknackery, Niello, O, Okimono, Ovolo, Palmette, Parure, Paternoster, Paua, Pawa, Pectoral, Pendant, Picot, Pipe, Pompom, Pompo(o)n, Pounce, Pralltriller, Prettify, Prunt, Purfle, Quatrefoil, Rel(l)ish, Rocaille, Rococo, Spangle, Tassel, Tettix, Tiki, Tool, Torque, Torsade, Tracery, Trappings, Trill, Trimming, Trinket, Triquetra, Turn, Wally, Water-leaf, Whigmaleerie, Whigmaleery

Ornate Baroque, Churrigueresque, Dressy, Elaborate, Fancy, Florid, Flowery

▷ **Ornate** *may indicate* an anagram

Ornithologist Audubon, Birdman

Orotund Bombastic, Grandiose, Pompous, Rhetorical, Sonant

Orphan Annie, Foundling, Topsy, Ward

Orpiment Arsenic, Zarnich

Orpington Buff, Hen

Ort Bit, Crumb, Morsel, Remnant

Orthodox Cocker, Conventional, Hardshell, Proper, Sound, Standard

Orthorhombic Enstatite

Ortolan Bird, Bunting, Rail

Oscar Award, O, Wilde

Oscillate, Oscillation, Oscillator Dynatron, Excitor, Fluctuate, Librate, Parasitic, Rock, Seiche, Squeg, Swing, Vibrate, Waver

Osier Red, Reed, Sallow, Willow

Osmium Os

Osmosis Reverse

Osprey Fish-hawk, Ossifrage, Pandion

Osseous Bony, Hard, Skeletal, Spiny

Ostensibly Apparent, External, Seeming

Ostentation, Ostentatious Camp, Display, Dog, Eclat, Epideictical, Extravagant, Fantoosh, Flamboyant, Flash(y), Flaunt, Florid, Flourish, Garish, Gaudy, Highfalutin(g), Parade, Pomp, Ponc(e)y, Pretence, Puff, > **SHOW(ING)**, Side, Splash, Swank, Tacky, Tulip

Ostracise, Ostracism Banish, Blackball, Boycott, Cut, Exclude, Exile, Petalism, Potsherd, Snub, Taboo, Tabu

Ostrich Em(e)u, Estrich, Estridge, Nandoo, Nandu, Ratite, Rhea, Struthio(nes), Titanis

Othello Moor, Morisco

Other(wise), Others Additional, Aka, Alia, Alias, Allo-, Alternative, Besides, Different, Distinct, Else, Et al, Etc, Excluding, Former, Further, Rest, Significant

Other things Alia

▷ **Otherwise** *may indicate* an anagram

Otiose Idle, Indolent, Ineffective, Lazy, Needless, Superfluous

Otis Bustard

Otter Edal, Paravane, Tarka

Otto Attar, Chypre, Mahratta

Ottoman Osmanli, Porte, Rumelia, Turk

Oubliette Dungeon, Pit, Prison

Ouch Brooch, Ornament, Ow

Ought All, Should

Ouida Ramee

Ounce Cat, Fluid, Liang, Oz, Panther, Tael, Uncial

Our(selves) Us, We

Ousel *see* OUZEL

Oust Depose, Dislodge, Eject, Evict, Expel, Fire, Supplant, Unnest

Out Absent, Aglee, Agley, Asleep, Aus, Begone, Bowl, Dated, En ville, Exposed, External, Forth, Haro, Harrow, Hors, Oust, Skittle, Striking, Stump, Taboo, Uit, Unfashionable, Up, York

Out *may indicate* an anagram

Out and out Absolute, Arrant, Rank, Sheer, Stark, Teetotal, Thorough, Totally, Utter

Outback Backblocks, Bundu, The mulga

Outbreak Epidemic, Eruption, Explosion, Flare-up, Plague, Putsch, Rash, Recrudescence

Outburst Access, Blurt, Bluster, Boutade, Evoe, Explosion, Fit, Flaw, Furore, Fusillade, Gush, Gust, Paroxysm, Passion, Philippic, Salvo, Storm, Tantrum, Tumult, Volley

Outcast Cagot, Discard, Eta, Exile, Exul, Ishmael, Leper, Mesel, Pariah, Rogue

Outcome Aftermath, Consequence, Dénouement, Effect, Emergence, End, Event, > RESULT, Sequel, Upshot

Outcrop Basset, Blossom, Crag, Creston, Inlier, Mesa, Spur, Tarpit

Outcry Alew, Bray, > CLAMOUR, Halloo, Howl, Hue, Protest, Racket, Shright, Steven, Uproar, Utas

Outdated Archaic, Dinosaur, Effete, Feudal, Fossil, Obsolete, Outmoded, Passé, Square

Outdo Beat, Cap, Picnic, Surpass, Top, Trump, Worst

Outdoor(s) Alfresco, External, Garden, Open air, Plein-air

Outer External, Extrogenous, Magpie, Superficial, Top

Outfit(ter) Accoutrement, Catsuit, Ensemble, Equipage, Fitout, Furnish, Get-up, Haberdasher, Habit, Kit, Rig, Samfoo, Samfu, Strip, Suit, Team, Trousseau, Weed(s)

Outflow Anticyclone, Discharge, Effluence, Eruption, Surge

Outgoing Egression, Exiting, Extrovert, Open, Retiring

Outgrowth Ala(te), Aril, Bud, Enation, Epiphenomenon, Exostosis, Offshoot, Root-hair, Sequel, Trichome

Outhouse Lean to, Privy, Shed, Skilling, Skillion, Skipper, Stable

Outing Excursion, Jaunt, Junket, Picnic, Sortie, Spin, Spree, Treat, Trip, Wayzgoose

Outlandish Barbarous, Bizarre, Exotic, Foreign, Peregrine, Rum

Outlaw Allan-a-Dale, Attaint, Badman, Ban, Bandit(ti), Banish, Exile, Fugitive, Hereward, Horn, Proscribe, Robin Hood, Rob Roy, Ronin, Tory, Waive

Outlay Cost, Expense, Mise

Outlet Débouché, Egress, Escape, Estuary, Exit, Femerall, Market, Opening, Outfall, Overflow, Sluice, Socket, Spout, Tuyere, Tweer, Twier, Twire, Twyer(e), Vent

Outline Adumbration, Aperçu, Circumscribe, Configuration, Contorno,

Contour, Delineate, Digest, > **DRAFT**, Esquisse, Footprint, Layout, Note, Perimeter, Plan, Profile, Prospectus, Relief, Scenario, Schematic, Shape, Silhouette, Skeletal, Skeleton, Sketch, Summary, Syllabus, Synopsis, T(h)alweg', Trace

Outlook Casement, Perspective, Prospect, View, Vista, Weltanschauung

Outmoded Wasm

▷ **Out of** *may indicate* an anagram

Out of date Corny, Obs, Passé, Scrap, Square, Worn

Out of form Amorphous, Awry

Out of order Fritz

Out of sorts Cachectic, Nohow, Peevish, Poorly

▷ **Out of sorts** *may indicate* an anagram

Out of tune Discordant, Flat, Scordato, Scordatura

Outpost Colony, Picquet

Outpour(ing) Effuse, Flood, Flow, Gush, Libation, Stream, Torrent

Output Data, Get, Produce, Production, Turnout, Yield

▷ **Output** *may indicate* an anagram

Outrage(ous) Affront, Appal, Atrocity, Desecrate, Disgust, Egregious, Enorm(ity), Flagrant, Insult, OTT, Rich, Sacrilege, Scandal, Shocking, Ungodly, Violate

▷ **Outrageously** *may indicate* an anagram

Outright Clean, Complete, Entire, Point-blank, Utter

Outset Beginning, Start

Outshine Eclipse, Excel, Overshadow, Surpass

Outside Ab extra, Crust, Exterior, External, Front, Furth, Hors, Periphery, Rim, Rind, Rine, Surface

Outsider Alien, Bolter, Bounder, Cad, Extern, Extremist, Foreigner, Incomer, Oustiti, Palagi, Pariah, Ring-in, Stranger, Stumer, Unseeded, Upstart

Outsize Capacious, Giant, Gigantic, Huge, OS

Outskirts Edge, Fringe, Periphery, Purlieu

Outspoken Bluff, Blunt, Broad, Candid, Explicit, Forthright, Frank, Plain, Rabelaisian, Round, Vocal

Outstanding Ace, Beaut(y), Belter, Billowing, Bulge, Chief, Egregious, Eminent, Especial, Exceptional, Extant, First, Fugleman, Highlight, Humdinger, Impasto, Jut, Lulu, Marked, Matchless, Oner, Owing, Paragon, Phenomenal, Pièce de résistance, Prince, Prize, Prominent, Promontory, Prosilient, Proud, Purler, Relief, Relievo, Salient, Signal, Special, Squarrose, Star, Stellar, Strout, Superb, Tour de force, Unpaid, Unsettled

Outstrip Best, Cap, Cote, Distance, Exceed, Overtake

Outward Efferent, Extern(e), External, Extrinsic, Extrorse, Extrovert, Posticous, Postliminary, Superficial

Outweigh Preponderate

Outwit Baffle, Best, Circumvent, Dish, Euchre, Fox, Over-reach, > **THWART**, Trick

Outwork Demilune, Jetty, Moon, Tenail(le), Tenaillon

Outworn Decrepit, Obsolete, Used

Ouzel Ring, Water

Oval(s) Cartouche, Cassini, Ellipse, Henge, Navette, Obovate, Ooidal

Ovary Oophoron

Ovation Applause, Cheer, Standing

Oven(-like) Aga®, Calcar, Camp, Convection, Cul-de-four, Dutch, Electric, Furnace, Gas, Haybox, Horn(it)o, Kiln, Lear, Leer, Lehr, Lime kiln, Maori, Microwave, Muffle, Norwegian, Oast, Oon, Stove

Over Above, Across, Again, Atop, C, Clear, Done, Finished, Hexad, Left, Maiden, Of, On, Ore, Ort, Owre, Sopra, Spare, Superior, Surplus, Uber, Yon

Overact Burlesque, Emote, Ham, Hell, Hoke

Overactive Hyper

Overall(s) Boiler suit, Denims, Dungarees, Dust-coat, Fatigues, Smicket, Smock, Tablier

Overbearing Arrogant, Dogmatic, Domineering, High-muck-a-muck, Imperious, Insolent, Lordly

Overbid Gazump

Overcast Cloudy, Lowering, Sew, Sombre

Overcharge Clip, Extort, Fleece, Gyp, OC, Rack-rent, Rook, Rush, Soak, Sting

Overcoat Benjamin, Benny, British warm, > COAT, Crombie, Dolman, Grego, Inverness, Joseph, Paletot, Petersham, Pos(h)teen, Prince Albert, Raglan, Redingote, Spencer, Surtout, Tabard, Taglioni, Ulster, Warm, Wooden, Wrap-rascal

Overcome Beat, Bested, Conquer, Convince, Defeat, Hit for six, Kill, Master, Mither, Prevail, Quell, Speechless, Subdue, Subjugate, Superate, Surmount, Vanquish, Win

Overcrowd Congest, Jam, Pack

Overdo(ne) Exceed, Ham, Hokey, Hokum, OTT, Percoct, Tire

Overdose OD

Overdraft Red

Overdrawn *may indicate* 'red' outside another word

Overdress(ing) Dudism, Flossy, Overall

Overdue Behindhand, Belated, Excessive, Late

Overeat(ing) Binge, Gorge, Hypertrophy, Satiate

Overemphasize Rub in, Stress

Overfeed Gorge, Sate, Stuff

Overflow Lip, Nappe, Ooze, Ream, Redound, Spillage, Surfeit, Teem

Overfull Brimming, Hept

Overgrow(n) Ivy'd, Jungle, Ramp(ant), Rank, Rhinophyma

Overhang(ing) Beetle, Bulge, Cornice, > JUT, Project, Shelvy

Overhaul Bump, Catch, Overtake, Recondition, Revision, Service, Strip

Overhead(s) Above, Aloft, Ceiling, Cost, Exes, Hair(s), Headgear, Oncost, Rafter, Upkeep, Zenith

Overhear Catch, Eavesdrop, Tap

Overindulge(nt) Crapulent, Crass, Pig

Overjoy Elate, Thrill

Overland Portage

Overlap(ping) Correspond, Equitant, Imbricate, Incubous, Kern(e), Limbous, Obvolute, Stretto, Tace, Tasse

Overlay Ceil, Smother, Stucco, Superimpose, Veneer

Overlearned Pedantic

Overload Burden, Plaster, Strain, Surcharge, Tax

Overlook Condone, Disregard, Excuse, Forget, Miss, Pretermit, Superintend, Waive

Overlord Excess, Invasion

Overlying Incumbent, Jessant, Pressing

Overmuch Excessive, Surplus, Too, Undue

Overplay Ham, Hoke

Overpower(ing) Crush, Evince, Mighty, Onerous, Oppress, Overwhelm, Subdue, Surmount, Swelter, Whelm

Overpraise Adulate
Over-refined Dainty, Nice, Pernickety, Precious
Overrule Abrogate, Disallow, Veto
Overrun Exceed, Extra, Infest, Inundate, Invade, Swarm, Teem
Overseas Abroad, Colonial, Outremer
Oversee(r) Baas, Boss, Captain, Care, Deputy, Direct, Eyebrow, Foreman, Forewoman, Grieve, Handle, Induna, Moderator, Periscope, Steward, Supercargo, Survey(or)
Oversentimental Byronic, Slushy
Overshadow Cloud, Dominate, Eclipse, Obscure, Outclass
Overshoe Arctic, Galosh, Sandal, Snowboot
Oversight Blunder, Care, Error, Gaffe, Lapse, Neglect, Parablepsis
Overstate(ment) Embroider, Exaggerate, Hyperbole
Overstrained Epitonic
Overt Manifest, Patent, Plain, Public
Overtake Catch, For(e)hent, Lap, Leapfrog, Overget, Overhaul, > PASS, Supersede, Usurp
Overthrow Dash, Defeat, Demolish, Depose, Down, Labefact(at)ion, Ruin, Smite, Stonker, Subvert, Supplant, Topple, Unhorse, Usurp, Vanquish, Whemmle, Whommle, Whummle, Worst
Overture Advance, Carnival, Concert, Egmont, French, Hebrides, Intro, Italian, Leonora, Offer, > OPENING, Prelude, Propose, Sinfonia, Toccata, Toccatella, Toccatina
Overturn(ing) Catastrophe, Quash, Reverse, Tip, Topple, Up(set), Upend, Whemmle
Overvalue Exaggerate, Salt
Overweening Bashaw, Cocky, Excessive, Imperious, Presumptuous
Overweight Sunk
Overwhelm(ed), Overwhelming Accablé, Assail, > CRUSH, Defeat, Foudroyant, Inundate, KO, Mind-boggling, Oppress, Overcome, Scupper, Smother, Submerge, Swamp, Whup
Overwork(ed) Fag, Hackneyed, Ornament, Slog, Stale, Supererogation, Tax, Tire, Toil
Overwrought Frantic, Hysterical, Ore-rested, Ornate, Rococo
Ovid Naso
Ovum Egg, Oosphere, Seed
Owe(d), Owing Attribute, Due, OD
Owen Glendower
Owl(s) African, Barn, Barred, Blinker, Boobook, Brown, Bubo, Bunter, Chinese, Eagle, Elegant, English, Fish, Glimmergowk, Hawk, Hoo(ter), Horned, Howlet, Jenny, Little, Long-eared, Longhorn, Madge, Moper, Mopoke, Mopus, Night, Ogle, Parliament, Ruru, Saw-whet, Scops, Screech, Sea, Snowy, Strich, Striges, Strigiformes, Tawny, Wood
Own(er), Owning, Ownership Admit, Agnise, Confess, Domain, Dominium, Fess, Have, Hold, Mortmain, Nain, Of, Possess, Proper, Proprietor, Recognise, Reputed, Title, Use
Ox(en) Anoa, Aquinas, Aurochs, Banteng, Banting, Bison, Bonas(s)us, Buffalo, Bugle, Bullock, Cat(t)alo, Fee, Gaur, Gayal, Gyal, Kouprey, Mart, Musk, Neat, Ovibos, Rother, Sapi-utan, S(e)ladang, Steare, Steer, Stirk, Taurus, Ure, Urus, Water, Yak, Yoke, Zebu, Z(h)o
Oxford (group) Buchmanism, OU, Puseyism, Shoe
Oxhead Aleph

Oxidation, **Oxide** Alumina, Anatase, Ceria, Erbium, Eremacausis, Gothite, Gummite, Holmia, Kernite, Lithia, Magnesia, Nitrous, Psilomelane, Quicklime, Red lead, Rutile, Samarskite, Strontia, Thoria, Zaffer, Zaffre

Oxtail *may indicate* 'x'

Oxygen (and lack of) Anoxia, Epoxy, Liquid, Lox, Loxygen, O, Vital air

Oyer Hearing, Trial

Oyster (bed), **Oyster disease**, **Oyster-eater** Avicula, Bivalve, Bonamia, Bush, Cul(t)ch, Kentish, Lay, Mollusc, Native, Ostrea, Ostreophage, Pandore, Pearl, Plant, Prairie, Salsify, Scalp, Scaup, Seed(ling), Spat, Spondyl, Vegetable

Oyster-catcher Sea-pie

Oyster-plant Gromwell, Salsify

Oz Amos, Australia

Ozone Air, Atmosphere, Oxygen

P Papa, Parking, Penny, Piano, Prince

PA Aide

Pabulum Aliment, Cheer, Food, Fuel, Nourishment

Pace, **Pacemaker** Canter, Clip, Cracking, Dog-trot, Easter, Gait, Geometruc, Jog-trot, Lope, Measure, Military, Pari passu, Pioneer, > RATE, Roman, Scout's, Snail's, Spank, Speed, Stride, Stroll, Tempo, Tramp, Tread, Trot

Pachyderm Armadillo, Elephant, Hippo, Mastodon, Rhino

Pacific, **Pacify** Appease, Bromide, Conciliate, Dove, Ease, Irenic, Lull, Mild, Moderate, Ocean, Placate, Placid, Quiet, Serene, Soothe, Subdue, Sweeten, Tranquil

Pacifist CO, Conciliator, D(o)ukhobor, Dove

Pack(age), **Packed**, **Packing** Bale, Blister, Bobbery, Box, Bubble, Bundle, Cards, Cold, Compress, Congest, Cram, Crate, Crowd, Cry, Deck, Dense, Dunnage, Embox, Entity, Everest, Excelsior, Face, Fardel, Floe, Gasket, Gaskin, Glut, Hamper, Hunt, Ice, Jam, Kennel, Knapsack, Load, Matilda, Pair, > PARCEL, Pikau, Power, Pun, Rout, Rucksack, Set, Shiralee, Shrink-wrap, Steeve, Stow, Suits, Tamp, Tread, Troop, Truss, Wad, Wet, Wolf, Wrap

Packet Boat, Bundle, Deck, Liner, Mailboat, Mint, Parcel, Pay, Red, Roll, Sachet, Steam, Steamboat, Wage

Pack-horse Sumpter

Packman Chapman, Hawker, Hiker, Pedlar, Tinker

Pact Agreement, Alliance, Bargain, Bilateral, Cartel, Contract, Covenant, Locarno, Munich, Suicide, > TREATY, Warsaw

Pad(ding) Batting, Bombast, Brake, Bustle, Compress, Crash, Cushion, Dabber, Damper, Dossil, Enswathe, Expand, Falsies, Filler, Flat, Frog, Gumshield, Hard, Hassock, Horse, Ink, Launch, Leg-guard, Lily, Nag, Note, Numnah, Patch, Paw, Ped, Pillow, Pincushion, Plastron, Pledget, Plumper, Pouf(fe), Protract, Pudding, Pulvillus, Scratch, Shoulder, Stamp, Stuff, Sunk, Tablet, Thief, Touch, Tournure, Tylopod, Tympan, Velour(s), Velure, Wad, Wase, Writing

Paddington Bear, Station

Paddle, **Paddle boat**, **Paddle-foot** Canoe, Dabble, Doggy, Oar, Pinniped, Seal, Side-wheel, Spank, Splash, Stern-wheeler, Wade

Paddock Field, Frog, Holding, Meadow, Park, Sacrifice

Paddy, **Paddy field** Fury, Ire, Irishman, Mick, Pat(rick), Pet, Rag, Rage, Sawah, Tantrum, Temper, Wax

Padre Chaplain, Cleric, Father, Monk, Priest

Paean Hymn, Ode, Praise, Psalm

Paedophile Nonce

Pagan Animist, Atheist, Gentile, Gentoo, Godless, Heathen, Idolater, Infidel, Odinist, Paynim, Saracen

Page(s), **Pageboy** Back, Bellboy, Bellhop, Bleep, Boy, Buttons, Callboy, Centrefold, Flyleaf, Folio, Foolscap, Front, Gate-fold, Groom, Haircut, Home, Hornbook, Leaf, Messenger, Moth, Octavo, Op-ed, P, Pane, PP, Problem, Quarto,

Ream, Recto, Ro, Servant, Sheet, Side, Squire, Tear sheet, Tiger, Title, Varlet, Verso, Web, Yellow

Pageant Cavalcade, Pomp, Spectacle, Tattoo, Triumph

Pagoda Temple, To

Pah Pish, Tush, Umph

Paid *see* PAY

Pail Bucket, Kettle, Leglan, Leglen, Leglin, Piggin

Pain(ful), Pains Ache, Aggrieve, Agony, Ake, Algesis, Angina, Anguish, Arthralgia, Bad, Bale, Bedsore, Bitter, Bore, Bot(t), Bother, Burn, Colic, Cramp, Crick, Distress, Dole, Doleur, Dolour, Dool(e), Dysmenorhoea, Dysury, Eina, Excruciating, Fibrositis, Gip, Grief, Gripe, Growing, Gyp, Harrow, Heartburn, Hemialgia, > HURT, Ill, Kink, Laborious, Mal, Mastalgia, Mastodynia, Metralgia, Migraine, Misery, Mulligrubs, Myalgia, Neuralgia, Nociceptive, Pang, Persuant, Pest, Pleurodynia, Prick, Pungent, Rack, Raw, Referred, Sair, Sciatica, Smart, Sore, Sorrow, Splitting, Sten(d), Sting, Stitch, Strangury, Stung, Teen(e), Tene, Throe, Topalgia, Torment, Tormina, Torture, Twinge, Wrench, Wring

Pain *may indicate* bread (French)

Painkiller Aminobutene, Analgesic, Bute, Cocaine, Distalgesic, Enkephalin, Jadeite, Meperidine, Metopon, Morphine, Number, Pethidine

Painlessness Analgesia

Painstaking Assiduous, Careful, Diligent, Elaborate, Exacting, Meticulous, Sedulous, Studious, Thorough

Paint(ed), Painting Abstract, Acrylic, Action, Airbrush, Alla prima, Aquarelle, Arcimboldo, Art autre, Art deco, Artificial, Art nouveau, Ash Can School, Barbizon, Bice, Blottesque, Camaieu, Canvas, Cellulose, Chiaroscuro, Clair-obscure, Clobber, Coat, Colour, Cubism, Dadaism, Daub, Dayglo, Decorate, Depict, Diptych, Distemper, Duco, Eggshell, Emulsion, Enamel, Encaustic, Fard, Fauvism, Finery, Finger, Flemish, Fore-edge, Fresco, Fucus, Genre, Gild, Gloss, Gouache, Grease, Grisaille, Hard-edge, Historical, Impasto, Impressionism, Intimism(e), Intonaco, Intumescent, Lead, Limn, Luminous, Magilp, Matt, Megilp, Mehndi, Miniate, Miniature, Modello, Mona Lisa, Monotint, Mural, Naive, Neo-Impressionism, Nightpiece, Nihonga, Nocturne, Non-drip, Oaker, Ochre, Oil, Old Master, Oleo(graph), Op art, Orphism, Paysage, Pentimento, Pict, Picture, Pigment, Pinxit, Plein air, Pointillism(e), Portray, Poster, Post-Impressionism, Predella, Primitive, Quadratura, Raddle, Rosemaling, Roughstuff, Sand, Scenography, Scumble, Secco, Sfumato, Sien(n)ese, Skyscape, Spray, Stencil, Stereochrome, Still life, Stipple, Suprematism, Tablature, Tachism(e), Tall-oil, Tanka, Tempera, Tenebrism, Thangka, Tondo, Ukiyo-e, Umber, Umbrian, Vanitas, Veduta, Vorticism, War, Wax

Painted woman Courtesan, Harlot, Pict, Tart

Painter > ARTIST, Blaue Reiter, Colourist, Cubist, Decorator, Gilder, Illusionist, Impressionist, Limner, Miniaturist, Paysagist, Plein-airist, Pre-Raphaelite, Primitive, Sien(n)ese, Soutine, Sunday, Yeats

Pair(ing) Brace, Cooper, Couple(t), Duad, Duo, Dyad(ic), Exciton, Fellows, Geminate, Item, Jugate, Link, Match, Mate, Minimal, Ocrea, Pigeon, Pr, Span, Synapsis, Syndyasmian, Syzygy, Tandem, Thummim, Twa(e), Tway, Two, Urim, Yoke

Paisley Orange, Shawl

Pakistan(i) Pathan

Pal Ally, Amigo, Bud(dy), China, Chum, Comrade, Crony, Cully, Mate

Palace Alhambra, Basilica, Blenheim, Buckingham, Court, Crystal, Edo, Elysee, Escorial, Escurial, Fontainebleau, Forbidden City, Fulham, Gin, Holyrood, Holyroodhouse, Hotel, Istana, Lambeth, Lateran, Linlithgow, Louvre, Mansion, Nonsuch, Palatine, Picture, Pitti, Quirinal, St James's, Sans Souci, Schloss, Seraglio, Serail, Shushan, Topkapi, Trianon, Tuileries, Valhalla, Vatican, Versailles

Paladin Champion, Charlemagne, Defender, Douzeper, Fièrabras, Ganelon, >**KNIGHT**, Ogier, Oliver, Orlando, Rinaldo, Roland

Palanquin Doolie, Litter, Palkee, Palki, Sedan

Palatable, **Palatalized**, **Palate** Cleft, Dainty, Hard, Moulle, Relish, Roof, Sapid, Savoury, Soft, Taste, Toothsome, Uranic, Uraniscus, Uvula, Velum

Palatial Ornate, Splendid

Palatinate, **Palatine** Officer, Pfalz

Palaver Chatter, Debate, Parley, Powwow, >**TALK**

Pale, **Paling** Ashen, Blanch, Bleach, Cere, Dim, English, Etiolate(d), Fade, >**FAINT**, Fence, Ghostly, Haggard, Insipid, Jewish, Lily (white), Livid, Mealy, Ox-fence, Pallescent, Pastel, Peelie-wally, Picket, Sallow, Shilpit, Stang, Verge, Wan, Whey-faced, White, Wishy-washy

Paleography Diplomatics

Pal(a)eolithic Acheulean, Acheulian, Chellean, Gravettian, Levallois(ian), Lower, Madelenian, Magdalenian, Middle, Perigordian, Solutrean, Strepyan, Upper

Paleozoic Silurian

Palestine, **Palestinian** Amorite, Gadarene, Intifada, Israel, Pal, Per(a)ea, PLO, Samaria

Palette Board, Cokuloris

Palindrome, **Palindromic** Cancrine, Sotadic

Palisade Barrier, Fence, Fraise, Stacket, Stockade

Pall Bore, Cloy, Damper, Glut, Mantle, Mortcloth, Satiate, Shroud

Palladium Defence, Pd, Safeguard

Pallas Athene

Pallet Bed, Cot, Couch, Mattress, Tick

Palliate, **Palliative** Alleviate, Anetic, Ease, Extenuate, Lessen, Mitigate, Reduce, Relieve, Sedative

Pallid Anaemic, Ashen, Insipid, Pale, Wan, Waxy

Palm Accolade, Areca, Assai, Atap, Babassu, Bangalow, Betel, Buriti, Burrawang, Bussu, Cabbage, Calamus, Carna(h)uba, Carnauba, Chamaerops, Chiqui-chiqui, Coco, Cohune, Conceal, Coquito, Corozo, Corypha, Cycad, Date (tree), Doom, Doum, Elaeis, Euterpe, Fan, Feather, Fob, Foist, Gomuti, Gomuto, Groo-groo, Gru-gru, Hand, Ita, Itching, Ivory, Jip(p)i-Jap(p)a, Jipyapa, Jupati, Kentia, Kittul, Laurels, Loof, Looves, Macahuba, Macaw, Macoya, Moriche, Nikau, Nipa, Oil, Palmyra, Paxiuba, Peach, Pupunha, Raffia, Raphia, Rat(t)an, Royal, Sabal, Sago, Sugar, Talipat, Talipot, Thenar, Toddy, Triumph, Troelie, Troolie, Trooly, Trophy, Vola, Washingtonia, Wax, Wine, Zatia

Palmer Lilli, Pilgrim

Palmerston Pam

Palmistry Ch(e)irognomy

Palm-leaf Frond

Palpable Evident, Gross, Manifest, Patent, Plain, Tangible

Palpitate Flutter, Pulsate, Throb, Twitter, Vibrate

Palsy Bell's, Cerebral, Paralysis, Shakes

Paltry Bald, Cheap, Exiguous, Mean, Measly, Peanuts, Pelting, Petty, Poor, Puny

Scald, Scalled, Sorry, Tin(-pot), Tinny, Trashy, Trifling, Two-bit, Vile, Waff, Whiffet

Pamper(ed) Cocker, Coddle, Cosher, Cosset, Cuiter, Feather-bed, Gratify, High-fed, > INDULGE, Mollycoddle, Overfeed, Pet, Spoon-fed

Pamphlet Brochure, Catalogue, Chapbook, Leaflet, Notice, Sheet, Tract

Pan Agree, Auld Hornie, Bainmarie, Balit, Basin, Betel(-pepper), Braincase, Chafer, Dent, Dial, Drip, Dripping, Goat-god, Goblet, God, Hard, Ice-floe, Iron, Karahi, Ladle, Lavatory, Muffin, Nature-god, Pancheon, Panchion, Patella, Patina, Peter, Poacher, Preserving, Prospect, Roast, Salt, Search, Skid, Skillet, Slag, Slate, Spider, Vessel, Warming, Wo(c)k, Work

Panacea All-heal, Azoth, Catholicon, Cure(-all), Elixir, Ginseng, Parkleaves, Remedy, Tutsan

Panache Bravura, Crest, Dash, Flair, Paz(z)azz, Piz(z)azz, Plume, Pzazz, Show, Talent

Pancake Blin(i), Blintz(e), Burrito, Crêpe (suzette), Drop(ped)-scone, Flam(m), Flapjack, Flaune, Flawn, Fraise, Fritter, Froise, Pikelet, Poppadum, Quesadilla, Scotch, Slapjack, Spring roll, Suzette, Taco, Tortilla, Tostada, Waffle

Pancreas Sweetbread

Panda Bear-cat, Chi-chi, Chitwah, Common, Giant, Lesser, Red

Pandarus Go-between

Pandemonium Inferno

Pander Broker, Indulge, Pimp, Procurer, Toady

Pane Glass, Light, Panel, Quarrel, Quarry, Sheet

Panegyric Eulogy, Laudation, Praise, Tribute

Panel(ling) Adoption, Board, Cartouche, Children's, Dashboard, Fa(s)cia, Gore, Hatchment, Inset, Instrument, Jury, Lacunar, Mandorla, Mimic, Orb, Patch(board), People's, Rocker, Screen, Skreen, Solar, Stile, Stomacher, Tablet, Valance, Volet, Wainscot

Pang Achage, Ache, Crick, Qualm, Spasm, Stab, Stound, Twinge, Wrench

Pangloss Optimist

Pangolin Ant-eater, Manis

Panhandle(r) Beggar, W. Virginia

Panic Alar(u)m, Amaze, Consternation, Fear, Flap, Flat-spin, Fright, Funk, Guinea-grass, Lather, Millet, Raggee, Raggy, Ragi, Sauve qui peut, > SCARE, Scarre, Stampede, Stampedo, Stew, Tailspin, > TERROR

Panicle Thyrse

Panjandrum Bashaw

Pannier Basket, Cacolet, Corbeil, Dosser, Saddlebag, Skip, Whisket

Panoply Armour, Array, Pomp

Panorama, Panoramic Range, Scenery, Veduta, View, Vista

Pansy Gay, Heart's-ease, Herb-trinity, Kiss-me-quick, Nance, Powder-puff, Queer, Viola

Pant(s) Bags, Breeches, Capri, Cargo, Chaps, Chinos, Culottes, Deck, Dhoti, Drawers, Fatigues, Flaff, Gasp, Gaucho, Harem, Hot, Long johns, Longs, Parachute, Pech, Pedal-pushers, Pegh, Puff, Ski, Slacks, Smalls, Stovepipe, Sweat, Throb, Toreador, Training, Trews, Trousers, Wheeze, Yearn

Pantaloon Columbine, Dupe, Pants

Pantheism Idolatry, Immanency

Panther Bagheera, Black, Cat, Cougar, Grey, Jaguar, Leopard, Pink

Panties Briefs, Knickers, Scanties, Step-ins, Undies

Pantomime, Pantomime character Aladdin, Charade, Cheironomy, Dumb-show, Farce, Galanty, Harlequinade, Pierrot, Play

Pantry Buttery, Closet, Larder, Spence, Stillroom

Pap Dug, Mealie, Mush, Nipple, Teat, Udder

Papal, **Papist** Catholic, Clementine, Concordat, Guelf, Guelph, Pontifical, RC, Roman, Vatican

Paper(s), **Paperwork**, **Papery** Allonge, Art, Atlas, Ballot, Baryta, Bible, Blotting, Bond, Broadsheet, Broadside, Bromide, Brown, Building, Bumf, Bumph, Carbon, Cartridge, Cellophane®, Chad, Chinese, Chiyogami, Cigarette, Colombier, Command, Commercial, Confetti, Corrugated, Cream-laid, Cream-wove, Credentials, Crepe, Crown, Cutch, Daily, Decorate, Demy, Document, Dossier, Elephant, Emery, Emperor, Essay, Exam, File, Filter, Final, Flock, Folio, Foolscap, Fourdrinier, FT, Galley, Garnet, Gem, Glass(ine), Glumaceous, Grand Jesus, Graph, Greaseproof, Green, Guardian, Hieratica, India, Jesus, Journal, Kent cap, Kraft, Kutch, Lace, Laid, Lavatory, Legal cap, Linen, Litmus, Manifold, Manil(l)a, Marble, Mercantile, Mirror, MS, Munimenti, Music(-demy), News(print), Note, Oil, Onion-skin, Order, Packing, Pad, Page, Papillote, Papyrus, Parchment, Pickwick, Plotting, Position, Post, Pot(t), Pravda, Press, Print, Quair, Quarto, Quire, Rag, Ramee, Rami(e), Ream, Retree, Rhea, Rice, Rolled, Rolling, Royal, Satin, Saxe, Scent, Scotsman, Scrip, Scroll, Scrowl, Sheaf, Sheet, Silver, Slipsheet, Spoilt, Stamp, State, Sugar, Sun, Tabloid, Taffeta, Tap(p)a, Tar, TES, Test, Thesis, Thread, Tiger, Tissue, Today, Toilet, Torchon, Touch, Tracing, Trade, Transfer, Treatise, Treeware, Turmeric, Vellum, Velvet, Voucher, Walking, Waste, Watch, Wax(ed), Web, Whatman®, White, Willesden, Wood(chip), Worksheet, Wove, Wrapping, Writing, Zine

Paperback Limp(back)

Paper-cutting, **Paper-folding** Decoupage, Kirigami, Origami, Psaligraphy

Papier-mâché Carton-pierre, Flong

Par Average, Equate, Equivalent, > **NORMAL**, Scratch

Parable Allegory, Fable, Proverb

Parabola Arc, Curve, Hyperbola

Parachute, **Parachutist** Aigrette, Brake, Drag, Drogue, Extraction, Float, Golden, Jump, Para, Parabrake, Red Devil, Ribbon, Silk, Sky-diving, Skyman, Thistledown, Umbrella

Parade (ground) Air, Arcade, Cavalcade, Church, Concours d'elegance, Display, Dress, Drill, Easter, Emu, Flaunt, Gala, Hit, Identification. Procession, Identity, Maidan, March-past, Monkey-run, Pageantry, Passing-out, Pomp, Prom(enade), Sashay, Show, Sick, Ticker tape, Troop

Paradise Arcadia, Avalon, Bliss, Eden, Elysium, Fool's, Garden, Heaven, Lost, Malaguetta, Nirvana, Park, Regained, Shangri-la, Svarga, Swarga, Swerga, > UTOPIA

Paradox(ical) Absurdity, Cantor's, Contradiction, Dilemma, Electra, French, Gilbertian, Hydrostatic, Koan, Liar, Olber's, Puzzle, Russell's, Sorites, Twin, Zeno's

Paraffin Earthwax, Kerosene, Kerosine, Liquid, Ozocerite, Ozokerite, Photogen(e), Propane

Paragon Model, Non(e)such, Pattern, Pearl, Phoenix, Rose

Paragraph (mark) Balaam, Note, Passage, Piece, Pilcrow

Parakeet Parrot, Popinjay, Rosella

Parallax Annual, Daily, Diurnal, Geocentric, Heliocentric

Parallel Analog, Collimate, Corresponding, Equal, Even, Forty-ninth, Like

Parallelogram Rhomb

Paralysis, **Paralyse** Apoplexy, Cataplexy, Cramp, Curarise, Cycloplegia,

Diplegia, Halt, Hemiplegia, Infantile, Lithyrism, Monoplegia, Numbness, Palsy, Paraplegia, Paresis, Polio, Quadriplegia, Radial, Scram, Shock, Shut, Spastic, Spina bifida, Stun

Paramedic Ambulance-man

Paramilitary Phalangist, SAS, Sena

Paramount Chief, Dominant, Greatest, Overall, Premier, > SUPREME, Topless, Utmost

Paramour Franion, Gallant, Leman, Lover, Mistress, Thais

Paranormal Clairvoyant, ESP, Spiritual, Telekinesis

Parapet (space) Barbette, Bartisan, Bartizan, Battlement, Brisure, Bulwark, Crenel, Flèche, Machicolation, Merlon, Rampart, Redan, Surtout, Terreplein, Top, Wall

Paraphernalia Belongings, Equipment, Gear, Trappings

Parasite, Parasitic Ascarid, Autoecious, Babesiasis, Bilharzia, Biogenous, Biotroph, Bladder-worm, Bloodsucker, Bonamia, Bot, Candida, Coccus, Conk, Copepod, Crab-louse, Cryptosporidium, Cryptozoite, Dodder, Ectophyte, Endamoeba, Endophyte, Entophyte, Entozoon, Epiphyte, Epizoon, Facultative, Filarium, Flatworm, Flea, Gapeworm, Giardia, Gregarinida, Haematozoon, Hair-eel, Heartworm, Heteroecious, Hook-worm, Ichneumon, Inquiline, Isopod, Kade, Ked, Lackey, Lamprey, Leech, Leishmania, Licktrencher, Liverfluke, Louse, Lungworm, Macdonald, Mallophagous, Mistletoe, Monogenean, Necrotroph, Nematode, Nit, Obligate, Orobanche, Pinworm, Plasmodium, Puccinia, Pulix, Rafflesia, Redia, Rhipidoptera, Rickettsia, Roundworm, Schistosoma, Scrounger, Shark, Smut-fungus, Sponge(r), Sporozoa(n), Strepsiptera, Strongyle, Strongyloid, Stylops, Sucker, Symphile, Tapeworm, Tick, Toady, Toxoplasma, Trematode, Trencher-friend, Trencher-knight, Trichina, Trichomonad, Tryp(anosoma), Vampire, Viscum, Wheatworm, Worms

Parasol Awning, Brolly, En tout cas, Sunshade, Umbrella

Paratrooper Skyman

Parcel Allocate, Allot, Aret, Bale, Bundle, Holding, Lot, Package, Packet, Sort, Wrap

Parch(ed) Arid, Bake, Dry, Graddan, Roast, Scorched, Sere, Thirsty, Toast, Torrid

Parchment Diploma, Forel, Mezuzah, Panel, Papyrus, Pell, Pergameneous, Roll, Roule, Scroll, Sheepskin, Vegetable, Vellum, Virgin

Pard Leopard, Pal, Partner

Pardon(able), Pardoner Absolve, Amnesty, Anan, Assoil, Clear, Condone, Eh, Excuse, > FORGIVE, Grace, Mercy, Quaestionary, Qu(a)estor, Release, Remission, Remit, Reprieve, Venial, What

Pare Flaught, Flay, Peel, Shave, Skive, Sliver, Strip, Whittle

Parent(al) Ancestral, Father, Forebear, Genitor, Maternal, Mother, Paternal, Single, Storge

Parenthesis Aside, Brackets, Innuendo

Parhelion Sun-dog

Pariah Ishmael, Leper, Outcast, Pi(e)dog, Pyedog

Paris(ian), Parisienne Abductor, Athene, Elle, Gai, Gay, Grisette, Lutetia (Parisiorum), Lutetian, Maillotin, Midinette, Trojan

Parish Charge, District, Flock, Kirkto(w)n, Parischan(e), Parishen, Parochin(e), Peculiar, Province, Title

Parity Smithsonian

Park(ing) Algonquin, Amusement, Battery, Brecon Beacons, Business, Common, Country, Daintree, Dales, Dartmoor, Death Valley, Enclosure,

Etosha, Everglades, Exmoor, Fiordland, Forest, Fun, Game, Garage, Gardens, Grand Canyon, Green, Green lung, Grounds, Hwange, Hyde, Jasper, Jasper National, Jurassic, Kakadu, Kalahari Gemsbok, Katmai, Kejionkujik, Kobuk Valley, Kruger, Lake District, Lamington, Lung, Mammoth Cave, Mansfield, Mesa Verde, Motor, Mount Aspiring, Mount McKinley, Mount Rainier, Mungo, Nahanni National, Nairobi, National, Northumberland, Osterley, P, Paradise, Peak District, Phoenix, Pitch, Pittie-ward, Prater, Preserve, Rec, Regent's, Riding Mountain, Safari, Sanctuary, Sandown, Science, Sequoia, Sequoia National, Serengeti, Shenandoah, Shenandoah National, Siding, Snowdonia, Stand, Stop, Theme, Trailer, Tsavo, Valet, Wildlife, Wind, Wood Buffalo, Yard, Yellowstone, Yosemite

Parker Dorothy, Nos(e)y

Parkleaves Tutsan

Parley Confer, Discourse, Palaver, Speak, Tret

Parliament Addled, Althing, Barebones, Black, Boule, Bundestag, Commons, Congress, Cortes, Council, Cross-bench, Dail, Diet, D(o)uma, Drunken, Eduskunta, European, Folketing, House, Imperial, Knesset, Lack-learning, Lagt(h)ing, Landst(h)ing, Lawless, Legislature, Lok Sabha, Long, Lords, Majlis, Merciless, Mongrel, Odelst(h)ing, Political, Rajya Sabha, Reichsrat, Reichstag, Riksdag, Rump, St Stephens, Sanhedrin, Seanad, Seanad Eireann, Sejm, Short, Stannary, States-general, Stirthing, Stormont, Stort(h)ing, Thing, Tynwald, Tynwald (Court), Unicameral, Unlearned, Useless, Vidhan Sabha, Volkskammer, Volksraad, Westminster

Parliamentarian Cabinet, Fairfax, Ireton, Leveller, Member, MP, Roundhead, Whip

Parlour Beauty, Funeral, Lounge, Massage, Milking, Salon, Snug

Parnassus Museum, Verse

Parody Burlesque, Cod, Lampoon, Mock, Piss-take, Satire, Sendup, Skit, Spoof, Travesty

Parole Pledge, Promise, Trust, Word

Paronychia Agnail, Felon, Whitlow

Paroxysm Fit, Frenzy, Rapture, Spasm, Subintrant, Throe

Parricide Cenci

Parrot Amazon, Cockatoo, Conure, Copy, Flint, Green leek, Grey, Imitate, Kaka(po), Kea, Lorikeet, Lory, Lovebird, Macaw, Mimic, Nestor, Owl, Parakeet, Paroquet, Poll(y), Popinjay, Psittacine, Quarrion, Repeat, Rosella, Rote, Stri(n)gops, T(o)uraco

Parrot-bill Glory-pea

Parry Block, Counter, Defend, Dodge, Forestall, Parade, Riposte, Sixte, Tac-au-tac, Thwart, Ward

Parsee Zoroastrian

Parsimonious, **Parsimony** Cheese-paring, Mean, Narrow, Near(ness), Niggardly, Stingy, Tight

Parsley Apiol, Cicely, Dog, Kecks, Kex, Persillade, Pot-herb

Parsnip Buttered, Buttery, Dill, Masterwort, Sium, Skirret

Parson Clergyman, Cleric, Minister, Non juror, Pastor, Priest, Rector, Rev, Sky-pilot, Soul-curer, Yorick

Part(s), **Parting** Accession, Aliquot, Antimere, Area, Aught, Bulk, Bye, Cameo, Character, Chunk, Cog, Component, Constituent, Crack, Cue, Dislink, Diverge, Dole, Element, Episode, Escapement, Farewell, Fascicle, Fork, Fraction, Goodbye, Half, Instalment, Into, Lathe, Lead, Leave, Leg, Lill, Lilt, Lines, List, Livraison, Member, Meronym, Parcel, Passus, > PIECE, Portion, Primo,

Principal, Private, Proportion, Pt, Quota, Rape, Ratio, Region, Rive, Role, Scena, Scene, Secondo, Section, Sector, Segment, Separate, Serial, Sever, Shade, Share, Shed, Sleave, Sle(i)ded, > SOME, Spare, Split, Stator, Sunder, Synthon, Tithe, Unit, Vaunt, Voice, Walk on, Wrench

Partake(r) Allottee, Eat, Participate, Share

Parthenogenesis Deuterotoky, Thelytoky

Partial(ity), Partially Biased, Ex-parte, Fan, Favour, Halflins, Imbalance, Incomplete, One-sided, Predilection, Slightly, Unequal, Weakness

Participate Engage, Join, Partake, Share

Participle Dangling, Misrelated, Past, Perfect, Present

Particle(s) Alpha, Anion, Antineutron, Antiproton, Atom, Baryon, Beta, Bit, Boson, Corpuscle, Curn, Dander, Delta, Deuteron, Effluvium, Elementary, Fermion, Fleck, Fragment, Fundamental, Gauge boson, Gemmule, Globule, Gluon, Grain, Granule, Graviton, Hadron, Heavy, Higgs, Hyperon, Ion, J, Jot, J/psi, Kaon, Lambda, Lemail, Lemel, Lepton, Meson, Micelle, Microsome, Mite, Molecule, Mote, Muon, Neutrino, Neutron, Nibs, Nobiliary, Omega-minus, Parton, Photon, Pion, Plasmagene, Platelet, Positron, Prion, Proton, Psi(on), Quark, Radioactivity, Shower, Sigma, Sinter, Smithereen, Spark, Speck, Strange, Subatom, Tachyon, Tardyon, Tau neutrino, Tauon, Thermion, Tittle, Virion, W, Whit, WIMP, X-hyperon, Z

Parti-coloured Fancy, Motley, Piebald, Pied, Variegated

Particular Choosy, Dainty, > DETAIL, Endemic, Especial, Essential, Express, Fiky, Fog, Fussy, Item, Itself, London fog, Nice, Niffy-naffy, Own, Pea-souper, Peculiar, Pernickety, Pet, Point, Prim, Proper, > RESPECT, Special, Specific, Stickler, Strict, Stripe

Partisan Adherent, Axe, Biased, Carlist, Champion, Devotee, Factional, Fan, Irregular, Partial, Provo, Sider, Spear, Supporter, Yorkist

Partition(ed) Abjoint, Bail, Barrier, Brattice, Bretasche, Bulkhead, Cloison, Cubicle, Diaphragm, Dissepiment, Division, Hallan, Mediastinum, Parpane, Parpen(d), Parpent, Parpoint, Perpend, Perpent, Replum, > SCREEN, Scriene, Septum, Tabula, Wall, With

Partlet Hen, Overlaid

Partner(ship) Accomplice, Ally, Associate, Bidie-in, Butty, Cahoot(s), Coachfellow, Cohab(itee), Cohabitor, Colleague, Comrade, Confederate, Consort, Copemate, Couple, Dutch, Escort, E-W, Firm, Gigolo, Mate, N-S, Oppo, Pal, Pard, Sidekick, Silent, Sleeping, Sparring, Spouse, Stablemate, Stand, Symbiosis

Part of *may indicate* a hidden word

Partridge Bird, Chik(h)or, Chukar, Chukor, Covey, Quail, Red-legged, Tinamou, Ynambu

Party Acid house, Alliance, Apparat, Assembly, At-home, Ba'ath, Ball, Band, Barbecue, Bash, Beano, Bee, Bloc, Blowout, Body, Bottle, Bunfight, Bust, Caboodle, Camp, Carousal, Carouse, Caucus, Celebration, Clambake, Cocktail, Commando, Communist, Concert, Congress, Conservative, Contingent, Cookie-shine, Cooperative, Coterie, Cult, Democratic, Detail, Ding, Discotheque, Do, Drum, Faction, Falange, Federalist, Fest, Fête champêtre, Fête Galante, Fianna Fáil, Fine Gael, Firing, Funfest, Gala, Gang, Garden, Green, Greenback, Grumbletonian, Guelf, Guelph, Guilty, Hen, High heels, Hoedown, Hooley, Hoot(a)nannie, Hoot(a)nanny, Hootenannie, Hootenanny, House, Housewarming, Hurricane, Irredentist, Jol(lities), Junket, Junto, Kettledrum, Kitchen tea, Klat(s)ch, Knees-up, Kuomintang, L, Labour, Launch, Lib, Liberal, Love-in, Low heels, Luau, Mallemaroking, Mollie, Musicale,

National, Neck-tie, Octobrist, Opposition, Orgy, People's, Person, Petting, Plaid, Progressive, Prohibition, Pyjama, Rage, Rave, Rave-up, Razzle(-dazzle), Reception, Republican, Revel, Ridotto, Rocking, Rort, Rout, SDP, Search, Sect, Set, Shindig, Shine, Shivoo, Shower, Shower tea, Side, Slumber, Smoker, SNP, Soc(ialist), Social, Social credit, Social Democratic, Soiree, Spree, Squad(rone), Squadrone volante, Stag, Symposium, Tailgate, Tea, Teafight, Third, Thrash, Tory, Treat, Ultramontane, Unionist, United, Wafd, Warehouse, Whig, Whoop-de-do(o), Wine, Wingding, Working

Partygoer Raver, Reveller, Socialite

Party-piece Solo

Parvenu Arriviste, Upstart

Pascal Blaise, Pa, Pressure

Pash Crush, Devotion

Pasha Achmed, Dey, Emir, Ismet

Pass(ed), Passing, Pass on, Past Ago, Agon, Annie Oakley, Aorist, Approve, Arise, Arlberg, Before, Behind, Bernina, Beyond, Bolan, Botte, Brenner, Brief, By, Bygone, Caudine Forks, Cerro Vordo, Chal(l)an, Chilkoot, Chine, Chit(ty), Clear, Col, Cote, Cross, Cursory, Death, Defile, Delate, Demise, Diadron, Die, Disappear, Double, Elapse, Emit, Enact, End, Ensue, Ephemeral, Exceed, Exeat, Faena, Foist, Forby, Forgone, Former, Forward, Gap, Gate, Gha(u)t, Glencoe, Glide, Go, Great St Bernard, Gulch, Halse, Hand, Happen, Hause, Hospital, Impart, Impermanent, In transit, Jark, Khyber, Killiecrankie, Kloof, La Cumbre, Lap, Late, Lead, Long syne, Mesmerism, Migrate, Moravian Gate, Mount Cenis, Nek, Notch, Nutmeg, Nye, Occur, Oer, OK, Okay, Oke, Omit, One-time, Overhaul, Overshoot, Overslaugh, Overtake, Pa, Palm, Participle, Perish, Permeate, Permit, Perpetuate, Poll, Poort, Predicament, Preterit(e), Pretty, Proceed, Propagate, Pun(c)to, Qualify, Railcard, Reach, Reeve, Refer, Relay, Retroactive, Retrospect, Reverse, Roncesvalles, Safe conduct, St Bernard, St Gotthard, San Bernardino, Sanitation, Scissors, Senile, Serve, Shipka, Simplon, Since, Skim, Skip, Skirt, Slap, Sling, Snap, Spend, Stab, State Thermopylae, Thread, Through, Ticket, Tip, Transient, Transilient, Transitory Transmit, Transude, Travel, Triptyque, Troop, Uspallata, Veronica, Vet, Visa, Visé, Wall, Wayleave, Weather, While, Wrynose, Yesterday, Yesteryear, Ygoe

Passable Adequate, Fair, Navigable, Tolerable

Passage Adit, Airway, Aisle, Alley(way), Alure, Apostrophe, Arcade, Archway, Areaway, Arterial, Atresia, Breezeway, Bylane, Cadenza, Caponier(e), Career, Channel, Chute, Citation, Clause, Close, Coda, Conduit, Corridor, Creep, Crossing, Crush, Cundy, Dead-end, Deambulatory, Defile, Drake, Drift, Duct, Eel-fare, Episode, Excerpt, Extract, Fare, Fat, Fistula, Flat, Flight, Flue, Gallery, Gangway, Gap, Gat, Gate, Ginnel, Gut, Hall, Head, Inlet, Journey, Kyle, Lane, Lapse, Larynx, Loan, Lobby, Locus, Meatus, Melisma, Middle, Mona, Movement, Northeast, Northwest, Para(graph), Path, Pend, Pericope, Phrase, Pore, Portion, Prelude, Prose, Purple, Ride, Ripieno, Rite, Ritornell(o), Rough, Route, Sailing, Screed, Shaft, Shunt, Slap, Slype, Snicket, Sprue, Strait Street, Stretta, Stretto, Subway, Sump, Text, Thirl, Thorough(fare), Throat, Tour, Trachea, Trance, Transe, Transit(ion), Travel, Tunnel, Tutti, Undercast, Unseen, Ureter, Voyage, Way, Windpipe

▷ **Passage of arms** *may indicate* 'sleeve'

Passé Corny, Dated, Ex, Obsolete

Passenger(s) Cad, Commuter, Fare, Payload, Pillion, Rider, Slacker, Steerage, Straphanger, Transit, Traveller, Voyager, Way, Wayfarer

Passion(ate), Passionately Anger, Appetite, Ardour, Con fuoco, Fervour, Fire,

Flame, Frampold, Fury, Gust, Gutsy, Hate, Heat, Hot, Hunger, Hwyl, Ileac, Iliac, Intense, Ire, Irish, Kama, Love, Lust, Mania, Obsession, Oestrus, Rage, Reverent, Stormy, Sultry, Torrid, Violent, Warm, Wax, Wrath, Yen, Zeal

Passion-fruit Water-lemon

Passion play Oberammergau

Passive (stage) Apathetic, Dormant, Inert, Pathic, Patient, Pupa, Supine, Yielding

Pass out Faint, Graduate, Swarf, Swarve, Swoon

Passover Agadah, Haggada, Omer, Pesach

Passport Access, Clearance, Congé(e), ID, Key, Laissez-passer, Nansen, Navicert, Sea-letter, Visa, Visitor's

Password Code, Countersign, Logon, Nayword, Parole, Sesame, Shibboleth, Sign, Tessera, Watchword

Past *see* PASS

Pasta Agnolotti, Cannelloni, Capelletti, Cellentani, Conchiglie, Durum, Farfal, Farfel, Fedelini, Fettuc(c)ine, Fusilli, Gnocch(ett)i, Lasagna, Lasagne, Linguini, Macaroni, Manicotti, Noodles, Orzo, Penne, Perciatelli, Ravioli, Rigatoni, Ruote, Spaghetti, Spaghettina, Tagliarini, Tagliatelle, Tortelli(ni), Vermicelli, Ziti

Paste, Pasty Ashen, Batter, Beat, Berbere, Botargo, Boule, Bridie, Cerate, Clobber, Cornish, Dentifrice, Dough, Electuary, Fake, Filler, Fondant, Frangipane, Glue, Guarana, Hard, Harissa, Knish, Lute, Magma, Marzipan, Masala, Mastic, Miso, Mountant, Pale, Pallid, Pâté, Patty, Pearl-essence, Pie, Piroshki, Pirozhki, Poonac, Punch, Putty, Rhinestone, Rout, Slip, Slurry, Soft, Spread, Strass, Tahina, Tahini, Tapenade, Taramasalata, Wan

Pastern Hobble, Knee, Tether

Pastiche Cento, Collage, Medley, Patchwork, Potpourri

Pastille Jujube, Lozenge

Pastime Diversion, Game, Hobby, Recreation, Seesaw, Sport

Past master Champion, Expert, Historian, Pro

Past midnight 1 am

Pastor(al) Arcadia, Bucolic, Curé, Eclogue, Endymion, Idyl(l), Minister, Priest, Rector, Rural, Shepherd, Simple

Pastry Apfelstrudel, Baclava, Bakemeat, Baklava, Beignet, Bouchée, Brik, Calzone, Chausson, Choux, Clafoutis, Coquile, Creamhorn, Cream puff, Croustade, Cruller, Crust, Danish, Dariole, Dough, Eclair, Empanada, Feuilleté, Filo, Flaky, Flan, Frangipane, French, Gougère, Hamantasch, Millefeuille, Phyllo, Pie, Pie-crust, Pirog, Piroshki, Pirozhki, Profiterole, Puff, Quiche, Rough-puff, Rug(g)elach, Samosa, Shortcrust, Strudel, Tart, Turnover, Vol-au-vent

Pasture Alp, Eadish, Eddish, Feed, Fell, Fodder, Grassland, Graze, Herbage, Kar(r)oo, Lair, Lare, Lea, Lease, Leasow(e), Leaze, Ley, Machair, Mead(ow), Pannage, Potrero, Raik, Rake, Soum, Sowm, Tie, Transhume, Tye

▶ **Pasty** *see* PASTE

Pat Apt, Bog-trotter, Butter, Chuck, Clap, Dab, Glib, Lump, Print, Prompt, Rap, Slap, Tap

Patch(y) Bed, Bit, Cabbage, Clout, Coalsack, Cobble, Cooper, Court plaster, Cover, Friar, Fudge, > MEND, Mosaic, Nicotine, Pasty, Piebald, Piece, Plage, Plaque, Plaster, Pot, Purple, Shinplaster, Shoulder, Solder, Tingle, Tinker, Vamp, Variegated

Patchwork Cento, Miscellany, Mosaic, Piecing

Pate, Pâté Crown, Paste, Rillettes, Taramasalata, Terrine

Patent(ed) Breveté, Copyright, Evident, Letters, Licence, License, Obvious, Overt, Plain, Rolls

Pater(nity) Father, Filiation, Walter

Paterfamilias Coarb, Master

Path(way) Aisle, Allée, Alley, Arc, Berm, Berme, Boreen, Borstal(l), Bridle, Byroad, Causeway, Causey, Clickstream, Course, Eclipse, Embden-Meyerhof, Flare, Flight, Garden, Gate, Gennel, Ginnel, Glide, Lane, Ley, Locus, Mean-free, Metabolic, Orbit, Pad, Parabola, Primrose, Ride, Ridgeway, Route, Run, Runway, Sidewalk, Spurway, Stie, Sty(e), Swath(e), Tow, Track, Trail, Trajectory, Trod, Walkway, > WAY, Xystus

Pathan Pakhto, Pakhtu, Pashto, Pashtu, Pushto(o), Pushtu

Pathetic(ally) Doloroso, Drip, Forlorn, Piss-poor, Piteous, Poignant, Sad, Schnook, Touching

Pathfinder Compass, Explorer, Guide, Pioneer, Scout

Pathological Diseased, Gangrene, Morbid, Septic

Pathos Bathos, Pity, Sadness, Sob-stuff

Patience Calm, Endurance, Forbearance, Fortitude, Indulgence, Longanimity, Monument, Operetta, Solitaire, Stoicism, Virtue

Patient(s) Calm, Case, Clinic, Forbearing, Grisel(da), Grisilda, Invalid, Job, Long-suffering, Passive, Private, Resigned, Stoic, Subject, Ward

Patois Argot, Cant, Dialect, Gumbo, Jargon, Jive, Lingo, Scouse

Patriarch Aaron, Abraham, Abuna, Catholicos, Ecumenical, Elder, Enoch, Isaac, Levi, Maron, Methuselah, Nestor, Noah, Pope, Simeon, Venerable

Patrician Aristocrat, Noble, Senator

Patrick Mick, Paddy, Pat, Spens

Patrimony Ancestry, Estate, Heritage

Patriot(ic), Patriotism Cavour, Chauvinist, DAR, Emmet, Flag-waving, Flamingant, Garibaldi, Hereward, Irredentist, Jingoism, Loyalist, Maquis, Nationalist, Revere, Tell

Patrol Armilla, Guard, Outguard, Picket, Piquet, Prowl-car, Reconnaissance, Scout, Sentinel, Sentry-go, Shark, Shore, Turm

Patron(age), Patronise(d), Patronising Advowson, Aegis, Auspices, Benefactor, Business, Champion, Client, Customer, Donator, Egis, Fautor, Maecenas, Nepotic, Protector, Protégé, Provider, Shopper, > SPONSOR, Stoop, Stoup

Patsy Dupe, Hendren, Scapegoat, Stooge

Patter Backchat, Cant, Jargon, Lingo, Mag, Pitch, Rap, S(c)htick, Schtik, Spiel

Pattern(ed) Argyle, Bird's eye, Blueprint, Branchwork, Broché, Check, Chequer, Chladni figure, Clock, Design, Dévoré, Diaper, Diffraction, Dog's tooth, Draft, Egg and dart, Epitome, Example, Exemplar, Fiddle, Figuration, Format, Fractal, Fret, Gestalt, Grain, Grammadion, Greek key, Herringbone, Holding, Hound's tooth, Intarsia, Intonation, Koru, Matel(l)asse, Matrix, Meander, > MODEL, Moire, Mosaic, Norm, Paisley, Paradigm, Paragon, Pinstripe, Plan, Polka-dot, Pompadour, Precedent, Prototype, Queenstitch, Quincunx, Radiation, Raster, Shawl, Stencil, Symmetry, Syndrome, Tala, Tangram, Tattersall, Template, Tessella, Tessera, Tracery, Traffic, Tread, Type, Willow

Patty Bouchée, Pie

Paul Jones, Oom, Pry, Revere, Robeson, S, St

Pauline Day-boy, Perils

Paunch Belly, Corporation, Gut, Kite, Kyte, Pod, Rumen, Tripe, Tum

Pauper Bankrupt, Beggar, Have-not, Mendicant, Penniless

Pause Break, Breakpoint, Breather, Caesura, Cessation, Cesura, Comma, Desist, Er, Fermata, Hesitate, Interkinesis, Interregnum, Interval, Limma, Lull,

Pitstop, > RESPITE, Rest, Selah, Stop, Tacet, Time out

Pave(ment), **Paving** Causeway, Clint, Corsey, Crazy, Diaper, Granolith, Limestone, Path, Roadside, Set(t), Sidewalk, Tessellate, Travolator, Trottoir

Pavilion Ear, Gazebo, Jingling Johnny, Kiosk, Marquee, Tent

Paw Kangaroo, Maul, Mitt, Pad, Pat, Pud, Pug

Pawky Dry, Humorous, Shrewd, Sly

Pawn(shop) Agent, Betel, Chessman, Counter, Derby, Dip, Gage, Gallery, Hanging, Hock, Hostage, Isolated, Leaving-shop, Lumber, Monte-de-piété, Monti di pieta, Pan, Passed, Peacock, Piece, Pignerate, Pignorate, Pledge, Pop, Security, Siri, Spout, Tiddleywink, Tool, Wadset, Weed

Pawnbroker, **Pawnee** Hockshop, Lumberer, Moneylender, Nunky, Pledgee, Sheeny, Uncle, Usurer

Pax Peace, Truce

Pay(master), **Payment**, **Paid**, **Pay off**, **Pay out** Advertise, Agterskot, Amortise, Annat, Annuity, Ante, Arles, Atone, Basic, Batta, Blench, Bonus, Bukshee, Bukshi, Cain, Cashier, Cens, Cheque, COD, Commute, Compensate, Consideration, Damage, Defray, Disburse, Discharge, Dividend, Down, Dub, Emolument, Endow, Equalisation, Eric, Escot, Farm, Fee, Feu-duty, Finance, Foot, Fork out, Fund, Gale, Gate, Give, Grassum, Grave, Greenmail, Han(d)sel, Hazard, Hire, Hoot(oo), HP, Imburse, Kain, Kickback, Leads and lags, Lobola, Lobolo, Mail, Meet, Merchet, Metayage, Mise, Modus, Overtime, Payola, Pension, Pittance, Pony, Posho, Prebendal, Premium, Primage, Pro, Pro forma, Progress, Purser, Quarterage, Quit(-rent), Ransom, Redundancy, Refund, Remittance, Remuneration, Rent, Requite, Residual, Respects, Royalty, Salary, Satisfaction, Scot, Screw, Scutage, Settle, Severance, Shell, Shell out, Sick, Sink, Sold(e), Soul-scat, Soul-scot, > SPEND, Square, Stipend, Strike, Stump, Sub, Subscribe, Sweetener, Table, Take-home, Tar, Tender, Token, Tommy, Transfer, Treasure, Treat, Tribute, Truck, Unpurse, Usance, Veer, Wage, Wardcorn, X-factor

Pea(s) Carling, Chaparral, Chickling, Desert, D(h)al, Dholl, Egyptian, Garbanzo, Goober, Hastings, Legume, Mangetout, Marrow, Marrowfat, Passiform, Petit pois, Pigeon, Pulse, Rounceval, Split, String, Sturt's desert, Sugar

Peace(ful), **Peace-keeper**, **Peace organisation**, **Peace symbol** Ahimsa, Ataraxy, Calm, Ease, Frith, Halcyon, Interceder, Irenic(on), King's, Lee, Lull, Nirvana, Olive, Order, Pacific, Pax, Pbuh, Queen's, Quiet, Repose, Rest, Salem, Serene, Sh, Shalom, Siesta, Silence, Still, Tranquil, Truce, UN

Peacemaker ACAS, Arbitrator, Conciliator, Mediator, Trouble-shooter

Peach Blab, Cling, Clingstone, Dish, Dob, Freestone, Inform, Laetrile, Malakatoone, Melba, Melocoto(o)n, Nectarine, Oner, Quandang, Shop, Sneak, Split, Squeak, Stunner, Tattle, Tell, Victorine

Peachum Polly

Peacock Coxcomb, Dandy, Fop, Junonian, Muster, Paiock(e), Pajock(e), Pavo(ne), Pawn, Payock(e), Pown, Sashay

Peak(y) Acme, Aiguille, Alp, Apex, Ben, Cap, Climax, Comble, Communism, Crag, Crest, Darien, Drawn, Eiger, Gable, Gannett, Horn, Matterhorn, Mons, > MOUNTAIN, Nevis, Nib, Nunatak, Optimum, Pale, Petermann, Pikes, Pin, Pinnacle, Piton, Pyramidal, Rainier, Sallow, Snowdon, Spire, Stalin, Sukarno, Top, Tor, Visor, Widow's, Zenith

Peal Carillon, Chime, Clap, Toll, Triple

Peanut(s) Arnut, Chickenfeed, Goober, Groundnut, Monkey-nut, Pittance

Pear Aguacate, Alligator, Anchovy, Anjou, Asian, Avocado, Bartlett, Bergamot, Beurré, Blanquet, Carmelite, Catherine, Colmar, Conference, Cuisse-madame,

Pearl(s) | 500

Jargonelle, Muscadel, Muscatel, Musk, Nashi, Neli(e)s, Nelis, Perry, Poperin, Poppering, Poprin, Prickly, Pyrus, Queez-maddam, Seckel, Seckle, Taylor's Gold, Warden, William

Pearl(s), Pearly Barocco, Barock, Baroque, Cultured, False, Gem, Imitated, Jewel, Mabe, Margaret, Margaric, Nacrous, Olivet, Orient, Prize, Rope, Seed, Simulated, String, Sulphur, Unio(n)

Pear-shaped Obconic, Pyriform

Peasant Bonhomme, Boor, Bumpkin, Chouan, Churl, Clodhopper, Contadino, Cossack, Cottar, Cotter, Cott(i)er, Fellah(s), Fellahin, Hick, Jungli, Kern(e), Kisan, Kulak, M(o)ujik, Muzhik, Quashi(e), Raiyat, Roturier, Rustic, Ryot, Swain, Tyrolean, Volost, Whiteboy, Yokel

Pea-shaped Pisiform

Peat(y) Moss-litter, Sod, Turbary, Turbinacious, Turf, Yarfa, Yarpha

Pebble(s), Pebbly Banket, Bibble, Calculus, Cobblestone, Dornick, Dreikanter, Gallet, Gooley, Gravel, Psephism, Pumie, Pumy, Scree, Shingle, Ventifact

Peccadillo Mischief, Misdemeanour, Offence

Peccary Mexican hog

Peck Bill, Bushel, Dab, Forpet, Forpit, Gregory, Kiss, Lip, Lippie, Nibble, Pickle, Tap

Pecksniff Charity

Peculiar(ity) Appropriate, Characteristic, Distinct, Eccentric, Especial, Exclusive, Ferly, Funny, Idiosyncratic, Kink, Kooky, Odd, Own, Proper, Queer, Quirk, Singular, > SPECIAL, Specific, Strange, Unusual

▷ **Peculiar** *may indicate* an anagram

Pedagogue Academic, B.Ed, Teacher

Pedal Bike, Chorus, Cycle, Damper, Lever, P, Rat-trap, Soft, Sostenuto, Sustaining, Treadle, Treddle

Pedal-coupler Tirasse

Pedant(ic) Casaubon, Chop logic, Dogmatic, Dryasdust, Elucubrate, Inkhorn, Intellectual, Jobsworth, Lucubrate, Pedagogue, Pernickety, Pompous, Precisian, Quibbler, Scholastic, Sesquipedalian

Peddle, Pedlar Bodger, Boxwallah, Camelot, Chapman, Cheapjack, Colporteur, Drummer, Duffer, Hawk, Huckster, Jagger, Packman, Pedder, Pether, Sell, Smouch, Smouse(r), Sutler, Tallyman, Tink(er), Yagger

▷ **Peddling** *may indicate* an anagram

Pedestal Acroter(ion), Dado, Footstool, Pillar, Support

Pedestrian Banal, Commonplace, Dull, Earth-bound, Ganger, Hack, Hike, Itinerant, Jaywalker, Laborious, Mundane, Trite, Voetganger, Walker

Pedigree(s) Ancestry, Blood, Breeding, Descent, Genealogy, House, Lineage, Phylogeny, Stemma(ta), Stirps, Studbook, Thoroughbred, Whakapapa

Pediment Fronton

Peduncle Scape, Stalk

Peek Eye, Glance, Glimpse, Peep

Peel(er) Bark, Bobby, Candied, Decorticate, Desquamate, Exfoliate, Flype, Orange, Pare, PC, Pill, Rind, Rine, Scale, Shell, Skin, > STRIP, Tirr, Zest

▷ **Peeled** *may indicate* outside letter(s) to be removed from a word

Peep(er), Peephole Cheep, Cook, Crow, Glance, Gledge, Judas, Keek, Kook, Lamp, Nose, Peek, Pink, Pry, Spy, Squeak, Squint, Stime, Styme, Voyeur

Peer(age), Peers Archduke, Aristocrat, Backwoodsman, Baron(et), Burke, Coeval, Daimio, Doucepere, Douzeper(s), Duke, Earl, Egal, Elevation, Equal, Eyeball, Gynt, Life, Lord, Match, Noble, Paladin, Peregal, Pink, Rank, Representative, Scry, Spiritual, Squint, Stare, Stime, Styme, Temporal, Toot,

Tweer, Twire

Peerless Matchless, Nonpareil, Supreme

Peevish(ness) Capernoited, Captious, Crabby, Cross, Doddy, Frabbit, Frampal, Frampold, Franzy, Fretful, Lienal, Meldrew, Moody, Nattered, Petulant, Pindling, Protervity, Querulous, Shirty, Sour, Spleen, Teachie, Testy, Te(t)chy

Peewit Lapwing, Peewee

Peg Cheville, Cleat, Cotter-pin, Crawling, Die, Fix, Freeze, Knag, Leg, Margaret, Nail, Nog, Pin, Piton, Snort, Spigot, Spile, Square, Stengah, Stinger, Support, Tap, Tee, Thole, Tholepin, Thowel, Toggle, Tot, Tuning, Vent, Woffington

Pegboard Solitaire

Pelagic Deep-sea, Marine, Oceanic

Pelf Lucre, Mammon, Money, Notes, Riches

Pelican Alcatras, Bird, Crossing, Golden Hind, LA, Louisiana, Steganopode

Pellagra Maidism

Pellet Birdshot, Bolus, Buckshot, Bullet, Pill, Pithball, Prill, Slug

Pelt Assail, Clod, Fleece, Fur, Hail, Hide, Hie, Lam, Pepper, Random, Sealskin, Shower, Skin, Squail, Stone

Peltast Soldier, Targeteer

Pelvis Ilium, Pubis, Renal

Pen Ballpoint, Bamboo, Bic®, Biro®, Cage, Calamus, Cartridge, Catching, Confine, Coop, Corral, Crawl, Crow-quill, Cru(i)ve, Cub, Cyclostyle, Dabber, Data, Enclosure, Fank, Farm, Felt(-tipped), Fold, Fountain, Gaol, Gladius, Hen, Highlighter, Hoosegow, J, > JAIL, Keddah, Kraal, Lair, Light, Marker, Mew, Mure, Music, Piggery, Poison, Pound, Quill, Ree, Reed, Ring, Rollerball, Scribe, Stell, Stie, Stir, Sty(e), Stylet, Stylo, Stylograph, Stylus, Submarine, Swan, Tank, Write

Pen *may indicate* a writer

Penal(ize) Cost, Fine, Gate, Handicap, Huff, Mulct, Punitive, Servitude

Penalty Abye, Amende, Cost, Death, Eric, Fine, Fixed, Forfeit, Han(d)sel, Huff, Keltie, Kelty, Pain, Price, Punishment, Sanction, Wide

Penance Atonement, Shrift

Penates Lares

Pence D, P, Peter's

Penchant Predilection

Pencil Beam, Ca(l)m, Caum, Charcoal, Chinagraph®, Crayon, Draft, Draw, Eyebrow, Fusain, Grease, Harmonic, Ink, Keelivine, Keelyvine, Lead, Outline, Propelling, Slate, Stump, Styptic

Pendant Albert, Chandelier, Drop, Girandole, Laval(l)ière, Necklace, Poffle, Stalactite

Pending Imminent, In fieri, Unresolved, Until

Pendragon Uther

Pendulous, Pendulum Compensation, Dewlap, Foucault's, Metronome, Noddy, One-way, Swing, Wavering

Penetrate, Penetrating, Penetration Acumen, Acuminate, Bite, Bore, Bridgehead, Cut, Enpierce, Enter, Imbue, Impale, Incisive, Indent, Indepth, Infiltrate, Insight, Into, Intrant, Lance, Permeate, Pierce, Probe, Sagacious, Shear, Thrust, Touch, X-ray

Penguin Aeroplane, Anana, Auk, Blue, Emperor, Fairy, Gentoo, King, Korora, Little, Macaroni, Rock-hopper

Penicillin Fleming

Peninsula Alaska, Alte, Antarctic, Arabian, Ards, Arm, Avalon, Baja California, Balkan, Banks, Bataan, Black Isle, Boothia, Cape, Cape Cod, Cape Verde,

Chalcidice, Chersonese, Chukchi, Coromandel, Crimea, Deccan, Delmarva, East Cape, Eyre, Florida, Freycinet, Gallipoli, Galloway, Gaspé, Gower, Iberia(n), Indo-China, Istria, Jutland, Kamchatka, Kathiawar, Kintyre, Kola, Kowloon, Labrador, Leizhou, Liaodong, Liaotung, Lleyn, Luichow, Malay, Melville, Neck, Northland, Nova Scotia, Olympic, Otago, Palmer, Peloponnese, Portland, Promontory, Quiberon, Scandinavian, Seward, Sinai, Spit, Spur, Taimyr, Talmyr, Tasman, Taymar, The Lizard, Upper, Wilson's Promontory, Wirral, Yorke, Yucatan

Penis Archie, Cor(e)y, Dick, Dildo(e), Dipstick, Dong, Ferret, Giggle(stick), Horn, Jack, John Thomas, Knob, Membrum virile, Mojo, Pecker, Peezle, Percy, Phallus, Pillicock, Pintle, Pisser, Pizzle, Plonker, Prick, Rod, Roger, Schlong, Shaft, Stiffy, Tockley, Tonk, Tool, W(h)ang, Willie, Willy, Winkle, Yard, Zeppelin

Penitent(iary) Calaboose, Clink, Contrite, Gaol, Jail, Jug, Prison, Repenter, Rosary, Stir

Pennant, Pennon Banner, Broad, Bunting, Fane, Flag, Guidon, Streamer

Penniless Bankrupt, Boracic, Broke, Bust, Impecunious, Poor, Skint, Strapped

Penny Bean, Cartwheel, Cent, Copper, D, Dreadful, Gild, Honest, P, Pretty, Sen, Sou, Sterling, Stiver, Win(n), Wing

Penny-farthing Bicycle, Ordinary

Pension(er) Allowance, Ann(at), Annuitant, Board, Chelsea, Cod, Cor(r)ody, Gratuity, Guest-house, Half-board, Occupational, Payment, Personal, Retire, Serps, Stakeholder, Stipend, Superannuation

Pensive Dreamy, Moody, Musing, Thoughtful, Triste, Wistful

Pentateuch T(h)orah

Pentecost Whit(sun)

Penthouse Cat, Lean-to, Roof

Peon Peasant, Serf, Slave, Ticca

Peony Moutan

People Bods, Body, Chosen, Commonalty, Commons, Demos, Ecology, Enchorial, Flower, Folk, Fraim, Gens, Guild, Human, Inca, Inhabit, Janata, Kin, Land, Lapith, Lay, Man(kind), Men, Mob, Nair, Nation(s), Nayar, One, Peculiar, Personalities, Phalange, Populace, Proletariat(e), Public, Punters, Quorum, Race, Settle, Society, Souls, They, Tribe, Volk

Pep Buck, Dash, Enliven, Gism, Go, Jism, Jissom, Stamina, Verve, Vim

Pepper Alligator, All-spice, Ava, Betel, Bird, Black, Capsicum, Cayenne, Chilli, Condiment, Cubeb, Devil, Dittander, Dittany, Ethiopian, Green, Guinea, Jalapeno, Jamaica, Kava, Long, Malaguetta, Matico, Negro, Paprika, Pelt, Pim(i)ento, Piper, Red, Riddle, Sambal, Spice, Sprinkle, Sweet, Szechwan, Tabasco®, Wall, White, Yaqona, Yellow

Peppercorn Nominal

Peppermint Bull's Eye, Humbug, Pandrop

Per By, Each, Through

Perambulate, Perambulator Buggy, Expatiate, Pedestrian, Pram, Stroller, Wagon, Walker

Perceive, Perception, Perceptive Acumen, Alert, Anschauung, Apprehend, Astute, Clairvoyance, Clear-eyed, Cryptaesthetic, Descry, Dianoia, Discern, Divine, ESP, Extrasensory, Feel, Insight, Intelligence, Intuit(ion), Kinaesthesia, Notice, Observe, Pan(a)esthesia, Remark, > SEE, Sense, Sensitive, Sentience, Shrewd, Subliminal, Tact, Taste, Tel(a)esthesia, Telegnosis, Understanding

Percentage Agio, Commission, Contango, Cut, Mark-up, Proportion, Royalty,

Scalage, Share, Vigorish

Perch(ing) Aerie, Alight, Anabis, Bass, Comber, Eyrie, Fish, Fogash, Gaper, Insessorial, Lug, Perca, Pole, Roost, Ruff(e), Seat, Serranid, > SIT, Wall-eye, Zingel

Percolate, Percolation Filter, Infiltrate, Leach, Lixiviate, Ooze, Osmosis, Permeate, Seep, Sipe, Soak, Strain, Sype

Percussion (cap) Amorce, Chinese temple block, Idiophone, Impact, Knee, Knock, Thump, Timbrel

Percy Hotspur, Shelley

Perdition Ades, Hades

Peremptory Absolute, Decisive, Haughty, Imperative, Imperious

Perennial Continual, Enduring, Flower, Livelong, Perpetual, Recurrent

Perfect(ly), Perfection(ist) Absolute, Accomplish, Accurate, Acme, Apple-pie, Bloom, Complete, Consummation, Cross-question, Dead, Develop, Fare-thee-well, Finish, Flawless, Fulfil, Full, Holy, Ideal(ist), Impeccable, Intact, It, Mint, Par, Paragon, Past, Pat, Peace, Pedant, Point-device, Practice, Present, Pure, Quintessential, Refine, Siddha, Soma, Sound, Spot-on, Stainless, Sublime, The nines, Thorough, Three-pricker, Unblemished, Unqualified, Utopian, Utter, Whole, Witeless

Perfidy Betrayal, Falsehood, Treachery, Treason

Perforate(d), Perforation, Perforator Cribrate, Cribrose, Drill, Eyelet, Hole, > PIERCE, Prick, Punch, Puncture, Riddle, Trephine, Trocar

Perforce Necessarily, Needs

Perform(ed), Performer, Performing Achieve, Act(or), Appear, Artist(e), Basoche, Busk, Chansonnier, Discharge, Do, Enact, Entertainer, Execute, Exert, Exhibit, Fancy Dan, Fire-eater, Fulfil, Function, Geek, Hand, Headliner, Hersall, Implement, Interlocutor, Majorette, Make, Moke, On, Perpetrate, Player, Praxis, Recite, Render, Ripieno, Strongarm, Supererogate, Sword-swallower, Throw, Vaudevillian, Virtuoso

Performance Accomplishment, Achievement, Act, Auto, Bravura, Broadcast, Command, Concert, Dare, Deed, Demonstration, Discharge, Entracte, Execution, Gas, Gig, Hierurgy, Holdover, Hootenanny, Masterstroke, Matinee, One-night stand, Operation, Perpetration, Practice, Première, Production, Recital, Rehearsal, Rendering, Rendition, Repeat, Repertoire, Rigmarole, Scene, Show, Sneak preview, Solo, Specific, Spectacle, Stunt, Turn

Perfume (box) Aroma, Attar, Bergamot, Cassolette, Chypre, Civet, Cologne, C(o)umarin, Enfleurage, Fragrance, Frangipani, Incense, Ionone, Lavender (water), Linalool, Millefleurs, Muscone, Muskone, Myrrh, Opopanax, Orris, Orrisroot, Patchouli, Patchouly, Pomander, Potpourri, Redolence, > SCENT, Terpineol

Perfunctory Apathetic, Careless, Cursory, Indifferent, Token

Perhaps A(i)blins, Belike, Haply, Happen, May(be), Peradventure, Percase, Perchance, Possibly, Relative, Say, Yibbles

▷ **Perhaps** *may indicate* an anagram

Perigee Apsis, Epigeum

Peril(ous) > DANGER, Hazard, Jeopardy, Precarious, Risk, Threat, Yellow

Perimeter Boundary, Circuit, Circumference, Limits

Period(ic) Abbevillian, Acheulian, AD, Age, Alcher(ing)a, Annual, Aurignacian, Azilian, Cambrian, Carboniferous, Chalcolithic, Chukka, Chukker, Climacteric, Cooling off, Cretaceous, Critical, Curse, Cycle, Day, Devonian, Diapause, Dot, Dreamtime, > DURATION, Eocene, Epoch, Excerpt, Floruit, Full-stop, Glacial, Grace, Hercynian, Holocene, Horal, Incubation, Innings,

Interregnum, Jurassic, Kalpa, Latency, Latent, Lesson, Liassic, Limit,
Meantime, Meanwhile, Mesolithic, Mesozoic, Middle Kingdom, Miocene,
Monthly, Neocomian, Neolithic, Neozoic, Octave, Olde-worlde, Oligocene,
Ordovician, Paleolithic, Permian, Phanerozoic, Phase, Phoenix, Pleistocene,
Pliocene, Pre-Cambrian, Protohistory, Quarter, Quarternary, Reformation,
Refractory, Regency, Rent, Riss, Romantic, Safe, Season, Session, Sidereal,
Silurian, Span, Spell, Stage, Stop, Stretch, Synodic, Term, Tertiary, Trecento,
Triassic, Trimester, Usance, Window

Periodic(al) Catamenia, Comic, Digest, Economist, Etesian, Journal, Liassic,
Listener, Mag, New Yorker, Organ, Paper, Phase, Publication, Punch, Rambler,
Regency, Review, Solutrean, Solutrian, Spectator, Strand, Stretch, Tatter, Tract

Peripatetic Gadabout, Itinerant, Promenader, Travelling

Periphery Ambit, Bounds, Fringe, Outskirts, Surface

Periscope Eye(-stalk)

Perish(able), Perished, Perishing Brittle, > DIE, End, Ephemeral, Expire, Fade,
Forfair, Fungibles, Icy, Tine, Tint, Transitory, Tyne, Vanish

Periwinkle Apocynum, Blue, Myrtle

Perjure(d) Forswear, Lie, Mansworn

Perk(s), Perky Brighten, Chipper, Freshen, Jaunty, LV, Perquisite

Perm(anent) Abiding, Durable, Enduring, Eternal, Everlasting, Fixed, For
keeps, Full-time, Indelible, > LASTING, Marcel, Stable, Standing, Stative, Wave

Permeability, Permeate Infiltrate, Leaven, Magnetic, Osmosis, Penetrate,
Pervade, Seep

Permission, Permit(ted) Allow, Authorise, Carnet, Chop, Clearance, Congé(e),
Consent, Copyright, Enable, Grant, Lacet, Laisser-passer, Latitude, Leave,
Legal, Let, Liberty, Licence, License, Lief, Luit, Nihil obstat, Ok(e), Pace, Pass,
Placet, Planning, Power, Pratique, Privilege, Sanction, Stamp-note, Suffer,
Ticket, Triptyque, Visa, Vouchsafe, Way-leave, Wear

Pernicious Evil, Harmful, Lethal, Noisome, Pestilent, Wicked

Pernickety Fikish, Niggly

Peroration Pirlicue, Purlicue

Peroxide Bleach, Blonde, Colcothar

Perpendicular Aplomb, Apothem, Atrip, Cathetus, Erect, Normal, Orthogonal,
Plumb, Sheer, Sine, > UPRIGHT, Vertical

Perpetrate Commit, Effect, Execute

Perpetual Constant, Eternal, Incessant, Sempiternal

Perplex(ed), Perplexity Anan, Baffle, Bamboozle, Beset, Bewilder, Bother,
Buffalo, Bumbaze, Cap, Confound, Confuse, Embarrass, Feague, Floor,
Flummox, Knotty, Meander, Mystify, Nonplus, Out, Puzzle, Quizzical, Stump,
Tangle, Tickle, Tostication

Perquisite Ap(p)anage, Emolument, Extra, Gratuity, > PERK, Tip

Perrier Stoner

Perry Mason

Persecute, Persecution Afflict, Annoy, Badger, Crucify, Dragon(n)ades, Harass,
Haze, Intolerant, Oppress, Pogrom, Ride, Torment, Torture, Witch hunt

Persevere, Perseverance Assiduity, Continue, Fortitude, Insist, Patience,
Persist, Plug, Stamina, Steadfastness, Stick, Stickability, Tenacity

Persia(n) Babee, Babi, Bahai, Cyrus, Farsi, Iran(ian), Mazdean, Mede, Middle,
Pahlavi, Parasang, Parsee, Pehlevi, Pushtu, Samanid, Sassanid, Sohrab,
Xerxes, Zoroaster

Persimmon Kaki, Sharon fruit

Persist(ence), Persistent Adhere, Assiduity, Chronic, Continual, Diligent,

Doggedness, Endure, Importunate, Labour, Longeval, Lusting, Nag, Persevere, Press, Sedulous, Sneaking, Stick, Tenacity, Urgent

Person(s), **Personal(ly)** Alter, Being, Bird, Bod(y), Chai, Chal, Character, Chi, Cookie, Displaced, Entity, Everymen, Figure, First, Fish, Flesh, Head, Human, Individual, In propria persona, One, Own, Party, Passer-by, Pod, Private, Quidam, Second, Selfhood, Skate, Sod, Soul, Specimen, Tales, Third, Walla(h)

Personage, **Personality** Anima, Celeb(rity), Character, Charisma, Dignitary, Ego, Grandee, Identity, Jekyll and Hyde, Multiple, Noble, Notability, Panjandrum, Presence, Psychopath, Sama, Schizoid, Seity, Sel, Self, Sell, Split, Star, Tycoon, Viscerotonia

Personified, **Personification**, **Personify** Embody, Incarnate, Prosopop(o)eia, Represent

Personnel Employees, Hands, Liveware, Manpower, Staff

Perspective Attitude, Distance, Linear, Point of view, Proportion, Slant, View, Vista

Perspicacious Astute, Clear-sighted, Discerning, Keen, Shrewd

Perspiration, **Perspire**, **Perspiring** Aglow, Forswatt, Glow, Hidrosis, Sudor, Suint, Sweat, Swelter

Persuade(d), **Persuasion**, **Persuasive** Cajole, Coax, Cogent, Conviction, Convince, Disarm, Eloquent, Faith, Feel, Forcible, Geed, Get, Induce, Inveigle, Lead on, Move, Plausible, > PREVAIL, Religion, Soft sell, Suborn, Truckled, Wheedle, Winning

Pert(ness) Bold, Brisk, Cocky, Dicacity, Flippant, Forward, Fresh, Impertinent, Insolent, Jackanapes, Minx, Saucy, Tossy

Pertain Belong, Concern, Relate, Touch

Pertinacious Dogged, Obstinate, Persistent, Stickler, Stubborn

Pertinent Apropos, Apt, Fit, Germane, Relevant, Timely

Perturb(ation) Aerate, Confuse, Dismay, Disturb, Dither, State, Trouble, Upset, Worry

Peru(vian) Inca, PE, Quechua(n), Quichua(n)

Peruse, **Perusal** Examine, Inspect, Read, Scan, Scrutiny, > STUDY

Pervade, **Pervasion**, **Pervasive(ness)** Diffuse, Drench, Immanence, Permeate, Saturate

Perverse, **Perversion**, **Pervert(ed)** Aberrant, Abnormal, Algolagnia, Awry, Cam(stairy), Camsteary, Camsteerie, Cantankerous, > CONTRARY, Corrupt, Cussed, Deviate, Distort, Donsie, False, Gee, Kam(me), Kinky, Licentious, Misuse, Nonce, Paraphilia, Refractory, Sadist, Sicko, Stubborn, Thrawn, Traduce, Unnatural, Untoward, Uranism, Warp(ed), Wayward, Wilful, Wrest, Wry

▷ **Perverted** *may indicate* an anagram

Pessimism, **Pessimist(ic)** Alarmist, Bear, Crapehanger, Crepehanger, Cynic, Defeatist, Doomwatch, Doomy, Doubter, Downbeat, Fatalist, Glumbum, Jeremiah, Killjoy, Negative

Pest(er) Badger, Bedbug, Blight, Bot, > BOTHER, Brat, Breese, Bug, Dim, Disagreeable, Earbash, Fly, Fowl, Harass, Irritate, Mither, Mouse, Nag, Nudnik, Nuisance, Nun, Pize, Plague, Rotter, Scourge, Tease, Terror, Thysanoptera, Vermin, Weevil

Pesticide DDT, Derris, Heplachlor, Mouser, Permethrin, Synergist, Warfarin

Pestilence, **Pestilent** Curse, Epidemic, Evil, Lues, Murrain, Noxious, Outbreak, Pernicious, Plague

Pet Aversion, Cade, Canoodle, Caress, Chou, Coax, Coddle, Cosset, Dandle, Daut(ie), Dawt(ie), Dod, Dort, Ducky, Favourite, Fondle, Glumps, Hamster,

Huff, Hump, Ire, Jarta, Jo, Lallygag, Lapdog, Miff, Mouse, Neck, Pique, Rabbit, Smooch, Snog, Spat, Strum, Sulk(s), Tantrum, Teacher's, Tiff, Tout, Towt, Umbrage, Virtual, Yarta

Petal Ala, Keels, Labellum, Leaf, Standard, Vexillum

Petard Firework, Squib

Peter Aumbry, Bell, Dwindle, Grimes, Pan, Principle, Quince, Quint, Rabbit, Safe, Saint, Sellers, Simon, Simple, Wane, Weaken

Petite Dainty, Mignon, Small

Petition(er) Appeal, Beg, Boon, Crave, Entreaty, Millenary, Orison, Plaintiff, Postulant, Prayer, Representation, Request, Round robin, Solicit, Sue, Suit(or), Suppli(c)ant, Vesper

Pet-name Hypocorisma, Nickname, So(u)briquet

Petrel Bird, Mother Carey's chickens, Nelly, Prion, Procellaria, Stormbird, Stormy, Wilton's

Petrify(ing) Fossilise, Frighten, Lapidescent, Niobe, Numb, Ossify, Scare, Terrify

Petrol(eum) Cetane, Cutting, Diesel, Esso®, Ethyl, Fuel, Gas, High-octane, High-test, Ligroin, Maz(o)ut, Octane, Oilstone, Olein, Rock-tar, Unleaded, Vaseline

Petticoat Balmoral, Basquine, Crinoline, Female, Filabeg, Fil(l)ibeg, Jupon, Kilt, Kirtle, Phil(l)abeg, Phil(l)ibeg, Placket, Sarong, Shift, Underskirt, Wylie-coat

Pettifogger Lawmonger

Petty, Pettiness Baubling, Bumbledom, Childish, Little, Mean, Minor, Narrow, Niggling, Nyaff, One-horse, Parvanimity, Picayunish, Pimping, Puisne, Shoestring, Small, Small-minded, Stingy, Tin, Trivial, Two-bit

Petulance, Petulant Fretful, Huff, Moody, Peevish, Perverse, Procacity, Querulous, Sullen, Toutie, Waspish

Pew Box, Carrel, Chair, Seat, Stall

Pewter Trifle, Tutenag

Phalanger Cus-cus, Honey-mouse, Opossum, Petaurist, Possum, Sugar glider, Tait, Tarsipes, Tuan, Wambenger

Phalanx Cohort, Coterie, Legion

Phalarope Lobe-foot

Phallus Linga(m), Penis, Priapus

Phantasist, Phantasm Apparition, Chimera, Spectre, Werewolf

Phantom Apparition, Bogey, Bugbear, Eidolon, Idol, Incubus, Maya, Pepper's ghost, Shade, Spectre, Tut, Wraith

Pharaoh Amenhotep, Cheops, Egyptian, Rameses, Thutmose, Tut, Tutankhamen, Tutankhamun, Tyrant

Pharisee Formalist, Humbug, Hypocrite, Nicodemus

Pharmacist > CHEMIST, Dispenser, MPS, Preparator

Phase Colourm, Cycle, Form, Period, Post-boost, Quarter, REM, Stage, State, Synchronise, Transition

Pheasant Argus, Bird, Fireback, Junglefowl, Mona(u)l, Nide, Nye, Peacock, Ring-necked, Tragopan

Phenol Orcine, Orcinol, Resorcin, Xylenol

Phenomenon Autokinetic, Blip, Effect, Event, Figure ground, Flying saucer, Flysch, Heterography, Marvel, Miracle, Mirage, Paranormal, Psi, Reynaud's, Synergy

Phial Bologna, Bottle, Flask

Phil, Philip Fluter, Macedonia, Pip

Philander(er) Flirt, Lothario, Playboy, Toyer, > TRIFLE, Wolf, Womaniser

Philanthropist, **Philanthropy** Altruist, Benefactor, Carnegie, Charity, Coram, Donor, Humanist, Humanitarian, Nobel, Rockefeller, Samaritan, Shaftesbury, Tate, Wilberforce

Philately Timbromania

Phileas Fogg

Philip *see* PHIL

Philippic Diatribe, Invective, Tirade

Philippine(s) Bisayan, Igorot, Moro, PI, RP, Tagalog, Visayan

Philistine, **Philistinism** Artless, Ashdod, Barbarian, Foe, Gath, Gaza, Gigman, Goliath, Goth, Lowbrow, Podsnappery, Vandal

Philology Linguistics, Semantics, Speechcraft

Philosopher, **Philosophy** Activism, Ahimsa, Analytical, Animism, Anthrosophy, Antinomianism, Attitude, Averr(h)oism, Comtism, Conceptualism, Cracker-barrel, Deontology, Empiricism, Enlightenment, Epistemology, Ethics, Existentialism, Fatalism, Hedonism, Hobbism, Humanism, Idealism, Ideology, -ism, Linguistic, Logical atomism, Logos, Marxism, Materialism, Metempiricism, Monism, Moral(ist), Natural, Neoplatonism, Nihilism, Nominalism, Opinion, Peripatetic, Phenomenology, Populism, Positivism, Rationalism, Realism, Scientology, Shankara(-charya), Stoic, Synthetic, Taoism, Theism, Theosophy, Transcendentalism, Ultraism, Utilitarianism, Utopianism, Voluntarism, Yoga

PHILOSOPHERS

4 letters:
Aver
Ayer
Hume
Kant
Mach
Mill
Ryle
Sage
Weil
Wolf
Yogi
Zeno

5 letters:
Amiel
Bacon
Comte
Croce
Cynic
Dewey
Hegel
Locke
Paine
Plato
Quine
Renan
Smith
Sorel
Taine

6 letters:
Cicero
Engels
Godwin
Herder
Hobbes
Holist
I Ching
Kaizen
Ortega
Pascal
Popper
Pyrrho
Sartre
Scotus
Seneca
Thales

7 letters:
Abelard
Aquinas
Atomist
Bentham

Bergson
Casuist
Diderot
Eleatic
Emerson
Erasmus
Erigena
Herbart
Hypatia
Leibniz
Malthus
Marcuse
Mencius
Meng-tse
Russell
Sankhya
Sceptic
Schlick
Sensist
Sheffer
Sophist
Spencer
Spinoza
Steiner
Thomist
Vedanta

8 letters:
Avicenna
Berkeley
Boethius
Cyreniac
Diogenes
Eclectic
Epicurus
Foucault
Harrison
Megarian
Menippus
Neoteric
Occamist
Old Moore
Plotinus
Plutarch
Rousseau
Socrates
Xenophon

9 letters:
Academist
Aristotle
Bosanquet
Cartesian
Cleanthes

- Confucius
- Descartes
- Euhemerus
- Heidegger
- Leucippus
- Lucretius
- Nietzsche
- Ockhamist
- Rosminian
- Santayana
- Schelling
- Schoolman
- Whitehead

10 letters:
Anacharsis
Anaxagoras
Anaximenes
Antiochene
Antiochian
Apemanthus
Apollonius
Aristippus
Campanella
Chrysippus
Democritus
Empedocles
Heraclitus

Nominalist
Paracelsus
Parmenides
Protagoras
Pythagoras
Saint Simon
Swedenborg
Xenocrates
Xenophanes

11 letters:
Anaximander
Antisthenes
Kierkegaard

Montesquieu
Occam's razor

12 letters:
Callisthenes
Gymnosophist
Schopenhauer
Wittgenstein

13 letters:
Deipnosophist
Metaphysician

Philosophic(al) Rational, Resigned, Thoughtful, Tranquil

Philtre Aphrodisiac, Charm, Drug, Hippomanes, Potion

Phlegm(atic) Calm, Composed, Pituita(ry), Pituite, Stolid, Unperturbed, Unruffled

Phloem Leptome, Liber

Phobia Aversion, Dread, Fear, Thing

Phoebe, **Phoebus** Apollo, Artemis, Day-star, Deaconess, Moon, Selene, Sol, Sun

Phoenician Tripolitania

Phoenix Fum, Fung, Paragon, Self-begotten

Phone Bell, Blower, Call, Cellular, Dial, Intercom, Mobile, Moby, Pay, Ring, Smart, > TELEPHONE

Phonetic(s) Acoustic, Articulatory, Mouille, Oral, Palaeotype, Palatal, Plosion, Spoken, Symbol, Synaeresis

▷ **Phonetically** *may indicate* a word sounding like another

Phon(e)y Bogus, Charlatan, Counterfeit, Fake, Hokey, Impostor, Poseur, > SHAM, Specious, Spurious

▷ **Phony** *may indicate* an anagram

Phosphate Monazite, Torbernite, Vivianite, Wavellite, Xenotime

Phosphor(escent), **Phosphorescence**, **Phosphorus** Briming, Foxfire, Friar's lantern, Ignis fatuus, Jack o'lantern, Luminescent, Noctilucent, P, Pyrosome, Sarin, Tabun, Will o' the wisp

Photo(copy), **Photograph(y)**, **Photographic**, **Photo finish** Ambrotype, Angiogram, Beefcake, Calotype, Clog, Close-up, Composite, Contre-jour, Daguerrotype, Diazo, Duplicate, Enprint, Exposure, Ferroprint, Ferrotype, Film, Flash, Headshot, Heliochrome®, Heliotype, Hologram, Infra-red, Kallitype, Kirlian, Kodak®, Microdot, Microfilm, Microgram, Micrograph, Monochrome, Mugshot, Negative, Opaline, Panel, Picture, Pinhole, Platinotype, Positive, Print, Resorcin, Rotograph, Rotogravure, Schlieren, Sepia, Shoot, Shot, Shutterbug, Snap, Spirit, Still, Take, Talbotype, Time-lapse, Tintype, Tomography, Topo, Trimetrogon, Vignette, Wire, Woodburytype, Xerography, X-ray

Photographer Beaton, Brandt, Cameraman, Cameron, Cartier-Bresson, Daguerre, Fox Talbot, Paparazzo, Schlierin, Shutterbug

Phrase Asyndeton, Buzzword, Catch(word), Cliché, Comma, Expression, Heroic Hook, Laconism, Leitmotiv, Locution, Mantra, Noun, Phr, Refrain, Riff, Slogan, Tag, Term

Phrygian Midas

Phthisis Decay, TB
Phylactery Amulet, Talisman, Tefillin, Tephillin
Phyllopod Brine-shrimp
Physic(s) Cryogenics, Culver's, Cure, Dose, Geostatics, Health, Kinematics,
  Medicine, Nuclear, Nucleonics, Particle, Photometry, Purge, Remedy,
  Rheology, Science, Solid-state, Thermodynamics, Ultrasonics
Physical Bodily, Carnal, Corpor(e)al, Material, Natural, Tangible
Physician Allopath, Doctor, Galen, Hakim, Harvey, Hippocrates, Internist,
  Leech, Linacre, Lister, Medic(o), Mesmer, Mindererus, Paean, Paracelsus,
  Practitioner, Preceptor, Quack, Roget, Sézary, Stahl, Therapist, Time
Physicist Alfren, Ampere, Angstrom, Appleton, Archimedes, Avogadro,
  Becquerel, Bohr, Born, Bose, Bragg, Brewster, Carnot, Cockcroft, Coulomb,
  Crookes, Curie, Dalton, Davisson, Debye, Dirac, Einstein, Faraday, Fermi,
  Galileo, Gauss, Geiger, Giorgi, Hahn, Hawking, Heaviside, Heisenberg,
  Henry, Hertz, Hooke, Huygens, Joliot-Curie, Josephson, Joule, Kerv, Kirchhoff,
  Landau, Lawe, Lodge, Lorentz, Mach, Marconi, Newton, Oersted, Ohm,
  Oppenheimer, Pauli, Pic(c)ard, Planck, Popov, Rayleigh, Reaumur, Ro(e)ntgen,
  Rutherford, Schottky, Scientist, Sievert, Stark, Torricelli, Tyndall, Van Allen,
  Van der Waals, Volta, Watson-Watt, Weber, Wheeler, Young
Physiognomist, **Physiognomy** Face, Features, Lavater
Physiologist Pavlov
Physiotherapist Masseur
Physique Body, Build, Figure, Pyknic
Pi, **Pious** Craw-thumper, Devotional, Devout, Fraud, Gallio, God-fearing, Godly,
  Holy, Holy Willie, Mid-Victorian, Religiose, Sanctimonious, Savoury, Smug,
  Wise, Zaddik
Piaffe Spanish-walk
Pianist Anda, Arrau, Hambourg, Hess, Hofmann, Liszt, Mingus, Morton,
  Pachmann, Padarewski, Répétiteur, Tatum, Vamper, Virtuoso
Piano Baby grand, Bechstein, Boudoir grand, Celesta, Celeste, Concert grand,
  Cottage, Flugel, Forte, Grand, Honkytonk, Keyboard, Overstrung, P, Player,
  Prepared, Semi-grand, Softly, Steinway, Stride, Thumb, Upright
Piano-maker Erard
Picaroon Brigand, Corsair, Pirate, Rogue
Piccadilly Whist
Piccolo Ottavino
Pick(er), **Pickaxe**, **Picking**, **Pick up** Break, Choice, > **CHOOSE**, Cream, Cull, Elite,
  Flower, Gather, Glean, Gurlet, Hack, Hopper, Mattock, Nap, Nibble, Oakum,
  Plectrum, Pluck, Plum, Select, Single, Sort, Steal, Strum, Tong, Wale
Picked *may indicate* an anagram
Picket Demonstrate, Flying, Pale, Palisade, Protester, Stake, Tether, Tie
Pickings Harvest, Profits, Scrounging, Spoils
Pickle(r) Achar, Brine, Cabbage, Caper, Chow-chow, Chutney, Corn, Cure,
  Dilemma, Dill, Eisel, Esile, Gherkin, Girkin, Jam, Kimchi, Marinade, Marinate,
  Mess, Mull, Olive, Onion, Peculate, Peregrine, Piccalilli, > **PLIGHT**, Samp(h)ire,
  Scrape, Souse, Vinegar, Wolly
Picklock Oustiti, Peterman
Pick-me-up Bracer, Drink, Restorer, Reviver, Tonic
Pickpocket(s) Adept, Bung, Cly-faker, Cutpurse, Dip, Diver, Fagin, File, Nipper,
  Swell mob, Wire
Pick-up Arrest, Light o'love, Truck, Ute
Picnic Alfresco, Braaivleis, Burgoo, Clambake, Fun, Outing, Push-over, Spread,

Wase-goose, Wayzgoose

Picture(s) Anaglyph, Arpillera, Art, Bambocciades, Bitmap, Canvas, Collage, Cyclorama, Decoupage, Depict, Describe, Diptych, Drawing, Drypoint, Emblem, Epitome, Etching, Film, Flick, Fresco, Gouache, Graphic, Histogram, Icon, Identikit®, Imagery, Inset, Kakemono, Landscape, Likeness, Lithograph, Montage, Motion, Movie, Moving, Movy, Mugshot, Myriorama, Oil, Photo, Photofit, Photogram, Photomosaic, Photomural, Pin-up, Pix, Plate, Polyptych, Portrait, Predella, Prent, Presentment, Print, Retraitt, Retrate, Scene, Shadowgraph, Shot, Slide, Snapshot, Stereochrome, Stereogram, Stereograph, Stevengraph, Still-life, Table(au), Talkie, Thermogram, Tone, Topo, Transfer, Transparency, Vanitas, Veetograph, Vision, Votive, Vraisemblance, Word, Zincograph

Picturesque Idyllic, Scenic

Pidgin Chinook jargon, Creole, Fanagalo, Fanakalo, Japlish, New Guinea, Police Motu, Solomon Islands, Tok Pisin

Pie(s) Anna, Banoffee, Battalia, Bridie, Camp, Chewet, Cobbler, Cottage, Curry puff, Custard, Deep-dish, Easy, Flan, Hash, Humble, Madge, Mess, Mince, Mud, Mystery bag, Pandowdy, Pastry, Pasty, Patty, Périgord, Pica, Piet, Pirog, Pizza, Pyat, Pyet, Pyot, Quiche, Rappe, Resurrection, Shepherd's, Shoofly, Spoil, Squab, Stargaz(e)y, Star(ry)-gazy, Sugar, Tart, Tarte tatin, Torte, Tourtiere, Turnover, Tyropitta, Umble, Vol-au-vent, Warden

▷ **Pie** *may indicate* an anagram

Piebald Calico, Dappled, Motley, Pied, Pinto, Skewbald

Piece(s) Add, Bishop, Bit, Blot, Cameo, Cannon, Cent, Charm, > **CHESSMAN**, Chip, Chunk, Coin, Companion, Component, Concerto, Conversation, Crumb, Domino, End, Extract, Flitters, Fragment, Frust, Gat, Goring, > **GUN**, Haet, Hait, Hunk, Item, Join, Mammock, Medaillons, Mite, Money, Morceau, Morsel, Museum, Nip, Novelette, Oddment, Off-cut, Ort, Part, Party, Patch, Pawn, Period, Peso, Pistareen, Pole, > **PORTION**, Recital, Scliff, Scrap, Section, Set, Shard, Sherd, Skliff, Slice, Sliver, Sou, Speck, String, Stub, Swatch, Tait, Tate, Tile, Toccata, Truncheon, Wedge

Pièce de résistance Star-turn

Piecemeal, Piecework Gradually, Intermittent, Jigsaw, Serial, Tut

Pie-crust Coffin, Lid, Pastry

Pied-à-terre Nest, Pad

Pieman Shepherd

Pier(s) Anta, Groyne, Jetty, Jutty, Landing, Mole, Plowman, Quay, Slipway, Swiss roll, Wharf

Pierce(d), Piercer, Piercing Accloy, Awl, Broach, Cleave, Cribrose, Dart, Drill, Endart, Fenestrate(d), Gimlet, Gore, Gride, Gryde, Hull, Impale, Jag, Keen, Lance, Lancinate, Lobe, Move, Needle, Penetrate, Perforate, Pike, Poignant, Punch, Puncture, Riddle, Rive, Shrill, Skewer, Slap, Sleeper, Spear, Spike, Spit, Stab, Steek, Stiletto, Sting, Thirl, Thrill(ant)

Piety Devotion, Purity, Sanctity

Piffle Bilge, Codswallop, Hogwash, Tommy-rot, Twaddle

Pig(s), Piggy, Pigskin Anthony, Babe, Babirusa, Baconer, Barrow, Bartholomew, Bessemer, Bland, Boar, Bonham, British lop, Bush, Captain Cooker, Doll, Duroc, Elt, Farrow, Fastback, Football, Gadarene, Gilt, Gloucester, Glutton, Gride, Grumphie, Guffie, Guinea, Gus, Ham, Hog, Ingot, Iron, Javelina, Kentledge, Kintledge, Lacombe, Landrace, Lard, Large black, Large white, Lingot, Long, Middle white, Napoleon, Old Spot, Peccary, Policeman, Pork(er), Razorback, Rosser, Runt, Saddleback, Shoat, Shot(e), Shott, Slip, Snowball,

Sounder, Sow, Squealer, Sucking, Suid(ae), Tamworth, Tayassuid, Tithe, Toe, Tootsie, Vietnamese pot-bellied, Warthog, Welsh, Yelt

Pig-disease Bullnose

Pigeon Archangel, Barb, Bird, Cape, Capuchin, Carrier, Clay, Cropper, Culver, Cumulet, Dove, Fairy swallow, Fantail, Goura, Gull, Homer, Homing, Horseman, Jacobin, Kuku, Manumea, Nun, Owl, Passenger, Peristeronic, Pouter, Ringdove, Rock(er), Roller, Ront(e), Ruff, Runt, Scandaroon, Solitaire, Spot, Squab, Squealer, Stock-dove, Stool, Talkie-talkee, Tippler, Tooth-billed, Tumbler, Turbit, Wonga-wonga, Zoozoo

Pigeonhole Classify, Compartment, File, Postpone, Shelve, Slot, Stereotype

Pigeon-house Columbary, Cote, Dovecot(e)

Pig-food Mast, Swill

Pig-iron Kentledge, Kintledge

Pigment(ation) Anthoclore, Anthocyan(in), Argyria, Betacyanin, Bilirubin, Biliverdin, Bister, Bistre, Bronzing, Cappagh-brown, Carmine, Carotene, Carotenoid, Carotin, Carotinoid, Chloasma, Chlorophyll, Chrome, Chromogen, Cobalt, Colcothar, Colour, Crocus, Dye, Etiolin, Flake-white, Flavin(e), Fucoxanthin, Gamboge, Gossypol, Haem, H(a)ematin, H(a)emocyanin, H(a)emoglobin, Hem(e), Iodopsin, Lamp-black, Lithopone, Liverspot, Lutein, Luteolin, Madder, Melanin, Monastral®, Naevus, Nigrosine, Ochre, Opsin, Orpiment, Paris-green, Phthalocyanine, Phycobilin, Phycoerythrin, Phycophaein, Phycoxanthin, Phytochrome, Porphyrin, Pterin, Quercetin, Realgar, Red lead, Respiratory, Retinene, Rhiboflavin, Rhodopsin, Scheele's green, Sepia, Sienna, Sinopia, Smalt, Tapetum, Tempera, Terre-verte, Tincture, Toner, Ultramarine, Umber, Urobilin, Urochrome, Verditer, Viridian, Whitewash, Xanthophyll, Xanthopterin(e), Zinc white

Pigtail Braid, Cue, Plait, Queue

Pi jaw Cant

Pike Assegai, Crag, Dory, Fogash, Gar(fish), Ged, Gisarme, Glaive, Hie, Holostei, Javelin, Lance, Luce, Partisan, Pickerel, Ravensbill, Scafell, Snoek, Spear, Speed, Spontoon, Vouge, Walleyed

Pilaster see PILLAR

Pile(d), Piles, Piling Agger, Amass, Atomic, Bing, Bomb, Camp-sheathing, Camp-shedding, Camp-sheeting, Camp-shot, Clamp, Cock, Column, Crowd, Deal, Down, Emerods, Farmers, Fender, Fig, Floccus, Fortune, Galvanic, Hair, Haycock, Heap, Hept, Historic, Hoard, Load, Lot, Marleys, Mass, Nap, Post, Pyre, Raft, Reactor, Ream(s), Rouleau, Screw, Shag, Sheet, > STACK, Starling, Stilt, Trichome, Upheap, Voltaic, Wealth, Windrow, Wodge

Pile-driver Tup

Pilfer(ing) Crib, Filch, Finger, Maraud, Miche, Nick, Peculate, Pickery, Pickle, Pinch, Plagiarise, Plunder, Purloin, Snitch, > STEAL

Pilgrim(age) Aske, Childe Harold, Expedition, Fatima, Hadj(i), Haji, Hajj(i), Karbala, Kerbela, Loreto, Lourdes, Mecca, Palmer, Pardoner, Reeve, Scallop-shell, Shrine, Voyage, Yatra

Pill(s) Abortion, Ball, Beverley, Bitter, Bolus, Caplet, Capsule, Dex, Doll, Dose, Globule, Lob, Medication, Medicine, Number nine, Peel, Pellet, Pep, Pilula, Pilule, Placebo, Poison, Protoplasmal, Radio, Sleeping, Spansule, Tablet, Troche, Trochisk, Upper

Pillage Booty, Devastate, Plunder, Ransack, Rapine, Ravage, Razzia, Robbery, Sack, Spoil

Pillar(ed), Pillars Anta, Apostle, Atlantes, Baluster, Balustrade, Boaz, Canton, Caryatides, Cippus, Columel, Column, Earth, Eustyle, Gendarme, Hercules,

Herm, Impost, Islam, Jachin, Lat, Man, Modiolus, Monolith, Newel, Nilometer, Obelisk, Pedestal, Peristyle, Pier, Post, Respond, Stalactite, Stalagmite, Stoop, Telamon, Tetrastyle, Trumeau

Pill-box Hat, Inro

Pillion Cushion, Pad, Rear

Pillory Cang(ue), Cippus, Crucify, Jougs, Little-ease, Pelt, Satirise, Slam

Pillow(case) Bear, Beer, Bere, Bolster, Cod, Cow, Cushion, Headrest, Hop, Lace, Pad, Pulvinar

Pilot Ace, Airman, Auto(matic), Aviator, Captain, > **CONDUCT**, Experimental, George, Govern, Guide, Hobbler, Lead, Lodesman, Lodestar, Palinure, Palinurus, Pitt, Prune, Shipman, Steer, Test, Tiphys, Trial, Usher, Wingman

Pimento Allspice

Pimp Apple-squire, Bludger, Fancyman, Fleshmonger, Hoon, Mack, Pandarus, Pander, Ponce, Procurer, Solicit, Souteneur

Pimpernel Bastard, Bog, Scarlet, Water, Wincopipe, Wink-a-peep, Yellow

Pimple, **Pimply** Blackhead, Botch, Bubukle, Button, Gooseflesh, Grog-blossom, Hickey, Horripilation, Papula, Plook, Plouk, Pock, Pustule, Quat, Rumblossom, Rum-bud, Spot, Tetter, Uredinial, Wen, Whelk, Whitehead, Zit

Pin Bayonet, Belaying, Bolt, Brooch, Cotter, Curling, Dowel, Drawing, Drift, End, Fasten, Fid, Firing, Fix, Gam, Gudgeon, Hair, Hairgrip, Hob, Joggle, Kevel, King, Nail, Needle, Nog, Panel, Peg, Pintle, Pivot, Preen, Rivet, Rolling, Safety, Scarf, SCART, Scatter, Shear, Skewer, Skittle, Skiver, Spike, Spindle, Split, Staple, Stick, Stump, Swivel, Taper, Thole, Thumbtack, Tre(e)nail, U-bolt, Woolder, Wrest, Wrist

Pinafore Apron, Brat, HMS, Overall, Pinny, Save-all, Tire

Pince-nez Nose-nippers

Pincers Chela, Claw, Forceps, Forfex, Nipper, Tweezers

Pinch(ed) Arrest, Bit, Bone, Chack, Constrict, Cramp, Crimp, Crisis, Emergency, Gaunt, Misappropriate, Nab, Nick, Nim, Nip, Peculate, Peel, Pilfer, Pocket, Pook(it), Prig, Pugil, Raft, Rob, Scrimp, Scrounge, Skimp, Smatch, Snabble, Snaffle, Sneak, Sneap, Sneeshing, Snuff, Squeeze, > **STEAL**, Swipe, Tate, Tweak, Twinge

Pine(s), **Pining** Arolla, Bristlecone, Celery, Cembra, Chile, Cluster, Cone, Conifer, Cypress, Droop, Dwine, Earn, Erne, Fret, Ground, Hone, Hoop, Huon, Jack, Japanese umbrella, Jeffrey, Kauri, Languish, Languor, Loblolly, Lodgepole, Long, Longleaf, Monkey-puzzle, Moon, Norfolk Island, Norway, Nut, Oregon, Parana, Picea, Pitch, Radiata, Red, Scotch, Scots, Screw, Softwood, Spruce, Starve, Stone, Sugar, Tree, Umbrella, Urman, Waste, White, Yearn

Pineapple Anana, Bomb, Bromelia, Grenade, Pina, Poll, Sorosis, Tillandsia

Ping Knock, Whir(r)

Pinguin Anana(s)

Pinion Fetter, Penne, Pinnoed, Secure, Shackle, Wing

Pink Blush, Carolina, Castory, Clove, Colour, Coral, Dianthus, Dutch, Emperce, FT, Fuchsia, Gillyflower, Knock, Lake, Lychnis, Moss, Mushroom, Oyster, Peach-blow, Peak, Perce, Pierce, Pompadour, Pounce, Rose(ate), Ruddy, Salmon, Scallop, Shell, Shocking, Shrimp, Spigelia, Spit, Stab, Tiny

Pinnacle Acme, Apex, Crest, Crown, Height, Needle, Pinnet, Summit

Pinniped Seal

Pin-point Focus, Highlight, Identify, Isolate, Localise

Pint(s) Cab, Jar, Log, Reputed

Pintail Duck, Smeath, Smee(th)

Pin-up Cheesecake, Dish, Star

Pioneer Baird, Bandeirante, Blaze, Boone, Colonist, Emigrant, Explore, Fargo, Fleming, Frontiersman, Harbinger, Innovator, Lead, Marconi, Oecist, Pathfinder, Planter, Rochdale, Sandgroper, Settler, Spearhead, Trail-blazer, Trekker, Voortrekker, Waymaker, Wells

Pious *see* PI

Pip Ace, Acinus, Blackball, Bleep, Hip, Hump, Phil, Pyrene, Seed, Star

Pipe(s), **Piper**, **Pipeline**, **Piping** Antara, Aorta, Aulos, Balance, Barrel, Blub, Boatswain's, Bong, Briar, Broseley, Bubble, Calabash, Call, Calumet, Chanter, Cheep, Cherrywood, Chibouk, Chibouque, Chillum, Churchwarden, Clay, Cob, Conduit, Corncob, Crane, Cutty, Down, Downcomer, Drain, Drill, Dry riser, Duct, Dudeen, Dudheen, Ell, Escape, Exhaust, Faucet, Feed, Fistula, Flue, Flute, Gage, Gedact, Gedeckt, Hawse, Hod, Hogger, Hooka(h), Hose, Hubble-bubble, Hydrant, Indian, Irish, Jet, Kalian, Kelly, Mains, Manifold, Marsyas, Meerschaum, Mirliton, Montre, Narghile, Narg(h)il(l)y, Nargile(h), Oat(en), Oboe, Organ, Ottavino, Pan, Peace, Pepper, Pibroch, Piccolo, Pied, Pifferaro, Pitch, Poverty, Pule, Qanat, Quill, Rainwater, Recorder, Ree(d), Rise, Riser, Sack-doudling, Salicional, Sennit, Serpent, Service, Sewer, Shalm, Shawm, Shrike, Siphon, Skirl, Sluice, Soil, Squeak, Stack, Standpipe, Stopcock, Stummel, Syrinx, Tail, Throttle, Tibia, Tootle, Trachea, Tremie, Tube, Tubule, Tweet, U-bend, Uillean(n), Union, Uptake, U-tube, Vent, Volcanic, Waste, Water(-spout), Weasand, Whistle, Woodnote

Pipefish Sea-adder

Pipe-laying Graft

Pipit Bird, Skylark, Titlark

Pippin Apple, Orange, Ribston

Pipsqueak Nobody

Piquancy, **Piquant** Pungent, Racy, Relish, Salt, Sharp, Spicy, Tangy

Pique Dod, Huff, Resentment, Titillate

Piracy, **Pirate**, **Piratical** Algerine, Barbarossa, Blackbeard, Boarder, Bootleg, Brigand, Buccaneer, Buccanier, Cateran, Condottier, Conrad, Corsair, Crib, Dampier, Fil(l)ibuster, Flint, Hijack, Hook, Kidd, Lift, Loot, Morgan, Picaro(on), Pickaroon, Plagiarise, Plunder, Rakish, Rover, Sallee-man, Sallee-rover, Sea-king, Sea-rat, Sea-robber, Silver, Skull and crossbones, Smee, Steal, Teach, Thief, Viking, Water-rat, Water-thief

Piranha Caribe, Characinoid, Piraya

Pistillate Female

Pistol Air, Ancient, Automatic, Barker, Barking-iron, Colt®, Dag, Derringer, Gat, > GUN, Hackbut, Horse, Luger®, Pepperbox, Petronel, Puffer, Revolver, Rod, Saloon, Shooter, Starter, Starting, Very, Water, Weapon

Piston Four-stroke, Plunger, Ram, Trunk

Pit(ted) Abyss, Alveolus, Antrum, Bottomless, Catch, Cave, Cesspool, Chasm, Cloaca, Colliery, Crater, Den, Depression, Depth, Dungmere, Ensile, Fossa, Fovea, Foxhole, Hangi, Heapstead, Hell, Hole, Hollow, Inferno, Inspection, Khud, Lacunose, Lime, Mark, Match, Measure, > MINE, Mosh, Orchestra, Parterre, Pip, Play, Pock, Pock-mark, Potato, Punctate, Putamen, Pyrene, Ravine, Scrobicule, Silo, Soakaway, Solar plexus, Stone, Sump, Tar, Tear, Trap, Trou-de-loup

Pitch(ed) Absolute, Asphalt, Atilt, Attune, Bitumen, Burgundy, Coal-tar, Concert, Crease, Diamond, Dive, Ela, Elect, Encamp, Erect, Establish, Fever, Fling, Fork, Ground, International, Intonation, Key, Labour, Length, Level, Lurch, Maltha, Mineral, Nets, Neume, Patter, Peck, Perfect, Philosophical, Piceous, Pight, Pin, Plong(e), Plunge, Pop, Resin, Rock, Ruff(e), Sales, Scend,

Seel, Send, Shape, Sling, Slope, Soprarino, Spiel, Stoit, Tar, Tessitura, Tilt, Tone Tonemic, Tonus, Tremolo, Tune, Vibrato, Wicket, Wood
Pitchblende Cleveite
Pitcher(-shaped) Aryt(a)enoid, Ascidium, Bowler, Cruse, Ewer, Jug, Steen, Urceolus
Pitchfork Hurl, Toss
Pitfall Danger, Hazard, Trap
Pith(y) Ambatch, Aphorism, Apo(ph)thegm, Core, Down, Essence, Gnomic, Hat-plant, Heart, Marrow, Medulla, Moxa, Nucleus, Rag, Succinct, Terse
Pithead Broo, Brow, Minehead
Pithless Thowless
Pitiless Flint-hearted, Hard, Ruthless
Piton Rurp
Pitt Chatham
Pity, **Piteous**, **Pitiful** Ah, Alack, Alas, Commiseration, > COMPASSION, Mercy, Pathos, Rue, Ruth(ful), Seely, Shame, Sin, Sympathy
Pivot(al) Ax(i)le, Central, Focal, Fulcrum, Gooseneck, Gudgeon, Kingbolt, Revolve, Rotate, Slue, > SWIVEL, Trunnion, Turn, Wheel
Pixie Brownie, Elf, Fairy, Gremlin, Sprite
Pizza Calzone, Pepperoni
Placard Affiche, Bill, Playbill, Poster
Placate Appease, Conciliate, Pacify, Propitiate, Soothe
Place Ad loc, Aim, Allocate, Berth, Bro, Decimal, Deploy, Deposit, Fix, Habitat, Hither, Howf, Identify, Impose, > IN PLACE OF, Install, Job, Joint, Juxtapose, Lay, Lieu, Locality, Locate, Locus, Pitch, Plat, Plaza, Point, Posit, > POSITION, Put, Realm, Region, Resting, Scene, Second, Set, Site, Situate, Situation, Spot, Stead, Sted(e), Stedd(e), Stratify, Town, Vendome
Placid Cool, Easy, Easy-osy, Quiet, Tame, Tranquil
Plagiarise, **Plagiarist** Copy, Crib, Lift, Pirate, Steal
Plague (spot) Annoy, Bane, Bedevil, Black death, Boil, Bubonic, Burden, Cattle, Curse, Dog, Dun, Goodyear, Goujeers, Harry, Infestation, Locusts, Lues, Murrain, Murran, Murrin, Murrion, Pest, Pester, Pox, Press, Scourge, Tease, Token, Torture, Try, Vex
Plaid Maud, Roon, Shepherd's, Tartan, Wales
Plain(s) Abraham, Archimedes, Artless, Ascetic, Au naturel, Bald, Banat, Bare, Blatant, Broad, Campagna, Campo, Candid, Carse, Ceará, Chryse, Clavius, Clear, Cook, Dowdy, Downright, Dry, Esdraelon, Evident, Explicit, Flat, Flood, Girondist, Gran Chaco, Great, Homely, Homespun, Inornate, Kar(r)oo, Lande, Langrenus, Llano, Lombardy, Lowland, Maidan, Manifest, Marathon, Mare, Monochrome, Nullarbor, Obvious, Ocean of storms, Oceanus Procellarum, Olympia, > ORDINARY, Outspoken, Overt, Packstaff, Pampa(s), Paramo, Patent, Pikestaff, Playa, Polje, Prairie, Prose, Ptolemaeus, Purbach, Sabkha(h), Sabkha(t), Sailing, Salisbury, Savanna(h), Secco, Serengeti, Sharon, Simple, Sodom, Spoken, Staked, Steppe, Tableland, Thessaly, Tundra, Vega, Veldt, Visible, Walled
Plainsman Llanero
Plainsong Ambrosian, Chant
Plaint(ive) Complaint, Dirge, Lagrimoso, Lament, Melancholy, Sad, Whiny
Plaintiff Doe, Impeacher, Litigant, Suer
Plait Braid, Crimp, Cue, Frounce, Furbelow, Goffer, Intertwine, Pigtail, Plica, Plight, Queue, Ruche, Sennit, Sinnet, Splice
Plan(ned), **Planner**, **Planning** Aim, American, Angle, Architect, Arrange,

Axonometric, Blueprint, Brew, Budget, Care, Chart, Commission, Complot, Contingency, Contrive, Dalton, Dart, Deliberate, Delors, Design, Desyne, Device, Devise, Diagram, Draft, Drawing, Elevation, Engineer, European, Family, Five-Year, Floor, Format, Galveston, Game, Ground, Hang, Ichnography, Idea, Idee, Instal(l)ment, Intent, Lay(out), Leicester, Map, Marshall, Master, Mastermind, Mean, Outline, Pattern, Pipe-dream, Plat, Plot, Ploy, Policy, Premeditate, Prepense, Procedure, Programme, Project, Projet, Proposal, Protraction, Rapacki, Scenario, Schedule, Scheme, Schlieffen, Spec(ification), Stratagem, Strategy, Subterfuge, System, Tactician, Town, Wheeze

Plane Aero(dyne), Air, > **AIRCRAFT**, Airliner, Airship, Bandit, Block, Boeing, Bomber, Bus, Camel, Canard, Cartesian, Chenar, Chinar, Comet, Concorde, Crate, Dakota, Datum, Delta-wing, Even, Facet, Fault, Fillester, Fillister, Flat, Focal, Galactic, Glider, Gotha, Homaloid, Hurricane, Icosahedron, Icosohedra, Inclined, Jack, Jet, Jointer, Jumbo, Level, Main, MIG, Mirage, Mosquito, Moth, Octagon, Perspective, Platanus, Polygon, Pursuit, Rocket, Router, Shackleton, Shave, Smooth, Sole, Spitfire, Spokeshave, Spy, Stealth (bomber), STOL, Surface, Sycamore, Tail, Taube, Thrust, Tow, Trainer, Tree, Trident, Trying, Viscount

Plane figure Endecagon, Hendecagon

Planet(s), Planetary Alphonsine, Ariel, Asteroid, Body, Cabiri, Ceres, Chiron, Constellation, Earth, Eros, Extrasolar, Georgian, Giant, Hyleg, Inferior, Inner, Jovian, Jupiter, Major, Mars, Mercury, Minor, Moon, Neptune, Pluto, Primary, Psyche, Quartile, Red, Satellitium, Saturn, Sphere, Starry, Sun, Superior, Terrestrial, Uranus, Venus, Vista, Vulcan, World

Plangent Mournful

Plank Board, Chess, Deal, Duckboard, Garboard, Plonk, Sarking, Slab, Spirketting, Straik, Strake, Stringer, Weatherboard, Wood, Wrest

Plankton Neuston, Pelagic, Red tide, Seston, Spatfall

Plant(s), Plant part Acrogen, Annual, Anther, Bed, Biennial, Biota, CAM, Cotyledon, Cultigen, Cultivar, Dibble, Ecad, Embed, Endogen, Enrace, Epiphyte, Establish, Factory, Fix, Forb, Growth, G(u)ild, Halophyte, Herbarium, House, Insert, Instil, Inter, Labiate, Land, Lathe, Machinery, Ornamental, Phloem, Pilot, Power, Sensitive, Sere, Shrub, Simple, Sow, Succulent, Therophyte, Tree, Vegetal, Vegetation, Works

PLANTS

3 letters: Dal, Kex, Meu, Pia, Rue, Set, Til, Udo, Urd, Yam

4 letters: Alga, Aloe, Anil, Arum, Deme, Fern, Grex, Herb, Ixia, Kali, Loco, More, Nard, Ombu, Rhus, Sego, Sola, Sunn, Taro, Thea, Vine, Weld, Wort, Yarr

5 letters: Ajwan, Anise, Anona, Aroid, Benni, Blite, Boree, Buchu, Bucku, Bugle, Calla, Canna, Chufa, Clary, Clote, Cress, Fouat

Fouet
Gemma
Glaux
Gorse
Guaco
Hosta
Inula
Jalap
Kenaf
Kudzu
Lotus
Lurgi
Medic
Morel
Murva
Musci
Orpin
Orris
Oshac
Panax
Sedge
Sedum
Spink
Tetra
Timbo
Urena

6 letters:
Acacia
Acorus
Ajowan
Alisma
Alpine
Annona
Arnica
Bablah
Betony
Burnet
Cactus
Cassia
Catnep
Cnicus
Cosmea
Cosmos
Cowpea
Croton
Datura
Derris
Dodder
Exacum
Exogen
Fat hen

Gnetum
Hyssop
Iberis
Knawel
Madder
Mallow
Manioc
Medick
Mimosa
Moorva
Nerium
Nettle
Nuphar
Orchis
Orpine
Pachak
Protea
Rattle
Reseda
Retama
Rubber
Sesame
Silene
Smilax
Spider
Spurge
Spurry
Squill
Styrax
Teasel
Thrift
Tulipa
Tutsan
Yarrow
Zinnia

7 letters:
Alkanet
All-good
Allseed
Alyssum
Brinjal
Burdock
Caltrop
Cardoon
Carduus
Carline
Cat's ear
Chervil
Dasheen
Dioecia
Dittany

Dogbane
Ephedra
Felwort
Filaree
Fly-trap
Freesia
Frogbit
Gentian
Gerbera
Haemony
Henbane
Ipomoea
Isoetes
Lantana
Lucerne
Lychnis
Madwort
Mahonia
Manihot
Melilot
Mercury
Mullein
Nemesia
Nigella
Nonsuch
Opuntia
Palmiet
Pareira
Petunia
Puccoon
Ragwort
Rhodora
Ruellia
Saffron
Salfern
Salsola
Sampire
Sanicle
Scandix
Setwall
Skirret
Spignel
Spiraea
Spurrey
Stapela
Statice
Syringa
Tagetes
Thallus
Triffid
Tritoma
Vanilla

Vervain
Weigela
Zedoary

8 letters:
Acanthus
Agrimony
Angelica
Arenaria
Asphodel
Bindi-eye
Buckbean
Buplever
Camomile
Canaigre
Centaury
Costmary
Cyclamen
Diandria
Dielytra
Dogberry
Dumbcane
Feverfew
Fluellin
Foxglove
Fumitory
Geophyte
Gesnaria
Gnetales
Gromwell
Hag-taper
Henequen
Hepatica
Hibiscus
Larkspur
Lavender
Mandrake
Mariposa
Monstera
Oleander
Opopanax
Plumbago
Psilotum
Putchock
Ratsbane
Roly-poly
Samphire
Scammony
Sea-blite
Self-heal
Silphium
Sparaxis

Spergula
Stapelia
Staragen
Starwort
Tamarisk
Tritonia
Tuberose
Tuckahoe
Wait-a-bit
Wormseed

9 letters:
Adderwort
Andromeda
Arrowhead
Arrowroot
Artemisia
Artillery
Aubrietia
Bald-money
Brooklime
Broom-rape
Butterbur
Celandine
Colocasia
Coltsfoot
Cordaites
Coreopsis
Coriander
Dittander
Erythrina
Euphorbia
Eyebright
Fenugreek
Germander

Groundsel
Herb-paris
Hoarhound
Horehound
Horse-tail
Liver-wort
Lousewort
Mare's-tail
Moneywort
Moschatel
Ouviranda
Patchouli
Pearlwort
Penstemon
Pimpernel
Portulaca
Rafflesia
Rocambole
Santoline
Screwpine
Spearmint
Spearwort
Spikenard
Stone-crop
Sweet-gale
Tomatillo
Tormentil
Wake-robin
Wincopipe
Wolf's bane
Woundwort

10 letters:
Alexanders
Ampelopsis

Angiosperm
Aspidistra
Astralagus
Dyer's-broom
Earth-smoke
Five-finger
Fraxinella
Fritillary
Goat-sallow
Goat's-thorn
Goat-willow
Goldilocks
Icosandria
Immortelle
Maidenhair
Mignonette
Parkleaves
Pentstemon
Rest-harrow
Salicornia
Touch-me-not
Tropophyte
Yellowroot

11 letters:
Acidanthera
Bear's-breech
Bristle-fern
Callitriche
Convolvulus
Dusty-miller
Hurtleberry
Incarvillea
Loosestrife
Meadowsweet

Nancy-pretty
Pelargonium
Schizophyte
Sempervivum
Swiss cheese
Thallophyte
Thimbleweed
Tous-les-mois
Wintergreen

12 letters:
Adam's flannel
Epacridaceae
Midsummermen
Morning glory
Parsley-piert
Pasqueflower
Phytobenthos
Resurrection
Southernwood
Venus flytrap
Wandering jew
Water-soldier

13 letters:
Townhall clock
Traveller's joy

14 letters:
Chincherinchee
Lords and ladies
Shepherd's purse

Plantagenet Angevin, Broom
Plantain Mato(o)ke, Ribwort, Waybread
Plantation Arboretum, Bosket, Bosquet, Estate, Grove, Hacienda, Pen, Pinetum, Ranch, Tara, Vineyard
Plant disease Anthracnose, Bunt, Club-root, Curlytop, Frogeye, Psillid yellows, Rosette, Smut, Sooty mould
Planted In, Under
Planter Dibber, Farmer, Settler, Trowel
Plaque Calculus, Dental, Plateau, Scale
Plasma Dextran, Sigmond
Plaster(ed) Bandage, Blister, Blotto, Butterfly clip, Cake, Cataplasm, Clam, Clatch, Compo, Court, Daub, Diachylon, Diachylum, Drunk, Emplastrum, Fresco, Gesso, Grout, Gypsum, Intonaco, Leep, Lit, Mud, Mustard, Oiled, Parge(t), Porous, Poultice, Render, Roughcast, Scratch-coat, Screed, Secco, Shellac, Sinapism, Smalm, Smarm, Smear, Sowsed, Staff, Sticking, Stookie, Stucco, Teer

Plastic Bakelite®, Cel(luloid), Cling film, Ductile, Fablon®, Fictile, Fluon, Formica®, Ionomer, Laminate, Loid, Lucite®, Melamine, Perspex®, Plexiglass®, Pliant, Polyethylene, Polystyrene, Polythene, Polyvinyl, PVC, Reinforced, Styrene, Styrofoam®, Teflon®, Urea-formaldehyde, Vinyl, Wet-look, Yielding

▷ **Plastic** *may indicate* an anagram

Plastic surgeon McIndoe

Plastic surgery Neoplasty, Otoplasty, Rhinoplasty

Plate(s), **Plated**, **Platelet**, **Plating** Acierage, Ailette, Angle, Anode, Armadillo, Armour, Ashet, Baffle, Bakestone, Baleen, Batten, Brass, Butt, Chamfrain, Chape, Charger, Chrome, Coat, Coccolith, Communion, Copper, Cramper, Cribellum, Ctene, Dasypus, Deadman, Denture, Diaphragm, Disc, Dish, Echo, Electro, Electrotype, Elytron, Elytrum, Enamel, Entoplastron, Escutcheon, Face, Fashion, Fine, Fish, Flatware, Foil, Frog, Frons, Futtock, Glacis, Gold, Graal, Ground, Gula, Half, Home, Horseshoe, Hot, Illustration, L, Lame, Lamella, Lamina, Lanx, Latten, Licence, Mascle, Mazarine, Nail, Nef, Neural, Nickel, Notum, Number, Ortho, Osteoderm, Paten, Patina, Patine, Pauldron, Peba, Petri, Phototype, Planometer, Plaque, Plastron, Platter, Pleximeter, Poitrel, Prescutum, Print, Quarter, Race, Registration, Riza, Rove, Salamander, Scale, Screw, Scrim, Scutcheon, Scute, Scutum, Seg, Selling, Sheffield, Shield, Sieve, Silver, Slab, Soup, Spacer, Spoiler, Squama, Steel, Stencil, Stereo(type), Sternite, Strake, Surface, Swash, T, Tablet, Tace, Tasse(l), Tectonic, Tergite, Terne, Theoretical, Tin(ware), Torsel, Touch, Trade, Trencher, Trophy, Tsuba, Tuill(ett)e, Tymp, Urostegite, Vane, Vanity, Vassail, Vessail, Vessel, Wall, Water, Web, Wet, Whirtle, Whole, Wortle, Wrap(a)round, Zincograph

Plateau Altiplano, Deccan, Eifel, Field, Fjeld, Had(h)ramaut, Highland, Highveld, Horst, Kalahari, Kar(r)oo, La Mancha, Langres, Laurentian, Mat(t)o Grosso, Mesa Verde, Meseta, Nilgiris, Ozark, Paramo, Piedmont, Puna, Shan, Shillong, Tableland, The Kimberleys, Ustyurt

Platform Accommodation, Almemar, Bandstand, Barbette, Base, Bema, Bier, Catafalque, Catwalk, Crane, Crow's nest, Dais, Deck, Dolly, Drilling, Emplacement, Entablement, Estrade, Exedra, Exhedra, Flake, Footpace, Footplate, Foretop, Gangplank, Gantry, Gauntree, Gauntry, Gravity, Hustings, Kang, Landing stage, Machan, Oil, Pad, Paint-bridge, Pallet, Perron, Plank, Podium, Predella, Production, Programme, Pulpit, Raft, Rig, Rostrum, Round-top, Scaffold, Shoe, Skidway, Soapbox, Space, Sponson, > **STAGE**, Stand, Stereobate, Stoep, Stylobate, Tee, Terminal, Thrall, Ticket, Top, Traverser, Tribunal, Tribune, Turntable, Wharf

Platinum Pt, Ruthenium, Sperrylite

Platitude Bromide, Cliché, Truism

Platocephalus Flat-headed

Platonic, **Platonist** Academician, Ideal, Spiritual

Platoon Company, Squad, Team

Platter Dish, EP, Graal, Grail, Lanx, LP, Plate, Record, Salver, Trencher

Platypus Duckbill, Duck-mole, Water mole

Plausible, **Plausibility** Cogent, Credible, Fair, Glib, Oil, Probable, Proball, Sleek, Smooth, Specious

Play(ing) Accompany, Active, Amusement, Antic, Antigone, Brand, Bust, Candida, Caper, Charm, Chronicle, Clearance, Crucible, Curtain-raiser, Daff, Dandle, Docudrama, Drama, Echo, Endgame, Equus, Escapade, Everyman, Extended, Fair, Finesse, Foul, Frisk, Frolic, Fun, Gamble, Gambol, Game, Ghosts, Hamlet, Harp, Holiday, Inside, Interlude, Jam, Jape, Jest, Jeu, Kinderspiel, Kitchen-sink, Laik, Lake, Latitude, Lear, Leeway, Licence, Lilt,

Long, Loot, Macbeth, Mask, Masque, Match, Medal, Melodrama, Miracle, Monodrama, Morality, Mousetrap, Mummers, Mysteries, Nativity, Nurse, Oberammergau, One-acter, Orestaia, Othello, Parallel, Passion, Perform, Personate, Portray, Prank, Pretend, Recreation, Represent, Riff, Role, Rollick, Romp, Room, Rope, RUR, Satyr, Saw, Shadow, Shoot, Sketch, Sport, Stage, Straight, Strain, Strike up, Stroke, Strum, Tolerance, Tonguing, Toy, Tragedy, Tragicomedy, Trifle, Tweedle, Twiddle, Two-hander, Vamp, Vent, Whitechapel, Word

Play *may indicate* an anagram

Playback Echo, Repeat, Replay

Playboy Hedonist, Rake, Roué

Player(s) Actor, Athlete, Back, Black, Brass, Bugler, Busker, Cast, CD, Centre, Colt, Contestant, Defenceman, DVD, E, East, ENSA, Equity, Fiddle, Flanker, Fullback, Gary, Ghetto-blaster, Goalie, Half, Half-back, Half-forward, Harlequin, Hooker, Infielder, It, Juke-box, Kest, Linebacker, Lineman, Lion, Lock, Longstop, Lutanist, Lutenist, Man, Midfield, Mid-on, Mime, Musician, Musician(er), N, Nero, North, Ombre, Onside, Orpheus, Pagliacci, Participant, Pianola®, Pitcher, Pocket, Pone, Pro, Prop, Quarterback, Record, Rover, S, Scrape, Scratch, Scrum half, Seagull, Secondo, Seed, Shamateur, Shortstop, Side, South, Split end, Stand-off, Stand-off half, Stereo, Striker, Strings, Strolling, Super, Sweeper, Team, Thespian, Tight end, Troubador, Troupe, Upright, Utility, Virtuosi, W, Walkman®, West, White, Wing, Winger, Wingman

Playfair Code

Playfellow Actor, Chum, Companion

Playful Arch, Coy, Frisky, Humorous, Kittenish, Ludic, Merry, Piacevole, Scherzo, Skittish, Sportive

Playgirl Actress, Electra

Playgoer Groundling

Playground Close, Garden, Park, Rec(reational), Rectangle, Theatre, Tot lot, Yard

Playhouse Amphitheatre, Cinema, Theatre, Wendy

Playsuit Rompers

Playwright Aeschylus, Albee, Anouilh, Arden, Ayckbourn, Barrie, Barry, Beaumarchais, Beaumont, Beckett, Behan, Bellow, Bennett, Besier, Bolt, Brecht, Chekhov, Congreve, Corneille, Coward, Dekker, Delaney, > **DRAMATIST**, Dramaturge, Dramaturgist, Drinkwater, Dryden, Euripides, Feydeau, Fletcher, Frayn, Fry, Gems, Genet, Goldoni, Gorky, Harwood, Hay, Ibsen, Jonson, Marlowe, Massinger, Menander, Miller, Molière, Mortimer, O'Casey, Odets, O'Neill, Orton, Osborne, Pinero, Pinter, Pirandello, Priestley, Racine, Rattigan, Rostard, Scriptwriter, Shaw, Sheridan, Sherry, Simpson, Sophocles, Stoppard, Storey, Strindberg, Synge, Tate, Terence, Thespis, Travers, Vanbrugh, Webster, Wesker, Wilde

Plea Appeal, Claim, Defence, Entreaty, Excuse, Exoration, Non contendere, Orison, Placitum, Prayer, Rebuttal, Rebutter, Rogation, Suit

Plead(er) Answer, Argue, Beg, Entreat, > **IMPLORE**, Intercede, Litigate, Moot, Vakeel, Vakil

Please(d), Pleasant, Pleasing, Pleasure(-seeker) Aggrate, Agreeable, Alcina, Algolagnia, Amene, Amuse, Arride, Benign, Bitte, Braw, Cheerful, Chuffed, Comely, Comfort, Content, Cute, Delectation, Delice, Delight, Do, Euphonic, Fair, Felicitous, Fit, Flatter, Fun, Genial, Glad, Gladness, Gratify, Hedonism, Jammy, Joy, Kama, Kindly, Lepid, List, Oblige, Piacevole, Primrose path,

Prithee, Prythee, Queme, Satisfy, Suit, Tasty, Tickle, Tickle pink, Treat, Vanity, Voluptuary, Wally, Will, Winsome, Wrapped, Xanadu List

Pleasure-garden, **Pleasure-ground** Lung, Oasis, Park, Policy, Ranelagh, Tivoli

Pleat Accordion, Box, Crimp, Fold, French, Frill, Goffer, Gusset, Inverted, Kick, Knife, Plait, Pranck(e), Prank, Sunburst, Sunray

Pleb(eian) Common, Essex man, Homely, Laic, Ordinary, Roturier

Pledge Affidavit, Arles, Band, Betroth, Bond, Borrow, Bottomry, Dedicate, Deposit, Earnest(-penny), Engage, Fine, Gage, Guarantee, Hock, Hypothecate, Impignorate, Mortgage, Oath, Pass, Pawn, Pignerate, Pignorate, Plight, Promise, Propine, Sacrament, Security, Stake, Surety, Teetotal, Toast, Troth, Undertake, Vow, Wad, Wed

Pleiades Alcyone, Celaeno, Electra, Maia, Merope, Sterope, Taygete

Plenitude Stouth and routh

Plentiful, **Plenty** Abounding, Abundance, Abundant, Ample, Bags, Copious, Copy, Easy, Excess, Foison, Fouth, Ful(l)ness, Fushion, Galore, Goshen, Lashings, Lots, Oodles, Pleroma, Profusion, Quantity, Riches, Rife, Routh, Rowth, Scouth, Scowth, Slue, Sonce, Sonse, Umpteen

Plenum Spaceless

Pliable, **Pliant** Amenable, Flexible, Limber, Limp, Lithe, Malleable, Plastic, Sequacious, Supple, Swack, Swank

▶ **Pliers** *see* **PLY**

Plight Betrothal, Case, Misdight, Peril, Pickle, Pledge, State, Troth

Plimsoll(s) Dap, Gutty, Gym-shoe, Line, Mutton-dummies, Sandshoe, Tacky

Plinth Acroter, Base, Block, Socle, Stand, Zocco

Plod(der) Drudge, Ploughman, Traipse, Tramp, Trog, Trudge

Plonk Rotgut, Wine

Plop Cloop, Drop, Fall, Plap, Plump

Plot(s) Allotment, Babington, Bed, Brew, Carpet, Chart, Cliché, Connive, Conspiracy, Conspire, Covin, Covyne, Engineer, Erf, Erven, Frame-up, Graden, Graph, Gunpowder, Imbroglio, Intrigue, Locus, Lot, Machination, Map, Meal-tub, Odograph, Pack, Patch, Plan, Plat, Popish, Rye-house, Scenario, > **SCHEME**, Sect(ion), Seedbed, Shot, Site, Story, Taluk, Terf, Turf, Web

Plotter Artist, Cabal, Camarilla, Catesby, Conspirator, Engineer, Oates, Scheme

Plough(man), **Ploughed**, **Ploughing** Arable, Ard, Arval, Big Dipper, Breaker, Bull tongue, Chamfer, Charles's wain, Contour, Dipper, Disc, Drail, Drill, Ear, Earth-board, Ere, Fail, Fallow, Farmer, Feer, Flunk, Gadsman, Gang, Great bear, Harrow, Lister, Middlebreaker, Middlebuster, Mouldboard, Piers, Pip, Push, Rafter, Rib, Ridger, Rive, Rotary, Rove, Sand, Scooter, Septentrion(e)s, Sill, Sow, Stump-jump, Swing, Till(er), Trench, Triones, Wheel

Plough-cleaner Pattle, Pettle

Ploughshare Co(u)lter, Sock

Ploughwise Boustrophedon

Plover Bud, Lapwing, Pretincole, Prostitute, Stand, Tewit, Wing

Plowman Piers

Ploy Brinkmanship, Dodge, M(a)cGuffin, Manoeuvre, Stratagem, Strike, Tactic, Wile

Pluck(ing), **Plucky** Avulse, Bare, Carphology, Cock, Courage, Deplume, Epilate, Evulse, Floccillation, Gallus, Game, > **GRIT**, Guts, Loot, Mettle, Pick, Pinch, Pip, Pizzicato, Plectron, Plectrum, Ploat, Plot, Plunk, Pook(it), Pouk(it), Pull, Race, Scrappy, Snatch, Spin, Spirit, Spunk, Summon, Tug, Twang, Tweak, Tweeze, Yank

Plug Ad, Banana, Block, Bung, Caulk, Chew, Commercial, Dam, DIN, Dook,

Dossil, Dottle, Douk, Fipple, Fother, Gang, Glow, Go-devil, Hype, Jack, Lam, Operculum, Pessary, Phono, Prod, Promote, Publicity, Ram, Rawlplug®, Recommendation, Safety, Spark(ing), Spile, Spiling, Stop(per), Stopple, Strobili, Suppository, Tampion, Tap, Tent, Tompion, Vent, Wage, Wander, Wedge

Plum Bullace, Cherry, Choice, Damask, Damson, Gage, Greengage, Ground, Japanese, Kaki, Mammee-sapota, Marmalade, Maroon, Mirabelle, Mussel, Myrobalan, Naseberry, Persimmon, Proin(e), Pruin(e), Prune, Quetsch, Raisin, Sapodilla, Sebesten, Victoria

Plumage, **Plume** Aigrette, Crest, Eclipse, Egret, Feather, Hackle, Mantle, Panache, Preen, Ptilosis, Quill

Plumb(er) Bullet, Dredge, Fathom, Lead(sman), Perpendicular, Plummet, Sheer, Sound, Test, True, Vertical

Plumbago Graphite, Wad(d), Wadt

Plummet Dive, Drop, Lead, > **PLUNGE**

Plump(er) Bold, Bonnie, Bonny, Buxom, Choose, Chubbed, Chubby, Cubby, Dumpy, Embonpoint, Endomorph, Fat, Fleshy, Flop, Fubsy, Full, Lie, Matronly, Opt, Plank, Plonk, Plop, Podgy, Portly, Roll-about, Rolypoly, Rotund, Round, Rubenesque, Sonsie, Sonsy, Soss, Souse, Squab, Squat, Stout, Swap, Swop, Tidy, Well-fed

Plunder(er) Berob, Booty, Depredate, Despoil, Devastate, Escheat, Fleece, Forage, Freebooter, Gut, Harry, Haul, Herriment, Herryment, Hership, Loot, Maraud, Peel, Pill(age), Privateer, > **RANSACK**, Rape, Rapparee, Raven, Ravin, Ravine, Reave, Reif, Reive, Rieve, Rifle, Rob, Sack, Scoff, Shave, Skoff, Spoil(s), Spoliate, Sprechery, Spuilzie, Spuly(i)e, Spulzie, Swag

Plunge(r) Dasher, Demerge, Dive, Douse, Dowse, Duck, Enew, Immerge, Immerse, La(u)nch, Nose-dive, Plummet, Plump, Raker, Send, Sink, Souse, Swoop, Thrust

Plural Multiply, Pl

Plus Addition, And, Gain, More, Positive

Plush(ed) Die, Luxurious, Smart, Tint, Velour, Velvet

Pluto(crat), **Plutonic** Abyssal, Dis, Hades, Hypogene, Nob, Pipeline, Underground

Plutonium Pu

Ply, **Plier(s)** Bend, Birl, Cab, Exercise, Exert, Gondoliers, Importune, Layer, Practise, Run, Trade, Wield

Plying *may indicate* an anagram

PM Addington, Afternoon, Arvo, Asquith, Attlee, Autopsy, Bute, Cabinet-maker, Chatham, De Valera, Disraeli, Gladstone, Major, Melbourne, Peel, Pitt, Portland, Premier, > **PRIME MINISTER**, Salisbury, Taoiseach

Pneumonia Visna

Poach Cook, Encroach, Filch, Lag, Steal, Trespass

Pochard Duck, Scaup

Pocket Air, Appropriate, Bag, Bin, Cavity, Cly, Cup, Enclave, Fob, Glom, Hideaway, Hip, Jenny, Misappropriate, Patch, Placket, Plaid-neuk, Pot, Pouch, Purloin, Purse, Sac, Sky, Slash, Sling, Slit, Steal, Take, Watch

Pod(s) Babul, Bean, Belly, Carob, Chilli, Dividivi, Engine, Gumbo, Lablab, Lomentum, Neb-neb, Okra, Pipi, Pregnant, Siliqua, Tamarind, Vanilla

Podgy Roly-poly

Poem(s), **Poetry** Acmeism, Acrostic, Aeneid, Alcaic, Anthology, Awdl, Ballad(e), Beowulf, Bestiary, Byliny, Caccia, Canzone, Cargoes, Cento, Choliamb, Choriamb, Cicada, Cinquain, Complaint, Concrete, Decastich, Dit(t),

Dithyramb, Divan, Dizain, Doggerel, Duan, Dunciad, Eclogue, Elegy, Elene, Epic(ede), Epigram, Epilogue, Epithalamium, Epode, Epopee, Epopoeia, Epos, Epyllion, Erotic, Fifteener, Finlandia, Gauchesco, Georgic, Ghazal, Graveyard, Haikai, Haiku, Heptastich, Heroic, Hexastich, Hokku, Hull, Hypermeter, Idyll, If, Iliad, Imagism, Jazz, Lay, Limerick, Logaoedic, London, Mahabharata(m), Mahabharatum, Melic, Metaphysical, Metre, Mock-heroic, Monostich, Nostos, Ode, Palinode, Paracrostic, Parnassus, Pastoral, Penill(ion), Pentastich, Poesy, Prelude, Prose, Prothalamion, Punk, Purana, Qasida, Quatorzain, Quatrain, Quire, Ramayama, Rat-rhyme, Renga, Rhapsody, Rig-Veda, Rime, Rondeau, Rondel, Rubai(yat), Rune, Scazon (iambus), Senryu, Sestina, Sijo, Sirvente, Song, Sonnet, Spondee, Stanza, Stornello, Symphonic, Tanka, Telestich, Temora, Tercet, Tetrastich, Title, Tone, Triolet, Tristich, Verse, Versicle, Villanelle, Voluspa, Voluspe, Waka
Poet(s) Bard(ling), Cavalier, Cumberland, Cyclic, Elegist, Georgian, Iambist, Imagist, Lake, Laureate, Layman, Lyrist, Maker, Meistersinger, Metaphysical, Metrist, Minnesinger, Minstrel, Mistral, Monodist, Odist, Parnassian, Performance, PL, Pleiade, Poetaster, Rhymer, Rhymester, Rhymist, Rymer, Scald, Scop, Skald, Smart, Sonneteer, Spasmodic, Thespis, Tragic, Trench, Troubadour, Trouvère, Trouveur, Vers librist(e), Water

POETS

2 letters:
AE

3 letters:
Gay
Poe

4 letters:
Abse
Blok
Cory
Dyer
Gray
Gunn
Hogg
Hood
Hugo
Hunt
Lang
Omar
Ovid
Owen
Pope
Rowe
Rumi
Tate
Vega

5 letters:
Arion
Auden
Blair
Blake
Burns
Byron
Cadou
Carew
Cinna
Clare
Dante
Donne
Eliot
Frost
Gower
Griot
Heine
Hesse
Homer
Horne
Hulme
Iqbal
Keats
Keyes
Lewis
Logue
Lorca
Lucan
Makar
Marot
Meyer

Moore
Nashe
Noyes
Plath
Pound
Prior
Rilke
Rishi
Sachs
Tasso
Theon
Yeats
Young

6 letters:
Arnold
Austin
Barham
Barnes
Belloc
Brecht
Brooke
Butler
Clough
Cowper
Crabbe
Dowson
Dryden
Dunbar
Ennius

George
Glycon
Goethe
Graves
Hesiod
Horace
Hughes
Landor
Larkin
Lawman
Lowell
Milton
Morris
Motion
Ossian
Pindar
Racine
Sappho
Seaman
Shanks
Sidney
Tagore
Thomas
Villon
Virgil
Waller

7 letters:
Addison
Alcaeus

Aretino
Ariosto
Beddoes
Belleau
Bridges
Caedmon
Campion
Chapman
Chaucer
Collins
Corinna
Cynwulf
Emerson
Flaccus
Flecker
Heredia
Herrick
Hopkins
Housman
Juvenal
Layamon
Martial
Marvell
Montale
Newbolt
Orpheus
Pushkin
Ronsard
Russell
Sassoon
Service

Shelley
Sitwell
Skelton
Sotades
Southey
Spender
Spenser
Statius
Terence
Thomson
Vaughan
Whitman

8 letters:
Anacreon
Betjeman
Brentano
Browning
Campbell
Catullus
Cummings
Cynewulf
Davenant
Day Lewis
De la Mare
Hamilton
Kynewulf
Laforgue
Langland
Leopardi
Lovelace

Macaulay
Mallarmé
Menander
Petrarch
Rossetti
Schiller
Shadwell
Stephens
Suckling
Taliesin
Tennyson
Thompson
Traherne
Tyrtaeus
Verlaine
Whittier

9 letters:
Aeschylus
Bunthorne
Coleridge
Euripides
Goldsmith
Lamartine
Lucretius
Marinetti
Masefield
Quasimodo
Shenstone
Simonides
Sophocles

Stevenson
Swinburne

10 letters:
Baudelaire
Chatterton
Drinkwater
Fitzgerald
Longfellow
Propertius
Tannhauser
Theocritus
Wordsworth

11 letters:
Apollinaire
Archilochus
Asclepiades
Maeterlinck
Pherecrates

12 letters:
Archilochian
Aristophanes

14 letters:
Dante Alighieri

15 letters:
Ettrick Shepherd

Poetaster Della-Cruscan
Poetess Ingelow, Orinda
Poet laureate Motion, PL
Poetry *see* POEM
Poignant Acute, Biting, Haunting, Keen, Pungent, Stirring, Touching
Point(ed), Pointer, Points Accumulation, Ace, Acerose, Acro-, Aculeate, Aim, Ainode, Antinode, Antler, Apex, Aphelion, Apogee, Appui, Apse, Apsis, Bar, Barb, Barrow, Bisque, Boiling, Break(ing), Brownie, Calk, Cape, Cardinal, Cash, Centre, Choke, Clou, Clue, Colon, Comma, Compass, Compensation, Cone, Conic, Corner, Cover, Crisis, Critical, Crux, Culmination, Cultrate, Curie, Cursor, Cusp, Cuss, Cutting, Decimal, Degree, Detail, Dew, Diamond, Direct, Dot, Dry, E, Ear, End, Entry, Epanodos, Epee, Equant, Equinoctial, Eutectic, Exclamation, Fang, Fastigiate, Feature, Fesse, Fielder, Firing, Fitch(e), Five, Fixed, Flash, Focal, Focus, Foreland, Fourteen, Freezing, Fulcrum, Gallinas, Game, Germane, Gist, Gnomon, Gold, Hastate, Head, High, Hinge, Hint, Home-thrust, Ideal, Index, Indicate, Indicator, Intercept, Ippon, Isoelectric, Jester, Keblah, Kiblah, Kip(p), Knub, Lace, Lagrangian, Lance, Lead, Limit, Lizard, Locate, Locus, Low, Mandelbrot set, Mark, Match, Melting, Metacentre, Microdot, Moot, Mucro, N, Nail, Nasion, Near, Neb, Needle, Neel, Ness, Nib, Nocking, Node, Nodus, Nombril, Now, Nub, Obelion, Obelisk, Objective,

Opinion, Ord, Particle, Peak, Pedal, Penalty, Perigee, Perihelion, Perilune, Pin, Pinch, Pinnacle, Place, Power, Pressure, Promontory, Prong, Prow, Punctilio, Punctual, Punctum, Purpose, Radix, Rallying, Ras, Reef, Respect, Rhumb, Rhumbline, S, Sample, Saturation, Scribe, Seg(h)ol, Set, Shaft, Sheva, Show, Shy, Silly, Socket, Sore, Spearhead, Spicate, Spick, Spike, Spinode, Spinulose, Stage, Stagnation, Starting, Stationary, Steam, Sticking, Stigme, Stiletto, Sting, Stipule, Strong, Sum, Suspension, Synapse, Tacnode, Talking, Taper, Tax, Technicality, Tine, > **TIP**, Tongue, Train, Transition, Trig, Trigger, Triple, Turning, Urde(e), Urdy, Use, Vane, Vanishing, Vantage, Verge, Verse, Vertex, Vowel, Voxel, W, Weak, Yad, Yield, Yuko

Pointless Blunt, Curtana, Flat, Futile, Inane, Inutile, Muticous, Otiose, Stupid, Vain

Point of honour Pundonor

Poise Aplomb, Balance, Composure, P, Serenity

Poison(er), Poisoning, Poisonous Abron, Aconite, Acrolein, Adamsite, Aflatoxin, Aldrin, Amanita, Antiar, Apocynum, Aqua-tofana, Arsenic, Aspic, Atropia, Atropin(e), Bane, Barbasco, Belladonna, Boletus, Borgia, Botulism, Brom(in)ism, Brucine, Bufotalin, Cacodyl, Cadaverine, Calabar-bean, Cannabin, Cicuta, Colchicine, Coniine, Contact, Cowbane, Coyotillo, Curare, Curari, Cyanide, Cyanuret, Datura, Daturine, Deadly nightshade, Digitalin, Dioxin, Dumbcane, Durban, Echidnine, Embolism, Emetin(e), Envenom, Ergotise, Fluorosis, Flybane, Flypaper, Food, Formaldehyde, Gelsemin(in)e, Gila, Gossypol, Hebenon, Hebona, Hemlock, Henbane, Hydragyrism, Hydrastine, Hyoscyamine, Iodism, Lead, Lewisite, Limberneck, Lindane, Lobeline, Locoweed, Malevolent, Manchineal, Mandragora, Mephitic, Mezereon, Miasma, Mineral, Monkshood, Muscarine, Mycotoxin, Nerve gas, Neurine, Neurotoxin, Neutron, Nicotine, Noogoora burr, Noxious, Obeism, Ouabain, Ourali, Ourari, Paraquat®, Paris green, Phallin, Phalloidin, Phosphorism, Picrotoxin, Pilocarpine, Plumbism, Ptomaine, Py(a)emia, Raphania, Ratsbane, Rot, Safrole, Salicylism, Samnitis, Santonin, Sapraemia, Sarin, Sassy wood, Saturnism, Saxitoxin, Septic(aemia), Solanine, Solpuga, Soman, Stibine, Stibium, Stonefish, Strophanthus, Strychnine, Sugar of lead, Surinam, Systemic, Tanghin, Tanghinin, Tetro(do)toxin, Thebaine, Thorn-apple, Timbo, Toxaphene, Toxic, Toxicology, Toxicosis, Toxin, Toxoid, Trembles, Tropine, Tutu, Upas, Urali, Uroshiol, Venefic, Venin, Venom(ous), Veratridine, Veratrin(e), Viperous, Virose, Virous, Virulent, Wabain, Warfarin, Wolfsbane, Woorali, Woorara, Wourali, Yohimbine

Poke, Poky Bonnet, Broddle, Chook, Garget, Itchweed, Jab, Jook, Meddle, Mock, Nousle, Nudge, Nuzzle, Ombu, Peg, Pick, Pote, Pouch, Powter, > **PRISON**, > **PROD**, Prog, Proke, Punch, Root(le), Rout, Rowt, Sporan, Stab, Thrust

Poker (work) Bugbear, Curate, Draw, Game, High-low, Mistigris, Penny ante, Pyrography, Red-hot, Salamander, Strip, Stud(-horse), Tickler, Tine

Poland PL, Sarmatia

Polar, Pole(s), Poler Anode, Antarctic, Arctic, Boom, Bowsprit, Bum(p)kin, Caber, Celestial, Copernicus, Cowl-staff, Cracovian, Crossbar, Extremity, Fishgig, Fizgy, Flagstaff, Flagstick, Galactic, Gas, Geomagnetic, Janker, Kent, Liberty, Lug, Magnetic, Mast, May, N, Nadir, Negative, Nib, North, Periscian, Po, Polack, Positive, Punt, Quant, Quarterstaff, Racovian, Range, Ricker, Ripeck, Rood, Ry(e)peck, S, Shaft, Slav, South, Spar, Sprit, Staff, Stang, Starosta, Stilt, Sting, Stobie, Telegraph, Terrestrial, Thyrsos, Thyrsus, Topmast, Totem, Vegetal, Zenith

▷ **Polar** *may indicate* with a pole

Polaris Rhodanic, Rocket, Star

Polecat Ferret, Fitch, Fitchet, Foulmart, Foumart, Weasel

Polemic(al) Argument, Controversy, Debate, Eristic(al)

Police(man), Policewoman Babylon, Bear, Beast, Bizzy, Black and Tans, Blue, Bluebottle, Bobby, Bog(e)y, Bull, Busy, Carabinero, Carabiniere, Catchpole, Centenier, Cheka, Chekist, CID, Constable, Cop(per), Cotwal, Crusher, Detective, Dibble, Druzhinnik, Europol, Filth, Flatfoot, Flattie, Flic, Flying Squad, Force, Fuzz, Garda, Gendarme, Gestapo, Gill, G-man, Guard, Gumshoe, Harmanbeck, Heat, Hermandad, Inspector, Interpol, Jamadar, Jemadar, John Hop, Keystone, Kitchen, Kotwal, Limb, Mata-mata, Met(ropolitan), Military, Morse, Mountie, MP, Mulligan, Nabman, Nark, Ochrana, Officer, OGPU, Ovra, Patrolman, PC, Peeler, Peon, Pig, Polis, Polizei, Porn squad, Posse (comitatus), Prefect, Provincial, Puppy-walker, Ranger, Redbreast, Redcap, Regulate, RIC, Riot, Robert, Rosser, Rozzer, RUC, Sbirro, SC, Secret, Securitate, Securocrat, Sepoy, Shamus, Sleeping, Slop, Smokey, Sowar(ry), Special, Stasi, State trooper, Super, Sureté, Sweeney, Texas Rangers, T(h)anadar, The Bill, The Law, Thirdborough, Thought, Trap, Vice squad, Vigilante, Walloper, Wolly, Woodentop, Zabtieh, Zaptiah, Zaptieh, Zomo

Police car Black Maria, Panda, Patrol, Prowl

Police station Copshop, Lock-up, Tana, Tanna(h), Thana(h), Thanna(h), Watchhouse

Policy Assurance, Ballon d'essai, CAP, Comprehensive, Course, Demesne, Endowment, Expedience, Floating, Good neighbour, Insurance, Knock for knock, Laisser-faire, Lend-lease, Line, Method, Open(-sky), Plank, Platform, Pork-barrel, Practice, Programme, Reaganism, Revanchism, Scorched earth, Stop-go, Tack, Tactics, Ticket, Traditional, Valued

Polish(ed), Polisher Beeswax, Black, Blacklead, Bob, Bruter, Buff, Bull, Burnish, Chamois, Complaisant, Edit, Elaborate, Elegant, Emery, Enamel, Finish, French, Furbish, Gentlemanly, Glass, Gloss, Heelball, Hone, Inland, Lap, Lustre, Nail, Perfect, Planish, Polite, Pumice, Refinement, Refurbish, Rottenstone, Rub, Sand, Sandblast, Sandpaper, Sejm, Sheen, Shellac, Shine, Slick, Slickenside, Supercalender, Tutty, Urbane, Veneer, Wax

Polite Civil, Courteous, Genteel, Grandisonian, Mannered, Suave, Urbane, Well-bred

Politic(al), Politics Apparat, Body, Chartism, Civic, Diplomacy, Discreet, Expedient, Falange, Fascism, Gesture, Leftism, Party, Poujadism, Power, Practical, Public, Radicalism, Rightism, State, Statecraft, Tactful, Wise

Politician(s) Bright, Carpet-bagger, Catiline, Chesterfield, Congressman, Demagogue, Demo(crat), Diehard, Disraeli, Eden, Evita, Green, Incumbent, Independent, Ins, Isolationist, Laski, Left, Legislator, Liberal, Log-roller, MEP, Minister, Moderate, MP, Parliamentarian, Parnell, Politico, Polly, Puppet, Rad, Rep, Senator, Socialist, Statesman, Statist, Tadpole, Taper, TD, Tory, Trotsky, Unionist, Veep, Warhorse, Whig, Wilberforce

Poll(ing) Ballot, Bean, Canvass, Count, Cut, Deed, Dod, Election, Exit, Gallup, Head, Humlie, Hummel, Lory, MORI, Nestor, Not(t), Opinion, Parrot, Pineapple, Pow, Push, Scrutiny, Straw, Votes

▷ **Poll** *may indicate* a first letter

Pollack Fish, Lob, Lythe

Pollard Doddered

Pollen, Pollinate(d), Pollination Anemophilous, Beebread, Dust, Errhine, Farina, Fertilised, My(i)ophily, Witch-meal, Xenia

Pollenbrush Scopa

Pollex Thumb
Pollster Psephologist
Pollute(d), Pollutant, Pollution Adulterate, Contaminate, Defile, Dirty, File, Foul, Impure, Infect, Miasma, Noise, Nox, Oil slick, Rainout, Soil, Soilure, Stain, Sully, Taint, Violate, Waldsterben
Polly Flinders, Parrot, Peachum
Polo Chukka, Marco, Mint, Navigator
Polonium Po
Poltergeist Apport, Ghost, Spirit, Trouble-house
Poltroon Coward, Craven, Dastard, Scald, Scaramouch
Polyandry Nair
Polygraph Lie-detector
Polymath Knowall, Toynbee
Polymer Elastomer, Isotactic, Lignin, Oligomer, Resin, Silicone, Tetramer, Trimer
Polymorphic Multiform, Proteus, Variform
Polynesian Moriori, Tahitian, Tongan
Polyp(s) Alcyonaria, Hydra, Hydranth, Nematophore, Obelia, Sea-anemone, Tumour
Polyphony Counterpoint
Polystyrene Expanded
Polyzoan Sea-mat
Pom Choom
Pomander Pounce(t)-box
Pomegranate Punica, Punic apple
Pommel Beat, Knob, Pound, Pummel
Pomp(ous) Big, Bombastic, Budge, Ceremonial, Display, Dogberry, Euphuistic, Fustian, Grandiloquent, Grandiose, Heavy, Highfalutin(g), High-flown, High-muck-a-muck, High-sounding, Hogen-mogen, Inflated, Orotund, Ostentatious, Pageantry, Parade, Pretentious, Solemn, Splendour, Starchy, State, Stilted, Stuffy, Turgid
Pom-pom Ball, Tassel
Ponce Pander, Solicit, Souteneur
Poncho Ruana
Pond(s) Dew, Dub, Hampstead, Lakelet, Lentic, Mill, Pool, Pound, Puddle, Settling, Slough, Stank, Stew, Tank, Turlough, Vivarium, Viver
Ponder(ous) Brood, Cogitate, Contemplate, Deliberate, Heavy, Laboured, Mull, Muse, Perpend, Poise, Pore, Reflect, Ruminate, > **THINK**, Vise, Volve, Weight(y), Wonder
Poniard Bodkin, > **DAGGER**, Dirk, Stiletto
Pontiff, Pontifical, Pontificate Aaron, Aaronic, Antipope, Dogmatise, Papal
Pontoon Blackjack, Bridge, Caisson, Chess, Game, Twenty one, Vingt-et-un
Pony Canuck, Cayuse, Cow, Dales, Dartmoor, Eriskay, Exmoor, Fell, Garran, Garron, Gen(n)et, GG, Griffin, Griffon, Gryfon, Gryphon, Jennet, Jerusalem, Mustang, New Forest, One-trick, Pit, Polo, Pownie, Sable Island, Shanks', Sheltie, Shetland, Show, Tangun, Tat(too), Timor, Welsh, Welsh mountain, Western Isles
Poodle Barbet, Swan
Pooh Bah, Bear, Pugh, Winnie, Yah
Pool Backwater, Bank, Bethesda, Billabong, Birthing, Bogey hole, Cenote, Cess, Collect, Combine, Dub, Dump, Flash, Flow, Gene, Jackpot, Jacuzzi®, Kitty, Lido, Lin(n), Meer, Mere, Mickery, Mikvah, Mikveh, Millpond, Moon, Natatorium,

Piscina, Piscine, Plash, Plesh, Plunge, > **POND**, Reserve, Share, Siloam, Snooker, Spa, Stank, Sump, Tank, Tarn, Water(ing) hole, Wave

Poor(ly) Bad, Bare, Base, Bijwoner, Breadline, Buckeen, Bywoner, Catchpenny, Cheapo, Churchmouse, Conch, Cronk, Destitute, Gritty, Hard-up, Have-nots, Hopeless, Humble, Hungry, Ill(-off), Impecunious, Indigent, Lazarus, Lean, Low, Low-downer, Meagre, Mean, Needy, Obolary, Pauper, Peaky, Poxy, Roinish, Rop(e)y, Roynish, Sad, Scrub, Shabby, Shitty, Sober, Sorry, Sub, Thin, Third-rate, Trashy, Undeserving, Unwell, Wattle, Wishy-washy

Poor *may indicate* an anagram

Poorhouse Union, Workhouse

Pooter Nobody, Nonentity

Pop (off), **Popper**, **Popping** Bang, Brit, Burst, Cloop, Crease, Die, Father, Fr, Gingerbeer, Hip-hop, Hock, Insert, Lumber, Mineral, Nip, Pater, Pawn, Pledge, Population, Press-stud, Punk, Sherbet, Soda, Splutter, Weasel

Pop *may indicate* an anagram

Pope(s) Adrian, Alexander, Atticus, Benedict, Black, Boniface, Clement, Dunciad, Eminence, Fish, Great Schism, Gregory, Hildebrand, Holiness, Innocent, Joan, Leo, Papa, Pius, Pontiff, Ruff(e), Schism, Sixtius, Theocrat, Tiara, Urban, Vatican, Vicar of Christ

Pop-gun Bourtree-gun

Popinjay Barbermonger, Coxcomb, Dandy, Fop, Macaroni, Prig, Skipjack

Poplar Abele, Aspen, Balsam, Cottonwood, Lombardy, Trembling, White

Poppet Valve

Poppy Argemone, Bloodroot, Blue, California, Chicalote, Coquelicot, Corn, Diacodin, Eschscholtzia, Field, Flanders, Horned, Iceland, Matilija, Mawseed, Opium, Papaver, Plume, Ponceau, Prickly, Puccoon, Rhoeadales, Shirley, Tall, Welsh

Poppycock Bosh, Nonsense, Rubbish

Popular(ity) Common, Cult, Demotic, Enchorial, General, Grass roots, Heyday, Hit, In, Laic, Lay, Mass, Plebeian, Prevalent, Public, Successful, Tipped, Trendy, Vogue

Population, **Populace** Catchment, Census, Demography, Inhabitants, Malthusian, Mass, Mob, > **PEOPLE**, Public, Universe

Porcelain Arita, Artificial, Bamboo, Belleek®, Blanc-de-chine, Celadon, Chelsea, China, Coalport, Crackle(ware), Crown Derby, Dresden, Eggshell, Famille, Famille jaune, Famille noir, Famille rose, Famille verte, Goss, Hard-paste, Hizen, Imari, Jasper, Jasper(ware), Limoges, Lithophane, Meissen, Minton, Parian, Sèvres, Softpaste, Spode, Sung

Porch Galilee, Lanai, Stoa, Stoep, Veranda(h)

Porcupine Hedgehog, Urson

Pore Browse, Hole, Hydrathode, Lenticel, Muse, Ostium, Outlet, Ponder, Stoma, Study

Porgy Braise, Scup(paug)

Pork Bacon, Boar, Brawn, Chap, Crackling, Flitch, Griskin, Ham, Pancetta, Salt, Scrapple, Scruncheon, Scrunchion, Spare-rib, Tenderloin

Porn(ography), **Pornographic** Curiosa, Erotica, Hard, Hard-core, Jazz mag, Rhyparography, Soft, Soft-core

Porous Cellular, Permeable, Pumice, Sponge

Porpoise Bucker, Dolphin, Mereswine, Pellach, Pellack, Pellock, Phocaena, Sea pig, Sea swine

Porridge Berry, Bird, Brochan, Brose, Burgoo, Busera, Crowdie, Drammach, Drammock, Gaol, Grits, Grouts, Gruel, Hominy, Kasha, Mabela, Mahewu,

Mealie pap, Oaten, Oatmeal, Parritch, Pease-brose, Polenta, Pottage, Praiseach, Sadza, Samp, Sentence, Skilly, Stirabout, Stretch, Sup(p)awn, Time, Ugali

Porridge stick Thible, Thivel

Port(s) Beeswing, Carry, Cinque, Container (terminal), Entrepot, Free, Gate, Geropiga, > **HARBOUR**, Haven, Hithe, Hythe, Induction, Larboard, Left, Manner, Mien, Parallel, Tawny, Treaty, Wine

PORTS

3 letters:
Abo
Ayr
Gao
Hué
Rio
Rye

4 letters:
Acre
Aden
Akko
Amoy
Apia
Baku
Bari
Boma
Cobh
Cork
Deal
Dill
Elat
Faro
Gary
Hilo
Hull
Icel
I-pin
Kiel
Kobe
Kure
Lima
Linz
Naha
Oban
Omsk
Oran
Oslo
Oulu
Perm
Pori
Pula

Puri
Ruse
Safi
Said
Sfax
Suez
Susa
Suva
Tema
Tyre
Vigo
Wick
Wuhu

5 letters:
Akaba
Anzio
Aqaba
Arhus
Arica
Aulis
Bahia
Barry
Basra
Batum
Belem
Bharu
Blyth
Brest
Cadiz
Cairo
Canea
Colon
Dakar
Davao
Derry
Dilli
Dover
Duala
Dubai
Eilat
Elath

Emden
Gabes
Galle
Gavie
Genoa
Ghent
Gijon
Goole
Haifa
Hania
Izmir
Jaffa
Jambi
Jedda
Jidda
Kerch
Kochi
Larne
Leith
Lulea
Mainz
Malmo
Masan
Merca
Miami
Mocha
Mokpu
Narva
Newry
Omaha
Osaka
Ostia
Palos
Ponce
Poole
Pusan
Pylos
Rabat
Rouen
Saida
Sakai
Salto

Selby
Sidon
Skien
Split
Surat
Susah
Tampa
Tanga
Tunis
Turku
Vaasa
Varna
Visby
Vlore
Volos
Yalta
Yeisk
Yeysk
Yibin

6 letters:
Aarhus
Abadan
Agadir
Albany
Alborg
Ancona
Andong
Annaba
Balbao
Bastia
Batumi
Bergen
Bilbao
Blanca
Bombay
Bootle
Boston
Bremen
Burgas
Cairns
Calais

Callao
Candia
Cannes
Canton
Cavite
Chania
Cochin
Cuiaba
Cuyaba
Da Nang
Danzig
Darwin
Dieppe
Djambo
Douala
Dunbar
Dundee
Durban
Durres
Elblag
Galata
Galati
Gdansk
Gdynia
Harbin
Havana
Hobart
Ichang
Iloilo
Inchon
Jaffna
Jarrow
Juneau
Kalmar
Kisumu
Lepaya
Lobito
Lubeck
Mackay
Madras
Malaga
Manaos
Manaus
Manila
Matadi
Menado
Mersin
Mobile
Mumbai
Muscat
Namibe
Nantes

Napier
Naples
Narvik
Nassau
Nelson
Ningbo
Ningpo
Nizhni
Odense
Odessa
Oporto
Ostend
Padang
Patras
Peoria
Pesaro
Quincy
Rabaul
Ragusa
Recife
Rijeka
Rimini
Rostov
Samara
Samsun
Santos
Sasebo
Savona
Skikda
Smyrna
Sousse
Speyer
St John
St Malo
St Paul
Suakin
Sydney
Tacoma
Timaru
Tobruk
Toulon
Tromso
Tyumen
Velsen
Venice
Vyborg
Weihai
Whitby
Wismar
Wonsan
Yantai

7 letters:
Aalborg
Abidjan
Ajaccio
Almeria
Antalya
Antibes
Antwerp
Aracaju
Astoria
Augusta
Averiro
Bayonne
Berbera
Bristol
Buffalo
Calabar
Cam Ranh
Canopus
Catania
Changde
Chilung
Cologne
Colombo
Conakry
Corinth
Corunna
Cotonou
Dunedin
Dunkirk
El Minya
Ephesus
Esbjerg
Foochow
Funchal
Geelong
Grimsby
Halifax
Hamburg
Harwich
Heysham
Hodeida
Horsens
Houston
Incheon
Iquique
Iquitos
Kaolack
Karachi
Kavalta
Kherson
Kinsale

Kolding
Kowloon
Kuching
La Plata
Latakia
Legaspi
Le Havre
Lepanto
Livorno
Lorient
Makurdi
Marsala
Massaua
Massawa
Maulman
Memphis
Messina
Milazzo
Mombasa
Moulman
Munster
Nanning
Neusatz
Newport
Niigata
Niteroi
Novi Sad
Oakland
Okayama
Onitsha
Otranto
Pahsien
Palermo
Pelotas
Phocaea
Piraeus
Qingdao
Randers
Rangoon
Rapallo
Rosario
Rostock
Runcorn
Salerno
Sao Luis
Seattle
Sekondi
Setubal
Seville
Shantou
Shantow
Sinuiji

Stettin
St John's
St Louis
Sukhumi
Swansea
Tampico
Tangier
Taranto
Trabzon
Trapani
Trieste
Tripoli
Ushuaia
Wanxian
Wenchow
Wenzhou
Whyalla
Yakutsk
Yichang

8 letters:
Aberdeen
Acapulco
Alicante
Arbroath
Auckland
Badalona
Barletta
Batangas
Benghazi
Benguela
Bordeaux
Boulogne
Brindisi
Brisbane
Caesaria
Cagliari
Calcutta
Changsha
Cheribou
Chimbote
Chingtao
Chongjun
Cuxhaven
Drogheda
Dunleary
El Ferrol
Elsinore
Falmouth
Flushing
Freetown
Gisborne

Gonaives
Goteborg
Greenock
Haiphong
Hakodate
Hamilton
Hangzhou
Harfleur
Hartford
Hastings
Helsinki
Holyhead
Honolulu
Iraklion
Istanbul
Jayapura
Jinjiang
Kanazawa
Kawasaki
Keflavik
Kingston
Klaipeda
La Coruna
La Guaira
La Guyara
La Spezia
Les Cayes
Limassol
Mariupol
Matanzas
Mayaguez
Monrovia
Montreal
Murmansk
Mytilene
Nagasaki
Nan-ching
Newhaven
Nha Trang
Novgorod
Nykøbing
Pago Pago
Paramibo
Pavlodar
Paysandu
Penzance
Pevensey
Plymouth
Pnom Penh
Pozzuoli
Qui Nhong
Ramsgate

Salvador
Samarang
Sandakan
San Diego
Sandwich
Santarem
Savannah
Schiedam
Semarang
Shanghai
Sorrento
Stockton
Syracuse
Szczecin
Taganrog
Takoradi
Tarshish
Tauranga
Teresina
Tjirebon
Tsingtao
Valdivia
Valencia
Veracruz
Victoria
Wanganui
Weymouth
Yarmouth
Yokohama
Yokosuka
Zaanstad

9 letters:
Anchorage
Angostura
Annapolis
Antserana
Archangel
Baltimore
Barcelona
Bhavnagar
Carnarvon
Cartagena
Cherbourg
Chisimaio
Cleveland
Constanta
Dartmouth
Den Helder
Dordrecht
Dubrovnik
Ellesmere

Esperance
Europoort
Famagusta
Fishguard
Fleetwood
Flensburg
Fortaleza
Fremantle
Gallipoli
Gateshead
Gravesend
Guataquil
Hangchoio
Helsinger
Hiroshima
Immingham
Inhambane
Jasselton
Kagoshima
Kirkcaldy
Kozhikode
Kronstadt
Las Palmas
Lowestoft
Magdeburg
Mahajanga
Mangalore
Maracaibo
Mariehamn
Marseille
Matamoros
Matsuyama
Melbourne
Milwaukee
Morecambe
Newcastle
Nuku'alofa
Palembang
Phnom Penh
Pontianak
Port Louis
Port Sudan
Rotterdam
Santa Cruz
Santander
Schleswig
Sheerness
Singapore
Stavanger
St George's
St Nazaire
Stornoway

Stralsund
Stranraer
Takamatsu
Taomasina
Tarragona
Trebizond
Trondheim
Tynemouth
Volgograd
Weihaiwei
Whangerei
Zamboanga
Zeebrugge

10 letters:
Alexandria
Belize City
Birkenhead
Bratislava
Bridgeport
Bridgetown
Caernarvon
Casablanca
Charleston
Cheboksary
Chittagong
Cienfuegos
Copenhagen
Corrientes
East London
Felixstowe
Folkestone
Fray Bentos
Georgetown
Gothenburg
Hammerfest
Hartlepool
Herakleion

Joao Pessoa
Karlskrona
Khabarovsk
Khota Bharu
Kitakyushu
La Rochelle
Launceston
Los Angelos
Louisville
Matozinhos
Montevideo
Mostaganem
New Bedford
New Orleans
Norrkoping
Paramaribo
Pittsburgh
Pontevedra
Port Gentil
Portobello
Portsmouth
Port Talbot
Providence
Queenstown
Sacramento
Santa Marta
Sebastopol
Sevastopol
Sunderland
Talcahuano
Thunder Bay
Townsville
Valparaiso
Willemsted

11 letters:
Baranquilla
Bremerhaven

Cheng-chiang
Dares Salaam
Grangemouth
Helsingborg
Hermonpolis
Kaliningrad
Makhachkala
New Plymouth
Newport News
Nuevo Laredo
Pointe-Noire
Porto Alegre
Punta Arenas
Rockhampton
San Fernando
Scarborough
Shimonoseki
Southampton
Telukketong
Trincomalee
Vlaardingen
Vladivostok

12 letters:
Angtofagasta
Bandjarmasin
Bandjermasin
Barranquilla
Buenaventura
Chandemagore
Ciudad Bolwar
Dun Laoghaire
Jacksonville
Kota Kinabalu
Kristiansand
Milford Haven
Philadelphia
Pointe-a-Pitre

Ponta Delgada
Port Adelaide
Port Harcourt
Prince Rupert
Rio de Janeiro
San Francisco
San Sebastian
Santo Domingo
South Shields
St Petersburg
Tanjungpriok
Thessaloniki
Ujung Pandang
Usti nad Labem

13 letters:
Charlottetown
Corpus Christi
Florianopolis
Great Yarmouth
Ho Chi Minh City
Port Elizabeth
Tandjungpriok
Trois Rivieres
Wilhelmshaven

14 letters:
Mina Hassen Tani
Santiago de Cuba

15 letters:
Alexandroupolis
Sault Saint Marie

16 letters:
Reggio di Calibria

Portable Lapheld, Laptop, Palmtop
Portend, Portent(ous) Augur, Awesome, Bode, Dire, Omen, Phenomenon, Presage, > WARN(ING)
Porter Ale, Bearer, Bellboy, Bellhop, Bummaree, Caddie, Caddy, Cole, Concierge, Coolie, Door-keeper, Doorman, Dvornik, Entire, Hamaul, Ham(m)al, Humper, Janitor, October, Ostiary, Red-cap, Stout
Portfolio Holding
Portico Colonnade, Decastyle, Distyle, Dodecastyle, Exedra, Loggia, Narthex, Parvis(e), Porch, Propylaeum, Prostyle, Stoa, Veranda(h), Xystus
Portion Aliquot, Ann(at), Bit, Deal, Distribute, Dole, Dose, Dotation, Fraction, Fragment, Helping, Heritage, Hunk, Instalment, Jointure, Lot, Measure, Mess, Modicum, Nutlet, Ounce, > PART, Piece, Ratio, Scantle, Scantling, Section, Segment, Serving, Share, Size, Slice, Something, Spoonful, Tait, Taste, Tate,

Tittle, Tranche, Wodge

Portland Bill, Cement, Stone

Portly Ample, Corpulent, Gaucie, Gaucy, Gawcy, Gawsy, Stout

Portmanteau Bag, Combination, Holdall, Valise

Portrait(ist) Carte de visite, Depiction, Drawing, Eikon, Icon, Identikit, Ikon, Image, Kit-cat, Lely, Likeness, Painting, Retraitt, Retrate, Sketch, Vignette

Portray(al) Caricature, Depict, Describe, Feature, Image, Limn, Paint, Render, Represent, > SHOW

Portsmouth Pompey

Portugal, **Portuguese** Lusitania(n), Luso-, Macanese, Senhor

Pose(r), **Poseur** Aesthete, Affect(ation), Arabesque, Asana, Ask, Contrapposto, Drape, Lotus, Mannequin, Man(n)ikin, Masquerade, Model, Place, Plastique, Posture, Pretend, Problem, Propound, Pseud, Sit, Stance, Sticker, Tickler

Poseidon Earthshaker

Posh Classy, Grand, Lah-di-dah, Ornate, Ritzy, Swanky, Swish, U

Position Asana, Attitude, Bearing(s), Close, Codille, Delta, Emplacement, Enfilade, False, Fixure, F(o)etal, Foothold, Fowler's, Grade, Instal, Lay, Lie, Location, Locus, Lodg(e)ment, Lotus, Missionary, Mudra, Office, Open, Pass, Peak, Place, Plant, Point, Pole, Post, Put, Recumbent, Root, Seat, Set(ting), Sextile, Sims, Site, Situ, Situs, Stance, Standing, Standpoint, Station, Status, Strategic, Syzygy, Tagmeme, Thesis, Tierce, Trendelenburg's, Viewpoint

Positive, **Positivist** Absolute, Anode, Assertive, Categorical, > CERTAIN, Comte, Definite, Emphatic, False, Plus, Print, Sure, Thetic, Upbeat, Yang, Yes

Posse Band, Mob, Vigilantes

Possess(ed), **Possession(s)**, **Possessive** Adverse, Apostrophe, Asset, Aver, Bedevil, Belonging(s), Demonic, Driven, Energumen, Estate, Have, Haveour, Haviour, Heirloom, His, Hogging, Know, Lares (et) penates, Mad, Obsessed, Occupation, > OWN, Sasine, Seisin, Sprechery, Substance, Tenancy, Usucap(t)ion, Vacant, Worth

Possible, **Possibility**, **Possibly** Able, Contingency, Feasible, Likely, Maybe, Mayhap, Off-chance, Peradventure, Perchance, Perhaps, Posse, Potential, Prospect, Resort, Viable, Will

▷ **Possibly** *may indicate* an anagram

Possum Burramys, Cataplexy, Opossum, Ringtail, Sugar glider, Sugar squirrel, Tait

Post(s), **Postage** Affix, After, Assign, Bitt, Bollard, Carrick bitt, Command, Correspondence, Dak, Dawk, Delivery, Dragon's teeth, Emily, Excess, Finger, First, Flagpole, Graded, Gradient, Guardhose, Hitching, Hurter, Jamb, Joggle, King, Last, Listening, Log, Mail, Mast, Newel, Observation, Outstation, Pale, Paling, Parcel, Pendant, Penny, Picket, Pile, Piling, Piquet, Placard, Place, Plant, Plum, Pole, Position, Presidio, Puncheon, Pylon, Queen, Quintain, Quoin, Registered, Remit, Residency, RM, Seat, Send, Snubbing, Spile, Staff, Staging, Stake, Starting, Station, Stell, Stoop, Stoup, Studdle, Term(inal), Tom, Tool, Trading, Upright, Vacancy, Waymark, Winning

Postcard(s) Deltiology

Poster Advertisement, Affiche, Bill, Broadsheet, Placard, Playbill, Sender

Posterior Behind, Bottom, Jacksie, Jacksy, Later, Lumbar, Pygal, Rear, Tail

Post-free Franco

Postman, **Postmaster**, **Postwoman** Carrier, Courier, Emily, Hill, Messenger, Nasby, Pat, Portionist, Sorter

Postmark Frank

Post mortem Autopsy, Enquiry, Necropsy

Postpone(ment) Adjourn, Contango, Defer, Delay, Frist, Hold over, Long-finger, Moratorium, Mothball, Pigeon-hole, Postdate, Prorogue, Reprieve, Respite, Shelve, Stay, Suspend, Withhold

Postulant Candidate, Noumenon, Novice

Postulate Assert, Assume, Claim, Propound

Posture(r), **Posturing** Affectation, Asana, Attitude, Birkie, Camp, Carriage, Decubitus, Deportment, Mudra, Pose, Pretence, Site, Stance, Vorlage

Posy Bouquet, Buttonhole, Corsage, Nosegay, Tussiemussie, Tuzzi-muzzy

Pot(s), **Potting**, **Potty** Abridge, Aludel, Bankroll, Basil, Belly, Cafetière, Cannabis, Casserole, Ca(u)ldron, Ceramic, Chamber, Chanty, Chatti, Chatty, Chimney, Cocotte, Crewe, Crock(ery), Crucible, Cruse(t), Cupel, Delf(t), Dixie, Ewer, Flesh, Gage, Gallipot, Ganja, Gazunder, Grass, Hash(ish), Helmet, Hemp, In off, Inurn, Jardinière, Jordan, Kettle, Kitty, Livery, Lobster, Lota(h), Maiolica, Majolica, Marijuana, Marmite, Melting, Ming, Olla, Olpe, Pan, Papper, Pat, Pint, Pipkin, Planter, Po, Pocket, Poot, Posnet, > **POTTERY**, Pounce, Pout, Prize, Quart, Samovar, Shoot, Skeet, Skillet, Steamer, Stomach, Tajine, Tea, Test, Throw, Togine, Trivet, Tureen, Urn, Vial, Ware, Wash, Wok

Potash Kalinite, Polverine, Sylvine, Sylvite

Potassium K, Kalium, Pearl ash, Saleratus, Saltpetre

Potation Dram, Drink

Potato(es) Batata, Chat, Couch, Datura, Duchesse, Early, Fluke, Hashbrowns, Hog, Hole, Hot, Irish, Jersey, Kidney, Kumara, Lyonnaise, Mash, Murphy, Parmentier, Peel-and-eat, Pratie, Praty, Roesti, Rumbledethump(s), Seed, Solanum, Stovies, Sweet, Tatie, Tattie, Teddy, Tuber, Ware, White, Yam

Pot-bearer Trivet

Pot-bellied Kedge, Kedgy, Kidge, Paunchy, Portly, Stout

Potboiler Hob

Pot-boy Basil, Ganymede, Scullion

Potent(ate) Dynamic, Emeer, Emir, Emperor, Huzoor, Influential, Kinglet, Mogul, Nawab, Panjandrum, Powerful, Ras, Ruler, Satrap, Squirearch, Sultan

Potential(ly) Action, Capacity, Electric, Electrode, In posse, Ionization, Making(s), Manqué, Possible, Promise, Resting, Scope, Viable

> **Potentially** *may indicate* an anagram

Pothole(r) Giant's kettle, Spelunker

Pot-house Shebeen, Tavern

Potion Dose, Draught, Drink, Dwale, Love, Mixture, Philtre, Tincture

Pot-pourri Hotchpotch, Medley, Pasticcio, Salmi

Potsherd Ostracon, Ostrakon

Pottage Berry

Potter Cue, Dabbity, Dabble, Dacker, Daidle, Daiker, Dibble, Dilly-dally, Dodder, Etruscan, Fettle, Fiddle, Footer, Footle, Fouter, Gamesmanship, Harry, Idle, Mess, Minton, Muck, Niggle, One-upmanship, Plouter, Plowter, Spode, Thrower, Tiddle, Tink(er), Troke, Truck, Wedgewood, Wedgwood

> **Potter** *may indicate* a snooker-player

Pottery Agatewear, Bank, Basalt, Bisque, Celadon, Ceramet, Ceramic, China, Creamware, Crock, Crouch-ware, Dabbity, Delf(t), Earthenware, Encaustic, Etruria, Faience, Flatback, Gombroon, Granitewear, Hollowware, Jomon, Lustreware, Maiolica, Majolica, Ming, Pebbleware, Raku, Red-figured, Satsuma, Scroddled, Sgraffito, Slab, Slipware, Smalto, Spode, Spongeware, Stoneware, Studio, Sung, Terra sigillata, Ware, Wedgwood®, Wemyss, Whieldon

Pouch(ed) Bag, Brood, Bum-bag, Bursa, Caecum, Cheek, Cisterna, Codpiece,

Diverticulum, Fanny pack, Gill, Jockstrap, Marsupial, Poke, Purse, Sac, Scrip, Scrotum, Spleuchan, Sporran, Tobacco

Poultice Application, Cataplasm, Embrocation, Epithem(a), Lenient, Plaster

Poultry Dorking, Fowl, Gallinaceous, Poot, Pout, Welsummer

Poultry disease Keel, Scaly-leg, Vent gleet

Pounce Claw, Jump, Lunge, Powder, Sere, Souse, Sprinkle, Swoop, Talon

Pound(er) Ache, As, Bar, Bash, Batter, Beat, Bombard, Bradbury, Bray, Broadpiece, Bruise, Catty, Contund, Coop, Drub, Embale, Enclosure, Ezra, Fold, Green, Hammer, Hatter, Imagist, Intern, Iron man, Jail, Kiddle, Kidel, Kin, Knevell, L, Lam, Lb, Lock, Mash, Nevel, Nicker, Oncer, One-er, Oner, Pale, Pen, Penfold, Pestle, Pin, Pindar, Pinfold, Powder, Pulverise, Pun, Quid, Quop, Rint, Smacker, Sov(ereign), Squid, Stamp, Strum, Tenderise, Thump, Tower, Weight

Pour Be mother, Birl(e), Bucket, Cascade, Circumfuse, Decant, Diffuse, Flood, Flow, Jaw, Jirble, Libate, Rain, Seil, Shed, Sile, Skink, Spew, Stream, Teem, Turn, Vent, Weep, Well

Pout Bib, Blain, Brassy, Eel, Fish, Horn(ed), Mope, Mou(e), Scowl, Sulk, Tout, Towt, Whiting

Poverty Beggary, Dearth, Deprivation, Illth, Indigence, > LACK, Locust years, Need, Penury, Poortith, Puirtith, Squalor, Want

Powder(ed), Powdery Alumina, Amberite, Araroba, Baking, Ballistite, Boracic, Calamine, Chalk, Cosmetic, Crocus, Culm, Curry, Custard, Cuttlefish, Dentifrice, Dover's, Dust, Dusting, Explosive, Face, Floury, Fulminating, Giant, Glaucous, Goa, Gregory, Grind, Gun, Hair, Kohl, Levigate, Lithia, Litmus, Lupulin, Meal, Mould-facing, Moust, Mu(i)st, Pemoline, Percussion, Persian, Plate, Pollen, Pounce, Priming, Prismatic, Projecting, Pruinose, Pulver, Pulvil, Putty, Rachel, Rochelle, Rottenstone, Rouge, Saleratus, Seidlitz, Seme(e), Sherbet, Silver iodide, Sitosterol, Smeddum, Smokeless, Snuff, Spode, Spodium, Talc(um), Thimerosal, Toner, Tooth, Triturate, Tutty, Washing, Zein

Power(ful), Powers Ability, Able, Aeon, Aggrandisement, Almighty, Amandla, Arm, Attorney, Autarchy, Authority, Axis, Big, Chakra, Cham, Charisma, Clairvoyance, Clout, Cogency, Command, Corridor, Cube, Danger, Despotic, Diadem, Dioptre, Dominion, Effective, Eminence, Eminence grise, Empathy, Empery, Energy, Eon, Exponent, Facility, Faculty, Fire, Flower, Force, Force majeure, Geothermal, Grey, Hefty, Hegemony, High, Hildebrandic, Horse, Hot, Hp, Hydroelectric, Imperium, Influence, Kami, Kilowatt, Log, Logarithm, Lusty, Mana, Mastery, Megalomania, Might, Mogul, Motive, Motor, Movers and shakers, Muscle, Nature, Nth, Nuclear, Od-force, Omnificent, Omnipotent, Option, P, Panjandrum, People, Pester, Plenipotency, Posse, Potency, Prepollence, Prepotent, Puissant, Punch, Regime, Resolving, Siddhi, Sinew, Solar, Soup, Stamina, Staying, Steam, Stiff, Stopping, Strength, > STRONG, Supercharge, Supreme, Suzerain, Teeth, Telling, Throne, Tidal, Tycoon, Tyrone, Valency, Vertu(e), Vigour, Vis, Volt, Vroom, Water, Watt, Wattage, Wave, Weight, Wind, World

Powerless Diriment, Downa-do, Freewheel, Hamstrung, Helpless, Impotent, Impuissant, Incapable, Unable, Unarmed, Weak

Powwow Confab, Conference, Council, Meeting

Pox Orf, Pize

Practical, Practicable Active, Brass tacks, Doable, Easy-care, Hard-boiled, Joker, No-nonsense, Nuts and bolts, On, Pragmatic, Realist(ic), Realpolitik, Rule of thumb, Sensible, Shrewd, Useful, Utilitarian, Viable, Virtual

Practice, Practise, Practitioner, Practised Abuse, Adept, Custom, Distributed, Do, Drill, Enure, Exercise, General, Group, Habit, Inure, Ism, Keep, Knock-up,

Massed, Meme, Nets, Operate, Order, Ply, Policy, Praxis, Private, Prosecution, Pursuit, Rehearsal, Rehearse, Restrictive, Rite, Rut, Sadhana, Sharp, Target, Teaching, Test-run, Trade, Tradition, Train, Trial, Ure, Usage, Use

Pragmatic, Pragmatist Ad hoc, Busy, Dogmatic, Humanist, Meddling, Officious, Realist

Prairie IL, Illinois, Llano, Plain, Savanna, Steppe, Tundra, Veldt

Prairie dog Whippoorwill, Wishtonwish

Praise(worthy) Acclaim, Adulation, Alleluia, Allow, Anthem, Applause, Belaud, Bless, Blurb, Bouquet, Butter, Carol, Citation, CL, Commend(ation), Compliment, Dulia, Encomium, Envy, Eulogise, Eulogium, Eulogy, Exalt, Extol, Gloria, Glory, Hero-worship, Herry, Hery(e), Hosanna, Hymn, Hype, Incense, Kudos, Laud, Lip service, Lo(o)s, Meritorious, Panegyric, Puff(ery), Rap, Roose, Tribute

Pram Carriage, Cart, Scow

Prance Brank, Canary, Caper, Cavort, Galumph, Gambol, Jaunce, Jaunse, Prank(le), Swagger, Tittup, Trounce

Prang Accident, Crash, Smash, Whale

Prank(s) Attrap, Bedeck, Bedizen, Caper, Dido, Escapade, Fredaine, Frolic, Gaud, Jape, Lark, Mischief, Rag, Reak, Reik, Rex, Rig, Spoof, Trick, Vagary

Praseodymium Pr

Prat Bottom, > **STUPID PERSON**

Prate Babble, Boast, Haver, Talk

Prattle Babble, Blat(her), Chatter, Gab(nash), Gas, Gibber, Gossip, Gup, Lalage, Patter, Smatter, Yap

Prawn Banana, Dublin Bay, Scampi, School, Shrimp

Pray(ing) Appeal, Beg, Beseech, Daven, > **ENTREAT**, Impetrate, Intone, Invoke, Kneel, Mantis, Solicit, Wrestle

Prayer (book), Prayers Acoemeti, Act, Amidah, Angelus, Ardas, Ave (Maria), Bead, Beadswoman, Bede, Bene, Bidding, Breviary, Collect, Common, Confiteor, Cry, Cursus, Daven, Deus det, Devotion, Eleison, Embolism, Entreaty, Epiclesis, Euchologion, Evensong, Geullah, Grace, Hail Mary, Hallan-shaker, Imam, Intercession, Invocation, Kaddish, Khotbah, Khotbeh, Khutbah, Kol Nidre, Kyrie, Kyrie eleison, Lauds, Litany, Lord's, Lychnapsia, Ma(c)hzor, Mantis, Mat(t)ins, Mincha(h), Missal, Musaf, Novena, Orant, Orarium, Orison, Our Father, Paternoster, Patter, Petition, Phylactery, Placebo, Plea, Proseucha, Proseuche, Puja, Requiem, Requiescat, Rogation, Rosary, Salat, Secret, Shema, Siddur, State, Stations of the Cross, Suffrage, Te igitur, Tenebrae, Triduum, Venite, Yajur-Veda, Yizkov

Prayer *may indicate* one who begs

Preach(er) Ainger, Boanerges, Devil-dodger, Dominican, Donne, Ecclesiastes, Evangelist, Exhort, Gospeller, Graham, Holy Roller, Itinerant, Knox, Lecture, Mar-text, Minister, Moody, > **MORALISE**, Patercove, Pontificate, Postillate, Predicant, Predicate, Predikant, Priest, Prophet, Pulpiteer, Rant, Spintext, Spurgeon, Teach

Preamble Introduction, Preface, Proem, Prologue

Precarious Dangerous, Parlous, Perilous, Risky, Touch and go, Trickle, Uncertain, Unsteady

Precaution Care, Fail-safe, Guard, In case, Prophylaxis, Safeguard

Precede(nce), Precedent Antedate, Example, Forego, Forerun, Head, Herald, Pas, Predate, Preface, Priority, Protocol

Precept Adage, Canon, Commandment, Maxim, Motto, Saw

Precession Larmor

Precinct(s) Ambit, Area, Banlieue, Close, Courtyard, District, Environs, Pedestrian, Peribolos, Region, Shopping, Temenos, Verge, Vihara

Precious Adored, Chary, Chichi, Costly, Dear, Dearbought, Ewe-lamb, La-di-da, Murr(h)a, Owre, Precise, Rare, Valuable

Precipice Bluff, Cliff, Crag, Krans, Kran(t)z, Sheer

Precipitate, Precipitation, Precipitous Abrupt, Accelerate, Cause, Deposit, Hailstone, Headlong, Impetuous, Launch, Lees, Pellmell, Pitchfork, Rash, Sca(u)r, Sheer, Shoot, Sleet, Snowflake, Start, > **STEEP**, White

Precis Abstract, Aperçu, Epitome, Résumé, Summary

Precise(ly), Precisian, Precision Absolute, Accurate, Dry, Exact, Explicit, Fine-drawn, Literal, Minute, Nice(ty), Particular, Perfect, Plumb, Point-device, Prig, Prim, Punctilious, Spang, Specific, Starchy, Stringent, Succinct, Surgical, Tight, Very

Preclude Bar, Debar, Estop, Foreclose, Hinder, Impede, Prevent

Precocious Advanced, Bratpack, Forward, Premature

Preconception Ideating

Precursor Avant-courier, Forerunner, Harbinger

Predator(y) Carnivore, Eagle, Fox, Glede, Harpy-eagle, Jackal, Kestrel, Kite, Lycosa, Marauder, Predacious, Puma, Tanrec, Tarantula, Tenrec

Pre-dawn Antelucan, Ante lucem

Predecessor Ancestor, Forebear, Foregoer

Predestined Doomed, Fated, Tramway

Predicament Box, Dilemma, Embarrassment, Embroglio, Hobble, Hole, Jam, Pass, Peril, Pickle, Plight, Quandary, Scrape, Spot

Predict(ion), Predictable, Predictor Augur, Belomancy, Bet, Damn, Divination, Forecast, Foreordain, Foresay, Foreshadow, Foreshow, Forespeak, Foretell, Forsay, Horoscope, Nap, Necromancy, Portend, Presage, Previse, Prognosis, Prophecy, Prophesy, Regular, Second-guess, Soothsayer

Predilection Fancy, Liking, Prejudice, Taste, Tendency

Predisposition Aptitude, Inclination, Parti-pris, Tendency

Predominate Abound, Govern, Overshadow, Prevail, Reign

Pre-eminence, Pre-eminent Arch, Foremost, Palm, Paramount, Primacy, Supreme, Topnotch, Unique

Pre-empt Enter

Preen Perk, Primp, Prink, Prune

Prefab(ricated) Quonset

Preface Foreword, Herald, Intro, Preamble, Precede, Proem, Prolegomenon, Usher

Prefect Pr(a)eposter, Prepositor

Prefer(ence), Preferred Advance, Choose, Discriminate, Elect, Faard, Faurd, Favour, Imperial, Incline, Lean, Liquidity, Predilect(ion), Prefard, Priority, Proclivity, Promote, Sooner, Stocks, Taste, Will

Prefix Eka, Introduce, Name

Pregnancy, Pregnant Big, Clucky, Cyesis, Ectopic, Enceinte, Fertile, Gestation, Gravid(a), Great, Heavy, Knocked-up, Phantom, Pseudocyesis, Pudding-club, Stomack, With child

Prehistoric Ancient, Azilian, Beakerfolk, Brontosaurus, Cambrian, Clovis, Cro-magnon, Eocene, Folsom, Mound Builder, Ogygian, Primeval, Primitive, Pteranodon, Pterodactyl(e), Pterosaur, Saurian, Sinanthropus, Stonehenge, Titanosaurus, Trilith(on)

Prejudice(d) Bias, Bigotry, Derry, Discrimination, Down, Illiberal, Impede, Injure, Insular, Intolerance, Partiality, Parti pris, Preoccupy, Prepossession,

Racism

Prelate Archiepiscopal, Cardinal, Churchman, Exarch, Monsignor, Odo, Priest

Preliminary Draft, Exploration, Heat, Initial, Introductory, Precursory, Previous, Prodrome, Prolusion, Rough, Title-sheet

Prelude Entree, Forerunner, Intrada, Overture, Proem(ial), Ritornell(e), Ritornello

Premature Early, Precocious, Pre(e)mie, Premy, Previous, Slink, Untimely, Untimeous

Premedication Atropia

Premeditate Anticipate, Foresee, Plan

Premier Chief, Leader, Main, PM, > **PRIME MINISTER**, Tojo

Premise(s) Assumption, Datum, Epicheirema, Ground, Hypothesis, Inference, Lemma, Postulate, Property, Proposition, Reason

Premium Ap, Bond, Bonus, Discount, Grassum, Pm, Reward, Scarce, Share

Premonition Hunch, Omen, Presentiment, Prodromal, Warning

Preoccupation, **Preoccupied**, **Preoccupy** Absorb, Abstracted, Distrait, Engross, Hang-up, Intent, Obsess, Thing

Prepaid Pro-forma, Sae

Prepare(d), **Preparation** Address, A la, Arrange, Attire, Boun, Bowne, Busk, Calver, Cock, Concoct, Cooper, Countdown, Decoct, Did, Do, Dress, Edit, Forearm, Game, Groom, Ground, Inspan, Key, Lay, Legwork, Lotion, Measure, Mobilise, Parasceve, Prime, Procinct, Prothesis, Provide, Psych, > **READY**, Rehearsal, Ripe, Rustle up, Set, Spadework, Stand-to, Suborn, Train, Truss, Warm-up, Whip up, Yare

> **Prepare(d)** *may indicate* an anagram

Preponderance, **Preponderant**, **Preponderate** Important, Majority, Outweigh, Paramount, Prevalence, Sway

Preposition Premise

Prepossessing, **Prepossession** Attractive, Fetching, Predilection, Winsome

Preposterous Absurd, Chimeric, Foolish, Grotesque, Unreasonable

> **Preposterous** *may indicate* a word reversed

Pre-Raphaelite Rossetti, Waterhouse

Prerequisite Condition, Essential, Necessity, Sine qua non

Prerogative Faculty, Franchise, Liberty, Privilege, Right

Presage Abode, Foresight, Omen, Portend, Presentiment, Prophesy

Presbyter(ian) Berean, Blue, Cameronian, Covenanter, Elder, Knox, Macmillanite, Moderator, Sacrarium, Whig(gamore)

Prescient Clairvoyant, Fly

Prescribe Appoint, Assign, Dictate, Enjoin, Impose, Ordain, Rule, Set

Prescription Cipher, Decree, Direction, Formula, Medicine, R, Rec, Receipt, Ritual, Specific

Presence Aspect, Bearing, Closeness, Company, Debut, Hereness, Real, Shechinah, Shekinah, Spirit

Present(ation), **Presented**, **Presenter**, **Presently** Ad sum, Anchorman, Anon, Assists, Autocutie, Award, Bestow, Bonsela, Boon, Bounty, Box, Breech, By, Cadeau, Congiary, Coram, Current, Debut, Dee-jay, Deodate, DJ, Donate, Dotal, Douceur, Dower, Emcee, Endew, Endow, Endue, Enow, Etrenne, Existent, Fairing, Feature, Front-man, Gie, > **GIFT**, Give, Going, Grant, Gratuity, Hand, Here, Hodiernal, Inst, Introduce, Largess(e), Linkman, MC, Mod, Nonce, Now, Nuzzer, On hand, Porrect, Potlach, Pr, Prevailing, Produce, Proffer, Pro-tem, Put, Render, Show, Slice, Tip, Today, Vee-jay, Xenium, Yeven

Preserve(d), **Preservative**, **Preserver** Bottle, Burnettize, Can, Chill, Confect,

Confiture, Corn, Creosote, Cure, Dehydrate, Dry, Eisel, Embalm, Fixative, Formaldehyde, Formalin, Freeze, Guard, Hain, Hesperides, Jam, Jerk, Keep, Kinin, Kipper, Konfyt, Kyanise, Life, > **MAINTAIN**, Marmalade, Mummify, Pectin, Peculiar, Piccalilli, Pickle, Pot, Powellise, Salt, Salve, Saut, Souse, Store, Stratify, Stuff, Tanalith, Tanalized, Tar, Tin, Vinegar, Waterglass

Preside(nt) Abe, Adams, Banda, Carter, Chair, Childers, Cleveland, Coolidge, Coty, Dean, De Gaulle, Director, Eisenhower, Ford, Garfield, Grant, Harding, Harrison, Hoover, Ike, Johnson, Kennedy, Kruger, Lead, Lincoln, Madison, Moderator, Nixon, Old Hickory, P, Peron, Polk, Pompidou, Pr(a)eses, Prexy, Roosevelt, Sa(a)dat, Speaker, Superintendent, Supervisor, Taft, Tito, Truman, Tyler, Veep, Washington, Wilson

Press(ed), Pressing, Pressure Acute, Aldine, Armoire, Atmospheric, Bar, Bench, Blackmail, Blood, Bramah, Button, Cabinet, Chivvy, Clarendon, Closet, Clothes, Coerce, Cram, Crease, Crimp, Critical, Crowd, Crush, Cupboard, Cylinder, Dragoon, Drill, Dun, Durable, Duress, Duresse, Enforcement, Enslaye, Exigent, Filter, Fluid, Fly, Force, Fourth estate, Goad, Greenmail, Gutter, Hasten, Head, Heat, Herd, Hie, Hug, Hustle, Hydraulic, Impact, Important, Importune, Inarm, Iron, Isobar, Jam, Jostle, Knead, Leverage, Lie, Lobby, Mangle, Megabar, Microbar, Mill, Minerva, Newspapers, Obligate, Onus, Osmotic, PA, Partial, Pascal, Peer, Permanent, Persist, Piezo-, Ply, Prease, Printing, Private, Psi, Pump, > **PUSH**, Racket, Ram, Ratpack, Record, Recruit, Reporter, Ridge, Roll, Rotary, Rounce, Rush, Samizdat, Screw, Scrooge, Scrouge, Scrowdge, Scrum, Serr(e), Sit, Speed, Spur, Squash, Squeeze, Stop, Strain(t), Straint, Stress, Tension, Thlipsis, Threap, Threep, Throng, Throttle, Thrutch, Torr, Tourniquet, Turgor, > **URGE**, Urgence, Urgency, Vanity, Vapour, Vice, Waid(e), Wardrobe, Weight, Wine, Wring, Yellow

Press agent Flack, Spin doctor

Press-gang Force, Impress, Shanghai

Pressman Ed, PRO, Reporter, Twicer

Prestidigitate(r) Conjure, Juggle, Legerdemain, Magician, Palm

Prestige, Prestigious Cachet, Credit, Distinguished, Fame, Influence, Kudos, Notable, Status

Presume, Presumably, Presumption, Presumptuous Allege, Arrogant, Audacity, Believe, Bold, Brass, Cocksure, Cocky, Doubtless, > **EXPECT**, Familiar, Forward, Gall, Impertinent, Insolent, Liberty, Outrecuidance, Pert, Probably, Suppose, Uppish, Whipper-snapper

Pretence, Pretend(er), Pretext Act, Affect(ation), Afflict, Assume, Blind, Bluff, Charade, Charlatan, Claim, Claimant, Cover, Cram, Dissemble, Dissimulate, Excuse, False, Feign, Feint, Gondolier, Hokum, Humbug, Hypocrisy, Impostor, Jactitation, Kid(stakes), Lambert Simnel, Let-on, Make-believe, Malinger, Masquerade, Obreption, Old, Parolles, Perkin Warbeck, Pose, Profess, Pseud(o) Quack, Sham, Simulate, Stale, Stalking-horse, Subterfuge, Suppose, Warbeck, Young

Pretension, Pretentious(ness) Arty, Bombast, Chi-chi, Fantoosh, Fustian, Gaudy, Grandiose, High-falutin(g), Kitsch, La-di-da, Orotund, Ostentatious, Overblown, Paraf(f)le, Pompous, Pseud(o), Sciolism, Showy, Snobbish, Squirt, Tat, Tattie-peelin, Tinhorn, Toffee-nosed, Uppity, Wanky, Whippersnapper

Pretty Attractive, Becoming, Chocolate-box, Comely, Cute, Dear, Decorate, Dish, Elegant, Fair(ish), Fairway, Inconie, Incony, Keepsaky, Looker, Moderately, Pass, Peach, Picturesque, Primp, Quite, Sweet, Twee, Winsome

Prevail(ing) Dominate, Endure, Go, Induce, Persist, Persuade, Predominant, Preponderate, Reign, Ring, Triumph, Victor, Win

Prevalent Catholic, Common, Dominant, Endemic, Epidemic, Obtaining, Rife, Widespread

Prevaricate, **Prevarication** Equivocate, Hedge, Lie, Runaround, Stall, Whittie-whattie

Prevent(ive) Avert, Bar, Debar, Deter, Disenable, Embar, Estop, Foreclose, Forfend, Help, Impound, Inhibit, Keep, Let, Obstruct, Obviate, Preclude, Prophylactic, Stop, Theriac, Trammel

Preview Sneak, Trailer, Vernissage

Previous(ly) Afore, Already, Before, Earlier, Ere(-now), Fore, Foreran, Former, Hitherto, Once, Prior

Prey Booty, Feed, Kill, Pelt, Plunder, Predate, Proul, Prowl, Quarry, Raven, Ravin(e), Soyle, Spreagh, Victim

Price(d), **Pricing**, **Price-raising** Appraise, Assess, Charge, Consequence, Contango, > COST, Dearth, Due, Evens, Exercise, Expense, Fee, Fiars, Hammer, Hire, Intervention, Issue, Limit, List, Loco, Market, Offer, Packet, Perverse, Predatory, Prestige, Quotation, Quote, Rate, Regrate, Reserve, Shadow, Song, Spot, Starting, Street value, Striking, Trade, Unit, Upset, Value, Vincent, Weregild, Wergeld, Wergild, Worth, Yardage

Prick(ed), **Prickle**, **Prickly** Acanaceous, Accloy, Argemone, Arrect, Bearded, Brakier, Bramble, Brog, Bunya, Cactus, Cloy, Cnicus, Echinate, Goad, Gore, Hedgehog, Hedgepig, Impel, Inject, Jab, Jook, Juk, Kali, Penis, Perse, Pierce, Prod, Puncture, Rowel, Rubus, Ruellia, Seta, Setose, Smart, Spicula, Spinate, Stab, Star-thistle, Stimulus, Sting, Tattoo, Tatu, Teasel, Thistle, Thorn, Tingle, Urge

Prickly heat Miliaria

Prickly-pear Opuntia, Tuna

Pride Bombast, Brag, Conceit, Elation, Esprit de corps, Glory, Hauteur, Hubris, Inordinate, Lions, London, Machismo, Plume, Preen, Purge, Triumphalism, Vainglory, Vanity

Priest(ess), **Priests** Aaron, Abaris, Abbess, Abbot, Ananias, Annas, Archimandrite, Bacchae, Bacchantes, Baptes, Becket, Bonze, Brahmin, Cardinal, Clergyman, Cleric, Cohen, Concelebrant, Corybant(es), Curé, Dalai Lama, Druid, Eli, Elisha, Father, Fetial, Flamen, Fr, Habacuc, Habakkuk, Hero, Hieratic, Hierophant, High, H(o)ungan, Io, Jethro, Lack-Latin, Lama, Laocoon, Levite, Lucumo, Mage, Magus, Mallet, Mambo, Marabout, Metropolitan, Minister, Missionary, Monsignor, Mufti, Norma, Oratorian, Padre, Papa, Parson, Pastor, Patercove, Patrico, Pawaw, Père, Pontifex, Pontiff, Pope, Pope's knight, Powwow, Pr, Preacher, Prelate, Presbyter, Prior(ess), Pythia, Rabbi, Rebbe, Rector, Rev, Sacerdotal, Salian, Savonarola, Seminarian, Shaman, Shaveling, Sky pilot, Spoiled, Tohunga, Vicar, Vivaldi, Worker, Zadok

Prig Dandy, Fop, Humbug, Nimmer, Pilfer, Prude, Puritan

Prim Demure, Mun, Neat, Old-maidish, Perjink, Preceese, Precise, Proper, Starchy

Primacy, **Primate** Ape, Aye-aye, Bandar, Bigfoot, Biped, Bishop, Bush baby, Cardinal, Ebor, Gibbon, Hanuman, Hominid, Jackanapes, King-kong, Loris, Macaque, Magot, Mammal, Marmoset, > MONKEY, Orang, Pongid, Potto, Prosimian, Protohuman, Quadruman, Ramapithecus, Rhesus, Sifaka, Tarsier

Prima donna Diva, Patti, Star

Prim(a)eval Ancient, Prehistoric, Primitive

Prime(r), **Primary**, **Priming** Arm, Basic, Bloom, Cardinal, Charging, Chief, Choice, Claircolle, Clearcole, Clerecole, Closed, Detonator, Direct, Donat, Donet, Election, Enarm, First, Flower, Heyday, Mature, Open, Original,

Paramount, Peak, Radical, Remex, Sell-by-date, Supreme, Thirteen, Tip-top, Totient, Totitive, Valuable, Windac, Windas, Ylem

Prime Minister Asquith, Attlee, Baldwin, Balfour, Begin, Bute, Canning, Chamberlain, Chatham, Dewan, Disraeli, Diwan, Eden, Grand Vizier, Grey, Home, Leaderene, North, Number Ten, Peel, Pitt, PM, Premier, Shastri, Tanaiste, Taoiseach, Thatcher, Walpole

Primitive Aborigine, Amoeba, Antediluvian, Arabic, Archaic, Atavistic, Barbaric, Caveman, Crude, Early, Evolué, Fundamental, Naive, Neanderthal, Neolithic, Old, Persian, Primordial, Pro, Prothyl(e), Protomorphic, Protyl(e), Radical, Rudimentary, Savage, Subman, Turkish, Uncivilised, Ur

Primordial Blastema, Fundamental, Original

Primrose, Primula Evening, League, Oenothera, Onagra, Ox-lip, Pa(i)gle, Rosebery, Vicar, Yellow

Prince(ly) Ahmed, Albert, Ameer, Amir, Amphitryon, Anchises, Arjuna, Atheling, Barnmecide, Black, Cadmus, Caliph, Chagan, Charming, Crown, Czarevich, Elector, Equerry, Eugene, Florizel, Fortinbras, Gaekwar, Gospodar, Guicowar, Hal, Highness, Hospodar, Huzoor, Igor, Inca, Infante, Khan, Ksar, Lavish, Lucumo, Maharaja, Margrave, Meleager, Merchant, Mir, Mirza, Nawab, Nizam, Noble, Otto, P, Pantagruel, Pendragon, Pirithous, Porphyrogenite, Potentate, Rainier, Rajah, Rana, Ras, Rasselas, Ratoo, Ratu, Regal, RH, Rudolph, Rupert, Serene, Sharif, Shereef, Sherif, Siegfried, Student, Tengku, Tereus, Tsar(evich), Tunku, Upper Roger

Princess Andromache, Andromeda, Anne, Ariadne, Begum, Creusa, Czarevna, Czarista, Danae, Di(ana), Electra, Electress, Eudocia, Europa, Hermione, Hesione, Ida, Imogen, Infanta, Iseult, Isolde, Jezebel, Maharanee, Maharani, Pocahontas, Procne, Rani, Regan, Tou Wan, Tsarevna, Tsarista, Turandot

Principal Arch, Capital, Central, > CHIEF, Decuman, Especial, First, Foremost, Head, Leading, Main(stay), Major, Mass, Protagonist, Ringleader, Staple, Star

Principality Andorra, Lichtenstein, Moldavia, Monaco, Muscovy, Wales, Wal(l)achia

Principle(s), Principled Animistic, Anthropic, Archimedes, Axiom, Basis, Bernouilli, Brocard, Canon, Carnot, Code, Cosmological, Criterion, Cui bono, Cy pres, D'Alembert's, Doctrine, Dogma, Element, Entelechy, Essential, Exclusion, Fermat's, First, Fourier, Gause's, Generale, Germ, Ground rule, Guideline, Heisenberg, Honourable, Huygen's, Key, Law, Least time, Le Chatelier's, Logos, Methodology, Organon, Ormazd, Ormuzd, Pauli-exclusion, Peter, Plank, Platform, Pleasure, Precept, Prescript, Rationale, Reality, Reason, Reciprocity, Relativity, Remonstrance, Rudiment, Rule, Sakti, Seed, Shakti, Spirit, Summum bonum, Tenet, Theorem, Ticket, Uncertainty, Verification, Vital, Yang, Yin

Prink Beautify, Bedeck, Dress

Print(er), Printing Baskerville, Batik, Benday, Bromide, Calotype, Caveman, Caxton, Chapel, Chromo, Cibachrome, Cicero, Collotype, Contact, Copperplate, Dab, Dot matrix, Electrothermal, Elzevir, Engrave, Etching, Ferrotype, Fine, Flexography, Font, Gravure, Gurmukhi, Gutenberg, Half-tone, Hectograph, Heliotype, Image, Impact, Impress, Incunabula, India, Ink-jet, Intaglio, Italic, Jobbing, Laser, Letterpress, Letterset, Line, Line-engraving, Lino-cut, Lithograph, Logotype, Lower-case, Matrix, Mimeograph®, Monotype®, Moon, Non-impact, Off-line, Offset, Old-face, Oleo, Oleograph, Opaline, Phototype, Plate, Platinotype, Positive, Press, Publish, Remarque, Report, Reproduction, Retroussage, Rotogravure, Samizdat, Screen, Serigraph, Ship, Silk-screen, Small, Smoot, Splash, Spore, Stamp, Stenochrome, Stonehand,

Strike, Thermal, Three-colour, Trichromatic, Typesetter, Typothetae, Whorl, Woodburytype, Woodcut, Xerography, Xylograph, Zincograph

Printing-press Rounce

Prior(ity) Abbot, Afore, Antecedent, Anterior, Aperture, Earlier, Former, Hitherto, Monk, Overslaugh, Pre-, Precedence, Prefard, Preference, Previous, Privilege, Shutter, Triage

Prise *see* PRIZE

Prism(s), Prismatic Catadioptric, Iriscope, Nicol, Periaktos, Rhombohedron, Spectrum, Teinoscope, Wollaston

Prison Albany, Alcatraz, Bagnio, Barracoon, Bastille, Bin, Bird, Boob, Bridewell, Brig, Brixton, Bullpen, Cage, Can, Cell, Chillon, Chok(e)y, Clink, Club, College, Confine, Cooler, Coop, Counter, Dartmoor, Dispersal, Dungeon, Durance, Fleet, Fotheringhay, Gaol, Glass-house, Guardhouse, Guardroom, Gulag, Hokey, Holloway, Hoos(e)gow, Hulk(s), Internment, > JAIL, Jug, Kitty, Limbo, Lob's pound, Lock-up, Logs, Lumber, Marshalsea, Massymore, Mattamore, Maze, Newgate, Nick, Oflag, Open, Panopticon, Pen, Penitentiary, Pentonville, Pit, Poke(y), Porridge, Pound, Princetown, Quad, Quod, Rasp-house, Reformatory, Roundhouse, Scrubs, Shop, Sing-sing, Slammer, Spandau, Stalag, State, Stir, Strangeways, The Leads, Tol(l)booth, Tower, Tronk, Wandsworth, Wormwood Scrubs

Prisoner Canary-bird, Captive, Collegian, Collegiate, Con(vict), Detainee, Detenu, Hostage, Inmate, Internee, Jailbird, Lag, Lifer, Political, POW, Trustee, Trusty, Yardbird, Zek

Pristine Fire-new, Fresh, New, Original, Unmarked, Unspoiled

Private(ly) Ain, Aside, Atkins, Auricular, Buccaneer, Byroom, Clandestine, Close, Closet, Conclave, Confidential, Enisle(d), Esoteric, Homefelt, Hush-hush, In camera, Individual, Inner, Intimate, Non-com, Own, Personal, Piou-piou, Poilu, Proprietary, Pte, Rank(er), Retired, Sanction, Sapper, Secret, Several, > SOLDIER, Squaddie, Sub rosa, Tommy

Privateer(s) Buccaneer, Corsair, Freebooter, Marque(s), Pirate

Privation Hardship, Penury, Want

Privileg(ed) Birthright, Blest, Charter, Curule, Enviable, Exempt, Favour, Franchise, Freedom, Indulgence, Insider, Liberty, Mozarab, Nomenklatura, Octroi, Parliamentary, Patent, Prerogative, Pryse, Regale, Regalia, Right, Sac

Privy Apprised, Can, Closet, Intimate, Jakes, John, Loo, Necessary, Reredorter, Secret, Sedge, Siege

Prize(s), Prizewinner, Prized Acquest, Apple, Archibald, Assess, Award, Best, Booby, Booker, Bravie, Capture, Champion, Consolation, Creach, Cup, Dux, Efforce, > ESTEEM, Force, Garland, Goncourt, Grice, Honour, Jackpot, Jemmy, Lever, Lot, Money, Nobel, Palm, Pearl, Pewter, Pie, Plum, Plunder, Pot, Pulitzer, Purse, Ram, Reprisal, > REWARD, Scalp, Ship, Spreaghery, Sprechery, Stakes, Taonga, Tern, Treasure, Trophy, Turner, Value

Pro Aye, Coach, For, Harlot, Moll, Paid, Tramp, Yea, Yes

Pro *see* PROSTITUTE

Probable, Probability Apparent, Belike, Conditional, Ergodic, Feasible, Likely, Marginal, Mathematical, Possible, Posterior, Verisimilar

Probation(er) Novice, Novitiate, Stibbler, Test, Trainee, Trial

Probe Antenna, Bore, Bougie, Canopus, Cassini, Corot, Delve, Dredge, Explore, Fathom, Feeler, Fossick, Galileo, Giotto, Inquire, Investigate, Magellan, Mariner, Mars Surveyor, Pelican, Pioneer, Poke, Pump, > SEARCH, Seeker, Sonde, Sound, Space, Stardust, Stylet, Tent, Thrust, Tracer, Venera

Probity Honour, Integrity, Justice

Problem(s) Acrostic, BO, Boyg, Brainteaser, Crisis, Crux, Dilemma, Egma, Enigma, Facer, Glitch, Handful, Hang-up, Headache, Hitch, Hurdle, Indaba, Knot(ty), Koan, Miniature, Musive, Net, Nuisance, Obstacle, Pons asinorum, Poser, Quandary, Question, Re, Rebus, Riddle, Rider, Snag, Sorites, Sum, Teaser, Thing, Tickler, Toughie, Trouble, Tsuris, Yips

Problem-solving Synectics

Proboscis Haustellum, Promuscis, Snout, Trunk

Proceed(s), **Proceeding**, **Procedure** Acta, Afoot, Algorithm, Continue, Course, Do, Drill, Emanate, Fand, Flow, Fond, Goes, Haul, Issue, Machinery, March, Mechanics, Method, Mine, MO, Modal, Move, On, Pass, Practice, Praxis, Process, Profit, Protocol, Punctilio, Pursue, Put, Rake, Return, Rite, Ritual, Routine, Sap, Steps, System, Take, Use, Yead(s), Yede, Yeed

Process(ing), **Procession**, **Processor** Acromion, Action, Additive, Ala, Ambarvalia, Axon, Ben Day, Bessemer, Bosch, Castner, Catalysis, Cavalcade, Cortège, Cyanide, Demo, Diagonal, Front-end, Haber, Handle, Managing, Markov, Method, Moharram, Mond, Motorcade, Muharram, Odontoid, Open hearth, -osis, Pageant, Parade, Parallel, Paseo, Photosynthesis, Pipeline, Planar, Pomp, Primary, Recycle, Screen, Secondary, Series, Silkscreen, Skimmington, Solvay, Speciation, Sterygoid, String, Subtractive, Thermite, Thought, Torchlight, Train, Treat, Trial, Turn(a)round, Unit, Xiphoid, Zygomatic

Proclaim, **Proclamation** Announce, Annunciate, Ban, Blaze, Blazon, Boast, Broadsheet, Cry, Edict, Enounce, Enunciate, Herald, Indiction, Kerygma, Oyez, Preconise, Predicate, Profess, Publish, Ring, Shout, Trumpet, Ukase

Procrastinate, **Procrastinating** Defer, Delay, Dilatory, Dilly-dally, Linger, Pettifog, Postpone, Shelve, Temporise, Vacillate

Procreate Beget, Engender, Generate, Initiate

Procrustean Conformity

Proctor Agent, King's, Monitor, Prog, Proxy, Queen's

Procurator, **Procure(r)** Achieve, Aunt, Crimp, Earn, Get, Induce, Naunt, Obtain, Pander, Pilate, Pimp, Sort, Suborn

Prod Cattle, Egg, Goad, Impel, Jab, Job, Jog, Nudge, Poke, Pote

Prodigal Costly, Lavish, Profligate, Spendall, Unthrift, Wanton, Wasteful, Waster

Prodigious, **Prodigy** Abnormal, Amazing, Huge, Immense, Infant, Monster, Monument, Mozart, Phenomenal, Portentous, Tremendous, Wonder, Wonderwork, Wunderkind

Produce(r), **Producing** Afford, Breed, Cause, Create, Crop, Ean, Edit, Effect, Engender, Evoke, Exhibit, Extend, Fruit, Generate, Get, Grow, Home-grown, Impresario, Issue, Kind, Make, Offspring, Onstream, Originate, Output, Propage, Propound, Raise, Son, Spawn, Stage, Supply, Teem, Throw, Wares, Whelp, Yield

▷ **Produces** *may indicate* an anagram

Product(ion), **Productive(ness)**, **Productivity** Actualities, Apport, Artefact, Ashtareth, Ashtaroth, Astarte, Bore, Coefficient, Commodity, Drama, End, Factorial, Fecund, Fertile, Fruit, Genesis, Global, Handiwork, Harvest, Net domestic, Net national, Output, Outturn, Pair, Partial, Prolific, Result, Rich, Scalar, Show, Speiss, Uberous, Uberty, Vector, Waste, Work, Yield

▷ **Production** *may indicate* an anagram

Proem Foreword, Overture, Pre, Preface

Profane, **Profanation**, **Profanity** Coarse, Coprolalia, Desecrate, Impious, Irreverent, Sacrilege, Unholy, Violate

Profess(ed), **Professor** Absent-minded, Academic, Adjoint, Admit, Asset, Avow, Challenger, Claim, Declare, Disney, Emeritus, Higgins, Hodja, Kho(d)ja, Know-all, Ostensible, Own, Practise, Pundit, Regent, Regius, RP, STP, Visiting

Profession(al) Admission, Assurance, Buppy, Business, Career, Creed, Expert, Métier, Practitioner, Pretence, Pursuit, Regular, Salaried, Skilled, Trade, Vocation, Yuppie

Proffer Give, Present, Proposition, Tender

Proficiency, **Proficient** Able, Adept, Alert, Dan, Expert, Forte, Past master, Practised, Skill, Technique

Profile Analysis, Contour, Cross, Half-face, Long, Loral, Low, Outline, Silhouette, Sketch, Statant, T(h)alweg, Vignette

Profit(able), **Profiteer**, **Profits** Advantage, Arbitrage, Asset, Avail, Benefit, Boot, Bunce, Cere, Clear, Divi(dend), Economic, Edge, Emblements, Emoluments, Exploit, Fat, Gain, Graft, Gravy, Grist, Gross, Income, Increment, Issue, Jobbery, Juicy, Leech, Lucrative, Makings, Margin, Melon, Milch cow, Mileage, Moneymaker, Net, Pay(ing), Perk, Pickings, Preacquisition, Rake-off, Return, Reward, Royalty, Spoils, Use, Usufruct, Utile, Utility, Vail

Profligate Corinthian, Corrupt, Degenerate, Dissolute, Extravagant, Lecher, Libertine, Lorel, Losel(l), Oatmeal, Rakehell, Reprobate, Roué, Spend-all, Wastrel

Profound Altum, Bottomless, Complete, Deep, Intense, Recondite

Profuse, **Profusion** Abundant, Copious, Excess, Free, Galore, Lavish, Liberal, Lush, Quantity, Rank, Rich, Two-a-penny

Progenitor, **Progenitrix** Ancestor, Ma, Predecessor, Sire, Stock

Progeny Children, Descendants, Fruit, Issue, Offspring, Seed

Prognosis Forecast, Prediction

Prognosticate, **Prognostication** Augur, Foretell, Omen, Predict, Presage, Prophesy

Program(ming), **Programming language**, **Programmer** Ada, Algol, Applet, Basic, BIOS, Bloatware, Boot, Bot, Cancelbot, Chatbot, Cobol, Coder, Columbus, CU See Me, Debugger, Dictionary, Est, Executive, Firmware, Fortran, Freeware, Inputter, Java®, Linear, Linker, LISP, Loader, Logic, LOGO, Object, Package, Parser, Pascal, PROLOG, PROM, Router, Screensaver, Search engine, Shell, Small-talk, SNOBOL, Software, Source, Spellchecker, Spreadsheet, SQL, Sustaining, Systems, Telnet, Translator, Utility, Web browser, Web crawler, Worm

Programme Agenda, Broadcast, Card, Chat show, Code, Documentary, Docusoap, Dramedy, Est, Event, Faction, Fly-on-the-wall, Infotainment, Linear, Mockumentary, PDL, Phone-in, Plan, Playbill, Prank, Regimen, Report, Schedule, Scheme, Sepmag, Show, Sitcom, Sked, Soap, Software, Syllabus, System, Telecast, Telethon, Timetable

Progress(ive), **Progression** > ADVANCE, Afoot, Arithmetic, Avant garde, Course, Fabian, Flow, Forge, Forward, Forward-looking, Gain, Geometric, Go, Growth, Harmonic, Headway, Incede, Liberal, Move, Onwards, Paraphonia, Pilgrim's, Prosper, Rack, Rake's, Reformer, Roll, Run, Sequence, Series, Step, Vaunce, Way, Yead, Yede, Yeed

Prohibit(ed), **Prohibition(ist)** Ban, Block, Debar, Dry, Embargo, Estop, Forbid, Hinder, Index, Injunct, Interdict, Noli-me-tangere, Off-limits, Prevent, Pussyfoot, Rahui, Suppress, Taboo, Tabu, Verboten, Veto

Project(ile), **Projecting**, **Projection**, **Projector** Aim, Ammo, Assignment, Astral, Astrut, Ball, Ballistic, Beetle, Bullet, Butt, Buttress, Cam, Cast, Catapult, Channel, Cinerama®, Cog, Conceive, Condyle, Conic, Console,

Corbel, Coving, Crossette, Cutwater, Denticle, Diascope, Discus, Eaves, Echinus, Elance, Enterprise, Episcope, Excrescence, Exsert, Extrapolate, Fet(ter)lock, Flange, Gair, Gore, Guess, Hangover, Helicity, Hoe, Homolosine, Hurtle, Inion, Jut, Kern, Knob, Ledge, Lobe, Lug, Magic lantern, Malleolus, Manhattan, Mercator, Mitraille, Mollweide, Mucro, Mutule, Nab, Nose, Nunatak(er), Olecranon, Opaque, Orillion, Orthogonal, Orthographic, Outcrop, Outjet, Outjut, Outshot, Overhang, Overhead, Oversail, Peter's, Pitch, Planetarium, Planisphere, Polyconic, Pork barrel, Prickle, Promontory, > **PROTRUDE**, Proud(er), Quillon, Raguly, Roach, Rocket, Sail, Salient, Sally, Sanson-Flamsteed, Scaw, Scheme, Screen, Shelf, Shrapnel, Sinusoidal, Skaw, Snag, Snout, Spline, Sponson, Sprocket, Spur, Squarrose, Stand out, Stereopticon, Stick out, Tang, Tappet, Tenon, Throw, Toe, Tracer, Trimetric, Trippet, Trunnion, Turnkey, Turtleback, Tusk, Umbo, Undertaking, Villus, Vitascope, Zenithal

Prolapse Procidence

Proletarian, **Proletariat** People, Plebeian, Popular

Proliferate Expand, Increase, Multiply, Propagate, Snowball

Prolific Abounding, Fecund, Fertile, Fruitful, Profuse, Teeming

Prolix(ity) Lengthy, Prosaic, Rambling, Rigmarole, Verbose, Wire-draw, Wordy

Prologue Introduce, Preface

Prolong(ed) Extend, Lengthen, Protract, Sostenuto, Spin, Sustain

Prom(enade) Alameda, Boulevard, Cakewalk, Catwalk, Crush-room, Esplanade, Front, Mall, Parade, Paseo, Pier, Sea-front, Stroll, > **WALK**

Prometheus Fire

Promethium Pm

Prominence, **Prominent** Antitragus, Blatant, Bold, Colliculus, Condyle, Conspicuous, Egregious, Emphasis, Featured, Gonion, High profile, Important, Insistent, Luminary, Manifest, Marked, Obtrusive, Outstanding, Salient, Signal, Teat, Toot, Tragus

Promiscuous, **Promiscuity** Casual, Fast, Free, Indiscriminate, Light, Mixed, Motley, Pell-mell, Slapper, Trollop, Whoredom

Promise, **Promising** Accept, Assure, Augur, Auspicious, Avoure, Behest, Behight, Behote, Bode, Coming, Compact, Covenant, Engagement, Foretaste, Guarantee, Hecht, Hest, Hete, Hight, IOU, Likely, Manifest, Parole, Pledge, Plight, Pollicitation, Potential, Recognisance, Recognizance, Rosy, Sign, Sponsor, Swear, Tile, Undertake, Vow, Warranty, Word

Promised land Beulah, Canaan, Israel

Promissory note IOU, PN

Promontory Bill, Cape Sable, Cliff, Flamborough Head, Foreland, Giant's Causeway, Hatteras, Headland, Hoe, Hogh, Mull, Naze, Ness, Nose, Peak, Pillars of Hercules, Spit, The Lizard, Tintagel Head

Promote(r), **Promotion** Adman, Advance, > **ADVERTISE**, Advocate, Aggrandise, Aid, Assist, Blurb, Boost, Campaign, Dog and pony show, Elevate, Encourage, Exponent, Foment, Foster, Further, Help, Hype, Increase, Make, Pracharak, Prefer, Prelation, Promulgate, Provoke, Queen, Rear, Remove, Run, Salutary, Sell, Sponsor, Spruik, Stage, Step, Subserve, Tendencious, Tendentious, Upgrade, Uplead, Uprate

Prompt(er), **Promptly**, **Promptness** Actuate, Alacrity, Autocue®, Believe, Celerity, Chop-chop, Cue, Egg, Expeditious, Frack, Idiot-board, Immediate, Incite, Inspire, Instigate, Move, On-the-nail, Opposite, Pernicious, Premove, Punctual, Quick, Ready, Speed(y), Spur, Stimulate, Sudden, Tight, Tit(e), Titely, Tyte, Urgent

Promulgate Preach, Proclaim, Publish, Spread

Prone Apt, Groof, Grouf, Grovel, Liable, Lying, Prostrate, Recumbent, Subject, Susceptible

Prong Fang, Fork, Grain, Peg, Tang, Tine

Pronghorn Cabrie, Cabrit

Pronoun Personal, Reciprocal, Relative

Pronounce(d), **Pronouncement** Adjudicate, Affirm, Articulate, Assert, Asseveration, Clear, Conspicuous, Declare, Definite, Dictum, Emphatic, Enunciate, Fiat, Indefinite, Marked, Opinion, Palatalise, Pontificate, Recite, Utter, Velarise, Vocal, Voice, Vote

Pronto PDQ

Pronunciation Betacism, Cacoepy, Delivery, Diction, Etacism, Itacism, Lallation, Orthoepy, Phonetics, Plateasm, Proclitic, Received, Rhotacism, Sound, Tense

Proof Apagoge, Argument, Bona fides, Confirmation, Direct, Evidence, Firm, Foundry, Galley, Godel's, Indirect, Positive, Preif(e), Probate, Pull, Quality, Refutation, Remarque, Reproduction, Resistant, Revision, Secure, Slip, Strength, Test, Tight, Token, Trial, Upmake, Validity

Prop Airscrew, Bolster, Buttress, Clothes, Crutch, Dog-shore, Fulcrum, Leg, Loosehead, Misericord(e), Pit, Point d'appui, Punch(eon), Rance, Rest, Shore, Sprag, Spur, Staff, Stay, Stempel, Stemple, Stilt, Stoop, Stoup, Studdle, Stull, > SUPPORT, Tighthead, Trig, Underpin

Propaganda, **Propagandist** Agitprop, Ballyhoo, Black, Brainwashing, Chevalier, Doctrine, Exponent, Goebbels, Grey, Promotion, Psyop, Psywar, Publicity, Slogan, Spin doctor, White

Propagate, **Propagator** Breed, Dispread, Generate, Graft, Hatch, Increase, Produce, Promulgate, Provine, Spread, Tan-bed

Propel(ler) Airscrew, Ca', Drive, Fin, Frogmarch, Launch, Leg, Lox, > MOVE, Oar, Paddle, Pedal, Project, Push, Rotor, Row, Screw, Throw

Propensity Aptness, Bent, Inclination, Penchant, Tendency

Proper(ly) Ain, Convenance, Correct, Decent, Decorous, Due, Eigen, En règle, Ethical, > FIT, Genteel, Governessy, Kosher, Noun, Ought, Own, Pakka, Pathan, Prim, Pucka, Pukka, Puritanic, Real, Seemly, Suitable, Tao, Trew, True, Veritable, Well

Property Assets, Attribute, Aver, Belongings, Chattel, Chose, Contenement, Dead-hand, Demesne, Des res, Dowry, Effects, Enclave, Escheat, Escrow, Estate, Fee, Feu, Flavour, Fonds, Freehold, Goods, Hereditament, Hot, Hotchpot, Immoveable, Inertia, Intellectual, Jointure, Leasehold, Living, Means, Mortmann, Paraphernalia, Peculium, Personal, Personalty, Premises, Private, Public, Quale, Quality, Real, Stock, Stolen, Theft, Time-share, Timocracy, Trait, Usucapion, Usucaption

Prophesy, **Prophet(ess)**, **Prophetic** Amos, Augur, Bab, Balaam, Calchas, Cassandra, Daniel, Deborah, Divine, Druid, Elias, Elijah, Elisha, Ezekiel, Ezra, Fatal, Fatidical, Forecast, Foretell, Former, Geomancer, Habakkuk, Haggai, Hosea, Is, Isa, Is(a)iah, Jeremiah, Joel, Jonah, Latter, Mahdi, Mahound, Major, Malachi, Mani, Mantic, Micah, Minor, Mohammed, Mopsus, Mormon, Moses, Nahum, Nathan, Nostradamus, Obadiah, Old Mother Shipton, Ominous, Oracle, Portend, Predictor, Prognosticate, Pythoness, Seer, Sibyl, Tipster, Tiresias, Vatic, Vaticinate, Voluspa, Zachariah, Zarathistra, Zechariah, Zephaniah, Zoroaster, Zwickau

Prophylactic, **Prophylaxis** Inoculation, Preventive, Serum, Vaccine, Variolation

Propitiate Appease, Atone, Pacify, Reconcile, Sop

Propitious Benign, Favourable, Lucky

Proponent Advocate, Backer, Partisan

Proportion(ate) Commensurable, Dimension, Inverse, Portion, Pro rata, Quantity, Quota, Ratio, Reason, Regulate, Relation, Sine, Size, Soum, Sowm

Proposal, Propose Advance, Bid, Bill, Canvass, Eirenicon, Feeler, Irenicon, Mean, Motion, Move, Nominate, Offer, Overture, Plan, Pop, Proffer, Propound, Recommend, Resolution, Scheme, Slate, Submission, > SUGGEST, Table, Tender, Volunteer, Woot, Would

Proposition Asses' bridge, Axiom, Convertend, Corollary, Deal, Disjunction, Ergo, Hypothesis, Identical, Lemma, Overture, Pons asinorum, Porism, Premise, Premiss, Rider, Sorites, Spec, Superaltern, Theorem, Thesis

Propound Advocate, Purpose, State

Proprietor, Propriety Correctitude, Decorum, Etiquette, Grundy, Keeper, Lord, Master, Owner, Patron, Rectitude

Prosaic Common, Drab, Flat, Humdrum, Tedious, Workaday

Proscenium Forestage

Proscribe Exile, Outlaw

Prose, Prosy Euphuism, Haikai, Polyphonic, Purple, Saga, Stich, Verbose, Version, Writing

Prosecute, Prosecutor, Prosecution Allege, Avvogadore, Charge, Crown, Fiscal, Furtherance, Impeach, Indict, Practise, Public, Sue, Wage

Proselytise(r), Proselytism Indoctrination, Propagandism, Souper

Prospect(or) Bellevue, Explore, Forty-niner, Fossick, Look-out, Mine, Opportunity, > OUTLOOK, Panorama, Perspective, Pleases, Possibility, Reefer, Scenery, Search, Sourdough, View, Vista, Visto, Wildcatter

Prospectus Menu, Pathfinder

Prosper(ity), Prosperous Blessed, Blossom, Boom, Fair, Fat cat, Flourish, Get ahead, Heyday, Mérimée, Palmy, > SUCCEED, Thee, Thrift, Thrive, Up, Warison, Wealth, Welfare, Well-heeled, Well-to-do

Prostitute, Prostitution Brass, Bulker, Callet, Catamite, Chippie, Cockatrice, Cocotte, Debase, Dell, Demi-mondaine, Dolly-mop, Doxy, Fancy woman, Fille de joie, Harlot, Hetaera, Hetaira, Hierodule, Ho, Hooker, Jailbait, Loose-fish, Loose woman, Madam, Magdalen(e), Moll, Mutton, Night-walker, Plover, Pole-cat, Pro, Punk, Quail, Quiff, Rent-boy, Road, Rough trade, Scrubber, Shippie, Slap, Social evil, Stew, Streetwalker, Strumpet, Tart, Trull, Venture, Wench, Whore

Prostrate, Prostration Collapse, Exhausted, Fell, Flat, Flatling, Ko(w)tow, Laid, Obeisance, Overcome, Procumbent, Prone, Repent, Throw

Protactinium Pa

Protean Amoebic, Fusible, Variable

Protect(ed), Protection, Protector Adonise, Aegis, Alexin, Arm, Armour, Asylum, Auspice, Bastion, Bestride, Bield, Buckler, Chaffron, Chain mail, Chamfrain, Chamfron, Charm, Cherish, Cloche, Coat, Cocoon, Coleor(r)hiza, Conserve, Cover, Covert, Cromwell, Cushion, Danegeld, Data, Defend, Defilade, Degauss, Egis, Enamel, Entrenchment, Escort, Estacade, Faun, Flank, Gobo, Groundsheet, Guard(ian), Gumshield, Hedge, House, Hurter, Immune, Inalienable, Indemnify, Insure, Keckle, Keep, Kickback, Lee, Mac(k)intosh, Mail, Male, Mollycoddle, Mother, Mouthpiece, Mudguard, Muniment, Noll, Nosey, Oliver, Orillion, Overall, Parados, Patent, Patron, Police, Pomander, Preserve, Rabbit's foot, Redome, Revetment, Ride shotgun, Safeguard, Sandbag, Save, Schanse, Schan(t)ze, Screen, Scug, Shadow, Sheathing, Sheeting, Shelter, > SHIELD, Skug, Splashback, Splashboard, Splasher,

Starling, Sunscreen, Talisman, Tribute, Tutelar, Umbrella, Underseal, Vaccine, Ward(ship), Warhead, Warrant, Weatherboard, Weatherstrip, Windbreaker, Windshield, Wing, Write

Protégé Pupil, Tutee, Ward

Protein Abrin, Actin, Actomyosin, Adipsin, Alanine, Albumen, Albumin, Aleuron(e), Allergen, Amandine, Analogon, Angiotensin, Antibody, Aquaporin, Avidin, Bradykinin, Calmodulin, Capsid, Capsomere, Caseinogen, Ceruloplasmin, Collagen, Complement, Conchiolin, Conjugated, Cytokine, Dystrophin, Elastin, Enzyme, Factor VIII, Ferritin, Fibrin, Fibrinogen, Fibroin, Flagellin, Gelatin, Gliadin(e), Glob(ul)in, Glutelin, Gluten, Haemoglobin, Haptoglobin, Histone, Hordein, Immunoglobulin, Incaparina, Interferon, Interleukin, Lactalbumin, Lectin, Legumin, Leptin, Leucin(e), Lewy bodies, Luciferin, Lymphokine, Lysin, Meat, Mucin, Myogen, Myoglobin, Myosin, Opsin, Opsonin, Ossein, Ovalbumin, Pepsin(e), Peptide, Phaseolin, Prion, Prolamin(e), Properdin, Protamine, Proteose, Prothrombin, Quorn®, Renin, Repressor, Ribosome, Sclerotin, Sericin, Serum albumin, Serum globulin, Single-cell, Soya, Spectrin, Spongin, Tempeh, Thrombogen, Toxalbumin, Transferrin, Tropomyosin, Troponin, TSP, Tubulin, Vitellin, Zein

Protest(er) Andolan, Aver, Avouch, Black Bloc(k), Clamour, Come, Démarche, Demo, Demonstrate, Demur, Deprecate, Dharna, Dissent, Expostulate, Gherao, Go-slow, Hartal, Inveigh, Lock-out, Luddite, March, Moonlighter, Nimby, Object, Outcry, Picket, Plea, Refus(e)nik, Remonstrate, Sit-in, Squawk, Squeak, Squeal, Suffragette, Work-to-rule

Protestant Amish, Anabaptist, Anglo, Calvin, Congregationalism, Covenanter, Cranmer, Dissenter, Evangelic, Gospeller, Huguenot, Independent, Lady, Loyalist, Lutheran, Mennonite, Methodist, Moravian, Neo-orthodoxy, Nonconformist, Oak-boy, Orangeman, Peep o' day Boys, Pentecostal, Pietism, Prod, Puritan, Religioner, Sacramentarian, Stundist, Swaddler, Wasp, Wesleyan

Protocol Agreement, Code, Convention, Etiquette, Genevan, Point-to-Point

Proton Nucleon, Quark

Protoplasm(ic) Coenocyte, Coenosarc, Cytode, Sarcode

Prototype Blueprint, Exemplar, Model, Original, Pattern

Protozoa(n) Am(o)eba, Foraminifer, Giardia, Globigerina, Gregarine, Heliozoan, Infusoria, Leishmania, Mastigophoran, Moner(a), Moneron, Paramecium, Peritricha, Radiolaria, Rhizopod, Thrichomonad, Trophozoite, Trypanosome, Volvox, Vorticella

Protract(ed) Delay, > EXTEND, Lengthen, Livelong, Prolong

Protrude, Protrusion Bulge, Eventration, Exsert, Jut, Pop, Pout, Project, Pseudopodium, Rectocele, Strout, Tel

Protuberance, Protuberant Apophysis, Bulge, Bump, Burl, Condyle, Crankle, Gibbous, Hump, Knap, Knob, Malleolus, Node, Papillose, Papule, Spadix, Swelling, Tragus, Tuber, Tubersity, Venter

Proud Arrogant, Boaster, Cocky, Conceited, Dic(k)ty, Elated, Flush, Haughty, Haut, Level, Lordly, Orgulous, Protruding, Superb, Vain

Prove(d), Proving Apod(e)ictic, Argue, Ascertain, Assay, Attest, Authenticate, Aver, Confirm, Convince, Deictic, Evince, Justify, > PROOF, Quote, > SHOW, Substantiate, Test

Proverb Adage, Axiom, Byword, Gnome, Maxim, Paroemia, Saw

Proverbial *may refer to* the biblical Proverbs

Provide(d), Provident(ial) Afford, Allow, Arrange, Besee, Bring, Cater, Compare, Conditional, Endow, Equip, Far-seeing, Fend, Find, Furnish, Generate, Give,

Grubstake, Heaven sent, If, Lay on, Maintain, Proviso, Purvey, Serve, So, Sobeit, > **SUPPLY**, Suttle

Province, Provincial(ism) Acadia, Alberta, Anjou, Antwerp, Aquitaine, Area, Chinghai, Connacht, Dauphine, District, Drenthe, Eparchy, Eritrea, Exclave, Eyalet, Forte, Friesland, Gamsu, Gascony, Gaul, Gauteng, Gelderland, Groningen, Guangdong, Guelderland, Guienne, Guyenne, Hainau(l)t, Hebel, Helvetia, Henan, Hesse-Nassau, Hubei, Hunan, Ifni, Illyriaim, Insular, Jehol, Jiangsu, Jiangxi, Jiazhou, Jilin, Kaliningrad, Kansu, Kiangsu, Kiaochow, Kirin, Kosovo, Kwazulu, Land, Languedoc, Leinster, Liaoning, Liege, Limousin, Limpopo, Livonia, Lorraine, Lusitania, Lyonnais, Manitoba, Marche, Maritime, Mofussil, Mpumalanga, Munster, Namur, Narrow, Natal, New Brunswick, Ning(h)sia, Nivernais, Nome, Normandy, North Brabant, North West (frontier), Oblast, Ontario, Orange Free State, Orleanais, Otago, Overijssel, Palatinate, Pale, Paphlagonia, Patavinity, Petrographic, Picardy, Poitou, Prairie, Provence, Punjab, Qinghai, Quebec, Realm, Regional, R(h)aetia, Roussillon, Rural, Sanjak, Santa Cruz, Saskatchewan, Satrapy, Shaanx, Shandong, Shansi, Shantung, Shanxi, Shensi, Shoa, Sichuan, Sikang, Sind, Sircar, South Holland, Subah, Suburban, Syrophoenicia, Szechwan, Territory, Tirol, Touraine, Transvaal, Tsinghai, Tyrol, Ulster, Utrecht, Vilayet, Western, West Prussia, Yunnan, Zeeland, Zhejiang

Provision(s), Provisional Acates, A(p)panage, Board, Fodder, Insolvency, Jointure, Larder, Makeshift, Proggins, Scran, Skran, Stock, Supply, Suttle, Viands, Viaticum, Victuals

Proviso, Provisional Caution, Caveat, Clause, Condition, Interim, IRA, On trial, Reservation, Salvo, Stipulation, Temporary, Tentative

Provocation, Provocative, Provoke Agacant, Alluring, Egg, Elicit, Erotic, Exacerbate, Excite, Flirty, Harass, Incense, Induce, Inflame, Instigate, Irk, Irritate, Needle, Nettle, Occasion, Pique, Prompt, Raise, Red rag, Sedition, Spark, Stimulate, Tar, Tease, Urge, Vex, Wind up

Provost Dean, Keeper, Marshal, Warden

Prow Bow, Cutwater, Fore, Nose, Prore, Stem

Pro-war Hawk

Prowess Ability, Bravery, Forte, Fortitude

Prowl(er) Hunt, Lurch, Lurk, Mooch, Prole, Rache, Ramble, Ratch, Roam, Rove, Snoke, Snook, Snowk, Tenebrio, Tom

Proxime accessit Next best

Proximity Handiness

Proxy Agent, Attorn, Deputy, PP, Regent, Sub, Surrogate, Vicar, Vice

Prude(nce), Prudent, Prudery Bluenose, Canny, Caution, Circumspect, Comstocker, Conservative, Discreet, Discretion, Foresight, Frugal, Grundyism, Judicious, Metis, Mrs Grundy, Politic, Prig, Prissy, Provident, Sage, Sensible, Sparing, Strait-laced, Strait-lacer, Thrifty, Tight-laced, Vice-nelly, Victorian, Ware, Wary, Well-advised, Wise

Prune(r) Bill-hook, Dehorn, Lop, Plum, Proign, Proin(e), Reduce, Reform, Secateur, Shred, Sned, Thin, Trim

Prunella Hedge-sparrow, Self-heal

Prurient Avaricious, Itchy, Lewd, Obscene

Prussia(n) Blue, Junker, Pruce, Spruce, Westphalian

Pry Ferret, Force, Lever, Meddle, Nose, Paul, Peep, Question, Search, Snoop, Stickyback, Toot

Psalm Anthem, Cantate, Chant, Chorale, Hallel, Hymn, Introit, Jubilate, Metrical, Miserere, Neck-verse, Paean, Penitential, Proper, Ps, Song, Tone,

Tract, Venite

Pseud(o) Bogus, Mock, Posy, Sham, Spurious

Pseudonym Aka, Alias, Allonym, Anonym, Pen-name, Stage-name

Pshaw Chut, Pooh, Tilley-valley, Tilly-fally, Tilly-vally

Psyche Ego, Self, Soul, Spirit, Superego

Psychiatrist, Psychologist Adler, Alienist, Clare, Coué, Ellis, Freud, Headshrinker, Jung, Laing, Rat-tamer, Reich, Shrink, Trick-cyclist

Psychic, Psychosis ESP, Korsakoff's, Lodge, Medium, Seer, Telekinesis, Telepathic

Psychological, Psychology, Psychologist Analytical, Behaviourism, Clinical, Depth, Dynamic, Educational, Experimental, Eysenck, Gestalt, Hedonics, Humanistic, Industrial, Latah, Occupational, Organisational, Piaget, Social, Structural

Psychosis, Psychotic Korsakoff's, Manic-depressive, Organic

Ptarmigan Rype

Ptomaine Neurine

Pub Bar, Beerhall, Beverage room, Boozer, Chequers, Free-house, Gin-palace, Houf(f), House, Howf(f), Inn, Jerry-shop, Joint, Local, Mughouse, Pothouse, Potshop, Rubbidy, Rubbity, Shanty, Tavern, Tiddlywink

Puberty Adolescence, Hebetic, Teens

Pubescence Tomentum

Public Apert, Bar, Civil, Common, Demos, General, Inn, Lay, Limelight, National, Open, Out, Overt, Populace, State, Vulgar, World

Publican Ale-keeper, Bung, Host, Landlord, Licensee, Tapster, Taverner

Publication Announcement, Bluebook, Broadsheet, Edition, Ephemera, Exposé, Festschrift, Issue, >JOURNAL, Lady, Mag, Organ, Pictorial, Samizdat, Tabloid, Tatler, Tract, Tribune, Yearbook

Publicist, Publicity Ad(vert), Airing, Ballyhoo, Coverage, Exposure, Flack, Glare, Headline, Hype, Leakage, Limelight, Notoriety, Plug, PRO, Promotion, Propaganda, Réclame, Spin-doctor, Splash

Publish(er), Published, Publishing, Publicise Air, Blaze, Cape, Delator, Desktop, Disclose, Edit, Electronic, Evulgate, Gollancz, Issue, Noise, OUP, Out, Pirate, Plug, Post, Print(er), Proclaim, Propagate, Put about, Release, Run, Vanity, Vent, Ventilate

Puck Disc, Elf, Lob, Sprite, Squid

Pucker(ed) Cockle, Contract, Gather, Plissé, Purse, Ruck, Shir(r), Wrinkle

Pud Fin, Paw

Pudding Afters, Baked Alaska, Bakewell, Black, Blancmange, Blood, Brown Betty, Cabinet, Charlotte, Christmas, Clootie dumpling, College, Custard, Dessert, Drisheen, Duff, Dumpling, Eve's, Flummery, Fritter, Fromenty, Frumenty, Furme(n)ty, Furmity, Haggis, Hasty, Hodge, Hog's, Kugel, Mealie, Milk, Nesselrode, Panada, Pandowdy, Parfait, Pease, Plum, Popover, Rice, Roly-poly, Sago, Semolina, Sowens, Sponge, Spotted dick, Stickjaw, Stodge, Suet, Summer, Sundae, Sweet, Tansy, Tapioca, Umbles, White hass, White hause, White hawse, Yorkshire, Zabaglione

Puddle Collect, Dub, Flush, Pant, Plash, Plouter, Plowter, Pool, Sop

Puff(ed), Puffer, Puffy Advertise, Blouse, Blow, Blowfish, Blurb, Bouffant, Breath, Chuff, Chug, Drag, Encomist, Eulogy, Exsufflicate, Fag, Flaff, Flatus, Fluffy, Fuff, Globe-fish, Grampus, Gust, Hype, Lunt, Pech, Pegh, Pluffy, Plug, Powder, Recommend, Skiff, Slogan, Steam, Swell, Toke, Waff, Waft, Waif, Whiff, Whiffle

Puffin Fratercula, Rockbird, Sea-parrot, Tammie Norie, Tam Noddy

Pug(ilist) Belcher, Boxer, Bruiser, Carlin, Fancy, Fistic, Monkey

Pugnacious Aggressive, Belligerent, Combative

Puke Retch, Sick, Vomit

Pukka Authentic, Genuine, Real, True

Pulchritude Beauty, Cheese-cake, Grace

Pull (up) Adduce, Attraction, Crane, Drag, Draw, Earn, Force, Haul, Heave, Heeze, Hook, > INFLUENCE, Lug, Mousle, Pluck, Rein, Ring, Rove, Rug, Saccade Sally, Sole, Sool(e), Sowl(e), Stop, Tit, Tow, Trice, Tug, Undertow, Wrest, Yank

Pulley Block, Capstan, Idle(r), Jack-block, Swig, Trice, Trochlea, Truckle

Pullover Jersey, Jumper, Sweater, Sweatshirt, Tank-top, Windcheater

Pullulate Teem

▶ **Pull up** *see* PULL

Pulp Cellulose, Chyme, Chymify, Crush, Flong, Gloop, Kenaf, Marrow, Mash, Mush, Pap, Paste, Pomace, Pound, Puree, Rot, Rubbish, Squeeze, Squidge, Wood

Pulpit(e) Ambo(nes), Lectern, Mimbar, Minbar, Pew, Rostrum, Tent, Tub, Wood

Pulsate Beat, Palpitate, Quiver, Throb, Vibrate

Pulse Alfalfa, > BEAN, Beat, Calavance, Caravance, Chickpea, D(h)al, Dholl, Dicrotic, Flageolet, Garbanzo, Gram, Groundnut, Ictus, Lentil, Lucerne, Pea, Rhythm, Sain(t)foin, Soy beans, Sphygmus, Sync, Systaltic, Systole, Throb

Pulverise Calcine, Comminute, Contriturate, Demolish, Grind, > POUND, Powder

Puma Catamount, Cougar, Mountain lion, Panther

Pummel(ling) Beat, Drub, Fib, Knead, Nevel, Pound, Tapotement, Thump

▷ **Pummelled** *may indicate* an anagram

Pump Bellows, Bowser, Centrifugal, Chain, Compressor, Cross-question, Donkey, Drive, Electromagnetic, Elicit, Feed, Filter, Force, Grease-gun, Grill, Heart, Heat, Hydropult, Inflate, Knee-swell, Lift, Mud, Nodding-donkey, Parish, Petrol, Piston, Pulsometer, Question, Rotary, Scavenge, Shoe, Stirrup, Stomach, Suction, Turbine, Vacuum, Water, Wind

Pumphandle Sweep

Pumpkin Butternut, Cashaw, Gourd, Pampoen, Quash, Queensland blue

Pun Calembour, Clinch, Equivoque, Paragram, Paronomasia, Quibble, Ram, Wordplay

Punch(ed) Antic, Biff, Blow, Boff, Bolo, Box, Bradawl, Bumbo, Card, Centre, Chad, Check, Chop, Clip, Cobbler's, Dry-beat, Fib, Fid, Fist(ic), Gang, Glogg, Haymaker, Hit, Hook, Horse, Jab, Key, Kidney, Knobble, Knubble, KO, Lander, Mat, Milk, Nail set, Nubble, One-er, Overhand, Perforate, Pertuse, Planter's, Plug, Poke, Polt, Pommel, Pounce, Prod, Pummel, Rabbit, Roundhouse, Rum, Rumbo, Slosh, Sock, Sting(o), Stoush, Sucker, Suffolk, Sunday, Swop, Upper-cut, Wap, Wind, Zest

Punctilious Exact, Formal, Nice, Particular, Picked, Precise, Prim, Stickler

Punctual(ity) Politesse, Prompt, Regular

Punctuate, Punctuation (mark) Apostrophe, Bracket, Close, Colon, Comma, Duckfoot quote, Emphasize, Guillemet, Interabang, Interrobang, Interrupt, Mark, Semicolon

Puncture(d) Bore, Centesis, Criblé, Cribrate, Deflate, Drill, Flat, Hole, Lumbar, Perforate, Pierce, Prick, Scarify

Pundit Egghead, Expert, Guru, Maven, Oracle, Sage, Savant, Swami, Teacher

Pungency, Pungent Acid, Acrid, Acrolein, Alum, Ammonia, Bite, Bitter, Caustic, Hot, Mordant, Nidorous, Piquant, Poignant, Point, Racy, Sair, Salt, Spice, Sting, Tangy, Witty

Punish(ed), **Punishing**, **Punishment** Amerce, Attainder, Baffle, Bastinado, Beat, Birch, Brasero, Cane, Capital, Cart, Castigate, Chasten, Chastise, Come-uppance, Commination, Corporal, Correct, Cucking-stool, Dam(nation), Defrock, Desert(s), Detention, > DISCIPLINE, Fatigue, Fine, Flog, Gantlope, Gate, Gauntlet, Gruel, Hellfire, Hiding, Horsing, Hot seat, Imposition, Impot, Interdict, Jankers, Jougs, Keelhaul, Knout, Laldie, Laldy, Lambast(e), Lines, Log, Marmalise, Necklace, Nemesis, Pack-drill, Pandy, Penalise, Penance, Penology, Perdition, Picket, Pillory, Pine, Rap, Reprisal, Retribution, Ruler, Scaffold, Scath, Scourge, Sentence, Six of the best, Smack, Smite, Spank, Spif(f)licate, Stocks, Strafe, Straff, Strap, Strappado, Swinge(ing), Talion, Tar and feather, Toco, Toko, Tophet, Treadmill, Trim, Tron, Trounce, Tumbrel, Tumbril, Visit, War(r)ison, What for, Whip, Ywrake, Ywroke

Punish *may indicate* an anagram

Punk Goop, Inferior, Neer-do-well, Nobody, Touchwood, Worthless

Punnet Basket, Thug

Punt(er), **Punting** Antepost, Back, Bet, Gamble, Kent, Kick, Pound, Quant, Turfite, Wager

Puny Frail, Inferior, Petty, Reckling, Runtish, Scram, Shilpit, Sickly, Small, Weak

Pup(py) Cub, Whelp

Pupa Chrysalis, Exarate, Neanic, Nymph, Obtect

Pupil Abiturient, Apple, Apprentice, Boarder, Cadet, Catechumen, Dayboy, Disciple, Etonian, Exit, Eyeball, Follower, Gyte, Junior, L, Monitor, Prefect, Preppy, Protégé(e), Scholar, Senior, Student, Tutee, Ward

Pupil *may refer to* an eye

Puppet(eer) Bunraku, Creature, Doll, Dummy, Faineant, Fantoccini, Glove, Guignol, Jack-a-lent, Judy, Mammet, Marionette, Mawmet, Mommet, Motion(-man), Pageant, Pawn, Pinocchio, Promotion, Punch(inello), Quisling, Rod, Tool

Purchase(r), **Purchasing** Acquisition, Bargain, Buy, Coff, Compulsory, Earn, Emption, Gadsden, Get, Grip, Halliard, Halyard, Hold, Layaway, > LEVERAGE, Louisiana, Parbuckle, Perquisitor, Secure, Shop, Toehold

Pure, **Purity** Absolute, Cando(u)r, Cathy, Chaste, Chiarezza, Clean(ly), Cosher, Fine, Good, Holy, Immaculate, Incorrupt, Innocent, Intemerate, Inviolate, Kathy, Kosher, Lily, Lilywhite, Maidenhood, Me(a)re, Net(t), Pristine, Quintessence, Sanctity, Sheer, Simon, Simple, Sincere, Snow-white, Stainless, True, Unalloyed, Vertue, Virgin, Virtue, White

Puree Coulis, Fool

Purgative, **Purge** Aloes, Aloetic, Araroba, Cacoon, Calomel, Cascara, Cassia, Castor-oil, Catharsis, Cholagogue, Colquintida, Croton, Delete, Diacatholicon, Diarrh(o)ea, Drastic, Elaterin, Elaterium, Eliminate, Eluant, Emetic, Enos®, Erase, Evacuant, Exonerate, Expiate, Flux, Gleichschaltung, Hiera-picra, Hydragogue, Ipecacuanha, Ipomoea, Jalap, Jalop, Laxative, McCarthyism, Physic, Picra, Pride's, Relaxant, Scour, Scur, Senna, Soil, Turbith, Turpeth, Wahoo

Purification, **Purifier**, **Purify(ing)** Absolve, Bowdlerise, Catharsis, Clay, Clean(se), Depurate, Despumate, Dialysis, Distil, Edulcorate, Elution, Exalt, Expurgate, Filter, Fine, Gas-lime, Green vitriol, Lustre, Lustrum, Niyama, Refine, Retort, Samskara, Sanctify, Scorify, Scrub, Try

Puritan(ical) Bible belt, Bluenose, Digger(s), Ireton, Ironsides, Pi, Pilgrim, Plymouth Colony, Precisian, Prude, Prynne, Roundhead, Seeker, Strait-laced, Traskite, Waldenses, Wowser, Zealot

Purl(er) Cropper, Eddy, Fall, Knit, Ripple, Stream

Purloin Abstract, Annex, Appropriate, Lift, Nab, Pilfer, Snaffle, Sneak, Steal

Purple Amarantin(e), Amethyst, Assai, Aubergine, Burgundy, Cassius, Chlamys, Claret, Corkir, Cudbear, Dubonnet, Eminence, Golp(e), Heather, Heliotrope, Hyacinthine, Imperial, Indigo, Korkir, Lavender, Lilac, Magenta, Mallow, Mauvin(e), Mulberry, Murrey, Orcein, Orcin(e), Orcinol, Pance, Pansy, Plum, Pompadour, Pontiff, Porporate, Proin(e), Puce, Puke, Punic, Purpurin, Rhodopsin, Royal, Solferino, Tyrian, Violet, Visual

Purport Bear, Claim, Drift, Feck, Mean, Tenor

Purpose Advertent, Aim, Avail, Cautel, Design, Ettle, Goal, Here-to, > INTENT, Mean(ing), Meant, Mint, Motive, Object, Plan, Point, Raison d'être, > REASON, Resolution, Resolve, Sake, Telic, Telos, Tenor, Use

Purposeless Dysteleology, Otiose

Purr Curr, Rumble

Purse Ad crumenam, Bag, Bung, Caba, Clutch, Crease, Crumenal, Fisc, Fisk, Long Melford, Mermaid's, Pocket, Prim, Privy, Prize, Public, Pucker, Spleuchan, Sporran, Wallet, Whistle

▷ **Pursed** *may indicate* one word within another

Pursue(r), **Pursuit** Alecto, Business, Chase, Chivvy, Course, Dog, Follow, Follow up, Hobby, Hot-trod, Hound, Hunt, Line, Practice, Practise, Proceed, Prosecute, Quest, Scouring, Stalk, Trivial

Purulent Mattery

Purvey(or) Cater, Provide, Provisor, Sell, Supply

Pus Empyema, Matter, Purulence, Quitter, Quittor

Push(er), **Push in** Airscrew, Barge, Birr, Boost, Bunt, Butt, Detrude, Drive, Edge, Effort, Elbow, Fire, Horn, Hustle, Impulse, Invaginate, Jostle, Motivation, Nose Nudge, Nurdle, Obtrude, Pitchfork, Plod, Ply, Press, Promote, Propel, Railroad, Ram, Sell, > SHOVE, Snoozle, Subtrude, Thrust, Urge

Pushchair Baby buggy®, Buggy, Stroller, Trundler

Pushover Doddle, Soda

Pusillanimous Coward, Timid, Weak, Weak-kneed, Yellow

Puss(y) Amentum, > CAT, Catkins, Face, Galore, Hare, Malkin, Mouth, Rabbit, Septic

Pussyfoot Dry, Equivocate, Inch, Paw, Steal, TT

Pustule Blotch, Pimple

Put (off; on; out; up) Accommodate, Add, Bet, Cup, Daff, Defer, Dish, Do, Don, Douse, Implant, Impose, Incommode, Inn, Lade, Lodge, Lump, Oust, Pit, Place, Plonk, Set, Smore, Snuff, Station, Stow

Put away Sheathe, Store, Stow

Put down Abase, Degrade, Demean, Disparage, Floor, Humiliate, Land, Snuff, Write

▷ **Put off** *may indicate* an anagram

Putrefaction, **Putrefy(ing)**, **Putrid** Addle, Bitter, Corrupt, Decay, Fester, Olid, Rot, Sepsis, Septic

Putt(ing) Gimme, Gobble, Green, Hash, Pigeon, Sink, > STUPID PERSON

Putter Chug, Club

Put together Assemble, Compile, Synthesize

Puzzle(r) Acrostic, Baffle, Bemuse, Bewilder, Brainteaser, Chinese, Confuse, Conundrum, Crossword, Crux, Egma, Elude, Enigma, Fox, Glaik, Gravel, Intrigue, Jigsaw, Kittle, Logogriph, Magic pyramid, Mind-bender, Monkey, Mystify, Nonplus, Perplex, Ponder, Pose(r), Rebus, Riddle, Rubik's cube®, Sorites, Sphinx, Stick(l)er, Stump, Tangram, Tickler, Wordsearch, Wordsquare

Pygmy Atomy, Dwarf, Negrillo, Negrito, Pyknic, Thumbling
Pyjamas Baby-doll, Churidars, Jimjams
Pyramid Cheops, Chephren, Frustum, Population, Stack, Teocalli
Pyre Bale(-fire), Bonfire, Brasero, Darga, Gha(u)t
Pyrenean Basque
Pyrites Fool's gold, Iron, Mispickel, Mundic, White
Pyrotechnics Arson, Fireworks
Pyroxene Aegirine, Aegirite, Diopside
Pyrus Service-tree
Pythagoras Samian
Pythian (seat) Delphic, Tripod
Python Anaconda, Diamond, Kaa, > SNAKE, Zombi(e)

Qq

Q Koppa, Quebec, Question
QC Silk
Qua As
Quack Charlatan, Crocus, Dulcamara, Empiric, Fake, Homeopath, > IMPOSTOR, Katerfelto, Mountebank, Pretender, Saltimbanco
Quad(rangle) Close, Complete, Compluvium, Court, Em, En, Horse, Pane
Quadrilateral Lambeth, Tetragon, Trapezium, Trapezoid
Quadrille Dance, Lancers, Matador(e), Pantalon
Quaff Carouse, Drink, Imbibe
Quagmire Bog, Fen, Imbroglio, Marsh, Morass, Swamp, Wagmoire
Quail Asteria, Bevy, Bird, Blench, Bob-white, Button, Caille, Colin, Flinch, Harlot, Hen, Quake, Shrink, Tremble
Quaint Cute, Naive, Odd, Old-world, Picturesque, Strange, Twee, Wham, Whim(sy)
Quake(r), Quaking Aminadab, Broad-brim, Dither, Dodder, Fox, Friend, Fry, Hicksite, Obadiah, Penn, Quail, Seism, Shake(r), Shiver, > TREMBLE, Tremor, Trepid
Qualification, Qualified, Qualify Able, Adapt, Adverb, Capacitate, Caveat, Competent, Condition, Degree, Diplomatic, Entitle, Fit, Graduate, Habilitate, Meet, Pass, Proviso, Restrict, Temper, Versed
Quality Aroma, Attribute, Body, Calibre, Cast, Charisma, Essence, Fabric, Fame, First water, Five-star, Flavour, Grade, Inscape, It, Kite-mark, Long suit, Mystique, Pitch, Premium, Primary, Property, Q, Quale, Reception, Sort, Standard, Stature, Style, Substance, Suchness, Thew, Thisness, Timbre, Tone, Up-market, Vinosity, Virgin, Virtu(e), Water, Worth
Qualm Compunction, Misgiving, Scruple
Quandary Dilemma, Fix, Predicament, Trilemma
Quantity > AMOUNT, Analog(ue), Batch, Bundle, Capacity, Deal, Dose, Feck, Fother, Hundredweight, Idempotent, Intake, Jag, Lock, Lot, Mass, Measure, Melder, Myriad, Nonillion, Number, Ocean(s), Operand, Parameter, Parcel, Peck, Plenty, Posology, Pottle, Qs, Qt, Quire, Quota, Quotient, Ream, Scalar, Slather, Slew, Slue, Sum, Surd, Tret, Unknown, Vector, Warp, Whips
Quantum Graviton, Phonon, Photon
Quarantine Isolate, Lazarette
Quark Flavo(u)r, Strange
Quarrel(some) Affray, Aggress, Altercate, Arrow, Barney, Barratry, Barretry, Bate, Bicker, Brabble, Brattle, Brawl, Breach, Breeze, Broil, Brulyie, Brulzie, Bust-up, Cagmag, Cantankerous, Carraptious, Cat and dog, Caterwaul, Chance-medley, Chide, Clash, Combative, Contretemps, Difference, Disagree, Dispute, Dust-up, Eristic, Estrangement, Exchange, Fall out, Feisty, Fracas, Fractious, Fratch(et)y, Fray, Hassle, Issue, Jar, Loggerheads, Outcast, Outfall, Pugnacious, Ragbolt, Row, Spat, Squabble, Tiff, Tink, Vendetta, Wap, Whid, Wrangle

Quarry, **Quarry face** Chalkpit, Chase, Game, Heuch, Mine, Pit, Prey, Scabble, Scent, Stone pit, Victim

Quart Winchester

Quarter(ing), **Quarters** Airt, Barrio, Billet, Canton(ment), Casern(e), Chinatown, Clemency, Close, Coshery, District, Dorm, E, Empty, Enclave, Fardel, Farl, First, Focsle, Forecastle, Forpet, Forpit, Fourth, Ghetto, Ham(s), Harbour, Haunch, Last, Latin, Medina, > MERCY, N, Note, Oda, Pity, Point, Principium, Quadrant, Region, S, Season, Sector, Tail, Trimester, W, Wardroom, Warp, Winter

Quarter-day LD

Quarterdeck *may indicate* a suit of cards

Quartet Foursome, Mess, Tetrad

Quartz Agate, Amethyst, Bristol diamond, Buhrstone, Cacholong, Cairngorm, Chalcedony, Chert, Citrine, Flint, Granophyre, Jasp(er), Morion, Onyx, Plasma, Prase, Rainbow, Rose, Rubasse, Sapphire, Silex, Silica, Smoky, Stishovite, Tiger-eye, Tonalite, Whin Sill

Quash Abrogate, Annul, Quell, Recant, Scotch, Subdue, Suppress, Terminate, Void

Quaver(ing) Shake, Tremulous, Trill, Vibrate, Warble

Quay Bund, Levee, Wharf

Queasy Delicate, Nauseous, Squeamish

Quebec Q

Queen(ly) Adelaide, African, Alcestis, Alexandra, Anna, Anne, Artemesia, Atossa, Balkis, Beauty, Bee, Begum, Bess, Boadicea, Boudicca, Brunhild(e), Camilla, Candace, Card, Caroline, Cleopatra, Closet, Clytemnestra, Coatcard, Dido, Drag, Drama, Eleanor(a), Ellery, Ena, ER, Esther, FD, Gertrude, Guinevere, Hatshepset, Hatshepsut, Hecuba, Helen, Hera, Here, Hermione, Hippolyta, HM, Isabel, Isabella, Ishtar, Isolde, Jocasta, Juno, King, Leda, Maam, Mab, Maeve, Marie Antoinette, Mary, Matilda, May, Medb, Mobled, Monarch, Nance, Nefertiti, Omphale, Pance, Pansy, Parr, Paunce, Pawnce, Pearly, Penelope, Persephone, Phaedram, Prince, Proserpina, Qu, R, Ranee, Rani, Regal, Regina(l), Sara, Semiramis, Sheba, Sultana, Titania, Victoria, Virgin, Warrior

Queen Anne Mrs Morley

Queer(ness) Abnormal, Berdash, Bizarre, Crazy, Cure, Curious, Fey, Fie, Fifish, Gay, Nance, Nancy, > ODD, Outlandish, Peculiar, Pervert, Poorly, Quaint, Rum, Spoil, Uranism, Vert

Quell Alegge, Allay, Calm, Quiet, Repress, Subdue, Suppress

Quench Assuage, Cool, Extinguish, Satisfy, Slake, Slo(c)ken, Sta(u)nch, Yslake

Query *see* QUESTION

Quest Goal, Graal, Grail, Hunt, Pursuit, Venture

Question(ing), **Questionnaire** Appose, Ask, Bi-lateral, Burning, Catechise, Chin, Contest, Conundrum, Cross-examine, Debrief, Dichotomous, Direct, Dispute, Dorothy Dixer, Doubt, Erotema, Eroteme, Erotesis, Examine, Fiscal, Good, Grill, Heckle, Impeach, Impugn, Indirect, Information, Innit, Interpellation, Interrogate, Interview, Koan, Leading, Loaded, Maieutic, Matter, Open, Oppugn, Pop, Pose, Previous, Probe, Problem, Pump, Q, Qu, Quaere, Quiz, Rapid-fire, Refute, Rhetorical, Riddle, Speer, Speir, Survey, Suspect, Tag, Teaser, Tickler, Vexed, West Lothian, WH, What, Worksheet

Questionable Ambiguous, Dubious, Fishy, Socratic

Question-master Interrogator, Socrates, Torquemada, Ximenes

Queue Braid, Breadline, Cercus, Crocodile, Cue, Dog, File, Kale, > LINE, Pigtail,

Plait, Plat, Stack, Tail(back), Track

Quibble(r), Quibbling Balk, Carp, Carriwitchet, Casuist, Cavil, Chicaner, Dodge, Elenchus, Equivocate, Hairsplitting, Nitpick, Pedantry, Pettifoggery, Prevaricate, Pun, Quiddity, Quillet, Quirk, Sophist

Quiche Flan, Tart

Quick(en), Quickening, Quicker, Quickly, Quickness Accelerate, Acumen, Adroit, Agile, Alive, Allegr(ett)o, Animate, Apace, Breakneck, Breathing, Brisk Celerity, Chop-chop, Citigrade, Cito, Con moto, Core, Cracking, Cuticle, Dappe Deft, Enliven, Existent, Expeditious, Express, Fastness, Festination, Foothot, Gleg, Hasten, Hie, High-speed, Hotfoot, Impulsive, Jiffy, Keen, Lickety-split, Living, Mercurial, Mistress, Mosso, Nailbed, Nimble, Nippy, Pdq, Piercing, Piu mosso, Post-haste, Prestissimo, Presto, Prompt, Pronto, Rapid, Rath(e), Ready, Rough and ready, Schnell, Sharp, Skin, Slippy, Smart, Snappy, Snort, Sodain(e) Soon, Spry, Streamline, Sudden, Swift, Swith, Tout de suite, Trice, Up tempo, Veloce, Vital, Vite, Vivify, Wikiwiki, Yare

Quicksand Flow, Syrtis

Quicksilver Mercury

Quid Chaw, Chew, L, Nicker, Oner, Plug, Pound, Quo, Sov, Tertium, Tobacco

Quid pro quo Mutuum, Tit-for-tat

Quiescence, Quiescent Calm, Di(o)estrus, Inactive, Inert, Latent, Still

Quiet(en), Quietly Accoy, Allay, Appease, Barnacle, Calm, Compose, Conticent, Doggo, Ease, Easeful, Easy, Encalm, Entame, Gag, Grave, Kail, Laconic, Loun(d), Low, Lown(d), Low-profile, Lull, Meek, Mp, Muffle, Mute, P, Pacify, Pauciloquent, Pause, Peace, Piano, Pipe down, QT, Reserved, Reticent, Sedate, Settle, Sh, Shtoom, Silence, Sitzkrieg, Sly, Sober, Soothe, Sotto voce, Still, Stum(m), Subact, Subdued, Tace, Taciturn, Tranquil, Wheesht, Whish, Whisht, Whist

Quill Calamus, Feather, Float, Plectre, Plectron, Plectrum, Plume, Remex

Quillwort Isoetes

Quilt(ed), Quilting Comfort(er), Continental, Counterpane, Cover, Crazy, Doona®, Duvet, Echo, Eiderdown, Futon, Kantha, Matel(l)asse, Patchwork, Trapunto

Quince Bael, Bel, Bengal, Bhel, Flowering, Japanese, Japonica

Quinine China, Crown-bark, Kina, Quina, Tonic

Quinsy Angina, Cynanche, Garget, Squinancy

Quintessence Heart, Pith

Quintet Pentad, Trout

Quip Carriwitchet, Crack, Epigram, Gibe, Jest, Jibe, Joke, Taunt, Zinger

Quirk Concert, Foible, Idiosyncrasy, Irony, Kink, Twist

Quisling Collaborator, Traitor

Quit(s) Abandon, Absolve, Ap(p)ay, Cease, Desert, Even(s), Go, Leave, Meet, Resign, > **STOP**

Quite Actually, All, Ap(p)ay, Clean, Dead, Enough, Enow, Fairly, Fully, Precisely, Real, Right, Sheer, Very

Quiver(ing) Aspen, Quake, Shake, Sheath, The yips, Tremble, Tremolo, Tremor, Tremulate, Trepid, Vibrant, Vibrate

Qui vive Go-go

Quixote, Quixotic Don, Errant, Impractical

Quiz Bandalore, Bee, Catechism, Examine, Interrogate, I-spy, Mastermind, Oddity, Probe, Pump, Question, Smoke, Trail, Yo-yo

Quizzical Curious, Derisive, Odd, Queer, Socratic

Quod Can, Clink, Jail, Prison

Quoit Disc(us), Disk, Ring
Quondam Once, Sometime, Whilom
Quorum Minyan
Quota Numerus clausus, Proportion, Ration, Share
Quotation, **Quote(d)**, **Quote** Adduce, Citation, Cite, Co(a)te, Duckfoot, Epigraph, Evens, Extract, Forward, Instance, Name, Price, Recite, Reference, Say, Scare, Soundbite, Tag, Verbatim, Wordbite
Quoth Co, Said
Quotient Achievement, Intelligence, Kerma, Quaternion, Ratio, Respiratory

Rr

R Arithmetic, King, Queen, Reading, Recipe, Right, Romeo, Run, Writing

Rabbi Dayan, Mashgiah, Rav, Rebbe

Rabbit Angora, Astrex, Brer, British lop, Buck, Bun(ny), Chat, Con(e)y, Cottontail, Daman, Dassie, Doe, Earbash, Harp, Haver, Hyrax, Jabber, Jack, Klipdas, Long white, Lop-eared, Marmot, Muff, Nest, Novice, Oarlap, Palaver, Patzer, Prate, Rattle, Rex, Rock, Snowshoe, Tapeti, Terricole, Waffle, Welsh, White, Witter, Yak, Yap, Yatter

Rabble Canaille, Clamjamphrie, Clanjamfray, Colluvies, Crowd, Doggery, Galere, Herd, Hoi-polloi, Horde, Legge, Mob, Raffle, Rag-tag, Rascaille, Rascal, Riff-raff, Rout, Scaff-raff, Shower, Tag, Tagrag

Rabelaisian Pantagruel, Panurge

Rabid, Rabies Extreme, Frenzied, Hydrophobia, Lyssa, Mad, Raging, Virulent

Raccoon Coati, Panda, Procyon

Race(course), Racing, Race meeting Aintree, Ancestry, Arms, Ascot, Autocross, Belt, Boat, Boskop, Breed, Broose, Brouze, Bumping, Career, Catadrome, Caucus, Cesarewitch, Chantilly, Chase, Claiming, Classic, Cone, Contest, Corso, Country, Course, Current, Cursus, Cyclo-cross, Dash, Derby, Doggett's Coat and Badge, Dogs, Doncaster, Drag, Dromos, Egg and spoon, Enduro, Epsom, Event, Fastnet, Flapping, Flat, Flow, Fun-run, Generation, Ginger, Goodwood, Grand National, Grand Prix, Handicap, Hare and hounds, Harness, Herrenvolk, Hialeah, Hippodrome, Human(kind), Hurry, Inca, Indy, Indy Car, Kermesse, Kind, Lampadedromy, Lampadephoria, Leat, Leet, Leger, Le Mans, Lick, Lignage, Line(age), Longchamps, Madison, Man, Marathon, Master, Meets, Mile, Motocross, > **NATIONAL**, Newmarket, Nursery, Nursery stakes, Oaks, Obstacle, One-horse, Paceway, Palio, Paper chase, Pattern, Picnic, Plate, Pluck, Point-to-point, Potato, Pursuit, Rallycross, Rallying, Rapids, Rat, Redcar, Regatta, Relay, Rill, Rod, Ronne, Roost, Sack, St Leger, Scramble, Scratch, Scud, Scurry, Seed, Selling, Shan, Slalom, Slipstream, Sloot, Slot-car, Sluit, Speedway, Sprint, Stakes, Steeplechase, Stem, Stirp(s), Stirpes, Stock, Strain, Streak, Strene, Sweepstake, Tail, Taste, Tear, Thousand Guineas, Three-legged, Tide, Torch, Torpids, Towcester, Tribe, Trotting, TT, Turf, Two-horse, Two Thousand Guineas, Velodrome, Volsungs, Walking, Walk-over, Waterway, Wetherby, Wetter, Whid, White, Wincanton

Racehorse, Racer Eclipse, Filly, Go-kart, Hare, Maiden, Novice, Plater, Red Rum, Steeplechaser, Trotter

Raceme Corymb, Panicle

Racial (area) Apartheid, Colour, Ethnic, Ghetto, Quarter

Rack Agonise, Bin, Cloud, Cratch, Drier, Flake, Frame, Hack, Hake, Plate, Pulley, Roof, Stretcher, Toast, Torment, Torture

Racket(eer) Bassoon, > **BAT**, Battledore, Bloop, Brattle, Caterwaul, Chirm, Clamour, Crime, Deen, Din, Discord, Earner, > **FIDDLE**, Gyp, Hubbub, Hustle, > **NOISE**, Noisiness, Protection, Ramp, Rort, Sokaiya, Stridor, Swindle, Tumult, Uproar, Utis

Racy Ethnic, Piquant, Pungent, Ribald, Salty, Spicy, Spirited

Rad Rem

Radar Angel, AWACS, Beacon, DEW line, Doppler, Gadget, Gee, Gull, Lidar, Loran, Monopulse, Navar, Rebecca-eureka, Shoran, Surveillance, Teleran®, Tracking

Raddle Hurdle, Ochre, Red

Radial Quadrant, Rotula, Spoke

Radiance, Radiant Actinic, Aglow, Aureola, Beamish, Brilliant, Gleam(y), Glory, Glow, Happy, Lustre, Refulgent, Shechina, Sheen, Shekinah

Radiate, Radiating, Radiation, Radiator Actinal, Adaptive, Air-colour, Beam, Bremsstrahlung, C(h)erenkov, Disseminate, Dosimetry, Effuse, Emanate, Emit, Exitance, Fluorescence, Gamma, Glow, Hawking, Heater, Infrared, Ionizing, Isohel, Laser, Millirem, Pentact, Photon, Pulsar, Quasar, Rem(s), Rep, Roentgen, > SHINE, Sievert, Spherics, Spoke, Stellate, Stray, SU, Sun, Synchroton, Terrestrial, Ultra violet, UVA, UVB, Van Allen, Visible

Radical Allyl, Amide, Amyl, Aryl, Benzil, Benzoyl, Bolshevist, Bolshie, Butyl, Calumba, Carbene, Cetyl, Dyad, Ester, Extreme, Fundamental, Gauchist, Genre-busting, Glyceryl, Glycosyl, Hydroxy, Innate, Isopropyl, Leftist, Leveller, Ligand, Maximalist, Methyl, Montagnard, Nitryl, Oxonium, Parsnip, Phenyl, Phosphonium, Pink, Propyl, Red, Revolutionary, Rhizocaul, Root, Rudiment, Sulfone, Sulphone, Trot(sky), Uranyl, Vinyl, Whig, Xylyl

Radio Boom-box, Cat's whisker, CB, Cellular, Citizen's band, Crystal set, Digital, Ether, Gee, Ghetto-blaster, Local, Loudspeaker, Marconigraph, Receiver, Reflex, Set, Simplex, Sound, Steam, Talkback, Tranny, Transceiver, Transistor, Transmitter, Transponder, Walkie-talkie, Walkman®, Walky-talky, Wireless

Radioactive, Radioactivity Actinide, Americium, Astatine, Bohrium, Cobalt 60, Emanation, Fall-out, Hot, Nucleonics, Plutonium, Radon, Steam, Thorium, Uranite

Radiogram Cable, Telegram, Wire

Radish Charlock, Mooli, Runch

Radium Ra

Radius Long, Schwarzschild, Short

Radon Rn

Raffia Rabanna

Raffle(s) Burglar, Draw, Lottery, Sweepstake

Raft(ing) Balsa, Catamaran, Float, Kontiki, Life, Pontoon, Whitewater

Rafter Barge-couple, Beam, Chevron, Jack, Joist, Ridge, Spar, Timber

Rag(ged), Rags Bait, Bate, Clout, Coral, Daily, Deckle, Dud(s), Duddery, Duddie, Duster, Fent, Figleaf, Glad, Guyed, Haze, Kid, Lap(pie), Lapje, Mop, Nose, Paper, Red, Remnant, Revel, Rivlins, Roast, Rot, S(c)hmatte, Scold, Scrap, > SHRED, Slate, Slut, Splore, Tack, Tat(t), Tatter(demalion), Tatty, Taunt, > TEASE, Tiger, Tongue, Uneven

▷ **Rag(ged)** *may indicate an anagram*

Rage, Raging > ANGER, Ardour, Bait, Bate, Bayt, Chafe, Conniption, Explode, Fashion, Fierce, Fit, Fiz(z), Fume, Furibund, Furore, Fury, Gibber, Go, Ire, Mode, Monkey, Paddy(-whack), Passion, Pelt, Pet, Pique, Rabid, Rail, Ramp, Rant, Road, Snit, Storm, Tear, Temper, Ton, Trolley, Utis, Wax, Wrath

Raglan Sleeve

Ragout Compot, Goulash, Haricot, Stew

Rag-picker Bunter

Raid(er) Assault, Attack, Baedeker, Bodrag, Bust, Camisado, Chappow, Commando, Corporate, Dawn, Do, For(r)ay, Imburst, Incursion, Inroad, Inrush,

Invade, Jameson, Maraud, March-treason, Mosstrooper, Pict, Pillage, Plunder, Ram, Ransel, Razzia, Reive, Sack, Scrump, Skrimp, Skrump, Smash-and-grab, Sortie, Spreagh, Storm, Viking

Rail(er), Railing Abuse, Amtrack, Arm, Arris, Balustrade, Ban, Banister, > **BAR**, Barre, Barrier, Bird, Bullhead, Cloak, Conductor, Coot, Corncrake, Crake, Criticise, Dado, Fender, Fiddle, Fife, Flanged, Flat-bottomed, Flow, Gush, Insult, Inveigh, Light, Live, Metal, Neckerchief, Notornis, Parclose, Picture, Pin, Plate, Post, Pulpit, Rag, Rate, Rave, Rung, Scold, Slang-whang, Slate, Slip, Snash, Sneer, Sora, Soree, Spar, T, Taffrail, Takahe, Taunt, Thersites, Third, Towel, Train, Vituperation, Weka

Raillery Badinage, Banter, Chaff, Persiflage, Sport

Railroad, Railway Amtrak, BR, Bulldoze, Cable, Cash, Coerce, Cog, Cremaillère, Dragoon, El, Elevated, Funicular, GWR, Inclined, L, Light, Lines, LMS, LNER, Loop-line, Maglev, Marine, Metro, Monorail, Mountain, Narrow-gauge, Rack, Rack and pinion, Rly, Road, Rollercoaster, Ropeway, ROSCO, Ry, Scenic, SR, Stockton-Darlington, Switchback, Telpher-line, Track, Train, Tramline, Tramway, Trans-Siberian, Tube, Underground

Railwayman Driver, Guard, NUR, Stephenson, Stoker

Raiment Apparel, Clothes, Garb, Ihram

Rain(y) Acid, Brash, Deluge, Drizzle, Hyad(e)s, Hyetal, Mistle, Mizzle, Oncome, Onding, Onfall, Pelt, Pluviose, Pluvious, Pour, Precipitation, Right, Roke, Scat, Seil, Serein, Serene, Shell, Shower, Sile, Silver thaw, Skiffle, Skit, Smir(r), Smur, Soft, Spat, Spet, Spit, Storm, Thunder-plump, Virga, Weep, Wet, Yellow

Rainbow(-maker) Arc, Bifrost, Bruise, Dew-bow, Indescence, Iris, Moon-bow, Spectroscope, Sunbow, Sundog, Water-gall, Weather-gall, White

Raincoat Burberry®, Gaberdine, Mac, Mino, Oils(kins), Slicker, Waterproof

Raingauge Ombrometer, Udometer

Rain-maker Indra

Rain tree Saman

Raise(d), Raising Advance, Aggrade, Attollent, Boost, Build, Cat, Coaming, Cock, Collect, Elate, > **ELEVATE**, Emboss, Enhance, Ennoble, Erect, Escalate, Exalt, Extol, Fledge, Grow, Heave, Heezie, Heft, High, Hike, Hoist, Increase, Jack, Key, Leaven, Lift, Mention, Overcall, Perk, Rear, Regrate, Repoussé, Revie, Rouse, Saleratus, Siege, Sky, Snarl, Step-up, Sublimate, Upgrade, Weigh

Rake, Raker, Rakish Casanova, Comb, Corinthian, Croupier, Dapper, Dissolute, Enfilade, Jaunty, Lecher, Libertine, Lothario, Raff, Reprobate, Rip, Roué, Scan, Scour, Scowerer, Scratch, Strafe, Stubble, Swash-buckler, Swinge-buckler, Wagons

Rale Crepitus, Rattle

Rally, Rallying-point Autocross, Autopoint, Badinage, Banter, Demo, Gather, Jamboree, Meeting, Mobilise, Monte Carlo, Muster, Oriflamme, Persiflage, Recover, Rely, Rest, Risorgimento, Roast, Rouse, Scramble

Ralph Imp, Nader, Rackstraw

Ram Aries, Battering, Buck, Bunt, Butter, Corvus, Crash, Drive, Hidder, Hydraulic, Mendes, Pun, Sheep, Stem, Tamp, Tup, Wether

Ramble(r), Rambling Aberrant, Aimless, Digress, Incoherent, Liana, Liane, Rigmarole, Roam, Rose, Rove, Skimble-skamble, Sprawl, Stray, Stroll, Vagabond, Wander

Rameses Pharaoh

Ramp Bank, Gradient, Helicline, Incline, Slipway, Slope

Rampage Fury, Spree, Storm, Warpath

Rampant Lionel, Predominant, Profuse, Rearing, Rife

Rampant *may indicate* an anagram or a reversed word
Rampart Abat(t)is, Brisure, Butt, Defence, Fortification, Parapet, Terreplein, Vallum, Wall
Ramrod Gunstick
Ramshackle Decrepit, Heath Robinson, Rickety, Rickle
Ranch Bowery, Corral, Dude, Farm, Hacienda, Spread
Rancid Frowy, Reast(y), Reest(y), Sour, Turned
Rancour Gall, Hate, Malice, Resentment, Spite
Rand Border, R, Roon
Random Accidental, Aleatoric, Arbitrary, > **AT RANDOM**, Blind, Casual, Desultory, Fitful, > **HAPHAZARD**, Harvest, Hit-or-miss, Hobnob, Indiscriminate, Scattershot, Sporadic, Stochastic
Random(ly) *may indicate* an anagram
Range(r), Rangy Align, Ambit, Andes, Atlas, AZ, Ballpark, Band, Bowshot, Bushwhack, Capsule, Carry, Cheviot, Compass, Cotswolds, Course, Darling, Diapason, Dispace, Dolomites, Dynamic, Err, > **EXTENT**, Eye-shot, Flinders, Forest, Gamut, Glasgow, Gunshot, Hamersley, Harmonic, Helicon, Himalayas, Interquartile, Ken(ning), Kolyma, Ladakh, Leggy, Limit, Line, Long, Massif, Middleback, > **MOUNT**, Orbit, Oven, Owen Stanley, Palette, Point-blank, Prairie, Purview, Rake, Reach, Register, Repertoire, Rifle, Roam, Rocket, Scale, Scope, Sc(o)ur, Selection, Short, Sierra, Sloane, Spectrum, Sphere, Stove, Strzelecki, Tape, Tessitura, Teton, Texas, Tier, Urals, Waldgrave, Wasatch, Waveband, Woomera
Rank(s) Arrant, Ayatollah, Begum, Brevet, Caste, Category, Cense, Classify, Cornet, Curule, Degree, Dignity, Downright, Earldom, Estate, Etat(s), Flight sergeant, Grade, Graveolent, Gross, High, Hojatoleslam, Hojatolislam, Majority, Olid, Parage, Percentile, Place, Range, Rate, Rooty, Row, Seed, Seigniorage, Sergeant, Serried, Shoulder-strap, Sort, Standing, > **STATION**, Status, Substantive, Taxi, Tier, > **TITLE**, Titule, Utter, Viscount
Rankle Chafe, Gall, Irritate, Nag
Ransack Fish, Loot, Pillage, Plunder, Rifle, Ripe, Rob, Rummage
Ransom King's, Redeem, Release, Rescue
Rant(er), Ranting Bombast, Declaim, Fustian, Ham, Harangue, Rail, Rodomontade, Scold, Spout, Spruik, Stump, Thunder, Tub-thump
Rap(ped) Blame, Censure, Chat, Clour, Gangsta, Halfpenny, Knock, Ratatat, Shand, Strike, Swapt, Tack, Tap
Rapacious Accipitrine, Esurient, Exorbitant, Greedy, Harpy, Kite, Predatory, Ravenous, Ravine
Rape Abuse, Assault, Belinda, Cole-seed, Colza, Creach, Creagh, Date, Deflower, Despoil, Gangbang, Hundred, Lock, Lucretia, Navew, Oilseed, Plunder, Statutory, Stuprate, Thack, Tow, Violate
Rapid(ity), Rapidly Chute, Dalle, Double-quick, Express, Fast, Meteoric, Mosso, Presto, Pronto, Quick-fire, Riffle, Sault, Shoot, Skyrocket, Speedy, Stickle, Swift, Tantivy, Veloce, Wildfire
Rapier Sword, Tuck
Rappel Abseil
Rapport Accord, Affinity, Agreement, Harmony
Rapprochement Detente, Reconciliation
Rapt Riveted
Raptor Eagle, Kestrel, Osprey, Standgale, Staniel, Stannel, Stanyel, Stooper
Rapture, Rapturous Bliss, > **DELIGHT**, Ecstasy, Elation, Joy, Trance
Rare, Rarity Blue moon, Curio, Earth, Geason, Infrequent, Intemerate, One-off,

Rear, Recherché, Scarce, Seeld, Seld(om), Singular, > **UNCOMMON**, Uncooked, Underdone, Unusual

Rarefied Thin

Rascal(ly) Arrant, Bad hat, Cad, Cullion, Cur, Deer, Devil, Gamin, Hallian, Hallion, Hallyon, > **KNAVE**, Limner, Loon, Losel, Low, Nointer, Rip, Rogue, Scallywag, Scamp, Scapegrace, Schelm, Skeesicks, Skellum, Skelm, Smaik, Spalpeen, Tinker, Toe-rag, Varlet, Varmint, Villain

Rash(er) Acne, Bacon, Barber's, Brash, Collop, Daredevil, Eruption, Erysipelas, Exanthem(a), Fast, Foolhardy, Harum-scarum, > **HASTY**, Headlong, Hives, Hotspur, Ill-advised, Impetigo, Impetuous, Imprudent, Impulsive, Lardo(o)n, Lichen, Madbrain, Madcap, Miliaria, Morphew, Nappy, Nettle, Outbreak, Overhasty, Precipitate, Purpura, Reckless, Roseola, Rubella, Sapego, Scarlatina, Serpigo, Spots, Tetter, Thoughtless, Unheeding, Unthinking, Urticaria

Rasp(er) File, Grate, Odontophore, Risp, Rub, Scrape, Scroop, Xyster

Raspberry Berate, Black(cap), Boo, Bronx-cheer, Etaerio, Hindberry, Razz

Rastafarian Dread

Rat(s), Ratty Agouta, Bandicoot, Blackleg, Blackneb, Boodie, Brown, Bug-out, Camass, Cane, Cur, Defect, Desert, Fink, Footra, Foutra, Geomyoid, Gym, Heck, Hydromys, Informer, Kangaroo, Mall, Maori, Mole, Moon, Norway, Pack, Poppycock, Potoroo, Pshaw, Pup(py), Renegade, Renegate, Rice, Rink, Rodent, Roland, Rot(ten), Scab, Sewer, Shirty, Squeal, Stinker, Turncoat, Vole, Water, Wharf, Whiskers, White, Wood

Rat-catcher Cat, Ichneumon, Mongoose, Pied Piper

Rate(s), Rating A, Able, Apgar, Appreciate, Assess, Base, Basic, Bit, Carpet, Castigate, Cess, Classify, Cost, Count, Credit, Deserve, Erk, Estimate, Evaluate, Exchange, Grade, Headline, Hearty, Hurdle, Incidence, ISO, Lapse, Leading, Mate's, Mortality, Mortgage, MPH, Octane, Ordinary, OS, Pace, Penalty, Percentage, PG, Piece, Poor, Prime (lending), Rag, Rebuke, Red, Refresh, Reproof, Rocket, Row, Sailor, Scold, > **SET**, Slew, > **SPEED**, Standing, Starting, Surtax, TAM, Tax, Tempo, Tog, U, Upbraid, Value, Water, Wig, World-scale, X

Rather Degree, Fairly, Gey, Instead, Lief, Liever, Loor, More, Prefer, Pretty, Some(what), Sooner, Yes

Ratify Amen, Approve, Confirm, Pass, Sanction, Validate

Ratio Advance, Albedo, Aspect, Bypass, Cash, Compression, Cosine, Distinctiveness, Duplicate, Focal, Fraction, Golden, Gyromagnetic, Inverse, Liquidity, Loss, Mass, Neper, PE, Pi, Pogson, Poisson's, Position, Proportion, Protection, Quotient, Reserve, Savings, Signal-to-noise, Sin(e), Slip, Tensor, Trigonometric

Ration(s) Allocate, Apportion, Compo, Dole, Etape, Iron, K, Quota, Restrict, Scran, Share, Short commons, Size

Rational(isation) A posteriori, Dianoetic, Level-headed, Logical, Lucid, Matter-of-fact, Sane, Sensible, Sine, Sober, Tenable

Rationale Motive

Rattle (box), Rattling Chatter, Clack, Clank, Clap, Clatter, Clitter, Conductor, Crescelle, Crotalaria, Death, Demoralise, Disconcert, Gas-bag, Hurtle, Jabber, Jangle, Jar, Maraca, Natter, Nonplus, Rale, Rap, Red, Reel, Rhonchus, Ruckle, Sabre, Shake, Sistrum, Sunn, Tirl, Upset, Yellow

Raucous Guttural, Hoarse, Loud, Strident

Ravage Depredation, Desecrate, Despoil, Havoc, Pillage, Prey, Ruin, Sack, Waste

Rave, Raving Boil, Enthuse, Praise, Redwood, Redwud, Storm, Ta(i)ver, Tear

Ravel Disentangle, Explain, Involve, Snarl, Tangle

Raven(ous) Black, Corbel, Corbie, Corvine, Croaker, Daw, Grip, Hugin, Munin, Unkindness

Ravine Arroyo, Barranca, Barranco, Canada, Chasm, Chine, Clough, Coulee, Couloir, Dip, Flume, Ghyll, Gorge, Grike, Gulch, Gully, Kedron, Khor, Khud, Kidron, Kloof, Lin(n), Nal(l)a, Nallah, Nulla(h), Pit

Ravish Constuprate, Debauch, Defile, Devour, Rape, Stuprate, Transport, Violate

Raw Brut, Chill, Coarse, Crude, Crudy, Damp, Fresh, Greenhorn, Natural, Recruit, Rude, Uncooked, Wersh

Raw-boned Gaunt, Lanky, Lean, Randle-tree

Ray(s), Rayed Actinic, Alpha, Beam, Beta, Canal, Cathode, Cosmic, Death, Delta, Diactine, Dun-cow, Eagle, Electric, Extraordinary, Fish, Gamma, Grenz, Guitarfish, Homelyn, Manta, Medullary, Monactine, Numbfish, Ordinary, Polyact, Positive, R, Radius, Re, Roentgen, Roker, Röntgen, Sawfish, Sea-devil, Sephen, Shaft, Skate, Starburst, Stick, Sting, Stingaree, Tetract, Thornback, Torpedo, Vascular

Rayon Acetate, Faille, Viscose

Raze Annihilate, Bulldoze, Demolish, Destroy, Level

Razor(-maker) Cut-throat, Occam, Safety

Razorbill Murre

Razor-fish Solen

Razz Raspberry

RE Sappers

Re About, Rhenium, Touching

Reach(ed) Ar(rive), Attain, Boak, Boke, Carry, Come, Get out, Hent, Hit, Key-bugle, Lode, Octave, Peak, Raught, Rax, Retch, Ryke, Seize, Stretch, Touch, Win

Reach-me-downs Slop-clothing

React(or), Reaction(ary) Allergy, Anaphylaxis, Answer, Backlash, Backwash, Behave, Blimp, Blowback, Bourbon, Breeder, Bristle, Bummer, CANDU, Catalysis, Chain, Chemical, Converter, Convertor, Core, Counterblast, Dark, Dibasic, Diehard, Diels-Adler, Dinosaur, Double-take, Falange, Fast(-breeder), Feedback, Fission, Flareback, Furnace, Fusion, Gas-cooled, Graphite, Gut, Hydrolysis, Imine, Insulin, Interplay, Junker, Kickback, Knee-jerk, Light, Magnox, Neanderthal, Nuclear, Outcry, Oxidation, Photolysis, Pile, Poujade, Reciprocate, Recoil, Redox, Repercussion, Respond, Reversible, Rigid, Sensitive, Solvolysis, Spallation, Sprocket, Swing-back, Thermal, Thermonuclear, Tokamak, Vaccinia, Wassermann, Water

Reactionary *may indicate* reversed or an anagram

Read(ing) Bearing, Browse, Decipher, Decode, Exegesis, First, Grind, Grounden, Haftarah, Haphtarah, Interpret, Learn, Lection, Lesson, Lu, Maftir, Maw, Pericope, Peruse, Pore, Rad, Rennet-bag, Scan, Second, See, Solve, Speed, Stomach, > **STUDY**, Third, Vell, Ycond

Reader(s) ABC, Alidad(e), Bookworm, Document, Editor, Epistoler, Homeridae, Lay, Lector, Primer, Silas Wegg, Tape, Taster

Readiest, Readily, Readiness, Ready Alacrity, Alamain, Alert, Amber, Apt, Atrip, Available, Boun, Bound, Brass, Cash, Conditional, Dough, Eager, Early, Eftest, Fettle, Fit, Forward, Game, Geared-up, Gelt, Go, Keyed, Latent, Lolly, Masterman, Money, On, Predy, Prepared, Present, Prest, Primed, Prompt, Reckoner, Ripe, Set, Soon, Spot, Turnkey, Usable, Wherewithal, Willing, Yare, Yark

Readjust Mend, Regulate, Retrue

Readymade Bought, Precast, Prepared, Prêt-à-porter, Slops, Stock, Store
Reagent Analytical, Grignard, Ninhydrin, Reactor, Schiff's, Titrant
Real, Reality, Realities, Really Actual, Bona-fide, Coin, Deed, De facto, Dinkum
Dinky-di(e), Earnest, Echt, Ens, Entia, Entity, Essence, > GENUINE, Honest,
Indeed, Mackay, McCoy, McKoy, Naive, Ontic, Quite, Royal, Simon Pure, Sooth
Sterling, Substantial, Tangible, Tennis, Thingliness, True, Verismo, Verity,
Very, Virtual
Realgar Rosaker, Zarnec, Zarnich
Realise, Realisation, Realism, Realistic Achieve, Attain, Attuite, Cash, Dirty,
Down-to-earth, Embody, Encash, Fetch, Fruition, Fulfil, Learn, Magic, Naive,
Practical, Sell, Sense, Suss, Understand
▶ **Realities, Reality** *see* REAL
Realm Domain, Dominion, Field, Kingdom, Land, Region, Special(i)ty, UK
Ream Bore, Foam, Froth, Paper, Printer's, Rime, Screed
Reap(er) Binder, Crop, Death, Earn, Gather, Glean, Harvest, Scythe, Shear,
Sickleman, Solitary, Stibbler
Reappear(ance) Emersion, Materialise, Recrudesce
Rear(ing) Aft, Back(side), Background, Baft, Behind, Breeches, Bring-up, Bunt,
Cabré, Catastrophe, Derrière, Foster, Haunch, Hind, Hindquarters, Loo, Natch
Nousell, Nurture, Prat, > RAISE, Serafile, Serrefile, Tonneau
Rearmament Moral
Rearrange(ment) Adjust, Anagram, Ectopia, Reorder
Reason(able), Reasoning A fortiori, Analytical, Apagoge, A priori, Argue,
Argument, Basis, Call, Cause, Colour, Consideration, Deduce, Expostulate,
Fair, Ground(s), Hypophora, Ijtihad, Inductive, Intelligent, Justification, Logic
Logical, Logistics, Logos, Mind, Moderate, Motive, Noesis, Petitio principii,
Plausible, Point, Practical, Pretext, Pro, Proof, Pure, Purpose, Ratiocinate,
Rational(e), Sanity, Sense, Sensible, Settler, Syllogism, Synthesis, Temperate,
Think, Why, Wit
Reave Despoil, Reif, Rob, Spoil
Rebate Diminish, Lessen, Refund, Repayment
Rebecca Sharp
Rebel(lion), Rebellious Aginner, Apostate, Arian, Beatnik, Bolshy, Boxer, Cade,
Contra, Croppy, Danton, Diehard, Disobedient, Emeute, Fifteen, Forty-five,
Frondeur, Glendower, Hampden, Hereward the Wake, Iconoclast, Insurgent,
Insurrection, IRA, Jacobite, Jacquerie, Kick, Luddite, Mutine(er), Mutiny,
Oates, Putsch, Rebecca, Recalcitrant, Recusant, Reluct, Resist, Revolt, Rise,
Rum, Scofflaw, Sedition, Sepoy, Spartacus, Steelboy, Straw, Tai-ping, Ted,
Titanism, Tyler, Venner, Warbeck, Whiteboy, Zealot
▷ **Rebellious** *may indicate* a word reversed
Rebirth Palingenesis, Renaissance, Revival, Samsara
Rebound Backfire, Bounce, Cannon, Elastic, Recoil, Repercussion, Ricochet,
Snapback
Rebuff Check, Cold-shoulder, Noser, Quelch, Repulse, Retort, Rubber, Sneb,
Snib, Snub
Rebuke Admonish, Berate, Check, Chide, Earful, Lecture, Neb, Objurgate, Rap,
Rate, Razz, Reprimand, Reproof, Reprove, Rollick, Scold, Score, Slap, Slate,
Snib, Snub, Strop, Threap, Threep, Tick off, Trim, Tut, Upbraid, Wig
Rebut Disprove, Refute, Repulse, Retreat
Recalcitrant Mulish, Obstinate, Unruly, Wilful
Recall(ing) Annul, Eidetic, Encore, Evocative, Partial, Reclaim, Recollect,
Redolent, Remember, Remind, Reminisce, Repeal, Retrace, Revoke, Total,

Unsay, Withdraw

Recant(ation) Disclaim, Palinode, Retract, Revoke

Recap(itulate), **Recapitulation** Epanodos, Summarise

Recapture Rescue

Recast *may indicate* an anagram

Recce *see* RECONNAISSANCE

Recede Decline, Ebb, Lessen, Regress, Shrink, Withdraw

Receipt(s) Acknowledge, Chit, Docket, Recipe, Revenue, Take, Voucher

Receive(d), **Receiver** Accept, Accoil, Admit, Aerial, Antenna, Assignee, Bailee, Dipole, Dish, Donee, Ear, Fence, Get, Grantee, Greet, Hydrophone, Inherit, Intercom, Official, Pernancy, Phone, Pocket, Radio, Reset, Responser, Responsor, Roger, Set, Take, Tap, Transistor, Wide

Recent(ly) Alate, Current, Fresh, Hot, Just, Late, Modern, New, Yesterday, Yestereve, Yesterweek

Receptacle Ash-tray, Basket, Bin, Bowl, Box, Ciborium, Container, Cyst, Hell-box, Locket, Loom, Monstrance, Receiver, Reliquary, Relique, Reservatory, Sacculus, Spermatheca, Tank, Thalamus, Tidy, Tore, Torus, Trash can

Reception, **Receptive** Accoil, At home, Bel-accoyle, Couchée, Court, Durbar, Entertainment, Greeting, Helpdesk, Infare, Kursaal, Levée, Open, Ovation, Pervious, Ruelle, Saloon, Sensory, Soirée, Teleasthetic, Welcome

Recess(ion) Alcove, Antrum, Apse, Apsidal, Apsis, Bay, Bole, Bower, Break, Closet, Columbarium, Corrie, Cove, Croze, Dinette, Ebb, Embrasure, Exedra, Fireplace, Grotto, Hitch, Inglenook, Interval, Loculus, Mortise, > NICHE, Nook, Oriel, Outshot, Rabbet, Rebate, Respite, Rest, Slump, Withdrawal

Recess *may indicate* 'reversed'

Rechabite TT

Réchauffé Hachis, Hash, Salmi

Recidivist Relapser

Recidivist *may indicate* 'reversed'

Recipe Dish, Formula, Prescription, R, Receipt, Take

Recipient Assignee, Beneficiary, Disponee, Grantee, Heir, Legatee, Receiver

Reciprocal, **Reciprocate** Corresponding, Elastance, Exchange, Inter(act), Mutual, Repay, Return

Recital, **Recitation(ist)**, **Recite(r)** Ave, Concert, Declaim, Diseuse, Enumerate, Incantation, Litany, Monologue, Parlando, Quote, Reading, Reel, Relate, Rhapsode, Say, Sing, Tell

Reckless(ness) Blindfold, Careless, Catiline, Desperado, Desperate, Devil-may-care, Gadarene, Harum-scarum, Hasty, Headfirst, Headlong, Hell-bent, Irresponsible, Madcap, Perdu(e), Ramstam, Rantipole, > RASH, Slapdash, Temerity, Ton-up, Wanton, Wildcat

Reckless *may indicate* an anagram

Reckon(ing) Assess, Bet, Calculate, Cast, Census, Computer, Consider, Count, Date, Doomsday, Estimate, Fancy, Figure, Guess, Number, Rate, Settlement, Shot, Tab

Reclaim(ed), **Reclamation** Assart, Empolder, Impolder, Innings, Novalia, Polder, Recover, Redeem, Restore, Swidden, Tame, Thwaite

Recline Lean, Lie, Lounge, Rest

Recluse Anchor(et), Anchorite, Ancress, Eremite, Hermit, Solitaire

Recognise(d), **Recognition** Accept, Acknow(ledge), Admit, Anagnorisis, Appreciate, Ascetic, Cit(ation), Exequatur, Identify, Isolated, Ken, > KNOW, Nod, Oust, Own, Reward, Salute, Scent, Standard, Voice, Wat, Weet

Recoil Backlash, Bounce, Kick(back), Quail, Rebound, Redound, Repercussion,

Resile, Reverberate, Shrink, Shy, Spring, Start

Recollect(ion) Anamnesis, Memory, Pelmanism, Recall, > **REMEMBER**, Reminisce

▷ **Recollection** *may indicate* an anagram

Recommend(ation) Advise, Advocate, Counsel, Direct, Endorse, Exhort, Nap, Promote, Rider, Suggest, Testimonial, Tip, Tout

Recompense Cognisance, Deodand, Deserts, Expiate, Guerdon, Pay, Remunerate, Repayment, Requite, Restitution, Reward

Reconcile(d) Adapt, Adjust, Affrended, Atone, Harmonise, Henotic, Make up, Mend

Recondite Difficult, Esoteric, Mystic, Obscure, Occult, Profound

Reconnaissance, **Reconnoitre** Case, Investigate, Recce, Scout, Survey

Reconstitute, **Reconstitution** Diagenesis

Reconstruction Perestroika

Record(er), **Record company**, **Recording** Album, Ampex, Analogue, Annal(ist), Archive, Archivist, Audit trail, Aulos, Bench-mark, Black box, Blue Riband, Book, Campbell-Stokes, Can, Cartulary, Casebook, CD, Chart, Chronicle, Clickstream, Clog-almanac, Coat(e), Daybook, Diary, Dictaphone®, Dictograph®, Digital, Disc, Document, Dossier, Eloge, Elpee, EMI, Endorsement, English flute, Enter, Entry, EP, Ephemeris, Estreat, Ever, Filater, File, Film, Flight, Flute, Form, Forty-five, Gram, Hansard, Helical scan, Hierogrammat, History, Incremental, Indie, Journal, Lap-chart, Ledger, List, Log, Logbook, LP, Mark, Maxi-single, Memento, Memo(randum), Memorial, Memorise, Meter, Mind, Minute, Mono, Noctuary, Notate, Notch, Note, Odometer, Pass book, Platter, Playback, Pressing, Previous, Protocol, Public, Quipo, Quipu, Quote, Rapsheet, Rec, Regest, Register, Release, Roll, Score(board), Seven-inch, Seventy-eight, Shellac, Single, Spectogram, Sphygmogram, Stenotype®, Tachograph, Tally, Tallyman, Tape, Thirty-three, Toast, Trace, Track, Transcript, Travelog, Trip, Twelve-inch, VERA, Vid(eo), Videotape, Vote, Wax, Wire, Wisden, Worksheet, Write

Record-holder Champion, Sleeve

Record-player DJ, Stereo

Recount Describe, Enumerate, > **NARRATE**, Relate, Tell

Recourse Access, Resort

Recover(y) Amend, Clawback, Comeback, Common, Convalescence, Cure, Dead cat bounce, Get over, Lysis, Over, Perk, Pull through, Rally, Reclaim, Recoup, Redeem, Regain, Repaint, Replevin, Replevy, Repo(ssess), Rescript, Rescue, Resile, > **RETRIEVE**, Revanche, Salvage, Salve, Second-wind, Spontaneous, Upswing

Recreate, **Recreation** Diversion, Hobby, Palingenesia, Pastime, Play, Revive, Sport

Recriminate, **Recrimination** Ruction

Recruit(s) Attestor, Bezonian, Choco, Conscript, Crimp, Draft, Employ, Engage, Enlist, Enrol, Headhunt, Intake, Muster, Nignog, Nozzer, Press, Rookie, Sprog, Volunteer, Wart, Yobbo

Rectangle, **Rectangular** Golden, Matrix, Oblong, Quad, Square

Rectifier, **Rectify** Adjust, Amend, Dephlegmate, Redress, Regulate, > **REMEDY**, Right, Silicon

Recto Ro

Rector R

Rectum Tewel

Recuperate Convalesce, Rally, Recover

Recur(rent), **Recurring** Chronic, Quartan, Quintan, Recrudesce, Repeated, Repetend, Return

Recurrent *may indicate* 'reversed'

Red(den), **Redness** Admiral, Alizarin, Angry, Archil, Ashamed, Auburn, Beet, Bilirubin, Blush, Bolshevik, Brick, Burgundy, C, Carmine, Carroty, Castory, Cent, Cerise, Cherry, Chica, Chinese, Choy-root, Chrome, Cinnabar, Claret, Coccineous, Commo, Communist, Congo, Copper, Coquelicot, Coral, Corallin(e), Corkir, Cramesy, Cremosin, Crimson, Crocoite, Cuprite, Cyanin, Damask, Debit, Duster, Embarrassed, Eosin, Eric, Erik, Erythema, Flame, Flaming, Florid, Flush, Foxy, Garnet, Geranium, Ginger, Gory, Grog-blossom, Gu(les), Guly, Hat, Henna, Herring, Incarnadine, Indian, Inflamed, Infra, Inner, Intertrigo, Jacqueminot, Keel, Kermes, Korkir, Lac-lake, Lake, Lateritious, Left(y), Lenin, Letter, Magenta, Maoist, Maroon, Marxist, Menshevik, Miniate, Minium, Modena, Murrey, Neaten, Orchel, Orchilla-weed, Orseille, Oxblood, Phenol, Pillar-box, Plethoric, Plum, Pompeian, Ponceau, Poppy, Pyrrhous, Raddle, Radical, Raspberry, Raw, Realgar, Rhodamine, Rhodopsin, Ridinghood, Roan, Rosaker, Rose, Rot, Rouge, Roy, Rubefy, Rubella, Rubescent, Rubicund, Rubric, Ruby, Ruddle, Ruddy, Rufescent, Russ(e), Russet, Russian, Rust(y), Rutilant, Sang-de-boeuf, Sanguine, Santalin, Sard, Scarlet, Sericon, Setter, Solferino, Stammel, Tape, Tidy, Tile, Titian, Trot, Trotsky, Turacin, Turkey, Tyrian, Venetian, Vermeil, Vermilion, Vermily, Vinaceous, Wallflower, Wine

Red *may indicate* an anagram

Redcoat Rust, Soldier

Redeem(er), **Redemption** Cross, Liberate, Mathurin, Messiah, Ransom, Retrieve, Salvation, Save

Red-faced Coaita, Florid, Flushed

Red-head Auburn, Blue(y), Carroty, Commissar, Mao, Rufus

Red herring Soldier

Redirect Sublimate

Rediscovered *may indicate* an anagram

Redolent Aromatic, Fragrant, Reeking, Suggestive

Redoubtable Stalwart

Redress Amends, Offset, Recompense, Rectify, Remedy, Right

Redshank Gambet, Totanus

Redskin Indian, Tomato

Red spot Tika

Reduce(r), **Reduced**, **Reduction** Abatement, Allay, Alleviate, Amortize, Attenuate, Beggar, Beneficiate, Clip, Commute, Condense, Contract, Cut, Cutback, Damping, Debase, Decimate, Decrease, Decrement, Demote, Deoxidate, Deplete, Depreciation, Detract, Devalue, Diminish, Diminuendo, Discount, Downsize, Draw-down, Epitomise, Foreshorten, Grind, Jeff, Kinone, >LESSEN, Lite, Markdown, Mitigate, Moderate, Palliate, Pot, Pulp, Put, Quinol, Razee, Remission, Retrench, Rundown, Scant, Shade, Shorten, Shrinkage, Slash, Strain, Taper, Telescope, Thin, Weaken, Write-off

Redundancy, **Redundant** Frill, Futile, Needless, Otiose, Pleonasm, Superfluous, Surplus

Redwood Amboyna, Mahogany, Sanders, Wellingtonia

Reed Arundinaceous, Broken, Calamus, Free, Oboe, Papyrus, Pipe, Quill, Raupo, Rush, Sedge, Seg, Sley, Spear, Sudd, Syrinx, Thatch, Twill, Whistle

Reef Atoll, Barrier, Bioherm, Bombora, Cay, Coral, Fringing, Great Barrier, Key, Knot, Lido, Motu, Saddle, Sca(u)r, Skerry, Witwatersrand

Reefer Cigarette, Jacket, Joint

Reek Emit, Exude, Stink

Reel Bobbin, Dance, Eightsome, Hoolachan, Hoolican, News, Pirn, Spin, Spool, Stagger, Strathspey, Sway, Swift, Swim, Totter, Virgina, Wheel, Whirl, Wintle

Refectory Frater

Refer Advert, Allude, Assign, Cite, Direct, Mention, Pertain, Relate, Remit, Renvoi, Renvoy, See, Submit, Touch, Trade

Referee Arbiter, Commissaire, Mediate, Oddsman, Official, Ref, Umpire, Voucher, Whistler, Zebra

Reference Allusion, Apropos, Character, Coat, Grid, Index, Innuendo, Mention, Passion, Quote, Regard, Renvoi, Respect, Retrospect, Testimonial, Vide

Referendum Mandate, Plebiscite, Vox populi

Refill Replenish

Refine(d), Refinement, Refiner(y) Alembicate, Attic, Catcracker, Couth, Cultivate, Culture, Distinction, Elaborate, Elegance, Exility, Exquisite, Genteel, Grace, Nice, Nicety, Polish(ed), Polite, Précieuse, Pure, Rare(fy), Recherché, Saltern, Sieve, Sift, Smelt, Sophisticated, Spirituel, Sublimate, Subtilise, Tasteful, Try, U, Urbane, Veneer

Reflect(ing), Reflection, Reflective, Reflector Albedo, Blame, Catoptric, Cat's eye®, Cats-eye, Chaff, Chew, Cogitate, > CONSIDER, Echo, Glass, Glint, Image, Meditate, Mirror, Muse, Nonspecular, Ponder, Ricochet, Ruminate, Spectacular, Speculum, Symmetrical, Tapetum, Thought

Reflex Achilles, Babinski, Bent, Cancrizans, Knee-jerk, Patellar, Pavlovian, Re-entrant, Single-lens, Tic

Reform(er) Amend, Apostle, Beveridge, Bloomer, Calvin, Chartism, Chastise, Correct, Enrage, Fry, Ghandi, Gradualism, Howard, Hussite, Improve, Knox, Land, Lollard, Luther, Meiji, Melanchthon, Mend, Mucker, New Deal, Owenite, PR, Progressionist, Protestant, Proudhon, Puritan, Rad(ical), Really, Recast, Reclaim, Reconstruction, Rectify, Regenerate, Resipiscence, Ruskin, Satyagraha, Savonarola, Syncretise, Tariff, Transmute, Tyndale, Wycliffe, Young Turk, Zwingli

▷ **Reform(ed)** *may indicate* an anagram

Reformatory Borstal, Magdalen(e)

Refract(ion), Refractive, Refractor(y) Anaclastic, Double, Firestone, Obstinate, Perverse, Prism, Recalcitrant, Refringe, Restive, Stubborn, Sullen, Wayward

Refrain Abstain, Alay, Avoid, Bob, Burden, Chorus, Desist, Epistrophe, Fa-la, Forbear, Hemistich, Mantra, O(v)erword, Repetend, Ritornello, Rumbelow, Rum(p)ti-iddity, Rum-ti-tum, Spare, Tag, Tirra-lirra, Tirra-lyra, Turn again, Undersong, Wheel

Refresh(ment), Refresher Air, Bait, Be(a)vers, Buffet, Cheer, Elevenses, Enliven, Food, Four-hours, Nap, New, Nourishment, Purvey, Refection, Reflect, Refocillate, Reinvigorate, Renew, Repast, Restore, Revive, Seltzer, Shire, Slake, Water

Refrigerator Chill, Chiller, Cooler, Deep freeze, Esky®, Freezer, Freon, Fridge, Ice-box, Minibar, Reefer

Refuge Abri, Ark, Asylum, Bolthole, Burrow, Dive, Fastness, Funkhole, Girth, Grith, Harbour, Haven, Hideaway, Hole, Holt, Home, Hospice, Oasis, Port, Reefer, Resort, Retreat, Sheet-anchor, > SHELTER, Soil, Stronghold, Women's

Refugee DP, Economic, Escapist, Fugitive, Grenzganger, Huguenot, Reffo

Refund Clawback, Repayment

▷ **Refurbished** *may indicate* an anagram

Refusal, Refuse Attle, Bagasse, Ba(u)lk, Bilge, Bin, Black, Blackball, Boycott,

Bran, Brash, Breeze, Brock, Bull, Bunkum, Cane-trash, Chaff, Clap-trap, Crane, Crap, Cul(t)ch, Debris, Decline, Denay, Deny, Disown, Draff, Drivel, Dross, Dunder, Dung, Eighty-six, Fag-end, Fenks, Fiddlesticks, Finks, First, Flock, Frass, Garbage, Gob, Guff, Hards, Hogwash, Hold-out, Hurds, Husk, Interdict, Jib, Junk, Knickknackery, Knub, Lay-stall, Leavings, Litter, Lumber, Mahmal, Marc, Megass(e), Midden, Mullock, Mush, Nay(-say), Nill, No, Noser, Nould, Nub, Offal, Off-scum, Orts, Pellet, Pigwash, Pot all, Punk, Radwaste, Raffle, Rape(cake), Rat(s), Rebuff, Recrement, Recusance, Red(d), Redargue, Reest, Regret, Reneg(u)e, Renig, Rot, > **RUBBISH**, Ruderal, Scaff, Scrap, Scree, Scum, Sewage, Shant, Shell heap, Slag, Sordes, Spurn, Sullage, Sweepings, Swill, Tinpot, Tip, Toom, Tosh, Trade, Trash, Tripe, Trock, Troke, Trumpery, Turndown, Twaddle, Unsay, Utter, Wash, Waste, Wastrel

Re-fused *may indicate* an anagram

Refutation, **Refute** Deny, Disprove, Elench(us), Rebut, Redargue, Refel

Regain Recover, Revanche

Regal *see* **ROYAL**

Regalia > **CIGAR**, Mound, Orb, Sceptre

Regard(ing) As to, Attention, Care, Consider, > **ESTEEM**, Eye, Gaum, Look, Observe, Odour, Pace, Rate, Re, Respect, Revere, Sake, Steem, Value, Vis-à-vis

Regardless Despite, Heedless, Irrespective, Notwithstanding, Rash, Uncaring, Unmindful, Willy-nilly

Regatta Head of the river, Henley

Regenerate Restore

Regent Interrex, Ruler, Viceroy

Regent's Park Zoo

Reggae Ska

Regicide Ireton, Macbeth

Regime(n) Administration, Control, Diet(etics), Method, Reich

Regiment Black Watch, Buffs, Colour(s), Discipline, Greys, Ironsides, Lifeguard, Monstrous, Nutcrackers, Organise, RA, RE, REME, Rifle, Royals, Tercio, Tertia

Regiment *may indicate* an anagram

Region Arctogaea, > **AREA**, Asir, Belt, Brittany, Bundu, Camargue, Chiasma, Climate, Clime, Critical, D, District, E, End, F, Hinterland, Holarctic, Hundred, Lothian, Lusitania, Lycia, Lydia, Macao, Macedonia, Maghreb, Manchuria, Masuria, Matabeleland, Mauretania, Mecklenburg, Mesopotamia, Midi, Molise, Murcia, Mysia, Namaqualand, Negeb, Negev, Nejd, New Castile, New Quebec, Nubia, Nuristan, Offing, Ogaden, Old Castile, Opher, Oriental, Ossetia, Oudh, Pannonia, Pargana, Part, Pergunnah, Piedmont, Province, Quart(er), Realm, Refugium, Ruthenia, Sector, Sogdiana, Stannery, Strathclyde, Subtopia, Tagma, Territory, Tetrarchate, Thule, Tract, Tundra, Ultima Thule, Umbria, Variable, Vaud, Weald, Zone

Register(ing), **Registration**, **Registry** Actuarial, Almanac, Annal, Cadastral, Cadastre, Calendar, Cartulary, Cash, Census, Check-in, Diptych, Enlist, Enrol, Enter, Gross, Handicap, Index, Indicate, Inscribe, Inventory, Land, Ledger, List, Lloyd's, Log, Matricula, Menology, NAI, Net, Note, Notitia, Parish, Park, Patent, Read, Record, Reg(g)o, Rent-roll, Roll, Roule, Score, Ship's, Soprano, Terrier, Voice

Registrar Actuary, Greffier, Protocolist, Recorder, Specialist

Regress(ion) Backslide, Recidivism, Revert

Regret(ful), **Regrettable** Alack, Alas, Apologise, Deplore, Deprecate, Ewhow, Forthwink, Ichabod, Lackaday, Lament, Mourn, Otis, Pity, Remorse, Repentance, Repine, > **RUE**, Ruth, Sorrow, Tragic

Regular(ity), Regularly Clockwork, Constant, Custom, Episodic, Even, Giusto, Goer, Habitual, Habitué, Hourly, Insider, Methodic, Nine-to-five, Normal, Often, Orderly, Orthodox, Patron, Peloria, Periodic, Rhythmic, Routine, Set, Smooth, > **STANDARD**, Stated, Statutory, Steady, Strict, Symmetric, Uniform, Usual, Yearly

Regulate, Regulation, Regulator Adjust, Appestat, Bye-law, Code, Control, Correction, Curfew, Customary, Direct, Gibberellin, Governor, Guide, King's, Logistics, Metrostyle, Order, Ordinance, Police, Queen's, Rule, Snail, Square, Standard, Statute, Stickle, Stopcock, Sumptuary, Thermostat, Valve

Regulus Matte

Regurgitation Trophallaxis

Rehabilitate, Rehabilitation Cure, Orthotics, Physio(therapy), Repone

Rehearsal, Rehearse Band-call, Dress, Drill, Dry-block, Dry-run, Dummy-run, Practice, Practise, Preview, Recite, Repeat, Trial

Reichenbach Falls, Od

Reign Era, Govern, Meiji, Prevail, Raine, Realm, Restoration, > **RULE**

Reimburse(ment) Indemnity, Recoup, Redress, Repay

Rein(s) Bearing, Check, Control, Curb, Free, Gag, Leading strings, Lumbar, Restrain

Reindeer Blitzen, Caribou, Comet, Cupid, Dancer, Dasher, Donner, Moss, Prancer, Rudolf, Tarand, Vixen

Reinforce(ment) Aid, Augment, Bolster, Boost, Brace, Buttress, Cleat, Line, Negative, Partial, Plash, Pleach, Recruit, Reserve, > **STRENGTHEN**, Support, Tetrapod, Underline

Reinstate Repone

Reinvigorate Recruit

Reiterate(d), Reiteration Battology, Emphasize, Ostinato, Plug, > **REPEAT**

Reject(ion) Abhor, Abjure, Athetise, Bin, Blackball, Brush off, Cast, Cast off, Deny, Dice, Discard, Disclaim, Discount, Disdain, Diss, Elbow, Export, Flout, Frass, Iconoclasm, Jilt, Kest, Kill, Knock-back, Ostracise, Oust, Outcast, Outtake, Pip, Plough, Rebuff, Recuse, Refuse, Reny, Repel, Reprobate, Repudiate, Repulse, Scout, Scrub, Spet, Spin, Spit, > **SPURN**, Sputum, Thumbs-down, Turndown, Veto

Rejoice, Rejoicing Celebrate, Exult, Festivity, Gaude, Glory, Joy, Maffick, Sing

Rejoin(der), Rejoined Answer, Counter, Relide, Reply, Response, Retort, Reunite

Rejuvenation Shunamitism

Relapse Backslide, Deteriorate, Recidivism, Regress, Revert, Sink

Relate(d), Relation(ship), Relative Account, Affair, Affine, Affinity, Agnate, Akin, Allied, Antibiosis, Appertain, Associate, Blood, Brer, Brisure, Cognate, Commensal, Concern, Connection, Connexion, Consanguinity, Coosen, Cousin, Coz, Deixis, Dispersion, Eme, Enate, False, Formula, German(e), Granny, Heterogeneous, Homologous, Impart, Industrial, Item, Kin, Kinsman, Labour, Liaison, Link, Love-hate, Mater, Material, Matrix, Mutualism, Narrative, One-to-one, Osculant, Pertain, Phratry, Pi, Plutonic, Poor, Privity, > **PROPORTION**, Proxemics, Public, Race, Rapport, Rapprochement, Ratio, Reciprocity, Recite, Recount, Rede, Refer(ence), Relevant, Respect(s), Sib(b), Sibbe, Sibling, Sine, Sybbe, Symbiosis, Syntax, Tale, Tell, Who

Relating to Of

Relax(ation), Relaxant, Relaxed Abate, Atony, Autogenics, Calm, Chalone, Chill out, Com(m)odo, Contrapposto, Degage, Detente, Diversion, Downbeat, Ease, Easy-going, Flaccid, Gallamine, Icebreaker, Laid-back, Leisured, Lesh states, Lighten, > **LOOSEN**, Mellow out, Mitigate, Peace, Relent, Relief, Remit, Rest, Slacken, Sleep, Toneless, Unbend, Unknit, Unrein, Untie, Unwind, Veg out

Relaxed *may indicate* an anagram

Relay(er) Convey, Medley, Race, Shift, Tell, Telstar, Torch-race

Relay(ing) *may indicate* an anagram

Release Abreact, Announcement, Bail, Catharsis, Clear, Day, Death, Deliver(y), Desorb, Disburden, Discharge, Disclose, Disengage, Disimprison, Dismiss, Disorb, Emancipate, Enfree, Excuse, Exeem, Exeme, Extricate, Exude, Free, Handout, Happy, > **LIBERATE**, Manumit, Merciful, Moksa, Parole, Press, Quietus, Quittance, Relinquish, Ripcord, Soft, Spring, Tre corde, Unconfine, Uncouple, Undo, Unhand, Unleash, Unloose, Unpen, Unshackle, Unteam, Untie

Relegate Banish, Consign, Demote, Exile, Sideline, Stellenbosch

Relent Bend, Mollify, Soften, Yield

Relentless Cruel, Hard, Hardface, Inexorable, Pitiless, Rigorous, Stern

Relevance, **Relevant** Ad rem, Applicable, Apposite, Apropos, Apt, Bearing, Germane, Material, Pertinent, Point, Valid

Reliable, **Reliance** *see* **RELY**

Relic Antique, Ark, Artefact, Fly-in-amber, Fossil, Leftover, Memento, Neolith, Remains, Sangraal, Sangrail, Sangreal, Souvenir, Survival

Relict Survivor, Widow

Relief, **Relieve(d)** Aid, Air-lift, Allay, Allegeance, Alleviate, Alms, Anaglyph, Anastatic, Anodyne, Assistance, Assuage, Bas, Beet, Beste(a)d, Bete, Cameo, Cavo-relievo, Comfort, Cure, Détente, Ease(ment), Emboss, Emollient, Free, Grisaille, High, Indoor, Let-up, Lighten, Low, Lucknow, Mafeking, On the parish, Outdoor, Palliate, Phew, Photo, Pog(e)y, Reassure, Redress, Remedy, Replacement, Repoussé, Reprieve, > **RESCUE**, Respite, Retirement, Rid, Spare, Spell, Stand-in, Stiacciato, Succour, Taper, Tax, Tondo, Toreutics, Wheugh, Whew, Woodcut

Religion, **Religious (sect)** Animism, Baha'i, Biblist, Bogomil, Buddhism, Camaldolite, Cargo cult, Carthusian, Celestine, Christadelphian, Christianity, Cistercian, Coenobite, Confucianism, Congregant, Creed, Culdee, Denomination, Devout, Din, Doctrine, Druse, Druz(e), Faith, Falun Gong, Familist, Gilbertine, Gnosticism, God-squad, Gueber, Guebre, Hadith, Hare Krishna, Has(s)id, Hieratic, Hospital(l)er, Ignorantine, Islam, Ismaili, Jain(a), Jansenism, Jehovah's Witness, Jesuit, Jewry, Judaism, Lamaism, Loyola, Lutheran, Macumba, Mahatma, Manichee, Maoism, Mazdaism, Mazdeism, Missionary, Missioner, Mithraism, Moony, Mormonism, New Light, Nun, Opium, Orphism, Pagan, Pantheist, Parseeism, Parsism, Pi, Piarist, Pietà, Postulant, Premonstratensian, Progressive, Rastafarian, Reformation, Resurrectionist, Revealed, Revivalism, Sabbatarian, Sabian, Sacramentarian, Santeria, Scientology®, Serious, Shaker, Shamanism, Shango, Shiism, Shinto(ism), Sikhism, Sodality, Solifidian, Sons of Freedom, Spike, Sunna, Swedenborgian, Taoism, Theatine, Theology, Tractarianism, Tsabian, Utraquist, Voodooism, Whore, Wicca, Zabian, Zarathustric, Zealous, Zend-avesta, Zoroaster, Zwinglian

Religious book Bible, Koran, Missal, NT, OT, Sefer, Tantra, Targum, T(h)orah

Relinquish Abdicate, Cede, Demit, Discard, Drop, Forlend, Remise, Waive(r), Yield

Reliquary Chef, Encolpion, Encolpium, Simonious, Tope

Relish(ing) Botargo, Catsup, Chakalaka, Chow-chow, Condiment, Enjoy,

Flavour, Gentleman's, Gout, Gust(o), Ketchup, Lap(-up), Lust, Opsonium, Palate, Pickle, Sapid, Sar, Sauce, Savour, Seasoning, Tang, Tooth, Worcester sauce, Zest

Reluctant Averse, Backward, Chary, Circumspect, Grudging, Half-hearted, Laith, Loth, Nolition, Renitent, Shy, Unwilling

Rely, **Reliance**, **Reliant**, **Reliable** Addiction, Authentic, Bank, Confidence, Constant, > COUNT, Dependent, Found, Hope, Jeeves, Lean, Loyal, Mensch, Presume, Pukka, Rest, Safe, Secure, Solid, Sound, Sponge, Stand-by, Staunch, Trustworthy, Trusty, Unfailing

Remain(der), **Remaining**, **Remains** Abide, Ash(es), Balance, Bide, Continue, Corse, Dreg(s), Dwell, Embers, Estate, Exuviae, Fag-end, Kreng, Last, Late, Lave Left, Lie, Locorestive, Manet, Nose, Oddment, Orts, Other, Outstand, Persist, Relic(ts), Reliquae, > REMNANT, Residue, Rest, Ruins, Scourings, Scraps, Stay, Stick, Stub, Surplus, Survive, Tag-end, Talon, Tarry, Wait, Wreck(age)

Remark Aside, Barb, Bromide, Comment(ary), Descry, Dig, Epigram, Generalise Mention, Noise, > NOTE, Notice, Obiter dictum, Observe, Platitude, Pleasantry, Reason, Sally, Shot, State

Remarkable, **Remarkably** Amazing, Arresting, Beauty, Bodacious, Conspicuous, Dilly, Egregious, Extraordinary, Heliozoan, Legendary, Lulu, Mirable, Notendum, Noteworthy, Phenomenal, Rattling, > SIGNAL, Singular, Some, Striking, Tall, Unco, Uncommon, Visible

Remedial, **Remedy** Aid, An mo, Antacid, Antibiotic, Antidote, Antiodontalgic, Antispasmodic, Arcanum, Arnica, Azoth, Bach, Bach flower, Basilicon, Calomel, Catholicon, Corrective, Cortisone, > CURE, Dinic, Drug, Elixir, Femiter, Feverfew, Fumitory, Ginseng, Heal, Ipecac, Leechdom, Medicate, Medicine, Moxa, Nosode, Nostrum, Palliative, Panacea, Panpharmacon, Paregoric, Poultice, Provisional, Rectify, Redress, Repair, Rescue, Salutory, Salve, Simillimum, Simple, Specific, Taraxacum, Therapeutic, Tonga, Treatment, Tutsan

Remember(ing), **Remembrance** Bethink, Commemorate, Con, Mem, Memorial, Memorise, Mention, Mneme, Recall, Recollect, Remind, Reminisce, Retain, Rosemary, Souvenir

▷ **Remember** *may indicate* RE-member, viz. Sapper

Remind(er) Aftertaste, Aide-memoire, Bookmark, Evocatory, Evoke, Jog, Keepsake, Mark, Memento, Memo, Mnemonic, Mnemotechnic, Monition, Nudge, Phylactery, Prod, Prompt, Souvenir, Token

Reminiscence(s), **Reminiscent** Ana, Evocative, Memory, Recall, Recollect, Remember, Retrospect

Remiss Careless, Derelict, Lax, Lazy, Negligent, Tardy

Remission Abatement, Absolution, Acceptilation, Indulgence, Pardon, Pause, Spontaneous

Remit Excuse, Forward, Pardon, Postpone

Remnant Butt, End, Fent, Heeltap, Left-over, Odd-come-short, Offcut, Relic, > REMAINDER, Rump, Trace, Vestige

Remonstrate Argue, Complain, Expostulate, Protest, Reproach

Remorse Angst, Ayenbite, Breast-beating, Compunction, Contrition, Had-i-wist, Pity, > REGRET, Rue, Ruing, Ruth, Sorrow

Remote Aloof, Aphelion, Back blocks, Backveld, Backwater, Backwood, Bullamakanka, Bundu, > DISTANT, Far flung, Forane, Inapproachable, Insular, Irrelevant, Jericho, Long(inquity), Out(part), Outback, Scrub, Secluded, Shut-out, Slightest, Surrealistic, Unlikely, Withdrawn, Woop woop

Remount(s) Remuda

Removal, Remove(d) Abduct, Ablation, Abstract, Apocope, Asport, Banish, Blot, Circumcision, Clear, Couch, Declassify, Dele(te), Depilate, Depose, Deracinate, Detach, Detract, Dishelm, Dislodge, Disloign, Dispel, Doff, Efface, Eject, Eloi(g)n, Emend, Eradicate, Erase, Esloyne, Estrange, Evacuate, Evict, Exalt, Excise, Extirpate, Extradite, Extricate, Far, Flit, Huff, Nick, Razee, Redline, Remble, Rid, Scratch, Sequester, Shift, Spirit, Sublate, Subtract, Supplant, Transfer, Transport, Unperson, Unseat, Uproot

Remuneration Pay, Return, Reward, Salary, Solde

Remus Uncle

Renaissance Awakening, Cinquecento, High, Quattrocento, Revival

Rend Cleave, Harrow, Lacerate, Rip, Rive, Rupture, Tear

Render(ing) Construe, Deliver, Do, Gie, Give, Interpretation, Make, Melt, Pebble-dash, Plaster, Provide, Recite, Represent, Restore, Setting, Tallow, Try, Yeve

Rendezvous Date, Meeting, Philippi, Tryst, Venue

Rendition Account, Delivery, Interpretation, Translation

Rene Descartes

Renegade, Renege Apostate, Default, Defector, Deserter, Rat(ton), Traitor, Turncoat

Renegade *may indicate* a word reversal

Renew(al) Instauration, Neogenesis, Palingenesis, Refresh, Replace, Resumption, Retrace, Revival, Urban

Rennet Steep, Vell

Renounce, Renunciation Abandon, Abdicate, Abjure, Abnegate, Disclaim, Disown, For(e)go, For(e)say, Forfeit, Forisfamiliate, Forsake, Forswear, Kenosis, Outclaim, Quitclaim, Recede, Relinquish, Renay, Retract, Sacrifice

Renovate(d), Renovation Duff, Face-lift, Instauration, Makeover, Refurbish, Renew, Repair, Restore, Revamp

Renown(ed) Fame, Glory, Illustrious, Kudos, Lustre, Notoriety, Prestige, Stardom

Rent(er), Renting Broken, Charge, Cornage, Cost, Crack, Cranny, Cuddeehih, Cuddy, Division, Economic, Fair, Farm, Fee, Fissure, Gale, Gavel, Ground, > HIRE, Lease, Let, List, Mail, Market, Occupy, Peppercorn, Quit-rent, Rack, Rip, Rived, Riven, Screed, Seat, Slit, Split, Stallage, Subtenant, Tare, Tenant, Tithe, Tore, Torn, Tythe, White

Reorganise Rationalise

Reorganised *may indicate* an anagram

Reorientate Rabat

Repair(s), Repairer, Reparation Amend(s), Anaplasty, Assythement, Botch, Cobble, Damages, Darn, Doctor, Excision, Fettle, Fitter, Go, Haro, Harrow, Jury rig, > MEND, Overhaul, Patch, Piece, Recompense, Redress, Refit, Reheel, Remedy, Renew, Renovate, Repoint, Resort, Restore, Retouch, Revamp, Running, Satisfaction, Stitch, Ulling, Vamp, Volery

Repartee Backchat, Badinage, Banter, Persiflage, Rejoinder, Retort, Riposte, Wit

Repast Bever, Collection, Food, Meal, Tea, Treat

Repay(ment) Avenge, Compensate, Quit, Refund, Requite, Retaliate, Reward, Satisfaction

Repeal Abrogate, Annul, Cancel, Rescind, Revoke

Repeat(edly), Repetition, Repetitive Again, Alliteration, Anadiplosis, Anaphora, Ancora, Battology, Belch, Bis, Burden, Burp, Copy, Ditto(graphy), Duplicate, > ECHO, Echolalia, Encore, Epanalepsis, Epistrophe, Epizuexis,

Eruct, Facsimile, Habitual, Harp, Image, Imitate, Ingeminate, Iterate, Iterum, Leit-motiv, Merism, Ostinato, Palillogy, Parrot, Passion, Perpetuate, Playback, Polysyndeton, Recite(r), Redo, Refrain, Regurgitate, Reiterate, Renew, Rep, Repetend, Reprise, Rerun, Retail, Rondo, Rosalia, Rote, Same(y), Screed, Segno, Symploce, Tautology, Tautophony, Thrum, Verbigerate

Repel(lent) Estrange, Harsh, Offensive, Rebarbative, Reject, Repulse, Revolt, Squalid, Turn-off, Ug(h), Ward

Repent(ant), **Repentance** Metanoia, Penitent, Regret, Rue, Sackcloth, Yamim Nora'im

Repercussion Backlash, Backwash, Effect, Impact, Recoil

Repertoire, **Repertory** Company, Depot, Rep, Store

▷ **Repetition** *see* REPEAT

Replace(ment), **Replaceable**, **Replacing** Change, Deputise, Diadochy, For, Pre-empt, Prosthesis, Raincheck, Refill, Replenish, Restore, Stand-in, Substitute, Supersede, Supplant, Surrogate, Taxis, Transform, Transliterate, Understudy

Replay Action, Instant, Iso(lated), Segno

Replenish Refill, Refresh, Revictual, Stock, Supply, Top

Replete, **Repletion** Awash, Full, Gorged, Plenitude, Plethora, Sated, Satiation

Replica Clone, Copy, Duplicate, Facsimile, Image, Repetition, Spit

Reply Accept, Answer, Churlish, Duply, Over, Rejoinder, Rescript, Response, Retort, Roger, Surrebut, Surrebutter, Surrejoin, Triply

Report(er) Account, Announce, Auricular, Bang, Blacksmith, Bruit, Bulletin, Cahier, Clap, Columnist, Comment, Commentator, Correspondent, Court, Cover, Crack, Crump, Cub, Debrief, Disclose, Dispatch, Dissertation, Explosion, Fame, Fireman, Grapevine, Hansard, Hearsay, Jenkins, Journalist, Legman, Libel, News, Newshawk, Newshound, Newsman, Noise, Pop, Pressman, Protocol, Relate, Relay, Representation, Repute, Return, Roorback, Rumour, Sitrep, Sound(bite), Staffer, State(ment), Stringer, Tale, > TELL, Thesis, Transcribe, Tripehound, Troop, Update, Weather, Whang, Wolfenden, Write up

▷ **Reported** *may indicate* the sound of a letter or word

Repose Ease, Kaif, Kef, Kif, Lie, Lig, Peace, Relax, > REST, Serenity

Repository Ark, Cabinet, Container, Genizah, Reservoir, Sepulchre, Vault

Reprehend Blame, Censure, Criticise, Rebuke, Warn

Represent(ation), **Representative**, **Represented** Agent, Ambassador, Anaconic, Caricature, Client, Commercial, Cross-section, Delegate, Depict, Deputation, Describe, Display, Drawing, Drummer, Effigy, Elchee, Eltchi, Emblem, Embody, Emissary, Example, Figurative, Image, John Bull, Legate, Lobby, Map, Mimesis, Mouthpiece, MP, Personate, Personify, Portray, Proportional, Quintessence, Rep, Resemble, Salesman, Senator, Shop steward, Simulacrum, Spokesman, Stand-in, Steward, Symbolic, Syndic, Tableau, Tiki, Transcription, Typical, Vakeel, Vakil, Vehicle

▷ **Represented** *may indicate* an anagram

Repress(ed) Check, Curb, Pent, Quell, Sneap, Stifle, Stultify, Subjugate, Withhold

Reprieve Delay, Postpone, Relief, Respite

Reprimand Admonish, Bounce, Carpet, > CENSURE, Chew out, Chide, Dressing-down, Earful, Jobe, Lace, Lambast, Lecture, Rark up, Rating, Rebuke, Reproof, Rocket, Rollicking, Slate, Strafe, Targe, Tick off, Tongue-lashing, Wig

Reprint Copy, Paperback, Replica

Reprisal(s) Marque, Retaliation, Revenge

Reproach Blame, Braid, Byword, Chide, Discredit, Dispraise, Exprobate, Gib, Mispraise, Odium, Opprobrium, Rebuke, Ronyon, Runnion, Scold, Shend, Sloan, Stigma, Taunt, Truant, Upbraid, Upcast, Yshend

Reprobate Cur, Lost soul, Outcast, Rascal, Scallywag, Scamp

Reprocess Re-make

Reproduce(r), **Reproduction**, **Reproductive (organ)** Amphimixis, Ape, Apomixis, Archegonium, Carpel, Clone, Copy, Counterfeit, Depict, Ectype, Edition, Etch, Eugenics, Gamogenesis, Gemmate, Homogenesis, Isospory, Megaspore, Meristematic, Mono, Multiply, Oogamy, Ozalid®, Parthogenesis, Phon(e)y, Playback, Proliferate, Propagate, Pullulation, Refer, Replica, Roneo®, Schizogony, Seminal, S(h)akti, Simulate, Spermatia, Stereo, Strobilation, Syngamy, Syngenesis

▸ **Reproduce** *may indicate* an anagram

Reproof, **Reprove** Admonish, Berate, Chide, Correction, Correption, Lecture, Rate, Rebuff, Rebuke, Scold, Sloan, Tut, Upbraid

Reptile, **Reptilian** Agamid, Alligarta, Alligator, Base, Basilisk, Caiman, Cayman, Chameleon, Chelonian, Creeper, Crocodile, Diapsid, Dicynodont, Dinosaur, Galliwasp, Goanna, Herpetology, Lacertine, Lizard, Mamba, Pteranodon, Pterodactyl, Rhynchocephalian, Sauroid, > SNAKE, Squamata, Synapsid, Tegu(exin), Thecodont, Therapsid, Theriodontia, Tortoise, Tuatara, Tuatera, Turtle, Worm

Republic Banana, Federal, Fifth, First, Fourth, People's, State, Third

REPUBLICS

1 letter:	Congo	Bharat	7 letters:
R	Czech	Brazil	Adharca
	Egypt	Bukavu	Albania
3 letters:	Gabon	Buryat	Algeria
RMM	Ghana	France	Andorra
UAR	Haiti	Gambia	Armenia
	India	Greece	Bashkir
4 letters:	Italy	Guinea	Belarus
Chad	Kenya	Guyana	Bolivia
Cuba	Khmer	Ingush	Burundi
Eire	Libya	Israel	Chechen
Fiji	Malta	Kalmyk	Chuvash
Iran	Nauru	Latvia	Comoros
Iraq	Niger	Malawi	Croatia
Komi	Palau	Mexico	Ecuador
Laos	Sakha	Myanma	Estonia
Mali	Sudan	Panama	Finland
Peru	Syria	Poland	Georgia
Togo	Tatar	Rwanda	Germany
Tuva	Yakut	Second	Hungary
	Yemen	Serbia	Iceland
5 letters:	Zaire	Turkey	Ireland
Adhar		Udmurt	Jibouti
Altai	6 letters:	Uganda	Kalmuck
Belau	Adygai	Weimar	Khakass
Benin	Adygei	Zambia	Lebanon
Chile	Angola		Liberia

- Moldova
- Myanmar
- Namibia
- Nigeria
- Romania
- Senegal
- Somalia
- Surinam
- Tunisia
- Ukraine
- Uruguay
- Vanuatu
- Vietnam

8 letters:
- Botswana
- Bulgaria
- Cambodia
- Cameroon
- Chechnya
- Colombia
- Dagestan
- Djibouti
- Dominica
- Esthonia
- Honduras
- Karelian
- Kiribati
- Malagasy
- Maldives

Mongolia
Pakistan
Paraguay
Portugal
Roumania
Sinn Fein
Slovakia
Slovenia
Sri Lanka
Tanzania
Zimbabwe

9 letters:
Argentina
Badakshan
Cape Verde
Costa Rica
Dominican
Guatemala
Indonesia
Kazakstan
Lithuania
Macedonia
Mauritius
Nicaragua
San Marino
Singapore
Venezuela

10 letters:
Azerbaijan
Bangladesh
Belorussia
El Salvador
Gorno-Altai
Kara-Kalpak
Kazakhstan
Kyrgyzstan
Madagascar
Mauritania
Montenegro
Mordvinian
Mozambique
North Korea
North Yemen
South Korea
Tajikistan
Ubang-Shari
Uzbekistan
Yugoslavia

11 letters:
Afghanistan
Burkino-Faso
Byelorussia
Cote d'Ivoire
Philippines
Sierra Leone
South Africa

Switzerland
West Germany

12 letters:
Guinea-Bissau
Turkmenistan

13 letters:
Bashkortostan
North Ossetian

15 letters:
Kabardino-Balkar
United Provinces

16 letters:
Congo-Brazzaville
Karachai-
  Cherkess

17 letters:
Bosnia-
  Herzegovina
Mari El-
  Nakhichevan
Sao Tomele
  Principe
Trinidad and
  Tobago

Republican Antimonarchist, Democrat, Fenian, Fianna Fail, Girondist, IRA, Iraqi, Leveller, Montagnard, Mugwump, Plato, Red, Sansculotte, Sansculottic, Sinn Fein, Whig

Repudiate Abjure, Deny, Discard, Disclaim, Disown, Ignore, Recant, Reject, Renounce, Repel, Retract

Repugnance, **Repugnant** Abhorrent, Alien, Disgust, Distaste, Fulsome, Horror, Loathing, Revulsion

Repulse, **Repulsive** Grooly, Lo(a)th, Off-putting, Rebuff, Rebut, Refel, Refuse, Repel, Repugnant, Slimy, Squalid, Ugly, Vile

Reputable, **Reputation**, **Repute(d)** Bubble, Dit, Estimate, Fame, Good, Izzat, Loos, Los, Name, Note, Notoriety, Odour, Opinion, Prestige, Putative, Regard, Renown, Said, Sar, > **STANDING**, Stink, Trustworthy

Request Adjure, Appeal, Apply, Ask, Beg, Desire, Entreaty, Invite, Petition, Plea, Prayer, Solicit, Supplication

Requiem Agnus dei, Mass

Require(d), **Requirement** Charge, Crave, De rigueur, Desire, Enjoin, Entail, Exact, Expect, Incumbent, Lack, Necessity, Need, Prerequisite

Requisite, **Requisition** Commandeer, Due, Embargo, Essential, Indent, Necessary, Needful, Order, Press, Simplement

Rescind Abrogate, Annul, Recant, Remove, Repeal

Rescue Aid, Air-sea, Deliver, Free, Liberate, Ransom, Recover, Recower, Redeem,

Regain, Relieve, Reprieve, Retrieve, Salvage, Salvation, > SAVE

Research(er) Boffin, Delve, Dig, Enquiry, Explore, Fieldwork, Investigate, Legwork, Market, Motivation(al), Operational, Pioneer, Sus(s), Think-tank

Resell Scalp

Resemblance, Resemble, Resembling Affinity, Apatetic, Approach, Assonant, Dead ringer, Likeness, -oid, -opsis, Replica, Similitude, Simulate

Resent(ful), Resentment Anger, Bridle, Chippy, Choler, Cross, Derry, Dudgeon, Grudge, Indignation, Ire, Jaundiced, Malign, Miff, Pique, Rankle, Smart, Spite, Umbrage

Reservation, Reserve(d), Reservist(s) Aloof, Arrière-pensée, Backlog, Bashful, Book, By, Caveat, Central, Cold, Demiss, Detachment, Distant, Earmark, Engage, Ersatz, Except, Fall-back, Fort Knox, Gold, Hold, Husband, Ice, Indian, Introvert, Landwehr, Layby, Locum, Mental, Militiaman, Nature, Nest-egg, Nineteenth man, Proviso, Qualification, Reddendum, Res, Rest, Restraint, Retain, Reticence, Retiring, Rez, Salvo, Sanctuary, Save, Scenic, Scruple, Set aside, Special, Stand-by, Stand-offishness, Starch, Stash, Stock(pile), TA(men), Uncommunicate, Understudy, Warren, Waves, Withhold

Reservoir Basin, Cistern, G(h)ilgai, Gilgie, Header tank, Repository, Rybinsk, Service, Stock, Sump, Tank, Water tower

Reset Taxis

Reside(nce), Resident(s) Abode, Address, Amban, Chequers, Commorant, Consulate, Denizen, Dwell, Embassy, Establishment, Expatriate, Exurbanite, Gremial, Guest, Home, In, Indweller, Inholder, Inmate, Intern, Ledger, Lei(d)ger, Lieger, Liveyer(e), Lodger, Metic, Occupant, Pad, Parietal, Permanent, Resiant, Settle, Sojourn, Stay, Tenant, Up, Vicinage, Villager, Yamen

Residual, Residue Ash, Astatki, Boneblack, Calx, Caput, Chaff, Cinders, Coke, Crud, Dottle, Draff, Dregs, Expellers, Greaves, Leavings, Mazout, Mortuum, Remainder, Remanent, Remnant, Slag, Slurry, Snuff, Vinasse

Resign(ed), Resignation Abandon, Abdicate, Demit, Fatalism, Heigh-ho, Leave, Meek, > QUIT, Reconcile, Stoic, Submit

Resilience, Resilient Bounce, Buoyant, Elastic, Flexible, Recoil, Springy

Resin Acaroid, Acrylic, Agila, Alkyd, Amber, Amine, Amino, Anime, Arar, Asaf(o)etida, Bakelite®, Balsam, Bal(sa)m of Gilead, Benjamin, Benzoin, Bursera, Cannabin, Cannabis, Caranna, Carauna, Charas, Cholestyramine, Churrus, Colophony, Conima, Copai(ba), Copaiva, Copal(m), Coumarone, Courbaril, Cymene, Dam(m)ar, Dammer, Dragon's blood, Elaterite, Elemi, Epoxy, Frankincense, Galbanum, Galipot, Gambi(e)r, Gamboge, Glyptal, Guaiacum, Gum, Hasheesh, Hashish, Hing, Jalapin, Kino, Labdanum, Lac, Ladanum, Lignaloes, Mastic, Melamine, Methacrylate, Myrrh, Olibanum, Opopanax, Perspex®, Phenolic, Phenoxy, Plastisol, Podophyllin, Polycarbonate, Polyester, Polymer, Polysterene, Polyvinyl, Propolis, Retinite, Roset, Rosin, Rosit, Rozet, Rozit, Sagapenum, Sandarac(h), Saran®, Scammony, Shellac, Storax, Styrax, Synthetic, Takamaka, Taxin, Urea, Vinyl, Xylenol

Resist Bristle, Buck, Combat, Contest, Defy, Face, Fend, Gainstrive, Impede, Oppose, Redound, Reluct, Stand (pat), Toughen, > WITHSTAND

Resistance, Resistant, Resistor Barretter, Bleeder, Ceramal, Cermet, Chetnik, Coccidiostat, Combat, Drag, Element, Friction, Hostile, Immunity, Impediment, Internal, Invar, Klendusic, Klepht, Maquis, Maraging, Megohm, Microhm, Negative, Obstacle, Ohm, Passive, Pat, Pull, R, Radiation, Reluctance, Renitent, Resilient, Rheostat, Sales, Satyagraha, Soul-force, Specific, Stability, Stand, Stonde, Stubborn, Tough

Resolute, Resolution Analysis, Bold, Cast-iron, Casuistry, Courage, Decided, Decision, Denouement, Determined, Doughty, > FIRM, Fortitude, Granite, Grim, Grit, Hardiness, Insist, Joint, Pertinacity, Promotion, Rede, Resolve, Stable, Stalwart, Staunch, Stout, Strength, Sturdy, Telic, Tenacity, Unbending, Valiant, Willpower

Resolve(d), Resolver Analyse, Calculate, Decide, Declare, > DETERMINE, Deux et machina, Factorise, Fix, Hellbent, Intent, Nerve, > PURPOSE, Settle, Steadfast, Tenacity, Vow, Will

▷ **Resolved** *may indicate* an anagram

Resonance, Resonant Canorous, Electromer, Morphic, Orotund, Parallel, Ringing, Sonorous, Timbre, Vibrant

Resort Centre, Dive, Etaples, Expedient, Frame, Frequent, Haunt, Hove, Hydro, Invoke, Lair, Last, Las Vegas, Lowestoft, Morecambe, Nassau, Paignton, Pau, Pis aller, Rapallo, Recourse, Repair, Riviera, Southend, Spa(w), Stand by, Use, Watering place, Zermatt

▷ **Resort(ing)** *may indicate* an anagram

Resound(ing) Echo, Plangent, Reboant, Reboation, Reverberate, Ring

Resource(s), Resourceful Assets, Beans, Bottom, Chevisance, Clever, Enterprise, Faculty, Funds, Gumption, Human, Ingenious, Input, Inventive, Means, Natural, Sharp, Stock-in-trade, > VERSATILE, Wealth

Respect(ed), Respectable, Respectful Admire, Ahimsa, Aspect, Behalf, Consider, Decent, Deference, Devoir, Duty, Esteem, Gigman, Homage, > HONOUR, Intent, Kempt, Latria, Obeisant, Officious, Pace, Particular, Preppy, Prestige, Proper, Reference, Regard, Relation, Reputable, Revere, Sir, S(t)irrah, U, Venerate, Wellborn, Well-thought-of, Wise, Worthy

Respirator, Respire, Respiration Artificial, Blow, Breathe, Exhale, Gasmask, Inhale, Iron lung, Pant, Snorkel

Respite Break, Breather, Frist, Interval, Leisure, Let up, Pause, Reprieve, Rest, Stay, Truce

Respond, Response, Responsive Amenable, Answer, Antiphon, Comeback, Conditioned, Echo, Feedback, Flechman, Grunt, Immune, Kneejerk, Kyrie, Litany, Nastic, Pavlovian, Photonasty, React(ion), Reflex, Reply, Repost, Retort Rheotaxis, Rheotropism, Rise, Synapte, Syntonic, Tender, Thigmotropic, Tic, Tropism, Unconditioned, Voice, Warm

Responsibility, Responsible Anchor, Answerable, Baby, Blame, Buck, Charge, Culpable, Dependable, Diminished, Duty, Frankpledge, Hot seat, Incumbent, Instrumental, Liable, Mea culpa, Onus, Pigeon, Sane, Solid, Stayman, Trust

Rest (day) Alt, Anchor, Avocation, Balance, Bed, Beulah, Break, Breather, Calm, Catnap, Cetera, Comma, Depend, Dwell, Ease, Easel, Etc, Fermata, Feutre, Fewter, Gite, Half-time, Halt, Inaction, Jigger, Lave, Lean, Lie, Lie-in, Light, Lodge, Loll, Lound, Lyte, Nap, Nooning, Others, Overlie, Pause, Quiescence, Quiet, Relache, Relax, Rely, Remainder, Repose, Requiem, Residue, Respite, Sabbath, Siesta, > SLEEP, Slide, Sloom, Slumber, Spell, Spider, Stopover, Support, Surplus, Time out, Y-level

Re-start Da capo

Restaurant, Restaurateur Automat, Beanery, Bistro, Brasserie, British, Cabaret, Cafe, Canteen, Chew'n'spew, Chip-shop, Chophouse, Commissary, Cook shop, Creperie, Diner, Eatery, Eating-house, Estaminet, Greasy spoon, Grill, Grillroom, Grub shop, Luncheonette, Maxim's, Noshery, Padrone, Rathskeller, Ratskeller, Roadhouse, Rotisserie, Slap-bang, Steakhouse, Takeaway, Taqueria, Taverna, Teahouse, Tearoom, Teashop, Trattoria

Rest-home Aggie, Hospice

Resting-place Bed, Couch, Dharmsala, Gite, Grave, Inn, Khan, Serai, She'ol, Stage

Restitute, **Restitution** Amends, Apocatastasis, Reparation, Restore, Return

Restive, **Restless(ness)** Chafing, Chorea, Fikish, Free-arm, Itchy, Jactitation, Toey, Unsettled

Restless *may indicate* an anagram

Restoration, **Restorative**, **Restore(d)** Cure, Descramble, Heal, Mend, Pentimento, Pick-me-up, Postliminy, Rally, Recondition, Redeem, Redintegrate, Redux, Refurbish, Regenerate, Rehabilitate, Rejuvenate, Remedial, Renew, Renovate, Repone, Restitute, Resuscitate, Retouch, Revamp, Revive, Stet, Tonic

Restrain(ed), **Restraint** Abstinence, Ban, Bate, Bit, Bottle, Branks, Bridle, Cage, Chain, Chasten, > CHECK, Cohibit, Compesce, Confinement, Contain, Control, Cramp, Curb, Dam, Decorum, Detent, Dry, Duress, Embargo, Enfetter, Estoppel, Freeze, Halt, Hamshackle, Handcuffs, Harness, Heft, Hinder, Hopple, Impound, Inhibit, Jess, Lid, Low-key, Manacle, Measure, Mince, Moderation, Muzzle, Quiet, Rein, Repress, Restrict, Ritenuto, Shackle, Sober, Sobriety, Squeeze, Stay, Stent, Stint, Straitjacket, Temper, Tether, Tie, Trash

Restrict(ed), **Restriction** Band, Bar, Bind, Bit, Burden, Cage, Catch, Censorship, Chain, Circumscribe, Closet, Condition, Cord, Corset, Cramp, Curb, DORA, Fence, Fold, Gate, Ground, Guard, Hamper, Hidebound, Hobble, Inhibit, Intern, Kennel, Let, > LIMIT, Lock, Mere, Narrow, Net, Nick, Pale, Parochial, Pen, Pent, Pier, Pin, Pot-bound, Private, Proscribed, Qualify, Regulate, Rein, Rope, Safety belt, Scant, Seal, Section, Selected, Shackle, Snare, Squeeze, Stenopaic, Stent, Stint, Stop, Straiten, Stunt, Tether, Tie

Restructure, **Restructuring** Perestroika

Result(s) Aftermath, Ans(wer), Bring, Causal, Consequence, Effect, Emanate, End, Ensue, Entail, Event, Eventuate, Finding, Fruict, Fruits, Issue, Karmic, Knock-on, Lattermath, > OUTCOME, Outturn, Pan, Proceeds, Quotient, Sequel, Side-effect, Sum, Upshot, Wale

Resume, **Résumé** Continue, Pirlicue, Purlicue, Summary

Resurrect(ion) Anabiosis, Rebirth, Revive, Zomb(ie)

Resuscitate(d), **Resuscitation** Mouth-to-mouth, Quicken, Redivivus, Restore, Revive

Retail(er) Chandler, Dealer, > NARRATE, Sell, Shopkeeper, Tell

Retain(er), **Retains** Brief, Contain, Deposit, Fee, Hold, Hold-all, Keep, Panter, Pantler, Reserve, Retinue, Servant

Retaliate, **Retaliation** Avenge, Counter, Lex talionis, Quid pro quo, Quit(e), Redress, Repay, Reprisal, Requite, Retort, Talion

Retard(ed) Arrest, Brake, Cretin, Encumber, Hinder, Slow

Retch Boak, Bock, Boke, Cowk, Gap, Heave, Keck, Reach, Vomit

Reticence, **Reticent** Clam, Coy, Dark, Reserve, Restraint, Secretive, Shy, Taciturn

Reticule, **Reticulum** Bag, Carryall, Dragnet, Lattice, Net

Retina Detached, Fovea, Macula lutea

Retinue Company, Cortège, Equipage, Following, Meiney, Meinie, Meiny, Sowarry, Suite

Retire(d), **Retiree**, **Retirement**, **Retiring** Abed, Aloof, Baccare, Backare, Backpedal, Blate, Bowler-hat, Cede, Coy, Depart, Ebb, Emeritus, Essene, Former, Leave, Lonely, Modest, Mothball, Nun, Outgoing, Pension, Perfing, Private, Quit, Recede, Recluse, Reserved, Resign, Retract, Retread, Retreat, Retrocedent, Roost, Rusticate, Scratch, Shy, Superannuate, Unassertive,

Withdraw

▷ **Retirement** *may indicate* 'bed' around another word, or word reversed

Retort Alembic, Comeback, Courteous, Quip, Repartee, > REPLY, Retaliate, Riposte, Still, Tu quoque

Retract(ion) Backpedal, Backtrack, Disavow, Epanorthosis, Palinode, Recall, Recant, Renounce, Revoke

Retreat Abbey, Arbour, Ashram(a), Asylum, Backpedal, Backwater, Bower, Bug, Camp David, Cell, Cloister, Convent, Crawfish, Dacha, Departure, Donjon, Girth, Grith, Hermitage, Hideaway, Hide-out, Hole, Interstadial, Ivory-tower, Katabasis, Lair, Lama(sery), Mew, Monastery, Nest, Neuk, Nook, Recede, Recoil, Recu(i)le, Redoubt, Reduit, Refuge, Retire, Retraite, Right-about, Rout, Shelter, Skedaddle, Stronghold, Withdraw

Retribution Come-uppance, Deserts, Nemesis, Revenge, Reward, Utu, Vengeance

Retrieve(r), **Retrieval** Access, Bird-dog, Field, Gundog, Labrador, Read-out, Recall, Recoup, Recover, Redeem, Rescue, Salvage

Retroflex Cacuminal

Retrograde Backward, Deasi(u)l, Deasoil, Decadent, Decline, Hindward, Rearward, Regrede

Retrospect(ive) Contemplative, Ex post facto, Hindsight, Regardant

Return(s) Agen, Bricole, Census, Comeback, Day, Diminishing, Dividend, Elect Er, Extradite, Gain, Pay, Proceeds, Profit, Rebate, Rebound, Recur, Redound, Regress, Reject, Render, Rent, Repay, Replace, Reply, Requital, Respond, Restitution, Restore, Retour, Revenue, Reverse, Revert, Riposte, Takings, Tax, Traffic, > YIELD

Rev Gun, Minister

Reveal(ing), **Revelation** Advertise, Air, Apocalyptic, Bare, Betray, Bewray, Confess, Descry, Disclose, Discover, Discure, > DIVULGE, Epiphany, Exhibit, Explain, Expose, Giveaway, Hierophantic, Impart, Indicate, Ingo, Kythe, Leak, Let on, Manifest, Open, Satori, > SHOW, Spill, Tell-tale, Unclose, Uncover, Unfold, Unheal, Unmask, Unveil

Revel(ling), **Revelry** Ariot, Bacchanalia, Bend, Carnival, Carouse, Comus, Dionysian, Feast, Gloat, Glory, Joy, Merriment, Orgy, Rant, Rejoice, Riot, Roister, Rollicks, Rout, Saturnalia, Splore, Swig, Upsee, Ups(e)y, Wallow, Wassail, Whoopee

Reveller Bacchant, Birler, Corybant, Guisard, Guiser, Maenad, Merrymaker, Orgiast, Silenus

Revenant Fetch, Ghost, Spectre

Revenge(ful) Aftergame, Avenge, Commination, Goel, Grenville, Montezuma's Reprise, Requite, Retaliation, Revanche, Ultion, Utu, Vindictive

Revenue Capital, Finance, Fisc(al), Fisk, Income, Inland, Internal, Jag(h)ir, Jaghire, Prebend, Primitiae, Rent, Taille, Tax, Turnover, Zamindar, Zemindar

Reverberate Echo, Recoil, Reflect, Repercuss, Resound

Revere(nce) Admire, Awe, Bostonian, Dread, Dulia, Esteem, Hallow, Hery, Homage, > HONOUR, Hyperdulia, Latria, Obeisance, Paul, Respect, Venerate

Reverie Daydream, Dream(iness), Fantasy, Memento

Revers Lap(p)el

Reversal, **Reverse**, **Reversing**, **Reversion** Antithesis, Antonym, Arsy-versy, Atavism, Back(slide), Change-over, Chiasmus, Commutate, Counter(mand), Escheat, Evaginate, Exergue, Flip, Inversion, Misfortune, > OPPOSITE, Overturn, Palindrome, Pile, Regress, Revoke, Rheotropic, Switchback, Tails, Throwback, Transit, Turn, Un-, Undo, U-turn, Verso, Vice versa, Volte-face

Revert Annul, Backslide, Regress, Relapse, Resort, Retrogress, Return
Review(er) Appeal, Censor, Critic, Critique, Editor, Encomium, Feuilleton, Footlights, Inspect, Judicial, Magazine, March-past, Notice, Pan, Recapitulate, Repeat, Revise, Rundown, Spithead, Summary, Survey, Write-up
Review *may indicate* an anagram or a reversed word
Revile, **Reviling** Abuse, Execrate, Inveigh, Rail, Rayle, Vilify, Vituperate
Revise(r), **Revision** Alter, Amend, Correct, Diaskeuast, Edit, Peruse, Reappraise, Reassess, Recense, Reform, Rev, Update
Revise(d) *may indicate* an anagram
Revival, **Revive**, **Revivify**, **Reviving** Araise, Enliven, Gothic, Greek, Rake up, Rally, Reanimate, Reawake(n), Rebirth, Redintegrate, Refresh, Rekindle, Renaissance, Renascent, Renew, Renovate, Restore, Resurrect, Resuscitate, Risorgimento, Romantic, Rouse, Wake
Revoke Abrogate, Cancel, Countermand, Negate, > **RECALL**, Repeal, Rescind
Revolt(ing), **Revolution(ary)** Agitator, Agitprop, American, Anarchist, Apostasy, Appal, Bloodless, Bolivar, Bolshevik, Bolshevist, Boxer, Bulldog, Cade, Castro, Chartist, Che, Chinese, Circle, Commune, Coup d'etat, Cultural, Cycle, Danton, Dervish, Disgust, Emeute, Emmet, Engels, Enrage, February, Fenian, Foul, French, Girondin, Girondist, Glorious, Green, Grody, Guevara, Gyration, Industrial, Inqilab, > **IN REVOLT**, Insurgent, Insurrection, Intifada, IRA, Jacobin, Jacquerie, Komitaji, Lap, Lenin, Marat, Marx, Maximalist, Maypole, Minimalist, Montagnard, Mountain, Mutiny, Nauseating, Nihilist, Orbit, Outbreak, Palace, Paris commune, Peasants, Poujadist, Putsch, Radical, > **REBEL(LION)**, Red, Red Shirt, Reformation, Riot, Rise, Robespierre, Roll, Rotation, Round, Run, Russian, Sandinista, Sansculotte(rie), Sedition, Sicilian vespers, Spartacus, Syndicalism, Thermidor, Trot(sky), Twist, Up(rise), > **UPRISING**, Velvet, Villa, Wat Tyler, Weatherman, Whirl, Wolfe Tone, Young Turk, Zapata
Revolutionary *may indicate* 'reversed'
Revolve(r), **Revolving** Carrier, Catherine wheel, Centrifuge, Colt®, Gat, Girandole, Grindstone, > **GUN**, Gyrate, Iron, Klinostat, Lathe, Maelstrom, Peristrephic, Pistol, Pivot, Roller, Rotate, Rotifer, Rotor, Roundabout, Run, Six-shooter, Tone, Turn(stile), Turntable, Turret, Wheel, Whirl(igig), Whirlpool
Revue Follies
Reward Albricias, Bonus, Bounty, Compensate, Consideration, Desert, Emolument, Fee, Guerdon, Head money, Medal, Meed, Payment, Premium, Price, Prize, Profit, Purse, Recompense, Reguerdon, Remuneration, Requital, Requite, S, Shilling, Tribute, Wage, War(r)ison
Reword Edit, Paraphrase
Reworking Rifacimento
Rex Priam, R
Reynolds Joshua, PRA
Rhapsodic, **Rhapsody** Ecstasy, Epic, Music, Unconnected
Rhea Em(e)u, Nandoo, Nandu, Ostrich
Rhenium Re
Rhesus Bandar, Macaque, Monkey
Rhetoric(al) Anaphora, Apophasis, Aureate, Bombast, Chiasmus, Ecbole, Eloquence, Enantiosis, Epistrophe, Erotema, Eroteme, Erotesis, Euphemism, Hendiadys, Hypallage, Hyperbole, Oratory, Paral(e)ipsis, Peroration, Platform, Pleonasm, Syllepsis, Synoeciosis, Trivium
Rhino Blunt, Bread, Cash, Lolly, Loot, > **MONEY**, Tin
Rhinoceros Baluchitherium, Keitloa, Square-lipped, White

Rhodes, **Rhodesia(n)** Cecil, Colossus, Ridgeback, Scholar, Zimbabwe
Rhodium Rh
Rhubarb Pie-plant, Rhapontic, Rheum, Rot, Spat
Rhyme(s), **Rhymer**, **Rhyming** Assonance, Clerihew, Closed couplet, Couplet, Crambo, Cynghanedd, Doggerel, Eye, Feminine, Head, Identical, Internal, Male, Masculine, Measure, Near, Nursery, Pararhyme, Perfect, Poetry, Rich, Riding, Rime riche, Rondel, Royal, Runic, Sight, Slang, Slant, Tail(ed), Tercet, Terza-rima, Thomas, Triple, > **VERSE**, Virelay, Vowel
Rhythm(ic) Agoge, Alpha, Asynartete, Backbeat, Beat, Beta, Bo Diddley beat, Breakbeat, Cadence, Circadian, Duple, Hemiol(i)a, In-step, Meter, Movement, Oompah, Pulse, Pyrrhic, Rove-over, Rubato, Scotch catch, Scotch snap, Sdrucciola, Singsong, Sprung, Swing, Syncopation, Tala, Talea, > **TEMPO**, Time, Voltinism
Rib(bed), **Ribbing**, **Rib-joint** Bar, Chaff, Chiack, Chip, Chyack, Cod, Costa, Cross-springer, Dutch, Eve, False, Fin, Floating, Futtock, Groin, Intercostal, Lierne, Nervate, Nervular, Nervure, Ogive, Persiflage, Rack, Rag, Rally, Short, Spare, Springer, Subcosta, Taunt, Tease, Tierceron, Tracery, True, Wife
Ribald(ry) Balderdash, Bawdy, Coarse, Scurrilous, Smut, Sotadic, Vulgar
Ribbon Band, Bandeau, Blue, Bow, Braid, Caddis, Caddyss, Cordon, Fattrels, Ferret, Fillet, Grosgrain, Hatband, Infula, Multistrike, Pad, Petersham, Radina, Rein, Soutache, Taenia, Tape, Teniate, Tie, Torsade, Yellow
Ribless Ecostate
Rice Arborio, Basmati, Bir(i)yani, Brown, Canada, Carnaroti, Elmer, Entertainer, Indian, Kedgeree, Miracle, Paddy, Patna, Pilaf, Pilau, Pilaw, Pillau, Reis, Risotto, Spanish, Sushi, Twigs, Water, Wild
Rich(es) Abounding, Abundant, Affluent, Amusing, Bonanza, Comic, Copious, Croesus, Dives, Edmund, Edwin, Fat, Feast, Fertile, Flush, Fruity, Full, Golconda, Haves, Heeled, High, Larney, Loaded, Lush, Luxurious, Mammon, Moneybags, Moneyed, Nabob, Oberous, > **OPULENT**, Plenteous, Plush, Plutocrat, Resonant, Rolling, Sumptuous, Toff, Vulgarian, > **WEALTHY**, Well-heeled, Well-to-do
Richard Angevin, Burbage, Dick(y), Lionheart, Rick, Roe
Richthofen Red Baron
Rick (burning) Goaf, Sprain, Swingism, Wrench
Rickets, **Rickety** Dilapidated, Rachitis, Ramshackle, Shaky, Unsound
▷ **Rickety** *may indicate* an anagram
Rickshaw Pedicab, Tuktuk
Ricochet Boomerang, Glance, Rebound
Rid Clear, Deliver, Ditch, Eliminate, Eradicate, Expunge, Free, Obviate, Offload, Purge, Scrub, Shot
Riddle Boulter, Charade, Colander, Dilemma, Enigma, Koan, Logogriph, Pepper, Perforate, Permeate, Puzzle, Screen, Searce, Search, Sieve, Sift, Siler, Sorites, Strain, Tems(e), Trommel
Ride, **Riding** Annoy, Aquaplane, Bareback, Bestride, Big dipper, Bruise, Canter, Coast, Crog(gy), Cycle, District, Division, Drive, Equitation, Field, Hack, Harass, Haute école, Hitchhike, Merry-go-round, Mount, Pick(-a-)back, Pickpack, Piggyback, Postil(l)ion, Rape, Revere's, Roadstead, Rollercoaster, Sit, Spin, Stang, Switchback, Third, Trot, Weather, Welter, Wheelie, Whip, White-knuckle
Rider(s) Addendum, Adjunct, Appendage, Attachment, Boundary, Cavalier, Charioteer, Circuit, Codicil, Condition, Corollary, Dispatch, Equestrian, Eventer, Freedom, Gaucho, Godiva, Guidon, Haggard, Horseman, Jockey,

Lochinvar, Messenger, Peloton, Postil(l)ion', Proviso, PS, Revere, Spurrer, Walkyrie

Ridge Alveolar, Anthelix, Antihelix, Arete, Arris, As(ar), Balk, Bank, Baulk, Berm, Bur(r), Carina, Chine, Clint, Costa, Crease, Crest, Crista, Cuesta, Darling Range, Drill, Drum(lin), Dune, Esker, Fret, Gonys, Gyrus, Hammock, Hoe, Hogback, Horst, Hummock, Interfluve, Keel, Knur(l), Ledge, Linch, Lynchet, Mid-Atlantic, Mid-ocean, Missionary, Nek, Nut, Oceanic, Pressure, Promontory, Ramp, Rand, Raphe, Razor-back, Reef, Rib, Rig, Rim, Sastruga, Screw-thread, Serac, Serpentine, Shoulder, Sowback, Torus, Varix, Verumontanum, Vimy, Wale, Weal, Whelp, Whorl, Windrow, Withers, Wrinkle, Yardang, Zastruga

Ridicule, **Ridiculous** Absurd, Badinage, Bathos, Chaff, Cockamamie, Deride, Derisory, Egregous, Foolish, Gibbet, Gibe, Gird, Guy, Haze, Jibe, Josh, Laughable, Ludicrous, Mimic, Mock, Paradox, Pasquin, Pillory, Pish, Pooh-pooh, Raillery, Rich, Roast, Satire, Scoff, Scout, Screwy, Sight, Silly, Skimmington, Taunt, Travesty

Ridinghood Nithsdale, Red

Riding-master RM

Riding-school Manège

Rife Abundant, Manifest, Numerous, Prevalent

Riffle Rapid

Riff-raff Canaille, Hoi polloi, Mob, Populace, Rag-tag, Scaff, Scum, Trash

Rifle Air, Armalite®, Bone, Browning, Bundook, Burgle, Calic, Carbine, Chassepot, Enfield, Enfield musket, Express, Garand, > **GUN**, Kalashnikov, Lee Enfield, Loot, Martini®, Martini-Henry, Mauser®, MI, Minié, Pea, Petronel, Pilfer, Ransack, Remington, Repeater, Rob, Ruger, Shiloh, Springfield, Winchester®

Rift Altercation, Chasm, Crevasse, Fault, Fissure, Gap, Gulf, Split

Rig(ging) Accoutre, Attire, Bermuda, Drilling, Equip, Feer, Gaff, Get-up, Gunter, Hoax, Jack-up, Mainbrace, Manipulate, Marconi, Martingale, Oil, Outfit, Panoply, Ratline, Ropes, Schooner, Semisubmersible, Slant, Sport, Stack, Standing, Strip, Swindle, Tackle, Trull, Wanton

Rigged *may indicate* an anagram

Right(en), **Rightness**, **Rights** Accurate, Advowson, Ancient lights, Angary, Appropriate, Appurtenance, Befit, Blue-pencil, BNP, Bote, Cabotage, Champart, Civil, Claim, Competence, Conjugal, Conservative, Copyhold, > **CORRECT**, Cor(r)ody, Coshery, Cure, Curtesy, Customer, De jure, Dexter, Direct, Divine, Doctor, Droit, Due, Easement, Eminent domain, Emphyteusis, Equity, Esnecy, Estover, Ethical, Exactly, Faldage, Farren, Fascist, Feu, Fire-bote, Fitting, Forestage, Franchise, Free-bench, Freedom, Gay, Germane, Gunter, Haybote, Hedge-bote, Human, Infangthief, Interest, Isonomy, Iure, Junior, Jural, Jus, Leet, Legit, Letters patent, Liberty, Lien, Maritage, Meet, Miner's, Moral, Naam, New, Ninepence, Off, Offhand, Offside, OK, Okay, Oke, Okey-dokey, Option, Ortho-, Oughtness, Paine, Passant, Pat, Patent, Performing, Ploughbote, Pose, Postliminy, Prerogative, Primogeniture, Priority, Prisage, Privilege, Proper, Property, Pukka, R, Rain, Reason, Recourse, Rectify, Rectitude, Redress, Remainder, Remedy, Repair, Rt, Sac, Sake, Side, So, Soc, Squatter's, Stage, Starboard, Stillicide, Tao, Tenants', Terce, Ticket, Title, Trivet, True, Turbary, User, Usucap(t)ion, Usufruct, Venville, Vert, Warren, Womens'

Right-angle(d) Orthogonal

Righteous(ness) Devout, Good, Just, Moral, Pharisee, Prig, Rectitude,

Sanctimonious, Tzaddik, Virtuous
Right-hand Dexter, E, Far, Recto, RH, Ro
Right-winger Falangist, Neo-fascist
Rigid(ity) Acierated, Catalepsy, Craton, Extreme, Fixed, Formal, Hard and fast, Hard-set, Hard-shell, Hidebound, Inflexible, Renitent, Rigor, Set, Slavish, Starch(y), Stern, Stiff, Stretchless, Strict, Stringent, Tense, Turgor
Rigmarole Nonsense, Palaver, Paraphernalia, Protocol, Ragman, Ragment, Riddlemeree, Screed
Rigorous, Rigour Accurate, Austere, Cruel, Exact, Firm, Hard, Inclement, Iron-bound, Stern, Strait, Strict, Stringent
Rile Anger, Annoy, Harry, Irritate, > NETTLE, Vex
▷ **Rile(y)** *may indicate* an anagram
Rill Purl, Sike
Rim Atlantic, Border, Chimb, Chime, Edge, Felloe, Felly, Flange, Kelyphitic, > LIP, Margin, Pacific, Strake, Verge
Rime Crust, Frost, Hoar, Rhyme, Rhythm
Rind Bark, Peel, Skin
Ring(ed), Ringer, Ringing, Rings Anchor, Angelus, Annual, Annulus, Anthelion, Arcus, Arena, Band, Bangle, Bell, Broch, Brogh, Call, Cambridge, Carabiner, Cartel, Cartouche, Change, Chime, Circinate, Circle, Circlet, Circlip, Circus, Claddagh, Clam, Clang, Clink, Coil, Collet, Cordon, Corona, Corral, Corrida, Crawl, Cricoid, Cringle, Cromlech, Cycle, Cyclic, Dead, Death's head, Dial, Dicyclic, Ding, Disc, Dohyo, Dong, D(o)uar, Draupnir, Echo, Encircle, Encompass, Engagement, Enhalo, Enlace, Environ, Enzone, Eternity, Extension, Eyelet, Fainne, Fairlead(er), Fairy, Ferrule, Fisherman, Fistic(uffs), Gas, Gimmal, Gird(le), Girr, Gloriole, Groin, Grom(m)et, Growth, Grummet, Guard, Gyges, Gymmal, Gyre, Halo, Hob, > HOOP, Hoop-la, Hula-hoop, Ideal, Inner, Inorb, Involucre, Jougs, Jow, Karabiner, Kartell, Keeper, Key, Knell, Knock-out, Kraal, Lifebelt, Link, Loop, Luned, Lute, Magpie, Manacle, Manilla, Marquise, Mourning, Napkin, Newton's, Nibelung, Nose, O, Orb, Outer, Pappus, Peal, Pele, Pen, Phone, Ping, Piston, Potato, Price, Prize, Puteal, Quoit, Resonant, Resound, Retaining, Round, Rove, Rundle, Runner, Scarf, Scrunchy, Seal, Signet, Slinger, Slip, Snap-link, Solomon, Sound, Spell, Split, Stemma, Stemme, Stonehenge, Surround, Swivel, Syndicate, Tang, Tattersall, Teething, Terret, Territ, Thimble, Timbre, Ting, Tingle, Tink, Tinnitius, Tintinnabulate, Toe, Token, Toll, Toplady, Tore, Torquate, Torques, Torret, Torus, Travelling, Tree, Trochus, Turret, Tweed, Varvel, Vervel, Vice, Vortex, Wagnerian, Washer, Wedding, Welkin, Withe, Woggle, Zero
Ring-dance Carol
Ring-leader Bell-wether, Fugleman, Instigator
Ringlet Curl(icue), Lock, Tendril, Tress
Ringmaster Wagner
Ringworm Serpigo, Tinea
Rinse Bathe, Blue, Cleanse, Douche, Sind, Sine, Swill, Synd, Syne, Tint, Wash
Riot(er), Riotous(ly), Riots Anarchy, Brawl, Clamour, Demo, Deray, Gordon, Hilarious, Hubbub, Luddite, Medley, Melee, Nicker, Orgy, Pandemonium, Peterloo, Petroleur, Porteous, Profusion, Quorum, Race, Rag, Rebecca, Rebel, Roaring, Roister, Rout, Rowdy, Ruction, Ruffianly, Scream, Swing, Tumult
▷ **Rioters, Riotous** *may indicate* an anagram
Rip(ping) Basket, Buller, Cur, Grand, Handful, Horse, Lacerate, Rent, Rep, Splendid, Tear, Tide, Topnotch, To-rend, Unseam
Ripe, Ripen(ing) Auspicious, Full, Mature, Mellow, Rathe, Ready

Riposte Repartee, Retaliate, Retort

Ripple Bradyseism, Fret, Overlap, Popple, Purl, Undulation, Wave, Wavelet, Wrinkle

Rippling *may indicate* an anagram

Rise(r), Rising Advance, Appreciate, Ascend, Assurgent, Bull, Butte, Cause, Dutch, Easter, Eger, Elevation, Emerge, Emeute, Eminence, Erect, Escalate, Hance, Hauriant, Haurient, Heave, Heliacal, Hike, Hill, Hummock, Hunt's up, Improve, Increase, Insurgent, Intumesce, Jibe, Knap, Knoll, Lark, Levee, Levitate, Lift, Mount, Mutiny, Orient, Peripety, Prove, Putsch, Rear, Resurgent, Resurrection, > REVOLT, Saleratus, Scarp, Sklim, Soar, Stand, Stie, Sty, Surface, Surge, The Fifteen, Tor, Tower, Transcend, Up, Upbrast, Upburst, Upgo, Uprest, Upsurge, Upswarm, Upturn, Well

Risk(y) Actuarial, Adventure, Back, Calculated, Chance, Compromise, > DANGER, Daring, Dice, Dicy, Emprise, Endanger, Fear, Gamble, Game, Hairy, Hazard, Imperil, Jeopardy, Liability, Peril, Precarious, Security, Shoot the works, Spec, Touch and go, Touchy, Unsafe, Venture

Risorgimento Renaissance

Risqué Blue, Racy, Salty, Scabrous, Spicy

Rissole(s) Cecils, Croquette, Faggot, Quennelle, Veggieburger

Rite(s) Asperges, Bora, Ceremony, Exequies, Initiation, Liturgy, Nagmaal, Obsequies, Powwow, Ritual, Sacrament, Sarum use, Superstition, York

Ritual Agadah, Arti, Ceremony, Chanoyu, Customary, Formality, Haggada, Lavabo, Liturgy, Mumbo-jumbo, Puja, Rite, Sacring, Seder, Social, Use

Rival(ry), Rivals Absolute, Acres, Aemule, Binocular, Compete, Emulate, Emule, Envy, Fo(n)e, > MATCH, Needle, Opponent, Retinal, Touch, Vie

River Ea, Estuary, Flood, Flower, Fluvial, Potamic, R, Riverain, Runner, Stream, Tributary, Waterway

RIVERS

2 letters:	Lot	Aras	Huon
Ob	Lys	Arno	Idle
Po	Nar	Aude	Isar
Xi	Ord	Avon	Iser
	Red	Back	Isis
3 letters:	San	Beni	Juba
Aar	Tay	Bomu	Kama
Aln	Tet	Dart	Kill
Axe	Ure	Deva	Kura
Ayr	Usk	Doon	Kwai
Bug	Wye	Dove	Lahn
Cam		Earn	Lech
Dee	**4 letters:**	Ebbw	Lena
Don	Abus	Ebro	Liao
Ems	Abzu	Eden	Lune
Esk	Acis	Eder	Maas
Exe	Adur	Elbe	Main
Fal	Aire	Erne	Meta
Fly	Alma	Esla	Milk
Han	Alph	Eure	Mino
Inn	Amur	Gila	Mole
Lee	Aran	Gota	Nene

Neva	Congo	Rhone	Crouch
Nile	Cross	Rogue	Cydnus
Nith	Dasht	Saône	Dalles
Oder	Desna	Seine	Danube
Ohio	Douro	Shari	Dawson
Oise	Drava	Shire	Donets
Ouse	Drave	Siret	Duddon
Oxus	Duero	Skien	Durack
Prut	Dvina	Slave	Finlay
Ruhr	Eblis	Snake	Fraser
Saar	Firth	Snowy	Gambia
Sava	Fleet	Somme	Ganges
Soar	Forth	Spree	Glomma
Spey	Gogra	Staff	Granta
Styx	Green	Stour	Hodder
Swan	Havel	Swale	Hudson
Swat	Indre	Tagus	Humber
Taff	Indus	Tamar	Iguacu
Tana	Isere	Tapti	Irtish
Tarn	James	Tarim	Irwell
Tees	Jumna	Teign	Itchen
Teme	Juruá	Terek	Japura
Test	Kasai	Tiber	Javari
Tyne	Kenga	Tisza	Javary
Uele	Kuban	Tobol	Jhelum
Ural	Lethe	Trent	Jordan
Vaal	Liard	Tweed	Kagera
Waal	Loire	Volga	Kennet
Wear	Marne	Volta	Kistna
Xero	Mbomu	Warta	Kolyma
Yalu	Meuse	Weser	Komati
Yare	Minho	Xiang	Liffey
Yate	Mosel	Xingu	Mamoré
Yser	Mulla	Yaqui	Medway
Yuan	Mures	Yarra	Mekong
Yuen	Namoi	Yssel	Mersey
	Negro	Yukon	Mohawk
	Neman		Molopo
5 letters:	Niger	**6 letters:**	Morava
Abana	Ogowe	Amazon	Murray
Acton	Onega	Angara	Neckar
Adige	Oreti	Arzina	Neisse
Afton	Peace	Atbara	Nyeman
Agate	Pearl	Barcoo	Ogooue
Aisne	Pecos	Barrow	Orange
Aldan	Pelly	Bio-bio	Orwell
Apure	Piave	Calder	Ottawa
Argun	Pison	Canton	Pahang
Avoca	Plate	Chenab	Parana
Boyne	Purus	Clutha	Peneus
Cauca	Rance	Colima	Platte
Chari	Rhine	Croton	Pripet
Clyde			

Rakaia
Ribble
Riffle
Rother
Sabine
Salado
Sambre
Santee
Severn
Struma
Sutley
Swanee
Tanana
Tarsus
Teviot
Thames
Ticino
Tigris
Tugela
Tyburn
Ubangi
Ussuri
Vardar
Vitava
Wabash
Wairau
Wensum
Wharfe
Wupper
Yarrow
Yellow

7 letters:
Acheron
Aruwimi
Berezua
Bermejo
Caqueta
Cauvery
Chagres
Cocytus
Damodar
Darling
Derwent
Detroit
Dnieper
Dubglas
Durance
Ettrick
Fitzroy
Garonne
Genesee

Gironde
Guapore
Helmand
Hooghly
Huang He
Hwangho
Iguassu
Irawadi
Kanawha
Krishna
Lachlan
Limpopo
Lualaba
Madeira
Manning
Maranon
Maritsa
Mataura
Meander
Moselle
Narbada
Narmada
Niagara
Orinoco
Orontes
Pechora
Pharpar
Potomac
Red Deer
Rubicon
Sabrina
Salinas
Salween
Salzach
Sanders
Scheldt
Senegal
Shannon
Songhua
St Croix
Swannee
Tapajos
Thomson
Ucayali
Uruguay
Vistula
Waikato
Washita
Welland
Yangtse
Yenisey
Zambesi

8 letters:
Amu Darya
Anderson
Apurimac
Araguaia
Araguaya
Blue Nile
Canadian
Cherwell
Chindwin
Clarence
Columbia
Daintree
Demerara
Dneister
Dordogne
Flinders
Franklin
Gascoyne
Godavari
Granicus
Guadiana
Klondike
Kootenay
Maeander
Mahanadi
Menderes
Missouri
Mitchell
Okanagan
Okavango
Okovango
Ouachita
Pactolus
Paraguay
Parnaiba
Putamayo
Rio Negro
Safid Rud
Saguenay
Suwannee
Syr Darya
Tonle Sap
Torridge
Toulouse
Tunguska
Victoria
Volturno
Wanganui
Windrush
Zhu Jiang

9 letters:
Ashburton
Billabong
Churchill
Crocodile
Euphrates
Irrawaddy
Kuskokwim
Mackenzie
Magdalena
Murchison
Parnahiba
Pilcomayo
Porcupine
Qu'Appelle
Rangitata
Richelieu
Rio Branco
Rio Grande
Salambria
Santa Cruz
White Nile
Wisconsin

10 letters:
Black Volta
Blackwater
Chao Phraya
Courantyne
Great Slave
Housatonic
Kizil Irmak
Phlegethon
Rangitaiki
Rangitikei
St Lawrence
White Volta
Yesil Irmak

11 letters:
Aegospotami
Assiniboine
Brahmaputra
Cooper Creek
Lesser Slave
Madre de Dios
Mississippi
Monongahela
Shatt-el-Arab
Susquehanna
Yellowstone

River-bank | 588

River-bank, **Riverside** Brim, Carse, Riparian

River-bed Thalweg

River-mouth Firth, Frith

Rivet Bolt, Clinch, Clink, Concentrate, Explosive, Fasten, Fix, Pean, Peen, Stud, Transfix

Rivulet Beck, Brook, Burn, Gill, Rill, Runnel, Strand

RNA > DNA, Messenger, Riboromal, Ribosome, Ribozyme, Transcribe, Transfer, Uracil

Roach Fish, Red-eye

Road(s), **Roadside**, **Road surface** A, A1, Access, Anchorage, Arterial, Asphalt, Autobahn, Autopista, Autostrada, Ave(nue), B, Beltway, Boulevard, Burma, Carriageway, Causeway, Cloverleaf, Coach, Concession, Corduroy, Corniche, Course, Cul-de-sac, Dirt, Driveway, Escape, Exit, Expressway, Fairway, Feeder, Fly-over, Fly-under, Foss(e) Way, Freeway, Grid, Hampton, Highway, Horseway, Kerb, Lane, Loan, Loke, Mall, Metal, M1, Motorway, Orbital, Overpass, Parkway, Path, Pike, Post, Private, Rd, Relief, Ride, Ridgeway, Ring, > ROUTE, Royal, Service, Shoulder, Shunpike, Skid, Slip, Speedway, Spur(way), St(reet), Switchback, Tarmac, Tar-seal, Thoroughfare, Tobacco, Toby, Track(way), Trunk, Turning, Turnpike, Underpass, Unmade, Verge, Via, Way

Road-block Barrier, Cone, Jam, Toll

Road-keeper Way-warden

Road-maker Drunkard, Macadam, Navigator, Telford, Wade

Roam Extravagate, Peregrinate, Rake, Ramble, Rove, Stray, Wander, Wheel

Roan Barbary, Bay, Horse, Leather, Schimmel, Strawberry

Roar(ing) Bawl, Bell(ow), Bluster, Boom, Boys, Cry, Forties, Guffaw, Laugh, Roin, Rote, Rout, Royne, Thunder, Tumult, Vroom, Wuther, Zoom

Roast Bake, Barbecue, Baste, Birsle, Brent, Cabob, Cook, Crab, Crown, Decrepitate, Grill, Kabob, Pan, Ridicule, Scald, Scathe, Sear, Slate, Tan, Torrefy

Rob(bed), **Robber(y)** Abduct, Bandalero, Bandit, Barabbas, Bereave, Blag, Brigand, Burgle, Bust, Cabbage, Cacus, Cateran, Clyde, Dacoit, Dakoit, Daylight, Depredation, Despoil, Do, Drawlatch, Fake, Filch, Fleece, Flimp, Footpad, Gilderoy, Heist, Hership, Highjack, High toby, Highwayman, Hijack, Hold-up, Hustle, Job, Ladrone, Land-pirate, Larceny, Latrocinium, Latron, Loot, Mill, Mosstrooper, Pad, Pandoor, Pandour, Pillage, Pinch, Piracy, Pluck, Plunder, Procrustes, Rapine, Reave, Reft, Reive, Rieve, Rifle, Roberdsman, Robertsman, Roll, Rover, Roy, Rubbet, Rustler, Sack, Sciron, Screw, Short change, Sinis, Skinner, Smash and grab, Snaphaunch, Spoliation, > STEAL, Steaming, Stick-up, Sting, Swindle, Thief, Toby, Turn-over, Turpin

Robe(s) Alb, Amice, Amis, Attrap, Camis, Camus, Cassock, Chimer, Chrisom(-cloth), Christom, Dalmatic, Dolman, > DRESS, Gown, Ihram, Jilbab, Kanzu, Khalat, Khilat, Kill(a)ut, Kimono, Mantle, Parament, Parliament, Pedro, Peplos, Pontificals, Regalia, Rochet, Saccos, Sanbenito, Soutane, Sticharion, Stola, Stole, Talar, Tire, Vestment, Yukata

Robert Bob(by), Bridges, Browning, Burns, Cop, Flic, Peel, Rab, Rob

Robin Adair, American, Bird, Cock, Day, Goodfellow, Hob, Hood, Puck(-hairy), Ragged, Redbreast, Reliant, Round, Ruddock, Starveling, Wake

Robot Android, Automaton, Cyborg, Dalek, Golem, Nanobot, Puppet, RUR, Telechir

Robust Hale, Hardy, Healthy, Hearty, Iron, Lusty, Muscular, Sound, Stalwart, Sthenic, Stout, Strapping, Sturdy, Vigorous

Roc Bird, Ruc, Rukh

Rock(s), Rocker, Rocking, Rocky Acid, Ages, Agitate, Astound, Cap, Cock, Country, Cradle, Dogger, Edinburgh, Erathem, Erratic, Garage, Gib(raltar), Heavy metal, Hybrid, Mantle, Marciano, Matrix, Native, Nunatak(kr), Permafrost, Petrology, Platform, Plymouth, Punk, Quake, Reel, Reggae, Reservoir, Rip-rap, Rudaceous, Sally, Sedimentary, > SHAKE, Shoogle, Showd, Soft, Stonehenge, Stun, Sway, Swee, Swing, Ted, Teeter, Totter, Unstable, Unsteady, Wall, Weeping, Wind, Windsor

ROCKS

2 letters:
Aa

3 letters:
Gem
Jow
Tor

4 letters:
Bell
Crag
Gang
Glam
Jura
Lava
Lias
Noup
Reef
Sill
Sima
Trap
Tufa
Tuff
Zoic

5 letters:
Ayers
Brash
Calpe
Chair
Chalk
Chert
Cliff
Craig
Elvan
Emery
Flint
Geode
Glass

Krans
Loess
Magma
Nappe
Scalp
Scree
Shale
Slate
Solid
Stone
Trass
Uluru
Wacke

6 letters:
Albite
Aplite
Arkose
Banket
Basalt
Dacite
Diapir
Dunite
Flaser
Flysch
Fossil
Gabbro
Gangue
Garnet
Gibber
Gneiss
Gossan
Gozzan
Inlier
Kingle
Marble
Masada
Norite
Oolite

Oolith
Ophite
Pelite
Pluton
Pumice
Rognon
Sarsen
Schist
Sinter
Skerry
Sklate
S. Peter
Stonen
Synroc
Tephra

7 letters:
Aquifer
Archean
Arenite
Boulder
Breccia
Clastic
Cuprite
Cyanean
Diamond
Diorite
Eucrite
Fastnet
Felsite
Geofact
Granite
Greisen
Lignite
Lorelei
Marlite
Minette
Molasse
Moraine

Needles
Olivine
Ophites
Outcrop
Outlier
Peridot
Picrite
Remanie
Rhaetic
Sinking
Spilite
Syenite
Thulite
Tripoli
Wenlock

8 letters:
Adularia
Aegirine
Andesite
Aphanite
Archaean
Asbestos
Basanite
Brockram
Burstone
Calcrete
Calc-tufa
Calc-tuff
Ciminite
Diabasic
Dolerite
Dolomite
Eclogite
Eklogite
Elvanite
Eutaxite
Fahlband
Footwall

- Ganister
- Hepatite
- Hornfels
- Idocrase
- Inchcape
- Isocline
- Laterite
- Lenticle
- Lopolith
- Mesolite
- Mudstone
- Mylonite
- Obsidian
- Peperino
- Petuntse
- Phyllite
- Pisolite
- Plutonic
- Porphyry
- Psammite
- Psephite
- Ragstone
- Regolith
- Rhyolite
- Rocaille
- Roe-stone
- Saxatile
- Saxonite
- Scorpion
- Sunstone
- Taconite
- Tarpeian
- Tephrite
- The Olgas
- Tonalite
- Trachyte
- Trappean
- Volcanic
- Xenolith

9 letters:
- Anticline
- Argillite
- Batholite
- Batholith
- Bentonite

- Bluestone
- Buhrstone
- Claystone
- Cockhorse
- Colluvium
- Cornstone
- Dalradian
- Diatomite
- Dolostone
- Eddystone
- Evaporite
- Firestone
- Flagstone
- Flowstone
- Gannister
- Goslarite
- Granulite
- Greensand
- Greystone
- Greywacke
- Hornstone
- Impactite
- Intrusion
- Ironstone
- Laccolite
- Laccolith
- Limestone
- Meteorite
- Mica-slate
- Migmatite
- Monadnock
- Monocline
- Monzonite
- Mortstone
- Mugearite
- Natrolite
- Neocomian
- Ophiolite
- Ottrelite
- Pegmatite
- Phonolite
- Phosphate
- Pleonaste
- Propylite
- Protogine
- Quartzite

- Sandstone
- Saprolite
- Scablands
- Schistose
- Siltstone
- Soapstone
- Tachylyte
- Theralite
- Tinguaite
- Toadstone
- Travertin
- Underclay
- Variolite
- Ventifact
- Vulcanite
- Whinstone
- Whunstane
- Zechstein

10 letters:
- Ailsa Craig
- Amygdaloid
- Camptonite
- Epidiorite
- Foundation
- Granophyre
- Greenstone
- Grey-wether
- Hypabyssal
- Ignimbrite
- Kersantite
- Kimberlite
- Lherzolite
- Limburgite
- Mica-schist
- Novaculite
- Orthophyre
- Palagonite
- Peridotite
- Phenocryst
- Pitchstone
- Pyroxenite
- Rupestrian
- Schalstein
- Serpentine
- Sparagmite

- Stinkstone
- Stonebrash
- Syntagmata
- Teschenite
- Touchstone
- Travertine
- Troctolite

11 letters:
- Agglomerate
- Amphibolite
- Annabergite
- Anorthosite
- Carbonatite
- Geanticline
- Halleflinta
- Lamprophyre
- Monchiquite
- Napoleonite
- Nephelinite
- Phillipsite
- Pyroclastic
- Symplegades

12 letters:
- Babingtonite
- Baltic Shield
- Granodiorite
- Grossularite
- Slickenslide
- Stromatolite
- Syntagmatite
- Thunderstone

13 letters:
- Hypersthenite

14 letters:
- Roche moutonnée

18 letters:
- Scandinavian Shield

Rock-boring Pholas
Rock-cress Arabis
Rocket Arugula, Booster, Capsule, Carpet, Congreve, Dame's, Delta, Drake, Dressing down, Dyer's, Engine, Eruca, Flare, Ion, Jato, London, Multistage, Onion, Posigrade, Reprimand, Reproof, Retro, Rockoon, Salad, SAM, Sea,

Skylark, Soar, Sonde, Sounding, Step, Stephenson, Take-off, Thruster, Tourbillion, Ullage, Upshoot, V1, Vernier, Von Braun, Wall, Warhead, Weld, Yellow, Zero stage

Rock-living Rupicoline, Saxatile, Saxicoline, Saxicolous

Rock-pipit Sea-lark

Rocky *may indicate* an anagram

Rococo Baroque, Fancy, Ornate, Quaint

Rod(-shaped), Rodlike, Rods Aaron's, Baculiform, Bar, Barbel(l), Barre, Birch, Caduceus, Caim, Came, Can, Cane, Centre, Connecting, Control, Cue, Cuisenaire, Dipstick, Divining, Dowser, Drain, Ellwand, Fasces, Filler, Fin-ray, Firearm, Fisher, Fishing, Fly, Fuel, Gun, Handspike, Jacob's staff, Kame, King, Laver, Lightning, Linchpin, Lug, Moses, Napier's bones, Nervure, Newel, Notochord, Perch, Pin, Pistol, Piston, Pitman, Pointer, Pole, Pontie, Pontil, Ponty, Probang, Puntee, Punty, Raddle, Regulating, Rhabdoid, Rhabdus, Rood, Scollop, Shaft, Sounding, Spindle, Spit, Stadia, Stair, Stanchion, Staple, Stave, Stay-bolt, Stick, Strickle, Switch, Tension, Tie, Track, Triblet, Tringle, Trocar, Twig, Urochord, Ventifact, Verge, Virgate, Virgulate, Wand, Welding, Withe

Rod-bearer Lictor

Rode Raid

Rodent Acouchi, Acouchy, Ag(o)uti, Bandicoot, Bangsring, Banxring, Beaver, Biscacha, Bizcacha, Bobac, Bobak, Boomer, Capybara, Cavy, Chickaree, Chincha, Chinchilla, Chipmunk, Civet, Coypu, Cricetus, Dassie, Deer-mouse, Delundung, Dormouse, Fieldmouse, Gerbil(le), Glires, Glutton, Gnawer, Gopher, Groundhog, Guinea pig, Ham(p)ster, Hedgehog, Hog-rat, Hutia, Hyrax, Jerboa, Jird, Lemming, Marmot, Mole rat, Mouse, Murid, Mus, Musk-rat, Musquash, Ochotona, Ondatra, Paca, Porcupine, Potoroo, Rat, Ratel, Ratton, Renegade, Runagate, Sciurine, Sewellel, Shrew, S(o)uslik, Spermophile, Springhaas, Springhase, Squirrel, Taguan, Taira, Tuco-tuco, Tucu-tuco, Vermin, Viscacha, Vole, Woodchuck, Woodmouse

Roderick Random, Usher

Rodomontade Bluster, Boast, Bombast, Brag, Gas

Roe Avruga, Caviar(e), Coral, Fry, Melt, Milt(z), Pea, Raun, Rawn

Roger Ascham, Bacon, Jolly, OK, Rights

Rogue, Roguish(ness) Arch, Bounder, Charlatan, Chiseller, Drole, Dummerer, Elephant, Espiegle(rie), Ganef, Ganev, Ganof, Gonif, Gonof, Greek, Gypsy, Hedge-creeper, Hempy, Herries, Imp, Knave, Latin, Limmer, Monkey, Panurge, Picaresque, Picaroon, Pollard, Poniard, Rapparee, Ra(p)scal(l)ion, Riderhood, Savage, Scamp, Schellum, Schelm, Skellum, Sleeveen, Slip-string, Sly, Swindler, Varlet, Villain, Wrong'un

Roil Agitate, Annoy, Churn, Provoke, Vex

Roister(er) Blister, Carouse, Ephesian, Revel, Rollick, Scourer, Scowrer, Swashbuckler, Swinge-buckler

Role Bit, Cameo, Capacity, Function, Metier, > **PART**, Prima-donna, Stead, Title, Travesty

Roll(ed), Roller, Roll-call, Rolling, Rolls Absence, Bagel, Bap, Barrel, Beigel, Billow, Bolt, Bridge, Brioche, Butterie, Calender, Cambridge, Chamade, Comber, Convolv(ut)e, Cop, Couch, Court, Croissant, Cylinder, Dandy, Drum, Dutch, Electoral, Enswathe, Eskimo, Even, Fardel, Fardle, Flatten, Forward, Furl, Go, Hotdog, Inker, Involute, Labour, List, Loaded, Lurch, Makimono, Mangle, Mano, Matricula, Motmot, Moving, Music, Muster, Notitia, Opulent, Paradiddle, Patent, Paupiette, Pay, Petit-pain, Piano, Pigeon, Pipe, Platen, Rafale, Ragman, Record, Reef, Reel, Register, Ren, Rent, Revolute, Revolve,

Rhotacism, Ring, Road, Rob, Rolag, Roster, Rota, Rotate, Rotifer, Roulade, Rouleau, RR, Rub-a-dub, Rumble, Run, Sausage, Schnecke(n), Skin up, Snap, Somersault, Spool, Spring, Sway, Swell, Swiss, Table, Tandem, Taxi, Temple, Tent, Terrier, Toilet, Tommy, Trill, Trindle, Trundle, Victory, Volume, Volutation, Wad, Wallow, Wamble, Waul, Wave, Wawl, Web, Welter, Western, Wince, Wrap

Rollick(ing) Frolic, Gambol, Romp, Sport

▷ **Rollicking** *may indicate* an anagram

Roly-poly Chubby

Roman Agricola, Agrippa, Calpurnia, Candle, Catholic, Cato, Consul, CR, Crassus, Decemviri, Decurion, Empire, Flavian, Galba, Holiday, Italian, Jebusite, Latin, Maecenas, Papist, Patrician, PR, Quirites, Raetic, RC, Retarius, Rhaetia, Road, Scipio, Seneca, Sulla, Tarquin, Tiberius, Type, Uriconian, Volsci

Romance, **Romantic (talk)** Affair, Amorous, Byronic, Casanova, Catalan, Dreamy, Fancy, Fantasise, Fib, Fiction, Gest(e), Gothic, Historical, Invention, Ladin(o), Ladinity, Langue d'oc(ian), Langue d'oil, Langue d'oui, Lie, Neo-Latin, Novelette, Poetic, Quixotic, R(o)uman, Stardust, Tale

▶ **Romanian** *see* RO(U)MANIAN

Romanov Nicholas

▶ **Romany** *see* GYPSY

Romeo Casanova, Montagu, Swain

Romp(ing) Carouse, Escapade, Fisgig, Fizgig, Frisk, Frolic, Hoyden, Randy, Rig, Sport, Spree

Ron Glum, Moody

Rondo Rota

Rontgen R, X-ray

Roo Joey

Roof (edge), **Roofing** Belfast, Bell, Ceil, Cl(e)ithral, Cover, Curb, Divot, Dome, Drip, Eaves, French, Gable, Gambrel, Hardtop, Hip(ped), Home, Imperial, Jerkin-head, Leads, Mansard, Monopitch, Palate, Pavilion, Pent, Pitched, Pop-top, Porte-cochère, Rigging, Saddle, Saddleback, Shingle, Skillion, Skirt, Span, Sun(shine), Tectiform, Tectum, Tegula, Thatch, Thetch, Tiling, Top, Uraniscus

Roof-climber Stegopholist

Roofless Hypaethral, Upaithric

Rook Bird, Castle, Cheat, Crow, Fleece, Fool, Overcharge, R, Swindle

Rookie Beginner, Colt, Galoot, Greenhorn, Nignog, Novice, Recruit, Tyro

Room(s), **Roomy** Antechamber, Anteroom, Apadana, Apartment, Assembly, Attic, Ben, Berth, Bibby, Boardroom, Boiler, Boudoir, Bower, But, Cabin(et), Camarilla, Camera, Capacity, Casemate, CC, Ceiling, Cell, Cellar, Cenacle, Chamber, Changing, Chat, Chaumer, Closet, Cockloft, Commodious, Compartment, Conclave, Consulting, Control, Cubicle, Cuddy, Cutting, Dark, Day, Delivery, Digs, Dissecting, Divan, Dojo, Drawing, Dressing, Durbar, Elbow, End, Engine, Ex(h)edra, Extension, Foyer, Gap, Garret, Genizah, Green, Grill, Gun, Herbarium, Incident, Kiva, Kursaal, Lab, Latitude, Laura, Lavra, Lebensraum, Leeway, Library, Living, Locker, Lodge, Loft, Loo, Lounge, Margin, Megaron, Misericord(e), Mould-loft, Music, Oda, Operations, Orderly, Oriel, Pad, Palm Court, Panic, Parlour, Parvis, Penetralia, Pentice, Pentise, Powder, Priesthole, Private, Projection, Property, Public, Pump, Reception, Recitation, Recovery, Recreation, Rest, Rm, Robing, Rumpus, Sacristy, Salle, Salon, Sanctum, Scope, Scriptorium, Scullery, Serdab, Servery, Shebang, Single, Single-end, Sitkamer, Smoking, Snug, Solar, Solarium, > SPACE, Spacious,

Spare, Spence, Spheristerion, Staff, Standing, Steam, Still, Stock, Stowage, Street, Strong, Studio, Study, Suite, Sun, Tap, Tea, Tiring, Tool, Twin, Ullage, Utility, Vestiary, Vestry, Voorkamer, Waiting, Ward, Wash, Wiggle, Work, Zeta

Roost(er) Cock, Perch, Siskin, Sit

Root(ing), Roots Beet, Buttress, Calumba, Cassava, Cheer, Contrayerva, Costus, Cube, Culver's, Dasheen, Delve, Deracinate, Derris, Dig, Eddo, Elacampane, Eradicate, Eringo, Eryngo, Etymic, Extirpate, Fibrous, Foundation, Gelseminine, Ginseng, Grass, Grout, Grub, Heritage, Horseradish, Hurrah, Implant, Irradicate, Jalap, Jicama, Lateral, Licorice, Mallee, Mandrake, Mangold, Mishmee, Mishmi, Mooli, More, Myall, Nousle, Nuzzle, Origins, Orris, Pachak, Pneumatophore, Poke, Prop, Pry, Putchock, Putchuk, Race, Radical, Radish, Radix, Repent, Rhatany, Rhizic, Rhizoid, Rhizome, Scorzonera, Senega, Sessile, Setwall, Snuzzle, Source, Square, Stock, Tap, Taro, Tuber, Tuberous, Tulip, Turbith, Turnip, Turpeth, Vetiver, Yam, Zedoary

Rootless Psilotum

Rope(s) Abaca, Backstay, Ba(u)lk, Becket, Bind, Bobstay, Boltrope, Brail, Breeching, Bunt-line, Cable, Cablet, Colt, Cord, Cordage, Cordon, Cringle, Downhaul, Drag, Earing, Fake, Fall, Flemish coil, Fore-brace, Foresheet, Forestay, Funicular, Futtock-shroud, Gantline, Grist, Guest, Guide, Guy, Halliard, Halser, Halter, Halyard, Hawser, Hawser-laid, Headfast, Inhaul, Jack-stay, Jeff, Jump, Kernmantel, Knittle, Ladder, Lanyard, Lasher, Lashing, Lasso, Line, Longe, Lunge, Mainbrace, Mainsheet, Manil(l)a, Marlin(e), Messenger, Monkey, Mooring, Nettle, Nip, Noose, Oakum, Outhaul, Painter, Parbuckle, Pastern, Prolonge, Prusik, Rawhide, Reef point, Riata, Roband, Robbin, Rode, Runner, Sally, Seal, Selvagee, Sennit, Sheet, Shroud, Sinnet, Span, Spancel, Spun-yarn, Stay, Sternfast, Stirrup, String, Sugan, Swifter, Tackle, Tail, Tether, Tie, Timenoguy, Tippet, Tow(line), Trace, Trail, Triatic, Triatic stay, Vang, Wanty, Warp, Widdy, Wire

Rosalind Ganymede

Rosary Beads, Mala, Paternoster

Rose(-red), Rosie, Rosy Albertine, Amelanchier, Aurorean, Avens, Bear's-foot, Blooming, Bourbon, Breare, Briar, Brier, Cabbage, Canker, Ceiling, Cherokee, China, Christmas, Compass, Corn, Damask, Dog, Eglantine, Eglatère, England, Floribunda, Geum, Golden, G(u)elder, Hellebore, Hybrid, Jack, Jacque, Jacqueminot, Lal(age), Lancaster, Lee, Moss, Multiflora, Musk, Noisette, Opulus, Peace, Petra, Pink, Potentilla, Promising, Provence, Province, Provincial, Provine, Pyrus, Quillaia, Quillaja, Rambler, Red(dish), Remontant, Rhodo-, Rock, Rugosa, Snowball, Sprinkler, Standard, Sweetbrier, Tea, Tokyo, Tudor, White, Whitethorn, York

Rose-apple Jamboo, Jambu

Rose-bay Oleander

Rosette Buttonhole, Chou, Cockade, Favour, Patera, Rosula

Rosin Colophony, Resin, Roset, Rosit, Rozet, Rozit

Rosinante Jade

Roster List, Register, Scroll, Table

Rostrum Ambo, Bema, Lectern, Podium, Pulpit, Tribune

Rot(ten), Rotting Addle, Baloney, Boo, Bosh, Botrytis, Bull, Caries, Carious, Corrode, Corrupt, Crown, Daddock, Decadent, > **DECAY**, Decompose, Decrepitude, Degradable, Dotage, Dry, Eat, Erode, Fester, Foot, Foul, Kibosh, Manky, Mildew, Noble, Nonsense, Poppycock, Poxy, Punk, Putid, Putrefy, Putrid, Rail, Rancid, Rank, Rat, Ret, Ring, Rust, Sapropel, Septic, Soft, Sour, Squish, Twaddle, Wet

Rotate, Rotating, Rotation, Rotator Feather, Gyrate, Lay-farming, Optical, Pivot, Pronate, Rabat(te), Reamer, Revolve, Roll, Selsyn, Trundle, Turn, Turntable, Twiddle, Vorticose, Wheel, Windmill

Rote Heart, Memory, Recite, Routine

Rotor Auxiliary, Flywheel, Impeller

▸ **Rotten** *see* ROT

▹ **Rotten** *may indicate* an anagram

Rotter Cad, Knave, Stinker, Swine

Rotund Chubby, Corpulent, Plump, Round, Stout

Rotunda Pantheon

Roué Debauchee, Decadent, Libertine, Profligate, Rake(-shame), Rip

Rouge Blush, Gild, Jeweller's, Raddle, Redden, Reddle, Ruddy

Rough(en), Roughly, Roughness About, Approximate, Asper(ate), Burr, C, Ca, Choppy, Circa, Coarse, Craggy, Crude, Exasperate, Frampler, Grained, Gross, Gruff, Gurly, Gusty, Hard, Harsh, Hispid, Hoodlum, Hooligan, Impolite, Imprecise, Incondite, Inexact, Irregular, Jagged, Karst, Keelie, Kokobeh, Muricate, Push, Ragged, Ramgunshoch, Raspy, Raucle, Rip, Risp, Robust, Row, Rude, Rugged, Rusticate, Rusty, Sandblast, Scabrid, Sea, Shaggy, Sketchy, Some, Spray, Spreathe, Squarrose, Stab, Strong-arm, Swab, Tartar, Tearaway, Ted, Textured, Uncut, Violent, Yahoo

Roughage Ballast, Bran, Fodder

Rough breathing Asper, Rale, Wheeze

Roughcast Harl

▹ **Roughly** *may indicate* an anagram

Roulette Russian

Ro(u)manian, Rumanian Ro, R(o)uman, Vlach, Wal(l)achian

Round(ness) About, Ammo, Ball, Beat, Bombe, Bout, Cartridge, Catch, Circle, Complete, Cycle, Dome, Doorstep, Figure, Full, Global, Globate, Hand, Jump-off, Lap, Leg, Milk, O, Oblate, Orb, Orbicular, Orbit, Ought, Patrol, Peri-, Pirouette, Plump, Qualifying, Quarter, Quarter-final, Rev, Ring, Robin, Roly-poly, Ronde, Rondure, Rota, Rotund, Route, Routine, Rundle, Rung, Salvo, Sandwich, Sarnie, Sellinger's, Semi-final, Shot, Skirt, Slice, Sphaer, Sphere, Spherical, Spiral, Step, Table, Tour, Tubby, U-turn

▹ **Round** *may indicate* a word reversed

Roundabout Ambages, Approximately, Bypass, Carousel, Circle, Circuit, Circumambient, Circumbendibus, Circus, Devious, Eddy, > INDIRECT, Merry-go-round, Peripheral, Rotary, Tortuous, Turntable, Waltzer, Whirligig

Round building Tholos, Tholus

Rounders Patball

Round-mouth Hag

Round-up Bang-tail muster, Collate, Corner, Corral, Gather, Herd, Rodeo, Spiral

Roup Auction, Croak, Pip, Roop

Rouse, Rousing Abrade, Abraid, Abray, Amo(o)ve, Animate, Beat, Bestir, Emotive, Enkindle, Firk, Flush, Hearten, Heat, Innate, Kindle, Rear, Send, Stimulate, Suscitate, Unbed, Waken, Whip

Rousseau Emile

Rout Clamour, Debacle, Defeat, Drub, Fleme, Flight, Hubbub, Hurricane, Rabble, Retreat, Rhonchal, Snore, Thiasus, Upsee, Upsey, Upsy, Vanquish, Whoobub

Route Avenue, Byroad, Causeway, Course, Direction, Itinerary, Line, Ling, Path, Red, Road, Stock, Track, Trade, Via, Way

Routine Automatic, Day-to-day, Drill, Everyday, Grind, Groove, Habitual,

Ho-hum, Jogtrot, Pattern, Perfunctory, Pipe-clay, Red tape, Rota, Rote, Round, Rut, S(c)htick, Schtik, Treadmill, Workaday

Rove(r), **Roving** Car, Discursive, Enrange, Errant, Gad, Globetrotter, Marauder, Nomad, Proler, Prowl, Ralph, Range, > ROAM, Slub(b), Stray, Vagabond, Varangarian, Viking, Wander

Row(er) Align, Altercation, Arew, Argue, Argument, Bank, Barney, Bedlam, Bobbery, Bow, Brattle, Cannery, Colonnade, Death, Debate, Deen, Din, Dispute, Dust-up, Feud, File, Fireworks, Food, Fyle, Hullabaloo, Line(-up), Noise, Note, Oar, Paddle, Parade, Peripteral, Pull, Quarrel, Rammy, Range, Rank, Raunge, Remigate Tone, Rew, Rhubarb, Rotten, Ruction, Rumpus, Scene, Scull, Series, Set, Shindig, Shindy, Shine, Skid, Spat, Splore, Stern, Street, Stridor, Stroke, Stushie, Sweep, Terrace, Tier, Tiff, Torpid, Wetbob, Wherryman

Rowan Ash, Quicken

Rowdy, **Rowdiness** Cougan, Hooligan, Loud, Noisy, Rorty, Rough, Roughhouse, Ruffian, Scourer, Scozza, Skinhead, Stroppy, Unruly, Uproarious

Roy Rob

Royal(ty), **Royalist** Academy, Angevin, Basilical, Battle, Bourbon, Emigré, Exchange, Fee, Hanoverian, Imperial, Imposing, Inca, Kingly, King's man, Majestic, Malignant, Palatine, Payment, Pharaoh, Plantagenet, Prince, Princess, Purple, Queenly, Regal, Regis, Regius, Regnal, Sail, Sceptred, Society

Rub(bing), **Rubber(y)**, **Rub out** Abrade, Attrition, Balata, Buff, Buna®, Bungie, Bungy, Bunje(e), Bunjie, Bunjy, Butyl, Calk, Calque, Camelback, Caoutchouc, Chafe, Cold, Condom, Corrade, Corrode, Cow gum®, Crepe, Cul(t)ch, Destroy, Dunlop®, Ebonite, Efface, Elastic, Elastomer, Embrocate, Emery, Erase, Factice, Fawn, Foam, Fray, Fret, Friction, Fridge, Frottage, Fudge, Funtumia, Gall, Galoch, Goodyear®, Grate, Graze, Grind, Guayule, Gum elastic, Gutta-percha, Hale, Hard, Hevea, India, Inunction, Irritate, Isoprene, Jelutong, Lagos, Latex, Leather, Masseur, Negrohead, Neoprene, Nuzzle, Obstacle, Para, Polish, Pontianac, Pontianak, Root, Safe, Sandpaper, Scour, Scrub, Scuff, Seringa, Silastic®, Smoked, Sorbo®, Sponge, Stroke, Synthetic, Towel, Trace, Ule, Vulcanite, Wild, Wipe, Xerotripsis

Rubbed *may indicate* an anagram

Rubbish Balls, Brack, Bull, Bunkum, Clap-trap, Cobblers, Debris, Dre(c)k, Drivel, Fiddlesticks, Garbage, Grot, Grunge, Hogwash, Kak, Landfill, Leavings, Litter, Mullock, Nonsense, Phooey, Raff, Raffle, > REFUSE, Stuff, Tinpot, Tip, Tom(fool), Tosh, Trade, Tripe, Trouch, Twaddle

Rubbish heap Dump, Lay-stall, Sweepings, Toom

Rubble Brash, Debris, Detritus, Moellon, Random, Remains, Riprap, Talus

Rubidium Rb

Ruby Agate, Balas, Brazilian, Colorado, Cuprite, Oriental, Pigeon's blood, Port, Red, Star

Ruck Furrow, Scrum, Wrinkle

Rucksack Backpack, Bergen, Pikau

Ruction Ado, Fuss, Quarrel

Rudder Budget, Helm, Steerer

Ruddle Lemnian

Ruddy Bally, Bloody, Flashy, Florid, Red, Roseate, Rubicund, Sanguine

Rude Abusive, Barbaric, Bestial, Bumpkin, Callow, Churlish, Coarse, Discourteous, Elemental, Goustrous, Green, Ill-bred, Impolite, Indecorous, Inficete, Ingram, Ingrum, Insolent, Ocker, Offensive, Peasant, Raw, Risque, Rough, Simple, Surly, Unbred, Uncomplimentary, Uncourtly, Unlettered, Unmannered, Vulgar

Rudiment(ary), Rudiments ABC, Absey, Anlage, Beginning, Element, Embryo, Foundation, Germ(en), Germinal, Inchoate, Seminal, Vestige

Rudolph Hess, Reindeer

Rue(ful) Boulevard, Dittany, Harmala, Harmel, Herb of grace, Mourn, Regret, Repent, Ruta, Sorry

Ruff Collar, Crest, Fraise, Frill, Partlet, Pope, Rabato, Rebato, Ree, Trump

Ruffian Apache, Bashi-bazouk, Brute, Bully, Cut-throat, Desperado, Goon(da), Highbinder, Hoodlum, Hooligan, Keelie, Larrikin, Lout, Miscreant, Mohock, Myrmidon, Phansigar, Plug-ugly, Raff, Rowdy, Skinhead, Sweater, Tearaway, Thug, Toe-ragger, Trailbaston, Tumbler

Ruffle(d) Bait, Dishevel, Falbala, Flounce, Fluster, Fret, > FRILL, Gather, Irritate, Jabot, Peplum, Rouse, Ruche, Rumple, Shirty, Tousle

▷ **Ruffle** *may indicate* an anagram

Rug Afghan, Bearskin, Carpet, Drugget, Ensi, Flokati, Gabbeh, Hearth, Herez, Heriz, Kelim, K(h)ilim, Kirman, Lap robe, Mat, Maud, Numdah, Oriental, Prayer, Runner, Rya, Scatter, Travelling

Rugby (player) Back, Fifteen, Forward, Harlequin, Lion, Pack, Quin, RU, Scrum, Sevens, Threequarter, Wing

Rugged Craggy, Harsh, Knaggy, Rough, Strong

Ruin(ed), Ruins Annihilate, Blast, Blight, Blue, Carcase, Collapse, Corrupt, Crash, Crock, Damn, Decay, Defeat, Demolish, Despoil, Destroy, Devastate, Disfigure, Dish, Disrepair, Dogs, Doom, Downcome, Downfall, End, Fordo, Hamstring, Heap, Hell, Insolvent, Inure, Kaput(t), Kibosh, Loss, Mar, Mocers, Mother's, Overthrow, Petra, Pot, Puckerood, Ravage, Reck, Relic, Scotch, Scupper, Scuttle, Shatter, Sink, Smash, Spill, > SPOIL, Stramash, Subvert, Undo, Unmade, Ur, Violate, Whelm, Woe, Wrack

▷ **Ruined** *may indicate* an anagram

Rule(r), Rules, Ruling Abbasid, Alexander, Algorithm, Align, Ameer, Amir, Archduke, Ardri(gh), Aristocrat, Arret, Article, Atabeg, Atabek, Autocrat, Bajayet, Bajazet, Ban, Bey, Bismarck, Bodicea, Bosman, Boudicca, Bretwalda, Britannia, Burgrave, Bylaw, Caesar, Caligula, Caliph, Calliper, Canon, Caractacus, Castro, Catapan, Caudillo, Chagan, Chain, Cham, Chandragupta, Charlemagne, Cheops, Chogyal, Cleopatra, Club-law, Code, Condominium, Constitution, Control, Cosmocrat, Criterion, Cromwell, Czar, Decree, Dergue, Despot, Dewan, Dey, Dictator, Diwan, Doge, Domineer, Dominion, Duce, Dynast, Elector, Emir, Emperor, Empire, Establishment, Estoppel, Ethnarch, Etiquette, Exarch, Fatwa, Feint, Fetwa, Fleming's, Formation, Formula, Franco, Fuhrer, Gaekwar, Gag, Gaikwar, Genghis Khan, Gerent, Global, Golden, Govern, Govern-all, Ground, Haile Selassie, Heptarch, Herod, Hespodar, Hierarch, Hitler, Home, Hoyle, Hyleg, Imam, Inca, Jackboot, Jamshid, Jamshyd, Judges, K, Kabaka, Kaiser, Khan, Khedive, King, Law, Leibniz's, Lesbian, Lex, Lindley, Liner, Maharaja, Majority, Mameluke, Manchu, Matriarchy, Maxim, McNa(u)ghten, Mede, Meteyard, Method, Mikado, Ministrate, Mir, Miranda, Mistress, Mogul, Monarch, Montezuma, Motto, Mpret, Mudir, Naismith's, Napoleon, Nawab, Negus, Nero, Netiquette, Nizam, Norm(a), Oba, Ochlocrat, Oligarch, Omayyad, Oppress, Ordinal, Overlord, Padishah, Parallel, Parallelogram, Pasha, Pendragon, Pericles, Peshwa, Pharaoh, Phase, Phrase-structure, Pie, Plantocrat, Plumb, Plutocrat, Podesta, Pope, Potentate, Precedent, Precept, Prescript, President, Prester John, Prevail, Prince, Principate, Principle, Protocol, Pye, Queen, Queensberry, R, Rafferty's, Raine, Raj(ah), Rajpramukh, Rana, Realm, Rector, Regal, Regent, Regula, Reign, Rewrite, Rex, Ring, Rubric, Sachem, Sagamore, Saladin, Sassanid,

Satrap, Scammozzi's, Serkali, Setting, Shah, Shaka, Sheik, Sherif, Shogun, Sirdar, Slide, Sophi, Sophy, Souldan, Sovereign, Squier, Squire, Stadtholder, Stalin, Standard, Statute, Stratocrat, Suleiman, Sultan, Sutra, Suzerain, Swaraj, Sway, Synarchy, Tamerlane, Ten-minute, Tenno, Ten-yard, Tetrarch, Thearchy, Three, Thumb, Toparch, Transformation(al), Trapezoid, Tsar, T-square, Tutankhamun, Tycoon, Tyrant, Umayyad, Vali, Viceroy, Wali, Wield, Zamorin

Rule-book Code, Pie, Pye

Rum(mer) Abnormal, Bacardi, Bay, Cachaca, Daiquiri, Demerara, Eerie, Eery, Glass, Grog, Island, Jamaica, Odd(er), Peculiar, Quaint, Queer, Screech, Strange, Tafia, Weird

Rumanian *see* RO(U)MANIAN

Rumble, **Rumbling** Borborygmus, Brool, Curmurring, Drum-roll, Groan, Growl, Guess, Lumber, Mutter, Rumour, Thunder, Tonneau, Twig

Ruminant, **Ruminate** Antelope, Cabrie, Camel, Cavicornia, Champ, Chew, Contemplate, Cow, Gemsbok, Gnu, Goat, Meditate, Merycism, Nyala, Okapi, Pecora

Rummage Delve, Fish, Foray, Jumble, Powter, Ransack, Root, Rootle, Scavenge, Search, Tot

Rummy Canasta, Cooncan, Game, Gin, Queer

Rumour Breeze, Bruit, Buzz, Canard, Cry, Fame, Furphy, > GOSSIP, Grapevine, Hearsay, Kite, Kite-flying, Mail, Noise, On-dit, Pig's-whisper, Report, Repute, Say-so, Smear, Tale, Talk, Underbreath, Unfounded, Vine, Voice, Whisper, Word

Rump Arse, Bottom, Buttocks, Croup(e), Croupon, Crupper, Curpel, Derriere, Parliament, Podex, Pygal, Steak, Uropygium

Rumple Corrugate, Crease, Mess, Tousle, Wrinkle

Rumpus Commotion, Riot, Row, Ruction, Shindig, Shindy, Shine, Stushie, Tirrivee, Uproar

Run(ning), **Run away**, **Run into**, **Run off**, **Runny**, **Runs** Admin(ister), Arpeggio, Bleed, Bolt, Break, Bunk, Bye, Career, Chase, Coop, Corso, Course, Cresta, Cross-country, Current, Cursive, Cut, Dash, Decamp, Direct, Double, Drive, Dry, Dummy, Escape, Extra, Fartlek, Flee, Flit, Flow, Fly, Follow, Fun, Fuse, Gad, Gallop, Gauntlet, Go, Green, Ground, Hare, Haste(n), Hennery, Hie, Home, Idle, Jog, Jump bail, Ladder, Lauf, Leg, Leg bye, Lienteric, Lope, Manage, Marathon, Melt, Milk, Mizzle, Mole, Molt, Neume, Now, On, On-line, Operate, Pace, Paper chase, Pelt, Ply, Pour, Print, Purulent, R, Race, Range, Red, Renne, Rin, Romp, Roulade, Rounder, Ruck, Scamper, Scapa, Scarper, Schuss, Scud, Scutter, Scuttle, See, Sequence, Shoot, Single, Skate, Skedaddle, Ski, Skid, Skirr, Skitter, Slalom, Slide, Smuggle, Spew, Split, Spread, Sprint, Sprue, Squitters, Stampede, Straight, Streak, Stream, Taxi, Tear, Tenor, Tie-breaker, Trial, Trickle, Trill, Trot

Runaway Drain, Easy, Escapee, Fugitive, Fugue, Refugee

Run down Asperse, Belie, Belittle, Calumniate, Denigrate, Derelict, Dilapidated, Infame, Knock, Low, Obsolesce(nt), Poorly, Rack, Résumé, Scud, Tirade, Traduce

Rune, **Runic** Ash, Futhark, Futhorc, Futhork, Kri, Ogham, Spell, Thorn, Wen, Wyn(n)

Rung Crossbar, Roundel, Rundle, Stave, Step, Tolled, Tread

Runner(s) Atalanta, Bean, Blade, Bow Street, Carpet, Coe, Courser, Deserter, Emu, Field, Geat, Gentleman, Gillie-wetfoot, Harrier, Hatta, Hencourt, Internuncio, Lampadist, Leg bye, Legman, Messenger, Miler, Milk, Mohr,

Mousetrap, Nurmi, Owler, Rug, > **RUN(NING)**, Sarmentum, Scarlet, Series, Slipe, Smuggler, Stolon, Stream, Trial

▷ **Running**, **Runny** *may indicate* an anagram

Runt Dilling, Oobit, Oubit, Reckling, Scalawag, Scrog, Smallest, Titman, Woobut, Woubit

Run through Impale, Pierce, Rehearsal

Runway Airstrip, Drive, Slipway, Strip, Tarmac®

Run wild Lamp, Rampage

Rupee(s) Lac, Lakh, Re

Rupert Bear

Rupture Breach, Burst, Crack, Hernia, Rend, Rhexis, Rift, Split

Rural Agrarian, Agrestic, Boo(h)ai, Boondocks, Bucolic, Country, Cracker-barrel Forane, Georgic, Hick, Mofussil, Platteland, Praedial, Predial, Redneck, Rustic Sticks, The Shires, Wops-wops

Ruse Artifice, Decoy, Dodge, Engine, Hoax, Pawk, Stratagem, > **TRICK**

Rush(ed) Accelerate, Barge, Bolt, Bustle, Career, Charge, Dart, Dash, Eriocaulon, Expedite, Faze, Feese, Feeze, Feze, Fly, Frail, Friar, Gad, Gold, Gust, Hare, Hasten, High-tail, > **HURRY**, Hurtle, Jet, Juncus, Lance, Lash, Leap, Luzula, Moses, Onset, Palmiet, Pellmell, Phase, Pheese, Pheeze, Phese, Plunge Precipitate, Railroad, Rampa(u)ge, Rash, Rayle, Reed, Rip, Scamp(er), Scirpus, Scour, Scud, Scurry, Sedge, Spate, Speed, Stampede, Star(r), Streak, Streek, Surge, Swoop, Swoosh, Tear, Thrash, Thresh, Tilt, Torrent, Tule, Viretot, Zap, Zoom

Rusk Zwieback

Russell AE, Bertrand, Jack

Russet Rutile

Russia(n), **Russian headman**, **Russian villagers** Apparatchik, Ataman, Belorussian, Beria, Bolshevik, Boris, Boyar, Byelorussian, Chukchee, Chukchi Circassian, Cossack, D(o)ukhobor, Dressing, Esth, Igor, Ingush, Ivan, Kabardian, Kalmuk, Kalmyck, Leather, Lett, Mari, Menshevik, Mingrel(ian), Minimalist, Mir, Muscovy, Octobrist, Osset(e), Red, Romanov, Rus, Russ(niak) Russki, Ruthene, Salad, Serge, Slav, Stakhanovite, SU, Thistle, Udmurt, Uzbeg Uzbek, Vladimir, Vogul, White, Yakut, Yuri, Zyrian

Rust(y) Aeci(di)um, Blister, Brown, Corrode, Cor(ro)sive, Erode, Etch, Ferrugo, Iron oxide, Iron-stick, Maderise, Oxidise, Puccinia, Rubiginous, Soare, Stem, Teleutospore, Telium, Uredine, Uredo, Verdigris, Yellow

Rust-fungus Aecidiospore

Rustic Arcady, Bacon, Bor(r)el(l), Bucolic, Bumpkin, Chawbacon, Churl, Clodhopper, Clown, Corydon, Cracker-barrel, Culchie, Damon, Doric, Forest, Georgic, Hayseed, Hick, Hillbilly, Hind, Hob, Hobbinoll, Hodge, Homespun, Idyl(l), Pastorale, Peasant, Pr(a)edial, Put(t), Rube, Rural, Strephon, Swain, Sylvan, Villager, Villatic, Yokel

▷ **Rustic** *may indicate* an anagram

Rusticate Banish, Seclude

Rustle(r), **Rustling** Abactor, Crinkle, Duff, Fissle, Frou-frou, Gully-raker, Poach Speagh(ery), Sprechery, Steal, Stir, Susurration, Swish, Thief, Whig

Rust-proof Zinced

Rut Channel, Furrow, Groove, Heat, Routine, Sulcus, Track

Ruth Babe, Compassion, Mercy, Pity, Remorse

Ruthenium Ru

Rutherfordium Rf

Ruthless Brutal, Cruel, Dog eat dog, Fell, Hard, Hardball, Hard-bitten

Rwanda(n) Tutsi
Rye Gentleman, Grain, Grass, Spelt, Whisky

Ss

S Ogee, Saint, Second, Sierra, Society, South, Square
SA It, Lure
Sabbatarian Wee Free
Sabbath Juma, Lord's Day, Rest-day, Shabbat, Sunday, Witches
Sabbatical Leave
Sabine Horace, Women
Sable American, Black, Jet, Negro, Pean, Zibel(l)ine
Sabotage, **Saboteur** Destroy, Frame-breaker, Ratten, Spoil, Treachery,
　Undermine, Vandalise, Wrecker
Sabre, **Sabre rattler** Jingo, Sword, Tulwar
Sabrina Severn
Sac Air, Allantois, Amnion, Aneurism, Aneurysm, Bag, Bladder, Bursa, Caecum,
　Cisterna, Cyst, Embryo, Follicla, Pericardium, Peritoneum, Pod, Scrotum,
　Spermatheca, Tylose, Tylosis, Vesica, Vocal, Yolk
Saccharine Dulcite, Dulcose
Sack(cloth), **Sacking** Bag, Bed, Boot, Bounce, Budget, Burlap, Can, Cashier,
　Chasse, Chop, Congé, Congee, Dash, Depredate, Despoil, Discharge, Doss, Fire,
　Gunny, Havoc, Hop-pocket, Jute, Knap, Lay waste, Loot, Mailbag, Maraud,
　Mitten, Pillage, Plunder, Poke, Push, Rapine, Reave, Replace, Road, Rob,
　Sanbenito, Sherris, Sherry, Spoliate, Vandalise
▷ **Sacks** *may indicate* an anagram
Sacrament Baptism, Communion, Confirmation, Eucharist, Extreme unction,
　Housel, Lord's supper, Matrimony, Nagmaal, Orders, Penance, Promise,
　Reconciliation, Ritual, Unction, Viaticum
Sacred, **Sacred place** Adytum, Churinga, Hallowed, Heart, Hierurgy, Holy,
　Ineffable, Nine, Omphalos, Padma, Pietà, Sacrosanct, Sanctum, Taboo, Tapu,
　Temenos
Sacrifice Alcestic, Cenote, Forego, Gambit, Hecatomb, Holocaust, Immolate,
　Iphigenia, Isaac, Lay down, Molech, Moloch, Oblation, > OFFERING, Peace
　offering, Relinquish, Sati, Suovetaurilia, Supreme, Surrender, Suttee,
　Taurobolium, Tophet, Vicarious, Victim
Sacrilege, **Sacrilegious** Blaspheme, Impiety, Profane, Violation
Sacristan, **Sacristy** Diaconicon, Sceuophylax, Sexton
Sacrosanct Inviolable
Sad(den), **Sadly**, **Sadness** Alas, Attrist, Blue, Con dolore, Dejected, Desolate,
　Disconsolate, Dismal, Doleful, Dolour, Downcast, Drear, Dull, Dumpy,
　Heartache, Lovelorn, Low, Lugubrious, Mesto, Oh, Plangent, Sorrowful, Sorry,
　Tabanca, Tearful, Tear-jerker, Threnody, Tragic, Triste, Tristesse, Unhappy,
　Wan, Wo(e)begone
Saddle (bag, cloth, girth, pad) Alforja, Aparejo, Arson, Burden, Cantle, Cinch,
　Col, Crupper, Demipique, Lumber, Numnah, Oppress, Pack, Pad, Panel,
　Pigskin, Pilch, Pillion, Seat, Sell(e), Shabrack, Shabracque, Side, Stock, Tree,
　Western

Saddle-bow Arson
Saddler Whittaw(er)
Sadie Thompson
Sadism, **Sadistic** Algolagnia, Cruel
Sadly *may indicate* an anagram
Safari Expedition, Hunt
Safe(ty) Active, Allright, Almery, Ambry, Coolgardie, Copper-bottomed, Delouse, Deposit, GRAS, Harmless, Immunity, Impunity, Inviolate, Keister, Night, Passive, Peter, Reliable, Roadworthy, Sanctuary, Secure, Sound, Strong-box, Strongroom, Sure, Whole-skinned, Worthy
Safeguard Bulwark, Caution, Ensure, Fail-safe, Frithborh, Fuse, Hedge, Palladium, Protection, Register, Ward
Saffron Crocus, Yellow
Sag(gy) Decline, Dip, Droop, Hang, Hogged, Lop, Slump, Swayback, Wilt
Saga Aga, Chronicle, Edda, Epic, Icelandic, Laxdale, Legend, Odyssey, Volsunga
Sagacity Commonsense, Depth, Elephant, Judgement, Sapience, Wisdom
Sage(s) Abaris, Aquinian, Bactrian, Bias, Carlyle, Cheronian, Chilo(n), Clary, Cleobulus, Confucius, Counsellor, Greybeard, Hakam, Herb, Imhotep, Jerusalem, Maharishi, Mahatma, Malmesbury, Manu, Mirza, Orval, Pandit, Periander, Philosopher, Pittacus, Rishi, Salvia, Savant, Seer, Seven, Solon, Tagore, Thales, Wiseacre, Wood
Sage-brush Nevada
Sahib Pukka
Said Co, Emir, Port, Quo(th), Related, Reputed, Spoken, Stated
▸ **Said** *may indicate* 'sounding like'
Sail(s), **Sailing** Bunt, Canvas, Circumnavigate, Cloth, Coast, Course, Cross-jack, Cruise, Drag, Drift, Fan, Fore(course), Fore-and-aft, Full, Gaff(-topsail), Genoa, Goose-wing, Head, Jib, Jigger, Jut, Lateen, Leech, Luff, Lug, Moon, Moonraker, Muslin, Navigate, Parachute spinnaker, Peak, Plain, Plane, Ply, Rag, Reef, Rig, Ring-tail, Royal, Sheet, Spanker, Spencer, Spinnaker, Spritsail, Square, Staysail, Steer, Studding, Stun, Suit, Top(-gallant), Top-hamper, Van, Vela, Wardrobe, Water, Yard
Sailor(s) AB, Admiral, Anson, Argonaut, Blue-jacket, Boatman, Boatswain, Bosun, Budd, Commodore, Crew, Deckhand, Drake, Evans, Freshwater, Galiongee, Gob, Greenhand, Grommet, Hat, Hearties, Helmsman, Hornblower, Hydronaut, Jack, Janty, Jauntie, Jaunty, Jonty, Khalasi, Killick, Killock, Kroo(boy), Krooman, Kru(boy), Kruman, Lascar, Leadsman, Limey, Loblolly boy, Lt, Lubber, Mariner, Matelot, Matlo(w), Middy, MN, Nelson, Noah, NUS, Oceaner, OS, Polliwog, Pollywog, Popeye, Powder monkey, Privateer, Rating, RN, Salt, Seabee, Seacunny, Sea-dog, Sea-lord, > **SEAMAN**, Serang, Shellback, Sin(d)bad, Stowaway, Submariner, Tar, Tarp(aulin), Tarry-breeks, Tindal, Triton, Waister, Wandering, Water-dog, Yachtsman
Saint(ly), **Saints** Agatha, Agnes, Aidan, Alban, Alexis, Alvis, Ambrose, Andrew, Anselm, Anthony, Asaph, Audrey, Augustine, Barbara, Barnabas, Bartholomew, Basil, Bees, Benedict, Bernard, Boniface, Brandan, Brendan, Bridget, Brigid, Canonise, Canonize, Catharine, Cecilia, Chad, Christopher, Clement, Columba(n), Crispian, Crispin(ian), Cuthbert, Cyr, David, Denis, Denys, Diego, Dominic, Dorothea, Dunstan, Dymphna, Elmo, Eloi, Elvis, Eulalie, Francis, Genevieve, George, Gertrude, Giles, Hagiology, Hallowed, Helena, Hilary, Hilda, Hugh, Ignatius, James, Jerome, John, Joseph, Jude, Just, Kentigern, Kevin, Kilda, Latterday, Lawrence, Leger, Leonard, Linus, Loyola, Lucy, Luke, Malo, Margaret, Mark, Martha, Martin, Matthew, Michael,

Monica, Mungo, Nicholas, Ninian, Odyl, Olaf, Oswald, Pancras, Patrick, Patron, Paul(inus), Peter, Pi, Pillar, Plaster, Polycarp, Quentin, Regulus, Ride, Rishi, Roch, Ronan, Roque, Rosalie, Rule, S, Sebastian, Severus, Simeon, Simon, SS, St, Stanislaus, Stephen, Sunday, Swithin, Templar, Teresa, Thecia, Theresa, Thomas, Tobias, Ursula, Valentine, Veronica, Vincent, Vitus, Walstan, Wilfred, William, Winifred

St Anthony's Fire Ergotism, Erysipelas

St Elmo's Fire Corona discharge, Corposant

St James Scallop-shell

St Jerome Hieronymic

St John's bread Carob

St Lucia WL

St Paul's Wren-ch

St Vincent WV

Sake Account, Behalf, Cause, Drink

Sal Volatile

Salacious, **Salacity** Lewd, Lust, Obscene, Scabrous

Salad Burnet, Caesar, Calaloo, Calalu, Chef's, Chicon, Corn, Cos, Cress, Cucumber, Days, Endive, Escarole, Fennel, Finnochio, Finoc(c)hio, Frisée, Fruit, Greek, Guacamole, Lactuca, Lamb's lettuce, Lettuce, Lovage, Mesclum, Mesclun, Mixture, Niçoise, Purslane, Radicchio, Radish, Rampion, Rocket, Rojak, Roquette, Russian, Salmagundi, Salmagundy, Slaw, Tabbouleh, Tabbouli, Tomato, Waldorf, Word

▷ **Salad** *may indicate* an anagram

Salamander Axolotl, Congo eel, Ewt, Hellbender, Lizard, Menopome, Mole, Mudpuppy, Olm, Proteus, Siren, Snake, Spring-keeper

Salami, **Salami technique** Fraud, Peperoni

Salary Emolument, Fee, Hire, Pay, Prebend, Screw, Stipend, > WAGE

Sale(s) Auction, Cant, Car-boot, Clearance, Farm-gate, Fire, Garage, Jumble, Market, Outroop, Outrope, Raffle, Retail, Roup, Rummage, Subhastation, Trade, Turnover, Venal, Vend, Vendue, Vent, Voetstoets, Voetstoots, Warrant, Wash, White, Wholesale

Saleroom Pantechnicon

Salesman Agent, Assistant, Bagman, Broker, Buccaneer, Bummaree, Counterhand, Drummer, Huckster, Loman, Pedlar, Rep, Retailer, Tallyman, Tout, Traveller

Salient Coign, Jut, Projection, Prominent, Redan, Spur

Saliva Drool, Parotid, Ptyalism, Sial(oid), Slobber, Spawl, Spit(tle), Sputum

Sallow Adust, Pallid, Pasty, Sale, Sauch, Wan

Sally Aunt, Boutade, Charge, Dash, Escape, Excursion, Flight, Foray, Issue, Jest, Mot, Pleasantry, Quip, Sarah, Sortie, Witticism

Salmagundi Mess

Salmon Alevin, Atlantic, Australian, Baggit, Blueback, Blue-cap, Boaz, Burnett, Chinook, Chum, Cock, Coho(e), Dog, Dorado, Grav(ad)lax, Grilse, Humpback, Kelt, Keta, King, Kipper, Kokanee, Lax, Ligger, Lox, Masu, Mort, Nerka, Oncorhynchus, Ouananiche, Par(r), Peal, Pink, Quinnat, Red, Redfish, Rock, Samlet, Shedder, Skegger, Slat, Smelt, Smolt, Smout, Smowt, Sockeye, Sparling, Spirling, Sprod

Salon, **Saloon** Barrel-house, Car, Hall, Honkytonk, Last chance, Lounge, Pullman, Sedan, Shebang, Tavern

Salt(s), **Salty** AB, Acid, Alginate, Aluminate, Andalusite, Aspartite, Attic, Aurate, Azide, Base, Bath, Bicarbonate, Bichromate, Borate, Borax, Brackish,

Brine, Bromate, Bromide, Capr(o)ate, Caprylate, Carbamate, Carbonate, Carboxylate, Cerusite, Chlorate, Chlorite, Chromate, Citrate, Complex, Corn, Cure(d), Cyanate, Cyclamate, Datolite, Deer lick, Diazonium, Dichromate, Dioptase, Dithionate, Double, Enos, Epsom, Ferricyanide, Formate, Glauber, Glutamate, Halite, Halo-, Health, Hydrochloride, Hygroscopic, Iodide, Ioduret, Isocyanide, Lactate, Lake-basin, Lithate, Liver, Magnesium, Malate, Malonate, Manganate, Matelot, Microcosmic, Monohydrate, Mucate, Muriate, NaCl, Nitrate, Nitrite, Oleate, Osm(i)ate, Oxalate, Palmitate, Pandermite, Perchlorate, Periodate, Phosphate, Phosphite, Phthalate, Picrate, Piquancy, Plumbate, Plumbite, Potassium, Powder, Propionate, Pyruvate, Rating, Resinate, Rochelle, Rock, Rosinate, Sailor, Sal ammoniac, Salify, Sal volatile, Saut, Sea-dog, Seafarer, Seasoned, Sebate, Selenate, Smelling, Soap, Sodium, Solar, Stannate, Stearate, Suberate, Succinate, Sulfite, Sulphate, Sulphite, Sulphonate, Table, Tannate, Tantalate, Tartrate, Tellurate, Thiocyanate, Thiosulphate, Titanate, Tungstate, Uranin, Urao, Urate, Vanadate, Volatile, Water-dog, White, Wit(ty), Xanthate

Salt meat Mart

Saltpetre Caliche, Chile, Cubic, Nitre, Norway

Salt-water Sea

Salubrious Healthy, Sanitary, Wholesome

Salutary Beneficial, Good, Wholesome

Salutation, **Salute** Address, Ave, Banzai, Barcoo, Bid, Cap, Cheer, Command, Coupé(e), Curtsey, Embrace, Feu de joie, Fly-past, Genuflect, Greet, Hail, Hallo, Halse, Homage, Honour, Jambo, Kiss, Present, Salaam, Salvo, Sieg Heil, Toast, Tribute, Wassail

Salvador Dali

Salvage Dredge, Lagan, Ligan, Reclaim, Recover, Recycle, Rescue, Retrieve, Tot

Salvation(ist) Booth, Redemption, Rescue, Soterial, Yeo

Salve Anele, Anoint, Assuage, Ave, Lanolin(e), Lotion, Ointment, Remedy, Saw, Tolu, Unguent, Weapon

Salver Tray, Waiter

Salvo Fusillade, Salute, Volley

Sal volatile Hartshorn

Sam Browse, Soapy, Uncle, Weller

Samara Ash-key

Samaritan Good

Samarium Sm

Same(ness) Ae, Agnatic, Contemporaneous, Do, Egal, Ejusd(en), Equal, Ib(id), Ibidem, Id, Idem, Identical, Identity, Ilk, Iq, Like, One, Thick(y), Thilk, Uniform, Ylke

Samovar Urn

Samoyed Dog, Uralian, Uralic

Sample, **Sampling** Biopsy, Blad, Browse, Example, Fare, Foretaste, Handout, Matched, Muster, Pattern, Pree, Prospect, Quadrat, Quota, Scantling, Specimen, Spread, Stratified, Swatch, Switch, > **TASTE**, Transect, Try

Samuel Pepys, Smiles

Samurai Ronin

Sam Weller *may indicate* the use of 'v' for 'w' or vice versa

Sanctify Consecrate, Purify, Saint

Sanctimonious Banbury, Creeping Jesus, Devout, Goody-goody, Pi, Religiose, Righteous, Saintly

Sanction Allow, Appro, Approbate, Approof, Approve, Authorise, Bar,

Countenance, Endorse, Imprimatur, Mandate, OK, Pass, Pragmatic, Ratify, Sustain

Sanctities, **Sanctity** Halidom, Holiness, Hollidam, Sonties

Sanctuary, **Sanctum** Adytum, Asylum, By-room, Cella, Ch, Church, Frithsoken, Frithstool, Girth, Grith, Holy, Kaaba, Lair, Naos, Oracle, Penetralia, Preserve, Refuge, Sacellum, Sacrarium, > **SHELTER**, Shrine, Tabernacle, Temple

Sand(bank), **Sandbar**, **Sands**, **Sandy** Alec, Alex, Areg, Arena(ceous), Arenose, Arkose, As, Atoll, Bar, Barchan(e), Bark(h)an, Beach, Caliche, Dene, Desert, Dogger Bank, Down, Dudevant, Dune, Dupin, Eremic, Erg, Esker, Foundry, Gat, George, Ginger, Goodwin, Grain, Granulose, Hazard, Light, Loess, Machair, Nore, Oil, Overslaugh, Podsol, Podzol, Portlandian, Psammite, Ridge, Sabulous, Sawney, Seif, Shelf, Shoal, Shore, Singing, Tar, Tee, Time, Tombolo

Sandal(s) Alpargata, Buskin, Calceamentum, Chappal, Espadrille, Flip-flop, Ganymede, Geta, Huarache, Jelly, Patten, Pump, Talaria, Thong, Zori

Sandalwood Algum, Almug, Chypre, Pride, Santal

Sandarac Arar

Sander Pike-perch

Sandhurst RMA

Sand-loving Ammophilous, Psammophil

Sandpiper Bird, Dunlin, Knot, Oxbird, Ree, Ruff, Sandpeep, Stint, Terek

Sandstone Arkose, Dogger, Fa(i)kes, Flysch, Grit, Hassock, Itacolumite, Kingle, Molasse, New Red, Old Red, Quartzite, Red

Sandstorm Haboob, Tebbad

Sandwich Bruschetta, Butty, Club, Croque-monsieur, Cuban, Doorstep, Earl, Hamburger, Island, Jeely piece, Open, Piece, Roti, Round, Sarney, Sarnie, Smorbrod, Smorgasbord, Smorrebrod, Stottie, Sub, Submarine, Thumber, Toastie, Triple-decker, Twitcher, Victoria, Wad

▷ **Sandwich(es)** *may indicate* a hidden word

Sane, **Sanity** Compos mentis, Formal, Healthy, Judgement, Rational, Reason, Sensible, Wice

Sangfroid Aplomb, Cool, Poise

Sanguine Confident, Hopeful, Optimistic, Roseate, Ruddy

Sanitary Hygienic, Salubrious, Sterile

Sanskrit Purana, Ramayana, Sutra, Upanishad, Vedic

Santa Claus Abonde, Kriss Kringle

Sap Benzoin, Bleed, Cremor, Drain, Enervate, Entrench, Ichor, Juice, Laser, Latex, Lymph, Mine, Mug, Pulque, Ratten, Resin, Roset, Rosin, Rozet, Rozit, Secretion, Soma, Sura, Swot, Undermine, Weaken

Sapid Flavoursome, Savoury, Tasty

Sapience, **Sapient** Discernment, Sage, Wisdom

Sapling Ash-plant, Ground-ash, Plant, Tellar, Teller, Tiller, Youth

Sapper(s) Miner, RE

Sapphire Star, White

Sappho Lesbian

Sapwood Alburnum

Sarah Battle, Camp, Sal

Sarcasm, **Sarcastic** Antiphrasis, Biting, Cutting, Cynical, Derision, Irony, Mordacious, Mordant, Pungent, Quip, Quotha, Sarky, Satire, Sharp, Smartmouth, Snide, Sting, Wisecrack

Sardine Fish, Sard

Sardonic Cutting, Cynical, Ironical, Scornful, Wry

Sargasso Ore, Sea(weed)

Sark Chemist, CI, Shirt
Sarong Sulu
SAS Red Devils
Sash Baldric(k), Band, Belt, Burdash, Cummerbund, Obi, Scarf, Window
Sassaby Tsessebe
Sassenach English, Lowlander, Pock-pudding
Satan Adversary, Apollyon, Arch-enemy, Cram, > DEVIL, Eblis, Evil One, Lucifer, Shaitan, Tempter
Satchel Bag, Scrip
Sate(d), **Satiate** Cloy, Glut, Replete, Sad, Surfeit
Satellite Adrastea, Ananke, Ariel, Artificial, Astra, Atlas, Attendant, Aussat, Belinda, Bianca, Bird, Callisto, Calypso, Camenae, Carme, Charon, Communications, Comsat®, Cordelia, Cosmic, Cressida, Deimos, Desdemona, Despina, Dione, Disciple, Early bird, Earth, Echo, Elara, Enceladus, Europa, Explorer, Fixed, Follower, Galatea, Galilean, Ganymede, Geostationary, Helene, Henchman, Himalia, Hipparchus, Hyperion, Iapetus, Intelsat, Io, Janus, Lackey, Larissa, Leda, Lysithea, Meteorological, Metis, Mimas, Miranda, Moon, Mouse, Nereid, Oberon, Ophelia, Orbiter, Pan, Pandora, Pasiphae, Phobos, Phoebe, Portia, Prometheus, Puck, Rhea, Rosalind, Sinope, Sputnik, Syncom, Telesto, Telstar, Tethys, Thalassa, Thebe, Tiros, Titan, Titania, Triton, Umbriel, Weather
Satin *see* SILK
Satire, **Satirical**, **Satirist** Arbuthnot, Archilochus, Burlesque, Butler, Candide, Chaldee, Dryden, Horace, Iambographer, Juvenal, Lampoon, Lash, Lucian, Menippean, Mockery, Pantagruel, Parody, Pasquil, Pasquin(ade), Pope, Raillery, Sarky, Sotadic, Spoof, Squib, Swift, Travesty
Satisfaction, **Satisfactory**, **Satisfy(ing)**, **Satisfactorily** Agree, Ah, Ap(p)ay, Appease, Assuage, Atone, Change, Compensation, Complacent, > CONTENT, Defrayment, Enough, Feed, Fill, Fulfil, Glut, Gratify, Indulge, Jake, Job, Liking, Meet, OK, Pacation, Palatable, Pay, Please, Propitiate, Qualify, Redress, Repay, Replete, Sate, Satiate, Serve, Settlement, Slake, Square, Suffice, Tickety-boo, Well
Saturate(d) Drench, Glut, Imbue, Impregnate, Infuse, Permeate, > SOAK, Sodden, Steep, Waterlog
Saturday Holy
Saturn God, Kronos, Lead, Planet, Rocket
Satyr Faun, Leshy, Lesiy, Libertine, Marsyas, Pan, Silen(us), Woodhouse, Woodwose
Sauce, **Saucy** Alfredo, Allemanse, Apple, Arch, Baggage, Barbecue, Béarnaise, Béchamel, Bigarade, Bold(-faced), Bolognese, Bordelaise, Bourguignonne, Bread, Brown, Caper, Carbonara, Catchup, Catsup, Chasseur, Chaudfroid, Cheek, Chilli, Condiment, Coulis, Cranberry, Cream, Cumberland, Custard, Dapper, Dip, Dressing, Enchilada, Espagnole, Fenberry, Fondue, Fu yong, Fu yung, Gall, Garum, Gravy, Hard, Hoisin, Hollandaise, Horseradish, HP®, Impudence, Jus, Ketchup, Lip, Malapert, Marinade, Marinara, Matelote, Mayonnaise, Melba, Meunière, Mint, Mirepoix, Mole, Mornay, Mousseline, Nam pia, Nerve, Newburg, Nuoc mam, Oxymal, Oyster, Panada, Parsley, Passata, Peart, Pert, Pesto, Piri-piri, Pistou, Ravigote, Relish, Remoulade, Rouille, Roux, Sabayon, Sal, Salpicon, Salsa, Salsa verde, Sambal, Sass, Satay, Shoyu, Soja, Soubise, Soy, Soya, Stroganoff, Sue, Supreme, Sweet and sour, Tabasco®, Tamari, Tartar(e), Tomato, Topping, Tossy, Velouté, Vinaigrette, White, Wine, Worcester, Worcestershire

Sauceboat-shaped Scaphocephalate

Saucepan Chafer, Goblet, Skillet, Stockpot

Saucer Ashtray, Discobolus, UFO

Sauna Bath, Sudatorium, Sudorific

Saunter Amble, Dander, Lag, Mosey, Promenade, Roam, Shool, Stroll, Toddle

Sausage(s) Andouillette, Banger, Black pudding, Blood, Boerewors, Bologna, Boudin, Bratwurst, Cervelat, Cheerio, Chipolata, Chorizo, Cumberland, Devon, Drisheen, Frankfurter, Hot dog, Kishke, Knackwurst, Knockwurst, Liver(wurst), Mortadella, Mystery bag, Pep(p)eroni, Polony, Salami, Sav(eloy), Snag(s), String, White pudding, Wiener(wurst), Wienie, Wurst, Zampone

Sausage-shaped Allantoid

Savage Ape, Barbarian, Boor, Brute, Cannibal, Cruel, Feral, Fierce, Grim, Gubbins, Immane, Inhuman, Maul, Noble, Sadistic, Truculent, Vitriolic, Wild

Savanna Plain, Sahel

Savant Expert, Mahatma, Sage, Scholar

Save, Saving(s) Bank, Bar, Besides, But, Capital, Conserve, Deposit, Economy, Except, Hain, Hoard, Husband, ISA, Keep, Layby, National, Nest egg, Nirlie, Nirly, PEPS, Preserve, Put by, Reclaim, Redeem, Relieve, Reprieve, > **RESCUE**, Reskew, Sa', Salt, Salvage, Scrape, Scrimp, Shortcut, Slate club, Spare, Stokvel, Succour, TESSA, Unless

Saviour Deliverer, Jesu(s), Messiah, Redeemer

Savour(ed), Savoury Aigrette, Bouchée, Canapé, Devils-on-horseback, Essence, Fag(g)ot, Flavour, Olent, Ramekin, Relish, Resent, Sair, Sapid, Sar, Smack, Starter, Tang, > **TASTE**, Vol au vent

Savoy Cabbage, Opera

Saw Adage, Aphorism, Apothegm, Azebiki, Back, Band, Beheld, Bucksaw, Buzz, Chain, Circular, Cliché, Compass, Coping, Cross-cut, Crown, Cut, Dictum, Dovetail, Dozuki, Flooring, Frame, Fret, Gang, Glimpsed, Gnome, Grooving, Hack, Hand, Jig, Keyhole, Legend, Log, Maxim, Met, Motto, Pad, Panel, Paroemia, Pitsaw, Proverb, Pruning, Quarter, Rabbeting, Rack, Ribbon, Rip, Ryoba, Sash, Saying, Scroll, Serra, Skil®, Skip-tooth, Slogan, Span, Spied, Stadda, Stone, Sweep, Tenon, Trepan, Trephine, Whip, Witnessed

Sawbones Surgeon

Saw-toothed Runcinate

Saxifrage Burnet, Golden, Heuchera, London Pride, St Patrick's cabbage

Saxon Cedric, Hengist, Wend

Say, Saying(s) Adage, Agrapha, Allege, Aphorism, Apophthegm, Apostrophise, Articulate, Axiom, Beatitude, Bon mot, Bromide, Byword, Cant, Catchphrase, Cliché, Declare, Dict(um), Eg, Enunciate, Epigram, Express, Fadaise, Gnome, Impute, Logia, Logion, > **MAXIM**, Mean, Mot, Mouth, Observe, Predicate, Pronounce, Proverb, Put, Quip, Recite, Rede, Relate, Remark, Report, Saine, Saw, Sc, Sententia, > **SPEAK**, Suppose, Sutra, Utter, Voice, Word

▷ **Say, Saying(s)** *may indicate* a word sounding like another

Scab(by) Blackleg, Crust, Eschar, Leggism, Leprose, Mangy, Rat, Scald, Scall, Sore, Strike-breaker

Scabbard Frog, Pitcher, Sheath, Tsuba

Scabies Itch, Psora, Scotch fiddle

Scabrous Harsh, Rough, Thersites

Scaffold(ing), Scaffolder Gallows, Gantry, Hoarding, Putlock, Putlog, Rig, Spiderman, Stage

Scald Blanch, Burn, Leep, Ploat, Plot

Scale, Scaly Analemma, API gravity, Ascend, Balance, Baumé, Beaufort,

Binet- Simon, Bismar, Brix, Bud, Burnham, Celsius, Centigrade, Ceterach, Chromatic, > CLIMB, Desquamate, Diagonal, Diatonic, Douglas, Elo, Escalade, Fahrenheit, Flake, Full, Furfur, Gamme, Gamut, Ganoid, Gapped, Gauge, Gravity, Gunter's, Hexachord, Humidex, Indusium, Interval, Kelvin, Ladder, Lamina, Layer, Leaf, Lepid, Lepidote, Leprose, Libra, Ligule, Likert, Lodicule, Loricate, Magnitude, Major, Mercalli, Mesel, Minor, Mohs, Munsell, Natural, Nominal, Octad, Ordinal, Palea, Palet, Patagium, Peel, Pentatonic, Pholidosis, Placoid, Plate, Platform, Ramentum, > RANGE, Rankine, Ratio, Réaumur, Regulo, Richter, Scan, Scarious, Scent, Scincoid, Scurf, Scutellate, Shin, Skink, Sliding, Speel, Squama, Squame(lla), Submediant, Tegmentum, Tegula, Tonal, Tridymite, Tron(e), Vernier, Wage, Wentworth, Wind

Scallop(ed) Bivalve, Clam, Coquille, Crenate, Escalop, Frill, Gimp, Mush, Pecten, Vandyke

Scallywag Rascal, Scamp, Skeesicks

Scalp Cut, Scrape, Skin, Trophy

Scalpel Bistoury, Knife

Scam Ramp

Scamp Fripon, Imp, Limb, Lorel, Lorrell, Losel, Lozell, Neglect, > RASCAL, Reprobate, Rip, Rogue, Scallywag, Skeesicks

Scamper Gambol, Lamp, Run, Scurry, Skedaddle, Skelter, Skitter

Scan(ning), **Scanner** CAT, CT, Examine, Helical, Interlaced, OCR, Optical, Peruse, PET, Rake, Raster, Scrutinise, Sector, SEM, Sequential, SPET, Survey, Tomography, Ultrasound, Vertical, Vet

Scandal(ous), **Scandalise** Belie, Canard, Commesse, Disgrace, Exposé, Gamy, Hearsay, Muck-raking, Opprobrium, Outrage, Shame, Slander, Stigma, Stink, Watergate

Scandinavian Dane, Finn, Laplander, Lapp, Nordic, Norseland, Northman, Olaf, Runic, Squarehead, Swede, Varangian, Viking

Scandium Sc

Scant(y) Bare, Brief, Exiguous, Ihram, Jejune, Jimp, Poor, Scrimpy, Short, Shy, Skimpy, Slender, Spare, Sparse, Stingy

Scapegoat Butt, Fall-guy, Hazazel, Joe Soap, Patsy, Stooge, Target, Victim, Whipping-boy

Scapula Blade, Omoplate

Scar(face) Al, Blemish, Cheloid, Cicatrix, Cliff, Craig, Epulotic, Hilum, Keloid, Leucoma, Leukoma, Mark, Pockmark, Stigma, Ulosis, Wipe

Scarab Beetle, Gem

Scarce(ly), **Scarcity** Barely, Dear, Dearth, Famine, Few, Hardly, Ill, Lack, Rare, Scanty, Seldom, Short, Strap, Uncommon, Want

Scare(mongering), **Scaring** Alarmist, Alert, Amaze, Fleg, Fright, Gally, Gliff, Hairy, Panic, Skeer, Spook, Startle

Scarecrow Bogle, Bugaboo, Dudder, Dudsman, Gallibagger, Gallibeggar, Gallicrow, Gallybagger, Gallybeggar, Gallycrow, Malkin, Mawkin, Potato-bogle, Ragman, S(h)ewel, Tattie-bogle

Scarf Babushka, Belcher, Cataract, Comforter, Cravat, Curch, Doek, Dupatta, Fichu, Hai(c)k, Haique, Headsquare, Hyke, Lambrequin, Madras, Mantilla, Muffettee, Muffler, Neckatee, Nightingale, Orarium, Pagri, Palatine, Pashmina, Pugg(a)ree, Rail, Rebozo, Sash, Screen, Stole, Tallith, Tippet, Trot-cosy, Trot-cozy, Vexillum

Scarifier Scuffler

Scarlet Cinnabar, Cochineal, Crimson, Pimpernel, Pink, Ponceau, Red, Vermilion

Scarper Bunk, Run, Shoo, Welsh

Scat Aroint, Dropping

Scathe, **Scathing** Mordant, Sarcastic, Savage, Severe, Vitriolic

Scatter(ed), **Scattering** Bestrew, Broadcast, Diaspora, Disject, Dispel, > DISPERSE, Dissipate, Flurr, Interspace, Litter, Rout, Scail, Skail, Sow, Sparge, Splutter, Sporadic, Spread, Sprinkle, Squander, Straw, Strew

Scatterbrain(ed) Dippy, Ditsy

Scavenge(r) Dieb, Forage, Hunt, Hy(a)ena, Jackal, Rake, Ratton, Rotten, Scaffie, Sweeper, Totter

Scenario Outline, Plot, Script

Scene(ry) Arena, Boscage, Coulisse, Decor, Flat(s), Landscape, Locale, Prop, Prospect, Set, Set piece, Sight, Site, Sketch, Stage, Tableau, Tormenter, Tormentor, Transformation, Venue, View

Scent Aroma, Attar, Chypre, Cologne, Eau de cologne, Essence, Fragrance, Frangipani, Fumet(te), Gale, Moschatel, Nose, Odour, Orris, Ottar, Otto, Perfume, Sachet, Smell, Spoor, Vent, Waft, Wind

Scentless Anosmia

Sceptic(al), **Scepticism** Agnostic, Cynic, Doubter, Incredulous, Infidel, Jaundiced, Nihilistic, Pyrrho(nic), Sadducee, Solipsism

Schedule Agenda, Calendar, Itinerary, Prioritise, Programme, Register, Slot, Table, Timescale, Timetable

Scheme(r), **Scheming** Colour, Concoct, Conspire, Crafty, Cunning, Dare, Darien, Dart, Decoct, Devisal, Diagram, Dodge, Draft, Gin, Honeytrap, Intrigue, Jezebel, Machiavellian, Machinate, Manoeuvre, Nostrum, Pilot, > PLAN, Plat, Plot, Project, Proposition, Purpose, Put-up job, Racket, Ruse, Stratagem, System, Table, Wangle, Wheeze

Schism(atic) Disunion, Division, Eastern, Great, Greek, Heterodox, Rent, Split, Western

Schizo(phrenia) Catatonic, Dementia praecox, Hebephreni

Schmaltz Goo, Slush

Schmieder S

Schmuck Gunsel

Schnapps Enzian

Scholar, **Scholast** Abelard, Academic, Alumni, Atticus, BA, Bookman, Boursier, Catachumen, Clergy, Clerisy, Clerk, Commoner, Demy, Disciple, Erasmus, Erudite, Etonian, Exhibitioner, Extern(e), Externat, Goliard, Graduate, Grecian, Hafiz, Inkhorn, Jowett, Literate, Littérateur, MA, Mal(l)am, Masorete, Noter, Occam Ulama, Pauline, Plutarch, Polymath, Pupil, Rhodes, Sap, Savant, Schoolboy, Sizar, Soph, > STUDENT, Tabardar, Taberdar, Taberder, Tom Brown

Scholarship Bursary, Education, Erudition, Exhibition, Grant, Learning, Lore, Mass, Rhodes

School Academy, Ampleforth, Approved, Ashlan, Barbizon, Bauhaus, Beacon, Benenden, Bluecoat, Board, Boarding, Charm, Charterhouse, Chartreux, Chautauqua, Cheder, Choir, Church, Classical, Coed, Community, Composite, Comprehensive, Conservative, Conservatoire, Conservatory, Cool, Correspondence, Council, Crammer, Cult, Dada, Dame, Day, Direct grant, Dojo, Downside, Drama, Drill, Driving, Dual, Educate, Elementary, Essenes, Eton, Exercise, External, Faith, Fettes, Finishing, First, Flemish, Frankfurt, Free, Gam, Giggleswick, Gordonstoun, Grade, Grammar, Grant-aided, Grant-maintained, Group, Gymnasien, Gymnasium, Harrow, Heder, Hedge, High, Historical, Honour, Hospital, Hostel, Hypermodern, Independent, Industrial, Infant, Institute, Integrated, Intermediate, Ionic, Jim Crow,

Junior, Kailyard, Kaleyard, Kant, Kindergarten, Lake, Lancing, Language, Life, List D, Loretto, Lower, LSE, Lycée, Madrassah, Magnet, Mahayana, Maintained, Maintaining, Manchester, Mannheim, Marlborough, Middle, National, Night, Normal, Nursery, Oundle, Palaestra, Parnassian, Parochial, Pensionnat, Perse, Piano, Play, Pod, Poly, Porpoises, Prep, Preparatory, Primary, Private, Progymnasium, Provided, Public, RADA, Ragged, RAM, Ramean, Real, Reformatory, Repton, Residential, Rhodian, Roedean, Rossall, Rydal, Sabbath, Sadducee, Satanic, Scandalous, Sciences, Scul, Scull(e), Secondary(-modern), Sect, Seminary, Separate, Shoal, Single-sex, Ski, Slade, Song, Spasmodic, Special, State, Stonyhurst, Stowe, Style, Summer, Sunday, Teach, Tonbridge, Trade, > TRAIN, Tutor, Upper, Voluntary(-aided), Voluntary-controlled, Wellington, Whales, Winchester, Yeshiva

Schoolboy, **Schoolgirl** Carthusian, Coed, Colleger, East, Etonian, Fag, Gait, Geit, Gyte, Miss, Monitor, Oppidan, Petty, Stalky, Wykehamist

School-leaver Abiturient

Schoolmaam, **Schoolman**, **Schoolmaster**, **Schoolmistress** Beak, Dominie, Duns, Holofernes, Miss, Occam, Orbilius, Pedagogue, Pedant, Sir, Squeers, Teacher, Ursuline

Schooner Glass, Hesperus, Prairie, Ship, Tern

Sciatica Hip-gout

Science Anatomy, Anthropology, Art, Astrodynamics, Astrophysics, Atmology, Axiology, Biology, Botany, Chemistry, Cognitive, Computer, Dismal, Domestic, Earth, Electrodynamics, Eth(n)ology, Euphenics, Exact, Geology, Information, Life, Mechanics, Natural, Noble, Nomology, Ology, Ontology, Optics, Pedagogy, Physical, Physics, Policy, Political, Rocket, Rural, Skill, Social, Soft, Soil, Sonics, Stinks, Stylistics, Tactics, Technics, Technology

Science fiction Cyberpunk

Scientist Alchemist, Anatomist, Archimedes, Aston, Astronomer, Atomist, Boffin, BSc, Cavendish, Climatologist, Copernicus, Curie, Dalton, Davy, Dopper, Einstein, Expert, Faraday, Fourier, FRS, Galileo, Geodesist, Harvey, Heaviside, Kennelly, Lodge, Lovell, Newton, Oersted, Pascal, Pasteur, Pauli, Piccard, Potamologist, Reaumur, Researcher, Volta

Scimitar Acinaciform, Sword

Scintillate Dazzle, Emicate, Gleam, Glitter, > SPARKLE

Scion Graft, Imp, Offspring, Sprig, Sprout

Scissors Clippers, Criss-cross, Cutters, Forfex, Nail, Probe, Shears

Scoff Belittle, Boo, Chaff, Deride, Dor, Eat, Feast, Flout, Food, Gall, Gibe, Gird, Gobble, > JEER, Mock, Rail, Rib, Ridicule, Roast, Scaff, Scorn, Sneer, Taunt

Scold(ing) Admonish, Berate, Callet, Catamaran, Chastise, Chide, Clapperclaw, Cotquean, Do, Earful, Flite, Flyte, Fuss, Jaw(bation), Jobation, Lecture, Nag, Objurgate, Philippic, Rant, Rate, > REBUKE, Reprimand, Reprove, Revile, Rouse on, Row, Sas(s)arara, Sis(s)erary, Slang, Slate, Termagant, Threap, Threep, Through-going, Tick-off, Tongue-lash, Trimmer, Upbraid, Virago, Wig, Xant(h)ippe, Yaff, Yankie, Yap

Sconce Candlestick, Crown, Forfeit, Head, Ice, Nole

Scone Drop, Girdle

Scoop Bale, Dipper, Exclusive, Gouge, Grab, Hollow, Ladle, Lap, Pale, Shovel, Trowel

Scope Ambit, Diapason, Domain, Elbow-room, Extent, Freedom, Gamut, Ken, Latitude, Leeway, Play, Purview, Range, Remit, Room, Rope, Scouth, Scowth, Size, Sphere

Scorch(er) Adust, Blister, Brasero, > BURN, Char, Destroy, Frizzle, Fry, Parch,

Scouther, Scowder, Scowther, Sear, Singe, Soar, Speed, Swale, Swayl, Sweal, Sweel, Torrefy, Torrid, Wither

Score Apgar, Behind, Bill, Birdie, Bradford, Bye, Capot, Chase, Conversion, Count, Crena, Debt, Eagle, Etch, Full, Groove, Hail, Honours, Ingroove, Ippon, Law, Magpie, Make, Music, Net, Nick, Notation, Notch, Partitur(a), Peg, Pique, Point, Record, Repique, Rit(t), Rouge, Run, Rut, Scotch, Scratch, Scribe, Scrive, Set, Single, Spare, Stria, String, Sum, Tablature, > **TALLY**, Twenty, Vocal, Waza-ari, Win

Score-board, **Score-sheet** Card, Telegraph

▷ **Scoring** *may indicate* an anagram

Scorn(ful) Arrogant, Bah, Contempt, Contumely, Deride, Despise, Dis(s), Disdain, Dislike, Flout, Geck, Haughty, Insult, Meprise, Mock, Opprobrium, Putdown, Rebuff, Ridicule, Sarcastic, Sardonic, Sarky, Scoff, Scout, Sdaine, Sdeigne, Sneer, Spurn, Wither

Scorpion Book, Chelifer, False, Father-lasher, Pedipalp(us), Vinegarroon, Water Whip

Scot(sman), **Scots(woman)**, **Scottish** Angus, Antenati, Berean, Blue-bonnet, Bluecap, Caledonian, Celt, Clansman, Covenanter, Duni(e)wassal, Dunniewassal, Erse, Fingal, Gael, Highland, Ian, Jock, Kelt, Kiltie, Kitty, Knox, Laird, Lallan(s), Lot, Lowland, Luckie, Lucky, Mac, Mon, Peght, Pict, Ross, Sandy, Säwn(e)y, Shetlander, Stuart, Tartan, Tax, Teuchter, Torridonian

Scotch(man) Censor, Dish, Distiller, Glenlivet®, Notch, Score, Scratch, Thwart, Usquebaugh, Whisky

Scot-free Wreakless

Scotland Alban(y), Albion, Caledonia, Gaeltacht, Gaidhealtachd, Lallans, Lothian, NB, Norland, Scotia

Scoundrel Cur, Fink, Knave, Reprobate, Scab, Smaik, Varlet, > **VILLAIN**

Scour Beat, Depurate, Full, Holystone, Purge, Quarter, Scrub

▷ **Scour** *may indicate* an anagram

Scourge Bible-thumper, Cat, Discipline, Flagellate, Knout, Lash, Pest, > **PLAGUE** Scorpion, Whip, Wire

Scout Akela, Beaver, Bedmaker, Colony, Disdain, Explorer, Flout, Guide, King's, Outrider, Pathfinder, Pickeer, Pioneer, Queen's, Reconnoitre, Rover, Runner, Scoff, Scorn, Scourer, Scurrier, Scurriour, Sea, Sixer, Spial, Spyal, Talent, Tenderfoot, Tonto, Track, Vedette, Venture

Scowl(ing) Frown, Glower, Gnar, Lour, Lower, Sullen

Scrabble Paw

Scrag(gy) Bony, Dewitt, Ewe-necked, Neck, Scrawny

Scram Begone, Hence, Scat, Shoo

Scramble Addle, Clamber, Encode, Grubble, Hurry, Mêlée, Mix, Motocross, Muss(e), Scamble, Sprattle, Sprawl, Swerve

Scrap(s), **Scrappy** Abandon, Abrogate, > **BIT**, Cancel, Conflict, Cutting, Discard, Dump, > **FIGHT**, Fisticuffs, Fragment, Fray, Iota, Jot, Mêlée, Mellay, Morceau, Morsel, Odd, Off-cut, Ort, Ounce, Papier colle, Patch, Piece, Pig's-wash, Rag, Rase, Raze, Remnant, Scarmoge, Scissel, Scissil, Scrub, Set-to, Shard, Sherd, Shred, Skerrick, Skirmish, Snap, Snippet, Spall, Tait, Tate, Tatter, Titbit, Trash, Truculent, Whit

Scrap book Album, Grangerism

Scrap box Tidy

Scrape(r) Abrade, Agar, Bark, Clat, Claw, Comb, Curette, D and C, Erase, Escapade, Grate, Graze, Harl, Hoe, Hole, Jar, Kowtow, Lesion, Lute, Predicament, Racloir, Rake, Rasorial, Rasp, Rasure, Raze, Razure, Saw,

Scalp, Scart, Scrat(ch), Scroop, Scuff, Shave, Skimp, Skive, Squeegee, Strake, Stridulate, Strigil, Xyster

Scraping noise Curr, Scroop

Scrap merchant Didakai, Didakei, Diddicoi, Diddicoy, Didicoi, Didicoy, Gold-end-man, Totter

Scratch(es), Scratched Annul, Cancel, Cla(u)t, Claw, Cracked heels, Curry, Devil, Efface, Eradicate, Erase, Grabble, Graze, Nick, Par, Periwig, Quit, Race, Rase, Rasp, Rast, Root, Satan, Scarify, Scart, Score, Scrab(ble), Scram(b), Scrape, Scrattle, Scrawm, Scrawp, Scrooch, Scrorp, Scrub, Spag, Streak, Striation, Tease, Teaze, Wig

Scratch(ed) *may indicate* an anagram

Scrawl Doodle, Scribble, Squiggle

Scream(er) Bellow, Cariama, Caterwaul, Comedian, Comic, Cry, Eek, Headline, Hern, Kamichi, Laugh, Priceless, Primal, Riot, Scare-line, Screech, Seriema, Shriek, Skirl, Squall, Sutch, Yell

Scree Bahada, Bajada, Eluvium, Talus

Screech(ing) Cry, Screak, Screich, Screigh, Scriech, Scritch, Skreigh, Skriech, Skriegh, Ululant, Whoot

Screed Megillah, Ms, Plastered, Tirade

Screen(s) Abat-jour, Arras, Backstop, Blind(age), Block, Blue, Boss, Brise-soleil, Camouflage, Chancel, Check, Chick, Cinerama®, Cloak, Cornea, Coromandel, Cover, Cribble, Curtain, Divider, Dodger, Eyelid, Festoon-blind, Fire, Fluorescent, Glib, Gobo, Grille, Hallan, Help, Hide, Hoard, Hoarding, Iconostas(is), Intensifying, Jube, Lattice, Mantelet, Mask, Nintendo, Nonny, Obscure, Organ, Over-cover, Parclose, Partition, Part-off, Pella, Purdah, Radar, Retable, Riddle, Rood, Scog, Sconce, Scope, > **SHADE**, Shelter, Shield, Shoji, Show, Sift, Sight, Silver, Skug, Small, Smoke, Split, Sunblock, Televise, Tems, Touch, Transenna, Traverse, Umbrella, VDU, Vet, Wide, Windbreak, Window, Windshield, Winnow

Screw Adam, Allen, Archimedes, Butterfly, Cap, Coach, Countersunk, Double-threaded, Dungeoner, Extort, Female, Grub, Ice, Interrupted, Jailer, Jailor, Lag, Lead, Levelling, Lug, Machine, Male, Micrometer, Miser, Monkey-wrench, Niggard, Perpetual, Phillips®, Prop(ellor), Robertson, Salary, Skinflint, Spiral, Thumb(i)kins, Twin, Twist, Vice, Worm

Screwdriver Pozidriv®, Ratchet, Stubby, Tweaker

Scribble Doodle, Pen, Scrawl

Scribe Clerk, Ezra, Mallam, Scrivener, Sopherim, Tabellion, Writer, WS

Scrimmage Bully, Maul, Mêlée, Rouge, Scrap, Skirmish, Struggle

Scrimp Economise, Pinch, Save, Scrape, Skrimp

Script Book, Calligraphy, Gurmukhi, Hand, Hiragana, Italic, Jawi, Kana, Libretto, Linear A, Linear B, Lines, Lombardic, Miniscule, Nagari, Nastalik, Nastaliq, Ogam, Ronde, Scenario, Screenplay, Shooting, Writing

Scripture(s), Scriptural version Adi Granth, Agadah, Antilegomena, Avesta, Bible, Gemara, Gematria, Gospel, Granth (Sahib), Guru Granth, Haggada(h), Hermeneutics, Hexapla, Holy book, Holy writ, Koran, K'thibh, Lesson, Lotus Sutra, Mishna(h), OT, Rig-veda, Smriti, Tantra, Targum, Testament, Upanishad, Veda, Vedic, Verse, Vulgate

Scrofula Crewels, Cruel(l)s, King's evil, Struma

Scroll(-work) Cartouche, Dead Sea, Gohonzon, Makimono, Megillah, Mezuza(h), Parchment, Pell, Roll, Roul(e), Scrow, Sefer Torah, Torah, Turbinate, Vitruvian, Volume, Volute

Scrooge Blagueur, Miser

Scrounge(r) Blag, Bludge(r), Borrow, Bot, Cadge, Forage, Freeload, Layabout, Ligger, Scunge, Sponge

Scrub(ber) Cancel, Chaparral, Cleanse, Dele(te), Gar(r)igue, Hog, Holystone, Loofa(h), Luffa, Mallee, Masseur, Negate, Pro, Rub, Scour, Tart

▷ **Scrub** *may indicate* 'delete'

Scruff(y) Dog-eared, Grubby, Nape, Raddled, Tatty, Uncombed, Untidy

Scrum Maul, Mob, Rouge, Ruck

Scrummy, Scrumptious Delectable, Delicious, Toothy, Yum-yum

Scrunt Carl

Scruple(s), Scrupulous Compunction, Conscience, Doubt, Meticulous, Nicety, Precise, Punctilious, Qualm, Queasy, Righteous, Stickle

Scrutinise, Scrutiny Check, Docimasy, Examine, Inspect, Observe, Peruse, Pore, Pry, > SCAN, Study

Scud East, Scoot, Spark, Spindrift, Spoom, Spoon, Spray

Scuff Brush, Shuffle

Scuffle Bagarre, Brawl, Scarmage, Skirmish, Struggle, Tussle

▷ **Scuffle** *may indicate* an anagram

Scull Oar, Row

Sculpt(ure) Acrolith, Aeginetan, Bas-relief, Boast, Bronze, Calvary, Canephor(a), Canephore, Canephorus, Carve, Chryselephantine, Della-robbia Figure, Kore, Kouros, Mobile, Nude, Pergamene, Pieta, Relief, Relievo, Sc, Scabble, Scapple, Shape, Stabile, > STATUARY, Topiary

Sculptor Arp, Artist, Bartholdi, Bernini, Brancusi, Canova, Cellini, Daedalus, Della Robbia, Donatello, Giacometti, Gibbons, Gill, Hepworth, Klippel, Landseer, Michelangelo, Myron, Nollekens, Paclozzi, Phidias, Pisano, Praxiteles, Pygmalion, Rodin, Scopas, Stevens, Wheeler

Scum Confervoid, Dregs, Dross, Epistasis, Glass-gall, Kish, Legge, Mantle, Mother, Rabble, Sandiver, Scorious, Slag, Slime, Spume, Sullage

Scupper Drain, Ruin, Scuttle, Sink

Scurf, Scurvy Dander, Dandriff, Dandruff, Furfur, Horson, Lepidote, Leprose, Scabrous, Scall, Scorbutic, Whoreson, Yaw(e)y, Yaws

Scurrilous Fescennine, Profane, Ribald, Sotadic, Thersites, Vulgar

Scurry Beetle, Hurry, Scamper, Scutter, Skedaddle, Skelter

Scut Fud, Tail

Scute Plate

Scuttle Abandon, Dan, Hod, Purdonium, Scoop, Scrattle, Scupper, Sink, Wreck

Scythe Bushwhacker, Cut, Hook, Sickle, Sieth, Snath(e), Snead, Sneath, Sned

Sea(s) Adriatic, Aegean, Amundsen, Andaman, Arabian, Arafura, Aral, Azov, Baltic, Banda, Barents, Beam, Beaufort, Bellingshausen, Benthos, Bering, Billow, Biscay, Bismarck, Black, Blue, Bosp(h)orus, Brine, Briny, Caribbean, Caspian, Celebes, Celtic, Ceram, Channel, China, Chukchi, Coral, Dead, Ditch, Drink, Euphotic, Euripus, Euxine, Flores, Galilee, Great, Greenland, Head, Herring-pond, High, Hudson Bay, Icarian, Inland, Ionian, Irish, Japan, Java, Kara, Kattegat, Labrador, Laptev, Ler, Ligurian, Main, Mare, Marmara, Marmora, Med, Mediterranean, Narrow, Nordenskjold, North, Norwegian, > OCEAN, Offing, Offshore, Oggin, Okhotsk, Pelagic, Philippine, Polynya, Quantity, Red, Ross, Sargasso, Seven, Skagerrak, South, South China, Spanish main, Strand, Sulu, Tasman, Tethys, Thalassic, Tiberias, Tide, Tide-rip, Timor, Tyrrhenian, Waddenzee, Water, Weddell, White, Yellow, Zee

Sea-anemone Actinia, Zoantharia

Sea-bear Fur-seal, Otary, Seal, Seecatchie

Sea-beast Ellops, Manatee

Sea-bream Carp, Fish, Porgie, Porgy, Tai
Sea-cow Dugong, Lamantin, Manatee, Rhytina, Sirenian
Sea-cucumber Bêche-de-mer, Trepang
Sea-dog Salt, Tar
Sea-ear Abalone, Paua
Sea-fight Naumachy
Seafood Crab, Crevette, > FISH, Lobster, Prawn, Shrimp, Zooplankton
Sea-front, **Seaside** Beach, Coast(line), Esplanade, Littoral, Orarian,
Prom(enade)
Sea-god Neptune, Nereus, Triton
Sea-green Glaucous, Incorruptible, Robespierre
Sea-horse Hippocampus, Hippodame, Lophobranchiate, Morse, Pipefish,
Tangie
Seal(s), **Seal box** Airtight, Appose, Bachelor, Bladdernose, Bull(a), Cachet,
Cap, Caulk, Chesterfield, Chop, Clinch, Close, Cocket, Common, Consign,
Crab-eater, Cylinder, Eared, Earless, Elephant, Emblem, Fob, Fur, Gasket,
Great, Greenland, Hair, Harbour, Harp, Hermetic, Hooded, Hudson, Impress,
Jark, Lute, Monk, Obsign, O-ring, Otary, Phoca, Pinnipedia, Pintadera, Pod,
Privy, Proof, Quarter, Ribbon, Ringed, Rookery, Saddleback, Sea-bear, Sealch,
Sea-leopard, Sealgh, Seecatch(ie), Selkie, Sigil, Signet, Silkie, Silky, Size,
Skippet, Solomon's, Sphragistic, Stamp, Tar, Wafer, Washer, Water, Weddell,
Whitecoat, Womb, Zalophus
Sea-legs Balance, Pleons
Sea-level Geoid
Sea-lily Crinoid, Palmatozoa
Seam Channel, Commissure, Fell, French, Furrow, Join, Layer,
Middle-stitching, Monk's, Sew, Suture, Welt
Seaman, **Seamen** AB, Crew, Jack, Lascar, Lubber, Mariner, OD, Ordinary, PO, RN,
> SAILOR, Salt, Swabby, Tar
Sea-mat Flustra, Hornwrack
Sea-matiness Gam
Sea-monster Kraken, Merman, Wasserman
Sea-mouse Bristle-worm
Séance Communication, Session, Sitting
Sea-parrot Puffin
Sear Brand, Burn, Catch, Cauterise, Frizzle, Parch, Scath(e), Scorch, Singe,
Wither
Search(ing) Beat, Comb, Dragnet, Examine, Ferret, Fingertip, > FORAGE,
Fossick, Frisk, Global, Grope, Home, Hunt, Indagate, Inquire, Jerk, Jerque,
Kemb, Manhunt, Perquisition, Perscrutation, Probe, Proll, Prospect, Proul,
Prowl, Quest, Rake, Rancel, Ransack, Ransel, Ranzel, Ravel, Ripe, Root, Rootle,
Rummage, Scan, Scour, Scur, Sker, Skirr, Snoop, Strip, Thumb, Trace, Zotetic
Sea-rover Norseman, Viking
Sea-serpent, **Sea-snake** Ellops, Hydrophidae, Phoca
Seaside see SEA-FRONT
Sea-slug Bêche-de-mer, Trepang
Sea-snail Neritidae
Season(able), **Seasonal**, **Seasoned**, **Seasoning** Accustom, Age, Aggrace,
Autumn, Betimes, Christmas, Close, Condiment, Devil, Dress, Duxelles,
Easter, Enure, Etesian, Fall, Fennel, Festive, Flavour, Garlic, G(h)omasco,
Growing, Hiems, High, In, Inure, Lent, Marjoram, Master, Mature, Nutmeg,
Open, Paprika, Pepper, Powellise, Practised, Ripen, Salt, Sar, Seal, Seel, Seil,

Sele, Silly, Solstice, Spice, Spring, Summer(y), Tahini, Ticket, Tide, Time, Whit, Winter, Xmas

Sea-squirt Ascidian, Cunjevoi

Seat Backside, Banc, Banquette, Bench, Bleachers, Booster, Borne, Bosun's chair, Bottom, Box, Bucket, Bum, Bunker, Buttocks, Canapé, Centre, Chair, Chaise longue, Coit, Couch, Creepie, Croup(e), Croupon, Cushion, Davenport, Deckchair, Derriere, Dick(e)y, Dicky, Divan, Ejector, Epicentre, Faldistory, Faldstool, Foundation, Fud, Fundament, Gradin, Hall, Home, Hot, Houdah, Howdah, Humpty, Hurdies, Jump, Knifeboard, Love, Marginal, Marquise, Mercy, Misericord, Natch, Nates, Ottoman, Palanquin, Palfrey, Perch, Pew, Pillion, Pit, Pouffe, Ringside, Rumble, Rumble-tumble, Rump, Saddle, Safe, Sagbag, Sedes, Sedile, Sedilium, See, Sell, Settee, Settle, Siege, Siege Perilous, Sliding, Sofa, Squab, Stool, Strapontin, Subsellium, Sunk(ie), Sunlounger, Synthronus, Throne, Tonneau, Window, Woolsack

Sea-urchin Asteria, Echinus, Pluteus, Whore's egg

Sea-vampire Manta

Sea-wall Bulwark, Dyke, Groyne

Sea-weed Agar, Alga(e), Arame, Badderlock, Bladderwort, Bladderwrack, Carrag(h)een, Ceylon moss, Chondrus, Conferva, Coralline, Cystocarp, Desmid, Diatom, Driftweed, Dulse, Enteromorpha, Fucus, Gulfweed, Heterocontae, Hornwrack, Kelp, Kilp, Kombu, Konbu, Laminaria, Laver, Lemon-weed, Nori, Nullipore, Oarweed, Ore, Peacock's tail, Phyco-, Porphyra, Redware, Rockweed, Sargasso, Seabottle, Sea-furbelow, Sea-lace, Sea-lettuce, Sea-mat, Sea-moss, Sea-tangle, Seaware, Sea-whistle, Sea-wrack, Tang, Tetraspore, Ulva, Varec(h), Vraic, Wakame, Wakane, Ware, Wrack

Sea-wolf Pirate

Sea-worm Palolo, Spunculid

Sebastian Coe

Secede, **Secession(ist)** Adullamite, Antiburgher, Defy, Desert, Dissident, Flamingant, Sever, Splinter

Seclude, **Seclusion** Cloister, Incommunicado, Isolate, Maroon, Nook, Privacy, Purdah, Quarantine, Retiracy, Retreat, Secret, Sequester, Shyness, Solitude

Second(s), **Secondary** Abet, Alternative, Another (guess), Appurtenance, Assist, Back(er), Beta, Coming, Comprimario, Deuteragonist, Ephemeris, Flash, Friend, Imperfect, Indirect, Inferior, Instant, Jiffy, Latter, Leap, Lesser, Minor, Mo(ment), Nature, Other, Pig's-whisper, Redwood, Runner-up, Sec, Shake, Share, Side(r), Sight, Silver, Split, Subsidiary, Support, Tick, Trice, Twinkling, Wind

Second-best Worsted

▸ **Second-class** *see* SECOND-RATE

Second coming Parousia

Second earth Antichthon

Second-hand Hand-me-down, Hearsay, Preloved, Reach-me-down, Re-paint, Tralatitious, Used, Vicarious

Second-rate, **Second-class** B, Inferior, Mediocre

Second-sight Deuteroscopy, Divination, Tais(c)h

Second tine Bay, Bez

Second-year student Semi(e)(-bajan), Sophomore

Secrecy, **Secret(s)**, **Secretive** Apocrypha, Arcana, Arcane, Arcanum, Backstairs, Cabbalistic, Cagey, Clam, Clandestine, Closet, Code, Conventicle, Covert, Cryptadia, Cryptic, Crypto, Dark, Dearn, Deep, Deep-laid, Dern, Devious, Esoteric, Hidden, Hidling, Hidlin(g)s, Hole and corner, Hugger-mugger,

Hush-hush, Hushy, Inly, Inmost, Latent, Mysterious, Mystical, Mystique, Open, Oyster, Password, Penetralia, Petto, > **PRIVATE**, Privity, Privy, QT, Rune, Scytale, Shelta, Silent, Sly, State, Stealth, Sub rosa, Tight-lipped, Top, Trade, Unbeknown, Undercover, Underhand, Undescried, Unknown, Unre(a)d, Unrevealed, Untold

Secretary Aide, Amanuensis, Chancellor, Chronicler, CIS, Desk, Desse, Famulus, Home, Minuteman, Moonshee, Munshi, Notary, Parliamentary, Permanent, Private, Scrive, Social, Steno(grapher), Stenotyper, Temp

Secretary-bird Messenger, Serpent-eater

Secrete, **Secretion** Aequorin, Allomone, Apocrine, Autacoid, Cache, Castor, Chalone, Cuckoo-spit, Discharge, Emanation, Exude, Hide, Hormone, Juice, Lac, Lerp, Melatonin, Mucus, Musk, Osmidrosis, Pruina, Renin, Resin, Rheum, Saliva, Sebum, Secern, Smegma, Spit(tle), Trypsin

Secret society see SECT

Sect(arian), **Secret society** Abelite, Adamite, Ahmadiy(y)ah, Albigenses, Amish, Anabaptist, Assassin, Babee, Babi, Bahai, Bigendian, Brahmin, Cabal, Cainite, Calixtine, Camorra, Cathar, Clan, Clapham, Covenantes, Crypto, Cult, Cynic, Danite, Darbyite, Dissenter, Docate(s), Donatist, Druse, Druze, Dunkard, Dunker, Ebionite, Encratite, Essene, Familist, Gheber, Ghebre, Giaour, Gnostic, Group, Gueber, Guebre, Gymnosophist, Harmonist, Harmonite, Hassid, Hauhau, Hemerobaptist, Hesychast, Hillmen, Illuminati, Ismaili, Jacobite, Jansenist, Karaite, Karmathian, Little-endian, Lollard, Macedonian, Macmillanite, Mandaean, Marcionite, Maronite, Monothelite, Montanist, Moonie, Mormon, Mucker, Muggletonian, Nazarine, Ophites, Order, Partisan, Patripassian, Paulician, Perfectionist, Pharisee, Philadelphian, Phrygian, Picard, Pietist, Plymouth Brethren, Plymouthite, Porch, Pure Land, Rappist, Ribbonism, Sabbatian, Sabian, Sadducee, Sandeman, School, Schwenkfelder, Seekers, Senus(s)i, Seventh Day Adventist, Sex, S(h)aiva, Shaker, Shembe, Shia(h), Soka Gakkai, Sons of Freedom, Therapeutae, Tunker, Ultraquist, Unitarian, Valdenses, Vaudois, Wahabee, Wahabi(i)te, Waldenses, Yezdi, Yezidee, Yezidi, Zealot, Zen, Zezidee

Section, **Sector** Caesarian, Chapter, Classify, Conic, Cross, Cut, Division, Ellipse, Eyalet, Gan, Golden, Gore, Hyperbola, Lith, Lune, Meridian, Metamere, Mortice, Movement, Octant, Outlier, Panel, Passus, > **PIECE**, Platoon, Private, Public, Quarter, Rhythm, Rib, Segment, Severy, Slice, Stage, Ungula, Unit, Warm, Zenith, Zone

Secular Earthly, Laic, Non-CE, Profane, Temporal, Worldly

Secure, **Security** Anchor, Assurance, Bag, Bail, Band, Bar, Batten, Belay, Bellwether, Bolt, Bond, Bottomry, Buck Rogers, Calm, Catch, Cement, Chain, Cheka, Cinch, Clamp, Clasp, Clench, Clinch, Close, Cocoon, Collateral, Collective, Consols, Cushy, Debenture, Dunnage, Engage, Ensure, Equity, Establishment, Fasten, Fastness, Fortify, Frap, Fungibles, Gilt, Grith, Guarantee, Guy, Hypothec, Immune, Indemnity, Invest(ment), Knot, Lace, Land, Lash, Latch, Lien, Listed, Lock, Lockaway, Long-dated, Longs, Medium-dated, Mortgage, Nail, National, Obtain, Patte, Pin, Pledge, Pot, Pre-empt, Preference, Protect, Quad, Rope, Rug, > **SAFE**, Safety, Settle, Snell, Snug, Social, Sound, Stable, Stanchion, Staple, Staylace, Stock, Strap, Sure(ty), Tack, Take, Tie, Tight, Trap, Trice, Warrant, Watertight, Wedge, Win

Sedan Battle, Brougham, Chair, Jampan(i), Jampanee, Litter, Palanquin, Palkee, Palki, Saloon

Sedate Calm, Cool, Decorous, Dope, Douce, Drug, Sad, Serene, Sober(sides), Staid, Stand

Sedative Amytal®, Anodyne, Aspirin, Barbitone, Bromide, Chloral, Depressant, Hypnic, Laurel water, Lenitive, Lupulin, Meprobamate, Metopryl, Miltown, Narcotic, Nembutal®, Opiate, Paraldehyde, Pethidine, Phenobarbitone, Premed(ication), Scopolamine, Seconal®, Soothing, Thridace, Valerian, Veronal

Sedentary Inactive, Sessile, Stationary

Sedge Carex, Chufa, Grey, Seg, Xyris

Sediment Alluvium, Chalk, Deposit, Dregs, F(a)eces, Fecula, Foots, Grounds, Grouts, Lees, Molasse, Placer, Residue, Salt, Sapropel, Silt, Sludge, Terrigenous, Till, Turbidite, Varve, Warp

Sedition, **Seditious** Incitement, Insurrection, Revolt, Riot, Treason

Seduce(r), **Seductive** Allure, Betray, Bewitch, Bribe, Cuckold-maker, Debauch, Dishonour, Entice, Honeyed, Honied, Jape, Lothario, Luring, Mislead, Pull, Siren, Slinky, Tempt, Trepan, Undo, Wrong

▷ **Seduce** *may indicate* one word inside another

See(ing) Acknow, Apostolic, Barchester, Behold, Bishopric, C, Consider, Deek, Descry, Diocesan, Discern, Durham, Ecce, Ely, Episcopal, Eye, Glimpse, Holy, La, Lo, Meet, Norwich, Notice, Observe, Papal, Perceive, Realise, Remark, Ripon, Rumble, Since, Sodor and Man, Spae, Spot, Spy, Truro, Twig, Understand, V, Vatican, Vid(e), View, Vision, Visit, Voila, Witness, York

Seed(s), **Seedy** Achene, Argan, Arilli, Arillode, Ash-key, Bean, Ben, Best, Bonduc, Cacoon, Caraway, Carvy, Cebadilla, Cevadilla, Chickpea, Cocoa, Colza, Coriander, Corn, Crabstone, Cum(m)in, Dragon's teeth, Embryo, Endosperm, Ergot, Favourite, Fern, Germ, Grain, Gritty, Issue, Ivory-nut, Kernel, Lima, Lomentum, Mangy, Miliary, Niger, Nucellous, Nut, Offspring, Ovule, Pea, Pinon, Pip, Poorly, Poppy, Sabadilla, Scuzz, Semen, Seminal, Sesame, Shabby, Shea-nut, Silique, Sorus, Sow, Sperm, Spore, Terminator, Zoosperm

Seed-case Aril, Bur(r), Endopleura, Husk, Pea(s)cod, Pod, Testa, Theca

Seed-leaf Cotyledon

Seedsman Driller, Nurseryman, Sower

Seek(er) Ask, Beg, Busk, Chase, Court, Endeavour, Ferret out, Pursue, Quest, Scur, Search, Skirr, Solicit, Suitor

Seem(ingly) Appear, Look, Ostensible, Purport, Quasi, Think

Seemly Comely, Decent, Decorous, Fit, Suitable

Seep Dribble, Exude, Leak, Ooze, Osmose, Percolate

Seer Augur, Auspex, Eye, Melampus, Nahum, Observer, Oculiform, Onlooker, Prescience, Prophet, Sage, Sibyl, Soothsayer, T(e)iresias, Witness, Zoroaster

Seesaw Bascule, Teeter(-totter), Tilt, Vacillate, Wild mare

Seethe(d) Boil, Bubble, Churn, Ferment, Simmer, Smoulder, Sod

Segment Antimere, Arthromere, Cut, Division, Gironny, Gyronny, Intron, Lacinate, Lobe, Merome, Merosome, Metamere, Part, Pig, Propodeon, Prothorax, Scliff, Share, Shie, Skliff, Somite, Split, Sternite, Syllable, Tagma, Telson, Trochanter, Urite, Uromere

Segregate, **Segregation** Apartheid, Exile, Insulate, Intern, > **ISOLATE**, Jim Crow, Seclude, Separate

Seidlitz Powder, Rochelle

Seismic Terremotive

Seismograph Tromometer

Seize, **Seizure** Angary, Apprehend, Areach, Arrest, Assume, Attach(ment), Bag, Bone, Capture, Claw, Cleek, Cly, Collar, Commandeer, Confiscate, Distrain, Distress, Extent, For(e)hent, > **GRAB**, Grip, Hend, Impound, Impress, Maverick, Na(a)m, Nab, Nap, Nim, Poind, Possess, Pot, Raid, Replevy, Rifle, Sequestrate,

Smug, Tackle, Trover, Usurp, Wingding

Seldom Infrequent, Rare, Unoften

Select(ion), **Selecting**, **Selector** Assortment, Bla(u)d, Cap, Casting, Choice, Choose, Classy, Cull, Darwinism, Discriminate, Draft, Draw, Eclectic, Edit, Elite, Excerpt, Exclusive, Extract, Favour, Garble, Inside, K, Kin, Nap, Natural, Pericope, > PICK, Pot-pourri, Prefer, Recherché, Sample, Seed, Sex, Single, Sort, Stream, Tipster, Triage, UCCA

Selenium Se, Zorgite

Self Atman, Auto, Character, Ego, Person, Psyche, Seity, Sel, Soul

Self-confidence Aplomb, Ego

Self-contained Absolute, Reticent, SC, Taciturn

Self-contradictory Absurd, Irish

Self-control, **Self-discipline** Ascesis, Encraty, Modesty, Patience, Restraint, Temper(ance)

Self-defence *see* MARTIAL (ARTS)

Self-esteem Amour-propre, Conceit, Confidence, Egoism, Pride

Self-evident Axiom, Manifest, Obvious, Patent, Truism, Truth

Self-existence Solipsism

Self-fertilisation, **Self-origination** Aseity, Autogamy

Self-governing Autonomy, Idior(r)hythmic, Kabele, Kebel, Puritanism, Swaraj

Self-help Smiles

Self-important, **Self-indulgent**, **Self-interested** Aristippus, Arrogant, Chesty, Cocky, Conceited, Immoderate, Jack-in-office, Licentious, Narcissistic, Pompous, Pragmatic, Profligate, Solipsist, Sybarite

Selfish(ness) Avaricious, Egoist, Grabby, Greedy, Hedonist, Mean, Solipsism

Selfless(ness) Non-ego, Tuism

Self-limiting Kenotic

Self-origination *see* SELF-FERTILISATION

Self-pollinating Cl(e)istogamic

Self-possession Aplomb, Composure, Cool, Nonchalant

Self-satisfied, **Self-satisfaction** Complacent, Narcissism, Smug, Tranquil

Self-service Automat, Buffet, Cafeteria, Supermarket

Self-sufficiency Absolute, Autarky, Complete

Self-taught Autodidact

Sell(er), **Selling** Apprize, Auction, Barter, Bear, Betray, Catch, Chant, Chaunt, Cope, Costermonger, Direct, Dispose, Do, Fancier, Flog, Go, Hard, Have, Hawk, Hustle, Inertia, Knock down, Market, Marketeer, Menage, Merchant, Missionary, Oligopoly, Pardoner, Peddle, Peddler, Pick-your-own, Purvey, Push, Pyramid, Rabbito(h), Realise, Rep, Retail, Ruse, Simony, Soft, Stall-man, Sugging, Switch, > TRADE, Vend

Selvage Border, Edge, Roon

Semantics General, Generative, Interpretive, Notional, Onomasiology

Semaphore Signal, Tic-tac, Wigwag

Semblance Aspect, Likeness, Sign, Verisimilitude

Semen Jis(so)m, Milt, Spunk

Semi-conductor Germanium, LED, Thryristor

Seminar(y) Class, Colloquium, Group, Theologate, Tutorial, Workshop

Semiotics Syntactics

Semi-paralysis Dyaesthesia

Semitic Accadian, Akkadian, Ammonite, Amorite, Arab, Aramaic, Canaanite, Chaldean, Geez, Jewish, Phoenician

Semitone Pycnon

Senate Council, Curia, Seanad (Eireann)

Senator Antiani, Cicero, Elder, Legislator, Solon

Send, Sent Consign, > DESPATCH, Disperse, Emit, Entrance, Issue, Launch, Mail, Order, Post, Rapt, Ship, Transmit, Transport

Send back Refer, Remand, Remit, Return

Send down Lower, Rusticate

Send up Chal(l)an, Lampoon, Promote

Senegal SN

Senescence Age

Senile, Senility Caducity, Dementia, Disoriented, Doddery, Doitit, Dotage, Eild, Eld, Gaga, Nostology, Twichild

Senior Aîné, Doyen, Elder, Father, Grecian, Mayor, Père, Primus, Superior, Upper

Senna Bladder

Senor(a) Caballero, Don(a), Hidalga, Hidalgo

Sensation(al) Acolouthite, Anoesis, Aura, Blood, Commotion, Emotion, Empfindung, Feeling, Gas, Impression, Lurid, Melodrama, Par(a)esthesia, Pyrotechnic, Shocker, Shock-horror, Showstopper, Splash, Stir, Styre, Synaesthesia, Thrill, Tingle, Vibes, Wow, Yellow

Sense, Sensual, Sensing Acumen, Aura, Carnal, Coherence, Common, Dress, ESP, Faculty, Feel, Gross, Gumption, Gustation, Hearing, Horse, Idea, Import, Instinct, Intelligence, Intuition, Lewd, Meaning, Nous, Olfactory, Palate, Perceptual, Rational, Receptor, Remote, Rumble-gumption, Rumgumption, Rum(m)el-gumption, Rum(m)le-gumption, Sight, Sixth, Slinky, Smell, Sybarite, Synesis, Taste, Touch, Voluptuary, Voluptuous, Wisdom, Wit

Senseless Absurd, Anosmia, Illogical, Inane, Mad, Numb, Stupid, Stupor, Unconscious, Unwise

Sensible Aware, Dianoetic, Down to earth, Prudent, Raisonné, Rational, Sane, Solid, Well-balanced

Sensitive, Sensitivity Algesia, Alive, Allergic, Atopy, Dainty, Delicate, Erethism, Erogenous, Hypaesthesia, Keen, Nesh, Nociceptive, Orthochromatic, Passible, Sympathetic, Tactful, Tender, Thermaesthesia, Thin-skinned, Ticklish, Touchy(-feely), Vulnerable

Sensor Detector, Palpi, Remote

Sentence(s) Assize, Bird, Carpet, Clause, Closed, Commit, Complex, Compound, Condemn, Custodial, Death, Decree(t), Deferred, Doom, Fatwah, Indeterminate, Judgement, Life, Matrix, Open, Pangram, Paragraph, Period(ic), Porridge, Predicate, Rap, Rheme, Rune, Simple, Stretch, Suspended, Swy, Tagmene, Time, Topic, Verdict, Versicle, Weigh off

Sententious Concise, Gnomic, Laconic, Pithy, Pompous, Terse

Sentiment(al), Sentimentality Byronism, Corn, Cornball, Drip, Feeling, Goo, Govey, Gucky, Gush, Hokey, Icky, Maudlin, Mawkish, Mind, Mush, Namby-pamby, Nostalgia, Opinion, Romantic, Rose-pink, Rosewater, Saccharin, Schmaltzy, Sloppy, Smoochy, Soppy, Spoony, Sugary, Tear-jerker, Traveller, Treacly, Twee, View, Weepy, Yucky

Sentry Custodian, Guard, Jaga, Picket, Sentinel, Vedette, Vidette, Watch

Separate(d), Separation, Separately Abstract, Asunder, Atmolysis, Avulsion, Comma, Compartmentalise, Cull, Cut, Decollate, Decompose, Decouple, Deduct, Deglutinate, Demarcate, Demerge, Detach, Dialyse, Diastasis, Diazeuxis, Diremption, Disally, Discerp, Disconnect, Discrete, Disjunction, Dissociate, Distance, Distinct, Disunite, Divide, Division, Divorce, Eloi(g)n, Elute, Elutriate, Esloin, Estrange, Filter, Grade, Heckle, Hive, Hyphenate, Insulate, Intervene, Isolate, Judicial, Laminate, Lease, Legal, Monosy, Part,

Particle, Peel off, Piece, Prescind, Ramify, Red(d), Rift, Scatter, Schism, Screen, Scutch, Secern, Segregate, Sequester, Sever, Several, Shed, Shore, Shorn, Sift, Sleave, Sle(i)ded, Solitary, Sort, > **SPLIT**, Steam-trap, Stream, Sunder, Sundry, Tems(e), Tmesis, Try, Twin(e), Unclasp, Unravel, Winnow, Wrench, Yandy

Sepia Cuttle, Ink

Seppuku Hara-kiri, Hari-kari

Septic Poisonous, Rotting

Septimus Small

Septum Mediastinum

Sepulchral, **Sepulchre** Bier, Cenotaph, Charnel, Crypt, Funeral, Monument, Pyramid, Tomb, Vault, Whited

Sequel After-clap, Consequence, Effect, Outcome, Suite

Sequence Agoge, Algorithm, Byte, Chronological, Continuity, Continuum, Escape, Fibonacci, Intervening, Intron, Line, Main, Order, Peptide, Polar, Program(me), Routine, Run, Seriatim, Series, Signal, Succession, Suit, Suite, Train, Vector

Sequester, **Sequestrate** Confiscate, Esloin, Esloyne, Impound, Isolate, Retire, Seclude, Separate

Sequin Paillette, Zecchino

Sequoia Redwood

Seraph Abdiel, > **ANGEL**

Serb(ian) Chetnik

Sere Arid, > **DRY**, Scorch, Wither

Serenade(r) Aubade, Charivari, Horning, Love song, Minstrel, Nocturne, Shivaree, Sing-song, Wait, Wake

Serene, **Serenity** Calm, Composed, Impassive, Placid, Repose, Sangfroid, Sedate, Smooth, > **TRANQUIL**

Serf(dom) Adscript, Bondman, Ceorl, Churl, Helot, Manred, > **SLAVE**, Thete, Thrall, Vassal, Velle(i)nage

Serge Russian, Say

Sergeant Buzfuz, Colour, Cuff, Drill, Havildar, Kite, Lance, > **NCO**, Platoon, RSM, Sarge, SL, SM, Staff, Technical, Troy

Serial Episode, Feuilleton, Heft, Livraison

Series Actinide, Actinium, Balmer, Catena, Chain, Concatenation, Continuum, Course, Cycle, Cyclus, Electromotive, Enfilade, Engrenage, En suite, Episode, Ethylene, Fibonacci, Fourier, Geometric, Gradation, Harmonic, Homologous, Lanthanide, Line, Links, Loop, Maclaurin's, Methane, Neptunium, Partwork, Power, > **PROGRESSION**, Radioactive, Rest, Routine, Rubber, Run, Sequence, Ser, Sitcom, String, Succession, Suit, Taylor's, Thorium, Time, Tone, Train, Uranium, World

Serious(ly) Critical, Earnest, Grave, Gravitas, Heavy, Important, Major, Momentous, Pensive, Sad, Serpentine, Sober, Solemn, Sombre, Staid, Straight(-faced), Very

Sermon Address, Discourse, Gatha, Homily, Lecture, Preachment, Spital

Serow Goral, Thar

Serpent(ine) Adder, Amphisbaena, Anguine, Apepi, Apophis, Asp, Aspic(k), Basilisk, Boa, Caduceus, Cockatrice, Dipsas, Firedrake, Midgard, Nagas, Ophiolite, Ouroboros, Peridotite, Retinalite, Sea-snake, Shesha, > **SNAKE**, Traitor, Uraeus, Viper, Wyvern

Serrate(d) Diprionidian, Saw, Scallop, Serried

Serum Antilymphocyte, Antitoxin, ATS, Fluid, Humoral, Opsonin, Senega

Serval Bush-cat

Servant, Serve(r) Attendant, Ayah, Batman, Bearer, Bedder, Bedmaker, Between-maid, Boot-catcher, Boots, Boy, Butler, Caddie, Chaprassi, Chuprassy, Civil, Columbine, Cook, Daily, Domestic, Dromio, Drudge, Employee, Factotum, Famulus, File, Flunkey, Footboy, Footman, Friday, Gehazi, G(h)illie, Gip, Gully, Gyp, Haiduk, Handmaid, Helot, Henchman, Heyduck, Hireling, Iras, Jack, Jack-slave, Jeames, Khansama(h), Khidmutgar, Khitmutgar, Kitchen-knave, Lackey, Lady's maid, Lazy Susan, Maid, Major-domo, Man, Man Friday, Menial, Minion, Myrmidon, Nethinim, Obedient, Page, Pantler, Person, Postman, Public, Retainer, Retinue, Scout, Scrub, Scullion, Servitor, Sewer, Skip, Slavey, Soubrette, Steward, Tapsman, Tendance, Theow, Thete, Tiger, Tweeny, Underling, Vails, Vales, Valet, Valkyrie, Varlet, Vassal, Waiter, Wash-rag, Weller

Serve, Service(s) Ace, Act, Active, Amenity, Answer, Arriage, Asperges, Assist, ATS, Attendance, Avail, Benediction, Breakfast, Candlemas, Cannonball, Ceefax®, China, Civil, Communion, Community, Complin(e), Corvée, Credo, Devotional, Dinnerset, Diplomatic, Dish, Divine, Do, Dow, Drumhead, Duty, Ecosystem, Employ, Evensong, Facility, Fault, Fee, Feudal, Fish, Foreign, Forensic, Forward, > **FUNCTION**, Further, Go, Help, Helpline, Hour, Ka(e), Kol Nidre, Let, Line, Ling, Lip, Litany, Liturgy, Mass, Mat(t)ins, Memorial, Mincha, Minister, Ministry, Missa, National, Nocturn, Nones, Oblige, Office, Oracle, Overarm, Overhaul, Pass, Pay, Personal, Pit stop, Possum, Pottery, Prime, Proper, Public, RAF, Requiem, Rite, RN, Room, Sacrament, Secret, Selective, Senior, Sext, Shacharis, Shaharith, Shuttle, Silver, Social, Sorb, Stead, Sted, Sue, Tableware, Tea, Tenebrae, Trental, Uncork, Under-arm, Use, Utility, Vespers, Wait, Waiterage, Watch-night, Worship, Yeoman('s)

Service-book Hymnal, Hymnary, Missal, Triodion

▷ **Serviceman** *may indicate* a churchman

Servile, Servility Abasement, Base, Crawling, Knee, Lickspittle, Menial, Obsequious, Slavish, Slimy, Suck-hole, Sycophantic, Truckle

Serving Helping, Heuristic, Portion

Servitude Bondage, Domination, Peonism, Slavery, Thrall, Vassalry, Yoke

Sesame Gingelly, Gingili, Grapple-plant, Jinjilli, Semsem, Tahini, Til

Session(s) Bout, Executive, Galah, Jam, Kirk, Meeting, Nightshift, Petty, Poster, Quarter, Rap, Round, Séance, Sederunt, Settle, Sitting, Term

Set(ting) (down; in; off; out; up) Activate, Adjust, Appoint, Arrange, Batch, Bent, Bezel, Boun, Brooch, Cabal, Cake, Case, Cast, Chaton, Class, Claw, Clique, Cliveden, Closed, Coagulate, Cock, Cockshy, Collection, Collet, Comp(ositor), Companion, Compose, Congeal, Context, Coterie, Couvert, Crew, Crystal, Cyclorama, Data, Dead, Decline, Decor, Detonate, Diorama, Dispose, Earnest, Earth, Environment, Establish, Explode, Film, Fit, Flagstone, Flash, Flat(s), Found, Garniture, Geal, Gel, Genome, Group, Harden, Ilk, Incut, Infinite, Jee, Jeel, Jell(y), Jet, Kit, Laid, Land, Lay, Leg, Locale, Locate, Lot, Mandelbrot, Milieu, Mise en scène, Monture, Mournival, Nest, Occident, Open, Ordered, Ordinate, Ouch, Parure, Permanent, Physique, Pitch, Place(ment), Plant, Plaste, Ply, Posed, Posit, Power, Put, Radio, Ready, Receiver, Relay, Rigid, Rooted, Rubber, Saw, Scenery, Series, Showcase, Sink, Smart, Solidify, Squad, Stand, Stationed, Stede, Stell, Stick, Stiffen, Still, Stream, Subscriber, Suit, Suite, Surround, Synchronize, Tar, Tea, Team, Teeth, Televisor, Telly, Tiffany, Till, Toilet, Trigger, Truth, Tube, Venn (diagram), Weather, Wide-screen, Yplast

Setback Bodyblow, Checkmate, Hiccup, Jolt, Relapse, Retard, Retreat, Reversal, Scarcement, Sickener, Tes, Vicissitude

Setter Cement, Comp, Dog, English, Gordon, Gundog, Irish, Pectin, Red, Smoot

Sphinx, Trend

Settle(d), **Settler**, **Settlement** Adjust, Agree, Alight, Appoint, Arrange, Ascertain, Ausgleich, Avenge, Balance, Bandobast, Bed, Bench, Boer, Borghetto, Bundobust, Bustee, Camp, Clear, Clench, Clinch, Colonial, Colonise, Colony, Compose, Compound, Compromise, Crannog, Decide, Defray, Determine, Diktat, Discharge, Dispose, Dorp, Dowry, Ekistics, Encamp, Endow, Ensconce, Entail, Establish, Expat, Faze, Feeze, Fix, Foot, Foreclose, Gravitate, Gridironer, Guilder, Habitant, Illegitimate, Informal, Jointure, Kibbutz, Land, Ledge, Light, Lyte, Manyat(t)a, Merino, Mission, Moshav, Nahal, Nest, Nestle, Oecist, Oikist, Opt, Outpost, Over, Pa(h), Pakka, Pale, Patroon, Pay, Peise, Penal, Perch, Pheazar, Pheese, Pheeze, Phese, Pilgrim, Pioneer, Placate, Planter, Populate, Port Arthur, Port Nicholson, Presidio, Pucka, Pueblo, Pukka, Rancheria, Rancherie, Readjust, Reduction, Reimburse, Remit, Reside, Resolve, Rest, Sate, Satisfaction, Secure, Sedimentary, Set fair, Shagroon, Silt, Smoot, Sofa, Soldier, Solve, Soweto, Square, State, Still, Straits, Subside, Taurus, Township, Ujamaa, Utu, Vest(ed), Viatical, Voortrekker

Settlement *may indicate* an anagram

Settler *may indicate* a coin

Set upon Assail, Attack, Sick

Seven(th) Ages, Days, Dials, Great Bear, Hebdomad, Hepta-, Hills, Magnificent, Nones, Pleiad(es), S, Sages, Seas, Septenary, Septimal, Sins, Sisters, Sleepers, Stars, Wonders, Zeta

Seventy S

Sever Amputate, Cut, Detach, Divide, Sunder

Several Divers, Many, Multiple, Some, Sundry

Severe(ly), **Severity** Acute, Bad, Caustic, Chronic, Cruel, Dour, Draconian, Drastic, Eager, Extreme, Grave, Grievous, Gruel(ling), Hard, > **HARSH**, Ill, Inclement, Morose, Penal, Rhadamanthine, Rigo(u)r, Roaring, Roundly, Serious, Sharp, Snell(y), Sore, Spartan, Stern, Strict, Swingeing

Sew(ing), **Sew up** Baste, Clinch, Cope, Embroider, Fell, Machine, Mitre, Overcast, Overlock, Run, Seam, Seel, Stitch, Tack, Whip

Sewage, **Sewer** Cesspool, Cloaca, Culvert, Dorcas, > **DRAIN**, Effluence, Jaw-box, Jaw-hole, Mimi, Needle, Privy, Shore, Soil, Sough, Soughing-tile, Waste

Sex(y) Bed-hopping, Coupling, Cunnilingus, Erotic, Fair, Favours, Fellatio, Female, Foreplay, Fornication, French, Gam(ic), Gamahuche, Gamaruche, Gender, Hanky-panky, Hump, Incest, Intercourse, Kind, Libidinous, Libido, Lingam, Lumber, Male, Mate, Nookie, Oomph, Opposite, Oral, Paedophilia, Pederasty, Phat, Priapean, Race, Randy, Raunchy, Rut(ish), Safe, Salacious, Screw, Sect, Steamy, Sultry, Teledildonics, Troilism, Unprotected, Venereal, Venery, VI, Voluptuous, Weaker

Sex appeal It, Oomph, SA

Sexcentenarian Shem

Sexless Agamogenetic, Atoke, N, Neuter

Sextet Over, Six

Sexton Blake, Fossor, Sacristan, Shammes, Warden

Seychelles SY

Sh P, Quiet

Shabby Base, Buckeen, Dog-eared, Down-at-heel, Fusc(ous), Grotty, Mangy, Mean, Moth-eaten, Oobit, Oorie, Oubit, Ourie, Outworn, Owrie, Raunch, Scaly, Scruffy, Seedy, Shoddy, Squalid, Tacky, Tatty, Worn, Woubit

Shack Heap, Hideout, Hovel, Hut

Shackle(s) Bilboes, Bind, Bracelet, Chain, Entrammel, Fetter(lock), Gyve,

Hamper, Irons, Manacle, Restrict, Tie, Trammel, Yoke

Shad Allice, Allis, Fish, Twait(e)

Shaddock Grapefruit, Pomelo

Shade(d), Shades, Shading, Shadow, Shady Adumbrate, Arbour, Arcade, Awning, Blend, Blind, Bongrace, Bowery, Brise-soleil, Brocken spectre, Buff, Cast, Chiaroscuro, Chroma, Cloche, Cloud, Cross-hatch, Degree, Dis, Dog, Dubious, Eclipse, Eye, Five o'clock, Galanty, Gamp, Ghost, Gradate, Gray, Hachure, Hell, Herbar, Hint, Hue, Inumbrate, Larva, Lee, Melt, Mezzotint, Nuance, Opaque, Overtone, Parasol, Phantom, Presence, Rain, Ray-Bans®, Satellite, Screen, Shroud, Sienna, Silhouette, Silvan, Skia-, Soften, Spectre, Spirit, Stag, Sunglasses, Swale, Swaly, Tail, Tinge, Tint, Tone, Ugly, Umbra(tile), Umbrage(ous), Underhand, Velamen, Velar(ium), Velum, Visor

Shadowless Ascian

Shaft(ed), Shafting Arbor, Arrow, Axle tree, Barb, Barrow-train, Beam, Capstan, Cardan, Chimney, Column, Crank, Cue, Diaphysis, Disselboom, Dolly, Drive, Fil(l), Fust, Idler, Incline, Journal, Lamphole, Limber, Loom, Mandrel, Mandril, Manhole, Moon pool, Moulin, Parthian, Passage, Pile, Pit, Pitch, Pole, Propeller, Quill (drive), Ray, Scape, Scapus, Shank, Snead, Spindle, Staff, Stairwell, Stale, Steal(e), Steel, Stele, Stem, Stulm, Sunbeam, Thill, Tige, Trave, Upcast, Well, Winning, Winze

Shag Cronet, Hair, Intercourse, Nap, Pile, Scart(h), Skart(h), Tire, Tobacco

Shaggy Ainu, Comate, Hairy, Hearie, Hirsute, Horrid, Horror, Nappy, Rough, Rugged, Shock, Shough, Tatty, Untidy

Shah Ruler, Sophi, Sophy

Shake(n), Shakes, Shaky Ague(-fit), Astonish, Brandish, Coggle, Concuss, Dabble, Dick(e)y, Didder, Dither, Dodder, > **DT'S**, Feeble, Groggy, Hod, Hotch, Jar, Jiggle, Joggle, Jolt, Jounce, Judder, Jumble, Milk, Mo, Nid-nod, Press flesh, Quake, Quiver, Quooke, Rattle, Rickety, Rickle, > **ROCK**, Rouse, Shimmer, Shiver, Shock, Shog, Shoogle, Shudder, Succuss(ation), Sweat, Tremble, Tremolo, Tremor, Tremulous, Trill(o), Tumbledown, Undulate, Vibrate, Vibrato, Wag, Waggle, Wind, Wobble, Wonky

▷ **Shake** *may indicate* an anagram

Shakedown Blackmail, Chantage, Pallet

Shakespeare Bard, Will, WS

Shale Blaes, Fa(i)kes, Kerogen, Rock, Till, Torbanite

Shall Sal

Shallot C(h)ibol, Onion, Scallion, Sybo(e), Sybow

Shallow(s) Ebb, Flat, Fleet, Flew, Flue, Justice, Neritic, Shoal, Slight, Superficial

Sham Apocryphal, Bluff, Bogus, Braide, Charade, Counterfeit, Deceit, Fake, > **FALSE**, Hoax, Idol, Impostor, Mimic, Mock, Phony, Pinchbeck, Postiche, Potemkin, Pretence, Pseudo, Repro, Simulated, Snide, Spurious

Shamble(s) Abattoir, Bauchle, Butchery, Mess, Shuffle, Totter, Tripple

Shame(ful), Shame-faced Abash, Aidos, Chagrin, Contempt, Crying, Degrade, Discredit, Disgrace, Dishonour, Embarrass, Fi donc, Fie, Gross, Hangdog, Honi, Humiliate, Ignominy, Infamy, Inglorious, Modesty, Mortify, Pity, Pudency, Pudor, Pugh, Shend, Sin, Slander, Stain, Stigma, Yshend

Shameless Audacious, Brash, Immodest, Ithyphallic

Shampoo(ing) Massage, Tripsis, Wash

Shandy Drink, Sterne, Tristram

Shanghai Abduct, Kidnap, Trick

Shank Leg, Shaft, Steal(e), Steel, Steil, Stele, Strike

Shanty, Shanty town Boatsong, Bothy, Bustee, Cabin, Dog-hole, Favela,

Forebitter, Hutment, Lean-to, Pondok, Sea, Shack, Song

Shape(d), Shapely, Shaping Blancmange, Boast, Bruting, Cast, Contour, Face, Fashion, Figure, Form, Format, Geoid, Gnomon, Headquarters, Hew, Holohedron, Jello, Model, Morph, > MOULD, Net, Pendentive, Ream, Rhomb(us), Scabble, Sculpt, Spile, Tromino, Turn, Whittle, Wrought, Zaftig, Zoftig

Shapeless Amorphous, Chaos, Dumpy, Indigest, Vague

Shard Fragment, Sliver, Splinter

Share(d), Shares, Sharing Allocation, Allotment, Apportion, Blue-chip, Bovate, Cahoots, Chop, Co, Cohabit, Coho(e), Common, Communal, Contango, Culter, Cut, Deferred, Divi(dend), Divide, Divvy, Dole, Dutch, Equity, Finger, Golden, Impart, Interest, Job, Kaffer, Kaf(f)ir, Kangaroo, Lion's, Market, Moiety, Odd lot, Ordinary, Oxgang, Oxgate, Oxland, Parcener, > PART, Partake, Participate, Penny, PIBS, Plough, Plough-iron, Portion, Prebend, Pref(erred), Preference, Pro rata, Prorate, Quarter, Quota, Rake off, Ration, Rug, Rundale, Scrip, Security, Shr, Slice, Snack, Snap, Sock, Split, Stock, Taurus, Teene, Time, Tranche, Two-way, Whack

Shareholder Stag

Shark Angel, Basking, Beagle, Blue, Bluepointer, Bonnethead, Bronze-whaler, Carpet, Cestracion, Cow, Demoiselle, Dog(fish), Flake, Fox, Gummy, Hammerhead, Houndfish, Huss, Lemonfish, Loan, Mackerel, Mako, Miller's dog, Monkfish, Noah, Nurse, Penny-dog, Plagiostomi, Porbeagle, Requiem, Rhin(e)odon, Rigg, Sail-fish, Saw, School, Sea-ape, Sea-lawyer, Sharp, Shovelhead, Smoothhound, Soupfin, Squaloid, Swindler, Thrasher, Thresher, Tiger, Tope, Usurer, Whale, Wobbegong, Zygaena

Sharkskin Shagreen

Sharp(er), Sharpen(er), Sharpness Abrupt, Accidental, Acerose, Acidulous, Acrid, Aculeus, Acumen, Acuminate, Acute, Alert, Angular, Arris, Bateless, Becky, Benchstone, Bitter, Brisk, Cacuminous, Cheat, Clear, Coticular, Cutting, Dital, Edge(r), Fine, Fly, Gleg, Grind, Hone, Hot, Keen, Kurtosis, Massé, Oilstone, Penetrant, Peracute, Piquant, Poignant, Pronto, Pungent, Razor, Rogue, Rook, Set, Shrewd, Snap, Snell, Sour, Spicate, Strop, Swindler, Tart, Testy, Tomium, Twenty-twenty, Vivid, Volable, Whet

Sharpshooter Bersaglier, Franc-tireur, Sniper, Tirailleur, Voltigeur

Shatter(ing) Astone, Break, Brisance, Craze, Dash, Explode, Shiver, Smash, Smithereen, Splinter, Unnerve

Shave(r), Shaving(s) Barb(er), Excelsior, Filings, Flake, Grain, Moslings, Pare, Plane, Pogonotomy, Poll, Raze, Scrape, Skive, Sliver, Splinter, Swarf, Todd, Tonsure, Whittle

Shaw Artie, Green, Spinn(e)y, Wood

Shawl Afghan, Buibui, Cashmere, Chuddah, Chuddar, Dopatta, Dupatta, Fichu, India, Kaffiyeh, Kashmir, Mantilla, Maud, Paisley, Partlet, Prayer, Serape, Stole, Tallis, Tallit(ot), Tallith, Tonnag, Tozie, Tribon, Whittle, Wrap(per), Zephyr

She A, Hoo

Sheaf Aplustre, Bundle, Folder, Gait, Garb(e), Gerbe, Mow, Shock, Thr(e)ave

Shear(s), Shearer Clip, Cut, Fleece, Greasy, Pinking, Poll, Ring(er), Shave, Snips, Trim, Wind

Sheath Axolemma, Capsule, Case, Cocoon, Coleorhiza, Condom, Cover, Extine, Fingerstall, Glume, Medullary, Myelin, Neurilemma, Neurolemma, Oc(h)rea, Perineurium, Periosteum, Quiver, Rhinotheca, Root, Scabbard, Spathe, Thecal, Thumbstall, Vagina, Volva, Wing

Sheave Bee, Clevis

Shed(ding), Shedder Autotomy, Barn, Cast, Cho(u)ltry, Coducity, Depot, Discard, Doff, Drop, Ecdysis, Effuse, Emit, Exuviate, Hangar, Hovel, Hut, Infuse, Lair, Lean-to, Linhay, Linny, Mew, Milking, Moult, Outhouse, Pent, Potting, Salmon, Shearing, Shippen, Shippon, Shuck, Skeo, Skillion, Skio, Slough, Sow, Spend, Spent, Spill, Tilt, Tool

Sheen Glaze, Gloss, Luminance, Lustre, Patina, Schiller, Shine

Sheep(ish) Ammon, Ancon(es), Aoudad, Argali, Barbary, Bell(wether), Bharal, Bident, Bighorn, Black, Blackface, Blate, Border Leicester, Broadtail, Burhel, Burrel(l), Caracul, Cheviots, Coopworth, Corriedale, Cotswold, Coy, Crone, Dinmont, Dorset Down, Dorset Horn, Down, Drysdale, Embarrassed, Ewe, Exmoor, Fank, Fat-tailed, Flock, Fold, Hair, Hampshire, Hampshire Down, Hangdog, Herdwick, Hidder, Hirsel, Hog(g), Hogget, Jacob, Jemmy, Jumbuck, Karakul, Kent, Kerry Hill, Lamb, Lanigerous, Leicester, Lincoln, Lo(a)ghtan, Loghtyn, Lonk, Marco Polo, Masham, Merino, Mor(t)ling, Mouf(f)lon, Mountain, Muflon, Mug, Mus(i)mon, Mutton, Oorial, Ovine, Oxford Down, Perendale, Portland, Ram, Rambouillet, Romeldale, Romney Marsh, Rosella, Ryeland, Scottish Blackface, Shearling, Shorthorn, > SHY, Soay, Southdown, Spanish, Stone('s), Suffolk, Sumph, Swaledale, Teeswater, Teg(g), Texel, Theave, Trip, Tup, Two-tooth, Udad, Urial, Vegetable, Welsh Mountain, Wensleydale, Wether, Wiltshire Horn, Woollyback, Yow(e), Yowie

Sheep disease Blue tongue, Braxy, Dunt, Gid, Hoove, Louping-ill, Orf, Rubbers, Scrapie, Sturdy, Swayback, Variola, Water-brain, Wildfire, Wind

Sheepdog Collie, Huntaway, Maremma

Sheepfold Fank, Pen

Sheepskin Basan, Caracul, Karakul, Mouton, Roan, Wool

Sheeptrack Terracette

Sheer Absolute, Clear, Main, Mere, Peekaboo, Plumb, Precipitous, Pure, Simple, Stark, Steep, Swerve, Thin, Utter

Sheet(s), Sheeting Balance, Cellophane, Cere-cloth, Cerement, Charge, Chart, Clean, Crime, Cutch, Dope, Expanse, Film, Flow, Fly, Folio, Foolscap, Heft, Ice, Inset, Leaf, Membrane, Nappe, Out-hauler, Page, Pot(t), Pour, Proof, Prospectus, Ream, Rope, Sail, Scandal, Scratch, Shroud, Stern, Stratus, Taggers, Tarpaulin(g), Tear, Tentorium, Terne, Thunder, Time, Title, Web, White, Winding

Sheet-anchor Letter-weight, Paperweight

Sheet-iron Taggers, Terne(plate)

Sheikdom Bahrein, Dubai

Shekel Mina, Sickle

Sheldrake Bergander

Shelf, Shelve(s) Bank, Bar, Bracket, Continental, Counter, Credence, Delay, Dresser, Étagère, Hob, Ice, Ledge, Leeboard, Mantle, Overmantel, Postpone, Rack, Retable, Ross Ice, Shunt, Sidetrack, Sill, Spinsterhood, Whatnot, Windowsill

Shell(ed), Shellfish Abalone, Acorn-shell, Admiral, Ambulacrum, Ammo, Argonaut, Balamnite, Balanus, Balmain bug, Bivalve, Blitz, Boat, Bombard, Buckie, Camera, Capiz, Capsid, Carapace, Cartridge, Casing, Chank, Chelonia, Chitin, Clam, Clio, Coat-of-mail, Cochlea, Cockle, Cohog, Conch, Cone, Copepoda, Cover, Cowrie, Cowry, Crab, Crustacea, Cuttlefish, Dariole, Deerhorn, Dentalium, Dop, Drill, Electron, Escallop, Eugarie, Foraminifer, Framework, Frustule, Globigerina, Haliotis, Hull, Husk, Hyoplastron, Isopoda, Lamp, Langouste, Limacel, Limpet, Lobster, Lorica, Lyre, Malacostraca,

Midas's ear, Mollusc, Monocoque, Moreton Bay bug, Mother-of-pearl, Murex, Music, Mussel, Nacre, Nautilus, Ormer, Ostracod, Ostrea, Otter, Oyster, Paua, Pawa, Peag, Peak, Pea(s)cod, Pecten, Pereia, Periostracum, Periwinkle, Pipi, Pipsqueak, Plastron, Pod, Prawn, Projectile, Purple, Putamen, Quahog, Razor, Sal, Scalarium, Scallop, Scollop, Sea-ear, Sea-pen, Shale, Shard, Sheal, Sheel, Shiel, Shill, Shock, Shot, Shrapnel, Shrimp, Shuck, Sial, Smoke-ball, Spend, Spindle, Star, Stomatopod, Stonk, Straddle, Strafe, Stromb(us), Swan-mussel, Tear, Test(a), Thermidor, Toheroa, Tooth, Top, Torpedo, Trivalve, Turbo, Turritella, Tusk, Univalve, Valency, Venus, Wakiki, Wampum, Whelk, Whiz(z)bang, Winkle, Xenophya, Yabbie, Yabby, Zimbi

Shelled Cracked, Kernel

Shelled *may indicate* an anagram

Shell money Wakiki, Wampum, Zimbi

Shelter Abri, Anderson, Asylum, Awn, Awning, Belee, Bender, Bield, Billet, Blind, Blockhouse, Booth, Bunker, Burladero, Butt, Cab, Carport, Casemate, Cot(e), Cove, Covert, Coverture, Defence, Dodger, Donga, Dripstone, Dug-out, Fall-out, Garage, Gunyah, Harbour, Haven, Hithe, Hospice, Hostel, House, Hovel, Humpy, Hut, Hutchie, Kipsie, Lee, Lee-gage, Loun, Lound, Lown, Lownd, Mai mai, Mission, Morrison, Nodehouse, > **REFUGE**, Retreat, Roof, Sanctuary, Scog, Sconce, Scoog, Scoug, Screen, Scug, Shed, Shiel(ing), Shroud, Skug, Snowshed, Stell, Storm-cellar, Succah, Sukkah, Summerhouse, Tax, Tent, Testudo, Tortoise, Tupik, Twigloo, Umbrage, Weather, Wheelhouse, Wi(c)kiup, Wickyup, Wil(t)ja, Windbreak

Shemozzle Debacle

Shenanigan Antic

Shepherd(ess) Abel, Acis, Amaryllis, Amos, Bergère, Bo-peep, Chloe, Clorin, Conduct, Corin, Corydon, Cuddy, Daphnis, Dorcas, Drover, Endymion, Escort, Ettrick, German, Good, Grubbinol, Gyges, Herdsman, Hobbinol, Lindor, Marshal, Menalcas, Padre, Pastor(al), Pastorella, Phebe, Sheepo, Strephon, Tar-box, Thenot, Thyrsis, Tityrus

Sheriff Bailiff, Deputy, Earp, Grieve, Land-dros(t), Lawman, Process-server, Shireman, Shirra, Shrievalty, Viscount

Sherry Amoroso, Bristol milk, Cobbler, Cyprus, Doctor, Fino, Gladstone, Jerez, Manzanilla, Oloroso, Palo cortado, Sack, Solera, Whitewash, Xeres

Sherwood Anderson, Forest

Shibboleth Password

Shield(s), **Shield-shaped** Ablator, Achievement, Aegis, Ancile, Armour, Arms, Baltic, Biological, Bodyguard, Box, Buckler, Canadian, Cartouche, Clypeus, Defend, Dress, Escutcheon, Fence, Gobo, Guard, Gyron, Hatchment, Heat, Hielaman, Insulate, Laurentian, Lozenge, Mant(e)let, Mask, Pavis(e), Pelta, Protect, Ranfurly, Riot, Rondache, Scandinavian, Screen, Scute, Scutum, Sheffield, Sternite, Targe(t), Thyroid, Vair, Visor

Shift(er), **Shifty** Amove, Astatic, Back, Blue, Budge, Change, Chemise, Core, Cymar, Day, Devious, Displace, Dogwatch, Doppler, Einstein, Evasive, Expedient, Fend, Function, Graveyard, Great Vowel, Hedging, Lamb, Landslide, Linen, Louche, Move, Night, Nighty, Paradigm, Red, Relay, Remove, Rota, Ruse, Scorch, Sell, Shirt, Shovel, Shunt, Simar(re), Slicker, Slip(pery), Sound, Spell, Split, Stagehand, Stick, Stint, Swing, Tour, Transfer, Tunic, Turn, Vary, Veer, Warp

Shift(ing) *may indicate* an anagram

Shilling Bob, Deaner, Falkiner, Hog, King's, Queen's, S, Teston

Shilly-shally Whittie-whattie

Shimmer(ing) Chatoyant, Glint, Glitter, Iridescence, Shine
▷ **Shimmering** *may indicate* an anagram
Shin Clamber, Climb, Cnemial, Leg, Shank, Skink, Swarm
Shindig, Shindy Bobbery, Row, Rumpus, Shivoo, Uproar
Shine(r), Shining, Shiny Aglow, Beam, Bright, Buff, Burnish, Deneb, Effulge, Excel, Flash, Gleam, Glimmer, Glisten, Glitzy, Gloss, > GLOW, Irradiant, Japan, > LAMP, Leam, Leme, Lucent, Luminous, Lustre, Mouse, Nitid, Phosphoresce, Polish, Radiator, Refulgent, Relucent, Resplend, Rutilant, Skyre, Sleek, Twinkle, Varnish
Shingle(s), Shingly Beach, Chesil, Cut, Dartre, Dartrous, Gravel, Herpes, Herpetic, Shake, Shale, Stone, Zona, Zoster
Shinpad Greave
Shinty Caman, Camanachd
▷ **Shiny** *may indicate* a star
Ship(ping) Boat, Container, Convoy, Cruiser, > DISPATCH, Embark, Export, Flagship, Flatboat, Her, Hulk, Jolly, Keel, Man, Marine, MV, Post, Privateer, Prize, Prow, Raft, Ram, Sail, Saique, She, Smack, SS, Tall, Transport, Tub, Vessel, Victualling, Weather

● **SHIPS**

1 letter:	Long	Laker	6 letters:
Q	Nina	Liner	Argosy
	Pink	Moses	Banker
2 letters:	Pont	Oiler	Barque
PT	Pram	Pinky	Bateau
	Prau	Pinto	Bawley
3 letters:	Proa	Plate	Beagle
Ark	Ro-ro	Praam	Bethel
Cat	Saic	Prore	Bireme
Cog	Scow	Pucan	Borley
Dow	Snow	Razee	Bounty
Fly	Tern	Rover	Caique
Hoy	Trow	Sabot	Carack
Kit	Yawl	Scoot	Carvel
Red	Zulu	Screw	Castle
		Scull	Coaler
4 letters:	5 letters:	Shell	Cobble
Argo	Aviso	Skiff	Codder
Bark	Barge	Slave	Cooper
Brig	Broke	Sloop	Crayer
Buss	Camel	Tramp	Curagh
Cock	Canoe	Troop	Cutter
Cott	Coble	U-boat	Decker
Dhow	Coper	Umiak	Dingey
Dory	Crare	Wager	Dinghy
Duck	Dandy	Whiff	Dogger
Fire	Dingy	Xebec	Droger
Flat	Drake	Yacht	Dromon
Grab	Ferry	Zabra	Drover
Isis	Funny	Zebec	Dugout
Koff	Ketch		Flying

Frigot
Galiot
Galley
Gay-you
Goldie
Hooker
Howker
Jigger
Launch
Lorcha
Lugger
Masula
Monkey
Mother
Nuggar
Packet
Pedalo
Pequod
Pinkie
Pirate
Pitpan
Pulwar
Puteli
Randan
Sampan
Sandal
School
Schuit
Schuyt
Settee
Slaver
Tanker
Tartan
Tender
Tonner
Torpid
Trader
Trek-ox
Turret
Whaler
Wherry
Zebeck

7 letters:
Belfast
Bidarka
Bumboat
Capital
Caravel
Carrack
Carract
Carrect

Catboat
Clipper
Coaster
Collier
Coracle
Counter
Currach
Curragh
Dredger
Drifter
Drogher
Dromond
Factory
Felucca
Flattop
Flyboat
Frigate
Gabbard
Gabbart
Galleon
Galliot
Galloon
Geordie
Gondola
Gunboat
Jetfoil
Kontiki
Liberty
Lymphad
Masoola
Mistico
Monitor
Mudscow
Oomiack
Patamar
Pelican
Pinnace
Piragua
Pirogue
Polacca
Polacre
Pontoon
Revenge
Sculler
Shallop
Sharpie
Steamer
Stew-can
Tartane
Titanic
Trawler
Trireme

Tugboat
Vedette
Victory
Vidette

8 letters:
Acapulco
Bilander
Billyboy
Cabotage
Corocore
Corocoro
Corvette
Dahabieh
Faldboat
Foldboat
Galleass
Galliass
Gallivat
Hoveller
Indiaman
Ironclad
Longboat
Longship
Mackinaw
Mary Rose
Masoolah
Merchant
Monohull
Mosquito
Pinafore
Savannah
Schooner
Shanghai
Showboat
Training

9 letters:
Bucentaur
Catamaran
Cutty Sark
Dahabeeah
Dahabiyah
Dahabiyeh
Dromedary
First-rate
Freighter
Frigatoon
Hydrofoil
Klondiker
Klondyker
Lapstrake

Lapstreak
Leviathan
Lightship
Mayflower
Minelayer
Monoxylon
Multihull
Outrigger
Peter-boat
Shear-hulk
Sheer-hulk
Steamboat
Submarine
Vaporetto
Whale-back
Whaleboat

10 letters:
Brigantine
Golden Hind
Hydroplane
Icebreaker
Knockabout
Mine-hunter
Paddleboat
Quadrireme
Santa Maria
Trekschuit
Triaconter
Windjammer

11 letters:
Barquentine
Bellerophon
Berthon-boat
Cockleshell
Dreadnought
Merchantman
Minesweeper
Pentaconter
Quinquereme
Side-wheeler
Skidbladnir
Submersible
Supertanker
Three-decker
Three-master
Torpedo boat

12 letters:
East Indiaman
Fore-and-after

- Great Eastern
- Marie Celeste

Stern-wheeler
Tangle-netter

13 letters:
Paddle steamer

14 letters:
Ocean greyhound

Shipmate Crew, Hearty, Sailor
Shipping line P and O
Ship's biscuit Dandyfunk, Dunderfunk
Shipshape Apple-pie, Neat, Orderly, Tidy, Trim
Shipwreck Split
Shire County
Shirk(er) Cuthbert, Dodge, Embusqué, Evade, Funk, Malinger, Mike, Pike, Poler, Scrimshank, Skive, Skrimshank, Slack, Soldier
Shirt Black, Boiled, Brown, Bush, Calypso, Camese, Camise, Chemise, Choli, Cilice, Dasheki, Dashiki, Dick(e)y, Dress, Fiesta, Garibaldi, Grandad, Hair, Hawaiian, Hoodie, Jacky Howe, Kaftan, Kaross, K(h)urta, Nessus, Non-iron, Parka, Partlet, Polo, Red, Safari, Sark, Serk, Shift, Smock, Sports, Stuffed, Subucula, Swan(n)dri®, Sweat, T
Shiva Destroyer
Shiver(ing), **Shivers**, **Shivery** Aguish, Break, Chitter, Crumble, Dash, Dither, Fragile, Frisson, Grew, Grue, Malaria, Nither, Oorie, Ourie, Owrie, Quake, Quiver, > **SHAKE**, Shatter, Shrug, Shudder, Smash, Smither, Smithereens, Splinter, Timbers, Tremble
▷ **Shiver(ed)** *may indicate* an anagram
Shoal Bar, Fish, Quantity, Reef, Run, School, Shallows, Shelf, Tail
Shock(ed), **Shocker**, **Shocking** Acoustic, Aghast, Agitate, Anaphylactic, Appal, Astound, Astun, Awhape, Bombshell, Brunt, Bunch, Consternate, Culture, Defibrillate, Disgust, Dorlach, Dreadful, Drop, Earthquake, ECT, Egregious, Electric, Epatant, Epiphenomenon, Fleg, Floccus, Forelock, Gait, Galvanism, Gobsmack, Hair, Horrify, Impact, Infamous, Insulin, Jar, Jolt, Live, Mane, Mop, Outrage, Poleaxe, Putrid, Recoil, Return, Revolt, Rick(er), Scandal(ise), Seismic, Shaghaired, Shake, Sheaf, Shell, Shilling, Shook, Stagger, Start(le), Stitch, Stook, Stound, Stun, Thermal, Trauma, Turn
Shock-absorber Buffer, Oleo, Snubber
▷ **Shocked** *may indicate* an anagram
Shod Calced
Shoddy Cagmag, Catchpenny, Cheap, Cheapjack, Cheapo, Cloth, Cowboy, Drecky, Gimcrack, Imitation, Oorie, Ourie, Owrie, Rag-wool, Ropy, Schlock, > **SHABBY**, Tatty, Tawdry, Tinny
Shoe(s) Accessory, Arctic, Athletic, Ballet, Balmoral, Bauchle, Blocked, Boat, Boot, Brake, Brogan, Brogue, Brothel creepers, Buskin, Calceate, Calk(er), Calkin, Casuals, Caulker, Cawker, Charlier, Chaussures, Chopin(e), Clodhopper, Clog, Co-respondent, Court, Creeper, Dap, Deck, Espadrille, Flattie, Galoche, Galosh, Gatty, Geta, Ghillie, Golosh, Gumshoe, Gym, High-low, High tops, Hot, Hush-puppies®, Jandal®, Jellies, Kletterschue, Kurdaitcha, Launch(ing), Loafer, Mary-Janes®, Mocassin, Moccasin, Muil, Mule, Open-toe, Oxford, Oxonian, Panton, Patten, Peeptoe, Pennyloafer, Pile, Plate, Plimsole, Plimsoll, Poulaine, Pump, Rivlin, Rope-soled, Rubbers, Rullion, Sabaton, Sabot, Saddle, Safety, Sandal, Sandshoe, Sannie, Scarpetto, Shauchle, Skid, Skimmer, Slingback, Slip-on, Slipper, Slip-slop, Sneaker, Snow, Sock, Soft, Solleret, Spike, Stoga, Stogy, Suede, Tackies, Takkies, Tennis, Tie, Topboot, Track, Trainer, Upper, Vamp(er), Veld-schoen, Veldskoen, Velskoen, Vibram®, Vibs, Wagon lock, Wedgie, Welt, Winkle-picker, Zori
Shoeless Barefoot, Discalced

Shoemaker Blacksmith, Clogger, Cobbler, Cordiner, Cordwainer, Cosier, Cozier, Crispi(a)n, Farrier, Gentle craft, Leprechaun, Sachs, Smith, Snob, Soutar, Souter, Sowter, Sutor

Shoe-string Cheap, Lace, Pittance

Shoe-toe Poulaine

Shoo Away, Begone, Hoosh, Off, Scat(ter), Voetsek

Shoot(er), Shooting Ack-ack, Airgun, Arrow, Bine, Bostryx, Braird, Breer, Bud, Bulbil, Catapult, Chit, Cyme, Dart(le), Delope, Discharge, Drib, Elance, Enate, Eradiate, Film, Fire, Flagellum, Germ, Germain(e), Germen, Germin(ate), Glorious twelfth, > GUN, Gunsel, Head-reach, Hurl, Imp, Layer, Limb, Loose, Offset, Photocall, Photograph, Pluff, Plug, Poot, Pop, Pot, Pout, Ramulus, Rapids, Ratoon, Riddle, Rod, Rove, Runner, Septembriser, Skeet, Snap, Snipe, Spire, Spirt, Spout, Spray, Sprout, Spurt, Spyre, Start, Stole, Stolon, Strafe, Sucker, Tellar, Teller, Tendril, Tiller, Trap, Turion, Twelfth, Twig, Udo, Vimen, Wand, Weapon, Wildfowler, Zap

Shop(s), Shopper Agency, Arcade, Atelier, Betray, Boutique, Bucket, Buy, Chain, Charity, Chippy, Closed, Coffee, Commissary, Co-op, Cop, Corner, Cut-price, Dairy, Delicatessen, Denounce, Dolly, Duddery, Duka, Duty-free, Emporium, Factory, Galleria, Gift, Grass, In bond, Inform, Luckenbooth, Machine, Mall, Mall-rat, Market, Megastore, Muffler, Off-licence, Open, Opportunity, Outlet, Parlour, Patisserie, Personal, Precinct, Print, PX, Retail, RMA, Salon, Sex, Shambles, Share, Shebang, Spaza, Squat, > STORE, Studio, Sundry, Superette, Supermarket, Superstore, Swap, Tally, Tea, Thrift, Tommy, Tuck, Union, Vintry, Warehouse, Works

Shopkeeper British, Butcher, Chemist, Clothier, Gombeen-man, Greengrocer, Grocer, Haberdasher, Hosier, Ironmonger, Merchant, Newsagent, Provisioner, Retailer, Stationer, Tradesman

Shoplift(er) Boost, Heist

Shore Bank, Beach, Buttress, Coast, Coastline, Coste, Eustatic, Foreside, Landfall, Littoral, Offing, Prop, Rance, Rivage, Saxon, Seaboard, Strand, Strandline, Support

Short(en), Shortly Abbreviate, Abridge, Abrupt, Anon, Apocope, Brief, Brusque, Commons, Compendious, Concise, Contract, Crisp, Cross, Curt, Curtail, Curtal, Diminish, Drink, Eftsoons, Epitomise, Ere-long, Fubsy, Fuse, Inadequate, Lacking, Laconical, Light, Limited, Low, Mini, Near, Nip, Nutshell, Pudsey, Punch, Pyknic, Reduce, Reef, Retrench, Scanty, Scarce, Shrift, Shy, Soon, Sparse, Spirit, Squab, Squat, Squat(ty), Staccato, Stint, Stocky, Strapped, Stubby, Succinct, Syncopate, Systole, Taciturn, Teen(s)y, Temporaneous, Terse, Tight, Tot, Towards, Transient, Wee

Shortage Dearth, Deficit, Drought, Famine, Lack, Need, Paucity, Scarcity, Sparsity, Wantage

Short circuit Varistor

Shortcoming Weakness

Shorthand Gregg, Outline, Phonographic, Pitman, Speedwriting®, Stenotypy, Tachygraphy, Tironian, Tironian notes, Triphone, Weblish

Short-headed Brachycephal

Short-lived Ephemeral, Fragile, Meson, Transitory

Shorts Bermuda, Board, Boxer, Briefs, Culottes, Cycling, Hot pants, Kaccha, Lederhosen, Plus-fours, Stubbies®, Trunks

Short-sight Myopia, Myosis

Short-winded Breathless, Concise, Puffed, Purfled, Pursy, Succinct

Shot(s) Aim, All-in, Ammo, Approach, Attempt, Backhand, Ball, Barrage,

Bisque, Blank, Blast, Bricole, Bull, Bullet, Burl, Canna, Cannonball, Cartridge, Case, Chain, Chatoyant, Chip, Cover, Crab, Crack, Daisy cutter, Dink, Dolly, Dram, Draw, Drop, Dunk, Exhausted, Forehand, Gesse, Glance, Go, Grape, Guess, Gun-stone, Hook, Jump, Langrage, Langrel, Langridge, Longjenny, Magpie, Marksman, Massé, Matte, Money, Mulligan, Multi-coloured, Noddy, Parthian, Parting, Passing, Pelican, Pellet, Penalty, Phiff, Photo, Plant, Pop, Pot, Puff, Rid, Round, Safety, Salvo, Scratch, Shy, Sighter, Silk, Six, Slam-dunk, Slap, Slice, Slug, Slung, Sped, Spell, Spent, Square cut, Stab, Still, Throw, Tonic, Tracking, Trial, Try, Turn, Volley, Warning, Wrist

Should Ought

Shoulder(-blade) Carry, Cold, Crossette, Epaule, Frozen, Hard, Hump, Omohyoid, Omoplate, Pick-a-back, Roadside, Scapula, Shouther, Soft, Spald, Spall, Spaul(d), Speal, Spule, Tote, Withers

Shout(er), Shouting Barrack, Bawl, Bellock, Bellow, Boanerges, Call, Claim, Clamour, Cry, Din, Exclaim, Geronimo, Heckle, Hey, Hoi(cks), Holla, Holla-ho(a), Holler, Hollo, Holloa, Hooch, Hosanna, Howzat, Hue, Parnell, Rah, Rant, Root, Round, Sa sa, Treat, Trumpet, Vociferate, Whoop, Yell(och), Yippee, Yoohoo, Yorp

Shove Barge, Birr, Elbow, Jostle, Push, Ram, Spoon, Thrust

Shovel Backhoe, Dustpan, Hat, Main, Peel, Power, Scoop, Shool, Spade, Steam, Trowel, Van

Show(ing), Shown, Showy Anonyma, Appearance, Aquacade, Bench, Betray, Branky, Broadcast, Brummagem, Burlesque, Cabaret, Chat, Circus, Come, Con, Cruft's, Demo(nstrate), Depict, Diorama, Display, Do, Dressy, Dumb, Effeir, Effere, Endeictic, Entertainment, Epideictic, Establish, Evince, > **EXHIBIT**, Expo, Extravaganza, Exude, Facade, Fair, Fangled, Farce, Flamboyant, Flash, Flaunt, Floor, Galanty, Game, Garish, Gaudy, Gay, Give, Glitz(y), Gloss, Horse, Indicate, Jazzy, Kismet, Light, Loud, Manifest, Matinée, Meritricious, Minstrel, Musical, Naumachy, Ostensible, Ostentatious, Pageant, Panel game, Pantomime, Parade, Patience, Performance, Phen(o), Point, Pomp, Portray, Pretence, Pride, Procession, Prog(ramme), Project, Prominence, Prove, Pseudery, Puff, Puppet, Quiz, Raree, Razzmatazz, Reality, Represent, Reveal, Revue, Road, Roll-out, Rushes, Screen, Shaw, Sight, Sitcom, Slang, Soap, Son et lumière, Specious, Spectacle, Splash, Splay, Stage, Stunt, Talk, Tamasha, Tattoo, Tawdry, Telethon, Theatrical, Three-man, Tinhorn, Unbare, Uncover, Usher, Vain, Variety, Vaudeville, Veneer, Wear, Wild west, Zarzuela

Showdown Confrontation, Crunch

Shower Douche, Exhibitor, Flurry, Hail, Indicant, Indicator, Kitchen tea, Meteor, Party, Pelt, Pepper, Precipitation, Rain, Scat, Scouther, Scowther, Skat, Skit, Snow, Spat, Spet, Spit, Splatter, Spray, Sprinkle, Ticker tape

▷ **Showers** *may indicate* an anagram

Showgirl Evita, Nanette

▷ **Showing, Shown in** *may indicate* a hidden word

Showman Bailey, Barnum, Entertainer, Goon, Impresario, Lord Mayor, MC, Ringmaster

Show-off Exhibitionist, Extrovert, Jack the lad, Peacock, Poseur, Sport, Swagger, Swank

Showpiece Flagship

Show-place Exhibition, Olympia, Pavilion, Theatre

Shrapnel Fragment, Shell, Splinter

Shred Clout, Filament, Grate, Julienne, Mammock, Mince, Mummock, Rag, Screed, Swarf, Tag, Ta(i)ver, Tatter, Thread, To-tear, Wisp

Shrew Bangsring, Banxring, Callet, Catamaran, Elephant, Fury, Hellcat, Kate, Marabunta, Nag, Otter, Pygmy, Show, Solenodon, Sondeli, Sorex, Spitfire, Squirrel, Tana, Termagant, Tree, Trull, Tupaia, Virago, Vixen, Xant(h)ippe, Yankie, Yenta

Shrewd Acute, Arch, Argute, Artful, Astucious, Astute, Callid, Canny, Clued-up, Cute, File, Gnostic, Gumptious, Hard-nosed, Judicious, Knowing, Pawky, Politic, Sagacious, Sapient(al), Wily, Wise

Shriek Cry, Scream, Scrike, Shright, Shrike, Shrill, Shritch, Skirl, Yell

Shrift Attention, Penance, Short

Shrike Bird, Butcher-bird

Shrill Argute, High, Keen, Piping, Reedy, Screech, Sharp, Skirl, Treble

Shrimp(s) Fairy, Freshwater, Krill, Mantis, Midge, Opossum, Potted, Prawn, Runt, Sand, Skeleton, Small, Spectre, Squill(a), Stomatopod

Shrine Adytum, Altar, Dagoba, Dargah, Delphi, Fatima, Feretory, Harem, Holy, Joss house, Kaaba, Marabout, Martyry, Naos, Pagoda, Reliquary, Scrine, Scryne, Stupa, Tabernacle, Temple, Tope, Vimana, Walsingham

Shrink(age), Shrinking, Shrunk Alienist, Analyst, Blanch, Blench, Boggle, Cling, Compress, Constringe, Contract, Cour, Cower, Creep, Crine, Cringe, Dare, Decrew, Depreciate, Dread, Dwindle, Flinch, Funk, Gizzen, Less, Nirl, > PSYCHIATRIST, Pycnosis, Quail, Recoil, Reduce, Sanforised, Shrivel, Shrug, Shy, Sphacelate, Timid, Violet, Wane, Wince, Wizened

Shrivel(led) Cling, Crine, Desiccate, Dry, Nirl, Parch, Scorch, Scrump, Sear, Shrink, Skrimp, Skrump, Tabid, Welk, Wither, Wizened, Writhled

Shropshire Salop

Shroud(s) Chadri, Chuddah, Chuddar, Cloak, Cloud, Conceal, Cover, Futtock, Grave-cloth, Pall, Rigging, Screen, Sheet, Sindon, Turin, Veil, Winding-sheet, Wrap

Shrub(bery) Aalii, Acacia, Alhagi, Andromeda, Aphelandra, Arboret, Arbutus, Aucuba, Azalea, Barberry, Beautybrush, Bosky, Bottlebrush, Brere, Brush, Buaze, Buazi, Buckthorn, Buddleia, Bullace, > BUSH, Camellia, Caper, Cascara, Clianthus, Cola, Coprosma, Coyotillo, Crossandra, Cytisus, Daphne, Dead-finish, Deutzia, Dogwood, Epacris, Eriostemon, Fatsia, Feijoa, Firethorn, Frangipani, Frutex, Fynbos, Gardenia, Garrya, Gorse, Guayule, Hakea, Hardhack, Hebe, Henna, Hibiscus, Hop-tree, Horizontal, Inkberry, Jaborandi, Jasmine, Jessamine, Jetbread, Jojoba, Joshua tree, Juniper, Kat, Krameria, Lantana, Laurustine, Lavender, Ledum, Lignum, Manoao, Maqui(s), Matico, Melaleuca, Mesquit, Mimosa, Mistletoe, Monte, Myrica, Myrtle, Nabk, Ninebark, Ocotillo, Olea(cea), P(a)eony, Parkleaves, Patchouli, Pittosporum, Pituri, Plant, Poinsettia, Privet, Protea, Pyracantha, Pyxie, Qat, Rhatany, Rhododendron, Rhus, Rock rose, Romneya, Rue, Ruta, Salal, Savanna(h), Savin(e), Schefflera, Senna, Shadbush, Shallon, Skimmia, Smilax, Southernwood, Spekboom, Spicebush, Steeplebush, Sumach, Supplejack, Sweetsop, Tamarisk, Tea-tree, Thyme, Titi, Toyon, Tutsan, Tutu, Undergrowth, Wahoo, Waratah, Ya(u)pon, Yupon, Zamia

Shrug Discard, Toss

Shudder(ing) Abhor, Ashake, Frisson, Grew, Grise, Grue, Horror, Jerk, Quake, Shake, Spasm, Tremble

Shuffle(d) Dodge, Drag, Hedge, Make, Mix, Palter, Permute, Redeployment, Riffle, Scuff, Shamble, Shauchle, Stack

Shuffle(d) *may indicate* an anagram

Shun Attention, Avoid, Eschew, Evade, Forbear, Ignore, Ostracise, Secede, > SPURN

Shunt Move, Shelve, Shuttle, Side-track

Shut(s), Shut (down; in; out; up) Bar, Close, Confined, Coop, Debar, Embar, Emure, Fasten, Fend, Impale, Impound, Latch, Lay-off, Lock, Rid, Scram, Seal, Shet, Slam, Spar, Steek, Telescope, Tine, To

Shutter(s) Blind, Dead-lights, Douser, Jalousie, Louvre, Persiennes, Shade

Shuttle Alternate, Commute, Drawer, Flute, Go-between, Orbiter, Shoot, Shunt, Space, Tat(t), Weave

Shy Bashful, Blate, Blench, Cast, Catapult, Chary, Coy, Deficient, Demure, Farouche, Flinch, Funk, Heave, Jerk, Jib, Laithfu', Leery, Lob, Mim, Mims(e)y, Rear, Recoil, Reserved, Reticent, Retiring, Sheepish, Shrinking, Skeigh, Start, Thraw, Throw, Timid, Tongue-tied, Toss, Try, Verecund, Violet, Willyard, Willyart, Withdrawn

Siamese, Simaese twins Chang, Eng, Seal-point, T(h)ai

Siberian Chukchi, Ostiak, Ostyak, Samo(y)ed, Tungus, Vogul, Yakut

Sibilant Hissing, Whistling

Sibling Brother, German, Kin, Sister

Sibyl Oracle, Prophetess, Seer, Soothsayer, Witch

Sicilian Sicanian, Trinacrian

Sick(en), Sickening, Sickliness, Sickly, Sickness Aegrotat, Affection, Ague, Ail, Bad, Bends, Cat, Chalky, Chunder, Colic, Crapulence, Crook, Decompression, Delicate, Disorder, Donsie, Gag, Hangover, Icky, Ill, Infection, Leisure, Maid-pale, Mal, Mawkish, Morbid, Morning, Motion, Mountain, Nauseous, Pale, Peaky, Pestilent, Pindling, Plague, Puly, Puna, Queachy, Queasy, Queechy, Radiation, Regorge, Repulsive, Retch, Serum, Shilpit, Sleeping, Soroche, Space, Spue, Squeamish, Sweating, Travel, Twee, Uncle Dick, Valetudinarian, Virus, Vomit, Wamble-cropped, Wan

Sick bay San

Sickle(-shaped) Falcate, Falx, Hook, Scythe

Side Abeam, Airs, Ally, Beam, Blind, Border, Branch, Camp, Cis-, Distaff, Edge, Effect, Eleven, English, Epistle, Ex intraque parte, Facet, Flank, Flip, Gospel, Gunnel, Hand, Hypotenuse, Iliac, Lateral, Lee(ward), Left, Off, On, OP, Pane, Part, Partisan, Party, Port, Pretension, Profile, Prompt, Rave, Reveal, Right, Rink, Silver, Slip, Spear, Starboard, Swank, > TEAM, Weak, Wind, Windward, Wing, XI

Sideboard(s) Beauf(f)et, Buffet, Cellaret, Commode, Credence, Credenza, Dresser, Whiskers

Side-effect, Side-issue Fall-out, Logograph, Logogriph, Offshoot, Secondary, Spin-off

Side-line Hobby, Lye, Siding, Spur

Side-step Crab, Dodge, Evade, Hedge, Maori, Volt

Side-track Distract, Divert, Shunt

Sidewalk Crab, Footpath, Pavement

Sideways Askance, Indirect, Laterally, Laterigrade, Oblique

Siding Alliance, Byway, Lie, Lye, Spur

Sidle Edge, Passage

Siege (work) Alamo, Beleaguer, Beset, Blockade, Gherao, Investment, Ladysmith, Leaguer, Mafeking, Obsidional, Perilous, Poliorcetic, Ravelin, Surround

Siesta Nap, Noonday, Nooning

Sieve, Sift(ing) Analyse, Bolt(er), Boult(er), Bunting, Colander, Coliform, Cribble, Cribrate, Cribrose, Cullender, Eratosthenes, Ethmoid, Filter, Molecular, Riddle, Screen, Searce, Search, Separate, Siler, Strain, Sye, Tamis,

Tammy, Tems(e), Trommel, Try, Winnow

Sigh Exhale, Heave, Lackaday, Long, Moan, Sough, Suspire, Welladay

Sight(ed) Aim, Barleycorn, Bead, Conspectuity, Eye(ful), Eyesore, Glimpse, Ken, Long, Oculated, Panoramic, Peep, Prospect, Range, Rear, Riflescope, Scene, Scotopia, Second, See, Short, Spectacle, Taish, Vane, > VIEW, Visie, Vision, Vista

Sight-screen Eyelid

Sightseer, Sightseeing Lionise, Observer, Rubberneck, Tourist, Tripper, Viewer

Sign(s), Signing, Signpost Accidental, Ache, Addition, Ale-stake, Ampassy, Ampersand, Aquarius, Archer, Aries, Arrow, Auspice, Autograph, Badge, Balance, Beck, Beckon, Board, Brand, Bull, Bush, Call, Cancer, Capricorn, Caract, Caret, Chevron, Clue, Coronis, Crab, Cross, Cue, Dactylology, Diacritic, Di(a)eresis, Diphone, Division, DS, Earmark, Emblem, Endeixis, Endorse, Endoss, Enlist, Evidence, Exit, Fascia, Fish, Gemini, Gesture, Goat, Grammalogue, Hallmark, Hamza(h), Harbinger, Hex, Hieroglyphic, Hint, Ideogram, Indian, Indicate, Indication, Indicium, Initial, Inscribe, Ivy-bush, Leo, Lexigram, Libra, Local, Logogram, Minus, Multiplication, Negative, Neume, Nod, Notice, Obelisk, Obelus, Omen, Peace, Phraseogram, Pisces, Plus, Positive, Presa, Presage, Prodromus, Radical, Ram, Rest, Rune, Sacrament, Sagittarius, Sain, Scorpio, Segno, Semeion, Shingle, Show, Sigil, Sigla, Signal, Star, Subscribe, Subtraction, Superscribe, Symbol, Symptom, Syndrome, Tag, Taurus, Tic(k)tac(k), Tilde, Titulus, Token, Trace, Triphone, Twins, Umlaut, V, Vestige, Virgo, Vital, Warning, Waymark, Word, Zodiac

Signal(ler) Alarm, Aldis lamp, Alert, Amber, Assemble, Baud, Beacon, Bell, Bleep, Bugle, Buzz, Chamade, Code, Compander, Compandor, Cone, Cue, Detonator, Diaphone, Distress, Earcon, Flag, Flagman, Flare, Flash, Fog, Gantry, Gesticulate, Gong, Griffin, Gun, Harmonic, Heliograph, Heliostat, Herald, Hooter, Horse and hattock, Icon, Important, Interrupt, Interval, Luminance, Mark, Mase, Megafog, Message, Modem, Morse, Navar, NICAM, Notation, Noted, Output, Password, Peter, Pinger, Pip, Pulsar, Radio, Renowned, Reveille, Robot, Salient, Semaphore, Semiology, Singular, Smoke, Sonogram, SOS, Spoiler, Squawk, Taps, Target, Tchick, Telegraph, Teles(e)me, Thumb, Tic(k)-tac(k), Time, Traffic, Troop, Very, Video, V-sign, Waff, Waft, Wave, Wave-off, Wigwag

Signature Alla breve, Autograph, By-line, Digital, Hand, John Hancock, John Henry, Key, Mark, Onomastic, Specimen, Subscription, Time

Signet Ring, Seal, Sigil, Sphragistics

Significance, Significant Cardinal, Consequence, Emblem, Great, Impact, Important, Indicative, Key, Magnitude, Material, Matter, Meaningful, Milestone, Moment(ous), Noted, Noteworthy, Other, Paramount, Pith, Pregnant, Salient, Special, Telling

Signify Bemean, Denote, Imply, Indicate, Intimate, Matter, > MEAN, Represent

Sign language Ameslan, Semaphore, Tic(k)tac(k)

Sikh(ism) Granth, Kaccha, Kangha, Kara, Kesh, Khalsa, Kirpan, Mazhbi, Mechanised, Nanak, (Ranjit) Singh

Silas Uncle, Wegg

Silence(r), Silent Amyclaean, Choke-pear, Clam, Clamour, Conticent, Creepmouse, Dumbstruck, Earplug, Gag, Hesychastic, Hist, Hush, Hushkit, Mim(budget), Muffler, Mum(p), Mumchance, Mute, Obmutescent, Omertà, Quench, Quiesce, > QUIET, Reticence, Shtoom, Shush, Speechless, Still, Sulky, Tace(t), Tacit(urn), Throttle, Tight-lipped, Wheesh(t), Whis(h)t

Silhouette Contour, Outline, Planform, Profile, Shadow figure, Shadowgraph, Shape, Skyline

Silica(te) Albite, Analcite, Andalusite, Chabazite, Chert, Cristobalite, Datolite, Diopside, Dioptase, Float-stone, Harmotome, Hiddenite, Humite, Iolite, Kieselguhr, Kyanite, Monticellite, Montmorillonite, Olivine, Opal, Penninite, Pinite, Rhodonite, Riebeckite, Saponite, Scapolite, Silex, Staurolite, Tridymite Tripoli, Ultrabasic, Vermiculite, Vitreous, Zeolite

Silicon Chip, Si

Silk(y), Silk screen Alamode, Atlas, Barathea, Brocade, Bur(r), Charmeuse®, Chenille, Chiffon, Cocoon, Corn, Crape, Crepe, Duchesse, Dupion, Faille, Fibroin, Filature, Filoselle, Florence, Florentine, Flosh, Floss, Flox, Foulard, Gazar, Gazzatum, Georgette, Gimp, Glossy, KC, Kincob, Lustrine, Lustring, Lutestring, Makimono, Malines, Marabou(t), Matelasse, Mercery, Moiré, Ninon, Oiled, Organza, Ottoman, Paduasoy, Parachute, Peau de soie, Pongee, Prunella, Prunelle, Prunello, Pulu, Raw, Samite, Sars(e)net, Satin, Schappe, Seal(ch), Sendal, Seric, Sericeous, Sericite, Serigraph, Shalli, Shantung, Sien-tsan, Sleave, Sleek, Sle(i)ded, Slipper satin, Smooth, Spun, Surah, Tabaret Tabby, Taffeta, Tasar, Thistledown, Tiffany, Tram, Tulle, Tussah, Tusseh, Tusser, Tussore, Vegetable, Velvet, Wild

Silkworm (eggs), Silkworm disease Bombyx, Eria, Graine, Multivoltine, Muscardine, Sericulture, Tussore

Sill Ledge, Straining, Threshold

Silly, Silliness Absurd, Anserine, Brainless, Buffer, Crass, Cuckoo, Daft, Dandy, Ditsy, Divvy, Dumb, Fatuous, Folly, Fool, Footling, Frivolous, Goopy, Goosey, Gormless, Hen-witted, Idiotic, Imbecile, Inane, Inept, Infield(er), Liminal, Mid-off, Mid-on, Mopoke, Puerile, Season, Simple, Soft(y), Spoony, > **STUPID**, Tripe, Wacky

▷ **Silly** *may indicate* relating to a sill

Silt Alluvium, Deposit, Dregs, Land, Lees, Residue, Sullage, Varve

Silver(skin) Ag, Albata, Alpac(c)a, Arg(ent), Argyria, Cardecue, Cerargyrite, Diana's tree, Free, Fulminating, German, Grey, Horn, Luna, Nickel, One-legged, Pakt(h)ong, Parcel-gilt, Pegleg, Piastre, Plate, Plateresque, Ruby, Stephanite, Sterling, Sycee, Thaler

▷ **Silver** *may indicate* a coin

Silversmith Demetrius, Lamerie, Plater

Simian Apelike, Catar(r)hine

Similar(ity) Analog(ue), Analogical, Corresponding, Equivalent, Etc, Homoeoneric, Homogeneous, Homologous, Homonym, Kindred, > **LIKE**, Parallel, Patristic, Resemblance, Samey, Suchlike

Similitude Parable

Simmer Bubble, Poach, Seethe, Stew

Simon Bolivar, Cellarer, Magus, Peter, Pure, Simple

Simper Bridle, Giggle, Smirk

Simple(r), Simplicity, Simplify, Simply Aefa(u)ld, Afa(w)ld, Arcadian, Artless, Austere, Bald, Bare, Basic, Crude, Doddle, Doric, > **EASY**, Eath(e), Elegant, ESN, Ethe, Facile, Fee, Folksy, Gomeral, Gotham, Green, Herb(alist), Herborist, Homespun, Idyllic, Incomposite, Inornate, Jaap, Japie, Mere, Moner(on), Naive(té), Naked, Niaiserie, Noddy, One-fold, Open and shut, Ordinary, Paraphrase, Pastoral, Peter, Plain, Pleon, Provincial, Pure, Reduce, Rustic, Saikless, Sapid, Semplice, Sheer, Silly, Simon, Spartan, Stupid, Tout court, Woollen

Simpleton Abderite, Airhead, Cokes, Cuckoo, Duffer, Flat, Fool, Gaby, Gomeral, Gomeril, Greenhorn, Juggins, Spoon, > **STUPID PERSON**, Wiseacre, Zany

Simulate, Simulating Affect, Anti, Feign, Pretend

Simultaneous Coinstantaneous, Contemporaneous, Synchronous, Together

Sin(ful) Aberrant, Accidie, Acedia, Actual, Anger, Avarice, Besetting, Bigamy, Covetousness, Crime, Deadly, Debt, Depravity, Envy, Err, Evil, Folly, Gluttony, Hamartiology, Harm, Hate, Impious, Lapse, Lust, Misdeed, Misdoing, Mortal, > **OFFENCE**, Original, Peccadillo, Piacular, Pride, Scape, Scarlet, Shirk, Sine, Sloth, Transgress, Trespass, Unrighteous, Venial, Vice, Wicked, Wrath, Wrong

Sinai Horeb, Mount

Since Ago, As, Meantime, Seeing, Sens, Sinsyne, Sith(en), Whereas

Sincere(ly), **Sincerity** Bona-fide, Candour, Earnest, Entire, Frank, Genuine, Heartfelt, Honest, Open, Real(ly), True, Verity, Whole-hearted

Sinclair Lewis, Upton

Sine Versed

Sinecure Bludge, Commendam

Sinew(y) Fibre, Ligament, Nerve, String, Tendinous, Tendon

Sinful *see* **SIN**

Sing(ing) Barbershop, Bel canto, Bhajan, Carol, Chant, Cheep, Chorus, Coloratura, Community, Cough, Croon, Crow, Diaphony, Diddle, Doo-wop, Glee club, Gorgia, Hum, Inform, Intone, Karaoke, Kirtan, La-la, Lilt, Melic, Parlando, Peach, Pen(n)illion, Pipe, Plainchant, Rand, Rant, Rap, Record, Render, Scat, Second(o), Solmization, Sprechgesang, Sprechstimme, Squeal, Tell, Thrum, Trill, Troll, Vocalise, Warble, Yodel

Singe Burn, Char, Scorch

Singer Alto, Balladeer, Bard, Baritone, Bass, Bing, Bird, Blondel, Callas, Canary, Cantabank, Cantatrice, Cantor, Car, Carreras, Caruso, Castrato, Chaliapin, Chanteuse, Chantor, Chazan, Cher, Chorister, Coloratura, Comprimario, Crooner, Dawson, Diva, Dylan, Ella, Falsetto, Folk, Gleemaiden, Gleeman, Grass, Haz(z)an, Heldentenor, Isaac, Kettle, Lark, Lauder, Lead, Lind, Lorelei, Lulu, Mathis, Melba, Minstrel, Oscine, Patti, Pitti, Precentor, Prima donna, Qawwal, Robeson, Session, Sinatra, Siren, Snitch, Songstress, Soprano, Soubrette, Stoolie, Succentor, Swan, Tatiana, Tenor, Torch, Treble, Troubador, Vocalist, Voice, Wait, Warbler

Single, **Singly** Ace, Aefa(u)ld, Aefawld, Alone, Azygous, Bachelor, Celibate, Discriminate, EP, Exclusive, Feme sole, Matchless, Monact, Mono, Odd, One-off, Only, Pick, Run, Sole, Solitary, Spinster, Unattached, Uncoupled, Unique, Unwed, Versal, Yin

Single-cell Protista

Single-chambered Monothalamous

Singlestick Sword

Singlet Tunic, Vest

Singular(ity) Curious, Especial, Exceptional, Extraordinary, Ferly, Naked, Odd, Once, One, Peculiar, Queer(er), Rare, > **UNIQUE**, Unusual

Singultus Hiccup

Sinister Bend, Dark, Dirke, Evil, L, Left, Lh, Louche, > **OMINOUS**

Sink(ing), **Sunken** Basin, Bog, Cadence, Carbon, Cower, Delapse, Depress, Descend, Devall, Dip, Down, Drain, Draught-house, Drink, Drop, Drown, Ebb, Flag, Founder, Gravitate, Heat, Hole, Immerse, Invest, Jawbox, Kitchen, Lagan, Laigh, Lapse, Ligan, Merger, Pad, Pot, Prolapse, Put(t), Relapse, Sag, Scupper, Scuttle, Set, Settle, Shipwreck, Slump, Steep-to, Sty, Submerge, Subside, Swag, Swamp

Sinner Evildoer, Malefactor, Offender, Reprobate, Trespasser

Sinuous Curvy, Ogee, Slinky, Snaky, Wavy, Winding

Sinus Cavity, Recess

Sip(ping) Delibate, Haporth, Libant, Sample, Sowp, Sup, Taste, Tiff(ing)

Siphon Draw, Rack, Soda, Suck, Transfer

Sir Dan, Dom, K, Knight, Kt, Lord(ing), Sahib, Signor, Sirrah, Stir, Stirra(h), Towkay, Tuan

Sire Beget, Father, Get

Siren Alarm, Alert, Diaphone, Enchanter, Femme fatale, Hooter, Houri, Leucosia, Ligea, Lorelei, Mermaid, Oceanides, Parthenope, Salamander, Teaser, Temptress, Vamp

Sirenian Dugong, Lamantin, Manatee, Manati, Sea-cow

Sirloin Backsey

Sirree Bo

Sisal Agave

Siskin Aberdevine, Bird, Finch

Sister(s) Anne, Beguine, Lay, Minim, > **NUN**, Nurse, Out, Religeuse, Sib, Sibling, Sis, Sob, Soul, Swallow, Theatre, Titty, Ursuline, Verse, Weird

Sisyphean Uphill

Sit(ter), Sitting Bestride, Clutch, Dharna, Duck, Gaper, Lit de justice, Model, MP, Perch, Pose, Reign, Represent, Roost, Séance, Sejeant, Session, Squat

Site, Siting Area, Brownfield, Building, Camp, Feng shui, Greenfield, Home-page, Location, Lot, Pad, Place, Plot, Rogue, Sacred, Silo, Spot, Stance

Situation Ballpark, Berth, Cart, Case, Catch, Catch-22, Cliff-hanger, Contretemps, Cow, Dilemma, Galère, Hole, Job, Lie, Location, Lurch, Matrix, Niche, No-win, Office, Plight, Position, Post, Scenario, Schmear, Schmeer, Set-up, Shebang, Showdown, Status quo, Sticky wicket, Strait, Where, Worst case

Six(th) Digamma, French, German, Half(-a)dozen, Hexad, Italian, Neapolitan, Prime, Senary, Sestette, Sextet, Sice, Size, Vau, VI

Six counties NI

Six days Hexa(e)meron

Six feet Fathom

Sixpence Bender, Kick, Slipper, Tanner, Tester(n), Testril(l), Tizzy, VID, VIP, Zack

Sixteen Sweet

Sixty Degree, Threescore

Size(able) Amplitude, Area, Bulk, Calibre, Countess, Demy, Displacement, > **EXTENT**, Format, Girth, Glair, Glue, Gum, Imperial, Measure, Physique, Plus, Pot(t), Princess, Proportion, Tempera, Tidy, Trim

Sizzle Fry, Hiss, Scorch

Skate(r), Skateboarder, Skating Blade, Bob, Cheap, Choctaw, Cousins, Curry, Dean, Figure, Fish, Free, Grommet, In-line, Maid, Mohawk, Rock(er), Roller, Rollerblade®, Runner, Speed

Skedaddle Shoo, Vamoose

Skein Hank, Hasp

Skeleton, Skeletal Anatomy, Atomy, Axial, Bones, Cadaverous, Cadre, Cage, Coenosteum, Corallite, Corallum, Family, Framework, Key, Ossify, Outline, Scenario, Sclere, Tentorium

Sketch(y) Cameo, Character, Charade, Croquis, Delineate, Diagram, Doodle, Draft, > **DRAW**, Ebauche, Esquisse, Illustration, Limn, Line, Maquette, Modello, Outline, Pencilling, Playlet, Pochade, Précis, Profile, Skit, Summary, Tenuous, Thumbnail, Trick, Vignette, Visual

Skew Agee, Ajee, Oblique, Sheer, Squint, Swerve, Veer

Skewer Brochette, En brochette, Prong, Spit, Transfix

Ski(ing) Aquaplane, Glide, Glissade, Hot-dog, Langlauf, Mogul, Nordic, Schuss,

Super G, Telemark, Vorlage, Wedeln

Skid Aquaplane, Drift, Jackknife, Side-slip, Slew, Slide, Slip, Slither, Spinout

Skidding *may indicate* an anagram

Skiff Canoe, Dinghy, Outrigger

Skill(ed), Skilful Ability, Able, Ace, Address, Adept, Adroit, Art, Bravura, Canny, Chic, Competence, Craft, Deacon, Deft, Dextrous, Enoch, Expertise, Facility, Feat, Finesse, Flair, Gleg, Habile, Hand, Handicraft, Handy, Hend, Hot, Ingenious, Knack, Know-how, Knowing, Lear(e), Leir, Lere, Masterly, Masterpiece, Mean, Mistery, Mystery, Mystique, Practised, Proficient, Prowess, Quant, Resource, Savvy, Science, Skeely, Sleight, Soft, Speciality, Tactics, Talent, Technic, Technique, Touch, Trade, Trick, Versed, Virtuoso

Skim Cream, Despumate, Flit, Glide, Graze, Plane, Ream, Scan, Scud, Scum, Skiff, Skitter

Skimp Restrict, Scamp, Scrimp, Stint

Skin(s) Agnail, Armour, Bark, Basan, Basil, Box-calf, Calf, Callus, Case, Cere, Chevrette, Coat, Corium, Cortex, Crackling, Cutaneous, Cuticle, Cutis, Deacon, Deer, Derm(a), Dermatome, Dermis, Dewlap, Disbark, Ectoderm, Enderon, Epicanthus, Epicarp, Epidermis, Eschar, Excoriate, Exterior, Fell, Film, Flaught, Flay, Flench, Flense, Flinch, Forel, Fourchette, Goldbeater's, Hangnail, Hide, Jacket, Kip, Kirbeh, Leather, Membrane, Muktuk, Nebris, Pachyderm, Parfleche, Peau, Peel, Pell, Pellicle, Pelt, Perinychium, Plew, Plu(e), Prepuce, Pteryla, Rack, Rape, Rind, Scalp, Scarskin, Serosa, Shell, Shoder, Spetch, Strip, Tegument, Tulchan, Veneer, Water-bouget, Wattle, Woolfell

Skin disease, Skin trouble Boba, Boil, Buba, Causalgia, Chloasma, Chloracne, Cowpox, Cradle cap, Cyanosis, Dartre, Dermatitis, Dermatosis, Dyschroa, EB, Ecthyma, Erysipelas, Exanthem(a), Favus, Flay, Framboesia, Gum rash, Herpes, Hives, Ichthyosis, Impetigo, Leishmaniasis, Lichen, Livedo, Lupus vulgaris, Mal del pinto, Mange, Miliaria, Morphew, Morula, Patagium, Pemphigus, Pinta, Pityriasis, Prurigo, Psoriasis, Pyoderma, Rash, Red-gum, Ringworm, Rosacea, Rose-rash, St Anthony's Fire, Sapego, Scabies, Sclerodermia, Scurvy, Seborrhoea, Serpigo, Strophulus, Telangiectasis, Tetter, Tinea, Vaccinia, Verruca, Verruga, Vitiligo, Xanthoma, Xerodermia, Yaws, Yawy

Skinflint Dryfist, Miser, Niggard, Pinch-gut, Scrooge, Tightwad

Skinful Drunk, Sausage

Skinhead Not, Punk, Scalp

Skink Seps

Skinny Barebone, Bony, Dermal, Emaciate, Lean, Scraggy, Thin, Weed

Skint Broke, Ghat, Penniless, Stony

Skip(ped), Skipper Boss, Caper, Captain, Cavort, Drakestone, Dumpster, Elater, Frisk, Hesperian, Jump, Jumping-mouse, Lamb, Luppen, Miss, Omit, Patroon, Ricochet, Saury, Scombresox, Spring, Tittup, Trounce(r)

Skirl Humdudgeon, Pibroch, Pipe, Screigh

Skirmish(er) Brush, Dispute, Escarmouche, Fray, Pickeer, Spar, Tirailleur, Velitation

Skirt(ing) Bases, Bell, Border, Bouffant, Cheongsam, Circle, Coat, Crinoline, Culotte(s), Dado, Dirndl, Edge, Fil(l)ibeg, Fringe, Fustanella, Fustanelle, Girl, Gore, Grass, Harem, Hobble, Hoop, Hug, Hula, Kilt, Lamboys, Lava-lava, Marge, Mini, Mopboard, Pareo, Pareu, Pencil, Peplum, Petticoat, Philibeg, Pinafore, Piu-piu, Plinth, Puffball, Ra-ra, Rim, Sarong, Sidestep, Stringboard, Tace, Tail, Taslet, Tasse(t), Tonlet, Tutu, Wrap(a)round, Wrapover

Skit Lampoon, Parody, Sketch

Skittish Coy, Curvetting, Frisky, Restless
Skittle(s) Bayle, Bowl, Kail(s), Kayle, Kingpin, Ninepin, Pin, Spare
Skive(r) Absentee, Scrimshank, Shirk
Skivvy Drudge, Slave
Skrimshank Bludge, Skive
Skulk Lurk, Mooch, Shool
Skull Bregma(ta), Calvaria, Cranium, Fontanel, Head, Malar, Maz(z)ard, Obelion, Occiput, Pannikell, Phrenology, Scalp, Sinciput
Skullcap Ya(r)mulka, Yarmulke, Zucchetto
Skunk Atoc, Atok, Hognosed, Polecat, Teledu, Zoril(lo)
Sky(-high) Air, Azure, Blue, Canopy, Carry, E-layer, Element, Empyrean, Ether, Firmament, Heaven, Lift, Loft, Mackerel, Occident, Octa, Uranus, Welkin
Sky-diver Para
Skylark Aerobatics, Bird
Skylight Abat-jour, Aurora, Comet, Lunette, Star
Skyline Horizon, Rooftops
Sky-pilot Chaplain, Vicar
Slab Briquette, Bunk, Bunk(er), Cake, Chunk, Dalle, Hawk, Ledger, Marver, Metope, Mihrab, Mud, Paving-stone, Planch, Plank, Sclate, Sheave, Slate, Slice Stela, Stelene, Tab, Tile
Slack(en), Slackness Abate, Careless, Crank, Dilatory, Dross, Ease, Easy-going, Glen, Idle, Lax(ity), Let-up, Loose, Malinger, Nerveless, Relax, Release, Remiss, Shirk, Skive, Slow, Surge, Unscrew, Veer
Slag Basic, Calx, Cinder, Dross, Scoria, Scum, Sinter, Tart
Slake Abate, Cool, Quench, Refresh, Satisfy
Slalom Super-G
Slam Crash, Criticise, Dad, Grand, Little, Pan(dy), Small, Sock, Swap, Swop, Vole, Wap
Slander(ous) Asperse, Backbite, Calumny, Defame, Derogatory, Detraction, Disparage, Libel, Malediction, Malign, Missay, Mud, Obloquy, Sclaunder, Smear, Traduce, Vilify, Vilipend
Slang Abuse, Argot, Back, Berate, Cant, Colloquial, Ebonics, Flash, Jargon, Lingo, Nadsat, Parlyaree, Polari, Rhyming, Slate, Tsotsitaal, Velan, Zowie
Slant(ed), Slanting Angle, Asklent, Atilt, Bevel, Bias, Brae, Cant, Careen, Chamfer, Clinamen, Diagonal, Escarp, Oblique, Prejudice, Slew, > **SLOPE**, Splay Squint, Talus, Tilt, Virgule
Slap Clatch, Clout, Cuff, Make-up, Pandy, Piston, Sclaff, Scud, Skelp, Smack, Spat, Tape, Twank
Slapdash Careless, Hurried, Random
Slash(ed) Chive, Cut, Gash, Hack, Jag, Lacerate, Laciniate, Leak, Oblique, Rash, Rast, Reduce, Scorch, Scotch, Separatrix, Slit, Solidus, Wee
Slat(s) Fish, Jalousie, Louvre
Slate, Slaty Cam, Countess, Credit, Criticise, Decry, Double, Duchess, Duchy, Enter, Griseous, Imperial, Killas, Knotenschiefer, Lady, Marchioness, Ottrelite Pan, Peggy, Polishing, Princess, Queen, Rag(g), Roof, Schalstein, Shingle, Slat, Small, Tomahawk, Viscountess
Slater Hellier, Insect
Slattern Bag, Besom, Drab, Drazel, Frump, Mopsy, Sloven, Slummock, Sozzle, Traipse, Trapes, Trollop
Slaughter(house), Slaughterer Abattoir, Behead, Bleed, Bloodshed, Butcher, Carnage, Decimate, Hal(l)al, Holocaust, Jhatka, Kill, Mactation, > **MASSACRE**, S(c)hechita(h), Scupper, Shambles, Shechita(h), Shochet, Smite

Slav Bohunk, Croat, Czech, Kulak, Polabian, Serb, Sorb, Wend(ic)

Slave(ry), **Slaves** Addict, Aesop, Aida, Androcles, Barracoon, Blackbird, Bond, Bond(s)man, Bondwoman, Bordar, Boy, Caliban, Coffle, Contraband, Dogsbody, Drudge, Drug, Dulocracy, Dulosis, Esne, Galley, Gibeonite, Helot, Hierodule, Mameluke, Mamluk, Marmaluke, Maroon, Minion, Odalisk, Odali(s)que, Peasant, Pr(a)edial, Rhodope, Serf, Servitude, Spartacus, Terence, Theow, Thersites, Thete, Thrall, Topsy, Vassal, Villein, Wage, White, Yoke

Slave-driver, **Slave-owner** Assam, Task-master

Slaver Bespit, Dribble, Drivel, Drool, Slobber, Spawl

Slay(er), **Slaying** Destroy, Execute, Ghazi, > KILL, Mactation, Murder, Quell, Saul, Slaughter

Sleazy Flimsy, Scuzzy, Seamy, Sordid, Squalid, Thin

Sled(ge), **Sleigh(-ride)** Bob, Dray, Hurdle, Hurly-hacket, Kibitka, Komatik, Lauf, Luge, Mud-boat, Polack, Pulk(h)(a), Pung, Skidoo®, Slipe, Stoneboat, Tarboggin, Toboggan, Train, Travois

Sleek Bright, Shine, Silky, Smarm, Smooth, Smug

Sleep, **Sleeper(s)**, **Sleepiness**, **Sleeping**, **Sleepy** Beauty, Bed, Bivouac, Blet, Car, Catnap, Coma, Couchette, Crash, Cross-sill, Cross-tie, Dormant, Dormient, Doss, Doze, Drowse, Earring, Endymion, Epimenides, Gum, Hibernate, Hypnology, Hypnos, Kip, Lethargic, Lie, Morpheus, Nap, Narcolepsy, Nod, Over, Paradoxical, Petal, Psychopannychism, REM, Repast, Repose, Rest, Rip Van Winkle, Rough, Sandman, Seven, Shuteye, Skipper, Sloom, Slumber, Snooz(l)e, Somnolent, Sopor(ose), Sownd, Swone, Tie, Torpid, Twilight, Wink, Zizz

Sleeping place Bed, Cot, Dormitory, Kang

Sleepless Wake-rife, Wauk-rife

Sleep-walking Noctambulation

Sleet Graupel, Hail

Sleeve (opening) Arm(hole), Batwing, Bishop's, Bush, Collet, Cover, Dolman, Gatefold, Gigot, Gland, Leg-o'-mutton, Liner, Magyar, Manche, Pagoda, Pudding, Querpo, Raglan, Sabot, Scye, Slashed, Trunk, Turnbuckle, Wind

Sleigh *see* SLED

Sleight Artifice, Conjury, Cunning, Dodge, Legerdemain, Trick

Slender(ness) Asthenic, Ectomorph, Elongate, Exiguity, Exility, Fine, Flagelliform, Flimsy, Gracile, Jimp, Leptosome, Loris, Narrow, Skinny, Slight, Slim, Small, Spindly, Stalky, Styloid, Svelte, Sylph, Tenuous, Trim, Waif

Sleuth Bloodhound, Detective, Dick, Eye, Lime-hound, Lyam(-hound), Lyme(-hound)

Slew Number, Skid, Slide, Twist

Slice Cantle, Chip, Collop, Cut, Doorstep, Fade, Frustrum, Piece, Rasure, Round, Sector, Segment, Share, Sheave, Shive, Slab, Sliver, Tranche, Wafer, Whang

Slice of *may indicate* a hidden word

Slick Adroit, Glim, Oil, Smooth, Suave

Slide Chute, Cursor, Diapositive, Drift, Ease, Glissando, Hair, Hirsle, Ice-run, Illapse, Lantern, Mount, Pulka, Schuss, Skid, Skite, Slip, Slippery dip, Slither, Snowboard, Transparency

Slight(ly) Affront, Belittle, Cold shoulder, Cut, Detract, Disparage, Disregard, Facer, Flimsy, Halfway, Insult, Misprise, Neglect, Nominal, Pet, Petty, Rebuff, Remote, > SLENDER, Slim, Slimsy, Slur, Small, Smattering, Sneaking, Snub, Subtle, Superficial, Sylphine, Tenuous, Thin, Tiny, Wee, Wispy

Slim Bant, Jimp, Macerate, Reduce, Slender, Slight, Sylph, Tenuous, Thin

Slime, **Slimy** Glair, Glit, Guck, Gunk, Mother, Muc(o)us, Myxomycete, Oily, Ooze, Sapropel, Slake, Sludge, Uliginous

Sling Balista, Catapult, Drink, Fling, Hang, Parbuckle, Prusik, Support, Toss, Trebuchet

Slink Lurk, Skulk, Slope

Slip(ped), **Slipping**, **Slips** Boner, Cover, Cutting, Disc, Docket, Drift, EE, Elapse, Elt, Engobe, Error, Faux pas, Fielder, Form, Freudian, Glide, Glissade, Infielder, Label, Landslide, Lapse, Lapsus linguae, Lath, Lauwine, Mistake, Muff, Nod, Oversight, Parapraxis, Petticoat, Pink, Prolapse, Ptosis, Quickset, Rejection, Relapse, Run, Scape, Sc(h)edule, Scoot, Set, Shim, Sin, Ski, Skid, Skin, Skite, Slade, Slidder, Slide, Slither, Slive, Spillican, Stumble, Surge, Ticket, Trip, Tunicle, Underskirt, Unleash, Wage(s)

Slipper(s) Baboosh, Babouche, Babuche, Baffies, Calceolate, Carpet, Eel, Japanese, Mocassin, Moccasin, Moyl, Mule, Pabouche, Pampootie, Pantable, Pantof(f)le, Panton, Pantoufle, Pump, Rullion, Runner, Ski, Sledge, Sneaker, Sock

Slippery Foxy, Glid, Icy, Lubric, Shady, Shifty, Skidpan, Slick

Slipshod Careless, Hurried, Jerry, Lax, Slapdash, Slatternly, Sloppy, Slovenly, Toboggan

▷ **Slipshod** *may indicate* an anagram

Slit Buttonhole, Cranny, Cut, Fent, Fissure, Fitchet, Gash, Gill, Loop, Pertus(at)e Placket, Placket-hole, Race, Rit, Scissure, Spare, Speld(er), Vent

Slithy Tove

Sliver Flake, Fragment, Moslings, Rove, Shaving, Slice, Splinter, Trace

Slob(ber) Drool, Lout, Slaver, Smarm, Wet

Sloe Blackthorn, Slae

Slog(ger) Drag, Strike, Swink, Swot, Traipse, Tramp, Trape, Trudge, Yacker, Yakka, Yakker

Slogan Amandla, Byword, Catchword, Jai Hind, Mot(to), Phrase, Rallying-cry, Slughorn(e), Tapline, Warcry, Watchword

Sloop Cutter, Hoy, Ship

Slop(s) Cop(per), Gardyloo, Jordeloo, Muck, Policeman, Rossers, Rozzers, Schmaltz, Sop, Spill, Swill

Slope(s), **Sloping** Acclivity, Angle, Anticline, Bahada, Bajada, Bank, Batter, Bevel, Borrow, Borstal(l), Brae, Breast, Chamfer, Cuesta, Declivity, Delve, Diagonal, Dry, Escarp, Fla(u)nch, Geanticline, Glacis, Grade, Gradient, Heel, Hill, Incline, Kant, Lean, Natural, Nursery, Oblique, Pent, Periclinal, Pitch, Rake, Ramp, Rollway, Scarp, Schuss, Scrae, Scree, Shelve, Sideling, Skewback, Slant, Slippery, Slipway, Splay, Steep, Stoss, Talus, Tilt, Verge, Versant, Weather

Sloppily, **Sloppy** Lagrimoso, Lowse, Madid, Mushy, Remiss, Schmaltzy, Slapdash, Slipshod, Sloven, Slushy, Untidy

▷ **Sloppy** *may indicate* an anagram

Slosh(y) Dowse, Fist, Splash, Wet

Slot(ted) Expansion, Graveyard, Groove, Hasp, Hesp, Hole, Key, Keyway, Mortice, Mortise, Seat, Slit, Swanmark, Time

Sloth(ful) Accidie, Acedia, Ai, Bradypus, Edentate, Ground, Idle, Inaction, Indolent, Inertia, Lazy, Lie-abed, Megatherium, Mylodon, Slugabed, Sweer(t), Sweered, Sweir(t), Three-toed, Unau

Slot machine One-armed bandit, Pokey, Pokie

Slouch Mooch, Mope, Slump

Slough(ing) Cast, Despond, Ecdysis, Eschar, Exuviae, Lerna, Marish, Marsh, Morass, Paludine, Shed, Shuck, Swamp

Sloven(ly) Careless, Dag(gy), D(r)aggle-tail, Frowsy, Grobian, Jack-hasty, Rag-doll, Ratbag, Slaister, Slammakin, Slammerkin, Slattern, Sleazy, Slipshod

Slubberdegullion, Slubberingly, Slummock, Streel, Untidy

Slow(ing), Slower, Slowly Adagio, Allargando, Andante, Brady, Brake, Broad, Calando, Crawl, Dawdle, Deliberate, Dilatory, Dull, Dumka, ESN, Flag, Gradual, Inchmeal, Lag, Langram, Larghetto, Largo, Lash, Lassu, Late, Lean-witted, Leisurely, Lentando, Lento, Lifeless, Loiter, Meno mosso, Obtuse, Pedetentous, Rall(entando), Rein, Reluctant, Retard, Ribattuta, Ritardando, Ritenuto, Slack, Slug, Sluggish, Snaily, Solid, Stem, Tardigrade, Tardive, Tardy

Slow-match Portfire

Sludge Activated, Gunge, Mire, Muck, Sapropel

Slug(s) Ammo, Bêche-de-mer, Blow, Bullet, Cosh, Drink, Limaces, Limax, Linotype®, Mollusc, Nerita, Pellet, Shot, Snail, Trepang

Sluggard Drone, Lazy, Lie-abed, Lusk, Unau

Sluggish Dilatory, Drumble, Idler, Inactive, Inert, Jacent, Lacklustre, Laesie, Languid, Lazy, Lentor, Lethargic, Lug, Phlegmatic, Saturnine, Sleepy, > SLOW, Stagnant, Tardy, Torpid, Unalive

Sluice Aboideau, Aboiteau, Drain, Gutter, Koker, Penstock, Rinse, Sasse

Slum Basti, Bustee, Busti, Cabbagetown, Ghetto, Pavela, Rookery, Shanty, Slurb, Warren

Slumber Doze, Drowse, Nap, Nod, Sleep, Sloom, Snooze

Slump Decrease, Depression, Deteriorate, Dip, Flop, Recession, Sink, Slouch

Slur(ring) Defame, Drawl, Innuendo, Libel, Opprobrium, Slight, Smear, Synaeresis, Tie

Slush Bathos, Boodle, Bribe, Drip, Money, Mush, Pap, Slop, Sposh, Swash

Slut Candle, Dollymop, Draggle-tail, Dratchell, Drazel, Floosie, Harlot, Slattern, Sow, Tart, Traipse, Trapes, Trollop

Sly Christopher, Clandestine, Coon, Covert, Cunning, Foxy, Furtive, Leery, Peery, Reynard, Shifty, Sleekit, Sleeveen, Slicker, Stealthy, Subtle, Tinker, Tod, Tricky, Weasel, Wily

Slyly *may indicate* an anagram

Smack(er) Buss, Cuff, Flavour, Foretaste, Fragrance, Hooker, Kiss, Lander, Lips, Pra(h)u, Relish, Salt, Saut, Skelp, Slap, Slat, Smatch, Smouch, Soupçon, Spank, Spice, Splat, Tack, > TANG, Taste, Thwack, Tincture, Trace, X, Yawl

Small (thing) Ateleiosis, Atom, Bantam, Beer, Bijou, Bittie, Bitty, Centesimal, Curn, Denier, Diminutive, Dinky, Drib, Elfin, Few, Fry, Grain, Haet, Ha'it, Half-pint, Handful, Holding, Insect, Ion, Leet, Lilliputian, Limited, Lite, > LITTLE, Lock, Low, Meagre, Measly, Midget, Mignon, Miniature, Minikin, Minute, Mite, Modest, Modicum, Peerie, Peewee, Petit(e), Petty, Pigmean, Pigmy, Pink(ie), Pinky, Pint-size, Pittance, Pocket, Poky, Poujadist, Rap, Reduction, Runt, S, Santilla, Scattering, Scrump, Scrunt, Scut, Shrimp, Single, Skerrick, Slight, Slim, Smattering, Smidge(o)n, Smidgin, Smithereen, Smout, Soupçon, Sprinkling, Spud, Stim, Stunted, Tad, Thin, Tidd(l)y, Tiny, Titch(y), Tittle, Tot(tie), Totty, Trace, Trivial, Unheroic, Wee, Weedy, Whit

Smallest Least, Minimal, Runt

Smallholder, Smallholding Croft, Nursery, Rundale, Share-cropper, Stead

Small-minded(ness) Parvanimity, Petty

Smallness Exiguity, Exility, Paucity

Smallpox Alastrim, Variola

Smarm(y) Oil, Smoothie, Unctuous

Smart(en), Smartest Ache, Acute, Alec, Astute, Best, Bite, Chic, Classy, Clever, Cute, Dandy, Dapper, Dressy, Elegant, Flash, Flip, Fly, Groom, Gussy up, Kookie, Kooky, Natty, Neat, Nifty, Nip, Nobby, Pac(e)y, Pacy, Posh, Preen, Primp, Prink, Pusser, Raffish, Rattling, Ritzy, Saucy, Slick, Sly, Smoke, Smug, Snappy,

Soigné(e), Spiff, Sprauncy, Sprightly, Spruce, Sprush, Spry, Sting, Swagger, Sweat, Swish, Tiddley, Tippy, Titivate, Toff, U, Well-groomed, Wiseacre

Smash(ed), Smasher, Smashing Atom, Bingle, Brain, Break, Crush, Demolish, Devastate, Dish, Forearm, High, Jarp, Jaup, Kaput, Kill, Lulu, Shatter, Shiver, Slam, Squabash, Stave, Super, Terrific, Tight, To-brake, > WRECK

Smash(ed) *may indicate an anagram*

Smear Assoil, Bedaub, Besmirch, Blur, Borm, Cervical, Clam, Daub, Defile, Denigrate, Discredit, Drabble, Enarm, Gaum, Gild, Gorm, Lick, Oil, Pap(anicolaou), Pay, Plaster, Slairg, Slaister, Slake, Slather, Slime, Slubber, Slur, Smalm, Smarm, Smudge, Sully, Teer, Traduce, Wax

Smell(ing), Smelly Aroma, Asafoetida, BO, Caproate, Effluvium, Empyreuma, Fetor, F(o)etid, Fug, Gale, Gamy, Graveolent, Guff, Hing, Honk, Hum, Mephitis, Miasm(a), Musk, Nidor, Niff, Nose, Odour, Olent, Olfact(ory), Osmatic, Perfume, Pong, Ponk, Pooh, Rank, Redolent, Reech, Reek, Sar, Savour, > SCENT, Sniff, Snifty, Snook, Snuff, Steam, Stench, Stifle, Stink, Tang, Whiff

Smelling salts Sal volatile

Smelt(ing) Atherinidae, Melt, Salmon, Scoria, Sparling, Speiss, Spirling

Smile(s), Smiling Agrin, Beam, Cheese, Favour, Gioconda, Grin, Rictus, Samuel, Self-help, Simper, Smirk

Smirk Grimace, Simper

Smite, Smitten Assail, Enamoured, Hit, Strike, Strook

Smith Adam, Farrier, FE, Forger, Hammerman, Mighty, Stan, Vulcan, Wayland

Smithy Forge, Smiddy, Stithy

Smock Blouse, Chemise, Drabbet, Gather, Shift, Slop, Smicket

Smoke(r), Smoking, Smoky Blast, Bloat, Censer, Chain, Chillum, > CIGAR(ETTE), Cure, Fog, Fuliginous, Fume, Funk, Gasper, Hemp, Incense, Indian hemp, Inhale, Kipper, Latakia, Lum, Lunt, Mainstream, Manil(l)a, Nicotian, Passive, Peat reek, Pother, Pudder, Puff, Reech, Reek, Reest, Roke, Smeech, Smeek, Smoor, Smoulder, Smudge, Snout, Toke, Vapour, Viper, Water, Whiff, Wreath

Smoke-hating Misocapnic

Smoking-room Divan

Smollett Tobias

▶ **Smooch** *see* SMOUCH

Smooth(e), Smoother, Smoothly Bland, Brent, Buff, Chamfer, Clean, Clockwork, Dress, Dub, Easy, Even, Fettle, File, Flat, Fluent, Glabrous, Glare, Glassy, Glib, Goose, Iron, Legato, Level, Levigate, Linish, Mealy-mouthed, Mellifluous, Oil, Plane, Plaster, Rake, Roll, Rub, Sand(er), Satiny, Scrape, Sleek, Slick, Slickenslide, Slur, Smug, Snod, Sostenuto, Streamlined, Suave, Swimmingly, Terete, Terse, Trim, Urbane

Smooth-haired Lissotrichous

Smother Burke, Choke, Muffle, Oppress, Overlie, Smoor, Smore, Smoulder, Stifle, Suppress

Smouch Cheat, Kiss, Lallygag, Lollygag, Neck

Smoulder Burn, Seethe

Smudge Blur, Dab, Offset, Slur, Smear, Smooch, Stain

Smug Complacent, Conceited, Goody-two-shoes, Neat, Oily, Pi, Sanctimonious, Self-satisfied, Trim

Smuggle(d), Smuggler, Smuggling Body-packer, Bootleg, Contraband, Contrabandist, Donkey, Fair trade, Gunrunning, Moonshine, Mule, Owler, Rum-runner, Run, Secrete, Steal, Traffic

Smut(ty) Bawdy, Blight, Blue, Brand, Burnt-ear, Coom, Filth, Grime, Racy, Soot, Speck, Stinking

Smut-fungus Basidia, Ustilago

Snack Bever, Bhelpuri, Bite, Blintz, Breadstick, Brunch, Butty, Canapé, Chack, Crudités, Elevenses, Entremets, Four-by-two, Gorp, Meze, Nacket, Nibble, Nocket, Nooning, Nuncheon, Pdkos, Pie, Popcorn, Rarebit, Refreshment, Samo(o)sa, Sandwich, Sarnie, Savoury, Tapa, Taste, Toast(y), Vada, Voidee, Wada, Zakuska

Snaffle Bit, Bridoon, Grab, Purloin

Snag Catch, Contretemps, Drawback, Hindrance, Hitch, Impediment, Knob, Nog, Obstacle, Remora, Rub, Snubbe, Stub, Tear

Snail Brian, Cowrie, Cowry, Dew, Dodman, Escargot, Garden, Gasteropod, Giant African, Helix, Hodmandod, Limnaea, Lymnaea, Nautilus, Nerite, Planorbis, Pond, Ramshorn, Roman, Slow, Slug, Strombus, Unicorn-shell, Univalve, Wallfish, Whelk, Wing

Snake Adder, Aesculapian, Amphisbaena, Anaconda, Anguine, Anguis, Apod(e), Asp, Bandy-bandy, Berg-adder, Blacksnake, Blind, Blue-racer, Boa, Boma, Boomslang, Brown, Bull, Bush-master, Camoodi, Carpet, Cerastes, Clotho, Coachwhip, Cobra, Coluber, Congo, Constrictor, Copperhead, Coral, Corn, Cottonmouth, Cribo, Crotalidae, Daboia, Death-adder, Dendrophis, Diamond(-back), Dipsas, Dugite, Elaps, Ellops, Fer-de-lance, Garter, Glass, Grass, Habu, Hamadryad, Hognose, Homorelaps, Hoop, Horned viper, Horsewhip, Hydra, Indigo, Jararaca, Jararaka, Joe Blake, Kaa, K(a)rait, King (cobra), Lachesis, Langaha, Mamba, Massasauga, Meander, Milk, Mocassin, Moccasin, Mulga, Naga, Naia, Naja, Ophidian, Pipe, Pit-viper, Plumber's, Puff-adder, Python, Racer, Rat, Rattler, Reptile, Ribbon, Ringhals, Ringneck, Rinkhals, River jack, Rock, Sand viper, Seps, > SERPENT, Sidewinder, Slowworm, Smooth, Spitting, Squamata, Sucuruju, Surucucu, Taipan, Takshaka, Thirst, Thread, Tiger, Timber rattlesnake, Tree, Uraeus, Vasuki, Viper, Water (moccasin), Whip, Wind, Worm

Snake-charmer Lamia

Snake-in-the-grass Peacher, Rat, Traitor

Snake-root Senega

Snap(per), **Snappy**, **Snap up** Autolycus, Bite, Break, Brittle, Camera, Click, Cold, Crack, Cross, Curt, Edgy, Fillip, Girnie, Glom, Gnash, Hanch, Knacker, Knap, Livery, Mugshot, Photo, Photogene, Scotch, Snack, Snatch, Spell, Still, Tetchy, Vigour

Snare Bait, Benet, Engine, Enmesh, Entrap, Gin, Grin, Hook, Illaqueate, Inveigle, Net, Noose, Rat-trap, Springe, Springle, Toil, > TRAP, Trapen, Trepan, Web, Weel, Wire

Snarl(ing) Chide, Complicate, Cynic, Enmesh, Girn, Gnar(l), Gnarr, Growl, Grumble, Knar, Knot, Snap, Tangle, Yirr

Snatch Claucht, Claught, Excerpt, Fragment, Glom, Grab, Kidnap, Nip, Pluck, Race, Rap, Rase, Raunch, Refrain, Snippet, Song, Spell, Strain, Take, Tweak, Wrap, Wrest

Snatch *may indicate* the first letter of a word

Snazzy Cat

Snead Snath

Sneak(y) Area, Carry-tale, Clipe, Clype, Inform, Lurk, Mumblenews, Nim, Peak, Scunge, Skulk, Slink, Slip, Slyboots, Snitch, Snoop, Split, Steal, Stoolie, Surreptitious, Tell(-tale), Underhand

Sneer(ing) Barb, Critic, Cynical, Fleer, Gibe, Jeer, Scoff, Smirk, Snide

Sneeze (at), **Sneezing** Atishoo, Neese, Neeze, Ptarmic, Scorn, Sternutation

Snick Click, Cut, Edge, Glance

Snicker Snigger, Titter, Whinny

Snide Bitchy, Shand

Sniff Inhale, Nose, Nursle, Nuzzle, Scent, Smell, Snivel, Snort, Snuffle, Vent, Whiff

Snigger Giggle, Laugh, Snicker, Snirtle, Titter, Whicker

Snip(pet) Bargain, Cert, Clip, Cut, Doddle, Piece, Sartor, Snatch, Snick, Tailor

Snipe(r) Bird, Bushwhacker, Criticise, Franc-tireur, Gutter, Heather-bleat(er), Heather-bluiter, Heather-blutter, Pick off, Scape, Shoot, Walk, Wisp

Snitch Conk, Konk, Nose

Snivel Blubber, Snotter, Snuffle, Weep, Whine

Snob(bery), Snobbish Cobbler, Crispin, High-hat, Inverted, Scab, Side, Snooty, Soutar, Souter, Sowter, Toffee-nose, Vain, Vamp

Snooker Pool, Stimie, Stimy, Stym(i)e

Snoop(er) Meddle, Nose, Pry, Tec

Snooty Bashaw, Snob(bish)

Snooze Calk, Caulk, Dove, Doze, Nap, Nod, Siesta, Sleep

Snore, Snoring Rhonchus, Rout, Snort, Stertorous, Zz

Snort(er) Drink, Grunt, Nare, Nasal, Roncador, Snore, Toot

Snot(ty) Mucoid

Snout Bill, Boko, Cigar, Gasper, Gruntie, Informer, Muzzle, Nose, Nozzle, Proboscis, Schnozzle, Tinker, Tobacco, Wall

Snow(y), Snowstorm Brig, Buran, Cocaine, Coke, Corn, Cornice, Crud, Firn, Flake, Flurry, Graupel, Half-pipe, Heroin, Marine, Mogul, Neve, Nival, Niveous, Oncome, Onding, Powder, Red, Sastruga, Spotless, Stall, Virga, White-out, Wintry, Wreath, Yellow, Zastruga

Snowball Accelerate, Cramp-bark, Cumulative, Guelder-rose, Increase, Magnify, Opulus, Pelt, Rose

Snowdrop Avalanche

Snowflake Leucojum, St Agnes' flower

Snow-goose Wav(e)y

Snowman Abominable, Eskimo, Junkie, Sherpa, Yeti

Snowmobile Sno-cat

Snowshoe Bear paw, Racket, Racquet

Snub Cut, Diss, Go-by, Lop, Pug, Put-down, Quelch, Rebuff, Reproof, Retroussé, Set-down, Short, Slap, Slight, Sloan, Sneap, Snool, Wither

Snuff(le) Asarabacca, Dout, Errhine, Extinguish, Maccabaw, Maccaboy, Maccoboy, Ptarmic, Pulvil, Rappee, Smother, Snaste, Sneesh(an), Sniff, Snift, Snush, Tobacco, Vent

Snuffbox Anatomical, Mill, Mull

Snug(gle) Burrow, Cose, > COSY, Couthie, Couthy, Croodle, Cubby, Cuddle, Embrace, Lion, Neat, Nestle, Nuzzle, Rug, Snod, Tight, Trim

So Argal, Ergo, Forthy, Hence, Sae, Sic(h), Sol, Therefore, This, Thus, True, Very, Yes

Soak Bate, Bath(e), Beath, Bewet, Bloat, Blot, Buck, Cree, Deluge, Drench, Drink, Drook, Drouk, Drown, Drunk, Duck, Dunk, Embay, Embrue, Fleece, Grog, Imbrue, Infuse, Lush, Macerate, Marinate, Mop, Oncome, Permeate, Rait, Rate, Ret(t), Rinse, Saturate, Seep, Sipe, Sog, Sop, Souce, Souse, Sows(s)e, Steep, Sype, Thwaite, Toper, Wet

Soap(y), Soap opera Cake, Carbolic, Castile, Eluate, Flake, Flannel, Flattery, Green, Joe, Lather, Marine, Metallic, Moody, Mountain, Pears®, Pinguid, Saddle, Saponaceous, Saponin, Sawder, Slime, Soft, Spanish, Suds, Sudser, Sugar, Syndet, Tablet, Tall-oil, Toheroa, Toilet, Washball, Windsor, Yellow

Soapstone French chalk, Steatite, Talc

Soar(ing) Ascend, Essorant, Fly, Glide, Hilum, Rise, Tower, Zoom

Sob (stuff) Blub(ber), Boohoo, Goo, Gulp, Lament, Singult, Singultus, Snotter, Wail, Weep, Yoop

Sober(sides) Abstemious, Calm, Demure, Pensive, Sedate, Staid, Steady, TT

Sobriquet Byname, Cognomen, Nickname, To-name

So-called Alleged, Nominal, Soi-disant

Sociable, Sociability Affable, Cameraderie, Chummy, Cosy, Extravert, Extrovert, Folksy, Friendly, Genial, Gregarious

Social(ise) Convivial, Hobnob, Hui, Mingle, Mix, Musicale, Phatic, Tea-dance, Yancha

Socialism, Socialist Ba'(a)th, Champagne, Chartist, Dergue, Engels, Fabian, Fourierism, Guild, ILP, International, Lansbury, Left(y), Marxism, Menchevik, Menchevist, National, Nihilism, Owen(ist), Owenite, Pinko, Red, Revisionist, St Simonist, Sandinista, Spartacist, Utopian, Webb

Socialite Deb

Society Affluent, Association, Beau monde, Benefit, Body, Broederbond, Building, Camorra, Carbonari, Class, Club, College, Company, Conger, Co-op, Cooperative, Culture, Danite, Defenders, Dorcas, Eleutheri, Elite, Elks, Fabian, Fashion, Foresters, Freemans, Freemasons, Friendly, Friends, Glee club, Grotian, Group, Guilds, Haut monde, Hetairia, High, Humane, Illuminati, Institute, Invincibles, John Birch, Ku-klux-klan, Kyrle, Law, Linnean, Lodge, Mafia, Malone, Masonic, Mau-mau, Menage, Molly Maguire, National, Oddfellows, Oral, Orangemen, Oratory, Order, Permissive, Phi Beta Kappa, Plunket, Plural, Pop, Provident, Repertory, Ribbonism, Rosicrucian, Rotary, Royal, S, School, Secret, Soc, Soroptomist, Sorority, Stakeholder, Tammany, Theosophical, Toc H, Ton, Tong, Triad, U, Whiteboy, World

Sociologist Weber

Sock(s) Argyle, Argyll, Biff, Bobby, Bootee, Digital, Hose(n), Punch, Rock, Slipper, Slosh, Strike, Tabi, Walk, Wind

Socket Acetabulum, Alveole, Budget, Gudgeon, Hollow, Hosel, Hot shoe, Jack, Nave, Ouch, Pod, Point, Port, Power-point, Shoe, Strike, Torulus, Whip

Sock-eye Nerka, Salmon

Socrates, Socratic Ironist, Maieutics, Sage

Sod Clump, Delf, Delph, Divot, Gazo(o)n, Mool, Mould, Mouls, Scraw, Sward, Turf

Soda, Sodium Acmite, Arfvedsonite, Baking, Barilla, Bicarb, Caustic, Club, Cream, La(u)rvikite, Na, Natrium, Natron, Reh, Saleratus, Splash, Trona, Washing

Sofa Canapé, Chesterfield, Couch, Daybed, Divan, Dos-à-dos, Dosi-do, Ottoman, Settee, Squab, Tête-à-tête

So far As, As yet, Until, Yonder

Soft(en), Softener, Softening, Softly Amalgam, Anneal, B, BB, Blet, Boodle, Calm, Casefy, Cedilla, Cree, Dim, Dolcemente, Doughy, Ease, Emolliate, Emollient, Flabby, Gentle, Hooly, Humanise, Intenerate, Lash, Lax, Lenient, Lenition, Limp, Low, Macerate, Malacia, Malax(ate), Malleable, Mardarse, Mardie, Mease, Mellow, Melt, Mild, Milksop, Mitigate, Modulate, Mollify, Mollities, Morendo, Mulch, Mush(y), Mute, Neale, Nesh, Option, P, Palliate, Pastel, Piano, Plushy, Porous, Propitiate, Rait, Rate, Relent, Scumble, Sentimental, Silly, Slack, Squashy, Squidgy, Squishy, Sumph, Talcose, Temper, >**TENDER**, Tone, Velvet, Weak

Softness Lenity

Software Firewall, Firmware, Groupware, Middleware, Parser, Payware, Shareware, Spreadsheet, Stiffware, Vaccine, Windows

Sog(gy) Sodden

Soil(ed), Soily Acid, Adscript, Agrology, Agronomy, Alkali(ne), Alluvium, Azonal, Bedraggle, Chemozem, Clay, Cohesive, Defile, Desecrate, Desert, Dinge, Dirt(y), Discolour, Earth, Edaphic, Frictional, Gault, Glebe, Grey, Grimy, Ground, Gumbo, Hotbed, Humus, Illuvium, Intrazonal, Lair, Land, Latosol, Lithosol, Loam, Loess, Lome, Loss, Mire, Mool, Mo(u)ld, Mud, Mulch, Mull, Night, Peat, Ped, Pedalfer, Pedocal, Pedology, Phreatic, Planosol, Podsol, Podzol, Prairie, Pure, Regar, Regolith, Regosol, Regur, Rendzina, Rhizosphere, Root-ball, Sal, Sedentary, Smudge, Smut, Solonchak, Solonetz, Solum, Soot, Stain, Stonebrash, Sub, Sully, Tarnish, Tash, Terrain, Terricolous, Tilth, Top, Tschernosem, Udal, Umber, Virgin, Yarfa, Yarpha, Zonal

Soirée Drum, Levee, Musicale

Sojourn Abide, Respite, Stay, Tarry

Sol G, Soh, Sun

Solace Cheer, Comfort

Solar(ium) Heliacal, Tannery

Sold Had

Solder Blaze, Join, Spelter, Tin, Weld

Soldier(s) Achilles, Alpini, Amazon, Ant, Anzac, Army, Arna(o)ut, Askari, Atkins, ATS, Banner, Bashi-Bazouk, Battalion, Bersaglier(e), Bluff, Bod, Bombardier, Borderer, Botha, Brave, Brigade, Buff-coat, Buff-jerkin, Butter-nut, Cadet, Caimac(am), Campaigner, Cannon-fodder, Car(a)bineer, Car(a)binier, Cataphract, Centinel(l), Centonel(l), Centurion, Chasseur, Chindit, Chocko, Choco, Chocolate, Cohort, Colonel, Colours, Commando, Confederate, Contingent, Cornet, Corp(s), Cossack, Crusader, Cuirassier, Ded, Desert rat, Detail, Dog-face, Doughboy, Draftee, Dragoon, Dugout, Emmet, Engineer, Enomoty, Evzone, Fag(g)ot, Federal, Fencibles, Fighter, Flanker, Foederatus, Foot, Forlorn-hope, Fugleman, Fusilier, Fuzzy-wuzzy, Fyrd, Gallo(w)glass, Galoot, General, GI, Gippo, Goorkha, Grenadier, Grim dig, Grunt, Guardee, Guardsman, Guerilla, Gurkha, Gyppo, Hackbuteer, Hobbler, Hoplite, Hussar, Immortal, Impi, Inf(antry), Iron Duke, Ironside, Irregular, Jackman, Janissary, Janizary, Jawan, Joe, Johnny Reb(el), Kaimakam, Kern(e), Kitchener, Knight, Lancer, Landsknecht, Lansquenet, Lashkar, Leatherneck, Legionary, Legionnaire, Levy, Line, Linesman, Lobster, Maniple, Martinet, Men-at-arms, Miles (gloriosus), Militiaman, Miner, Minuteman, Musketeer, Nahal, Naik, Nasute, Nizam, Non-com, Old moustache, OR, Orderly, Palatine, Palikar, Pandoor, Pandour, Paratroop, Partisan, Peltast, Peon, Perdu(e), Persevere, Phalanx, Pikeman, Piou-piou, Pistoleer, Platoon, Poilu, Point man, Pongo, Post, POW, Private, Rajput, Ranger, Rank(er), Rank and file, Rapparree, Rat-tail, Reb, Redcoat, Reformado, Regiment, Regular, Reiter, Reservist, Retread, Rifleman, Rutter, Sabre, Saddler, Sammy, Samurai, SAS, Sebundy, Sentinel, Sepoy, Serviceman, Signaller, Silladar, Snarler, So(d)ger, Soldado, Sowar(ee), Sowarry, Spearman, Squaddie, Squaddy, Stalhelm(er), Stormtrooper, Strelitz, Subaltern, Swad(dy), Sweat, Targeteer, Tarheel, Templar, Terrier, Territorial, Timariot, Tin, Tommy, Toy, Train-band, Trencher, Trooper, Troops, Turco(pole), Uhlan, Unknown, Velites, Vet(eran), Voltigeur, Volunteer, Wagon, Warhorse, Warmonger, Warrior, Whitecoat, Yardbird, Yeoman, Zouave

▷ **Soldiers** *may indicate* bread for boiled eggs

Sole, Solitaire, Solitary Alone, Anchoret, Anchorite, Clump, Convex,

Dover, Dropped, Fish, Incommunicado, Lemon, Lonesome, Megrim, Merl, Meunière, Monastical, Monkish, Only, Pad, Palm, Patience, Pelma, Planta(r), Plantigrade, Platform, Recluse, Scaldfish, Single(ton), Skate, Slip, Smear-dab, Tap, Thenar, Tread, Unique, Vibram®, Vola

Solemn Agelast, Austere, Devout, Earnest, Grave, Gravitas, Impressive, Majestic, Owlish, Po-faced, Sacred, Sedate, Serious, Sober, Sobersides

Solent Lee

Solicit Accost, Approach, Ask, Attract, Bash, > **BEG**, Canvass, Commission, Cottage, Importun(at)e, Plead, Ply, Proposition, Speer, Speir, Tout, Woo

Solicitor(s) Advocate, Attorney, Avoué, Beggar, Canvasser, Hallanshaker, Law-agent, Lawyer, Notary, Side-bar, SL, Tout, Trull, Writer to the Signet, WS

Solid(arity), **Solidify** Cake, Chunky, Clot, Clunky, Compact, Comradeship, Concrete, Cone, Congeal, Consolidate, Cube, Cylinder, Dense, Enneahedron, Firm, Foursquare, Freeze, Frustrum, Fuchsin(e), Gel, Hard, Holosteric, Impervious, Masakhane, Merbromin, Octahedron, Pakka, Petrarchan, Platonic, Polyhedron, Prism, Pucka, Pukka, Robust, Set, Skatole, Stilbene, Sublimate, Substantial, Tetrahedron, Thick, Unanimous

Solipsism Egotism, Panegoism

Solitude Privacy, Seclusion

Solo Aria, Cadenza, Cavatine, Concertante, Lone, Monodrama, Monody, Ombre, One-man, Scena, Variation

Solon Sage

So long Cheerio, Ciao, Goodbye, Tata

Solstice Summer, Tropic, Winter

Soluble Alkaline, Surfactant

Solution Acetone, Alkali, Ammonia, Amrit, > **ANSWER**, Austenite, Benedict's, Collodion, Colloidal, Dakin's, Dobell's, Eclairassement, Electrolyte, Elixir, Emulsion, Eusol, Fehling's, Final, Key, Leachate, Limewater, Lixivium, Lye, Oleoresin, Rationale, Reducer, Ringer's, Rinse, Saline, Solid, Solvent, Soup, Standard, Suspensoid, Tincture, Titrate, Viscose

Solution *may indicate* an anagram

Solve(d), **Solver** Assoil, Casuist, Clear, Crack, Decode, Holmes, Loast, Loose, Read(er), Suss out, Troubleshoot, Unclew, Undo, Unriddle

Solvent Acetaldehyde, Acetone, Afloat, Alcahest, Aldol, Alkahest, Anisole, Aqua-regia, Banana oil, Cleanser, Cyclohexane, Cyclopentane, Decalin, Diluent, Dioxan(e), Eleunt, Eluant, Ether, Funded, Furan, Hexane, Ligroin, Megilp, Menstruum, Methanol, Methylal, Naphtha, Paraldehyde, Picoline, Protomic, Pyridine, Sound, Stripper, Terebene, Terpineol, Tetrachloromethane, Thinner, Thiophen, Toluene, Toluol, Trike, Trilene, Turpentine

Sombre Dark, Drab, Drear, Dull, Gloomy, Grave, Morne, Subfusc, Subfusk, Sullen, Triste

Some Any, Arrow, Ary, Certain, Divers, Few, One, Part, Portion, Quota, These, They, Wheen

Some *may indicate* a hidden word

Somebody Dignitary, Name, Notable, One, Person, Quidam, Someone, > **VIP**

Somehow Somegate

Somehow *may indicate* an anagram

Somersault Barani, Deltcher, Flip(-flap), Flip-flop, Handspring, Pitchpole, Pitchpoll

Something Aliquid, Chattel, Matter, Object, Summat, What, Whatnot

Sometime(s) Erstwhile, Ex, Former, Occasional, Off and on, Quondam

Somewhat Bit, -ish, Mite, Partly, Quasi, Quite, Rather

Somewhere Somegate

Son Boy, Descendant, Disciple, Epigon(e), Fils, Fitz, Lad, Lewis, M(a)c, Offspring, Prodigal, Progeny, Scion

Song Air, Amoret, Anthem, Antistrophe, Aria, Art, Aubade, Ayre, Ballad, Ballant, Ballata, Barcarol(l)e, Belter, Berceuse, Bhajan, Blues, Brindisi, Burden, Burthen, Cabaletta, Calypso, Cancionero, Canticle, Cantilena, Canzona, Canzone, Canzonet(ta), Carmagnole, Carol, Catch, Cavatina, Chanson, Cha(u)nt, Come-all-ye, Conductus, Corn-kister, Cycle, Descant, Dirge, Dithyramb, Ditty, Epithalamion, Epithalamium, Fado, Fit, Flamenco, Folk, Forebitter, Glee, Gorgia, Gradual, Hillbilly, Hum, Hymeneal, Hymn, Internationale, Jug(-jug), Lament, Lay, Lied(er), Lilt, Lullaby, Lyric, Madrigal, Magnificat, Marseillaise, Matin, Melic, Melisma, Melody, Mento, Negro spiritual, Noel, Number, Nunc dimittus, Oat, Paean, Pane, Part, Patter, Pennillion, Plain, Plaint, Plantation, Prick, Prothalamion, Prothalamium, Psalm, Qawwali, Rap, Recitativo, Relish, Rhapsody, Rispetto, Roulade, Roundelay, Rune, Scat, Sea-shanty, Secular, Serenade, Shanty, Siren, Sirvente, Skolion, Sososholoza, Spiritual, Stave, Strain, Strophe, Swan, Taps, Tenebrae, Theme, Torch, Trill, Tune, Villanella, Volkslied, Warble, Wassail, Waulking, Yodel, Yodle

Songbook Cancionero, Hymnal, Kommersbuch, Libretto, Psalter

Songsmith, Songwriter Dowland, Espla, Foster, Kern, Minot, Zappa

Sonnet Amoret, Elizabethan, English, Italian, Miltonic, Petrarch(i)an, Shakespearean, Shakespearian, Spenserian

Sonometer Monochord

Soon(er) Anon, Directly, Erelong, Lief, OK, Oklahoma, Presently, Shortly, Tight, Timely, Tit(ely), Tite, Tyte

Soot(y) Colly, Coom, Crock, Fuliginous, Gas black, Grime, Lampblack, Smut, Speck

Soothe, Soothing Accoy, Allay, Anetic, Anodyne, Appease, Assuage, Bucku, Calm, Compose, Demulcent, Dulcet, Emollient, Irenic, Lenitive, Lull, Mellifluous, Mollify, Pacific, Paregoric, Poultice, Quell, Rock

Soothsayer Astrologer, Augur, Calchas, Chaldee, Divine, Forecaster, Haruspex, Melampus, Oracle, Picus, Prophet, Pythoness, > SEER, Shipton, Tiresias

Sop Appease, Berry, Douceur, Rait, Ret, Sponge

Sophist(ic) Casuist, Elenchic, Quibbler

Sophisticate(d) Blasé, Boulevardier, City slicker, Civilised, Cosmopolitan, Couth, Doctor, High-end, Patrician, Polished, Sative, Slicker, Svelte, Urbane, Worldly

▷ **Sophoclean** *may indicate* Greek (alphabet, etc)

Sophomore Semie

Soporific Barbiturate, Bromide, Drowsy, Halothane, Hypnotic, Lullaby, Narcotic, Opiate, Sedative, Tedious

Soppiness, Soppy Maudlin, Schwarmerei, Sloppy, Slushy

Soprano Castrato, Crespin, Descant, Lind, Patti, Treble

Sorb Wend

Sorcerer, Sorceress, Sorcery Angakok, Ashipu, Circe, Conjury, Diablerie, Hoodoo, Kadaitcha, Kurdaitcha, Lamia, Mage, Magian, Magic(ian), Magus, Medea, Merlin, Morgan le Fay, Mother Shipton, Necromancer, Obi, Pishogue, Shaman, Sortilege, Venefic(ious), Voodoo, Warlock, Witch, Wizard

Sordid Base, Low-life, Scungy, Seamy, Sleazy, Squalid, Vile

Sore(ly), Sores Abrasion, Anthrax, Bitter, Blain, Boil, Canker, Chancre, Chap,

Chilblain, Cold, Dearnly, Felon, Gall, Impost(h)ume, Ireful, Kibe, Quitter, Quittor, Raw, Running, Rupia(s), Saddle, Sair, Shiver, Sitfast, Surbate, Ulcer(s), Whitlow, Wound

Sore throat Garget, Prunella, Quinsy, Tonsillitis

Sorghum Milo

Sorrel Common, French, Hetty, Mountain, Oca, Roman, Sheep, Soar(e), Sore, Sourock

Sorrow(ful) Affliction, Distress, Dole, Dolente, Dolour, Emotion, Fee-grief, > **GRIEF**, Lament, Misery, Nepenthe, Penance, Pietà, Remorse, Rue, Triste, Wae, Waugh, Wirra, Woe, Yoop

Sorry Ashamed, Contrite, Miserable, Oops, Penitent, Pitiful, Poor, Regretful, Relent, Wretched

Sorry *may indicate* an anagram

Sort(ing) Arrange, Brand, Breed, Category, Character, Classify, Collate, Drive, Grade, > **KIND**, Nature, Pranck(e), Prank, Sift, Species, Stamp, Tidy, Triage, Type, Variety

Sortie Attack, Foray, Mission, Outfall, Raid, Sally

Sorts *see* OUT OF SORTS

So-so Average, Indifferent, Mediocre, Middling

So to speak Quasi

So to speak *may indicate* 'sound of'

Sotto voce Murmur, Whisper

Soubriquet *see* SOBRIQUET

Sough Rustle, Sigh

Soul(ful) Alma, Ame, Anima, Animist, Atman, Ba, Bardo, Brevity, Deep, Entelechy, Eschatology, Expressive, Heart, Inscape, Larvae, Lost, Manes, Object, Person, Pneuma, Psyche, Saul, Shade, Spirit, Universal

Sound(ed), **Soundness**, **Sound system** Accurate, Ach-laut, Acoustic, Affricate, Albemarle, Alveolar, Amphoric, Audio, Bay, Bleep, Blow, Boing, Bong, Cacophony, Chime, Chirr(e), Chord, Chug, Clam, Clang, Clink, Clop, Clunk, Continuant, Dah, Dental, Dit, Dive, Dolby®, Echo, Euphony, Fast, Fathom, Fere, Fettle, Fit, Good, Hale, Harmonics, Healthy, Hearty, Hi-fi, Ich-laut, Inlet, Knell, Kyle, Labiodental, Lo-fi, Long Island, Lucid, Mach, Madrilene, McMurdo, Mersey, Milford, Mouillé, Music, Narrow, > **NOISE**, Onomatopaeia, Oompah, Optical, Orthodox, Palatal, Palato-alveolar, Pamlico, Paragog(u)e, Peal, Pectoriloquy, Phone(me), Phonetic, Phonic, Phonology, Pitter(-patter), Plap, Plink, Plonk, Plop, Plosion, Plumb, Plummet, Plunk, Probe, Puget, Put-put, Quadraphonic(s), Quadrophonic(s), Rale, Rational, Real, Reliable, Ring, Roach, Robust, Rong, Rumble, Rustle, Sabin, Safe, Sandhi, Sane, S(c)hwa, Scoresby, Sensurround®, Skirl, Solid, Sonance, Sone, Souffle, Sough, Sowne, Splat, Stereo, Stereophony, Strait, Surround, Swish, Tamber, Tannoy®, Thorough, Timbre, Ting, Tone, Toneme, Trig, Triphthong, Trumpet, Twang, Ultrasonic(s), Unharmed, Uvular, Valid, Voice, Vowel, Wah-wah, Watertight, Well, Whistle, Whole(some), Whump, Wolf

Sounder Echo, Lead

Soundproof Deaden

Sound-track Dubbing, Stripe

Soup Alphabet, Avgolemono, Bird's nest, Bisk, Bisque, Borsch, Bouillabaisse, Bouillon, Brewis, Broth, Burgoo, Chowder, Cock-a-leekie, Consommé, Duck, Garbure, Gazpacho, Gomb(r)o, Gruel, Gumbo, Harira, Hoosh, Julienne, Kail, Kale, Madrilene, Marmite, Mess, Minestrone, Mock turtle, Mulligatawny, Oxtail, Palestine, Pea(se), Pot-au-feu, Pot(t)age, Primordial, Puree, Ramen,

Rubaboo, Sancoche, Shchi, Shtchi, Skilligalee, Skilligolee, Skilly, Skink, Stock, Tattie-claw, Toheroa, Turtle, Vichyssoise

▷ **Soup** *may indicate* an anagram

Soupçon Thought, Touch

Sour(puss) Acerb, Acescent, Acid, Acidulate, Alegar, Bitter, Citric, Crab, Esile, Ferment, Moody, Stingy, Subacid, > TART, Turn, Verjuice, Vinegarish

Source Authority, Basis, Bottom, Centre, Database, Derivation, Egg, Fons, Font, Fount, Fountain-head, Germ, Head-stream, Literary, Mine, Mother, Origin, Parent, Pi, Pion, Point, Provenance, Quarry, Reference, Rise, Riverhead, Root, Seat, Seed, Spring, Springhead, Urn, Well, Wellhead, Wellspring, Widow's cruse, Ylem

Sour milk Curds, Smetana, Whey, Whig, Yogh(o)urt

Souse Beath, Duck, Immerse, Pickle, Plunge, Soak, Spree, Steep

South(ern), **Southerner** Austral, Dago, Decanal, Decani, Deep, Dixieland, Meridian, Meridional, S

South Africa(n) Azania, Bantu, Caper, Ciskei, Grikwa, Griqua, Hottentot, Kaf(f)ir, Qwaqwa, SA, Springbok, Swahili, Xhosa, ZA, Zulu

South American Araucanian, Arawak, Argentino, Aymara, Bolivian, Carib, Chibcha, Chilean, Galibi, Guarani, Inca, Jivaro, Kechua, Llanero, Mam, Mapuchi, Mochica, Quechua, SA, Tapuyan, Tupi

Southwark Boro'

Souvenir Keepsake, Memento, Relic, Remembrance, Scalp, Token, Trophy

Sovereign(ty), **Sovereign remedy** Anne, Autocrat, Bar, Condominium, Couter, Dominant, ER, Goblin, Haemony, Harlequin, Imperial, Imperium, James, King, L, Liege, Nizam, Pound, Quid, Royalty, Ruler, Shiner, Supreme, Swaraj, Synarchy, Thick'un, Thin'un

Soviet Circassian, Council, Estonian, Russian, Supreme, Volost

Sow(ing) Catchcrop, Elt, Foment, Gilt, Inseminate, Plant, Scatter, Seed, Sprue, Strew, Yelt

Soya Tempe(h)

Spa Baden, Baden-Baden, Bath, Buxton, Evian, Godesberg, Harrogate, Hydro, Kurhaus, Kursaal, Leamington, Vichy

Space(d), **Spacing**, **Spacious**, **Space man** Abyss, Acre, Area, Areola, Bay, Bracket, Breathing, Cellule, Cishinar, Clearing, C(o)elom, Compluvium, Concourse, Contline, Crookes, Cubbyhole, Deep, Diastema, Distal, Distance, Elbow-room, Esplanade, Ether, Exergue, Expanse, Extent, Footprint, Forecourt, Freeband, Gap, Glade, Glenn, Goaf, Gob, Gutter, Hair, Hash(mark), Headroom, Homaloid, Indention, Inner, Intergalactic, Interplanetary, Interstellar, Interstice, Invader, Kerning, Killogie, Kneehole, Lacuna, Lair, Lebensraum, Legroom, Life, Logie, Lumen, Lunar, Lung, Machicolation, Maidan, Metope, Mihrab, Muset, Musit, Orbit, Outer, Peridrome, Personal, Plenum, Pomoerium, Priest hole, Proportional, Quad, Retrochoir, > ROOM, Ruelle, Sample, Sheets, Shelf room, Slot, Spandrel, Spandril, Step, Storage, Third, Topological, Tympanum, Ullage, Uncluttered, Vacuole, Vacuum, Vast, Vector, Void

Spacecraft, **Space agency**, **Space object**, **Spaceship**, **Space station** Apollo, Capsule, Columbia, Deep Space, Explorer, Galileo, Genesis, Giotto, Lander, LEM, Luna, Lunik, Mariner, MIR, Module, NASA, Orbiter, Pioneer, Probe, Quasar, Ranger, Salyut, Shuttle, Skylab, Soyuz, Sputnik, Starship, Tardis, Viking, Vostok, Voyager, Zond

Space walk EVA

Spade Breastplough, Caschrom, Cas crom, Castrato, Detective, Flaughter, Graft, Loy, Negro, Paddle, Pattle, Pettle, Pick, S, Shovel, Slane, Spit, Suit, Turf,

Tus(h)kar, Tus(h)ker, Twiscar
Spain E, Hesperia, Iberia
Spalpeen Sinner
Span Age, Arch, Attention, Bestride, Bridge, Chip, Ctesiphon, Extent, Life, Memory, Range
Spangle(d) Avanturine, Aventurine, Glitter, Instar, O, Paillette, Sequin
Spaniard, **Spanish** Alguacil, Alguazil, Andalusian, Barrio, Basque, Cab, Caballero, Carlist, Castilian, Catalan, Chicano, Dago, Don, Fly, Grandee, Hidalgo, Hispanic, Jose, Main, Mestizo, Mozarab, Pablo, Papiamento, Señor, Spic(k), Spik
Spaniel Blenheim, Cavalier, Clumber, Cocker, Crawler, Creep, Dog, Fawner, Field, Irish (water), King Charles, Maltese, Papillon, Placebo, Skip-kennel, Springer, Sussex, Tibetan, Toad-eater, Toady, Toy, Water, Welsh springer
Spank(ing) Cob, Paddywhack, Rapid, Scud, Slap, Slipper, Sprack
Spanner Arc, Box, Bridge, Clapper, Key, Ring, Shifter, Socket, Torque, Wrench
Spar Barytes, Blue John, Boom, Bowsprit, Box, Cauk, Cawk, Fight, Gaff, Iceland, Jib-boom, Mainyard, Manganese, Martingale, Mast, Nail-head, Outrigger, Rafter, Rail, Ricker, Schiller, Shearleg, Sheerleg, Snotter, Spathic, Sprit, Steeve, Stile, Tabular, Triatic, Whiskerboom, Whiskerpole, Yard
Spare, **Sparing** Angular, Cast-off, Dup(licate), Economical, Free, Frugal, Gash, Gaunt, Hain, Lean, Lenten, Other, Pardon, Reserve, Rib, Save, Scant, Skimp, Slender, Stint, Subsecive, Thin
Spark Animate, Arc, Beau, Blade, Bluette, Dandy, Flash, Flaught, Funk, Ignescent, Kindle, Life, Muriel, Scintilla, Smoulder, Spunk, Trigger, Vital, Zest
Sparkle(r), **Sparkling** Aerated, Aventurine, Coruscate, Diamanté, Effervesce, Elan, Emicate, Fire, Fizz, Flicker, Frizzante, Glamour, Glint, Glisten, Glitter, Life, Pétillant, Scintillate, Seltzer, Seltzogene, Spangle, Spritzig, Spumante, Twinkle, Verve, Witty, Zap
Sparrow Bird, Cape, Isaac, Java, Junco, Mah-jong(g), Mossie, Passerine, Piaf, Prunella, Spadger, Speug, Sprug, Sprug(gy), Titling
Sparrow-grass Asparagus, Sprue
Sparse Meagre, Rare, Scant, Thin
Spartan(s) Austere, Basic, Enomoty, Hardy, Helot, Heraclid, Lacedaemonian, Laconian, Lysander, Menelaus, Severe, Valiant
Spasm(odic) Blepharism, Chorea, Clonus, Cramp, Crick, Fit(ful), Hiccup, Hippus, Hyperkinesis, Intermittent, Irregular, > JERK, Kink, Laryngismus, Nystagmus, Paroxysm, Periodical, Start, Tetany, Throe, Tonic, Tonus, Trismus, Twinge, Twitch, Writer's cramp
Spasmodic *may indicate* an anagram
Spastic Athetoid, Clonic, Jerky
Spat(s) Bicker, Brattle, Gaiters, Legging, Quarrel, Shower, Tiff
Spate Flood, Sluice, Torrent
Spatter Disject, Ja(u)p, Scatter, Splash, Splosh, Spot, Sprinkle
Spattered *may indicate* an anagram
Spawn(ing), **Spawning place** Anadromous, Blot, Fry, Progeny, Propagate, Redd, Roud, Seed, Spat, Spet, Spit
Speak(er), **Speaking** Address, Articulate, Broach, Chat, Cicero, Collocuter, Communicate, Converse, Coo, Declaim, Dilate, Discourse, Diseur, Dwell, Effable, Elocution, Eloquent, Expatiate, Express, Extemporise, Filibuster, Intercom, Intone, Inveigh, Jabber, Jaw, Lip, Loq, Mang, Mention, Mike, Mina, Mouth, Mouthpiece, Nark, Open, Orate, Orator, Palaver, Parlance, Parley, Pontificate, Prate, Preach, Prelector, Rhetor, > SAY, Sayne, Spout, Spruik,

Squawk box, Stump, Talk, Tannoy®, Tongue, Trap, Tub-thumper, Tweeter, Utter, Voice, Waffle, Witter, Word

Speakeasy Fluent, Shebeen

Spear Ash, Asparagus, Assagai, Assegai, Dart, Gad, Gavelock, Gig, Gungnir, Hastate, Impale, Javelin, Lance(gay), Launcegaye, Leister, Morris-pike, Partisan, Pierce, Pike, Pilum, Skewer, Spike, Trident, Trisul(a), Waster

Spear-rest Feutre, Fewter

Special Ad hoc, Constable, Designer, Distinctive, Extra, Important, Notable, Notanda, Particular, Peculiar, S, Specific

Specialise, **Specialist(s)** Authority, Concentrate, Connoisseur, Consultant, ENT, Expert, Illuminati, Maestro, Major, Quant, Recondite, Technician

Species Class, Genre, Genus, Kind, Pioneer, Strain, Taxa

Specific(ally), **Specified**, **Specify** As, Ascribe, Assign, Concretize, Cure, Define, Detail, Explicit, Full-blown, Itemise, Medicine, Namely, Precise, Remedy, Sp, Special, State, Stipulate, The, Trivial

Specimen(s) Example, Exempla, Imago, Model, Sample, Slide, Swab, Topotype, Type

Specious False, Glib, Hollow, Pageant, Plausible, Spurious

Speck(led) Atom, Bit, Dot, Fleck, Floater, Freckle, Gay, Muscae volitantes, Particle, Peep(e), Pip, Spot, Spreckle, Stud

Spectacle(d), **Spectacles**, **Spectacular** Arresting, Barnacles, Bifocals, Blazers, Blinks, Bossers, Cheaters, Colourful, Epic, Escolar, Giglamps, > **GLASSES**, Goggles, Horn-rims, Nose-nippers, Oo, Optical, Outspeckle, Pageant, Pince-nez, Pomp, Preserves, Raree-show, Scene, Show, Sight, Son et lumière, Sunglasses, Tamasha, Tattoo, Trifocal, Varifocals

Spectator(s) Bystander, Dedans, Etagère, Eyer, Gallery, Gate, Groundling, Kibitzer, Observer, Onlooker, Standerby, Witness

Spectograph Aston

Spectral, **Spectre** Apparition, Boggle, Bogy, Brocken, Eidolon, Empusa, Ghost, Idola, Iridal, Malmag, Phantasm, Phantom, Phasma, Spirit, Spook, Tarsier, Walking-straw, Wraith

Spectrum Absorption, Band, Continuous, Emission, Iris, Optical, Rainbow, Sunbow, Sundog, Visible, X-ray

Speculate, **Speculative**, **Speculator**, **Speculation** Agiotage, Arbitrage, Bear, Better, Bull, Conjecture, Flier, Flyer, Gamble, Guess, Ideology, If, Imagine, Meditate, Notional, Operate, Pinhooker, Shark, Stag, Theoretical, Theorise, Theory, Thought, Trade, Wonder

Speech, **Speech element** Accents, Address, Argot, Articulation, Bunkum, Burr, Curtain, Delivery, Dialect, Diatribe, Diction, Direct, Discourse, Dithyramb, Drawl, Eloge, English, Eulogy, Filibuster, Free, Gab, Glossolalia, Harangue, Idiolect, Idiom, Inaugural, Indirect, Jargon, Keynote, King's, Lallation, > **LANGUAGE**, Lingua franca, Litany, Maiden, Monologue, Morph(eme), Motherese, Musar, Oblique, Oral, Oration, Parabasis, Parle, Peroration, Phasis, Philippic, Phonetics, Prolocution, Prolog(ue), Queen's, Reported, Rhetoric, Sandhi, Scanning, Screed, Sermon, Side, Slang, Soliloquy, Stemwinder, Stump, Tagmeme, Talk, Taxeme, Tirade, Tongue, Vach, Visible, Voice, Wawa, Whistle-stop

Speech defect, **Speech disease** Dysarthria, Dysphasia, Dysphoria, Echolalia, Idioglossia, Lisp, Palilalia, Paralalia, Paraphasia, Pararthria, Psellism, Stammer, Stutter

Speechless Alogia, Dumb, Dumbstruck, Inarticulate, Mute, Silent, Tongue-tied

Speed(ily), **Speedy** Accelerate, Alacrity, Amain, Amphetamine, Apace, Average,

Bat, Belive, Belt, Breakneck, Burn, Celerity, Clip, Dart, Despatch, DIN, Dispatch, Expedite, Fangy, Fast, Film, Fleet, Further, Gait, Gallop, Goer, Group, Gun, Haste, Hie, Hotfoot, Hypersonic, Induce, Instantaneous, Knot, Landing, Lick, Mach, Merchant, MPH, > **PACE**, Phase, Pike, Post-haste, Pronto, Race, Rapidity, Rate, RPS, Rush, Scorch, Scud, Scurr, Skirr, Soon, Spank, Split, Stringendo, Supersonic, Swift, Tach, Tear, Tempo, Ton up, V, Velocity, Vroom, Wave, Whid, Wing

Speedwell Brooklime, Fluellin, Germander, Veronica

Spelaean Troglodyte

Spelk Skelf, Splinter

Spell(ing) Abracadabra, Bewitch, Bout, Cantrip, Charm, Conjuration, Do, Elf-shoot, Enchantment, Entrance, Fit, Go, Gri(s)-gri(s), Hex, Incantation, Innings, Jettatura, Juju, Knur, > **MAGIC**, Need-fire, Nomic, Open sesame, Orthography, Period, Philter, Philtre, Phonetic, Pinyin, Relieve, Ride, Romaji, Run, Rune, Scat, Shot, Signify, Snap, Snatch, Sorcery, Sp, Span, Spasm, Splinter, Stint, Stretch, Tack, Tour, Trick, Turn, Weird, Whammy, Witchcraft

Spelling-book ABC, Grimoire

Spencer Topcoat, Tracy, Vest

Spend(er), Spending Anticipate, Birl, Blue, Boondoggling, Consume, Deplete, Disburse, Exhaust, Fritter, Lash out, Live, Outlay, Pass, Pay, Shopaholic, Splash, Splash out, Splurge, Ware

Spendthrift Essex man, High-roller, Prodigal, Profligate, Profuser, Scattergood, Wastrel

Spent Consumed, Dead, Done, Expended, Stale, Tired, Used, Weak, Weary

Sperm Seed, Semen

Spew Eject, Emit, Gush, Spit, Vomit

Sphagnum Moss, Peat

Sphere, Spherical Armillary, Celestial, Discipline, Element, Field, Firmament, Globe, Mound, Orb(it), Planet, Prolate, Province, Realm, Schwarzschild, Theatre, Wheel

Sphinx Hawk-moth, Oracle, Riddler

Spice, Spicy Amomum, Anise, Aniseed, Aryl, Cardamom, Cardamon, Cardamum, Cassareep, Cassaripe, Cinnamon, Clove, Clow, Coriander, Cubeb, Cum(m)in, Dash, Devil, Garam masala, Ginger, Mace, Malaguetta, Marjoram, Masala, Myrrh, Nutmeg, Oregano, Paprika, Peppercorn, Pimento, Piperic, Piquant, Salsa verde, Season, Stacte, Staragen, Tamal(e), Tamara, Tansy, Tarragon, Taste, Turmeric, Vanilla, Variety

Spick Dink, Neat, Spike, Tidy

Spicule Sclere, Tetract

Spider(s) Anancy, Ananse, Arachnid, Aranea, Araneida, Arthrapodal, Attercop, Bird, Black widow, Bobbejaan, Cardinal, Cheesemite, Chelicerate, Citigrade, Diadem, Epeira, Epeirid, Ethercap, Ettercap, Funnel-web, Harvester, Harvestman, House, Hunting, Huntsman, Jumping, Katipo, Lycosa, Mite, Money, Mygale, Orb-weaver, Pan, Phalangid, Podogona, Pycnogonid, Red, Redback, Rest, Ricinulei, Saltigrade, Scorpion, Solifugae, Solpuga, Spinner, Strap, Tarantula, Telary, Trapdoor, Violin, Water, Wolf, Zebra

Spiderwort Tradescantia

Spiel Spruik

Spignel Baldmoney, Meu

Spigot Bung, Plug, Tap

Spike(d) Barb, Brod, Calk, Calt(h)rop, Chape, Cloy, Crampon, Ear, Fid, Foil, Gad, Goad, Grama, Herissé, Icicle, Impale, Lace, Locusta, Marlin(e), Nail, > **PIERCE**,

Point, Pricket, Prong, Puseyite, Rod, Sharp, Shod, Skewer, Spadix, Spear, Spicate, Spicule, Spire, Strobiloid, Tang, Thorn, Tine

Spill(age) Divulge, Drop, Fidibus, Jackstraw, Lamplighter, Leakage, Let, Overflow, Overset, Reveal, Scail, Scale, Shed, Skail, Slop, Stillicide, Taper, Tumble

Spin(ner), Spinning Aeroplane, Arabian, Arachne, Bielmann, Birl, Camel, Centrifuge, Cribellum, Cut, Day trip, Dextrorse, DJ, Flat, Flip, Gimp, Googly, Gymp, Gyrate, Gyre, Gyroscope, Hurl, Isobaric, Lachesis, Mole, Nun, Peg-top, Pirouette, Pivot, PR, Precess, Prolong, Purl, Rev(olve), Ride, Rotate, Royal, Screw, Side, Sinistrorse, Slide, Spider, Stator, Strobic, Swirl, Swivel, Throstle, Tirl, Toss, Trill, Twirl, Twist, Wheel, Whirl, Work

Spinach Florentine, Orach(e), Popeye

Spinal (chord), Spine, Spiny Acromion, Aculeus, Areole, Backbone, Barb, Chine, Coccyx, Column, Doorn, Dorsal, Epidural, Muricate, Myelon, Notochord, Ocotillo, Prickle, Quill, Rachial, Ray, R(h)achis, Thorn, Tragacanth

Spindle(-shanks), Spindly Arbor, Bobbin, Capstan, Fusee, Fusiform, Fusil, Mandrel, Pin, Scrag, Staff, Triblet

▸ **Spine** *see* SPINAL

Spinel Balas, Picotite

Spineless Muticous, Timid, Weak

Spinn(e)y Coppice, Shaw, Thicket

Spinning-wheel Chark(h)a

Spinster Discovert, Feme sole, Old maid, Tabby

Spiral Archimedes, Cochlea, Coil, Dexiotropic, Dextrorse, Ekman, Gyrate, Helical, Helix, Hyperbolic, Inflationary, Logarithmic, Loxodromical, Screw, Scroll, Sinistrorse, Spin, Tailspin, Turbinate, Volute, Whorl, Wind

Spire(-shaped) Broach, Flèche, Peak, Shaft, Steeple, Thyrsoid

Spirit(s), Spirited Ahriman, Akvavit, Alcohol, Ammonia, Angel, Animal, Animation, Applejack, Apsaral, Aquavit, Aqua vitae, Arak, Arch(a)eus, Ardent, Ariel, Arrack, Asmoday, Astral, Bitters, Blithe, Boggart, Bogle, Brandy, Bravura, Brio, Brollachan, Buggan(e), Buggin, Cant, Cherub, Courage, Creature, Crouse, Daemon, Dash, Deev, Deva, Distillation, Div, Djinn(i), Domdaniel, > **DRINK**, Dryad, Duende, Duppy, Dybbuk, Eblis, Eidolon, Elan, Element(al), Emit, Empusa, Entrain, Erdgeist, Esprit, Essence, Ethos, Eudemon, Fachan, Faints, Familiar, Feints, Feisty, Feni, Fenny, Fetich(e), Fetish, Fettle, Fight, Firewater, Fuath, Gamy, Geist, Geneva, Genie, Genius, > **GHOST**, Ghoul, Ginger, Ginn, Gism, Glastig, Glendoveer, Go, Grappa, Gremlin, Grit, Grog, Gumption, Gytrash, Hartshorn, Heart, Hollands, Holy, Huaca, Imp, Incubus, Indwelt, Jann, Jinn(i), Jinnee, Jism, Ka, Kachina, Kelpie, Kindred, Kirsch, Kobold, Larva, Lemur(e), > **LIQUOR**, Lively, Loki, Manes, Manito(u), Manitu, Mare, Marid, Metal, Meths, Methyl(ated), Mettle, Mindererus, Mobbie, Mobby, Morale, Nain rouge, Neutral, Nis, Nix, Nobody, Numen, Ondine, Orenda, Panache, Paraclete, Party, Pecker, Pep, Peri, Pernod®, Petrol, Phantom, Pluck(y), Pneuma, Poltergeist, Pooka, Potato, Poteen, Presence, Proof, Psyche, Puck, Python, Racy, Rakee, Raki, Rakshas(a), Rectified, Rosicrucian, Ruin, Rum(bullion), Rye, Salt, Samshoo, Samshu, Saul, Schnapps, Seraph, Shade, Shadow, Shaitan, She'ol, Short, Smeddum, Soul, Spectre, Spright, Sprite, Spunk, Steam, Strunt, Surgical, Sylph, Tafia, Tangie, Taniwha, Team, Tequila, Tokoloshe, Ton, Turpentine, Turps, Undine, Verve, Vigour, Vim, Vodka, Voodoo, Water horse, Weltgeist, White, Wili, Wine, Witblits, Wood, Wraith, Zeitgeist, Zephon, Zing, Zombie

Spiritless Craven, Dowf, Insipid, Languid, Meek, Milksop, Poor, Tame, Vapid

Spirit-level Vial
Spiritual(ism), Spiritualist Aerie, Aery, Coon-song, Ecclesiastic, Ethereous, Eyrie, Eyry, Incorporeal, Negro, Planchette, Platonic, Psychic, Table-rapping, Table-turning
Spirt Gush, Jet, Rush
Spit(ting), Spittle Barbecue, Broach, Chersonese, Dead ringer, Dribble, Drool, Emptysis, Eructate, Expectorate, Fuff, Gob, Golly, Gooby, Goss, Grill, Hawk, Hockle, Impale, Jack, Lookalike, Peninsula, Ras, Ringer, Rotisserie, Saliva, Skewer, Slag, Spade(ful), Spawl, Spear, Sputter, Sputum, Tombolo, Yesk, Yex
Spite(ful) Backbite, Bitchy, Catty, Grimalkin, Harridan, Irrespective, Malevolent, Malgrado, Malice, Mau(l)gre, Mean, Petty, Pique, Rancour, Spleen, Venom, Waspish
Spitfire Cacafogo, Cacafuego, Wildcat
Spittoon Cuspidor(e)
Spiv Lair, Rorter
Splash Blash, Blue, Dabble, Dash, Dog, Drip, Feature, Flouse, Fl(o)ush, Gardyloo, Jabble, Ja(u)p, Jirble, Paddle, Plap, Plop, Plowter, Sket, Slosh, Slush, Soda, Sozzle, Spairge, Spat(ter), Spectacle, Splat(ch), Splatter, Splodge, Splosh, Splotch, Spray, Spree, Squatter, Swash, Swatter, Water, Wet
Splay(ed) Flew, Flue, Patte(e), Spread
Spleen Acrimony, Bite, Lien, Melt, Milt(z), Pip, Stomach, Vitriol, Wrath
Splendid, Splendour Ah, Braw, Brilliant, Bully, Capital, Champion, Clinker, Dandy, Eclat, Effulgent, Excellent, Fine, Finery, Fulgor, Gallant, Garish, Glitterand, Glittering, Glorious, Glory, Gorgeous, Grand(eur), Grandiose, Ha, Heroic, Lustrous, Majestic, Mooi, Noble, Palatial, Panache, Pomp, Proud, Radiant, Rich, Ripping, Royal, Stunning, Super(b), Wally
Splice(d) Braid, Eye, Join, Knit, Mainbrace, Wed
▷ **Spliced** *may indicate* an anagram
Splint Airplane, Banjo, Brace, Cal(l)iper, Splenial, T
Splinter(s) Bone-setter, Breakaway, Flinder, Fragment, Matchwood, Shatter, Shiver, Skelf, Sliver, Spale, Spall, Speel, Spelk, Spell, Spicula, Spill
Split Axe, Banana, Bifid, Bifurcate, Bisect, Break, Burst, Chasm, Chine, Chop, Clint, Clove(n), Crack, Crevasse, Cut, Departmentalise, Disjoin, Distrix, > **DIVIDE**, Division, Divorce, End, Fissile, Fissure, Flake, Fork(ed), Fragment, Grass, Lacerate, Partition, Red(d), Rift(e), Rip, Rive, Russian, Ryve, Schism, Scissor, Segregate, Separate, Septemfid, Sever, Share, Skive, Slit, Sliver, Spall, Spalt, Speld, Tattle, Tmesis, Told, To-rend, To-tear, Wedge
▷ **Split** *may indicate* a word to become two; one word inside another; or a connection with Yugoslavia
Splodge, Splotch Blot, Drop, Splash
Splurge Binge, Indulge, Lavish, Spend, Splash, Spree
Splutter Chug, Expectorate, Fizz, Gutter, Spray, Stammer
Spoil(s), Spoilt Addle, Agrise, Agrize, Agryze, Blight, Blunk, Booty, Botch, Bribe, Coddle, Corrupt, Crool, > **DAMAGE**, Dampen, Deface, Defect, Deform, Dish, Foul, Hames, Harm, Impair(ed), Indulge, Loot, Maderise, Maltreat, Mar, Mardy, Muck, Mutilate, Mux, Pamper, Pet, Pickings, Pie, Plunder, Prize, Queer, Rait, Rate, Ravage, Ret, Rot, Ruin, Scupper, Spuly(i)e, Swag, Taint, Tarnish, Vitiate, Wanton, Winnings
▷ **Spoil(ed), Spoilt** *may indicate* an anagram
Spoilsport Damper, Killjoy, Party pooper, Wet blanket, Wowser
Spoke(s) Concentric, Radius, Ray, Rung, Said, Sed, Strut
▷ **Spoken** *may indicate* the sound of a word or letter

Spokesman Foreman, Mouthpiece, Orator, Prophet, Representative

Spoliation, Spoliative Devastation, Pillage, Plunder, Predatory, Reif

Sponge(r), Spongy Alcoholic, Ambatch, Argentine, Battenburg, Bum, Cadge, Cake, Cleanse, Diact, Diploe, Fozy, Free-loader, Glass-rope, Hexact, Hyalonema, Leech, Lig, Lithistid(a), Loofa(h), Madeira, Madeleine, Mermaid's glove, Mooch, Mop, Mouch, Mump, Parasite, Parazoa, Pentact, Poachy, Porifera(n), Quandong, Rhabdus, Sarcenchyme, Scambler, Schnorrer, Scrounge, Shark, Shool, Siphonophora, Smell-feast, Sooner, Sop, Sucker, Swab, Sycophant, Tetract, Tiramisu, Tylote, Vegetable, Velamen, Venus's flowerbasket, Wangle, Wipe, Zimocca, Zoophyte

Spongewood Sola

Sponsor(ship) Aegis, Angel, Auspice, Backer, Egis, Finance, Godfather, Godparent, Gossip, Guarantor, Lyceum, Patron, Surety

Spontaneous Aleatoric, Autonomic, Gratuitous, Immediate, Impromptu, Impulsive, Instant, Intuitive, Natural, Ultroneus, Unasked, Unpremeditated, Unprompted

Spoof Chouse, Cozenage, Deception, Delusion, Fallacy, > HOAX, Imposture, Ramp, Swindle, Trick

Spook(s), Spooky CIA, Eerie, Fantom, Frightening, Ghost, Phantom, Shade

Spool Bobbin, Capstan, Pirn, Reel, Trundle

Spoon(ful), Spoon-shaped Apostle, Canoodle, Cochlear, Deflagrating, Dollop, Dose, Gibby, Greasy, Labis, Ladle, Mote, Neck, Rat-tail, Runcible, Scoop, Scud, Server, Snuff, Spatula, Sucket, Trolling, Woo, Wooden

Spoonerism Marrowsky, Metathesis

Spoor Trace, Track, Trail

Sporadic Fitful, Isolated, Occasional, Patchy

Spore (case) Conidium, Ex(t)ine, Fungus, Glomerule, Lenticel, Seed, Sorus, Telium, Uredinium

Sporran Pock

Sport(s), Sporting, Sportive Aikido, Amusement, Angling, Aquatics, Autocross, Basho, Blood, Bonspiel, Breakaway, Brick, Bungee-jumping, By-form, Contact, Curling, Cyclo-cross, Daff, Dalliance, Dally, Deviant, Drag-racing, Extreme, Field, Freak, Frisky, Frolic, Fun, > GAME, Gent, Gig, Hang-gliding, In, Joke, Karate, Kickboxing, Korfball, Laik, Lake, Langlauf, Lark, Merimake, Merry, Morph, Mutagen, Octopush, Orienteering, Pal, Pancratium, Paragliding, Parakiting, Parapenting, Parasailing, Parascending, Paraskiing, Polo, Rallycross, Recreate, Rogue, RU, Rules, Shinny, Shinty, Skijoring, Snowboarding, Softball, Spectator, Speedball, Speed-skating, Speedway, Squash, Steeplechase, Sumo, Tailing, Tournament, Tourney, Toy, Trampolining, Trapshooting, Wakeboarding, Water polo, Wear, Weightlifting, Windsurfing, Winter, Wrestling

▷ **Sport(s)** *may indicate* an anagram

Sportsman, Sportsmen All-rounder, Athlete, Blue, Corinthian, Hunter, Nimrod, Pentathlete, Pitcher, Shamateur, Shikaree, Shikari

Spot(s), Spotted, Spotting, Spotty Ace, Acne, Area, Areola, Areole, Baily's beads, Bausond, Bead, Beauty, Befoul, Blackhead, Blain, Blemish, Blind, Blip, Blob, Blot, Blotch(ed), Blur, Brind(l)ed, Carbuncle, Caruncle, Cash, Check, Cloud, Colon, Comedo, Corner, Curn, Cyst, Dance, Dapple(-bay), Dick, Discern, Discover, Dot, Drop, Eruption, Espy, Eye, Facula, Flat, Fleck, Floater, Fogdog, Foxed, Freak, Freckle, Furuncle, G, Gay, Gräfenberg, Gricer, Guttate, High, Hot, Jam, Leaf, Lentago, Location, Loran, Mackle, Macle, Macul(at)e, Mail, Meal, Measly, Microdot, Milium, Moil, Mole, Morbilli, Mote, Motty, Muscae volitantes, Naevoid, Note, Notice, Ocellar, Ocellus, Paca, Papule, Paraselene, Pardal, Parhelion, Patch, Peep(e), Penalty, Petechia, Pied, Pimple, Pin, Pip, Place, Plook, Plot, Plouk, Pock, Punctuate, Pupil, Pustule, Quat, Radar, Rash, Recognise, Red, Rose-drop, Scotoma, Situation, Skewbald, Smut, Soft, Speck(le), Speculum, Splodge, Spy, Stigma, Sully, Sun, Taint, Tar, Tight, Touch, Trouble, Weak, Whelk, Whitehead, X, Yellow, Zit

Spotless Clean, Immaculate, Virginal

Spotlight Ace, Baby, Bon-bon, Brute, Maxi-brute

Spot on To a t

Spouse Companion, Consort, F(i)ere, Hubby, Husband, Mate, Oppo, Partner, Pheer, Pirrauru, Significant other, Wife, Xant(h)ippe

Spout(er) Adjutage, Erupt, Gargoyle, Geyser, Grampus, Gush, Impawn, Jet, Mouth, Nozzle, Orate, Pawn, Pourer, Raile, Rote, Spurt, Stream, Stroup, Talk, Tap, Vent

Sprain(ed) Crick, Rax, Reckan, Rick, Stave, Strain, Wrench, Wrick

Sprat Brit, Fish, Garvie, Garvock

Sprawl Loll, Scramble, Sprangle, Spread, Stretch, Urban

Spray Aerosol, Aigrette, Atomiser, Buttonhole, Corsage, Cyme, Egret, Fly, Hair, Mace®, Nasal, Posy, Rose, Rosula, Shower, Sparge, Spindrift, Splash, Spoondrift, Sprent, Sprig, Sprinkle, Spritz, Strinkle, Syringe, Twig

Spray *may indicate* an anagram

Spread(ing), Spreader Air, Apply, Banquet, Bestrew, Beurre, Blow-out, Branch, Bush, Butter, Carpet, Centre, Contagious, Couch, Coverlet, Coverlid, Deploy, Diffract, Diffuse, Dilate, Disperse, Dissemination, Distribute, Divulge, Double, Drape, Dripping, Elongate, Emanate, Expand, Extend, Fan, Feast, Flare, Guac(h)amole, Honeycomb, Jam, Lay, Marge, Marmite®, Metastasis, Multiply, Nutter, Oleo, Open, Overgrow, Paste, Pâté, Patent, Patulous, Perfuse, Pervade, Picnic, Propagate, Radiate, Ran, Run, Scale, Set, Sheet, Slather, Smear, Smorgasbord, Sow, Span, Speld, Spelder, Spillover, Splay, Sprawl, Spray, Straddle, Straw, Stretch, Strew, Strow, Suffuse, Systemic, Tath, Teer, Unfold, Unguent, Vegemite®, Widen, Wildfire

Spread *may indicate* an anagram

Spree Bat, Beano, Bender, Binge, Bum, Bust, Carousal, Frolic, Jag, Jamboree, Juncate, Junket, Lark, Loose, Randan, Rantan, Razzle(-dazzle), Revel, Rouse, Splore, Tear, Ups(e)y

Sprig Brad, Branch, Cyme, Nail, Sien, Spray, Syen, Twig, Youth

Sprightly Agile, Airy, Chipper, Jaunty, Mercurial

Spring(s), Springtime, Springy Aganippe, Alice, Arise, Bolt, Bounce, Bound, Box, Bunt, Cabriole, Caper, Capriole, Castalian, Cavort, Cee, Coil, Dance, Elastic, Eye, Fount(ain), Gambado, Germinate, Geyser, Grass, Hair, Helix, Hippocrene, Hop, Hot, Jump, Leaf, Leap, Lent, Lep, Litt, Low-water, May, Mineral, Originate, Persephone, Pierian, Pounce, Prance, Primavera, Prime, Resilient, Ribbon, Rise, Saddle, Season, Skip, Snap, Spa, Spang, Spaw, Stem, Stot, Submarine, Sulphur, Thermae, Thermal, Trampoline, Valve, Vault, Vaute, Vawte, Vernal, Voar, Ware, Watch, Waterhole, Weeping, Well(-head), Whip, Winterbourne

Spring(y) *may indicate* an anagram

Springbok Amabokoboko

Springless Telega

Springtail Apterygota

Sprinkle(r), Sprinkling Asperge, Aspergill(um), Bedash, Bedrop, Bescatter, Caster, Dredge, Dust, Hyssop, Lard, Pouncet, Powder, Rose, Scatter,

Scouthering, Shower, Sow, Spa(i)rge, Spatter, Splash, Spray, Spritz, Strinkle
Sprint(er) Burst, Dash, Race, Rash, Run, Rush, Wells
Sprite Apsaras, Croquemitaine, Echo, Elf, Fairy, Fiend, Genie, Goblin, Gremlin, Hobgoblin, Icon, Ondine, Puck, Spirit, Troll, Trow, Umbriel, Undine
Sprout Braird, Breer, Brussels, Bud, Burgeon, Chit, Crop, Eye, Germ(inate), Grow, Pullulate, Shoot, Spire, Tendron, Vegetate
Spruce Dapper, Engelmann, Natty, Neat, Norway, Picea, Pitch-tree, Prink, Shipshape, Sitka, Smart, Spiff, Tidy, Tree, Trim, Tsuga, White
Spry Active, Agile, Constance, Dapper, Nimble, Volable
Spud Murphy, Potato, Spade, Tater, Tatie
Spume Eject, Foam, Froth, Lather, Spet, Spit
Spunk Courage, Grit, Pluck, Tinder
Spur Accourage, Activate, Calcar(ate), Encourage, Fame, Fire, Galvanise, Goad, Heel, Incite, Limb, Lye, Needle, Offset, Prick, Rippon, Rowel, Shoot, Spica, Stimulus, Strut, Stud, Tar, Urge
Spurge (tree) Candelilla, Croton, Euphorbia, Kamala, Poinsettia, Ricinus
Spurious Adulterine, Apocryphal, Bogus, Counterfeit, Dog, False, Phoney, Pseudo, Sciolism
▷ **Spurious** *may indicate* an anagram
Spurn Despise, Disdain, Ignore, Jilt, Reject, > **SCORN**, Shun
Spurt Burst, Forge, Geyser, Jet, Outburst, Pump, Spout
Sputter Fizzle, Spit, Splutter, Stutter
Spy(ing), **Spies** Agent, Beagle, Caleb, CIA, Cicero, Curtain-twitcher, Descry, Dicker, Emissary, Espionage, Fink, Fuchs, Informer, Keeker, Mata Hari, MI, Mole, Mouchard, Nark, Nose, Operative, Pimp, Plant, Pry, Recce, Scout, See, Setter, Shadow, Sinon, Sleeper, Spetsnaz, Spook, Tout, Wait
Spyhole Eyelet, Judas-hole, Oillet, Peephole
Squab Chubby, Cushion, Obese
Squabble Argue, Bicker, Brabble, Quarrel, Rhubarb, Row, Scrap
Squad(ron) Band, Blue, Company, Crew, Death, Drugs, Escadrille, Fifteen, Firing, Flying, Fraud, Hit, Nahal, Platoon, Red, Snatch, Vice, White, Wing
Squalid, **Squalor** Abject, Colluvies, Dickensian, Dinge, Dingy, Filth, Frowsy, Grungy, Poverty, Scuzzy, Seedy, Sleazy, Slum(my), Slurb, Sordid
Squall Blast, Blow, Chubasco, Commotion, Cry, Drow, Flaw, Flurry, Gust, Line, Sumatra, Wail, White, Yell, Yowl
Squander Blow, Blue, Fritter, Frivol, Lash, Mucker, Slather, Splash, Splurge, Ware, > **WASTE**
Square(d), **Squares** Agree, Anta, Ashlar, Ashler, Bang, Barrack, Belgrave, Berkeley, Block, Bribe, Chequer, Compone, Compony, Corny, Deal, Dinkum, Even(s), Fair, Fog(e)y, Forty-nine, Fossil, Four, Gobony, Grey, Grosvenor, Latin, Least, Leicester, Level, Magic, Market, Meal, Mitre, Nasik, Neandert(h)aler, Nine, Norma, Old-fashioned, Palm, Passé, Pay, Perfect, Piazza, Place, Platz, Plaza, Quad(rangle), Quadrate, Quarry, Quits, Red, Rood, S, Set(t), Sloane, Solid, Squier, Squire, Straight, T, Tee, Times, Traditionalist, Trafalgar, Try, Unhip
Squash(y) Adpress, Butternut, Conglomerate, Crush, Gourd, Kia-ora, Knead, Marrow, Mash, Obcompress, Oblate, Pattypan, Press, Pulp, Shoehorn, Silence, Slay, Slew, Slue, Soft, Squeeze, Squidge, Squidgy, Suppress, Torpedo
Squat(ter) Bywoner, Crouch, Croup(e), Dumpy, Fubby, Fubsy, Hunker, Pudsey, Pyknic, Rook, Ruck, Sit, Spud, Stubby, Stumpy, Swatter, Usucaption
Squaw Kloo(t)chman
Squawk Cackle, Complain, Cry, Scrauch, Scraugh

Squeak(er) Cheep, Creak, Narrow, Peep, Pip, Scroop, Shoat, Squeal

Squeal(er) Blow, Eek, Howl, Inform, Pig, Screech, Sing, Sneak, Tell, Wee, Yelp

Squeamish(ness) Delicate, Disgust, Missish, Nervous, Prudish, Queasy, Reluctant

Squeeze Bleed, Chirt, Coll, Compress, Concertina, Constrict, Cram, Credit, Crowd, Crush, Dispunge, Exact, Express, Extort, Hug, Jam, Mangle, Milk, Preace, Press, Sandwich, Sap, Scrooge, Scrouge, Scrowdge, Scruze, Shoehorn, Squash, Squish, Sweat, Thrutch, Thumbscrew, Wring

Squelch Gurgle, Squash, Squish, Subdue

Squib Banger, Damp, Firework, Lampoon

Squid Calamari, Calamary, Cephalopod, Ink-fish, Loligo, Mortar, Nautilus, Octopus, Sleeve fish

Squiffy Drunk, Tiddley

Squiggle *may indicate an anagram*

Squint(ing) Boss-eyed, Cast, Cock-eye, Cross-eye, Glance, Gledge, Glee, Gley, Hagioscope, Heterophoria, Louche, Proptosis, Skellie, Skelly, Sken, Squin(n)y, Strabism, Swivel-eye, Vergence, Wall-eye

Squire Armiger(o), Beau, Donzel, Escort, Hardcastle, Headlong, Land-owner, Scutiger, Swain, Western, White

Squirm(ing) Fidget, Reptation, Twist, Worm, Wriggle, Writhe

Squirrel, Squirrel's nest Aye-aye, Boomer, Bun, Cage, Chickaree, Chipmuck, Chipmunk, Dray, Drey, Flickertail, Flying, Fox, Gopher, Grey, Ground, Hackee, Hoard(er), Meerkat, Petaurist, Phalanger, Red, Sciuroid, Sewellel, Skug, S(o)uslik, Spermophile, Taguan, Vair, Zizel

Squirt(er) Chirt, Cockalorum, Douche, Jet, Scoosh, Scoot, Skoosh, Spirt, Spout, Spritz, Urochorda, Wet, Whiffet, Whippersnapper

Sri Lanka(n) Ceylon, Cingalese, CL, Serendip, Sinhalese, Vedda

St Saint, Street

Stab Bayonet, Crease, Creese, Dag, Effort, Go, Gore, Guess, Jab, Knife, Kreese, Kris, Lancinate, Pang, Pierce, Pink, Poniard, Prick, Prong, Stick, Stiletto, Wound

Stabilise(r), Stability Aileron, Balance, Emulsifier, Even, Maintain, Pax Romana, Peg, Permanence, Plateau, Poise, Steady, Tail panel

Stable(s) Augean, Balanced, Barn, Byre, Certain, Constant, Durable, Equerry, Equilibrium, Firm, Livery, Loose box, Manger, Mews, Poise, Secure, Solid, Sound, Stall, Static(al), Steadfast, Steady, Stud, Sure

Stableman Groom, Lad, Ostler

Stachys Betony

Stack(s) Accumulate, A gogo, Chimney, Clamp, Cock, End, Funnel, Heap, Lum, > PILE, Rick, Shock, Staddle

Stadium Arena, Ballpark, Bowl, Circus, Circus Maximus, Coliseum, Hippodrome, Speedway, Velodrome

Staff Alpenstock, Ash-plant, Bato(o)n, Bourdon, Burden, Caduceus, Cane, Crook, Crosier, Cross(e), Crozier, Crutch, Cudgel, Entourage, Equerry, Etat-major, Faculty, Ferula, Ferule, Flagpole, General, Linstock, Lituus, Mace, Omlah, Pastoral, Personnel, Pike, Pole, Rod, Runic, Sceptre, Seniority, Skeleton, Stave, Stick, Taiaha, Tapsmen, Tau, Thyrsus, Truncheon, Verge, Wand, Workers, Workforce

Stag Actaeon, Brocket, Buck, Deer, For men, Imperial, Line, Male, Party, Royal, Rutter, Ten-pointer, Wapiti

Stage Act, Anaphase, Apron, Arena, Bardo, Bema, Boards, Catasta, Centre, Chrysalis, Committee, Diligence, Dog-leg, Estrade, Fare, Fargo, Fit-up, Grade,

Juncture, Key, Landing, Leg, Level, Metaphase, Milestone, Moment, Mount, Oidium, Phase, Phasis, Pier, Pin, Platform, Point, Prophase, Proscenium, PS, Puberty, Report, Rostrum, Scene, Sensorimeter, Sound, Stadium, Step, Stor(e), Subimago, Theatre, Thrust, Transition, Trek, Yuga

Stage-coach Diligence, Thoroughbrace

Stagecraft Pinafore

Stagehand Flyman, Grip

Stagger(ed) Alternate, Amaze, Astichous, Awhape, Daidle, Falter, Floor, Lurch, Recoil, Reel, Rock, Shock, Stoiter, Stot(ter), Stumble, Sway, Teeter, Thunderstricken, Thunderstruck, Titubate, Tolter, Totter, Wamble, Wintle

▷ **Staggered** *may indicate* an anagram

Stagirite, **Stagyrite** Aristotle

Stagnant, **Stagnation** Foul, Inert, Scummy, Stasis, Static

Staid Decorous, Demure, Formal, Grave, Matronly, Prim, Sad, Sober, Stick-in-the-mud

Stain(er) Aniline, Bedye, Besmirch, Blemish, Blob, Blot, Blotch, Discolour, Dishonour, Dye, Embrue, Ensanguine, Eosin, Fox, Gram's, Grime, Imbrue, Iodophile, Keel, Maculate, Mail, Meal, Mote, Portwine, Slur, Smirch, Smit, Soil, Splodge, Splotch, Stigma, Sully, Taint, Tarnish, Tinge, Tint, Vital, Woad

Stair(case), **Stairs** Apples, Apples and pears, Caracol(e), Cochlea, Companionway, Escalator, Flight, Perron, Rung, Spiral, Step, Tread, Turnpike, Vice, Wapping, Winding

Stake(s) Ante, Bet, Claim, Gage, Holding, Impale, Impone, Interest, Lay, Loggat, Mark, Mise, Paal, Pale, Paliform, Paling, Palisade, Peel, Peg, Pele, Picket, Pile, Play, Post, Pot, Punt, Put, Rest, Revie, Risk, Septleva, Spike, Spile, Stang, Stob, Straddle, Sweep, Tether, Vie, Wager, Welter

Stalactite Dripstone, Dropstone, Helictite, Lansfordite, Soda straw

Stale Aged, Banal, Flat, Fozy, Frowsty, Fusty, Hackneyed, Handle, Hoary, Mouldy, Musty, Old, Pretext, Rancid, Urine, Worn

▷ **Stale** *may indicate* an obsolete word

Stalemate Deadlock, Dilemma, Hindrance, Impasse, Mexican standoff, Saw-off, Standoff, Tie, Zugswang

Stalk(s) Anthophore, Bun, Cane, Caulicle, Follow, Funicle, Garb(e), Gynophore, Ha(u)lm, Keck(s), Kecksey, Keksye, Kex, Ommatophore, Pedicel, Pedicle, Peduncle, Petiole, Petiolule, Phyllode, Pursue, Rush, Scape, Seta, Shaw, Spear, Spire, Stem, Sterigma, Stipe(s), Stride, Strig, Strut, Stubble, Stump, Trail, Yolk

Stalking-horse Stale

Stall(s) Arrest, Bay, Booth, Box, Bulk, Crib, > DELAY, Floor, Flypitch, Hedge, Kiosk, Loose-box, Orchestra, Pen, Pew, Prebendal, Seat, Shamble, Sideshow, Stand, Starting, Stasidion, Temporise, Trap, Traverse, Travis, Trevis(s), Whip

Stallion Cooser, Cuisser, Cusser, Entire, > HORSE, Stag, Staig, Stonehorse, Stud

Stalwart Anchor-man, Buirdly, Firm, Manful, Robust, Sturdy, Trusty, Valiant

Stamen(ed) Androecium, Octandria, Polyandria

Stamina Endurance, Fibre, Fortitude, Guts, Last, Stamen, Stay, Steel

Stammer(ing) Balbutient, Er, Hesitate, Hum, Psellism, Sputter, Stumble, > STUTTER, Waffle

Stamp(s), **Stamped** Appel, Cast, Character, Date(r), Die, Enface, Frank, Imperforate, Impress, Imprint, Incuse, Label, Matchmark, Mint, Pane, Penny black, Perfin, Philately, Pintadera, Postage, Press(ion), Rubber, Seal, Seebeck, Se-tenant, Signet, Spif, Strike, Swage, Tête-bêche, Touch, Touchmark, Trading, Trample, Tread, Tromp, Type

Stamp-collecting Philately, Timbrology, Timbrophily

Stampede Debacle, Flight, Panic, Rampage, > RUSH

Stance Attitude, Pose, Position, Posture

Stand(ing), Stand for, Stand up Apron, Arraign, Attitude, Base, Be, Bear, Bide, Binnacle, Bipod, Bristle, Brook, Canterbury, Caste, Confrontation, Cradle, Crease, Dais, Degree, Desk, Dock, Dree, Dumb-waiter, Easel, Etagère, Face, Foothold, Freeze, Gantry, Gueridon, Hard, Hob, Insulator, Klinostat, Last, Lazy Susan, Lectern, Leg, Music, Nef, Odour, One-night, Ovation, Pedestal, Place, Plant, Podium, Pose, Position, Pou sto, Prestige, Promenade, Protest, Qua, Rack, Rank, Regent, Remain, Represent, Repute, Rise, Stall, Statant, Station, > STATUS, Stay, Stillage, Stock, Stool, Straddle, Straphang, Stroddle, Strut, Table, Tantalus, Taxi, Teapoy, Terrace, > TREAT, Tree, Tripod, Trivet, Umbrella, Upright, Whatnot

Standard(s) Banner, Base, Baseline, Basic, Benchmark, Bogey, British, Canon, CAT, Classic(al), Cocker, Colour(s), Criterion, Double, Eagle, English, Ethics, Examplar, Example, Exemplar, Flag, Ga(u)ge, Gold, Gonfalon, Guidon, Ideal, Labarum, Level, Living, Model, Norm(a), Normal, Numeraire, Old Glory, Oriflamme, Par, Parker Morris, Pennon, Principle, Rate, Regular, Rod, Rose, Routine, Royal, > RULE, Silver, Spec(ification), Staple, Sterling, Stock, Time, Touchstone, Tricolour, Troy, Two-power, Usual, Valuta, Vexillum, Yardstick

Standard-bearer Alferez, Cornet, Ensign, Vexillary

Stand-by Adminicle, Reserve, Substitute, Support, Understudy

Stand-in Double, Locum, Stunt man, Sub(stitute), Surrogate, Temp, Understudy

Standish Miles

Stand-off(ish) Aloof, Remote, Reserved, Stalemate, Upstage

Standpoint Angle

Standstill Deadset, Halt, Jam

Stanley Baldwin, Knife, Rupert

Stannic Tin

Stanza Ballad, Elegiac, Envoi, Envoy, Heroic, Ottava, Poem, Sixaine, Spenserian, Staff, Stave, Tetrastich, Verse

Staple Basic, Bread, Chief, Maize, Pin, Wool

Star(s) Aster(isk), Body, Celebrity, Constant, Constellation, Cynosure, Double, Exploding, Falling, Feather, Feature, Film, Fixed, Flare, Giant, Headline, Hero, Hexagram, Idol, Lead, Lion, Mogen David, Movie, Multiple, Pentacle, Personality, Pip, Pointer, Principal, Pulsating, Shell, Shine, Shooting, Sidereal, Solomon's seal, Spangle, Starn(ie), Stellar, Stern, Swart, (The) Pointers, Top-liner, Ultraviolet, Variable, Vedette

STARS

3 letters:
Dog
Sol

4 letters:
Argo
Beta
Dark
Grus
Lode
Lyra
Mira

Nova
Pavo
Pole
Ursa
Vega
Vela
Zeta

5 letters:
Acrux
Agena
Algol

Alpha
Ceres
Comet
Delta
Deneb
Draco
Dubhe
Dwarf
Gamma
Hyads
Indus
Lupus

Mensa
Merak
Mizar
Norma
North
Polar
Radio
Rigel
Rigil
Spica
Theta
Venus

Virgo
Wagon
Whale

6 letters:
Alioth
Alkaid
Altair
Aquila
Auriga
Binary
Bootes
Carbon
Carina
Castor
Cygnus
Dorado
Esther
Etoile
Fornax
Galaxy
Hyades
Lizard
Megrez
Merope
Meteor
Mullet
Octans
Phecda
Plough
Pollux
Psyche
Pulsar

Puppis
Quasar
Saturn
Sirius
Sothis
Uranus
Vesper
Volans

7 letters:
Antares
Calaeno
Canopus
Capella
Cepheus
Chamber
Columba
Dolphin
Epsilon
Estoile
Evening
Gemingo
Lucifer
Morning
Neutron
Perseus
Phoenix
Polaris
Procyon
Proximo
Regulus
Sabaism
Serpens

Sterope
Triones
Wagoner

8 letters:
Achernar
Arcturus
Barnard's
Circinus
Denebola
Equuleus
Hesperus
Magnetar
Mira Ceti
Pegasean
Phosphor
Pleiades
Praesepe
Red dwarf
Red giant
Scorpius
Synastry
Waggoner

9 letters:
Aldebaran
Andromeda
Bellatrix
Big Dipper
Black hole
Centaurus
Collapsar
Delphinus

Fire-drake
Fomalhaut
Meteorite
Ophiuchus
Pentagram
Rigil-Kent
Supernova
Wolf-Rayet

10 letters:
Betacrucis
Betelgeuse
Betelgeuze
Brown dwarf
Cassiopeia
Orion's belt
Phosphorus
Supergiant
White dwarf

11 letters:
Circumpolar

12 letters:
Little Dipper

13 letters:
Southern Cross

14 letters:
Proxima centaur

Starboard Right

Starch(y), **Starch producer** Amyloid, Arrowroot, Cassava, Ceremony, Congee, Conjee, Coontie, Coonty, Cycad, Farina, Fecula, Formal, Glycogen, Manioc, Maranta, Pentosan, Stamina, Statolith, Tapioca, Tous-les-mois

Stare Eyeball, Fisheye, Gape, Gapeseed, Gawp, Gaze, Geek, Goggle, Gorp, Look, Outface, Peer, Rubberneck

Starfish Asterid, Asteroid(ea), Bipinnaria, Brittlestar, Ophiurid, Radiata

Star-gaze(r), **Star-gazing** Astrodome, Astronomy, Copernicus

Stark Apparent, Austere, Bald, Bare, Gaunt, Harsh, Naked, Nude, Sheer, Stiff, Utterly

Starling Bird, Murmuration, Pastor, Stare

Star of Bethlehem Chincherinchee, Chinkerinchee

Start(ed), **Starter** Ab ovo, Abrade, Abraid, Abray, Activate, Actuate, Begin, Boggle, Bot, Broach, Bug, Bump, Chance, Commence, Crank, Create, Crudites, Dart, Ean, Embryo, Face-off, False, Fire, Flinch, Float, Flush, Flying, Found, Gambit, Gan, Genesis, Getaway, Gun, Handicap, Head, Hot-wire, Impetus, Imprimis, Incept(ion), Initiate, Instigate, Institute, Intro, Jerk, Jump, Jump-off, Kick-off, L, Lag, Launch, Lead, Off, Offset, Onset, Ope(n), Ord, Origin, Outset,

Preliminary, Prelude, Proband, Put-up, Reboot, Resume, Roll, Rouse, Scare, Set off, Shy, Slip, Snail, Spring, Spud, String, Tee-off, Wince

Start *may indicate* an anagram or first letter(s)

Startle, **Startling** Alarm, Bewilder, Disturb, Eye-opener, Flush, Frighten, Magical, Rock, Scare

Starvation, **Starve(d)**, **Starving** Anorexia, Anoxic, Bant, Clem, Cold, Deprive, Diet, Famish, Inanition, Macerate, Perish, Pine, Undernourished

Starving *may indicate* an 'o' in the middle of a word

State(s) Affirm, Alabama, Alaska, Alle(d)ge, Andorra, Aread, Arizona, Ark(ansas), Arrede, Assert, Assever, Attest, Aver, Avow, Bahar, Balkan, Belize, Benin, Brunei, Buffer, California, Carolina, Case, Chad, Cite, Client, Colorado, Commonwealth, Condition, Confederate, Conn(ecticut), Country, Critical, Cutch, Dakota, Declare, Del(aware), Dependency, Dixie, Dubai, Durango, Emirate, Empire, Etat, Ethiopia, Federal, Fettle, Fla, Flap, Florida, Free, Ga, Gabon, Georgia, Ghana, Guatemala, Gulf, Habitus, Hawaii, Hesse, Honduras, Humour, Ia, Idaho, Illinois, Indiana, Iowa, Jalisco, Jamahiriya, Jharkand, Jigawa, Johore, Jumhouriya, Kalat, Kano, Kansas, Karnataka, Kashmir, Kedah, Kelantan, Kentucky, Kerala, Khelat, Kingdom, Kogi, Kutch, Kuwait, Kwara, Land, Lesh, Louisiana, Madras, Maine, Malawi, Malay, Manipur, Maranhao, Maryland, Mass(achusetts), Md, Me, Meghalaya, Mess, Mewar, Mi(chigan), Michoacán, Minas Gerais, Minnesota, Mississippi, Missouri, Mizovam, Montana, Morelos, Mysore, Nagaland, Name, Nanny, Nation, Native, Nayarit, NC, Nebraska, Negri Sembilan, Nevada, New Hampshire, New Jersey, New Mexico, New South Wales, New York, Nirvana, Nuevo Léon, NY, Oaxaca, Ogun, Ohio, Oklahoma, Oman, Ondo, Orange Free, Oregon, Orissa, Osun, Oyo, Pa, Pahang, Palatinate, Papal, Para, Paraiba, Parana, Penang, Pennsylvania, Perak, Perlis, Pernambucio, Piaui, Plateau, Plight, Police, Pradesh, Predicament, Predicate, Premise, Pronounce, Protectorate, Prussia, Puebla, Punjab, Puppet, Qatar, Quantum, Queensland, Queretaro, Quintana Roo, Rajasthan, Realm, Reich, Republic, RI, Rivers, Rogue, Rondonia, Roraima, Saarland, Sabah, St Kitts and Nevis, St Vincent, Samoa, San Luis Potosi, Santa Catarina, Sao Paulo, Sarawak, Satellite, Saxony(-Anholt), Say, Schleswig-Holstein, Selangor, Sergipe, Sikkim, Slave, Sokoto, Sonora, Sorry, South Australia, South Carolina, South Dakota, Sparta, Standing, Steady, Styria, Succession, Swat, Tabasco, Tamaulipas, Tamil Nadu, Tanganyika, Tasmania, Tennessee, T(e)rengganu, Texas, Threeness, Thuringia, Tiaxcala, Tocantina, Togo, Ton(g)kin(g), Travancore, Tripura, Trucial, Udaipur, UK, Uncle Sam, Union, United, US, Ut, Utah, Uttaranchai, Utter Pradesh, Va, Vatican City, Venezuela, Veracruz, Vermont, Victoria, Virginia, Washington, Welfare, West Virginia, Wis(consin), Wyoming, Yucatan, Zacatecas

Stated *may indicate* a similar sounding word

Stately, **Stately home** August, Dome, Grand, Imposing, Majestic, Mansion, Noble, Regal

Statement Account, Affidavit, Aphorism, Assertion, Attestation, Avowal, Bill, Bulletin, Communiqué, Deposition, Dictum, Diktat, Encyclical, Evidence, Expose, Factoid, Generalisation, Indictment, Invoice, Jurat, Manifesto, Mission, Outline, Paraphrase, Pleading, Press release, Profession, Pronouncement, Proposition, Protocol, Quotation, Release, Remonstrance, Report, Sentence, Soundbite, Sweeping, Testimony, Truism, Utterance, Verb

Stateroom Bibby, Cabin

Statesman American, Attlee, Botha, Briand, Bright, Canning, Cato, Clarendon, Diplomat, Disraeli, Draco, Elder, Flaminius, Franklin, Genro, Georgian,

Gladstone, Gracchi, Grotius, Guy, Kissinger, Kruger, Lafayette, Lie, North, Politician, Politico, Seneca, Smuts, Stein, Talleyrand, Tasmanian, Thiers, Walpole, Wealsman, Yankee

Static Atmospherics, Becalmed, Electricity, Inert, Maginot-minded, Motionless, Sferics, Stationary

Station(s) Action, Base, Berth, Birth, Camp, Caste, CCS, Comfort, Crewe, Deploy, Depot, Dressing, Euston, Filling, Fire, Garrison, Gas, Halt, Head, Hill, Hilversum, Ice, Lay, Location, Marylebone, Outpost, Panic, Petrol, Pitch, Place, Plant, Point, Police, Polling, Post, Power, Quarter, Radio, Rank, Relay, Rowme, Seat, Service, Sheep, Sit, Space, Stance, Stand, Status, Stond, Subscriber, Tana, Tanna(h), Terminus, Testing, Thana(h), Thanna(h), Tracking, Triangulation, Victoria, Waterloo, Waverley, Way, Weather, Work

Stationary Fasten, Fixed, Immobile, Parked, Sessile, Stable, Static

Stationer(y), Stationery-case Continuous, Papeterie

Statistic(ian), Statistics Actuary, Descriptive, Fermi-Dirac, Figure, Gradgrind, Graph, Lod, Number, Parametric, Percentage, Quantum, Sampling, Student's t, Vital

Statuary, Statue(tte) Acrolith, Bronze, Bust, Colossus (of Rhodes), Discobolus, Effigy, Figure, Figurine, Galatea, Idol, Image, Kore, Kouros, Liberty, Memnon, Monument, Oscar, Palladium, Pietà, Sculpture, Sphinx, Stonework, Tanagra, Torso, Xoanon

Stature Growth, Height, Inches, Rank

Status Beacon, Caste, Class, Political, > POSITION, Prestige, Quo, Rank, Standing

Statute Act, Capitular, Chapter 7, Chapter 11, Decree, Edict, Law, Novels

Staunch Amadou, Leal, Resolute, Steady, Stem, Stout, Styptic, Watertight

Stave Break, Dali, Forestall, Lag, Slat, Stanza, Ward

Stay(s) Alt, Avast, Bide, Board, Bolster, Cohab(it), Corselet, Corset, Embar, Endure, Fulcrum, Gest, Guy, Hawser, Indwell, Jump, Lie, Lig, Linger, Lodge, Manet, Moratorium, Piers, Prop, > REMAIN, Reprieve, Restrain, Settle, Sist, Sleepover, Sojourn, Stem, Stop off, Stop-over, Strut, Sustain, Tarry, Triatic, Villeggiatura

Stay-at-home Indoor, Tortoise

STD Aids, Herpes, Telephone, VD

Steadfast Changeless, Constant, Firm, Implacable, Resolute, Sad, Stable

Steady Andantino, Ballast, Beau, Boyfriend, Changeless, Composer, Constant, Even, Faithful, Firm, Girlfriend, Measured, Regular, Rock, Stabilise, Stable, Unswerving

Steak Carpet-bag, Chateaubriand, Chuck, Fillet, Flitch, Garni, Mignon, Minute, Pope's eye, Porterhouse, Rump, Slice, Tartare, T-bone, Tenderloin, Tournedos, Vienna

Steal(ing) Abstract, Bag, Bandicoot, Bone, Boost, Cabbage, Cly, Condiddle, Convey, Creep, Crib, Duff, Embezzle, Filch, Glom, Grab, Half-inch, Heist, Hotting, Joyride, Kidnap, Knap, Lag, Liberate, Lift, Loot, Mag(g), Mahu, Mill, Naam, Nam, Nap, Nick, Nim, Nip, Nym, Peculate, Pilfer, Pillage, Pinch, Piracy, Plagiarise, Plunder, Poach, Prig, Proll, Purloin, Ram-raid, Remove, Rifle, Rob, Rustle, Scrump, Skrimp, Smug, Snaffle, Snatch, Sneak, Snitch, Souvenir, Swipe, Take, Theft, Thieve, Tiptoe, TWOC, Whip

Stealth(y) Art, Catlike, Covert, Cunning, Furtive, Obreption, Surreptitious, Tiptoe

Steam(ed), Steamy Boil, Condensation, Cushion, Dry, Fume, Gaseous, Het, Humid, Live, Mist, Porn, Radio, Roke, Sauna, Spout, Vapor, Vapour, Wet

Steamer, Steamboat Kettle, Showboat, Side-wheeler, SS, Str, Tramp, Turbine

Steam-hammer Ram

Steed Charger, Horse, Mount

Steel(y) Acierate, Adamant, Bethlehem, Blade, Blister, Bloom, Brace, Carbon, Cast, Chrome, Chromium, Cold, Concrete, Crucible, Damascus, Damask, High-carbon, High-speed, Magnet, Manganese, Maraging, Martensite, Metal, Mild, Nickel, Pearlite, Ripon, Rolled, Sorbite, Spray, Stainless, Structural, Sword, Toledo, Tool, Tungsten, Vanadium, Wootz

Steelyard Bismar

Steep Abrupt, Arduous, Brent, Costly, Embay, Expensive, High-pitched, Hilly, Krans, Krantz, Kranz, Macerate, Marinade, Marinate, Mask, Precipice, Precipitous, Rait, Rapid, Rate, Ret, Saturate, Scarp, > SHEER, Soak, Sog, Souse, Stey, Stickle, Tan

Steeple(jack) Spiderman, Spire, Turret

Steer(er), Steering Ackerman, Airt, Buffalo, Bullock, Cann, Castor, Con(n), Cox, Direct, > GUIDE, Helm, Navaid, Navigate, Ox, Pilot, Ply, Power, Rudder, Stot, Whipstaff, Zebu

Stem Alexanders, Arrow, Axial, Biller, Bine, Bole, Caudex, Caulicle, Caulome, Check, Cladode, Cladophyll, Confront, Corm, Culm, Dam, Epicotyl, Floricane, Ha(u)lm, Kex, Pedicle, Peduncle, Pin, Pseudaxis, Rachis, R(h)achilla, Rhachis, Rhizome, Rise, Rod, Sarment, Scapus, Seta, Shaft, Shank, Sobole(s), Spring, Stalk, Staunch, Stipe, Stolon, Stopple, Straw, Sympodium, Tail

Stench F(o)etor, Funk, Miasma, Odour, Smell, Stink, Whiff

Stencil Copy, Duplicate, Mimeograph®, Pochoir

Stenographer, Stenography Amanuensis, Secretary, Shorthand, Typist

Step(s) Act, Balancé, Chassé, Choctaw, Corbie, Curtail, Dance, Démarche, Echelon, Escalate, False, Flight, Fouetté, Gain, Gait, Glissade, Goose, Grecian, Greece, Grees(e), Greesing, Grese, Gressing, Griece, Grise, Grize, Halfpace, Lavolt, Lock, Measure, Move, Notch, Pace, Pas, Pas de souris, Phase, Pigeon's wing, Quantal, Raiser, Ratlin(e), Rattlin(e), Rattling, Roundel, Roundle, Rung, Shuffle, Slip, Stage, Stair, Stalk, Stile, Stope, Stride, Toddle, Trap, Tread, Trip, Unison, Waddle, Walk, Whole, Winder

Stephen Martyr, Stainless

Stepmother Novercal

Stepney Spare

Steppe Kyrgyz, Llano, Plain

Stereo Personal

Stereotype(d) Hackney, Ritual

Sterile, Sterilise(r), Sterility Acarpous, Aseptic, Atocia, Autoclave, Barren, Dead, Fruitless, Impotent, Infertile, Neuter, Pasteurise, Spay

Sterling Excellent, Genuine, Pound, Silver, Sound

Stern Aft, Austere, Counter, Dour, Flinty, Grim, Hard, Implacable, Iron, Isaac, Nates, Poop, Rear, Relentless, Rugged, Stark, Strict, Tailpiece, Transom

Steroid Anabolic, Androsterone, Calciferol, Cortisone, Dexamethasone, Ergosterol, Fusidic, Lumisterol, Mifepristone, Nandrolone, Predniso(lo)ne, Spironolactone, Testosterone

Sterol Stigmasterol

Stertorous Snore

Stet Restore

Stevedore Docker, Dockhand, Longshoreman, Stower, Wharfinger

Stevenson RLS, Tusitala

Stew(ed), Stews Bagnio, Bath, Blanquette, Boil, Bordel(lo), Bouillabaisse, Bouilli, Braise, Bredie, Brothel, Burgoo, Carbonade, Carbonnade, Casserole,

Cassoulet, Cholent, Chowder, Coddle, Colcannon, Compot(e), Daube, Flap, Fuss, Goulash, Haricot, Hash, Hell, Hot(ch)pot(ch), Irish, Jug, Lather, Lobscouse, Maconochie, Matapan, Matelote, Mulligan, Navarin, Olla podrida, Osso bucco, Paddy, Paella, Pepperpot, Pot-au-feu, Pot-pourri, Ragout, Ratatouille, Rubaboo, Salmi, Sass, Scouse, Seethe, Simmer, Slumgullion, Squiffy, Stie, Stove, Stovies, Sty, Succotash, Sweat, Swelter, Tajine, Tatahas, Tzimmes, Zamzawed, Zarzuela

Steward Butler, Cellarer, Chamberlain, Chiltern Hundreds, Dewan, Factor, Hind, Malvolio, Manciple, Maormor, Mormaor, Official, Oswald, Panter, Purser, Reeve, Seneschal, Sewer, Shop, Smallboy, Sommelier, Waiter

▷ **Stewed** *may indicate* an anagram

Stibnite Antimony, Kohl

Stick(ing) (out), **Sticks**, **Sticky**, **Stuck** Adhere, Affix, Agglutinant, Aground, Ash, Ashplant, Atlatl, Attach, Bamboo, Bastinado, Bat, Baton, Bauble, Bayonet, Bludgeon, Bond, Boondocks, Caman, Cambrel, Cammock, Cane, Celery, Cement, Chalk, Chapman, Clag, Clam(my), Clarty, Clave, Cleave, Cling, Clog, Club, Cocktail, Cohere, Coinhere, Composing, Control, Crab, Crosier, Cross(e), Crotch, Crozier, Crummack, Crummock, Cue, Distaff, Divining-rod, Dog, Dure, Endure, Fag(g)ot, Firewood, Flak, Founder, Fuse, Gad(e), Gaid, Gambrel, Gelatine, Glair, Gliadin, Glit, Glue, Goad, Gold, Goo, Gore, Ground-ash, Gum, Gunge, Gunk, Harpoon, Hob, Hurley, Immobile, Impale, Inhere, Isinglass, Jab, Jam, Jut, Kebbie, Kid, Kierie, Kindling, Kip, Kiri, Knitch, Knobkerrie, Ko, Lance, Lath(i), Lathee, Lentisk, Limy, Lug, Message, Minder, Molinet, Orange, Parasitic, Paste, Penang-lawyer, Persist, Phasmid, Piceous, Pierce, Piolet, Plaster, Pogo, Pole, Posser, Protrude, Protuberant, Pugol, Quarterstaff, Rash, Ratten, Rhubarb, Rhythm, Rod, Ropy, Scouring, Seat, Shillela(g)h, Shooting, Size, Ski, Smudge, Spanish windlass, Spear, Spurtle, Squail(er), Staff, Stand, Stang, Stob, Stodgy, Supplejack, Swagger, Switch, Swizzle, Swordstick, Tacamahac, Tack(y), Tally, Tar, Thick, Throwing, Toddy, Truncheon, Trunnion, Twig, Vare, Viscid, Viscous, Waddy, Wait, Walking, Wand, White, Woolder, Woomera(ng)

Sticker Araldite®, Barnacle, Bur, Glue, Label, Limpet, Partisan, Poster, Slogan

Stickler Pedant, Poser, Problem, Purist, Rigid, Rigorist, Tapist

Stiff, **Stiffen(er)**, **Stiffening**, **Stiffness** Anchylosis, Angular, Ankylosis, Baleen, Bandoline, Brace, Buckram, Budge, Corpse, Corpus, Dear, Defunct, Expensive, Formal, Frore(n), Frorn(e), Gammy, Goner, Grommet, Gut, Hard, Lignin, Mort, Myotonia, Petrify, Pokerish, Prim, Ramrod, Rigid, Rigor, Rigor mortis, Sad, Set, Shank-iron, Size, Solid, Starch, Stark, Stay, Steeve, Stieve, Stilted, Stoor, Stour, Stowre, Sture, Trubenize®, Unbending, Whalebone, Wigan, Wooden

Stifle Crush, Dampen, Funk, Muffle, Scomfish, Smore, Smother, Stive, Strangle

Stigma(tise) Blemish, Brand, Carpel, Discredit, Note, Slur, Smear, Spot, > **STAIN**, Wound

Stile Gate, Steps, Sty

Stiletto Bodkin, Heel, Knife

Still Accoy, Airless, Alembic, Assuage, Becalm, Calm, Check, Current, Doggo, Ene, Even(ness), Freeze-frame, Higher, Howbe, However, Hush, Illicit, Inactive, Inanimate, Inert, Kill, Languid, Limbec(k), Lull, Motionless, Nevertheless, Patent, Peaceful, Photograph, Placate, Placid, Posé, Pot, Quiescent, Quiet, Resting, Silent, Snapshot, Soothe, Stagnant, Static, Stationary, Though, Yet

Stilt Avocet, Bird, Poaka, Prop, Scatch

Stilted Formal, Pedantic, Stiff, Unruffled, Wooden

Stimulant, Stimulate, Stimulus Activate, Adrenaline, Antigen, Arak, Arouse, Auxin, Benny, Caffeine, Cinder, Clomiphene, Coca, Conditioned, Coramine, Cue, Dart, Digitalin, Digoxin, Egg, Energise, Evoke, Excitant, Fillip, Fuel, Galvanize, Ginger, Goad, Hormone, Incite, Innerve, Inspire, Irritate, Jog, Key, K(h)at, Kick, L-dopa, Mneme, Motivate, Nikethamide, Oestrus, Oxytocin, Paraphilia, Pemoline, Pep, Philtre, Pick-me-up, Piquant, Pituitrin, Prod, Promote, Provoke, Psych, Qat, Rim, Roborant, > ROUSE, Rowel, Rub, Sassafras, Sensuous, Spur, Sting, Stir, Tannin, Tar, Theine, Tickle, Titillate, Tone, Tonic, Unconditioned, Upper, Whet(stone), Wintergreen, Winter's bark

Sting(ing) Aculeate, Barb, Bite, Cheat, Cnida, Goad, Nematocyst, Nettle(tree), Overcharge, Perceant, Piercer, Poignant, Prick, Pungent, Rile, Scorpion, Sephen, Smart, Spice, Stang, Stimulus, Surcharge, Tang, Trichocyst, Urent, Urtica

Sting-ray Sephen, Trygon

Stingy Cheeseparing, Chintzy, Close, Costive, Hard, Illiberal, Mean, Miserly, Narrow, Near, Niggardly, Nippy, Parsimonious, Skimpy, Snippy, Snudge, Tight(wad), Tight-arse

Stingy *may indicate* something that stings

Stink(er), Stinking, Stinks Abroma, Atoc, Atok, Brock, Cacodyl, Crepitate, Desman, Fetor, Foumart, Guff, Heel, Hellebore, Malodour, Mephitis, Miasma, Ming, Niff, Noisome, Rasse, Reek, Rich, Science, > SMELL, Sondeli, Stench, Teledu

Stinkbird Hoa(c)tzin

Stint Chore, Economise, Limit, Scamp, Scantle, Scrimp, Share, Skimp

Stipend Ann(at), Annexure, Pay, Prebend, Remuneration, Salary, Wages

Stipulate, Stipulation Clause, Condition, Covenant, Insist, Provision, Proviso, Rider, Specify

Stipule Ocrea

Stir(red), Stirring Accite, Admix, Ado, Afoot, Agitate, Amo(o)ve, Animate, Annoy, Bird, Bother, Bustle, Buzz, Can, Churn, Cooler, Excite, Foment, Furore, Fuss, Gaol, Hectic, Impassion, Incense, Incite, Inflame, Instigate, Insurrection, Intermix, Jee, Jog, Kitty, Limbo, Live, > MIX, Move, Noy, Paddle, Penitentiary, Poss, Pother, > PRISON, Prod, Provoke, Quad, Quatch, Quetch, Quinche, Qui(t)ch, Quod, Rabble, Rear, Roil, Rouse, Roust, Rummage, Rustle, Sod, Steer, Styre, Swizzle, To-do, Upstart, Wake

Stir(red), Stirring *may indicate* an anagram

Stirrup (guard) Bone, Footrest, Footstall, Iron, Stapes, Tapadera, Tapadero

Stitch (up) Bargello, Basket, Baste, Blanket, Blind, Box, Buttonhole, Cable, Chain, Couching, Crewel, Crochet, Cross, Daisy, Embroider, Feather, Fell, Flemish, Florentine, Garter, Gathering, Grospoint, Hem, Herringbone, Honeycomb, Insertion, Kettle, Knit, Lazy daisy, Lock, Monk's seam, Moss, Needle, Open, Overcast, Overlock, Pearl, Petit point, Pinwork, Plain, Purl, Queen, Rag, Railway, Rib, Rope, Running, Saddle, Satin, Screw, Sew, Slip, Spider, Stab, Stay, Steek, Stem, Stockinette, Stocking, Straight, Sutile, Suture, Tack, Tailor's tack, Tent, Topstitch, Vandyke, Whip, Whole

Stock(ed), Stocks, Stocky Aerie, Aery, Ambulance, Amplosome, Barometer, Blue-chip, Bouillon, Bree, Breech, Brompton, Buffer, But(t), Capital, Carry, Cattle, Choker, Cippus, Congee, Conjee, Court-bouillon, Cravat, Dashi, Debenture, Delta, Die, Endomorph, Equip, Fumet, Fund, Gamma, Gear(e), Government, Graft, Gun, Handpiece, He(a)rd, Hilt, Hoosh, Industrial, Intervention, Inventory, Joint, Just-in-time, Kin, Larder, Laughing, Line, Little-ease, Locuplete, Omnium, Pigeonhole, Preferred, Pycnic, Race, Ranch,

Recovery, Rep(ertory), Replenish, Reserve, Rolling, Root, Scrip, Seed, Shorts, Soup, Squat, Staple, Steale, Steelbow, Stirp(e)s, > **STORE**, Strain, Stubby, Supply, Surplus, Talon, Tap, Team, Tie, Utility, Virginia

Stockade Barrier, Eureka, Zare(e)ba, Zereba, Zeriba

Stocking(s) Bas, Boot-hose, Fishnet, Hogger, Hose, Leather, Legwarmer, Moggan, Netherlings, Nylons, Seamless, Sheer, Sock, Spattee, Support, Tights

Stockman, **Stockbroker** Broker, Jobber, Neatherd

Stodge, **Stodgy** Dull, Filling, Heavy

Stoic(al) Impassive, Job, Logos, Patient, Philosophical, Plato, Porch, Seneca(n), Spartan, Stolid, Zeno

Stoke(r), **Stokes** Bram, Coal-trimmer, Fire(man), Fuel, S, Shovel

Stole(n) Bent, Epitrachelion, Hot, Maino(u)r, Manner, Manor, Nam, Orarion, Orarium, Reft, Scarf, Staw, Tippet, Tweedle

Stolid Deadpan, Dull, Impassive, Phlegmatic, Po(-faced), Thickset, Wooden

Stomach(ic) Abdomen, Abomasum, Accept, Appetite, Belly, Bible, Bingy, Bonnet, Bread-basket, Brook, C(o)eliac, Corporation, Epigastrium, Epiploon, Fardel-bag, Gaster, Gizzard, Gut, Heart, Jejunum, King's-hood, Kite, Kyte, Little Mary, Manyplies, Mary, Maw, Mesaraic, Midriff, Omasum, Paunch, Potbelly, Propodon, Proventriculus, Psalterium, Pylorus, Read, Rennet, Reticulum, Rumen, Stick, Swagbelly, > **SWALLOW**, Tripe, Tum, Tun-belly, Urite, Vell, Venter, Wame, Washboard, Wem, Zingiber

Stomach-ache Colic, Colitis, Collywobbles, Giardiasis, Gripe, Gutrot, Mulligrubs

Stone(d), **Stone age**, **Stones**, **Stony** Blotto, Drunk, Henge, Imposing, Ink, Inukshuk, Lucky, Lydian, Mort, Niobe(an), Pelt, Precious, Rolling, Sermon, Standing, Step(ping), Through, Touch

STONES

2 letters:	Lode	Flint	Sneck
St	Onyx	Gooly	Stela
	Opal	Grape	Stele
3 letters:	Plum	Jewel	Topaz
Gem	Ragg	Kenne	Wacke
Hog	Sard	Lapis	Wyman
Pit	Skew	Logan	
Rag	Slab	Menah	**6 letters:**
Tin	Soap	Metal	Amazon
	Tile	Mocha	Ashlar
4 letters:	Trap	Paste	Ashler
Bath		Prase	Baetyl
Blue		Pumie	Bezoar
Celt	**5 letters:**	Quern	Brinny
Door	Agate	Quoin	Chesil
Flag	Amber	Quoit	Chisel
Hone	Balas	Rubin	Cobble
Horn	Beryl	Rufus	Coping
Iron	Black	Rybat	Cultch
Jasp	Chalk	Satin	Dolmen
Kerb	Chert	Scone	Flusch
Lias	Coade	Scree	Fossil
Lime	Culch	Slate	Gibber
	Drupe		

Gooley
Goolie
Gravel
Humite
Jargon
Jasper
Kidney
Kingle
Ligure
Lithic
Menhir
Metate
Mosaic
Muller
Nutlet
Oamaru
Paving
Pebble
Pot-lid
Pumice
Pyrene
Rip-rap
Samian
Sarsen
Scarab
Summer
Tanist
Yonnie

7 letters:
Asteria
Avebury
Blarney
Bologna
Boulder
Breccia
Callais
Cat's eye
Chuckie
Curling
Girasol

Granite
Hyacine
Hyalite
Jargoon
Lia-fail
Lithoid
Moabite
Olivine
Parpane
Parpend
Parpent
Pennant
Peridot
Perpend
Perpent
Petrous
Pudding
Purbeck
Putamen
Rocking
Rosetta
Sardine
Sardius
Sarsden
Scaglia
Schanse
Schanze
Smaragd
Staddle
Tektite
Telamon
Thunder
Tripoli
Urolith

8 letters:
Aerolite
Aerolith
Amethyst
Asteroid
Baguette

Cabochon
Calculus
Cinnamon
Cromlech
Cryolite
Ebenezer
Elf-arrow
Endocarp
Essonite
Ganister
Girasole
Lapidate
Megalith
Menamber
Monolith
Nephrite
Omphalos
Onychite
Parpoint
Peastone
Petrosal
Phengite
Pisolite
Portland
Rollrich
Sapphire
Sardonyx
Scalpins
Schantze
Specular
Tonalite
Voussoir

9 letters:
Alabaster
Asparagus
Cairngorm
Carnelian
Cholelith
Chondrite
Cornelian

Crossette
Dichroite
Firestone
Gannister
Greensand
Hessonite
Hoarstone
Lithiasis
Meteorite
Paleolith
Pipestone
Rubicelle
Scagliola
Trilithon
Turquoise
Ventifact

10 letters:
Adamantine
Alectorian
Aragonites
Chalcedony
Draconites
Enhydritic
Foundation
Gastrolith
Grey-wether
Kimberlite
Lherzolite
Lithophyte
Pearlstone
Rhinestone

11 letters:
Peristalith

12 letters:
Carton-pierre
Philosopher's

Stone-crop Orpin(e), Sedum, Succulent
Stone-pusher Sisyphus
Stone-thrower Bal(lista), Catapult, David, Mangonel, Onager, Perrier, Sling, Trebuchet
Stone-wall(er) Block, Mule, Revet
Stone-worker Jeweller, Knapper, Sculptor
Stooge Butt, Cat's-paw, Feed, Straight man
Stook(s) Sheaf, Stack, Thr(e)ave
Stool Buffet, Coppy, Cracket, Creepie, Cricket, Cucking, Curule, Cutty, Ducking, Faeces, Hassock, Milking, Music, Piano, Pouf(fe), Repentance, Seat,

Sir-reverence, Step, Stercoral, Sunkie, Taboret, Tripod, Tripos, Turd

Stoop Bend, Condescend, C(o)urb, Daine, Deign, Incline, Porch, Slouch

Stop(page), **Stopcock**, **Stopper**, **Stopping** Abort, An(n)icut, Arrest, Avast, Bait, Ba(u)lk, Bide, Blin, Block, Brake, Buffer, Bung, Canting-coin, > **CEASE**, Cessation, Chapter, Check, Checkpoint, Cheese, Cholestasis, Clarabella, Clarino, Clarion, Clog, Close, Colon, Comfort, Comma, Conclude, Cork, Coupler, Cremo(r)na, Cremorne, Cromorna, Cut, Deactivate, Debar, Demurral, Desist, Deter, Devall, Diapason, Diaphone, Discontinue, Discourage, Dit, Dolce, Dot, Dulciana, Echo, Embargo, End, Field, Fifteenth, Flag, Flue, Flute, Foreclose, Foundation, Fr(a)enum, Freeze, Full, Gag, Gamba, Gemshorn, Glottal, Gong, Halt, Hamza(h), Hartal, Hinder, Hitch, Ho, Hold, Hoy, Intermit, Ischuria, Jam, Kibosh, Let-up, Lill, Lin, Lute, Media, Mutation, Nasard, Oboe, Obturate, Occlude, Oppilate, Organ, Outspan, Pause, Period, Piccolo, Pit, Plug, Point, Poop, Preclude, Prevent, Principal, Prorogue, Pull-in, Pull over, Pull-up, Punctuate, Quash, Quint, Quit, Racket, Red, Reed, Refrain, Register, Rein, Remain, Request, Rest, Salicet, Scotch, Screw-top, Semi-colon, Sese, Sesqualtera, Sext, Sist, Snub, Solo, Spigot, Stall, Stanch, Standstill, Stash, Stasis, Station, Staunch, Stay, Stive, Strike, Subbase, Subbass, Suction, Supersede, Suppress, Suspend, Tab, Tamp(ion), Tap, Tenuis, Terminate, Toby, Toho, Truck, Voix celeste, Vox angelica, Vox humana, Waldflute, Waldhorn, Waypoint, When, Whistle, Whoa

Stopgap Caretaker, Gasket, Gaskin, Interim, Makeshift, Temporary

Storage, **Store(house)**, **Store** Accumulate, Arsenal, Backing, Barn, Bin, Bottle, Bottom drawer, Boxroom, Bunker, Buttery, Cache, Cell, Cellar, Chain, Clamp, Clipboard, Convenience, Co-op(erative), Co-operative, Cootch, Core, Cupboard, Cutch, Database, Deli, Dene-hole, Dépanneur, Department(al), Depository, Depot, Dime, Discount, Dolia, Dolly-shop, Elevator, Emporium, Ensile, Entrepot, Etape, Fund, Garner, Genizah, Girnal, Glory hole, Go-down, Granary, Groceteria, > **HOARD**, Hold, Hope chest, House, Humidor, Husband, Hypermarket, Imbarn, Larder, Lastage, Lazaretto, Liquor, Lumber room, Magazine, Main, Mart, Mattamore, Memory, Mine, Morgue, Mothball, Mow, Multiple, Nest-egg, Off-licence, Package, Pantechnicon, Pantry, Pithos, Provision, Pumped, Rack(ing), RAM, Repertory, Reposit, ROM, Sector, > **SHOP**, Silage, Silo, Spence, Spooling, Springhouse, Squirrel, Stack, Stash, Stock, Stockroom, Stow, Superbaza(a)r, Superette, Supermarket, Supply, Tack-room, Tank, Thesaurus, Tithe-barn, Tommy-shop, Virtual, Volutin, Warehouse, Woodshed, Woodyard, Wool (shed)

▸ **Storey** see **STORY**

Stork Adjutant, Antigone, Argala, Bird, Jabiru, Marabou(t), Marg, Saddlebill, Wader, Wood, Wood ibis

Stork's bill Erodium

Storm(y) Ablow, Adad, Assail, Attack, Baguio, Blizzard, Bluster, Bourasque, Brouhaha, Buran, Calima, Charge, Cyclone, Devil, Dirty, Dust, Electric, Enlil, Expugn, Furore, Gale, Gusty, Haboob, Hurricane, Ice, Magnetic, Monsoon, Onset, Oragious, Rage(ful), Raid, Rain, Rampage, Rant, Rave, Red spot, Rugged, Rush, Shaitan, Snorter, Squall, Sumatra, Tea-cup, Tebbad, Tempest, Tornade, Tornado, Tropical, Unruly, Violent, Weather, Willy-willy, Wroth, Zu

▹ **Stormy** *may indicate* an anagram

Story, **Storyline**, **Storey**, **Stories** Account, Allegory, Anecdote, Apocrypha, Arthuriana, Attic, Bar, Basement, Baur, Bawr, Biog, Blood and thunder, Chestnut, Clearstory, Clerestory, Cock and bull, Conte, Cover, Decameron, Edda, Epic, Episode, Etage, Exclusive, Exemplum, Fable, Fabliau, Fib, Fiction,

Flat, Floor, Folk-tale, Gag, Geste, Ghost, Hard-luck, Heptameron, Hitopadesa, Horror, Idyll, Iliad, Jataka, Lee, Legend, Lie, Mabinogion, Marchen, Mezzanine, Myth(os), Mythus, Narrative, Nouvelle, Novel(la), Oratorio, Parable, Passus, Pentameron, Plot, Rede, Report, Romance, Rumour, Saga, Scoop, Script, Serial, SF, Shaggy dog, Shocker, Short, Smoke-room, Sob, Spiel, Spine-chiller, Splash, Stage, Success, Tale, Tall, Thread, Thriller, Tier, Triforium, Upper, Version, Yarn

Story-teller Aesop, Fibber, Griot, Liar, Munchausen, Narrator, Raconteur, Shannachie, Tusitala

Stoup Benitier, Bucket, Vessel

Stout(ness) Ale, Beer, Black velvet, Burly, Chopping, Chubby, Embonpoint, Endomorph, Entire, Fat, Fubsy, Hardy, Humpty-dumpty, Lusty, Manful, Milk, Obese, Overweight, Porter, Portly, Potbelly, Robust, Stalwart, Stalworth, Sta(u)nch, Strong, Stuggy, Sturdy, Substantial, Tall, Velvet

Stove Baseburner, Break, Calefactor, Cockle, Cooker, Furnace, Gasfire, Oven, Potbelly, Primus®, Range, Salamander

Stow Cram, Flemish (down), Load, Pack, Rummage, Stack, Stash, Steeve

Strabismus Squint

Straddle Bestride, Strodle

Strafe Bombard, Shell, Shoot

Straggle(r), Straggly Estray, Gad, Meander, Ramble, Rat-tail, Spidery, Sprawl, Stray, Wander

Straight(en), Straightness Align, Bald, Beeline, Correct, Die, Direct, Downright, Dress, Frank, Gain, Het(ero), Home, Honest, Lank, Legit, Level, Neat, Normal, Orthotropous, Rectilineal, Rectitude, Righten, Sheer, Slap, Tidy, True, Unbowed, Uncurl, Unlay, Upright, Veracious, Virgate

Straight edge Lute, Ruler

Straightforward Candid, Direct, Easy, Even, Forthright, Honest, Jannock, Level, Plain sailing, Pointblank, Simple

Straight-haired Leiotrichous

Strain(ed), Strainer, Straining Agonistic, Ancestry, Aria, Breed, Carol, Clarify, Colander, Distend, Drawn, Effort, Exert, Filter, Filtrate, Fit, Fitt(e), Force, Fray, Fytt(e), Intense, Kind, Melody, Milsey, Molimen, Music, Note, Overtask, Passus, Percolate, Plus, Pressure, Pull, Purebred, Rack, Raring, Reck(an), Retch, Rick, Seep, Seil(e), Set, Shear, Sieve, Sift, Sile, Stape, Start, Stock, Streak, Stress, Stretch, Sye, Tamis, Tammy, Tax, Tenesmus, Tense, Tension, Threnody, Try, Tune, Unease, Vein, Vice, Work, Wrick

Strait(s) Bab el Mandeb, Basilan, Bass, Bering, Bosp(h)orus, Canso, Channel, Condition, Cook, Crisis, Cut, Dardanelles, Davis, Denmark, Desperate, Drake Passage, Euripus, Formosa, Foveaux, Gat, Gibraltar, Golden Gate, Gut, Hormuz, Hudson, Johor, Juan de Fuca, Kattegat, Kerch, Korea, Kyle, Little Belt, Lombok, Mackinac, Magellan, Malacca, Menai, Messina, Mona Passage, Narrow, North Channel, Otranto, Palk, Predicament, Soenda, Solent, Sound, St, Sumba, Sunda, Taiwan, Tatar, Tiran, Torres, Tsugaru, Windward Passage

Straiten(ed) Impecunious, Impoverish, Poor, Restrict

Strait-laced Blue-nosed, Narrow, Primsie, Puritan, Stuffy

Strand(ed) Abandon, Aground, Bank, Beach, Desert, Fibre, Haugh, Hexarch, Isolate, Lock, Maroon, Neaped, Ply, Rice, Rope, Shore, Sliver, Thread, Three-ply, Tress, Wisp

Strange(ness), Stranger Alien, Aloof, Amphitryon, Curious, Eerie, Exotic, Foreign, Fraim, Frem(d), Fremit, Frenne, Funny, Guest, Malihini, New, Novel, Odd(ball), Outlandish, Outsider, Quare, Queer, Rum, S, Screwy, Selcouth, Singular, Tea-leaf, Uncanny, Unco, Uncommon, Unked, Unket, Unkid, Unused,

Unusual, Wacky, Weird, Wondrous

▷ **Strange** *may indicate* an anagram

Strangle(r) Choke, Garotte, Jugulate, Suppress, Throttle, Thug(gee)

Strap(ping) Able-bodied, Band, Barber, Beat, Bowyangs, Brail, Braw, Breeching, Browband, Crupper, Cuir-bouilli, Curb, Deckle, Girth, Halter, Harness, Holdback, Jess, Jock(ey), Larrup, Lash, Ligule, Lorate, Lore, Manly, Martingale, Nicky-tam, Octopus, Pandy, Rand, Rein, Robust, Shoulder, Sling, Spider, Strop, Surcingle, Suspender, T, Tab, Taws(e), T-bar, Thong, Throatlash, Throatlatch, Trace, Tump-line, Wallop, Watch

Stratagem, Strategist, Strategy Artifice, Clausewitz, Coup, Deceit, Device, Dodge, Exit, Fetch, Finesse, Fraud, Heresthetic, Kaupapa, Masterstroke, Maximum, Minimax, Plan, Rope-a-dope, > **RUSE**, Scheme, Scorched earth, Sleight, Subterfuge, Tactic(s), Tactician, Trick, Wile

Stratum, Strata Bed, Coal Measures, Kar(r)oo, Layer, Neogene, Permian, Schlieren, Seam, Syncline

Straw(s), Strawy Balibuntal, Boater, Buntal, Chaff, Cheese, Halm, Hat, Haulm, Hay, Insubstantial, Last, Leghorn, Monkey-pump, Nugae, Oaten, Panama, Parabuntal, Pea(se), Pedal, Short, Sipper, Stalk, Stramineous, Strammel, Strummel, Stubble, Trifles, Wisp, Ye(a)lm

Strawberry Barren, Birthmark, Fragaria, Garden, Hautbois, Hautboy, Potentilla, Wild

Stray Abandoned, Chance, Depart, Deviate, Digress, Err, Forwander, Foundling, Gamin, Maverick, Meander, Misgo, Pye-dog, Ramble, Roam, Sin, Straggle, Streel, Traik, Unowned, Waff, Waif, Wander

Streak(ed), Streaker, Streaky Archimedes, Bended, Blue, Brindle, Comet, Flaser, Flash, Fleck, Freak, Hawked, Highlights, Lace, Layer, Leonid, Lowlight, Mark, Merle, Mottle, Primitive, Race, Run, Schlieren, Seam, Shot, Striate, Striga, Strip(e), Vein, Venose, Vibex, Waif, Wake, Wale, Yellow

Stream Acheron, Anabranch, Arroyo, Beam, Beck, Bogan, Bourne, Burn, Consequent, Course, Current, Driblet, Fast, Flow, Flower, Freshet, Gulf, Gush, Headwater, Influent, Jet, Kill, Lade, Lane, Leet, Logan, Meteor, Nala, Obsequent, Pokelogan, Pour, Pow, Riffle, Rill, River, Rivulet, Rubicon, Run, Runnel, Sike, Slough, Spruit, Star, Streel, Subsequent, Syke, The Fleet, Thrutch, Tide-race, Torrent, Tributary, Trickle, Trout, Watercourse, Water-splash, Winterbourne

Streamer Banderol(e), Bandrol, Banner(all), Bannerol, Pennon, Pinnet, Ribbon, Tape, Vane

Streamline(d), Streamliner Clean, Fair, Fairing, Simplify, Sleek, Slim

Street Alley, Ave(nue), Bowery, Broad, Carey, Carnaby, Cato, Causey, Champs Elysées, Cheapside, Civvy, Close, Corso, Court, Crescent, Downing, Drive, Easy, Fleet, Gate, Grub, Harley, High(way), Kármán vortex, Lane, Lombard, Main, Meuse, Mews, One-way, Parade, Paseo, Queer, Road, Sesame, Side, Sinister, St, Strand, Terrace, Thoroughfare, Threadneedle, Throgmorton, Two-way, Vortex, Wall, Wardour, Watling, Way, Whitehall

Street arab Mudlark

Streetcar Desire, Tram

Strength(en), Strengthening Afforce, Ausforming, Bant, Beef, Brace, Brawn, Build, Confirm, Consolidate, Enable, Energy, Field, Foison, Force, Forte, Fortify, Freshen, Grit, Heart, Herculean, Horn, Intensity, Iron, Line, Main, Man, Might, Munite, Muscle, Nerve, > **POWER**, Prepotence, Pre-stress, Proof, Reinforce, Roborant, Sinew, Spike, Stamina, Steel, Sthenia, Stoutness, > **STRONG**, Tensile, Thews, Titration, Ultimate, Unity, Vim, Yield

Strenuous Arduous, Effort, Exhausting, Hard, Laborious, Vehement

Strephon Rustic, Wooer

Stress(ed) Accent, Arsis, Birr, Brunt, Emphasis, Ictus, Impress, Italicise, Marcato, Orthotonesis, Oxytone, Paroxytone, Post-traumatic, Primary, Proof, PTSD, Rack, Ram, Rhythm, RSI, Sentence, Sforzando, Shear, Strain, Taut, Tense, > TENSION, Try, Underline, Underscore, Urge, Wind shear, Word, Yield (point)

Stretch(able), Stretched, Stretcher, Stretching Belt, Brick, Crane, Distend, Draw, Ectasis, Eke, Elastic, Elongate, Expanse, Extend, Extensile, Farthingale, Fib, Frame, Give, Gurney, Lengthen, Litter, Narrows, Outreach, Pallet, Pandiculation, Porrect, Procrustes, Prolong, Protend, Pull, Rack, Rax, > REACH, Sentence, Shiner, Span, Spell, Spread, Spreadeagle, Strain, Taut, Tend, Tense, Tensile, Tenter, Term, Time, Tract, Tractile, Tree, Trolley

Striate Lineolate, Vein

Stricken Beset, Hurt, Overcome, Shattered

Strict Dour, Harsh, Literal, Medic, Narrow, Orthodox, Penal, Proper, Puritanical, Rigid, Rigorous, Severe, Spartan, Stern, Strait(-laced), Stringent

Stride Gal(l)umph, Leg, Lope, March, Pace, Piano, Stalk, Sten, Straddle, Stroam, Strut, Stump

Strident Brassy, Grinding, Harsh, Raucous, Screech

Strife Bargain, Barrat, Colluctation, Conflict, Conteck, Contest, Discord, Disharmony, Dissension, Feud, Food, Friction, Ignoble, Scrap(ping), Sturt

Strike(r), Striking, Strike out Affrap, Air, Alight, Annul, Appulse, Arresting, Attitude, Backhander, Baff, Band, Bandh, Bang, Bash, Bat, Baton, Batsman, Batter, Beat, Belabour, Better, Biff, Black, Bla(u)d, Bonanza, Bop, Buff, Buffet, Bund(h), Butt, Cane, Catch, Chime, Chip, Clap, Clash, Clatch, Clip, Clock, Clout, Club, Cob, Collide, Constitutional, Coup, Cue, Cuff, Dad, Dent, Dev(v)el, Ding, Dint, Dismantle, Distingué, Douse, Dowse, Dramatic, Drive, Dush, Eclat, Evenement, Fet(ch), Fillip, Firk, Fist, Flail, Flog, Frap, General, Get, Go-slow, Gowf, Hail, Hartal, Head-butt, > HIT, Horn, Hour, Hunger, Ictus, Illision, Impact, Impinge, Impress, Jarp, Jaup, Jole, Joll, Joule, Jowl, Knock, Lam, Lambast, Laser, Lay(-off), Lightning, Match, Middle, Notable, Noticeable, Official, Out, Pash, Pat(ter), Pat, Pean, Peen, Pein, Pene, Percuss, Picket, Pize, Plectrum, Pronounced, Pummel, Punch, Ram, Rap, Remarkable, Rolling, Roquet, Salient, Scrub, Scutch, Shank, Sideswipe, Sitdown, Sit-in, Slam, Slap, Slat, Slog, Slosh, Smack, Smash, Smite, Sock, Souse, Sowce, Sowse, Spank, Stayaway, Stop(page), Stub, Swap, Swat, Swinge, Swipe, Swop, Sympathy, Tan, Tapotement, Tat, Thump, Tip, Token, Tonk, Tripper, Unconstitutional, Unofficial, Walk-out, Wallop, Wap, Whack, Whang, Whap, Wherrit, Who does what, Whomp, Whop, Wick, Wildcat, Wipe, Wondrous, Zap

Strike-breaker Blackleg, Fink, Rat, Scab

String(s), Stringy Band, Beads, Bootlace, Bow, Bowyang, Cello, Chalaza, Chanterelle, Cord, Cosmic, Creance, Cremaster, Drill, Enfilade, Fiddle, Fillis, First, G, Glass, Gut, Henequin, Heniquin, Hypate, Idiot, Injection, Keyed, Lace, Lag, Lichanos, Macramé, Mese, Necklace, Nete, Nicky-tam, Paramese, Pledget, Production, Proviso, Purse, Quint, Ripcord, Rope, Second, Series, Shoe(-tie), Sinewy, Snare, Straggle, Strand, Sympathetic, Team, Tendon, Thairm, Tie, Tough, Train, Trite, Viola, Violin, Wreathed

String-course Moulding, Table

Stringent Extreme, Rigid, Severe, Strict, Urgent

Strip(ped), Stripper, Striptease Airfield, Armband, Band, Bare, Bark, Batten, Belt, Bereave, Blowtorch, Casparian, Chippendale, Comic, Cote, Defoliate,

Stripe(d) | 674

Denude, Deprive, Derobe, Despoil, Devest, Disbark, Dismantle, Dismask, Disrobe, Divest, Drag, Ecdysiast, Ecdysis, Ecorché, Fannel(l), Fiche, Film, Flashing, Flaught, Flay, Fleece, Flench, Flense, Flight, Flinch, Flounce, Flype, Furring, Gaza, Goujon, Hatband, Infula, Jib, Label, Landing, Lap-dancer, Lardon, Lath, Ledge, Linter, List, Littoral, Loading, Maniple, Median, Mobius, Panhandle, Parting, Peel, Pillage, Pluck, Pull, Puttee, Puttie, Rand, Raunch, Raw, Ribbon, Ring-bark, Roon, Royne, Rumble, Rund, Runway, Screed, Scrow, Shear, Shed, Shim, Shuck, Skin, Slat, Slit, Sliver, Spellican, Spilikin, Spill(ikin), Splat, Splent, Spline, Splint, Splinter, Spoil, Straik, Strake, Strap, Streak, Strop, Sugar soap, Swath, Sweatband, Tack, Tee, Thong, Tirl, Tirr, Uncase, Undeck, Undress, Unfrock, Unrig, Unrip, Unvaile, Valance, Weather, Widow, Zone

Stripe(d) Band, Bausond, Candy, Chevron, Cingulum, Cove, Endorse, Lance-jack, Laticlave, Line, List, Magnetic, > **NCO**, Ombré, Pale, Paly, Pin, Pirnie, Pirnit, Slash, Snip, Straik, Strake, Streak, Stroke, Tabaret, Tabby, Tiger, Tragelaph(us), Vitta, Weal

Strive, **Striving** Aim, Aspire, > **ATTEMPT**, Contend, Endeavour, Enter, Kemp, Labour, Nisus, Pingle, Press, Strain, Struggle, Toil, Try, Vie

Stroke Apoplex(y), Backhander, Bat, Bisque, Blow, Boast, Breast, Butterfly, Caress, Carom, Chip, Chop, Counterbuff, Coup, Coy, Crawl, Dash, Dint, Dog(gy)-paddle, Down-bow, Drear(e), Drere, Dropshot, Effleurage, Estrarnazone, Exhaust, Feat, Flick, Fondle, Foozle, Forehand, Glance, Ground, Hairline, Hand(er), Ictus, Inwick, Jenny, Jole, Joll, Joule, Jowl, Knell, Knock, Lash, Lightning, Like, Line, Loft, Long jenny, Loser, Massé, Oarsman, Oblique, Odd, Off-drive, Outlash, Palp, Paw, Pot-hook, Pull, Punto reverso, Put(t), Reverso, Ridding straik, Roquet, Rub, Scart, Scavenge, Sclaff, Scoop, Seizure, Sheffer's, Short jenny, Sider, Sixte, Slash, Smooth, Solidus, Spot, Strike, Stripe, Sweep, Swipe, Tact, Tittle, Touch, Touk, Trait, Trudgen, Trudgeon, Tuck, Upbow, Virgule, Wale, Whang

Stroll(er), **Strolling** Ambulate, Bummel, Dander, Daun(d)er, Dawner, Flanerie, Flaneur, Idle, Lounge, Ramble, Saunter, Stravaig, Stray, Toddle, Walk, Walkabout, Wander

Strong(est) Able, Brawny, Cast-iron, Doughty, Durable, F, Firm, Fit, Forceful, Forcible, Forte, Full-blown, Hale, Heady, Hercules, Humming, Husky, Intense, Mighty, Nappy, Pithy, Pollent, Potent, Powerful, Pungent, Racy, Rank, Robust, Samson, Solid, Stalwart, Stark, Steely, Sthenic, Stiff, Stout, Str, Strapping, > **STRENGTH**, Sturdy, Substantial, Suit, Tarzan, Tenable, Thesis, Thickset, Trusty, Vegete, Vehement, Vigorous, Violent, Virile, Well-built, Well-set, Ya(u)ld

Stronghold Acropolis, Aerie, Bastion, Castle, Citadel, Eyrie, Eyry, Fastness, Fortress, Keep, Kremlin, Redoubt, Tower

Strontium Sr

Strop Leather, Sharpen, Strap

Struck Aghast, Raught, Smitten

Structural, **Structure** Allotrope, Analysis, Anatomy, Armature, Building, Catafalque, Cold frame, Compage(s), Data, Deep, Edifice, Erection, Fabric, Fairing, Format(ion), Formwork, Frame, Galea, Heterarchy, Hyperbolic, Hyperfine, Ice-apron, Kekulé, Lantern, Macrocosm, Mole, Organic, Palmation Pediment, Pergola, Phloem, Physique, Pod, Power, Protein, Retinaculum, Set-up, Shape, Skeleton, Sponson, Sporocarp, Squinch, Starling, Stylobate, Surface, Syntax, System, Tectonic, Telomere, Texas, Texture, Trochlea, Undercarriage

Struggle Agon(ise), Agonistes, Buckle, Camp, Chore, Class, Conflict, Contend,

Contest, Cope, Debatement, Effort, Endeavour, Fight, Flounder, Grabble, Grapple, Kampf, Labour, Luctation, Mill, Pingle, Rat-race, Reluct, Scrape, Scrimmage, Scrum, Scrummage, Scuffle, Slugfest, Sprangle, > **STRIVE**, Toil, Tug, Tussle, Uphill, Vie, War(sle), Wrestle

Struggle *may indicate* an anagram

Strum Thrum, Tweedle, Vamp

Strumpet Cocotte, Harlot, Hiren, Lorette, Paramour, Succubus, Wench

Strut(ter), **Strutting** Bracket, Brank, Bridging, Cock, Dolphin striker, Flounce, Haught(y), Jet, Kingrod, Longeron, Martingale boom, Member, Nervure, Peacock, Pown, Prance, Prop, Scotch, Shore, Spur, Stalk, Stretcher, Strunt, Swagger, Swank, Tail-boom, Tie-beam

Stuart Anne, James, Pretender

Stub(by) Butt, Counterfoil, Dout, Dowt, Dumpy, Squat, Stob, Stocky

Stubble Ar(r)ish, Bristle, Designer, Hair, Ill-shaven, Stump

Stubborn(ness) Adamant, Bigoted, Contumacious, Cussed, Diehard, Dogged, Entêté, Hard(-nosed), Hidebound, Intransigent, Inveterate, Moyl(e), Mulish, Mumpsimus, Obdurate, Obstinate, Opinionated, Ornery, Ortus, Pertinacious, Perverse, Recalcitrant, Reesty, Refractory, Rigwiddie, Rigwoodie, Self-willed, Stiff, Stout, Tenacious, Thrawn, Wrong-headed

Stuck Fast, Glued, Jammed, Set, Stopped, Wedged

Stuck-up Chesty, Highty-tighty, Hoity-toity, La(h)-di-da(h), Proud, Sealed, Vain

Stud(ded) Boss, Cooser, Cripple, Cu(i)sser, Farm, Frost, He-man, Knob, Nail, Press, Race, Rivet, Seg, Set, Shear, Sire, Stop

Student(s) Alphabetarian, Alumnus, Apprentice, Bajan, Bejant, Bursar, Bursch(en), Cadet, Catachumen, Class, Coed, Commoner, Dan, Dig, Disciple, Dresser, Dux, Exchange, Exhibitioner, Extensionist, External, Form, Fresher, Freshman, Gownsman, Graduand, Green welly, Gyte, Ikey, Internal, Junior, Kommers, Kyu, > **LEARNER**, Magistrand, Matie, Mature, Medical, Nomologist, NUS, Opsimath, Ordinand, Oxonian, Peking duck, Pennal, Plebe, Poll, Postgraduate, Preppy, Pupil, Reader, Sap, > **SCHOLAR**, Self-taught, Semi, Seminar, Seminarian, Shark, Sizar, Sizer, Smug, Softa, Soph(omore), Sophister, Subsizar, Swot, Templar, Tiro, Tosher, Trainee, Tuft, Tukkie, Tutee, Wedge, Wonk, Wooden wedge, Wrangler, Year

Studio(s) Atelier, Bottega, Elstree, Gallery, Pinewood, Workshop

Study, **Studied**, **Studies**, **Studious** Analyse, Bone, Brown, Carol, Case, Classics, Con(ne), Conscious, Consider, Course, Cram, Den, Dig, Etude, Feasibility, Field, Gen up, Learn, Liberal, Lucubrate, Media, Motion, Mug, Mull, Muse, Nature, Perusal, Peruse, Pilot, Pore, Post-doctoral, Probe, Read, Recce, Reconnoitre, Research, Reverie, Revise, Sanctum, Sap, Scan, Scrutinise, Specialize, Stew, Swot, Take, Time and motion, Trade-off, Tutorial, Typto, Voulu, Work

Stuff(iness), **Stuffing**, **Stuffy** Airless, Bombast, Canvas, Close, Cloth, Codswallop, Cram, Crap, Dimity, Farce, Feast, Fiddlesticks, Fill, Force, Forcemeat, Frows(t)y, Frowzy, Fug, Gear, Gobble, Gorge, Guff, Havers, Hooey, Horsehair, Hot, Lard, Line, Linen, > **MATERIAL**, Matter, Musty, No-meaning, Nonsense, Overeat, Pad, Pang, Panne, Pompous, Ram, Replete, Rot, Salpicon, Sate, Satiate, Scrap, Sob, Stap, Steeve, Stew, Stifling, Taxidermy, Trig, Upholster, Wad, Youth

Stultify Repress, Ridicule, Smother

Stumble Blunder, Bobble, Err, Falter, Flounder, Founder, Lurch, Peck, Snapper, Stoit, Titubate, Trip

Stump(ed), **Stumps**, **Stumpy** Black, Butt, Clump, Fag-end, Floor, More, Nog, Nonplus, Orate, Runt, Scrag, Snag, Snooker, Squab, St, Staddle, Stob, Stock,

Stool, Stub(ble), Stud, Tortillon, Tramp, Truncate, Wicket

Stun(ning), Stunned Astonish, Astound, Awhape, Bludgeon, Concuss, Cosh, Daze, Dazzle, Deafen, Donnard, Donnert, Dove, Drop-dead, Glam, KO, Shell-shocked, Shock, Stoun, Stupefy, Taser®

Stunner Belle, Bobby-dazzler, Cheese, Cosh, Doozy, KO, Peach, Taser®

Stunt(ed) Aerobatics, Confine, Droichy, Dwarf, Escapade, Feat, Gimmick, Hot-dog, Hype, Jehad, Jihad, Loop, Nirl, Puny, Ront(e), Runt, Ruse, Scroggy, Scrub(by), Scrunt(y), Stub, Trick, Wanthriven, Wheelie

Stupefaction, Stupefy(ing) Amaze(ment), Assot, Benumb, Dozen, Dumbfound Etherise, Fuddle, Hocus, Narcoses, Numb, Stonne, Stun

Stupid, Stupid person Dense, Dull(ard), Fatuous, Foolish, Gormless, Gross, Inane, Insensate, Mindless, Natural, Obtuse, Silly, Thick, Torpid, Vacuous

STUPID PERSON

3 letters:
Ass
Auf
Bob
Cod
Daw
Dim
Div
Fon
Git
Jay
Lob
Log
Nit
Oaf
Owl
Put
Sap
Sot
Twp
Yap

4 letters:
Berk
Bete
Bobb
Bozo
Burk
Cake
Calf
Clod
Clot
Cony
Coof
Coot
Daft
Dill

Dite
Doat
Does
Dolt
Dorb
Dork
Dote
Dozy
Flat
Fogy
Fool
Fozy
Gaby
Gaga
Geck
Gelt
Goat
Goof
Goon
Goop
Gouk
Gowk
Gull
Gump
Hash
Jerk
Lown
Meff
Mome
Mong
Mook
Mutt
Nana
Nerd
Nerk
Nong
Nurd

Ouph
Poon
Poop
Prat
Putt
Putz
Rook
Simp
Stot
Tony
Twit
Warb
Yo-yo
Zany

5 letters:
Blent
Bobby
Booby
Brute
Bumbo
Chick
Chump
Clunk
Cokes
Crass
Cuddy
Cully
Dicky
Divvy
Dorba
Dubbo
Dumbo
Dummy
Dunce
Dweeb
Eejit

Fogey
Galah
Golem
Goofy
Goose
Hoser
Idiot
Kerky
Klutz
Looby
Loony
Lowne
Moron
Neddy
Ninny
Noddy
Ocker
Ouphe
Patch
Prune
Quo-he
Schmo
Simon
Snipe
Spoon
Stock
Stupe
Sumph
Taver
Twerp
Waldo
Wally
Yampy

6 letters:
Bampot
Boodle

Buffer
Cretin
Cuckoo
Cuddie
Dawney
Dickey
Dimwit
Dodkin
Donkey
Doofus
Dottle
Drongo
Gaupus
Gunsel
Ignaro
Ingram
Ingrum
Josser
Lummox
Lurden
Nidget
Nig-nog
Nincum
Nitwit
Noodle
Nudnik
Numpty
Oxhead
Schlep
Schmoe
Scogan
Sucker
Taiver
Thicko
Tosser
Tumphy
Turkey
Turnip
Wommit
Wooden
Zombie

7 letters:
Airhead
Asinico
Asinine

Barmpot
Becasse
Buffoon
Charlie
Damfool
Dawbake
Dim bulb
Dizzard
Donnard
Donnart
Donnerd
Donnert
Gomeral
Gomeril
Gubbins
Half-wit
Haverel
Insulse
Jackass
Juggins
Jughead
Lurdane
Mafflin
Mampara
Muggins
Palooka
Pillock
Pinhead
Plonker
Pot-head
Saphead
Schmock
Schmuck
Schnook
Scoggin
Thickie
Tosspot
Want-wit
Wazzock

8 letters:
Abderian
Abderite
Anserine
Baeotian
Besotted

Blockish
Boeotian
Bonehead
Boofhead
Clodpole
Clodpoll
Crackpot
Deadhead
Dickhead
Dipstick
Dodipoll
Donnered
Dotterel
Dottrell
Dumbbell
Flathead
Gobshite
Goofball
Goose-cap
Imbecile
Knobhead
Liripipe
Liripoop
Lunkhead
Maffling
Meathead
Moon-calf
Omadhaun
Pea-brain
Shot-clog
Softhead
Tom-noddy
Wiseacre
Woodcock

9 letters:
Beccaccia
Blockhead
Braindead
Capocchia
Chipochia
Clarthead
Desipient
Doddipoll
Doddypoll
Dottipoll

Dumb-cluck
Gothamite
Half-baked
Ignoramus
Insipient
Jobernowl
Lamebrain
Malt-horse
Schlemiel
Schlemihl
Simpleton
Thickhead
Woodentop

10 letters:
Analphabet
Changeling
Dummelhead
Dunderhead
Dunderpate
Headbanger
Loggerhead
Muttonhead
Nincompoop
Sheepshead
Thimblewit
Touchstone
Woodenhead

11 letters:
Chowderhead
Featherhead
Hare-brained
Knucklehead
Leather-head
Ninny-hammer
Simple Simon
Thick-witted
Van der Merwe

12 letters:
Featherbrain
Hammerheaded
Shatterbrain

Stupidity Goosery, Hebetude, Thickness, Torpor
Stupor Catatony, Coma, Daze, Dwa(u)m, Fog, Lethargy, Narcosis, Trance
Sturdy Burly, Dunt, Gid, Hardy, Hefty, Lubbard, Lubber, Lusty, Stalwart,
   Staunch, Steeve, Stieve, Strapping, Strong, Stuffy, Thickset, Turnsick, Vigorous
Sturgeon Beluga, Ellops, Fish, Huso, Osseter, Sevruga, Sterlet

Stutter Hesitate, Stammer
Sty Frank, Hovel, Pen
Stye Eyesore, Hordeolum
Style(s), **Stylish**, **Stylist** Adam, A la, A-line, Band, Barocco, Barock, Baroque, Biedermeier, Blow-dry, Burin, Call, Cantilena, Carry-on, Chic, Chinoiserie, Chippendale, Class, Cultism, Cut, Dapper, Dash, Decor, Decorated, Demotic, Diction, Directoire, Dub, Elan, Elegance, Empire, Entitle, Euphuism, Execution, Face, Farand, > FASHION, Finesse, Flamboyant, Flossy, Form(at), Genre, Gnomon, Gongorism, Gothic, Grace, Gr(a)ecism, Grand, Groovy, Hair-do, Hand, Hepplewhite, Hip, Homeric, House, International (Gothic), Intitule, Katharev(o)usa, Lapidary, Manner, Marivaudage, Mod(e), Modish, Natty, New, Nib, Nifty, Old, Panache, Pattern, Pen, Perm, Perpendicular, Personal, Phrase, Pistil, Pointel, Port, Post-modernism, Preponderant, Probe, Queen Anne, Rakish, Rank, Regency, Rococo, Romanesque, Sheraton, Silk, Snazzy, Spiffy, Sporty, Street, Swish, Taste, Term, Title, Ton, Tone, Touch, Traditional, Tuscan, Uncial, Vogue, Way
Stymie Thwart
Styptic Alum, Amadou, Matico, Sta(u)nch
Suave Bland, Debonair, Oily, Smooth, Unctuous, Urbane
Sub Advance, Due, Submarine, Subordinate, U-boat, Under
Sub-atomic Mesic
Subconscious Inner, Instinctive, Not-I, Subliminal, Suppressed
Sub-continent India
Subdivision Arm, Branch, Oblast, Sanjak, Senonian, Wapentake
Subdominant Fah
Subdue(d) Abate, Adaw, Allay, Chasten, Conquer, Cow, Crush, Dant(on), Daunt(on), Dominate, Entame, Lick, Low-key, Master, Mate, Mute, Overpower, > QUELL, Quieten, Reduce, Refrain, Slow, Sober, Subact, Suppress, Tame, Under
Subfusc, **Subfusk** Dim, Dressy, Dusky, Evening, Sombre
Subhuman Apeman, Bestial
Subject(s), **Subjection**, **Subject to** Amenable, Art, Bethrall, Caitive, Case, Citizen, Contingent, Core, Cow, Donne(e), Enthrall, Foundation, Gist, Hobby, Hobby-horse, Inflict, Liable, Liege(man), Matter, National, On, Overpower, PE, People, Poser, Rayah, RE, RI, Serf, Servient, Servitude, Sitter, Slavery, Snool, Submit, Suit, > THEME, Thirl, Thrall, Topic, Under, Vassal
Subjugate Enslave, Master, Oppress, Overcome, Reduce, Repress, Suppress
Sublieutenant Cornet
Sublimate(r) Aludel, Cleanse, Suppress, Transfer
Sublime August, Empyreal, Grand, Great, Lofty, Majestic, Outstanding, Perfect, Porte, Splendid
Submarine Diver, Innerspace, Nautilus, Pig-boat, Polaris, Sub, U-boat, Undersea, X-craft
▷ **Submarine** *may indicate* a fish
Submerge(d) Dip, Dive, Drown, Embathe, Engulf, Imbathe, Lemuria, Overwhelm, Ria, Sink, Take, Whelm
Submissive, **Submit** Acquiesce, Bow, Capitulate, Comply, Defer, Docile, File, Knuckle, Meek, Obedient, Obtemperate, Passive, Pathetic, Refer, Render, Resign, Snool, Stoop, Succumb, Truckle, > YIELD
Subordinate Adjunct, Dependent, Flunky, Inferior, Junior, Minion, Myrmidon, Offsider, Postpone, Secondary, Second banana, Servient, Stooge, Subject, Subservient, Subsidiary, Surrender, Under(ling), Underman, Under-strapper, Vassal

Subscribe(r), Subscription Abonnement, Approve, Assent, Conform, Due, Pay, Sign(atory), Signature, Undersign, Underwrite

Subsequent(ly) Anon, Consequential, Future, Later, Next, Postliminary, Since, Then, Ulterior

Subservient Kneel, Obedient, Obsequious

Subside, Subsidence, Subsidy Abate, Adaw, Aid, Assuage, Bonus, Diminish, Ebb, Grant, Sink, Sit, Swag

Subsidiary, Subsidise Auxiliar(y), By(e), Feather-bed, Junior, Secondary, Side, Spin-off, Succursal

Subsist(ence) Batta, Bread-line, Dole, Keep, Live, Maintain, Rely, Survive

Substance, Substantial Ambergris, Anethole, Antithrombin, Antitoxin, Blocky, Body, Calyx, Cermet, Chalone, Chemzyne, Chitin, Chromatin, Colloid, Considerable, Content, Cosmin(e), Ectocrine, Ectoplasm, Elemi, Essential, Excipient, Extender, Exudate, Fabric, Fixative, Getter, Gist, Gluten, Gossypol, Gravamen, Growth, Guanazolo, Hearty, Hefty, Indol, Inhibitor, Iodoform, Iodophor, Isatin(e), Isomer, Lecithin, Leucotriene, Linin, Luciferin, Material, Matter, Meaning, Meat(y), Metol, Mineral, Mole, Morphogen, Mucigen, Murr(h)ine, Mutagen, Naloxone, Neurotoxin, Orgone, Papier mâché, Phlogiston, Polymer, Protyl(e), Purin(e), Queen (bee), Quid, Reality, Resin, Sense, Solid, Stuff, Sum, Surfactant, Sympathin, Tabasheer, Tabashir, Tangible, Tusche, Viricide, Volutin

Substandard Infra dig, Off, Poor, Schlo(c)k, Second, Small

Substantial *see* SUBSTANCE

Substantiate Confirm, Flesh, Prove, Strengthen, Support

Substantive Direct, Noun

Substitute, Substitution Acting, Carborundum®, Change, Changeling, Commute, Creamer, Deputy, Dextran, Double, Dub, Emergency, Ersatz, -ette, Euphemism, Eusystolism, Exchange, Fill-in, Improvise, Instead, Lieu(tenant), Locum, Makeshift, Metonymy, Pinch-hit, Proxy, Regent, Relieve, Replace, Represent, Reserve, Resolution, Ringer, Seth, Simulacrum, Stand-in, Stead, Stopgap, Subrogate, Succedaneum, Surrogate, Switch, Swop, Synthetic, Understudy, Vicar(ial), Vicarious

Substructure Base, Foundation, Keelson, Platform, Podium

Subterfuge Artifice, Chicane, Evasion, Hole, Manoeuvre, Off-come, Ruse, Strategy, Trick

Subterranean Concealed, Mattamore, Sunken, Underground, Weem

Subtle(ty) Abstruse, Alchemist, Crafty, Fine(spun), Finesse, Ingenious, Nice, Nice(ty), Refinement, Sly, Thin, Wily

Subtle difference Nuance

Subtract(ion) Commission, Deduct, Discount, Sum, Take, Tithe, Withdraw

Suburb Banlieue, Environs, Exurbia, Faubourg, Garden, Outskirts, Purlieu, Subtopia

Subversion, Subvert Fifth column, Overthrow, Reverse, Sabotage, Sedition, Treasonous, Undermine, Upset

Subway Metro, Passage, Tube, Underground

Succeed, Success(ful), Success(ful) Accomplish, Achieve, Arrive, Blockbuster, Boffo, Breakthrough, Chartbuster, Contrive, Coup, Eclat, Effective, Efficacious, Fadge, Felicity, Flourish, Follow, Fortune, Gangbuster, Get, Go, Hit, Hotshot, Inherit, Killing, Landslide, Luck, Made, Manage, Masterstroke, Mega, Midas touch, Offcome, Pass, Prevail, Procure, Prosper, Purple patch, Reach, Replace, Riot, Score, Seal, Seel, Sele, Sell out, Soaraway, Socko, Speed, Stardom, Superstar, Sure thing, Tanistry, Triumph, Up, Up and coming, Upstart, Vault,

Weather, W(h)iz(z)kid, Win, Wow, Wunderkind

Succession Apostolic, Chain, Cognate, Dead men's shoes, Line, Order, Reversion, Sequence, Seriatim, Series, Suite

Successor Co(m)arb, Deluge, Descendant, Ensuite, Epigon(e), Heir, Incomer, Inheritor, Khalifa, Next, Syen

Succinct Brief, Cereus, Compact, Concise, Houseleek, Laconic, Pithy, Short

Succour Aid, Assist, Help, Minister, Relieve, Rescue, Sustain

Succulent Agave, Cactus, Echeveria, Juicy, Lush, Rich, Saguaro, Sappy, Spekboom, Tender, Toothy

Succumb Capitulate, Fall, Go under, Surrender, Yield

Such Like, Sae, Sike, Similar, That

Suck(er), Sucking Absorb, Acetabular, Acetabulum, Amphistomous, Antlia, Aphis, Aspirator, Ass, Bull's eye, Culicidae, Dracula, Drink, Dupe, Fawn, Fellatio, Gnat, Graff, Graft, Gull, Haustellum, Haustorium, Hoove, Lamia, Lamprey, Leech, Liquorice, Mammal, Monotremata, Mouth, Mug, Muggins, Osculum, Patsy, Plunger, Remora, Rook, Shoot, Siphon, Slurp, Smarm, Spire, Spyre, Straw, Surculus, Swig, Sycophant, Tellar, Teller, Tick, Tiller, Toad-eater, Turion, Vampire

Suckle Feed, Mother, Nourish, Nurse, Nurture

Suction Adhere, Pump, Siphon

Sud(s) Foam, Sapples

Sudanese Mahdi, Nuba

Sudden(ly) Abrupt, Astart, Astert, Extempore, Ferly, Fleeting, Foudroyant, Fulminant, Hasty, Headlong, Impulsive, Overnight, Rapid, Slap, Sodain, Subitaneous, Subito, Swap, Swop, Unexpected

Sue Ask, Beseech, Dun, Entreat, Implead, Implore, Litigate, Petition, Pray, Process, Prosecute, Woo

Suede Split

Suffer(er), Suffering Abide, Aby(e), Ache, Affliction, Agonise, Auto, Be, > **BEAR**, Brook, Calvary, Cop, Die, Distress, Dree, Dukkha, Endurance, Endure, Feel, Gethsemane, Golgotha, Grief, Hardship, Have, Incur, Let, Luit, Martyr, Pain, Passible, Passion, Passive, Patible, Patience, Pellagrin, Permit, Pine, Plague, Purgatory, Stand, Stomach, Sustain, Thole, Tolerate, Toll, Torment, Trial, Tribulation, Undergo, Use, Victim

Suffering remnant Macmillanite

Suffice, Sufficient Adequate, Ample, Basta, Do, Due, Enough, Enow, Experimental, Run to, Satisfy, Serve

Suffix Enclitic

Suffocate Asphyxiate, Choke, Smoor, Smore, Smother, Stifle, Strangle, Throttle

Suffrage(tte) Ballot, Feminist, Franchise, Manhood, Vote

Suffuse Colour, Glow, Imbue, Saturate, Spread

Sugar(y), Sugar cane Aldohexose, Aldose, Amygdalin, Arabinose, Barley, Beet, Blood, Brown, Candy, Cane, Caramel, Carn(e), Cassonade, Caster, Cellobiose, Cellose, Chaptalise, Confectioner's, Daddy, Demerara, Deoxyribose, Dextrose, Disaccharide, Flattery, Fructose, Fucose, Furanose, Galactose, Gallise, Glucose, Glucosoric, Goo(r), Granulated, Grape, Gur, Heroin, Hexose, Honeydew, Hundreds and thousands, Iced, Icing, Inulin, Invert, Jaggary, Jaggery, Jagghery, Lactose, Laevulose, Loaf, Lump, Maltose, Manna, Mannose, Maple, Money, Monosaccharide, Muscovado, Nectar, Palm, Panocha, Pentose, Penuche, Raffinose, Rhamnose, Ribose, Saccharine, Saccharoid, Simple, Sis, Sorbose, Sorg(h)o, Sorghum, Sparrow, Spun, Sweet, Trehala(se), Triose, White, Wood, Xylose

Sugar-daddy Lyle, Tate

Suggest(ion), **Suggestive** Advance, Advice, Advise, Connote, Counter-proposal, Cue, Hint, Idea, Imply, Innuendo, Insinuate, Intimate, Mention, Modicum, Moot, Posit, Prompt, Proposal, Propound, Provocative, Racy, Raise, Recommend, Redolent, Reminiscent, Risqué, Smacks, Soft core, Suspicion, Touch, Trace, Undertone, Wind, Wrinkle

Suicide Felo-de-se, Hara-kiri, Hari-kari, Kamikaze, Lemming, Lethal, Sati, Seppuku, Shinju, Suttee

Suit Action, Adapt, Adjust, Agree, Answer, Apply, Appropriate, Become, Befit, Beho(o)ve, Bequest, Beseem, Birthday, Boiler, Cards, Case, Cat, Clubs, Conform, Courtship, Demob, Diamonds, Dittos, Diving, Do, Drapes, Dress, Effeir, Effere, Etons, Fadge, Fashion, Fit, G, Garb, Gee, Gree, Hearts, Hit, Jump, Lis pendens, Long, Lounge, Major, Mao, Match, Minor, Monkey, NBC, Noddy, Orison, Outcome, Paternity, Petition, Plaint, Play, Plea, Please, Point, Prayer, Pressure, Process, Pyjama, Quarterdeck, Queme, Romper(s), Safari, Sailor, Salopettes, Samfoo, Samfu, Satisfy, Serve, Shell, Siren, Skeleton, Slack, Space, Spades, Strong, Sun, Sunday, Supplicat, Sweat, Swim, Tailleur, Three-piece, Track, Trouser, Trumps, Tsotsi, Twin, Two-piece, Uniform, Union, Wet, Zoot

Suitable Apposite, Appropriate, Apropos, Apt, Becoming, Capable, Congenial, Consonant, Convenance, Convenient, Due, Expedient, > FIT, Giusto, Keeping, Meet, Opportune, Relevant, Seasonal, Seemly, Very, Worthy

Suite Allemande, Apartment, Chambers, Ensemble, Entourage, Hospitality, Lounge, Nutcracker, Partita, Retinue, Rooms, Serenade, Set, Skybox, Tail, Three-piece, Train, Two-piece

Suitor Beau, Gallant, John Doe, Lover, Petitioner, Pretender, Suppli(c)ant, Swain, Wooer

Sulk(y), **Sulkiness** B(r)oody, Dod, Dort, Gee, Glout(s), Glower, Glum, Grouchy, Grouty, Grumps, Huff, Hump, Jinker, Mardy, Maungy, Mope, Mulligrubs, Mump, Pet, Pique, Pout, Spider, Strunt, Stuffy, Stunkard, Sullen, Tout(ie), Towt, Umbrage

Sullen Dorty, Dour, Farouche, Glum(pish), Grim, Moody, Peevish, Stunkard, Sulky, Surly, Truculent

Sully Assoil, Bedye, Besmirch, Blot, Defile, Glaur(y), Smear, Smirch, Smutch, Soil, Tarnish, Tar-wash

Sulphate, **Sulphide** Alum, Alunite, Blende, Bluestone, Bornite, Copperas, Coquimbite, Glance, Melanterite, Pyrites, Zarnec, Zarnich

Sulphur Baregine, Brimstone, Hepar, Oleum, S, Stannite, Thionic

Sultan(a), **Sultanate** Brunei, Caliph, Emir, Grand Seignoir, Grand Turk, Hen, Kalif, Oman, Osman, Padishah, Roxane, Saladin, Soldan, Suleiman, Tippoo, Tipu, Wadai

Sultry Humid, Sexy, Smouldering, Steamy, Tropical

Sum(s), **Sum up** Add(end), Aggregate, All, Amount, Arsmetric, Bomb, Connumerate, Encapsulate, Foot, Logical, Lump, Number, Perorate, Plumule, > QUANTITY, Re-cap, Refund, Remittance, Reversion, Solidum, Total, Vector

Summarize, **Summary** Abridge, Abstract, Aperçu, Bird's eye, Brief, Compendium, Condense, Conspectus, Digest, Docket, Epitome, Gist, Instant, Memo, Minute, Offhand, Outline, Overview, Precis, Recap, Resume, Résumé, Round-up, Syllabus, Synopsis, Tabloid, Tabulate, Tabulation, Wrap-up

Summer(time) Aestival, August, BST, Computer, Estival, Indian, Lintel, Luke, Prime, St Luke's, St Martin's, Season, Solstice, Totter

Summerhouse Belvedere, Chalet, Conservatory, Folly, Gazebo

Summit Acme, Acri-, Apex, Braeheid, Brow, Climax, Conference, > CREST,

Crown, Height, Hillcrest, Jole, Peak, Pike, Pinnacle, Spire, Vertex, Vertical, Yalta

Summon(s) Accite, Arrière-ban, Azan, Beck(on), Call, Cist, Cital, Citation, Command, Conjure, Convene, Convent, Drum, Evoke, Garnishment, Gong, Hail, Invocation, Muster, Order, Page, Post, Preconise, Rechate, Recheat, Reveille, Signal, Sist, Ticket, Warn, Warrant, Whoop, Writ

Sumo Makunouchi

Sump Bilge, Drain, Pool, Sink

Sumpter Led horse, Pack-horse

Sumptuous Expensive, Lavish, Palatial, Rich(ly), Superb

Sun(-god), Sunlight, Sunny, Sunshine Albedo, Amen-Ra, Amon-Ra, Apollo, Ashine, Aten, Bright, Cheer, Combust, Daily, Day(star), Dry, Earthshine, Glory, Heater, Helio(s), Helius, Horus, Mean, Midnight, New Mexico, Paranthelion, Parhelion, Pet-day, Phoebean, Photosphere, Ra, Radiant, Rays, Re, Rising, Shamash, Sol(ar), Soleil, Sonne, Surya, Svastika, Swastika, Tabloid, Tan, Titan, UV

Sunbathe Apricate, Bask, Brown, Tan

Sunbeam Car, Ray

Sunburn Bronze, Combust, Peeling, Tan

Sunday Advent, Best, Cantate, Care, Carle, Carling, Dominical, Easter, Fig, Jubilate, Judica, Laetare, Lord's Day, Lost, Low, Mid-Lent, Mothering, Orthodox, Palm, Passion, Quadragesima, Quasimodo, Quinquagesima, Refection, Refreshment, Remembrance, Rogation, Rose, Rush-bearing, S, Septuagesima, Sexagesima, Stir-up, Tap-up, Trinity, Whit

Sunday school SS

Sunder Divide, Divorce, Part, Separate, Sever, Split

Sundew Drosera, Eyebright

Sundial Analemma, Gnomon, Solarium

Sundry Divers, Several, Various

Sunflower Kansas, KS

Sunglasses Shades

▶ **Sun-god** see SUN

▶ **Sunken** see SINK

Sunrise, Sun-up Aurora, Cosmical, Dawn, East

Sunset Acronical, Evening

Sunshade Awning, Brise-soleil, Canopy, Chi(c)k, Cloud, Parasol, Umbrella

Sunspot Facula, Freckle, Macula

Sunstroke Heliosis, Siriasis

Sunwise Deasi(u)l, Deasoil, Deis(h)eal, Eutropic

Sun-worshipper Heliolater

Sup Dine, Eat, Feast, Sample, Sip, Swallow

Super A1, Arch, Extra, Fab(ulous), Great, Grouse, Ideal, Lulu, Paramount, Superb, Terrific, Tip-top, Tops, Walker-on, Wizard

Superadded Advene

Superb A1, Concours, Fine, Grand, Great, Majestic, Peerless, Phat, Splendid, Top-notch

Supercilious Aloof, Arrogant, Bashaw, Cavalier, Haughty, Lordly, Snide, Sniffy, Snooty, Snotty, Snouty, Superior, Toffee-nosed, Upstage

Superficial Cosmetic, Cursenary, Cursory, Dilettante, Exterior, Facile, Glib, Outside, Outward, Overlying, Perfunctory, Shallow, Sketchy, Skindeep, Smattering, Veneer

▷ **Superficial(ly)** may indicate a word outside another

Superfluous, Superfluity Cheville, De trop, Extra, Lake, Mountain, Needless, Otiose, Pleonastic, Plethora, Redundant, Spare, Unnecessary

Superhuman Bionic, Herculean, Heroic, Supernatural

Superintend(ent) Boss, Director, Foreman, Guide, Janitor, Oversee(r), Preside, Sewer, Supercargo, Surveillant, Warden, Zanjero

Superior(ity) Abbess, Abeigh, Above, Advantage, Aloof, Atop, Better, Brahmin, Choice, Condescending, Custos, De luxe, Dinger, Eminent, Excellent, Exceptional, Finer, Herrenvolk, High-grade, Lake, Liege, Mastery, Morgue, Mother, Nob, Outstanding, Over, Paramount, Predominance, Prestige, Pretentious, Prior, Superordinate, Supremacy, Swell, Top(-loftical), Transcendent(al), U, Udal, Upper(most), Uppish, Upstage

Superlative Best, Exaggerated, Peerless, Smasheroo, Supreme, Utmost

Superman Batman, Bionic, Titan, Ubermensch

Supermarket Co-op, Fund, GUM, Self service, Store

Supernatural Divine, Eerie, Fey, Fie, Fly, Gothic, Kachina, Mana, Metaphysical, Paranormal, Sharp, Siddhi, Uncanny, Unearthly, Wight

Supernova Plerion

Supernumerary Additional, Corollary, Extra, Mute, Orra

Supersede Replace, Stellenbosch, Supplant

Superstition Aberglaube, Abessa, Fable, Folk-lore, Freet, Myth, Uncertainty

Superstructure Mastaba(h)

Supertonic Ray

Supervise(d), Supervision, Supervisor Administer, Chaperone, Check, Direct, Engineer, Floorwalker, Foreman, Grieve, Handle, Honcho, Invigilate, Manager, Officiate, Overman, Oversee(r), Probation, Shopwalker, Stage-manage, Targe, Under, Walla(h)

Supine Inactive, Inert, Lying, Protract

Supper Dinner, > **DRINK(ER)**, Hawkey, Hockey, Horkey, Last, Meal, Nagmaal, Repast, Soirée

Supplant Displace, Exchange, Oust, Replace, Substitute, Supersede

Supple Compliant, Leish, Limber, Lissom(e), > **LITHE**, Loose, Loose-limbed, Pliable, Souple, Wan(d)le, Wannel, Whippy

Supplement(ary) Addend(um), Addition, And, Annex(e), Appendix, Augment, Auxiliary, Codicil, Colour, Eche, Eke, Extra, Incaparina, Paralipomena, Postscript, Relay, Ripienist, Ripieno, Weighting

Supplicant, Supplicate Beg, Entreat, Importune, Invoke, Petition, Plead, Request, Schnorr, Sue

Supplier, Supplies, Supply Accommodate, Advance, Afford, Cache, Cater, Commissariat, Contribute, Crop, Endue, Equip, Excess, Exempt, Feed, Fill, Find, Fit, Foison, Fund, Furnish, Give, Grist, Grubstake, Heel, Holp(en), Indue, Issue, Lend, Lithely, Mains, Materiel, Pipeline, Plenish, Ply, > **PROVIDE**, Provision, Purvey, RASC, Retailer, Serve, Source, Stake, Stock, > **STORE**, Viands, Vintner, Water, Widow's cruse, Yield

Support(er), Supporting Abacus, Abet, Abutment, Adherent, Adminicle, Advocate, Affirm, Aficionado, Aid, Aidance, Aliment(ative), Ally, Ammunition, Anchor, Ancillary, Andiron, Anta, Appui, Arch, Arm, Assistant, Axle, Back(bone), Back-up, Baculum, Baluster, Banister, Bankroll, Barrack, Barre, Base, Batten, Beam, Bear, Befriend, Belt, Bibb, Bier, Bolster, Boom, Bouclée, Bra, Brace, Bracket, Brassiere, Breadwinner, Breast-summer, Bridge, Bridgeboard, Buttress, C(ee)-spring, Chair, Champion, Chaptrel, Clientele, Column, Confirm, Console, Corbel, Corbel-table, Cornerstone, Countenance, Cradle, Cross-beam, Crutch, Dado, Diagrid, Dog-shore, Doula,

Easel, Encourage, Endorse, Endow, Engager, Espouse, Family, Fan, Favour, Fid, Finance, Flying buttress, Fly-rail, Footrest, Footstool, For, Gamb, Gantry, Garter, Girder, Glia, Grass roots, Groundswell, Harpin(g)s, Headrest, Help, Henchman, Horse, Hound, Idealogue, Impost, Income, Instantiate, Ite, Jack, Jockstrap, Joist, Keep, Kingpost, Knee, Knighthead, Lectern, Leg, Lierne, Lifebelt, Lifebuoy, Lobby, Loper, Loyalist, Mahlstick, Mainstay, Maintain, Makefast, Miserere, Misericord(e), Monial, Moral, Mortsafe, Nervure, Neuroglia, -nik, Nourish, Paranymph, Parawalker, Partisan, Partizan, Partners, Patronage, Pedestal, Pessary, Pier, Pillar, Pin, Plinth, Poppet, Post, Potent, Price, Prop, Proponent, Prop-root, PTA, Pull-for, Purlin(e), Purlins, Pylon, Raft, Rally round, Reinforce, Relieve, Respond, Rest, Rind, Rod, Roof-plate, Root, Royalist, Rynd, Samaritan, Sanction, Sawhorse, Second, Shore, Skeg, Skeleton, Skewput, Skid, Sleeper, Sling, Snotter, Socle, Solidarity, Splat, Splint, Sponson, Sprag, Spud, Staddle, Staddlestone, Staff, Staging, Stake, Stalwart, Stanchion, Stand(-by), Stay, Steady, Stem(pel), Step, Stick, Stirrup, Stool, Stringer, Strut, Stylobate, Subscribe, Subsidy, Succour, Suffragist, Summer, Suppedaneum, Suspender, Sustain, Tailskid, Tee, Telamon, Tendril, Third, Tie, Tige, Torsel, Trabecula, Tress(el), Trestle, Tripod, Trivet, Truss, Underlay, Underpin, Understand, Unipod, Uphold, Upkeep, Viva, Waterwings, Y-level, Zealot

Suppose(d), Supposition An, Assume, Believe, Expect, Guess, Hypothetical, Idea, If, Imagine, Imply, Opine, Presume, Putative, Said, Sepad, Theory

Suppress(ion) Abolish, Adaw, Burke, Cancel, Censor, Clampdown, Crush, Cushion, Ecthlipsis, Elide, Elision, Gleichschaltung, Hush-up, Mob(b)le, Quash, Quell, Quench, Restrain, Silence, Smother, Squash, Stifle, Submerge, Subreption, Throttle

Suppurate, Suppuration Diapyesis, Discharge, Exude, Fester, Maturate, Ooze, Pus, Pyorrhoea, Rankle

Supreme, Supremacy, Supremo Apical, Baaskap, Caudillo, Consummate, Kronos, Leader, Napoleon, Overlord, Paramount, Peerless, Regnant, Sovereign, Sublime, Sudder, Superlative, Top, Utmost, White

Surcharge Addition, Extra, Tax

Surd Voiceless

Sure(ly) Assured, Ay, Bound, Cert(ain), Confident, Definite, Doubtless, Firm, Infallible, Know, Pardi(e), Pardy, Perdie, Positive, Poz, Safe, Secure, Shoo-in, Sicker, Syker, Uh-huh, Yep, Yes

Surety Bail, Frithborth, Guarantee, Mainprise, Security, Sponsional

Surf(er) Breach, Breaker, Grommet, Rollers, Rote, Sea, Waxhead

Surface Aerofoil, Appear, Area, Arise, Camber, Control, Day, Dermal, Dermis, Emerge, Epigene, Exterior, External, Face, Facet, Flock, Macadam, Meniscus, Outcrop, Outward, Paintwork, Patina, Pave, Plane, Reveal, Rise, Salband, Side, Skin, Soffit, Spandrel, Superficial, Superficies, Tarmac®, Tar-seal, Texture, Top, Toroid, Worktop

Surf-boat Masoola(h), Masula

Surfeit(ed) Blasé, Cloy, Excess, Glut, Overcloy, Plethora, Satiate, Stall, Staw

▷ **Surfer** *may indicate* programming

Surge Billow, Boom, Drive, Gush, Onrush, S(c)end, Seethe, Storm, Sway, Swell

Surgeon Abernethy, BCh, BS, CHB, CM, Doctor, House, Lister, Medic, Operator, Orthopod, Plastic, Sawbones, Staff, Tang, Vet(erinary)

Surgery Anaplasty, Cosmetic, Facelift, Keyhole, Knife, Laparotomy, Laser, Medicine, Nip and tuck, Nose job, Op, Open-heart, Osteoplasty, Plastic, Prosthetics, Reconstructive, Repair, Spare-part, Ta(g)liacotian, Zolatrics

Surly Bluff, Cantankerous, Chough, Chuffy, Churl(ish), Crabby, Crusty, Cynic, Glum, Gruff, Grum, Grumpy, Rough, Sullen, Truculent

Surmise Extrapolate, Guess, Imagine, Infer, Presume, Suppose

Surmount Beat, Climb, Conquer, Crest, Master, Overcome, Scan, Superate, Tide, Transcend

Surname Cognomen, Patronymic

Surpass Bang, Beat, Best, Cap, Cote, Ding, Eclipse, Efface, Exceed, Excel, Outdo, Outgun, Out-Herod, Outreach, Outshine, Outstrip, Overtop, Transcend

Surplice Cotta, Ephod, Rochet, Sark, Serk, Vakass

Surplus Excess, Extra, Glut, Lake, Mountain, Out-over, Over, Overage, Overcome, Remainder, Rest, Spare, Surfeit

Surprise(d), **Surprising** Alert, Amaze, Ambush, Arrah, Astonish, Bewilder, Blimey, Boilover, Bombshell, By Jove, Caramba, Catch, Confound, Coo, Cor, Crick(e)y, Crikey, Criminé, Cripes, Criv(v)ens, Dear, Eye-opener, Gadso, Gee, Geewhiz, Gemini, Geminy, Gemony, Gobsmacked, Golly, Good-lack, Gorblimey, Gordon Bennett, Gosh, Ha, Hah, Hallo, Heavens, Heck, Heh, Hello, Hey, Ho, Jeepers, Jeez(e), Law, Lawks, Lor, Lordy, Lummy, Marry, Musha, My, Obreption, Och, Odso, Omigod, Oops, Open-mouthed, Overtake, Phew, Pop-eyed, Really, Sheesh, Shock, Singular, Spot, Stagger, Startle, Strewth, Struth, Stun, Sudden, Treat, Turn-up, Uh, Whew, Whoops, Wonderment, Wow, Wrongfoot, Yikes, Yow, Zinger, Zowie

Surrealist Bizarre, Dali, Ernst, Grotesque, Magritte, Man Ray, Miro

Surrender Capitulate, Cave-in, Cession, Enfeoff, Extradite, Fall, Forego, Forfeit, Handover, Hulled, Kamerad, Naam, Recreant, Release, Relinquish, Remise, Rendition, Submit, Succumb, Waive, > **YIELD**

Surreptitious Clandestine, Covert, Fly, Furtive, Secret, Sly, Stealthy, Underhand

Surrey Carriage, Sy

Surrogate Agent, Depute, Deputy, Locum, Proxy

Surround(ed), **Surrounding(s)** Ambient, Amongst, Architrave, Background, Bathe, Bego, Beset, Bundwall, Circumvallate, Circumvent, Compass, Doughnutting, Ecology, Embail, Encase, > **ENCIRCLE**, Enclave, Enclose, Encompass, Enfold, Envelop, Environ, Enwrap, Fence, Gherao, Gird, Hedge, Hem in, Impale, Invest, Mid, Orb, Orle, Outflank, Outside, Perimeter, Setting, Wall

Surtees Jorrocks, Sponge

Surveillance, **Survey(ing)**, **Surveyor** Behold, Cadastre, Case, Conspectus, Dialler, Domesday, Doomwatch, Espial, Examination, Eye, Geodesy, Groma, Look-see, Once-over, Ordnance, Patrol, Poll, Quantity, Recce, Reconnaissance, Regard, Review, Scan, Scrutiny, Stakeout, Straw poll, Supervision, Terrier, Theodolite, Triangulate, Trilateration, Vigil, Watch

Survival, **Survive**, **Surviving**, **Survivor** Cope, Die hard, Endure, Extant, Finalist, Hibakusha, Last, Leftover, Outdure, Outlast, Outlive, Outwear, Overlive, Persist, Relic(t), Ride, Street-wise, Viability, Warhorse, Weather

Susan Lazy

Susceptible, **Susceptibility** Anaphylaxis, Impressionable, Liable, Receptive, Vulnerable

Suspect, **Suspicion**, **Suspicious** Askance, Breath, Dodgy, Doubt, Dubious, Fishy, Grain, Guess, Hint, Hunch, Jalouse, Jealous, Leery, Misdeem, Misdoubt, Misgiving, Mislippen, Mistrust, Modicum, Notion, Paranoia, Queer, Scent, Smatch, Soupçon, Thought, Tinge, Whiff

▷ **Suspect**, **Suspicious** *may indicate* an anagram

Suspend(ed), **Suspense**, **Suspension** Abate, Abeyance, Adjourn, Anabiosis,

Anti-shock, Cliffhanger, Colloid, Dangle, Defer, Delay, Dormant, Freeze, Ground, > HANG, Hydraulic, Independent, Intermit, Mist, Moratorium, Nailbiter, Pensile, Poise, Prorogue, Put on ice, Reprieve, Respite, Rub out, Rusticate, Sideline, Sol, Stand off, Swing, Tenterhooks, Truce, Withhold

▷ **Suspended** *may indicate* 'ice' (on ice) at the end of a down light

Sussex Rape

Sustain(ed), **Sustaining**, **Sustenance** Abide, Afford, Aliment, Bear, Constant, Depend, Endure, Food, Keep, Last, Maintain, Nutrient, Nutriment, Pedal, Prolong, Sostenuto, Succour, Support, Tenuto, Upbear

Sutler Vivandière

Suture Button, Catgut, Cobbler, Lambda, Pterion, Purse-string, Stitch

Suzanne, **Suzie** Lenglen, Wong

Svelte Lithe, Slender, Slim

Swab Dossil, Dry, Mop, Pledget, Scour, Sponge, Squeegee, Stupe, Tampon, Tompon, Wipe

Swaddle, **Swaddling** Bind, Envelop, Incunabula, Swathe, Wrap

Swag Booty, Encarpus, Festoon, Haul, Loot, Maino(u)r, Manner, Matilda, Shiralee, Toran(a)

Swagger(er), **Swaggering** Birkie, Bluster, Boast, Brag, Bragadisme, Bravado, Bucko, Cock, Crow, Jaunty, Matamore, Nounce, Panache, Pra(u)nce, Roist, Roll, Rollick, Roul, Royster, Ruffle, Side, Strive, Swank, Swash(-buckler), Tigerism

Swain Amoretti, Beau, Churl, Corin, Damon, Hind, Lover, Rustic, Shepherd, Strephon, Wooer

Swallow(able), **Swallowing** Aerophagia, Ariel, Barn, Bird, Bolt, Cliff, Consume, Deglutition, Devour, Down, Drink, Eat, Endue, Englut, Engulf, Engulph, Esculent, Glug, Gobble, Gula, Gulp, Hirundine, Incept, Ingest, Ingulf, Ingurgitate, Itys, Lap, Martin, Martlet, Progne, Quaff, Shift, Sister, Slug, Stomach, Swig, Take, Take off

Swamp(y) Bog, Bunyip, Cowal, Cypress, Deluge, Dismal, Drown, Engulf, Everglade, Flood, Great Dismal, Inundate, Lentic, Lerna, Lerne, Loblolly, Mar(i)sh, Morass, Muskeg, Okavango, Okefenokee, Overrun, Overwhelm, Paludal, Quagmire, Slash, Slough, Sudd, Uliginous, Urman, Vlei, Vly, Wetland

Swan(s) Avon, Bewick's, Bird, Black, Cob, Cygnet, Cygnus, Game, Leda, Lindor, Mute, Pen, Seven, Seward, Song, Stroll, Trumpeter, Whistling, Whooper, Whooping

Swank(y) Boast, Lugs, Pretentious, Side, Style

Swan-song Finale, Last air

Swap, Swop > BARTER, Chop, Commute, Exchange, Scorse, Switch, Trade, Truck

▷ **Swap(ped)** *may indicate* an anagram

Sward Grass, Green, Lawn, Sod, Turf

Swarm(ing) Abound, Alive, Bike, Bink, Byke, Cast, Cloud, Crowd, Flood, Geminid, Hoatching, Host, Hotter, Infest, Meteor, Overrun, Pullulate, Rife, Shin, Shoal, Throng

Swarthy Dark, Dusky, Melanotic

Swash Swig, Swill

Swash-buckler Adventurer, Boaster, Braggart, Gascon, Swordsman

Swastika Filfot, Fylfot, Gamma(dion), Hakenkreuz

▶ **Swat** *see* SWOT

Swathe Bind, Enfold, Enroll, Swaddle, Wrap

Sway(ing) Careen, Carry, Command, Diadrom, Domain, Dominion, Flap, Fluctuate, Govern, Hegemony, Influence, Lilt, Oscillate, Prevail, Reel, Reign, Rock, Roll, Rule, Shog, Shoogle, Swag, Swale, Swee, Swing(e), Teeter, Titter,

Totter, Vacillate

Swear(ing), **Swear word** Attest, Avow, Coprolalia, Curse, Cuss, Depose, Execrate, Expletive, Invective, Jurant, Juratory, Oath, Pledge, Plight, Rail, Sessa, Tarnal, Tarnation, Verify, Vow

Sweat(ing), **Sweaty** Apocrine, Beads, Clammy, Cold, Diaphoresis, Excrete, Exude, Flop, Forswatt, Glow, Hidrosis, Lather, Ooze, Osmidrosis, > **PERSPIRE**, Secretion, Slave, Stew, Sudament, Sudamina, Sudate, Swelter

Sweater Aran, Argyle, Circassian, Circassienne, Cowichan, Fair Isle, Gansey, Guernsey, Indian, Jersey, Polo, Pullover, Roll-neck, Siwash, Skivvy, Slip-on, Slop-pouch, Sloppy Joe, Turtleneck, Woolly

Swede Nordic, Rutabaga, Scandinavian, Turnip

Sweeney Police, Todd

Sweep(er), **Sweeping(s)** Besom, Broad, Broom, Brush, Chimney, Chummy, Clean, Curve, Debris, Detritus, Expanse, Extensive, Lash, Libero, Lottery, Net, Oars, Pan, Phasing, Police-manure, Range, Scavenger, Scud, Sling, Snowball, Soop, Sooterkin, Street, Stroke, Surge, Swathe, Vacuum, Waft, Well, Wide

Sweepstake Draw, Gamble, Lottery, Raffle, Tattersall's, Tombola

Sweet(s), **Sweetener**, **Sweetmeat**, **Sweetness** Adeline, Afters, Alcorza, Aldose, Amabile, Aspartame, Barley sugar, Bombe, Bonbon, Bonus, Brandyball, Bribe, Bull's eye, Burnt-almonds, Butterscotch, Candy, Candyfloss, Caramel, Chaptalise, Charity, Charming, Cherubic, Choc(olate), Choccy, Cloying, Coconut ice, Comfit, Confect(ion), Confetti, Confiserie, Confit, Conserve, Crème, Cute, Cyclamate, > **DESSERT**, Dolce, Dolly, Dolly mixture, Douce(t), Dowset, Dragée, Dulcet, Dulcitude, Elecampane, Flummery, Fondant, Fool, Fragrant, Fresh, Fudge, Glucose, Glycerin, Gob-stopper, Goody, Gum(drop), Gundy, Hal(a)vah, Halva, Honey(ed), Humbug, Hundreds and thousands, Ice, Icky, Indican, Jelly baby, Jelly bean, Jube, Jujube, Kiss, Lavender, Lemon drop, Licorice, Liquorice, Lollipop, Lolly, Lozenge, Luscious, Marchpane, Marshmallow, Marzipan, Melodious, Mint, Mousse, Muscavado, Nectared, Noisette, Nonpareil, Nougat, Pandrop, Pastille, Pea, Peardrop, Pet, Pick'n'mix, Pie, Praline, Pud(ding), Redolent, Rock, Romic, Saccharin(e), Scroggin, Seventeen, Sillabub, Sixteen, Solanine, Soot(e), Sop, Sorbet, Spice, Split, Stickjaw, Sucker, Sucrose, Sugar, Sugarplum, Syllabub, Syrupy, Tablet, Taffy, Tart, Thaumatin, Toffee, Torte, Trifle, Truffle, Turkish delight, Twee, Uses, William, Winsome, Xylitol, Zabaglione

Sweetbread Bur(r), Inchpin, Pancreas

Sweetheart Amoret, Amour, Beau, Dona(h), Dowsabel(l), Doxy, Dulcinea, Flame, Follower, Honey(bunch), Honeybun, Jarta, Jo(e), Lass, Leman, Lover, Masher, Neaera, Peat, Romeo, Steady, Toots(y), True-love, Valentine, Yarta, Yarto

Sweet-seller Butcher, Confectioner

Swell(ing) Adenomata, Ague-cake, Anasarca, Aneurysm, Apophysis, Bag, Bellying, Berry, Billow, Blab, Blister, Bloat, Blow, Boil, Boll, Bolster, Botch, Braw, Bubo, Bulb, Bulge, Bump, Bunion, Capellet, Carnosity, Cat, Chancre, Chilblain, Clour, Cratches, Curb, Cyst, Dandy, Desmoid, Diapason, Dilate, > **DISTEND**, Dom, Don, Eche, Ectasia, Eger, Elephantiasis, Enhance, Entasis, Epulis, Excellent, Farcy-bud, Frog, Gall, Gathering, Gent, Goiter, Goitre, Gout, Grandee, Ground, H(a)ematoma, Heave, Heighten, Hove, Hydrocele, Hydroma, Hygroma, Increase, Inflate, Intumesce, Kibe, L, Lampas(se), Lampers, Louden, Lump, Macaroni, Mouse, Nodule, Odontoma, Oedema, OK, Onco-, Ox-warble, Parotitis, Plim, Plump, Protrude, Protuberance, Proud, Pulvinus, Rise, Roil, Scirrhus, Scleriasis, Sea, Shinsplints, Splenomegaly, Strout, Struma, Stye,

Surge, Teratoma, Toff, Torose, Torulose, Tragus, Tuber(cle), Tumescence, Tumour, Tympany, Upsurge, Varicocele, Venter, Wallow, Warble, Wen, Whelk, Windgall, Xanthoma

▷ **Swelling** *may indicate* a word reversed

Swelter(ing) Perspire, Stew, Sweat, Tropical

Swerve, **Swerving** Bias, Broach, Careen, Deflect, Deviate, Lean, Sheer, Shy, Stray, Swee, Swing, Warp, Wheel

Swift(ly) Apace, Bird, Dean, Dromond, Fleet, Flock, Hasty, Martlet, Newt, Nimble, Presto, Prompt, Pronto, Quick, > **RAPID**, Reel, Slick, Spanking, Velocipede, Wight

Swig Drink, Gulp, Nip, Scour, Swill, Tighten

Swill Guzzle, Leavings, Rubbish, Slosh, Swash

▷ **Swilling** *may indicate* an anagram

Swim(ming) Bathe, Bogey, Bogie, Crawl, Dip, Float, Naiant, Natatorial, Paddle, Reel, Run, Skinny-dip, Soom, Synchro(nized), Trudgen, Whirl

▷ **Swim** *may indicate* an anagram

Swimmer Bather, Cichlid, Duckbill, Duckmole, Dugong, Frogman, Leander, Pad(d)le, Paidle, Planula, Pleopod, Pobble, Terrapin, Trudgen, Webb

▷ **Swimmer** *may indicate* a fish

Swimming costume Bathers, Bikini, Cossie, Maillot, Monokini, One-piece, Tanga, Tankini, Tog, Trunks

Swindle(r) Beat, Bite, Bucket-shop, Bunco, Bunkosteerer, Cajole, Champerty, > **CHEAT**, Chouse, Con, Crimp, Defraud, Diddle, Do, Escroc, Fiddle, Finagle, Fineer, Fleece, Fraud, Gazump, Gip, Goose-trap, Graft, Grifter, Gyp, Hocus, Hoser, Hustler, Leg, Leger, Long-firm, Magsman, Mountebank, Mulct, Nobble, Peter Funk, Plant, Racket, Ramp, Rig, Rogue, Scam, Sell, Shark, Sharper, Shicer, Shyster, Skelder, Skin, Skin game, Sting, Stitch-up, Stumer, Suck, Swiz(z), Trick, Twist, Two-time

Swine(herd) Boar, Brute, Cad, Eumaeus, Gadarene, Heel, Hog, Peccary, Pig, Porcine, Pork, Rotter, Sounder, Sow, Sybotic

Swing(er), **Swinging** Colt, Dangle, Flail, Hang, Hep, Kip(p), Lilt, Metronome, Mod, Music, Oscillate, Pendulate, Pendulum, Rock, Rope, Shoogie, Shuggy, Slew, Swale, Sway, Swee, Swerve, Swey, Swipe, Trapeze, Vibratile, Voop, Wave, Wheel, Whirl, Yaw

Swipe(s) Backhander, Beer, Haymaker, Steal, Strike, Tap-lash

Swirl Eddy, Purl, Swoosh, Tourbill(i)on, Twist, Whirl

▷ **Swirling** *may indicate* an anagram

Swish Cane, Frou-frou, Rustle, Smart, Whir, Whisper

Swiss Genevese, Ladin, Roll, Tell, Vaudois

Switch(ed), **Switches**, **Switching** Birch, Change, Convert, Crossbar, Cryotron, Dimmer, Dip, Exchange, Gang, Hairpiece, Knife, Legerdemain, Mercury, Message, Pear, Replace, Retama, Rocker, Rod, Scutch, Thyristor, Time, Toggle, Trip, Tumbler, Twig, Wave, Zap

▷ **Switched** *may indicate* an anagram

Switzerland CH, Helvetia

Swivel Caster, Pivot, Root, Rotate, Spin, Terret, Territ, Torret, Turret, Wedein

Swiz Chiz(z)

Swollen Blown, Bollen, Bombe, Bulbous, Full, Gourdy, Gouty, Incrassate, Nodose, Puffy, Tumid, Turgescent, Turgid, Varicose, Ventricose, Vesiculate

Swoon Blackout, Collapse, Deliquium, Dover, Dwa(l)m, Dwaum, Faint

Swoop Descend, Dive, Glide, Plummet, Souse

▶ **Swop** *see* **SWAP**

Sword(-like), **Swordplay** Andrew Ferrara, Anelace, Angurvadel, Anlace, Arondight, Assegai, Balisarda, Balmung, Bilbo, Blade, Brand, Brandiron, Broad(sword), Brondyron, Caliburn, Cemitare, Claymore, Colada, Court, Curtal-ax, Curtana, Curtax, Cutlass, Daisho, Damascene, Damaskin, Damocles, Dance, Dirk, Duranda(l), Durindana, Ensate, Ensiform, Epée, Espada, Estoc, Excalibur, Falchion, Faulchi(o)n, Firangi, Foil, Forte, Fox, Gladius, Glaive, Gleave, Glorious, Hanger, Iai-do, Jacob's staff, Joyeuse, Katana, Kendo, Khanda, Kirpan, Kreese, Kris, Kukri, Kusanagi, Machete, Mandau, Merveilleuse, Mimming, Montanto, Morglay, Nothung, Parang, Philippan, Rapier, Rosse, Sabre, Samurai, Schiavone, Schlager, Scimitar, Semita(u)r, Shabble, Shamshir, Sharp, Sigh, Simi, Skene-dhu, Smallsword, Spadroon, Spirtle, Spit, Spurtle(blade), Steel, Toasting-iron, Toledo, Tuck, Tulwar, Two-edged, Waster, Whinger, Whiniard, Whinyard, White-arm, Xiphoid, Yatag(h)an

Sword-bearer, **Swordsman**, **Swordswoman** Aramis, Athos, Blade, Brenda(n), D'Artagnon, Fencer, Frog, Gladiator, Matador, Porthos, Selictar, Spadassin, Spadroon, Spartacus, Swashbuckler, Zorro

Sword-dancer Matachin

Swordfish Espada, Istiophorus, Xiphias

Sword-swallower Samite

Swot Dig, Grind, Kill, Mug, Read up, Smug, Stew, Strike, Swat

Sybarite Aristippus, Epicure, Hedonist, Voluptuary

Sycamore Acer, Maple, Plane, Tree

Sycophant(ic) Apple polisher, Brown-nose, Claqueur, Crawler, Creeper, Damocles, Fawner, Gnathonic, Lickspittle, Parasite, Pickthank, Placebo, Toad-eater, Toady, Yesman

Syllabary Hiragana, Kana, Katakana

Syllable(s) Acatalectic, Anacrusis, Aretinian, Nonsense, Om, Tonic

Syllabus Program(me), Prospectus, Résumé, Summary, Table

Syllogism Argument, Conclusion, Deduction, Enthymeme, Epicheirema

Sylph Ariel, Nymph

Symbol(ic), **Symbols**, **Symbolism**, **Symbolist** Acrophony, Agma, Algebra, Allegory, Ampersand, Aniconic, Ankh, Apostrophus, Aramanth, Asterisk, Badge, Cachet, Caret, Cedilla, Character, Chord, Choropleth, Cipher, Clef, Colon, Crest, Daffodil, Decadent, Del, Descriptor, Diesis, Dingbat, Double-axe, Eagle, Emblem, Emoticon, Eng, Equal, Fertility, Grammalogue, Grapheme, Hash, Heitiki, Hieroglyph, Hierogram, Hiragana, Ichthus, Icon, Iconography, Ideogram, Index, Kalachakra, Kanji, Length mark, Lexigram, Logo(gram), Logograph, Mandala, Mark, Menorah, Metaphor, Mezuzah, Minus, Mogen David, Moral, Motif, Mystical, Nabla, Neum(e), Nominal, Notation, Obelus, Om, One, Ouroborus, Paragraph, Pentacle, Phonetic, Phonogram, Phraseogram, Pi, Pictograph, Plus, Presa, Redon, Rose, Rune, Segno, Semicolon, Semiotic, Shamrock, Sigla, Sign, Slur, Smiley, Star of David, Status, Svastika, Swastika, Syllabary, Syllabogram, Synthetism, Tag, Talisman, Thistle, Tiki, Tilde, Token, Totem, Trademark, Triskele, Triskelion, Type, Uraeus, Wild card, Yoni

Symmetric(al), **Symmetry** Balance, Digonal, Diphycercal, Even, Harmony, Isobilateral, Mirror, Pseudocubic, Radial, Regular, Skew

Sympathetic, **Sympathise(r)**, **Sympathy** Approval, Commiserate, Commiseration, Compassion, Condole(nce), Condone, Congenial, Crypto, Empathy, Fellow-traveller, Humane, Par, Pity, Rapport, Ruth, Side, Vicarious

Symphony Concert, Eroica, Fifth, Jupiter, Manfred, Music, New World, Opus,

Pastoral, Sinfonia, Sinfonietta, Unfinished

Symposium Assembly, Conference, Synod

Symptom(s) Epiphenomenon, Feature, Indicia, Merycism, Mimesis, Prodrome, Semiotic, Sign, Syndrome, Token, Trait, Withdrawal

Synagogue Beit Knesset, Beth Knesseth, Shul, Temple

Synchronise(r) Coincide, Genlock, Tune

Syncopated, Syncopation, Syncope Abridged, Breakbeat, Revamp, Vasovagal, Zoppa, Zoppo

Syndicate Associate, Cartel, Combine, Mafioso, Pool, Ring, Stokvel

Syndrome Adams-Stokes, Asperger's, Carpal tunnel, Cerebellar, Characteristic, China, Chronic fatigue, Compartment, Cri du chat, Crush, Cushing's, Down's, Empty nest, Fetal alcohol, Fragile X, Goldenhar's, Gorlin, Guillain-Barré, Gulf War, Hutchinson-Gilford, Jerusalem, Klinefelter's, Korsakoff's, Locked-in, Marfan, ME, Menières, Munch(h)ausen's, Nonne's, Overuse, Pattern, POS, Postviral, Prader-Willi, Premenstrual, Proteus, Reiter's, Reye's, SARS, Sezary, Sick building, Sjogren's, Stevens-Johnson, Stockholm, Stokes-Adams, Sturge-Weber, Tall-poppy, Temperomandibular, TMJ, Tourette's, Toxic shock, Turner's, Wag the Dog, Wernicke-Korsakoff, Wobbler, XYY

Synod Assembly, Conference, Convocation, Whitby

Synonym(ous) Comparison, Reciprocal

Synopsis Abstract, Blurb, Conspectus, Digest, Outline, Résumé, Schema, >**SUMMARY**

Syntax Grammar

Synthesis Amalgam, Aperture, Fusion, Merger

Synthesizer Moog®, Vocoder, Wind

Synthetic Empirical, Ersatz, Fake, False, Mock, Plastic, Polyamide, Silicone, Spencerian

Syphilis Chancre, Lues, Pip

Syrian Aramaean, Aramaic, Druse, Druz(e), Hittite, Hurrian, Levantine, Phoenician

Syringe(s) Douche, Flutes, Harpoon, Hypo, Hypodermic, Needle, Reeds, Spray, Squirt, Wash, Works

Syrphid Hoverfly

Syrup Capillaire, Cassis, Cocky's joy, Corn, Diacodion, Diacodium, Flattery, Golden, Grenadine, Linctus, Maple, Molasses, Moskonfyt, Orgeat, Quiddany, Rob, Sorghum, Sugar, Treacle

System(s), Systematic ABO, An mo, Bertillon, Binary, Braille, Code, Compander, Continental, Copernican, Cosmos, Course, Crystal, Decimal, Delsarte, Dewey (Decimal), Distributed, Early warning, Economy, Eocene, Ergodic, Establishment, Expert, Feudal, Formal, Giorgi, Grading, Harvard, HLA, Iastic, Immune, Imprest, Imputation, Inertial, Kalamazoo, Life-support, Limbic, Linear, Loop, Lymphatic, Madras, Merit, >**METHOD**, Metric, Microcosm, Midi, Miocene, Nervous, Network, Nicam, Notation, Octal, Operating, Order, Organon, Panel, Periodic, Permian, Pleiocene, Plenum, Points, Process, Ptolemaic, Purchase, Quota, Realtime, Regime, Regular, Respiratory, Root, Scheme, Scientific, Servo, SI, Sofar, Solar, Sonar, Sound, Spoils, Sprinkler, Squish lip, Stack(ing), Staff, Stanislavski, Star, Structure, Studio, Tally, Ternary, Theory, Tommy, Touch, Trias(sic), Truck, Turnkey, Tutorial, Two-party, Universe, Vestibular, Warehousing, Water, Weapon

Tt

T Bone, Junction, Potence, Tango, Tau-cross, Tee, Time, Toc(k)

Tab Bill, Check, > **LABEL**, Ring-pull, Stay-on, Tally, Trim

Tabby Blabbermouth, Brindled, > **CAT**, Gossip, Mottled, Spinster, Striped, Trout

Tabitha Gazelle

Table(-like) Alphonsine, Altar, Board, Bradshaw, Breakfast, Calendar, > **CHART**, Coffee, Console, Contingency, Counter, Credence, Credenza, Decision, Desk, Diagram, Dinner, Dolmen, Draw-leaf, Draw-top, Dressing, Drop-leaf, Drum, Ephemeris, Experience, Food, Gateleg, Glacier, Graph, Green-cloth, Gueridon, High, Imposing, Index, Key, League, Life, Light, > **LIST**, Lord's, Mahogany, Matrix, Mensa(l), Mesa, Monopode, Mortality, Multiplication, Occasional, Operating, Pembroke, Periodic, Piecrust, Pier, Plane, Platen, Pool, Prothesis, Pythagoras, Reckoner, Refectory, Roll, Round, Rudolphine, Sand, Schedule, Scheme, Slab, Sofa, Spoon, Stall, Statistical, Stone, Taboret, Tabular, Tea, Te(a)poy, Tide, Times, Toilet, Trestle, Trolley, Truth, Twelve, Washstand, Water, Whirling, Wool, Workbench, Writing

Tableau Semantic

Tablecloth Damask, Linen

Table-land Barkly, Kar(r)oo, Mesa, Plateau, Puna

Table-list Memo, Menu

Tablet Abacus, Album, Aspirin, Caplet, Eugebine, Graphics, Hatch, Medallion, Opisthograph, Osculatory, Ostracon, Ostrakon, > **PAD**, > **PILL**, Pilule, Plaque, Slate, Stele, Stone, Tombstone, Torah, Triglyph, Triptych, Troche, Trochisk, Ugarit, Votive

Table-talker Deipnosophist

Table-turner Tartar

Table-ware China, Cutlery, Silver

Taboo, Tabu Ban(ned), Bar, Blackball, Forbidden, Incest, Non dit, No-no, Unclean

Tacit, Taciturn(ity) Implicit, Laconic, Mumps, Oyster, Silent, Understood

Tack(y) Baste, Beat, Brass, Cheesy, Cinch, Clubhaul, Cobble, Gybe, Leg, Martingale, Nail, Saddlery, Salt-horse, > **SEW**, Sprig, Stirrup, Tailor's, Veer, Wear, White-seam, Yaw, Zigzag

Tackle Accost, Approach, Attempt, Beard, Bobstay, Burton, Claucht, Claught, Clevis, Clew-garnet, Collar, Dead-eye, Fishing, Garnet, Gear, Haliard, Halyard, Harness, Jury-rig, Rig, Rigging, Scrag, Straight-arm, Topping-lift

Tact, Tactful Delicacy, Diplomacy, Diplomatic, Discreet, Discretion, Politic, Savoir-faire

Tactic(s) Audible, Finesse, Hardball, Manoeuvre, Masterstroke, Plan, Ploy, Ruse, Salami, Shock, > **STRATEGY**, Strong-arm, Zwischenzug

Tactless(ness) Blundering, Brash, Crass, Gaffe, Gauche, Indelicate, Maladroit

Tadpole Ascidian, Polliwig, Polliwog, Pollywig, Pollywog, Porwiggle

Taffy Thief, Toffee, Welshman

Tag Aglet, Aiguillette, Cliché, Dog, Electronic, End, Epithet, > **FOLLOW**, Kabaddi,

Kimball, Label, Price, Question, Quote, Remnant, Tab, > TICKET, Treasury

Tail, Tailpiece Apocopate, > APPENDAGE, Bob, Brush, Caudal, Cercal, Cercus, Coda, Codetta, Colophon, Cue, Dock, Empennage, Fan, Fee, Flag, Floccus, > FOLLOW, Fud, Liripoop, Parson's nose, Pole, Pope's nose, PS, Queue, Rumple-bane, Scut, Seat, Stag, Stern, Telson, > TIP, Train, Uro(some), Uropygium, Women

Tailless Acaudal, An(o)urous, Fee-simple

Tail-lobes Anisocercal

Tailor(ed) Adapt, Bespoke, Bushel, Cabbager, Couturier, Cutter, Darzi, Durzi, Epicene, Feeble, Flint, Merchant, Nine, Outfitter, Pick-the-louse, Pricklouse, Sartor, Seamster, Snip, Starveling, Style, Whipcat, Whipstitch

▷ **Tailor** *may indicate* an anagram

Taint(ed) Besmirch, Blemish, Fly-blown, High, Infect, Leper, Off, Poison, > SPOIL, Stain, Stigma, Tinge, Trace, Unwholesome

Taiwan RC

Take(n), Take in, Taking(s), Take over Absorb, > ACCEPT, Adopt, Assume, Attract, Bag, Beg, Bite, Bone, Borrow, Bottle, > CAPTURE, Catch, Claim, Cop, Coup, Detract, Dishy, Distrain, Entr(y)ism, Exact, Expropriate, Get, Grab, Handle, Haul, Hent, House, Howe, Huff, Incept, Ingest, Mess, Misappropriate, Nick, Occupy, Pocket, Quote, R, Rec, Receipt, Receive, Recipe, Reverse, Rob, Seise, Sequester, Ship, Smitten, Snatch, Sneak, > STEAL, Stomach, Subsume, Swallow, Sweet, Swipe, Toll, Trump, Turnover, Usher, Usurp, Wan, Winsome, Wrest

Take away, Take off Aph(a)eresis, Asport, Carry-out, Deduct, Dock, Doff, Esloin, Exenterate, Expropriate, Jato, Parody, Parrot, Press-gang, Shanghai, Skit, Subtract, Vertical, VTO(L)

Take care Guard, See, Tend, Watch

▷ **Taken up** *may indicate* reversed

Take part Act, Engage, Side

Talbot House Toc H

Talc Potstone, Rensselaerite, Soapstone, Steatite, Venice

Tale(s) Allegory, Blood, Boccaccio, Conte, Decameron, Edda, Fable, Fabliau, Fairy, Fairy story, Fiction, Folk, Gag, Geste, Hadith, Iliad, Jataka, Jeremiad, Legend, Lie, Mabinogion, Maise, Ma(i)ze, Marchen, Mease, Milesian, Narrative, Odyssey, Old wives', Pentameron, Rede, Saga, Sandabar, Score, Sinbad, Sind(a)bad, Sob-story, Spiel, > STORY, Tradition, Traveller's, Weird

Tale-bearer, Tale-teller Gossip, Grass, Informer, Sneak, Tattler, Tusitala

Talent(ed) Ability, Accomplishment, Aptitude, Bent, Dower, Faculty, Flair, Forte, Genius, Gift, Ingenium, Knack, Long suit, Nous, Prodigy, Schtick, Strong point, Versatile, Virtuoso, W(h)iz(z), Whiz-kid

Talion Reprisal

Talisman Amulet, Charm, Saladin, Sampo, Scarab, Telesm

Talk(ing), Talking point, Talker, Talks Ana, Articulate, Babble, Bibble-babble, Blab, Blague, Blat, Blather, Blether-skate, Cant, Chalk, Chat, Chinwag, Chirp, Circumlocution, Colloquy, Commune, Confabulate, Confer, Converse, Coo, Cross, Descant, Dialog(ue), Diatribe, Dilate, Discourse, Diseur, Dissert, Double, Earbash, Earful, Express, Fast, Filibuster, Froth, Gab, Gabble, Gabnash, Gas, Gibber, Gossip, Grandiloquence, Guff, Harp, Imparl, Jabber, Jargon, Jaw, Jazz, Korero, Lip, Logorrhoea, Macrology, Mang, Maunder, Mince, Monologue, Motormouth, Nashgab, Natter, Noise, Omniana, Palabra, Palaver, Parlance, Parley, Patter, Pawaw, Pep, Perorate, Phraser, Pidgin, Pillow, Pitch, Potter, Powwow, Prate, Prattle, Presentation, Prose, Proximity, Ramble, Rap, Rigmarole, Rote, SALT, Shop, Slang(-whang), Small, Soliloquy, > SPEAK, Spiel,

Spout, Straight, Sweet, Table, Tachylogia, Topic, Turkey, Twaddle, Twitter, Unbosom, Up(s), Utter, Vocal, Waffle, Witter, Wongi, Wrangle, Yabber, Yack, Yak, Yalta, Yammer, Yap, Yatter

Talkative Chatty, Fluent, Gabby, Garrulous, Gash, Glib, Loquacious, Vocular, Voluble

Tall Etiolated, Exaggerated, Hie, High, Hye, Lanky, Lathy, Leggy, Lofty, Long, Procerity, Randle-tree, Rantle-tree, Tangle, Taunt, Tower, Towery

Tallboy Chest, Dresser

Tallow Greaves, Hatchettite, Lead-arming, Mineral, Vegetable, Wax

Tally > AGREE, Census, Correspond, Count, Match, Nickstick, Notch, Record, > SCORE, Stick, Stock, Tab, Tag

Talmud Gemara, Mishna

Talon Claw, Ogee, Single

Talus Scree

Tamarind Assam

Tamasha Fuss, To-do

Tame Amenage, Break, Docile, Domesticate, Lapdog, Mansuete, Meek, Mild, Safe, Snool, Subdue

Tammany Hall, Sachem

Tamp, Tampon Plug

Tamper(ing) Bishop, Cook, Doctor, Fake, Fiddle, Meddle, Medicate, Monkey, Nobble, Phreaking

Tam-tam Gong

Tan(ned), Tanned skin, Tanning Adust, Bablah, Babul, Bark, Basil, Beige, Bisque, Boarding, Bronze, > BROWN, Canaigre, Catechu, Furan, Furfuran(e), Insolate, Lambast, Leather, Neb-neb, Paste, Pipi, Puer, Pure, Spank, Sun, Sunbathe, Tenné, Umber, Val(l)onia, Valonea, Ybet

Tandem Duo, Randem

Tang Relish, Smack, Taste

Tangent Ratio, Slope, Touching

Tangible Concrete, Palpable, Plain, Solid, Tactual

Tangle Alga, Badderlock, Burble, Dulse, Embroil, Entwine, Fank, Fankle, Heap, Implication, Ket, > KNOT, Labyrinth, Laminaria, Lutin, Mat, Mix, Nest, Oarweed, Ore, Perplex, Pleach, > RAVEL, Sea-girdle, Seaweed, Skean, Skein, Snarl, Taigle, Taut(it), Tawt, Thicket, Varec

Tangled *may indicate* an anagram

Tank Abrams, Alligator, Amphibian, Aquarium, Belly, Casspir, Centurion, Cesspool, Challenger, Chieftain, Cistern, Drop, Feedhead, Float, Flotation, Gasholder, Header, Keir, Kier, Mouse, Panzer, Pod, Quiescent, > RESERVOIR, Ripple, Sedimentation, Septic, Sherman, Shield pond, Sponson, Sump, Surge, Think, Tiger, Valentine, Vat, Ventral, Vivarium, Whippet

Tankard Blackjack, Peg, Pewter, Pot, Stein, Tappit-hen

Tanker Bowser, Lorry, Oiler

Tanner(y) Bender, Currier, Kick, Solarium, Sunbather, Sunshine, Tawery, Tester(n), 'VId', Zack

Tannin Catechu

Tantalise Entice, Tease, Tempt, Torture

Tantalum Ta

Tantivy Alew, Halloo

Tantrum Hissyfit, Paddy, Pet, Rage, Scene, Tirrivee, Tirrivie

Tanzania EAT

Tap(ping), Taps Accolade, Bibcock, Blip, Broach, Bug, Cock, Col legno, Drum,

Faucet, Flick, Hack, Mag, Milk, Mixer, Monitor, Paracentesis, Pat, Patter, Percuss, Petcock, > RAP, Spigot, Spinal, Stopcock, Stroup, Tack, Tat, Tit, Touk, Tuck, Water

Tape Chrome, DAT, > DRINK, Duct, Ferret, Finish, Gaffer, Grip, Idiot, Incle, Inkle, Insulating, Magnetic, Masking, Measure, Metal, Narrowcast, Paper, Passe-partout, Perforated, Punched, Record, Red, Scotch, Sellotape®, Shape, Sticky, Ticker, Video, Welding

Taper(ed), **Tapering** Diminish, Fastigiate, Featheredge, Fusiform, Lanceolate, Morse, Narrow, Nose, Subulate, Tail

Tapestry Alentous, Arras(ene), Aubusson, Bayeux, Bergamot, Crewel-work, Dosser, Gobelin, Hanging, Oudenarde, Petit point, Tapet

Tapeworm Echinococcus, Hydatid, Measle, Scolex, Taenia, Teniasis

Tapioca Cassava, Pearl, Yuca, Yucca

Tapir Anta, S(e)ladang

Tar, **Tar product** AB, Bitumen, Coal, Creosote, Egg, Gladwellise, Gob, Indene, Maltha, Matelot, Matlo, Mineral, Naphtha, Needle, OS, Parcel, Pay, Picamar, Picene, Pine, Pitch, Rating, Retene, Sailor, Salt, Uintahite, Uintaite, Wood, Xylol

Tardy Behindhand, Dilatory, Late, > SLOW

Tare Tine, Vetch

Target > AIM, Blank, Butt, Clout, Cockshy, Dart, Drogue, End, Hit, Home, Hub, Inner, Magpie, Mark, Motty, > OBJECT, Outer, Pelta, Pin, Prey, Prick, Quintain, Sitter, Sitting, Tee, Victim, Wand

Tariff List, Preferential, Protective, Rate, Revenue, Zabeta

Tarnish Defile, Discolour, Soil, Stain, Sully, Taint

Taro Arum, Coc(c)o, Dasheen, Eddo

Tarot Arcana

Tarpaulin Weathercloth

Tarragon Staragen

Tarry Bide, Dally, Leng, > LINGER, Stay, Sticky

Tarsier Malmag

Tarsus Saul

Tart Acetic, Acid, Bakewell, Broad, Charlotte, Cocotte, Croquante, Cupid, Custard, Dariole, Doxy, Duff, Flam(m), Flan, Flawn, Frock, Harlot, Hussy, Jade, Lemony, Mirliton, Moll, Mort, Nana, > PIE, Pinnace, Piquant, Pro, Quean, Quiche, Quine, > SHARP, Slapper, Slut, Snappy, Sour, Stew, Strumpet, Tatin, Tramp, Treacle, Trull, Unsweet

Tartan Argyle, Argyll, Maud, Plaid, Set(t), Trews

Tartar Argal, Argol, Beeswing, Calculus, Crust, Hell, Plaque, Rough, Scale, Tam(b)erlane, Zenocrate

Tashkent Uzbek

Task Assignment, Aufgabe, > CHORE, Duty, Errand, Exercise, Fag, Imposition, Mission, Ordeal, Pensum, Stint, Thankless, Vulgus

Tasmania Apple Isle, Van Diemen's Land

Tassel Pompom, Toorie, Tourie, Tsutsith, Tuft

Taste(ful), **Taster**, **Tasty** Acquired, Aesthetic, Appetite, Degust, Delibate, Delicious, Discrimination, > EAT, Fashion, Flavour, Form, Gout, Gust, Gustatory, Hint, Lekker, Lick, Palate, Penchant, Pica, Pree, Refinement, Relish, > SAMPLE, Sapor, Sar, Savour, S(c)hme(c)k, Sip, Smack, Smatch, Snack, Soupçon, Stomach, Succulent, Tang, Titbit, Toothsome, > TRY, Vertu, Virtu, Wine

Tasteless Appal, Brassy, Fade, Flat, Insipid, Stale, Tacky, Vapid, Vulgar, Watery,

Wearish, Wersh

Tat, **Tatter**, **Tatty** Rag, Ribbon, Roon, Scrap, Shred, Tag, Tan, Untidy

Tattie-bogle Scarecrow

Tattle(r) Blab, Chatter, Gash, > GOSSIP, Prate, Rumour, Sneak, Snitch, Totanus, Willet

Tattoo Devil's, Drum, Edinburgh, Moko, Rataplan, Row-dow, Tat

Tatum Art

Taught Up

Taunt Dig, Fling, Gibe, Gird, > JEER, Rag, Ridicule, Twight, Twit

Taut Stiff, Tense

Tavern Bar, Bodega, Bousing-ken, Bush, Fonda, > INN, Kiddleywink, Kneipe, Mermaid, Mitre, Mughouse, Pothouse, Shebeen, Taphouse

Taw Alley, Ally, Marble

Tawdry Catchpenny, > CHEAP, Flashy, Gaudy, Raffish, Sleazy, Tatty, Tinsey

Tawny Brindle, Dusky, Fawn, Fulvous, Mulatto, Port, Tan

Tawse Cat, Lash, Thong, Whip

Tax(ing), **Taxation** ACT, Agist, Aid, Alms-fee, Assess, Capitation, Carbon, Carucage, Cense, Cess, > CHARGE, Corporation, Council, Custom, Danegeld, Direct, Duty, Energy, EPT, Escot, Escuage, Exact, Excise, Exercise, EZT, Gabelle, Geld, Gift, Head, Hidage, Impose, Imposition, Impost, Impute, Indirect, Inheritance, IR, Jaghir(e), Jagir, Land, Levy, Likin, Lot, Murage, Negative, Octroi, Operose, Overwork, Pavage, PAYE, Peter-pence, Poll, Poundage, Primage, Property, Proportional, PT, Punish, Purchase, Rate, Regressive, Road, Rome-pence, Sales, Scat(t), Scot (and lot), Scutage, Sess, SET, Sin, Single, Skat, Stealth, Stent, Streetage, Stumpage, Super, Taille, Tallage, Talliate, Tariff, Task, Teind, Tithe, Tobin, Toilsome, Toll, Tonnage, Tribute, Try, Turnover, Unitary, Value-added, VAT, Wattle, Wealth, Weary, White rent, Windfall, Window, Withholding, Zakat

Tax area Tahsil, Talooka, Taluk(a)

Tax-collector, **Taxman** Amildar, Cheater, Exciseman, Farmer, Gabeller, Inspector, IR(S), Publican, Stento(u)r, Tithe-proctor, Tollman, Undertaker, Zemindar

Taxi Cab, Hackney, Samlor, Zola Budd

Taxidermist Venus

Taxman *see* TAX-COLLECTOR

TB Scrofula

TE Lawrence, Ross, Shaw

Tea Afternoon, Assam, Beef, Black, Bohea, Brew, Brick, Bush, Cambric, Camomile, Caper, Ceylon, Cha, Chamomile, Chanoyu, China, Chirping-cup, Congo(u), Cream, Cuppa, Darjeeling, Earl Grey, Grass, Green, Gunfire, Gunpowder, Herb(al), High, Hyson, Indian, Jasmine, K(h)at, Kitchen, Labrador, Lapsang, Lapsang Souchong, Leaves, Ledum, Lemon, Malt, Manuka, Marijuana, Maté, Mexican, Mint, Morning, New Jersey, Oolong, Orange pekoe, Oulong, Paraguay, Pekoe, Post and rail, Pot, Qat, Red-root, Rooibos, Rosie Lee, Russian, Senna, Souchong, Stroupach, Stroupan, Switchel, Tay, Thea, Theophylline, Twankay, Yerba (de Maté)

Teach(er), **Teaching (material)**, **Teachings** Acharya, Adjoint, Agrege, AMMA, Apostle, Barbe, Beale, BEd, Bhagwan, Buss, Catechist, Chalkface, > COACH, Con(ne), Didactic, Didascalic, Docent, Doctrine, Dogma, Dominie, Dressage, Edify, > EDUCATE, Educationalist, Edutainment, EIS, ELT, Explain, Faculty, Froebel, Gerund-grinder, Gooroo, Gospel, Governess, Guru, Head, Heuristic, Hodja, Inculcate, Indoctrinate, Inform, Instil, Instruct, Ism, Kho(d)ja, Kumon

(Method), Lair, Lancasterian, Larn, Lear(e), Lecturer, Leir, Lere, Maam, Maggid, Magister, Maharishi, Mahavira, Mallam, Marker, Marm, Master, Maulvi, Mentor, Miss, Mistress, Molla(h), Monitor, Montessorian, Moola(h), Moolvi(e), Mufti, Mullah, Munshi, Mystagogue, Nuffield, Paedotribe, Pedagogue, Pedant, Pr(a)efect, Preceptor, Privat-docent, Proctor, Prof, Prog, PT, Pupil, Rabbi, Realia, Rebbe, Remedial, Rhetor, Scholastic, Schoolman, Scribe, Sensei, Show, Sir, Smriti, Socrates, Sophist, Staff, Starets, Staretz, Sunna, Supply, Swami, Tantra, Team, Train(er), Tutelage, Tutor, Usher

Teach-in Seminar

Teahouse Sukiya

Teak African, Bastard, White

Team Bafana bafana, Colts, Crew, Dream, Ecurie, Eleven, Equipe, Farm, Fifteen, Outfit, Oxen, Panel, Possibles, Probables, Relay, Scrub, > SIDE, Span, Special, Squad, Squadron, Staff, Tiger, Troupe, Turnout, Unicorn, United, XI

Tea-party Boston, Bunfight, Cookie-shine, Drum, Kettledrum, Shine

Teapot Billycan, Cadogan, Samovar

Tear(s), Tearable, Tearful, Tearing Beano, Claw, Crocodile, Divulsion, Drop, Eye-drop, Eye-water, Greeting, Hurry, Lacerate, Laniary, Pelt, Ranch, Rash, Reave, > REND, Rheum, Rip, Rive, Rume, Scag, Screed, Shred, Snag, Split, Spree, Tire, Waterworks, Wet, Worry, Wrench, Wrest

Tearaway Get, Hothead, Ned

Tear-jerker Onion

Tear-pit Crumen, Larmier

Tease, Teasing Arch, Backcomb, Badinage, Bait, Banter, Card, Chaff, Chap, Chiack, Chip, Chyack, Cod, Grig, Guy, Hank, Imp, Ironic, Itch, Josh, Kemb, Kid, Mag, Mamaguy, Nark, Persiflage, > RAG, Raillery, Rally, Razz, Rib, Rot, Strip, > TANTALISE, Toaze, Torment(or), Twilly, Twit, Worrit

Teasel Dipsacus, Valerian

Teat Dug, Dummy, Mamilla, Mastoid, Nipple, Pap, Soother, Tit

Tea-time Chat

Teaze Gig, Moze

Technetium Tc

Technical, Technician, Technique Adept, Alexander, Artisan, Brushwork, College, Delphi, Execution, Foley artist, Footsteps editor, Kiwi, Know-how, Manner, > METHOD, Operative, Salami, Sandwich, Science, Toe and heel

Technology, Technological High, State of the art, Stealth

Ted(dy) Bodgie, Dexter, Ducktail, Moult, Widgie, Yob

Tedium, Tedious Boring, Chore, Deadly, Doldrums, Drag, Dreich, Dull, Ennui, Heaviness, Long, Longspun, Longueur, Monotony, Operose, Prosy, Soul-destroying, > TIRING, Twaddle, Wearisome, Yawn

Tee Hub, Umbrella

Teem(ing) Abound, Bustling, Empty, Great, Pullulate, Swarm

Teenager Adolescent, Bobbysoxer, Junior, Juvenile, Minor, Mod, Rocker, Sharpie, Skinhead, Youth

▶ **Teeth** *see* TOOTH

Teething ring Coral

Teetotal(ler) Abdar, Blue Ribbon, Nephalist, Rechabite, Temperate, TT, Water-drinker, Wowser

Tegument Seed coat

Telecommunications Cellnet®, Vodafone®

Telegram, Telegraph Bush, Cable, Ems, Grapevine, Greetings, International, Message, Moccasin, Mulga wire, Singing, Telex, Wire

Telepathy, Telepathic Clairvoyance, ESP, Seer
Telephone Ameche, ATLAS, Bell, Blower, BT, Call, Cellphone, Centrex, Cordless, Dial, Dog and bone, GRACE, Handset, Horn, Intercom, Line, Lo-call®, Mercury, Mobile, Pay-station, Pdq, > **PHONE**, POTS, Ring, Squawk box, STD, Textphone, Touch-tone, Vodafone®, Wire
Teleprinter Creed
Telescope Altazimuth, Binocle, Cassegrain(ian), Collimator, Coudé, Electron, Finder, Galilean, Gemini, Glass, Gregorian, Heliometer, Hubble, Intussuscept, Meniscus, Newtonian, Night-glass, Optical, Palomar, Perspective, Radio, Reflector, Refractor, Schmidt, Shorten, Snooperscope, Spyglass, Stadia, Terrestrial, Tube, X-ray, Zenith
Teletext® Ceefax®, Oracle®
Television, Telly Box, Cable, Digital, Diorama, Event, Goggle box, Image orthicon, ITV, MAC, PAL, Pay, Plumbicon®, Projection, RTE, Satellite, SECAM, Set, Small screen, Subscription, Tree and branch, Tube, > **TV**, Video
Tell Acquaint, Announce, Apprise, Archer, Beads, Blab, Break, Clipe, Clype, Compt, Direct, > **DISCLOSE**, Divulge, Grass, Impart, Inform, > **NARRATE**, Noise, Notify, Number, Recite, Recount, Relate, Report, Retail, Rumour, Sneak, Snitch, Spin, Teach, William
Tellurium Te
Temerity Cheek, Gall, Impertinence, Imprudence, Impudence, Incaution, Rashness, Recklessness
Temper, Temperate Abstemious, Abstinent, Allay, Anneal, Assuage, Attune, Balmy, Bile, Blood, Calm, Choler, Comeddle, Continent, Dander, Delay, Ease, Fireworks, Flaky, Irish, Leaven, > **MILD**, Mitigate, Moderate, Modify, > **MOOD**, Neal, Paddy, Paddywhack, Pet, Radge, Rage, Season, Short fuse, Snit, Sober, Soften, Spitfire, Spleen, Strop, Swage, Tantrum, Techy, Teen, Teetotal, Tetchy, Tiff, Tone, Trim, Tune
Temperament(al) Bent, Blood, Choleric, Crasis, Disposition, Equal, Just, Kidney, Mean-tome, Melancholy, Mettle, Moody, > **NATURE**, Neel, Over-sensitive, Phlegmatic, Prima donna, Sanguine, Unstable, Viscerotonia
Temperance Moderation, Pledge, Rechabite
Temperature Absolute, Celsius, Centigrade, Chambré, Colour, Critical, Curie, Dew point, Fahrenheit, Fever, Flashpoint, Heat, Heterothermal, Hyperthermia, Kelvin, Regulo, Restrictive, Room, T, Thermodynamic, Weed, Weid
Tempest(uous) Bourasque, Euraquilo, Euroclydon, Gale, High, Marie, > **STORM(Y)**
Temple, Temple gate Adytum, Amphiprostyle, Artemis, Capitol, Cella, Chapel, Church, Delphi, Delubrum, Ephesus, Fane, Gompa, Gurdwara, Haffet, Haffit, Heroon, Inner, Mandir(a), Masjid, Middle, Monopteron, Monopteros, Mosque, Museum, Naos, Nymphaeum, Pagod(a), Pantheon, Parthenon, > **SHRINE**, Shul(n), Teocalli, Teopan, Torii, Vihara, Wat
Tempo Agoge, Rate, > **RHYTHM**, Rubato
Temporary Acting, Caretaker, Cutcha, Ephemeral, Hobjob, Interim, Kutcha, Locum, Makeshift, Pro tem, Provisional, Short-term, Stopgap, Temp, Transient, Transitional
Temporise(r) Politique
Tempt(ation), Tempting, Tempter, Temptress Allure, Apple, Bait, Beguile, Beset, Circe, Dalilah, Decoy, Delilah, > **ENTICE**, Eve, Groundbait, Impulse, Lure, Providence, Satan, Seduce, Siren, Snare, Tantalise, Test, Tice, Trial
Ten Commandments, Decad, Dectet, Decury, Denary, Googol, 10, Iota, Tera-,

Tribes, X

Tenacious, Tenacity Clayey, Determined, Dogged, Fast, Guts, Hold, Intransigent, Persevering, Persistent, Resolute, Retentive, Sticky

Tenancy, Tenant(s) Censuarius, Cosherer, Cottar, Cotter, Cottier, Dreng, Feuar, Feudatory, Gravelman, Homage, Ingo, Inhabit, Leaseholder, Lessee, > **LODGER**, Metayer, Occupier, Periodic, Rentaller, Renter, Secure, Shorthold, Sitting, Socager, Socman, Sokeman, Suckener, Tacksman, Valvassor, Vassal, Vavasour, Visit

Tend Care, Dress, Herd, Incline, Lean, Liable, Nurse, Prone, Run, Shepherd, Verge

Tendency Apt, Bent, Bias, Central, Conatus, Drift, Genius, Idiosyncrasy, Import, Militant, Penchant, Proclivity, Propensity, Trend

Tender(iser), Tenderly, Tenderness Affettuoso, Amoroso, Bid, Bill, Coin, Con amore, Crank, Dingey, Ding(h)y, Fond, Frail, Gentle, Green, Humane, Jolly-boat, Legal, Nesh, Nurse, > **OFFER**, Painful, Papain, Pinnace, Prefer, Present, Proffer, Proposal, Quotation, Red Cross, Sair, Shepherd, > **SOFT**, Sore, SRN, Submit, Sympathy, Tendre

Tenderfoot Babe, Chechacho, Chechako, Cub, Greenhorn, Innocent

Tenderloin Psoas, Undercut

Tendon Achilles, Aponeurosis, Hamstring, Kangaroo, Leader, Paxwax, Sinew, String, Vinculum, Whitleather

Tendril(led) Capreolate, Cirrose, Cirrus, Tentacle

Tenement(s) Dominant, Land, Rook, Tack

Tenet Adiaphoron, Creed, > **DOCTRINE**, Dogma

Tenfold Decuple

Tennis Close, Court, Deck, Lawn, LTA, Real, Royal, Set, Sphairistike, Squash, Table, Wimbledon

Tenon Cog, Dovetail, Lewis

Tenor Course, Domingo, > **DRIFT**, Effect, Ferreras, Gigli, Gist, Heroic, Pavarotti, Purport, Singer, T, Tide, Timbre, Trial, Vein

Tense Aor, Aorist, Case, Clench, Drawn, Edgy, Electric, Essive, Imperfect, Keyed up, Mood(y), Nervy, Overstrung, Past, Perfect, Pluperfect, Preterit, Preterite, Rigid, Simple, Stiff, Strained, Stressed(-out), Strict, T, > **TAUT**, Uptight

Tensing Sherpa

Tension Creative, High, Isometrics, Isotonic, Meniscus, Nerviness, Premenstrual, > **STRAIN**, Stress, Stretch, Surface, Tone, Tonicity, Tonus, Yips

Tent Bell, Bivvy, Cabana, Douar, Dowar, Duar, Kedar, Kibitka, Marquee, Oxygen, Pavilion, Probe, Pup, Red wine, Ridge, Shamiana(h), Shamiyanah, Shelter, Tabernacle, Teepee, Tepee, Tilt, Tipi, Top, Topek, Trailer, Tupek, Tupik, Wigwam, Wine, Y(o)urt

Tentacle Actinal, Cirrate, Feeler, Hectocotylus, Horn, Lophophore

Tentative Empirical, Experimental, Gingerly, Peirastic

Tent-dweller, Tent-maker Camper, Indian, Kedar, Omar, St Paul

Tenth Disme, Teind, Tithe

Ten Thousand Toman

Tenuous Frail, Slender, Slight, Thin, Vague

Tenure Blench, Burgage, Copyhold, Cottier(ism), Drengage, Fee-farm, Feu, Frankalmoi(g)n(e), Frank-fee, Gavelkind, Leasehold, Manorial, Occupation, Raiyatwari, Rundale, Runrig, Ryotwari, Socage, > **TERM**, Vavasory, Venville, Zemindar

Tepid Laodicean, Lukewarm

Terbium Tb

Terete Centric(al)

Term(s), **Terminal**, **Termly** Air, Anode, Buffer, Cathode, Coast, Coste, Designate, Desinant, Distal, Distributed, > EPITHET, Euphemism, Expression, Final, Gnomon, Goal, Half, Hilary, Inkhorn, Intelligent, Law, Lent, Major, Michaelmas, Middle, Minor, > PERIOD, Rail(head), Real, Removal, Sabbatical, Semester, Session, Stint, Stretch, Trimester, Trimestrial, Trinity, Ultimatum, Waterloo, > WORD, Work station, Zeroth

Termagant Jade, Shrew, Shrow, Spitfire, Vixen

Terminate, **Termination**, **Terminus** Abort, Axe, Conclude, Depot, Desinent, Earth, > END, Expiry, > FINISH, Goal, Liquidate, Naricorn, Railhead, Suffix

Termite Duck-ant

Tern Egg-bird, Scray, Three

Terrace Barbette, Beach, Bench, Linch, Lynchet, Offset, Perron, Shelf, Stoep, Tarras, Undercliff, Veranda(h)

Terra-cotta Tanagra

Terrain Area, Landscape, Scablands, Tract

Terrapin Diamondback, Emydes, Emys, Slider, Turtle

Terrible, **Terribly** Appalling, Awful, Deadly, Fell, Frightful, Ghastly, Horrible, Much, Odious, Very

Terrible person Humgruffi(a)n, Ivan, Ogre

Terrier Aberdeen, Airedale, Apsos, Australian, Bedlington, Black and tan, Border, Boston, Bull, Catalogue, Cesky, Dandie Dinmont, Fox, Griffon, Irish, Jack Russell, Kerry blue, Lakeland, Maltese, Manchester, Norfolk, Norwich, Pinscher, Pit bull, Ratter, Register, Scotch, Scottie, Scottish, Sealyham, Silky, Skye, Soft-coated wheaten, Staffordshire bull, Sydney silky, TA, Tibetan, Welsh, West Highland, West Highland white, Westie, Wire-haired, Yorkshire

Terrific, **Terrified**, **Terrify(ing)** Affright, Aghast, Agrise, Agrize, Agryze, Appal, Awe, Blood-curdling, Enorm, Fear, Fine, Fley, Gast, Helluva, Huge, Overawe, > PETRIFY, Scare, Superb, Unman, Yippee

Territory Abthane, Ap(p)anage, Colony, Domain, Dominion, Duchy, Emirate, Enclave, Exclave, Goa, Indian, Latium, Lebensraum, Manor, Margravate, No-man's-land, Northern, Northwest, Nunavut, Palatinate, Panhandle, Papua, Petsamo, Principate, Protectorate, Province, Realm, > REGION, Scheduled, Sphere, Sultanate, Ter(r), Trust, Union, Yukon

Terror(s) Blue funk, Bugaboo, Bugbear, Eek, > FEAR, Fright, Holy, Imp, Night, Panic, Skrik

Terrorist Alarmist, Al Fatah, Anarchist, Bogeyman, Bomber, Bully, Cagoulard, Desperado, Dynamitard, Eta, Grapo, Hijacker, Ku Klux Klan, Mau-mau, Maximalist, Mountain, Nightrider, Nihilist, Pirate, PLO, Provo, Red Brigade, Robespierre, Ustashi

Terry Ellen, Towel

Terse Abrupt, Brusque, Curt, Laconic, Pithy, Precise, Succinct

Tertiary Cainozoic, Eocene, Miocene, Oligocene, Palaeogene, Pliocene

Tessellation Mosaic

Test(er), **Testing** Achievement, Acid, Alpha, Ames, Amniocentesis, Apgar, Appro, Aptitude, Assay, Audition, Barany, Bench, Bender, Benedict, Beta, Blood, Breath, Breathalyser®, Brinell, Candle, Canopy, Check, Chi-square, Cis-trans, Cloze, Conn(er), Coomb's, Crash, Criterion, Crucial, Crucible, Crunch, Dick, Docimastic, Driving, Dummy-run, Eprouvette, Examine, Exercise, Experiment, Field, Flame, Frog, Ink-blot, Intelligence, International, Litmus, Mann-Whitney, Mantoux, Mazzin, Means, Medical, MOT, Mug, Neckverse, Needs, Objective, Oral, Ordalian, > ORDEAL, Pale, Pap,

Papanicolaou, Paraffin, Patch, Paternity, Performance, Personality, PH, Pilot, Pons asinorum, Pree, Preeve, Preif, Preve, Probe, Projective, Proof, Prove, Proving-ground, Pyx, Q-sort, Qualification, Quiz, Rally, Reagent, Road, Rorschach, SAT, Scalogram, Schick's, Schilling, Schutz-Charlton, Scratch, Screen, Shadow, Shibboleth, Showdown, Shroff, Sign, Significance, Sixpence, Skin, Slump, Smear, Smoke, Snellen, Sound, Spinal, Stanford-Binet, Stress, Tempt, Tensile, Touch, Touchstone, Trial, Trier, Trior, Try, Turing, Ultrasonic, Viva, Wassermann's, Wilcoxon, Zack

Testament Bible, Covenant, Hagographa, Heptateuch, Hexateuch, Hornolog(o)umena, Midrash, New, Old, Pentateuch, Scripture, Septuagint, Tanach, Targum, Will

Testicle(s) Ballocks, Balls, Bollix, Bollocks, Cobblers, Cojones, Gool(e)y, Goolie, Knackers, Monkey-gland, Monorchid, Nads, Nuts, Ridgel, Ridgil, Rig(gald), Rocks, Stone

Testify, Testimonial, Testimony Character, Chit, Declare, Depone, Deposition, > EVIDENCE, Rap, Scroll, Tribute, Viva voce, Witness

Testy, Tetchy Cross, Narky, Peevish, Ratty

Tetanus Lockjaw

Tête-a-tête Collogue, Confab, Hobnob, Twosome

Tether Cord, Endurance, Hitch, Noose, Picket, Seal, Stringhalt, > TIE

Tetrahedrite Fahlerz, Fahlore

Tetrarchy Iturea

Tetrasyllabic Paeon

Tetrode Resnatron

Teuton(ic) Erl-king, German, Goth, Herren, Vandal

Texas Ranger

Text(s), Textbook ABC, Body, Brahmana, Church, Codex, Donat, Ennage, Greeked, Harmony, Libretto, Mandaean, Mantra, Mezuzah, Octapla, Op-cit, Philology, Plain, Pyramid, Quran, Responsa, Rubric, Script, S(h)astra, Shema, > SUBJECT, Sura, Sutra, Tefillin, Tephillin, Tetrapla, Thesis, Topic, Tripitaka, Typography, Upanis(h)ad, Variorium, Vulgate, Zohar

Textile Cloth, Fabric, Mercy

Texture Constitution, Feel, Fiber, Fibre, Grain, Open, Wale, Weave, Woof

Thai(land) Karen, Lao(s), Mon, Shan, Siam

Thalamus Optic

Thallium Tl

Thames Father, Tamesis

Than And

Thane Banquo, Ross

Thank(s), Thankful, Thanksgiving Appreciate, Collins, Deo gratias, Gloria, Grace, Gramercy, Grateful, Gratitude, Kaddish, Mercy, Roofer

Thankless Ingrate, Vain

That (is), That one As, Cestui, Das heisst, Dh, Exists, How, Ie, Ille, Namely, Que, Sc, Such, Thence, Thon(der), What, Which, Yon, Yt

Thatch(er), Thatching At(t)ap, Daych, Hair, Heard, Hear(i)e, Hele, Hell, Mane, PM, Reed, Straw, Thack, Theek, Wig

Thaw Debacle, Defreeze, Defrost, > MELT, Melt-water, Relax

▷ **Thaw** *may indicate* 'ice' to be removed from a word

The Der, Die, El, Il, La, Le, Los, T', Ye, Ze

Theatre(s), Theatrical(ity) Abbey, Adelphi, Balcony, Broadway, Camp, Cinema, Circle, Coliseum, Criterion, Crucible, Drama, Event, Everyman, Field, Fringe, Gaff, Gaiety, Globe, Grand Guignol, Great White Way, Hall, Haymarket,

Hippodrome, Histrionic, House, Kabuki, La Scala, Legitimate, Little, Lyceum, Melodramatic, Mermaid, Music-hall, National, News, Nickelodeon, Noh, Odeon, Odeum, Operating, OUDS, Palladium, Panache, Pennygaff, Pit, Playhouse, Political, Rep(ertory), Sadler's Wells, Shaftesbury, Sheldonian, Shop, Stage, Stalls, Stoll, Straw-hat, Street, Summer stock, Total, Touring, Vic, Windmill, Zarzuela

Theatregoer Circle, Gallery, Gods, Pit, Stalls

Theft, Thieving Appropriation, Burglary, Heist, Identity, Kinchinlay, Larceny, Maino(u)r, Manner, Petty larceny, Pilfery, Plagiarism, Plunder, Pugging, Ram-raid, Robbery, Stealth, Stouth(rief), > THIEF, Touch, TWOC

Their Her

Theist Believer, Unitarian

Them 'Em, Hem, Tho

Theme Burden, Crab canon, Donnée, Fugue, Idea, Leitmotiv, Lemma, Lemmata, > MELODY, Motif, Peg, Question, > SUBJECT, Text, Topic, Topos

Then(ce) Away, Next, Since, So, Syne, Thereupon, Tho

> **The northern** *may indicate* t'

Theodolite Diopter, Dioptre, Groma, Tacheometer, Tachymeter, Transit

Theologian, Theologist, Theology Abelard, Aquinas, Barth, Calvin, Christology, Colet, DD, Divine, Erastus, Eschatology, Eusebius, Exegetics, Genevan, Hase, Infralapsarian, Irenics, Jansen, Kierkegaard, Knox, Liberation, Moral, Mullah, Natural, Newman, Niebuhr, Origen, Paley, Pectoral, Pelagius, Pusey, Rabbi, Religious, Sacramentarian, Schoolman, Scotus, Softa, STP, Supralapsarian, Tertullian, Ulema, Universalist

Theorem, Theoretical, Theorist, Theory Academic, Atomic, Automata, Bayes(ian), Bernouilli's, Big bang, Binomial, Bohr, Boo-hurrah, Catastrophe, Chaos, Conspiracy, Corpuscular, Darwinian, Decision, Deduction, Dependency, Dictum, Domino, Dow, Einstein, Empiricism, Epigenesist, Exponential, Fermat's (last), Galois, Game, Gauge, Germ, Gödel's, Grotian, Guess, Holism, Hypothesis, Ideal, Identity, Ideology, Information, Ism(y), James-Lange, Kinetic, Laingian, Lamarckism, Lemma, MAD, Model, Monism, Mythical, Nernst heat, Notion, Number, Object relations, Perturbation, Poynting, Probability, Proof, Pure, Pythagoras, Quantity, Quantum, Relativity, Satisfaction, Set, Speculative, Steady state, String, System, Tachyon, TOE, Tychism, Vulcanist, Wasm, Wave, Wholism, Wolfian

Therapeutic, Therapy Aura-Soma, Aversion, Behaviour, Bowen, Cellular, Chavuttithirumal, Chelation, Cognitive, Cognitive-behavioural, Colour, Combination, Craniosacral, Crystal (healing), Curative, Curietherapy, Deep, Dianetics, Electric shock, Electroconvulsive, Family, Faradism, Fever, Flotation, Gemstone, Gene, Gestalt, Group, Hellerwork, HRT, Hypnosis, Implosive, Insight, Larval, Light, Live cell, Logop(a)edics, Looyenwork, Magnetic, Metamorphic technique, MLD, Movement, Music, Narco, Natal, Natural, Non directive, Occupational, ORT, Osteopathy, Past life, Pattern, Physical, Polarity, Pressure, Primal, Primal (scream), Psychodrama, Radiation, Radio, Radium, Rainbow, Reflexology, Regression, Reichian, Reiki, Relaxation, Retail, Rogerian, Rolfing, Root-canal, Sanatory, Scientology®, Scream, Sex, SHEN, Shiatsu, Shiatzu, Shock, Sound, Speech, Speleotherapy, Supportive, Thalassotherapy, Theriacal, Thermotherapy, Touch, > TREATMENT, Water cure, X-ray, Zone

There(after), Thereby, Thereupon Holla, Ipso facto, Present, Thither, Thon, Upon, Y, Yonder

Therefore Argal, Ergo, Forthy, Hence, So, Why

Thermometer Aethrioscope, Centesimal, Clinical, Gas, Glass, Maximum and minimum, Psychrometer, Pyrometer, Resistance, Thermograph, Water, Wet and dry bulb, Wet bulb

Thermoplastic Cel(luloid), Resin

Thesaurus Dictionary, Lexicon, Roget, Treasury

These Thir

Theseus Champion

Thesis Argument, Dissertation, Doctorial, Theme

Thespian > ACTOR, Ham, Performer

Thessalonian Lapith

They A

Thick(en), Thickening, Thickener, Thickness, Thickset Abundant, Algin, Burly, Bushy, Callosity, Callus, Clavate, Cloddy, Cruddle, Curdle, Dense, Dextrin(e), Dumose, Engross, Grist, Grouty, Grume, Guar, Gum, Hyperostosis, Incrassate, Inspissate, Kuzu, Liaison, Lush, Nuggety, Panada, Roux, Sclerosis, > SOLID, Soupy, Squat, Stumpy, > STUPID, Thieves, This, Thixotropic, Waulk, Wooden, Xantham

Thick-coated Atheromatous

Thicket Bosk, Brake, Brush, Cane-brake, Chamisal, Chapparal, Coppice, Copse, Dead-finish, Greve, Grove, Macchie, Maquis, Queach, Reedrand, Reedrond, Salicetum, Shola

Thick-lipped Labrose

Thick-skinned Armadillo, Callous, Pachyderm, Tough

Thief, Thieves, Thievish Abactor, Autolycus, Blood, Chummy, Coon, Corsair, Cutpurse, Dismas, Dysmas, Filcher, Flood, Footpad, Freebooter, Furacious, Ganef, Gestas, Heist, Hotter, Huaquero, Ice-man, Jackdaw, Kiddy, Kondo, Larcener, Light-fingered, Limmer, Looter, Mag, Montith, Nip(per), Nuthook, Pad, Peculator, Pilferer, Pirate, Plagiarist, Poacher, Poddy-dodger, Prig, Raffles, River-rat, > ROBBER, Rustler, St Nicholas's clerks, Shark, Shop-lifter, Sneak, Sticky fingers, Taffy, Taker, Tea-leaf, Thick

Thigh Femoral, Gaskin, Ham, Haunch, Hock, Meros

Thin(ner) Acetone, Attenuate, Bald, Bony, Cull, Dilute, Ectomorph, Emaciated, Enseam, Fine, Fine-drawn, Flimsy, Gaunt, Hairline, Hair('s-)breadth, Inseem, Lanky, Lean, Matchstick, Mawger, Puny, Rackabones, Rangy, Rare, Rarefied, Reedy, Scant, Scraggy, Scrannel, Scrawny, Sheer, Sieve, Skeletal, Skimpy, Skinking, Slender, Slim, Slimline, Slink, > SPARE, Sparse, Spindly, Stilty, Stringy, Subtle, Taper, Tenuous, Turps, Wafer, Washy, Waste, Watch, Water(y), > WEAK, Weedy, Whirtle, Wiry, Wispy, Wortle, Wraith

Thing(s) Alia, Article, Chattel, Chose, Doodah, Doofer, Entia, Fetish, Fixation, It, Item, Jingbang, Job, Last, Material, Matter, Noumenon, > OBJECT, Obsession, Paraphernalia, Phobia, Res, Tool, Vision, Whatnot

Thingummy Dingbat, Dinges, Doodah, Doofer, Doohickey, Gubbins, Whatsit, Yoke

Think(er), Thinking Associate, Believe, Brain, Brood, Casuistry, Cogitate, Conjecture, Consider, Contemplant, > CONTEMPLATE, Deem, Deliberate, Descartes, Dianoetic, Divergent, Esteem, Fancy, Fear, Feel, Fogramite, Ghesse, Gnostic, Guess, Hegel, Hold, > IMAGINE, Judge, Lateral, Meditate, Mentation, Mindset, Mull, Muse, Opine, Pensive, Philosopher, Phrontistery, Ponder, Pore, Presume, Ratiocinate, Rational, Reckon, Reflect, Reminisce, Ruminate, Synectics, Trow, Vertical, Ween, Wishful

Thin-skinned Sensitive

Third, Third rate Bronze, C, Eroica, Gamma, Gooseberry, Interval, Mediant,

Picardy, Quartan, Tertiary, Tertius, Tierce, Trisect

Third man Abel, Lime

Thirst(y) Adry, > CRAVE, Dives, Drought, Drouth, Dry, Hydropic, Nadors, Pant, Polydipsia, Thrist

Thirteen Baker's dozen, Devil's dozen, Long dozen, Riddle, Triskaidekaphobia, Unlucky

Thirty Lambda

Thirty nine books All-OT, OT

This Hic, Hoc, The, Thick, Thilk, Thir

Thistle Canada, Carduus, Carline, Cnicus, Dayshell, Echinops, Milk, Musk, Russian, Safflower, Scotch, Sow, Spear, Star, Thrissel, Thristle

This year Ha

Thomas Aquinas, Arnold, Christadelphian, De Quincey, Didymus, Doubting, Dylan, Erastus, Hardy, Loco, Parr, Rhymer, Tompion, True, Turbulent

Thong Babiche, Jandal®, Lash, Latchet, Leather, Lore, Riem, Shoe-latchet, > STRAP, Taws(e), Whang, Whip

Thor Thunderer

Thorax Chest, Peraeon, Pereion, Scutellum, Throat

Thorium Th

Thorn(y) Acantha, Bael, Bel, Bhel, Bramble, Briar, Coyotillo, Doom, Edh, Eth, Irritation, Jerusalem, Mahonia, Mayflower, Nabk, Nebbuk, Nebe(c)k, > NEEDLE, Pricker, Prickle, Slae, Spine, Spinescent, Spinulate, Trial, Wagn'bietjie, Y, Ye, Zare(e)ba, Zariba, Zeriba

Thorn-apple Jimpson-weed

Thornless Inerm

Thorough(ly) A fond, Complete, Deep, Even-down, Firm, Fully, Ingrained, Inly, Out, Out and out, Painstaking, Pakka, Pucka, Pukka, Ripe, Root and branch, Searching, Sound, Strict, Total, Tout à fait, Up

Thoroughbred Arab, Bloodstock, Pedigree

Thoroughfare Avenue, Broadway, Causeway, Freeway, Highway, Parkway, > ROAD, Street

Those Thaim, Them, Tho, Yon

Thou M, Mil

Though Albe, Albeit, All-be, Ever, Tho, Whenas

Thought(s), Thoughtful(ness) Avisandum, Broody, Censed, Cerebration, Cogitation, Concept, Considerate, Contemplation, Dianoetic, Felt, Idea, Innate, Kind, Maieutic, Mind, Musing, Notion, Opinion, Pensée, Pensive, Philosophy, Reflection, Rumination, Second

Thoughtless Blindfold, Careless, Heedless, Improvident, Incogitant, Inconsiderate, Pillock, > RASH, Reckless, Remiss, Scatter-brained, Vacant, Vain

Thousand(s) Chiliad, Gorilla, K, Lac, Lakh, M, Millenary, Millennium, Myriad, Plum, Toman

Thracian Spartacus

Thrall Captive, Esne, Serf, Slave

Thrash(ing) > BEAT, Belabour, Belt, Bepelt, Binge, Bless, Cane, Dress, Drub, Flail, Flog, Jole, Joll, Joule, Jowl, Lace, Laidie, Laidy, Lambast, Larrup, Lather, Leather, Lick, Marmelise, Paste, Ploat, Quilt, Slog, Smoke, Strap-oil, Swat, Tank, Targe, Thraiping, Towel, Trim, Trounce, Wallop, Whale, Whap, Writhe

Thread, Threadlike Acme screw, Ariadne, Bar, Bottom, Bride, Buttress, Chalaza, Chromatid, Chromatin, Chromosome, Clew, Clue, Cop(pin), Cord, Coventry blue, Eel-worm, End, Fibre, Filament, File, Filiform, Filose, Filoselle, Float, Flourishing, Gold, Gossamer, Heddle, Ixtle, Lace, Lap, Lingel, Lingle, Link,

Lisle, Lurex®, Meander, Mycellum, Nematode, Nematoid, Organzine, Pack, Pearlin(g), Pick, Plasmodesm, Ravel, Reeve, Sacred, Screw, Sellers screw, Seton, Silver, Single, > **STRAND**, Stroma, Suture, Tassel, Tendril, Theme, Thrid, Thrum, Trace, Tram, Trundle, Tussore, Twine, Warp, Watap, Wax(ed), Weft, Whitworth, Whitworth screw, Wick, > **WIND**, Wisp, Worm

Threadbare Hackneyed, Napless, Shabby, Worn

Threadworm Nemathelminth, Strongyl, Vinegar-eel

Threat(en), Threatened, Threatening Baleful, Blackmail, Bluster, Coerce, Comminate, Face, Fatwa, Fraught, Greenmail, Greymail, Hazard, Impend, Imperil, Loom, > **MENACE**, Minacious, Minatory, Mint, Omen, Overcast, Overhang, Parlous, Peril, Portent, Ramp, Sabre-rattling, Shore, Strongarm, Ugly, Veiled, Warning

Three, Threefold, Three-wheeler, Thrice Graces, Har, Harpies, Jafenhar, Leash, Muses, Musketeers, Pairial, Pair-royal, Prial, Ter, Tern, Terzetta, Thrice, Thridi, Tid, T.i.d, Tierce, Tray, Trey, Triad, Tricar, Triennial, Trifid, Trigon, Trilogy, Trinal, Trine, Trinity, Trio, Triple, Triptote, Troika

Three-D(imensional) Lenticular, Stereopsis

Three-day Triduan, Triduum

Threehalfpence Dandiprat, Dandyprat

Three-handed Cutthroat

Three-headed Cerberus, Geryon

Three hundred B, Carpet

Three-legged IOM, Triskele, Triskelion

Threepence, Threepenny bit Tickey, Tray, Trey, Treybit

Three-year old Staggard

Threnody Dirge, Epicede, > **LAMENT**

Thresh Beat, Flail, Separate

Threshold Absolute, Brink, Cill, Difference, Doorstep, Limen, Liminal, Sill, Tax, Verge

▶ **Thrice** see **THREE**

Thrift(y) Economy, Frugal, Husbandry, Oeconomy, Sea-grass, Sea-pink, Virtue

Thrill(er), Thrilling Atingle, Buzz, Delight, Dindle, Dinnle, Dirl, Dread, Dynamite, Emotive, > **ENCHANT**, Excite, Film noir, Frisson, Gas, Jag, Kick, Page-turner, Perceant, Plangent, Pulsate, Pulse, Quiver, Sensation, Thirl, Tinglish, Tremor, Vibrant, Whodunit

Thrive Batten, Blossom, Boom, Do, Fl, > **FLOURISH**, Flower, Grow, Mushroom, > **PROSPER**, Succeed, Thee

Throat(y) Craw, Crop, Deep, Dewlap, Fauces, Gorge, Gular, Gullet, Guttural, Hot coppers, Jugular, Maw, Pereion, Pharynx, Prunella, Quailpipe, Red lane, Roopit, Roopy, Strep, Swallet, Thrapple, Thropple, Throttle, Weasand, Wesand, Whistle, Windpipe

Throb(bing) Beat, Palpitate, Pant, Pit-a-pat, Pulsate, Quop, Stang, Tingle, Vibrato

▷ **Throbbing** *may indicate* an anagram

Throe(s) Agony, Pang, Paroxysm

Thrombosis Deep-vein

Throne Bed-of-justice, Cathedra, Episcopal, Gadi, Mercy-seat, Peacock, Rule, Seat, See, Siege, Tribune

Throng(ing) Crowd, Flock, Host, Press, Resort, Swarm

Throttle > **CHOKE**, Gar(r)otte, Gun, Mug, Regulator, Scrag, Silence, Stifle, Strangle, Strangulate, Thrapple, We(a)sand

Through, Throughout Along, Ana, By, Dia-, During, Everywhere, Over, Passim,

Per, Pr, Sempre, Sic passim, To, Trans, Via, Yont

Throw(n) *see* TOSS

Throwback Atavism, Echo

Throw (up), **Thrower**, **Throw-out** Bin, Cast-off, Chunder, Discobolus, Egesta, Emesis, Jettison, Puke, Spew, Squirt, Squit

Thrush Ant, Aphtha, Bird, Chat, Fieldfare, Hermit, Homescreetch, Mavis, Missel, Mistle, Pitta, Prunella, Redwing, Sprue, Turdine, Veery

Thrust, **Thruster** Aventre, Bear, Boost, Botte, Burn, Detrude, Dig, Drive, Elbow, Exert, Extrude, Flanconade, Foin, > FORCE, Gist, Hay, Imbroc(c)ata, Impulse, Job, Lunge, Montant(o), Obtrude, Oust, Pass, Passado, Peg, Perk, Pitchfork, Poke, Potch(e), Pote, Probe, Propel, Pun, Punto, > PUSH, Put, Remise, Repost, Run, Shoulder, Shove, Single-stock, Sock, Sorn, Squat, Stap, Stick, Stoccado, Stoccata, Stock, Stuck, Thrutch, Tilt, Tuck

Thud Drum, Dump, Flump, Phut, Plod, Thump

Thug(s) Goon(da), Gorilla, Gurrier, Hoodlum, Loord, Ninja, Ockers, Phansigar, Plug-ugly, Roughneck, SS, Strangler, Ted, Tityre-tu, Tsotsi

Thule Ultima

Thulium Tm

Thumb Bally, Green, Hitch, Midget, Ovolo, Pollex, Scan, Tom

Thump(ing) Blow, Bonk, Clobber, Cob, Crump, Da(u)d, Drub, Dub, Hammer, Knevell, Knock, Nevel, Oner, Paik, > POUND, Pummel, Slam, Slosh, Souse, Swat, Swingeing, Thud, Trounce, Tund, Whud

Thunder(ing), **Thunderstorm** Bolt, Boom, Clap, Coup de foudre, Donnerwetter, Foudroyant, Foulder, Fulminate, Intonate, Lei-king, Pil(l)an, Raiden, > ROAR, Rumble, Summanus, Tempest, Thor, Tonant

Thursday Chare, Holy, Maundy, Sheer, Shere

Thus Ergo, Sic, So, Therefore

Thwart Baffle, Balk, > CROSS, Dash, Dish, Foil, Frustrate, Hamstring, Hogtie, Obstruct, Outwit, Pip, Prevent, Scotch, Snooker, Spike, Spite, Stonker, Stymie, Transverse

Thy Yourn

Thyme Basil, Lemon, Water

Thyroid Goitre, Myxodema

Tiara Cidaris, Crownet

Tiberius Gracchus

Tibetan Lamaist, Naga, Sherpa, Sitsang

Tic Vocal

Tick, **Tick off** Acarida, Acarus, Beat, Bloodsucker, Check, > CHIDE, Click, Cr, > CREDIT, Deer, HP, Idle, Instant, Jar, Ked, Mattress, Mile, Mo, Moment, Ricinulei, Second, Strap, Worm

Ticket(s) Billet, Bone, Brief, Carnet, Commutation, Complimentary, Coupon, Day, Docket, Dream, Excursion, Kangaroo, Label, Meal, One-day, One-way, Parking, Pass, Pass-out, Pawn, Platform, Raffle, Raincheck, Return, Scratchcard, Season, Single, Soup, Split, Straight, Stub, Supersaver, > TAG, Tempest, Tessera(l), Through, Tix, Transfer, Tyburn, Unity, Voucher, Walking, Zone

Ticket-seller Scalper

Tickle, **Ticklish** Amuse, Delicate, Divert, Excite, Gratify, Gump, > ITCH, Kittle, Queasy, Thrill, Titillate

Tiddler Brit, Tom

Tide, **Tidal** Current, Drift, Eagre, Easter, Eger, Estuary, Flood, High, High water, Lee, Low, Marigram, Neap, Red, Rising, Roost, Sea, Seiche, Slack water, Spring,

Surge, Trend, Wave

Tide-gate Aboideau, Aboiteau, Weir

Tidings Gospel, > NEWS, Rumour, Word

Tidy Comb, Considerable, Curry, Do, Fair, Fettle, Groom, Kempt, Large, Neat, > ORDER, Pachyderm, Predy, Preen, Primp, Red(d), Slick, Snug, Sort, Spruce, Trim, Valet

Tie, Tying Ascot, Attach, Barcelona, Berth, Bind, Black, > BOND, Bootlace, Bow, Bowyang, Cable, Cope, Cravat, Cup, Dead-heat, Drag, Draw, Four-in-head, Frap, Halter, Handicap, Harness, Holdfast, Kipper, > KNOT, Lash, Level, Ligament, Ligate, Ligature, Link, Marry, Match, Moor, Neck and neck, Oblige, Obstriction, Old School, Oop, Oup, Overlay, Raffia, Restrain, Rod, Scarf, School, Score draw, Semifinal, Shackle, Shoelace, Shoestring, Sleeper, Slur, Solitaire, Soubise, Splice, Stake, Strap, String, Tawdry-lace, Tether, Trice, Truss, Unite, White, Windsor

Tier Apron, Bank, Gradin(e), Knotter, Layer, Rank, Stage, Storey

Tierce Leash, Tc

Tiff Bicker, Contretemps, Difference, Dispute, Feed, Feud, Huff, Miff, Skirmish, Spat, Squabble

Tiffany Gauze

Tiger Bengal, > CAT, Clemenceau, Demoiselle, Lily, Machairodont, Machairodus, Margay, Paper, Sabre-tooth, Smilodon, Tamil, Tasmanian, Woods

Tight(en), Tightness, Tights Boozy, Bosky, Brace, Cinch, Close(-hauled), Constriction, Cote-hardie, > DRUNK, Fishnet, Fleshings, High, Hose, Jam, Leggings, Leotards, Lit, Loaded, Maillot, Mean, Merry, Niggardly, Oiled, Pang, Pantihose, Phimosis, Pickled, Pinch(penny), Plastered, Prompt, Proof, Rigour, Snug, Squiffy, Stenosis, > STINGY, Stinko, Strict, Stringent, Swift, Swig, Taut, Tense, Tipsy, Trig, Woozy

Tightrope(-walker) Aerialist, Blondin, Equilibrist, Funambulist, Petauriste

Tightwad Cheapskate, > MISER, Scrooge

Tile(d), Tiles Antefix, Arris, Azulejo, Carpet, Chapeau, Dalle, Derby, Dutch, Encaustic, Field, > HAT, Imbrex, Imbricate, Lid, Lino, Ostracon, Ostrakon, Peever, Quarrel, Quarry, Rag(g), Rooftop, Sclate, Shingle, Slat, > SLATE, Tegula, Tessella, Tessera, Titfer, Topper, Wall, Wally

Till Cashbox, Checkout, Coffer, Ear, Eulenspiegel, Farm, Hasta, Hoe, Husband, Lob, Peter, > PLOUGH, Set, Unto

Tiller Gardener, Helm, Ploughman, Rotavator, Wheel

Tilt Awning, Bank, Camber, Cant, Cock, Dip, Heel, Hut, Joust, Just, > LIST, Quintain, Rock, Tip, Unbalance

Timber Apron, Balk, Batten, Beam, Bond, Bridging, Cant-rail, Carapa, Chess, Clapboard, Compass, Coulisse, Cross-tree, Cruck, Dwang, Elmwood, Flitch, Four-by-two, Futchel, Futtock, Greenheart, Hardwood, Harewood, Intertie, Iroko, Ironwood, Joist, Knee, Knighthead, Lauan, Ligger, Lintel, Log, Lumber, Nogging, Nothofagus, Plank-sheer, Purlin(e), Putlock, Putlog, Pyengadu, Radiata, Ramin, Rib, Ridgepole, Roundwood, Rung, Sandalwood, Sapele, Sapodilla, Satinwood, Scantling, Shook, Shorts, Sissoo, Skeg, Sneezewood, Softwood, Souari, Stemson, Stere, Sternpost, Sternson, Straddle, Stull, Stumpage, Summer, Swing-stock, Towing-butts, Transom, Trestletree, Two-by-four, Wale, Wallplate, Weatherboard, Whitewood, > WOOD, Yang

Timbre Clang, Klang(farbe), Register, > TENOR, Tone

Time(s), Timer Access, Agoge, Apparent, Assymetric, Astronomical, Autumn, Awhile, Bird, BST, Central, Chronic, Chronometer, Chronon, Clock, Closing, Common, Compound, Connect, Core, Counter, Date, Day, Dead, Decade,

Dimension, Double, Duple, Duration, Early, Eastern, Eastern Standard, Egg-glass, Enemy, Eon, Ephemeris, Epoch, Equinox, Era, European, Eve(ning), Extra, Father, Flexitime, Forelock, Free, Full, Gest, Glide, Half, Healer, High, Horologe, Hour, Hourglass, Hr, Idle, Imprisonment, Injury, Innings, Instant, Interlude, Jiff, Juncture, Kalpa, Latent, Lay-day, Lead, Lean, Leisure, Life, Lighting-up, Lilac, Local, Mean, Menopause, Metronome, Mountain standard, Multiple, Needle, Nonce, Nones, Occasion, Oft, > **ON TIME**, Opening, Pacific, Paralysis, Part, Period, Phanerozoic, Pinger, Porridge, Post, Prelapsarian, Prime, Proper, Quadruple, Quality, Question, Quick, Reaction, Real, Reaper, Recovery, Response, Reverberation, Rhythm, Sandglass, Seal, > **SEASON**, Seel, Seil, Semeion, Serial, Session, Shelf-life, Sidereal, Sight, Simple, Sith(e), Slow, Solar, Solstice, Space, Span, Spare, Spell, Spin, Split, Spring, Standard, Stoppage, Stopwatch, Stound, Stownd, Stretch, Summer, Sundial, Sundown, Sythe, T, Tem, Tempo, Tempore, Tense, Thief, Three-four, Thunderer, Tick, Tid, Tide, Trice, Triple, Turnaround, Two-four, Universal, Usance, While, Winter, X, Yonks, Zero

Timebomb Demographic

Time-keeper, **Timepiece** Ben, Chronometer, Clock, Hourglass, Ref, Sand-glass, Sundial, Ticker, Tompion, Watch

Timeless Eternal, Nd, Undying

Timely Appropriate, Apropos, Happy, Opportune, Pat, Prompt

Timescale Geological

Time-server Prisoner, Trimmer

Timetable Bradshaw, > **CHART**, Schedule

Timid, **Timorous** Afraid, Aspen, Bashful, Blate, Chicken, Cowardly, Eerie, Eery, Faint-hearted, Fearful, Hare, Hen-hearted, Milquetoast, Mouse, Mous(e)y, Pavid, Pigeon-hearted, Pusillanimous, Quaking, Schnok, Shrinking, > **SHY**, Skeary, Sook, Yellow

Timothy Cat's-tail, Grass, Phleum

Tin(ned), **Tinfoil**, **Tinny** Argentine, Block, Britannia metal, Can, Cash, Debe, Dixie, Maconochie, Mess, > **MONEY**, Moola(h), Ochre, Plate, Rhino, Sn, Stannary, Stannic, Stream, Tain, Tole

Tincture Arnica, Bufo, Chroma, Elixir, Fur, Infusion, Laudanum, Metal, Or, Sericon, Sol, Spice, Taint, Tenné, Vert

Tinder Amadou, Faggot, Fuel, Funk, Punk, Spark, Spunk, Touchwood

Tine Antler, Bay, Cusp, Grain, Prong, Snag, Surroyal, Trey

Tinge(d) Dye, Eye, Flavour, Gild, > **HUE**, Infuscate, Taint, Tincture, Tone, Touch

Tingle, **Tingling** Dinnle, Dirl, Paraesthesia, Prickle, Thrill, Throb, Tinkle

Tinker Bell, Caird, Coster, Didakai, Didakei, Diddicoy, Didicoy, Didikoi, > **FIDDLE**, Gypsy, Mender, Pedlar, Potter, Prig, Putter, Repair, Sly, Snout, Tamper, Tramp, Traveller

Tinkle Pink

Tinsel(ly) Clinquant, Gaudy, Glitter, O, Spangle, Turkey

Tint Colour, Henna, Hue, Pigment, > **STAIN**, Tinct, Tinge, Woad

Tiny Atto-, Baby, Diddy, Dwarf, Ha'it, Infinitesimal, Itsy-bitsy, Lilliputian, Minikin, Minim, Mite, Negligible, Petite, Small, Smidgeon, Teeny, Tiddl(e)y, Tiddy, Tim, Tine, Tottie, Totty, Toy, Wee

Tip, **Tipping** Apex, Arrowhead, Ash-heap, Asparagus, Backshish, Baksheesh, Batta, Beer-money, Bonsel(l)a, Bonus, B(u)onamono, Cant, Cert, Chape, Counsel, Coup, Cowp, Crown, Cue, Cumshaw, Douceur, Dump, Extremity, Fee, Felt, Ferrule, Filter, Forecast, Glans, Gratillity, Gratuity, Heel, > **HINT**, Hunch, Inkle, Iridise, Lagniappe, Largess(e), List, Mess, Middenstead, Nap, Noop,

Ord, Perk, Perquisite, Point, Pointer, Pour, Pourboire, Previse, Prong, Straight, Suggestion, Summit, Tag, Tail, Tilt, Toom, Touch, Tronc, Vail, Vales, Whisper, Wink, Wrinkle

Tippet Cape, Fur, Scarf

Tipple Bib, Booze, > DRINK, Paint, Pot, Poteen

Tipster Prophet, Tout

Tipsy Bleary, Boozy, Bosky, > DRUNK, Elevated, Moony, Nappy, Oiled, On, Rocky, Screwed, Slewed, Slued, Squiffy, Wet

▷ **Tipsy** *may indicate* an anagram

Tiptoe Digitigrade

Tirade Diatribe, Invective, Jobation, Laisse, Philippic, Rand, Rant, Screed, Slang

Tire(d), **Tiredness**, **Tiring** All-in, Beat, Bore, Bushed, Caparison, Deadbeat, Dress, Drowsy, > EXHAUST, Fag, Fagged out, Fatigue, Flag, Fordid, Fordod, Forjeskit, Frazzle, Gruel, Irk, Jade, Lassitude, Limp, ME, Overspent, Pall, Poop, Puggled, > ROBE, Rubber, Sap, Shagged, Sicken, Sleepry, Sleepy, Spent, Swinkt, Tax, Tedious, Wabbit, Wappend, Weary, Wrecked

Tiresome Boring, Exhausting, Humdrum, Pill, Tedious, Vexing

Tirl Rattle, Risp, Strip, Turn

▸ **Tiro** *see* TYRO

Tissue Adenoid, Adhesion, Adipose, Aerenchyma, Aponeurosis, Archesporium, Callus, Carbon, Cartilage, Cementum, Chalaza, Cheloid, Chlorenchyma, Coenosarc, Collagen, Collenchyma, Commissure, Conducting, Connective, Cortex, Dentine, Diploe, Epimysium, Epineurium, Epithelium, Eschar, Evocator, Fabric, Fascia, Flesh, Gamgee, Gauze, Gleba, Glia, Granulation, Gum, Heteroplasia, Histogen, Histoid, Infarct, Keloid, Kleenex®, Lamina, Lies, Ligament, Luteal, Lymphoid, Macroglia, Marrow, Matrix, Mechanical, Medulla, > MEMBRANE, Meristem, Mesophyll, Mestom(e), Mole, Myelin(e), Myocardium, Neuroglia, Nucellus, Olivary, Pack, Palisade, Pannus, Paper, Papilla, Parenchyma, Periblem, Perichylous, Peridesmium, Perimysium, Perinephrium, Perineurium, Perisperm, Phellogen, Phloem, Pith, Placenta, Plerome, Polyarch, Pons, Primordium, Prosenchyma, Prothallis, Pterygium, Pulp, Radula, Sarcenet, Sars(e)net, Scar, Sclerenchyma, Sequestrum, Sinew, Soft, Somatopleure, Stereome, Stroma, Submucosa, Suet, Tarsus, Tela, Tendon, Tonsil, Tunica, Vascular, Velum, Web, Wound, Xylem, Zoograft

Tit, **Tit-bit(s)** Analecta, Canape, Crested, Currie, Curry, Delicacy, Dug, Nag, Nipple, Nun, Pap, Quarry, Sample, Scrap, Snack, Teat, Tug, Twitch, Willow, Wren, Zakuska

Titan(ic), **Titaness** Atlas, Colossus, Cronos, Cronus, Drone, Enormous, Giant, Huge, Hyperion, Kronos, Leviathan, Liner, Oceanus, Phoebe, Prometheus, Rhea, Themis, Vast

Titanium, **Titanite** Sagenite, Sphene, Ti

Tit for tat Deserts, Revenge, Talion

Tithe Disme, Dyzemas, Frankpledge, Teind, Tenth

Titian Abram, Auburn

Titillate Delight, Excite, Tickle

Titivate Primp

Title Abbe, > ADDRESS, Ag(h)a, Antonomasia, Appellative, Bahadur, Baroness, Baronet, Bart, Bhai, Bretwalda, Calif, Caliph, Caption, Charta, Chogyal, Claim, Conveyance, Count(ess), Courtesy, Credit, Dan, Datin, Datuk, Dauphin, Dayan, Deeds, Devi, Dom, Don, Don(n)a, Dowager, Dub, Duchess, Duke, Earl, Effendi, Eminence, Epithet, Esquire, Excellency, Fra, Frau(lein), Gospodin, Gyani, Hafiz, Handle, Header, Heading, Headline, Hojatoleslam, Hon,

Honour, Imperator, Interest, Kalif, Kaliph, Kaur, King, Lady, Lala, Lemma,
> **LIEN**, Lord, Mal(l)am, Marchesa, Marchese, Marquess, Marquis, Master,
Masthead, Maulana, Memsahib, Meneer, Mevrou, Miladi, Milady, Milord,
Mirza, Mr(s), Name, Nizam, Nomen, Padishah, Peerage, Pir, Polemarch, Prefix,
Prince(ss), Queen, > **RANK**, Reb, Reverence, Reverend, > **RIGHT**, Rubric, Sahib,
Sama, San, Sardar, Sayid, Senhor(a), Señor(a), Shri, Singh, Sir, Sirdar, Son,
Sowbhagyawati, Sri, Stratum, Tannie, Tenno, Torrens, Tycoon, V, Worship

Title-holder Cartouche, Champion, Landlord, Noble

Titmouse Bird, Hickymal, Mag, Reedling, Tit

Titter Giggle, Snigger, Tehee

Tittle Jot

Titus Oates

Tizz(y) Pother, Spin, Tanner, Testril, Vld

TNT Explosive, Trotyl

To(wards) At, Beside, Inby, Onto, Prone, Shet, Shut, Till

Toad(y) Bootlicker, Bufo, Bumsucker, Cane, Clawback, Cocksucker, Crapaud,
Crawler, Fawn, Frog, Horned, Jackal, Jenkins, Knot, Lackey, Lick-platter,
Lickspittle, Midwife, Minion, Natterjack, Nototrema, Paddock, Parasite,
Pick-thank, Pipa, Placebo, Platanna, Puddock, Queensland cane, Sook,
Spade-foot, Surinam, Sycophant, Tree, Tuft-hunter, Walking, Xenopus,
Yesman

Toadstool Amanita, Death-cap, Death-cup, Destroying angel, Fly agaric,
> **FUNGUS**, Grisette, Horsehair, Paddock-stool, Parrot, Sulphur tuft, Verdigris,
Wax cap

Toast(er) Bacchus, Bell, Birsle, Brindisi, > **BROWN**, Bruschetta, Bumper, Cheers,
Chin-chin, Crostini, Crouton, French, Gesundheit, Grace-cup, Grill, Health,
Iechyd da, Kiaora, L'chaim, Lechayim, Loyal, Melba, Pledge, Pop up, Propose,
Prosit, Round, Scouther, Scowder, Scowther, Sentiment, Sippet, Skoal, Slainte,
Slainte mha(i)th, Soldier, Sunbathe, Wassail, Zwieback

Toastmaster MC, Symposiarch

Tobacco, Tobacco-field Alfalfa, Bacchi, Baccy, Bird's eye, Broadleaf, Burley,
Canaster, Capa, Caporal, Cavendish, Chew, Dottle, Filler, Honeydew,
Killikinnick, Kinnikinick, Latakia, Mundungus, Nailrod, Navy-cut,
Negro-head, Nicotian, Nicotine, Niggerhead, Perique, Pigtail, Plug, Quid,
Rapper, Régie, Returns, Shag, Sneesh, Snout, Snuff, Straight cut, Stripleaf,
Turkish, Twist, Vega, Virginia, Weed

Toboggan Sled(ge), Sleigh

Toby Dog, Highwayman, Jug

Tocsin Alarm, Siren

Today Hodiernal, Now, Present

Toddle(r) Baim, Gangrel, Mite, Tot, Totter, Trot, Waddle

Toddy Arrack, > **DRINK**, Sura, Whisky

To-do Sensation, Stir

Toe(s) Dactyl, Digit, Fissiped, Hallux, Hammer, Piggy, Pinky, Pointe, Poulaine,
Prehallux, Tootsie

Toff Nob, Nut, Swell

Toffee Banket, Butterscotch, Caramel, Cracknel, Gundy, Hard-bake,
Hokey-pokey, Humbug, Tom-trot

Toga Palla

Together Among, At-one, Atone, Attone, En bloc, En masse, Gathered, Infere,
> **JOINT**, Pari-passu, Sam, Unison, Wed, Y, Yfere, Ysame

Toggle Fastener, Netsuke

Togs Clothes, Gear, Rig, Strip

Toil(s) Drudge, Fag, Industry, > **LABOUR**, Mesh, Net, Seine, Sisyphus, Sweat, Swink, Tela, Tew, Trap, Trauchle, Travail, Tug, Web, > **WORK**, Wrest, Yacker, Yakka, Yakker

Toilet Can, Chemical, Coiffure, John, Lat(rine), > **LAVATORY**, Loo, Necessary house, Necessary place, Pot, Powder room, WC

Token Buck, Check, Counter, Coupon, Disc, Double-axe, Emblem, Gift, Indication, > **MEMENTO**, Nominal, Portend, Seal, Sign, Signal, Symbol, Symptom, Tessera, Valentine

Tolerable Acceptable, Bearable, Mediocre, Passable, So-so

Tolerance, Tolerant, Tolerate(d) Abear, Abide, > **ALLOW**, Bear, Broadminded, Brook, Endure, Enlightened, Hack, Had, Immunological, Latitude, > **LENIENT**, Lump, Mercy, Permit, Stand, Stick, Stomach, Studden, Suffer, Support, Thole, Wear, Zero

Toll Chime, Customs, Due, Duty, Excise, Joll, Joule, Jowl, Light-dues, Octroi, Pierage, Pike, Pontage, Rates, > **RING**, Scavage, Streetage, Tariff, Tax

Tom(my) Atkins, Bell, Bowling, Bread, Brown, > **CAT**, Collins, Edgar, Gib, Grub, Gun, He-cat, Jerry, Jones, Mog(gy), Nosh, Peeping, Private, Pte, Puss, Ram-cat, Sawyer, Snout, Soldier, Stout, Thos, Thumb, Tiddler, Tucker

Tomato Beef(steak), Cherry, Gooseberry, Husk, Love-apple, Plum, Portuguese, Strawberry, Tamarillo, Tree, Wolf's peach

Tomb(stone) Burial, Catacomb, Catafalque, Cenotaph, Cist, Coffin, Dargah, Durgah, Grave, Hypogeum, Kistvaen, Marmoreal, Mastaba, Mausoleum, Megalithic, Monument, Pyramid, > **SEPULCHRE**, Sepulture, Serdab, Shrine, Speos, Tell el Amarna, Tholos, Tholus, Through-stone, Treasury, Vault

Tombola Draw, Lottery, Raffle

Tomboy Gamine, Gilpey, Gilpy, Hoyden, Ladette, Ramp, Romp

Tome > **BOOK**, Volume

Tomfoolery Caper, Fandangle, Shenanigan

Tomorrow Future, Manana, Morrow

Tompion Watchman

Tom Snout Tinker

Ton(age) C, Chic, Displacement, Freight, Gross, Hundred, Long, Measurement, Metric, Register, Shipping, Short, T

Tone, Tonality Brace, Dialling, Engaged, Fifth, Harmonic, Hum, Inflection, Key, Klang, Ninth, Partial, Qualify, Quarter, Resultant, Ringing, Side, > **SOUND**, Strain, Temper, Tenor, Timbre, Touch, Trite, Whole

Tong(s) Curling, Lazy, Wafer

Tongue Brogue, Burr, Chape, Clack, Clapper, Doab, Double, Final, Forked, Glossa, Glossolalia, Jinglet, > **LANGUAGE**, Languet(te), Lap, Ligula, Lill, Lingo, Lingulate, Mother, Organ, Radula, Ranine, Rasp, Red rag, Single, Spit, Tab, Triple, Voice, Vulgar

Tongue-tied Mush-mouthed

Tongue-twister Jaw-breaker, Shibboleth

Tonic Bracer, C(h)amomile, Doh, Key, Mease, Medicinal, Mishmee, Mishmi, Myrica, Oporice, Pareira brava, Pick-me-up, Quassia, Refresher, Roborant, Sage tea, Sarsaparilla, Solfa

▷ **Tonic** *may indicate* a musical note

Tonsil, Tonsillitis Amygdala, Antiaditis, Pharyngeal, Quinsy

Tonsure(d) Epilate, Haircut, Peel, Pield

Tony Bête, Chic, Fool, Smart

Too Als(o), As well, Besides, Eke, Excessive, Item, Likewise, Moreover, Oer, Over,

Overly, Plus, Troppo

Took Naam, Nam, Set, Stole, Wan, Won

Tool Adze, Aiguille, Auger, Awl, Ax(e), Beetle, Bevel, Billhook, Bit, Broach, Brog, Bur(r), Burin, Calipers, Catspaw, Chaser, Chisel, Chopper, Clippers, Croze, Dibber, Dibble, Die, Dolly, Drawknife, Drawshave, Drift(pin), Eatche, Edge, Elsin, Eolith, Facer, Fid, File, Firmer, Float, Float-stone, Former, Fraise, Froe, Frow, Fuller, Gad, Gimlet, Go-devil, Gouger, Grapnel, Grattoir, Graver, Hammer, Hardy, Hob, Hoe, Husker, > IMPLEMENT, Insculp, > INSTRUMENT, Iron, Jackhammer, Jemmy, Jim Crow, Jointer, Laster, Loggerhead, Loom, Lute, Machine, Mallet, Marlin(e)spike, Microlith, Mitre square, Moon-knife, Muller, Nippers, Oustiti, Outsiders, Palaeolith, Pattle, Pawn, Penis, Percussion, Pestle, Pick, Picklock, Pitchfork, Piton, Plane, Pliers, Plunger, Power, Pricker, Property, Prunt, Punch, Puncheon, Rabble, Rasp, Reamer, Ripple, Roll(er), Rounder, Router, Sander, Saw, Scalpel, Scauper, Scissors, Scorper, Scraper, Screwdriver, Scriber, Scutch, Scythe, Seamset, Secateurs, Shoder, Sickle, Slater, Sleeker, Snake, Spanner, Spirit-level, Spitsticker, Spokeshave, Strickle, Strike, Strimmer®, Swage, Swingle, Swipple, Tint, Tjanting, Triblet, Trowel, Try square, Tweezers, Twibill, Upright, Vibrator, Vice, Wimble, Wrench

Toot(er) Blow, Horn, Parp, Trumpet

Tooth(ed), Toothy, Teeth Bicuspid, Bit, Buck, Bunodont, Canine, Carnassial, Chactodon, Cheek tooth, Cog, Cott's, Crena(te), Ctenoid, Cusp, Denticle, Dentin(e), Dentures, Egg, Eye, False, Fang, Gam, Gat, Gnashers, Grinder, Heterodont, Impacted, Incisor, Ivory, Joggle, Laniary, Milk, Mill, Molar, Nipper, Odontoid, Orthodontics, Overbite, Pawl, Pearly gates, Pectinate, Peristome, Permanent, Phang, Plate, Pre-molar, Prong, Ratch, Scissor, Secodont, Sectorial, Serration, Set, Snaggle, Sprocket, Store, Sweet, Trophi, Tush, Tusk, Uncinus, Upper, Wallies, Wang, Wiper, Wisdom, Wolf, Zalambdodont

Toothache, Tooth troubles Caries, Odontalgia

Toothless Edentate, Gummy, Pangolin

Toothpaste Dentifrice

Top (drawer; hole; line; notcher), Topmost, Topper Ace, Acme, A1, Altissimo, Apex, Apical, Behead, Best, Better, Big, Blouse, Blouson, Boob tube, Brow, Bustier, Cacumen, Cap, Capstone, Ceiling, Coma, Cop, Coping, Corking, Cream, > CREST, Crista, Crop, Crown, Culmen, De capo, Decollate, Diabolo, Dog, Dome, Double, Drawer, Dreid(e)l, Elite, Execute, Fighting, Finial, Flip, Gentry, Gyroscope, Halterneck, Hard, Hat, > HEAD, Height, Hummer, Humming, Imperial, Jumper, Lid, Nun, One-er, Optimate, Orb, Parish, > PEAK, Peerie, Peery, Peg, Peplos, Peplus, Pinnacle, Pitch, Replenish, Ridge, Roof, Sawyer, Screw, Secret, Shaw, Shirt, Skim, Slay, Soft, Spinning, Star, Summit, Superate, Superb, Supernal, Supreme, Supremo, Surface, Sweater, Tambour, Targa, Teetotum, Texas, Tile, Trash, T-shirt, Turbinate, Up(most), Uppermost, V, Vertex, Whipping, Whirligig

Top *may indicate* first letter

Topaz Citrine, Colorado, Occidental, Oriental, Pycnite, Rose, Scottish, Spanish

Topcoat Finish, Overcoat, Ulster

Tope(r) Boozer, Bouser, Dagaba, Dagoba, > DRUNK, Sot, Tosspot

Topic(al) Head, Hobbyhorse, Item, Motion, Shop, Subject, Text, > THEME

Top-knot Tuft

Topping Grand, Icing, Meringue, Pepperoni, Piecrust, Streusel

Topple Oust, Overbalance, Overturn, Tip, Upend, > UPSET

Topsy Parentless

Topsy-turvy Careen, Cockeyed, Inverted, Summerset, Tapsalteerie, Tapsleteerie

Torch Brand, Cresset, Flambeau, Hards, Hurds, Lamp, Lampad, Link, Olympic, Plasma, Roughie, Tead(e), Wisp

Torch-bearer Usherette

Toreador Escamillo, Matador, Picador, Torero

Torment(ed), Tormentor Agony, Anguish, Bait, Ballyrag, Bedevil, Butt, Cruciate, Crucify, Curse, Distress, Excruciate, Frab, Gehenna, Grill, Harass, Hell, Martyrdom, Molest, Nag, Nettle, Pang, Pine, Plague, > RACK, Sadist, Tantalise, Tease

Tornado Cyclone, Twister, Waterspout

Toronto Hogtown

Torpedo Bangalore, Bomb, Fish, Ray, Subroc, Tin fish, Weapon

Torpedo-guard Crinoline

Torpid, Torpor Accidie, Acedia, Comatose, Dormant, Inertia, Languid, Lethargic, Sluggish, Slumbering

Torrent Flood, Spate

Torrid Amphiscian, Hot, Sultry, Tropical

Torsk Cusk

Tortilla Pancake, Taco

Tortoise Chelonia, Emydes, Emys, Galapagos, Giant, Hic(c)atee, Kurma, Pancake, Snapping-turtle, Terrapin, Testudo, Timothy, Turtle, Water

Tortoiseshell Epiplastra, Hawksbill, Testudo

Tortuous Ambagious, Twisty, Winding

▷ **Tortuous** *may indicate* an anagram

Torture, Torture chamber, Torture instrument Agonise, Auto-da-fé, Bastinade, Bastinado, Boot, Bootikin, Catasta, Chinese burn, Chinese water, Crucify, Engine, Excruciate, Flageolet, Fry, Gadge, Gauntlet, Gyp, Iron maiden, Knee-cap, Naraka, Persecute, Pilliwinks, Pine, Pinniewinkle, Pinnywinkle, > RACK, Sadism, Scaphism, Scarpines, Scavenger, Scavenger's daughter, Scourge, Strappado, Tantalise, Third degree, Thumbscrew, Tumbrel, Tumbril, Water, Wheel, Wrack

▷ **Tortured** *may indicate* an anagram

Torturer Torquemada

Torus Disc, Stellarator

Tory Abhorrer, Blimp, Blue, C, Opposition, Right, Tantivy, Unionist

Toss(ing), Throw(n) Abject, Bandy, Bounce, Buck, Bung, Buttock, Cant, Canvass, Cast, Catapult, > CHUCK, Cottabus, Crabs, Cross-buttock, Dad, Daud, Deal, Disconcert, Elance, Estrapade, Falcade, > FLING, Flip, Flump, Flutter, Flying (head)-mare, Free, Full, Gollum, Haunch, Heave, Hipt, Hoy, > HURL, Jack, Jact(it)ation, Jaculation, Jeff, Juggle, Jump, Lance, Lob, Loft, Pash, Pitch, Purl, Put(t), Round-arm, Seamer, Shy, Slat, Sling, Unhorse, Unseat, Upcast

Toss-up Cross and pile, Heads or tails

Tot Add, Babe, Bairn, > CHILD, Dop, Dram, Infant, Mite, Nightcap, Nip(per), Nipperkin, Slug, Snifter, Snort, Tad

Total, Toto Absolute, Aggregate, All(-out), Amount, Balance, Be-all, > COMPLETE, Entire, Gross, Lot, Sum, Tale, Tally, Unqualified, Utter, Whole

Totalitarian Autocrat, Despot, Etatiste, Fascist

Tote Bear, > CARRY, Yomp

Totem Fetish, Icon, Image, Pole

Tottenham Hotspur

Totter Abacus, Daddle, Daidle, Didakai, Didakei, Did(d)icoy, Didicoi, Halt, Ragman, Rock, > STAGGER, Swag, Sway, Topple, Waver

Touch(ed), Touching, Touchy Accolade, Adjoin, Affect, Anent, Badass, Barmy,

Cadge, Captious, Carambole, Caress, Carom, Common, Concern, Connivent, Contact, Contiguous, Emove, > **FEEL**, Finger, Finishing, Flick, Fondle, Haptic, Huffy, > **IN TOUCH**, Iracund, Irascible, J'adoube, Liaison, Libant, Loan, Loco, Midas, Miffy, Near, Nie, Nigh, Nudge, Palp, Pathetic, Paw, Potty, Re, Sense, Shade, Skiff, Soft, Sore, Spice, > **SPOT**, Tactile, Tactual, Tag, Tangible, Tap, Taste, Tat, Tickle, Tig, Tinderbox, Tinge, Titivate, Trace, Trait, Tuck, Vestige

Touchline Tangent

Touchstone Basanite, Criterion, Norm, Standard

Touchwood Absit omen, Monk, Punk, Spunk, Tinder

Tough(en) Adamantine, Anneal, Apache, Arduous, Ballsy, Burly, > **HARD**, Hard-boiled, Hard-nosed, Hardy, Heavy duty, He-man, Hood, Hoodlum, Husky, Indurate, Knotty, Leathern, Leathery, Nut, Pesky, Rambo, Rigwiddie, Rigwoodie, Roughneck, Sinewy, Spartan, Steely, Stiff, String, Sturdy, Teuch, Thewed, Tityre-tu, Virile

Toupee Hairpiece, Rug, Tour, > **WIG**

Tour(er), Tourist Barnstorm, Circuit, Cook's, Emmet, Excursion, Grand, Grockle, GT, Holiday-maker, Itinerate, > **JOURNEY**, Lionise, Mystery, Outing, Parra, Posting, Roadie, Rubberneck, Safari, Swing, Tiki, > **TRAVEL**, Trip(per), Viator, Whistle-stop

Tourmaline Schorl, Zeuxite

Tournament American, Basho, Bonspiel, Carousel, Drive, Event, Jereed, Jerid, Joust, Just, Ladder, Plate, Pro-am, Round robin, Royal, Super Twelve, Swiss, Tilt, Tourney, Wimbledon

Tourniquet Garrot, Throttle, Torcular

Tousle Dishevel, Rumple

Tout Barker, Laud, Ply, Praise, Runner, Solicit, Toot

Tow(ing) Aquaplane, Button, Fibre, > **HAUL**, Pull, > **ROPE**, Ski, Skijoring, Stupe, Track

Towards *see* **TO**

Towel Dry, Jack, Nappy, Roller, Rub, Sanitary, Tea, Terry, Turkish

Tower Aspire, Atalaya, Babel, Barbican, Bastille, Bastion, Belfry, Bell, Bloody, Brattice, Brettice, Brogh, Campanile, Conning, Control, Cooling, Donjon, Dungeon, Edifice, Eiffel, Fly, Fortress, Gantry, Garret, Gate, Giralda, Gopura(m), Guérite, Horologium, Ivory, Keep, Leaning, Loom, Maiden, Martello, Minar(et), Monument, Mooring, Mouse, Nuraghe, Nurhag, Overtop, Peel, Pinnacle, Pound, Pylon, Rear, Rise, Rolandseck, Rood, Round, Sail, Sears, Shot, Sikhara, Silo, Ski-lift, Space Needle, Specula, Spire, Stealth, Steeple, Tête-de-pont, Texas, Tractor, Tugboat, > **TURRET**, Victoria, Watch, Water, Yagura, Ziggurat, Zikkurat

Town, Township Boom, Borgo, Borough, Bourg, Burg(h), City, Conurbation, County, Deme, Dormitory, Dorp, Favella, Garrison, Ghost, Ham(let), Intraurban, Market, Municipal, Nasik, One-horse, Podunk, Pueblo, Satellite, Shanty, Staple, Tinsel, Tp, Twin, Urban, Wick

Townee, Townsman Cad, Cit(izen), Dude, Freeman, Oppidan, Philister, Resident

Town hall Prytaneum

Toxaemia Eclampsia

Toxic(ity), Toxin Abrin, Antigen, Botulin, Cadaverine, Coumarin, Curare, Deadly, Dioxan, Eclampsia, Fluorin(e), Lethal, Muscarine, Phalloidin, Phenol, Phenothiazine, Psoralen, Ricin, Sepsis, Serology, Venin, Venomous, Virulence, Zootoxin

Toy Bauble, Bull-roarer, Cockhorse, Cyberpet, Dally, Dandle, Doll, Executive,

Faddle, Finger, Flirt, Frisbee®, Gewgaw, Golly, Gonk, Jack-in-the-box, Jumping-jack, Kaleidoscope, Kickshaw, Knack, Lego®, Noah's ark, Novelty, Paddle, Pantine, Peashooter, Plaything, Praxinoscope, Rattle, Scooter, Shoofly, Skipjack, Taste, Teddy, Thaumatrope, > **TRIFLE**, Trinket, Tu(r)ndun, Whirligig, Yoyo, Zoetrope

Trace Atom, Cast, Derive, Describe, Draft, Draw, Dreg, Echo, Footprint, Ghost, > **HINT**, Leaf, Limn, Mark, Memory, Outline, Relic, Relict, Remnant, Scintilla, Semblance, Sign, Smack, Soupçon, Strap, > **TOUCH**, Track, Vestige, Whiff, Whit

Tracery Filigree

Track(s), **Tracker**, **Tracking**, **Trackman** Aintree, Band, B-road, Caterpillar®, Cinder, Circuit, Course, Dog, DOVAP, Drift, Ecliptic, El, Fast, Fettler, Footing, Gaudy dancer, Hunt, Ichnite, Ichnolite, Inside, Lane, Ley, Line, Loipe, Loopline Mommy, Monitor, Monza, > **PATH**, Persue, Piste, Pug, Pursue, Race, Raceway, Rail, Railway, Rake, Ridgeway, Route, Run, Rut, Siding, Sign, Skidway, Sleuth, Slot, Sonar, Speedway, Spoor, Tan, Tan-ride, Taxi, Tenure, Tideway, > **TRAIL**, Trajectory, Tram, Tramline, Tramroad, Tramway, Tread, Trode, Tug(boat), Twin, Wake, Wallaby, Way, Y

Tract(able), **Tracts** Area, Belt, Bench, Clime, Colporteur, Common, Dene, Enclave, Flysheet, Lande, Leaflet, Monte, Moor, Olfactory, > **PAMPHLET**, Prairie, Province, Purlieu, Pusey, Region, Screed, Taluk, Tawie, Terrain, Wold

Tractarian(ism) Newman, Oxford movement, Pusey(ism)

Tractor Bulldozer, Cat, Caterpillar®, Fendalton, Pedrail, Remuera, Skidder, Tower

Trade(r), **Tradesman**, **Trading** Arb(itrageur), Banian, Banyan, Bargain, Barter, Bricks and clicks, Bun(n)ia, Burgher, Business, Cabotage, Calling, Carriage, Chaffer, Chandler, Chapman, Cheapjack, Coaster, Comanchero, > **COMMERCE**, Coster, Costermonger, Crare, Crayer, Deal(er), Easterling, Errand, Exchange, Factor, Fair, Floor, Free, Handle, Horse, Hosier, Hot, Importer, Indiaman, Industry, Insider, Ironmonger, Jobber, Legrolling, Line, Merchant, Métier, Middleman, Mister, Monger, Mystery, Outfitter, Paralleling, Pitchman, Ply, Rag, Retailer, Roundtripping, Scalp, Screen, Sell, Simony, Slave, Stallenger, Stallinger, Stationer, Sutler, Suttle, > **SWAP**, Traffic, Transit, Trant, Truck, Union, Vaisya, Vend, Wholesaler, Wind

Trademark Brand, Chop, Idiograph, Label, Logo, Tm

Trade Union ASLEF, COHSE, Local, Solidarity, Syndicalism, UNISON, USDAW

Trading money, **Trading post** Cabotage, Fort, Wampum

Tradition(s), **Traditional(ist)** Ancestral, Classical, Convention, Custom(ary), Eastern, Folkway, Hadith, Heritage, Legend, Lore, Mahayana, Misoneist, Old guard, Old-school, Orthodox, Pharisee, Pompier, Practice, Purist, Suburban, Time-honoured, Trad, Tralaticious, Tralatitious

Traduce Abuse, Asperse, Defame, Impugn, Malign, Smear, Vilify

Traffic, **Traffic pattern** Barter, Broke, Cabotage, Clover-leaf, Commerce, Contraflow, Deal, Negotiate, Passage, Run, Smuggle, Through, Trade, Truck, Vehicular

Tragedian, **Tragedy**, **Tragic** Aeschylus, Buskin, Calamity, Cenci, Corneille, Dire, > **DRAMA**, Euripides, Macready, Melpomene, Oedipean, Oresteia, Otway, Pathetic, Seneca, Sophoclean, Thespian, Thespis

Trail(er), **Trailing** Abature, Audit, Bedraggle, Caravan, Condensation, Creep, Drag, Draggle, Follow, Ipomaea, Lag, Liana, Liane, Nature, Oregon, Path, Persue, Preview, Promo(tion), Pursue, Repent, Runway, Santa Fe, Scent, Shadow, Sign, Sleuth, Slot, Spoor, Stream, Streel, Tag, Trace, > **TRACK**, Trade, Traipse, Trape, Trauchle, Trayne, Troad, Vapour, Vine, Virga, Wake

Train(er), Training Advanced, APT, BR, Breed, Caravan, Cat, Cavalcade, Circuit, Coach, Commuter, Condition, Cortège, Diesel, Direct, Discipline, Dog, Dressage, Drill, Drive, Educate, Entourage, Enure, Epicyclic, Eurostar®, Exercise, Express, Fartlek, Field, Flier, Flight simulator, Freightliner®, Fuse, Gear, Ghan, Ghost, Gravy, Grounding, GWR, Handle(r), Instruct, Intercity®, Interval, Jerkwater, Journey, Liner, Link, LMS, LNER, Loco, Longe, Lunge, Maglev, Mailcar, Manège, Manrider, Mein(e)y, Meinie, Mentor, Milk, Nopo, Nurture, Nuzzle, Omnibus, Orient Express, Owl, Pack, Paddy, PE, Pendolino, Potty, Practise, > **PREPARE**, Procession, PT, Puffer, Puff-puff, Push-pull, Q, Queue, Rattler, Rehearse, Retinue, Road, Roadwork, Rocket, Ry, Sack, > **SCHOOL**, Series, Shoe, Shuttle service, Siege, Sinkansen, Skill centre, Sloid, Sloyd, Sowarree, Sowarry, Special, SR, Steer, String, Suite, Tail, Tame, > **TEACH**, Through, Tire, Tirocinium, Track shoe, Trail, Tube, Wage, Wagon, Wave, Way

Train(ed) *may indicate* an anagram

Trainee > **APPRENTICE**, Cadet, Cub, Learner, Ordinand, Rookie, Rooky

Train-spotter Gricer

Trait Characteristic, Feature, Knack, Ph(a)enotype, Strain, Thew, Trick

Traitor Benedict Arnold, Betrayer, Casement, Dobber-in, Joyce, Judas, Judas Maccabaeus, Nid(d)ering, Nid(d)erling, Nithing, Proditor, Quisling, Renegade, Reptile, Tarpeian, Traditor, Treachetour, Turncoat, Viper, Wallydraigle, Weasel

Trajectory Parabola, Track

Trammel *may indicate* an anagram

Tramp, Trample Bog-trotter, Bum, Caird, Clochard, Clump, Crush, Derelict, Dero, Dingbat, Dosser, Estragon, Footslog, Freighter, Gadling, Gook, Hike, Hobo, Knight of the road, Meff, Override, Overrun, Pad, Piker, Plod, Poach, Potch(e), Rover, Scorn, Ship, Splodge, Sundowner, Swagman, > **TINKER**, Toe-rag(ger), Track, Traipse, Tread, Trek, Trog, Tromp, Truant, Trudge, Tub, Vagabond, Vagrant, Weary Willie

Trampoline Trampet(te)

Trance Catalepsy, Cataplexy, Goa, Narcolepsy

Tranche Gold, Reserve

Tranquil(lity) Ataraxy, Calm, Composure, Easy, Halcyon, Lee, Quietude, Sedate, > **SERENE**

Tranquillise(r) Appease, Ataractic, Ataraxic, > **CALM**, Diazepam, Downer, Hypnone, Hypnotic, Librium®, Nervine, Nitrazepam, Oxazepam, Placate, Satisfy, Soothe, Still, Valium®

Transaction(s) Affair, Agio, Brokerage, Deal, Escrow, Fasti, Leaseback, Tr

Transcend(ent), Transcendental(ist) Excel, Mystic, Overtop, Surpass, Thoreau

Transcribe, Transcript Copy, Rescore, Tenor, > **TRANSLATE**, Transume

Transfer Alien, Alienate, > **ASSIGN**, Attorn, Calk, Cede, Communize, Consign, Convey(ance), Credit, Crosstalk, Decal, Demise, Devolve, Download, Exchange, Explant, Hive off, Make over, Mancipation, Metathesis, Mortmain, Nuclear, On-lend, Pass, Photomechanical, Provection, Reassign, Redeploy, Remit, Remove, Repot, Second, Settlement, Transduction, Transfection, Uproot, Virement

Transferred *may indicate* an anagram

Transfix Impale, Rivet, > **SKEWER**, Spear, Spit

Transform(ation), Transformer Alter, Apotheosis, Balun, Change, Fourier, Lorentz, Metamorphism, Metamorphose, Metamorphosis, Metaplasia, Metastasis, Morphing, Permute, Rectifier, Sea change, Tinct, Toupee, Transmogrify, Wig

Transform(ed) *may indicate* an anagram

Transfusion Apheresis

Transgress(ion) Encroach, Err, Infringe, Offend, Overstep, Peccancy, > SIN, Violate

Transient, **Transit(ion)**, **Transitory** Brief, Ephemeral, Fleeting, Fly-by-night, Forbidden, Fugacious, Hobo, Metabasis, Passage, Passing, Provisional, Seque, T, Temporary

Transistor Drift, Epitaxial, Field-effect, Junction

Translate, **Translation**, **Translator** Calque, Construe, Convert, Coverdale, Crib, Explain, Free, Horse, Interpret, In vitro, Jerome, Key, Linguist, Loan, Machine, Metaphrase, Paraphrase, Pinyin, Polyglot, Pony, Reduce, Render, Rendition, Rhemist, Simultaneous, Targum, Tr, Transcribe, Transform, Trot, Unseen, Version(al), Vulgate, Wycliffe

▷ **Translate(d)** *may indicate* an anagram

Transmigrate, **Transmigration** Exodus, Metempsychosis, Passage, Trek

Transmit(ter), **Transmitted**, **Transmission** Air, Allele, Automatic, Band, Beacon, Broadband, > BROADCAST, Cable, Carry, CB, Communicate, Conduct, Consign, Contagion, Convection, Convey, Facsimile, Filler, Forward, Gearbox, Gene, Heredity, Impart, Intelsat, Manual, Microphone, Modem, Nicol, Permittivity, Propagate, Racon, Radiate, Radio, Receiver, Simplex, Simulcast, Sonabuoy, Synchronous, Tappet, Telecast, Telegony, Telemetry, Teleprinter, Televise, Telex, Tiros, Traduce, Traject, Tralaticious, Tralatitious, UART, Uplink, Upload, Walkie-talkie

Transom Reverse, Traverse

Transparent, **Transparency** Adularia, Clear, Crystal(line), Diaphanous, Dioptric, Glassy, Glazed, Hyaloid, Iolite, Leno, Limpid, Lucid, Luminous, Patent, Pellucid, Sheer, Slide, Tiffany

Transpire Happen, Occur

Transplant Allograft, Anaplasty, Graft, Repot, Reset, Shift

Transport(ed), **Transporter**, **Transportation** Active, Argo, Bear, Bike, Broomstick, BRS, Bus, Cargo, Carract, > CARRY, Cart, Charm, Convey, Delight, Ecstasy, Electron, Eloin, Enrapt, Enravish, Entrain, Esloin, Estro, Freight, Haul(age), Helicopter, Jerrican, Joy, Kurvey, Lug, Maglev, Mambrane, Monorail, Palanquin, Pantechnicon, Public, Put, Rape, Rapine, Rapture, Roadster, Ship, Shuttle, Sidecar, Sledge, Supersonic, Tanker, Tote, Trap, Tuktuk, Waft, Wheels, Wireway

Transpose, **Transposition** Anagram, Commute, Convert, Invert, Metathesis, Shift, Spoonerism, Switch, Tr

▷ **Transposed** *may indicate* an anagram

Transsexual Invert

Transubstantiate, **Transubstantiation** Capernaite

Transverse Across, Crosscut, Diagonal, Obliquid, Thwart

Transvest(it)ism, **Transvestite** Berdache, Berdash, Cross-dressing, Eonist

Tranter Dolly

Trap(s), **Trapdoor**, **Trapped**, **Trappings** Ambush, > BAGGAGE, Bags, Belongings, Booby, Buckboard, Bunker, Carriage, Catch, Catch-pit, Clapnet, Corner, Cru(i)ve, Deadfall, Death, Decoy, Dogcart, Downfall, Eelset, Emergent, Ensnare, Entrain, Fall, Fit-up, Fly, Flypaper, Frame-up, Fyke, Gig, Gin, Gob, Grin, Hatch, Ice-bound, Jinri(c)ksha(w), Keddah, Kettle, Kheda, Kiddle, Kidel, Kipe, Kisser, Knur(r), Light, Lime, > LUGGAGE, Lure, Mesh, Mouth, Net, Nur(r), Paraphernalia, Pitfall, Plant, Police, Pot, Poverty, Putcheon, Putcher, Quicksand, Radar, Regalia, Sand, Scruto, > SNARE, Speed, Spell, Spider, Springe, Stake-net, Star, Steam, Stench, Sting, Stink, Sun, Tangle, Tank,

Teagle, Toil, Tonga, Trou-de-loup, Two-wheeler, U, U-bend, Vampire, Web, Weel, Weir, Wire

Trapezist Leotard

Trapper Carson, Voyageur

Trash(y) Bosh, Deface, Dre(c)k, Garbage, Junk, Kitsch, Pulp, > **RUBBISH**, Schlock, Scum, Tinpot, Vandalise, White, Worthless

Trauma Insult, Shock

Travel(ler), Travelling Backpack, Bagman, Bushwhacker, Commercial, Commute, Crustie, Crusty, Drive, Drummer, Fare, Fellow, Fly, Fogg, Gipsen, Gipsy, Gitano, Globe-trotter, Go, Gulliver, Gypsy, Hike, Interrail, Itinerant, Journey, Long-haul, Marco Polo, Meve, Migrant, Motor, Move, Mush, New Age, Nomad, Passenger, Passepartout, Peregrination, Peripatetic, Pilgrim, Ply, Polo, Pootle, Range, Rep, Ride, Rom(any), Rove, Safari, Sail, Salesman, Samaritan, Space, > **TOUR**, Trek, Tripper, Tsigane, Viator, Voyage, Wanderjahr, Wayfarer, Wend, Wildfire, Zigan

Traverse Cross, Girdle, Measure, Quest, Trace

Travesty Burlesque, Charade, Distortion, Parody, Show, Skit

Trawl Drag-net, Hose-net, Net

Tray Antler, Bottle-slide, Carrier, Case, Charger, Coaster, Gallery, Joe, Lazy Susan, Plateau, > **SALVER**, Shower, Tea, Trencher, Voider, Waiter

Treacherous, Treachery Deceit, Delilah, Fickle, Ganelon, Guile, Insidious, Judas-kiss, Knife, Mala fide, Medism, Perfidious, Punic, Quicksands, Serpentine, Sleeky, Snaky, Trahison, Traitor, > **TREASON**, Two-faced, Viper

Treacle Black(jack), Butter, Molasses, Venice

Tread Clamp, Clump, Dance, Pad, Step, Stramp, Track, Trample

Treason Betrayal, High, Insurrection, Lèse-majesté, Lese-majesty, Perduellion, Petty, Sedition, > **TREACHERY**

Treasure(r), Treasury Banker, Bursar, Cache, Camerlengo, Camerlingo, Cherish, Chest, Cimelia, Coffer, Ewe-lamb, Exchequer, Fisc(al), Fisk, Godolphin, Golden, Heritage, Hoard, Montana, Palgrave, Pork barrel, > **PRIZE**, Procurator, Purser, Relic, Riches, Steward, Taonga, Thesaurus, Trove

Treat, Treatment Action, Acupuncture, Allopathy, Antidote, Archilowe, Arenation, Aromatherapy, Balneotherapy, Beano, Besee, Capitulate, Care, Chemotherapy, Chiropractic, Condition, Course, Cryotherapy, Cupping, Cure, Deal, Detox(ification), Dialysis, Do, > **DOCTOR**, Dose, Dress, Dutch, Enantiopathy, Entertain, Est, Facial, Faith-healing, Fango, Figuration, Foment, Frawzery, Handle, Holistic, Homeopathy, HRT, Hydrotherapy, Hypnotherapy, Immunotherapy, Intermediate, Jin shin do, Kenny, Laser, Manage, Medicate, Moxibustion, Naturopathy, Negotiate, Opotherapy, Osteopathy, > **OUTING**, Pasteur, Pedicure, Pelotherapy, Physic, Physiotherapy, Pie, Probiotics, Process, Prophylaxis, Psychoanalysis, Psychotherapy, Radiotherapy, Regale, Rehab(ilitation), Rest cure, Root, Secretage, Serotherapy, Shout, Shrift, Smile, > **STAND**, Tablet, Tebilise®, Thalassotherapy, Themotherapy, Therapy, Titbit, Traction, Twelve-step, Usance, Use, Vet

Treated *may indicate* an anagram

Treatise Almagest, Commentary, Didache, Discourse, Dissertation, Essay, Monograph, Pandect, Prodrome, Summa, Tract(ate), Upanishad, Vedanta

Treaty Agreement, Alliance, Assiento, Concordat, Covenant, Entente, Jay's, Lateran, Maastricht, North Atlantic, > **PACT**, Private, Protocol, Rijswijk, Utrecht, Verdun, Versailles, Yorktown

Treble Castrato, Choirboy, Chorist(er), Pairial, Soprano, > **TRIPLE**, Triune, Voice

Tree(s) Actor, > **ANCESTRY**, Axle, Beam, Boom, Bosk, Bottle, Clump, Conifer,

Trees | 718

Coppice, Corner, Deciduous, Decision, Dendrology, Descent, Family, Fault, Fringe, Gallows, Genealogical, Grove, Hang, Hardwood, Jesse, Nurse, Pedigree, Pole, Rood, Roof, Sawyer, Shoe, Softwood, Staddle, Stemma, Summer, Timber, Tyburn, Vista, > **WOOD**

TREES

2 letters:	Eugh	5 letters:	Kauri
Bo	Gean	Abele	Khaya
Ti	Hule	Abies	Kiaat
	Jack	Ackee	Kokum
3 letters:	Kaki	Afara	Larch
Ash	Kiri	Agila	Lemon
Asp	Kola	Alamo	Lilac
Bay	Lime	Alder	Lotus
Bel	Lote	Alnus	Mahoe
Ben	Mako	Anona	Mahua
Box	Meal	Areca	Mahwa
Cow	Milk	Argan	Mamey
Elm	Ming	Aspen	Maple
Fir	Mott	Banak	Matai
Gum	Mowa	Beech	Melia
Ita	Nipa	Belah	Motte
Jak	Olea	Birch	Mugga
Koa	Ombu	Bodhi	Mulga
Mot	Palm	Boree	Mvule
Nim	Pine	Butea	Myall
Oak	Pipe	Cacao	Ngaio
Oil	Pith	Carap	Nikau
Sal	Plum	Cedar	Nyssa
Tea	Poon	Ceiba	Opepe
Til	Rain	China	Osier
Ule	Rata	Cocoa	Palas
Wax	Rhus	Cocus	Palay
Yew	Rimu	Coral	Panax
	Sack	Ebony	Pecan
4 letters:	Shea	Elder	Pinon
Acer	Silk	Fagus	Pipal
Aloe	Sloe	Fever	Pipul
Amla	Soap	Flame	Pitch
Arar	Sorb	Fruit	Plane
Atap	Tawa	Grass	Quina
Bael	Teak	Guava	Ramin
Bhel	Teil	Hakea	Roble
Bito	Titi	Hazel	Rowan
Cade	Toon	Hevea	Sabal
Coco	Tung	Holly	Saman
Cola	Tutu	Iroko	Sassy
Dali	Upas	Jambu	Scrog
Dhak	Yang	Jarul	Silva
Dika		Judas	Smoke
Dita		Karri	Sumac

Taxus
Thorn
Thuja
Thuya
Tilia
Tsuga
Tuart
Tulip
Vitex
Wahoo
Wilga
Withy
Xylem
Yacca
Yulan
Zaman
Zamia

6 letters:
Abroma
Acacia
Alerce
Angico
Annona
Antiar
Arbute
Arolla
Babaco
Balsam
Banyan
Baobab
Bilian
Bombax
Bonsai
Bo-tree
Buriti
Cadaga
Cadagi
Carapa
Carica
Cashew
Cembra
Cerris
Chaste
Chenar
Cherry
Chinar
Citron
Coffee
Cordon
Cornel
Cornus

Damson
Deodar
Diana's
Dragon
Durian
Durion
Emblic
Feijoa
Fustet
Fustic
Gallus
Garjan
Gidgee
Gidjee
Gingko
Ginkgo
Glinap
Gnetum
Gopher
Guango
Gurjun
Gympie
Illipe
Illipi
Jarool
Jarrah
Joshua
Jujube
Kamala
Kamela
Karaka
Karite
Kowhai
Laurel
Lebbek
Linden
Locust
Longan
Loquat
Lucuma
Lungah
Macoya
Mallee
Manuka
Mastic
Mazard
Mimosa
Missel
Mopane
Mopani
Myrtle
Nutmeg

Obeche
Orange
Padauk
Padouk
Pagoda
Papaya
Pawpaw
Peepul
Pepper
Platan
Pomelo
Poplar
Popple
Protea
Puriri
Quince
Red-bud
Ricker
Roucou
Rubber
Sabicu
Sallow
Samaan
Sapele
Sapium
Sapota
Saxaul
She-oak
Sinder
Sorrel
Souari
Spruce
Styrax
Sumach
Sunder
Sundra
Sundri
Tallow
Tamanu
Tewart
Titoki
Tooart
Totara
Tupelo
Waboom
Wandoo
Wicken
Wicopy
Willet
Willow
Witgat
Yarran

Zamang

7 letters:
Ailanto
Amboina
Arbutus
Avodire
Bebeeru
Bilimbi
Bilsted
Bubinga
Buck-eye
Bursera
Cajeput
Cajuput
Calamus
Camphor
Camwood
Canella
Carbeen
Cassava
Catalpa
Champac
Champak
Chayote
Coquito
Corylus
Corypha
Cumquat
Daddock
Dagwood
Dogwood
Dryades
Durmast
Geebung
Genipap
Gluinap
Gumtree
Hickory
Hog-plum
Holm-oak
Jipyapa
Kumquat
Lacquer
Lagetto
Lentisk
Logwood
Lumbang
Madrono
Mahaleb
Manjack
Marasca

Margosa
Mazzard
Mesquit
Moringa
Morrell
Pereira
Pimento
Platane
Pollard
Populus
Quassia
Quicken
Quillai
Quinain
Radiata
Rampick
Rampike
Redwood
Rock elm
Saksaul
Sandbox
Saouari
Sapling
Sausage
Sequoia
Seringa
Service
Shittah
Sourgum
Soursop
Spindle
Sundari
Trumpet
Varnish
Wallaba
Wirilda
Witchen
Wych-elm
Xylopia
Zelkova

8 letters:
Aguacate
Algaroba
Aquillia
Bangalay
Bangalow
Basswood
Benjamin
Bergamot
Berrigan
Blackboy

Blimbing
Bountree
Bourtree
Breadnut
Brigalow
Calabash
Cinchona
Cinnamon
Cocoplum
Coolabah
Coolibah
Corkwood
Crabwood
Cudgerie
Dendroid
Dracaena
Espalier
Flittern
Fraxinus
Garcinia
Ghost-gum
Gnetales
Guaiacum
Hagberry
Hornbeam
Huon-pine
Igdrasil
Ironbark
Ironwood
Jelutong
Kingwood
Laburnum
Lacebark
Lecythis
Loblolly
Magnolia
Mahogany
Makomako
Mangrove
Manna-ash
Mesquite
Mulberry
Ocotillo
Oiticica
Oleaceae
Oleaster
Palmetto
Pandanus
Pichurim
Pinaster
Pithtree
Pyinkado

Quandang
Quandong
Quantong
Quillaia
Quillaja
Raintree
Rambutan
Rangiora
Rewa-rewa
Sago-palm
Sandarac
Santalum
Sapindus
Sapucaia
Sea grape
Shagbark
Simaruba
Snowball
Snowdrop
Soapbark
Sourwood
Standard
Stinging
Sweet gum
Sweetsop
Sycamine
Sycamore
Sycomore
Tamarack
Tamarind
Tamarisk
Taxodium
Umbrella
Whitegum
Wine-palm
Ygdrasil

9 letters:
Agila-wood
Ailantous
Albespine
Angophora
Azedarach
Bilimbing
Bitternut
Blackbutt
Blackwood
Bloodwood
Bolletrie
Boobialla
Bully-tree
Bulwaddee

Burrawary
Butternut
Caliatour
Caliature
Candlenut
Canoewood
Carambola
Casuarina
Chempaduk
Cherimoya
Chincapin
Chinkapin
Coachwood
Cordyline
Courbaril
Cupressus
Eaglewood
Evergreen
Firewheel
Flame-leaf
Greenwood
Grevillea
Hackberry
Ivory palm
Jacaranda
Kahikatea
Krummholz
Kurrajong
Lancewood
Lemonwood
Macadamia
Marmalade
Mirabelle
Mockernut
Monkeypot
Naseberry
Nux vomica
Paloverde
Paperbark
Paulownia
Persimmon
Pistachio
Pitch-pine
Poinciana
Ponderosa
Pontianac
Quebracho
Rauwolfia
Rose-apple
Sapodilla
Sassafras
Satinwood

Shellbark
Simarouba
Star-anise
Star-apple
Stinkwood
Tacamahac
Terebinth
Toothache
Torchwood
Wagenboom
Wayfaring
Whitebeam
Whitewood
Wych-hazel
Yggdrasil
Zebrawood

10 letters:
Arbor Vitae
Blackbully
Breadfruit
Bulletwood
Buttonball
Calamondin
Calliature
Candle-wood
Cannonball
Chamaerops

Chaulmugra
Cheesewood
Chinaberry
Chinquapin
Cottonwood
Cowrie-pine
Eucalyptus
Fiddlewood
Flamboyant
Flindersia
Frangipani
Green-heart
Hackmatack
Ilang-ilang
Jaboticaba
Jippi-jappa
Letter-wood
Lilly-pilly
Macrocarpa
Manchineel
Mangabeira
Mangosteen
Marblewood
Nithofagus
Palisander
Paper birch
Pohutukawa
Quercitron

Ribbonwood
Sandalwood
Sappanwood
Silk-cotton
Silverbell
Sneezewood
Spotted gum
Strawberry
Traveller's
Turpentine
Witch-hazel
Witgatboom
Woollybutt
Yellowwood
Ylang-ylang

11 letters:
Appleringie
Cabbage-palm
Chaulmougra
Chokecherry
Cryptomeria
Dipterocarp
Eriodendron
Flamboyante
Fothergilla
Gingerbread
Honey locust

Jesuit's bark
Leatherwood
Lignum vitae
Liquidambar
Maceranduba
Metasequoia
Pomegranate
Purpleheart
Shittimwood
Sitka spruce
Stringybark

12 letters:
Hercules' club
Liriodendron
Mammee-sapota
Masseranduba
Monkey-puzzle
Washingtonia
Wellingtonia

13 letters:
Paper-mulberry

14 letters:
Western hemlock

Tree-climber, Tree-dweller Monkey, Opossum, Sciurus, Squirrel, Unau
Tree disease Dutch elm, Waldsterben
Tree-man Ent
Tree-moss Usnea
Tree-paeony Moutan
Tree-pecker Picus
Tree-shrew Tana
Trefoil Bird's foot, Clover, Hop, Lotos, Lotus
Trek Hike, Journey, Leg, Odyssey, Safari, Yomp
Trellis Espalier, Lattice, Pergola, Treillage, Treille
Tremble, Trembling, Tremor Aftershock, Ashake, Butterfly, Dither, Dodder, Foreshock, Hotter, Intention, Judder, Moonquake, Palpitate, Quail, Quake, Quaver, Quiver, Seismal, > **SHAKE**, Shiver, Shock, Shudder, Stound, Temblor, Trepid, Twitchy, Vibrant, Vibrate, Vibration, Vibratiuncle, Vibrato, Wobble, Wuther, Yips
Tremendous Big, Enormous, Howling, Immense, Marvellous
Tremolo Bebung, Trillo
▶ **Tremor** *see* TREMBLE
Tremulous Dithering, Hirrient, Quaking, Shaky, Timorous
Trench(er) Boyau, Cunette, Cuvette, Delf, Delph, Dike(r), > **DITCH**, Dyke(r), Encroach, Fleet, Foss(e), Foxhole, Fur(r), Furrow, Grip, Gullet, Gutter, Leat, Line, Mariana, Moat, Oceanic, Outwork, Rill, Rille, Ring-dyke, Robber, Salient, Sap, Shott, Slit, Sod, Sondage

Trenchant Acid, Cutting

Trend(y) Bent, Bias, Chic, Climate, Drift, Fashion, Hep, In, Mainstream, New Age(r), Newfangled, Pop, Posey, Rage, Right-on, Style, Swim, Tendency, Tendenz, Tenor, Tide, Tonnish

Trespass(ing) Aggravated, Encroach, Errant, Hack, Impinge, Infringe, Offend, Peccancy, Sin, Trench, Wrong

Tress(es) Curl, Lock, Ringlet, Switch, Tallent

Trestle Sawhorse

Triad Chord

Trial Adversity, Affliction, Appro, Approbation, Approval, Assize, Attempt, Bane, Bernoulli, Bout, Clinical, Corsned, Court-martial, Cow, Cross, Dock, Essay, > **EXPERIMENT**, Field, Fitting, Hearing, Nuremberg, Ordeal, Pilot, Pree, Probation, Proof, Rehearsal, Scramble, Sheepdog, Show, Taste, Time

Triangle(d), Triangular Acute, Bermuda, Circular, Cosec, Deltoid, Equilateral, Eternal, Gair, Golden, Gore, Gyronny, Isosceles, Obtuse, Pascal's, Pedimental, Pendentive, Pyramid, Rack, Right-angled, Scalene, Similar, Spherical, Trigon, Tromino, Warning

Trias(sic) Bunter, Keuper, Muschelkalk, Rhaetic

Tribe(s), Tribal, Tribesmen Amalekite, Ammonites, Ashanti, Asher, Benjamin, Celt, Cherokee, Clan(nish), Creek, Dan, Dinka, Dynasty, Edomites, Ephraim, Family, Gad, Gens, Gentes, Gentilic, Gond, Goth, Hapu, Helvetii, Hittite, Horde, Hottentot, Ibo, Iceni, Israelite, Issachar, Jat, Judah, Kaffir, Kenite, Kurd, Lashkar, Levi, Lost, Manasseh, Masai, Moabite, Mongol, Moro, Naga, Naphtali, Nation, Nervii, Ngati, Ostrogoths, Pathan, Phyle, > **RACE**, Reuben, Riff, Rod, Sakai, Salian, Schedule, Senones, Senussi, Sept, Shawnee, Silures, Simeon, Standloper, Tasaday, Teuton, Trinobantes, Vandals, Wolof, Wyandot(te), X(h)osa, Zebulun

Tribune, Tribunal Aeropagus, Bema, Bench, > **COURT**, Divan, Employment, Forum, Hague, Industrial, Leader, Platform, Rienzi, Rota, Star-chamber, Waitangi

Tributary Affluent, Bogan, Branch, Creek, Fork

Tribute Cain, Capelline, Citation, Commemoration, Compliment, Dedication, Deodate, > **DUE**, Epitaph, Festschrift, Gavel, Heriot, Homage, Kain, Memento, Ode, Panegyric, Peter's pence, > **PRAISE**, Rome-penny, Scat(t), Tax, Toast, Wreath, Wroth

Trice Flash, Instant

Trichosanthin Q

Trick(ed), Trickery, Tricks(ter), Tricky Antic, Art, Artifice, Attrap, Awkward, Bamboozle, Begunk, Book, Bunco, Bunko, Cantrip, Capot, Catch, Cheat, Chicane(ry), Chouse, Claptrap, Cod(-act), Cog, Confidence, Coyote, Crook, Davenport, Deception, Deck, Delicate, Delude, Device, Dirty, > **DO**, > **DODGE**, Dupe, Elf, Elfin, Elvan, Fard, Feat, Fetch, Fiddle, Finesse, Flam, Flim-flam, Fob, Fox, Fraud, Fun, Game, Gaud, Gleek, Glike, Guile, Had, Hey presto, Hoax, Hocus(-pocus), Hoodwink, Hornswoggle, Hum, Illude, Illusion, Illywhacker, Jadery, Jockey, John, Kittle, Knack, Lark, Magsman, Mislead, Monkey, Monkey-shine, Nap, Nasruddin, Palter, Parlour, Pass, Pawk, Pleasantry, Pliskie, Prank, Prestige, Put-on, Quick, Ramp, Raven, Reak, Reik, Rex, Rig, Ropery, Roughie, Ruse, Scam, Sell, Set-up, Shanghai, Shavie, Shenanigan, Shifty, Shill, Skin-game, Skite, Skul(l)duggery, Skylark, Slam, Sleight, Slight, Slinter, Spoof, Stall, Stint, Subterfuge, Sug, Swiftie, Thimble-rig, Three-card, Ticklish, Trap, Tregetour, Trump, Turn, Tweedler, Undercraft, Underplot, Vole, Wangle, Wheeze, Wile, Wrinkle

Trick *may indicate* an anagram

Trickle Drib(ble), Driblet, Dropple, Leak, Rill, Seep

Trickless Misère

Triclinic Anorthic

Trident Fork, Plane, Trisul(a)

Trifle(s), Trifling Bagatelle, Banal, Baubee, Bauble, Bibelot, Birdseed, Bit, Cent, Chickenfeed, Coquette, Dabble, Dalliance, > **DALLY**, Denier, Desipient, Do, Doit, Faddle, Falderal, Fallal, Fattrell, Feather, Fewtril, Fiddle, Fig, Fingle-fangle, Flamfew, Fleabite, Flirt, Folderol, Fool, Footle, Fribble, Frippery, Fritter, Frivol, Gewgaw, Idle, Iota, Kickshaw, Knick-knack, Luck-penny, Mite, Nick-nacket, Niff-naff, Nothing, Nugae, Nugatory, Nyaff, Palter, Paltry, Peanuts, Peddle, Peppercorn, Petty, Philander, Picayune, Piddle, Piffle, Pin, Pingle, Pittance, Play, Potty, Quelquechose, Quiddity, Quiddle, Slight, Small beer, Smatter, Song, Sport, Stiver, Strae, Straw, Sundry, Sweet Fanny Adams, Tiddle, Toy, Trinket, Trivia, Whifflery, Whim-wham, Whit

Trig(onometry) Neat, Sech, Spherical, Tosh, Trim

Trigger Activate, Detent, Hair, Instigate, Kryton, Pawl, Precipitate, Schmitt, Start, Touch off

Trill(ed), Triller, Trilling Burr, Churr, Hirrient, Quaver, Ribattuta, Roll, Staphyle, Trim, Twitter, Warble

Trilobite Olenellus, Olenus, Paradoxide

Trim(med), Trimmer, Trimming Ballast, Bleed, Braid, Bray, Chipper, Clip, Dapper, Dinky, Dress, Ermine, Face, Falbala, Fettle, File, Froufrou, Garni, Garnish, Garniture, Gimp, Guimpe, Macramé, Macrami, Marabou, Neat, Net(t), Ornament, Pare, Passament, Passement(erie), Pipe, Plight, Posh, Preen, Proign, Proyn(e), Pruin(e), Prune, Robin, Ruche, Sax, Sett, Shipshape, Smirk, Smug, Sned, Snod, > **SPRUCE**, Straddle, Stroddle, Strodle, Stylist, Svelte, Tiddley, > **TIDY**, Time-server, Torsade, Trick, Whippersnipper, Wig

Trinidadian Carib

Trinitarian, Trinity Mathurin(e), Triad, Trimurti, Triune, Word

Trinket(s) Bauble, Bibelot, Bijou(terie), Charm, Fallal, Nicknack, Toy, Trankum, Trumpery

Trio Catch, Graces, Skat, Terzetto

Trip(per) Awayday, Cruise, Dance, Day, Ego, Errand, > **FALL**, Field, Flight, Flip, Guilt, Head, High, Jolly, Journey, Junket, Kilt, Link, Outing, Pleasure, Power, Ride, Round, Run, Sail, Sashay, Spin, Spurn, > **STUMBLE**, Tour, Trek, Trial, Voyage

> **Trip** *may indicate* an anagram

Tripe Abracadabra, Bosh, Caen, Entrails, Offal, Rot

Triple, Triplet Codon, Hemiol(i)a, Sdrucciola, Ternal, Tiercet, Treble, Trifecta, Trilling, Trin(e), Tripling

Tripod Cat, Cortina, Highhat, Oracle, Triangle, Trippet, Trivet

Triptych Volet

Trishaw Cycle

Trite Banal, Boilerplate, Cornball, Corny, Hackneyed, Hoary, Laughable, Novelettish, Platitude, Rinky-dink, Stale, Stock, Time-worn

Triton Eft, Evet, Ewt, Trumpet-shell

Triumph(ant) Cock-a-hoop, Codille, Cowabunga, Crow, Eureka, Exult, Glory, Impostor, Killing, Oho, Olé, Ovation, Palm, Victorious, > **WIN**

Triumvir Caesar, Crassus, Pompey

Trivet Tripod, Trippet

Trivia(l), Triviality Adiaphoron, Bagatelle, Balaam, Bald, > **BANAL**, Footling,

Frippery, Frothy, Futile, Idle, Inconsequential, Light, Minutiae, Nitpicking, Nothingism, Paltry, Pap, Peppercorn, Pettifoggery, Petty, Picayune, Piddling, Piffling, Shallow, Small, Small beer, Small fry, Snippety, Squirt, Squit, Toy(s), Vegie

Trochee Choree

Troglodyte Ape, Caveman, Hermit, Spelean, Wren

Trojan Aeneas, Agamemnon, Dardan, Iliac, Priam, Teucrian, Troic

Troll > FISH, Gnome, Rove, Spoon, Trawl, Warble

Trolley Brute, Cart, Dolly, Gurney, Hostess, Shopping, Tea, Traymobile, Truck, Trundler

▸ **Trollop** see LOOSE WOMAN

Trombone Posaune

Troop(s), Trooper Alpini, Band, BEF, Brigade, Company, Depot, Detachment, Guard, Horde, Household, Logistics, Midianite, Militia, Pultan, Pulton, Pultoon, Pultun, SAS, School, Shock, Sowar, State, Storm, Subsidiary, Tp, Turm(e)

Troopship Transport

Trophy Adward, Ashes, > AWARD, Belt, Cup, Emmy, Memento, Palm, > PRIZE, Scalp, Schneider, Spoils, Tourist, TT

Tropic(al) Cancer, Capricorn, Derris, Jungle, Neogaea, Sultry

Trot(ter), Trot out Air, Crib, Crubeen, Job, Jog, Passage, Pettitoes, Piaffe, Pony, Ranke, Red(-shirt), Rising, Tootsie

Troth Perfay, Troggs

Trotsky(ist) Entr(y)ism, Leon, Militant Tendency

Troubador Blondel, Griot, Manrico, Minstrel, Singer, Sordello

Trouble(s), Troublemaker, Troublesome Ache, Ado, Affliction, Aggro, Agitate, Ail, Alarm, Annoy, Bale, Barrat, Beset, > BOTHER, Bovver, Brickle, Burden, Care, Coil, Concern, Debate, Disaster, Disquiet, Distress, Disturb, Dog, Dolour, Eat, Esclandre, Exercise, Fash, Fashious, Finger, Firebrand, Fossick, Gram(e), Grief, Hag-ride, Harass, Harry, Hassle, Hatter, Heat, Heist, Hellion, Hot water, Howdyedo, Hydra, Inconvenience, Infest, > IN TROUBLE, Jam, Kiaugh, Mess, Mixer, Moil, Molest, Noy, Perturb, Pester, Plague, Poke, Reck, Rub, Scrape, Shake, Shtuck, Soup, Spiny, Stir, Storm, Sturt, Tartar, Teen, Teething, Thorny, Tine, Toil, Trial, Tsouris, Tsuris, Turn-up, Tyne, Unsettle, Vex, > WORRY

Trouble-free Gallio

Trouble-shooter Ombudsman

▷ **Troublesome** may indicate an anagram

Trough Back, Bed, Bucket, Buddle, Channel, Chute, Culvert, Graben, Hod, Hutch, Langmuir, Launder, Leachtub, Manger, Pneumatic, Puerto Rico, Stock, Straik, Strake, Syncline, Troffer, Tundish, Tye, Watering

Trounce > BEAT, Hammer, Thump

Trouser(s) Bags, Bell-bottoms, Bloomers, Breeches, Capri pants, Churidars, Clam-diggers, Continuations, Cords, Corduroys, Cossacks, Culottes, Daks, Denims, Drainpipe, Drawers, Ducks, Dungarees, Eel-skins, Flannels, Flares, Galligaskins, Gaskins, Gauchos, Hip-huggers, Hipsters, Inexpressibles, Innominables, Jeans, Jodhpurs, Kaccha, Ke(c)ks, Knee cords, Lederhosen, Longs, Loons, Moleskins, Overalls, Oxford bags, Palazzo (pants), Palazzos, Pantaloons, Pants, Pedal pushers, Pegtops, Plus-fours, Plus-twos, Reach-me-downs, Salopettes, Shalwar, Ski pants, Slacks, Stovepipes, Strides, Strossers, Sweatpants, Trews, Trouse, Unmentionables, Unutterables, Utterless

Trout Aurora, Brook, Brown, Bull, Coral, Finnac(k), Finnock, Fish, Gillaroo,

Hag(fish), Herling, Hirling, Kamloops, Peal, Peel, Phinnock, Pogies, Quintet, Rainbow, Salmon, Sewen, Sewin, Speckled, Splake, Steelhead, Togue, Whitling

Trow Faith, Meseems

Trowel Float

Troy Ilium, Sergeant, T, Weight

Truant Absentee, AWOL, Dodge, Hooky, Kip, Mich(e), Mitch, Mooch, Mouch, Wag

Truce Armistice, Barley, Ceasefire, Fainites, Fains, Interlude, Pax, Stillstand, Treague, Treaty

Truck Bakkie, Bogie, Breakdown, Business, Cattle, Cocopan, Dealings, Dolly, Dumper, Flatbed, Forklift, Haul, Hopper, Journey, > **LORRY**, Low-loader, Pallet, Panel, Pick-up, Semi, Sound, Stacking, Tipper, Tow(ie), Traffic, Trolley, Trundle, Ute, Utility, Van, Wrecker

Trudge Footslog, Jog, Lumber, Pad, Plod, Stodge, Stramp, Taigle, Traipse, Trash, Trauchle, Trog, Vamp

True Accurate, Actual, Apodictic, Candid, Constant, Correct, Exact, Factual, Faithful, Genuine, Honest, Indubitable, Leal, Literal, Loyal, Platitude, Plumb, Pure, Real, Realistic, Richr, Right, Sooth, Very

Truffle Tuber, Tuberaceae

Trug Basket, Wisket

Truly Certainly, Certes, Fegs, Forsooth, Honestly, Indeed, Surely, Verily, Yea

Trump(s), **Trumpet(er)** Agami, Alchemy, Alchymy, Armstrong, Bach, Blare, Blast, Bray, Buccina, Bugle(r), Call, Card, Clarion, Conch, Cornet, Corona, Crow, Daffodil, Ear, Elephant, Fanfare, Hallali, Honours, > **HORN**, Invent, Jew's, Last, Lituus, Long ten, Lur(e), Lurist, Manille, Marine, Megaphone, > **NO TRUMP**, Proclaim, Ram's-horn, Rant, Resurrect, Ruff, Salpingian, Salpinx, Satchmo, Sennet, Shofar, Shophar, Slug-horn, Speaking, Surpass, Tantara, Tantarara, Tar(at)antara, Theodomas, Tiddy, Triton, Triumph

Trumpery Fattrels, Jimcrack, Paltry, Trashy

Truncate(d) Abrupt, Cut, Dock, Shorten

Truncheon Billie, Billy, Blackjack, Cosh, Night-stick, Warder

Trundle Hump, Trill, Troll

Trunk(s) Aorta(l), A-road, Body, Bole, Box, Bulk, Bus, But(t), Cabin, Carcase, Chest, Coffer, Hose, Imperial, Log, Peduncle, Pollard, Portmanteau, Portmantle, Proboscis, Ricker, Road, Saratoga, Shorts, STD, Stock, Stud, Synangium, Torso, Valise, Wardrobe

Truss > **BIND**, Ligate, Oop, Oup, Sheaf, Tie, Upbind

Trust(y), **Trusting**, **Trustworthy** Active, Affy, Authentic, Belief, Care, Cartel, Charge, Charitable, Combine, Confide, Credit, Dependable, Discretionary, > **FAITH**, Fiduciary, Gullible, Honest, Hope, Investment, Leal, Lippen, Loyal, National, NT, Reliable, Reliance, Rely, Repose, Reputable, Sound, Special, Split, Staunch, Tick, Trojan, Trow, True, Trump, Unit

Trustee Agent, Executor, Fiduciary, Pensioneer, Tr

Truth(ful), **Truism** Accuracy, Alethic, Axiom, Bromide, Cliché, Cold turkey, Dharma, Dialectic, > **FACT**, Facticity, Forsooth, Gospel, Home, Honesty, Idea(l), Logical, Maxim, Naked, Pravda, Reality, Sooth, Soothfast, Troggs, Veraity, Veridical, Verisimilitude, Verity, Vraisemblance

Try(ing) Aim, Approof, Assay, Attempt, Audition, Bash, Bid, Birl, Burden, Burl, Conative, Contend, Crack, Effort, Empiric(utic), > **ENDEAVOUR**, Essay, Examine, Experiment, Fand, Fish, Fling, Foretaste, Go, Harass, Hard, Hear, Impeach, Importunate, Irk, Offer, Ordalium, Practise, Pree, Prieve, Push-over, > **SAMPLE**, Seek, Shot, Sip, Stab, Strain, Strive, Taste, Tax, Tempt, Test, Touchdown, Whirl

Tryst Date, Rendezvous

Tsar(ist) Alexis, Emperor, Godunov, Octobrist, Ruler

TT Rechabite

Tub(by), **Tubbiness**, **Tub-thumper** Ash-leach, Back, Bath, Boanerges, Bran, Corf, Cowl, Dan, Diogenes, Dolly, Endomorph, Firkin, Keeve, Kid, Kieve, Kit, Luckydip, Mashing, Meat, Pin, Podge, Pot-bellied, Pudge, Pulpit, Stand, Swill, Tun, Twin, Vat, Wash

Tuba Bombardon, Euphonium

Tube, **Tubing**, **Tubular** Acorn, Arteriole, Artery, Barrel, Blowpipe, Bronchus, Burette, Calamus, Camera, Canaliculus, Cannula, Capillary, Casing, Catheter, Cathode-ray, Cave, Conduit, Crookes, Digitron, Diode, Discharge, Drain, Drift, Dropper, Duct, Electron, Endiometer, Epididymis, Eustachian, Extension, Fallopian, Fistula, Fulgurite, Geissler, Germ, Grommet, Hose, Iconoscope, Image(orthicon), Inner, Kinescope, Klystron, Macaroni, Malpighian, Matrass, Metro, Neural, Nixie, Orthicon, Oval, Oviduct, Pentode, Picture, Pilot-static, > PIPE, Pipette, Pitot, Pitot-static, Pneumatic, Pollen, Promethean, Salpinx, Saticon®, Saucisse, Saucisson, Schnorkel, Shadow-mask, Shock, Sieve, Siphon, Siphonet, Siphonostele, Siphuncle, Skelp, Skiatron, Sleeve, Snorkel, Spaghetti, Speaking, Spout, Staple, Static, Stent, Storage, Straw, Strobotron, Subway, Sucker, Swallet, Telescope, Teletron, Television, Terete, Test, Tetrode, Thyratron, Tile, Torpedo, Torricellian, Trachea, Triniscope, Trocar, Trochotron, Trunk, Tunnel, Tuppenny, U, Underground, Ureter, Urethra, Vacuum, Vas, VDU, Vein, Vena, Venturi, Video, Vidicon®, Worm, X-ray

Tuber(s) Arnut, Arracacha, Bulb, Chufa, Coc(c)o, Dahlia, Dasheen, Earth-nut, Eddoes, Mashua, Oca, Potato, Salep, Taproot, Taro, Yam

Tuberculosis Consumption, Crewels, Cruel(l)s, Decline, King's evil, Lupus, Phthisis, Scrofula, White plague

Tuck Dart, Friar, Gather, Grub, Kilt, Pin, Pleat, Scran, Truss, Tummy

Tuesday Hock, Pancake, Shrove, Super

Tuft(ed) Amentum, Beard, C(a)espitose, Candlewick, Catkin, Cluster, Coma, Comb, Cowlick, Crest, Dollop, Flaught, Floccus, Flock, Goatee, Hassock, Knop, Lock, Pappus, Penicillate, Quiff, Scopate, Shola, Tait, Tassel, Tate, Toorie, Toupee, Tourie, Tussock, Tuzz, Whisk

Tug Drag, Haul, Jerk, Lug, Pug, > PULL, Rive, Saccade, Ship, Sole, Soole, Sowl(e), Tit, Tow, Towboat, Yank

Tui Poebird

Tuition Masterclass, Seminal

Tully Cicero

Tumble, **Tumbler** Acrobat, Cartwheel, Drier, Fall, > GLASS, Header, Pitch, Popple, Purl, Realise, Spill, Stumble, Tailer, Topple, Trip, Twig, Voltigeur, Welter

▷ **Tumble** *may indicate* an anagram

Tumbledown Decrepit, Dilapidated, Ramshackle, Rickle, Ruinous

Tumbril Caisson

Tummy Belly, Colon, Mary, Paunch, Pod

Tummy-ache Colic, Gripe, Tormina

Tumour Adenoma, Anbury, Angioma, Angiosarcoma, Astroblastoma, Astrocytoma, Burkitt('s) lymphoma, Cancer, Carcinoid, Carcinoma, Carcinosarcoma, Chondroma, Condyloma, Crab(-yaws), Dermoid, Encanthis, Encephaloma, Enchondroma, Endothelioma, Epulis, Exostosis, Fibroid, Fibroma, Ganglion, Germinoma, Gioblastoma, Glioma, Granuloma, Grape, > GROWTH, Gumma, Haemangioma, Haematoma, Hepatoma, Lipoma, Lymphoma, Medullablastoma, Melanoma, Meningioma, Mesothelioma,

Metastasis, Mole, Myeloma, Myoma, Myxoma, Neoplasm, Nephroblastoma, Neuroblastoma, Neuroma, Odontoma, -oma, Oncology, Osteoclastoma, Osteoma, Osteosarcoma, Papilloma, Polypus, Retinoblastoma, Rhabdomyoma, Sarcoma, Scirrhous, Secondary, Seminoma, Steatoma, Struma, Syphiloma, Talpa, Teratoma, Thymoma, Wart, Warthin's, Wen, Wilm's, Windgall, Wolf, Xanthoma, Yaw

Tumult Brattle, Brawl, Coil, Deray, Ferment, Fracas, Hirdy-girdy, Hubbub, Hurly-burly, Reird, Riot, > ROAR, Romage, Rore, Stoor, Stour, Stowre, Stramash, Tew, > UPROAR

Tumulus Barrow, Mote, Motte

Tun Cask, Keg

Tundra Barren Grounds, Barren Lands

Tune(s), **Tuneful**, **Tuner**, **Tuning** Adjust, Air, Aria, Canorous, Carillon, Catch, Choral, Dump, Earworm, Etude, Fine, Fork, Harmony, Hornpipe, Jingle, Key, Maggot, Measure, Melisma, > MELODY, Old Hundred, > OUT OF TUNE, Peg, Port, Potpourri, Raga, Rant, Ranz-des-vaches, Signature, Snatch, Song, Spring, Strain, Sweet, Syntonise, Temper, Temperament, Theme, Tone, Tweak

Tungstate, **Tungsten** Scheelite, W, Wolfram

Tunic Ao dai, Caftan, Chiton, Choroid, Cote-hardie, Dalmatic, Dashiki, Gymslip, Hauberk, Kabaya, Kaftan, Kameez, K(h)urta, Salwar kameez, > SINGLET, Surcoat, Tabard, Toga

Tunicate Salpa

Tunnel(ler) Blackwall, Bore, Channel, Chunnel, Condie, Countermine, Culvert, Cundy, Earthworm, Euro, Gallery, Head, Mine, Qanat, Rotherhithe, Simplon, Smoke, Stope, Subway, Syrinx, Tube, Underpass, Water, Wind, Wormhole

Tunny Bonito, Tuna

Turban Bandanna, Hat, Mitral, Pagri, Puggaree, Puggery, Puggree, Sash, Scarf, Tulipant

Turbid Cloudy, Dense, Drumly, Roily

Turbine Francis, Gas, Impulse, Ram air, Reaction, Steam, Wind

Turbulence, **Turbulent** Becket, Bellicose, Buller, Factious, Fierce, Rapids, Stormy, Unruly

> **Turbulent** *may indicate* an anagram

Turf Caespitose, Clod, Divot, Earth, Fail, Feal, Flaught, > GRASS, Greensward, Peat, Screw, > SOD, Sward

Turk(ish) Anatolian, Bashaw, Bashkir, Bey, Bimbashi, Bostangi, Byzantine, Caimac(am), Crescent, Effendi, Golden Horde, Grand, Gregory, Horse(tail), Irade, Kaimakam, Kazak(h), Kurd, Mameluke, Mutessarif(at), Omar, Osman(li), Ottamite, Ottoman, Ottomite, Rayah, Scanderbeg, Selim, Seljuk(ian), Seraskier, Spahi, Tartar, Tatar, Timariot, Usak, Uzbeg, Uzbek, Yakut, Young

Turkey, **Turkey-like** Anatolia, Brush, Bubbly(-jock), Cold, Curassow, Eyalet, Flop, Gobbler, Norfolk, Plain, Scrub, Sultanate, Talegalla, Talk, TR, Trabzon, Vulturn

Turmeric Curcumine

Turmoil Chaos, Din, Ferment, Stoor, Stour, Tornado, Tracasserie, Tumult, > UPROAR, Welter

> **Turn(ing)** *may indicate* an anagram

Turn(ing), **Turned away**, **Turned up**, **Turns** Acescent, Act, Addle, Advert, Antrorse, Apostrophe, Apotropaic, Avert, Bad, Bank, Become, Bend, Buggins, Bump, Canceleer, Cancelier, Caracol(e), Careen, Cartwheel, Cast, Chainé, Chandelle, Change, Char(e), Chore, Christiana, Christie, Christy, Churn, Cock,

Coil, Crank(le), Cuff, Curd(le), Curve, Defect, Deflect, Demi-volt(e), Detour, Deviate, Dig, Digress, Divert, Ear, Earn, Elbow, Evert, Fadge, Flip, Forfend, Go, Good, Gruppetto, Hairpin, Handbrake, Head-off, Hie, High, Hinge, Hup, Immelmann, Influence, Innings, Intussuscept, Invert, Jar, Jink, Keel, Kick, Laeotropic, Lodging, Lot, Luff, Mohawk, Number, Obvert, Parallel, Parry, Penchant, Pivot, Plough, Pronate, Prove, PTO, Quarter, Quersprung, Rebut, Refer, Refract, Remuage, Retroflex, Retroussé, Retrovert, Rev, Revolt, Ride, Riffle, Rocker, Roll, Root, > **ROTATE**, Rote, Roulade, Rout, Routine, Screw, Secund, Sheer, > **SHOT**, Shout, Sicken, Skit, Slew, Slue, Solstice, Sour, > **SPELL**, Spin, Spot, Sprain, Star, Start, Stem, Step, Swash, Swing, Swivel, Telemark, Three-point, Throw, Tiptilt, Tirl, Torque, Transpose, Trend, Trick, Trie, Trochilic, Turtle, Twiddle, Twist, U, Uey, Up, Veer, Versed, Version, Vertigo, Volta, Volte-face, Volutation, Wap, Warp, Wedein, Wend, Went, > **WHEEL**, Whelm, Whirl, Whorl, Wimple, Wind, Wrest, Wriggle, Zigzag

Turn-coat Apostate, Cato, Defector, Quisling, Rat, Renegade, Tergiversate, Traitor

Turner Axle, Lana, Lathe, Painter, Pivot, Rose-engine, Spanner, Worm, Wrench

Turning point Crisis, Crossroads, Landmark, Watershed

Turnip(-shaped) Baggy, Bagie, Hunter, Jicama, Napiform, Navew, Neep, Prairie, Rutabaga, > **STUPID PERSON**, Swede, Tumshie

Turnkey Gaoler, Jailer

Turn-out Eventuate, Gathering, Product, Rig, Splay, Style

Turn over Capsize, Careen, Flip, Inversion, Production, PTO, Somersault, TO, Up-end

Turnpike Highway, Toll

Turnstile Tourniquet

Turntable Rota, Rotator

Turpentine Galipot, Rosin, Thinner, Turps, Venice

Turquoise Bone, Fossil, Ligure, Occidental, Odontolite, Turkey stone

Turret(ed) Barmkin, Bartisan, Garret, Louver, Louvre, Pepperbox, Sponson, > **TOWER**, Turriculate

Turtle, Turtle head Bale, Calipash, Calipee, Chelone, Diamondback, Emys, Floor, Green, Hawk(s)bill, Inverted, Leatherback, Loggerhead, Matamata, Mossback, Mud, Musk, Ridley, Screen, Snapper, Snapping, Soft-shelled, Stinkpot, Terrapin, Thalassian

Tusk Gam, Horn, Ivory, Tooth, Tush

Tusker Dicynodont, Elephant, Mastodon

Tussle Giust, Joust, Mêlée, Scrimmage, Scrum, Scuffle, Skirmish, Touse, Touze, Towse, Towze, Tuilyie, Wrestle

Tussock Hassock, Niggerhead, Tuft

Tut(-tut) Och, Pooh

Tutelary Guardian, Protector

Tutor Abbé, Aristotle, Ascham, Bear, > **COACH**, Crammer, Don, Instruct, Leader, Mentor, Preceptor, Répétiteur, Supervisor, Teacher

Tuxedo DJ

TV Baird, Box, Cable, Digital, Idiot-box, Lime Grove, Monitor, PAL, Pay, Reality, SECAM, Sky, Tele, > **TELEVISION**, Telly, Tube, Video

Twaddle Blether, Drivel, Rot, Slipslop, Tripe

Twang Nasal, Pluck, Plunk, Rhinolalia

Tweak Pluck, Twiddle, Twist, Twitch

Tweed(y) Donegal, Harris®, Homespun, Lovat, Raploch

Tweet Chirrup

Twelfth, Twelve Apostles, Dozen, Epiphany, Glorious, Grouse, Midday, Midnight, N, Night, Noon, Ternion, Twal

Twenty, Twenty-sided Icosahedron, Score, Vicenary, Vicennial, Vicesimal, Vigesimal

Twenty-five Pony, Quartern

Twenty-four Thr(e)ave

Twerp Pipsqueak

Twice *see* TWO

Twice-yearly Biennial, Equinox

Twiddle Fidget, Twirl

Twig(s) Besom, Birch, Cotton, Cow, Dig, Grasp, Kow, Osier, Realise, Reis, Rice, Rumble, Sarment, See, Sprig, Sticklac, Switch, Understand, Walking, Wand, Wattle, Wicker, Withe

Twilight Astronomical, Civil, Cockshut, Crepuscular, Demi-jour, Dusk, Gloam(ing), Gotterdämmerung, Nautical, Summerdim

Twill Cavalry, Chino

Twin(s) Asvins, Castor, Coetaneous, Conjoined, Didymous, Dioscuri, Ditokous, Dizygotic, Double, Fraternal, Gemel, Hemitrope, Identical, Isogeny, Kindred, Macle, Monozygotic, Pigeon-pair, Pollux, Siamese, Tweedledee, Tweedledum

Twine Braid, Coil, Cord, Inosculate, Packthread, Sisal, Snake, String, Twist, Wreathe

Twinge Pang, Scruple, Stab

Twinkle, Twinkling Glimmer, Glint, Mo(ment), > SPARKLE, Starnie, Trice

Twirl Spin, Swivel, Tirl, Tirlie-wirlie, Trill, Twiddle, Twizzle, Whirl

Twirling *may indicate* an anagram

Twist(ed), Twister, Twisting, Twisty Anfractuous, Askant, Askew, Baccy, Becurl, Bought, Braid, Card-sharper, Chisel, Coil, Contort, Convolution, Crinkle, Crinkum-crankum, Crisp, Cue, Curl(icue), Cyclone, Deform, Detort, Distort, > DODGE, Entwine, Garrot, Helix, Imposture, Kink, Mangulate, Mat, Möbius strip, Oliver, Pandanaceous, Plait, Quirk, Raddle, Ravel, Rick, Rogue, Rotate, Rove, Serpent, Skew, Slew, Slub(b), Slue, Snake, Snarl, Spin, Spiral, Sprain, Squiggle, Squirm, Swivel, Tendril, Thrawn, Torc, Tornado, Torque, Torsade, Torsion, Torticollis, Tortile, Turn, Tweak, Twiddle, Twine, Twirl, Typhoon, Valgus, Volvulus, Wamble, Warp, Welkt, Wigwag, Wind, Wound-wrap, Wrast, Wreathe, Wrench, Wrest, Wrethe, Wrick, Wriggle, Wring, Writhe, Wry, Zigzag

Twisted, Twisting *may indicate* an anagram

Twit, Twitter Chaff, Cherup, Chirrup, Dotterel, Gear(e), Giber, > JEER, Stupid, Taunt, Tweet, Warble

Twitch(ing), Twitchy Athetosis, Clonic, Grass, Jerk, Life-blood, Start, Subsultive, Tic, Tig, Tit, Tweak, Twinge, Vellicate, Yips

Two(some), Twice Bice, Bis, Bisp, Both, Brace, Couple(t), Deuce, Double, Duad, Dual, Duet, Duo, Dyad, > PAIR, Swy, Tête-à-tête, Twain, Twins, Twister

Two-edged Ancipitous

Two-faced Dihedral, Dorsiventral, Hypocritical, Janus, Redan

Two-gallon Peck

Two-headed Amphisbaenic, Dicephalous, Orthos

Two hundred H

Two hundred and fifty E, K

Two-master Brig

Two-rayed Diactinal

Two-sided Bilateral, Equivocatory

Two thousand Z

Two-up Kip, Swy
Two-wheeler Bicycle, Scooter
Tycoon Baron, Empire-builder, Magnate, Mogul, Plutocrat, Shogun
Type(s), Typing A, Agate, Aldine, Antimony, Antique, B, Balaam, Baskerville, Bastard, Bembo, Black-letter, Blood, Bodoni, Body, Bold face, Bourgeois, Braille Brand, Brevier, Brilliant, Canon, Caslon, Category, Character, Chase, Cicero, Clarendon, Class, Columbian, Condensed, Cut, Egyptian, Elite, Elzevir, Em, Emblem, Emerald, English, Face, Font, Form(e), Founder's, Fount, Fraktur, Fudge, Garamond, Gem, Genre, Gent, Gothic, Great primer, Gutenberg, Hair, Ilk, Image, Kern(e), Key, Kidney, Kind, Late-star, Ligature, Light-faced, Longprimer, Ludlow, Minion, Modern, Moon, Mould, Non-pareil, Norm, Old English, Old-face, Old Style, Paragon, Pattern, Pearl, Peculiar, Personality, Pi, Pica, Pie, Plantin, Point, Primer, Print, Quad(rat), Roman, Ronde, Ruby, Sanserif, Secretary, Semibold, Serif, Serological, > **SORT**, Sp, Species, Spectral, Stanhope, Style, Times, Tissue, Touch, Version
▷ **Type of** *may indicate* an anagram
Typewriter Golfball, Portable, Stenograph, Stenotype®, Varityper®
Typhoid, Typhus Camp-fever, Tick-borne
Typhoon Cyclone, Hurricane, Monsoon, Tornado, Wind
Typical Average, Characteristic, Classic, Echt, Normal, Representative, Standard, Symbolic, True-bred, Usual
Typist Audio, Printer, Temp
Tyrannise(d) Domineer, Lord, Under
Tyrant, Tyranny, Tyrannical Absolutism, Autocrat, Caligula, Despot, Dictator, Drawcansir, Gelon, Herod, Lordly, Nero, Oppressor, Pharaoh, Sardanapalus, Satrap, Stalin, Totalitarian, Tsar, Yoke
Tyre Balloon, Cross-ply, Cushion, Michelin, Pericles, Pneumatic, Radial, Radial(-ply), Recap, Remould, Retread, Shoe, Sidewall, Slick, Snow, Spare, Tread, Tubeless, Whitewall
Tyro Beginner, Ham, > **NOVICE**, Rabbit, Rookie, Rooky, Starter
Tyrolese R(h)aetian

Uu

U, **U-type** Gent, Unicorn, Universal, Uranium
Ubiquitous Everywhere, Omnipresent
Udder Bag, Dug
Ugandan Obote
Ugly Cow, Customer, Eyesore, Foul, Gorgon, Gruesome, Hideous, Homely, Huckery, Loth, Mean, Ominous, Plain
Ugrian Ostiak, Ostyak, Samo(y)ed, Vogul
UK GB
Ukase Decree
Ukraine Ruthene, UR
Ulcer(ous) Abscess, Aphtha, Bedsore, Canker, Chancroid, Decubitus, Duodenal, Gastric, Helcoid, Noli-me-tangere, Noma, Peptic, Phagedaena, Rodent, Rupia, Sore, Varicose, Wolf
Ulster NI, Overcoat, Raincoat, Ulad
Ulterior External, Hidden
Ultimate Absolute, Basic, Deterrent, Eventual, Final, Furthest, Last, Maximum, So, Supreme, Thule
Ultra Drastic, Extreme, Radical
Ultra-modern Space age
Ultra-republican Leveller
Ulysses Bloom, Grant, Odysseus
Umbellifer(ous) Angelica, Arnut, Car(r)away, Dill, Honewort, Narthex, Pig-nut, Seseli
Umber Burnt, Mottled, Raw, Waved
Umbrage Offence, Pique, Resentment, Shade
Umbrella(-shaped) Bubble, Bumbershoot, Chatta, Gamp, Gingham, Gloria, Mush(room), Nuclear, Parasol, Sunshade, Tee
Umbria Eugubine, Iguvine
Umpire Arb(iter), Byrlawman, Daysman, Decider, Judge, Oddjobman, Odd(s)man, Overseer, Oversman, Referee, Rule, Stickler, Thirdsman
Unabashed Bare-faced, Brazen, Shameless
Unable Can't, Incapable
Unaccented Atonic, Proclitic
Unacceptable Non-U, Not on, Out, Stigmatic
Unaccompanied A cappella, Alone, High-lone, Secco, Single, Solo, Solus
Unaccustomed Desuetude, New
Unadorned Bald
Unadulterated Sincere
Unaffected Artless, Genuine, Homely, Natural, Plain, Sincere, Unattached
Unaided Single-handed, Solo
Unaltered Constant, Same
Unambiguous Univocal
Unanimous Accord, Nem con

Unanswerable Erotema, Irrefragable, Irrefutable
Unarguable Erotema
Unarmed Inerm, Naked, Vulnerable
Unashamed Blatant, Brazen, Open
Unassigned Adespota, Anonymous
Unassuming Lowly
Unattached Freelance, Loose
Unattractive Drac(k), Lemon, Minger, Plain, Plug-ugly, Rebarbative, Seamy, Ugly
Unattributable Anon
Unauthentic Plagal
▷ **Unauthentic** *may indicate* an anagram
Unavail(able), Unavailing Bootless, Futile, Ineluctable, Lost, No use, Off, Useless, Vain
Unavoidable Inevitable, Necessary, Perforce
Unaware Heedless, Ignorant, Incognisant, Innocent, Oblivious
Unbalanced Asymmetric, Deranged, Doolalli, Doolally, Loco, Lopsided, Uneven
Unbearable Bassington, Intolerable
Unbeaten All-time
Unbecoming, Unbefitting Improper, Infra dig, Shabby, Unfitting, Unseemly, Unsuitable, Unworthy
Unbelievable, Unbeliever Agnostic, Atheist, Cassandra, Doubter, Giaour, Heathen, Incredible, Infidel, Pagan, Painim, Paynim, Sceptic, Tall, Zendik
Unbent Relaxed
Unbiased Fair, Impartial, Just, Neutral, Objective, Unattainted
Unblemished Spotless, Vestal
Unblinking Alert, Astare, Fearless
Unborn Future, Unbred
Unbowed In-kneed, Resolute
Unbreakable Infrangible, Inviolate
Unbridled Fancy free, Footloose, Lawless, Uncurbed, Unrestricted, Unshackled, Untramelled
Unburden Confide, Offload, Relieve, Unload
Uncanny Eerie, Eldritch, Extraordinary, Geason, Rum, Spooky, Weird
Uncastrated Stone
Uncertain(ty) Blate, Broken, Chancy, Chary, Contingent, Delicate, Dicey, Dither, Doubtful, Dubiety, Grey, Heisenberg, Hesitant, Iffy, Indeterminate, Indistinct, Irresolute, Peradventure, Queasy, Risky, Slippery, Tentative, Vor
▷ **Uncertain** *may indicate* an anagram
Unchallengeable, Unchallenge(d) Irrecusable, Sackless
Unchangeable, Unchanged, Unchanging As is, Enduring, Eternal, Idempotent, Immutable, Monotonous, Pristine, Stable, Standpat
Uncharacteristic Atypical
Uncharged Neutral, Neutron
Unchaste Corrupt, Immodest, Immoral, Impure, Lewd, Wanton
Unchecked Rampant
Uncivil(ised) Barbaric, Benighted, Boondocks, Discourteous, Disrespectful, Giant-rude, Goth, Heathen, Impolite, Military, Rude, Rudesby
Uncle Abbas, Afrikaner, Arly, Bob, Dutch, Eme, Nunky, Oom, Pawnbroker, Pop-shop, Remus, Sam, Tio, Tom, Usurer, Vanya
Unclean Defiled, Dirty, Impure, Obscene, Ordure, Squalid, Tabu, T(e)refa(h)
Unclear Ambitty, Hazy, Nebulous, Obscure

Unclothed Bald, Nude
Uncloven Soliped
Uncommitted Laodicean
Uncommon Rare, Strange, Unusual
Uncommon(ly) *may indicate* an anagram
Uncommunicative Reserved, Tight-lipped
Uncompanionable Threesome
Uncomplimentary Blunt
Uncomprehending Anan, Ignorant
Uncompromising Cutthroat, Hardline, Hardshell, Intransigent, Rigid, Strict, Ultra
Unconcealed Open, Pert
Unconcerned Bland, Careless, Casual, Cold, Indifferent, Insouciant, Nonchalant, Strange
Unconditional Absolute, Free, Pure
Unconnected Asyndetic, Detached, Disjointed, Off-line
Unconscious(ness) Asleep, Catalepsy, Cold, Comatose, Instinctive, Non-ego, Not-I, Subliminal, Trance, Under
Unconsidered Impetuous, Rash
Uncontrolled Atactic, Free, Incontinent, Loose, Loose cannon, Wild
Unconventional Beatnik, Bohemian, Drop-out, Eccentric, Gonzo, Heretic, Heterodox, Informal, Irregular, Offbeat, Original, Outlandish, Outré, Raffish, Unorthodox
Unconventional *may indicate* an anagram
Unconverted Neat
Unconvincing Farfet(ched), Lame, Thin
Uncoordinated Asynergia, Ataxic, Awkward, Clumsy
Uncorrect Stet
Uncouth(ness) Backwoodsman, Bear, Crude, Gothic, Inelegant, Rough, Rube, Rude, Rugged, Uncivil
Uncover(ed) Bare, Disclose, Dismask, Expose, Inoperculate, Open, Overt, Peel, Reveal, Shave, Shill, Shuck, Uncap, Unveil
Unction, Unctuous(ness) Anele, Balm, Chrism, Extreme, Oil(y), Ointment, Oleaginous, Ooze, Smarm, Soapy
Uncultivated, Uncultured Artless, Bundu, Fallow, Ignorant, Philistine, Rude, Tramontane, Wild
Undamaged Intact, Sound, Whole
Undated Sine die
Undecided Doubtful, Moot, Non-committal, Open-ended, Pending, Pendulous, Uncertain, Wavering
Undefiled Chaste, Clean, Pure, Virgin
Undeniable Fact, Incontestable, Irrefutable
Under Aneath, Below, Beneath, Hypnotized, Sotto, Sub-, Unconscious
Underarm Axilla, Lob
Underburnt Samel
Under-butler Bread-chipper
Undercarriage Bogie, Chassis
Undercoat Base, Primer
Undercooked Rare, Raw, Samel
Undercover Espionage, Secret, Veiled
Undercurrent Acheron, Undertone, Undertow
Underdevelopment Ateleiosis

Underdog Cerberus, Loser, Victim

▶ **Undergarment** *see* UNDERWEAR

Undergo Bear, Dree, Endure, Solvate, Sustain

Undergraduate Fresher, L, Pup, Sizar, Sophomore, Student, Subsizar, Tuft

Underground (group) Basement, Catacomb, Cellar, Hell, Hypogaeous, Irgun, Kiva, Macchie, Maquis, Mattamore, Metro, Phreatic, Pict, Plutonia, Pothole, Secret, Souterrain, Subsoil, Subterranean, Subway, Tube

Undergrowth Brush, Chaparral, Firth, Frith, Scrub

Underhand Dirty, Haunch, Insidious, Lob, Oblique, Secret, Sinister, Sly, Sneaky, Surreptitious

Underlease Subtack

Underline Emphasise, Insist

Underling Bottle-washer, Cog, Inferior, Jack, Menial, Munchkin, Subordinate

Underlying Subjacent

Undermine Erode, Fossick, Sap, Subvert, Tunnel, Weaken

Undernourished Puny, Starveling

Underpass Simplon, Subway

Underside Bed, Soffit

Understand(able), **Understanding** Accept, Acumen, Agreement, Apprehend, Capeesh, Clear, Cognisable, Comprehend, Conceive, Concept, Cotton-on, Deal, Dig, Enlighten, Entente, Exoteric, Fathom, Follow, Gather, Gauge, Gaum, Geddit, Gorm, Grasp, Have, Head, Heels, Insight, Ken, Kind, Knowhow, Learn, Light, Omniscient, Pact, Plumb, Rapport, Rapprochement, Realise, Savey, Savvy, See, Sense, Sole, Substance, Tolerance, Treaty, Tumble, Twig, Uptak(e), Wisdom, Wit

Understate(d), **Understatement** Litotes, M(e)iosis, Subtle

Understood Implicit, OK, Perspicuous, Roger, Tacit, Unspoken

Understudy Deputy, Double, Stand-in, Sub

Undertake, **Undertaking** Attempt, Contract, Covenant, Enterprise, Feat, Guarantee, Pledge, Promise, Scheme, Shoulder, Venture, Warranty

Undertaker Entrepreneur, Mortician, Obligor, Sponsor, Upholder

Under-ten Unit, Yarborough

Undertone Murmur, Rhubarb, Sotto voce

Underwater Demersal

Underwear Balbriggan, Bloomers, Bodice, Body, Body stocking, Body suit, Bra(ssiere), Briefs, Broekies, Camiknickers, Camisole, Chemise, Chemisette, Chuddies, Combinations, Combs, Corset, Dainties, Drawers, (French) knickers, Frillies, Girdle, Innerwear, Jump, Linen, Lingerie, Linings, Long Johns, Pantalets, Pantaloons, Panties, Pantihose, Panty girdle, Petticoat, Scanties, Semmit, Shift, Shorts, Singlet, Skivvy, Slip, Smalls, Stays, Step-ins, Subucula, Suspenders, Tanga, Teddy, Thermal, Underdaks, Undergarments, Underpants, Undershirt, Underthings, Undies, Unmentionables, Vest, Wyliecoat, Y-fronts

Underworld Chthonic, Criminal, Hades, Hell, Lowlife, Mafia, Shades, Tartar(e), Tartarus, Tartary

Underwrite, **Underwritten** Assure, Endorse, Guarantee, Insure, Lloyds, PS

Undeserving Immeritous

Undesirable Kibitzer

Undeveloped Backward, Depauperate, Green, Inchoate, Latent, Nubbin, Ridge, Ridgil, Ridgling, Rig, Riggald, Riglin(g), Rudimentary, Seminal

Undifferentiated Thalliform, Thallus

Undigested Crude

Undignified (end) Disaster, Foot, Improper, Infra dig, Unseemly

Undiluted Neat, Pure, Sheer, Straight
Undiminished Entire, Intact, Whole
Undiplomatic Brusque, Tactless
Undisciplined Hothead, Rule-less, Rulesse, Sloppy, Unruly, Wanton
Undisclosed Hidden, In petto
Undisguised Apert, Clear, Plain
Undistinguished Plebeian
Undivided Aseptate, Complete, Entire, Indiscrete, One
Undo(ing) Annul, Defeat, Destroy, Disconnect, Downfall, Dup, Poop, Poupe, Release, Ruin, Unravel
Undoctored Neat
Undone Arrears, Left, Postponed, Ran, Ruined
Undoubtedly Certes, Ipso facto, Positively, Sure
Undress(ed) Bare, Disarray, Disrobe, En cuerpo, Expose, Négligé, Nude, Nue, Peel, Querpo, Raw, Rough, Self-faced, Spar, Strip, Unapparelled
Undulate, Undulating Billow, Nebule, Ripple, Roll, Wave
Unduly *may indicate* an anagram
Undyed Greige
Undying Amaranthine, Eternal
Unearth(ly) Astral, Dig, Discover, Disentomb, Exhumate, Indagate
Unease, Uneasiness, Uneasy Angst, Anxious, Creeps, Disquiet, Inquietude, Itchy, Malaise, Restive, Shy, Tense, The willies, Uptight, Windy, Womble-cropped
Unedifying Idle
Unembarrassed Blasé, Dégagé
Unemotional Bland, Cool, Iceberg, Matter-of-fact, Sober, Stolid
Unemployed, Unemployment Drone, Idle, Latent, Lay-off, Redundant, Residual, Stalko, Surfie
Unending Chronic, Eternal, Lasting, Sempiternal
Unenlightened Ignorant, Nighted
Unenthusiastic Damp, Tepid
Unenveloped Achlamydeous
Unequal(led) Aniso-, Disparate, Non(e)such, Scalene, Unjust
Unerring Dead, Exact, Precise
Unestablished Free
Unethical Amoral, Corrupt, Immoral
Uneven(ness) Accident, Blotchy, Bumpy, Erose, Irregular, Jaggy, Patchy, Ragged, Scratchy
Unevenly *may indicate* an anagram
Unexceptional Ordinary, Workaday
Unexpected(ly) Abrupt, Accidental, Adventitious, Fortuitous, Inopinate, Snap, Sodain(e), Sudden, Turn-up, Unawares, Unwary
Unexperienced Strange
Unexplained Obscure
Unfading Evergreen, Immarcescible
Unfailing Sure
Unfair Bias(s)ed, Crook, Dirty, Inclement, Invidious, Mean, Partial
Unfaithful Disloyal, Godless, Infidel, Traitor, Two-timing
Unfamiliar New, Quaint, Strange
Unfashionable Cube, Dowdy, Out(moded), Out-of-date, Passe, Square
Unfashionable *may indicate* 'in' to be removed
Unfavourable Adverse, Ill, Inimical, Poor, Untoward

Unfeeling Adamant, Callous, Cold, Cruel, Dead, Hard, Inhuman(e), Insensate, Robotic

Unfinished Crude, Inchoate, Raw, Scabble, Scapple, Stickit

Unfit(ting) Cronk, Disabled, Faulty, Ill, Impair, Inept, Outré, Trefa, Tre(i)f, Unable

▷ **Unfit** *may indicate* an anagram

Unfixed Isotropic, Loose

Unfledged Gull

Unflinching Fast, Staunch

Unfold Deploy, Display, Divulge, Evolve, Interpret, Open, Relate, Spread

Unforced Voluntary

Unforeseen Accident, Sudden

Unfortunate(ly) Accursed, Alack, Alas, Hapless, Ill-starred, Luckless, Shameless, Sorry, Unlucky

Unfounded Groundless

Unfriendly Aloof, Antagonistic, Asocial, Chill(y), Cold, Fraim, Fremd, Fremit, Hostile, Icy, Remote, Surly

Unfruitful Abortive, Barren, Sterile

Unfulfilled Manqué

Ungainly Awkward, Gawkish, Uncouth, Weedy

Ungenerous Small

Ungodliness, Ungodly Impiety, Pagan, Perfidious, Profane

Ungracious Cold, Offhand, Rough, Rude

Ungrammatical Anacoluthia

Ungrateful Ingrate, Snaky

Unguent Nard, Pomade, Salve

Ungulate Antelope, Dinoceras, Eland, Equidae, Hoofed, Moose, Rhino, Ruminantia, Takin, Tapir, Tylopoda

Unhappily, Unhappy, Unhappiness Blue, Depressed, Disconsolate, Dismal, Distress, Doleful, Downcast, Down-hearted, Dysphoria, Glumpish, Love-lorn, Lovesick, Miserable, Sad, Sore, Tearful, Unlief, Upset

▷ **Unhappily** *may indicate* an anagram

Unharmed Safe, Scatheless

Unharness Outspan

Unhealthy Bad, Clinic, Diseased, Epinosic, Insalubrious, Morbid, Noxious, Peaky, Prurient, Sickly

Unholy Profane, Wicked

Unhurried Patient

Uniat Maronite, Melchite

Unicorn Ch'i-lin, Coin, Monoceros, Moth, Myth, Narwhal

Unidentified Anon, Anonym(ous), Incognito, Ligure

Unification, Unify(ing) Henotic, Integrate, Risorgimento, Unite

Uniform Abolla, Battledress, Consistent, Dress, Equable, Equal, Even, Flat, Forage-cap, Homogeneous, Homomorphic, Identical, Khaki, Kit, Livery, Regimentals, Regular, Rig, Robe, Same, Sole, Standard, Steady, Strip, Unvaried

Unimaginative Banausic, Literalistic, Pedestrian, Pooter

Unimpaired Entire, Intact, Sound

Unimportant Cog, Expendable, Fiddling, Footling, Frivolous, Idle, Immaterial, Inconsequent, Inconsiderable, Insignificant, MacGuffin, Makeweight, Minnow, Minutiae, Negligible, Nugatory, Peripheral, Petty, Small-time, Trifling, Trivia(l)

Unimpressible Cynical

Uninformed Ingram
Uninhabited Bundu, Deserted, Lonely
Uninhibited Bold, Raunchy
Uninspired Humdrum, Pedestrian, Pompier, Tame
Unintelligent Dumb, Obtuse, Stupid
Unintelligible Arcane, Code, Greek
Unintentional Inadvertent
Uninterested, Uninteresting Apathetic, Bland, Dreary, Dry, Dull, Grey, Incurious, Nondescript
Uninterrupted Constant, Continuous, Incessant, Running, Steady
Uninvited Gatecrasher, Interloper, Intruder, Sorner, Trespasser, Umbra
Union(ist) Affiance, Allegiance, Alliance, Anschluss, Art, Association, Bed, Benelux, Bond, Close, Combination, Company, Concert, Confederacy, Covalency, Craft, Credit, Customs, Diphthong, Economic, Enosis, Ensemble, Equity, EU, European, Fasciation, Federal, Federation, French, Frithgild, Fusion, Group, Guild, Heterogamy, Horizontal, Impanation, Industrial, Knight of labour, Liaison, Liberal, Link-up, Management, Marriage, Match, Merger, NUM, Nuptials, NUR, NUS, NUT, Pan-American, Parabiosis, Pearl, RU, Rugby, Samiti, Sex, Sherman, Solidarity, Soviet, Splice, Sponsal, Student, Symphysis, Syngamy, Synizesis, Synostosis, Synthesis, Syssarcosis, Teamsters, > **TRADE UNION**, TU, U, UNISON, USDAW, Uxorial, Verein, Vertical, Vienna, Wedding, Wedlock, Wield, Zollverein, Zygosis
Unique(ness) Alone, A-per-se, Hacceity, Inimitable, Irreplaceable, Lone, Matchless, Nonesuch, Nonpareil, Nonsuch, One-off, Only, Peerless, Rare, Singular, Sole, Sui generis
Unisex(ual) Epicene, Hermaphrodite
Unison Chorus, Harmony, One, Sync
Unit Abampere, Absolute, Ace, Amp, Angstrom, Archine, Archiphoneme, Bar, Bargaining, Barn, Base, Baud, Becquerel, Bioblast, Biogen, Biophor(e), Bit, Brigade, Byte, Cadre, Candela, Cell, Centimorgan, Centipoise, Chaldron, Chronon, Codon, Congius, Corps, Coulomb, Crith, Cusec, Dalton, Daraf, Darcy, Debye, Degree, Denier, Derived, Dessiatine, Detachment, DIN, Dioptre, Division, Dobson, Dol, Dyne, Echelon, Ecosystem, Electromagnetic, Electron, Electrostatic, Element, Em, EMU, En, Energid, Ensuite, Episome, Erg, Erlang, Farad, Feedlot, Fermi, Field, Flight, Foot-candle, Foot-lambert, Foot-pound, Foot-ton, Fresnel, Fundamental, Gal, Gauss, Gestalt, GeV, Gigabit, Gigaflop, Gigahertz, Gigawatt, Gilbert, Glosseme, Gram, Grav, Gray, Hartree, Henry, Hertz, Hide, Hogshead, Holon, Ion, Item, Jansky, Joule, K, Kelvin, Kilderkin, Kilerg, Kilowatt, Lambert, Langley, Last, League, Lexeme, Lumen, Lux, Maceral, Magneton, Man-hour, Maxwell, Measure, Megabyte, Megahertz, Megaton, Megawatt, Megohm, Message, Metre, Mho, Micella, Micelle, Microcurie, Microinch, Micron, Mil, Module, Mole, Monad, Monetary, Mongo(e), Morgen, Morpheme, Mutchkin, Neper, Nepit, Nest, Newton, Nit, Octa, Oersted, Ohm, Okta, Organ, Panzer, Parasang, Pascal, Ped, Pennyweight, Peripheral, Phoneme, Phot, Phyton, Pixel, Ploughgate, Point, Poise, Poundal, Power, Practical, Probit, Protoplast, RA, Radian, Rem, Remen, Rep, Ro(e)ntgen, Rutherford, Sabin, Sealed, Second, Secure, Semeion, Sememe, Shed, SI, Siemens, Sievert, Singleton, Sink, Slug, Sone, Steradian, Stere, Stilb, Stock, Stoke(s), Strontium, Syllable, Syntagm(a), TA, Tagmeme, Terabyte, Terminal, Tesla, Tetrapody, Tex, Therblig, Therm, Tog, Token, Torr, Vanitory, Vanity, Var, Vara, Volt, Wall, Watt, Weber, Wing, X, Yrneh
Unitarian Arian, Paulian, Racovian, Socinian

Unite(d) Accrete, Bind, Coalesce, Combine, Concordant, Connate, Connect, Consolidate, Consubstantiate, Covalent, Fay, Federal, Federalise, Federate, Fuse, Gene, Injoint, Inosculate, Join, Kingdom, Knit, Lap, Link, Marry, Meint, Meng, Ment, Merge, Meynt, Ming, Nations, Oop, Oup, Siamese, Solid, States, Tie, > WED, Weld, Yoke

United Ireland Fine Gael

United Kingdom Old Dart, UK

Unity Harmony, One, Solidarity, Sympathy, Togetherness

Univalent Monatomic

Universal, Universe All, Catholic, Cosmos, Creation, Ecumenic(al), Emma, Expanding, General, Global, Infinite, Inflationary, Island, Macrocosm, Mandala, Microcosm, Sphere, U, Via Lactea, World(wide)

University Academe, Academy, Alma mater, Aston, Berkeley, Bonn, Brown, Campus, Civic, College, Columbia, Cornell, Exeter, Gown, Harvard, Ivy League, Open, OU, Oxbridge, Pennsylvania, Princeton, Reading, Redbrick, St Andrews, Sorbonne, Varsity, Whare wananga, Yale

Unjust(ified) Groundless, Inequity, Iniquitous, Invalid, Tyrannical

Unkempt Dishevelled, Greebo, Mal soigné, Raddled, Raggle-taggle, Scody, Scuzzy, Shaggy

Unknown Agnostic, Anon, A.N.Other, Hidden, Ign, Incog(nito), N, Nobody, Noumenon, Occult, Quantity, Secret, Soldier, Strange, Symbolic, Tertium quid, Warrior, X, Y

Unleavened Azymous

Unless Nisi, Save, Without

Unliable Exempt

Unlicensed Illicit

Unlike(ly) Difform, Disparate, Dubious, Far-fetched, Improbable, Inauspicious, Long shot, Outsider, Remote, Tall, Unlich

Unlimited Almighty, Boundless, Indefinite, Measureless, Nth, Universal, Vast

Unlisted Ex-directory

Unload Disburden, Discharge, Drop, Dump, Jettison, Land, Strip

Unlock(ed) Bald

Unlucky Donsie, Hapless, Ill(-starred), Inauspicious, Infaust, Jonah, Misadventure, Misfallen, S(c)hlimazel, Stiff, Thirteen, Untoward, Wanchancie, Wanchancy

Unman Castrate

Unmannerly Crude, Discourteous, Impolite, Low bred, Rude

Unmarried Bachelor, Common-law, Single, Spinster

Unmask Expose, Rumble

Unmatched Bye, Champion, Orra, Unique

Unmentionable(s) Bra, Foul, Secret, > UNDERWEAR, Undies

Unmindful Heedless, Oblivious

Unmistakable Clear, Manifest, Plain

Unmitigated Absolute, Arrant, Sheer, Ultra

Unmixed Me(a)re, Neat, Nett, Pure, Raw, Straight

Unmoved, Unmoving Adamant, Doggo, Firm, Serene, Static, Stolid

Unnamed Anon

Unnatural Abnormal, Affected, Cataphysical, Contrived, Eerie, Flat, Geep, Irregular, Strange

▷ **Unnaturally** *may indicate* an anagram

Unnecessary De trop, Extra, Gash, Gratuitous, Needless, Otiose, Redundant, Superfluous

Unnerve, Unnerving Discouraging, Eerie, Rattle
Unobserved Backstage, Sly, Unseen
Unobtrusive Low profile
Unoccupied Empty, Idle, Vacant, Void
Unofficial Fringe, Wildcat
Unoriginal Banal, Copy, Derivative, Imitation, Plagiarised, Slavish
Unorthodox Heretic, Heterodox, Maverick, Off-the-wall, Unconventional
Unorthodox *may indicate* an anagram
Unpaid Amateur, Brevet, Hon(orary), Outstanding, Voluntary
Unpaired Azygous, Bye
Unpalatable Acid, Bitter, Unsavoury
Unparalleled Supreme, Unique
Unpartitioned Aseptate
Unperturbed Bland, Calm, Serene
Unplanned Impromptu, Improvised, Spontaneous
Unpleasant, Unpleasant person Cow, Creep, Fink, God-awful, Grim, Grotty, Harsh, Horrible, Icky, Invidious, Nasty, Obnoxious, Odious, Offensive, Painful, Pejorative, Rank, Rebarbative, Shady, Shitty, Shocker, Snarky, Sticky, Toerag, Wart
Unploughed Lea-rig
Unpolluted Sterile
Unpopular Hat(e)able
Unpractical Futile, Orra
Unpredictable Aleatory, Dicy, Erratic, Maverick, Wild card
Unprepared Ad lib, Extempore, Impromptu, Last minute, Unready
Unpretentious Quiet
Unprincipled Amoral, Dishonest, Irregular, Reprobate, Unscrupulous
Unproductive Arid, Atokal, Atokous, Barren, Dead-head, Eild, Fallow, Futile, Lean, Poor, Shy, Sterile, Yeld, Yell
Unprofitable Bootless, Fruitless, Lean, Thankless
Unprogressive Inert, Square
Unprotected Exposed, Nude, Vulnerable
Unpublished Inedited
Unpunctual Tardy
Unqualified Absolute, Entire, Outright, Perfect, Profound, Pure, Quack, Sheer, Straight, Thorough, Total, Utter
Unquestionably, Unquestioning Absolute, Certain, Doubtless, Implicit
Unravel Construe, Disentangle, Feaze, Fray, Solve
Unready Unripe
Unreal(istic) Eidetic, En l'air, Escapist, Fake, Fancied, Illusory, Insubstantial, Mirage, Oneiric, Phantom, Phon(e)y, Planet Zog, Pseudo, Romantic, Sham, Spurious
Unreasonable, Unreasoning Absurd, Bigot, Extreme, Illogical, Irrational, Misguided, Perverse, Rabid, Steep
Unrecognised Incognito, Inconnu, Invalid, Thankless, Unsung
Unrefined Coarse, Common, Crude, Earthy, Gur, Impure, Rude, Vul(g), Vulgar
Unrehearsed Extempore, Impromptu
Unrelenting Implacable, Remorseless, Severe, Stern
Unreliable Dodgy, Dubious, Erratic, Fair-weather, Fickle, Flighty, Fly-by-night, Shonky, Unstable, Wankle, Wonky
Unremarkable Nondescript
Unremitting Dogged, Intensive

Unresponsive Cold, Frigid, Nastic, Rigor
Unrest Discontent, Ferment
Unrestrained Effusive, Extravagant, Free, Hearty, Homeric, Immoderate, Incontinent, Lax, Lowsit, Rampant, Wanton, Wild
Unreturnable Ace
Unrighteousness Adharma
Unrivalled Nonesuch
Unromantic Classic(al), Mundane
Unruffled Calm, Placid, Serene, Smooth, Tranquil
Unruly Anarchic, Bodgie, Buckie, Camstairy, Camsteary, Camsteerie, Coltish, Exception, Fractious, Lawless, Obstreperous, Ragd(e), Raged, Ragged, Rambunctious, Rampageous, Rattlebag, Riotous, Tartar, Turbulent, Turk, Wanton, Wayward, Zoo
▷ **Unruly** *may indicate* an anagram
Unsafe Deathtrap, Fishy, Insecure, Perilous, Precarious, Vulnerable
Unsatisfactory, **Unsatisfying** Bad, Lame, Lousy, Meagre, Rocky, Thin, Wanting
Unsavoury Epinosic
Unscramble Decode, Decrypt
Unscripted Ad lib
Unscrupulous Rascally, Slippery
Unseasonable, **Unseasoned** Green, Murken, Raw, Untimely
Unseat Depose, Dethrone, Oust, Overset, Overthrow, Throw
Unseemly Coarse, Improper, Incivil, Indecent, Indign, Seedy, Untoward
Unselfish Altruist, Generous
Unsent Square
Unsettle(d) Faze, Homeless, Hunky, Indecisive, Nervous, Outstanding, Queasy, Restive, Troublous
▷ **Unsettled** *may indicate* an anagram
Unsexy N, Neuter
Unsheltered Bleak, Exposed, Homeless
Unsight(ed), **Unsightly** Eyeless, Hideous, Repulsive, Ugly
Unsinning Impeccable, Pure
Unskilled Awkward, Dilutee, Gauche, Green, Inexpert, Rude
Unsmiling Agelastic
Unsociable Anchoretic, Grouchy, Solitary, Stay-at-home
Unsophisticated Alf, Boondocks, Boonies, Bushie, Cornball, Corny, Cracker-barrel, Direct, Down-home, Faux-naif, Hillbilly, Homebred, Homespun, Inurbane, Jaap, Jay, Naive, Provincial, Rube, Verdant
Unsound Barmy, Infirm, Invalid, Shaky, Wildcat, Wonky
▷ **Unsound** *may indicate* an anagram
Unsparing Severe
Unspeakable Dreadful, Ineffable, Nefandous
Unspecific General, Generic, Vague
Unspoiled, **Unspoilt** Innocent, Natural, Perfect, Pristine, Pure
Unspoken Silent, Tacit
Unstable, **Unsteady** Anomic, Astatic, Bockedy, Casual, Crank, Crank(y), Dicky, Erratic, Flexuose, Flexuous, Fluidal, Giddy, Groggy, Infirm, Insecure, Labile, Rickety, Shaky, Shifty, Slippy, Tickle, Tottery, Totty, Variable, Volatile, Walty, Wambling, Wankle, Warby, Wobbly
Unstated Concordat, Tacit, Unknown
▶ **Unsteady** *see* UNSTABLE
Unstressed Enclitic

Unstuck *may indicate* an anagram
Unsubstantial Aeriform, Airy, Flimsy, Paltry, Shadowy, Slight, Thin, Yeasty
Unsuccessful Abortive, Futile, Manqué, Vain
Unsuitable Impair, Improper, Inapt, Incongruous, Inexpedient, Malapropos, Unbecoming, Unfit
Unsupported Astylar, Floating, Unfounded
Unsure Hesitant, Tentative
Unsurpassed All-time, Best, Supreme
Unsuspecting Credulous, Innocent, Naive
Unsweetened Brut, Natural
Unsymmetrical Heterauxesis(m), Irregular, Lopsided
Unsympathetic Short shrift
Unthinking Mechanical
Untidy Daggy, Dowd(y), Frowzy, Litterbug, Ragged, Raunchy, Scruff(y), Slipshod, Slovenly, Tatty
Untidy *may indicate* an anagram
Untie Free, Undo, Unlace
Until Hasta
Untilled Fallow
Untiring Assiduous
Untold Secret, Umpteen, Unread, Unred, Vast
Untouchable Burakumin, Dalit, Harijan, Immune, Sancrosanct, Sealed
Untouched Intact, Inviolate, Pristine, Virgin
Untrained *may indicate* 'BR' to be removed
Untried New, Virgin
Untrue, Untruth Apocryphal, Eccentric, Fabrication, Faithless, False(hood), Lie, Prefabrication, Unleal
Untrustworthy Dishonest, Fickle, Fly-by-night, Mamzer, Momzer, Shifty, Sleeky, Tricky
Untypical Anomalous, Isolated, Unusual
Unused, Unusable Impracticable, New, Over, Wasted
Unusual(ly) Abnormal, Atypical, Exceptional, Extra(ordinary), Freak, New, Novel, Odd, Out-of-the-way, Outre, Particular, Rare, Remarkable, Singular, Special, > STRANGE, Unco, Unique, Untypical, Unwonted
Unusual *may indicate* an anagram
Unutterable Ineffable
Unvarying Constant, Eternal, Stable, Static, Uniform
Unveil Expose, Honour
Unvoiced Surd
Unwanted De trop, Exile, Gooseberry, Nimby, Outcast, Sorn
Unwavering Steadfast
Unwed Celibate, Single
Unwelcome, Unwelcoming Frosty, Icy, Lulu, Obtrusive, (Persona) Non grata
Unwell Ailing, Crook, Dicky, Ill, Impure, Poorly, Quazzy, Queasy, Seedy, Shouse, Toxic
Unwholesome Miasmous, Morbid, Noxious
Unwieldy Cumbersome, Elephantine
Unwilling(ness) Averse, Disinclined, Intestate, Loth, Nolition, Nolo, Obdurate, Perforce, Reluctant
Unwind Relax, Straighten, Unreave, Unreeve
Unwind *may indicate* an anagram
Unwinnable Catch 22

Unwise Foolish, Ill-advised, Impolitic, Imprudent, Inexpedient, Injudicious, Rash

Unwitting Accidental, Nescient

Unwonted Inusitate

Unworkable Impossible, Inoperable

Unworried Carefree

Unworthy Below, Beneath, Indign, Inferior

Unwritten Verbal

Unyielding Adamant, Eild, Firm, Hardline, Inexorable, Inextensible, Intransigent, Obdurate, Rigid, Steely, Stubborn, Tough, Unalterable

Unyoke Outspan

Up(on), Upturned, Upper, Uppish A, Acockbill, Afoot, Antidepressant, Arrogant, Astir, Astray, Astride, Cloud-kissing, Euphoric, Heavenward, Hep, Horsed, Incitant, Off, On, Primo, Range, Ride, Riding, Risen, Skyward, Speed, > UPPER CLASS, Vamp, Ventral

Up-anchor Atrip, Weigh

Upbeat Anacrusis, Arsis

Upbraid Abuse, Rebuke, Reproach, Reprove, Scold, Storm, Twit

Upcountry Anabasis, Inland

Update Brief, Renew, Report

Upheaval Cataclysm, Chaos, Eruption, Rummage, Seismic, Stir

▷ **Upheld** *may indicate* 'up' in another word

Uphill Arduous, Borstal, Sisyphean

Uphold Assert, Defend, Maintain

Upholstery Lampas, Moquette, Trim

Upkeep Support

Upland(s) Alps, Downs, Hilly, Wold

Uplift Boost, Edify, Elate, Elevation, Exalt, Hoist, Levitation, Sky

Upper class, Upper crust Aristocrat, County, Crachach, Nobility, Patrician, Posh, Sial, Top-hat, Tweedy, U

Upright(s), Uprightness Aclinic, Anend, Apeak, Apeek, Aplomb, Arrect, Atrip, Erect, Goalpost, Honest, Incorrupt, Jamb, Joanna, Merlon, Moral, Mullion, Orthograde, Perpendicular, Piano, Pilaster(s), Post, Rectitude, Roman, Splat, Stanchion, Stares, Stile, Stud, Vertical, Virtuous

Uprising Incline, Intifada, Rebellion, Revolt, Tumulus

Uproar(ious) Ballyhoo, Bedlam, Blatancy, Brouhaha, Charivari, Clamour, Clangour, Collieshangie, Commotion, Cry, Din, Dirdam, Dirdum, Durdum, Emeute, Ferment, Flaw, Fracas, Furore, Garboil, Hell, Hoopla, Hubbub(oo), Hullabaloo, Hurly(-burly), Katzenjammer, Madhouse, Noise, Noyes, Outcry, Pandemonium, Racket, Raird, Reird, Riotous, Roister, Romage, Rowdedow, Rowdydow(dy), Ruckus, Ruction, Rumpus, Stramash, Turmoil, Whoobub

Uproot Deracinate, Eradicate, Evict, Outweed, Supplant, Weed

Upset(ting) Aggrieve, Alarm, Bother, Capsize, Catastrophe, Choked, Coup, Cowp, Crank, Derange, Dip, Discomboberate, Discombobulate, Discomfit, Discomfort, Discommode, Disconcert, Dismay, Disquiet, Distraught, Disturb, Dod, Eat, Fuss, Inversion, Keel, Miff, Nauseative, Offend, Overthrow, Overturn, Perturb, Pip, Pother, Purl, Rattle, Rile, Ruffle, Rumple, Sad, Seel, Shake, Sore, Spill, Tapsalteerie, Tip, Topple, Trauma, Undo, Unsettled

▷ **Upset** *may indicate* an anagram; a word upside down; or 'tes'

Upshot Outcome, Result, Sequel

Upside down Inverted, Resupinate, Tapsie-teerie, Topsy-turvy

Upstart Buckeen, Jumped-up, Mushroom, Parvenu, Vulgarian

Upstart *may indicate* 'u'
Upstream Thermal
Upsurge Thrust, Waste
Uptake Shrewdness, Understanding, Wit
Up to Till, Until
Up-to-date Abreast, Contemporary, Current, Mod, New-fashioned, Right-on, State-of-the-art, Swinging, Topical, Trendy
Upwards Acclivious, Aloft, Antrorse, Cabré
Uranium Pitchblende, U, Yellowcake
Urban Civic, Megalopolis, Municipal, Town
Urbane Civil, Debonair, Refined, Townly
Urchin Arab, Brat, Crinoid, Crossfish, Cystoid, Echinoderm, Echinoidea, Echinus, Gamin, Guttersnipe, Gutty, Heart, Mudlark, Nipper, Pluteus, Ragamuffin, Sand-dollar, Sea, Sea-egg, Spatangoidea, Spatangus, Street-arab, Townskip
Urge, Urgent Admonish, Ca, Coax, Constrain, Crying, Dire, Drive, Egg, Enjoin, Exhort, Exigent, Goad, Hard, Hie, Hoick, Hunger, Hurry, Id, Immediate, Impel, Impulse, Incense, Incite, Insist(ent), Instance, Instigate, Itch, Kick, Libido, Nag, Peremptory, Persuade, Press(ing), Prod, Push, Set on, Spur, Strong, Threapit, Threepit, Wanderlust, Whig, Yen
▶**Urgent** *may indicate* 'Ur-gent', viz. Iraqi
Uriah Hittite, Humble, Umble
Urinal Bog, John, Jordan, > **LAVATORY**, Loo, Pissoir
Urinate, Urine Chamber-lye, Emiction, Enuresis, Lant, Leak, Micturition, Oliguria, Pee, Piddle, Piss, Planuria, Relieve, Slash, Stale, Strangury, Tiddle, Werris (Creek), Widdle
Urn(s), Urn-shaped Cinerarium, Ewer, Grecian, Olla, Ossuary, Samovar, Storied, Tea, Urceolate, Vase
Us 's, UK, Uns, We
Usage, Use(r), Used, Utilise Application, Apply, Avail, Boot, Consume, Custom, Deploy, Dow, > **EMPLOY**, End, Ex, Exercise, Exert, Expend, Exploit, Flesh, Habit, Hand-me-down, Inured, Manner, Ply, Practice, Sarum, Spare, Spent, Sport, Take, Tradition, Treat, Ure, Wield, With, Wont
Useful Asset, Availing, Commodity, Dow, Expedient, Invaluable
Useless Base, Bung, Cumber, Dead-wood, Dud, Empty, Futile, Gewgaw, Grotty, Idle, Inane, Ineffective, Lame, Lemon, Nonstarter, Otiose, Plug, Sculpin, Sterile, Swap, US, Vain, Void, Wet
Usher Black Rod, Chobdar, Commissionaire, Conduct(or), Doorman, Escort, Guide, Herald, Huissier, Macer, Rod, Show, Steward
Usual Common, Customary, Habit(ual), Natural, Normal, Ordinary, Routine, Rule, Solito, Stock, Typical, Wont
Usurer, Usury Gombeen, Loanshark, Moneylender, Note-shaver, Shark, Uncle
Usurp(er) Abator, Arrogate, Encroach, Invade
Ut As, Doh, Utah
Utah Ut
Utensil(s) Batterie, Battery, Chopsticks, Colander, Cookware, Corer, Fish-kettle, Fork, Funnel, Gadget, Grater, Gridiron, Implement, Instrument, Knife, Mandolin(e), Ricer, Scoop, Skillet, Spatula, Spoon, Things, Tool, Zester
▶**Utilise** *see* **USE**
Utilitarian Benthamite, Mill, Practical, Useful
Utility Elec(tricity), Expected, Gas, Public, Water
Utmost Best, Extreme, Farthest, Maximum, Nth

Utopia(n) Adland, Cloud-cuckoo-land, Ideal, Pantisocracy, Paradise, Perfect, Shangri-la

Utter(ance), Uttered, Utterly Absolute, Accent, Agrapha, Agraphon, Aread, Arrant, Cry, Dead, Deliver, Dictum, Dog, Downright, Ejaculate, Emit, Enunciate, Express, Extreme, Glossolalia, Issue, Judgement, Lenes, Lenis, Mint, Most, Oracle, Pass, Phonate, Pronounce, Pure, Quo(th), Rank, Rap, Rattle, Remark, Saw, > SAY, Sheer, Stark, State, Syllable, Tell, Vend, Vent, Very, Voice

Uvula Staphyle

Vv

V Anti, Bomb, Del, Five, Nabla, See, Sign, Verb, Verse, Versus, Victor(y), Volt, Volume

Vacancy, **Vacant** Blank, Empty, Glassy, Hole, Hollow, Inane, Place, Space, Vacuum

Vacation Holiday, Leave, Non-term, Outing, Recess, Trip, Voidance

Vaccination, **Vaccine** Antigen, Bacterin, Cure, HIB, Jenner, MMR, Sabin, Salk, Serum, Subunit

Vacillate, **Vacillating** Dither, Feeble, Hesitate, Shilly-shally, Trimmer, Wabble, Wave(r)

Vacuous Blank, Empty, Toom, Vacant

Vacuum Blank, Cleaner, Dewar, Emptiness, Magnetron, Nothing, Plenum, Thermos®, Torricellian, Ultra-high, Void

Vade-mecum Ench(e)iridion, Notebook

Vagabond Bergie, Gadling, > GYPSY, Hobo, Landlo(u)per, Rapparee, Romany, Rover, Runabout, Runagate, Tramp

Vagrant Beachcomber, Bum, Bummer, Caird, Crusty, Derro, Dosser, Drifter, Gangrel, Gang-there-out, Goliard, Gypsy, Hobo, Landlo(u)per, Lazzarone, Nomad, Patercove, Rinthereout, Rogue, Romany, Scatterling, Strag, Straggle, Stroller, Swagman, Tinker, > TRAMP, Truant, Walker

Vague(ness) Amorphous, Bleary, Blur, Confused, Dim, Equivocal, Hazy, Ill-defined, Ill-headed, Indeterminate, Indistinct, Loose, Mist, Nebulous, Shadowy, Woolly-minded

Vaguely *may indicate* an anagram

Vain Bootless, Coxcomb, Coxcomical, Egoistic, Empty, Fruitless, > FUTILE, Hollow, Idle, Peacock, Profitless, Proud, Strutting, Useless, Vogie

Vainglory Panache

Valance Pand, Pelmet

Vale Addio, Adieu, Cheerio, Coomb, Dean, Dedham, Dene, Ebbw, Enna, Glen, Ta-ta, Tempé, Valley

Valediction, **Valedictory** Apopemptic, Cheerio, Farewell

Valentine Card, Sweetheart

Valerian All-heal, Cetywall, Greek, Red, Setuale, Setwale, Setwall, Spur

Valet Aid, Andrew, Gentleman's gentleman, Jeames, Jeeves, Man, Passepartout, Quint, Servant, Skip-kennel

Valetudinarian Hypochondriac, Invalid

Valiant Brave, Doughty, Heroic, Resolute, Stalwart, Stouthearted, Wight

Valid(ate) Confirm, Establish, Just, Legal, Rational, Sound

Valise Bag, Case, Dorlach, Satchel

Valkyrie Brynhild

Valley Ajalon, Aosta, Baca, Barossa, Bekaa, Bolson, Clough, Comb(e), Coomb, Cwm, Dale, Dargle, Dean, Death, Defile, Dell, Den, Dene, Dingle, Dip, Drowned, Dry, Gehenna, Ghyll, Glen, Graben, Great Glen, Great Rift, Grindelwald, Hanging, Haugh, Heuch, Hollow, Hope, Humiliation, Hutt,

Ladin, Lagan, Lallan, Nemean, Olympia, Ravine, Rhondda, Ria, Rift, San Fernando, Silicon, Slack, Slade, Strath(spey), Tempe, Tophet, Trossachs, Umbria, Valdarno, Vale, Vallambrosa, Water

Valour Bravery, Courage, Heroism, Merit, Prowess

Valuable, Valuation, Value Absolute, Acid, Appraise, Appreciate, Apprize, Assess(ment), Asset, Bargain, Calibrate, Carbon, Checksum, Cherish, CIF, Cop, Cost, Crossover, Denomination, Equity, Esteem, Estimate, Expected, Face, Feck, Hagberg, Intrinsic, Limit, Market, Modulus, Net present, Net realizable, Nominal, Nuisance, Omnium, Par, pH, Place, Precious, Present, Price, Prize, Prys, Quartile, Rarity, Rate, Rateable, Rating, Regard, Residual, Respect, Rogue, Salt, Sentimental, Set, Steem, Stent, Store, Street, Surrender, Taonga, Time, Treasure, Valuta, > **WORTH**

Valueless Bum, Fig, Mare's nest, Orra, Useless, Worthless

Valve Acorn, Air, Aortic, Ball, Bicuspid, Bleed, Butterfly, Check, Clack, Cock, Drawgate, Dynatron, Escape, Exhaust, Flip-flop, Foot, Gate, Induction, Magnetron, Mitral, Mixing, Needle, Non-return, Pallet, Pentode, Petcock, Piston, Poppet, Pulmonary, Puppet, Radio, Resnatron, Safety, Seacock, Semilunar, Shut-off, Sleeve, Slide, Sluice, Sluicegate, Snifter, Snifting, Stopcock, Suction, Tap, Tetrode, Thermionic, Throttle, Thyratron, Triode, Turncock, Vacuum, Ventil, Vibroton

Vamoose Abscond, Decamp, Scat, Scram

Vamp Adlib, Charm, Rehash, Seduce, Siren, Strum, Twiddle

Vampire Bat, Dracula, False, Ghoul, Lamia, Lilith, Pontianak, Stringes

Van(guard) Advance, Box-car, Brake, Camper, Cart, Delivery, Dormobile®, Forefront, Foremost, Front, Furniture, Guard's, Head, Kombi®, Lead, Leader(s), Lorry, Loudspeaker, Luggage, Meat wagon, Panel, Panel-truck, Pantechnicon, Patrol-wagon, Prison, Removal, Spearhead, Truck, Ute, Wagon

Vanadium V

Vandal(ise), Vandalism Desecrate, Hooligan, Hun, Loot, Pillage, Ravage, Rough, Sab(oteur), Sack, Saracen, Skinhead, Slash, Trash

Vandyke Beard, Painter

Vane(s) Dog, Fan, Guide, Rudder, Telltale, Vexillum, Weather(cock), Web, Wind(tee), Wing

Vanessa Butterfly

Vanilla Pinole

Vanish(ed) Cease, Disappear, Disperse, Dissolve, Evanesce(nt), Evaporate, Extinct, Faint(ed), Mizzle, Slope, Unbe

Vanity Amour-propre, Arrogance, Ego, Esteem, Futility, Pomp, Pretension, Pride, Self-conceit, Self-esteem

Vanquish Beat, Conquer, Floor, Master, Overcome

Vantage (point) Ascendancy, Coign(e), Height

Vaporise, Vapour Boil, Cloud, Effluent, Fog, Fume, Halitus, Iodine, Miasma, Mist, Reek, Roke, > **STEAM**, Steme, Water

▶ **Variable, Variance, Variant, Variation** *see* **VARY**

Varicose Haemorrhoids

▶ **Varied, Variety** *see* **VARY**

▷ **Varied** *may indicate* an anagram

Variegate(d) Calico, Dappled, Flecked, Fretted, Motley, Mottle, Pied, Rainbow, Skewbald, Tissue

▷ **Variety of** *may indicate* an anagram

Various Divers(e), Manifold, Multifarious, Separate, Several, Sundry

Various years Vy

Varlet Cad, Knave

Varnish(ing) Arar, Bee-glue, Copal, Cowdie-gum, Dam(m)ar, Desert, Dope, Dragon's-blood, Glair, Japan, Lacquer, Lentisk, Nail, Nibs, Oil, Resin, Sandarac, Shellac, Spirit, Tung-oil, Tung-tree, Vernis martin, Vernissage

Vary(ing), Variable, Variance, Variant, Variation, Varied, Variety Ablaut, Aelotropy, Alter, Amphoteric, Assortment, Breed, Brew, Cepheid, Change, Chequered, Colour, Contrapuntal, Counterpoint, Daedal(e), Dedal, Dependent, Differ, Discrepancy, Diverse, Diversity, Dummy, Eclectic, Enigma, Farraginous, Fickle, Fluctuating, Form, Grid, Iid, Inconsistent, Inconstant, Independent, Isochor, Isopleth, Line, Medley, Mix, Morph, Morphosis, Multifarious, Multiplicity, Mutable, Nuance, Olio, Omniform, Orthogenesis, Parametric, Partita, Protean, Random, Remedy, Response, Smorgasbord, Sort, Species, Spice, Sport, Stirps, Stochastic, Strain, Timeserver, Tolerance, Twistor, Var, Versatile, Versiform, Version, Vicissitude, Vl, Wane, Wax, X, Y, Z

Vase Bronteum, Canopus, Cornucopia, Diota, Hydria, Jardiniere, Kalpis, Lecythus, Lekythos, Moon flask, Murr(h)a, Portland, Pot, Potiche, Stamnos, Urn, Vessel

Vassal Client, Daimio, Feoffee, Lackey, Liege, Man, Manred, Servant, Vavaso(u)r

Vast(ness) Big, Cosmic, Cyclopic, Enormous, Epic, Extensive, Huge(ous), Immense, Mighty, Monumental, Ocean, Prodigious

Vat Back, Barrel, Blunger, Chessel, Copper, Cowl, Cuvee, Fat, Girnel, Keir, Kier, Pressfat, Stand, Tank, Tan-pit, Tub, Tun, Winefat

Vatican Rome, V

Vaudeville Zarzuela

Vaughan Silurist

Vault(ed), Vaulting Arch, Barrel, Cavern, Cellar, Chamber, Clear, Cross, Crypt, Cul-de-four, Cupola, Dome, Dungeon, Fan, Firmament, Fornicate, Groin, Hypogeum, Jump, Kiva, Leap(frog), Lierne, Ossuary, Palm, Pend, Pendentive, Pole, Rib, Safe, Sepulchre, Severy, Shade, Souterrain, Tholus, Tomb, Tunnel, Underpitch, Wagon, Weem, Wine

Vault *may indicate* an anagram

Vaunt Boast, Brag, Crow

Veal Escalope, Fricandeau, Galantine, Scallop, Schnitzel, Wiener schnitzel

Vector, Vector operator Dyad, Nabla, Phasor, Polar, Radius

Veer Bag, Boxhaul, Broach, Deviate, Draw, Gybe, Splay, Swerve, Tack, Turn, Wear, Yaw

Vegetable(s) Alexanders, Allium, Artichoke, Asparagus, Aubergine, Beans, Beet(root), Borecole, Brassica, Broccoli, Cabbage, Calabrese, Calaloo, Calalu, Cardoon, Carrot, Castock, Cauliflower, Celeriac, Celery, Chard, Chicory, Chiffonade, Chive, Choko, Chufa, Cocoyam, Colcannon, Cole, Collard, Corn-on-the-cob, Coulis, Courgette, Crout, Cucumber, Custock, Daikon, Endive, Escarole, Eschalot, Fennel, Finocchio, Flora, Gherkin, Greens, Guar, Hastings, Inert, Ingan, Jerusalem artichoke, Jicama, Kale, Kohlrabi, Kumara, Kumera, Lablab, Leek, Legume(n), Lettuce, Macedoine, Mangel(-wurzel), Mangetout, Mangold, Marrow(-squash), Mirepoix, Mooli, Navew, Neep, Oca, Okra, Okro, Olitory, Onion, Orach(e), Parsnip, Pea(se), Pepper, Pimento, Plant, Potato, Pottage, Pratie, Primavera, Pulse, Pumpkin, Quinoa, Radicchio, Radish, Rapini, Ratatouille, Rocambole, Root, Rutabaga, Sabji, Salad, Salsify, Samphire, Sauce, Sauerkraut, Savoy, Scorzonera, Shallot, Sibol, Sium, Skirret, Sorrel, Spinach(-beet), Spinage, Sprouts, Spud, Squash, Succotash, Swede, Sweet corn, Sweet potato, Taro, Tomato, Tonka-bean, Triffid, Turnip, Udo, Wort, Yam, Zucchini

Vegetable extract Solanine

Vegetarian Herbivore, Maigre, Meatless, Parev(e), Parve, Pythagorean, Vegan, Veggie

Vegetate, **Vegetator**, **Vegetation** Alga, Brush, Cover, Flora, Gar(r)igue, Greenery, Herb, Maquis, Quadrat, Scrub, Stagnate, Sudd, Transect

Vehemence, **Vehement(ly)** Amain, Ardent, Fervid, Forcible, Frenzy, Heat, Hot, Intense, Violent

Vehicle Ambulance, Amtrack, Artic, Articulated, ATV, Autocycle, Autorickshaw, Brake, Brancard, Buckboard, Buggy, Bus, Cab, Camper, Car, Caravan, Carry-all, Cart, Channel, Chariot, Commercial, Conveyance, Crate, Curricle, Cycle, Dennet, Dog-cart, Dormobile®, Dray, Duck, Dune buggy, Estate car, Fiacre, Float, Fly, Four-by-four, Four-seater, Gharri, Gharry, Gladstone, Go-cart, Go-kart, Go-Ped®, Gritter, Growler, Half-track, Hansom, Hatchback, Hearse, Hovercraft, Jeep®, Jeepney, Jet-Ski, Jingle, Jinker, Jitney, Juggernaut, Kago, Kart, Koneke, Landau, Land Rover, Launch, LEM, Limber, Litter, Lorry, Machine, Means, Medium, Micro-scooter, Minibus, Minicab, Minivan, Motor, Multipurpose, Norimon, Offroad, Paddock-basher, Pantechnicon, Pedicab, Penny-farthing, People carrier, People-mover, Perambulator, Personnel carrier, Phaeton, Pick-up, Quad, Recreational, Re-entry, Ricksha(w), Runabout, Samlor, Sand-yacht, Scow, Shay, Shuttle, Sidecar, Skibob, Skidoo®, Sled(ge), Sleigh, Sno-Cat®, Snowmobile, Snowplough, Soyuz, Spider, Stanhope, Station wagon, Steam-car, Sulky, Surrey, Tarantas(s), Taxi, Tempera, Three-wheeler, Tipcart, Tip-up, Tonga, Tracked, Tractor, Trailer, Tram, Transporter, Trap, Tricar, Tricycle, Trishaw, Troika, Trolley, Trolleybus, Truck, Tuk tuk, Tumble-car(t), Tumbril, Turbo, Two-seater, Two-wheeler, Unicycle, Ute, Utility, Vahana, Velocipede, Vespa, Volante, Wagon, Wheelbarrow, Wrecker

Veil Burk(h)a, Calyptra, Chad(d)ar, Chador, Chuddah, Chuddar, Cover, Curtain, Envelop, Hejab, Hijab, Humeral, Kalyptra, Kiss-me, Lambrequin, Mantilla, Mist, Obscure, Purdah, Sacramental, Scene, Veale, Volet, Weeper, Wimple, Yashmak

Vein Artery, Azygas, Basilic, Coronary, Costa, Diploic, Epithermal, Fahlband, Gate, Hemiazygous, Innominate, Jugular, Ledge, Lode, Mainline, Media, Midrib, Mood, Nervure, Organic, Percurrent, Portal, Postcava, Precava, Pulmonary, Rake, Rib, Saphena, Sectorial, Spur, Stockwork, Stringer, Style, Thread, Varicose, Varix, Vena, Venule, Vorticose

Vellum Cutch, Kutch, Parchment

Velocity Angular, Escape, Mustard, Muzzle, Orbital, Radial, Rate, Speed, Terminal, V

Velvet Bagheera, Chenille, National, Panné, Pile, Three-pile, Velour, Velure

Venal Corruptible, Mercenary, Sale

Vend(or) Hawk, Pedlar, Rep, Sammy, Sell, Sutler

Vendetta Feud

Veneer Facade, Gloss, Varnish

Venerable Aged, August, Bede, Guru, Hoary, Sacred, Sage, Vintage

Venerate, **Veneration** Adore, Awe, Douleia, Dulia, Hallow, Homage, Idolise, Latria, Revere, Worship

Venereal NSU, VD

Venery Chase

Venetian Blind, Doge, Gobbo, Polo

Vengeance, **Vengeful** Commination, Erinyes, Reprisal, Ultion, Vindictive, Wannion, Wrack, Wreak

Venison Cervena, Deer

Venom(ous) Gall, Gila, Jamestown-weed, Jim(p)son-weed, Poison, Rancour, Solpuga, Spite, Toxic, Virus

Vent Airway, Aperture, Belch, Chimney, Emit, Express, Fumarole, Issue, Ostiole, Outlet, Smoker, Solfatara, Spiracle, Undercast, Wreak

Venter Uterus

Ventilate, Ventilator Air, Air-brick, Air-hole, Discuss, Express, Louvre, Plenum, Shaft, Voice, Windsail, Windway, Winze

Venture(d) Ante, Chance, Dare, Daur, Durst, Flutter, Foray, Handsel, Hazard, Jump, Opine, Presume, Promotion, Risk, Spec, Throw

Venue Bout, Locale, Place, Showground, Stadium, Tryst, Visne

Venus Cohog, Cytherean, Hesper(us), Love, Lucifer, Morning-star, Phosphorus, Primavera, Quahog, Rokeby, Vesper

Venus fly-trap Dionaea

Veracity, Veracious Accurate, Factual, Sincere, Truth(ful)

Veranda(h) Balcony, Gallery, Lanai, Patio, Piazza, Porch, Sleep-out, Stoep, Stoop, Terrace

Verb(al), Verbs Active, Argy-bargy, Auxiliary, Causative, Conative, Copula, Ergative, Infinitive, Intransitive, Irregular, Modal, Passive, Phrasal, Preterite, Stative, Transitive, Vb, Word-of-mouth

Verbascum Mullein

Verbatim Literally

Verbena Vervain

Verbose, Verbosity Padding, Prolix, Talkative, Wordy

Verdant Lush

Verdict Decision, Formal, Judg(e)ment, Majority, Open, Opinion, Pronouncement, Resolution, Ruling, Special

Verdigris Aeruginous, Patina

Verge Border, Brink, > EDGE, Hard shoulder, Incline, Long paddock, Rim

Verger Beadle, Pew-opener

Verify Affirm, Ascertain, Check, Confirm, Crosscheck, Prove, Validate

Verily Yea

Verisimilitude Artistic, Authenticity, Credibility

Verity Fact, Sooth, Truth

Vermifuge Cow(h)age, Cowitch

Vermilion Cinnabar, Minium, Red

Vermin(ous) Carrion, Catawampus, Lice, Mice, Ratty, > RODENT, Scum

Vermouth Absinthiated, French, It(alian), Martini®

Vernacular Common, Dialect, Idiom, Jargon, Lingo, Native, Patois

Veronica Hebe, Hen-bit, Speedwell

Verruca Wart

Versatile Adaptable, All-rounder, Flexible, Handy, Protean, Resourceful

Verse(s), Versed Dactyl, Free, Linked, Logaoedic, Passus, Poetry, Political, Reported, > RHYME

VERSES

1 letter:	4 letters:	Epos	Sijo
V	Awdl	Hymn	Song
	Blad	Neck	Vers
	Duan	Poem	
3 letters:	Epic	Rime	
Fit			

Versed sine

5 letters:
Blank
Blaud
Canto
Comus
Epode
Gazal
Haiku
Hokku
Ionic
Lyric
Meter
Poesy
Renga
Rubai
Spasm
Stave
Tanka
Tract
Triad

Miurus
Octave
Pantun
Rondel
Scazon
Stanza
Strain
Tercet

6 letters:
Adonic
Ballad
Burden
Ghazal
Ghazel
Gnomic
Haikai
Heroic
Jingle
Laisse

7 letters:
Alcaics
Couplet
Dimeter
Elegiac
Epigram
Fabliau
Huitain
Leonine
Pantoum
Pennill
Prosody
Pythian
Rondeau
Sapphic
Sestina
Sestine
Sixaine
Stiches
Strophe
Tiercet
Triolet
Tripody

8 letters:
Cinquain
Clerihew
Doggerel
Glyconic
Kyrielle
Madrigal
Nonsense
Pindaric
Quatrain
Rhopalic
Rove-over
Rubaiyat
Scansion
Senarius
Sirvente
Terzetta
Trimeter
Tristich
Versicle

9 letters:
Amphigory
Asclepiad
Beatitude
Dithyramb
Ditrochee
Goliardic
Hexameter
Macaronic
Monometer
Octameter

Octastich
Saturnian
Stornello
Terza rima
Vers libre

10 letters:
Asynartete
Catalectic
Cynghanedd
Fescennine
Mock-heroic
Ottava rima
Pennillion
Pentameter
Rhyme-royal
Serpentine
Tetrameter
Tetrastich
Villanelle

11 letters:
Acatalectic
Alexandrine
Hudibrastic
Riding-rhyme
Septenarius

12 letters:
Archilochian
Hudibrastics

Versed sine Sagitta
Versifier Lyricist, Poetaster, Rhymer, Rhymester
Version Account, Adaptation, Authorised, Cover, Edition, Form, Paraphrase, Rede, Rendering, Rendition, Revision, Translation
Vertebra(e), Vertebrate Agnathan, Amniote, Amphioxus, Ascidian, Atlas, Axis, Bone, Centrum, Cervical, Chordae, Cyclostome, Dorsal, Gnathostome, Ichthyopsida, Lamprey, Lumbar, Placoderm, Reptile, Sauropsida, Spondyl, Tetrapod, Tunicata, Vermis
Vertex Apex, Crest, Crown, Summit, Zenith
Vertical Apeak, Apeek, Atrip, Erect, Lapse, Montant, Ordinate, Perpendicular, Plumb, Prime, Sheer, Standing, Stemmed, Stile, Upright
Vertigo Dinic, Dizziness, Fainting, Giddiness, Megrim, Nausea, Staggers, Whirling
Verve Dash, Energy, Go, Panache, Vigour
Very (good, well) A1, Ae, Assai, Awfully, Boffo, Bonzer, Boshta, Boshter, Dashed, Def, Ever, Extreme(ly), Fell, Frightfully, Gey, Grouse, Heap, Hellova, Helluva, Highly, Jolly, Light, Mighty, Molto, Much, OK, Opt, Precious, Precise, Purler, Real, Right, Self same, So, Sore, Stinking, Très, Utter, V, VG, Way
Vesicle Ampul, Bladder

Vespers Evensong, Lychnic, Placebo, Sicilian
Vessel > BOAT, Capillary, Container, Craft, Dish, Pressure, Receptacle, Seed,
> SHIP, Utensil, Vascular

VESSELS

3 letters:
Bin
Cog
Cup
Dow
Fat
Obo
Pan
Pig
Pyx
Tub
Urn
Vas
Vat

4 letters:
Bowl
Buss
Cask
Cowl
Dhow
Etna
Font
Grab
Horn
Lota
Olpe
Skin
Snow
Vase
Vein
Vena
Vial
Zulu

5 letters:
Aorta
Blood
Cogue
Crare
Crewe
Crock
Cruet
Cupel
Dandy
Dixie

Gourd
Ketch
Laver
Lotah
Mazer
Oiler
Pokal
Quart
Round
Scoop
Shell
Stean
Steen
Stoop
Stoup
Tazza
Varix
Xebec
Zabra

6 letters:
Aludel
Argyle
Argyll
Artery
Beaker
Bicker
Bouget
Bucket
Carafe
Carboy
Chatty
Copper
Crayer
Dinghy
Dogger
Dolium
Elutor
Flagon
Frigot
Galiot
Galley
Goblet
Goglet
Guglet
Humpen

Kettle
Lorcha
Mortar
Noggin
Retort
Rumkin
Sampan
Sconce
Shippo
Situla
Steane
Tassie
Trough
Tureen
Venule
Wherry

7 letters:
Amphora
Ampulla
Canteen
Chalice
Cistern
Costrel
Creamer
Cresset
Cuvette
Cyathus
Dredger
Drifter
Felucca
Frigate
Galleon
Galliot
Gurglet
Jugular
Mudscow
Patamar
Pinnace
Pitcher
Polacca
Precava
Steamer
Tankard
Terreen
Washpot

8 letters:
Calabash
Cauldron
Ciborium
Colander
Coolamon
Crucible
Cucurbit
Decanter
Figuline
Galleass
Galliass
Gallipot
Gallivat
Jerrican
Longboat
Monteith
Pancheon
Panchion
Pannikin
Sinusoid

9 letters:
Alcarraza
Autoclave
Bucentaur
Calandria
Casserole
Cullender
Destroyer
Hydrofoil
Tappit-hen

10 letters:
Bathyscaph
Deep-sinker
Jardinière
Triaconter

11 letters:
Aspersorium
Bathyscaphe

12 letters:
Lachrymatory

Vest Beset, Confer, Gilet, Modesty, Semmit, Singlet, Skivvy, Spencer, Sticharion, String, Undercoat, Undershirt, Waistcoat

Vestibule Anteroom, Atrium, Entry, Exedra, Foyer, Hall, Lobby, Narthex, Oeil-de-boeuf, Porch, Portico, Pronaos, Tambour

Vestige Hint, Mark, Mention, Shadow, Sign, Trace

Vestment Alb, Canonicals, Chasuble, Chimar, Chimer(e), Cotta, Dalmatic, Ephod, Fannel, Fanon, Garb, > GARMENT, Maniple, Mantelletta, Omophorion, Pallium, Parament, Ph(a)elonian, Pontificals, Raiment, Rational, Rochet, Rocquet, Sakkos, Sticharion, Stole, Surplice, Tunic(le)

Vestry Common, Sacristy, Select

Vet(ting), Veterinary, Vets Check, Doc(tor), Examine, Ex-serviceman, Inspect, OK, Screen, Veteran, Zoiatria, Zootherapy

Vetch Bitter, Ers, Fitch, Kidney, Locoweed, Milk, Tare, Tine

Veteran BL, Expert, GAR, Master, Oldster, Old sweat, Old-timer, Old 'un, Retread, Seasoned, Soldier, Stager, Stalwart, Stalworth, Vet, War-horse

▷ **Veteran** *may indicate* 'obsolete'

Veto Ban, Bar, Debar, Item, Local, Negative, Pocket, Reject, Taboo, Tabu

Vex(ing), Vexed Anger, Annoy, Bother, Chagrin, Debate, Fret, Gall, Grieve, Harass, Irritate, Madden, Mortify, Pester, Rankle, Rile, Sore, Spite, Tease, Torment, Trouble, Worrisome

Vexation(s) Barrator, Chagrin, Drat, Grief, Nuisance, Pique, Spite, Trouble

Vexatious Trying

Vexillum Web

Via By, Per, Through

Viable Economic, Going, Healthy, Possible

Vial Spirit-level

Viand Cate

Vibrant, Vibration Chatter, Energetic, Harmonogram, Plangent, Resonant, Rumble, Uvular

Vibrate, Vibration(s) Atmosphere, Diadrom, Dinnle, Dirl, Flutter, Fremitus, Hotter, Jar, Judder, Oscillate, Pulse, Quake, Resonance, Seiche, Shimmy, Shudder, Thrill, Throb, Tingle, Tremble, Tremor, Trill, Twinkle, Wag, Whir(r)

Viburnum Opulus

Vicar Apostolic, Bray, Choral, Elton, Forane, General, Incumbent, Lay, Pastoral, Plenarty, Primrose, Rector, Rev(erend), Trimmer

Vice Clamp, Crime, Deputy, Eale, Evil, Greed, Iniquity, Instead, Jaws, Regent, Second (in command), > SIN

Vice-president Croupier, Veep

Viceroy Khedive, Nawab, Provost, Satrap, Willingdon

Vichy water Eau

Vicinity Area, Environs, Hereabouts, Locality, Neighbourhood, Region

Vicious Flagitious, Hotbed

Victim Abel, Angel, Butt, Casualty, Dupe, Fashion, Frame, Host, Lay-down, Mark, Martyr, Nebbich, Neb(b)ish, Pathic, Patsy, Pigeon, Prey, Quarry, Sacrifice, Scapegoat

Victor(y) Banzai, Beater, Cadmean, Captor, Champ(ion), Conqueror, Conquest, Epinicion, Epinikion, Flagship, Fool's mate, Gree, Gris, Hallelujah, Hugo, Jai, Kobe, Landslide, Lepanto, Ludorum, Mature, Moral, Nike, Palm, Philippi, Pyrrhic, Runaway, Scalp, Signal, Triumph, VE (day), Vee, Vic, Walk-away, Walkover, Win(ner)

Victoria(n) Aussie, Plum, Prig, Station

Victualler Caterer, Grocer, Licensed, Purveyor, Supplier, Vivandiere

Video Digital, Interactive, Laser vision, Minitel, Pixelation, Promo, Reverse, Scratch, Still, Vera

Vie Compete, Contend, Emulate, Strive

Vienna Wien

Vietnamese Cham

View(er) Aim, Angle, Aspect, Belief, Bird's eye, Cineaste, Consensus, Consider, Cosmorama, Dekko, Dogma, Doxy, Endoscope, Exploded, Eye, Facet, Gander, Glimpse, Grandstand, Helicopter, Idea, Introspect, Kaleidoscope, Landscape, Line, Notion, Opinion, Optic®, Outlook, Pan, Panorama, Point, Private, Profile, > **PROSPECT**, Scan, Scape, Scene(ry), See, Sight, Skyscape, Slant, Specular, Standpoint, Stereoscope, Strain, Synop(sis), Tenet, Terrain, Thanatopsis, Theory, Vantage-point, Veduta, Vista, Visto, Watch, Witness, Worm's eye

Viewpoint Attitude, Belvedere, Grandstand, Perspective, Sight

Vigil, Vigilant(e) Awake, Aware, Deathwatch, Eve, Guardian angel, Hawk-eyed, Lyke-wake, Pernoctate, Wake, Wake-rife, Wary, Watch, Whitecap

Vignette Print, Profile, Sketch

Vigorous(ly), Vigour Athletic, Bant, Billy-o, Billy-oh, Birr, Blooming, Brisk, Con brio, Drastic, Elan, Emphatic, Energetic, Flame, Forceful, Furioso, Go, Green, Heart(y), Heterosis, Hybrid, Lush, Lustihood, Lusty, P, Pep, Pith, Potency, Punchy, Pzazz, Racy, Rank, Robust, Round, Rude, Spirit, Sprack, Sprag, Steam, Sthenic, Stingo, Strength, Strong, Thews, Tireless, Tone, Tooth and nail, Trenchant, Vegete, Vim, Vitality, Vivid, Voema, Zip

> **Vigorously** *may indicate* an anagram

Viking Dane, Norseman, Rollo, R(y)urik, Varangian

Vile Base, Corrupt, Depraved, Dregs, Durance, Earthly, Mean, Offensive, Scurvy, Vicious

Vilify Smear

Villa Bastide, Chalet, Dacha, House

Village Aldea, Auburn, Burg, Clachan, Corporate, Dorp, Endship, Global, Gram, Greenwich, Hamlet, Kaik, Kainga, Kampong, Kraal, Manyat(t)a, Mir, Pueblo, Rancheria, Rancherie, Shtetl, Skara Brae, Thorp(e), Ujamaa, Vill, Wick

Villain(y) Baddy, Bluebeard, Bravo, Crim(inal), Crime, Dastard, Dog, Heavy, Iago, Knave, Macaire, Miscreant, Mohock, Nefarious, Ogre, Reprobate, Rogue, Scab, Scelerat, Scoundrel, Skelm, Tearaway, Traitor

Villein Bordar, Churl, Serf

Vim Go, Vigour, Vitality, Zing

Vincent Van Gogh

Vindicate, Vindication Absolve, Acquit, Apologia, Avenge, Clear, Compurgation, Darraign(e), Darrain(e), Darrayn, Defend, Deraign, Justify

Vindictive Hostile, Malevolent, Repay(ing), Spiteful, Vengeful

Vine(yard) Ampelopsis, Ayahuasco, Balloon, Balsam apple, Bine, Bush rope, Chateau, Clinging, Clos, Colocynth, Cru, Cubeb, Cypress, Dodder, Domaine, Grapery, Hop, Idaean, Kangaroo, Kudzu, Lawyer, Liana, Martha's, Matrimony, Muskmelon, Naboth's, Quinta, Russian, Sarsaparilla, Stephanotis, Supplejack, Swallowwort, Trumpet, Turpeth, Vitis, Wonga-wonga, Yam, Yquem

Vinegar Acetic, Acetum, Alegar, Balsam, Eisel(l), Esile, Malt, Oxymel, Tarragon, Wine, Wood

Vintage Classic, Crack, Cru, Old, Quality

Viola, Violet African, Alto, Amethyst, Archil, Crystal, Dame's, Dog, Dog's tooth, Gamba, Garden, Gentian, Gridelin, Hesperis, Ianthine, Indole, Ionone, Kiss-me, Mauve, Methyl, Neapolitan, Orchil, Pansy, Parma, Prater,

Saintpaulia, Shrinking, Sweet, Tenor, Visual, Water

Violate, Violating, Violation Abuse, Breach, Contravene, Defile, Desecrate, Fract, Infraction, > **INFRINGE**, March-treason, Outrage, Peccant, Rape, Ravish, Stuprate, Transgress, Trespass

Violence, Violent(ly) Amain, Attentat, Berserk, Brutal, Drastic, Extreme, Fierce, Flagrant, Force, Frenzied, Furious, Heady, Het, High, Hot, Mighty, Onset, Rage, Rampage, Rampant, Rough, Rough stuff, Rude, Severe, Slap, Stormy, Ta(r)tar, Tearaway, Terrorism, Thuggery, Tinderbox, Vehement, Vie, Wrath

▸ **Violet** *see* VIOLA

Violin(ist), Violin-maker, Violin-shaped Alto, Amati, Cremona, Fiddle, Griddle, Gu(e), Guarneri(us), Guarnieri, Kennedy, Kit, Kubelik, Leader, Luthier, Menuhin, Nero, Oistrakh, Paganini, Pandurate, Rebeck, Rote, Stradivarius

VIP Bashaw, Bigshot, Bigwig, Brass, Cheese, Cob, Effendi, Envoy, Grandee, Imago, Magnate, Magnifico, Mugwump, Nabob, Nib, Nob, Pot, Snob, Someone, Swell, Tuft, Tycoon, Worthy

Viper Asp, Gaboon, Horned, Pit, Rattlesnake, Russell's, Sand, Saw-scaled, > **SNAKE**, Traitor, Villain

Virago Amazon, Battle-axe, Beldam(e), Harpy, Shrew

Virgil Maro

Virgin(al), Virginity Airline, Blessed, Celibate, Chaste, Cherry, Extra, Intact, Maiden, Maidenhead, Maidenhood, May, New, Parthenos, Pietà, Pucel(l)age, Pucelle, Pure, Queen, Snood, Tarpeia, Untainted, Vestal

Virginia(n) Creeper, Old Dominion, Tuckahoe, Va, Wade

Virile, Virility Energetic, Machismo, Macho, Manly, Red-blooded

Virtu Curio

Virtue(s), Virtuous Angelic, Assay-piece, Attribute, Cardinal, Caritas, Charity, Chastity, Continent, Dharma, Efficacy, Ethical, Excellent, Faith, Fortitude, Good, Goody-goody, Grace, Hope, Justice, Moral(ity), Natural, Patience, Plaster-saint, Principal, Prudence, Qua, Say-piece, Temperance, Theological, Upright, Worth

Virtuosity, Virtuoso Artist, Bravura, Excellence, Executant, Maestro, Paganini, Savant

Virulent Acrimonious, Deadly, Hostile, Malign, Noxious, Toxic, Vitriolic, Waspish

Virus Antigen, Arbovirus, Bacteriophaze, Capsid, Contagium, Coxsackie, EB, Ebola, Echo, Epstein-Barr, Filterable, Fowlpest, Germ, Granulosis, Hantavirus, Herpes, HIV negative, HIV positive, Lassa, Latent, Leaf-mosaic, Lentivirus, Michelangelo, Oncogen, Parainfluenza, Parvo(virus), Pathogen, Peach-yellow, Picornavirus, Polyoma, Prophage, Reovirus, Retrovirus, Rhabdovirus, Rhinovirus, Ross River, Rotavirus, SARS, Shingles, Slow, Street, SV40, Varicella, Virion, Zoster

Visa Transit

Viscera Bowels, Entrails, Giblets, Guts, Harigal(d)s, Haslet, Innards, Omentum, Splanchnic, Umbles, Vitals

Viscount Vis

Viscous (liquid), Viscosity Glaireous, Gluey, Gummy, Slab, Sticky, Stoke, Tacky, Tar, Thick, Thixotropic

Visible Clear, Conspicuous, Evident, Explicit, Obvious

Visigoth Asaric

Vision(ary) Aery, Aisling, Apparition, Beatific, Bourignian, Double, Dream(er), Emmetropia, Fancy, Idealist, Image, Kef, Moonshine, Mouse-sight, Mystic, Ocular, Phantasm(a), Phantom, Pholism, Photopia, Rainbow-chaser,

Romantic, Seeing, Seer, Sight, Stereo, Sweven, Tunnel, Twenty-twenty
Visit(or) Affliction, Alien, Caller, ET, Event, First-foot, Frequent, Gam, Guest, Habitue, Haunt, Health, Kursaal, Manuhic, Prison, See, Sightseer, Stranger, Take
Visor, **Vizor** Eyeshade, Mesail, Mezail, Umbrel, Umbr(i)ere, Umbril, Vent(ayle)
Vista Enfilade, Outlook, Scene, View
Visual(ise) Envisage, Ocular, Optical, Visible
Vital(ity) Alive, Central, Critical, Crucial, Energy, Esprit, Essential, Existent, Foison, Gusto, Indispensable, Key, Kick, Life-blood, Linchpin, Lung, Mites, Momentous, Necessary, Oomph, Organ, Pizzazz, Salvation, Sap, Viable, Vigour, Zing, Zoetic
Vitals Numbles, Umbles, Viscera
Vitamin(s) A, Aneurin, Axerophthol, B, Bioflavonoid, Biotin, C, Calciferol, Calcitriol, Citrin, Cobalamin, D, E, Ergocalciferol, Folacin, H, Inositol, K, Linoleic, Menadione, Menaquinone, Niacin, P, Pan(to)thenol, Phylloquinone, Phytonadione, Pyridoxine, Retinene, Retinol, Riboflavin, Ribose, Thiamin(e), Tocopherol, Torulin, Tretinoin
Vitiate(d) Flaw(ed)
Vitreous Glassy, Hyaline
Vitriol(ic) Acid, Acrimonious, Biting, Blue, Caustic, Green, Mordant, White
Vituperate Abuse, Berate, Castigate, Censure, Defame, Inveigh, Lash, Rail, Scold
Viva Oral
Vivacity, **Vivacious** Animation, Brio, Esprit, Exuberant, Spirit, Verve
Vivid Bright, Brilliant, Dramatic, Eidectic, Fresh, Graphic, Keen, Live, Pictorial, Picturesque, Sharp, Violent
Vixen Catamaran, Harridan, Shrew, Virago
Viz Sc, Videlicet
Vizier Pheazar, Wazir
Vizor *see* VISOR
Vocabulary Active, Glottochronology, Idiolect, Idioticon, Jargon, (Kata)kana, Lexicon, Lexis, Meta-language, Nomenclator, Passive, Wordbook
Vocal(isation), **Vocalist** Articulate, Eloquent, Minstrel, Oral, Singer, Sprechgesang
Vocation Call, Métier, Mission, Priesthood, Profession, Shop
Vociferous(ly) Clamant, Loud, Ore rotundo, Strident
Vogue Chic, Day, > FASHION, It, Mode, Rage, Style, Ton
Vogul Ugrian, Ugric
Voice(d) Active, Air, Alto, Ancestral, Bass, Chest, Contralto, Countertenor, Edh, Emit, Eth, Express, Falsetto, Glottis, Harp, Head, Lyric, Mezzo-soprano, Mouth, Opinion, Passive, Phonic, Pipe, Presa, Quill, Say, Sonant, Soprano, Speak, Spinto, Sprechstimme, Steven, Syrinx, Tais(c)h, Tenor, Throat, Tone, > TONGUE, Treble, Utter, White
Voiceless Aphonia, Aphony, Dumb, Edh, Eth, Mute, Silent, Tacit
Void Abyss, Annul, Belch, Blank, Chasm, Defeasance, Defecate, Diriment, Empty, Evacuate, Gap, Hollow, Inane, Invalid, Irritate, Lapse, Nullify, Quash, Space, Vacuum
Volatile Excitable, Explosive, Latin, Live(ly), Mercurial, Temperamental, Terpene
Volcanic, **Volcano** Aa, Agglomerate, Amygdale, Andesite, Aniakchak, Antisana, Aragats, Ararat, Askja, Aso(san), Cameroon, Chimborazo, Citlaltépetl, Comoros, Cone, Conic, Corcovado, Cotopaxi, Demavend, Egmont, El Misti,

Vole | 756

Erclyas Dagi, Erebus, Etna, Fernando de Noronha, Fuji, Fumarole, Haleakala, Hekla, Hornito, Huasca(ra)n, Ice, Idocrase, Igneous, Ignimbrite, Iliamna, Ischia, Iwo Jima, Katmai, Kauai, Kazbek, Kilimanjaro, Krakatoa, Lassen Peak, Lipari, Maui, Mauna Kea, Mauna Loa, Mayon, Misti, Mofette, Montserrat, Mount Erebos, Mount Katmai, Mount St Helens, Mt Suribachi, Mud, National Park, Nevada de Colima, Nevada de Toluca, Nyamuragira, Nyiragongo, Obsidian, Okmok, Olympus Mons, Paricutin, Pele, Pelée, Pico de Teide, Pico de Teyde, Plinian, Popocatepetl, Pozz(u)olana, Pumice, Puy, Puzzolana, Ruapehu, St Helena, St Helens, St Kilda, Salse, Sandblow, Semeroe, Semeru, Shield, Soffioni, Solfatara, Soufrière Hills, Stromboli, Taal, Tambora, Tangariro, Taraniki, Thira, Tolima, Trass, Tuff, Vesuvius, Warrumbungle Range

Vole Arvicola, Muskrat, Musquash, Ondatra
Volition Velleity, Will
Volley Barrage, Boom, Broadside, Platoon, Salvo, Tirade, Tire
Volt(age) BeV, Bias, HT
Voltaire Arouet
Volte face U-turn
Voluble Fluent, Glib
Volume Band, Barrel, Book, Bushel, Capacity, CC, Code(x), Content, Critical, Cubage, Gallon, Hin, Loudness, Mass, Ml, Molecular, Omnibus, Peck, Pint, Quart, Quart(o), Roll, Roul(e), Size, Space, Specific, Stere, Swept, Tidal, Tome, Vol
Voluntary, Volunteer Enlist, Fencible, Free, Free-will, Honorary, Offer, Postlude, Reformado, Spontaneous, Tender, Tennessee, Terrier, TN, Ultroneous, Yeoman
Voluptuary, Voluptuous Carnal, Hedonist, Houri, Luscious, Sensuist, Sensuous, Sybarite
Volute Helix, Roll
Vomit(ing) Anacatharsis, Barf, Boak, Boke, Cascade, Cat, Chunder, Disgorge, Egist, Egurgitate, Emesis, Fetch-up, Haematemesis, Honk, Keck, Parbreak, Posset, Puke, Ralph, Regurgitate, Retch, Rolf, Spew, Throw up, Upchuck
Voodoo Charm, Jettatura, Kurdaitcha, Macumba, Mambo, Obeah, Sorcery, Zombi(e)
Voracious, Voracity Bulimia, Edacity, Gluttony, Greed, Ravenous, Serrasalmo
Vortex Charybdis, Eddy, Gyre, Trailing, Whirlpool
Votary Adherent, Cenobite, Devotee, Disciple, Fan, Nun, Swinger, Zealot
Vote(r), Votes, Voting Alternative, Aye, Ballot, Block, Card, Casting, Choose, Colonist, Coopt, Cross, Cumulative, Division, Donkey, Fag(g)ot, Floating, Franchise, Free, Grey, Informal, Mandate, Nay, No, Opt, People, Placet, Plebiscite, Plump, Plural, Poll, Postal, Pot-wabbler, Pot-waller, Pot-walloner, Pot-walloper, Pot-wobbler, PR, Preferential, Referendum, Return, Scrutiny, Side, Straw(-poll), Suffrage, Swinging, Tactical, Ten-pounder, Theta, Ticket, Token, Transferable, Voice, X, Yea, Yes
Vote-catcher Pork
Vouch(er), Vouchsafe Accredit, Assure, Attest, Book token, Chit, Coupon, Endorse, Gift, Guarantee, Luncheon, Meal-ticket, Receipt, Ticket, Token, Warrant
Voussoir Quoin, Wedge
Vow Baptismal, Behight, Behot(e), Earnest, Ex voto, Hecht, Hest, I do, Nuncupate, > OATH, Pledge, Plight, Promise, Simple, Solemn, Swear, Troth, Vum
Vowel(s) Ablaut, Anaptyxis, Aphesis, Breve, Cardinal, Diphthong, Gradation,

Indeterminate, Monophthong, Mutation, Point, Rhyme, S(c)hwa, Seg(h)ol, Svarabhakti, Triphthong

Voyage(r) Anson, Course, Cruise, Launch, Maiden, Passage, Peregrinate, Sinbad, Travel

Voyeur Scopophiliac

VTOL Convertiplane

Vulcan(ite) Blacksmith, Ebonite, Fire, Mulciber, Spock, Wayland

Vulgar(ian) Banausic, Barbaric, Base, Blatant, Blue, Brassy, Buffoon, Canaille, Cheap, Cit, Coarse, Common, Crude, Demotic, Flash, Forward, Gaudy, General, Gent, Gross, Heel, Hussy, Ignorant, Indecent, Laddish, Lewd, Low(-life), Naff, Obscene, Ostentatious, Pandemian, Plebby, Plebeian, Popular, Proletarian, Raffish, Riff-raff, Scaff, Tacky, Tawdry, Threepenny, Tiger, Tink, Upstart, Vulg

Vulnerable Exposed, Open, Susceptible, Unguarded, Wide-open

Vulture Aasvogel, Bird, Buzzard, California (condor), Condor, Culture, Falcon, Gallinazo, Gier, Griffon, Gripe, Grype, Lammergeier, Lammergeyer, Ossifrage, Predator, Turkey, Urubu, Zopilote

Ww

W Watt, West, Whisky, Women

Wad(ding) Batting, Lump, Pad, Pledget, Roll, Swab, Wodge

Waddle Toddle, Waggle

Waddy Club, Cowboy, Stick

Wade(r), Wading Antigropelo(e)s, Curlew, Dikkop, Egret, Flamingo, Gallae, Godwit, Grallatorial, Greenshank, Heron, Ibis, Jacksnipe, Limpkin, Oyster-catcher, Paddle, Phalarope, Plodge, Sarus, Seriema, Shoebill, Splodge, Stilt(bird), Terek, Virginia

Waesucks Ewhow, O(c)hone

Wafer Biscuit, Cracker, Crisp, Gaufer, Gaufre, Gofer, Gopher, Host, Papad, Seal

Waff Flap, Flutter, Wave

Waffle Adlib, Blather, Equivocate, Gas, Gaufer, Gaufre, Gofer, Gopher, Hedge, Poppycock, Prate, Rabbit

Waft(ing) Airborne, Aura, Blow, Drift, Float

Wag(gish), Waggle Arch, Card, Comedian, Facetious, Joker, Lick, Niddle-noddle, Nod, Rogue, Shake, Sway, Wit(snapper), Wobble

Wage(s) Ante, Fee, Hire, Living, Meed, Minimum, Pay, Portage, Practise, Prosecute, Rate, Salary, Screw, Subsistence

Wage-earner Breadwinner, Employee, Proletariat(e)

Wager Ante, Back, > BET, Gamble, Lay, Pascal's, Stake, Wed

Wagon(er) Ar(a)ba, Aroba, Bootes, Boxcar, Brake, Buck, Buckboard, Buggy, Caisson, Carriage, Cart, Cattle truck, Chuck, Cocopan, Conestoga, Corf, Covered, Democrat, Dray, Flatcar, Fourgon, Gambo, Go-cart, Hopper, Hutch, Low-loader, Mammy, Paddy, Palabra, Patrol, Plaustral, Police, Prairie schooner, Rave, Reefer, Rubberneck, Shandry, Station, Tank, Tartana, Telega, Tender, Trap, Trekker, Truck, Van, Victoria, Wain, Water

Waif Arab, Foundling, Jetsam, Stray, Victoria, Wastrel, Water, Weft

Wail(er) Banshee, Bawl, Blubber, Howl, Keen, Lament, Moan, Skirl, Threnody, Threnos, Ululate, Vagitus, Wah-wah, Yammer

Wain Cart, Dray, Wagon

Waist(band) Belt, Cummerbund, Girdlestead, Girth, Hour-glass, Middle, Midship, Obi, Sash, Shash, Wasp, Zoster

Waistcoat Gilet, Jerkin, Lorica, MB, Pressure, Sayon, Shawl, Vest, Weskit

Wait(er) Abid(e), Ambush, Barista, Bide, Busboy, Butler, Buttle, Carhop, Commis, Cupbearer, Dally, Delay, Estragon, Expect, Flunkey, Frist, Garçon, Hang on, Hesitate, Hover, Interval, Khidmutgar, Lime, Linger, Lurch, Maitre d', Maitre d'hôtel, Minority, Omnibus, Pannier, Pause, Remain, Serve(r), Sommelier, Stay, Steward, Suspense, Taihoa, Tarry, Tend(ance), Tray, Vladimir, Wine, Won

Waitress Hebe, Miss, Mousme(e), Nippy, Server

Waive Abandon, Defer, Overlook, Postpone, Relinquish, Renounce

Wake(n) Abrade, Abraid, Abray, Aftermath, Alert, American, Animate, Arouse, Astern, Deathwatch, Excite, Hereward, Keen, Knock-up, Like, Lyke, Prod, Rear,

> **ROUSE**, Train, Wash

Waldo Emerson

Wale(r) Prop, Ridge, Weal

Wales Cambria, Cymru, Dyfed, Principality

Walk(er), **Walking**, **Walkabout**, **Walkway** Alameda, Alley, Alure, Amble, Ambulate, Arcade, Berceau, Birdcage, Charity, Cloister, Clump, Constitutional, Dander, Dauner, Emu, Esplanade, EVA, Expatiate, Flanerie, Frescade, Gait, Gallery, Ghost, Go, Gradient, Gressorial, Heel and toe, Hike, Hookey, Hump, Lambeth, Leg, Lumber, Mainstreeting, Mall, March, Mince, Mosey, Pace, Pad, Pasear, Paseo, Passage, Path, Ped, Perambulate, Pergola, Pipe-opener, Prance, Prom(enade), Rack, Ramble, Rampart, Random, Routemarch, Sashay, Shamble, Sidle, Slommock, Space, Spanish, Sponsored, Stalk, Step, Striddle, Stroll, Strut, Stump, Terrace, Toddle, Tramp, Trash, Travolator, Tread, Trog, Truck, Trudge, Turn, Wend, Widow's, Xyst

Walk-over Doddle, Pie, Scratch

Wall Antonine, Bail, Bailey, Barrier, Berlin, Berm, Cavity, Cell, Chinese, Climbing, Countermure, Curtain, Dado, Dam, Dike, Dry-stone, Enceinte, Epispore, Exine, Fail-dike, Fourth, Fronton, Frustule, Gable, Great, Hadrian's, Hanging, Hangman, Head, Immure, Intine, Mahjongg, Mani, Merlon, Myocardium, Non-bearing, Parapet, Parietal, Parie(te)s, Parpane, Parpen(d), Parpent, Parpoint, Partition, Party, Peribolos, Pericarp, Perpend, Perpent, Pleuron, Puteal, Qibla, Retaining, Revet(ment), Ring, Roman, Roughcast, Sea, Septum, Severus, Side, Somatopleure, Spandrel, Spandril, Street, Tambour, Tariff, Trumeau, Vallation, Vallum, Video, Wa', Wailing, Western, Zooecia

Wallaby Brusher, Dama, Kangaroo, Pad(d)ymelon, Pademelon, Quokka, Tammar, Whiptail

Wallah Competition

Wallaroo Euro

Wall-covering, **Wallpaper** Anaglypta®, Arras, Burlap, Flock, Lincrusta, Paper, Tapestry, Tapet

Waller Fats, Mason

Wallet Billfold, Case, Notecase, Pochette, Pocket-book, Purse, Scrip

Wallflower Crucifer, Dowd(y), Pariah

Wall-game Eton, Mahjongg

Wallop Bash, Baste, Batter, Beat, Biff, Clout, Cob, > **HIT**, Lam, Lounder, Polt, Pound, Slog, Strap, Swinge, Tan, Tat, Trounce

Wallow(ing) Bask, Flounder, Luxuriate, Revel, Roll, Splash, Swelter, Tolter, Volutation, Welter

Wall-painting Fresco, Graffiti, Grisaille

Wallpaper *see* **WALL-COVERING**

Wall-plate Tassel, Torsel

Wall-support Beam, Foundation, Pier, Rear-arch, Rere-arch

Wally Dipstick

Walnut Black, Butternut, Hickory, Juglans, Satin, White

Walrus Morse, Moustache, Pinniped, Rosmarine, Sea-horse, Tash

Walter Bruno, Mitty, Pater, Scott

Waltz Anniversary, Blue Danube, Boston, Dance, Hesitation, Rotate, Valse

Wampum Peag, Shell-money

Wan Pale, Pallid, Pasty, Sanguine, Sorry

Wanchancy Unlucky

Wand Baton, Caduceus, Rod, Runic, Stick, Thyrse, Thyrsus, Vara, Vare

Wander(er), **Wandering** Aberrance, Amble, Bedouin, Berber, Bum, Caird,

Delirious, Desultory, Deviate, Digress, Divagate, Drift, Errant, Estray, Evagation, Excursive, Expatiate, Extravagate, Gad(about), Grope, Hobo, Jew, Landloper, Maunder, Meander, Meandrian, Mill, Moon, Nomad(e), Odysseus, Pedder, Peregrine, Peripatetic, Polar, Rache, Ramble, Range, Ratch, Roamer, Romany, Room, Rove, Solivagant, Stooge, Straggle, Stravaig, Stray, Strayve, Streel, Stroam, Stroll, Swan, Ta(i)ver, Tramp, Troll, Tuareg, Vagabond, Vagrant Vague, Waif, Wend, Wheel, Wilder, Wolves

▷ **Wandering** *may indicate* an anagram

Wane Decline, Decrease, Diminish, Ebb

Wangle Arrange, Finagle, Trick

Want(ing), Wants Absence, Conative, Covet, Crave, Dearth, Defect, Deficient, Derth, Desiderata, > **DESIRE**, Destitution, Envy, Hardship, Indigent, Itch, Lack, Long, Mental, Need, Penury, Require, Scarceness, Scarcity, Shortfall, Shy, Void, Wish, Yen

Wanton(ness) Bona-roba, Cadgy, Chamber, Cocotte, Colt's tooth, Deliberate, Demirep, Filly, Flirt-gill, Gammerstang, Giglet, Giglot, Gillflirt, Hussy, Jay, Jezebel, Jillflirt, Lewd, Licentious, Loose, Nice, Protervity, Rig, Roué, Slut, Smicker, Sportive, Sybarite, Toyish, Twigger, Unchaste, Wayward

Wap Blow, Knock, Strike

War(fare), Wars American Civil, American Independence, Ares, Armageddon, Arms, Attrition, Barons', Bate, Battle, Biological, Bishop, Chemical, Civil, Clash, Class, Cod, Cold, Combat, Conflict, Crescentade, Crimean, Crusade, Electronic, Emergency, Feud, > **FIGHT**, Flame, Food, Franco-Prussian, Fray, Germ, Gigantomachy, Great, Guer(r)illa, Gulf, Holy, Hostilities, Hot, Hundred Years', Information, Internecine, Jehad, Jenkins' ear, Jihad, Jugurthine, Korean, Krieg, Mars, Mexican, Napoleonic, Nuclear, Opium, Peasants', Peloponnesian, Peninsular, Phony, Price, Private, Psychological, Punic, Push-button, Queen Anne's, Rebellion, Revolutionary, Roses, Russo-Japanese Secession, Seven Years', Six Day, Social, Spam, Spanish-American, Spanish Civil, Star, Stoush, Sword, Terrapin, Theomachy, Thirty Years', Total, Trench, Trojan, Turf, Vietnam, Winter, World, Yom Kippur

Warble(r) Carol, Chiff-chaff, Chirl, Fauvette, Peggy, Record, Rel(l)ish, Trill, Vibrate, Yodel, Yodle

War-chant, War-cry Alalagmos, Haka, Slogan

Ward (off) Artemus, Averruncate, Care, Casual, Charge, Defend, District, Fend, Guard, Hand-off, Maternity, Nightingale, Oppose, Parry, Protégé, Pupil, Soc, Soken, Vintry, Wear, Weir

Warden Caretaker, Concierge, Constable, Crossing, Curator, Custodian, Game, Guardian, Keeper, Maori, Meter maid, Ranger, Septimus, Spooner, Steward, Traffic, Way

Warder Beefeater, Gaoler, Guardian, Keeper, Provost, Screw, Turnkey, Twirl

Wardrobe Almirah, Capsule, Closet, Clothes, Garderobe, Outfit, Vestuary

Ware(s) Arretine, Beware, Biscuit, Cameo, Canton, Chelsea, China, Etruria, Faience, Goods, Lustre, Merchandise, Palissy, Samian, Sanitary, Satsuma, Shippo, Truck, Wemyss

Warehouse Bonded, Data, Depository, Entrepôt, Freight-shed, Go-down, Hong, Store

▶ **Warfare** *see* **WAR**

War-game Kriegs(s)piel

War-god Ares, Mars, Tiu, Tiw, Tyr

Warhead Atomic, Supremo

Warhorse Charger, Destrier, Fighter

Wariness, Wary Ca'canny, Cagey, Careful, Cautel, Caution, Chary, Discreet, Distrust, Guarded, Leery, Mealy-mouthed, Prudent, Sceptical, Tentie, Tenty, Vigilant

Warlike Battailous, Bellicose, Gung-ho, Lachlan, Martial, Militant

Warlord Haw-haw, Kitchener, Shogun

Warm(er), Warming, Warmth Abask, Admonish, Air, Ardour, Balmy, British, Calefacient, Calid(ity), Chambré, Cordial, Empressement, Enchafe, Fervour, Foment, Gemutlich, Genial, Global, Glow, > HEAT, Hot, Incalescent, Kang, Lew, Logic, Loving, Muff, Muggy, Mull, Tepid, Thermal, Toast, Toasty

Warm-blooded Homothermal, Homothermic, Homothermous, Idiothermous

Warmonger Hawk

Warn(ing) Admonish, Alarum, Alert, Amber, Aposematic, Apprise, Beacon, Bleep, Buoy, Caution, Caveat, Caveat emptor, Commination, Cone, Counsel, Document, Early, En garde, Example, Foghorn, Fore, Foretoken, Gardyloo, Garnishment, Harbinger, Hazchem, Heads up, Hoot, Horn, Klaxon, Larum, Lesson, Light, Maroon, Monition, Nix, Nota bene, Notice, Omen, Pi-jaw, Portent, Premonitory, Presage, Prodromal, Profit, Rumble strip, Scaldings, Scarborough, Sematic, Shore, Signal, Storm, Tattler, Threat, Tip-off, Token, Vigia, Vor, Yellow card

Warner Alarm, Fore, Plum, Siren

Warp(ed) Bias, Buckle, Cast, Contort, Distort, Kam, Kedge, Pandation, Time, Twist, Weft

Warpath Rampage

Warped *may indicate* an anagram

Warrant(y) Able, Authorise, Bench, Caption, Certificate, Death, Detainer, Distress, General, Guarantee, Justify, Mittimus, Permit, Precept, Royal, Search, Sepad, Special, Swear, Transire, Vouch, Warn

Warren Burrow, Colony, Hastings

Warrior Achilles, Agamemnon, Ajax, Amazon, Anzac, Berserk(er), Brave, Cossack, Crusader, Eorl, Fianna, Fighter, Geronimo, Ghazi, Heimdall, Housecarl, Impi, Myrmidon, Nestor, Rainbow, Rajpoot, Rajput, Samurai, Soldier, Tatar, Unknown, Warhorse, Zulu

Warship Battleship, Castle, Cog, Corvette, Cruiser, Destroyer, Drake, Dromon(d), Frigate, Invincible, Man-o-war, Mine-layer, Monitor, Privateer, Ram, Wooden Walls

Wart(y) Anbury, Angleberry, Blemish, Keratose, Muricate, Plantar, Tuberous, Verruca, Wen

Warwick Kingmaker

Wary *see* WARINESS

Was Erat, Existed, Lived, Past

Wash(ed), Washer, Washing (up), Wash out Ablution, Affusion, Alluvion, Bath, Bay(e), Bidet, Bubble-dancing, Bur(r), Calcimine, Circlip, Clean(se), Cradle, D, Dashwheel, Dele(te), Dip, Edulcorate, Elute, Elutriate, Enema, Fen, Flush, Freshen, Gargle, Grommet, Grummet, Irrigate, Kalsomine, Lap, > LAUNDER, Lave, Leather, Lip, Lotion, Marsh, Maundy, Mop, Nipter, Pan, Pigswill, Poss, Purify, Rinse, Scrub, Shampoo, Shim, Sind, Sloosh, Sluice, Soogee, Soojee, Soojey, Squeegie, Stream, Sujee, Swab, Synd, Tie, Toilette, Top and tail, Twin tub, Tye, Wake, Wudu, Yellow

Washbasin, Washtub, Washhouse Copper, Lavabo, Steamie

Washerman, Washerwoman Dhobi, Laundress

Washington Wa

Wasn't Nas, Wasna

Wasp(ish) Appledrain, Bembex, Bink, Bite, Chalcid, Cuckoo-fly, Cynipidae, Cynips, Digger, European, Fig, Fretful, Gall(-fly), Gold, Hornet, Horntail, Hoverfly, Irritable, Marabunta, Mason, Miffy, Muddauber, Paper, Peevish, Pompilid, Potter, Ruby-tail, Sand, Seed, Solitary, Spider, Velvet ant, Vespa, Wood, Yellow jacket

Wasp's nest Bike, Bink, Byke

Wassail Carouse, Pledge, Toast

Wast Wert

Wastage, Waste(d), Wasting, Wasteland Atrophy, Blue, Cesspit, Cirrhosis, Consume, Contabescent, Cotton, Crud, Culm, Decay, Dejecta, Desert, Detritus, Devastate, Dilapidate, Dissipate, Dross, Dung, Dwindle, Dwine, Dystrophy, Effluent, Egesta, Emaciate, Erode, Estrepe, Excrement, Exhaust, Expend, Exudate, Faeces, Flue, Forpine, Fribble, Fritter, Garbage, Gash, Gob, Gunge, Haggard, Havoc, Hazardous, Knub, Lavish, Loose, Lose, Loss, Low-level, Marasmus, Merino, Misspent, Moor, Moulder, Muir, Mullock, Mungo, Natural, Novalia, Nub, Nuclear, Offal, Oller, Ordure, Pellagra, Phthisis, Pigswill, Pine, Prodigalise, Radioactive, Rammel, Ravage, Recrement, Red mud, Red tape, > REFUSE, Reif, Rubble, Ruderal, Schappe, Scissel, Scoria, Scrap, Sewage, Slag, Slurry, Spend, Spill, Spoil(age), Squander, Sullage, Syntexis, Tabes, Tailing, Thin, Ureal, Urine, Uropoiesis, Vast, Wanze, Wear, Wilderness, Yearn

▷ **Wasted** *may indicate* an anagram

Wastrel Idler, Profligate, Scattergood, Spend-all, Spendthrift, Stalko, Vagabond

Watch(er) Accutron®, Analog(ue), Analogon, Argus, Await, Bark, Behold, Bird-dog, Black, Clock, Coastguard, Cock-crow, Digital, Dog, Espy, Fob, Glom, Gregory, Guard, Half-hunter, Huer, Hunter, Kettle, Latewake, Lever, Lo, Look, Look-out, Middle, Monitor, Morning, Nark, Neighbourhood, Night, Nit, Note, Nuremberg egg, Observe, Overeye, Patrol, Pernoctation, Posse, Quartz, Regard, Repeater, Rolex®, Scout, Sentinel, Sentry, Shadow, Spectate, Spotter, Stemwinder, Surveillance, Tend, Ticker, Timekeeper, Timepiece, Timer, Tompion, Tout, Turnip, Vedette, > VIGIL, Voyeur, Wait, Wake, Wrist(let)

Watch-chain Albert, Slang

Watch-control Escapement

Watchful(ness) Alert, Aware, Care, Dragon, Ira, Jealous, Vigilant, Wary

Watchman Bellman, Charley, Charlie, Chok(e)y, Cho(w)kidar, Guard, Sentinel, Sentry, Speculator, Tompion, Viewer

Watch-tower Atalaya, Barbican, Beacon, Mirador, Sentry-go

Watchword Cry, Password, Shibboleth, Slogan

Water(ed), Waters, Watery Adam's ale, Adam's wine, Amrit, Apollinaris, Aq(ua), Aquatic, Aqueous, Barley, Bayou, Bedabble, Bilge, Bound, Brine, Broads, Brook, Burn, Canal, Cancer, Chresard, Chuck, Cold, Compensation, Conductivity, Dead, Deaw, Deg, Demersal, Dew, Dill, Dilute, Dribble, Drinking, Eau, Ebb, Echard, Element, Ennerdale, Epilimnion, Euphotic, Evian®, First, Flood, Ford, Fossil, Gallise, Gallize, Ganga jal, Grey, Gripe, Ground, Hard, Heavy, Hectum, Hellespont, High, Holy, Hot, Hungary, Hydatoid, Irrigate, Javel(le), Kuroshio, Kyle, Lagoon, Lagune, Lake, Lant, Lavender, Leachate, Lentic, Light, Limnology, Lithia, Lode, Lotic, Lough, Low, Lubricated, Lymph, Meteoric, Mineral, Miner's inch, Moiré, Nappe, North, Oasis®, Oedema, Overfall, Pawnee, Pee, Perrier®, Phreatic, Pisces, Polly, Polynia, Polynya, Poppy, Potash, Potass, Pump, Purest, Quinine, Rain, Rapids, Rate, Reach, Rip, Riverine, Rose, Runny, Rydal, Saltchuck, Scorpio, Sea, Seltzer, Sera, Serous, Serum, Shower, Simpson, Skinkling, Slack, Slick, Sluice, Soda, Sodden, Soft, Solent, Sound, Souse, Stream, Surface, Table, Tam, Tap, Tar, Territorial, Thin, Tide, Toilet,

Tonic, Urine, Vadose, Vichy, Viscous, Vlei, Vly, Wash(y), Weak, Wee, Whey, White, White coal, Wild, Wishy-washy

Waterbaby Moses, Tom

Water-boa Anaconda

Water-boatman Notonecta

Water-brash Pyrosis

Water-buckets Noria

Water-carrier Aqueduct, Bheestie, Bheesty, Bhistee, Bhisti, Bucket, Carafe, Chatty, Furphy, Hose, Hydra, Kirbeh, Pail, Pitcher

Water-chestnut Saligot

Water-colour Aquarelle, Painting, Pastel, RI

Water-course Arroyo, Billabong, Canal, Ditch, Dyke, Falaj, Furrow, Gutter, Khor, Lead, Nala, Nulla, Rean, Rhine, Riverway, Shott, Spruit, Wadi, Whelm

Water-device Shadoof, Shaduf

Water-diviner Dowser, Hydrostat

Waterfall Angel (Falls), Cataract, Churchill, Chute, Cuquenan, Force, Foss, Iguaçú, Kabiwa, Kaieteur, Kile, Lasher, Lin(n), Mardel, Mtarazi, Niagara, Overfall, Rapid, Sault, Sutherland, Takakkaw, Tugela, Victoria, Yellowstone, Yosemite

Water-fern Marsilea, Salvinia

Water-gate Penstock, Sluice, Sluse

Water-god Aleion, Aleyin, Alpheus

Water-hen Gallinule

Water-hole Bore, Gilgai, Oasis

Water-lily Lotus, Nenuphar, Nuphar, Spatterdock

Waterloo Rout

Waterman Aquarius, Bargee, Ferryman, Oarsman

Water-monster Nicker

Water-nymph Kelpie, Kelpy, Naiad, Ondine, Rusalka

Water-parsnip Sium, Skirret

Water-plant Alisma, Aquatic, Cress, Crowfoot, Elodea, Gulfweed, Lace-leaf, Lattice-leaf, Nelumbo, Nenuphar, Nuphar, Ouvirandra, Pontederia, Quillwort, Reate, Sea-mat, Sedge, Seg, Stratiotes, Urtricularia, Vallisneria

Waterproof, **Water-tight** Caisson, Caulk, Cofferdam, Dampcourse, Dubbin(g), Groundsheet, Loden, Mac, Mino, Oilers, Oilskin, Pay, Seaworthy, Stank, Sta(u)nch, Tarp, Waders

Water-rat Arvicola, Musk-rat, Ratty, Vole

Watershed Divide, Hilltop

Water-spout Gargoyle, Geyser, Hurricano

Water-sprite Kelpie, Kelpy, Nix(ie), Nixy, Tangie, Undine, Water-nymph

Water supply Dewpond, H, Hydrant, Spring, Tank, Tap

Waterway Aqueduct, Billabong, Canal, Channel, Culvert, Ditch, Igarapé, Illinois, Intracoastal, Lode, River, Sound, Straight, Suez

Water-wheel Noria, Pelton, Sakia, Saki(y)eh

Wattle(s) Acacia, Boobialla, Boree, Dewlap, Gills, Mimosa, Mulga, Sallow, Savanna, Snot

Wave(s), **Waved**, **Wavelength**, **Wavy** Alfven, Alpha, Beachcomber, Beam, Beck, Beta, Billow, Bore, Bow, Brain, Brandish, Breaker, Carrier, Circular polarisation, Clapotis, Comber, Complex, Continuous, Crenulate, Crest, Crime, Crimp, Cymotrichous, De Broglie, Decuman, Delta, Dominant, Dumper, Electromagnetic, Finger, Flap, Flaunt, Float, Flote, Flourish, Gesticulate, Gravitational, Gravity, Graybeard, Ground, Groundswell, Gyrose, Harmonic,

Haystack, Heat, Hertzian, Internal, Ionospheric, Lee, Long, Longitudinal, Marcel, Matter, Medium, Mexican, Nebule, New, Oundy, Peristalsis, Perm(anent), Plunger, Primary, Pulse, Radar, Radiation, Radio, Rayleigh, Repand, Rip, Ripple, Roller, Rooster, Sastrugi, Scrub, Sea, Secondary, Seiche, Seismic, Shock, Short, Sine, Sky, Snaky, Soliton, Sound, Spiller, Square, Squiggle, Standing, Stationary, Stream, Supplementary, Surf, Surge, Sway, Tabby, Theta, Third, Thought, Tidal, Tidal bore, Tide, Train, Transverse, Travelling, Tsunami, Ultrasonic, Undate, Unde, Undulate, Vermicular, Waffle, Waft, Wag, Waive, Wash, Waw, Whitecap, White-horse, Wigwag

▷ **Wave(s)** *may indicate* an anagram

Wave-band Channel

Wave-detector Coherer

Wavelength Band, De Broglie

Waver(ing), Waverer Dither, Falter, Flag, Gutter, Halt, Hesitate, Oscillate, Stagger, Sway, Swither, Teeter, Trimmer, Vacillate, Waffle, Wet, Wow

Wax(ed), Waxing, Waxy Adipocere, Ambergris, Appal, Bate, Bees, Bone, Brazilian, Candelilla, Carna(h)uba, Cere, Ceresin, Cerumen, Chinese, Cobbler's, Cutin, Earth, Effuse, Enseam, Gr(e)aves, Grow, Heelball, Honeycomb, Increase, Increscent, Inseam, Ire, Japan, Kiss, Lecithin, Lipide, Livid, Lost, Lyrical, Mineral, Montan, Mummy, Ozocerite, Ozokerite, Paraffin, Parmacitie, Pela, Petroleum, Propolis, Pruina, Rage, Seal, Sealing, Spermaceti, Suberin, Tallow, Tantrum, Temper, Toxaphene, Vegetable, White, Yielding

Waxwing Cedar-bird, Icarus

Way(s), Wayside Access, Agate, Appian, Autobahn, Avenue, Borstal(l), Bypass, Companion, Course, Crescent, Direction, Door, Draw, E, Each, Entrance, Family, Fashion, Flaminian, Foss(e), Gate, Habit, Hatch, Hedge, High, Hither, How, Lane, Manner, Means, Method, Milky, Mo, Mode, Modus, N, Pass, Path, Pennine, Permanent, Pilgrim's, Procedure, Railroad, Regimen, Ridge, > ROAD, Route, S, Sallypost, St(reet), Style, System, Taoism, Third, Thoroughfare, Thus, Trace, Trail, Troade, Turnpike, Underpass, Untrodden, Via, W, Wise

Wayfarer Commuter, Piepowder, Pilgrim, Traveller, Voyager

Waylay Accost, Ambuscade, Ambush, Beset, Bushwhack, Buttonhole, Molest, Obstruct, Stick up

Way-out Advanced, Bizarre, Egress, Esoteric, Exit, Exotic, Extreme, Offbeat, Trendy

Wayward Capricious, Disobedient, Errant, Erratic, Loup-the-dyke, Obstreperous, Perverse, Stray, Unruly, Wilful

We I and I, Oo, Royal, Us

Weak(er), Weaken(ing), Weakest, Weakness Achilles' heel, Acrasia, Antimnemonic, Aphesis, Appal, Arsis, Asthenia, Attenuate, Blot, Brickle, Brittle, Cachexia, Cataplexy, Chink, Cripple(d), Debile, Debilitate, Decrease, Delay, Delicate, Dilute, Disable, Effete, Emasculate, Enervate, Enfeeble, Entender, Fade, Faible, Failing, Faint, Fatigue, Feeble, Fissile, Flag, Flaw, Flimsy, Foible, Fragile, Frail(tee), Frailty, Give, Gone, Ham, Hamartia, Helpless, Honeycomb, Impair, Impotence, Infirm, Knock-kneed, Labefaction, Lassitude, Leptosomatic, Low, Low ebb, Meagre, Mild, Milk and water, Myasthenia, Namby-pamby, Pale, Pall, Paraparesis, Paresis, Puny, Push-over, Pusillanimous, Reckling, Reduce, Simp, Slack, Tenuous, Thesis, Thin, Thready, Tottery, Unable, Underdog, Undermine, Unnerve, Unstable, Vapid, Velleity, Vessel, Vulnerability, W, Washy, Water(y), Wish(y)-wash(y), Wuss(y)

Weakling Dilling, Drip, Milksop, Nerd, Nisgul, Reed, Softie, Wuss

Weal Ridge, Stripe, Wealth, Welfare, Welt, Whelk

Wealth(y) Abundance, Affluence, Bullion, Croesus, Fat-cat, Fortune, Golconda, Jet-set, Klondike, Klondyke, Load(s'a), Loaded, Lolly, Mammon, Means, Mine, Mint, Moneyed, Nabob, Opulence, Ore, Pelf, Plutocrat, Reich, Rich, Ritzy, Solid, Substance, Treasure, Untold, Well-heeled, Well-off, Well-to-do

Wean Ablactation, Bairn, Spain, Spane, Spean

Weapon Airgun, Alderman, Arbalest, Arblast, Arm, Armalite®, Arquebus(e), Arrow, Arsenal, Assegai, Ataghan, Backsword, Ballista, Baton, Battleaxe, Bayonet, Bazooka, Bill, Binary, Blowgun, Blowpipe, Bludgeon, Bolo, Bomb, Bondook, Broadsword, Caliver, Calthrop, Caltrap, Caltrop, Carbine, Catapult, Catchpole, Cestus, Chainshot, Club, Co(e)horn, Cosh, Creese, Cudgel, Culverin, Cutlass, Dag(ger), Dart, Derringer, Deterrent, Doodlebug, Dragon, Dragoon, Duster, Elf-arrow, Enfield, Estoc, Excalibur, Flail, Flamethrower, Flintlock, Forty-five, Fougade, Fougasse, Gad(e), Gaid, Gingal(l), Gisarme, Glaive, Grenade, Halberd, Halbert, Harpoon, Harquebus, Hoplology, Howitzer, Javelin, Jingal, Katana, Knife, Knuckleduster, Kris, Lance, Life-preserver, Longbow, Long-range, Machete, Mangonel, Manrikigusari, Matchet, Mauser®, Maxim, Mere, Missile, Morgenstern, Mortar, Munition, Musket, Nuclear, Nuke, Nunchaku (sticks), Onager, Orgue, Partisan, Pea-shooter, Petrary, Petronel, Pike, Pilum, Pistol, Poleaxe, Quarterstaff, Revolver, Rifle, Sabre, Saker, Sandbag, Sarbacane, Shotgun, Sidearm, Skean-dhu, Skene-dhu, Slingshot, Smallsword, Snickersnee, Sparke, Sparth, Spat, Spontoon, Sten, Stiletto, Sting, Stinkpot, Sword, Taiaha, Taser®, Theatre, Throw-stick, Tomboc, Torpedo, Traditional, Trebuchet, Trident, Truncheon, V1, Vou(l)ge, Whirl-bat, Whorl-bat

Wear(ing), **Wear Out** Abate, Ablative, Abrade, Air, Attrition, Chafe, Corrade, Corrode, Deteriorate, Detrition, Efface, Erode, Erosion, Fashion, For(e)spend, Fray, Frazzle, Fret, Garb, Impair, In, Pack, Scuff, Sport, Stand, Tedy, Utility

▶ **Wear** *may indicate* the NE (eg Sunderland)

Weariness, **Wearisome**, **Weary** Beat, Bejade, Bore, Cloy, Dog-tired, Ennui, Ennuyé, Exhaust, Fag, Fatigate, Fatigue, Harass, Hech, Irk, Jade, Lacklustre, Lassitude, Pall, Puny, Ramfeezle, Sleepy, Spent, Tire, Trash, Try, Tucker, Wabbit, Worn

Weasel Beech-marten, Cane, Delundung, Ermine, Ferret, Glutton, Grison, Kolinsky, Marten, Mink, Mustela, Pekan, Polecat, Stoat, Taira, Tayra, Vermin, Whitterick, Whit(t)ret, Whittrick, Wolverine, Woodshock

Weather, **Weather forecast** Atmosphere, Climate, Cyclone, Discolour, Ecoclimate, Elements, El Nino, Endure, Met, Sky, Stand, Survive, Tiros, Undergo, Withstand

Weathercock Barometer, Fane, Vane

Weave(r), **Weaves**, **Weaving** Arachne, Basket, Cane, Complect, Entwine, Finch, Fishnet, Folk, Heald, Heddle, Interlace, Lace, Lease, Leno, Lion, Loom, Marner, Pick, Plain, Raddle, Ripstop, Rya, Shuttle, Sparrow, Spider, Splice, Taha, Texture, Throstle, Tissue, Tweel, Twill, Twine, Wabster, Waggle, Webster, Zigzag

Weaver-bird Amadavat, Avadavat, Quelea, Rice-bird, Taha

Web(bed), **Webbing**, **Web-footed**, **Web-site** Aranea, Fissipalmate, Food, Fourchette, Infomediary, Internet, Mat, Maze, Mesh(work), Offset, Palama, Palmate, Palmiped, Patagium, Pinnatiped, Retiary, Skein, Snare, Spider, Tear, Tela, Tissue, Toil, Totipalmate, World Wide

Webster Spider, Weaver

Wed(ding), **Wedlock** Alliance, Bet, Diamond, Espousal, Golden, Hymen, Join, Knobstick, Link, Marriage, Marry, Mate, Matrimony, Me(i)nt, Meng(e), Meynt, Ming, Monkey's, Nuptials, Pair, Penny, Ruby, Shotgun, Silver, Spousal,

> **UNION**, Unite, White, Y

Wedge(d) Accretionary, Canting-coin, Chock, Chunk, Cleat, Cotter, Cuneal, Doorstop, Feather, Forelock, Gagger, Gib, Impacted, Jack, Jam, Key, Niblick, Pitching, Prop, Quoin, Sand, Scotch, Shim, Sphenic, Stick, Trig, Vomerine, Voussoir, Whipstock

Wedgwood Benn, China®

Wednesday Ash, Midweek, Pulver, Spy

Wee Leak, Little, Pee, Sma(ll), Tiny, Urinate, Widdle

Weed(y) Adderwort, Agrestal, Alga, Allseed, Anacharis, Arenaria, Bedstraw, Bell-bind, Blinks, Burdock, Carpetweed, Catch, Charlock, Chickweed, Chlorella, Cigar(ette), Cissy, Clover, Cobbler's pegs, Cockle, Colonist, Coltsfoot, Corncockle, Couch, Daisy, Dallop, Darnel, Dock, Dollop, Dulse, Elodea, Ers, Fag, Fat hen, Femitar, Fenitar, Fucoid, Fumitory, Groundsel, Helodea, Hoe, Indian, Joe-pye, Knapweed, Knawel, Knot-grass, Lemna, Mare's-tail, Marijuana, Matfelon, Mayweed, Nard, Nettle, Nipplewort, Nostoc, Onion, Oxygen, Paterson's curse, Pearlwort, Pilewort, Piri-piri, Plantain, Potamogeton, Purslane, Ragi, Ragwort, Reate, Rest-harrow, Ribwort, Ruderal, Runch, Sagittaria, Sargasso, Scal(l)awag, Scallywag, Senecio, Softy, Sorrel, Spurge, Spurrey, Sudd, Sun-spurge, Swine's-cress, Tansy, Tare, Thistle, Tine, Tobacco, Tormentil, Twitch, Ulotrichale, Ulva, Vetch, Viper's bugloss, Wartcress, Widow's, Winnow, Yarr

Weedkiller Arsenic, Atrazine, Dalapon, Diquat, Diuron, Herbicide, Paraquat®, Selective, Simazine

Week(ly) Ember, Expectation, Great, Hebdomadary, Holy, Orientation, Ouk, Oulk, Passion, Periodical, Rag, Rogation, Sennight, Working

Weekday Feria

Weekend K, Sat, Sun

Weep(er), **Weepy**, **Wept** Bawl, Blubber, Cry, Grat, Greet, Lachrymose, Lament, Loser, Maudlin, Niobe, Ooze, Pipe, Screet, Seep, Sob, Wail

Weevil Anthonomous, Bean, Boll, Bug, Cornworm, Curculio, Diamond-beetle, Grain, Insect, Pea, Rice, Seed

Weft Roon, Shot, Texture, Warp, Woof

Weigh(ing), **Weigh down**, **Weight(y)** All-up, Apothecaries', Arroba, Artal, As, Atomic, Avoirdupois, Balance, Bantam, Baric, Bob, Bulk, Burden, Candie, Candy, Cantar, Carat, Catty, Cental, Centner, Clove, Consider, Count, Counterpoise, Cruiser, Ct, Dead, Decagram(me), Deliberate, Derham, Dirham, Dirhem, Drail, Dumbbell, Emphasis, Equivalent, Feather, Fother, G, Gerah, Grain, Gram, Grammage, Gross, Heft, Importance, Impost, Incumbent, Journey, Kandy, Kantar, Kat(i), Katti, Kerb, Khat, Kin, Kip, Last, Libra, Lisp(o)und, Load, Mark, Massive, Maund, Metage, Mina, Mna, Molecular, Moment, Mouse, Nail, Nett, Obol, Oke, Onerous, Oppress, Ounce, Overpoise, Oz, Pease, Peaze, Peck, Peise, Peize, Perpend, Peyse, Pikul, Plummet, Poise, Ponderal, Pood, Pound, Pregnant, Preponderance, Prey, Pud, Pudge, Quintal, Recul, Rod, Rotolo, Sash, Scruple, Seer, Semuncia, Ser, Sinker, Sit, Slang, Slung-shot, Stone, Stress, Talent, Tare, Throw, Tical, Tod, Tola, Ton(nage), Tonne, Tophamper, Troy, Trutinate, Unce, Unmoor, Welter, Wey, Wt

Weighing machine Bismar, Scales, Steelyard, Tron(e)

Weightless Agravic

Weight-lifter Crane, Lewis, Windlass

Weir Cauld, Dam, Garth, Kiddle, Kidel, Lasher, Pen, Watergate

Weird Bizarre, Curious, Dree, Eerie, Eery, Eldritch, Kookie, Offbeat, Spectral, Strange, Supernatural, Taisch, Uncanny, Zany

Welch, Welsh Abscond, Cheat, Default, Embezzle, Levant, Rat, Reneg(u)e, Renig, Skedaddle, Weasel

Welcome, Welcoming Aloha, Ave, Bel-accoyle, Ciao, Embrace, Entertain, Glad-hand, Greet, Haeremai, Hallo, Halse, Hello, Hi, Hospitable, How, Hullo, Karanga, Powhiri, Receive, Reception, Salute, Yellow-ribbon

Weld(ing) Arc, Explosion, Fillet, Friction, Gas, Join, Merge, MIG, Resistance, Seam, Sinter, Stud, Tack, TIG, Ultrasonic, Unite

Welfare Advantage, Alms, Benison, Ha(y)le, Heal, Health, Sarvodaya, Social, Weal

Welkin Firmament, Sky

Well (done) Artesian, Atweel, Aweel, Bien, Bore(hole), Bravo, Cenote, Development, Dropping, Dry hole, Euge, Famously, Fine, Fit, Gas, Gasser, Good, Gosh, Gusher, Hale, > **HEALTHY**, Hot, Inkpot, Kapa haka, Law, My, Namma hole, Odso, Oh, Oil, Phreatic, Potential, Pump, So, Source, Spa, Spring, Sump, Surge, Um, Upflow, Zemzem

Wellbeing Atweel, Bien-être, Comfort, Euphoria, Euphory, Good, Health, Oomph, Welfare

Well-bred Genteel

Well-built Sturdy, Tight

Well-covered Chubby, Padded

Well-curb Puteal

Welles Orson

Wellington, Welly Accelerate, Boot, Green, Gumboot, Iron Duke, Nosey

Well-known Famous, Illustrious, Notorious, Notour, Prominent

Well-off Affluent, Far, Rich, Wealthy

Well part Bucket, Shadoof, Shaduf

Wells Bombardier, Fargo, Sadler's

Well-wisher Friend

Welsh *see* WELCH

Welsh(man) Briton, Brittonic, Brython, Cake, Cambrian, Celtic, Cog, Cym(ric), Cymry, Dai, Ebbw, Emlyn, Evan, Fluellen, Gareth, Harp, Idris, Ifor, Keltic, P-Celtic, P-Keltic, Rabbit, Rarebit, Rees, Rhys, Sion, Taffy, Tudor, W

Wen Cyst, Talpa, Tumour, Wart

Wench Blowze, Court, Girl, Gouge, Hussy, Maid, Ramp, Rig, Smock, Strumpet

Wend Meander, Sorb, Steer

Wendy Darling, House

Went Left

Werewolf Loup-garou, Lycanthrope, Nazi, Turnskin, Vampire

Wesleyan Epworth, Methodist

West(ern), Westerly Ang mo, Far, Favonian, Hesperian, Mae, Middle, Movie, Oater, Occidental, Ponent, Spaghetti, Sunset, W, Wild

West African Fantee, Fanti, Kroo, Wolof

> **West end** *may indicate* 't' *or* 'W1'

West Indian Carib, Creole, Jamaican, Taino

Westminster SW1

Wet(ting) Bedabble, Bedraggled, Clammy, Daggle, Damp, Dank, Dew, Dip, Douse, Dowse, Drench, Drip(ping), Drook, Drouk, Embrue, Enuresis, Feeble, Humect, Humid, Hyetal, Imbue, Irrigate, Irriguous, Madefy, Madid, Marshy, Moil, Moist(en), Molly, Namby-pamby, Pee, Piddle, Pouring, Rainy, Ret(t), Roral, Roric, Runny, Saturate, Shower, Simp(leton), Sipe, Sluice, > **SOAK**, Sodden, Sopping, Sour, Steep, Tiddle, Tipsy, Urinate, Wat, Wee, Widdle, Wimpy, Wringing

Whack(ed) Belt, Bemaul, Biff, Deadbeat, Joll, Joule, Jowl, Lambast, Lounder, Swish, Thump

Whale(meat), Whaling Baleen, Beaked, Beluga, Black, Blower, Blubber, Blue, Bottlehead, Bottlenose, Bowhead, Bull, Cachalot, Calf, Cetacea(n), Cete, Cow, Cowfish, Dolphin, Dorado, Fall, Fin(back), Finner, Gam, Glutton, Grampus, Greenland, Grey, Greyback, Humpback, Killer, Kreng, Leviathan, Manatee, Minke, Monodon, Mysticeti, Narwhal, Odontoceti, Paste, Physeter, Pilot, Pod, Porpoise, Right, Rorqual, School, Scrag, Sea-canary, Sea-unicorn, Sei, Social, Sperm, Spouter, Sulphur-bottom, Thrasher, Toothed, Toothless, White, Zeuglodon(t)

▷ **Whale** *may indicate* an anagram

Whalebone Busk

Whaler Ahab, Harpooner, Ship, Specksioneer, Specktioneer, Waister

Whales' meat Clio

Wham Bang, Collide

Whang Blow, Flog, Thrash, Whack

Wharf(inger) Dock(er), Jetty, Key, Landing, Pier, Quay, Roustabout, Rouster, Staith(e)

What Anan, Eh, How, Pardon, Que, Siccan, That, Which

Whatnot, What's-its-name Dinges, Dingus, Doings, Etagère, Gismo, Jiggamaree, Jiggumbob, Thingamy, Thingumajig, Thingumbob, Thingummy, Timenoguy

Wheat Amelcorn, Blé, Bulg(h)ur, Cone, Couscous, Cracked, Durum, Einkorn, Emmer, Federation, Fromenty, Frumenty, Furme(n)ty, Furmity, Grain, Hard, Mummy, Rivet, Sarrasin, Sarrazin, Seiten, Semolina, Sharps, Soft, Spelt, Spring, Triticum, Winter

Wheatsheaf Bale, Gerbe, Stook

Wheedle Banter, Barney, Blandish, Butter up, Cajole, Coax, Cog, Cuiter, Cuittle, Flatter, Inveigle, Tweedle, Whilly(whaw)

Wheel(er) Balance, Bedel, Bevel, Bogy, Buff(ing), Caracol(e), Caster, Castor, Catherine, Chain, Chark(h)a, Circle, Cistern, Crown, Cycle, Daisy, Disc, Driving, Emery, Epicycloidal, Escape, Fan, Felloe, Felly, Ferris, Fifth, Fortune, Gear, Grinding, Helm, Hurl, Idle(r), Jagger, Kick, Lantern, Magnate, Medicine, Mortimer, Nabob, Nose, Paddle, Pattern, Pedal, Pelton, Perambulator, Persian, Pin, Pinion, Pitch, Pivot, Planet, Potter's, Prayer, Pulley, Rag, Ratchet, Rhomb, Roll, Rotate, Roulette, Rowel, Sheave, Snail, Spider, Spinning, Sprocket, Spur, Star, Steering, Stepney, Stitch, Tail, Throwing-table, Tread, Trindle, Trochus, Trolley, Truckle, Trundle, > TURN, Tympan(um), Water, Web, Wharve, Wire, Worm, Zoetrope

Wheelbarrow Monotroch

Wheelhouse Caravan, Paddle-box

Wheel-hub Axle, Nave

Wheelman Cyclist, Ixion

Wheelwright Spokesman

Wheeze Asthma, Jape, Joke, Pant, Ploy, Rale, Reak, Reik, Rhonchus, Ruse, Stridor, Trick, Whaisle, Whaizle

Whelk Buckie, Limpet, Shellfish, Stromb, Triton

Whelm Nalla(h), Nulla(h)

Whelp Bear, Bra(t)chet, Pup

When(ever) Although, As, If, Once, Though, Time

Where(abouts) Location, Neighbourhood, Place, Site, Vicinity, Whaur, Whither

Wherefore Cause, Reason, Why

Whereupon So, When
Wherewithal Finance, Means, Money, Needful, Resources
Wherry Barge, Rowboat
Whet(stone) Coticular, Excite, Hone, Sharpen, Stimulate
Whether Conditional, If
Whey Serum, Whig
Which(ever), Which is Anyway, As, QE, Whatna, Whilk, Who
Whiff Breath, Cigarette, Gust, Hum, Puff, Redolence, Smatch, Sniff, Trace, Waft
Whig Adullamite, Jig, Rascal, Tory, Whey
While Although, As, Interim, Since, Space, Span, Though, Throw, Time, When, Whenas, Yet
Whim(s), Whimsical, Whimsy Bizarre, Caprice, Conceit, Crotchet, Fad, Fancy, Fantastic, Fey, Flisk, Impulse, Kicksy-wicksy, Kink, Notion, Quaint, Quirk, Tick, Toy, Vagary
Whimper Cry, Grizzle, Mewl, Pule, Snivel, Whine
Whin Furze, Gorse, Ulex
Whine, Whinge Cant, Carp, Complain, Cry, Grumble, Kvetch, Mewl, Moan, Peenge, Pule, Snivel, Whimper, Yammer
Whinny Neigh, Nicker, Whicker
Whip(ped), Whip out, Whipping Beat, Braid, Brede, Bullwhack, Bullwhip, Cat, Cat o' nine tails, Chabouk, Chantilly, Chastise, Chief, Cilium, Colt, Crop, Drive, Feague, Firk, Five-line, Flagellate, Flagellum, Flay, Gad, Hide, Jambok, Knout, K(o)urbash, Larrup, > LASH, Leather, Limber, Lunge, Quirt, Rawhide, Riem, Scourge, Sjambok, Slash, Steal, Stock, Strap-oil, Swinge, Swish, Switch, Taw, Thong, Three-line, Trounce, Welt, West country, Whap, Whop
Whippersnapper Dandiprat, Dandyprat, Pup, Squirt
Whirl(er), Whirling Bullroarer, Circumgyrate, Dervish, Eddy, Gyrate, > IN A WHIRL, Pivot, Reel, Spin, Swing, Swirl, Vortex, Vortical, Vorticose, Vortiginous, Whirry
Whirlpool Eddy, Gulf, Gurge, Maelstrom, Moulin, Sea purse, Swelchie, Vorago, Vortex, Weel, Wiel
Whirlwind Cyclone, Dust devil, Eddy, Sand-devil, Tornado, Tourbillion, Typho(o)n, Vortex, Willy-willy
Whisk Chowri, Chowry, Swish, Switch, Whid, Whip
Whisker(s) Beard, Beater, Burnsides, Cat's, Dundreary, Hackle, Hair, Moustache, Mutton-chop, Samuel, Satyric tuft, Side(-boards), Side-burns, Vibrissa
Whisk(e)y Alcohol, Barley-bree, Barley-broo, Barley-broth, Bond, Bourbon, Canadian, Cape Smoke, Chain lighting, Corn, Cratur, Crayther, Creature, Fife, Fire-water, Hard tack, Highball, Hokonui, Hoo(t)ch, Irish, Malt, Monongahela, Moonshine, Morning, Mountain dew, Nip, Peat-reek, Pot(h)een, Ragwater, Red eye, Rye, Scotch, Sourmash, Spunkie, Tanglefoot, Tarantula juice, Usquebaugh, Wheech, Whiss
> **Whisky** *may indicate an anagram*
Whisper Breath(e), Bur(r), Hark, Hint, Innuendo, Murmur, Round, Rumour, Rustle, Sigh, Stage, Susurrus, Tittle, Undertone
Whist Dummy, Hush, Long, Quiet, Sh, Short, Solo
Whistle(r) Blow, Boatswain's, Calliope, Feedback, Flageolet, Hiss, Marmot, Penny, Ping, Pipe, Ref, Siffle(ur), Sowf(f), Sowth, Steam, Stop, Stridor, Swab(ber), Tin, Toot, Tweedle, Tweet, Warbler, Wheeple, Wheugh, Whew, Whiffle, Wolf
Whit Atom, Doit, Figo, Haet, Iota, Jot, Particle, Pentecost, Point, Red cent, Straw

White(n), **Whitener**, **Whiteness** Agene, Agenise, Alabaster, Albedo, Albescent, Albino, Albugineous, Albumen, Argent, Ashen, Au lit, Bakra, Blameless, Blanch, Blanco, Bleach, Buckra, Cabbage, Calm, Cam, Camstone, Candid, Candour, Canescent, Canities, Caucasian, Caum, China, Chinese, Christmas, Cliffs, Collar, Company, Dealbate, Egg, Elephant, Ermine, European, Fang, Fard, Feather, Flag, Flake, French, Glair, Gwen(da), Gwendolen, Honorary, Hore, House, Innocent, Ivory, Large, Leucoma, Lie, Lily, Livid, Man, Marbled, Mealy, Niveous, Opal, Oyster, Pakeha, Pale(face), Pallor, Paper, Paris, Pearl, Poor, Pure, Redleg, Russian, Sclerotic, Selborne, Sheep, Silver, Small, Snow(y), Spanish, Taw, Vitiligo, Wan, Wedding, Zinc

Whitefish Menominee

Whitefriars Alsatia

Whitehall Ministry

Whitehead Milium

White horses Skipper's daughters

White man Anglo, Ba(c)kra, Buckra, Caucasian, Gub(bah), Haole, Honkie, Honky, Kabloona, Larney, Mzungu, Occidental, Ofay, Pakeha, Paleface, Redleg Redneck, Umlungu, WASP

Whitewash Calcimine, Excuse, Kalsomine, Lime, Skunk, Trounce

Whitlow Ancome, Felon, Panaritium, Paronychia

Whitsun Pinkster, Pinxter

Whittle Carve, Pare, Sharpen

Whizz Wheech

Who As, Doctor

Whodunit Mystery

Whole, **Wholehearted**, **Wholeness**, **Wholly** All, Eager, Entire(ty), Entity, Fully, Hale, Indiscrete, Intact, Integer, Integrity, Largely, Lot, Sum, Systemic, Thoroughly, Total, Unbroken, Uncut

Wholesale(r) Cutprice, En bloc, Engrosser, Jobber, Root and branch, Supplier, Sweeping

Wholesome Clean, Good, Healthy, Physical, Sound

Whoop(er), **Whooping cough** Alew, Celebrate, Chincough, Crane, Cry, Excite, Kink(cough), Kink-hoast, Pertussis, Swan, War

Whoopee Carouse, Evoe, Hey-go-mad, Roister

Whoosh Birr, Swish

Whopper, **Whopping** Barn, Crammer, Huge, Immense, Jumbo, Lie, Lig, Oner, Out and outer, Scrouger, Slapper, Slockdolager, Soc(k)dalager, Soc(k)dolager, Soc(k)doliger, Soc(k)dologer, Sogdolager, Sogdoliger, Sogdologer, Stonker, Tale Taradiddle

Whore Drab, Harlot, Loose woman, Pinnace, Pro, Quail, Road, Strumpet, Tart

Whorl Corolla, Eucyclic, Spiral, Swirl, Verticil, Volute

Why Reason, Yogh

Wick Farm, Rush, Snaste, Vill(age)

Wicked(ness) Adharma, Atrocity, > **BAD**, Candle, Criminal, Cru(i)sie, Crusy, Depravity, Devilish, Evil, Facinorous, Flagitious, Goaty, Godless, Heinous, High-viced, Immoral, Impious, Improbity, Iniquity, Lantern, Nefarious, Night-light, Ponerology, Pravity, Rush, Satanic, Scelerate, Sin(ful), Taper, Turpitude, Unholy, Vile

▷ **Wicked** *may indicate* containing a wick

Wicker(work) Basketry, Sale, Seal

Wicket Gate, Hatch, Infield, Pitch, Square, Sticky, Stool, Stump, Yate

Wicket-keeper Stumper

Wide, Widen(ing), Width Abroad, Ample, Bay, Broad, Dilate, Drib, Eclectic, Expand, Extend, Far, Flanch, Flange, Flare, Flaunch, Ga(u)ge, General, Latitude, Miss, Prevalent, Roomy, Spacious, Spread, Sundry, Sweeping, Vast

Wide-awake Alert, Fly, Hat, Wary, Watchful

Widespread Catholic, Diffuse, Epidemic, Extensive, General, Pandemic, Panoramic, Prevalent, Prolate, Rife, Routh(ie), Sweeping

Widow(ed) Bereft, Black, Dame, Dowager, Golf, Grass, Hempen, Jointress, Relict, Sati, Sneerwell, Suttee, Vidual, Viduous, Whydah-bird, Widdy

Wield Brandish, Control, Exercise, Handle, > **MANIPULATE**, Ply, Sound

Wife, Wives Bride, Concubine, Consort, Devi, Dutch, Enid, Evadne, Feme, Feme covert, Fiere, Frau, Haram, Harem, Harim, Helpmate, Helpmeet, Hen, Her indoors, Kali, Kickie-wickie, Kicksy-wicksy, Kloo(t)chman, Lakshmi, Little woman, Mate, Memsahib, Missis, Missus, Mrs, Mummer's, Partner, Penelope, Pirrauru, Potiphar's, Rib, Seraglio, Spouse, Squaw, Trophy, Trouble and strife, Umfazi, Ux(or), W

Wig Adonis, Bagwig, Bob(wig), Brigadier, Brutus, Buzz-wig, Cadogan, Campaign, Carpet, Cauliflower, Caxon, Chevelure, Chide, Cockernony, Dalmahoy, Fright, Full-bottomed, Gizz, Gooseberry, Gorgone, Gregorian, Hair(piece), Heare, Jas(e)y, Jazey, Jiz, Macaroni, Major, Periwig, Peruke, Postiche, Ramil(l)ie(s), Rate, Reprimand, Rug, Scold, Scratch, Sheitel, Spencer, Targe, Tie, Toupee, Toupet, Tour

Wiggle, Wiggly Jiggle, Scoleciform, Wobble, Wriggle

Wight Man, Vectis

Wigwam Te(e)pee

Wild Aberrant, Agrestal, Barbarous, Berserk, Bundu, Bush, Chimeric, Crazy, Dionysian, Earl, Errant, Erratic, Farouche, Feral, Frantic, Frenetic, Haggard, Hectic, Lawless, Mad(cap), Manic, Meshugge, Myall, Natural, Rampant, Raver, Riotous, > **SAVAGE**, Unmanageable, Unruly, Violent, Warrigal, West, Woolly

> **Wild(ly)** *may indicate* an anagram

Wild beast Eyra, Sapi-utan, Scrubber

Wildcat Lion, Manul, Ocelot, Strike, Tiger

Wilderness Bush, Desert, Ruderal, Sinai, Solitude, Waste

Wild goose Chase, Greylag

Wild oats Haver

Wile, Wily Art, Artful, Artifice, Astute, Braide, > **CUNNING**, Deceit, Foxy, Peery, Ruse, Shifty, Shrewd, Slee, > **SLY**, Spider, Stratagem, Streetwise, Subtle, Trick, Versute, Wide

Wilful Deliberate, Headstrong, Heady, Obstinate, Recalcitrant, Wayward

Will, Willing(ly) Alsoon, Amenable, Bard, Bequeath, Bewildered, Bill(y), Complaisant, Compliant, Conation, Content, Desire, Devise, Fain, Force, Free, Game, General, Hay, Holographic, Leave, Legator, Leve, Lief, Lieve, Living, Noncupative, Obedient, On, Please, Prone, Purpose, Raring, Rather, Ready, Receptive, Scarlet, Soon, Spirit, Swan, Testament, Testate, Volition, Voluntary, Volunteer, Way, Wimble, Woot

> **Will** *may indicate* an anagram

William(s) Bill(y), Conqueror, Occam, Orange, Pear, Rufus, Silent, Sweet, Tell, Tennessee

Will o' the wisp Fen-fire, Friar's lantern, Ignis-fatuus, Jack o'lantern, Min min, Nightfire, Rush

Willow(ing), Willowy Crack, Diamond, Lissom(e), Lithe, Osier, Poplar, Port Jackson, Pussy, Salix, Sallow, Sauch, Saugh, Supple, Twilly, Weeping, Withy

Willpower Ab(o)uha, Determination, Strength

Willy-nilly Nolens volens, Perforce
Wilt Decline, Droop, Fade, Flag, Sap, Shalt, Wither
Wiltshireman Moonraker
▸ **Wily** *see* WILE
Wimple Gorget, Meander, Ripple, Turn
▷ **Wimple** *may indicate* an anagram
Win(ner), Winning Achieve, > BEAT, Capot, Champion, Conciliate, Conquer, Cup, Cute, Decider, Disarming, Dormie, Dormy, Earn, Endearing, First, Gain, Gammon, Hit, Jackpot, Land, Laureate, Lead, Medallist, Motser, Motza, Nice, Pile, Pot, Prevail, Profit, Purler, Repique, Result, Rubicon, Shoo-in, Slam, Snip, Success, Sweet, Take, > TRIUMPH, Up, Vellet, Velvet, Victor(y), Vole, Walk over, Wrest
Wince Blench, Cringe, Flinch, Recoil
Winch Crab, Crane, Jack, Windlass
Winchester® Rifle
Wind(er), Winding(s), Windy Aeolian, Air, Airstream, Ambages, Anabatic, Anfractuous, Anti-trade, Aquilo(n), Argestes, Auster, Backing, Baguio, Bend, Berg, Bise, Blore, Blow, Bluster, Bora, Boreas, Bottom, Bourasque, Brass, Breeze, Brickfielder, Buran, Burp, Buster, Cape doctor, Capstan, Carminative, Caurus, Chili, Chill, Chinook, Coil, Colic, Cordonazo, Corus, Crank, Creeky, Curl, Cyclone, Downwash, Draught, Draw, Dust devil, Easterly, Etesian, Euraquilo, Euroclydon, Eurus, Evagation, Favonian, Favonius, Fearful, Firn, Flatulence, Flatus, Flaw, Fo(e)hn, Gale, Gas, G(h)ibli, Gregale, Gust, Haboob, Harmattan, Heaves, Hurricane, Hurricano, Jet stream, Kamseen, Katabatic, K(h)amsin, Knee-swell, Levant(er), Libecc(h)io, Libs, Link, Meander, Meltemi, Mistral, Monsoon, Muzzler, Nervous, Noreast, Norther, Nor(th)wester(ly), Noser, Notus, Pampero, Periodic, Ponent, Poop, Prevailing, Puna, Purl, Quill, Reeds, Reel, Rip-snorter, Roll, Samiel, Sciroc, Scirocco, Screw, Sea, Second, Series, Serpentine, Shamal, Shimaal, Simoom, Simoon, Sinuous, Sirocco, Slant, Snake, Snifter, Snorter, Solano, Solar, Sough, Souther, Southerly buster, Spiral, Spool, Squall, Stellar, Sumatra, Surface, Swirl, Tail, Tehuantepecer, Thread, Throw, Tornado, Tortuous, Tourbillon, Trade, Tramontana, Trend, Turn, Twaddle, Twine, Twister, Twisty, Typhon, Typhoon, Vayu, Veer, Veering, Ventose, Volturnus, Waffle, Weave, Wester, Westerly, Whirlblast, White squall, Williwaw, Willy-willy, Winch, Woold, Wrap, Wreathe, Wrest, Wuthering, Zephyr(us), Zonda
Windbag Balloon, Bore, Drogue, Prattler, Whoopee cushion, Zeppelin
Windfall Bonanza, Buckshee, Caduac, Fortune, Godsend, Manna
Windflower Anemone
Windlass Differential, Spanish, Whim, Winch
Windmill Post, Smock, Whirligig
Window(s) Atmosphere, Bay, Bow, Casement, Catherine-wheel, Companion, Compass, Day, Deadlight, Dormer, Dream-hole, Eye, Eyelids, Fanlight, Fenestella, Fenestra, French, Gable, Garret, Glaze, Guichet, Jalousie, Jesse, Judas, Lancet, Lattice, Launch, Loop-light, Louver, Louvre, Lozen, Lucarne, Lunette, Luthern, Lychnoscope, Marigold, Mezzanine, Mirador, Monial, Mullion, Oculus, Oeil-de-boeuf, Ogive, Orb, Oriel, Ox-eye, Pane, Pede, Picture, Porthole, Quarterlight, Radio, Re-entry, Rosace, Rose, Sash, Sexfoil, Spyhole, Storm, Transom, Trellis, Ventana, Weather, Wheel, Wicket, Windock, Winnock
Window-bar, Window-fastening Astragal, Espagnolette
Windpipe Bronchus, Gular, Throat, Trachea, Weasand

Windscale Beaufort
Windsock Drogue, Sleeve
Windswept Scud
Wind-up End, Fright, Liquidate, Span
Windward Ahold, Aloof, Laveer, Luff, Up
Wine Bin, Cup, Essence, Fortified, Low, Must, Piece, Premier cru, Prisage, Rotgut, Rouge, The grape, Vat, Vintage

WINES

2 letters:
It

3 letters:
Dao
Red
Sec
Tun
Vin

4 letters:
Asti
Brut
Cava
Hock
Mull
Palm
Pipe
Port
Race
Rosé
Rosy
Sack
Sekt
Stum
Tent
Tutu
Vino

5 letters:
Anjou
Anker
Biddy
Blanc
Bombo
Comet
Cuvée
Gallo
Macon
Medoc
Mirin
Mosel

Negus
Pinot
Plonk
Rhine
Rioja
Soave
Straw
Syrah
Table
Tavel
Toddy
Tokay
White
Xeres

6 letters:
Barley
Barolo
Barsac
Beaune
Bishop
Bubbly
Canary
Claret
Ginger
Graves
Lisbon
Malaga
Merlot
Muscat
Piment
Plotty
Red Ned
Shiraz

7 letters:
Alicant
Amoroso
Auslese
Bastard
Catawba
Chablis

Chateau
Chianti
Cowslip
Demi-sec
Dessert
Eiswein
Fendant
Icewine
Madeira
Malmsey
Margaux
Marsala
Moselle
Oenomel
Orvieto
Pomerol
Pommard
Retsina
Rhenish
Sangria
Terroir
Vouvray

8 letters:
Bordeaux
Bucellas
Buckfast®
Burgundy
Cabernet
Champers
Charneco
Dubonnet®
Espumoso
Essencia
Frascati
Gluhwein
Jerepigo
Kabinett
Log-juice
Malvasia
Malvesie
Montilla

Mountain
Muscadel
Muscadet
Muscatel
Oenology
Pinotage
Pradikat
Red biddy
Resinata
Rheingau
Riesling
Sancerre
Sangaree
Sauterne
Semillon
Spätlese
Spumante
St Julien
Sylvaner
Verdelho
Vermouth

9 letters:
Bacharach
Bardolino
Champagne
En primeur
Falernian
Gladstone
Hermitage
Hippocras
Hoccamore
Inglenook
Lambrusco
Languedoc
Loll-shrob
Malvoisie
Meersault
Muscadine
Ordinaire
Pinot noir
Sauvignon

Sauvignon
Sparkling
St Emilion
Tafelwein
Tarragona
Zinfandel

10 letters:
Beaujolais
Bull's blood
Chambertin
Chardonnay
Constantia
Elderberry
Genevrette
Hochheimer
Loll-shraub

Manzanilla
Montrachet
Muscadelle
Napa Valley
Peter-see-me
Piesporter
Vinho verde

11 letters:
Amontillado
Dom Perignon
Niersteiner
Pouilly-Fume
Rudesheimer
Scuppernong
Steinberger

12 letters:
Johannisberg
Marcobrunner
Supernaculum
Valpolicella
Vin ordinaire

13 letters:
Beerenauslese
Entre-Deux-Mers
Liebfraumilch
Pouilly-Fousse

14 letters:
Gewürztraminer
Johannisberger

15 letters:
Lachryma Christi

17 letters:
Cabernet
 Sauvignon
Chateaux
 cardboard
Nuits Saint
 Georges

20 letters:
Trockenbeeren-
 auslese

Wine-cellar, **Wine-shop** Bistro, Bodega, Vault, Vaut(e)
Wine-glass Flute
Wine-making Gallising, Remuage
Wing(ed), **Winger**, **Wings**, **Wing-like** Aerofoil, Ala(r), Alula, Annexe, Appendage, Arm, Bastard, ▷ **BIRD**, Branch, Canard, Cellar, Corium, Coulisse, Delta, Dipteral, El(l), Elevon, Elytral, Elytriform, Elytron, Elytrum, Fender, Flap, Flew, Flex, Flipper, Flying, Forward, Gull, Halteres, Hurt, Left, Limb, Parascenia, Parascenium, Patagium, Pennate, Pennon, Pinero, Pinion, Pip, Pterygoid, Putto, Right, Rogallo, Sail, Samariform, Scent-scale, Segreant, Seraphim, Split, Standard, Sweepback, Sweptback, Sweptwing, Swift, Swingwing, Tailplane, Tectrix, Tegmen, Transept, Van, Vol(et), Wound(ed)
Winged sandals Talaria
▷ **Winger** *may indicate* a bird
Wing-footed Aliped, Fleet, Swift
Wingless Apteral
Wink (at) Atone, Bat, Condone, Connive, Eyelid, Flicker, Ignore, Instant, Nap, Nictitate, Pink, Twinkle
Winnie Pooh
Winnow Fan, Riddle, Separate, Sift, Van, Wecht
Winsome Bonny, Engaging, Gay, Pleasant
Winter, **Wintry** Blackthorn, Bleak, Brumal, Cold, Dec, Fimbul, Frigid, Frore, Hibernate, Hiemal, Hiems, Hodiernal, Jack Frost, Jasmine, Nuclear, Snowy, W
Winter cherry Chinese lantern
Wintergreen Sarcodes
Winter pear Nelis
Winter-sport Ski
Wipe (out), **Wiping** Abolish, Abrogate, Absterge, Amortise, Cancel, Cleanse, Demolish, Destroy, Deterge, Dicht, Dight, Eradicate, Expunge, Hanky, Mop, Nose-rag, Null, Purge, Raze, Reroussage, Slorm, Sponge, Tersion, Tissue
Wire(s), **Wiry** Aerial, Barb(ed), Cable, Cat's whiskers, Chicken, Coil, Earth, Fencing, Filament, Filar, File, Heald, Heddle, High, Kirschner, Lean, Lecher, Live, Marconigram, Mil, Nichrome®, Nipper, Piano, Pickpocket, Razor, Sevice, Shroud, Sinewy, Snake, Solenoid, Spit, Staple, Stilet, Strand, String, Stylet, Telegram, Telegraph, Thoth, Thread, Trace

Wireless (operator), Wireless part Baffle, Set, Sparks, Valve

Wise(acre), Wisdom Advisedly, Ancient, Astute, Athena, Athene, Canny, Depth, Ernie, Ganesa, Gothamite, Hep, Hindsight, Judgement, Judicious, Learned, Long-headed, Lore, Manner, Mimir, Minerva, Norman, Oracle, Owl, Penny, Philosopher, Philosophy, Politic, Polymath, Prajna, Profound, Prudence, Sagacity, Sage, Salomonic, Sapience, Savvy, Shrewd, Smartie, Solomon, Solon, Sophia, Wice

Wisecrack Dig, One-liner

Wise man Balthazar, Caspar, Heptad, Melchior, Nestor, Sage, Sapient, Seer, Solomon, Swami, Thales, Tohunga, Worldly

Wish(es) Crave, Death, Desiderate, > DESIRE, Hope, List, Long, Pant, Pleasure, Precatory, Regards, Velleity, Want, Yearn

Wishbone Furcula, Marriage-bone, Merrythought, Skipjack

Wishy-washy Bland, Feeble, Insipid, Irresolute, Milksop, Weak, Wheyey

Wisp(y) Cirrate, Frail, Scrap, Shred, Virga, Wase

Wit(s), Witticism, Witty Acumen, Attic, Badinage, Banter, Brevity, Commonsense, Concetto, Cunning, Dry, Epigram, Esprit, Estimation, Eutrapelia, Eutrapely, Facetious, Fantasy, Hartford, Humour, Imagination, Intelligence, Irony, Jest, Jeu d'esprit, Joke, Marbles, Marinism, Memory, Mind, Mot, Mother, Native, Nous, Pawky, Pun, Repartee, Rogue, Sally, Salt, Saut, Sconce, > SENSE, Shaft, Smart, Videlicet, Viz, Wag, Weet, Wisecrack, Word-play

Witch(craft) Broomstick, Cantrip, Carline, Circe, Coven, Craigfluke, Crone, Cutty Sark, Enchantress, Ensorcell, Galdragon, Glamour, Goety, Gramary(e), Gyre-carlin, Hag, Hecat(e), Hex, Invultuation, Lamia, Magic, Medea, Myal(ism), Necromancy, Night-hag, Obeahism, Obiism, Pythoness, Salem, Selim, Sibyl, Sieve, Sorceress, Speller, Sycorax, Trout, Valkyrie, Vaudoo, Vilia, Voodoo, Weird, Wicca

Witch-doctor Boyla, Medicine man, Mganga, Obi, Pawaw, Powwow, Sangoma, Shaman

Witch-hazel Fothergilla, Platan(e), Winter-bloom

Witch-hunter McCarthy

With And, By, Con, Cum, Hereby, In, Mit, Of, Plus, W

Withdraw(al), Withdrawn Abdicate, Alienate, Aloof, Cold turkey, Cry off, Detach, Disengage, Distrait, Enshell, Evacuate, Hive off, Inshell, Introvert, Offish, Palinode, Preserve, Recant, Recoil, Repair, Resile, Reticent, Retire, Retract(ion), Retreat, Revoke, Revulsion, Scratch, Secede, Sequester, Shrink, Shy, Stand down, Subduct, Unreeve, Unsay

Wither(ed), Withering, Withers Arefy, Atrophy, Blight, Burn, Corky, Die, Droop, Dry, Evanish, Fade, Forpine, Googie, Languish, Marcescent, Miff, Nose, Scram, Sere, Shrink, Shrivel, Welk, Welt

Withershins Eastlin(g)s

> **With gaucherie** *may indicate* an anagram

Withhold(ing) Abstain, Conceal, Curt, Deny, Detain, Detinue, Hide, Keep, > RESERVE, Trover

Within Enclosed, Endo-, Immanent, Indoors, Inside, Interior, Intra

With it Hep, Hip, Syn, Trendy, W

Without Bar, Beyond, Ex, Lack(ing), Less, Minus, Orb, Outdoors, Outside, Sans, Save, Sen, Senza, Sine, X

> **Without** *may indicate* one word surrounding another

> **Without restraint** *may indicate* an anagram

Without stimulus Nastic

Withstand Blight, Brave, Contest, Defy, Endure, Oppose, Resist, Weather

Witness Attest, Bystander, Compurgator, Crown, Deponent, Depose, Evidence, Expert, Hostile, Jehovah's, Martyr, Material, Muggletonian, Observe, Obtest, Onlooker, Proof, > SEE, Testament, Teste, Testify, Testimony

Witness-box Peter, Stand

▶ **Witticism** *see* WIT

Wizard (priest) Archimage, Carpathian, Conjuror, Expert, Gandalf, Hex, Magician, Merlin, Oz, Prospero, Shaman, Sorcerer, Super, Warlock, > WITCH-DOCTOR

Wizen(ed) Dehydrate, Dry, Sere, Shrivel, Sphacelate, Wither

Woad Anil, Dye, Indigo, Isatis, Pastel, Pastil

Wobble, Wobbling, Wobbly Chandler's, Coggle, Precess, Quaver, Reel, Rock, Shoggle, Shoogle, Totter, Tremble, Trillo, Unstable, Wag, Waggle, Walty, Waver, Wibble

Wodehouse Plum

Woe(ful) Alack, Alas, Bale, Bane, Distress, Doole, Dule, Ewhow, Gram, Grief, Jeremiad, Lack-a-day, Misery, Pain, Plague, > SORROW, Torment, Tribulation, Unhappy

Wolf(ish), Wolf-like Akela, Assyrian, Bolt, Cancer, Casanova, Coyote, Cram, Dangler, Earth, Engorge, Fenrir, Fenris, Gorge, Grey, Ise(n)grim, Lobo, Lone, Lothario, Lupine, Luster, Lycanthrope, MI, Michigan, Pack, Prairie, Rake, Ravenous, Red, Rip, Roué, Rout, Rye, Scoff, Sea, Strand, Tasmanian, Thylacine, Tiger, Timber, Wanderer, Were, Whistler

Wolfram Tungsten

Wolf's bane Aconite, Friar's-cap

Wolseley Sir Garnet

Woman(hood), Women Anile, Bellibone, Besom, Biddy, Bimbo, Bint, Boiler, Broad, Cailleach, Callet, Chai, Chapess, Chook, Citess, Crone, Cummer, Dame, Daughter, Distaff, Doe, Dona(h), Dorcas, Doris, Drab, Eve, F, Fair, Fair sex, > FEMALE, Feme, Flapper, Floozy, Frail, Frow, Gammer, Gimmer, Gin, Girl, Gyno-, -gyny, Harpy, Harridan, Hen, Her, Inner, Jade, Jane, Lady, Liberated, Lilith, Lorette, Madam(e), Mademoiselle, Maenad, Mary, Miladi, Milady, Mob, Mort, Ms, Muliebrity, Pandora, Peat, Pict, Piece, Piece of goods, Placket, Popsy, Quean, Queen, Ramp, Rib, Ribibe, Ronyon, Rudas, Runnion, Sabine, Sakti, Scarlet, Shakti, She, Skirt, Sort, Squaw, Tail, Tedesca, Tib, Tiring, Tit, Tottie, Totty, Trot, Umfazi, Vahine, Wahine, Weaker sex, Wifie

Womaniser Casanova, Lady-killer, Poodle-faker, Wolf

Womb Belly, Matrix, Metritis, Side, Uterus, Ventricle

Women's club, Women's lib S(h)akti, Soroptimist

Won Chon, W

Wonder(s) Admire, Agape, Amazement, AR, Arkansas, Arrah, Awe, Colossus, Ferly, Grape-seed, Marle, > MARVEL, Meteor, Mirabilia, Miracle, Muse, Nine-day, Phenomenon, Prodigy, Seven, Speculate, Stupor, Suppose, Surprise, Wheugh, Whew, Wow

Wonderful(ly) Amazing, Bees' knees, Bitchin(g), Chinless, Épatant, Fantastic, Far-out, Ferly, Geason, Gee-whiz, Glorious, Gramercy, Great, Keen, Lal(l)apalooza, Magic, Mirable, Old, Purely, Ripping, Smashing, Sublime, Superb

Wonder-worker Fakir, Thaumaturgist, Thaumaturgus

Wonky Cockeyed

Wont(ed) Accustomed, Apt, Custom, Habit, Shan't, Used, Winna

Woo(er) Address, Beau, Carve, Court, Seduce, Suitor, Swain

Wood(en), Woodland, Woody Arboretum, Batten, Beam, Board, Boord(e),

Brake, Cask, Channel, Chipboard, Clapboard, Conductor, Dead, Deadpan, Expressionless, Fathom, Fire, Fish, Funk, Furious, Gantry, Gauntree, Hanger, Hard, Hyle, Kindling, Knee, Lath, Lumber, Nemoral, Nemorous, Offcut, Pallet, Plastic, Pulpwood, Punk, Silvan, Slat, Spinney, Splat, Spline, Splint, Stolid, Sylvan, Three-ply, Timber, Tinder, Touch, Treen, Trees, Twiggy, Vert, Xylem, Xyloid

WOOD

3 letters:
Ash
Box
Cam
Elm
Log
Mad
Red

4 letters:
Beef
Bent
Bowl
Carr
Cord
Cork
Deal
Eugh
Gapó
Holt
Iron
King
Lana
Lima
Lime
Rata
Rock
Shaw
Soft
Spar
Wild
Yang

5 letters:
Agila
Algum
Almug
Balsa
Bavin
Beech
Cedar
Copse
Drive

Ebony
Elfin
Firth
Frith
Green
Grove
Heben
Hurst
Igapó
Iroko
Jarul
Joist
Kokra
Lance
Maple
Mazer
Myall
Opepe
Peach
Plane
Ramin
Rowan
Sapan
Spoon
Stink
Taiga
Thorn
Tiger
Tulip
Zante
Zebra

6 letters:
Alerce
Bamboo
Beaver
Birnam
Bocage
Brazil
Canary
Carapa
Cheese
Citron

Citrus
Dingle
Forest
Fustet
Fustic
Fustoc
Gaboon
Gopher
Jarool
Jarrah
Letter
Lignum
Loggat
Manuka
Miombo
Obeche
Orache
Orange
Paddle
Poplar
Raddle
Sabele
Sabicu
Sandal
Sapele
Sappan
Sissoo
Sponge
Tallow
Waboom
Walnut
Wandoo
Yellow

7 letters:
Amboina
Baywood
Boscage
Brassie
Cambium
Coppice
Dudgeon
Dunnage

Duramen
Gambrel
Gumwood
Hadrome
Hickory
Leopard
Meranti
Palmyra
Paranym
Pimento
Sanders
Sapwood
Shawnee
Shittim
Wallaba

8 letters:
Agalloch
Alburnum
Basswood
Bushveld
Caatinga
Coulisse
Harewood
Hornbeam
Kingwood
Laburnum
Ligneous
Mahogany
Pyengadu
Pyinkado
Rosewood
Sapucaia
Shagbark
Southern
Tamarack

9 letters:
Briarwood
Butternut
Caliature
Campeachy
Cocuswood

- Eaglewood
- Fruitwood
- Heartwood
- Ivorywood
- Krummholz
- Matchwood
- Partridge
- Porcupine

Quebracho
Satinwood

10 letters:
Afrormosia
Blockboard
Bulletwood
Calamander

Candlewood
Chittagong
Coromandel
Fiddlewood
Greenheart
Hackmatack
Nettle-tree
Palisander

Springwood
Summerwood

11 letters:
Lignum-vitae
Sanderswood
Slippery elm

▷ **Wood** *may indicate* an anagram (in sense of mad)

Wood-carver Bodger, Gibbons, Whittler

Woodchuck Bobac, Marmot

Woodcock Becasse, Beccaccia, Snipe

Woodlouse Isopod, Oniscus, Slater

Woodman Ali (Baba), Feller, Forester, Hewer, Logger, Lumberjack, Sawyer

Woodpecker Bird, Flicker, Hickwall, Picarian, Rainbird, Sapsucker, Saurognathae, Witwall, Woodwale, Yaffle

Wood-pigeon Bird, Cushat, Que(e)st, Qu(o)ist

Wood-sorrel Oca

Wood-tar Furan, Furfuran

Woodwind Bassoon, Clarinet, Cornet, Flute, Oboe, Piccolo, Pipe, Recorder, Reed

Woodwork(er) Sloid, Sloyd, Tarsia, Termite

Woodworm Gribble, Termes

Wookey Stalactite

Wool(len), Woolly Alpaca, Angora, Aran, Ardil, Bainin, Barège, Beige, Berlin, Botany, Bouclé, Calamanco, Cardi(gan), Cashmere, Cas(s)imere, Clip, Cotton, Crutchings, Daglock, Delaine, Doeskin, Dog, Doily, Down, Doyley, Drugget, Duffel, Fadge, Fingering, Fleece, Flock, Frib, Frieze, Fuzz, Glass, Greasy, Guernsey, Hank, Hause-lock, Hogget, Indumentum, Jaeger, Jersey, Kashmir, Ket, Lanate, Laniferous, Lanigerous, Lanose, Lock, Loden, Merino, Mineral, Mortling, Moul, Mullein, New, Noil(s), Nun's-veiling, Offsorts, Oo, Pashm, Pelage, Persian, Qiviut, Rock, Rolag, Sagathy, Saxon, Say, Shahtoosh, Shalloon, Shamina, Shetland, Shoddy, Skein, Slipe, Slip-on, Slub, Spencer, Staple, Steel, Strouding, Swansdown, Tamise, Tammy, Thibet, Three-ply, Tod, Tricot, Tweed, Twin set, Vicuna, Virgin, Wire, Wood, Worcester, Yarn, Zephyr, Zibel(l)ine

Wool-gather(er), Woolgathering Argo, Dreamer, Reverie

Wool-holder, Woolsack Bale, Distaff

Woolly-bear Tiger-moth, Woubit

Wool-oil Yolk

Wooster Bertie

Woozy Drunk, Vague, Woolly

Worcester Wigorn

Word(s), Wording, Wordy Appellative, Bahuvrihi, Buzz, Cheville, Claptrap, Clipped, Code, Comment, Content, Dick, Dit(t), Echoic, Embolalia, Enclitic, Epos, Etymon, Faith, Four-letter, Function, Ghost, Grace, Hard, Heteronym, Hint, Homograph, Homonym, Household, Hyponym, > **IN A WORD**, > **IN TWO WORDS**, Janus, Jonah, Key, Last, Lexeme, Lexicon, Lexis, Loan, Logia, Logos, Long-winded, Lyrics, Mantra, Message, Morpheme, Mot, Neologism, News, Nonce, Nonsense, Noun, Oracle, Order, Palabra, Paragram, Parole, Paroxytone, Particle, Perissology, Phrase, Piano, Pledge, Pleonasm, Polysemen, Portmanteau, Preposition, Prolix, Promise, Pronoun, Reserved, Rhematic, Rumour, Saying, Selah, Semantics, Signal, Subtitle, Surtitle, Term, Tetragram,

Text, Trigger, Trope, Typewriter, Verb, Verbiage, Verbose, Vogue, Warcry, Weasel, Wort, Written

Word-blindness Alexia, Dyslexia

Word-play Charade, Paronomasia, Pun

Workable Feasible, Practical

Workaholic, **Work(er)**, **Working(-class)**, **Workmen**, **Works**, **Workman(ship)**
Act(ivate), Ant, Appliqué, Apronman, Artefact, Artel, Artifact, Artificer, Artisan, Beaver, Bee, Blue-collar, Bohunk, Boondoggle, Bull, Business, Careerist, Casual, Char, Chargehand, Chore, Claim, Clock, Coolie, Corvée, Crew, Darg, Do, Dog, Dogsbody, Droil, Drudge, Drug, Dung, Earn, Effect, Effort, Em, Erg(ataner), Ergatoid, Erg-nine, Ergon, Ergonomics, Erg-ten, Eta, Evince, Exercise, Exploit, Factotum, Facture, Fat, Fettler, Field, Floruit, Fret, Fuller, > **FUNCTION**, Gastarbeiter, Gel, Go, Graft, Grass, Grind, Grisette, Hand, Harness, Hat, Hobo, Horse, Hunky, Industry, Innards, Job, Journeyman, Key, Knead, Kolhoznik, Labour, Laid, Luddite, Lump, Machinist, Man, Manipulate, Manpower, Mechanic, Meng, Menial, Midinette, Mine, Ming, MO, Moider, Moil, Moonlight, Movement, Navvy, Neuter, Number, Oeuvre, On, Op, Opera(tion), Operative, Operator, Opus, Opusc(u)le, Outside, Ouvrier, Ox, Parergon, Part, Peasant, Peg, Pensum, Peon, Ply, Portfolio, Potboiler, Practise, Production, Prole(tariat), Prud'homme, Public, Pursuit, Red-neck, Rep, Ride, Robot, Roughneck, Rouseabout, Roustabout, Run, Samiti, Satisfactory, Scabble, Scapple, Serve, Service, Servile, Shift, Shop, Situation, Slogger, Smithy, Social, Staff, Stakhanovite, Stevedore, Stint, Strap, Straw, Strive, Support, Surface, Swaggie, Swagman, Sweat, Swink, Take, Tamper, Task, Temp, Tenail(le), Tenaillon, Termite, Tew, Tick, Till, Toccata, Toil, Toreutic, Travail, Treatise, Trojan, TU, Tut, Typto, Uphill, Wage plug, Walla(h), Wark, White-collar, Wobblies, Yacker, Yakka, Yakker

Work-basket, **Workbox** Caba(s), Nécessaire

Workbench Siege

Workhouse Casual ward, Spike, Union

Working *may indicate* an anagram

Working-party Bee, Quilting-bee, Sewing-bee, Squad

Workmate Yokefellow

Work out Deduce

Works, **Workshop** Atelier, Engine, Factory, Forge, Foundry, Garage, Hacienda, Hangar, Innards, Lab, Mill, Passage, Plant, Public, Shed, Shop, Skylab, Smithy, Studio, Sweatshop, Telecottage, Time, Tin, Upper

Workshy Sweer(ed), Sweert, Sweir(t)

World(ly), **Worldwide** Carnal, Chthonic, Cosmopolitan, Cosmos, Dream, Earth, Fleshly, Fourth, Free, Ge, Globe, Kingdom, Lay, Lower, Mappemond, Microcosm, Mondaine, Mondial, Mould, Mundane, Nether, New, Old, Orb, Other, Oyster, Planet, Possible, Secular, Sensual, Society, Sphere, Spirit, Temporal, Terra, Terrene, Terrestrial, Third, Universe, Vale, Web, Welt

Worm(-like), **Worms**, **Wormy** Acorn, Anguillula, Annelid, Annulata, Apod(e), Apodous, Army, Arrow, Articulata, Ascarid, Bilharzia, Bladder, Blind, Blood, Bob, Bootlace, Brandling, Bristle, Caddis, Capeworm, Caseworm, Catworm, Cestode, Cestoid, Chaetopod, Clamworm, Copper, Dew, Diet, Diplozoon, Edge, Enteropneust, Fan, Filander, Filaria, Flag, Flat, Fluke, Galley, Gape, Gilt-tail, Gordius, Gourd, Guinea, Hair-eel, Hairworm, Heartworm, Helminth, Hemichordata, Hookworm, Horsehair, Idle, Inchworm, Leech, Liver-fluke, Lob, Lumbricus, Lytta, Maw, Measuring, Merosome, Miner's, Mopani, Nematoda, Nematode, Nemertea, Nereid, Night-crawler, Oligochaete,

Paddle, Palmer, Palolo, Paste-eel, Peripatus, Piper, Planarian, Platyhelminth, Polychaete, Ragworm, Ribbon, Roundworm, Sabella, Sand-mason, Schistosome, Scoleciform, Scolex, Seamouse, Serpula, Servile, Ship, Sipunculacea, Sipunculoidea, Stomach, Strawworm, Strongyl(e), Taenia, Tag-tail, Taint, Tapeworm, Tenioid, Teredo, Termite, Threadworm, Tiger tail, Tongue, Toxocara, Trematode, Trichina, Trichin(ell)a, Trichinosed, Triclad, Tube, Tubifex, Turbellaria, Vermiform, Vinegar, Vinegar eel, Wheat-eel, Wheatworm, Whipworm

Wormkiller Anthelmintic, Santonin

Wormwood Absinth, Appleringie, Artemisia, Mugwort, Santonica, Southernwood

Worn (out) Attrite, Bare, Decrepit, Detrition, Effete, Epuisé, Exhausted, Forfairn, Forfoughten, Forjaskit, Forjeskit, Frazzled, Knackered, Old, On, Passé, Raddled, Rag, Seedy, Shabby, Shot, Spent, Stale, Tired, Traikit, Trite, Used, Weathered, Whacked

Worried, **Worrier**, **Worry** Agonise, Angst, Annoy, Anxiety, Badger, Bait, Beset, Bother, Care(worn), Cark, Chafe, Concern, Deave, Deeve, Distress, Disturb, Dog, Eat, Exercise, Feeze, Frab, Fret, Fuss, Harass, Harry, Headache, Hyp, Inquietude, Knag, Nag, Perturb, Pester, Pheese, Pheeze, Phese, Pingle, Pium, Preoccupy, Rile, Sool, Stew, Tew, Touse, Towse, Trouble, Unease, Unnerve, Vex, Wherrit, Worn

▷ **Worried** *may indicate* an anagram

Worse(n) Adversely, Degenerate, Deteriorate, Exacerbate, Impair, Inflame, Pejorate, Regress, War(re), Waur

Worship(per) Adore, Adulation, Ancestor, Angelolatry, Autolatry, Bless, Churchgoer, Cult, Deify, Devotion, Douleia, Dulia, Epeolatry, Exercise, Fetish, Glorify, Gurdwara, Happy-clappy, Henotheism, Hero, Idolatry, Idolise, Latria, Lauds, Lionise, Liturgics, Lordolatry, Mariolatry, Oncer, Orant, Praise, Puja, Revere, Sabaism, Sakta, Service, Shacharis, Shakta, Sun, Synaxis, Thiasus, Vaishnava, Venerate, Votary, Wodenism

Worst Beat, Best, Defeat, Get, Nadir, Outdo, Overpower, Pessimum, Rock-bottom, Scum, Severest, The pits, Throw, Trounce

Worsted Caddis, Caddyss, Challis, Coburg, Genappe, Lea, Ley, Serge, Shalli, Tamin(e), Whipcord

▷ **Worsted** *may indicate* an anagram

Wort Laser, Parkleaves, Plant, Tutsan

Worth(while), **Worthy**, **Worthies** Admirable, Asset, Be, Cop, Cost, Deserving, Eligible, Estimable, Feck, > MERIT, Nine, Notable, Substance, Tanti, Use, Value, Venerable, Virtuous, Wealth

Worthless (person) Base, Beggarly, Bilge, Blown, Bodger, Bootless, Bum, Catchpenny, Cheapjack, Crumb, Cypher, Damn, Despicable, Docken, Dodkin, Doit, Doitkin, Draffish, Draffy, Dreck, Dross, Fallal, Footra, Fouter, Foutre, Frippery, Gimcrack, Gingerbread, Glop, Gubbins, Hilding, Javel, Jimcrack, Left, Light, Lorel, Lorrell, Losel, Lozell, Manky, Mare's nest, Mud, Nugatory, Nyaff, Obol, Orra, Otiose, Paltry, Pin, Poxy, Punk, Raca, Rag, Rap, Riffraff, Rubbishy, Scabby, Scum, Shinkin, Shotten, Siwash, Sorry, Straw, Tinhorn, Tinpot, Tinsel, Tittle, Toerag, Trangam, Trashy, Trumpery, Tuppenny, Twat, Two-bit, Twopenny, Useless, Vain, Vile, Waff, Wanworthy, Wauff

Wotchermean Anan

Would be Assumed, Pseudo, Soi-disant

Wouldn't Nould(e)

Wound(ed) Battery, Bite, Bless, Blighty, Bruise, Chagrin, Coiled, Crepance,

Cut, Dere, Engore, Flesh, Ganch, Gash, Gaunch, Gore, Harm, Hurt, Injury, Lacerate, Lesion, Maim, Molest, Mortify, Offend, Pip, Sabre-cut, Scab, Scar, Scath, Scotch, Scratch, Shoot, Snaked, Snub, Sore, Stab, Sting, Trauma, Twined, Umbrage, Vuln, Vulnerary, Walking, Wing, Wint

Woven Faconne, Knitted, Pirnit, Textile, Wattle

Wow Amaze, Howl, My, Success

Wrack Destroy, Downfall, Kelp, Ore, Torment, Varec(h), Vengeance

Wraith Apparition, Fetch, Ghost, Phantom, Shadow, Spectre

Wrangle(r), Wrangling Altercate, Argie-bargie, > ARGUE, Bandy, Bicker, Brangle, Broil, Dispute, Haggle, Mathematical, Rag, Second, Senior, Vitilitigation

Wrap(per), Wrapping, Wrap up Amice, Amis, Bind, Body, Bubble, Bundle, Cellophane®, Cere, Clingfilm, Cloak, Clothe, Cocoon, Conclude, Emboss, Enfold, Enrol(l), Ensheath(e), Envelop(e), Foil, Folio, Furl, Hap, Hem, Kimono, Kraft, Lag, Lap, Mail, Mob, Muffle, Negligee, Nori, Parcel, Roll, Rug, Shawl, Sheath(e), Stole, Swaddle, Swathe, Throw, Tinfoil, Tsutsumu, Velamen, Wap, Wimple

Wrasse Conner, Cunner, Parrot-fish, Scar

Wrath Anger, Cape, Fury, Ire, Passion, Vengeance

Wreak Avenge, Indulge, Inflict

Wreath(e) Adorn, Anadem, Bridal, Chaplet, Coronal, Crown, Entwine, Festoon, Garland, Laurel, Lei, Torse, Tortile, Twist

Wreathe(d) Hederated

Wreck(age), Wrecked, Wrecker Blotto, Crab, Debris, Demolish, Devastate, Flotsam, Founder, Goner, Hesperus, Hulk, Lagan, Ligan, Loss, Luddite, Mutilate, Nervous, Ruin(ate), Sabotage, Shambles, Shatter, Sink, Smash, Subvert, Torpedo, Trash, Wrack

Wrecked *may indicate* an anagram

Wren Architect, Bird, Golden-crested, Hannah, Jenny, Kinglet, Rifleman-bird, Sailor, Willow

Wrench Allen, Bobbejaan, Box, Fit, Jerk, Lug, Mole, Monkey, Pin, Pipe, Pull, Socket, Spanner, Spider, Sprain, Stillson®, Strain, Strap, T-bar, Tear, Torque, Twist, Windlass, Wrest

Wrestle(r), Wrestling All-in, Antaeus, Arm, Basho, Catch-as-catch-can, Catchweight, Clinch, Featherweight, Flying mare, Folding-press, Freestyle, Full-nelson, Grapple, Grovet, Half-nelson, Hammerlock, Haystacks, Headlock, Hip-lock, Indian, Judo, Knee-drop, Makunouchi, Milo, Monkey climb, Mud, Nelson, Niramiai, Ozeki, Palaestral, Pancratium, Pinfall, Posting, Rikishi, Sambo, Stable, Struggle, Sumo, Sumotori, Tag, Tag (team), Tussle, Whip, Wraxle, Wristlock, Writhe, Yokozuna

Wretch(ed) Bally, Blackguard, Blue, Caitiff, Chap-fallen, Cullion, Donder, Forlorn, Git, Hapless, Lorn, Low, Measly, Miser, Miserable, Peelgarlic, Pilgarlick, Pipsqueak, Pitiable, Poltroon, Poor, Punk, Rat, Scoundrel, Scroyle, Seely, Snake, Unblest, Wo(e), Woeful

Wretched *may indicate* an anagram

Wriggle Hirsle, Shimmy, Squirm, Twine, Wiggle, Writhe

Wring(er) Drain, Extort, Mangle, Screw, Squeeze, Twist

Wrinkle(d), Wrinkly Clue, Cockle, Corrugate, Crease, Crepy, Crimple, Crimpy, Crinkle, Crow's-foot, Crumple, Fold, Frounce, Frown, Frumple, Furrow, Gen, Groove, Headline, Hint, Idea, Line, Lirk, Plissé, Plough, Pucker, Purse, Ridge, Rimple, Rivel, Rop(e)y, Ruck(le), Rugose, Rumple, Runkle, Seamy, Shrivel, Sulcus, Time-worn, Tip, Whelk

Wrist Carpus, Radialia, Shackle-bone

Writ(s) Audita querela, Capias, Certiorari, Cursitor, Dedimus, Distringas, Elegit, Fieri facias, Filacer, Habeas corpus, Holy, Injunction, Jury process, Latitat, Law-burrows, Mandamus, Mise, Mittimus, Noverint, Praemunire, Process, Quo warranto, Replevin, Scirefacias, Significat, Subpoena, Summons, Supersedeas, Supplicavit, Tolt, Venire, Venire facias, Warrant

Write(r), Writing Allograph, Amphigory, Annotator, Apocrypha, > **AUTHOR**, Automatic, Ballpoint, Biographer, Biro®, Bloomsbury Group, Book-hand, Boustrophedon, Calligraphy, Causerie, Cento, Charactery, Clerk, Clinquant, Collectanea, Columnist, Copperplate, Creative, Cuneiform, Cursive, Diarist, Dite, Draft, > **DRAMATIST**, Elohist, Endorse, Endoss, Engross, Epigrammatise, Epistle, > **ESSAYIST**, Expatiate, Festschrift, Fist, Form, Formulary, Freelance, Ghost, Gongorism, Graffiti, Grammatology, Graphite, Hack, Hairline, Hand, Haplography, Hieratic, Hieroglyphics, Hiragana, Indite, Ink, Inkhorn-mate, Ink-jerker, Inkslinger, Inscribe, Join-hand, Jot(tings), Journalese, Journalist, Journo, Kalakana, Kaleyard School, Kana, Kanji, Katakana, Keelivine, Keelyvine, Leader, Lexigraphy, Lexis, Linear A, Lipogram, Litterateur, Longhand, Lucubrate, Marivaudage, Minoan, Mirror, Ms(s), Nesk(h), Nib, Notary, Notate, Novelese, > **NOVELIST**, Paragraphia, Pasigraphy, Pen, Pencil, Penmanship, Penne, Penny-a-liner, Pentel®, Picture, Pinyin, Planchette, > **POET**, Polemic, Pot-hook, Proser, Pseudepigrapha, Purana, Purple patch, Quill, Roundhand, Samizdat, Sanskrit, Sci-fi, Scissorer, Scratch, Screed, Screeve, Scribe, Scrip(t), Scripture, Scrivener, Scrow, Scytale, Secretary, Shaster, Shastra, Sign, Sling-ink, Space, Spirit, Stichometry, Style, Subscript, Superscribe, Sutra, Syllabary, Syllabic, Syllabism, Syngraph, Tantra, Transcribe, Treatise, Tushery, Uncial, Wordsmith, Zend-Avesta

WRITERS

3 letters:
APH
Eco
Lee
Paz
Poe
RLS

4 letters:
Amis
Asch
Aymé
Bede
Behn
Bolt
Cary
Dahl
Elia
Gide
Hope
Hugo
Hunt
King
Lamb
Lang
Loos
Loti
Lyly
Mann
More
Nash
Opie
Ovid
Pope
Saki
Sand
Shaw
Snow
Ward
West
Zola

5 letters:
Acton
Albee
Auden
Ayres
Bates
Blake
Caine
Camus
Corvo
Crane
Defoe
Doyle
Dumas
Eliot
Ellis
Genet
Gogol
Gorky
Gosse
Greer
Grimm
Hardy
Harte
Henty
Hesse
Heyer
Homer
Hoyle
Ibsen
Innes
James
Joyce
Kafka
Lewis
Lodge
Lorca
Mason
Milne
Munro
Musil
Nashe
Orczy
Ouida
Pater
Paton
Pliny
Pound
Powys
Reade
Renan
Rilke
Sagan
Scott

Seuss
Shute
Spark
Stark
Stein
Swift
Synge
Twain
Verne
Vidal
Waugh
Wells
White
Wilde
Woolf
Yates
Yonge

6 letters:
Ambler
Arnold
Artaud
Asimov
Austen
Balzac
Baring
Barrie
Belloc
Bellow
Borges
Borrow
Braine
Bronte
Buchan
Bunyan
Butler
Capote
Cicero
Clarke
Conrad
Cowper
Cronin
Daudet
Dryden
Engels
Fowles
France
Gibbon
Goethe
Graves
Greene
Heller

Hobbes
Hughes
Huxley
Jerome
Jonson
Le Fanu
London
Lucian
Lytton
Mailer
Malory
Mannin
Miller
Milton
Morgan
Nerval
Onions
Orwell
Proust
Racine
Runyon
Ruskin
Sapper
Sappho
Sayers
Sendac
Sewell
Smiles
Steele
Sterne
Stoker
Storey
Thomas
Updike
Virgil
Walton
Wilder

7 letters:
Addison
Aldrich
Aretino
Bagehot
Ballard
Beckett
Bennett
Bentley
Boileau
Boswell
Burgess
Carlyle
Chaucer

Chekhov
Cobbett
Colette
Collins
Cookson
Coppard
Corelli
Cranmer
Deeping
Dickens
Drabble
Dreiser
Durrell
Emerson
Fenelon
Forster
Gissing
Golding
Haggard
Herbert
Hichens
Johnson
Kipling
Lardner
Marryat
Maugham
Mauriac
Mérimée
Mitford
Moravia
Murdoch
Nabokov
Naipaul
Peacock
Pushkin
Pynchon
Ransome
Rostand
Rushdie
Saroyan
Sassoon
Shelley
Simenon
Sitwell
Surtees
Terence
Thoreau
Tolkien
Tolstoy
Travers
Wallace
Walpole

Wharton
Whitman
Wyndham

8 letters:
Andersen
Beaumont
Bradbury
Browning
Caldwell
Cartland
Chandler
Childers
Christie
Constant
De la Mare
Disraeli
Faulkner
Fielding
Flaubert
Forester
Goncourt
Ishiguro
Kingsley
Langland
Lawrence
Mannheim
Meredith
Perrault
Plutarch
Proudhon
Rabelais
Rattigan
Remarque
Rousseau
Salinger
Schiller
Sillitoe
Smollett
Stendhal
Taffrail
Traherne
Trollope
Turgenev
Voltaire
Williams

9 letters:
Aeschylus
Ainsworth
Blackmore
Boccaccio

- Burroughs
- Cervantes
- Dos Passos
- Du Maurier
- Edgeworth
- Goldsmith
- Hawthorne
- Hemingway
- Isherwood
- Lermontov
- Linklater
- Mackenzie
- Madariaga

Mansfield
Martineau
Oppenheim
Pasternak
Priestley
Santayana
Sholokhov
Steinbeck
Stevenson
Thackeray
Wodehouse

10 letters:
Ballantyne
Chesterton
Dostoevsky
Fitzgerald
Galsworthy
Mandeville
Maupassant
Richardson

11 letters:
Machiavelli
Maeterlinck

Shakespeare

12 letters:
Aristophanes
Solzhenitsyn

13 letters:
Chateaubriand
Sackville-West

15 letters:
Somerset
Maugham

Write-off Amortise, Annul, Cancel, Scrap
Writhe, Writhing Athetosis, Contort, Curl, Scriggle, Squirm, Thraw, Twist, Wriggle
▷ **Writhing** *may indicate* an anagram
Writing-case Kalamdan
Writing-room Scriptorium
Wrong Aggrieve, Agley, Amiss, Astray, Awry, Bad, Bum, Chout, Delict, Disservice, Err, Fallacious, False, Falsism, Harm, Ill, Immoral, Improper, Incorrect, Injury, Mischief, Misintelligence, Misled, Mistake(n), Misuse, Nocent, Offbase, Offend, Peccadillo, Perverse, Private, Public, Sin(ful), Tort, Transgress, Unethical, Unright, Unsuitable, Withershins, Wryly, X
▷ **Wrong** *may indicate* an anagram
Wrong opinion Cacodoxy
Wrought (up) Agitated, Beaten, Carved, Created, Excited, Filigree, Freestone, Shaped
Wrung Twisted, Withers
Wry Askew, Contrary, Devious, Distort, Droll, Grimace, Ironic
Wryneck Iynx, Jynx, Torticollis, Yunx
Wycliffian Lollard
Wyoming Wy

X(-shaped) Buss, By, Chi, Christ, Cross, Decussate, Drawn, Kiss, Ten, Times, Unknown, X-ray
Xant(h)ippe Battle-axe, Dragon
Xenon Xe
Xerophyte, **Xerophytic** Cactus, Cereus, Mesquite, Tamaricaceae, Tamarisk
Xhosan Caffre, Kaf(f)ir
Ximenes Cardinal
Xmas *see* CHRISTMAS
X-ray Angiogram, Anticathode, C(A)T-scanner, Cholangiography, Emi-Scanner, Encephalogram, Encephalograph, Fermi, Grenz, Mammogram, Plate, Pyelogram, Radioscopy, Rem, Roentgen, Sciagram, Screening, Skiagram, Tomography, Venogram, Xeroradiography
Xylophone Marimba, Sticcado, Sticcato

Yy

Y Samian, Unknown, Yankee, Yard, Year, Yen, Yttrium

Yacht Britannia, Dragon, Ice, Keelboat, Ketch, Knockabout, Land, Maxi, Sailboat, Sand

Yachtsman, **Yachtsmen** Chichester, RYS

Yak Gup, Talk

Yale® Key, Lock

Yam Adjigo, Batata, Breadroot, Camote, Dioscorea, Diosgenin, Kumara

Yank(ee) Bet, Carpetbagger, Hitch, Jerk, Jonathan, Lug, Northerner, Pluck, Pull, Rug, Schlep(p), So(o)le, Sowl(e), > **TUG**, Tweak, Twitch, Wrench, Wrest

▷ **Yank** *may indicate* an anagram

Yap Bark, Yelp

Yard Area, CID, Close, Court, Farm-toun, Garden, Haw, Hof, Kail, Knacker's, Main, Marshalling, Mast, Measure, Navy, Patio, Poultry, Prison, Ree(d), Scotland, Spar, Sprit, Steel, Stick, Stride, Switch, Tilt, Timber, Victualling, Y, Yd

Yarn(s) Abb, Berlin, Bouclé, Caddice, Caddis, Chenille, Clew, Clue, Cop, Cord, Crewel, Fib, Fibroline, Fingering, Genappe, Gimp, Gingham, Guimp(e), Gymp, Homespun, Jaw, Knittle, Knot, Lay, Lea, Ley, Line, Lisle, Lurex®, Marl, Merino, Mohair, Nylon, Organzine, Orlon®, Ply, Rigmarole, Ripping, Rogue's, Rope, Saxony, Schappe, Sennit, Sinnet, Skein, Spun, Story, Strand, Tale, Taradiddle, Thread, Thrid, Thrum(my), Tram, Warp, Weft, Woof, Wool, Worsted, Zephyr

Yarrow Milfoil

Yashmak Veil

Yaw(s) Boba, Buba, Deviate, Framboesia, Lean, Morula, Tack, Veer

Yawn(ing) Boredom, Chasmy, Fissure, Gant, Gape, Gaunt, Greys, Hiant, Oscitation, Pandiculation, Rictus

Yea Certainly, Truly, Verily, Yes

Year(ly), **Years** A, Age, Anno, Annual, Anomalistic, Astronomical, Calendar, Canicular, Civil, Common, Cosmic, Decennium, Donkey's, Dot, Ecclesiastical, Egyptian, Embolismic, Equinoctial, Financial, Fiscal, Gap, Great, Hebrew, Holy, Indiction, Julian, Leap, Legal, Light, Lunar, Lunisolar, Natural, PA, Perfect, Platonic, Riper, Sabbatical, School, Sidereal, Solar, Sothic, Summer, Sun, Tax, Theban, Time, Towmon(d), Towmont, Tropical, Twelvemonth, Vintage, Wander

Yearbook Annual

Yearling Colt, Hogget, Stirk, Teg

Yearn(ing) Ache, Ake, Aspire, Brame, Burn, Covet, Crave, Curdle, Desire, Erne, Greed, Hanker, Hone, > **LONG**, Nostalgia, Pant, Pine, Sigh

▷ **Yearning** *may indicate* an anagram

Year's end Dec

Yeast Barm, Bees, Brewer's, Ferment, Flor, Leaven, Saccharomycete, Torula, Vegemite®

Yell Cry, Hue, Shout, Skelloch, Thunder, Tiger, Waul, Yoick

Yellow(ish) Abram, Amber, Anthoclore, Auburn, Back, Beige, Bisque, Bistre,

Buff, Butternut, Cadmium, Canary, Chicken, Chrome, Citrine, Cowardly, Craven, Curcumin(e), Daffodil, Etiolin, Fallow, Fever, Filemot, Flavescent, Flavin(e), Flavon, Flaxen, Fulvous, Gamboge, Gold, Icteric, Isabel(le), Isabella, Jack, Jaundiced, Lammer, Lemon(y), Lupulin, Lutein, Lutescent, Mustard, Nankeen, Naples, Oaker, Ochery, Ochre(y), Or(eide), Oroide, Pages, Peril, Pink, Primrose, Queen's, River, Saffron, Sallow, Sand, Sear, Spineless, Straw, Sulphur, Tawny, Topaz, Tow, Vitelline, Weld, Xanthous, Yolk

Yellowhammer Bunting, Yeldring, Yeldrock, Yite, Yoldring

Yellow-wood Gopher

Yelp Cry, Squeal, Whee, Ya(w)p

Yemeni Adeni, Saba, Sabean, Sheba

Yen Desire, Itch, Longing, Urge, Y, Yearn

Yeoman Beefeater, Exon, Goodman, Goodwife, Salvation

Yep OK, Yes

Yes Ay(e), Da, Indeed, Ja, Jokol, Nod, OK, Oke, Quite, Sure, Truly, Uh-huh, Wilco, Yea, Yokul, Yup

Yesterday Démodé, Eve, Hesternal, Pridian

Yet But, Even, How-be, Moreover, Nay, Nevertheless, Now, Still, Though

Yeti Abominable snowman, Sasquatch

Yew Taxus

Yibbles A(i)blins

Yield(ing) Abandon, Afford, Bend, Bow, Breed, Capitulate, Catch, Cede, Come, Comply, Concede, Crack, Crop, Defer, Dividend, Docile, Ductile, Easy, Elastic, Exert, Facile, Flaccid, Flexible, Give, Harvest, Interest, Knuckle, Knuckle under, Meek, Meltith, Mess, Output, Pan, Pay, Pliant, Produce, Redemption, Relent, Render, Return, Sag, Soft, > **SUBMIT**, Succumb, Surrender, Susceptible, Truckle, Weak-kneed

Yodel Song, Warble

Yoga, Yogi As(h)tanga, Bear, Bhakti, Fakir, Hatha, Maha, Power, Raja, Sid(d)ha, Sivananda

Yog(h)urt Madzoon, Matzoon, Tzatziki

Yoke Bow, Cang(ue), Collar, Couple, Harness, Inspan, Jugal, Oxbow, Pair, Span, Square, Tucker

Yokel Boor, Bumpkin, Chaw(-bacon), Clumperton, Hayseed, Hick, Jake, Jock, Peasant, Rustic

Yolk Parablast, Vitellicle, Vitellus, Yellow

Yon(der) Distant, Further, O'erby, Thae, There, Thether, Thither

Yore Agone, Olden, Past

Yorick Sterne

York(shire), Yorkshireman Batter, Bowl, Ebor, Pudding, Ridings, Tyke

Yorker Tice

You One, Sie, Thee, Thou, Usted, Ye

Young (person), Youngster, Youth(ful) Adolescent, Ageless, Amorino, Bev(an), Bodgie, Boy, Boyhood, Brigham, Bub, Buckie, Calf-time, Ch, Charver, Chick, Chicken, Child, Chile, Cockerel, Cockle, Colt, Comsomol, Cornstalk, Cub, DJ, Early, Ephebe, Ephebus, Esquire, Flapper, Fledgling, Foetus, Fry, Gigolo, Gilded, Gillet, Girl, Gunsel, Halfling, Hebe, Hobbledehoy, Immature, Imp, Infant, Issue, Junior, Juvenal, Juvenesce, Juvenile, Keral, Kid, Kiddo, Kiddy, Kipper, Knave-bairn, Komsomol, Lad, Lamb, Latter-day, Leaping-time, Less, Litter, Little, Loretta, Middle, Minor, Misspent, Mod, Mormon, Nance, Neanic, Neophyte, Nestling, New, New Romantic, Nipper, Nymph, Plant, (Pre-)pubescent, Progeny, Protégé(e), Punk, Pup, Sapling, Scent,

Scion, Shaveling, Shaver, Skinhead, Slip, Son, Spawn, Sprig, Springal(d), Stripling, Swain, Syen, Ted, Teenager, Teens, Teenybopper, Toyboy, Vernal, Well-preserved, Whelp, Whippersnapper, Wigga, Wigger, Yippy, Yoof, Yopper, Younker, Yumpie, Yuppie

Younger, Youngest Baby, Benjamin, Cadet, Last born, Less, Minimus, Seneca, Wallydrag, Wallydraigle, Yr

Your(s) Thee, Thine, Thy

▸ **Youth** *see* YOUNG PERSON

Yo-yo Bandalore

Ytterbium Yb

Yttrium Y

Yucatan Maya

Yucca Adam's needle

Yucky Gooey, Grooly, Sickly, Sticky

Yugoslav Croat(ian), Serb, Slovene, Ustashi

Yukon YT

Yuletide Advent, Dec, Noel, Xmas

Zz

Z Izzard, Izzet, Zambia, Zebra

Zamenhof Esperanto

Zander Fogash, Sander

Zany Bor(r)el, Comic, Cuckoo, Idiotic, Mad

Zeal(ous) Ardour, Bigotry, Devotion, Eager, Enthusiasm, Evangelic, Fervour, Fire, Perfervid, Study

Zealot Bigot, Devotee, Fan(atic), St Simon, Votary

Zebra Convict, Quagga

Zenith Acme, Apogee, Height, Pole, Summit

Zeno Colonnade, Elea, Stoic

Zeolite Analcime, Analcite, Gmelinite

Zephyr Breeze, Wind

Zeppelin Airship, Balloon, Dirigible

Zero Absolute, Blob, Cipher, Donut, Ground, Nil, Nothing, Nought, O, Status, Z

Zest Condiment, Crave, Élan, Gusto, Pep, Piquancy, Relish, Spark, Spice, Tang, Zap, Zing

Ziegfeld Flo

Zigzag Crémaillère, Crinkle-crankle, Dancette, Feather-stitch, Indent, Major Mitchell, Ric-rac, Slalom, Stagger, Switchback, Tack, Traverse, Yaw

Zinc Blende, Gahnite, Mossy, Sherardise, Spelter, Sphalerite, Tutenag, Tutty, Willemite, Wurtzite, Zn

Zip(per) Dash, Energy, Fastener, Fly, Go, Oomph, Presto, Stingo, Vim, Vivacity, Whirry, Zero

Zircon Hyacinth, Jacinth, Jargo(o)n

Zirconium Baddeleyite, Zr

Zither Cithara, Kantela, Kantele, Koto

Zodiac(al) Aquarius, Archer, Aries, Bull, Cancer, Capricorn, Counter-glow, Crab, Fish, Gegenschein, Gemini, Goat, Horoscope, Leo, Libra, Lion, Ophiuchus, Pisces, Ram, Sagittarius, Scales, Scorpio(n), Taurus, Twins, Virgin, Virgo, Watercarrier

Zola Budd, Emile, Nana, Realism

Zombie Catatonic, Dolt, Robot

Zone(s) Abyssal, Acid, Anacoustic, Area, Band, Bathyal, Belt, Benioff, Buffer, Canal, Climate, Collision, Comfort, Convergence, Crumple, Drop, Economic, Ecotone, End, Enterprise, Erogenous, Euro, Exclusion, F layer, Fracture, Free, Fresnel, Frigid, Hadal, Hot, Impact, Krumhole, Low velocity, Neutral, No-fly, Nuclear-free, Precinct, > REGION, Rift, Ring, Sahel, Sector, Shear, Skip, Smokeless, Stratopause, Strike, Subduction, Temperate, Time, Tolerance, Torrid, Tundra, Twilight

Zoo Bedlam, Circus, Menagerie, Vivarium, Whipsnade

Zoologist, Zoology Biologist, Botanist, Cetology, Naturalist

Zoom Close-up, Speed

Zoroastrian Gabar, Gheber, Ghebre, Gueber, Guebre, Magus, Mazdaist,

Zulu | 790

Mazdean, Ormazd, Ormuzd, Parsee, Parsi
Zulu Chaka, Impi, Inkatha, Matabele, Niger, Shaka, Warrior
Zut Crimini

BRADFORD'S CROSSWORD LISTS

Crossword lists

A a

Abbreviations

CLASSIFIED ADVERTISEMENTS

Abbreviation	Meaning
AMC *or* amc	All mod cons
Deps	Deposit
Exc *or* excl	Excluding
F/f	Furnished flat
GCH	Gas central heating
Inc *or* incl	Including
Pcm	Per calendar month
Pw	Per week

LONELY HEARTS COLUMN ABBREVIATIONS

Abbreviation	Meaning
GSOH	Good sense of humour
GWM	Gay white male
LTR	Long term relationship
NS *or* N/S	Non-smoker
SOH	Sense of humour
SWF	Single white female
VGSOH	Very good sense of humour
WLTM	Would like to meet
WSOH	Weird *or* wicked sense of humour

OTHER ABBREVIATIONS

1 letter:		
A	M	Y
B	N	Z
C	O	
D	P	**2 letters:**
E	Q	AA
F	R	Aa
G	S	AB
H	T	A/C
I	U	AC
K	V	A/c
L	W	Ac
	X	AD

OTHER ABBREVIATIONS (CONTINUED)

Ae	BO	CU
A/F	Bo	Cu
AF	Bp	CV
Af	B/R	CW
AG	BR	D/A
AH	Br	DA
AI	B/S	DB
AK	BS	DC
AL	BT	DD
A/M	Bt	DE
AM	BV	D/F
Am	B/W	DF
AN	BW	DG
A/O	Bx	Dg
AO	Bz	DI
AP	C/A	DJ
AQ	CA	DM
Aq	Ca	D/O
AR	CB	DO
Ar	Cb	Do
AS	CC	D/P
AT	Cc	DP
At	CD	DR
AU	C/d	Dr
AV	Cd	DS
Av	CE	DU
A-v	CF	Du
AZ	C/f	DV
Az	Cf	D/W
BA	CG	Ea
BB	Cg	EC
BC	CH	Ed
B/D	Ch	EE
BD	CI	Ee
Bd	CJ	Eg
B/E	CM	EI
BE	C/N	EN
Bé	CO	Eo
B/F	C/o	EP
BJ	Co	Ep
Bk	CP	EQ
B/L	Cp	Eq
BL	CQ	ER
Bl	CR	ET
BM	Cr	EU
Bm	CS	EV
Bn	CT	Ex
B/O	Ct	Ez

OTHER ABBREVIATIONS (CONTINUED)

FA	HJ	KC
Fa	HK	Kc
FC	HL	KD
Fc	HM	KE
FD	HO	KG
FI	Ho	Kg
FL	HP	Kn
FI	HQ	KP
FM	HR	Kr
Fm	Hr	KS
FO	HS	KT
Fo	HT	Kt
FP	Ht	KV
Fp	HV	KW
Fr	HW	Ky
Fs	Ia	LA
FT	IC	La
Ft	I/c	Lb
Fv	ID	L/C
FX	Id	LC
GA	IE	Lc
Ga	Ie	LD
GB	IF	Ld
Gb	IG	LE
GC	IL	LF
GG	IM	LG
GI	IN	Lg
Gi	In	LH
Gk	I/O	Lh
GM	IP	LI
GO	IQ	LJ
GP	Iq	LL
GQ	IR	Ll
Gr	Ir	Ln
GS	Is	LO
GT	IT	L/P
Gu	It	LP
Gv	IU	LT
Ha	Iv	Lt
HC	JA	LU
Hd	JC	LV
HE	JD	Lv
HF	JJ	LW
Hf	JP	MA
HG	Jr	MB
Hg	Jt	Mb
HH	KB	MC
HI	Kb	MD

OTHER ABBREVIATIONS (CONTINUED)

Md	Nr	Pm
ME	NS	PN
Me	Ns	PO
MF	NT	PP
Mf	NV	Pp
MG	NY	PQ
MI	NZ	Pq
Mi	OB	PR
Mk	Ob	Pr
ML	OC	PS
MM	O/c	Ps
Mm	OD	PT
MN	OE	Pt
MO	Oe	PW
Mo	OF	PX
MP	OG	QB
Mp	Og	QC
MR	OH	Qe
MS	OJ	QF
MT	OK	Ql
Mt	OM	QM
MU	ON	Qm
MV	OP	Qn
Mv	Op	QR
MW	OR	Qr
MX	OS	QS
MY	OT	Qs
NA	OU	Qt
N/a	Oz	Qv
NB	PA	Qy
Nb	Pa	RA
NC	PB	RC
ND	P/C	Rc
Nd	PC	RD
NE	Pc	Rd
N/F	PD	RE
NF	Pd	RF
NG	PE	Rf
NH	Pf	RH
NI	PG	Rh
NJ	Pg	RI
NL	Ph	RL
NI	PI	RM
NM	PK	Rm
Nm	Pk	RN
No	PL	RP
NP	PI	RQ
Np	PM	RR

OTHER ABBREVIATIONS (CONTINUED)

RS	TT	Wg
RT	TU	Wl
Rt	TV	WK
RU	TX	Wk
RV	UA	WO
Rv	UC	W/o
RW	Uc	WP
SA	UK	WR
Sa	UN	Wt
Sb	UP	WV
SC	UR	WY
Sc	U/S	Xn
SD	US	XO
Sd	Us	Xt
SF	UT	YC
Sf	UU	Yd
SG	UV	Yr
Sg	VA	YT
SI	Va	ZB
SJ	VB	
SK	Vb	**3 letters:**
Sk	VD	AAA
S/L	Vd	AAM
SL	VF	AAP
SI	VG	ABA
SM	Vg	ABC
SO	VI	ABH
SP	Vi	Abl
Sp	VJ	ABM
Sq	VL	Abp
Sr	Vl	ABS
SS	VO	ABV
St	Vo	ACA
SU	VP	ACC
SV	VR	Acc
Sv	VS	ACM
SW	Vs	ACT
Sw	Vt	ACW
TA	Vv	ADC
TB	VW	ADD
Tb	WA	ADH
TC	WB	Adj
TD	Wb	Adm
TG	WC	ADO
Tg	Wc	Adv
TM	WD	AEA
TN	Wd	AEC
Tr	Wf	Aet

OTHER ABBREVIATIONS (CONTINUED)

AEW	AOB	BAR
AFB	AOC	Bar
AFC	AOH	BBC
Afg	AOR	BBL
AFK	APB	BBQ
AFL	APR	BBS
AFM	Apr	BCA
AFN	APT	BCC
Afp	Apt	BCD
AFV	ARA	BCE
AGC	ARC	BCF
AGM	Arg	BCG
AGN	Ark	BCh
AGR	Arm	BCL
Agr	Arr	BCS
Agt	ART	BDA
AHQ	ARV	Bde
AIA	ASA	Bdl
AID	ASB	BDS
AIF	ASL	Bds
AIH	Asl	BEA
AIM	ASM	BEd
AIR	AST	BEF
AIS	ASW	BEM
AJA	ATB	BeV
AJC	ATC	BFA
Aka	ATK	BFI
Ala	ATM	BFN
Alb	Atm	BHP
Ald	ATN	Bhp
ALF	ATP	Bid
Alg	ATV	BIM
Alk	AUC	BIS
ALP	Aug	Bkg
ALS	AUS	Bks
ALU	Aus	BLL
AMA	AUT	BMA
AMF	AVC	BMI
AMM	Ave	BMJ
AMP	AVM	BMR
Amp	Avn	BMX
Amt	AWA	BNA
AMU	AWS	BNP
Amu	AWU	BOD
ANA	AZT	Bol
ANC	BAF	BOT
ANU	BAK	Bot
ANZ	BAL	BPC

OTHER ABBREVIATIONS (CONTINUED)

BPE	Cap	Cie
Bpi	CAR	Cif
BPR	CAS	CIM
Bps	CAT	CIO
Bpt	Cat	Cir
BRB	CAV	CIS
BRE	CAW	CIT
Bro	CBC	Cit
BRT	CBD	CJA
BSB	CBE	CJD
BSC	CBI	CLC
BSc	CBR	CMG
BSE	CBS	Cml
BSF	CBT	CMV
BSI	Ccc	CNA
BSL	CCD	CND
Bs/L	CCF	CNG
Bsl	CCJ	CNN
BSP	CDC	CNR
BSS	CDE	CNS
BST	Cdf	CoA
BSW	Cdn	COD
BTG	CDR	COI
BTh	Cdr	Col
Btl	CDT	Com
BTU	CDU	Con
Btu	CDV	COO
BTW	CER	CoO
Bty	CET	COP
BUF	CFB	Cor
Bul	CFC	COS
Bur	CFD	Cos
BVA	CFE	Cot
BVM	Cfi	COV
BWD	CFL	Coy
BWG	CFS	CPA
BWR	CGI	CPD
BWV	CGM	Cpd
CAA	CGS	CPI
CAB	CGT	Cpi
CAE	ChB	Cpl
CAF	ChE	CPO
CAI	Chg	CPR
CAL	ChM	CPS
Cal	CIA	Cps
CAM	CIB	CPU
Can	CID	CQB
CAP	CIE	CRE

OTHER ABBREVIATIONS (CONTINUED)

CRI	DDR	DPP
CRM	DDS	Dpt
CRO	Deb	DPW
CRP	Dec	DSC
CRT	Def	DSc
CSA	Deg	DSM
CSB	Del	DSO
CSC	Dem	Dsp
Csc	Den	DSS
CSE	Dep	DST
CSF	DES	DTI
CSM	DET	DTL
CSR	DFC	DTP
CSS	DFM	DT's
CST	DHA	DTT
CSV	DHB	Dur
CTC	DHS	DVD
Ctn	Din	DVM
CTO	Dip	DVT
CTR	Dir	DWP
Cts	DIY	Dwt
CTU	DLL	EAS
CTV	DLR	EBS
CVA	Dlr	EBU
CVO	DMA	EBV
CVS	DMD	ECB
CWA	DMF	ECG
Cwo	DMK	ECR
CWS	DMS	ECS
Cwt	DMs	ECT
CWU	DMT	EDC
CYA	DMZ	EDI
CYF	DNR	EDM
DAB	DNS	EDT
Dak	DOA	EEA
Dan	DOC	EEC
DAP	Doc	EEG
DAR	DOD	EFA
DAT	DOE	EFL
Dat	DoH	EGM
DBE	DoI	EHF
Dbh	DOM	EHO
DBS	Dom	EHV
DCB	Doz	EIA
DCC	DPB	EIB
DCF	DPH	EKG
DCL	Dpi	ELF
DCM	DPM	ELT

OTHER ABBREVIATIONS (CONTINUED)

Emf	Exr	FSH
EMS	Ext	Fth
EMU	FAA	Ft-l
Emu	FAB	Fur
EMV	FAI	FWD
Enc	FAO	Fwd
ENG	FAQ	FYI
Eng	Faq	FZS
ENO	FAS	GAA
Ens	FBA	GAI
ENT	FBI	GAL
EOC	FBL	Gal
Eom	FBW	GBE
EPA	FCA	GBH
EPG	FCC	GBS
Eph	FCO	GCA
EPO	FDA	GCB
EPP	Fdm	GCE
EPR	FDP	GCF
Eps	FDR	GDP
EPZ	Feb	GDR
EQC	Fec	Gds
ERA	Fed	Gen
Erf	Fem	Ger
ERM	FET	GeT
ERO	Ffa	GeV
ERS	FIA	GHB
ESA	Fig	GHQ
ESB	Fin	GIS
Esd	Fla	GLA
ESL	Fld	GLC
ESN	FMD	Gld
ESO	FMS	GMB
ESP	Fob	GMC
Esq	FoC	Gmc
ESR	FoE	GMO
EST	Fol	GMT
Est	For	GNC
Esu	FPA	GNP
ETA	FPO	Gns
Etc	Fps	GOC
ETD	FRG	GOM
ETF	Fri	GOP
Eth	Frl	Gov
Ety	FRS	GPI
EVA	Frt	GPO
EWO	FSA	GPS
Exc	FSB	GPU

OTHER ABBREVIATIONS (CONTINUED)

GRF	Hts	IMS
Gro	HUD	Inc
GSM	HWM	IND
Gsm	Hyp	Ind
GSR	IAA	INF
GST	IAF	INS
GTC	IAP	Ins
Gtd	IAS	IOC
GUM	IBA	IOM
Gyn	IBF	IOW
HAA	ICA	IPA
Hab	ICC	IPO
HAC	ICE	IRA
Hag	Ice	IRC
HBC	ICI	IRD
HBM	ICJ	Ire
HCF	ICS	IRL
HCG	ICT	IRM
Hcp	ICU	IRO
HDL	IDA	IRS
Heb	Ida	IRW
Her	IDB	ISA
HEU	IDC	ISD
HEW	IDD	Isl
HGH	IDN	ISM
Hgt	IDP	ISP
HGV	IEA	ITA
Hhd	IEE	Ita
HIE	IFA	ITC
HIH	IFC	ITN
HIM	IFF	ITO
HIV	IFP	ITU
HJS	IFR	ITV
HMG	IFS	IUD
HMI	IGC	IUS
HMS	IGM	IVF
HNC	IGY	IVR
HND	IHC	IWC
Hon	Iid	IWW
Hos	IJC	JAG
HPV	III	Jam
HRE	ILO	Jan
HRH	ILR	JAP
HRT	ILS	Jap
HSE	ILU	Jas
HSH	IMF	JCD
HSM	IMO	JCL
HST	Imp	JCR

OTHER ABBREVIATIONS (CONTINUED)

JCS	LED	MCS
Jer	LEO	MDF
JFK	Lev	MDR
JIT	LGV	MDS
Jnd	Lhd	MEC
Jnr	Lib	MEd
Jon	Liq	Med
JSA	Lit	MEP
JSD	LLB	Mer
JUD	LLD	Met
Jud	LLM	Mex
Jul	LMS	MEZ
Jun	LNG	MFA
JWV	LOL	Mfd
Kan	Loq	Mfg
KBE	LPG	MFH
KCB	LPO	Mfr
Kčs	LPS	MGB
Ken	LRT	Mgr
KeV	LSD	MHA
KIT	LSE	MHC
KKK	LSI	MHD
Knt	LSO	MHG
Kph	LSZ	MHR
KRL	LTA	MIA
KWh	Ltd	Mic
KZN	LTR	Mid
Lab	LUV	Mil
LAC	Lux	Min
Lam	LVP	MIP
LAN	Lwl	MIT
Lat	LWM	Mkt
LBD	MAC	MLA
Lbf	Mac	MLC
LBJ	Mag	MLD
LBO	Maj	MLF
LBV	Mal	MLG
Lbw	Mar	MLR
LCD	Mat	MMC
Lcd	Max	Mmf
LCJ	MBA	MMM
LCL	MBE	MMP
Lcm	MBO	MMV
Ldg	MCB	MNA
LDL	MCC	MOB
LDR	MCG	MoC
LDS	MCh	MOD
LEA	MCP	Mod

OTHER ABBREVIATIONS (CONTINUED)

MOH	NCC	NRC
MOI	NCM	NRL
Mol	NCO	NRN
Mon	NCP	NRT
MOR	NDE	NRV
Mor	NDP	NSB
MOS	NDT	NSF
MOT	NEB	NSG
MPC	NEC	NSU
MPG	NEG	NSW
Mpg	Neg	Nth
Mph	Neh	NTO
MPP	NEP	NTP
MPS	Nev	NTS
MPV	NFA	NUJ
MRA	NFB	NUM
MRC	NFL	Num
MRE	NFS	NUR
MRI	NFT	NUS
MRM	NFU	NUT
MRP	NGA	NVQ
Msb	NGC	NWT
MSC	NGF	NYC
MSc	NGk	NZC
MSD	NGL	NZE
MSF	NGO	NZR
MSG	NHI	OAP
MSI	NHL	OAS
Msl	NHS	OAU
MSM	NIC	Obb
MSP	NII	OBE
MSS	NLC	Obj
MST	NLF	Obs
Mtg	NLS	OCD
MTV	NLW	OCR
Mus	NMR	OCS
MVD	NNP	Oct
MVO	NOI	ODA
MVP	Nom	ODI
MVS	Nos	OED
Nah	Nov	OEM
NAI	NPA	OFM
NAS	NPC	OFS
Nat	NPD	OFT
NAV	NPL	OHG
NBA	NPV	Ohv
NBC	NQA	OIC
NBG	NRA	OLG

OTHER ABBREVIATIONS (CONTINUED)

OMM	PGA	Psi
OMS	PGD	PSK
ONC	PGR	PSL
OND	PHC	PSS
Ono	PhD	PST
ONS	PHS	PSV
Ont	PID	PTA
ONZ	P-i-n	Pte
OPC	Pkg	Ptg
Ops	Pkt	PTN
Org	PKU	PTO
OSA	PLA	Pts
OSB	Plc	Pty
OSD	PLO	Pub
OSF	PLP	PVA
OSI	PLR	PVC
OST	PLU	PVR
OTC	PMG	PVS
OTE	PMI	Pvt
OTT	PMS	PWA
Ozs	PMT	PWR
PAC	PNI	Pwt
Pac	POB	QCA
Pal	POD	QCD
Pan	POE	QED
Par	POL	QEF
PAU	Pol	QFD
PAX	POM	Qld
PBX	POP	QMC
PCB	Pop	QMG
PCC	POS	QMS
Pcm	Pos	QMV
PCP	POW	Qqv
PCR	Ppd	QSM
Pct	PPE	QSO
PCV	Ppm	Qto
PDA	PPP	QTS
Pdl	Ppr	Qty
Pdq	PPS	Que
PDR	PRB	RAC
PEI	Prn	Rad
Pen	PRO	RAE
PEP	PRP	RAF
PER	Prs	RAM
PET	PRT	Ram
Pet	PRW	RAN
Pfa	Psf	RAR
PFI	PSG	RAS

OTHER ABBREVIATIONS (CONTINUED)

RBE	RPC	SCR
RCA	RPG	Scr
RCD	RPI	SDI
Rcd	Rpm	SDP
RCL	RPS	SEC
RCM	Rps	Sec
RCN	Rpt	SEN
RCO	RPV	Sen
RCP	RRP	Seq
RCS	RSA	SFA
RCT	RSC	SFO
Rct	RSG	SFW
RDA	RSI	Sgd
RDC	RSJ	Sgt
RDS	RSL	SHA
RDX	RSM	SHF
Ref	RSV	SHM
Reg	RTA	SIB
Rel	RTC	Sig
REM	RTE	SIN
Rep	RTF	Sin
Res	RTR	SIS
Rev	RTT	SIT
RFC	RUC	SJA
RGB	RUG	SJC
RGN	Rwd	SJD
RGS	Rwy	Skt
Rgt	SAC	SLD
RHA	SAD	Sld
Rhd	SAE	SLR
RHG	Sae	SMD
RHS	SAm	SMP
RIA	Sam	SMS
RIC	SAR	SMV
RIP	SAS	SNG
Rit	SAT	SNP
Rly	SAW	Snr
RMA	SBA	Sob
RME	SBE	Soc
Rmm	SBS	SOE
RMS	SBU	Sol
Rms	ScD	Som
RMT	SCE	SOP
RNR	SCG	Sop
RNZ	Sch	SPA
ROC	Sci	SpA
Rom	SCM	SPD
Rot	SCP	SPF

OTHER ABBREVIATIONS (CONTINUED)

Spp	Tdc	UBR
SPR	Tdm	UCL
Spt	TES	UCT
SQA	Tex	UDA
SQL	TGV	UDC
Sqn	ThB	UDI
Sqq	ThD	UDR
SRA	THI	UFO
Sra	THX	UGC
SRN	TIA	UHF
SRO	Tid	UHT
SSB	Tim	Ukr
SSC	TIR	Ult
SSD	Tit	UNA
SSM	TKO	UNO
SSN	TLA	UPC
SSP	TLC	UPI
Ssp	TLS	URC
SSR	TMI	URL
ST	TMT	Uru
Sta	TMV	USA
STC	Tng	USB
STD	Tob	USM
Std	Tox	USN
Ste	TPI	USO
Stg	Tpr	USP
Sth	TQM	USS
Stk	TRC	USW
STP	TRH	UTC
Str	Trs	UV-A
STV	TSB	UV-B
Sub	TSE	UVF
Suf	TSH	UWT
Sun	TSO	VAD
Sup	Tsp	VAR
SUV	TTA	Var
VQ	TTL	VAT
Syn	TUC	Vat
Syr	TUF	VCR
TAB	TVM	VDC
Tab	TVP	VDT
TAC	TVR	VDU
TAI	TXT	Ven
Tan	Typ	Vet
Tbc	UAE	VGA
Tbs	UAM	VHF
TBT	UAR	VHS
TCM	UAV	VIP

OTHER ABBREVIATIONS (CONTINUED)

VIR	WVS	ASDE
Vis	WWF	ASIO
Viz	WWI	Assn
VLA	WWW	ASSR
VLF	Wyo	Asst
VMD	XUV	ASTM
VMI	YBA	Astr
Voc	YHA	At no
Vol	Yrs	A to J
VPL	YTS	Attn
VRI	ZCC	Atty
Vsb	ZPG	At wt
VSO		AUEW
VTR	**4 letters:**	Aust
WAN	ACCA	Avdp
War	ACCC	AWRE
WBA	ACER	BAOR
WBC	ACGI	Bapt
WBO	ACII	Bart
WBU	ACLU	BBBC
WCC	Actg	BBFC
WDA	ACTT	BCAR
WDM	ACTU	BCNU
WEA	ADFA	BCNZ
Wed	ADHD	BCom
Wef	Advt	Beds
WEU	AECL	Belg
WFF	AFTN	BEng
Whf	AICC	BFPO
WHO	Alas	Biog
Whr	ALCM	Biol
Wig	Alta	Bkcy
Wis	AMDG	Bkpt
WLM	Amer	Bldg
WMD	Anat	BLit
Wmk	Anim	Blvd
WMO	Anon	BMus
WOF	ANSI	BNFL
WOW	AOCB	BOAC
WPA	AONB	Braz
WPB	Apoc	BRCS
WPC	APRA	Brig
Wpm	Arch	Brit
WST	ARCM	Bros
WTC	ARCS	BSSc
WTG	Ariz	Bulg
WTO	ARSM	BYOB
W Va	Asap	CABE

OTHER ABBREVIATIONS (CONTINUED)

Camb	CRAC	Esth
Cant	Cres	Et al
Caps	Crim	Exec
Capt	Crit	Exod
Card	CSCE	Exor
CART	CSYS	Ezek
CATV	DATV	FACE
CBSO	DBib	FAHA
CCEA	DBMS	Fath
CCMA	DCMG	Fcap
CCRC	DCMS	FCCA
CCTA	DCVO	FCII
CCTV	DDSc	F Eng
CDNA	Decd	FIDE
Cdre	DEng	Fl dr
CEGB	Dent	Flem
CEng	Dept	Fl oz
CGBR	DETR	FMCG
Chap	Deut	FMRI
Chem	DfEE	Foll
Ches	DFID	FONE
Chin	DHSS	FRCM
CICA	Diag	FRCO
CIFE	Dial	FRCP
CIGS	Diam	FRCS
C in C	DMAC	FRGS
Cllr	DMSO	FRPS
Cmdr	DMus	FRSC
CMEA	DOCG	Ft-lb
CNAA	DTLR	FWIW
CNAR	DVLA	GAIN
C of E	Ebor	Gall
C of I	EBRD	GCHQ
C of S	Eccl	GCMG
Colo	Ecol	GCSE
Comr	Econ	GCVO
Cong	ECSC	Gdns
Conj	Ecua	Genl
Conn	EFIS	Geod
Cons	EFTS	Geog
Coop	Encl	Geol
Corp	ENEA	Geom
CPAG	Engr	Glos
CPRE	Epis	GmbH
CPSA	EPNS	GMTA
CPSU	ERCP	GnRH
CPVE	ERDF	GNVQ
CQSW	ESRC	Govt

OTHER ABBREVIATIONS (CONTINUED)

GPMU	IPCC	MIHL
GPRS	IRAS	Minn
Grad	IRBM	Misc
Gram	ISBN	Miss
Gr wt	ISDN	MMDS
GSOH	ISSN	MmHg
GSVQ	ISSP	MMus
Guat	Isth	Mont
Guin	Ital	MPLA
HAND	IUCD	MRBM
Hdbk	Josh	MRCA
HDTV	Junc	MRIA
HFEA	Junr	MRNA
HFMD	JurD	MRSA
Hind	Kcal	MRSC
HMAS	KCMG	Msgr
HMCS	KCVO	MTBE
HMSO	KISS	MTBF
Hond	KStJ	MTNG
HSRC	LACW	MusB
HTLV	LAIA	MusD
HTML	Lb tr	MusM
HTTP	L/Cpl	MVDI
Hung	Lgth	MVSc
IAAF	LH-RH	Myth
IAEA	Ling	NAHT
IARU	Lith	NAIC
Ibid	LMVD	Natl
IBRD	Long	NCCL
ICAO	LRSC	NCEA
ICBM	LTNS	NCIS
ICSH	LTSA	NCVO
ICTZ	Luth	Nebr
IDDM	LVAD	NEDC
IFAD	Macc	NERC
IGBP	MAgr	Neth
IKBS	MAOI	Neut
ILEA	Marq	NFWI
IMCO	Masc	NIHE
IMHO	Mass	NKGB
Inbd	Math	NKVD
Incl	Matt	Norm
INLA	MCom	Norw
INRI	MCPS	NRMA
Inst	MDMA	Nt wt
Intl	Meth	NYSE
Intr	Mich	NZEF
IOOF	MICR	NZEI

OTHER ABBREVIATIONS (CONTINUED)

NZLR	Pres	RNLI
NZMA	Priv	RNVR
NZOM	Prob	RNZN
NZPA	Proc	ROFL
NZRN	Prod	Ronz
NZSE	Prof	RRNA
NZSO	Prog	RRSP
Obad	Pron	RSGB
Obdt	Prot	RSNO
OCAM	Prov	RSNZ
OECD	Prox	RSPB
OEEC	PSBR	RSVP
OHMS	Psia	RUOK
Okla	Psid	Russ
Oreg	Psig	SABC
Orig	PSIS	SABS
Orth	PSNI	SACC
OSCE	PSTN	SACP
Oxon	PTFE	SAfr
PABX	PTSD	Sans
Part	Quad	SARS
Pass	Quot	Sask
Patd	RAAF	SATB
Path	RACQ	SAYE
PAYE	RAEC	SCID
Payt	Rall	Scot
PCOS	RAMC	SCQF
PDSA	RAOC	S Dak
Penn	RASC	SDLP
Perf	RAVC	SDRs
Peta	RCAF	Secy
Phar	RCMP	SEED
Phil	Rcpt	SEPA
PHLS	RCVS	Sept
Phon	Recd	Seqq
PHSE	Rect	SGML
Phys	Regd	Shpt
Pizz	Regt	SIDS
Plur	Rept	Sing
PNdB	Retd	SIPS
Port	Revd	SLBM
Poss	RFID	SLCM
POST	RFLP	SLSC
PPTA	RIBA	SNCF
Pred	RICS	SOHF
Pref	RNAS	Span
Prem	RNIB	SPCK
Prep	RNID	Spec

OTHER ABBREVIATIONS (CONTINUED)

Sp gr	USSR	Assoc
Sp ht	V aux	BArch
SPQR	VCJD	Barit
Srta	VDQS	BBSRC
SSHA	Vers	BECTU
SSRI	Vert	Berks
SSSI	Visc	BLitt
SSTA	VLBI	BPhil
Stat	VLCC	Bucks
Stbd	VLSI	Calif
Stge	Vols	Cambs
Stir	V Rev	CCANZ
STUC	VSOP	Chron
Subj	Vulg	Cifci
Suff	Wash	CITES
Supt	WFTU	CMIIW
Surg	Wisd	Comdg
Surv	Wkly	Comdr
Suth	WKND	Comdt
SVGA	WLTM	Const
SWFF	WRAC	Contd
SWOT	WRAF	Cosec
SYHA	WRNS	Cotan
TATT	Wrnt	Cryst
TAVR	WRVS	CSIRO
TCAS	WSSD	Cwlth
Tech	WWII	Denom
Temp	XLNT	DipAD
Tenn	Xnty	DipEd
Terr	YMCA	DLitt
TGWU	YMHA	DPhil
TIGR	Yugo	Epiph
TPWS	YWCA	Epist
Trig	YWHA	Equiv
T-RNA	ZAMS	Et seq
TTFN	Zech	Ex div
TTYL	Zeph	Ex lib
Tues	Zool	Ex off
Turk		Exptl
TVEI	**5 letters:**	FASSA
TVNZ	A'asia	FRACP
TVRO	Accel	FRACS
UKCC	Aeron	FRCVS
ULCC	AFAIK	FRICS
Unit	AFNOR	Front
Univ	AMICE	FRSNZ
UPVC	AMIEE	FYROM
USAF	Archd	Genit

OTHER ABBREVIATIONS (CONTINUED)

Gloss	MPhil	Topog
GMDSS	MTech	TRALI
H and c	Mt Rev	Trans
Hants	Mycol	Treas
Hdqrs	NAACP	UKAEA
Herts	Navig	UNHCR
Horol	NIDDM	V and A
ICFTU	NLLST	Venez
ichth	Nottm	Visct
MarE	Notts	WAAAF
MinE	NSAID	Warks
MunE	NSPCC	Westm
ncog	NZCER	Whsle
ndef	NZRFU	Wilts
ndic	OFris	Worcs
ndiv	Op cit	WRAAC
nfin	PAGAD	WRAAF
n mem	Paren	WRANS
norg	PPARC	Yorks
nter	Presb	
ntro	Propr	**6 letters:**
rreg	Pseud	AARNet
Kbyte	RAFVR	Abbrev
Lancs	R and R	AFL-CIO
Leics	Réaum	AFRAeS
Lieut	Ref Ch	A into G
Lincs	Repub	Am-dram
LittB	RNWMP	Approx
LittD	RNZAF	Arccos
L'pool	RSFSR	Archbp
Lt Cdr	RSPCA	Archit
Lt Col	Rt Hon	Arcsin
Lt Gen	SAARC	Arctan
Lt Gov	SARFU	Astrol
Maced	Sergt	Att Gen
Madag	SGHWR	Attrib
Manuf	SHEEP	BPharm
MArch	SMATV	Cantab
March	SQUID	CertEd
Maths	Stacc	Colloq
Mbyte	Subst	Com Ver
MEcon	Suffr	Confed
Metal	Switz	Covers
Middx	Synop	DipCom
MLitt	Theol	DipMet
Moham	Theos	EBITDA
Mol wt	Thess	Eccles
Morph	Thurs	Ecclus

OTHER ABBREVIATIONS (CONTINUED)

Geneal
GOC-in-C
Hon Sec
IChemE
Illust
IMechE
IMNSHO
Imperf
Imp gal
Interj
IONARC
Lib Dem
Loc cit
Maj Gen
MIMinE
MIMunE
NATFHE
Nem con
Neurol
Non seq
Northd
NZEFIP
Obstet
Pat Off
Petrog
Petrol
Philem
Philol
Philos
Photog
Prelim
QARANC
Rev Ver
ROFLOL

Rt Revd
Sgt Maj
Sociol
S of Sol
Sqn Ldr
Staffs
UNCTAD
Ut dict

7 letters:
AFSLAET
Anthrop
Austral
Auth Ver
Bibliog
Brig Gen
Cantuar
Co Derry
Contrib
Decresc
Embryol
Entomol
E Sussex
Intrans
Lexicog
Mineral
New Test
Nol pros
Non pros
Oceanog
Old Test
OTPOTSS
Pat pend
P/E ratio

Physiol
Psychol
Reg prof
Rom Cath
Technol
TE score
Verb sap

8 letters:
AMIChemE
AMIMechE
Archaeol
Co Durham
In loc cit
Meteorol
Ornithol
TCA cycle

9 letters:
Bacteriol
Northants
Pharmacol

10 letters:
Cur adv vult
DipChemEng
Ophthalmol
Palaeontol
Psychoanal

11 letters:
IYKWIMAITYD

Acids

SPECIFIC ACIDS

2 letters:
PH

3 letters:
DNA
HCL
RNA

4 letters:
Dopa
Uric

5 letters:
Auric
Boric
Caro's

L-dopa
Malic
Mucic
Oleic
Orcin
Trona

SPECIFIC ACIDS (CONTINUED)

6 letters:
Acetic
Adipic
Bromic
Capric
Cholic
Citric
Cyanic
Erucic
Formic
Gallic
Lactic
Lauric
Leucin
Lipoic
Maleic
Niacin
Nitric
Oxalic
Pectic
Phenol
Picric
Quinic
Sialic
Sorbic
Tannic
Tiglic
Valine

7 letters:
Abietic
Alginic
Benzoic
Butyric
Caproic
Cerotic
Chloric
Chromic
Creatin
Ellagic
Ferulic
Folacin
Fumaric
Fusidic
Guanine
Malonic
Meconic
Muramic

Nitrous
Orcinol
Prussic
Pteroic
Pyruvic
Racemic
Sebacic
Selenic
Silicic
Stannic
Stearic
Suberic
Terebic
Titanic
Valeric
Xanthic
Xylonic

8 letters:
Abscisic
Ascorbic
Aspartic
Butanoic
Caprylic
Carbamic
Carbolic
Carbonic
Chlorous
Cinnamic
Creatine
Cresylic
Crotonic
Cyclamic
Decanoic
Ethanoic
Fulminic
Glutamic
Glyceric
Glycolic
Guanylic
Hexanoic
Hippuric
Itaconic
Linoleic
Lysergic
Manganic
Muriatic
Myristic

Nonanoic
Palmitic
Phthalic
Rhodanic
Succinic
Tantalic
Tartaric
Telluric
Tungstic
Tyrosine
Valproic

9 letters:
Aqua-regia
Citruline
Citydylic
Dichromic
Hydrazoic
Hydriodic
Isocyanic
Linolenic
Methanoic
Nalidixic
Nicotinic
Panthenic
Pentanoic
Propanoic
Propenoic
Pyroboric
Saccharic
Salicylic
Sassolite
Selenious
Sulphonic
Sulphuric

10 letters:
Aquafortis
Asparagine
Barbituric
Dithionous
Dodecanoic
Glucoronic
Glutaminic
Hyaluronic
Methionine
Pelargonic
Perchloric

SPECIFIC ACIDS (CONTINUED)

Phosphoric
Proprionic
Pyrogallic
Ricinoleic
Sulphurous
Thiocyanic
Tryptophan

11 letters:
Arachidonic
Decanedioic
Ethanedioic
Ferricyanic
Ferrocyanic
Gibberellic
Hydnocarpic
Hydrobromic
Methacrylic
Octanedioic
Pantothenic
Permanganic
Phosphorous

Ribonucleic
Sarcolactic
Taurocholic

12 letters:
Aminobenzoic
Chloroacetic
Hydrochloric
Hydrofluoric
Hypochlorous
Indoleacetic
Persulphuric
Phenylalanin
Polyadenalic
Prostacyclin
Pyroligneous
Spiraeic acid
Terephthalic

13 letters:
Galactosamine
Glacial acetic
Heptadecanoic

Indolebutyric
Phenylalanine
Platinocyanic
Prostaglandin
Pyrosulphuric
Thiosulphuric

14 letters:
Hypophosphoric
Metaphosphoric
Polyphosphoric
Pyrophosphoric

15 letters:
Hypophosphorous
Orthophosphoric
Trichloroacetic

16 letters:
Deoxyribonucleic
Para-aminobenzoic

TYPES OF ACID

4 letters:
Acyl
Pyro

5 letters:
Amide
Amino
Fatty
Folic
Iodic
Lewis

Osmic

7 letters:
Dibasic
Mineral
Nucleic
Peracid

8 letters:
Periodic

9 letters:
Polybasic

10 letters:
Carboxylic

12 letters:
Dicarboxylic

14 letters:
Polycarboxylic

AMINO ACIDS

6 letters:
Lysine
Serine

7 letters:
Alanine
Cystine
Glycine
Leucine

Proline

8 letters:
Arginine

9 letters:
Ethionine
Glutamine
Histidine

Ornithine
Threonine

10 letters:
Citrulline
Isoleucine

16 letters:
Triiodothyronine

Actaeon's hounds

4 letters:
Agre
Alce
Nape

5 letters:
Aello
Arcas
Lacon
Ladon
Thous

6 letters:
Canace
Dromas
Lachne
Lebros
Leucon
Sticte

Theron
Tigris

7 letters:
Asbolus
Cyprius
Dorceus
Harpyia
Hylaeus
Laelaps
Lycisce

8 letters:
Agriodus
Arethusa
Harpalus
Hylactor
Melampus
Melaneus

Oribasus
Poemenis
Pterelas

9 letters:
Pamphagus

10 letters:
Ichnobates
Theridamas

11 letters:
Nebrophonus

12 letters:
Melanchaetes

13 letters:
Oresistrophus

Actors

MALE

3 letters:
Lee, *Bruce*
Lee, *Christopher*
Rey, *Fernando*

4 letters:
Cook, *Peter*
Dean, *James*
Ford, *Harrison*
Hope, *Bob*
Hurt, *John*
Kean, *Edmund*
Peck, *Gregory*
Penn, *Sean*
Roth, *Tim*
Shaw, *Glen Byam*
Tati, *Jacques*
Wood, *Elijah*

5 letters:
Allen, *Woody*
Bates, *Alan*
Boyer, *Charles*

Brody, *Adrien*
Caine, *Michael*
Flynn, *Errol*
Fonda, *Henry*
Gabin, *Jean*
Gable, *Clark*
Grant, *Cary*
Hanks, *Tom*
Hardy, *Oliver*
Irons, *Jeremy*
Kelly, *Gene*
Lloyd, *Harold*
Mason, *James*
Miles, *Bernard*
Mills, *John*
Moore, *Dudley*
Neill, *Sam*
Niven, *David*
Quinn, *Anthony*
Tracy, *Spencer*
Wayne, *John*

6 letters:
Beatty, *Warren*
Bogart, *Humphrey*
Brando, *Marlon*
Brooks, *Mel*
Burton, *Richard*
Cagney, *James*
Callow, *Simon*
Carrey, *Jim*
Cleese, *John*
Cooper, *Chris*
Cooper, *Gary*
Coward, *Noel*
Cruise, *Tom*
De Niro, *Robert*
De Sica, *Vittorio*
Dexter, *John*
Fields, *WC*
Finney, *Albert*
Gibson, *Mel*
Howard, *Leslie*
Howard, *Trevor*
Hudson, *Rock*

MALE (CONTINUED)

Irving, *Henry*
Jacobi, *Derek*
Jolson, *Al*
Keaton, *Buster*
Keitel, *Harvey*
Kemble, *John*
Laurel, *Stan*
Lugosi, *Bela*
Massey, *Raymond*
Morley, *Robert*
Neeson, *Liam*
Newman, *Paul*
Oldman, *Gary*
O'Toole, *Peter*
Pacino, *Al*
Quayle, *Anthony*
Reagan, *Ronald*
Welles, *Orson*

7 letters:
Astaire, *Fred*
Bennett, *Alan*
Bogarde, *Dirk*
Branagh, *Kenneth*
Burbage, *Richard*
Carlyle, *Robert*
Chaplin, *Charlie*
Clooney, *George*
Connery, *Sean*
Costner, *Kevin*
Douglas, *Kirk*
Douglas, *Michael*
Garrick, *David*

Gielgud, *John*
Hackman, *Gene*
Hoffman, *Dustin*
Hopkins, *Anthony*
Hordern, *Michael*
Karloff, *Boris*
McQueen, *Steve*
Mitchum, *Robert*
Olivier, *Laurence*
Redford, *Robert*
Robbins, *Tim*
Robeson, *Paul*
Sellers, *Peter*
Shepard, *Sam*
Stewart, *James*
Ustinov, *Peter*

8 letters:
Barrault, *Jean-Louis*
Belmondo, *Jean-Paul*
Crawford, *Michael*
DiCaprio, *Leonardo*
Eastwood, *Clint*
Guinness, *Alec*
Harrison, *Rex*
Kingsley, *Ben*
Laughton, *Charles*
Macready, *William*
McGregor, *Ewan*
McKellen, *Ian*
Redgrave, *Michael*
Robinson, *Edward G*
Scofield, *Paul*

Stallone, *Sylvester*
Travolta, *John*
Von Sydow, *Max*

9 letters:
Barrymore, *John*
Chevalier, *Maurice*
Depardieu, *Gerard*
Fairbanks, *Douglas Jr*
Fairbanks, *Douglas Snr*
Humphries, *Barry*
Lancaster, *Burt*
Nicholson, *Jack*
Pleasence, *Donald*
Radcliffe, *Daniel*
Valentino, *Rudolph*

10 letters:
Richardson, *Ralph*
Sutherland, *Donald*

11 letters:
Mastroianni, *Marcello*
Weissmuller, *Johnny*

12 letters:
Attenborough, *Richard*
Stanislavsky, *Konstantin*

14 letters:
Schwarzenegger, *Arnold*

FEMALE

3 letters:
Bow, *Clara*

4 letters:
Gish, *Lillian*
Qing, *Jian*
West, *Mae*

5 letters:
Brice, *Fanny*
Close, *Glenn*
Davis, *Bette*

Davis, *Geena*
Davis, *Judy*
Dench, *Judi*
Evans, *Edith*
Fonda, *Jane*
Garbo, *Greta*
Kelly, *Grace*
Lange, *Jessica*
Leigh, *Vivien*
Lenya, *Lotte*
Lopez, *Jennifer*
Loren, *Sophia*

Smith, *Maggie*
Terry, *Ellen*
Welch, *Raquel*

6 letters:
Arnaud, *Yvonne*
Bardot, *Brigitte*
Foster, *Jodie*
Harlow, *Jean*
Hiller, *Wendy*
Hunter, *Holly*
Keaton, *Diane*

ACTORS, FEMALE (CONTINUED)

Kemble, *Fanny*
Kidman, *Nicole*
Mirren, *Helen*
Monroe, *Marilyn*
Moreau, *Jeanne*
Robson, *Flora*
Rogers, *Ginger*
Seyrig, *Delphine*
Streep, *Meryl*
Suzman, *Janet*
Taylor, *Elizabeth*
Temple, *Shirley*
Theron, *Charlize*
Weaver, *Sigourney*

7 letters:
Bergman, *Ingrid*
Colbert, *Claudette*
Deneuve, *Catherine*
Dunaway, *Faye*
Gardner, *Ava*

Garland, *Judy*
Hepburn, *Audrey*
Hepburn, *Katharine*
Huppert, *Isabelle*
Jackson, *Glenda*
McKenna, *Siobhan*
Roberts, *Julia*
Siddons, *Sarah*
Winslet, *Kate*

8 letters:
Ashcroft, *Peggy*
Bankhead, *Tallulah*
Crawford, *Joan*
Dietrich, *Marlene*
Grenfell, *Joyce*
Lawrence, *Gertrude*
Lockwood, *Margaret*
MacLaine, *Shirley*
Mercouri, *Melina*
Minnelli, *Liza*

Pfeiffer, *Michelle*
Pickford, *Mary*
Redgrave, *Vanessa*
Sarandon, *Susan*
Signoret, *Simone*
Thompson, *Emma*
Whitelaw, *Billie*

9 letters:
Bernhardt, *Sarah*
Plowright, *Joan*
Streisand, *Barbra*
Thorndike, *Sybil*
Zeta-Jones, *Catherine*

10 letters:
Rutherford, *Margaret*
Woffington, *Peg*
Zellwegger, *Renée*

Terms of affection

3 letters:
Pet

4 letters:
Babe
Baby
Bean
Dear
Doll
Lamb
Love
Star

5 letters:
Angel
Babes
Goose
Honey
Kitty
Lover
Petal
Puppy
Sugar
Tiger

Toots

6 letters:
Flower
Kitten
Muppet
Poppet
Sweets
Weasel

7 letters:
Beloved
Chicken
Darling
Dearest
Dear one
Pet lamb
Pumpkin
Treacle

8 letters:
Kitty cat
Little 'un
Loved one

Munchkin
Precious
Princess
Pussycat
Treasure
Truelove

9 letters:
Bunnykins
Dearheart
Little one
Pepperpot

10 letters:
Honey bunny
Sweetheart
Sweetie pie

11 letters:
Fluffy bunny

12 letters:
Chicken bunny

Agriculturalists

4 letters:
Coke, *Thomas William*
Tull, *Jethro*

5 letters:
Lawes, *Sir John Bennet*
Young, *Arthur*

6 letters:
Carver, *George Washington*

7 letters:
Borlaug, *Norman Ernest*
Burbank, *Luther*

8 letters:
Bakewell, *Robert*

9 letters:
McCormick, *Cyrus Hall*

12 letters:
Boussingault, *Jean-Baptiste Joseph*

Agricultural terms

2 letters:
EE

3 letters:
Agr
Bed
Box
BST
CAP
Cot
Cow
Cut
Dag
Dip
Dry
End
Ewe
Fan
Hay
Hoe
Hog
Hut
Kye
Lea
Ley
Mob
Mow
NFU
Pen
Pig
Pug
Ram
RAS
Rig
Run

Rye
Set
Sow
Sty
Tag
Ted
Teg
Tup
Van
Win

4 letters:
Bail
Bale
Balk
Barn
Beam
Bone
Boss
Bull
Byre
Calf
Chip
Clip
Cock
Comb
Come
Coop
Corn
Cote
Crib
Crop
Cull
Disc
Dogy

Drag
Dump
Dung
Duty
Fall
Farm
Feed
Fire
Foal
Fold
Frib
Gang
Grow
Hack
Ha-ha
Hame
Heel
Herd
Hind
Hops
IFAD
Lair
Lamb
Land
Leaf
Lime
List
Loan
Mare
Marl
Mash
Meal
Milk
Muck

Oast
Oats
Pest
Plow
Poll
Pook
Rabi
Rape
Raze
Rean
Reap
Rear
Reen
Rich
Rick
Ring
Salt
Seed
Shaw
Shed
Show
Sick
Silo
Slop
Soil
Sole
Sour
Span
Spit
Spud
Stub
Till
Toun
Turn
Unit
Wain
Walk
Wisp
Yard
Yeld
Yoke

5 letters:
Baler
Bench
Board
Bogle
Brake
Cadet
Calve

Capon
Carry
Cavie
Chaff
Chalk
Check
Churn
Chute
Clamp
Clear
Cling
Close
Cocky
Colon
Cover
Crawl
Croft
Dairy
Daych
Dogie
Dress
Drift
Drill
Drove
Field
Flail
Flake
Flush
Force
Frame
Frost
Fruit
Glean
Grain
Grass
Graze
Grist
Haunt
Heart
Hedge
Hodge
Horse
Hough
Hovel
Jembe
Kraal
Lands
Lease
Levee
Lodge

Milch
Mulch
Oxbow
Paddy
Plaas
Plant
Poley
Punch
Quern
Quick
Raise
Ranch
Range
Rodeo
Rogue
Rural
Share
Sheaf
Shear
Sheep
Shoat
Shock
Shook
Shote
Singe
Sloot
Spell
Stack
Stale
Stall
Stand
Stile
Stirk
Stock
Stook
Store
Straw
Strip
Swath
Swede
Sweep
Swill
Tally
Tilth
Tolly
Trash
Tribe
Truck
Wheat

6 letters:
Animal
Apiary
Arable
Bail up
Barley
Barren
Barrow
Barton
Binder
Candle
Cattle
Cereal
Cheque
Clutch
Colter
Corral
Cotton
Cowboy
Cowman
Cowpat
Cradle
Cratch
Crutch
Culler
Cut out
Dobbin
Drover
Duster
Eatage
Enrich
Ensile
Fallow
Farmed
Farmer
Farrow
Fatten
Feeder
Fleece
Fodder
Foison
Forage
Furrow
Garner
Gavage
Grange
Grease
Greasy
Grieve
Harrow

Haw-haw
Haymow
Heeler
Heifer
Hen run
Herder
Hockey
Hogget
Hopper
Hummel
Hurdle
Incult
Kharif
Lea-rig
Linhay
Lister
Litter
Manger
Manure
Meadow
Mealie
Mellow
Middle
Mielie
Milker
Mistal
Moshav
Muster
Pakahi
Parity
Pastor
Pigpen
Pigsty
Pleugh
Plough
Porker
Rancho
Ratoon
Reaper
Reddle
Ringer
Ripple
Roller
Ruddle
Run off
Runway
Scythe
Seeder
Shamba
Shears

Shed up
Sheepo
Sheuch
Shorts
Sickle
Silage
Smudge
Spider
Spread
Stable
Stitch
Stover
Summer
Swathe
Take up
Tar boy
Tedder
Thrash
Thresh
Titman
Vinery
Winnow
Winter
Zoo doo

7 letters:
Breaker
Break in
Breeder
Bucolic
Calving
Chamber
Combine
Compost
Conacre
Contact
Coulter
Cowbell
Cowherd
Cowshed
Crofter
Cropper
Culture
Daglock
Dockage
Drummer
Earmark
Exhaust
Farming
Fatling

Feedbag
Feedlot
Fertile
Florist
Foaling
Freshen
Fruiter
Granary
Grazier
Grazing
Grow bag
Haggard
Harvest
Haycock
Hayfork
Hayrick
Hayseed
Hencoop
Hennery
Herbage
Hogwash
Infield
Kolkhoz
Lairage
Lambing
Lay down
Lazy bed
Machair
Milkman
Milling
Multure
Nest box
Nest egg
Nitrate
Nitrify
Oil cake
Orchard
Organic
Paddock
Pannage
Parlour
Pasture
Piggery
Pinfold
Planter
Pork pig
Poultry
Poverty
Prairie
Predial

Produce
Pruning
Rattoon
Reaping
Rearing
Reclaim
Round up
Scarify
Shedder
Shed out
Show day
Skirter
Sleeper
Soilage
Sovkhoz
Sprayer
Staddle
Station
Stubble
Subsoil
Swidden
Swipple
Tankage
Tillage
Topsoil
Tractor
Tumbrel
Turbary
Upgrade
Vintage
Wigging
Windrow
Wrangle
Wrestle
Yarding

8 letters:
Abattoir
Agrarian
Agrestal
Agrology
Agronomy
Apiarian
Apiarist
Barnyard
Bone meal
Butchery
Caponize
Cash crop
Checkrow

Chin ball
Churning
Cockatoo
Cockerel
Corncrib
Cornhusk
Cow cocky
Creamery
Crofting
Dairying
Dairyman
Dieldrin
Ditching
Domestic
Drainage
Dressing
Elevator
Empty cow
Ensilage
Farm hand
Farmland
Farmyard
Fishmeal
Flushing
Foremilk
Forestry
Fruitage
Fumatory
Generous
Geoponic
Goatherd
Hacienda
Handfeed
Hatchery
Haymaker
Haystack
Haywagon
Headland
Henhouse
Herdsman
Home farm
Hot fence
Huntaway
Irrigate
Lamb down
Land girl
Land-poor
Landside
Loosebox
Marginal

Maverick
Milkmaid
Moorburn
Mowburnt
Muckrake
Muirburn
Muleteer
Outfield
Overcrop
Pastoral
Perchery
Pharming
Pigswill
Plant out
Plougher
Poundage
Praedial
Preserve
Property
Quickset
Richness
Root crop
Rotation
Seed corn
Seminary
Set-aside
Shambles
Shed hand
Sheep-dip
Shepherd
Shieling
Soil bank
Spreader
Stabling
Stampede
Steading
Stockman
Stubbled
Swanherd
Sweatbox
Systemic
Thresher
Top-dress
Town milk
Two-tooth
Unbolted
Vineyard
Vintager
Voorskot
Watering

Wayleggo
Wool clip
Woolshed
Workfolk
Wrangler
Zamindar
Zemindar

9 letters:
Aftermath
Agterskot
Beastings
Beestings
Bell sheep
Bellyband
Biestings
Biosafety
Breakaway
Broadcast
Bunkhouse
Butterfat
Canebrake
Cane piece
Catalogue
Catch crop
Cattleman
Cleanskin
Cornfield
Corn shock
Corn shuck
Cornstalk
Cover crop
Cultivate
Dairymaid
Dead stock
Depasture
Dog tucker
Enclosure
Expellers
Extensive
Farmstead
Fertilize
Field corn
Field tile
Flystrike
Free-range
Geoponics
Gleanings
Grassland
Hand glass

Hand-piece
Hard wheat
Harvester
Haymaking
Home-grown
Homestead
Hop-picker
Husbandry
Intensive
Intercrop
Livestock
Moldboard
Mole drain
No-tillage
Overgraze
Overstock
Pasturage
Pesticide
Phosphate
Pitchfork
Ploughboy
Ploughing
Ploughman
Poulterer
Provender
Rangeland
Rice field
Rotary hoe
Rotovator
Scarifier
Scourings
Seed drill
Sharecrop
Shearling
Sheepcote
Sheepfold
Sheep race
Sheepwalk
Shrinkage
Side-dress
Slaughter
Soft wheat
Stall-feed
Stock unit
Stock whip
Stockyard
Sundowner
Sunk fence
Swineherd
Tea garden

Thrashing
Threshing
Ventilate
Vernalize
Water-sick
Winnowing
Wool table
Zamindari

10 letters:
Apiculture
Aviculture
Battery hen
Bull tongue
Cattle-cake
Cattle-grid
Cattle prod
Cattle-stop
Corn circle
Corn-picker
Cotton belt
Cotton cake
Cottonseed
Cowfeteria
Crop circle
Crutchings
Cultivable
Cultivated
Cultivator
Deep-litter
Disc harrow
Disc plough
Dry farming
Energy crop
Fertilizer
Fire blight
Fumatorium
Gang plough
Hamshackle
Harvesting
Harvestman
Heading dog
Herd tester
Husbandman
Impregnate
Irrigation
Land reform
Ley farming
Mouldboard
Nitro-chalk

Plantation
Poultryman
Quernstone
Rouseabout
Roustabout
Seed potato
Self-feeder
Semination
Showground
Stockhorse
Stockroute
Stump ranch
Turkey nest
Underdrain
Ungrateful
Unimproved
Virgin soil
Wine grower
Winterfeed
Wool cheque
Woolgrower

11 letters:
Agriculture
Agrobiology
Aquaculture
Aquiculture
Catching pen
Chamberhand
Compostable
Crop-dusting
Cultivation
Dogleg fence
Estate agent
Extractions
Factory farm
Full-mouthed
Green manure
Harvest home
Head station
Hedge laying
Hobby farmer
Hydroponics
Insecticide
Latifundium
Mariculture
Milking shed
Monoculture
Mule skinner
Pastoralist

Ploughshare
Ploughstaff
Pomiculture
Reclamation
Sericulture
Sharefarmer
Share-milker
Stock saddle
Subirrigate
Submarginal
Tank farming
Tattie-bogle
Top dressing
Vinedresser
Viniculture
Viticulture
Water meadow
Windlestraw
Winter wheat
Zero grazing

12 letters:
Agribusiness
Agricultural
Agrochemical
Agroforestry
Break feeding
Broiler house
Citriculture
Cotton picker
Crop rotation
Cutting horse
Double-dumped
Forcing house
Furfuraceous
Market garden
Mixed farming
Muck spreader
Rotary plough
Sharecropper
Shearing gang
Shearing shed
Sheep station
Slash-and-burn
Slaughterman
Smallholding
Staddlestone
Strong-eye dog
Taranaki gate
Ten-acre block

Tenant farmer
Transhumance
Trash farming
Uncultivated

13 letters:
Anthropophyte
Double digging
Freezing works
Middlebreaker
Pumice country
Sheepshearing
Strip cropping
Stubble-jumper
Thremmatology

14 letters:
Cottonseed meal
Holding paddock
Milking machine

Slaughterhouse
Terminator seed

15 letters:
Animal husbandry
Butterfat cheque
Cooperative farm
Gentleman-farmer
Green revolution
Market gardening
Nonagricultural
Stump-jump plough

16 letters:
Combine harvester
Contour ploughing
Rabbit-proof fence
Sacrifice paddock
Soil conservation
Threshing machine

17 letters:
Aerial top dressing
Potassium chloride
Soldier settlement

18 letters:
Subsistence farming

19 letters:
Bovine somatotrophin
Shifting cultivation

20 letters:
Stock and station agent

24 letters:
Common Agricultural
   Policy

Aircraft

TYPES OF AIRCRAFT

3 letters:
Jet
MIG
SST

4 letters:
Moth
STOL
VTOL
Wing

5 letters:
Avion
Blimp
Camel
Comet
Drone
Gotha
Jumbo
Rigid
Stuka
Taube

6 letters:
Auster
Bomber
Canard
Chaser
Fokker
Galaxy
Glider
Hunter
Mirage
Ramjet
Tanker
Tri-jet

7 letters:
Airship
Aviette
Balloon
Biplane
Chopper
Fighter
Harrier
Heinkel
Jump jet

Parasol
Penguin
Propjet
Sopwith
Trident

8 letters:
Aerodyne
Aerostat
Airliner
Autogiro
Autogyro
Brabazon
Concorde
Gyrodyne
Jetliner
Jet plane
Jumbo jet
Mosquito
Oerlikon
Scramjet
Seaplane
Skiplane
Spitfire

Types of Aircraft (continued)

Triplane
Turbofan
Turbojet
Viscount
Warplane
Zeppelin

9 letters:
Amphibian
Autoflare
Coleopter
Cyclogiro
Delta-wing
Dirigible
Doodlebug
Fixed-wing
Freighter
Hurricane
Lancaster
Liberator
Microlite
Monoplane
Orthopter
Rotaplane

Sailplane
Semi-rigid
Swept-wing
Swing-wing
Taxiplane
Turboprop

10 letters:
Dive bomber
Flying boat
Flying wing
Hang-glider
Helicopter
Microlight
Multiplane
Tankbuster

11 letters:
Intercepter
Interceptor
Lifting body
Ornithopter
Turboramjet

12 letters:
Night fighter
Sopwith Camel
Stealth plane
Stratotanker
Troop carrier

13 letters:
Convertaplane
Convertiplane
Convertoplane
Fighter-bomber
Hot-air balloon
Light aircraft
Messerschmitt
Stealth bomber
Stratocruiser

16 letters:
Gas-filled balloon

17 letters:
Helicopter gunship

Aircraft Parts

3 letters:
Fin
Pod
Tab

4 letters:
Body
Cowl
Flap
Hold
Horn
Keel
Nose
Slat
Tail
Wing

5 letters:
Cabin
Pylon
Rotor

Waist

6 letters:
Basket
Canopy
Elevon
Engine
Galley
Pusher
Ramjet
Rudder
Turret

7 letters:
Aileron
Airlock
Athodyd
Blister
Bomb bay
Capsule
Chassis

Cockpit
Cowling
Fairing
Gondola
Jet pipe
Nacelle
Spinner
Spoiler
Trim tab
Winglet
Wing tip

8 letters:
Aerofoil
Airframe
Air scoop
Airscrew
Anti-icer
Arrester
Black box
Bulkhead

AIRCRAFT PARTS (CONTINUED)

Drop tank
Elevator
Fuel tank
Fuselage
Heat sink
Joystick
Longeron
Pulsejet
Tailskid

9 letters:
Air-intake
Altimeter
Astrodome
Autopilot
Bombsight
Clamshell
Dashboard
Empennage
Engine pod
Jet engine
Main plane
Nose wheel
Pitot tube

Propeller
Tailplane
Tail wheel

10 letters:
Astrohatch
Cantilever
Flight deck
Hydroplane
Launch shoe
Stabilizer

11 letters:
Afterburner
Horn balance
Landing gear
Slinger ring

12 letters:
Control stick
Ejection seat
Inclinometer
Landing light
Ramjet engine

Trailing edge

13 letters:
Aerostructure
All-flying tail
Control column
Launching shoe
Undercarriage

14 letters:
Flight recorder

15 letters:
Instrument panel

16 letters:
Aerometeorograph

17 letters:
Artificial horizon

18 letters:
Auxiliary power unit

Airline flight codes

Code	Airline
AA	American Airlines
AC	Air Canada
AF	Air France
AH	Air Algerie
AI	Air India
AJ	Air Belgium
AM	Aeromexico
AQ	Aloha Airlines (Hawaii)
AR	Aerolineas Argentinas
AY	Finnair
AZ	Alitalia
BA	British Airways
BD	British Midland
BY	Britannia Airways
CA	Air China
CO	Continental Airlines

Code	Airline
CP	Canadian Airlines International
CT	Air Sofia
CU	Cubana
CY	Cyprus Airways
DA	Air Georgia
DI	Deutsche BA
DL	Delta Airlines
DX	Danish Air Transport
EI	Aer Lingus
EK	Emirates
FE	Royal Khmer Airlines
FI	Icelandair
FR	Ryanair
GF	Gulf Air
GH	Ghana Airways
GM	Air Slovakia
HA	Hawaiian Airlines
IB	Iberia
IC	Indian Airlines
IL	Istanbul Airways
IR	Iran Air
JA	Air Bosnia
JE	Manx Airlines
JG	Air Greece
JL	Japan Airlines
JM	Air Jamaica
JU	JAT (Yugoslavia)
KL	KLM
KQ	Kenya Airways
KU	Kuwait Airways
LG	Luxair
LH	Lufthansa
LV	Albanian Airlines
LY	El Al
MA	Malev (Hungary)
MS	Egyptair
NG	Lauda Air (Austria)
NH	All Nippon Airlines
NV	Northwest Territorial Airways (Canada)
NW	Northwest Airlines (USA)
NY	Air Iceland
NZ	Air New Zealand

Code	Airline
OA	Olympic Airlines (Greece)
OG	Go
OK	Czech Airlines
OS	Austrian Airlines
OU	Croatia Airlines
OV	Estonian Air
PC	Fiji Air
PK	Pakistan International Airlines
PS	Ukraine International Airlines
QF	Qantas
QR	Qatar Airways
QS	Tatra Air (Slovakia)
QU	Uganda Airlines
QZ	Zambia Airways
RG	Varig (Brazil)
RM	Air Moldova
RO	Tarom (Romania)
RR	Royal Air Force
SA	South African Airways
SK	SAS (Scandinavian Airlines, Sweden)
SN	Sabena Belgian World Airlines
SQ	Singapore Airlines
SR	Swissair
SU	Aeroflot (Russia)
TE	Lithuanian Airlines
TK	Turkish Airlines
TP	TAP Air Portugal
TT	Air Lithuania
TW	TWA (USA)
UA	United Airlines (USA)
UK	KLM UK
UL	Sri Lankan Airlines
UM	Air Zimbabwe
US	USAir
VS	Virgin Atlantic Airways
WN	Southwest Airlines (USA)
WT	Nigeria Airways
WX	Cityjet (Ireland)
ZB	Monarch Airlines (UK)

Airports

3 letters:
JFK
Lod

4 letters:
Dyce
Faro
Lydd
Orly
Sfax
Wick

5 letters:
Logan
Luton
McCoy
O'Hare

6 letters:
Dulles
Gander
Gerona
Lympne

7 letters:
Ataturk
Dalaman
Entebbe
Gatwick
Kennedy
Kerkyra
Lincoln
Shannon

8 letters:
Beauvais
Ciampino
G Marconi
Heathrow
Idlewild
Keflavik
McCarran
Mohamed V
Schiphol
Stansted

9 letters:
Ben Gurion
Charleroi
Fiumicino
Jose Marti
Marco Polo
Peninsula
Prestwick
Queen Alia
Turnhouse

10 letters:
Hellenikon
King Khaled
Louis Botha
Reina Sofia
Will Rogers

11 letters:
Ninoy Aquino

12 letters:
Benito Juarez
Chiang Kai She
Indira Gandhi
Jomo Kenyatta
Norman Manley
Papola Casale
Queen Beatrix
Santos Dumont
Simon Bolivar

13 letters:
Grantley Adams
King Abdul Aziz

14 letters:
Galileo Galilei
Lester B Pearson
Luis Munoz Marin

15 letters:
Charles De Gaulle
General Mitchell
Leonardo da Vinci
Murtala Muhammed
Sir Seretse Khama

17 letters:
Cristoforo Colombo
Houari Boumedienne

Alcoholic drinks

2 letters:
It

3 letters:
Ale
Ava
Cup
Dop
Gin
Kir
Mum

Rum
Rye
Vin

4 letters:
Asti
Bock
Dram
Flip
Grog
Kava

Kvas
Malt
Mead
Nipa
Port
Purl
Raki
Sack
Saké
Saki
Soma

Sour
Sura
Tent
Yill

5 letters:
Bingo
Bombo
Bumbo
Cider
Cyder
Glogg
Haoma
Julep
Kefir
Kvass
Mâcon
Mauby
Meath
Medoc
Meths
Mobby
Mulse
Nappy
Negus
Perry
Pombe
Punch
Quass
Rakee
Rummy
Sling
Stout
Toddy
Vodka
Xeres

6 letters:
Arrack
Bishop
Burton
Busera
Caudle
Cauker
Chaser
Cooler
Cooper
Doctor
Eggnog
Enzian

Frappé
Gimlet
Grappa
Kephir
Kirsch
Kümmel
Meathe
Nobbie
Pastis
Pernod®
Posset
Pulque
Samshu
Shandy
Sherry
Stingo
Strega
Waragi
Yaqona
Zythum

7 letters:
Absinth
Akvavit
Alcopop
Amoroso
Aquavit
Bacardi
Campari®
Chablis
Chianti
Cinzano®
Cobbler
Curaçao
Curaçoa
Daquiri
Eggflip
Fustian
Italian
Liqueur
Malmsey
Martini®
Oenomel
Oloroso
Pilsner
Pink gin
Ratafia
Sangria
Scrumpy
Sherris

Shnapps
Shooter
Slammer
Sloe gin
Stengah
Swizzle
Tequila
Tio Pepe®

8 letters:
Absinthe
Aleberry
Anisette
Apéritif
Bordeaux
Burgundy
Calvados
Champers
Charneco
Ciderkin
Cocktail
Cold duck
Daiquiri
Dog's nose
Dubonnet®
Geropiga
Gin sling
Gluhwein
Highball
Home brew
Hydromel
Mahogany
Palm wine
Pilsener
Red biddy
Resinata
Resinate
Rice beer
Rice wine
Riesling
Sangaree
Skokiaan
Snowball
Spritzer
Tequilla
Vermouth
Witblitz

9 letters:
Applejack

Aqua-vitae
Ayahuasco
Badminton
Buck's fizz
Champagne
Cuba libre
Hard cider
Hippocras
Lambswool
Manhattan
Metheglin
Mint julep
Nor'wester
Sauternes
Slivovitz
Snakebite
Sundowner
Whisky mac

10 letters:
Bloody Mary
Chartreuse®
Ginger wine
Malt liquor
Maraschino
Mulled wine
Piña colada
Pousse-café
Shandygaff
Spruce beer
Tom Collins

11 letters:
Aguardiente
Benedictine
Black and tan
Black velvet
Boiler-maker

Half-and-half
Irish coffee
Niersteiner
Screwdriver

12 letters:
Gaelic coffee
Humpty-dumpty
Marcobrunner
Old-fashioned
Tome-and-Jerry

14 letters:
Elderberry wine
French vermouth
John Barleycorn

15 letters:
Italian vermouth

See also:
➤ **Beers** ➤ **Cocktails** ➤ **Liqueurs** ➤ **Spirits** ➤ **Whiskies** ➤ **Wines**

Alcohols

4 letters:
Diol

5 letters:
Cetyl
Ethal
Ethyl
Meths
Nerol

6 letters:
Cresol
Lauryl
Mescal
Phytol
Propyl

Sterol

7 letters:
Borneol
Choline
Ethanol
Mannite
Xylitol

8 letters:
Acrolein
Aldehyde
Catechol
Farnesol
Fusel-oil
Geraniol

Glycerin
Inositol
Linalool
Mannitol
Methanol
Sorbitol

9 letters:
Glycerine
Isopropyl
Mercaptan

11 letters:
Cholesterol
Citronellol
Sphingosine

Algae

3 letters:
Red

4 letters:
Kelp

5 letters:
Brown
Dulse
Fucus

Alkalis

Green
Jelly
Laver
Wrack

6 letters:
Desmid
Diatom
Fucoid
Lichen
Nostoc
Volvox

7 letters:
Euglena
Isokont
Oarweed
Seaweed
Valonia

8 letters:
Anabaena
Carageen

Conferva
Gulfweed
Plankton
Pleuston
Rockweed
Sargasso
Sea wrack
Ulothrix

9 letters:
Carrageen
Chlorella
Irish moss
Prokaryon
Sargassum
Sea tangle
Spirogyra
Star-jelly
Stonewort

10 letters:
Carragheen

Sea lettuce

11 letters:
Blanketweed
Iceland moss
Protococcus

12 letters:
Bladderwrack
Heterocontae
Reindeer moss
Ulotrichales
Zooxanthella

13 letters:
Blackfish weed
Phytoplankton

14 letters:
Dinoflagellate

16 letters:
Neptune's necklace

Alkalis

5 letters:
Borax

6 letters:
Emetin
Harmin
Potash

7 letters:
Betaine
Brucine
Codeine
Emetine
Harmine
Narceen
Quinine
Tropine

8 letters:
Hyoscine
Lobeline
Narceine
Nicotine
Piperine
Thebaine
Veratrin

9 letters:
Bebeerine
Berberine
Capsaicin
Ephedrine
Gelsemine
Guanidine
Harmaline
Reserpine
Rhoeadine

Sparteine
Veratrine
Yohimbine

10 letters:
Colchicine
Papaverine

11 letters:
Apomorphine
Gelseminine
Scopolamine
Theobromine
Vinblastine
Vincristine

12 letters:
Theophylline

Alloys

5 letters:
Brass
Invar®
Monel
Potin
Steel
Terne

6 letters:
Albata
Alnico®
Babbit
Billon
Bronze
Cermet
Chrome
Latten
Magnox
Marmem
Occamy
Oreide
Ormolu
Oroide
Pewter
Tambac
Tombac
Tombak

7 letters:
Amalgam
Chromel
Nimonic
Nitinol
Paktong

Platina
Shakudo
Similor
Spelter
Tutenag

8 letters:
Electron
Electrum
Gunmetal
Kamacite
Manganin®
Nichrome®
Orichalc
Stellite®
Zircaloy
Zircoloy

9 letters:
Bell metal
Duralumin®
Magnalium
Permalloy
Pinchbeck
Platinoid
Shibuichi
Type metal
White gold
Zircalloy

10 letters:
Bell bronze
Constantan
Misch metal

Nicrosilal
Osmiridium
Soft solder

11 letters:
Babbit metal
Cupronickel
Ferronickel
Monell metal

12 letters:
Ferrosilicon
Nickel silver
Nimonic alloy

13 letters:
Brazing solder
Ferrochromium
Magnolia metal
Platiniridium
Speculum metal

14 letters:
Britannia metal
Ferromanganese
Phosphor bronze
Sterling silver

15 letters:
Ferromolybdenum

24 letters:
Austenitic stainless steel

Alphabets

RELATED VOCABULARY

3 letters:
ITA

4 letters:
Kana
Ogam

5 letters:
Cufic
Kanji
Kufic
Latin
Ogham
Roman

6 letters:
Brahmi
Glagol
Hangul
Nagari
Pinyin
Romaji

RELATED VOCABULARY (CONTINUED)

7 letters:
Braille
Futhark
Futhorc
Futhork
Glossic
Grantha
Linear A
Linear B
Pangram

8 letters:
Cyrillic
Hiragana
Katakana
Logogram
Phonetic

9 letters:
Logograph
Syllabary

10 letters:
Devanagari
Estrangelo
Glagolitic
Lexigraphy

11 letters:
Estranghelo

ARABIC LETTERS

Alif
Bā
Tā
Thā
Jīm
Ḥā
Khā
Dāl
Dhāl
Rā

Zā
Sīn
Shīn
Ṣād
Ḍād
Ṭā
Ẓā
`Ain
Ghain
Fā

Qāf
Kāf
Lām
Mīm
Nūn
Hā
Wāw
Yā

GREEK LETTERS

Alpha
Beta
Chi
Delta
Epsilon
Eta
Gamma
Iota

Kappa
Lambda
Mu
Nu
Omega
Omicron
Phi
Pi

Psi
Rho
Sigma
Tau
Theta
Upsilon
Xi
Zeta

HEBREW LETTERS

Aleph
Ayin
Ain
Beth
Daleth
Daled
Gimel
He
Heth
Cheth
Kaph

Koph
Qoph
Lamed
Lamedh
Mem
Nun
Pe
Resh
Sadhe
Sade
Tsade

Samekh
Shin
Sin
Tav
Taw
Teth
Vav
Waw
Yod
Yodh
Zayin

COMMUNICATIONS CODE WORDS FOR THE ALPHABET

Alpha	Juliet	Sierra
Bravo	Kilo	Tango
Charlie	Lima	Uniform
Delta	Mike	Victor
Echo	November	Whiskey
Foxtrot	Oscar	X-Ray
Golf	Papa	Yankee
Hotel	Quebec	Zulu
India	Romeo	

English and American equivalences

English	American
Aeroplane	Airplane
American football	Football
Antenatal	Prenatal
Aubergine	Egg plant
Autumn	Fall
Bad-tempered	Mean
Banknote	Bill
Bat	Paddle
Benefit	Welfare
Bin *or* dustbin	Trashcan
Biscuit	Cookie
Black pudding	Blood sausage
Blinds	Shades
Bonnet	Hood
Boot	Trunk
Braces	Retainer
Braces	Suspenders
Breve	Double whole note
Broad bean	Fava bean
Building society	Savings and loan
Burgle	Burglarize
Candy floss	Cotton candy
Car	Automobile
Car park	Parking lot
Chemist	Drug store
Chips	French fries
Clothes peg	Clothes pin
Coffin	Casket
Condom	Rubber
Cornflour	Corn starch

English	American
Courgette	Zucchini
Crisps	Chips *or* potato chips
Crossroads	Intersection
Crotchet	Quarter note
Current account	Checking account
Curtains	Drapes
Cutlery	Flatware *or* silverware
CV	Résumé
Dialing code	Area code
Dinner jacket	Tuxedo
Double cream	Heavy cream
Drapery	Dry goods
Draughts	Checkers
Drawing pin	Thumb tack
Dressing gown	Robe
Dummy	Pacifier *or* soother
Engaged tone	Busy signal
Estate agent	Realtor
Estate car	Station wagon
Fire lighter	Fire starter
First floor	Second floor
Flat	Apartment
Flick knife	Switch blade
Football	Soccer
Foyer	Lobby
Fringe	Bangs
Garden	Yard
Gear lever	Stick shift
Goose pimples	Goose bumps
Ground floor	First floor
Hair grip	Bobby pin
Hairpin bend	Switchback
Handbag	Purse
Hessian	Burlap
High street	Main street
Holiday	Vacation
Indicator	Blinker
Invigilator	Proctor
Ironmonger	Hardware store
Jam	Jelly
Janitor	Caretaker
Lawyer	Attorney
Lift	Elevator

English	**American**
Mangetout	Snowpea
Mate	Friend
Merry-go-round	Carousel
Methylated spirits	Denatured alcohol
Mince	Ground beef
Minim	Half note
Nappy	Diaper
Neat	Straight
Noughts and crosses	Tick-tack-toe
Nursery	Kindergarten
Off licence	Liquor store
Paraffin	Kerosene
Pavement	Sidewalk
Pepper	Bell pepper
Petrol	Gas *or* gasoline
Pissed	Drunk
Plait	Braid
Plasterboard	Dry lining
Plot	Lot
Porridge	Oatmeal
Postcode	Zip code
Postman	Mail man
Pub *or* public house	Bar
Public school	Private school
Purse	Pocketbook
Pushchair	Stroller
Quaver	Eighth note
Quilt *or* eiderdown	Comforter
Railway	Railroad
Receptionist	Desk clerk
Reverse charge	Collect
Ring road	Beltway
Roll *or* bap	Bun
Rubber	Eraser
Rubbish	Trash *or* garbage
Semibreve	Whole note
Semi-detached	Duplex
Semiquaver	Sixteenth note
Shop	Store
Silencer	Muffler
Skip	Dumpster
Skirting board	Baseboard
Sleeper	Tie

English	American
Slowcoach	Slowpoke
Soft drink	Soda
Spanner	Wrench
Spring onion *or* salad onion	Scallion
State school	Public school
Stream	Creek
Surgical spirit	Rubbing alcohol
Sweet	Candy
Tap	Faucet
Tarmac	Asphalt
Telegram	Wire
Thread	Cotton
Tights	Pantihose
Timber	Lumber
Torch	Flashlight
Town centre	Downtown
Trainers	Sneakers
Tram	Streetcar
Trousers	Pants
Turn up	Cuff
VAT	Sales tax
Vest	Undershirt
Waistcoast	Vest
Windscreen	Windshield

American football teams

11 letters:
New York Jets
St Louis Rams

12 letters:
Buffalo Bills
Chicago Bears
Detroit Lions

13 letters:
Dallas Cowboys
Denver Broncos
Houston Texans
Miami Dolphins
New York Giants

14 letters:
Atlanta Falcons

Oakland Raiders

15 letters:
Baltimore Ravens
Cleveland Browns
Green Bay Packers
Seattle Seahawks
Tennessee Titans

16 letters:
Arizona Cardinals
Carolina Panthers
Kansas City Chiefs
Minnesota Vikings
New Orleans Saints
San Diego Chargers

17 letters:
Cincinnati Bengals
Indianapolis Colts

18 letters:
New England Patriots
Philadelphia Eagles
Pittsburgh Steelers
Tampa Bay Buccaneers
Washington Redskins

19 letters:
Jacksonville Jaguars

23 letters:
San Francisco Forty-
   niners

Amphibians

3 letters:
Eft
Olm

4 letters:
Frog
Hyla
Newt
Pipa
Rana
Toad

5 letters:
Anura
Guana
Siren
Snake

6 letters:
Desman
Hassar

7 letters:
Axolotl
Crapaud
Proteus
Tadpole
Urodela
Urodele

8 letters:
Bullfrog
Caecilia
Cane toad
Congo eel
Mud puppy
Tree frog
Urodelan

9 letters:
Ambystoma
Caecilian

Hairy frog
Salientia

10 letters:
Amblystoma
Batrachian
Hellbender
Natterjack
Salamander

11 letters:
Goliath frog
Midwife toad
Surinam toad

16 letters:
Brown-striped frog

18 letters:
Queensland cane toad

Ancient cities

2 letters:
Ur

3 letters:
Bam

4 letters:
Coba
Rome
Susa
Troy
Tula
Tyre
Uruk

5 letters:
Aksum
Argos
Bosra
Copán
Hatra
Huari
Kabah

Khiva
Labna
Mitla
Moche
Nemea
Petra
Sayil
Shloh
Tegea
Tikal
Tultm
Uxmal

6 letters:
Athens
Byblos
Delphi
Jabneh
Jamnia
Megara
Napata
Nippur
Sardis

Sikyon
Sparta
Thebes
Ugarit
Xlapak

7 letters:
Antioch
Babylon
Bukhara
Cahokia
Corinth
Eleusis
El Tajin
Ephesos
Ephesus
Mayapan
Miletus
Mycenae
Mykenae
Nineveh
Olympia
Pompeii

Angels

Samaria
Sybaris

8 letters:
Carthage
Cihuatán
Damascus
Palenque
Pergamon
Pergamum
Sigiriya
Tashkent

Thysdrus

9 letters:
Byzantium
Perepolis
Samarkand
Sukhothai

10 letters:
Alexandria
Carchemish
Heliopolis
Hierapolis

11 letters:
Chichén Itzá
Machu Picchu
Polonnaruwa

12 letters:
Anuradhapura

13 letters:
Halicarnassus

14 letters:
Constantinople

Angels

ANGELS

5 letters:
Ariel
Uriel

6 letters:
Abdiel
Arioch
Azrael
Belial
Rimmon
Uzziel

7 letters:
Asmadai
Gabriel
Israfel
Lucifer
Michael
Raphael
Zadkiel
Zephiel

8 letters:
Apollyon
Ithuriel

9 letters:
Beelzebub

10 letters:
Adramelech

ANGELIC ORDERS

6 letters:
Angels
Powers

7 letters:
Thrones
Virtues

8 letters:
Cherubim
Seraphim

9 letters:
Dominions

10 letters:
Archangels
Princedoms

11 letters:
Dominations

14 letters:
Principalities

Animals

RELATED WORDS

Ant	Formic
Ass	Asinine
Bear	Ursine
Bee	Apian
Bird	Avian *or* ornithic
Bull	Taurine
Cat	Feline
Crab	Cancroid
Crow	Corvine
Deer	Cervine
Dog	Canine
Dove	Columbine
Eagle	Aquiline
Elephant	Elephantine
Falcon	Falconine
Fish	Piscine *or* icthyoid
Fowl	Gallinaceous
Fox	Vulpine
Goat	Caprine *or* hircine
Goose	Anserine *or* anserous
Gull	Larine
Hare	Leporine
Hawk	Accipitrine
Horse	Equine
Lion	Leonine
Lynx	Lyncean
Mite *or* tick	Acaroid
Monkey	Simian
Ox	Bovine
Parrot	Psittacine
Peacock	Pavonine
Pig	Porcine
Puffin	Alcidine
Seal	Phocine
Sheep	Ovine
Snake	Serpentine, anguine, ophidian, *or* colubrine
Swallow	Hirundine
Wasp	Vespine
Wolf	Lupine

COLLECTIVE ANIMALS

Antelopes	Herd
Apes	Shrewdness
Asses	Pace *or* herd
Badgers	Cete
Bears	Sloth
Bees	Swarm *or* grist
Birds	Flock, congregation, flight, *or* volery
Bitterns	Sedge *or* siege
Boars	Sounder
Bucks	Brace *or* lease
Buffaloes	Herd
Capercailzies	Tok
Cats	Clowder
Cattle	Drove *or* herd
Choughs	Chattering
Colts	Rag
Coots	Covert
Cranes	Herd, sedge, *or* siege
Crows	Murder
Cubs	Litter
Curlews	Herd
Curs	Cowardice
Deer	Herd
Dolphins	School
Doves	Flight *or* dule
Ducks	Paddling *or* team
Dunlins	Flight
Elk	Gang
Fish	Shoal, draught, haul, run, *or* catch
Flies	Swarm *or* grist
Foxes	Skulk
Geese	Gaggle *or* skein
Giraffes	Herd
Gnats	Swarm *or* cloud
Goats	Herd *or* tribe
Goldfinches	Charm
Grouse	Brood, covey, *or* pack
Gulls	Colony
Hares	Down *or* husk
Hawks	Cast
Hens	Brood

COLLECTIVE ANIMALS (CONTINUED)

Herons	Sedge *or* siege
Herrings	Shoal *or* glean
Hounds	Pack, mute, *or* cry
Insects	Swarm
Kangaroos	Troop
Kittens	Kindle
Lapwings	Desert
Larks	Exaltation
Leopards	Leap
Lions	Pride *or* troop
Mallards	Sord *or* sute
Mares	Stud
Martens	Richesse
Moles	Labour
Monkeys	Troop
Mules	Barren
Nightingales	Watch
Owls	Parliament
Oxen	Yoke, drove, team, *or* herd
Partridges	Covey
Peacocks	Muster
Pheasants	Nye *or* nide
Pigeons	Flock *or* flight
Pigs	Litter
Plovers	Stand *or* wing
Pochards	Flight, rush, bunch, *or* knob
Ponies	Herd
Porpoises	School *or* gam
Poultry	Run
Pups	Litter
Quails	Bevy
Rabbits	Nest
Racehorses	Field *or* string
Ravens	Unkindness
Roes	Bevy
Rooks	Building *or* clamour
Ruffs	Hill
Seals	Herd *or* pod
Sheep	Flock
Sheldrakes	Dopping
Snipe	Walk *or* wisp
Sparrows	Host

COLLECTIVE ANIMALS (CONTINUED)

Starlings	Murmuration
Swallows	Flight
Swans	Herd *or* bevy
Swifts	Flock
Swine	Herd, sounder, *or* dryft
Teal	Bunch, knob, *or* spring
Whales	School, gam, *or* run
Whelps	Litter
Whiting	Pod
Wigeon	Bunch, company, knob, *or* flight
Wildfowl	Plump, sord, *or* sute
Wolves	Pack, rout, *or* herd
Woodcocks	Fall

HABITATIONS

Ant	Ant hill *or* formicary
Badger	Set *or* sett
Beaver	Lodge
Bee	Hive *or* apiary
Bird	Nest
Eagle	Aerie *or* eyrie
Fish	Redd
Fox	Earth
Otter	Holt
Pig	Sty
Puffin	Puffinry
Rabbit	Warren
Rook	Rookery
Seal	Sealery
Squirrel	Drey *or* dray
Termite	Termitarium
Wasp	Vespiary *or* bike

MALE

Ass	Jack
Bird	Cock
Cat	Tom
Deer	Hart *or* stag
Donkey	Jack
Duck	Drake

MALE (CONTINUED)

Elephant	Bull
Falcon	Tercel *or* tiercel
Ferret	Hob
Fowl	Cock
Fox	Dog
Goat	Billy *or* buck
Goose	Gander
Hare	Buck
Horse	Stallion
Kangaroo	Buck *or* old man
Lobster	Cock
Ox	Bull
Peafowl	Peacock
Pig	Boar
Rabbit	Buck
Reindeer	Buck
Ruff	Ruff
Sheep	Ram *or* tup
Swan	Cob
Weasel	Whittret
Whale	Bull

FEMALE

Ass	Jenny
Bird	Hen
Cat	Tabby
Deer	Doe *or* hind
Dog	Bitch
Donkey	Jenny
Elephant	Cow
Ferret	Gill *or* jill
Fowl	Hen
Fox	Vixen
Goat	Nanny
Hare	Doe
Horse	Mare
Leopard	Leopardess
Lion	Lioness
Lobster	Hen
Mink	Sow
Ox	Cow

FEMALE (CONTINUED)

Peafowl	Peahen
Pig	Sow
Rabbit	Doe
Ruff	Reeve
Sheep	Ewe
Swan	Pen
Tiger	Tigress
Whale	Cow
Wolf	Bitch
Wren	Jenny

YOUNG

Bear	Cub
Bird	Chick, fledgling, fledgeling, *or* nestling
Butterfly	Caterpillar, chrysalis, *or* chrysalid
Cat	Kitten
Cod	Codling
Deer	Fawn
Dog	Pup *or* puppy
Duck	Duckling
Eagle	Eaglet
Eel	Elver *or* grig
Elephant	Calf
Falcon	Eyas
Ferret	Kit
Fish	Fry *or* fingerling
Fox	Kit *or* cub
Frog	Tadpole
Goat	Kid *or* yeanling
Goose	Gosling
Hare	Leveret
Herring	Alevin, brit, *or* sparling
Horse	Foal, colt, *or* filly
Kangaroo	Joey
Lion	Cub
Moth	Caterpillar
Owl	Owlet
Ox	Calf
Pig	Piglet
Pigeon	Squab

YOUNG (CONTINUED)

Salmon	Alevin, grilse, parr, *or* smolt
Seal	Pup
Sheep	Lamb *or* yeanling
Sprat	Brit
Swan	Cygnet
Tiger	Cub
Toad	Tadpole
Whale	Calf
Wolf	Cub *or* whelp

See also:
➤ **Amphibians ➤ Birds ➤ Dinosaurs ➤ Fish ➤ Insects ➤ Invertebrates**
➤ **Extinct mammals ➤ Parasites ➤ Reptiles**

Anniversaries

Year	Traditional	Modern
1st	Paper	Clocks
2nd	Cotton	China
3rd	Leather	Crystal *or* glass
4th	Linen *or* silk	Electrical appliances
5th	Wood	Silverware
6th	Iron	Wood
7th	Wool *or* copper	Desk sets
8th	Bronze	Linen *or* lace
9th	Pottery *or* china	Leather
10th	Tin *or* aluminium	Diamond jewellery
11th	Steel	Fashion jewellery *or* accessories
12th	Silk	Pearls *or* coloured gems
13th	Lace	Textile *or* furs
14th	Ivory	Gold jewellery
15th	Crystal	Watches
20th	China	Platinum
25th	Silver	Sterling silver
30th	Pearl	Diamond
35th	Coral *or* jade	Jade
40th	Ruby	Ruby
45th	Sapphire	Sapphire
50th	Gold	Gold
55th	Emerald	Emerald
60th	Diamond	Diamond

Antelopes

3 letters:
Elk
Gnu
Kob

4 letters:
Kudu
Oryx
Puku
Suni
Thar
Topi

5 letters:
Addax
Bongo
Bubal
Eland
Goral
Kaama
Nagor
Nyala
Oribi
Sable
Saiga
Sasin
Serow
Takin

6 letters:
Dikdik

Duiker
Duyker
Dzeren
Impala
Inyala
Koodoo
Lechwe
Nilgai
Nilgau
Ourebi
Pallah
Pygarg
Reebok
Rhebok

7 letters:
Blaubok
Blesbok
Bloubok
Bubalis
Chamois
Chikara
Gazelle
Gemsbok
Gerenuk
Grysbok
Kongoni
Madoqua
Nylghau
Sassaby

Stembok

8 letters:
Bluebuck
Bontebok
Bushbuck
Hartbees
Pale-buck
Reedbuck
Steenbok
Stemback
Tsessebe

9 letters:
Blackbuck
Prongbuck
Pronghorn
Sitatunga
Situtunga
Steinbock
Tragelaph
Waterbuck

10 letters:
Hartebeest
Wildebeest

12 letters:
Klipspringer

Antibiotics

7 letters:
Opsonin

8 letters:
Colistin
Neomycin
Nystatin

9 letters:
Kanamycin
Mitomycin
Oxacillin
Polymixin

Rifamycin

10 letters:
Bacitracin
Gentamicin
Gramicidin
Lincomycin
Lineomycin
Rifampicin
Terramycin®
Tyrocidine

11 letters:
Actinomycin
Cloxacillin
Doxorubicin
Doxycycline
Interleukin
Methicillin
Tyrothricin

12 letters:
Erythromycin
Griseofulvin
Streptomycin

Tetracycline

Spectinomycin

15 letters:
Oxytetracycline

13 letters:
Cephalosporin

14 letters:
Streptothricin

Antiques terms

3 letters:
Bow
FSA

4 letters:
Adam
Buhl

5 letters:
Bulla
Curio
Inlay
Relic
Resto
Spode
Style
Tudor

6 letters:
Boulle
Branks
Bureau
Bygone
Flacon
Gothic
Period
Rococo
Sconce
Settle

7 letters:
Antique
Baroque
Charger
Curiosa

Diptych
Dresser
Gadroon
Godroon
Kiwiana
Netsuke
Regency
Snuffer
Tallboy

8 letters:
Baluster
Coalport
Ephemera
Jacobean
Snuffbox

9 letters:
Antiquary
Antiquate
Bed warmer
Davenport
Fleurette
George III
Marquetry
Porcelain
Queen Anne
Washstand

10 letters:
Art Nouveau
Bellarmine
Blue willow
Escritoire
Escutcheon

Four-poster
Secretaire
Victoriana

11 letters:
Antiquarian
Antiquities
Chinoiserie
Chippendale
Collectable
Cromwellian
Hepplewhite
Museum piece
Period piece
Renaissance

12 letters:
Apostle spoon
Elgin marbles
Gateleg table
Sanction mark
Welsh dresser

13 letters:
Drop-leaf table
Early Georgian
Fiddle pattern
Neo-classicism

14 letters:
Collector's item
William and Mary

15 letters:
English Heritage

Anteaters and other edentates

2 letters:
Ai

5 letters:
Sloth

6 letters:
Numbat

7 letters:
Echidna
Tamandu

8 letters:
Aardvark
Anteater
Pangolin
Tamandua

9 letters:
Armadillo

13 letters:
Scaly anteater
Spiny anteater

14 letters:
Banded anteater
Lesser anteater

Ants, bees and wasps

3 letters:
Ant
Bee

4 letters:
Wasp

5 letters:
Emmet
Minga

7 letters:
Army ant
Blue ant
Bull ant
Bull Joe
Hive bee
Termite
Wood ant

8 letters:
Gall wasp
Honey ant
Honeybee
Horntail

Kootchar
Mason bee
Sand wasp
Slave ant
White ant
Wood wasp

9 letters:
Amazon ant
Bumblebee
Cuckoo bee
Driver ant
Humblebee
Killer bee
Mason wasp
Mining bee
Mud dauber
Native bee
Sirex wasp
Velvet ant

10 letters:
Bulldog ant
Digger wasp

Flower wasp
Pharaoh ant

11 letters:
Honeypot ant
Sugarbag fly

12 letters:
Carpenter bee
Cicada hunter
Ichneumon fly
Legionary ant
Policeman fly
Ruby-tail wasp
Yellow jacket

13 letters:
Ichneumon wasp
Leafcutter ant
Leafcutter bee

17 letters:
Spider-hunting wasp

Four Horsemen of the Apocalypse

White (*Christ*)
Red (*War*)

Black (*Famine*)

Pale (*Death*)

The Twelve Apostles

4 letters:
John
Jude

5 letters:
James (*the Great*)
James (*the Less*)
Peter

Simon

6 letters:
Andrew
Philip
Thomas

7 letters:
Matthew

8 letters:
Matthias

11 letters:
Bartholomew

Apples

4 letters:
Crab
Fuji
John
Lobo
Love
Pome
Snow

5 letters:
Pyrus
Sugar
Thorn

6 letters:
Balsam
Biffin
Codlin
Elstar
Empire
Idared
Mammee
Medlar
Pippin
Pomace
Pomroy
Rennet
Russet
Sunset

7 letters:
Baldwin
Bramley
Codling
Costard
Custard

Pomeroy
Ribston
Ruddock
Spartan
Sturmer
Winesap

8 letters:
Braeburn
Greening
Jonagold
Jonathan
Jonathon
Pearmain
Pink Lady
Reinette
Ribstone
Sweeting

9 letters:
Alligator
Charlotte
Crab apple
Discovery
Grenadier
Jenneting
Nonpareil
Quarenden
Quarender
Redstreak
Royal Gala

10 letters:
Quarantine
Quarrender
Red Ellison

Sops-in-wine

11 letters:
Charles Ross
Granny Smith
James Grieve
Leather-coat
Quarrington

12 letters:
Greensleeves
Laxton Superb
Prince Albert
Red Delicious

13 letters:
Lord Lambourne
Seek-no-further

14 letters:
Blenheim Orange
Egremont Russet
Rosemary Russet

15 letters:
Golden Delicious

16 letters:
Cox's orange pippin

17 letters:
Worcester Pearmain

Types of arch

3 letters:
Gee

4 letters:
Keel
Ogee
Skew

5 letters:
Acute
Hance
Ogive
Roman
Vault

6 letters:
Gothic

Haunch
Lancet
Lierne
Marble
Norman
Portal
Soffit
Trajan

7 letters:
Pointed
Squinch

8 letters:
Cross-rib
Intrados

9 letters:
Admiralty
Arblaster
Archivolt
Ctesiphon
Horseshoe
Triumphal

10 letters:
Proscenium

11 letters:
Counterfort

Archaeology

ARCHAEOLOGICAL PERIODS

6 letters:
Ice age
La Tène
Minoan

7 letters:
Azilian
Iron Age

8 letters:
Asturian
Helladic

9 letters:
Acheulean
Acheulian

Bronze Age
Levallois
Mycenaean
Neolithic
Solutrean

10 letters:
Eneolithic
Gravettian
Mesolithic
Mousterian

11 letters:
Aurignacian
Magdalenian

New Stone Age
Old Stone Age

12 letters:
Chalcolithic
Levalloisian
Palaeolithic

13 letters:
Neo-Babylonian
Old Babylonian

15 letters:
Châtelperronian

ARCHAEOLOGICAL TERMS

4 letters:
Celt
Cist
Core
Kist

5 letters:
Baulk
Blade
Burin
Cairn
Flake

Flint
Henge
Mound
Pylon
Stela
Stele

ARCHAEOLOGICAL TERMS (CONTINUED)

6 letters:
Arcade
Barrow
Bogman
Cirque
Dolmen
Eolith
Larnax
Vallum

7 letters:
Callais
Caveman
Hogback
Ley line
Neolith
Obelisk
Patella
Retouch
Sondage
Tumulus

8 letters:
Bifacial
Cartouch
Cromlech
Graffito
Hillfort
Megalith
Palmette
Palstave
Tribrach

9 letters:
Acropolis
Alignment
Bracteate
Cartouche
Earthwork
Hut circle
Microlith

10 letters:
Souterrain

11 letters:
Clovis point
Cross-dating
Stone circle

12 letters:
Robber trench
Stratigraphy

15 letters:
Archeomagnetism

16 letters:
Archaeomagnetism

17 letters:
Radiocarbon dating

Archbishops of Canterbury

3 letters:
Oda

4 letters:
Lang, *Cosmo*
Laud, *William*
Pole, *Reginald*
Rich, *Edmund*
Tait, *Archibald*
Wake, *William*

5 letters:
Abbot, *George*
Carey, *George*
Deane, *Henry*
Islip, *Simon*
Juxon, *William*
Kempe, *John*
Moore, *John*
Serio, *Sigeric*

6 letters:
Anselm

Becket, *Thomas à*
Benson, *Edward*
Coggan, *Frederick*
Fisher, *Geoffrey*
Howley, *William*
Hutton, *Matthew*
Justus
Lyfing
Mepham, *Simon*
Morton, *John*
Offord, *John*
Parker, *Matthew*
Pecham, *John*
Potter, *John*
Ramsey, *Arthur*
Robert of *Jumieges*
Runcie, *Robert*
Secker, *Thomas*
Sumner, *John*
Sutton, *Charles*
Temple, *Frederick*
Temple, *William*

Walden, *Roger*
Walter, *Hubert*
Warham, *William*

7 letters:
Aelfric
Arundel, *Thomas*
Baldwin
Cranmer, *Thomas*
Dunstan
Eadsige
Grindal, *Edmund*
Herring, *Thomas*
Langham, *Simon*
Langton, *Stephen*
Le Grant, *Richard*
Longley, *Charles*
Nothelm
Richard of *Dover*
Sheldon, *Gilbert*
Stigand
Sudbury, *Simon*
Tatwine

Tenison, *Thomas*
William *of Corbeil*
Wulfred

8 letters:
Aelfheah
Aelfsige
Bancroft, *Richard*
Boniface *of Savoy*
Ceolnoth
Chichele, *Henry*
Davidson, *Randall*
D'Escures, *Ralph*
Honorius
Lanfranc
Mellitus
Plegmund
Reynolds, *Walter*

Sancroft, *William*
Stafford, *John*
Theobald *of Bec*
Whitgift, *John*
Williams
Wulfhelm

9 letters:
Aethelgar
Aethelred
Augustine
Breguwine
Courtenay, *William*
Deusdedit
Feologild
Kilwardby, *Robert*
Stratford, *John*
Theodorus

Tillotson, *John*

10 letters:
Aethelhelm
Aethelnoth
Beorhthelm
Bourgchier, *Thomas*
Cornwallis, *Frederick*
Cuthbeorht
Jaenbeorht
Laurentius
Whittlesey, *William*
Winchelsey, *Robert*

11 letters:
Aethelheard
Beorhtweald
Bradwardine

Architecture

ARCHITECTURAL STYLES

5 letters:
Doric
Ionic
Roman
Saxon
Tudor

6 letters:
Empire
Gothic
Norman
Rococo
Tuscan

7 letters:
Art Deco
Baroque
Bauhaus
Moderne
Moorish
Morisco
Mudéjar
Regency
Saracen

8 letters:
Colonial

Georgian
Jacobean

9 letters:
Brutalist
Byzantine
Classical
Composite
Decorated
Edwardian
Mannerist
Modernist
Palladian
Queen-Anne
Victorian

10 letters:
Art Nouveau
Corinthian
Federation
Louis Seize
Romanesque
Transition

11 letters:
Elizabethan

Louis Quinze
Louis Treize
Renaissance

12 letters:
Early English
Greek Revival
New brutalist
Transitional

13 letters:
Functionalism
Gothic Revival
Louis Quatorze
Neoclassicist
Perpendicular
Postmodernist

14 letters:
Churrigueresco
Early Christian

15 letters:
Churrigueresque

18 letters:
International Style

Architectural terms

3 letters:
Hip

4 letters:
Drum
Naos
Rise

5 letters:
Giant
Order
Shaft
Shell
Stria

6 letters:
Filler
Florid
Fluted
Hipped
Invert
Lierne
Lintel
Listed
Loggia
Member
Module
Return
Rhythm
Soffit
Spring
Storey
String
Summer

7 letters:
Abuttal
Astylar
Bolster
Bracket
Castled
Engaged
Galilee
Profile

Rampant
Respond
Stilted
Subbase
Surbase

8 letters:
Abutment
Colossal
Cradling
Diastyle
Diminish
Dipteral
Foliated
Galleria
King post
Lanceted
Moresque
Postiche
Prostyle
Shafting
Stringer
Tail beam
Trabeate
Tympanic

9 letters:
Composite
Crenelate
Discharge
Elevation
Eurhythmy
Floor plan
Floreated
Floriated
Foliation
Hexastyle
Hypostyle
Imbricate
Pulvinate
Queen post
Rendering
Rusticate
Springing

Stylobate
Tailpiece
Trabeated

10 letters:
Cloistered
Crenellate
Flamboyant
Ground plan
Imbricated
Joggle post
Polychromy
Pulvinated
Sexpartite
Summer tree

11 letters:
Castellated
Cinquecento
Denticulate
Fenestrated
High-pitched
Orientation

12 letters:
String course

13 letters:
Architectonic
Architectural
Springing line
Supercolumnar

14 letters:
Architectonics
Springing point

15 letters:
Underpitch vault

17 letters:
Intercolumniation
Ribbon development

ARCHITECTURAL FEATURES

3 letters:
Bow
Cap
Die
Ell
Fan
Rib
Web

4 letters:
Anta
Apse
Arch
Balk
Band
Base
Bead
Beak
Case
Cove
Cusp
Cyma
Dado
Drip
Foil
Jube
Naos
Neck
Ogee
Pace
Pier
Quad
Reed
Sill
Stoa
Term
Tore
Xyst

5 letters:
Aisle
Ancon
Apsis
Arris
Atlas
Attic
Cella
Cheek

Choir
Coign
Conch
Congé
Crown
Doors
Facet
Facia
Gable
Garth
Glyph
Groin
Gutta
Hance
Helix
Label
Newel
Niche
Ogive
Oriel
Ovolo
Patio
Porch
Pylon
Quirk
Quoin
Ridge
Shaft
Spire
Splay
Stela
Stele
Stria
Table
Talon
Tenia
Thumb
Torus
Truss
Vault
Verge

6 letters:
Abacus
Ancone
Arcade
Atrium
Baguet

Belfry
Bezant
Billet
Binder
Breast
Broach
Byzant
Canopy
Casing
Cellar
Coffer
Coigne
Column
Concha
Corbel
Cordon
Corona
Coving
Crenel
Cullis
Cupola
Dentil
Ectype
Exedra
Facade
Facial
Fascia
Fillet
Finial
Flèche
Frieze
Garret
Gazebo
Gradin
Griffe
Grotto
Haunch
Hipped
Impost
Lacuna
Leaded
Listel
Loggia
Louvre
Metope
Mutule
Offset
Perron

ARCHITECTURAL FEATURES (CONTINUED)

Piazza
Pillar
Plinth
Podium
Portal
Reglet
Relief
Return
Reveal
Rosace
Scotia
Screen
Soffit
Squint
Summer
Taenia
Trophy
Turret
Tympan
Volute

7 letters:
Acroter
Annulet
Antefix
Apteral
Balcony
Bezzant
Bracket
Caisson
Calotte
Capital
Cavetto
Ceiling
Channel
Chaplet
Chevron
Corbeil
Cornice
Crochet
Crocket
Cushion
Echinus
Entasis
Fantail
Fascial
Festoon
Fluting

Footing
Frustum
Gadroon
Gallery
Gambrel
Godroon
Hip roof
Landing
Lantern
Lucarne
Mansard
Meander
Minaret
Mullion
Narthex
Necking
Obelisk
Parapet
Pendant
Perpend
Portico
Postern
Reeding
Respond
Rosette
Rotunda
Roundel
Squinch
Steeple
Strigil
Tambour
Telamon
Tracery
Trefoil
Tribune
Trumeau
Veranda

8 letters:
Acanthus
Accolade
Apophyge
Arcature
Astragal
Atlantes
Baguette
Baluster
Banderol

Bannerol
Basement
Buttress
Caryatid
Casement
Chapter
Cloister
Crenelle
Cresting
Crossing
Crow step
Curb roof
Cymatium
Dancette
Dogtooth
Extrados
Fanlight
Fenestra
Gable end
Gargoyle
Gorgerin
Headwork
Imperial
Intrados
Keystone
Moulding
Ogee arch
Pedestal
Pediment
Pinnacle
Platform
Predella
Semidome
Shafting
Skew arch
Skylight
Spandrel
Spandril
Springer
Tellamon
Terminal
Terminus
Transept
Traverse
Triglyph
Tympanum
Verandah
Vignette

ARCHITECTURAL FEATURES (CONTINUED)

9 letters:
Anthemion
Archivolt
Arcuation
Baldachin
Banderole
Bay window
Bilection
Bolection
Bow window
Cartouche
Choir loft
Colonnade
Corbeille
Decastyle
Dripstone
Embrasure
Footstall
Gatehouse
Headstone
Helicline
Hood mould
Hypophyge
Medallion
Modillion
Onion dome
Penthouse
Peristyle
Poppyhead
Roman arch
Strap work
Stylobate
Triforium

10 letters:
Ambulatory
Arc-boutant
Architrave
Ballflower

Belt course
Cantilever
Cinquefoil
Clerestory
Corbel step
Corbie-step
Egg and dart
Fan tracery
Fenestella
Gothic arch
Hagioscope
Lancet arch
Norman arch
Propylaeum
Quadrangle
Quatrefoil
Rose window
Saddleback
Saddle roof
Sash window
Scrollwork
Stereobate
Wagon vault
Water table

11 letters:
Amphistylar
Barge couple
Barge course
Barrel vault
Bed moulding
Bottom house
Brattishing
Columbarium
Corbie gable
Curtail step
Curtain wall
Cuspidation
Entablature

Gable window
Half landing
Oeil-de-boeuf
Oriel window
Tunnel vault

12 letters:
Articulation
Columniation
Egg and anchor
Egg and tongue
Frontispiece
Lancet window
Palm vaulting
Porte-cochere
Quarter round
String course

13 letters:
Amphiprostyle
Compass window
French windows
Machicolation

14 letters:
Catherine wheel
Flying buttress
Straining piece

15 letters:
Underpitch vault

16 letters:
Long-and-short work

17 letters:
Whispering gallery

ARCHITECTS

3 letters:
Oud, *Jacobus Johann Pieter*
Pei, *I(eoh) M(ing)*

4 letters:
Adam, *James*

Adam, *Robert*
Adam, *William*
Kahn, *Louis I(sadore)*
Kent, *William*
Loos, *Adolf*
Nash, *John*

Shaw, *Richard Norman*
Webb, *Aston*
Webb, *Philip*
Wood, *John*
Wren, *Christopher*

ARCHITECTS (CONTINUED)

5 letters:
Aalto, *Alvar*
Baker, *Herbert*
Barry, *Charles*
Bryce, *David*
Dance, *George*
Doshi, *Balkrishna Vithaldas*
Dudok, *Willem Marinus*
Engel, *Johann Carl Ludwig*
Gaudí, *Antonio*
Gibbs, *James*
Gilly, *Friedrich*
Horta, *Victor*
Jones, *Inigo*
Levau, *Louis*
Moore, *Charles Willard*
Nervi, *Pier Luigi*
Pugin, *Augustus* (*Welby Northmore*)
Scott, *George Gilbert*
Scott, *Giles Gilbert*
Soane, *John*
Tange, *Kenzo*
Terry, (*John*) *Quinlan*
Utzon, *Jorn*
Wyatt, *James*

6 letters:
Boulle, *Etienne-Louis*
Breuer, *Marcel Lajos*
Burton, *Decimus*
Casson, *Hugh* (*Maxwell*)
Coates, *Wells Wintemute*
Foster, *Norman*
Fuller, (*Richard*) *Buckminster*
Geddes, *Patrick*
Giotto (*di Bondone*)
Howard, *Ebenezer*
Lasdun, *Denys*
Ledoux, *Claude Nicolas*
Lescot, *Pierre*
Nissen, *Godber*
Paxton, *Joseph*
Perret, *Auguste*
Pisano, *Andrea*

Pisano, *Nicola*
Pollio, *Marcus Vitruvius*
Repton, *Humphrey*
Rogers, *Richard*
Romano, *Giulio*
Scopas
Serlio, *Sebastiano*
Smirke, *Robert*
Spence, *Basil* (*Unwin*)
Street, *George Edmund*
Stuart, *James*
Vasari, *Giorgio*
Voysey, *Charles* (*Francis Annesley*)
Wagner, *Otto*
Wright, *Frank Lloyd*

7 letters:
Alberti, *Leon Battista*
Asplund, *Erik Gunnar*
Behrens, *Peter*
Berlage, *Hendrick Petrus*
Bernini, *Gian Lorenzo*
Burnham, *David Hudson*
Candela, *Felix*
Columbo, *David*
Da Vinci, *Leonardo*
De l'Orme, *Philibert*
Gabriel, *Ange-Jacques*
Garnier, *Tony* (*Antoine*)
Gibberd, *Frederick*
Gilbert, *Cass*
Gropius, *Walter*
Guarini, *Guarino*
Holland, *Henry*
Ictinus
Imhotep
Johnson, *Philip Cortelyou*
Lethaby, *William Richard*
Lorimer, *Robert Stodart*
Lutyens, *Edwin*
Maderna, *Carlo*
Maderno, *Carlo*
Mansart, *François*
Mansart, *Jules Hardouin*
Neumann, *Johann Balthasar*

Orcagna (*Andrea di Cionne*)
Peruzzi, *Baldassare Tommaso*
Poelzig, *Hans*
Raphael
Renwick, *James*
Thomson, *Alexander* (*Greek*)
Venturi, *Robert*
Vignola, *Giacomo*

8 letters:
Bramante, *Donato*
Chambers, *William*
Daedalus
De Brosse, *Salomon*
Di Cambio, *Arnolfo*
Erickson, *Arthur Charles*
Hamilton, *Thomas*
Hawkmoor, *Nicholas*
Hoffmann, *Josef*
Jacobsen, *Arne*
Niemeyer, *Oscar*
Palladio, *Andrea*
Piranesi, *Giambattista*
Playfair, *William Henry*
Rietveld, *Gerrit Thomas*
Saarinen, *Eero*
Schinkel, *Karl Friederich*
Smythson, *Robert*
Sottsass, *Ettore Jr*
Soufflot, *Jacques Germain*
Stirling, *James*
Sullivan, *Louis* (*Henri*)
Vanbrugh, *John*
Yamasaki, *Minoru*

9 letters:
Anthemias *of Tralles*
Bartholdi, *Frédéric August*
Borromini, *Francesco*
Cockerell, *Charles Robert*
Da Cortona, *Pietro*
Da Cortona, *Pietro Berrettini*

ARCHITECTS (CONTINUED)

Da Vignola, *Giacomo Barozzi*
Di Giorgio, *Francesco*
Haussmann, *Georges Eugene*
Hawksmoor, *Nicholas*
Labrouste, *(Pierre Francois) Henri*
Mackmurdo, *Arthur Heygate*
Macquarie, *Lachlan*
Sansovino, *Jacopo*
Van Campen, *Jacob*
Vitruvius
Von Erlach, *Johann Bernhard Fischer*

10 letters:
Chermayeff, *Serge*
Mackintosh, *Charles Rennie*
Mendelsohn, *Eric*
Michelozzo
Sanmicheli, *Michele*
Trophonius
Van der Rohe, *Ludwig Mies*
Van de Velde, *Henry*
Waterhouse, *Alfred*

11 letters:
Abercrombie, *(Leslie) Patrick*

Butterfield, *William*
Callicrates
Churriguera, *Don Jose*
De Cuvillies, *Francois*
Le Corbusier
Van Doesburg, *Theo*

12 letters:
Brunelleschi, *Filippo*
Michelangelo
Viollet-le-Duc, *Eugène Emmanuel*

14 letters:
Von Hildebrandt, *Johann Lukas*

Armour

4 letters:
Cush
Jack
Mail
Tace
Umbo

5 letters:
Armet
Bevor
Cuish
Culet
Curat
Fauld
Jupon
Nasal
Petta
Tasse
Visor
Vizor

6 letters:
Beaver
Byrnie
Camail
Corium
Couter
Crinet

Cuisse
Curiet
Gorget
Greave
Gusset
Helmet
Jamber
Poleyn
Secret
Taslet
Tasset
Thorax
Tonlet
Tuille
Voider

7 letters:
Ailette
Basinet
Besagew
Brasset
Buckler
Casspir
Corslet
Cuirass
Hauberk
Jambart
Jambeau

Lamboys
Panoply
Placcat
Placket
Poitrel
Roundel
Sabaton
Ventail

8 letters:
Barbette
Bascinet
Chaffron
Chamfron
Chanfron
Chausses
Corselet
Gauntlet
Jazerant
Pauldron
Pavloron
Plastron
Pouldron
Solleret
Spaudler
Vambrace

9 letters:
Chamfrain
Garniture
Habergeon
Jesserant
Lance rest
Nosepiece

Sword belt
Vantbrass

10 letters:
Brigandine
Cataphract
Coat-of-mail

11 letters:
Breastplate
Genouillère
Mentonnière

Art

ART STYLES AND MOVEMENTS

2 letters:
Op

3 letters:
Pop

4 letters:
Clip
Dada
Deco
Fine
Kano

5 letters:
Cobra
Dedal
Nabis
Tatum
Virtu

6 letters:
Bonsai
Brücke
Cubism
Daedal
Gothic
Kitsch
Rococo
Trouvé
Ukiyo-e

7 letters:
Art Deco
Baroque
Bauhaus
Dadaism
Daedale

De Stijl
Fauvism
Flemish
Kinetic
Minimal
Montage
New Wave
Norwich
Nouveau
Optical
Orphism
Plastic
Realism
Relievo
Sienese
Tachism
Trivium

8 letters:
Abstract
Futurism
Mandorla
Nazarene
Tachisme
Trecento

9 letters:
Mannerism
Modernism
Primitive
Still-life
Symbolism
Tenebrism
Toreutics
Vorticism

10 letters:
Arte Povera
Art Nouveau
Bloomsbury
Classicism
Commercial
Conceptual
Decorative
Jugendstil
Naturalism
Postmodern
Quadratura
Quadrivium
Romanesque
Surrealism
Synthetism

11 letters:
Chiaroscuro
Divisionism
Performance
Perigordian
Pointillism
Psychedelic
Romanticism
Suprematism
Synchronism
Trompe l'oeil

12 letters:
Clair-obscure
Clare-obscure
Neoclassical

13 letters:
Expressionism
Impressionism

ART STYLES AND MOVEMENTS (CONTINUED)

Impressionist
Neoclassicism
Neoplasticism
Postmodernism
Pre-Raphaelite

14 letters:
Abstractionism

Barbizon School
Constructivism
Der Blaue Reiter

16 letters:
Neoimpressionism

17 letters:
Postimpressionism

21 letters:
Abstract expressionism

ART EQUIPMENT

3 letters:
Ink

5 letters:
Brush
Chalk
Easel
Glaze
Paint

6 letters:
Canvas
Crayon
Ground
Pastel
Pencil

7 letters:
Acrylic
Palette
Spatula
Varnish

8 letters:
Airbrush
Charcoal
Fixative
Oil paint
Paintbox
Spray gun

9 letters:
Lay figure

10 letters:
Linseed oil
Paintbrush
Sketchbook

11 letters:
Watercolour

12 letters:
Drawing paper
Palette knife

Arthurian legend

CHARACTERS IN ARTHURIAN LEGEND

4 letters:
Bors

5 letters:
Nimue

6 letters:
Arthur
Elaine
Gawain
Merlin
Modred

7 letters:
Caradoc
Galahad
Gawayne
Igraine
Launfal
Tristan
Viviane

8 letters:
Bedivere
Lancelot
Parsifal

Perceval
Tristram

11 letters:
Morgan Le Fay

14 letters:
Gareth of Orkney
Launcelot du Lac
Uther Pendragon

16 letters:
The Lady of the Lake

PLACES IN ARTHURIAN LEGEND

6 letters:
Avalon

7 letters:
Astolat

Camelot

8 letters:
Tintagel

9 letters:
Lyonnesse

11 letters:
Glastonbury

Artists

3 letters:
Arp, *Hans*
Arp, *Jean*
Cox, *David*
Dou, *Gerrit*
Fry, *Roger*
Gui, *Xia*
Nay, *Ernst Wilhelm*
Ray, *Man*

4 letters:
Bell, *Vanessa*
Boyd, *Arthur*
Caro, *Anthony*
Cuyp, *Aelbert*
Dadd, *Richard*
Dalí, *Salvador*
Doré, *Gustave*
Dufy, *Raoul*
Etty, *William*
Gabo, *Naum*
Gill, *Eric*
Goya (y Lucientes),
  Francisco José de
Gris, *Juan*
Gros, *Antoine Jean*
Hals, *Frans*
Hunt, *William Holman*
John, *Augustus*
John, *Gwen*
Klee, *Paul*
Kuei, *Hsia*
Kuyp, *Aelbert*
Lely, *Peter*
Marc, *Franz*
Miró, *Joan*
Nash, *Paul*
Opie, *John*

Phiz (*Hablot Knight
  Browne*)
Reni, *Guido*
Rosa, *Salvator*
West, *Benjamin*
Zorn, *Anders*

5 letters:
Aiken, *John MacDonald*
Appel, *Karel*
Bacon, *Francis*
Bakst, *Leon Nikolayevich*
Beuys, *Joseph*
Blake, *Peter*
Blake, *William*
Bosch, *Hieronymus*
Brown, *Ford Madox*
Burra, *Edward*
Corot, *Jean Baptiste
  Camille*
Crane, *Walter*
Crome, *John*
Danby, *Francis*
David, *Jacques Louis*
Degas, *Hilaire Germain
  Edgar*
Denis, *Maurice*
Dulac, *Pierre Charles*
Dürer, *Albrecht*
Ensor, *James*
Ernst, *Max*
Freud, *Lucian*
Gorky, *Arshile*
Grant, *Duncan*
Greco, *El*
Grosz, *George*
Hirst, *Damien*
Hoare, *William*
Homer, *Winslow*

Hooch, *Pieter de*
Johns, *Jasper*
Kitaj, *Ron B(rooks)*
Klimt, *Gustav*
Kline, *Franz*
Leech, *John*
Léger, *Fernand*
Lewis, *Wyndham*
Lippi, *Filippino*
Lotto, *Lorenzo*
Lowry, *L(awrence)
  S(tephen)*
Manet, *Edouard*
Monet, *Claude Oscar*
Moore, *Henry*
Morse, *Samuel Finley
  Breese*
Moses, *Grandma*
Munch, *Edvard*
Myron
Nolan, *Sidney*
Nolde, *Emil*
Orpen, *Sir William*
Oudry, *Jean Baptiste*
Pilon, *Germain*
Piper, *John*
Puget, *Pierre*
Redon, *Odilon*
Riley, *Bridget*
Rodin, *Auguste*
Runge, *Philipp Otto*
Seago, *Edward*
Shahn, *Ben*
Sloan, *John*
Smith, *David*
Steen, *Jan*
Steer, *Philip Wilson*
Stoss, *Veit*
Tatum, *Mary*

Watts, *George Frederick*
Zumbo, *Gaetano Giulio*

6 letters:
Albers, *Josef*
Andrei, *Rublev*
Andrei, *Rublyov*
Benton, *Thomas Hart*
Boudin, *Eugène*
Braque, *Georges*
Buffet, *Bernard*
Butler, *Reg*
Calder, *Alexander*
Callot, *Jacques*
Campin, *Robert*
Canova, *Antonio*
Clouet, *François*
Clouet, *Jean*
Copley, *John*
Coypel, *Antoine*
De Goya, *Francisco*
Derain, *André*
De Wint, *Peter*
Dobell, *William*
D'Orsay, *Count Alfred
   Guillaum Gabriel*
Eakins, *Thomas*
Fuseli, *Henry*
Gérard, *François*
Giotto (*di Bondone*)
Greuze, *Jean Baptiste*
Guardi, *Francesco*
Haydon, *Benjamin
   Robert*
Hopper, *Edward*
Houdon, *Jean Antoine*
Ingres, *Jean Auguste
   Dominique*
Knight, *Laura*
Lebrun, *Charles*
Le Nain, *Antoine*
Le Nain, *Louis*
Le Nain, *Mathieu*
Mabuse, *Jan*
Martin, *John*
Massys, *Quentin*
Millet, *Jean François*
Moreau, *Gustave*
Morris, *William*
Newman, *Barnett*

O'Keefe, *Georgia*
Orozco, *José Clemente*
Palmer, *Samuel*
Pisano, *Andrea*
Pisano, *Giovanni*
Pisano, *Nicola*
Potter, *Paulus*
Ramsay, *Allan*
Renoir, *Pierre Auguste*
Ribera, *Jusepe de*
Rivera, *Diego*
Romano, *Giulio*
Romney, *George*
Rothko, *Mark*
Rubens, *Peter Paul*
Scopas
Sendak, *Maurice*
Sesshu, *Toyo*
Seurat, *Georges*
Signac, *Paul*
Sisley, *Alfred*
Sluter, *Claus*
Stubbs, *George*
Tanguy, *Yves*
Tatlin, *Vladimir*
Tissot, *James Jacques
   Joseph*
Titian
Turner, *J(oseph)
   M(allord) W(illiam)*
Vasari, *Giorgio*
Villon, *Jacques*
Warhol, *Andy*
Wilson, *Richard*
Wright, *Joseph*
Zeuxis

7 letters:
Alberti, *Leon Battista*
Allston, *Washington*
Apelles
Audubon, *John James*
Balthus (*Balthasar
   Klossowski de Rola*)
Bellini, *Giovanni*
Bernini, *Gian Lorenzo*
Bomberg, *David*
Bonheur, *Rosa*
Bonnard, *Pierre*
Borglum, *Gutzon*

Boucher, *Francois*
Brassaï, *Gyula*
Bruegel, *Jan*
Bruegel, *Pieter*
Cassatt, *Mary*
Cellini, *Benvenuto*
Cézanne, *Paul*
Chagall, *Marc*
Chardin, *Jean-Baptiste
   Siméon*
Cimabue, *Giovanni*
Collier, *John*
Courbet, *Gustave*
Cranach, *Lucas*
Daumier, *Honoré*
Da Vinci, *Leonardo*
De Hooch, *Pieter*
De Hoogh, *Pieter*
Delvaux, *Paul*
Duchamp, *Marcel*
Epstein, *Jacob*
Flaxman, *John*
Fouquet, *Jean*
Gauguin, *Paul*
Gibbons, *Grinling*
Hobbema, *Meindert*
Hockney, *David*
Hofmann, *Hans*
Hogarth, *William*
Hokusai, *Katsushika*
Holbein, *Hans*
Hoppner, *John*
Kneller, *Godfrey*
Kossoff, *Leon*
Lindsay, *Norman Alfred
   William*
Lorrain, *Claude*
Maillol, *Aristide*
Martini, *Simone*
Matisse, *Henri*
Memlinc, *Hans*
Memling, *Hans*
Millais, *John Everett*
Morisot, *Berthe*
Morland, *George*
Murillo, *Bartolomé
   Esteban*
Nattier, *Jean Marc*
Orcagna, (*Andrea di
   Cionne*)

Pasmore, *Victor*
Patinir, *Joachim*
Peruzzi, *Baldassare*
Pevsner, *Antoine*
Phidias
Picabia, *Francis*
Picasso, *Pablo*
Pigalle, *Jean Baptiste*
Pissaro, *Camille*
Pollock, *Jackson*
Poussin, *Nicolas*
Proesch, *Gilbert*
Prud'hon, *Pierre Paul*
Rackham, *Arthur*
Raeburn, *Henry*
Raphael
Rouault, *Geroges*
Sargent, *John Singer*
Schiele, *Egon*
Sickert, *Walter Richard*
Soutine, *Chaim*
Spencer, *Stanley*
Teniers, *David*
Tiepolo, *Giambattista*
Uccello, *Paolo*
Utamaro, *Kitigawa*
Utrillo, *Maurice*
Van Dyck, *Anthony*
Van Eyck, *Jan*
Van Gogh, *Vincent*
Van Rijn, *Rembrandt Harmensz*
Vecchio, *Palma*
Vermeer, *Jan*
Watteau, *Jean Antoine*
Zeuxian
Zoffany, *Johann*

8 letters:
Angelico, *Fra*
Annigoni, *Pietro*
Auerbach, *Frank*
Beckmann, *Max*
Boccioni, *Umberto*
Bramante, *Donato*
Brancusi, *Constantin*
Breughel, *Jan*
Breughel, *Pieter*
Bronzino, *Agnolo*
Brueghel, *Jan*

Brueghel, *Pieter*
Carracci, *Agostino*
Carracci, *Annibale*
Carracci, *Ludovico*
Chadwick, *Lynn*
Daubigny, *Charles François*
De La Tour, *Georges*
Delaunay, *Robert*
De Ribera, *José*
Di Cosimo, *Piero*
Di Duccio, *Agostino*
Drysdale, *George Russell*
Dubuffet, *Jean*
Eastlake, *Sir Charles Lock*
Ghiberti, *Lorenzo*
González, *Julio*
Hamilton, *Richard*
Jongkind, *Johan Barthold*
Jordaens, *Jacob*
Kirchner, *Ernst Ludwig*
Landseer, *Edwin*
Lawrence, *Thomas*
Leighton, *Frederic*
Leonardo
Lipchitz, *Jacques*
Lysippus
Magritte, *René*
Malevich, *Kasimir Severinovich*
Mantegna, *Andrea*
Masaccio (*Thomasso Giovanni di Simone Guidi*)
Mondrian, *Piet*
Munnings, *Alfred*
Nevinson, *Christopher Richard Wynne*
Paolozzi, *Eduardo*
Passmore, *George*
Patenier, *Joachim*
Perugino, *Pietro*
Piranesi, *Giambattista*
Pissarro, *Camille*
Pontormo, *Jacopo Carucci*
Reynolds, *Joshua*
Rossetti, *Dante Gabriel*
Rousseau, *Henri Julien*

Rousseau, *Théodore*
Ter Borch, *Gerard*
Topolski, *Feliks*
Van Goyen, *Jan*
Vasarely, *Victor*
Veronese, *Paolo*
Whistler, *James Abbott McNeill*
Zurbarán, *Francisco*

9 letters:
Altdorfer, *Albrecht*
Bartholdi, *Frédéric August*
Beardsley, *Aubrey Vincent*
Bonington, *Richard Parkes*
Canaletto (*Giovanni Antonio Canal*)
Carpaccio, *Vittore*
Cavallini, *Pietro*
Constable, *John*
Correggio, *Antonio Allegri da*
Da Cortona, *Pietro*
Da Messina, *Antonello*
De Chirico, *Giorgio*
De Kooning, *Willem*
Delacroix, *Eugène*
Delaroche, *Paul*
Donatello (*Donato di Betto Bardi*)
Feininger, *Lyonel*
Fragonard, *Jean Honoré*
Friedrich, *Caspar David*
Géricault, *Théodore*
Giorgione, *Giorgio Barbarelli*
Grünewald, *Isaak*
Hiroshige, *Ando*
Kandinsky, *Wassily*
Kauffmann, *Angelica*
Kokoschka, *Oscar*
Kuniyoshi, *Utagawa*
Lehmbruck, *Wilhelm*
Mestrovic, *Ivan*
Nicholson, *Ben*
Nollekens, *Joseph*
Oldenburg, *Claes*

Pisanello
Rembrandt (*Rembrandt Harmensz van Rijn*)
Rodchenko, *Alexander Mikhailovich*
Roubiliac, *Louis-François*
Roubillac, *Louis-François*
Siqueiros, *David Alfaro*
Thornhill, *James*
Velázquez, *Diego Rodríguez de Silva y*

10 letters:
Alma-Tadema, *Lawrence*
Archipenko, *Aleksandr Porfiryevich*
Arcimboldo, *Giuseppe*
Bonnington, *Richard Parkes*
Botticelli, *Sandro*
Buonarroti, *Michelangelo*
Burne-Jones, *Edward*
Da Corregio, *Antonio Allegri*
Da Fabriano, *Gentile*
De Vlaminck, *Maurice*
Giacometti, *Alberto*
Guillaumin, *Armand*
Mackintosh, *Charles Rennie*
Michelozzo, *Michelozzi*
Modigliani, *Amedeo*
Moholy-Nagy, *László*
Polyclitus
Polygnotus

Praxiteles
Rowlandson, *Thomas*
Schongauer, *Martin*
Schwitters, *Kurt*
Signorelli, *Luca*
Sutherland, *Graham*
Tintoretto, *Jacopo*
Van der Goes, *Hugo*
Van de Velde, *Adriaen*
Van de Velde, *Willem*

11 letters:
Bartolommeo, *Fra*
Callimachus
De Chavannes, *Pierre Puvis*
Del Barbiere, *Domenico*
Della Robbia, *Andrea*
Della Robbia, *Luca*
Domenichino (*Domenico Zampien*)
Ghirlandaio, *Domenico*
Giambologna (*Jean de Boulogne*)
Terbrugghen, *Hendrik*
Thorvaldsen, *Bertel*
Van Ruisdael, *Jacob*
Van Ruysdael, *Salomen*
Vigée-Lebrun, *Élisabeth*

12 letters:
Da Caravaggio, *Michelangelo Merisi*
De Champaigne, *Philippe*
Della Quercia, *Jacopa*
Fantin-Latour, *Henri*

Gainsborough, *Thomas*
Lichtenstein, *Roy*
Michelangelo (*Michelagniolo di Lodovico Buonarriti*)
Parmigianino (*Girolano Francesco Maria Mazzola*)
Pinturicchio (*Bernardino di Betto*)
Rauschenberg, *Robert*
Van der Weyden, *Rogier*
Winterhalter, *Franz Xaver*

13 letters:
Del Pollaiuolo, *Antonio*
Del Pollaiuolo, *Piero*
Del Verrocchio, *Andrea*
Di Buoninsegna, *Duccio*
Messerschmidt, *Franz Xavier*

14 letters:
Da Castelfranco, *Giorgione*
Della Francesca, *Piero*
Gaudier-Brzeska, *Henri*

16 letters:
Gilbert and George

17 letters:
De Toulouse-Lautrec, *Henri Marie Raymond*

Asteroids

4 letters:
Eros
Juno

5 letters:
Ceres

6 letters:
Hermes
Pallas

8 letters:
Hesperia
Phaethon

Astrology terms

2 letters:
MC

3 letters:
Air

4 letters:
Cusp
Fire

5 letters:
Earth
Fixed
House
Stars
Trine
Water

6 letters:
Aspect
Square
Zodiac

7 letters:
Element
Mutable
Sun sign

8 letters:
Cardinal
Quintile
Star sign

9 letters:
Ascendant

Ascendent
Horoscope
Midheaven

10 letters:
Birthchart
Descendant
Descendent
Opposition

11 letters:
Conjunction
Satellitium

12 letters:
Ruling planet

Astronomers

4 letters:
Hale, *Alan*
Oort, *Jan*

5 letters:
Brahe, *Tycho*
Encke, *Johann Franz*
Hoyle, *Sir Fred(erick)*
Jeans, *Sir James Hopwood*
Meton
Reber, *Grote*
Roche, *Edouard*

6 letters:
Bessel, *Friedrich Wilhelm*
Halley, *Edmund*
Hewish, *Antony*
Hubble, *Edwin*
Kepler, *Johannes*

Lovell, *Sir (Alfred Charles) Bernard*

7 letters:
Bradley, *James*
Cassini, *Giovanni*
Celsius, *Anders*
Eudoxus
Galileo, *Galilei*
Huggins, *Sir William*
Khayyam, *Omar*
Laplace, *Pierre Simon de*
Lockyer, *Sir Joseph Norman*
Ptolemy (*Claudius Ptolemaeus*)

8 letters:
Almagest
Callipic
Herschel, *Caroline*

Herschel, *William*

9 letters:
Eddington, *Sir Arthur*
Flamsteed, *John*
Leverrier, *Urbain Jean Joseph*
Sosigenes

10 letters:
Copernicus, *Nicolas*
Hipparchus
Tycho Brahe

11 letters:
Aristarchus

12 letters:
Eratosthenes

13 letters:
Schwarzschild, *Karl*

Astronomy terms

3 letters:
Jet
Ray

4 letters:
Apse
Coma
Cusp
Limb
Mass
Node
Nova
Pole
Ring
Star
Tide

5 letters:
Apsis
Basin
Burst
Comet
Crust
Dwarf
Epoch
Flare
Giant
Lunar
Maria
Nadir
Orbit
Quiet
Rupes
Saros
Solar
Space
Spray
Train

6 letters:
Albedo
Aurora
Bolide
Colure
Corona
Cosmic
Crater
Ejecta

Facula
Galaxy
Merger
Meteor
Nebula
Octant
Plages
Quasar
Rising
Spinar
Syzygy
Zenith

7 letters:
Apapsis
Apolune
Appulse
Aureola
Aureole
Azimuth
Cluster
Ellipse
Equator
Equinox
Farside
Inertia
Ingress
New moon
Nucleus
Perigee
Plerion
Primary
Quarter
Radiant
Sextile
Spicule
Stellar
Sunspot

8 letters:
Aerolite
Altitude
Analemma
Aphelion
Asteroid
Cislunar
Crescent
Dynamics

Emersion
Evection
Filament
Fireball
Loadstar
Lodestar
Mass loss
Meridian
Nearside
Northing
Nutation
Parallax
Red giant
Regolith
Rotation
Solstice
Southing
Spherule
Universe

9 letters:
Aerospace
Anthelion
Black drop
Black hole
Chondrite
Collapsar
Companion
Cosmogony
Cosmology
Eccentric
Ecosphere
Ephemeris
Exosphere
Flocculus
Immersion
Light year
Magnitude
Meteorite
Meteoroid
Moonquake
Obliquity
Percentre
Periapsis
Planetary
Planetoid
Polar axis
Protostar

Ring plain
Satellite
Secondary
Shell star
Spacetime
Star cloud
Supernova
Variation
White hole

10 letters:
Achondrite
Aerosphere
Almacantar
Almucantar
Astrobleme
Atmosphere
Barycentre
Binary star
Brown dwarf
Elongation
Extinction
Inequality
Insolation
Ionosphere
Luminosity
Mesosphere
Metal ratio
Oblateness
Opposition
Periastron
Perihelion
Precession
Prominence
Quadrature
Revolution
Supergiant
Terminator
Tidal force
Triple star
White dwarf

11 letters:
Apocynthion
Chemosphere
Circumlunar
Circumpolar
Circumsolar
Colour index
Conjunction

Culmination
Evolved star
Gravitation
Heliosphere
Inclination
Inner planet
Major planet
Metallicity
Meteor storm
Missing mass
Neutron star
Observatory
Occultation
Open cluster
Outer planet
Photosphere
Protogalaxy
Protoplanet
Radio source
Retardation
Singularity
Solar system
Stellar wind
Troposphere

12 letters:
Asteroid belt
Chromosphere
Interstellar
Lunar eclipse
Mass transfer
Meteor shower
Multiple star
Planetesimal
Plasmasphere
Proper motion
Sidereal time
Solar eclipse
Spectral type
Sunspot cycle
Supercluster
Telluric line
Thermosphere
Tidal capture
Total eclipse
Tropical year
Variable star

13 letters:
Blue straggler

Circumstellar
Constellation
Magnetosphere
Moving cluster
Red supergiant
Scintillation
Seyfert galaxy
Solar constant
Solar spectrum
Spectral class
Sublunar point
Subsolar point
Symbiotic star
Synodic period
Tidal friction
Universal time

14 letters:
Annular eclipse
Aurora borealis
Escape velocity
Galactic centre
Inferior planet
Interplanetary
Molecular cloud
Northern lights
Partial eclipse
Reciprocal mass
Southern lights
Superior planet
Total magnitude
Vertical circle
Zenith distance

15 letters:
Aurora australis
Cepheid variable
Galactic equator
Meridian passage
Meteoroid stream
Nucleosynthesis
Orbital elements
Orbital velocity
Planetary system
Ptolemaic system
Strömgren sphere
Substellar point
Visual magnitude

16 letters:
Copernican system
Galactic rotation
Naked singularity
Penumbral eclipse
Stellar evolution
Stellar structure

17 letters:
Cooordinate system
Physical libration
Pulsating universe
Pulsating variable
Shepherd satellite
Terrestrial planet

18 letters:
Chandrasekhar limit
Heliocentric system
North celestial pole
Northern hemisphere
North polar distance
Planetary alignment
Quasi-stellar object
South celestial pole
Southern hemisphere
South polar distance
Velocity dispersion

19 letters:
Cataclysmic variable

Oscillating universe
Schwarzschild radius

20 letters:
Effective temperature

23 letters:
Transient lunar
  phenomena

24 letters:
Precession of the
  equinoxes

See also:
➤ **Asteroids** ➤ **Regions of the atmosphere** ➤ **Comets** ➤ **Galaxies**
➤ **Meteor showers** ➤ **Planets** ➤ **Satellites** ➤ **Stars and constellations**

Athletic events

5 letters:
Relay

6 letters:
Discus
Hammer

7 letters:
Hurdles
Javelin
Shot put
Walking

8 letters:
High jump
Long jump
Marathon

9 letters:
Decathlon
Pole vault
Triathlon

10 letters:
Heptathlon

Pentathlon
Triple jump

12 letters:
Half marathon
Orienteering
Steeplechase

19 letters:
Cross-country running

Regions of the atmosphere

10 letters:
Ionosphere
Mesosphere
Ozone layer

11 letters:
Ozonosphere
Troposphere

12 letters:
Stratosphere
Thermosphere

Aviation terms

3 letters:
SBA
Yaw

4 letters:
Bank
Bunt
Crab
Dive
Gate
Hunt
Loop
Mach
Rake
Roll
Spin
Taxi
Trim

5 letters:
Ditch
Glide
Pilot
Pitch
Stack
Stall

6 letters:
Cruise
Drogue
Redeye
Reheat
Runway

7 letters:
Air miss
Airside
Batsman
Ceiling
Copilot
Feather
Landing
Loading

Overfly
Takeoff
Taxiway
Yaw axis

8 letters:
Airspeed
Anhedral
Approach
Attitude
Clearway
Dihedral
Flameout
In-flight
Landside
Nose dive
Roll axis
Sideslip
Snap roll
Subsonic
Tailspin
Wide-body
Wingover

9 letters:
Autopilot
Chandelle
Crash-dive
Crash-land
Fly-by-wire
Immelmann
Navigator
Overshoot
Pitch axis
Power dive
Sonic boom

10 letters:
Aerobatics
Barrel roll
Bird strike
Flight path
Shockstall

Supersonic
Undershoot

11 letters:
Air corridor
Groundspeed
Vapour trail
Victory roll

12 letters:
Approach path
Autorotation
Belly landing
Boarding pass
Redeye flight
Sound barrier

13 letters:
Charter flight
Contact flight
Head-up display
Immelmann turn

14 letters:
Automatic pilot
Holding pattern
Pancake landing

15 letters:
Scheduled flight

17 letters:
Air traffic control

20 letters:
Standard beam
  approach

23 letters:
Flight management
  systems

B b

Back words

2 letters:
Ah / Ha
Am / Ma
At / Ta
Eh / He
Em / Me
Er / Re
Ha / Ah
He / Eh
Ho / Oh
Ma / Am
Me / Em
Mp / Pm
No / On
Oh / Ho
On / No
Pm / Mp
Re / Er
Ta / At

3 letters:
And / Dna
Are / Era
Bad / Dab
Bag / Gab
Ban / Nab
Bat / Tab
Ben / Neb
Bid / Dib
Big / Gib
Bin / Nib
Bog / Gob
Boy / Yob
Bud / Dub
Bun / Nub
Bus / Sub
But / Tub
Cam / Mac
Cor / Roc
Dab / Bad
Dag / Gad
Dal / Lad

Dam / Mad
Dew / Wed
Dib / Bid
Dim / Mid
Dna / And
Dog / God
Doh / Hod
Don / Nod
Dot / Tod
Dub / Bud
Eel / Lee
Era / Are
Gab / Bag
Gad / Dag
Gal / Lag
Gas / Sag
Gel / Leg
Gib / Big
Git / Tig
Gob / Bog
God / Dog
Got / Tog
Gum / Mug
Gut / Tug
Hay / Yah
Hod / Doh
Jar / Raj
Lad / Dal
Lag / Gal
Lap / Pal
Lee / Eel
Leg / Gel
Mac / Cam
Mad / Dam
Map / Pam
May / Yam
Mid / Dim
Mug / Gum
Nab / Ban
Nap / Pan
Neb / Ben

Net / Ten
Nib / Bin
Nip / Pin
Nit / Tin
Nod / Don
Not / Ton
Now / Won
Nub / Bun
Owt / Two
Pal / Lap
Pam / Map
Pan / Nap
Par / Rap
Pat / Tap
Pay / Yap
Per / Rep
Pin / Nip
Pit / Tip
Pot / Top
Pus / Sup
Put / Tup
Raj / Jar
Rap / Par
Rat / Tar
Raw / War
Rep / Per
Roc / Cor
Rot / Tor
Sag / Gas
Saw / Was
Sub / Bus
Sup / Pus
Tab / Bat
Tap / Pat
Tar / Rat
Ten / Net
Tig / Git
Tin / Nit
Tip / Pit
Tod / Dot
Tog / Got

Ton / Not
Top / Pot
Tor / Rot
Tub / But
Tug / Gut
Tup / Put
Two / Owt
War / Raw
Was / Saw
Way / Yaw
Wed / Dew
Won / Now
Yah / Hay
Yam / May
Yap / Pay
Yaw / Way
Yob / Boy

4 letters:
Abut / Tuba
Agas / Saga
Ajar / Raja
Auks / Skua
Avid / Diva
Bard / Drab
Bats / Stab
Bird / Drib
Bonk / Knob
Brag / Garb
Buns / Snub
Burg / Grub
Buts / Stub
Cram / Marc
Dart / Trad
Deem / Meed
Deep / Peed
Deer / Reed
Deus / Sued
Dial / Laid
Diva / Avid
Doom / Mood
Door / Rood
Drab / Bard
Draw / Ward
Dray / Yard
Drib / Bird
Dual / Laud
Edam / Made
Edit / Tide
Emir / Rime

Emit / Time
Ergo / Ogre
Et al / La te
Evil / Live
Flog / Golf
Flow / Wolf
Gals / Slag
Garb / Brag
Girt / Trig
Gnat / Tang
Gnus / Sung
Golf / Flog
Grub / Burg
Gulp / Plug
Gums / Smug
Guns / Snug
Hoop / Pooh
Keel / Leek
Keep / Peek
Knob / Bonk
Laid / Dial
Lair / Rial
Late / Etal
Laud / Dual
Leek / Keel
Leer / Reel
Liar / Rail
Live / Evil
Loop / Pool
Loot / Tool
Macs / Scam
Made / Edam
Maps / Spam
Marc / Cram
Mart / Tram
Maws / Swam
Meed / Deem
Meet / Teem
Mood / Doom
Moor / Room
Naps / Span
Nets / Sten
Nips / Spin
Nuts / Stun
Ogre / Ergo
Pals / Slap
Pans / Snap
Part / Trap
Paws / Swap
Peed / Deep

Peek / Keep
Pees / Seep
Pets / Step
Pins / Snip
Plug / Gulp
Pooh / Hoop
Pool / Loop
Pots / Stop
Prat / Tarp
Rail / Liar
Raja / Ajar
Raps / Spar
Rats / Star
Reed / Deer
Reel / Leer
Rial / Lair
Rime / Emir
Rood / Door
Room / Moor
Saga / Agas
Saps / Spas
Scam / Macs
Seep / Pees
Skua / Auks
Slag / Gals
Slap / Pals
Smug / Gums
Snap / Pans
Snip / Pins
Snot / Tons
Snub / Buns
Snug / Guns
Spam / Maps
Span / Naps
Spar / Raps
Spas / Saps
Spat / Taps
Spin / Nips
Spit / Tips
Spot / Tops
Stab / Bats
Star / Rats
Sten / Nets
Step / Pets
Stew / Wets
Stop / Pots
Stub / Buts
Stun / Nuts
Sued / Deus
Sung / Gnus

Back words

Swam / Maws
Swap / Paws
Sway / Yaws
Swot / Tows
Tang / Gnat
Taps / Spat
Tarp / Prat
Teem / Meet
Tide / Edit
Time / Emit
Tips / Spit
Tons / Snot
Tool / Loot
Tops / Spot
Tort / Trot
Tows / Swot
Trad / Dart
Tram / Mart
Trap / Part
Trig / Girt
Trot / Tort
Tuba / Abut
Ward / Draw
Wets / Stew
Wolf / Flow
Yard / Dray
Yaws / Sway

5 letters:
Debut / Tubed
Decaf / Faced
Decal / Laced
Deeps / Speed
Denim / Mined
Devil / Lived
Draws / Sward
Faced / Decaf
Fires / Serif
Keels / Sleek
Knits / Stink
Laced / Decal
Lager / Regal
Leper / Repel
Lever / Revel
Lived / Devil
Loops / Spool
Loots / Stool

Mined / Denim
Nonet / Tenon
Pacer / Recap
Parts / Strap
Pools / Sloop
Ports / Strop
Rebut / Tuber
Recap / Pacer
Regal / Lager
Remit / Timer
Repel / Leper
Revel / Lever
Rones / Senor
Señor / Roñes
Serif / Fires
Sleek / Keels
Sloop / Pools
Smart / Trams
Snaps / Spans
Snips / Spins
Spans / Snaps
Speed / Deeps
Spins / Snips
Spool / Loops
Spots / Stops
Sprat / Tarps
Stink / Knits
Stool / Loots
Stops / Spots
Stows / Swots
Strap / Parts
Straw / Warts
Strop / Ports
Sward / Draws
Swots / Stows
Tarps / Sprat
Tenon / Nonet
Timer / Remit
Trams / Smart
Tubed / Debut
Tuber / Rebut
Warts / Straw

6 letters:
Denier / Reined
Diaper / Repaid
Drawer / Reward

Looter / Retool
Pilfer / Reflip
Pupils / Slipup
Recaps / Spacer
Redraw / Warder
Reflip / Pilfer
Reflow / Wolfer
Reined / Denier
Reknit / Tinker
Rennet / Tenner
Repaid / Diaper
Retool / Looter
Reward / Drawer
Sleets / Steels
Slipup / Pupils
Sloops / Spools
Snoops / Spoons
Spacer / Recaps
Spools / Sloops
Spoons / Snoops
Sports / Strops
Steels / Sleets
Strops / Sports
Tenner / Rennet
Tinker / Reknit
Warder / Redraw
Wolfer / Reflow

7 letters:
Amaroid / Diorama
Deifier / Reified
Deliver / Reviled
Dessert / Tressed
Diorama / Amaroid
Gateman / Nametag
Nametag / Gateman
Reified / Deifier
Reknits / Stinker
Reviled / Deliver
Stinker / Reknits
Tressed / Dessert

8 letters:
Desserts / Stressed
Redrawer / Rewarder
Rewarder / Redrawer
Stressed / Desserts

Bacteria

4 letters:
MRSA

5 letters:
Cocci
Staph
Strep

6 letters:
Aerobe

Vibrio

7 letters:
Bacilli
Lysogen

8 letters:
Listeria
Pathogen
Spirilla

10 letters:
Salmonella

11 letters:
Pasteurella

13 letters:
Streptococcus

Types of bag

3 letters:
Bum
Cod
Ice
Net
Sea
Tea

4 letters:
Body
Caba
Cool
Dime
Grip
Poke
Port
Sack
Tote

5 letters:
Amaut
Amowt
Bulse
Cabas
Dilli
Dilly
Ditty
Doggy
Jelly
Jiffy®
Nunny
Pikau

Pouch
Purse
Scrip
Water

6 letters:
Bergen
Carpet
Clutch
Duffel
Kitbag
Oxford
Sachet
Saddle
Sponge
Tucker
Valise
Vanity
Wallet

7 letters:
Alforja
Carrier
Daypack
Dorothy
Handbag
Holdall
Satchel
Shopper
Sporran
Weekend
Workbag

8 letters:
Backpack
Carryall
Crumenal
Knapsack
Pochette
Reticule
Ridicule
Rucksack
Shoulder
Sleeping
Suitcase
Survival

9 letters:
Briefcase
Carpetbag
Gladstone
Haversack
Overnight
Saddlebag
Vanity box

10 letters:
Diplomatic
Portmantle
Portmantua
Sabretache
Vanity case

11 letters:
Portmanteau

Ballets

5 letters:
Manon
Rodeo

6 letters:
Bolero
Carmen
Façade
Ondine
Onegin
Parade

7 letters:
Giselle
Masques
Orpheus

8 letters:
Coppélia
Firebird
Les Noces

Serenade
Swan Lake

9 letters:
Les Biches
Spartacus

10 letters:
Cinderella
La Bayadère
Nutcracker
Petroushka

11 letters:
Billy the Kid

12 letters:
Les Sylphides
Rite of Spring
Scheherezade

14 letters:
Romeo and Juliet
Sleeping Beauty

16 letters:
Enigma Variations
La Fille mal gardée

17 letters:
Appalachian Spring

18 letters:
L'après-midi d'un faune

19 letters:
La Boutique Fantasque

20 letters:
Midsummer Night's
  Dream

Ballet steps and terms

3 letters:
Pas

4 letters:
Jeté
Plié

5 letters:
Adage
Battu
Brisé
Coupé
Decor
Passé
Tombé

6 letters:
Adagio
Aplomb
Ballon
Chassé
Croisé
Dégagé

Ecarté
En l'air
Failli
Ouvert
Pointe
Relevé

7 letters:
Allegro
Allongé
Balancé
Ciseaux
Déboulé
Échappé
Emboîté
Soutenu
Turn-out

8 letters:
Absolute
Abstract
Assemblé
Attitude

Ballonné
Ballotté
Batterie
Cabriole
Demi-plié
En dedans
En dehors
En pointe
Figurant
Glissade
Pas coupé
Romantic
Sickling
Sur place
Temps lié
Toe-dance

9 letters:
Arabesque
Ballerina
Battement
Classical
Cou-de-pied

Détournée
Dévelopée
Elevation
Entrechat
Pas de chat
Pas de deux
Pirouette
Raccourci
Temps levé
Variation

10 letters:
Changement
Demi-pointe
En couronne
Foudroyant
Grand écart
Grande plié
Pas ciseaux
Pas de brisé
Pas échappé
Soubresaut
Tour en l'air

11 letters:
Ballet blanc
Contretemps
Pas ballotté
Pas de bourée
Pas de chassé
Ports de bras
Rond de jambe
Terre à terre

12 letters:
Ballet de cour
Croisé devant
Enchaînement
Gargouillade

13 letters:
Ballet d'action
En tire-bouchon
Pas de sissonne
Temps de cuisse
Temps de flèche

14 letters:
Benesh notation

Croisé derrière
Entrée de ballet
Premier danseur
Prima ballerina
Temps de poisson
Temps dévelopée

15 letters:
Cecchetti method

16 letters:
Pas de bourée couru
Première danseuse
Stepanov notation
Von Laban notation

17 letters:
Changement de pieds
Fouetté en tournant

21 letters:
Défilé de corps de ballet

22 letters:
Prima ballerina assoluta

Ballgames

4 letters:
Golf

5 letters:
Fives

6 letters:
Boules
Hockey
Soccer
Squash
Tennis

7 letters:
Bowling
Croquet
Hurling
Netball
Pinball

Pyramid
Snooker

8 letters:
Baseball
Football
Goalball
Handball
Korfball
Lacrosse
Pushball
Rounders
Subbuteo®

9 letters:
Badminton
Bagatelle
Billiards
Crazy golf

Paintball
Punchball

10 letters:
Volleyball

11 letters:
Bumble-puppy

12 letters:
Bar billiards

15 letters:
Australian Rules
Pocket billiards

16 letters:
American football
Canadian football
Piggy in the middle

Baseball teams

11 letters:
Chicago Cubs
New York Mets

12 letters:
Boston Red Sox
Texas Rangers

13 letters:
Anaheim Angels
Atlanta Braves
Detroit Tigers
Houston Astros
Montreal Expos

14 letters:
Florida Marlins

Minnesota Twins
New York Yankees
San Diego Padres

15 letters:
Chicago White Sox
Cincinnatti Reds
Colorado Rockies
Seattle Mariners
Toronto Blue Jays

16 letters:
Baltimore Orioles
Cleveland Indians
Kansas City Royals
Milwaukee Brewers

Oakland Athletics
St Louis Cardinals

17 letters:
Los Angeles Dodgers
Pittsburgh Pirates
Tampa Bay Devil Rays

18 letters:
San Francisco Giants

19 letters:
Arizona Diamondbacks

20 letters:
Philadelphia Phillies

Bats

5 letters:
Fruit

6 letters:
Kalong

7 letters:
Noctule
Vampire

8 letters:
Serotine

9 letters:
Flying fox
Horseshoe

10 letters:
Hammerhead

11 letters:
Barbastelle
Pipistrelle

12 letters:
False vampire

13 letters:
Insectivorous

Famous battles

Aboukir Bay *or* Abukir Bay	1798
Actium	31 B.C.
Agincourt	1415
Alamo	1836
Arnhem	1944
Atlantic	1939-45
Austerlitz	1805
Balaklava *or* Balaclava	1854
Bannockburn	1314
Barnet	1471
Bautzen	1813
Belleau Wood	1918

Blenheim	1704
Borodino	1812
Bosworth Field	1485
Boyne	1690
Britain	1940
Bulge	1944-45
Bull Run	1861;1862
Bunker Hill	1775
Cannae	216 B.C.
Crécy	1346
Culloden	1746
Dien Bien Phu	1954
Edgehill	1642
El Alamein	1942
Falkirk	1298; 1746
Flodden	1513
Gettysburg	1863
Guadalcanal	1942-3
Hastings	1066
Hohenlinden	1800
Imphal	1944
Inkerman	1854
Issus	333 B.C.
Jemappes	1792
Jena	1806
Killiecrankie	1689
Kursk	1943
Ladysmith	1899-1900
Le Cateau	1914
Leipzig	1813
Lepanto	1571
Leyte Gulf	1944
Little Bighorn	1876
Lützen	1632
Manassas	1861; 1862
Mantinea or Mantineia	418 B.C.; 362 B.C.
Marathon	490 B.C.
Marengo	1800
Marston Moor	1644
Missionary Ridge	1863
Naseby	1645
Navarino	425 B.C.
Omdurman	1898
Passchendaele	1917

Philippi	42 B.C.
Plains of Abraham	1759
Plassey	1757
Plataea	479 B.C.
Poltava	1709
Prestonpans	1745
Pydna	168 B.C.
Quatre Bras	1815
Ramillies	1706
Roncesvalles	778
Sadowa *or* Sadová	1866
Saint-Mihiel	1918
Salamis	480 B.C.
Sedgemoor	1685
Sempach	1386
Shiloh	1862
Shipka Pass	1877-78
Somme	1916; 1918
Stalingrad	1941-42
Stamford Bridge	1066
Stirling Bridge	1297
Tannenberg	1410; 1914
Tewkesbury	1471
Thermopylae	480 B.C.
Tobruk	1941; 1942
Trafalgar	1805
Trenton	1776
Verdun	1916
Vitoria	1813
Wagram	1809
Waterloo	1815
Ypres	1914; 1915; 1917; 1918
Zama	202 B.C.

Bays

2 letters:
MA

3 letters:
Ise

4 letters:
Pigs

Vigo
Wick

5 letters:
Algoa
Bonny
Byron
Casco

Dvina
False
Fleet
Fundy
Glace
Green
Hawke
Herne

Horse
James
Korea
Milne
Omura
Osaka
Shark
Sligo
Suvla
Table
Tampa
Tokyo
Urado

6 letters:
Abukir
Ariake
Baffin
Bantry
Bengal
Biscay
Botany
Broken
Callao
Colwyn
Daphne
Dublin
Galway
Golden
Hawke's
Hudson
Jervis
Lobito
Manila
Mobile
Newark
Tasman
Toyama
Tralee
Ungava
Vyborg
Walvis

7 letters:
Aboukir
Cape Cod
Delagoa
Delogoa
Dundalk
Florida
Jiazhou
Montego
Moreton
New York
Pegasus
Poverty
Setúbal
Swansea
Thunder
Walfish
Whitley

8 letters:
Biscayne
Buzzards
Cardigan
Delaware
Georgian
Hangzhou
Quiberon
San Pedro
Santiago

9 letters:
Bay of Acre
Bay of Pigs
Bombetoka
Discovery
Encounter
Famagusta
Frobisher
Guanabara
Inhambane
Kuskokwim
Magdalena

Morecambe
St Austell

10 letters:
Bay of Cádiz
Bay of Fundy
Bay of Vlorë
Caernarvon
Carmarthen
Chesapeake
Cienfuegos
Guantánamo
Lützow-Holm

11 letters:
Bay of Bengal
Bay of Biscay
Bay of Gdansk
Bay of Naples
Bay of Plenty
Port Phillip

12 letters:
Bay of Kaválla
Narragansett
San Francisco

13 letters:
Bay of Campeche
Bay of St Michel
Corpus Christi
Massachusetts
Passamaquoddy

14 letters:
Bay of Gibraltar

16 letters:
Bay of Trincomalee

18 letters:
Bay of Espírito Santo

Beans and other pulses

3 letters:
Red

4 letters:
Dhal
Gram
Lima

Mung
Navy
Soya

Types of bed

5 letters:
Black
Bobby
Broad
Field
Green
Pinto

6 letters:
Adsuki
Adzuki
Butter
French
Kidney
Lentil
Runner
String

7 letters:
Haricot
Snow pea

8 letters:
Borlotti
Chick pea
Garbanzo
Split pea

9 letters:
Black-eyed
Cannelini
Flageolet
Mangetout
Petit pois
Pigeon pea

Puy lentil
Red kidney
Red lentil

11 letters:
Green lentil

12 letters:
Black-eyed pea
Marrowfat pea
Sugar snap pea

17 letters:
Continental lentil

Types of bed

3 letters:
Air
Box
Cot
Day
Mat

4 letters:
Bunk
Camp
Cott
Crib
Kang
Lilo®
Loft
Sofa
Twin

5 letters:
Berth
Couch
Divan
Field
Futon

Water

6 letters:
Cradle
Double
Litter
Murphy
Pallet
Put-u-up
Single
Sleigh

7 letters:
Amenity
Charpoy
Feather
Folding
Hammock
Trestle
Truckle
Trundle

8 letters:
Apple-pie

Bassinet
Captain's
Carrycot
Foldaway
Hospital
King-size
Mattress
Platform

9 letters:
Couchette
King-sized
Paillasse
Palliasse
Queen-size
Shake down
Stretcher

10 letters:
Four-poster
Queen-sized

11 letters:
Procrustean

Beers

3 letters:
Ale
Ice
IPA
Keg
Nog

4 letters:
Bock
Mild
Nogg
Pils

5 letters:
Fruit
Guest
Heavy
Lager
Light
Plain
Sixty
Stout
Wheat

6 letters:
Eighty
Export
Gueuze
Kaffir
Kölsch
Lambic

Porter
Shandy
Stingo

7 letters:
Draught
Pale ale
Pilsner
Real ale
Seventy
Shebean
Shebeen
Special

8 letters:
Brown ale
Home-brew
Light ale
Pilsener
Trappist

9 letters:
Christmas
Milk stout
Rauchbier
Weissbier

10 letters:
Barley wine
Sweet stout
Weizenbier

11 letters:
Black and tan
Boilermaker
Half-and-half

12 letters:
Bière de Garde
Christmas ale
India Pale Ale

13 letters:
Sixty shilling

14 letters:
Eighty shilling

15 letters:
Cask-conditioned
Seventy shilling

17 letters:
Bottle-conditioned

18 letters:
Cask-conditioned ale

20 letters:
Bottle-conditioned ale

Beetles

3 letters:
Bee
Dor
May
Oil

4 letters:
Bark
Cane
Dorr
Dung
Flea
Gold

Huhu
June
King
Leaf
Mall
Maul
Pill
Rose
Rove
Stag

5 letters:
Bacon

Black
Click
Clock
Jewel
Roach
Snout
Tiger
Water

6 letters:
Batler
Carpet
Chafer

Diving
Dor-fly
Elater
Gregor
Ground
Hammer
Larder
Mallet
May bug
Museum
Potato
Scarab
Sexton
Sledge
Spider
Weevil

7 letters:
Asiatic
Blister
Burying
Cabinet
Cadelle
Carrion
Elytron
Elytrum
Firefly
Goldbug
Goliath
Hop-flea
Hornbug
June bug
Ladybug

Leather
Skelter
Soldier
Vedalia

8 letters:
Ambrosia
Bum-clock
Cardinal
Colorado
Curculio
Darkling
Glow-worm
Hercules
Japanese
Ladybird
Longhorn
Māori bug
Scarabee
Skipjack
Snapping
Tortoise
Wireworm

9 letters:
Buprestus
Cantharis
Carpet bug
Christmas
Cockroach
Furniture
Goldsmith
Kekerengu
Longicorn

Pea weevil
Pinchbuck
Scavenger
Timberman
Tumble-bug
Whirligig
Woodborer

10 letters:
Bean weevil
Boll weevil
Bombardier
Churchyard
Cockchafer
Deathwatch
Dumbledore
Long-horned
Rhinoceros
Rose chafer
Spanish fly
Turnip-flea

11 letters:
Bloody-nosed
Typographer

12 letters:
Buzzard-clock
Sledge-hammer

16 letters:
Devil's coach-horse

Bible

BOOKS OF THE BIBLE: OLD TESTAMENT

3 letters:
Job

4 letters:
Amos
Ezra
Joel
Ruth

5 letters:
Hosea
Jonah
Kings
Micah
Nahum

6 letters:
Daniel
Esther

Exodus
Haggai
Isaiah
Joshua
Judges
Psalms
Samuel

7 letters:
Ezekiel

BOOKS OF THE BIBLE: OLD TESTAMENT (CONTINUED)

Genesis
Malachi
Numbers
Obadiah

8 letters:
Habakkuk
Jeremiah
Nehemiah

Proverbs

9 letters:
Leviticus
Zechariah
Zephaniah

10 letters:
Chronicles

11 letters:
Deuteronomy

12 letters:
Ecclesiastes
Lamentations

13 letters:
Song of Solomon

BOOKS OF THE BIBLE: NEW TESTAMENT

4 letters:
Acts
John
Jude
Luke
Mark

5 letters:
James
Peter
Titus

6 letters:
Romans

7 letters:
Hebrews
Matthew
Timothy

8 letters:
Philemon

9 letters:
Ephesians

Galatians

10 letters:
Colossians
Revelation

11 letters:
Corinthians
Philippians

13 letters:
Thessalonians

BOOKS OF THE BIBLE: APOCRYPHA

5 letters:
Tobit

6 letters:
Baruch
Esdras
Judith
Wisdom

8 letters:
Manasseh

9 letters:
Maccabees

14 letters:
Ecclesiasticus

Song of the Three

16 letters:
Daniel and Susanna

20 letters:
Daniel, Bel and the
   Snake

CHARACTERS IN THE BIBLE

3 letters:
Dan
Eve
Gad
Ham
Job
Lot

4 letters:
Abel
Adam
Ahab
Amos
Boaz
Cain
Cush
Enos

Esau
Ezra
Jael
Jehu
Joab
Joel
John
Jude
Kush

CHARACTERS IN THE BIBLE (CONTINUED)

Leah
Levi
Luke
Mark
Mary
Noah
Paul
Ruth
Saul
Seth
Shem

5 letters:
Aaron
Ammon
Asher
David
Dinah
Dives
Elias
Enoch
Hagar
Herod
Hiram
Hosea
Isaac
Jacob
James
Jesse
Jonah
Jonas
Jubal
Judah
Laban
Magus
Micah
Moses
Nahum
Naomi
Peter
Sarah
Simon
Tobit
Uriah

6 letters:
Andrew
Balaam

Baruch
Belial
Caspar
Daniel
Dorcas
Elijah
Elisha
Esther
Gideon
Gilead
Haggai
Hannah
Isaiah
Jephte
Jethro
Joseph
Joshua
Josiah
Judith
Martha
Midian
Miriam
Naboth
Nathan
Nimrod
Philip
Rachel
Reuben
Salome
Samson
Samuel
Simeon
Thomas
Zilpah

7 letters:
Abigail
Abraham
Absalom
Ananias
Deborah
Delilah
Ephraim
Ezekiel
Gabriel
Goliath
Ishmael
Japheth

Jezebel
Lazarus
Malachi
Matthew
Meshach
Obadiah
Rebecca
Solomon
Susanna
Thadeus
Zachary
Zebedee
Zebulun

8 letters:
Abednego
Barabbas
Benjamin
Caiaphas
Habakkuk
Hezekiah
Issachar
Jephthah
Jeremiah
Jeroboam
Jonathan
Lot's wife
Manasseh
Matthias
Melchior
Mordecai
Naphtali
Nehemiah
Potiphar
Shadrach
Thaddeus
Zedekiah

9 letters:
Ahasuerus
Balthazar
Bathsheba
Beelzebub
Boanerges
Nabonidus
Nathanael
Nicodemus
Tubal-cain

CHARACTERS IN THE BIBLE (CONTINUED)

Zachariah
Zacharias
Zechariah
Zephaniah

10 letters:
Achitophel
Ahithophel
Belshazzar
Holofernes
Methuselah
Virgin Mary

11 letters:
Bartholomew
Gog and Magog
Jehoshaphat
Jesus Christ
Melchizedek
Prodigal Son

12 letters:
Melchisedech
Queen of Sheba

13 letters:
Good Samaritan
Judas Iscariot
Mary Magdalene

14 letters:
John the Baptist
Nebuchadnezzar
Nebuchadrezzar
Tetragrammaton
Whore of Babylon

PLACE NAMES IN THE BIBLE

2 letters:
On

4 letters:
Aram
Cana
Eden
Gath
Gaza
Moab

5 letters:
Babel
Horeb
Judah
Judea
Ophir
Sodom

6 letters:
Ararat
Bashan
Canaan

Goshen
Judaea
Shiloh
Shinar
Tadmor
Tophet

7 letters:
Antioch
Calvary
Galilee
Gehenna
Jericho
Samaria
Shittim
Topheth

8 letters:
Aceldama
Bethesda
Golgotha
Gomorrah

Gomorrha
Nazareth

9 letters:
Arimathea
Bethlehem
Capernaum
Jerusalem
Land of Nod

10 letters:
Arimathaea
Gethsemane
Wilderness

12 letters:
Garden of Eden
Rabbath Ammon

18 letters:
Land of milk and honey

TYPES OF BIBLE

2 letters:
AV
NT
OT
RV

3 letters:
RSV

4 letters:
Whig

5 letters:
Douai

Douay
Itala

6 letters:
Cramer
Family
Geneva

TYPES OF BIBLE (CONTINUED)

Gideon
Gospel
Italic
Missal
Tanach
Targum
Wyclif
Zurich

7 letters:
Bamberg
Hexapla
Mazarin
Midrash
Peshito

Psalter
Tyndale
Vulgate

8 letters:
Cromwell
Mazarine
Peshitta
Peshitto
Polyglot
Wycliffe

9 letters:
Apocrypha
Coverdale
King James

Taverners

10 letters:
Pentateuch
Septuagint

12 letters:
Antilegomena

14 letters:
Revised Version

16 letters:
King James version

Bicycles

BICYCLE PARTS

4 letters:
Bell

5 letters:
Pedal
Wheel

6 letters:
Saddle

7 letters:
Pannier
Rat-trap

8 letters:
Crossbar
Mudguard

9 letters:
Kickstand
Saddlebag

10 letters:
Handlebars
Mileometer
Stabilizer

11 letters:
Bicycle pump

12 letters:
Bicycle chain

TYPES OF BICYCLE

3 letters:
BMX

6 letters:
Tandem

7 letters:
Bicycle
Chopper

8 letters:
Roadster

9 letters:
Autocycle

10 letters:
Boneshaker
Fairy cycle
Velocipede

12 letters:
Exercise bike
Mountain bike

13 letters:
Penny-farthing

Biochemists

3 letters:
Dam, *Henrik Carl Peter*

4 letters:
Cori, *Carl Ferdinand*
Cori, *Gerti*
Funk, *Casimir*
Funk, *Kazimierz*
Katz, *Bernard*

5 letters:
Bloch, *Konrad Emil*
Boyer, *Herbert*
Cohen, *Stanley*
Doisy, *Edward Adelbert*
Krebs, *Sir Hans Adolf*
Monod, *Jaques Lucien*
Moore, *Stanford*
Ochoa, *Severo*
Stein, *William H(oward)*
Synge, *Richard*

6 letters:
Beadle, *George Wells*
De Duve, *Christian*

Domagk, *Gerhard*
Florey, *Sir Howard Walter*
Holley, *Robert W(illiam)*
Martin, *Archer*
Mullis, *Kary Banks*
Oparin, *Alexandr*
Porter, *Rodney Robert*
Sanger, *Frederick*
Sumner, *James B(atcheller)*

7 letters:
Buchner, *Eduard*
Edelman, *Gerald M(aurice)*
Fleming, *Sir Alexander*
Gilbert, *Walter*
Hopkins, *Sir Frederick Gowland*
Kendrew, *John C(owdery)*
Khorana, *Har Gobind*
Macleod, *John James Richard*

Rodbell, *Martin*
Stanley, *Wendell Meredith*
Waksman, *Selman Abraham*
Warburg, *Otto Heinrich*

8 letters:
Anfinsen, *Christian Boehmer*
Chargaff, *Erwin*
Kornberg, *Arthur*
Meyerhof, *Otto Fritz*
Northrop, *John H(oward)*

9 letters:
Bergstrom, *Sune K(arl)*
Butenandt, *Adolf Friedrich Johann*
Ferdinand, *Max Perutz*
Nirenberg, *Marshall W(arren)*

10 letters:
Samuelsson, *Bengt*

Biology

BRANCHES OF BIOLOGY

6 letters:
Botany

7 letters:
Ecology
Zoology

8 letters:
Biometry
Cytology
Genetics
Taxonomy

9 letters:
Histology

10 letters:
Biophysics
Biostatics
Morphology
Organology
Somatology
Teratology

11 letters:
Aerobiology
Agrobiology
Biodynamics
Cryobiology

12 letters:
Astrobiology
Bacteriology

Biochemistry
Biogeography
Cytogenetics
Microbiology
Oceanography
Organography
Parasitology
Photobiology
Radiobiology
Sociobiology
Stoichiology

13 letters:
Actinobiology
Chronobiology
Palaeontology
Photodynamics

BIOLOGY TERMS

3 letters:
DNA
Egg
RNA

4 letters:
Bone
Cell
Gene
Ovum
Root
Seed
Skin
Soil

5 letters:
Blood
Class
Clone
Fruit
Genus
Gland
Gonad
Order
Organ
Sperm
Spore
Virus

6 letters:
Albino
Allele
Dorsal
Embryo
Enzyme
Family
Flower
Foetus
Fossil
Fungus
Gamete
Growth
Hybrid
Muscle
Phylum
Pollen
Zygote

7 letters:
Aerobic
Biomass
Diploid
Haploid
Hormone
Kingdom
Meiosis
Mitosis
Nucleus
Osmosis
Progeny
Protein
Puberty
Species
Ventral
Vitamin

8 letters:
Anterior
Bacteria
Division
Dominant
Heredity
Mutation
Parasite
Pathogen
Pectoral
Predator
Ribosome
Skeleton

9 letters:
Anaerobic
Cytoplasm
Diffusion
Digestion
Ecosystem
Epidermis
Evolution
Excretion
Food chain
Gestation
Life cycle
Ovulation
Pollution
Posterior
Pregnancy

Recessive
Symbiosis

10 letters:
Chromosome
Conception
Copulation
Krebs cycle
Metabolism
Protoplasm
Vertebrate
Viviparous

11 letters:
Allelomorph
Blood vessel
Circulation
Codominance
Cold-blooded
Environment
Germination
Inheritance
Pollination
Propagation
Respiration
Warm-blooded
X-chromosome
Y-chromosome

12 letters:
Assimilation
Fermentation
Invertebrate
Menstruation
Reproduction
Spermatozoon

13 letters:
Agglutination
Binary fission
Fertilization
Hermaphrodite
Metamorphosis
Nitrogen cycle
Translocation
Transpiration

14 letters:
Photosynthesis

BIOLOGY TERMS (CONTINUED)

Poikilothermic

16 letters:
Natural selection

17 letters:
Circulatory system
Ribose nucleic acid

18 letters:
Sexual reproduction

19 letters:
Asexual reproduction

20 letters:
Deoxyribonucleic acid

BIOLOGISTS

3 letters:
May, *Robert McCredie*
Orr, *John Boyd*

4 letters:
Berg, *Paul*
Koch, *Robert*

5 letters:
Crick, *Francis Harry
   Compton*
Krebs, *Hans Adolf*

6 letters:
Beadle, *George Well*
Carrel, *Alexis*
Carson, *Rachel*
Claude, *Albert*

Darwin, *Charles (Robert)*
Harvey, *William*
Huxley, *Andrew Fielding*
Huxley, *Julian*
Huxley, *Thomas Henry*
Mendel, *Gregor*
Morgan, *Thomas Hunt*
Watson, *James Dewey*

7 letters:
Fleming, *Alexander*
Haeckel, *Ernst Heinrich*
Pasteur, *Louis*

8 letters:
Delbrück, *Max*
Dulbecco, *Renato*

Franklin, *Rosalind*
Linnaeus
Von Linné, *Carl*

9 letters:
Baltimore, *David*
Von Haller, *Albrecht*

10 letters:
Denisovich, *Trofim*
Dobzhansky, *Theodosius*

14 letters:
Van Leeuwenhoek,
   Anton

See also:
➤ **Bacteria** ➤ **Enzymes** ➤ **Hormones** ➤ **Membranes** ➤ **Proteins** ➤ **Sugars**

Birds

2 letters:
Ka

3 letters:
Ani
Auk
Boo
Cob
Emu
Fum
Jay
Kae
Kea
Maw

Mew
Nun
Oil
Owl
Pea
Pie
Ree
Roc
Ruc
Tit
Tui

4 letters:
Barb

Chat
Cirl
Cobb
Coly
Coot
Crax
Crow
Dove
Emeu
Erne
Eyas
Fung
Gled
Guan

Guga
Gull
Hawk
Hern
Huma
Ibis
Iynx
Jynx
Kagu
Kaka
Kite
Kiwi
Knot
Koel
Kora
Lark
Loon
Lory
Lyre
Mina
Monk
Myna
Otis
Pavo
Pawn
Pern
Piet
Pink
Pown
Pyot
Rail
Rhea
Roch
Rook
Ruff
Runt
Ruru
Rype
Shag
Smee
Sora
Swan
Taha
Tara
Teal
Tern
Tody
Tuli
Weka
Whio

Whip
Wren
Xema
Yale
Yite

5 letters:
Agami
Ardea
Ariel
Bennu
Booby
Bosun
Capon
Chook
Colin
Colly
Cooee
Crake
Crane
Diver
Egret
Finch
Fleet
Galah
Galar
Glede
Goose
Goura
Grebe
Heron
Hobby
Homer
Isaac
Junco
Kight
Liver
Lowan
Macaw
Madge
Manch
Mavis
Merle
Micky
Mimus
Mohua
Monal
Mulga
Murre
Mynah

Nandu
Nelly
Noddy
Ousel
Ouzel
Ox-eye
Peggy
Pekan
Pewit
Picus
Piper
Pipit
Pitta
Poaka
Poker
Potoo
Prion
Quail
Quest
Quist
Raven
Reeve
Rifle
Robin
Rotch
Ryper
Saker
Scape
Scart
Scaup
Scops
Scray
Scrub
Serin
Shama
Sitta
Skart
Snipe
Solan
Soree
Spink
Sprug
Squab
Stare
Stilt
Stint
Stork
Sugar
Swift
Sylph

Terek
Tewit
Topaz
Twite
Umber
Umbre
Urubu
Veery
Vireo
Wader
Whaup
Widow
Wonga
Yaffa

6 letters:
Amazon
Aquila
Avocet
Avoset
Bantam
Barbet
Bishop
Bittor
Bittur
Bonxie
Boubou
Brolga
Bulbul
Canary
Chough
Chukar
Condor
Conure
Corbie
Coucal
Cuckoo
Culver
Curlew
Cushat
Darter
Dikkop
Dipper
Drongo
Duiker
Dunlin
Duyker
Elanet
Evejar
Falcon

Fulmar
Gambet
Gander
Gannet
Garuda
Gentle
Gentoo
Gillar
Go-away
Godwit
Gooney
Goslet
Grakle
Grouse
Hagden
Hagdon
Haglet
Hermit
Hoopoe
Houdan
Jabiru
Jaçana
Jaegar
Jaeger
Kakapo
Karoro
Kereru
Kokako
Kotare
Kotuku
Lahore
Lanner
Leipoa
Linnet
Lintie
Locust
Loriot
Lourie
Lungie
Magpie
Martin
Menura
Merlin
Merops
Missel
Mistle
Monaul
Mopoke
Mossie
Motmot

Musket
Nandoo
Oriole
Osprey
Parrot
Parson
Pavone
Peahen
Peewee
Peewit
Pernis
Petrel
Phoebe
Pigeon
Pipipi
Plover
Pouter
Progne
Puffin
Pukeko
Pullet
Queest
Quelea
Quoist
Redcap
Reeler
Roller
Scamel
Scarth
Scaury
Scraye
Sea-cob
Sea-mew
Seapie
Shrike
Simara
Simorg
Simurg
Siskin
Skarth
Smeath
Soland
Sorage
Strich
Sultan
Sylvia
Tailor
Takahe
Tarcel
Tassel

Tauhou
Tewhit
Thrush
Tom-tit
Toucan
Towhee
Trogon
Turaco
Turbit
Tyrant
Tystie
Verdin
Wading
Walker
Waxeye
Weaver
Whidah
Whydah
Willet
Woosel
Yaffle
Ynambu
Yucker
Zoozoo

7 letters:
Amokura
Anhinga
Antbird
Apostle
Apteryx
Axebird
Babbler
Bécasse
Bittern
Bittour
Blighty
Bluecap
Blue-eye
Blue jay
Bluetit
Boobook
Bullbat
Bunting
Buphaga
Bushtit
Bustard
Buzzard
Cacique
Cariama

Catbird
Chewink
Chicken
Coal tit
Coletit
Colibri
Corella
Cotinga
Courlan
Courser
Cowbird
Creeper
Crombec
Cropper
Cumulet
Diamond
Dinorus
Dottrel
Dovekie
Dunnock
Emu-wren
Fantail
Fern-owl
Fig-bird
Finfoot
Flicker
Frigate
Gobbler
Goburra
Gorcrow
Goshawk
Grackle
Grallae
Hacklet
Hadedah
Hagbolt
Hagdown
Halcyon
Hemipod
Hoatzin
Humming
Ice-bird
Jacamar
Jackdaw
Jacobin
Kahawai
Kamichi
Kestrel
Killdee
Kinglet

Lapwing
Leghorn
Limpkin
Manakin
Marabou
Maribou
Martlet
Mesites
Minivet
Mudlark
Ortolan
Oscires
Ostrich
Pandion
Peacock
Peafowl
Pelican
Penguin
Phoenix
Pickmaw
Piculet
Pinnock
Pintado
Pintail
Pochard
Pockard
Poe-bird
Poy-bird
Quetzal
Rainbow
Rasores
Redpoll
Redwing
Regulus
Rooster
Rosella
Rotchie
Ruddock
Sakeret
Sawbill
Scooper
Scourie
Sea-mell
Seriema
Simurgh
Sirgang
Sitella
Skimmer
Skylark
Snow-cap

Birds

Soldier
Spadger
Sparrow
Squacco
Staniel
Stinker
Sturnus
Sunbird
Swallow
Tanager
Tarrock
Tattler
Teacher
Teuchat
Tiercel
Tinamou
Titanis
Titlark
Titling
Tokahea
Totanus
Touraco
Tumbler
Tweeter
Vulture
Vulturn
Wagtail
Warbler
Waxbill
Waxwing
Whooper
Widgeon
Wimbrel
Witwall
Wood hen
Woosell
Wren-tit
Wrybill
Wryneck
Yang-win

8 letters:
Aasvogel
Accentor
Adjutant
Aigrette
Alcatras
Altrices
Amadavat
Aquiline

Arapunga
Avadavat
Barnacle
Bee-eater
Bellbird
Blackcap
Bluebird
Blue duck
Blue-wing
Boatbill
Boattail
Bobolink
Bobwhite
Buln-buln
Bush wren
Capuchin
Caracara
Cardinal
Cargoose
Cheewink
Chirn-owl
Cockatoo
Coquette
Curassow
Dabchick
Didapper
Dip-chick
Dobchick
Dotterel
Estridge
Fauvette
Fernbird
Firebird
Fish-hawk
Flamingo
Gambetta
Gang-gang
Garefowl
Garganey
Great tit
Greenlet
Grosbeak
Guacharo
Hackbolt
Hangbird
Hangnest
Hawfinch
Hazelhen
Hemipode
Hernshaw

Hill myna
Hoactzin
Hornbill
Kakariki
Killdeer
Kingbird
Kiskadee
Koromako
Landrail
Lanneret
Laverock
Longspur
Lorikeet
Lovebird
Lyrebird
Magotpie
Makomako
Māori hen
Marsh tit
Megapode
Mire-drum
Miromiro
Morepork
Murrelet
Nightjar
Nuthatch
Ovenbird
Oxpecker
Paradise
Parakeet
Peetweet
Percolin
Petchary
Pheasant
Philomel
Pihoihoi
Podargus
Poorwill
Puffbird
Quarrian
Quarrion
Rainbird
Rallidae
Redshank
Redstart
Reedbird
Reedling
Reed-wren
Ricebird
Rifleman

Birds

Ringdove
Ringtail
Riroriro
Rock dove
Sandpeep
Scolopar
Screamer
Shake-bag
Shoebill
Silktail
Skua-gull
Snowbird
Stanniel
Starling
Struthio
Surfbird
Swiftlet
Tantalus
Tapacolo
Tapaculo
Teru-tero
Thrasher
Thresher
Throstle
Tick-bird
Titmouse
Tom-noddy
Toucanet
Tragopan
Trembler
Troopial
Troupial
Umbrella
Umbrette
Water-hen
Weka rail
Wheatear
Whimbrel
Whinchat
Whitecap
White-eye
Woodchat
Woodcock
Wood ibis
Woodlark
Woodwale
Yoldring

9 letters:
Accipiter

Aepyornis
Albatross
Aylesbury
Baldicoot
Baltimore
Beccaccia
Beccafico
Bergander
Blackbird
Blackcock
Blackhead
Blackpoll
Bowerbird
Brambling
Broadbill
Brown duck
Brown kiwi
Bullfinch
Campanero
Cassowary
Chaffinch
Chatterer
Chickadee
Coachwhip
Cockateel
Cockatiel
Cormorant
Corncrake
Crocodile
Crossbill
Currawong
Cushie-doo
Dowitcher
Estreldid
Fieldfare
Fig-pecker
Firecrest
Fledgling
Francolin
Friarbird
Frogmouth
Gallinule
Gerfalcon
Gier-eagle
Goldcrest
Goldfinch
Goosander
Grassquit
Green leek
Grenadier

Guillemot
Happy Jack
Helldiver
Heronshaw
Icteridae
Impundulu
Jacksnipe
Kittiwake
Lintwhite
Mallemuck
Merganser
Mistletoe
Mollymawk
Mousebird
Nighthawk
Nutjobber
Olive-back
Ossifraga
Ossifrage
Pardalote
Parrakeet
Partridge
Peaseweep
Peregrine
Phalarope
Pictarnie
Pied goose
Policeman
Porphyrio
Ptarmigan
Razorbill
Redbreast
Red grouse
Riflebird
Ring ouzel
Rosy finch
Salangane
Sandpiper
Sapsucker
Scansores
Sea-turtle
Secretary
Seedeater
Sheldrake
Shoveller
Silvereye
Skunk-bird
Snakebird
Solitaire
Spoonbill

Standgale
Stock dove
Stonechat
Storm-cock
Swart-back
Swordbill
Talegalla
Thickhead
Thick-knee
Thornbill
Trochilus
Trumpeter
Turnstone
Volucrine
Water rail
Willow tit
Wind-hover
Xanthoura

10 letters:
Aberdevine
Banded rail
Bearded tit
Bell magpie
Bishopbird
Black robin
Bluebreast
Blue grouse
Bluethroat
Brain-fever
Bubbly-jock
Budgerigar
Bush canary
Bush shrike
Butter-bump
Cape pigeon
Chiffchaff
Crested tit
Demoiselle
Dickcissel
Didunculus
Dollarbird
Ember-goose
Eyas-musket
Flycatcher
Fringillid
Goatsucker
Gobemouche
Grassfinch
Greenfinch

Greenshank
Guinea fowl
Hen harrier
Honeyeater
Honey guide
Hooded crow
Jungle fowl
Kingfisher
Kookaburra
Magpie lark
Marsh-robin
Meadowlark
Night heron
Noisy miner
Nutcracker
Pettichaps
Pettychaps
Piwakawaka
Pratincole
Quaker-bird
Racket-tail
Rafter-bird
Regent-bird
Rhampastos
Rhinoceros
Roadrunner
Rockhopper
Rock pigeon
Saddleback
Saddlebill
Sage grouse
Sanderling
Sandgrouse
Sand martin
Scandaroon
Shearwater
Sheathbill
Sicklebill
Silverbill
Snowy egret
Song thrush
Spatchcock
Stone-snipe
Sun bittern
Tailorbird
Tanagridae
Tree-runner
Tropicbird
Turtledove
Water crake

Water ouzel
Wattlebird
Weaverbird
Whisky-jack
Whisky-john
White heron
Wild turkey
Wonga-wonga
Woodpecker
Wood pigeon
Yaffingale
Yellowlegs
Yellowtail
Yellowyite
Zebra finch

11 letters:
Black cuckoo
Black grouse
Bokmakierie
Bristlebird
Butcherbird
Button quail
Cape sparrow
Carrion crow
Coppersmith
Corn bunting
Gnatcatcher
Grallatores
Green plover
Grey warbler
Happy family
Honeysucker
House martin
Hummingbird
Java sparrow
King penguin
Leatherhead
Lily-trotter
Magpie goose
Meadow pipit
Mockingbird
Moss-bluiter
Moss-cheeper
Nightingale
Pied wagtail
Plain turkey
Plantcutter
Pyrrhuloxia
Reed bunting

Reed warbler
Scissortail
Snow bunting
Song sparrow
Stone curlew
Storm petrel
Stymphalian
Tawny pippit
Thunderbird
Titipounamu
Tree creeper
Tree sparrow
Wall creeper
Water thrush
Whitethroat
Wonga pigeon
Woodcreeper
Woodswallow
Wood warbler
Yellow-ammer
Zebra parrot

12 letters:
Bronze-pigeon
Brown creeper
Bustard quail
Capercaillie
Capercailzie
Chimney swift
Cliff swallow
Collared dove
Cuckoo-shrike
Drongo-cuckoo
Drongo-shrike
Flower-pecker
Golden oriole
Hedge sparrow
Homing pigeon
Honey creeper
House sparrow
Marsh harrier
Missel thrush
Mistle thrush
Mosquito hawk
Mountain duck
Mourning dove
Murray magpie
Painted finch
Pallid cuckoo
Paradise duck

Peppershrike
Piping shrike
Plains turkey
Putangitangi
Ring-dotterel
Ringed plover
Ruffed grouse
Sage-thrasher
Sedge warbler
Serpent-eater
Spotted crake
Standard-wing
Stonechatter
Stormy petrel
Throstle-cock
Whippoorwill
Willow grouse
Willy wagtail
Yellowhammer
Yellow-yowley

13 letters:
Bushman's clock
Chaparral cock
Cock-of-the-rock
Crow blackbird
Gouldian finch
Long-tailed tit
Major Mitchell
Numidian crane
Oyster-catcher
Pipiwharauroa
Plantain-eater
Settler's clock
Swamp pheasant
Topknot pigeon
Whistling duck
White cockatoo
Whooping crane
Willow warbler

14 letters:
Banded dotterel
Bird of paradise
Chimney swallow
Cockatoo-parrot
Emperor penguin
Manx shearwater
Noisy friarbird
Ortolan bunting

Pheasant coucal
Pie-billed grebe
Ringneck parrot
Robin redbreast
Satin bowerbird
Scarlet tanager
Superb blue wren
Superb lyrebird
Tawny frogmouth
Woodchat shrike

15 letters:
American ostrich
Australian crane
Baltimore oriole
Blackbacked gull
Blue-wattled crow
Boat-billed heron
Cape Barren goose
Chipping sparrow
Chuck-will's-widow
Demoiselle crane
Green woodpecker
Laughing jackass
Native companion
Purple gallinule
Rainbow lorikeet
Red-backed shrike
Regent bowerbird
Shining starling

16 letters:
Black-fronted tern
Californian quail
Cardinal grosbeak
Loggerhead shrike
Metallic starling
New Zealand pigeon
Piping crow-shrike
Regent honeyeater
Spotted sandpiper
White-fronted tern

17 letters:
Great crested grebe
Pectoral sandpiper
Port Lincoln parrot
Spotted flycatcher

18 letters:
Bronze-winged cuckoo
Great northern diver
Grey-crowned babbler
Red-backed sandpiper
Red-legged partridge
Ring-necked pheasant

19 letters:
Leadbeater's cockatoo
Purple-breasted finch

20 letters:
Great brown kingfisher
Yellowtail kingfisher

22 letters:
Sulphur-crested
  cockatoo

EXTINCT BIRDS

3 letters:
Moa

4 letters:
Dodo
Huia

5 letters:
Piopio

8 letters:
Great auk
Notornis

9 letters:
Solitaire

11 letters:
Archaeornis

Ichthyornis

13 letters:
Archaeopteryx

15 letters:
Passenger pigeon

See also:
➤ **Ducks** ➤ **Types of fowl** ➤ **Hawks** ➤ **Birds of prey** ➤ **Sea birds**

Birthstones

Month	Stone
January	Garnet
February	Amethyst
March	Aquamarine, Bloodstone
April	Diamond
May	Emerald
June	Pearl, Alexandrite, Moonstone
July	Ruby
August	Peridot, Sardonyx
September	Sapphire
October	Opal, Tourmaline
November	Topaz
December	Turquoise, Zircon

Biscuits

3 letters:
Nut
Sea
Tea

4 letters:
Farl
Kiss
Rusk

Soda
Tack

5 letters:
Marie
Matzo
Pilot
Ship's
Wafer
Water

6 letters:
Cookie
Empire
Oliver
Parkin
Perkin

7 letters:
Bannock
Bourbon
Cracker
Fairing
Oatcake
Osborne
Pig's ear
Pretzel
Ratafia
Rich tea

Tararua

8 letters:
Captain's
Charcoal
Cracknel
Flapjack
Hardtack
Macaroon
Mattress
Poppadom
Poppadum
Zwieback

9 letters:
Abernethy
Dandyfunk
Digestive
Garibaldi
Ginger nut
Jaffa cake®
Lebkuchen
Petit four
Shortcake
Sweetmeal

10 letters:
Bath Oliver
Brandy snap
Butterbake
Crispbread
Dunderfunk
Florentine
Ginger snap
Love letter
Shortbread

12 letters:
Caramel wafer
Cream cracker
Langue de chat

13 letters:
Graham cracker

14 letters:
Gingerbread man

18 letters:
Chocolate digestive

Shades from black to white

3 letters:
Ash
Jet

4 letters:
Grey
Iron

5 letters:
Black
Cream
Ebony
Ivory
Pearl

Putty
Raven
Sable
Slate
Stone
White

6 letters:
Pewter
Silver

8 letters:
Charcoal
Eggshell

Gunmetal
Off-white
Platinum

9 letters:
Steel grey

10 letters:
Pitch-black

11 letters:
Oyster white

Blemishes

3 letters:
Zit

4 letters:
Boil
Mole
Scab
Scar
Spot
Wart

5 letters:
Stain

6 letters:
Callus
Naevus
Pimple

7 letters:
Freckle
Pustule
Verruca

8 letters:
Pockmark

9 letters:
Birthmark
Blackhead
Carbuncle
Whitehead

12 letters:
Dicoloration

14 letters:
Strawberry mark

Blood cells

9 letters:
Haemocyte
Leucocyte
Macrocyte
Microcyte
Polymorph

10 letters:
Lymphocyte

11 letters:
Erythrocyte
Poikilocyte

12 letters:
Reticulocyte

24 letters:
Phagocytic white blood
  cell

Shades of blue

3 letters:
Sky

4 letters:
Aqua
Bice
Cyan
Navy
Nile
Saxe
Teal

5 letters:
Azure
Clear
Perse
Royal
Saxon
Slate
Steel

6 letters:
Berlin
Cantab
Cobalt
Indigo
Oxford
Petrol
Pewter
Powder
Saxony
Welkin

7 letters:
Celeste
Duck-egg
Gentian
Nattier
Peacock
Watchet

8 letters:
Bleuâtre
Caesious
Cerulean
Eggshell
Electric
Lavender
Mazarine
Midnight
Prussian
Sapphire
Stafford
Wedgwood®

9 letters:
Cambridge
Germander
Robin's egg
Turquoise

10 letters:
Aquamarine
Copenhagen
Cornflower

Heliotrope
Periwinkle

11 letters:
Clair de lune
Lapis lazuli
Ultramarine

Board games

2 letters:
Go

3 letters:
I-go

4 letters:
Ludo

5 letters:
Chess
Halma

6 letters:
Cluedo®

7 letters:
Reversi

8 letters:
Chequers
Draughts
Monopoly®
Scrabble®

9 letters:
Acey-deucy
Bagatelle
Parcheesi®
Solitaire

10 letters:
Backgammon

Kriegspiel
Speed chess

11 letters:
Fox and geese

14 letters:
Lightning chess
Nine men's morris
Shove-halfpenny

15 letters:
Chinese chequers

16 letters:
Snakes and ladders

Boats and ships

1 letter:
Q

2 letters:
MY
PT
VJ

3 letters:
Ark
Cat
Cog
Cot
Dow
Gig
Hoy
MTB
Red
Tub
Tug

4 letters:
Argo
Bark
Brig
Buss
Cock
Dhow
Dory
Duck
Grab
Junk
Koff
Maxi
Nina
Pink
Pont
Pram
Prau
Proa
Punt

Raft
Ro-ro
Saic
Scow
Snow
Tall
Tern
Trow
Yawl
Zulu

5 letters:
Aviso
Barge
Broke
Camel
Canal
Canoe
Coble
Coper

113

Crare
Dandy
Dingy
Drake
E-boat
Ferry
Funny
Jolly
Kayak
Ketch
Keteh
Laker
Liner
Moses
Oiler
Pinky
Pinto
Prore
Púcán
Razee
Sabot
Scoot
Screw
Scull
Shell
Skiff
Sloop
Swamp
Tramp
U-boat
Umiak
Whiff
Xebec
Yacht
Zabra
Zebec

6 letters:
Argosy
Banker
Barque
Bateau
Bawley
Beagle
Bethel
Bireme
Boatel
Borley
Bounty
Caïque

Carack
Carvel
Castle
Coaler
Cobble
Cooper
Crayer
Cutter
Decker
Dingey
Dinghy
Dogger
Droger
Dromon
Drover
Dugout
Flotel
Frigot
Galiot
Galley
Gay-you
Hooker
Jigger
Launch
Lorcha
Lugger
Masula
Narrow
Nuggar
Oomiak
Packet
Pedalo
Pequod
Pinkie
Pirate
Pitpan
Pulwar
Puteli
Randan
Rowing
Sampan
Sandal
Schuit
Schuyt
Sealer
Settee
Slaver
Tanker
Tartan
Tender

Tonner
Torpid
Trader
Whaler
Wherry
Zebeck

7 letters:
Airboat
Belfast
Bidarka
Bumboat
Capital
Caravel
Carrack
Carract
Carrect
Catboat
Clipper
Coaster
Collier
Coracle
Counter
Crabber
Cruiser
Currach
Curragh
Dredger
Drifter
Drogher
Dromond
Factory
Felucca
Fishing
Floatel
Flyboat
Foyboat
Frigate
Gabbard
Gabbart
Galleas
Galleon
Galliot
Galloon
Geordie
Gondola
Gunboat
Jet-boat
Jetfoil
Liberty

Lymphad
Man o' war
Masoola
Mistico
Monitor
Mudscow
Oomiack
Patamar
Pelican
Pinnace
Piragua
Pirogue
Polacca
Polacre
Pontoon
Revenge
Rowboat
Sailing
Scooter
Shallop
Sharpie
Steamer
Stew-can
Tartane
Titanic
Torpedo
Towboat
Trawler
Trireme
Tugboat
Vedette
Victory
Vidette
Warship

8 letters:
Acapulco
Bilander
Billyboy
Cabotage
Cockboat
Corocore
Corocoro
Corvette
Dahabieh
Faldboat
Faltboat
Fireboat
Flatboat
Foldboat

Galleass
Galliass
Gallivat
Hoveller
Ice yacht
Indiaman
Ironclad
Keelboat
Lifeboat
Longboat
Longship
Mackinaw
Man-of-war
Mary Rose
Masoolah
Merchant
Monohull
Outboard
Pinafore
Sailboat
Savannah
Schooner
Shanghai
Showboat
Skipjack
Surfboat
Trimaran

9 letters:
Auxiliary
Bucentaur
Catamaran
Cutty Sark
Dahabeeah
Dahabiyah
Dahabiyeh
Destroyer
Dromedary
First-rate
Freighter
Frigatoon
Houseboat
Hydrofoil
Klondiker
Klondyker
Lapstrake
Lapstreak
Leviathan
Lightship
Mayflower

Minelayer
Monoxylon
Motorboat
Multihull
Outrigger
Oysterman
Peter-boat
Powerboat
Shear-hulk
Sheer-hulk
Speedboat
Steamboat
Steamship
Submarine
Troopship
Vaporetto
Whale-back
Whaleboat

10 letters:
Bathyscape
Bathyscaph
Battleship
Bermuda rig
Brigantine
Cockleboat
Golden Hind
Hydroplane
Icebreaker
Knockabout
Minehunter
Motor yacht
Paddleboat
Quadrireme
Santa Maria
Trekschuit
Triaconter
Windjammer

11 letters:
Barquantine
Barquentine
Bathyscaphe
Bellerophon
Berthon-boat
Bulk carrier
Cockleshell
Dreadnaught
Dreadnought
Merchantman

Minesweeper
Penteconter
Quinquereme
Sidewheeler
Skidbladnir
Submersible
Supertanker
Threedecker
Three-master
Weathership

12 letters:
Cabin cruiser

See also:
➤ **Parts of ships**

Fore-and-after
Great Eastern
Landing craft
Marie Celeste
Motor torpedo
Square-rigger
Stern-wheeler

13 letters:
Battlecruiser
Paddle steamer
Revenue cutter
Ship of the line

14 letters:
Ocean greyhound
Vaucluse junior

15 letters:
Aircraft carrier
Destroyer escort

16 letters:
Pocket battleship

20 letters:
Torpedo-boat destroyer

Parts of the body

Part of the body	Technical name	Related adjective
Abdomen	-	Abdominal
Adenoids	Pharyngeal tonsil	Adenoid *or* adenoidal
Alimentary canal	-	-
Ankle	Talus	-
Anus	-	Anal
Appendix	Vermiform appendix	Appendicular
Arm	Brachium	Brachial
Armpit	Axilla	Axillary
Artery	-	Arterial
Back	-	Dorsal
Belly	Venter	Ventral
Bladder	Urinary bladder	Vesical
Blood	-	Haemal, haemic, *or* haematic
Bone	Os	Osseous, osteal, *or* osteoid
Brain	Encephalon	Cerebral
Breast	-	-
Buttocks	Nates	Natal *or* gluteal
Caecum	-	Caecal
Calf	-	-
Capillary	-	Capillary
Cervix	-	Cervical
Cheek	Gena	Genal
Chest	-	Pectoral

Part of the body	Technical name	Related adjective
Chin	-	Genial *or* mental
Clitoris	-	Clitoral
Colon	-	Colonic
Duodenum	-	Duodenal
Ear	-	Aural
Elbow	-	-
Epiglottis	-	Epiglottal
External ear	Auricle *or* pinna	-
Eye	-	Ocular *or* ophthalmic
Eyebrow	-	Superciliary
Eyelash	Cilium	Ciliary
Eyelid	-	Palpebral
Fallopian tube	Oviduct	Oviducal *or* oviductal
Finger	-	Digital
Fingernail	-	Ungual *or* ungular
Fist	-	-
Follicle	-	Follicular
Fontanelle *or* fontanel	-	-
Foot	Pes	Pedal
Forearm	-	Cubital
Forehead	-	Frontal
Foreskin	Prepuce	Preputial
Gall bladder	-	-
Gland	-	Adenoid
Glottis	-	Glottic
Groin	-	Inguinal
Gullet	Oesophagus	Oesophageal
Gum	Gingiva	Gingival
Hair	-	-
Half-moon	Lunula *or* lunule	-
Hamstring	-	Popliteal
Hand	Manus	Manual
Hard palate	-	-
Head	Caput	Capital
Heart	-	Cardiac
Heel	-	-
Hip	-	-
Ileum	-	Ileac *or* ileal
Inner ear *or* internal ear	Labyrinth	-
Instep	-	-
Intestine	-	Alvine
Jaw	-	Gnathic *or* gnathal
Jejunum	-	Jejunal

Part of the body	Technical name	Related adjective
Jugular vein	-	-
Kidney	-	Renal or nephritic
Knee	Genu	Genicular
Knuckle	-	-
Labia majora	-	Labial
Labia minora	-	Labial
Large intestine	-	-
Leg	Crus	Crural
Lip	-	Labial
Liver	-	Hepatic
Loin	Lumbus	Lumbar
Lung	-	Pulmonary
Lymph cell	Lymphocyte	-
Lymph node	-	-
Midriff	Diaphragm	-
Mons pubis	-	-
Mons veneris	-	-
Mouth	-	Stomatic
Nape	Nucha	Nuchal
Navel or omphalos	Umbilicus	Umbilical
Neck	Cervix	Cervical
Nerve	-	Neural
Nerve cell	Neuron or neurone	Neuronic
Nipple or teat	Mamilla or papilla	Mamillary
Nose	-	Nasal
Nostril	Naris	Narial or narine
Occiput	-	Occipital
Ovary	-	Ovarian
Pancreas	-	Pancreatic
Penis	-	Penile
Pharynx	-	Pharyngeal
Pubes	-	Pubic
Rectum	-	Rectal
Red blood cell	Erythrocyte	Erythrocytic
Ribcage	-	-
Scalp	-	-
Scrotum	-	Scrotal
Shin	-	-
Shoulder	-	-
Side	-	-
Skin	Cutis	Cutaneous
Small intestine	-	-
Soft palate	-	-

Part of the body	Technical name	Related adjective
Sole	-	Plantar
Spleen	-	Lienal *or* splenetic
Stomach	-	Gastric
Tear duct	Lacrimal duct	-
Temple	-	Temporal
Tendon	-	-
Testicle	-	Testicular
Thigh	-	Femoral *or* crural
Thorax	-	Thoracic
Throat	-	Guttural, gular, *or* jugular
Thumb	Pollex	Pollical
Toe	-	-
Toenail	-	Ungual *or* ungular
Tongue	Lingua	Lingual *or* glottic
Tonsil	-	Tonsillar *or* tonsillary
Torso	-	-
Transverse colon	-	-
Trunk	-	-
Umbilical cord	Umbilicus	-
Ureter	-	Ureteral *or* ureteric
Urethra	-	Urethral
Vagina	-	Vaginal
Vein	Vena	Venous
Vocal cords	Glottis	Glottal
Voice box	Larynx	Laryngeal
Vulva	-	Vulval, vulvar, *or* vulvate
Waist	-	-
White blood cell	Leucocyte	Leucocytic
Windpipe	Trachea	Tracheal *or* tracheate
Womb	Uterus	Uterine
Wrist	Carpus	-

See also:
➤ **Blood cells** ➤ **Bodily humours** ➤ **Bones** ➤ **Parts of the brain** ➤ **Parts of the ear** ➤ **Parts of the eye** ➤ **Glands** ➤ **Parts of the heart** ➤ **Membranes** ➤ **Muscles** ➤ **Nerves** ➤ **Organs** ➤ **Teeth** ➤ **Veins**

Bombs

4 letters:
Atom
Nail

5 letters:
A-bomb
Mills

6 letters:
Fusion
Petrol

7 letters:
Cluster
Grenade
Neutron
Nuclear
Plastic

8 letters:
Bouncing
Hydrogen

10 letters:
Incendiary

11 letters:
Blockbuster
Depth charge
Hand grenade
Stun grenade

15 letters:
Molotov cocktail

16 letters:
Bangalore torpedo

Bones

Bone	Nontechnical name
Astragalus	Anklebone
Calcaneus	Heel bone
Carpal	Wrist
Carpus	Wrist
Centrum	-
Clavicle	Collarbone
Coccyx	-
Costa	Rib
Cranium	Brainpan
Cuboid	-
Ethmoid	-
Femur	Thighbone
Fibula	-
Frontal bone	-
Hallux	-
Humerus	Funny
Hyoid	-
Ilium	-
Incus	Anvil
Innominate bone	Hipbone
Ischium	-
Malar	Cheek
Malleus	Hammer
Mandible	Lower jawbone
Mastoid	-
Maxilla	Upper jawbone

Bone	Nontechnical name
Metacarpal	-
Metatarsal	-
Metatarsus	-
Nasal	Nose
Occipital bone	-
Parietal bone	-
Patella	Kneecap
Pelvis	-
Phalanx	-
Pubis	-
Radius	-
Rib	-
Sacrum	-
Scapula	Shoulder blade
Skull	-
Sphenoid	-
Spinal column *or* spine	Backbone
Stapes	Stirrup
Sternum	Breastbone
Talus	Anklebone
Tarsal	-
Tarsus	-
Temporal bone	-
Tibia	Shinbone
Trapezium	-
Ulna	-
Vertebra	-
Vertebral column	Backbone
Zygomatic bone	Cheekbone

Books

TYPES OF BOOK

3 letters:
Log

4 letters:
A to Z
Hymn
Road
Song

5 letters:
Album
Atlas
Bible
Comic
Diary
Novel
Score

6 letters:
Annual
Gradus
Jotter
Ledger
Manual
Missal
Phrase
Prayer

TYPES OF BOOK (CONTINUED)

Primer
Reader

7 letters:
Almanac
Anatomy
Bibelot
Cookery
Grammar
Journal
Lexicon
Logbook
Novella
Ordinal
Peerage
Psalter
Service
Speller
Statute
Who's who

8 letters:
Armorial
Baedeker
Bestiary
Breviary
Brochure
Casebook

Copybook
Exercise
Grimoire
Handbook
Notebook
Register
Textbook
Wordbook
Workbook
Yearbook

9 letters:
Anthology
Biography
Catalogue
Catechism
Companion
Directory
Formulary
Gazetteer
Guidebook
Monograph
Novelette
Reference
Scrapbook
Storybook
Thesaurus
Vade mecum

10 letters:
Compendium
Dictionary
Lectionary
Miscellany
Prospectus
Sketchbook

11 letters:
Coffee-table
Commonplace
Concordance

12 letters:
Confessional
Dispensatory
Encyclopedia
Graphic novel

13 letters:
Autobiography
Encyclopaedia
Pharmacopoeia

18 letters:
Telephone directory

PARTS OF A BOOK

4 letters:
Back
Leaf
Page
Tail

5 letters:
Blurb
Cover
Folio
Index
Plate
Proem
Recto
Spine
Verso

6 letters:
Errata
Gutter
Margin
Rubric

7 letters:
Binding
Chapter
Flyleaf
Preface
Prelims
Wrapper

8 letters:
Addendum
Appendix

Contents
Endpaper
Epigraph
Epilogue
Fore-edge
Foreword
Glossary
Prologue
Slipcase

9 letters:
Afterword
Half-title
Interleaf
Title page

PARTS OF A BOOK (CONTINUED)

10 letters:
Back matter
Corrigenda
Dedication
Dust jacket
Postscript

11 letters:
Front matter
Running head

12 letters:
Bibliography
Frontispiece

Illustration
Introduction
Prolegomenon

15 letters:
Acknowledgments

Botany

BRANCHES OF BOTANY

8 letters:
Algology
Bryology
Mycology

9 letters:
Carpology

10 letters:
Dendrology
Floristics

11 letters:
Agrostology
Astrobotany
Ethnobotany
Phytography
Pteridology

12 letters:
Archeobotany
Palaeobotany

Phytogenesis

13 letters:
Archaeobotany

14 letters:
Phytogeography
Phytopathology

17 letters:
Palaeoethnobotany

BOTANY TERMS

3 letters:
Key
Nut
Sap

4 letters:
Axil
Axis
Bulb
Corm
Leaf
Pith
Root
Seed
Stem

5 letters:
Auxin
Berry
Calyx
Fruit

Hilum
Ovary
Ovule
Sepal
Shoot
Spore
Stoma
Style
Testa
Tuber
Xylem

6 letters:
Anther
Carpel
Corona
Cortex
Flower
Lamina
Legume
Phloem

Pistil
Pollen
Raceme
Runner
Spadix
Stamen
Stigma
Stolon

7 letters:
Cambium
Corolla
Cuticle
Plumule
Radicle
Rhizome
Root cap
Rosette
Seed pod
Tropism

BOTANY TERMS (CONTINUED)

8 letters:
Filament
Lenticel
Meristem
Root hair
Seedcase

9 letters:
Cotyledon
Epidermis
Foliation
Guard cell
Gynaecium
Mesophyll
Micropyle
Operculum

10 letters:
Abscission
Androecium
Geotropism
Integument

Receptacle
Root nodule
Seed vessel
Sporangium

11 letters:
Androgynous
Archegonium
Chlorophyll
Chloroplast
Dicotyledon
Germination
Pollination
Seed capsule

12 letters:
Hydrotropism
Phototropism

13 letters:
Inflorescence
Monocotyledon

Translocation
Transpiration

14 letters:
Nastic movement
Photosynthesis
Vascular bundle

15 letters:
Self-pollination
Spongy mesophyll
Wind pollination

16 letters:
Cross-pollination

17 letters:
Insect pollination
Palisade mesophyll

22 letters:
Vegetative reproduction

BOTANISTS

3 letters:
Ray, *John*

5 letters:
Banks, *Joseph*
Brown, *Robert*

6 letters:
Carver, *George
  Washington*

Darwin, *Charles* (*Robert*)
Hooker, *Joseph Dalton*
Hooker, *William Jackson*
Mendel, *Gregor Johann*

7 letters:
Bellamy, *David* (*James*)
De Vries, *Hugo*
Eichler, *August Wilhelm*

8 letters:
Linnaeus
Von Linné, *Carl*

10 letters:
De Candolle, *Auguste
  Pyrame*
Tradescant, *John*

See also:
➤ **Algae** ➤ **Ferns** ➤ **Fungi** ➤ **Grasses** ➤ **Lilies** ➤ **Mosses** ➤ **Palms** ➤ **Plants**
➤ **Parts of plants** ➤ **Sea-weeds** ➤ **Shrubs** ➤ **Trees**

Bottles

5 letters:
Flask
Gourd
Phial
Water

6 letters:
Carboy
Caster
Flacon
Flagon

Lagena
Nansen
Stubby
Woulfe

7 letters:
Ampulla
Feeding

Half-jack
Hot-water
Screw top

10 letters:
Pycnometer
Soda siphon

8 letters:
Decanter
Demijohn

9 letters:
Miniature

11 letters:
Vinaigrette

Boxes

4 letters:
Case
Coin
Deed
Nest
Poor
Wine

5 letters:
Bulla
Chest
Ditty
Glory
Glove
Grass
Music
Trunk

6 letters:
Ballot

Carton
Casket
Coffer
Coffin
Hatbox
Haybox
Saggar
Vanity
Window

7 letters:
Bandbox
Caisson
Cracket
Honesty
Keister
Pillbox
Pouncet
Saltbox

Sandbox
Soapbox

8 letters:
Dispatch
Matchbox
Paintbox
Solander

9 letters:
Cartouche
Papeterie
Strongbox
Tinderbox

10 letters:
Desiccator

11 letters:
Packing case

Boxing weights

Weight	Amateur	Professional
Light flyweight	48 kg	49 kg
Flyweight	51 kg	51 kg
Bantamweight	54 kg	53.5 kg
Featherweight	57 kg	57 kg
Junior lightweight	-	59 kg
Lightweight	60 kg	61 kg
Light welterweight	63.5 kg	63.5 kg
Welterweight	67 kg	66.6 kg
Light middleweight	71 kg	70 kg
Middleweight	75 kg	72.5 kg
Light heavyweight	81 kg	79 kg

Weight	Amateur	Professional
Cruiserweight	-	88.5 kg
Heavyweight	91 kg	+88.5 kg
Superheavyweight	+91 kg	-

Parts of the brain

6 letters:
Vermis

8 letters:
Amygdala
Cerebrum
Meninges
Midbrain
Thalamus

9 letters:
Brainstem

10 letters:
Afterbrain
Broca's area
Cerebellum
Grey matter
Pineal body

11 letters:
Frontal lobe
Hippocampus
Pons Varolli
White matter

12 letters:
Diencephalon
Hypothalamus
Infundibulum
Limbic system
Optic chiasma
Parietal lobe
Temporal lobe

13 letters:
Central sulcus
Choroid plexus
Mamillary body
Occipital lobe

Wernicke's area

14 letters:
Cerebral cortex
Corpus callosum
Myelencephalon
Pituitary gland
Substantia alba
Third ventricle

15 letters:
Fourth ventricle

16 letters:
Cerebral aqueduct
Medulla oblongata

18 letters:
Cerebrospinal fluid

Breads

3 letters:
Bap
Bun
Cob
Nan
Pan
Rye

4 letters:
Corn
Loaf
Naan
Puri
Roll
Roti
Soda

5 letters:
Bagel
Black
Brown
Matza
Matzo
Pitta
Plain
Plait
White

6 letters:
Beigel
Coburg
Damper
French
Gluten

Hallah
Indian
Matzah
Matzoh
Muffin

7 letters:
Bloomer
Brioche
Buttery
Challah
Chapati
Granary®
Long tin
Paratha
Stollen
Wheaten

8 letters:
Baguette
Barm cake
Chapatti
Ciabatta
Corn pone
Focaccia
Poppadom
Poppadum
Quartern
Split tin
Tortilla

9 letters:
Barmbrack
Batch loaf
Croissant
Farmhouse
Fruit loaf
Schnecken
Sourdough
Square tin
Wholemeal

10 letters:
Billy-bread

Bridge roll
Johnny cake
Unleavened
Whole-wheat

11 letters:
Cottage loaf
French stick

12 letters:
Griddlebread
Half-quartern
Pumpernickel

Bridges

BRIDGES

4 letters:
Skye
Tyne

5 letters:
Tower

6 letters:
Humber
London
Rialto
Severn

7 letters:
Rainbow

8 letters:
Brooklyn
Waterloo

9 letters:
Forth Road
Halfpenny

10 letters:
Golden Gate
Millennium
Oakland Bay

11 letters:
Westminster

12 letters:
Forth Railway

13 letters:
Bridge of Sighs
Sydney Harbour

17 letters:
Clifton Suspension

19 letters:
Gateshead Millennium

TYPES OF BRIDGE

4 letters:
Deck
Snow
Turn

5 letters:
Pivot
Swing
Truss

6 letters:
Bailey

7 letters:
Balance
Bascule
Clapper
Flyover
Pontoon
Viaduct

8 letters:
Aqueduct

9 letters:
Box-girder

10 letters:
Cantilever
Drawbridge
Footbridge
Suspension

11 letters:
Cable-stayed

12 letters:
Counterpoise

Shades of brown

3 letters:
Bay
Dun
Tan

4 letters:
Buff
Drab
Ecru
Fawn
Fusc
Rust
Sand
Sore
Teak

5 letters:
Abram
Amber
Beige
Camel
Cocoa
Cream
Hazel
Henna
Khaki
Liver
Mocha
Mousy
Sable
Sepia
Soare

Taupe
Tawny
Tenné
Umber

6 letters:
Almond
Auburn
Bisque
Bistre
Bronze
Burnet
Coffee
Copper
Fallow
Ginger
Nutmeg
Rufous
Russet
Sienna
Sorrel
Walnut

7 letters:
Biscuit
Brindle
Caramel
Caromel
Filemot
Fulvous
Fuscous
Neutral

Oatmeal
Oxblood
Vandyke

8 letters:
Brunette
Chestnut
Cinnabar
Cinnamon
Mahogany
Mushroom
Nutbrown
Philamot

9 letters:
Butternut
Chocolate
Seal brown

10 letters:
Burnt umber
Café au lait
Coromandel
Terracotta
Testaceous

11 letters:
Burnt sienna

13 letters:
Tortoiseshell

Schools of Buddhism

3 letters:
Zen

4 letters:
Jodo
Soto

5 letters:
Foism
Geluk
Kagyü
Sakya

6 letters:
Rinjai
Tendai

7 letters:
Lamaism
Nyingma

8 letters:
Hinayana
Mahayana
Nichiren

9 letters:
Theravada
Vajrayana

10 letters:
Soka Gakkai

16 letters:
Pure Land Buddhism

Bugs

4 letters:
Lace

5 letters:
Māori
Mealy
Stink
Water

6 letters:
Bedbug
Chinch
Cicada
Cicala

Damsel
Debris
Shield

7 letters:
Kissing
Spittle

9 letters:
Harlequin

10 letters:
Froghopper
Leaf-hopper

Pond-skater

11 letters:
Water skater

12 letters:
Water boatman
Water strider

13 letters:
Spittle insect
Water scorpion

Buildings and monuments

5 letters:
Kaaba

6 letters:
Big Ben
Louvre
Masada

7 letters:
Beehive
Knossos
Kremlin
Lateran
Vatican

8 letters:
Alhambra
Barbican
Cenotaph
Monument
Pentagon
Taj Mahal

9 letters:
Charminar

Hermitage

10 letters:
White House

11 letters:
Eiffel Tower
Scone Palace

12 letters:
Althorp House
Mansion House

13 letters:
Arc de Triomphe
Crystal Palace
Elysées Palace
Forbidden City
Holyroodhouse
Lambeth Palace
Longleat House
Nelson's Column
Tower of London

14 letters:
Admiralty House
Blenheim Palace

15 letters:
Angel of the North
Edinburgh Castle

16 letters:
Buckingham Palace
Cleopatra's Needle
Kensington Palace
Westminster Abbey

17 letters:
Saint James's Palace

18 letters:
Hampton Court Palace
Houses of Parliament
Leaning Tower of Pisa
Palace of Versailles

19 letters:
Empire State Building

Business people

4 letters:
Benz, *Karl Friedrich*
Bond, *Alan*
Boot, *Sir Jesse*
Cook, *Thomas*
Ford, *Henry*
Jobs, *Steven Paul*
Shah, *Eddy*
Tate, *Sir Henry*

5 letters:
Astor, *Lord John Jacob*
Dawes, *Charles Gates*
Dyson, *James*
Flynt, *Larry*
Forte, *Lord Charles*
Frick, *Henry Clay*
Gates, *Bill*
Getty, *Jean Paul*
Grade, *Michael*
Heinz, *Henry John*
Honda, *Soichiro*
Jones, *Digby*
Krupp, *Friedrich*
Laker, *Sir Freddie*
Lyons, *Sir Joseph*
Marks, *Lord Simon*
Rolls, *Charles Stewart*
Royce, *Sir Henry*
Sieff, *Lord Israel*
Sugar, *Alan*
Zeiss, *Carl*

6 letters:
Ashley, *Laura*
Austin, *Lord Herbert*
Boeing, *William Edward*
Butlin, *Billy*

Conran, *Sir Terence*
Cunard, *Sir Samuel*
Dunlop, *John Boyd*
Farmer, *Sir Tom*
Hammer, *Armand*
Hanson, *Lord James*
Hilton, *Conrad Nicholson*
Hoover, *William Henry*
Hughes, *Howard*
Hulton, *Sir Edward*
Lipton, *Sir Thomas*
Monday, *Sir Robert Ludwig*
Morris, *William Richard (Viscount Nuffield)*
Ogilvy, *David*
Packer, *Kerry*
Ratner, *Gerald Irving*
Turner, *Ted*
Warner, *Harold*

7 letters:
Agnelli, *Giovanni*
Barclay, *Robert*
Branson, *Sir Richard*
Bugatti, *Ettore*
Burrell, *Sir William*
Cadbury, *George*
Citroën, *André Gustave*
Douglas, *Donald*
Kennedy, *Joseph Patrick*
Maxwell, *Robert*
Murdoch, *Rupert*
Onassis, *Aristotle*
Roddick, *Dame Anita Lucia*
Tiffany, *Charles Lewis*

8 letters:
Birdseye, *Clarence*
Carnegie, *Andrew*
Christie, *James*
Guinness, *Sir Benjamin Lee*
Michelin, *André*
Olivetti, *Adriano*
Pulitzer, *Joseph*
Rowntree, *Joseph*
Sinclair, *Sir Clive*
Southeby, *John*
Zaharoff, *Sir Basil*

9 letters:
Firestone, *Harvey Samuel*
Sainsbury, *Lord Aan*
Selfridge, *Harry Gordon*
Woolworth, *Frank Winfield*

10 letters:
Rothschild, *Meyer Amschel*
Vanderbilt, *Cornelius*

11 letters:
Beaverbrook, *Lord Max*
Harvey-Jones, *Sir John Henry*

12 letters:
Rockerfeller, *John Davison*

Butterflies and moths

2 letters:
Io

3 letters:
Bag
Bee

Fox
Nun
Owl
Wax

4 letters:
Arch
Bell
Blue
Goat
Hawk

Butterflies and moths

Leaf
Luna
Meal
Puss
Wave

5 letters:
Argus
Atlas
Brown
Comma
Eggar
Egger
Flour
Ghost
Gipsy
Grass
Gypsy
Heath
House
Owlet
Snout
Swift
Thorn
Tiger
Tinea
Umber
White
Y-moth

6 letters:
Antler
Apollo
Bogong
Bugong
Burnet
Carpet
Codlin
Copper
Dagger
Ermine
Herald
Kitten
Lackey
Lappet
Lichen
Magpie
Morpho
Muslin
Noctua

Pieris
Psyche
Sphinx
Thecla
Turnip
Veneer
Winter
Yellow

7 letters:
Abraxas
Bagworm
Buff-tip
Cabbage
Clothes
Codling
Drinker
Emperor
Festoon
Hook-tip
Kallima
Leopard
Lobster
Monarch
Noctuid
Old lady
Peacock
Pug-moth
Ringlet
Silver-Y
Skipper
Stamper
Sulphur
Thistle
Tortrix
Tussock
Unicorn
Vanessa
Zygaena

8 letters:
Bobowler
Bombycid
Cardinal
Cecropia
Cinnabar
Dart-moth
Geometer
Goldtail
Grayling

Hesperid
Oak-Egger
Peppered
Saturnia
Silkworm
Sphingid
Tapestry
Tineidae
Vapourer
Wainscot

9 letters:
Arctiidae
Brimstone
Brown-tail
Carpenter
Clearwing
Cleopatra
Geometrid
Honeycomb
Notodonta
Orange-tip
Pyralidae
Saturniid
Scavenger
Underwing
Wall brown

10 letters:
Common blue
Death's-head
Fritillary
Gate-keeper
Hairstreak
Large white
Leafroller
Polyphemus
Privet hawk
Red admiral
Silverspot
Small white
Yellowtail

11 letters:
Diamondback
Hummingbird
Large copper
Meadow brown
Painted lady
Swallowtail

Butterflies and moths

12 letters:
Cabbage white
Cactoblastis
Kentish glory
Lymantriidae
Marbled white
Red underwing
Sallow-kitten
Speckled wood
White admiral

13 letters:
Clouded yellow
Mother-of-pearl
Mother Shipton
Mourning cloak
Processionary
Purple emperor

14 letters:
Two-tailed pasha

15 letters:
Yellow underwing

16 letters:
Camberwell beauty
Clifden nonpareil
Tiger swallowtail

C c

Cakes and pastries

3 letters:
Nut
Oil
Pan
Set

4 letters:
Baba
Farl
Kush
Pone
Puff
Puri
Rock
Roti
Rout
Rusk
Slab
Soul
Tart

5 letters:
Angel
Babka
Cream
Donut
Fairy
Farle
Fudge
Genoa
Lardy
Latke
Layer
Poori
Pound
Rosti
Scone
Sushi
Tansy
Tipsy
Torte
Wafer

6 letters:
Almond
Carrot
Cherry
Coburg
Cotton
Dainty
Dundee
Eccles
Eclair
Gateau
Girdle
Hockey
Johnny
Jumbal
Jumble
Kuchen
Marble
Muffin
Parkin
Simnel
Sponge
Tablet
Waffle
Wonder
Yumyum

7 letters:
Baklava
Banbury
Bannock
Brioche
Brownie
Carcake
Chapati
Chupati
Coconut
Cruller
Crumpet
Cupcake
Fritter
Galette

Jannock
Jumbles
Kruller
Linseed
Madeira
Oatmeal
Pancake
Paratha
Pavlova
Pikelet
Pomfret
Ratafia
Rum baba
Savarin
Stollen
Teacake
Vetkoek
Wedding

8 letters:
Agnus dei
Birthday
Black bun
Chapatti
Chillada
Chupatty
Doughnut
Dumpling
Flapjack
Macaroon
Meringue
Mince pie
Napoleon
Pandowdy
Sandwich
Seedcake
Teabread
Tortilla
Turnover

9 letters:
Angel food

Barmbrack
Chocolate
Christmas
Chupattie
Clapbread
Cream puff
Croquette
Drop scone
Fruitcake
Kuglehopf
Lamington
Madeleine
Panettone
Petit four
Puftaloon
Queencake
Sally Lunn
Swiss roll

10 letters:
Battenberg
Battenburg
Coffee kiss
Devil's food
Frangipane
Frangipani
Koeksister
Ladyfinger
Pontefract
Puftaloona
Religieuse
Upside-down

11 letters:
Gingerbread
Hot cross bun
Linzer torte
Profiterole
Sachertorte

12 letters:
Bakewell tart
Buckwheat bun
Danish pastry
French pastry
Maid of honour
Millefeuille
Singing hinny
Sponge finger

13 letters:
Genoese sponge

14 letters:
Selkirk bannock
Victoria sponge

17 letters:
Black forest gateau

Camera parts

6 letters:
Tripod

7 letters:
Hot shoe
Shutter

8 letters:
Flash gun
Lens hood
Sprocket
Zoom lens

9 letters:
Amplifier
Macro lens

10 letters:
Autowinder
Viewfinder

12 letters:
Synchroflash

13 letters:
Accessory shoe

Extension ring
Iris diaphragm
Telephoto lens
Wide-angle lens

14 letters:
Automatic focus
Intervalometer

17 letters:
Automatic exposure

Types of camera

3 letters:
Box

4 letters:
Cine

6 letters:
Candid
Reflex
Webcam

7 letters:
Brownie
Compact

Digital
Pinhole
Process

8 letters:
Polaroid

9 letters:
Automatic
Camcorder
Miniature

Steadicam

10 letters:
Programmed

12 letters:
Subminiature

Canals

4 letters:
Erie
Göta
Kiel
Suez

5 letters:
Grand

6 letters:
Moscow
Panama
Twente

7 letters:
Corinth
Welland

8 letters:
Berezina

9 letters:
Champlain

10 letters:
Caledonian
Grand Union
Mittelland
Rhine-Herne

11 letters:
Bridgewater
Canal du Midi
Dortmund-Ems
Houston Ship

12 letters:
Canal do Norte

14 letters:
Manchester Ship

17 letters:
Canal de São Gonçalo
New York State Barge

Caps

3 letters:
Mob
Taj
Tam

4 letters:
Blue
Caul
Coif
Cope
Cowl
Flat
Kepi

5 letters:
Beret
Chaco
Chape
Cloth
Kippa
Mutch
Pagri
Quoif

Shako
Toque
Tuque
Turk's

6 letters:
Abacot
Amorce
Barret
Berret
Biggin
Blakey
Calpac
Chapka
Cornet
Czapka
Dunce's
Forage
Gandhi
Granny
Jockey
Juliet

Kalpak
Kipput
Kiss-me
Morion
Pileus
Pinner
Square
Toorie

7 letters:
Bathing
Bellhop
Bendigo
Biretta
Bycoket
Calotte
Calpack
Chapeau
Chechia
Fatigue
Grannie
Kippoth

Liberty
Monteer
Montero
Morrion
Newsboy

8 letters:
Balmoral
Baseball
Capeline
Chaperon
Garrison
Havelock
Monmouth
Phrygian

Puggaree
Schapska
Skullcap
Stocking
Thinking
Trencher
Yarmulka
Yarmulke
Zuchetto

9 letters:
Balaclava
Glengarry
Trenchard

10 letters:
Cockernony
Kilmarnock

11 letters:
Bonnet-rouge
Deerstalker
Kiss-me-quick
Mortar-board
Tam-o'-shanter

12 letters:
Cheese-cutter
Davy Crockett

Capes

3 letters:
Cod
Hoe
May
Ras

4 letters:
Fear
Hogh
Horn
Naze
Race
Roca
Scaw
Skaw

5 letters:
Byron
Canso
North
Parry

Sable
Sandy
Verde
Wrath

6 letters:
Helles
Lizard
Reinga
Sontag
Ushant

7 letters:
Agulhas
Comorin
Delgado
Leeuwin
Matapan
Runaway
Western

8 letters:
Farewell
Flattery
Good Hope
Hatteras
Palatine

9 letters:
Canaveral
Dungeness
Guardafui
Lindisnes
Southwest
St Vincent
Trafalgar

10 letters:
Finisterre

11 letters:
Fairweather

Capitals

Capital	Country, region, state, etc
Abidjan	Ivory Coast
Abu Dhabi	United Arab Emirates
Abuja	Nigeria
Accra	Ghana

Capital	Country, region, state, etc
Acra	Hunger
Addis Ababa	Ethiopia
Adelaide	South Australia
Agana	Guam
Albany	New York (state capital)
Algiers	Algeria
Amman	Jordan
Amsterdam	Netherlands
Andorra la Vella	Andorra
Ankara	Turkey
Annapolis	Maryland
Antananarivo	Madagascar
Antioch	Ancient Syria
Apia	Samoa
Ashkhabad	Turkmenistan
Asmara	Eritrea
Astana	Kazakhstan
Asunción	Paraguay
Athens	Greece
Atlanta	Georgia
Austin	Texas
Baghdad	Iraq
Baku	Azerbaijan
Bamako	Mali
Bandar Seri Begawan	Brunei
Bangalore	Karnataka
Bangkok	Thailand
Bangui	Central African Republic
Banjul	Gambia
Barnaul	Altai
Basseterre	St. Kitts and Nevis
Bastia	Corsica
Baton Rouge	Louisiana
Beijing *or* Peking	People's Republic of China
Beirut *or* Beyrouth	Lebanon
Belfast	Northern Ireland
Belgrade	Yugoslavia (Serbia and Montenegro)
Belmopan	Belize
Berlin	Germany
Berne	Switzerland
Bishkek	Kyrgyzstan
Bissau	Guinea-Bissau

Capital	Country, region, state, etc
Bloemfontein	Judicial capital of South Africa
Bogotá	Colombia
Bonn	Federal Republic of Germay (formerly)
Brasília	Brazil
Bratislava	Slovakia
Brazzaville	Congo (Republic of)
Bridgetown	Barbados
Brisbane	Queensland
Brno	Moravia
Bruges	West Flanders
Brussels	Belgium
Bucharest	Romania
Budapest	Hungary
Buenos Aires	Argentina
Bujumbura	Burundi
Caen	Basse-Normandie
Cagliari	Sardinia
Cairo	Egypt
Calcutta	West Bengal
Cali	Valley of the Cauca, Colombia
Canberra	Australia
Cape Town	Legislative capital of South Africa
Caracas	Venezuela
Cardiff	Wales
Cartagena	Bolivar
Castries	St. Lucia
Cayenne	French Guiana
Charleston	West Virginia
Colombo	Sri Lanka
Conakry *or* Konakry	Guinea
Copenhagen	Denmark
Cordoba	Cordoba
Dakar	Senegal
Damascus	Syria
Darwin	Northern Territory, Australia
Delhi	India
Dhaka *or* Dacca	Bangladesh
Dili	East Timor
Djibouti *or* Jibouti	Djibouti *or* Jibouti
Dodoma	Tanzania
Doha	Qatar
Douglas	Isle of Man

Capital	Country, region, state, etc
Dublin	Republic of Ireland
Dushanbe	Tajikistan
Edinburgh	Scotland
Enugu	Enugu
Faro	The Algarve
Fongafale	Tuvalu
Fort-de-France	Martinique
Freetown	Sierra Leone
Funafuti	Tuvalu
Funchal	Madeira
Gaborone	Botswana
Georgetown	Guyana
Guatemala City	Guatemala
Hanoi	Vietnam
Harare	Zimbabwe
Havana	Cuba
Helsinki	Finland
Heraklion *or* Eraklion	Crete
Hobart	Tasmania
Honiara	Solomon Islands
Honolulu	Hawaii
Ibadan	Oyo State, Nigeria
Ipoh	Perak
Islamabad	Pakistan
Istanbul *or* Constantinople	Turkey (formerly)
Jakarta *or* Djakarta	Indonesia
Jerusalem	Israel
Jos	Plateau (central Nigeria)
Kabul	Afghanistan
Kampala	Uganda
Karachi	Sind
Katmandu *or* Kathmandu	Nepal
Khartoum *or* Khartum	Sudan
Kiel	Schleswig-Holstein
Kiev	Ukraine
Kigali	Rwanda
Kingston	Jamaica
Kingstown	St. Vincent and the Grenadines
Kinshasa	Congo (Democratic Republic of)
Kirkwall	Orkney Islands
Kishinev	Moldova
Kobe	Honshu
Koror	Palau

Capital	Country, region, state, etc
Kuala Lumpur	Malaysia
Kuwait	Kuwait
Lagos	Nigeria (formerly)
La Paz	Administrative capital of Bolivia
Lassa *or* Lhasa	Tibet
Leningrad, St Petersburg, *or* Petrograd	Russia (formerly)
Libreville	Gabon
Lilongwe	Malawi
Lima	Peru
Lisbon	Portugal
Little Rock	Arkansas
Ljubljana	Slovenia
Lomé	Togo
London	United Kingdom
Luanda	Angola
Lusaka	Zambia
Luxembourg	Luxembourg
Madrid	Spain
Majuro	Marshall Islands
Malabo	Equatorial Guinea
Malé	Maldives
Managua	Nicaragua
Manama	Bahrain
Manila	Philippines
Maputo	Mozambique
Maseru	Lesotho
Mathura	Braj Bhoomi
Mbabane	Swaziland
Memphis	Egypt, Old Kingdom
Mexico City	Mexico
Minsk	Belarus
Mogadishu	Somalia
Monaco-Ville	Monaco
Monrovia	Liberia
Montevideo	Uruguay
Moroni	Comoros
Moscow	Russia
Muscat	Oman
Nairobi	Kenya
Nashville	Tennessee
Nassau	Bahamas
Ndjamena	Chad

Capital	Country, region, state, etc
Niamey	Niger
Nicosia	Cyprus
Nineveh	Ancient Assyrian empire
Nouakchott	Mauritania
Nuku'alofa	Tonga
Nuuk	Greenland
Olympia	Washington state
Oslo	Norway
Ottawa	Canada
Ouagadougou	Burkina-Faso
Palermo	Sicily
Palikir	Micronesia
Panama City	Panama
Pandemonium *or* Pandaemonium	Hell
Paramaribo	Suriname
Paris	France
Persepolis	Ancient Persia
Phnom Penh	Cambodia
Pishpek	Kirghizia
Port-au-Prince	Haiti
Port Louis	Mauritius
Port Moresby	Papua New Guinea
Port of Spain	Trinidad and Tobago
Porto Novo	Benin
Port Vila	Vanuatu
Prague	Czech Republic
Praia	Cape Verde
Pretoria	Administrative capital of South Africa
Pristina	Kosovo (Federal Republic of Yugoslavia)
Providence	Rhode Island
Pyongyang	North Korea
Quito	Ecuador
Rabat	Morocco
Reykjavik	Iceland
Riga	Latvia
Rio	Rio de Janeiro
Rio Branco	Acre
Riyadh	Saudi Arabia
Rome	Italy
Roseau	Dominica

Capital	Country, region, state, etc
Samarkand	Mongol Empire (14th century)
San`a	Yemen
San José	Costa Rica
San Juan	Puerto Rico
San Marino	San Marino
San Salvador	El Salvador
Santiago	Chile
Santo Domingo	Dominican Republic
São Tomé	São Tomé and Principe
Sarajevo	Bosnia and Herzegovina
Sendai	Tohoku
Seoul	South Korea
Singapore	Singapore
Skopje	Macedonia
Sofia	Bulgaria
Sokoto	Sokoto
St. George's	Grenada
St. John's	Antigua and Barbuda
Stockholm	Sweden
Stuttgart	Baden-Württemberg
Sucré	Legislative and judicial capital of Bolivia
Susa	Ancient Persia (Achaemenid dynasty)
Suva	Fiji
Taipei	Taiwan
Tallinn	Estonia
Tarawa	Kiribati
Tashkent	Uzbekistan
Tbilisi	Georgia
Tegucigalpa	Honduras
Tehran *or* Teheran	Iran
Tel Aviv	Israel
Thebes	Ancient Egypt (18th dynasty)
Thimphu *or* Thimbu	Bhutan
Tirana	Albania
Tokyo	Japan
Topeka	Kansas
Trebizond	Trebizond
Tripoli	Libya
Tunis	Tunisia
Ufa	Bashkiria
Ulan Bator	Mongolia

Capital	Country, region, state, etc
Vaduz	Liechtenstein
Valladolid	Castilla-Léon
Valletta	Malta
Vatican City	Vatican City
Victoria	Seychelles
Vienna	Austria
Vientiane	Laos
Vilnius	Lithuania
Warsaw	Poland
Washington DC	United States of America
Wellington	New Zealand
Windhoek	Namibia
Winnipeg	Manitoba
Xanthus	Ancient Lycia
Xian	Shaanxi
Yamoussoukro	Côte d'Ivoire
Yangon (Rangoon)	Myanmar (Burma)
Yaoundé *or* Yaunde	Cameroon
Yaren	Nauru
Yerevan	Armenia
Zagreb	Croatia

Cars

TYPES OF CAR

2 letters:
BL
GT
MG
RR
VW

3 letters:
Cab
Elf

4 letters:
Audi
Biza
Drag
Fiat
Ford
Kart

Lada
Limo
Merc
Mini
Opel
Tank

5 letters:
Astra
Buick
Coupé
Panda
Prowl
Racer
Rolls
Sedan
Skoda
Squad

Stock
Turbo

6 letters:
Beetle
Bubble
Bumper
Dodgem®
Estate
Hearse
Hot-rod
Lancia
Morris
Patrol
Ragtop
Roller
Sports
Tourer

TYPES OF CAR (CONTINUED)

7 letters:
Bugatti
Company
Cortina
Daimler
Formula
Hardtop
Hillman
Lagonda
Sunbeam
Veteran
Vintage

8 letters:
Cadillac
Dragster
Drophead
Fastback
Mercedes
Roadster

9 letters:
Cabriolet
Hatchback
Landaulet
Landrover
Limousine

Notchback
Two-seater

10 letters:
Subcompact

11 letters:
Convertible
Stretch-limo

12 letters:
Station wagon
Three-wheeler

CAR PARTS

3 letters:
Fan
Top

4 letters:
Axle
Body
Boot
Bulb
Coil
Cowl
Door
Fuse
Gear
Hood
Horn
Jack
Lock
Plug
Roof
Seat
Sump
Tank
Trim
Tyre
Wing

5 letters:
Brake
Choke
Crank

Light
Pedal
Valve
Wheel

6 letters:
Air bag
Big end
Bonnet
Bumper
Clutch
Engine
Fascia
Fender
Gasket
Grille
Heater
Hubcap
Piston
Points
Towbar
Window

7 letters:
Ammeter
Ashtray
Battery
Bearing
Chassis
Exhaust
Fan belt

Fog lamp
Fuse box
Gearbox
Hard top
Mud flap
Oil pump
Soft top
Springs
Starter
Sunroof
Wing nut

8 letters:
Brake pad
Camshaft
Cylinder
Demister
Dipstick
Flywheel
Headrest
Ignition
Manifold
Odometer
Radiator
Seat belt
Silencer
Sprocket
Tailgate
Tailpipe
Wheel nut

CAR PARTS (CONTINUED)

9 letters:
Crankcase
Dashboard
Fuel gauge
Gear lever
Gearshift
Generator
Handbrake
Headlight
Indicator
Little end
Milometer
Oil filter
Petrol cap
Radius arm
Rear light
Taillight
Wheel trim

10 letters:
Alternator
Brake light
Bucket seat
Crankshaft
Disc brakes
Door handle
Driveshaft

Mileometer
Petrol tank
Safety belt
Spare wheel
Suspension
Torsion bar
Wheel brace
Windscreen
Wing mirror

11 letters:
Accelerator
Anti-roll bar
Carburettor
Distributor
Hazard light
Luggage rack
Numberplate
Parcel shelf
Petrol gauge
Speedometer

12 letters:
Cylinder head
Parking light
Sunshine roof
Transmission

13 letters:
Connecting rod
Shock absorber
Steering wheel

14 letters:
Automatic choke
Childproof lock
Convertible top
Distributor cap
Radiator grille
Rear-view mirror
Reversing light
Steering column
Universal joint

15 letters:
Windscreen wiper

16 letters:
Glove compartment
Oil-pressure gauge

18 letters:
Catalytic converter

INTERNATIONAL CAR REGISTRATION LETTERS

Letter(s)	Country
A	Austria
ADN	Yemen
AFG	Afghanistan
AL	Albania
AND	Andorra
AUS	Australia
B	Belgium
BD	Bangladesh
BDS	Barbados
BG	Bulgaria
BH	Belize
BR	Brazil
BRN	Bahrain
BRU	Brunei

INTERNATIONAL CAR REGISTRATION LETTERS (CONTINUED)

Letter(s)	Country
BS	Bahamas
BUR	Myanmar
C	Cuba
CDN	Canada
CH	Switzerland
CI	Côte d'Ivoire
CL	Sri Lanka
CO	Colombia
CR	Costa Rica
CY	Cyprus
CZ	Czech Republic
D	Germany
DK	Denmark
DOM	Dominican Republic
DY	Benin
DZ	Algeria
E	Spain
EAK	Kenya
EAT	Tanzania
EAU	Uganda
EC	Ecuador
ES	El Salvador
ET	Egypt
ETH	Ethiopia
EW	Estonia
F	France
FIN	Finland
FJI	Fiji
FL	Liechtenstein
FR	Faeroe Islands
GB	United Kingdom
GBA	Alderney
GBG	Guernsey
GBJ	Jersey
GBM	Isle of Man
GBZ	Gibraltar
GCA	Guatemala
GH	Ghana
GR	Greece
GUY	Guyana
H	Hungary

INTERNATIONAL CAR REGISTRATION LETTERS (CONTINUED)

Letter(s)	Country
HK	Hong Kong
HKJ	Jordan
HR	Croatia
I	Italy
IL	Israel
IND	India
IR	Iran
IRL	Republic of Ireland
IRQ	Iraq
IS	Iceland
J	Japan
JA	Jamaica
K	Cambodia
KWT	Kuwait
L	Luxembourg
LAO	Laos
LAR	Libya
LB	Liberia
LS	Lesotho
LT	Lithuania
LV	Latvia
M	Malta
MA	Morocco
MAL	Malaysia
MC	Monaco
MEX	Mexico
MS	Mauritius
MW	Malawi
N	Norway
NA	Netherlands Antilles
NIC	Nicaragua
NL	Netherlands
NZ	New Zealand
OMAN	Oman
P	Portugal
PA	Panama
PE	Peru
PK	Pakistan
PL	Poland
PNG	Papua New Guinea
PY	Paraguay

INTERNATIONAL CAR REGISTRATION LETTERS (CONTINUED)

Letter(s)	Country
RA	Argentina
RB	Botswana
RC	Taiwan
RCA	Central African Republic
RCB	Congo Republic
RCH	Chile
RH	Haiti
RI	Indonesia
RIM	Mauritania
RL	Lebanon
RM	Madagascar
RMM	Mali
RO	Romania
ROK	South Korea
ROU	Uruguay
RP	Philippines
RSM	San Marino
RU	Burundi
RUS	Russian Federation
RWA	Rwanda
S	Sweden
SD	Swaziland
SGP	Singapore
SK	Slovakia
SME	Surinam
SN	Senegal
SWA	Namibia
SY	Seychelles
SYR	Syria
T	Thailand
TG	Togo
TN	Tunisia
TR	Turkey
TT	Trindad and Tobago
USA	United States of America
V	Vatican City
VN	Vietnam
WAG	Gambia
WAL	Sierra Leone
WAN	Nigeria
WD	Dominica

INTERNATIONAL CAR REGISTRATION LETTERS (CONTINUED)

Letter(s)	Country
WG	Grenada
WL	St. Lucia
WS	Western Samoa
WV	St. Vincent and the Grenadines
YU	Yugoslavia
YV	Venezuela
Z	Zambia
ZA	South Africa
ZRE	Zaire
ZW	Zimbabwe

Cards

CARD GAMES

3 letters:
Loo
Nap

4 letters:
Faro
Skat
Snap
Solo

5 letters:
Cinch
Monte
Ombre
Poker
Rummy
Stops
Whist

6 letters:
Boston
Bridge
Casino
Chemmy
Écarté
Euchre
Hearts
Piquet

Quinze
Switch

7 letters:
Bezique
Canasta
Cooncan
Old maid
Pinocle
Pontoon
Seven up

8 letters:
Baccarat
Canfield
Conquian
Cribbage
Gin rummy
Napoleon
Patience
Penuchle
Penuckle
Pinochle
Slapjack

9 letters:
Blackjack
Solo whist

Spoilfive
Stud poker

10 letters:
Strip poker

11 letters:
Chemin-de-fer
Five hundred
Rouge et noir

12 letters:
Rubber bridge

13 letters:
Auction bridge
Happy families

14 letters:
Contract bridge

15 letters:
Duplicate bridge

16 letters:
Trente et quarante

17 letters:
Beggar-my-neighbour

BRIDGE TERMS

4 letters:
East
Ruff
Slam
West

5 letters:
Dummy
North
South
Trick
Trump

6 letters:
Double
Rubber

7 letters:
Finesse
No-trump

8 letters:
Contract
Redouble

9 letters:
Grand slam
Singleton
Small slam

10 letters:
Little slam
Vulnerable
Yarborough

POKER TERMS

3 letters:
See
Shy

4 letters:
Ante
Pair

5 letters:
Flush
Raise

8 letters:
Showdown
Stand pat
Straddle
Straight

9 letters:
Full house

10 letters:
Royal flush

13 letters:
Straight flush

OTHER CARD TERMS

3 letters:
Ace
Cut

4 letters:
Deal
Deck
Hand
Jack
King
Suit

Trey
Wild

5 letters:
Clubs
Deuce
Joker
Knave
Queen

6 letters:
Hearts
Revoke
Spades

8 letters:
Diamonds
Face card

9 letters:
Court card

Carnivores

3 letters:
Cat
Dog
Fox

4 letters:
Bear
Coon
Eyra
Lion
Lynx

Mink
Puma
Wolf

5 letters:
Civet

Carnivores

Dhole
Dingo
Genet
Hyena
Otter
Ounce
Panda
Potto
Rasse
Ratel
Sable
Skunk
Stoat
Tayra
Tiger
Zibet

6 letters:
Badger
Bobcat
Chetah
Corsac
Cougar
Coyote
Ermine
Fennec
Ferret
Grison
Hyaena
Jackal
Jaguar
Kit fox
Margay
Marten
Nanook
Ocelot
Racoon
Red fox
Serval
Teledu
Weasel

7 letters:
Caracal
Cheetah
Genette
Glutton
Grey fox
Grizzly
Leopard
Linsang
Meerkat
Panther
Polecat
Raccoon
Rooikat
Sun bear
Zorilla
Zorille

8 letters:
Aardwolf
Carcajou
Grey wolf
Kinkajou
Kolinsky
Mongoose
Sea otter
Swift fox
Tiger cat
Warrigal
Zibeline

9 letters:
Arctic fox
Binturong
Black bear
Brown bear
Cacomixle
Catamount
Hog badger
Honey bear
Ichneumon

Native dog
Palm civet
Polar bear
Silver fox
Sloth bear
Wolverine

10 letters:
Cacomistle
Desert lynx
Giant panda
Jaguarondi
Jaguarundi
Kodiak bear
Otter shrew
Pine marten
Prairie dog
Raccoon dog
Strandwolf
Timber wolf

11 letters:
Grizzly bear
Prairie wolf
Snow leopard
Stone marten
Sweet marten

12 letters:
Catamountain
Cat-o'-mountain
Cinnamon bear
Mountain lion
Spotted hyena

13 letters:
Hognosed skunk
Laughing hyena

See also:
➤ **Breeds of cat** ➤ **Breeds of dog**

Carpets and rugs

5 letters:
Kilim

6 letters:
Durrie
Kirman
Numdah
Wilton

7 letters:
Ingrain

8 letters:
Aubusson
Chenille

9 letters:
Axminster
Broadloom
Flat-woven

10 letters:
Bukhara rug

Persian rug

12 letters:
Turkey carpet

13 letters:
Kidderminster
Persian carpet

14 letters:
Brussels carpet

Carriages and carts

3 letters:
Cab
Car
Fly
Gig
Rig

4 letters:
Bier
Cart
Chay
Coch
Drag
Ekka
Pung
Shay
Sled
Trap
Wain

5 letters:
Bandy
Brake
Buggy
Coach
Coupé
Ratha
Sulky
Tonga
Wagon

6 letters:
Berlin

Britka
Calash
Chaise
Charet
Dennet
Do-si-do
Drosky
Fiacre
Gharry
Go-cart
Hansom
Herdic
Landau
Limber
Pochay
Random
Remise
Sledge
Spider
Surrey
Tandem
Troika
Whisky

7 letters:
Berline
Britska
Britzka
Calèche
Cariole
Caroche
Chariot
Chassis

Dogcart
Dos-a-dos
Droshky
Growler
Norimon
Phaeton
Tilbury
Vetture
Vis-à-vis
Voiture
Whiskey

8 letters:
Barouche
Brougham
Cape cart
Carriage
Carriole
Carryall
Clarence
Curricle
Equipage
Pochaise
Quadriga
Rickshaw
Rockaway
Sociable
Stanhope
Tarantas
Victoria

9 letters:
Britschka

Buckboard
Cabriolet
Gladstone
Horseless
Jaunty car
Landaulet
Tarantass
Wagonette
Whirligig

10 letters:
Four-in-hand
Post chaise
Stagecoach
Tim-whiskey

11 letters:
Hurly-hacket
Jaunting car

12 letters:
Covered wagon

13 letters:
Désobligeante
Spider phaeton

14 letters:
Conestoga wagon

15 letters:
Prairie schooner

Cartoon characters

3 letters:
Doc
Ren
Tom

4 letters:
Dino
Kyle
Stan

5 letters:
Bambi
Bluto
Dopey
Dumbo
Goofy
Happy
Itchy
Jerry
Kenny
Pluto
Snowy

6 letters:
Bam-Bam
Boo-Boo
Grumpy
Krusty
Popeye
Shaggy
Sleepy
Sneezy

Stimpy
Tigger
Tintin
Top Cat

7 letters:
Bashful
Cartman
Muttley
Pebbles
Swee' Pea

8 letters:
Olive Oyl
Scratchy
Yogi Bear

9 letters:
Betty Boop
Daffy Duck
Elmer Fudd
Scooby-Doo
Sylvester
Tweety-Pie

10 letters:
Donald Duck
Roadrunner

11 letters:
Bart Simpson
Betty Rubble

Lisa Simpson
Mickey Mouse
Minnie Mouse
Ned Flanders
Sideshow Bob
Wile E Coyote
Yosemite Sam

12 letters:
Barney Rubble
Homer Simpson
Marge Simpson

13 letters:
Dick Dastardly
Maggie Simpson
Officer Dibble
The Hooded Claw
Winnie the Pooh

14 letters:
Foghorn Leghorn
Fred Flintstone
Speedy Gonzalez

15 letters:
Penelope Pitstop
Wilma Flintstone

19 letters:
Groundskeeper Willie

Cases

3 letters:
Box
Pod

4 letters:
Aril
Beer
Bere
Etui
Flan
Grip
Hull
Husk
Port

5 letters:
Ascus
Blimp
Burse
Calyx
Chase
Crate
Crust
Etwee
Frame
Ocrea
Theca
Trunk
Volva

6 letters:
Basket
Chitin
Cocoon
Locket
Lorica
Manche
Ochrea
Penner
Quiver
Sheath
Telium
Valise
Walise
Wallet

7 letters:
Cabinet
Capsule
Compact
Elytron
Hanaper
Hold-all
Humidor
Keister
Nacelle
Sheathe
Six-pack
Sporran
Wardian

8 letters:
Bundwall
Canister
Cartouch
Cellaret
Dispatch
Flapjack
Indusium
Nutshell
Scabbard
Tantalus
Tea-chest
Vasculum

9 letters:
Cartouche
Cartridge
Chrysalis
Croustade
Housewife
Papeterie

10 letters:
Canterbury
Phylactery
Sabretache

12 letters:
Plummer-block

Castles

3 letters:
Man

4 letters:
Cheb
Drum
More
Rait
Trim

5 letters:
Aydon
Blois
Cabra

Cahir
Conwy
Corfe
Dinan
Hever
Leeds
Spain
Torún
Vaduz

6 letters:
Brodie
Dublin

Durham
Farney
Forfar
Glamis
Kilkea
Ludlow
Raglan
Rithes
Stuart

7 letters:
Amboise
Arundel

Ashford
Barnard
Beeston
Belvoir
Blarney
Braemar
Calzean
Canossa
Chillon
Colditz
Crathes
Culzean
Despair
Harlech
Lincoln
Otranto
Schloss
Skipton
St Mawes
Warwick
Windsor

8 letters:
Balmoral
Balvenie
Bamburgh
Bastille
Berkeley
Bunraity
Carbonek
Darnaway
Doubting
Egremont
Elephant

Elsinore
Kilkenny
Killaghy
Leamaneh
Malahide
Malperdy
Monmouth
Pembroke
Portlick
Rackrent
Richmond
Stirling
Stokesay
Taymouth
Tintagel
Urquhart
Wartburg

9 letters:
Beaumaris
Dangerous
Dunnottar
Dunsinane
Edinburgh
Esterháza
Inverness
Kilravock
Lancaster
Leicester
Pendennis
Restormel
Sherborne
Trausnitz
Vincennes

10 letters:
Caernarfon
Caerphilly
Carmarthen
Heidelberg
Kenilworth
Launceston
Pontefract

11 letters:
Aberystwyth
Carisbrooke
Eilean Donan
Gormenghast
Scarborough

12 letters:
Berkhamstead
Caerlaverock
Château-Raoul
Dunstaffnage
Fotheringhay
Herstmonceux
Rock of Cashel

13 letters:
Ballindalloch
Carrickfergus

14 letters:
Ashby de la Zouch

16 letters:
Berwick-upon-Tweed

Breeds of cat

3 letters:
Rex

4 letters:
Manx

5 letters:
Tabby

6 letters:
Angora
Havana

7 letters:
Burmese
Persian
Ragdoll
Siamese
Turkish

9 letters:
Himalayan
Maine coon

10 letters:
Abyssinian

11 letters:
Colourpoint
Russian blue

13 letters:
Bengal leopard
Tortoiseshell

Famous cats

3 letters:
Tom

4 letters:
Bast
Jinx

5 letters:
Bucky
Felix
Fritz
Hodge
Salem

6 letters:
Arthur
Bastet
Ginger

Huckle
Muessa
Selima
Top Cat

7 letters:
Bagpuss
Lucifer
Slipper

8 letters:
Garfield
Lady Jane
Scratchy
Snowball

9 letters:
Mehitabel

Mistigris
Thomasina
Tobermory

10 letters:
Grizabella
Heathcliff

11 letters:
Bombalurina
Cat in the Hat
Cheshire Cat
Mungojerrie
Puss-in-Boots
Snagglepuss

13 letters:
Fat Freddy's Cat

Cattle

BREEDS OF CATTLE

4 letters:
Aver
Gyal
Neat
Nout
Nowt
Soum
Sowm
Stot

5 letters:
Devon
Heard
Kerry
Kraal
Kyloe
Luing
Owsen
Store

6 letters:
Ankole
Catalo
Dexter

Durham
Jersey
Rother
Sussex

7 letters:
Brahman
Cattalo
Kouprey
Lairage
Lincoln
Red Poll

8 letters:
Alderney
Ayrshire
Charbray
Friesian
Galloway
Gelbvieh
Guernsey
Hereford
Highland
Holstein

Limousin
Longhorn
Normandy

9 letters:
Charolais
Friesland
Illawarra
Red Polled
Shorthorn
Simmental
Teeswater

10 letters:
Africander
Brown Swiss
Charollais
Piemontese
Simmenthal
Welsh black

11 letters:
Chillingham

BREEDS OF CATTLE (CONTINUED)

12 letters:
Norwegian Red

13 letters:
Aberdeen Angus
Texas longhorn

14 letters:
Belted Galloway
Santa Gertrudis

16 letters:
Blonde d'Aquitaine

Holstein Friesian
Meuse-Rhine-Ijssel

18 letters:
Illawarra shorthorn

CATTLE AND OTHER ARTIODACTYLS

2 letters:
Ox
Zo

3 letters:
Cow
Dzo
Elk
Gnu
Goa
Kob
Pig
Yak
Zho

4 letters:
Axis
Boar
Bull
Deer
Gaur
Goat
Ibex
Kudu
Oont
Oryx
Pudu
Sika
Stag
Tahr
Thar
Zebu

5 letters:
Addax
Argal
Ariel
Bison
Bongo

Bubal
Camel
Eland
Gayal
Goral
Izard
Jacob
Llama
Moose
Nagor
Nyala
Okapi
Oribi
Saiga
Serow
Sheep
Takin

6 letters:
Alpaca
Aoudad
Argali
Bharal
Chital
Dik-dik
Duiker
Duyker
Impala
Koodoo
Nilgai
Reebok
Rhebok
Sambar
Sambur
Vicuña
Wapiti

7 letters:
Alpacca

Blaubok
Blesbok
Brocket
Bubalis
Buffalo
Bushpig
Carabao
Caracul
Caribou
Chamois
Gazelle
Gemsbok
Gerenuk
Giraffe
Grysbok
Guanaco
Jumbuck
Karakul
Kongoni
Kouprey
Markhor
Mouflon
Muntjac
Muntjak
Nilghau
Nylghau
Peccary
Red deer
Roe deer
Sassaby
Wart hog
Water ox

8 letters:
Antelope
Babirusa
Boer goat
Bontebok
Boschbok

CATTLE AND OTHER ARTIODACTYLS (CONTINUED)

Bushbuck
Markhoor
Moufflon
Mule deer
Musk deer
Reedbuck
Reindeer
Steenbok
Wild boar

9 letters:
Blacktail
Dromedary
Hartbeest
Marshbuck
Mouse deer
Pronghorn
Razorback
Springbok

Waterbuck

10 letters:
Camelopard
Chevrotain
Hartebeest
Jacob sheep
Wildebeest

11 letters:
Barking deer
Cape buffalo
Kashmir goat

12 letters:
Hippopotamus
Klipspringer
Mountain goat
Water buffalo

13 letters:
Bactrian camel
Sable antelope

14 letters:
Père David's deer

15 letters:
White-tailed deer

16 letters:
Chinese water deer

17 letters:
Harnessed antelope
Rocky Mountain goat

See also:
➤ **Cows** ➤ **Breeds of pig** ➤ **Breeds of sheep**

Types of chair

3 letters:
Pew
Tub

4 letters:
Bath
Camp
Cane
Club
Deck
Easy
Form
Pouf
Wing

5 letters:
Bench
Sedan
Stool
Súgán
Swing

6 letters:
Barrel
Basket
Bosun's
Carver
Corner
Curule
Dining
Estate
Garden
Jampan
Morris
Pouffe
Rocker
Settle
Swivel
Throne

7 letters:
Beanbag
Berbice
Bergère

Dos-à-dos
Folding
Guérite
Hassock
Jampani
Lounger
Ottoman
Rocking
Windsor

8 letters:
Armchair
Bar stool
Bentwood
Birthing
Campaign
Captain's
Cathedra
Electric
Fauteuil
Jampanee
Recliner

Straight
Wainscot

9 letters:
Banquette
Butterfly
Director's
Highchair
Opsitbank
Reclining

10 letters:
Bucket seat
Fiddle-back
Ladder-back
Music stool
Piano stool
Wheelchair
Window seat

11 letters:
Gestatorial

12 letters:
Milking stool

13 letters:
Shooting stick
Windsor rocker

14 letters:
Platform rocker

Champagne bottles

Bottle	Capacity
Magnum	2 bottles
Jeroboam	2 magnums
Rehoboam	3 magnums
Methuselah	4 magnums
Salmanazar	6 magnums
Balthazar	8 magnums
Nebuchadnezzar	10 magnums

Channels

3 letters:
Fox

5 letters:
North

6 letters:
Queen's

7 letters:
Bristol

English
Yucatán

8 letters:
Spithead

9 letters:
St George's

10 letters:
Mozambique

11 letters:
Solway Firth

12 letters:
Saint George's

14 letters:
Molucca Passage

Cheeses

3 letters:
Ewe
Fet
Oka
Pot

4 letters:
Blue
Brie
Curd
Edam
Feta

Goat
Hard
Skyr
Tofu
Yarg

5 letters:
Caboc
Cream
Derby
Esrom
Fynbo
Goats'
Gouda
Islay
Kenno
Quark
Samsø

6 letters:
Cantal
Chèvre
Damson
Dunlop
Ermite
Junket
Orkney
Romano
Tilsit

7 letters:
Boursin
Chaumes
Cheddar
Chessel
Cottage
Crowdie
Fontina
Gjetost
Gruyère
Havarti
Kebbock
Kebbuck
Limburg
Munster
Mycella
Ricotta
Sapsago

Stilton

8 letters:
American
Bel Paese
Blue vein
Cheshire
Emmental
Halloumi
Huntsman
Muenster
Parmesan
Pecorino
Raclette
Taleggio
Tornegus
Vacherin
Vignotte

9 letters:
Amsterdam
Appenzell
Blue Vinny
Camembert
Emmenthal
Ilchester
Jarlsberg
Killarney
Leicester
Limburger
Lymeswold
Mousetrap
Neuchatel
Port-Salut
Provolone
Reblochon
Roquefort
Sage Derby
Saint Agur

10 letters:
Blue Vinney

Bonchester
Caerphilly
Cambazolla
Canestrato
Danish blue
Dolcelatte
Emmentaler
Gloucester
Gorgonzola
Lanark Blue
Lancashire
Mascarpone
Mozzarella
Neufchâtel
Red Windsor
Stracchino

11 letters:
Blue Stilton
Coulommiers
Dunsyre Blue
Emmenthaler
Ribblesdale
Wensleydale

12 letters:
Bavarian blue
Bleu de Bresse
Caciocavallo
Fromage frais
Monterey jack
Red Leicester

13 letters:
Bleu d'Auvergne

14 letters:
Blue Shropshire

16 letters:
Double Gloucester

Famous chefs

3 letters:
Hom, *Kenneth*

4 letters:
Diat, *Louis*
Gray, *Rose*
Kerr, *Graham*

Puck, *Wolfgang*
Roux, *Albert*
Roux, *Michel*
Spry, *Constance*

5 letters:
Beard, *James*
Blanc, *Raymond*
David, *Elizabeth*
Floyd, *Keith*
Leith, *Prue*
Nairn, *Nick*
Sardi, *Vincent*
Smith, *Delia*
Soyer, *Alexis*
Stein, *Rick*
White, *Marco Pierre*

6 letters:
Mrs Beeton
Bocuse, *Paul*
Elliot, *Rose*
Farmer, *Fannie*

Lawson, *Nigella*
Oliver, *Jamie*
Patten, *Marguerite*
Ramsay, *Gordon*
Rhodes, *Gary*
Slater, *Nigel*

7 letters:
Grigson, *Jane*
Harriot, *Ainsley*
Jaffrey, *Madhur*

8 letters:
Craddock, *Fanny*
Grossman, *Loyd*
Mosimann, *Anton*
Paterson, *Jennifer*

9 letters:
Carluccio, *Antonio*
Claiborne, *Craig*
Delmonico, *Lorenzo*
Escoffier, *Auguste*
McCartney, *Linda*
Prudhomme, *Paul*

13 letters:
Dickson-Wright, *Clarissa*

15 letters:
Worrall-Thompson,
  Anthony

21 letters:
Fearnley-Whittingstall,
  Hugh

Chemical elements

Chemical element	Symbol	Atomic number
Hydrogen	H	1
Helium	He	2
Lithium	Li	3
Beryllium	Be	4
Boron	B	5
Carbon	C	6
Nitrogen	N	7
Oxygen	O	8
Fluorine	F	9
Neon	Ne	10
Sodium	Na	11
Magnesium	Mg	12
Aluminium *or* aluminum	Al	13
Silicon	Si	14
Phosphorus	P	15
Sulphur *or* sulfur	S	16
Chlorine	Cl	17
Argon	Ar	18
Potassium	K	19
Calcium	Ca	20
Scandium	Sc	21
Titanium	Ti	22
Vanadium	V	23

Chemical element	Symbol	Atomic number
Chromium	Cr	24
Manganese	Mn	25
Iron	Fe	26
Cobalt	Co	27
Nickel	Ni	28
Copper	Cu	29
Zinc	Zn	30
Gallium	Ga	31
Germanium	Ge	32
Arsenic	As	33
Selenium	Se	34
Bromine	Br	35
Krypton	Kr	36
Rubidium	Rb	37
Strontium	Sr	38
Yttrium	Y	39
Zirconium	Zr	40
Niobium	Nb	41
Molybdenum	Mo	42
Technetium	Tc	43
Ruthenium	Ru	44
Rhodium	Rh	45
Palladium	Pd	46
Silver	Ag	47
Cadmium	Cd	48
Indium	In	49
Tin	Sn	50
Antimony	Sb	51
Tellurium	Te	52
Iodine	I	53
Xenon	Xe	54
Caesium *or* cesium	Cs	55
Barium	Ba	56
Lanthanum	La	57
Cerium	Ce	58
Praseodymium	Pr	59
Neodymium	Nd	60
Promethium	Pm	61
Samarium	Sm	62
Europium	Eu	63
Gadolinium	Gd	64
Terbium	Tb	65
Dysprosium	Dy	66

Chemical elements

Chemical element	Symbol	Atomic number
Holmium	Ho	67
Erbium	Er	68
Thulium	Tm	69
Ytterbium	Yb	70
Lutetium or lutecium	Lu	71
Hafnium	Hf	72
Tantalum	Ta	73
Tungsten or wolfram	W	74
Rhenium	Re	75
Osmium	Os	76
Iridium	Ir	77
Platinum	Pt	78
Gold	Au	79
Mercury	Hg	80
Thallium	Tl	81
Lead	Pb	82
Bismuth	Bi	83
Polonium	Po	84
Astatine	At	85
Radon	Rn	86
Francium	Fr	87
Radium	Ra	88
Actinium	Ac	89
Thorium	Th	90
Protactinium	Pa	91
Uranium	U	92
Neptunium	Np	93
Plutonium	Pu	94
Americium	Am	95
Curium	Cm	96
Berkelium	Bk	97
Californium	Cf	98
Einsteinium	Es	99
Fermium	Fm	100
Mendelevium	Md	101
Nobelium	No	102
Lawrencium	Lr	103
Rutherfordium	Rf	104
Dubnium	Db	105
Seaborgium	Sg	106
Bohrium	Bh	107
Hassium	Hs	108
Meitnerium	Mt	109

Chemistry

BRANCHES OF CHEMISTRY

7 letters:
Nuclear
Organic
Zymurgy

8 letters:
Chemurgy
Kinetics
Physical

9 letters:
Inorganic

10 letters:
Analytical

12 letters:
Biochemistry
Geochemistry
Zoochemistry

13 letters:
Cytochemistry
Stoichiometry

14 letters:
Astrochemistry
Histochemistry
Neurochemistry
Petrochemistry

Phonochemistry
Photochemistry
Phytochemistry
Radiochemistry

15 letters:
Immunochemistry
Stereochemistry
Thermochemistry

16 letters:
Electrochemistry
Magnetochemistry

CHEMISTRY TERMS

2 letters:
PH

3 letters:
Fat
Gas
Ion
Oil
Ore

4 letters:
Acid
Atom
Base
Bond
Foam
Fuel
Mole
Salt
Soap

5 letters:
Alloy
Anion
Anode
Chain
Ester
Ether
Inert

Metal
Solid
Sugar

6 letters:
Alkali
Alkane
Cation
Dilute
Fusion
Isomer
Liquid
Proton

7 letters:
Alcohol
Cathode
Crystal
Element
Fission
Formula
Halogen
Isotope
Mineral
Mixture
Monomer
Neutral
Neutron

Nucleus
Organic
Plastic
Polymer
Reagent
Soluble
Solvent
Valency

8 letters:
Analysis
Catalyst
Compound
Electron
Emulsion
Equation
Inert gas
Molarity
Molecule
Noble gas
Nonmetal
Reaction
Solution

9 letters:
Allotrope
Amino acid
Corrosion

CHEMISTRY TERMS (CONTINUED)

Diffusion
Electrode
Fatty acid
Inorganic
Insoluble
Ionic bond
Metalloid
Oxidation
Reduction
Saturated
Synthesis

10 letters:
Atomic mass
Combustion
Hydrolysis
Ionization
Lanthanide
Litmus test
Suspension

11 letters:
Alkali metal

Evaporation
Hydrocarbon
Precipitate
Sublimation
Unsaturated

12 letters:
Atomic number
Boiling point
Carbohydrate
Concentrated
Condensation
Covalent bond
Distillation
Electrolysis
Fermentation
Melting point

13 letters:
Chain reaction
Periodic table
Radioactivity
Redox reaction

14 letters:
Brownian motion
Chromatography
Electrovalency
Saponification

15 letters:
Crystallization
Transition metal

16 letters:
Rare-earth element

17 letters:
Van der Waals forces

18 letters:
Alkaline earth metal

20 letters:
Substitution reaction

CHEMISTS

4 letters:
Auer, *Karl*
Caro, *Heinrich*
Davy, *Humphrey*
Hall, *Charles Martin*
Hill, *Archibald Vivian*
Kipp, *Petrus Jacobus*
Mond, *Ludwig*
Swan, *Joseph Wilson*
Todd, *Alexander Robert*
Urey, *Harold Clayton*

5 letters:
Abney, *William*
Adams, *Roger*
Aston, *Francis William*
Baumé, *Antoine*
Black, *James (Whyte)*
Black, *Joseph*
Bosch, *Carl*
Boyle, *Robert*
Brown, *Herbert Charles*

Curie, *Marie*
Curie, *Pierre*
Dakin, *Henry*
Debye, *Peter Joseph Wilhelm*
Dewar, *James*
Dumas, *Jean-Baptiste André*
Eigen, *Manfred*
Ernst, *Richard Robert*
Haber, *Fritz*
Henry, *William*
Hooke, *Robert*
Libby, *Willard Frank*
Nobel, *Alfred Bernhard*
Prout, *William*
Soddy, *Frederick*

6 letters:
Barton, *Derek*
Brandt, *Georg*
Bunsen, *Robert Wilhelm*

Calvin, *Melvin*
Carver, *Geroge Washington*
Dalton, *John*
Draper, *John William*
Liebig, *Justus*
Morley, *Edward Williams*
Müller, *Paul Hermann*
Mullis, *Kary Banks*
Nernst, *Walther Hermann*
Perutz, *Max Ferdinand*
Porter, *George*
Proust, *Joseph Louis*
Ramsay, *William*
Schiff, *Hugo*
Solvay, *Ernest*
Tizard, *Henry*
Werner, *Alfred*
Wöhler, *Friedrich*
Woulfe, *Peter*

CHEMISTS (CONTINUED)

7 letters:
Abelson, *Philip*
Andrews, *Thomas*
Bergius, *Friedrich (Karl Rudolph)*
Buchner, *Eduard*
Castner, *Hamilton Young*
Crookes, *William*
Faraday, *Michael*
Fischer, *Emil Hermann*
Fischer, *Ernst Otto*
Fischer, *Hans*
Gadolin, *Johan*
Gomberg, *Moses*
Guthrie, *Samuel*
Hodgkin, *Dorothy Crowfoot*
Leblanc, *Nicolas*
Macadam, *John*
Ostwald, *Wilhelm*
Pasteur, *Louis*
Pauling, *Linus Carl*
Piccard, *Jean Félix*
Scheele, *Karl Wilhelm*
Seaborg, *Glenn Theodore*
Von Babo, *Lambert*
Warburg, *Otto Heinrich*

Ziegler, *Carl*

8 letters:
Beckmann, *Ernst Otto*
Grignard, *Victor*
Langmuir, *Irving*
Mulliken, *Robert Sanderson*
Newlands, *John Alexander*
Sabatier, *Paul*
Silliman, *Benjamin*
Smithson, *James*
Sorensen, *Soren Peter Lauritz*
Van't Hoff, *Jacobus Hendricus*
Woodward, *R(obert) B(urns)*

9 letters:
Arrhenius, *Svante August*
Butenandt, *Adolf Frederick Johann*
Cavendish, *Henry*
Cornforth, *John Warcup*
Gay-Lussac, *Joseph Louis*
Lavoisier, *Antoine Laurent*

Pelletier, *Pierre Joseph*
Priestley, *Joseph*
Prigogine, *Ilya*
Von Baeyer, *Johann Friedrich Wilhelm Adolf*
Von Hevesy, *George*
Zsigmondy, *Richard Adolf*

10 letters:
Chardonnet, *(Louis Marie) Hilaire Bernigaud*
Erlenmeyer, *Emil*
Mendeleyev, *Dmitri Ivanovich*
Van Helmont, *Jean Baptiste*

13 letters:
Von Stradonitz, *(Friedrich) August Kekulé*

25 letters:
Von Nagyrapolt Szent-Gyorgyi, *Albert*

See also:
➤ **Acids** ➤ **Alcohols** ➤ **Alkalis** ➤ **Alloys** ➤ **Chemical elements**
➤ **Compounds** ➤ **Crystals** ➤ **Hydrocarbons** ➤ **Minerals** ➤ **Molecules**
➤ **Ores** ➤ **Salts** ➤ **Silicas and silicates** ➤ **Subatomic particles** ➤ **Sugars**

Chess pieces

Piece	Abbreviation
Bishop	B
King	K
King's bishop	KB
King's knight	KN
King's rook	KR
Knight	N
Pawn	P

Piece	Abbreviation
Queen	Q
Queen's bishop	QB
Queen's knight	QN
Queen's rook	QR

Types of china

4 letters:
Goss
Ming
Waly
Ware

5 letters:
Delft
Derby
Hizen
Imari
Seric
Spode®

Wally

6 letters:
Kaolin
Minton

7 letters:
Crackle
Dresden
Limoges
Meissen

8 letters:
Coalport
Eggshell
Etrurian
Wedgwood®

9 letters:
Cameoware
Porcelain

10 letters:
Rockingham
Willowware

Christian denominations and sects

5 letters:
Amish

7 letters:
Mormons

9 letters:
Adventism
Calvinism
Methodism
Quakerism
Shakerism

10 letters:
Anabaptism

11 letters:
Anglicanism
Catholicism
Lutheranism

12 letters:
Coptic Church

Unitarianism

13 letters:
Baptist Church
Protestantism
Salvation Army

14 letters:
Evangelicalism
Maronite Church
Moravian Church
Orthodox Church
Pentecostalism

15 letters:
Byzantine Church
Episcopal Church
Latter-day Saints
Presbyterianism

16 letters:
Christian Science
Plymouth Brethren

Roman Catholicism
Society of Friends

17 letters:
Congregationalism
Jehovah's Witnesses
Unification Church

18 letters:
Christadelphianism
New Jerusalem Church

19 letters:
Dutch Reformed Church
Greek Orthodox Church
Seventh-Day Adventism

21 letters:
Eastern Orthodox
  Church
Russian Orthodox
  Church

Cinema and television

2 letters:
TV

3 letters:
Act
BBC
Cue
Fan
ITV
Set

4 letters:
Cast
Crew
Film
Hero
Mike
Part
Play
Plot
Role
Shot
Show
Star
Unit

5 letters:
Actor
Cable
Drama
Enact
Extra
Flick
Movie
Odeon
Oscar
Radio
Scene
Telly
Video

6 letters:
Camera
Ceefax
Cinema
Comedy
Critic
Make up

Movies
Rushes
Screen
Script
Serial
Series
Sit com
Studio
Talkie
TV show

7 letters:
Actress
Cartoon
Compere
Feature
Film set
Flicker
Heroine
Musical
Network
Perform
Phone-in
Pop star
Portray
Present
Produce
Sponsor
Tragedy
Trailer

8 letters:
Audience
Bioscope
Chat show
Cinerama
Comedian
Director
Festival
Film crew
Film star
Fruit pie
Newsreel
Pictures
Premiere
Producer
Quiz show
Tape deck

Telecast
Telefilm

9 letters:
Blue movie
Broadcast
Cameraman
Character
Direction
Entertain
Exhibitor
Fillm club
Film actor
Film extra
Film-strip
Flash-back
Goggle-box
Guest star
Interview
Movie-goer
Movie show
Movie star
Performer
Photoplay
Programme
Projector
Recording
Rehearsal
Soap opera
Spectacle
Title role
Voice-over

10 letters:
Commercial
Crowd scene
Home-movies
Horror film
Horse opera
Microphone
Movie actor
Needle time
Newscaster
Newsreader
On location
Performing
Production
Screenplay

Cities

Silent film
Television
The critics

Show business
Silver screen
Technicolour

Continuity girl
Feature picture
Features editor
Moving pictures
Question master
Supporting cast
Supporting film
Supporting part
Supporting role
Television play
Third Programme

11 letters:
Broadcaster
Credit title
Documentary
Echo chamber
Entertainer
Feature film
Performance
Picture show
Radio caster
Sound effect
Talking film

13 letters:
Chinese puzzle
Cinematograph
Cine projector
Clapperboards
Continuity man
Entertainment
Global village
Motion picture
Nouvelle Vague
Picture palace
Tape recording
Telerecording
Television set
Videocassette
Video recorder

15 letters:
Animated cartoon
Cable television
Cinematographer
Cinematographic
Documentary film
French subtitles
Peak viewing time
Situation comedy
Slapstick comedy
Spot advertising

12 letters:
Academy award
Cinéma vérité
Clapperboard
Film festival
Picture house
Scriptwriter

14 letters:
Cinematography
Closed circuits

Cities

4 letters:
Baku
Bari
Bonn
Brno
Cork
Gifu
Giza
Graz
Homs
Hull
Ipoh
Kano
Kiel
Kiev
Kobe
Lima
Lodz
Nice
Omsk
Oran
Oslo

Riga
Rome

5 letters:
Accra
Adana
Amman
Basle
Basra
Belem
Berne
Bursa
Cairo
Chiba
Dacca
Davao
Delhi
Essen
Genoa
Gorky
Haifa
Halle

Hanoi
Izmir
Kabul
Kazan
Kyoto
Lagos
La Paz
Leeds
Lyons
Malmo
Mecca
Miami
Milan
Mosul
Omaha
Osaka
Padua
Paris
Patna
Perth
Poona
Quito

Rabat
Sakai
Seoul
Sofia
Surat
Tampa
Tokyo
Tomsk
Tunis
Turni

6 letters:
Aachen
Abadan
Aleppo
Ankara
Asmara
Athens
Austin
Baroda
Beirut
Berlin
Bilbao
Bochum
Bogota
Bombay
Boston
Bremen
Cracow
Dallas
Dayton
Denver
Dublin
Dundee
Durban
El Paso
Frunze
Fukoka
Fushun
Gdansk
Geneva
Harbin
Havana
Ibadan
Indore
Jaipur
Kanpur
Kansas
Khulna
Kumasi

Lahore
Lisbon
London
Luanda
Lübeck
Lusaka
Madras
Madrid
Magpur
Málaga
Malang
Manila
Mexico
Moscow
Multan
Munich
Mysore
Nantes
Naples
Newark
Odessa
Oporto
Ottawa
Oxford
Panama
Peking
Penang
Poznan
Prague
Puebla
Quebec
Santos
Shiraz
St Paul
Sydney
Tabriz
Taipei
Talinn
Toledo
Venice
Verona
Vienna
Warsaw
Zagreb
Zürich

7 letters:
Abidjan
Algiers
Antwerp

Atlanta
Baghdad
Bangkok
Barnaul
Belfast
Bologna
Brescia
Bristol
Buffalo
Caracas
Cardiff
Chengtu
Chicago
Cologne
Colombo
Córdoba
Corunna
Detroit
Donetsk
Dresden
Firenze
Foochow
Glasgow
Gwalior
Hamburg
Hanover
Houston
Irkutsk
Isfahan
Jakarta
Kalinin
Karachi
Kharkov
Kowloon
Kwangju
La Plata
Leipzig
Lucknow
Managua
Memphis
Messina
Mombasa
Nairobi
Nanking
New York
Oakland
Palermo
Phoenix
Rangoon
Rosario

Cities

San Jose
San Juan
Santa Fe
Sapporo
Saratov
Seattle
Seville
Soochow
Stettin
St Louis
Taranto
Tbilisi
Teheran
Tel Aviv
Toronto
Trieste
Tripoli
Utrecht

8 letters:
Aberdeen
Adelaide
Amritsar
Auckland
Augsburg
Belgrade
Bordeaux
Bradford
Brasilia
Brisbane
Brussels
Budapest
Bulawayo
Cagliari
Calcutta
Campinas
Canberra
Capetown
Columbus
Coventry
Curitiba
Damascus
Dortmund
Duisborg
Edmonton
Florence
Gorlovka
Hague, The
Haiphong
Hamilton

Hangchow
Helsinki
Honolulu
Istanbul
Katmandu
Katowice
Khartoum
Kingston
Kinshasa
Kumamoto
Kweiyang
Mandalay
Mannheim
Montreal
Murmansk
Nagasaki
Oklahoma
Peshawar
Plymouth
Portland
Port Said
Pretoria
Pyongang
Richmond
Salonika
Salt Lake
San Diego
Santiago
Sao Paulo
Sarajevo
Shanghai
Sholapur
Srinagar
Tashkent
Tientsin
Toulouse
Winnipeg
Yokohama

9 letters:
Ahmedabad
Allahabad
Amagasaki
Amsterdam
Archangel
Asahikawa
Astrakhan
Baltimore
Bangalore
Barcelona

Brunswick
Bucharest
Cambridge
Cartagena
Chengchow
Chihuahua
Cleveland
Des Moines
Edinburgh
Fort Worth
Frankfurt
Guatemala
Guayaquil
Hamamatsu
Hiroshima
Hyderabad
Jerusalem
Karlsruhe
Krasnodar
Kuibyshev
Kwangchow
Las Palmas
Leicester
Leningrad
Liverpool
Magdeburg
Maracaibo
Marrakesh
Melbourne
Milwaukee
Nuremburg
Reykjavik
Rotterdam
Salisbury
Samarkand
Saragossa
Sheffield
Singapore
Stockholm
Stuttgart
Vancouver
Volgograd
Wuppertal

10 letters:
Addis Ababa
Alexandria
Baton Rouge
Birmingham
Bratislava

Canterbury
Casablanca
Chittagong
Cincinnati
Coimbatore
Copenhagen
Düsseldorf
Gothenburg
Jamshedpur
Krivoi Roig
Los Angeles
Louisville
Manchester
Marseilles
Monte Video
New Orleans
Nottingham
Pittsburgh
Portsmouth
Rawalpindi
Sacramento
San Antonio

Strasbourg
Sunderland
Sverdlovsk
Tananarive
Valparaiso
Washington
Wellington

11 letters:
Baranquilla
Braunshweig
Buenos Aires
Chelyabinsk
Dar-es-Salaam
Guadalajara
Kuala Lumpur
Mar del Plata
Novosibirsk
Pondicherry
Rostov-on-Don
San Salvador
Southampton
Vladivostok

12 letters:
Barquisimeto
Bloemfontein
Indianapolis
Jacksonville
Johannesburg
Magnitogorsk
Philadelphia
Port-au-Prince
Rio de Janeiro
San Francisco
Santo Domingo
Stoke-on-Trent

13 letters:
Gelsenkirchen
Karl-Marx-Stadt
Port Elizabeth
Shihkiachwang
Wolverhampton

14 letters:
Dnepropetrovsk

Clothing

ARTICLES OF CLOTHING

3 letters:
Aba
Alb
Tie

4 letters:
Abba
Body
Bubu
Coat
Gown
Haik
Hose
Izar
Kilt
Muff
Rami
Robe
Sari
Sash
Shoe

Slop
Sock
Toga
Vest
Wrap

5 letters:
Abaya
Ao dai
Apron
Burka
Burqa
Cardy
Chaps
Cimar
Cotta
Dress
Ephod
Fanon
Frock
Gilet

Glove
Ihram
Jupon
Kanga
Kanzu
Levis
Pilch
Plaid
Ramée
Ramie
Ruana
Saree
Shawl
Shift
Shirt
Smock
Stola
Stole
Tanga
Thong
Tunic

ARTICLES OF CLOTHING (CONTINUED)

6 letters:
Barrow
Basque
Bikini
Blouse
Bodice
Bolero
Boubou
Braces
Caftan
Cardie
Chador
Chimer
Cilice
Coatee
Cossie
Dirndl
Dolman
Exomis
Garter
Halter
Jacket
Jerkin
Jersey
Jibbah
Jubbah
Jumper
Kaftan
Kameez
Kaross
Khanga
Kimono
Kittel
Mantle
Mitten
Peplos
Rochet
Sarong
Serape
Shorts
Skivvy
Tabard
Tallit
Tights
Trunks
T-shirt
Zephyr

7 letters:
Baldric
Blouson
Bourkha
Burnous
Bustier
Busuuti
Catsuit
Chapeau
Chuddah
Chuddar
Chudder
Costume
Dashiki
Djibbah
Doublet
Exomion
Hauberk
Leotard
Maillot
Manteau
Necktie
Nightie
Overall
Pajamas
Paletot
Pallium
Partlet
Pelisse
Pyjamas
Rompers
Shalwar
Singlet
Soutane
Sporran
Surcoat
Sweater
Tank top
Tunicle
Unitard
Wrapper
Yashmac
Yashmak

8 letters:
Bathrobe
Bodysuit
Cardigan

Chasuble
Chausses
Codpiece
Dalmatic
Galluses
Gambeson
Himation
Jump suit
Negligée
Overcoat
Pashmina
Peignoir
Pelerine
Pullover
Scapular
Surplice
Swimsuit
Tee shirt

9 letters:
Cover-slut
Dungarees
Housecoat
Loincloth
Mandilion
Mandylion
Nightgown
Overskirt
Pantihose
Pantyhose
Sanbenito
Waistcoat

10 letters:
Chaparajos
Chaparejos
Cote-hardie
Cummerbund
Jeistiecor
Kummerbund
Nightdress
Nightshirt
Oversleeve
Salopettes
Suspenders

11 letters:
Bathing suit

ARTICLES OF CLOTHING (CONTINUED)

Bib and brace
Breechcloth
Dreadnought

12 letters:
Body stocking
Dressing gown
Undergarment

14 letters:
Bathing costume
Swimming trunks

15 letters:
Swimming costume

PARTS OF CLOTHING

3 letters:
Arm
Hem
Leg

4 letters:
Cuff
Hood
Seam
Tail
Yoke

5 letters:
Dicky
Jabot
Lapel

Train
Waist

6 letters:
Armlet
Bodice
Collar
Gusset
Lining
Pocket
Sleeve

7 letters:
Armhole
Flounce
Hemline

8 letters:
Neckline
Shoulder

9 letters:
Epaulette
Waistline

10 letters:
Buttonhole

11 letters:
Patch pocket
Shawl collar

TYPES OF CLOTHING

4 letters:
Hose

5 letters:
Mufti
Slops

6 letters:
Armour
Civies
Livery
Samfoo

7 letters:
Civvies
Hosiery
Uniform
Weepers

8 letters:
Black tie

Fatigues
Froufrou
Knitwear
Lingerie
Neckwear
Skivvies
Swimwear
White tie

9 letters:
Beachwear
Clericals
Coveralls
Long-coats
Millinery
Nightwear
Sackcloth
Separates
Underwear

10 letters:
Canonicals
Fancy dress
Sportswear

11 letters:
Baby clothes
Coordinates
Long clothes
Underthings
Widow's weeds

12 letters:
Evening dress
Morning dress
Nightclothes
Overgarments

TYPES OF CLOTHING (CONTINUED)

13 letters:
Academic dress

Highland dress
Undergarments

16 letters:
Swaddling clothes

See also:
➤ **Caps** ➤ **Coats and cloaks** ➤ **Dresses** ➤ **Hats** ➤ **Hoods** ➤ **Jackets**
➤ **Scarves** ➤ **Shirts** ➤ **Shoes and boots** ➤ **Skirts** ➤ **Socks and tights**
➤ **Suits** ➤ **Sweaters** ➤ **Ties and cravats** ➤ **Trousers and shorts**
➤ **Underwear**

Types of cloud

3 letters:
Fog

4 letters:
Haze
Mist

5 letters:
Storm

6 letters:
Cirrus
Nimbus

7 letters:
Cumulus
Stratus

8 letters:
Water-dog
Woolpack

9 letters:
Goat's hair
Mare's tail

11 letters:
Altocumulus
Altostratus

False cirrus
Thunderhead

12 letters:
Cirrocumulus
Cirrostratus
Cumulonimbus
Nimbostratus

13 letters:
Fractocumulus
Fractostratus
Stratocumulus

Types of club

3 letters:
Bat

4 letters:
Cosh
Kiri
Mace
Maul
Mell
Mere
Meri
Patu
Polt

5 letters:
Basto
Lathi

Waddy

6 letters:
Alpeen
Cudgel
Kierie
Priest

7 letters:
Bourdon

8 letters:
Bludgeon
Shillala
Trunnion

9 letters:
Blackjack
Knobstick
Truncheon

10 letters:
Knobkerrie
Nightstick
Nulla-nulla
Shillelagh

12 letters:
Quarterstaff

13 letters:
Life preserver

Clubs

3 letters:
RAC

4 letters:
Bath
Golf

5 letters:
Disco
Slate
Youth

6 letters:
Brook's
Cotton
Drones
Guards
Jockey
Kitcat
Monday
Reform
Rotary
Savage
Savile
White's

7 letters:
Adelphi
Almack's
Boodles
Carlton
Cavalry
Country
Garrick
Hampden
Jacobin
Kiwanis
Leander
Variety

8 letters:
Atheneum
Hell-fire
Rotarian

9 letters:
Athenaeum
Beefsteak

10 letters:
Crockford's

Devonshire
Landsdowne
Oddfellows
Travellers

11 letters:
Army and Navy
Caterpillar
Discotheque

12 letters:
Conservative

13 letters:
Junior Carlton
Thatched House

14 letters:
Constitutional
United Services

15 letters:
National Liberal

Coats and cloaks

3 letters:
Aba
Box
Car
Fur
Mac
Top

4 letters:
Abba
Capa
Cape
Cope
Hair
Hood
Jack
Jump
Mack
Polo

Rail
Sack
Seal
Tail
Tent
Toga
Warm
Wool

5 letters:
Abaya
Acton
Amice
Dress
Frock
Grego
Jelab
Jemmy
Jupon

Lammy
Loden
Manta
Palla
Parka
Pilch
Sagum
Tails

6 letters:
Abolla
Achkan
Afghan
Anarak
Anorak
Capote
Chimer
Coatee
Covert

Dolman
Domino
Duffel
Duster
Fleece
Fun fur
Jacket
Jerkin
Joseph
Kaross
Lammie
Mantle
Parkee
Peplum
Poncho
Raglan
Riding
Tippet
Trench
Tuxedo
Ulster
Vestry
Visite

7 letters:
Admiral
Burnous
Cassock
Chimere
Chlamys
Chuddah
Chuddar
Crombie®
Cutaway
Galabea
Galabia
Hacking
Jellaba
Manteel
Mantlet
Matinee
Morning
Mozetta
Paenula
Paletot
Pallium
Peacoat
Pelisse
Posteen
Rocklay

Rokelay
Sarafan
Slicker
Snorkel
Spencer
Surcoat
Surtout
Swagger
Topcoat
Zamarra
Zamarro

8 letters:
Barathea
Bathrobe
Benjamin
Burberry®
Burnoose
Burnouse
Capuchin
Cardinal
Chasuble
Djellaba
Galabieh
Gambeson
Hall-robe
Haqueton
Himation
Jellabah
Jodhpuri
Mackinaw
Mantelet
Mantilla
Overcoat
Peignoir
Poshteen
Raincoat
Revestry
Scapular
Sherwani
Taglioni
Tailcoat
Vestiary

9 letters:
Balmacaan
Caracalla
Chlamydes
Coat dress
Djellabah

Gabardine
Gaberdine
Gallabeah
Greatcoat
Hacqueton
Housecoat
Inverness
Macintosh
Newmarket
Opera hood
Pea jacket
Petersham
Redingote
Sheepskin
Sou'wester
Undercoat

10 letters:
Fearnaught
Fearnought
Gallabiyah
Gallabiyeh
Mackintosh
Opera cloak
Roquelaure
Ulsterette
Waterproof
Windjammer
Wrap-rascal

11 letters:
Dreadnaught
Dreadnought
Swallowtail

12 letters:
Chesterfield
Dressing gown
Mousquetaire
Paludamentum
Prince Albert

13 letters:
Swallow-tailed

Cocktails

3 letters:
Cup
Kir
Nog

4 letters:
Nogg

5 letters:
Bumbo
Glogg
Julep
Punch
Sling
Twist

6 letters:
Atomic
Caudle
Cooler
Crusta
Eggnog
Gibson
Gimlet
Mojito
Orgasm
Rickey
Zombie

7 letters:
Bellini
Cobbler
Collins
Egg flip
Fustian
Martini

Negroni
Oenomel
Pink gin
Sangria
Sazerac
Sidecar
Stengah
Stinger
Swizzle

8 letters:
Aperitif
Bullshot
Cold duck
Daiquiri
Gin sling
Highball
Pink lady
Sangaree
Sillabub
Snowball
Spritzer
Syllabub

9 letters:
Alexander
Americano
Buck's fizz
Claret cup
Cuba libre
Manhattan
Margarita
Milk punch
Mint julep
Rusty Nail
Whisky mac

White lady

10 letters:
Bloody Mary
Dry martini
Moscow Mule
Piña colada
Tom Collins

11 letters:
Black velvet
Screwdriver
Whiskey sour

12 letters:
Black Russian
Old-fashioned

13 letters:
Long Island Tea
Planter's punch

14 letters:
Singapore sling

15 letters:
Brandy Alexander

16 letters:
Harvey Wallbanger

23 letters:
Slow Screw Against the
  Wall

Coffees

4 letters:
Java

5 letters:
Black
Brown
Decaf
Irish

Latte
Mocha
White

6 letters:
Gaelic
Kenyan

7 letters:
Arabica
Instant
Robusta
Turkish

8 letters:
Café noir

Coins

Espresso

9 letters:
Americano
Brazilian
Colombian
Macchiato

10 letters:
Café au lait
Cappuccino
Costa Rican
Mochaccino

11 letters:
Continental
Frappuccino

French roast
Skinny latte

12 letters:
Blue mountain

13 letters:
Decaffeinated

Coins

1 letter:
D

2 letters:
As
DM
Kr
Rd
Xu

3 letters:
Ban
Bar
Bob
Cob
Dam
Ecu
Fen
Fil
Fin
Flu
Hao
Jun
Kip
Lat
Lei
Lek
Leu
Lev
Lew
Mil
Mna
Moy
Ore
Pul
Pya
Red

Sen
Sol
Som
Sou
Won
Yen
Zuz

4 letters:
Anna
Baht
Bani
Birr
Buck
Cedi
Cent
Chon
Dibs
Dime
Doit
Dong
Dram
Duro
Euro
Fiat
Fils
Inti
Jack
Jane
Jiao
Kina
Kobo
Kuna
Kyat
Lari
Lion
Lira

Loti
Maik
Mark
Merk
Mina
Obol
Para
Paul
Peag
Peni
Peso
Pice
Pula
Puli
Punt
Rand
Real
Reis
Rial
Riel
Rock
Ryal
Sene
Slog
Spur
Tael
Taka
Tala
Toea
Vatu
Yuan
Zack

5 letters:
Agora
Angel
Asper

Aurar
Baiza
Bekah
Belga
Bodle
Broad
Brown
Butat
Butut
Chiao
Colon
Conto
Crore
Crown
Daric
Dibbs
Dinar
Dobra
Ducat
Eagle
Eyrir
Franc
Fugio
Gerah
Groat
Grosz
Haler
Krona
Krone
Kroon
Kurus
Laari
Laree
Leone
Liard
Litas
Livre
Louis
Lyart
Maile
Manat
Maneh
Mohur
Mongo
Mopus
Naira
Nakfa
Ngwee
Noble
Obang

Oscar
Paisa
Paolo
Pence
Pengo
Penie
Penni
Penny
Plack
Pound
Razoo
Rider
Royal
Ruble
Rupee
Sceat
Scudo
Scute
Semis
Sente
Shand
Soldo
Souon
Sucre
Sycee
Tenge
Thebe
Tical
Ticky
Tolar
Toman
Tyiyn
Zaire
Zimbi
Zloty

6 letters:
Aureus
Balboa
Bawbee
Bender
Bezant
Boddle
Byzant
Canary
Centas
Copeck
Couter
Dalasi
Danace

Deaner
Décime
Denier
Derham
Dirham
Dirhem
Dodkin
Dollar
Double
Drachm
Ekuele
Escudo
Filler
Florin
Forint
Gilder
Gourde
Guinea
Gulden
Halala
Heller
Hryvna
Jitney
Kobang
Koruna
Kroner
Kroona
Kwacha
Kwanza
Lepton
Likuta
Loonie
Makuta
Mancus
Markka
Mawpus
Pa'anga
Pagoda
Pataca
Pennia
Peseta
Pesewa
Qintar
Rappen
Rouble
Rupiah
Santum
Satang
Sceatt
Seniti

Coins

Sequin
Shekel
Sickle
Siglos
Stater
Stiver
Stotin
Talent
Tanner
Tester
Teston
Thaler
Tickey
Toonie
Tugrik
Turner
Vellon
Wakiki

7 letters:
Afghani
Austral
Bolivar
Cardecu
Carolus
Centavo
Chetrum
Cordoba
Crusado
Drachma
Ekpwele
Guarani
Guilder
Hryvnya
Jacobus
Joannes
Kreuzer
Lemoira
Metical
Millime
Milreis
Moidore
Ostmark
Ouguiya
Patrick
Piastre
Piefort

Pistole
Pollard
Quarter
Quetzal
Ringgit
Ruddock
Rufiyaa
Sextans
Solidus
Spanker
Tambala
Testoon
Testril
Thrimsa
Thrymsa
Tughrik
Unicorn
Xerafin

8 letters:
Brockage
Cardecue
Cruzeiro
Denarius
Doubloon
Ducatoon
Emalengi
Farthing
Groschen
Johannes
Kreutzer
Llangeni
Louis d'or
Maravedi
Millieme
Napoleon
Ngultrum
Picayune
Pistolet
Planchet
Portague
Portigue
Quadrans
Rigmarie
Semuncia
Sesterce
Shilling

Skilling
Solidare
Stotinka
Xeraphim
Zecchino

9 letters:
Boliviano
Britannia
Centesimo
Dandiprat
Dandyprat
Didrachma
Dupondius
Luckpenny
Pistareen
Rennminbi
Rix-dollar
Rose noble
Schilling
Sovereign
Spur-royal
Yellowboy
Zwanziger

10 letters:
Broadpiece
Chervonets
Krugerrand
Portcullis
Reichsmark

11 letters:
Deutschmark
Sword-dollar
Tetradrachm

12 letters:
Antoninianus

13 letters:
Rennminbi yuan

18 letters:
Maria Theresa dollar

Collective nouns

Noun	Collective Noun
Actors	Company
Aldermen	Bench, guzzle
Bakers	Tabernacle
Bishops	Bench
Critics	Shrivel
Directors	Board
Eggs	Clutch
Flowers	Bouquet
Inventions	Budget
Judges	Bench
People	Audience, crowd, congregation, horde, mob
Poems	Garland
Policemen	Posse
Prisoners	Gang
Remedies	Rabble
Rumours	Nest
Sailors	Crew
Ships	Fleet
Stories	Anthology
Thieves	Gang
Workmen	Gang

Collectors and enthusiasts

Collector/enthusiast	Object
Ailurophile	Cats
Arctophile	Teddy bears
Audiophile	High-fidelity sound reproduction
Automobilist	Cars
Bibliophile	Books
Brolliologist	Umbrellas
Campanologist	Bell-ringing
Cartophilist	Cigarette cards
Cruciverbalist	Crosswords
Deltiologist	Picture postcards
Discophile	Gramophone records
Fusilatelist	Phonecards
Herbalist	Herbs
Lepidopterist	Moths and butterflies

Colleges

Collector/enthusiast	Object
Medallist	Medals
Numismatist	Coins
Oenophile	Wine
Paranumismatist	Coin-like objects
Philatelist	Stamps
Phillumenist	Matchbox labels
Phraseologist	Phrases
Scripophile	Share certificates
Vexillologist	Flags
Zoophile	Animals

Colleges

3 letters:
New

4 letters:
City
Dana
Eton
Fife
Iona
Reed
Snow
Taft
York

5 letters:
Bates
Chase
Clare
Green
Jesus
Keble
King's
Oriel
Peace
Ripon
Salem
Smith
Union
Wells

6 letters:
Bethel
Boston

Darwin
Durham
Exeter
Geneva
Girton
Gordon
Hebrew
Ithaca
Merton
Queen's
Selwyn
Thomas
Vassar
Wadham

7 letters:
Amherst
Aquinas
Balliol
Barnard
Bedford
Bermuda
Bowdoin
Chatham
Christ's
Concord
Cornell
Cypress
Douglas
Downing
Emerson
Erskine
Kellogg

Linacre
Lincoln
New Hall
Newnham
St Anne's
St Cross
St Hugh's
St John's
St Paul's
Trinity
Wolfson

8 letters:
All Souls
Bryn Mawr
Carleton
Columbia
Emmanuel
Findhorn
Hamilton
Hastings
Hertford
Homerton
Illinois
Imperial
Lewisham
Longwood
Magdalen
Meredith
Monmouth
National
Nuffield
Pembroke

183

Comedians

Robinson
St Hilda's
St Peter's

Wellesley
Worcester

Regent's Park
Springfield
Trinity Hall

9 letters:
Brasenose
Churchill
Clare Hall
Claremont
Gateshead
Guildford
Hampshire
Haverford
Kalamazoo
Lafayette
Magdalene
Manhattan
Mansfield
Newcastle
St Antony's
St Edmund's
Templeton

10 letters:
Chesapeake
Goldsmith's
Greyfriars
Heidelberg
Hughes Hall
Huntingdon
Middlebury
Paul Smith's
Peterhouse
Somerville
St Stephen's
University
Washington

11 letters:
Blackfriars
Campion Hall
Fitzwilliam
King Alfred's

12 letters:
Christ Church
Sidney Sussex
St Benet's Hall
St Catharine's
St Catherine's
St Edmund Hall
Wycliffe Hall

13 letters:
Corpus Christi
Lucy Cavendish

16 letters:
Gonville and Caius
Harris Manchester
Lady Margaret Hall

See also:
➤ **Academic degrees** ➤ **Education terms** ➤ **Ivy League universities**
➤ **Oxbridge colleges** ➤ **Schools** ➤ **Types of school**

Comedians

3 letters:
Dee, *Jack*
Fry, *Stephen*
Ray, *Ted*
Wax, *Ruby*

4 letters:
Ali G
Ball, *Lucille*
Barr, *Roseanne*
Cook, *Peter*
Dodd, *Ken*
Hill, *Benny*
Hill, *Harry*
Hope, *Bob*
Hudd, *Roy*
Idle, *Eric*
Marx, *Chico*
Marx, *Groucho*

Marx, *Harpo*
Marx, *Zeppo*
Sims, *Joan*
Took, *Barry*
Wall, *Max*
Wise, *Ernie*
Wood, *Victoria*

5 letters:
Allen, *Dave*
Allen, *Woody*
Askey, *Arthur*
Benny, *Jack*
Borge, *Victor*
Brand, *Jo*
Bruce, *Lenny*
Burns, *George*
Chase, *Chevy*
Cohen, *Sacha Baron*

Cosby, *Bill*
Drake, *Charlie*
Elton, *Ben*
Emery, *Dick*
Goons, *The*
Hardy, *Jeremy*
Hardy, *Oliver*
Henry, *Lenny*
Hicks, *Bill*
Horne, *Kenneth*
James, *Sidney*
Jones, *Griff Rhys*
Jones, *Spike*
Jones, *Terry*
Leary, *Denis*
Lewis, *Jerry*
Lloyd, *Harold*
Moore, *Dudley*
Myers, *Mike*

Oddie, *Bill*
Palin, *Michael*
Pryor, *Richard*
Robey, *Sir George*
Sayle, *Alexei*
Smith, *Linda*
Smith, *Mel*
Starr, *Freddie*
Sykes, *Eric*
Worth, *Harry*

6 letters:
Abbott, *Bud*
Abbott, *Russ*
Bailey, *Bill*
Barker, *Ronnie*
Carrey, *Jim*
Cleese, *John*
Coogan, *Steve*
Cooper, *Tommy*
Dawson, *Les*
De Vito, *Danny*
Fields, *W(illiam) C(laude)*
French, *Dawn*
Garden, *Graeme*
Howerd, *Frankie*
Izzard, *Eddie*
Junkin, *John*
Keaton, *Buster*
Laurel, *Stan*
Laurie, *Hugh*
Lehrer, *Tom*
Martin, *Steve*
Mayall, *Rik*
Merton, *Paul*
Murphy, *Eddie*
Proops, *Greg*
Reeves, *Vic*

Ullman, *Tracey*
Wisdom, *Norman*

7 letters:
Aykroyd, *Dan*
Baddiel, *David*
Belushi, *John*
Bentine, *Michael*
Bremner, *Rory*
Carrott, *Jasper*
Chaplin, *Charlie*
Chapman, *Graham*
Charles, *Craig*
Corbett, *Ronnie*
Crystal, *Billy*
Edwards, *Jmmey*
Enfield, *Harry*
Everett, *Kenny*
Feldman, *Marty*
Gervais, *Ricky*
Goodman, *John*
Grammer, *Kelsey*
Hancock, *Tony*
Handley, *Tommy*
Jacques, *Hattie*
Manning, *Bernard*
Matthau, *Walter*
Newhart, *Bob*
Rushton, *Willie*
Secombe, *Harry*
Sellers, *Peter*
Tarbuck, *Jimmy*
Toksvig, *Sandi*
Ustinov, *Sir Peter*

8 letters:
Coltrane, *Robbie*
Connolly, *Billy*

Costello
Edmonson, *Adrian*
Goldberg, *Whoopi*
Groening, *Matt*
Milligan, *Spike*
Mortimer, *Bob*
Sadowitz, *Jerry*
Saunders, *Jennifer*
Seinfeld, *Jerry*
Sessions, *John*
Williams, *Kenneth*
Williams, *Robin*

9 letters:
Humphries, *Barry*
Monkhouse, *Bob*
Morecombe, *Eric*
Whitfield, *June*

10 letters:
Pete and Dud
Stephenson, *Pamela*
Whitehouse, *Paul*

11 letters:
Monty Python
Terry-Thomas

12 letters:
Brooke-Taylor, *Tim*

14 letters:
Rowan and Martin

15 letters:
The Marx Brothers
The Three Stooges

Comets

4 letters:
Wild

7 letters:
Halley's

8 letters:
Borrelly
Hale-Bopp

Kohoutek

9 letters:
Hyakutake
Oort cloud

11 letters:
Swift-Tuttle

13 letters:
Shoemaker-Levy

19 letters:
Schwassmann-
  Wachmann

Commonwealth members

4 letters:
Fiji

5 letters:
Ghana
India
Kenya
Malta
Nauru
Samoa
Tonga

6 letters:
Belize
Brunei
Canada
Cyprus
Guyana
Malawi
Tuvalu
Uganda
Zambia

7 letters:
Grenada
Jamaica
Lesotho
Namibia

Nigeria
St Lucia
Vanuatu

8 letters:
Barbados
Botswana
Cameroon
Dominica
Kiribati
Malaysia
Maldives
Pakistan
Sri Lanka
Tanzania
Zimbabwe

9 letters:
Australia
Mauritius
Singapore
Swaziland
The Gambia

10 letters:
Bangladesh
Mozambique

New Zealand
Seychelles
The Bahamas

11 letters:
Sierra Leone
South Africa

13 letters:
United Kingdom

14 letters:
Papua New Guinea
Solomon Islands

15 letters:
St Kitts and Nevis

17 letters:
Antigua and Barbuda
Trinidad and Tobago

25 letters:
St Vincent and The
   Grenadines

Communications

2 letters:
IT
PA

3 letters:
BCD
Cue
Dah
Dit
Dot
DVD
FAQ
Fax
FTP
IAP
ICT

ISP
LAN
Net
Out
TMT
URL
WAN
WAP
Web
XML

4 letters:
Alfa
Byte
CCTA
Code

Dash
Data
E-CRM
E-FIT
HTML
Java
Link
Mail
Mast
Over
Page
SGML
Site
Spam
WiFi
Worm

5 letters:
Bleep
Carry
Comms
Crier
Datum
DOVAP
Email
Flame
GMDSS
Inbox
Media
Modem
Pager
Radar
Radio
Stamp
Telex
Virus

6 letters:
Aerial
Browse
Cipher
Codify
Convey
Decode
Direct
Encode
Letter
Mayday
Medium
Nettie
Newbie
Outbox
Return
Server
Trojan
Usenet

7 letters:
Bleeper
Browser
Courier
Decrypt
DEW line
Digital
Dossier
En clair
Encrypt

Entropy
Evernet
E-wallet
Lurking
Message
Meta tag
Nethead
Netizen
Network
Tapping
Webcast
Web page
Website

8 letters:
Anti-site
Blocking
Boob tube
Chatroom
Codeword
Computer
Coverage
Data bank
Database
Decipher
Diaphone
Dispatch
Disperse
E-address
Envelope
E-payment
Ethernet
Firewall
Internet
Intranet
Listen in
Minidish
New media
Postmark
Register
Registry
Semaphor
Wireless

9 letters:
Aldis lamp
Bandwidth
Bluetooth
Broadband
Cybercafé

Digital TV
Direction
Directory
E-commerce
Facsimile
Frequency
Hypertext
Mass media
Morse code
Paperless
Royal Mail
Satellite
Snail mail
Telephone
Time-stamp

10 letters:
Beam aerial
Come across
Correspond
Dead letter
Degenerate
Fax machine
JavaScript
Media event
Memorandum
Multimedia
Netiquette
Silicon Fen
Ticker tape
Ultrafiche
Undirected

11 letters:
Address book
Chain letter
Communicate
Cryptograph
Dactylology
Mailing list
Mobile phone
Safe surfing
Silicon Glen

12 letters:
Cause célèbre
Conversation
Cryptography
Email address
Registration

Silicon Alley
Silver surfer

13 letters:
Bandspreading
Communication
Communicative
Correspondent
Cryptanalysis
Dead letter box
Dispatch rider
Online banking
Rural delivery
Satellite dish
Silicon Valley

14 letters:
Conversational
Correspondence
Electronic mail
Registered post

16 letters:
Recorded delivery

17 letters:
Branch instruction
Desktop publishing
General Post Office

18 letters:
Bottom-up processing
Exclusive OR circuit
Wireless networking

20 letters:
Digital versatile disk

21 letters:
Information technology

23 letters:
Internet Service
   Provider

Compass points

Compass Point	Abbreviation
North	N
North by East	N by E
North North East	NNE
North East by North	NE by N
North East	NE
North East by East	NE by E
East North East	ENE
East by North	E by N
East	E
East by South	E by S
East South East	ESE
South East by East	SE by E
South East	SE
South East by South	SE by S
South South East	SSE
South by East	S by E
South	S
South by West	S by W
South South West	SSW
South West by South	SW by S
South West	SW
South West by West	SW by W
West South West	WSW
West by South	W by S
West	W
West by North	W by N

Compass Point	Abbreviation
West North West	WNW
North West by West	NW by W
North West	NW
North West by North	NW by N
North North West	NNW
North by West	N by W

Cardinal point	Related adjective
North	Arctic *or* boreal
East	Oriental
South	Meridional *or* austral
West	Occidental *or* hesperidan

Composers

CLASSICAL COMPOSERS

3 letters:
Bax, *Arnold*

4 letters:
Adam, *Adolphe*
Arne, *Thomas*
Bach, *Carl Philipp Emanuel*
Bach, *Johann Christian*
Bach, *Johann Christoph Friedrich*
Bach, *Johann Sebastian*
Bach, *Wilhelm Friedemann*
Berg, *Alban*
Blow, *John*
Bull, *John*
Byrd, *William*
Cage, *John*
Dima, *Gheorghe*
Ives, *Charles*
Lalo, *Édouard*
Nono, *Luigi*
Orff, *Carl*
Pärt, *Arvo*
Peri, *Jacopo*
Raff, *Joachim*
Ward, *David*
Weir, *Judith*
Wolf, *Hugo*

5 letters:
Adams, *John*
Alwyn, *William*
Auber, *Daniel François Espirit*
Auric, *Georges*
Balfe, *Michael William*
Berio, *Luciano*
Biber, *Heinrich*
Bizet, *Georges*
Bliss, *Arthur*
Bloch, *Ernest*
Boito, *Arrigo*
Boyce, *William*
Brian, *Havergal*
Bruch, *Max*
Crumb, *George*
D'Indy, *Vincent*
Dukas, *Paul*
Dupré, *Marcel*
Dutch, *Jan Pieterszoon Sweelinck*
Elgar, *Edward*
Fauré, *Gabriel*
Field, *John*
Finzi, *Gerald*
Glass, *Philip*
Gluck, *Christoph Willibald*
Grieg, *Edvard*

Harty, *Sir (Herbert) Hamilton*
Haydn, *Franz Joseph*
Haydn, *Michael*
Henze, *Hans Werner*
Holst, *Gustav*
Ibert, *Jacques*
Jones, *Daniel*
Lawes, *Henry*
Lawes, *William*
Lehár, *Franz*
Liszt, *Franz*
Lloyd, *George*
Locke, *Matthew*
Loewe, *Karl*
Lully, *Jean Baptiste*
Nyman, *Michael*
Ogdon, *John*
Parry, *Hubert*
Prout, *Ebenezer*
Ravel, *Maurice*
Reger, *Max*
Reich, *Steve*
Rieti, *Vittorio*
Rossi, *Luigi*
Satie, *Erik*
Smyth, *Ethel*
Sousa, *John Philip*
Suppe, *Franz von*
Tosti, *Francesco Paolo*

CLASSICAL COMPOSERS (CONTINUED)

Verdi, *Giuseppi*
Watts, *Isaac*

6 letters:
Alfven, *Hugo*
Arnold, *Malcolm*
Azione
Barber, *Samuel*
Bartók, *Béla*
Boulez, *Pierre*
Brahms, *Johannes*
Bridge, *Frank*
Burney, *Charles*
Busoni, *Ferruccioni*
Carter, *Eliot*
Carver, *Robert*
Casals, *Pablo*
Chopin, *Frédéric*
Clarke, *Jeremiah*
Coates, *Eric*
Czerny, *Karl*
Davies, *Peter Maxwell*
Delius, *Frederick*
Doráti, *Antal*
Duparc, *Henri*
Dvořák, *Antonín*
Enesco, *Georges*
Farmer, *John*
Flotow, *Friedrich Freiherr von*
Franck, *César*
German, *Sir Edward*
Glière, *Reinhold*
Glinka, *Mikhail Ivanovich*
Gounod, *Charles François*
Gurney, *Ivor*
Halévy, *Fromental*
Handel, *George Frederick*
Harris, *Roy*
Hummel, *Johann Nepomuk*
Joplin, *Scott*
Kodály, *Zoltán*
Lassus, *Orlandus*
Ligeti, *György*
Mahler, *Gustav*
Martin, *Frank*

Mingus, *Charles*
Morley, *Thomas*
Mozart, *Leopold*
Mozart, *Wolfgang Amadeus*
Ogolon
Rameau, *Jean Philippe*
Rubbra, *Edmund*
Schütz, *Heinrich*
Straus, *Oscar*
Tallis, *Thomas*
Thomas, *Ambroise*
Varèse, *Edgar*
Varèse, *Edgard*
Wagner, *Richard*
Walton, *William*
Webern, *Anton*

7 letters:
Albéniz, *Isaac*
Allegri, *Gregorio*
Antheil, *George*
Bantock, *Granville*
Bellini, *Vincenzo*
Bennett, *Richard Rodney*
Berlioz, *Hector*
Berners, *Gerald*
Borodin, *Aleksandr Porfirevich*
Britten, *Benjamin*
Brubeck, *Dave (David Warren)*
Copland, *Aaron*
Corelli, *Arcangelo*
Debussy, *Claude*
De Falla, *Manuel*
Delibes, *Léo*
De Lisle, *Claude Joseph Rouget*
Des Prés, *Josquin*
Di Lasso, *Orlando*
Dowland, *John*
Duruflé, *Maurice*
Gibbons, *Orlando*
Górecki, *Henryk*
Ireland, *John*
Janáček, *Leoš*
Joachim, *Joseph*

Knussen, *Oliver*
Krommer, *Franz*
Kubelik, *Raphael*
Lambert, *Constant*
Lutyens, *Elisabeth*
Martinů, *Bohuslav*
Menotti, *Gian Carlo*
Milhaud, *Darius*
Nicolai, *Carl Otto Ehrenfried*
Nielsen, *Carl*
Poulenc, *Francis*
Puccini, *Giacomo*
Purcell, *Henry*
Purnell, *Alton*
Quilter, *Roger*
Rodrigo, *Joaquín*
Romberg, *Sigmund*
Rossini, *Gioacchino Antonio*
Roussel, *Albert*
Salieri, *Antonio*
Schuman, *William*
Simpson, *Robert*
Smetana, *Bedřich*
Stainer, *John*
Strauss, *Johann*
Strauss, *Richard*
Tartini, *Giuseppe*
Tavener, *John*
Thomson, *Virgil*
Tippett, *Michael*
Vivaldi, *Antonio*
Warlock, *Peter*
Weelkes, *Thomas*
Wellesz, *Egon*
Xenakis, *Yannis*

8 letters:
Alaleona, *Domenico*
Albinoni, *Tomaso*
Benjamin, *Arthur*
Berkeley, *Lennox*
Bonporti, *Francesco Antonio*
Bruckner, *Anton*
Chabrier, *Emmanuel*
Chausson, *Ernest*

CLASSICAL COMPOSERS (CONTINUED)

Cimarosa, *Domenico*
Couperin, *François*
De Lassus, *Roland*
Gabrieli, *Andrea*
Gabrieli, *Giovanni*
Gershwin, *George*
Gesualdo, *Carlo*
Glazunov, *Aleksandr Konstantinovich*
Goossens, *Eugene*
Grainger, *Percy*
Granados, *Enrique*
Holliger, *Heinz*
Honegger, *Arthur*
Korngold, *Erich*
Kreutzer, *Conradin*
Maconchy, *Elizabeth*
Marcello, *Benedetto*
Marenzio, *Luca*
Martland, *Steve*
Mascagni, *Pietro*
Massenet, *Jules Émile Frédéric*
Messager, *André*
Messiaen, *Olivier*
Musgrave, *Thea*
Ockeghem, *Johannes*
Paganini, *Niccolò*
Panufnik, *Andrzej*
Respighi, *Ottorino*
Schnabel, *Artur*
Schubert, *Franz*
Schumann, *Clara*
Schumann, *Robert*
Scriabin, *Aleksandr Nikolayvich*
Sessions, *Roger*
Sibelius, *Jean*
Stanford, *Charles*
Taverner, *John*
Telemann, *Georg Philipp*
Von Weber, *Carl Maria*
Williams, *Ralph Vaughan*

9 letters:
Balakirev, *Mily Alexeyevich*
Bernstein, *Leonard*

Bocherini, *Luigi*
Boulanger, *Nadia*
Broughton, *Bruce*
Buxtehude, *Dietrich*
Carpenter, *John Alden*
Chaminade, *Cecile*
Cherubini, *Luigi*
De Machaut, *Guillaume*
Donizetti, *Gaetano*
Dunstable, *John*
Dutilleux, *Henri*
Ginastera, *Alberto*
Hildegard *of Bingen*
Hindemith, *Paul*
Klemperer, *Otto*
MacMillan, *James*
Meyerbeer, *Giacomo*
Offenbach, *Jacques*
Pachelbel, *Johann*
Pergolesi, *Giovanni Battista*
Prokofiev, *Sergei Sergeyevich*
Scarlatti, *Alessandro*
Scarlatti, *Domenico*
Schnittke, *Alfred*
Takemitsu, *Toru*
Tortelier, *Paul*
Von Flotow, *Friedrich*
Whitehead, *Gillian*
Zemlinsky, *Alexander*

10 letters:
Canteloube, *Joseph*
De Victoria, *Tomás Luis*
Monteverdi, *Claudio*
Mussorgsky, *Modest Petrovich*
Paderewski, *Ignace Jan*
Palestrina, *Giovanni Pierluigi da*
Penderecki, *Krzystof*
Ponchielli, *Amilcare*
Praetorius, *Michael*
Rawsthorne, *Alan*
Rubinstein, *Anton Grigorevich*
Saint-Saëns, *Camille*

Schoenberg, *Arnold*
Sculthorpe, *Peter*
Stravinsky, *Igor Fyodorovich*
Villa-Lobos, *Heitor*
Williamson, *Malcolm*

11 letters:
Birtwhistle, *Harrison*
Butterworth, *George*
Charpentier, *Gustave*
Charpentier, *Marc-Antoine*
Frescobaldi, *Girolamo*
Fürtwangler, *Wilhelm*
Humperdinck, *Englebert*
Leoncavallo, *Ruggiero*
Lutosławski, *Witold*
Mendelssohn, *Fanny*
Mendelssohn, *Felix*
Rachmaninov, *Sergei Vassilievich*
Stockhausen, *Karlheinz*
Szymanowski, *Karol*
Tchaikovsky, *Pyotr Ilyich*
Theodorakis, *Mikis*
Von Dohnányi, *Ernst*
Wolf-Ferrari, *Ermanno*

12 letters:
Dallapiccola, *Luigi*
Khachaturian, *Aram Ilich*
Rostropovich, *Mstislav Leopoldovich*
Shostakovich, *Dmitri Dmitriyevich*
Van Beethoven, *Ludwig*

14 letters:
Jaques-Dalcroze, *Émile*
Rimsky-Korsakov, *Nikolai Andreyevich*

15 letters:
Coleridge-Taylor, *Samuel*

POPULAR COMPOSERS, SONGWRITERS, AND LYRICISTS

4 letters:
Baez, *Joan*
Bart, *Lionel*
Brel, *Jacques*
Cahn, *Sammy*
Duke, *Vernon*
Hart, *Lorenz*
John, *Elton*
Kern, *Jerome (David)*
King, *Carole*
Mann, *Barry*
Monk, *Thelonious (Sphere)*
Rice, *Tim*
Webb, *Jimmy*
Weil, *Cynthia*

5 letters:
Arlen, *Harold*
Barry, *John*
Bowie, *David*
Brown, *Nacio Herb*
Cohan, *George*
Cohen, *Leonard*
Dixon, *Willie*
Dylan, *Bob*
Handy, *W(illiam) C(hristopher)*
Jarre, *Maurice*
Jobim, *Antonio Carlos*
Loewe, *Frederick*
Pomus, *Doc*
Shore, *Howard*
Simon, *Paul*
Styne, *Jule*
Weill, *Kurt*

6 letters:
Berlin, *Irving*
Coward, *Noel*
Dozier, *Lamont*
Foster, *Stephen*
Goffin, *Gerry*
Herman, *Jerry*
Jagger, *Mick*
Lehrer, *Tom*
Lennon, *John*
Lerner, *Alan Jay*
Lieber, *Jerry*
McColl, *Ewan*
McColl, *Kirsty*
McHugh, *Jimmy*
Nelson, *Willie*
Porter, *Cole*
Strong, *Barrett*
Waites, *Tom*
Warren, *Harry*
Wilson, *Brian*

7 letters:
Gilbert, *W(illiam) S(chwenck)*
Guthrie, *Woody*
Holland, *Brian*
Holland, *Eddie*
Johnson, *Robert*
Loesser, *Frank*
Mancini, *Henry*
Manilow, *Barry*
Novello, *Ivor*
Rodgers, *Richard*
Romberg, *Sigmund*
Stoller, *Mike*
Youmans, *Vincent*

8 letters:
Gershwin, *George*
Hamlisch, *Marvin*
Mitchell, *Joni*
Morrison, *Van*
Richards, *Keith*
Robinson, *William 'Smokey'*
Sondheim, *Stephen*
Sullivan, *Arthur*
Williams, *Hank*
Williams, *John*

9 letters:
Bacharach, *Burt*
Bernstein, *Leonard*
Ellington, *Duke*
Goldsmith, *Jerry*
Ledbetter, *Huddie 'Leadbelly'*
McCartney, *Paul*
Strayhorn, *Billy*
Toussaint, *Allen*
Van Heusen, *Johnny*
Whitfield, *Norman*

10 letters:
Carmichael, *Hoagy*
Goldenthal, *Elliot*
Livingston, *Jay*

11 letters:
Hammerstein, *Oscar*
Lloyd-Webber, *Andrew*

13 letters:
Kristofferson, *Kris*

Compounds

3 letters:
Azo

4 letters:
Alum
EDTA
Enol

Haem
Heme
TEPP
Urea

5 letters:
Allyl

Amide
Amino
Azide
Azine
Azole
Diazo
Diene

Dimer
Diode
Erbia
Ester
Furan
Halon
Imide
Imine
Lipid
Olein
Oxide
Oxime
Potin
Pyran
Sarin
Tabun
Thiol
Trona
Vinyl

6 letters:
Acetal
Alkane
Alkene
Arsine
Baryta
Borane
Calque
Cetane
Chrome
Cresol
Epimer
Fluate
Glycol
Halide
Haloid
Hexene
Isatin
Isomer
Ketone
Lithia
Niello
Phenol
Pinene
Potash
Purine
Pyrone
Retene
Silane
Speiss

Tartar
Tetryl
Thymol
Triene
Trimer
Uranyl

7 letters:
Acetone
Acridin
Aglycon
Ammonia
Benzene
Betaine
Bromide
Caliche
Calomel
Camphor
Carbide
Chelate
Choline
Cinerin
Creatin
Cumarin
Cyanide
Diamine
Diazine
Diazole
Dioxide
Dvandva
Epoxide
Erinite
Ethanol
Eugenol
Fenuron
Flavone
Hormone
Hydrate
Hydride
Indican
Indoxyl
Lactate
Menthol
Metamer
Monomer
Nitrite
Oxazine
Peptone
Polymer
Protein

Quassia
Quinoid
Quinone
Realgar
Skatole
Steroid
Sulfide
Syncarp
Taurine
Terpene
Toluene
Tritide
Uridine
Wolfram

8 letters:
Acridine
Aglycone
Aldehyde
Alizarin
Arginine
Butyrate
Catenane
Chloride
Chromene
Coenzyme
Coumarin
Creatine
Cyanogen
Datolite
Dieldrin
Dopamine
Farnesol
Fluoride
Glycogen
Hydroxyl
Indoform
Isologue
Ketoxime
Lecithin
Massicot
Melamine
Monoxide
Pentosan
Peroxide
Piperine
Ptomaine
Pyrazole
Rock-alum
Rotenone

Selenate
Silicide
Siloxane
Sodamide
Stilbene
Sulphide
Sulphone
Tautomer
Tetroxid
Thiazide
Thiazine
Thiazole
Thiotepa
Thiourea
Titanate
Triazine
Triazole
Trilling
Tyramine
Urethane
Xanthate
Xanthine
Zirconia

9 letters:
Aflatoxin
Alicyclic
Aliphatic
Anhydride
Biguanide
Carbazole
Carnitine
Cellulose
Cementite
Cortisone
Deuteride
Dipeptide
Disulfram
Endorshin
Ferrocene

Flavanone
Glycoside
Guanosine
Haematein
Histamine
Hydrazide
Hydroxide
Imidazole
Impsonite
Ionophore
Monoamine
Pentoxide
Phenoxide
Pheromone
Phosphide
Piperonal
Polyamine
Porphyrin
Qinghaosu
Quercetus
Quinidine
Serotonin
Tetroxide
Veratrine

10 letters:
Amphoteric
Argyrodite
Dimethoate
Disulphide
Enkephalin
Isocyanate
Lumisterol
Mercaptide
Nucleoside
Phenocaine
Picrotoxin
Piperazine
Piperidine
Propionate

Putrescine
Tatpurusha
Thimerosal
Tocopherol

11 letters:
Acetanilide
Amphetamine
Coprosterol
Dimercaprol
Electrolyte
Fluorescein
Ghitathione
Hydrocarbon
Neostigmine
Sesquioxide

12 letters:
Carbohydrate
Formaldehyde
Haematoxylin
Hydroquinone
Permanganate
Polyurethane
Triglyceride
Trimethadine

13 letters:
Catecholamine
Cycloheximide
Isoproterenol
Metronidazole
Nortriptyline
Trinucleotide

14 letters:
Oxyhaemoglobin
Polycarboxylic
Polyunsaturate
Trohalomethane

Computer games

3 letters:
Jak

4 letters:
Doom
Halo

6 letters:
Driver
Far Cry

7 letters:
RockMan

Top Spin

8 letters:
Half-Life
Max Payne
Ragnarok

Star Wars
Warcraft
Xenosaga

9 letters:
Ace Combat
Bejeweled
Guild Wars
Homeworld
Spy Hunter

10 letters:
Call of Duty
Dragon Fire
Fight Night
Fire Emblem
Primal Rage
Redemption
Terminator

11 letters:
Ghost Master
Ninja Gaiden

12 letters:
Age of Wonders
Apocalyptica
City of Heroes
Return to Arms
Viewtiful Joe

13 letters:
Rise of Nations

14 letters:
Ace Yeti Trapper
Ancient Empires
Backyard Skater
Beyond Divinity

Grand Theft Auto
Massive Assault
Prince of Persia

15 letters:
Freedom Fighters
Pro Rugby Manager
Red Dead Revolver
Samurai Warriors

16 letters:
Sonic the Hedgehog
Unreal Tournament

18 letters:
Railsport Challenge
Supermario Brothers

Computers

COMPUTER PARTS

3 letters:
ALU
CPU
MTU
VDU

4 letters:
Case
Chip
DIMM
Disk
DRAM
Port
SIMM

5 letters:
Modem
Mouse
SDRAM

6 letters:
DDR-RAM
Memory
Screen
Webcam

7 letters:
Console
Counter
Encoder
Monitor
Printer
Scanner
Speaker
USB port

8 letters:
Disk unit
Emulator
Joystick
Keyboard
LCD panel

9 letters:
Cartridge
Digitizer
Disk drive
DVD reader
DVD writer
Hard drive
Interface

Processor
Sound card
Trackball

10 letters:
CD-rewriter
CD-Rom drive
Control key
Daisywheel
Floppy disk
Transistor

11 letters:
Line printer
Motherboard
Multiplexor
Optical disk

12 letters:
Coaxial cable
Graphics card
Laser printer

13 letters:
Digital camera

COMPUTER PARTS (CONTINUED)

14 letters:
Flatbed scanner
Microprocessor
Optical scanner

16 letters:
Magnetic tape unit

17 letters:
Integrated circuit

Visual display unit

18 letters:
Digital audio player

19 letters:
Arithmetic logic unit
Printed circuit board

21 letters:
Central processing unit

22 letters:
Optical character reader

24 letters:
Analogue-digital
   converter

COMPUTER TERMS

2 letters:
AI
I/O
IT
PC

3 letters:
Bit
Bpi
Bug
Bus
CAD
CAE
CAI
CAL
CAM
CAT
CBT
CIM
COL
COM
DAC
DMA
DOS®
Dpi
DTP
FAT
FTP
Gif
ICL
IDE
Job
LAN
OCR
OEM

PDA
Pdf
RAM
ROM
Run
SAM
USB
WAN
WAP
XML

4 letters:
ADSL
Area
Bomb
Boot
Byte
Cast
CISC
Code
Data
Dump
Echo
Edit
Exit
File
Flag
Gate
Giga-
GIGO
Host
HTML
Icon
IKBS
ISDN

Jpeg
Kilo-
Load
Loop
Mega-
Menu
Midi
Mpeg
Node
Open
PROM
RISC
SCSI
SGML
Sort
UNIX®
WIMP
Word
Worm

5 letters:
Array
ASCII
Brain
CD-Rom
Clock
Crash
Cyber
Cycle
Datel®
Digit
Earom
E-mail
Eniac
EPROM

COMPUTER TERMS (CONTINUED)

ERNIE
Field
Flops
Fuzzy
Input
JANET
Key in
Log in
Macro
Micro
Patch
Pixel
Queue
Rerun
Reset
Sense
Stack
Store
Tally
Tower
Virus
Voxel
Warez

6 letters:
Access
Analog
Applet
Backup
Buffer
Bundle
Busbar
CADCAM
CADMAT
Caster
Cookie
Cursor
Device
Driver
Duplex
Earcon
EBCDIC
Editor
EEPROM
Figure
Hacker
Holmes
Hot key

Infect
Kludge
Laptop
Legacy
Linker
Log out
Module
Online
OR gate
Output
Packet
Parser
Prompt
Read in
Reboot
Record
Scroll
Server
Sprite
String
SWITCH
Syntax
System
TAURUS
Toggle
Uptime
Window
Wizard

7 letters:
ActiveX
Address
AND gate
Capture
Chipset
Clip art
Command
Corrupt
Counter
Databus
Default
Desktop
Digital
Freenet
Gateway
Install
Keyword
Lapheld

Manager
Measure
Network
NOR gate
NOT gate
Numlock
Offline
Package
Palette
Palmtop
Pointer
Power up
Process
Program
Read out
Routine
Run time
Time out
Utility
Vaccine
WYSIWIG
Wysiwyg

8 letters:
Analogue
Assemble
Autosave
Backbone
Beta-test
Black box
Calculus
Checksum
Chiphead
Compiler
Constant
Data bank
Database
Digitize
Document
Download
Downsize
Down time
Emulator
Estimate
Extranet
Fail-safe
Filename
Firewall

COMPUTER TERMS (CONTINUED)

FireWire
Firmware
Freeware
Function
Gigabyte
Graphics
Hard card
Hard copy
Hardware
Idle time
Internet
Intranet
Kilobyte
Language
Liveware
Location
Megabyte
Morphing
NAND gate
Optimize
Overflow
Password
Platform
Portable
Printout
Protocol
Pushdown
Realtime
Reckoner
Skinning
Software
TALISMAN
Terabyte
Terminal
Topology
Tristate
Variable
Wild card

9 letters:
Algorithm
Alpha-test
Assembler
Authoring
Bandwidth
Bluetooth
Bootstrap
Broadband

Bus master
Calculate
Character
Co-routine
Cybercafé
Cyberpunk
Debugging
Directory
Dithering
Dot matrix
Ecommerce
Flowchart
Groupware
Handshake
Hard-wired
Hypertext
Interface
Interrupt
Logic bomb
Mainframe
Multi-user
Parameter
Power down
Procedure
Processor
Retrieval
Shareware
Smart card
Statement
Tetrabyte
Trackball
Underflow
User group

10 letters:
3D graphics
Access time
Address bus
Compatible
Core memory
Cyberspace
Encryption
Fileserver
Hypermedia
Initialize
Integrator
Linked list
Main memory

Menu-driven
Patch board
Programmer
README file
Robustness
Scratchpad
Stand-alone
Subroutine
Throughput
Transcribe
Translator
Transputer
Voice input
Webcasting

11 letters:
Antialising
Base address
Binary digit
Bits per inch
Cache memory
Clickstream
Computerate
Computerize
Concordance
Cut and paste
Cybernetics
Data capture
Dots per inch
File manager
Function key
Help screens
Input device
Input/output
Instruction
Interactive
Interpreter
Machine code
Mail bombing
Multiaccess
NAND circuit
Parity check
Screensaver
Spreadsheet
Superserver
Systems disk
Time sharing
Trackerball

COMPUTER TERMS (CONTINUED)

Work station

12 letters:
Architecture
Backing store
Digital fount
Disassembler
Dumb terminal
Error message
Expert system
Global search
Housekeeping
Logic circuit
Minicomputer
Mobile device
Remote access
Reserved word
Search engine
Shell program
Telesoftware
World Wide Web

13 letters:
Audio response
Bulletin board
Configuration
Data structure
Decision table
Escape routine
Expansion slot
Memory mapping
Microcomputer
Multi-threaded
Neurocomputer
Object program
Query language
Queuing theory
Source program
Storage device
Supercomputer
Turnkey system
Virtual memory
Voice response
Word processor

14 letters:
Binary notation
Communications

Condition codes
Cross assembler
Data processing
Data protection
Digital imaging
Digital mapping
Document reader
Electronic mail
Hybrid computer
Magnetic bubble
Microprocessor
Neural computer
Number-cruncher
Plug compatible
Read only memory
Source document
Teleprocessing
Text processing
User-defined key
Virtual address
Virtual reality
Virtual storage
Volatile memory
Web development

15 letters:
Absolute address
Archival storage
Automatic repeat
Batch processing
Command language
Computer science
Control commands
Digital computer
Fifth-generation
Machine learning
Machine readable
Operating system
Packet-switching
Palmtop computer
Storage capacity
Store and forward
Systems analysis

16 letters:
Analogue computer
Assembly language
Computer graphics

Digital watermark
Distributed logic
Electronic office
Hand-held computer
Image enhancement
Interactive video
Local area network
Logic programming
Low-level language
Multiprogramming
Notebook computer
Personal computer
Program generator
Program statement
Sequential access
Serial processing
Voice recognition

17 letters:
Branch instruction
Desktop publishing
Development system
Front-end processor
High-level language
Speech recognition
Top-down processing
Visual programming

18 letters:
Application program
Bottom-up processing
Database management
Direct memory access
Exclusive OR circuit
Incremental plotter
Machine translation
Parallel processing
Random access memory
Real-time processing
Serial access memory

19 letters:
Computer-aided design
Computer typesetting
Direct-access storage
Disk operating system®
Hexadecimal notation
Incremental recorder

COMPUTER TERMS (CONTINUED)

Intelligent terminal
Polymorphic function
Programming language
Random-access storage
Software engineering

20 letters:
Computer aided trading
Computer conferencing
Concurrent processing
Dataflow architecture
Electronic publishing
File transfer protocol
Restricted users group

21 letters:
Computer-aided
  learning
Computer-aided
  teaching
Computer-based
  training
Decision support
  system
Information technology

22 letters:
Artificial intelligence
Graphical user interface

23 letters:
Computer-aided
  management

24 letters:
Computer-aided
  engineering
Computer-aided
  instruction
Computer-aided
  manufacture
Computer-assisted
  learning
Computer input on
  microfilm

25 letters:
Distributed array
  processor
Windows icons menus
  pointers

26 letters:
Programmable read
  only memory

28 letters:
Random Instruction Set
  Computer

29 letters:
Complex instruction set
  computer
Computer integrated
  manufacture
Original equipment
  manufacturer
Reduced instruction set
  computer
Small Computer
  Systems Interface

31 letters:
Intelligent knowledge-
  based system

32 letters:
Floating-point
  operations per second

33 letters:
Computer-aided design
  and manufacture

34 letters:
Electronic flight
  information systems

41 letters:
Extended binary-coded
  decimal-interchange
  code

COMPUTER SCIENTISTS

4 letters:
Cray, *Seymour*

5 letters:
Aiken, *Howard*
Gates, *Bill*

6 letters:
Eckert, *John Presper*

Turing, *Alan Mathison*

7 letters:
Babbage, *Charles*
Mauchly, *John W.*

8 letters:
Lovelace, *Ada (Countess of)*

Sinclair, *Clive*

9 letters:
Hollerith, *Herman*

10 letters:
Berners-Lee, *Tim*
Von Neumann, *John*

See also:
➤ **Computer games** ➤ **Internet domain names** ➤ **Programming languages**

Containers for liquid

3 letters:
Can
Jar
Jug
Keg
Tin

4 letters:
Cask
Tube

5 letters:
Flask
Gourd
Tinny

6 letters:
Barrel

Bottle
Carafe
Carton
Coldie
Firkin
Flagon
Magnum
Stubby

7 letters:
Amphora
Ampulla
Pitcher
Polypin

8 letters:
Decanter

Hogshead
Jeroboam
Rehoboam
Screw-top
Tantalus

9 letters:
Balthazar
Miniature

10 letters:
Half-bottle
Methuselah
Salmanazar

14 letters:
Nebuchadnezzar

Confectionery

3 letters:
Gem
Gum

4 letters:
Jube
Kiss
Mint
Rock

5 letters:
Candy
Dolly
Fudge
Halva
Lolly
Taffy

6 letters:
Bonbon
Button
Cachou
Comfit
Confit
Dainty
Dragée

Halvah
Humbug
Jujube
Nougat
Sorbet
Sundae
Tablet
Toffee

7 letters:
Brittle
Caramel
Fondant
Gumdrop
Halavah
Lozenge
Panocha
Praline
Sherbet
Truffle

8 letters:
Acid drop
All-sorts
Bull's eye
Licorice

Lollipop
Marzipan
Noisette
Pastille
Peardrop
Scroggin
Stickjaw

9 letters:
Blackball
Chocolate
Fruit drop
Jelly baby
Jelly bean
Lemon drop
Liquorice
Marchpane

10 letters:
Brandyball
Candyfloss
Chewing gum
Coconut ice
Gob-stopper
Nanaimo bar
Peppermint

Pick and mix
Soft-centre

11 letters:
Barley sugar
Boiled sweet
Marshmallow
Toffee apple

12 letters:
Burnt-almonds
Butterscotch

13 letters:
Fruit pastille

14 letters:
Turkish delight

20 letters:
Hundreds and
  thousands

Continents

4 letters:
Asia

6 letters:
Africa
Europe

9 letters:
Australia

10 letters:
Antarctica

12 letters:
North America
South America

Cookery

GENERAL COOKERY TERMS

3 letters:
Fry
Ice

4 letters:
Bake
Bard
Boil
Chef
Cook
Dice
Ghee
Jerk
Lard
Luau
Mash
Mask
Meze
Rise
Roux
Soup
Stew
Whip

5 letters:
Au jus

Barde
Baste
Broth
Cured
Dough
Farci
Flour
Fumet
Glacé
Glaze
Grate
Gravy
Grill
Icing
Knead
Ladle
Offal
Paste
Poach
Purée
Roast
Sauce
Sauté
Steam
Stock

Sweat
Tikka
Yeast

6 letters:
Au lait
Barbie
Batter
Blanch
Braise
Coddle
Commis
Corned
Creole
Entrée
Fajita
Fillet
Flambé
Fondue
Goujon
Lardon
Leaven
Mornay
Panada
Potage
Ragout

GENERAL COOKERY TERMS (CONTINUED)

Season
Sippet
Smoked

7 letters:
À la king
À la mode
Caterer
Cobbler
Cuisine
Curried
Custard
Garnish
Giblets
Goulash
Lardoon
Liaison
Marengo
Marmite
Newburg
Parboil
Rissole
Roulade
Supreme
Timbale
Topping

8 letters:
Au gratin
Barbecue
Browning
Chasseur
Colander
Consommé

Cookbook
Dressing
En croute
Gelatine
Julienne
Marinade
Marinate
Meunière
Mirepoix
Scramble
Tandoori
Teriyaki
Unsmoked

9 letters:
Antipasto
Au naturel
Blackened
Carbonado
Casserole
Char-grill
Cook-chill
Entremets
Fricassee
Lyonnaise
Macedoine
Oven-ready
Salipicon
Tenderize
Undressed
Wholemeal

10 letters:
Caramelise

Jardinière
Médaillons
Medallions
Parmentier
Provençale
Rijstaffel
Royal icing
Stroganoff
Unleavened
Wholewheat

11 letters:
Chafing dish
Cookery book
En brochette
Graham flour
Hors d'oeuvre

12 letters:
Boil-in-the-bag
Confectioner
Sweet-and-sour

13 letters:
Silver service

14 letters:
Cuisine minceur
Wholemeal flour

15 letters:
Nouvelle cuisine

CUISINES AND COOKING STYLES

4 letters:
Ital
Thai

5 letters:
Balti
Greek
Halal
Tapas
Vegan

6 letters:
French
Indian
Kosher
Tex-Mex

7 letters:
Chinese
Italian
Mexican
Seafood

Sichuan
Turkish

8 letters:
Fast food
Japanese
Szechuan

9 letters:
Cantonese
Caribbean

CUISINES AND COOKING STYLES (CONTINUED)

Malaysian
Provençal

10 letters:
Cordon bleu
Indonesian
Vegetarian

11 letters:
Californian
Home cooking

12 letters:
Haute cuisine

13 letters:
Gutbürgerlich

International
Mediterranean

14 letters:
Cuisine minceur

15 letters:
Nouvelle cuisine

Countries

4 letters:
Chad
Cuba
Fiji
Iran
Iraq
Laos
Mali
Oman
Peru
Togo

5 letters:
Belau
Benin
Chile
Congo
Egypt
Gabon
Ghana
Haiti
India
Italy
Japan
Kenya
Libya
Malta
Nauru
Nepal
Niger
Qatar
Samoa
Spain
Sudan
Syria

Tonga
Wales
Yemen

6 letters:
Angola
Belize
Bhutan
Brazil
Brunei
Canada
Cyprus
France
Gambia
Greece
Guinea
Guyana
Israel
Jordan
Kuwait
Latvia
Malawi
Mexico
Monaco
Norway
Panama
Poland
Russia
Rwanda
Serbia
Sweden
Taiwan
Turkey
Tuvalu
Uganda

Zambia

7 letters:
Albania
Algeria
Andorra
Armenia
Austria
Bahamas
Bahrain
Belarus
Belgium
Bolivia
Burundi
Comoros
Croatia
Denmark
Ecuador
England
Eritrea
Estonia
Finland
Georgia
Germany
Grenada
Hungary
Iceland
Jamaica
Lebanon
Lesotho
Liberia
Moldova
Morocco
Myanmar
Namibia

Countries

Nigeria
Romania
Senegal
Somalia
St Lucia
Surinam
Tunisia
Ukraine
Uruguay
Vanuatu
Vietnam

8 letters:
Barbados
Botswana
Bulgaria
Cambodia
Cameroon
Colombia
Djibouti
Dominica
Ethiopia
Honduras
Kiribati
Malaysia
Mongolia
Pakistan
Paraguay
Portugal
Scotland
Slovakia
Slovenia
Sri Lanka
Tanzania
Thailand
Zimbabwe

9 letters:
Argentina
Australia
Cape Verde
Costa Rica
East Timor
Greenland
Guatemala

Indonesia
Kirghizia
Lithuania
Macedonia
Mauritius
Nicaragua
San Marino
Singapore
Swaziland
Venezuela

10 letters:
Azerbaijan
Bangladesh
El Salvador
Kazakhstan
Luxembourg
Madagascar
Mauritania
Micronesia
Montenegro
Mozambique
New Zealand
North Korea
Puerto Rico
Seychelles
South Korea
Tajikistan
Uzbekistan
Yugoslavia

11 letters:
Afghanistan
Burkina-Faso
Côte d'Ivoire
Netherlands
Philippines
Saudi Arabia
Sierra Leone
South Africa
Switzerland
Vatican City

12 letters:
Guinea-Bissau

Turkmenistan

13 letters:
American Samoa
Czech Republic
Liechtenstein
United Kingdom

14 letters:
Papua New Guinea
Solomon Islands

15 letters:
Marshall Islands
Northern Ireland
St Kitts and Nevis

16 letters:
Equatorial Guinea

17 letters:
Antigua and Barbuda
Dominican Republic
Republic of Ireland
Trinidad and Tobago

18 letters:
Republic of Maldives
São Tomé and Principe
United Arab Emirates

20 letters:
Bosnia and Herzegovina

21 letters:
United States of America

22 letters:
Central African Republic
People's Republic of
   China

25 letters:
St Vincent and the
   Grenadines

See also:
➤ **Commonwealth members** ➤ **Dependencies** ➤ **Members of the**
European Union ➤ **Republics**

Counties

ENGLISH COUNTIES

4 letters:
Kent

5 letters:
Devon
Essex

6 letters:
Dorset
Durham
Surrey

7 letters:
Bristol
Cumbria
Norfolk
Rutland
Suffolk

8 letters:
Cheshire
Cornwall
Somerset

9 letters:
Berkshire

Hampshire
Wiltshire

10 letters:
Derbyshire
East Sussex
Lancashire
Merseyside
Shropshire
West Sussex

11 letters:
Isle of Wight
Oxfordshire
Tyne and Wear

12 letters:
Bedfordshire
Lincolnshire
Warwickshire
West Midlands

13 letters:
Greater London
Herefordshire

Hertfordshire
Staffordshire
West Yorkshire

14 letters:
Cambridgeshire
Leicestershire
Northumberland
North Yorkshire
South Yorkshire
Worcestershire

15 letters:
Buckinghamshire
Gloucestershire
Nottinghamshire

16 letters:
Northamptonshire

17 letters:
Greater Manchester

21 letters:
East Riding of Yorkshire

FORMER ENGLISH COUNTIES

4 letters:
Kent

5 letters:
Devon
Essex

6 letters:
Dorset
Durham
Surrey

7 letters:
Norfolk
Rutland

8 letters:
Cheshire

Cornwall
Somerset

9 letters:
Berkshire
Hampshire
Wiltshire

10 letters:
Cumberland
Derbyshire
East Sussex
Lancashire
Shropshire
West Sussex

11 letters:
East Suffolk

Oxfordshire
Westmorland
West Suffolk

12 letters:
Bedfordshire
Lincolnshire
Warwickshire

13 letters:
East Yorkshire
Greater London
Herefordshire
Hertfordshire
Staffordshire
West Yorkshire

FORMER ENGLISH COUNTIES (CONTINUED)

14 letters:
Leicestershire
Northumberland
North Yorkshire
Worcestershire

15 letters:
Buckinghamshire
Gloucestershire
Nottinghamshire

16 letters:
Northamptonshire

25 letters:
Huntingdon and
  Peterborough

26 letters:
Cambridgeshire and Isle
  of Ely

SCOTTISH COUNTIES

4 letters:
Fife

5 letters:
Angus
Moray

6 letters:
Orkney

7 letters:
Falkirk

8 letters:
Highland
Shetland
Stirling

10 letters:
Dundee City

Eilean Siar
Inverclyde
Midlothian

11 letters:
East Lothian
Glasgow City
West Lothian

12 letters:
Aberdeen City
East Ayrshire
Renfrewshire
Western Isles

13 letters:
Aberdeenshire
Argyll and Bute
North Ayrshire

South Ayrshire

15 letters:
City of Edinburgh
Perth and Kinross
Scottish Borders

16 letters:
Clackmannanshire
East Renfrewshire
North Lanarkshire
South Lanarkshire

18 letters:
East Dunbartonshire
West Dunbartonshire

19 letters:
Dumfries and Galloway

FORMER SCOTTISH COUNTIES

4 letters:
Bute
Fife

5 letters:
Angus
Banff
Moray
Nairn

6 letters:
Argyll
Dundee
Orkney

7 letters:
Glasgow
Kinross

8 letters:
Aberdeen
Ayrshire
Roxburgh
Shetland

9 letters:
Caithness
Edinburgh

10 letters:
Banffshire

Kincardine
Midlothian
Nairnshire
Perthshire
Sutherland

11 letters:
East Lothian
Lanarkshire
West Lothian

12 letters:
Berwickshire
Kinross-shire
Peeblesshire

FORMER SCOTTISH COUNTIES (CONTINUED)

Renfrewshire
Selkirkshire
Wigtownshire

13 letters:
Aberdeenshire
Dumfriesshire
Roxburghshire

Stirlingshire

14 letters:
Dunbartonshire
Inverness-shire

15 letters:
Kincardineshire

Ross and Cromarty

16 letters:
Clackmannanshire

18 letters:
Kirkcudbrightshire

WELSH COUNTIES (POST-1998)

5 letters:
Conwy
Powys

7 letters:
Cardiff
Gwynedd
Newport
Swansea
Torfaen
Wrexham

8 letters:
Anglesey
Bridgend

10 letters:
Caerphilly
Ceredigion
Flintshire

12 letters:
Blaenau Gwent
Denbighshire

13 letters:
Merthyr Tydfil
Monmouthshire
Pembrokeshire

15 letters:
Carmarthenshire
Neath Port Talbot
Vale of Glamorgan

16 letters:
Rhondda, Cynon, Taff

FORMER WELSH COUNTIES

5 letters:
Clwyd
Dyfed
Gwent
Powys

7 letters:
Gwynedd

12 letters:
Mid Glamorgan

13 letters:
West Glamorgan

14 letters:
South Glamorgan

NORTHERN IRISH COUNTIES

4 letters:
Down

6 letters:
Antrim
Armagh

Tyrone

9 letters:
Fermanagh

11 letters:
Belfast City
Londonderry

15 letters:
Londonderry City

REPUBLIC OF IRELAND COUNTIES

4 letters:
Cork
Mayo

5 letters:
Cavan
Clare
Kerry
Laois

Louth
Meath
Sligo

REPUBLIC OF IRELAND COUNTIES (CONTINUED)

6 letters:
Carlow
Dublin
Galway
Offaly

7 letters:
Donegal

Kildare
Leitrim
Wexford
Wicklow

8 letters:
Kilkenny
Limerick

Longford
Monaghan

9 letters:
Roscommon
Tipperary
Waterford
Westmeath

Cows

2 letters:
Zo

3 letters:
Dun
Zho

4 letters:
Zebu

5 letters:
Colly
Kyloe
Milch
Mooly

See also:
➤ **Cattle**

Muley
Stirk

6 letters:
Crummy
Dexter
Heifer
Jersey
Mulley
Rother

7 letters:
Kouprey
Redpoll

8 letters:
Alderney
Galloway
Guernsey
Hereford

9 letters:
Charolais
Red Sindhi
Simmental
Teeswater

11 letters:
Rother-beast

Crafts

5 letters:
Batik

6 letters:
Sewing

7 letters:
Crochet
Macramé
Pottery
Weaving

8 letters:
Basketry
Ceramics

Knitting
Knotwork
Quilling
Quilting
Spinning
Tapestry

9 letters:
Decoupage
Patchwork

10 letters:
Crewelwork
Embroidery

Raffia work
Sugarcraft
Wickerwork

11 letters:
Calligraphy
Cloisonnage
Dressmaking
Needlepoint

12 letters:
Basket-making

15 letters:
Flower arranging

Cricketers

3 letters:
Dev, *Kapil*
Fry, *C(harles) B(urgess)*
May, *Peter*

4 letters:
Ames, *Leslie*
Bird, *Richard 'Dicky'*
Boon, *David*
Hick, *Graham*
Khan, *Imran*
Lara, *Brian*
Lock, *Tony*
Snow, *John*
Vaas, *Chaminda*

5 letters:
Croft, *Colin*
Evans, *Godfrey*
Gooch, *Graham*
Gough, *Darren*
Gower, *David*
Grace, *W(illiam) G(ilbert)*
Greig, *Tony*
Hobbs, *Sir Jack*
Knott, *Alan*
Laker, *Jim*
Lloyd, *Clive Hubert*
Marsh, *Rodney*
Patil, *Sandeep*
   Madhusuda
Singh, *Harbhajan*
Smith, *M(ichael) J(ohn)*
   K(night)
Tyson, *Frank*
Walsh, *Courtney*
Warne, *Shane*
Waugh, *Mark*
Waugh, *Steve*

6 letters:
Akhtar, *Shoaib*
Bailey, *Trevor*
Barnes, *Sydney*
Benaud, *Richie*
Bishan, *Bedi*
Border, *Allan*
Botham, *Ian*

Cronje, *Hansie*
Dexter, *Ted*
Donald, *Allan*
Dravid, *Rahul*
Flower, *Andrew*
Garner, *Joel*
Hadlee, *Sir Richard*
Hayden, *Matthew*
Haynes, *Desmond*
Hutton, *Sir Len*
Kallis, *Jacques*
Kambli, *Vinod*
Kumble, *Anil*
Laxman, *V(angipurappu)*
   V(enkata) S(ai)
Lillee, *Dennis*
Loader, *Peter*
Mankad, *Mulvantrai*
   Himatlal 'Vinoo'
McCabe, *Stanley*
Olonga, *Henry*
Rhodes, *Jonty*
Sehwag, *Virender*
Sobers, *Sir Garfield*
Styris, *Scott*
Thorpe, *Graham*
Turner, *Glenn*
Wardle, *Johnny*
Weekes, *Sir Everton*
Younis, *Waqar*

7 letters:
Ambrose, *Curtly*
Boycott, *Geoffrey*
Bradman, *Sir Donald*
Compton, *Denis*
Cowdrey, *Sir Colin*
Fleming, *Stephen*
Ganguly, *Saurav*
Ganguly, *Sourav*
Gatting, *Mike*
Hammond, *Walter*
Hussein, *Nasser*
Jardine, *Douglas*
Larwood, *Harold*
McGrath, *Glenn*
Miandad, *Javed*
O'Reilly, *Bill*

Pollock, *Shaun*
Srinath, *Javagal*
Statham, *Brian*
Stewart, *Alec*
Thomson, *Jeffrey*
Trueman, *Fred*
Tufnell, *Phil*
Umrigar, *Pahelam*
   Ratanji
Wadekar, *Ajit Laxman*
Walcott, *Sir Clyde*
Worrell, *Sir Frank*

8 letters:
Amarnath, *Lala*
Amarnath, *Mohinder*
Amarnath, *Surinder*
Atherton, *Mike*
Brearley, *Michael*
Chappell, *Greg*
Chappell, *Ian*
Gavaskar, *Sunil*
Graveney, *Tom*
Houghton, *Dave*
Lindwall, *Ray*
Marshall, *Malcolm*
Mohammad, *Hanif*
Richards, *Viv*

9 letters:
D'Oliveira, *Basil Lewis*
Gilchrist, *Adam*
Gillespie, *Jason*
Greenidge, *Gordon*
Manjrekar, *Sanjay Vijay*
Ranatunga, *Arjuna*
Sutcliffe, *Herbert*
Tendulkar, *Sachin*
Underwood, *Derek*

10 letters:
Azharuddin,
   Mohammed
Barrington, *Ken*
Greatbatch, *Mark*
Jayasuriya, *Sanath*
Vengsarkar, *Dilip*
   Balwant

11 letters:
Heyhoe-Flint, *Rachel*
Trescothick, *Marcus*

12 letters:
Inzamam-ul-Haq
Muralitharan, *Muttiah*
Ranjitsinhji, *K(umar)
S(hri)*

13 letters:
Chandrasekhar,
*Bhagwat
Subramaniam*

Cricket terms

2 letters:
In

3 letters:
Bat
Bye
Cut
Out
Pad
Run
Six

4 letters:
Bail
Ball
Bowl
Duck
Edge
Four
Hook
Over
Pull
Seam
Slip
Spin
Wide

5 letters:
Ashes
Catch
Drive
Extra
Glide
Gully
Mid on
Pitch
Stump
Sweep
Swing

Umpie

6 letters:
Appeal
Bowled
Bowler
Bumper
Caught
Covers
Crease
Glance
Googly
Leg bye
Long on
Maiden
Mid off
No ball
On side
Opener
Run out
Single
Umpire
Wicket
Yorker

7 letters:
Batsman
Bouncer
Century
Declare
Fielder
Fine leg
Innings
Leg side
Leg slip
Long leg
Long off
Off side
Stumped

8 letters:
Boundary
Chinaman
Follow on
Full toss
Leg break
Off break
Short leg
Third man

9 letters:
Fieldsman
Hit wicket
Mid wicket
Square leg
Test match

10 letters:
Cover point
Extra cover
Fast bowler
Maiden over
Silly mid on
Twelfth man

11 letters:
Silly mid off

12 letters:
Wicketkeeper

13 letters:
Nightwatchman

14 letters:
Opening batsman

15 letters:
Leg before wicket

Crime terms

2 letters:
Do
Go

3 letters:
Job
Rap
Sin

4 letters:
Abet
Gaol
Heat
Jail
Life
Rape
View

5 letters:
Admit
Alibi
Arson
Atone
Bribe
Caper
Cough
Crime
Do for
Fraud
Guilt
Panel
Remit
Steal
Sting
Theft
Thief

6 letters:
Acquit
Bigamy
Charge
Commit
Degree
Detect
Exposé
Felony
Finger
Guilty

Hijack
Incest
Indict
Infect
Murder
Piracy
Punish
Record
Turn in
Verbal
Wanted

7 letters:
Assault
Battery
Bribery
Burglar
Confess
Convict
Cover-up
Find out
Forgery
Impeach
Larceny
Mugging
Offence
Penance
Pentito
Perjury
Robbery
Soldier
Treason
Villain

8 letters:
Acqittal
Barratry
Burglary
Conspire
Criminal
Homicide
Infamous
Innocent
Litigate
Murderer
Offender
Penology
Poaching

Prisoner
Sabotage
Thriller
Tu quoque
War crime

9 letters:
Accessory
Admission
Blackmail
Blasphemy
Criminate
Desertion
Detective
Extortion
Guiltless
Hate crime
Implicate
Innocence
Inside job
Penal code
Pilfering
Principal
Red-handed
Terrorism
Vandalism
Whodunnit
Wrongdoer

10 letters:
Accomplice
Accusation
Bail bandit
Commission
Commitment
Conspiracy
Conviction
Corruption
Cybercrime
Delinquent
Entrapment
Indictable
Indictment
Kidnapping
Litigation
Misconduct
Perpetrate
Petty theft

Punishment
Recidivism

11 letters:
Conspirator
Criminology
Delinquency
Hooliganism
Incriminate
Infanticide
Investigate
Law-and-order
Lawlessness
Premeditate

12 letters:
Death penalty

Denunciation
Embezzlement
Extraditable
Life sentence
Manslaughter
Misadventure
Misdemeanour

13 letters:
Drug smuggling
Housebreaking
Identity theft
Premeditation
Reinvestigate
Transgression

15 letters:
Computer hacking
Crime passionnel
Victimless crime

16 letters:
Bill of indictment
Private detective

17 letters:
Capital punishment

19 letters:
Justifiable homicide

20 letters:
Identification parade

Crime writers

3 letters:
Poe, *Edgar Allan*

4 letters:
Vine, *Barbara*

5 letters:
Block, *Lawrence*
Doyle, *Arthur Conan*
James, *P(hyllis) D(orothy)*

6 letters:
Rankin, *Ian*

Sayers, *Dorothy L(eigh)*

7 letters:
Bateman, *Colin*
Grisham, *John*
Hiaasen, *Carl*
Rendell, *Ruth*
Simenon, *Georges*
Wallace, *Edgar*

8 letters:
Chandler, *Raymond*

Christie, *Agatha*
Connelly, *Michael*
Connolly, *John*
Cornwell, *Patricia*

9 letters:
Brookmyre, *Christopher*
Highsmith, *Patricia*

10 letters:
Wiesenthal, *Simon*

Critics

4 letters:
Frye, *Northrop*
Ross, *Jonathan*
Said, *Edward*
Self, *Will*
Shaw, *George Bernard*

5 letters:
Bloom, *Harold*
Booth, *Wayne*
Burke, *Kenneth*
Carey, *John*

De Man, *Paul*
Greer, *Bonnie*
Greer, *Germaine*
Hegel, *Georg W(ilhelm) F(riedrich)*
Lodge, *David*
Plato
Ronay, *Egon*
Tynan, *Kenneth*
Weber, *Max*
Woolf, *Virginia*

6 letters:
Barker, *Harley Granville*
Berlin, *Isaiah*
Bhabha, *Homi K.*
Brooks, *Cleanth*
Clarke, *Oz*
Gulden, *Jilly*
Horace
Lawson, *Mark*
Leavis, *F(rank) R(aymond)*
Milnes, *Rodney*

Morley, *Paul*
Norman, *Barry*
Norman, *Emma*
Orwell, *George*
Parker, *Dorothy*
Paulin, *Tom*
Ruskin, *John*
Sartre, *Jean-Paul*
Sewell, *Brian*
Sontag, *Susan*

7 letters:
Bakhtin, *Mikhail*
Barthes, *Roland*
Carlyle, *Thomas*

Chomsky, *Noam*
Derrida, *Jacques*
Forster, *E(dward)*
  M(organ)
Kermode, *Frank*
Nabokov, *Vladimir*

8 letters:
Benjamin, *Walter*
Bradbury, *Malcolm*
Eagleton, *Terry*
Foucault, *Michel*
Longinus
Plotinus
Sedgwick, *Eve Kosofsky*

9 letters:
Aristotle
Showalter, *Elaine*
Winterson, *Jeanette*

10 letters:
De Beauvior, *Simone*
Greenblatt, *Stephen*
Lewis-Smith, *Victor*

11 letters:
Bogdanovich, *Peter*

12 letters:
Wittgenstein, *Ludwig*

Types of cross

3 letters:
Red
Tau

4 letters:
Ankh
Crux
Iona
Iron
Rood
Tree

5 letters:
Fiery
Greek
Latin
Papal
Pommé
Rouen

6 letters:
Ansate
Barbée
Botone
Celtic
Chiasm
Fitché
Fleury
Fylfot
Geneva
George

Graded (Calvary)
Moline
Pattée
Potent
Raguly
Trefly

7 letters:
Botonne
Calvary
Chiasma
Eleanor
Maltese
Patonce
Potence
Rarulée
Saltier
Saltire

8 letters:
Cercelée
Crosslet
Crucifix
Globical
Holy rood
Lorraine
Military
Millvine
Pectoral
Quadrate
Southern

St Peter's
Svastika
Swastika
Victoria

9 letters:
Encolpion
Jerusalem
St Andrew's
St George's

10 letters:
Canterbury
Clover-leaf
Crux ansata
St Anthony's

11 letters:
Constantine
Patriarchal

12 letters:
Pattée formée

13 letters:
Cross crosslet

14 letters:
Archiepiscopal

15 letters:
Russian Orthodox

Crustaceans

4 letters:
Crab
Craw

5 letters:
Koura
Krill
Maron
Prawn

6 letters:
Cyprid
Cypris
Isopod
Scampi
Scampo
Shrimp
Slater

7 letters:
Camaron
Copepod
Cyclops
Decapod
Foot-jaw
Gribble
Lobster
Macrura
Squilla

8 letters:
Amphipod

Barnacle
Cirriped
Cirripid
Crawfish
Crayfish
Cumacean
Decapoda
King crab
Land crab
Nauplius
Pagurian
Sand flea
Scorpion

9 letters:
Beach flea
Cirripede
Euphausia
Fishlouse
King prawn
Langouste
Ostracoda
Phyllopod
Schizopod
Sea spider
Water flea
Woodlouse

10 letters:
Brachyuran
Cladoceran

Hermit crab
Oyster crab
Robber crab
Sand hopper
Sand shrimp
Spider crab
Stomatopod

11 letters:
Langoustine
Rock lobster

12 letters:
Branchiopoda
Entomostraca
Spiny lobster

13 letters:
Goose barnacle
Horseshoe crab
Malacostracan
Norway lobster
Opossum shrimp
Rhizocephalan
Soft-shell crab

14 letters:
Dublin Bay prawn

16 letters:
Freshwater shrimp

Crystals

4 letters:
Lead
Rock
Spar

5 letters:
Beryl
Druse
Glass
Macle
Nicol
Prism

Purin

6 letters:
Liquid
Purine
Quartz

7 letters:
Baccara
Cumarin
Epitaxy

8 letters:
Baccarat
Coumarin
Dendrite
Jarosite
Melamine
Pinacoid
Pinakoid
Sorbitol
Trichite
Trilling

9 letters:
Hemitrope
Love-arrow
Rubicelle
Snowflake
Xenocryst

10 letters:
Phenocryst
Rhinestone
Watch-glass

12 letters:
Enantiomorph

15 letters:
Allotriomorphic

Cups

2 letters:
FA

4 letters:
UEFA

5 letters:
Davis
Fairs
Rider
Ryder
World

8 letters:
America's
Calcutta
European

Cups and other drinking vessels

3 letters:
Cup
Mug
Nut
Pot
Tig
Tot
Tyg

4 letters:
Dish
Horn

5 letters:
Calix
Cruse
Cylix
Glass
Hanap
Kylix
Tazza

6 letters:
Beaker
Copita
Cotyle
Fingan
Finjan
Goblet
Loving
Noggin
Porrón
Quaich
Rhyton
Tassie

7 letters:
Canteen
Chalice
Cyathus
Scyphus
Stirrup
Tankard
Tea-dish

Tumbler

8 letters:
Pannikin
Schooner
Tantalus
Tastevin

9 letters:
Cantharus
Demitasse
Moustache

10 letters:
Monstrance

11 letters:
Water bottle

14 letters:
Champagne flute

Cupboards and cabinets

4 letters:
Safe

5 letters:
Ambry
Chest
Press
Shelf
Stand

6 letters:
Buffet
Bureau
Closet
Dooket
Drawer
Larder
Locker
Lowboy
Pantry

7 letters:
Armoire
Cabinet
Commode
Console
Dresser
Étagère
Highboy
Tallboy
Vitrine
Whatnot

8 letters:
Bookcase
Cellaret
Credenza
Wardrobe

9 letters:
Garderobe
Sideboard

10 letters:
Canterbury
Chiffonier

11 letters:
Chiffonnier

12 letters:
Chest-on-chest
Clothes-press
Welsh dresser

13 letters:
Court cupboard
Credence table
Filing cabinet
Medicine chest

14 letters:
Chest of drawers
Coolgardie safe

Currencies

Country	Currency
Afghanistan	Afghani
Albania	Lek
Algeria	Algerian dinar
Andorra	Euro
Angola	Kwanza
Antigua and Barbuda	East Caribbean dollar
Argentina	Peso
Armenia	Dram
Australia	Australian dollar
Austria	Euro
Azerbaijan	Manat
Bahamas	Bahamian dollar
Bahrain	Dinar
Bangladesh	Taka
Barbados	Barbados dollar
Belarus	Rouble
Belgium	Euro
Belize	Belize dollar
Benin	CFA franc

Country	**Currency**
Bhutan	Ngultrum
Bolivia	Boliviano
Bosnia-Herzegovina	Convertible marka
Botswana	Pula
Brazil	Real
Brunei	Brunei dollar
Bulgaria	Lev
Burkina-Faso	CFA franc
Burundi	Burundi franc
Cambodia	Riel
Cameroon	CFA franc
Canada	Canadian dollar
Cape Verde	Escudo
Central African Republic	CFA franc
Chad	CFA franc
Chile	Peso
China	Yuan
Colombia	Peso
Comoros	Comorian franc
Congo (Democratic Republic of)	Congolese franc
Congo (Republic of)	CFA franc
Costa Rica	Cólon
Côte d'Ivoire	CFA franc
Croatia	Kuna
Cuba	Peso
Cyprus	Pound
Czech Republic	Koruna
Denmark	Krone
Djibouti	Djibouti franc
Dominica	East Caribbean dollar
Dominican Republic	Peso
East Timor	US dollar
Ecuador	US dollar
Egypt	Pound
El Salvador	Cólon
Equatorial Guinea	CFA franc
Eritrea	Nakfa
Estonia	Kroon
Ethiopia	Birr
Fiji	Fiji dollar
Finland	Euro
France	Euro
French Guiana	French franc

Country	Currency
Gabon	CFA franc
Gambia	Dalasi
Germany	Euro
Ghana	Cedi
Greece	Euro
Greenland	Danish krone
Grenada	East Caribbean dollar
Guatemala	Quetzal
Guinea	Guinea franc
Guinea-Bissau	CFA franc
Guyana	Guyana dollar
Haiti	Gourde
Honduras	Lempira
Hungary	Forint
Iceland	Krona
India	Rupee
Indonesia	Rupiah
Iran	Rial
Iraq	Dinar
Ireland (Republic of)	Euro
Israel	Shekel
Italy	Euro
Jamaica	Jamaican dollar
Japan	Yen
Jordan	Dinar
Kazakhstan	Tenge
Kenya	Shilling
Kirghizia	Som
Kiribati	Australian dollar
Kosovo	Dinar; euro
Kuwait	Dinar
Kyrgyzstan	Som
Laos	Kip
Latvia	Lat
Lebanon	Pound
Lesotho	Loti
Liberia	Liberian dollar
Libya	Dinar
Liechtenstein	Swiss franc
Lithuania	Litas
Luxembourg	Euro
Macedonia	Denar
Madagascar	Malagasy franc

Country	Currency
Malawi	Kwacha
Malaysia	Ringgit
Maldives (Republic of)	Rufiyaa
Mali	CFA franc
Malta	Lira
Marshall Islands	U.S. dollar
Mauritania	Ouguiya
Mauritius	Rupee
Mexico	Peso
Micronesia	U.S. dollar
Moldova	Leu
Monaco	French franc
Mongolia	Tugrik
Montenegro	Euro
Montserrat	East Caribbean dollar
Morocco	Dirham
Mozambique	Metical
Myanmar	Kyat
Namibia	Namibian dollar
Nauru	Australian dollar
Nepal	Rupee
Netherlands	Euro
New Zealand	New Zealand dollar
Nicaragua	Córdoba
Niger	CFA franc
Nigeria	Naira
North Korea	Won
Norway	Krone
Oman	Rial
Pakistan	Rupee
Palau	U.S. dollar
Panama	Balboa
Papua New Guinea	Kina
Paraguay	Guarani
Peru	New sol
Philippines	Philippine peso
Poland	Zloty
Portugal	Euro
Qatar	Riyal
Romania	Leu
Russia	Rouble
Rwanda	Rwanda franc
St. Kitts and Nevis	East Caribbean dollar

Country	Currency
St. Lucia	East Caribbean dollar
St. Vincent and the Grenadines	East Caribbean dollar
Samoa	Tala
San Marino	Euro
São Tomé and Principe	Dobra
Saudi Arabia	Riyal
Senegal	CFA franc
Seychelles	Rupee
Sierra Leone	Leone
Singapore	Singapore dollar
Slovakia	Koruna
Slovenia	Tolar
Solomon Islands	Solomon Islands dollar
Somalia	Shilling
South Africa	Rand
South Korea	Won
Spain	Euro
Sri Lanka	Rupee
Sudan	Dinar
Surinam	Guilder
Swaziland	Lilangeni
Sweden	Krona
Switzerland	Swiss franc
Syria	Pound
Taiwan	Taiwan dollar
Tajikistan	Somoni
Tanzania	Shilling
Thailand	Baht
Togo	CFA franc
Tonga	Pa'anga
Trinidad and Tobago	Trinidad and Tobago dollar
Tunisia	Dinar
Turkey	Turkish lira
Turkmenistan	Manat
Tuvalu	Australian dollar
Uganda	Shilling
Ukraine	Hryvna
United Arab Emirates	Dirham
United Kingdom	Pound sterling
United States of America	U.S. dollar
Uruguay	Peso
Uzbekistan	Sum
Vanuatu	Vatu

Country	Currency
Vatican City	Euro
Venezuela	Bolívar
Vietnam	Dong
Yemen	Riyal
Yugoslavia (Serbia)	Dinar
Zambia	Kwacha
Zimbabwe	Zimbabwe dollar

Types of curry

4 letters:
Dhal
Phal

5 letters:
Balti
Bhuna
Kofta
Korma
Tikka

6 letters:
Achari

Bhoona
Chasni
Karahi
Madras
Masala
Pathia

7 letters:
Biryani
Dhansak
Dopiaza
Jaipuri
Nentara

Pasanda
Red thai

8 letters:
Jalfrezi
Tandoori
Vindaloo

9 letters:
Green thai
Mussalman
Rogan josh

Cutting tools

3 letters:
Axe
Bit
Saw

4 letters:
Adze
Sawn

5 letters:
Dicer
Lance
Mower

6 letters:
Carver
Chisel
Grater
Jigsaw
Padsaw
Ripsaw
Scythe
Shaver
Shears
Sickle

7 letters:
Chopper

Cleaver
Coulter
Handsaw
Scissor

8 letters:
Engraver

9 letters:
Secateurs

11 letters:
Ploughshare

D d

Dams

4 letters:
Guri
Hume
Pati

5 letters:
Aswan
Nurek
Rogun

6 letters:
Hoover

Inguri
Itaipu
Kariba
Vaiont

7 letters:
Benmore

8 letters:
Chapetón

9 letters:
Aswan High

10 letters:
Glen Canyon

11 letters:
Grand Coulee
Three Gorges

13 letters:
Grande Dixence
Vishvesvaraya

16 letters:
Syncrude Tailings

Dance

DANCES

3 letters:
Fan
Gig
Hay
Hey
Ice
Jig
Lap
Pas
Poi
Sun
Tap
Toe
War

4 letters:
Alma
Ball
Barn
Bump
Clog
Dump
Fado

Folk
Foot
Frug
Giga
Go-go
Haka
Hora
Hula
Jive
Jota
Juba
Juke
Kolo
Lion
Mosh
Nach
Pogo
Polo
Reel
Shag
Slam
Spin
Stag

Step
Taxi
Trip

5 letters:
Belly
Bogle
Brawl
Break
Caper
Carol
Ceroc®
Conga
Disco
Dolin
Fling
Furry
Galop
Ghost
Gigue
Gopak
Horah
Limbo

DANCES (CONTINUED)

Loure
Mambo
Mooch
Natch
Paspy
Pavan
Paven
Pavin
Polka
Raver
Round
Rumba
Salsa
Samba
Shake
Skank
Snake
Stomp
Strut
Sword
Tango
Twist
Valse
Vogue
Volta
Waltz
Whirl

6 letters:
Almain
Apache
Ballet
Bolero
Boogie
Boston
Branle
Canary
Cancan
Cha-cha
Do-si-do
Fading
Floral
German
Gigolo
Hustle
Jump-up
Kathak
Lavolt

Maenad
Maxixe
Minuet
Morris
Nautch
Oberek
Pavane
Petipa
Redowa
Shimmy
Spring
Square
Trophe
Valeta
Veleta
Zapata

7 letters:
Baladin
Ballant
Beguine
Bourrée
Bransle
Brantle
Calypso
Cantico
Capuera
Carioca
Coranto
Cossack
Country
Courant
Csardas
Czardas
Farruca
Forlana
Foxtrot
Furlana
Gavotte
Hailing
Hetaera
Hetaira
Hoedown
Lambada
Lancers
Ländler
Lavolta
Macaber

Macabre
Mazurka
Moresco
Morisco
Morrice
Moshing
Musette
Old-time
One-step
Pericon
Planxty
Polacca
Pyrrhic
Ridotto
Romaika
Roundel
Roundle
Sardana
Sashaya
Saunter
Shuffle
St Vitus
Tanagra
Tordion
Trenise
Two-step
Ziganka

8 letters:
Baladine
Ballroom
Bayadère
Boogaloo
Bunny hug
Cachucha
Cakewalk
Canticoy
Capoeira
Chaconne
Corybant
Coryphee
Cotillon
Courante
Egg-dance
Excuse-me
Fandango
Flamenco
Flip-flop

DANCES (CONTINUED)

Galliard
Habanera
Hay-de-guy
Haymaker
Heythrop
Hoolican
Hornpipe
Hula-hula
Irish jig
Joncanoe
Junkanoo
Kantikoy
Kazachok
Kazatzka
Lindy hop
Macarena
Marinera
Matachin
Medicine
Merengue
Murciana
Orchesis
Pierette
Rigadoon
Rigaudon
Robotics
Ronggeng
Saraband
Snowball
Soft-shoe
Trippant
Trucking
Vogueing

9 letters:
Allemande
Ballabile
Bergamask
Bergomask
Bossa nova
Breakdown
Butterfly
Caballero
Cha-cha-cha
Cotillion
Ecossaise

Eightsome
Farandole
Formation
Gallopade
Hoolachan
Jitterbug
Kathakali
Malagueña
Pas de deux
Paso doble
Passepied
Paul Jones
Polonaise
Poussette
Quadrille
Quickstep
Ring-shout
Roundelay
Siciliano
Sink-a-pace
Tambourin
Tripudium
Variation
Zapateado

10 letters:
Antimasque
Carmagnole
Charleston
Cinque-pace
Corroboree
Gay Gordons
Hay-de-guise
Hay-de-guyes
Hey-de-guise
Hokey cokey
Nautch-girl
Passamezzo
Petronella
Saltarello
Seguidilla
Sicilienne
Sinke-a-pace
Strathspey
Tarantella
Trenchmore

Tripudiate
Turkey trot
Tyrolienne

11 letters:
Antistrophe
Black bottom
Body popping
Buck and wing
Comprimario
Contradance
Contredanse
Cracovienne
Lambeth walk
Palais glide
Passacaglia
Pastourelle
Schottische
Shimmy-shake
Terpsichore
Varsovienne

12 letters:
Bharat Natyam
Labanotation
Passemeasure
Passy-measure
Robot dancing
Saltatorious
Virginia reel

13 letters:
Eightsome reel
Highland fling

14 letters:
Jack-in-the-green
Strip the willow

18 letters:
Sir Roger de Coverley

20 letters:
Dashing White Sergeant

GENERAL DANCE STEPS AND TERMS

3 letters:
Pas
Set

4 letters:
Time

5 letters:
Glide
Score
Steps

6 letters:
Chassé

Dosido
In step
Phrase
Rhythm

7 letters:
Pas seul
Routine
Shuffle

8 letters:
Keep step
Sequence
Slip step

9 letters:
Out of step
Promenade

10 letters:
Grand chain
Pigeonwing

11 letters:
Pas de basque
Progressive

12 letters:
Choreography

See also:
➤ **Ballets** ➤ **Ballet steps and terms**

Academic degrees

Degree	Abbreviation
Bachelor of Agriculture	BAgr
Bachelor of Arts	BA
Bachelor of Commerce	BCom
Bachelor of Dental Surgery	BDS
Bachelor of Divinity	BD
Bachelor of Education	BEd
Bachelor of Engineering	BEng
Bachelor of Law	BL
Bachelor of Laws	LLB
Bachelor of Letters	BLitt
Bachelor of Medicine	BM *or* MB
Bachelor of Music	BMus, MusB, *or* MusBac
Bachelor of Pharmacy	BPharm
Bachelor of Philosophy	BPhil
Bachelor of Science	BSc
Bachelor of Surgery	BS
Diploma in Education	DipEd
Doctor of Dental Surgery *or* Science	DDS *or* DDSc
Doctor of Divinity	DD
Doctor of Laws	LLD
Doctor of Letters *or* Literature	DLitt *or* LittD
Doctor of Medicine	MD

Degree	Abbreviation
Doctor of Music	DMus, MusD, *or* MusDoc
Doctor of Philosophy	PhD
Higher National Certificate	HNC
Higher National Diploma	HND
Master of Arts	MA
Master of Education	MEd
Master of Laws	LLM
Master of Letters	MLitt
Master of Music	MMus
Master of Philosophy	MPhil
Master of Science	MSc
Master of Surgery	MCh
Master of Technology	MTech
Ordinary National Certificate	ONC
Ordinary National Diploma	OND

Dependencies

4 letters:
Guam
Niue

5 letters:
Aruba
Macau (S.A.R.)
Undof

6 letters:
Jersey

7 letters:
Bermuda
Mayotte
Reunion
Tokelau

8 letters:
Anguilla
Guernsey
Hong Kong (S.A.R.)
Jan Mayen
Svalbard
West Bank

9 letters:
Aksai Chin

East Timor
Gaza Strip
Gibraltar
Greenland
Isle of Man
Wake Atoll

10 letters:
Antarctica
Guadeloupe
Martinique
Montserrat
Puerto Rico

11 letters:
Baker Island
Cook Islands
Kingman Reef
Saint Helena

12 letters:
Bouvet Island
Cocos Islands
Europa Island
Faroe Islands
French Guiana
Golan Heights

Jarvis Island
New Caledonia
Palmyra Atoll

13 letters:
American Samoa
Bassas da India
Cayman Islands
Howland Island
Islas Malvinas
Johnston Atoll
Midway Islands
Navassa Island
Norfolk Island
Virgin Islands
Western Sahara

14 letters:
Keeling Islands
Paracel Islands
Spratly Islands
Tromelin Island

15 letters:
Christmas Island
Coral Sea Islands
Falkland Islands

French Polynesia
Glorioso Islands
Pitcairn Islands
Wallisand Futuna

16 letters:
Clipperton Island
Juan de Nova Island

19 letters:
Netherlands Antilles

20 letters:
British Virgin Islands

21 letters:
Turks and Caicos Islands

22 letters:
Northern Mariana
  Islands
Saint Pierre and
  Miquelon

24 letters:
Ashmore and Cartier
  Islands

27 letters:
British Indian Ocean
  Territory

29 letters:
Heard Island and
  McDonald Islands

31 letters:
French Southern and
  Antarctic Lands

38 letters:
South Georgia and the
  South Sandwich
  Islands

Deserts

4 letters:
Gobi
Thar

6 letters:
Gibson
Libyan
Mohave
Mojave
Nubian
Sahara

7 letters:
Arabian
Atacama
Kara Kum

8 letters:
Kalahari
Kyzyl Kum

9 letters:
Dasht-e-Lut
Dasht-i-Lut

10 letters:
Great Sandy
Rub'al Khali

11 letters:
Death Valley

13 letters:
Great Victoria

15 letters:
Taklimakan Shama

Desserts and sweet dishes

3 letters:
Ice
Pav
Pud

4 letters:
Duff
Eve's
Fool
Milk
Plum
Rice
Sago
Suet

Tart
Whip

5 letters:
Black
Bombe
Coupe
Crème
Crêpe
Hasty
Jello
Jelly
Kulfi
Pease

Slump
Sweet
Tansy
Torte

6 letters:
Afters
Blintz
Gâteau
Haggis
Junket
Kissel
Mousse
Panada

Detectives 228

Pashka
Sorbet
Sowens
Sponge
Stodge
Summer
Sundae
Trifle
Yogurt

7 letters:
Cabinet
Caramel
Cassata
Cobbler
College
Compote
Crumble
Custard
Dessert
Fondant
Fritter
Furmety
Furmity
Panocha
Parfait
Pavlova
Popover
Pudding
Sabayon
Soufflé
Spumone
Spumoni
Steamed
Strudel
Tapioca
Tartlet

8 letters:
Bavarois
Cocktail
Dumpling
Flummery
Fromenty
Fruit cup
Frumenty
Furmenty
Ice cream
Pandowdy
Plum duff
Queen ofs
Roly-poly
Semolina
Sillabub
Stickjaw
Syllabub
Tiramisu
Vacherin
Water ice

9 letters:
Charlotte
Christmas
Cranachan
Shortcake
White hass
Yorkshire

10 letters:
Blancmange
Brown Betty
Cheesecake
Fruit salad
Nesselrode
Peach Melba
Shoofly pie
White hause
White hawse

Zabaglione

11 letters:
Athole Brose
Atholl Brose
Baked Alaska
Banana split
Crème brûlée
Easter-ledge
Spotted dick
Tutti-frutti

12 letters:
Butterscotch
Crème caramel
Crêpe suzette
Île Flottante

13 letters:
Bavarian cream
Marrons glacés

14 letters:
Bread and butter
Charlotte russe

15 letters:
Clootie dumpling

16 letters:
Death by chocolate

17 letters:
Black Forest gateau
Mississippi mud pie

18 letters:
Knickerbocker glory
Neapolitan ice cream

Detectives

7 letters:
Maigret
Taggart

8 letters:
Ironside

Sam Spade

9 letters:
Dick Tracy
Donald Lam
Joe Friday

Lew Archer
Nancy Drew
Nero Wolfe

10 letters:
Jane Marple

Mike Hammer
Paul Temple
Perry Mason

11 letters:
Charlie Chan
Ellery Queen
Father Brown
Jim Bergerac
Jim Rockford
Lord Peter Wimsey
Travis McGee

12 letters:
Sergeant Cuff
Simon Templar

13 letters:
Albert Campion
C Auguste Dupin
Hercule Poirot
Jonathan Creek
Kinky Friedman
Philip Marlowe

14 letters:
Brother Cadfael
Charlie Resnick
Inspector Morse
Inspector Rebus
Sherlock Holmes

15 letters:
Eddie Shoestring
Inspector Bucket
Lieutenant Kojak

16 letters:
Inspector Wexford

17 letters:
Inspector Clouseau
Inspector Lestrade
Lieutenant Columbo
Marcus Didius Falco

19 letters:
Commissario Brunetti

Diarists

3 letters:
Nin, *Anaïs*

4 letters:
Gide, *André*

5 letters:
Frank, *Anne*
Pepys, *Samuel*

6 letters:
Burney, *Fanny*
Evelyn, *John*

7 letters:
Kilvert, *Francis*

8 letters:
Fielding, *Helen* (*Bridget Jones*)
Townsend, *Sue* (*Adrian Mole*)

9 letters:
Delafield, *E.M.*

Grossmith, *George and Weedon* (*Charles Pooter*)

10 letters:
Wordsworth, *Dorothy*

11 letters:
Rivers-Moore, *Marion*

12 letters:
Bashkirtseff, *Marie*

Dinosaurs

8 letters:
Allosaur
Mosasaur
Stegodon
Theropod

9 letters:
Apatosaur
Hadrosaur
Iguanodon
Oviraptor
Pterosaur
Stegodont

Stegosaur
Trachodon

10 letters:
Allosaurus
Ankylosaur
Brontosaur
Ceratosaur
Dimetrodon
Diplodocus
Dromiosaur
Elasmosaur
Iguanodont

Megalosaur
Mosasaurus
Plesiosaur
Pteranodon
Titanosaur

11 letters:
Apatosaurus
Atlantosaur
Brachiosaur
Dolichosaur
Hadrosaurus
Ichthyosaur

Pterodactyl
Stegosaurus
Triceratops
Tyrannosaur

12 letters:
Ankylosaurus
Brontosaurus

Ceratosaurus
Dromiosaurus
Elasmosaurus
Megalosaurus
Plesiosaurus
Titanosaurus
Velociraptor

13 letters:
Atlantosaurus
Brachiosaurus
Compsognathus
Dolichosaurus
Ichthyosaurus
Protoceratops
Tyrannosaurus

Film directors

3 letters:
Lee, *Spike*
Ray, *Satyajit*

4 letters:
Coen, *Ethan*
Coen, *Joel*
Ford, *John*
Hall, *Peter*
Hill, *George Roy*
Lang, *Fritz*
Lean, *David*
Penn, *Arthur*
Reed, *Carol*
Roeg, *Nicholas*
Tati, *Jacques*
Weir, *Peter*
Wise, *Robert*

5 letters:
Allen, *Woody*
Brook, *Peter*
Capra, *Frank*
Carné, *Marcel*
Clair, *René*
Dante, *Joe*
Demme, *Johnathan*
Gance, *Abel*
Hawks, *Howard*
Ivory, *James*
Kaige, *Chen*
Kazan, *Elia*
Leigh, *Mike*
Loach, *Ken*
Lucas, *George*
Lumet, *Sidney*
Lynch, *David*
Malle, *Louis*

Pabst, *G(eorge)*
   W(ilhelm)
Reitz, *Edgar*
Roach, *Hal*
Scott, *Ridley*
Stone, *Oliver*
Vadim, *Roger*
Wajda, *Andrei*
Yimou, *Zhang*

6 letters:
Altman, *Robert*
Badham, *John*
Beatty, *Warren*
Besson, *Luc*
Brooks, *Mel*
Buñuel, *Luis*
Burton, *Tim*
Corman, *Roger*
Cuarón, *Alfonso*
Curtiz, *Michael*
Donner, *Richard*
Forbes, *Bryan*
Forman, *Milös*
Frears, *Stephen*
Godard, *Jean-Luc*
Guitry, *Sacha*
Herzog, *Werner*
Huston, *John*
Jarman, *Derek*
Jordan, *Neil*
Kasdan, *Lawrence*
Landis, *John*
Lester, *Richard*
Méliès, *Georges*
Mendes, *Sam*
Miller, *George*
Miller, *Jonathon Wolfe*

Ophüls, *Max*
Pagnol, *Marcel*
Parker, *Alan*
Powell, *Michael*
Reiner, *Carl*
Reiner, *Rob*
Renoir, *Jean*
Rohmer, *Eric*
Romero, *George*
Siegal, *Don*
Welles, *Orson*
Wilder, *Billy*
Winner, *Michael*

7 letters:
Aldrich, *Robert*
Asquith, *Anthony*
Bergman, *Ingmar*
Boorman, *John*
Bresson, *Robert*
Cameron, *James*
Campion, *Jane*
Chabrol, *Claude*
Cocteau, *Jean*
Coppola, *Francis Ford*
De Mille, *Cecil B(lount)*
De Palma, *Brian*
De Sicca, *Vittoria*
Edwards, *Blake*
Fellini, *Federico*
Fleming, *Victor*
Forsyth, *Bill*
Gilliam, *Terry*
Jackson, *Peter*
Kaufman, *Philip*
Kubrick, *Stanley*
McBride, *Jim*
Nichols, *Mike*

Olivier, *Laurence*
Pollack, *Sydney*
Puttnam, *David*
Redford, *Robert*
Resnais, *Alain*
Ritchie, *Guy*
Robbins, *Tim*
Russell, *Ken*
Sturges, *Preston*
Wenders, *Wim*

8 letters:
Anderson, *Lindsay*
Columbus, *Christopher*
Eastwood, *Clint*
Friedkin, *William*
Grierson, *John*
Griffith, *D(avid) W(ark)*
Kurosawa, *Akira*
Levinson, *Barry*
Merchant, *Ismail*
Minnelli, *Vincente*
Pasolini, *Pier Paolo*
Polanski, *Roman*

Pudovkin, *Vsevolod*
Scorsese, *Martin*
Truffaut, *François*
Visconti, *Luchino*
Zemeckis, *Robert*

9 letters:
Almódovar, *Pedro*
Antonioni, *Michelangelo*
Armstrong, *Gillian*
Carpenter, *John*
Dovzhenko, *Aleksandr Petrovitch*
Greenaway, *Peter*
Hitchcock, *Alfred*
Mizoguchi, *Kenji*
Peckinpah, *Sam*
Preminger, *Otto*
Spielberg, *Steven*
Stevenson, *Robert*
Tarantino, *Quentin*
Tarkovsky, *Andrei*
Tavernier, *Bertrand*
Zinnemann, *Fred*

10 letters:
Bertolucci, *Bernardo*
Cronenberg, *David*
Eisenstein, *Sergei Mikhailovich*
Fassbinder, *Rainer Werner*
Kieslowski, *Krzysztof*
Mankiewicz, *Joseph*
Rossellini, *Roberto*
Soderbergh, *Steven*
Zeffirelli, *Franco*

11 letters:
Bogdanovich, *Peter*
Mackendrick, *Alexander*
Pressburger, *Emeric*
Riefenstahl, *Leni*
Schlesinger, *John*
Von Stroheim, *Erich*

12 letters:
Attenborough, *Richard*
Von Sternberg, *Joseph*

The Twelve Disciples

4 letters:
John
Jude

5 letters:
James (*the Great*)
James (*the Less*)
Judas

Peter
Simon

6 letters:
Andrew
Philip
Thomas

7 letters:
Matthew

11 letters:
Bartholomew

Diseases

2 letters:
CD
ME
MS
TB
VD

3 letters:
ALD

BSE
CFS
Flu
Gid
Haw
Pip
Pox
Rot
TSE

Wog

4 letters:
Acne
Ague
AIDS
Boba
Bots
Bunt

Clap
Cold
Conk
Gout
Kuru
Loco
Lues
Lyme
Roup
Scab
Yaws

5 letters:
Bang's
Brand
Braxy
Ebola
Edema
Ergot
Favus
Gapes
Lupus
Lurgi
Lurgy
Mesel
Mumps
Ngana
Palsy
Pinta
Polio
Pott's
Sprue
Surra
Tinea
Weil's

6 letters:
Anbury
Angina
Asthma
Blight
Blotch
Cancer
Canker
Caries
Chagas'
Chorea
Cowpox
Crohn's
Cruels

Dartre
Dengue
Dropsy
Eczema
Farcin
Goitre
Grapes
Graves'
Heaves
Herpes
Income
Iritis
Johne's
Lampas
Mad cow
Meazel
Mildew
Morbus
Nagana
Oedema
Otitis
Paget's
Q fever
Quinsy
Rabies
Sapego
Scurvy
Spavin
Still's
Sweeny
Thrush
Typhus
Ulitis
Urosis
Warble
Zoster

7 letters:
Anthrax
Apraxia
Ascites
Bright's
British
Bulimia
Caisson
Cholera
Coeliac
Colitis
Crewels
Dourine

Earache
Founder
Glue ear
Hansen's
Hard pad
Hydatid
Icterus
Lampers
Leprosy
Lockjaw
Lumbago
Maidism
Malaria
Marburg
Measles
Megrims
Mooneye
Moor-ill
Murrain
Myiasis
Pébrine
Pinkeye
Porrigo
Prurigo
Purples
Purpura
Quittor
Ratbite
Rickets
Roaring
Rosette
Rubella
Scabies
Scrapie
Sequela
Serpigo
Sitfast
Sycosis
Tetanus
Tetters
Typhoid
Uraemia
Uveitis
Variola
Wilson's

8 letters:
Addison's
Alastrim
Anorexia

Aortitis
Beriberi
Blackleg
Bornholm
Bull nose
Bursitis
Carditis
Clubroot
Coxalgia
Cushing's
Cynanche
Cystitis
Diabetes
Dutch elm
Economo's
Epilepsy
Ergotism
Fishskin
Fowl pest
Glanders
Glaucoma
Grand mal
Gummosis
Hidrosis
Hodgkin's
Hookworm
Impetigo
Jaundice
Kala-azar
Loose-cut
Lumpy jaw
Lymphoma
Mastitis
Menières
Minamata
Myopathy
Myxedema
Osteitis
Pellagra
Petit mal
Phthisis
Phytosis
Pleurisy
Progeria
Pullorum
Rachitis
Raynaud's
Red water
Reynaud's
Rhinitis

Ringbone
Ringworm
Rose-rash
Sciatica
Scrofula
Seedy toe
Shingles
Smallpox
Staggers
Suppeago
Swayback
Swinepox
Syphilis
Tay-Sachs
Toe crack
Trachoma
Trembles
Venereal
Vincent's
Vulvitis
Windgall
Zoonosis

9 letters:
Acariasis
Arthritis
Bilharzia
Brown lung
Calenture
Chancroid
Chin cough
Chloracne
Chlorosis
Christmas
Cirrhosis
Dhobi itch
Diarrhoea
Diathesis
Distemper
Dysentery
Emphysema
Enteritis
Exanthema
Gastritis
Glossitis
Gonorrhea
Hepatitis
Ideopathy
Influenza
Ixodiasis

Kawasaki's
Laminitis
Lathyrism
Leucaemia
Leukaemia
Loose smut
Malanders
Milk fever
Myxoedema
Nephritis
Nephrosis
Newcastle
Pellagrin
Pemphigus
Phlebitis
Pneumonia
Porphyria
Psoriasis
Pyorrhoea
Retinitis
Sand crack
Sapraemia
Scratches
Siderosis
Silicosis
Sinusitis
Splenitis
Strangles
Sunstroke
Synovitis
Tarantism
Tick fever
Trichosis
Tularemia
Urticaria
Vaginitis
Vagotonia
Varicosis
Varioloid
Whistling

10 letters:
Absinthism
Acromegaly
Alcoholism
Alzheimer's
Amoebiasis
Asbestosis
Ascariasis
Autoimmune

Diseases

Babesiosis
Bagassosis
Bell's palsy
Black Death
Broken wind
Bronchitis
Byssinosis
Cellulitis
Chickenpox
Common cold
Dandy-fever
Dermatitis
Diphtheria
Ebola virus
Erysipelas
Fibrositis
Filariasis
Framboesia
Gingivitis
Gonorrhoea
Heartwater
Hemophilia
Hepatitis A
Hepatitis B
Hog cholera
Ichthyosis
Impaludism
Laryngitis
Lassa fever
Leuchaemia
Limber-neck
Lou Gehrig's
Louping ill
Mallanders
Mallenders
Meningitis
Moniliasis
Muscardine
Narcolepsy
Neuropathy
Ornithosis
Parkinson's
Pityriasis
Rinderpest
Salmonella
Scarlatina
Scleriasis
Seborrhoea
Shell shock
Springhalt

Stomatitis
Stringhalt
Swamp fever
Swine fever
Texas fever
Tularaemia
Urethritis
Valvulitis

11 letters:
Anthracosis
Brittle-bone
Brucellosis
Cardiopathy
Consumption
Dead fingers
Farmer's lung
Green monkey
Haemophilia
Hebephrenia
Huntington's
Hypothermia
Jungle fever
Kwashiorkor
Listeriosis
Myxomatosis
Parasitosis
Pharyngitis
Psittacosis
Rickettsial
Salpingitis
Scleroderma
Scrub typhus
Septicaemia
Spina bifida
Spondylitis
Thoroughpin
Tonsillitis
Trench fever
Trench mouth
Trichinosis
Utriculitis
Yellow fever

12 letters:
Aeroneurosis
Anaplasmosis
Appendicitis
Athlete's foot
Avitaminosis

Bilharziasis
Bilharziosis
Black measles
Bush sickness
Constipation
Cor pulmonale
Encephalitis
Endocarditis
Enterobiasis
Fascioliasis
Finger and toe
Foot-and-mouth
Furunculosis
Gallsickness
Herpes zoster
Hoof-and-mouth
Legionnaire's
Milk sickness
Molybdenosis
Motor neurone
Osteomalacia
Osteoporosis
Pericarditis
Quarter crack
Ratbite fever
Sarcomatosis
Scarlet fever
Schizothymia
Sclerodermia
Shaking palsy
Sheep measles
Splenomegaly
Spotted fever
Thalassaemia
Tuberculosis
Typhoid fever
Uncinariasis

13 letters:
Actinomycosis
Blind staggers
Bronchiolitis
Bubonic plague
Elephantiasis
Enterocolitis
Genital herpes
German measles
Greensickness
Herpes simplex
Labyrinthitis

Leichmaniasis
Leishmaniasis
Leishmaniosis
Leptospirosis
Lupus vulgaris
Moon blindness
Non-A hepatitis
Non-B hepatitis
Osteomyelitis
Poliomyelitis
Polycythaemia
Reye's syndrome
Salmonellosis
Schizophrenia
Serum sickness
Syringomyelia
Toxoplasmosis
Tsutsugamushi
Undulant fever
Whooping cough

14 letters:
Bulimia nervosa
Cardiomyopathy
Coal miner's lung
Conjunctivitis
Cystic fibrosis
Diverticulitis
Encephalopathy
Glandular fever
Histoplasmosis
Hypothyroidism
Kaposi's sarcoma
Leucodystrophy
Onchocerciasis
Osteoarthritis
Pneumoconiosis
Relapsing fever
Rheumatic fever
Senile dementia
Spirochaetosis
Sporotrichosis
Swine vesicular
Trichomoniasis
Trichophytosis
Variola porcina
Vincent's angina
Vulvovaginitis

15 letters:
Agranulocytosis
Ancylostomiasis
Ankylostomiasis
Anorexia nervosa
Atherosclerosis
Blackwater fever
Burkitt lymphoma
Double pneumonia
Equine distemper
Gastroenteritis
Pleuropneumonia
Schistosomiasis
Strongyloidosis
Sydenham's chorea
Trypanosomiasis

16 letters:
Actinodermatitis
Anchylostomiasis
Arteriosclerosis
Bronchopneumonia
Burkitt's lymphoma
Creutzfeldt-Jakob
Erythroblastosis
Ménière's syndrome
Myasthenia gravis
Paratyphoid fever
Saint Vitus's dance
Sleeping sickness
Strongyloidiasis
Sweating sickness
Tourette syndrome

17 letters:
Encephalomyelitis
Haemoglobinopathy
Huntington's chorea
Multiple sclerosis
Muscular dystrophy
Osteitis deformans
Presenile dementia
Radiation sickness
Sickle-cell anaemia

18 letters:
Cerebellar syndrome
Coccidioidomycosis

Exophthalmic goitre
Glomerulonephritis
Lupus erythematosus
Pelvic inflammatory
Toxic shock syndrome

19 letters:
Infectious hepatitis
Korsakoff's psychosis
Non-Hodgkin's
  lymphoma
Rheumatoid arthritis

20 letters:
Adrenoleukodystrophy
Carpal tunnel syndrome
Necrotising fasciitis

21 letters:
Decompression sickness

22 letters:
Chronic fatigue
  syndrome

23 letters:
Bacillary white
  diarrhoea
Equine infectious
  anaemia
Infectious
  mononucleosis

24 letters:
Myalgic
  encephalomyelitis

25 letters:
Rocky Mountain
  spotted fever
Seasonal affective
  disorder

30 letters:
Bovine spongiform
  encephalopathy

Dishes

3 letters:
Fry
Pan
Pie
Poi

4 letters:
Dent
Flan
Fool
Hash
Lanx
Mess
Olla
Paté
Puri
Soba
Soss
Soup
Stew
Taco
Tofu
Udon

5 letters:
Balti
Belle
Bhaji
Bitok
Brawn
Brose
Broth
Champ
Chips
Crêpe
Curry
Cutie
Daube
Dolma
Fry-up
Gomer
Grits
Kasha
Kebab
Kibbe
Knish
Kofta
Korma

Laksa
Maror
Paten
Patin
Patty
Pilaf
Pilao
Pilau
Pilaw
Pilow
Pizza
Poori
Quorn®
Raita
Ramen
Roast
Rojak
Salad
Salmi
Sango
Satay
Sushi
Tamal
Thali
Tikka
Toast

6 letters:
Apollo
Bharta
Blintz
Bredie
Bridie
Burgoo
Canapé
Coddle
Cook-up
Croute
Cuscus
Diable
Entrée
Faggot
Fondue
Haggis
Hotpot
Houmus
Hummus
Humous

Kimchi
Kishke
Laggen
Laggin
Luggie
Mousse
Muesli
Nachos
Omelet
Paella
Pakora
Panada
Patera
Patine
Pilaff
Pirogi
Pot pie
Quiche
Ragout
Salmis
Samosa
Sanger
Sarmie
Scampi
Scouse
Sowans
Sowens
Subgum
Tagine
Tamale
Tsamba
Won ton

7 letters:
Biriani
Bobotie
Bouchée
Burrito
Calzone
Ceviche
Chafing
Charger
Cocotte
Comport
Compote
Crowdie
Crubeen
Crumble

Custard
Cuvette
Dariole
Dhansak
Dopiaza
Egg roll
Epergne
Fajitas
Falafel
Fel-a-fel
Flasket
Foo yong
Foo Yung
Friture
Goulash
Grav lax
Lasagne
Mousaka
Navarin
Padella
Polenta
Pottage
Poutine
Ramekin
Rarebit
Ravioli
Risotto
Rissole
Roulade
Sashimi
Scallop
Seviche
Skirlie
Sosatie
Soufflé
Stir-fry
Stottie
Stovies
Tartlet
Tempura
Terrine
Timbale
Tostada

8 letters:
Brandade
Caponata
Chop suey
Chow mein
Consommé

Coolamon
Coq au vin
Coquille
Couscous
Crostini
Dolmades
Entremes
Escargot
Feijoada
Fish cake
Gado-gado
Halloumi
Kedgeree
Keftedes
Kickshaw
Kouskous
Kreplach
Kromesky
Matelote
Mazarine
Meat loaf
Mirepoix
Moussaka
Omelette
Pandowdy
Pannikin
Pastrami
Pirozhki
Porridge
Pot-au-feu
Pot roast
Quenelle
Raclette
Ramequin
Salpicon
Sandwich
Shashlik
Sillabub
Souvlaki
Steak pie
Sukiyaki
Syllabub
Teriyaki
Tomalley
Tortilla
Tsatsiki
Tzatziki
Yakimono
Yakitori

9 letters:
Carbonara
Casserole
Cassoulet
Compotier
Croquette
Curry puff
Egg-fo-yang
Enchilada
Entremets
Forcemeat
Fricassee
Galantine
Game chips
Gravad lax
Guacamole
Hamburger
Howtowdie
Irish stew
Jambalaya
Lobscouse
Madrilène
Manicotti
Matelotte
Mutton pie
Osso bucco
Pastitsio
Pepper pot
Reistafel
Rijstafel
Schnitzel
Scotch egg
Scotch pie
Shashlick
Souvlakia
Succotash
Surf 'n' turf
Tyropitta
Vol-au-vent

10 letters:
Avgolemono
Baked beans
Blanquette
Bombay duck
Bruschetta
Cacciatore
Cottage pie
Coulibiaca
Couscousou

Doner kebab
Egg-foo-yung
Fish finger
Fish supper
Hotchpotch
Jugged hare
Koulibiaca
Laver bread
Minestrone
Mixed grill
Nasi goreng
Parmigiana
Provencale
Quesadilla
Red pudding
Rijsttafel
Salmagundi
Salmagundy
Sauerkraut
Scaloppine
Scaloppini
Shish kebab
Smørrebrød
Spitchcock
Spring roll
Stroganoff
Vegeburger

11 letters:
Buck-rarebit
Caesar salad
Chicken Kiev
Clam chowder
Cock-a-leekie
Corn chowder
Cullen skink
Frankfurter
French toast

Fritto misto
Gefilte fish
Hominy grits
Olla podrida
Palm-oil chop
Ratatouille
Saltimbocca
Sauerbraten
Sausage roll
Scotch broth
Smorgasbord
Spanakopita
Spanish rice
Spanokopita
Suet pudding
Vichyssoise
Welsh rabbit

12 letters:
Cheeseburger
Club sandwich
Cockie-leekie
Cornish pasty
Eggs Benedict
Fish and chips
Forfar bridie
Gefüllte fish
Mulligatawny
Open sandwich
Pease pudding
Prawn cracker
Shepherd's pie
Steak tartare
Taramasalata
Veggieburger
Waldorf salad
Welsh rarebit
White pudding

13 letters:
Prairie oyster
Rumbledethump
Salade niçoise
Scrambled eggs
Toad-in-the-hole

14 letters:
Beef bourguinon
Beef stroganoff
Chilli con carne
Lobster Newburg
Macaroni cheese
Mock turtle soup
Quiche lorraine
Rumbledethumps

15 letters:
Bubble and squeak
Ploughman's lunch

16 letters:
Blanquette de veau
Lancashire hotpot
Lobster thermidor
Yorkshire pudding

17 letters:
Angels-on-horseback
Cauliflower cheese
Devils-on-horseback
Steak-and-kidney pie

18 letters:
Boeuf bourguignonne

21 letters:
Steak-and-kidney
   pudding

Divination

METHODS OF DIVINATION

4 letters:
Dice

5 letters:
Runes

Tarot

6 letters:
I Ching

7 letters:
Dowsing
Scrying

METHODS OF DIVINATION (CONTINUED)

9 letters:
Astrology
Palmistry
Sortilege
Tea leaves

10 letters:
Numerology

12 letters:
Clairvoyance

13 letters:
Crystal gazing

MEANS OF DIVINATION

Name	Object used
Ailuromancy	Cats
Alphitomancy	Wheat *or* barley cakes
Arachnomancy	Spiders
Astragalomancy	Dice
Bibliomancy	Passages from books
Cartomancy	Cards
Catoptromancy	Mirror
Ceromancy	Melted wax
Chiromancy	Hands
Cleidomancy	Suspended key
Crithomancy	Freshly baked bread
Cromniomancy	Onions
Crystallomancy	Crystal ball
Dactylomancy	Suspended ring
Geomancy	Earth, sand, *or* dust
Hippomancy	Horses
Hydromancy	Water
Lampadomancy	Oil lamps
Lithomancy	Precious stones
Lychnomancy	Flames of wax candles
Molybdomancy	Molten lead
Necromancy	The dead
Oneiromancy	Dreams
Ornithomancy	Birds
Pegomancy	Sacred pool
Pyromancy	Fire *or* flames
Radiesthesia	Pendulum
Rhabdomancy	Rod *or* wand
Sciomancy	Ghosts
Tasseography	Tea leaves
Theomancy	God
Tyromancy	Cheese

Breeds of dog

3 letters:
Cur
Lab
Pom
Pug

4 letters:
Barb
Bush
Chow
Dane
Kuri
Peke
Puli
Stag
Tosa

5 letters:
Akita
Alans
Apsos
Boxer
Brach
Cairn
Coach
Corgi
Husky
Spitz
Spoor

6 letters:
Afghan
Bandog
Barbet
Beagle
Blanch
Borzoi
Briard
Chenet
Cocker
Collie
Eskimo
Goorie
Kelpie
Messan
Pariah
Poodle
Pye-dog

Saluki
Scotch
Setter
Shough
Sleuth
Talbot
Teckel
Vizsla
Westie
Yorkie

7 letters:
Basenji
Boerbul
Bouvier
Brachet
Bulldog
Courser
Griffon
Harrier
Lurcher
Maltese
Maremma
Mastiff
Mongrel
Pointer
Prairie
Raccoon
Samoyed
Sapling
Scottie
Shar-Pei
Sheltie
Shih-tzu
Showghe
Spaniel
Terrier
Volpino
Whippet

8 letters:
Aardwolf
Aberdeen
Airedale
Alsatian
Blenheim
Bratchet
Carriage

Chow-chow
Doberman
Elkhound
Foxhound
Huntaway
Keeshond
Komondor
Labrador
Landseer
Malamute
Malemute
Papillon
Pekinese
Pembroke
Pinscher
Samoyede
Scottish
Sealyham
Springer
Warragal
Warrigal

9 letters:
Buckhound
Chihuahua
Coonhound
Dachshund
Dalmatian
Deerhound
Gazehound
Great Dane
Greyhound
Kerry blue
Lhasa apso
Pekingese
Red setter
Retriever
Schnauzer
Staghound
St. Bernard
Wolfhound

10 letters:
Bedlington
Bloodhound
Blue cattle
Blue heeler
Bruxellois

Fox terrier
Otterhound
Pomeranian
Rottweiler
Schipperke
Tripehound
Weimaraner
Welsh corgi

11 letters:
Afghan hound
Basset hound
Bichon Frise
Bull mastiff
Bull terrier
Irish setter
Jack Russell
Rough collie
Skye terrier
Sleuthhound
Sydney silky

12 letters:
Belvoir hound
Border collie
Cairn terrier
Field spaniel
Gordon setter
Irish terrier
Japanese tosa
Newfoundland
Saint Bernard
Water spaniel
Welsh terrier
West Highland

13 letters:
Affenpinscher

Alpine spaniel
Bearded collie
Border terrier
Boston terrier
Cocker spaniel
Dandie Dinmont
English setter
French bulldog
Scotch terrier
Sussex spaniel

14 letters:
Clumber spaniel
Egyptian basset
German shepherd
Irish wolfhound
Norfolk terrier
Norwich terrier
Pit bull terrier

15 letters:
Aberdeen terrier
Airedale terrier
Alaskan malamute
Blenheim spaniel
Blue Gascon hound
Cuban bloodhound
Golden retriever
Highland terrier
Japanese spaniel
Lakeland terrier
Mexican hairless
Sealyham terrier
Springer spaniel

16 letters:
Australian cattle
Doberman pinscher

Italian greyhound
Kerry blue terrier
Persian greyhound
Pyrenean mountain
Russian wolfhound
Shetland sheepdog
Yorkshire terrier

17 letters:
Australian terrier
Bedlington terrier
Dobermann-pinscher
Irish water spaniel
Labrador retriever
Manchester terrier
Norwegian elkhound
Wire-haired terrier

18 letters:
Black-and-tan terrier
Jack Russell terrier
King Charles spaniel
Old English sheepdog
Rhodesian ridgeback

20 letters:
Dandie Dinmont terrier
Queensland blue heeler

22 letters:
American pit bull terrier
Australian silky terrier
Norfolk springer spaniel

24 letters:
Staffordshire bull terrier
West Highland white
  terrier

Types of drama

2 letters:
No

3 letters:
Noh

5 letters:
Farce

6 letters:
Comedy
Kabuki
Sitcom
Sketch

7 letters:
Tragedy

8 letters:
Jacobean

9 letters:
Kathakali
Melodrama
Soap opera

Dramatists

10 letters:
Shadow play

11 letters:
Kitchen sink
Mystery play
Passion play
Tragicomedy

12 letters:
Costume drama
Costume piece

Grand Guignol
Morality play

13 letters:
Street theatre

14 letters:
Revenge tragedy

15 letters:
Comedy of manners
Situation comedy

16 letters:
Commedia dell'arte
Theatre of cruelty

17 letters:
Restoration Comedy

18 letters:
Theatre of the absurd

Dramatists

2 letters:
Fo, *Dario*

3 letters:
Fry, *Christopher Harris*
Gay, *John*
Kyd, *Thomas*

4 letters:
Amos, *Robert*
Bond, *Edward*
Ford, *John*
Gray, *Oriel*
Hare, *David*
Inge, *William Motter*
Lyly, *John*
Shaw, *George Bernard*

5 letters:
Albee, *Edward*
Behan, *Brendan*
Eliot, *T(homas) S(tearns)*
Esson, *Louis*
Friel, *Brian*
Genet, *Jean*
Gogol, *Nikolai*
Havel, *Václav*
Hayes, *Alfred*
Ibsen, *Henrik*
Lorca, *Federico Garcia*
Mamet, *David*
Odets, *Clifford*
Orton, *Joe*
Otway, *Thomas*

Synge, *John Millington*
Udall, *Nicholas*
Wilde, *Oscar*
Yeats, *W(illiam) B(utler)*

6 letters:
Adamov, *Arthur*
Beynon, *Richard*
Brecht, *Bertolt*
Bridie, *James (Osborne Henry Mavor)*
Brieux, *Eugene*
Coward, *Noël (Pierce)*
Dekker, *Thomas*
De Vega, *Lope*
Dryden, *John*
Greene, *Robert*
Hebbel, *(Christian) Friedrich*
Hewett, *Dorthy*
Howard, *Sidney*
Jonson, *Ben*
Kaiser, *George*
Lawler, *Ray*
Miller, *Arthur*
Oakley, *Barry*
O'Casey, *Sean*
O'Neill, *Eugene (Gladstone)*
Pinero, *Arthur Wing*
Pinter, *Harold*
Porter, *Hal*
Racine, *Jean Baptiste*
Sartre, *Jean-Paul*

Seneca, *Lucius Annaeus*
Wilder, *Thornton*

7 letters:
Anouilh, *Jean*
Beckett, *Samuel*
Chapman, *George*
Chekhov, *Anton Pavlovich*
Gilbert, *W(illiam) S(chwenk)*
Goldoni, *Carlo*
Heywood, *Thomas*
Hibberd, *Jack*
Ionesco, *Eugène*
Kushner, *Tony*
Marlowe, *Christopher*
Marston, *John*
Molière
Osborne, *John*
Patrick, *John*
Plautus, *Titus Maccius*
Pushkin, *Aleksander Sergeyevich*
Romeril, *John*
Rostand, *Edmond*
Russell, *Willy*
Seymour, *Alan*
Shaffer, *Peter*
Shepard, *Sam*
Soyinka, *Wole*
Terence
Webster, *John*

243

Dresses

8 letters:
Beaumont, *Francis*
Congreve, *William*
Fletcher, *John*
Lochhead, *Liz*
Menander
Rattigan, *Terence Mervyn*
Schiller, *Johann Christoph Friedrich*
Shadwell, *Thomas*
Sheridan, *Richard Brinsley*
Sherwood, *Robert*
Stoppard, *Tom*
Vanbrugh, *Sir John*
Wedekind, *Frank*
Williams, *Tennessee*
Wycherly, *William*

9 letters:
Aeschylus
Ayckbourn, *Alan*
Bleasdale, *Alan*
Corneille, *Pierre*
De la Barca, *Pedro Calderón*
Euripides
Giraudoux, (*Hippolyte*) *Jean*
Goldsmith, *Oliver*
Hauptmann, *Gerhart Johann Robert*
Massinger, *Philip*
Middleton, *Thomas*
Sackville, *Thomas*
Sophocles
Von Goethe, *Johann Wolfgang*

10 letters:
Drinkwater, *John*
Galsworthy, *John*
Pirandello, *Luigi*
Strindberg, *August*
Williamson, *David Keith*

11 letters:
Maeterlinck, *Maurice*
Shakespeare, *William*
Von Schiller, *Johann Christoph Friedrich*

12 letters:
Aristophanes
Beaumarchais, *Pierre Augustin Caron de*

14 letters:
De Beaumarchais, *Pierre Augustin Caron*

Dresses

4 letters:
Coat
Midi
Sack
Sari

5 letters:
Burka
Pinny
Saree
Shift
Tunic

6 letters:
Caftan
Chiton
Dirndl
Jumper
Kaftan
Kimono
Mantua
Muu-muu

Nighty
Sheath

7 letters:
Busuuti
Chemise
Gymslip
Nightie
Sweater
Tea gown
Wedding

8 letters:
Ballgown
Cocktail
Negligée
Peignoir
Pinafore
Sundress

9 letters:
Cheongsam

Maxidress
Minidress
Nightgown
Nightrobe
Overdress

10 letters:
Microdress
Nightdress
Nightshirt
Shirtdress
Shirtwaist

11 letters:
Riding habit

12 letters:
Shirtwaister

13 letters:
Button-through
Mother Hubbard

Soft drinks

3 letters:
Cha
Pop
Tea

4 letters:
Bull
Coke®
Cola
Kola
Maté
Milk
Soda

5 letters:
Cocoa
Crush
Float
Juice
Pekoe
Pepsi®
Polly
Salop
Shake
Shrub
Tizer®
Tonic
Vimto®
Water

6 letters:
Bovril®
Cassis
Coffee
Koumis
Kumiss
Nectar
Oolong
Orgeat
Ribena®
Squash

See also:
➤ **Coffees** ➤ **Teas**

Tisane

7 letters:
Cordial
Guarana
Herb tea
Koumiss
Koumyss
Limeade
Mineral
Perrier®
Seltzer
Sherbet

8 letters:
Ambrosia
Coca-Cola®
Fruit tea
Iron brew
Lemonade
Lemon tea
Lucozade®
Persicot
Root beer
Smoothie
Spremuta
Switchel

9 letters:
Chocolate
Cream soda
Gingerade
Ginger ale
Grenadine
Milk shake
Orangeade
Soda water

10 letters:
Apple juice
Buttermilk

Fruit juice
Ginger beer
Lolly water
Russian tea
Vichy water

11 letters:
Barley water
Bitter lemon
Lemon squash
Lime cordial
Orange juice
Soapolallie
Tomato juice

12 letters:
Hot chocolate
Ice-cream soda
Mineral water
Perrier water®
Sarsaparilla
Seltzer water

13 letters:
Prairie oyster

14 letters:
Herbal infusion

15 letters:
Alcohol-free beer
Grapefruit juice

16 letters:
Non-alcoholic beer

17 letters:
Peppermint cordial

19 letters:
Dandelion and burdock

Drugs and drug terms

1 letter:
E
Q

2 letters:
Do
LD
OD

3 letters:
Ana
Cop
DET
DMT
Eve
Fix
Hit
Hop
Ice
INH
Jag
Kif
LSD
Man
MLD
PCP®
Pop
Pot
STP
Tab
Tea

4 letters:
Acid
Adam
Alum
Bang
Blow
Bong
Bust
Bute
Buzz
Coke
Dopa
Dope
Dose
Drop
Gear

Gone
Goof
Hard
Hash
Head
Hemp
High
Hype
Junk
Kick
Line
Mass
Nail
Narc
Oral
Sida
Soft
Soma
Toke
Toot
Trip
Unit
User
Wine
Wrap

5 letters:
Aloes
Aloin
Benny
Bhang
Candy
Crack
Crank
Dagga
Ganja
Grass
Habit
Hocus
Hop up
Intal®
Joint
L-dopa
Lit up
Local
Mummy
NSAID
Opium

Poppy
Quina
Roach
Route
Rutin
Salep
Salop
Salts
Score
Smack
Smoke
Snort
Speed
Stash
Stuff
Sugar
Sulfa
Taxol
Tonic
Upper
Vomit
Wafer

6 letters:
Amulet
Amytal®
Ativan®
Bombed
Bromal
Bummer
Burned
Charas
Cocain
Cook up
Curare
Curari
Dealer
Dosage
Downer
Dragée
Dry out
Elixir
Emetic
Get off
Heroin
Hooked
Inulin
Ipecac

Jack up
Joypop
Junkie
Kaolin
Liquor
Loaded
Make it
Mescla
Monkey
Mummia
Nod out
Normal
Number
Opiate
Peyote
Pituri
Popper
Prozac®
Pusher
Reefer
Remedy
Saloop
Skin up
Spaced
Spirit
Spliff
Squill
Step on
Stoned
Sulpha
Turn on
Valium®
Viagra®
Wasted
Weight
Zonked

7 letters:
Anodyne
Araroba
Argyrol®
Aspirin
Atabrin
Atebrin®
Atropin
Blocker
Botanic
Calomel
Cardiac
Cascara

Charlie
Chillum
Churrus
Cocaine
Codeine
Crank up
Damiana
Dapsone
Ecbolic
Ecstasy
Errhine
Ethical
Eucaine
Exhaust
Extract
Guarana
Hashish
Hemagog
Hemlock
Henbane
Hepatic
Hophead
Hyped up
Hypnone
Insulin
Jellies
Kaoline
Librium®
Linctus
Metopon
Miltown®
Mixture
Mogadon®
Morphia
Nervine
Patulin
Pep pill
Pessary
Placebo
Pothead
Quinine
Reactor
Rhatany
Salicin
Seconal®
Shoot up
Skin-pop
Smashed
Steroid
Styptic

Suramin
Swacked
Synergy
Tetanic
Topical
Trional
Turpeth
Vehicle
Veronal®
Vinegar
Wrecked

8 letters:
Acidhead
Adjuvant
Antabuse®
Antidote
Aromatic
Atabrine®
Ataraxic
Atropine
Autacoid
Bacterin
Banthine
Barbital
Benadryl®
Bioassay
Blockade
Caffeine
Cannabis
Cinchona
Cohobate
Comedown
Cortisol
Curarine
Designer
Diazepam
Diuretic
Emulsion
Endermic
Ephedrin
Excitant
External
Fentanyl
Freebase
Goofball
Hyoscine
Hypnotic
Inhalant
Ketamine

Krameria
Laetrile
Laudanum
Laxative
Lenitive
Mainline
Mersalyl
Mescalin
Methadon
Miticide
Moonrock
Morphine
Naloxone
Narcotic
Nembutal®
Neomycin
Nepenthe
Nicotine
Nystatin
Opium den
Overdose
Oxytocic
Pectoral
Positive
Psilocin
Pulmonic
Reaction
Relaxant
Retrovir®
Rifampin
Roborant
Salicine
Santonin
Scammony
Scopolia
Sedative
Serevent®
Snowball
Spansule
Specific
Switch on
Terebene
Tetronal
Thiazide
Tincture
Tolerant
Valerian
Vesicant
Viricide
Wormseed

Zerumbet

9 letters:
Acyclovir
Addiction
Addictive
Analeptic
Analgesic
Angel dust
Anovulant
Antrycide
Arsenical
Ataractic
Attenuant
Augmentin
Azedarach
Barbitone
Berberine
Biguanide
Botanical
Bring down
Busulphan
Calmative
Captopril
Carbachol
Cathartic
Cisplatin
Clozapine
Corticoid
Cortisone
Crackhead
Cyclizine
Cytotoxin
Decoction
Demulcent
Digitalis
Dramamine®
Electuary
Ephedrine
Excipient
Expellant
Expellent
Febrifuge
Foscarnet
Frusemide
Galenical
Glycoside
Goa powder
Hemagogue
Ibuprofen

Inotropic
Iprindole
Isoniazid
Jaborandi
Lorazepam
Magistral
Marihuana
Marijuana
Menstruum
Mepacrine
Merbromin
Mercurial
Mescaline
Methadone
Mydriasis
Novocaine®
Nux vomica
Officinal
Oleoresin
Paludrine®
Paregoric
Pethidine
Phenytoin
Practolol
Purgative
Quercetin
Quercitin
Quinidine
Quinquina
Reserpine
Resolvent
Revulsive
Safflower
Scopoline
Senna leaf
Senna pods
Sensitise
Sensitize
Signature
Smackhead
Soporific
Spaced out
Speedball
Stimulant
Strung out
Sudorific
Synergism
Synergist
Tamoxifen
Temazepam

Drugs and drug terms

Teniacide
Teniafuge
Totaquine
Tricyclic
Trinitrum
Verapamil
Vermifuge
Vulnerary
Wych hazel
Yohimbine

10 letters:
Abirritant
Absorption
Acetanilid
Agrypnotic
Alterative
Amantadine
Ampicillin
Anesthetic
Antagonist
Antibiotic
Antiemetic
Antimonial
Antipyrine
Anxiolytic
Astringent
Atracurium
Bacitracin
Belladonna
Benzedrine®
Benzocaine
Biological
Bufotenine
Chalybeate
Cholagogue
Cimetedine
Cimetidine
Cinchonine
Clofibrate
Clomiphene
Cold turkey
Colestipol
Confection
Connection
Convulsant
Dependency
Depressant
Disulfiram
Ergotamine

Ethambutol
Euphoriant
Formestane
Get through
Haemagogue
Helminthic
Hemostatic
Hypodermic
Imipramine
Indapamide
Isoniazide
Ivermectin
Lethal dose
Long-acting
Medication
Mefloquine
Meperidine
Methyldopa
Mickey Finn
Nalbuphine
Nifedipine
Nitrazepam
Painkiller
Palliative
Papaverine
Parenteral
Penicillin
Pentaquine
Phenacaine
Phenacetin
Phenformin
Potash alum
Potentiate
Prednisone
Preventive
Primaquine
Probenecid
Propanolol
Psilocybin
Quinacrine
Rifampicin
Salbutamol
Selegiline
Sialagogue
Sialogogue
Side effect
Space cadet
Speedfreak
Spermicide
Stramonium

Sucralfate
Taeniacide
Taeniafuge
Terramycin®
Thiouracil
Unofficial
Vesicatory
Witch hazel
Withdrawal
Zidovudine

11 letters:
Acetanilide
Acriflavine
Adiaphorous
Allopurinol
Aminobutene
Amphetamine
Amyl nitrite
Anaesthetic
Antifebrile
Antimycotic
Antipyretic
Antitussive
Aphrodisiac
Apomorphine
Barbiturate
Beta-blocker
Bitter aloes
Bupivacaine
Cantharides
Carbimazole
Carminative
Chloroquine
Chrysarobin
Cinnarizine
Clenbuterol
Clindamycin
Contrayerva
Deserpidine
Diamorphine
Diaphoretic
Distalgesic
Embrocation
Emmenagogue
Expectorant
Fluconazole
Gemfibrozil
Haemostatic
Haloperidol

Hyoscyamine
Ipecacuanha
Ipratropium
Isoxsuprine
Laughing gas
Magic bullet
Masticatory
Meprobamate
Neuroleptic
Nikethamide
Paracetamol
Paraldehyde
Pentamidine
Pentazocine
Pravastatin
Propranolol
Proprietary
Psychedelic
Psychodelic
Purple heart
Restorative
Sanguinaria
Scopolamine
Sensitivity
Short-acting
Succedaneum
Suppository
Suppurative
Thalidomide
Theobromine
Tolbutamide
Tous-les-mois
Trituration
Tropomyosin
Tumefacient
Vasodilator
Vinblastine
Vincristine

12 letters:
ACE inhibitor
Alexipharmic
Alpha-blocker
Anthelmintic
Antimalarial
Antiperiodic
Arsphenamine
Azathioprine
Chlorambucil
Control group

Cyclopropane
Cyclosporin-A
Decongestant
False saffron
Fluidextract
Fluphenazine
Glue-sniffing
Gonadotropin
Guanethidine
Hallucinogen
Idiosyncrasy
Incompatible
Indomethacin
Intoxicating
Mecamylamine
Methaqualone
Methotrexate
Mifepristone
Nitrous oxide
Perphenazine
Physotigmine
Prednisolene
Prescription
Promethazine
Prophylactic
Psychoactive
Radio mimetic
Recreational
Solvent abuse
Sorbefacient
Spermatocide
Streptomycin
Stupefacient
Tetracycline
Tranquilizer
Trimethoprim
Venepuncture
Venipuncture

13 letters:
Abortifacient
Amitriptyline
Anaphrodisiac
Anthelminthic
Antihistamine
Antispasmodic
Carbamazepine
Contraceptive
Co-trimoxazole
Depressomotor

Knockout drops
Magic mushroom
Materia medica
Mind-expanding
Penicillamine
Phencyclidine
Phenothiazine
Pyrimethamine
Sulphadiazine
Sympatholytic
Tachyphylaxis
Thiabendazole
Tranquilliser
Tranquillizer
Triamcinolone
Vasoinhibitor
Vinca alkaloid

14 letters:
Anticonvulsant
Antidepressant
Antimetabolite
Antiphlogistic
Bendrofluozide
Benzodiazepine
Bronchodilator
Butyrhophenone
Cascara sagrada
Chlorothiazide
Chlorpromazine
Chlorpropamide
Chlorthalidone
Contraindicate
Dimenhydrinate
Flucloxacillin
Hydrocortisone
Hypersensitive
Mean lethal dose
Mercaptopurine
Norethisterone
Over-the-counter
Pentobarbitone
Phenacyclidine
Phenobarbitone
Phenylbutazone
Rochelle powder
Seidlitz powder
Sulfamethazine
Sulphadimidine
Sulphanilamide

Sulphathiozole
Sulphisoxazole

15 letters:
Acetophenetidin
Alkylating agent
Anticholinergic
Bioavailability
Chloramphenicol
Dinitrogen oxide
Local anesthetic
Methamphetamine
Phenolphthalein
Psychotomimetic
Seidlitz powders
Shooting gallery
Sodium Pentothal®
Sympathomimetic
Vasoconstrictor

16 letters:
Anti-inflammatory
Blow someone's mind

Chemoprophylaxis
Chlordiazepoxide
Hypodermic needle
Local anaesthetic
Median lethal dose
Thiopental sodium

17 letters:
Calcium antagonist
Chlortetracycline
Dextroamphetamine
Diethyltryptamine
General anesthetic
Hypodermic syringe
Immunosuppressive
Minimum lethal dose
Pentylenetetrazol
Thiopentone sodium

18 letters:
Dimethyltryptamine
General anaesthetic
Intermediate-acting

Withdrawal symptoms

19 letters:
Acetylsalicylic acid
Sodium pentabarbital

20 letters:
Pentobarbitone sodium

21 letters:
Procaine hydrochloride

23 letters:
Meperidene
 hydrochloride

24 letters:
Lysergic acid
 diethylamide

28 letters:
Nonsteroidal anti-
 inflammatory

Ducks

4 letters:
Blue
Musk
Smee
Smew
Sord
Surf
Teal
Wood

5 letters:
Eider
Ruddy
Scaup

6 letters:
Garrot
Hareld
Herald
Runner
Scoter
Smeath
Smeeth
Tufted

Wigeon

7 letters:
Flapper
Gadwall
Mallard
Muscovy
Pintail
Pochard
Spatula
Widgeon

8 letters:
Bald-pate
Garganey
Mandarin
Oldsquaw
Paradise
Shelduck
Shoveler

9 letters:
Aylesbury
Bargander

Bergander
Golden-eye
Goosander
Greenhead
Harlequin
Sheldduck
Shoveller
Sprigtail
Whistling

10 letters:
Bufflehead
Canvasback
Long-tailed
Shieldrake
Surfscoter

11 letters:
Ferruginous

12 letters:
Velvet scoter

Snow White's seven dwarfs

3 letters:
Doc

5 letters:
Dopey

Happy

6 letters:
Grumpy
Sleepy

Sneezy

7 letters:
Bashful

Dyes

3 letters:
Azo
Vat

4 letters:
Anil
Chay
Choy
Ikat
Kohl
Wald
Weld
Woad
Wold

5 letters:
Batik
Chaya
Chica
Congo
Eosin
Grain
Henna
Shaya
Sumac
Woald

6 letters:
Archil
Battik
Cobalt
Corkir
Crotal
Direct
Flavin

Fustic
Fustoc
Gambir
Indigo
Kamala
Kermes
Korkir
Madder
Orcein
Orchel
Orchil
Raddle
Sumach
Tannin
Tie-dye

7 letters:
Alkanet
Camwood
Crocein
Crottle
Cudbear
Engrain
Flavine
Fuchsin
Gambier
Indican
Indoxyl
Indulin
Magenta
Para-red
Puccoon
Sunfast
Valonia

8 letters:
Catechin
Cinnabar
Fuchsine
Indamine
Induline
Mauveine
Nigrosin
Orchella
Purpurin
Pyronine
Safranin
Stone-rag
Stone-raw
Turnsole
Xanthium
Xylidine

9 letters:
Cochineal
Envermeil
Incardine
Indirubin
Myrobalan
Nigrosine
Phthalein
Primuline
Quinoline
Rhodamine
Rosanilin
Safranine
Tropaelin

Dyes

10 letters:
Anthracene
Azobenzine
Carthamine
Quercitron
Resorcinol

See also:
➤ **Pigments**

Rosaniline
Tartrazine

13 letters:
Anthraquinone
Canthaxanthin

14 letters:
Dinitrobenzene

15 letters:
Phenolphthalein

E e

Parts of the ear

5 letters:
Ancus
Incus
Pinna

6 letters:
Meatus
Stapes
Tragus

7 letters:
Cochlea
Eardrum
Ear lobe

Malleus
Saccule
Utricle

8 letters:
Tympanum

10 letters:
Oval window

11 letters:
Round window

12 letters:
Organ of Corti

13 letters:
Auditory canal
Auditory nerve

14 letters:
Eustachian tube

16 letters:
Tympanic membrane

18 letters:
Semicircular canals

21 letters:
External auditory canal

Layers of the earth's crust

4 letters:
Sial
Sima

7 letters:
Oceanic

8 letters:
Basement

11 letters:
Continental
Lithosphere
Lower mantle
Upper mantle

13 letters:
Asthenosphere

14 letters:
Transition zone

24 letters:
Mohorovicíc
  discontinuity

Specific eating habits

Food	Name of habit
Fellow humans	Anthropophagic *or* anthropophagous
Bees	Apivorous
Other members of the same species	Cannibalistic
Meat	Carnivorous

Food	Name of habit
Fruit	Carpophagous, frugivorous, *or* fruitarian
Dead and rotting flesh	Carrion
Dung	Coprophagous
Earth	Geophagous
Plants	Herbivorous
Wood	Hylophagous
Insects	Insectivorous
Mud	Limivorous
Large pieces of food	Macrophagous
Only one food	Monophagous
Fungi	Mycetophagous
Ants	Myrmecophagous
Nectar	Nectarivorous
Nuts	Nucivorous
Meat and plants	Omnivorous
Raw food	Omophagic *or* omophagous
Fish	Piscivorous
Gods	Theophagous
No animal products	Vegan
No flesh	Vegetarian
Animals	Zoophagous

Ecclesiastical terms

1 letter:
R
S
V
X
Y

2 letters:
BV
CE
DG
DV
HC
MS
PB
PP
RR
Sr
SS

St
VG
VW
Xn
XP
Xt

3 letters:
Abp
Alb
BVM
Cup
Dip
Fra
God
IDN
IHS
Lay
LDS

Mgr
Nun
Par
Pie
Pit
Pix
Pye
Pyx
Rev
See
Sta
STD
Ste
Sun
Use
Ven
Vow
WCC
Zen

4 letters:
Abbé
Alms
Ambo
Amen
Apse
Bans
Bapt
Beat
Bell
Cell
Chap
C of E
Cope
Cowl
Crib
Cure
Dame
Dean
Dove
Ebor
Eccl
Fall
Fold
Font
Hadg
Hajj
Halo
Holy
Host
Hymn
Idol
Kirk
Laic
Lent
Mass
Monk
None
Pall
Revd
Rite
Rood
Rule
Sain
Seal
Sext
Sign
Sion
Slip
Suff

Text
Veil
V Rev
Wake
Whit
Xmas
Xnty
YMCA
Yule
YWCA
Zion

5 letters:
Abbey
Abbot
Agape
Allah
Altar
Ambry
Amice
Amish
Angel
Banns
Bedel
Bible
Bless
Canon
Carol
Catho
Cense
Chant
Choir
Clerk
Close
Cloth
Credo
Creed
Cross
Cruet
Crypt
Curse
Deify
Deism
Deist
Deity
Demon
Denom
Devil
Dirge
Dogma

Dowry
Druid
Elder
Elect
Epiph
Exeat
Faith
Flock
Friar
Frock
Glebe
Glory
Godly
Grace
Hindu
Hours
House
Islam
Jesus
Jewry
Karma
Koran
Laity
Laver
Maker
Manna
Manse
Matin
Miter
Mitre
Mt Rev
Myrrh
Nones
Offer
Order
Padre
Pagan
Papal
Paten
Patin
Pietà
Piety
Plate
Prior
Psalm
Pyxis
Rabbi
Saint
Satan
Stall

Stole
Stoop
Stoup
Suffr
Synod
Teind
Tithe
Title
Trump
Vigil
Wafer

6 letters:
Abbacy
Abbess
Advent
Almuce
Anoint
Anthem
Archbp
Assume
Aumbry
Austin
Beadle
Bishop
Cantor
Censer
Chapel
Cherub
Chrism
Christ
Church
Clergy
Cleric
Coming
Common
Crèche
Curacy
Curate
Curtal
Deacon
Devout
Divine
Dossal
Dragon
Easter
Eparch
Exarch
Exodus
Father

Ferial
Friary
Fundie
Gloria
Gnosis
God man
Godson
Gospel
Gradin
Hallow
Harrow
Heaven
Hebrew
Heresy
Homily
Housel
Hymnal
Impose
Intone
Israel
Jesuit
Jewish
Judaic
Lavabo
Lector
Legend
Lenten
Lesson
Litany
Living
Marian
Martyr
Matins
Maundy
Mormon
Mosaic
Moslem
Mosque
Mother
Muslim
Novice
Nuncio
Oblate
Octave
Office
Old man
Ordain
Orders
Papacy
Papism

Papist
Parish
Parson
Pastor
Patron
Paynim
Person
Postil
Prayer
Preach
Priest
Priory
Proper
Pulpit
Purify
Purple
Quaker
Redeem
Revert
Ritual
Rosary
Rt Revd
Rubric
Sacral
Sacred
Schism
Season
Secret
Sermon
Server
Sexton
Shiite
Shinto
Shrine
Shroud
Simony
Sinful
Sinner
Sister
Solemn
Stigma
Sufism
Sunday
Suttee
Talmud
Tantra
Taoism
Te Deum
Temple
Theism

Tippet
Tongue
Venite
Verger
Vesper
Vestal
Vestry
Virgin
Votary
Warden

7 letters:
Aaronic
Acolyte
Agrapha
Ampulla
Anagoge
Apostle
Article
Ascetic
Asperse
Atheism
Atheist
Bahaism
Bambino
Baptism
Baptist
Baptize
Benison
Blessed
Brother
Canonry
Cantuar
Cassock
Cenacle
Chalice
Chancel
Chantry
Chapter
Chrisom
Classis
Cluniac
Collate
Collect
College
Commune
Confess
Confirm
Conform
Convent

Council
Counsel
Crosier
Crozier
Deanery
Decanal
Defrock
Deified
Devotee
Diocese
Dissent
Dominie
Element
Epistle
Eremite
Errancy
Evangel
Evil One
Expiate
Frontal
Genesis
Gentile
Glorify
Gnostic
Godhead
Godhood
Halidom
Hassock
Heathen
Holy day
Holy Joe
Hosanna
Idolize
Immerse
Incense
Infulae
Inspire
Introit
Jainism
Jehovah
Judaism
Kenosis
Kerygma
Kirkman
Labarum
Lady Day
Laicize
Liturgy
Low Mass
Lustral

Madonna
Maniple
Martyry
Mattins
Maurist
Messiah
Minster
Miracle
Mission
Monkery
Monkish
Mortify
Mourner
Movable
Mystery
Notitia
Nunhood
Nunnery
Old Nick
Oratory
Ordinal
Our Lady
Parlour
Paschal
Pauline
Peccant
Penance
Pietism
Pilgrim
Pontiff
Prebend
Prelacy
Prelate
Present
Primacy
Primate
Profane
Prophet
Proverb
Provide
Puritan
Ramadan
Recluse
Rectory
Regular
Reredos
Respond
Retable
Revival
Sabbath

Sacring
Sanctum
Sanctus
Saviour
Secular
Sedilia
Service
Species
Sponsor
Spousal
Station
Stylite
Tantric
Titulus
Tribune
Trinity
Unction
Unfrock
Vatican
Vespers
Whitsun
Worship
Xmas Day
Yule log
Zionism

8 letters:
Abbatial
Ablution
Advowson
Affusion
Agnus Dei
Alleluia
Altar boy
Anathema
Anglican
Antiphon
Beadsman
Bedesman
Benefice
Brownist
Buddhism
Buddhist
Canonist
Canonize
Canon law
Canticle
Cathedra
Catholic
Celibacy

Cellarer
Cenobite
Chancery
Chapelry
Chaplain
Charisma
Chasuble
Cherubim
Choirboy
Christen
Ciborium
Clerical
Cloister
Coenacle
Colloquy
Creation
Crucifix
Deaconry
Dedicate
Devotion
Diaconal
Dies Irae
Diocesan
Diriment
Disciple
Disfrock
Docetism
Doxology
Druidess
Druidism
Ecce Homo
Ecclesia
Emmanuel
Empyrean
Epiphany
Epistler
Evensong
Expiable
Faithful
Footpace
Fraction
Frontlet
Galilean
Gallican
Godchild
God's acre
Godsquad
Guardian
Hail Mary
Hallowed

Heavenly
Hierarch
Hieratic
High Mass
Holiness
Holy City
Holy Land
Holy rood
Holy Week
Hymn book
Immanent
Immanuel
Jacobite
Jubilate
Lavatory
Libellee
Lord's Day
Lustrate
Lutheran
Man of God
Maronite
Marriage
Menology
Ministry
Miserere
Mohammed
Monachal
Monastic
Monition
Monkhood
Nativity
Oblation
Offering
Ordinand
Ordinary
Orthodox
Paradise
Parament
Parclose
Pastoral
Pelagian
Penitent
Pericope
Piacular
Postlude
Priestly
Prophesy
Province
Psalmody
Redeemer

Registry
Response
Reverend
Rigorism
Rogation
Sacristy
Sanctify
Sanctity
Sarum use
Scapular
Sentence
Separate
Silenced
Simoniac
Sinecure
Son of God
Suffrage
Superior
Tantrism
Tertiary
Thurible
Thurifer
Tithable
Traditor
Transept
Unchurch
Unhallow
Veronica
Versicle
Vesperal
Vestment
Viaticum
Vicarage
Vicarial

9 letters:
Adoration
Alleluiah
Allelujah
Ambrosian
Antiphony
Apostolic
Archangel
Aspersion
Augustine
Avoidance
Baptistry
Beelzebub
Bishopric
Blasphemy

Born-again
Calvinism
Calvinist
Candlemas
Canonical
Cantorial
Capitular
Catechism
Catechize
Cathedral
Celebrant
Celestial
Christian
Christmas
Churchman
City of God
Claustral
Clergyman
Clericals
Cloistral
Coadjutor
Coenobite
Collation
Collative
Collegium
Comforter
Commendam
Communion
Conciliar
Confessor
Confirmed
Dalai Lama
Damnation
Deaconess
Dei gratia
Diaconate
Dimissory
Directory
Discalced
Dissenter
Dog collar
Dominical
Easter Day
Ecumenism
Epiclesis
Episcopal
Establish
Eucharist
Exarchate
Expectant

Expiation
Expiatory
Formalism
Formulary
Godfather
Godmother
Godparent
Gospeller
Graveyard
Hagiarchy
Halloween
Hallowmas
Hermitage
Hierarchy
High altar
Holocaust
Holy Ghost
Holy Grail
Holy water
Homiletic
Immersion
Impeccant
Incensory
Incumbent
Institute
Interdict
Jerusalem
Last rites
Lay sister
Libellant
Liturgics
Liturgist
Love feast
Low Sunday
Martinmas
Martyrdom
Mercy seat
Methodism
Methodist
Millenary
Miscreant
Missioner
Monastery
Mortal sin
Novitiate
Obedience
Offertory
Officiant
Officiate
Our Father

Out sister
Paraclete
Parochial
Parsonage
Pastorate
Patriarch
Patrimony
Patristic
Patrology
Patroness
Pentecost
Perdition
Pluralism
Plurality
Pluralize
Polyptych
Precentor
Preceptor
Predicant
Prelatism
Presbyter
Proselyte
Provision
Quakerism
Recession
Reconcile
Reconvert
Reformism
Religieux
Religious
Reliquary
Remission
Ritualism
Ritualize
Rubrician
Rural dean
Sacrament
Sacrarium
Sacrifice
Sacrilege
Sacristan
Saint's day
Salvation
Sanctuary
Scientist
Seneschal
Shintoism
Solemnize
Spiritual
Succentor

Succursal
Suffragan
Surrogate
Sutteeism
Synagogue
Testament
Tradition
Translate
Venerable
Venial sin
Vestryman
Vicariate
Yom Kippur

10 letters:
Act of faith
Allhallows
Altar cloth
Amen corner
Antinomian
Antiphonal
Apostolate
Archbishop
Archdeacon
Archpriest
Asceticism
Ascription
Assumption
Athanasian
Bar mitzvah
Benedicite
Benedictus
Canonicals
Canonicate
Canonicity
Canto fermo
Catechumen
Ceremonial
Chancellor
Childermas
Churchgoer
Circumcise
Cloistered
Conference
Confessant
Confession
Confirmand
Conformist
Conformity
Connection

Consecrate
Consistory
Conventual
Dedication
Deo gratias
Deo volente
Devotional
Discipline
Ecumenical
Enthusiasm
Enthusiast
Episcopacy
Episcopate
Evangelism
Evangelist
Evangelize
Fellowship
Fenestella
Free Church
Gnosticize
Good Friday
Gospel oath
Hagiolatry
Halleluiah
Hallelujah
Hierocracy
High Church
High Priest
Holy Family
Holy orders
Holy Spirit
Homiletics
Horologium
House group
House of God
Idolatrize
Impanation
Impeccable
Insufflate
Intinction
Invitatory
Invocation
Irreligion
Lammastide
Last Supper
Lay brother
Lectionary
Limitarian
Liturgical
Lord's table

Magnificat
Metropolis
Millennium
Miscreance
Misericord
Missionary
Mother's Day
Ordination
Palm Sunday
Pancake Day
Pilgrimage
Pontifical
Prayer book
Preachment
Prebendary
Presbytery
Priesthood
Profession
Protestant
Providence
Provincial
Puritanism
Religieuse
Requiescat
Reredorter
Responsory
Retrochoir
Reunionist
Revelation
Revivalism
Revivalist
Sacerdotal
Sacrosanct
Sanctified
Sanctitude
Scriptures
Secularize
Sexagesima
Shrovetide
Sisterhood
Solifidian
Subreption
Subsellium
Superaltar
Tabernacle
Twelfth Day
Unhallowed
Unhouseled
Versicular
Vigil light

Visitation
Whit Monday
Whit Sunday

11 letters:
All Souls' Day
Antependium
Antiphonary
Archdiocese
Aspersorium
Augustinian
Benediction
Beneficiary
Blasphemous
Book of hours
Brotherhood
Calefactory
Cardinalate
Catholicism
Celtic cross
Christening
Christingle
Churchwoman
Clericalism
Cockleshell
Coessential
Commandment
Communicant
Communicate
Contemplate
Conventicle
Convocation
Crucifixion
Evangelical
Externalism
Gloria Patri
Glossolalia
Goddaughter
Hare Krishna
House church
Immanentism
Impropriate
Incarnation
Incorporeal
Independent
Institution
Irreligious
Jesus Christ
Judgment Day
Lord of Hosts

Lord's Prayer
Lord's Supper
Martyrology
Millenarian
Monasticism
Monseigneur
Mother of God
Oecumenical
Parish clerk
Parishioner
Paschal Lamb
Passiontide
Passion Week
Patron saint
Pelagianism
Pentecostal
Preparation
Priestcraft
Prodigal Son
Proselytize
Protomartyr
Purificator
Rastafarian
Recessional
Ritualistic
Sabbatarian
Sacramental
Sanctus bell
Scriptorium
Stabat Mater
Sursum corda
Temporality
Thaumaturge
Twelfthtide
Whitsuntide
Year of grace
Zen Buddhism

12 letters:
Advent Sunday
All Saints' Day
Anathematize
Annunciation
Apostolic See
Archdeaconry
Ascension Day
Ash Wednesday
Body of Christ
Chapel of ease
Chapterhouse

Christmas Day
Christmas Eve
Churchwarden
Circuit rider
Concelebrate
Confessional
Confirmation
Confucianism
Congregation
Deconsecrate
Disestablish
Dispensation
Ecclesiastic
Ecclesiology
Eleanor Cross
Episcopalian
Episcopalism
Good Shepherd
Heteroousian
Holy Saturday
Holy Thursday
Immersionism
Independency
Intercession
Judgement Day
Kyrie eleison
Last Judgment
Messeigneurs
Metropolitan
Ministration
Most Reverend
New Testament
Non-Christian
Obedientiary
Old Testament
Palingenesis
Patriarchate
Presbyterian
Presentation
Presentative
Procathedral
Processional
Providential
Quadragesima
Real presence
Residentiary
Rogation Days
Satisfaction
Satisfactory
Septuagesima

Spirituality
Spiritualize
Spy Wednesday
Subapostolic
Subscription
Sunday school
Superhumeral
Thanksgiving
Traducianism
Twelfth Night
Very Reverend
Vicar general
Well dressing
Winding sheet

13 letters:
Allhallowtide
Apostles' Creed
Archbishopric
Archidiaconal
Ascensiontide
Autocephalous
Baptism of fire
Burnt offering
Canonical hour
Contemplation
Contemplative
Corpus Christi
Credence table
Day of Judgment
Divine service
Ecclesiolatry
Excommunicate
Gift of tongues
Glorification
Holy Communion
Incardination
Last Judgement
Mater dolorosa
Metrical psalm
Mortification
Nonpractising
Passion Sunday
Premillennial
Protestantism
Quadragesimal
Quinquagesima
Right Reverend
Roman Catholic
Sacerdotalism

Salvation Army
Sanctuary lamp
Shrove Tuesday
Spoiled priest
Trinity Sunday
Unconsecrated

14 letters:
Archidiaconate
Archiepiscopal
Article of faith
Day of Judgement
Ecclesiastical
Exclaustration
Extracanonical
Fundamentalism
Gregorian chant
Indifferentism
Intercommunion
Maundy Thursday
Millenarianism
Orthodox Church
Parish register
Peculiar people
Pontifical Mass
Rastafarianism
Recording Angel
Reverend Mother
Sacramentalism
Sacramentarian
Territorialism

15 letters:
Act of contrition
Archiepiscopate
Athanasian Creed
Church of England
Dominical letter
Ecclesiasticism
Excommunication
Father confessor
General Assembly
Jehovah's Witness
Mothering Sunday
Presbyterianism
Ten Commandments

16 letters:
Apostolic Fathers
Blessed Sacrament

Church of Scotland
Patriarchal cross
Premillennialism
Prince of Darkness
Saint Swithin's Day
Sustentation fund

17 letters:
Communion of saints
Established Church

Saint Andrew's Cross
Speaking in tongues

18 letters:
College of Cardinals
Establishmentarian
Stations of the Cross

19 letters:
Gloria in Excelsis Deo

22 letters:
World Council of
  Churches

27 letters:
Ecclesiastical
  Commissioners
Purification of the Virgin
  Mary

Economics

BRANCHES OF ECONOMICS

7 letters:
Welfare

10 letters:
Agronomics
Industrial

11 letters:
Cliometrics

12 letters:
Econometrics

14 letters:
Macroeconomics
Microeconomics

15 letters:
Economic history

ECONOMICS TERMS

2 letters:
HP

3 letters:
Bid
GDP
GNP
Pay
PEP
Tax
UBR
VAT

4 letters:
Bank
Boom
Cash
Debt
Duty
Hire
Loan
MCAs
Mint
PAYE
PSBR

Rent
Shop
Wage

5 letters:
Asset
Lease
Money
Price
Sales
Share
Slump
Stock
Trade
Trust
Yield

6 letters:
Barter
Budget
Cartel
Credit
Demand
Export
Import

Income
Labour
Lender
Market
Merger
Patent
Picket
Profit
Retail
Salary
Saving
Supply
Tariff
Wealth

7 letters:
Autarky
Boycott
Capital
Dumping
Duopoly
Embargo
Finance
Freight
Funding

ECONOMICS TERMS (CONTINUED)

Hedging
Holding
Invoice
Lockout
Payroll
Pension
Premium
Revenue
Subsidy
Surplus
Synergy
Trustee
Utility

8 letters:
Base rate
Capacity
Consumer
Currency
Discount
Dividend
Earnings
Employee
Employer
Exchange
Freeport
Hoarding
Hot money
Interest
Junk bond
Monopoly
Mortgage
Offshore
Overtime
Producer
Recovery
Supplier
Takeover
Taxation
Tax haven
Training

9 letters:
Commodity
Deflation
Franchise
Free rider
Free trade

Income tax
Insurance
Liability
Liquidity
Means test
Mediation
Middleman
Net profit
Oligopoly
Overheads
Piecework
Portfolio
Rationing
Recession
Recycling
Reflation
Trademark
Unit trust

10 letters:
Automation
Bankruptcy
Bear market
Bull market
Capitalism
Closed shop
Commission
Depression
Divestment
Employment
Fiscal drag
Fiscal year
Fixed costs
Forfaiting
Game theory
Green money
Insolvency
Investment
Monetarism
Pawnbroker
Production
Redundancy
Share issue
Tax evasion
Trade union
Wholesaler

11 letters:
Arbitration
Capital good
Central bank
Competition
Consumption
Cooperative
Corporation
Devaluation
Durable good
Expenditure
Fixed assets
Foreclosure
Gross profit
Index-linked
Indirect tax
Intangibles
Legal tender
Liquid asset
Liquidation
Money supply
Overheating
Overmanning
Pension fund
Poverty trap
Premium bond
Public works
Pump priming
Revaluation
Savings bank
Self service
Shareholder
Share market
Shop steward
Social costs
Speculation
Stagflation
Stockbroker
Stock market
Stop-go cycle
Transaction
Underwriter

12 letters:
Balance sheet
Black economy
Bridging loan
Buyer's market

ECONOMICS TERMS (CONTINUED)

Clearing bank
Common market
Consumer good
Cost of living
Customs union
Depreciation
Deregulation
Discount rate
Disinflation
Dutch disease
Earned income
Entrepreneur
Exchange rate
Fiscal policy
Five-Year Plan
Gold standard
Hard currency
Hire purchase
Human capital
Interest rate
Joint venture
Labour market
Laisser faire
Laissez faire
Mercantilism
Merchant bank
Mixed economy
Moonlighting
National debt
Pay-as-you-earn
Productivity
Profit margin
Rent controls
Risk analysis
Soft currency
Stock control
Tax avoidance
Terms of trade
Trade barrier
Unemployment
Welfare state

13 letters:
Budget deficit
Business cycle
Credit squeeze
Discount house
Financial year

Free trade area
Free trade zone
Futures market
Income support
Invisible hand
Listed company
Market failure
Multinational
Primary sector
Privatization
Profitability
Profit sharing
Protectionism
Public finance
Public utility
Ratchet effect
Seller's market
Sequestration
Service sector
Stock exchange
Unit of account
Value-added tax
Variable costs
Wage restraint

14 letters:
Balanced budget
Balance of trade
Barriers to exit
Command economy
Commercial bank
Corporation tax
Credit controls
Current account
Deposit account
Disequilibrium
Economic growth
Economic policy
Fringe benefits
Full employment
Gains from trade
Government bond
Hyperinflation
Infrastructure
Inheritance tax
Mass production
Monetary policy
National income

Nondurable good
Planned economy
Public interest
Quality control
Regional policy
Self-employment
Simple interest
Specialization
Tangible assets
Unearned income
Venture capital
Working capital

15 letters:
Barriers to entry
Building society
Diversification
Fixed investment
Friendly society
Marginal revenue
Marginal utility
Nationalization
National product
Per capita income
Private property
Purchasing power
Rationalization
Self-sufficiency
Share price index

16 letters:
Demand management
Disposable income
Division of labour
Economies of scale
Industrial estate
Industrial policy
Industrial sector
Instalment credit
Intangible assets
Invisible balance
Management buy-out
Medium of exchange
Retail price index
Standard of living

17 letters:
Balance of payments

ECONOMICS TERMS (CONTINUED)

Chamber of Commerce
Cost effectiveness
Cost-push inflation
Economic sanctions
Free-market economy
Gilt-edged security
Industrial dispute
International debt
Joint-stock company
Private enterprise
Public expenditure
Subsidiary company

18 letters:
Diminishing returns
Environmental audit
Import restrictions
Inflationary spiral
Perfect competition
Personal equity plan
Socio-economic group
Trade-weighted index

19 letters:
Cost-benefit analysis
Deindustrialization
Demand-pull inflation
Industrial relations
Labour theory of value
Macroeconomic policy
Microeconomic policy
Progressive taxation
Stabilization policy
Supply-side economics
Unemployment benefit
Uniform business rate
Vertical integration
Worker participation

20 letters:
Collective bargaining
Comparative advantage
Greenfield investment
Gross domestic product
Gross national product
Imperfect competition
Information agreement
Profit-and-loss account
Rational expectations
Residual
  unemployment
Seasonal
  unemployment

21 letters:
Foreign exchange
  market
Forward exchange
  market
Horizontal integration
International reserves
Polluter pays principle
Voluntary
  unemployment

22 letters:
Conspicuous
  consumption
Institutional investors
Prices and incomes
  policy
Recommended retail
  price
Research and
  development
Structural
  unemployment

23 letters:
Fixed exchange-rate
  system
Foreign exchange
  controls

25 letters:
Intellectual property
  right
Natural rate of
  unemployment
Public-sector debt
  repayment
Restrictive labour
  practice

26 letters:
Floating exchange-rate
  system

27 letters:
Medium-term financial
  strategy
Monetary
  compensatory
  amounts

28 letters:
International
  competitiveness

30 letters:
National insurance
  contributions

32 letters:
Public-sector borrowing
  requirement

ECONOMICS SCHOOLS AND THEORIES

7 letters:
Chicago
Marxism

8 letters:
Austrian

9 letters:
Classical

10 letters:
Monetarism

11 letters:
Physiocrats
Reaganomics
Rogernomics
Thatcherism

12 letters:
Keynesianism
Mercantilism
Neoclassical

13 letters:
NeoKeynesians

ECONOMISTS

4 letters:
Hume, *David*
Marx, *Karl*
Mill, *James*
Mill, *John Stuart*
Ward, *Dame Barbara
  (Mary)*
Webb, *Sidney*
West, *Arthur Lewis*

5 letters:
Passy, *Frédéric*
Smith, *Adam*
Weber, *Max*

6 letters:
Angell, *Norman*
Bright, *John*
Cobden, *Richard*
Delors, *Jacques*
Frisch, *Ragnar*
George, *Henry*
Jevons, *William Stanley*
Keynes, *John Maynard*
Laffer, *Arthur*

Monnet, *Jean*
Pareto, *Vilfredo*
Turgot, *Anne Robert
  Jacques*
Veblen, *Thorstein*

7 letters:
Bagehot, *Walter*
Cournot, *Augustin*
D' Oresme, *Nicole*
Douglas, *C(lifford)
  H(ugh)*
Kuznets, *Simon*
Leacock, *Stephen Butler*
Malthus, *Thomas Robert*
Quesnay, *François*
Ricardo, *David*
Toynbee, *Arnold*
Wootton, *Barbara
  (Frances)*

8 letters:
Beccaria, *Cesare
  Bonesana*
Friedman, *Milton*

Mansholt, *Sicco Leendert*
Marshall, *Alfred*
Phillips, *A(lban) W(illiam)
  H(ousego)*
Von Hayek, *Friedrich
  August*

9 letters:
Beveridge, *William
  Henry*
Galbraith, *J(ohn)
  K(enneth)*
Tinbergen, *Jan*

10 letters:
De Sismondi, *Jean
  Charles Léonard
  Simonde*
Papandreou, *Andreas
  (George)*
Schumacher, *Ernst
  Friedrich*
Schumpeter, *Joseph*

Education terms

2 letters:
UE

3 letters:
COP
Don
Dux

GCE
GPS
Jig
LMS
ONC
PTA
SCE

Set
Wag

4 letters:
Co-ed
CPVE
Crib

Dean
Exam
Fail
GCSE
Gown
Hall
Hood
Mich
Pass
Pipe
SATS
Term
Test
Year

5 letters:
Class
Dunce
Entry
Essay
Expel
Flunk
Gaudy
Grade
Grant
Hooky
House
Lines
Lycée
Mitch
Mocks
Pandy
Resit
Shell
Sizar
Stage
Tutee
Tutor
Union

6 letters:
A level
Alumna
Bedder
Binary
Bursar
Campus
Credit
Degree
Docent

Fellow
Ferule
Greats
Higher
Honors
Hookey
Incept
Infant
Junior
Master
Matric
O grade
O level
Pedant
Porter
Reader
Recess
Rector
Regent
Remove
Report
Second
Senate
Senior
Stream
Thesis
Truant
Warden

7 letters:
Adviser
Advisor
Alumnus
Banding
Battels
Boarder
Bursary
Crammer
Deanery
Dominie
Donnish
Dropout
Educate
Faculty
Federal
Fresher
Honours
Janitor
Lecture
Marking

Midterm
Prefect
Prelims
Primers
Proctor
Provost
Seminar
Session
Subject
Teach-in
Tuition

8 letters:
A bursary
Academic
Accredit
Aegrotat
B bursary
Comedown
Commoner
Delegacy
Dunce cap
Emeritus
Exercise
External
Freshman
Graduand
Graduate
Headship
Homework
Internal
Key stage
Lecturer
Manciple
Mistress
Parietal
Redbrick
Remedial
Semester
Send down
Sorority
Transfer
Tutorial
Wrangler

9 letters:
Assistant
Associate
Bubs grade
Bursarial

Catalogue
Catchment
Classmate
Classroom
Collegial
Collegian
Detention
Education
Extension
Gymnasium
Moderator
Muck-up day
Principal
Professor
Reception
Registrar
Rusticate
Schoolman
Sixth form
Sophomore
Speech day
Sports day
Statement
Trimester

10 letters:
Assignment
Bursarship
Chancellor
Collegiate
Coursework
Curricular
Curriculum
Department
Easter term
Eleven-plus
Exhibition
Extramural
Fellowship
Graded post
Graduation
Grant-in-aid
Headmaster
High school
Hilary term
Imposition
Instructor
Intramural
Invigilate
Prepositor

Prospectus
Readership
Recreation
Sabbatical
Scholastic
Schoolmarm
Supervisor
Transcript
Unstreamed

11 letters:
Coeducation
Convocation
Educational
Examination
Housefather
Housemaster
Housemother
In residence
Invigilator
Lower school
Matriculate
Trinity term
Upper school

12 letters:
Accumulation
Chapterhouse
Commencement
Congregation
Core subjects
Dissertation
Exhibitioner
Headmistress
Open learning
Postgraduate
Privatdocent
Schoolleaver
Schoolmaster
Self-educated
Subprincipal

13 letters:
Advanced level
Baccalaureate
Boarding house
Cuisenaire rod®
Full professor
Lowerclassman
Matriculation

Mature student
Ordinary grade
Ordinary level
Professoriate
Schoolteacher
Standard Grade
Summa cum laude
Undergraduate

14 letters:
Common Entrance
Family grouping
Headmastership
Liaison officer
Michaelmas term
Sandwich course
Schoolmistress
Student teacher
Tutorial system
Vice chancellor

15 letters:
Advisory teacher
Cross-curricular
Extracurricular
Grant-maintained
Hall of residence
Interscholastic
Refresher course
Regius professor
Tertiary bursary

16 letters:
Campus university
Further education
Headmistress-ship
Junior common room
Middle common room
Senior common room
Sixth-form college
Vertical grouping

17 letters:
Level of attainment
Literae humaniores
Local examinations
School Certificate
Visiting professor

18 letters:
Great Public Schools
National Curriculum
Punishment exercise
University entrance

19 letters:
Conductive education
Record of achievement
Summative assessment

20 letters:
Continuous assessment

23 letters:
Nuffield teaching
  project

Standard assessment
  tasks

24 letters:
Certificate of Proficiency
Local management of
  schools
Parent teacher
  association

27 letters:
Ordinary National
  Certificate

29 letters:
General Certificate of
  Education

University entrance
  examination

30 letters:
Scottish Certificate of
  Education

35 letters:
Certificate of Pre-
  vocational Education

38 letters:
General Certificate of
  Secondary Education

Electronics terms

3 letters:
Bar
Bus
CCD
Eye
Key
LCD
LED
Pad

4 letters:
Bell
Bulb
Card
Chip
Coil
Cord
Dial
Disc
Duct
Flex
Fuse
Gate
Gobo
Jack
Lead
Lobe
Loop
Mike

Neon
Plug
Port
Slug
Tube
Wire

5 letters:
Array
Balun
Cable
Choke
Clock
Coder
Diode
Donor
Drain
Latch
Maser
Mixer
Motor
Plate
Shunt
Spool
Tuner
Valve
Wafer
Wiper

6 letters:
Aerial
Bridge
Buffer
Busbar
Button
Buzzer
Bypass
Carbon
Driver
Feeder
Heater
Mosaic
Needle
Outlet
Phasor
Pick-up
Radome
Scaler
Screen
Sensor
Sheath
Sleeve
Slicer
Socket
Stator
Stylus
Switch
Triode

Woofer

7 letters:
Acetate
Adaptor
Antenna
Battery
Bimorph
Booster
Breaker
Bushing
Capstan
Charger
Chassis
Chopper
Clipper
Console
Counter
Coupler
Crystal
Display
Divider
Element
Emitter
Exciter
Excitor
Fuse box
Gyrator
Harness
Igniter
Krytron
Limiter
Mag tape
Monitor
Negator
Pentode
Reactor
Scanner
Speaker
Tetrode
Tone arm
Trimmer
Tweeter

8 letters:
Acceptor
Black box
Detector
Diffuser
Digitron

Envelope
Expander
Filament
Heat sink
Ignitron
Inverter
Live wire
Magic eye
Neon lamp
Orthicon
Radiator
Receiver
Recorder
Repeater
Resistor
Rheostat
Sleeving
Slip ring
Solenoid
Varactor
Varistor
Vibrator

9 letters:
Amplifier
Autometer
Autotimer
Bolometer
Call alarm
Capacitor
Cartridge
Choke coil
Component
Condenser
Conductor
Contactor
Delay line
Drift tube
Dummy load
Dynamotor
Equalizer
Flame lamp
Fluxmeter
Hygristor
Image tube
Kinescope
Labyrinth
Leyden jar
Light bulb
Magnetron

Metal tape
Microchip
Nixie tube
Optophone
Phono plug
Phototube
Pilot lamp
Plugboard
Plumbicon
Power pack
Rectifier
Reflector
Resnatron
Resonator
Sequencer
Spark coil
Tesla coil
Thyratron
Thyristor
Turntable
Voltmeter
Wattmeter

10 letters:
Acorn valve
Alternator
Banana plug
Breadboard
Camera tube
Chrome tape
Commutator
Comparator
Compressor
Controller
Coulometer
Esaki diode
Goniometer
Harmonizer
Hydrophone
LCD display
LED display
Microphone
Mimic panel
Moving coil
Multimeter
NOT circuit
Oscillator
Patch board
Photodiode
P-n junction

Push button
Radio valve
Reproducer
Rhumbatron
Screen grid
Servomotor
Shadow mask
Sodium lamp
Solar panel
Stabilizer
Suppressor
Switchgear
Thermistor
Time switch
Transducer
Transistor
Trip switch
Vacuum tube
Variometer
Voltameter
Wander plug
Welding rod
Zener diode

11 letters:
Anticathode
Autochanger
Cat's whisker
Cold cathode
Electric eye
Faraday cage
Interrupter
Junction box
Knife switch
Loading coil
Loudspeaker
Microswitch
Motherboard
NAND circuit
Open circuit
Picture tube
Ring circuit
Silicon chip
Space heater
Storage tube
Strobe tuner
Switchboard
Tickler coil
Transformer
Tunnel diode

Voltammeter

12 letters:
Bow collector
Circuit board
Coaxial cable
Electrometer
Electron tube
Friction tape
Magnetic tape
Microcircuit
Oscillograph
Oscilloscope
Preamplifier
Squirrel cage
Standard cell
Toggle switch

13 letters:
Crystal pick-up
Discharge tube
Discriminator
Electric motor
Image orthicon
Induction coil
Low-pass filter
Mercury switch
Multivibrator
Potentiometer
Quartz crystal
Record-changer
Rhombic aerial
Ripple control
Semiconductor
Tumbler switch

14 letters:
Band-pass filter
Circuit breaker
Heating element
High-pass filter
Image converter
Induction motor
Long-wire aerial
Magnetic pick-up
Magnetic stripe
Mesh connection
Motor generator
Noise generator
Peltier element

Power amplifier
Printed circuit
Schmitt trigger
Servomechanism
Star connection
Television tube
Trickle charger
Turbogenerator
Universal motor
Voltage divider

15 letters:
Alloyed junction
Autotransformer
Bleeder resistor
Bridge rectifier
Cavity resonator
Class-A amplifier
Class-B amplifier
Class-C amplifier
Crystal detector
Drift transistor
Electric circuit
Local oscillator
Majority carrier
Minority carrier
Phototransistor
Shuttle armature
Signal generator
Thermionic valve

16 letters:
Carbon microphone
Gas-discharge tube
Image intensifier
Potential divider
Ribbon microphone
Silicon rectifier
Smoothing circuit
Sodium-vapour lamp
Spark transmitter
Spectrum analyser
Synchronous motor
Transmission line

17 letters:
Crystal microphone
Electrostatic lens
Equivalent circuit
Full-wave rectifier

Ground-plane aerial
Integrated circuit
Lightning arrester
Photoelectric cell

18 letters:
Dynatron oscillator
Electronic ignition
I-type semiconductor
Junction transistor
Light-emitting diode
Lightning conductor
Travelling-wave tube

19 letters:
Epitaxial transistor

Parametric amplifier
Parametric equalizer
Pulse height analyser
Seven-segment display

20 letters:
Liquid-crystal display
Multichannel analyser
Operational amplifier
Relaxation oscillator
Synchronous converter

21 letters:
Electric-discharge lamp
Field-effect transistor
Residual current device

22 letters:
Electrostatic generator
Intrinsic semiconductor

24 letters:
Analogue-digital
   converter

26 letters:
Silicon-controlled
   rectifier

32 letters:
Steam-generating
   heavy-water reactor

Embroidery stitches

3 letters:
Fly

4 letters:
Back
Barb
Coil
Fern
Post
Rice
Stem

5 letters:
Briar
Catch
Chain
Coral
Cross
Daisy
Greek
Satin
Split

6 letters:
Basque
Beaded
Berlin
Cast on
Cretan
Crewel

Damask
Eyelet
Ladder
Scroll

7 letters:
Berwick
Blanket
Bullion
Chevron
Chinese
Convent
Feather
Kloster
Outline
Plaited
Running
Russian
Sampler
Sham Hem

8 letters:
Pekinese
Scottish
Wheatear

9 letters:
Arrowhead
Crow's-foot
Lazy Daisy

Open Chain
Quilt Knot

10 letters:
Buttonhole
Casalguidi
French Knot
German Knot
Portuguese
Roman Chain
Whipped Fly

11 letters:
Caterpillar
Double Cross
Herringbone
Montenegrin
Renaissance
Ribbed Wheel
Threaded Fly
Whipped Back
Whipped Stem
Zigzag Chain

12 letters:
Ghiordes Knot
Russian Cross
Twisted Chain
Whipped Chain

Emperors

13 letters:
Buttonhole Bar
Closed Feather
Porto Rico rose

14 letters:
Crossed corners
Feathered Chain

Whipped Running

15 letters:
Buttonhole Wheel
Threaded Running

16 letters:
Closed Buttonhole

17 letters:
Crossed Buttonhole
Threaded Arrowhead
Woven Spider's Wheel

18 letters:
Twisted Lattice Band

Emperors

TITLES OF EMPERORS

3 letters:
Imp
Rex

4 letters:
Inca
King
Tsar

5 letters:
Kesar
Mpret
Negus
Rosco
Ruler
Shang
Tenno

6 letters:
Kaiser
Keasar
Mikado
Purple
Sultan

9 letters:
Sovereign

FAMOUS EMPERORS

3 letters:
Leo

4 letters:
John
Ming
Nero
Otho
Otto
Pu-yi
Wu Di

5 letters:
Akbar
Asoka
Babur
Gaius
Henry
Jimmu
Kesar
Meiji
Negus
Nerva
Pedro

Rosco
Shang
Tenno
Titus

6 letters:
Caesar
George
Joseph
Kaiser
Keaser
Trajan
Valens
Yong Lo

7 letters:
Akihito
Charles
Francis
Gratian
Hadrian
Leopold
Lothair
Menelik

Severus
William

8 letters:
Agramant
Augustan
Augustus
Caligula
Claudius
Commodus
Hirohito
Matthias
Napoleon
Octavian
Qian Long
Theodore
Tiberius
Valerian
Xuan Zong

9 letters:
Agramante
Atahualpa
Aurangzeb

FAMOUS EMPERORS (CONTINUED)

Bonaparte
Caracalla
Diomitian
Ferdinand
Frederick
Heraclius
Justinian
Montezuma
Shah Jahan
Vespasian
Vitellius

10 letters:
Barbarossa
Dessalines

Diocletian
Franz Josef
Kublai Khan
Maximilian
Theodosius
Theophilus
Wenceslaus

11 letters:
Charlemagne
Constantine
Genghis Khan
Valentinian

13 letters:
Akbar the Great
Antoninus Pius
Haile Selassie
Peter the Great

16 letters:
Germanicus Caesar

17 letters:
Napoleon Bonaparte
Ras Tafari Makonnen

19 letters:
Frederick Barbarossa

Branches of engineering

5 letters:
Civil
Naval

6 letters:
Mining

7 letters:
Genetic
Nuclear
Process
Traffic

8 letters:
Chemical
Military
Sanitary

9 letters:
Aerospace

10 letters:
Automotive
Electrical
Ergonomics
Hydraulics
Mechanical
Production
Structural

11 letters:
Electronics
Geotechnics

12 letters:
Aerodynamics
Aeronautical
Agricultural
Astronautics
Cosmonautics
Mechatronics

13 letters:
Computer-aided
Environmental
Fluid dynamics

14 letters:
Bioengineering

Entertainment

TYPES OF ENTERTAINMENT

3 letters:
Gig

4 letters:
Agon
Ball

Fair
Fête
Film
Gala
Play
Rave

Show

5 letters:
Dance
Farce
Feast

TYPES OF ENTERTAINMENT (CONTINUED)

Gaudy
Levee
Magic
Opera
Party
Revue
Rodeo

6 letters:
Ballet
Circus
Comedy
Kermis
Masque
Review
Soiree

7 letters:
Airshow
Banquet
Busking
Cabaret
Ceilidh
Charade
Concert
Ice show
Karaoke
Kirmess
Musical
Reading
Recital
Ridotto
Tragedy
Variety
Waltzer

8 letters:
All-dayer
Après-ski
Aquashow
Carnival
Cotillon
Juggling
Operetta
Road show
Sideshow
Singsong
Zarzuela

9 letters:
Conjuring
Cotillion
Fireworks
Floor show
Light show
Melodrama
Music hall
Pantomime
Raree show
Reception
Slide show
Video game

10 letters:
Acrobatics
Aerobatics
All-nighter
Antimasque
Escapology
Exhibition
Masked ball
Puppet show

Recitation
Shadow play
Striptease
Vaudeville
Whist drive

11 letters:
Bear-baiting
Fashion show
Funambulism
Galanty show
Garden party
Slot machine
Wall of death

12 letters:
Bullfighting
Cockfighting
Minstrel show
Pyrotechnics
Son et lumière

13 letters:
Burlesque show
Street theatre
Ventriloquism

14 letters:
Warehouse party

16 letters:
Tightrope-walking

18 letters:
Command performance

TYPES OF ENTERTAINER

4 letters:
Diva
Fool

5 letters:
Actor
Clown
Mimic

6 letters:
Artist
Busker
Dancer
Guiser
Jester
Mummer
Singer

7 letters:
Acrobat
Actress
Artiste
Auguste
Juggler
Trouper
Tumbler

TYPES OF ENTERTAINER (CONTINUED)

8 letters:
Comedian
Conjurer
Funnyman
Gracioso
Jongleur
Magician
Minstrel
Musician
Show girl
Stripper

9 letters:
Fire eater
Harlequin
Lion tamer
Performer
Puppeteer
Raconteur
Strongman
Tragedian

10 letters:
Chorus girl
Comedienne
Go-go dancer
Prima donna
Ringmaster
Unicyclist

11 letters:
Equilibrist
Funambulist
Illusionist
Merry-andrew
Stripteaser
Tragedienne

12 letters:
Circus artist
Escapologist
Exotic dancer
Impersonator

Organ-grinder
Snake charmer
Vaudevillian

13 letters:
Bareback rider
Contortionist
Impressionist
Trapeze artist
Ventriloquist

14 letters:
Prima ballerina
Sword swallower

15 letters:
Strolling player
Tightrope walker

17 letters:
Quick-change artist

PLACES OF ENTERTAINMENT

3 letters:
Zoo

4 letters:
Hall
Lido

5 letters:
Arena
Disco

6 letters:
Big top
Cinema
Circus
Museum

7 letters:
Funfair
Gallery

Marquee
Niterie
Stadium
Theatre

8 letters:
Ballroom
Carnival
Coliseum
Waxworks

9 letters:
Bandstand
Bingo hall
Colosseum
Dance hall
Music hall
Nightclub
Nightspot

10 letters:
Auditorium
Fairground
Opera house
Social club
Vaudeville

11 letters:
Concert hall

12 letters:
Amphitheatre

13 letters:
Leisure centre

15 letters:
Amusement arcade

Enzymes

3 letters:
ACE

5 letters:
Lyase
Lysin
Renin

6 letters:
Cytase
Kinase
Ligase
Lipase
Mutase
Papain
Pepsin
Rennin
Urease
Zymase

7 letters:
Amylase
Apyrase
Casease
Cyclase
Enolase
Erepsin
Guanase
Hydrase
Inulase
Lactase
Maltase
Oxidase
Pectase
Pepsine
Plasmin
Ptyalin
Trypsin

8 letters:
Aldolase
Arginase
Bromelin
Catalase
Diastase
Elastase
Esterase
Lysozyme
Nuclease
Permease
Protease
Steapsin
Thrombin

9 letters:
Amylopsin
Autolysin
Bromelain
Cathepsin
Cellulase
Deaminase
Hydrolase
Invertase
Isomerase
Oxygenase
Reductase
Sulfatase
Trehalase
Urokinase

10 letters:
Allosteric
Kallikrein
Luciferase
Peroxidase
Polymerase

Proteinase
Saccharase
Subtilisin
Sulphatase
Tyrosinase

11 letters:
Carboxylase
Chymopapain
Collagenase
Dipeptidase
Histaminase
Phosphatase
Restriction
Transferase

12 letters:
Asparaginase
Carbohydrase
Chimotrypsin
Enterokinase
Fibrinolysin
Flavoprotein
Ribonuclease
Transaminase

13 letters:
Decarboxylase
Oxdoreductase
Streptokinase
Transcriptase

14 letters:
Cholinesterase
Pectinesterase
Streptodornase
Thromboplastin

Equestrianism

EQUESTRIAN EVENTS AND SPORTS

4 letters:
Hunt
Oaks
Polo

5 letters:
Ascot
Derby
Joust

Plate

7 letters:
Classic

EQUESTRIAN EVENTS AND SPORTS (CONTINUED)

Jump-off
Meeting

8 letters:
Dressage
Eventing
Gymkhana
Races, the

9 letters:
Badminton
Cavalcade
Puissance

10 letters:
Picnic race
Saint Leger
Sweepstake

11 letters:
Buckjumping
Horse racing
Race meeting
Showjumping
Sweepstakes

12 letters:
Claiming race
Point-to-point

Steeplechase

13 letters:
Grand National
Harness racing
Kentucky Derby
Nursery stakes

16 letters:
Three-day eventing

18 letters:
One Thousand Guineas
Two Thousand Guineas

CLASSIC ENGLISH HORSE RACES

Race	Course	Distance
One Thousand Guineas (fillies)	Newmarket	One mile
Two Thousand Guineas (colts)	Newmarket	One mile
Derby (colts)	Epsom	One and a half miles
The Oaks (fillies)	Epsom	One and a half miles
St. Leger (colts and fillies)	Doncaster	One and three quarter miles

HORSE RACING TERMS

3 letters:
Nap

4 letters:
Away
Card
Colt
Draw
Flat
Gate
Head
Neck
Pole
Post
Turf
Wire

5 letters:
Break
Chase
Fence
Filly
Going
Handy
Pacer
Place
Plate
Sweat
Track

6 letters:
Boring
Chaser
Come in

Course
Faller
Finish
Flight
Hurdle
Impost
Jockey
Length
Maiden
Novice
Plater
Scurry
Stakes
Stayer

7 letters:
Also-ran

HORSE RACING TERMS (CONTINUED)

Classic
Each way
Furlong
Meeting
Paddock
Roughie
Scratch
Starter
Steward
Stretch
Sweat up
Trainer
Weigh in

8 letters:
Dead heat
Distance
Handicap
Hurdling
Milepost
Race card
Straight
Ticktack
Unplaced
Walkover
Yearling

9 letters:
Allowance

Break away
Dope sheet
Objection
Pacemaker
Short head

10 letters:
Apprentice
Flat jockey
Flat racing
Green horse
Jockey Club
Jump jockey
Pacesetter
Silver ring

11 letters:
Accumulator
Daily double
Handicapper
Harness race
Home stretch
Photo finish
Selling race
Winning post

12 letters:
Auction plate
Claiming race

Home straight
National Hunt
Point-to-point
Starting gate
Starting post
Steeplechase
Straightaway
Trotting race

13 letters:
Blanket finish
Starting price
Unseated rider

14 letters:
Across-the-board
Starting stalls

15 letters:
Ante post betting
Stewards' inquiry

16 letters:
Clerk of the course
Clerk of the scales

19 letters:
Under starter's orders

TYPES OF JUMP

4 letters:
Gate
Wall

6 letters:
Planks

8 letters:
Hog's back

9 letters:
Water jump

10 letters:
Double oxer
Triple bars

11 letters:
Narrow stile

12 letters:
Post and rails

13 letters:
Brush and rails
Parallel poles

Members of the European Union

1958	Belgium
1958	France
1958	Germany
1958	Italy
1958	Luxembourg
1958	The Netherlands
1973	Denmark
1973	Republic of Ireland
1973	United Kingdom
1981	Greece
1986	Portugal
1986	Spain
1995	Finland
1995	Sweden
1995	Austria
2004	Cyprus
2004	Czech Republic
2004	Estonia
2004	Hungary
2004	Latvia
2004	Lithuania
2004	Malta
2004	Poland
2004	Slovakia
2004	Slovenia

Explosives

2 letters:
HE

3 letters:
Cap
SAM
TNT

4 letters:
Mine

5 letters:
Agene
Jelly
Petar

6 letters:
Amatol
Dualin
Petard
Semtex®
Tetryl
Tonite
Trotyl

7 letters:
Ammonal
Cordite
Dunnite
Grenade
Warhead

8 letters:
Cheddite
Fireball
Firedamp
Firework
Landmine
Melinite
Roburite
Xyloidin

9 letters:
Gelignite
Guncotton
Gunpowder
Xyloidine

10 letters:
Aquafortis
Euchlorine

11 letters:
Firecracker

12 letters:
Thunderflash

14 letters:
Nitroglycerine

15 letters:
Trinitrobenzene

16 letters:
Bangalore torpedo

Parts of the eye

3 letters:
Rod

4 letters:
Cone
Iris
Lens

5 letters:
Fovea
Pupil

6 letters:
Cornea
Retina
Sclera

7 letters:
Choroid
Eyeball

8 letters:
Chorioid

9 letters:
Blind spot

10 letters:
Optic nerve

11 letters:
Ciliary body
Conjunctiva

12 letters:
Ocular muscle
Vitreous body

13 letters:
Aqueous humour

14 letters:
Retinal vessels
Vitreous humour

18 letters:
Suspensory ligament

Afflictions of the eye

6 letters:
Iritis
Miosis
Myosis
Nebula
Xeroma

7 letters:
Leucoma
Scotoma
Thylose
Tylosis
Wall-eye

8 letters:
Cataract
Coloboma
Diplopia
Glaucoma
Hemiopia

Synechia
Thylosis
Trachoma

9 letters:
Amblyopia
Ametropia
Ceratitis
Entropion
Keratitis
Lippitude
Micropsia
Nystagmus
Retinitis
Scotomata

10 letters:
Asthenopia
Nyctalopia
Presbyopia

Stigmatism
Strabismus
Teichopsia
Tritanopia

11 letters:
Aniseikonia
Astigmatism
Hemeralopia
Hemianopsia

12 letters:
Exophthalmus

13 letters:
Anisomatropia
Hypermetropia
Xerophthalmia

F f

Fabrics

3 letters:
Abb
Fur
Net
Rep
Say
Web

4 letters:
Aida
Baft
Ciré
Cord
Doek
Drab
Duck
Felt
Fent
Gair
Haik
Harn
Huck
Hyke
Ikat
Jean
Kelt
Knit
Lace
Lamé
Lawn
Leno
Line
Mull
Nude
Rund
Shag
Silk
Slop
Sulu
Tick
Wool

5 letters:
Atlas
Baize
Batik
Beige
Binca
Budge
Chino
Crape
Crash
Crepe
Denim
Dobby
Drill
Duroy
Fanon
Foulé
Frisé
Gauze
Gunny
Haick
Honan
Jaspe
Kanga
Kente
Khadi
Khaki
Kikoi
Linen
Lisle
Llama
Loden
Lurex®
Lycra®
Moiré
Mongo
Mungo
Ninon
Orlon®
Panne
Perse

Piqué
Plaid
Plush
Poult
Rayon
Satin
Scrim
Serge
Slops
Stuff
Stupe
Surah
Surat
Surge
Tabby
Tamin
Tammy
Terry
Tibet
Toile
Towel
Tulle
Tweed
Tweel
Twill
Union
Voile
Wigan

6 letters:
Aertex®
Alpaca
Angora
Armure
Barège
Battik
Beaver
Bouclé
Broche
Burlap
Burnet
Burrel

Byssus
Caddis
Calico
Camlet
Camlot
Canvas
Chintz
Cilice
Cloqué
Coburg
Cotton
Coutil
Crepon
Cubica
Cyprus
Dacron®
Damask
Devoré
Dimity
Domett
Dossal
Dossel
Dowlas
Dralon®
Duffel
Duffle
Dupion
Durrie
Etamin
Faille
Fannel
Fleece
Frieze
Gloria
Greige
Gurrah
Haique
Harden
Herden
Hodden
Humhum
Hurden
Jersey
Kersey
Khanga
Kincob
Lampas
Madras
Medley
Melton

Merino
Mohair
Mongoe
Moreen
Muslin
Nankin
Oxford
Pongee
Poplin
Rateen
Ratine
Runner
Russel
Russet
Samite
Satara
Sateen
Saxony
Sendal
Shalli
Sherpa
Shoddy
Sindon
Soneri
Stroud
Tamine
Tartan
Thibet
Tricot
Tussah
Tusser
Velour
Velure
Velvet
Vicuna
Wadmal
Wincey
Winsey

7 letters:
Abattre
Acrilan®
Alepine
Baracan
Batiste
Brocade
Bunting
Cabbage
Cambric
Camelot

Challie
Challis
Cheviot
Chiffon
Crombie
Cypress
Delaine
Dhurrie
Doeskin
Dornick
Drabbet
Drapery
Droguet
Drugget
Duvetyn
Etamine
Façonné
Fannell
Fishnet
Flannel
Foulard
Fustian
Galatea
Genappe
Gingham
Gore-Tex®
Grogram
Hessian
Holland
Hopsack
Jaconet
Jamdani
Khaddar
Kitenge
Leather
Lockram
Marabou
Mockado
Nankeen
Oilskin
Organza
Orleans
Ottoman
Paisley
Percale
Rabanna
Raploch
Raschel
Ratteen
Rattine

Sacking
Sagathy
Satinet
Schappe
Silesia
Sinamay
Spandex
Stammel
Suiting
Tabaret
Tabinet
Taffeta
Ticking
Tiffany
Tussore
Veiling
Velours
Viyella®
Wadmaal
Webbing
Woolsey
Worsted
Zanella

8 letters:
Algerine
American
Armozeen
Armozine
Arresine
Bagheera
Barathea
Barracan
Bayadere
Bird's-eye
Bobbinet
Brocatel
Buckskin
Cameline
Cashmere
Casimere
Celanese
Chambray
Chamelot
Chenille
Ciclaton
Corduroy
Corporal
Coteline
Coutille

Cretonne
Diamanté
Drabette
Duchesse
Dungaree
Duvetine
Duvetyne
Eolienne
Gambroon
Gossamer
Homespun
Jacquard
Jeanette
Lambskin
Lava-lava
Lustring
Mackinaw
Mantling
Marcella
Marocain
Mazarine
Moleskin
Moquette
Nainsook
Organdie
Osnaburg
Paduasoy
Pashmina
Prunella
Prunelle
Prunello
Rodevore
Sarcenet
Sarsenet
Shabrack
Shalloon
Shantung
Sheeting
Shirting
Sicilian
Spun silk
Swanskin
Tabbinet
Tarlatan
Terylene®
Toilinet
Whipcord
Wild silk
Zibeline

9 letters:
Balzarine
Bengaline
Bombasine
Bombazine
Calamanco
Cassimere
Cerecloth
Charmeuse®
Ciclatoun
Corporale
Cottonade
Crepoline
Crimplene®
Crinoline
Evenweave
Farandine
Filoselle
Folk weave
Gaberdine
Georgette
Grenadine
Grosgrain
Haircloth
Horsehair
Huckaback
Indiennes
Levantine
Mandylion
Marseille
Matelassé
Messaline
Nun's cloth
Organzine
Paramatta
Penistone
Percaline
Persienne
Petersham
Piña cloth
Polyester
Ravenduck
Sailcloth
Satinette
Sharkskin
Silkaline
Stockinet
Swan's-down
Tarpaulin
Towelling

Tricotine
Velveteen
Wire gauze
Worcester
Zibelline

10 letters:
Balbriggan
Broadcloth
Brocatelle
Candlewick
Farrandine
Fearnaught
Fearnought
Ferrandine
Florentine
India print
Kerseymere
Lutestring
Marseilles
Monk's cloth
Mousseline
Needlecord
Parramatta

Peau de soie
Polycotton
Ravensduck
Seersucker
Shabracque
Sicilienne
Tattersall
Toilinette
Tuftaffeta
Winceyette

11 letters:
Abercrombie
Cheesecloth
Cloth of gold
Covert cloth
Dotted Swiss
Drap-de-berry
Dreadnought
Hammercloth
Harris Tweed®
Interfacing
Kendal green
Marquisette

Poult-de-soie
Sempiternum
Stockinette
Stretch knit
Swiss muslin

12 letters:
Brilliantine
Cavalry twill
Crepe de chine
Donegal tweed
Leather-cloth
Slipper satin

13 letters:
Cotton flannel
Gros de Londres
Jacquard weave
Linsey-woolsey

14 letters:
Paisley pattern

See also:
➤ **Materials** ➤ **Types of silk**

The Fates

6 letters:
Clotho

7 letters:
Atropos

8 letters:
Lachesis

Fencing terms

4 letters:
Mask
Volt

5 letters:
Carte
Feint
Guard
Parry
Piste
Prime
Reach

Sabre
Sixte
Terce
Touch

6 letters:
Bracer
Octave
Parade
Quarte
Quinte
Tierce

Touché

7 letters:
Seconde
Septime

9 letters:
Backsword
Repechage

11 letters:
Singlestick

Ferns

3 letters:
Oak

4 letters:
Hard
Lady
Male
Tara
Tree

5 letters:
Beech
Cycad
Filmy
Grape
Marsh
Ponga
Punga
Royal
Sword

6 letters:
Azolla
Meadow
Nardoo
Pteris
Shield
Silver

7 letters:
Bladder
Bracken
Buckler
Cyathea
Elkhorn
Filices
Isoetes
Osmunda
Parsley
Polypod
Walking
Wall rue
Woodsia

8 letters:
Adiantum
Aspidium
Barometz
Bungwall
Ceterach
Cinnamon
Fishbone
Marsilea
Marsilia
Moonwort
Mosquito
Mulewort
Pillwort

Rachilla
Schizaea
Staghorn

9 letters:
Asparagus
Asplenium
Bird's nest
Cryptogam
Dicksonia
Filicales
Rock brake

10 letters:
Maidenhair
Pepperwort
Spleenwort
Venus's-hair

11 letters:
Hart's-tongue

12 letters:
Adder's-tongue
Nephrolepsis
Ophioglossum

13 letters:
Scolopendrium

Festivals

3 letters:
Mod
Tet

4 letters:
Feis
Gaff
Holi
Mela
Noel
Obon
Puja
Utas
Yule

5 letters:
Doseh
Druid
Hosay
Litha
Mabon
Miraj
Pasch
Pesah
Pooja
Purim
Seder
Vesak
Wesak

6 letters:
Adonia
Ashora
Bairam
Dewali
Divali
Diwali
Easter
Eostra
Fringe
Hosein
Imbolc
Lammas
Ostara

Fibres

Pardon
Pesach
Pongal
Poojah
Shrove
Yomtov

7 letters:
Al Hijra
Baisaki
Beltane
Gregory
Harvest
Holy-ale
Kermess
Kermiss
Kirmess
Lady-day
Lemural
Lemuria
Matsuri
Palilia
Potlach
Samhain
Vinalia

8 letters:
Al Hijrah
Baisakhi
Bayreuth
Biennale

Cerealia
Chanukah
Dassehra
Dionysia
Encaenia
Epiphany
Hanukkah
Hock-tide
Id-al-fitr
Panegyry
Passover
Shabuath
Shavuath
Yuletide

9 letters:
Aldeburgh
Candlemas
Chanukkah
Church-ale
Crouchmas
Hallowmas
Navaratra
Navaratri
Pentecost
Thargelia
Up-Helly-Aa

10 letters:
Ambarvalia
Childermas

Eisteddfod
Lughnasadh
Lupercalia
Merry-night
Michaelmas
Quirinalia
Saturnalia
Semi-double
Shrovetide
Terminalia
Visitation

11 letters:
Anthesteria

12 letters:
All Saints' Day
Circumcision
Lailat-ul-Qadr
Lesser Bairam
Panathenaean
Rosh Hashanah
Simchat Torah
Thesmophoria

13 letters:
Corpus Christi
Laylat-al-Miraj

Fibres

3 letters:
Tow

4 letters:
Bass
Bast
Coir
Flax
Hemp
Herl
Jute
Noil
Pita
Pons
Pulu

Rami
Rhea

5 letters:
Abaca
Buaze
Bwazi
Istle
Ixtle
Kapok
Kenaf
Noils
Nylon
Orlon®
Ramee

Viver
Watap

6 letters:
Aramid
Arghan
Cotton
Cuscus
Dralon®
Kevlar®
Kittul
Strick

7 letters:
Acrilan®

288

Acrylic
Cantala
Filasse
Funicle
Gore-Tex®
Monofil
Pontine
Tampico
Whisker

8 letters:
Elastane
Henequen
Henequin
Monomode
Peduncle
Piassaba
Piassava
Sunn-hemp

Toquilla

9 letters:
Courtelle®

11 letters:
Monkey-grass

Figures of speech

5 letters:
Irony

6 letters:
Aporia
Climax
Simile
Tmesis
Zeugma

7 letters:
Analogy
Kenning
Litotes
Meiosis
Sarcasm

8 letters:
Allusion
Anaphora
Chiasmus
Emphasis
Metaphor
Metonymy
Oxymoron
Pleonasm

9 letters:
Apophasis
Hendiadys
Hypallage
Hyperbole
Inversion
Prolepsis
Syllepsis

10 letters:
Anastrophe
Antithesis
Apostrophe
Epanaphora
Gemination
Hyperbaton
Paralipsis
Repetition
Spoonerism

11 letters:
Anacoluthia
Anadiplosis
Antiphrasis
Antonomasia
Aposiopesis
Catachresis

Exclamation
Malapropism
Paraleipsis
Parenthesis
Periphrasis
Prosopopeia
Synechdoche

12 letters:
Alliteration
Epanorthosis
Onomatopoeia
Polysyndeton
Prosopopoeia

14 letters:
Circumlocution

15 letters:
Personification

16 letters:
Hysteron proteron

18 letters:
Rhetorical question

Film and television

1 letter:
A
U

2 letters:
AA
PG

3 letters:
BFI
CGI
Cut
Dub

Pan
SFX
Zap

4 letters:
BBFC
Boom
Edit
Emmy
Grip
HDTV
IMAX
Sync
TiVo

5 letters:
Anime
BAFTA
Cameo
Frame
Oscar
Short
Weepy

6 letters:
Action
Biopic
B movie
Co-star
Editor
Gaffer
Razzie
Repeat
Romcom
X-rated

7 letters:
Animate
Backlot
Betacam
Cable TV
Credits
Fleapit
Footage
Key grip
Prequel
Ratings

Trailer
Western
Zapping

8 letters:
Actioner
Art house
Britpack
Game show
Long shot
Stuntman
Subtitle
Talk show
Typecast

9 letters:
Animation
Big screen
Bollywood
Celluloid
Cinematic
Digital TV
Docu-drama
Flashback
Footprint
Hollywood
LCD screen
Reality TV
Road movie
Satellite
Set-top box
Stop-frame

10 letters:
Access card
Adult movie
Blue screen
Body double
Chick flick
Flat screen
Home cinema
Neorealism
Screen test
Slow motion
Snuff movie
Soundtrack
Stop-motion

Storyboard
Video nasty
Widescreen

11 letters:
Channel-surf
Chapter stop
Cinemascope
Cliffhanger
Freeze-frame
Reality show
Satellite TV
Small screen
Synthespian

12 letters:
Animatronics
Cinematheque
Plasma screen
Screenwriter
Slasher movie
Sneak preview

13 letters:
Interactive TV
Motion capture
Remote control
Satellite dish

14 letters:
Channel-surfing
Postproduction
Shooting script
Special effects

16 letters:
Spaghetti western

17 letters:
Digital television

19 letters:
Satellite television

21 letters:
Interactive television

Fireworks

3 letters:
SIB

4 letters:
Cake
Mine
Pioy

5 letters:
Gerbe
Peeoy
Pioye
Squib
Wheel

6 letters:
Banger
Fizgig
Maroon
Petard
Rocket

7 letters:
Cracker
Serpent

8 letters:
Fountain
Pinwheel
Sparkler

9 letters:
Girandole
Skyrocket
Whizzbang

10 letters:
Cherry bomb

11 letters:
Bengal light
Roman candle
Tourbillion

14 letters:
Catherine wheel

First names

BOYS

3 letters:
Abe
Alf
Ali
Ben
Bob
Dan
Don
Ger
Gus
Guy
Ian
Jan
Jim
Joe
Kim
Len
Leo
Luc
Max
Nat
Ned
Nye
Ray
Reg
Rex
Roy

Sam
Sid
Tam
Ted
Tim
Tom
Val
Vic
Viv
Wal
Wim

4 letters:
Abel
Abie
Adam
Alan
Aldo
Amos
Andy
Avis
Bart
Bert
Bill
Carl
Chad
Clem

Dave
Dick
Dirk
Drew
Duke
Earl
Egon
Eric
Evan
Ewan
Fred
Gene
Gert
Gwyn
Hans
Hugh
Hugo
Iain
Ivan
Ivor
Jack
Jake
Jean
Jeff
Jock
John
José

BOYS (CONTINUED)

Josh	Abdul	Émile
Juan	Adolf	Enoch
Karl	Ahmed	Ernie
Kurt	Aidan	Ernst
Leon	Alain	Errol
Luca	Alfie	Felix
Luke	Algie	Frank
Marc	Alvin	Franz
Mark	André	Fritz
Matt	Angus	Garry
Mick	Anton	Garth
Mike	Artur	Gavin
Muir	Barry	Geoff
Neal	Basil	Georg
Neil	Benny	Giles
Nick	Bernd	Guido
Noel	Bobby	Harry
Olaf	Boris	Hasan
Otto	Brian	Heinz
Owen	Bruce	Henri
Paco	Bruno	Henry
Paul	Caleb	Hiram
Pepe	Carlo	Inigo
Pete	Cecil	Jacky
Phil	Celio	Jacob
Raul	Chris	Jaime
Rémy	Cliff	Jakob
Rene	Clive	Jamal
Rhys	Colin	James
Rick	Cyril	Jamie
Rolf	Cyrus	Jason
Rory	Danny	Jerry
Ross	Darby	Jesse
Rudi	D'Arcy	Jesús
Ryan	David	Jimmy
Sa'id	Davie	Jorge
Saul	Denis	Jules
Sean	Derek	Keith
Stan	Diego	Kevin
Theo	Dodie	Klaus
Toby	Dylan	Lance
Tony	Eamon	Lenny
Walt	Eddie	Lewis
Will	Edgar	Lloyd
Yves	Elias	Louis
	Eliot	Luigi
5 letters:	Ellis	Manny
Aaron	Elmer	Marco

BOYS (CONTINUED)

Mario	Arthur	Harvey
Marty	Arturo	Hector
Miles	Aubrey	Helmut
Moses	Austin	Hilary
Myles	Aylwin	Horace
Niall	Barney	Howard
Nicky	Benoît	Hubert
Nigel	Billie	Hugues
Orson	Calvin	Hunter
Oscar	Carlos	Ingram
Pablo	Caspar	Irving
Paddy	Cedric	Isaiah
Paolo	Claude	Israel
Pedro	Connor	Jackie
Perce	Conrad	Jasper
Percy	Damian	Javier
Perry	Daniel	Jeremy
Peter	Darsey	Jerome
Piero	Deepak	Johann
Ralph	Dermot	Joseph
Robin	Didier	Joshua
Rodge	Dieter	Josiah
Roger	Donald	Julian
Romeo	Dougal	Julien
Rufus	Dudley	Julius
Serge	Dugald	Jürgen
Simon	Duncan	Justin
Steve	Dustin	Kenelm
Tariq	Dwight	Larrie
Terry	Edmund	Laurie
Tomás	Edward	Leslie
Vijay	Egbert	Lester
Vince	Enrico	Lionel
Wayne	Ernest	Lucius
	Esmond	Ludwig
6 letters:	Eugene	Luther
Adrian	Fergus	Magnus
Adrien	Gareth	Mahmud
Albert	Gaston	Manuel
Aldous	George	Marcel
Alexis	Gerald	Marcus
Alfred	Gideon	Marius
Andrés	Gilles	Martin
Andrew	Gordon	Melvin
Antony	Graham	Melvyn
Archie	Gregor	Merlin
Arnaud	Hamish	Mervyn
Arnold	Harold	Michel

BOYS (CONTINUED)

Mickey	**7 letters:**	Herbert
Miguel	Abraham	Horatio
Murray	Alberto	Ibrahim
Nathan	Alfonso	Jacques
Norman	Alfredo	Jeffrey
Norris	Alister	Joachim
Oliver	Ambrose	Joaquin
Osbert	Andreas	Kenneth
Oswald	Anthony	Lachlan
Petrus	Antoine	Laurent
Philip	Antonio	Leonard
Pierre	Baldwin	Leopold
Rainer	Barnaby	Lindsey
Rashid	Bernard	Lorenzo
Reuben	Bertram	Luciano
Robert	Brendan	Malcolm
Rodney	Cameron	Matthew
Roland	Carlton	Maurice
Ronald	Charles	Maxwell
Rupert	Charlie	Michael
Samuel	Clement	Montagu
Sanjiv	Clemmie	Murdoch
Selwyn	Desmond	Mustafa
Sergio	Diarmid	Neville
Sidney	Dominic	Nicolas
Stefan	Douglas	Norbert
Steven	Ebeneza	Obadiah
Stuart	Edmondo	Olivier
Sydney	Edoardo	Pascual
Thomas	Édouard	Patrice
Trevor	Emanuel	Patrick
Ulrich	Erasmus	Placido
Victor	Estéban	Quentin
Vikram	Étienne	Raphael
Vivian	Ezekiel	Raymond
Wallis	Fabrice	Richard
Walter	Filippo	Rodrigo
Warner	Francis	Rolando
Warren	Gabriel	Rudolph
Werner	Geordie	Rudyard
Wesley	Georges	Russell
Wilbur	Geraint	Sigmund
Willie	Gerhard	Solomon
Willis	Giacomo	Spencer
Xavier	Gilbert	Stanley
Yasser	Giorgio	Stefano
Yehudi	Godfrey	Stephan
	Gregory	Stephen

Boys (CONTINUED)

Stewart
Terence
Thibaut
Thierry
Timothy
Umberto
Valerie
Vaughan
Vincent
Wallace
Wilfred
Wilhelm
William
Windsor
Winston
Wyndham
Youssef

8 letters:
Abdullah
Alasdair
Alastair
Aloysius
Augustus
Benedict
Benjamin
Bernabas
Bernardo
Bertrand
Charlton
Clarence
Claudius
Clifford
Consuelo
Cuthbert
Dietrich
Emmanuel
Fabrizio
Farquhar

Fernando
François
Geoffrey
Giovanni
Giuliano
Giuseppe
Heinrich
Hercules
Humphrey
Johannes
Jonathan
Lancelot
Laurence
Lawrence
Leonardo
Llewelyn
Marcello
Matthias
Matthieu
Montague
Morrison
Mortimer
Muhammed
Nicholas
Octavius
Odysseus
Percival
Philippe
Reginald
Roderick
Salvador
Santiago
Sherlock
Silvanus
Sinclair
Somerset
Stéphane
Theodore
Timothée

Wolfgang

9 letters:
Alejandro
Alexander
Alexandre
Alphonsus
Archibald
Augustine
Christian
Cornelius
Dominique
Ethelbert
Ferdinand
Francesco
Frederick
Friedrich
Gottfried
Grégoire
Guillaume
Marmaduke
Nathaniel
Peregrine
Sebastian
Sébastien
Siegfried
Sylvester

10 letters:
Alessandro
Christophe
Maximilian
Montgomery

11 letters:
Bartholomew
Christopher

Girls

3 letters:
Ada
Amy
Ana
Ann
Bab

Bea
Bel
Dot
Ena
Eva
Eve

Fay
Flo
Gay
Ger
Ina
Isa

GIRLS (CONTINUED)

Jan
Joy
Kay
Kim
Kit
Liz
Lyn
May
Meg
Nan
Net
Pam
Pat
Peg
Pen
Pip
Pru
Rae
Sal
Sis
Sue
Tam
Una
Ute
Val
Zoe

4 letters:
Alba
Ally
Alma
Anke
Anna
Anne
Babs
Bess
Beth
Cara
Ciss
Cleo
Dawn
Dora
Edna
Ella
Elma
Elsa
Emma
Enid

Gail
Gill
Gina
Gita
Gwen
Hope
Inge
Iona
Iris
Jane
Jean
Jess
Jill
Joan
Judy
June
Kate
Leah
Lena
Lily
Lisa
Lois
Lola
Lucy
Lynn
Mary
Maud
Myra
Nell
Nina
Nita
Olga
Oona
Rene
Rita
Romy
Rosa
Rose
Ruby
Ruth
Sara
Tess
Tina
Vera
Zara

5 letters:
Abbie

Adele
Aggie
Agnes
Ailie
Ailsa
Alice
Aline
Anita
Annie
April
Avril
Beata
Becca
Bella
Berry
Beryl
Betsy
Betty
Biddy
Carla
Carol
Cathy
Celia
Chloe
Chris
Clara
Clare
Coral
Corin
Daisy
D'Arcy
Delia
Diana
Diane
Dilys
Dinah
Dolly
Donna
Doris
Edith
Edwin
Effie
Elise
Eliza
Ellen
Ellis
Elsie
Emily

GIRLS (CONTINUED)

Ethel	Maeve	Tanya
Faith	Magda	Tatum
Fanny	Mamie	Thora
Fiona	Marge	Tilly
Fleur	Margo	Tracy
Flora	Maria	Vicky
Freda	Marie	Viola
Gerda	Marta	Wanda
Ginny	Marty	Wendy
Grace	Maude	
Greta	Mavis	**6 letters:**
Hazel	Merle	Agatha
Heidi	Milly	Aileen
Helen	Mitzi	Alexis
Helga	Moira	Alicia
Hetty	Molly	Alison
Hilda	Morag	Althea
Honor	Moray	Amanda
Irene	Morna	Amelia
Isaac	Myrna	Amélie
Jacky	Nancy	Andrea
Janet	Nanny	Angela
Janey	Naomi	Arabel
Jayne	Nelly	Arline
Jenny	Netty	Astrid
Jesse	Nicky	Athene
Josie	Nicol	Audrey
Joyce	Norma	Aurora
Julie	Patty	Bertha
Karen	Paula	Bianca
Katja	Pearl	Billie
Kitty	Peggy	Blaise
Laura	Penny	Brenda
Laure	Polly	Bryony
Leila	Renée	Carmen
Leona	Rhoda	Carole
Libby	Rhona	Carrie
Liese	Sadie	Cécile
Linda	Sally	Céline
Lindy	Sandy	Cherry
Lorna	Sarah	Cheryl
Lotte	Sofia	Claire
Lucia	Sonia	Concha
Luisa	Sonja	Daphne
Lydia	Susan	Davina
Lynne	Susie	Debbie
Mabel	Sybil	Denise
Madge	Tania	Dianne

GIRLS (CONTINUED)

Doreen	Lottie	Sharon
Dulcie	Louisa	Sheena
Easter	Louise	Sheila
Edwina	Madhur	Silvia
Eileen	Maggie	Simone
Eilidh	Maisie	Sophia
Elaine	Marcia	Sophie
Elinor	Margie	Stella
Elisha	Marian	Sylvia
Elodie	Marina	Tamsin
Elvira	Marion	Thelma
Emilia	Martha	Tricia
Esther	Maxine	Trixie
Eunice	Minnie	Trudie
Evadne	Miriam	Ulrike
Evelyn	Monica	Ursula
Fatima	Morgan	Verity
Gertie	Morrie	Violet
Gladys	Morris	Vivian
Gloria	Morven	Winnie
Gretel	Muriel	Yvette
Gwenda	Myrtle	Yvonne
Hannah	Nadine	
Hattie	Nessie	**7 letters:**
Hélène	Nettie	Abigail
Hester	Nicola	Adriana
Hilary	Nicole	Alfreda
Imogen	Noelle	Annabel
Indira	Odette	Annette
Ingrid	Oonagh	Antonia
Isabel	Oriana	Ariadne
Isobel	Paloma	Aurelia
Isolde	Pamela	Barbara
Jackie	Petula	Belinda
Jamila	Phoebe	Bernice
Janice	Rachel	Bettina
Jeanne	Raquel	Blanche
Jemima	Regina	Bridget
Jessie	Renata	Bronwen
Joanna	Robina	Camilla
Joanne	Rowena	Camille
Judith	Roxana	Candida
Juliet	Sabina	Carolyn
Kirsty	Sabine	Cecilia
Krista	Salome	Celeste
Lesley	Sandra	Chantal
Lilian	Selina	Charity
Lolita	Serena	Charlie

GIRLS (CONTINUED)

Chrissy
Christy
Clarice
Claudia
Colette
Corinna
Corinne
Cynthia
Deborah
Deirdre
Dolores
Dorothy
Eleanor
Elspeth
Estella
Eugenia
Fenella
Florrie
Flossie
Frances
Gertrud
Gillian
Giselle
Gwyneth
Harriet
Heather
Isadora
Jessica
Jocelyn
Josette
Juliana
Justine
Katrina
Kirstie
Kristin
Lavinia
Leonora
Letitia
Lillian
Lindsey
Linette
Lucille
Lucinda
Manuela
Margery
Marilyn
Martina
Martine

Matilda
Maureen
Melanie
Melissa
Mildred
Mirabel
Miranda
Modesty
Myfanwy
Natalie
Natasha
Ophelia
Ottilie
Pauline
Perdita
Petrina
Phyllis
Queenie
Rebecca
Roberta
Rosalie
Sabrina
Shelagh
Shelley
Shirley
Siobahn
Susanna
Suzanne
Theresa
Valerie
Vanessa
Yolande

8 letters:
Adrienne
Angeline
Arabella
Beatrice
Beverley
Brigitta
Brigitte
Carlotta
Carolina
Caroline
Cathleen
Catriona
Charmian
Claribel

Clarissa
Claudine
Clemence
Collette
Conchita
Consuela
Cordelia
Cressida
Danielle
Dominica
Dorothea
Drusilla
Euphemia
Felicity
Florence
Francine
Georgina
Gertrude
Hermione
Isabelle
Iseabail
Jeanette
Jeannine
Jennifer
Juliette
Kathleen
Lorraine
Madeline
Magdalen
Marcella
Margaret
Marianne
Marigold
Marjorie
Mercedes
Meredith
Michaela
Michelle
Patience
Patricia
Penelope
Perpetua
Primrose
Prudence
Prunella
Rosalind
Rosamund
Rosemary

GIRLS (CONTINUED)

Samantha
Scarlett
Theodora
Veronica
Victoria
Violette
Virginia
Virginie
Winifred

9 letters:
Alejandra
Alexandra
Anastasia
Anastasie
Annabella
Cassandra
Catherina
Catherine
Charlotte
Christina
Christine
Constance

Elizabeth
Esmerelda
Francesca
Françoise
Gabrielle
Genevieve
Geraldine
Gwendolyn
Henrietta
Jacquetta
Josephine
Katharine
Madeleine
Magdalene
Millicent
Mirabelle
Nicolette
Phillippa
Priscilla
Rosabella
Sempronia
Seraphina
Stephanie

Veronique

10 letters:
Alessandra
Antoinette
Christabel
Christelle
Christiana
Christiane
Clementine
Concepción
Emmanuelle
Jacqueline
Lieselotte
Margherita
Marguerite
Petronella
Wilhelmina

11 letters:
Bernadettte
Constantine

Fish

2 letters:
Ai
Id

3 letters:
Aua
Ayu
Bar
Bib
But
Cat
Cod
Cow
Dab
Dib
Dog
Eel
Gar
Ged
Hag
Ice

Ide
Koi
Lax
Lob
Par
Pod
Ray
Rig
Sar
Tai
Top

4 letters:
Bass
Blay
Bley
Brim
Brit
Butt
Carp
Cero

Chad
Char
Chub
Chum
Coho
Cray
Cusk
Dace
Dare
Dart
Dory
Fugu
Gade
Goby
Gump
Hake
Harl
Hoki
Huso
Huss
Jack

Fish

Kelt
Keta
Lant
Leaf
Ling
Luce
Lump
Maid
Maze
Moki
Mort
Opah
Orfe
Parr
Peal
Peel
Pike
Pogy
Pope
Pout
Raun
Rawn
Rigg
Rudd
Ruff
Scad
Scar
Scat
Scup
Seer
Seir
Shad
Sild
Slip
Snig
Sole
Star
Tope
Trot
Tuna
Tusk
Woof

5 letters:
Ablet
Ahuru
Allis
Angel
Apode
Barra

Basse
Betta
Bleak
Bream
Brill
Bully
Capon
Charr
Cisco
Clown
Cobia
Cohoe
Coley
Cuddy
Danio
Dorad
Doras
Doree
Dorse
Elops
Elver
Fluke
Gadus
Gibel
Grunt
Guppy
Jewie
Jurel
Koaea
Laker
Lance
Loach
Lythe
Maise
Maize
Manta
Masus
Mease
Molly
Moray
Murre
Murry
Nerka
Padle
Perai
Perca
Perch
Pilot
Piper
Pirai

Platy
Pogge
Porae
Porgy
Powan
Prawn
Roach
Roker
Ruffe
Saith
Sargo
Saury
Scrod
Sewen
Sewin
Shark
Sheat
Skate
Slope
Smelt
Snoek
Snook
Solen
Speck
Sprat
Sprod
Tench
Tetra
Toado
Togue
Torsk
Trout
Tunny
Umber
Wahoo
Whiff
Wirra
Witch
Yabby
Zebra

6 letters:
Alevin
Allice
Anabas
Angler
Araara
Archer
Ballan
Barbel

Fish

Belone
Beluga
Bigeye
Blenny
Bonito
Bounce
Bowfin
Braise
Braize
Bumalo
Burbot
Callop
Caplin
Caranx
Caribe
Cheven
Clupea
Cockle
Comber
Conger
Conner
Cottus
Cudden
Cuddie
Cuddin
Cunner
Cuttle
Darter
Dentex
Diodon
Dipnoi
Discus
Doctor
Dorado
Dun-cow
Finnac
Finnan
Flying
Fogash
Fumado
Gadoid
Garvie
Gilgie
Goramy
Grilse
Groper
Gulper
Gunnel
Gurami
Gurnet

Haddie
Hapuka
Hapuku
Hassar
Inanga
Jerker
Jilgie
Kelpie
Kipper
Kokopu
Labrus
Lancet
Launce
Lizard
Louvar
Lunker
Mad Tom
Mahsir
Maomao
Marari
Marlin
Meagre
Medaka
Medusa
Megrim
Milter
Minnow
Morgay
Mudcat
Mullet
Murena
Nerite
Nigger
Oyster
Paddle
Paidle
Pakoko
Parore
Parrot
Patiki
Pholas
Pillie
Piraña
Piraya
Plaice
Podley
Pollan
Porgie
Puffer
Rawaru

Red cod
Redfin
Remora
Robalo
Roughy
Runner
Saithe
Salmon
Samlet
Samson
Sander
Sardel
Sargus
Sauger
Saurel
Scampi
Sea-bat
Sea-owl
Seeder
Serran
Shanny
Sheath
Shiner
Skelly
Sparid
Sucker
Tailor
Tarpon
Tautog
Toitoi
Tomcod
Trygon
Turbot
Twaite
Ulicon
Ulikon
Vendis
Weever
Wirrah
Wrasse
Yabbie
Zander
Zingel

7 letters:
Alewife
Anchovy
Anemone
Asterid
Azurine

Batfish
Beardie
Bellows
Bergylt
Bloater
Bluecap
Blue cod
Boxfish
Brassie
Buffalo
Bummalo
Cabezon
Capelin
Catfish
Cavalla
Cavally
Ceviche
Cichlid
Codfish
Copepod
Cowfish
Crappie
Croaker
Crucian
Crusian
Cutlass
Dogfish
Eelfare
Eelpout
Escolar
Findram
Finnack
Finnock
Flattie
Garfish
Garpike
Garvock
Geelbek
Gemfish
Goldeye
Gourami
Grouper
Growler
Grunion
Gudgeon
Gurnard
Gwiniad
Gwyniad
Haddock
Hagdown

Hagfish
Halibut
Herling
Herring
Hirling
Hogfish
Homelyn
Houting
Ichthys
Inconnu
Javelin
Jewfish
Kahawai
Keeling
Koi carp
Kokanee
Lampern
Lamprey
Lampuki
Lantern
Lingcod
Lobster
Lyomeri
Mahseer
Medacca
Merling
Mojarra
Mooneye
Morwong
Mudfish
Muraena
Oarfish
Old-wife
Oolakan
Opaleye
Osseter
Oulakan
Oulicon
Panchax
Pandora
Pegasus
Pigfish
Pinfish
Piranha
Pollack
Pollock
Pomfret
Pompano
Ragfish
Rasbora

Ratfish
Rat-tail
Redfish
Rock cod
Rorqual
Sand dab
Sand eel
Sardine
Sawfish
Scalare
Scallop
Sculpin
Sea bass
Sea-cock
Sea-dace
Sea-moth
Sea-pike
Sea-star
Sea-wife
Sillock
Skegger
Skipper
Skitter
Sleeper
Snapper
Sockeye
Sparoid
Speldin
Sterlet
Sunfish
Surgeon
Teleost
Tiddler
Tilapia
Titling
Torgoch
Torpedo
Ulichon
Vendace
Walleye
Warehou
Whipray
Whiting
Wide-gab

8 letters:
Albacore
Anableps
Arapaima
Asteroid

Atherine	Gobiidae	Rosefish
Ballahoo	Goldfish	Saibling
Bay trout	Graining	Sailfish
Billfish	Grayling	Saltfish
Black cod	Hackbolt	Sardelle
Blind eel	Hairtail	Scabbard
Bloodfin	Halfbeak	Sciaenid
Blowfish	Hard-head	Scorpion
Blueback	Holostei	Scuppaug
Bluefish	Hornbeak	Sea bream
Bluegill	Hornpout	Sea-devil
Blue moki	Jackfish	Sea horse
Blue nose	John Dory	Sea-lemon
Boarfish	Kabeljou	Sea perch
Bonefish	Kelpfish	Sea raven
Brisling	Killfish	Sea robin
Bullhead	Kingfish	Sea snail
Bullhorn	Kingklip	Sea trout
Cabezone	Kukukuma	Sergeant
Cabrilla	Lionfish	Serranus
Cardinal	Luderick	Skipjack
Cavefish	Lumpfish	Smear-dab
Characid	Lungfish	Snake-eel
Characin	Mackerel	Sparling
Chimaera	Mahi-mahi	Stenlock
Climbing	Mangrove	Stingray
Coalfish	Manta ray	Stonecat
Corkwing	Mata Hari	Sturgeon
Cucumber	Menhaden	Tarakihi
Cyprinid	Milkfish	Tarwhine
Dealfish	Monkfish	Teraglin
Devil ray	Moonfish	Terakihi
Dragonet	Mulloway	Tilefish
Drumfish	Nannygai	Toadfish
Eagle-ray	Nennigai	Trevalla
Escallop	Nine-eyes	Trevally
Eulachon	Oulachon	Tropical
Fallfish	Paradise	Tubenose
Fighting	Patutuki	Tullibee
Filefish	Pickerel	Weakfish
Flatfish	Pilchard	Whitling
Flathead	Pipefish	Wobegong
Flounder	Pirarucu	Wolffish
Four-eyed	Redbelly	Wollamai
Four-eyes	Red bream	Wollomai
Frogfish	Rock bass	
Ganoidei	Rock-cook	**9 letters:**
Gillaroo	Rockfish	Alfonsino
Gilthead	Rockling	Amberjack
Goatfish	Roncador	Anabantid

Fish

Anchoveta
Angelfish
Argentine
Barracuda
Black bass
Blackfish
Blindfish
Bony bream
Bull trout
Butterfly
Cascadura
Ceratodus
Chaetodon
Chavender
Clingfish
Clupeidae
Coregonus
Coryphene
Devilfish
Gaspereau
Glassfish
Globefish
Goldfinny
Goldsinny
Golomynka
Goosefish
Greenbone
Greenling
Grenadier
Haberdine
Hornyhead
Hottentot
Houndfish
Ichthyoid
Jacksmelt
Jewelfish
Kabeljouw
Killifish
Labyrinth
Lamper eel
Latimeria
Lemon sole
Menominee
Mudhopper
Neon tetra
Pikeperch
Placoderm
Porbeagle
Porcupine
Quillback

Red mullet
Red salmon
Roussette
Sand lance
Scaldfish
Schnapper
Scorpaena
Selachian
Shubunkin
Siluridae
Slickhead
Snailfish
Snakehead
Snipefish
Solenette
Spadefish
Spearfish
Speldring
Stargazer
Steelhead
Steenbras
Stingaree
Stockfish
Stone bass
Stonefish
Surfperch
Surmullet
Swellfish
Swordfish
Swordtail
Thornback
Threadfin
Tittlebat
Tommy ruff
Topminnow
Trachinus
Troutfish
Trunkfish
Whitebait
White-bass
Whitefish
Wobbegong
Wobbygong
Wreckfish
Yellowfin

10 letters:
Archerfish
Barracoota
Barracouta

Barramunda
Barramundi
Bitterling
Black bream
Black perch
Bombay duck
Bottlehead
Brook trout
Brown trout
Butterfish
Candlefish
Cockabully
Coelacanth
Coral trout
Cornetfish
Cyclostome
Damselfish
Demoiselle
Dollarfish
Etheostoma
Fingerling
Flutemouth
Giant perch
Groundling
Guitarfish
Horned pout
King salmon
Lumpsucker
Māori chief
Maskalonge
Maskanonge
Maskinonge
Midshipman
Mirror carp
Mossbunker
Mudskipper
Needlefish
Nurse-hound
Ouananiche
Paddlefish
Pakirikiri
Parrotfish
Pearl perch
Rabbitfish
Red emperor
Red snapper
Ribbonfish
Rock salmon
Rudderfish
Scopelidae

Fish

Sea lamprey
Sea-poacher
Sea-surgeon
Serrasalmo
Sheepshead
Shovelnose
Silverfish
Silverside
Springfish
Squeteague
Teleostome
Titarakura
Tommy rough
Tripletail
Yellow jack
Yellowtail

11 letters:
Bluefin tuna
Chondrostei
Dolly Varden
Electric eel
Golden perch
Istiophorus
Lake herring
Lepidosiren
Maskallonge
Moorish idol
Murray perch
Muskellunge
Ostracoderm
Oxyrhynchus
Plagiostome
Pumpkinseed
Salmon trout
Scolopendra
Sea scorpion
Seventy-four
Silver belly
Silversides

Sleeper goby
Smooth hound
Soldierfish
Stickleback
Stone roller
Surgeonfish
Triggerfish
Trumpetfish
Whiting pout
Yellow-belly

12 letters:
Baggie minnow
Ballan-wrasse
Elasmobranch
Father lasher
Heterosomata
Histiophorus
Mangrove Jack
Miller's thumb
Mouthbreeder
Native salmon
Orange roughy
Ox-eye herring
Plectognathi
Rainbow trout
River lamprey
Silver salmon
Skipjack tuna
Squirrelfish
Walleyed pike
Yarra herring

13 letters:
Armed bullhead
Black kingfish
Black rockfish
Brown bullhead
Chinook salmon
Climbing perch

Flying gurnard
Horse mackerel
Leatherjacket
Northern porgy
Quinnat salmon
Sailor's choice
Sergeant Baker
Sergeant major
Speckled trout

14 letters:
Largemouth bass
Orange chromide
School mackerel
Smallmouth bass

15 letters:
Crossopterygian
Freshwater bream
Siamese fighting
Spanish mackerel
Spotted mackerel

16 letters:
Australian salmon

17 letters:
Queensland halibut

18 letters:
Queensland kingfish
Queensland lungfish

19 letters:
Queensland trumpeter

22 letters:
Short-spined sea
  scorpion

See also:
➤ **Seafood** ➤ **Sharks**

Flags

7 letters:
Saltire

8 letters:
Lone Star
Old Glory
Swastika

9 letters:
Betsy Ross
Blue Peter
Maple Leaf
Red Dragon
Red Duster
Rising Sun
Tricolore
Tricolour

Union Jack

10 letters:
Blue Ensign
Bonnie Blue
Jolly Roger
Lonely Star
Single Star

11 letters:
Golden Arrow
White Duster

12 letters:
Federal Cross
Herring Salad
Stars and Bars

13 letters:
Southern Cross

14 letters:
Flag of the South

15 letters:
Cross of St George
Hammer and Sickle
Stainless Banner
Stars and Stripes

18 letters:
Skull and crossbones

Flowers

4 letters:
Aloe
Arum
Cyme
Disa
Flag
Gold
Gool
Gule
Irid
Iris
Lily
Pink
Rose

5 letters:
Agave
Aster
Brook
Bugle
Camas
Daisy
Enemy
Hosta
Lotus
Lupin
Oxlip

Padma
Pansy
Peony
Phlox
Poppy
Stock
Tansy
Toran
Tulip
Umbel
Yulan

6 letters:
Acacia
Adonis
Arabis
Azalea
Betony
Cactus
Camash
Camass
Corymb
Crants
Crocus
Dahlia
Gollan
Henbit

Madder
Maguey
Mallow
Nuphar
Onagra
Orchid
Paeony
Pompom
Pompon
Protea
Safety
Scilla
Sesame
Silene
Smilax
Spadix
Tassel
Torana
Vernal
Violet
Yarrow
Zinnia

7 letters:
Aconite
Alyssum
Anemone

Arbutus
Astilbe
Begonia
Bugloss
Burdock
Campion
Cowslip
Dog rose
Freesia
Fumaria
Gentian
Gilt-cup
Glacier
Godetia
Golland
Gowland
Hemlock
Ipomoea
Jasmine
Jonquil
Kikumon
Lobelia
Melilot
Petunia
Picotee
Primula
Quamash
Ragweed
Rampion
Saffron
Sulphur
Verbena

8 letters:
Abutilon
Acanthus
Amaranth
Argemone
Asphodel
Aubretia
Aubrieta
Bignonia
Bindi-eye
Bluebell
Camellia
Camomile
Carolina
Clematis
Cyclamen
Daffodil

Floscule
Foxglove
Gardenia
Geranium
Gillyvor
Glory-pea
Harebell
Hepatica
Hibiscus
Hyacinth
Kok-sagyz
Larkspur
Lavender
Magnolia
Mandrake
Marigold
Marjoram
Myosotis
Oleander
Oxtongue
Primrose
Samphire
Scabious
Snowdrop
Stapelia
Sweet pea
Trollius
Tuberose
Turnsole
Valerian
Wisteria
Woodbine

9 letters:
Amaryllis
Aubrietia
Bald-money
Belamoure
Buttercup
Calendula
Carnation
Celandine
Chamomile
Clianthus
Columbine
Dandelion
Desert pea
Digitalis
Edelweiss
Eglantine

Gessamine
Gladiolus
Groundsel
Hellebore
Hollyhock
Hydrangea
Jessamine
Melampode
Monkshood
Narcissus
Pimpernel
Pre-vernal
Rudbeckia
Santonica
Saxifrage
Speedwell
Strobilus
Sunflower
Tiger lily
Water lily

10 letters:
Aspidistra
Bellamoure
Busy Lizzie
Cornflower
Coronation
Delphinium
Gypsophila
Heart's-ease
Heliotrope
Immortelle
Marguerite
Nasturtium
Oxeye daisy
Pentstemon
Poinsettia
Snapdragon
Stavesacre
Sweetbrier
Tibouchine
Touch-me-not
Wallflower
Willowherb

11 letters:
Bog asphodel
Bur-marigold
Cotoneaster
Forget-me-not

Gilliflower
Gillyflower
Guelder-rose
London pride
Loose-strife
Meadowsweet
Ragged robin
Wintergreen
Wood anemone

12 letters:
Hortus siccus
Morning-glory
None-so-pretty

Old man's beard
Sweet william
Tradescantia

13 letters:
African violet
Babe-in-a-cradle
Bougainvillea
Chrysanthemum
Grape hyacinth
Passionflower

14 letters:
Black-eyed Susan

Cardinal flower
Cooktown orchid
Love-in-idleness

15 letters:
Christmas cactus
Lily of the valley
Michaelmas daisy
Sturt's desert pea

16 letters:
Deadly nightshade
Love-lies-bleeding
Scarlet pimpernel

See also:
➤ **Lilies**

Flies

3 letters:
Bee
Bot
Fly
Fox

4 letters:
Bulb
Bush
Cleg
Deer
Dung
Frit
Gnat
Horn
Moth
Pium
Zimb

5 letters:
Alder
Aphid
Aphis
Baker
Black
Brize
Crane
Drake
Drone

Flesh
Fruit
Hover
Musca
Nymph
Onion
Sedge
Snake
Snipe
Zebub

6 letters:
Blowie
Botfly
Breese
Breeze
Caddis
Carrot
Dayfly
Dragon
Gadfly
Mayfly
Medfly
Motuca
Mutuca
Needle
Pomace
Robber
Stable

Thrips
Tipula
Tsetse
Tzetze
Warble
Willow

7 letters:
Antlion
Beetfly
Blowfly
Brommer
Bushfly
Chalcid
Cluster
Diptera
Gallfly
Grannom
Harvest
Hessian
Lantern
Mangold
Sandfly
Spanish
Tabanid
Tachina
Vinegar
Watchet

8 letters:
Assassin
Bedstead
Blackfly
Dutchman
Glossina
Greenfly
Horsefly
Housefly
Lacewing
Mosquito
Ox-warble
Scorpion
Simulium
Stonefly
Whitefly

9 letters:
Bean aphid
Bee killer
Blue-arsed
Damselfly

Dobsonfly
Dragonfly
Greenhead
Homoptera
Ichneumon
Jock Scott
Sciaridae
Screwworm
Syrphidae

10 letters:
Bluebottle
Cecidomyia
Drosophila
Plant louse
Silverhorn

11 letters:
Apple blight
Buffalo gnat
Greenbottle
Plecopteran

12 letters:
Cheesehopper
Green blowfly
Jenny-spinner
Trichopteran

13 letters:
Cheese skipper
Daddy-longlegs

14 letters:
American blight

15 letters:
Welshman's button

18 letters:
Mediterranean fruit

19 letters:
Devil's darning-needle

Football

TERMS USED IN (ASSOCIATION) FOOTBALL

2 letters:
FA

3 letters:
Bar
Cap
Net
Nil
SFA

4 letters:
Back
FIFA
Foul
Goal
Half
Mark
Pass
Post
Save
Shot
Trap

UEFA
Wall
Wing

5 letters:
Cross
Derby
Dummy

6 letters:
Corner
Cut out
Goalie
Lay off
Nutmeg
One-two
Onside
Square
Tackle
Winger

7 letters:
Booking
Bye kick
Caution
Dribble
Forward
Goal net
Kick off
Offside
Own goal
Penalty
Playoff
Red card
Referee
Striker
Sweeper
Throw in

8 letters:
Crossbar
Defender
Free kick

Terms used in (Association) Football (continued)

Fullback
Full time
Goal area
Goal kick
Goalpost
Halfback
Half time
Handball
Left back
Linesman
Long ball
Midfield
Pass-back
Reserves
Route One
Spot kick
Transfer
Wall pass

9 letters:
Aggregate
Breakaway
Clearance
Extra time
Finishing
Inswinger
Non-league
Promotion

Right back
Score draw
Target man
Touchline

10 letters:
Ballplayer
Ballwinner
Catenaccio
Centre half
Corner kick
Goalkeeper
Injury time
Inside left
Midfielder
Penalty box
Relegation
Sending-off
Six-yard box
Substitute
Yellow card

11 letters:
Half way line
Inside right
Offside trap
Ordering-off
Outside left

Penalty area
Penalty kick
Penalty spot
Six-yard line

12 letters:
Centre circle
Outside right
Stoppage time

13 letters:
Centre forward
International
Sliding tackle
Total football

14 letters:
Aggregate score
Direct free kick

15 letters:
Penalty shoot-out

16 letters:
Indirect free kick
Professional foul

Terms used in Australian Rules Football

3 letters:
AFL

4 letters:
Goal
Mark
Rove
Ruck

5 letters:
Flank
Footy
Point
Rover

6 letters:
Behind

Rub out
Stanza

7 letters:
Quarter
Throw in

8 letters:
Boundary
Eighteen, the
Follower
Free kick
Guernsey
Half-back
Handball
Shepherd
Stab kick

9 letters:
Ruckrover
Scrimmage

10 letters:
Back pocket
Behind line
Behind post
Goal umpire
Shirt front

11 letters:
Aussie Rules
Field umpire
Half-forward
Interchange

Terms used in Australian Rules Football (continued)

12 letters:
Twentieth man

13 letters:
Forward pocket

Nineteenth man

14 letters:
Aerial ping-pong

24 letters:
Australian Football
League

Terms used in American Football

3 letters:
Run

4 letters:
Down
Line
Pass
Play
Punt
Rush
Sack
Snap

5 letters:
Blitz
Block
Guard

6 letters:
Center
Kicker
Punter
Safety
Tackle

7 letters:
Defense
End zone
Lineman
Offense
Pigskin
Shotgun

8 letters:
Complete
Football
Fullback
Gridiron
Halfback
Overtime
Tight end
Turnover

9 letters:
Backfield
Field goal
Scrimmage
Secondary
Super Bowl

Touchback
Touchdown

10 letters:
Cornerback
Incomplete
Line backer
Point after

11 letters:
Quarterback
Running back
Special team

12 letters:
Defensive end
Interception
Wide receiver

13 letters:
Defensive back

15 letters:
Line of scrimmage

Football clubs

European Football Clubs

4 letters:
Ajax
Genk
Lyon
Roma

5 letters:
Lazio
Parma

6 letters:
Brugge
Lierse
Monaco

7 letters:
AC Milan
Beveren
Brondby
FC Porto

Hamburg

8 letters:
Besiktas
Juventus
Valencia

9 letters:
AEK Athens
Barcelona

EUROPEAN FOOTBALL CLUBS (CONTINUED)

Celta Vigo
Feyenoord
Stuttgart
Villareal

10 letters:
Anderlecht
Dynamo Kiev
Heerenveen
Inter Milan
Olympiacos
Real Madrid

11 letters:
Ferencvaros
Galatasaray

Rapid Vienna
RCD Mallorca

12 letters:
Bayern Munich
Dinamo Zagreb
PSV Eindhoven
Real Sociedad
Sparta Prague

13 letters:
Austria Vienna
Panathenaikos

14 letters:
Paris St Germain

15 letters:
Lokomotiv Moscow
Red Star Belgrade
Steaua Bucharest

16 letters:
Borussia Dortmund
Partizan Belgrade

17 letters:
Deportivo La Coruna

18 letters:
Olympique Marseille

UK FOOTBALL CLUBS

Club	Nickname	Ground
Aberdeen	Dons	Pittodrie
Arsenal	Gunners	Highbury
Aston Villa	Villa	Villa Park
Birmingham City	-	-
Blackburn Rovers	Rovers	Ewood Park
Bolton	Trotters	-
Bradford	-	-
Bristol City	Robins	-
Burnley	-	-
Cardiff	-	-
Celtic	Celts, Hoops	Parkhead
Charlton	Addicks	The Valley
Chelsea	Pensioners	Stamford Bridge
Coventry City	-	-
Crewe	-	-
Crystal Palace	Glaziers	-
Derby County	Rams	-
Dundee	Dark Blues	Dens Park
Dundee United	Tangerines	Tannadice
Dunfermline Athletic	Pars	East End Park
Everton	Toffee Men	Goodison Park
Fulham	Cottagers	Craven Cottage
Gillingham	-	-
Hearts	Jambos, Jam Tarts	Gorgie Road

UK FOOTBALL CLUBS (CONTINUED)

Club	Nickname	Ground
Hibernian	Hibs, Hibees	Easter Road
Inverness Caley Thistle	-	-
Ipswich	-	-
Kilmarnock	Killie	-
Leeds United	-	Elland Road
Leicester City	Filberts	Filbert Street
Leyton Orient	Orient	-
Liverpool	Reds	Anfield
Livingston	Livi	-
Manchester City	City	Maine Road
Manchester United	Reds, Red Devils	Old Trafford
Middlesbrough	Boro	-
Millwall	Lions	The Den
Motherwell	Steelmen, Well	Fir Park
Newcastle	Magpies, Toon	St James Park
Norwich	Canaries	-
Nottingham Forest	Forest	-
Partick Thistle	Jags	Firhill
Peterborough	Posh	-
Portsmouth	Pompey	-
Preston	-	-
Queen of the South	-	-
Queen's Park Rangers	QPR	-
Rangers	Gers, Light Blues	Ibrox
Reading	-	-
Rotherham	-	-
St Johnstone	-	-
St Mirren	-	Love Street
Sheffield United	Blades	-
Sheffield Wednesday	-	-
Southampton	Saints	-
Stenhousemuir	-	-
Stoke	Potteries	-
Sunderland	-	Stadium of Light
Tottenham Hotspur	Spurs	White Hart Lane
Tranmere Rovers	-	-
Walsall	-	-
Watford	-	-
West Bromwich Albion	-	-
West Ham	Hammers	-

UK FOOTBALL CLUBS (CONTINUED)

Club	Nickname	Ground
Wigan	-	-
Wimbledon	Dons	-
Wolves	-	-

Footballers

3 letters:
Law, *Dennis*

4 letters:
Ball, *Alan*
Best, *George*
Dean, *Dixie*
Didi
Duff, *Damien*
Figo, *Luis*
Gray, *Eddie*
Hunt, *Roger*
Owen, *Michael*
Pele
Repp, *Johnny*
Rush, *Ian*
Zoff, *Dizo*

5 letters:
Adams, *Tony*
Banks, *Gordon*
Giggs, *Ryan*
Giles, *John*
Greig, *John*
Henry, *Thierry*
Hurst, *Geoff*
Moore, *Bobby*
Pires, *Robert*
Rossi, *Paulo*

6 letters:
Agathe, *Didier*
Baggio, *Roberto*
Barnes, *John*
Baxter, *Jim*
Bowles, *Stan*
Cooper, *Davie*
Crespo, *Hernan*
Cruyff, *Johann*

Finney, *Tom*
Ginola, *David*
Graham, *George*
Gullit, *Ruud*
Hansen, *Alan*
Heskey, *Emil*
Hoddle, *Glen*
Horton, *Jim*
Keegan, *Kevin*
Lawton, *Tommy*
Mackay, *Dave*
McNeil, *Billy*
McStay, *Paul*
Muller, *Gerd*
Puskas, *Ferenc*
Robson, *Brian*
Seaman, *David*
Stiles, *Nobby*
St John, *Ian*
Viduka, *Mark*
Vieira, *Patrick*
Wright, *Billy*
Wright, *Ian*
Yashin, *Lev*
Zidane, *Zinedine*

7 letters:
Alberto, *Carlos*
Beckham, *David*
Bremner, *Billy*
Cantona, *Eric*
Charles, *Joun*
DiCanio, *Paulo*
Eusebio
Francis, *Trevor*
Gemmell, *Archie*
Gemmell, *Tommy*
Gilzean, *Alan*
Greaves, *Jimmy*

Larsson, *Henrik*
Lineker, *Gary*
Lorimer, *Peter*
Mannion, *Wilf*
McCoist, *Ally*
Platini, *Michel*
Rivaldo
Ronaldo
Scholes, *Paul*
Shearer, *Alan*
Shilton, *Peter*
Souness, *Graeme*
Toshack, *John*
Waddell, *Willie*

8 letters:
Bergkamp, *Dennis*
Charlton, *Bobby*
Charlton, *Jack*
Dalglish, *Kenny*
Fontaine, *Just*
Heighway, *Steve*
Jennings, *Pat*
Johnston, *Willie*
Maradona, *Diego*
Matthaus, *Lothar*
Socrates

9 letters:
Archibald, *Steve*
Collymore, *Stan*
DiStefano, *Alfredo*
Gascoigne, *Paul*
Henderson, *Willie*
Jairzinho
Johnstone, *Jimmy*
Klinsmann, *Jurgen*
Lofthouse, *Nat*
Van Basten, *Marco*

10 letters:
Battistuta, *Gabriel*
Djourkaeff, *Youri*
McClintock, *Frank*

Ronaldinho
Schillacci, *Toto*

11 letters:
Beckenbauer, *Franz*

12 letters:
Blanchflower, *Danny*

13 letters:
Van Nistelrooy, *Ruud*

Foreign words and phrases

3 letters:
Ami
Jeu
Mot

4 letters:
À bas
Abbé
Doge
Gene
In re
Lied
Vivo

5 letters:
Ab ovo
Addio
À deux
Ad hoc
Adios
Ad lib
Ad rem
Adsum
À gogo
Aidos
Apage
Arras
Assai
Buffo
Ca ira
Canto
Corno
Desto
Dolce
Domus
École
Étude
Grave
Largo
Lento
Lycée

Mores
Obiit
Per se
Plaza
Pleno
Reich
Salle
Segno
Segue
Sordo
Tacet
Torte
Tutti
Usine

6 letters:
Abattu
Abrege
Agrege
Allons
Aperçu
À terre
Aubade
Au fait
Au fond
Avanti
Avenir
Bel air
Bêtise
Bon mot
Bon ton
Cortes
Crible
Da capo
Dégagé
Déja vu
De jure
Der Tag
Emptor
En fête
Fi donc

Flèche
Giusto
Grazia
Ibidem
In vivo
Legato
Lieder
Maison
Mañana
Nobile
Ottava
Palais
Posada
Presto
Rubato
Sempre
Subito
Tenuto
Torero
Troppo
Vivace

7 letters:
Acharne
Ad astra
Ad finem
Ad litem
À droite
Ad vivum
Affaire
Affiche
Agaçant
À gauche
Agitato
À jamais
À la mode
Alcaide
Alcalde
Al conto
Altesse
Animato

A priori
À quatre
Attacca
Au mieux
Auslese
Bas bleu
Battuta
Berceau
Bonjour
Bonsoir
Bourrée
Bravura
Calando
Cantina
Canzona
Canzone
Caramba
Chambre
Chanson
Château
Chez moi
Clavier
Codetta
Comedia
Con brio
Con moto
Couloir
Cui bono
D'accord
Danseur
Ébauche
En prise
En route
Ex aequo
Fagotto
Farceur
Fermata
Friture
Furioso
Gestalt
Giocoso
Gouache
Haut ton
Ich dien
In utero
In vacuo
In vitro
Ländler
Laus Deo
Märchen

Morceau
Morendo
Palazzo
Pas seul
Peccavi
Pension
Pesante
Piacere
Plafond
Pomposo
Pro rata
Qui vive
Ragazza
Rathaus
Rigsdag
Riksdag
Rondeau
Rondino
Rosalio
Roulade
Schloss
Sine die
Sordino
Sub rosa
Tant pis
Vibrato

8 letters:
Abat jour
Abat-voix
Ad summum
Agaçerie
Agrément
À la carte
Alta moda
Apéritif
A piacere
Après ski
À quoi bon
Au gratin
Au revoir
Autobahn
Aux armes
À volonté
Banlieue
Bel canto
Bien-être
Bona fide
Bout-rime
Chez nous

Col legno
Con amore
Con fuoco
Coryphée
Cum laude
Dal segno
Danseuse
Déjeuner
Démarche
Deus vult
Dies irae
Distrait
Doloroso
Duettino
Enceinte
Entresol
Estancia
Et cetera
Excerpta
Ex gratia
Faubourg
Fine Gael
Gendarme
Grand mal
Hacienda
Hic jacet
Idée fixe
Leggiero
Maestoso
Maggiore
Mala fide
Mal de mer
Mandamus
Mea culpa
Moderato
Mon repos
Mot juste
Ostinato
Par avion
Parlando
Parlante
Pro forma
Raisonné
Rara avis
Ripiendo
Ritenuto
Sayonara
Scordato
Semplice
Serenata

Sobranje
Spianato
Staccato
Sub poena
Trouvère
Una corda
Vorspiel

9 letters:
À bon droit
Aborigine
A cappella
Ad hominem
Ad libitum
Ad nauseum
Ad valorem
A fortiori
Alla breve
Alma mater
Âme perdue
Anschluss
Antipasto
À outrance
Arc-en-ciel
Aria buffa
Assez bien
Au courant
Au naturel
Au secours
Ausgleich
Autopista
Autoroute
Bal masque
Beaux arts
Beaux yeux
Bel esprit
Belle amie
Ben venuto
Bête noire
Bon marché
Bon vivant
Bon viveur
Bon voyage
Bundesrat
Bundestag
Buona sera
Cantabile
Carpe diem
Cauchemar
Cave canem

Centumvir
Coup d'état
Das heisst
Dei gratia
De rigeuer
Dolce vita
En famille
En passant
Et tu, Brute
Flute-a-bec
Folketing
Gemütlich
Glissando
Grandioso
Grand prix
Haut monde
Inter alia
Ipse dixit
Ipso facto
Landsting
Leitmotiv
Mardi Gras
Meden agan
Mezza voce
Nisi prius
Obbligato
Objet d'art
Pari passu
Pas de deux
Passepied
Per capita
Per contra
Petit four
Piacevole
Piangendo
Politburo
Pro patria
Pro re nata
Ricercare
Rus in urbe
Scherzoso
Sforzando
Siciliana
Sine prole
Smerzando
Solfeggio
Sostenuto
Sotto voce
Spiritoso
Sub judice

Sub specie
Succès fou
Tant mieux
Taoiseach
Tête-à-tête
Tout à fait
Tout court
Vers libre
Volkslied
Vox humana

10 letters:
À bon marché
Absente reo
Ad absurdum
Ad vizandum
Affettuoso
Aficionado
Alla Franca
Allargando
All tedesca
Anno Domini
Art nouveau
Au pis aller
Autostrada
Avant garde
Bar mitzvah
Bêche-de-mer
Ben trovato
Billet doux
Bon appetit
Buon giorno
Café au lait
Camino real
Canto fermo
Canzonetta
Certiorari
Cinquepace
Confiserie
Con sordini
Con spirito
Cordon bleu
Danke schön
Deo gratias
Deo volente
Dernier cri
Eisteddfod
Feuilleton
Fianna Fáil
Forte piano

Foreign words and phrases

Gesundheit
In excelsis
In extremis
Jardinière
Jus commune
Jus gentium
Lebensraum
Magnum opus
Mezzo forte
Mezzo piano
Nom-de-plume
Opera buffa
Ottava rima
Perdendosi
Pied-à-terre
Plat du jour
Ponticello
Prima facie
Prix unique
Pro hac vice
Quid pro quo
Recitativo
Ritardando
Ritornelle
Ritornello
Scherzando
Scordatura
Seguidilla
Semper idem
Sens unique
Sine qua non
Stringendo
Sui generis
Table d'hôte
Terra firma
Thé dansant
Tiergarten
Tout de même
Tremolando
Ultra vires
Urbi et orbi
Villanella

11 letters:
Accelerando
Ad infinitum
Aetatis suae
Aide-mémoire
Allez-vous en
Alto-relievo

Amor patriae
Amour-propre
À nos moutons
A posteriori
Arcades ambo
Arrivederci
Au contraire
Avec plaisir
À votre santé
Belle époque
Bien entendu
Bonne bouche
Boutonnière
Capriccioso
Carte du jour
Cavo-relievo
Che sera sera
Comme il faut
Concertante
Contra punto
Contredanse
Coram populo
Crème brûlée
Dail Eireann
Decrescendo
Degringoler
De haut en bas
De profundis
Ex hypothesi
Ex post facto
Femme fatale
Fieri facias
Fin de siècle
Fritto misto
Hasta mañana
In medias res
In principio
Lèse majesté
Lignum vitae
Litterateur
Mise en scène
Motu proprio
Musica ficta
Ne plus ultra
Nihil obstat
Nom de guerre
Nous verrons
Obiter dicta
Objet trouvé
Opera bouffe

Papier-mâché
Pas de quatre
Pax vobiscum
Politbureau
Raison d'être
Rellentando
Savoir-faire
Schottische
Smörgasbord
Summum bonum
Tempo giusto
Tempus fugit
Tertium quid
Tout le monde
Und so weiter
Vivacissimo

12 letters:
Acciaccatura
Amicus curiae
Ancien régime
Ante meridiem
Appassionata
Appoggiatura
À quatre mains
Arrière-garde
Ave atque cale
Ballon d'essai
Basso-relievo
Buenas noches
Carte blanche
Cause célèbre
Caveat emptor
Compos mentis
Concertstück
Conseil d'état
Contra mundum
Crème caramel
Degringolade
Donnerwetter
Doppelganger
Eppur si muove
Experto crede
Fait accompli
Ferae naturae
Feu d'artifice
Force majeure
Gesellschaft
Glockenspiel
Habeas corpus

Haute couture
Homme du monde
Honoris causa
Hors concours
Hors de combat
Hors d'oeuvres
Hotel de ville
Laissez-faire
Lapsus calami
Lite pendente
Mezzo-relievo
Modus vivendo
Obiter dictum
Opéra comique
Piobaireachd
Pollice verso
Porte-cochère
Porte-monnaie
Quelque chose
Rien ne va plus
Salle à manger
Sauve qui peut
S'il vous plait
Terminus a quo
Zigeunerlied

13 letters:
Ab urbe condita
Aggiornamento
À la bonne heure
À propos de rien
Ariston metron
Arrière pensée
Avant-gardiste
Avis au lecteur
Basso profondo
Champs Élysées
Cogito ergo sum

Corps de ballet
Corpus delicti
Couleur de rose
Crème de menthe
Croix de guerre
Cum grano salis
Deux ex machina
Éminence grise
Exempli gratia
Ex proprio motu
Faites vos jeux
Fête champêtre
Force de frappe
Hasta las vista
In vino veritas
Laissez-passer
Lapsus linguae
Magna cum laude
Mirabile dictu
Modus operandi
Multum in parvo
Nolens vivendi
Noli-me-tangere
Nolle prosequi
Nouvelle Vague
Nulli secundus
Palais de danse
Poisson d'avril
Ponsa asinorum
Quartier latin
Schadenfreude
Succès d'estime
Summa cum laude
Très au sérieux

14 letters:
A minori ad majus
Annus mirabilis

Auf Wiedersehen
Bureau de change
Ceteris paribus
Crème de la crème
Deuxième Bureau
Dis aliter visum
Divide et impera
Dolce far niente
Double entendre
Ejusdem generis
Enfant terrible
Et in Arcadia ego
Facile princeps
Hapax legomenon
Homme d'affaires
In loco parentis
Ipsissima verba
Maxima cum laude
Ne obliviscaris
Obiit sine prole
Petit bourgeois
Terminus ad quem
Terra incognita
Tertius gaudens
Valet de chambre

15 letters:
Ad misericordiam
Amende honorable
À propos de bottes
Argumentum ad rem
Cherchez la femme
Cordon sanitaire
Crime passionnel
Gaudeamus igitur
Mutatis mutandis
Persona non grata
Rem acu tetigisti

Fossils

5 letters:
Amber

6 letters:
Eozoon
Olenus

7 letters:
Exuviae
Ichnite
Zoolite

8 letters:
Ammonite
Baculite

Blastoid
Calamite
Conchite
Conodont
Eohippus
Mosasaur
Pliosaur
Ram's horn

Scaphite
Solenite
Volulite
Volutite
Wood-opal

9 letters:
Belemnite
Buccinite
Ceratodus
Chondrite
Cordaites
Encrinite
Goniatite
Ichnolite
Miliolite
Muscalite
Nummulite
Ostracite
Patellite
Phytolite

Serpulite
Stigmaria
Strombite
Tellinite
Trilobite
Turbinate
Turrilite

10 letters:
Blastoidea
Eurypterus
Graptolite
Lingulella
Mosasauros
Orthoceras
Osteolepis
Plesiosaur
Pliohippus
Pterygotus
Sigillaria
Snakestone

11 letters:
Gongiatites
Ichthyolite
Ostracoderm

12 letters:
Pythonomorph
Sinanthropus
Stromatolite
Uintatherium

13 letters:
Titanotherium
Zinganthropus

14 letters:
Conchyliaceous

15 letters:
Ichthyodurolite

Types of fowl

3 letters:
Cob
Hen
Ree

4 letters:
Cock
Coot
Duck
Gnow
Kora
Nene
Smew
Swan
Teal

5 letters:
Capon
Chock
Chook
Eider
Ember
Goose
Layer
Quail

Reeve
Rumpy
Scaup
Solan

6 letters:
Ancona
Bantam
Boiler
Brahma
Cochin
Eirack
Guinea
Houdan
Jungle
Pullet
Rumkin
Sitter
Sultan
Sussex
Tappit
Turkey
Wigeon

7 letters:
Campine
Chicken
Dorking
Gadwall
Greylag
Hamburg
Leghorn
Mallard
Minorca
Moorhen
Partlet
Pintado
Pintail
Pochard
Poulard
Redhead
Rooster
Sawbill
Sea duck
Sumatra
Whooper
Widgeon

Fruits

8 letters:
Baldpate
Blue duck
Cockerel
Hamburgh
Langshan
Marsh hen
Megapode
Musk duck
Mute swan
Pheasant
Screamer
Shelduck
Shoveler
Wood duck

9 letters:
Black swan
Blue goose
Eider duck
Faverolle
Goldeneye
Goosander
Merganser

Orpington
Partridge
Pertelote
Ruddy duck
Scaup duck
Snow goose
Welsummer
Wyandotte

10 letters:
Andalusian
Australorp
Bufflehead
Burrow-duck
Canvasback
Chittagong
Mallee fowl
Spatchcock
Spitchcock

11 letters:
Bewick's swan
Brissle-cock
Brush turkey
Canada goose

Magpie goose
Muscovy duck
Scrub turkey
Whooper swan

12 letters:
Greylag goose
Mandarin duck
New Hampshire
Paradise duck
Plymouth Rock
Velvet scoter

13 letters:
Barnacle goose
Buff Orpington
Harlequin duck
Trumpeter swan
Whistling swan

14 letters:
American wigeon
Rhode Island Red

Fruits

3 letters:
Fig
Haw
Hep
Hip
Hop
Jak

4 letters:
Akee
Bael
Bito
Date
Gage
Gean
Jack
Kaki
Kiwi
Lime
Pear
Pepo

Plum
Pome
Sloe
Sorb
Star
Tuna
UGLI®

5 letters:
Anana
Anona
Apple
Assai
Berry
Bread
Choko
Gourd
Grape
Guava
Jaffa
Lemon

Lichi
Lotus
Mango
Melon
Nancy
Naras
Nashi
Nelis
Olive
Papaw
Peach
Prune
Rowan
Whort

6 letters:
Almond
Ananas
Babaco
Banana
Banian

Banyan
Carica
Casaba
Cherry
Chocho
Citron
Citrus
Damson
Durian
Durion
Emblic
Feijoa
Kiwano®
Lichee
Litchi
Longan
Loquat
Lychee
Mammee
Medlar
Narras
Nelies
Orange
Papaya
Pawpaw
Pepino
Pepper
Pomelo
Pruine
Quince
Raisin
Russet
Samara
Sapota
Sharon
Squash
Sweety
Tomato
Wampee

7 letters:
Apricot
Avocado
Bramble
Bullace
Cedrate
Chayote
Crab-nut
Cumquat
Geebung

Genipap
Kumquat
Leechee
Litchee
Manjack
Morello
Naartje
Passion
Pimento
Pinguin
Poperin
Pumpkin
Pupunha
Ruddock
Satsuma
Soursop
Sultana
Sweetie
Tangelo
Winesap

8 letters:
Abricock
Apricock
Bergamot
Bilberry
Blimbing
Boxberry
Calabash
Dewberry
Fraughan
Goosegog
Hagberry
Hastings
Hedgehog
Kalumpit
Mandarin
May apple
Minneola
Mulberry
Physalis
Plantain
Rambutan
Sebesten
Shaddock
Sunberry
Sweetsop
Tamarind
Tayberry
Victoria

9 letters:
Algarroba
Apple-john
Asian pear
Aubergine
Bakeapple
Beach plum
Blaeberry
Blueberry
Cantaloup
Canteloup
Carambola
Chempaduk
Cherimoya
Cranberry
Greengage
Haanepoot
Hackberry
Jackfruit
Japan plum
Love apple
Mirabelle
Muskmelon
Myrobalan
Naseberry
Nectarine
Neesberry
Ogen melon
Ortanique
Persimmon
Pineapple
Plumdamas
Poppering
Raspberry
Rockmelon
Sapodilla
Saskatoon
Shadberry
Snowberry
Sour gourd
Star-apple
Tamarillo
Tangerine
Tomatillo
Victorine
Whimberry

10 letters:
Blackberry
Breadfruit

Fungi

Calamondin
Canteloupe
Cherimoyer
Clementine
Cloudberry
Elderberry
Galia melon
Gooseberry
Granadilla
Grapefruit
Grenadilla
Jargonelle
Loganberry
Mangosteen
Pick-cheese
Redcurrant
Scaldberry
Sour cherry
Strawberry
Tree tomato
Watermelon
Youngberry

11 letters:
Anchovy pear
Avocado pear
Black cherry
Blood orange
Boysenberry

Chokecherry
Heart cherry
Hesperidium
Huckleberry
Jaffa orange
Marionberry
Navel orange
Pampelmoose
Pampelmouse
Pomegranate
Pompelmoose
Pompelmouse
Prickly pear
Salmonberry
Sweet cherry
Winter melon

12 letters:
Bartlett pear
Bergamot pear
Blackcurrant
Cassaba melon
Concord grape
Custard apple
Serviceberry
Victoria plum
White currant
Whortleberry
Williams pear

13 letters:
Alligator pear
Honeydew melon
Morello cherry
Sapodilla plum
Seville orange

14 letters:
Cape gooseberry
Conference pear
Queensland blue
Worcesterberry

15 letters:
Beurre Hardy pear
Bigarreau cherry
Bon Chretien pear
Cantaloupe melon
Charentais melon

16 letters:
Blackheart cherry
Strawberry tomato

17 letters:
Chinese gooseberry

Fungi

3 letters:
Cup

4 letters:
Bunt
Rust
Smut

5 letters:
Black
Ergot
Favus
Honey
Jelly
Morel
Mould
Mucor

Spunk
Yeast

6 letters:
Agaric
Amadou
Dry rot
Elf-cup
Empusa
Ink-cap
Mildew
Miller
Peziza
Torula
Wax cap
Wet rot

7 letters:
Amanita
Blewits
Boletus
Bracket
Candida
Jew's ear
Milk cap
Monilia
Phallus
Pythium
Russula
Tarspot
Truffle

8 letters:
Ambrosia

Bootlace
Clubroot
Death cap
Death-cup
Fuss-ball
Fuzz-ball
Merulius
Mushroom
Noble rot
Puccinia
Puckfist
Puffball
Rhizopus
Rhytisma
Sariodes
Sickener
Tremella
Tuckahoe
Ustilago

9 letters:
Beefsteak
Blackknot
Cramp ball
Earthstar
Eumycetes
Funnel cap

Horsehair
Mucorales
Shaggy cap
Stinkhorn
Toadstool

10 letters:
Gibberella
Liberty cap
Oak-leather
Orange-peel
Rust fungus
Shoestring
Sooty mould
Yellow rust

11 letters:
Anthracnose
Aspergillus
Chantarelle
Chanterelle
Cladosporum
Craterellus
Ithyphallus
Jelly fungus
Penicillium
Phycomycete

Saprolegnia
Sulphur tuft
Velvet shank

12 letters:
Cryptococcus
Discomycetes
Horn of plenty
Hypersarcoma
Trichophyton
Wood hedgehog

13 letters:
Bracket fungus
Magic mushroom
Saccharomyces
Witches' butter

14 letters:
Wood woollyfoot

15 letters:
Bird's-nest fungus
Dermatophytosis
Destroying angel

Furies

6 letters:
Alecto

7 letters:
Megaera

9 letters:
Tisiphone

Furniture

TYPES OF FURNITURE

6 letters:
Canopy
Litter
Screen
Tester

7 letters:
Bedpost
Epergne
Lectern
Trolley

8 letters:
Bedstead
Hatstand
Vanitory

9 letters:
Coatstand
Footstool
Girandola
Girandole
Hallstand

Headboard
Washstand

10 letters:
Dumbwaiter
Vanity unit

11 letters:
Cheval glass

TYPES OF FURNITURE (CONTINUED)

13 letters:
Longcase clock
Umbrella stand

16 letters:
Grandfather clock
Grandmother clock

FURNITURE STYLES

5 letters:
Saxon
Tudor

6 letters:
Empire
Gothic
Norman
Shaker

7 letters:
Art Deco
Bauhaus
Puritan
Regency

8 letters:
Georgian
Jacobean
Medieval

9 letters:
Cape Dutch
Edwardian
Queen Anne
Victorian

10 letters:
Louis Seize

11 letters:
Elizabethan

Louis Quinze
Louis Treize
New Georgian
Restoration

12 letters:
Greek Revival
Second Empire

13 letters:
Louis Quatorze

14 letters:
William and Mary

FURNITURE DESIGNERS

4 letters:
Adam, *Robert*
Heal, *Ambrose*
Kent, *William*

5 letters:
Aalto, *Alvar*
Bevan, *Charles*
Jones, *Inigo*
Jones, *William*
Klint, *Kaara*
Marot, *Daniel*

Phyfe, *Duncan*
Pugin, *Augustus*
Smith, *George*

6 letters:
Breuer, *Marcel Lajos*
Burges, *William*
Morris, *William*
Voysey, *Charles*

8 letters:
Sheraton, *Thomas*

9 letters:
Pergolesi, *Michael
  Angelo*

10 letters:
Mackintosh, *Charles
  Rennie*

11 letters:
Chippendale, *Thomas*
Hepplewhite, *George*

G g

Galaxies

4 letters:
Arp's

5 letters:
Bode's
Draco
Dwarf
Giant
Helix
Radio
Virgo

6 letters:
Baade's
Carafe
Carina
Cygnus
Fornax
Maffei
Quasar
Spiral
Zwicky

7 letters:
Barbon's
Cluster
Garland

Pancake
Regular
Seyfert
Spindle

8 letters:
Aquarius
Barnard's
Bear's Paw
Black Eye
Circinus
Holmberg
Lacertid
Milky Way
Papillon
Pinwheel
Reinmuth
Sculptor
Seashell
Sombrero

9 letters:
Andromeda
Blue fuzzy
Capricorn
Cartwheel
Centaurus

Great Wall
Irregular

10 letters:
Elliptical
Horologium
Local Group

12 letters:
Supercluster

13 letters:
Burbidge Chain

15 letters:
Exclamation Mark

17 letters:
Ambartsumian's Knot

19 letters:
Mini Magellanic cloud

20 letters:
Large Magellanic Cloud
Small Magellanic Cloud

Games

2 letters:
Eo
Go
RU

3 letters:
Cat
Hob
Loo
Maw

Nap
Nim
Pit
Put
Swy
Tag
Tig
War

4 letters:
Base
Brag
Bull
Crap
Dibs
Fa-fi
Faro
Goff
Golf

Grab
I-spy
Keno
Kino
Loto
Ludo
Main
Mora
Polo
Pool
Putt
Ruff
Scat
Skat
Snap
Solo
Taws
Vint

5 letters:
Bingo
Bocce
Bowls
Catch
Chess
Cinch
Craps
Darts
Fives
Goose
Halma
House
Jacks
Keeno
Lotto
Lurch
Merel
Meril
Monte
Morra
Noddy
Novum
Omber
Ombre
Poker
Quino
Rebus
Roque
Rummy
Shogi

Spoof
Tarok
Tarot
Trugo
Two-up
Whisk
Whist

6 letters:
Animal
Basset
Beetle
Boston
Boules
Casino
Chemmy
Clumps
Crambo
Ecarté
Euchre
Fantan
Footer
Gammon
Gobang
Gomoku
Hockey
Hoopla
Hurley
Kitcat
Merell
Pelota
Piquet
Quinze
Quoits
Raffle
Shinny
Shinty
Soccer
Socker
Squash
Tipcat
Uckers
Vigoro

7 letters:
Anagram
Ba'spiel
Bezique
Braemar
Camogie

Canasta
Cassino
Charade
Codille
Conkers
Coon-can
Croquet
Curling
Diabolo
Hangman
Hurling
In-and-In
Jai Alai
Jukskei
Kabaddi
Lottery
Mahjong
Mancala
Marbles
Matador
Muggins
Netball
Old Maid
Pachisi
Pallone
Peekabo
Pharaoh
Pinball
Plafond
Primero
Rackets
Reversi
Ring taw
Seven-up
Snooker
Squails
Statues
Tangram
Vingt-un
War game

8 letters:
Acrostic
All-fours
Baccarat
Bumpball
Canfield
Charades
Chouette
Cottabus

Cribbage
Dominoes
Fivepins
Football
Forfeits
Handball
Klondike
Klondyke
Korfball
Leapfrog
Mah-jongg
Monopoly®
Ninepins
Nintendo®
Octopush
Pachinko
Pall-mall
Pastance
Patience
Peekaboo
Pegboard
Penneech
Penneeck
Penuchle
Petanque
Ping-pong
Pinochle
Pintable
Pope Joan
Reversis
Rolypoly
Roulette
Rounders
Sack race
Scrabble®
Skipping
Skittles
Slapjack
Softball
Sphairee
Subbuteo®
Teetotum
Tray-trip
Tredille
Trictrac
Verquere
Verquire
Wall game

9 letters:
Badminton
Bagatelle
Billiards
Black-cock
Black-jack
Broomball
Crossword
Duplicate
Fillipeen
Hopscotch
Jingo-ring
Lanterloo
Level-coil
Logogriph
Matrimony
Mistigris
Mumchance
Newmarket
Or mineral
Paintball
Parcheesi®
Pelmanism
Punchball
Quadrille
Quidditch®
Simon says
Solitaire
Spoilfive
Stoolball
Tip-and-run
Tredrille
Twenty-one
Vegetable
Vingt-et-un

10 letters:
Angel-beast
Basketball
Bouillotte
Candlepins
Cat's cradle
Deck tennis
Dumb Crambo
Five-stones
Handy-dandy
Horseshoes
Jackstones
Jackstraws
Knurr-spell

Lansquenet
Paddleball
Phillipina
Phillipine
Philopoena
Spillikins
Tablanette
Tchoukball
Thimblerig
Tricktrack
Troll-madam
Trou-madame
Volley-ball

11 letters:
Barley-brake
Battleships
Bumble-puppy
Catch-the-ten
Hide-and-seek
Racquetball
Rouge et noir
Sancho-pedro
Shovelboard
Speculation
Tick-tack-toe
Tiddlywinks
Troll-my-dame

12 letters:
Bar billiards
Caber tossing
Commonwealth
Consequences
Housey-housey
Jigsaw puzzle
Knur and spell
One-and-thirty
Pitch-and-toss
Shuffleboard
Span-farthing
Troll-my-dames

13 letters:
Blind man's buff
French cricket
Musical chairs
Postman's knock
Prisoner's base
Scavenger hunt

Gases

14 letters:
British bulldog
Crown and anchor
Ducks and drakes
Follow-my-leader
Shove-halfpenny
Snip-snap-snorum
Three-card monte

15 letters:
Chinese whispers
Crossword puzzle
King of the castle
Russian roulette
The Minister's Cat
Twenty questions

16 letters:
Trente-et-quarante

17 letters:
Noughts and crosses

See also:
➤ **Board games** ➤ **Chess pieces** ➤ **Computer games**

Gases

1 letter:
H
O

2 letters:
BZ
CN
CS
He
Kr
Ne
RN
VX

3 letters:
Air
CNG
LNG
LPG
Nox
SNG

4 letters:
Coal
Damp
Flue
Mace®
Neon
Tail
Tear
Town

5 letters:
Argon
Calor®

Ether
Marsh
Nerve
Ozone
Radon
Sarin
Soman
Tabun
Water
Xenon

6 letters:
Arsine
Biogas
Bottle
Butane
Butene
Ethane
Ethene
Ethine
Helium
Ketene
Oilgas
Olefin
Oxygen
Plasma
Sewage
Silane
Thoron
V-agent

7 letters:
Ammonia
Argonon
Blister

Bottled
Coal-oil
Crypton
Fluorin
Krypton
Methane
Mofette
Mustard
Natural
Olefine
Propane
Propene
Stibine

8 letters:
Chlorine
Cyanogen
Diborane
Etherion
Ethylene
Firedamp
Fluorine
Hydrogen
Laughing
Lewisite
Nitrogen
Phosgene
Producer

9 letters:
Acetylene
Afterdamp
Butadiene
Chokedamp
Phosphine

Propylene
Protostar
Solfatara
Synthesis
Whitedamp

10 letters:
Diphosgene
Greenhouse

11 letters:
Methylamine
Nitric oxide

12 letters:
Carbonic-acid
Diazomethane
Electrolytic
Formaldehyde

Nitrous oxide
Oxyacetylene

13 letters:
Carbon dioxide
Methyl bromide
Vinyl chloride

14 letters:
Carbon monoxide
Hydrogen iodide
Methyl chloride
Sulphur dioxide

15 letters:
Hydrogen bromide
Nitrogen dioxide
Nitrogen mustard

16 letters:
Hydrogen chloride
Hydrogen fluoride
Hydrogen sulphide
Synthetic natural

17 letters:
Compressed natural
Tetrafluoroethene

18 letters:
Liquefied petroleum

19 letters:
Tetrafluoroethylene

23 letters:
Dichlorodifluoro-
  methane

Gemstones

2 letters:
ID

3 letters:
Jet

4 letters:
Jade
Onyx
Opal
Ruby
Sard

5 letters:
Agate
Balas
Beryl
Idaho
Pearl
Prase
Topaz

6 letters:
Garnet
Iolite
Jargon
Jasper

Jaspis
Morion
Plasma
Pyrope
Quartz
Sphene
Spinel
Zircon

7 letters:
Cat's-eye
Citrine
Diamond
Emerald
Girasol
Girosol
Helidor
Jacinth
Jadeite
Jargoon
Kunzite
Peridot
Sardine
Smaragd

8 letters:
Adularia

Amethyst
Corundum
Diopside
Fire opal
Girasole
Hawk's-eye
Heliodor
Hyacinth
Melanite
Menilite
Peridote
Sapphire
Sardonyx
Sunstone
Titanite

9 letters:
Almandine
Amazonite
Andradite
Aventurin
Black opal
Cairngorm
Carnelian
Cornelian
Cymophane
Demantoid

Hessonite
Hiddenite
Liver opal
Moonstone
Morganite
Moss agate
Rhodolite
Rubellite
Spodumene
Starstone
Tiger's eye
Turquoise
Uvarovite

10 letters:
Andalusite
Aquamarine
Avanturine
Aventurine
Bloodstone
Chalcedony
Chrysolite

Heliotrope
Indicolite
Indigolite
Odontolite
Rhinestone
Rose quartz
Staurolite
Topazolite
Tourmaline

11 letters:
Alexandrite
Chrysoberyl
Chrysoprase
Lapis lazuli
Smoky quartz
Spessartite
Verd antique
Vesuvianite

12 letters:
Colorado ruby

Dumortierite
Grossularite
Spanish topaz

13 letters:
Bone turquoise
Colorado topaz
Water sapphire
White sapphire

15 letters:
Oriental emerald

17 letters:
Oriental almandine

20 letters:
Madagascar
  aquamarine
New Zealand
  greenstone

Famous generals

3 letters:
Ike (*Dwight David
  Eisenhower*)
Lee, *Robert E*(*dward*)

5 letters:
Booth, *William*
Condé, *Louis de
  Bourbon, Prince de*
De Wet, *Christian*
Grant, *Ulysses Simpson*
Smuts, *Jan*
Wolfe, *James*

6 letters:
Custer, *George
  Armstrong*
Franco, *Francisco*
Gordon, *Charles George*
Joshua
Leslie, *David*
Napier, *Lord Robert*
Patton, *George*
Pompey

Raglan, *Fitzroy James
  Henry Somerset*
Rommel, *Erwin*
Scipio, *Publius Cornelius*

7 letters:
Agrippa, *Marcus
  Vipsanius*
Allenby, *Viscount
  Edmund*
Crassus, *Marcus Licinius*
Gamelin, *Maurice
  Gustave*
Hadrian
Sherman, *William
  Tecumseh*
Turenne

8 letters:
Agricola, *Gnaeus Julius*
De Gaulle, *Charles
  (André Joseph Marie)*
Hannibal
Marshall, *George Catlett*

Montcalm, *Louis Joseph
  de*
Napoleon (*Bonaparte*)
Pershing, *Johh Joseph*
Shrapnel, *Henry*
Stilwell, *Joseph Warren*
Stratton, *Charles
  Sherwood*
Tom Thumb (*Charles
  Sherwood Stratton*)

9 letters:
Agamemnon
Antigonus
Antipater
Boulanger, *George Ernest
  Jean Marie*
Kitchener, *Earl Herbert*
Lafayette, *Marie Joseph,
  Marquis de*
Macarthur, *Douglas*

10 letters:
Alcibiades

Cornwallis, *Charles,*   Eisenhower, *Dwight*   Holofernes
  Marquis   *D(avid) (Ike)*

Geography

BRANCHES OF GEOGRAPHY

5 letters: Hydrology   Chorography
Human   Orography   Climatology
                        Political   Geopolitics
7 letters: Meteorology
Geology   **10 letters:**   Vulcanology
Orology   Demography
                        Glaciology   **12 letters:**
8 letters: Oceanology   Biogeography
Pedology   Seismology   Oceanography
Physical   Topography

9 letters: **11 letters:**   **13 letters:**
Chorology   Cartography   Geomorphology

GEOGRAPHY TERMS AND FEATURES

3 letters: Basin   Mantle
Bay   Beach   Sierra
Col   Cliff   Spring
Cwm   Crust   Steppe
Map   Delta   Suburb
Tor   Fault   Tundra
                        Fjord
4 letters: Glade   **7 letters:**
Core   Levée   Climate
Crag   Ocean   Contour
Dyke   Ridge   Culvert
Fell   Scree   Equator
Glen   Stack   Erosion
Loch   Veldt   Estuary
Reef   Glacier
Rill   **6 letters:**   Isobath
Spit   Canyon   Isohyet
Spur   Cirque   Isthmus
Tarn   Coombe   Meander
Veld   Corrie   Moraine
Wadi   Crater   New town
                        Desert   Rivulet
5 letters: Ice cap   Sand bar
Arête   Isobar   Savanna
Atlas   Jungle   Subsoil
Atoll   Lagoon   Topsoil

GEOGRAPHY TERMS AND FEATURES (CONTINUED)

Tropics
Tsunami
Volcano
Wetland

8 letters:
Crevasse
Eastings
Headland
Isotherm
Latitude
Oriental
Salt flat
Salt lake
Sandbank
Sand dune
Savannah
Snow line

9 letters:
Antipodes
Continent
Coral reef
Dormitory
Epicentre
Green belt
Longitude
Northings
North Pole
Pollution
Relief map
South Pole

Temperate
Waterfall
Watershed
Whirlpool

10 letters:
Atmosphere
Earthquake
Escarpment
Flood plain
Glaciation
Irrigation
Occidental
Ozone layer
Permafrost
Rainforest
Rain shadow
Rift valley
River basin
Third World
Water cycle
Water table
Weathering

11 letters:
Conurbation
Environment
Watercourse

12 letters:
Conservation
Urbanization

13 letters:
Afforestation
Deforestation
Global warming
Grid reference
Hanging valley
Precipitation

14 letters:
Infrastructure
Longshore drift
Ordnance Survey
Plate tectonics

15 letters:
Desertification

16 letters:
Continental drift
Continental shelf
Greenhouse effect

18 letters:
Mercator projection
Northern hemisphere
Southern hemisphere

21 letters:
International Date Line

GEOGRAPHERS

6 letters:
Kremer, *Gerhard*
Strabo

7 letters:
Hakluyt, *Richard*
Ptolemy

8 letters:
Mercator, *Gerardus*

9 letters:
Mackinder, *Sir Halford John*
Pausanias

10 letters:
Somerville, *Mary*

See also:
➤ **Canals** ➤ **Capes** ➤ **Capitals** ➤ **Channels** ➤ **Cities** ➤ **Continents**
➤ **Countries** ➤ **Deserts** ➤ **Layers of the earth's crust** ➤ **Hills** ➤ **Islands and island groups** ➤ **Lakes, lochs and loughs** ➤ **Peninsulas** ➤ **Ports** ➤ **Rivers**
➤ **Seas and oceans** ➤ **Sounds** ➤ **Straits** ➤ **Towns** ➤ **Volcanoes**
➤ **Waterfalls**

Geology

GEOLOGICAL ERAS

8 letters:
Cenozoic
Mesozoic

10 letters:
Palaeozoic

11 letters:
Precambrian

GEOLOGICAL PERIODS

7 letters:
Permian

Silurian
Tertiary
Triassic

Ordovician
Quaternary

8 letters:
Cambrian
Devonian
Jurassic

10 letters:
Cretaceous

13 letters:
Carboniferous

EPOCHS OF THE CENOZOIC ERA

6 letters:
Eocene

8 letters:
Holocene
Pliocene

10 letters:
Palaeocene

7 letters:
Miocene

9 letters:
Oligocene

11 letters:
Pleistocene

See also:
➤ **Layers of the earth's crust** ➤ **Minerals** ➤ **Types of rock** ➤ **Types of stone**

Giants and giantesses

2 letters:
Og

Hymir
Idris
Magog
Mimir
Talos
Talus
Thrym

Urizen

3 letters:
Gog

7 letters:
Antaeus
Cyclops
Despair
Gabbara
Geirred
Goliath
Harapha
Skrymir

4 letters:
Anak
Bran
Otus
Ymir

6 letters:
Coltys
Cottus
Gefion
Krasir
Pallas
Tityus
Triton
Typhon

5 letters:
Argus
Balan
Balor
Cacus

8 letters:
Ascapart
Bellerus
Briareus
Colbrand

Cormoran
Cyclopes
Ferragus
Hrungnir
Slaygood

9 letters:
Alcyoneus
Archiloro

Colbronde
Enceladus
Ephialtes
Gargantua
Lestrigon
Leviathan
Rounceval
Tregeagle
Tryphoeus

10 letters:
Pantagruel
Patagonian
Polyphemus

11 letters:
Alifanfaron
Blunderbore
Galligantus

Glands

3 letters:
Oil

4 letters:
Silk

5 letters:
Green
Liver
Lymph
Mucus
Ovary
Scent
Sweat

6 letters:
Ink-sac
Pineal
Tarsel
Testis
Thymus
Tonsil

7 letters:
Adenoid
Adrenal
Cowper's

Eccrine
Mammary
Musk-sac
Nectary
Parotid
Parotis
Thyroid

8 letters:
Apocrine
Conarium
Exocrine
Lacrimal
Pancreas
Pope's eye
Prostate
Salivary
Testicle

9 letters:
Digestive
Endocrine
Epiphysis
Helocrine
Lachrymal
Melbomian
Pituitary

Sebaceous
Uropygial

10 letters:
Bartholin's
Hypophysis
Osmeterium
Suprarenal

11 letters:
Colleterial
Paranephros
Parathyroid
Prothoracic

12 letters:
Hypothalamus

13 letters:
Bulbourethral

18 letters:
Islets of Langerhans

19 letters:
Islands of Langerhans

Types of glass

3 letters:
Cut

4 letters:
Eden

Jena
Lead
Milk
Spun
Vita

Wire

5 letters:
Crown
Flint

Float
Paste
Plate
Pyrex®
Silex
Smalt

6 letters:
Bottle
Cullet
Quartz
Smalto
Strass

7 letters:
Baccara
Crookes
Crystal
Favrile

Lalique
Murrine
Opaline
Perlite
Schmelz
Stained
Tektite
Tiffany
Triplex®
Vitrail

8 letters:
Baccarat
Murrhine
Obsidian
Pearlite
Venetian
Volcanic

9 letters:
Fulgurite
Lanthanum
Tachilite
Tachylite
Tachylyte
Waterford

10 letters:
Avanturine
Aventurine
Calcedonio
Latticinio
Millefiori
Mousseline
Pitchstone

12 letters:
Vitro-di-trina

Gods and Goddesses

AZTEC

3 letters:
Atl

4 letters:
Tena

5 letters:
Innan
Itzli
Teteo

6 letters:
Atlaua
Paynal
Tlaloc
Xolotl

7 letters:
Amimitl
Ehecatl
Omacatl
Xilonen

8 letters:
Camaxtli

Centeotl
Chantico
Mayahuel
Mixcoatl
Patecatl
Techlotl
Tonatiuh
Tzapotla
Xippilli

9 letters:
Coatlicue
Cochimetl
Ixtlilton
Techalotl
Tzintetol
Tzontemoc
Xipe Totec
Xiuhcoatl

10 letters:
Acolmiztli
Chiconahui
Cihuacoatl
Nanauatzin

Omecihuatl
Xochipilli

11 letters:
Huehueteotl
Itzpapalotl
Ometecuhtli
Tepeyollotl
Tlazolteotl
Uixtociuatl
Xiuhteuctli

12 letters:
Chicomecoatl
Coyolxauhqui
Malinalxochi
Quetzalcoatl
Tecciztecatl
Tezcatlipoca
Tlaltecuhtli
Xochiquetzal
Yacatecuhtli

13 letters:
Acolnahuacatl

Aztec (continued)

Huixtocihuatl
Ilamatecuhtli
Macuilxochitl

14 letters:
Chicomexochtli
Itzlacoliuhque
Mictlantecutli

Tonacatecuhtli

15 letters:
Centzonuitznaua
Chalchiuhtlicue
Chalchiutotolin
Chalmecacihuilt
Huitzilopochtli

16 letters:
Mictlantecihuatl

17 letters:
Chalchiuhtlatonal

21 letters:
Tlahuixcalpantecuhtli

Celtic

3 letters:
Anu
Dôn
Lir

4 letters:
Áine
Badb
Bíle
Bodb
Dana
Danu
Donn
Ériu
Esus
Fand
Llyr
Lugh
Medb
Ogma

5 letters:
Artio

Balor
Banba
Bóand
Dagda
Epona
Mabon
Macha
Midir
Núadu

6 letters:
Bécuma
Brigid
Nemain
Sirona

7 letters:
Belenus
Nechtan
Sequana
Taranis

8 letters:
Ceridwen
Manannán
Morrígan
Nemetona
Rhiannon
Rosmerta
Sucellus
Teutates

9 letters:
Arianhrod
Blodeuedd
Cernunnos
Manawydan

11 letters:
Nantosuelta
Óengus Mac Óc

14 letters:
Lleu Llaw Gyffes
Vagdavercustis

Egyptian

2 letters:
Ra
Re

3 letters:
Set

4 letters:
Isis
Maat
Ptah

5 letters:
Horus
Thoth

6 letters:
Amen-Ra
Anubis
Hathor
Osiris

7 letters:
Serapis

GREEK

Aeolus	Winds
Aphrodite	Love and beauty
Apollo	Light, youth, and music
Ares	War
Artemis	Hunting and the moon
Asclepius	Healing
Athene *or* Pallas Athene	Wisdom
Bacchus	Wine
Boreas	North wind
Cronos	Fertility of the earth
Demeter	Agriculture
Dionysus	Wine
Eos	Dawn
Eros	Love
Fates	Destiny
Gaea *or* Gaia	The earth
Graces	Charm and beauty
Hades	Underworld
Hebe	Youth and spring
Hecate	Underworld
Helios	Sun
Hephaestus	Fire and metalworking
Hera	Queen of the gods
Hermes	Messenger of the gods
Horae *or* the Hours	Seasons
Hymen	Marriage
Hyperion	Sun
Hypnos	Sleep
Iris	Rainbow
Momus	Blame and mockery
Morpheus	Sleep and dreams
Nemesis	Vengeance
Nike	Victory
Pan	Woods and shepherds
Poseidon	Sea and earthquakes
Rhea	Fertility
Selene	Moon
Uranus	Sky
Zephyrus	West wind
Zeus	King of the gods

Gods and Goddesses 340

HINDU

4 letters:
Agni
Devi
Kali
Kama
Maya
Rama
Siva

5 letters:
Durga
Indra
Shiva
Ushas

6 letters:
Brahma

Ganesa
Varuna
Vishnu

7 letters:
Hanuman
Krishna
Lakshmi

INCAN

3 letters:
Apo

4 letters:
Inti

5 letters:
Huaca
Supay

6 letters:
Chasca
Ekkeko
Illapa

7 letters:
Paricia

Punchau
Vichama

8 letters:
Catequil
Cocomama
Coniraya
Copacati
Zaramama

9 letters:
Apu Illapu
Cavillaca
Mama Allpa
Mama Cocha
Mama Oello
Mama Pacha

Pariacaca
Urcaguary
Viracocha

10 letters:
Apu Punchau
Mama Quilla
Manco Capac
Pachacamac

11 letters:
Apocatequil

13 letters:
Chasca Coyllur
Ka-Ata-Killa Kon

MAYAN

2 letters:
Ix

3 letters:
Kan
K'in

4 letters:
Acan
Acat
Alom
Chac
Naum
Zotz

5 letters:
Ah Kin

Ah Mun
Ajbit
Balam
Bitol
Cauac
Cizin
Ixtab
Mulac
Tohil
Votan
Yaluk

6 letters:
Ah Peku
Ah Puch
Chamer
Coyopa

Cum Hau
Ghanan
Ixchel
Kianto
Tzakol

7 letters:
Ac Yanto
Ahau-Kin
Ah Ciliz
Ahmakiq
Ah Tabai
Ahulane
Cakulha
Ekchuah
Hunab Ku
Hun Came

MAYAN (CONTINUED)

Hurakan
Itzamna
Xaman Ek
Yum Caax

8 letters:
Ah Cancum
Ah Cun Can
Ah Cuxtal
Ah Hulneb
Cabaguil
Camaxtli
Camazotz
Caprakan
Colel Cab
Gucumatz
Ixzaluoh
Kukulcan

9 letters:
Ah Chuy Kak
Akhushtal
Chibirias
Hacha'kyum
Kan-xib-yui
Tlacolotl

10 letters:
Ah Chun Caan
Ah Muzencab
Ah Uuc Ticab
Hun Hunahpu
Kinich Ahau

11 letters:
Alaghom Naom
Cit Bolon Tum

Itzananohk`u
Ix Chebel Yax
Kan-u-Uayeyab
Nohochacyum

12 letters:
Backlum Chaam
Buluc Chabtan
Chac Uayab Xoc

13 letters:
Ah Bolom Tzacab
Colop U Uichkin

14 letters:
Ah Uincir Dz'acab

NORSE

3 letters:
Hel
Tyr

4 letters:
Frey
Hela
Idun
Loki
Odin
Thor
Tyrr

5 letters:
Aegir
Aesir
Bragi
Freya
Freyr
Frigg
Njord
Norns
Othin
Vanir

6 letters:
Balder

Freyja
Frigga
Ithunn
Njorth

7 letters:
Heimdal

8 letters:
Heimdall

9 letters:
Heimdallr

ROMAN

Aesculapius	Medicine
Apollo	Light, youth, and music
Aurora	Dawn
Bacchus	Wine
Bellona	War
Bona Dea	Fertility
Ceres	Agriculture
Cupid	Love
Cybele	Nature

ROMAN (CONTINUED)

Diana	Hunting and the moon
Faunus	Forests
Flora	Flowers
Janus	Doors and beginnings
Juno	Queen of the gods
Jupiter *or* Jove	King of the gods
Lares	Household
Luna	Moon
Mars	War
Mercury	Messenger of the gods
Minerva	Wisdom
Neptune	Sea
Penates	Storeroom
Phoebus	Sun
Pluto	Underworld
Quirinus	War
Saturn	Agriculture and vegetation
Sol	Sun
Somnus	Sleep
Trivia	Crossroads
Venus	Love
Victoria	Victory
Vulcan	Fire and metalworking

Golfers

3 letters:
Els, *Ernie*

4 letters:
Lyle, *Sandy*

5 letters:
Braid, *James*
Faldo, *Nick*
Furyk, *Jim*
Hagen, *Walter*
Hogan, *Ben*
Jones, *Bobby*
Lopez, *Nancy*
Snead, *Sam*
Woods, *Tiger*

6 letters:
Carner, *JoAnne*
Foster, *Mark*
Garcia, *Sergio*
Gibson, *Althea*
Lawrie, *Paul*
Nelson, *Byron*
Norman, *Greg*
Palmer, *Arnold*
Player, *Gary*
Vardon, *Harry*
Watson, *Tom*

7 letters:
Bradley, *Pat*
Jacklin, *Tony*
Sarazen, *Gene*

Stewart, *Payne*
Trevino, *Lee*
Woosnam, *Ian*

8 letters:
Crenshaw, *Ben*
Nicklaus, *Jack*
Olazabal, *José-Maria*
Torrance, *Sam*
Zaharias, *Babe*

9 letters:
Whitworth, *Kathy*

11 letters:
Ballesteros, *Severiano*
Montgomerie, *Colin*

Golf terms

3 letters:
Ace
Bag
Cup
Cut
Lag
Lie
Par
Pin
Run
Tee
Top

4 letters:
Ball
Chip
Club
Draw
Duff
Fade
Fore
Grip
Half
Heel
Hole
Hook
Iron
Loft
Pull
Putt
Thin
Trap
Wood
Yips

5 letters:
Apron
Blade
Bogey
Carry
Divot
Drive
Eagle
Fluff
Gimme
Green
Hosel
Links

Rough
Round
Score
Shaft
Shank
Slice
Spoon
Swing
Tiger
Wedge

6 letters:
Bandit
Birdie
Borrow
Bunker
Caddie
Course
Dormie
Driver
Foozle
Hazard
Honour
Marker
Putter
Rabbit
Sclaff
Single
Stance
Stroke
Stymie
Waggle

7 letters:
Air shot
Fairway
Midiron
Scratch
Trolley

8 letters:
Approach
Back nine
Four-ball
Foursome
Green fee
Half shot
Handicap

Long iron
Medal tee
Plus twos
Recovery
Sand trap
Slow play
Take-away

9 letters:
Albatross
Backswing
Caddie car
Clubhouse
Downswing
Front nine
Greensome
Hole in one
Ladies' tee
Match play
Medal play
Pitch shot
Plus fours
Sand wedge
Score card
Short iron
Sweetspot
Threesome

10 letters:
Better-ball
Local rules
Stroke play

11 letters:
Casual water
Green keeper
Pitch and run
Play through

12 letters:
Driving range
Fresh air shot
Putting green

13 letters:
Pitching wedge
Practice swing
Rub of the green

14 letters:
Nine-hole course
Nineteenth hole

15 letters:
Royal and Ancient

16 letters:
Stableford system

Gorgons

6 letters:
Medusa

Stheno

7 letters:
Euryale

Types of government

Absolutism	By an absolute ruler
Anarchy	Absence of government
Aristocracy	By nobility
Autarchy *or* autocracy	By an unrestricted individual
Bureaucracy	By officials
Communalism	By self-governing communities
Constitutionalism	According to a constitution
Corporatism	By corporate groups
Democracy	By the people
Despotism	By a despot or absolute ruler
Diarchy *or* dyarchy	By two rulers
Dictatorship	By dictator
Ergatocracy	By the workers
Gerontocracy	By old people
Gynaecocracy *or* gynarchy	By women
Hagiocracy *or* hagiarchy	By holy men
Heptarchy	By seven rulers
Hexarchy	By six rulers
Hierocracy *or* hierarchy	By priests
Imperialism	By an emperor or empire
Isocracy	By equals
Meritocracy	By rulers chosen according to ability
Mobocracy	By the mob
Monarchy	By monarch
Monocracy	By one ruler
Nomocracy	By rule of law
Ochlocracy	By mob
Octarchy	By eight rulers
Oligarchy	By the few

Pantisocracy	By all equally
Pentarchy	By five rulers
Plutocracy	By the rich
Pornocracy	By whores
Ptochocracy	By the poor
Quangocracy	By quangos
Slavocracy	By slaveholders
Squirearchy *or* squirarchy	By squires
Stratocracy	By the army
Technocracy	By experts
Tetrarchy	By four rulers
Theocracy *or* thearchy	By a deity
Triarchy	By three rulers
Tyranny	By a tyrant

The Graces

6 letters:
Aglaia

Thalia

10 letters:
Euphrosyne

Grammatical cases

6 letters:
Dative

7 letters:
Elative
Oblique

8 letters:
Ablative
Agentive

Ergative
Genitive
Illative
Locative
Vocative

9 letters:
Objective

10 letters:
Accusative
Nominative
Possessive
Subjective

12 letters:
Instrumental

Grand Prix circuits

5 letters:
Monza

6 letters:
Monaco
Sepang
Suzuka

7 letters:
Bahrain

8 letters:
Shanghai

9 letters:
Catalunya

10 letters:
Albert Park

11 letters:
Hungaroring
Nurburgring
Silverstone

12 letters:
Indianapolis

13 letters:
Francorchamps

14 letters:
Hockenheimring
Jose Carlos Pace

16 letters:
Enzo e Dino Ferrari
Gilles Villeneuve
Nevers-Magny Cours

Grapes

3 letters:
Fox

5 letters:
Gamay
Pinot
Steen
Syrah
Tokay
Viura

6 letters:
Malbec
Merlot
Muscat
Shiraz
Spanna

7 letters:
Aligoté
Barbera
Catawba
Concord
Furmint
Hamburg
Malmsey
Sercial

8 letters:
Cabernet
Cinsault
Delaware
Dolcetto
Garnacha
Grenache
Hamburgh
Hanepoot

Honeypot
Malvasia
Malvesie
Marsanne
Moscatel
Muscadel
Muscatel
Nebbiolo
Pinotage
Riesling
Ruländer
Sémillon
Silvaner
Sylvaner
Verdelho
Viognier

9 letters:
Colombard
Haanepoot
Lambrusco
Malvoisie
Mourvèdre
Muscadine
Pinot gris
Pinot noir
Sauvignon
Scheurebe
Trebbiano
Ugni blanc
Véronique
Zinfandel

10 letters:
Chardonnay
Hárslevelü
Kékfrankos

Muscadelle
Negroamoro
Pinot blanc
Sangiovese
Sweet-water
Verdicchio

11 letters:
Chenin blanc
Pinot grigio
Scuppernong
Seyval blanc
Tempranillo

12 letters:
Laski rizling
Olasz rizling

13 letters:
Cabernet franc
Montepulciano
Müller-thurgau
Rhine riesling
Spätburgunder

14 letters:
Gewürztraminer
Sauvignon blanc
Tokay-Pinot Gris
Welschriesling

15 letters:
Grüner veltliner

17 letters:
Cabernet sauvignon

Grasses

3 letters:
Eel
Lop
Oat
Poa
Rye
Saw
Seg
Tef

4 letters:
Alfa
Bent
Cane
Cord
Crab
Culm
Dari
Diss
Doob
Dura
Hair
Kans
Knot
Lyme
Milo
Rami
Reed
Rice
Rips
Rusa
Salt
Snow
Stag
Star
Tape
Teff
Tell
Wire
Worm

5 letters:
Alang
Avena
Bahia
Blady
Canna
Chess

Cogon
Couch
Cutty
Dhura
Doura
Durra
Emmer
Flote
Goose
Grama
Halfa
Heath
Jawar
Jowar
Kunai
Lemon
Maize
Manna
Melic
Oryza
Pamir
Panic
Peach
Plume
Quack
Quick
Ramee
Ramie
Roosa
Sedge
Sisal
Spear
Spelt
Starr
Stipa
Storm
Sword
Wheat
Witch

6 letters:
Bamboo
Barley
Bennet
Bladey
Bromus
Buffel
Canary

Carpet
Clover
Cotton
Cuscus
Darnel
Dhurra
Eddish
Fescue
Fiorin
Jawari
Jowari
Kikuyu
Lalang
Lolium
Lucern
Marram
Marrum
Melick
Millet
Pampas
Phleum
Puszta
Quitch
Redtop
Ribbon
Scurvy
Scutch
Sesame
Toetoe
Toitoi
Twitch
Zoysia

7 letters:
Alfalfa
Bermuda
Bristle
Buffalo
Cannach
Clivers
Esparto
Feather
Foxtail
Heather
Johnson
Locusta
Lucerne
Matweed

Quaking
Sacaton
Sea-reed
Sorghum
Squitch
Timothy
Vetiver
Wallaby
Whangee
Whitlow
Wild oat
Wild rye
Zizania
Zostera

8 letters:
Barnyard
Cat's tail
Cleavers
Dactylis
Dogstail

Eelwrack
Elephant
Flinders
Kangaroo
Khuskhus
Materass
Paspalum
Rye-grass
Scorpion
Spinifex
Teosinte

9 letters:
Bluegrass
Cocksfoot
Corkscrew
Danthonia
Deergrass
Gama-grass
Harestail
Job's tears

Porcupine
Snowgrass
Sour-gourd
Sugar cane
Triticale

10 letters:
Brome-grass
Citronella
Cochlearia
Cortaderia
Miscanthus
Pennisetum
Persicaria

12 letters:
Kentucky blue
Squirrel-tail
Yorkshire fog

Famous Greeks

4 letters:
Ajax
Nike

5 letters:
Homer
Momus
Timon
Zorba

6 letters:
Epirus
Euclid
Nestor
Nostos

Strabo

7 letters:
Orestes
Paestum
Pelopid
Perseus
Theseus

8 letters:
Achilles
Diomedes
Leonidas
Xenophon

9 letters:
Agamemnon
Aristides
Isocrates
Patroclus
Spartacus
Thersites

10 letters:
Archimedes
Pythagoras

11 letters:
Epaminondas

Shades of green

3 letters:
Pea
Sea

4 letters:
Aqua
Cyan
Jade
Lime

Nile
Pine
Teal

5 letters:
Apple
Olive

6 letters:
Almond
Citron

7 letters:
Avocado
Celadon
Emerald
Lincoln

8 letters:
Eau de nil

9 letters:
Pistachio
Turquoise

10 letters:
Aquamarine
Chartreuse

Guns

2 letters:
HA

3 letters:
BAR
Dag
Gat
Ray
Tea
Uzi®
Zip

4 letters:
Bren
Burp
Colt
Owen
Pump
Riot
Sten
Stun
Tier

5 letters:
Flame
Fusil
Lewis
Luger®
Maxim
Radar
Rifle
Saker
Siege
Spear
Spray
Taser®
Tommy

6 letters:
Ack-ack
Archie
Barker
Bofors
Breech
Falcon
Fowler
Garand
Gingal
Jezail
Jingal
Magnum®
Mauser
Minnie
Minute
Mortar
Musket
Pistol
Pom-pom
Quaker
Roscoe
Squirt
Staple
Swivel
Tupelo

7 letters:
Bazooka
Bulldog
Bundook
Caliver
Carbine
Coehorn
Gatling
Gingall
Hackbut
Long Tom

Machine
Noonday
Pedrero
Pelican
Perrier
Shotgun

8 letters:
Amusette
Armalite®
Arquebus
Biscayan
Browning
Culverin
Deringer
Electron
Elephant
Falconet
Firelock
Howitzer
Oerlikon
Paderero
Paterero
Pederero
Petronel
Pistolet
Repeater
Revolver
Starting
Sterling
Thompson

9 letters:
Archibald
Automatic
Big Bertha
Brown Bess
Carronade

Chassepot
Chokebore
Derringer
Escopette
Flintlock
Forty-five
Harquebus
Matchlock
Morris Meg
Musketoon
Sarbacane
Snaphance
Sterculia

10 letters:
Scatter-gun
Self-cocker

Six-shooter
Smoothbore
Snaphaunce

11 letters:
Blunderbuss
Garand rifle
Kalashnikov
Stern-cannon
Stern-chaser
Thirty eight

12 letters:
Anti-aircraft
Breech-loader
Enfield rifle
Fowlingpiece
Martini-Henry®

Mitrailleuse
Muzzle-loader
Trench mortar

13 letters:
Sub-machine-gun

15 letters:
Winchester rifle

16 letters:
Springfield rifle

21 letters:
Thompson sub-machine
  gun®

Gymnastic events

4 letters:
Beam

5 letters:
Rings

7 letters:
High bar

10 letters:
Horse vault

11 letters:
Pommel horse

12 letters:
Parallel bars

13 letters:
Horizontal bar

14 letters:
Asymmetric bars
Floor exercises
Side horse vault

18 letters:
Rhythmic gymnastics

H h

Hairstyles

2 letters:
DA

3 letters:
Bob
Bun

4 letters:
Afro
Crop
Perm
Pouf

5 letters:
Plait
Wedge

6 letters:
Marcel

Mullet

7 letters:
Beehive
Bunches
Buzz cut
Chignon
Corn row
Crew cut
Flat top
Mohican
Pageboy
Pigtail
Shingle

8 letters:
Bouffant
Eton crop

Ponytail
Razor-cut
Skinhead

9 letters:
Duck's arse
Pompadour

10 letters:
Dreadlocks
Feather-cut
French roll
Marcel wave

11 letters:
French pleat

13 letters:
Permanent wave

Harpies

5 letters:
Aello

7 letters:
Celaeno

Ocypete

Hats

3 letters:
Cap
Fez
Lum
Mob
Nab
Red
Taj
Tam
Tin
Tit
Top

4 letters:
Coif
Hard
Hood
Kepi
Poke
Silk
Sola
Tile
Topi
Ugly
Veil

5 letters:
Akuba
Ascot
Beany
Beret
Boxer
Busby
Crown
Curch
Derby
Envoy
Gibus

Mitre
Mutch
Opera
Pagri
Paper
Pilos
Salet
Shako
Snood
Solah
Straw
Tammy
Terai
Tiara
Topee
Toque
Tuque
Visor
Vizor

6 letters:
Akubra®
Anadem
Barret
Basher
Beanie
Beaver
Boater
Bonnet
Bowler
Breton
Calash
Calpac
Castor
Cloche
Cocked
Coolie
Cornet
Cowboy
Diadem
Fedora
Gaucho
Heaume
Helmet
Hennin
Kalpak
Lum-hat
Mobcap
Morion
Panama

Pilion
Pinner
Safari
Sailor
Salade
Sallet
Shacko
Shovel
Slouch
Sunhat
Titfer
Toorie
Topper
Tourie
Trilby
Turban
Wimple

7 letters:
Bandana
Bandeau
Basinet
Biretta
Bluecap
Caleche
Calotte
Calpack
Capouch
Capuche
Chaplet
Circlet
Commode
Coronet
Cossack
Crusher
Curchef
Earmuff
Flat cap
Frontal
Hattock
Homburg
Kufiyah
Laurels
Leghorn
Matador
Montero
Petasus
Picture
Pillbox
Pilleus

Plateau
Pork-pie
Profile
Puritan
Skimmer
Songkok
Stetson
Sundown
Tarbush
Tricorn

8 letters:
Babushka
Balmoral
Bandanna
Bascinet
Bearskin
Berretta
Blackcap
Capotain
Cloth cap
Coonskin
Dunce cap
Fool's cap
Frontlet
Havelock
Headband
Kaffiyeh
Keffiyeh
Mountie's
Mushroom
Nightcap
Planter's
Puggaree
Ramilies
Runcible
Skullcap
Snap-brim
Sola-topi
Sombrero
Tarboosh
Tarboush
Trencher
Tricorne
Tyrolean
Watch cap
Yarmulke

9 letters:
Astrakhan

353

Balaclava
Billycock
Bollinger
Broadbrim
Cartwheel
Cockle-hat
Dunstable
Forage cap
Gandhi cap
Glengarry
Headdress
Juliet cap
Nor'wester
Peaked cap
Ramillies
Shower cap
Sou'wester
Stovepipe
Sugarloaf

Sunbonnet
Tarbouche
Tarpaulin
Ten-gallon
Wide-awake

10 letters:
Balibuntal
Bluebonnet
Chimneypot
Fascinator
Liberty cap
Pith helmet
Poke bonnet
Sola-helmet

11 letters:
Baseball cap
Crash helmet

Deerstalker
Dolly Varden
Kamelaukion
Mortarboard
Phrygian cap
Stocking cap
Tam-o'-shanter
Trencher cap

12 letters:
Cheese cutter
Fore-and-after
Steeple-crown

15 letters:
Balaclava helmet

Hawks

4 letters:
Eyas
Kite
Nyas
Soar
Sore

5 letters:
Eagle
Hobby
Marsh
Soare

6 letters:
Auceps
Elanet
Falcon
Keelie
Lanner
Merlin
Musket
Osprey

Sorage
Tarsal
Tarsel
Tassel
Tercel

7 letters:
Buzzard
Cooper's
Goshawk
Haggard
Harrier
Kestrel
Sparrow
Staniel
Tarsell
Tiersel

8 letters:
Caracara
Lanneret
Ringtail

Tercelet

9 letters:
Gerfalcon
Gier-eagle
Ossifraga
Ossifrage
Peregrine
Sore-eagle
Wind-hover

10 letters:
Hen harrier

11 letters:
Accipitrine
Lammergeier

12 letters:
Marsh harrier

Parts of the heart

5 letters:
Aorta

6 letters:
Atrium
Septum

7 letters:
Auricle

8 letters:
Vena cava

9 letters:
Ventricle

13 letters:
Bicuspid valve
Pulmonary vein

14 letters:
Semilunar valve
Tricuspid valve

15 letters:
Pulmonary artery

Heraldry terms

2 letters:
Or

3 letters:
Bar
Fur
Vol

4 letters:
Bars
Base
Bend
Coue
Fess
File
Fret
Golp
Lion
Lyon
Orle
Pale
Pall
Paly
Pean
Pile
Semé
Urdé
Vair
Vert
Yale

5 letters:
Azure
Baton
Chief

Crest
Cross
Crown
Eagle
Fesse
Field
Flory
Fusil
Giron
Golpe
Gules
Gyron
Label
Party
Rebus
Sable
Scarp
Semée
Torse
Trick
Urdée

6 letters:
Argent
Armory
Bezant
Blazon
Byzant
Canton
Charge
Checky
Couped
Coward
Dexter
Empale

Erased
Ermine
Falcon
Fecial
Fetial
Fillet
Fleury
Herald
Impale
Lionel
Lodged
Mascle
Moline
Mullet
Naiant
Norroy
Pallet
Parted
Potant
Potent
Proper
Sejant
Shield
Verdoy
Voided
Volant
Vorant
Wreath
Wyvern

7 letters:
Annulet
Armiger
Bandeau
Bearing

355

Bezzant
Bordure
Cadency
Chaplet
Chevron
Compone
Compony
Coronet
Dormant
Endorse
Gardant
Garland
Gironny
Griffon
Gyronny
Issuant
Leopard
Lozenge
Lozengy
Martlet
Nascent
Nombril
Passant
Purpure
Quarter
Rampant
Red Hand
Roundel
Roundle
Salient
Saltire
Sea lion
Sejeant
Statant
Trangle
Trundle
Urinant

8 letters:
Bendwise
Blazonry
Caboched
Cicerone
Couchant
Crescent
Crosslet
Emblazon
Guardant
Hauriant
Heraldic
Mantling
Naissant
Octofoil
Opinicus
Ordinary
Segreant
Sinister
Tressure
Trippant
Umbrated

9 letters:
Abatement
Dimidiate
Displayed
Embattled
Hatchment
Quartered
Quarterly
Regardant
Scutcheon
Supporter

10 letters:
Bloody Hand
Bluemantle
Cinquefoil

Clarenceux
Coat armour
Coat of arms
Cockatrice
Cognisance
Cognizance
Difference
Escutcheon
Fleur-de-lis
Fleur-de-lys
King-of-arms
Lambrequin
Portcullis
Pursuivant
Quartering

11 letters:
Achievement
Canting arms
Clarencieux
Spread eagle
Subordinary

12 letters:
Bend sinister
Inescutcheon

13 letters:
College of arms
Matriculation
Officer of arms
Voided lozenge

14 letters:
Armes parlantes
Counter-passant
Lyon King of Arms
Sun in splendour

Herbs, spices and seasonings

3 letters:
Bay
Oca
Pia
Rue

4 letters:
Dill
Forb
Mace
Mint
Miso
Moly

Sage
Salt
Wort

5 letters:
Anise
Avens

Herbs, spices and seasonings

Basil
Chive
Clove
Cress
Cumin
Eruca
Inula
Maror
Medic
Orval
Senna
Shoyu
Tacca
Tansy
Thyme
Typha
Yerba

6 letters:
Bennet
Borage
Capers
Chilli
Cummin
Exacum
Fennel
Ferula
Garlic
Ginger
Hyssop
Lovage
Madder
Nam pla
Nutmeg
Origan
Purpie
Savory
Sesame
Sorrel
Tamari
Wasabi
Willow
Yarrow

7 letters:
Aconite
Aniseed
Arugula
Bayleaf
Canella

Chervil
Cilanto
Coconut
Comfrey
Dittany
Felicia
Gentian
Gunnera
Madwort
Mustard
Oregano
Origane
Paprika
Parsley
Saffron
Salsify
Vervain

8 letters:
Allspice
Angelica
Bergamot
Cardamom
Centaury
Cinnamon
Costmary
Feverfew
Fireweed
Fluellin
Galangal
Knapweed
Mandrake
Marjoram
Origanum
Plantain
Purslane
Rosemary
Soapwort
Soy sauce
Staragen
Szechuan
Szechwan
Tarragon
Turmeric
Valerian
Wormwood

9 letters:
Asafetida
Calendula

Chamomile
Coriander
Echinacea
Eyebright
Fenugreek
Fish sauce
Galingale
Germander
Haworthia
Kalanchoe
Lamb's ears
Laserwort
Poppy seed
Pussytoes
Red pepper
Rhizocarp
Rocambole
Rodgersia
Soya sauce
Spearmint
Star anise
Tormentil

10 letters:
Asafoetida
Cassia bark
Lemon grass
Peppercorn
Pipsissewa
Rest-harrow
Sesame seed

11 letters:
Black pepper
Caraway seed
Coconut milk
Curry powder
Fines herbes
Garam masala
Laserpicium
Sweet cicely
White pepper

12 letters:
Aristolochia
Ornithogalum
Southernwood

13 letters:
Cayenne pepper
Good-King-Henry
Sunflower seed

14 letters:
Kaffir lime leaf

15 letters:
Alligator pepper

Five spice powder

18 letters:
Sichuan peppercorns

Labours of Hercules

The slaying of the Nemean lion
The slaying of the Lernaean hydra
The capture of the hind of Ceryneia
The capture of the wild boar of Erymanthus
The cleansing of the Augean stables
The shooting of the Stymphalian birds
The capture of the Cretan bull
The capture of the horses of Diomedes
The taking of the girdle of Hippolyte
The capture of the cattle of Geryon
The recovery of the golden apples of Hesperides
The taking of Cerberus

Heroes

3 letters:
Cid

4 letters:
Aitu
Ajax
Eric
Finn
Kami
Lion
Tell

5 letters:
Faust
Jason

6 letters:
Amadis
Cyrano
Fingal
Hector
Kaleva
Nestor
Oliver

Onegin
Roland
Rustem
Rustum
Sigurd

7 letters:
Alcides
Beowulf
Couplet
Lothair
Marmion
Paladin
Perseus
Rinaldo
Saladin
Tancred
Theseus
Tristam
Tristan
Ulysses
Volsung

8 letters:
Achilles
Crockett
Heracles
Hercules
Hiawatha
Leonidas
Meleager
Owlglass
Parsifal
Pericles
Roderego
Roderick
Superman
Tristram

9 letters:
Agamemnon
Cuchulain
Garibaldi
Lochinvar
Owleglass
Owspiegle
Siegfried

10 letters:
Cuchullain
Howleglass
Owlspiegle

11 letters:
Bellerophon
Finn MacCool
Tam o'Shanter
Triptolemus

White knight

13 letters:
Vercingetorix

Hills

3 letters:
How
Kip
Kop
Law
Man
Nab
Tel

4 letters:
Bent
Chin
Cone
Kipp
Knot
Loma
Mesa
Pike
Pnyx
Sion
Tara
Tell
Zion

5 letters:
Bluff
Cleve
Gebel
Horst
Jebel
Kopje
Morro

Pingo
Wolds

6 letters:
Arafar
Broken
Calvan
Coteau
Djebel
Mendip
Wrekin

7 letters:
Beverly
Caelian
Capitol
Drumlin
Hammock
Ludgate
Mamelon
Merrick
Nanatak
Silbury
Viminal

8 letters:
Aventine
Cheviots
Chiltern
Golgotha
Highgate
Lavender

Palatine
Pennines
Quirinal

9 letters:
Areopagus
Esquiline
Grampians
Helvellyn
Janiculum
Monadnock
Monticule
Quantocks

10 letters:
Capitoline
Lammermuir
North Downs
Saddleback
Tweedsmuir

11 letters:
Crag-and-tail
Otway Ranges

12 letters:
Golan Heights

16 letters:
Mount Lofty Ranges

Hindu denominations and sects

6 letters:
Saktas

8 letters:
Saivaism

11 letters:
Hare Krishna
Vaishnavism

Historians

4 letters:
Bede, *the Venerable*
Livy
Oman, *Sir Charles William Chadwick*

5 letters:
Acton, *John Emerich Edward Dalberg*
Green, *John Richard*
Pliny (*the Elder*)
Renan, (*Joseph*) *Ernest*
Wells, *H(erbert) G(eorge)*

6 letters:
Arrian
Bryant, *Sir Arthur* (*Wynne Morgan*)
Buckle, *Henry Thomas*
Camden, *William*

Froude, *James Anthony*
Gibbon, *Edward*
Gildas
Taylor, *A(lan) J(ohn) P(ercivale)*
Thiers, (*Louis*) *Adolphe*

7 letters:
Asellio, *Sempronius*
Carlyle, *Thomas*
Sallust
Starkey, *David*
Tacitus
Toynbee, *Arnold Joseph*

8 letters:
Macaulay, *Thomas Babbington*
Plutarch

Ponsonby, *Lord Arthur*
Strachey, (*Giles*) *Lytton*
Xenophon

9 letters:
Herodotus
Suetonius
Trevelyan, *G(eorge) M(acaulay)*

10 letters:
Thucydides

11 letters:
Trevor-Roper, *Hugh*

13 letters:
Knickerbocker, *Diedrick*

History

HISTORICAL CHARACTERS

3 letters:
Lee, *Robert E(dward)*

4 letters:
Cody, *William Frederick*
Cook, *Captain James*
Dong, *Mao Ze*
Khan, *Genghis*
King, *Martin Luther*
Polo, *Marco*

5 letters:
Drake, *Francis*
El Cid
James, *Jesse*
Jesus
Lenin, *Vladimir Ilyich*
Oates, *Lawrence Edward Grace*
Scott, *Robert Falcon*

6 letters:
Borgia, *Lucrezia*
Brutus
Buddha
Caesar, *Julius*
Cortés, *Hernando*
Custer, *George Armstrong*
Fawkes, *Guy*
Gandhi, *Mahatma*
Hickok, *James Butler*
Hickok, *Wild Bill*
Hitler, *Adolf*
Luther, *Martin*
Nelson, *Horatio*
Pompey
Stalin, *Joseph*
Stuart, *Charles Edward*
Wright, *Orville and Wilbur*
Zapata, *Emiliano*

7 letters:
À Becket, *Thomas*
Gagarin, *Yuri*
Guevara, *Che*
Lincoln, *Abraham*
Raleigh, *Walter*
Saladin
Trotsky, *Leon*
Tse-tung, *Mao*
Wallace, *William*

8 letters:
Augustus
Boadicea
Boudicca
Columbus, *Christopher*
Crockett, *Davy*
Cromwell, *Oliver*
Geronimo
Hannibal
Hiawatha
Mohammed

HISTORICAL CHARACTERS (CONTINUED)

Muhammad
Pericles
Rasputin, *Grigori
Efimovich*
Selassie, *Haile*
Socrates

9 letters:
Bonaparte, *Napoleon*
Churchill, *Winston*
Cleopatra
Garibaldi, *Giuseppe*
Joan of Arc
Montezuma
Mussolini, *Benito*

10 letters:
Antoinette, *Marie*
Crazy Horse
Mark Antony

Washington, *George*

11 letters:
Billy the Kid
Buffalo Bill
Charlemagne
Nightingale, *Florence*
Sitting Bull

12 letters:
Attila the Hun
Captain Oates
Clive *of India*
De Torquemada, *Tomás*

14 letters:
Alfred the Great
Robert the Bruce
The Black Prince

15 letters:
Hereward the Wake
Ivan the Terrible

16 letters:
Duke *of Wellington*
Gordon *of Khartoum*
Lawrence *of Arabia*

17 letters:
Alexander the Great
Catherine the Great
Mary, *Queen of Scots*

19 letters:
Bonnie Prince Charlie
Richard the Lionheart
Warwick the Kingmaker
William the Conqueror

HISTORICAL EVENTS

4 letters:
D-day

5 letters:
Alamo

7 letters:
Boer War
Cold War

8 letters:
Civil War
Crusades
Waterloo

9 letters:
Agincourt
Armistice
Great Trek
Hiroshima
Holocaust
Korean War
Long March
Trafalgar
Watergate

10 letters:
Black Death
Crimean War
Depression
Magna Carta
Suez Crisis
Vietnam War

11 letters:
Diet of Worms
Gordon Riots
Great Schism
Pearl Harbor
Reformation
Renaissance
Restoration

12 letters:
Bloody Sunday
Crystal Night
Easter Rising
Indian Mutiny
Potato Famine
Risorgimento

13 letters:
General Strike
Gunpowder Plot
Kristallnacht
Reign of Terror
Spanish Armada

14 letters:
Boston Tea Party
Boxer Rebellion
Napoleonic Wars
Norman Conquest
Peasants' Revolt
South Sea Bubble
Thirty Years' War
Wars of the Roses

15 letters:
Hundred Years War
Munich Agreement
Spanish Civil War
Wall Street Crash

16 letters:
American Civil War
Battle of Hastings

HISTORICAL EVENTS (CONTINUED)

French Revolution
Peterloo Massacre

17 letters:
Gettysburg Address
Great Fire of London
Hungarian Uprising
Jacobite Rebellion
Russian Revolution

18 letters:
Cultural Revolution
Glorious Revolution

Spanish Inquisition
Treaty of Versailles

20 letters:
Industrial Revolution
Night of the Long Knives

22 letters:
The War between the
   States

23 letters:
Charge of the Light
   Brigade
Tiananmen Square
   Massacre

25 letters:
Declaration of
   Independence

26 letters:
Saint Valentine's Day
   Massacre

Types of home

2 letters:
Ho

3 letters:
Cot
Hut
Inn
Mas

4 letters:
Bush
Casa
Chez
Cote
Crib
Dail
Digs
Drum
Flat
Gite
Hall
Home
Iglu
Keys
Mews
Pent
Rath
Safe
Semi
Slum
Tent

Tied
Town
York

5 letters:
Adobe
Booth
Cabin
Croft
Dacha
Dower
Frame
Hogan
Hotel
House
Hovel
Igloo
Lodge
Lords
Manor
Manse
Motel
Opera
Ranch
Shack
Tepee
Tower
Tudor
Tupek
Tupik
Usher

Villa
Wendy
Whare

6 letters:
Bhavan
Bhawan
Biggin
Bunker
Castle
Chalet
Custom
Des res
Duplex
Flotel
Garret
Grange
Hostel
Insula
Maison
Mobile
Mud hut
Orange
Palace
Prefab
Priory
Shanty
Stuart
Tavern
Wigwam

7 letters:
Althing
Barrack
Bastide
Caboose
Caravan
Chamber
Chapter
Charnel
Château
Commons
Convent
Cottage
Council
Crannog
Customs
Deanery
Embassy
Fashion
Flatlet
Habitat
Halfway
Hanover
Harbour
Knesset
Mansion
Meeting
Osborne
Rectory
Schloss
Starter
Stately
Terrace
Theatre
Trailer
Trinity
Windsor

8 letters:
Boarding

Bungalow
Burghley
Camboose
Clearing
Dwelling
Hacienda
Lagthing
Log cabin
Longleat
Montagne
Rest-home
Somerset
Tenement
Vicarage

9 letters:
Admiralty
Apartment
Bedsitter
Bundestag
But and ben
Clapboard
Consulate
Doss house
Farmhouse
Flophouse
Houseboat
Lancaster
Long house
Mattamore
Odelsting
Parsonage
Penthouse
Roadhouse
Show house
Single-end
Town house
Tree house

10 letters:
Back-to-back
Black house
Brownstone
Chatsworth
Commercial
Guest house
Heartbreak
Maisonette
Odelsthing
Parliament
Pied-à-terre
Studio flat

11 letters:
Cottage flat
Plantagenet
Shooting box

12 letters:
Broadcasting
Chattel house
Lake dwelling
Motor caravan
Weatherboard

13 letters:
Boarding house

14 letters:
Cape Cod cottage

15 letters:
Board-and-shingle
Duplex apartment

17 letters:
Bachelor apartment

Homophones

2 letters:
Be / Bee
By / Buy
Hi / High
Ho / Hoe
In / Inn

Lo / Low
Mo / Mow
No / Know
Oh / Owe
Pa / Pah
Pi / Pie

So / Sew
To / Two
We / Wee

3 letters:
Ail / Ale

Air / Heir
Ale / Ail
All / Awl
Arc / Ark
Ark / Arc
Awe / Ore
Awl / All
Aye / Eye
Baa / Bah
Bad / Bade
Bah / Baa
Bay / Bey
Bee / Be
Bey / Bay
Bow / Bough
Boy / Buoy
Bur / Burr
But / Butt
Buy / By
Can / Cannes
Coo / Coup
Cox / Cocks
Dam / Damn
Daw / Door
Dew / Due
Die / Dye
Doe / Dough
Due / Dew
Dug / Doug
Dun / Done
Dye / Die
Ewe / Yew
Eye / Aye
Few / Phew
Fin / Finn
Fir / Fur
For / Four
Fur / Fir
Gym / Jim
Haw / Whore
Hay / Hey
Hew / Hue
Hey / Hay
Him / Hymn
Hoe / Ho
Hue / Hew
Inn / In
Ion / Iron
Jam / Jamb
Jim / Gym

Key / Quay
Lax / Lacks
Lay / Ley
Lea / Leigh
Led / Lead
Lee / Lea
Ley / Lay
Lie / Lye
Loo / Lieu
Low / Lo
Lye / Lie
Mat / Matt
Mow / Mo
Nap / Knap
Nay / Neigh
Née / Nay
Net / Nett
New / Knew
Nix / Nicks
Nob / Knob
Not / Knot
Nun / None
Oar / Ore
Ode / Owed
One / Won
Ore / Oar
Our / Hour
Owe / Oh
Pah / Pa
Par / Parr
Pax / Packs
Pea / Pee
Pee / Pea
Per / Purr
Pie / Pi
Rap / Wrap
Red / Read
Rex / Wrecks
Roe / Row
Row / Roe
Rye / Wry
Sac / Sack
Set / Sett
Sew / So
Sic / Sick
Son / Sun
Spa / Spar
Sty / Stye
Sue / Sioux
Sum / Some

Sun / Son
Tax / Tacks
Tic / Tick
Toe / Tow
Ton / Tun
Too / To
Tor / Tore
Tow / Toe
Tun / Ton
Two / To
Urn / Earn
Use / Ewes
War / Wore
Wax / Whacks
Way / Whey
We'd / Weed
Wee / We
Wen / When
Wet / Whet
Wig / Whig
Win / Whin
Wit / Whit
Woe / Whoa
Won / One
Wry / Rye
Yew / Ewe

4 letters:
Airy / Eyrie
Alms / Arms
Ante / Anti
Anti / Ante
Aran / Arran
Arms / Alms
Away / Aweigh
Bade / Bad
Bail / Bale
Bait / Bate
Bald / Balled
Bale / Bail
Ball / Bawl
Balm / Barm
Bang / Bhang
Bare / Bear
Bark / Barque
Barm / Balm
Base / Bass
Bass / Base
Bate / Bait
Bawd / Board

Bawl / Ball	Cork / Caulk	Gael / Gale
Bays / Baize	Cote / Coat	Gaff / Gaffe
Bean / Been	Coup / Coo	Gage / Gauge
Bear / Bare	Cows / Cowes	Gait / Gate
Beat / Beet	Crew / Crewe	Gale / Gael
Beau / Bow	Curb / Kerb	Gall / Gaul
Been / Bean	Damn / Dam	Gate / Gait
Beer / Bier	Dane / Deign	Gaul / Gall
Beet / Beat	Days / Daze	Gays / Gaze
Bell / Belle	Daze / Days	Gaze / Gays
Berg / Burg	Dear / Deer	Gibe / Jibe
Bier / Beer	Deer / Dear	Gild / Guild
Bite / Bight	Dire / Dyer	Gill / Jill
Blew / Blue	Done / Dun	Gilt / Guilt
Blue / Blew	Door / Daw	Guys / Guise
Boar / Bore	Dost / Dust	Hail / Hale
Bode / Bowed	Doug / Dug	Hair / Hare
Bold / Bowled	Dual / Duel	Hale / Hail
Bole / Bowl	Duct / Ducked	Hall / Haul
Boos / Booze	Duel / Dual	Hare / Hair
Bore / Boar	Dust / Dost	Hart / Heart
Born / Borne	Dyer / Dire	Haul / Hall
Bosh / Boche	Earn / Urn	Heal / Heel
Bowl / Bole	Eddy / Eddie	Hear / Here
Brae / Bray	Eves / Eaves	Heel / Heal
Bray / Brae	Ewes / Use	Heir / Air
Bred / Bread	Fain / Feign	Herd / Heard
Buoy / Boy	Fair / Fare	Here / Hear
Burg / Berg	Fare / Fair	Hide / Hied
Burr / Bur	Fate / Fête	Hied / Hide
Bury / Berry	Faun / Fawn	High / Hi
Butt / But	Fawn / Faun	Hire / Higher
Call / Caul	Feat / Feet	Hoar / Whore
Cash / Cache	Feet / Feat	Hoes / Hose
Cast / Caste	Fête / Fate	Hold / Holed
Caul / Call	Find / Fined	Hole / Whole
Cede / Seed	Finn / Fin	Hose / Hoes
Cell / Sell	Firs / Furze	Hour / Our
Cent / Scent	Flaw / Floor	Hymn / Him
Choc / Chock	Flea / Flee	Idle / Idol
Cite / Sight	Flee / Flea	Idol / Idle
Coal / Kohl	Flew / Flue	Iron / Ion
Coat / Cote	Flex / Flecks	Isle / Aisle
Coax / Cokes	Floe / Flow	Jamb / Jam
Coin / Coign	Flow / Floe	Jibe / Gibe
Cops / Copse	Flue / Flew	Jill / Gill
Copt / Copped	Fold / Foaled	Kail / Kale
Copy / Kopje	Foul / Fowl	Kale / Kail
Cord / Chord	Four / For	Kerb / Curb
Core / Corps	Fowl / Foul	Knap / Nap

Knew / New
Knob / Nob
Knot / Not
Know / No
Kohl / Coal
Lade / Laid
Laid / Lade
Lain / Lane
Lama / Llama
Lane / Lain
Laps / Lapse
Laud / Lord
Lava / Larva
Lawn / Lorn
Lays / Laze
Laze / Leys
Lead / Led
Leaf / Lief
Leak / Leek
Leek / Leak
Lent / Leant
Levy / Levee
Leys / Laze
Liar / Lyre
Lief / Leaf
Lieu / Loo
Limb / Limn
Limn / Limb
Load / Lode
Loan / Lone
Lode / Lowed
Lone / Loan
Loos / Lose
Loot / Lute
Lord / Laud
Lorn / Lawn
Lose / Loos
Lute / Loot
Lynx / Links
Lyre / Liar
Made / Maid
Maid / Made
Mail / Male
Main / Mane
Male / Mail
Mane / Main
Mare / Mayor
Mark / Marque
Mask / Masque
Matt / Mat

Maze / Maize
Mead / Meed
Mean / Mien
Meat / Meet
Meed / Mead
Meet / Mete
Mete / Meet
Mews / Muse
Mien / Mean
Mind / Mined
Minx / Minks
Mist / Missed
Mite / Might
Moan / Mown
Moat / Mote
Mode / Mowed
Moor / More
More / Moor
Morn / Mourn
Mote / Moat
Mown / Moan
Muse / Mews
Must / Mussed
Nave / Knave
Need / Knead
Neil / Kneel
Nell / Knell
Nett / Net
None / Nun
Nose / Knows
Oral / Aural
Ours / Hours
Owed / Ode
Pact / Packed
Pail / Pale
Pain / Pane
Pair / Pear
Pale / Pail
Pall / Paul
Pane / Pain
Pare / Pair
Parr / Par
Past / Passed
Paul / Pall
Pawl / Pall
Pawn / Porn
Paws / Pause
Peak / Peek
Peal / Peel
Pear / Pair

Peat / Pete
Peek / Peak
Peel / Peal
Peer / Pier
Pete / Peat
Phew / Few
Pier / Peer
Plum / Plumb
Pole / Poll
Poll / Pole
Poof / Pouffe
Pore / Pour
Porn / Pawn
Pour / Pore
Pray / Prey
Prey / Pray
Pros / Prose
Purl / Pearl
Purr / Per
Quay / Key
Rack / Wrack
Rain / Rein
Rapt / Wrapped
Raze / Raise
Read / Red
Reed / Read
Rein / Rain
Rest / Wrest
Ring / Wring
Rite / Right
Road / Rode
Roam / Rome
Rode / Road
Role / Roll
Roll / Role
Rome / Roam
Rood / Rude
Room / Rheum
Root / Route
Rose / Rows
Rota / Rotor
Rote / Wrote
Rows / Rouse
Rude / Rood
Rues / Ruse
Ruff / Rough
Rung / Wrung
Ruse / Rues
Sack / Sac
Sail / Sale

Sale / Sail
Sane / Seine
Seam / Seem
Sear / Seer
Seed / Cede
Seek / Sikh
Seem / Seam
Seen / Scene
Seer / Sear
Sell / Cell
Serf / Surf
Sett / Set
Shoe / Shoo
Shoo / Shoe
Sick / Sic
Side / Sighed
Sign / Sine
Sikh / Seek
Sine / Sign
Size / Sighs
Slay / Sleigh
Sloe / Slow
Slow / Sloe
Soar / Sore
Sold / Soled
Sole / Soul
Some / Sum
Sore / Soar
Sort / Sought
Soul / Sole
Spar / Spa
Spec / Speck
Step / Steppe
Stye / Sty
Styx / Sticks
Surf / Serf
Swat / Swot
Swot / Swat
Tact / Tacked
Tail / Tale
Tale / Tail
Talk / Torque
Tare / Tear
Taut / Taught
Team / Teem
Tear / Tier
Teem / Team
Tern / Turn
Tick / Tic
Tide / Tied

Tied / Tide
Tier / Tear
Time / Thyme
Tire / Tyre
Toad / Towed
Told / Tolled
Tore / Tor
Tuba / Tuber
Tuna / Tuner
Turn / Tern
Tyre / Tire
Vain / Vein
Vale / Veil
Vane / Vain
Veil / Vale
Vein / Vain
Vial / Viol
Viol / Vial
Wade / Weighed
Wail / Whale
Wain / Wane
Wait / Weight
Wale / Whale
Wane / Wain
Ward / Warred
Ware / Where
Warn / Worn
Watt / What
Wave / Waive
Weak / Week
Wear / Ware
Weed / We'd
Week / Weak
Weld / Welled
Were / Whirr
What / Watt
When / Wen
Whet / Wet
Whey / Way
Whig / Wig
Whin / Win
Whit / Wit
Whoa / Woe
Who's / Whose
Wile / While
Wine / Whine
Won't / Wont
Wood / Would
Wore / War
Worn / Warn

Wrap / Rap
Yaws / Yours
Yoke / Yolk
Yolk / Yoke
Yore / You're
Your / Yore
Yule / You'll

5 letters:
Aisle / Isle
Aloud / Allowed
Altar / Alter
Alter / Altar
Arran / Aran
Auger / Augur
Aught / Ought
Augur / Auger
Aural / Oral
Baize / Bays
Balmy / Barmy
Barmy / Balmy
Baron / Barren
Based / Baste
Baste / Based
Beach / Beech
Beech / Beach
Belle / Bell
Berry / Bury
Berth / Birth
Betel / Beetle
Bhang / Bang
Bight / Bite
Birth / Berth
Board / Bored
Boche / Bosh
Booze / Boos
Bored / Board
Borne / Born
Bough / Bow
Bowed / Bode
Brake / Break
Bread / Bred
Break / Brake
Brews / Bruise
Brood / Brewed
Brows / Browse
Bruit / Brute
Brute / Bruit
Build / Billed
Cache / Cash

Calve / Carve
Canon / Cannon
Carat / Carrot
Carve / Calve
Caste / Cast
Caulk / Cork
Cause / Cores
Chard / Charred
Cheap / Cheep
Check / Czech
Cheep / Cheap
Chews / Choose
Chock / Choc
Choir / Quire
Chord / Cord
Chute / Shoot
Claws / Clause
Climb / Clime
Clime / Climb
Cocks / Cox
Coign / Coin
Cokes / Coax
Copse / Cops
Cores / Cause
Corps / Core
Court / Caught
Cowes / Cows
Cozen / Cousin
Creak / Creek
Creek / Creak
Crewe / Crew
Crews / Cruise
Crude / Crewed
Czech / Check
Deign / Dane
Derek / Derrick
Dough / Doe
Douse / Dowse
Dowse / Douse
Draft / Draught
Draws / Drawers
Droop / Drupe
Drupe / Droop
Eaves / Eves
Eddie / Eddy
Eerie / Eyrie
Eyrie / Eerie
Faint / Feint
Feign / Fain
Feint / Faint

Fined / Find
Flair / Flare
Flare / Flair
Floor / Flaw
Flour / Flower
Franc / Frank
Frank / Franc
Frays / Phrase
Friar / Frier
Frier / Friar
Furze / Firs
Gaffe / Gaff
Gauge / Gage
Gauze / Gores
Gores / Gauze
Grate / Great
Great / Grate
Groan / Grown
Groin / Groyne
Grown / Groan
Guest / Guessed
Guide / Guyed
Guild / Gild
Guilt / Gilt
Guise / Guys
Guyed / Guide
Heard / Herd
Heart / Hart
Hertz / Hurts
Hoard / Horde
Holed / Hold
Horde / Hoard
Horse / Hoarse
Hours / Ours
Hurts / Hertz
Islet / Eyelet
Knave / Nave
Knead / Need
Kneel / Neil
Knell / Nell
Knows / Nose
Kooky / Cookie
Kopje / Copy
Lacks / Lax
Lager / Laager
Lapse / Laps
Larva / Lava
Leach / Leech
Leads / Leeds
Leant / Lent

Least / Leased
Leech / Leach
Leeds / Leads
Leigh / Lea
Levee / Levy
Lewes / Lewis
Lewis / Lewes
Liken / Lichen
Links / Lynx
Llama / Lama
Lowed / Lode
Maize / Maze
Manor / Manner
Mayor / Mare
Medal / Meddle
Metal / Mettle
Meter / Metre
Metre / Meter
Might / Mite
Mined / Mind
Miner / Minor
Minks / Minx
Minor / Mynah
Moose / Mousse
Mourn / Morn
Mowed / Mode
Mucus / Mucous
Mynah / Minor
Naval / Navel
Navel / Naval
Neigh / Nay
Nicks / Nix
Night / Knight
Ought / Aught
Paced / Paste
Packs / Pax
Paste / Paced
Pause / Paws
Pawed / Pored
Peace / Piece
Pearl / Purl
Pedal / Peddle
Phlox / Flocks
Piece / Peace
Place / Plaice
Plain / Plane
Plane / Plain
Pleas / Please
Plumb / Plum
Pored / Pawed

Prays / Praise
Prise / Prize
Prize / Prise
Prose / Pros
Putty / Puttee
Quire / Choir
Raise / Raze
Reams / Rheims
Reign / Rain
Retch / Wretch
Revue / Review
Rheum / Room
Right / Write
Roads / Rhodes
Rotor / Rota
Rough / Ruff
Rouse / Rows
Route / Root
Sauce / Source
Saver / Savour
Scene / Seen
Scent / Cent
Scull / Skull
Seine / Sane
Semen / Seaman
Sewer / Sower
Shake / Sheik
Shear / Sheer
Sheer / Shear
Sheik / Shake
Shire / Shyer
Shoot / Chute
Shyer / Shire
Sighs / Size
Sight / Cite
Sioux / Sue
Skull / Scull
Soled / Sold
Sonny / Sunny
Sower / Sewer
Spade / Spayed
Speck / Spec
Staid / Stayed
Stair / Stare
Stake / Steak
Stalk / Stork
Stare / Stair
Steak / Stake
Steal / Steel
Steel / Steal

Sties / Styes
Stile / Style
Stoop / Stoup
Stork / Stalk
Story / Storey
Stoup / Stoop
Styes / Sties
Style / Stile
Suite / Sweet
Sunny / Sonny
Sweet / Suite
Sword / Soared
Tacks / Tax
Taper / Tapir
Tapir / Taper
Tenor / Tenner
Their / They're
There / Their
Threw / Through
Throe / Throw
Throw / Throe
Thyme / Time
Titan / Tighten
Towed / Toad
Troop / Troupe
Trust / Trussed
Tuber / Tuba
Tuner / Tuna
Venus / Venous
Waist / Waste
Waive / Wave
Waste / Waist
Waver / Waiver
Weald / Wield
Weigh / Way
Whale / Wale
Where / Ware
Which / Witch
While / Wile
Whine / Wine
Whirl / Whorl
Whirr / Were
White / Wight
Whole / Hole
Whore / Hoar
Whorl / Whirl
Whose / Who's
Wield / Weald
Wight / White
Witch / Which

World / Whirled
Would / Wood
Wrack / Rack
Wrest / Rest
Wring / Ring
Write / Right
Wrote / Rote
Wrung / Rung
You'll / Yule
You're / Yore
Yours / Yaws

6 letters:
Ascent / Assent
Assent / Ascent
Aweigh / Away
Balled / Bald
Baring / Bearing
Barque / Bark
Barren / Baron
Beetle / Betel
Billed / Build
Bolder / Boulder
Border / Boarder
Bowled / Bold
Breach / Breech
Breech / Breach
Brewed / Brood
Bridal / Bridle
Bridle / Bridal
Briton / Britain
Broach / Brooch
Brooch / Broach
Browse / Brows
Bruise / Brews
Callus / Callous
Cannes / Can
Cannon / Canon
Canvas / Canvass
Carrot / Carat
Caster / Castor
Castor / Caster
Caught / Court
Cellar / Seller
Censer / Censor
Censor / Censor
Cereal / Serial
Chased / Chaste
Chaste / Chased
Chilli / Chilly

369

Chilly / Chilli
Choler / Collar
Choose / Chews
Citrus / Citrous
Claude / Clawed
Clause / Claws
Clawed / Claude
Coarse / Course
Collar / Choler
Conker / Conquer
Cookie / Kooky
Copped / Copt
Corral / Chorale
Course / Coarse
Cousin / Cozen
Coward / Cowered
Crewed / Crude
Cruise / Crews
Cygnet / Signet
Cymbal / Symbol
Cyprus / Cypress
Denary / Deanery
Desert / Dessert
Dollar / Dolour
Dolour / Dollar
Ducked / Duct
Elicit / Illicit
Ensure / Insure
Ernest / Earnest
Eyelet / Islet
Father / Farther
Fillip / Philip
Fisher / Fissure
Flecks / Flex
Flocks / Phlox
Floury / Flowery
Flower / Flour
Foaled / Fold
Freeze / Frieze
Frieze / Freeze
Gallop / Gallup
Gallup / Gallop
Gamble / Gambol
Gambol / Gamble
Geezer / Geyser
Geyser / Geezer
Gilder / Guilder
Grater / Greater
Groyne / Groin
Hangar / Hanger

Hanger / Hangar
Hansom / Handsome
Heroin / Heroine
Higher / Hire
Hoarse / Horse
Hookah / Hooker
Hooker / Hookah
Insure / Ensure
Invade / Inveighed
Kernel / Colonel
Knight / Night
Laager / Lager
Leader / Lieder
Leased / Least
Lessen / Lesson
Lesson / Lessen
Lichen / Liken
Lieder / Leader
Lumbar / Lumber
Lumber / Lumbar
Manner / Manor
Marque / Mark
Marten / Martin
Martin / Marten
Masque / Mask
Meddle / Medal
Medlar / Meddler
Mettle / Metal
Missed / Mist
Mousse / Moose
Mucous / Mucus
Muscle / Mussel
Mussed / Must
Mussel / Muscle
Oriole / Aureole
Packed / Pact
Pallet / Palette
Passed / Past
Patten / Pattern
Peddle / Pedal
Pedlar / Peddler
Petrel / Petrol
Petrol / Petrel
Philip / Fillip
Phrase / Frays
Pistil / Pistol
Pistol / Pistil
Plaice / Place
Please / Pleas
Pouffe / Poof

Praise / Prays
Profit / Prophet
Puttee / Putty
Quarts / Quartz
Quartz / Quarts
Racket / Racquet
Ranker / Rancour
Revere / Revers
Revers / Revere
Review / Revue
Rheims / Reams
Rhodes / Roads
Rigger / Rigour
Rigour / Rigger
Ringer / Wringer
Roomer / Rumour
Rumour / Roomer
Savour / Saver
Schema / Schemer
Seaman / Semen
Seller / Cellar
Serial / Cereal
Sighed / Side
Signet / Cygnet
Sleigh / Slay
Slight / Sleight
Soared / Sword
Sought / Sort
Source / Sauce
Spayed / Spade
Stayed / Staid
Steppe / Step
Sticks / Styx
Storey / Story
Strait / Straight
Sucker / Succour
Sundae / Sunday
Sunday / Sundae
Symbol / Cymbal
Tacked / Tact
Taught / Taut
Tenner / Tenor
They're / Their
Throne / Thrown
Thrown / Throne
Tolled / Told
Torque / Talk
Troupe / Troop
Venous / Venus
Waists / Wastes

Waiver / Waver
Warred / Ward
Wastes / Waists
Weight / Wait
Welled / Weld
Wether / Whether
Whacks / Wax
Wither / Whither
Wrecks / Rex
Wretch / Retch
Wright / Right

7 letters:
Allowed / Aloud
Aureole / Oriole
Bearing / Baring
Boarder / Border
Boulder / Bolder
Britain / Briton
Callous / Callus
Canvass / Canvas
Ceiling / Sealing
Cession / Session
Charred / Chard
Chorale / Corral
Citrous / Citrus
Clanger / Clangour
Coarser / Courser
Colonel / Kernel
Conquer / Conker
Council / Counsel
Counsel / Council
Courser / Coarser
Cowered / Coward
Cubical / Cubicle
Cubicle / Cubical
Currant / Current
Current / Currant
Cypress / Cyprus
Deanery / Denary
Derrick / Derek
Descent / Dissent
Dessert / Desert
Dissent / Descent
Draught / Draft
Drawers / Draws
Earnest / Ernest
Elusive / Illusive
Farther / Father
Fissure / Fisher

Flowery / Floury
Gorilla / Guerrilla
Greater / Grater
Greaves / Grieves
Grieves / Greaves
Guessed / Guest
Guilder / Gilder
Heroine / Heroin
Humerus / Humorous
Illicit / Elicit
Literal / Littoral
Manikin / Mannequin
Marshal / Martial
Martial / Marshal
Meddler / Medlar
Morning / Mourning
Mustard / Mustered
Nightly / Knightly
Palette / Pallet
Pattern / Patten
Peddler / Pedlar
Pervade / Purveyed
Prophet / Profit
Racquet / Racket
Radical / Radicle
Radicle / Radical
Rancour / Ranker
Reining / Reigning
Schemer / Schema
Sealing / Ceiling
Session / Cession
Slaying / Sleighing
Sleight / Slight
Storied / Storeyed
Succour / Sucker
Summary / Summery
Summery / Summary
Through / Threw
Tighten / Titan
Trooper / Trouper
Trouper / Trooper
Trussed / Trust
Weather / Wether
Weighed / Wade
Whether / Wether
Whirled / World
Whither / Wither
Wrapped / Rapt
Wringer / Ringer

8 letters:
Brighten / Brighton
Brighton / Brighten
Clangour / Clanger
Discreet / Discrete
Discrete / Discreet
Formally / Formerly
Formerly / Formally
Handsome / Hansom
Humorous / Humerus
Illusive / Elusive
Knightly / Nightly
Lineally / Linearly
Linearly / Lineally
Littoral / Literal
Mourning / Morning
Mustered / Mustard
Overseas / Oversees
Oversees / Overseas
Populace / Populous
Populous / Populace
Purveyed / Pervade
Reigning / Reining
Sterling / Stirling
Stirling / Sterling
Storeyed / Storied
Straight / Strait
Windlass / Windless
Windless / Windlass

9 letters:
Guerrilla / Gorilla
Inveighed / Invade
Lightning / Lightening
Mannequin / Manikin
Principal / Principle
Principle / Principal
Sleighing / Slaying
Veracious / Voracious
Voracious / Veracious

10 letters:
Complement /
  Compliment
Compliment /
  Complement
Councillor / Counsellor
Counsellor / Councillor
Indiscreet / Indiscrete
Indiscrete / Indiscreet

Lightening / Lightning
Stationary / Stationery
Stationery / Stationary

13 letters:
Complementary /
  Complimentary

Complimentary /
  Complementary

Hoods

4 letters:
Coif
Cope
Cowl

5 letters:
Amaut
Amice
Amowt
Pixie
Snood

6 letters:
Almuce
Apache
Biggin
Calash
Mantle

7 letters:
Bashlik
Calèche
Capuche
Jacobin

8 letters:
Calyptra
Capeline
Capuccio
Chaperon
Trot-cozy

9 letters:
Balaclava
Chaperone
Trot-cosey

Hormones

3 letters:
Sex

5 letters:
Auxin
Kinin

6 letters:
Growth

7 letters:
Gastrin
Inhibin
Insulin
Relaxin
Steroid
Thyroid

8 letters:
Androgen
Autacoid
Bursicon
Ecdysone
Estrogen
Florigen
Glucagon
Juvenile

Oestriol
Oestrone
Oxytocin
Secretin
Thymosin

9 letters:
Adrenalin®
Corticoid
Cortisone
Cytokinin
Endocrine
Melatonin
Oestrogen
Prolactin
Secretion
Serotonin
Thyroxine

10 letters:
Adrenaline
Calcitonin
Intermedin
Lactogenic
Lipotropin
Oestradiol

11 letters:
Aldosterone
Angiotensin
Epinephrine
Gibberellin
Luteinizing
Parathyroid
Progestogen
Somatomedin
Thyrotropin
Vasopressin

12 letters:
Androsterone
Antidiuretic
Biosynthesis
Corpus luteum
Gonadotropin
Luteotrophin
Noradrenalin
Pancreozymin
Progesterone
Secretagogue
Somatostatin
Somatotropin
Stilboestrol

Testosterone
Thyrotrophin

13 letters:
Gonadotrophic
Gonadotrophin
Noradrenaline
Prostaglandin
Somatotrophin

14 letters:
Corticosteroid
Corticosterone
Enterogastrone
Erythropoietin
Hydrocortisone

15 letters:
Cholecystokinin
Gibberellic acid

16 letters:
Triiodothyronine

18 letters:
Thyroid-stimulating

19 letters:
Deoxycorticosterone
Follicle-stimulating

20 letters:
Adrenocorticotrophic

22 letters:
Chorionic
   gonadotrophin

26 letters:
Trichlorophenoxyacetic
   acid

27 letters:
Interstitial-cell-
   stimulating
Luteinizing hormone-
   releasing

Horses

TYPES/BREEDS OF HORSE

2 letters:
Kt

3 letters:
Ass
Bay
Cob
Don
Dun
Nag
Pad
Pot
Rip
Tit

4 letters:
Arab
Aver
Barb
Colt
Dale
Deli
Fell
Foal
Hack
Jade
Mare
Plug

Pole
Pony
Post
Prad
Roan
Shan
Snow
Stud
Taki
Turk
Weed
Wild
Yale
Yaud

5 letters:
Airer
Arion
Arkle
Batak
Bevis
Bidet
Borer
Caple
Capul
Crock
Favel
Filly

Genet
Huçul
Iomud
Konik
Lokai
Morel
Neddy
Night
Pacer
Pinto
Poler
Punch
Rogue
Screw
Seian
Shire
Spiti
Steed
Tacky
Takhi
Waler
Wheel
White
Zebra

6 letters:
Ambler
Basuto

TYPES/BREEDS OF HORSE (CONTINUED)

Bayard
Breton
Bronco
Brumby
Calico
Canuck
Cayuse
Chaser
Cooser
Crollo
Curtal
Cusser
Danish
Exmoor
Favell
Garran
Garron
Gennet
Gidran
Hogget
Hunter
Jennet
Kanuck
Keffel
Lampos
Morgan
Mudder
Nonius
Novice
Pad-nag
Plater
Poster
Quagga
Randem
Remuda
Roarer
Rouncy
Runner
Sabino
Saddle
Shagya
Sorrel
Stayer
String
Summer
Tandem
Tarpan
Tracer

Vanner
Viatka

7 letters:
Beetewk
Bobtail
Burmese
Cavalry
Charger
Clipper
Courser
Cow pony
Criollo
Cuisser
Dappled
Eclipse
Eventer
Finnish
Flemish
Gelding
Hackney
Hobbler
Jutland
Kabarda
Klepper
Liberty
Manipur
Marengo
Marocco
Marwari
Morocco
Mustang
Palfrey
Piebald
Quarter
Rhenish
Saddler
Sheltie
Shirazi
Smudish
Spanker
Starter
Strelet
Suffolk
Sumpter
Swallow
Swinger
Trigger

Trooper
Walking
Wheeler
Yamoote
Zeeland
Zmudzin

8 letters:
Aquiline
Ardennes
Balearic
Bangtail
Bathorse
Boerperd
Camargue
Clay-bank
Cocktail
Dartmoor
Destrier
Eohippus
Fell pony
Friesian
Galloway
Gulf Arab
Highland
Holstein
Hyperion
Karabair
Karabakh
Karadagh
Kochlani
Limousin
Lusitano
Palomino
Polo pony
Schimmel
Shetland
Skewbald
Sleipnir
Springer
Stalking
Stallion
Stibbler
Turkoman
Warhorse
Warragal
Warragle
Warragul

TYPES/BREEDS OF HORSE (CONTINUED)

Warregal
Warrigal
Welsh Cob
Whistler
Yarraman
Yearling

9 letters:
Akhal-Teke
Anglo-Arab
Appaloosa
Black Bess
Brabançon
Caballine
Carthorse
Clavileno
Coldblood
Connemara
Dales pony
Drayhorse
Esthonian
Fjord pony
Gringolet
Groningen
Houyhnhnm
Icelandic
Kladruber
Knabstrup
Miohippus
Mongolian
Oldenburg
Packhorse
Percheron
Pinzgauer
Racehorse
Rosinante
Rozinante
Schleswig
Tarbenian

Timor pony
Trakehner
Warmblood
Welsh pony
Workhorse

10 letters:
Andalusian
Bloodstock
Bucephalus
Buckjumper
Buttermilk
Clydesdale
Copenhagen
Gelderland
Hafflinger
Hanoverian
Kathiawari
Lipizzaner
Lippizaner
Pliohippus
Polish Arab
Przewalski
Show jumper
Stockhorse
Svadilfari
Zemaitukas

11 letters:
Anglo-Norman
High-stepper
Iceland pony
Mecklenburg
Merychippus
Persian Arab
Przewalski's
Running mate

12 letters:
Cleveland Bay
Dartmoor pony
Dutch Draught
Gudbrandsdal
Hambletonian
Highland pony
North Swedish
Orlov Trotter
Shetland pony
Standard Bred
Suffolk Punch
Thoroughbred

13 letters:
Hyracotherium
Kurdistan pony
New Forest pony
Russian saddle
Spanish Jennet
Stalking-horse

14 letters:
American Saddle
Polish Half-bred
Yorkshire Coach

15 letters:
American Quarter
Orlov Rostopchin
Swedish Ardennes

16 letters:
Tennessee Walking

17 letters:
Welsh Mountain pony

18 letters:
Polish Thoroughbred

LEGENDARY/FICTIONAL/HISTORICAL HORSES

5 letters:
Boxer

6 letters:
Bayard
Flicka
Silver

7 letters:
Pegasus
Trigger

8 letters:
Champion
Hercules
Mister Ed
Sleipnir
Traveler

9 letters:
Black Bess
El Fideldo

Incitatus
Rosinante

10 letters:
Bucephalus

11 letters:
Black Beauty

HORSE COLOURS

3 letters:
Bay
Dun

4 letters:
Grey
Roan

5 letters:
Black
Cream
Mealy

Pinto

6 letters:
Albino
Dapple
Sorrel

7 letters:
Piebald

8 letters:
Blue roan

Chestnut
Claybank
Palomino
Skewbald

10 letters:
Dapplegrey
Fleabitten

14 letters:
Strawberry roan

HORSE MARKINGS

4 letters:
Snip
Sock
Star

5 letters:
Blaze

6 letters:
Stripe

7 letters:
Coronet

8 letters:
Stocking

9 letters:
White face

HORSE GAITS

4 letters:
Lope
Pace
Rack
Trot
Walk

5 letters:
Amble

6 letters:
Canter
Gallop
Prance

7 letters:
Jog trot

10 letters:
Rising trot

Single-foot

11 letters:
Sitting trot

12 letters:
Extended trot

Horses

HORSE PARTS

3 letters:
Bar
Haw
Toe

4 letters:
Back
Dock
Frog
Heel
Hock
Hoof
Mane
Neck
Poll
Sole
Tail
Tusk
Wall

5 letters:
Croup
Ergot
Flank
Loins
Shank

6 letters:
Barrel
Croupe
Gaskin
Haunch
Muzzle
Saddle
Sheath

7 letters:
Brisket
Counter
Forearm
Foreleg
Gambrel
Off-fore
Off-hind
Pastern
Quarter
Shannon
Withers

8 letters:
Buttress
Chestnut
Coupling

Diagonal
Forehand
Forelock
Near-fore
Near-hind

9 letters:
Hamstring
White line

10 letters:
Cannon bone
Chin groove
Coffin bone
Splint bone

11 letters:
Coronet band
Second thigh
Stifle joint

12 letters:
Fetlock joint
Forequarters

PEOPLE ASSOCIATED WITH HORSES

3 letters:
Lad

5 letters:
Coper
Groom
Rider

6 letters:
Buster
Cowboy
Hussar
Jockey
Knight
Ostler

7 letters:
Cavalry
Currier
Equerry

Equites
Farrier
Knacker
Picador
Rustler
Saddler
Trainer

8 letters:
Cavalier
Coachman
Horseman
Wrangler

9 letters:
Caballero
Chevalier
Postilion
Postrider

Stable lad

10 letters:
Equestrian
Horsewoman
Jockey Club
Roughrider

12 letters:
Broncobuster
Equestrienne

14 letters:
Horse whisperer

TACK AND EQUIPMENT AND THEIR PARTS

3 letters:
Bar
Bit

4 letters:
Bard
Boot
Curb
Flap
Rein
Spur
Tack
Wisp

5 letters:
Barde
Cinch
Girth
Plate
Skirt
Trace

6 letters:
Bridle
Cantle
Day rug
Gag-bit
Halter
Numnah
Pelham
Pommel
Roller
Saddle
Twitch

7 letters:
Bridoon
Crupper
Curb bit
Gambado
Harness
Kneecap
Nosebag
Snaffle

Stirrup
Trammel

8 letters:
Blinkers
Browband
Cavesson
Chamfron
Hockboot
Hoof pick
Lip strap
Mane comb
Night rug
Noseband
Saddlery
Sliphead
Tail comb

9 letters:
Body brush
Breeching
Check rein
Curb chain
Curb reins
Curry comb
Front arch
Headpiece
Horseshoe
Nosepiece
Overcheck
Pad saddle
Saddlebag
Surcingle
Tailguard
Trappings

10 letters:
Cheek-piece
Crownpiece
Dandy brush
Girth strap
Kimblewick
Martingale
Sidesaddle

Snaffle bit
Stirrup bar
Throatlash
Water brush

11 letters:
Bearing rein
Breastplate
Saddlecloth
Stirrup iron
Summer sheet
Swingletree
Tail bandage
Throatlatch
Whiffletree
Whippletree

12 letters:
Anti-sweat rug
Double bridle
Plain snaffle
Stable rubber
Sweat scraper
Underblanket

13 letters:
Fulmer snaffle
New Zealand rug

14 letters:
Hackamore plate
Stirrup leather
Twisted snaffle

15 letters:
Weymouth curb bit

16 letters:
Split-eared bridle

20 letters:
Double-jointed snaffle

21 letters:
Jointed egg-butt snaffle

HORSES, RHINOS AND OTHER PERISSODACTYLS

3 letters:
Ass

4 letters:
Mule

5 letters:
Horse
Kiang
Kulan
Tapir

Zebra

6 letters:
Donkey
Onager

7 letters:
Keitloa

8 letters:
Chigetai

Elephant

9 letters:
Dziggetai

10 letters:
Rhinoceros

13 letters:
White elephant

See also:
➤ **Types/breeds of horse**

Household items

3 letters:
Bib
Box
Cup
Fan
Gas
Hob
Jar
Key
Log
Mop
Mug
Pan
Peg
Pot
Rug
Tap
Tin

4 letters:
Beam
Bell
Bowl
Bulb
Case
Coal
Dish
Door
Ewer
Flue

Fork
Fuel
Gong
Hi-fi
Hose
Iron
Jamb
Lamp
Lift
Lock
Oven
Pail
Pipe
Plug
Safe
Sash
Seat
Sink
Soap
Soda
Sofa
Spit
Tank
Tidy
Tile
Tray
Vase
Zarf

5 letters:
Apron
Ashet
Basin
Bench
Besom
Bidet
Blind
Board
Broil
Brush
Caddy
Chore
Cigar
Clock
Cloth
Cover
Crock
Cruet
Cruse
Diota
Doily
Duvet
Flask
Frame
Glass
Grate
Hinge
Juice
Knife

Ladle
Latch
Linen
Mixer
Mural
Paint
Panel
Poker
Quilt
Radio
Sheet
Shelf
Sieve
Spoon
Stove
Straw
Timer
Tongs
Torch
Towel
Trunk
Whisk

6 letters:
Aerial
Ash-bin
Ash-can
Awning
Basket
Beaker
Biggin
Bleach
Bluing
Boiler
Bucket
Bunker
Burner
Candle
Caster
Coffer
Colmar
Cooker
Cradle
Damper
Dishes
Dolium
Drawer
Duster
Egg-cup
Fender

Fiasco
Fingan
Flacon
Flagon
Fridge
Frieze
Gas-jet
Gas tap
Geyser
Grater
Hamper
Handle
Hearth
Heater
Ice-box
Jumble
Kaross
Kettle
Ladder
Lagena
Lintel
Locker
Log bin
Louvre
Mangle
Menage
Mincer
Mobile
Napkin
Patina
Pelmet
Pillow
Plaque
Polish
Pouffe
Pulley
Rhyton
Salver
Saucer
Scales
Sconce
Shovel
Shower
Skewer
Sponge
Starch
String
Switch
Teapot
Teaset

Tea-urn
Toy box
Trivet
Tureen
Vessel
Washer
Window
Wiring

7 letters:
Adaptor
Amphora
Ashtray
Bath tub
Bedding
Blanket
Bolster
Bouquet
Cake tin
Canteen
Ceiling
Chalice
Chamois
Chimney
Chopper
Cistern
Cleaver
Coaster
Coconut
Crystal
Cushion
Cutlery
Deed box
Dish mop
Doorway
Dustbin
Dust-pan
Faience
Fitting
Fixture
Furbish
Furnace
Fuse box
Gas-ring
Griddle
Hammock
Heating
Hickory
High tea
Hip bath

Household items

Holdall
Keyhole
Lacquer
Lagging
Lantern
Lattice
Matches
Oil lamp
Overall
Padella
Parquet
Pass-key
Pie-dish
Pitcher
Platter
Play pen
Pottery
Ramekin
Roaster
Samovar
Sanctum
Service
Serving
Shelves
Skillet
Spatula
Spy-hole
Stamnos
Steamer
Stewpot
Sundial
Sweeper
Tankard
Tea-cosy
Tea tray
Thermos
Thimble
Ticking
Toaster
Toby jug
Tool kit
Transom
Trellis
Trolley
Tumbler
Utensil
Valance
Varnish
Washday
Washtub

Worktop
Wringer

8 letters:
Atomiser
Ballcock
Barbecue
Bassinet
Bath cube
Bath soap
Bed cover
Bed linen
Bell pull
Billy can
Bird bath
Bookends
Cache-pot
Canister
Casement
Cauldron
Cigar box
Colander
Coverlet
Cream jug
Crockery
Cupboard
Cuspidor
Cut glass
Decanter
Doorbell
Doorknob
Doorpost
Doorstep
Doorstop
Driptray
Eggslice
Eggspoon
Eggtimer
Eggwhisk
Emulsion
Fanlight
Filament
Fireside
Firewood
Fixtures
Flat iron
Flour bin
Fly paper
Food-mill
Fuse-wire

Gallipot
Gas-meter
Handbell
Handrail
Hangings
Hip flask
Hollands
Homespun
Hot-plate
Immerser
Jelly bag
Jewel box
Kickshaw
Kindling
Linoleum
Matchbox
Mattress
Meatsafe
Monogram
Moth ball
Moulding
New broom
Ornament
Ovenware
Painting
Pannakin
Paraffin
Patty pan
Pendulum
Pipe rack
Pocelain
Polisher
Portrait
Pot plant
Radiator
Rosebowl
Saucepan
Scissors
Scrubber
Shoehorn
Shredder
Shutters
Side-door
Sink unit
Sitz bath
Skylight
Slop bowl
Slop pail
Snuff box
Soap dish

Soapsuds
Soft soap
Solarium
Spice jar
Spittoon
Squeezer
Strainer
Sunblind
Surround
Tablemat
Tapestry
Tea chest
Tea cloth
Teaspoon
Trapdoor
Underlay
Wainscot
Water jug
Water tap
Wig-block
Wireless
Yale lock

9 letters:
Ansaphone
Auto-timer
Baking tin
Barometer
Bath salts
Bath towel
Bay window
Bedspread
Beer glass
Blank door
Cakestand
Cantharus
Casserole
Chandlier
Chinaware
Cigarette
Clepsydra
Coffee cup
Container
Corkscrew
Crossbeam
Cullender
Demitasse
Desk light
Detergent
Directory

Dishcloth
Dish towel
Distemper
Dog basket
Doorplate
Drainpipe
Dust-sheet
Dutch oven
Dutch wife
Egg beater
Egg slicer
Eiderdown
Facecloth
Face towel
Fire alarm
Fireguard
Fire irons
Firelight
Fireplace
Fish knife
Fish slice
Flower pot
Foodmixer
Front door
Fruit bowl
Fruit dish
Frying pan
Gas burner
Gas cooker
Girandole
Glass door
Gold plate
Gravy boat
Hand towel
Hourglass
Housewife
Housework
Japanning
Jewel case
Joss-stick
Lamplight
Lampshade
Lampstand
Letterbox
Light bulb
Log basket
Loving cup
Master key
Mousetrap
Objet d'art

Panelling
Partition
Patchwork
Phone book
Pie-funnel
Place-card
Porringer
Punchbowl
Radiogram
Safety pin
Salad bowl
Sauceboat
Serviette
Shakedown
Shoeblack
Shower cap
Side light
Silver-wax
Slop basin
Soup plate
Soup spoon
Spin-drier
Sponge-bag
Staircase
Statuette
Steam iron
Steel wool
Storm door
Stovepipe
Sugar bowl
Swing door
Table lamp
Tableware
Tea kettle
Tea-waggon
Telephone
Threshold
Timepiece
Tinder-box
Tin opener
Toast-rack
Toilet bag
Underfelt
Wall clock
Wall light
Wallpaper
Washbasin
Washboard
Water butt
Water cock

Water pipe
Water tank
Wax polish
Whitewash
Window box
Wine glass

10 letters:
Abstergent
Alarm clock
Anthracite
Apple-cover
Baking bowl
Baking tray
Bedclothes
Bedsprings
Bellarmine
Boot polish
Bread board
Breadknife
Butter dish
Candelabra
Cassolette
Chafing pan
Chopsticks
Clothes peg
Coal-bucket
Coal-bunker
Coat-hanger
Coffee mill
Curtain rod
Deep-freeze
Dinner gong
Dishwasher
Doorhandle
Drawing pin
Dutch clock
Featherbed
Finger bowl
Fire-basket
Fire-escape
Firescreen
Fish kettle
Floor-cloth
Forcing bag
Fruit-knife
Glass-cloth
Gramophone
Grand piano
Hollow ware

Knickknack
Lamp socket
Letter-rack
Loose cover
Matchstick
Milk bottle
Mixing bowl
Musical box
Mustard pot
Napkin ring
Night-light
Nutcracker
Oven gloves
Paint-brush
Paper knife
Pepper mill
Percolator
Persian rug
Persiennes
Photograph
Pillowcase
Pillow slip
Pilot light
Pin cushion
Plate glass
Plate piece
Pot scourer
Pot scraper
Power point
Rain barrel
Ration book
Rolling pin
Rose-window
Salt cellar
Sealing wax
Silverware
Soap flakes
Soap powder
Spirit lamp
Step ladder
Storage jar
Strip-light
Tablecloth
Table-knife
Table-linen
Tablespoon
Tea service
Television
Thermostat
Time-switch

Tobacco jar
Toilet roll
Toilet soap
Toothbrush
Toothpaste
Transistor
Trinket box
Vanity lamp
Ventilator
Waffle-iron
Wall-socket
Warming pan
Washbasket
Wassai bowl
Watchglass
Water clock
Whisk broom
Window-pane
Window-sash
Window-seat
Window-sill
Wine basket
Wine bottle
Wine cooler
Wooden ware
Work basket
Worry beads

11 letters:
Airtight jar
Baking sheet
Broom handle
Butter-knife
Candelabrum
Candlestick
Centrepiece
Chafing dish
Cheese board
China figure
Chinoiserie
Clothes line
Clothes pole
Coal scuttle
Cookery book
Cooling tray
Counterpane
Cuckoo clock
Curtain hook
Curtain rail
Curtain ring

Dessert fork
Door-knocker
Earthenware
Eating irons
Elbowgrease
Family album
Firelighter
First-aid box
Floor polish
French chalk
Garden party
Garden swing
Hearth brush
Kitchen sink
Kitchen unit
Laundry room
Light switch
Linen basket
Loving spoon
Mantelpiece
Meat chopper
Meat cleaver
Metal polish
Non-stick pan
Oil painting
Oriental rug
Paperweight
Picture rail
Plant-holder
Pocket flask
Primus stove
Pudding bowl
Pumice stone
Record album
Roasting tin
Rotary whisk
Sauce bottle
Scouring pad
Serving dish
Shopping bag
Shower-cloth
Silver plate
Silver spoon
Skeleton key
Sliding door
Spring clean
Storm window
Table napkin
Tape measure
Tea-strainer

Thermometer
Vacuum flask
Vinaigrette
Washing line
Washing soap
Washing soda
Water closet
Water heater
Window blind
Window frame
Window-light
Wintergreen
Wooden spoon
Work-surface
Wrought iron

12 letters:
Adhesive tape
Antimacassar
Apron-strings
Ball of string
Bedside light
Bottle-opener
Bottom drawer
Bread curtain
Candleholder
Candle-sconce
Carpet beater
Carriage lamp
Carving-knife
Cheese-grater
Chiming clock
Chimney piece
Chimney-stack
Cigarette box
Clothes-brush
Clothes-drier
Clothes-horse
Companion set
Convex mirror
Cooking range
Dessert spoon
Disinfectant
Double boiler
Electric fire
Electric iron
Electric lamp
Extractor fan
Firelighters
Fireside seat

Flower holder
French polish
Hot water tank
Ironing board
Kettle-holder
Labour-saving
Light fitting
Looking-glass
Lunch counter
Magazine rack
Mulligatawny
Paraffin lamp
Passe-partout
Perambulator
Picnic basket
Picnic hamper
Picture frame
Place-setting
Pudding basin
Radiant plate
Record-player
Reel of cotton
Reel of thread
Refrigerator
Serving hatch
Serving spoon
Stain remover
Standard lamp
Swizzle stick
Table lighter
Table service
Talcum powder
Tape-recorder
Thermos flask
Toasting fork
Turkish towel
User-friendly
Visiting card
Washing board
Washing cloth

13 letters:
Backscratcher
Blanket stitch
Blotting paper
Candle snuffer
Carpet sweeper
Carriage clock
Chopping-block
Chopping-board

Clothes basket
Cocktail stick
Darning-needle
Dinner service
Draught screen
Electric mixer
Electric razor
Emulsion paint
Feather duster
Fire-resistant
Food processor
Household gods
Hurricane lamp
Lawn sprinkler
Microwave oven
Mowing-machine
Petrol lighter
Pinking-shears
Preserving-pan
Saratoga trunk
Sewing-machine
Smoothing iron
Soldering iron

Storage heater
Vacuum-cleaner
Venetian blind
Washing powder
Water softener

14 letters:
Cartridge-paper
Casement-window
Central heating
Chinese lantern
Cocktail shaker
Coconut-matting
Corrugated iron
Cut-throat razor
Electric cooker
Electric kettle
Electric shaver
Hot-water bottle
Hot-water system
Household goods
Household linen
Insulating tape
Kitchen utensil

Knitting-needle
Knives and forks
Luncheon basket
Pair of scissors
Patchwork quilt
Pressure-cooker
Scrubbing-brush
Spring cleaning
Spring mattress
Washing-machine

15 letters:
Cigarette holder
Combination lock
Corrugated paper
Electric blanket
Electric toaster
Immersion heater
Knitting-machine
Pencil sharpener
Photograph album
Weighing machine

Bodily humours

5 letters:
Blood

6 letters:
Phlegm

9 letters:
Black bile

10 letters:
Yellow bile

Huts

4 letters:
Shed
Skeo
Skio
Tilt

5 letters:
Banda
Booth
Bothy
Cabin
Hogan

Humpy
Igloo
Shack
Sheal
Shiel
Wilja

6 letters:
Bothie
Bustee
Chalet
Gunyah

Mia-mia
Nissen
Pondok
Rancho
Shanty
Succah
Sukkah
Tolsel
Tolsey
Tolzey
Wigwam
Wikiup

Wiltja
Wurley

Wanigan
Wickiup

Wannigan

9 letters:
Pondokkie
Rancheria

7 letters:
Choltry
Quonset®
Shebang

8 letters:
Rondavel
Shealing
Shieling

Hydrocarbons

3 letters:
Wax

5 letters:
Alkyl
Arene
Diene
Gutta
Halon
Hexyl
Phene
Xylol

6 letters:
Aldrin
Alkane
Alkene
Alkyne
Butane
Butene
Cetane
Cubane
Decane
Dioxin
Ethane
Hexane
Hexene
Indene
Nonane

Octane
Picene
Pyrene
Retene
Xylene

7 letters:
Amylene
Benzene
Heptane
Ligroin
Naphtha
Olefine
Pentane
Pentene
Polyene
Propane
Styrene
Terpene
Toluene

8 letters:
Camphane
Camphene
Carotene
Diphenyl
Hexylene
Isoprene
Limonene

Paraffin
Squalene
Stilbene
Triptane

9 letters:
Acetylene
Butadiene
Isobutane
Isooctane
Pentylene

10 letters:
Asphaltite
Mesitylene

11 letters:
Cycloalkane
Cyclohexane
Hatchettite
Naphthalene

12 letters:
Cyclopropane
Phenanthrene

15 letters:
Cyclopentadiene

I i

Types of inflammation

3 letters:
Sty

4 letters:
Acne
Noma
Stye

5 letters:
Croup
Felon

6 letters:
Ancome
Angina
Bunion
Eczema
Garget
Iritis
Otitis
Quinsy
Thrush
Ulitis

7 letters:
Colitis
Ecthyma
Founder
Ignatis
Onychia
Pinkeye
Prurigo
Sunburn
Sycosis
Tylosis
Whitlow

8 letters:
Adenitis
Aortisis
Bursitis
Carditis

Cystisis
Fibrosis
Hyalitis
Mastitis
Metritis
Mycetoma
Myelitis
Myositis
Neuritis
Orchitis
Osteitis
Ovaritis
Phlegmon
Pleurisy
Pyelitis
Rachitis
Rhinitis
Uvulitis
Windburn

9 letters:
Arteritis
Arthritis
Balanitis
Cheilitis
Enteritis
Gastritis
Glossitis
Keratitis
Laminitis
Nephritis
Parotitis
Phlebitis
Phrenitis
Pneumonia
Proctitis
Pyorrhoea
Retinitis
Scleritis
Sinusitis
Splenitis
Strumitis

Synovitis
Typhlitis
Vaginitis

10 letters:
Asbestosis
Bronchitis
Cellulitis
Cervicitis
Dermatitis
Erysipelas
Fibrositis
Gingivitis
Hepatitis A
Hepatitis B
Intertrigo
Laryngitis
Meningitis
Oophoritis
Ophthalmia
Paronychia
Phlegmasia
Stomatitis
Tendinitis
Thrombosis
Tracheitis
Urethritis
Valvulitis
Vasculitis

11 letters:
Blepharitis
Farmer's lung
Mastoiditis
Myocarditis
Peritonitis
Pharyngitis
Prostatitis
Salpingitis
Shin splints
Spondylitis
Thoroughpin

Thyroiditis
Tonsillitis

12 letters:
Appendicitis
Encephalitis
Endocarditis
Folliculitis
Misenteritis
Osteoporosis
Pancreatitis
Pericarditis
Polyneuritis
Swimmer's itch

13 letters:
Enterocolitis
Labyrinthitis
Osteomyelitis
Perihepatitis
Perinephritis
Periodontisis
Perityphlitis
Tenosynovitis

14 letters:
Conjunctivitis
Diverticulitis
Osteoarthritis

Vincent's angina

15 letters:
Gastroenteritis

16 letters:
Bronchopneumonia

17 letters:
Encephalomyelitis
Meningocephalitis

Inhabitants

Place	Inhabitant
Aberdeen	Aberdonian
Afghanistan	Afghan
Alabama	Alabaman *or* Alabamian
Alaska	Alaskan
Albania	Albanian
Alberta	Albertan
Algeria	Algerian
Alsace	Alsatian
American continent	American
American Samoa	American Samoan
Amsterdam	Amsterdammer
Anatolia	Anatolian
Andorra	Andorran
Angola	Angolan
Anjou	Angevin
Antigua	Antiguan
Argentina	Argentine *or* Argentinian
Arizona	Arizonan
Arkansas	Arkansan *or* (*informal*) Arkie
Armenia	Armenian
Asia	Asian
Assam	Assamese
Assyria	Assyrian
Australia	Australian *or* (*informal*) Aussie
Austria	Austrian
Azerbaijan	Azerbaijani *or* Azeri
Babylon	Babylonian

Place	Inhabitant
Bahamas	Bahamian
Bahrain	Bahraini
Bali	Balinese
Bangladesh	Bangladeshi
Barbados	Barbadian, Bajan (*informal*), or Bim (*informal*)
Barbuda	Barbudan *or* Barbudian
Bavaria	Bavarian
Belarus *or* Byelorussia	Belarussian *or* Byelorussian
Belau	Belauan
Belgium	Belgian
Benin	Beninese *or* Beninois
Berlin	Berliner
Bhutan	Bhutanese
Birmingham	Brummie
Bohemia	Bohemian
Bolivia	Bolivian
Bordeaux	Bordelais
The Borders	Borderer
Bosnia	Bosnian
Boston	Bostonian *or* (*U.S. slang*) Bean-eater
Botswana	Botswanan
Brazil	Brazilian
Bristol	Bristolian
British Columbia	British Columbian
Brittany	Breton
Bulgaria	Bulgarian
Burgundy	Burgundian
Burkina-Faso	Burkinabe
Burma	Burmese
Burundi	Burundian
Byzantium	Byzantine
California	Californian
Cambodia	Cambodian
Cambridge	Cantabrigian
Cameroon	Cameroonian
Canada	Canadian *or* (*informal*) Canuck
Canada, Maritime Provinces	Downeaster
Cape Verde	Cape Verdean
Castile	Castilian
Catalonia	Catalan
The Caucasus	Caucasian

Place	**Inhabitant**
Cayman Islands	Cayman Islander
Chad	Chadian *or* Chadean
Chicago	Chicagoan
Chile	Chilean
China	Chinese
Circassia	Circassian
Colombia	Colombian
Colorado	Coloradan
Comoros Islands	Comorian
Connecticut	Nutmegger
Congo Republic	Congolese
Cork	Corkonian
Cornwall	Cornishman, Cornishwoman
Corsica	Corsican
Costa Rica	Costa Rican
Côte d'Ivoire	Ivorian *or* Ivorean
Croatia	Croat *or* Croatian
Cuba	Cuban
Cumbria	Cumbrian
Cyprus	Cypriot
Czechoslovakia	Czechoslovak *or* Czechoslovakian
Czech Republic	Czech
Delaware	Delawarean
Delphi	Pythian
Denmark	Dane
Devon	Devonian
Djibouti	Djiboutian *or* Djiboutien
Dominica	Dominican
Dominican Republic	Dominican
Dublin	Dubliner
Dundee	Dundonian
East Timor	East Timorese
Ecuador	Ecuadorean *or* Ecuadoran
Edinburgh	Edinburgher
Egypt	Egyptian
El Salvador	Salvadoran, Salvadorean, *or* Salvadorian
England	Englishman, Englishwoman
Ephesus	Ephesian
Equatorial Guinea	Equatorian
Eritrea	Eritrean
Estonia	Estonian

Place	Inhabitant
Place	**Inhabitant**
Ethiopia	Ethiopian
Europe	European
Euzkadi	Basque
Faeroe Islands	Faeroese
Falkland Islands	Falkland Islanders *or* Falklander
Fife	Fifer
Fiji	Fijian
Finland	Finn
Flanders	Fleming
Florence	Florentine
Florida	Floridian
France	Frenchman, Frenchwoman
French Guiana	Guianese
Friesland	Frisian
Friuili	Friulian
Gabon	Gabonese
Galicia	Galician
Galilee	Galilean
Galloway	Gallovidian
Galway	Galwegian
Gambia	Gambian
Gascony	Gascon
Genoa	Genoese
Georgia (country)	Georgian
Georgia (U.S. state)	Georgian
Germany	German
Ghana	Ghanaian *or* Ghanian
Glasgow	Glaswegian
Greece	Greek
Greenland	Greenlander
Grenada	Grenadian
Guam	Guamanian
Guatemala	Guatemalan
Guinea	Guinean
Guyana	Guyanese *or* Guyanan
Haiti	Haitian
Havana	Habanero
Hawaii	Hawaiian
Hesse	Hessian
Honduras	Honduran
Hungary	Hungarian *or* Magyar
Hyderabad state	Mulki
Ibiza	Ibizan

Place	**Inhabitant**
Iceland	Icelander
Idaho	Idahoan
Illinois	Illinoian *or* Illinoisian
India	Indian
Indiana	Indianan, Indianian, *or* (*informal*) Hoosier
Indonesia	Indonesian
Iowa	Iowan
Iran	Iranian
Iraq	Iraqi
Ireland	Irishman, Irishwoman
Isle of Man	Manxman, Manxwoman
Israel	Israeli
Italy	Italian
Jamaica	Jamaican
Japan	Japanese
Java	Javanese
Jordan	Jordanian
Kansas	Kansan
Karelia	Karelian
Kazakhstan	Kazakh
Kent (East)	Man, Woman of Kent
Kent (West)	Kentish Man, Woman
Kentucky	Kentuckian
Kenya	Kenyan
Kirghizia	Kirghiz
Korea	Korean
Kuwait	Kuwaiti
Lancashire	Lancastrian
Lancaster	Lancastrian
Laos	Laotian
Latvia	Latvian *or* Lett
Lebanon	Lebanese
Liberia	Liberian
Libya	Libyan
Liechtenstein	Liechtensteiner
Lincolnshire	Yellow belly (*dialect*)
Lithuania	Lithuanian
Liverpool	Liverpudlian *or* (*informal*) Scouse *or* Scouser
Lombardy	Lombard
London	Londoner *or* Cockney
Los Angeles	Angeleno

Place	Inhabitant
Louisiana	Louisianan *or* Louisianian
Luxembourg	Luxembourger
Lyon	Lyonnais
Macao	Macaonese
Macedonia	Macedonian
Madagascar	Madagascan *or* Malagasy
Madrid	Madrileño, Madrileña
Maine	Mainer *or* Downeaster
Majorca	Majorcan
Malawi	Malawian
Malaya	Malayan
Malaysia	Malaysian
Maldive Islands	Maldivian
Malta	Maltese
Manchester	Mancunian
Manitoba	Manitoban
Marquesas Islands	Marquesan
Mars	Martian
Marseilles	Marsellais
Marshall Islands	Marshall Islander
Martinique	Martiniquean
Maryland	Marylander
Massachusetts	Bay Stater
Mauritania	Mauritanian
Mauritius	Mauritian
Melanesia	Melanesian
Melbourne	Melburnian
Mexico	Mexican
Michigan	Michigander, Michiganite, *or* Michiganian
Micronesia	Micronesian
Milan	Milanese
Minnesota	Minnesotan
Mississippi	Mississippian
Missouri	Missourian
Moldavia	Moldavian
Monaco	Monegasque
Mongolia	Mongolian
Montana	Montanan
Montenegro	Montenegrin
Montserrat	Montserratian
Moravia	Moravian
Morocco	Moroccan

Place	Inhabitant
Moscow	Muscovite
Mozambique	Mozambican
Namibia	Namibian
Naples	Neapolitan
Nauru	Nauruan
Nebraska	Nebraskan
The Netherlands	Dutchman, Dutchwoman
New Brunswick	New Brunswicker
Newcastle upon Tyne	Geordie
New England	New Englander or (*informal*) Yankee or Downeaster
Newfoundland	Newfoundlander or (*informal*) Newfie
Newfoundland fishing village	Outporter
New Hampshire	New Hampshirite
New Jersey	New Jerseyan or New Jerseyite
New Mexico	New Mexican
New South Wales	New South Welshman, New South Welshwoman
New York	New Yorker or Knickerbocker
New Zealand	New Zealander or (*informal*) Kiwi or Enzedder
Nicaragua	Nicaraguan
Niger	Nigerien
Nigeria	Nigerian
Normandy	Norman
North Carolina	North Carolinian or Tarheel
North Dakota	North Dakotan
Northern Ireland	Northern Irishman, Northern Irishwoman
Northern Territory	Territorian
Northern Territory, north part of	Top Ender
North Korea	North Korean
Northumbria	Northumbrian
Norway	Norwegian
Nova Scotia	Nova Scotian or (*informal*) Bluenose
Ohio	Ohioan
Okinawa	Okinawan
Oklahoma	Oklahoman or (*slang*) Okie
Oman	Omani
Ontario	Ontarian or Ontarioan
Oregon	Oregonian

Place	Inhabitant
Orkney	Orcadian
Oxford	Oxonian
Pakistan	Pakistani
Palestine	Palestinian
Panama	Panamanian
Papua New Guinea	Papua
Paraguay	Paraguayan
Paris	Parisian *or* Parisienne
Pennsylvania	Pennsylvanian
Persia	Persian
Perth	Perthite
Peru	Peruvian
The Philippines	Filipino
Poland	Pole
Pomerania	Pomeranian
Portugal	Portuguese
Prince Edward Island	Prince Edward Islander
Provence	Provençal
Prussia	Prussian
Puerto Rico	Puerto Rican
Qatar	Qatari
Quebec	Quebecer, Quebecker, *or* Quebecois
Queensland	Queenslander
Rhode Island	Rhode Islander
Rhodes	Rhodian
Rhodesia	Rhodesian
Rio de Janeiro	Cariocan
Romania	Romanian
Rome	Roman
Russian Federation	Russian
Ruthenia	Ruthenian
Rwanda	Rwandan
Samaria	Samaritan
San Marino	San Marinese *or* Sammarinese
Sardinia	Sardinian
Saskatchewan	Saskatchewanian
Saudi Arabia	Saudi *or* Saudi Arabian
Savoy	Savoyard
Saxony	Saxon
Scandinavia	Scandinavian
Scotland	Scot, Scotsman, Scotswoman, *or* Caledonian

Place	Inhabitant
Scottish Highlands	Highlander *or* (*old-fashioned*) Hielanman
Senegal	Senegalese
Serbia	Serb *or* Serbian
Seychelles	Seychellois
Shetland	Shetlander
Sierra Leone	Sierra Leonean
Sind	Sindhi
Singapore	Singaporean
Slovakia	Slovak
Slovenia	Slovene *or* Slovenian
Solomon Islands	Solomon Islander
South Africa	South African
South Australia	South Australian *or* (*informal*) Croweater
South Carolina	South Carolinian
South Dakota	South Dakota
South Korea	South Korean
Spain	Spaniard
Sri Lanka	Sri Lankan
Sudan	Sudanese
Suriname	Surinamese
Swaziland	Swazi
Sweden	Swede
Switzerland	Swiss
Sydney	Sydneysider
Sydney, Western suburbs of	Westie
Syria	Syrian
Taiwan	Taiwanese
Tajikistan	Tajik
Tanzania	Tanzanian
Tasmania	Tasmanian *or* (*informal*) Tassie *or* Apple Islander
Tennessee	Tennessean
Texas	Texan
Thailand	Thai
Thessalonika	Thessalonian
Tibet	Tibetan
Togo	Togolese
Tonga	Tongan
Tobago	Tobagan *or* Tobagonian
Trinidad	Trinidadian
Troy	Trojan

Place	Inhabitant
Tunisia	Tunisian
Turkey	Turk
Turkmenistan	Turkmen
Tuscany	Tuscan
Tuvalu	Tuvaluan
Tyneside	Geordie
Tyre	Tyrian
Uganda	Ugandan
Ukraine	Ukrainian
Ulster	Ulsterman, Ulsterwoman
Umbria	Umbrian
United Kingdom	Briton, Brit (*informal*), *or* Britisher
United States of America	American *or* (*informal*) Yank *or* Yankee
Uruguay	Uruguayan
Utah	Utahan *or* Utahn
Uzbekistan	Uzbek
Venezuela	Venezuelan
Venice	Venetian
Vermont	Vermonter
Victoria	Victorian
Vienna	Viennese
Vietnam	Vietnamese
Virginia	Virginian
Wales	Welshman, Welshwoman
Washington	Washingtonian
Wearside	Mackem
Wessex	West Saxon
Western Australia	Western Australian, Westralian, *or* (*informal*) Sandgroper
Western Sahara	Sahwari
West Virginia	West Virginian
Winnipeg	Winnipegger
Wisconsin	Wisconsinite
Wyoming	Wyomingite
Yemen	Yemeni
Yorkshire	Yorkshireman, Yorkshirewoman
The Yukon	Yukoner
Zaire	Zairean
Zambia	Zambian
Zanzibar	Zanzibari
Zimbabwe	Zimbabwean

Insects

TYPES OF INSECT

3 letters:
Ant
Bee
Bot
Fly
Lac
Nit
Wax

4 letters:
Crab
Flea
Gnat
Grig
Kutu
Lice
Mite
Moth
Pium
Tick
Wasp
Weta
Zimb

5 letters:
Aphis
Cimex
Emmet
Louse
Midge
Ox-bot
Scale
Stick
Zebub

6 letters:
Acarid
Breeze
Capsid
Chigoe
Cicada
Cicala
Cootie
Day-fly
Earwig
Gadfly

Hopper
Hornet
Locust
Looper
Mantid
Mantis
Mayfly
Psocid
Psylla
Punkie
Redbug
Sawfly
Scarab
Slater
Spider
Tettix
Thrips
Walker
Weevil

7 letters:
Antlion
Buzzard
Chalcid
Chigger
Cornfly
Cricket
Daphnid
Ergates
Firefly
Gallfly
Grayfly
Hive-bee
Humbuzz
Katydid
Ladybug
Odonata
Oestrus
Oniscus
Phasmid
Pill-bug
Pyralis
Sandfly
Spectre
Stylops
Termite

8 letters:
Alderfly
Bollworm
Bookworm
Caseworm
Circutio
Coccidae
Crane-fly
Dipteras
Firebrat
Gall-wasp
Glossina
Horntail
Horsefly
Inchworm
Itchmite
Lacewing
Ladybird
Lygus bug
Mealybug
Metabola
Milliped
Mosquito
Myriapod
Puss-moth
Reduviid
Ruby-tail
Scarabee
Sheep ked
Silkworm
Snowflea
Stinkbug
Stonefly
Waterbug
Wheel bug
Whitefly
Wireworm
Woodworm

9 letters:
Ametabola
Body louse
Booklouse
Caddis-fly
Centipede
Clipshear

TYPES OF INSECT (CONTINUED)

Cochineal
Cockroach
Compodeid
Crab louse
Croton bug
Damselfly
Dobsonfly
Dragonfly
Ephemeron
Hemiptera
Homoptera
Mecoptera
Millepede
Millipede
Rearhorse
Sheep tick
Tabanidae
Tiger-moth
Woodlouse

10 letters:
Apterygota
Bark mantis
Bluebottle
Caddis worm
Cankerworm
Casebearer
Chironomid
Clipshears
Cockchafer
Coleoptera

Collembola
Fan-cricket
Fen-cricket
Froghopper
Harvestman
Leaf-cutter
Leafhopper
Mallophaga
Orthoptera
Phylloxera
Plant-louse
Pond-skater
Psocoptera
Rhipiptera
Silverfish
Springtail
Thysanuran
Treehopper
Web spinner

11 letters:
Apple maggot
Bristletail
Cabbageworm
Dermopteran
Grasshopper
Greenbottle
Hymenoptera
Mole cricket
Neuropteran
Tiger-beetle

Trichoptera

12 letters:
Bishop's mitre
Dictyopteran
Heteropteran
Rhipidoptera
Strepsiptera
Sucking louse
Thousand-legs
Thysanoptera
Walking stick

13 letters:
Cotton stainer
Daddy-long-legs
Jenny-longlegs
Leatherjacket
Measuring worm
Praying mantis
Staphylinidae

15 letters:
German cockroach
Tent caterpillar

16 letters:
Periodical cicada

19 letters:
Seventeen-year locust

PARTS OF INSECTS

3 letters:
Jaw

4 letters:
Coxa

5 letters:
Femur
Ileum
Notum
Scape
Snout
Thigh
Tibia

6 letters:
Air sac
Arista
Cercus
Cirrus
Corium
Glossa
Labium
Labrum
Ligula
Proleg
Scutum
Stigma
Tarsus

Tegmen
Thorax

7 letters:
Antenna
Clasper
Clypeus
Elytron
Gonopod
Hamulus
Maxilla
Ocellus
Pedicel
Trachea

PARTS OF INSECTS (CONTINUED)

8 letters:
Forewing
Mandible
Pronotum
Spiracle

9 letters:
Flagellum
Proboscis
Prothorax
Pulvillus
Scutellum
Spinneret

Underwing

10 letters:
Acetabulum
Epicuticle
Exocuticle
Haustellum
Hemelytron
Mesothorax
Metathorax
Ovipositor
Prosternum
Trochanter

11 letters:
Compound eye
Endocuticle
Ventriculus

14 letters:
Proventriculus

16 letters:
Malpighian tubule

See also:
➤ **Ants, bees and wasps** ➤ **Beetles** ➤ **Bugs** ➤ **Butterflies and moths**
➤ **Flies**

Types of instrument

3 letters:
Fan

4 letters:
Celt
Clam
Fork
Mike
Prog
Rasp
Rote
Tram

5 letters:
Brake
Fleam
Float
Gadge
Groma
Meter
Miser
Probe
Sonde
Wecht

6 letters:
Bougie

Broach
Etalon
Scythe
Strobe
Trocar

7 letters:
Alidade
Cadrans
Caltrop
Curette
Forceps
Pelican
Pointel
Probang
Scriber
Sextant
Spatula
Strigil
Swazzle
Swingle
Swozzle
Syringe
Trammel

8 letters:
Ablative

Barnacle
Diagraph
Dividers
Ecraseur
Odometer
Otoscope
Oximeter
Quadrant
Scissors
Strickle
Trephine
Waywiser

9 letters:
Alphonsin
Astrolabe
Atmometer
Auxometer
Barometer
Baryscope
Bolometer
Coelostat
Crows-bill
Cymograph
Dermatome
Dip-circle
Dropsonde

Eriometer
Haemostat
Heliostat
Hodometer
Konimeter
Machmeter
Manometer
Marigraph
Megascope
Metronome
Nocturnal
Potometer
Raspatory
Retractor
Rheometer
Tasimeter
Telemeter
Telescope
Tellurian
Tellurion
Tenaculum
Tonometer
Tripmeter
Voltmeter
Wavemeter

10 letters:
Almacantar
Almucantar
Altazimuth
Anemometer
Ceilometer
Clinometer
Colposcope

Cryophorus
Cystoscope
Fibrescope
Hydrometer
Hydroscope
Hygrometer
Hypsometer
Micrometer
Microphone
Pilliwinks
Protractor
Radiosonde
Spirograph
Spirometer
Tachigraph
Tachometer
Tensometer
Theodolite
Tribometer
Voltameter

11 letters:
Auxanometer
Chronograph
Chronometer
Chronoscope
Helicograph
Jacob's staff
Laparascope
Pinnywinkle
Polarimeter
Rocketsonde
Seismograph
Solarimeter

Stauroscope
Stethoscope
Stroboscope
Synthesizer
Tacheometer
Tensiometer
Thermometer

12 letters:
Aethrioscope
Bronchoscope
Cephalometer
Keraunograph
Myringoscope
Penetrometer
Pinniewinkle
Respirometer
Scarificator
Sensitometer
Spectroscope
Synchroscope
Turbidimeter
Zenith-sector

13 letters:
Tachistoscope

14 letters:
Interferometer
Ophthalmoscope

16 letters:
Sphygmomanometer

Insults and terms of abuse

2 letters:
'ho

3 letters:
Cow
Git
Mug
Nit
Oaf

4 letters:
Berk

Bozo
Clod
Clot
Coot
Dope
Dork
Drip
Fool
Geek
Jerk
Loon
Mong

Nerd
Nurd
Ogre
Prat
Scab
Slag
Tart
Twit
Wimp
Wuss

5 letters:
Bitch
Chump
Clown
Devil
Divvy
Dumbo
Dummy
Dunce
Dweeb
Eejit
Galah
Goose
Idiot
Moron
Ninny
Plank
Rogue
Twerp
Twirp
Wally
Whore

6 letters:
Cretin
Dimwit

Donkey
Doofus
Heifer
Mincer
Minger
Muppet
Nitwit
Numpty
Rascal
Thicko
Wretch

7 letters:
Airhead
Article
Bushpig
Cabbage
Charlie
Chicken
Chuckie
Dumb-ass
Fathead
Halfwit
Pillock
Plonker
Scutter

Slapper

8 letters:
Bonehead
Dipstick
Doughnut
Imbecile
Numskull
Pea-brain
Scrubber

9 letters:
Bird-brain
Blockhead
Lamebrain
Numbskull
Scoundrel
Simpleton
Thickhead

10 letters:
Nincompoop

12 letters:
Cheeky monkey

Internet domain names

Abbreviation	Top-level domain (TLD)
.co	Commercial company (used with country)
.com	Commercial company
.net	Company *or* organization
.org	Organization, usually nonprofit
.edu	Educational establishment
.eu	European Union
.gov	US government organization
.mil	US military
.int	International organization
.arpa	Internet infrastructure

Abbreviation	New TLDs (2000)
.aero	Air-transport industry
.biz	Business
.coop	Cooperative
.info	General use

Abbreviation	**New TLDs (2000)**
.museum	Museum
.name	Individual user
.pro	Professionals (accountants, lawyers, etc.)

Abbreviation	**Country TLDs**
.ac	Ascension Island
.ad	Andorra
.ae	United Arab Emirates
.af	Afghanistan
.ag	Antigua and Barbuda
.ai	Anguilla
.al	Albania
.am	Armenia
.an	Netherlands Antilles
.ao	Angola
.aq	Antarctica
.ar	Argentina
.as	American Samoa
.at	Austria
.au	Australia
.aw	Aruba
.az	Azerbaijan
.ba	Bosnia and Herzegovina
.bb	Barbados
.bd	Bangladesh
.be	Belgium
.bf	Burkina Faso
.bg	Bulgaria
.bh	Bahrain
.bi	Burundi
.bj	Benin
.bm	Bermuda
.bn	Brunei Darussalam
.bo	Bolivia
.br	Brazil
.bs	Bahamas
.bt	Bhutan
.bv	Bouvet Island
.bw	Botswana
.by	Belarus
.bz	Belize
.ca	Canada

Abbreviation	Country TLDs
.cc	Cocos (Keeling) Islands
.cd	Congo, Democratic Republic of the
.cf	Central African Republic
.cg	Congo, Republic of
.ch	Switzerland
.ci	Côte d'Ivoire
.ck	Cook Islands
.cl	Chile
.cm	Cameroon
.cn	China
.co	Colombia
.cr	Costa Rica
.cu	Cuba
.cv	Cap Verde
.cx	Christmas Island
.cy	Cyprus
.cz	Czech Republic
.de	Germany
.dj	Dijibouti
.dk	Denmark
.dm	Dominica
.do	Dominican Republic
.dz	Algeria
.ec	Ecuador
.ee	Estonia
.eg	Egypt
.eh	Western Sahara
.er	Eritrea
.es	Spain
.et	Ethiopia
.fi	Finland
.fj	Fiji
.fk	Falkland Islands (Malvina)
.fm	Micronesia, Federal State of
.fo	Faroe Islands
.fr	France
.ga	Gabon
.gd	Grenada
.ge	Georgia
.gf	French Guiana
.gg	Guernsey
.gh	Ghana

Abbreviation	Country TLDs
.gi	Gibraltar
.gl	Greenland
.gm	Gambia
.gn	Guinea
.gp	Equatorial Guinea
.gr	Greece
.gs	South Georgia and the South Sandwich Islands
.gt	Guatemala
.gu	Guam
.gw	Guinea-Bissau
.gy	Guyana
.hk	Hong Kong
.hm	Heard and McDonald Islands
.hn	Honduras
.hr	Croatia/Hrvatska
.ht	Haiti
.hu	Hungary
.id	Indonesia
.ie	Ireland
.il	Israel
.im	Isle of Man
.in	India
.io	British Indian Ocean Territory
.iq	Iraq
.ir	Iran (Islamic Republic of)
.is	Iceland
.it	Italy
.je	Jersey
.jm	Jamaica
.jo	Jordan
.jp	Japan
.ke	Kenya
.kg	Kyrgyzstan
.kh	Cambodia
.ki	Kiribati
.km	Comoros
.kn	Saint Kitts and Nevis
.kp	Korea, Democratic People's Republic
.kr	Korea, Republic of
.kw	Kuwait
.ky	Cayman Islands

Abbreviation	Country TLDs
.kz	Kazakhstan
.la	Lao People's Democratic Republic
.lb	Lebanon
.lc	Saint Lucia
.li	Liechtenstein
.lk	Sri Lanka
.lr	Liberia
.ls	Lesotho
.lt	Lithuania
.lu	Luxembourg
.lv	Latvia
.ly	Libyan Arab Jamahiriya
.ma	Morocco
.mc	Monaco
.md	Moldova, Republic of
.mg	Madagascar
.mh	Marshall Islands
.mk	Macedonia, Former Yugoslav Republic
.ml	Mali
.mm	Myanmar
.mn	Mongolia
.mo	Macau
.mp	Northern Mariana Islands
.mq	Martinique
.mr	Mauritania
.ms	Montserrat
.mt	Malta
.mu	Mauritius
.mv	Maldives
.mw	Malawi
.mx	Mexico
.my	Malaysia
.mz	Mozambique
.na	Namibia
.nc	New Caledonia
.ne	Niger
.nf	Norfolk Island
.ng	Nigeria
.ni	Nicaragua
.nl	Netherlands
.no	Norway

Abbreviation	Country TLDs
.np	Nepal
.nr	Nauru
.nu	Niue
.nz	New Zealand
.om	Oman
.pa	Panama
.pe	Peru
.pf	French Polynesia
.pg	Papua New Guinea
.ph	Philippines
.pk	Pakistan
.pl	Poland
.pm	St. Pierre and Miquelon
.pn	Pitcairn Island
.pr	Puerto Rico
.ps	Palestinian Territories
.pt	Portugal
.pw	Palau
.py	Paraguay
.qa	Qatar
.re	Reunion Island
.ro	Romania
.ru	Russian Federation
.rw	Rwanda
.sa	Saudi Arabia
.sb	Soloman Islands
.sc	Seychelles
.sd	Sudan
.se	Sweden
.sg	St. Helena
.si	Slovenia
.sj	Svalbard and Jan Mayen Islands
.sk	Slovak Republic
.sl	Sierra Leone
.sm	San Marino
.sn	Senegal
.so	Somalia
.sr	Suriname
.st	Sao Tome and Principe
.sv	El Salvador
.sy	Syrian Arab Republic
.sz	Swaziland
.tc	Turks and Caicos Islands

Abbreviation	Country TLDs
.td	Chad
.tf	French Southern Territories
.tg	Togo
.th	Thailand
.tj	Tajikistan
.tk	Tokelau
.tm	Turkmenistan
.tn	Tunisia
.to	Tongo
.tp	East Timor
.tr	Turkey
.tt	Trinidad and Tobago
.tv	Tuvalu
.tw	Taiwan
.tz	Tanzania
.ua	Ukraine
.ug	Uganda
.uk	United Kingdom
.um	US Minor Outlying Islands
.us	United States
.uy	Uruguay
.uz	Uzbekistan
.va	Holy See (City Vatican State)
.vc	Saint Vincent and the Grenadines
.ve	Venezuela
.vg	Virgin Islands (British)
.vi	Virgin Islands (USA)
.vn	Vietnam
.vu	Vanuatu
.wf	Wallis and Futuna Islands
.ws	Western Samoa
.ye	Yemen
.yt	Mayotte
.yu	Yugoslavia
.za	South Africa
.zm	Zambia
.zw	Zimbabwe

Invertebrates

3 letters:
Lug

4 letters:
Clam
Cone
Kina
Pipi
Worm

5 letters:
Ameba
Bardi
Bardy
Coral
Cunje
Gaper
Leech
Polyp
Squid
Ugari

6 letters:
Amoeba
Bardie
Chiton
Cockle
Cuttle
Mussel
Oyster
Quahog
Sea mat
Sea pen
Sponge
Tellin
Teredo

7 letters:
Bivalve
Blubber
Catworm
Crinoid
Daphnia
Decapod
Eelworm
Lobworm
Lugworm
Mollusc

Octopus
Piddock
Ragworm
Rotifer
Scallop
Sea lily
Sea wasp
Sunstar
Trepang
Tubifex

8 letters:
Ammonite
Annelida
Argonaut
Bryozoan
Clamworm
Cunjevoi
Echinoid
Gapeworm
Lancelet
Lungworm
Milleped
Nautilus
Parazoan
Pauropod
Pumpworm
Red coral
Sandworm
Sea mouse
Shipworm
Starfish
Tapeworm
Tube worm
Whipworm
White cat
Zoophyte

9 letters:
Amphioxus
Anthozoan
Arrowworm
Arthropod
Belemnite
Brandling
Centipede
Clabby-doo
Clappy-doo

Comb jelly
Cone shell
Devilfish
Earthworm
Gastropod
Hard-shell
Hydrozoan
Jellyfish
Lamp shell
Millepede
Millipede
Peritrich
Poriferan
Razor clam
Round clam
Roundworm
Sea slater
Sea squirt
Sea urchin
Soft-shell
Trilobite
Tusk shell
Water bear
Wheatworm
White worm
Woodborer

10 letters:
Animalcule
Balmain bug
Bêche-de-mer
Bluebottle
Brachiopod
Ctenophore
Cuttlefish
Echinoderm
Euripterid
Eurypterid
Gasteropod
Graptolite
Guinea worm
Horseleech
Liver fluke
Otter shell
Paddle worm
Protostome
Razor-shell
Scyphozoan

Sea anemone
Seed oyster
Stony coral
Tardigrade
Tooth shell
Venus shell
Vinegar eel
Water louse

11 letters:
Animalculum
Bladder worm
Bluff oyster
Feather star
Globigerina
Sea cucumber
Stomach worm
Vinegar worm
Water slater

12 letters:
Box jellyfish
Chicken louse
Gastropodart
Onychophoran
Trochelminth
Venus's-girdle

13 letters:
Crown-of-thorns
Hard-shell clam
Paper nautilus
Precious coral
Soft-shell clam
Water measurer

14 letters:
Pearly nautilus

15 letters:
Coat-of-mail shell

16 letters:
Water stick insect

17 letters:
Blue-ringed octopus
Chambered nautilus

18 letters:
Portuguese man-of-war
Venus's flower basket

21 letters:
Crown-of-thorns starfish

See also:
➤ **Insects** ➤ **Shellfish** ➤ **Snails, slugs and other gastropods** ➤ **Spiders and other arachnids** ➤ **Worms**

Moslem denominations and sects

4 letters:
Shia

5 letters:
Druse
Druze
Imami
Shiah
Sunni

Zaidi

6 letters:
Nizari
Shiite
Sufism

7 letters:
Isma'ili

8 letters:
Alawites
Wahabism

9 letters:
Alaouites
Wahhabism

Islands and island groups

2 letters:
TT

3 letters:
Aru
Cos
Diu
Fyn
Hoy

Kos
Man
May
Rat
Rum
Sea
Yap

4 letters:
Amoy
Aran
Arru
Attu
Bali
Biak
Bute
Calf

Cebú
Coll
Cook
Cuba
Dogs
Eigg
Elba
Erin
Fair
Fiji
Guam
Heat
Herm
Holm
Holy
Hova
Idse
Iona
Java
Jolo
Jura
Keos
King
Line
Long
Mahé
Malé
Maui
Mazu
Mona
Motu
Muck
Mull
Niue
Oahu
Rhum
Rona
Ross
Saba
Sark
Seil
Skye
Truk
Uist
Ulva
Unst
Wake
Yell

5 letters:
Aland
Apple
Arran
Aruba
Banka
Banks
Barra
Batan
Belau
Belle
Bioko
Bohol
Bonin
Caldy
Canna
Capri
Ceram
Cheju
Chios
Clare
Cocos
Coney
Coral
Corfu
Crete
Delos
Disko
Ellis
Faial
Farne
Faroe
Fayal
Foula
Funen
Gigha
Haiti
Handa
Ibiza
Islay
Isola
Jerba
Kauai
Kiska
Kuril
Lanai
Lewis
Leyte
Longa
Luing

Lundy
Luzon
Maewo
Malta
Matsu
Melos
Nauru
Naxos
Nevis
North
Oland
Ormuz
Panay
Páros
Pemba
Qeshm
Qishm
Reil's
Rhode
Samar
Samoa
Samos
Saria
Seram
South
Spice
Sumba
Sunda
Thera
Thule
Timor
Tiree
Tombo
Tonga
Turks
Upolu
Whale
White
Wight
Youth
Zante

6 letters:
Achill
Aegean
Aegina
Amager
Andros
Avalon
Azores

Baffin
Banaba
Bangka
Barrow
Bikini
Borneo
Bounty
Butung
Caicos
Canary
Canvey
Cayman
Ceylon
Chiloé
Cyprus
Devil's
Diomed
Djerba
Easter
Ellice
Euboea
Flores
Fraser
Hainan
Harris
Hawaii
Hobart
Honshu
Hormuz
Icaria
Imbros
Indies
Insula
Ionian
Ischia
Ithaca
Jersey
Kiushu
Kodiak
Kosrae
Kurile
Kyushu
Labuan
Laputa
Lemnos
Lesbos
Leucas
Leukas
Levkás
Lipari

Lizard
Lombok
Madura
Majuro
Marajó
Mercer
Mersea
Midway
Negros
Ogygia
Orkney
Paphos
Patmos
Penang
Pharos
Philae
Pladdy
Ponape
Quemoy
Raasay
Ramsey
Rhodes
Rialto
Rjukyu
Robben
Ryukyu
Safety
Saipan
Saltee
Savaii
Scilly
Scyros
Sicily
Skerry
Skomer
Skyros
Snares
Soemba
Soenda
Staffa
Staten
St. John
Stroma
Summer
Tahiti
Taiwan
Thanet
Thásos
Tobago
Tresco

Tubuai
Tuvalu
Unimak
Ushant
Veneti
Virgin
Walney

7 letters:
Aeolian
Aldabra
Amboina
Andaman
Antigua
Austral
Bahamas
Baranof
Barbuda
Bardsey
Basilan
Battery
Bedloe's
Bermuda
Bonaire
British
Cartier
Celebes
Channel
Chatham
Cipango
Corsica
Crannog
Curaçao
Cythera
Diomede
Emerald
Eriskay
Faeroes
Falster
Flannan
Frisian
Fur Seal
Gambier
Gilbert
Gotland
Grenada
Hawaiki
Hayling
Heimaey
Howland

Iceland
Ireland
Iwo Jima
Jamaica
Kerrera
Laaland
La Palma
Leeward
Liberty
Lismore
Lofoten
Lolland
Madeira
Majorca
Masbate
Mayotte
Mindoro
Minorca
Molokai
Moreton
Mykonos
Nicobar
Norfolk
Oceania
Okinawa
Orcades
Orkneys
Palawan
Palmyra
Phoenix
Rathlin
Réunion
Roanoke
Rockall
Salamis
San Juan
Sao Tomé
Scalpay
Sheppey
Shikoku
Skikoku
Society
Socotra
Solomon
St. Croix
Stewart
St. Kilda
St. Kitts
St. Lucia
Sumatra

Sumbawa
Surtsey
Tenedos
Tokelau
Tortola
Tortuga
Tuamotu
Tutuila
Vanuatu
Visayan
Volcano
Waihake
Western
Wrangel
Zealand
Zetland

8 letters:
Alcatraz
Alderney
Aleutian
Anglesey
Anguilla
Antilles
Atlantis
Auckland
Balearic
Barbados
Bathurst
Billiton
Blefuscu
Bora Bora
Bornholm
Canaries
Caroline
Catalina
Choiseul
Colonsay
Cyclades
Dominica
Falkland
Farquhar
Flinders
Foulness
Friendly
Gothland
Gottland
Guernsey
Hamilton
Hebrides

Hokkaido
Hong Kong
Jan Mayen
Kangaroo
Kermadec
Krakatau
Krakatoa
Ladrones
Lavongai
Lilliput
Lord Howe
Luggnagg
Mackinac
Mainland
Maldives
Mallorca
Marianas
Marquesa
Marshall
Melville
Mindanao
Miquelon
Moluccas
Mustique
Pelagian
Pitcairn
Portland
Pribilof
Principe
Sakhalin
Sardinia
Schouten
Shetland
Sjælland
Skokholm
Soembawa
Somerset
Sporades
Sri Lanka
St. Helena
St. Martin
Sulawesi
Sverdrup
Tasmania
Tenerife
Terceira
Thousand
Thursday
Trinidad
Tsushima

Unalaska
Venetian
Victoria
Viti Levu
Windward
Zanzibar

9 letters:
Admiralty
Alexander
Andreanof
Anticosti
Antipodes
Ascension
Barataria
Benbecula
Calf of Man
Chichagof
Christmas
Elephanta
Ellesmere
Falklands
Fortunate
Galápagos
Governors
Greenland
Hainan Tao
Halmahera
Innisfree
Jamestown
Kerguelen
Lampedusa
Lanzarote
Macquarie
Manhattan
Margarita
Marquesas
Mascarene
Mauritius
Melanesia
Nantucket
New Guinea
North Uist
Polynesia
Rangitoto
Rarotonga
Runnymede
Sao Miguel
Shetlands
Singapore

Sjaelland
South Uist
Stromboli
St. Tudwal's
St. Vincent
Teneriffe
Trobriand
Vancouver
Vanua Levu
Walcheren

10 letters:
Basse-Terre
Bermoothes
Campobello
Cape Breton
Cephalonia
Corregidor
Dodecanese
Formentera
Grand Manan
Grand Terre
Grenadines
Heligoland
Hispaniola
Isle Royale
Kiritimati
Langerhans
Madagascar
Manitoulin
Marinduque
Martinique
Micronesia
Montserrat
New Britain
New Georgia
New Ireland
Pescadores
Poor Knight
Samothrace
Seychelles
Three Kings
West Indies
Whitsunday

11 letters:
Dry Tortugas
Florida Keys
Glubdubdrib
Grand Bahama

Grand Canary
Grande-Terre
Guadalcanal
Lakshadweep
Lindisfarne
Mount Desert
New Siberian
Pantelleria
Philippines
San Salvador
Southampton
South Orkney
Spitsbergen

12 letters:
Bougainville
Cassiterides
Glubbdubdrib
Greater Sunda
Marie Galante
New Caledonia
Newfoundland
Nusa Tenggara
Prince Edward
San Cristóbal
Santa Barbara
South Georgia
Torres Strait

13 letters:
Espíritu Santo
Forneaux Group
Fuerteventura
Juan Fernández
New Providence
Prince of Wales
Santa Catalina
South Shetland
St. Christopher

14 letters:
D'Entrecasteaux
Franz Josef Land
Lesser Antilles
Lewis and Harris
Queen Charlotte
Queen Elizabeth
Tristan da Cunha
Turks and Caicos
Vestmannaeyjar

15 letters:
Greater Antilles
Lewis with Harris
Wallis and Futuna

16 letters:
French West Indies
Heard and McDonald

17 letters:
Andaman and Nicobar

Fernando de Noronha

19 letters:
Netherlands Antilles

Ivy League universities

4 letters:
Yale

5 letters:
Brown

7 letters:
Cornell

Harvard

8 letters:
Columbia

9 letters:
Princeton

16 letters:
Dartmouth College

24 letters:
University of
   Pennsylvania

J j

Jackets

3 letters:
Bed
Cag
Mao
Pea
Tux

4 letters:
Baju
Boxy
Bush
Coat
Eton
Flak
Life
Mess
Sack

5 letters:
Acton
Bania
Biker
Cymar
Denim
Duvet
Gilet
Grego
Jupon
Nehru
Parka
Pilot
Polka
Shell
Shrug
Simar
Tunic
Wamus
Water

6 letters:
Amauti
Anorak

Báinín
Banian
Banyan
Basque
Battle
Blazer
Bolero
Bomber
Cagoul
Combat
Dinner
Dolman
Donkey
Jerkin
Kagool
Lumber
Monkey
Reefer
Sacque
Safari
Sports
Strait
Tabard
Tuxedo
Wammus
Wampus
Zouave

7 letters:
Amautik
Barbour®
Blouson
Cagoule
Doublet
Fustian
Hacking
Leather
Mae West
Matinée
Norfolk
Reefing
Simarre

Smoking
Spencer
Vareuse

8 letters:
Camisole
Cardigan
Gambeson
Gendarme
Haqueton
Mackinaw
Mandarin
Tailcoat
Toreador

9 letters:
Habergeon
Hacqueton
Newmarket
Pourpoint
Shortgown
Waistcoat

10 letters:
Body warmer
Bumfreezer
Carmagnole
Fearnought
Hug-me-tight
Windjammer

11 letters:
Afghanistan
Windbreaker®
Windcheater

12 letters:
Lumberjacket
Mackinaw coat

Jazz musicians

3 letters:
Bix

4 letters:
Getz, *Stanley 'Stan'*
Pine, *Courtney*
Shaw, *Artie*

5 letters:
Basie, *William*
Davis, *Miles (Dewey)*
Haden, *Charles (Edward)*
Tatum, *Art (Arthur Tatum)*

6 letters:
Bechet, *Leon Bismarcke*
Bechet, *Sidney*
Blakey, *Art(hur)*

Garner, *Erroll*
Gordon, *Dexter*
Mingus, *Charles 'Charlie'*
Oliver, *Joseph*
Waller, *Fats (Thomas Waller)*

7 letters:
Brubeck, *Dave*
Coleman, *Ornette*
Hampton, *Lionel*
Hawkins, *Coleman*
Jarrett, *Keith*
Vaughan, *Sarah (Lois)*

8 letters:
Coltrane, *John (William)*
Marsalis, *Wynton*

Peterson, *Oscar (Emmanuel)*

9 letters:
Carpenter, *John Alden*
Christian, *Charlie*
Dankworth, *John (Philip William)*
Grappelli, *Stéphane*
Lyttelton, *Humphrey*

10 letters:
Count Basie
Fitzgerald, *Ella*
King Oliver

Jazz terms

3 letters:
Gig

4 letters:
Band
Cool
Jazz
Jive
Riff
Skin

5 letters:
Combo
Jazzy
Major
Minor
Sound
Stomp
Swing

Vocal

6 letters:
Hepcat
Jazz up
Number
Vibist

7 letters:
Bassist
Big band
Hipster
Jug band
Sideman
Stomper

8 letters:
Slap bass
Vocalist

9 letters:
Augmented
Jitterbug
Mouldy fig
Ring-shout
Saxophone

10 letters:
Added sixth
Diminished
Jam session
Ninth chord
Vibraphone

13 letters:
Eleventh chord

15 letters:
Thirteenth chord

Types of jazz

3 letters:
Bop

4 letters:
Free
Scat
Trad

5 letters:
Swing

6 letters:
Modern

7 letters:
Hard bop
Ragtime

8 letters:
Highlife

9 letters:
Afro-Cuban
Dixieland
Gutbucket
West Coast

10 letters:
Mainstream
New Orleans

11 letters:
Barrelhouse
Thirdstream
Traditional

12 letters:
Boogie-woogie
Western swing

Jewish denominations and sects

7 letters:
Zionism

8 letters:
Hasidism

9 letters:
Chasidism

Hassidism

10 letters:
Chassidism

13 letters:
Reform Judaism

14 letters:
Liberal Judaism

15 letters:
Orthodox Judaism

19 letters:
Conservative Judaism

Judges

3 letters:
Ito, *Lance A(llan)*

4 letters:
Coke, *Sir Edward*
More, *Sir Thomas*

5 letters:
Draco
Solon
Woolf, *Lord Henry*

6 letters:
Gideon
Holmes, *Oliver Wendell*

Hutton, *Lord* (*James*)
 Brian (*Edward*)
Irvine, *Lord Alexander*
Mackay, *Lord James*

7 letters:
Deborah
De Burgh, *Hubert*
Denning, *Lord Alfred*
Jephtha
Pickles
Roy Bean
Solomon

8 letters:
Falconer, *Lord Charles*

Hailsham, *Viscount*
 Quintin McGarel Hogg
Jeffreys, *Lord George*
Marshall, *Thurgood*

9 letters:
Judge Judy

10 letters:
Elwyn-Jones, *Lord*
 Frederick

13 letters:
Judge 'Joe' Dredd
Pontius Pilate

K k

Kings

2 letters:
ER
Og

3 letters:
Asa
Ine
Lir
Log
Lud
Roi
Zog

4 letters:
Agag
Agis
Ahab
Brut
Ceyx
Cnut
Cole
Edwy
Fahd
Jehu
Lear
Nudd
Numa
Offa
Olaf
Saul

5 letters:
Balak
Brute
Creon
Cyrus
David
Edgar
Edwin
Gyges
Herod
Hiram

Idris
Ixion
James
Lludd
Louis
Midas
Minos
Mpret
Negus
Ninus
Penda
Priam
Rufus
Uther

6 letters:
Aegeus
Alfred
Alonso
Amasis
Arthur
Attila
Baliol
Brutus
Canute
Cheops
Clovis
Darius
Duncan
Edmund
Egbert
Farouk
Fergus
Harold
Hyksos
Lucomo
Ludwig
Memnon
Nestor
Oberon
Ogyges
Paphos

Philip
Ramses
Rhesus
Xerxes

7 letters:
Acestes
Baldwin
Balliol
Beowulf
Busiris
Caradoc
Cecrops
Croesus
Elidure
Evander
Kenneth
Macbeth
Malcolm
Oedipus
Ptolemy
Pyrrhus
Rameses
Servius
Solomon
Stephen
Tarquin
Umberto

8 letters:
Cambyses
Cophetua
Endymion
Ethelred
Hezekeah
Jereboam
Jonathan
Leonidas
Menander
Menelaus
Milesian
Odysseus

Rehoboam
Tantalus
Thyestes
Tigranes
Zedekiah

9 letters:
Agamemnon
Ahasuerus
Alexander
Athelstan
Bretwalda
Brian Boru
Conchobar
Cunobelin

Cymbeline
Ethelbert
Florestan
Frederick
Gargantua
Pygmalion
Ras Tafari
Tarquinus
Vortigern
Wenceslas

10 letters:
Belshazzar
Cadwaladar
Caractacus

Ozymandias
Wenceslaus

11 letters:
Charlemagne
Hardicanute
Jehoshaphat
Sennacherib

12 letters:
Wayland Smith

14 letters:
Nebuchadnezzar
Uther Pendragon

Kitchen equipment

3 letters:
Aga®
Pot
Wok

4 letters:
Fork
Olla
Oven

5 letters:
Grill
Knife
Ladle
Mould
Ricer
Sieve
Spoon
Whisk

6 letters:
Barbie
Cooker
Girdle
Grater
Juicer
Kettle
Masher
Peeler
Scales
Tagine

Teapot

7 letters:
Blender
Cake tin
Chip pan
Flan tin
Griddle
Loaf tin
Poacher
Ramekin
Skillet
Spatula
Spurtle
Steamer
Tandoor
Timbale
Toaster

8 letters:
Barbecue
Colander
Egg whisk
Icing bag
Jelly bag
Pot-au-feu
Saucepan
Strainer
Teaspoon

9 letters:
Bain-marie
Cafetiere
Casserole
Coffeepot
Corkscrew
Egg beater
Fish slice
Frying pan
Gravy boat
Mandoline
Mezzaluna
Microwave
Sauce boat
Tin-opener

10 letters:
Baking tray
Bread knife
Chopsticks
Liquidizer
Mixing bowl
Nutcracker
Pepper mill
Percolator
Rolling pin
Rotisserie
Tablespoon
Tenderizer

11 letters:
Cooling rack
Wooden spoon

12 letters:
Bottle opener
Carving knife
Deep fat fryer
Dessertspoon
Double boiler
Measuring jug

Pastry cutter
Toasting fork

13 letters:
Chopping board
Coffee grinder
Food processor
Ice-cream maker
Lemon squeezer
Microwave oven

14 letters:
Double saucepan
Juice extractor

15 letters:
Fan-assisted oven
Mortar and pestle

17 letters:
Batterie de cuisine

Knights

3 letters:
Kay

4 letters:
Bors

5 letters:
Guyon
Pinel

6 letters:
Bliant
Cambel
Gareth
Gawain
Lionel
Melius
Modred
Ritter

7 letters:
Accolon
Artegal
Caradoc
Galahad
Launfal
Orlando
Paladin
Tristan

8 letters:
Alphagus
Banneret
Bedivere
Calidore
Lancelot
Maecenas
Palmerin
Parsifal
Perceval

Percival
Tristram
Vavasour

9 letters:
Aguecheek
Britomart
Caballero
Launcelot
Lochinvar
Lohengrin
Pharamond
Valvassor

10 letters:
Tannhauser

11 letters:
Perceforest

Knitting stitches

3 letters:
Box
Rib

4 letters:
Moss
Seed
Slip

5 letters:
Cable

6 letters:
Garter

7 letters:
Layette

8 letters:
Pavilion
Stocking

9 letters:
Garter rib

10 letters:
Double moss
Double seed
Mistake rib

Moss panels

11 letters:
Diagonal rib

Roman stripe

13 letters:
Fisherman's rib

Knots

3 letters:
Bow
Tie

4 letters:
Bend
Flat
Loop
Love
Mesh
Reef
Slip
Wale
Wall

5 letters:
Hitch
Mouse
Picot
Quipu
Thumb
Water

6 letters:
Clinch
French
Granny
Lover's
Prusik
Shroud
Square

7 letters:
Barrell
Bowknot
Bowline
Cat's paw
Crochet
Diamond
Gordian
Rosette
Running
Sailor's
Windsor

8 letters:
Hangman's
Overhand
Slipknot
Surgeon's
Truelove

9 letters:
Bowstring
Half-hitch
Sheet bend
Swab hitch
Turk's-head

10 letters:
Becket bend
Clove hitch
Fisherman's

Girth hitch
Hawser bend
Monkey fist
Sheepshank
Stevedore's
Truelover's

11 letters:
Carrick bend
Englishman's
Magnus hitch
Timber hitch

12 letters:
Harness hitch
Rolling hitch
Weaver's hitch

13 letters:
Figure of eight
Matthew Walker
Slippery hitch

14 letters:
Blackwall hitch
Englishman's tie
Fisherman's bend
Running bowline

L l

Lakes, lochs and loughs

2 letters:
No

3 letters:
Ard
Awe
Ewe
Tay
Van
Zug

4 letters:
Bala
Biel
Bled
Chad
Como
Earn
Erie
Erne
Eyre
Fyne
Kivu
Mead
Ness
Nyos
Taal
Tana
Thun
Tien

5 letters:
Allen
Atlin
Cowan
Frome
Garda
Gatún
Huron
Ilmen
Léman
Leven

Lochy
Lower
Malar
Meech
Morar
Mungo
Mweru
Myall
Nam Co
Neagh
Nyasa
Onega
Patos
Playa
Poopó
Pskov
Sevan
Sween
Tahoe
Taupo
Tsana
Urmia
Volta

6 letters:
Albert
Annecy
Argyle
Averno
Baikal
Barlee
Bitter
Broads
Cayuga
Corrib
Edward
Geneva
Kariba
Ladoga
Laggan
Linnhe
Lomond

Lugano
Malawi
Miveru
Mobutu
Nakura
Nam Tso
Nasser
Oneida
Peipus
P'o-yang
Rudolf
Saimaa
Te Anau
Tekapo
Tummel
Vanern
Zürich

7 letters:
Amadeus
Aral Sea
Avernus
Axolotl
Balaton
Belfast
Dead Sea
Iliamna
Katrine
Koko Nor
Kuku Nor
Lucerne
Managua
Manapua
Nipigon
Ontario
Rannoch
Rotonia
Toronto
Torrens
Turkana

8 letters:
Balkhash
Bodensee
Carnegie
Dongting
Gairdner
Grasmere
Issyk-Kul
Kootenay
Lake Aral
Maggiore
Manitoba
Menindee
Menteith
Michigan
Naumachy
Okanagan
Onondaga
Regillus
Reindeer
Superior
Titicaca
Tonle Sap
Torridon
Veronica
Victoria
Wakatipu
Wanawaka
Winnipeg

9 letters:
Athabasca
Athabaska
Bangweulu

Champlain
Constance
Ennerdale
Everglade
Great Bear
Great Salt
Innisfree
Killarney
Macquarie
Manapouri
Maracaibo
Naumachia
Neuchâtel
Nicaragua
Nipissing
Saint John
Serbonian
Thirlmere
Trasimene
Trasimono
Ullswater
Wairarapa
Wast Water
Winnebago
Ysselmeer

10 letters:
Buttermere
Caspian Sea
Clearwater
Great Lakes
Great Slave
Hawes Water
Ijsselmeer

Miraflores
Mistassini
Okeechobee
Okefenokee
Saint Clair
Serpentine
Tanganyika
Washington
Windermere

11 letters:
Great Bitter
Lesser Slave
Stanley Pool

12 letters:
Derwentwater
Little Bitter
Memphremagog
Sea of Galilee
Waikaremoana

13 letters:
Bassenthwaite
Coniston Water
Crummock Water
Pontchartrain

14 letters:
Disappointment
Ennerdale Water
Lake of the Woods

Languages

AFRICAN LANGUAGES

2 letters:
Ga
Gã

3 letters:
Edo
Ewe
Ibo
Luo
Tiv

Twi

4 letters:
Akan
Beni
Bini
Efik
Fang
Fula
Hutu

Igbo
Krio
Lozi
Luba
Nama
Nuba
Nupe
Pedi
Susu
Zulu

AFRICAN LANGUAGES (CONTINUED)

5 letters:
Bemba
Chewa
Duala
Dyula
Fanti
Fulah
Galla
Ganda
Hausa
Kongo
Masai
Moore
Mossi
Nyoro
Pondo
Sango
Shona
Sotho
Swazi
Temne
Tigré
Tonga
Venda
Wolof
Xhosa

6 letters:
Berber
Coptic
Damara
Fulani
Grikwa
Griqua
Herero
Ibibio
Kabyle
Kikuyu
Nyanja
Ovambo
Rwanda
Somali
Tsonga
Tswana
Tuareg
Yoruba

7 letters:
Adamawa
Amharic
Ashanti
Bambara
Barotse
Bashkir

Kirundi
Luganda
Malinke
Maninke
Namaqua
Ndebele
Sesotho
Songhai
Swahili

8 letters:
Chichewa
Fanagalo
Fanakalo
Kingwana
Malagasy
Matabele
Tigrinya
Tshiluba

9 letters:
Afrikaans
Hottentot

13 letters:
Northern Sotho

ASIAN LANGUAGES

3 letters:
Lao
Mon

4 letters:
Ainu
Cham
Moro
Naga
Nuri
Shan
Thai
Urdu

5 letters:
Dinka
Farsi
Gondi

Hindi
Karen
Kazak
Khmer
Malay
Oriya
Tamil
Tatar
Uigur
Uzbek
Yakut

6 letters:
Abkhaz
Adygei
Adyghe
Afghan
Arabic

Bihari
Brahui
Buriat
Buryat
Divehi
Evenki
Hebrew
Kafiri
Kalmyk
Kazakh
Korean
Lahnda
Lepcha
Manchu
Mishmi
Mongol
Nepali
Ostyak

ASIAN LANGUAGES (CONTINUED)

Pashto
Pushto
Pushtu
Sindhi
Telegu
Telugu
Tungus
Uighur

Ossetic
Punjabi
Sogdian
Tadzhik
Tagalog
Tibetan
Turkman
Turkmen

Turkoman

9 letters:
Abkhazian
Cantonese
Kabardian
Malayalam
Mongolian
Sinhalese

7 letters:
Abkhazi
Aramaic
Balochi
Baluchi
Bengali
Burmese
Chinese
Chukchi
Chuvash
Dzongka
Iranian
Kalmuck
Kannada
Khalkha
Kirghiz
Kurdish
Marathi

8 letters:
Armenian
Assamese
Balinese
Canarese
Chukchee
Filipino
Gujarati
Gujerati
Gurkhali
Japanese
Javanese
Kanarese
Kashmiri
Mahratti
Mandarin
Ossetian
Tadzhiki

10 letters:
Circassian
Hindostani
Hindustani
Kara-Kalpak
Kazan Tatar
Malayalaam
Vietnamese

11 letters:
Azerbaijani
Hindoostani

15 letters:
Bahasa Indonesia

AUSTRALASIAN LANGUAGES

4 letters:
Krio
Motu

5 letters:
Dinka
Māori

6 letters:
Aranda
Fijian
Papuan
Samoan

Tongan

7 letters:
Moriori
Nauruan
Pintubi

8 letters:
Gurindji
Hawaiian
Hiri Motu
Tuvaluan
Warlpiri

9 letters:
Kamilaroi

10 letters:
Beach-la-Mar
Police Motu

13 letters:
Neo-Melanesian

20 letters:
Solomon Islands Pidgin

Languages

EUROPEAN LANGUAGES

4 letters:
Erse
Komi
Lapp
Manx

5 letters:
Czech
Dutch
Greek
Ladin
Vogul
Welsh

6 letters:
Basque
Bokmål
Breton
Cymric
Danish
French
Gaelic
German
Kymric
Ladino
Lallan
Magyar
Polish
Romany
Shelta
Slovak
Udmurt
Votyak
Zyrian

7 letters:
Catalan
Cornish
English
Finnish
Flemish
Frisian
Gagauzi
Italian
Lallans
Latvian
Lettish
Maltese
Mingrel
Mordvin
Nynorsk
Romanes
Romansh
Russian
Samoyed
Slovene
Sorbian
Spanish
Swedish
Turkish
Yiddish

8 letters:
Albanian
Bohemian
Cheremis
Croatian
Estonian

Faeroese
Friulian
Galician
Georgian
Karelian
Landsmål
Lusatian
Romanian
Romansch

9 letters:
Alemannic
Bulgarian
Castilian
Cheremiss
Hungarian
Icelandic
Norwegian
Provençal
Sardinian
Ukrainian

10 letters:
Lithuanian
Macedonian
Mingrelian
Portuguese
Serbo-Croat

12 letters:
Byelorussian

13 letters:
Serbo-Croatian

NORTH AMERICAN LANGUAGES

3 letters:
Fox
Ute

4 letters:
Crow
Erie
Hopi
Zuñi

5 letters:
Aleut

Creek
Haida
Huron
Osage
Piute
Sioux
Taino

6 letters:
Abnaki
Apache

Cayuga
Eskimo
Micmac
Mixtec
Mohave
Mohawk
Mojave
Navaho
Navajo
Nootka
Ojibwa

NORTH AMERICAN LANGUAGES (CONTINUED)

Oneida
Paiute
Pawnee
Pequot
Seneca

7 letters:
Arapaho
Caddoan
Catawba
Chinook
Choctaw
Mahican
Mohican
Shawnee
Tahltan
Tlingit

8 letters:
Aleutian

Algonkin
Cherokee
Cheyenne
Comanche
Delaware
Iroquois
Kwakiutl
Menomini
Nez Percé
Okanagan
Okanogan
Okinagan
Onondaga
Sahaptan
Sahaptin
Seminole
Shoshone
Shoshoni

9 letters:
Algonquin
Blackfoot
Chickasaw
Inuktitut
Sahaptian
Tuscarora
Winnebago

11 letters:
Assiniboine
Massachuset
Narraganset

12 letters:
Narragansett

13 letters:
Massachusetts

SOUTH AMERICAN LANGUAGES

4 letters:
Tupi

6 letters:
Aymara
Galibi
Kechua

7 letters:
Guarani
Nahuatl
Quechua
Quichua
Zapotec

8 letters:
Chibchan

10 letters:
Araucanian

ANCIENT LANGUAGES

4 letters:
Avar
Ge'ez
Inca
Maya
Norn
Pali

5 letters:
Aztec
Ionic
Koine
Latin
Mayan
Oscan

Punic
Vedic

6 letters:
Gothic
Hebrew
Libyan
Lycian
Lydian
Sabean
Syriac

7 letters:
Avestan
Avestic

Chaldee
Edomite
Elamite
Hittite
Pahlavi
Pehlevi
Pictish
Sabaean
Umbrian
Venetic
Wendish

8 letters:
Akkadian
Assyrian

ANCIENT LANGUAGES (CONTINUED)

Egyptian
Ethiopic
Etruscan
Faliscan
Frankish
Illyrian
Messapïc
Old Norse
Phrygian
Sanskrit
Scythian
Sumerian
Thracian
Ugaritic
Volscian

9 letters:
Canaanite
Langue d'oc
Messapian
Sabellian
Tocharian
Tokharian

10 letters:
Anglo-Saxon
Babylonian
Gallo-Roman
Himyaritic
Langue d'oïl
Phoenician

11 letters:
Celtiberian
Langobardic
Old Prussian
Osco-Umbrian

12 letters:
Ancient Greek
Gallo-Romance

13 letters:
Old High German

14 letters:
Thraco-Phrygian

17 letters:
Old Church Slavonic

ARTIFICIAL LANGUAGES

3 letters:
Ido

7 letters:
Volapuk

Volapük

9 letters:
Esperanto

11 letters:
Interlingua

LANGUAGE GROUPS

3 letters:
Gur
Kwa
San

5 letters:
Bantu
Carib
Indic
Mande
Mayan
Munda
Nguni
Norse
Ugric
Yuman

6 letters:
Altaic
Baltic

Celtic
Chadic
Cymric
Dardic
Eskimo
Finnic
Italic
Na-Déné
Pahari
Salish
Siouan
Turkic
Uralic

7 letters:
Caddoan
Hamitic
Iranian
Khoisan
Nilotic

Oceanic
Romance
Saharan
Semitic
Sinitic
Sudanic
Voltaic

8 letters:
Albanian
Arawakan
Armenian
Cushitic
Germanic
Hellenic
Mongolic
Mon-Khmer
Penutian
Rhaetian
Salishan

LANGUAGE GROUPS (CONTINUED)

Slavonic
Tungusic
Wakashan

9 letters:
Algonkian
Anatolian
Brythonic
Caucasian
Chari-Nile
Dravidian
Indo-Aryan
Iroquoian
Muskogean
Semi-Bantu

10 letters:
Algonquian
Athabascan
Athabaskan
Athapascan
Athapaskan
Australian

Benue-Congo
Canaanitic
Hindustani
Melanesian
Muskhogean
Niger-Congo
Polynesian
Sanskritic
Shoshonean
Uto-Aztecan

11 letters:
Afro-Asiatic
East Iranian
Indo-Iranian
Indo-Pacific
Kordofanian
Micronesian
Nilo-Saharan
Pama-Nyungan
Sino-Tibetan
Tupi-Guarani
West Iranian

12 letters:
Austronesian
East Germanic
Indo-European
Tibeto-Burman
West Atlantic
West Germanic
West Slavonic

13 letters:
Austro-Asiatic
Hamito-Semitic
North Germanic
Semito-Hamitic

16 letters:
Malayo-Polynesian

20 letters:
Trans-New Guinea
  phylum

Law

LAW TERMS

2 letters:
On

3 letters:
Ban
Bar
CAV
Doe
Dot
Jus
Run
Sue
Try
Use

4 letters:
Abet
Able
Aver

Avow
Bail
Bond
Case
Cite
Deed
Eyre
Fact
Feme
File
Find
Flaw
Free
Gist
Hear
Heir
Jury
Land
Lien

Mise
Mute
Nisi
Nude
Oath
Open
Oyer
Plea
Real
Rest
Riot
Rout
Rule
Sign
Sine
Soke
Sole
Suit
Term

Law terms (continued)

Tort
Udal
Upon
User
View
Waif
Ward
Will
Writ

5 letters:
Abate
Adopt
Adult
Agist
Alibi
Array
Avoid
Award
Baron
Bench
Brief
Bring
Cause
Cheat
Chose
Close
Costs
Count
Court
Covin
Culpa
Demur
Devil
Donee
Donor
Dower
Droit
Enter
Estop
Evict
Folio
Grant
Grith
Heres
In fee
In rem
Issue

Joint
Judge
Jural
Jurat
Juror
Lapse
Libel
Limit
Manus
Mesne
Moral
Naked
Novel
Offer
Overt
Panel
Parol
Party
Petit
Petty
Plead
Posse
Privy
Proof
Prove
Pupil
Remit
Reply
Retry
Salvo
Sound
Squat
Stale
Swear
Tales
Tenor
Thing
Title
Trial
Venue
Waive
Waste
Wrong

6 letters:
Abator
Accrue
Accuse

Acquit
Action
Affirm
Affray
Allege
Amerce
Answer
Appeal
Assets
Assign
Attach
Attorn
Bailee
Bailor
Bigamy
Capias
Caveat
Cessor
Charge
Come on
Common
Custom
Cy pres
Decree
Defeat
De jure
Delict
Demand
Depose
Devise
Digest
Disbar
Docket
Domain
Duress
Enjoin
Equity
Escrow
Estray
Extend
Extent
Factor
Fiscal
Forest
Guilty
Haeres
Holder
In banc

LAW TERMS (CONTINUED)

Infant
Infirm
Injury
Intent
Junior
Jurist
Laches
Lawyer
Legist
Maihem
Malice
Matter
Mayhem
Merger
Merits
Motion
Nonage
Owelty
Pardon
Plaint
Prayer
Prefer
Queen's
Recoup
Rejoin
Relief
Remand
Remise
Report
Rescue
Retain
Return
Review
Ruling
Saving
Script
Socage
Suitor
Surety
Tender
Termer
Termor
Trover
Vacant
Vacate
Vendee
Vendor
Verify

Versus
Viewer
Waiver

7 letters:
Accused
Ad litem
Affiant
Alienee
Alienor
Alimony
Amnesty
Ancient
Approve
Arraign
Assault
Attaint
Bailiff
Bencher
Bequest
Capital
Caption
Case law
Caution
Circuit
Codicil
Commute
Condemn
Condone
Connive
Convene
Convert
Coroner
Counsel
Cruelty
Culprit
Custody
Damages
Damnify
Default
Defence
Deodand
Deraign
Detinue
Devolve
Dies non
Dismiss
Dissent

Dowable
Earnest
Empanel
Engross
Escheat
Estreat
Examine
Execute
Exhibit
Ex parte
Fiction
Filiate
Finding
Foreign
Foreman
Forfeit
Garnish
Grantee
Grantor
Hearing
Hearsay
Heiress
Heritor
Impanel
Implead
Ingoing
In posse
Inquest
Joinder
Juryman
Jus soli
Justice
Justify
Larceny
Lawsuit
Law term
Lex loci
Manager
Mandate
Mens rea
Misuser
Movable
Nol. pros.
Non pros.
Nonsuit
Obscene
Onerous
Opening

LAW TERMS (CONTINUED)

Portion
Precept
Presume
Privity
Probate
Proceed
Process
Purview
Recital
Recover
Relator
Release
Replevy
Residue
Reverse
Scandal
Session
Settlor
Several
Slander
Sound in
Stand by
Succeed
Summary
Summons
Suo jure
Suo loco
Swear in
Tenancy
Testate
Testify
Triable
Verdict
Vesture
Vitiate
Voucher
Warrant
Witness

8 letters:
Abeyance
Absolute
Act of God
Advocate
Alienate
Alluvion
Appellee
Assessor

Assignee
Assignor
Attorney
Avulsion
Bailable
Bailment
Bailsman
Bankrupt
Barratry
Barretry
Bequeath
Bondsman
Caveator
Chambers
Chancery
Citation
Complete
Compound
Contempt
Contract
Copyhold
Covenant
Darraign
Dead hand
Decedent
Deed poll
Demurrer
Deponent
Detainer
Disannul
Disclaim
Distrain
Distress
Dividend
Dotation
Estoppel
Estovers
Evidence
Executor
Felo de se
Feme sole
Fiducial
Forensic
Forjudge
Fungible
Gravamen
Guardian
Hand down

Handling
Heirship
Heritage
Hung jury
Hypothec
In camera
In escrow
Innuendo
Insanity
In specie
Instruct
In venter
Ipso jure
Issuable
Jeopardy
Jointure
Judgment
Judicial
Juratory
Juristic
Law Lords
Litigant
Mandamus
Material
Mistrial
Mittimus
Monopoly
Mortmain
Moveable
Novation
Nuisance
Oblivion
Occupant
Ordinary
Parcener
Peculium
Personal
Petition
Pleading
Post-obit
Premises
Presents
Promisee
Promisor
Propound
Pursuant
Question
Rebutter

LAW TERMS (CONTINUED)

Recorder
Recovery
Relation
Replevin
Reporter
Reprieve
Schedule
Scienter
Sentence
Sergeant
Serjeant
Solatium
Solution
Spinster
Stranger
Stultify
Subpoena
Sui juris
Swear out
Tenantry
Tipstaff
Tortious
Transfer
Traverse
Trespass
Tribunal
Variance
Voidable
Voir dire
Warranty

9 letters:
Abandonee
Accessary
Accessory
Accretion
Adjective
Adminicle
Affidavit
Affiliate
Alienable
Annulment
Appellant
Appellate
Appendant
Arbitrary
Assumpsit
Attainder

Authentic
Authority
Avoidance
Bailiwick
Barrister
Blasphemy
Bona fides
Briefless
Cartulary
Cassation
Challenge
Champerty
Collusion
Committal
Commonage
Common law
Competent
Complaint
Condition
Contumacy
Coparceny
Counselor
Coverture
Criminate
Custodian
Customary
Debatable
Declarant
Defalcate
Defendant
Demandant
Desertion
Determine
Devisable
Diligence
Disaffirm
Discharge
Discommon
Discovert
Discovery
Disforest
Distraint
Effectual
Equitable
Evocation
Exception
Execution
Executory

Executrix
Exemplify
Extradite
Fiduciary
Filiation
Foreclose
Forejudge
Garnishee
Gavelkind
Grand jury
Guarantee
Heritable
Immovable
Imperfect
Indemnity
Indenture
Instanter
Intention
Interdict
Intervene
Intestate
Jointress
Judge-made
Judgement
Judicable
Judiciary
Juridical
Jurywoman
Law French
Leasehold
Litigable
Mortgagee
Muniments
Nisi prius
Nolle pros.
Non liquet
Not guilty
Obreption
Occupancy
Onomastic
Pecuniary
Petit jury
Petty jury
Plaintiff
Pleadings
Precedent
Prescribe
Principal

LAW TERMS (CONTINUED)

Privilege
Proponent
Prosecute
Public law
Pupillage
Quitclaim
Recaption
Re-examine
Reference
Refresher
Rejoinder
Remission
Res gestae
Residuary
Sequester
Servitude
Severable
Severance
Signatory
Sine prole
Solemnity
Solicitor
Specialty
Stand down
Statement
Stipulate
Subrogate
Summation
Summing-up
Surcharge
Surrender
Testament
Testimony
Under oath
Venireman
Vexatious
Vindicate
Voluntary
Volunteer

10 letters:
Absente reo
Acceptance
Accusation
Actionable
Admissible
Advocation
Alienation

Ambulatory
Appearance
Assignment
Attachment
Automatism
Beneficial
Bill of sale
Case stated
Certiorari
Cessionary
Chargeable
Chartulary
Civil death
Coexecutor
Cognisable
Cognisance
Cognizable
Cognizance
Commitment
Commutable
Competence
Competency
Conclusion
Confiscate
Connivance
Consensual
Consortium
Constitute
Contraband
Contractor
Conversion
Conveyance
Convincing
Coparcener
Copyholder
Counsellor
Crown court
Cur. adv. vult
Dead letter
Decree nisi
Defamation
Defeasible
Deposition
Disinherit
Disorderly
Distrainee
Distringas
Emblements

Expectancy
Extinguish
Feme covert
Gratuitous
Ground rent
Hereditary
Homologate
Impartible
Impediment
In articles
Incapacity
In chancery
Inducement
Injunction
In personam
Institutes
Instrument
Intendment
Interplead
Inter vivos
Invalidate
Judicative
Judicatory
Judicature
Jus gentium
Left-handed
Lex scripta
Limitation
Lis pendens
Litigation
Magistrate
Memorandum
Misjoinder
Moratorium
Morganatic
Negligence
Next friend
Nonjoinder
Obligation
Perception
Peremptory
Personalty
Petitioner
Possessory
Predispose
Pre-emption
Preference
Prima facie

LAW TERMS (CONTINUED)

Private law
Privileged
Prize court
Proceeding
Propositus
Prosecutor
Recognisee
Recognisor
Recognizee
Recognizor
Repetition
Resolutive
Respondent
Returnable
Secularise
Secularize
Separation
Settlement
Smart money
Spoliation
Stated case
Statute law
Stillicide
Submission
Subreption
Surplusage
Suspension
Third party
Tort-feasor
Trial court
Ultra vires
Unilateral
Vindictive
Wager of law

11 letters:
Affiliation
Affirmation
Arbitration
Beneficiary
Commutation
Complainant
Composition
Constituent
Contentious
Continuance
Coparcenary
Corpus juris

Counterpart
Countersign
County court
Declaration
Declaratory
Dereliction
Descendable
Descendible
Disafforest
Discontinue
Distributee
Disturbance
Encumbrance
Enfranchise
Engrossment
Examination
Expropriate
Fieri facias
Forbearance
Fornication
Garnishment
Hypothecate
Incompetent
Incorporeal
Incriminate
Inheritance
Inquisition
Judges' rules
Jury process
Jus naturale
Justiciable
Law merchant
Leaseholder
Lex talionis
Locus standi
Maintenance
Malfeasance
Mare clausum
Mare liberum
Ministerial
Misfeasance
Mispleading
Necessaries
Nonfeasance
Nudum pactum
Port of entry
Presentment
Presumption

Preterition
Procuration
Procuratory
Prohibition
Prosecution
Protonotary
Provocation
Quo warranto
Replication
Reservation
Res judicata
Restitution
Scire facias
Self-defence
Sequestrate
Special case
Subrogation
Substantive
Surrebuttal
Surrebutter
Unalienable
Unavoidable
Ward of court
Year and a day

12 letters:
Accusatorial
Amicus curiae
Bona vacantia
Chance-medley
Chief justice
Codification
Compurgation
Constructive
Contributory
Conventional
Co-respondent
Coroner's jury
Counterclaim
Cross-examine
Denunciation
Determinable
Distribution
Earnest money
Encumbrancer
Extraditable
Force majeure
Grand larceny

Law terms (continued)

Habeas corpus
Incapacitate
Indefeasible
Instructions
Interpleader
Jail delivery
Jurisconsult
Jurisprudent
Jus sanguinis
Justice court
Manslaughter
Misadventure
Notary public
Obiter dictum
Onus probandi
Pendente lite
Petit larceny
Petty larceny
Prescription
Prothonotary
Real property
Receivership
Recognisance
Recognizance
Surrejoinder
Testamentary
Traffic court
Unappealable
Uncovenanted
Unwritten law
Venire facias
Verification

13 letters:
A mensa et thoro
Articled clerk
Attorney-at-law
Body corporate
Breach of trust
Burden of proof
Certification
Change of venue
Civil marriage
Consideration
Consolidation
Corpus delicti
Countercharge
Determination

Documentation
Eminent domain
Extrajudicial
First offender
Inferior court
Inquisitorial
Interlocutory
Irrepleviable
Jurisprudence
Juvenile court
King's evidence
Legal medicine
Lex non scripta
Nolle prosequi
Paraphernalia
Paterfamilias
Paternity suit
Petty sessions
Premeditation
Primogeniture
Probable cause
Process-server
Question of law
Recrimination
Res adjudicata
Right of common
Self-executing
Sequestration
Sergeant at law
Serjeant at law
Treasure-trove

14 letters:
Arrest judgment
Barrister-at-law
Chamber counsel
Counselor-at-law
Decree absolute
Direct evidence
Examine-in-chief
Family Division
Fideicommissum
Irreplevisable
Justices in eyre
Mental disorder
Napoleonic Code
Nolo contendere
Non prosequitur

Plea bargaining
Posse comitatus
Property centre
Public defender
Public nuisance
Question of fact
Representation
State's evidence
Summary offence
Time immemorial
Ultimogeniture
Unincorporated
Utter barrister

15 letters:
Attorney general
Bill of attainder
Breach of promise
Carnal knowledge
Coroner's inquest
Disorderly house
Due process of law
Fideicommissary
Imprescriptable
Interrogatories
Non compos mentis
Official Referee
Oyer and terminer
Private nuisance
Quarter sessions
Res ipsa loquitur
Special pleading
Writ of execution

16 letters:
Affiliation order
Anton Piller order
Bill of indictment
Blasphemous libel
Breach of the peace
Conscience clause
Deferred sentence
Demisit sine prole
Dies non juridicus
Exemplary damages
Flagrante delicto
Forensic medicine
Goods and chattels

LAW TERMS (CONTINUED)

Magistrates' court
Mental impairment
Personal property
Public prosecutor
Restraining order
Statement of claim
Territorial court
Transitory action
Unlawful assembly
Without prejudice

17 letters:
Arrest of judgement
Compliance officer
Curia advisari vult
Disorderly conduct
False imprisonment
Insurable interest
Judgment by default
Justice of the peace
Persistent cruelty

18 letters:
Clerk to the justices

Corpus Juris Civilis
Cumulative evidence
In flagrante delicto
Judicial separation
Particulars of Claim
Pecuniary advantage
Place of safety order

19 letters:
Administration order
Challenge to the array
Challenge to the polls
Prosecuting attorney
Restrictive covenant
Specific performance
Summary jurisdiction

20 letters:
Court of first instance
Criminal conversation
Medical jurisprudence
Obtaining by deception
Psychopathic disorder
Statutory declaration

Voluntary arrangement

21 letters:
Indeterminate sentence
Unreasonable
  behaviour

22 letters:
Affiliation proceedings
Contributory
  negligence
Divorce from bed and
  board

23 letters:
Letters of administration

24 letters:
Diminished
  responsibility

26 letters:
Certificate of
  incorporation

CRIMINAL LAW TERMS

5 letters:
Arson
Entry
Felon
Force
Theft
Thief
Utter

6 letters:
Felony
Suborn

7 letters:
Battery
Embrace
Forgery
Impeach
Perjure
Perjury

Riot Act
Robbery

8 letters:
Bailment
Burglary
Embracer
Infamous
True bill

9 letters:
Acquittal
Deception
Embraceor
Embracery
Felonious
Personate

10 letters:
Hard labour

Indictable
Indictment

12 letters:
Misdemeanant
Misdemeanour

13 letters:
Housebreaking

14 letters:
False pretences
Penal servitude

16 letters:
Actual bodily harm

18 letters:
Grievous bodily harm
Malice aforethought

PROPERTY LAW TERMS

3 letters:
Fee

4 letters:
Oust
Tail

5 letters:
Entry

6 letters:
Assure
Convey
Demise
Divest
Entail
Estate
Ouster
Result
Revert
Seisin
Seizin
Tenure
Vested

7 letters:
Abutter
Adverse
Appoint
Chattel
Deforce
Demesne
Descent
Devisee
Devisor
Enfeoff
Fee tail
Fixture
Heirdom

8 letters:
Abuttals
Amortise
Amortize
Disseise
Dominion
Dominium
Easement
Freehold
Heirloom
Hotchpot
Messuage
Remitter
Riparian
Survivor
Warranty

9 letters:
Abatement
Accession
Ademption
Appointee
Appointor
Disentail
Ejectment
Fee simple
Heir-at-law
Intrusion
Mortgager
Mortgagor
Partition
Party wall
Reconvert
Remainder
Reversion
Severalty

10 letters:
Betterment

Freeholder
Particular
Perpetuity
Transferee
Transferor

11 letters:
Advancement
Appointment
Chattel real
Reversioner
Transferrer

12 letters:
Appurtenance
Dilapidation
Heir apparent
Heriditament
Remainderman

13 letters:
Administrator

14 letters:
Administration
Vested interest

15 letters:
Abstract of title
Chattel personal
Unity of interest

16 letters:
Dominant tenement
Servient tenement

18 letters:
Equity of redemption
Power of appointment

SCOTS LAW TERMS

3 letters:
Feu

5 letters:
Agent
Poind

Pupil
Tutor

6 letters:
Assize
Decern

Delict
Depone
Desert
Fiscal
Notour
Repone

Scots law terms (continued)

Sasine
Wadset

7 letters:
Aliment
Curator
Decreet
Feu duty
Mandate

8 letters:
Advocate
Continue
Defender
Hypothec
Law agent
Location
Lockfast
Poinding
Thirlage

9 letters:
Approbate
Avizandum
Interdict
Not proven
Tradition

10 letters:
Alimentary
Arrestment
Crown agent
Declarator
Repetition

11 letters:
Assignation
Fire raising
Sequestrate
Warrant sale

12 letters:
Interlocutor
Precognition

13 letters:
District court

14 letters:
Advocate Depute
Condescendence
Notour bankrupt
Sheriff officer

16 letters:
Culpable homicide
Multiplepoinding
Procurator fiscal

21 letters:
Approbate and
  reprobate

22 letters:
Justice of the peace
  court

Law sittings

6 letters:
Easter
Hilary

7 letters:
Trinity

10 letters:
Michaelmas

Types of leather

3 letters:
Kid
Kip

4 letters:
Buff
Calf
Cuir
Hide
Napa
Roan
Yuft

5 letters:
Mocha
Nappa
Suede

6 letters:
Corium
Deacon
Levant
Nubuck®
Oxhide
Patent
Rexine®
Russia

Shammy

7 letters:
Box-calf
Chamois
Cowhide
Dogskin
Hog-skin
Kip-skin
Morocco
Pigskin
Rawhide
Saffian

8 letters:
Buckskin
Cabretta
Capeskin
Cheverel
Cordovan
Cordwain
Deerskin
Marocain

Maroquin
Rough-out
Shagreen

9 letters:
Chevrette
Horsehide
Sharkskin
Sheepskin

10 letters:
Checklaton
Shecklaton

11 letters:
Cuir-bouilli
Whitleather

Lilies

3 letters:
Day

4 letters:
Aloe
Arum
Corn
Lent
Lote
Sego

5 letters:
Calla
Camas
Lotus
Padma
Regal
Tiger
Water
Yucca

6 letters:
Camash
Camass
Canada
Crinum
Easter

Jacob's
Nerine
Nuphar
Smilax
Zephyr

7 letters:
African
Candock
Madonna
Nelumbo
Quamash

8 letters:
Asphodel
Galtonia
Martagon
Nenuphar
Phormium
Plantain
Trillium
Turk's cap
Victoria

9 letters:
Amaryllis

Colchicum
Colocasia
Herb-paris
Kniphofia

10 letters:
Agapanthus
Aspidistra
Belladonna
Fleur de lys
Haemanthus

11 letters:
Convallaria

12 letters:
Annunciation
Hemerocallis
Skunk cabbage
Solomon's seal

14 letters:
Chincherinchee

15 letters:
Star of Bethlehem

Liqueurs

3 letters:
Kir

4 letters:
Ouzo

5 letters:
Anise
Crème
Hogan
Kirsh

Mobby
Noyau

6 letters:
Enzian

Glayva®
Kahlua
Kümmel
Malibu®
Midori
Mobbie
Oedema
Pastis
Pernod®
Strega®

7 letters:
Curaçao
Persico
Ratafee
Ratafia
Sambuca

8 letters:
Advocaat
Amaretto
Anisette

Calvados
Drambuie®
Galliano®
Geropiga
Prunelle
Sambucca
Tia Maria®

9 letters:
Cointreau®
Mirabelle
Van der Hum

10 letters:
Chartreuse
Frangelico
Hogan-mogen
Maraschino
Pousse-café

11 letters:
Benedictine

Kirshwasser

12 letters:
Cherry brandy
Crème de cacao
Grand Marnier®
Kirschwasser

13 letters:
Amendoa Amarga
Crème de menthe
Eau des creoles
Peach schnapps

14 letters:
Veuve Jacquolot

15 letters:
Southern Comfort®

17 letters:
Bailey's Irish Cream®

Literature

LITERATURE TERMS

2 letters:
SF

4 letters:
Coda
Epic
Myth
Plot
Saga

5 letters:
Beats
Cento
Drama
Essay
Fable
Gloss
Maxim
Motif
Novel
Roman
Story

Theme
Trope
Verse

6 letters:
Bathos
Comedy
Gothic
Legend
Parody
Pathos
Satire
Simile
Sketch
Theory
Thesis

7 letters:
Bombast
Byronic
Chiller
Conceit

Epistle
Epitaph
Erasure
Faction
Fantasy
Homeric
Imagery
Janeite
Joycean
Kenning
Lampoon
Novella
Polemic
Realism
Subplot
Subtext
Tragedy

8 letters:
Allegory
Allusion
Anti-hero

LITERATURE TERMS (CONTINUED)

Aphorism
Archaism
Augustan
Causerie
Dialogue
Epilogue
Exegesis
Fabulist
Foreword
Futurism
Horatian
Jacobean
Kailyard
Kiddy lit
Metaphor
Narrator
Oxymoron
Pastiche
Pastoral
Samizdat
Swiftian
Vignette

9 letters:
Amphigory
Antinovel
Anti-roman
Brechtian
Bricolage
Cyberpunk
Decadence
Derridian
Dialectic
Discourse
Gongorism
Hellenism
Invective
Melodrama
Modernism
Narrative
Novelette
Pot-boiler

10 letters:
Amphigouri
Bakhtinian
Belletrist
Ciceronian

Classicism
Denouement
Dickensian
Johnsonian
Journalese
Juvenalian
Kafkaesque
Laurentian
Lawrentian
Mock-heroic
Mythopoeia
Naturalism
Nom de plume
Palindrome
Paraphrase
Picaresque
Plagiarism
Post-theory
Roman à clef
Short story
Spoonerism
Surrealism

11 letters:
Black comedy
Campus novel
Courtly love
Fantastique
Festschrift
Fin de siècle
Foucauldian
Hagiography
Historicism
Littérateur
Metafiction
Narratology
Pornography
Queer theory
Romanticism
Tragicomedy

12 letters:
Alliteration
Bibliography
Bodice-ripper
Hermeneutics
Magic realism
Metalanguage

New criticism
Nouveau roman
Onomatopoeia
Splatterpunk

13 letters:
Angry Young Men
Belles-lettres
Bildungsroman
Carnivalesque
Celtic Revival
Colloquialism
Expressionism
Marxist theory
Postmodernism
Structuralism
Sturm und Drang

14 letters:
Beat Generation
Bowdlerization
Cut-up technique
Deconstruction
Double entendre
Feminist theory
Figure of speech
Locus classicus
Lost Generation
Magical realism
New historicism
Science fiction

15 letters:
Bloomsbury group
Comedy of manners
Epistolary novel
Historical novel
Intertextuality
Post-colonialism

16 letters:
Commedia dell'arte
Death of the author
Hudibrastic verse
Sentimental novel
Socialist realism

LITERATURE TERMS (CONTINUED)

17 letters:
Interior monologue
Literary criticism
Post-structuralism

Restoration comedy

19 letters:
Cultural materialism

21 letters:
Signifier and signified
Stream of consciousness

LITERARY CHARACTERS

Character	Book	Author
Captain Ahab	Moby Dick	Herman Melville
Aladdin	The Arabian Nights' Entertainments	Traditional
Alice	Alice's Adventures in Wonderland, Through the Looking-Glass	Lewis Carroll
Bridget Allworthy	Tom Jones	Henry Fielding
Squire Allworthy	Tom Jones	Henry Fielding
Blanch Amory	Pendennis	William Makepeace Thackeray
Harry Angstrom	Rabbit, Run et al.	John Updike
Artful Dodger	Oliver Twist	Charles Dickens
Jack Aubrey	Master and Commander et al.	Patrick O'Brian
Aunt Polly	Tom Sawyer	Mark Twain
Joe Bagstock	Dombey and Son	Charles Dickens
David Balfour	Kidnapped, Catriona	Robert Louis Stevenson
Mrs. Bardell	The Pickwick Papers	Charles Dickens
Barkis	David Copperfield	Charles Dickens
Jake Barnes	The Sun Also Rises	Ernest Hemingway
Adam Bede	Adam Bede	George Eliot
Seth Bede	Adam Bede	George Eliot
Laura Bell	Pendennis	William Makepeace Thackeray
Elizabeth Bennet	Pride and Prejudice	Jane Austen
Jane Bennet	Pride and Prejudice	Jane Austen
Kitty Bennet	Pride and Prejudice	Jane Austen
Lydia Bennet	Pride and Prejudice	Jane Austen
Mary Bennet	Pride and Prejudice	Jane Austen
Mr. Bennet	Pride and Prejudice	Jane Austen
Mrs. Bennet	Pride and Prejudice	Jane Austen
Edmund Bertram	Mansfield Park	Jane Austen
Julia Bertram	Mansfield Park	Jane Austen
Lady Bertram	Mansfield Park	Jane Austen

LITERARY CHARACTERS (CONTINUED)

Character	Book	Author
Maria Bertram	Mansfield Park	Jane Austen
Sir Thomas Bertram	Mansfield Park	Jane Austen
Tom Bertram	Mansfield Park	Jane Austen
Biddy	Great Expectations	Charles Dickens
Charles Bingley	Pride and Prejudice	Jane Austen
Stephen Blackpool	Hard Times	Charles Dickens
Anthony Blanche	Brideshead Revisited	Evelyn Waugh
Leopold Bloom	Ulysses	James Joyce
Molly Bloom	Ulysses	James Joyce
Mr. Boffin	Our Mutual Friend	Charles Dickens
Mrs. Boffin	Our Mutual Friend	Charles Dickens
Farmer Boldwood	Far from the Madding Crowd	Thomas Hardy
Josiah Bounderby	Hard Times	Charles Dickens
Madeline Bray	Nicholas Nickleby	Charles Dickens
Alan Breck	Kidnapped, Catriona	Robert Louis Stevenson
Sue Bridehead	Jude the Obscure	Thomas Hardy
Miss Briggs	Vanity Fair	William Makepeace Thackeray
Dorothea Brooke	Middlemarch	George Eliot
Mr. Brooke	Middlemarch	George Eliot
Mr. Brownlow	Oliver Twist	Charles Dickens
Daisy Buchanan	The Great Gatsby	F. Scott Fitzgerald
Rosa Bud	Edwin Drood	Charles Dickens
Billy Budd	Billy Budd, Foretopman	Herman Melville
Mr. Bulstrode	Middlemarch	George Eliot
Bumble	Oliver Twist	Charles Dickens
Mrs. Cadwallader	Middlemarch	George Eliot
Carker	Dombey and Son	Charles Dickens
Richard Carstone	Bleak House	Charles Dickens
Sydney Carton	A Tale of Two Cities	Charles Dickens
Mr. Casaubon	Middlemarch	George Eliot
Casby	Little Dorrit	Charles Dickens
Flora Casby	Little Dorrit	Charles Dickens
Dunstan Cass	Silas Marner	George Eliot
Godfrey Cass	Silas Marner	George Eliot
Lady Castlewood	Henry Esmond	William Makepeace Thackeray
Lord Castlewood	Henry Esmond	William Makepeace Thackeray
Holden Caulfield	The Catcher in the Rye	J. D. Salinger

LITERARY CHARACTERS (CONTINUED)

Character	Book	Author
Chadband	Bleak House	Charles Dickens
Constance Chatterley	Lady Chatterley's Lover	D. H. Lawrence
The Cheeryble Brothers	Nicholas Nickleby	Charles Dickens
Edward Chester	Barnaby Rudge	Charles Dickens
Sir James Chettam	Middlemarch	George Eliot
Chuffey	Martin Chuzzlewit	Charles Dickens
Frank Churchill	Emma	Jane Austen
Jonas Chuzzlewit	Martin Chuzzlewit	Charles Dickens
Martin Chuzzlewit	Martin Chuzzlewit	Charles Dickens
Ada Clare	Bleak House	Charles Dickens
Angel Clare	Tess of the D'Urbervilles	Thomas Hardy
Arthur Clennam	Little Dorrit	Charles Dickens
Humphry Clinker	Humphry Clinker	Tobias Smollett
William Collins	Pride and Prejudice	Jane Austen
Benjy Compson	The Sound and the Fury	William Faulkner
David Copperfield	David Copperfield	Charles Dickens
Emily Costigan	Pendennis	William Makepeace Thackeray
Bob Cratchit	A Christmas Carol	Charles Dickens
Henry Crawford	Mansfield Park	Jane Austen
Mary Crawford	Mansfield Park	Jane Austen
Bute Crawley	Vanity Fair	William Makepeace Thackeray
Miss Crawley	Vanity Fair	William Makepeace Thackeray
Mrs. Bute Crawley	Vanity Fair	William Makepeace Thackeray
Pitt Crawley	Vanity Fair	William Makepeace Thackeray
Rawdon Crawley	Vanity Fair	William Makepeace Thackeray
Sir Pitt Crawley	Vanity Fair	William Makepeace Thackeray
Septimus Crisparkle	Edwin Drood	Charles Dickens
Vincent Crummles	Nicholas Nickleby	Charles Dickens
Jerry Cruncher	A Tale of Two Cities	Charles Dickens
Robinson Crusoe	Robinson Crusoe	Daniel Defoe
Captain Cuttle	Dombey and Son	Charles Dickens
Sebastian Dangerfield	The Ginger Man	J. P. Donleavy
Fitzwilliam Darcy	Pride and Prejudice	Jane Austen
Charles Darnay	A Tale of Two Cities	Charles Dickens
Elinor Dashwood	Sense and Sensibility	Jane Austen

LITERARY CHARACTERS (CONTINUED)

Character	Book	Author
John Dashwood	Sense and Sensibility	Jane Austen
Margaret Dashwood	Sense and Sensibility	Jane Austen
Marianne Dashwood	Sense and Sensibility	Jane Austen
Mrs. Henry Dashwood	Sense and Sensibility	Jane Austen
Dick Datchery	Edwin Drood	Charles Dickens
Fancy Day	Under The Greenwood Tree	Thomas Hardy
Lady Catherine de Bourgh	Pride and Prejudice	Jane Austen
Stephen Dedalus	A Portrait of the Artist as a Young Man, Ulysses	James Joyce
Sir Leicester Dedlock	Bleak House	Charles Dickens
Lady Dedlock	Bleak House	Charles Dickens
Madame Defarge	A Tale of Two Cities	Charles Dickens
Dick Dewy	Under The Greenwood Tree	Thomas Hardy
Mr. Dick	David Copperfield	Charles Dickens
Jim Dixon	Lucky Jim	Kingsley Amis
William Dobbin	Vanity Fair	William Makepeace Thackeray
Mr. Dombey	Dombey and Son	Charles Dickens
Florence Dombey	Dombey and Son	Charles Dickens
Don Quixote	Don Quixote de la Mancha	Miguel de Cervantes
Arabella Donn	Jude the Obscure	Thomas Hardy
Lorna Doone	Lorna Doone	R. D. Blackmore
Amy Dorrit or Little Dorrit	Little Dorrit	Charles Dickens
Fanny Dorrit	Little Dorrit	Charles Dickens
Tip Dorrit	Little Dorrit	Charles Dickens
William Dorrit	Little Dorrit	Charles Dickens
Edwin Drood	Edwin Drood	Charles Dickens
Bentley Drummle	Great Expectations	Charles Dickens
Catriona Drummond	Catriona	Robert Louis Stevenson
Alec D'Urberville	Tess of the D'Urbervilles	Thomas Hardy
Tess Durbeyfield	Tess of the D'Urbervilles	Thomas Hardy
Catherine Earnshaw	Wuthering Heights	Emily Brontë
Hareton Earnshaw	Wuthering Heights	Emily Brontë
Hindley Earnshaw	Wuthering Heights	Emily Brontë
Anne Elliot	Persuasion	Jane Austen
Elizabeth Elliot	Persuasion	Jane Austen

Literary Characters (continued)

Character	Book	Author
Sir Walter Elliot	Persuasion	Jane Austen
Em'ly	David Copperfield	Charles Dickens
Eppie	Silas Marner	George Eliot
Esmeralda	Notre Dame de Paris	Victor Hugo
Beatrix Esmond	Henry Esmond	William Makepeace Thackeray
Henry Esmond	Henry Esmond	William Makepeace Thackeray
Estella	Great Expectations	Charles Dickens
Bathsheba Everdene	Far from the Madding Crowd	Thomas Hardy
Jane Eyre	Jane Eyre	Charlotte Brontë
Fagin	Oliver Twist	Charles Dickens
Andrew Fairservice	Rob Roy	Sir Walter Scott
Donald Farfrae	The Mayor of Casterbridge	Thomas Hardy
Jude Fawley	Jude the Obscure	Thomas Hardy
Edward Ferrars	Sense and Sensibility	Jane Austen
Huck or Huckleberry Finn	Tom Sawyer, Huckleberry Finn	Mark Twain
Miss Flite	Bleak House	Charles Dickens
Julia Flyte	Brideshead Revisited	Evelyn Waugh
Sebastian Flyte	Brideshead Revisited	Evelyn Waugh
Phileas Fogg	Around the World in Eighty Days	Jules Verne
Man Friday	Robinson Crusoe	Daniel Defoe
Sarah Gamp	Martin Chuzzlewit	Charles Dickens
Joe Gargery	Great Expectations	Charles Dickens
Jay Gatsby	The Great Gatsby	F. Scott Fitzgerald
Walter Gay	Dombey and Son	Charles Dickens
Solomon Gills	Dombey and Son	Charles Dickens
Louisa Gradgrind	Hard Times	Charles Dickens
Thomas Gradgrind	Hard Times	Charles Dickens
Tom Gradgrind	Hard Times	Charles Dickens
Mary Graham	Martin Chuzzlewit	Charles Dickens
Edith Granger	Dombey and Son	Charles Dickens
Dorian Gray	The Picture of Dorian Gray	Oscar Wilde
Mr. Grewgious	Edwin Drood	Charles Dickens
Mrs. Grundy	Speed the Plough	T. Morton
Ben Gunn	Treasure Island	Robert Louis Stevenson
Chris Guthrie	Sunset Song et al.	Lewis Grassic Gibbon

LITERARY CHARACTERS (CONTINUED)

Character	Book	Author
Ham	David Copperfield	Charles Dickens
Richard Hannay	The Thirty-nine Steps et al.	John Buchan
Emma Haredale	Barnaby Rudge	Charles Dickens
John Harmon	Our Mutual Friend	Charles Dickens
James Harthouse	Hard Times	Charles Dickens
Miss Havisham	Great Expectations	Charles Dickens
Sir Mulberry Hawk	Nicholas Nickleby	Charles Dickens
Jim Hawkins	Treasure Island	Robert Louis Stevenson
Bradley Headstone	Our Mutual Friend	Charles Dickens
Heathcliff	Wuthering Heights	Emily Brontë
Uriah Heep	David Copperfield	Charles Dickens
Michael Henchard	The Mayor of Casterbridge	Thomas Hardy
Lizzy Hexam	Our Mutual Friend	Charles Dickens
Betty Higden	Our Mutual Friend	Charles Dickens
Sherlock Holmes	The Adventures of Sherlock Holmes et al.	Sir Arthur Conan Doyle
Humbert Humbert	Lolita	Vladimir Nabokov
Mr. Hyde	The Strange Case of Dr. Jekyll and Mr. Hyde	Robert Louis Stevenson
Injun Joe	Tom Sawyer	Mark Twain
Ishmael	Moby Dick	Herman Melville
Jaggers	Great Expectations	Charles Dickens
John Jarndyce	Bleak House	Charles Dickens
Bailie Nicol Jarvie	Rob Roy	Sir Walter Scott
John Jasper	Edwin Drood	Charles Dickens
Jeeves	My Man Jeeves et al.	P. G. Wodehouse
Dr. Jekyll	The Strange Case of Dr. Jekyll and Mr. Hyde	Robert Louis Stevenson
Mrs. Jellyby	Bleak House	Charles Dickens
Mrs. Jennings	Sense and Sensibility	Jane Austen
Jim	Huckleberry Finn	Mark Twain
Lord Jim	Lord Jim	Joseph Conrad
Jingle	The Pickwick Papers	Charles Dickens
Jo	Bleak House	Charles Dickens
Cissy Jupe	Hard Times	Charles Dickens
Joseph K.	The Trial	Franz Kafka
George Knightley	Emma	Jane Austen
Krook	Bleak House	Charles Dickens
Kurtz	Heart of Darkness	Joseph Conrad
Will Ladislaw	Middlemarch	George Eliot

LITERARY CHARACTERS (CONTINUED)

Character	Book	Author
Helena Landless	Edwin Drood	Charles Dickens
Neville Landless	Edwin Drood	Charles Dickens
Edgar Linton	Wuthering Heights	Emily Brontë
Isabella Linton	Wuthering Heights	Emily Brontë
Dr. Livesey	Treasure Island	Robert Louis Stevenson
Tertius Lydgate	Middlemarch	George Eliot
Rob Roy Macgregor	Rob Roy	Sir Walter Scott
Randle P. McMurphy	One Flew Over the Cuckoo's Nest	Ken Kesey
Abel Magwitch	Great Expectations	Charles Dickens
Dr. Manette	A Tale of Two Cities	Charles Dickens
Lucie Manette	A Tale of Two Cities	Charles Dickens
Madame Mantalini	Nicholas Nickleby	Charles Dickens
The Marchioness	The Old Curiosity Shop	Charles Dickens
Jacob Marley	A Christmas Carol	Charles Dickens
Philip Marlowe	The Big Sleep et al.	Raymond Chandler
Silas Marner	Silas Marner	George Eliot
Stephen Maturin	Master and Commander et al.	Patrick O'Brian
Oliver Mellors	Lady Chatterley's Lover	D. H. Lawrence
Merdle	Little Dorrit	Charles Dickens
Mrs. Merdle	Little Dorrit	Charles Dickens
Wilkins Micawber	David Copperfield	Charles Dickens
Walter Mitty	The Secret Life of Walter Mitty	James Thurber
Lord Mohun	Henry Esmond	William Makepeace Thackeray
Monks	Oliver Twist	Charles Dickens
Dean Moriarty	On the Road	Jack Kerouac
Professor Moriarty	The Adventures of Sherlock Holmes et al.	Sir Arthur Conan Doyle
Dinah Morris	Adam Bede	George Eliot
Murdstone	David Copperfield	Charles Dickens
Mrs. Grundy	Hard Times	Charles Dickens
Baron Münchhausen	Münchhausen, Baron, Narrative of His Marvellous Travels	R. E. Raspe
Nancy	Oliver Twist	Charles Dickens
Little Nell	The Old Curiosity Shop	Charles Dickens
Captain Nemo	Twenty Thousand Leagues under the Sea	Jules Verne

LITERARY CHARACTERS (CONTINUED)

Character	Book	Author
Kate Nickleby	Nicholas Nickleby	Charles Dickens
Nicholas Nickleby	Nicholas Nickleby	Charles Dickens
Ralph Nickleby	Nicholas Nickleby	Charles Dickens
Newman Noggs	Nicholas Nickleby	Charles Dickens
Susan Nipper	Dombey and Son	Charles Dickens
Kit Nubbles	The Old Curiosity Shop	Charles Dickens
Gabriel Oak	Far from the Madding Crowd	Thomas Hardy
Glorvina O'Dowd	Vanity Fair	William Makepeace Thackeray
Major O'Dowd	Vanity Fair	William Makepeace Thackeray
Mrs. O'Dowd	Vanity Fair	William Makepeace Thackeray
Francis Osbaldistone	Rob Roy	Sir Walter Scott
Rashleigh Osbaldistone	Rob Roy	Sir Walter Scott
George Osborne	Vanity Fair	William Makepeace Thackeray
Pancks	Little Dorrit	Charles Dickens
Sancho Panza	Don Quixote de la Mancha	Miguel de Cervantes
Sal Paradise	On the Road	Jack Kerouac
Passepartout	Around the World in Eighty Days	Jules Verne
Pecksniff	Martin Chuzzlewit	Charles Dickens
Charity Pecksniff	Martin Chuzzlewit	Charles Dickens
Mercy Pecksniff	Martin Chuzzlewit	Charles Dickens
Peggoty	David Copperfield	Charles Dickens
Arthur Pendennis	Pendennis	William Makepeace Thackeray
Helen Pendennis	Pendennis	William Makepeace Thackeray
Pew	Treasure Island	Robert Louis Stevenson
Samuel Pickwick	The Pickwick Papers	Charles Dickens
Ruth Pinch	Martin Chuzzlewit	Charles Dickens
Tom Pinch	Martin Chuzzlewit	Charles Dickens
Pip or Philip Pirrip	Great Expectations	Charles Dickens
Herbert Pocket	Great Expectations	Charles Dickens
Charles Pooter	The Diary of a Nobody	G. and W. Grossmith
Martin Poyser	Adam Bede	George Eliot
Mrs. Poyser	Adam Bede	George Eliot
Fanny Price	Mansfield Park	Jane Austen

LITERARY CHARACTERS (CONTINUED)

Character	Book	Author
J. Alfred Prufrock	Prufrock and Other Observations	T. S. Eliot
Pumblechook	Great Expectations	Charles Dickens
Quasimodo	Notre Dame de Paris	Victor Hugo
Queequeg	Moby Dick	Herman Melville
Daniel Quilp	The Old Curiosity Shop	Charles Dickens
Roderick Random	Roderick Random	Tobias Smollett
Riah	Our Mutual Friend	Charles Dickens
Rogue Riderhood	Our Mutual Friend	Charles Dickens
Fanny Robin	Far from the Madding Crowd	Thomas Hardy
Mr. Rochester	Jane Eyre	Charlotte Brontë
Barnaby Rudge	Barnaby Rudge	Charles Dickens
Lady Russell	Persuasion	Jane Austen
Charles Ryder	Brideshead Revisited	Evelyn Waugh
Tom Sawyer	Tom Sawyer	Mark Twain
Scrooge	A Christmas Carol	Charles Dickens
Amelia Sedley	Vanity Fair	William Makepeace Thackeray
Jos Sedley	Vanity Fair	William Makepeace Thackeray
Tristram Shandy	The Life and Opinions of Tristram Shandy	Laurence Sterne
Becky or Rebecca Sharp	Vanity Fair	William Makepeace Thackeray
Bill Sikes	Oliver Twist	Charles Dickens
Long John Silver	Treasure Island	Robert Louis Stevenson
Harold Skimpole	Bleak House	Charles Dickens
Sleary	Hard Times	Charles Dickens
Smike	Nicholas Nickleby	Charles Dickens
Harriet Smith	Emma	Jane Austen
Winston Smith	1984	George Orwell
Augustus Snodgrass	The Pickwick Papers	Charles Dickens
Hetty Sorrel	Adam Bede	George Eliot
Lady Southdown	Vanity Fair	William Makepeace Thackeray
Mrs. Sparsit	Hard Times	Charles Dickens
Dora Spenlow	David Copperfield	Charles Dickens
Wackford Squeers	Nicholas Nickleby	Charles Dickens
Starbuck	Moby Dick	Herman Melville
Lucy Steele	Sense and Sensibility	Jane Austen
James Steerforth	David Copperfield	Charles Dickens

LITERARY CHARACTERS (CONTINUED)

Character	Book	Author
Lord Steyne	Vanity Fair	William Makepeace Thackeray
Esther Summerson	Bleak House	Charles Dickens
Dick Swiveller	The Old Curiosity Shop	Charles Dickens
Mark Tapley	Martin Chuzzlewit	Charles Dickens
Tartuffe	Tartuffe	Molière
Mr. Tartar	Edwin Drood	Charles Dickens
Tarzan	Tarzan of the Apes	Edgar Rice Burroughs
Becky Thatcher	Tom Sawyer	Mark Twain
Montague Tigg	Martin Chuzzlewit	Charles Dickens
Tiny Tim	A Christmas Carol	Charles Dickens
Mrs. Todgers	Martin Chuzzlewit	Charles Dickens
Toots	Dombey and Son	Charles Dickens
Traddles	David Copperfield	Charles Dickens
Squire Trelawney	Treasure Island	Robert Louis Stevenson
Fred Trent	The Old Curiosity Shop	Charles Dickens
Job Trotter	The Pickwick Papers	Charles Dickens
Betsey Trotwood	David Copperfield	Charles Dickens
Sergeant Troy	Far from the Madding Crowd	Thomas Hardy
Tulkinghorn	Bleak House	Charles Dickens
Tracy Tupman	The Pickwick Papers	Charles Dickens
Thomas Tusher	Henry Esmond	William Makepeace Thackeray
Oliver Twist	Oliver Twist	Charles Dickens
Gabriel Varden	Barnaby Rudge	Charles Dickens
Dolly Varden	Barnaby Rudge	Charles Dickens
Mr. Veneering	Our Mutual Friend	Charles Dickens
Mrs. Veneering	Our Mutual Friend	Charles Dickens
Diggory Venn	Return of the Native	Thomas Hardy
Diana Vernon	Rob Roy	Sir Walter Scott
Rosamond Vincy	Middlemarch	George Eliot
Johann Voss	Voss	Patrick White
Eustacia Vye	Return of the Native	Thomas Hardy
George Warrington	Pendennis	William Makepeace Thackeray
Dr. Watson	The Adventures of Sherlock Holmes et al.	Sir Arthur Conan Doyle
Silas Wegg	Our Mutual Friend	Charles Dickens
Sam Weller	The Pickwick Papers	Charles Dickens
Wemmick	Great Expectations	Charles Dickens
Frank Wentworth	Persuasion	Jane Austen

LITERARY CHARACTERS (CONTINUED)

Character	Book	Author
Agnes Wickfield	David Copperfield	Charles Dickens
George Wickham	Pride and Prejudice	Jane Austen
Damon Wildeve	Return of the Native	Thomas Hardy
Bella Wilfer	Our Mutual Friend	Charles Dickens
John Willoughby	Sense and Sensibility	Jane Austen
Nathaniel Winkle	The Pickwick Papers	Charles Dickens
Dolly Winthrop	Silas Marner	George Eliot
Allan Woodcourt	Bleak House	Charles Dickens
Emma Woodhouse	Emma	Jane Austen
Mr. Woodhouse	Emma	Jane Austen
Bertie Wooster	My Man Jeeves et al.	P. G. Wodehouse
Eugene Wrayburn	Our Mutual Friend	Charles Dickens
Jenny Wren	Our Mutual Friend	Charles Dickens
Clym Yeobright	Return of the Native	Thomas Hardy
Thomasin Yeobright	Return of the Native	Thomas Hardy
Yossarian	Catch-22	Joseph Heller
Yuri Zhivago	Doctor Zhivago	Boris Pasternak
Zorba or Alexis Zorbas	Zorba the Greek	Nikos Kazantzakis

See also:
➤ **Diarists** ➤ **Dramatists** ➤ **Musketeers** ➤ **Novelists** ➤ **Poetry**
➤ **Shakespeare** ➤ **Works of literature and music** ➤ **Writers**

Lizards

3 letters:
Eft
Jew

4 letters:
Abas
Gila
Newt
Sand
Tegu
Wall
Worm

5 letters:
Agama
Anole
Draco
Gecko

Guana
Skink
Snake
Tokay
Varan

6 letters:
Anguis
Goanna
Horned
Iguana
Komodo
Leguan
Moloch
Worral
Worrel

7 letters:
Bearded
Frilled
Geckone
Lacerta
Leguaan
Monitor
Perenty
Stellio
Tuatara
Tuatera
Zandoli

8 letters:
Basilisk
Dinosaur
Hatteria
Menopome

Mosasaur
Perentie
Stellion
Sungazer
Teguexin
Whiptail

9 letters:
Blindworm

Chameleon
Galliwasp
Mastigure

10 letters:
Chuckwalla
Glass snake
Hellbender
Kabaragoya

Mosasaurus

11 letters:
Amphisboena
Blue-tongued
Brontosurus

12 letters:
Komodo dragon

Famous locomotives

7 letters:
Mallard

9 letters:
Blue Peter
Britannia
City Class
Hall Class
King Class

10 letters:
Black Class

The General

11 letters:
Golden Arrow
West Country

12 letters:
General Stamp
Merchant Navy
Schools Class

14 letters:
Flying Scotsman

15 letters:
Coronation Class
Midland Compound

16 letters:
Duke of Gloucester

19 letters:
Thomas the Tank Engine

Boroughs of London

5 letters:
Brent

6 letters:
Barnet
Bexley
Camden
Ealing
Harrow
Merton
Newham
Sutton

7 letters:
Bromley
Croydon
Enfield
Hackney

Lambeth

8 letters:
Haringey
Havering
Hounslow
Kingston
Lewisham
Richmond

9 letters:
Greenwich
Islington
Redbridge
Southwark

10 letters:
Hillingdon

Wandsworth

11 letters:
Westminster

12 letters:
Tower Hamlets

13 letters:
Waltham Forest

18 letters:
Barking and Dagenham

20 letters:
Hammersmith and
  Fulham
Kensington and Chelsea

455

Famous lovers

Famous lovers

Antony and Cleopatra
Bonnie (Parker) and Clyde (Barrow)
Richard Burton and Elizabeth Taylor
Julius Caesar and Cleopatra
Casanova
Cathy and Heathcliffe
Dante and Beatrice
Darby and Joan
Dido and Aeneas
Don Juan
Edward VIII and Wallis Simpson
Eloise and Abelard
Harlequin and Columbine
Hero and Leander
Jane Eyre and Edward Rochester
Lancelot and Guinevere
Lochinvar and Ellen

Napoleon and Josephine
Scarlett O'Hara and Rhett Butler
Orpheus and Eurydice
Paris and Helen of Troy
Pelleas and Melisande
Petrarch and Laura
Porgy and Bess
Pyramus and Thisbe
Robin Hood and Maid Marian
Romeo and Juliet
Rosalind and Orlando
Samson and Delilah
Tosca and Cavarodossi
Tristan and Isolde
Troilus and Cressida
Zeus and Hera

M m

Extinct mammals

6 letters:
Apeman
Quagga
Tarpan

7 letters:
Aurochs
Mammoth

8 letters:
Creodont
Eohippus
Irish elk
Mastodon

9 letters:
Dinoceras
Dinothere
Megathere

10 letters:
Glyptodont
Uintathere

11 letters:
Nototherium
Titanothere

12 letters:
Chalicothere

13 letters:
Dryopithecine

14 letters:
Baluchitherium
Labyrinthodont

15 letters:
Sabre-toothed cat

17 letters:
Australopithecine
Sabre-toothed tiger

See also:
➤ **Anteaters and other edentates** ➤ **Antelopes** ➤ **Bats** ➤ **Carnivores**
➤ **Breeds of cat** ➤ **Cattle** ➤ **Cows** ➤ **Breeds of dog** ➤ **Horses** ➤ **Marsupials**
➤ **Monkeys, apes and other primates** ➤ **Breeds of pig** ➤ **Rabbits and**
hares ➤ **Rodents** ➤ **Seals** ➤ **Sea mammals** ➤ **Breeds of sheep** ➤ **Shrews**
and other insectivores ➤ **Whales and dolphins**

Types of mania

Mania	Object
Ablutomania	Washing
Agoramania	Open spaces
Ailuromania	Cats
Andromania	Men
Anglomania	England
Anthomania	Flowers
Apimania	Bees
Arithmomania	Counting
Automania	Solitude
Autophonomania	Suicide
Balletomania	Ballet
Ballistomania	Bullets
Bibliomania	Books

Mania	Object
Chionomania	Snow
Choreomania	Dancing
Chrematomania	Money
Cremnomania	Cliffs
Cynomania	Dogs
Dipsomania	Alcohol
Doramania	Fur
Dromomania	Travelling
Egomania	Your self
Eleuthromania	Freedom
Entheomania	Religion
Entomomania	Insects
Ergasiomania	Work
Eroticomania	Erotica
Erotomania	Sex
Florimania	Plants
Gamomania	Marriage
Graphomania	Writing
Gymnomania	Nakedness
Gynomania	Women
Hamartiomania	Sin
Hedonomania	Pleasure
Heliomania	Sun
Hippomania	Horses
Homicidomania	Murder
Hydromania	Water
Hylomania	Woods
Hypnomania	Sleep
Ichthyomania	Fish
Iconomania	Icons
Kinesomania	Movement
Kleptomania	Stealing
Logomania	Talking
Macromania	Becoming larger
Megalomania	Your own importance
Melomania	Music
Mentulomania	Penises
Micromania	Becoming smaller
Monomania	One thing
Musicomania	Music
Musomania	Mice
Mythomania	Lies
Necromania	Death

Mania	Object
Noctimania	Night
Nudomania	Nudity
Nymphomania	Sex
Ochlomania	Crowds
Oikomania	Home
Oinomania	Wine
Ophidiomania	Reptiles
Orchidomania	Testicles
Ornithomania	Birds
Phagomania	Eating
Pharmacomania	Medicines
Phonomania	Noise
Photomania	Light
Plutomania	Great wealth
Potomania	Drinking
Pyromania	Fire
Scribomania	Writing
Siderodromomania	Railway travel
Sitomania	Food
Sophomania	Your own wisdom
Thalassomania	The sea
Thanatomania	Death
Theatromania	Theatre
Timbromania	Stamps
Trichomania	Hair
Verbomania	Words
Xenomania	Foreigners
Zoomania	Animals

Marsupials

3 letters:
Roo

4 letters:
Dama
Marl
Tait
Tuan
Uroo

5 letters:
Bilby
Damar

Koala
Mardo
Marlu
Pongo
Quoll
Tungo
Yapok

6 letters:
Badger
Bobuck
Boodie

Cuscus
Glider
Jerboa
Kowari
Merrin
Mongan
Numbat
Possum
Quenda
Quokka
Tammar
Toolah

Tungoo
Warabi
Wogoit
Wombat
Woylie
Yapock

7 letters:
Bettong
Biggada
Dalgite
Dalgyte
Dasyure
Dibbler
Dunnart
Kultarr
Mulgara
Munning
Ningaui
Opossum
Potoroo
Wallaby
Wild cat
Wurrung
Yallara

8 letters:
Boongary
Burramys
Dasyurid
Duckbill
Forester
Kangaroo
Karrabul
Macropod
Platypus
Ringtail
Squeaker
Tiger cat
Toolache
Wallaroo
Wintarro
Wuhl-wuhl

9 letters:
Bandicoot
Boodie rat
Didelphia
Koala bear
Larapinta

Native cat
Pademelon
Petaurist
Phalanger
Thylacine
Wambenger

10 letters:
Antechinus
Diprotodon
Honey mouse
Native bear
Noolbenger
Notoryctes
Paddymelon
Phascogale
Red wallaby
Rock possum
Satanellus

11 letters:
Diprotodont
Fairy possum
Flying mouse
Hare-wallaby
Honey possum
Nototherium
Pygmy glider
Pygmy possum
Rat kangaroo
Red kangaroo
Rock wallaby
Sugar glider
Tcharibeena

12 letters:
Agile wallaby
Black wallaby
Fluffy glider
Grey forester
Marsupial cat
Parma wallaby
Pitchi-pitchi
River wallaby
Sandy wallaby
Scrub wallaby
Swamp wallaby
Tree kangaroo

13 letters:
Brush kangaroo
Feather glider
Marsupial mole
Rufous wallaby
Sooty kangaroo
Striped possum
Tasmanian wolf
Ursine dasyure

14 letters:
Banded anteater
Brown bandicoot
Flying squirrel
Forest kangaroo
Gunn's bandicoot
Jerboa kangaroo
Jungle kangaroo
Mallee kangaroo
Marsupial mouse
Mountain possum
Plains kangaroo
Ringtail possum
Squirrel glider
Tasmanian devil
Tasmanian tiger

15 letters:
Barred bandicoot
Bennett's wallaby
Brush-tail possum
Desert bandicoot
Flying phalanger
Golden bandicoot
Naked-nose wombat
Rabbit bandicoot
Whiptail wallaby

16 letters:
Antelope kangaroo
Hairy-nosed wombat
Musky rat-kangaroo
Red-necked wallaby
Ringtailed possum
Spotted native cat

17 letters:
Antilopine wallaby
Brindled bandicoot
Brush-tailed possum

Cannings' little dog
Desert-rat kangaroo
Great grey kangaroo
Grey's brush wallaby
Leadbeater's possum
Northern native cat
Pretty-face wallaby
Rufous rat-kangaroo

18 letters:
Black-faced kangaroo
Black-tailed wallaby
Brush-tailed bettong
Brush-tailed wallaby
Duck-billed platypus
Jerboa pouched mouse
Long-eared bandicoot
Long-nosed bandicoot
Pig-footed bandicoot

19 letters:
Darling Downs dunnart
Eastern brush wallaby
Eastern grey kangaroo
Green ringtail possum
Lesueur's rat-kangaroo

Mountain pygmy
   possum
Short-eared bandicoot
Short-nosed bandicoot
Western grey kangaroo
Yellow-bellied glider

20 letters:
Bennett's tree kangaroo
Burrowing rat-kangaroo
Rabbit-eared bandicoot

21 letters:
Lumholtz's tree
   kangaroo
Ring-tailed rock wallaby
Short-nosed rat
   kangaroo

22 letters:
Bridled nail-tail wallaby
Lemuroid ringtail
   possum
Northern brown
   bandicoot

Southern brown
   bandicoot
Yellow-footed
   antechinus

23 letters:
Crescent nail-tail
   wallaby
Mountain brushtail
   possum
Northern nail-tail
   wallaby
Yellow-footed rock
   wallaby

24 letters:
Tasmanian barred
   bandicoot

25 letters:
Crest-tailed marsupial
   mouse

26 letters:
Herbert River ringtail
   possum

Martial arts

MARTIAL ARTS

4 letters:
Judo
Sumo

5 letters:
Iai-do
Kendo
Kyudo

6 letters:
Aikido
Karate
Kung fu
Tukido®

7 letters:
Hapkido
Ju jitsu

Ju-jutsu

8 letters:
Capoeira
Iai-jutsu
Jiu jitsu
Karate-do
Muay Thai
Ninjitsu
Ninjutsu
Wing Chun

9 letters:
Tae kwon-do
Yari-jutsu

10 letters:
Jeet Kune Do

Kick boxing
Naginata-do
Thai boxing

11 letters:
Tai chi chuan

12 letters:
Tai chi qi gong
Tomiki aikido

13 letters:
Goju Kai karate
Goju Ryu karate
Hung Gar kung fu
Sumo wrestling
Wado Ryu karate

MARTIAL ARTS (CONTINUED)

14 letters:
Ishin Ryu karate
Sankukai karate
Shito Ryu karate
Shotokai karate
Shotokan karate
Shukokai karate
Wing Tsun kung fu

16 letters:
Crane style kung fu
Ta Sheng Men kung fu
Tiger style kung fu

17 letters:
Monkey style kung fu

18 letters:
Kyokushinkai karate

24 letters:
Praying Mantis style
 kung fu

MARTIAL ARTS TERMS

Term	Meaning
Basho	Sumo turnament
Bo	Staff
Bogu	Kendo armour
Bokuto	Kendo wooden sword
Budo *or* bushido	Warrior's way
Dan	Black belt grade
Do	Kendo breastplate
-do	The way
Dohyo	Sumo ring
Dojo	Practice room or mat
Gi	Suit
Hachimaki *or* tenugui	Kendo headcloth
Hakama	Divided skirt
Ippon	One competition point
Jiu-kumite	Freestyle karate competition
-jutsu	Fighting art
-ka	Student
Kama	Hand sickle
Kata	Sequence of techniques
Katana	Kendo sword
Katsu	Resuscitation techniques
Keikogi	Kendo jacket
Kesho-mawashi	Embroidered sumo apron
Ki, chi *or* qi	Inner power
Kiai	Yell accompanying movement
Kihon	Repetition of techniques
Kote	Kendo gauntlets
Kyu	Student grade
Makiwara	Practice block
Mawashi	Sumo fighting belt
Men	Kendo mask

MARTIAL ARTS TERMS (CONTINUED)

Term	Meaning
Nage-waza *or* tachi-waza	Ju jitsu competition
Naginata	Curved-blade spear
Ne-waza	Ju jitsu competition
Ninin-dori	Aikido competition
Ninja	Japanese trained assassin
Nunchaku	Hinged flails
Obi	Coloured belt
Ozeki	Sumo champion
Qi gong	Breath control
Randori kyoghi	Aikido competition
Rikishi	Sumo wrestler
Rokushakubo	Six-foot staff
Ryu	Martial arts school
Sai	Short trident
Samurai	Japanese warrior caste
Sensei	Teacher
Shinai	Kendo bamboo sword
Sifu	Teacher
Suneate	Naginata shin guards
Tanto randori	Aikido competition
Tare	Kendo apron
Te	Hand fighting
Ton-fa *or* tui-fa	Hardwood weapon
Tsuna	Sumo grand champion's belt
Waza-ari	Half competition point
Yari	Spear
Yokozuna	Sumo grand champion
Zanshin	Total awareness

Materials

3 letters:
Say

4 letters:
Lamé
Lawn
Tape
Wool

5 letters:
Crash

Toile
Twill

6 letters:
Canvas
Cermet
Coburg
Dimity
Russel
Soneri

Tusser

7 letters:
Batiste
Cambric
Ceramic
Chiffon
Galatea
Genappe
Hessian

Oilskin
Sagathy

Toilinet

Swansdown
Tarpaulin
Towelling
Worcester

8 letters:
Cretonne
Gossamer
Homespun
Illusion
Jeanette
Marocain
Moquette
Prunella

9 letters:
Calamanco
Cellulose
Charmeuse®
Fibrefill
Gaberdine
Macintosh
Pina-cloth
Polyester
Sackcloth

10 letters:
Fibreglass
Toilinette
Winceyette

12 letters:
Stockingette

Mathematics

BRANCHES OF MATHEMATICS

4 letters:
Pure

6 letters:
Conics

7 letters:
Algebra
Applied

8 letters:
Analysis
Calculus
Geometry
Topology

9 letters:
Set theory

10 letters:
Arithmetic
Game theory
Nomography
Statistics

11 letters:
Group theory

12 letters:
Number theory
Trigonometry

13 letters:
Chaos geometry

14 letters:
Boolean algebra

16 letters:
Integral calculus

17 letters:
Euclidean geometry
Numerical analysis
Probability theory

18 letters:
Analytical geometry
Coordinate geometry

20 letters:
Differential calculus
Non-Euclidean
  geometry

MATHEMATICAL TERMS

2 letters:
Pi

3 letters:
Arc
Log
Odd
Set
Sum

4 letters:
Area
Axis
Base
Cone
Cube
Cusp
Even
Mean
Mode
Node

Plus
Root
Sine
Surd
Zero

5 letters:
Angle
Chord
Curve
Digit

Mathematical Terms (continued)

Graph
Helix
Index
Locus
Minus
Power
Prism
Proof
Ratio
Solid
Torus
Union
Value
X-axis
Y-axis
Z-axis

6 letters:
Binary
Circle
Cosine
Cuboid
Denary
Equals
Factor
Matrix
Median
Number
Oblong
Origin
Radian
Radius
Scalar
Secant
Sector
Sphere
Square
Subset
Vector
Volume

7 letters:
Average
Decagon
Decimal
Ellipse
Formula
Hexagon

Integer
Nonagon
Octagon
Open set
Polygon
Product
Rhombus
Scalene
Tangent

8 letters:
Addition
Algorism
Binomial
Constant
Cosecant
Cube root
Cylinder
Diagonal
Diameter
Division
Equation
Fraction
Function
Heptagon
Infinity
Integral
Operator
Parabola
Parallel
Pentagon
Quadrant
Quotient
Triangle
Variable

9 letters:
Algorithm
Closed set
Cotangent
Factorial
Frequency
Hyperbola
Isosceles
Logarithm
Numerator
Operation
Rectangle

Remainder
Slide rule
Trapezium

10 letters:
Acute angle
Concentric
Co-ordinate
Hemisphere
Hypotenuse
Octahedron
Percentage
Polyhedron
Polynomial
Real number
Reciprocal
Right angle
Semicircle
Square root

11 letters:
Coefficient
Denominator
Equilateral
Exponential
Icosahedron
Obtuse angle
Prime number
Probability
Reflex angle
Subtraction
Tetrahedron
Venn diagram

12 letters:
Common factor
Dodecahedron
Intersection
Universal set

13 letters:
Circumference
Complex number
Mandelbrot set
Natural number
Ordinal number
Parallelogram
Perfect number
Quadrilateral

MATHEMATICAL TERMS (CONTINUED)

14 letters:
Cardinal number
Multiplication
Proper fraction
Rational number
Vulgar fraction

15 letters:
Imaginary number

16 letters:
Improper fraction
Irrational number
Natural logarithm

Recurring decimal
Strange attractor

17 letters:
Common denominator
Pythagoras' theorem
Quadratic equation

18 letters:
Significant figures

19 letters:
Right-angled triangle

20 letters:
Cartesian coordinates
Lowest common
  multiple

21 letters:
Simultaneous equations

23 letters:
Lowest common
  denominator

MATHEMATICIANS

3 letters:
Dee, *John*
Lie, *Marius Sophus*

4 letters:
Hero
Kahn, *Herman*
Weyl, *Hermann*
Zeno (*of Elea*)

5 letters:
Aiken, *Howard
  Hathaway*
Bondi, *Hermann*
Boole, *George*
Comte, *Isidore Auguste*
Euler, *Leonhard*
Gauss, *Karl Friedrich*
Gibbs, *Josiah Willard*
Gödel, *Kurt*

6 letters:
Agnesi, *Maria Gaetana*
Ampère, *André Marie*
Balmer, *Johann Jakob*
Bessel, *Friedrich Wilhelm*
Briggs, *Henry*
Cantor, *Georg*
Cauchy, *Augustin Louis*
Cayley, *Arthur*
Cocker, *Edward*

Darwin, *George Howard*
Euclid
Fermat, *Pierre De*
Gunter, *Edmund*
Halley, *Edmund*
Jacobi, *Karl Gustav Jacob*
Napier, *John*
Newton, *Isaac*
Pappus *of Alexandria*
Pascal, *Blaise*
Peirce, *Charles Sanders*
Penney, *William George*
Taylor, *Brook*
Thales
Turing, *Alan Mathison*
Wiener, *Norbert*

7 letters:
Babbage, *Charles*
D'Oresme, *Nicole*
Eudoxus *of Cnidus*
Fourier, *Jean Baptiste
  Joseph*
Galileo
Hawking, *Stephen
  William*
Hilbert, *David*
Khayyám, *Omar*
Laplace, *Pierre Simon*
Leibniz
Pearson, *Karl*

Penrose, *Roger*
Poisson, *Siméon Denis*
Ptolemy
Pytheas
Riemann, *Georg
  Friedrich Bernhard*
Russell, *Bertrand*
Shannon, *Claude*

8 letters:
Archytas
Clausius, *Rudolf Julius*
Dedekind, *Julius Wilhelm
  Richard*
De Fermat, *Pierre*
Einstein, *Albert*
Goldbach, *Christian*
Hamilton, *William
  Rowan*
Lagrange, *Joseph Louis*
Legendre, *Adrien Marie*
Lovelace, *Ada*
Mercator, *Gerardus*
Playfair, *John*
Poincaré, *Jules Henri*

9 letters:
Bernoulli, *Daniel*
Bernoulli, *Jacques*
Bernoulli, *Jean*
Descartes, *René*

MATHEMATICIANS (CONTINUED)

Dirichlet, *Peter Gustav Lejeune*
Dunstable, *John*
Fibonacci, *Leonardo*
Minkowski, *Hermann*
Whitehead, *Alfred North*

10 letters:
Apollonius *of Perga*
Archimedes
Diophantus

Kolmogorov, *Andrei Nikolaevich*
Pythagoras
Torricelli, *Evangelista*
Von Neumann, *John*

11 letters:
Anaximander
Lobachevsky, *Nikolai Ivanovich*
Von Leibnitz, *Gottfried Wilhelm*

12 letters:
De Maupertuis, *Pierre Louis Moreau*
Eratosthenes

13 letters:
Regiomontanus, *Johann Müller*

14 letters:
Le Rond Alembert, *Jean*

Types of meal

3 letters:
Tea

5 letters:
Feast
Lunch
Snack
Tapas

6 letters:
Barbie
Brunch
Buffet

Dinner
Picnic
Supper
Tiffin

7 letters:
Banquet
Fish fry
High tea

8 letters:
Barbecue
Cream tea

Luncheon

9 letters:
Beanfeast
Breakfast
Elevenses

11 letters:
Smorgasbord

12 letters:
Afternoon tea

Types and cuts of meat

3 letters:
Ham
Leg
Rib

4 letters:
Beef
Chop
Duck
Game
Hock
Hogg
Lamb
Loin
Pork

Rack
Rump
Spam®
Veal

5 letters:
Bacon
Chuck
Chump
Devon
Gigot
Goose
Hough
Liver
Mince

Offal
Round
Scrag
Shank
Skirt
Steak
T-bone
Tripe

6 letters:
Breast
Collar
Cutlet
Fillet
Gammon

467

medals**Medals**

Haslet
Hogget
Kidney
Lights
Mutton
Oxtail
Pigeon
Polony
Saddle
Salami
Tongue
Turkey

7 letters:
Beef-ham
Brisket
Charqui
Chicken
Chorizo
Gristle
Numbles
Sausage
Saveloy
Sirloin
Topside
Venison

8 letters:
Bath chap
Cervelat
Chitlins
Cold cuts
Escalope

Forehock
Lamb's fry
Noisette
Oxtongue
Parma ham
Pastrami
Pemmican
Pheasant
Pope's eye
Salt pork
Shoulder
Sparerib
Undercut

9 letters:
Bockwurst
Boerewors
Bratwurst
Chipolata
Chitlings
Entrecôte
Foreshank
Pepperoni
Tournedos

10 letters:
Chuck steak
Corned beef
Crown roast
Knackwurst
Knockwurst
Liverwurst
Médaillons

Mortadella
Prosciutto
Rolled lamb
Silverside
Sweetbread
Tenderloin

11 letters:
Baron of beef
Minute steak
Parson's nose
Square slice

12 letters:
Black pudding
Chitterlings
Liver sausage
Lorne sausage
Luncheon meat
Stewing steak

13 letters:
Chateaubriand
Colonial goose
Square sausage

16 letters:
Porterhouse steak

17 letters:
Cumberland sausage

Medals

9 letters:
Iron Cross

10 letters:
Bronze Star
Silver Star

11 letters:
George Cross
Purple Heart

13 letters:
Croix de Guerre
Legion of Merit
Royal Red Cross
Victoria Cross

14 letters:
Légion d'Honneur

20 letters:
Militaire Willemsorde

25 letters:
Congressional Medal of
 Honor
Distinguished Service
 Cross
Distinguished Service
 Order

Medicine

BRANCHES OF MEDICINE

5 letters:
Legal
Space

6 letters:
Sports

7 letters:
Anatomy
Myology
Nuclear
Otology
Surgery
Urology

8 letters:
Aviation
Etiology
Forensic
Internal
Nosology
Oncology
Physical
Posology
Serology
Tocology
Tokology
Virology

9 letters:
Aetiology
Anaplasty
Andrology
Angiology
Audiology
Chiropody
Dentistry
Midwifery
Neurology
Nostology
Nutrition
Optometry
Orthotics
Osteology

Pathology
Radiology
Rhinology

10 letters:
Balneology
Cardiology
Embryology
Exodontics
Geratology
Geriatrics
Gynecology
Hematology
Immunology
Industrial
Nephrology
Obstetrics
Odontology
Orthoptics
Pediatrics
Preventive
Proctology
Psychiatry
Psychology
Toxicology
Trichology
Veterinary

11 letters:
Biomedicine
Dermatology
Diagnostics
Eccrinology
Endodontics
Gerontology
Gynaecology
Haematology
Laryngology
Neonatology
Oral hygiene
Orthodontia
Orthopedics
Osteoplasty
Paediatrics

Physiatrics
Stomatology
Syphilology
Venereology

12 letters:
Anaesthetics
Bacteriology
Epidemiology
Neuroanatomy
Neurosurgery
Orthodontics
Orthopaedics
Periodontics
Pharyngology
Rheumatology
Therapeutics

13 letters:
Dental hygiene
Dental surgery
Endocrinology
Genitourinary
Materia medica
Morbid anatomy
Ophthalmology
Physiotherapy
Speech therapy

14 letters:
Neuropathology
Otolaryngology
Plastic surgery
Psychoanalysis
Symptomatology

15 letters:
Bioastronautics
Encephalography
Immunochemistry
Neurophysiology
Neuropsychiatry

BRANCHES OF MEDICINE (CONTINUED)

16 letters:
Gastroenterology
Spare-part surgery

17 letters:
Electrophysiology
Hydrotherapeutics
Veterinary science

18 letters:
Neuroendocrinology

19 letters:
Electrotherapeutics

MEDICAL PRACTITIONERS AND SPECIALISTS

2 letters:
GP

3 letters:
Vet

5 letters:
Nurse

6 letters:
Doctor
Extern
Intern
Matron
Physio

7 letters:
Dentist
Externe
Interne
Midwife
Orderly
Surgeon

8 letters:
Houseman
Optician
Resident

9 letters:
Anatomist
Dietitian
Internist
Myologist
Orthotist
Otologist
Paramedic
Registrar
Therapist
Urologist

10 letters:
Consultant
Etiologist
Exodontist
Geriatrist
Nosologist
Oncologist
Orthoptist
Serologist
Virologist

11 letters:
Aetiologist
Andrologist
Audiologist
Chiropodist
Endodontist
Neurologist
Optometrist
Orthopedist
Osteologist
Pathologist
Radiologist
Rhinologist

12 letters:
Anaesthetist
Balneologist
Cardiologist
Embryologist
Geriatrician
Gynecologist
Hematologist
Immunologist
Junior doctor
Nephrologist
Neurosurgeon
Nutritionist
Obstetrician
Odontologist

Orthodontist
Orthopaedist
Pediatrician
Proctologist
Psychiatrist
Psychologist
Radiographer
Toxicologist
Trichologist
Veterinarian

13 letters:
Dental surgeon
Dermatologist
Diagnostician
District nurse
Gerontologist
Gynaecologist
Haematologist
Health visitor
Laryngologist
Neonatologist
Oral hygienist
Paediatrician
Psychoanalyst
Syphilologist
Venereologist

14 letters:
Bacteriologist
Barefoot doctor
Epidemiologist
House physician
Hydrotherapist
Neuroanatomist
Nursing officer
Pharyngologist
Plastic surgeon
Rheumatologist

MEDICAL PRACTITIONERS AND SPECIALISTS (CONTINUED)

15 letters:
Dental hygienist
Endocrinologist
Ophthalmologist
Physiotherapist
Speech therapist

16 letters:
Neuropathologist
Otolaryngologist

17 letters:
Forensic scientist
Neurophysiologist
Neuropsychiatrist
Veterinary surgeon

18 letters:
Gastroenterologist

19 letters:
Electrophysiologist
General practitioner

20 letters:
Laboratory technician

21 letters:
Occupational therapist

MEDICAL AND SURGICAL INSTRUMENTS AND EQUIPMENT

4 letters:
Swab

5 letters:
Clamp
Curet
Drain
Lance
Probe
Sling
Sound
Stupe

6 letters:
Bedpan
Canula
Lancet
Needle
Splint
Stylet
Suture
Trepan
Trocar

7 letters:
Bandage
Cannula
Catling
Curette
Forceps
Packing
Scalpel
Scanner
Syringe
Wet pack

8 letters:
Bistoury
Catheter
Heat lamp
Hemostat
Iron lung
Otoscope
Pulmotor®
Speculum
Trephine

9 letters:
Aspirator
CT scanner
Cymograph
Depressor
Endoscope
Fetoscope
Haemostat
Inhalator
Kymograph
Nebulizer
Pacemaker
Perimeter
Raspatory
Retractor
Rheometer
Skiascope
Stretcher

10 letters:
CAT scanner
Colposcope
Compressor
Cystoscope

Fiberscope
Fibrescope
Gonioscope
Hypodermic
Inspirator
Microscope
Orthoscope
Oxygen mask
Oxygen tent
Respirator
Rhinoscope
Spirograph
Spirometer
Tourniquet
Urinometer
Ventilator

11 letters:
Arthroscope
Cardiograph
Colonoscope
Fluoroscope
Gamma camera
Gastroscope
Laparoscope
Nephroscope
Plaster cast
Pneumograph
Proctoscope
Retinoscope
Stethoscope
Stomach pump
X-ray machine

MEDICAL AND SURGICAL INSTRUMENTS AND EQUIPMENT (CONTINUED)

12 letters:
Bronchoscope
Laryngoscope
Resuscitator
Sphygmograph
Thoracoscope
Urethroscope

13 letters:
Defibrillator
Encephalogram
Esophagoscope
Kidney machine
Pharyngoscope
Pneumatometer
Röntgenoscope

Styptic pencil

14 letters:
Oesophagoscope
Ophthalmoscope
Roentgenoscope
Specimen bottle

15 letters:
Artificial heart
Dialysis machine
Electromyograph

16 letters:
Artificial kidney
Heart-lung machine
Hypodermic needle

Sphygmomanometer

17 letters:
Hypodermic syringe
Ultrasound scanner

18 letters:
Electrocardiograph
Life-support machine

19 letters:
Clinical thermometer

21 letters:
Electroencephalograph

BRANCHES OF ALTERNATIVE MEDICINE

7 letters:
Massage
Shiatsu

8 letters:
Hypnosis

9 letters:
Herbalism
Iridology
Radionics

10 letters:
Homeopathy

Osteopathy

11 letters:
Acupressure
Acupuncture
Biofeedback
Homoeopathy
Kinesiology
Moxibustion
Naturopathy
Reflexology

12 letters:
Aromatherapy

Chiropractic
Hydrotherapy
Hypnotherapy

16 letters:
Bach flower remedy

17 letters:
Autogenic training

18 letters:
Alexander technique

PEOPLE IN MEDICINE

4 letters:
Bell, *Sir Charles*
Drew, *Charles*
Jung, *Carl*
Koch, *Robert*
Lind, *James*
Mayo, *Charles*
Reed, *Walter*
Ross, *Sir Ronald*
Salk, *Jonas E(dward)*

5 letters:
Broca, *Paul*
Bruce, *Sir David*
Cajal, *Santiago Ramon y*
Crick, *Francis*
Curie, *Marie*
Freud, *Sigmund*
Galen
Henle, *Friedrich*
Kenny, *Elizabeth*
Krebs, *Sir Edwin*

Leach, *Penelope*
Lower, *Richard*
Osler, *Sir William*
Paget, *Sir James*
Remak, *Robert*
Sharp, *Phillip*
Spock, *Benjamin*
Steno, *Nicolaus*

6 letters:
Barton, *Clara*

PEOPLE IN MEDICINE (CONTINUED)

Bichat, *Marie*
Bishop, *Michael*
Bright, *Richard*
Carrel, *Alexis*
Cavell, *Edith Louisa*
Cooper, *Sir Astley*
Cuvier, *Georges*
Fernel, *Jean*
Finsen, *Niels*
Garrod, *Sir Archibald*
Harvey, *William*
Hunter, *John*
Inglis, *Elsie*
Jenner, *Edward*
Lister, *Joseph*
Manson, *Sir Patrick*
Mesmer, *Franz Anton*
Mullis, *Kary*
Pavlov, *Ivan*
Sanger, *Margaret*
Treves, *Sir Frederick*
Varmus, *Harold*
Watson, *James*
Watson, *John*
Willis, *Thomas*

7 letters:
Addison, *Thomas*
Axelrod, *Julius*
Banting, *Sir Frederick*
Barnard, *Christiaan*
Bethune, *Henry Norman*
Burkitt, *Denis*
Cushing, *Harvey*
Ehrlich, *Paul*

Eijkman, *Christian*
Fleming, *Sir Alexander*
Gilbert, *William*
Hodgkin, *Dorothy*
Hodgkin, *Thomas*
Laennec, *Rene*
Laveran, *Charles*
Linacre, *Thomas*
MacEwen, *Sir William*
McIndoe, *Sir Archibald*
Medawar, *Sir Peter*
Nicolle, *Charles*
Pasteur, *Louis*
Röntgen, *Wilhelm Conrad*
Seacole, *Mary Jane*
Simpson, *Sir James Young*
Warburg, *Otto*
Winston, *Lord Robert*

8 letters:
Anderson, *Elizabeth Garrett*
Avicenna
Beaumont, *William*
Billroth, *Theodor*
Charnley, *Sir John*
Delbruck, *Max*
Duchenne, *Guillaume*
Dulbecco, *Renato*
Flemming, *Sir Alexander*
Geronimo
Jex-Blake, *Sophia*
Leishman, *Sir William*

Magendie, *Francois*
Malpighi, *Marcello*
Morgagni, *Giovanni*
Pattison, *Dorothy*
Stoppard, *Miriam*
Sydenham, *Thomas*
Tournier, *Paul*
Vesalius

9 letters:
Alzheimer, *Alois*
Bartholin, *Erasmus*
Blackwell, *Elizabeth*
Boerhaave, *Hermann*
Dupuytren, *Guillaume*
Dutrochet, *Henri*
Hahnemann, *Samuel*
Mackenzie, *Sir James*
Parkinson, *James*

10 letters:
Fracastoro, *Girolamo*
Greenfield, *Susan*
Langerhans, *Paul*
Paracelsus
Stephenson, *Elsie*

11 letters:
Hippocrates
Livingstone, *David*
Nightingale, *Florence*
Szent-Gyorgi, *Albert*

12 letters:
Erasistratus

Membranes

3 letters:
Haw

4 letters:
Dura

5 letters:
Exine
Mater

6 letters:
Amnion
Cornea
Extine
Intima
Intine
Meninx
Mucosa
Mucous

Pleura
Sclera
Serosa
Serous
Tympan

7 letters:
Chorion
Choroid

Decidua
Hyaloid
Periost
Putamen

8 letters:
Axilemma
Ependyma
Frenulum
Indusium
Patagium
Pericarp
Pia mater
Synovial
Tympanic
Vacuolar

9 letters:
Arachnoid
Dura mater
Endostium
Involucre
Mesentery
Tonoplast
Vitelline

10 letters:
Periosteum
Peritoneum
Sarcolemma

11 letters:
Chromoplast
Conjunctiva
Dissepiment
Endocardium

Endometrium
Mediastinum
Nictitating
Pericardium
Pericranium
Peritonaeum
Third eyelid
Trophoblast

12 letters:
Schneiderian

13 letters:
Choroid plexus
Perichondrium

15 letters:
Chorioallantois

Metals

Metal	Symbol
Actinium	Ac
Aluminium	Al
Americium	Am
Antimony	Sb
Barium	Ba
Berkelium	Bk
Beryllium	Be
Bismuth	Bi
Cadmium	Cd
Caesium *or* cesium	Cs
Calcium	Ca
Californium	Cf
Cerium	Ce
Chromium	Cr
Cobalt	Co
Copper	Cu
Curium	Cm
Dysprosium	Dy
Einsteinium	Es
Erbium	Er
Europium	Eu
Fermium	Fm

Metals

Metal	Symbol
Francium	Fr
Gadolinium	Gd
Gallium	Ga
Germanium	Ge
Gold	Au
Hafnium	Hf
Holmium	Ho
Indium	In
Iridium	Ir
Iron	Fe
Lanthanum	La
Lawrencium	Lr
Lead	Pb
Lithium	Li
Lutetium	Lu
Magnesium	Mg
Manganese	Mn
Mendelevium	Md
Mercury	Hg
Molybdenum	Mo
Neodymium	Nd
Neptunium	Np
Nickel	Ni
Niobium	Nb
Nobelium	No
Osmium	Os
Palladium	Pd
Platinum	Pt
Plutonium	Pu
Polonium	Po
Potassium	K
Praseodymium	Pr
Promethium	Pm
Protactinium	Pa
Radium	Ra
Rhenium	Re
Rhodium	Rh
Rubidium	Rb
Ruthenium	Ru
Samarium	Sm
Scandium	Sc
Silver	Ag
Sodium	Na

Metal	Symbol
Strontium	Sr
Tantalum	Ta
Technetium	Tc
Terbium	Tb
Thallium	Tl
Thorium	Th
Thulium	Tm
Tin	Sn
Titanium	Ti
Tungsten *or* wolfram	W
Uranium	U
Vanadium	V
Ytterbium	Yb
Yttrium	Y
Zinc	Zn
Zirconium	Zr

Meteor showers

6 letters:
Boötes
Cetids
Lyrids
Ursids
Velids

7 letters:
Corvids
Cygnids
Hydrids
Leonids
Librids
Mensids
Normids
Piscids
Puppids
Scutids
Taurids

8 letters:
Aquilids
Arietids
Aurigids
Cancrids
Geminids
Orionids
Pavonids
Pegasids
Perseids

9 letters:
Aquariids
Craterids
Draconids
Eridanids
Herculids
Scorpiids
Virginids

10 letters:
Centaurids
Phoenicids
Sextantids

11 letters:
Andromedids
Quadrantids
Triangulids

12 letters:
Capricornids
Monocerotids
Sagittariids
Ursa Majorids

13 letters:
Canis Minorids

14 letters:
Coma Berenicids

Military ranks

2 letters:
AB
AC
AM
BO
CO
FM
FO
Lt
MO
OS
PO
QM
RA
SM
VA
WO

3 letters:
ACM
Adm
AVM
Cdr
Col
COS
Cpl
CPO
CSM
Gen
LAC
Maj
NCO
Pte
RSM
Sgt
SMO

4 letters:
Brig
Capt
Cdre
C-in-C
Corp
Genl
L-Cpl
MRAF
Sub L

5 letters:
Flt Lt
G Capt
Lt-Col
Lt-Gen
Major
Sergt

6 letters:
Col Sgt
Flt Sgt
Lt-Comm
Maj-Gen
Marine
Sqn-Ldr

7 letters:
Admiral
Captain
Colonel
General
Marshal
Private

8 letters:
Corporal
Sergeant

9 letters:
Brigadier
Commander
Commodore
Drum major
Subaltern

10 letters:
Able rating
Able seaman
Air marshal
Air officer
Lieutenant
Midshipman

11 letters:
Aircraftmen
Rear admiral
Vice admiral

12 letters:
Air commodore
Chief of staff
Field marshal
Field officer
Fleet admiral
Group captain
Major general
Petty officer
Pilot officer

13 letters:
Branch officer
Flying officer
Lance corporal
Leading rating
Master aircrew
Quartermaster
Sergeant major
Staff sergeant
Sublieutenant
Wing commander

14 letters:
Air vice-marshal
Colour sergeant
Flight engineer
Flight mechanic
Flight sergeant
Medical officer
Ordinary rating
Ordinary seaman
Squadron leader
Warrant officer

15 letters:
Air chief marshal
Chief technician

16 letters:
Able-bodied seaman
Commander in chief
Flight lieutenant
Junior technician
Second lieutenant

17 letters:
Admiral of the fleet

Chief petty officer
Commanding officer
Lieutenant colonel
Lieutenant general
Senior aircraftman

18 letters:
Leading aircraftman

19 letters:
Acting sublieutenant

Commissioned officer
Lieutenant commander

20 letters:
Company sergeant
  major
Senior medical officer

22 letters:
Fleet chief petty officer

Noncommissioned
  officer

23 letters:
Regimental sergeant
  major

25 letters:
Marshal of the Royal Air
  Force

Minerals

4 letters:
Gang
Mica
Opal
Sard
Spar
Talc
Trap
Urao

5 letters:
Agate
Balas
Beryl
Borax
Chert
Emery
Flint
Fluor
Mafic
Nitre
Prase
Topaz
Trona
Umber

6 letters:
Acmite
Albite
Augite
Blende
Galena
Gangue
Garnet
Glance

Gypsum
Halite
Hauyne
Illite
Jargon
Jasper
Lithia
Norite
Nosean
Pinite
Pyrite
Quartz
Rutile
Schorl
Silica
Sphene
Spinel
Tincal
Zircon

7 letters:
Alunite
Amalgam
Anatase
Apatite
Axinite
Azurite
Barytes
Bauxite
Biotite
Bornite
Brucite
Calcite
Calomel
Catseye

Cuprite
Cyanite
Diamond
Dysodil
Epidote
Euclase
Eucrite
Fahlore
Felspar
Gahnite
Göthite
Gummite
Hessite
Ice spar
Jadeite
Jargoon
Kainite
Kernite
Kunzite
Kyanite
Leucite
Mellite
Mullite
Nacrite
Olivine
Pennine
Peridot
Pyrites
Realgar
Rosaker
Sylvine
Sylvite
Thorite
Thulite
Tripoli

Turgite
Ulexite
Uralite
Uranite
Uranium
Zeolite
Zincite
Zoisite
Zorgite

8 letters:
Adularia
Allanite
Analcime
Analcite
Andesine
Ankerite
Antimony
Aphanite
Asbestos
Autunite
Blue john
Boehmite
Boracite
Braunite
Brookite
Calamine
Cerusite
Chlorite
Chromite
Cinnabar
Cleveite
Corundum
Crocoite
Cryolite
Datolite
Dendrite
Diallage
Diaspore
Diopside
Dioptase
Disthene
Dolomite
Dysodile
Dysodyle
Epsomite
Erionite
Euxenite
Fayalite
Feldspar

Flinkite
Fluorite
Galenite
Galinite
Gibbsite
Goethite
Graphite
Gyrolite
Hematite
Hyacinth
Idocrase
Ilmenite
Iodyrite
Jarosite
Lazulite
Lazurite
Lewisite
Limonite
Massicot
Melilite
Metamict
Mimetite
Monazite
Nephrite
Noselite
Orpiment
Petuntse
Petuntze
Prehnite
Pyroxene
Resalgar
Rock-salt
Sanidine
Saponite
Siderite
Smaltite
Smectite
Sodalite
Stannite
Stibnite
Stilbite
Taconite
Tenorite
Titanite
Troilite
Xenotime
Zaratite

9 letters:
Alabaster

Allophane
Amazonite
Amphibole
Anglesite
Anhydrite
Anorthite
Aragonite
Argentite
Atacamite
Blackjack
Blacklead
Carnelian
Carnotite
Celestine
Celestite
Cerussite
Chabazite
Cheralite
Chondrule
Cobaltine
Cobaltite
Coccolite
Columbate
Columbite
Covellite
Elaeolite
Enhydrite
Enstatite
Erythrite
Fibrolite®
Fluorspar
Gehlenite
Germanite
Geyserite
Gmelinite
Goslarite
Haematite
Harmotome
Hercynite
Hiddenite
Kaolinite
Kermesite
Kieserite
Magnesite
Magnetite
Malachite
Manganite
Marcasite
Margarite
Marialite

479

479

Minerals

Microlite
Microlith
Millerite
Mispickel
Mizzonite
Monzonite
Moonstone
Muscovite
Natrolite
Nepheline
Nephelite
Niccolite
Nitratine
Olivenite
Ottrelite
Ozocerite
Ozokerite
Pargasite
Pectolite
Periclase
Pericline
Phenacite
Phenakite
Pleonaste
Polianite
Pollucite
Powellite
Proustite
Rhodonite
Rubellite
Scapolite
Scheelite
Scolecite
Spodumene
Sylvanite
Tantalite
Tremolite
Troostite
Tungstite
Turquoise
Uraninite
Uvarovite
Variscite
Vulpinite
Wavellite
Wernerite
Willemite
Witherite
Wulfenite
Zinkenite

10 letters:
Actinolite
Alabandine
Alabandite
Andalusite
Bastnasite
Calaverite
Carnallite
Chalcocite
Chessylite
Chrysolite
Chrysotile
Colemanite
Cordierite
Crocoisite
Dyscrasite
Forsterite
Gadolinite
Garnierite
Glauconite
Halloysite
Heulandite
Honey-stone
Hornblende
Indicolite
Indigolite
Jamesonite
Laurdalite
Meerschaum
Microcline
Oligoclase
Orthoclase
Perovskite
Phosgenite
Polybasite
Polyhalite
Pyragyrite
Pyrolusite
Pyroxenite
Pyrrhotine
Pyrrhotite
Redruthite
Riebeckite
Ripidolite
Samarskite
Sapphirine
Serpentine
Smaragdite
Sperrylite
Sphalerite

Staurolite
Tennantite
Thaumasite
Thenardite
Thorianite
Tiemannite
Torbernite
Tourmaline
Triphylite
Vanadinite
Wolframite
Zinckenite

11 letters:
Alexandrite
Amblygonite
Annabergite
Apophyllite
Baddeleyite
Bastnaesite
Cassiterite
Cerargyrite
Chiastolite
Chrysoberyl
Clay mineral
Clinochlore
Crocidolite
Dendrachate
Franklinite
Greenockite
Hypersthene
Josephinite
Labradorite
Lapis lazuli
Molybdenite
Pentlandite
Phosphorite
Piedmontite
Pitchblende
Psilomelane
Pyrargyrite
Sillimanite
Smithsonite
Tetradymite
Vermiculite
Vesuvianite
Ythro-cerite

12 letters:
Arfvedsonite

Missiles

Arsenopyrite
Babingtonite
Bismuthinite
Chalcanthite
Chalcopyrite
Cristobalite
Dumortierite
Feldspathoid
Fluorapatite

Hemimorphite
Pyromorphite
Pyrophyllite
Senarmontite
Skutterudite
Strontianite
Synadelphite
Tetrahedrite
Wollastonite

13 letters:
Bismuth glance
Clinopyroxene
Cummingtonite
Rhodochrosite

15 letters:
Montmorillonite

Missiles

3 letters:
SAM
SSM
UAM

4 letters:
Ammo
Ball
Bolt
Bomb
Dart
ICBM
MIRV
Scud
Shot
SLBM
SLCM
Styx
Thor

5 letters:
Arrow
Atlas
Bolas
Kiley
Kyley
Kylie
Onion
Shell
Spear
Titan

6 letters:
Bullet

Cruise
Dum-dum
Exocet
Guided
Pellet
Rocket
Tracer

7 letters:
Dingbat
Grenade
Harpoon
Patriot
Polaris
Quarrel
Torpedo
Trident
Warhead

8 letters:
Air-to-air
Buzz bomb
Maverick
Pershing
Poseidon
Snowball
Standoff

9 letters:
Ballistic
Boomerang
Doodlebug
Fléchette

Minuteman
Smart bomb

10 letters:
Blue streak
Flying bomb
Side-winder

11 letters:
Interceptor

12 letters:
Surface to air

13 letters:
Anti-ballistic

16 letters:
Surface to surface

17 letters:
Sea-launched cruise

25 letters:
Intercontinental ballistic

26 letters:
Submarine-launched
 ballistic

43 letters:
Multiple independently
 targeted re-entry
 vehicle

Molecules

3 letters:
DNA

5 letters:
Codon
Dimer
Kinin

6 letters:
Chiral
Hapten
Isomer
Ligand
Trimer

7 letters:
Carbene
Monomer

Peptide
Polymer
Uridine

8 letters:
Acceptor
Cavitand
Coenzyme
Cofactor
Replicon

9 letters:
Buckyball
Cobalamin
Fullerene
Long-chain
Metameric

Semantide

10 letters:
Metabolite

11 letters:
Chromophore
Closed chain
Footballene

12 letters:
Enantiomorph
Stereoisomer

14 letters:
Polysaccharide

Monastic orders

6 letters:
Sangha

7 letters:
Cluniac
Saivite
Shaolin

8 letters:
Basilian
Trappist
Vaisnava

9 letters:
Capuchins
Carmelite
Celestine
Dominican

Mathurins
Red Friars

10 letters:
Bendictine
Carthusian
Cistercian
Feuillants
Franciscan

11 letters:
Augustinian
Bridgettine
Camaldolese
Gilbertines
Tironensian
White Canons

12 letters:
Redemptorist
Trinitarians

14 letters:
Knights Templar
Premonstratian

17 letters:
Christian Brothers
Premonstratensian
Visitation Sisters

20 letters:
Mendicant Augustinian

Monks

3 letters:
Dan
Dom

4 letters:
Bede
Lama

5 letters:
Abbot
Arhat
Black
Bonze
Bruno
Friar
Prior

6 letters:
Austin
Bhikhu
Culdee
Jerome
Mendel
Oblate
Sangha

7 letters:
Beghard

Brother
Caedmon
Caloyer
Cluniac
Félibre
Hegumen
Jacobin
Maurist

8 letters:
Acoemeti
Basilian
Cenobite
Jacobite
Olivetan
Pelagian
Rasputin
Salesian
Talapoin
Theatine
Trappist

9 letters:
Celestine
Coenobite
Dominican
Gyrovague
Hesychast

Thelemite
Thelonius

10 letters:
Bernardine
Carthusian
Cistercian
Hildebrand
Norbertine
Savonarola

11 letters:
Abbey-lubber
Augustinian
Benedictine
Bonaventura
Ignorantine
Mekhitarist
Tironensian

12 letters:
Bethlehemite
Mechitharist

13 letters:
Archimandrite
Thomas à Kempis

Monkeys, apes and other primates

3 letters:
Pug
Sai

4 letters:
Douc
Leaf
Mico
Mona
Nala
Saki
Tana
Titi
Zati

5 letters:
Cebus
Chimp
Diana
Drill
Green
Indri
Jocko
Lemur
Loris
Magot
Midas
Orang
Sajou
Silen

Toque

6 letters:
Aye-aye
Baboon
Bandar
Bonnet
Chacma
Coaita
Colugo
Galago
Gelada
Gibbon
Grison
Grivet
Guenon

Howler
Indris
Jackey
Langur
Macaco
Malmag
Monkey
Rhesus
Sagoin
Saguin
Sifaka
Simpai
Spider
Tee-tee
Uakari
Vervet
Wou-wou
Wow-wow

7 letters:
Cebidae
Colobus
Gorilla
Guereza
Hanuman
Hoolock
Jacchus
Macaque
Meerkat

Mycetes
Nasalis
Ouakari
Sagouin
Saimiri
Sapajou
Siamang
Silenus
Tamarin
Tarsier
Wistiti

8 letters:
Bushbaby
Capuchin
Durukuli
Entellus
Mandrill
Mangabey
Marmoset
Ouistiti
Squirrel
Talapoin
Wanderoo

9 letters:
Hylobates
Orang-utan
Phalanger

Proboscis

10 letters:
Barbary ape
Chimpanzee
Cynomolgus
Jackanapes
Silverback

11 letters:
Douroucouli
Flying lemur
Green monkey
Orang-outang
Platyrrhine

12 letters:
Bonnet monkey
Howler monkey
Rhesus monkey
Slender loris
Spider monkey

14 letters:
Squirrel monkey

15 letters:
Proboscis monkey

Monsters

3 letters:
Orc

4 letters:
Eten
Ogre

5 letters:
Ettin
Giant
Harpy
Hydra
Lamia
Snark
Teras
Troll
Yowie

6 letters:
Alecto
Bunyip
Dragon
Erebus
Geryon
Gorgon
Kraken
Medusa
Moloch
Nessie
Scylla
Simorg
Simurg
Sphinx
Typhon
Wyvern

7 letters:
Caliban
Chimera
Cyclops
Grendel
Simurgh
Taniwha
Vampire
Wendego
Wendigo
Werwolf
Ziffius

8 letters:
Asmodeus
Behemoth
Cerberus

Chimaera
Mastodon
Minotaur
Opinicus
Stegodon
Typhoeus
Werewolf

9 letters:
Dinoceras

Fire-drake
Leviathan
Stegosaur
Wasserman

10 letters:
Cockatrice
Hippogriff
Jabberwock
Sarsquatch

11 letters:
Chichevache
Hippocampus
Triceratops

12 letters:
Bandersnatch
Frankenstein

Mosses

3 letters:
Fog
Hag

4 letters:
Club
Hagg
Peat
Rose

5 letters:
Agate
Irish
Marsh
Usnea

6 letters:
Ceylon
Hypnum
Lichen
Litmus

7 letters:
Acrogen
Iceland
Lycopod
Muscoid
Parella
Spanish

8 letters:
Reindeer

Sphagnum
Staghorn

9 letters:
Carrageen
Lecanoram
Wolf's claw

10 letters:
Carragheen
Fontinalis

11 letters:
Polytrichum
Selaginella

Motor sports

7 letters:
Karting

8 letters:
Rallying
Speedway

9 letters:
Autocross
Motocross

10 letters:
Drag racing
Rallycross
Scrambling

11 letters:
Motor racing

13 letters:
Motor rallying

14 letters:
Stock car racing

16 letters:
Motor-cycle racing

Mountaineers

5 letters:
Munro, *Sir HT*

6 letters:
Conway, *Sir Martin*
Harrer, *Heinrich*
Norgay, *Tenzing*
Willss, *Sir Alfred*

7 letters:
Corbett, *JR*
Hillary, *Sir Edmund*
Mallory, *George*
Messner, *Reinhold*
Shipman, *Eric*
Simpson, *Joe*
Whymper, *Edward*
Workman, *Fannie Bullock*

8 letters:
Petzoldt, *Paul*

9 letters:
Bonington, *Chris*

10 letters:
Freshfield, *DW*

Mountains

2 letters:
K2

3 letters:
Apo
Ida
Kaf
Ore

4 letters:
Alai
Blue
Bona
Cook
Etna
Fuji
Harz
Hoss
Isto
Jaya
Jura
Meru
Nebo
Oeta
Ossa
Rigi
Rosa
Viso
Zeil

5 letters:
Abora
Adams
Aldan

Altai
Amara
Andes
Aneto
Arber
Athos
Atlas
Badon
Black
Blanc
Coast
Corno
Djaja
Eiger
Ellis
Ghats
Green
Guyot
Hekla
Horeb
Idris
Kamet
Kenya
Leone
Logan
Marcy
Munro
Ozark
Rocky
Rydal
Sinai
Siple
Slide

Snowy
Table
Tabor
Tatra
Teide
Tyree
Urals
Welsh
White

6 letters:
Amhara
Anadyr
Arafat
Ararat
Averno
Balkan
Bogong
Carmel
Cho Oyu
Dragon
Egmont
Elbert
Elberz
Elbrus
Erebus
Gilead
Hermon
Hoggar
Hoosac
Kunlin
Lhotse
Makalu

Mountains

486

Mourne
Musala
Negoiu
Ortles
Pamirs
Pelion
Pisgah
Pocono
Robson
Scopus
Sorata
Steele
Tasman
Taunus
Taurus
Vernon
Vosges
Zagros

7 letters:
Aorangi
Aragats
Arcadia
Belukha
Bernina
Brocken
Buffalo
Calvary
Cariboo
Cascade
Chianti
Corbett
Dapsang
Everest
Helicon
Kennedy
Khingan
Lebanon
Lucania
Manaslu
Markham
Nan Shan
Olympus
Palomar
Perdido
Pilatus
Rainier
Rhodope
Scafell
Selkirk

Skiddaw
Snowdon
Sperrin
Stanley
Sudeten
Toubkal
Travers
Troglav
Whitney
Wicklow
Zard Kuh

8 letters:
Anai Mudi
Ben Nevis
Cambrian
Cevennes
Demavend
Estrella
Grampian
Hymettus
Illimani
Jungfrau
Kinabalu
King Peak
Klínovec
Leibnitz
McKinley
Mitchell
Mulhacén
Pennines
Pyrenees
Rushmore
Skalitsy
Smólikas
St Helen's
Taraniki
Tien Shan
Vesuvius
Victoria
Waun Fach
Wrangell

9 letters:
Aconcagua
Allegheny
Annapurna
Apennines
Argentera
Ben Lomond

Blackburn
Blue Ridge
Cairngorm
Catskills
Caucasian
Connemara
Corcovado
Demavrand
Dolomites
El Capitan
Emi Koussi
Grampians
Guadalupe
Helvellyn
Highlands
Himalayas
Hindu Kush
Inselberg
Jebel Musa
Karakoram
Kings Peak
Kosciusko
Lenin Peak
Longs Peak
Mansfield
Marmolada
Mont Blanc
Nanda Devi
Narodnaya
Parnassus
Pikes Peak
Puy de Dôme
Rock Creek
Sugarloaf
Tirich Mir
Vancouver
Venusberg
Weisshorn
Woodroffe
Zugspitze

10 letters:
Arakan Yoma
Ben Macdhui
Blanca Peak
Cantabrian
Carpathian
Delectable
Dhaulagiri
Erymanthus

Erzgebirge
Gannet Peak
Grand Teton
Great Gable
Harney Peak
Horselberg
Kongur Shan
Laurentian
Masharbrum
Matterhorn
Monte Corno
Montserrat
Pentelikon
Piz Bernina
Pobeda Peak
Puncak Jaya
Puy de Sancy
St Michael's
Tengri Khan
Timpanogos
Waddington
Washington
Wellington

11 letters:
Adirondacks
Alaska Range
Appalachian
Aran Fawddwy
Bartle Frere
Bimberi Peak
Brooks Range
Drakensberg
Fairweather
Gerlachovka

Kilimanjaro
Kolyma Range
Munku-Sardyk
Nanga Parbat
Salmon River
Scafell Pike
Schneekoppe
Sierra Madre
Sir Sandford

12 letters:
Albert Edward
Cascade Range
Citlaltépetl
Godwin Austen
Gran Paradiso
Kanchenjunga
Ruahine Range
Sierra Nevada
Slieve Donard
Tararua Range
Ulugh Muztagh
Victoria Peak
Vinson Massif
Western Ghats

13 letters:
Carmarthen Van
Carrantuohill
Clingman's Dome
Croagh Patrick
Flinders Range
Grossglockner
Humphreys Peak
Kangchenjunga

Massif Central
Mount of Olives
Petermann Peak
San Bernardino

14 letters:
Bohemian Forest
Carnarvon Range
Finsteraarhorn
Hamersley Range
Kaikoura Ranges
Kommunizma Peak
Liverpool Range
Musgrove Ranges
Ruwenzori Range
Stirling Ranges

15 letters:
Cerro de Mulhacén
Uncompahgre Peak

16 letters:
Blue Mountain Peak
Macdonnell Ranges
Thabana Ntlenyana

17 letters:
Continental Divide
Sir Wilfrid Laurier
Transylvanian Alps

19 letters:
Macgillicuddy's Reeks

Famous murderers

4 letters:
Cain
Gacy, *John*
Gein, *Ed*
Ruby, *Jack*
West, *Fred*
West, *Rosemary*

5 letters:
Booth, *John Wilkes*
Brady, *Ian*

Ellis, *Ruth*

6 letters:
Bonney, *William*
Borden, *Lizzie*
Corday, *Charlotte*
Graham, *Barbara*
Manson, *Charles*
Oswald, *Lee Harvey*
Pearce, *Charlie*
Sirhan, *Sirhan*

7 letters:
Chapman, *Mark*
Crippen, *Hawley*
Gilmore, *Gary*
Hindley, *Myra*
Huntley, *Ian*
Macbeth
Panzram, *Carl*
Shipman, *Harold*
Wuornos, *Aileen*

8 letters:
Chessman, *Caryl*
Christie, *John*

9 letters:
Bible John
Hauptmann, *Bruno*
Sutcliffe, *Peter*

11 letters:
Billy the Kid

13 letters:
Jack the Ripper

14 letters:
Leopold and Loeb

17 letters:
The Moors Murderers

18 letters:
The Boston Strangler
The Yorkshire Ripper

Muscles

3 letters:
Abs
Lat
Pec

4 letters:
Pecs
Quad

5 letters:
Psoas
Teres
Tonus

6 letters:
Biceps
Flexor
Pathos
Rectus
Smooth
Soleus
Tensor
Thenar

7 letters:
Agonist
Ciliary
Deltoid
Dilator
Erecter
Erector
Evertor
Gluteus
Iliacus
Laxator
Levator
Pylorus
Rotator

Sarcous
Scalene
Sthenic
Triceps

8 letters:
Abductor
Adductor
Effector
Elevator
Extensor
Glutaeus
Kreatine
Masseter
Occlusor
Omohyoid
Opponent
Pectoral
Peroneus
Platysma
Pronator
Risorius
Scalenus
Serratus
Splenial
Striated

9 letters:
Arytenoid
Attollens
Cremaster
Depressor
Diaphragm
Digastric
Hamstring
Perforans
Quadratus
Retractor

Sartorius
Sphincter
Supinator
Suspensor
Tenaculum
Trapezius
Voluntary

10 letters:
Antagonist
Buccinator
Compressor
Contractor
Corrugator
Perforatus
Protractor
Quadriceps
Sarcolemma
Suspensory

11 letters:
Accelerator
Accessorius
Constrictor
Lumbricalis
Rhomboideus

13 letters:
Gastrocnemius

14 letters:
Gluteus maximus
Peroneal muscle

15 letters:
Latissimus dorsi

Muses

Calliope	Epic poetry
Clio	History
Erato	Love poetry
Euterpe	Lyric poetry and music
Melpomene	Tragedy
Polyhymnia	Singing, mime, and sacred dance
Terpsichore	Dance and choral song
Thalia	Comedy and pastoral poetry
Urania	Astronomy

Mushrooms and other edible fungi

3 letters:
Cep

5 letters:
Enoki
Horse
Hypha
Magic
Morel

6 letters:
Agaric
Blewit
Button
Hyphal
Ink-cap
Meadow
Oyster
Waxcap

7 letters:
Blewits

Parasol
Porcini
Porcino
Truffle

8 letters:
Penny-bun
Puffball
Shiitake

9 letters:
Fly agaric
Gyromitra

10 letters:
Champignon
Lawyer's wig
Liberty cap
Shaggymane

11 letters:
Chanterelle

Velvet shank

12 letters:
Black truffle
Horn of plenty
Scotch bonnet
Shaggy ink cap
White truffle

13 letters:
Straw mushroom

14 letters:
Button mushroom
Meadow mushroom
Oyster mushroom

15 letters:
Wood ear mushroom

16 letters:
Shiitake mushroom

Music

CLASSICAL MUSIC GENRES

5 letters:
Early
Salon

6 letters:
Galant
Gothic
Rococo
Serial

7 letters:
Ars nova
Baroque

CLASSICAL MUSIC GENRES (CONTINUED)

8 letters:
Romantic

9 letters:
Classical

10 letters:
Ars antiqua
Minimalist

Twelve-tone

11 letters:
Nationalist
Renaissance

12 letters:
Dodecaphonic

Neoclassical
Post-romantic

13 letters:
Expressionist
Impressionist
Music concrète

TYPES OF COMPOSITION

3 letters:
Air
Duo

4 letters:
Aria
Duet
Lied
Mass
Raga
Reel
Song
Trio

5 letters:
Canon
Dirge
Dumka
Elegy
Étude
Fugue
Galop
Gigue
March
Motet
Nonet
Octet
Opera
Polka
Psalm
Suite
Waltz

6 letters:
Anthem
Ballet

Bolero
Chorus
Lament
Medley
Minuet
Pavane
Septet
Sextet
Sonata

7 letters:
Ballade
Bourrée
Cantata
Canzona
Canzone
Chorale
Czardas
Fantasy
Gavotte
Ländler
Mazurka
Partita
Passion
Pibroch
Prelude
Quartet
Quintet
Requiem
Romance
Scherzo
Toccata

8 letters:
Barceuse
Canticle

Cavatina
Chaconne
Concerto
Fantasia
Galliard
Hornpipe
Madrigal
Nocturne
Notturno
Operetta
Oratorio
Overture
Part song
Pastiche
Phantasy
Rhapsody
Ricercar
Rigadoon
Rigadoun
Serenade
Sonatina
Symphony
Tone poem

9 letters:
Allemande
Bagatelle
Barcarole
Capriccio
Ecossaise
Farandole
Impromptu
Interlude
Passepied
Pastorale
Polonaise

TYPES OF COMPOSITION (CONTINUED)

Quadrille
Ricercare
Singspiel
Song cycle

10 letters:
Albumblatt
Canzonetta
Concertino
Grand opera
Humoresque
Opera buffa
Opera seria

Strathspey
Trio sonata

11 letters:
Concertante
Contradance
Contredanse
Passacaglia
Schottische
Sinfonietta

12 letters:
Concertstück

Divertimento

13 letters:
Symphonic poem

14 letters:
Concerto grosso
Divertissement

19 letters:
Sinfonia concertante

POPULAR MUSIC TYPES

3 letters:
AOR
Bop
Dub
Pop
Rag
Rai
Rap
Ska

4 letters:
Folk
Funk
Go-go
Goth
Jazz
Loco
Punk
Rave
Rock
Romo
Soca
Soul
Trad
Zouk

5 letters:
Bebop
Blues
Cajun
Cu-bop
Disco

Dream
Early
House
Indie
Kwela
Muzak®
Neume
P-funk
Piped
Ragga
Salon
Salsa
Sokah
Swing

6 letters:
Bebung
Doo-wop
Fusion
Gagaku
Garage
Gospel
Gothic
Grunge
Hip-hop
Jungle
Khayal
Marabi
Motown®
New Age
Reggae
Techno

Thrash
Trance
Zydeco

7 letters:
Ambient
Bhangra
Britpop
Calypso
Ceilidh
Chamber
Country
Gangsta
Hardbag
Hardbop
Klezmer
New Wave
Pibroch
Qawwali
Ragtime
Skiffle
Soukous
Trip hop
Ziganka

8 letters:
Acid jazz
Acid rock
Bluebeat
Concrete
Cool jazz
Flamenco

POPULAR MUSIC TYPES (CONTINUED)

Folk rock
Free jazz
Glam rock
Hardcore
Hard rock
High life
Jazz-funk
Jazz-rock
Karnatak
Lollipop
Mariachi
Mbaqanga
Punk rock
Trad jazz

9 letters:
Acid house
Bluegrass
Bubblegum
Dixieland
Folk music
Hillbilly
Honky-tonk
Rock'n'roll
Spiritual
Surf music

Swingbeat
Technopop
Warehouse

10 letters:
Chopsticks
Death metal
Gangsta rap
Gothic rock
Heavy metal
Hindustani
Industrial
Merseybeat
Modern jazz
New Country
Rockabilly
Rocksteady
Urban blues
World music

11 letters:
Country rock
Harmolodics
Motor rhythm
New romantic
Psychobilly

Raggamuffin
Rock and roll
Stadium rock
Third stream
Thrash metal

12 letters:
Boogie-woogie
Country blues

13 letters:
Detroit techno

14 letters:
Mainstream jazz
New Orleans jazz
Rhythm and blues

15 letters:
Musique concrete
Progressive rock

17 letters:
Country and western

MUSICAL EXPRESSIONS AND TEMPO INSTRUCTIONS

Instruction	Meaning
Accelerando	With increasing speed
Adagio	Slowly
Agitato	In an agitated manner
Allegretto	Fairly quickly or briskly
Allegro	Quickly, in a brisk, lively manner
Amoroso	Lovingly
Andante	At a moderately slow tempo
Andantino	Slightly faster than andante
Animato	In a lively manner
Appassionato	Impassioned
Assai	(in combination) very
Calando	With gradually decreasing tone and speed
Cantabile	In a singing style
Con	(in combination) with
Con affeto	With tender emotion

Musical expressions and tempo instructions (continued)

Instruction	Meaning
Con amore	Lovingly
Con anima	With spirit
Con brio	Vigorously
Con fuoco	With fire
Con moto	Quickly
Crescendo	Gradual increase in loudness
Diminuendo	Gradual decrease in loudness
Dolce	Gently and sweetly
Doloroso	In a sorrowful manner
Energico	Energetically
Espressivo	Expressively
Forte	Loud or loudly
Fortissimo	Very loud
Furioso	In a frantically rushing manner
Giocoso	Merry
Grave	Solemn and slow
Grazioso	Graceful
Lacrimoso	Sad and mournful
Largo	Slowly and broadly
Larghetto	Slowly and broadly, but less so than largo
Legato	Smoothly and connectedly
Leggiero	Light
Lento	Slowly
Maestoso	Majestically
Marziale	Martial
Mezzo	(in combination) moderately
Moderato	At a moderate tempo
Molto	(in combination) very
Non troppo or non tanto	(in combination) not too much
Pianissimo	Very quietly
Piano	Softly
Più	(in combination) more
Pizzicato	(in music for stringed instruments) to be plucked with the finger
Poco or un poco	(in combination) a little
Pomposo	In a pompous manner
Presto	Very fast
Prestissimo	Faster than presto
Quasi	(in combination) almost, as if

MUSICAL EXPRESSIONS AND TEMPO INSTRUCTIONS (CONTINUED)

Instruction	Meaning
Rallentando	Becoming slower
Rubato	With a flexible tempo
Scherzando	In jocular style
Sciolto	Free and easy
Semplice	Simple and unforced
Sforzando	With strong initial attack
Smorzando	Dying away
Sospirando	`sighing', plaintive
Sostenuto	In a smooth and sustained manner
Sotto voce	Extremely quiet
Staccato	(of notes) short, clipped, and separate
Strascinando	Stretched out
Strepitoso	Noisy
Stringendo	With increasing speed
Tanto	(in combination) too much
Tardo	Slow
Troppo	(in combination) too much
Vivace	In a brisk lively manner
Volante	`flying', fast and light

MUSICAL MODES

Final note	
I Dorian	D
II Hypodorian	A
III Phrygian	E
IV Hypophrygian	B
V Lydian	F
VI Hypolydian	C
VII Mixolydian	G
VIII Hypomixolydian	D
IX Aeolian	A
X Hypoaeolian	E
XI Ionian	C
XII Hypoionian	G

MUSICAL INSTRUMENTS

2 letters:
Ax
Gu

3 letters:
Axe
Gue
Kit
Lur
Oud
Saz
Uke
Zel

4 letters:
Bell
Crwd
Drum
Fife
Gong
Harp
Horn
Kora
Koto
Lure
Lute
Lyre
Moog®
Oboe
Pipa
Pipe
Rate
Reed
Rote
Sang
Tuba
Vina
Viol
Whip
Zeze

5 letters:
Aulos
Banjo
Bongo
Bugle
Cello
Chime
Clave

Cobza
Conga
Corno
Crowd
Crwth
Dobro®
Flute
Guiro
Gusla
Gusle
Gusli
Kazoo
Mbira
Naker
Nebel
Ngoma
Organ
Piano
Quena
Rebec
Regal
Sanko
Sansa
Sarod
Shalm
Shawm
Sitar
Tabla
Tabor
Tibia
Veena
Viola
Zanze
Zinke

6 letters:
Antara
Cither
Citole
Cornet
Cymbal
Euphon
Fiddle
Flugel
Guitar
Kanoon
Maraca
Poogye

Racket
Rebeck
Ribibe
Sancho
Santir
Santur
Shalme
Sittar
Spinet
Syrinx
Tabour
Tam-tam
Timbal
Tom-tom
Trigon
Tymbal
Vielle
Violin
Zither
Zufolo

7 letters:
Alphorn
Althorn
Bagpipe
Bandore
Bandura
Baryton
Bassoon
Bazooka
Bodhrán
Celesta
Celeste
Cembalo
Chikara
Cithara
Cithern
Cittern
Clarion
Clavier
Console
Cornett
Cowbell
Cymbalo
Dichord
Dulcian
Fagotto
Flutina

MUSICAL INSTRUMENTS (CONTINUED)

Gamelan
Gittern
Hautboy
Helicon
High-hat
Kalimba
Kantela
Kantele
Kithara
Klavier
Lyricon
Mandola
Marimba
Musette
Ocarina
Pandora
Pandore
Pandura
Pianola®
Piccolo
Poogyee
Posaune
Rackett
Sackbut
Sambuca
Samisen
Santour
Sarangi
Saxhorn
Saxtuba
Serpent
Sistrum
Tambour
Tambura
Theorbo
Timbrel
Timpani
Trumpet
Tympani
Tympany
Ukelele
Ukulele
Vihuela
Violone
Vocoder
Whistle
Zuffolo

8 letters:
Angklung
Archlute
Autoharp®
Bagpipes
Barytone
Bass drum
Bass viol
Bouzouki
Calliope
Canorous
Carillon
Charango
Cimbalom
Cimbalon
Clarinet
Clarsach
Clavecin
Cornetto
Cornpipe
Cromorna
Cromorne
Crumhorn
Cymbalon
Dulcimer
Gemshorn
Guarneri
Guimbard
Handbell
Hautbois
Hornpipe
Humstrum
Jew's-harp
Keyboard
Key-bugle
Langspel
Lyra viol
Mandolin
Manzello
Martenot
Melodeon
Melodica
Melodion
Mirliton
Ottavino
Panpipes
Phorminx
Polyphon

Psaltery
Recorder
Reco-reco
Reed pipe
Side drum
Slughorn
Spinette
Sticcado
Sticcato
Surbahar
Tamboura
Tamburin
Tenoroon
Theremin®
Triangle
Trombone
Virginal
Vocalion
Zambomba
Zampogna

9 letters:
Accordion
Alpenhorn
Baby grand
Balalaika
Bandoneon
Baryulele
Böhm flute
Bombardon
Castanets
Chalumeau
Cornemuse
Decachord
Euphonium
Flageolet
Flexatone
Gittarone
Gran cassa
Gutbucket
Harmonica
Harmonium
Idiophone
Kent-bugle
Krummhorn
Langspiel
Mandoline
Monochord

MUSICAL INSTRUMENTS (CONTINUED)

Mouth-harp
Nose flute
Octachord
Orpharion
Pantaleon
Pastorale
Polyphone
Reed organ
Saxophone
Seraphine
Slughorne
Snare drum
Sopranino
Stockhorn
Trompette
Washboard
Welsh harp
Wood block
Wurlitzer®
Xylophone
Xylorimba

10 letters:
Basset horn
Bass guitar
Bullroarer
Chitarrone
Clavichord
Concertina
Contrabass
Cor anglais
Didgeridoo
Double bass
Flugelhorn
French horn
Gramophone
Grand piano
Hurdy-gurdy
Kettledrum
Mellophone
Mouth organ
Oboe d'amore
Ophicleide

Orpheoreon
Pantachord
Shakuhachi
Sousaphone
Squeeze-box
Steam organ
Stylophone
Symphonium
Tambourine
Thumb piano
Vibraphone

11 letters:
Aeolian harp
Bach trumpet
Barrel organ
Chordophone
Clairschach
Contrabasso
Drum machine
English horn
Harmoniphon
Harpsichord
Heckelphone
Hunting horn
Nickelodeon
Orchestrina
Orchestrion
Phonofiddle
Player piano
Slide guitar
Square piano
Steel guitar
Straduarius
Synthesizer
Trump-marine
Viola d'amore
Violincello
Violoncello

12 letters:
Boudoir grand
Chamber organ

Chapman stick®
Chinese block
Clavicembalo
Concert grand
Cottage piano
Glockenspiel
Hammond organ®
Harmoniphone
Metallophone
Oboe da caccia
Penny whistle
Sarrusophone
Stock and horn
Stradivarius
Tromba-marina
Tubular bells
Uillean pipes
Upright piano
Viola da gamba

13 letters:
Contrabassoon
Contrafagotto
Double bassoon
Ondes Martenot
Panharmonicon
Physharmonica
Spanish guitar

14 letters:
Electric guitar
Glass harmonica
Hawaiian guitar
Portative organ
Viola da braccio

15 letters:
Electronic organ

16 letters:
Pedal steel guitar

See also:
➤ **Composers** ➤ **Instruments in a full orchestra** ➤ **Jazz musicians** ➤ **Jazz terms** ➤ **Types of jazz** ➤ **Musical notes and rests** ➤ **Works of literature and music**

Musketeers

5 letters:
Athos

6 letters:
Aramis

7 letters:
Porthos

9 letters:
D'Artagnan

Mythology

CHARACTERS IN CLASSICAL MYTHOLOGY

2 letters:
Io

4 letters:
Ajax
Dido
Echo
Leda

5 letters:
Atlas
Circe
Helen
Ixion
Jason
Medea
Midas
Minos
Muses
Niobe
Orion
Paris
Priam
Remus
Sibyl

6 letters:
Adonis
Aeneas
Castor
Charon
Europa
Hector
Hecuba
Icarus

Medusa
Pollux
Psyche
Semele
Thisbe

7 letters:
Actaeon
Amazons
Arachne
Ariadne
Calypso
Electra
Galatea
Jocasta
Oedipus
Orestes
Orpheus
Pandora
Perseus
Pyramus
Romulus
Silenus
Theseus
Ulysses

8 letters:
Achilles
Antigone
Atalanta
Callisto
Daedalus
Eurydice
Ganymede
Heracles

Hercules
Menelaus
Odysseus
Penelope
Pleiades
Sisyphus
Tantalus
Tiresias

9 letters:
Agamemnon
Andromeda
Argonauts
Cassandra
Narcissus
Pygmalion

10 letters:
Andromache
Cassiopeia
Hippolytus
Hyacinthus
Persephone
Polydeuces
Polyphemus
Prometheus
Proserpina

12 letters:
Clytemnestra

14 letters:
Hermaphroditus

PLACES IN CLASSICAL MYTHOLOGY

4 letters:
Styx
Troy

5 letters:
Hades
Lethe

6 letters:
Erebus
Thebes

7 letters:
Acheron
Colchis
Elysium
Helicon
Olympus

8 letters:
Tartarus

9 letters:
Parnassus

10 letters:
Phlegethon

19 letters:
Islands of the Blessed

MYTHOLOGICAL CREATURES

3 letters:
Elf
Fay
Nix
Orc
Roc

4 letters:
Faun
Fury
Peri

5 letters:
Afrit
Dryad
Dwarf
Fairy
Genie
Giant
Harpy
Hydra
Jinni
Kylin
Lamia
Naiad
Nixie
Nymph
Oread
Pixie
Satyr
Siren
Sylph
Troll

6 letters:
Afreet
Bunyip
Djinni
Djinny
Dragon
Geryon
Goblin
Gorgon
Hobbit
Jinnee
Kelpie
Kraken
Merman
Nereid
Scylla
Sphinx

7 letters:
Banshee
Centaur
Chimera
Cyclops
Echidna
Erlking
Gremlin
Grendel
Griffin
Griffon
Gryphon
Mermaid
Oceanid
Phoenix

Tricorn
Unicorn

8 letters:
Basilisk
Behemoth
Cerberus
Chimaera
Minotaur

9 letters:
Charybdis
Hamadryad
Hobgoblin
Impundulu
Leviathan
Tokoloshe
Wood nymph

10 letters:
Cockatrice
Hippogriff
Hippogryph
Leprechaun
Salamander
Water nymph

11 letters:
Androsphinx
Hippocampus

CHARACTERS IN NORSE MYTHOLOGY

3 letters:
Ask
Lif

4 letters:
Atli

5 letters:
Mimir
Regin

6 letters:
Fafnir
Gudrun
Gunnar
Sigurd

7 letters:
Andvari
Sigmund
Wayland

8 letters:
Brynhild
Gutthorn
Hreidmar

10 letters:
Lifthrasir

PLACES IN NORSE MYTHOLOGY

3 letters:
Hel

4 letters:
Hela

6 letters:
Asgard
Utgard

7 letters:
Asgarth
Bifrost
Midgard

8 letters:
Midgarth
Niflheim

Valhalla

9 letters:
Jotunheim

10 letters:
Jotunnheim

See also:
➤ Actaeon's hounds ➤ Ancient cities ➤ Arthurian legend ➤ The Fates ➤ Giants and giantesses ➤ Gods and Goddesses ➤ Gorgons ➤ The Graces ➤ Famous Greeks ➤ Harpies ➤ Labours of Hercules ➤ Monsters ➤ Muses ➤ Rivers of Hell ➤ Seven against Thebes ➤ Seven wonders of the ancient world

N n

Nerves

4 letters:
Axon

5 letters:
Cyton
Nidus
Optic
Ulnar
Vagus

6 letters:
Bouton
Facial
Myelon
Radial

7 letters:
Cranial
Excitor
Sciatic
Synapse

8 letters:
Acoustic
Ganglion

9 letters:
Depressor
Epicritic
Trochlear

10 letters:
Commissure
Perikaryon
Trigeminal

11 letters:
Octulomotor
Solar plexus

12 letters:
Baroreceptor
Electrotonus

13 letters:
Proprioceptor

Newspapers and magazines

2 letters:
GQ
OK

3 letters:
FHM
Red
She
Viz
Zoo

4 letters:
Best
Chat
Chic
Elle
Mind
Mojo
More
Nuts
Time
Word

5 letters:
Bella
Blick
Bliss
Hello
Metro
Prima
Punch
Ta Nea
Uncut
Vogue
Which
Wired
Woman

6 letters:
El Pais
Forbes
Granta
Loaded
Nature
Pepper

Record
The Sun
War Cry

7 letters:
Company
Die Welt
Die Zeit
Esquire
Fortune
Hustler
Le Monde
Mayfair
Newsday
Options
Playboy
The Face
The Lady
The Star
Time Out
Tribune

Newspapers and magazines

8 letters:
Big Issue
Campaign
Gay Times
Il Giorno
La Stampa
Le Figaro
Navy News
Newsweek
New Woman
Observer
The Oldie
The Onion
The Times
USA Today

9 letters:
Classic FM
Dagbladet
Daily Mail
Daily Star
Expressen
Ideal Home
L'Humanité
New Yorker
Smash Hits
The Lancet
The Tablet
The Tatler
Total Film
Woman's Own

10 letters:
Asian Times
Daily Sport
Denver Post
Film Review
France-Soir
Il Giornale
Irish Times
La Lanterne
Libération
Private Eye
Racing Post
Radio Times
Sunday Mail
Sunday Post
Vanity Fair

11 letters:
Bild Zeitung
Boston Globe
Daily Mirror
De Telegraaf
El Periodico
Marie Claire
Melody Maker
Miami Herald
Morning Star
New York Post
Ouest France
Sunday Sport
Sunday World
The European
The Guardian
The Scotsman
The Universe
Woman's Realm

12 letters:
Angling Times
Boston Herald
Cosmopolitan
Daily Express
Family Circle
Fortean Times
History Today
Il Messaggero
La Repubblica
La Voix du Nord
New Scientist
New Statesman
New York Times
Nursing Times
Poetry Review
Seattle Times
Sunday Herald
Sunday Mirror
Sunday People
The Economist
The Spectator
Woman and Home
Woman's Weekly

13 letters:
Evening Herald
Horse and Hound
Just Seventeen
Mother and Baby

Reader's Digest
The Bookseller
The Watchtower
Wales on Sunday
Woman's Journal

14 letters:
Chicago Tribune
Daily Telegraph
Financial Times
France-Dimanche
House and Garden
Kansas City Star
Literary Review
News of the World
Publishing News
The Independent
The Sunday Times
Washington Post

15 letters:
Algemeen Dagblad
Berliner Zeitung
Chicago Sun-Times
Evening Standard
Exchange and Mart
Express on Sunday
Harpers and Queen
Homes and Gardens
Los Angeles Times
The Mail on Sunday

16 letters:
Dazed and Confused
Detroit Free Press
Diario de Noticias
Houston Chronicle
Irish Independent
National Enquirer
New York Daily News
Scotland on Sunday
The People's Friend
The Scots Magazine

17 letters:
Corriere della Sera
Dallas Morning News
New Musical Express
Sunday Independent
Wall Street Journal

18 letters:
National Geographic
The Sunday Telegraph

20 letters:
Orange County Register
Philadelphia Enquirer

21 letters:
British Medical Journal
San Francisco Chronicle

22 letters:
The Independent on
  Sunday

26 letters:
International Herald
  Tribune
The Times Literary
  Supplement

28 letters:
Frankfurter Allgemeine
  Zeitung

Ranks of nobility

RANKS OF BRITISH NOBILITY (IN ORDER OF PRECEDENCE)

Royal duke
Royal duchess
Duke
Duchess
Marquess

Marquis
Marchioness
Earl
Countess
Viscount

Viscountess
Baron
Baroness
Baronet

RANKS OF FOREIGN NOBILITY

5 letters:
Boyar
Count

6 letters:
Prince

7 letters:
Grandee
Marquis
Vicomte

8 letters:
Archduke
Burgrave
Countess
Marchesa
Marchese
Margrave
Marquise
Princess

9 letters:
Grand duke

Landgrave

10 letters:
Margravine
Vicomtesse

11 letters:
Archduchess
Landgravine

12 letters:
Grand duchess

Musical notes and rests

British name	American name
Breve	Double-whole note
Semibreve	Whole note
Minim	Half note
Crotchet	Quarter note
Quaver	Eighth note
Semiquaver	Sixteenth note
Demisemiquaver	Thirty-second note
Hemidemisemiquaver	Sixty-fourth note

Novelists

2 letters:
Mo, *Timothy*
Oë, *Kenzaburo*

3 letters:
Eco, *Umberto*
Lee, *Harper*
Lee, *Laurie*
Nye, *Robert*
Rao, *Raja*

4 letters:
Amis, *Kingsley*
Amis, *Martin*
Behn, *Aphra*
Bely, *Andrei*
Böll, *Heinrich*
Boyd, *William*
Buck, *Pearl*
Cela, *Camilo José*
Dunn, *Nell*
Fast, *Howard*
Ford, *Ford Madox*
Ford, *Richard*
Gide, *André*
Gold, *Herbert*
Gray, *Alasdair*
Hill, *Susan*
Hogg, *James*
Hope, *Anthony*
Hugo, *Victor (Marie)*
Jong, *Erica*
King, *Francis*
King, *Stephen*
Levi, *Primo*
Mann, *Thomas*
Okri, *Ben*
Puzo, *Mario*
Read, *Piers Paul*
Rhys, *Jean*
Roth, *Henry*
Saki
Sand, *George*
Snow, *C(harles) P(ercy)*
Uris, *Leon*
Wain, *John*
West, *Morris*
West, *Rebecca*

Wouk, *Herman*
Zola, *Emile*

5 letters:
Adams, *Douglas*
Adams, *Richard*
Anand, *Mulk Raj*
Banks, *Iain*
Banks, *Lynne Reid*
Barth, *John*
Bates, *H(erbert) E(rnest)*
Bowen, *Elizabeth*
Bragg, *Melvin*
Brink, *André*
Brown, *George Douglas*
Brown, *George Mackay*
Byatt, *A(ntonia) S(usan)*
Camus, *Albert*
Carey, *Peter*
Crane, *Stephen*
Defoe, *Daniel*
Desai, *Anita*
Doyle, *Arthur Conan*
Doyle, *Roddy*
Duffy, *Maureen*
Dumas, *Alexandre*
Eliot, *George*
Elkin, *Stanley*
Ellis, *Alice Thomas*
Elton, *Ben*
Figes, *Eva*
Frame, *Janet Paterson*
Frayn, *Michael*
Gogol, *Nikolai Vasilievich*
Gorky, *Maxim*
Gosse, *Edmund*
Grass, *Günter (Wilhelm)*
Hardy, *Thomas*
Hesse, *Hermann*
Heyer, *Georgette*
Hines, *Barry*
Hoban, *Russell*
Hulme, *Keri*
Innes, *Hammond*
James, *Henry*
James, *P(hyllis) D(orothy)*
Joyce, *James*
Kafka, *Franz*

Keane, *Molly*
Kesey, *Ken*
Lewis, *(Harry) Sinclair*
Llosa, *Mario Vargos*
Lodge, *David*
Lowry, *(Clarence) Malcolm*
Lurie, *Alison*
Marsh, *Ngaio*
Moore, *Brian*
Newby, *P(ercy) H(oward)*
Oates, *Joyce Carol*
O'Hara, *John*
Orczy, *Baroness Emmuska*
Ouida
Ozick, *Cynthia*
Paton, *Allan*
Peake, *Mervyn*
Powys, *John Cowper*
Queen, *Ellery*
Rolfe, *Frederick William*
Scott, *Walter*
Selby, *Hubert Jr*
Shute, *Nevil*
Simon, *Claude*
Smith, *Iain Crichton*
Smith, *Zadie*
Spark, *Muriel*
Stead, *C K*
Stein, *Gertrude*
Stone, *Robert*
Stowe, *Harriet Elizabeth Beecher*
Swift, *Graham*
Swift, *Jonathan*
Toole, *John Kennedy*
Tuohy, *Frank*
Twain, *Mark*
Tyler, *Anne*
Verne, *Jules*
Vidal, *Gore*
Waugh, *Evelyn*
Wells, *H(erbert) G(eorge)*
Welsh, *Irvine*
Welty, *Eudora*
White, *Antonia*
White, *Patrick*

White, *T(erence) H(anbury)*
Wilde, *Oscar*
Wolfe, *Thomas Clayton*
Wolfe, *Tom*
Wolff, *Tobias*
Woolf, *Virginia*
Yerby, *Frank*

6 letters:
Achebe, *Chinua*
Aldiss, *Brian*
Ambler, *Eric*
Archer, *Jeffrey*
Asimov, *Isaac*
Atwood, *Margaret*
Austen, *Jane*
Barker, *Elspeth*
Barker, *Pat*
Barnes, *Julian*
Bawden, *Nina*
Bellow, *Saul*
Berger, *John*
Berger, *Thomas*
Binchy, *Maeve*
Bowles, *Paul*
Braine, *John*
Brontë, *Anne*
Brontë, *Charlotte*
Brontë, *Emily (Jane)*
Brophy, *Brigid*
Buchan, *John*
Bunyan, *John*
Burney, *Fanny*
Butler, *Samuel*
Capote, *Truman*
Carter, *Angela*
Cather, *Willa*
Clarke, *Arthur C(harles)*
Cleary, *Jon*
Condon, *Richard*
Conrad, *Joseph*
Cooper, *James Fenimore*
Cooper, *Jilly*
Cooper, *William*
Davies, *(William) Robertson*
De Sade, *Marquis*
Didion, *Joan*
Farmer, *Philip José*

Fowles, *John*
Fraser, *Antonia*
French, *Marilyn*
Fuller, *Roy*
Gaddis, *William*
Garner, *Helen*
Gibbon, *Lewis Grassic*
Godden, *(Margaret) Rumer*
Godwin, *William*
Graham, *Winston*
Graves, *Robert*
Greene, *Graham*
Hailey, *Arthur*
Heller, *Joseph*
Hilton, *James*
Holtby, *Winifred*
Horgan, *Paul*
Howard, *Elizabeth Jane*
Hughes, *Thomas*
Hunter, *Evan*
Huxley, *Aldous*
Irving, *John*
Kaplan, *Johanna*
Kelman, *James*
Le Fanu, *Sheridan*
Le Guin, *Ursula*
Lively, *Penelope*
London, *Jack*
Mailer, *Norman*
Malouf, *David*
Massie, *Allan*
McEwan, *Ian*
Miller, *Henry*
Mosley, *Nicholas*
O'Brien, *Edna*
Orwell, *George*
Passos, *John Roderigo Dos*
Porter, *Harold*
Porter, *Katherine Anne*
Powell, *Anthony*
Proulx, *E Annie*
Proust, *Marcel*
Sartre, *Jean-Paul*
Sayers, *Dorothy L(eigh)*
Sharpe, *Tom*
Singer, *Isaac Bashevis*
Spring, *Howard*
Sterne, *Laurence*

Stoker, *Bram*
Storey, *David*
Styron, *William*
Symons, *Julian*
Trevor, *William*
Updike, *John*
Upward, *Edward (Falaise)*
Walker, *Alice*
Warner, *Marina*
Warren, *Robert Penn*
Weldon, *Fay*
Wesley, *Mary*
Wilder, *Thornton*
Wilson, *A(ndrew) N(orman)*
Wright, *Richard Nathaniel*

7 letters:
Ackroyd, *Peter*
Alvarez, *Al*
Angelou, *Maya*
Ballard, *J(ames) G(raham)*
Barstow, *Stanley*
Bedford, *Sybille*
Bennett, *(Enoch) Arnold*
Burgess, *Anthony*
Burrows, *Edgar Rice*
Calvino, *Italo*
Canetti, *Elias*
Clavell, *James*
Coetzee, *J(ohn) M(ichael)*
Colette
Collins, *(William) Wilkie*
Connell, *Evan*
Cookson, *Catherine*
DeLillo, *Don*
De Vries, *Peter*
Dickens, *Charles (John Huffam)*
Dickens, *Monica*
Dinesen, *Isak*
Drabble, *Margaret*
Durrell, *Gerald*
Durrell, *Laurence*
Fleming, *Ian*

Novelists

Forster, E(dward) M(organ)
Forsyth, Frederick
Francis, Dick
Gaskell, Elizabeth
Gibbons, Stella
Gilliat, Penelope
Gissing, George
Glasgow, Ellen
Golding, William (Gerald)
Goldman, William
Grisham, John
Haggard, Rider
Hartley, L(eslie) P(oles)
Hazzard, Shirley
Hurston, Zora Neale
Kennedy, Margaret
Kerouac, Jack
Kipling, Rudyard
Kundera, Milan
Lamming, George
Le Carré, John
Lehmann, Rosamond
Lessing, Doris
MacLean, Alistair
Mahfouz, Naguib
Malamud, Bernard
Manning, Olivia
Márquez, Gabriel García
Marryat, Frederick
Maugham, Somerset
Mauriac, Francois
Mishima, Yukio
Mitford, Nancy
Murdoch, Iris
Nabokov, Vladimir Vladimirovich
Naipaul, V(idiadhar) S(urdjprasad)
Peacock, Thomas Love
Pynchon, Thomas
Raphael, Frederic
Renault, Mary
Rendell, Ruth
Richler, Mordecai
Robbins, Harold
Rushdie, (Ahmed) Salman
Saroyan, William

Shelley, Mary
Shields, Carol
Simenon, Georges
Stewart, J(ohn) I(nnes) M(ackintosh)
Stewart, Mary
Süskind, Patrick
Tennant, Emma
Theroux, Paul
Tolkien, J(ohn) R(onald) R(euel)
Tolstoy, Leo
Tranter, Nigel
Tremain, Rose
Tutuola, Amos
Walpole, Horace
Wharton, Edith
Wilding, Michael

8 letters:
Abrahams, Peter
Aldridge, James
Apuleius, Lucius
Beerbohm, Max
Bradbury, Malcolm
Bradford, Barbara Taylor
Brittain, Vera
Brookner, Anita
Bulgakov, Mikhail Afanaseyev
Cartland, Barbara
Chandler, Raymond
Christie, Agatha (Mary Clarissa)
Correlli, Maria
Davidson, Lionel
De Balzac, Honoré
Deighton, Len
De Laclos, Pierre Choderlos
De Quincy, Thomas
Disraeli, Benjamin
Donleavy, J(ames) P(atrick)
Faulkner, William
Fielding, Helen
Fielding, Henry
Flaubert, Gustave
Forester, C(ecil) S(cott)
Freeling, Nicholas

Galloway, Janice
Gordimer, Nadine
Guterson, David
Heinlein, Robert A(nson)
Ishiguro, Kazuo
Jhabvala, Ruth Prawer
Keneally, Thomas
Kingsley, Charles
Lawrence, D(avid) H(erbert)
Macauley, Rose
MacInnes, Colin
Melville, Herman
Meredith, George
Michener, James A(lbert)
Mitchell, Julian
Mitchell, Margaret
Moorcock, Michael
Morrison, Toni
Mortimer, John
Mortimer, Penelope
Oliphant, Margaret
Ondaatje, Michael
Remarque, Erich Maria
Salinger, J(erome) D(avid)
Sillitoe, Alan
Smollett, Tobias George
Stendhal
Trollope, Anthony
Trollope, Joanna
Turgenev, Ivan Sergeyevich
Voltaire
Vonnegut, Kurt
Zamyatin, Evgeny Ivanovich

9 letters:
Blackmore, R(ichard) D(oddridge)
Bleasdale, Alan
Bromfield, Louis
Burroughs, William
Delafield, E M
Du Maurier, Daphne
Edgeworth, Maria
Feinstein, Elaine
Gerhardie, William Alexander

Goldsmith, *Oliver*
Goncharov, *Ivan Aleksandrovich*
Grossmith, *George*
Grossmith, *Weedon*
Hawthorne, *Nathaniel*
Hemingway, *Ernest*
Highsmith, *Patricia*
Isherwood, *Christopher*
Lermontov, *Mikhail Yurievich*
MacDonald, *George*
MacKenzie, *Compton*
MacKenzie, *Henry*
Mankowitz, *(Cyril) Wolf*
McCullers, *Carson*
McLaverty, *Bernard*
Mitchison, *Naomi*
Monsarrat, *Nicholas*
O'Flaherty, *Liam*
Pasternak, *Boris Leonidovich*
Pratchett, *Terry*
Priestley, *J(ohn) B(oynton)*
Pritchett, *V(ictor) S(awdon)*
Radcliffe, *Ann*
Schreiner, *Olive*

Sholokhov, *Mikhail Alexandrovich*
Steinbeck, *John*
Stevenson, *Robert Louis*
Thackeray, *William Makepeace*
Von Goethe, *Johann Wolfgang*
Wa Thiong'o, *Ngugi*
Winterson, *Jeanette*
Wodehouse, *P(elham) G(renville)*
Yourcenar, *Marguerite*

10 letters:
Bainbridge, *Beryl*
Ballantyne, *R(obert) M(ichael)*
Benedictus, *David*
Brooke-Rose, *Christina*
Chesterton, *G(ilbert) K(eith)*
De Beauvoir, *Simone*
Dostoevsky, *Fyodor Mikhailovich*
Fairbairns, *Zöe*
Fitzgerald, *F(rancis) Scott (Key)*
Fitzgerald, *Penelope*

Galsworthy, *John*
Markandaya, *Kamala*
McIlvanney, *William*
Richardson, *Dorothy*
Richardson, *Samuel*
Van der Post, *Laurens*
Vansittart, *Peter*
Waterhouse, *Keith*

11 letters:
Auchincloss, *Louis*
De Cervantes, *Miguel*
Di Lampedusa, *Guiseppe Tomasi*

12 letters:
De Maupassant, *Guy*
Kazantazakis, *Nikos*
Solzhenitsyn, *Alexander Isayevich*

13 letters:
Alain-Fournier
Sackville-West, *Vita*

14 letters:
Compton-Burnett, *Ivy*
De Saint-Exupéry, *Antoine*

Nuts

3 letters:
Cob

4 letters:
Cola
Kola
Mast
Pine
Rhus

5 letters:
Acorn
Areca
Arnut
Beech
Betel
Hazel

Lichi
Pecan

6 letters:
Acajou
Almond
Bauple
Brazil
Cashew
Cobnut
Illipe
Lichee
Litchi
Lychee
Marron
Monkey
Peanut

Pignut
Supari
Walnut

7 letters:
Arachis
Babassu
Coquina
Filberd
Filbert
Hickory
Praline
Prawlin

8 letters:
Chestnut
Earthnut

Nuts

Hazelnut
Quandong
Sapucaia

9 letters:
Amygdalus
Barcelona
Beech-mast
Butternut
Chincapin

Chinkapin
Coco de mer
Groundnut
Macadamia
Mockernut
Pistachio
Sassafras

10 letters:
Chinquapin

Pine kernel
Queensland

12 letters:
Bertholletia

13 letters:
Dwarf chestnut

O o

Occupations

2 letters:
AB
BA
CA
DD
GP
MA
MC
MD
MO
MP
Mr
PA
PM

3 letters:
BSc
CID
Deb
Doc
Don
Dux
Fan
Guy
Job
Kid
Lad
Man
Mrs
Nun
Pay
Rep
Sir
Spy

4 letters:
Aide
Babe
Baby
Bard
Beak
Bear

Beau
Boss
Bull
Chap
Char
Chef
Cook
Crew
Cure
Dean
Demy
Dick
Diva
Doxy
Dyer
Feed
Firm
Girl
G-man
Hack
Hand
Head
Hero
Hobo
Host
Lass
Lead
Magi
Maid
Miss
Monk
Page
Peer
Peon
Poet
Pope
Sage
Salt
Seer
Serf
Silk

Star
Tyro
Wage
Ward
Whip

5 letters:
Abbot
Actor
Ad-man
Adult
Agent
Baker
Belle
Boots
Bosun
Boxer
Buyer
Caddy
Cadet
Canon
Chief
Chips
Clerk
Coach
Crier
Crone
Crony
Crook
Decoy
Demon
Devil
Diver
Donor
Doyen
Dummy
Dutch
Elder
Envoy
Extra
Fakir
Felon

Fence
Fifer
Friar
Galen
Garbo
Ghost
Gipsy
Grass
Guard
Guest
Guide
Hewer
Issue
Judge
Juror
Laird
Limey
Local
Locum
Loser
Lover
Luter
Madam
Major
Maker
Maori
Mason
Mayor
Medic
Miner
Minor
Model
Nanny
Navvy
Nurse
Odist
Owner
Padre
Party
Pilot
Pin-up
Piper
Posse
Prior
Proxy
Pupil
Quack
Quill
Rabbi
Racer

Rider
Rishi
Rival
Rover
Saver
Sawer
Scout
Sewer
Slave
Smith
Sower
Staff
Tenor
Thief
Tiler
Tommy
Tramp
Tuner
Tutor
Uhlan
Usher
Valet
Vicar
Viner
Wench
Witch
Woman
Yokel
Youth

6 letters:
Abbess
Ad-mass
Air ace
Airman
Albino
Alumna
Archer
Artist
Au pair
Aurist
Author
Backer
Bandit
Banker
Barber
Bargee
Barker
Barman
Batman

Batter
Beadle
Bearer
Beater
Beggar
Beldam
Berber
Bishop
Boffin
Bookie
Bowman
Broker
Bugler
Bursar
Busker
Butler
Cabbie
Caddie
Caller
Camper
Cantor
Captor
Career
Carter
Carver
Casual
Censor
Cleric
Client
Codist
Co-heir
Consul
Coolie
Cooper
Copier
Copper
Co-star
Coster
Couper
Cowboy
Creole
Critic
Curate
Cutler
Cutter
Damsel
Dancer
Deacon
Dealer
Debtor

Deputy	Het-man	Miller
Divine	High-up	Minion
Docker	Hippie	Mister
Doctor	Hosier	Moiler
Double	Hunter	Monger
Dowser	Hussar	Moppet
Draper	Hymner	Mortal
Drawer	Ice-man	Mummer
Driver	Inmate	Munshi
Drudge	Intern	Musico
Duenna	Jailer	Mystic
Editor	Jester	Nannie
Ensign	Jet set	Native
Escort	Jobber	Norman
Eskimo	Jockey	Notary
Etcher	Joiner	Novice
Expert	Jumper	Nudist
Fabler	Junior	Nuncio
Factor	Junker	Oboist
Feeder	Keener	Odd job
Fellow	Keeper	Office
Fitter	Killer	Oilman
Flunky	Lackey	Optime
Flyman	Lancer	Oracle
Forger	Lascar	Orator
Friend	Lawyer	Ostler
Fuller	Leader	Outlaw
Gaffer	Lector	Packer
Gagman	Legate	Parson
Ganger	Lender	Pastor
Gaoler	Lessee	Patron
Garcon	Levite	Pedlar
Gaucho	Limner	Penman
German	Living	Pen-pal
Gigolo	Lodger	Picket
Gillie	Lutist	Pieman
Glazer	Lyrist	Pirate
Glover	Mahout	Pitman
Golfer	Maiden	Plater
Graver	Marine	Player
Grocer	Marker	Pommie
Grower	Master	Porter
Gunman	Matron	Potter
Gunner	Medico	Prater
Hatter	Medium	Priest
Hawker	Member	Punter
Healer	Menial	Purser
Helper	Mentor	Ragman
Herald	Mercer	Ranger
Hermit	Mikado	Rating

Reader
Reaper
Rector
Regius
Rhymer
Rigger
Ringer
Rioter
Robber
Rookie
Runner
Sailor
Sapper
Sartor
Savage
Savant
Sawyer
Scorer
Scouse
Scribe
Sea-dog
Sealer
Seaman
Second
Seller
Senior
Sentry
Server
Sexton
Shadow
Sheila
Shower
Shrink
Singer
Sister
Skater
Skivvy
Skyman
Slater
Slavey
Slayer
Sleuth
Smoker
Sniper
Soutar
Souter
Sowter
Sparks
Squire
Status

Stoker
Suitor
Sutler
Tailor
Talent
Tanner
Tartar
Tarvet
Taster
Tatter
Teller
Tenant
Teuton
Tiller
Tinker
Tinner
Toiler
Trader
Truant
Turner
Tycoon
Typist
Tyrant
Umpire
Urchin
Usurer
Valuer
Vanman
Vendor
Verger
Victor
Viking
Waiter
Walk-on
Warden
Warder
Weaver
Welder
Whaler
Winner
Wizard
Worker
Wright
Writer
Yeoman

7 letters:
Abetter
Abigail
Acolyte

Acrobat
Actress
Actuary
Admiral
Adviser
Almoner
Alumnus
Amateur
Analyst
Apostle
Arbiter
Artisan
Artiste
Assayer
Athlete
Attache
Auditor
Aviator
Bailiff
Ballboy
Bandman
Barmaid
Baronet
Bassist
Bedouin
Beldame
Bellboy
Bellhop
Big name
Big shot
Bit-part
Blender
Boarder
Boatman
Bookman
Bouncer
Breeder
Brigand
Builder
Burglar
Bushman
Butcher
Buttons
Callboy
Calling
Cambist
Captain
Captive
Carrier
Cashier

Caulker
Caveman
Cellist
Chemist
Chindit
Chorist
Citizen
Cleaner
Climber
Clippie
Coalman
Cobbler
Cockney
Colleen
Collier
Colonel
Commere
Company
Compere
Comrade
Convert
Convict
Co-pilot
Copyist
Copyman
Coroner
Corsair
Cossack
Counsel
Courier
Cowherd
Cowpoke
Creator
Crofter
Crooner
Cropper
Curator
Custode
Cyclist
Danseur
Daysman
Debater
Denizen
Dentist
Diviner
Dominie
Doorman
Dragoon
Drayman
Dresser

Driller
Drummer
Dustman
Elogist
Embassy
Entrant
Equerry
Escapee
Escaper
Esquire
Farceur
Farcist
Farrier
Fiddler
Fighter
Fireman
Flagman
Flapper
Flesher
Florist
Footboy
Footman
Footpad
Foreman
Founder
Frogman
Furrier
Gambler
Gate-man
General
Ghillie
Glazier
Gleaner
Grown up
Gun moll
Gymnast
Handler
Hangman
Harpist
Haulier
Head boy
Headman
Heckler
Heiress
Heroine
Hipster
Histrio
Hostess
Hymnist
Imagist

Invalid
Jack-tar
Janitor
Jemedar
Juggler
Junkman
Justice
Knacker
Knitter
Learner
Lineman
Linkboy
Linkman
Lockman
Look-out
Lorimer
Maestro
Magnate
Mailman
Manager
Mariner
Marshal
Masseur
Matador
Matelot
Meatman
Midwife
Milkman
Mobsman
Mobster
Modiste
Monitor
Moulder
Mourner
Mudlark
Navarch
Newsboy
Newsman
Oarsman
Oculist
Officer
Old salt
Omnibus
Oratrix
Orderly
Page-boy
Painter
Partner
Passman
Patient

Occupations

Patroon
Pearler
Peasant
Pianist
Picador
Pierrot
Pilgrim
Pioneer
Planner
Planter
Plumber
Poacher
Poetess
Pollman
Poloist
Pontiff
Poor man
Pop idol
Pop star
Post-boy
Postman
Prefect
Prelate
Premier
Presser
Primate
Printer
Privado
Private
Proctor
Proofer
Prophet
Protégé
Provost
Prowler
Puddler
Punster
Pursuer
Railman
Rancher
Rat race
Realtor
Redskin
Referee
Refugee
Regular
Remover
Rentier
Rescuer
Reserve

Retinue
Rich man
Routine
Rustler
Saddler
Sagaman
Samurai
Sandman
Scalper
Scenist
Scholar
Scraper
Sea-cook
Sea-king
Sea-lord
Sea-wolf
Seminar
Senator
Servant
Service
Settler
Sevitor
Sharper
Shearer
Sheriff
Shopman
Shopper
Showman
Skinner
Skipper
Soldier
Soloist
Soprano
Spartan
Speaker
Spinner
Sponsor
Spotter
Stand-by
Starlet
Starman
Starter
Station
Steward
Stipend
Student
Supremo
Surgeon
Swagman
Tapster

Teacher
Tipster
Tourist
Trainee
Trainer
Trapper
Trawler
Tripper
Trooper
Trouper
Tumbler
Turfman
Veteran
Viceroy
Vintner
Visitor
Warrior
Webster
Whipper
Wiseman
Witness
Wolf cub
Woodman
Woolman
Workman

8 letters:
Abductor
Adherent
Adjutant
Advocate
Aeronaut
Alderman
Alienist
Allopath
Ambivert
Anchoret
Armorist
Armourer
Arranger
Assassin
Assessor
Attacker
Attorney
Axemaker
Bagmaker
Banjoist
Bankrupt
Banksman
Bargeman

Baritone
Beadsman
Bedesman
Bedmaker
Beginner
Bigamist
Blackleg
Blind man
Boardman
Bohemian
Bondsman
Boniface
Borrower
Botanist
Bowmaker
Boxmaker
Boy scout
Brakeman
Brunette
Bummaree
Cabin boy
Call-girl
Canoness
Cardinal
Castaway
Ceramist
Chairman
Chambers
Champion
Chandler
Chaperon
Chaplain
Choirboy
Cicerone
Cicisbeo
Civilian
Claimant
Clansman
Classman
Clerkess
Clothier
Co-author
Comedian
Commando
Commoner
Compiler
Composer
Conjurer
Convener
Corporal

Coryphee
Cottager
Courtier
Coxswain
Creditor
Croupier
Cupmaker
Cutpurse
Dairyman
Danseuse
Dead-head
Deck-hand
Delegate
Deserter
Designer
Detainee
Dictator
Diet cook
Diocesan
Diplomat
Director
Disciple
Dogsbody
Domestic
Dragoman
Druggist
Duettist
Educator
Elegiast
Embalmer
Emeritus
Emigrant
Emissary
Employee
Engineer
Engraver
Epic poet
Essayist
Eulogist
Examinee
Executor
Explorer
Exponent
Fabulist
Factotum
Falconer
Fanfaron
Fanmaker
Farm hand
Ferryman

Figurant
Film idol
Filmstar
Finalist
Finisher
Fishwife
Flatfoot
Flautist
Floorman
Forester
Forgeman
Freshman
Front-man
Fugitive
Fusilier
Gangsman
Gangster
Gaolbird
Gardener
Garroter
Gendarme
Goatherd
Governor
Gownsman
Graduate
Guardian
Gunsmith
Ham actor
Handmaid
Handyman
Hatmaker
Hawkshaw
Haymaker
Head cook
Head girl
Headship
Hebraist
Helmsman
Henchman
Herdsman
Hijacker
Hired gun
Hired man
Hireling
Home help
Horseman
Hotelier
Houseboy
Hula girl
Huntsman

Idyllist
Importer
Inceptor
Informer
Initiate
Inkmaker
Inventor
Islander
Jailbird
Jet pilot
Jeweller
Jongleur
Juvenile
Knife-boy
Labourer
Land-girl
Landlady
Landlord
Landsman
Lapidary
Law agent
Lawgiver
Lawmaker
Laywoman
Lecturer
Licensee
Life-peer
Linesman
Linguist
Listener
Logician
Loiterer
Looker-on
Lumberer
Luminary
Lyricist
Magician
Mandarin
Mapmaker
Marauder
Marksman
Masseuse
Mechanic
Mediator
Melodist
Mercator
Merchant
Milkmaid
Millgirl
Millhand

Milliner
Minister
Ministry
Minstrel
Mistress
Modeller
Moralist
Motorist
Muleteer
Muralist
Murderer
Musician
Narrator
Naturist
Neophyte
Netmaker
Newcomer
News-hawk
Nightman
Norseman
Novelist
Objector
Occupant
Official
Onlooker
Op artist
Operator
Opponent
Optician
Oratress
Ordinand
Organist
Overlord
Overseer
Pardoner
Parodist
Party man
Passer-by
Patentee
Penmaker
Perfumer
Perjurer
Picaroon
Pilferer
Pillager
Plagiary
Poetling
Poisoner
Polisher
Pontifex

Position
Potmaker
Practice
Preacher
Pressman
Prioress
Prisoner
Prizeman
Producer
Promoter
Prompter
Psychist
Publican
Pugilist
Purveyor
Quarrier
Radar man
Rag trade
Ragwoman
Receiver
Recorder
Reformer
Reporter
Resident
Retailer
Retainer
Reveller
Revenant
Reviewer
Rewriter
Ridleman
Rivetter
Road-gang
Rotarian
Rugmaker
Saboteur
Salesman
Salvager
Satirist
Sawbones
Sawsmith
Sciolost
Scullion
Sculptor
Seafarer
Seedsman
Selector
Sentinel
Sergeant
Shepherd

Shipmate
Shopgirl
Showgirl
Side-kick
Sidesman
Silk gown
Sketcher
Sky-scout
Small fry
Smuggler
Solitary
Songster
Sorcerer
Spaceman
Spearman
Speed cop
Sprinter
Stageman
Star turn
Stockman
Storeman
Stowaway
Stranger
Stripper
Stroller
Stunt man
Superior
Superman
Supplier
Surveyor
Survivor
Swagsman
Tallyman
Taxpayer
Teddy boy
Teenager
Thatcher
Thespian
Thurifer
Tin miner
Tinsmith
Tom Thumb
Tone post
Top brass
Toreador
Torturer
Townsman
Trainman
Trappist
Tripeman

Tunester
Unionist
Union man
Vagabond
Valuator
Vanguard
Vigilate
Virtuoso
Vocalist
Vocation
Waitress
Ward maid
Wardress
Watchman
Waterman
Wayfarer
Wet nurse
Wheelman
Whiphand
Whipjack
Whittler
Wig maker
Woodsman
Workfolk
Workgirl
Workhand
Wrangler
Wrestler
Yodeller

9 letters:
Aborigine
Absconder
Aerialist
Alchemist
Anatomist
Anchoress
Anchorite
Annotator
Announcer
Annuitant
Antiquary
Apologist
Applicant
Appraiser
Arch-enemy
Architect
Archivist
Art critic
Art dealer

Artificer
Assistant
Associate
Astronaut
Attendant
Authoress
Authority
Automaton
Axlesmith
Balladist
Ballerina
Bargainer
Barrister
Barrow-boy
Beefeater
Bee keeper
Beermaker
Beggarman
Bellmaker
Biologist
Bit player
Boatswain
Bodyguard
Bodymaker
Boilerman
Boltsmith
Bookmaker
Bootblack
Bootmaker
Bradmaker
Brass hats
Brigadier
Buccaneer
Bunny girl
Bus driver
Bush pilot
Byrewoman
Bystander
Cab driver
Cabin crew
Café owner
Cakemaker
Cameraman
Candidate
Canvasser
Cardsharp
Caretaker
Carpenter
Casemaker
Celebrity

Cellarman	Debutante	Gem cutter
Centurion	Decorator	Geologist
Chain gang	Defendant	Girl guide
Charterer	Dependent	Gladiator
Charwoman	Designate	Gluemaker
Chauffeur	Desk clerk	Go-between
Choralist	Detective	Goldsmith
Chorus boy	Dialogist	Gondolier
Clergyman	Dietician	Governess
Clinician	Dispenser	Grapevine
Clogmaker	Dog walker	Grenadier
Coadjutor	Dollmaker	Guarantor
Coal miner	Dramatist	Guardsman
Coenobite	Drum major	Guerrilla
Colleague	Drysalter	Guest star
Collector	Ecologist	Guitarist
Columnist	Economist	Gunrunner
Combatant	Embezzler	Handsewer
Commander	Emolument	Harbinger
Commodore	Enamelist	Harbourer
Companion	Enchanter	Harlequin
Concierge	Engrosser	Harmonist
Concubine	Entourage	Harpooner
Conductor	Errand boy	Harvester
Confessor	Espionage	Head clerk
Confidant	Estimator	Herbalist
Conqueror	Exchanger	Hillbilly
Conscript	Exchequer	Hired hand
Constable	Exciseman	Hired help
Contender	Executive	Historian
Contralto	Eye doctor	Home maker
Cornerboy	Fieldwork	Homeopath
Cosmonaut	Figurante	Hottentot
Cost clerk	Film actor	House dick
Costumier	Film extra	Housemaid
Court fool	Film maker	Husbandry
Couturier	Financier	Hypnotist
Covergirl	Fire guard	Immigrant
Crackshot	First mate	Innkeeper
Cracksman	Fisherman	Inscriber
Crayonist	Foreigner	In service
Cricketer	Foundling	Inside man
Cupbearer	Free lance	Inspector
Custodian	Freemason	Interview
Cutthroat	Fruiterer	Ironminer
Cymbalist	Furnisher	Ironsmith
Daily help	Garreteer	Jay walker
Day-labour	Garrotter	Jitterbug
Deaconess	Gas fitter	Jobholder
Dean of men	Gazetteer	Key worker

Kidnapper
Lacemaker
Lady's maid
Lampmaker
Lampooner
Land agent
Land force
Landowner
Landreeve
Land shark
Larcenist
Launderer
Laundress
Lawmonger
Lay figure
Lay reader
Lay sister
Legionary
Lensmaker
Librarian
Lifeguard
Linotyper
Liontamer
Lip-reader
Liveryman
Loan agent
Lockmaker
Locksmith
Log-roller
Lord mayor
Lowlander
Lumberman
Machinist
Major domo
Major poet
Make-up man
Male model
Male nurse
Man-at-arms
Man Friday
Medallist
Mendicant
Mercenary
Mesmerist
Messenger
Middleman
Minor poet
Model girl
Monitress
Moonraker

Mortician
Muscleman
Musketeer
Mythmaker
Navigator
Neighbour
Newsagent
Newshound
Nursemaid
Occultist
Odd job man
Office boy
Old master
Old stager
Ombudsman
Operative
Osteopath
Otologist
Outfitter
Panellist
Pantomime
Paparazzo
Part-owner
Passenger
Patrolman
Patroness
Paymaster
Paysagist
Pedagogue
Pen friend
Pen pusher
Pensioner
Performer
Personnel
Phone girl
Physician
Physicist
Picksmith
Pierrette
Pistoleer
Pitwright
Plaintiff
Plasterer
Ploughboy
Ploughman
Plunderer
Poetaster
Policeman
Pop artist
Pop singer

Portrayer
Portreeve
Possessor
Postulant
Postwoman
Poulterer
Precentor
Precursor
Prelector
Presbyter
President
Priestess
Principal
Privateer
Professor
Profiteer
Prud'homme
Publicist
Publisher
Puppeteer
Raconteur
Rainmaker
Ransacker
Ranzelman
Ratefixer
Ratepayer
Recordist
Reference
Registrar
Residency
Rhymester
Ringsider
Roadmaker
Rocketeer
Rocket man
Ropemaker
Roundsman
Rum runner
Rural dean
Sackmaker
Sacristan
Safemaker
Sailmaker
Sales girl
Sales team
Sassenach
Scarecrow
Scavenger
Scenarist
Schoolma'm

Scrapegut
Scribbler
Scrivener
Sea-lawyer
Secretary
Seneschal
Sentryman
Seraskier
Serenader
Sermonist
Servitude
Shoemaker
Signaller
Signalman
Situation
Skin diver
Solicitor
Songsmith
Sonneteer
Sophister
Sophomore
Sorceress
Soubrette
Space crew
Speedster
Spider man
Spokesman
Sportsman
Stagehand
Stage idol
Star gazer
Statesman
Stationer
Steersman
Stevedore
Strike pay
Subaltern
Sub-editor
Subsitute
Suffragan
Swineherd
Tablemaid
Tailoress
Tap dancer
Tax evader
Tentmaker
Test pilot
Therapist
Timberman
Toolsmith

Town clerk
Towncrier
Tradesman
Traveller
Tribesman
Trumpeter
Tympanist
Undergrad
Usherette
Violinist
Volunteer
Wassailer
Waxworker
Weekender
Wheelsman
Winemaker
Woodreeve
Workwoman
Yachtsman
Youngster
Zitherist
Zoologist

10 letters:
Able seaman
Accomplice
Accountant
Advertiser
Aeronomist
Agrologist
Agronomist
Aide-de-camp
Air hostess
Air steward
Amanuensis
Ambassador
Anglo-Saxon
Anvilsmith
Apothecary
Apprentice
Arbitrator
Archbishop
Archdeacon
Archpriest
Aristocrat
Astrologer
Astronomer
Auctioneer
Audit clerk
Au pair girl

Babe in arms
Baby sitter
Ballet girl
Ballplayer
Bandmaster
Bank robber
Baseballer
Bassoonist
Bear leader
Beautician
Bellringer
Benefactor
Billbroker
Billposter
Biochemist
Biographer
Blacksmith
Bladesmith
Blockmaker
Bludgeoner
Bluebottle
Bluejacket
Boatwright
Bogtrotter
Bombardier
Bonesetter
Bonus clerk
Bookbinder
Book dealer
Bookfolder
Bookholder
Bookkeeper
Bookseller
Bookwright
Bootlegger
Brain drain
Brakemaker
Brass smith
Bricklayer
Brickmaker
Broom maker
Brushmaker
Bulb grower
Bumbailiff
Bureaucrat
Burlesquer
Camera team
Campaigner
Cartoonist
Cat breeder

Cat burglar
Catechumen
Cavalryman
Ceramicist
Chainmaker
Chairmaker
Chancellor
Changeling
Chargehand
Charity boy
Chauffeuse
Chorus girl
Chronicler
Cider maker
Cigar maker
Claim agent
Clapper boy
Cloakmaker
Clockmaker
Clocksmith
Clog dancer
Cloisterer
Cloistress
Clothmaker
Clubmaster
Coachmaker
Coastguard
Co-director
Collar-work
Coloratura
Colporteur
Comedienne
Commandant
Commission
Competitor
Compositor
Concertist
Consultant
Contestant
Contractor
Controller
Copyreader
Copywriter
Corn doctor
Cornettist
Coryphaeus
Councillor
Counsellor
Country boy
Countryman

Couturiere
Cover agent
Crackbrain
Cultivator
Customs man
Cytologist
Day tripper
Demoiselle
Dilettante
Dirty nurse
Disc jockey
Discounter
Discoverer
Dishwasher
Dispatcher
Dog breeder
Donkey work
Doorkeeper
Dramatizer
Dramaturge
Dressmaker
Drug pusher
Drummer boy
Dry cleaner
Duty roster
Early riser
Empiricist
Equestrian
Evangelist
Eye witness
Fabricator
Faith curer
Farmer's boy
Fellmonger
Fictionist
Film editor
Firemaster
Fire raiser
Fishmonger
Flag bearer
Flight crew
Flower girl
Folk singer
Footballer
Foot doctor
Forecaster
Forerunner
Forty-niner
Frame maker
Freebooter

Fund raiser
Gamekeeper
Game warden
Garage hand
Gatekeeper
Gatewright
Geisha girl
Geneticist
Geochemist
Geographer
Glassmaker
Glossarist
Goalkeeper
Gold beater
Gold digger
Goldworker
Grammarian
Grand prior
Groceryman
Gubernator
Gunslinger
Hall porter
Handmaiden
Handshaker
Hatchetman
Headhunter
Headmaster
Head porter
Head waiter
Hedgesmith
Henchwoman
Highlander
High priest
Highwayman
Hitchhiker
Holy orders
Honorarium
Horn player
Horologist
House agent
Husbandman
Impresario
Incendiary
Inhabitant
Inquisitor
Instructor
Iol painter
Ironmaster
Ironmonger
Ironworker

Jewel thief	Monopolist	Poet-priest
Job printer	Moonshiner	Politician
Journalist	Motley fool	Postmaster
Junk dealer	Mouthpiece	Prebendary
Kennelmaid	Naturalist	Priesthood
Kitchenboy	Nautch girl	Prima donna
Kitchenman	Naval cadet	Private eye
Knifesmith	Negotiator	Procurator
Land holder	Neutralist	Programmer
Land jobber	Newscaster	Prolocutor
Landlubber	News editor	Proprietor
Land pirate	Newsvendor	Prospector
Land waiter	Newswriter	Proveditor
Lapidarist	Night float	Questioner
Laundryman	Night nurse	Quizmaster
Law officer	Notability	Railwayman
Lay brother	Nurseryman	Raw recruit
Leading man	Obituarist	Recitalist
Legislator	Occupation	Researcher
Liberty man	Pallbearer	Retirement
Librettist	Pantomimic	Revenue man
Licentiate	Pantry maid	Revivalist
Lieutenant	Papermaker	Rhapsodist
Lighterman	Park keeper	Ringmaster
Lime burner	Park ranger	Roadmender
Linotypist	Pastrycook	Ropedancer
Lobsterman	Pathfinder	Ropewalker
Lock keeper	Pawnbroker	Safeblower
Loggerhead	Peacemaker	Sales clerk
Loomworker	Pearl diver	Sales force
Lumberjack	Pearly king	Saleswoman
Machineman	Pedestrian	Saltworker
Magistrate	Pediatrist	Sand-dancer
Mail robber	Pedicurist	Scientists
Management	Penologist	Scrutineer
Manageress	Perruquier	Sculptress
Manicurist	Personnage	Sea-captain
Manservant	Petitioner	Seamstress
Medical man	Pharmacist	Second mate
Medicaster	Piano tuner	Sematicist
Message boy	Piccoloist	Seminarian
Midshipman	Pickpocket	Sempstress
Militiaman	Piermaster	Serologist
Millwright	Plagiarist	Serviceman
Mind-curist	Platelayer	Session man
Mind healer	Playbroker	Shanghaier
Mindreader	Playwright	Shipwright
Ministress	Playwriter	Shopfitter
Missionary	Poet-artist	Shopkeeper
Model maker	Poet-farmer	Signwriter

Songstress
Sound mixer
Spacewoman
Specialist
Speculator
Spy catcher
Staff nurse
Starmonger
Steelmaker
Steepljack
Step dancer
Stewardess
Stick-up man
Stockrider
Stocktaker
Stonemason
Storesmith
Strategist
Submariner
Subscriber
Supercargo
Supervisor
Supplicant
Swordsmith
Symphonist
Syncopator
Tally clerk
Tallywoman
Taskmaster
Taxi driver
Technician
Technocrat
Televiewer
Tenderfoot
Third party
Tilewright
Timekeeper
Trafficker
Translator
Tripehound
Tripewoman
Trombonist
Troubadour
Tweedledee
Tweedledum
Typesetter
Typing pool
Underagent
Understudy
Undertaker

Vegetarian
Versemaker
Versesmith
Veterinary
Vice-consul
Vice-master
Victualler
Vine grower
Wage earner
Wage worker
Wainwright
Watchmaker
Water guard
Wharfinger
Wholesaler
Winebibber
Winewaiter
Wireworker
Woodcarver
Woodcutter
Woodworker
Wool carder
Wool comber
Wool sorter
Wool winder
Workfellow
Working man
Workmaster
Workpeople
Worshipper

11 letters:
Abecedarian
Academician
Accompanist
Actor's agent
Antiquarian
Appointment
Army officer
Astrologist
Astronomist
Audio typist
Backroom boy
Bag snatcher
Bank cashier
Bank manager
Bargemaster
Basketmaker
Beauty queen
Bell founder

Beneficiary
Billsticker
Bingo caller
Bird fancier
Bird watcher
Board member
Body builder
Body servant
Boilermaker
Boilersmith
Breadwinner
Bridgemaker
Broadcaster
Bronzesmith
Bullfighter
Bushfighter
Businessman
Candlemaker
Car salesman
Chamberlain
Chambermaid
Charcoalist
Cheerleader
Cheesemaker
Chiropactor
Chiropodist
Choirmaster
Clairvoyant
Clergywoman
Coachwright
Co-authoress
Coffinmaker
Cognoscenti
Commentator
Congressman
Conspirator
Contributor
Conveyancer
Co-ordinator
Coppersmith
Court jester
Crane driver
Crimewriter
Crown lawyer
Cub reporter
Cypher clerk
Day labourer
Dean of women
Delivery man
Demographer

Distributor
Double agent
Draughtsman
Drill master
Drug peddler
Duty officer
Electrician
Embroiderer
Enlisted man
Entertainer
Estate agent
Etymologist
Executioner
Extortioner
Factory hand
Faith healer
Field worker
Fifth column
Fighting man
Filing clerk
Fingersmith
Fire brigade
Fire watcher
Flag captain
Flag officer
Flat dweller
Flying squad
Foot soldier
Fruit picker
Funambulist
Functionary
Galley slave
Gamesmaster
Gentlewoman
Ghostwriter
Ginger group
Glass blower
Glass cutter
Grave digger
Greengrocer
Gunman's moll
Haberdasher
Hairdresser
Hair stylist
Hammersmith
Handservant
Hardwareman
Head teacher
Hedgepriest
High sheriff

High society
Home crofter
Horse doctor
Horse trader
Housemaster
Housemother
Housewright
Ice-cream man
Illuminator
Illusionist
Illustrator
Infantryman
Interpreter
Interviewer
Iron founder
Kitchenmaid
Lamplighter
Landscapist
Land steward
Laundrymaid
Leading lady
Leaseholder
Ledger clerk
Leter writer
Lifeboatman
Locum tenens
Lollipop man
Lord Provost
Lorry driver
Madrigalist
Maidservant
Mandolinist
Manipulator
Masquerader
Master baker
Matinee idol
Mechanician
Medicine man
Merchantman
Metalworker
Method actor
Military man
Millionaire
Mimographer
Miniaturist
Momorialist
Money lender
Moonlighter
Mother's help
Mountaineer

Music critic
Naval rating
Needlewoman
Neurologist
Night hunter
Night porter
Night sister
Night worker
Novelettist
Numismatist
Office party
Onion Johnny
Optometrist
Ornamentist
Orthopedist
Palaestrian
Pamphleteer
Panelbeater
Panel doctor
Papal nuncio
Paperhanger
Paragrapher
Parish clerk
Parlourmaid
Pathologist
Pearlfisher
Pearly queen
Penny-a-liner
Petrologist
Philatelist
Philologist
Philosopher
Phonologist
Piece worker
Police cadet
Policewoman
Portraitist
Predecessor
Prizewinner
Probationer
Proof reader
Protagonist
Purseholder
Questionist
Quill driver
Radiologist
Rag merchant
Rank and file
Rear admiral
Relic monger

Research man
Rhetorician
River keeper
Roadsweeper
Rocket pilot
Rugby player
Safebreaker
Safecracker
Sandwichman
Saxophonist
School nurse
Scorekeeper
Scoutmaster
Scrap dealer
Scythesmith
Search party
Secret agent
Semaphorist
Semi-skilled
Senior clerk
Sharebroker
Sheep farmer
Shepherdess
Shipbuilder
Ship's cooper
Ship's tailor
Ship's writer
Shop steward
Silversmith
Sinologoist
Sister tutor
Slaughterer
Slave trader
Smallholder
Sociologist
Space doctor
Spacewriter
Speechmaker
Stage player
Stagewright
Stallholder
Stenotypist
Stereotyper
Stipendiary
Stockbroker
Stockfarmer
Stockjobber
Stonecutter
Storekeeper
Storyteller

Straight man
Stripteaser
Subordinate
Surrebutter
Swordmaster
Talent scout
Taxidermist
Telegrapher
Telepathist
Telephonist
Terpsichore
Testimonial
Ticket agent
Toastmaster
Tobacconist
Tommy Atkins
Tooth doctor
Tooth drawer
Town planner
Toxophilite
Train bearer
Train robber
Transcriber
Travel agent
Tree surgeon
Truck farmer
Typographer
Upholsterer
Van salesman
Versemonger
Vine dresser
Viola player
War reporter
Washerwoman
Water doctor
Water finder
Welfare work
Whalefisher
Wheelwright
White-collar
White hunter
Witch doctor
Woodshopper
Wool stapler
Working girl
Xylophonist
Youth leader

12 letters:
Actor-manager

Advance party
Air commodore
Aircraftsman
Air-sea rescue
Ambulance man
Anaesthetist
Armour bearer
Artilleryman
Balladmonger
Ballad singer
Ballet dancer
Bibliologist
Bibliopegist
Body snatcher
Booking clerk
Bookstitcher
Border sentry
Bottlewasher
Boulevardier
Bridgemaster
Brigade major
Cabinet maker
Calligrapher
Camp follower
Candlewright
Caricaturist
Carpet bagger
Carpet fetter
Cartographer
Casual labour
Cattle lifter
Cerographist
Check-weigher
Chicken thief
Chief cashier
Chief justice
Chief mourner
Chief of staff
Chimney sweep
Chirographer
Churchwarden
Circuit rider
Civil servant
Civil service
Clarinettist
Clerk of works
Coachbuilder
Coatguardman
Collaborator
Commissioner

Occupations

Confectioner
Conquistador
Contemporary
Corn chandler
Costermonger
Customs clerk
Deep-sea diver
Demonstrator
Desk sergeant
Doctor's round
Dramaturgist
Ecclesiastic
Electrotyper
Elocutionist
Entomologist
Entrepreneur
Escapologist
Exhibitioner
Experimenter
Ex-serviceman
Exterminator
Family doctor
Father figure
Field-marshal
Figure dancer
Filed officer
Filibusterer
Film director
Film producer
First officer
First reserve
Flying column
Flying doctor
Footplateman
Garret master
General agent
Geriatrician
Globetrotter
Grandstander
Group captain
Guest speaker
Gynecologist
Headmistress
Headshrinker
Heir apparent
High official
Hockey player
Holidaymaker
Hotel manager
Housebreaker

Houseekeeper
Housepainter
Hydropathist
Immunologist
Impersonator
Improvisator
Instructress
Intermediary
Jazz musician
Junior rating
Juvenile lead
King's counsel
Kitchen staff
Knifegrinder
Knifethrower
Lady superior
Landed gentry
Land surveyor
Law stationer
Lay-out artist
Leader writer
Leathernecks
Legal adviser
Lexicologist
Line sergeant
Literary hack
Literary lion
Lithographer
Longshoreman
Loss adjuster
Maid of honour
Maitre d'hotel
Major-general
Make-up artist
Man of letters
Man of science
Manual worker
Manufacturer
Mass-producer
Master-at-arms
Mastersinger
Metallurgist
Metropolitan
Mezzo soprano
Mineralogist
Money-changer
Monographist
Motorcyclist
Musicologist
Naval officer

Newspaperman
Notary public
Nutritionist
Obstetrician
Office bearer
Office junior
Pastoral poet
Patent office
Pediatrician
Penitentiary
Petty officer
Photographer
Physiologist
Plant manager
Ploughwright
Plumber's mate
Poet laureate
Post graduate
Postmistress
Practitioner
Press officer
Principal boy
Prison warder
Prison worker
Quarrymaster
Racing driver
Radiodontist
Radiographer
Receptionist
Restaurateur
Retaining fee
Sales manager
Scene-painter
Scene-shifter
Schoolmaster
Screenwriter
Scriptwriter
Scullery maid
Sister german
Site engineer
Snake-charmer
Social worker
Soil mechanic
Sole occupant
Special agent
Speechwriter
Spiritualist
Sportscaster
Sports master
Sportswriter

Staff officer
Stage manager
Statistician
Steel erector
Stenographer
Stereotypist
Stonedresser
Stormtrooper
Street-trader
Tax-collector
Technologist
Telegraph boy
Telephone man
Tennis player
Test engineer
Theatre nurse
Ticket holder
Ticket writer
Top executive
Trained nurse
Trichologist
Trick-cyclist
Troutbreeder
Undermanager
Vaudevillist
Vice-director
Vice-governor
Vicie-admiral
Warehouseman
Water-diviner
Wind musician
Wine merchant
Wood-engraver
Worker priest
Working party
Workmistress
Works manager

13 letters:
Alongshoreman
Antique dealer
Archaeologist
Articled clerk
Audio-engineer
Barber-surgeon
Campanologist
Church officer
Civil engineer
Common law wife
Contortionist

Contrabandist
Cook-housemaid
Cotton spinner
Counter-jumper
Craftsmanship
Cryptographer
Dancing master
Dental surgeon
District nurse
Feature editor
Fellow-servant
Fencing master
Fortune-teller
Guardian angel
Gynaecologist
Harbour master
Health visitor
Industrialist
Lady-in-waiting
Lexicographer
Lift attendant
Lighthouseman
Livery servant
Lollipop woman
Maid-of-all-work
Master builder
Master mariner
Nightwatchman
Office manager
Old-clothes man
Poultry farmer
Printer's devil
Prison visitor
Process server
Rag-and-bone-man
Rent collector
Reseach worker
Scrap merchant
Ship's chandler
Shop assistant
Shop detective
Skeleton staff
Skilled worker
Slave labourer
Still-room maid
Street sweeper
Toastmistress
Traffic warden
Universal aunt
Window cleaner

Window dresser

14 letters:
Accomplishment
Apprenticeship
Audiometrician
Black marketeer
Bus conductress
Casual labourer
Charcoal burner
Chimney sweeper
Clerical worker
Coastguardsman
Commissionaire
Common informer
Dramatic critic
Elder statesman
Hotel detective
House decorator
House detective
King's messenger
Labour exchange
Maintenance man
Market gardener
Marriage broker
Matron of honour
Mining engineer
Munition worker
Naval architect
Nursing officer
Opposite number
Opthalmologist
Prison governor
Reverend Mother
Ship's carpenter
Sports reporter
Stage carpenter
Stamp collector
Standard bearer
Station manager
Store detective
Street musician
Superintendent
Tobacco planter
Trouble shooter
Turf accountant
Valet de chambre

15 letters:
Blastfurnaceman

Officials

Bow street runner
Colliery manager
Commission agent
Crossing sweeper
Customs official
District visitor
Father Christmas
Funeral director
Gentleman farmer
Gentleman's usher

Gossip columnist
Jack-of-all-trades
Old-age pensioner
One-parent family
Planning officer
Police constable
Programme seller
Queen's messenger
Research chemist
Shorthand typist

Shorthand writer
Slave trafficker
Stretcher bearer
Surrogate father
Surrogate parent
Ticket collector
Tight-rope walker
Under-cover agent
Youth club leader

Officials

2 letters:
MC
SL

3 letters:
Aga
GOC

4 letters:
Agha
Cigs
Dean
Exon
Imam
Prog
Suit

5 letters:
Amban
Chair
Ephor
Imaum
Jurat
Mayor
Mirza
Sewer
Usher

6 letters:
Ataman
Beadle
Bursar
Censor
Consul
Datary
Deacon

Hetman
Keeper
Lictor
Master
Notary
Purser
Sexton
Syndic
Verger
Warden
Yeoman

7 letters:
Agistor
Attaché
Bailiff
Coroner
Darogha
Equerry
Filacer
Filazer
Hayward
Jamadar
Jemadar
Jemidar
Marshal
Mueddin
Pooh-Bah
Proctor
Provost
Sheriff
Speaker
Steward
Tribune

8 letters:
Bimbashi
Black rod
Chairman
Claviger
Cursitor
Decurion
Delegate
Mandarin
Palatine
Tipstaff
Verderer
Whiffler

9 letters:
Apparitor
Catchpole
Catchpoll
Commissar
Constable
Ealdorman
Escheator
Exciseman
Gauleiter
Intendant
Jobsworth
Landdrost
Moderator
Ombudsman
Polemarch
Precentor
President
Principal
Tahsildar
Treasurer
Waldgrave

10 letters:
Ambassador
Bumbailiff
Bureaucrat
Chairwoman
Chancellor
Magistrate
Postmaster
Procurator
Proveditor
Pursuivant
Silentiary
Subchanter
Supercargo
Tidewaiter
Timekeeper

11 letters:
Chairperson
Chamberlain
Functionary
Infirmarian
Shop steward

12 letters:
Commissioner
Jack-in-office
Remembrancer

13 letters:
Quartermaster

14 letters:
Provost-marshal

15 letters:
Plenipotentiary

16 letters:
Procurator fiscal
Public prosecutor
Returning officer

17 letters:
Compliance officer

Oils

3 letters:
Gas
Nim
Nut

4 letters:
Bone
Coal
Corn
Fuel
Musk
Neem
Oleo
Palm
Poon
Soya
Tung
Yolk

5 letters:
Ajwan
Argan
Attar
Benne
Benni
Clove
Colza
Crude
Fixed
Fusel

Heavy
Maize
Olive
Pulza
Rosin
Savin
Shale
Sperm
Spike
Stand
Train
Whale

6 letters:
Ajowan
Banana
Canola
Carapa
Carron
Castor
Croton
Diesel
Drying
Elaeis
Jojoba
Neroli
Peanut
Ramtil
Savine
Semsem

Sesame
Virgin

7 letters:
Butyrin
Cajeput
Cajuput
Camphor
Coconut
Dittany
Gingili
Linalol
Linseed
Lumbang
Menthol
Mineral
Mustard
Myrrhol
Naphtha
Picamar
Retinol
Ricinus
Tea tree
Vitriol

8 letters:
Bergamot
Camphire
Cod-liver
Gingelli

Gingelly
Lavender
Linalool
Macassar
Oiticica
Paraffin
Pristane
Rapeseed

9 letters:
Groundnut
Neat's foot
Parathion
Patchouli
Sassafras
Spikenard

Star-anise
Sunflower
Vegetable

10 letters:
Citronella
Cottonseed
Eucalyptus
Peppermint
Sandalwood
Turpentine
Ylang-ylang

11 letters:
Camphorated
Chaulmoogra

Chinese wood
Wintergreen

12 letters:
Benzaldehyde

13 letters:
Pentyl acetate
Sunflower seed

14 letters:
Glutaraldehyde

15 letters:
Evening primrose

Shades of orange

4 letters:
Gold

5 letters:
Amber
Ochre

Peach

9 letters:
Grenadine
Tangerine

10 letters:
Terracotta

11 letters:
Burnt sienna

Instruments in a full orchestra

4 letters:
Gong
Harp
Oboe
Tuba

5 letters:
Cello
Flute
Piano
Viola

6 letters:
Violin

7 letters:
Bassoon
Celesta
Piccolo
Timpani
Trumpet

8 letters:
Bass-drum
Clarinet
Trombone

9 letters:
Snare drum
Xylophone

10 letters:
Cor anglais
Double bass
French horn

11 letters:
Violoncello

12 letters:
Tubular bells

13 letters:
Contra-bassoon

Ores

3 letters:
Tin
Wad

4 letters:
Alga
Wadd

6 letters:
Copper
Glance

7 letters:
Bauxite
Bornite
Niobite
Oligist
Peacock
Realgar

8 letters:
Calamine
Cerusite
Crocoite
Galenite
Ilmenite
Limonite
Smaltite
Tenorite

9 letters:
Coffinite
Haematite
Hedyphane
Ironstone
Phacolite
Proustite
Stream-tin

10 letters:
Calaverite

Chalcocite
Horseflesh
Iridosmine
Melaconite
Sphalerite
Stephanite

11 letters:
Pitchblende
Psilomelane
Pyrargyrite

12 letters:
Babingtonite
Chalcopyrite
Pyromorphite
Tetrahedrite

15 letters:
Stilpnosiderite

Organs

3 letters:
Ear
Fin

4 letters:
Gill

5 letters:
Cort's
Ctene
Gonad
Liver
Serra

6 letters:
Carpel
Feeler
Fundus
Kidney
Radula
Spleen
Stamen
Syrinx

Thymus
Tongue
Tonsil
Uterus
Viscus
Vitals

7 letters:
Isomere
Medulla
Nectary
Oogonia
Saprobe
Viscera

8 letters:
Hapteron
Pancreas
Placenta
Pulmones
Receptor
Tentacle
Tympanum

9 letters:
Sensillum
Spinneret

10 letters:
Nephridium
Ovipositor
Parapodium
Photophore
Sporangium
Sporophore

11 letters:
Archegonium

12 letters:
Exteroceptor

13 letters:
Chemoreceptor
Photoreceptor

Economic organizations and treaties

2 letters:
EU

3 letters:
CAP
CBI
ECO
EEA
EMS
EMU
IFC
ILO
IMF
TUC
WTO

4 letters:
ACAS
CACM
ECSC
EFTA
GATT
NEDC
OECD
OPEC

5 letters:
LAFTA
NAFTA
UNIDO

6 letters:
ECOSOC
ECOWAS
UNCTAD

7 letters:
CARICOM
CARIFTA
COMECON

8 letters:
Advisory

9 letters:
World Bank

12 letters:
Conciliation

Treaty of Rome

13 letters:
European Union

14 letters:
Lomé agreements

16 letters:
Maastricht Treaty

18 letters:
Bretton Woods System

19 letters:
Office of Fair Trading
Trades Union Congress

20 letters:
European Economic
    Area

21 letters:
And Arbitration Service
European Monetary
    Union

22 letters:
Caribbean Free Trade
    Area
European Investment
    Bank
European Monetary
    System
World Trade
    Organization

23 letters:
Single European Market
    Act

24 letters:
Common Agricultural
    Policy
Economic and Social
    Council
European Coal
    Organization

25 letters:
International Monetary
    Fund

27 letters:
Central American
    Common Market

28 letters:
European Free Trade
    association

29 letters:
European Coal and Steel
    Community

30 letters:
Confederation of British
    Industry
Monopolies and
    Mergers Commission

31 letters:
European Monetary
    Cooperation Fund
European Regional
    Development Fund
International Finance
    Corporation
International Labour
    Organization
North American Free
    Trade Agreement

33 letters:
Caribbean Community
    and Common Market
General Agreement on
    Tariffs and Trade
Latin American Free
    Trade Association

34 letters:
Council for Mutual
    Economic Assistance
National Economic
    Development Council

36 letters:
Economic Community
Of West African States

40 letters:
New Zealand and
Australia Free Trade
Agreement

41 letters:
Organization of
Petroleum Exporting
Countries

43 letters:
European Bank for
Reconstruction and
Development

44 letters:
United Nations
Conference on Trade
and Development

46 letters:
United Nations
Industrial

Development
Organization

48 letters:
International Bank for
Reconstruction and
Development
Organization for
Economic
Cooperation and
Development

Oxbridge colleges

3 letters:
New

5 letters:
Clare
Green
Jesus
Keble
King's
Oriel

6 letters:
Darwin
Exeter
Girton
Merton
Queen's
Selwyn
Wadham

7 letters:
Balliol
Christ's
Downing
Kellogg
Linacre
Lincoln
New Hall
Newnham
St Anne's

St Cross
St Hugh's
St John's
Trinity
Wolfson

8 letters:
All Souls
Emmanuel
Homerton
Magdalen
Nuffield
Pembroke
Robinson
St Hilda's
St Peter's

9 letters:
Brasenose
Churchill
Clare Hall
Magdalene
Mansfield
St Antony's
St Edmund's
Templeton
Worcester

10 letters:
Greyfriars

Hughes Hall
Peterhouse
Somerville
St Stephen's
University

11 letters:
Blackfriars
Campion Hall
Fitzwilliam
Regent's Park
Trinity Hall

12 letters:
Christ Church
Sidney Sussex
St Benet's Hall
St Catharine's
St Catherine's
St Edmund Hall
Wycliffe Hall

13 letters:
Corpus Christi
Lucy Cavendish

16 letters:
Gonville and Caius
Harris Manchester
Lady Margaret Hall

P p

Palms

3 letters:
Ita

4 letters:
Atap
Coco
Date
Doum
Nipa

5 letters:
Areca
Assai
Betel
Bussu
Macaw
Nikau
Ratan
Sabal

6 letters:
Buriti
Corozo
Elaeis

Gomuti
Gomuto
Gru-gru
Jupati
Kentia
Macoya
Raffia
Raphia
Rattan
Trooly

7 letters:
Babassu
Calamus
Coquito
Corypha
Euterpe
Jipyapa
Moriche
Palmyra
Paxiuba
Pupunha
Talipat

Talipot
Troelie
Troolie

8 letters:
Carnauba
Date tree
Groo-groo
Jipi-Japa
Macahuba

9 letters:
Burrawang
Carnahuba

10 letters:
Chamaerops
Jippi-Jappa

12 letters:
Chiqui-chiqui
Washingtonia

Papers

3 letters:
Art
Rag
Wax

4 letters:
Bond
Chad
Demy
Exam
File
Laid
Note

Rice
Test
Wove

5 letters:
Bible
Brown
Crepe
Crown
Emery
Flock
Glass
Graph

Green
India
Kraft
Linen
Sheet
Sugar
Touch
Waste
Waxed
White

6 letters:
Ballot

Baryta
Carbon
Filter
Garnet
Litmus
Manila
Retree
Tissue
Toilet
Vellum

7 letters:
Bromide
Manilla
Papyrus

Torchon
Tracing
Whatman®
Writing

8 letters:
Document
Foolscap
Glassine
Turmeric
Wrapping

9 letters:
Cartridge
Chiyogami

Cigarette
Cream-laid
Cream-wove
Hieratica
Onion-skin
Papillote
Parchment
Willesden

10 letters:
Cellophane®

11 letters:
Greaseproof

Parasites

3 letters:
Bot
Ked
Nit

4 letters:
Conk
Flea
Kade
Tick
Tryp

5 letters:
Leech
Louse
Worms

6 letters:
Coccus
Dodder
Isopod
Viscum

7 letters:
Ascarid
Bonamia
Candida
Copepod
Epizoon
Giardia
Hair-eel

Lamprey
Pinworm
Stylops

8 letters:
Entozoon
Epiphyte
Filarium
Hook-worm
Lungworm
Nematode
Puccinia
Sporozoa
Tapeworm
Trichina

9 letters:
Bilharzia
Ectophyte
Endamoeba
Endophyte
Entophyte
Heartworm
Ichneumon
Inquiline
Macdonald
Mistletoe
Orobanche
Rafflesia
Roundworm
Sporozoan

Strongyle
Trematode

10 letters:
Autoecious
Babesiasis
Liverfluke
Monogenean
Plasmodium
Rickettsia
Smut-fungus
Toxoplasma

11 letters:
Bladder-worm
Cryptozoite
Gregarinida
Haematozoon
Schistosoma
Strongyloid
Trypanosoma

12 letters:
Heteroecious
Licktrencher
Mallophagous
Rhipidoptera
Strepsiptera

15 letters:
Cryptosporidium

Parliaments

4 letters:
Dail
Diet
Rump
Sejm

5 letters:
Lords
Thing

6 letters:
Cortes
Majlis
Seanad

7 letters:
Althing
Commons
Knesset

Lagting
Riksdag
Tynwald

8 letters:
Congress
Lagthing
Lok Sabha
Stannary
Stormont
Storting

9 letters:
Barebones
Bundestag
Eduskunta
Folketing
Landsting

Odelsting
Reichstag
Sanhedrin
Stirthing
Storthing

10 letters:
Landsthing
Rajya Sabha
St Stephens

11 letters:
Volkskammer
Westminster

13 letters:
Seanad Eireann

Types of pasta

4 letters:
Pipe
Zita
Ziti

5 letters:
Penne
Ruote

6 letters:
Ditali

7 letters:
Bavette
Fusilli
Gnocchi
Lasagne
Lumache
Noodles
Ravioli

Spätzle

8 letters:
Bucatini
Farfalle
Linguine
Macaroni
Rigatoni
Spaetzle
Taglioni

9 letters:
Agnolotti
Fettucine
Fettucini
Spaghetti

10 letters:
Bombolotti
Cannelloni

Cellentani
Conchiglie
Fettuccine
Gnocchetti
Lasagnette
Tortellini
Tortelloni
Vermicelli

11 letters:
Cappelletti
Maultaschen
Orecchiette
Pappardelle
Tagliatelle
Tortiglioni

12 letters:
Paglia e fieno

Types of pastry

4 letters:
Filo
Puff
Suet

5 letters:
Choux

Flaky

8 letters:
Hot water

9 letters:
Rough puff

10 letters:
Pâte brisée
Pâte sucrée
Shortcrust

14 letters:
Pâte feuilletée

Peninsulas

4 letters:
Ards
Cape
Eyre
Kola

5 letters:
Gaspé
Gower
Lleyn
Malay
Sinai
Yorke

6 letters:
Alaska
Avalon
Balkan
Bataan
Crimea
Deccan
Iberia
Istria
Palmer

Tasman
Wirral

7 letters:
Arabian
Boothia
Cape Cod
Chukchi
Florida
Iberian
Jutland
Kintyre
Kowloon
Leizhou

8 letters:
Delmarva
East Cape
Labrador
Melville

9 letters:
Antarctic
Cape Verde

Gallipoli
Indo-China
Kamchatka
Kathiawar
The Lizard

10 letters:
Chalcidice
Chersonese
Nova Scotia

11 letters:
Peloponnese

12 letters:
Scandinavian

14 letters:
Baja California

17 letters:
Wilson's Promontory

Peoples

AFRICAN PEOPLES

3 letters:
Edo
Ewe
Ibo
Luo
Rif

San
Tiv
Twi

4 letters:
Akan
Boer

Efik
Fang
Fula
Hutu
Igbo
Lozi

AFRICAN PEOPLES (CONTINUED)

Luba
Moor
Munt
Mzee
Nama
Nuba
Nuer
Nupe
Pedi
Riff
Rifi
Susu
Tshi
Xosa
Zulu

5 letters:
Bantu
Bemba
Bintu
Chewa
Dinka
Duala
Dyula
Fanti
Fingo
Fulah
Galla
Ganda
Hausa
Ibibi
Kongo
Lango
Mande
Masai
Mende
Mossi
Muntu
Negro
Nguni
Nilot
Nyoro
Oromo
Pigmy
Pondo
Pygmy
Shluh
Shona

Sotho
Swazi
Temne
Tonga
Tutsi
Venda
Wolof
Xhosa

6 letters:
Basuto
Beento
Berber
Damara
Grikwa
Griqua
Hamite
Herero
Ibibio
Kabyle
Kenyan
Kikuyu
Libyan
Malawi
Malian
Nilote
Nubian
Nyanja
Ovambo
Somali
Tsonga
Tswana
Tuareg
Watusi
Yoruba

7 letters:
Angolan
Ashanti
Baganda
Bambara
Barbary
Barotse
Basotho
Biafran
Bushman
Cairene
Flytaal

Gambian
Ghanian
Gullash
Lesotho
Lowveld
Maghreb
Maghrib
Malinke
Maninke
Mashona
Mosotho
Namaqua
Ndebele
Shilluk
Songhai
Swahili
Voltaic
Watutsi
Yoruban
Zairean

8 letters:
Botswana
Cushitic
Eritrean
Gabonese
Ghanaian
Khoikhoi
Liberian
Mandingo
Matabele
Moroccan
Namibian
Negrillo
Shangaan
Sudanese
Transkei
Tunisian

9 letters:
Congolese
Ethiopian
Gazankulu
Hottentot

AFRICAN PEOPLES (CONTINUED)

Rhodesian
Transvaal

Mozambican

12 letters:
Carthaginian

10 letters:
Abyssinian

11 letters:
Rastafarian
Strandloper

ASIAN PEOPLES

3 letters:
Hui
Hun
Jat
Lao
Mon

4 letters:
Ainu
Arab
Cham
Chin
Dani
Dard
Dyak
Gond
Jain
Kurd
Mede
Moro
Motu
Naga
Nair
Nuri
Shan
Sikh
Sind
Thai
Turk

5 letters:
Dayak
Hindu
Kafir
Karen
Kazak
Khmer
Kisan
Malay
Mogul

Munda
Nayar
Nogay
Oriya
Parsi
Sindh
Tajik
Tamil
Tatar
Uigur
Uzbek
Vedda
Yakut

6 letters:
Beduin
Bihari
Buryat
Cumans
Essene
Evenki
Fulani
Gurkha
Harsha
Igorot
Jewish
Kalmyk
Kazakh
Khalsa
Lepcha
Lycian
Lydian
Mazhbi
Mishmi
Mongol
Parsee
Pashto
Pathan
Pushto
Pushtu

Sabean
Semite
Sherpa
Sindhi
Tadjik
Tartar
Telegu
Tongan
Tungus
Uighur
Veddah

7 letters:
Adivasi
Adivisi
Amorite
Balochi
Baluchi
Bashkir
Bedouin
Bengali
Bisayan
Burmese
Chinese
Chukchi
Chuvash
Cossack
Elamite
Harijan
Hittite
Hurrian
Israeli
Kalmuck
Kassite
Maratha
Maratta
Negrito
Panjabi
Punjabi
Sabaean

ASIAN PEOPLES (CONTINUED)

Samoyed
Saracen
Sogdian
Tadzhik
Tagalog
Talaing
Turkmen
Visayan

8 letters:
Accadian
Akkadian
Canarese
Chaldean
Chukchee
Ephesian

Gujarati
Gujerati
Igorrote
Kanarese
Kashmiri
Mahratta
Sumerian
Turanian

9 letters:
Amalekite
Bakhtyari
Chaldaean
Dravidian
Kabardian
Sinhalese

Tocharian
Tokharian

10 letters:
Andamanese
Babylonian
Ephraimite
Kara-Kalpak
Kshatriyas
Montagnard
Phoenician

11 letters:
Palestinian

AUSTRALASIAN PEOPLES

5 letters:
Dayak
Māori

6 letters:
Aranda

7 letters:
Tagalog

8 letters:
Gurindji

9 letters:
Aborigine

10 letters:
Melanesian
Polynesian

CENTRAL AND SOUTH AMERICAN INDIAN PEOPLES

2 letters:
Ge

4 letters:
Inca
Maya
Tupi

5 letters:
Aztec
Carib
Chimú

6 letters:
Aymara
Chibca
Kechua
Makuna
Mixtec
Toltec

7 letters:
Guarani
Nahuatl

Quechua
Quichua
Zapotec

8 letters:
Arawakan

10 letters:
Araucanian
Cashinahua

INUIT PEOPLES

5 letters:
Aleut
Inuit
Yupik

6 letters:
Innuit

8 letters:
Aleutian

13 letters:
Caribou Eskimo

EUROPEAN PEOPLES

4 letters:
Celt
Dane
Finn
Gaul
Goth
Jute
Komi
Lapp
Manx
Pict
Pole
Scot
Slav
Sorb
Turk
Wend

5 letters:
Angle
Aryan
Azeri
Croat
Cymry
Czech
Dutch
Frank
Gipsy
Greek
Gypsy
Iceni
Irish
Kymry
Latin
Norse
Saxon
Swede
Swiss
Vlach
Welsh

6 letters:
Basque
Belgae
Breton
Briton
Bulgar
Cimbri

Dorian
Eolian
French
Gaelic
Gascon
German
Goidel
Ingush
Ionian
Magyar
Norman
Ostyak
Sabine
Salain
Slovak
Teuton
Ugrian
Vandal
Viking
Volsci
Votyak
Walach

7 letters:
Achaean
Achaian
Aeolian
Azorean
Brython
Catalan
Chechen
Cornish
English
Fleming
Frisian
Iberian
Latvian
Lombard
Maltese
Mordvin
Russian
Samnite
Samoyed
Serbian
Silures
Slovene
Swabian
Walloon

8 letters:
Albanian
Alemanni
Armenian
Austrian
Bavarian
Cheremis
Corsican
Croatian
Ephesian
Estonian
Etrurian
Etruscan
Faeroese
Galician
Georgian
Hellenic
Illyrian
Karelian
Lusatian
Prussian
Romanian
Scythian
Sephardi
Sicilian
Thracian
Tyrolese
Visigoth

9 letters:
Aragonese
Ashkenazi
Bulgarian
Castilian
Celtiberi
Cheremiss
Esthonian
Icelandic
Langobard
Norwegian
Ostrogoth
Provençal
Sabellian
Sardinian
Ukrainian

10 letters:
Andalusian

EUROPEAN PEOPLES (CONTINUED)

Anglo-Saxon
Burgundian
Carinthian
Lithuanian
Macedonian
Portuguese

11 letters:
Anglo-Norman
Azerbaijani
Belorussian
Celtiberian
Montenegrin

12 letters:
Indo-European
Luxembourger

13 letters:
Bosnian Muslim

NATIVE AMERICAN TRIBES

3 letters:
Fox
Ute

4 letters:
Cree
Crow
Dene
Hopi
Hupa
Inca
Iowa
Maya
Moki
Pima
Pomo
Sauk
Tewa
Tico
Tiwa
Tupi
Yuma
Zuni

5 letters:
Aztec
Blood
Caddo
Cajun
Campa
Carib
Creek
Haida
Huron
Kansa
Kiowa
Lipan
Miami
Moqui

Olmec
Omaha
Osage
Ponca
Sioux
Teton
Wappo
Yaqui
Yuchi
Yuman
Yunca

6 letters:
Abnaki
Apache
Aymara
Biloxi
Cayuga
Cocopa
Dakota
Dogrib
Kechua
Kichai
Lakota
Mandan
Micmac
Mistec
Mixtec
Mohave
Mohawk
Mojave
Navaho
Navajo
Nootka
Oglala
Ojibwa
Oneida
Ostiak
Ottawa

Paiute
Papago
Pawnee
Pequot
Pericu
Piegan
Plains
Pueblo
Quakaw
Quapaw
Salish
Santee
Sarcee
Seneca
Siwash
Toltec
Warrau
Yanqui

7 letters:
Abenaki
Arapaho
Araucan
Arikara
Caddoan
Catawba
Chibcha
Chilcal
Chinook
Choctaw
Hidatsa
Kutenai
Mahican
Mapuche
Mohegan
Mohican
Nahuatl
Natchez
Ojibway

NATIVE AMERICAN TRIBES (CONTINUED)

Orejone
Palouse
Pontiac
Quechua
Quichua
Senecan
Serrano
Shawnee
Stonies
Tlingit
Tonkawa
Wichita
Wyandot
Yalkama

8 letters:
Aguaruna
Algonkin
Cherokee
Cheyenne
Chippewa
Comanche
Delaware
Flathead
Illinois
Iroquois
Kickapoo
Kootenai
Kootenay
Kwakiutl
Malecite
Menomini
Mikasuki
Mogollon

Muskogee
Nez Percé
Okanagon
Onondaga
Powhatan
Seminole
Shoshone
Shoshoni
Shushwap

9 letters:
Algonkian
Algonquan
Algonquin
Apalachee
Ashochimi
Blackfoot
Chickasaw
Chipewyan
Chippeway
Karankawa
Manhattan
Melungeon
Menominee
Mescalero
Muskogean
Penobscot
Potawatom
Suquamash
Tsimshian
Tuscarora
Wampanoag
Winnebago
Wyandotte

10 letters:
Algonquian
Athabascan
Bella Coola
Leni-Lenapé
Miniconjou
Minnetaree
Montagnais
Montagnard
Muskhogean
Root-digger
Tarahumara

11 letters:
Assiniboine
Kiowa Apache
Massachuset
Minneconjou
Narraganset
Susquehanna

12 letters:
Mound Builder
Pasamaquoddy

13 letters:
Northern Piute
Southern Piute
Susquehannock

14 letters:
Northern Paiute
Southern Paiute

Philosophy

PHILOSOPHICAL SCHOOLS AND DOCTRINES

5 letters:
Deism

6 letters:
Monism
Taoism
Theism

7 letters:
Animism
Atomism
Dualism
Fideism
Marxism
Realism
Thomism

8 letters:
Cynicism
Fatalism
Hedonism
Humanism
Idealism
Nihilism
Stoicism

PHILOSOPHICAL SCHOOLS AND DOCTRINES (CONTINUED)

9 letters:
Platonism
Pluralism

10 letters:
Eleaticism
Empiricism
Kantianism
Nominalism
Positivism
Pragmatism
Pyrrhonism
Scepticism
Utopianism

11 letters:
Determinism
Hegelianism

Materialism
Rationalism

12 letters:
Behaviourism
Cartesianism
Confucianism
Epicureanism
Essentialism
Neo-Platonism

13 letters:
Conceptualism
Immaterialism
Phenomenalism
Scholasticism
Structuralism

14 letters:
Existentialism
Logical atomism
Pythagoreanism
Sensationalism
Utilitarianism

15 letters:
Aristotelianism
Conventionalism
Critical realism

16 letters:
Consequentialism

17 letters:
Logical positivism

PHILOSOPHERS

2 letters:
Xi, *Chu*
Zi, *Lao*
Zi, *Xun*
Zu, *Han Fei*

4 letters:
Ayer, *A(lfred) J(ules)*
Cato, *Marcus Porcius*
Hume, *David*
Kant, *Immanuel*
Mach, *Ernst*
Marx, *Karl*
Mill, *James*
Mill, *John Stuart*
More, *Henry*
Mo-Zi
Reid, *Thomas*
Ryle, *Gilbert*
Vico, *Giovanni Battista*
Weil, *Simone*
Wolf, *Friedrich August*

5 letters:
Amiel, *Henri Frédéric*
Bacon, *Francis*
Bacon, *Roger*

Bayle, *Pierre*
Benda, *Julien*
Bruno, *Giordano*
Buber, *Martin*
Burke, *Edmund*
Comte, *Auguste*
Croce, *Benedetto*
Dewey, *John*
Frege, *Gottlob*
Fromm, *Erich*
Godel, *Kurt*
Green, *T(homas) H(ill)*
Hegel, *Georg Wilhelm
    Friedrich*
Iqbal, *Muhammad*
James, *William*
Locke, *John*
Lully, *Ramón*
Moore, *G(eorge)
    E(dward)*
Paine, *Thomas*
Paley, *William*
Plato
Rawls, *John*
Renan, *(Joseph) Ernest*
Royce, *Josiah*
Smith, *Adam*

Sorel, *Georges*
Taine, *Hippolyte Adophe*

6 letters:
Adorno, *Theodor
    Wiesengrund*
Agnesi, *Maria Gaetana*
Arendt, *Hannah*
Austin, *J(ohn)
    L(angshaw)*
Berlin, *Isaiah*
Carnap, *Rudolf*
Cicero, *Marcus Tallius*
Cousin, *Victor*
Engels, *Friedrich*
Eucken, *Rudolph
    Christoph*
Fichte, *Johann Gottlieb*
Ficino, *Marsilio*
Gasset, *José Ortega y*
Godwin, *William*
Herder, *Johann Gottfried*
Herzen, *Aleksandr
    Ivanovich*
Hobbes, *Thomas*
Langer, *Suzanne*
Lukács, *Georg*

Philosophers (continued)

Magnus, *Albertus*
Marcel, *Gabriel*
Newton, *Isaac*
Ortega (y Gasset), *José*
Pascal, *Blaise*
Peirce, *Charles Sanders*
Popper, *Karl*
Pyrrho
Sartre, *Jean-Paul*
Scotus, *John Duns*
Seneca, *Lucius Annaeus*
Tagore, *Rabindranath*
Tarski, *Alfred*
Thales

7 letters:
Abelard, *Peter*
Aquinas, *Thomas*
Bentham, *Jeremy*
Bergson, *Henri Louis*
Bradley, *F(rancis)*
  H(erbert)
Buridan, *Jean*
Derrida, *Jacques*
Diderot, *Denis*
Emerson, *Ralph Waldo*
Erasmus, *Desiderius*
Erigena, *John Scotus*
Fechner, *Gustav Theodor*
Gentile, *Giovanni*
Gorgias
Haeckel, *Ernst Heinrich*
Hah-Levi, *Judah*
Hartley, *David*
Herbart, *Johann*
  Friedrich
Herbert, *Edward*
Husserl, *Edmund*
Hypatia
Jaspers, *Karl*
Judaeus, *Philo*
Leibniz, *Gottfried*
  Wilhelm
Malthus, *Thomas Robert*
Marcuse, *Herbert*
Masaryk, *Tomáš*
  Garrigue
Mencius

Meng-tse
Murdoch, (*Jean*) *Iris*
Proclus
Ricoeur, *Paul*
Russell, *Bertrand*
Sankara
Sankhya
Schlick, *Moritz*
Spencer, *Herbert*
Spinoza, *Baruch*
Steiner, *Rudolf*
Tillich, *Paul Johannes*
Tolstoy, *Leo*

8 letters:
Al-Farabi, *Mohammed*
  ibn Tarkhan
Averroës
Avicenna
Berkeley, *George*
Boethius, *Anicius*
  Manlius Severinus
Cassirer, *Ernst*
Cudworth, *Ralph*
Davidson, *Donald*
De Suárez, *Francisco*
Diogenes
Eberhard, *Johann*
  August
Epicurus
Foucault, *Michel*
Gassendi, *Pierre*
Hamilton, *William*
Harrison, *Frederic*
Leopardi, *Giacomo*
Maritain, *Jacques*
Menippus
Plotinus
Plutarch
Poincaré, *Jules Henri*
Porphyry
Ramanuja
Rousseau, *Jean Jacques*
Shankara
Socrates
Spengler, *Oswald*
Strawson, *Peter*

Voltaire, *François-Marie*
  Arouet de
Von Hayek, *Friedrich*
  August
Williams, *Bernard*
Xenophon
Zhuangzi

9 letters:
Althusser, *Louis*
Aristotle
Berdyayev, *Nikolai*
  Aleksandrovich
Bosanquet, *Bernard*
Chuang-tzu
Cleanthes
Confucius
Copleston, *Frederick*
  (Charles)
De Chardin, *Pierre*
  Teilhard
Descartes, *René*
De Unamuno, *Miguel*
Epictetus
Euhemerus
Feuerbach, *Ludwig*
  Andreas
Heidegger, *Martin*
Helvétius, *Claude Adrien*
Hutcheson, *Francis*
Leucippus
Lévy-Bruhl, *Lucien*
Lucretius
Nietzsche, *Friedrich*
  Wilhelm
Santayana, *George*
Schelling, *Friedrich*
  Wilhelm Joseph Von
Von Herder, *Johann*
  Gottfried
Whitehead, *A(lfred)*
  N(orth)

10 letters:
Anacharsis
Anaxagoras
Anaximenes
Apemanthus

PHILOSOPHERS (CONTINUED)

Apollonius
Aristippus
Baumgarten, *Alexander Gottlieb*
Campanella, *Tommaso*
Chrysippus
Chrysostom, *Dio*
Churchland, *Paul*
Cumberland, *Richard*
De Beauvoir, *Simone*
Democritus
Empedocles
Heraclitus
Ibn-Gabirol, *Solomon*
Ibn-Khaldun
Maimonides
Parmenides
Protagoras
Pythagoras
Schweitzer, *Albert*
Swedenborg, *Emanuel*
Xenocrates
Xenophanes
Zeno *of Elea*

11 letters:
Anaximander
Antisthenes
Bonaventura

De Condillac, *Étienne Bonnot*
Heracleides
Kierkegaard, *Søren Aabye*
Machiavelli, *Niccolò*
Malebranche, *Nicolas*
Montesquieu, *Charles de Secondat (Baron de la Brède et de)*
Reichenbach, *Hans*
Von Leibnitz, *Gottfried Wilhelm*
Von Schlegel, *Friedrich*

12 letters:
Callisthenes
De Fontenelle, *Bernard le Bovier*
De Saint-Simon, *Comte*
Merleau-Ponty, *Maurice*
Schopenhauer, *Arthur*
Theophrastus
Von Pufendorf, *Samuel*
Von Schelling, *Friedrich Wilhelm Joseph*
Wittgenstein, *Ludwig Josef Johann*
Zeno *of Citium*

13 letters:
De Montesquieu, *Baron de la Brède et*
Van Orman Quine, *Willard*

14 letters:
Della Mirandola, *Giovanni Pico*
Nicholas *of Cusa*
Rosmini-Serbati, *Antonio*
Schleiermacher, *Friedrich Ernst Daniel*
Shankaracharya

15 letters:
Le Rond d'Alembert, *Jean*
William *of Ockham*

16 letters:
Marsilius *of Padua*

18 letters:
De Caritat Condorcet, *Marie Jean Antoine Nicholas*
St Augustine *of Hippo*

Phobias

Phobia	Object
Acerophobia	Sourness
Achluophobia	Darkness
Acrophobia	Heights
Aerophobia	Air
Agoraphobia	Open spaces
Aichurophobia	Points
Ailurophobia	Cats
Akousticophobia	Sound
Algophobia	Pain
Amakaphobia	Carriages
Amathophobia	Dust
Androphobia	Men

Phobia	Object
Anemophobia	Wind
Anginophobia	Narrowness
Anthropophobia	Man
Antlophobia	Flood
Apeirophobia	Infinity
Aquaphobia	Water
Arachnophobia	Spiders
Asthenophobia	Weakness
Astraphobia	Lightning
Atephobia	Ruin
Aulophobia	Flute
Bacilliphobia	Microbes
Barophobia	Gravity
Basophobia	Walking
Batrachophobia	Reptiles
Belonephobia	Needles
Bibliophobia	Books
Brontophobia	Thunder
Cancerophobia	Cancer
Cheimaphobia	Cold
Chionophobia	Snow
Chrematophobia	Money
Chronophobia	Duration
Chrystallophobia	Crystals
Claustrophobia	Closed spaces
Cnidophobia	Stings
Cometophobia	Comets
Cromophobia	Colour
Cyberphobia	Computers
Cynophobia	Dogs
Demonophobia	Demons
Demophobia	Crowds
Dermatophobia	Skin
Dikephobia	Justice
Doraphobia	Fur
Eisoptrophobia	Mirrors
Electrophobia	Electricity
Enetephobia	Pins
Entomophobia	Insects
Eosophobia	Dawn
Eremophobia	Solitude
Ereuthophobia	Blushing
Ergasiophobia	Work

Phobia	Object
Genophobia	Sex
Geumaphobia	Taste
Graphophobia	Writing
Gymnophobia	Nudity
Gynophobia	Women
Hadephobia	Hell
Haematophobia	Blood
Hamartiophobia	Sin
Haptophobia	Touch
Harpaxophobia	Robbers
Hedonophobia	Pleasure
Helminthophobia	Worms
Hodophobia	Travel
Homichlophobia	Fog
Homophobia	Homosexuals
Hormephobia	Shock
Hydrophobia	Water
Hypegiaphobia	Responsibility
Hypnophobia	Sleep
Ideophobia	Ideas
Kakorraphiaphobia	Failure
Katagelophobia	Ridicule
Kenophobia	Void
Kinesophobia	Motion
Kleptophobia	Stealing
Kopophobia	Fatigue
Kristallophobia	Ice
Laliophobia	Stuttering
Linonophobia	String
Logophobia	Words
Lyssophobia	Insanity
Maniaphobia	Insanity
Mastigophobia	Flogging
Mechanophobia	Machinery
Metallophobia	Metals
Meteorophobia	Meteors
Misophobia	Contamination
Monophobia	One thing
Musicophobia	Music
Musophobia	Mice
Necrophobia	Corpses
Nelophobia	Glass
Neophobia	Newness

Phobia	Object
Nephophobia	Clouds
Nosophobia	Disease
Nyctophobia	Night
Ochlophobia	Crowds
Ochophobia	Vehicles
Odontophobia	Teeth
Oikophobia	Home
Olfactophobia	Smell
Ommatophobia	Eyes
Oneirophobia	Dreams
Ophidiophobia	Snakes
Ornithophobia	Birds
Ouranophobia	Heaven
Panphobia	Everything
Pantophobia	Everything
Parthenophobia	Girls
Pathophobia	Disease
Peniaphobia	Poverty
Phasmophobia	Ghosts
Phobophobia	Fears
Photophobia	Light
Pnigerophobia	Smothering
Poinephobia	Punishment
Polyphobia	Many things
Potophobia	Drink
Pteronophobia	Feathers
Pyrophobia	Fire
Russophobia	Russia
Rypophobia	Soiling
Satanophobia	Satan
Selaphobia	Flesh
Siderophobia	Stars
Sitophobia	Food
Spermaphobia	Germs
Spermatophobia	Germs
Stasiphobia	Standing
Stygiophobia	Hell
Taphephobia	Being buried alive
Technophobia	Technology
Teratophobia	Giving birth to a monster
Thaasophobia	Sitting
Thalassophobia	Sea
Thanatophobia	Death

Phobia	Object
Theophobia	God
Thermophobia	Heat
Tonitrophobia	Thunder
Toxiphobia	Poison
Tremophobia	Trembling
Triskaidekaphobia	Thirteen
Xenophobia	Strangers *or* foreigners
Zelophobia	Jealousy
Zoophobia	Animals

Photography terms

3 letters:
Cam
Pan
TTL

4 letters:
Cock
Film
Gate
Gobo
Grip
Load
Shot
Stop

5 letters:
Blimp
Crane
Dolly
F-stop
Set up
Track
T-stop

6 letters:
Mosaic
Screen
Target
Tripod
Unipod

7 letters:
Hot shoe
Key grip

Release
Saticon
Shutter
T-number
Vidicon

8 letters:
Cassette
Film pack
Lens hood
Long shot
Orthicon
Snapshot
Stop down
Zoom lens

9 letters:
Amplifier
Cameraman
Cartridge
Cokuloris
Ferrotype
Film speed
Macro lens
Objective
Paparazzo
Plumbicon

10 letters:
Autowinder
Camera tube
Focal plane
Iconoscope
Viewfinder

Vignetting

11 letters:
Caméra stylo
Focus puller
Large-format

12 letters:
Cable release
Depth of focus
Synchroflash
Tracking shot

13 letters:
Accessory shoe
Cinematograph
Delayed action
Extension ring
Image orthicon
Telephoto lens
Wide-angle lens

14 letters:
Automatic focus
Kinetheodolite
Pan and tilt head
Shooting script

18 letters:
Hyperfocal distance

19 letters:
Photoreconnaissance

Physics

BRANCHES OF PHYSICS

5 letters:
Solar

6 letters:
Atomic
Optics
Sonics

7 letters:
Applied
Nuclear
Quantum
Statics

8 letters:
Dynamics
Kinetics
Particle
Rheology

9 letters:
Acoustics
Cosmology
Harmonics
Magnetics

Magnetism
Mechanics

10 letters:
Biophysics
Cryogenics
Geophysics
High-energy
Nucleonics
Photometry
Pneumatics
Solid-state

11 letters:
Aerostatics
Electronics
Mesoscopics
Theoretical
Thermometry
Ultrasonics

12 letters:
Aerodynamics
Astrophysics
Macrophysics

Microphysics
Spectroscopy

13 letters:
Thermostatics

14 letters:
Electrostatics
Low-temperature
Magnetostatics
Thermodynamics

15 letters:
Condensed-matter

16 letters:
Electromagnetism
Quantum mechanics

17 letters:
Superaerodynamics

20 letters:
Statistical mechanics

PHYSICS TERMS

3 letters:
Ohm

4 letters:
Atom
Fuse
Lens
Mass
Muon
Volt
Watt
Wave
X-ray

5 letters:
Anion
Diode
Earth

Farad
Field
Force
Hertz
Joule
Laser
Meson

6 letters:
Ampere
Baryon
Cacion
Charge
Energy
Fusion
Kelvin
Lepton
Matter

Moment
Newton
Pascal
Proton
Vacuum

7 letters:
Calorie
Coulomb
Current
Decibel
Density
Fission
Gravity
Hyperon
Impetus
Inertia
Neutron

PHYSICS TERMS (CONTINUED)

Nucleon
Nucleus
Ohm's law
Quantum
Tension

8 letters:
Angstrom
Electron
Friction
Gamma ray
Half-life
Infrared
Momentum
Neutrino
Particle
Red shift
Spectrum
Velocity

9 letters:
Amplifier
Becquerel
Boyle's law
Conductor
Cosmic ray
Cyclotron
Diffusion
Frequency
Generator
Microwave
Radiation
Radio wave
Viscosity

10 letters:
Antimatter
Cathode ray
Charles' law
Convection
Inductance
Reflection
Refraction
Relativity
Resistance
Rutherford
Thermostat
Transistor
Wavelength

11 letters:
Capacitance
Diffraction
Electricity
Tau particle
Transformer
Ultraviolet

12 letters:
Acceleration
Fluorescence
Luminescence

13 letters:
Direct current
Doppler effect
Kinetic energy
Radioactivity
Semiconductor

Superfluidity

14 letters:
Brownian motion
Planck constant
Surface tension

15 letters:
Centre of gravity
Planck's constant
Potential energy

16 letters:
Centrifugal force
Centripetal force
Terminal velocity

17 letters:
Static electricity
Subatomic particle
Superconductivity

18 letters:
Alternating current
Electromotive force

19 letters:
Potential difference

20 letters:
Simple harmonic
  motion

PHYSICISTS

3 letters:
Lee, *Tsung-Dao*
Ohm, *Georg Simon*

4 letters:
Abbe, *Ernst*
Bohr, *Aage Niels*
Bohr, *Niels (Henrik David)*
Born, *Max*
Bose, *Jagadis Chandra*
Bose, *Satyendra Nath*

Hahn, *Otto*
Hess, *Victor Francis*
Kerr, *John*
Lamb, *Willis Eugene*
Lawe, *William C*
Mach, *Ernst*
Néel, *Louis*
Rabi, *Isidor Isaac*
Snow, *C(harles) P(ercy)*
Swan, *Joseph Wilson*

Ting, *Samuel Chao
  Chung*
Wien, *Wilhelm*
Yang, *Chen Ning*

5 letters:
Aston, *Francis William*
Auger, *Pierre*
Basov, *Nikolai*
Bethe, *Hans Albrecht*
Bloch, *Felix*

PHYSICISTS (CONTINUED)

Bothe, *Walter*
Boyle, *Robert*
Bragg, *Sir William Henry*
Braun, *Karl Ferdinand*
Curie, *Marie*
Curie, *Pierre*
Debye, *Peter Joseph Wilhelm*
Dewar, *James*
Dirac, *Paul Adrien Maurice*
Fabry, *Charles*
Fermi, *Enrico*
Fuchs, *Klaus*
Gauss, *Carl Friedrich*
Gibbs, *Josiah Willard*
Henry, *Joseph*
Hertz, *Gustav*
Hertz, *Heinrich Rudolph*
Hooke, *Robert*
Jeans, *James Hopwood*
Joule, *James Prescott*
Lodge, *Oliver*
Pauli, *Wolfgang*
Popov, *Alexander Stepanovich*
Sègre, *Emilio*
Stark, *Johannes*
Volta, *Alessandro*
Weber, *Wilhelm Eduard*
Young, *Thomas*

6 letters:
Alfren
Alfvén, *Hannes Olaf Gösta*
Ampère, *André Marie*
Barkla, *Charles Glover*
Binnig, *Gerd*
Carnot, *Nicolas Leonard Sadi*
Cooper, *Leon*
Cronin, *James Watson*
Dalton, *John*
Franck, *James*
Frisch, *Otto*
Geiger, *Hans*
Giorgi, *Filippo*

Glaser, *Donald Arthur*
Graham, *Thomas*
Kelvin, *William Thomson*
Landau, *Lev Davidovich*
Newton, *Isaac*
Pascal, *Blaise*
Perrin, *Jean Baptiste*
Picard, *Jean*
Planck, *Max (Karl Ernst Ludwig)*
Powell, *Celic*
Talbot, *William Henry Fox*
Teller, *Edward*
Townes, *Charles Hard*
Walton, *Ernest Thomas Sinton*
Wigner, *Eugene Paul*
Wilson, *Charles Thomson Rees*
Yukawa, *Hideki*
Zwicky, *Fritz*

7 letters:
Alvarez, *Luis Walter*
Babinet, *Jacques*
Bardeen, *John*
Bravais, *Auguste*
Broglie, *Maurice*
Charles, *Jacques*
Compton, *Arthur Holly*
Coulomb, *Charles Augustin De*
Crookes, *William*
Doppler, *C(hristian) J(ohann)*
Faraday, *Michael*
Fechner, *Gustav*
Feynman, *Richard*
Fresnel, *Augustin*
Galilei, *Galileo*
Galileo
Gell-Man, *Murray*
Gilbert, *William*
Goddard, *Robert Hutchings*
Hawking, *Stephen William*
Heitler, *Walter*

Huygens, *Christiaan*
Kapitza, *Piotr Leonidovich*
Langley, *Samuel Pierpont*
Laplace, *Pierre Simon*
Lippman, *Gabriel*
Lorentz, *Hendrik Antoon*
Marconi, *Guglielmo*
Maxwell, *James Clerk*
Meitner, *Lise*
Milikin, *Robert*
Moseley, *Henry Gwyn-Jeffreys*
Oersted, *Hans Christian*
Penrose, *Roger*
Piccard, *Auguste*
Prandtl, *Ludwig*
Purcell, *Edward Mill*
Réaumur, *René Antoine Ferchault De*
Richter, *Burton*
Röntgen, *Wilhelm Konrad Von*
Seaborg, *Glenn*
Szilard, *Leo*
Thomson, *Benjamin*
Thomson, *George Paget*
Thomson, *Joseph John*
Tyndall, *John*
Von Laue, *Max Theodor Felix*
Wheeler, *John Archibald*

8 letters:
Anderson, *Carl David*
Anderson, *Elizabeth Garrett*
Anderson, *Philip Warren*
Ångström, *Anders Jonas*
Appleton, *Edward*
Avogadro, *Amedeo*
Blackett, *Patrick Maynard Stuart*
Brattain, *Walter Houser*
Brewster, *David*
Bridgman, *Percy*
Chadwick, *James*

PHYSICISTS (CONTINUED)

Cherwell, *Frederick Alexander Lindemann*
Clausius, *Rudolf*
Davisson, *Clinton Joseph*
Einstein, *Albert*
Foucault, *Jean Bernard Léon*
Gassendi, *Pierre*
Ipatieff, *Vladimir Nikolaievich*
Lawrence, *Ernest Orlando*
McMillan, *Edwin*
Mullikin, *Robert Sanderson*
Oliphant, *Mark Laurence Elwin*
Poincaré, *Jules Henri*
Rayleigh, *John William Strutt*
Roentgen, *Wilhelm Konrad*
Sakharov, *Andrei*
Shockley, *William Bradfield*
Siegbahn, *Kai*
Van Allen, *James*
Von Mayer, *Julius Robert*
Weinberg, *Steven*
Zworykin, *Vladimir Kosma*

9 letters:
Arrhenius, *Svante August*
Becquerel, *Antoine Henri*
Bernoulli, *Daniel*
Boltzmann, *Ludwig*
Cavendish, *Henry*
Cherenkov, *Pavel Alekseyevich*
Cockcroft, *John Douglas*
De Coulomb, *Charles Augustin*
Eddington, *Arthur Stanley*
Gay-Lussac, *Joseph Louis*
Heaviside, *Oliver*
Josephson, *Brian David*
Kirchhoff, *Gustav*
Lindemann, *Frederick*
Michelson, *Albert*
Von Békésy, *Georg*
Von Eötvös, *Roland*

10 letters:
Archimedes
Barkhausen, *Heinrich Georg*
Fahrenheit, *Gabriel Daniel*
Heisenburg, *Werner Karl*
Richardson, *Owen Willans*

Rutherford, *Ernest*
Torricelli, *Evangelista*
Watson-Watt, *Robert Alexander*

11 letters:
Chamberlain, *Owen*
Joliot-Curie, *Irène*
Oppenheimer, *J(ulius) Robert*
Schrödinger, *Erwin*
Van de Graaff, *R(obert) J(emison)*
Van der Waals, *Johannes Diderik*
Von Guericke, *Otto*

12 letters:
Von Helmholtz, *Hermann Ludwig Ferdinand*

13 letters:
Von Fraunhofer, *Joseph*

14 letters:
Le Rond Alembert, *Jean*

15 letters:
Kamerlingh-Onnes, *Heike*

See also:
➤ **Molecules** ➤ **Subatomic particles**

Breeds of pig

5 letters:
Duroc
Welsh

8 letters:
Cheshire
Landrace
Pietrain
Tamworth

9 letters:
Berkshire
Hampshire

10 letters:
Large Black
Large White
Saddleback
Small White

11 letters:
Middle White

12 letters:
Chester White

17 letters:
Gloucester Old Spot

20 letters:
Vietnamese pot-bellied

Pigments

3 letters:
Hem

4 letters:
Haem
Heme

5 letters:
Ochre
Opsin
Sepia
Smalt
Umber

6 letters:
Bister
Bistre
Chrome
Cobalt
Flavin
Lutein
Madder
Naevus
Pterin
Sienna

7 letters:
Argyria
Carmine
Carotin
Etiolin
Flavine

Gamboge
Melanin
Sinopia
Tapetum
Tempera

8 letters:
Carotene
Gossypol
Iodopsin
Luteolin
Orpiment
Retinene
Verditer
Viridian

9 letters:
Anthocyan
Bilirubin
Chromogen
Colcothar
Lamp-black
Lithopone
Liverspot
Nigrosine
Porphyrin
Quercetin
Rhodopsin
Urochrome

10 letters:
Anthoclore
Betacyanin
Biliverdin
Carotenoid
Carotinoid
Hemocyanin
Hemoglobin
Paris-green
Terre-verte

11 letters:
Anthocyanin
Chlorophyll
Fucoxanthin
Haemocyanin
Haemoglobin
Phytochrome
Rhiboflavin
Xanthophyll

12 letters:
Cappagh-brown
Phycoxanthin
Xanthopterin

13 letters:
Phycoerythrin
Xanthopterine

14 letters:
Phthalocyanine

Pirates

4 letters:
Smee

7 letters:
Ben Gunn

8 letters:
Black Dog
Blind Pew

Mary Read
Redbeard

9 letters:
Anne Bonny
Thomas Tew

10 letters:
Barbarossa

Blackbeard
Calico Jack

11 letters:
Captain Hook
Edward Teach
Sir Henry Morgan
Jean Laffite
John Rackham

12 letters:
Sir Francis Drake

13 letters:
Basil Ringrose

14 letters:
Captain Pugwash
Long John Silver
William Dampier

18 letters:
Bartholomew Roberts
William (Captain) Kidd

Places and their nicknames

Place	Nickname
Aberdeen	The Granite City
Adelaide	The City of Churches
Amsterdam	The Venice of the North
Birmingham	Brum *or* the Venice of the North
Boston	Bean Town
Bruges	The Venice of the North
California	The Golden State
Chicago	The Windy City
Dallas	The Big D
Detroit	The Motor City
Dresden	Florence on the Elbe
Dublin	The Fair City
Dumfries	Queen of the South
Edinburgh	Auld Reekie *or* the Athens of the North
Florida	The Sunshine State
Fraserburgh	The Broch
Fremantle	Freo
Glasgow	The Dear Green Place
Hamburg	The Venice of the North
Indiana	The Hoosier State
Iowa	The Hawkeye State
Ireland	The Emerald Isle
Jamaica	J.A. *or* the Yard
Jerusalem	The Holy City
Kentucky	The Bluegrass State
Kuala Lumpur	K.L.
London	The Big Smoke *or* the Great Wen
Los Angeles	L.A.
New Jersey	The Garden State
New Orleans	The Crescent City *or* the Big Easy
New South Wales	Ma State
New York (City)	The Big Apple
New York (State)	The Empire State
New Zealand	Pig Island

Place	Nickname
North Carolina	The Tarheel State
Nottingham	Queen of the Midlands
Oklahoma	The Sooner State
Pennsylvania	The Keystone State
Philadelphia	Philly
Portsmouth	Pompey
Prince Edward Island	Spud Island
Queensland	Bananaland *or* the Deep North (*both derogatory*)
Rome	The Eternal City
San Francisco	Frisco
Southeastern U.S.A.	Dixie, Dixieland, *or* the Deep South
Tasmania	Tassie *or* the Apple Isle
Texas	The Lone Star State
Utah	The Beehive State
Venice	La Serenissima

Planets

4 letters:
Mars

5 letters:
Earth
Pluto

Venus

6 letters:
Saturn
Uranus

7 letters:
Jupiter
Mercury
Neptune

Plants

3 letters:
Dal
Kex
Meu
Pia
Rue
Set
Til
Udo
Urd
Yam

4 letters:
Alga
Aloe
Anil

Deme
Fern
Forb
Herb
Ixia
Kali
Loco
More
Nard
Ombu
Rhus
Sego
Sola
Sunn
Taro
Thea

Vine
Yarr

5 letters:
Ajwan
Anise
Aroid
Benni
Blite
Boree
Buchu
Bucku
Bugle
Calla
Canna
Clary

Plants

Clote
Cress
Fouat
Fouet
Gemma
Glaux
Gorse
Guaco
Hosta
Inula
Jalap
Kenaf
Kudzu
Lathe
Lotus
Lurgi
Medic
Morel
Murva
Musci
Orpin
Orris
Oshac
Panax
Sedge
Sedum
Spink
Tetra
Timbo
Urena

6 letters:
Acacia
Acorus
Ajowan
Alisma
Alpine
Arnica
Bablah
Betony
Burnet
Cactus
Cassia
Catnep
Cnicus
Cosmea
Cosmos
Croton
Datura
Derris

Dodder
Exogen
Gnetum
Hyssop
Iberis
Knawel
Madder
Mallow
Medick
Mimosa
Moorva
Nerium
Nettle
Nuphar
Orchis
Orpine
Pachak
Phloem
Protea
Rattle
Reseda
Retama
Rubber
Sesame
Silene
Smilax
Spider
Spurge
Spurry
Squill
Styrax
Teasel
Thrift
Tulipa
Tutsan
Yarrow

7 letters:
Alkanet
All-good
Allseed
Alyssum
Brinjal
Burdock
Caltrop
Cardoon
Carduus
Carline
Cat's ear
Chervil

Dasheen
Dioecia
Dittany
Ephedra
Filaree
Fly-trap
Freesia
Frogbit
Gentian
Gerbera
Haemony
Henbane
Ipomoea
Isoetes
Lantana
Lucerne
Lychnis
Mahonia
Melilot
Mercury
Mullein
Nemesia
Nigella
Nonsuch
Opuntia
Palmiet
Pareira
Petunia
Ragwort
Rhodora
Ruellia
Saffron
Salfern
Salsola
Sampire
Sanicle
Scandix
Setwall
Skirret
Spignel
Spiraea
Spurrey
Stapela
Syringa
Tagetes
Thallus
Triffid
Tritoma
Vanilla
Vervain

Zedoary

8 letters:
Acanthus
Agrimony
Angelica
Arenaria
Asphodel
Bindi-eye
Buckbean
Buplever
Camomile
Canaigre
Centaury
Costmary
Diandria
Dielytra
Dumbcane
Fluellin
Fumitory
Geophite
Gesnaria
Gnetales
Gromwell
Hag-taper
Henequen
Hepatica
Hibiscus
Larkspur
Lavender
Mandrake
Monstera
Oleander
Opopanax
Plumbago
Psilotum
Putchock
Ratsbane
Roly-poly
Samphire
Scammony
Self-heal
Silphium
Sparaxis
Spergula
Stapelia
Staragen
Starwort
Tamarisk
Tritonia

Tuberose
Tuckahoe
Wait-a-bit

9 letters:
Adderwort
Andromeda
Arrowroot
Artemisia
Aubrietia
Bald-money
Brooklime
Broom-rape
Butterbur
Colocasia
Coltsfoot
Cordaites
Coreopsis
Coriander
Dittander
Erythrina
Euphorbia
Eyebright
Fenugreek
Germander
Groundsel
Herb-paris
Horse-tail
Liver-wort
Lousewort
Mare's-tail
Moneywort
Moschatel
Patchouli
Pimpernel
Portulaca
Rocambole
Screwpine
Spearmint
Spearwort
Spikenard
Stone-crop
Sweet-gale
Tomatillo
Tormentil
Wake-robin
Wincopipe
Wolf's bane

10 letters:
Alexanders
Angiosperm
Aspidistra
Astralagus
Dyer's-broom
Earth-smoke
Five-finger
Fraxinella
Fritillary
Goat-sallow
Goats-thorn
Goat-willow
Goldilocks
Icosandria
Maidenhair
Mignonette
Parkleaves
Rest-harrow
Salicornia
Touch-me-not
Tropophyte
Yellowroot

11 letters:
Acidanthera
Bears-breech
Bristle-fern
Callitriche
Convolvulus
Dusty-miller
Hurtleberry
Loosestrife
Meadowsweet
Nancy-pretty
Schizophyte
Sempervivum
Thallophyte

12 letters:
Adam's flannel
Epacridaceae
Midsummermen
Morning glory
Parsley-piert
Pasqueflower
Phytobenthos
Resurrection
Southernwood
Water-soldier

Parts of plants

13 letters:
Townhall clock

14 letters:
Chincherinchee

Lords and ladies
Shepherd's purse

See also:
➤ Algae ➤ Botany ➤ Ferns ➤ Flowers ➤ Fungi ➤ Grasses ➤ Lilies
➤ Mosses ➤ Palms ➤ Parts of plants ➤ Sea-weeds ➤ Shrubs ➤ Trees

Parts of plants

3 letters:
Bud
Lip
Pod

4 letters:
Cyme
Head
Leaf
Root
Seed
Spur
Stem

5 letters:
Bract
Calyx
Costa
Fruit
Glume
Joint
Lemma
Ovary
Ovule
Palea
Petal
Sepal
Spike
Stoma
Style
Tepal
Torus
Umbel
Xylem

6 letters:
Anther
Bulbil

Carpel
Catkin
Caulis
Corymb
Floret
Phloem
Pistil
Pollen
Raceme
Rachis
Sheath
Spadix
Spathe
Stamen
Stigma
Tassel

7 letters:
Blossom
Corolla
Foliage
Nectary
Panicle
Pedicel
Root cap
Seed pod
Taproot

8 letters:
Cyathium
Filament
Nucellus
Offshoot
Peduncle
Perianth
Placenta
Root hair
Spikelet

Thalamus

9 letters:
Capitulum
Dichasium
Epidermis
Guard cell
Gynoecium
Internode
Involucel
Involucre
Micropyle
Pollinium
Secundine

10 letters:
Androecium
Anthophore
Carpophore
Commissure
Hypanthium
Receptacle

11 letters:
Clinandrium
Gametophore
Monochasium
Pollen grain

12 letters:
Hibernaculum

13 letters:
Inflorescence

14 letters:
Floral envelope
Vascular bundle

Poetry

POETRY AND PROSODY TERMS

3 letters:
Bob

4 letters:
Foot
Iamb

5 letters:
Arsis
Canto
Envoi
Envoy
Epode
Ictus
Ionic
Metre
Octet
Paeon
Rhyme
Wheel

6 letters:
Adonic
Alcaic
Cesura
Cretic
Dactyl
Dipody
Iambic
Iambus
Octave
Rhythm
Septet
Sestet
Stanza
Tercet

7 letters:
Anapest
Cadence
Cadency
Caesura
Couplet
Distich
Elision
Paeonic

Pyhrric
Quintet
Refrain
Sapphic
Sestina
Sextain
Spondee
Stichic
Strophe
Triplet
Trochee

8 letters:
Amoebean
Anapaest
Bacchius
Choriamb
Dactylic
Dieresis
Eye rhyme
Pindaric
Quatrain
Quintain
Scansion
Spondaic
Trochaic

9 letters:
Amoebaean
Anacrusis
Anapestic
Assonance
Diaeresis
Free verse
Full rhyme
Half-rhyme
Hemistich
Hexameter
Long metre
Macaronic
Octameter
Pararhyme
Rime riche
Terza rima
Tetrapody
Unstopped

Vers libre

10 letters:
Amphibrach
Amphimacer
Anapaestic
Blank verse
Catalectic
Choriambus
Consonance
Consonancy
End-stopped
Heptameter
Heptastich
Hypermeter
Ottava rima
Pentameter
Pentastich
Rhyme royal
Short metre
Tetrabrach
Tetrameter
Tetrastich

11 letters:
Alexandrine
Antistrophe
Common metre
Enjambement
Jabberwocky
Rhyme scheme

12 letters:
Alliteration
Ballad stanza
Leonine rhyme
Onomatopoeia
Perfect rhyme
Sprung rhythm

13 letters:
Closed couplet
Common measure
Feminine rhyme
Heroic couplet
Internal rhyme

POETRY AND PROSODY TERMS (CONTINUED)

Syllabic metre

15 letters:
Masculine ending

19 letters:
Stress-syllabic metre

14 letters:
Accentual metre
Feminine ending
Masculine rhyme
Verse paragraph

16 letters:
Spenserian stanza

22 letters:
Accentual-syllabic
  metre

17 letters:
Quantitative metre

POETRY MOVEMENTS AND GROUPINGS

8 letters:
Imagists

11 letters:
Petrarchans
The Movement

14 letters:
Liverpool Poets

9 letters:
Decadents
Lake Poets
Romantics

12 letters:
Alexandrians

17 letters:
Metaphysical Poets

10 letters:
Symbolists

13 letters:
Georgian Poets

19 letters:
Scottish Chaucerians

POETS

2 letters:
AE
HD

3 letters:
Gay, *John*
Paz, *Octavio*
Poe, *Edgar Allan*

4 letters:
Abse, *Dannie*
Beer, *Patricia*
Blok, *Alexander
  Alexandrovich*
Cory, *William Johnson*
Dunn, *Douglas*
Dyer, *Sir Edward*
Gray, *Thomas*
Gunn, *Thom*
Hill, *Geoffrey*
Hogg, *James*
Hood, *Thomas*
Hugo, *Victor Marie*
Hunt, (*James Henry*)
  Leigh

Lang, *Andrew*
Muir, *Edwin*
Nash, *Ogden*
Ovid
Owen, *Wilfred*
Pope, *Alexander*
Rich, *Adrienne*
Rowe, *Nicholas*
Rumi, *Jelaluddin*
Tate, (*John Orley*) *Allen*
Vega, (*Garcilaso de la*)
Webb, *Francis Charles*

5 letters:
Aiken, *Conrad* (*Potter*)
Arion
Auden, *W*(*ystan*) *H*(*ugh*)
Blair, *Robert*
Blake, *William*
Burns, *Robert*
Byron, (*George Gordon*)
Cadou, *René-Guy*
Carew, *Thomas*
Cinna, *Gaius Helvius*

Clare, *John*
Dante (*Alighieri*)
Donne, *John*
Duffy, *Carol Ann*
Eliot, *T*(*homas*) *S*(*tearns*)
Frost, *Robert* (*Lee*)
Gower, *John*
Heine, *Heinrich*
Henri, *Adrian*
Hesse, *Hermann*
Homer
Horne, *Richard Henry*
  ('*Hengist*')
Hulme, *Thomas Ernest*
Iqbal, *Sir Mohammed*
Keats, *John*
Keyes, *Sidney*
Lewis, *Cecil Day*
Logue, *Christopher*
Lorca, *Federigo Garcia*
Lucan (*Marcus Annaeus
  Lucanus*)
Marot, *Clément*
Meyer, *Conrad Ferdinand*

POETS (CONTINUED)

Moore, *Marianne*
Nashe, *Thomas*
Noyes, *Alfred*
O'Hara, *Frank*
Perse, *Saint-John*
Plath, *Sylvia*
Pound, *Ezra (Loomis)*
Prior, *Matthew*
Raine, *Kathleen*
Rilke, *Rainer Maria*
Sachs, *Hans*
Scott, *Sir Walter*
Smart, *Christopher*
Smith, *Stevie*
Tasso, *Torquato*
Theon
Wyatt, *Thomas*
Yeats, *W(illiam) B(utler)*
Young, *Edward*

6 letters:
Adcock, (*Karen*) *Fleur*
Arnold, *Matthew*
Austin, *Alfred*
Barham, *Richard Harris*
Barnes, *William*
Belloc, *Hilaire*
Bishop, *Elizabeth*
Brecht, *Bertolt Eugen Friedrich*
Brooke, *Rupert (Chawner)*
Brooks, *Gwendolyn*
Butler, *Samuel*
Carver, *Raymond*
Clough, *Arthur Hugh*
Cowper, *William*
Crabbe, *George*
Dowson, *Ernest Christopher*
Dryden, *John*
Dunbar, *William*
Dutton, *Geoffrey*
Elliot, *Ebenezer*
Éluard, *Paul*
Empson, *William*
Ennius, *Quintus*
George, *Stefan*

Glycon
Goethe, *Johann Wolfgang Von*
Graves, *Robert*
Heaney, *Seamus*
Hesiod
Horace
Hughes, *Ted*
Jonson, *Ben*
Landor, *Walter Savage*
Larkin, *Philip*
Lawman
Lowell, *Amy*
Lowell, *Robert*
Millay, *Edna St Vincent*
Milton, *John*
Morgan, *Edwin*
Morris, *Sir Lewis*
Motion, *Andrew*
Neruda, *Pablo*
Ossian
Patten, *Brian*
Pindar
Porter, *Peter*
Racine, *Jean*
Rhymer, *Corn Law*
Riding, *Laura*
Sappho
Seaman, *Sir Owen*
Shanks, *Edward*
Sidney, *Sir Philip*
Tagore, *Sir Rabindranath*
Thomas, *Dylan (Marlais)*
Thomas, *Edward*
Thomas, *R(onald) S(tuart)*
Trench, *Frederick Herbert*
Villon, *François*
Virgil
Waller, *Edmund*
Wright, *Judith*

7 letters:
Addison, *Joseph*
Alcaeus
Angelou, *Maya*
Aretino, *Pietro*
Ariosto, *Ludovico*

Beddoes, *Thomas*
Belleau, *Rémy*
Blunden, *Edmund*
Bridges, *Robert Seymour*
Brodsky, *Joseph*
Caedmon
Campion, *Thomas*
Causley, *Charles*
Chapman, *George*
Chaucer, *Geoffrey*
Collins, *William*
Corinna
Cynwulf
De Vigny, *Alfred Victor*
Emerson, *Ralph Waldo*
Flaccus, *Horace (Quintus Horatius)*
Flecker, *James Elroy*
Herbert, *George*
Heredia, *José María*
Herrick, *Robert*
Hodgson, *Ralph*
Hopkins, *Gerard Manley*
Housman, *A(lfred) E(dward)*
Johnson, *Samuel*
Juvenal
Khayyam, *Omar*
Kipling, (*Joseph*) *Rudyard*
Layamon
Leonard, *Tom*
MacCaig, *Norman*
MacLean, *Sorley*
Martial
Marvell, *Andrew*
McGough, *Roger*
Mistral, *Frédéric*
Newbolt, *Sir Henry John*
Orpheus
Pushkin, *Aleksander Sergeyevich*
Rimbaud, *Arthur*
Roethke, *Theodore Huebner*
Ronsard, *Pierre de*
Russell, *George William*
Sassoon, *Siegfried*

POETS (CONTINUED)

Schwarz, *Delmore*
Seifert, *Jaroslav*
Service, *Robert William*
Shelley, *Percy Bysshe*
Sitwell, *Edith*
Skelton, *John*
Southey, *Robert*
Spender, *Stephen*
Spenser, *Edmund*
Statius, *Publius Papinius*
Stevens, *Wallace*
Terence (*Publius Terentius Afer*)
Thomson, *James*
Vaughan, *Henry*
Vaughan, *William*
Walcott, *Derek*
Whitman, *Walt*

8 letters:
Anacreon
Berryman, *John*
Betjeman, *John*
Browning, *Elizabeth Barrett*
Browning, *Robert*
Campbell, *Thomas*
Catullus, *Gaius Valerius*
Clampitt, *Amy*
Cummings, *E(dward) E(stlin)*
Cynewulf
Davenant, *Sir William*
De la Mare, *Walter*
Ginsberg, *Allen*
Hamilton, *William*
Henryson, *Robert*
Jennings, *Elizabeth*
Kavanagh, *Patrick*
Kynewulf
Langland, *William*
Leopardi, *Giacomo*
Lovelace, *Richard*

Macauley, *Thomas*
MacNeice, *Louis*
Mallarmé, *Stéphane*
Menander
Petrarch
Rossetti, *Christina Georgina*
Rossetti, *Dante Gabriel*
Schiller, (*Johann Cristoph) Friedrich (Von)*
Shadwell, *Thomas*
Stephens, *James*
Suckling, *John*
Taliesin
Tennyson, *Lord Alfred*
Thompson, *Francis*
Traherne, *Thomas*
Tyrtaeus
Verlaine, *Paul*
Whittier, *John Greenleaf*

9 letters:
Aeschylus
Bunthorne, *Reginald*
Coleridge, *Samuel Taylor*
De Camoëns, *Luis Vaz*
Dickinson, *Emily*
Doolittle, *Hilda (H D)*
Euripides
Goldsmith, *Oliver*
Lamartine, *Alphone Marie Loius De*
Lucretius
Marinetti, *Emilio Filippo Tommaso*
Masefield, *John*
Quasimodo, *Salvatore*
Rochester, (*John Wilmot*)
Rosenberg, *Isaac*
Shenstone, *William*
Simonides (*of Ceos*)
Sophocles

Stevenson, *Robert Louis Balfour*
Swinburne, *Algernon Charles*
Von Goethe, *Johann Wolfgang*

10 letters:
Akhamatova, *Anna*
Baudelaire, *Charles Pierre*
Chatterton, *Thomas*
Cumberland, *Richard*
Drinkwater, *John*
Fitzgerald, *Edward*
Fitzgerald, *Robert*
Longfellow, *Henry Wadsworth*
MacDiarmid, *Hugh*
Propertius, *Sextus*
Szymborska, *Wislawa*
Tannhauser
Theocritus
Wordsworth, *William*

11 letters:
Apollinaire, *Guillaume*
Archilochus
Asclepiades
Callimachus
De Lamartine, *Alphonse Marie Louis de Prat*
Maeterlinck, *Maurice*
Shakespeare, *William*
Von Schiller, *Johann Christoph Friedrich*

12 letters:
Aristophanes
De La Fontaine, *Jean*

15 letters:
Ettrick Shepherd

Poisons

POISONOUS SUBSTANCES AND GASES

4 letters:
Bane
Lead
Tutu
Upas

5 letters:
Aspic
Conin
Ergot
Sarin
Sassy
Soman
Timbo
Urali

6 letters:
Aldrin
Antiar
Arsine
Cicuta
Conine
Curare
Curari
Datura
Dioxin
Emetin
Hebona
Ourali
Ourari
Phenol
Wabain

7 letters:
Aconite
Amanita
Aniline
Arsenic
Atropin
Benzene
Brucine
Cacodyl
Coniine
Cowbane
Cyanide
Emetine

Hebenon
Hemlock
Henbane
Lindane
Neurine
Ouabain
Phallin
Red lead
Safrole
Solpuga
Stibine
Stibium
Surinam
Tanghin
Tropine
Woorali
Woorara
Wourali

8 letters:
Acrolein
Adamsite
Apocynum
Atropine
Barbasco
Botulism
Cyanogen
Cyanuret
Daturine
Death cap
Dumbcane
Foxglove
Gossypol
Laburnum
Lewisite
Lobeline
Locoweed
Methanol
Mezereon
Nerve gas
Oleander
Paraquat
Phosgene
Pokeroot
Pokeweed
Ratsbane

Samnitis
Santonin
Sasswood
Solanine
Thallium
Thebaine
Uroshiol
Urushiol
Veratrin
Warfarin

9 letters:
Aflatoxin
Afterdamp
Baneberry
Benzidine
Coyotillo
Digitalin
Echidnine
Fly agaric
Gelsemine
Monkshood
Muscarine
Nux vomica
Poison gas
Poison ivy
Poison oak
Pokeberry
Sassy wood
Saxitoxin
Stonefish
Tanghinin
Toxaphene
Veratrine
Whitedamp
Wolf's-bane
Yohimbine

10 letters:
Aqua-tofana
Belladonna
Cadaverine
Colchicine
Cyanic acid
Death angel
Hydrastine

Poisonous substances and gases (continued)

Liberty cap
Limberneck
Manchineel
Mandragora
Mustard gas
Oxalic acid
Paris green
Phalloidin
Picrotoxin
Stavesacre
Strychnine
Tetrotoxin
Thorn apple

11 letters:
Agent Orange
Black bryony
Calabar-bean
Death camass
Dog's mercury
Gelseminine
Hyoscyamine
Pilocarpine
Poison elder
Prussic acid
Staggerbush
Sugar of lead
Veratridine

12 letters:
Allyl alcohol
Formaldehyde
Lead monoxide
Noogoora burr
Poison sumach
Strophanthus
Tetrodotoxin
Water hemlock
Zinc chloride

13 letters:
Dieffenbachia
Mercuric oxide
Methyl bromide
Poison dogwood
Silver nitrate
Sodium cyanide

14 letters:
Carbon monoxide
Castor-oil plant
Hydrogen iodide
Mountain laurel

15 letters:
Arsenic trioxide
Barium hydroxide

Black nightshade
Destroying angel
Hydrogen cyanide
Indian liquorice
Nitrogen dioxide
Osmium tetroxide
Woody nightshade

16 letters:
Carbon disulphide
Deadly nightshade
Hydrogen fluoride
Hydrogen sulphide
Mercuric chloride
Potassium cyanide

19 letters:
Sodium fluoroacetate
Tetramethyldiarsine

21 letters:
Potassium
  permanganate

25 letters:
Antimony potassium
  tartrate

Types of poisoning

4 letters:
Lead

6 letters:
Iodism

7 letters:
Bromism

8 letters:
Botulism

Ergotism
Plumbism
Ptomaine

9 letters:
Fluorosis
Saturnism

10 letters:
Digitalism
Salmonella

11 letters:
Hydrargyria
Listeriosis
Phosphorism

12 letters:
Mercurialism
Strychninism

Political parties

AUSTRALIA

20 letters:
Australian Labor Party

23 letters:
Liberal Party of Australia

24 letters:
National Party of
Australia

AUSTRIA

3 letters:
FPÖ
ÖVP
SPÖ

12 letters:
Freedom Party
People's Party

14 letters:
Socialist Party

BELGIUM

2 letters:
PS
SP
VB

3 letters:
CVP
PRL
PSC
PVV

5 letters:
Ecolo

6 letters:
Agalev

11 letters:
Flemish Bloc

16 letters:
French Green Party

17 letters:
Flemish Green Party

19 letters:
Flemish Liberal Party

20 letters:
French Socialist Party

21 letters:
Flemish Socialist Party

24 letters:
French Liberal Reform
Party

26 letters:
French Social Christian
Party

27 letters:
Flemish Social Christian
Party

CANADA

11 letters:
Reform Party

12 letters:
Liberal Party

13 letters:
Bloc Quebecois

17 letters:
Social Credit Party

18 letters:
New Democratic Party

23 letters:
Progressive
Conservative

DENMARK

1 letter:
V

2 letters:
CD

FP
KF
RV
SD
SF

3 letters:
KrF

8 letters:
Liberals

DENMARK (CONTINUED)

13 letters:
Progress Party

14 letters:
Left Socialists

15 letters:
Centre Democrats
Radical Liberals
Social Democrats

21 letters:
Christian People's Party

Socialist People's Party

24 letters:
Conservative People's
  Party

FINLAND

2 letters:
KP
SD

3 letters:
KOK
SFP
SMP

4 letters:
SKDL

10 letters:
Green Party

11 letters:
Centre Party

17 letters:
Finnish Rural Party

19 letters:
Swedish People's Party

21 letters:
Democratic Alternative
Social Democratic Party

22 letters:
National Coalition Party

30 letters:
Finnish People's
  Democratic League

FRANCE

2 letters:
PC
PR
PS

3 letters:
RDR
UDF

13 letters:
National Front

14 letters:
Communist Party
Socialist Party

15 letters:
Republican Party

19 letters:
Rally for the Republic

23 letters:
Union for French
  Democracy

GERMANY

3 letters:
CDU
CSU
FDP
PDS
SPD

10 letters:
Green Party

19 letters:
Free Democratic Party

20 letters:
Christian-Social Union

21 letters:
Social Democratic Party

24 letters:
Christian-Democratic
  Union

26 letters:
Party of Democratic
  Socialism

GREECE

2 letters:
ND

5 letters:
PASOK

12 letters:
New Democracy

14 letters:
Politiki Aniksi

15 letters:
Political Spring

19 letters:
Greek Communist Party

28 letters:
Pan-Hellenic Socialist
  Movement

INDIA

1 letter:
I

3 letters:
BJP

8 letters:
Congress

9 letters:
Janata Dal

20 letters:
Bharitiya Janata Party

IRISH REPUBLIC

8 letters:
Fine Gael

10 letters:
Fianna Fáil

11 letters:
Labour Party

14 letters:
Democratic Left

20 letters:
Progressive Democrats

ISRAEL

5 letters:
Likud

11 letters:
Labour Party

ITALY

3 letters:
PDS

11 letters:
Centre Union
Forza Italia

14 letters:
Northern League

16 letters:
National Alliance

22 letters:
Christian Democrat
  Party

24 letters:
Democratic Party of the
  Left

JAPAN

7 letters:
Komeito

21 letters:
Social Democratic Party

22 letters:
Liberal Democratic Party

24 letters:
Democratic Socialist
  Party

LUXEMBOURG

2 letters:
PD

3 letters:
PCS

4 letters:
POSL

14 letters:
Communist Party

15 letters:
Democratic Party

20 letters:
Christian Social Party

31 letters:
Luxembourg Socialist
  Workers' Party

MALTA

16 letters:
Malta Labour Party

Nationalist Party

MEXICO

3 letters:
PAN
PRD
PRI

19 letters:
National Action Party

25 letters:
Revolutionary Workers'
  Party

30 letters:
Party of the Democratic
  Revolution

31 letters:
Institutional
  Revolutionary Party

THE NETHERLANDS

3 letters:
CDA
VVD

4 letters:
PvdA

11 letters:
Labour Party

25 letters:
Christian Democratic
  Appeal

34 letters:
People's Party for
  Freedom and
  Democracy

NEW ZEALAND

11 letters:
Labour Party

13 letters:
National Party

NORTHERN IRELAND

4 letters:
SDLP

8 letters:
Sinn Féin

23 letters:
Democratic Unionist
  Party

27 letters:
Official Ulster Unionist
  Party

30 letters:
Social Democratic and
  Labour Party

PORTUGAL

2 letters:
PS

3 letters:
CDS
PRD
PSD

14 letters:
Socialist Party

21 letters:
Social Democratic Party

22 letters:
Democratic Renewal
  Party

27 letters:
Democratic Social
  Centre Party

SOUTH AFRICA

3 letters:
ANC
PAC

13 letters:
National Party

19 letters:
Inkatha Freedom Party

21 letters:
Pan-Africanist Congress

23 letters:
African National
  Congress

SPAIN

2 letters:
HB
IU
PP

3 letters:
CiU
PNV

4 letters:
PSOE

10 letters:
United Left

12 letters:
People's Party

13 letters:
Herri Batasuna

16 letters:
Convergencia i Uni

21 letters:
Socialist Workers' Party

22 letters:
Basque Nationalist Party

SWEDEN

3 letters:
SAP

9 letters:
Left Party

10 letters:
Green Party

11 letters:
Centre Party

12 letters:
Liberal Party

13 letters:
Moderate Party

24 letters:
Christian Democratic
  Party

27 letters:
Social Democratic
  Labour Party

TURKEY

3 letters:
PKK

4 letters:
ANAP

13 letters:
True Path Party

15 letters:
Motherland Party

19 letters:
Kurdish Workers' Party

29 letters:
Social Democratic
  Populist Party

UNITED KINGDOM (MAINLAND)

10 letters:
Plaid Cymru

11 letters:
Labour Party

16 letters:
Liberal Democrats

21 letters:
Scottish National Party

28 letters:
Conservative and
Unionist Party

UNITED STATES OF AMERICA

15 letters:
Democratic Party
Republican Party

Politicians

4 letters:
Eden, *Sir (Robert)*
Anthony

5 letters:
Laski, *Harold Joseph*

6 letters:
Bright, *John*

7 letters:
Parnell, *Charles Stewart*
Trotsky, *Leon*

8 letters:
Disraeli, *Benjamin*

11 letters:
Wilberforce, *William*

12 letters:
Chesterfield, *Philip
Dormer Stanhope*

See also:
➤ **U.S. Presidents ➤ Prime Ministers**

Popes

Pope	Pontificate
Peter	Until c.64
Linus	C.64-c.76
Anacletus	C.76-c.90
Clement I	C.90-c.99
Evaristus	C.99-c.105
Alexander I	C.105-c.117
Sixtus I	C.117-c.127
Telesphorus	C.127-c.137
Hyginus	C.137-c.140
Pius I	C.140-c.154
Anicetus	C.154-c.166
Soter	C.166-c.175
Eleutherius	175-89
Victor I	189-98
Zephyrinus	198-217

Pope	Pontificate
Callistus I	217-22
Urban I	222-30
Pontian	230-35
Anterus	235-36
Fabian	236-50
Cornelius	251-53
Lucius I	253-54
Stephen I	254-57
Sixtus II	257-58
Dionysius	259-68
Felix I	269-74
Eutychianus	275-83
Caius	283-96
Marcellinus	296-304
Marcellus I	308-09
Eusebius	310
Miltiades	311-14
Sylvester I	314-35
Mark	336
Julius I	337-52
Liberius	352-66
Damasus I	366-84
Siricius	384-99
Anastasius I	399-401
Innocent I	402-17
Zosimus	417-18
Boniface I	418-22
Celestine I	422-32
Sixtus III	432-40
Leo I	440-61
Hilarus	461-68
Simplicius	468-83
Felix III (II)	483-92
Gelasius I	492-96
Anastasius II	496-98
Symmachus	498-514
Hormisdas	514-23
John I	523-26
Felix IV (III)	526-30
Boniface II	530-32
John II	533-35
Agapetus I	535-36
Silverius	536-37

Pope	Pontificate
Vigilius	537-55
Pelagius I	556-61
John III	561-74
Benedict I	575-79
Pelagius II	579-90
Gregory I	590-604
Sabinianus	604-06
Boniface III	607
Boniface IV	608-15
Deusdedit or Adeodatus I	615-18
Boniface V	619-25
Honorious I	625-38
Severinus	640
John IV	640-42
Theodore I	642-49
Martin I	649-54
Eugenius I	654-57
Vitalian	657-72
Adeotatus II	672-6
Donus	676-78
Agatho	678-81
Leo II	682-83
Benedict II	684-85
John V	685-86
Cono	686-87
Sergius I	687-701
John VI	701-05
John VII	705-07
Sisinnius	708
Constantine	708-15
Gregory II	715-31
Gregory III	731-41
Zacharias	741-52
Stephen II (not consecrated)	752
Stephen II (III)	752-7
Paul I	757-67
Stephen III (IV)	768-72
Hadrian I	772-95
Leo III	795-816
Stephen IV (V)	816-17
Paschal I	817-24
Eugenius II	824-27
Valentine	827

Pope	Pontificate
Gregory IV	827-44
Sergius II	844-47
Leo IV	847-55
Benedict III	855-58
Nicholas I	858-67
Hadrian II	867-72
John VIII	872-82
Marinus I	882-84
Hadrian III	884-85
Stephen V (VI)	885-91
Formosus	891-96
Boniface VI	896
Stephen VI (VII)	896-97
Romanus	897
Theodore II	897
John IX	898-900
Benedict IV	900-03
Leo V	903
Sergius III	904-11
Anastasius III	911-13
Lando	913-14
John X	914-28
Leo VI	928
Stephen VII (VIII)	928-31
John XI	931-35
Leo VII	936-39
Stephen IX	939-42
Marinus II	942-46
Agapetus II	946-55
John XII	955-64
Leo VIII	963-65
Benedict V	964-66
John XIII	965-72
Benedict VI	973-74
Benedict VII	974-83
John XIV	983-84
John XV	985-96
Gregory V	996-99
Sylvester II	999-1003
John XVII	1003
John XVIII	1004-09
Sergius IV	1009-12
Benedict VIII	1012-24

Popes

Pope	Pontificate
John XIX	1024-32
Benedict IX (first reign)	1032-44
Sylvester III	1045
Benedict IX (second reign)	1045
Gregory VI	1045-46
Clement II	1046-47
Benedict IX (third reign)	1047-48
Damasus II	1048
Leo IX	1048-54
Victor II	1055-57
Stephen IX (X)	1057-58
Nicholas II	1059-61
Alexander II	1061-73
Gregory VII	1073-85
Victor III	1086-87
Urban II	1088-99
Paschal II	1099-1118
Gelasius II	1118-19
Callistus II	1119-24
Honorious II	1124-30
Innocent II	1130-43
Celestine II	1143-44
Lucius II	1144-45
Eugenius III	1145-53
Anastasius IV	1153-54
Hadrian IV	1154-59
Alexander III	1159-81
Lucius III	1181-85
Urban III	1185-87
Gregory VIII	1187
Clement III	1187-91
Celestine III	1191-98
Innocent III	1198-1216
Honorious III	1216-27
Gregory IX	1227-41
Celestine IV	1241
Innocent IV	1243-54
Alexander IV	1254-61
Urban IV	1261-64
Clement IV	1265-68
Gregory X	1271-76
Innocent V	1276
Hadrian V	1276

Pope	Pontificate
John XXI	1276-77
Nicholas III	1277-80
Martin IV	1281-85
Honorious IV	1285-87
Nicholas IV	1288-92
Celestine V	1294
Boniface VIII	1294-1303
Benedict XI	1303-04
Clement V	1305-14
John XXII	1316-34
Benedict XII	1334-42
Clement VI	1342-52
Innocent VI	1352-62
Urban V	1362-70
Gregory XI	1370-78
Urban VI	1378-89
Boniface IX	1389-1404
Innocent VII	1404-06
Gregory XII	1406-15
Martin V	1417-41
Eugenius IV	1431-47
Nicholas V	1447-55
Callistus III	1455-58
Pius II	1458-64
Paul II	1464-71
Sixtus IV	1471-84
Innocent VIII	1484-92
Alexander VI	1492-1503
Pius III	1503
Julius II	1503-13
Leo X	1513-21
Hadrian VI	1522-23
Clement VII	1523-34
Paul III	1534-49
Julius III	1550-55
Marcellus II	1555
Paul IV	1555-59
Pius IV	1559-65
Pius V	1566-72
Gregory XIII	1572-85
Sixtus V	1585-90
Urban VII	1590
Gregory XIV	1590-91

Pope	Pontificate
Innocent IX	1591
Clement VIII	1592-1605
Leo XI	1605
Paul V	1605-21
Gregory XV	1621-23
Urban VIII	1623-44
Innocent X	1644-55
Alexander VII	1655-67
Clement IX	1667-69
Clement X	1670-76
Innocent XI	1676-89
Alexander VIII	1689-91
Innocent XII	1691-1700
Clement XI	1700-21
Innocent XIII	1721-24
Benedict XIII	1724-30
Clement XII	1730-40
Benedict XIV	1740-58
Clement XIII	1758-69
Clement XIV	1769-74
Pius VI	1775-99
Pius VII	1800-23
Leo XII	1823-29
Pius VIII	1829-30
Gregory XVI	1831-46
Pius IX	1846-78
Leo XIII	1878-1903
Pius X	1903-14
Benedict XV	1914-22
Pius XI	1922-39
Pius XII	1939-58
John XXIII	1958-63
Paul VI	1963-78
John Paul I	1978
John Paul II	1978-

Ports

3 letters:
Abo
Ayr
Goa

Hué
Rio
Rye

4 letters:
Acre
Aden
Akko

579

Ports

Amoy
Apia
Baku
Bari
Cebu
Cóbh
Cork
Deal
Dill
Elat
Hilo
Hull
Icel
Kiel
Kobe
Lima
Lomé
Oban
Omsk
Oran
Oslo
Perm
Pula
Puri
Riga
Said
Suez
Suva
Tyre
Vigo
Wick

5 letters:
Accra
Aqaba
Arhus
Arica
Aulis
Barry
Basra
Batum
Beira
Belem
Brest
Cádiz
Cairo
Colón
Dakar
Derry
Dilli

Dover
Dubai
Eilat
Emden
Galle
Genoa
Gijón
Haifa
Izmir
Jaffa
Jedda
Jidda
Kerch
Kochi
Lagos
Larne
Leith
Lulea
Macao
Malmo
Mocha
Newry
Osaka
Ostia
Poole
Pusan
Rabat
Salto
Sidon
Sligo
Split
Surat
Tampa
Tokyo
Tunis
Turku
Visby
Yalta

6 letters:
Aarhus
Abadan
Agadir
Albany
Ancona
Ashdod
Bastia
Batumi
Beirut
Belize

Bergen
Bilbao
Bissau
Bombay
Bootle
Boston
Bremen
Burgas
Calais
Callao
Cannes
Canton
Cochin
Danzig
Darwin
Dieppe
Duluth
Dundee
Durban
Elblag
Galata
Galway
Gdańsk
Gdynia
Harbin
Havana
Hobart
Iloilo
Inchon
Juneau
Kisumu
Kuwait
Lisbon
Lobito
London
Luanda
Lübeck
Madras
Malaga
Manama
Manaus
Manila
Maputo
Mobile
Muscat
Nantes
Naples
Narvik
Nassau
Nelson

Ports

Odense
Odessa
Oporto
Ostend
Padang
Quincy
Ragusa
Recife
Rimini
Rostov
Santos
Smyrna
St Malo
Sydney
Tacoma
Tallin
Venice
Whitby
Yangon

7 letters:
Abidjan
Ajaccio
Algiers
Antibes
Antwerp
Augusta
Bangkok
Belfast
Bristol
Buffalo
Cardiff
Catania
Chicago
Cologne
Colomba
Colombo
Conakry
Corinth
Dunedin
Dunkirk
Ephesus
Esbjerg
Foochow
Funchal
Geelong
Glasgow
Grimsby
Halifax
Hamburg

Harwich
Incheon
Iquique
Iquitos
Karachi
Kinsale
Kowloon
Latakia
Legaspi
Le Havre
Lerwick
Livorno
Lorient
Marsala
Messina
Milazzo
Mombasa
Munster
Newport
New York
Oakland
Okayama
Palermo
Piraeus
Rangoon
Rapallo
Rosario
Rostock
Runcorn
Salerno
San Juan
Seattle
Seville
Stettin
Swansea
Tallinn
Tampico
Tangier
Taranto
Trieste
Tripoli
Ushuaia
Wexford
Wicklow

8 letters:
Aberdeen
Acapulco
Alicante
Arbroath

Auckland
Batangas
Bathurst
Benghazi
Bordeaux
Boulogne
Brindisi
Brisbane
Cagliari
Calcutta
Cape Town
Djibouti
Flushing
Freetown
Geropiga
Göteborg
Greenock
Hamilton
Harfleur
Helsinki
Holyhead
Honolulu
Istanbul
Kanazawa
Kawasaki
Keflavik
Kingston
La Coruña
La Guaira
Limassol
Limerick
Monrovia
Montreal
Murmansk
Nagasaki
Newhaven
Paramibo
Penzance
Pevensey
Plymouth
Portland
Port Said
Ramsgate
Rosslare
Salvador
San Diego
Sandwich
Savannah
Schiedam
Shanghai

Syracuse
Szczecin
Takoradi
Valencia
Veracruz
Weymouth
Yokohama

9 letters:
Amsterdam
Anchorage
Angostura
Annapolis
Archangel
Baltimore
Barcelona
Cartagena
Cherbourg
Dartmouth
Dubrovnik
Dunkerque
Ellesmere
Esperance
Europoort
Famagusta
Fishguard
Fleetwood
Fremantle
Gallipoli
Gateshead
Gravesend
Guayaquil
Immingham
Inhambane
Kao-hsiung
Kirkcaldy
Las Palmas
Liverpool
Lowestoft
Marseille
Melbourne
Mogadishu
Morecambe
Newcastle
Phnom Penh
Port Louis
Port Sudan

Reykjavik
Rotterdam
Santander
Schleswig
Sheerness
Singapore
Stavanger
Stockholm
Stornoway
Stranraer
Tarragona
Trondheim
Tynemouth
Vancouver
Volgograd
Walvis Bay
Waterford
Zeebrugge

10 letters:
Alexandria
Birkenhead
Bratislava
Bridgetown
Caernarfon
Cap-Haitien
Casablanca
Charleston
Chittagong
Copenhagen
East London
Folkestone
Fray Bentos
Georgetown
Gothenburg
Hammerfest
Launceston
Los Angeles
Mogadiscio
Montego Bay
Montevideo
New Orleans
Portsmouth
Port Talbot
Queenstown
Sevastopol
Sunderland

Townsville
Valparaíso
Wellington

11 letters:
Buenos Aires
Dar es Salaam
Grangemouth
Londonderry
Mar del Plata
Port Moresby
Punta Arenas
Scarborough
Southampton
Trincomalee
Vladivostok

12 letters:
Barranquilla
Buenaventura
Dún Laoghaire
Jacksonville
Milford Haven
Port Adelaide
Port au Prince
Rio de Janeiro
San Francisco
San Sebastian
Santo Domingo
South Shields

13 letters:
Ellesmere Port
Great Yarmouth
Ho Chi Minh City
Hook of Holland
Port Elizabeth
Tandjungpriok

14 letters:
Vishakhapatnam

15 letters:
Saint Petersburg

17 letters:
Newcastle upon Tyne

Potatoes

4 letters:
Cara

5 letters:
Wilja

6 letters:
Estima
Romano

7 letters:
Desiree
Marfona
Roseval

8 letters:
Catriona

9 letters:
Charlotte
Kerr's Pink
Maris Bard

10 letters:
Arran Comet
Arran Pilot
King Edward
Maris Piper

11 letters:
Jersey Royal

12 letters:
Arran Victory
Golden Wonder

Pentland Dell
Pink Fir Apple

13 letters:
Pentland Crown
Ulster Sceptre

14 letters:
Pentland Squire
Sharpe's Express

15 letters:
Belle de Fontenay
Pentland Javelin

Pottery

4 letters:
Delf
Ming
Raku
Sung
Ware

5 letters:
China
Delft
Spode

6 letters:
Bisque
Wemyss

7 letters:
Celadon
Ceramic
Etruria
Faience
Satsuma

8 letters:
Flatback
Gombroon
Majolica
Slipware
Wedgwood®
Whieldon

9 letters:
Agatewear
Creamware
Stoneware

10 letters:
Crouch-ware
Hollowware
Spongeware

11 letters:
Granitewear

U.S. Presidents

President	Party	Term of office
1. George Washington	Federalist	1789-97
2. John Adams	Federalist	1797-1801
3. Thomas Jefferson	Democratic Republican	1801-1809
4. James Madison	Democratic Republican	1809-1817
5. James Monroe	Democratic Republican	1817-25

President	Party	Term of office
6. John Quincy Adams	Democratic Republican	1825-29
7. Andrew Jackson	Democrat	1829-37
8. Martin Van Buren	Democrat	1837-41
9. William Henry Harrison	Whig	1841
10. John Tyler	Whig	1841-45
11. James K. Polk	Democrat	1845-49
12. Zachary Taylor	Whig	1849-50
13. Millard Fillmore	Whig	1850-53
14. Franklin Pierce	Democrat	1853-57
15. James Buchanan	Democrat	1857-61
16. Abraham Lincoln	Republican	1861-65
17. Andrew Johnson	Republican	1865-69
18. Ulysses S. Grant	Republican	1869-77
19. Rutherford B. Hayes	Republican	1877-81
20. James A. Garfield	Republican	1881
21. Chester A. Arthur	Republican	1881-85
22. Grover Cleveland	Democrat	1885-89
23. Benjamin Harrison	Republican	1889-93
24. Grover Cleveland	Democrat	1893-97
25. William McKinley	Republican	1897-1901
26. Theodore Roosevelt	Republican	1901-1909
27. William Howard Taft	Republican	1909-13
28. Woodrow Wilson	Democrat	1913-21
29. Warren G. Harding	Republican	1921-23
30. Calvin Coolidge	Republican	1923-29
31. Herbert C. Hoover	Republican	1929-33
32. Franklin D. Roosevelt	Democrat	1933-45
33. Harry S. Truman	Democrat	1945-53
34. Dwight D. Eisenhower	Republican	1953-61
35. John F. Kennedy	Democrat	1961-63
36. Lyndon B. Johnson	Democrat	1963-69
37. Richard M. Nixon	Republican	1969-74
38. Gerald R. Ford	Republican	1974-77
39. James E. Carter, Jr	Democrat	1977-81
40. Ronald W. Reagan	Republican	1981-89
41. George H. W. Bush	Republican	1989-93
42. William J. Clinton	Democrat	1993-2001
43. George W. Bush	Republican	2001-

Birds of prey

3 letters:
Ern
Owl

4 letters:
Erne
Gled
Hawk
Kite
Ruru

5 letters:
Eagle
Glede
Hobby
Saker

6 letters:
Condor
Falcon
Lanner
Merlin
Mopoke
Osprey

7 letters:
Barn owl
Boobook
Buzzard
Goshawk
Harrier
Hawk owl
Hoot owl

Kestrel
Red kite
Vulture

8 letters:
Brown owl
Bush-hawk
Caracara
Duck hawk
Falconet
Karearea
Sea eagle
Snowy owl
Tawny owl

9 letters:
Accipiter
Bald eagle
Eagle-hawk
Fish eagle
Gerfalcon
Gier-eagle
Gyrfalcon
Horned owl
Little owl
Ossifraga
Ossifrage
Wind-hover

10 letters:
Hen harrier
Screech owl

11 letters:
Chicken hawk
Cooper's hawk
Golden eagle
Lammergeier
Lammergeyer
Sparrowhawk

12 letters:
Honey buzzard
Long-eared owl
Marsh harrier

13 letters:
Bateleur eagle
Secretary bird
Turkey buzzard

14 letters:
Bearded vulture

15 letters:
Montagu's harrier
Peregrine falcon

16 letters:
Wedge-tailed eagle

17 letters:
Australian goshawk

18 letters:
Rough-legged buzzard

Prime Ministers

BRITISH PRIME MINISTERS

Prime Minister	Party	Term of office
Robert Walpole	Whig	1721-42
Earl of Wilmington	Whig	1742-43
Henry Pelham	Whig	1743-54
Duke of Newcastle	Whig	1754-56
Duke of Devonshire	Whig	1756-57
Duke of Newcastle	Whig	1757-62
Earl of Bute	Tory	1762-63

BRITISH PRIME MINISTERS (CONTINUED)

Prime Minister	Party	Term of office
George Grenville	Whig	1763-65
Marquess of Rockingham	Whig	1765-66
Duke of Grafton	Whig	1766-70
Lord North	Tory	1770-82
Marquess of Rockingham	Whig	1782
Earl of Shelburne	Whig	1782-83
Duke of Portland	Coalition	1783
William Pitt	Tory	1783-1801
Henry Addington	Tory	1801-04
William Pitt	Tory	1804-06
Lord Grenville	Whig	1806-7
Duke of Portland	Tory	1807-09
Spencer Perceval	Tory	1809-12
Earl of Liverpool	Tory	1812-27
George Canning	Tory	1827
Viscount Goderich	Tory	1827-28
Duke of Wellington	Tory	1828-30
Earl Grey	Whig	1830-34
Viscount Melbourne	Whig	1834
Robert Peel	Conservative	1834-35
Viscount Melbourne	Whig	1835-41
Robert Peel	Conservative	1841-46
Lord John Russell	Liberal	1846-52
Earl of Derby	Conservative	1852
Lord Aberdeen	Peelite	1852-55
Viscount Palmerston	Liberal	1855-58
Earl of Derby	Conservative	1858-59
Viscount Palmerston	Liberal	1859-65
Lord John Russell	Liberal	1865-66
Earl of Derby	Conservative	1866-68
Benjamin Disraeli	Conservative	1868
William Gladstone	Liberal	1868-74
Benjamin Disraeli	Conservative	1874-80
William Gladstone	Liberal	1880-85
Marquess of Salisbury	Conservative	1885-86
William Gladstone	Liberal	1886
Marquess of Salisbury	Conservative	1886-92
William Gladstone	Liberal	1892-94
Earl of Rosebery	Liberal	1894-95

BRITISH PRIME MINISTERS (CONTINUED)

Prime Minister	Party	Term of office
Marquess of Salisbury	Conservative	1895-1902
Arthur James Balfour	Conservative	1902-05
Henry Campbell-Bannerman	Liberal	1905-08
Herbert Henry Asquith	Liberal	1908-15
Herbert Henry Asquith	Coalition	1915-16
David Lloyd George	Coalition	1916-22
Andrew Bonar Law	Conservative	1922-23
Stanley Baldwin	Conservative	1923-24
James Ramsay MacDonald	Labour	1924
Stanley Baldwin	Conservative	1924-29
James Ramsay MacDonald	Labour	1929-31
James Ramsay MacDonald	Nationalist	1931-35
Stanley Baldwin	Nationalist	1935-37
Arthur Neville Chamberlain	Nationalist	1937-40
Winston Churchill	Coalition	1940-45
Clement Attlee	Labour	1945-51
Winston Churchill	Conservative	1951-55
Anthony Eden	Conservative	1955-57
Harold Macmillan	Conservative	1957-63
Alec Douglas-Home	Conservative	1963-64
Harold Wilson	Labour	1964-70
Edward Heath	Conservative	1970-74
Harold Wilson	Labour	1974-76
James Callaghan	Labour	1976-79
Margaret Thatcher	Conservative	1979-90
John Major	Conservative	1990-97
Tony Blair	Labour	1997-

AUSTRALIAN PRIME MINISTERS

Prime minister	Party	Term of office
Edmund Barton	Protectionist	1901-03
Alfred Deakin	Protectionist	1903-04
John Christian Watson	Labor	1904
George Houston Reid	Free Trade	1904-05
Alfred Deakin	Protectionist	1905-08
Andrew Fisher	Labor	1908-09

AUSTRALIAN PRIME MINISTERS (CONTINUED)

Prime Minister	Party	Term of office
Alfred Deakin	Fusion	1909-10
Andrew Fisher	Labor	1910-13
Joseph Cook	Liberal	1913-14
Andrew Fisher	Labor	1914-15
William Morris Hughes	National Labor	1915-17
William Morris Hughes	Nationalist	1917-23
Stanley Melbourne Bruce	Nationalist	1923-29
James Henry Scullin	Labor	1929-31
Joseph Aloysius Lyons	United	1931-39
Earle Christmas Page	Country	1939
Robert Gordon Menzies	United	1939-41
Arthur William Fadden	Country	1941
John Joseph Curtin	Labor	1941-45
Joseph Benedict Chifley	Labor	1945-49
Robert Gordon Menzies	Liberal	1949-66
Harold Edward Holt	Liberal	1966-67
John McEwen	Country	1967-68
John Grey Gorton	Liberal	1968-71
William McMahon	Liberal	1971-72
Edward Gough Whitlam	Labor	1972-75
John Malcolm Fraser	Liberal	1975-83
Robert James Lee Hawke	Labor	1983-91
Paul Keating	Labor	1991-96
John Howard	Liberal	1996-

CANADIAN PRIME MINISTERS

Prime Minister	Party	Term of office
John A. MacDonald	Conservative	1867-73
Alexander Mackenzie	Liberal	1873-78
John A. MacDonald	Conservative	1878-91
John J.C. Abbot	Conservative	1891-92
John S.D. Thompson	Conservative	1892-94
Mackenzie Bowell	Conservative	1894-96
Charles Tupper	Conservative	1896
Wilfrid Laurier	Liberal	1896-1911
Robert Borden	Conservative	1911-20
Arthur Meighen	Conservative	1920-21

CANADIAN PRIME MINISTERS (CONTINUED)

Prime Minister	Party	Term of office
William Lyon Mackenzie King	Liberal	1921-26
Arthur Meighen	Conservative	1926
William Lyon Mackenzie King	Liberal	1926-30
Richard Bedford Bennet	Conservative	1930-35
William Lyon Mackenzie King	Liberal	1935-48
Louis St. Laurent	Liberal	1948-57
John George Diefenbaker	Conservative	1957-63
Lester Bowles Pearson	Liberal	1963-68
Pierre Elliott Trudeau	Liberal	1968-79
Joseph Clark	Conservative	1979-80
Pierre Elliott Trudeau	Liberal	1980-84
John Turner	Liberal	1984
Brian Mulroney	Conservative	1984-93
Kim Campbell	Conservative	1993
Joseph Jacques Jean Chrétien	Liberal	1993-

NEW ZEALAND PRIME MINISTERS

Prime Minister	Party	Term of office
Henry Sewell	-	1856
William Fox	-	1856
Edward William Stafford	-	1856-61
William Fox	-	1861-62
Alfred Domett	-	1862-63
Frederick Whitaker	-	1863-64
Frederick Aloysius Weld	-	1864-65
Edward William Stafford	-	1865-69
William Fox	-	1869-72
Edward William Stafford	-	1872
William Fox	-	1873
Julius Vogel	-	1873-75
Daniel Pollen	-	1875-76
Julius Vogel	-	1876

NEW ZEALAND PRIME MINISTERS (CONTINUED)

Prime Minister	Party	Term of office
Harry Albert Atkinson	-	1876-77
George Grey	-	1877-79
John Hall	-	1879-82
Frederick Whitaker	-	1882-83
Harry Albert Atkinson	-	1883-84
Robert Stout	-	1884
Harry Albert Atkinson	-	1884
Robert Stout	-	1884-87
Harry Albert Atkinson	-	1887-91
John Ballance	-	1891-93
Richard John Seddon	Liberal	1893-1906
William Hall-Jones	Liberal	1906
Joseph George Ward	Liberal/National	1906-12
Thomas Mackenzie	National	1912
William Ferguson Massey	Reform	1912-25
Francis Henry Dillon Bell	Reform	1925
Joseph Gordon Coates	Reform	1925-28
Joseph George Ward	Liberal/National	1928-30
George William Forbes	United	1930-35
Michael Joseph Savage	Labour	1935-40
Peter Fraser	Labour	1940-49
Sidney George Holland	National	1949-57
Keith Jacka Holyoake	National	1957
Walter Nash	Labour	1957-60
Keith Jacka Holyoake	National	1960-72
John Ross Marshall	National	1972
Norman Eric Kirk	Labour	1972-74
Wallace Edward Rowling	Labour	1974-75
Robert David Muldoon	National	1975-84
David Russell Lange	Labour	1984-89
Geoffrey Palmer	Labour	1989-90
Mike Moore	Labour	1990
Jim Bolger	National	1990-97
Jenny Shipley	National	1997-99
Helen Clark	Labour	1999-

Programming languages

1 letter:
C

3 letters:
Ada
RPG
SQL

4 letters:
Java
LISP
LOGO
Perl

5 letters:
Algol
BASIC
Basic
COBOL
CORAL
FORTH
OCCAM

6 letters:
Pascal
PROLOG

Simula
SNOBOL

7 letters:
FORTRAN
Haskell

9 letters:
Smalltalk

10 letters:
Postscript

Proteins

4 letters:
Zein

5 letters:
Abrin
Actin
Opsin
Prion
Renin
Ricin

6 letters:
Avidin
Capsid
Enzyme
Fibrin
Globin
Gluten
Lectin
Leptin
Myosin
Ossein

7 letters:
Adipsin
Albumen
Albumin
Aleuron
Amyloid
Elastin
Fibroin

Gliadin
Hordein
Keratin
Legumin
Opsonin
Sericin
Spongin
Tubulin

8 letters:
Aleurone
Amandine
Collagen
Cytokine
Ferritin
Globulin
Prolamin
Spectrin
Troponin
Vitellin

9 letters:
Capsomere
Flagellin
Myoglobin
Ovalbumin
Phaseolin
Prolamine
Properdin
Protamine
Repressor

Sclerotin

10 letters:
Actomyosin
Apoprotein
Bradykinin
Calmodulin
Caseinogen
Conchiolin
Dystrophin
Factor VIII
Fibrinogen
Interferon
Lymphokine
Thrombogen
Toxalbumin

11 letters:
Angiotensin
Haptoglobin
Interleukin
Lactalbumin
Transferrin
Tropomyosin

12 letters:
Lactoprotein
Serum albumin

13 letters:
Ceruloplasmin
Serum globulin

14 letters:
Immunoglobulin

16 letters:
Alpha-fetoprotein

Canadian provinces

Province	Abbreviation
Alberta	AB
British Columbia	BC
Manitoba	MB
New Brunswick	NB
Newfoundland	NF
Northwest Territories	NWT
Nova Scotia	NS
Nunavut	NU
Ontario	ON
Prince Edward Island	PE
Quebec	PQ
Saskatchewan	SK
Yukon Territory	YT

South African provinces and provincial capitals

Province	Capital
Eastern Cape	Bisho
Free State	Bloemfontein
Gauteng	Johannesburg
KwaZulu-Natal	Pietermaritzburg
Limpopo	Pietersburg
Mpumalanga	Nelspruit
North-West	Mafikeng
Northern Cape	Kimberley
Western Cape	Cape Town

Psychology

BRANCHES OF PSYCHOLOGY

5 letters:
Child

6 letters:
Social

8 letters:
Analytic
Clinical
Hedonics

10 letters:
Industrial
Psychiatry

BRANCHES OF PSYCHOLOGY (CONTINUED)

11 letters:
Comparative
Educational

12 letters:
Experimental

13 letters:
Developmental
Psychometrics
Psychophysics

14 letters:
Organizational
Parapsychology

15 letters:
Neuropsychology

16 letters:
Psychophysiology

17 letters:
Psycholinguistics

PSYCHOLOGY TERMS

2 letters:
Id

3 letters:
Ego

4 letters:
Anal
Mind
Self

5 letters:
Angst
Mania

6 letters:
Phobia
Psyche
Stress
Trauma

7 letters:
Anxiety
Complex
Persona

8 letters:
Alter ego
Analysis

Delusion
Dementia
Fixation
Hypnosis
Hysteria
Neurosis
Paranoia
Superego
Syndrome

9 letters:
Death wish
Extrovert
Introvert
Obsession
Psychosis

10 letters:
Compulsion
Depression
Regression
Repression

11 letters:
Inkblot test
Personality
Sublimation
Unconscious

12 letters:
Conditioning
Freudian slip
Group therapy
Hypochondria
Subconscious

13 letters:
Consciousness
Primal therapy
Psychosomatic
Rorschach test
Schizophrenia

14 letters:
Electra complex
Gestalt therapy
Oedipus complex
Psychoanalysis

18 letters:
Inferiority complex
Persecution complex

19 letters:
Personality disorder
Primal scream therapy

PSYCHOLOGISTS

4 letters:
Coué, *Émile*
Jung, *Carl Gustav*

5 letters:
Adler, *Alfred*
Freud, *Sigmund*
Fromm, *Erich*
James, *William*

Janet, *Pierre Marie Félix*
Luria, *Alexander
  Romanovich*
Reich, *Wilhelm*
Wundt, *Wilhelm Max*

PSYCHOLOGISTS (CONTINUED)

6 letters:
Hering, *Ewald*
Horney, *Karen*
Köhler, *Wolfgang*
Müller, *Johannes Peter*
Pavlov, *Ivan Petrovich*
Piaget, *Jean*
Watson, *John*

7 letters:
Eysenck, *Hans Jürgen*
Fechner, *Gustav Theodor*
Skinner, *B(urrhus)*
  F(rederic)

9 letters:
Thorndike, *Edward Lee*

10 letters:
Ebbinghaus, *Hermann*

11 letters:
Münsterberg, *Hugo*

Shades of purple

4 letters:
Plum
Puce
Wine

5 letters:
Lilac
Mauve
Pansy
Royal

6 letters:
Claret
Indigo

Tyrian
Violet

7 letters:
Carmine
Gentian
Heather
Magenta

8 letters:
Amethyst
Burgundy
Dubonnet
Lavender

Mulberry

9 letters:
Aubergine
Peach-blow

10 letters:
Heliotrope
Periwinkle

11 letters:
Gentian blue

Q q

Queens

3 letters:
Mab
May

4 letters:
Anna
Anne
Bess
Dido
Juno
Leda
Mary

5 letters:
Helen
Maeve
Sheba

6 letters:
Atossa
Balkis
Esther
Hecuba
Isabel

Ishtar
Isolde

7 letters:
Camilla
Candace
Eleanor
Jocasta
Matilda
Omphale
Titania

8 letters:
Adelaide
Alcestis
Boadicea
Boudicca
Brunhild
Caroline
Eleanora
Gertrude
Hermione
Penelope

Phaedram
Victoria

9 letters:
Alexandra
Artemesia
Brunhilde
Cleopatra
Elizabeth
Guinevere
Hippolyta
Nefertiti
Semiramis

10 letters:
Hatshepset
Hatshepsut
Persephone
Proserpina

15 letters:
Marie Antoinette

R r

Rabbits and hares

4 letters:
Cony
Hare
Pika

5 letters:
Coney

6 letters:
Rabbit

10 letters:
Arctic hare
Cottontail
Jack rabbit

11 letters:
Belgian hare

12 letters:
Angora rabbit
Snowshoe hare

14 letters:
Snowshoe rabbit

Races

2 letters:
TT

4 letters:
Boat
Milk
Oaks

5 letters:
Derby
Palio

6 letters:
Le Mans

7 letters:
St Leger

8 letters:
Olympics
RAC Rally

10 letters:
Epsom Derby
Royal Ascot

11 letters:
Admiral's Cup
America's Cup

12 letters:
Melbourne Cup
National Hunt
Tour de France

13 letters:
Dubai World Cup
Grand National
Kentucky Derby
Manx Grand Prix

15 letters:
Monte Carlo Rally

17 letters:
Cheltenham Gold Cup

Shades of red

3 letters:
Bay

4 letters:
Foxy
Pink
Plum
Puce

Rose
Rosy
Ruby
Rust
Wine

5 letters:
Coral

Flame
Flesh
Gules
Henna
Liver
Peach
Poppy
Sandy

6 letters:
Auburn
Cerise
Cherry
Claret
Copper
Damask
Ginger
Maroon
Russet
Titian
Turkey

7 letters:
Carmine
Carroty
Coppery
Crimson

Fuchsia
Magenta
Old rose
Oxblood
Roseate
Scarlet
Tea rose
Vermeil

8 letters:
Baby pink
Burgundy
Cardinal
Chestnut
Cinnabar
Cyclamen
Dubonnet
Mulberry

9 letters:
Carnation
Grenadine
Peach-blow
Raspberry
Shell pink
Vermilion

10 letters:
Oyster pink
Salmon pink
Strawberry
Terracotta

11 letters:
Burnt sienna

Regimental nicknames

Regiment	Nickname
Army Service Corps	Ally Sloper's Cavalry
21st SAS	Artist's Rifles
13th Hussars	Baker's Dozen
2nd Dragoon Guards	The Bays
Royal Leicestershire Regiment	Bengal Tigers
17th Lancers	Bingham's Dandies
Royal Dragoons	Birdcatchers
7th Dragoon Guards	Black Horse
North Staffordshire Regiment	Black Knots
50th Foot Regiment	Blind *or* Dirty Half Hundred
Manchester Regiment	Bloodsuckers
11th Foot	Bloody Eleventh
4th/7th Royal Dragoon Guards	Blue Horse
Royal Horse Guards	Blues
Royal Scots Greys	Bubbly Jocks
3rd Foot	Buffs, Nutcrackers *or* Resurrectionists
4th (Royal Irish) Dragoon Guards	Buttermilks
26th & 90th Foot	Cameronians *or* Scottish Rifles
3rd Prince of Wales Dragoon Guards	Carabineers, Carbs *or* Tichborne's Own
55th Foot	Castle Reeves
Royal Army Medical Corps	Castor Oil Dragoons

Regiment	Nickname
11th Hussars (Prince Albert's Own)	Cherry Pickers *or* Cherubims
Coldstream Guards	Coldies
8th (King's Royal Irish) Hussars	Cross Belts
17th/21st Lancers	Death *or* Glory Boys
9th (Queen's Royal) Lancers	Delhi Spearmen
7th Armoured Division	Desert Rats
Inns of Court Regiment	Devil's Own
46th Foot (Duke of Cornwall's Light Infantry)	Docs *or* Red Feathers
18th (Queen Mary's Own) Hussars	Drogheda Light Horse
33rd Foot (Duke of Wellington's)	Duke's
Royal Scots Fusiliers	Earl of Mar's Grey Breeks
15th (The King's) Hussars	Eliott's Tailors
Territorial Army Emergency Reserve	Ever Readies
40th (XL) Foot	Excellers
68th Foot (Durham Light Infantry)	Faithful Durhams
Royal Berkshire Regiment	Farmers' Boys
87th Foot (Royal Irish Fusiliers)	Faugh-a-ballagh Boys *or* Old Fogs
15th (King's) Hussars	Fighting Fifteenth
5th Foot (Royal Northumberland Fusiliers)	Fighting Fifth
9th Foot (Royal Norfolk Regiment)	Fighting Ninth, Holy Boys *or* Norfolk Howards
Worcestershire Regiment	Firms
Welsh Regiment	First Invalids
Queen's Royal Regiment (West Surrey)	First Tangerines
Royal Ulster Rifles	Fitch and Grenadiers
54th Foot (Dorset Regiment)	Flamers
Gloucestershire Regiment	Fore and Aft
42nd Foot (Black Watch)	Forty-Twas
Royal Scots (1st Foot)	First and Wurst
Royal Highland Fusiliers	Fusil Jocks
Royal Horse Artillery	Galloping Gunners
3rd (King's Own) Hussars	Galloping Third
Gordon Highlanders	Gay Gordons
70th Foot (East Surrey)	Glasgow Greys
Highland Light Infantry	Glesca Keelies

Regiment	Nickname
5th (Princess Charlotte of Wales) Dragoon Guards	Green Horse
Alexandra Princess of Wales Own Yorkshire Regiment	Green Howards
King's Royal Rifle Corps	Green Jackets
21st (Empress of Indian's) Lancers	Grey Lancers
Royal Scots Greys	Greys
Royal Hampshire Regiment	Hampshire Tigers
33rd Foot (Duke of Wellington's Regiment)	Havercake Lads
Royal Army Veterinary Corps	Horse Doctors
17th (Duke of Cambridge's Own) Lancers	Horse Marines
South Wales Borderers	Howard's Greens
Royal Army Pay Corps	Ink Slingers
King's Royal Rifle Corps	Jaegers
Royal Marines	Jollies
Scots Guards	Kiddies
King's Own Scottish Borderers	Kokky-Olly Birds *or* Kosbies
King's Own Yorkshire Light Infantry	Kolis *or* Koylies
32nd Foot (Duke of Cornwall's Light Infantry)	Lacedaemonians
47th Foot	Lancashire Lads *or* The Loyal Regiment
8th Foot (King's Regiment)	Leather Hats
Oxfordshire & Buckinghamshire Light Infantry	Light Bobs
13th Hussars	Lily Whites
Irish Guards	Micks
Lancashire Fusiliers	Minden Boys
Royal Army Service Corps	Moke Train
Wiltshire Regiment	Moonrakers
4th (Royal Irish) Dragoon Guards	Mounted Micks
Royal Engineers	Mudlarks
Royal Marines	Neptune's Bodyguard
Welsh Regiment	Old Agamemnons
Gloucestershire Regiment	Old Braggs
53rd Foot (King's Shropshire Light Infantry)	Old Brickdusts *or* Old Five and Threepennies
3rd (Prince of Wales's) Dragoon Guards	Old Canaries
12th Foot (Suffolk Regiment)	Old Dozen

Regiment	Nickname
Grenadier Guards	Old Eyes
87th Foot (Royal Irish Fusiliers)	Old Fogs
7th (Queen's Own) Hussars	Old Saucy Seventh
Sherwood Foresters	Old Stubborns
35th Foot	Orange Lilies
4th (Queen's Own) Hussars	Paget's Irregular Horse
Bedfordshire & Hertfordshire Regiment	Peacemakers
90th Foot (Cameronians)	Perthshire Grey Breeks
Royal Lincolnshire Regiment	Poachers
56th Foot	Pompadours
77th Foot	Pot-Hooks
South Staffordshire Regiment	Pump and Tortoise
Royal Army Pay Corps	Quill Drivers
5th (Royal Irish) Lancers	Red Breasts
Royal Horse Artillery	Right of the Line
91st Foot (Argyll & Sutherland Highlanders)	Rorys
Royal (1st) Dragoons	Royals
65th Foot (York & Lancaster Regiment)	Royal Tigers
2nd Dragoon Guards (Queen's Boys)	Rusty Buckles
Grenadier Guards	Sand Bags
39th Foot (Dorsetshire Regiment)	Sankey's Horse
Royal Engineers	Sappers
6th Foot (Royal Warwickshire Fusiliers)	Saucy Sixth
16th (Queen's Royal) Lancers	Scarlet Lancers
6th (Inniskilling) Dragoons	Skiffingers
5th Royal Inniskilling Dragoon Guards	Skins
17th (Duke of Cambridge's Own) Lancers	Skull and Crossbones
Gloucestershire Regiment	Slashers
15th Foot (East Yorkshire Regiment)	Snappers
Wiltshire Regiment	Springers
1st Northamptonshire Regiment	Steel Backs
7th (Princess of Wales's Royal) Lancers	Strawboots
12th (Prince of Wales's Royal) Lancers	Supple Twelfth

Regiment	Nickname
Rifle Brigade	Sweeps
Welsh Guards	Taffys
93rd Foot (2nd Battalion Argyll & Sutherland Highlanders)	Thin Red Line
30th Foot (East Lancashire Regiment)	Three Tens
Life Guards	Tin Bellies *or* The Tins
Yorkshire & Lancashire Regiment	Twin Roses
55th Foot (Border Regiment)	Two Fives
44th Foot (Essex Regiment)	Two Fours
20th Foot (Lancashire Fusiliers)	Two Tens
69th Foot	Ups and Downs
Royal Warwickshire Fusiliers	Warwickshire Lads
20th Hussars	The X's
31st Foot (East Surrey Regiment)	Young Buffs
7th (Queen's Own) Hussars	Young Eyes

Administrative regions

FRENCH REGIONS

6 letters:
Alsace
Centre

7 letters:
Corsica

8 letters:
Auvergne
Brittany
Burgundy
Limousin
Lorraine
Picardie

9 letters:
Aquitaine

10 letters:
Rhône-Alpes

11 letters:
Île-de-France
Pays de Loire

12 letters:
Franche-Comté
Midi-Pyrénées

14 letters:
Basse-Normandie

Haute-Normandie

15 letters:
Nord-Pas-de-Calais
Poitou-Charentes

16 letters:
Champagne-Ardenne

19 letters:
Languedoc-Roussillon

22 letters:
Provence-Alpes-Côte
  d'Azur

FRENCH DÉPARTEMENTS

3 letters:
Ain
Lot
Var

4 letters:
Aube
Aude
Cher
Eure
Gard

Gers
Jura
Nord
Oise
Orne
Tarn

FRENCH DÉPARTEMENTS (CONTINUED)

5 letters:
Aisne
Corse
Doubs
Drôme
Indre
Isère
Loire
Marne
Meuse
Paris
Rhône
Saône
Somme
Yonne

6 letters:
Allier
Ariège
Cantal
Creuse
Essone
Gayane
Landes
Loiret
Lozère
Manche
Sarthe
Savoie
Vendée
Vienne
Vosges

7 letters:
Ardèche
Aveyron
Bas Rhin
Corrèze
Cote d'Or

Gironde
Hérault
Mayenne
Moselle
Niveres
Réunion

8 letters:
Ardennes
Calvados
Charente
Dordogne
Haut Rhin
Morbihan
Val d'Oise
Vaucluse
Yvelines

9 letters:
Finistère
Puy de Dôme

10 letters:
Deux Sèvres
Eure et Loir
Guadeloupe
Haute Loire
Haute Marne
Loir et Cher
Martinique
Val de Marne

11 letters:
Côtes du Nord
Hautes Alpes
Haute Savoie
Haute Vienne
Pas de Calais

12 letters:
Haute Garonne
Hauts de Seine
Indre et Loire
Lot et Garonne
Maine et Loire
Saône et Loire
Seine et Marne

13 letters:
Ille et Vilaine
Seine Maritime
Tarn et Garonne

14 letters:
Alpes Maritimes
Bouches du Rhône
Hautes Pyrénées

15 letters:
Loire Atlantique
Seine Saint Denis

16 letters:
Charente Maritime
Meurthe et Moselle

18 letters:
Pyrénées Orientales

19 letters:
Pyrénées Atlantiques
Territoire de Belfort

20 letters:
Alpes de Haute
   Provence

GERMAN STATES

6 letters:
Berlin
Bremen
Hessen
Saxony

7 letters:
Bavaria
Hamburg

8 letters:
Saarland

9 letters:
Thuringia

11 letters:
Brandenburg
Lower Saxony

GERMAN STATES (CONTINUED)

12 letters:
Saxony-Anhalt

16 letters:
Baden-Württemberg

17 letters:
Schleswig-Holstein

19 letters:
Rhineland-Palatinate

20 letters:
North Rhine-Westphalia

24 letters:
Mecklenburg-West
   Pomerania

ITALIAN REGIONS

5 letters:
Lazio

6 letters:
Marche
Molise
Puglia
Sicily
Umbria
Veneto

7 letters:
Abruzzo

Liguria
Tuscany

8 letters:
Calabria
Campania
Lombardy
Piedmont
Sardinia

10 letters:
Basilicata

11 letters:
Valle d'Aosta

13 letters:
Emilia-Romagna

17 letters:
Trentino-Alto Adige

19 letters:
Friuli-Venezia Giulia

ITALIAN PROVINCES

4 letters:
Asti
Bari
Como
Enna
Lodi
Pisa
Roma

5 letters:
Aosta
Cuneo
Forlì
Lecce
Lecco
Lucca
Nuoro
Parma
Pavia
Prato
Rieti
Siena
Terni

Udine

6 letters:
Ancona
Arezzo
Chieti
Foggia
Genova
Latina
Matera
Milano
Modena
Napoli
Novara
Padova
Pesaro
Ragusa
Rimini
Rovigo
Savona
Teramo
Torino
Trento

Varese
Verona

7 letters:
Belluno
Bergamo
Bologna
Bolzano
Brescia
Caserta
Catania
Cosenza
Cremona
Crotone
Ferrara
Firenze
Gorizia
Imperia
Isernia
L'Aquila
Livorno
Mantova
Messina

Administrative regions

ITALIAN PROVINCES (CONTINUED)

Palermo
Perugia
Pescara
Pistoia
Potenza
Ravenna
Salerno
Sassari
Sondrio
Taranto
Trapani
Treviso
Trieste
Venezia
Vicenza
Viterbo

8 letters:
Avellino
Brindisi

Cagliari
Grosseto
La Spezia
Macerata
Oristano
Piacenza
Siracusa
Verbania
Vercelli

9 letters:
Agrigento
Benevento
Catanzaro
Frosinone
Pordenone

10 letters:
Campobasso

11 letters:
Alessandria

12 letters:
Ascoli Piceno
Massa Carrara
Reggio Emilia
Vibo Valentia

13 letters:
Caltanissetta

16 letters:
Reggio di Calabria

21 letters:
Repubblica di San
  Marino

SPANISH REGIONS

5 letters:
Ceuta

6 letters:
Aragón
Madrid
Murcia

7 letters:
Galicia
La Rioja
Melilla
Navarra

8 letters:
Asturias

9 letters:
Andalucía
Cantabria
Catalonia

11 letters:
Extremadura

12 letters:
Castilla-León

13 letters:
Basque Country
Canary Islands

15 letters:
Balearic Islands

16 letters:
Castilla-La Mancha

18 letters:
Valencian Community

SPANISH PROVINCES

4 letters:
Jaén
León
Lugo

5 letters:
Álava
Ávila
Cádiz

Ceuta
Soria

6 letters:
Burgos
Cuenca
Girona
Huelva
Huesca

Lleida
Madrid
Málaga
Murcia
Orense
Teruel
Toledo
Zamora

SPANISH PROVINCES (CONTINUED)

7 letters:
Almerìa
Badajoz
Cácares
Cordoba
Granada
La Rioja
Melilla
Navarra
Segovia
Sevilla
Vizcaya

8 letters:
Albacete
Alicante

Asturias
La Coruna
Palencia
Valencia
Zaragoza

9 letters:
Alhucemas
Balearics
Barcelona
Cantabria
Castellón
Guipúzcoa
Las Palmas
Salamanca
Tarragona

10 letters:
Chafarinas
Ciudad Real
Pontevedra
Valladolid

11 letters:
Gualalajara

15 letters:
Vélez de la Gomera

19 letters:
Santa Cruz de Tenerife

See also:
➤ **Canadian provinces** ➤ **Countries** ➤ **South African provinces and provincial capitals** ➤ **States and territories** ➤ **Swiss cantons** ➤ **New Zealand territories**

Religion

RELIGIONS

4 letters:
Babi
Druz
Jain

5 letters:
Baha'i
Druse
Druze
Hasid
Islam
Jaina
Jewry
Sunna

6 letters:
Babism
Culdee
Gueber
Guebre
Hadith

Hassid
Jesuit
Loyola
Sabian
Shaker
Shango
Shembe
Shinto
Taoism
Voodoo
Zabian

7 letters:
Animism
Baha'ism
Bogomil
Ismaili
Jainism
Judaism
Lamaism
Macumba

Mahatma
Orphism
Parsism
Piarist
Sikhism
Tsabian
Yezidis

8 letters:
Buddhism
Druidism
Hinduism
Lutheran
Manichee
Mazdaism
Mazdeism
Paganism
Santeria
Satanism
Theatine

RELIGIONS (CONTINUED)

9 letters:
Celestine
Coenobite
Hindooism
Jansenism
Mithraism
Mormonism
Pantheist
Shamanism
Shintoism
Utraquist
Voodooism
Zoroaster

10 letters:
Carthusian
Cistercian

Gilbertine
Heliolatry
Hospitaler
Manicheism
Zend-avesta

11 letters:
Camaldolite
Hare Krishna
Hospitaller
Ignorantine
Manichaeism
Mithraicism
Ryobu Shinto
Scientology®
Zoroastrism

12 letters:
Christianity
Confucianism
Zarathustric

13 letters:
Sons of Freedom
Tractarianism

14 letters:
Rastafarianism
Zoroastrianism

15 letters:
Christadelphian
Jehovah's Witness

RELIGIOUS BOOKS

2 letters:
Lu

4 letters:
Veda

5 letters:
Bible
Koran
Li Chi
Quran
Torah

6 letters:
Granth
I Ching

Talmud

7 letters:
Rigveda
Su Ching

8 letters:
Ayurveda
Ramayana
Samaveda
Shi Ching
Tipitaka

9 letters:
Adi Granth
Apocrypha

Atharveda
Siddhanta
Tripitaka
Yajurveda

11 letters:
Mahabharata

12 letters:
Bhagavad-Gita
Book of Mormon
New Testament
Old Testament

15 letters:
Guru Granth Sahib

RELIGIOUS BUILDINGS

5 letters:
Abbey
Kaaba
Marae

6 letters:
Bethel
Chapel
Church

Mosque
Temple

7 letters:
Convent

8 letters:
Gurdwara

9 letters:
Cathedral
Monastery
Synagogue

10 letters:
Tabernacle

Religion

RELIGIOUS CLOTHING

3 letters:
Alb

4 letters:
Coif
Cope
Cowl

5 letters:
Amice
Cotta
Habit
Mitre

6 letters:
Almuce
Chimar
Chimer
Cornet
Guimpe
Peplos
Peplus
Rochet

Tippet
Wimple

7 letters:
Biretta
Calotte
Capuche
Cassock
Chimere
Gremial
Infulae
Maniple
Mozetta
Pallium
Soutane

8 letters:
Berretta
Capouche
Chasuble
Dalmatic
Mozzetta
Scapular

Surplice

9 letters:
Clericals
Dog collar
Shovel hat
Surcingle
Zucchetto

10 letters:
Canonicals

11 letters:
Mantelletta
Pontificals

12 letters:
Superhumeral

14 letters:
Clerical collar

RELIGIOUS FESTIVALS

4 letters:
Holi
Lent

5 letters:
Hirja
Purim
Wesak

6 letters:
Advent
Diwali
Easter
Pesach

7 letters:
Ramadan
Shavuot
Succoth
Sukkoth
Trinity
Whitsun
Yuan Tan

8 letters:
Al Hijrah
Baisakhi
Bodhi Day
Chanukah
Dussehra
Epiphany
Hanukkah
Id-ul-Adha
Id-ul-Fitr
Passover
Rogation

9 letters:
Candlemas
Ching Ming
Christmas
Eid ul-Adha
Eid ul-Fitr
Pentecost
Rama Naumi
Yom Kippur

10 letters:
Good Friday
Michaelmas
Palm Sunday
Sexagesima

11 letters:
Dhammacakka
Hola Mohalla

12 letters:
Ascension Day
Ash Wednesday
Janamashtami
Lailat ul-Qadr
Moon Festival
Quadragesima
Rosh Hashanah
Septuagesima

13 letters:
Corpus Christi
Lailat ul-Barah

RELIGIOUS FESTIVALS (CONTINUED)

Passion Sunday
Quinquagesima
Raksha Bandhan
Shrove Tuesday

14 letters:
Day of Atonement
Mahashivaratri
Maundy Thursday
Winter Festival

18 letters:
Dragon Boat Festival
Feast of Tabernacles
Guru Nanak's Birthday

20 letters:
Lailat ul-Isra Wal Mi'raj

See also:
➤ **Angels** ➤ **Four Horsemen of the Apocalypse** ➤ **The Twelve Apostles**
➤ **Archbishops of Canterbury** ➤ **Bible** ➤ **Schools of Buddhism**
➤ **Christian denominations and sects** ➤ **The Twelve Disciples**
➤ **Ecclesiastical terms** ➤ **Gods and Goddesses** ➤ **Hindu denominations
and sects** ➤ **Moslem denominations and sects** ➤ **Jewish denominations
and sects** ➤ **Monks** ➤ **Monastic orders** ➤ **Religious movements**
➤ **Religious orders** ➤ **Saints**

Religious movements

Adidam (The Way of the Heart)
African Methodist Episcopalian
  Church
Alcoholics Anonymous
AME Church
Amish
Ananda Church of Self Realization
Ananda Marga Yoga Society
Anglo-Israelism
Assemblies of God
Association for Research and
  Enlightenment
Atheism
Atherius Society
Aum Shinrikyo
Baha'i Faith
Baptists, Primitive
Baptists, Southern
Bogomils
Boston Church of Christ
Branch Davidians
Branhamism
British-Israelism
Brownsville Revival
Bruderhof
Buddhism
Call to Renewal (Christians for a New
  Political Vision)

Calvary Chapel
Campus Crusade for Christ
Candomble
Cao Daism
Channeling
Charismatic Movement
Chen Tao (The Right Way)
Children of God
Christadelphians
Christian and Missionary Alliance
Christian Coalition
Christian Identity Movement
Christian Reconstructionism
Christian Reformed Church in
  America
Christian Science
Christianity in Japan
Church in Island Pond
Church of God International
Church of Satan
Church of Set
Church of the Nazarene
Church of the New Jerusalem
Church Universal and Triumphant
Concerned Christians
Course in Miracles
Deepak Chopra
Discordianism

Divine Light Mission
Druids
Druse
Druze
Eckankar
Elan Vital
Est
Falun Gong (Religious Freedom in China)
Father Divine
Feng Shui
First Church of Christ, Scientist
Foundation of Human Understanding
Foursquare Gospel Church
Freemasonry
Fundamentalism
Ghebers
Gnosticism
Guebres
Hare Krishnas
Hasidism
Healthy, Happy, Holy Organization
Heaven's Gate
Hinduism
Holy Order of MANS
Holy Spirit Association for the Unification of World Christianity
Huguenots
Hussites
Hutterian Brethern of New York, Inc.
I Am
Institute of Noetic Sciences
Integral Yoga
International Church of Scientology
International Church of the Foursquare Gospel
International Churches Of Christ
International Peace Mission Movement
International Raelian Religion
International Society for Krishna Consciousness
ISKCON
Islam
Israeli School of Universal Practical Knowledge (The Twelve Tribes)
Jainism
Jehovah's Witnesses
Jesus Army

Jesus Fellowship Church
Jesus People USA
Jonestown
Kabbalah
Karaites
Knights of Columbus
Konkokyo
Lamaism
Landmark Education
Latter Day Saints
Latter Rain Movement
Lifespring
Local Church
Macumba Maitreya
Manichaeism
Masada
Masons
Mazdaism
Mazdeism
Meher Baba Groups
Mennonites
Messianic Jewish Alliance of America
Methodist Church
Millennium Prophecies
Mithraism
Moody Bible Institute
Moody Church
Moonies
Moral Rearmament
Moravian Church
Mormonism (LDS)
MOVE
Movement for the Restoration of the Ten Commandments of God
Movement of Spiritual Inner Awareness
MSIA
Nation of Islam
Nation of Yahweh
National Baptist Convention
Native American Religions
Nazarene
Neo-Paganism
Neturei Karta (Guardians of the City)
New Age
New Creation Christian Community
New Thought
Nichiren Shoshu
Northeast Kingdom Community Church

Nubian Islamic Hebrews
Old Catholicism
Oneida Movement
Opus Dei
Order of the Solar Temple
Osho
Oxford
Paramahansa Yogananda
Parseeism
Parsiism
Pentacostalism
Peoples Temple
Philadelphia Church of God
Primitive Baptists
Process Church of the Final Judgment
Promise Keepers
Puseyism
Quakers
Raelians
Rajnesshism
Ramakrishna Order of the Vendanta
   Society
Ramtha's School of Enlightenment
Rastafarianism
Rebirthing
Religious Science (United Church of)
Reorganized Church Of Jesus Christ
   of Latter Day Saints
Restoration Movement
Restoration of the Ten
   Commandments of God
Roman Catholicism
Rosicrucian Order (AMORC)
Sabbatarian
Sabians
Sacramentarians
Sahaja Yoga
Salem Witch Trials
Salvation Army
Santeria
Satanism
Scientific Pantheism
Scientology
Secular Humanism
Seicho No Ie
Self-Realization Fellowship
Seventh-Day Adventists
Shakers
Shamanism
Shambhala International

Shinreikyo
Shinto
Shirdi Sai Baba
Sikh Dharma
Sikhs
Silva Mind Control *or* Silva Method
Snake Handlers
Society of Friends
Soka Gakkai
Solar Temple
Southern Baptists
Southern Christian Leadership
   Conference (SCLC)
Spiritual Discovery (Suma Ching Hai)
Spiritualism
Sri Chinmoy
Sukyo Mahikari
Suma Ching Hai
Swedenborgianism
Synanon
Synchronicity Contemporary
   Meditation
Taoism
Tenrikyo
The Brethren
The Church of God (Seventh Day)
The Church of Jesus Christ of Latter
   Day Saints
The Family
The Forum
The Process
The Temple of Set
The Way International (the way)
The Zarathushtrian Assembly
Theosophy
Toronto Blessing
Tractarianism
Transcendental Meditation
Twelve Tribes
Two X Twos
Unarius Academy of Science
Unification Church
Unitarian Universalist
United Church of Religious Science
United Methodist Church
United Pentacostal Church
   International
United Society of Believers
Unity School of Christianity
Universal Life Church

Universal Negro Improvement Association
Universal Peace Mission Movement
Urantia Brotherhood
Vendanta Society
Vineyard Churches
Voodooism
Watchtower and Bible Tract Society
Wicca
Willow Creek Community Church
Woman's Christian Temperance Union
Worldwide Church of God
Zen Buddhism
Zionism
Zoroastrianism

Religious orders

Assumptionist (A.A.)
Augustinian (O.S.A.)
Barnabite Fathers
Benedictine (O.S.B)
Bridgitine (C.S.B)
Brothers of St Gabriel
Brothers of St John of God
Brothers of the Christian Schools (F.S.C.)
Camaldolese Benedictines
Canossian Daughters of Charity
Carmelite (O.C., O.C.D., O.C.D.S.)
Carthusian (O. Cart.)
Celestine
Cenacle Sisters
Christian Brothers
Cistercian (O. Cist.)
Claretian Missionaries
Congregation Marians
Congregation of the Holy Cross (C.S.C.)
Cordeliers
Daughters of St Francis of Assisi
Daughters of St Mary of Providence
Daughters of St Paul
Dervish
Divine Word Missionaries (D.V.M.)
Dominican (O.P.)
Felician Sisters
Franciscan (O.F.M.)
Handmaids of the Precious Blood
Hare Krishna (International Society for Krishna Consciousness *or* I.S.K.C.O.N.)
Institute of Charity (Rosminians) (I.C.)
Jesuits (S.J.)
Lasallian Brothers
Little Brothers of the Good Shepherd
Little Sisters of the Poor
Loretto nuns
Marianists
Marist Fathers and Brothers
Maryknoll
Missionaries of Charity (M.C.)
Missionaries of the Sacred Heart (M.S.C.)
Norbertines (C.R.P.)
Oblates (O.M.I.)
Observants
Passionists (C.P.)
Piarists
Poor Clares
Poor Sisters of Nazareth
Redemptorists (C.S.S.R.)
Resurrectionists (C.R.)
Salesians
Salesians of Don Bosco (S.D.B.)
Salvatorians
Servites
Sisters of Charity
Sisters of Mercy (R.S.M.)
Sisters of Notre Dame de Namur (S.N.D., S.N.D. de N.)
St Joseph Sisters (C.S.J./S.S.J.)
Sulpicians (P.S.S.)
Trappists (O.C.R., O.C.S.O.)
Ursuline Sisters

Reptiles

2 letters:
Go

3 letters:
Asp
Boa

4 letters:
Habu

5 letters:
Adder
Agama
Anole
Cobra
Gecko
Krait
Mamba
Racer
Skink
Snake
Swift
Tokay
Viper

6 letters:
Agamid
Caiman
Cayman
Dugite
Dukite
Elapid
Freshy
Garial
Gavial
Goanna
Iguana
Leguan
Lizard
Moloch
Python
Saltie
Taipan
Turtle

7 letters:
Camoodi
Frillie

Gharial
Monitor
Ngarara
Perenty
Rattler
Tuatara

8 letters:
Anaconda
Bungarra
Cerastes
Moccasin
Perentie
Pit viper
Rat snake
Ringhals
Sea snake
Slowworm
Terrapin
Tortoise

9 letters:
Alligator
Blindworm
Blue racer
Boomslang
Box turtle
Bull snake
Chameleon
Crocodile
Deaf adder
Galliwasp
Hamadryad
Hawksbill
Hoop snake
Jew lizard
King cobra
King snake
Milk snake
Mud turtle
Puff adder
Rock snake
Sand viper
Sphenodon
Tree snake
Whip snake

10 letters:
Bandy-bandy
Black snake
Blind snake
Blue tongue
Brown snake
Bushmaster
Chuckwalla
Copperhead
Coral snake
Death adder
Fer-de-lance
Glass snake
Grass snake
Horned toad
Kabaragoya
Loggerhead
Massasauga
Rock python
Sand lizard
Sidewinder
Tiger snake
Wall lizard
Water snake
Worm lizard

11 letters:
Amphisbaena
Carpet snake
Constrictor
Cottonmouth
Diamondback
Gaboon viper
Garter snake
Gila monster
Gopher snake
Green turtle
Horned viper
Indigo snake
Leatherback
Mallee snake
Rattlesnake
Smooth snake
Thorn lizard
Thorny devil

12 letters:
Diamond snake

Reptiles

Flying dragon
Flying lizard
Hognose snake
Komodo dragon
Komodo lizard

13 letters:
Bearded dragon
Bearded lizard
Bicycle lizard
Cycling lizard
Diamond python
Frilled lizard
Giant tortoise
Mountain devil
Water moccasin

14 letters:
Boa constrictor
Cobra de capello
Harlequin snake
Leathery turtle
Malayan monitor
Snapping turtle

15 letters:
Hawksbill turtle
Schneider python

16 letters:
Loggerhead turtle

17 letters:
Amethystine python
Diamondback turtle
Frill-necked lizard
Soft-shelled turtle

18 letters:
Saltwater crocodile

19 letters:
Diamondback terrapin
Freshwater crocodile

20 letters:
Red-bellied black snake

See also:
➤ **Dinosaurs** ➤ **Lizards** ➤ **Snakes**

Republics

3 letters:
UAR

4 letters:
Chad
Cuba
Eire
Fiji
Iran
Komi
Laos
Mali
Peru
Togo

5 letters:
Belau
Benin
Chile
Czech
Egypt
Gabon
Ghana
Haiti
Italy
Khmer
Malta

Nauru
Niger
Palau
Sudan
Syria
Yemen
Zaire

6 letters:
Angola
Bukavu
Gambia
Guinea
Guyana
Ingush
Israel
Kalmuk
Latvia
Malawi
Mexico
Myanma
Panama
Rwanda
Serbia
Turkey
Weimar
Zambia

7 letters:
Albania
Algeria
Andorra
Bashkir
Belarus
Bolivia
Burundi
Chechen
Comoros
Croatia
Ecuador
Estonia
Finland
Hungary
Iceland
Kalmuck
Khakass
Lebanon
Liberia
Moldova
Myanmar
Namibia
Nigeria
Romania
Senegal
Somalia

Surinam
Tunisia
Ukraine
Uruguay
Vanuatu
Vietnam

8 letters:
Botswana
Bulgaria
Cambodia
Cameroon
Chechnya
Colombia
Dagestan
Djibouti
Dominica
Esthonia
Honduras
Karelian
Kiribati
Malagasy
Maldives
Mongolia
Paraguay
Sinn Fein
Slovakia

Slovenia
Sri Lanka
Tanzania
Udmurtia
Zimbabwe

9 letters:
Argentina
Cape Verde
Costa Rica
Dominican
Guatemala
Indonesia
Kazakstan
Lithuania
Macedonia
Mauritius
Nicaragua
San Marino
Venezuela

10 letters:
Azerbaijan
Bangladesh
Belorussia
El Salvador
Kazakhstan

Kyrgyzstan
Madagascar
Mauritania
Montenegro
Mordvinian
Mozambique
Tajikistan
Ubang-Shari
Yugoslavia

11 letters:
Afghanistan
Byelorussia
Philippines
Sierra Leone
Switzerland

12 letters:
Guinea-Bissau
Turkmenistan

13 letters:
Bashkortostan

17 letters:
Bosnia-Herzegovina

Resins

3 letters:
Gum
Lac

4 letters:
Arar
Hing
Kino
Urea

5 letters:
Amber
Amino
Copai
Copal
Damar
Elemi
Epoxy
Myrrh

Roset
Rosin
Rosit
Rozet
Rozit
Saran®

6 letters:
Balsam
Charas
Conima
Copalm
Dammar
Dammer
Gambir
Mastic
Storax
Styrax

7 letters:
Acaroid
Benzoin
Caranna
Carauna
Churrus
Copaiba
Copaiva
Galipot
Gambier
Gamboge
Glyptal
Hashish
Jalapin
Ladanum
Polymer
Shellac
Xylenol

8 letters:
Bakelite®
Benjamin
Cannabin
Galbanum
Guaiacum
Hasheesh
Melamine
Olibanum
Opopanax
Phenolic

Propolis
Retinite
Sandarac
Scammony
Takamaka

9 letters:
Asafetida
Courbaril
Polyester
Sagapenum

Sandarach

10 letters:
Asafoetida

11 letters:
Podophyllin

12 letters:
Dragon's blood
Frankincense

Rice and other cereals

4 letters:
Bran
Corn
Oats
Ragi
Sago

5 letters:
Maize
Wheat

6 letters:
Millet

7 letters:
Oatmeal
Tapioca

8 letters:
Couscous
Wild rice

9 letters:
Brown rice
Patna rice

10 letters:
Indian rice

11 letters:
Arborio rice
Basmati rice
Bulgur wheat

13 letters:
Long grain rice

14 letters:
Short grain rice

Rivers

2 letters:
Ob
Po
Si
Xi

3 letters:
Aar
Ain
Aln
Axe
Ayr
Bug
Cam
Dee
Don

Ems
Esk
Exe
Fal
Fly
Han
Hsi
Inn
Lee
Lot
Nar
Ord
Red
San
Tay
Tet

Ure
Usk
Var
Wye

4 letters:
Abus
Abzu
Acis
Adur
Aire
Alma
Alph
Amur
Aran
Aras

Arno
Aube
Aude
Avon
Back
Beni
Bomu
Cher
Dart
Deva
Doon
Dove
Drin
Earn
Ebbw
Ebro
Eden
Eder
Elbe
Erne
Esla
Eure
Gila
Göta
Huon
Idle
Isar
Iser
Isis
Juba
Kama
Kill
Kura
Kwai
Lahn
Lech
Lena
Liao
Lune
Maas
Main
Meta
Milk
Miño
Mole
Nene
Neva
Nile
Nith
Oder

Ohio
Oise
Ouse
Oxus
Prut
Ruhr
Saar
Sava
Save
Soar
Spey
Styx
Swan
Swat
Taff
Tana
Tarn
Tees
Teme
Test
Tyne
Uele
Ural
Vaal
Waal
Wear
Xero
Yalu
Yare
Yate
Yser
Yüan
Yüen

5 letters:
Abana
Acton
Adige
Afton
Agate
Aisne
Aldan
Apure
Argun
Avoca
Benue
Boyne
Cauca
Chari
Clyde

Congo
Cross
Dasht
Desna
Doubs
Douro
Drava
Drave
Duero
Dvina
Eblis
Firth
Fleet
Forth
Gogra
Green
Havel
Indre
Indus
Isère
James
Jumna
Juruá
Kabul
Kasai
Kenga
Kuban
Lethe
Liard
Lippe
Loire
Marne
Meuse
Minho
Mosel
Mulla
Namoi
Negro
Neman
Niger
Ogowe
Onega
Oreti
Peace
Pearl
Pecos
Pelly
Piave
Pison
Plate

Purús
Rance
Rhein
Rhine
Rhône
Rogue
Saône
Seine
Shari
Shiré
Siang
Siret
Skien
Slave
Snake
Snowy
Somme
Spree
Staff
Stour
Swale
Tagus
Tamar
Tapti
Tarim
Teign
Terek
Tiber
Tisza
Tobol
Trent
Tweed
Volga
Volta
Warta
Weser
Xiang
Xingú
Yaqui
Yarra
Yonne
Yssel
Yukon

6 letters:
Albany
Allier
Amazon
Anadyr
Angara

Arzina
Atbara
Barcoo
Barrow
Bío-Bío
Calder
Canton
Chenab
Clutha
Crouch
Cuiaba
Cydnus
Danube
Dawson
Donets
Duddon
Durack
Finlay
Fraser
Gambia
Ganges
Glomma
Granta
Hodder
Hsiang
Hudson
Humber
Iguaçú
IJssel
Irtish
Irtysh
Irwell
Itchen
Japurá
Javari
Javary
Jhelum
Jordan
Kagera
Kaveri
Kennet
Kolyma
Komati
Liffey
Mamoré
Medway
Mekong
Mersey
Mohawk
Molopo

Morava
Moskva
Murray
Neckar
Neisse
Nelson
Nyeman
Ogooué
Orange
Orwell
Ottawa
Pahang
Paraná
Pripet
Rakaia
Ribble
Riffle
Rother
Sabine
Salado
Saluda
Sambre
Santee
Severn
Struma
Sutlej
Sutley
Swanee
Tanana
Tarsus
Teviot
Thames
Ticino
Tigris
Tugela
Tyburn
Ubangi
Ussuri
Vardar
Vienne
Vltava
Wabash
Wairau
Wensum
Wharfe
Yarrow
Yellow

7 letters:
Acheron

Alabama
Aruwimi
Bermejo
Caquetá
Cauvery
Chagres
Cocytus
Damodar
Darling
Derwent
Detroit
Dnieper
Dubglas
Durance
Ettrick
Fitzroy
Garonne
Genesee
Gironde
Guaporé
Helmand
Hooghly
Huang He
Hwangho
Iguassú
Irawadi
Kanawha
Krishna
Lachlan
Limpopo
Lualaba
Madeira
Manning
Marañón
Maritsa
Mataura
Meander
Moselle
Narmada
Niagara
Orinoco
Orontes
Paraíba
Pechora
Pharpar
Potomac
Rubicon
Sabrina
Salinas
Salween

Salzach
Sanders
Scheldt
Senegal
Shannon
Songhua
Swannee
Tapajós
Thomson
Ucayali
Uruguay
Vistula
Waikato
Washita
Welland
Yangtse
Yangtze
Yenisei
Yenisey
Zambese
Zambesi
Zambezi

8 letters:
Amu Darya
Anderson
Apurimac
Araguaia
Arkansas
Berezina
Blue Nile
Canadian
Charente
Cherwell
Chindwin
Clarence
Colorado
Columbia
Daintree
Delaware
Demerara
Dneister
Dniester
Dordogne
Flinders
Franklin
Gascoyne
Godavari
Guadiana
Illinois

Kentucky
Klondike
Kootenai
Kootenay
Maeander
Mahanadi
Menderes
Missouri
Mitchell
Okanagan
Okavango
Ouachita
Pactolus
Paraguay
Parnaíba
Putamayo
Rio Negro
Safid Rud
Saguenay
Savannah
Suwannee
Syr Darya
Torridge
Toulouse
Tunguska
Victoria
Volturno
Wanganui
Windrush
Zhu Jiang

9 letters:
Ashburton
Athabaska
Billabong
Churchill
Crocodile
Des Moines
Essequibo
Euphrates
Irrawaddy
Kuskokwim
Mackenzie
Macquarie
Magdalena
Magdelana
Minnesota
Murchison
Parnahiba
Pilcomayo

Porcupine
Qu'Appelle
Rangitata
Richelieu
Rio Branco
Rio Grande
Saint John
Salambria
Santa Cruz
Tennessee
Tocantins
White Nile
Wisconsin

10 letters:
Black Volta
Blackwater

Chao Phraya
Courantyne
Housatonic
Kizil Irmak
Phlegethon
Rangitaiki
Rangitikei
Sacramento
Saint Croix
St Lawrence
White Volta

11 letters:
Assiniboine
Brahmaputra
Connecticut
Cooper Creek

Lesser Slave
Madre de Dios
Mississippi
Monongahela
Shatt-al-Arab
Susquehanna
Yellowstone

12 letters:
Cooper's Creek
Guadalquivir
Murrumbidgee
Saskatchewan

13 letters:
Little Bighorn
Saint Lawrence

Rivers of Hell

4 letters:
Styx (River of Oath)

5 letters:
Lethe (River of Forgetfulness)

7 letters:
Acheron (River of Woe)
Cocytus (River of Lament)

10 letters:
Phlegethon (River of Fire)

Types of rock

2 letters:
Aa

3 letters:
Gem
Gib
Jow
Tor

4 letters:
Bell
Clay
Coal
Crag
Gang
Glam
Grit
Jura

Lava
Lias
Noup
Reef
Sill
Sima
Trap
Tufa
Tuff
Zoic

5 letters:
Ayers
Brash
Calpe
Chair
Chalk
Chert

Cliff
Craig
Elvan
Flint
Geode
Glass
Krans
Loess
Magma
Nappe
Scalp
Scree
Shale
Skarn
Slate
Solid
Stone
Trass

619

Types of rockTypes of rock

Uluru
Wacke

6 letters:
Aplite
Arkose
Banket
Basalt
Dacite
Diapir
Dunite
Flaser
Flysch
Fossil
Gabbro
Gangue
Gibber
Gneiss
Gossan
Gozzan
Gravel
Hyboid
Inlier
Kingle
Marble
Masada
Norite
Oolite
Pelite
Pluton
Pumice
Rognon
Sarsen
Schist
Sinter
Skerry
Sklate
S. Peter
Stonen
Synroc
Tephra

7 letters:
Aquifer
Boulder
Breccia
Clastic
Cuprite
Cyanean
Diamond

Diorite
Eucrite
Fastnet
Felsite
Granite
Greisen
Lignite
Lorelei
Marlite
Minette
Molasse
Moraine
Needles
Nunatak
Olivine
Ophites
Outcrop
Outlier
Peridot
Picrite
Remanie
Rhaetic
Sinking
Spilite
Syenite
Thulite
Tripoli
Wenlock

8 letters:
Adularia
Aegirine
Andesite
Aphanite
Basanite
Brockram
Burstone
Calcrete
Calc-tufa
Calc-tuff
Ciminite
Diabasic
Dolerite
Dolomite
Eclogite
Eklogite
Elvanite
Eutaxite
Fahlband
Felstone

Ganister
Hepatite
Hornfels
Idocrase
Inchcape
Laterite
Lopolith
Mesolite
Mudstone
Mylonite
Obsidian
Peperino
Perknite
Petuntse
Phyllite
Pisolite
Plutonic
Plymouth
Porphyry
Psammite
Psephite
Ragstone
Regolith
Rhyolite
Rocaille
Roe-stone
Saxatile
Saxonite
Scorpion
Sunstone
Taconite
Tarpeian
Tephrite
The Olgas
Tonalite
Trachyte
Trappean
Xenolith

9 letters:
Anticline
Argillite
Batholite
Bentonite
Bluestone
Buhrstone
Claystone
Cockhorse
Colluvium
Cornstone

Types of rock

Dalradian
Eddystone
Edinburgh
Evaporite
Firestone
Flowstone
Gannister
Gibraltar
Goslarite
Granulite
Graywacke
Greensand
Greystone
Greywacke
Hornstone
Impactite
Intrusion
Ironstone
Laccolite
Laccolith
Limestone
Meteorite
Migmatite
Monadnock
Monocline
Monzonite
Mortstone
Mugearite
Natrolite
Neocomian
Nunatakkr
Ophiolite
Ottrelite
Pegmatite
Petrology
Phonolite
Phosphate
Pleonaste
Protogine
Quartzite
Reservoir
Sandstone

Saprolite
Scablands
Schistose
Siltstone
Soapstone
Tachylyte
Theralite
Tinguaite
Toadstone
Travertin
Variolite
Vulcanite
Whinstone
Whunstane
Zechstein

10 letters:
Ailsa Craig
Amygdaloid
Anthracite
Camptonite
Epidiorite
Foundation
Granophyre
Greenstone
Hypabyssal
Ignimbrite
Kersantite
Kimberlite
Lherzolite
Limburgite
Novaculite
Palagonite
Peridotite
Permafrost
Phenocryst
Pitchstone
Pyroxenite
Rupestrian
Schalstein
Serpentine
Sparagmite

Stinkstone
Stonebrash
Stonehenge
Syntagmata
Teschenite
Touchstone
Travertine
Troctolite

11 letters:
Agglomerate
Amphibolite
Annabergite
Anorthosite
Carbonatite
Geanticline
Halleflinta
Lamprophyre
Monchiquite
Napoleonite
Nephelinite
Phillipsite
Pyroclastic
Sedimentary
Symplegades

12 letters:
Babingtonite
Conglomerate
Granodiorite
Grossularite
Hornblendite
Slickenslide
Stromatolite
Syntagmatite
Thunderstone

13 letters:
Hypersthenite

14 letters:
Roche moutonnée

See also:
➤ **Minerals** ➤ **Ores** ➤ **Types of stone**

Rodents

3 letters:
Mus
Rat

4 letters:
Cavy
Jird
Mara
Paca
Vole

5 letters:
Aguti
Bobac
Bobak
Civet
Coypu
Hutia
Hyrax
Kiore
Mouse
Murid
Ratel
Shrew
Taira

6 letters:
Agouti
Beaver
Boomer
Dassie
Gerbil
Glires
Gopher
Hog-rat
Jerbil
Jerboa
Marmot
Nutria
Ratton
Suslik
Taguan

7 letters:
Acouchi
Acouchy
Cane rat
Chincha
Glutton
Hamster
Lemming
Mole rat
Muskrat
Ondatra
Pack rat
Potoroo
Souslik

8 letters:
Banxring
Biscacha
Bizcacha
Black rat
Brown rat
Capybara
Chipmunk
Cricetus
Dormouse
Gerbille
Hampster
Hedgehog
Māori rat
Musquash
Ochotona
Sciurine
Sewellel
Squirrel
Tucotuco
Tucu-tuco
Viscacha
Vizcacha
Water rat
White rat

9 letters:
Bandicoot
Bangsring

Chickaree
Deer mouse
Delundung
Desert rat
Groundhog
Guinea pig
Jerboa rat
Norway rat
Porcupine
Water vole
Woodchuck

10 letters:
Chinchilla
Dargawarra
Fieldmouse
House mouse
Springhaas
Springhase

11 letters:
Fox squirrel
Kangaroo rat
Pocket mouse
Red squirrel
Spermophile

12 letters:
Grey squirrel
Harvest mouse
Hopping mouse
Jumping mouse
Pocket gopher

14 letters:
Flying squirrel
Ground squirrel

16 letters:
White-footed mouse

20 letters:
Spinifex hopping mouse

Roman numerals

Numeral	Equivalent
A	50
B	300
C	100
D	500
E	250
F	40
G	400
H	200
I	1
K	250
L	50
M	1000
N	90
O	11
P	400
Q	500
R	80
S	7 or 70
T	160
V	5
X	10
Y	150
Z	2000

The seven hills of Rome

7 letters:
Caelian
Viminal

8 letters:
Aventine
Palatine
Quirinal

9 letters:
Esquiline

10 letters:
Capitoline

Types of roof

3 letters:
Hip

4 letters:
Bell
Dome

5 letters:
Gable
Skirt

6 letters:
French
Hipped

Pop-top
Saddle
Thatch
Thetch

7 letters:
Belfast

Gambrel
Hardtop
Mansard
Shingle

8 letters:
Imperial
Pavilion

9 letters:
Monopitch

10 letters:
Jerkin-head

12 letters:
Porte-cochère

Ropes

3 letters:
Guy
Tow

4 letters:
Balk
Cord
Fall
Jeff
Line
Stay
Vang

5 letters:
Baulk
Brail
Cable
Guide
Lasso
Longe
Lunge
Riata
Sheet
Sugan
Trace
Wanty
Widdy

6 letters:
Cablet
Cordon
Earing

Halser
Halter
Hawser
Inhaul
Marlin
Prusik
Roband
Robbin
Runner
Shroud
String
Tackle

7 letters:
Bobstay
Cringle
Halyard
Lanyard
Marline
Mooring
Outhaul
Painter
Pastern
Rawhide
Stirrup
Swifter
Towline
Triatic

8 letters:
Backstay
Boltrope

Bunt-line
Downhaul
Forestay
Gantline
Halliard
Headfast
Jack-stay
Prolonge
Selvagee
Spun-yarn

9 letters:
Breeching
Foresheet
Mainbrace
Mainsheet
Reef point
Sternfast
Timenoguy

10 letters:
Hawser-laid
Kernmantel

11 letters:
Triatic stay

13 letters:
Futtock-shroud

Rugby terms

3 letters:
Try

4 letters:
Back
Ball
Mark
Maul
Pack
Pass
Punt
Ruck

5 letters:
Scrum

6 letters:
Centre
Hooker
Tackle
Winger

7 letters:
Back row
Flanker
Fly half
Forward
Knock on
Line-out
Penalty
Referee

8 letters:
Crossbar
Drop goal
Front row
Full back
Goalpost
Half back

9 letters:
Garryowen
Loose head
Scrum half
Scrummage

Second row
Tight head

10 letters:
Conversion
Five-eighth
Touch judge
Up and under

11 letters:
Lock forward
Outside half
Prop forward
Wing forward

12 letters:
Loose forward
Stand-off half
Three-quarter

18 letters:
Number eight forward

Rulers

TITLES OF RULERS

3 letters:
Ban
Bey
Dey
Mir
Oba
Raj
Rex

4 letters:
Amir
Cham
Czar
Doge
Duce
Duke
Emir
Imam
Inca

Khan
King
Pope
Raja
Rana
Rani
Shah
Tsar
Vali
Wali

5 letters:
Ameer
Ardri
Calif
Chief
Dewan
Diwan
Imaum

Kalif
Mogul
Mpret
Mudir
Nabob
Nawab
Negus
Nizam
Pacha
Pasha
Queen
Rajah
Ranee
Shaka
Sheik
Sophi
Sophy
Tenno

TITLES OF RULERS (CONTINUED)

6 letters:
Atabeg
Atabek
Caesar
Caliph
Chagan
Dergue
Despot
Dynast
Exarch
Führer
Kabaka
Kaiser
Khalif
Manchu
Mikado
Prince
Regent
Sachem
Satrap
Sharif
Sheikh
Sherif
Shogun
Sirdar
Squier
Squire
Sultan
Tycoon
Tyrant

7 letters:
Abbasid
Ardrigh

Bajayet
Bajazet
Catapan
Chogyal
Elector
Emperor
Empress
Gaekwar
Gaikwar
Jamshid
Jamshyd
Khedive
Lesbian
Monarch
Pharaoh
Podesta
Shereef
Souldan
Toparch
Viceroy

8 letters:
Archduke
Autocrat
Burgrave
Caudillo
Dictator
Ethnarch
Heptarch
Hierarch
Hospodar
Maharaja
Maharani

Mameluke
Mistress
Oligarch
Padishah
Sagamore
Sassanid
Suzerain
Tetrarch

9 letters:
Bretwalda
Cosmocrat
Dalai Lama
Maharajah
Maharanee
Ochlocrat
Pendragon
Plutocrat
Potentate
Sovereign
Vicereine

10 letters:
Aristocrat
Great Mogul
Plantocrat
Rajpramukh
Stadholder
Stratocrat

11 letters:
Stadtholder

FAMOUS RULERS

4 letters:
Nero

5 letters:
Herod
Lenin
Louis

6 letters:
Castro
Cheops

Franco
Hitler
Nasser
Stalin

7 letters:
Idi Amin
Saladin

8 letters:
Augustus

Bismarck
Boadicea
Boudicca
Caligula
Cromwell
De Gaulle
Hirohito
Nicholas
Pericles
Victoria

FAMOUS RULERS (CONTINUED)

9 letters:
Churchill
Cleopatra
Elizabeth
Mao Ze Dong
Montezuma
Mussolini
Tamerlane

10 letters:
Caractacus
Kublai Khan
Mao Tse-tung

11 letters:
Charlemagne
Genghis Khan
Prester John

Tamburlaine
Tutankhamen
Tutankhamun

12 letters:
Chandragupta
Julius Caesar

13 letters:
Haile Selassie
Peter the Great

14 letters:
Alfred the Great

15 letters:
Ivan the Terrible

17 letters:
Alexander the Great
Catherine the Great
Napoleon Bonaparte

18 letters:
Edward the Confessor

19 letters:
Richard the Lionheart
William the Conqueror

22 letters:
Suleiman the
  Magnificent

ENGLISH RULERS (IN CHRONOLOGICAL ORDER)

Saxons:
Egbert
Ethelwulf
Ethelbald
Ethelbert
Ethel(d)red I
Alfred the Great
Edward the Elder
Athelstan
Edmund (I)
Edred
Edwy
Edgar
Edward the Martyr
Ethel(d)red II (the
  Unready)
Edmund II (Ironside)

Danes:
Canute
Harold I
Hardecanute

Saxons:
Edward the Confessor
Harold II

Normans:
William (I) the
  Conqueror
William II Rufus
Henry I
Stephen

Plantagenets:
Henry II
Richard I The Lionheart
John
Henry III
Edward I
Edward II
Edward III
Richard II

Lancasters:
Henry IV
Henry V
Henry VI

Yorks:
Edward IV
Edward V
Richard III

Tudors:
Henry VII
Henry VIII
Edward VI
Lady Jane Grey
Mary (I)
Elizabeth (I)

Stuarts:
James I (VI of Scotland)
Charles I (Stuart)

**Commonwealth
Protectors:**
Oliver Cromwell
Richard Cromwell

(Stuarts)
Charles II
James II (Interregnum)
William III and Mary II
Anne

Hanovers:
George I
George II
George III

George IV
William IV
Victoria

Edward VII (Saxe-
   Coburg-Gotha)

Windsors:
George V

Edward VIII (abdicated)
George VI
Elizabeth II

SCOTTISH RULERS (IN CHRONOLOGICAL ORDER)

Kenneth (I) M(a)cAlpin
Donald
Constantine I
Aedh
Eocha
Donald
Constantine II
Malcolm I
Indulph
Dubh
Cuilean
Kenneth II
Constantine III

Malcolm II
Duncan I
Macbeth
Lulach
Malcolm III
Donald Bane
Duncan II
Donald Bane
Edmund
Edgar
Alexander I
David I
John Baliol

Robert (the) Bruce
David II
Robert II
Robert III
James I
James II
James III
James IV
James V
Mary (Queen of Scots)
James VI

Russian federal republics

VOLGA DISTRICT

6 letters:
Mari El

7 letters:
Mariy El

8 letters:
Mordovia
Udmurtia

9 letters:
Chuvashia
Mordvinia

10 letters:
Tartarstan

13 letters:
Bashkortostan

NORTHERN CAUCASUS

7 letters:
Adygeya

8 letters:
Chechnia
Chechnya
Dagestan

Kalmykia

10 letters:
Ingushetia

15 letters:
Northern Ossetia

17 letters:
Kabardino-Balkaria

18 letters:
Karachay-Cherkessia
North Ossetia-Alania

NORTHWESTERN RUSSIA

4 letters:
Komi

7 letters:
Karelia

SIBERIA

4 letters:
Tuva

8 letters:
Buryatia

9 letters:
Khakassia

5 letters:
Altay

RUSSIAN FAR EAST

5 letters:
Sakha

S s

Saints

Saint	Feast day
Agatha	5 February
Agnes	31 January
Aidan	31 August
Alban	22 June
Albertus Magnus	15 November
Aloysius (patron saint of youth)	21 June
Ambrose	7 December
Andrew (Scotland)	30 November
Anne	26 July
Anselm	21 April
Anthony *or* Antony	17 January
Anthony *or* Antony of Padua	13 June
Athanasius	2 May
Augustine of Hippo	28 August
Barnabas	11 June
Bartholomew	24 August
Basil	2 January
Bede	25 May
Benedict	11 July
Bernadette of Lourdes	16 April
Bernard of Clairvaux	20 August
Bernard of Menthon	28 May
Bonaventura *or* Bonaventure	15 July
Boniface	5 June
Brendan	16 May
Bridget, Bride *or* Brigid (Ireland)	1 February
Bridget *or* Birgitta (Sweden)	23 July
Catherine of Alexandria	25 November
Catherine of Siena (the Dominican Order)	29 April
Cecilia (music)	22 November
Charles Borromeo	4 November
Christopher (travellers)	25 July
Clare of Assisi	11 August
Clement I	23 November
Clement of Alexandria	5 December

Saint	Feast day
Columba *or* Colmcille	9 June
Crispin (shoemakers)	25 October
Crispinian (shoemakers)	25 October
Cuthbert	20 March
Cyprian	16 September
Cyril	14 February
Cyril of Alexandria	27 June
David (Wales)	1 March
Denis (France)	9 October
Dominic	7 August
Dorothy	6 February
Dunstan	19 May
Edmund	20 November
Edward the Confessor	13 October
Edward the Martyr	18 March
Elizabeth	5 November
Elizabeth of Hungary	17 November
Elmo	2 June
Ethelbert *or* Æthelbert	25 February
Francis of Assisi	4 October
Francis of Sales	24 January
Francis Xavier	3 December
Geneviève (Paris)	3 January
George (England)	23 April
Gertrude	16 November
Gilbert of Sempringham	4 February
Giles (cripples, beggars, and lepers)	1 September
Gregory I (the Great)	3 September
Gregory VII *or* Hildebrand	25 May
Gregory of Nazianzus	2 January
Gregory of Nyssa	9 March
Gregory of Tours	17 November
Hilary of Poitiers	13 January
Hildegard of Bingen	17 September
Helen *or* Helena	18 August
Helier	16 July
Ignatius	17 October
Ignatius of Loyola	31 July
Isidore of Seville	4 April
James	23 October
James the Less	3 May
Jane Frances de Chantal	12 December

Saint	Feast day
Jerome	30 September
Joachim	26 July
Joan of Arc	30 May
John	27 December
John Bosco	31 January
John Chrysostom	13 September
John Ogilvie	10 March
John of Damascus	4 December
John of the Cross	14 December
John the Baptist	24 June
Joseph	19 March
Joseph of Arimathaea	17 March
Joseph of Copertino	18 September
Jude	28 October
Justin	1 June
Kentigern *or* Mungo	14 January
Kevin	3 June
Lawrence	10 August
Lawrence O'Toole	14 November
Leger	2 October
Leo I (the Great)	10 November
Leo II	3 July
Leo III	12 June
Leo IV	17 July
Leonard	6 November
Lucy	13 December
Luke	18 October
Malachy	3 November
Margaret	20 July
Margaret of Scotland	10 June, 16 November (in Scotland)
Maria Goretti	6 July
Mark	25 April
Martha	29 July
Martin de Porres	3 November
Martin of Tours (France)	11 November
Mary	15 August
Mary Magdalene	22 July
Matthew *or* Levi	21 September
Matthias	14 May
Methodius	14 February
Michael	29 September
Neot	31 July

Saint	Feast day
Nicholas (Russia, children, sailors, merchants, and pawnbrokers)	6 December
Nicholas I (the Great)	13 November
Ninian	16 September
Olaf *or* Olav (Norway)	29 July
Oliver Plunket *or* Plunkett	1 July
Oswald	28 February
Pachomius	14 May
Patrick (Ireland)	17 March
Paul	29 June
Paulinus	10 October
Paulinus of Nola	22 June
Peter *or* Simon Peter	29 June
Philip	3 May
Philip Neri	26 May
Pius V	30 April
Pius X	21 August
Polycarp	26 January *or* 23 February
Rose of Lima	23 August
Sebastian	20 January
Silas	13 July
Simon Zelotes	28 October
Stanislaw *or* Stanislaus (Poland)	11 April
Stanislaus Kostka	13 November
Stephen	26 *or* 27 December
Stephen of Hungary	16 *or* 20 August
Swithin *or* Swithun	15 July
Teresa *or* Theresa of Avila	15 October
Thérèse de Lisieux	1 October
Thomas	3 July
Thomas à Becket	29 December
Thomas Aquinas	28 January
Thomas More	22 June
Timothy	26 January
Titus	26 January
Ursula	21 October
Valentine	14 February
Veronica	12 July
Vincent de Paul	27 September
Vitus	15 June
Vladimir	15 July
Wenceslaus *or* Wenceslas	28 September
Wilfrid	12 October

Salts

2 letters:
AB

4 letters:
Corn
NaCl
Rock
Soap
Urao

5 letters:
Azide
Borax
Urate

6 letters:
Aurate
Borate
Halite
Iodide
Malate
Mucate
Oleate
Osmate
Sebate
Sodium
Uranin

7 letters:
Bromate
Bromide
Caprate
Citrate
Cyanate
Formate
Glauber
Ioduret
Lactate
Lithate

Muriate
Nitrate
Nitrite
Osmiate
Oxalate
Picrate
Sulfite
Tannate

8 letters:
Alginate
Caproate
Cerusite
Chlorate
Chlorite
Chromate
Datolite
Malonate
Plumbite
Pyruvate
Resinate
Rochelle
Selenate
Stannate
Stearate
Suberate
Sulphate
Sulphite
Tartrate
Titanate
Vanadate
Xanthate

9 letters:
Aluminate
Aspartite
Caprylate
Carbamate
Carbonate

Cyclamate
Glutamate
Magnesium
Manganate
Palmitate
Periodate
Phosphate
Phthalate
Potassium
Succinate
Tellurate
Tungstate

10 letters:
Andalusite
Bichromate
Dithionate
Isocyanide
Pandermite
Propionate
Sulphonate

11 letters:
Bicarbonate
Carboxylate
Microcosmic
Monohydrate
Perchlorate
Sal ammoniac
Sal volatile
Thiocyanate

12 letters:
Ferricyanide
Thiosulphate

13 letters:
Hydrochloride

Satellites

EARTH

4 letters:
Moon

5 letters:
Astra (artificial)

Tiros (artificial)

JUPITER

2 letters:
Io

4 letters:
Leda
Teba

5 letters:
Carme
Elara
Karme
Metis

Thebe

6 letters:
Ananke
Europa
Metida
Pacife
Sinope

7 letters:
Amaltea
Gimalia

Himalia
Lisitea

8 letters:
Adrastea
Amalthea
Callisto
Galilean
Ganymede
Lysithia
Pasiphaë

SATURN

3 letters:
Pan

4 letters:
Rhea

5 letters:
Atlas
Dione
Janus
Mimas
Titan

6 letters:
Helene
Phoebe
Tethys

7 letters:
Calypso
Iapetus
Pandora
Telesto

8 letters:
Hyperion

9 letters:
Enceladus

10 letters:
Epimetheus
Prometheus

URANUS

4 letters:
Puck

5 letters:
Ariel

6 letters:
Bianca
Juliet
Oberon

Portia

7 letters:
Belinda
Caliban
Miranda
Ophelia
Sycorax
Titania
Umbriel

8 letters:
Cordelia
Cressida
Rosalind

9 letters:
Desdemona

NEPTUNE

5 letters:
Naian

6 letters:
Nereid

Triton

7 letters:
Despina
Galatea

Larissa
Proteus

8 letters:
Thalassa

MARS

6 letters:
Deimos

Phobos

PLUTO

6 letters:
Charon

Sauces

2 letters:
HP®

3 letters:
Soy

4 letters:
Fish
Hard
Mint
Mole
Soja
Soya
Wine

5 letters:
Apple
Bread
Brown
Caper
Cream
Curry
Fudge
Garum
Gravy
Melba
Pesto
Salsa
Satay

Shoyu
White

6 letters:
Cheese
Chilli
Coulis
Creole
Fondue
Fu yong
Fu yung
Hoisin
Mornay
Nam pla
Orange
Oxymal
Oyster
Panada
Pistou
Relish
Sambal
Tamari
Tartar
Tomato

7 letters:
À la king
Alfredo
Custard

Ketchup
Newburg
Nuoc mam
Parsley
Passata
Rouille
Sabayon
Soubise
Suprême
Tabasco®
Tartare
Velouté

8 letters:
Barbecue
Béchamel
Chasseur
Chow-chow
Fenberry
Marinara
Matelote
Meunière
Mirepoix
Piri-piri
Ravigote
Red pesto
Salpicon
Verjuice

Sausages

9 letters:
Allemanse
Béarnaise
Black bean
Bolognese
Carbonera
Chocolate
Cranberry
Enchilada
Espagnole
Rémoulade
Worcester

10 letters:
Bolognaise

Bordelaise
Chaudfroid
Cumberland
Mayonnaise
Mousseline
Piccalilli
Salad cream
Salsa verde
Stroganoff

11 letters:
Hollandaise
Horseradish
Vinaigrette

12 letters:
Brandy butter
Sweet-and-sour

13 letters:
Bourguignonne
Salad dressing

14 letters:
French dressing
Worcestershire

15 letters:
Russian dressing

Sausages

3 letters:
Sav

4 letters:
Lola

5 letters:
Black
Blood
Devon
Kiska
Kiske
Liver
Lorne
Lyons
Metts
Sujuk
Wurst

6 letters:
Banger
Garlic
Haggis
Hot dog
Kishka
Kishke
Lolita
Mirkas
Polony
Salami
Summer

Tuscan
Vienna
Wiener
Wienie

7 letters:
Abruzzo
Bologna
Cheerio
Chorizo
Frizzes
Kolbasa
Merguez
Saveloy
Soujouk
Yershig
Zampone

8 letters:
Cervelat
Chaurice
Chourico
Drisheen
Kielbasa
Lap chong
Lap chung
Linguica
Linguisa
Lop chong
Morcilla
Peperoni

Rohwurst
Teewurst
Toulouse

9 letters:
Andouille
Blutwurst
Bockwurst
Boerewors
Bratwurst
Chipolata
Cotechino
Knoblauch
Landjager
Lap cheong
Longanisa
Longaniza
Loukanika
Mettwurst
Pepperoni
Red boudin
Saucisson
Sulzwurst

10 letters:
Bauerwurst
Boerewurst
Bruehwurst
Cumberland
Knackwurst
Knockwurst

Landjaeger
Liverwurst
Mettwaurst
Mortadella
Potato korv
Weisswurst

11 letters:
Bauernwurst
Boudin blanc
Boudin rouge
Frankfurter
Genoa salami

Grutzewurst
Knublewurst
Kochwuerste
Pinkelwurst
Weisswurste
White boudin
Wienerwurst
Zungenwurst

12 letters:
Andouillette
Bierschinken
Black pudding

Fleischwurst
White pudding

13 letters:
Schinkenwurst

14 letters:
Braunschweiger
Lebanon bologna
Medisterpoelse

15 letters:
Katenrauchwurst

Scarves

4 letters:
Doek
Haik
Hyke

5 letters:
Curch
Fichu
Haick
Pagri
Stole

6 letters:
Cravat
Haique
Madras

Rebozo
Tippet

7 letters:
Belcher
Dupatta
Muffler
Orarium
Tallith

8 letters:
Babushka
Cataract
Mantilla
Neckatee

Palatine
Trot-cosy
Trot-cozy
Vexillum

9 letters:
Comforter
Muffettee

10 letters:
Lambrequin

11 letters:
Nightingale

Schools

3 letters:
RAM

4 letters:
Dada
Eton
RADA

5 letters:
Perse
Slade
Stowe

6 letters:
Fettes
Harrow
Oundle
Repton

7 letters:
Bauhaus
Flemish
Lancing
Loretto
Roedean
Rossall

8 letters:
Barbizon
Benenden
Downside
Mannheim

9 letters:
Chartreux
Frankfurt
Tonbridge

10 letters:
Ampleforth

Manchester
Stonyhurst
Wellington
Winchester

11 letters:
Giggleswick
Gordonstoun
Marlborough

12 letters:
Charterhouse

See also:
➤ **Academic degrees** ➤ **Colleges** ➤ **Education terms** ➤ **Ivy League universities** ➤ **Oxbridge colleges** ➤ **Types of school**

Types of school

3 letters:
CAT
CTC
GPS
LSE
Uni

4 letters:
Co-ed
Poly
Prep
Tech

5 letters:
Kindy
Lycée

6 letters:
Hostel
Kindie

7 letters:
Academe
Academy
College
Convent
Crammer
Nursery
Varsity
Yeshiva

8 letters:
Seminary

9 letters:
Alma mater
Day school
Gymnasien

Gymnasium
Institute
Ivy League
Madrassah
Palaestra

10 letters:
Chautauqua
Dame school
High school
Pensionnat
Prep school
University

11 letters:
Charm school
Choir school
Drama school
First school
Grade school
Hedge-school
List D school
Lower school
Mixed school
Night school
Open College
Polytechnic
Reformatory
State school
Trade school
Upper school

12 letters:
Church school
Conservatory
Infant school
Junior school
Kindergarten

Magnet school
Middle school
Multiversity
Normal school
Progymnasium
Public school
Ragged school
Reform school
Summer school
Sunday school

13 letters:
Community home
Comprehensive
Conservatoire
Convent school
Council school
Grammar school
Junior college
Nursery school
Primary school
Private school
Sabbath school
Special school

14 letters:
Approved school
Bluecoat school
Boarding school
Hospital school
National School
Open University
Schola cantorum
Separate school
Village college

15 letters:
Civic university

Community school
Composite school
Finishing school
Parochial school
Secondary school
Single-sex school
Tertiary college

16 letters:
Classical college
Community college
Elementary school
Grant-aided school
Integrated school
Maintained school
Sixth-form college
Technical college

17 letters:
Direct-grant school
Independent school
Preparatory school
Residential school
Technology college

18 letters:
College of education
District high school
Great Public Schools
Intermediate school

19 letters:
Collegiate institute
Comprehensive school
Land grant university

20 letters:
Correspondence school

21 letters:
City technology college
Grant-maintained
  school
Secondary modern
  school

27 letters:
College of advanced
  technology

Sea-weeds

3 letters:
Ore

4 letters:
Agar
Alga
Kelp
Kilp
Nori
Tang
Ulva
Ware

5 letters:
Algae
Arame
Dulse
Fucus
Kombu
Laver
Varec
Vraic
Wrack

6 letters:
Desmid
Diatom
Sea-mat
Varech
Wakame
Wakane

7 letters:
Oarweed
Redware
Sea-lace
Sea-moss
Seaware

8 letters:
Chondrus
Conferva
Gulfweed
Porphyra
Rockweed
Sargasso
Sea-wrack

9 letters:
Carrageen
Coralline
Cystocarp
Laminaria
Nullipore
Seabottle
Sea-tangle

10 letters:
Badderlock
Carragheen
Ceylon moss
Sea-lettuce
Sea-whistle

11 letters:
Bladderwort
Sea-furbelow

12 letters:
Bladderwrack
Enteromorpha
Heterocontae
Peacock's tail

Seals

4 letters:
Harp
Monk

5 letters:
Eared
Great
Otary
Phoca
Silky

6 letters:
Hooded
Hudson
Ringed

Sealch
Sealgh
Selkie
Silkie

7 letters:
Earless
Harbour
Sea-bear
Weddell

8 letters:
Elephant
Seecatch

Zalophus

9 letters:
Crab-eater
Greenland
Pintadera

10 letters:
Pinnipedia
Seecatchie

11 letters:
Bladdernose

Seas and oceans

3 letters:
Ler
Med
Red

4 letters:
Aral
Azov
Dead
Java
Kara
Ross
Sulu

5 letters:
Banda
Black
Ceram
China
Coral
Hadal
Irish
Japan
North
South
Timor
White

6 letters:
Abssal
Aegean
Arctic
Baltic
Bering
Biscay
Celtic
Euxine
Flores
Indian
Inland
Ionian
Laptev
Scotia
Tasman
Tethys
Yellow

7 letters:
Andaman
Arabian
Arafura
Barents
Caspian
Celebes
Channel
Chukchi
Euripus

Galilee
Icarian
Lincoln
Marmara
Marmora
Okhotsk
Pacific
Pelagic
Polynya
Solomon
Weddell

8 letters:
Adriatic
Amundsen
Atlantic
Beaufort
Bismarck
Bosporus
Hwang Hai
Labrador
Ligurian
Sargasso
Southern
Tiberias

9 letters:
Antarctic
Bosphorus

Caribbean
East China
Greenland
Hudson Bay
Melanesia
Norwegian
Polynesia
Skagerrak
Thalassic

10 letters:
Philippine
South China
Tyrrhenian

11 letters:
Herring-pond
Spanish main

12 letters:
East Siberian
Nordenskjöld

13 letters:
Mediterranean

14 letters:
Bellingshausen

Sea birds

3 letters:
Auk
Cob
Ern
Mew

4 letters:
Cobb
Coot
Erne
Gull
Shag
Skua
Tara
Titi

5 letters:
Booby
Kawau
Prion

6 letters:
Auklet
Fulmar
Gannet
Korora
Petrel
Scoter
Sea-cob
Sea-mew
Seapie
Takapu

7 letters:
Oldwife

Sea duck
Seagull
Taranui

8 letters:
Black cap
Blue shag
Fish hawk
Murrelet
Old squaw
Skua-gull
Surf duck

9 letters:
Albatross
Black shag
Cormorant
Guillemot
Ivory gull
Kittiwake
Razorbill

10 letters:
Gooney bird
Mutton bird
Sea swallow
Shearwater
Surf scoter

11 letters:
Blue penguin
Caspian tern
Frigate bird
Herring gull
Kahawai bird

Storm petrel

12 letters:
Fairy penguin
Glaucous gull
Man-of-war bird
Stormy petrel
Velvet scoter

13 letters:
Little penguin
Oystercatcher
Wilson's petrel

14 letters:
Black guillemot
Razor-billed auk

15 letters:
Black-backed gull

16 letters:
White-fronted tern

17 letters:
Little blue penguin

18 letters:
Wandering albatross

19 letters:
Mother Carey's chicken
Tasmanian mutton bird

21 letters:
Short-tailed shearwater

Seafood

3 letters:
Cod
Dab
Eel

4 letters:
Bass
Carp
Clam
Crab
Hake
Huss
Ling
Pike
Pipi
Pout
Shad
Sild
Sole
Tuna

5 letters:
Bream
Brill
Koura
Perch
Prawn
Roach
Shark
Skate
Snoek
Snook
Sprat
Squid
Trout
Tunny
Wahoo
Whelk
Witch
Yabby

6 letters:
Bonito
Callop
Cockle
Dorado
Kipper
Marron

Megrim
Mullet
Mussel
Oyster
Pillie
Plaice
Saithe
Salmon
Shrimp
Turbot
Winkle
Yabbie
Zander

7 letters:
Abalone
Anchovy
Bloater
Blue cod
Catfish
Codling
Crawbob
Craybob
Craydab
Dogfish
Gemfish
Haddock
Halibut
Herring
Jewfish
Kahawai
Lobster
Morwong
Mud crab
Octopus
Pollack
Pomfret
Queenie
Redfish
Sardine
Scallop
Scollop
Snapper
Sockeye
Whiting

8 letters:
Clawchie

Coalfish
Crawfish
Crayfish
Flounder
Grayling
John Dory
Kingfish
Lumpfish
Mackerel
Monkfish
Mulloway
Nannygai
Pilchard
Rockfish
Sand crab
Tarakihi
Teraglin
Terakihi
Tilefish
Trevally
Wolffish

9 letters:
Blackfish
Blue manna
Clabby-doo
Clappy-doo
Dover sole
King prawn
Lemon sole
Red salmon
Swordfish
Whitebait

10 letters:
Balmain bug
Barramundi
Butterfish
Parrotfish
Red snapper
Tiger prawn

11 letters:
Banana prawn
Blue swimmer
Langoustine
School prawn
Sea cucumber

Yellow belly

12 letters:
Queen scallop
Rainbow trout
Skipjack tuna

13 letters:
Moreton Bay bug
Norway lobster

14 letters:
Dublin Bay prawn

16 letters:
Australian salmon
Greenland halibut

18 letters:
Shovel-nosed lobster

Sea mammals

4 letters:
Seal

6 letters:
Dugong
Sea cow
Walrus

7 letters:
Manatee

Sea lion

8 letters:
Harp seal
Sea horse

9 letters:
Eared seal

10 letters:
Hooded seal

11 letters:
Earless seal

12 letters:
Elephant seal

Seasons

Season	Related adjective
Spring	Vernal
Summer	Aestival *or* estival
Autumn	Autumnal
Winter	Hibernal *or* hiemal

Seats

3 letters:
Box
Pew
Pit

4 letters:
Banc
Love
Sofa
Sunk

5 letters:
Bench
Chair
Couch

Dicky
Divan
Perch
Sedes
Siege
Squab
Stool

6 letters:
Bucket
Canapé
Dickey
Houdah
Howdah
Humpty

Pouffe
Rumble
Saddle
Settee
Settle
Sunkie
Throne

7 letters:
Ejector
Ottoman
Palfrey
Pillion
Tonneau

8 letters:
Sedilium
Woolsack

Deckchair
Faldstool
Palanquin

Subsellium
Sunlounger
Synthronus

9 letters:
Banquette
Bleachers
Davenport

10 letters:
Faldistory
Knifeboard
Strapontin

12 letters:
Chaise longue
Rumble-tumble

Seven against Thebes

6 letters:
Tydeus

9 letters:
Polynices

13 letters:
Parthenopaeus

8 letters:
Adrasyus
Capaneus

10 letters:
Amphiaraüs
Hippomedon

Shakespeare

CHARACTERS IN SHAKESPEARE

Character	Play
Sir Andrew Aguecheek	Twelfth Night
Antonio	The Merchant of Venice
Antony	Antony and Cleopatra, Julius Caesar
Ariel	The Tempest
Aufidius	Coriolanus
Autolycus	The Winter's Tale
Banquo	Macbeth
Bassanio	The Merchant of Venice
Beatrice	Much Ado About Nothing
Sir Toby Belch	Twelfth Night
Benedick	Much Ado About Nothing
Bolingbroke	Richard II
Bottom	A Midsummer Night's Dream
Brutus	Julius Caesar
Caliban	The Tempest
Casca	Julius Caesar
Cassio	Othello
Cassius	Julius Caesar
Claudio	Much Ado About Nothing, Measure for Measure

CHARACTERS IN SHAKESPEARE (CONTINUED)

Character	Play
Claudius	Hamlet
Cleopatra	Antony and Cleopatra
Cordelia	King Lear
Coriolanus	Coriolanus
Cressida	Troilus and Cressida
Demetrius	A Midsummer Night's Dream
Desdemona	Othello
Dogberry	Much Ado About Nothing
Edmund	King Lear
Enobarbus	Antony and Cleopatra
Falstaff	Henry IV Parts I and II, The Merry Wives of Windsor
Ferdinand	The Tempest
Feste	Twelfth Night
Fluellen	Henry V
Fool	King Lear
Gertrude	Hamlet
Gloucester	King Lear
Goneril	King Lear
Guildenstern	Hamlet
Hamlet	Hamlet
Helena	All's Well that Ends Well, A Midsummer Night's Dream
Hermia	A Midsummer Night's Dream
Hero	Much Ado About Nothing
Hotspur	Henry IV Part I
Iago	Othello
Jaques	As You Like It
John of Gaunt	Richard II
Juliet	Romeo and Juliet
Julius Caesar	Julius Caesar
Katharina *or* Kate	The Taming of the Shrew
Kent	King Lear
Laertes	Hamlet
Lear	King Lear
Lysander	A Midsummer Night's Dream
Macbeth	Macbeth
Lady Macbeth	Macbeth
Macduff	Macbeth
Malcolm	Macbeth
Malvolio	Twelfth Night

CHARACTERS IN SHAKESPEARE (CONTINUED)

Character	Play
Mercutio	Romeo and Juliet
Miranda	The Tempest
Oberon	A Midsummer Night's Dream
Octavius	Antony and Cleopatra
Olivia	Twelfth Night
Ophelia	Hamlet
Orlando	As You Like It
Orsino	Twelfth Night
Othello	Othello
Pandarus	Troilus and Cressida
Perdita	The Winter's Tale
Petruchio	The Taming of the Shrew
Pistol	Henry IV Part II, Henry V, The Merry Wives of Windsor
Polonius	Hamlet
Portia	The Merchant of Venice
Prospero	The Tempest
Puck	A Midsummer Night's Dream
Mistress Quickly	The Merry Wives of Windsor
Regan	King Lear
Romeo	Romeo and Juliet
Rosalind	As You Like It
Rosencrantz	Hamlet
Sebastian	The Tempest, Twelfth Night
Shylock	The Merchant of Venice
Thersites	Troilus and Cressida
Timon	Timon of Athens
Titania	A Midsummer Night's Dream
Touchstone	As You Like It
Troilus	Troilus and Cressida
Tybalt	Romeo and Juliet
Viola	Twelfth Night

PLAYS OF SHAKESPEARE

6 letters:
Hamlet
Henry V

7 letters:
Macbeth
Othello

8 letters:
King John
King Lear

9 letters:
Cymbeline
Henry VIII

Richard II

10 letters:
Coriolanus
Richard III
The Tempest

PLAYS OF SHAKESPEARE (CONTINUED)

11 letters:
As You Like It

12 letters:
Henry IV Part I
Henry VI Part I
Julius Caesar
Twelfth Night

13 letters:
Henry IV Part II
Henry VI Part II
Timon of Athens

14 letters:
Henry VI Part III
Romeo and Juliet
The Winter's Tale

15 letters:
Titus Andronicus

16 letters:
Love's Labour's Lost

17 letters:
Measure for Measure
The Comedy of Errors

18 letters:
Antony and Cleopatra
Troilus and Cressida

19 letters:
Much Ado About
    Nothing
The Merchant of Venice

The Taming of the
    Shrew

20 letters:
All's Well that Ends Well
Pericles, Prince of Tyre

21 letters:
A Midsummer Night's
    Dream

22 letters:
The Merry Wives of
    Windsor

23 letters:
The Two Gentlemen of
    Verona

POEMS OF SHAKESPEARE

7 letters:
Sonnets

14 letters:
Venus and Adonis

16 letters:
The Rape of Lucrece

20 letters:
The Passionate Pilgrim

22 letters:
The Phoenix and the
    Turtle

Sharks

3 letters:
Cow
Dog

4 letters:
Blue
Huss
Mako
Noah
Rigg
Tope

5 letters:
Angel
Gummy
Nurse
Tiger
Whale

6 letters:
Beagle
Carpet
School
Sea-ape
Whaler

7 letters:
Basking
Dogfish
Requiem
Reremai
Soupfin
Zygaena

8 letters:
Mackerel
Monkfish

Penny-dog
Rhinodon
Sailfish
Thrasher
Thresher

9 letters:
Angelfish
Grey nurse
Houndfish
Lemonfish
Porbeagle
Rhineodon
Seven-gill
Six-gilled
Wobbegong

10 letters:
Blue whaler
Bonnethead
Cestracion
Demoiselle
Hammerhead
Nursehound
Shovelhead

11 letters:
Blue pointer
Plagiostomi

Smoothhound

12 letters:
Bronze whaler

Breeds of sheep

4 letters:
Down
Kent
Lonk
Mule
Soay
Udad

5 letters:
Ammon
Ancon
Jacob
Lleyn
Texel
Urial

6 letters:
Aoudad
Argali
Bharal
Bident
Burhel
Burrel
Exmoor
Masham
Merino
Muflon
Musmon
Oorial
Orkney
Oxford

7 letters:
Ancones
Bighorn
Boreray
Burrell
Caracul
Cheviot
Colbred

Dinmont
Karakul
Lincoln
Loghtan
Loghtyn
Mouflon
Musimon
Ryeland
St. Kilda
Suffolk

8 letters:
Cheviots
Cotswold
Dartmoor
Drysdale
Herdwick
Loaghtan
Moufflon
Mountain
Polwarth
Portland
Shetland

9 letters:
Blackface
Blue-faced
Broadtail
Cambridge
Coopworth
Dalesbred
Fat-tailed
Hampshire
Hebridian
Kerry Hill
Leicester
Llanwenog
Marco Polo
Perendale
Romeldale

Rough Fell
Shorthorn
Southdown
Swaledale
Teeswater
Welsh Mule

10 letters:
Clun Forest
Corriedale
Dorset Down
Dorset Horn
Exmoor Horn
Hill Radnor
Shropshire

11 letters:
Île de France
Manx Loghtan
Norfolk Horn
Rambouillet
Romney Marsh
Wensleydale

12 letters:
British Texel

13 letters:
East Friesland
Hampshire Down
Mountain sheep
Rouge de l'Ouest
Welsh Halfbred
Welsh Mountain
Wiltshire Horn

14 letters:
British Vendéen
Devon Closewool
North Ronaldsay

15 letters:
Border Leicester
English Halfbred
Hexham Leicester
Lincoln Longwool
Oxfordshire Down

16 letters:
British Friesland
British Milksheep
British Oldenburg
Scottish Halfbred

17 letters:
British Charollais
Leicester Longwool
Scottish Blackface
Welsh Hill Speckled
White Face Dartmoor

18 letters:
Beulah Speckled-face
Black Welsh Mountain
British Bleu du Maine
South Wales Mountain
Whitefaced Woodland

19 letters:
Derbyshire Gritstone
North Country Cheviot
Wensleydale Longwool

20 letters:
Brecknock Hill Cheviot

24 letters:
Devon and Cornwall
   Longwool
Welsh Mountain Badger
   Faced

Shellfish

3 letters:
Mya
Top

4 letters:
Arca
Boat
Clam
Clio
Crab
Lamp
Paua
Pawa
Pipi
Tusk
Unio

5 letters:
Bulla
Capiz
Chank
Cohog
Conch
Cowry
Doris
Drill
Gaper
Helix
Koura
Murex
Olive
Ormer
Pinna

Polyp
Prawn
Razor
Sepia
Solen
Spoot
Squid
Turbo
Venus
Whelk
Yabby
Zimbi

6 letters:
Buckie
Chiton
Cockle
Cowrie
Cuttle
Limpet
Marron
Mussel
Ostrea
Oyster
Pecten
Pereia
Pholas
Poulpe
Purple
Quahog
Sea-ear
Sea-pen
Stromb

Tellen
Tellin
Teredo
Triton
Wakiki
Winkle
Yabbie

7 letters:
Abalone
Balanus
Bivalve
Crawbob
Craybob
Craydab
Isopoda
Lobster
Mud crab
Octopod
Octopus
Piddock
Quahaug
Scallop
Scollop
Sea-hare
Sea-slug
Toheroa
Torpedo
Trochus
Vitrina

8 letters:
Ammonite

Argonaut
Ark-shell
Chelonia
Clawchie
Copepoda
Crawfish
Crayfish
Deerhorn
Escallop
Haliotis
Nautilus
Ostracod
Pteropod
Sand crab
Saxicava
Sea-lemon
Shipworm
Strombus
Trivalve
Univalve
Xenophya

9 letters:
Balamnite
Belemnite
Blue manna
Clabby-doo
Clappy-doo
Cone-shell

Crustacea
Dentalium
Gastropod
King prawn
Langouste
Monocoque
Neopilina
Scalarium
Thermidor
Tusk-shell
Wing-shell

10 letters:
Acorn-shell
Amphineura
Cuttlefish
Gasteropod
Periwinkle
Razorshell
Scaphopoda
Stomatopod
Swan-mussel
Turritella
Wentletrap

11 letters:
Banana prawn
Blue swimmer
Foraminifer

Globigerina
Langoustine
Paper-sailor
School prawn
Soldier crab
Tectibranch
Trochophore

12 letters:
Malacostraca
Pelican's-foot

13 letters:
Lamellibranch
Moreton Bay bug
Norway lobster
Opisthobranch
Paper nautilus

14 letters:
Dublin Bay prawn
Pearly nautilus

16 letters:
Freshwater shrimp

18 letters:
Shovel-nosed lobster

Parts of ships

3 letters:
Bow
Gyn
Jib
Rig

4 letters:
Amas
Beam
Bung
Bunk
Deck
Foil
Foot
Gaff
Hank
Head

Helm
Hull
Keel
Line
Loof
Luff
Mast
Peak
Prow
Rode
Rope
Sail
Skin
Slot
Spar
Yard

5 letters:
Berth
Bilge
Bitts
Blade
Block
Cabin
Chine
Chock
Cleat
Flare
Genoa
Hatch
Hoist
Kedge
Leech
Lines

Loofe
Oakum
Screw
Sheet
Slide
Staff
Stern
Wheel
Winch

6 letters:
Anchor
Bridge
Burgee
Colors
Davite
Dinghy
Dorade
Drogue
Fender
Fiddle
Fo'c'sle
Frames
Galley
Gunnel
Jigger
Rudder
Sheave
Shroud

7 letters:
Ballast
Bearers
Bobstay
Boomkin
Buoyage
Capstan
Channel
Coaming
Cordage
Dunnage
Fardage
Fin keel
Gallows
Gudgeon
Gunwale
Halyard
Iron-jib
Jibboom
Jib stay

Nippers
Outhaul
Quarter
Raffees
Rigging
Sea cock
Snubber
Toe rail
Topmast
Trysail
Yard arm

8 letters:
Backstay
Boom-vang
Bowsprit
Bulkhead
Bulwarks
Ditty box
Fife rail
Foredeck
Foremast
Forepeak
Foresail
Forestay
Full keel
Headsail
Headstay
Jib sheet
Leeboard
Life boat
Lifeline
Life raft
Mainmast
Mainsail
Masthead
Moonsail
Poop deck
Porthole
Scuppers
Shear pin
Staysail
Storm jib
Telltale
Trip line

9 letters:
Bilge keel
Bilge pump
Bitter end

Cabin sole
Crow's nest
Deck plate
Gang plank
Hard chine
Hawse hole
King spoke
Lazarette
Lazyjacks
Lazysheet
Main sheet
Moonraker
Outrigger
Preventer
Royal mast
Sea-anchor
Sheathing
Spinnaker
Stanchion
Traveller

10 letters:
Anchor ball
Canoe stern
Figurehead
Fore castle
Jib netting
Jib topsail
Jigger-mast
Martingale
Mizzen mast
Mizzen sail
Riding sail
Rudder post
Sailing-rig
Sidelights
Turnbuckle

11 letters:
Anchor chain
Anchor light
Bosun's chair
Carline wood
Chafing gear
Foretopmast
Heaving line
Holding tank
Main topsail
Mooring line
Planing-hull

Sampson post
Spring lines
Towing light

12 letters:
Anchor locker
Bosun's locker
Charley noble
Companionway
Forestaysail
Hatch coaming
Kicking-strap
Reefing lines

13 letters:
Flame arrester
Iron-spinnaker
Running lights
Spinnaker boom
Spinnaker lift
Spinnaker pole
Stability sail

14 letters:
Anchor windlass
Courtesy ensign
Mizzen staysail

Running rigging

15 letters:
Running backstay

16 letters:
Painted waterline

17 letters:
Spinnaker pole lift

Shirts

3 letters:
Tee

4 letters:
Bush
Hair
Polo
Sark

5 letters:
Dress
Kurta

6 letters:
Banyan
Blouse

Boiled
Camise
Guimpe
Khurta
Skivvy
Sports
T-shirt

7 letters:
Chemise
Dashiki
Grandad
Kerbaya

8 letters:
Lava-lava
Swanndri®

9 letters:
Garibaldi
Jacky Howe

10 letters:
Overblouse

11 letters:
Middy blouse

13 letters:
Cover-shoulder

Shoes and boots

3 letters:
Dap
Tie

4 letters:
Boot
Clog
Flat
Geta
Muil
Mule
Pump
Sock

Soft
Spat
Vamp
Vibs
Zori

5 letters:
Court
Gatty
Plate
Sabot
Scuff

Spike
Stoga
Stogy
Suede
Track
Wader
Wedge
Welly

6 letters:
Arctic
Ballet

Bootee
Brogan
Brogue
Buskin
Chopin
Flatty
Gaiter
Galosh
Golosh
Jandal®
Lace-up
Loafer
Mukluk
Oxford
Panton
Patten
Racket
Rivlin
Saddle
Safety
Sandal
Sannie
Slip-on
Vamper
Vibram®
Wedgie

7 letters:
Blucher
Bottine
Casuals
Chopine
Cothurn
Creeper
Flattie
Galoche
Ghillie
Gumboot
Gumshoe
Gym shoe
High-low
Open-toe

Oxonian
Peeptoe
Racquet
Rubbers
Rullion
Sabaton
Slipper
Sneaker
Top boot
Trainer

8 letters:
Athletic
Balmoral
Crowboot
Deck shoe
Flip-flop
Golf shoe
Half boot
High heel
Jackboot
Larrigan
Mocassin
Moccasin
Moonboot
Overshoe
Pantofle
Platform
Plimsole
Plimsoll
Poulaine
Rock boot
Sandshoe
Snowshoe
Solleret
Stiletto
Velskoen

9 letters:
Ankle boot
Biker boot
Cothurnus
Court shoe

Doc Marten®
Field boot
Mary-Janes®
Pantoffle
Pantoufle
Rope-soled
Scarpetto
Slingback
Thigh boot
Track shoe
Veldskoen
Wedge heel

10 letters:
Bovver boot
Chukka boot
Cowboy boot
Espadrille
Kitten heel
Kurdaitcha
Tennis shoe
Veld-schoen

11 letters:
Hessian boot
Hobnail boot
Hush-puppies®
Running shoe

12 letters:
Co-respondent
Football boot
Kletterschue
Surgical boot
Training shoe
Winkle-picker

14 letters:
Brothel creeper
Wellington boot

15 letters:
Brothel creepers

Shrews and other insectivores

4 letters:
Mole

5 letters:
Shrew

6 letters:
Desman
Tenrec

7 letters:
Moon rat

9 letters:
Shrew mole
Solenodon
Tree shrew

10 letters:
Shrewmouse
Water shrew

13 letters:
Elephant shrew
Star-nosed mole

Shrubs

3 letters:
Box
Kat
Qat
Rue
Tea
Wax

4 letters:
Coca
Cola
Hebe
Nabk
Olea
Rhus
Rose
Ruta
Titi
Tutu

5 letters:
Aalii
Brere
Briar
Brier
Broom
Brush
Buaze
Buazi
Caper
Gorse
Hakea
Heath
Henna
Lilac

Maqui
Monte
Pyxie
Salal
Savin
Senna
Thyme
Toyon
Wahoo
Yacca
Yacka
Yapon
Yupon
Zamia

6 letters:
Acacia
Alhagi
Aucuba
Azalea
Bauera
Correa
Cotton
Crowea
Daphne
Fatsia
Feijoa
Frutex
Fynbos
Garrya
Jojoba
Laurel
Lignum
Manoao
Maquis

Matico
Mimosa
Myrica
Myrtle
Pituri
Privet
Protea
Savine
Sumach
Tawine
Tutsan
Yaupon

7 letters:
Arboret
Arbutus
Banksia
Boronia
Bramble
Bullace
Cascara
Cytisus
Dogwood
Emu bush
Epacris
Fuchsia
Geebong
Geebung
Heather
Hop-tree
Jasmine
Jibbong
Juniper
Lantana
Mesquit

Oleacea
Olearia
Rhatany
Romneya
Shallon
Skimmia
Tarwine
Tauhinu
Tea-tree
Waratah

8 letters:
Acanthus
Barberry
Bilberry
Black boy
Bluebush
Buddleia
Camellia
Clematis
Gardenia
Harhback
Hawthorn
Hibiscus
Inkberry
Jetbread
Laburnum
Lavender
Magnolia
Ninebark
Ocotillo
Oleander
Rock rose
Rosemary
Saltbush
Shadbush

Spekboom
Sweetsop
Tamarisk

9 letters:
Andromeda
Blueberry
Buckthorn
Clianthus
Coprosoma
Coyotillo
Cranberry
Daisy bush
Firethorn
Forsythia
Grevillea
Hydrangea
Jaborandi
Jessamine
Kerrawang
Liquorice
Melaleuca
Mistletoe
Patchouli
Poison ivy
Poison oak
Raspberry
Spicebush
Waxflower
Yacca bush

10 letters:
Blackthorn
Cottonbush
Cottonwood
Crossandra

Eriostemon
Frangipani
Gooseberry
Horizontal
Joshua tree
Laurustine
Mock orange
Parkleaves
Poinsettia
Potentilla
Pyracantha
Redcurrant
Strawberry
Supplejack

11 letters:
Beautybrush
Blanket bush
Bottlebrush
Honeysuckle
Pittosporum
Steeplebush

12 letters:
Blackcurrant
Rhododendron
Southernwood

13 letters:
Christmas bush
Crown-of-thorns

18 letters:
Geraldton waxflower

Seven deadly sins

4 letters:
Envy
Lust

5 letters:
Anger

Pride
Sloth

7 letters:
Avarice

8 letters:
Gluttony

12 letters:
Covetousness

Silicas and silicates

4 letters:
Opal

5 letters:
Chert
Silex

6 letters:
Albite
Humite
Iolite
Pinite

7 letters:
Kyanite
Olivine
Tripoli

Zeolite

8 letters:
Analcite
Datolite
Diopside
Dioptase
Saponite

9 letters:
Chabazite
Hiddenite
Penninite
Rhodonite
Scapolite
Tridymite

10 letters:
Andalusite
Float-stone
Kieselguhr
Staurolite
Ultrabasic

11 letters:
Vermiculite

12 letters:
Cristobalite
Monticellite

15 letters:
Montmorillonite

Types of silk

4 letters:
Corn
Flox
Pulu
Tram

5 letters:
Atlas
Crape
Crepe
Flosh
Floss
Gazar
Ninon
Satin
Seric
Surah
Tabby
Tasar
Tulle

6 letters:
Dupion
Faille
Kincob
Pongee
Samite
Sendal

Shalli
Sleave
Tussah
Tusseh
Tusser
Velvet

7 letters:
Alamode
Brocade
Chiffon
Foulard
Marabou
Organza
Ottoman
Sarsnet
Schappe
Tabaret
Taffeta
Tiffany
Tussore

8 letters:
Barathea
Chenille
Duchesse
Florence
Lustrine

Lustring
Makimono
Marabout
Paduasoy
Prunella
Prunelle
Prunello
Sarsenet
Shantung
Sien-tsan

9 letters:
Charmeuse®
Filoselle
Georgette
Matelasse
Parachute
Sericeous
Serigraph

10 letters:
Florentine
Lutestring
Peau de soie

11 letters:
Thistledown

Afflictions of the skin

4 letters:
Boba
Buba
Rash
Yaws

5 letters:
Favus
Hives
Mange
Pinta
Tinea

6 letters:
Cowpox
Dartre
Herpes
Livedo
Morula
Sapego
Scurvy
Tetter

7 letters:
Ecthyma

Prurigo
Rosacea
Scabies
Serpigo
Verruca
Verruga

8 letters:
Chloasma
Cyanosis
Dyschroa
Exanthem
Impetigo
Miliaria
Pyoderma
Ringworm
Rose-rash
Vaccinia
Vitiligo
Xanthoma

9 letters:
Chloracne
Exanthema

Pemphigus
Psoriasis

10 letters:
Dermatitis
Dermatosis
Erysipelas
Framboesia
Ichthyosis
Pityriasis
Seborrhoea
Strophulus

11 letters:
Mal del pinto

12 letters:
Sclerodermia

13 letters:
Leishmaniasis
Lupus vulgaris

Skirts

4 letters:
Bell
Full
Hoop
Hula
Kilt
Mini
Ra-ra
Tace
Tutu

5 letters:
A-line
Grass
Harem
Pareo
Pareu
Tasse

6 letters:
Dirndl
Hobble
Pencil
Peplum
Piu-piu
Riding
Sarong
Taslet
Tasset
Tonlet

7 letters:
Culotte
Divided
Filibeg
Lamboys

8 letters:
Bouffant
Culottes
Fillibeg
Half-slip
Lava-lava
Philibeg
Puffball
Wrapover

9 letters:
Cheongsam
Crinoline
Gabardine
Gaberdine
Maxiskirt
Midiskirt
Miniskirt
Overskirt

Petticoat
Waist-slip
Wraparound

10 letters:
Fustanella

Fustanelle
Microskirt
Underskirt
Wraparound

11 letters:
Drop-waisted

13 letters:
Button-through

Snails, slugs and other gastropods

4 letters:
Slug

5 letters:
Conch
Cowry
Murex
Ormer
Snail
Whelk

6 letters:
Cowrie
Limpet
Sea-ear
Triton
Winkle

7 letters:
Abalone
Sea hare
Sea slug

8 letters:
Ear shell
Top-shell

10 letters:
Nudibranch
Periwinkle
Roman snail
Wentletrap

13 letters:
Ramshorn snail

Snakes

3 letters:
Asp
Boa
Rat

4 letters:
Boma
Bull
Corn
Habu
Hoop
King
Milk
Naga
Naia
Naja
Pipe
Rock
Seps
Tree
Whip

5 letters:
Adder
Blind

Brown
Cobra
Congo
Coral
Cribo
Elaps
Glass
Grass
Krait
Mamba
Mulga
Racer
Tiger
Viper
Water

6 letters:
Carpet
Clotho
Daboia
Dipsas
Dugite
Ellops
Garter
Indigo

Karait
Python
Ribbon
Smooth
Taipan
Thirst
Uraeus
Vasuki

7 letters:
Camoodi
Coluber
Diamond
Hognose
Langaha
Rattler

8 letters:
Anaconda
Cerastes
Jararaca
Jararaka
Lachesis
Mocassin
Moccasin

Pit-viper
Ringhals
Ringneck
Rinkhals
Slowworm
Spitting
Sucuruju
Surucucu
Takshaka

9 letters:
Blue-racer
Boomslang
Coachwhip
Hamadryad

Horsewhip
King cobra
Kingsnake
Puff-adder
River jack
Sand viper

10 letters:
Bandy-bandy
Blacksnake
Bush-master
Copperhead
Death-adder
Dendrophis
Fer-de-lance

Homorelaps
Massasauga
Sidewinder

11 letters:
Amphisbaena
Cottonmouth
Diamond-back
Horned viper

13 letters:
Water moccasin

17 letters:
Timber rattlesnake

Snooker and billiards terms

1 letter:
D

3 letters:
Lag
Pot
Red
Top

4 letters:
Ball
Blue
Draw
Foul
Kick
Kiss
Pink
Rack
Rest
Side
Spot
Stun

5 letters:
Baize
Baulk
Black
Break
Brown
Carom

Chalk
Fluke
Frame
Green
In-off
Jenny
Massé
Nurse
Plant
Screw
White

6 letters:
Bridge
Cannon
Cue tip
Double
Hazard
Miscue
Pocket
Safety
Spider
Yellow

7 letters:
Bouclée
Bricole
Cue ball
Cushion
English

Scratch
Snooker

8 letters:
Free ball
Half-butt
Headrail
Spot ball
Triangle

9 letters:
Baulkline
Clearance
Long jenny
Plain ball

10 letters:
Drop cannon
Object ball
Short jenny

11 letters:
Whitechapel

12 letters:
Cue extension
Maximum break

13 letters:
Nursery cannon

Socks and tights

4 letters:
Hose
Sock

5 letters:
Putty
Stock

6 letters:
Anklet
Argyle
Nylons
Puttee
Stay-up

Tights

7 letters:
Bed sock
Maillot
Pop sock

8 letters:
Half-hose
Stocking

9 letters:
Ankle sock
Bobby sock

Legwarmer
Pantihose
Pantyhose

10 letters:
Slouch sock

12 letters:
Knee-high sock

13 letters:
Lisle stocking

Types of sofa

5 letters:
Couch
Divan
Futon
Squab

6 letters:
Canapé
Chaise
Day bed
Lounge

Settee
Settle

7 letters:
Bergère
Sofa bed
Vis-à-vis

8 letters:
Love seat

9 letters:
Davenport
Tête-à-tête

11 letters:
Studio couch

12 letters:
Chaise longue
Chesterfield

Sounds

4 letters:
Jura

5 letters:
Puget
Smith

6 letters:
Achill
Nootka
Tromsø

7 letters:
Mcmurdo
Milford
Pamlico

8 letters:
Plymouth
Scoresby
The Sound

9 letters:
Lancaster

10 letters:
Kilbrennan
King George

12 letters:
Sound of Sleat

14 letters:
Queen Charlotte

Spiders and other arachnids

3 letters:
Red

4 letters:
Bird
Mite
Tick
Wolf

5 letters:
Money
Water

6 letters:
Aranea
Chigoe
Diadem
Epeira
Jigger
Katipo
Lycosa
Mygale
Redbug
Violin

7 letters:
Chigger
Hunting
Jumping

Red-back
Solpuga
Spinner

8 letters:
Arachnid
Araneida
Attercop
Cardinal
Ethercap
Ettercap
Huntsman
Itch mite
Podogona
Sand flea
Trapdoor

9 letters:
Bobbejaan
Funnel-web
Harvester
Orb-weaver
Phalangid
Ricinulei
Tarantula

10 letters:
Bird spider

Black widow
Cheese mite
Harvestman
Pycnogonid
Spider mite
Wolf spider

11 letters:
House spider
Money spider
Vinegarroon
Water spider

12 letters:
Book scorpion
Jockey spider
Whip scorpion

13 letters:
Daddy-longlegs
False scorpion
Hunting spider
Jumping spider
Red-back spider

14 letters:
Cardinal spider
Trap-door spider

Spirits

3 letters:
Gin
Rum

4 letters:
Arak
Korn
Marc
Ouzo
Raki

5 letters:
Hooch
Rakee
Vodka

6 letters:
Arrack
Brandy
Cognac
Grappa
Kirsch
Mescal
Poitín
Poteen
Taffia
Whisky

7 letters:
Absinth
Akvavit

Aquavit
Bacardi®
Bitters
Dark rum
Palinka
Schnaps
Sloe gin
Tequila

8 letters:
Absinthe
Armagnac
Calvados
Eau de vie
Hollands

Sports

Schnapps
White rum

9 letters:
Applejack
Aqua vitae
Firewater

Framboise
Slivovitz
Triple sec

11 letters:
Aguardiente
Apple brandy

12 letters:
Kirschwasser

15 letters:
Applejack brandy

Sports

2 letters:
RU

4 letters:
Golf
Polo
Pool
Sumo

5 letters:
Bandy
Bowls
Darts
Fives
Rugby
Sambo
Skeet

6 letters:
Aikido
Boules
Boxing
Hockey
Hurley
Karate
Pelota
Quoits
Savate
Shinty
Soccer
Squash
Tennis

7 letters:
Angling
Archery
Camogie
Cricket
Croquet

Curling
Cycling
Fencing
Fishing
Gliding
Hurling
Jai alai
Kabbadi
Netball
Rackets
Snooker

8 letters:
Aquatics
Baseball
Coursing
Falconry
Football
Goalball
Handball
Korfball
Lacrosse
Octopush
Pétanque
Rounders
Shooting
Skittles
Softball
Speedway
Tug-of-war

9 letters:
Autocross
Badminton
Billiards
Decathlon
Ice hockey
Potholing
Skijoring

Skydiving
Stool ball
Triathlon
Water polo
Wrestling

10 letters:
Ballooning
Basketball
Candlepins
Cyclo-cross
Drag-racing
Fly-fishing
Fox-hunting
Gymnastics
Kickboxing
Lawn tennis
Paddleball
Paraskiing
Real tennis
Rugby union
Volleyball

11 letters:
Hang gliding
Parachuting
Paragliding
Parasailing
Rugby league
Table tennis
Windsurfing

12 letters:
Bullfighting
Cockfighting
Orienteering
Parascending
Pigeon racing
Rock climbing

Roller hockey
Speed-skating
Steeplechase
Trampolining
Trapshooting
Wakeboarding

13 letters:
Roller skating
Rugby football
Squash rackets
Tenpin bowling
Weightlifting

14 letters:
Gaelic football
Mountaineering
Sambo wrestling

15 letters:
Australian Rules
Greyhound racing

16 letters:
American football
Canadian football
Modern pentathlon

17 letters:
Five-a-side football

18 letters:
Clay pigeon shooting
Rhythmic gymnastics

19 letters:
Association football

23 letters:
Australian Rules football

See also:
➤ **American football teams** ➤ **Athletic events** ➤ **Ballgames** ➤ **Baseball teams** ➤ **Boxing weights** ➤ **Cricketers** ➤ **Equestrianism** ➤ **Fencing terms** ➤ **Football** ➤ **Football clubs** ➤ **Footballers** ➤ **Golfers** ➤ **Golf terms** ➤ **Grand Prix circuits** ➤ **Gymnastic events** ➤ **Martial arts** ➤ **Motor sports** ➤ **Rugby terms** ➤ **Snooker and billiards terms** ➤ **Sportspeople** ➤ **Swimming strokes** ➤ **Tennis terms** ➤ **Tennis players** ➤ **Water sports** ➤ **Winter sports**

Sportspeople

3 letters:
Coe, *Sebastian*

4 letters:
Anne, *Princess*
Dean, *Christopher*
Leng, *Virginia*
Lowe, *John*
Rose, *Sir Alec*
Ruth, *Babe*
Witt, *Katarina*

5 letters:
Blyth, *Sir Chay*
Curry, *John*
Davis, *Steve*
Ebdon, *Peter*
Lewis, *Carl*
Lewis, *Denise*
Meade, *Richard*
Orser, *Brian*
Ovett, *Steve*
Owens, *Jesse*
Smith, *Harvey*

Spitz, *Mark*
Stark, *Ian*
Viren, *Lasse*
Wells, *Allan*
White, *Jimmy*

6 letters:
Broome, *David*
Davies, *Sharron*
Foster, *Brendan*
Foster, *Tim*
Gunnel, *Sally*
Hendry, *Stephen*
Holmes, *Kelly*
Joiner, *Florence Griffith*
Jordan, *Michael*
Korbut, *Olga*
Martin, *Rhona*
Palmer, *Lucinda Prior*
Schenk, *Christaian*
Wilson, *Jockey*

7 letters:
Bristow, *Eric*

Cousins, *Robin*
Edwards, *Eddie 'The Eagle'*
Edwards, *Jonathan*
Fosbury, *Dick*
Francis, *Claire*
Freeman, *Cathy*
Higgins, *Alex 'Hurricane'*
Johnson, *Ben*
Pinsent, *Matthew*
Reardon, *Ray*
Simpson, *O(renthal) J(ames)*
Torvill, *Jayne*
Zvereva, *Ellina*

8 letters:
Boardman, *Chris*
Brabants, *Tim*
Chataway, *Christopher*
Christie, *Linford*
Comaneci, *Nadia*
Hamilton, *Scott*
Petrenko, *Viktor*

Redgrave, *Steve*
Thompson, *Daley*
Thorburn, *Cliff*

9 letters:
Bannister, *Roger*
Bullimore, *Tony*
Cracknell, *James*
Schumaker, *Michael*

10 letters:
Chichester, *Sir Francis*

11 letters:
Weissmuller, *Johnny*

Stars and constellations

STARS

3 letters:
Sol

4 letters:
Argo
Grus
Idol
Lyra
Mira
Pavo
Pole
Ursa
Vega
Vela

5 letters:
Acrux
Agena
Algol
Ceres
Deneb
Draco
Dubhe
Hyads
Indus
Lupus
Mensa
Merak
Mizar
Norma
North
Polar
Rigel
Rigil
Venus
Virgo
Wagon
Whale

6 letters:
Alioth
Alkaid
Altair
Aquila
Auriga
Boötes
Carina
Castor
Cygnus
Dorado
Esther
Fornax
Hyades
Megrez
Merope
Octans
Phecda
Plough
Pollux
Psyche
Puppis
Saturn
Sirius
Sothis
The Sun
Uranus
Vesper
Volans

7 letters:
Antares
Calaeno
Canopus
Capella
Cepheus
Columba
Dolphin
Lucifer

Phoenix
Polaris
Procyon
Proximo
Regulus
Serpens
Triones
Wagoner

8 letters:
Achernar
Arcturus
Barnard's
Canicula
Circinus
Denebola
Equuleus
Hesperus
Pegasean
Pleiades
Pointers
Praesepe
Scorpius
Waggoner

9 letters:
Aldebaran
Andromeda
Bellatrix
Betelgeux
Big Dipper
Centaurus
Delphinus
Fomalhaut
Ophiuchus
Wolf-Rayet

10 letters:
Betelgeuse

STARS (CONTINUED)

Betelgeuze
Cassiopeia
Mogen David
Orion's belt
The Dog Star

11 letters:
The Pointers
The Pole Star

12 letters:
Little Dipper

Solomon's seal
The North Star

14 letters:
Proxima centaur

CONSTELLATIONS

Latin name	English name
Andromeda	Andromeda
Antlia	Air Pump
Apus	Bird of Paradise
Aquarius	Water Bearer
Aquila	Eagle
Ara	Altar
Argo	Ship of the Argonauts
Aries	Ram
Auriga	Charioteer
Boötes	Herdsman
Caelum	Chisel
Camelopardalis	Giraffe
Cancer	Crab
Canes Venatici	Hunting Dogs
Canis Major	Great Dog
Canis Minor	Little Dog
Capricornus	Sea Goat
Carina	Keel
Cassiopeia	Cassiopeia
Centaurus	Centaur
Cepheus	Cepheus
Cetus	Whale
Chamaeleon	Chameleon
Circinus	Compasses
Columba	Dove
Coma Berenices	Bernice's Hair
Corona Australis	Southern Crown
Corona Borealis	Northern Crown
Corvus	Crow
Crater	Cup
Crux	Southern Cross
Cygnus	Swan
Cynosure	Dog's Tail

CONSTELLATIONS (CONTINUED)

Latin name	English name
Delphinus	Dolphin
Dorado	Swordfish
Draco	Dragon
Equuleus	Little Horse
Eridanus	River Eridanus
Fornax	Furnace
Gemini	Twins
Grus	Crane
Hercules	Hercules
Horologium	Clock
Hydra	Sea Serpent
Hydrus	Water Snake
Indus	Indian
Lacerta	Lizard
Leo	Lion
Leo Minor	Little Lion
Lepus	Hare
Libra	Scales
Lupus	Wolf
Lynx	Lynx
Lyra	Harp
Mensa	Table
Microscopium	Microscope
Monoceros	Unicorn
Musca	Fly
Norma	Level
Octans	Octant
Ophiuchus	Serpent Bearer
Orion	Orion
Pavo	Peacock
Pegasus	Winged Horse
Perseus	Perseus
Phoenix	Phoenix
Pictor	Easel
Pisces	Fishes
Piscis Austrinus	Southern Fish
Puppis	Ship's Stern
Pyxis	Mariner's Compass
Reticulum	Net
Sagitta	Arrow

CONSTELLATIONS (CONTINUED)

Latin name	English name
Sagittarius	Archer
Scorpius	Scorpion
Sculptor	Sculptor
Scutum	Shield
Serpens	Serpent
Sextans	Sextant
Taurus	Bull
Telescopium	Telescope
Triangulum	Triangle
Triangulum Australe	Southern Triangle
Tucana	Toucan
Ursa Major	Great Bear (contains the Plough or (U.S.) Big Dipper)
Ursa Minor	Little Bear or (U.S.) Little Dipper
Vela	Sails
Virgo	Virgin
Volans	Flying Fish
Vulpecula	Fox

States and territories

AUSTRALIAN STATES AND TERRITORIES

8 letters:
Tasmania
Victoria

10 letters:
Queensland

13 letters:
New South Wales

14 letters:
South Australia

16 letters:
Western Australia

17 letters:
Northern Territory

26 letters:
Australian Capital
    Territory

INDIAN STATES

3 letters:
Goa

5 letters:
Assam
Bihar

6 letters:
Kerala
Orissa
Punjab
Sikkim

7 letters:
Gujarat
Haryana
Manipur
Mizoram
Tripura

INDIAN STATES (CONTINUED)

8 letters:
Jharkand
Nagaland

9 letters:
Karnataka
Meghalaya
Rajasthan
Tamil Nadu

10 letters:
West Bengal

11 letters:
Maharashtra
Uttaranchal

12 letters:
Chhattisgarh
Uttar Pradesh

13 letters:
Andhra Pradesh
Madhya Pradesh

15 letters:
Himachal Pradesh
Jammu and Kashmir

16 letters:
Arunachal Pradesh

INDIAN UNION TERRITORIES

5 letters:
Delhi

10 letters:
Chandigarh

11 letters:
Daman and Diu
Lakshadweep
Pondicherry

19 letters:
Dadra and Nagar Haveli

24 letters:
Andaman and Nicobar
Islands

US STATES

State	Abbreviation	Zip code	Nickname	Capital
Alabama	Ala.	AL	Cotton	Montgomery
Alaska	Alas.	AK	Last Frontier	Juneau
Arizona	Ariz.	AZ	Apache	Phoenix
Arkansas	Ark.	AR	Wonder	Little Rock
California	Cal.	CA	Golden	Sacramento
Colorado	Colo.	CO	Centennial	Denver
Connecticut	Conn.	CT	Nutmeg	Hartford
Delaware	Del.	DE	Diamond	Dover
District of Columbia	D.C.	DC	-	-
Florida	Fla.	FL	Sunshine	Tallahassee
Georgia	Ga.	GA	Peach	Atlanta
Hawaii	Haw.	HI	Aloha	Honolulu
Idaho	Id. or Ida.	ID	Gem	Boise
Illinois	Ill.	IL	Prairie	Springfield
Indiana	Ind.	IN	Hoosier	Indianapolis
Iowa	Ia. or Io.	IA	Hawkeye	Des Moines
Kansas	Kan. or Kans.	KS	Sunflower	Topeka
Kentucky	Ken.	KY	Blue Grass	Frankfort
Louisiana	La.	LA	Pelican	Baton Rouge
Maine	Me.	ME	Pine Tree	Augusta
Maryland	Md.	MD	Free	Annapolis

US STATES (CONTINUED)

State	Abbreviation	Zip code	Nickname	Capital
Massachusetts	Mass.	MA	Bay	Boston
Michigan	Mich.	MI	Wolverine	Lansing
Minnesota	Minn.	MN	Gopher	St Paul
Mississippi	Miss.	MS	Magnolia	Jackson
Missouri	Mo.	MO	Show-me	Jefferson City
Montana	Mont.	MT	Treasure	Helena
Nebraska	Neb.	NE	Cornhusker	Lincoln
Nevada	Nev.	NV	Sagebrush	Carson City
New Hampshire	N.H.	NH	Granite	Concord
New Jersey	N.J.	NJ	Garden	Trenton
New Mexico	N.M. *or* N.Mex.	NM	Sunshine	Santa Fe
New York	N.Y.	NY	Empire	Albany
North Carolina	N.C.	NC	Tar Heel	Raleigh
North Dakota	N.D. *or* N.Dak.	ND	Sioux	Bismarck
Ohio	O.	OH	Buckeye	Columbus
Oklahoma	Okla.	OK	Sooner	Oklahoma City
Oregon	Oreg.	OR	Beaver	Salem
Pennsylvania	Pa., Penn., *or* Penna.	PA	Keystone	Harrisburg
Rhode Island	R.I.	RI	Little Rhody	Providence
South Carolina	S.C.	SC	Palmetto	Columbia
South Dakota	S.Dak.	SD	Coyote	Pierre
Tennessee	Tenn.	TN	Volunteer	Nashville
Texas	Tex.	TX	Lone Star	Austin
Utah	Ut.	UT	Beehive	Salt Lake City
Vermont	Vt.	VT	Green Mountain	Montpelier
Virginia	Va.	VA	Old Dominion	Richmond
Washington	Wash.	WA	Evergreen	Olympia
West Virginia	W.Va.	WV	Panhandle	Charleston
Wisconsin	Wis.	WI	Badger	Madison
Wyoming	Wyo.	WY	Equality	Cheyenne

US States: Year of Accession to the Union

State	Year of Accession
Alabama	1819
Alaska	1959
Arizona	1912
Arkansas	1836
California	1850
Colorado	1876
Connecticut	1788
Delaware	1787
District of Columbia	1889
Florida	1845
Georgia	1788
Hawaii	1959
Idaho	1890
Illinois	1818
Indiana	1816
Iowa	1846
Kansas	1861
Kentucky	1792
Louisiana	1812
Maine	1820
Maryland	1788
Massachusetts	1788
Michigan	1837
Minnesota	1858
Mississippi	1817
Missouri	1821
Montana	1889
Nebraska	1867
Nevada	1864
New Hampshire	1788
New Jersey	1787
New Mexico	1912
New York	1788
North Carolina	1789
North Dakota	1889
Ohio	1803
Oklahoma	1907
Oregon	1859
Pennsylvania	1787
Rhode Island	1790
South Carolina	1788

US States: Year of Accession to the Union (continued)

State	Year of Accession
South Dakota	1889
Tennessee	1796
Texas	1845
Utah	1896
Vermont	1791
Virginia	1788
Washington	1889
West Virginia	1863
Wisconsin	1848
Wyoming	1890

Types of stone

2 letters:
St

3 letters:
Gem
Hog
Pit
Rag
Tin

4 letters:
Bath
Blue
Celt
Door
Flag
Hone
Horn
Iron
Jasp
Kerb
Lias
Lime
Lode
Onyx
Opal
Plum
Ragg
Sard
Skew
Slab
Soap

Tile

5 letters:
Agate
Amber
Balas
Beryl
Black
Chalk
Chert
Coade
Culch
Drupe
Flint
Gooly
Grape
Jewel
Kenne
Lapis
Logan
Menah
Metal
Mocha
Niobe
Paste
Prase
Pumie
Quern
Quoin
Quoit
Rubin
Rufus

Rybat
Scone
Scree
Slate
Sneck
Stela
Stele
Topaz
Wacke
Wyman

6 letters:
Amazon
Ashlar
Ashler
Baetyl
Bezoar
Brinny
Cobble
Coping
Cultch
Dolmen
Flusch
Fossil
Gibber
Gooley
Goolie
Gravel
Humite
Jargon
Jasper
Kidney

Kingle
Ligure
Lithic
Menhir
Metate
Muller
Nutlet
Oamaru
Paving
Pebble
Pot-lid
Pumice
Pyrene
Rip-rap
Sarsen
Scarab
Summer
Tanist

7 letters:
Asteria
Avebury
Blarney
Bologna
Boulder
Breccia
Callais
Chuckie
Curling
Girasol
Granite
Hyacine
Hyalite
Jargoon
Lia-fail
Lithoid
Moabite
Niobean
Olivine
Parpane
Parpend
Parpent
Peridot
Perpend
Perpent
Petrous
Pudding
Purbeck

Putamen
Rocking
Rosetta
Sardine
Sarsden
Scaglia
Schanse
Schanze
Smaragd
Tektite
Telamon
Tripoli
Urolith

8 letters:
Aerolite
Aerolith
Amethyst
Asteroid
Baguette
Cabochon
Calculus
Cinnamon
Cromlech
Ebenezer
Elf-arrow
Endocarp
Essonite
Ganister
Girasole
Lapidate
Megalith
Menamber
Monolith
Nephrite
Omphalos
Onychite
Parpoint
Petrosal
Phengite
Portland
Rollrich
Sapphire
Sardonyx
Scalpins
Schantze
Tonalite
Voussoir

9 letters:
Alabaster
Asparagus
Cairngorm
Carnelian
Cholelith
Chondrite
Cornelian
Crossette
Dichroite
Firestone
Gannister
Greensand
Hessonite
Hoarstone
Lithiasis
Paleolith
Pipestone
Rubicelle
Scagliola
Trilithon
Turquoise
Ventifact

10 letters:
Adamantine
Alectorian
Aragonites
Chalcedony
Draconites
Enhydritic
Foundation
Gastrolith
Grey-wether
Kimberlite
Lherzolite
Lithophyte
Rhinestone

11 letters:
Peristalith

12 letters:
Carton-pierre
Philosopher's

See also:
➤ **Minerals** ➤ **Ores** ➤ **Types of rock**

Straits

4 letters:
Bass
Cook
Mena
Palk

5 letters:
Cabot
Davis
Dover
Kerch
Korea
Sumba

6 letters:
Bangka
Barrow
Bering
Hainan
Hecate
Hudson
Lombok
Madura
Taiwan
Tartar
Torres

7 letters:
Denmark
Dolphin
Euripus
Evripos
Florida

Formosa
Foveaux
Le Maire
Malacca
Molucca
Øresund

8 letters:
Bosporus
Makassar
Minch, The
Sound, The

9 letters:
Bosphorus
Great Belt
La Pérouse
Small Belt
Solent, The

10 letters:
Gut of Canso
Juande Fuca
Limfjorden
Little Belt
North Minch

11 letters:
Bab-el-Mandeb
Dardanelles
Kattegat, The
Little Minch
Mona Passage

12 letters:
Skagerrak, The

13 letters:
Strait of Canso
Strait of Sunda

14 letters:
Northumberland
Strait of Hormuz
Straits of Johor

15 letters:
Strait of Georgia
Strait of Malacca
Strait of Messina
Strait of Otranto
Straits of Harris
Windward Passage

16 letters:
Strait of Magellan

17 letters:
Passage of Colonsay
Strait of Belle Isle
Strait of Bonifacio
Straits of Mackinac

18 letters:
Strait of Juan de Fuca
Straits of Gibraltar

Subatomic particles

1 letter:
J
W
Z

3 letters:
Chi
Eta
Psi
Tau

4 letters:
Kaon
Muon
Pion

5 letters:
Axion
Boson
Gluon
Meson
Omega

Quark
Sigma
Tauon

6 letters:
Baryon
Hadron
Lambda
Lepton
Parton
Photon

Proton

Upsilon

9 letters:
Resonance

7 letters:
Fermion
Neutron
Tachyon

8 letters:
Electron
Monopole
Neutrino

10 letters:
Higgs boson

Sugars

3 letters:
Goo
Gur

4 letters:
Beet
Cane
Goor
Loaf
Lump
Milk
Palm
Wood

5 letters:
Brown
Candy
Grape
Icing
Maple
Sorgo
White

6 letters:
Aldose
Barley
Caster
Fucose
Hexose
Inulin
Invert

Ribose
Sorgho
Triose
Xylose

7 letters:
Caramel
Cellose
Glucose
Jaggary
Jaggery
Lactose
Maltose
Mannose
Panocha
Pentose
Penuche
Refined
Sorbose
Sorghum
Trehala

8 letters:
Demerara
Dextrose
Fructose
Furanose
Honeydew
Jagghery
Powdered

Rhamnose

9 letters:
Amygdalin
Arabinose
Cassonade
Galactose
Laevulose
Muscovado
Raffinose
Trehalose

10 letters:
Aldohexose
Cellobiose
Glucosoric
Granulated
Saccharine
Saccharoid

11 letters:
Deoxyribose

12 letters:
Crystallized
Disaccharide

14 letters:
Monosaccharide

Suits

3 letters:
Mao
Ski
Wet

4 letters:
Jump
Pant
Zoot

5 letters:
Anti-G
Dress
G-suit

Shell
Slack
Sweat

6 letters:
Boiler
Judogi
Lounge
Romper
Safari
Sailor
Sweats

7 letters:
Catsuit
Pajamas
Penguin
Pyjamas
Sunsuit
Trouser

8 letters:
Playsuit
Swimsuit

9 letters:
Buckskins

Spacesuit
Tracksuit

10 letters:
Three-piece

12 letters:
Evening dress
Morning dress

14 letters:
Double-breasted
Single-breasted

The supernatural

PEOPLE WITH SUPERNATURAL POWERS

3 letters:
Hag
Hex

4 letters:
Mage
Seer

5 letters:
Magus
Siren
Witch

6 letters:
Dowser
Medium
Shaman
Wizard

7 letters:
Diviner
Warlock

8 letters:
Conjurer
Exorcist
Magician
Sorcerer
Spaewife

9 letters:
Archimage
Enchanter
Rainmaker
Sorceress
Superhero

10 letters:
Channeller

Water witch
White witch

11 letters:
Clairvoyant
Enchantress
Necromancer
Thaumaturge
Witch doctor
Witch master

12 letters:
Clairaudient
Water diviner

13 letters:
Clairsentient
Fortune-teller

SUPERNATURAL CREATURES

3 letters:
Elf
Fay
God
Imp

4 letters:
Ogre
Peri

5 letters:
Angel
Demon

Devil
Dwarf
Fairy
Genie
Ghost
Ghoul
Giant

SUPERNATURAL CREATURES (CONTINUED)

Gnome
Golem
Jinni
Lamia
Pixie
Sylph
Troll
Zombi

6 letters:
Djinni
Djinny
Dybbuk
Goblin
Jinnee
Kelpie
Selkie
Silkie
Sprite
Wraith

Zombie

7 letters:
Banshee
Brownie
Goddess
Gremlin
Incubus
Kachina
Monster
Phantom
Sandman
Spectre
Vampire

8 letters:
Familiar
Succubus
Werewolf

9 letters:
Hobgoblin

10 letters:
Leprechaun
Little folk

11 letters:
Lycanthrope
Poltergeist

12 letters:
Little people

13 letters:
Guardian angel

14 letters:
Fairy godmother

SUPERNATURAL TERMS

3 letters:
ESP
Hex
Obi

4 letters:
Aura
Fate
Jinx
Juju
Mojo
Rune
Wand

5 letters:
Charm
Curse
Obeah
Ouija®
Sigil
Spell

6 letters:
Amulet
Apport

Fetish
Grigri
Hoodoo
Kismet
Séance
Voodoo

7 letters:
Evil eye
Philtre
Portent

8 letters:
Exorcism
Greegree
Grimoire
Gris-gris
Talisman

9 letters:
Ectoplasm
Magic wand
Pentagram
Telepathy

10 letters:
Black magic
Divination
Indian sign
Levitation
Magic spell
Necromancy
Possession
Sixth sense
Telegnosis
White magic
Xenoglossy

11 letters:
Abracadabra
Incantation
Magic circle
Premonition
Second sight
Telekinesis
The Black Art
Xenoglossia

12 letters:
Clairvoyance

SUPERNATURAL TERMS (CONTINUED)

Invultuation
Telaesthesia
Witching hour

13 letters:
Clairaudience
Psychokinesis

Reincarnation

14 letters:
Clairsentience
Cryptaesthesia
Parapsychology

17 letters:
Speaking in tongues

22 letters:
Extrasensory perception

Surgical operations

5 letters:
Graft
Taxis

6 letters:
Bypass

7 letters:
Section

8 letters:
Ablation
Avulsion
Cesarean
Colotomy
Face-lift
Liposuck
Lobotomy
Tenotomy
Vagotomy

9 letters:
Anaplasty
Autograft
Caesarean
Colectomy
Colostomy
Colpotomy
Costotomy
Curettage
Cystotomy
Ileostomy
Iridotomy
Leucotomy
Lithotomy
Lobectomy
Necrotomy

Neoplasty
Neurotomy
Osteotomy
Plication
Resection
Rhizotomy
Skin graft
Tummy tuck
Vasectomy
Zooplasty

10 letters:
Adenectomy
Amputation
Autoplasty
Biosurgery
Craniotomy
Cystectomy
Enterotomy
Episiotomy
Gastrotomy
Iridectomy
Keratotomy
Laparotomy
Lithotrity
Lumpectomy
Mastectomy
Myomectomy
Nephrotomy
Neurectomy
Ovariotomy
Phlebotomy
Pleurotomy
Rachiotomy
Sclerotomy
Strabotomy
Thymectomy

Transplant
Varicotomy

11 letters:
Anastomosis
Angioplasty
Arthrectomy
Cryosurgery
Débridement
Embolectomy
Embryectomy
Enterectomy
Enterostomy
Gastrectomy
Gastrostomy
Glossectomy
Hysterotomy
Laminectomy
Laryngotomy
Liposuction
Nephrectomy
Osteoclasis
Osteoplasty
Ovariectomy
Phlebectomy
Pneumectomy
Pylorectomy
Rhinoplasty
Splenectomy
Tenorrhaphy
Thoracotomy
Tracheotomy
Vaginectomy
Venesection

12 letters:
Arthroplasty

Circumcision
Dermabrasion
Fenestration
Heteroplasty
Hysterectomy
Keratoplasty
Microsurgery
Neurosurgery
Oophorectomy
Paracentesis
Pharyngotomy
Replantation
Tonsillotomy
Tracheostomy

13 letters:
Adenoidectomy
Dermatoplasty
Mastoidectomy
Pneumonectomy
Prostatectomy

Psychosurgery
Salpingectomy
Stomatoplasty
Sympathectomy
Thoracoplasty
Thyroidectomy
Tonsillectomy
Tubal ligation

14 letters:
Appendicectomy
Blepharoplasty
Cardiocentesis
Clitoridectomy
Coronary bypass
Electrosurgery
Keyhole surgery
Plastic surgery
Staphyloplasty
Xenotransplant

15 letters:
Cholecystectomy
Cosmetic surgery
Staphylorrhaphy

16 letters:
Caesarean section
Open-heart surgery
Radial keratotomy
Spare-part surgery

17 letters:
Commando operation
Gastroenterostomy
Haemorrhoidectomy

18 letters:
Gastroduodenostomy
Gender reassignment

Sweaters

4 letters:
Aran
Polo

5 letters:
V-neck

6 letters:
Indian
Jersey
Jumper
Siwash
Skivvy

7 letters:
V-necked

8 letters:
Cardigan
Cowichan
Crew-neck
Fairisle
Guernsey
Polo neck
Pullover
Rollneck

Slipover

9 letters:
Icelandic
Sloppy joe

10 letters:
Cowl-necked
Crew-necked
Sweatshirt
Turtleneck

Swellings

3 letters:
Wen

4 letters:
Bump
Cyst
Gout

Kibe
Lump
Stye

5 letters:
Mouse
Tuber

Whelk

6 letters:
Bunion
Epulis
Goiter
Goitre

Swimming strokes → Swiss cantons

Lampas
Oedema
Struma
Tumour
Warble

7 letters:
Blister
Chancre
Entasis
Lampers

8 letters:
Anasarca

Aneurysm
Capellet
Farcy-bud
Hematoma
Lampasse
Odontoma
Ox-warble
Pulvinus
Scirrhus
Teratoma
Tubercle
Windgall
Xanthoma

9 letters:
Adenomata
Apophysis
Chilblain
Haematoma
Hydrocele
Parotitis

10 letters:
Scleriasis

13 letters:
Elephantiasis

Swimming strokes

5 letters:
Crawl

7 letters:
Trudgen

8 letters:
Buttefly

9 letters:
Back crawl
Freestyle

10 letters:
Backstroke
Front crawl
Sidestroke

11 letters:
Doggy-paddle

12 letters:
Breaststroke

20 letters:
Inverted breaststroke

Swiss cantons

3 letters:
Uri
Zug

4 letters:
Bern
Jura
Vaud

5 letters:
Berne

6 letters:
Aargau
Genève
Glarus
Luzern
Schwyz
Ticino

Valais
Wallis
Zürich

7 letters:
Thurgau

8 letters:
Freiburg
Fribourg
Obwalden

9 letters:
Neuchâtel
Nidwalden
Solothurn

10 letters:
Basel-Stadt

Graubünden

11 letters:
Sankt Gallen

12 letters:
Schaffhausen

15 letters:
Basel-Landschaft

20 letters:
Appenzell-Innerrhoden

21 letters:
Appenzell-
  Ausserrhoden

Swords and other weapons with blades

4 letters:
Bill
Chiv
Dirk
Épée
Foil
Kris
Pike

5 letters:
Bilbo
Broad
Estoc
Jerid
Kendo
Knife
Kukri
Saber
Sabre
Skean
Spear
Sword

6 letters:
Anlace
Curtax
Dagger
Espada
Glaive
Gleave
Hanger
Jereed
Katana
Khanda
Kirpan
Parang
Rapier
Toledo
Tulwar

7 letters:
Anelace
Assagai
Assegai
Ataghan
Balmung
Bayonet
Curtana
Cutlass
Gladius
Halberd
Hatchet
Jerreed
Machete
Morglay
Poleaxe
Poniard
Semitar
Shabble
Spirtle
Spurtle
Whinger
Yatagan

8 letters:
Cemitare
Claymore
Curtal-ax
Falchion
Faulchin
Partisan
Schlager
Scimitar
Semitaur
Sgian-dhu
Skene-dhu
Spadroon
Spontoon

Stiletto
Stone axe
Tomahawk
Whiniard
Whinyard
White-arm
Yataghan

9 letters:
Arondight
Backsword
Balisarda
Battle-axe
Damascene
Excalibur
Faulchion
Jackknife
Schiavone

10 letters:
Angurvadel
Bowie knife
Broadsword
Smallsword
Swordstick

11 letters:
Sheath knife
Snickersnee
Trench knife

12 letters:
Spurtleblade
Sword bayonet

13 letters:
Andrew Ferrara

T t

Tables and desks

3 letters:
Bar

4 letters:
Desk

6 letters:
Buffet
Bureau
Carrel
Lowboy
Teapoy

7 letters:
Counter

8 letters:
Lapboard
Tea table

9 letters:
Card table
Davenport
Drum table

Side table
Wool table
Workbench
Worktable

10 letters:
Escritoire
Secretaire
Tea trolley
Traymobile

11 letters:
Coffee table
Dining table
Reading desk
Roll-top desk
Writing desk

12 letters:
Bedside table
Breakfast bar
Console table
Folding table

Gate-leg table
Kitchen table
Nest of tables
Pedestal desk
Snooker table
Trestle table
Writing table

13 letters:
Billiard table
Dressing table
Drop-leaf table
Pembroke table
Piecrust table

14 letters:
Breakfast table
Refectory table

15 letters:
Gate-legged table
Occasional table

Teas

4 letters:
Beef
Bush
Herb
Maté
Mint

5 letters:
Assam
Black
Bohea
China
Congo
Grass

Green
Hyson
Ledum
Lemon
Pekoe
Senna
Yerba

6 letters:
Ceylon
Congou
Herbal
Indian
Oolong

Oulong

7 letters:
Chanoyu
Chinese
Gunfire
Jasmine
Lapsang
Red-root
Rooibos
Russian
Twankay

8 letters:
Camomile
Earl Grey
Labrador
Paraguay
Souchong

9 letters:
Chamomile
Gunpowder

10 letters:
Darjeeling

11 letters:
Orange pekoe
Post-and-rail
Yerba de Maté

15 letters:
Lapsang Souchong

Teeth

5 letters:
Molar

6 letters:
Canine

7 letters:
Incisor

8 letters:
Premolar

9 letters:
Foretooth

11 letters:
Wisdom tooth

Tennis terms

3 letters:
Ace
Let
Lob
Net
Set

4 letters:
Ball
Chip
Game
Love

5 letters:
Court
Deuce
Fault
Match
Rally
Slice
Smash

6 letters:
Racket
Return
Server
Umpire

Volley

7 letters:
Doubles
Net cord
Racquet
Service
Singles
Topspin

8 letters:
Backhand
Baseline
Drop shot
Forehand
Line call
Linesman
Love game
Receiver
Set point
Sideline
Tie-break
Tramline
Undercut

9 letters:
Advantage

Clay court
Foot fault
Forecourt
Hard court

10 letters:
Break point
Cannonball
Centre line
Centre mark
Grass court
Half-volley
Lawn tennis
Tiebreaker

11 letters:
Double fault
Passing shot
Service line

12 letters:
Approach shot
Break of serve
Ground stroke
Mixed doubles

Tennis players

MALE

4 letters:
Ashe, *Arthur*
Borg, *Bjorn*
Cash, *Pat*
Moya, *Carlos*
Rios, *Marcelo*

5 letters:
Blake, *James*
Canas, *Guillermo*
Costa, *Albert*
Laver, *Rod*
Lendl, *Ivan*
Lloyd, *John*
Novak, *Jiri*
Perry, *Fred*
Roche, *Tony*
Safin, *Marat*
Vilas, *Guillermo*

6 letters:
Agassi, *Andre*
Becker, *Boris*
Edberg, *Stefan*
Henman, *Tim*
Hewitt, *Lleyton*
Rafter, *Pat*

7 letters:
Amitraj, *Vijay*
Connors, *Jimmy*
Emerson, *Roy*
Federer, *Roger*
Ferrero, *Juan Carlos*
Gambill, *Jan-Michael*
Maskell, *Dan*
McEnroe, *John*
Nastase, *Ilie*
Roddick, *Andy*

Sampras, *Pete*

8 letters:
Corretja, *Alex*
Gonzalez, *Fernando*
Grosjean, *Sebastien*
Newcombe, *John*
Rosewall, *Ken*
Rusedski, *Greg*
Schalken, *Sjeng*

10 letters:
Ivanisevic, *Goran*
Kafelnikov, *Yevgeny*
Nalbandian, *David*
Srichaphan, *Paradorn*

13 letters:
Philippoussis, *Mark*

FEMALE

4 letters:
Graf, *Steffi*
King, *Billie-Jean*
Wade, *Virginia*

5 letters:
Bueno, *Maria*
Court, *Margaret*
Dokic, *Jelena*
Evert, *Chris*
Jones, *Ann*
Rubin, *Chanda*
Seles, *Monica*
Stove, *Betty*

6 letters:
Barker, *Sue*
Casals, *Rosie*

Cawley, *Evonne*
Farina, *Silvia*
Hingis, *Martina*

7 letters:
Maleeva, *Magdalena*
Myskina, *Anastasia*
Novotna, *Jana*

8 letters:
Capriati, *Jennifer*
Mauresmo, *Amelie*
Sabatini, *Gabriela*
Williams, *Serena*
Williams, *Venus*

9 letters:
Clijsters, *Kim*

Davenport, *Lindsay*
Goolagong, *Evonne*
Pistolesi, *Anna*
Stevenson, *Alexandra*

10 letters:
Hantuchova, *Daniela*
Kournikova, *Anna*

11 letters:
Navratilova, *Martina*

13 letters:
Henin-Hardenne, *Justine*

14 letters:
Sanchez-Vicario,
  Arantxa

New Zealand territories

4 letters:
Niue

7 letters:
Tokelau

11 letters:
Cook Islands

12 letters:
Union Islands

14 letters:
Ross Dependency

Theatre terms

3 letters:
Act
Cue
Ham

4 letters:
Exit
Flat
Gods
Prop
Role

5 letters:
Flies
Fluff
House
Lines
Scene
Stage
Wings

6 letters:
Chorus
Circle
Corpse
Prompt
Script
Speech
Stalls

7 letters:
Curtain
Gallery
Overact

Resting
Scenery
Unities
Upstage

8 letters:
Crush bar
Entr'acte
Entrance
Juvenile
Offstage
Prompter
Scene bay
Thespian

9 letters:
Backstage
Downstage
Greenroom
Monologue
Noises off
Orchestra
Scene dock
Soliloquy
Soubrette
Stage door
Stagehand
Stage left

10 letters:
First night
Leading man
Opera house
Stage right

Understudy

11 letters:
Catastrophe
Curtain call
Greasepaint
Leading lady
Off-Broadway
Stage fright
Stage-struck

12 letters:
Front of house
Orchestra pit
Stage manager
Stage whisper

13 letters:
Coup de théâtre
Curtain-raiser
Curtain speech

14 letters:
Off-off-Broadway
Proscenium arch
Stage direction

16 letters:
Comédie Française
Dramatis personae
First-night nerves

17 letters:
Theatre-in-the-round

Ties and cravats

3 letters:
Boa
Tie

5 letters:
Ascot
Dicky
Fichu
Scarf
Stock
Stole

6 letters:
Bertha
Bow tie

Cravat
Madras
Rebozo

7 letters:
Foulard
Muffler
Necktie

8 letters:
Black tie
Carcanet
Dicky bow
Kerchief

White tie

9 letters:
Comforter
Neckcloth
School tie

10 letters:
Windsor tie

11 letters:
Falling band
Neckerchief

Time

RELATED VOCABULARY

2 letters:
AD
Am
BC
Mo
Pm

3 letters:
Age
Ago
Aye
Day
Due
E'en
E'er
Eld
Eos
Era
Ere
Eve
May
Oft
Old
Sec
Ult
Yet

4 letters:
Aeon
Ages
Anon
Ante
Date
Dawn
Dial
Dusk
Even
Ever
Fall
Fast
Fore
Ides
Inst
Jiff
July
June
Late
Lent
Moon
Morn
Next
Noel
Noon
Once

Over
Past
Post
Prox
Slow
Soon
Span
Term
Then
Tick
Tide
Till
Time
Unto
Week
When
Xmas
Year
Yore
Yule

5 letters:
Again
Annum
April
As yet
Brief

RELATED VOCABULARY (CONTINUED)

Clock
Cycle
Daily
Dekad
Delay
Diary
Early
Epact
Epoch
Fasti
Flash
Jiffy
Later
March
Matin
Month
Never
Night
Nonce
Nones
Often
Passe
Pause
Point
Prime
Prior
Purim
Ready
Shake
Sharp
Short
Since
So far
Space
Spell
Still
Style
Sunup
Tempo
Today
Trice
Until
Watch
While
Years
Young
Youth

6 letters:
Actual
Advent
Always
Annual
At once
August
Aurora
Autumn
Bairam
Brumal
Coeval
Coming
Crisis
Curfew
Decade
Dotage
During
Easter
Elapse
Ere now
Extant
Ferial
Friday
Future
Gnomon
Heyday
Hiemal
Hourly
Ice age
In time
Jet age
Julian
Lammas
Lapsed
Lately
Latest
Latish
Lustre
Manana
May day
Midday
Minute
Modern
Moment
Monday
Morrow
New day

O'clock
Off-day
Of late
Old age
One day
On time
Period
Presto
Pre-war
Prompt
Pronto
Rarely
Recent
Season
Second
Seldom
Sooner
Spring
Sudden
Summer
Sunday
Sunset
Timely
To date
Update
Vernal
Vesper
Weekly
Whilst
Winter
Yearly
Yester

7 letters:
Abiding
Ack emma
Ageless
Ages ago
All over
Almanac
Already
Ancient
Anytime
Archaic
At night
Bedtime
Belated
Betimes

RELATED VOCABULARY (CONTINUED)

Boyhood	Mid-week	**8 letters:**
By-and-by	Monthly	Abruptly
Calends	Morning	A long day
Century	Newborn	Antedate
Chiliad	New Year	As soon as
Current	Nightly	Biannual
Dawning	Noonday	Biennial
Daylong	October	Birthday
Day-peep	One-time	Biweekly
Daytime	Overdue	Blue moon
Diurnal	Pending	Brumaire
Dog days	Pip emma	Calendar
Earlier	Postwar	Civil day
Elapsed	Present	Darkling
Endless	Pro term	Date line
Epochal	Proximo	Daybreak
Equinox	Quarter	Daylight
Estival	Quondam	Deadline
Evening	Ramadan	December
Exactly	Ripe age	Derby day
Expired	Sabbath	Directly
Extinct	Secular	Dogwatch
Fast day	Shortly	Doomsday
Flag day	Sine die	Duration
Forever	Some day	Eggtimer
For good	Stretch	Enduring
For life	Sukkoth	Entr'acte
Harvest	Sundial	Epiphany
High day	Sundown	Eternity
History	Sunrise	Eventide
Holiday	Teenage	Evermore
Holy day	Tertian	Every day
Infancy	This day	Evil hour
Instant	Time-lag	Fast time
Interim	Time was	Feast day
Iron Age	Tonight	February
January	Too late	Fleeting
Journal	Too soon	Foredawn
Jubilee	Tuesday	Forenoon
Just now	Twinkle	Formerly
Kalends	Two two's	Frequent
Lady day	Unready	Gain time
Long ago	Up to now	Gloaming
Long run	Usually	Half hour
Lustrum	Weekday	Half past
Manhood	Weekend	Hanukkah
Manhour	Whereon	Hereunto
Matinal	Whitsun	Hibernal

RELATED VOCABULARY (CONTINUED)

High time
Hitherto
Hogmanay
Holy days
Holy week
Horology
Ill-timed
In a flash
In a trice
Infinity
In future
In no time
In season
Interval
Juncture
Keep time
Kill time
Lang syne
Last time
Last week
Lateness
Latterly
Leap year
Lifelong
Life-span
Lifetime
Livelong
Long time
Lord's day
Lose time
Lunation
Mark time
Mean time
Medieval
Menology
Meridian
Meteoric
Midnight
Momently
Natal day
New Style
Next week
Noontide
Noontime
Not often
November
Nowadays
Obsolete

Occasion
Ofttimes
Old times
On the dot
Our times
Passover
Pass time
Postdate
Postpone
Previous
Promptly
Punctual
Recently
Right now
Ringtime
Saturday
Seasonal
Seedtime
Semester
Solar day
Solstice
Some time
Space Age
Sporadic
Steel Age
Suddenly
Take time
Temporal
This week
Thursday
Timeless
Time-worn
Tomorrow
Too early
Twilight
Ultimate
Until now
Untimely
Up-to-date
Weeklong
Whenever
Year-book
Yearlong
Years ago
Yoretime
Yuletide

9 letters:
Adulthood
Afternoon
After that
After time
All at once
Antiquity
Atomic Age
At present
Bimonthly
Boxing Day
Bronze Age
Candlemas
Canicular
Centenary
Childhood
Christmas
Chronicle
Civil time
Civil year
Clepsydra
Continual
Crepuscle
Days of old
Dayspring
Decennary
Decennial
Decennium
Due season
Earliness
Early bird
Ember days
Empire Day
Ephemeral
Ephemeris
Epochally
Erstwhile
Ever since
Every hour
Far future
First time
Foregoing
Forthwith
Fortnight
From now on
Gnomonics
Golden Age
Great year

RELATED VOCABULARY (CONTINUED)

Gregorian
Hallowe'en
Hallowmas
Happy days
Hereafter
Honeymoon
Hourglass
Immediacy
Immediate
In a second
In due time
Instanter
Instantly
Interlude
In the past
Julian day
Lammas day
Later date
Latter day
Light year
Local time
Longevity
Long-lived
Long since
Long spell
Long while
Lunar year
Many a time
Many times
Mardi Gras
Martinmas
Mature age
Matutinal
Meanwhile
Mediaeval
Menstrual
Metronome
Midday sun
Middle age
Midsummer
Midwinter
Mistiming
Momentary
Monthlong
Nevermore
Nightfall
Nightlong
Nighttide

Night time
Nocturnal
Octenniel
Oftentime
Opportune
Out of date
Overnight
Pentecost
Perennial
Permanent
Postcenal
Preceding
Precisely
Premature
Presently
Quarterly
Quarter to
Quotidian
Recurrent
Regularly
Remote age
Right time
Saint's day
Salad days
Sandglass
Semestral
September
Short term
Short time
Solar time
Solar year
Sometimes
Space time
Spare time
Spend time
Stop watch
Swiss plan
Temporary
Temporize
Therewith
Till death
Time being
Time check
Time clock
Time flies
Time limit
Time of day
Timepiece

Times past
Timetable
To this day
Transient
Triennial
Twinkling
Two shakes
Upon which
Vicennial
Waste time
Wednesday
Well-timed
Wherefore
Whereunto
Whereupon
Wrong time
Yesterday

10 letters:
Afterwards
After which
Alarm clock
Allhallows
All the time
Anno Domini
At all times
At that time
At this time
Beforehand
Before long
Beforetime
Behindhand
Behind time
Better days
Break of day
Bygone days
By the clock
Centennial
Childermas
Chronogram
Chronology
Close of day
Common time
Consequent
Constantly
Continuous
Cosmic time
Crepuscule

RELATED VOCABULARY (CONTINUED)

Days gone by
Days of yore
Eastertide
Easter time
Evanescent
Eventually
Father's day
Father Time
Fiscal year
Fleetingly
Frequently
Futuristic
Generation
Good Friday
Half a jiffy
Half an hour
Half a shake
Hardly ever
Hebdomadal
Hebrew Year
Henceforth
Here and now
Heretofore
Historical
Immemorial
Incidental
In good time
Invariably
Isochronon
Julian year
Just in time
Lammastide
Last chance
Last minute
Lententide
Lunar month
Methuselah
Michaelmas
Middle-aged
Middle Ages
Midmorning
Millennium
Moratorium
Mother's day
Near future
Nick of time
Now or never
Occasional

Of the clock
Olden times
One fine day
On occasion
On the eve of
Palm Sunday
Posthumous
Prehistory
Present day
Previously
Proper time
Repeatedly
Retrospect
Ripe old age
Sabbath day
Seasonable
Semiweekly
Septennial
Sextennial
Short spell
Small hours
Soon enough
Springtide
Springtime
Subsequent
Summertide
Summertime
Thereafter
This minute
Time-keeper
Timeliness
Time signal
Time to come
Time to kill
Transitory
Tricennial
Triple time
Ultimately
Very seldom
Vespertime
Water clock
Wedding day
Whensoever
Whitmonday
Whitsunday
Wintertide
Wintertime
With the sun

Wristwatch
Years on end
Yesteryear

11 letters:
Adjournment
Adolescence
After-dinner
Against time
Ahead of time
All Fools day
All Souls day
Anachronism
Anniversary
At intervals
Bicentenary
Bygone times
Ceaselessly
Chronograph
Chronometer
Chronoscope
Coincidence
Concurrence
Continually
Crack of dawn
Crepuscular
Cuckoo clock
Day after day
Day and night
Day in day out
Dead of night
Endless time
Ever and a day
Ever and anon
Everlasting
Every moment
Fin de siècle
Flower of age
For evermore
Former times
Fortnightly
Gay Nineties
Golden hours
Good old days
Halcyon days
Half a second
Hebdomadary
Hereinafter

RELATED VOCABULARY (CONTINUED)

Ides of March
Immediately
In an instant
Incessantly
In due course
Inopportune
Intercalary
Interregnum
Judgment day
Lapse of time
Leisure time
Little while
Livelong day
Long-lasting
Long overdue
March of time
Microsecond
Middle years
Millisecond
Modern times
Momentarily
Morningtide
Morningtime
Never-ending
New Year's day
New Year's eve
Night and day
Once or twice
Opportunely
Opportunity
Out of season
Passion week
Penultimate
Perennially
Perfect year
Perpetually
Play for time
Point of time
Present time
Prime of life
Promptitude
Punctuality
Quadrennial
Quarter past
Rogation Day
Sands of time
Semi-monthly
Shining hour

Short notice
Some time ago
Split second
Straightway
Synchronism
Synchronize
Tempus fugit
Thenceforth
The other day
This morning
This very day
Time and tide
Time drags by
Time machine
Time to spare
Turret clock
Twelvemonth
Ultramodern
Waiting time
Whitsuntide
With the lark
Year of Grace

12 letters:
All of a sudden
All Saints Day
A long time ago
Ancient times
Annunciation
Antediluvian
Ante meridiem
Antemeridien
Armistice day
Ascension day
Ash Wednesday
Auld lang syne
Bide one's time
Calendar year
Christmas day
Christmas eve
Consequently
Contemporary
Course of time
Decisive hour
Decline of day
Donkey's years
Eleventh hour
Feast of Weeks

Following day
Fourth of July
From that time
Greek calends
Holy Thursday
In days of yore
Indian summer
Innocents day
In olden times
Intermission
Late in the day
Long-standing
Many a long day
Metachronism
Nychthemaron
Occasionally
Old-fashioned
Once in a while
On the instant
On the morroww
Parachronism
Periodically
Postdiluvian
Postmeridiem
Postponement
Postprandial
Quadrigesima
Quinquennial
Quinquennium
Rare occasion
Red letter day
Sempiternity
Sidereal time
Simultaneous
Stall for time
Standard time
Still of night
Stitch in time
Synodic month
Tercentenary
The dawn of day
Then and there
The year round
Time and again
Time-honoured
Timelessness
Time will tell
Turning point

RELATED VOCABULARY (CONTINUED)

Twelfth night
Twelve o'clock
Unseasonable
Witching hour
Without delay

13 letters:
Again and again
All Hallow's eve
April fool's day
Ascensiontide
At short notice
Broad daylight
Calendar month
Christmas-tide
Christmas-time
Chronographer
Chronological
Days of the week
Every few hours
Every few years
Every other day
Financial year
For the present
From the outset
From the word go
Generation gap
Getting on a bit
Golden jubilee
Golden wedding
Greenwich time
Michaelmas day
Old as the hills
Once upon a time
Passion Sunday
Quincentenary
Quinquagesima
Retrospective
Right up to date
Roman calendar
Round the clock
Shrove Tuesday
Silver jubilee
Silver wedding
Some of the time
Some other time
Sooner or later
Speaking clock

St Crispin's day
St Luke's summer
St Swithin's day
Summer holiday
Synchronology
The time is ripe
Time after time
Time marches on
Time of arrival
Time out of mind
Tomorrow night
Trinity Sunday
Tropical month
Turn of the year
Up-to-the-minute
Up with the lark
Vernal equinox
Week in, week out
Year in, year out

14 letters:
Advancing years
Before and after
Behind schedule
Breathing space
Chronometrical
Day in and day out
Daylight saving
Declining years
Diamond jubilee
Diamond wedding
During the night
Easter holidays
For ever and a day
For ever and ever
For the duration
From time to time
Fullness of time
Geological time
In ancient times
In course of time
Interval of time
In the afternoon
In the beginning
In the meanwhile
Julian calendar
Keep early hours
Maundy Thursday

Midsummer night
Month of Sundays
Pancake Tuesday
Past and present
Remembrance Day
Sabbatical year
Septuagenarian
Walpurgis night
Witches' Sabbath

15 letters:
Against the clock
Ahead of schedule
Chronologically
Contemporaneity
Contemporaneous
Continental time
Continuation day
Dominical letter
Equinoctial year
Every now and then
For a year and a day
Fourth dimension
How goes the enemy
In the nick of time
Month after month
Months and months
Months of the year
Mothering Sunday
Night after night
Once in a blue moon
Once in a lifetime
Put back the clock
Put the clock back
Retrospectively
Spur of the moment
St Valentine's day
Thanksgiving day
The morning after
This year of grace
Tomorrow evening
Tomorrow morning
World without end

16 letters:
Quartercentenary

GREGORIAN CALENDAR

January	May	September
February	June	October
March	July	November
April	August	December

JEWISH CALENDAR

Tishri	Shebat	Tammuz
Cheshvan	Adar	Av
Heshvan	Nisan	Ab
Kislev	Iyar	Elul
Tevet	Iyyar	
Shevat	Sivan	

MUSLIM CALENDAR

Muharram	Jumada I	Rhamadhan
Moharram	Jumada II	Ramazan
Safar	Rajab	Shawwal
Saphar	Shaban	Dhu'l-Qa'dah
Rabia I	Shaaban	Dhu'l-Hijjah
Rabia II	Ramadan	

FRENCH REVOLUTIONARY CALENDAR

Vendémiaire	Ventôse	Thermidor
Brumaire	Germinal	Fervidor
Frimaire	Floréal	Fructidor
Nivôse	Prairial	
Pluviôse	Messidor	

TIME ZONES

17 letters:
British Summer Time
Greenwich Mean Time
Yukon Daylight Time
Yukon Standard Time

19 letters:
Central Daylight Time
Central European Time
Central Standard Time
Eastern Daylight Time
Eastern Standard Time

Pacific Daylight Time
Pacific Standard Time

20 letters:
Atlantic Daylight Time
Atlantic Standard Time
Mountain Daylight Time
Mountain Standard Time

24 letters:
Newfoundland Daylight Time
Newfoundland Standard Time

Tobacco

TYPES OF TOBACCO

4 letters:
Shag

5 letters:
Snout
Snuff

6 letters:
Burley
Filler
Rappee

7 letters:
Caporal

Perique
Sumatra
Turkish

8 letters:
Canaster
Makhorka
Maryland
Virginia

9 letters:
Broadleaf
Fire-cured

Flue-cured

11 letters:
Cigar binder
Cigar filler

12 letters:
Cigar wrapper
Dark air-cured

14 letters:
Chewing tobacco
Cuban cigar leaf

TYPES OF CIGAR AND CIGARETTE

5 letters:
Breva
Claro
Stogy

6 letters:
Concha
Corona
Havana
Maduro

Manila
Roll-up
Stogey

7 letters:
Cheroot

8 letters:
Perfecto
Puritano

9 letters:
Cigarillo
Imperiale
Panatella

10 letters:
Tailor-made

11 letters:
Roll-your-own

PIPES

4 letters:
Clay

5 letters:
Briar
Peace

6 letters:
Hookah

7 letters:
Corncob

8 letters:
Calabash

10 letters:
Meerschaum

12 letters:
Churchwarden
Hubble-bubble

GENERAL SMOKING TERMS

3 letters:
Ash

4 letters:
Bowl

Butt
Pipe
Plug
Stem

5 letters:
Flint

6 letters:
Dottle

GENERAL SMOKING TERMS (CONTINUED)

Smoker
Splint

Rollings
Snuffbox

7 letters:
Ashtray
Humidor
Lighter
Makings
Matches
Pigtail

8 letters:
Calabash
Pipe rack

9 letters:
Filter tip
Smoke room

11 letters:
Pipe cleaner
Smoking room
Tobacconist

12 letters:
Tobacco pouch

13 letters:
Cigarette case
Smoking jacket

14 letters:
Cigarette paper

15 letters:
Cigarette holder

18 letters:
Smoking compartment

Tools

3 letters:
Awl
Axe
Bit
Gab
Gad
Hob
Hoe
Saw
Sax

4 letters:
Bosh
Comb
File
Fork
Froe
Frow
Hack
Hone
Maul
Pick
Rake
Spud

5 letters:
Auger
Borer
Broad
Burin

Clink
Croze
Drift
Drill
Drove
Facer
Float
Gavel
Kevel
Plane
Punch
Shave
Slick
Snake
Spade
Swage

6 letters:
Beetle
Bodkin
Broach
Chaser
Chisel
Comber
Cradle
Dibble
Fillet
Flange
Former
Fraise

Fuller
Gimlet
Gouger
Graver
Gympie
Hammer
Jumper
Mallet
Padsaw
Pestle
Pliers
Rabble
Ripple
Rocker
Router
Sander
Scutch
Scythe
Shears
Sickle
Spider
Stylus
Trepan
Trowel
Wimble
Wrench

7 letters:
Bolster
Dresser

Towns

Flatter
Ice pick
Jointer
Mattock
Nibbler
Nippers
Rabbler
Rounder
Scauper
Scorper
Scriber
Slasher
Spanner
Spudder

8 letters:
Allen key
Billhook
Bitstock
Clippers
Driftpin
Edge tool
Screw tap
Scutcher
Stiletto

9 letters:
Alligator
Drawknife
Drawshave
Eyeleteer

10 letters:
Bushhammer
Claw hammer
Cold chisel
Drill press
Hack hammer
Icebreaker
Jackhammer
Piledriver
Power drill
Tack hammer
Tilt hammer
Triphammer

11 letters:
Brace and bit
Centre punch
Countersink
Drove chisel
Hammer drill

Mitre square
Ploughstaff
Pruning hook
Screwdriver
Spitsticker

12 letters:
Diamond point
Firmer chisel
Floatcut file
Monkey wrench
Pitching tool
Sledgehammer

13 letters:
Rawhide hammer
Soldering iron

14 letters:
Ball-peen hammer
Knapping hammer
Percussion tool

15 letters:
Half-round chisel
Pneumatic hammer

Towns

3 letters:
Ems
Gao
Ife
Lod
Niš
Spa
Zug

4 letters:
Agen
Albi
Asti
Biel
Bury
Bute
Cheb
Cork
Deal
Edam

Eton
Genk
Györ
Hamm
Hove
Hyde
Kent
Lens
León
Lodi
Mayo
Melk
Mons
Mull
Niue
Oahu
Sale
Sfax
Skye
Thun

Toul
Trim
Tyre
Wick

5 letters:
Aarau
Aduwa
Ahwaz
Aksum
Alloa
Alost
Aosta
Arlon
Arras
Aruba
Ascot
Aswan
Aulis
Aydin

Balkh
Banff
Bohol
Capua
Cavan
Clare
Cluny
Conwy
Copán
Corby
Cowes
Crewe
Daman
Delft
Dinan
Doorn
Dubna
Egham
Elche
Elgin
Emmen
Ennis
Epsom
Esher
Faial
Flint
Gotha
Gouda
Hilla
Hotan
Ikeja
Ipsus
Irbid
Issus
Izmit
Jerez
Jinja
Kauai
Kells
Kerry
Korçë
Krems
Lahti
Laois
Leigh
Lewes
Leyte
Lorca
Louth
Luton

Luxor
Lydia
Maraş
Massa
Meath
Namur
Negev
Nikko
Niort
Noyon
Öland
Omagh
Ostia
Otago
Pavia
Pelée
Pemba
Płock
Ponce
Pydna
Qeshm
Rugby
Sedan
Sibiu
Sitka
Skien
Sligo
Stans
Ta`izz
Tomsk
Tours
Trier
Truro
Ujiji
Upolu
Vaduz
Vichy
Wigan
Youth
Ypres
Zarqa

6 letters:
Abydos
Actium
Aegina
Agadir
Almada
Al Marj
Amalfi

Anadyr
Antrim
Anyang
Armagh
Arnold
Ashdod
Assisi
Atbara
Aveiro
Ayodha
Bangor
Bastia
Batley
Battle
Bauchi
Bayeux
Bethel
Bingen
Biskra
Bodmin
Bolton
Bouaké
Brecon
Butung
Buxton
Can Tho
Carlow
Celaya
Cognac
Crosby
Cuenca
Dachau
Dawson
Denton
Deurne
Dinant
Dodona
Dudley
Dunoon
Eccles
Edessa
Edirne
Epping
Évreux
Flores
Forfar
Galway
Gibeon
Glarus
Guyana

Hameln
Harlow
Havant
Hawick
Huambo
Huesca
Hwange
Ilesha
Ilkley
Irvine
Kalisz
Kendal
Kirkby
Kiruna
Kokura
Kumasi
Labuan
Lashio
Latina
Lemnos
Lesbos
Lombok
Ludlow
Lugano
Lützen
Macapá
Maldon
Medway
Megara
Menton
Merano
Mérida
Miseno
Morley
Nablus
Nakuru
Nelson
Newark
Oakham
Offaly
Oldham
Örebro
Osijek
Ottawa
Owerri
Pernik
Phuket
Pleven
Poitou
Pudsey

Ragusa
Rashid
Rijeka
Sarnen
Schwyz
Sennar
Sestos
Seveso
Shache
Shiloh
Sintra
Slough
Sokoto
Soweto
Tarbes
Tivoli
Tralee
Tyumen
Verdun
Vienne
Warley
Welkom
Widnes
Woking
Zabrze
Zwolle

7 letters:
Airdrie
Alençon
Ålesund
Al Hufuf
Almadén
Altdorf
Amboise
Antibes
Appleby
Armenia
Arundel
Ashford
Augusta
Auxerre
Baalbek
Bacolod
Bamberg
Banbury
Bedford
Belfort
Bien Hoa
Blaydon

Bonaire
Burnley
Cabimas
Cambrai
Cannock
Carlton
Carrara
Caserta
Cassino
Chatham
Cholula
Chorley
Clacton
Clonmel
Colditz
Concord
Consett
Corinth
Cortona
Crawley
Crotone
Cwmbran
Cythera
Devizes
Dhahran
Donegal
Donetsk
Dongola
Douglas
Dundalk
Eleusis
Entebbe
Evesham
Exmouth
Falkirk
Falster
Fareham
Farnham
Fashoda
Felling
Fiesole
Görlitz
Gosport
Halifax
Harlech
Hasselt
Herisau
Heywood
Hoylake
Ipswich

699

Towns

Iqaluit
Karbala
Keswick
Khojent
Kildare
Kutaisi
La Línea
La Palma
Legnica
Leitrim
Lerwick
Leuctra
Lifford
Lisieux
Locarno
Lourdes
Louvain
Malvern
Margate
Matlock
Megiddo
Meissen
Melilla
Minorca
Morpeth
Moulins
Newbury
Newport
Newtown
Numidia
Okinawa
Olsztyn
Orvieto
Otranto
Paisley
Papeete
Peebles
Penrith
Pereira
Plovdiv
Punakha
Pushkin
Reading
Red Deer
Reigate
Renfrew
Runcorn
Sagunto
Saint-Lô
Segovia

Setúbal
Seville
Shakhty
Sheppey
Shkodër
Skipton
Sovetsk
Staines
Stanley
Swindon
Tampere
Tanagra
Taunton
Telford
Thapsus
Tobolsk
Torquay
Tripoli
Tutuila
Urmston
Üsküdar
Valence
Vellore
Walsall
Warwick
Watford
Wexford
Wicklow
Windsor
Wisbech
Woomera
Worksop
Wrexham
Zaandam
Zealand

8 letters:
Abeokuta
Aberdare
Abingdon
Amravati
Aquileia
Armidale
Aubusson
Aycliffe
Ballarat
Banstead
Barbados
Barnsley
Basildon

Bastogne
Beauvais
Bedworth
Benfleet
Beverley
Biarritz
Billiton
Boa Vista
Bornholm
Budapest
Buraydah
Caerleon
Calabria
Campania
Chamonix
Chartres
Chepstow
Chertsey
Cheshunt
Chigwell
Courtrai
Damietta
Dartford
Daventry
Demerara
Dewsbury
Dumfries
Ebbw Vale
El Faiyûm
Erlangen
Fribourg
Galloway
Golconda
Grantham
Guernica
Hamilton
Hastings
Hatfield
Hertford
Hinckley
Holyhead
Ilkeston
Jemappes
Junagadh
Keighley
Kerkrade
Kilkenny
Kirkwall
Le Cateau
Limerick

Llandaff
Llanelli
Longford
Lüneburg
Lyonnais
Mafikeng
Mainland
Maitland
Manassas
Maubeuge
Mézières
Mindanao
Monaghan
Monmouth
Montreux
Mufulira
Murmansk
Nanterre
Nazareth
Nijmegen
Nishapur
Normandy
Nuneaton
Omdurman
Paignton
Pembroke
Penzance
Peterlee
Piacenza
Piedmont
Portland
Redditch
Richmond
Rijswijk
Rochdale
Rothesay
Sabadell
Sarajevo
Seremban
Solihull
Spalding
Stafford
Subotica
Tamworth
Ternopol
Timbuktu
Touraine
Tübingen
Uxbridge
Viti Levu

Wallasey
Wallsend
Waterloo
Zlatoust
Zululand

9 letters:
Abbeville
Agrigento
Alcántara
Aldershot
Ambleside
Apeldoorn
Appenzell
Auschwitz
Aylesbury
Bebington
Beersheba
Bethlehem
Bethsaida
Blackpool
Bracknell
Brentwood
Brighouse
Capernaum
Castlebar
Chaeronea
Chantilly
Charleroi
Chernobyl
Chiengmai
Chinatown
Clydebank
Coleraine
Colwyn Bay
Deauville
Dodge City
Dolgellau
Doncaster
Dumbarton
Dunstable
Eastleigh
Elizabeth
Esslingen
Five Towns
Gällivare
Galwegian
Gelligaer
Godesberg
Gold Coast

Gütersloh
Halesowen
Harrogate
Inveraray
Jamestown
Kettering
Killarney
King's Lynn
Kitchener
Kitzbühel
Lambaréné
Lancaster
Le Creusot
Llandudno
Lockerbie
Long Eaton
Los Alamos
Lower Hutt
Lymington
Maidstone
Mansfield
Middleton
Mullingar
Neuchâtel
Newmarket
New Romney
Northwich
Ogbomosho
Paderborn
Palm Beach
Périgueux
Perpignan
Pharsalus
Pontypool
Portadown
Port Royal
Prestwich
Prestwick
Princeton
Roscommon
Rotherham
Saint Gall
Saint-Ouen
Salamanca
Santa Cruz
Sherborne
Solothurn
Sosnowiec
Southport
Stevenage

Stockport
Stralsund
Stranraer
Stretford
Surakarta
Tipperary
Tombstone
Tonbridge
Tourcoing
Tullamore
Vancouver
Viareggio
Wadi Halfa
Wad Medani
Waterford
Westmeath
Woodstock
Worcester
Wuppertal

10 letters:
Accrington
Altrincham
Amersfoort
Anderlecht
Austerlitz
Barnstaple
Bellinzona
Bennington
Bridgwater
Bromsgrove
Buckingham
Caerphilly
Canterbury
Carmarthen
Castleford
Chadderton
Cheltenham
Ciudad Real
Coatbridge
Colchester
Coldstream
Darjeeling
Darlington
Dorchester
Eisenstadt
Ffestiniog
Frauenfeld
Galashiels
Gettysburg

Gillingham
Glenrothes
Hammerfest
High Street
Huntingdon
Interlaken
Kalgoorlie
Kapfenberg
Kenilworth
Kilmarnock
Kragujevac
Letchworth
Leverkusen
Linlithgow
Livingston
Llangollen
Longbenton
Los Angeles
Maidenhead
Middelburg
Monte Carlo
Montego Bay
Motherwell
Neumünster
New Castile
New Ireland
Paramaribo
Pontefract
Pontypridd
Portlaoise
Regensburg
Ruda Śląska
Sacramento
Saint Croix
Saint-Denis
San Antonio
Scunthorpe
Shrewsbury
Simferopol
Tewkesbury
Trowbridge
Twickenham
Vijayawada
Warrington
Washington
Whitehorse
Winchester
Winterthur
Xochimilco

11 letters:
Aberystwyth
Aix-les-Bains
Alessandria
Armentières
Basingstoke
Cirencester
Clackmannan
Cumbernauld
Dawson Creek
Downpatrick
Enniskillen
Farnborough
Fort William
Glastonbury
Grande-Terre
Halberstadt
High Wycombe
Kanchipuram
Kigoma-Ujiji
Leatherhead
Marlborough
Mississauga
Missolonghi
Montbéliard
Montpellier
Nakhichevan
Northampton
Novosibirsk
Nyíregyháza
Prestonpans
Rambouillet
Saint-Brieuc
Saint David's
Saint Helena
Saint Helens
Saint Helier
Saint Pierre
San Fernando
Sharpeville
Sierra Leone
Stourbridge
Wanne-Eickel

12 letters:
Alice Springs
Anuradhapura
Ascoli Piceno
Beaconsfield
Bielsko-Biała

Bougainville
Cerro de Pasco
Chesterfield
Chilpancingo
Christchurch
East Kilbride
Huddersfield
Kristianstad
Loughborough
Luang Prabang
Macclesfield
Marie Galante
Matabeleland
Milton Keynes
Newtownabbey
Peterborough
Saint Austell
Saint-Étienne
Saint-Quentin
San Ildefonso
Schaffhausen
Secunderabad
Seringapatam
Skelmersdale
Valenciennes
Villahermosa
Villeurbanne
Wattenscheid
West Bromwich

13 letters:
Berchtesgaden
Blantyre-Limbe
Bury St Edmunds
Carrickfergus
Cayman Islands
Évian-les-Bains

Fontainebleau
Hertfordshire
Hradec Králové
Kidderminster
Leamington Spa
Lipari Islands
Llano Estacado
Lons-le-Saunier
Melton Mowbray
Merthyr Tydfil
Middlesbrough
New Providence
Northallerton
Ryukyu Islands
Southend-on-Sea

14 letters:
Annapolis Royal
Ashby-de-la-Zouch
Bishop Auckland
Château-Thierry
Griqualand East
Griqualand West
Hemel Hempstead
Henley-on-Thames
Mariánské Lázně
Saint Augustine
Tunbridge Wells
Wellingborough

15 letters:
Ashton-under-Lyne
Barrow-in-Furness
Burton-upon-Trent
Camborne-Redruth
Falkland Islands
Lewis with Harris

Neuilly-sur-Seine
Scottish Borders
Stratford-on-Avon
Sunbury-on-Thames
Sutton Coldfield
Weston-super-Mare

16 letters:
Alcazar de San Juan
Berwick-upon-Tweed
Eastern Townships
Houghton-le-Spring
Sutton-in-Ashfield
Welwyn Garden City

17 letters:
Talavera de la Reina

18 letters:
Aldridge-Brownhills
Newcastle-under-Lyme
Prince Edward Island
Saint-Maur-des-Fossés

19 letters:
Bismarck Archipelago
Charleville-Mézières
Dumfries and Galloway

21 letters:
Queenborough in
  Sheppey

28 letters:
Saint Vincent and the
  Grenadines

Torture

INSTRUMENTS OF TORTURE

4 letters:
Boot
Rack

5 letters:
Brake
Wheel

7 letters:
Scourge

10 letters:
Iron maiden
Pilliwinks
Thumbscrew

13 letters:
Cat-o'-nine-tails

14 letters:
Procrustean bed

TYPES OF TORTURE

5 letters:
Water

8 letters:
Gauntlet

9 letters:
Bastinado
Strappado
Water cure

12 letters:
Chinese water

Trade terms

2 letters:
CA
Co
HP
Rd

3 letters:
Bag
Bar
Bid
Bob
BOT
Buy
Cap
COD
Con
Dot
Due
Dun
EEC
Fee
IOU
Job
Lot
Ltd
Net
Oof
Owe
Par
Pay
Pit
Pro
Put
Rig
Sag
SET
Sum
Tag
Tax

Tin
Tip
VAT
Wad

4 letters:
Agio
Back
Bank
Bear
Body
Bond
Boom
Buck
Bulk
Bull
Bury
Call
Cant
Cash
Cess
Char
Chip
Coin
Co-op
Corn
Cost
Crop
Curb
Deal
Dear
Debt
Desk
Dibs
Dole
Drug
Dues
Dump
Dust

Duty
Earn
EFTA
Fair
Fees
Fine
Fire
Firm
Fisc
Free
Fund
Gain
Game
Gift
Gild
Gilt
Giro
Glut
Gold
Good
Haul
Hawk
Heap
Hire
Hive
Hold
Hype
Idle
IOUs
Item
Lend
Levy
Line
List
Loan
Long
Loss
Make
Mart

Meed
Milk
Mill
Mint
Nail
Note
Paid
Pawn
PAYE
Peag
Perk
Pool
Post
Rags
Raid
Rate
Reap
Rent
Risk
Roll
Roup
Ruin
Sack
Safe
Sale
Salt
Save
Scab
Sell
Shop
Sink
Slug
Sold
Stag
Swap
Tare
Task
Tick
Till
Tout
Vend
Visa
Wage
Ware
Work

5 letters:
Agent
Amass
Angel

Assay
Asset
At par
Audit
Baron
Batch
Beans
Bears
Bid up
Block
Blunt
Board
Bogus
Bones
Bonus
Boost
Booth
Brand
Brass
Broke
Bucks
Bulls
Bunce
Buyer
Buy up
By-bid
Cadge
Cargo
Cheap
Check
Chink
Chips
Chore
Clear
Clerk
Costs
Craft
Crash
Cycle
Debit
Depot
Dives
Dough
Dowry
Draft
Entry
Ernie
Exact
Files
Float

Forge
Funds
Gilts
Gnome
Goods
Gross
Guild
Hoard
House
Index
Ingot
Issue
Lease
Lucre
Maker
Means
Midas
Money
Ochre
Offer
Order
Owing
Panic
Paper
Piece
Pitch
Plant
Pound
Price
Prize
Purse
Queer
Quota
Quote
Rails
Rally
Rebuy
Remit
Repay
Rhino
Rocks
Salve
Scalp
Scoop
Score
Scrip
Set up
Share
Shark
Shift

Short
Skill
Slash
Slump
Smash
Smith
Snide
Spend
Spiel
Spots
Stake
Stall
Stand
Stint
Stock
Store
Strop
Tally
Taxes
Terms
Tithe
Token
Trade
Treat
Trend
Truck
Trust
Usury
Utter
Value
Venal
Wages
Wares
Welsh
Works
Worth
Yield

6 letters:
Abacus
Accept
Accrue
Admass
Afford
Agency
Agenda
Amount
Appeal
Arrear
Assets

At cost
Avails
Backer
Banker
Barker
Barter
Bazaar
Bearer
Boodle
Borrow
Bought
Bounce
Bounty
Bourse
Branch
Broker
Budget
Bureau
Bursar
Button
Buying
Buy out
Cambio
Career
Cartel
Cash in
Change
Charge
Cheque
Client
Coffer
Consol
Copper
Corner
Costly
Coupon
Cowrie
Credit
Crisis
Custom
Dealer
Deal in
Debtee
Debtor
Defray
Demand
Dicker
Drawer
Dunner
Emptio

Enrich
Equity
Errand
Estate
Excise
Expend
Export
Figure
Fiscal
Fold up
Freeze
Future
Garage
Gazump
Godown
Go slow
Gratis
Grease
Growth
Guinea
Haggle
Hammer
Hard up
Hawker
Import
Impose
Impost
In bulk
In cash
Income
In debt
In-tray
Jobber
Job lot
Labour
Leader
Ledger
Lender
Liable
Living
Luxury
Mammon
Merger
Minute
Moneys
Monger
Monies
Notice
Nugget
Octroi

Odd job
Odd lot
Office
On call
Oncost
On tick
Option
Outbid
Outcry
Outlay
Outlet
Output
Packet
Parity
Patron
Pauper
Pay day
Pay for
Paying
Pay-off
Payola
Pay out
Peddle
Pedlar
Picket
Pirate
Pledge
Plunge
Plutus
Pocket
Policy
Profit
Public
Purvey
Racket
Raffle
Rating
Ration
Realty
Rebate
Recoup
Redeem
Refund
Reject
Remedy
Render
Rental
Resale
Resell
Resign

Retail
Retire
Return
Reward
Rialto
Riches
Ruined
Salary
Save up
Saving
Sell up
Settle
Shares
Shorts
Silver
Simony
Smithy
Specie
Spiral
Sponge
Spread
Stable
Staker
Stocks
Strike
Sundry
Supply
Surtax
Swings
Tariff
Taxman
Teller
Tender
Tenths
Ticker
Ticket
Towage
Trader
Treaty
Tycoon
Unload
Unpaid
Usurer
Valuta
Vendor
Vendue
Wallet
Wampum
Wealth
Worker

Wright

7 letters:
Abscond
Account
Actuary
Allonge
Annuity
Arrears
Article
Atelier
Auction
Auditor
Automat
Average
Backing
Bad debt
Balance
Ballast
Banking
Bargain
Berries
Bidding
Bonanza
Bondage
Boycott
Bullets
Bullion
Bursary
Buy back
Cabbage
Calling
Cambist
Capital
Cash box
Cashier
Ceiling
Chapman
Charity
Chinker
Clinker
Coinage
Coining
Company
Concern
Consols
Contact
Convert
Coppers
Corn pit

Cottons	Guerdon	Pay rise
Counter	Half-day	Payroll
Croesus	Harvest	Payslip
Cumshaw	Haulage	Peddlar
Customs	Head tax	Pending
Cut-rate	Holding	Pension
Damages	Imports	Pet bank
Daybook	Inflate	Plunger
Dealing	In funds	Poll tax
Declare	Intrust	Poor man
Default	Invoice	Portage
Deficit	Iron men	Pre-empt
Deflate	Jingler	Premium
Deposit	Jobbers	Prepaid
Deviser	Jobbing	Pricing
Dockage	Jobless	Produce
Draw out	Journal	Profits
Due bill	Killing	Promote
Dumping	Land tax	Pro rata
Economy	Leading	Prosper
Effects	Lending	Provide
Embargo	Lettuce	Pursuit
Emption	Limited	Pyramid
Endorse	Lockout	Realize
Engross	Lombard	Realtor
Entrust	Long-run	Refusal
Expense	Lottery	Regrate
Exploit	Lump sum	Reissue
Exports	Manager	Release
Factory	Man-made	Requite
Failure	Mintage	Reserve
Fall due	Mission	Retiral
Finance	Moneyed	Returns
Flutter	Nest egg	Revenue
Foot lot	Net gain	Rich man
Foreman	Notions	Rigging
Forgery	Nummary	Rollers
For sale	Oddment	Room man
Fortune	On offer	Rouleau
Foundry	On terms	Royalty
Freebie	On trust	Sacking
Freight	Opening	Salable
Full lot	Opulent	Salt tax
Futures	Out-tray	Salvage
Gabelle	Package	Savings
Gift box	Parlour	Seconds
Go broke	Parvenu	Selling
Good buy	Payable	Sell out
Good sum	Pay cash	Service
Go under	Payment	Shekels

Shopman
Shopper
Skilled
Smelter
Solvent
Sponger
Squeeze
Stipend
Storage
Striker
Subsidy
Surplus
Swindle
Takings
Taxable
Tax-free
Terrier
The city
Tidy sum
Trade in
Trading
Traffic
Tranche
Trustee
Utility
Vacancy
Vending
Venture
Voucher
Walkout
War bond
Warrant
Wealthy
Welfare
Well off
Welsher
Wildcat
Workday

8 letters:
Above par
Accredit
Affluent
After tax
Agiotage
Agronomy
Amortize
Appraise
At a price
Auditing

Automate
Badly off
Bad money
Ballyhoo
Bankbook
Bank loan
Bank note
Bank roll
Bankrupt
Base coin
Basic pay
Bear pool
Bear raid
Beat down
Below par
Blackleg
Blue chip
Board lot
Boardman
Bondager
Boom town
Borrower
Boutique
Breakage
Brochure
Bull pool
Bull raid
Business
Buying in
Campaign
Carriage
Cashbook
Cash down
Cash sale
Circular
Clientry
Close out
Cold cash
Commands
Commerce
Consumer
Contango
Contract
Converts
Counting
Creditor
Credit to
Currency
Customer
Cut-price

Day shift
Dealings
Defrayal
Director
Disburse
Discount
Disposal
Dividend
Dry goods
Earnings
Embezzle
Employee
Employer
Emporium
Entrepot
Estimate
Evaluate
Exchange
Expended
Expenses
Exporter
Face ruin
Finances
Fire sale
Flat rate
Floorman
For a song
Free gift
Free port
Function
Gasworks
Gazetted
Gazumper
Gift shop
Gilt edge
Giveaway
Gold mine
Gold rush
Good will
Gratuity
Grow rich
Hallmark
Hard cash
Hard sell
Hardware
Hoarding
Homework
Hot money
Huckster
Importer

In arrear
Increase
Indebted
Industry
In pocket
Interest
In the red
Investor
Issuance
Issue par
Jeweller
Junkshop
Keep shop
Kitemark
Knitwork
Labourer
Lame duck
Largesse
Large sum
Legation
Levanter
Lifework
Live high
Live well
Long side
Low price
Low water
Make a bid
Make good
Manifest
Man power
Mark down
Material
Maturity
Merchant
Mint drop
Monetary
Moneybag
Moneybox
Monopoly
Mortgage
Net price
Net worth
No charge
Notation
Notecase
Oddments
Off price
On credit
On demand

On strike
Operator
Opulence
Ordinary
Overhaul
Overhead
Overseer
Overtime
Par value
Passbook
Pawn shop
Pay talks
Pin money
Pipeline
Pittance
Position
Post paid
Poundage
Practice
Premises
Price cut
Price war
Proceeds
Producer
Property
Prospect
Purchase
Put price
Quit rent
Rack rent
Rag trade
Rainy day
Receipts
Reckoner
Recorder
Recovery
Refinery
Register
Regrater
Rent-free
Rent roll
Requital
Reserves
Retailer
Retainer
Richesse
Richling
Round lot
Round sum
Ruch hour

Salaried
Saleroom
Salesman
Salt down
Sanction
Scalping
Scarcity
Schedule
Security
Self-made
Shipment
Shipyard
Shopping
Short-run
Showcase
Showroom
Sideline
Sinecure
Small sum
Soft cell
Solatium
Solidity
Solvency
Spending
Spot cash
Spot sale
Square up
Sterling
Sundries
Supertax
Supplies
Swapping
Takeover
Take stop
Tallyman
Taxation
Tax dodge
Taxpayer
Time bill
Tolbooth
Tool shop
Toolwork
Top price
Trade gap
Trade off
Treasure
Treasury
Turnover
Underbid
Undercut

Usufruct
Valorize
Valuable
Venality
Vendible
Vocation
Wash sale
Watchdog
Well-to-do
Wharfage
Workaday
Work late
Workroom
Workshop
Write off

9 letters:
Absconder
Ad valorem
Affiliate
Affluence
Aggregate
Allowance
Amount due
Appraisal
Arbitrage
Arrearage
Assigment
Avocation
Back shift
Bad cheque
Bank clerk
Bank stock
Barrow boy
Bartering
Bear panic
Blind pool
Board room
Bond issue
Bon marché
Bonus bond
Borrowing
Box office
Brand name
Breadline
Brokerage
Bucketing
Bull panic
Buy in bulk
By auction

By-bidding
By-product
Cable code
Cable rate
Call price
Cash grain
Catalogue
Cellarage
Cheapjack
Check rate
Clearance
Clientage
Clientele
Co-emption
Coin money
Commodity
Costerman
Cost price
Craftsman
Death duty
Debenture
Deduction
Defaulter
Deflation
Depositor
Dime store
Directors
Direct tax
Dirt-cheap
Discharge
Dishonour
Dismissal
Dollar gap
Draw wages
Drug store
Easy money
Easy terms
Economics
Economies
Economise
Emolument
Establish
Exchequer
Exciseman
Excise tax
Executive
Expansion
Expensive
Exploiter
Export tax

Extortion
Face value
Fair price
Fair trade
Fat profit
Fiat money
Financial
Financier
Firm offer
Firm price
Flash note
Flat broke
Flotation
Free trade
Full purse
Gilt-edged
Going rate
Gold piece
Good price
Greenback
Guarantee
Guarantor
Half-price
Handiwork
Hard goods
Hard money
Head buyer
Heavy cost
High price
High value
Holy stone
Hot market
Hush money
Import tax
In arrears
Incentive
Income tax
In deficit
Indemnity
Inflation
Insolvent
Insurance
In the city
Invention
Inventory
Job of work
Joint bank
Keep books
Knock down
Late shift

Legal bond	Poorly off	Spot grain
Liability	Portfolio	Spot price
Life's work	Pound note	Stability
Liquidate	Pourboire	Stamp duty
List price	Practical	Statement
Long purse	Priceless	Stock list
Lossmaker	Price list	Stockpile
Low-priced	Price ring	Stock rate
Luxury tax	Price rise	Strike pay
Mail order	Prime cost	Strongbox
Make a sale	Principal	Subsidize
Market day	Profiteer	Substance
Marketing	Promotion	Sumptuary
Means test	Purchaser	Surcharge
Middleman	Qualified	Sweatshop
Moneybags	Quittance	Sweet shop
Money belt	Quotation	Syndicate
Mortgagee	Ratepayer	Synthetic
Mortgager	Ready cash	Tax return
Neat price	Real wages	Technical
Negotiate	Recession	The actual
Net income	Reckoning	The market
Night safe	Reduction	The street
Officiate	Redundant	Tie-in sale
Off market	Reference	Timocracy
On account	Refinance	Tollbooth
On the nail	Reflation	Trade fair
Operative	Registrar	Trademark
Order book	Reimburse	Trade name
Outgoings	Repayment	Trade sale
Out of debt	Resources	Tradesman
Out of work	Restraint	Traffic in
Outworker	Sacrifice	Treadmill
Overdraft	Sale block	Treasurer
Overdrawn	Salesgirl	Undersell
Overheads	Sales talk	Union card
Overspend	Secretary	Unit trust
Patronage	Sell short	Unsalable
Patronize	Shift work	Unskilled
Pay dearly	Shop floor	Up for sale
Pay in kind	Short sale	Utilities
Paymaster	Short side	Utterance
Pecuniary	Sight bill	Valuation
Pecunious	Single tax	Vendition
Penniless	Situation	Wage claim
Penny wise	Soft goods	Wage scale
Petty cash	Sole agent	Warehouse
Piecework	Soundness	Wash sales
Piggy bank	Speculate	Wealth tax
Plutocrat	Spendings	Well-lined

Whitewash
Wholesale
Work force
Workhouse
Work study
World Bank

10 letters:
Acceptance
Accountant
Accounting
Accumulate
Adjustment
Advertiser
Appreciate
Apprentice
Assessment
At a bargain
At a premium
At the spear
Auctioneer
Auction off
Automation
Average out
Bank credit
Bankruptcy
Bearer bond
Bear market
Best seller
Bill broker
Bill of sale
Blood money
Bondholder
Bonus stock
Bookkeeper
Bucket shop
Bulk buying
Buy and sell
Buy futures
Calculator
Capitalism
Capitalist
Capitalize
Chain banks
Chain store
Chancellor
Chargeable
Chargehand
Cheapening
Cheap skate

Cheque book
Chrematist
Chrysology
Closed shop
Closing bid
Collateral
Colporteur
Commercial
Commission
Compensate
Conference
Consortium
Contraband
Cost centre
Coupon bond
Credit card
Credit slip
Curb broker
Curb market
Daily bread
Dead market
Deep in debt
Defalcator
Defrayment
Del credere
Deliquence
Demand bill
Department
Depository
Depreciate
Depression
Direct cost
Dirty money
Dividend on
Dollar bill
Dummy share
Dutch treat
Easy market
Economizer
Efficiency
Employment
Encumbered
End product
Enterprise
Estate duty
Eurodollar
Evaluation
Ex-dividend
Exorbitant
Exposition

False money
Fancy goods
Fancy price
Fancy stock
Filthy rich
First offer
Fiscal year
Fixed price
Fixed trust
Flat market
Floor price
Floor trade
Forced sale
Free gratis
Free market
Free sample
Free trader
Freightage
Full stocks
Funded debt
Give credit
Gold nugget
Go on strike
Go shopping
Government
Green pound
Grindstone
Half stocks
Handicraft
Hand market
Have in hand
Head office
Heavy purse
High-priced
Hold office
Honorarium
Import duty
Imposition
In business
Income bond
Incumbered
Incur a debt
Industrial
Insolvency
Instalment
In the black
In the money
Investment
Job-hunting
Joint bonds

Joint stock
Jumble sale
Laboratory
Lighterage
Liquidator
Livelihood
Living wage
Loan market
Long market
Long seller
Loss leader
Management
Man of means
Marked down
Marketable
Market hall
Mass market
Meal ticket
Member bank
Mercantile
Merchantry
Midas touch
Monetarism
Monetarist
Moneyed man
Money order
Monopolise
Monopolist
Moratorium
Negotiable
Never never
Nightshift
Nominal fee
Nominal par
Nonpayment
Note of hand
Numismatic
Obligation
Occupation
Off licence
Oil of palms
On the block
On the cheap
On the rocks
On the shelf
Opening bid
Open market
Out of funds
Overcharge
Paper money

Pawnbroker
Peppercorn
Percentage
Picket duty
Pig in a poke
Pilot plant
Plutocracy
Pocket book
Power plant
Pre-emption
Preference
Prepayment
Price index
Price level
Printworks
Prix unique
Production
Profession
Profitable
Prospector
Prospectus
Prosperity
Provide for
Purchasing
Pure profit
Put and call
Ration book
Ready money
Real estate
Recompense
Recoupment
Redeemable
Redundancy
Remittance
Remunerate
Repair shop
Reparation
Repository
Repurchase
Retail shop
Retirement
Rock bottom
Round trade
Run up a bill
Salability
Sales force
Saving bank
Saving game
Scrip issue
Second-hand

Securities
Serial bond
Settlement
Settle with
Share index
Shoestring
Shopkeeper
Shop window
Short bonds
Sick market
Skilled man
Slave trade
Slow market
Smart money
Soft market
Sole agency
Speciality
Speculator
Split shift
Spondulies
Statistics
Steelworks
Steep price
Stock issue
Stockpiles
Stony broke
Straitened
Stronghold
Strongroom
Sum of money
Swap horses
Take a flier
Taskmaster
Tax evasion
Technician
Technocrat
The needful
Thin margin
Third World
Ticker tape
Tour of duty
Trade board
Trade cycle
Trade guild
Trade price
Trade route
Trade union
Treaty port
Typewriter
Typing pool

Underwrite
Unemployed
Upset price
Wad of notes
Wage freeze
Wage policy
Walk of life
Wall Street
Waterworks
Wealthy man
Well afford
Well-heeled
Wholesaler
Window-shop
Working day
Work to rule
Written off

11 letters:
Accountancy
Account book
Acquittance
Advertising
Agriculture
Antique shop
Appointment
Asking price
Assemby line
Association
At face value
Auction ring
Bank account
Bank balance
Bank holiday
Bank manager
Bank of issue
Barclaycard
Bargain sale
Bear account
Bear the cost
Betting shop
Big business
Billionaire
Bill of costs
Black market
Blank cheque
Bonus scheme
Book-keeping
Bottom price
Bread winner

Brisk market
Budget price
Bull account
Businessman
Capital gain
Carbon paper
Cash account
Catallactic
Caught short
Central bank
Certificate
Chamberlain
Chancellery
Chemist shop
Chrysocracy
Circulation
Closing down
Come to terms
Commodities
Common stock
Company rule
Competition
Competitive
Comptometer
Consumption
Cool million
Co-operative
Copperworks
Corn in Egypt
Corporation
Cosing price
Cost-benefit
Counterfeit
Cover charge
Cum dividend
Custom house
Customs duty
Danger money
Defence bond
Demand curve
Demarcation
Deposit slip
Devaluation
Display case
Distributor
Dividend off
Double entry
Down payment
Drive a trade
Dutch aution

Earn a living
Economic law
Economic man
Economy size
Embarrassed
Endorsement
Established
Estate agent
Expenditure
Fabrication
Fetch a price
Filthy lucre
Fixed assets
Fixed income
Floor broker
Fluctuation
Foot the bill
Foreclosure
Free harbour
Future grain
Future price
Gingerbread
Gross income
Hard bargain
High finance
Horse market
Hypermarket
Impecunious
Indirect tax
Industrials
Inexpensive
Institution
Intercourse
Ironmongery
Joint return
Key industry
King's ransom
Lap of luxury
Legal tender
Liberty bond
Life savings
Line of goods
Liquidation
Local branch
Local office
Long account
Long service
Loose change
Machine-made
Machine shop

Made of money
Manufactory
Manufacture
Market place
Market price
Mass-produce
Merchandise
Millionaire
Minimum wage
Mint of money
Money broker
Money dealer
Money lender
Money's worth
Money to burn
Negotiation
Nest factory
Net interest
Net receipts
Nuisance tax
Numismatics
On easy terms
On good terms
On the market
Open account
Open-end bond
Out of pocket
Outstanding
Overpayment
Package deal
Paper credit
Partnership
Pay cash down
Pay on demand
Pay spot cash
Pay the piper
Piece of work
Pilot scheme
Place of work
Pocket money
Polytechnic
Possessions
Postal order
Pots of money
Poverty line
Poverty trap
Premium bond
Pretty penny
Price-fixing
Price freeze

Price spiral
Price ticket
Property tax
Proposition
Purchase tax
Put-up market
Queer Street
Quoted price
Raw material
Reserve bank
Resignation
Restriction
Retiring age
Risk capital
Rummage sale
Run into debt
Safe deposit
Sales ledger
Salesperson
Savings bank
Self-service
Sell at a loss
Sell forward
Sell futures
Sharebroker
Shareholder
Share ledger
Shopping bag
Short change
Short seller
Single entry
Sinking fund
Slot machine
Small change
Small trader
Sole emption
Speculation
Sponsorship
Stagflation
Stockbroker
Stock dealer
Stockholder
Stockjobber
Stock ledger
Stock market
Stockpiling
Stocktaking
Storekeeper
Subsistence
Supermarket

Take-home pay
Take-over bid
Tattersall's
Tax assessor
Tax gatherer
Technocracy
The have-nots
Tight budget
Tight market
Time bargain
Tired market
To the tune of
Trade school
Trading post
Transaction
Travel agent
Truck system
Undercharge
Underwriter
Vendibility
Wherewithal
Working life
Workmanlike
Workmanship
Works outing
World market

12 letters:
Active market
Ad valorem tax
Amalgamation
Amortization
Amortizement
Arithmometer
Auction stand
Balance sheet
Bank examiner
Bargain offer
Bargain price
Barter system
Be in business
Bill of lading
Board meeting
Board of Trade
Bond to bearer
Bottom dollar
Bottomry bond
Branch office
Broker's agent
Brokers board

Business deal
Business life
Businesslike
Buyer's market
Buying public
Callable bond
Capital gains
Capital goods
Capital stock
Cash and carry
Cash register
Casual labour
Catallactics
Circular note
Clearing bank
Common market
Compensation
Consumer good
Cook the books
Copartneship
Costermonger
Cost of living
Counting-room
Credit rating
Critical path
Currency note
Current price
Customs union
Denomination
Depreciation
Direct labour
Disbursement
Discount rate
Distribution
Dollar crisis
Durable goods
Early closing
Earned income
Econometrics
Economy drive
Entrepreneur
Exchange rate
Exhaust price
Extend credit
Extravagance
Fair exchange
Fill an office
First refusal
Fiscal policy
Fixed capital

Floating debt
Folding money
Foreign trade
Gate receipts
General store
Get rich quick
Going concern
Gold standard
Goods for sale
Great expense
Haberdashery
Hard currency
High pressure
Hire purchase
Hungry market
Impulse buyer
In conference
Indebtedness
Interest rate
Internal bond
In the gazette
Joint account
Keep accounts
Labour of love
Laissez-faire
Leather goods
Line of credit
Live in clover
Lively market
Long interest
Make a bargain
Make a fortune
Make delivery
Make one's pile
Manipulation
Manufacturer
Marginal cost
Mass-produced
Mercantilism
Monetization
Money changer
Money matters
Mortgage bond
National bank
Nearest offer
Nine till five
Nominal price
Nominal value
Nouveau riche
Odd-lot dealer

Offered price
Offer for sale
Office junior
Open-end trust
Opening price
Organization
Packing house
Pay as you earn
Pay in advance
Pegged market
Peg the market
Ply one's trade
Porte-monnaie
Pressure belt
Price ceiling
Price control
Price current
Price of money
Price rigging
Productivity
Professional
Profiteering
Profit margin
Profit motive
Purse strings
Rags to riches
Rate of growth
Redeployment
Regional bank
Remuneration
Remunerative
Reserve price
Retaining fee
Retrenchment
Rigged market
Rig the market
Rising prices
Rolling stock
Rubber cheque
Sale by outcry
Sale or return
Sales gimmick
Sales manager
Salesmanship
Satisfaction
Sell on credit
Severance pay
Share company
Shareholding
Short account

Show business
Slender means
Sliding scale
State lottery
Steady market
Sterling area
Stock company
Stock dealing
Stockholding
Stock in trade
Stockjobbery
Street market
Strike action
Strike it rich
Strong market
Superannuate
Sustain a loss
Tax collector
Tax exemption
Ten-cent store
The long green
Ticker market
Trade balance
Trade mission
Trading stamp
Travel agency
Treasury bill
Treasury note
Trial balance
Trustee stock
Unemployment
Variety store
Watered stock
Welfare State
Without a bean
Working class
Working order

13 letters:
Advertisement
Asset stripper
Bank messenger
Bank of England
Bank overdraft
Bank statement
Budget account
Budget surplus
Bulls and bears
Burial society
Business hours

Cash dispenser
Cash in advance
Cash on the nail
Clearance sale
Clearing-house
Commercialism
Commercialist
Company report
Concessionary
Confetti money
Confidence man
Consumer goods
Cost-effective
Counting-house
Credit account
Credit balance
Credit company
Credit squeeze
Crossed cheque
Current assets
Depressed area
Discount house
Discount store
Excess profits
Eye to business
Falling prices
Filing cabinet
Financial year
Fire insurance
Free-trade area
Fringe benefit
Going for a song
Impulse buying
Incorporation
Industrialism
In Queer Street
Life assurance
Life insurance
Lombard Street
Man of business
Millionairess
Modernisation
Money no object
Multinational
Multiple store
Parkinson's Law
Payment in kind
Payment in lieu
Penalty clause
Petticoat lane

Price increase
Private income
Private sector
Profitability
Profit and loss
Profit sharing
Protectionism
Protectionist
Public company
Purchase price
Raise the money
Rate for the job
Rates and texes
Regular income
Sellers market
Service charge
Small business
Small investor
Spending spree
Stock exchange
Strike breaker
Subcontractor
Tax-deductible
Trade discount
Trade unionism
Trade unionist
Trading estate
Value added tax
White elephant
Wild-cat strike

14 letters:
Accident policy
Asset stripping
Balance of trade
Bargain counter
Bill discounter
Capitalisation
Cash on delivery
Certain annuity
Clearance house
Company meeting
Concessionaire
Consumer demand
Corporation tax
Cost accountant
Cost accounting
Cost efficiency
Current account
Deposit account

Direct-debiting
Discount broker
Distressed area
Electricty bill
Expense account
Eye for business
Family business
Finance company
Free enterprise
Free of interest
Full employment
Gnomes of Zurich
Holding company
Imprest account
Inertia selling
Letter of credit
Lighting-up time
Limited company
Lloyd's register
Market research
Mass production
Merchant banker
Monthly payment
National income
National wealth
Ordinary shares
Over production
Over the counter
Penny-in-the-slot
Peppercorn rent
Peter principle
Private company
Production line
Pyramid selling
Quality control
Rate of exchange
Rate of interest
Second-hand shop
Shopping centre

Simple interest
Superannuation
Surrender value
Tariff reformer
Three mile limit
Under the hammer
Unearned income
Vending machine
Vested interest
Visible exports
Window shopping
Working capital

15 letters:
American Express
Bargain basement
Building society
Business as usual
Business circles
Business contact
Business manager
Business studies
Business venture
Capital gains tax
Carriage forward
Cash transaction
Closing-down sale
Commission agent
Company director
Company promoter
Complete annuity
Cottage industry
Deferred annuity
Deferred payment
Department store
Development area
Distress warrant
Dividend warrant
Do a roaring trade

Endowment policy
Entrepreneurial
Exchange control
Family allowance
Floating capital
Foreign exchange
Franking machine
Friendly society
Golden handshake
Income-tax demand
Income-tax rebate
Income-tax relief
Income-tax return
Insurance broker
Insurance policy
Investment trust
Invisible import
Labour intensive
Lightning strike
Marine insurance
Money for old rope
National savings
No-claim discount
Non-profit-making
Preference stock
Public ownership
Purchasing power
Registration fee
Regular customer
Reserve currency
Rock-bottom price
Service industry
Settle an account
Sleeping partner
Supply and demand
Suspense account
Under the counter
Unemployment pay
World of commerce

Trees

2 letters:
Bo
Ti

3 letters:
Ash
Asp

Bay
Bel
Ben
Box
Elm
Fig

Fir
Gum
Ita
Jak
Koa
Mot

Nim
Oak
Sal
Tea
Til
Ule
Wax
Yew

4 letters:
Acer
Akee
Aloe
Amla
Arar
Atap
Bael
Bhel
Bito
Boab
Bosk
Cade
Coco
Cola
Cork
Dali
Deal
Dhak
Dika
Dita
Eugh
Gean
Hule
Ilex
Jack
Kaki
Kiri
Kola
Lime
Lind
Lote
Mako
Ming
Mott
Mowa
Nipa
Ombu
Palm
Pear
Pine

Plum
Poon
Rata
Rhus
Rimu
Shea
Silk
Sloe
Sorb
Tawa
Teak
Teil
Titi
Toon
Tung
Tutu
Upas
Yang

5 letters:
Abele
Abies
Ackee
Afara
Alamo
Alder
Alnus
Anona
Apple
Areca
Argan
Aspen
Balsa
Beech
Belah
Belar
Birch
Bodhi
Boree
Bunya
Butea
Cacao
Carap
Carob
Cedar
Ceiba
China
Cocoa
Cocus
Coral

Ebony
Elder
Fagus
Fever
Flame
Guava
Hakea
Hazel
Hevea
Holly
Iroko
Jambu
Jarul
Judas
Karri
Kauri
Khaya
Kiaat
Kokum
Larch
Lemon
Lilac
Lotus
Mahoe
Mahua
Mahwa
Mamey
Mango
Maple
Marri
Matai
Melia
Motte
Mugga
Mulga
Mvule
Myall
Ngaio
Nyssa
Olive
Opepe
Osier
Palas
Palay
Panax
Papaw
Peach
Pecan
Pinon
Pipal

Pipul	Bo-tree	Jujube
Plane	Bottle	Kamala
Quina	Brazil	Kamela
Ramin	Buriti	Kanuka
Roble	Cadaga	Karaka
Rowan	Cadagi	Karite
Sabal	Carapa	Kowhai
Saman	Carica	Laurel
Sassy	Cashew	Lebbek
Scrog	Cassia	Linden
Silva	Cembra	Locust
Smoke	Cerris	Longan
Sumac	Chaste	Loquat
Taxus	Chenar	Lucuma
Thorn	Cherry	Macoya
Thuja	Chinar	Mallee
Thuya	Citron	Manuka
Tilia	Citrus	Mastic
Tsuga	Coffee	Mimosa
Tuart	Cordon	Mopane
Tulip	Cornel	Mopani
Vitex	Cornus	Myrtle
Wahoo	Deodar	Nutmeg
Wilga	Diana's	Obeche
Witch	Dragon	Orange
Xylem	Durian	Padauk
Yacca	Durion	Padouk
Yucca	Emblic	Pagoda
Yulan	Eumong	Papaya
Zaman	Eumung	Pawpaw
Zamia	Feijoa	Peepul
	Fustet	Pepper
6 letters:	Fustic	Platan
Abroma	Gallus	Pomelo
Acacia	Garjan	Poplar
Alerce	Gidgee	Popple
Almond	Gidjee	Protea
Angico	Gingko	Puriri
Annona	Ginkgo	Quince
Antiar	Glinap	Raffia
Arbute	Gnetum	Red-bud
Arolla	Gopher	Ricker
Balsam	Guango	Roucou
Banana	Gurjun	Rubber
Banyan	Gympie	Sabicu
Baobab	Illipe	Sallow
Bilian	Illipi	Samaan
Billar	Jarool	Sapele
Bombax	Jarrah	Sapium
Bonsai	Joshua	Sapota

Saxaul
She-oak
Sinder
Souari
Spruce
Stemma
Storax
Sumach
Sunder
Sundra
Sundri
Tamanu
Tewart
Titoki
Tooart
Totara
Tupelo
Waboom
Walnut
Wandoo
Wattle
Wicken
Willet
Willow
Witgat
Yarran
Zamang

7 letters:
Ailanto
Amboina
Apricot
Arbutus
Avodire
Bebeeru
Bilimbi
Bilsted
Bubinga
Buck-eye
Bursera
Cabbage
Cajeput
Cajuput
Calamus
Camphor
Camwood
Canella
Carbean
Carbeen
Catalpa

Champac
Champak
Chayote
Coconut
Coquito
Cork oak
Corylus
Corypha
Cumquat
Cypress
Daddock
Dagwood
Dogwood
Dryades
Durmast
Geebung
Genipap
Gluinap
Grey gum
Hemlock
Hickory
Holm-oak
Iron gum
Jipyapa
Juniper
Karbeen
Kumquat
Lacquer
Lagetto
Lentisk
Logwood
Lumbang
Madrono
Mahaleb
Manjack
Marasca
Margosa
Mazzard
Mesquit
Moringa
Morrell
Pereira
Pimento
Platane
Pollard
Populus
Quassia
Quicken
Quillai
Quinain

Radiata
Rampike
Redwood
Rock elm
Saksaul
Sandbox
Saouari
Sapling
Sausage
Sequoia
Seringa
Service
Shittah
Snow gum
Sourgum
Soursop
Spindle
Sundari
Tea-tree
Varnish
Wallaba
Wirilda
Witchen
Wych-elm
Xylopia
Zelkova

8 letters:
Aguacate
Algaroba
Aquillia
Bangalay
Bangalow
Banyalla
Basswood
Beefwood
Benjamin
Berrigan
Black boy
Black oak
Blimbing
Bountree
Bourtree
Breadnut
Brigalow
Bulwaddy
Calabash
Chestnut
Cinchona
Cinnamon

Cocoplum
Coolabah
Coolibah
Corkwood
Date palm
Dendroid
Dracaena
Espalier
Eucalypt
Flittern
Fraxinus
Garcinia
Ghost gum
Gnetales
Guaiacum
Hagberry
Hawthorn
Hoop pine
Hornbeam
Huon pine
Igdrasil
Ironbark
Ironwood
Jelutong
Kingwood
Laburnum
Lacebark
Lecythis
Loblolly
Magnolia
Mahogany
Makomako
Mangrove
Manna-ash
Mesquite
Mulberry
Ocotillo
Oiticica
Oleaceae
Oleaster
Palmetto
Pichurim
Pinaster
Pyinkado
Quandang
Quandong
Quantong
Quillaia
Quillaja
Quondong

Raintree
Rambutan
Rangiora
Rewa-rewa
Rivergum
Rosewood
Sago-palm
Sandarac
Santalum
Sapindus
Sapucaia
Scots fir
Sea grape
Silky oak
Simaruba
Soapbark
Sourwood
Stinging
Sweet gum
Sweetsop
Sycamine
Sycamore
Sycomore
Tamarack
Tamarind
Tamarisk
Taxodium
Umbrella
White ash
Whitegum
Witch elm
Ygdrasil

9 letters:
Agila-wood
Ailantous
Albespine
Angophora
Azedarach
Bauple nut
Bilimbing
Bimble box
Bitternut
Black bean
Blackbutt
Black pine
Blackwood
Bloodwood
Bolletrie
Boobialla

Bullwaddy
Bully-tree
Bulwaddee
Burrawang
Burrawary
Butternut
Caliatour
Caliature
Candlenut
Carambola
Casuarina
Cherimoya
Chile pine
Chincapin
Chinkapin
Coachwood
Cordyline
Courbaril
Cupressus
Currajong
Evergreen
Firewheel
Flame-leaf
Grasstree
Greenwood
Ground ash
Ground oak
Hackberry
Ivory palm
Jacaranda
Kahikatea
Kahikatoa
Krummholz
Kurrajong
Lancewood
Lemonwood
Macadamia
Melaleuca
Mockernut
Monkeypot
Naseberry
Native oak
Nux vomica
Paloverde
Paperbark
Paulownia
Persimmon
Piccabean
Pistachio
Pitch-pine

Poinciana
Ponderosa
Pontianac
Quebracho
Rauwolfia
Rose-apple
Sapodilla
Sassafras
Satinwood
Scots pine
Star-anise
Stinkwood
Tacamahac
Terebinth
Toothache
Torchwood
Wagenboom
Whitebeam
Whitewood
Yellow box
Yggdrasil
Zebrawood

10 letters:
Arbor Vitae
Bitterbark
Bitterbush
Blackbully
Bulletwood
Bullwaddie
Bunya-bunya
Calamondin
Calliature
Candle-wood
Cannonball
Celery pine
Chamaerops
Chaulmugra
Cheesewood
Chinaberry
Chinquapin
Cottonwood
Cowrie-pine
Douglas fir
Eucalyptus
Fiddlewood
Flamboyant
Flindersia
Flooded gum
Frangipani

Grapefruit
Green-heart
Hackmatack
Ilang-ilang
Jaboticaba
Jippi-jappa
Kentia palm
Letter-wood
Lilli pilli
Lilly pilly
Macrocarpa
Manchineel
Mangabeira
Mangosteen
Marblewood
Mudgerabah
Palisander
Paper birch
Pohutukawa
Quercitron
Ribbonwood
Sandalwood
Sappanwood
Silverbell
Sneezewood
Spotted gum
Strawberry
Tallowwood
Turpentine
Witch-hazel
Witgatboom
Woollybutt
Yellowwood
Ylang-ylang

11 letters:
Appleringie
Black wattle
Blanket-leaf
Cabbage-palm
Chaulmougra
Chokecherry
Cryptomeria
Dipterocarp
Eriodendron
Flamboyante
Fothergilla
Leatherwood
Lignum vitae
Liquidambar

Maceranduba
Mountain ash
Pomegranate
Purpleheart
Pussy willow
Radiata pine
River red gum
Scribbly gum
Shittimwood
Silver birch
Sitka spruce
Stringy-bark

12 letters:
Bangalow palm
Golden wattle
Gympie nettle
Hercules' club
Insignis pine
Liriodendron
Mammee-sapota
Masseranduba
Monkey puzzle
Monterey pine
Washingtonia

13 letters:
Camphor laurel
Celery-top pine
Horse chestnut
Moreton Bay ash
Moreton Bay fig
Paper-mulberry
Peppermint gum
Queensland nut
Weeping willow

14 letters:
Antarctic beech
Bunya-bunya pine
Cedar of Lebanon
Illawarra flame
Stinking wattle

15 letters:
Bastard mahogany
Cabbage tree palm

16 letters:
Tasmanian blue gum

17 letters:
Bat's wing coral-tree
Norfolk Island pine

18 letters:
Moreton Bay chestnut

Trousers and shorts

5 letters:
Cords
Jeans
Levis®
Loons
Slops
Trews

6 letters:
Breeks
Capris
Chinos
Denims
Flares
Slacks
Trouse

7 letters:
Combats
Joggers
Kachera
Pyjamas
Shalwar

8 letters:
Bloomers
Breeches
Britches
Culottes

Flannels
Hipsters
Hot pants
Jodhpurs
Knickers
Leggings
Overalls
Ski pants

9 letters:
Buckskins
Churidars
Corduroys
Dungarees
Loon pants
Plus fours
Trunk hose
Wranglers®

10 letters:
Capri pants
Cargo pants
Drainpipes
Hip-huggers
Lederhosen
Oxford bags
Pantaloons
Salopettes
Stovepipes

11 letters:
Bell-bottoms

12 letters:
Galligaskins
Gallygaskins
Palazzo pants
Pedal pushers
Smallclothes

13 letters:
Bermuda shorts
Cycling shorts
Spatterdashes
Toreador pants

14 letters:
Knickerbockers
Riding breeches

15 letters:
Jogging trousers

17 letters:
Sweat-suit trousers
Tracksuit trousers

Tumours

3 letters:
Wen
Yaw

4 letters:
Crab
Mole
Wart

5 letters:
Grape
Gumma
Myoma
Talpa
Wilm's

6 letters:
Anbury

Cancer
Epulis
Glioma
Lipoma
Myxoma
Struma

7 letters:
Adenoma

Angioma
Dermoid
Fibroid
Fibroma
Myeloma
Neuroma
Osteoma
Polypus
Sarcoma
Thymoma

8 letters:
Crab-yaws
Ganglion
Hepatoma
Lymphoma
Melanoma
Seminoma
Steatoma
Teratoma
Windgall

Xanthoma

9 letters:
Carcinoid
Carcinoma
Chondroma
Condyloma
Encanthis
Exostosis
Granuloma
Haematoma
Papilloma

10 letters:
Meningioma

11 letters:
Astrocytoma
Encephaloma
Gioblastoma
Haemangioma

12 letters:
Angiosarcoma
Endothelioma
Mesothelioma
Osteosarcoma

13 letters:
Neuroblastoma
Osteoclastoma

14 letters:
Carcinosarcoma
Retinoblastoma

15 letters:
Burkitt lymphoma
Medullablastoma

16 letters:
Burkitt's lymphoma

Typefaces

3 letters:
Gem

4 letters:
Pica
Quad
Ruby

5 letters:
Agate
Canon
Elite
Pearl
Roman
Ronde
Serif

6 letters:
Aldine
Caslon

Cicero
Gothic
Minion
Primer

7 letters:
Braille
Brevier
Elzevir
Emerald
Fraktur
Old-face
Paragon
Plantin
Quadrat

8 letters:
Bold face
Egyptian
Garamond

Old style
Sanserif
Semibold

9 letters:
Bourgeois
Brilliant
Clarendon
Columbian
Non-pareil

10 letters:
Longprimer

11 letters:
Baskerville
Black-letter
Great primer

U u

Underwear

3 letters:
Bra

4 letters:
Body
Vest

5 letters:
Pants
Shift
Teddy

6 letters:
Basque
Boxers
Briefs
Bustle
Corset
Garter
Girdle
Shorts
Trunks
T-shirt

7 letters:
Drawers
G-string
Pannier
Panties

Singlet
Step-ins
Y-fronts

8 letters:
Balmoral
Bloomers
Broekies
Camisole
Corselet
Half-slip
Knickers
Lingerie
Thermals

9 letters:
Brassiere
Crinoline
Jockstrap
Long johns
Petticoat
Suspender
Undervest
Union suit
Waist-slip

10 letters:
Chemisette

Garter belt
String vest
Underpants
Undershirt
Underskirt

11 letters:
Boxer shorts
Panty girdle
Undershorts

12 letters:
Body stocking
Camiknickers
Combinations
Underdrawers

13 letters:
Liberty bodice
Suspender belt

14 letters:
French knickers

15 letters:
Athletic support

17 letters:
Foundation garment

Units

1 letter:
K

2 letters:
SI

3 letters:
Amp
Bar

Bit
Erg
Gal
GeV
Lux
Mho
Mil
Nit

Ohm
Rem
Rep
Tog

4 letters:
Baud
Byte

Dyne
Foot
Gram
Gray
Hour
Inch
Mile
Octa
Okta
Phot
Pint
Slug
Sone
Torr
Volt
Watt
Yard

5 letters:
Crith
Cusec
Daraf
Darcy
Debye
Farad
Fermi
Gauss
Henry
Hertz
Joule
Litre
Lumen
Metre
Neper
Nepit
Ounce
Pixel
Pound
Quart
Remen
Sabin
Stilb
Stoke
Stone
Tesla

Therm
Weber
Yrneh

6 letters:
Dalton
Degree
Denier
Dobson
Gallon
Jansky
Kelvin
Kilerg
Lexeme
Micron
Morgen
Newton
Pascal
Probit
Radian
Second
Sememe
Stokes

7 letters:
Candela
Congius
Coulomb
Dioptre
Energid
Fresnel
Gigabit
Gilbert
Lambert
Man-hour
Maxwell
Megaton
Micella
Micelle
Minute
Oersted
Phoneme
Poundal
Rontgen
Semeion

Siemens
Sievert
Syntagm
Tagmeme

8 letters:
Abampere
Angstrom
Chaldron
Electron
Glosseme
Kilowatt
Magneton
Megabyte
Megawatt
Morpheme
Roentgen
Syntagma
Terabyte
Therblig

9 letters:
Becquerel
Kilderkin
Kilometre
Megahertz
Microinch
Steradian

10 letters:
Centimetre
Centipoise
Dessiatine
Microcurie
Millilitre
Millimetre
Nanosecond
Picosecond
Ploughgate
Rutherford

11 letters:
Centimorgan
Pennyweight

V v

Vegetables

3 letters:
Cos
Oca
Pea
Udo
Yam

4 letters:
Beet
Cole
Corn
Guar
Kail
Kale
Leek
Neep
Okra
Okro
Puha
Sium
Spud
Taro

5 letters:
Ackee
Beans
Chard
Chive
Choko
Chufa
Cress
Ingan
Mooli
Navew
Onion
Orach
Pease
Puwha
Savoy
Swede
Syboe

6 letters:
Adjigo
Allium
Batata
Bhindi
Calalu
Carrot
Celery
Daikon
Endive
Fennel
Frisee
Greens
Jicama
Kumara
Kumera
Lablab
Mangel
Marrow
Orache
Pepper
Potato
Pratie
Quinoa
Radish
Rapini
Sorrel
Sprout
Squash
Tomato
Turnip
Warran

7 letters:
Bok choy
Cabbage
Calaloo
Cardoon
Chayote
Chicory
Cocoyam
Collard

Gherkin
Lettuce
Mangold
Pak-choi
Parsnip
Pimento
Pumpkin
Rauriki
Romaine
Salsify
Shallot
Skirret
Spinach
Spinage
Sprouts

8 letters:
Baby corn
Beetroot
Brassica
Broccoli
Capsicum
Celeriac
Cucumber
Eggplant
Escarole
Eschalot
Hastings
Kohlrabi
Pimiento
Rutabaga
Samphire
Scallion
Zucchini

9 letters:
Artichoke
Asparagus
Aubergine
Broad bean
Calabrese
Corn salad

Courgette
Finocchio
Mangetout
Radicchio
Rocambole
Succotash
Sweet corn
Tonka-bean

10 letters:
Alexanders
Bean sprout
Beef tomato
Bell pepper
Cos lettuce
Salad onion
Scorzonera
Silver beet

See also:
➤ **Potatoes**

11 letters:
Cauliflower
Chinese leaf
Horseradish
Lady's finger
Oyster plant
Spinach-beet
Spring onion
Sweet potato

12 letters:
Cherry tomato
Corn on the cob
Lamb's lettuce
Mangel-wurzel
Marrow squash
Savoy cabbage
Spanish onion
Spring greens

13 letters:
Pe-tsai cabbage

14 letters:
Brussels sprout
Chinese cabbage
Globe artichoke
Iceberg lettuce

15 letters:
Vegetable marrow

16 letters:
Butternut pumpkin

18 letters:
Jerusalem artichoke

Types of vehicle

3 letters:
ATV
Bus
Cab
Car
Hog
JCB®
LEM
Ute
Van

4 letters:
Bike
Boat
Cart
Dray
Jeep®
Kago
Kart
Luge
Pram
Quad
Scow
Shay

Ship
Sled
Tank
Taxi
Tram
Trap

5 letters:
Artic
Brake
Buggy
Coach
Coupé
Crate
Cycle
Float
Hatch
Lorry
Moped
Ratha
Soyuz
Sulky
Tip-up
Tonga

Towie
Train
Truck
Turbo
Vespa
Wagon

6 letters:
Barrow
Camion
Camper
Chaise
Dennet
Fiacre
Gharri
Gharry
Go-cart
Go-kart
Hansom
Hearse
Jet ski
Jingle
Jinker
Jitney

Koneka
Koneke
Launch
Limber
Litter
Pick-up
Rocket
Samlor
Skibob
Skidoo®
Sledge
Sleigh
Sno-Cat®
Spider
Surrey
Tandem
Tanker
Telega
Tourer
Tricar
Troika
Tuk tuk
Vahana
Waggon

7 letters:
Amtrack
Bicycle
Caravan
Chariot
Dog-cart
Gritter
Growler
Jeepney
Kibitka
Komatik
Minibus
Minicab
Minivan
Norimon
Omnibus
Pedicab
Phaeton
Postbus
Railcar
Ricksha
Scooter
Sidecar
Tempera
Tipcart

Tracked
Tractor
Trailer
Tramcar
Travois
Trishaw
Trolley
Tumbrel
Tumbril
Utility
Volante
Wildcat

8 letters:
Aircraft
Brancard
Carriage
Carry-all
Curricle
Dustcart
Motorbus
Motorcar
Panda car
Rickshaw
Runabout
Scout car
Stanhope
Steam-car
Tarantas
Toboggan
Tow truck
Tricycle
Unicycle

9 letters:
Ambulance
Autocycle
Bulldozer
Cabriolet
Camper van
Charabanc
Dormobile®
Dump truck
Dune buggy
Estate car
Gladstone
Half-track
Hansom cab
Hatchback
Jaunty car

Jinriksha
Landaulet
Land Rover
Limousine
Low-loader
Milk float
Motorbike
Police car
Racing car
Road train
Sand-yacht
Spaceship
Sports car
Streetcar
Tarantass
Trail bike
Tumble-car
Wagonette

10 letters:
Black Maria
Fire engine
Hovercraft
Jinricksha
Jinrikisha
Juggernaut
Locomotive
Motorcycle
Panel truck
Post chaise
Roadroller
Shandrydan
Snowmobile
Snow plough
Spacecraft
Space probe
Stagecoach
Tank engine
Touring car
Trolleybus
Trolley car
Tumble-cart
Two-wheeler
Velocipede
Waggonette

11 letters:
Articulated
Caterpillar®
Delivery van

Dumper-truck
Jaunting car
Jinrickshaw
Landaulette
Light engine
Steamroller
Tipper lorry
Tipper truck
Wheelbarrow

12 letters:
Autorickshaw
Breakdown van
Double-decker

Garbage truck
Motorbicycle
Motor caravan
Motor scooter
Motor vehicle
Pantechnicon
Perambulator
Single-decker
Space capsule
Space shuttle
Station wagon
Three-wheeler
Troop carrier
Utility truck

13 letters:
Fork-lift truck
Paddock-basher
Penny-farthing
People carrier

14 letters:
Conestoga wagon
Off-road vehicle
Traction engine

16 letters:
Articulated lorry
Combine harvester

See also:
➤ **Aircraft** ➤ **Bicycles** ➤ **Boats and ships** ➤ **Cars** ➤ **Carriages and carts**
➤ **Famous locomotives**

Veins

4 letters:
Spur

6 letters:
Portal
Radius

7 letters:
Basilic
Femoral

Jugular
Saphena

8 letters:
Terminal
Vena cava

9 letters:
Arteriole

Pulmonary
Sectorial

10 letters:
Subclavian

11 letters:
Subscapular

Volcanoes

3 letters:
Apo
Aso
Puy

4 letters:
Etna
Fuji
Maui
Pelé
Taal

5 letters:
Askja

Elgon
Hekla
Kauai
Kenya
Mayon
Misti
Pelée
Teide
Teyde
Thira

6 letters:
Ararat

Asosan
Egmont
Erebus
Ischia
Katmai
Kazbek
Semeru
Tolima

7 letters:
Aragats
El Misti
Hornito

Volcanoes

Huascán
Iliamna
Iwo Jima
Ruapehu
Semeroe
Tambora

8 letters:
Antisana
Cameroon
Cotopaxi
Demavend
Krakatau
Krakatoa
Mauna Kea
Mauna Loa
St Helens
Taraniki
Vesuvius

9 letters:
Aniakchak
Corcovado

Haleakala
Helgafell
Huascarán
Paricutín
Pozzolana
Puzzolana
Soufrière
Stromboli
Suribachi
Tangariro

10 letters:
Chimborazo
Lassen Peak
Montserrat
Nyiragongo
Pozzuolana
Santa Maria

11 letters:
Erciyas Dagi
Kilimanjaro
Mount Katmai

Nyamuragira
Olympus Mons

12 letters:
Citlaltépetl
Ixtaccihuatl
Iztaccihuatl
National Park
Popocatépetl

13 letters:
Mount St. Helens

14 letters:
Nevado de Colima
Nevado de Toluca
Soufrière Hills
Tristan da Cunha

17 letters:
Warrumbungle Range

W w

Warfare terms

2 letters:
AB
GI
MP
RA
RE
RN

3 letters:
Arm
Axe
Bow
Cap
Cut
Dud
Foe
Gat
Gun
Hun
NCO
POW
RAF
Ram
Rat
Rod
Row
Sap
Spy
Sub
TNT
Tyr
Van
Vet
War

4 letters:
Ally
Ammo
Ares
Arms
Army
A-war

AWOL
Ball
Band
Barb
Bard
Bill
Bird
Bola
Bolt
Bomb
Bone
Bout
Bren
Butt
Camp
Club
Cock
Coif
Colt
Cosh
Dart
D-day
Dike
Dirk
Dove
Duck
Duel
Dump
Duty
Epee
Exon
Feud
File
Fire
Fish
Flak
Foil
Fort
Fray
Guns
Hate

Hawk
Helm
Hero
Hilt
Hold
Host
H-war
ICBM
Impi
Jack
Jamb
Jeep
Jock
Keep
Kill
Kris
Levy
Load
Lock
Mail
Mars
Mere
Mine
MIRV
Moat
Mole
Navy
Odin
Peel
Peon
Pike
Post
Rack
Rank
Rath
Riot
Rock
Rout
Rush
Shot
Slug

Spit
Spur
Stab
Tank
Tuck
Unit
WACS
Wage
Wall
Ward
WAVE
Wing
WRNS
Yomp
Zone
Zulu

5 letters:
AA gun
A-bomb
Aegis
Arena
Armed
Armet
Array
Arrow
At bay
At war
Baton
Beset
Blade
Blank
Blast
Blitz
Boche
Bolas
Brave
Broch
Buffs
Burst
Cadre
Chute
Clash
Corps
Cover
Ditch
Draft
Drive
Enemy
Feint

Fence
Field
Fight
Flail
Flank
Fleet
Foray
Fosse
Front
Fusee
Fusil
Grape
Guard
Harry
H-bomb
H-hour
Jerid
Jerry
Jihad
Jingo
Knife
Kukri
Lager
Lance
Leave
Luger
Melee
Mound
Muket
Onset
Orgue
Parry
Pavis
Plate
Poilu
Posse
Power
Provo
Rally
Range
Ranks
Rebel
Recce
Redan
Repel
Rifle
Rowel
Sally
Salvo
Scarp

Scene
Scout
Sepoy
Serve
Shaft
Shako
Shell
Shoot
Siege
Skean
Sling
Snake
Sowar
Spahi
Spear
Spike
Spray
Spurs
Squad
Staff
Steel
Stick
Stone
Storm
Sword
Targe
Tasse
Tommy
Train
Troop
Truce
U-boat
Uhlan
Visor
WAACS
WAAFS
Waddy
Woden
Wound
WRACS
Wrens

6 letters:
Abatis
Ack-ack
Action
Air arm
Air gun
Alpeen
Amazon

Ambush	Enlist	Oilcan
Animus	Ensign	Outfit
Anzacs	Escarp	Panzer
Archer	Escort	Parade
Archie	Exocet	Parole
Argosy	Fewter	Patrol
Armada	Flight	Pavise
Armour	Foeman	Pellet
Askari	Forage	Pepper
Assail	Forces	Petard
Attack	Gabion	Picket
Barbel	Galoot	Pierce
Barrel	Glacis	Pistol
Batman	Glaive	Pogrom
Battle	Gorget	Pompom
Beaver	Greave	Powder
Bellum	Gunner	Pow-pow
Big gun	Gun shy	Quiver
Billet	Gurkha	Rafale
Bomber	Gusset	Rajput
Breech	Hagbut	Ramrod
Bugler	Hammer	Rapier
Bullet	Hanger	Rappel
Bunker	Hanjar	Ray gun
Camail	Harass	Razzia
Cannon	Heaume	Rebuff
Casque	Helmet	Reduit
Castle	Hot war	Report
Casual	Hussar	Revolt
Charge	Impact	Rioter
Cohort	Impale	Rocket
Column	In arms	Rookie
Combat	Inroad	Salade
Convoy	Jereed	Sallet
Cordon	Jingal	Salute
Corium	Laager	Sangar
Creese	Labrys	Sapper
Cudgel	Lancer	Sconce
Cuisse	Legion	Scutum
Curfew	Lorica	Sentry
Curtal	Mailed	Set gun
Dagger	Maquis	Shield
Defeat	Marine	Slogan
Defend	Mauser	Sniper
Detail	Merlon	Sortie
Donjon	Minnie	Sparth
Dry run	Morion	Spying
Duello	Mortar	Strafe
Dugout	Muster	Strike
Dumdum	Muzzle	Swivel

Talion	Blowgun	Dragoon
Target	Boer War	Draught
Tenail	Bombard	Dry fire
Thrust	Bombing	Dudgeon
To arms	Booster	Dueller
Tocsin	Bravado	Dungeon
Toledo	Bren gun	Echelon
Tom-tom	Bricole	Enomoty
Trench	Brigade	Fall-out
Troops	Buckler	Fend off
Tulwar	Bulldog	Fighter
Turret	Bulwark	Firearm
Vallum	Caisson	Fortify
Valour	Caitiff	Fortlet
Vandal	Calibre	Foxhole
Victor	Caliver	Gallant
Volley	Caltrop	Gallery
War cry	Canonry	Gas bomb
War god	Cap-a-pie	Gas mask
Weapon	Carbine	Germ war
Womera	Carcass	Gisarme
Yeoman	Carrier	Go to war
Zouave	Cashier	Grapnel
	Cavalry	Grenade
7 letters:	Chamade	Gunboat
Abattis	Chamber	Gundeck
Advance	Charger	Gunfire
Air raid	Chicken	Gunlock
Amnesty	Citadel	Gunnage
Archery	Cold war	Gunnery
Armoury	Command	Gunning
Arsenal	Company	Gun park
Assault	Conchie	Gunplay
Assegai	Conquer	Gun port
Atom gun	Cordite	Gunroom
Atom war	Corslet	Gunshot
Baldric	Cossack	Hackbut
Barrack	Coupure	Halberd
Barrage	Courage	Handjar
Barrier	Courser	Harness
Bar shot	Crusade	Hatchet
Basinet	Cudgels	Hauberk
Bastion	Cuirass	Heroism
Battery	Curtain	Hessian
Bayonet	Curtana	Heyduck
Bazooka	Cutlass	Hold off
Beat off	Dastard	Holster
Bellona	Defence	Holy war
Big guns	Disband	Hostage
Big shot	Distaff	Invader

Jackman
Jambeau
Jankers
Javelin
Jollies
Jump jet
Knifing
Kremlin
Lambast
Lamboys
Longbow
Long Tom
Lookout
Lunette
Lyddite
Machete
Make war
Maniple
Mantlet
Marines
Martial
Matross
Megaton
Militia
Missile
Mission
Neutral
Offence
On guard
Open war
Outpost
Outwork
Paladin
Panoply
Parados
Parapet
Patriot
Pedrero
Petrary
Phalanx
Pikeman
Pillbox
Platoon
Poleaxe
Poniard
Private
Quarrel
Rampage
Rampart
Ravelin

Recruit
Red army
Redcoat
Redoubt
Regular
Repulse
Retreat
Riposte
Sabaoth
Sabaton
Salient
Samurai
Sandbag
Seabees
Section
Self bow
Service
Shoot at
Shooter
Shotgun
Soldier
Spartan
Sparthe
Spinner
Sten gun
Supremo
Tactics
Tear-gas
Tenable
Testudo
Theatre
The fray
Torpedo
Traitor
Trigger
Trooper
Tumbril
Uniform
Veteran
Victory
Wage war
War club
Ward off
War drum
Warfare
War game
Warhead
Warlike
Warlord
Warpath

Warring
Warrior
Warship
War song
Weapons
Wind gun
Woomera
Wounded
Yatagan
Yomping

8 letters:
Aceldama
Activate
Air force
Air rifle
Air-to-air
All-clear
Alliance
Ammo dump
Anabasis
Anti-mine
Arbalest
Armament
Armature
Armoured
Arms race
Arquebus
Art of war
Atom bomb
Attacker
Aventail
Ballista
Banderol
Barbette
Barbican
Barracks
Bartisan
Baselard
Battalia
Battling
Bear arms
Besieger
Betrayer
Blockade
Blowpipe
Bludgeon
Bomb rack
Bomb site
Brattice

Brickbat	File fire	Mailclad
Broadaxe	Fireball	Man-of-war
Browning	Fire bomb	Mantelet
Buckshot	Firelock	Marksman
Buttress	Fire upon	Martello
Buzzbomb	Flotilla	Massacre
Campaign	Fortress	Maxim gun
Casemate	Fugleman	Melinite
Catapult	Furlough	Militant
Cavalier	Fusilier	Military
Chaffron	Gambeson	Mobilize
Chamfron	Garrison	Morrison
Champion	Gauntlet	Muniment
Chasseur	Great War	Munition
Chivalry	Guerilla	Mushroom
Civil war	Gunflint	Musketry
Claymore	Gunmetal	Nerve gas
Cold feet	Gunpoint	Open fire
Commando	Gunsmith	Ordnance
Conflict	Gunstick	Orillion
Crossbow	Gunstock	Outguard
Cry havoc	Hang fire	Overkill
Culverin	Heavy gun	Pacifist
Cylinder	Hedgehog	Palisade
Defender	Herisson	Palstaff
Demilune	Hill fort	Palstave
Deserter	Hireling	Partisan
Destrier	Hornwork	Password
Division	Howitzer	Pauldron
Doughboy	Infantry	Petronel
Drum call	Informer	Pikehead
Drumfire	Invading	Poltroon
Drumhead	Invasion	Puncheon
Duellist	Ironclad	Quisling
Dynamite	Janizary	Quo vadis
Embattle	Jazerant	Recreant
Enfilade	Jingoism	Regiment
Enlistee	Jump area	Renegade
Entrench	Killadar	Repulsor
Envelope	Knuckles	Reserves
Errantry	Lancegay	Reveille
Escalade	Land-army	Revolver
Exercise	Land-mine	Ricochet
Falchion	Langrage	Rifleman
Falconet	Last post	Risalder
Fasthold	Launcher	Runagate
Fastness	Leon mine	Safehold
Fencible	Lewis gun	Scabbard
Field gun	Loophole	Scimitar
Fighting	Magazine	Sentinel

Shrapnel
Side arms
Siege cap
Skean dhu
Skirmish
Soldiery
Solleret
Space gun
Spadroon
Spearman
Spontoon
Squadron
Stabbing
Stalwart
Star Wars
Stave off
Stiletto
Stockade
Strafing
Strategy
Struggle
Surprise
Surround
Take arms
Tenaille
The front
The sword
Time bomb
Tomahawk
Tommy gun
Total war
Transfix
Trenches
Turnback
Turncoat
Turntail
Up in arms
Uprising
Vambrace
Vamplate
Vanguard
Vanquish
Vendetta
War cloud
Warcraft
War dance
Warfarer
War horse
War hound
War paint

War whoop
Waterloo
Wayfarer
Weaponry
World war
Yeomanry
Zero hour

9 letters:
Accoutred
Aggressor
Air-to-ship
Ambuscade
Arch enemy
Army corps
Army issue
Army lists
Arrowhead
Artillery
Assailant
Atomic gun
Atomic war
Attacking
Attrition
Automatic
Auto-rifle
Backplate
Ballistic
Banderole
Bandolier
Bastinado
Battalion
Battleaxe
Battlecry
Beachhead
Beefeater
Beleaguer
Bellicism
Bellicose
Big Bertha
Blackjack
Bloodshed
Bomb-happy
Bombs away
Bombshell
Bombsight
Booby trap
Boomerang
Broadside
Brown Bess

Brown bill
Camouflet
Cannonade
Cannoneer
Caparison
Carronade
Carry arms
Cartouche
Cartridge
Casemated
Castellan
Cease fire
Chain mail
Chain shot
Challenge
Chamfrain
Chassepot
Cold steel
Combatant
Combative
Conqueror
Conscript
Corselect
Crackshot
Cross fire
Defensive
Derringer
Desert rat
Deterrent
Detonator
Discharge
Doodlebug
Double sap
Drop a bomb
Earthwork
Embattled
Encompass
Enemy camp
Enemy fire
Escopette
Espionage
Explosive
Face guard
Fence wall
Field army
Fieldwork
Fire a shot
Firepower
Fireworks
First line

Flintlock	Manoeuvre	Ski troops
Flying sap	March past	Skyrocket
Fortalice	Matchlock	Sky troops
Fortified	Mercenary	Slaughter
Fourth arm	Militancy	Slingshot
Free-lance	Minefield	Slungshot
Front line	Minuteman	Small arms
Fulgurite	Monomachy	Small bore
Fusillade	Munitions	Small-shot
Gas attack	Musketeer	Smoke bomb
Gelignite	Musketoon	Soldierly
Gladiator	Needle gun	Soldier on
Grapeshot	Nose guard	Sonic mine
Grenadier	Nosepiece	Son of a gun
Guardsman	Offensive	Spearhead
Gun battle	Onslaught	Spring gun
Guncotton	Open order	Stand fire
Gunpowder	Operation	Stink bomb
Gun turret	Other side	Strategic
Habergeon	Overthrow	Subaltern
Harquebus	Panoplied	Submarine
Headpiece	Parachute	Super bomb
Heavy fire	Peel-house	Surprisal
Heroic act	Peel-tower	Surrender
Home Guard	Pikestaff	Swivel gun
Hostility	Prick-spur	Sword-play
Hydrobomb	Projector	Take sides
Incursion	Pugnacity	Tank corps
Incursive	Pyroxylin	Target day
In defence	Ram rocket	Task force
Ironbound	Rearguard	Tit for tat
Irregular	Rebel call	Torpedoed
Irruption	Rebellion	Torpedoer
Janissary	Rerebrace	Trainband
Jesserant	Ressalder	Trench gun
Katabasis	Rifle ball	Troopship
Keep guard	Rocket gun	Truncheon
Keep vigil	Rocket man	Under arms
Lance-jack	Roundhead	Under fire
Langridge	Round shot	Vigilante
Last ditch	Rowel spur	Volunteer
Legionary	Royal Navy	Warmonger
Levy war on	Sally port	War Office
Lie in wait	Saltpetre	War rocket
Lionheart	Sea battle	Watchword
Logistics	Seat of war	White flag
Long-range	Sentry box	Woomerang
Luftwaffe	Shellfire	Zumbooruk
Make war on	Signalman	
Man-at-arms	Single sap	

10 letters:

Activation	Carabineer	Lambrequin
Active army	Carry on war	Lay siege to
Active duty	Cavalryman	Life Guards
Active list	Coastguard	Light-armed
Adventurer	Coat of mail	Line of fire
Aerial bomb	Combat area	Loaded cane
Aerial mine	Combat team	Long knives
Aggression	Commandant	Lookout man
Aggressive	Contingent	Machine gun
Air Command	Cross-staff	Martiality
Air service	Cuirassier	Militarism
Ambushment	Declare war	Militarize
Ammunition	Defendable	Militiaman
Antagonism	Defensible	Missile man
Armageddon	Demobilize	Mob tactics
Armed force	Detachment	Mount guard
Armed guard	Direct fire	Mural crown
Armed truce	Dragonnade	Musket shot
Armigerous	Dragoonade	Mustard gas
Armipotent	Drawbridge	Napalm bomb
Arm's length	Drummer boy	No man's land
Atomic bomb	Embankment	Nuclear war
Atomic pile	Encampment	Obsidional
Atom-rocket	Engarrison	Occupation
Ballistics	Eprouvette	Old soldier
Barbed-wire	Escalation	On the march
Battle flag	Expedition	Operations
Battle hymn	Faint heart	Other ranks
Battle line	Fieldpiece	Over the top
Battlement	Field train	Oyster mine
Battleship	Fiery cross	Paratroops
Blitzkrieg	Fire trench	Percussion
Blockhouse	Firing area	Petrol bomb
Bold stroke	Flying bomb	Picket duty
Bombardier	Flying tank	Point blank
Bowie knife	Foot Guards	Portcullis
Box barrage	Foot rifles	Private war
Breastwork	Gatling gun	Projectile
Bridgehead	Ground fire	Raking fire
Brigandine	Ground mine	Rally round
Broadsword	Ground-zero	Raw recruit
Bugle corps	Halberdier	Resistance
Call to arms	Heavy-armed	Revolution
Camel corps	Impalement	Rifle range
Camouflage	Incendiary	Rocket bomb
Campaigner	Investment	Rocket fire
Cannon ball	Jingoistic	Rules of war
Cannon shot	Knighthood	Run-through
Cantonment	Knobkerrie	Second line
	Kriegspiel	Sentry duty

Serviceman
Shellshock
Shillelagh
Short-range
Siegecraft
Siege train
Six-shooter
Slit trench
Smallsword
Smooth bore
Spill blood
Stand guard
State of war
Strategist
Stronghold
Submachine
Sure as a gun
Sword fight
Swordstick
Sworn enemy
Take to arms
Tenderfoot
Ten-pounder
Test rocket
Touch paper
Trajectile
Trajectory
Under siege
Vanquisher
Volunteers
War goddess
Winchester

11 letters:
Air-to-ground
Anti-missile
Anti-tank gun
Area bombing
Armed combat
Armed forces
Armoured car
Auxiliaries
Barnstormer
Battle array
Battledress
Battlefield
Battle order
Battle plane
Battle royal
Beach master

Bersaglieri
Besiegement
Blockbuster
Bloody shirt
Blunderbuss
Bombardment
Bomber pilot
Bomb-release
Bow and arrow
Breastplate
British Army
British Navy
Buck private
Bulletproof
Buoyant mine
Bushwhacker
Camaraderie
Castellated
Castle guard
Caterpillar
Change sides
Combat train
Contentious
Countermine
Crack troops
Declaration
Demibastion
Depth charge
Dive-bombing
Emplacement
Enemy action
Engine of war
Enlisted man
Envelopment
Fighting man
Fire a volley
Fire tactics
Firing party
Firing squad
Firing table
First strike
Fission bomb
Flare rocket
Flying corps
Footed arrow
Footslogger
Foot soldier
Forced march
Force of arms
Friend or foe

Full harness
Full of fight
Gang warfare
Generalship
Germ warfare
Giant powder
Ground-to-air
Guerrillero
Guncarriage
Hair trigger
Hand grenade
Heavy armour
Heavy bomber
High dudgeon
Hill station
Horse Guards
Horse pistol
Hostilities
Infantrymen
Irish Guards
Iron rations
Land warfare
Light bomber
Lionhearted
Lochaber axe
Loggerheads
Look daggers
Magazine gun
Maginot line
Marine Corps
Might of arms
Military man
Mine thrower
Moral defeat
Mountain gun
Naval bomber
Naval forces
Nitre powder
Nitrocotton
Nuclear bomb
Open warfare
Pattern bomb
Peace treaty
Picket guard
Plate armour
Platoon fire
Postern gate
Powder grain
Provisional
Put to flight

Rallying cry
Rank and file
Rebel action
Reconnoitre
Recruitment
Regular army
Retro-rocket
Rolling fire
Safe-conduct
Safety catch
Scots Guards
Service call
Ship-to-shore
Shock troops
Shooting war
Shoot to kill
Shuttle raid
Signal Corps
Smell powder
Smoke screen
Sneak attack
Soldatesque
Soldierlike
Soldiership
Spent bullet
Stand at ease
Stand of arms
Step rockets
Stormtroops
Stray bullet
Subdivision
Swiss Guards
Sword in hand
Take by storm
Thin red line
Tommy Atkins
Torpedo boat
Trench knife
Trigger talk
True colours
Trusty sword
Under attack
Underground
Up and at them
Warlikeness
War of nerves
Warriorlike
War to end war
Water cannon
Wooden horse

Wooden walls

12 letters:
Acoustic mine
Anti-aircraft
Appeal to arms
Armour-plated
Army reserves
Artilleryman
Atomic cannon
Awkward squad
Banzai charge
Battering ram
Battleground
Beat a retreat
Belligerence
Breakthrough
Breechloader
Buccaneering
Bushfighting
Cannon fodder
Cannon's mouth
Civil defence
Council of war
Counter march
Court martial
Cut-and-thrust
Daggers drawn
Deadly weapon
Demi-culverin
Dumdum bullet
Dutch courage
Electron bomb
Encirclement
Engines of war
Entrenchment
Escaramouche
False colours
Field of blood
Flame-thrower
Floating mine
Flying column
Forward march
Fowling piece
Gladiatorial
Go over the top
Grand tactics
Ground forces
Guerrilla war
Guided weapon

Heavy dragoon
Home reserves
Homing rocket
Horse and foot
Horse marines
Hydrogen bomb
Lady from hell
Launching pad
Leathernecks
Light Brigade
Light dragoon
Line of action
Line of battle
Machicolated
Magnetic mine
March against
Marching song
Medical Corps
Medium bomber
Military zone
Mine detector
Mobilization
Moral courage
Moral support
Moral victory
Muzzle-loader
Naval militia
Naval reserve
Naval warfare
On the warpath
Parthian shot
Pearl Harbour
Picked troops
Pioneer corps
Plunging fire
Powder charge
Pyrotechnics
Quarterstaff
Reactivation
Religious war
Rifled cannon
Rifle grenade
Rocket attack
Second strike
Sharpshooter
Shock tactics
Shoulder a gun
Shoulder arms
Siege warfare
Signal rocket

Warfare terms

Single combat
Smoker rocket
Standing army
Stormtrooper
Stouthearted
Sudden attack
Supply troops
Sword bayonet
Tactical unit
Take the field
Theatre of war
Tooth and nail
Trench mortar
Trigger happy
Under the flag
Vertical fire
Virus warfare
Warmongering
White feather
Who goes there
Yellow streak

13 letters:
Active service
Andrew Ferrara
Armaments race
Armed conflict
Arms and the man
Army exercises
Articles of war
Assault course
Baptism of fire
Battle cruiser
Battle honours
Battle-scarred
Bayonet charge
Beleaguerment
Bomber command
Breechloading
British Legion
Cartridge-belt
Cavalry charge
Cheval-de-frise
Churchill tank
Cobelligerent
Combat fatigue
Comrade in arms
Counter-attack
Desert warfare
Disengagement

Dispatch-rider
Drill sergeant
Evasive action
Exocet missile
Field hospital
Field of battle
Fighter patrol
First world war
Flammenwerfer
Flying colours
Flying officer
Force de frappe
Foreign legion
Fortification
Generalissimo
Guard of honour
Guided missile
Gunnery school
High-explosive
Lance-corporal
Light infantry
Line of defence
Listening post
Machine gunner
Messerschmitt
Military Cross
Military Medal
Military tatoo
Mine detection
Mini-submarine
Muzzle loading
Non-resistance
Nuclear weapon
Order of battle
Order of the day
Passage of arms
Peninsular War
Pitched battle
Prisoner of war
Put to the sword
Quarter-gunner
Quartermaster
Reinforcement
Royal air force
Running battle
Sabre-rattling
Scorched earth
Senior service
Sergeant-major
Siegfried line

Staff-sergeant
Striking force
Sublieutenant
Sub-machine gun
Trench warfare
Two-edged sword
Unarmed combat
Victoria Cross
War department
War to the death
Wing commander
Yeoman service

14 letters:
Action stations
Airborne forces
Airborne troops
Aircraftswoman
Air Vice-Marshal
Ammunition dump
Army cadet force
Army manoeuvres
Barrage balloon
Battle stations
Blank-cartridge
Blockade runner
Captain-general
Cavalry officer
Chevaux-de-frise
Cloak-and-dagger
Coastal battery
Coastal command
Colonel-in-chief
Colour-sergeant
Comrades in arms
Conquering hero
Demobilisation
Field ambulance
Field artillery
Fifth columnist
Fighter command
Fight to a finish
Flag-lieutenant
Freedom fighter
Guerrilla chief
Guerrilla force
Heavy artillery
Horse artillery
Incendiary bomb
Liaison officer

Light artillery
Marching orders
Militarisation
Military police
Muzzle velocity
Non-operational
Nuclear warfare
Nuclear warhead
Operations room
Orderly officer
Ordinary seaman
Pincer movement
Powder magazine
Pyrrhic victory
Reconnaissance
Regimental band
Royal Artillery
Royal Engineers
Royal Fusiliers
Royal Tank Corps
Squadron-leader
Street fighting
Supreme command
Unknown soldier

Unknown warrior
Urban guerrilla
Warrant officer
Wars of the Roses
Winter quarters

15 letters:
Adjutant general
Air chief marshal
Aircraft carrier
Anderson shelter
Armed to the teeth
Armoured cruiser
Brigade of Guards
Chemical warfare
Displaced person
First lieutenant
Gentleman-at-arms
Grenadier Guards
Light machine-gun
Military mission
Military service
Molotov cocktail
Morrison shelter

Mulberry harbour
National defence
National service
Naval engagement
Naval operations
Non-commissioned
Observation post
Officer of the day
On active service
Orderly corporal
Orderly sergeant
Parachute troops
Rearguard action
Recruiting drive
Regimental march
Second-in-command
Spoils of victory
Sword-and-buckler
Telescopic sight
Territorial army

17 letters:
Up guards and at them

Water sports

6 letters:
Diving
Rowing

7 letters:
Sailing
Surfing

8 letters:
Canoeing
Swimming
Yachting

9 letters:
Canoe polo
Water polo

10 letters:
Skin diving

11 letters:
Aquabobbing
Parasailing
Water-skiing
Windsurfing

12 letters:
Powerboating

15 letters:
Powerboat racing

20 letters:
Synchronized
    swimming

Waterfalls

5 letters:
Angel
Pilao
Tysse

6 letters:
Iguaçú
Kabiwa
Mardel
Ormeli

Ribbon
Tugela

7 letters:
Mtarazi

Niagara
Roraima

Victoria
Yosemite

Sutherland

11 letters:
Yellowstone

8 letters:
Cuquenan
Itatinga
Kaieteur
Takakkaw

9 letters:
Churchill

13 letters:
Vestre Mardola

10 letters:
Cleve-Garth

Weapons

2 letters:
V1

3 letters:
Dag
Gad
Gun

4 letters:
Bill
Bolo
Bomb
Club
Cosh
Dart
Gade
Gaid
Kris
Mace®
Nuke
Spat
Sten

5 letters:
Arrow
Baton
Estoc
Flail
Maxim
Orgue
Pilum
Rifle
Sabre
Saker
Sting
Sword
Taser®
Vouge

6 letters:
Airgun
Binary
Cestus
Cohorn
Cudgel
Dagger
Gingal
Glaive
Jingal
Mauser®
Mortar
Musket
Napalm
Onager
Pistol
Sparke
Sparth
Taiaha
Tomboc
Voulge

7 letters:
Arblast
Assegai
Ataghan
Bayonet
Bazooka
Bondook
Caliver
Caltrap
Caltrop
Carbine
Coehorn
Cutlass
Dragoon
Enfield
Fougade

Gingall
Gisarme
Grenade
Halberd
Halbert
Harpoon
Javelin
Longbow
Machete
Matchet
Quarrel
Sandbag
Shotgun
Torpedo
Trident

8 letters:
Arbalest
Armalite®
Arquebus
Ballista
Blowpipe
Bludgeon
Calthrop
Catapult
Crossbow
Culverin
Death ray
Elf-arrow
Fougasse
Howitzer
Mangonel
Nunchaku
Partisan
Petronel
Revolver
Skean-dhu
Skene-dhu

Spontoon
Stiletto
Stinkpot
Whirl-bat
Whorl-bat

9 letters:
Arquebuse
Backsword
Battleaxe
Derringer
Doodlebug
Excalibur
Fléchette
Flintlock
Forty-five
Grapeshot
Greek fire
Harquebus

Poison gas
Sarbacane
Trebuchet
Trebucket
Truncheon

10 letters:
Broadsword
Mustard gas

11 letters:
Germ warfare
Morgenstern
Snickersnee

12 letters:
Flame-thrower
Quarterstaff
Rifle grenade

13 letters:
Knuckle-duster
Life-preserver
Maurikigusari

14 letters:
Nunchaku sticks

15 letters:
Chemical warfare

17 letters:
Biological warfare

22 letters:
Bacteriological warfare

Weather

WEATHER DESCRIPTIONS

3 letters:
Dry
Hot
Icy
Raw
Wet

4 letters:
Cold
Dull
Fine
Foul
Hazy
Mild

5 letters:
Balmy
Bland
Clear
Close
Dirty
Foggy

Fresh
Humid
Misty
Muggy
Nippy
Parky
Rainy
Snowy
Sunny
Windy

6 letters:
Arctic
Baking
Breezy
Clammy
Cloudy
Dreich
Filthy
Sticky
Stormy
Sultry

Wintry

7 letters:
Clement
Drizzly
Showery

8 letters:
Blustery
Freezing
Overcast
Thundery
Tropical

9 letters:
Inclement
Perishing
Scorching

10 letters:
Blistering

WEATHER PHENOMENA

3 letters:
Fog
Ice

4 letters:
Gale
Gust
Haar
Hail
Mist
Rain
Snow
Thaw
Wind

5 letters:
Cloud
Sleet
Smirr
Storm

6 letters:
Breeze
Freeze
Shower
Squall
Zephyr

7 letters:
Cyclone
Drizzle
Tempest
Thunder
Tornado
Tsunami
Typhoon

8 letters:
Acid rain
Cold snap
Heatwave
Pressure
Sunshine

9 letters:
Dust devil
Dust storm
Hurricane
Lightning
Peasouper
Sandstorm
Tidal wave
Whirlwind

10 letters:
Waterspout
Willy-willy

13 letters:
Ball lightning
Precipitation

14 letters:
Sheet lightning

METEOROLOGICAL TERMS

4 letters:
Scud

5 letters:
Front
Ridge
Virga

6 letters:
Isobar
Trough

7 letters:
Cyclone
Lee wave
Thermal

9 letters:
Cold front
Isallobar
Warm front

10 letters:
Depression
Heat-island

11 letters:
Anticyclone

13 letters:
Occluded front
Synoptic chart

GATHERERS OF WEATHER DATA

9 letters:
Dropsonde
Met. Office

10 letters:
Radiosonde
Weatherman

11 letters:
Weather ship

12 letters:
Meteorograph
Pilot balloon
Weatherwoman

14 letters:
Weather station

20 letters:
Meteorological Office

WEATHER MEASURING INSTRUMENTS

Instrument	Phenomenon measured
Anemometer	Wind velocity
Anemoscope	Wind direction
Atmometer	Rate of water evaporation into atmosphere
Barograph	Atmospheric pressure
Barometer	Atmospheric pressure
Baroscope	Atmospheric pressure
Hygrometer	Humidity
Maximum-minimum thermometer	Temperature variation
Nephoscope	Cloud velocity, altitude, and direction of movement
Psychrometer	Humidity
Rain gauge	Rainfall and snowfall
Rawinsonde	Atmospheric wind velocity
Stevenson's screen	Temperature
Sunshine recorder	Hours of sunshine
Thermometer	Temperature
Weathercock	Wind direction
Weather vane	Wind direction
Wet-and-dry-bulb thermometer	Humidity
Wind gauge	Wind velocity
Wind tee	Wind direction

See also:
➤ **Regions of the atmosphere** ➤ **Types of cloud** ➤ **Winds**

Weeds

3 letters:
Ers

4 letters:
Alga
Dock
Nard
Ragi
Sudd
Tare
Tine
Ulva
Yarr

5 letters:
Couch
Daisy
Dulse
Lemna
Reate
Runch
Tansy
Vetch

6 letters:
Blinks
Clover
Cockle

Dallop
Darnel
Dollop
Elodea
Fat hen
Fucoid
Indian
Joe-pye
Knawel
Nettle
Nostoc
Oxygen
Sorrel

Spurge
Twitch
Widow's
Winnow

7 letters:
Allseed
Burdock
Femitar
Fenitar
Helodea
Mayweed
Ragwort
Ruderal
Senecio
Spurrey
Thistle

8 letters:
Arenaria

Bedstraw
Bell-bind
Charlock
Fumitory
Knapweed
Matfelon
Pilewort
Piri-piri
Plantain
Purslane
Sargasso

9 letters:
Adderwort
Anacharis
Chickweed
Chlorella
Coltsfoot
Groundsel

Knot-grass
Mare's-tail
Pearlwort
Sun-spurge
Tormentil
Wartcress

10 letters:
Carpetweed
Corncockle
Nipplewort
Rest-harrow
Sagittaria

11 letters:
Potamogeton
Swine's-cress
Ulotrichale

Weights and measures

IMPERIAL SYSTEM

Linear	**Square**	**Weight**
Mile	Square mile	Ton
Furlong	Acre	Hundredweight
Rod	Square rod	Stone
Yard	Square yard	Pound, Ezra Loomis
Foot	Square foot	Ounce
Inch	Square inch	-
Mil	-	-

Land	**Volume**	**Liquid volume**
Square mile	Cubic yard	Gallon
Acre	Cubic foot	Quart
Square rod	Cubic inch	Pint
Square yard	-	Fluid ounce

METRIC SYSTEM

Linear	**Square**	**Weight**
Kilometre	Square kilometre	Tonne
Metre	Square metre	Kilogram
Centimetre	Square centimetre	Gram
Millimetre	Square millimetre	-

METRIC SYSTEM (CONTINUED)

Land	Volume	Liquid volume
Square kilometre	Cubic metre	Litre
Hectare	Cubic decimetre	Millilitre
Are	Cubic centimetre	-
-	Cubic millimetre	-

Whales and dolphins

4 letters:
Orca

6 letters:
Beluga
Dorado

7 letters:
Bowhead
Grampus
Narwhal
Rorqual

8 letters:
Bay whale
Cachalot
Greyback

Porpoise
Sei whale

9 letters:
Blackfish
Blue whale
Grey whale

10 letters:
Black whale
Minke whale
Pilot whale
Right whale
Sperm whale
White whale

11 letters:
Baleen whale
Killer whale

12 letters:
Toothed whale

13 letters:
Humpback whale
Sulphur-bottom

14 letters:
Greenland whale
Whalebone whale

17 letters:
Bottlenose dolphin

Whiskies

3 letters:
Rye

4 letters:
Corn
Malt

5 letters:
Blend
Grain

6 letters:
Poitín
Poteen
Redeye
Scotch

7 letters:
Blended
Bourbon
Hokonui
Shebean
Shebeen

8 letters:
Sour mash

10 letters:
Single malt
Vatted malt

12 letters:
Irish whiskey

Winds

4 letters:
Berg
Bise
Bora
Bura
Föhn
Gale
Gust
Puna

5 letters:
Blore
Buran
Eurus
Foehn
Gibli
Noser
Notus
Trade
Zonda

6 letters:
Aquilo
Auster
Baguio
Boreas
Ghibli
Haboob
Kamsin
Levant
Samiel
Sciroc
Simoom
Simoon
Solano

Squall
Wester
Zephyr

7 letters:
Aeolian
Aquilon
Bluster
Chinook
Cyclone
Draught
Etesian
Gregale
Kamseen
Khamsin
Meltemi
Mistral
Monsoon
Nor'east
Norther
Pampero
Shimaal
Sirocco
Snifter
Snorter
Souther
Sumatra
Tornado
Twister
Typhoon

8 letters:
Argestes
Easterly
Favonian

Favonius
Levanter
Libeccio
Scirocco
Williwaw
Zephyrus

9 letters:
Anti-trade
Dust devil
Euraquilo
Harmattan
Hurricane
Hurricano
Libecchio
Nor'wester
Volturnus

10 letters:
Cape doctor
Euroclydon
Rip-snorter
Tourbillon
Tramontana
Tramontane
Whirlblast
Willy-willy

11 letters:
White squall

13 letters:
Northwesterly

Windows

3 letters:
Bay
Bow

4 letters:
Rose
Sash

5 letters:
Gable
Jesse
Judas
Ogive
Oriel
Ox-eye
Storm

6 letters:
Dormer
French
Garret
Lancet
Monial
Oculus
Rosace

Wicket

7 letters:
Compass
Guichet
Lattice
Lucarne
Lunette
Luthern
Mullion
Picture
Transom
Trellis
Ventana
Weather

Windock
Winnock

8 letters:
Casement
Fanlight
Fenestra
Porthole

9 letters:
Companion
Deadlight
Dream-hole
Loop-light
Mezzanine

10 letters:
Fenestella

11 letters:
Lychnoscope
Oeil-de-boeuf

12 letters:
Quarterlight

14 letters:
Catherine-wheel

Wines

WINES

2 letters:
It

3 letters:
Dão

4 letters:
Asti
Brut
Cava
Gavi
Hock
Palm
Port
Rosé
Rosy
Sack
Sekt
Tent
Tutu

5 letters:
Anjou
Fitou
Lirac
Mâcon
Médoc
Mirin
Mosel

Pinot
Rhine
Rioja
Roero
Rueda
Rully
Soave
Straw
Syrah
Tavel
Tokay
Xeres

6 letters:
Bandol
Barley
Barolo
Barsac
Beaune
Cahors
Canary
Carema
Claret
Ginger
Graves
Lisbon
Málaga
Merlot
Mocker

Muscat
Quincy
Saumur
Sherry
Shiraz
Tokaji

7 letters:
Alicant
Amarone
Amoroso
Auslese
Banyuls
Bastard
Bucelas
Catawba
Chablis
Chianti
Cowslip
Eiswein
Essence
Fendant
Fleurie
Gaillac
Madeira
Malmsey
Margaux
Marsala
Moselle

WINES (CONTINUED)

Orvieto
Parrina
Pomerol
Pommard
Retsina
Rhenish
Vouvray

8 letters:
Bairrada
Bergerac
Bordeaux
Brouilly
Bucellas
Burgundy
Cabernet
Charneco
Condrieu
Dubonnet®
Espumoso
Essencia
Faugères
Frascati
Gigondas
Jerepigo
Jurançon
Kabinett
Malvasia
Malvesie
Montilla
Muscadel
Muscadet
Muscatel
Pauillac
Pinotage
Pradikat
Resinata
Riesling
Sancerre
Sauterne
Spätlese
Spumante
Verdelho

9 letters:
Bacharach
Bardolino
Bourgogne

Bourgueil
Champagne
Corbières
Côte Rôtie
Falernian
Fumé Blanc
Gattinara
Gladstone
Hermitage
Hoccamore
Lambrusco
Languedoc
Malvoisie
Meersault
Meursault
Minervois
Muscadine
Pinot noir
Sauternes
Sauvignon
St Emilion
Tarragona
Zinfandel

10 letters:
Barbaresco
Beaujolais
Bull's Blood
Chambertin
Chardonnay
Constantia
Elderberry
Genevrette
Hochheimer
Manzanilla
Montrachet
Peter-see-me
Piesporter
Rosé d'Anjou
Saint-Véran
Valdepeñas
Verdicchio
Vinho Verde

11 letters:
Amontillado
Crusted port
Egri Bikaver

Monbazillac
Niersteiner
Pinot Grigio
Pouilly-Fumé
Rosso Cònero
Rüdesheimer
Saint-Julien
Scuppernong
Steinberger

12 letters:
Asti Spumante
Barbera d'Albi
Barbera d'Asti
Colheita Port
Côtes du Rhône
Liqueur Tokay
Marcobrunner
Moscato d'Asti
Saint-Émilion
Saint-Estèphe
Valpolicella
Vin ordinaire
Vosne-Romanée

13 letters:
Blanc de blancs
Entre-Deux-Mers
Liebfraumilch
Liqueur Muscat
Mâcon-Villages
Pessac-Léognan
Pouilly-Fousse
Pouilly-Fuissé

14 letters:
Crémant d'Alsace
Crémant de Loire
Gewürztraminer
Johannisberger
Quarts de Chaume
Tokay-Pinot Gris

15 letters:
Crozes-Hermitage
Grange Hermitage
Lachryma Christi
Salice Salentino

WINES (CONTINUED)

16 letters:
Gevrey-Chambertin

17 letters:
Beaujolais nouveau
Bereich Bernkastel
Cabernet Sauvignon
Nuits-Saint-Georges

18 letters:
Blanquette de Limoux

Coteaux du Tricastin
Teroldego Rotaliano

20 letters:
Brunello di Montalcino
Côte de Beaune-Villages
Trockenbeerenauslese

21 letters:
Montepulciano
d'Abruzzo

23 letters:
Muscat de Beaumes-de-
Venise

25 letters:
Vino Nobile di
Montepulciano

WINE-PRODUCING AREAS

Area	Country
Ahr	Germany
Alsace	France
Alto Adige *or* Südtirol	Italy
Anjou	France
Argentina	-
Austria	-
Baden	Germany
Barossa Valley	Australia
Bordeaux	France
Bulgaria	-
Burgundy	France
California	U.S.A.
Chablis	France
Champagne	France
Chianti	Italy
Chile	-
Clare Valley	Australia
Coonawarra	Australia
Côte d'Or	France
Finger Lakes	U.S.A.
Franken	Germany
Friuli	Italy
Gisborne	New Zealand
Goulburn Valley	Australia
Greece	-
Hawkes Bay	New Zealand
Hessiches Bergstrasse	Germany
Hungary	-
Hunter Valley	Australia

WINE-PRODUCING AREAS (CONTINUED)

Area	Country
Languedoc	France
Loire	France
Margaret River	Australia
Marlborough	New Zealand
Martinborough	New Zealand
McLaren Vale	Australia
Mendocino	U.S.A.
Mittelrhein	Germany
Moldavia	-
Mornington Peninsula	Australia
Mosel-Saar-Ruwer	Germany
Nahe	Germany
Napa Valley	U.S.A.
Navarra	Spain
New York State	U.S.A.
Oregon	U.S.A.
Padthaway	Australia
Penedès	Spain
Piedmont	Italy
Portugal	-
Provence	France
Rheingau	Germany
Rheinhessen	Germany
Rheinpfalz	Germany
Rhône	France
Ribera del Duro	Spain
Rioja	Spain
Romania	-
Sicily	Italy
Sonoma	U.S.A.
South Africa	-
Switzerland	-
Touraine	France
Tuscany	Italy
Umbria	Italy
Valdepeñas	Spain
Veneto	Italy
Washington State	U.S.A.
Württemberg	Germany
Yarra Valley	Australia

WINE TERMS

2 letters:
AC
NV

3 letters:
AOC
DOC
Dry
LBV
QbA
QmP
Sec
TBA

4 letters:
Aszú
Brix
Brut
DOCG
Fino
Flor
Rosé
Sekt
VDQS

5 letters:
Baumé
Cream
Cuvée
Dolce
Plonk
Secco
Sweet
Tinto

6 letters:
Medium
Solera
Sur lie
Tannin

7 letters:
Amabile
Auslese
Crianza
Demi-sec
Eiswein
Malmsey
Oechsle

Oloroso
Organic
Passito
Recioto
Récolte
Reserva
Riserva
Terroir
Trocken
Vin gris
Vintage
Weingut

8 letters:
Ausbruch
Botrytis
Grand cru
Kabinett
Moelleux
Mousseux
Noble rot
Prädikat
Ruby Port
Spätlese
Spumante
Varietal
Vigneron
Vignoble

9 letters:
Abbocatto
Cru classé
Grosslage
Medium-dry
Pale cream
Pétillant
Puttonyos
Table wine
Tafelwein
Tawny Port
Vin de pays

10 letters:
Botrytized
Einzellage
Garrafeira
Manzanilla
Non-vintage

Premier cru
Second wine
Sin crianza
Vin de table

11 letters:
Amontillado
Dessert wine
Gran reserva
Halbtrocken
Late harvest
Medium-sweet
Weissherbst

12 letters:
Cru bourgeois
Vino da tavola

13 letters:
Beerenauslese
Estate bottled
Fortified wine
Qualitätswein
Sparkling wine

14 letters:
Vendage tardive
Vieilles vignes
Vin doux naturel

15 letters:
Pourriture noble
Sigle Quinta Port

17 letters:
Erzeugerabfüllung

18 letters:
Late-Bottled Vintage
Méthode champenoise

20 letters:
Appellation contrôlée
Trockenbeerenauslese
Winzergenossenschaft

22 letters:
Late-Bottled Vintage
  Port

WINE TERMS (CONTINUED)

Malolactic fermentation

24 letters:
Qualitätswein mit
  Prädikat

28 letters:
Appellation d'origine
  contrôlée

30 letters:
Vin Délimité de Qualité
  Supérieure

33 letters:
Denominazione di
  origine controllata

34 letters:
Qualitätswein
  bestimmter
  Anbaugebiet

43 letters:
Denominazione di
  origine controllata e
  garantita

Winter sports

4 letters:
Luge

6 letters:
Skiing
Slalom
Super-G

7 letters:
Curling
Skating

8 letters:
Biathlon

9 letters:
Bobsleigh
Ice hockey
Skijoring

10 letters:
Ice dancing
Ice skating
Skibobbing
Ski jumping

11 letters:
Tobogganing

12 letters:
Alpine skiing
Nordic skiing
Snowboarding
Speed skating

13 letters:
Figure skating

14 letters:
Downhill racing

Seven wonders of the ancient world

Colossus of Rhodes
Hanging Gardens of Babylon
Mausoleum of Halicarnassus
Pharos of Alexandria

Phidias' statue of Zeus at Olympia
Pyramids of Egypt
Temple of Artemis at Ephesus

Types of wood

3 letters:
Ash
Box
Elm
Fir
Koa
Oak
Red

Yew

4 letters:
Beef
Cade
Eugh
Iron
Lana

Lime
Pear
Pine
Poon
Rata
Teak
Toon
Yang

5 letters:
Agila
Algum
Almug
Apple
Balsa
Beech
Birch
Cedar
Ebony
Hazel
Heben
Iroko
Jarul
Kauri
Kiaat
Kokra
Larch
Maple
Myall
Olive
Opepe
Plane
Ramin
Rowan
Sapan
Sassy
Stink
Sumac
Thorn
Tulip
Zante

6 letters:
Alerce
Bamboo
Bog oak
Brasil
Brazil
Canary
Carapa
Cherry
Citron
Fustet
Fustic
Fustoc
Gaboon
Gopher
Jarool
Jarrah

Lignum
Locust
Miombo
Obeche
Orache
Orange
Padauk
Padouk
Poplar
Red fir
Red gum
Red oak
Sabele
Sabicu
Sandal
Sapele
Sappan
Sissoo
Sponge
Spruce
Sumach
Tupelo
Waboom
Walnut
Willow

7 letters:
Amboina
Amboyna
Assagai
Assegai
Baywood
Boxwood
Camwood
Cypress
Durmast
Gumtree
Gumwood
Hemlock
Hickory
Meranti
Nutwood
Palmyra
Pimento
Quassia
Sanders
Sapwood
Shawnee
Shittim
Wallaba

8 letters:
Agalloch
Alburnum
Basswood
Beefwood
Chestnut
Corkwood
Crabwood
Guaiacum
Guaiocum
Hardwood
Harewood
Hornbeam
Ironwood
Jelutong
Kingwood
Laburnum
Mahogany
Pulpwood
Pyengadu
Pyinkado
Red cedar
Rosewood
Sandarac
Sapucaia
Sasswood
Shagbark
Softwood
Southern
Sycamore
Tamarack
Tamarind

9 letters:
Briarwood
Butternut
Caliature
Campeachy
Coachwood
Eaglewood
Hackberry
Jacaranda
Lancewood
Partridge
Persimmon
Pitch pine
Quebracho
Satinwood
Scots pine
Shellbark

Stinkwood
Torchwood
Tulipwood
White pine
Whitewood
Zebrawood

10 letters:
Afrormosia
Bulletwood
Calamander
Candlewood
Coromandel
Durmast oak
Fiddlewood

Greenheart
Hackmatack
Marblewood
Nettle-tree
Orangewood
Palisander
Paraná pine
Ribbonwood
Sandalwood
Sappanwood
Sneezewood
Spotted gum
Summerwood
White cedar
Yellowwood

11 letters:
Black walnut
Lignum-vitae
Sanderswood
Slippery elm

13 letters:
Partridge-wood

15 letters:
African mahogany
Western red cedar

Works of literature and music

3 letters:
Job
Kim
She

4 letters:
Aida
Emma
Lulu
Maud

5 letters:
Brand
Comus
Faust
Fetes
Kipps
La Mer
Manon
Medea
Norma
Scoop
Tosca

6 letters:
Alcina
Amelia
Becket
Ben Hur
Carmen
En Saga

Ghosts
Hassan
Helena
Iberia
Jenufa
Lolita
Martha
Mignon
Nuages
Oberon
Otello
Rienzi
Rob Roy
Rokeby
Salome
Semele
Sylvia
Trilby
Utopia
Walden

7 letters:
Adonais
Aladdin
Amadeus
Babbitt
Beowulf
Camilla
Candida
Don Juan
Dracula

Electra
Erewhon
Euphues
Fidelio
Giselle
Ivanhoe
Lord Jim
Lycidas
Macbeth
Manfred
Marmion
Ma Vlast
Mazeppa
Messiah
Nabucco
Othello
Rebecca
Ring, The
Shirley
Sirenes
Ulysses
Volpone
Werther
Wozzeck

8 letters:
Adam Bede
Adam Zero
Alcestis
Anabasis
Antigone

Arabella
Bells, The
Born Free
Carnaval
Carnival
Catriona
Cenci, The
Coppelia
Cranford
Endymion
Everyman
Falstaff
Gloriana
Hay Fever
Hiawatha
Hudibras
Hyperion
Idiot, The
Idomeneo
Iliad, The
In the Wet
Iolanthe
Jane Eyre
King Lear
LA Boheme
L'Allegro
Lavengro
Les Noces
Lucky Jim
Moby Dick
Parsifal
Patience
Peer Gynt
Pericles
Rasselas
Sea Drift
Swan Lake
Tom Jones
Turandot
Villette
Waves, The

9 letters:
Aeneid, The
Agamemnon
Beau Geste
Billy Budd
Brigg Fair
Capriccio
Cavalcade

Checkmate
Choephori
Coningsby
Cox and Box
Critic, The
Cymbeline
Dandy Dick
Don Carlos
Dr Zhivago
Dubliners
East Lynne
Egoist, The
Eumenides
Euryanthe
Hard Times
Hobbit, The
I, Claudius
I Puritani
Kidnapped
Kubla Khan
Les Biches
Lohengrin
Mein Kampf
Men at Arms
Mikado, The
No Highway
On Liberty
Papillons
Prince, The
Pygmalion
Rigoletto
Rivals, The
Ruddigore
Saint Joan
Siegfried
Tom Sawyer
Venusberg
Vice Versa
Warden, The

10 letters:
All for Love
Animal Farm
Appalachia
Bleak House
Borough, The
Cannery Row
Casablanca
Cinderella
Citadel, The

Coriolanus
Das Kapital
Die Walkure
Don Quixote
Dunciad, The
Dynasts, The
Howards End
Il Seraglio
Inferno, The
In Memoriam
Intermezzo
I Pagliacci
Jamaica Inn
John Gilpin
Kenilworth
Kingdom, The
La Gioconda
La Traviata
Les Troyens
Lorna Doone
Lysistrata
My Fair Lady
My Son, My Son
Nelson Mass
Odyssey, The
Oedipus Rex
Only Way, The
On the Beach
Our Village
Pantagruel
Persuasion
Petroushka
Planets, The
Prelude, The
Prince Igor
Relapse, The
Rural Rides
Seagull, The
Seasons, The
Semiramide
Tannhauser
Tempest, The
Tono-Bungay
Trojans, The
Uncle Remus
Uncle Vanya
Vanity Fair
Vile Bodies
War Requiem
Water Music

Westward Ho

11 letters:
American, The
Apostles, The
As You Like It
Big Sleep, The
Black Beauty
Blue Bird, The
Boule de Suif
Cakes and Ale
Child Harold
Creation, The
Cruel Sea, The
Doll's House, A
Don Giovanni
Don Pasquale
Firebird, The
Georgics, The
Greenmantle
Harp Quartet
Hedda Gabler
High Windows
HMS Pinafore
Hymn of Jesus
I Like It Here
Il Penseroso
Il Trovatore
Jack and Jill
Journey's End
Judith Paris
Little Eyolf
Little Women
Loved One, The
Love for Love
Luisa Miller
Mary Poppins
Middlemarch
Minute Waltz
Mrs Dalloway
Mr Standfast
Newcomes, The
Now We Are Six
Noye's Fludde
Ode to Autumn
Oliver Twist
Peter Grimes
Peter Simple
Pippa Passes
Princess Ida

Princess, The
Puss in Boots
Redgauntlet
Rosmersholm
Salut d'Amour
Sea Symphony
Silas Marner
Sorcerer, The
South Riding
Stalky and Co
Stenka Razin
Tale of a Tub, A
Talisman, The
Tam o'Shanter
Trial by Jury
What Katy Did
Wild Duck, The
William Tell
Women in Love
Wrong Box, The

12 letters:
Alchemist, The
Anna Karenina
Antiquary, The
Apple Cart, The
Archduke Trio
Areopagitica
Ash Wednesday
Barnaby Rudge
Blithe Spirit
Brighton Rock
Buddenbrooks
Caretaker, The
Charley's Aunt
Cosi fan Tutte
Danse Macabre
Decameron, The
Dogs of War, The
Dombey and Son
Epithalamion
Eugene Onegin
Excursion, The
Four Quartets
Frankenstein
Golden Ass, The
Grand Duke, The
Guy Mannering
Handley Cross
Julius Caeser

Karelia Suite
Khovanschina
Kinderscenen
Kreisleriana
La Sonnambula
Le Pere Goriot
Les Huguenots
Les Sylphides
Linz Symphony
Little Dorrit
Locksley Hall
Lost Chord, The
Madame Bovary
Major Barbara
Manon Lescaut
Moll Flanders
Moonstone, The
Old Mortality
Owen Wingrave
Paradise Lost
Piers Plowman
Porgy and Bess
Precious Bane
Private Lives
Prothalamion
Rheingold, Das
Rip Van Winkle
Rogue Herries
Romany Rye, The
Sardanapalus
Spring Sonata
Trout Quintet
Twelfth Night
Valkyries, The
Whisky Galore

13 letters:
Albert Herring
Almayer's Folly
Andrea Chenier
Angel Pavement
Arms and the Man
Art of Fugue, The
Bab Ballads, The
Black Arrow, The
Black Mischief
Blue Danube, The
Boris Godounov
Brave New World
Cancer Ward, The

Carmina Burana
Chanson de Nuit
Clock Symphony
Crown Imperial
Death in Venice
Der Freischutz
Dido and Aeneas
Doctor Faustus
Doctor Zhivago
Fame is the Spur
Finnegan's Wake
Ghost Train, The
Gondoliers, The
Harold in Italy
Hatter's Castle
Jungle Book, The
Just So Stories
La Cenerentola
L'Elisir d'Amore
Mabinogion, The
Magic Flute, The
Magistrate, The
Mansfield Park
Metamorphosen
Nutcracker, The
Odessa File, The
Orb and Sceptre
Path to Rome, The
Peg Woffington
Private Angelo
Religio Medici
Schindler's Ark
Sketches by Box
Songs of Travel
Sons and Lovers
Stamboul Train
Tarka the Otter
Timon of Athens
Under Milk Wood
Utopia Limited
Virginians, The
White Devil, The
Winnie-the-Pooh
Winslow Boy, The
Zuleika Dobson

14 letters:
Ambassadors, The
Andrea del Sarto
Battle Symphony

Bee's Wedding, The
Book of Snobs, The
Brief Encounter
Chanson de Matin
Choral Symphony
Cider with Rosie
Claudius the God
Coral Island, The
Country Wife, The
Crotchet Castle
Darkness at Noon
Decline and Fall
Deep Blue Sea, The
Die Zauberflote
Ein Heldenleben
Emperor Quartet
Entertainer, The
Eroica Symphony
Forsyte Saga, The
Four Just Men, The
Gay Lord Quex, The
Golden Bough, The
Goodbye Mr Chips
Goodby to Berlin
Great Gatsby, The
Handful of Dust, A
Horse's Mouth, The
Jude the Obscure
Kreutzer Sonata
Le Morte d'Arthur
London Symphony
Loom of Youth, The
Lord of the Flies
Lord of the Rings
Lost Horizon, The
Lyrical Ballads
Madam Butterfly
Man and Superman
Masterman Ready
National Velvet
Nightmare Abbey
Nine Tailors, The
Of Human Bondage
Our Man in Havana
Passage to India
Peal Fishers, The
Pickwick Papers
Plain Dealer, The
Prague Symphony
Quentin Durward

Rhapsody in Blue
Rights of Man, The
Robinson Crusoe
Roderick Random
Romeo and Juliet
Separate Tables
Shropshire Lad, A
Siegfried Idyll
Sinister Street
Sins of my Old Age
Slavonic Dances
Spring Symphony
Stones of Venice
Time Machine, The
Town Like Alice, A
Tragic Symphony
Treasure Island
Tristram Shandy
Uncle Tom's Cabin
Venus and Adonis
Vicar of Bray, The
Voices of Spring
Water Babies, The
Widowers Houses
Winter's Tale, The
Woodlanders, The

15 letters:
African Queen, The
Allan Quatermain
Ariadne auf Naxos
Bartholomew Fair
Beggar's Opera, The
Child of our Time, A
Christmas Carol, A
Clarissa Harlowe
Dangerous Corner
Daphnis and Chloe
Divine Comedy, The
Emperor Concerto
Emperor Waltz, The
Essays of Elia, The
Faerie Queene, The
Fanny by Gaslight
Farewell to Arms, A
Frenchman's Creek
From the New World
Golden Legend, The
Gone with the Wind
Gotterdammerung

Haffner Symphony
Hansel and Gretel
Heartbreak House
Huckleberry Finn
Iceman Cometh, The
Invisible Man, The
Italian Symphony
Jupiter Symphony
Le Nozze di Figaro
Letters of Junius
Life for the Tsar, A
Look Back in Anger
Moonlight Sonata

Northanger Abbey
Old Wives Tale, The
Our Mutual Friend
Peregrine Pickle
Peter and the Wolf
Puck of Pook's Hill
Put out More Flags
Raindrop Prelude
Rite of Spring, The
Rupert of Hentzau
Samson Agonistes
Samson and Dalila
Scholar Gipsy, The

Serenade to Music
Simon Boccanegra
Soldier's Tale, The
Tanglewood Tales
Three Men in a Boat
Titus Andronicus
To the Lighthouse
Waiting for Godot
Waldstein Sonata
Weir of Hermiston
Woman in White, The
Yarrow Revisited
You Never Can Tell

Worms

3 letters:
Bob
Dew
Fan
Lob

4 letters:
Tube

5 letters:
Acorn
Arrow
Fluke
Leech
Lytta
Piper

6 letters:
Caddis
Guinea
Nereid
Paddle
Palmer
Palolo
Ribbon
Scolex
Taenia
Teredo
Tongue

7 letters:
Ascarid
Bladder

Bristle
Catworm
Cestode
Cestoid
Filaria
Gordius
Hair-eel
Ragworm
Sabella
Serpula
Stomach
Tag-tail
Tenioid
Triclad
Tubifex
Vinegar

8 letters:
Bootlace
Capeworm
Caseworm
Clamworm
Filander
Gilt-tail
Hairworm
Hookworm
Inchworm
Nematoda
Nematode
Nemertea
Paste-eel
Seamouse
Strongyl

Toxocara
Trichina
Wheat-eel
Whipworm

9 letters:
Bilharzia
Brandling
Diplozoon
Heartworm
Horsehair
Lumbricus
Peripatus
Planarian
Strawworm
Strongyle
Tiger tail
Trematode
Wheatworm

10 letters:
Anguillula
Liver-fluke
Polychaete
Threadworm

11 letters:
Oligochaete
Schistosome
Scoleciform
Trichinella
Trichinosed
Turbellaria

12 letters:
Enteropneust
Hemichordata

Night-crawler
Sipunculacea

13 letters:
Platyhelminth
Sipunculoidea

Writers

3 letters:
Eco, *Umberto*
Lee, *Sophia*
Paz, *Octavio*
Poe, *Edgar Allan*
RLS

4 letters:
Amis, *Martin (Louis)*
Asch, *Sholem*
Aymé, *Marcel*
Bede, *the Venerable*
Bolt, *Robert (Oxton)*
Cary, *(Arthur) Joyce Lunel*
Cole, *Babette*
Dahl, *Roald*
Fine, *Ann*
Gide, *André (Paul Guillaume)*
Hope, *Anthony (Sir Anthony Hope Hawkins)*
Hugo, *Victor Marie*
Hunt, *E(verette) Howard*
King, *Stephen (Edwin)*
Lamb, *Charles*
Loos, *Anita*
Loti, *Pierre*
Lyly, *John*
Mann, *Thomas*
More, *Henry*
Nash, *(Frederic) Ogden*
Opie, *Iona*
Ovid
Pope, *Alexander*
Saki *(Hector Hugh Munro)*
Sand, *George*
Shaw, *George Bernard*
Snow, *C(harles) P(ercy)*
Ward, *Mary Augusta*
West, *Nathanael*
Zola, *Émile*

5 letters:
Acton, *Sir Harold Mario*
Aesop
Albee, *Edward Franklin*
Auden, *W(ystan) H(ugh)*
Ayres, *Noreen*
Banks, *Lynn Reid*
Bates, *H(erbert) E(rnest)*
Blake, *William*
Blume, *Judy*
Burke, *Edmund*
Caine, *Sir (Thomas Henry) Hall*
Camus, *Albert*
Corvo, *Baron*
Crane, *Stephen*
Defoe, *Daniel*
Digby, *Anne*
Doyle, *Arthur Conan*
Dumas, *Alexandre*
Eliot, *T(homas) S(tearns)*
Ellis, *(Henry) avelock*
Genet, *Jean*
Gogol, *Nikolai Vasilevich*
Gorky, *Maxim*
Gosse, *Sir Edmund William*
Greer, *Germaine*
Grimm, *Wilhelm Carl*
Hardy, *Thomas*
Henry, *O (William Sydney Porter)*
Henty, *G(eorge) A(lfred)*
Hesse, *Hermann*
Heyer, *Georgette*
Homer
Ibsen, *Henrik*
Innes, *(Ralph) Hammond*
James, *Henry*
Jones, *Diana Wynne*
Joyce, *James (Augustine Aloysius)*
Kafka, *Franz*

Kempe, *Margery*
Lewis, *C(live) S(taples)*
Lodge, *David John*
Lorca, *Frederico García*
Mason, *Alfred Edward Woodley*
Milne, *A(lan) A(lexander)*
Munro, *H(ector) H(ugh)*
Musil, *Robert*
Nashe, *Thomas*
Ouida
Paine, *Tom*
Pater, *Walter Horatio*
Paton, *Alan*
Pepys, *Samuel*
Pliny
Pound
Powys, *John Cowper*
Reade, *Charles*
Renan, *(Joseph) Ernest*
Rilke, *Rainer Maria*
Sagan, *Françoise*
Scott, *Sir Walter*
Seuss, *Dr (Theodor Seuss Geisel)*
Shute, *Nevil*
Smith, *Dick King*
Spark, *Dame Muriel Sarah*
Stark, *Dame Freya Madeline*
Stein, *Gertrude*
Swift, *Jonathan*
Synge, *(Edmund) J(ohn) M(illington)*
Twain, *Mark (Samuel L Clemens)*
Verne, *Jules*
Waugh, *Evelyn (Arthur St John)*
Wells, *H(erbert) G(eorge)*

Wilde, *Oscar (Fingal O'Flahertie Wills)*
Woolf, *(Adeline) Virginia*
Yates, *Dornford*
Yonge, *Charlotte Mary*

6 letters:
Alcott, *Louisa May*
Ambler, *Eric*
Arnold, *Matthew*
Artaud, *Antonin Marie Joseph*
Ascham, *Roger*
Asimov, *Isaac*
Austen, *Jane*
Balzac, *Honoré de*
Baring, *Maurice*
Barrie, *J(ames) M(atthew)*
Belloc, *(Joseph) Hilaire (Pierre)*
Bellow, *Saul*
Blyton, *Enid (Mary)*
Borges, *Jorge Luis*
Borrow, *George Henry*
Braine, *John Gerard*
Bronte, *Emily Jane (Ellis Bell)*
Buchan, *John*
Bunyan, *John*
Butler, *Samuel*
Capote, *Truman*
Cicero, *Marcus Tullius*
Colfer, *Eoin*
Conrad, *Joseph*
Cowper, *William*
Cronin, *A(rchibald) J(oseph)*
Daudet, *Alphonse*
Dryden, *John*
Durrel, *Laurence George*
Engels, *Friedrich*
Fowles, *John (Robert)*
France, *Anatole*
Gibbon, *Edward*
Godwin, *William*
Goethe, *Johann Wolfgang von*
Graves, *Robert (Ranke)*
Greene, *(Henry) Graham*

Harris, *Joel Chandler*
Heller, *Joseph*
Hobbes, *Thomas*
Hughes, *Thomas*
Hutton, *R(ichard) H(olt)*
Huxley, *Aldous Leonard*
Inkpen, *Mike*
Irving, *Washington*
Jarvis, *Robin*
Jerome, *Jerome K(lapka)*
Jonson, *Ben(jamin)*
Le Fanu, *(Joseph) Sheridan*
London, *Jack*
Lucian
Lytton, *Bulwer*
Mailer, *Norman Kingsley*
Malory, *Thomas*
Mannin, *Ethel*
Miller, *Henry Valentine*
Milton, *John*
Morgan, *Edwin George*
Murphy, *Jill*
Nerval, *Gérard de*
Nesbit, *E(dith)*
Onions, *Charles Talbut*
Orwell, *George*
Parker, *Dorothy*
Proust, *Marcel*
Racine, *Jean*
Runyon, *Damon*
Ruskin, *John*
Sachar, *Louis*
Sapper *(H C McNeile)*
Sayers, *Dorothy L(eigh)*
Sewell, *Anna*
Smiles, *Samuel*
Steele, *Richard*
Sterne, *Laurence*
Storey, *David Malcolm*
Thomas, *Dylan Marlais*
Updike, *John Hoyer*
Virgil
Walton, *Izaac*
Wilder, *Laura Ingalls*
Wilson, *Jacqueline*

7 letters:
Addison, *Joseph*
Aldrich, *Thomas Bailey*

Aretino, *Pietro*
Beckett, *Samuel (Barclay)*
Bennett, *(Enoch) Arnold*
Bentley, *Edmund Clerihew*
Boileau, *Nicholas (Despréaux)*
Boswell, *James*
Burgess, *Anthony*
Carlyle, *Thomas*
Carroll, *Lewis (Charles Lutwidge Dodgson)*
Chaucer, *Geoffrey*
Chekhov, *Anton Pavlovich*
Cobbett, *William*
Colette, *(Sidonie-Gabrielle)*
Collins, *Wilkie (William)*
Coppard, *A(lfred) E(dgar)*
Corelli, *Marie*
Cranmer, *Thomas*
Cushman, *Karen*
Deeping, *(George) Warwick*
Dickens, *Charles (John Huffam)*
Drabble, *Margaret*
Dreiser, *Theodore Herman Albert*
Durrell, *Gerald Malcolm*
Emerson, *Ralph Waldo*
Erasmus, *Desiderius*
Fénelon, *François de Salignac de la Mothe*
Forster, *Margaret*
Gissing, *George Robert*
Golding, *Sir William Gerald*
Grahame, *Kenneth*
Haggard, *Sir H(enry) Rider*
Hazlitt, *William*
Herbert, *George*
Hichens, *Robert Smythe*
Johnson, *Samuel*
Kipling, *(Joseph) Rudyard*

Lardner, *Ring(gold Wilmer)*

Marryat, *(Captain) Frederick*

Maugham, *W(illiam) Somerset*

Mauriac, *François*

Mérimée, *Prosper*

Mitford, *Jessica Lucy*

Moravia, *Alberto*

Murdoch, *Dame (Jean) Iris*

Nabokov, *Vladimir*

Naipaul, *Sir V(idiadhar) S(urajprasad)*

Peacock, *Thomas Love*

Pullman, *Philip*

Pushkin, *Alexander*

Ransome, *Arthur Mitchell*

Riddell, *Chris*

Rostand, *Edmond*

Rowling, *J(oanne) K(athleen)*

Saroyan, *William*

Sassoon, *Siegfried Louvain*

Shelley, *Mary Wollstonecraft*

Simenon, *Georges Joseph Christian*

Sitwell, *Sir (Francis) Osbert*

Stephen, *Leslie*

Stewart, *Paul*

Surtees, *Robert Smith*

Terence

Thoreau, *Henry David*

Tolkien, *J(ohn) R(onald) R(euel)*

Tolstoy, *Count Leo Nikolayevich*

Travers, *Ben(jamin)*

Wallace, *(Richard Horatio) Edgar*

Walpole, *Sir Hugh Seymour*

Wharton, *Edith Newbold*

Whitman, *Walt(er)*

8 letters:

Andersen, *Hans Christian*

Beaumont, *Sir John*

Browning, *Robert*

Caldwell, *Erskine*

Chandler, *Raymond*

Childers, *(Robert) Erskine*

Christie, *(Dame) Agatha (Mary Clarissa)*

Constant, *Benjamin*

Coolidge, *Susan*

De la Mare, *Walter (John)*

Disraeli, *Benjamin*

Faulkner, *William*

Fielding, *Henry*

Flaubert, *Gustave*

Forester, *C(ecil) S(cott)*

Goncourt, *Jules*

Ishiguro, *Kazuo*

Kingsley, *Mary St Leger*

Lawrence, *T(homas) E(dward)*

Mannheim, *Baron Carl Gustav Emil*

Melville, *Herman*

Meredith, *George*

Morpurgo, *Michael*

Perrault, *Charles*

Plutarch

Rabelais, *François*

Rattigan, *Sir Terence Mervyn*

Remarque, *Erich Maria*

Rousseau, *Jean-Jacques*

Salinger, *J(erome) D(avid)*

Schiller, *(Johann Christoph) Friedrich (von)*

Smollett, *Tobias George*

Stendhal *(Marie-Henri Beyle)*

Taffrail *(Henry Taprell Dorling)*

Traherne, *Thomas*

Trollope, *Joanna*

Turgenev, *Ivan Sergeyevich*

Voltaire *(François Marie Arouet)*

Williams, *Tennessee*

9 letters:

Aeschylus

Ainsworth, *William Harrison*

Blackmore, *R(ichard) D(oddridge)*

Boccaccio, *Giovanni*

Brent-Dyer, *Elinor M(ary)*

Burroughs, *Edgar Rice*

Dos Passos, *John Roderigo*

Du Maurier, *Dame Daphne*

Edgeworth, *Maria*

Goldsmith, *Oliver*

Hawthorne, *Nathaniel*

Hemingway, *Ernest (Millar)*

Isherwood, *Christopher William Bradshaw*

Jefferson, *Thomas*

Lermontov, *Mikhail Yuriyevich*

Linklater, *Eric*

Mackenzie, *Sir (Edward Montague) Compton*

Madariaga, *Salvador de*

Mansfield, *Katherine*

McCullers, *Carson*

Oppenheim, *Edward Phillips*

Pasternak, *Boris Leonidovich*

Pratchett, *Terry*

Priestley, *J(ohn) B(oynton)*

Santayana, *George*

Sholokhov, *Mikhail Aleksandrovich*

Steinbeck, *John Ernest*

Stevenson, *Robert Louis Balfour*

Thackeray, *William Makepeace*

Wodehouse, *Sir P(elham) G(renville)*

Writers

10 letters:
Ballantyne, *Robert Michael*
Chesterton, *G(ilbert) K(eith)*
Dostoevsky, *Fyodor Mikhailovich*
Fitzgerald, *F(rancis) Scott (Key)*
Galsworthy, *John*
Richardson, *H(enry) H(andel)*

11 letters:
De Cervantes (Saavedra), *Miguel*

De Montaigne, *Michel Eyquem*
Machiavelli, *Niccolò*
Maeterlinck, *Count Maurice*
Shakespeare, *William*
Streatfield, *Noel*

12 letters:
Aristophanes
Chesterfield, *Lord*
De Mandeville, *Sir Jehan (or John)*
De Maupassant, (*Henri René Albert*) *Guy*
Solzhenitsyn, *Aleksandr Isayevich*

13 letters:
Sackville-West, *Vita (Victoria Mary)*

14 letters:
Wollstonecraft, *Mary*

15 letters:
De Chateaubriand, *Vicomte (François René)*

24 letters:
APH (*Sir Alan Patrick Herbert*)

See also:
➤ **Diarists** ➤ **Dramatists** ➤ **Novelists** ➤ **Poets** ➤ **Shakespeare**

Y y

Shades of yellow

4 letters:
Buff
Ecru
Gold

5 letters:
Amber
Beige
Lemon
Maize
Ochre
Straw
Topaz

6 letters:
Almond
Bisque

Bistre
Citron
Golden

7 letters:
Gamboge
Jasmine
Mustard
Nankeen
Oatmeal
Old gold
Saffron
Tea rose

8 letters:
Cinnamon

Daffodil
Eau de nil
Eggshell
Magnolia
Primrose

9 letters:
Butternut
Champagne

12 letters:
Canary yellow

13 letters:
Tortoiseshell

Z z

Signs of the Zodiac

Aquarius (the Water Carrier)
Aries (the Ram)
Cancer (the Crab)
Capricorn (the Goat)

Gemini (the Twins)
Leo (the Lion)
Libra (the Scales)
Pisces (the Fishes)
Sagittarius (the Archer)

Scorpio (the Scorpion)
Taurus (the Bull)
Virgo (the Virgin)

Chinese animal years

Chinese	English			Years		
Shu	Rat	1960	1972	1984	1996	2008
Niu	Ox	1961	1973	1985	1997	2009
Hu	Tiger	1962	1974	1986	1998	2010
Tu	Hare	1963	1975	1987	1999	2011
Long	Dragon	1964	1976	1988	2000	2012
She	Serpent	1965	1977	1989	2001	2013
Ma	Horse	1966	1978	1990	2002	2014
Yang	Sheep	1967	1979	1991	2003	2015
Hou	Monkey	1968	1980	1992	2004	2016
Ji	Cock	1969	1981	1993	2005	2017
Gou	Dog	1970	1982	1994	2006	2018
Zhu	Boar	1971	1983	1995	2007	2019

Zoology

BRANCHES OF ZOOLOGY

3 letters:
Shu

7 letters:
Zootomy

8 letters:
Cetology
Ethology

Zoometry

9 letters:
Mammalogy
Ophiology
Zoography

10 letters:
Entomology

Malacology

11 letters:
Arachnology
Herpetology
Ichthyology
Myrmecology
Ornithology
Primatology

BRANCHES OF ZOOLOGY (CONTINUED)

12 letters:
Protozoology
Zoogeography

13 letters:
Palaeozoology

14 letters:
Archaeozoology

ZOOLOGY TERMS

3 letters:
Fin

4 letters:
Gill
Prey
Pupa

5 letters:
Biped
Imago
Larva
Spawn
Spine

6 letters:
Caudal
Cocoon
Coelom
Colony
Dorsal
Raptor
Rodent
Sucker
Thorax

7 letters:
Abdomen

Antenna
Bivalve
Decapod
Primate
Reptile
Segment
Ventral

8 letters:
Anterior
Arachnid
Chordate
Dipteran
Edentate
Omnivore
Pectoral
Placenta
Predator
Ruminant
Skeleton

9 letters:
Amphibian
Appendage
Arthropod
Carnivore
Chrysalis
Gastropod

Herbivore
Marsupial
Migration
Passerine
Posterior
Protozoan
Quadruped

10 letters:
Crustacean
Echinoderm
Gasteropod
Parenchyma
Vertebrate

11 letters:
Aestivation
Hibernation
Insectivore

12 letters:
Coelenterate
Invertebrate
Lepidopteran

13 letters:
Metamorphosis

ZOOLOGISTS

5 letters:
Elton, *Charles Sutherland*

6 letters:
Cuvier, *Georges*
Darwin, *Charles (Robert)*
Kinsey, *Alfred Charles*
Lorenz, *Konrad Zacharias*
Morgan, *Thomas Hunt*

7 letters:
Dawkins, *Richard*
Driesch, *Hans Adolf Eduard*
Durrell, *Gerald (Malcolm)*
Lamarck, *Jean Baptiste Pierre Antoine De Monet*
Medawar, *Peter Brian*
Wallace, *Alfred Russel*

8 letters:
Kammerer, *Paul*

9 letters:
Lankester, *Edwin Ray*
Tinbergen, *Nikolaas*
Von Frisch, *Karl*
Zuckerman, *Solly*